THE HCSB

LIGHT SPEED

BIBLE

HOLMAN
**CHRISTIAN
STANDARD
BIBLE**®

WILLIAM PROCTOR, EDITOR

HOLMAN
BIBLE PUBLISHERS

Nashville, Tennessee

220.07 BIBLE—STUDY

Printed in Canada
1 2 3 4 5 6 7 8 09 08 07 06 05
SW

CONTENTS

Books of the Old Testament

Books of the New Testament

The Light Speed Bible Reading Program

Additional Material

PLAN OF SALVATION

What do you understand it takes for a person to go to Heaven?

Consider how the Bible answers this question: It's a matter of **FAITH**

F is for FORGIVENESS

We cannot have eternal life and heaven
without God's forgiveness.—**Read Ephesians 1:7a.**

A is for AVAILABLE

Forgiveness is available. It is—

• **Available for all.**	**—Read John 3:16.**
• **But not automatic.**	**—Read Matthew 7:21a.**

I is for IMPOSSIBLE

It is impossible for God to allow sin into heaven.

• **Because of who He is: God is loving and just.** **His judgment is against sin.**	**—Read James 2:13a.**
• **Because of who we are:** **Every person is a sinner.**	**—Read Romans 3:23.**

But how can a sinful person enter heaven, when God allows no sin?

T is for TURN

Turn means to repent.

• **Turn from something —sin and self.**	**—Read Luke 13:3b.**
• **Turn to Someone; trust Christ only.**	**—Read Romans 10:9.**

H is for HEAVEN

Heaven is eternal life.

• **Here**	**—Read John 10:10b.**
• **Hereafter**	**—Read John 14:3.**

How can a person have God's forgiveness, heaven and eternal life, and Jesus as personal Savior and Lord? By trusting in Christ and asking Him for forgiveness. Take the step of faith described by another meaning of FAITH: **F**orsaking **A**ll **I T**rust **H**im.

Prayer:

Lord Jesus, I know I am a sinner and have displeased You in many ways. I believe You died for my sin and only through faith in Your death and resurrection can I be forgiven.

I want to turn from my sin and ask You to come into my life as my Savior and Lord. From this day on, I will follow You by living a life that pleases You. Thank You, Lord Jesus for saving me. Amen.

After you have received Jesus Christ into your life, tell a Christian friend about this important decision you have made. Follow Christ in believer's baptism and church membership. Grow in your faith and enjoy new friends in Christ by becoming part of His church. There, you'll find others who will love and support you.

INTRODUCTION TO THE HOLMAN CHRISTIAN STANDARD BIBLE®

The Bible is God's revelation to man. It is the only book that gives us accurate information about God, man's need, and God's provision for that need. It provides us with guidance for life and tells us how to receive eternal life. The Bible can do these things because it is God's inspired Word, inerrant in the original manuscripts.

The Bible describes God's dealings with the ancient Jewish people and the early Christian church. It tells us about the great gift of God's Son, Jesus Christ, who fulfilled Jewish prophecies of the Messiah. It tells us about the salvation He accomplished through His death on the cross, His triumph over death in the resurrection, and His promised return to earth. It is the only book that gives us reliable information about the future, about what will happen to us when we die, and about where history is headed.

Bible translation is both a science and an art. It is a bridge that brings God's Word from the ancient world to the world today. In dependence on God to accomplish this sacred task, Holman Bible Publishers presents the Holman Christian Standard Bible, a new English translation of God's Word.

Textual base of the Holman CSB®

The textual base for the New Testament [NT] is the Nestle-Aland *Novum Testamentum Graece*, 27th edition, and the United Bible Societies' *Greek New Testament*, 4th corrected edition. The text for the Old Testament [OT] is the *Biblia Hebraica Stuttgartensia*, 5th edition. At times, however, the translators have followed an alternative manuscript tradition, disagreeing with the editors of these texts about the original reading.

Where there are significant differences among Hebrew [Hb] and Aramaic [Aram] manuscripts of the OT or among Greek [Gk] manuscripts of the NT, the translators have followed what they believe is the original reading and have indicated the main alternative(s) in footnotes. In a few places in the NT, large square brackets indicate texts that the translation team and most biblical scholars today believe were not part of the original text. However, these texts have been retained in brackets in the Holman CSB because of their undeniable antiquity and their value for tradition and the history of NT interpretation in the church. The Holman CSB uses traditional verse divisions found in most Protestant Bibles.

Goals of this translation

The goals of this translation are:

- to provide English-speaking people across the world with an accurate, readable Bible in contemporary English

- to equip serious Bible students with an accurate translation for personal study, private devotions, and memorization

- to give those who love God's Word a text that has numerous reader helps, is visually attractive on the page, and is appealing when heard

- to affirm the authority of Scripture as God's Word and to champion its absolute truth against social or cultural agendas that would compromise its accuracy

The name, Holman Christian Standard Bible, captures these goals: *Holman* Bible Publishers presents a new *Bible* translation, for *Christian* and English-speaking communities, which will be a *standard* in Bible translations for years to come.

Why is there a need for another English translation of the Bible?

There are several good reasons why Holman Bible publishers invested its resources in a modern language translation of the Bible:

1. Each generation needs a fresh translation of the Bible in its own language.

The Bible is the world's most important book, confronting each individual and each culture with issues that affect life, both now and forever. Since each new generation must be introduced to God's Word in its own language, there will always be a need for new translations such as the Holman Christian Standard Bible. The majority of Bible translations on the market today are revisions of translations from previous generations. The Holman CSB is a new translation for today's generation.

2. English, one of the world's greatest languages, is rapidly changing, and Bible translations must keep in step with those changes.

English is the first truly global language in history. It is the language of education, business, medicine, travel, research, and the Internet. More than 1.3 billion people around the world speak or read English as a primary or secondary language. The Holman CSB seeks to serve many of those people with a translation they can easily use and understand.

English is also the world's most rapidly changing language. The Holman CSB seeks to reflect recent changes in English by using modern punctuation, formatting, and vocabulary, while avoiding slang, regionalisms, or changes made specifically for the sake of political or social agendas. Modern linguistic and semantic advances have been incorporated into the Holman CSB, including modern grammar.

3. Rapid advances in biblical research provide new data for Bible translators.

This has been called the "information age," a term that accurately describes the field of biblical research. Never before in history has there been as much information about the Bible as there is today—from archaeological discoveries to analysis of ancient manuscripts to years of study and statistical research on individual Bible books. Translations made as recently as 10 or 20 years ago do not reflect many of these advances in biblical research. The translators have taken into consideration as much of this new data as possible.

4. Advances in computer technology have opened a new door for Bible translation.

The Holman CSB has used computer technology and telecommunications in its creation perhaps more than any Bible translation in history. Electronic mail was used daily and sometimes hourly for communication and transmission of manuscripts. An advanced Bible software program, Accordance®, was used to create and revise the translation at each step in its production. A developmental copy of the translation itself was used within Accordance to facilitate cross-checking during the translation process—something never done before with a Bible translation.

Translation Philosophy of the Holman CSB

Most discussions of Bible translations speak of two opposite approaches: formal equivalence and dynamic equivalence. Although this terminology is meaningful, Bible translations cannot be neatly sorted into these two categories any more than people can be neatly sorted into two categories according to height or weight. Holman Bible Publishers is convinced there is room for another category of translation philosophies that capitalizes on the strengths of the other two.

1. <u>Formal Equivalence:</u>

Often called "word-for-word" (or "literal") translation, the principle of formal equivalence seeks as nearly as possible to preserve the structure of the original language. It seeks to represent each word of the translated text with an exact equivalent word in the translation so that the reader can see word for word what the original human author wrote. The merits of this approach include its consistency with the conviction that the Holy Spirit did inspire the very words of Scripture in the original manuscripts. It also provides the English Bible student some access to the structure of the text in the original language. Formal equivalence can achieve accuracy to the degree that English has an exact equivalent for each word and that the grammatical patterns of the original language can be reproduced in understandable English. However, it can sometimes result in awkward, if not incomprehensible, English or in a misunderstanding of the author's intent. The literal rendering of ancient idioms is especially difficult.

2. Dynamic or Functional Equivalence:

Often called "thought-for-thought" translation, the principle of dynamic equivalence rejects a s misguided the desire to preserve the structure of the original language. It proceeds by distinguishing the meaning of a text from its form and then translating the meaning so that it makes the same impact on modern readers that the ancient text made on its original readers. Strengths of this approach include a high degree of clarity and readability, especially in places where the original is difficult to render word for word. It also acknowledges that accurate and effective translation requires interpretation. However, the meaning of a text cannot always be neatly separated from its form, nor can it always be precisely determined. A biblical author may have intended multiple meanings. In striving for readability, dynamic equivalence also sometimes overlooks some of the less prominent elements of meaning. Furthermore, lack of formal correspondence to the original makes it difficult to verify accuracy and thus can affect the usefulness of the translation for in-depth Bible study.

3. Optimal Equivalence:

In practice, translations are seldom if ever purely formal or dynamic but favor one theory of Bible translation or the other to varying degrees. Optimal equivalence as a translation philosophy recognizes that form cannot be neatly separated from meaning and should not be changed (for example, nouns to verbs or third person "they" to second person "you") unless comprehension demands it. The primary goal of translation is to convey the sense of the original with as much clarity as the original text and the translation language permit. Optimal equivalence appreciates the goals of formal equivalence but also recognizes its limitations.

Optimal equivalence starts with an exhaustive analysis of the text at every level (word, phrase, clause, sentence, discourse) in the original language to determine its original meaning and intention (or purpose). Then relying on the latest and best language tools and experts, the nearest corresponding semantic and linguistic equivalents are used to convey as much of the information and intention of the original text with as much clarity and readability as possible. This process assures the maximum transfer of both the words and thoughts contained in the original.

The Holman CSB uses optimal equivalence as its translation philosophy. When a literal translation meets these criteria, it is used. When clarity and readability demand an idiomatic translation, the reader can still access the form of the original text by means of a footnote with the abbreviation "Lit."

The gender language policy in Bible translation

Some people today ignore the Bible's teachings on distinctive roles of men and women in family and church and have an agenda to eliminate those distinctions in every arena of life. These people have begun a program to engineer the removal of a perceived male bias in the English language. The targets of this program have been such traditional linguistic practices as the generic use of "man" or "men," as well as "he," "him," and "his."

A group of Bible scholars, translators, and other evangelical leaders met in 1997 to respond to this issue as it affects Bible translation. This group produced the "Guidelines for Translation of Gender-Related Language in Scripture" (adopted May 27, 1997 and revised Sept. 9, 1997). The Holman Christian Standard Bible was produced in accordance with these guidelines.

The goal of the translators has not been to promote a cultural ideology but to faithfully translate the Bible. While the Holman CSB avoids using "man" or "he" unnecessarily, the translation does not restructure sentences to avoid them when they are in the text. For example, the translators have not changed "him" to "you" or to "them," neither have they avoided other masculine words such as "father" or "son" by translating them in generic terms such as "parent" or "child."

History of the Holman Christian Standard Bible

After several years of preliminary development, Holman Bible Publishers, the oldest Bible publisher in America, assembled an international, interdenominational team of 100 scholars, editors, stylists, and proofreaders, all of whom were committed to biblical inerrancy. Outside consultants and reviewers contributed valuable suggestions from their areas of expertise. An executive team then edited, polished, and reviewed the final manuscripts.

Traditional features found in the Holman CSB

In keeping with a long line of Bible publications, the Holman Christian Standard Bible has retained a number of features found in traditional Bibles:

1. Traditional theological vocabulary (such as *justification, sanctification, redemption*, etc.) has been retained since such terms have no translation equivalent that adequately communicates their exact meaning.
2. Traditional spellings of names and places found in most Bibles have been used to make the Holman CSB compatible with most Bible study tools.
3. Some editions of the Holman CSB will print the words of Christ in red letters to help readers easily locate the spoken words of the Lord Jesus Christ.
4. Nouns and personal pronouns that clearly refer to any person of the Trinity are capitalized.
5. Descriptive headings, printed above each section of Scripture, help readers quickly identify the contents of that section.
6. Small lower corner brackets: ⌞⌟ indicate words supplied for clarity by the translators (but see below, under <u>Substitution of words in sentences</u>, for supplied words that are not bracketed).
7. Two common forms of punctuation are used in the Holman CSB to help with clarity and ease of reading: em dashes (a long dash —) are used to indicate sudden breaks in thought or to help clarify long or difficult sentences. Parentheses are used infrequently to indicate words that are parenthetical in the original languages.

How certain names and terms are translated

The names of God

The Holman Christian Standard Bible OT consistently translates the Hebrew names for God as follows:

Holman CSB English:	Hebrew original:
God	*Elohim*
LORD	*YHWH (Yahweh)*

Lord	*Adonai*
Lord GOD	*Adonai Yahweh*
LORD of Hosts	*Yahweh Sabaoth*
God Almighty	*El Shaddai*

However, the Holman CSB OT uses Yahweh, the personal name of God in Hebrew, when a biblical text emphasizes Yahweh as a name: "His name is Yahweh" (Ps 68:4). Yahweh is used more often in the Holman CSB than in most Bible translations because the word LORD in English is a title of God and does not accurately convey to modern readers the emphasis on God's name in the original Hebrew.

The uses of Christ and Messiah

The Holman CSB translates the Greek word *Christos* ("anointed one") as either "Christ" or "Messiah" based on its use in different NT contexts. Where the NT emphasizes *Christos* as a name of our Lord or has a Gentile context, "Christ" is used (Eph 1:1 "Paul, an apostle of Christ Jesus…"). Where the NT *Christos* has a Jewish context, the title "Messiah" is used (Eph 1:12 "…we who had already put our hope in the Messiah"). The first use of "Messiah" in each chapter is also marked with a bullet referring readers to the Bullet Note at the back of most editions.

Place-names

In the original text of the Bible, particularly in the OT, a number of well-known places have names different from the ones familiar to contemporary readers. For example, "the Euphrates" often appears in the original text simply as "the River." In cases like this, the Holman Christian Standard Bible uses the modern name, "the Euphrates River," in the text without a footnote or lower corner brackets.

Substitution of words in sentences

A literal translation of the biblical text sometimes violates standard rules of English grammar, such as the agreement of subject and verb or person and number. In order to conform to standard usage, the Holman CSB has often made these kinds of grammatical constructions agree in English without footnotes or lower corner brackets.

In addition, the Greek or Hebrew texts sometimes seem redundant or ambiguous by repeating nouns where modern writing substitutes pronouns or by using pronouns where we would supply nouns for clarity and good style. When a literal translation of the original would make the English unclear, the Holman CSB sometimes changes a pronoun to its corresponding noun or a noun to its corresponding pronoun without a footnote or lower corner brackets. For example, Jn 1:42 reads: "And he brought Simon to Jesus . . ." The original Greek of this sentence reads: "And he brought him to Jesus."

Special Formatting Features

The Holman Christian Standard Bible has several distinctive formatting features:

1. OT passages quoted in the NT are set in boldface type. OT quotes consisting of two or more lines are block indented.

2. In dialogue, a new paragraph is used for each new speaker as in most modern publications.

3. Many passages, such as 1 Co 13, have been formatted as dynamic prose (separate block-indented lines like poetry) for ease in reading and comprehension. Special block-indented formatting has also been used extensively in both the OT and NT to increase readability and clarity in lists, series, genealogies and other parallel or repetitive texts.

4. Almost every Bible breaks lines in poetry using automatic typesetting programs with the result that words are haphazardly turned over to the next line. In the Holman

CSB, special attention has been given to break every line in poetry and dynamic prose so that awkward or unsightly word wraps are avoided and complete units of thought turn over to the next line. The result is a Bible page that is much more readable and pleasing to the eye.

5. Certain foreign, geographical, cultural, or ancient words are preceded by a superscripted bullet (•*Abba*) at their first occurrence in each chapter. These words are listed in alphabetical order at the back of the Bible under the heading **Holman CSB Bullet Notes**. A few important or frequently misunderstood words (•slaves) are marked with a bullet more than one time per chapter.

6. Italics are used in the text for a transliteration of Greek and Hebrew words ("*Hosanna*!" in Jn 12:13) and in footnotes for direct quotations from the biblical text and for words in the original languages (the footnote at Jn 1:1 reads: "The *Word* (Gk *logos*) is a title for Jesus...").

7. Since the majority of English readers do not need to have numbers and fractions spelled out in the text, the Holman CSB uses a similar style to that of modern newspapers in using Arabic numerals for the numbers 10 and above and in fractions, except in a small number of cases, such as when a number begins a sentence.

Footnotes

Footnotes are used to show readers how the original biblical language has been understood in the Holman Christian Standard Bible.

NT Textual Footnotes

NT textual notes indicate significant differences among Greek manuscripts (mss) and are normally indicated in one of three ways:

Other mss read _____
Other mss add _____
Other mss omit _____

In the NT, some textual footnotes that use the word "add" or "omit" also have square brackets before and after the corresponding verses in the biblical text (see the discussion above in the paragraph entitled "Textual base of the Holman CSB"). Examples of this use of square brackets are Mk 16:9-20, Jn 5:3-4, and Jn 7:53–18:11.

OT Textual Footnotes

OT textual notes show important differences among Hebrew manuscripts and among ancient OT versions, such as the Septuagint and the Vulgate. See the list of abbreviations on page xii for a list of other ancient versions used.

Some OT textual notes (like NT textual notes) give only an alternate textual reading. However, other OT textual notes also give the support for the reading chosen by the editors as well as for the alternate textual reading. For example, the Holman CSB text of Ps 12:7 reads:

You will protect us[a] from this generation forever.

The textual footnote for this verse reads:

[a]**12:7** Some Hb mss, LXX; other Hb mss read *him*

The textual note in this example means that there are two different readings found in the Hebrew manuscripts: some manuscripts read *us* and others read *him*. The Holman

CSB translators chose the reading *us*, which is also found in the Septuagint (LXX), and placed the other Hebrew reading *him* in the footnote.

Two other OT textual notes are:

Alt Hb tradition reads _____	a variation given by scribes in the Hebrew manuscript Tradition (known as *Kethiv/Qere* readings)
Hb uncertain	when it is uncertain what the original Hebrew text was

Other Kinds of Footnotes

Lit _____	a more literal rendering in English of the Hebrew, Aramaic, or Greek text
Or _____	an alternate or less likely English translation of the same Hebrew, Aramaic, or Greek text
=	an abbreviation for " it means" or "it is equivalent to"
Hb, Aram, Gk	the actual Hebrew, Aramaic, or Greek word is given using English letters
Hb obscure	the existing Hebrew text is especially difficult to translate
emend(ed) to _____	the original Hebrew text is so difficult to translate that competent scholars have conjectured or inferred a restoration of the original text based on the context, probable root meanings of the words, and uses incomparative languages

In some editions of the Holman Christian Standard Bible, additional footnotes clarify the meaning of certain biblical texts or explain biblical history, persons, customs, places, activities, and measurements. Cross-references are given for parallel passages or passages with similar wording, and in the NT, for passages quoted from the OT.

Commonly Used Abbreviations in the Holman CSB

A.D.	in the year of our Lord
alt	alternate
a.m.	from midnight until noon
Aram	Aramaic
Aq	Aquila
B.C.	before Christ
c.	circa
chap	chapter
DSS	Dead Sea Scrolls
Eng	English
Gk	Greek
Hb	Hebrew
Lat	Latin
Lit	Literally
LXX	Septuagint—an ancient translation of the Old Testament into Greek
MT	Masoretic Text
NT	New Testament
ms(s)	manuscript(s)
OT	Old Testament
p.m.	from noon until midnight
pl	plural
Ps(s)	psalm(s)
Sam	Samaritan Pentateuch
sg	singular
syn.	synonym
Sym	Symmachus
Syr	Syriac
Tg	Targum
Theod	Theodotian
v., vv.	verse, verses
Vg	Vulgate—an ancient translation of the Bible into Latin
vol(s).	volume(s)

The
Light Speed
Bible
Reading Program

*The Official Step-by-Step Guide
to Faster, More Effective
Whole Bible Reading and Study
with Maximum Comprehension*

1.
The Adventure of Whole Bible Reading

He sends His command throughout the earth;
His word runs swiftly.
Psalm 147:15

The Bible tells us that God is light and Jesus is the light of the world—the written, inspired Word of God beams this divine light on us. Or as the Psalmist has put it, "Your word is a lamp for my feet and a light on my path." [1]

In fact, throughout the Scriptures, the word "light" is often employed to describe God and His realm—a realm illuminated by ultimate truth, love, and joy. When God appears to human beings, His presence may be signaled by an indescribable, even blinding light—whether in the Shekinah glory, the burning bush of Moses, the star of Bethlehem, or the dazzling, life-changing radiance encountered by Paul on the road to Damascus.

Because we know this heavenly light also emanates from the pages of the Bible, the *Light Speed Bible* has been designed with the hope that God's miraculous light will be conveyed to the innermost recesses of *your* being through new and fresh channels. The limitations of human time will fade as you absorb the study principles in this introduction and then, in an exhilarating sweep of less than 24 hours, expose your mind and heart to every word and teaching of the Old and New Testaments. There will no longer be any need for you to wonder if you have read all of Habakkuk, the "begats," or the laws of Leviticus. Neither will there be a nagging suspicion that "I own several Bibles, but I don't think I've ever really made it through the entire text."

No Longer the Most-Owned, Least-Read Book

The Bible is arguably the most-owned but least-read book in the world—a disheartening observation for those who know that the Scriptures can revolutionize lives and societies. The goal of the *Light Speed Bible* is to change all that.

Specifically, this edition of the Bible has been created to make it easier for increasing numbers of people to read the *entire* Bible in a remarkably short period of time with good comprehension. If various national and international studies and surveys are to be believed, there is a great need for an effective, highly accessible strategy of whole Bible reading.

In the United States, the Bible is almost certainly the most-owned book, with 93 percent of American households owning at least one copy, and 84 percent owning more than one. [2] In fact, the median number of Bibles owned per household is four, according to a 2001 Gallup poll for the American Bible Society.

Yet Gallup polls also show that as few as six percent of teenage readers say they have read the Bible all the way through. As for adults, both Gallup and Barna surveys report that no more than one-quarter of the adults in the United States claim to have read the entire Bible.[3]

Our surveys with *Light Speed Bible* seminar participants suggest that the actual number of adult whole-Bible readers may be much smaller. For example, many regular Bible readers have responded with a "no" or a question mark when asked more specific questions about their Bible reading background. Negative or equivocal answers are especially common when these participants are questioned whether or not they have read little-known or infrequently studied books, such as Habakkuk, Nahum, Philemon, Jude, or Third John—or whether they have actually read, word for word, all the Old Testament laws, royal lists, and genealogies.

A similarly disheartening Bible reading situation exists in other countries. Among Canadian Christians, only 15 percent say they have read the Bible all the way through.[4] In Great Britain, most adults have a copy of the Bible at home, but nearly all say they never read it, according to the London *Times*. The trend also prevails in France, where three of four people say they have never read any part of the Bible, much less the entire text—and only half of the homes in France have a copy of the Bible.[5]

As a consequence of low Bible readership and study, Bible knowledge among Americans remains sub par, reports pollster George Gallup, Jr. He cites these representative responses from his surveys as proof:

- Less than half of American adults can name the first book of the Bible.

- Only 35 percent know the country that ruled Jerusalem in the time of Jesus.

- Only 40 percent can name the Holy Trinity.

- Only 42 percent know who delivered the Sermon on the Mount.

- A mere 35 percent can name the four Gospels.

Despite this lack of Bible reading and knowledge, 65 percent of Americans agree that the Bible answers all or most of the basic questions of life, according to Gallup. And a resounding 75 percent—three quarters of American adults—say they are either interested or somewhat interested in deepening their understanding of the Bible.

So Why Don't More People Read the Entire Bible?

From these surveys, it's clear that the cause of the failure to read the whole Bible is not a lack of interest or a rejection of scriptural authority. So what exactly *is* the underlying problem?

Certainly many people lack the personal discipline to complete the Bible from start to finish—especially on those reading programs that require months or even a full year to complete the entire text. But more important, *most people simply lack the reading know-how* necessary to read large segments of the Bible quickly and effectively. They plod along at the average reading speed of 200 to 250 words per minute or slower, when they could be moving through the pages with *enhanced comprehension* at 700 to 1,000 words per minute or faster.

This *Light Speed Bible* offers a study program that can empower anyone with at least seventh-grade reading ability to read *every word* of the *entire* Bible in *24 hours or less*—with good comprehension. Or if you want to start with the New Testament using the strategy, the average time it will take to read every word and phrase from Matthew 1 through Revelation 22 is about five hours. Furthermore, in accordance with *Light Speed Bible* principles, these total times include not just one but *three* passes through the entire text.

Our long-term goal with these techniques is to provide a "scriptural antidote" for those who complain that they either read too slowly or lack the patience or commitment to stick with a one-year reading program. With such a strategy, there is every reason to expect that the number of readers of the *whole* Bible could increase exponentially—from the current low numbers to 50 percent or more of the population within five years. And of course, as whole Bible reading surges, knowledge of scriptural content and teachings will explode.

The Many Benefits of the
Light Speed Bible Strategy

A common misconception is that if you are going to get the most out of the Bible, you must always read slowly. Yet a growing body of research and experience points in quite a different direction—namely, that *combining fast and slow reading will actually enrich Bible study.* A number of considerations are prompting this shift in thinking about studying and reading the Scriptures.

Study for Regular Bible Classes. In the first place, experienced Bible teachers typically say that to study the Bible most effectively, you should begin by reading the entire book to be studied. Then, when you focus verse-by-verse on the text, you'll understand the details better in a broader context.

Unfortunately, most Bible students don't follow this advice, and their failure often has nothing to do with objections to faster Bible reading. Instead, these common complaints echo in many Bible study classes, including those I have taught over the last 30 years: "I don't have time! ... It takes too long for me to read all the way through Acts (or the Psalms, or Genesis) ... I'm a slow reader ... Maybe I'll try to do it next week ... or next month."

Such objections impede effective Bible study because an initial reading of the entire book at a swift pace will almost always highlight important themes that the student may otherwise overlook. In support of this point, here are some observations from those who have attended our seminars:

> "By reading large chunks of the Old Testament in one flow, I was struck by the repeating cycles of sin, repentance, and God's patient responses."

"Faster reading in the first part of the Old Testament made the trend of declining human life spans jump out at me. I continue to reflect on what factors may have caused ancient people to live longer than we do."

"In the 10 minutes or so it took for the first two reading 'passes' using the *Light Speed Bible* technique, I was able to get a good overview of Genesis and formulate all sorts of interesting questions. Then I read every word of the whole book in another 40 minutes."

"It's amazing how often the word 'meditation' is used in the book of Psalms. Yet I never would have noted the frequency if I hadn't read the entire book in one sitting. I'm still considering what the word may mean for me in my own prayer life."

"After reading every word of the book of Luke in about a half hour, I saw that Jesus managed to do a lot more than I thought. For example, He did many more healings than I remembered."

"In going through all the Gospels in an afternoon, I realized that there are more variations in accounts of the same event than I had assumed—such as Jesus' birth or death. Since then, I've gone back and looked more closely at how those different reports fit together, and that's given me a much more complete picture of what actually happened."

"In reading the Gospel of John at one sitting, I noticed for the first time that Nicodemus plays a continuing role and actually seems to develop spiritually."

Cross-referencing. Faster reading of broad segments of text also encourages more frequent and effective cross-referencing during study. So, if you read through all the Gospels at one sitting, you'll almost certainly notice the first reference to the Beatitudes in Matthew 5. Then, as you continue reading through Mark and into Luke, you'll be quite likely to focus on Luke's version of the same teaching in Luke 6.

Meditation. A third benefit to faster reading is that it provides a context for more profound meditation on a short passage of Scripture. One student reported that she meditated for 10 minutes one morning on the first part of verse one in Psalm 23, "The Lord is my shepherd." As she reflected, she found her mind being drawn to New Testament passages and parables referring to Jesus as the good Shepherd, which she had recently read during a "Landmark Speed" session (see below).

In fact, faster reading *itself* can be meditative or devotional. A number of students have discovered that "cruising" through lengthy passages at speeds of 700 to 1,000 words per minute or faster (i.e., approximately one or two pages per minute in the *Light Speed Bible*) puts them into a heightened listening mode that God often uses to good effect in their lives.

Factual Comprehension. Many individual reports and speed-reading studies have revealed that factual comprehension does not decrease and may actually increase with greater reading speed.[6]

Although this point may seem to run against common sense, the evidence suggests otherwise, and you yourself may well become a positive case study for the principle of enhanced comprehension as your skills grow. To test your comprehension using the *Light Speed Bible* strategies, you will be given an opportunity to take a sample quiz on Genesis later in this instructional section.

Successful Whole Bible Reading. Faster reading makes it more likely that you'll read through the entire Bible, in contrast to those who have tried unsuccessfully to follow various one-year Bible-reading programs. With the *Light Speed Bible* approach, you'll avoid getting bogged down in Leviticus or Second Chronicles, or in the listing of genealogical descendants, or the lists of kings of Judah and Israel. Also, you'll be in a position to read through the entire Bible many times each year. At the same time, you will find that you have plenty of time left over for effective in-depth study of particular books or passages.

Enhanced Relaxation—and Even Better Health. Although reading the Bible, or any other book for that matter, at an accelerated pace may at first seem like stressful work, emerging scientific research suggests the opposite. For one thing, a number of scientific studies have shown that the act of reading in itself can reduce stress.[7]

On an even more fundamental level, the physical actions and mental skills employed in the *Light Speed Bible* approach can trigger the "relaxation response," which has been identified by Dr. Herbert Benson of the Harvard Medical School as the healthful antidote to the stress response.[8]

These triggers include the physical repetition of moving your hand, fingers, or a ruler or mechanical pointer down each column of the Bible text, page after page, and Bible book after book. Also, the steady downward and upward movement of the eyes, the rhythmic turning of Bible pages, and regular breathing[9] promote the relaxation response effect.

Studies conducted by Dr. Benson and other experts have shown that many types of steady mental or physical repetition, including walking, jogging, and cycling, can cause bodily changes that counter the stress response. Specifically, the stress response involves the release of the so-called fight-or-flight hormones and neurotransmitters, including epinephrine (adrenaline) and norepinephrine (noradrenaline). These secretions from the adrenal glands, which lie just above the kidneys, can cause narrowing of blood vessels, increase in blood pressure, and higher heart rate. Scores of serious illnesses, including heart disease, stroke, and various forms of pain, have been linked to a failure to manage stress.

But mental and physical techniques that trigger the relaxation response set off a cascade of bodily changes that effectively neutralize the stress response. According to the best current thinking, these techniques cause the release of nitric oxide (NO) in the body's cells. As the NO moves throughout the body and brain, it counteracts norepinephrine and other stress hormones. At the same time, the brain releases calming neurotransmitters, such as endorphins and dopamine, which have been associated with feelings of well-being and good health.

In evaluating the physical techniques employed in the *Light Speed Bible* program, including regular turning of pages at a steady clip and metronome-like movement of the hands, Dr. Benson said:

"Such repetitive physical movements—as well as mental repetition of a word, phrase, or Scripture verse—help break prior, unproductive patterns of thought. This shift of inner direction enhances health through beneficial physiological changes and also opens the person up mentally to fresh insights and experiences. Obviously, if you are exposing yourself to the Bible when you 'open up' in this way, your insights are likely to be positive and edifying."

To put this in biblical terms, employing the *Light Speed Bible* strategies may actu- ally take advantage of innate, God-given healing mechanisms that underlie many principles, observations, and pleas from the Psalms, Proverbs, and other sections of Scripture. Here are a few illustrations:

"He sent His word and healed them." *(Psalm 107:20)*

"I will never forget Your precepts, for You have given me life through them." *(Psalm 119:93)*

"I am severely afflicted; LORD, give me life through Your word." *(Psalm 119:107)*

"Consider how I love Your precepts; LORD, give me life, according to Your faithful love." *(Psalm 119:159)*

"Listen, my son. Accept my words, and you will live many years." *(Proverbs 4:10)*

"My son, pay attention to my words; listen closely to my sayings. Don't lose sight of them; keep them within your heart. For they are life to those who find them, and health to one's whole body." *(Proverbs 4:20-22)*

"There is one who speaks rashly, like a piercing sword; but the tongue of the wise brings healing." *(Proverbs 12:18)*

"Pleasant words are a honeycomb: sweet to the taste and health to the body." *(Proverbs 16:24)*

In other words, it's likely that the techniques employed with the *Light Speed Bible* will not only improve your Bible knowledge and stimulate your spiritual development, but may even tap into a scripturally recognized capacity to improve human health.

Does It Matter How Old or Young I Am?

Sometimes, those considering this approach to reading and study may object, "I really think I'm too old to learn a new reading technique."

Others may ask, "What about my educational level—is there a minimum amount of schooling I need?"

And parents may wonder, "Is it wise to introduce this approach to my elementary school child?"

There is no age or educational limitation on the *Light Speed Bible* technique. In the first place, the Holman Christian Standard Bible translation uses vocabulary appropriate for those who read at a seventh-grade level. In other words, there are no "hundred-dollar words" in this text.

As far as age levels are concerned, in seminars as well as in individual tutoring sessions, individuals in their seventies and eighties have benefited significantly from the program. At the other end of the age spectrum, sixth- and seventh-grade students have emerged as superior readers with high comprehension as they move through the Bible text at speeds in excess of 700 to 1,000 words per minute. Young students also find that that they can easily transfer their skills to schoolwork assignments and critical reading sections on standardized tests.

In general, scientific studies have shown that those taking a speed-reading course with instruction similar to that offered by the program can expect measurable beneficial changes in reading speed and eye movements.[10] Yet as we've already seen, increased speed typically involves no decrease—and in many cases, results in an increase—in comprehension. In short, this Bible has the potential to trigger a revolution, both in your own life and in that of your friends and loved ones. But what exactly *is* the *Light Speed Bible* technique, and how can you make use of it?

2.
The Four Speed Zones

The basic technique involves going through extensive sections of the specially designed *Light Speed Bible* text three times at declining rates of speed. You'll accomplish this by employing three *"speed zones"*: first, *Light Speed;* then, *Landmark Speed;* and finally, *Learning Speed.* This "triple-pass" technique is based on proven principles tested in *Light Speed Bible* seminars and tutorials that help maximize your speed *and* retention.

A fourth speed zone, *Meditative Speed,* is discretionary, depending on your particular study or devotional objectives. But this very slow speed often works best after you've first read through a particular passage using the faster pace required in the first three speed zones.

For example, in your private prayer sessions you may want to spend a half hour or longer meditating and "journaling" on the personal meaning for you of the words "receive" and "believe" in John 1:12. In such cases, you will almost always find it helpful first to read the entire Gospel of John—or even all four Gospels. This way, you'll be more likely to understand the overall biblical context before you sit down to focus on just one verse. Furthermore, you will be in a better position to understand commentaries or Bible word dictionaries.

In summary, combining the first three speed zones with slower study or meditation can make your times of reflection much richer. Fast, effective, broad-stroke reading always lays a solid groundwork to help you maximize the impact of the meditative zone. Both approaches are essential ingredients of serious Bible study.

Every Speed Zone Is a Study Zone

The first three reading speeds—Light, Landmark, and Learning—are designed to build familiarity with the text, stimulate questions, focus attention, and enhance speed and comprehension. Although we may call these "reading" speeds, they are also *study speeds* because readers who employ them almost always learn something at each speed that would often be missed at other reading rates.

In each of the first three speed zones, you will learn to increase your proficiency through the use of basic, proven tools of speed-reading. These include such techniques as using hand and finger movements or special straightedge devices to help you establish a steady, rhythmic reading pace. Such pacing will help you avoid regression (reading back over previously covered text) and minimize saccades, or jerky eye movements that impede reading efficiency.[11] You'll also learn how to choose the best reading location and position and establish your own personal reading plan. To maintain an optimum pace as you read, our studies have shown that it's best to avoid notetaking or underlining during the first three passes through the Scriptures.

Other study tools, unique features of this Bible not generally available with other standard editions, include special text features such as an "open," well-spaced format and an exceptionally high number of strategic headings, subheadings, and underlining. These have been designed specifically to help you maximize your reading speed and understanding of the text.

Now, here is a more detailed description of each speed zone. After you learn how each zone works—and after you practice regularly—your reading speed and comprehension should increase almost immediately.*

The First Zone: Light Speed

This first pass through the Bible text will almost certainly take you completely out of your normal reading comfort zone. The reason? You'll be skimming and scanning the text at such a high rate of speed that you can expect to take in no more than about 10 percent of the content, and usually you'll process an even smaller amount.

No, that's *not* a misprint. At the most, in this first phase you will indeed absorb a maximum of only about 10 percent of the information on each page, which typically will amount to a few key geographical references, names of characters, or other isolated facts.

In our seminars, participants often have to be warned about confused or flustered reactions they are likely to experience when first passing through this speed zone. Practically every new student of this method has this disconcerted response. One person even compared the feeling to taking a ride on a scary roller-coaster.

But we always caution students not to walk out of the room during the Light Speed Zone. In fact, this super-fast run-through of one or more books of the Bible is an absolutely essential first step for fast and effective Bible reading and study, and it actually can be a relaxing experience.

How fast should you move while in this Light Speed Zone?

> In the Light Speed Zone, the optimum speed is a *rate of about four seconds per page (two seconds per column), or 15 pages per minute.* (See the speed zone chart at the end of this section.)

Because moving so quickly through written text can be unsettling to those unaccustomed to speed-study techniques, feel free on your first few trial runs to slow this rate to around three to four seconds per column, or six to eight seconds per page. At that lower speed, you'll cover about eight to ten pages per minute. Then, after you become more comfortable moving at this pace, you can increase your speed to the target rate of four seconds per page (two seconds per column).

*Note: Throughout this book, it's assumed that the reader has no problem with dyslexia or any other reading or learning disability. Those with these conditions should seek professional medical advice.

At the preferred, four-seconds-per-page rate for the Light Speed Zone, you will complete *the entire Old and New Testaments in about an hour and a half.* Or if you prefer to limit this skimming-style reading to just one book—Genesis, for instance— you will spend a little over four minutes moving through the book in this first speed zone.

Getting Ready for the Highest Speed. Because of the high speeds involved in this first pass through the text, the greatest challenge many readers find is to turn the pages quickly enough to keep up the pace. As a result, before launching yourself into this first speed zone, you should first "break in" a new *Light Speed Bible* by going systematically through the text and bending the pages carefully back toward the spine so that the book opens easily. If you execute this "back-bending" process every 50 pages or so, the Bible will lie flatter while you read, and the pages will turn more easily.

Another important technique to facilitate your movement during this high-speed first pass is to position yourself physically so that you can turn the pages easily and quickly. This will mean finding a comfortable sitting position and perhaps placing the book on a flat surface so that it doesn't keep shifting or slipping in your hand or on your lap.

Also, most readers find that after turning one page, it's helpful to position the fingers immediately at the top of the *next* page to be turned. For this turning maneuver, you can use your right hand, or you can cradle the top of the text with your left forearm and use your left-hand fingers. Or you can use both hands if that works best for you.

The main idea is to get as comfortable as possible with the fast-turning procedure so that you develop a steady rhythm. The ample margins and other physical features of the *Light Speed Bible* have been designed and produced with these reading and page-turning considerations in mind.

Reaching Your Optimum Rhythm. As already indicated, the most important principle in experiencing the Light Speed Zone is to establish a regular, rhythmic rate of turning the pages and moving the eyes steadily down each column of text. Many readers have also discovered that it's helpful during this high-speed phase to focus on breathing regularly while scanning and page-turning. Feelings of stress and a sense of "working too hard" at reading can increase if you hold your breath or breathe erratically.

For example, you may find it comfortable to breathe out once as you complete one page (two columns); then, take in a breath at the beginning of the next page; next, breathe out again as you scan to the end of that second page and so on. But the breathing pace is up to you, so long as you keep your breathing regular and comfortable.

Finally, paying attention to regular breathing will help you trigger that physiologic antidote to the stress response—the relaxation response (see the previous discussion in section 1). Medical research has actually shown that regular breathing by itself has the capacity to set off the cascade of beneficial bodily chemicals and neu-rotransmitters that counter stress and promote better health and well-being.

Savor the Speed! Even for those who understand the mechanics of employing this Light Speed Zone, a common objection is, "I'm just rushing through the Bible. I'm not really reading anything!"

This comment is partially correct because in this first speed zone you *will* be mov-ing at high speed, and you won't be reading every word. But as you skim through, you will be absorbing the overall structure of the text, gaining familiarity with the factual content, and formulating questions that you will answer as you move into subsequent reading zones.

So remember: this first pass is not the end of the story! Rather, the Light Speed pass prepares you for increasing levels of comprehension and insight that will emerge later. Rather than getting frustrated, always keep in mind your three main goals while in the Light Speed Zone:

Goal # 1: Check the overall structure of the text. A basic goal in the Light Speed Zone is to get an overall sense of the structure of the Bible as a whole, or of a particular book of the Bible. Assume, for instance, that you've decided to read only Genesis. If you didn't know the chapter count before, after this quick pass you'll see that there are 50 chapters in the book. You'll also note that the book begins with the creation and ends with the account of Joseph in Egypt.

Goal # 2: Begin to make use of headings and subheadings. The headings and subheadings of the *Light Speed Bible* have been designed so that if you read them alone, you'll get a good idea—in effect, a summary—of the narrative flow and con-tent of the text.

As you read Genesis, for instance, you will probably note that much more is devoted to the story of Joseph than you realized before—about a quarter of the entire book of Genesis. Also, as your eyes move quickly over every page and focus on a scattering of the headings that punctuate the text, you'll pick up key names such as Adam, Abraham, Rebekah, Jacob, or Joseph. As you utilize the Light Speed Zone with other sections of the Bible, you'll gain a similar overview.

Goal # 3: Begin to formulate questions and goals. Finally, this first, high-speed pass through the text will help you begin the all-important process of *formulating questions* about the Bible that you want to answer in later reading, and *establishing study goals you want to achieve*.

One of the most important principles of efficient study and reading is to approach any written text in a state of high interest with an idea of the facts you want to find, concepts you want to explore, or questions you want to answer. With an alert, atten-tive, and even aggressive approach to the Bible, you'll find that your mind will tend to wander less and you will get maximum benefit from your reading.

In practical terms, here is a list of questions one student formulated for later study while she went through the book of Genesis at Light Speed:

   a. In exactly what sequence did God create the universe, the earth, and earth's creatures?

   b. What was the role of sin or disobedience to God in Genesis and what lessons can I learn?

   c. How *exactly* did Adam and Eve sin?

   d. What were the consequences of sin?

   e. What was the *real* problem between Cain and Abel?

   f. Why was the earth destroyed by a flood?

   g. What was the tower of Babylon (Babel) all about?

   h. Why was Abraham's relationship with God so special?

   i. What can I learn from that relationship?

   j. What kind of a father was Isaac?

   k. Was Jacob the kind of person I would like to have as a friend?

   l. Was Joseph an arrogant kid? How did he grow and mature spiritually as an adult?

Obviously, this particular student had no time to respond to these points in the fast-moving Light Speed Zone. But there was plenty of time to answer them during the next two passes.

As you become more comfortable moving at this very high speed—and *greater comfort will come with practice*—you'll find that your comprehension at this level will steadily increase. One reason is that as you travel again and again through the Bible at Light Speed, your familiarity with the text will mushroom exponentially. At the same time, you'll notice additional connections among different sections of Scripture. For example, one reader reported that at this speed, the subheadings fixed firmly in his mind the fact that Rebekah comes chronologically before Rachel, a sequence the reader had previously mixed up.

But perhaps the most important thing to keep in mind when you're moving through the text in the Light Speed Zone is that this is just the first step in fast, efficient reading. Remember: you'll still have at least two more passes at the text, and perhaps a fourth pass if you choose the optional Meditative Speed Zone. Also, you can repeat the process all over again as often as you like.

The Total Time Advantage. You'll find that when you add up the overall minutes or hours it takes you to move through a particular segment of text in all three speed zones, this *total time will be much faster* than that achieved by going through the text one time at the average reading speed of 200 to 250 words per minute. In fact, those who learn reading techniques at a *Light Speed Bible* seminar typically double or even triple their original speed before the end of one day. Also, comprehension tests show that those who follow the triple-pass approach usually retain more than traditional readers moving at much slower speeds.

Now let's move on to the second speed zone, Landmark Speed, which, though very fast by most standards, may seem to be creeping along after you've completed the Light Speed phase.

The Second Zone: Landmark Speed

This extremely important second pass—reminiscent of the stone landmarks laid by Jacob and Joshua to help the Israelites remember great events or encounters with God—also moves at a fast pace, though one much slower than that of Light Speed. What is the recommended rate for Landmark Speed?

> In the Landmark Speed Zone, the optimum speed is a *rate of about eight seconds per page (four seconds/column), or seven to eight pages per minute.* (See the speed zone chart at the end of this section.)

Many who shift down to this speed zone just after employing the much faster Light Speed rate feel as though they are race horses being restrained by an uncomfortable bridle. In fact, in most *Light Speed Bible* seminars, a number of participants almost always find themselves going through the text during Landmark Speed at about six seconds a page, or well above the recommended rate. The seminar leader may actually have to remind them to slow down. After they finish, the few who simply can't slow down are asked to start going through the assigned passage once again at the Landmark Speed Zone rate until everyone else has caught up with them.

Though the Landmark pace may seem rather slow after Light Speed, reading at the recommended Landmark speed rate of eight seconds per page will move you through the text at a clip of about 4,000 words per minute. At this speed, you will be able to complete *the entire Bible at Landmark Speed in about three to three-and-a-half hours.* Or if you are reading only Genesis, you would make it through the entire book in about nine to ten minutes.

This rate, which is fast but encourages a reasonable level of comprehension, allows your eyes to take in every major "landmark" in the text, including every heading and subheading and most of the strategically underlined words and passages.

Remember: No Regression! Certain additional techniques become important as the reading rate decreases to this slower Landmark Speed Zone level. For one thing, an essential, unwavering law of effective reading is that *you must not regress.* That is, you must not re-read sections of the text that you've already passed through, no matter how strong the temptation. A primary reason for slow, ineffectual reading with lower comprehension levels is the tendency to regress.

"But my mind wandered during that last paragraph!" you may object. "That could have been the key to understanding the whole passage! I have to go back over it!"

In fact, in almost every case, issues or facts contained in the section you missed will be covered again later in the text. Even if they are not, don't forget that this is just your second pass! You will have an opportunity to go back through the text *a third time* during the Learning Speed Zone at a reading rate considerably slower than your current Landmark Speed. In that final pass, you'll be able to look through the passages you missed in more detail.

Also, remember that there is no rule that says you have to limit yourself to reading the Bible three times! In part, that's what the fourth Meditative Speed Zone is all about: it's an invitation to encourage you to move at a snail's place if you like, as you memorize, study, or meditate on certain verses or words.

Ask Additional Questions. Another major purpose of the Landmark Speed Zone is that *you'll be in a strong position to formulate additional questions and study goals.* And remember that tackling the text with good questions or study objectives is an excellent strategy to ensure that you'll read with maximum attention and focus.

So if you think about it, missing some interesting material during the Landmark Speed Zone phase—and not going back to check it out immediately—can actually be a *good* thing. The omission will motivate you to search quickly for specific material in the next zone; also, by assuming that "search mode," you will be in a stronger position to increase your reading speed and study efficiency. In other words, you can expect your inefficient reading or wandering mind to work in your favor!

Hand-Pacing: A Tool to Reinforce Your Reading Rhythm. Another very useful technique for Landmark (and the slower Learning Speed) is the use of the fingers, the entire hand, or a mechanical aid such as a pencil or ruler to pace your reading. By moving your hand or a straight edge down each column, you'll also be less likely to regress in your reading. It's hard to keep that hand or ruler moving down when your eyes are moving upward, in the opposite direction!

Using the hands or a mechanical device as a pacer will help reinforce the rhythm of reading and page-turning. As in Light Speed, your goal should be to establish a regular breathing rate during Landmark Speed and to coordinate your breathing with your hand movements and page-turning. Again, these repetitive physical movements will enhance the relaxing, meditative, and healthful dimension of the *Light Speed Bible* experience.

See All Headings and Subheadings. The more often you enter the Landmark Speed Zone, the more expert you'll become in handling this high rate of reading. After using the triple-pass technique several times, most readers find that in the Landmark Speed Zone, they are able to read all headings and subheadings and can actually "see" the majority of words in the text.

After finishing the Landmark Speed Zone, several seminar participants made these observations:

"Reading all the Gospels at Landmark Speed gave me a much better picture of how hard it was for the disciples to catch on to what Jesus was trying to teach them."

"By focusing on the headings and subheadings, I got the best picture I've ever had of how Genesis is organized and how early history flows through the pages."

"Even though I was moving quickly, for the first time I understood how the inheritance system worked with the tribes of Israel. I saw that Jacob picked Joseph's two children, Manasseh and Ephraim, to receive equal portions with Jacob's other sons. To get this information, all I really had to do was look at the subheadings and underlining."

So in the Landmark Speed Zone, many people find that their comprehension increases significantly. Yet with the book of Genesis, the typical *Light Speed Bible* reader will spend a total of only about 12 to 14 minutes skimming and searching in the first two zones. Or with the book of Luke, the time required for the average person to complete the first two passes is approximately eight to nine minutes.

Finally, keep in mind that the first two zones are only the beginning. A third, extremely significant opportunity for Bible study and comprehension still remains—the Learning Speed Zone.

The Third Zone: Learning Speed

This third zone in the triple-pass strategy—the Learning Speed Zone—involves seeing every word and phrase in the text. What are the time recommendations for the most efficient reading with the greatest comprehension?

> In the Learning Speed Zone the optimum speed is a *rate of about 15 to 30 seconds per column or one to two pages per minute.* As your reading skills improve, your speed will increase from the lower to the upper range of this target rate—and beyond. (See the speed zone chart at the end of this section.)

In this third speed zone, depending on where you are operating in the recommended rate range, you can expect to take about *12 to 24 hours or a little longer to read every word of the Old and New Testaments.*

If you stay in the middle of the targeted reading range for Learning Speed, you'll move through at a pace of 1.5 pages (about 860 words) per minute.[*] In this mid-range, you will read every word of the book of Genesis in about 40 minutes; the entire Bible will require about 16 hours.

An Important Difference. In contrast to the other zones, an important difference with Learning Speed is that your basic goal is not just to take in every subheading and every underlined passage in the text, but *also to see every word and phrase in the Bible.*

The specific reading techniques that will maximize your comprehension and enjoyment of the text during this third pass include some of the same principles suggested under the discussion of Landmark Speed, plus a few additional points. These include:

Don't regress.

As with Landmark Speed, re-reading passages is the deadly enemy of full comprehension and efficient reading, especially at this stage of your study.

Establish a rhythmic pace.

Continue to use your fingers, the edge of your hand, a ruler or other straightedge, or a pencil to pace your eyes steadily down each column on each page. This approach, combined with regular breathing, will promote relaxation, reduce stress, and increase your energy levels and staying power.

Always assume a searching mindset.

In other words, in this third speed zone be on the lookout for answers to the questions or issues you've posed about the text, as well as for new information that might provide spiritual insights.

Listen for God's unexpected messages.

Be alert for passages or stories that suggest practical personal applications of biblical principles to your life or to the lives of friends and loved ones.

For example, you or someone you know may be wrestling with anxiety, but you may not quite remember where passages dealing with this problem are located. Reading at the Learning Speed rate—or even at the faster Landmark Speed—will almost certainly draw your eye to such passages as Matthew 6:25; or to Paul's famous antidote for anxiety in Philippians 4:6-7; or to Peter's short, powerful admonition: "... casting all your care upon Him, because He cares about you" (1 Peter 5:7).

Pray when you hit a "boring" passage.

When you encounter a section that seems uninteresting, such as a genealogical list, a catalog of ancient kings, a description of building materials, or a series of obscure Hebrew laws, immediately say a prayer:

---

*Note: At the mid-range Learning Speed (1.5 pages per minute), the total time needed to read through the entire Bible using all three of the main speed zones—Light, Landmark, and Learning—will be about 20 to 24 hours. Furthermore, you'll read or skim through many passages as often as three times.

"Lord, why did you put this material in here? I really don't think you're trying to turn me away, so show me what this means. Is there any application to my life today?"

You may not receive an immediate or complete answer. But the chances are that you'll start to receive a partial answer, which may be filled in as you meditate on these pages in the days and weeks ahead. And almost certainly, you'll read with more interest and expectancy.

More than one scintillating class has been taught on one set of passages that many new Bible readers skip over as potentially boring, such as Jesus' genealogies. Titles that come to mind could easily serve as questions or ideas formulated during a Light or Landmark Speed pass: "Possible Reasons for the Different Genealogies in Matthew and Luke"; or "Why Did Matthew Include Women in Jesus' Genealogical Line in Matthew?"; or "The Importance of the David Connection in Jesus' Family History."

Obviously, no reader will comprehend or understand every detail of any scriptural text after just three passes. Seasoned Bible students know that doesn't happen even after a lifetime of intensive study and multiple readings of different passages.

Still, after completing the triple-pass strategy only one time, most readers should score at least 70 percent on basic, factual multiple-choice evaluations, such as the quiz on Genesis provided in this instructional section. Other Bible comprehension quiz books are available through the *Light Speed Bible* seminar program.

The more often you read the entire text and check your comprehension through Bible class participation or factual quizzes, the more extensive your knowledge and memory of the Scriptures will become.

Finally, as already suggested, in-depth study of the Bible or leisurely meditation on certain passages, sections, or concepts will require moving at a much slower pace. That's why the *Light Speed Bible* program emphasizes the importance of the fourth speed zone—Meditative Speed—which we describe as "optional" mainly to signal that it can be accommodated to each reader's individual needs.

The Optional Fourth Zone: Meditative Speed

This slower speed zone, which has no suggested time or pacing limits, will suit those who want to spend additional time on a particular verse or passage. Common objectives during these sessions might include:

- in-depth study of one passage;

- deep reflection on a single Bible verse; or

- memorization of particular verses.

In-depth study. After employing the first three speeds, you will almost certainly encounter verses or passages that raise questions that can be answered only through slow, deliberate study. In fact, you might not even notice those passages without first reading them quickly in context.

After reading the entire context surrounding a particular passage, you'll be in a much stronger position to get the most out of in-depth study. For example, in the slow-study phase, you may want to do extensive cross-referencing of certain selected passages with other parts of the Bible. Again, a broad reading background of the entire Bible will greatly enhance your cross-referencing ability.

Also in this slowest speed zone, you may want to turn to commentaries and Bible dictionaries. In addition, unlike the recommendations for the first three passes, we encourage note-taking, outlining, and highlighting for those doing in-depth study in the Meditative Speed Zone.

Deep reflection. Deep reflection or meditation on the Bible may involve spending minutes or even hours focusing on one concept, principle, or verse. Biblical meditation should always be content-based or *linked directly to certain verses or passages of Scripture.* Again, an extensive reading and factual knowledge of the *whole* Bible will give you all sorts of insights and ideas about possible subject matter for meditation.

The Psalms, in particular, provide wonderful guidelines for meditation. For example, take the longest chapter in the Bible, Psalm 119. There, the psalmist tells us we should meditate on God's "precepts" and "ways" (v. 15); His "statutes" (v. 23); His "wonders" (v. 27); His "name" (v. 55); His "teaching" (v. 97); His "decrees" (v. 99); and His "promise" (v. 148).

What is the best way to become familiar with these many precepts, ways, teachings, decrees, and promises of God? Our knowledge of these qualities and communications of God comes primarily from reading *all* of His Word—and comprehending the basic facts of what we read.

Memorization. Verse 11 of Psalm 119 also provides us with perhaps the best rationale for slowing down so that we can commit the Bible to memory: "I have treasured Your word in my heart so that I may not sin against You."

But the Bible is so vast, and our time is so short. How can we select key verses to memorize?

One way is to consult an effective Bible memory plan, such as the Order of St. George Bible Memory Program (Bristol House). Such a program should first suggest memory techniques and then direct you to certain classic, essential verses, such as John 3:16, John 1:12, Romans 3:23, and the Ten Commandments. After you've developed a good foundation of memorization, the program you choose should challenge you to build a much more extensive Bible memory base.

But an important adjunct to any such program should always be a regular *whole Bible reading plan.* By exposing yourself to all of God's word, you'll find that you regularly encounter verses that are especially meaningful to you or someone you love, even though those verses may not be included in any formal memory program. When that happens, you can incorporate those verses as part of your own more personalized memorization plan.

* * *

As a reminder of the various reading speeds, you may find it helpful to consult the following "Speed Zone Chart." This chart summarizes techniques that are helpful in moving through each zone efficiently. Also, in the far right column you'll see the goals commonly linked to each zone—including those for the flexible Meditative Zone, which has no recommended time limits.

The format of the *Light Speed Bible* has been designed for accessibility to the text and content, enhanced reading speed, and maximum comprehension. The next section describes in more detail how this particular Bible makes maximum use of such features as accessible page layout, specially constructed headings and subheadings, and strategic underlining.

Light Speed Bible
Speed Zone Chart

SPEED ZONES	TECHNIQUES	TARGET READING RATE	GOALS
FIRST PASS: *LIGHT SPEED*	Focus on main headings, most sub-headings. Eyes should sweep entire text. Avoid note-taking.	Two seconds per column, *or* four seconds per page, *or* 15 pages per minute.	Get feel of overall text. Understand basic story line from majority of headings and subheadings. Raise key questions.
SECOND PASS: *LANDMARK SPEED*	Focus on all headings, subheadings, and most underlining. Again, eyes sweep entire text. Avoid note-taking.	Four seconds per column, *or* eight seconds per page, *or* seven to eight pages per minute.	Absorb more content. Read all headings, subheadings and underlined passages. Raise more questions.
THIRD PASS: *LEARNING SPEED*	See every word in text. Never regress. Avoid note-taking.	15 to 30 seconds per column, *or* one to two pages per minute.	Read every word in text. Score at least 70% on basic comprehension quiz.
OPTIONAL FOURTH PASS: *MEDITATIVE SPEED*	Reflect on the verse or passage as long as necessary. Take notes or make journal entries. Memorize verses, passages, or Bible organization, such as the books of the Bible in order.	As desired.	Do in-depth study of one verse or passage. In prayer times, meditate on Bible verse or passage. Commit Scripture to memory so that biblical principles become an ingrained part of your daily life.

3.
Designed for Speed and Comprehension

This special Bible is built for speed and accessibility in reading, handling, and comprehension. To this end, the text features:

- Main headings that always signal where the reader is located in a particular passage

- Explanatory subheadings, which, in themselves, help tell an abbreviated story of the main text

- The use of strategic underlining to draw the eye rapidly and efficiently through important biblical content and teachings

- A clear, open layout with optimum horizontal and vertical spacing to facilitate quicker identification of words, phrases, main themes and facts

- The use of boldface for Old Testament quotations in the New Testament

- The use of boxes or rectangles to signal written materials in the text, such as signs that were placed over Jesus on the cross

- An overall text design intended to conform to the latest scientific findings on how page and word presentation can enhance the effect of eye movements, attentiveness, and reading comprehension

Specifically, we have chosen a classic two-column text format, designed to encourage the eyes to travel straight down each column, with minimal need for wide peripheral vision or back-and-forth movement of the eyes on each text line. Using hand or straightedge pacing with this two-column format should help further reduce wasteful, jerky eye movements, which have been associated with slower, ineffective reading. As indicated earlier, certain scientific studies have shown that a major drag on fast, effective reading is "saccadic eye movements," or the tendency of the eye to jump around randomly as you read through a particular text.

In one study[12] the reading pace of a group of readers was tested in two ways. First, they read ordinary pages of printed text. Then, they read using a special reading mechanism that presented the text sequentially, one word or short phrase at a time, with the words always appearing on the same location in a visual field. In technical terms, this is known as "rapid serial visual presentation" or RSVP.[13]

The researchers found that the readers could read significantly faster with the special highlighting device that greatly limited the saccadic eye movements. In fact, almost half of the participants were timed on the device at the *maximum testable rate of more than 1,650 words per minute with 75 percent comprehension!*

Of course, such specialized highlighting devices aren't available for the average Bible reader. But the *Light Speed Bible* is designed to do the next best thing—to keep your eyes moving steadily and sequentially, with as little distraction and as much comprehension as possible, as your hand and eyes move steadily and rhythmically down each column of the text.

Also, in contrast to the format of many "dense" Bible texts, the greater vertical spacing or "leading" between each line in the *Light Speed Bible* has been chosen to facilitate reading speed and understanding, a choice that is consistent with recent findings published in a number of medical and scientific journals.[14]

Finally, most experienced readers know that when they are confronted with a solid block of text containing few paragraphs, subheadings, or other graphics, reading can become a struggle. Whenever possible, we have designed the format with the intention of avoiding such obstacles and making the reading experience easier and more fluid. One of the main tools we've used to achieve these ends has been the careful selection and placement of many headings and subheadings throughout the Bible text.

The Heading-Subheading Advantage

Although all of the above speed features in the design of this Bible are important, the free and abundant use of headings and subheadings may be the *most* important aid to increasing your reading efficiency.

The *Light Speed Bible* employs an unusually large number of headings, subheadings, and underlined passages for several reasons. In the first place, such features tend to stimulate increased interest in the text. Also, they make the details of the text more accessible and draw the reader more quickly and deeply into the narratives and teachings. The presence of so many highlights in the text serves the additional purpose of helping Bible students find buried passages more quickly.

A basic principle in the creation of this Bible has been to write the headings and subheadings in such a way that even if read alone without the underlying text, they will give you a coherent, capsule version of the overall narrative. As a result, many of the headings and subheadings are written as short, action sentences; they are sometimes drafted more like headlines in a newspaper than like normal Bible headings; and they lean toward extra detail in describing the action or main point that follows.

To understand how powerful this approach can be both for learning and fast reading, turn to the next section and look through the list of headings and subheadings in the book of Genesis. These headings and subheadings are taken from the actual text of the *Light Speed Bible*.

4.
Genesis in Headlines

Reading through the following headings and subheadings without even referring to the underlying text will provide you with a capsule version of the narrative of Genesis. In other words, reading *only* the headings and subheadings will inform you about such events and people as the sequence of creation; the early murderers in the Bible; and the life and adventures of Abraham, Isaac, Jacob, and Joseph.

When the headings, along with strategic underlining, are interspersed throughout the text itself, the result is a series of powerful biblical *"landmarks"* that make it much easier to read with greater comprehension and a better sense of the organization of the book.

As a preliminary exercise in using the *Light Speed Bible* methods, read the list this way: First, note the current time (to the second) before you begin to read this list. Then, use your hand to pace your eyes steadily down the page as you read. Don't regress, or look back over what you've previously read. You'll receive further instructions when you finish the list.

Genesis 1

The Creation

First Day: Light and Darkness

Second Day: Waters and Sky

Third Day: Land and Plants

Fourth Day: Sun and Moon

Fifth Day: Fish and Birds

Sixth Day: Land Animals, Humans

Genesis 2

Seventh Day: Rest

Man and Woman in Eden

Man Created

Garden Planted in Eden

Tree of Knowledge

Woman Created

Genesis 3

The Man and Woman Sin

The Serpent Strikes

The Woman and Adam Eat

Adam and the Woman Hide from God

God Punishes the Serpent

God Punishes the Woman

God Punishes Adam

Adam Names Eve
God Banishes Humans from the Garden

Genesis 4

Cain, Abel, and Seth
Cain versus Abel
Cain Banished
Cain's Children
Lamech: Another Killer
Seth Born

Genesis 5

From Adam to Noah
Enoch Never Died
Methuselah: the Oldest Man
Noah Born

Genesis 6

Noah and the Flood
Noah and the Ark

Genesis 7

The Flood Covers the Earth
Impact of the Deluge

Genesis 8

The Flood Recedes
The Lord's Promise

Genesis 9

God's Covenant with Noah
Noah's Sons
Noah Drunk
Noah's Curses and Blessings

Genesis 10

The Table of Nations
Descendants of Japheth
Descendants of Ham
Descendants of Shem

Genesis 11

The Tower of Babel
From Shem to Abram
The Family of Terah

Genesis 12

The Call of Abram
Abram Leaves Haran with Sarai and Lot

Abram and Sarai in Egypt
Pharaoh in Trouble with Sarai

<u>Genesis 13</u>
Abram and Lot Separate

<u>Genesis 14</u>
Abram Rescues Lot
Melchizedek Blesses Abram

<u>Genesis 15</u>
The Lord's Covenant with Abram

<u>Genesis 16</u>
The Birth of Ishmael
Angel's Promise to Hagar

<u>Genesis 17</u>
Abram is Named Abraham
The Sign of Circumcision
Sarai is Named Sarah

<u>Genesis 18</u>
A Son Promised to Sarah
The Three "Men"
Sarah Laughs
Abraham's Plea for Sodom
Abraham Negotiates with God

<u>Genesis 19</u>
Sodom and Gomorrah Destroyed
The Angels are Threatened
Sodom Condemned
Lot's Wife
Lot and His Daughters

<u>Genesis 20</u>
Abraham Deceives Abimelech

<u>Genesis 21</u>
The Birth of Isaac
Hagar and Ishmael Sent Away
God Saves Ishmael
A Treaty with Abimelech

<u>Genesis 22</u>
Abraham's Obedience Tested
Abraham Prepares to Sacrifice Isaac

Genesis 23
The Burial of Sarah
Abraham's Family Tomb at Hebron

Genesis 24
Isaac Marries Rebekah
Abraham's Servant Prays for Help

God's Answer: Rebekah

Family Marriage Discussions

Rebekah is Given to Isaac

Isaac Loves Rebekah

Genesis 25
Abraham's Other Wife and Sons
The Death of Abraham
Ishmael's Descendants
The Birth of Jacob and Esau
Esau Sells His Birthright
The Infamous Trade: Stew for the Family Future

Genesis 26
Isaac Deceives Abimelech
God's Promise to Isaac

Like Father, Like Son

Conflict over Water Rights
Isaac Moves

Isaac Moves Again—and God Appears

A Treaty with Abimelech
Esau Marries

Genesis 27
Jacob Steals Esau's Blessing
Jacob's Disguise

Jacob Deceives His Father, Isaac

Esau Devastated—and Enraged

Jacob Flees to Paddan-Aram
Esau Plots to Kill Jacob

Genesis 28
Jacob Flees

Esau Marries Again

Jacob's Dream at Bethel
God's Promise to Jacob

Jacob's Altar at Bethel

Genesis 29
Jacob Arrives at Paddan-Aram
Rachel Appears
Jacob Marries Leah and Rachel
Jacob's Marriage Deal with Laban
Laban Tricks Jacob
Jacob Finally Gets Rachel
Jacob's Many Children
Leah's First Four Sons

Genesis 30
Rachel Wants Children
Jacob's Two Sons by Bilhah
Jacob's Two Sons by Zilpah
Leah's Deal with Rachel: Two More Sons
Rachel's First Son—Joseph
Jacob's Flocks and Wealth Increase
Jacob's Genetic Experiment

Genesis 31
Jacob Flees from Laban
Jacob Plots His Escape
Laban Pursues Jacob
Laban Accuses Jacob
Jacob Angry at Laban
Jacob's Treaty with Laban

Genesis 32
Jacob Sends Gifts to Esau
Jacob Struggles with God
Jacob Becomes Israel

Genesis 33
Jacob and Esau Make Peace

Genesis 34
Revenge against Shechem
Dinah Raped
Shechem Wants to Marry Dinah
Jacob's Sons Deceive Shechem
Swords of Simeon and Levi
Jacob Rebukes His Sons

Genesis 35
Jacob's Return to Bethel
God Blesses Jacob
The Deaths of Rachel and Isaac

Benjamin Born, Rachel Dies

Twelve Sons of Jacob

Isaac's Death

Genesis 36

Descendants of Esau

Inhabitants of Seir

Rulers of Edom

Leaders of Clans of Esau

Genesis 37

Joseph's Dreams

Joseph Angers His Brothers

Jacob Rebukes Joseph

Joseph Sold into Slavery

Jacob Mourns Joseph

Joseph Sold to Potiphar

Genesis 38

Judah and Tamar

Disobedience of Er and Onan

Judah's Deceit

Tamar's Trickery

Tamar's Relations with Judah Revealed

Tamar's Twins

Genesis 39

Joseph in Potiphar's House

Trouble: Potiphar's Wife

Joseph Put in Prison

Genesis 40

Joseph Interprets Two Dreams

The Cup-bearer's Dream

The Baker's Dream

Genesis 41

Pharaoh's Dreams

Pharaoh Seeks an Interpretation

Pharaoh Sends for Joseph

Joseph Interprets

Joseph Made Ruler of Egypt

Seven Years of Plenty

Joseph's Two Sons

Seven Years of Famine

Now that you have reached the end of the list of the Genesis headings and sub-headings, note the minute and second that you've finished. Probably it's taken you about four to five minutes to complete the list, or about the time required to skim-read the entire book of Genesis at Light Speed.

Next, spend a few moments reflecting on what you've read. What new questions about the book came to your mind? What did you notice about the structure of the book? What important people "jumped" out at you from the text? What people or events piqued your interest in a new way? Did God seem to be speaking to you personally at any point?

You have now taken the first step in developing a fresh overview of the book of Genesis, but much more remains. For a fuller experience with this first book of the Bible—and with the *Light Speed Bible* approach—move on to the next section.

5.
Beginning at the Beginning:
Applying Your Skills to Genesis

For a further taste of how the *Light Speed Bible* actually works in practice, let's now take a trial run through the book of Genesis, using the techniques and principles described in this introduction.

All you need to test yourself is a timer, watch, or clock that measures seconds; a pen or pencil; and piece of paper to monitor your speed in each of the three speed zones.

The typical reader will take about two-and-a-half hours to get through Genesis one time at an average reading speed of 250 words per minute. If you read at the lower end of the average range, about 200 words per minute, it would take you even longer, about three hours, to get through Genesis once.

But with the *Light Speed Bible* approach, you won't have to struggle through the text for almost three hours. Instead, using the triple-pass technique outlined in the previous pages, your total time in reading Genesis should amount to only about 45 minutes to one hour. Furthermore, you will go through the text *three times* at declining rates of speed.

If you are interested in calculating your words-per-minute reading speed for all or different segments of Genesis, here are a couple of key average word counts to help you out. Although the exact number of words on each page varies, you can assume that the average wordage per page is 575. So if it takes you a minute to read one page, you're going at a rate of about 575 words per minute; or if you cover two pages, you're moving at the rate of about 1,150 words per minute.

Now, prepare for a trial run through the first book of the Bible. Sit in a comfortable position, with the Bible resting on your lap or a flat surface so that your eyes are at their usual reading distance from the pages. The text should be firmly in place so that both hands are free to move as you read. Be sure the lighting is right for easy reading. Your only necessary equipment is the timing device, pencil, and paper to monitor your speed and progress.

You're now ready to move on to *Step 1.* (*Note:* As you move through each step with Genesis, consult the "Speed Zone Chart" summarizing each of the three reading speed zones at the end of section 2.)

Step 1: First, Read Genesis at Light Speed

Write down the exact time—to the second—that you plan to begin reading. Now, put your pencil down. (Remember, during the first three speed zones, it's best not to use writing instruments that could tempt you to take notes. There will be plenty of time for note-taking later if you elect to use the Meditative Speed Zone.)

Now, you're ready to go.

Begin skim-reading at Light Speed when the seconds indicator reaches the starting time that you have chosen. You should spend *only about two seconds on each column, or four seconds per page*. The more you practice the *Light Speed Bible* method, the more accurate you'll become at timing the pace of your reading without the use of a watch or clock. But the main idea with this trial run through Genesis is to get used to what the different speed zones feel like at the recommended reading ranges.

After you finish page one, move on to page two; repeat your fast skimming of that page; and then go to page three. To facilitate a relaxed physical response throughout your body, breathe in a steady, comfortable rhythm and proceed with regular page-turning and up-and-down eye movements.

Also, remember the basic principles of effective speed-study reading—especially avoiding regression, or looking back over text that you've already covered.

At this fast pace don't worry if you feel at any point that you're losing track of the narrative. In the Light Speed Zone your main purpose is *not* to read all or even most of the text. Rather, your goals are threefold:

> *Goal #1:* Get a "feel" for *how the overall text is constructed*, including the length of the book, the number of chapters, and the general movement of the main narrative.

> *Goal #2:* See and understand *as many headings and subheadings as possible.* This approach will jumpstart your ability to comprehend subject matter during later passes through the text. (In section 4 you've already been exposed to the same list of headings and subheadings that you're about to read.)

> *Goal # 3:* Begin to *raise questions* that you'll try to answer in the next two passes because approaching a text with good questions is one of the most powerful secrets to reading fast with high comprehension. (For examples of questions, check the samples for Genesis listed in section 2.)

Above all, don't worry if you feel a little uncomfortable. It's inevitable that you'll sense some lack of control over the text at this super-fast speed. In fact, on the first few attempts, the Light Speed Zone reading rate pushes almost *everyone* out of his or her comfort zone. But after a little practice skimming at this high rate, you'll begin to reap considerable benefits, which will carry over to the next two passes.

By maintaining this rate through all of Genesis, you will cover about 37,000 words—the length of some short books—*in a little more than four minutes!* Yet with the *Light Speed Bible* method, you'll start to pick up important information from the text, and at the same time you can look forward to the opportunity to read back over the text *at least two additional times* at Landmark and Learning Speeds. In other words, it's helpful to keep perspective on the limited goals that you're trying to accomplish in this first speed zone.

At the end of this first pass, record exactly how long you took to move through the entire text. Keeping track of your times, especially at the beginning of this learning experience, will improve your accuracy in estimating how fast you're moving during later reading sessions. Also, by monitoring your progress on paper, you'll be more motivated to improve your skill and performance in subsequent readings.

On your first try, the chances are you won't make it through the entire book of Genesis in exactly the target range of four minutes. Even those experienced with this program may move a little slower than the Light Speed Zone target rate of four seconds per page. But eventually, as you practice the techniques and move through the text multiple times with the triple-pass approach, you'll find Light Speed becoming much more comfortable. It's also likely that you'll find God speaking to you in different ways each time you go through sections of the Bible at this unusual pace.

Step 2: Next, Read Genesis at Landmark Speed

On this second pass through the text, you should once again time yourself. But now, you'll be moving at a much slower rate—*about four seconds per column, or eight seconds per page* (a rate that translates to about seven to eight pages per minute). This should take you through the entire book of Genesis in about eight to nine minutes.

At this pace, you'll be able to pick up much more information than you could while moving at Light Speed, and, as a consequence, your comprehension will improve significantly. Also, you'll begin to formulate additional questions that you'll want to answer in the third speed zone, Learning Speed.

Your goal in the Landmark Speed Zone should be to focus on every heading and subheading in Genesis and on many of the strategically underlined words and passages. Many *Light Speed Bible* readers find that the second or third time they read a particular segment at Landmark Speed, they actually are able to see most words, even though they don't necessarily fully comprehend or absorb everything they see. This increased comprehension results from greater familiarity with the text and also improved skills in navigating the Landmark Speed Zone.

In this second pass, employ the tools and principles of effective Landmark Speed reading described in section 2. Here is a reminder of the basics:

- Use hand and finger movements or other physical pacing techniques to guide your eye steadily down each column at the target speed range of the Landmark Zone.

- Avoid regression.

- Don't underline or take notes.

To develop skill at estimating the number of seconds it takes you to finish each page, it may be helpful at this stage to check your watch occasionally as you read. When you finish your reading of Genesis at this pace, you should check your final time to see precisely how close you've come to the goal of about eight to nine minutes for the entire book.

If you hit the Landmark Speed Zone target of eight seconds per page exactly, you will make it through the entire book of Genesis in about eight-and-a-half minutes. In that case, you'll be moving at a reading rate of more than 4,300 words per minute, a considerable improvement over the average person's reading speed of 200 to 250 words per minute.

But still, when you move at such a fast speed in this early stage of your training, you'll miss significant facts and points in the text. All that will change and comprehension will soar when you move to the third speed zone.

Step 3: Finally, Read Genesis at Learning Speed

Again, have your timer and other recording materials at hand, and assume the same comfortable position with good lighting that you've been using in the first two zones.

As with the first two speed zones, it's best to avoid taking notes or underlining the text during Learning Speed, though you may want to insert a quick check mark in the margin to help you find a passage that you'd like to study later in more depth. Our studies have shown that taking notes or extensive underlining can reduce reading speed by half or even two-thirds of the time that can be achieved without such pencil use.

At Learning Speed, your pace will seem almost leisurely, even though you'll be reading in the range of *15 to 30 seconds per column, or about one to two pages per minute*. At the fast end of this range, or two pages per minute, you could finish all of Genesis in a little more than 30 minutes. That means you would be reading every word and phrase of the text at a rate of about 1,150 words per minute.

Furthermore, as you develop your skills, reading through the entire text of Genesis three times—at the fastest recommended rate in *all three* speed zones—will require *only about 45 minutes or a little longer.* In contrast, you'll recall, completing Genesis just once at an untrained, high-average reading rate of 250 words per minute would require about two-and-a-half hours, or more than triple the reading time required for the *Light Speed Bible* method.

In this third speed zone, even though the slowest recommended reading rate is about 575 words per minute, some students move quickly up to the 700 to 1000 w.p.m. range or even faster. Others may feel more comfortable increasing their speed at a somewhat slower pace.

But whatever approach you choose, when you use the *Light Speed Bible* program, you will move *much* faster than the average reading speed. And most likely, you'll feel at least as comfortable—and perhaps more comfortable—than you did when reading more slowly. Most important of all, you'll expose your mind and spirit to the word of God with greater frequency.

Every Word on Every Page. At Learning Speed, your objective is to take in every subheading and every underlined passage in Genesis and to see every word on every page. The very first time you try this speed, you will find that you are learning things about the Bible that you never knew before. As you move at this faster pace, new trends and relationships among facts will jump out at you.

For example, one student who had just read the Genesis text noticed for the first time that "light and darkness" were created on the first day of Creation, while the "sun and moon" were introduced on the fourth day. This observation led to further study as the student explored possible resolutions to this puzzle.

Another reader, who had studied the Bible for years, noted during a *Light Speed Bible* session that Lamech, one of Cain's descendants, was also a killer.

"Murder apparently ran in the family!" he said.

Still another reader was impressed that the patriarch Isaac seemed constitutionally oriented toward avoiding conflict. In Genesis 26, for instance, after a conflict over water rights, he moved several times to avoid direct confrontations. This insight led the student to do a further "character analysis" of Isaac and the other patriarchs.

The Comprehension Paradox. Practically every speed-reading program and course has supported the counterintuitive finding that reading faster actually enhances comprehension. This benefit highlights what we call the "comprehension paradox," which can be stated this way: *as you spend less time on each page, your knowledge of the contents of that page tends to increase—at least up to a certain point.*

After employing the triple-pass technique only one time, you will probably find that your comprehension of Bible content and context improves markedly. Specifically, your goal after moving through the Learning Speed Zone should be to score at least 70 percent on any basic Bible comprehension quiz that relates to the subject matter you've read.

So now that you have executed a triple-pass through all of Genesis, it's time to take the next step. How much do you recall? To find out, tackle the medium-hard Genesis Quiz in the next section.

6.
Test Your Comprehension:
A Genesis Quiz

This final section of this introduction includes the following 50-question, multiple-choice quiz on the book of Genesis. Answers, with references to appropriate Bible sources, are listed at the end of the quiz.

This quiz and others offered by the *Light Speed Bible* program serve several purposes by providing:

1. A means of testing your Bible comprehension *after* you read through the text using the triple-pass technique.

2. A tool that can be used *before* you read the Bible to help you frame issues and questions for later reading.

   Encountering preliminary questions that you can't answer will put you in more of a searching mode—and make the reading process more efficient and interesting.

3. An *ongoing* learning mechanism—or a test that you can take over and over to refresh your memory about Bible facts.

   We find that there are significant benefits when a person misses a particular question and then learns the correct answer, especially if he or she is exposed a number of times to the same question. In such cases, the individual rarely forgets the particular fact or teaching being tested.

   Or to use the words of the psalmist, the reading program plus the quiz can help you "hide in your heart" certain facts, concepts, or verses (Psalm 119:11).

4. A *fresh, detailed overview* of the organization of Genesis and other books, as well as the book's sequence of events.

   This knowledge will greatly enhance your ability to move quickly and accurately to different parts of a particular book, as well as through the Bible as a whole, during both devotional reading and in-depth study sessions.

   Note: Tests on other books of the Bible, including tests with varying levels of difficulty, are available through the *Light Speed Bible* program. (For contact information, see the box following the Genesis quiz.)

The level of difficulty of this comprehension test on Genesis is *medium-hard*. Some seasoned Bible students will be able to answer certain questions without even reading the text for this exercise because they have already read it many times before. On the other hand, most people will require a fresh reading to maximize their scores.

To find your score, multiply the number of questions you answer correctly by two. In other words, if you get 38 correct, you would multiply 38 times 2 for a score of 76.

A score of 90 or above is excellent; 80–89 is good; and 70–79 is satisfactory. But don't worry if you fail to reach the 70 level on your first try. First of all, this is not an easy test: that's why it has been designated as "medium-hard."

Also, remember that everyone begins at a different starting point in terms of personal Bible knowledge. Those who have been studying the Bible all their lives will be much more likely to score well than those who are reading the Scriptures for the first time. If this is just your first or second reading of Genesis and you get more than half of these relatively difficult questions right, you've made a good start in expanding your Bible knowledge.

In any event, by employing the *Light Speed Bible* strategy several times a year or more often, you'll find your Bible knowledge increasing dramatically, regardless of where you begin.

Now here is the medium-hard Genesis Quiz. You should allot 25 minutes to complete the 50 questions, or about 30 seconds per question.

Try to answer all the questions, but put a question mark next to those you're not sure about. That way, even if you get the answer right, you can go back over doubtful answers and firm up your knowledge. When you're finished, check all your answers against the answer page and consult the references to see exactly what the Bible text says.

THE GENESIS QUIZ

(Difficulty Level: Medium-Hard)

When answering, choose only one letter for each question.

1. What did God do on the first day of creation?
   a. He rested.
   b. He created the sun and moon.
   c. He separated the light from the darkness.
   d. He made the sky.
   e. He made the dry ground.

2. What did God do on the fifth day of creation?
   a. He made the fish.
   b. He made the dry land.
   c. He created chimpanzees and other non-human primates.
   d. He rested from his labors.
   e. He created the seed-bearing plants.

3. What did God tell Adam and Eve that they must not eat?
   a. A certain apple.
   b. All fruit in the garden of Eden.
   c. Fruit from the tree of life.
   d. Fruit offered by the serpent.
   e. Fruit from the tree of the knowledge and good and evil.

4. What curse did God place on the serpent?
   a. That he would be cast out of heaven.
   b. That he would have to crawl on his belly.
   c. That he would no longer be able to trick humans.
   d. That he would be known as Satan.
   e. That he would eventually be cast into the eternal fiery pit.

5. Cain became very angry because
   a. He was younger and had fewer blessings than his brother Abel.
   b. God loved Abel more.
   c. God had no regard for Cain and his offering.
   d. Adam showed favoritism toward Abel.
   e. Abel provoked him.

6. Lamech was
   a. A killer.
   b. A son of Cain.
   c. A son of Seth.

    d.   A musician.

    e.   The first metal-worker

7. Which of the following statements about Methuselah is UNtrue?

    a.   Was in the ancestral line of Seth.

    b.   Was Noah's grandfather.

    c.   Lived 969 years.

    d.   Held the biblical record for being the longest-living man.

    e.   None of the above—i.e., all statements are true.

8. Which of the following is NOT listed as one of the reasons that God decided to destroy the world with a flood?

    a.   The thoughts of humans were evil.

    b.   There was not one righteous person left on earth.

    c.   Violence was everywhere.

    d.   Corruption was everywhere.

    e.   None of the above—i.e., all are listed as reasons God decided to destroy the earth.

9. While Noah was in the ark, the rain fell on the earth for

    a.   One year.

    b.   Seven days.

    c.   Five months.

    d.   30 days and 30 nights.

    e.   40 days and 40 nights.

10. After the flood, God promised Noah

    a.   That the earth would only be destroyed again by fire.

    b.   That He would never destroy the earth again.

    c.   That He would never destroy anyone again by a flood.

    d.   That His rainbow would be a sign to Noah and every living creature of His promise not to destroy all living things again by a flood.

    e.   That His rainbow would be placed in the clouds as a permanent sign of His love for all peoples.

11. What was the immediate result of Ham's viewing of his father Noah's nakedness?

    a.   God cursed Ham.

    b.   Ham's brothers, Shem and Japheth, reprimanded Ham.

    c.   Noah announced a curse against Ham.

    d.   Noah announced a curse against Canaan.

    e.   God labeled drunkenness a sin.

12. After God confused human language at the tower of Babylon (Babel),

   a. People scattered over all the earth.
   b. The richness of human language encouraged humans to respect other cultures.
   c. It became impossible for people to form tribes or nations.
   d. Military conquest of other lands became unattainable.
   e. Respect for God's power increased significantly.

13. Abram was a descendant of

   a. Cain.
   b. Japeth.
   c. Shem.
   d. Ham.
   e. Lot.

14. God's blessings bestowed on Abram included:

   a. A promise that all peoples of the earth would be blessed through him.
   b. A promise of a great name.
   c. A promise that those who treated Abram with contempt would be cursed.
   d. All of the above.
   e. Only two of the above.

15. When a dispute broke out between the herdsmen of Abram and Lot,

   a. Abram ordered Lot to leave Canaan and take land in the Jordan Valley.
   b. Lot ordered Abram to stay in Canaan while he (Lot) took more fertile land.
   c. Pharaoh intervened and divided the land between them.
   d. The kings of Sodom and Gomorrah influenced Lot to join them.
   e. Abram gave Lot the right to choose the land where he would live.

16. After Abram rescued Lot from King Chedorlaomer and his allies,

   a. The king of Sodom attacked Abram.
   b. The king of Sodom offered Lot all the goods that Abram had recovered.
   c. King Melchizedek rewarded Abram with a tenth of all the goods that he (Abram) had recovered.
   d. Abram gave King Melchizedek a tenth of the goods that he (Abram) had captured.
   e. Abram built an altar to God.

17. God declared Abram righteous because

    a. He was the most righteous man in the land.
    b. He defended his family and his principles.
    c. He had faith.
    d. He had been chosen to lead his people to a promised land.
    e. He was the legitimate heir of Seth.

18. Ishmael was Abram's

    a. Nephew.
    b. Faithful servant.
    c. Son by Sarai.
    d. Son by Keturah, his wife after Sarai died.
    e. Son by Hagar.

19. God changed Abram's name to Abraham because He said Abram would be:

    a. The father of many nations.
    b. The ancestor of the Messiah.
    c. The mightiest of all ancient warriors.
    d. The main Old Testament example of faith.
    e. The first leader of Israel.

20. The outward sign of God's covenant or great promise to Abraham was

    a. Baptism of newborn children.
    b. Circumcision of all males immediately after birth.
    c. Circumcision of all males on the eighth day after birth.
    d. Circumcision of males and females.
    e. Dedication of new born children in the tabernacle.

21. When God told Abraham that his wife Sarai's name would be changed to Sarah and that she would give birth to a son even though she was 90 years old, Abraham:

    a. Laughed.
    b. Thanked God.
    c. Built an altar to God.
    d. Danced "to the Lord."
    e. Organized a great banquet.

22. God's promise of a son to Abraham was confirmed during:

    a. A visit by two male visitors.
    b. A visit by three male visitors.
    c. A visit by two angels in shining garments.
    d. A message to Abraham in a dream.
    e. A special vision of Sarah.

23. After an intense discussion with Abraham, God said that He:

    a. Would save Sodom and Gomorrah if only one righteous man could be found there.
    b. Would save Sodom and Gomorrah if only ten righteous men could be found there.
    c. Would not save Sodom and Gomorrah under any circumstances because they were so evil.
    d. Would consider saving Sodom and Gomorrah if Abraham continued to pray and lead a righteous life.
    e. Would save only Lot and his relatives and righteous friends—so long as they all promised never to sin again.

24. More than once, Abraham tried to protect himself by telling political rulers:

    a. That Sarah was his servant.
    b. That he and Sarah were divorced.
    c. That Sarah was his sister.
    d. That Sarah was his first cousin.
    e. That Sarah was Lot's wife.

25. After God told Abraham to offer his son Isaac as a sacrifice, Abraham

    a. Asked God to have mercy.
    b. Told Isaac what God had commanded.
    c. Sacrificed his son.
    d. Took his knife to kill Isaac.
    e. Brought a sacrificial ram up onto the mountain.

26. Abraham's family tomb was at

    a. The cave of Machpelah near Hebron in the land of Canaan, though Sarah was not buried there.
    b. The cave of Machpelah near Hebron in the land of Canaan, where Sarah was also buried.
    c. The cave of Machpelah at Ephraim in the land of Canaan, though Sarah was not buried there.
    d. The cave of Machpelah at Ephraim in the land of Canaan, where Sarah was also buried.
    e. The cave of Machpelah at Bethel in the land of Canaan, where all of Abraham's descendants were buried.

27. Israel's other name was

    a. Abraham.
    b. Isaac.
    c. Jacob.
    d. Joseph.
    e. Shem.

28. Isaac's wife was named

    a. Rachel.
    b. Rebekah.
    c. Sarah.
    d. Leah.
    e. Bilhah.

29. Jacob was

    a. An only child.
    b. One of twelve brothers.
    c. One of three half-brothers.
    d. An elder twin.
    e. A younger twin.

30. Jacob was accused of deceiving which of the following people twice?

    a. Abraham.
    b. Isaac.
    c. Esau.
    d. Laban.
    e. Rebekah.

31. Which of the following people is never recorded by Genesis as engaging in deception?

    a. Israel.
    b. Lamech.
    c. Abraham.
    d. Isaac.
    e. Laban.

32. Choose the correct chronological order, from first mention in Genesis to last, of the following women:

    a. Rachel, Rebekah, Sarai, Hagar, Tamar, Asenath.
    b. Sarai, Hagar, Rachel, Rebekah, Tamar, Asenath.
    c. Sarai, Rebekah, Tamar, Asenath, Rachel, Hagar.
    d. Sarai, Hagar, Rebekah, Rachel, Tamar, Asenath.
    e. Sarai, Hagar, Rachel, Rebekah, Tamar, Asenath.

33. Jacob argued or struggled with

    a. Laban.
    b. Esau.
    c. God.
    d. His sons.
    e. All of the above (a-d).

34. Jacob's sons, Simeon and Levi,

    a. Killed Shechem and Hamor.
    b. Deceived Shechem and Hamor.
    c. Became enraged when their sister, Dinah, was raped.
    d. Plundered the town where Dinah was raped.
    e. All of the above (a-d).

35. The last of Jacob's sons to be born was

    a. Ephraim
    b. Joseph.
    c. Benjamin.
    d. Asher.
    e. Dan.

36. Esau's other name was

    a. Ishmael.
    b. Seir.
    c. Korah.
    d. Beor.
    e. Edom

37. Joseph angered his brothers because of

    a. Jacob's partiality to Joseph.
    b. Joseph's apparent claim to be their ruler.
    c. Joseph's dreams.
    d. All of the above (a-c).
    e. Two of the above (a-c).

38. Tamar, who is also mentioned in the genealogy of Jesus (Matthew 1:3),

    a. Was the wife of one of Judah's son Er.
    b. Slept with Judah's son Onan.
    c. Was the mother of two of Judah's own children.
    d. Posed as a prostitute.
    e. All of the above (a-d).

39. Joseph was thrown into prison because

    a. The baker hated his dream interpretations.
    b. Potiphar found him to be an incompetent administrator.
    c. He was accused of a sexual offense.
    d. Pharaoh's staff regarded him as dangerous.
    e. He was accused of stealing.

40. Pharaoh called Joseph before him

    a. To interpret one of Pharaoh's dreams.
    b. To interpret two of Pharaoh's dreams.

    c.   Because he had heard Joseph was a smart administrator.

    d.   To stand trial on charges he had been disrespectful to Egyptian officials.

    e.   To award him a silver cup.

41. After Joseph became ruler of Egypt,

    a.   He was placed over everyone, including Pharaoh.

    b.   He faced seven years of famine and then seven years of plenty.

    c.   He had two sons, Manasseh and Ephron.

    d.   He bought all of the land of Egypt for Pharaoh.

    e.   He made five of his brothers his slaves.

42. When Joseph first encountered his brothers in Egypt, he

    a.   Welcomed them as long-lost members of his family.

    b.   Accused them.

    c.   Put five of them in prison.

    d.   Put a silver cup in Benjamin's luggage.

    e.   Asked about the welfare of his father, Jacob.

43. When the brothers returned to Egypt for a second visit after seeing their father, Jacob,

    a.   They brought Benjamin with them to a banquet thrown by Joseph.

    b.   They left Benjamin at home because Jacob was afraid for his welfare.

    c.   They tried to deceive Joseph by pretending that Benjamin had another name.

    d.   They offered to give Benjamin to the Egyptians in return for their own safe passage.

    e.   They were surprised because Joseph wept in front of them after he saw Benjamin.

44. When Pharaoh heard that Joseph's brothers had come to Egypt, he

    a.   Threatened to put them in prison.

    b.   Cautioned Joseph that family matters shouldn't distract him from his duties in Egypt.

    c.   Invited Jacob to Egypt.

    d.   Arranged for Jacob and his family to become his special slaves in Egypt.

    e.   Said they would be given all the food they needed as soon as they turned over their possessions to Pharaoh.

45. Which of the following was NOT a son of Jacob?

    a.   Levi.

    b.   Issachar.

    c.   Zebulun.

    d.   Gad.

    e.   Ephraim.

46. Jacob showed the greatest favor to

    a. Simeon.
    b. Levi.
    c. Ephraim.
    d. Manasseh.
    e. Reuben.

47. Which of the following did NOT inherit an equal portion of Jacob's land in Canaan?

    a. Gad.
    b. Ephraim.
    c. Manasseh.
    d. Simeon.
    e. Joseph.

48. After arriving in Egypt, Jacob's family settled in the land of

    a. Shiloh.
    b. Alexandria.
    c. Goshen.
    d. Hyskos.
    e. Paran.

49. When Jacob died,

    a. Joseph buried him in Egypt.
    b. Joseph buried him in Egypt, but instructed that Jacob's bones be taken to Canaan later and buried with his ancestors.
    c. Pharaoh presided over his burial at a state funeral in Egypt.
    d. Joseph left Egypt with many chariots and senior officers of Egypt and buried Jacob's body with his ancestors in Canaan.
    e. With Pharaoh's blessing, Joseph sent his brothers back to Canaan with Jacob's body, and they (the brothers) buried Jacob there with his ancestors.

50. After Jacob's death and burial

    a. Joseph's brothers found they had lost all fear of Joseph.
    b. Joseph agreed with Pharaoh that his brothers should become slaves.
    c. Joseph told his brothers, "What you planned for evil, God chose to punish."
    d. Joseph asked the people of Israel to take his bones with them when they finally left Egypt.
    e. Joseph died immediately, without seeing his grandchildren.

ANSWERS TO THE GENESIS QUIZ

(Difficulty Level: Medium-Hard)

1. c (Gn 1:4)	26. b (Gn 23:19-20)
2. a (Gn 1:20)	27. c (Gn 32:28)
3. e (Gn 2:17)	28. b (Gn 24:67)
4. b (Gn 3:14)	29. e (Gn 25:26)
5. c (Gn 4:5)	30. c (Gn 27:36)
6. a (Gn 4:23)	31. b (Gn 4:19; 5:25-31)
7. e (Gn 5)	32. d (Gn 11:29–41:45
8. b (Gn 6:9)	33. e (Gn 27–42)
9. e (Gn 7:12)	34. e (Gn 34)
10. d (Gn 9:13-15)	35. c (Gn 35:18)
11. d (Gn 9:25)	36. e (Gn 36:1)
12. a (Gn 11:9)	37. d (Gn 37)
13. c (Gn 11:10-26)	38. e (Gn 38)
14. d (Gn 12:2-3)	39. c (Gn 39:14)
15. e (Gn 13:9)	40. b (Gn 41:1-7)
16. d (Gn 14:20)	41. d (Gn 47:20)
17. c (Gn 15:6)	42. b (Gn 42:9)
18. e (Gn 16:15)	43. a (Gn 43:29)
19. a (Gn 17:5)	44. c (Gn 45:18)
20. c (Gn 17:12)	45. e (Gn 48)
21. a (Gn 17:17)	46. c (Gn 48:17-20)
22. b (Gn 18)	47. e (Gn 48)
23. b (Gn 18:32)	48. c (Gn 47:27)
24. c (Gn 12:19; 20:2)	49. d (Gn 50:7-13)
25. d (Gn 22:10)	50. d (Gn 50:25)

ENDNOTES

1. Psalm 119:105. See also 1 John 1:5; James 1:17; Psalm 27:1; John 8:12; 2 Corinthians 4:4.

2. George Gallup, Jr. *The Bible and the American People* (Princeton, NJ: The Princeton Religion Research Center, 2001).

3. Barna research is available at www.barna.org.

4. Canadian Bible Society, Toronto, ON. Published online at http//fredericton.anglican.org/cbs/faithcbh.html.

5. From a 2001 market research survey by TNS *Sofres*, cited in an April 29, 2003, release by the Seventh-day Adventist Church in Paris.

6. *Contemporary Educational Psychology* 24(2) (1999): 156–165. *Journal of General Psychology* 117(2) (1990): 153–9. *Journal of the American Optometry Association* 70(3) (1999): 171–81.

7. *Journal of Psychosomatic Research* 36(4) (1992): 361–70. *Obstetrics and Gynecology* 75(4) (1990): 649–55. *Journal of Psychosomatic Obstetrics and Gynaecology* 1996 17(4) (1996): 202–7. *Preventive Medicine* 25(3) (1996): 339–45.

8. For a sampling of Benson's research findings, see *Psychiatry* 37 (1974): 37–46. *New England Journal of Medicine* 300 (1979): 1424–29. *Harvard Business Review* 58 (1980): 82–92. *Timeless Healing: The Power and Biology of Belief* (New York: Scribner, 1996). *The Breakout Principle* (New York: Scribner, 2003, 2004).

9. *Journal of Trauma and Stress* 17(2) (2004): 143–7.

10. *Journal of the American Optometry Association* 70(3) (1999): 171–81.

11. *Vision Research* 32(5) (1992): 895–1202.

12. Ibid.

13. Oquist, Gustav, "Adaptive Rapid Serial Visual Presentation." (Master's Thesis) Language Engineering Programme, Uppsala University, Uppsala, Sweden. Dec. 2001. *Human Factors* 41(1) (1999): 106–17. *Optometry and Visual Science* 75(3) (1998): 191–6.

14. *Optometry and Visual Science* 81(7) (2004): 525–35. *Vision Research* 42(12) (2002): 499–512.

THE
OLD TESTAMENT

GENESIS

The Creation

1 <u>In the beginning God created the heavens and the earth.</u>

First Day: Light and Darkness

² Now the earth was[a] formless and empty, darkness covered the surface of the watery depths, and the Spirit of God was hovering over the surface of the waters. ³ Then God said, "Let there be light," and there was light. ⁴ God saw that the light was good, and God separated the light from the darkness. ⁵ God called the light "day," and He called the darkness "night." Evening came, and then morning: the first day.

Second Day: Waters and Sky

⁶ Then God said, "Let there be an expanse[b] between the waters, separating water from water." ⁷ So God made the expanse and separated the water under the expanse from the water above the expanse. And it was so. ⁸ God called the expanse "sky."[c] Evening came, and then morning: the second day.

Third Day: Land and Plants

⁹ Then God said, "Let the water under the sky be gathered into one place, and let the dry land appear." And it was so. ¹⁰ God called the dry land "earth," and He called the gathering of the water "seas." And God saw that it was good. ¹¹ Then God said, "Let the earth produce vegetation: seed-bearing plants, and fruit trees on the earth bearing fruit with seed in it, according to their kinds." And it was so. ¹² The earth brought forth vegetation: seed-bearing plants according to their kinds and trees bearing fruit with seed in it, according to their kinds. And God saw that it was good. ¹³ Evening came, and then morning: the third day.

Fourth Day: Sun and Moon

¹⁴ Then God said, "Let there be lights in the expanse of the sky to separate the day from the night. They will serve as signs for festivals and for days and years. ¹⁵ They will be lights in the expanse of the sky to provide light on the earth." And it was so. ¹⁶ God made the two great lights—the greater light to have dominion over the day and the lesser light to have dominion over the night—as well as the stars. ¹⁷ God placed them in the expanse of the sky to provide light on the earth, ¹⁸ to dominate the day and the night, and to separate light from darkness. And God saw that it was good. ¹⁹ Evening came, and then morning: the fourth day.

Fifth Day: Fish and Birds

²⁰ Then God said, "Let the water swarm with[d] living creatures, and let birds fly above the earth across the expanse of the sky." ²¹ So God created the large sea-creatures[e] and every living creature that moves and swarms in the water, according to their kinds. ᵢHe also createdᵢ every winged bird according to its kind. And God saw that it was good. ²² So God blessed them, "Be fruitful, multiply, and fill the waters of the seas, and let the birds multiply on the earth." ²³ Evening came, and then morning: the fifth day.

---

[a]**1:1-2** Or *When God began to create the sky and the earth,* ² *the earth was*   [b]**1:6** The Hb word for *expanse* is from a root meaning "to spread out, stamp, beat firmly," which suggests something like a dome; Jb 37:16-18; Is 40:22.   [c]**1:8** Or *"heavens"*   [d]**1:20** Lit *with swarms of*   [e]**1:21** Or *created sea monsters*

Sixth Day: Land Animals, Humans

24 Then God said, "Let the earth produce living creatures according to their kinds: livestock, creatures that crawl, and the wildlife of the earth according to their kinds." And it was so. 25 So God made the wildlife of the earth according to their kinds, the livestock according to their kinds, and creatures that crawl on the ground according to their kinds. And God saw that it was good.

26 Then God said, "Let Us make man in Our image, according to Our likeness. They will rule the fish of the sea, the birds of the sky, the animals, all the earth,[a] and the creatures that crawl[b] on the earth."

27 So God created man
   in His own image;
   He created him in the image
      of God;
   He created them male and female.

28 God blessed them, and God said to them, "Be fruitful, multiply, fill the earth, and subdue it. Rule the fish of the sea, the birds of the sky, and every creature that crawls[c] on the earth." 29 God also said, "Look, I have given you every seed-bearing plant on the surface of the entire earth, and every tree whose fruit contains seed. This food will be for you, 30 for all the wildlife of the earth, for every bird of the sky, and for every creature that crawls on the earth—everything having the breath of life in it. ⌊I have given⌋ every green plant for food." And it was so. 31 God saw all that He had made, and it was very good. Evening came, and then morning: the sixth day.

Seventh Day: God Rests

2 So the heavens and the earth and everything in them[d] were completed. 2 By the seventh[e] day, God completed His work that He had done, and He rested[f] on the seventh day from all His work that He had done. 3 God blessed the seventh day and declared it holy, for on it He rested from His work of creation.[g]

Man and Woman
in the Garden

God Creates Man

4 These are the records of the heavens and the earth, concerning their creation at the time[h] that the LORD God made the earth and the heavens. 5 No shrub of the field had yet ⌊grown⌋ on the land,[i] and no plant of the field had yet sprouted, for the LORD God had not made it rain on the land, and there was no man to work the ground. 6 But water would come out of the ground and water the entire surface of the land. 7 Then the LORD God formed the man out of the dust from the ground and breathed the breath of life into his nostrils, and the man became a living being.

God Plants Garden in Eden

8 The LORD God planted a garden in Eden, in the east, and there He placed the man He had formed. 9 The LORD God caused to grow out of the ground every tree pleasing in appearance and good for food, including the tree of life in the midst of the garden, as well as the tree of the knowledge of good and evil.

10 A river went[j] out from Eden to water the garden. From there it divided and became the source of four rivers.[k] 11 The name of the first is Pishon, which encircles the entire land of the Havilah, where there is gold. 12 Gold

---

a**1:26** Syr reads *sky, and over every animal of the land*   b**1:26** Lit *scurry*   c**1:28** Lit *and all scurrying animals that scurry*   d**2:1** Lit *and all their host*   e**2:2** Sam, LXX, Syr read *sixth*   f**2:2** Or *ceased*   g**2:3** Lit *work that God created to make*   h**2:4** Lit *creation on the day*   i**2:5** Or *earth*   j**2:10** Or *goes*   k**2:10** Lit *became four heads*

from that land is pure;[a] bdellium[b] and onyx[c] are also there. 13 The name of the second river is Gihon, which encircles the entire land of •Cush. 14 The name of the third river is the Tigris, which flows to the east of Assyria. And the fourth river is the Euphrates.

Tree of Knowledge

15 The LORD God took the man and placed him in the garden of Eden to work it and watch over it. 16 And the LORD God commanded the man, "You are free to eat from any tree of the garden, 17 but you must not eat[d] from the tree of the knowledge of good and evil, for on the day you eat from it, you will certainly die."

God Creates Woman

18 Then the LORD God said, "It is not good for the man to be alone. I will make a helper who is like him." 19 So the LORD God formed out of the ground each wild animal and each bird of the sky, and brought each to the man to see what he would call it. And whatever the man called a living creature, that was its name. 20 The man gave names to all the livestock, to the birds of the sky, and to every wild animal; but for the man[e] no helper was found who was like him. 21 So the LORD God caused a deep sleep to come over the man, and he slept. God took one of his ribs and closed the flesh at that place. 22 Then the LORD God made the rib He had taken from the man into a woman and brought her to the man. 23 And the man said:

This one, at last, is bone
  of my bone,
and flesh of my flesh;
this one will be called woman,
for she was taken from man.

24 This is why a man leaves his father and mother and bonds with his wife, and they become one flesh. 25 Both the man and his wife were naked, yet felt no shame.

The Temptation and the Fall

The Serpent Strikes

3 Now the serpent was the most cunning of all the wild animals that the LORD God had made. He said to the woman, "Did God really say, 'You can't eat from any tree in the garden'?"

2 The woman said to the serpent, "We may eat the fruit from the trees in the garden. 3 But about the fruit of the tree in the middle of the garden, God said, 'You must not eat it or touch it, or you will die.'"

4 "No! You will not die," the serpent said to the woman. 5 "In fact, God knows that when[f] you eat it your eyes will be opened and you will be like God,[g] knowing good and evil."

Woman and Adam Disobey and Eat

6 Then the woman saw that the tree was good for food and delightful to look at, and that it was desirable for obtaining wisdom. So she took some of its fruit and ate ⌊it⌋; she also gave ⌊some⌋ to her husband, ⌊who was⌋ with her, and he ate ⌊it⌋. 7 Then the eyes of both of them were opened, and they knew they were naked; so they sewed fig leaves together and made loincloths for themselves.

Adam and Woman Hide

8 Then the man and his wife heard the sound of the LORD God walking in the garden at the time of the evening breeze,[h] and they hid themselves from the LORD God among the trees of the

a2:12 Lit good   b2:12 A yellowish, transparent gum resin   c2:12 Identity of this precious stone uncertain   d2:17 Lit eat from it   e2:20 Or for Adam   f3:5 Lit on the day   g3:5 Or gods, or divine beings   h3:8 Lit at the wind of the day

garden. ⁹ So the LORD God called out to the man and said to him, "Where are you?"

¹⁰ And he said, "I heard You[a] in the garden, and I was afraid because I was naked, so I hid."

¹¹ Then He asked, "Who told you that you were naked? Did you eat from the tree that I had commanded you not to eat from?"

¹² Then the man replied, "The woman You gave to be with me—she gave me ⸤some fruit⸥ from the tree, and I ate."

¹³ So the LORD God asked the woman, "What is this you have done?"

And the woman said, "It was the serpent. He deceived me, and I ate."

God Punishes Serpent

¹⁴ Then the LORD God said to the serpent:

> Because you have done this,
> you are cursed more than
>   any livestock
> and more than any wild animal.
> You will move on your belly
> and eat dust all the days of your life.
> ¹⁵ I will put hostility between you
>   and the woman,
> and between your •seed
>   and her seed.
> He will strike your head,
> and you will strike his heel.

God Punishes Woman

¹⁶ He said to the woman:

> I will intensify your labor pains;
> you will bear children in anguish.
> Your desire will be for your husband,
> yet he will dominate you.

God Punishes Adam

¹⁷ And He said to Adam, "Because you listened to your wife's voice and ate from the tree about which I commanded you, 'Do not eat from it':

> The ground is cursed
>   because of you.
> You will eat from it by means of
>   painful labor[b]
> all the days of your life.
> ¹⁸ It will produce thorns and thistles
>   for you,
> and you will eat the plants
>   of the field.
> ¹⁹ You will eat bread[c] by the sweat
>   of your brow
> until you return to the ground,
> since you were taken from it.
> For you are dust,
>   and you will return to dust."

Adam Names Eve

²⁰ Adam named his wife Eve[d] because she was the mother of all the living. ²¹ The LORD God made clothing out of skins for Adam and his wife, and He clothed them.

God Banishes Humans from Garden

²² The LORD God said, "Since man has become like one of Us, knowing good and evil, he must not reach out, and also take from the tree of life, and eat, and live forever." ²³ So the LORD God sent him away from the garden of Eden to work the ground from which he was taken. ²⁴ He drove man out, and east of the garden of Eden He stationed •cherubim with a flaming, whirling sword to guard the way to the tree of life.

Cain, Abel, and Seth

Cain Murders Abel

4 Adam knew his wife Eve intimately, and she conceived and gave birth to Cain. She said, "I have had a male child with the LORD's help."[e] ² Then she also

---

gave birth to his brother Abel. Now Abel became a shepherd of a flock, but Cain cultivated the land. ³ In the course of time Cain presented some of the land's produce as an offering to the LORD. ⁴ And Abel also presented ⌊an offering⌋—some of the firstborn of his flock and their fat portions. The LORD had regard for Abel and his offering, ⁵ but He did not have regard for Cain and his offering. Cain was furious, and he was downcast.ᵃ

⁶ Then the LORD said to Cain, "Why are you furious? And why are you downcast?ᵇ ⁷ If you do right, won't you be accepted? But if you do not do right, sin is crouching at the door. Its desire is for you, but you must master it."

⁸ Cain said to his brother Abel, "Let's go out to the field."ᶜ And while they were in the field, Cain attacked his brother Abel and killed him.

⁹ Then the LORD said to Cain, "Where is your brother Abel?"

"I don't know," he replied. "Am I my brother's guardian?"

God Banishes Cain

¹⁰ Then He said, "What have you done? Your brother's blood cries out to Me from the ground! ¹¹ So now you are cursed ⌊with alienation⌋ from the ground that opened its mouth to receive your brother's blood you have shed.ᵈ ¹² If you work the land, it will never again give you its yield. You will be a restless wanderer on the earth."

¹³ But Cain answered the LORD, "My punishmentᵉ is too great to bear! ¹⁴ Since You are banishing me today from the soil, and I must hide myself from Your presence and become a restless wanderer on the earth, whoever finds me will kill me."

¹⁵ Then the LORD replied to him, "In that case,ᶠ whoever kills Cain will suffer vengeance seven times over."ᵍ And He placed a mark on Cain so that whoever found him would not kill him. ¹⁶ Then Cain went out from the LORD's presence and lived in the land of Nod, east of Eden.

The Line of Cain

¹⁷ Cain knew his wife intimately, and she conceived and gave birth to Enoch. Then Cain became the builder of a city, and he named the city Enoch after his son. ¹⁸ Irad was born to Enoch, Irad fathered Mehujael, Mehujael fathered Methushael, and Methushael fathered Lamech.

Lamech: Another Killer

¹⁹ Lamech took two wives for himself, one named Adah and the other named Zillah. ²⁰ Adah bore Jabal; he was the father of the nomadic herdsmen.ʰ ²¹ His brother was named Jubal; he was the father of all who play the lyre and the flute. ²² Zillah bore Tubal-cain, who made all kinds of bronze and iron tools. Tubal-cain's sister was Naamah.

²³ Lamech said to his wives:

> Adah and Zillah, hear my voice;
> wives of Lamech, pay attention
> to my words.
> For I killed a man for wounding me,
> a boy for striking me.
> ²⁴ If Cain is to be avenged
> seven times over,
> then for Lamech it will be seventy-seven times!

Seth Born

²⁵ Adam knew his wife intimately again, and she gave birth to a son and

---

ᵃ4:5 Lit *and his face fell*　ᵇ4:6 Lit *why has your face fallen*　ᶜ4:8 Sam, LXX, Syr, Vg; MT omits *Let's go out to the field*　ᵈ4:11 Lit *blood from your hand*　ᵉ4:13 Or *sin*　ᶠ4:15 LXX, Syr, Vg read *Not so!*　ᵍ4:15 Or *suffer severely*　ʰ4:20 Lit *the dweller of tent and livestock*

named him Seth, for ⌊she said,⌋ "God has given[a] me another child in place of Abel, since Cain killed him." 26 A son was born to Seth also, and he named him Enosh. At that time people began to call on the name of[b] the LORD.

From Adam to Noah

5 These are the family[c] records of the descendants of Adam. On the day that God created man,[d] He made him in the likeness of God; 2 He created them male and female. When they were created, He blessed them and called them man.[d]

3 Adam was 130 years old when he fathered ⌊a child⌋ in his likeness, according to his image, and named him Seth. 4 Adam lived 800 years after the birth of Seth, and he fathered sons and daughters. 5 So Adam's life lasted 930 years; then he died.

6 Seth was 105 years old when he fathered Enosh. 7 Seth lived 807 years after the birth of Enosh, and he fathered sons and daughters. 8 So Seth's life lasted 912 years; then he died.

9 Enosh was 90 years old when he fathered Kenan. 10 Enosh lived 815 years after the birth of Kenan, and he fathered sons and daughters. 11 So Enosh's life lasted 905 years; then he died.

12 Kenan was 70 years old when he fathered Mahalalel. 13 Kenan lived 840 years after the birth of Mahalalel, and he fathered sons and daughters. 14 So Kenan's life lasted 910 years; then he died.

15 Mahalalel was 65 years old when he fathered Jared. 16 Mahalalel lived 830 years after the birth of Jared, and he fathered sons and daughters. 17 So Mahalalel's life lasted 895 years; then he died.

18 Jared was 162 years old when he fathered Enoch. 19 Jared lived 800 years after the birth of Enoch, and he fathered sons and daughters. 20 So Jared's life lasted 962 years; then he died.

Enoch Never Died

21 Enoch was 65 years old when he fathered Methuselah. 22 And after the birth of Methuselah, Enoch walked with God 300 years and fathered sons and daughters. 23 So Enoch's life lasted 365 years. 24 Enoch walked with God, and he was not there, because God took him.

Methuselah: the Oldest Man

25 Methuselah was 187 years old when he fathered Lamech. 26 Methuselah lived 782 years after the birth of Lamech, and he fathered sons and daughters. 27 So Methuselah's life lasted 969 years; then he died.

Noah Born

28 Lamech was 182 years old when he fathered a son. 29 And he named him Noah, saying, "This one will bring us relief[e] from the agonizing labor of our hands, caused by the ground the LORD has cursed." 30 Lamech lived 595 years after Noah's birth, and he fathered sons and daughters. 31 So Lamech's life lasted 777 years; then he died.

32 Noah was 500 years old, and he fathered Shem, Ham, and Japheth.

Noah and the Flood

Sons of God and Daughters of Men

6 When mankind began to multiply on the earth and daughters were born to them, 2 the sons of God saw that the daughters of man[f] were beautiful, and they took any they chose as wives[g] for

---

a 4:25 The Hb word translated *given* sounds like the name *Seth*.   b 4:26 Or *to worship*, or *to proclaim* or *invoke the name of*   c 5:1 Lit *written family*   d 5:1,2 Or *Adam*   e 5:29 The Hb word translated *bring us relief* sounds like the name of *Noah*.   f 6:2 Or *the human women*   g 6:2 Or *women*

themselves. ³ And the LORD said, "My Spirit will not remainᵃ withᵇ mankind forever, because they are corrupt.ᶜ Their days will be 120 years." ⁴ The Nephilimᵈ were on the earth both in those days and afterwards, when the sons of God came to the daughters of man, who bore children to them. They were the powerful men of old, the famous men.

God's Judgment

⁵ When the LORD saw that man's wickedness was widespread on the earth and that every scheme his mind thought of was nothing but evil all the time, ⁶ the LORD regretted that He had made man on the earth, and He was grieved in His heart. ⁷ Then the LORD said, "I will wipe off the face of the earth: man, whom I created, together with the animals, creatures that crawl, and birds of the sky—for I regret that I made them." ⁸ Noah, however, found favor in the eyes of the LORD.

God Warns Noah

⁹ These are the family records of Noah. Noah was a righteous man, blameless among his contemporaries; Noah walked with God. ¹⁰ And Noah fathered three sons: Shem, Ham, and Japheth.

¹¹ Now the earth was corrupt in God's sight, and the earth was filled with violence.ᵉ ¹² God saw how corrupt the earth was, for all flesh had corrupted its way on the earth. ¹³ Then God said to Noah, "I have decided to put an end to all flesh, for the earth is filled with violenceᵉ because of them; therefore I am going to destroy them along with the earth.

Noah's Ark

¹⁴ "Make yourself an ark of goferᶠ wood. Make rooms in the ark, and cover

it with pitch inside and outside. ¹⁵ This is how you are to make it: The ark will be 450 feet long, 75 feet wide, and 45 feet high.ᵍ ¹⁶ You are to make a roof,ʰ finishing ⌞the sides of the ark⌟ to within 18 inchesⁱ ⌞of the roof.⌟ You are to put a door in the side of the ark. Make it with lower, middle, and upper ⌞decks⌟.

¹⁷ "Understand that I am bringing a deluge—floodwaters on the earth to destroy all flesh under heaven with the breath of life in it. Everything on earth will die. ¹⁸ But I will establish My covenant with you, and you will enter the ark with your sons, your wife, and your sons' wives. ¹⁹ You are also to bring into the ark two of every living thing of all flesh, male and female, to keep them alive with you. ²⁰ Two of everything—from the birds according to their kinds, from the livestock according to their kinds, and from every animal that crawls on the ground according to its kind—will come to you so that you can keep them alive. ²¹ Take with you every kind of food that is eaten; gather it as food for you and for them." ²² And Noah did this. He did everything that God had commanded him.

The Flood Covers the Earth

7 Then the LORD said to Noah, "Enter the ark, you and all your household, for I have seen that you ⌞alone⌟ are righteous before Me in this generation. ² You are to take with you seven pairs, a male and its female, of all the clean animals, and two of the animals that are not clean, a male and its female, ³ and seven pairs, male and female, of the birds of the sky—in order to keep •offspring alive on the face of the whole earth. ⁴ Seven days from now I will make it rain on the

ᵃ**6:3** Or *strive*   ᵇ**6:3** Or *in*   ᶜ**6:3** Lit *flesh*   ᵈ**6:4** Possibly means "fallen ones"; traditionally *giants*; Nm 13:31-33   ᵉ**6:11,13** Or *injustice*   ᶠ**6:14** Unknown species of tree; perhaps pine or cypress   ᵍ**6:15** Or *300 cubits long, 50 cubits wide, and 30 cubits high*   ʰ**6:16** Or *window*, or *hatch*; Hb uncertain   ⁱ**6:16** Lit *to a cubit*

earth 40 days and 40 nights, and I will wipe off the face of the earth every living thing I have made." [5] And Noah did everything that the LORD commanded him.

[6] Noah was 600 years old when the deluge came ⌊and⌋ water covered the earth. [7] So Noah, his sons, his wife, and his sons' wives entered the ark because of the waters of the deluge. [8] From the clean animals, unclean animals, birds, and every creature that crawls on the ground, [9] two of each, male and female, entered the ark with Noah, just as God had commanded him. [10] Seven days later the waters of the deluge came on the earth.

Impact of the Deluge

[11] In the six hundredth year of Noah's life, in the second month, on the seventeenth day of the month, on that day all the sources of the watery depths burst open, the floodgates of the sky were opened, [12] and the rain fell on the earth 40 days and 40 nights. [13] On that same day Noah along with his sons Shem, Ham, and Japheth, Noah's wife, and his three sons' wives entered the ark with him. [14] They ⌊entered it⌋ with all the wildlife according to their kinds, all livestock according to their kinds, every creature that crawls on the earth according to its kind, all birds, every fowl, and everything with wings according to their kinds. [15] Two of all flesh that has the breath of life in it entered the ark with Noah. [16] Those that entered, male and female of all flesh, entered just as God had commanded him. Then the LORD shut him in.

[17] The deluge continued 40 days on the earth; the waters increased and lifted up the ark so that it rose above the earth. [18] The waters surged and increased greatly on the earth, and the ark floated on the surface of the water. [19] Then the waters surged even higher on the earth, and all the high mountains under the whole sky were covered. [20] The mountains were covered as the waters surged ⌊above them⌋ more than 20 feet.[a] [21] All flesh perished—creatures that crawl on the earth, birds, livestock, wildlife, and all creatures that swarm[b] on the earth, as well as all mankind. [22] Everything with the breath of the spirit of life in its nostrils—everything on dry land died. [23] He wiped out every living thing that was on the surface of the ground, from mankind to livestock, to creatures that crawl, to the birds of the sky, and they were wiped off the earth. Only Noah was left, and those that were with him in the ark. [24] And the waters surged on the earth 150 days.

The Flood Recedes

8 God remembered Noah, as well as all the wildlife and all the livestock that were with him in the ark. God caused a wind[c] to pass over the earth, and the water began to subside. [2] The sources of the watery depths and the floodgates of the sky were closed, and the rain from the sky stopped. [3] The water steadily receded from the earth, and by the end of 150 days the waters had decreased significantly. [4] The ark came to rest in the seventh month, on the seventeenth day of the month, on the mountains of Ararat.[d]

[5] The waters continued to recede until the tenth month; in the tenth month, on the first day of the month, the tops of the mountains were visible. [6] After 40 days Noah opened the window of the ark that he had made, [7] and he sent out a raven. It went back and forth until the waters

had dried up from the earth. ⁸ Then <u>he sent out a dove</u> to see whether the water on the earth's surface had gone down, ⁹ but the dove found no resting place for her foot. She returned to him in the ark because water covered the surface of the whole earth. He reached out and brought her into the ark to himself. ¹⁰ So Noah waited seven more days and sent out the dove from the ark again. ¹¹ When the dove came to him at evening, there was a plucked olive leaf in her beak. So Noah knew that the water on the earth's surface had gone down. ¹² After he had waited another seven days, he sent out the dove, but she did not return to him again. ¹³ In the six hundred and first year,ᵃ in the first month, on the first day of the month, the water ⌊that had covered⌋ the earth was dried up. Then Noah removed the ark's cover and saw that the surface of the ground was drying. ¹⁴ By the twenty-seventh day of the second month, the earth was dry.

The LORD's Promise

¹⁵ Then God spoke to Noah, ¹⁶ "Come out of the ark, you, your wife, your sons, and your sons' wives with you. ¹⁷ Bring out every living thing of all flesh that is with you—birds, livestock, creatures that crawl on the ground—and they will spread over the earth and be fruitful and multiply on the earth." ¹⁸ So Noah, along with his sons, his wife, and his sons' wives, came out. ¹⁹ All wildlife, all livestock, every bird, and every creature that crawls on the earth came out of the ark by their groups.

²⁰ Then Noah built an altar to the LORD. He took some of every kind of clean animal and every kind of clean bird and offered •burnt offerings on the altar. ²¹ When the LORD smelled the pleasing aroma, He said to Himself, "<u>I will never again curse the ground because of man</u>, even though man's inclination is evil from his youth. And I will never again strike down every living thing as I have done.

²² As long as the earth endures,
    seedtime and harvest,
      cold and heat,
    summer and winter,
      and day and night
    will not cease."

God's Covenant with Noah

9 God blessed Noah and his sons and said to them, "Be fruitful and multiply and fill the earth. ² The fear and terror of you will be in every living creature on the earth, every bird of the sky, every creature that crawls on the ground, and all the fish of the sea. They are placed under your authority.ᵇ ³ <u>Every living creature will be food for you</u>; as ⌊I gave⌋ the green plants, I have given you everything. ⁴ However, you must not eat meat with its lifeblood in it. ⁵ I will require the life of every animal and every man for your life and your blood. <u>I will require the life of each man's brother for a man's life.</u>

⁶ Whoever sheds man's blood,
    his blood will be shed by man,
    for God made man
    in His image.

⁷ But you, be fruitful and multiply; spread out over the earth and multiply on it."

⁸ Then God said to Noah and his sons with him, ⁹ "Understand that I am confirming My covenant with you and your descendants after you, ¹⁰ and with every living creature that is with you—birds, livestock, and all wildlife of the earth

ᵃ**8:13** Dating from the birth of Noah   ᵇ**9:2** Lit *are given in your hand*

that are with you—all the animals of the earth that came out of the ark. ¹¹ I confirm My covenant with you that never again will all flesh be wiped out by the waters of a deluge; there will never again be a deluge to destroy the earth."

¹² And God said, "This is the sign of the covenant I am making between Me and you and every living creature with you, a covenant for all future generations: ¹³ I have placed My bow in the clouds, and it will be a sign of the covenant between Me and the earth. ¹⁴ Whenever I form clouds over the earth and the bow appears in the clouds, ¹⁵ I will remember My covenant between Me and you and every living creature of all flesh: water will never again become a deluge to destroy all flesh. ¹⁶ The bow will be in the clouds, and I will look at it and remember the everlasting covenant between God and every living creature of all flesh on earth." ¹⁷ God said to Noah, "This is the sign of the covenant that I have confirmed between Me and all flesh on earth."

Noah's Sons

¹⁸ Noah's sons who came out of the ark were Shem, Ham, and Japheth. Ham was the father of Canaan. ¹⁹ These three were Noah's sons, and from them the whole earth was populated.

Noah Drunk

²⁰ Noah, a man of the soil, was the first to plantᵃ a vineyard. ²¹ He drank some of the wine, became drunk, and uncovered himself inside his tent. ²² Ham, the father of Canaan, saw his father naked and told his two brothers outside. ²³ Then Shem and Japheth took a cloak and placed it over both their shoulders, and walking backwards, they covered their father's nakedness. Their faces were turned away, and they did not see their father naked.

Noah's Curses and Blessings

²⁴ When Noah awoke from his drinking and learned what his youngest son had done to him, ²⁵ he said:

Canaan will be cursed.
He will be the lowest of slaves
    to his brothers.

²⁶ He also said:

Praise the LORD, the God of Shem;
Canaan will beᵇ his slave.
²⁷ God will extendᶜ Japheth;
he will dwell in the tents of Shem;
Canaan will be his slave.

²⁸ Now Noah lived 350 years after the flood. ²⁹ So Noah's life lasted 950 years; then he died.

The Table of Nations

10 These are the family records of Noah's sons, Shem, Ham, and Japheth. They also had sons after the deluge.

Descendants of Japeth

² Japheth's sons: Gomer, Magog, Madai, Javan, Tubal, Meshech, and Tiras. ³ Gomer's sons: Ashkenaz, Riphath, and Togarmah. ⁴ And Javan's sons: Elishah, Tarshish, Kittim, and Dodanim.ᵈ ⁵ The coastland peoples spread out into their lands. These are ⌊Japheth's sons⌋ by their clans, in their nations. Each ⌊group⌋ had its own language.

Descendants of Ham

⁶ Ham's sons: Cush, Egypt, Put, and Canaan. ⁷ Cush's sons: Seba, Havilah,

---

ᵃ9:20 Or *Noah began to be a farmer and planted*   ᵇ9:26 As a prophecy; others interpret the verbs in vv. 26-27 as a wish or prayer: *let Canaan be . . .*   ᶜ9:27 The Hb word for *extend* sounds like *Japheth*.   ᵈ10:4 Some Hb mss, Sam, LXX read *Rodanim*; 1 Ch 1:7

Sabtah, Raamah, and Sabteca. And Raamah's sons: Sheba and Dedan.

⁸ Cush fathered Nimrod, who was the first powerful man on earth. ⁹ He was a powerful hunter in the sight of the LORD. That is why it is said, "Like Nimrod, a powerful hunter in the sight of the LORD." ¹⁰ His kingdom started with Babylon, Erech,ᵃ Accad,ᵇ and Calneh,ᶜ in the land of •Shinar.ᵈ ¹¹ From that land he went to Assyria and built Nineveh, Rehoboth-ir, Calah, ¹² and Resen, between Nineveh and the great city Calah.

¹³ Egypt fathered Ludim, Anamim, Lehabim, Naphtuhim, ¹⁴ Pathrusim, Casluhim (the Philistines came from them), and Caphtorim.

¹⁵ Canaan fathered Sidon his firstborn, and the Hittites, ¹⁶ the Jebusites, the Amorites, the Girgashites, ¹⁷ the Hivites, the Arkites, the Sinites, ¹⁸ the Arvadites, the Zemarites, and the Hamathites. Afterwards the Canaanite clans scattered. ¹⁹ The Canaanite border went from Sidon going toward Gerar as far as Gaza, and going toward Sodom, Gomorrah, Admah, and Zeboiim, as far as Lasha.

²⁰ These are Ham's sons, by their clans, according to their languages, in their own lands and their nations.

Descendants of Shem

²¹ And Shem, Japheth's older brother, also had children. Shem was the father of all the children of Eber. ²² Shem's sons were Elam, Asshur,ᵉ Arpachshad, Lud, and Aram.

²³ Aram's sons: Uz, Hul, Gether, and Mash.

²⁴ Arpachshad fatheredᶠ Shelah, and Shelah fathered Eber. ²⁵ Eber had two sons. One was named Peleg, for during his days the earth was divided; his brother was named Joktan. ²⁶ And Joktan fathered Almodad, Sheleph, Hazarmaveth, Jerah, ²⁷ Hadoram, Uzal, Diklah, ²⁸ Obal, Abimael, Sheba, ²⁹ Ophir, Havilah, and Jobab. All these were Joktan's sons. ³⁰ Their settlements extended from Mesha to Sephar, the eastern hill country.

³¹ These are Shem's sons by their clans, according to their languages, in their lands and their nations.

³² These are the clans of Noah's sons, according to their family records, in their nations. The nations on earth spread out from these after the flood.

The Tower of Babylon

11 At one time the whole earth had the same language and vocabulary.ᵍ ² As peopleʰ migrated from the east, they found a valley in the land of •Shinar and settled there. ³ They said to each other, "Come, let us make oven-fired bricks." They had brick for stone and asphalt for mortar. ⁴ And they said, "Come, let us build ourselves a city and a tower with its top in the sky. Let us make a name for ourselves; otherwise, we will be scattered over the face of the whole earth."

⁵ Then the LORD came down to look over the city and the tower that the •men were building. ⁶ The LORD said, "If, as one people all having the same language, they have begun to do this, then nothing they plan to do will be impossible for them. ⁷ Come, let Us go down there and confuseⁱ their languageʲ so that they will not understand one another's speech."ᵏ ⁸ So the LORD scattered them from there over the face of the whole earth, and they stopped building the city. ⁹ Therefore its name is called Babylon,ˡ

ᵃ**10:10** Or *Uruk*   ᵇ**10:10** Or *Akkad*   ᶜ**10:10** Or *and all of them*   ᵈ**10:10** Or *in Babylonia*   ᵉ**10:22** Or *Assyria*
ᶠ**10:24** LXX reads *fathered Cainan, and Cainan fathered*; Gn 11:12-13; Lk 3:35-36   ᵍ**11:1** Lit *one lip and the same words*   ʰ**11:2** Lit *they*   ⁱ**11:7** Or *confound*   ʲ**11:7** Lit *lip*   ᵏ**11:7** Lit *understand each man the lip of his companion*
ˡ**11:9** The Hb word for *confuse* sounds like *Babylon*.

for there the LORD confused the language of the whole earth, and from there the LORD scattered them over the face of the whole earth.

From Shem to Abram

¹⁰ These are the family records of Shem. Shem lived 100 years and fathered Arpachshad two years after the deluge. ¹¹ After he fathered Arpachshad, Shem lived 500 years and fathered ˌotherˌ sons and daughters. ¹² Arpachshad lived 35 yearsª and fathered Shelah. ¹³ After he fathered Shelah, Arpachshad lived 403 years and fathered ˌotherˌ sons and daughters. ¹⁴ Shelah lived 30 years and fathered Eber. ¹⁵ After he fathered Eber, Shelah lived 403 years and fathered ˌotherˌ sons and daughters. ¹⁶ Eber lived 34 years and fathered Peleg. ¹⁷ After he fathered Peleg, Eber lived 430 years and fathered ˌotherˌ sons and daughters. ¹⁸ Peleg lived 30 years and fathered Reu. ¹⁹ After he fathered Reu, Peleg lived 209 years and fathered ˌotherˌ sons and daughters. ²⁰ Reu lived 32 years and fathered Serug. ²¹ After he fathered Serug, Reu lived 207 years and fathered ˌotherˌ sons and daughters. ²² Serug lived 30 years and fathered Nahor. ²³ After he fathered Nahor, Serug lived 200 years and fathered ˌotherˌ sons and daughters. ²⁴ Nahor lived 29 years and fathered Terah. ²⁵ After he fathered Terah, Nahor lived 119 years and fathered ˌotherˌ sons and daughters. ²⁶ Terah lived 70 years and fathered Abram, Nahor, and Haran.

Family of Terah

²⁷ These are the family records of Terah. Terah fathered Abram, Nahor, and Haran, and Haran fathered Lot. ²⁸ Haran died in his native land, in Ur of the Chaldeans, during his father Terah's lifetime. ²⁹ Abram and Nahor took wives: Abram's wife was named Sarai, and Nahor's wife was named Milcah. She was the daughter of Haran, the father of both Milcah and Iscah. ³⁰ Sarai was barren; she had no child.

³¹ Terah took his son Abram, his grandson Lot (Haran's son), and his daughter-in-law Sarai, his son Abram's wife, and they set out together from Ur of the Chaldeans to go to the land of Canaan. But when they came to Haran, they settled there. ³² Terah lived 205 years and died in Haran.

The Call of Abram

12 The LORD said to Abram:

Go out from your land,
your relatives,
and your father's house
to the land that I will show you.
² I will make you into a great nation,
I will bless you,
I will make your name great,
and you will be a blessing.ᵇ
³ I will bless those who bless you,
I will curse those who treat you
with contempt,
and all the peoplesᶜ on earth
will be blessedᵈ through you.ᵉ

Abram, Sarai, and Lot Leave Haran

⁴ So Abram went, as the LORD had told him, and Lot went with him. Abram was 75 years old when he left Haran. ⁵ He took his wife Sarai, his nephew Lot, all the possessions they had accumulated, and the people he had acquired in Haran, and they set out for the land of Canaan. When they came to the land of

---

ª**11:12-13** LXX reads *years and fathered Cainan.* ¹³ *After he fathered Cainan, Arphachshad lived 430 years and fathered [other] sons and daughters, and he died. Cainan lived 130 years and fathered Shelah. After he fathered Shelah, Cainan lived 330 years and fathered [other] sons and daughters, and he died;* Gn 10:24; Lk 3:35-36 ᵇ**12:2** Or *great. Be a blessing!* ᶜ**12:3** Lit *clans* ᵈ**12:3** Or *will find blessing* ᵉ**12:3** Or *will bless themselves by you*

Canaan, ⁶ Abram passed through the land to the site of Shechem, at the oak of Moreh. At that time the Canaanites were in the land. ⁷ But the LORD appeared to Abram and said, "I will give this land to your •offspring." So he built an altar there to the LORD who had appeared to him. ⁸ From there he moved on to the hill country east of Bethel and pitched his tent, with Bethel on the west and Ai on the east. There he built an altar to the LORD and worshiped[a] Him. ⁹ Then Abram journeyed by stages to the •Negev.

Abram and Sarai in Egypt

¹⁰ There was a famine in the land, so Abram went down to Egypt to live there for a while because the famine in the land was severe. ¹¹ When he was about to enter Egypt, he said to his wife Sarai, "Look, I know what a beautiful woman you are. ¹² When the Egyptians see you, they will say, 'This is his wife.' They will kill me but let you live. ¹³ Please say you're my sister so it will go well for me because of you, and my life will be spared on your account." ¹⁴ When Abram entered Egypt, the Egyptians saw that the woman was very beautiful. ¹⁵ Pharaoh's officials saw her and praised her to Pharaoh, so the woman was taken to Pharaoh's house. ¹⁶ He treated Abram well because of her, and Abram acquired flocks and herds, male and female donkeys, male and female slaves, and camels.

Pharaoh in Trouble

¹⁷ But the LORD struck Pharaoh and his house with severe plagues because of Abram's wife Sarai. ¹⁸ So Pharaoh sent for Abram and said, "What have you done to me? Why didn't you tell me she was your wife? ¹⁹ Why did you say, 'She's my sister,' so that I took her as my wife? Now, here's your wife. Take her and go!" ²⁰ Then Pharaoh gave ⌊his⌋ men orders about him, and they sent him away, with his wife and all he had.

Abram and Lot Separate

13 Then Abram went up from Egypt to the •Negev—he, his wife, and all he had, and Lot with him. ² Abram was very rich[b] in livestock, silver, and gold. ³ He went by stages from the Negev to Bethel, to the place between Bethel and Ai where his tent had formerly been, ⁴ to the site where he had built the altar. And Abram worshiped[a] the LORD there.

⁵ Now Lot, who was traveling with Abram, also had flocks, herds, and tents. ⁶ But the land was unable to support them as long as they stayed together, for they had so many possessions that they could not stay together, ⁷ and there was quarreling between the herdsmen of Abram's livestock and the herdsmen of Lot's livestock. At that time the Canaanites and the Perizzites were living in the land.

⁸ Then Abram said to Lot, "Please, let's not have quarreling between you and me, or between your herdsmen and my herdsmen, since we are relatives.[c] ⁹ Isn't the whole land before you? Separate from me: if ⌊you go⌋ to the left, I will go to the right; if ⌊you go⌋ to the right, I will go to the left."

Lot Chooses

¹⁰ Lot looked out and saw that the entire Jordan Valley as far as[d] Zoar was well-watered everywhere like the LORD's garden and the land of Egypt. This was before God destroyed Sodom and Gomorrah. ¹¹ So Lot chose the entire Jordan

---

a12:8; 13:4 Or *proclaimed* or *invoked the name of*; lit *called on the name of*   b13:2 Lit *heavy*   c13:8 Lit *brothers*
d13:10 Lit *Valley as you go to*

Valley for himself. Then Lot journeyed eastward, and they separated from each other. ¹² Abram lived in the land of Canaan, but Lot lived in the cities of the valley and set up his tent near Sodom. ¹³ Now the men of Sodom were evil, sinning greatly[a] against the LORD.

¹⁴ After Lot had separated from him, the LORD said to Abram, "Look from the place where you are. Look north and south, east and west, ¹⁵ for I will give you and your •offspring forever all the land that you see. ¹⁶ I will make your offspring like the dust of the earth, so that if one could count the dust of the earth, then your offspring could be counted. ¹⁷ Get up and walk from one end of the land to the other, for I will give it to you."

¹⁸ So Abram moved his tent and went to live beside the oaks of Mamre at Hebron, where he built an altar to the LORD.

Abram Rescues Lot

14 In those days Amraphel king of •Shinar, Arioch king of Ellasar, Chedorlaomer king of Elam,[b] and Tidal[c] king of Goiim[d] ² waged war against Bera king of Sodom, Birsha king of Gomorrah, Shinab king of Admah, and Shemeber king of Zeboiim, as well as the king of Bela (that is, Zoar). ³ All of these came as allies to the Valley of Siddim (that is, the Dead Sea). ⁴ They were subject to Chedorlaomer for 12 years, but in the thirteenth year they rebelled. ⁵ In the fourteenth year Chedorlaomer and the kings who were with him came and defeated the Rephaim in Ashteroth-karnaim, the Zuzim in Ham, the Emim in Shaveh-kiriathaim, ⁶ and the Horites in the mountains of Seir, as far as El-paran by the wilderness.

⁷ Then they came back to invade En-mishpat (that is, Kadesh), and they defeated all the territory of the Amalekites, as well as the Amorites who lived in Hazazon-tamar.

⁸ Then the king of Sodom, the king of Gomorrah, the king of Admah, the king of Zeboiim, and the king of Bela (that is, Zoar) went out and lined up for battle in the Valley of Siddim ⁹ against Chedorlaomer king of Elam, Tidal king of Goiim, Amraphel king of Shinar, and Arioch king of Ellasar—four kings against five. ¹⁰ Now the Valley of Siddim contained many asphalt pits, and ⌊as⌋ the kings of Sodom and Gomorrah fled, ⌊some⌋ fell into them,[e] but the rest fled to the mountains. ¹¹ The ⌊four kings⌋ took all the goods of Sodom and Gomorrah and all their food and went on. ¹² They also took Abram's nephew Lot and his possessions, for he was living in Sodom, and they went on.

¹³ One of the survivors came and told Abram the Hebrew, who was at the oaks belonging to Mamre the Amorite, the brother of Eshcol and the brother of Aner. They were bound by a treaty with[f] Abram. ¹⁴ When Abram heard that his relative had been taken prisoner, he assembled[g] his 318 trained men, born in his household, and they went in pursuit as far as Dan. ¹⁵ And he and his servants deployed against them by night, attacked them, and pursued them as far as Hobah to the north of Damascus. ¹⁶ He brought back all the goods and also his relative Lot and his goods, as well as the women and the ⌊other⌋ people.

Melchizedek Blesses Abram

¹⁷ After Abram returned from defeating Chedorlaomer and the kings who

---

[a] **13:13** Lit *evil and sinful* [b] **14:1** A region in southwest Iran [c] **14:1** The name *Tidal* may be related to the Hittite royal name Tudhaliya. [d] **14:1** Or *nations* [e] **14:10** Sam, LXX read *fell there* [f] **14:13** Lit *were possessors of a covenant of* [g] **14:14** Sam; MT reads *poured out*

were with him, the king of Sodom went out to meet him in the Valley of Shaveh (that is, the King's Valley). ¹⁸ Then <u>Melchizedek, king of Salem, brought out bread and wine; he was a priest to God •Most High.</u> ¹⁹ He blessed him and said:

> Abram is blessed
>   by God Most High,
>   Creatorª of heaven and earth,
> ²⁰ and give praise toᵇ God Most High
>   who has handed over your enemies
>   to you.

And <u>Abram gave him a tenth of everything.</u>

²¹ Then the king of Sodom said to Abram, "Give me the people, but take the possessions for yourself."

²² But Abram said to the king of Sodom, "I have raised my hand in an oath to the LORD, God Most High, Creator of heaven and earth, ²³ that I will not take a thread or sandal strap or anything that belongs to you, so you can never say, 'I made Abram rich.' ²⁴ I will take nothingᶜ except what the servants have eaten. But as for the share of the men who came with me—Aner, Eshcol, and Mamre—they can take their share."

God's Covenant with Abram

15 After these events, the word of the LORD came to Abram in a vision:

> Do not be afraid, Abram.
> <u>I am your shield;</u>
> your reward will be very great.

² But Abram said, "Lord GOD, what can You give me, since I am childless and the heir of my house is Eliezer of Damascus?"ᵈ ³ Abram continued, "Look, You have given me no •offspring, so a slave born inᵉ my house will be my heir."

⁴ Now the word of the LORD came to him: "This one will not be your heir; instead, one who comes from your own bodyᶠ will be your heir." ⁵ He took him outside and said, "<u>Look at the sky and count the stars, if you are able to count them." Then He said to him, "Your offspring will be that ₍numerous₎.</u>"

Abram's Faith

⁶ <u>Abram believed the LORD, and He credited it to him as righteousness.</u>

⁷ He also said to him, "I am the LORD who brought you from Ur of the Chaldeans to give you this land to possess."

⁸ But he said, "Lord GOD, how can I know that I will possess it?"

⁹ He said to him, "Bring Me a three-year-old cow, a three-year-old female goat, a three-year-old ram, a turtledove, and a young pigeon."

¹⁰ So he brought all these to Him, split them down the middle, and laid the pieces opposite each other, but he did not cut up the birds. ¹¹ Birds of prey came down on the carcasses, but Abram drove them away. ¹² As the sun was setting, a deep sleep fell on Abram, and suddenly a terror and great darkness descended on him.

¹³ Then the LORD said to Abram, "Know this for certain: Your offspring will be strangers in a land that does not belong to them; they will be enslaved and oppressedᵍ 400 years. ¹⁴ However, I will judge the nation they serve, and afterwards they will go out with many possessions. ¹⁵ But you will go to your fathers in peace and be buried at a ripe old age. ¹⁶ In the fourth generation they will return here, for the iniquity of the Amorites has not yet reached its full measure."ʰ

¹⁷ When the sun had set and it was dark, a smoking fire pot and a flaming

---

ª**14:19** Or *Possessor* ᵇ**14:20** Or *and blessed be* ᶜ**14:24** Lit *Nothing to me* ᵈ**15:2** Hb obscure ᵉ**15:3** Lit *a son of* ᶠ**15:4** Lit *loins* ᵍ**15:13** Lit *will serve them and they will oppress them* ʰ**15:16** Lit *Amorites is not yet complete*

torch appeared and passed between the divided ⌊animals⌋. ¹⁸ On that day the LORD made a covenant with Abram, saying, "I give this land to your offspring, from the brook of Egypt to the Euphrates River:ᵃ ¹⁹ ⌊the land of⌋ the Kenites, Kenizzites, Kadmonites, ²⁰ Hittites, Perizzites, Rephaim, ²¹ Amorites, Canaanites, Girgashites, and Jebusites."

Hagar and Ishmael

Birth of Ishmael

16 Abram's wife Sarai had not borne him children. She owned an Egyptian slave named Hagar. ² Sarai said to Abram, "Since the LORD has prevented me from bearing children, go to my slave; perhaps I can have childrenᵇ by her." And Abram agreed to what Sarai said.ᶜ ³ So Abram's wife Sarai took Hagar, her Egyptian slave, and gave her to her husband Abram as a wife for him. ⌊This happened⌋ after Abram had lived in the land of Canaan 10 years. ⁴ He slept withᵈ Hagar, and she became pregnant. When she realized that she was pregnant, she looked down on her mistress. ⁵ Then Sarai said to Abram, "You are responsible for my suffering!ᵉ I put my slave in your arms,ᶠ and ever since she saw that she was pregnant, she has looked down on me. May the LORD judge between me and you."

⁶ Abram replied to Sarai, "Here, your slave is in your hands; do whatever you want with her."ᵍ Then Sarai mistreated her so much that she ran away from her.

Angel's Promise to Hagar

⁷ The Angel of the LORD found her by a spring of water in the wilderness, the spring on the way to Shur. ⁸ He said, "Hagar, slave of Sarai, where have you come from, and where are you going?"

She replied, "I'm running away from my mistress Sarai."

⁹ Then the Angel of the LORD said to her, "You must go back to your mistress and submit to her mistreatment."ʰ ¹⁰ The Angel of the LORD also said to her, "I will greatly multiply your •offspring, and they will be too many to count."

¹¹ Then the Angel of the LORD said to her:

You have conceived and will have
  a son.
You will name him Ishmael,ⁱ
for the LORD has heard
  your ⌊cry of⌋ affliction.
¹² This man will be ⌊like⌋ a wild ass.
  His hand will be against everyone,
  and everyone's hand will be
    against him;
  he will live at odds with all
    his brothers.

¹³ So she named the LORD who spoke to her: The God Who Sees,ʲ for she said, "Have I really seen here the One who sees me?"ᵏ ¹⁴ That is why she named the spring, "A Well of the Living One Who Sees Me."ˡ It is locatedᵐ between Kadesh and Bered.

¹⁵ So Hagar gave birth to Abram's son, and Abram gave the name Ishmael to the son Hagar had. ¹⁶ Abram was 86 years old when Hagar bore Ishmael to him.

Abram Becomes Abraham

17 When Abram was 99 years old, the LORD appeared to him, saying, "I am •God Almighty. Live in My presence and be devout. ² I will establish My cove-

---

ᵃ**15:18** Lit *the great river, the river Euphrates*   ᵇ**16:2** Lit *I will be built up*   ᶜ**16:2** Lit *Abram listened to the voice of Sarai*   ᵈ**16:4** Lit *He came to*   ᵉ**16:5** Or *May my suffering be on you*   ᶠ**16:5** Lit *bosom*   ᵍ**16:6** Lit *do to her what is good in your eyes*   ʰ**16:9** Lit *to mistreatment under her hand*   ⁱ**16:11** = God Hears   ʲ**16:13** Lit *her: You God Who Sees*   ᵏ**16:13** Hb obscure   ˡ**16:14** Hb *Beer-lahai-roi*   ᵐ**16:14** Lit *Look*

nant between Me and you, and I will multiply you greatly."

3 Then Abram fell to the ground,[a] and God spoke with him: 4 "As for Me, My covenant is with you, and you will become the father of many nations.[b] 5 Your name will no longer be Abram,[c] but your name will be Abraham,[d] for I will make you the father of many nations. 6 I will make you extremely fruitful and will make nations and kings come from you. 7 I will keep My covenant between Me and you, and your •offspring after you throughout their generations, as an everlasting covenant to be your God and the ₍God₎ of your offspring after you. 8 And to you and your offspring after you I will give the land where you are residing— all the land of Canaan—as an eternal possession, and I will be their God."

Sign of Circumcision

9 God also said to Abraham, "As for you, you and your offspring after you throughout their generations are to keep My covenant. 10 This is My covenant, which you are to keep, between Me and you and your offspring after you: Every one of your males must be circumcised. 11 You must circumcise the flesh of your foreskin to serve as a sign of the covenant between Me and you.[e] 12 Throughout your generations, every male among you at eight days old is to be circumcised. This includes a slave born in your house and one purchased with money from any foreigner. The one who is not your offspring, 13 a slave born in your house, as well as one purchased with money, must be circumcised. My covenant will be in your flesh as an everlasting covenant. 14 If any male is not

circumcised in the flesh of his foreskin, that man will be cut off from his people; he has broken My covenant."

Sarai Becomes Sarah

15 God said to Abraham, "As for your wife Sarai, do not call her Sarai, for Sarah[f] will be her name. 16 I will bless her; indeed, I will give you a son by her. I will bless her, and she will produce nations; kings of peoples will come from her."

God Promises a Son

17 Abraham fell to the ground,[a] laughed, and thought in his heart, "Can a child be born to a hundred-year-old man? Can Sarah, a ninety-year-old woman, give birth?" 18 So Abraham said to God, "If only Ishmael could live in Your presence!"

19 But God said, "No. Your wife Sarah will bear you a son, and you will name him Isaac.[g] I will confirm My covenant with him as an everlasting covenant for his offspring after him. 20 As for Ishmael, I have heard you. I will certainly bless him; I will make him fruitful and will multiply him greatly. He will father 12 tribal leaders, and I will make him into a great nation. 21 But I will confirm My covenant with Isaac, whom Sarah will bear to you at this time next year." 22 When He finished talking with him, God withdrew[h] from Abraham.

23 Then Abraham took his son Ishmael and all the slaves born in his house or purchased with his money—every male among the members of Abraham's household—and he circumcised the flesh of their foreskin on that very day, just as God had said to him. 24 Abraham

---

a 17:3,17 Lit fell on his face   b 17:4 Abraham was father not only of the Israelites, but also of the Ishmaelites, the Edomites, and the Midianites. Spiritually, he is the father of all believers; Gl 3:7,29.   c 17:5 = The Father Is Exalted   d 17:5 = Father of a Multitude   e 17:11 You in v. 11 is pl.   f 17:15 = Princess   g 17:19 = He Laughs   h 17:22 Lit went up, or ascended

was 99 years old when the flesh of his foreskin was circumcised, 25 and his son Ishmael was 13 years old when the flesh of his foreskin was circumcised. 26 On that same day Abraham and his son Ishmael were circumcised. 27 And all the men of his household—both slaves born in his house and those purchased with money from a foreigner—were circumcised with him.

Abraham's Three Visitors

18 Then the LORD appeared to Abraham at the oaks of Mamre while he was sitting in the entrance of his tent during the heat of the day. 2 He looked up, and he saw three men standing near him. When he saw them, he ran from the entrance of the tent to meet them and bowed to the ground. 3 Then he said, "My lord,[a] if I have found favor in your sight, please do not go on past your servant. 4 Let a little water be brought, that you may wash your feet and rest yourselves under the tree. 5 I will bring a bit of bread so that you may strengthen yourselves.[b] This is why you have passed your servant's ⌊way⌋. Later, you can continue on."

"Yes," they replied, "do as you have said."

6 So Abraham hurried into the tent and said to Sarah, "Quick! Knead three measures[c] of fine flour and make bread."[d] 7 Meanwhile, Abraham ran to the herd and got a tender, choice calf. He gave it to a young man, who hurried to prepare it. 8 Then Abraham took curds[e] and milk, and the calf that he had prepared, and set ⌊them⌋ before the men. He served[f] them as they ate under the tree.

Sarah Laughs

9 "Where is your wife Sarah?" they asked him.

"There, in the tent," he answered.

10 The LORD said, "I will certainly come back to you in about a year's time, and your wife Sarah will have a son!" Now Sarah was listening at the entrance of the tent behind him.

11 Abraham and Sarah were old and getting on in years.[g] Sarah had passed the age of childbearing.[h] 12 So she laughed to herself: "After I have become shriveled up and my lord is old, will I have delight?"

13 But the LORD asked Abraham, "Why did Sarah laugh, saying, 'Can I really have a baby when I'm old?' 14 Is anything impossible for the LORD? At the appointed time I will come back to you, and in about a year she will have a son."

15 Sarah denied it. "I did not laugh," she said, because she was afraid.

But He replied, "No, you did laugh."

Abraham's Plea for Sodom

16 The men got up from there and looked out over Sodom, and Abraham was walking with them to see them off. 17 Then the LORD said, "Should I hide from Abraham what I am about to do? 18 Abraham is to become a great and powerful nation, and all the nations of the earth will be blessed through him. 19 For I have chosen[i] him so that he will command his children and his house after him to keep the way of the LORD by doing what is right and just. This is how the LORD will fulfill to Abraham what He promised him." 20 Then the LORD said, "The outcry against Sodom and Gomorrah is immense, and their sin is extremely serious. 21 I will go down to see if what they have done justifies the cry that has come up to Me. If not, I will find out."

---

[a]18:3 Or My Lord, or The Lord   [b]18:5 Lit may sustain your heart   [c]18:6 Lit three seahs; about 21 quarts   [d]18:6 A round, thin, unleavened bread   [e]18:8 Or butter   [f]18:8 Lit was standing by   [g]18:11 Lit days   [h]18:11 Lit The way of women had ceased for Sarah   [i]18:19 Lit known

Abraham Negotiates with God

22 The men turned from there and went toward Sodom while Abraham remained standing before the LORD.ª 23 Abraham stepped forward and said, "Will You really sweep away the righteous with the wicked? 24 What if there are 50 righteous people in the city? Will You really sweep it away instead of sparing the place for the sake of the 50 righteous people who are in it? 25 You could not possibly do such a thing: to kill the righteous with the wicked, treating the righteous and the wicked alike. You could not possibly do that! Won't the Judge of all the earth do what is just?"

26 The LORD said, "If at Sodom I find 50 righteous people in the city, I will spare the whole place for their sake."

27 Then Abraham answered, "Since I have ventured to speak to the Lord— even though I am dust and ashes— 28 suppose the 50 righteous lack five. Will you destroy the whole city for lack of five?"

He replied, "I will not destroy ⌊it⌋ if I find 45 there."

29 Then he spoke to Him again, "Suppose 40 are found there?"

He answered, "I will not do ⌊it⌋ on account of 40."

30 Then he said, "Let the Lord not be angry, and I will speak further. Suppose 30 are found there?"

He answered, "I will not do ⌊it⌋ if I find 30 there."

31 Then he said, "Since I have ventured to speak to the Lord, suppose 20 are found there?"

He replied, "I will not destroy ⌊it⌋ on account of 20."

32 Then he said, "Let the Lord not be angry, and I will speak one more time. Suppose 10 are found there?"

He answered, "I will not destroy ⌊it⌋ on account of 10." 33 When the LORD had finished speaking with Abraham, He departed, and Abraham returned to his place.

The Destruction of Sodom and Gomorrah

19 The two angels entered Sodom in the evening as Lot was sitting at Sodom's •gate. When Lot saw ⌊them⌋, he got up to meet them. He bowed ⌊with his⌋ face to the ground 2 and said, "My lords, turn aside to your servant's house, wash your feet, and spend the night. Then you can get up early and go on your way."

"No," they said. "We would rather spend the night in the square." 3 But he urged them so strongly that they followed him and went into his house. He prepared a feast and baked unleavened bread for them, and they ate.

Angels Threatened

4 Before they went to bed, the men of the city of Sodom, both young and old, the whole population, surrounded the house. 5 They called out to Lot and said, "Where are the men who came to you tonight? Send them out to us so we can have sex •with them!"

6 Lot went out to them at the entrance and shut the door behind him. 7 He said, "Don't do ⌊this⌋ evil, my brothers. 8 Look, I've got two daughters who haven't had sexual relations with a man. I'll bring them out to you, and you can do whatever you wantᵇ to them. However, don't do anything to these men, because they have come under the protection of my roof."

9 "Get out of the way!" they said, adding, "This one came here as a foreigner,

---

ª**18:22** One ancient Jewish tradition reads *while the LORD remained standing before Abraham*   ᵇ**19:8** Lit *do what is good in your eyes* but he's acting like a judge! Now we'll do more harm to you than to them." They put pressure on Lot and came up to break down the door. ¹⁰ But the angels^a reached out, brought Lot into the house with them, and shut the door. ¹¹ They struck the men who were at the door of the house, both young and old, with a blinding light so that they were unable to find the door.

Sodom Condemned

¹² Then the angels^a said to Lot, "Do you have anyone else here: a son-in-law, your sons and daughters, or anyone else in the city who belongs to you? Get them out of this place, ¹³ for we are about to destroy this place because the outcry against its people is great before the LORD, and the LORD has sent us to destroy it."

¹⁴ So Lot went out and spoke to his sons-in-law, who were going to marry^b his daughters. "Get up," he said. "Get out of this place, for the LORD is about to destroy the city!" But his sons-in-law thought he was joking.

¹⁵ At the crack of dawn the angels urged Lot on: "Get up! Take your wife and your two daughters who are here, or you will be swept away in the punishment^c of the city." ¹⁶ But he hesitated, so because of the LORD's compassion for him, the men grabbed his hand, his wife's hand, and the hands of his two daughters. And they brought him out and left him outside the city.

¹⁷ As soon as the angels got them outside, one of them^d said, "Run for your lives! Don't look back and don't stop anywhere on the plain! Run to the mountains, or you will be swept away!"

¹⁸ But Lot said to them, "No, Lord^e—please. ¹⁹ Your servant has indeed found favor in Your sight, and You have shown me great kindness by saving my life. But I can't run to the mountains; the disaster will overtake me, and I will die. ²⁰ Look, this town is close enough for me to run to. It is a small place. Please let me go there—it's only a small place, isn't it?—so that I can survive."

²¹ And he said to him, "All right,^f I'll grant your request^g about this matter too and will not overthrow the town you mentioned. ²² Hurry up! Run there, for I cannot do anything until you get there." Therefore the name of the city is Zoar.^h

Lot's Wife

²³ The sun had risen over the land when Lot reached Zoar. ²⁴ Then the LORD rained burning sulfur on Sodom and Gomorrah from the LORD out of the sky. ²⁵ He overthrew these cities, the entire plain, all the inhabitants of the cities, and whatever grew on the ground. ²⁶ But his wife looked back and became a pillar of salt.

²⁷ Early in the morning Abraham went to the place where he had stood before the LORD. ²⁸ He looked down toward Sodom and Gomorrah and all the land of the plain, and he saw that smoke was going up from the land like the smoke of a furnace. ²⁹ So it was, when God destroyed the cities of the plain, He remembered Abraham and brought Lot out of the middle of the upheaval when He overthrew the cities where Lot had lived.

Lot's Daughters: Origin of Moab and Ammon

³⁰ Lot departed from Zoar and lived in the mountains along with his two daugh-

---

^a**19:10,12** Lit *men*   ^b**19:14** Lit *take*   ^c**19:15** Or *iniquity,* or *guilt*   ^d**19:17** LXX, Syr, Vg read *outside, they*   ^e**19:18** Or *My Lord,* or *My lords*   ^f**19:21** Or *Look!*   ^g**19:21** Lit *I will lift up your face*   ^h**19:22** *Zoar* is related to the word for *small place* in v. 20; its original name was Bela (Gn 14:2).

ters, because he was afraid to live in Zoar. Instead, he and his two daughters lived in a cave. 31 Then the firstborn said to the younger, "Our father is old, and there is no man in the land to sleep with us ⌊as is⌋ the custom of all the land. 32 Come, let's get our father to drink wine so that we can sleep with him and preserve our father's line." 33 So they got their father to drink wine that night, and the firstborn came and slept with her father; he did not know when she lay down or when she got up.

34 The next day the firstborn said to the younger, "Look, I slept with my father last night. Let's get him to drink wine again tonight so you can go sleep with him and we can preserve our father's line." 35 That night they again got their father to drink wine, and the younger went and slept with him; he did not know when she lay down or when she got up.

36 So both of Lot's daughters became pregnant by their father. 37 The firstborn gave birth to a son and named him Moab.a He is the father of the Moabites of today. 38 The younger also gave birth to a son, and she named him Ben-ammi.b He is the father of the Ammonites of today.

Abraham Deceives Abimelech

20 From there Abraham traveled to the region of the •Negev and settled between Kadesh and Shur. While he lived in Gerar, 2 Abraham said about his wife Sarah, "She is my sister." So Abimelech king of Gerar had Sarah brought to him.

3 But God came to Abimelech in a dream by night and said to him, "You are about to die because of the woman you have taken, for she is a married woman."c

4 Now Abimelech had not approached her, so he said, "Lord, would you destroy a nation even though it is innocent? 5 Didn't he himself say to me, 'She is my sister'? And she herself said, 'He is my brother.' I did this with a clear conscienced and cleane hands."

God Rescues Sarah

6 Then God said to him in the dream, "Yes, I know that you did this with a clear conscience.f I have also kept you from sinning against Me. Therefore I have not let you touch her. 7 Now return the man's wife, for he is a prophet, and he will pray for you and you will live. But if you do not return her, know that you will certainly die, you and all who are yours."

8 Early in the morning Abimelech got up, called all his servants together, and personallyg told them all these things; and the men were terrified.

9 Then Abimelech called Abraham in and said to him, "What have you done to us? How did I sin against you that you have brought such enormous guilt on me and on my kingdom? You have done things to me that should never be done." 10 Abimelech also said to Abraham, "What did you intend when you did this thing?"

11 Abraham replied, "I thought, 'There is absolutely no •fear of God in this place. They will kill me because of my wife.' 12 Besides, she really is my sister, the daughter of my father though not the daughter of my mother, and she became my wife. 13 So when God had me wander from my father's house, I said to her: Show your loyalty to me wherever we

a19:37 = From My Father   b19:38 = Son of My People   c20:3 Lit is possessed by a husband   d20:5 Lit with integrity of my heart   e20:5 Lit cleanness of my   f20:6 Lit with integrity of your heart   g20:8 Lit in their ears

go, and say about me: 'He's my brother.' "

14 Then Abimelech took sheep and cattle and male and female slaves, gave them to Abraham, and returned his wife Sarah to him. 15 Abimelech said, "Look, my land is before you. Settle wherever you want."a 16 And to Sarah he said, "Look, I am giving your brother 1,000 pieces of silver. It is a verification of your honorb to all who are with you. You are fully vindicated."

17 Then Abraham prayed to God, and God healed Abimelech, his wife, and his female slaves so that they could bear children, 18 for the LORD had completely closed all the wombs in Abimelech's household on account of Sarah, Abraham's wife.

The Birth of Isaac

21 The LORD came to Sarah as He had said, and the LORD did for Sarah what He had promised. 2 Sarah became pregnant and bore a son to Abraham in his old age, at the appointed time God had told him. 3 Abraham named his son who was born to him—the one Sarah bore to him—Isaac. 4 When his son Isaac was eight days old, Abraham circumcised him, as God had commanded him. 5 Abraham was 100 years old when his son Isaac was born to him.

6 Sarah said, "God has made me laugh, and everyone who hears will laugh with me." 7 She also said, "Who would have told Abraham that Sarah would nurse children? Yet I have borne himc a son in his old age."

Hagar and Ishmael Banished

8 The child grew and was weaned, and Abraham held a great feast on the day Isaac was weaned. 9 But Sarah saw the son mockingd—the one Hagar the Egyptian had borne to Abraham. 10 So she said to Abraham, "Drive out this slave with her son, for the son of this slave will not be a co-heir with my son Isaac!"

11 Now this was a very difficult thing fore Abraham because of his son. 12 But God said to Abraham, "Do not be concernedf about the boy and your slave. Whatever Sarah says to you, listen to her, because your •offspring will be traced through Isaac. 13 But I will also make a nation of the slave's son because he is your offspring."

14 Early in the morning Abraham got up, took bread and a waterskin, ⌊put them⌋ on Hagar's shoulders, and sent her and the boy away.g She left and wandered in the Wilderness of Beer-sheba. 15 When the water in the skin was gone, she left the boy under one of the bushes. 16 Then she went and sat down nearby, about a bowshot away, for she said, "I can't ⌊bear to⌋ watch the boy die!" So as she sat nearby, sheh wept loudly.

God Saves Ishmael

17 God heard the voice of the boy, and thei angel of God called to Hagar from heaven and said to her, "What's wrong, Hagar? Don't be afraid, for God has heard the voice of the boy from the place where he is. 18 Get up, help the boy up, and sustain him, for I will make him a great nation." 19 Then God opened her eyes, and she saw a well of water. So she went and filled the waterskin and gave the boy a drink. 20 God was with the boy, and he grew; he settled in the wilderness and became an archer. 21 He settled in the Wilderness of Paran, and his

---

a**20:15** Lit Settle in the good in your eyes   b**20:16** Lit a covering of the eyes   c**21:7** Sam, Tg Jonathan; MT omits him
d**21:9** LXX, Vg add Isaac her son   e**21:11** Lit was very bad in the eyes of   f**21:12** Lit Let it not be bad in your eyes
g**21:14** To "send away" a woman = divorce her; Dt 24:1. To "send away" a slave = free her; Dt 15:13.   h**21:16** LXX reads the boy   i**21:17** Or an

mother got a wife for him from the land of Egypt.

Abraham's Treaty with Abimelech

²² At that time Abimelech, with Phicol the commander of his army, said to Abraham, "God is with you in everything you do. ²³ Now swear to me here by God that you will not break an agreement with me or with my children and descendants. As I have kept faith with you, so you will keep faith with me and with the country where you are a resident alien."

²⁴ And Abraham said, "I swear ⌊it⌋." ²⁵ But Abraham complained to Abimelech because of the water well that Abimelech's servants had seized.

²⁶ Abimelech replied, "I don't know who did this thing. You didn't report anything to me, so I hadn't heard about it until today."

²⁷ Then Abraham took sheep and cattle[a] and gave them to Abimelech, and the two of them made a covenant. ²⁸ But Abraham had set apart seven ewe lambs from the flock. ²⁹ And Abimelech said to Abraham, "Why have you set apart these seven ewe lambs?"

³⁰ He replied, "You are to accept the seven ewe lambs from my hand so that this act[b] will serve as my witness that I dug this well." ³¹ Therefore that place was called Beer-sheba[c] because it was there that the two of them swore an oath. ³² After they had made a covenant at Beer-sheba, Abimelech and Phicol, the commander of his army, left and returned to the land of the Philistines.

³³ Abraham planted a tamarisk tree in Beer-sheba, and there he worshiped[d] the LORD, the Everlasting God. ³⁴ And Abraham lived as a foreigner in the land of the Philistines for many days.

The Sacrifice of Isaac

22 After these things God tested Abraham and said to him, "Abraham!"

"Here I am," he answered.

² "Take your son," He said, "your only ⌊son⌋ Isaac, whom you love, go to the land of Moriah, and offer him there as a •burnt offering on one of the mountains I will tell you about."

Abraham Prepares Sacrifice

³ So early in the morning Abraham got up, saddled his donkey, and took with him two of his young men and his son Isaac. He split wood for a burnt offering and set out to go to the place God had told him about. ⁴ On the third day Abraham looked up and saw the place in the distance. ⁵ Then Abraham said to his young men, "Stay here with the donkey. The boy and I will go over there to worship; then we'll come back to you." ⁶ Abraham took the wood for the burnt offering and laid it on his son Isaac. In his hand he took the fire and the sacrificial knife,[e] and the two of them walked on together.

⁷ Then Isaac spoke to his father Abraham and said, "My father."

And he replied, "Here I am, my son."

Isaac said, "The fire and the wood are here, but where is the lamb for the burnt offering?"

⁸ Abraham answered, "God Himself will provide[f] the lamb for the burnt offering, my son." Then the two of them walked on together.

---

[a] **21:27** A covenant or treaty was regularly ratified by animal sacrifice (Gn 8:20—9:9; 15:9-17; Ex 24:8) and often involved an exchange of gifts (1 Kg 15:19; Hs 12:1). The animals here could serve both purposes. [b] **21:30** Lit *that it* [c] **21:31** = Seven Wells, or Well of the Oath [d] **21:33** Or *proclaimed* or *invoked the name of*; lit *called on the name of* [e] **22:6** The same word is used in Jdg 19:29 and Pr 30:14. [f] **22:8** Lit *see*

⁹ When they arrived at the place that God had told him about, Abraham built the altar there and arranged the wood. He bound his son Isaacª and placed him on the altar, on top of the wood. ¹⁰ Then Abraham reached out and took the knife to slaughter his son.

¹¹ But the Angel of the LORD called to him from heaven and said, "Abraham, Abraham!"

He replied, "Here I am."

¹² Then He said, "Do not lay a hand on the boy or do anything to him. For now I know that you •fear God, since you have not withheld your only son from Me." ¹³ Abraham looked up and saw a ramᵇ caught by its horns in the thicket. So Abraham went and took the ram and offered it as a burnt offering in place of his son. ¹⁴ And Abraham named that place The LORD Will Provide,ᶜ so today it is said: "It will be providedᵈ on the LORD's mountain."

God Commends Abraham

¹⁵ Then the Angel of the LORD called to Abraham a second time from heaven ¹⁶ and said, "By Myself I have sworn, says the LORD: Because you have done this thing and have not withheld your only son,ᵉ ¹⁷ I will indeed bless you and make your •offspring as numerous as the stars in the sky and the sand on the seashore. Your offspring will possess the gates of their enemies. ¹⁸ And all the nations of the earth will be blessedᶠ by your offspring because you have obeyed My command."

¹⁹ Abraham went back to his young men, and they got up and went together to Beer-sheba. And Abraham settled in Beer-sheba.

Rebekah's Family

²⁰ Now after these things Abraham was told, "Milcah also has borne sons to your brother Nahor: ²¹ Uz his firstborn, his brother Buz, Kemuel the father of Aram, ²² Chesed, Hazo, Pildash, Jidlaph, and Bethuel." ²³ And Bethuel fathered Rebekah. Milcah bore these eight to Nahor, Abraham's brother. ²⁴ His concubine, whose name was Reumah, also bore Tebah, Gaham, Tahash, and Maacah.

Sarah's Burial

23 Now Sarah lived 127 years; ₓthese were allₓ the years of her life. ² Sarah died in Kiriath-arba (that is, Hebron) in the land of Canaan, and Abraham went in to mourn for Sarah and to weep for her.

³ Then Abraham got up from beside his dead ₓwifeₓ and spoke to the Hittites: ⁴ "I am a resident alien among you. Give me a burial site among you so that I can bury my dead."ᵍ

⁵ The Hittites replied to Abraham,ʰ ⁶ "Listen to us, lord.ⁱ You are God's chosen one among us. Bury your dead in our finest burial place.ʲ None of us will withhold from you his burial place for burying your dead."

Abraham's Family Tomb at Hebron

⁷ Then Abraham rose and bowed down to the Hittites, the people of the land. ⁸ He said to them, "If you are willing ₓfor meₓ to bury my dead, listen to me and ask Ephron son of Zohar on my behalf ⁹ to give me the cave of Machpelah that belongs to him; it is at the end of his field. Let him give it to me in your pres-

---

ª**22:9** Or perhaps *Isaac hand and foot* ᵇ**22:13** Some Hb mss, Sam, LXX, Syr, Tg; other Hb mss read *saw behind [him] a ram* ᶜ**22:14** Hb *Yahweh-yireh* ᵈ**22:14** Or *He will be seen* ᵉ**22:16** Sam, LXX, Syr, Vg add *from Me* ᶠ**22:18** Or *will bless themselves,* or *will find blessing* ᵍ**23:4** Lit *dead from before me* ʰ**23:5** Lit *Abraham, saying to him* ⁱ**23:6** Lit *my lord* ʲ**23:6** Or *finest graves*

ence, for the full price, as a burial place."

¹⁰ Ephron was present with the Hittites. So in the presence[a] of all the Hittites who came to the •gate of his city, Ephron the Hittite answered Abraham: ¹¹ "No, my lord. Listen to me. I give you the field, and I give you the cave that is in it. I give it to you in the presence[b] of my people. Bury your dead."

¹² Abraham bowed down to the people of the land ¹³ and said to Ephron in the presence[a] of the people of the land, "Please listen to me. Let me pay the price of the field. Accept it from me, and let me bury my dead there."

¹⁴ Ephron answered Abraham and said to him, ¹⁵ "My lord, listen to me. Land worth 400 •shekels of silver—what is that between you and me? Bury your dead." ¹⁶ Abraham agreed with Ephron, and Abraham weighed out to Ephron the silver that he had agreed to in the hearing of the Hittites: 400 shekels of silver at the current commercial rate. ¹⁷ So Ephron's field at Machpelah near Mamre—the field with its cave and all the trees anywhere within the boundaries of the field—became ¹⁸ Abraham's possession in the presence of all the Hittites who came to the gate of his city. ¹⁹ After this, Abraham buried his wife Sarah in the cave of the field at Machpelah near Mamre (that is, Hebron) in the land of Canaan. ²⁰ The field with its cave passed from the Hittites to Abraham as a burial place.

Isaac Marries Rebekah

24 Abraham was now old, getting on in years,[c] and the LORD had blessed him in everything. ² Abraham said to his servant, the elder of his household who managed all he owned,

"Place your hand under my thigh, ³ and I will have you swear by the LORD, God of heaven and God of earth, that you will not take a wife for my son from the daughters of the Canaanites among whom I live, ⁴ but will go to my land and my family to take a wife for my son Isaac."

⁵ The servant said to him, "Suppose the woman is unwilling to follow me to this land? Should I have your son go back to the land you came from?"

⁶ Abraham answered him, "Make sure that you don't take my son back there. ⁷ The LORD, the God of heaven, who took me from my father's house and from my native land, who spoke to me and swore to me, 'I will give this land to your •offspring'—He will send His angel before you, and you can take a wife for my son from there. ⁸ If the woman is unwilling to follow you, then you are free from this oath to me, but don't let my son go back there." ⁹ So the servant placed his hand under his master Abraham's thigh and swore an oath to him concerning this matter.

¹⁰ The servant took 10 of his master's camels and departed with all kinds of his master's goods in hand. Then he set out for the town of Nahor, Aram-naharaim. ¹¹ He made the camels kneel beside a well of water outside the town at evening. ⌊This was⌋ the time when the women went out to draw water.

Abraham's Servant Prays for Help

¹² "LORD, God of my master Abraham," he prayed, "grant me success today, and show kindness to my master Abraham. ¹³ I am standing here at the spring where the daughters of the men of the town are coming out to draw water. ¹⁴ Let the girl to whom I say, 'Please

---

[a]23:10,13 Lit ears   [b]23:11 Lit in the eyes of the sons   [c]24:1 Lit days

lower your water jug so that I may drink,' and who responds, 'Drink, and I'll water your camels also'—let her be the one You have appointed for Your servant Isaac. By this I will know that You have shown kindness to my master."

God's Answer: Rebekah

¹⁵ Before he had finished speaking, there was Rebekah—daughter of Bethuel son of Milcah, the wife of Abraham's brother Nahor—coming with a jug on her shoulder. ¹⁶ Now the girl was very beautiful, a young woman who had not known a man intimately. She went down to the spring, filled her jug, and came up. ¹⁷ Then the servant ran to meet her and said, "Please let me have a little water from your jug."

¹⁸ She replied, "Drink, my lord." She quickly lowered her jug to her hand and gave him a drink. ¹⁹ When she had finished giving him a drink, she said, "I'll also draw water for your camels until they have had enough to drink."ᵃ ²⁰ She quickly emptied her jug into the trough and hurried to the well again to draw water. She drew water for all his camels ²¹ while the man silently watched her to see whether or not the LORD had made his journey a success.

²² After the camels had finished drinking, the man took a gold ring weighing half a •shekel, and for her wrists two bracelets weighing 10 shekels of gold. ²³ "Whose daughter are you?" he asked. "Please tell me, is there room in your father's house for us to spend the night?"

²⁴ She answered him, "I am the daughter of Bethuel son of Milcah, whom she bore to Nahor." ²⁵ She also said to him, "We have plenty of straw and feed, and a place to spend the night."

²⁶ Then the man bowed down, worshiped the LORD, ²⁷ and said, "Praise the LORD, the God of my master Abraham, who has not withheld His kindness and faithfulness from my master. As for me, the LORD has led me on the journey to the house of my master's relatives."

Marriage Discussions

²⁸ The girl ran and told her mother's household about these things. ²⁹ Now Rebekah had a brother named Laban, and Laban ran out to the man at the spring. ³⁰ As soon as he had seen the ring, and the bracelets on his sister's wrists, and when he had heard his sister Rebekah's words—"The man said this to me!"—he went to the man. He was standing there by the camels at the spring.

³¹ Laban said, "Come, you who are blessed by the LORD. Why are you standing out here? I have prepared the house and a place for the camels." ³² So the man came to the house, and the camels were unloaded. Straw and feed were given to the camels, and water was brought to wash his feet and the feet of the men with him.

³³ A meal was set before him, but he said, "I will not eat until I have said what I have to say."

So Laban said, "Speak on."

³⁴ "I am Abraham's servant," he said. ³⁵ "The LORD has greatly blessed my master, and he has become rich. He has given him sheep and cattle, silver and gold, male and female slaves, and camels and donkeys. ³⁶ Sarah, my master's wife, bore a son to my master in herᵇ old age, and he has given him everything he owns. ³⁷ My master put me under this oath: 'You will not take a wife for my son from the daughters of the Canaanites in

ᵃ24:19 Lit *they are finished drinking*   ᵇ24:36 Sam, LXX read *his*

whose land I live ³⁸ but will go to my father's household and to my family to
take a wife for my son.' ³⁹ But I said to
my master, 'Suppose the woman will not
come back with me?' ⁴⁰ He said to me,
'The LORD before whom I have walked
will send His angel with you and make
your journey a success, and you will take
a wife for my son from my family and
from my father's household. ⁴¹ Then you
will be free from my oath if you go to my
family and they do not give ⌊her⌋ to
you—you will be free from my oath.'

⁴² "Today when I came to the spring, I
prayed: LORD, God of my master Abraham, if only You will make my journey
successful! ⁴³ I am standing here at a
spring. Let the virgin who comes out to
draw water, and I say to her: Please let
me drink a little water from your jug,
⁴⁴ and who responds to me, 'Drink, and
I'll draw water for your camels also'—let
her be the woman the LORD has appointed for my master's son.

⁴⁵ "Before I had finished praying in
my heart, there was Rebekah coming
with her jug on her shoulder, and she
went down to the spring and drew water. So I said to her: Please let me have
a drink. ⁴⁶ She quickly lowered her jug
from her ⌊shoulder⌋ and said, 'Drink,
and I'll water your camels also.' So I
drank, and she also watered the camels. ⁴⁷ Then I asked her: Whose daughter are you? She responded, 'The
daughter of Bethuel son of Nahor,
whom Milcah bore to him.' So I put the
ring on her nose and the bracelets on
her wrists. ⁴⁸ Then I bowed down, worshiped the LORD, and praised the LORD,
the God of my master Abraham, who
guided me on the right way to take the
daughter of my master's brother for his
son. ⁴⁹ Now, if you are going to show
kindness and faithfulness to my master,
tell me; if not, tell me, and I will go
elsewhere."ᵃ

Laban and Bethuel Agree

⁵⁰ Laban and Bethuel answered, "This
is from the LORD; we have no choice in
the matter.ᵇ ⁵¹ Rebekah is here in front of
you. Take ⌊her⌋ and go, and let her be a
wife for your master's son, just as the
LORD has spoken."

⁵² When Abraham's servant heard
their words, he bowed to the ground before the LORD. ⁵³ Then he brought out
objects of silver and gold, and garments,
and gave ⌊them⌋ to Rebekah. He also gave
precious gifts to her brother and her
mother. ⁵⁴ Then he and the men with
him ate and drank and spent the night.

When they got up in the morning, he
said, "Send me to my master."

⁵⁵ But her brother and mother said,
"Let the girl stay with us for about 10
days.ᶜ Then sheᵈ can go."

⁵⁶ But he responded to them, "Do not
delay me, since the LORD has made my
journey a success. Send me away so that
I may go to my master."

Rebekah Agrees

⁵⁷ So they said, "Let's call the girl and
ask her opinion."ᵉ

⁵⁸ They called Rebekah and said to her,
"Will you go with this man?"

She replied, "I will go." ⁵⁹ So they sent
away their sister Rebekah and her nurse,
and Abraham's servant and his men.

⁶⁰ They blessed Rebekah, saying to
her:

Our sister, may you become
thousands upon ten thousands.
May your offspring possess
the gates of theirᶠ enemies.

⁶¹ Then Rebekah and her young women got up, mounted the camels, and followed the man. So the servant took Rebekah and left.

Isaac Loves Rebekah

⁶² Now Isaac was returning from Beer-lahai-roi,ᵃ for he was living in the •Negev region. ⁶³ In the early evening, Isaac went out to walkᵇ in the field, and looking up, he saw camels coming. ⁶⁴ Rebekah looked up, and when she saw Isaac, she got down from her camel ⁶⁵ and asked the servant, "Who is that man in the field coming to meet us?"

The servant answered, "It is my master." So she took her veil and covered herself. ⁶⁶ Then the servant told Isaac everything he had done.

⁶⁷ And Isaac brought her into the tent of his mother Sarah and took Rebekah to be his wife. Isaac loved her, and he was comforted after his mother's death.

Abraham's Other Wife and Sons

25 Now Abraham took another wife, whose name was Keturah, ² and she bore him Zimran, Jokshan, Medan, Midian, Ishbak, and Shuah. ³ Jokshan fathered Sheba and Dedan. Dedan's sons were the Asshurim, Letushim, and Leummim. ⁴ And Midian's sons were Ephah, Epher, Hanoch, Abida, and Eldaah. All these were sons of Keturah. ⁵ Abraham gave everything he owned to Isaac. ⁶ And Abraham gave gifts to the sons of his concubines, but while he was still alive he sent them eastward, away from his son Isaac, to the land of the East.

Abraham's Death

⁷ This is the length of Abraham's life:ᶜ 175 years. ⁸ He took his last breath and died at a ripe old age, old and contented,ᵈ and he was gathered to his people. ⁹ His sons Isaac and Ishmael buried him in the cave of Machpelah near Mamre, in the field of Ephron son of Zohar the Hittite. ¹⁰ This was the field that Abraham bought from the Hittites. Abraham was buried there with his wife Sarah. ¹¹ After Abraham's death, God blessed his son Isaac, who lived near Beer-lahai-roi.

Ishmael's Descendants

¹² These are the family records of Abraham's son Ishmael, whom Hagar the Egyptian, Sarah's slave, bore to Abraham. ¹³ These are the names of Ishmael's sons; their names according to the family records are: Nebaioth, Ishmael's firstborn, then Kedar, Adbeel, Mibsam, ¹⁴ Mishma, Dumah, Massa, ¹⁵ Hadad, Tema, Jetur, Naphish, and Kedemah. ¹⁶ These are Ishmael's sons, and these are their names by their villages and encampments: 12 leadersᵉ of their clans.ᶠ ¹⁷ This is the lengthᵍ of Ishmael's life: 137 years. He took his last breath and died, and was gathered to his people. ¹⁸ And theyʰ settled from Havilah to Shur, which is opposite Egypt as you go toward Asshur. Heⁱ lived in opposition toʲ all his brothers.

Birth of Jacob and Esau

¹⁹ These are the family records of Isaac son of Abraham. Abraham fathered Isaac. ²⁰ Isaac was 40 years old when he took as his wife Rebekah daughter of Bethuel the Aramean from Paddan-aram, and sister of Laban the Aramean. ²¹ Isaac prayed to the LORD on behalf of his wife because she was barren. The LORD heard his prayer, and his wife Rebekah con-

ᵃ**24:62** = A Well of the Living One Who Sees Me; Gn 16:13-14 ᵇ**24:63** Or *pray,* or *meditate;* Hb obscure ᶜ**25:7** Lit *And these are the days of the years of the lives of Abraham that he lived* ᵈ**25:8** Sam, LXX, Syr read *full of days* ᵉ**25:16** Or *chieftains* ᶠ**25:16** Or *peoples* ᵍ**25:17** Lit *And these are the years* ʰ**25:18** LXX, Vg read *he* ⁱ**25:18** Ishmael and his descendants ʲ**25:18** Or *He settled down alongside of*

ceived. ²² But the children inside her struggled with each other, and she said, "Why is this happening to me?"ᵃ So she went to inquire of the LORD. ²³ And the LORD said to her:

> Two nations are in your womb;
> two people will ⌊come⌋ from you
>   and be separated.
> One people will be stronger
>   than the other,
> and the older will serve the younger.

²⁴ When her time came to give birth, there were indeed <u>twins in her womb</u>. ²⁵ The first one came out reddish,ᵇ covered with hairᶜ like a fur coat, and they named him <u>Esau</u>. ²⁶ After this, his brother came out grasping Esau's heel with his hand. So he was named <u>Jacob</u>.ᵈ Isaac was 60 years old when they were born.

Esau Sells His Birthright

²⁷ When the boys grew up, Esau became an expert hunter, an outdoorsman,ᵉ but Jacob was a quiet man who stayed at home.ᶠ ²⁸ Isaac loved Esau because he had a taste for wild game, but Rebekah loved Jacob.

Hard Deal: Stew for Legacy

²⁹ Once when Jacob was cooking a stew, Esau came in from the field, exhausted. ³⁰ He said to Jacob, "Let me eat some of that red stuff, because I'm exhausted." That is why he was ⌊also⌋ named Edom.ᵍ

³¹ Jacob replied, "First sell me your birthright."

³² "Look," said Esau, "I'm about to die, so what good is a birthright to me?"

³³ Jacob said, "Swear to me first." So he swore to Jacob and sold his birthright

to him. ³⁴ Then Jacob gave bread and lentil stew to Esau; he ate, drank, got up, and went away. So Esau despised his birthright.

Isaac Deceives Abimelech

26 There was another famine in the land in addition to the one that had occurred in Abraham's time. And Isaac went to Abimelech, king of the Philistines, at Gerar.

God's Promise to Isaac

² The LORD appeared to him and said, "Do not go down to Egypt. Live in the land that I tell you about; ³ stay in this land as a foreigner, and I will be with you and bless you. For I will give all these lands to you and your •offspring, and I will confirm the oath that I swore to your father Abraham. ⁴ I will make your offspring as numerous as the stars of the sky, I will give your offspring all these lands, and all the nations of the earth will be blessedʰ by your offspring, ⁵ because Abraham listened to My voice and kept My mandate, My commands, My statutes, and My instructions." ⁶ So Isaac settled in Gerar.

Like Father, Like Son

⁷ When the men of the place asked about his wife, he said, "She is my sister," for he was afraid to say "my wife," ⌊thinking⌋, "The men of the place will kill me on account of Rebekah, for she is a beautiful woman." ⁸ When Isaac had been there for some time, Abimelech king of the Philistines looked down from the window and was surprised to seeⁱ Isaac caressing his wife Rebekah.

ᵃ**25:22** Lit *If thus, why this I*   ᵇ**25:25** The Hb word for *reddish* sounds like the Hb word "Edom" (Gn 32:3).
ᶜ**25:25** The Hb word for *hair* sounds like the Hb word "Seir" (Gn 32:3).   ᵈ**25:26** = He Grasps the Heel   ᵉ**25:27** Lit *a man of the field*   ᶠ**25:27** Lit *man living in tents*   ᵍ**25:30** = Red   ʰ**26:4** Or *will bless themselves*   ⁱ**26:8** Or *and he looked and behold—*

⁹ Abimelech sent for Isaac and said, "So she is really your wife! How could you say, 'She's my sister'?"

Isaac answered him, "Because I thought I might die on account of her."

¹⁰ Then Abimelech said, "What is this you've done to us? One of the people could easily have slept with your wife, and you would have brought guilt on us." ¹¹ So Abimelech warned all the people with these words: "Whoever harms this man or his wife will certainly die."

Conflicts over Wells

¹² Isaac sowed seed in that land, and in that year he reapedª a hundred times ⌊what was sown⌋. The LORD blessed him, ¹³ and the man became rich and kept getting richer until he was very wealthy. ¹⁴ He had flocks of sheep, herds of cattle, and many slaves, and the Philistines were envious of him. ¹⁵ The Philistines stopped up all the wells that his father's slaves had dug in the days of his father Abraham, filling them with dirt. ¹⁶ And Abimelech said to Isaac, "Leave us, for you are much too powerful for us."ᵇ

Isaac Moves

¹⁷ So Isaac left there, camped in the valley of Gerar, and lived there. ¹⁸ Isaac reopened the water wells that had been dug in the days of his father Abraham and that the Philistines had stopped up after Abraham died. He gave them the same names his father had given them. ¹⁹ Moreover, Isaac's slaves dug in the valley and found a well of springᶜ water there. ²⁰ But the herdsmen of Gerar quarreled with Isaac's herdsmen and said, "The water is ours!" So he named the well Quarrelᵈ because they quarreled with him. ²¹ Then they dug another well

and quarreled over that one also, so he named it Hostility.ᵉ ²² He moved from there and dug another, and they did not quarrel over it. He named it Open Spacesᶠ and said, "For now the LORD has made room for us, and we will be fruitful in the land."

Isaac Moves Again—and God Appears

²³ From there he went up to Beersheba, ²⁴ and the LORD appeared to him that night and said, "I am the God of your father Abraham. Do not be afraid, for I am with you. I will bless you and multiply your offspring because of My servant Abraham."

²⁵ So he built an altar there, worshipedᵍ the LORD, and pitched his tent there. Isaac's slaves also dug a well there.

Treaty with Abimelech

²⁶ Then Abimelech came to him from Gerar with Ahuzzath his adviser and Phicol the commander of his army. ²⁷ Isaac said to them, "Why have you come to me? You hated me and sent me away from you."

²⁸ They replied, "We have clearly seen how the LORD has been with you. We think there should be an oath between two parties—between us and you. Let us make a covenant with you: ²⁹ You will not harm us, just as we have not harmed you but have only done what was good to you, sending you away in peace. You are now blessed by the LORD."

³⁰ So he prepared a banquet for them, and they ate and drank. ³¹ They got up early in the morning and swore an oath to each other.ʰ Then Isaac sent them on their way, and they left him in peace.

ª**26:12** Lit found   ᵇ**26:16** Or are more numerous than we are   ᶜ**26:19** Lit living   ᵈ**26:20** Hb Esek   ᵉ**26:21** Hb Sitnah   ᶠ**26:22** Hb Rehoboth   ᵍ**26:25** Or proclaimed or invoked the name of; lit called on the name of   ʰ**26:31** Lit swore, each man to his brother

[32] On that same day Isaac's slaves came to tell him about the well they had dug, saying to him, "We have found water!" [33] He called it Oath.[a] Therefore the name of the city is Beer-sheba[b] to this day.

Esau Marries

[34] When Esau was 40 years old, he took as his wives Judith daughter of Beeri the Hittite, and Basemath daughter of Elon the Hittite. [35] They made life bitter[c] for Isaac and Rebekah.

Jacob Steals Esau's Blessing

27 When Isaac was old and his eyes were so weak that he could not see, he called his older son Esau and said to him, "My son."

And he answered, "Here I am."

[2] He said, "Look, I am old and do not know the day of my death. [3] Take your ⌊hunting⌋ gear, your quiver and bow, and go out in the field to hunt some game for me. [4] Then make me the delicious food that I love and bring it to me to eat, so that I can bless you before I die."

[5] Now Rebekah was listening to what Isaac said to his son Esau. So while Esau went to the field to hunt some game to bring in, [6] Rebekah said to her son Jacob, "Listen! I heard your father talking with your brother Esau. He said, [7] 'Bring me some game and make some delicious food for me to eat so that I can bless you in the LORD's presence before I die.' [8] Now obey every order I give you, my son. [9] Go to the flock and bring me two choice young goats, and I will make them into a delicious meal for your father—the kind he loves. [10] Then take it to your father to eat so that he may bless you before he dies."

Jacob's Disguise

[11] Jacob answered Rebekah his mother, "Look, my brother Esau is a hairy man, but I am a man with smooth skin. [12] Suppose my father touches me. Then I will seem to be deceiving him, and I will bring a curse rather than a blessing on myself."

[13] His mother said to him, "Your curse be on me, my son. Just obey me and go get them for me."

[14] So he went and got them and brought them to his mother, and his mother made the delicious food his father loved. [15] Then Rebekah took the best clothes of her older son Esau, which were there at the house, and had her younger son Jacob wear them. [16] She put the goatskins on his hands and the smooth part of his neck. [17] Then she handed the delicious food and the bread she had made to her son Jacob.

Jacob Deceives Isaac

[18] When he came to his father, he said, "My father."

And he answered, "Here I am. Who are you, my son?"

[19] Jacob replied to his father, "I am Esau, your firstborn. I have done as you told me. Please sit up and eat some of my game so that you may bless me."

[20] But Isaac said to his son, "How did you ever find it so quickly, my son?"

He replied, "Because the LORD your God worked it out for me."

[21] Then Isaac said to Jacob, "Please come closer so I can touch you, my son. Are you really my son Esau, or not?"

[22] So Jacob came closer to his father Isaac. When he touched him, he said, "The voice is the voice of Jacob, but the hands are the hands of Esau." [23] He did not recognize him, because his hands

---

[a]**26:33** Hb *Shibah*   [b]**26:33** = Well of the Oath   [c]**26:35** Lit *And they became bitterness of spirit*

were hairy like those of his brother Esau; so he blessed him. ²⁴ Again he asked, "Are you really my son Esau?"

And he replied, "I am."

²⁵ Then he said, "Serve me, and let me eat some of my son's game so that I can bless you." Jacob brought it to him, and he ate; he brought him wine, and he drank.

²⁶ Then his father Isaac said to him, "Please come closer and kiss me, my son." ²⁷ So he came closer and kissed him. When Isaac smelledª his clothes, he blessed him and said:

> Ah, the smell of my son
> is like the smell of a field
> that the LORD has blessed.
> ²⁸ May God give to you—
> from the dew of the sky
> and from the richness of the land—
> an abundance of grain and new wine.
> ²⁹ May peoples serve you
> and nations bow down to you.
> Be master over your brothers;
> may your mother's sons bow down
> to you.
> Those who curse you
> will be cursed,
> and those who bless you
> will be blessed.

Esau Enraged

³⁰ As soon as Isaac had finished blessing Jacob and Jacob had left the presence of his father Isaac, his brother Esau arrived from the hunt. ³¹ He had also made some delicious food and brought it to his father. Then he said to his father, "Let my father get up and eat some of his son's game, so that you may bless me."

³² But his father Isaac said to him, "Who are you?"

He answered, "I am Esau your first-born son."

³³ Isaac began to tremble uncontrollably. "Who was it then," he said, "who hunted game and brought it to me? I ate it all before you came in, and I blessed him. Indeed, he will be blessed!"

³⁴ When Esau heard his father's words, he cried out with a loud and bitter cry and said to his father, "Bless me—me too, my father!"

³⁵ But he replied, "Your brother came deceitfully and took your blessing."

³⁶ So he said, "Isn't he rightly named Jacob?ᵇ For he has cheated me twice now. He took my birthright, and look, now he has taken my blessing." Then he asked, "Haven't you saved a blessing for me?"

³⁷ But Isaac answered Esau: "Look, I have made him a master over you, have given him all of his relatives as his servants, and have sustained him with grain and new wine. What then can I do for you, my son?"

³⁸ Esau said to his father, "Do you only have one blessing, my father? Bless me—me too, my father!" And Esau wept loudly.ᶜ

³⁹ Then his father Isaac answered him:

> Look, your dwelling place will be
> away from the richness of the land,
> away from the dew
> of the sky above.
> ⁴⁰ You will live by your sword,
> and you will serve your brother.
> But when you rebel,ᵈ
> you will break his yoke
> from your neck.

Jacob Flees

Esau Plots Murder

⁴¹ Esau held a grudge against Jacob because of the blessing his father had given him. And Esau determined in his heart:

ª**27:27** Lit *smelled the smell of*   ᵇ**27:36** = He Grasps the Heel   ᶜ**27:38** Lit *Esau lifted up his voice and wept*   ᵈ**27:40** Hb obscure

"The days of mourning for my father are approaching; then I will kill my brother Jacob."

⁴²When the words of her older son Esau were reported to Rebekah, she summoned her younger son Jacob and said to him, "Listen, your brother Esau is consoling himself by planning to kill you. ⁴³So now, my son, listen to me. Flee at once to my brother Laban in Haran, ⁴⁴and stay with him for a few days until your brother's anger subsides— ⁴⁵until your brother's rage turns away from you and he forgets what you have done to him. Then I will send for you and bring you back from there. Why should I lose you both in one day?"

⁴⁶So Rebekah said to Isaac, "I'm sick of my life because of these Hittite women. If Jacob marries a Hittite woman like one of them,ª what good is my life?"

Isaac's Blessing and Jacob's Escape

28 Isaac summoned Jacob, blessed him, and commanded him: "Don't take a wife from the Canaanite women. ²Go at once to Paddan-aram, to the house of Bethuel, your mother's father. Marry one of the daughters of Laban, your mother's brother. ³May •God Almighty bless you and make you fruitful and multiply you so that you become an assembly of peoples. ⁴May God give you and your •offspring the blessing of Abraham so that you may possess the land where you live as an alien, the land God gave to Abraham." ⁵So Isaac sent Jacob to Paddan-aram, to Laban son of Bethuel the Aramean, the brother of Rebekah, the mother of Jacob and Esau.

Esau Marries Again

⁶Esau noticed that Isaac blessed Jacob and sent him to Paddan-aram to get a wife there. When he blessed him, Isaac commanded Jacob not to marry a Canaanite woman. ⁷And Jacob listened to his father and mother and went to Paddan-aram. ⁸Esau realized that his father Isaac disapproved of the Canaanite women, ⁹so Esau went to Ishmael and married, in addition to his other wives, Mahalath daughter of Ishmael, Abraham's son. She was the sister of Nebaioth.

Jacob's Dream at Bethel

¹⁰Jacob left Beer-sheba and went toward Haran. ¹¹He reached a certain place and spent the night there because the sun had set. He took one of the stones from the place, put it there at his head, and lay down in that place. ¹²And he dreamed: A stairway was set on the ground with its top reaching heaven, and God's angels were going up and down on it.

God's Promise to Jacob

¹³The LORD was standing there beside him, saying, "I am the LORD, the God of your father Abraham and the God of Isaac. I will give you and your offspring the land that you are now sleeping on. ¹⁴Your offspring will be like the dust of the earth, and you will spread out toward the west, the east, the north, and the south. All the peoples on earth will be blessed through you and your offspring. ¹⁵Look, I am with you and will watch over you wherever you go. I will bring you back to this land, for I will not leave you until I have done what I have promised you."

Jacob's Altar

¹⁶When Jacob awoke from his sleep, he said, "Surely the LORD is in this place,

ª**27:46** Lit *of these daughters of the land*

and I did not know it." ¹⁷ He was afraid and said, "What an awesome place this is! This is none other than the house of God. This is the gate of heaven."

¹⁸ Early in the morning Jacob took the stone that was near his head and set it up as a marker. He poured oil on top of it ¹⁹ and named the place Bethel,ᵃ though previously the city was named Luz. ²⁰ Then Jacob made a vow: "If God will be with me and watch over me on this journey, if He provides me with food to eat and clothing to wear, ²¹ and if I return safely to my father's house, then the LORD will be my God. ²² This stone that I have set up as a marker will be God's house, and I will give to You a tenth of all that You give me."

Jacob Meets Rachel

29 Jacob resumed his journeyᵇ and went to the eastern country.ᶜ ² He looked and saw a well in a field. Three flocks of sheep were lying there beside it because the sheep were watered from this well. A large stone covered the opening of the well. ³ When all the flocksᵈ were gathered there, the ⌊shepherds⌋ would roll the stone from the opening of the well and water the sheep. The stone was then placed back on the well's opening.

⁴ Jacob asked the men at the well, "My brothers! Where are you from?"

"We're from Haran," they answered.

⁵ "Do you know Laban son of Nahor?" Jacob asked them.

They answered, "We know ⌊him⌋."

⁶ "Is he well?" Jacob asked.

"Yes," they said, "and here is his daughter Rachel, coming with his sheep."

⁷ Then Jacob said, "Look, it is still broad daylight. It's not time for the animals to be gathered. Water the flock, then go out and let them graze."

⁸ But they replied, "We can't, until all the flocks have been gathered and the stone is rolled from the well's opening. Then we will water the sheep."

First Meeting with Rachel

⁹ While he was still speaking with them, Rachel came with her father's sheep, for she was a shepherdess. ¹⁰ As soon as Jacob saw his uncle Laban's daughter Rachel with his sheep,ᵉ he went up and rolled the stone from the opening and watered his uncle Laban's sheep. ¹¹ Then Jacob kissed Rachel and wept loudly.ᶠ ¹² He told Rachel that he was her father's relative, Rebekah's son. She ran and told her father.

Jacob's Marriage Deal

¹³ When Laban heard the news about his sister's son Jacob, he ran to meet him, hugged him, and kissed him. Then he took him to his house, and Jacob told him all that had happened.

¹⁴ Laban said to him, "Yes, you are my own flesh and blood."ᵍ

After Jacob had stayed with him a month, ¹⁵ Laban said to him, "Just because you're my relative, should you work for me for nothing? Tell me what your wages should be."

Laban's Daughters

¹⁶ Now Laban had two daughters: the older was named Leah, and the younger was named Rachel. ¹⁷ Leah had delicateʰ eyes, but Rachel was shapely and beautiful. ¹⁸ Jacob loved Rachel, so he answered Laban, "I'll work for you seven years for your younger daughter Rachel."

ᵃ**28:19** = House of God   ᵇ**29:1** Lit Jacob picked up his feet   ᶜ**29:1** Lit the land of the children of the east
ᵈ**29:3** Sam, some LXX mss read flocks and the shepherds   ᵉ**29:10** Lit with the sheep of Laban his mother's brother
ᶠ**29:11** Lit and he lifted his voice and wept   ᵍ**29:14** Lit my bone and my flesh   ʰ**29:17** Or tender

¹⁹ Laban replied, "Better that I give her to you than to some other man. Stay with me." ²⁰ So Jacob worked seven years for Rachel, and they seemed like only a few days to him because of his love for her.

Laban Tricks Jacob

²¹ Then Jacob said to Laban, "Give me my wife, for my time is completed. I want to sleep with[a] her." ²² So Laban invited all the men of the place to a feast. ²³ That evening, Laban took his daughter Leah and gave her to Jacob, and he slept with her. ²⁴ And Laban gave his slave Zilpah to his daughter Leah as her slave.

²⁵ When morning came, there was Leah! So he said to Laban, "What is this you have done to me? Wasn't it for Rachel that I worked for you? Why have you deceived me?"

²⁶ Laban answered, "It is not the custom in this place to give the younger ₌daughter in marriage₌ before the firstborn. ²⁷ Complete this week ₌of wedding celebration₌, and we will also give you this ₌younger₌ one in return for working yet another seven years for me."

Jacob Gets Rachel

²⁸ And Jacob did just that. He finished the week ₌of celebration₌, and Laban gave him his daughter Rachel as his wife. ²⁹ And Laban gave his slave Bilhah to his daughter Rachel as her slave. ³⁰ Jacob slept with Rachel also, and indeed, he loved Rachel more than Leah. And he worked for Laban another seven years.

Jacob's Large Family

Leah's First Four Sons

³¹ When the LORD saw that Leah was unloved, He opened her womb; but Rachel was barren. ³² Leah conceived, gave birth to a son, and named him Reuben,[b] for she said, "The LORD has seen my affliction; surely my husband will love me now."

³³ She conceived again, gave birth to a son, and said, "The LORD heard that I am unloved and has given me this ₌son₌ also." So she named him Simeon.[c]

³⁴ She conceived again, gave birth to a son, and said, "At last, my husband will become attached to me because I have borne him three sons." Therefore he was named Levi.[d]

³⁵ And she conceived again, gave birth to a son, and said, "This time I will praise the LORD." Therefore she named him Judah.[e] Then Leah stopped having children.

Rachel Wants Children

30 When Rachel saw that she was not bearing Jacob ₌any children₌, she envied her sister. "Give me sons, or I will die!" she said to Jacob.

² Jacob became angry with Rachel and said, "Am I in God's place, who has withheld children[f] from you?"

Bilhah's Two Sons

³ Then she said, "Here is my slave Bilhah. Go sleep with her, and she'll bear ₌children₌ for me[g] so that through her I too can build ₌a family₌." ⁴ So Rachel gave her slave Bilhah to Jacob as a wife, and he slept with her. ⁵ Bilhah conceived and bore Jacob a son. ⁶ Rachel said, "God has vindicated me; yes, He has heard me and given me a son," and she named him Dan.[h]

⁷ Rachel's slave Bilhah conceived again and bore Jacob a second son. ⁸ Rachel

---

[a]**29:21** Lit *to go to*   [b]**29:32** = See, a Son; but sounds like Hb "has seen my affliction"   [c]**29:33** The name *Simeon* sounds like Hb "has heard."   [d]**29:34** The name *Levi* sounds like Hb "attached to."   [e]**29:35** The name *Judah* sounds like Hb "praise."   [f]**30:2** Lit *the fruit of the womb*   [g]**30:3** Lit *bear on my knees*   [h]**30:6** The name *Dan* sounds like Hb "has vindicated," or "has judged."

said, "In ⌊my⌋ wrestlings with God,[a] I have wrestled with my sister and won," and she named him Naphtali.[b]

Zilpah's Two Sons

[9] When Leah saw that she had stopped having children, she took her slave Zilpah and gave her to Jacob as a wife. [10] Leah's slave Zilpah bore Jacob a son. [11] Then Leah said, "What good fortune!"[c] and she named him Gad.[d]

[12] When Leah's slave Zilpah bore Jacob a second son, [13] Leah said, "I am happy that the women call me happy," so she named him Asher.[e]

Leah and Rachel Bargain

[14] Reuben went out during the wheat harvest and found some mandrakes in the field. When he brought them to his mother Leah, Rachel asked, "Please give me some of your son's mandrakes."

[15] But Leah replied to her, "Isn't it enough that you have taken my husband? Now you also want to take my son's mandrakes?"

"Well," Rachel said, "you can sleep with him tonight in exchange for your son's mandrakes."

Two More Sons and a Daughter for Leah

[16] When Jacob came in from the field that evening, Leah went out to meet him and said, "You must come with me, for I have hired you with my son's mandrakes." So Jacob slept with her that night.

[17] God listened to Leah, and she conceived and bore Jacob a fifth son. [18] Leah said, "God has rewarded me for giving my slave to my husband," and she named him Issachar.[f]

[19] Then Leah conceived again and bore Jacob a sixth son. [20] "God has given me a good gift," Leah said. "This time my husband will honor me because I have borne him six sons," and she named him Zebulun.[g] [21] Later, Leah bore a daughter and named her Dinah.

Rachel's First Son: Joseph

[22] Then God remembered Rachel. He listened to her and opened her womb. [23] She conceived and bore a son, and said, "God has taken away my shame." [24] She named him Joseph:[h] "May the LORD add another son to me."

Jacob's Flocks and Wealth

[25] After Rachel gave birth to Joseph, Jacob said to Laban, "Send me on my way so that I can return to my homeland. [26] Give me my wives and my children that I have worked for, and let me go. You know how hard I have worked for you."

[27] But Laban said to him, "If I have found favor in your sight, ⌊stay.⌋ I have learned by •divination that the LORD has blessed me because of you." [28] Then Laban said, "Name your wages, and I will pay them."

Jacob's Agricultural Experiment

[29] So Jacob said to him, "You know what I have done for you and your herds. [30] For you had very little before I came, but now your wealth has increased. The LORD has blessed you because of me. And now, when will I also do something for my own family?"

[31] Laban asked, "What should I give you?"

And Jacob said, "You don't need to give me anything. If you do this one

[a]30:8 Or *With mighty wrestlings*   [b]30:8 The name *Naphtali* sounds like Hb "my wrestling."   [c]30:11 Alt Hb tradition, LXX, Vg read *Good fortune has come*   [d]30:11 = Good Fortune   [e]30:13 = Happy   [f]30:18 *Issachar* sounds like Hb "reward."   [g]30:20 The name *Zebulun* sounds like Hb "honored."   [h]30:24 = He Adds

thing for me, I will continue to shepherd and keep your flock. [32] Let me go through all your sheep today and remove every sheep that is speckled or spotted, every dark-colored sheep among the lambs, and the spotted and speckled among the female goats. ⌊Such⌋ will be my wages. [33] In the future when you come to check on my wages, my honesty will testify for me. ⌊If I have⌋ any female goats that are not speckled or spotted, or any lambs that are not black, they will be considered stolen."

[34] "Good," said Laban. "Let it be as you have said."

[35] That day Laban removed the streaked and spotted male goats and all the speckled and spotted female goats— every one that had any white on it—and every dark-colored sheep among the lambs, and he placed his sons in charge of them. [36] He put a three-day journey between himself and Jacob. Jacob, meanwhile, was shepherding the rest of Laban's flock.

[37] Jacob then took branches of fresh poplar, almond, and plane wood, and peeled ⌊the bark⌋, exposing white stripes on the branches. [38] He set the peeled branches in the troughs in front of the sheep—in the water channels where the sheep came to drink. And the sheep bred when they came to drink. [39] The flocks bred in front of the branches and bore streaked, speckled, and spotted young. [40] Jacob separated the lambs and made the flocks face the streaked and the completely dark sheep in Laban's flocks. Then he set his own stock apart and didn't put them with Laban's sheep.

[41] Whenever the stronger of the flock were breeding, Jacob placed the branches in the troughs, in full view of the flocks, and they would breed in front of the branches. [42] As for the weaklings of the flocks, he did not put out the branches. So it turned out that the weak sheep belonged to Laban and the stronger ones to Jacob. [43] And the man became very rich.[a] He had many flocks, male and female slaves, and camels and donkeys.

Jacob Flees from Laban

31 Now Jacob heard what Laban's sons were saying: "Jacob has taken all that was our father's and has built this wealth from what belonged to our father." [2] And Jacob saw from Laban's face that his attitude toward him was not the same.

[3] Then the LORD said to him, "Go back to the land of your fathers and to your family, and I will be with you."

Jacob Plots His Escape

[4] Jacob had Rachel and Leah called to the field ⌊where⌋ his flocks were. [5] He said to them, "I can see from your father's face that his attitude toward me is not the same, but the God of my father has been with me. [6] You know that I've worked hard for your father [7] and that he has cheated me and changed my wages 10 times. But God has not let him harm me. [8] If he said, 'The spotted sheep will be your wages,' then all the sheep were born spotted. If he said, 'The streaked sheep will be your wages,' then all the sheep were born streaked. [9] God has taken your father's herds and given them to me.

[10] "When the flocks were breeding, I saw in a dream that the streaked, spotted, and speckled males were mating with the females. [11] In that dream the Angel of God said to me, 'Jacob!' and I said: Here I am. [12] And He said, 'Look up

---

[a]**30:43** Lit *The man spread out very much, very much*

and see: all the males that are mating with the flocks are streaked, spotted, and speckled, for I have seen all that Laban has been doing to you. [13] I am the God of Bethel, where you poured oil on the stone marker and made a solemn vow to Me. Get up, leave this land, and return to your native land.'"

[14] Then Rachel and Leah answered him, "Do we have any portion or inheritance in our father's household? [15] Are we not regarded by him as outsiders? For he has sold us and has certainly spent our money. [16] In fact, all the wealth that God has taken from our father belongs to us and to our children. So do whatever God has said to you."

[17] Then Jacob got up and put his children and wives on the camels. [18] He took all the livestock and possessions he had acquired in Paddan-aram, and he drove his herds to go to the land of his father Isaac in Canaan. [19] When Laban had gone to shear his sheep, Rachel stole her father's household idols. [20] And Jacob deceived[a] Laban the Aramean, not telling him that he was fleeing. [21] He fled with all his possessions, crossed the Euphrates, and headed for[b] the hill country of Gilead.

Laban Overtakes Jacob

[22] On the third day Laban was told that Jacob had fled. [23] So he took his relatives with him, pursued Jacob for seven days, and overtook him at Mount Gilead. [24] But God came to Laban the Aramean in a dream at night. "Watch yourself!" God warned him. "Don't say anything to Jacob, either good or bad."

Laban Accuses Jacob

[25] When Laban overtook Jacob, Jacob had pitched his tent in the hill country, and Laban and his brothers also pitched ⌊their tents⌋ in the hill country of Gilead. [26] Then Laban said to Jacob, "What have you done? You have deceived me and taken my daughters away like prisoners of war! [27] Why did you secretly flee from me, deceive me, and not tell me? I would have sent you away with joy and singing, with tambourines and lyres, [28] but you didn't even let me kiss my grandchildren and my daughters. You have acted foolishly. [29] I could do you great harm, but last night the God of your father said to me: 'Watch yourself. Don't say anything to Jacob, either good or bad.' [30] Now you have gone off because you long for your father—but why have you stolen my gods?"

[31] Jacob answered, "I was afraid, for I thought you would take your daughters from me by force. [32] If you find your gods with anyone ⌊here⌋, he will not live! Before our relatives, point out anything that is yours and take it." Jacob did not know that Rachel had stolen ⌊the idols⌋.

[33] So Laban went into Jacob's tent, then Leah's tent, and then the tents of the two female slaves, but he found nothing. Then he left Leah's tent and entered Rachel's. [34] Now Rachel had taken Laban's household idols, put them in the saddlebag of the camel, and sat on them. Laban searched the whole tent but found nothing.

[35] She said to her father, "Sir, don't be angry that I cannot stand up in your presence; I am having my monthly period." So Laban searched, but could not find the household idols.

Jacob Angry with Laban

[36] Then Jacob became incensed and brought charges against Laban. "What is my crime?" he said to Laban. "What is

---

[a]31:20 Lit *And he stole the heart of*　[b]31:21 Lit *and set his face to*

my sin, that you have pursued me? ³⁷ You've searched all my possessions! Have you found anything of yours? Put it here before my relatives and yours, and let them decide between the two of us. ³⁸ I've been with you these 20 years. Your ewes and female goats have not miscarried, and I have not eaten the rams from your flock. ³⁹ I did not bring you any of the flock torn by wild beasts; I myself bore the loss. You demanded ⌊payment⌋ from me for what was stolen by day or by night. ⁴⁰ There I was—the heat consumed me by day and the frost by night, and sleep fled from my eyes. ⁴¹ For 20 years I have worked in your household—14 years for your two daughters and six years for your flocks—and you have changed my wages 10 times! ⁴² If the God of my father, the God of Abraham, the Fear of Isaac, had not been with me, certainly now you would have sent me off empty-handed. But God has seen my affliction and my hard work,ᵃ and He issued His verdict last night."

Jacob's Treaty with Laban

⁴³ Then Laban answered Jacob, "The daughters are my daughters; the sons, my sons; and the flocks, my flocks! Everything you see is mine! But what can I do today for these daughters of mine or for the children they have borne? ⁴⁴ Come now, let's make a covenant, you and I. Let it be a witness between the two of us."

⁴⁵ So Jacob picked out a stone and set it up as a marker. ⁴⁶ Then Jacob said to his relatives, "Gather stones." And they took stones and made a mound, then ate there by the mound. ⁴⁷ Laban named the mound Jegar-sahadutha, but Jacob named it Galeed.ᵇ

⁴⁸ Then Laban said, "This mound is a witness between me and you today." Therefore the place was called Galeed, ⁴⁹ and ⌊also⌋ Mizpah,ᶜ for he said, "May the LORD watch between you and me when we are out of each other's sight. ⁵⁰ If you mistreat my daughters or take other wives, though no one is with us, understand that God will be a witness between you and me." ⁵¹ Laban also said to Jacob, "Look at this mound and the marker I have set up between you and me. ⁵² This mound is a witness and the marker is a witness that I will not pass beyond this mound to you, and you will not pass beyond this mound and this marker to do me harm. ⁵³ The God of Abraham, and the gods of Nahor—the gods of their fatherᵈ—will judge between us." And Jacob swore by the fear of his father Isaac. ⁵⁴ Then Jacob offered a sacrifice on the mountain and invited his relatives to eat a meal. So they ate a meal and spent the night on the mountain. ⁵⁵ᵉ Laban got up early in the morning, kissed his grandsons and daughters, and blessed them. Then Laban left to return home.

Jacob Sends Gifts to Esau

32 Jacob went on his way, and God's angels met him. ² When he saw them, Jacob said, "This is God's camp." So he called that place Mahanaim.ᶠ

³ Jacob sent messengers ahead of him to his brother Esau in the land of Seir, the country of Edom. ⁴ He commanded them, "You are to say to my lord Esau, 'This is what your servant Jacob says. I have been staying with Laban and have been delayed until now. ⁵ I have oxen, donkeys, flocks, male and female slaves. I have sent ⌊this message⌋ to inform my lord, in order to seek your favor.'"

ᵃ**31:42** Lit *and the work of my hands*   ᵇ**31:47** *Jegar-sahadutha* is Aram, and *Galeed* is Hb; both names = Mound of Witness   ᶜ**31:49** = Watchtower   ᵈ**31:53** Two Hb mss, LXX omit *the gods of their father*   ᵉ**31:55** Gn 32:1 in Hb   ᶠ**32:2** = Two Camps

⁶ When the messengers returned to Jacob, they said, "We went to your brother Esau; he is coming to meet you—and he has 400 men with him." ⁷ Jacob was greatly afraid and distressed; he divided the people with him into two camps, along with the flocks, cattle, and camels. ⁸ He thought, "If Esau comes to one camp and attacks it, the remaining one can escape."

⁹ Then Jacob said, "God of my father Abraham and God of my father Isaac, the LORD who said to me, 'Go back to your land and to your family, and I will cause you to prosper,' ¹⁰ I am unworthy of all the kindness and faithfulness You have shown Your servant. Indeed, I crossed over this Jordan with my staff, and now I have become two camps. ¹¹ Please rescue me from the hand of my brother Esau, for I am afraid of him; otherwise, he may come and attack me, the mothers, and their children. ¹² You have said, 'I will cause you to prosper, and I will make your •offspring like the sand of the sea, which cannot be counted.'"

¹³ He spent the night there and took part of what he had brought with him as a gift for his brother Esau: ¹⁴ 200 female goats, 20 male goats, 200 ewes, 20 rams, ¹⁵ 30 milk camels with their young, 40 cows, 10 bulls, 20 female donkeys, and 10 male donkeys. ¹⁶ He entrusted them to his slaves as separate herds and said to them, "Go on ahead of me, and leave some distance between the herds."

Jacob's Strategy

¹⁷ And he told the first one: "When my brother Esau meets you and asks, 'Who do you belong to? Where are you going? And whose ₗanimalsₗ are these ahead of you?' ¹⁸ then tell him, 'They belong to your servant Jacob. They are a gift sent to my lord Esau. And look, he is behind us.'"

¹⁹ He also told the second one, the third, and everyone who was walking behind the animals, "Say the same thing to Esau when you find him. ²⁰ You are to also say, 'Look, your servant Jacob is right behind us.'" For he thought, "I want to appease Esau with the gift that is going ahead of me. After that, I can face him, and perhaps he will forgive me."

²¹ So the gift was sent on ahead of him while he remained in the camp that night. ²² During the night Jacob got up and took his two wives, his two female slaves, and his 11 sons, and crossed the ford of Jabbok. ²³ He took them and brought them across the stream, along with all his possessions.

Jacob Struggles with God

²⁴ Jacob was left alone, and a man wrestled with him until daybreak. ²⁵ When the man saw that He could not defeat him, He struck Jacob's hip as they wrestled and dislocated his hip socket. ²⁶ Then He said to Jacob, "Let Me go, for it is daybreak."

But Jacob said, "I will not let You go unless You bless me."

²⁷ "What is your name?" the man asked.

"Jacob!" he replied.

Jacob Becomes Israel

²⁸ "Your name will no longer be Jacob," He said. "It will be Israelª because you have struggled with God and with men and have prevailed."

²⁹ Then Jacob asked Him, "Please tell me Your name."

But He answered, "Why do you ask My name?" And He blessed him there.

ª**32:28** The name *Israel* sounds like Hb "he struggled (with) God."

³⁰ Jacob then named the place Peniel,ᵃ "For," ⌞he said,⌟ "I have seen God face to face, and I have been delivered." ³¹ The sun shone on him as he passed by Penuelᵇ—limping on his hip. ³² That is why, to this day, the Israelites don't eat the thigh muscle that is at the hip socket: because He struck Jacob's hip socket at the thigh muscle.ᶜ

Jacob and Esau Make Peace

33 Now Jacob looked up and saw Esau coming toward him with 400 men. So he divided the children among Leah, Rachel, and the two female slaves. ² He put the female slaves first, Leah and her sons next, and Rachel and Joseph last. ³ He himself went on ahead and bowed to the ground seven times until he approached his brother.

⁴ But Esau ran to meet him, hugged him, threw his arms around him, and kissed him. Then they wept. ⁵ When Esau looked up and saw the women and children, he asked, "Who are these with you?"

He answered, "The children God has graciously given your servant." ⁶ Then the female slaves and their children approached ⌞him⌟ and bowed down. ⁷ Leah and her children also approached and bowed down, and then Joseph and Rachel approached and bowed down.

⁸ So Esau said, "What do you mean by this whole processionᵈ I met?"

"To find favor with you, my lord," he answered.

⁹ "I have enough, my brother," Esau replied. "Keep what you have."

¹⁰ But Jacob said, "No, please! If I have found favor with you, take this gift from my hand. For indeed, I have seen your face, ⌞and it is⌟ like seeing God's face, since you have accepted me. ¹¹ Please take my present that was brought to you, because God has been gracious to me and I have everything I need." So Jacob urged him until he accepted.

¹² Then Esau said, "Let's move on, and I'll go ahead of you."

¹³ Jacob replied, "My lord knows that the children are weak, and I have nursing sheep and cattle. If they are driven hard for one day, the whole herd will die. ¹⁴ Let my lord go ahead of his servant. I will continue on slowly, at a pace suited to the livestock and the children, until I come to my lord at Seir."

¹⁵ Esau said, "Let me leave some of my people with you."

But he replied, "Why do that? Please indulge me,ᵉ my lord."

¹⁶ On that day Esau started on his way back to Seir, ¹⁷ but Jacob went on to Succoth. He built a house for himself and stalls for his cattle; that is why the place was called Succoth.ᶠ ¹⁸ After Jacob came from Paddan-aram, he arrived safely at the Canaanite city of Shechem and camped in front of the city. ¹⁹ He purchased a section of the field from the sons of Hamor, Shechem's father, for 100 *qesitahs*,ᵍ where he had pitched his tent. ²⁰ And he set up an altar there and called it "God, the God of Israel."ʰ

Revenge against Shechem

Shechem Defiles Dinah

34 Dinah, Leah's daughter whom she bore to Jacob, went out to see some of the young women of the area. ² When Shechem son of Hamor the Hivite, a prince of the region, saw her, he took her and raped her. ³ He became infatuated with Dinah, daughter of Jacob. He loved the young girl and spoke

---

ᵃ**32:30** = Face of God   ᵇ**32:31** Variant of *Peniel*   ᶜ**32:32** Or *tendon*   ᵈ**33:8** Lit *camp*   ᵉ**33:15** Lit *May I find favor in your eyes*   ᶠ**33:17** = Stalls, or Huts   ᵍ**33:19** The value of this currency is unknown.   ʰ**33:20** Hb *El-Elohe-Israel*

tenderly to her.[a] 4 "Get me this girl as a wife," he told his father Hamor.

5 Jacob heard that Shechem had defiled his daughter Dinah, but since his sons were with his cattle in the field, he remained silent until they returned. 6 Meanwhile, Shechem's father Hamor came to speak with Jacob. 7 Jacob's sons returned from the field when they heard ιabout the incidentյ and were deeply grieved and angry. For Shechem had committed an outrage against Israel by sleeping with Jacob's daughter, and such a thing should not be done.

Shechem Wants to Marry Dinah

8 Hamor said to Jacob's sons, "My son Shechem is strongly attracted to your[b] daughter. Please give her to him as a wife. 9 Intermarry with us; give your daughters to us, and take our daughters for yourselves. 10 Live with us. The land is before you. Settle here, move about, and acquire property in it."

11 Then Shechem said to Dinah's father and brothers, "Grant me this favor,[c] and I'll give you whatever you say. 12 Set for me the compensation[d] and the gift; I'll give you whatever you ask me. Just give the girl to be my wife!"

Jacob's Sons Deceive Shechem

13 But Jacob's sons answered Shechem and his father Hamor deceitfully because he had defiled their sister Dinah. 14 "We cannot do this thing," they said to them. "Giving our sister to an uncircumcised man is a disgrace to us. 15 We will agree with you only on this condition: if all your males are circumcised as we are. 16 Then we will give you our daughters, take your daughters for ourselves, live with you, and become one people. 17 But

if you will not listen to us and be circumcised, then we will take our daughter and go."

18 Their words seemed good in the eyes of Hamor and his son Shechem. 19 The young man did not delay doing this, because he was delighted with Jacob's daughter. Now he was the most important in all his father's house. 20 So Hamor and his son Shechem went to the •gate of their city and spoke to the men there.

21 "These men are peaceful toward us," they said. "Let them live in our land and move about in it, for indeed, the region is large enough for them. Let us take their daughters as our wives and give our daughters to them. 22 But the men will agree to live with us and be one people only on this condition: if all our men are circumcised as they are. 23 Won't their herds, their possessions, and all their livestock become ours? Only let us agree with them, and they will live with us."

Swords of Simeon and Levi

24 All the able-bodied men[e] listened to Hamor and his son Shechem, and all the able-bodied men[f] were circumcised. 25 On the third day, when they were still in pain, two of Jacob's sons, Simeon and Levi, Dinah's brothers, took their swords, went into the unsuspecting city, and killed every male. 26 They killed Hamor and his son Shechem with their swords, took Dinah from Shechem's house, and went away. 27 Jacob's ιotherյ sons came to the slaughter and plundered the city because their sister had been defiled. 28 They took their sheep, cattle, donkeys, and whatever was in the city and in the field. 29 They captured all

---

[a]34:3 Lit spoke to her heart   [b]34:8 Hb your is pl, showing that Hamor is speaking to Jacob and his sons.   [c]34:11 Lit May I find favor in your eyes   [d]34:12 Or bride-price, or betrothal present   [e]34:24 Lit All who went out of the city gate   [f]34:24 Lit all the males who went out of the city gate

their possessions, children, and wives, and plundered everything in the houses.

Jacob Rebukes His Sons

³⁰ Then Jacob said to Simeon and Levi, "You have brought trouble on me, making me odious to the inhabitants of the land, the Canaanites and the Perizzites. We are few in number; if they unite against me and attack me, I and my household will be destroyed." ³¹ But they answered, "Should he have treated our sister like a prostitute?"

Jacob Returns to Bethel

35 God said to Jacob, "Get up! Go to Bethel and settle there. Build an altar there to the God who appeared to you when you fled from your brother Esau."

² So Jacob said to his family and all who were with him, "Get rid of the foreign gods that are among you. Purify yourselves and change your clothes. ³ We must get up and go to Bethel. I will build an altar there to the God who answered me in my day of distress. He has been with me everywhere I have gone."

⁴ Then they gave Jacob all their foreign gods and their earrings, and Jacob hid them under the oak near Shechem. ⁵ When they set out, a terror from God came over the cities around them, and they did not pursue Jacob's sons. ⁶ So Jacob and all who were with him came to Luz (that is, Bethel) in the land of Canaan. ⁷ Jacob built an altar there and called the place God of Bethelᵃ because it was there that God had revealed Himself to him when he was fleeing from his brother.

⁸ Deborah, Rebekah's nurse, died and was buried under the oak south of Bethel. So Jacob named it Oak of Weeping.ᵇ

God Blesses Jacob

⁹ God appeared to Jacob again after he returned from Paddan-aram, and He blessed him. ¹⁰ God said to him:

> Your name is Jacob;
> you will no longer be named Jacob,
> but Israel will be your name.

So He named him Israel. ¹¹ God also said to him:

> I am •God Almighty.
> Be fruitful and multiply.
> A nation, indeed an assembly
>   of nations,
> will come from you,
> and kings will descend from you.ᶜ
> 12   The land that I gave to Abraham
>   and Isaac
> I will give to you.
> And I will give the land
> to your descendants after you.

¹³ Then God withdrewᵈ from him at the place where He had spoken to him.

¹⁴ Jacob set up a marker at the place where He had spoken to him—a stone marker. He poured a drink offering on it and anointed it with oil. ¹⁵ Jacob named the place where God had spoken with him Bethel.

Deaths of Rachel and Isaac

Benjamin Born, Rachel Dies

¹⁶ They set out from Bethel. When they were still some distance from Ephrath, Rachel began to give birth, and her labor was difficult. ¹⁷ During her difficult labor, the midwife said to her, "Don't be afraid, for this is another son for you." ¹⁸ With her last breath—for she was dying—she named him Ben-oni,ᵉ but his father called him Benjamin.ᶠ ¹⁹ So Rachel died and was buried on the way to

---

ᵃ**35:7** Hb *El-bethel*   ᵇ**35:8** Hb *Allon-bacuth*   ᶜ**35:11** Lit *will come from your loins*   ᵈ**35:13** Lit *went up*   ᵉ**35:18** = Son of My Sorrow   ᶠ**35:18** = Son of the Right Hand

Ephrath (that is, Bethlehem). ²⁰ Jacob set up a marker on her grave; it is the marker at Rachel's grave to this day.

Twelve Sons of Jacob

²¹ Israel set out again and pitched his tent beyond the tower at Eder.ª ²² While Israel was living in that region, Reuben went in and slept with his father's concubine Bilhah, and Israel heard about it.

Jacob had 12 sons:

²³   Leah's sons were Reuben
        (Jacob's firstborn),
        Simeon, Levi, Judah,
        Issachar, and Zebulun.
²⁴   Rachel's sons were
        Joseph and Benjamin.
²⁵   The sons of Rachel's slave Bilhah
        were Dan and Naphtali.
²⁶   The sons of Leah's slave Zilpah
        were Gad and Asher.

These are the sons of Jacob, who were born to him in Paddan-aram.

Isaac's Death

²⁷ Jacob came to his father Isaac at Mamre in Kiriath-arba (that is, Hebron), where Abraham and Isaac had stayed. ²⁸ Isaac lived 180 years. ²⁹ He took his last breath and died, and was gathered to his people, old and full of days. His sons Esau and Jacob buried him.

Descendants of Esau

36 These are the family records of Esau (that is, Edom). ² Esau took his wives from the Canaanite women: Adah daughter of Elon the Hittite, Oholibamah daughter of Anah and granddaughterᵇ of Zibeon the Hivite; ³ and Basemath daughter of Ishmael and sister of Nebaioth. ⁴ Adah bore Eliphaz to Esau, Basemath bore Reuel, ⁵ and Oholibamah bore Jeush, Jalam, and Korah. These were Esau's sons, who were born to him in the land of Canaan.

⁶ Esau took his wives, sons, daughters, and all the people of his household, as well as his herds, all his livestock, and all the property he had acquired in Canaan; he went to a land away from his brother Jacob. ⁷ For their possessions were too many ⌊for them⌋ to live together, and because of their herds, the land where they stayed could not support them. ⁸ So Esau (that is, Edom) lived in the mountains of Seir.

⁹ These are the family records of Esau, father of the Edomites in the mountains of Seir.

¹⁰   These are the names of Esau's sons:
        Eliphaz son of Esau's wife Adah,
        and Reuel son of Esau's wife
        Basemath.
¹¹   The sons of Eliphaz were
        Teman, Omar, Zepho, Gatam,
        and Kenaz.
¹²   Timna, a concubine of Esau's son
        Eliphaz,
        bore Amalek to Eliphaz.
        These were the sons of Esau's wife
        Adah.
¹³   These are Reuel's sons:
        Nahath, Zerah, Shammah,
        and Mizzah.
        These were the sons of Esau's wife
        Basemath.
¹⁴   These are the sons of Esau's wife
        Oholibamah
        daughter of Anah
        and granddaughterᵇ of Zibeon:
        She bore Jeush, Jalam, and Korah
        to Edom.
¹⁵   These are the chiefs of Esau's sons:
        the sons of Eliphaz, Esau's firstborn:

ª**35:21** Or *beyond Migdal-eder*   ᵇ**36:2,14** Sam, LXX read *Anah son*

Chiefs Teman, Omar, Zepho,
  Kenaz,
16 Korah,[a] Gatam, and Amalek.
These are the chiefs of Eliphaz
in the land of Edom.
These are the sons of Adah.

17 These are the sons of Reuel,
  Esau's son:
Chiefs Nahath, Zerah, Shammah,
  and Mizzah.
These are the chiefs of Reuel
in the land of Edom.
These are the sons of Esau's wife
  Basemath.

18 These are the sons of Esau's wife
  Oholibamah:
Chiefs Jeush, Jalam, and Korah.
These are the chiefs of Esau's wife
  Oholibamah
daughter of Anah.
19 These are the sons of Esau
  (that is, Edom),
and these are their chiefs.

Sons of Seir

20 These are the sons of Seir
  the Horite,
the inhabitants of the land:
Lotan, Shobal, Zibeon, Anah,
21 Dishon, Ezer, and Dishan.
These are the chiefs of the Horites,
the sons of Seir, in the land
  of Edom.
22 The sons of Lotan were Hori
  and Heman.
Timna was Lotan's sister.
23 These are Shobal's sons:
Alvan, Manahath, Ebal, Shepho,
  and Onam.
24 These are Zibeon's sons:
Aiah and Anah.
This was the Anah who found
  the hot springs[b] in the wilderness

while he was pasturing the donkeys
  of his father Zibeon.
25 These are the children of Anah:
Dishon and Oholibamah
  daughter of Anah.
26 These are Dishon's sons:
Hemdan, Eshban, Ithran,
  and Cheran.
27 These are Ezer's sons:
Bilhan, Zaavan, and Akan.
28 These are Dishan's sons:
Uz and Aran.

29 These are the chiefs of the Horites:
Chiefs Lotan, Shobal, Zibeon, Anah,
30 Dishon, Ezer, and Dishan.
These are the chiefs of the Horites,
according to their divisions,
  in the land of Seir.

Rulers of Edom

31 These are the kings who ruled
  in the land of Edom
before any king ruled
  over the Israelites:
32 Bela son of Beor ruled in Edom;
the name of his city was Dinhabah.
33 When Bela died, Jobab son of Zerah
  from Bozrah ruled in his place.
34 When Jobab died, Husham
  from the land of the Temanites
  ruled in his place.
35 When Husham died, Hadad
  son of Bedad ruled in his place.
He defeated Midian in the field
  of Moab;
the name of his city was Avith.
36 When Hadad died, Samlah
  from Masrekah ruled in his place.
37 When Samlah died, Shaul
  from Rehoboth-on-the-River ruled
  in his place.
38 When Shaul died, Baal-hanan
  son of Achbor ruled in his place.

---

[a] **36:16** Sam omits *Korah*   [b] **36:24** Syr, Vg; Tg reads *the mules*; Hb obscure

³⁹ When Baal-hanan son of Achbor
　　died, Hadar^a ruled in his place.
　　His city was Pau,
　　　and his wife's name
　　　was Mehetabel
　　daughter of Matred daughter of Me-
　　zahab.

⁴⁰ These are the names
　　of Esau's chiefs,
　according to their families
　　and their localities,
　by their names:
　Chiefs Timna, Alvah, Jetheth,
⁴¹ Oholibamah, Elah, Pinon,
⁴² Kenaz, Teman, Mibzar,
⁴³ Magdiel, and Iram.
　These are Edom's chiefs,
　according to their settlements
　　in the land they possessed.
Esau^b was father of the Edomites.

Joseph's Dreams

37 Jacob lived in the land where his father had stayed, the land of Canaan. ² These are the family records of Jacob.

At 17 years of age, Joseph tended sheep with his brothers. The young man ⌊was working⌋ with the sons of Bilhah and Zilpah, his father's wives, and he brought a bad report about them to their father.

³ Now Israel loved Joseph more than his other sons because Joseph was a son ⌊born to him⌋ in his old age, and he made a robe of many colors^c for him. ⁴ When his brothers saw that their father loved him more than all his brothers, they hated him and could not bring themselves to speak peaceably to him.

⁵ Then Joseph had a dream. When he told it to his brothers, they hated him even more. ⁶ He said to them, "Listen to this dream I had: ⁷ There we were, binding sheaves of grain in the field. Suddenly my sheaf stood up, and your sheaves gathered around it and bowed down to my sheaf."

Joseph Angers His Brothers

⁸ "Are you really going to reign over us?" his brothers asked him. "Are you really going to rule us?" So they hated him even more because of his dream and what he had said.

⁹ Then he had another dream and told it to his brothers. "Look," he said, "I had another dream, and this time the sun, moon, and 11 stars were bowing down to me."

Jacob Rebukes Joseph

¹⁰ He told his father and brothers, but his father rebuked him. "What kind of dream is this that you have had?" he said. "Are your mother and brothers and I going to bow down to the ground before you?" ¹¹ His brothers were jealous of him, but his father kept the matter ⌊in mind⌋.

Joseph Sold into Slavery

¹² His brothers had gone to pasture their father's flocks at Shechem. ¹³ Israel said to Joseph, "Your brothers, you know, are pasturing ⌊the flocks⌋ at Shechem. Get ready. I'm sending you to them."

"I'm ready," Joseph replied.

¹⁴ Then Israel said to him, "Go and see how your brothers and the flocks are doing, and bring word back to me." So he sent him from the valley of Hebron, and he went to Shechem.

¹⁵ A man found him there, wandering in the field, and asked him, "What are you looking for?"

¹⁶ "I'm looking for my brothers," Joseph said. "Can you tell me where they are pasturing ⌊their flocks⌋?"

^a**36:39** Many Hb mss, Sam, Syr read *Hadad*　^b**36:43** Lit *He Esau*　^c**37:3** Or *robe with long sleeves*

[17] "They've moved on from here," the man said. "I heard them say, 'Let's go to Dothan.'" So Joseph set out after his brothers and found them at Dothan.

[18] They saw him in the distance, and before he had reached them, they plotted to kill him. [19] They said to one another, "Here comes that dreamer![a] [20] Come on, let's kill him and throw him into one of the pits. We can say that a vicious animal ate him. Then we'll see what becomes of his dreams!"

[21] When Reuben heard this, he tried to save him from them.[b] He said, "Let's not take his life." [22] Reuben also said to them, "Don't shed blood. Throw him into this pit in the wilderness, but don't lay a hand on him"—intending to rescue him from their hands and return him to his father.

[23] When Joseph came to his brothers, they stripped off his robe, the robe of many colors that he had on. [24] Then they took him and threw him into the pit. The pit was empty; there was no water in it.

[25] Then they sat down to eat a meal. They looked up, and there was a caravan of Ishmaelites coming from Gilead. Their camels were carrying aromatic gum, balsam, and resin, going down to Egypt.

[26] Then Judah said to his brothers, "What do we gain if we kill our brother and cover up his blood? [27] Come, let's sell him to the Ishmaelites and not lay a hand on him, for he is our brother, our ⌊own⌋ flesh." His brothers agreed. [28] When Midianite traders passed by, they pulled Joseph out of the pit and sold him for 20 pieces of silver to the Ishmaelites, who took Joseph to Egypt.

[29] When Reuben returned to the pit and saw that Joseph was not there, he tore his clothes. [30] He went back to his brothers and said, "The boy is gone! What am I going to do?"[c] [31] So they took Joseph's robe, slaughtered a young goat, and dipped the robe in its blood. [32] They sent the robe of many colors to their father and said, "We found this. Examine it. Is it your son's robe or not?"

Jacob Mourns Joseph

[33] His father recognized it. "It is my son's robe," he said. "A vicious animal has devoured him. Joseph has been torn to pieces!" [34] Then Jacob tore his clothes, put •sackcloth around his waist, and mourned for his son many days. [35] All his sons and daughters tried to comfort him, but he refused to be comforted. "No," he said. "I will go down to •Sheol to my son, mourning." And his father wept for him.

Joseph Sold to Potiphar

[36] Meanwhile, the Midianites sold Joseph in Egypt to Potiphar, an officer of Pharaoh and the captain of the guard.

Judah and Tamar

38 At that time Judah left his brothers and settled near an Adullamite named Hirah. [2] There Judah saw the daughter of a Canaanite named Shua; he took her as a wife and slept with her. [3] She conceived and gave birth to a son, and he named him Er. [4] She conceived again, gave birth to a son, and named him Onan. [5] She gave birth to another son and named him Shelah. It was at Chezib that[d] [e] she gave birth to him.

Disobedience of Er and Onan

[6] Judah got a wife for Er, his firstborn, and her name was Tamar. [7] Now Er, Judah's firstborn, was evil in the LORD's sight, and the LORD put him to death.

---

[a]**37:19** Lit *comes the lord of the dreams*   [b]**37:21** Lit *their hands*   [c]**37:30** Lit *And I, where am I going*   [d]**38:5** LXX reads *She was at Chezib when*   [e]**38:5** Or *He was at Chezib when*

8 Then Judah said to Onan, "Sleep with your brother's wife. Perform your duty as her brother-in-law and produce •offspring for your brother." 9 But Onan knew that the offspring would not be his; so whenever he slept with his brother's wife, he released his semen on the ground so that he would not produce offspring for his brother. 10 What he did was evil in the LORD's sight, so He put him to death also.

Judah's Deceit

11 Then Judah said to his daughter-in-law Tamar, "Remain a widow in your father's house until my son Shelah grows up." For he thought, "He might die too, like his brother." So Tamar went to live in her father's house.

Tamar's Trickery

12 After a long time[a] Judah's wife, the daughter of Shua, died. When Judah had finished mourning, he and his friend Hirah the Adullamite went up to Timnah to the sheepshearers. 13 Tamar was told, "Your father-in-law is going up to Timnah to shear his sheep." 14 So she took off her widow's clothes, veiled ⌊her face⌋, covered herself, and sat at the entrance to Enaim,[b] which is on the way to Timnah. For she saw that, though Shelah had grown up, she had not been given to him as a wife. 15 <u>When Judah saw her, he thought she was a prostitute</u>, for she had covered her face.

16 He went over to her and said, "Come, let me sleep with you," for he did not know that she was his daughter-in-law.

She said, "What will you give me for sleeping with me?"

17 "I will send you a young goat from my flock," he replied.

But she said, "Only if you leave something ⌊with me⌋ until you send it."

18 "What should I give you?" he asked.

She answered, "Your signet ring, your cord, and the staff in your hand." So he gave them to her and slept with her, and she got pregnant by him. 19 She got up and left, then removed her veil and put her widow's clothes back on.

20 When Judah sent the young goat by his friend the Adullamite in order to get back the items he had left with the woman, he could not find her. 21 He asked the men of the place, "Where is the cult prostitute who was beside the road at Enaim?"

"There has been no cult prostitute here," they answered.

22 So the Adullamite returned to Judah, saying, "I couldn't find her, and furthermore, the men of the place said, 'There has been no cult prostitute here.'"

23 Judah replied, "Let her keep ⌊the items⌋ for herself; otherwise we will become a laughingstock. After all, I did send this young goat, but you couldn't find ⌊her⌋."

Tamar's Relations with Judah Revealed

24 About three months later Judah was told, "Your daughter-in-law has been acting like a prostitute, and now she is pregnant."

"Bring her out!" Judah said. "Let her be burned ⌊to death⌋!"

25 As she was being brought out, she sent her father-in-law ⌊this message⌋: "I am pregnant by the man to whom these items belong." And she added, "Examine them. Whose signet ring, cord, and staff are these?"

26 Judah recognized ⌊them⌋ and said, "She is more in the right[c] than I, since I

---

[a] **38:12** Lit *And there were many days*   [b] **38:14** Or *sat by the mouth of the springs*   [c] **38:26** Or *more righteous*

did not give her to my son Shelah." And he did not know her intimately again.

Tamar's Twins

27 When the time came for her to give birth, there were twins in her womb. 28 As she was giving birth, one of them put out his hand, and the midwife took it and tied a scarlet ⌊thread⌋ around it, announcing, "This one came out first." 29 But then he pulled his hand back, and his brother came out. Then she said, "You have broken out ⌊first⌋!" So he was named Perez.ᵃ 30 Then his brother, who had the scarlet ⌊thread⌋ tied to his hand, came out, and was named Zerah.ᵇ

Joseph in Potiphar's House

39 Now Joseph had been taken to Egypt. An Egyptian ⌊named⌋ Potiphar, an officer of Pharaoh and the captain of the guard, bought him from the Ishmaelites who had brought him there. 2 The LORD was with Joseph, and he became a successful man, servingᶜ in the household of his Egyptian master. 3 When his master saw that the LORD was with him and that the LORD made everything he did successful, 4 Joseph found favor in his master's sight and became his personal attendant. Potiphar also put him in charge of his household and placed all that he owned under his authority.ᵈ 5 From the time that he put him in charge of his household and of all that he owned, the LORD blessed the Egyptian's house because of Joseph. The LORD's blessing was on all that he owned, in his house and in his fields. 6 He left all that he owned under Joseph's authority;ᵉ he did not concern himself with anything except the food he ate.

Trouble: Potiphar's Wife

Now Joseph was well-built and handsome. 7 After some timeᶠ his master's wife looked longingly at Joseph and said, "Sleep with me." 8 But he refused and said to his master's wife, "Look, my master does not concern himself with anything in his house, and he has put all that he owns under my authority.ᵍ 9 No one in this house is greater than I am. He has withheld nothing from me except you, because you are his wife. So how could I do such a great evil and sin against God?"

10 Although she spoke to Joseph day after day, he refusedʰ to go to bed with her. 11 Now one day he went into the house to do his work, and none of the household servants was there.ⁱ 12 She grabbed him by his garment and said, "Sleep with me!" But leaving his garment in her hand, he escaped and ran outside. 13 When she realized that he had left his garment with her and had run outside, 14 she called the household servants. "Look," she said to them, "my husband brought a Hebrew man to us to make fun of us. He came to me so he could sleep with me, and I screamed as loud as I could. 15 When he heard me screaming for help,ʲ he left his garment with me and ran outside."

16 She put Joseph's garment beside her until his master came home. 17 Then she told him the same story: "The Hebrew slave you brought to us came to me to make fun of me, 18 but when I screamed for help,ᵏ he left his garment with me and ran outside."

Joseph in Prison

19 When his master heard the story his wife told him—"These are the things

---

ᵃ38:29 = Breaking Out   ᵇ38:30 = Brightness of Sunrise; perhaps related to the scarlet thread   ᶜ39:2 Lit and he was   ᵈ39:4 Lit owned in his hand   ᵉ39:6 Lit owned in Joseph's hand   ᶠ39:7 Lit And after these things   ᵍ39:8 Lit owns in my hand   ʰ39:10 Lit did not listen to her   ⁱ39:11 Lit there in the house   ʲ39:15 Lit me raise my voice and scream   ᵏ39:18 Lit I raised my voice and screamed

your slave did to me"—he was furious
²⁰ and had him thrown into prison,
where the king's prisoners were confined. So Joseph was there in prison.

²¹ But the LORD was with Joseph and
extended kindness to him. He granted
him favor in the eyes of the prison warden. ²² The warden put all the prisoners
who were in the prison under Joseph's
authority,ᵃ and he was responsible for everything that was done there. ²³ The
warden did not bother with anything under Joseph's authority,ᵇ because the
LORD was with him, and the LORD made
everything that he did successful.

Joseph Interprets Two Prisoners' Dreams

40 After this, the king of Egypt's cupbearer and his baker offended
their master, the king of Egypt. ² Pharaoh
was angry with his two officers, the chief
cupbearer and the chief baker, ³ and put
them in custody in the house of the captain of the guard, in the prison where Joseph was confined. ⁴ The captain of the
guard assigned Joseph to them, and he
became their personal attendant. And
they were in custody for some time.ᶜ

⁵ The cupbearer and the baker of the
king of Egypt, who were confined in the
prison, each had a dream. Both had a
dream on the same night, and each
dream had its own meaning. ⁶ When Joseph came to them in the morning, he
saw that they looked distraught. ⁷ So he
asked Pharaoh's officers who were in
custody with him in his master's house,
"Why are your faces sad today?"

⁸ "We had dreams," they said to him,
"but there is no one to interpret them."

Then Joseph said to them, "Don't interpretations belong to God? Tell me
⸤your dreams⸥."

The Cupbearer's Dream

⁹ So the chief cupbearer told his dream
to Joseph: "In my dream there was a
vine in front of me. ¹⁰ On the vine were
three branches. As soon as it budded, its
blossoms came out and its clusters ripened into grapes. ¹¹ Pharaoh's cup was in
my hand, and I took the grapes,
squeezed them into Pharaoh's cup, and
placed the cup in Pharaoh's hand."

¹² "This is its interpretation," Joseph
said to him. "The three branches are
three days. ¹³ In just three days Pharaoh
will lift up your head and restore you to
your position. You will put Pharaoh's cup
in his hand the way you used to when
you were his cupbearer. ¹⁴ But when all
goes well for you, remember that I was
with you. Please show kindness to me by
mentioning me to Pharaoh, and get me
out of this prison. ¹⁵ For I was kidnapped
from the land of the Hebrews, and even
here I have done nothing that they
should put me in the dungeon."

The Baker's Dream

¹⁶ When the chief baker saw that the
interpretation was positive, he said to Joseph, "I also had a dream. Three baskets
of white bread were on my head. ¹⁷ In
the top basket were all sorts of baked
goods for Pharaoh, but the birds were
eating them out of the basket on my
head."

¹⁸ "This is its interpretation," Joseph
replied. "The three baskets are three
days. ¹⁹ In just three days Pharaoh will
lift up your head—from off you—and
hang you on a tree.ᵈ Then the birds will
eat the flesh from your body."ᵉ

²⁰ On the third day, which was Pharaoh's birthday, he gave a feast for all his
servants. He lifted up the heads of the
chief cupbearer and the chief baker:

ᵃ**39:22** Lit *prison in the hand of Joseph*   ᵇ**39:23** Lit *anything in his hand*   ᶜ**40:4** Lit *custody days*   ᵈ**40:19** Or *and impale you on a pole*   ᵉ**40:19** Lit *eat your flesh from upon you*

²¹ he restored the chief cupbearer to his position as cupbearer, and he placed the cup in Pharaoh's hand; ²² but he hanged[a] the chief baker, just as Joseph had explained to them. ²³ Yet the chief cupbearer did not remember Joseph; he forgot him.

Pharaoh's Dreams

41 Two years later Pharaoh had a dream: He was standing beside the Nile, ² when seven healthy-looking, well-fed cows came up from the Nile and began to graze among the reeds. ³ After them, seven other cows, sickly and thin, came up from the Nile and stood beside those cows along the bank of the Nile. ⁴ The sickly, thin cows ate the healthy, well-fed cows. Then Pharaoh woke up. ⁵ He fell asleep and dreamed a second time: Seven heads of grain, full and good, came up on one stalk. ⁶ After them, seven heads of grain, thin and scorched by the east wind, sprouted up. ⁷ The thin heads of grain swallowed up the seven full, good ones. Then Pharaoh woke up, and it was only a dream.

Pharaoh Seeks Interpretation

⁸ When morning came, he was troubled, so he summoned all the magicians of Egypt and all its wise men. Pharaoh told them his dreams, but no one could interpret them for him.

⁹ Then the chief cupbearer said to Pharaoh, "Today I remember my faults. ¹⁰ Pharaoh had been angry with his servants, and he put me and the chief baker in the custody of the captain of the guard. ¹¹ He and I had dreams on the same night; each dream had its own meaning. ¹² Now a young Hebrew, a slave of the captain of the guards, was with us there. We told him our dreams, he interpreted our dreams for us, and each had its own interpretation. ¹³ It turned out just the way he interpreted them to us: I was restored to my position, and the other man was hanged."

Pharaoh Sends for Joseph

¹⁴ Then Pharaoh sent for Joseph, and they quickly brought him from the dungeon. He shaved, changed his clothes, and went to Pharaoh.

¹⁵ Pharaoh said to Joseph, "I have had a dream, and no one can interpret it. But I have heard it said about you that you can hear a dream and interpret it."

¹⁶ "I am not able to," Joseph answered Pharaoh. "It is God who will give Pharaoh a favorable answer."[b]

Joseph Interprets

¹⁷ So Pharaoh said to Joseph: "In my dream I was standing on the bank of the Nile, ¹⁸ when seven well-fed, healthy-looking cows came up from the Nile and began to graze among the reeds. ¹⁹ After them, seven other cows—ugly, very sickly, and thin—came up. I've never seen such ugly ones as these in all the land of Egypt. ²⁰ Then the thin, ugly cows ate the first seven well-fed cows. ²¹ When they had devoured them, you could not tell that they had devoured them; their appearance was as bad as it had been before. Then I woke up. ²² In my dream I had also seen seven heads of grain, full and good, coming up on one stalk. ²³ After them, seven heads of grain—withered, thin, and scorched by the east wind—sprouted up. ²⁴ The thin heads of grain swallowed the seven full ones. I told this to the magicians, but no one can tell me what it means."

²⁵ Then Joseph said to Pharaoh, "Pharaoh's dreams mean the same thing. God

---

[a]**40:22** Or *impaled*   [b]**41:16** Or *"God will answer Pharaoh with peace [of mind]."*

has revealed to Pharaoh what He is about to do. 26 The seven good cows are seven years, and the seven good heads are seven years. The dreams mean the same thing. 27 The seven thin, ugly cows that came up after them are seven years, and the seven worthless, scorched heads of grain are seven years of famine.

28 "It is just as I told Pharaoh: God has shown Pharaoh what He is about to do. 29 Seven[a] years of great abundance are coming throughout the land of Egypt. 30 After them, seven years of famine will take place, and all the abundance in the land of Egypt will be forgotten. The famine will devastate the land. 31 The abundance in the land will not be remembered because of the famine that follows it, for the famine will be very severe. 32 Because the dream was given twice to Pharaoh, it means that the matter has been determined by God, and He will soon carry it out.

33 "So now, let Pharaoh look for a discerning and wise man and set him over the land of Egypt. 34 Let Pharaoh do this: Let him appoint overseers over the land and take one-fifth ⌊of the harvest⌋ of the land of Egypt during the seven years of abundance. 35 Let them gather all the ⌊excess⌋ food during these good years that are coming, store the grain under Pharaoh's authority as food in the cities, and preserve ⌊it⌋. 36 The food will be a reserve for the land during the seven years of famine that will take place in the land of Egypt. Then the country will not be wiped out by the famine."

Joseph Ruler of Egypt

37 The proposal pleased Pharaoh and all his servants. 38 Then Pharaoh said to his servants, "Can we find anyone like this, a man who has the spirit of God[b] in him?" 39 So Pharaoh said to Joseph, "Since God has made all this known to you, there is no one as intelligent and wise as you. 40 You will be over my house, and all my people will obey your commands.[c] Only with regard to the throne will I be greater than you." 41 Pharaoh also said to Joseph, "See, I am placing you over all the land of Egypt." 42 Pharaoh removed his signet ring from his hand and put it on Joseph's hand, clothed him with fine linen garments, and placed a gold chain around his neck. 43 He had Joseph ride in his second chariot, and ⌊servants⌋ called out before him, "Abrek!"[d] So he placed him over all the land of Egypt. 44 Pharaoh said to Joseph, "I am Pharaoh, but without your permission no one will be able to raise his hand or foot in all the land of Egypt." 45 Pharaoh gave Joseph the name Zaphenath-paneah and gave him a wife, Asenath daughter of Potiphera, priest at On.[e] And Joseph went throughout[f] the land of Egypt.

Joseph's Administration

46 Joseph was 30 years old when he entered the service of Pharaoh king of Egypt. Joseph left Pharaoh's presence and traveled throughout the land of Egypt.

Seven Years of Plenty

47 During the seven years of abundance the land produced outstanding harvests. 48 Joseph gathered all the ⌊excess⌋ food in the land of Egypt during the seven years and placed it in the cities. He placed the food in every city from the fields around it. 49 So Joseph stored up grain in such abundance—like the sand

---

a41:29 Lit Look! Seven   b41:38 Or Spirit of God, or spirit of the gods   c41:40 Lit will kiss your mouth   d41:43 Perhaps an Egyptian word meaning Attention!; others see it as a Hb word meaning Kneel!   e41:45 Or Heliopolis   f41:45 Or Joseph gained authority over

of the sea—that he stopped measuring it because it was beyond measure.

Joseph's Two Sons

[50] Two sons were born to Joseph before the years of famine arrived. Asenath daughter of Potiphera, priest at On,[a] bore ⌊them⌋ to him. [51] Joseph named the firstborn Manasseh, meaning, "God has made me forget all my hardship in my father's house." [52] And the second son he named Ephraim, meaning, "God has made me fruitful in the land of my affliction."

Seven Years of Famine

[53] Then the seven years of abundance in the land of Egypt came to an end, [54] and the seven years of famine began, just as Joseph had said. There was famine in every country, but throughout the land of Egypt there was food. [55] Extreme hunger came to all the land of Egypt, and the people cried out to Pharaoh for food. Pharaoh told all Egypt, "Go to Joseph and do whatever he tells you." [56] Because the famine had spread across the whole country, Joseph opened up ⌊all the storehouses⌋ and sold grain to the Egyptians, for the famine was severe in the land of Egypt. [57] The whole world came to Joseph in Egypt to buy grain, for the famine was severe all over the earth.

Joseph's Brothers in Egypt

42 When Jacob learned that there was grain in Egypt, he said to his sons, "Why do you keep looking at each other? [2] Listen," he went on, "I have heard there is grain in Egypt. Go down there and buy some for us so that we will live and not die." [3] So 10 of Joseph's brothers went down to buy grain from Egypt. [4] But Jacob did not send Joseph's brother Benjamin with his brothers, for he thought, "Something might happen to him."

Joseph Accuses His Brothers

[5] The sons of Israel were among those who came to buy grain, for the famine was in the land of Canaan. [6] Joseph was in charge of the country; he sold grain to all its people. His brothers came and bowed down before him with their faces to the ground. [7] When Joseph saw his brothers, he recognized them, but he treated them like strangers and spoke harshly to them.

"Where do you come from?" he asked.

"From the land of Canaan to buy food," they replied.

[8] Although Joseph recognized his brothers, they did not recognize him. [9] Joseph remembered his dreams about them and said to them, "You are spies. You have come to see the weakness[b] of the land."

[10] "No, my lord. Your servants have come to buy food," they said. [11] "We are all sons of one man. We are honest; your servants are not spies."

[12] "No," he said to them. "You have come to see the weakness of the land."

[13] But they replied, "We, your servants, were 12 brothers, the sons of one man in the land of Canaan. The youngest is now[c] with our father, and one is no longer living."

[14] Then Joseph said to them, "I have spoken:[d] 'You are spies!' [15] This is how you will be tested: As surely as Pharaoh lives, you will not leave this place unless your youngest brother comes here. [16] Send one of your number to get your brother. The rest of you will be imprisoned so that your words can be tested to see if they are true. If they are not, then

---

[a] **41:50** Or *Heliopolis* [b] **42:9** Lit *nakedness* [c] **42:13** Or *today* [d] **42:14** Lit *"That which I spoke to you saying*

as surely as Pharaoh lives, you are spies!"

Joseph Tests His Brothers

[17] So Joseph imprisoned them together for three days.

[18] On the third day Joseph said to them, "I •fear God—do this and you will live. [19] If you are honest men, let one of you[a] be confined to the guardhouse, while the rest of you go and take grain ⌊to relieve⌋ the hunger of your households. [20] Bring your youngest brother to me so that your words can be confirmed; then you won't die." And they consented to this.

[21] Then they said to each other, "It is plain that we are being punished for what we did to our brother. We saw his deep distress when he pleaded with us, but we would not listen. That is why this trouble has come to us."

[22] But Reuben replied: "Didn't I tell you not to harm the boy? But you wouldn't listen. Now we must account for his blood!"[b]

[23] They did not realize that Joseph understood them, since there was an interpreter between them. [24] He turned away from them and wept. Then he turned back and spoke to them. He took Simeon from them and had him bound before their eyes. [25] Joseph then gave orders to fill their containers with grain, return each man's money to his sack, and give them provisions for their journey. This order was carried out. [26] They loaded the grain on their donkeys and left there.

The Brothers Return Home

[27] At the place where they lodged for the night, one of them opened his sack to get feed for his donkey, and he saw his money there at the top of the bag.

[28] He said to his brothers, "My money has been returned! It's here in my bag." Their hearts sank. Trembling, they turned to one another and said, "What is this that God has done to us?"

Jacob Learns of the "Egyptian Lord"

[29] When they reached their father Jacob in the land of Canaan, they told him all that had happened to them: [30] "The man who is the lord of the country spoke harshly to us and accused us of spying on the country. [31] But we told him: We are honest men and not spies. [32] We were 12 brothers, sons of the same[c] father. One is no longer living, and the youngest is now[d] with our father in the land of Canaan. [33] The man who is the lord of the country said to us, 'This is how I will know if you are honest men: Leave one brother with me, take ⌊food to relieve⌋ the hunger of your households, and go. [34] Bring back your youngest brother to me, and I will know that you are not spies but honest men. I will then give your brother back to you, and you can trade in the country.'"

[35] As they began emptying their sacks, there in each man's sack was his bag of money! When they and their father saw their bags of money, they were afraid. [36] Their father Jacob said to them, "You have deprived me of my sons. Joseph is gone and Simeon is gone. Now you want to take Benjamin. Everything happens to me!"

[37] Then Reuben said to his father, "You can kill my two sons if I don't bring him back to you. Put him in my care,[e] and I will return him to you."

[38] But Jacob answered, "My son will not go down with you, for his brother is dead and he alone is left. If anything happens to him on your journey, you will

---

[a]**42:19** Lit *your brothers*   [b]**42:22** Lit *Even his blood is being sought*   [c]**42:32** Lit *of our*   [d]**42:32** Or *today*   [e]**42:37** Lit *hand*

bring my gray hairs down to •Sheol in sorrow."

Brothers Return to Egypt

43 Now the famine in the land was severe. ² When they had used up the grain they had brought back from Egypt, their father said to them, "Go back and buy us some food."

³ But Judah said to him, "The man specifically warned us: 'You will not see me again unless your brother is with you.' ⁴ If you will send our brother with us, we will go down and buy food for you. ⁵ But if you will not send him, we will not go, for the man said to us, 'You will not see me again unless your brother is with you.'"

⁶ "Why did you cause me so much trouble?" Israel asked. "Why did you tell the man that you had another brother?"

⁷ They answered, "The man kept asking about us and our family: 'Is your father still alive? Do you have ⌊another⌋ brother?' And we answered him accordingly. How could we know that he would say, 'Bring your brother here'?"

⁸ Then Judah said to his father Israel, "Send the boy with me. We will be on our way so that we may live, and not die—neither we, nor you, nor our children. ⁹ I will be responsible for him. You can hold me personally accountable!ª If I do not bring him back to you and set him before you, I will be guilty before you forever. ¹⁰ If we had not wasted time, we could have come back twice by now."

Jacob Agrees: Benjamin to Egypt

¹¹ Then their father Israel said to them, "If it must be so, then do this: Put some of the best products of the land in your packs and take them down to the man as a gift—some balsam and some honey, aromatic gum and resin, pistachios and almonds. ¹² Take twice as much money with you. Return the money that was returned ⌊to you⌋ in the top of your bags. Perhaps it was a mistake. ¹³ Take your brother also, and go back at once to the man. ¹⁴ May •God Almighty cause the man to be merciful to you so that he will release your other brother and Benjamin to you. As for me, if I am deprived of my sons, then I am deprived."

The Trip to Egypt

¹⁵ The men took this gift, double the amount of money, and Benjamin. They made their way down to Egypt and stood before Joseph.

¹⁶ When Joseph saw Benjamin with them, he said to his steward,ᵇ "Take the men to ⌊my⌋ house. Slaughter an animal and prepare it, for they will eat with me at noon." ¹⁷ The man did as Joseph had said and brought them to Joseph's house.

Feast at Joseph's Palace

¹⁸ But the men were afraid because they were taken to Joseph's house. They said, "We have been brought here because of the money that was returned in our bags the first time. They intend to overpower us, seize us, make us slaves, and take our donkeys." ¹⁹ So they approached Joseph's stewardᶜ and spoke to him at the doorway of the house.

²⁰ They said, "Sir, we really did come down here the first time only to buy food. ²¹ When we came to the place where we lodged for the night and opened our bags of grain, each one's money was at the top of his bag! It was the full amount of our money, and we have brought it back with us. ²² We have brought additional money with us to buy

---

ª**43:9** Lit *can seek him from my hand*　ᵇ**43:16** Lit *to the one who was over his house*　ᶜ**43:19** Lit *approached the one who was over the house*

food. We don't know who put our money in the bags."

23 Then the steward said, "May you be well. Don't be afraid. Your God and the God of your father must have put treasure in your bags. I received your money." Then he brought Simeon out to them. 24 The man brought the men into Joseph's house, gave them water to wash their feet, and got feed for their donkeys. 25 Since the men had heard that they were going to eat a meal there, they prepared their gift for Joseph's arrival at noon. 26 When Joseph came home, they brought him the gift they had carried into the house, and they bowed to the ground before him.

Joseph Questions His Brothers

27 He asked if they were well, and he said, "How is your elderly father that you told me about? Is he still alive?"

28 They answered, "Your servant our father is well. He is still alive." And they bowed down to honor him.

29 When he looked up and saw his brother Benjamin, his mother's son, he asked, "Is this your youngest brother that you told me about?" Then he said, "May God be gracious to you, my son." 30 Joseph hurried out because he was overcome with emotion for his brother, and he was about to weep. He went into an inner room to weep. 31 Then he washed his face and came out. Regaining his composure, he said, "Serve the meal."

32 They served him by himself, his brothers by themselves, and the Egyptians who were eating with him by themselves, because Egyptians could not eat with Hebrews, since that is abhorrent to them. 33 They were seated before him in order by age, from the firstborn to the youngest. The men looked at each other in astonishment. 34 Portions were served to them from Joseph's table, and Benjamin's portion was five times larger than any of theirs. They drank, and they got drunk with Joseph.

Joseph's Final Test

44 Then Joseph commanded his steward: "Fill the men's bags with as much food as they can carry, and put each one's money at the top of his bag. 2 Put my cup, the silver one, at the top of the youngest one's bag, along with his grain money." So he did as Joseph told him.

3 At morning light, the men were sent off with their donkeys. 4 They had not gone very far from the city when Joseph said to his steward, "Get up. Pursue the men, and when you overtake them, say to them, 'Why have you repaid evil for good?[a] 5 Isn't this the cup that my master drinks from and uses for •divination? What you have done is wrong!' "

The Silver Cup: Benjamin Accused

6 When he overtook them, he said these words to them. 7 They said to him, "Why does my lord say these things? Your servants could not possibly do such a thing. 8 We even brought back to you from the land of Canaan the money we found at the top of our bags. How could we steal gold and silver from your master's house? 9 If any of us is[b] found to have it, he must die, and we also will become my lord's slaves."

10 The steward replied, "What you have said is proper, but only the one who is found to have it will be my slave, and the rest of you will be blameless."

11 So each one quickly lowered his sack to the ground and opened it. 12 The

---

a 44:4 LXX adds *Why have you stolen my silver cup?*　　b 44:9 Lit *If your servants are* steward searched, beginning with the oldest and ending with the youngest, and the cup was found in Benjamin's sack. ¹³ Then they tore their clothes, and each one loaded his donkey and returned to the city.

¹⁴ When Judah and his brothers reached Joseph's house, he was still there. They fell to the ground before him. ¹⁵ "What is this you have done?" Joseph said to them. "Didn't you know that a man like me could uncover the truth by divination?"

¹⁶ "What can we say to my lord?" Judah replied. "How can we plead? How can we justify ourselves? God has exposed your servants' iniquity. We are now my lord's slaves—both we and the one in whose possession the cup was found."

¹⁷ Then Joseph said, "I swear that I will not do this. The man in whose possession the cup was found will be my slave. The rest of you can go in peace to your father."

Judah's Plea for Benjamin

¹⁸ But Judah approached him and said, "Sir, please let your servant speak personally to my lord.ᵃ Do not be angry with your servant, for you are like Pharaoh. ¹⁹ My lord asked his servants, 'Do you have a father or a brother?' ²⁰ and we answered my lord, 'We have an elderly father and a young brother, the child of his old age. The boy'sᵇ brother is dead. He is the only one of his mother's sons left, and his father loves him.' ²¹ Then you said to your servants, 'Bring him to me so that I can see him.' ²² But we said to my lord, 'The boy cannot leave his father. If he were to leave, his father would die.' ²³ Then you said to your servants, 'If your younger brother does not

come down with you, you will not see me again.'

²⁴ "This is what happened when we went back to your servant my father: We reported your words to him. ²⁵ But our father said, 'Go again, and buy us some food.' ²⁶ We told him, 'We cannot go down unless our younger brother goes with us. But if our younger brother isn't with us, we cannot see the man.' ²⁷ Your servant my father said to us, 'You know that my wife bore me two sons. ²⁸ One left—I said that he must have been torn to pieces—and I have never seen him again. ²⁹ If you also take this one from me and anything happens to him, you will bring my gray hairs down to •Sheol in sorrow.'

³⁰ "So, if I come to your servant my father and the boy is not with us—his life is wrapped up with the boy's life— ³¹ when he sees that the boy is not with us, he will die. Then your servants will have brought the gray hairs of your servant our father down to Sheol in sorrow. ³² Your servant became accountable to my father for the boy, saying, 'If I do not return him to you, I will always bear the guilt for sinning against ⌊you,⌋ my father.' ³³ Now please let your servant remain here as my lord's slave, in place of the boy. Let him go back with his brothers. ³⁴ For how can I go back to my father without the boy? I could not bear to seeᶜ the grief that would overwhelm my father."

Joseph Reveals His Identity

45 Joseph could no longer keep his composure in front of all his attendants,ᵈ so he called out, "Send everyone away from me!" No one was with him when he revealed his identity to his brothers. ² But he wept so loudly that the

---

ᵃ **44:18** Lit *speak a word in my lord's ears* ᵇ **44:20** Lit *His* ᶜ **44:34** Lit *boy lest I see* ᵈ **45:1** Lit *all those standing about him*

Egyptians heard it, and also Pharaoh's household heard it. ³ Joseph said to his brothers, "I am Joseph! Is my father still living?" But his brothers were too terrified to answer him.

⁴ Then Joseph said to his brothers, "Please, come near me," and they came near. "I am Joseph, your brother," he said, "the one you sold into Egypt. ⁵ And now don't be worried or angry with yourselves for selling me here, because God sent me ahead of you to preserve life. ⁶ For the famine has been in the land these two years, and there will be five more years without plowing or harvesting. ⁷ God sent me ahead of you to establish you as a remnant within the land and to keep you alive by a great deliverance.ᵃ ⁸ Therefore it was not you who sent me here, but God. He has made me a father to Pharaoh, lord of his entire household, and ruler over all the land of Egypt.

Joseph Sends for Jacob

⁹ "Return quickly to my father and say to him, 'This is what your son Joseph says: "God has made me lord of all Egypt. Come down to me without delay. ¹⁰ You can settle in the land of Goshen and be near me—you, your children, and grandchildren, your sheep, cattle, and all you have. ¹¹ There I will sustain you, for there will be five more years of famine. Otherwise, you, your household, and everything you have will become destitute."' ¹² Look! Your eyes and my brother Benjamin's eyes can see that it is I ι, Joseph,ι who amᵇ speaking to you. ¹³ Tell my father all about my glory in Egypt and about all you have seen. And bring my father here quickly."

¹⁴ Then Joseph threw his arms around Benjamin and wept, and Benjamin wept on his shoulder. ¹⁵ Joseph kissed each of his brothers as he wept,ᶜ and afterward his brothers talked with him.

Pharaoh Invites Jacob to Egypt

¹⁶ When the news reached Pharaoh's house, "Joseph's brothers have come," Pharaoh and his servants were pleased. ¹⁷ Pharaoh said to Joseph, "Tell your brothers, 'Do this: Load your animals and go on back to the land of Canaan. ¹⁸ Get your father and your households, and come back to me. I will give you the best of the land of Egypt, and you can eat from the richness of the land.' ¹⁹ You are also commanded, 'Do this: Take wagons from the land of Egypt for your young children, your wives, and bring your father here. ²⁰ Do not be concerned about your belongings, for the best of all the land of Egypt is yours.'"

²¹ The sons of Israel did this. Joseph gave them wagons as Pharaoh had commanded, and he gave them provisions for the journey. ²² He gave each of the brothers changes of clothes, but he gave Benjamin 300 pieces of silver and five changes of clothes. ²³ He sent his father the following: 10 donkeys carrying the best products of Egypt, and 10 female donkeys carrying grain, food, and provisions for his father on the journey. ²⁴ So Joseph sent his brothers on their way, and as they were leaving, he said to them, "Don't argue on the way."

"Joseph Is Still Alive!"

²⁵ So they went up from Egypt and came to their father Jacob in the land of Canaan. ²⁶ They said, "Joseph is still alive, and he is ruler over all the land of Egypt!" Jacob was stunned,ᵈ for he did not believe them. ²⁷ But when they told Jacob all that Joseph had said to them,

ᵃ45:7 Or keep alive for you many survivors ᵇ45:12 Lit that my mouth is ᶜ45:15 Lit brothers, and he wept over them ᵈ45:26 Lit Jacob's heart was numb

and when he saw the wagons that Joseph had sent to transport him, the spirit of their father Jacob revived.

²⁸ Then Israel said, "Enough! My son Joseph is still alive. I will go to see him before I die."

Jacob Leaves for Egypt

46 Israel set out with all that he had and came to Beer-sheba, and he offered sacrifices to the God of his father Isaac. ² That night God spoke to Israel in a vision: "Jacob, Jacob!" He said.

And Jacob replied, "Here I am."

³ God said, "I am God, the God of your father. Do not be afraid to go down to Egypt, for I will make you a great nation there. ⁴ I will go down with you to Egypt, and I will also bring you back. Joseph will put his hands on your eyes."ᵃ

⁵ Jacob left Beer-sheba. The sons of Israel took their father Jacob in the wagons Pharaoh had sent to carry him, along with their children and their wives. ⁶ They also took their cattle and possessions they had acquired in the land of Canaan. Then Jacob and all his children with him went to Egypt. ⁷ His sons and grandsons, his daughters and granddaughters, indeed all his •offspring, he brought with him to Egypt.

Jacob's Family in Egypt

⁸ These are the names of the Israelites, Jacob and his descendants, who went to Egypt:

Jacob's firstborn: Reuben.
⁹ Reuben's sons: Hanoch, Pallu, Hezron, and Carmi.
¹⁰ Simeon's sons: Jemuel, Jamin, Ohad, Jachin, Zohar, and Shaul, the son of a Canaanite woman.
¹¹ Levi's sons: Gershon, Kohath, and Merari.
¹² Judah's sons: Er, Onan, Shelah, Perez, and Zerah; but Er and Onan died in the land of Canaan.
Perez's sons: Hezron and Hamul.
¹³ Issachar's sons: Tola, Puvah,ᵇ Jashub,ᶜ and Shimron.
¹⁴ Zebulun's sons: Sered, Elon, and Jahleel.
¹⁵ These were Leah's sons born to Jacob in Paddan-aram, as well as his daughter Dinah. The total number of persons:ᵈ 33.
¹⁶ Gad's sons: Ziphion, Haggi, Shuni, Ezbon, Eri, Arodi, and Areli.
¹⁷ Asher's sons: Imnah, Ishvah, Ishvi, Beriah, and their sister Serah. Beriah's sons were Heber and Malchiel.
¹⁸ These were the sons of Zilpah— whom Laban gave to his daughter Leah—that she bore to Jacob: 16 persons.
¹⁹ The sons of Jacob's wife Rachel: Joseph and Benjamin.
²⁰ Manasseh and Ephraim were born to Joseph in the land of Egypt. They were born to him by Asenath daughter of Potiphera, a priest at On.ᵉ
²¹ Benjamin's sons: Bela, Becher, Ashbel, Gera, Naaman, Ehi, Rosh, Muppim, Huppim, and Ard.
²² These were Rachel's sons who were born to Jacob: 14 persons.
²³ Dan's son:ᶠ Hashum.
²⁴ Naphtali's sons: Jahzeel, Guni, Jezer, and Shillem.
²⁵ These were the sons of Bilhah, whom Laban gave to his daughter

---

ᵃ**46:4** = Joseph will close your eyes after you die   ᵇ**46:13** Sam, Syr read *Puah*; 1 Ch 7:1   ᶜ**46:13** Sam, LXX; MT reads *Iob*   ᵈ**46:15** Lit *All persons his sons and his daughters*   ᵉ**46:20** Or *Heliopolis*   ᶠ**46:23** Alt Hb tradition reads *sons*

Rachel. She bore to Jacob: seven persons. 26 The total number of persons belonging to Jacob— his direct descendants,[a] not including the wives of Jacob's sons—who came to Egypt: 66. 27 And Joseph's sons who were born to him in Egypt: two persons. All those of Jacob's household who had come to Egypt: 70[b] persons.

Jacob Arrives in Egypt

Joseph Greets Jacob

28 Now Jacob had sent Judah ahead of him to Joseph to prepare for his arrival[c] at Goshen. When they came to the land of Goshen, 29 Joseph hitched ⌊the horses to⌋ his chariot and went up to Goshen to meet his father Israel. Joseph presented himself to him, threw his arms around him, and wept for a long time.

30 Then Israel said to Joseph, "At last I can die, now that I have seen your face ⌊and know⌋ you are still alive!"

31 Joseph said to his brothers and to his father's household, "I will go up and inform Pharaoh, telling him: My brothers and my father's household, who were in the land of Canaan, have come to me. 32 The men are shepherds; indeed they raise livestock. They have brought their sheep and cattle and all that they have. 33 When Pharaoh addresses you and asks, 'What is your occupation?' 34 you are to say, 'Your servants, both we and our fathers, have raised livestock[d] from our youth until now.' Then you will be allowed to settle in the land of Goshen, since all shepherds are abhorrent to Egyptians."

Jacob Blesses Pharaoh

47 So Joseph went and informed Pharaoh: "My father and my brothers, with their sheep and cattle and all that they have, have come from the land of Canaan and are now in the land of Goshen."

2 He took five of his brothers and presented them before Pharaoh. 3 Then Pharaoh asked his brothers, "What is your occupation?"

And they said to Pharaoh, "Your servants, both we and our fathers, are shepherds." 4 Then they said to Pharaoh, "We have come to live in the land for a while because there is no grazing land for your servants' sheep, since the famine in the land of Canaan has been severe. So now, please let your servants settle in the land of Goshen."

5 Then Pharaoh said to Joseph, "⌊Now that⌋ your father and brothers have come to you, 6 the land of Egypt is open before you; settle your father and brothers in the best part of the land. They can live in the land of Goshen. If you know of any capable men among them, put them in charge of my livestock."

7 Joseph then brought his father Jacob and presented him before Pharaoh, and Jacob blessed Pharaoh. 8 Then Pharaoh said to Jacob, "How many years have you lived?"[e]

9 Jacob said to Pharaoh, "My pilgrimage has lasted 130 years. My years have been few and hard, and they have not surpassed the years of my fathers during their pilgrimages." 10 So Jacob blessed Pharaoh and departed from Pharaoh's presence.

11 Then Joseph settled his father and brothers in the land of Egypt and gave them property in the best part of the land, the land of Rameses, as Pharaoh

a **46:26** Lit *Jacob who came out from his loins*   b **46:27** LXX reads *75*; Ac 7:14   c **46:28** Lit *to give directions before him*   d **46:34** Lit *fathers, are men of livestock*   e **47:8** Lit *many are the days of the years*

had commanded. [12] And Joseph provided his father, his brothers, and all his father's household with food for their dependents.

Joseph's Leadership in the Famine

[13] But there was no food in that entire region, for the famine was very severe. The land of Egypt and the land of Canaan were exhausted by the famine. [14] Joseph collected all the money to be found in the land of Egypt and the land of Canaan in exchange for the grain they were purchasing, and he brought the money to Pharaoh's house. [15] When the money from the land of Egypt and the land of Canaan was gone, all the Egyptians came to Joseph and said, "Give us food. Why should we die here in front of you? The money is gone!"

[16] But Joseph said, "Give me your livestock. Since the money is gone, I will give you food in exchange for your livestock." [17] So they brought their livestock to Joseph, and he gave them food in exchange for the horses, the herds of sheep, the herds of cattle, and the donkeys. That year he provided them with food in exchange for all their livestock.

[18] When that year was over, they came the next year and said to him, "We cannot hide from our lord that the money is gone and that all our livestock belongs to our lord. There is nothing left for our lord except our bodies and our land. [19] Why should we perish here in front of you—both us and our land? Buy us and our land in exchange for food. Then we with our land will become Pharaoh's slaves. Give us seed so that we can live and not die, and so that the land won't become desolate."

Pharaoh Owns the Land

[20] In this way, Joseph acquired all the land in Egypt for Pharaoh, because every Egyptian sold his field since the famine was so severe for them. The land became Pharaoh's, [21] and Joseph moved the people to the cities[a] from one end of Egypt to the other. [22] The only land he didn't acquire was that of the priests, for it was their allotment from Pharaoh. They lived off[b] the allotment Pharaoh had given them; therefore they did not sell their land.

[23] Then Joseph said to the people, "Understand today that I have acquired you and your land for Pharaoh. Here is seed for you. Sow it in the land. [24] At harvest, you are to give a fifth of it to Pharaoh, and four-fifths will be yours as seed for the field and as food for yourselves, your households, and your dependents."

[25] And they said, "You have saved our lives. We have found favor in our lord's eyes and will be Pharaoh's slaves." [26] So Joseph made it a law, still in effect today in the land of Egypt, that a fifth ⌊of the produce⌋ belongs to Pharaoh. Only the priests' land does not belong to Pharaoh.

Israel Settles in Goshen

[27] Israel settled in the land of Egypt, in the region of Goshen. They acquired property in it and became fruitful and very numerous. [28] Now Jacob lived in the land of Egypt 17 years, and his life span was 147 years. [29] When the time drew near for him to die, he called his son Joseph and said to him, "If I have found favor in your eyes, put your hand under my thigh ⌊and promise me⌋ that you will deal with me in faithful love. Do not bury me in Egypt. [30] When I lie down with my fathers, carry me away

---

[a] **47:21** Sam, LXX, Vg read *and he made the people servants*   [b] **47:22** Lit *They ate*

from Egypt and bury me in their burial place."

Joseph answered, "I will do what you have asked."

³¹ And Jacob said, "Swear to me." So Joseph swore to him. Then Israel bowed ⌊in thanks⌋ at the head of his bed.ᵃ

Jacob Blesses Ephraim and Manasseh

48 Some time after this, Joseph was told, "Your father is weaker." So he set out with his two sons, Manasseh and Ephraim. ² When Jacob was told, "Your son Joseph has come to you," Israel summoned his strength and sat up in bed.

³ Jacob said to Joseph, "•God Almighty appeared to me at Luz in the land of Canaan and blessed me. ⁴ He said to me, 'I will make you fruitful and numerous; I will make many nations ⌊come from⌋ you, and I will give this land as an eternal possession to your descendants to come.' ⁵ Your two sons born to you in the land of Egypt before I came to you in Egypt are now mine. Ephraim and Manasseh belong to me just as Reuben and Simeon do. ⁶ Children born to you after them will be yours and will be recorded under the names of their brothers with regard to their inheritance. ⁷ When I was returning from Paddan, to my sorrow Rachel died along the way, some distance from Ephrath in the land of Canaan. I buried her there along the way to Ephrath," (that is, Bethlehem).

⁸ When Israel saw Joseph's sons, he said, "Who are these?"

⁹ And Joseph said to his father, "They are my sons God has given me here."

So Jacob said, "Bring them to me and I will bless them." ¹⁰ Now Jacob's eyesight was poor because of old age; he could hardlyᵇ see. Joseph brought them to him, and he kissed and embraced them. ¹¹ Israel said to Joseph, "I never expected to see your face ⌊again⌋, but now God has even let me see your •offspring." ¹² Then Joseph took them from his ⌊father's⌋ knees and bowed with his face to the ground.

Jacob Favors Ephraim

¹³ Then Joseph took them both—with his right hand Ephraim toward Israel's left, and with his left hand Manasseh toward Israel's right—and brought them to Israel. ¹⁴ But Israel stretched out his right hand and put it on the head of Ephraim, the younger, and crossing his hands, put his left on Manasseh's head, although Manasseh was the firstborn. ¹⁵ Then he blessed Joseph and said:

The God before whom my fathers
  Abraham and Isaac walked,
the God who has been
  my shepherd all my life
  to this day,
¹⁶ the Angel who has redeemed me
  from all harm—
may He bless these boys.
And may they be called
  by my name
and the names of my fathers
  Abraham and Isaac,
and may they grow to be numerous
  within the land.

¹⁷ When Joseph saw that his father had placed his right hand on Ephraim's head, he thought it was a mistakeᶜ and took his father's hand to move it from Ephraim's head to Manasseh's. ¹⁸ Joseph said to his father, "Not that way, my father! This one is the firstborn. Put your right hand on his head."

ᵃ**47:31** Or *Israel worshiped while leaning on the top of his staff* ᵇ**48:10** Lit *he was not able to* ᶜ**48:17** Or *he was displeased*; lit *head, it was bad in his eyes*

¹⁹ But his father refused and said, "I know, my son, I know! He too will become a tribe,ᵃ and he too will be great; nevertheless, his younger brother will be greater than he, and his offspring will become a populous nation."ᵇ ²⁰ So he blessed them that day with these words:

Israel will invoke blessings by you,
saying,
"May God make you like Ephraim
and Manasseh,"

putting Ephraim before Manasseh.

²¹ Then Israel said to Joseph, "Look! I am about to die, but God will be with you and will bring you back to the land of your fathers. ²² Over and above what I am giving your brothers, I am giving you the one mountain slopeᶜ that I took from the hand of the Amorites with my sword and bow."

Jacob Evaluates His Sons

49 Then Jacob called his sons and said, "Gather around, and I will tell you what will happen to you in the days to come.ᵈ

² Come together and listen,
    sons of Jacob;
    listen to your father Israel:

³ Reuben, you are my firstborn,
    my strength and the firstfruits
    of my virility,
    excelling in prominence,
    excelling in power.
⁴ Turbulent as water, you will
    no longer excel,
    because you got into your father's
    bed
    and you defiled it—heᵉ got
    into my bed.
⁵ Simeon and Levi are brothers;

their knives are vicious weapons.
⁶ May I never enter their council;
    may I never join their assembly.
    For in their anger they kill men,
    and on a whim
    they hamstring oxen.
⁷ Their anger is cursed,
    for it is strong,
    and their fury, for it is cruel!
    I will disperse them
    throughout Jacob
    and scatter them throughout Israel.

⁸ Judah, your brothers will praise
    you.
    Your hand will be on the necks
    of your enemies;
    your father's sons will bow down
    to you.
⁹ Judah is a young lion—
    my son, you return from the kill—
    he crouches; he lies down
    like a lion
    and like a lioness—who wants
    to rouse him?
¹⁰ The scepter will not depart
    from Judah,
    or the staff from between his feet,
    until He whose right it is comesᶠ
    and the obedience of the peoples
    belongs to Him.
¹¹ He ties his donkey to a vine,
    and the colt of his donkey
    to the choice vine.
    He washes his clothes in wine,
    and his robes in the blood
    of grapes.
¹² His eyes are darker than wine,
    and his teeth are whiter than milk.

¹³ Zebulun will live by the seashore
    and will be a harbor for ships,
    and his territory will be
    next to Sidon.

ᵃ48:19 Lit people ᵇ48:19 Lit a fullness of nations; perhaps a multitude of nations ᶜ48:22 Lit one shoulder; Hb Shechem, Joseph's burial place ᵈ49:1 Or in the last days ᵉ49:4 LXX, Syr, Tg read you ᶠ49:10 Or until tribute comes to him, or until Shiloh comes, or until He comes to Shiloh

¹⁴ Issachar is a strong donkey
lying down between the saddlebags.^a
¹⁵ He saw that his resting place
    was good
and that the land was pleasant,
so he leaned his shoulder to bear
    a load
and became a forced laborer.

¹⁶ Dan will judge his people
as one of the tribes of Israel.
¹⁷ He will be a snake by the road,
a viper beside the path,
that bites the horses' heels
so that its rider falls backwards.

¹⁸ I wait for Your salvation, LORD.

¹⁹ Gad will be attacked
    by ⌊marauding⌋ bands,
but he will attack their heels.

²⁰ Asher's^b food will be rich,
and he will produce royal delicacies.

²¹ Naphtali is a doe set free
that bears beautiful fawns.

²² Joseph is a fruitful vine,
a fruitful vine beside a spring;
its branches^c climb over the wall.^d
²³ The archers attacked him,
shot at him, and were hostile
    toward him.
²⁴ Yet his bow remained steady,
and his strong^e arms were made agile
by the hands of the Mighty One
    of Jacob,
by the name of^f the Shepherd,
    the Rock of Israel,
²⁵ by the God of your father
    who helps you,
and by the •Almighty who blesses
    you
with blessings of the heavens above,
blessings of the deep that lies below,

and blessings of the breasts
    and the womb.
²⁶ The blessings of your father excel
the blessings of my ancestors^g
and^h the bounty of the eternal hills.^d
May they rest on the head of Joseph,
on the crown of the prince
    of his brothers.

²⁷ Benjamin is a wolf; he tears
    ⌊his prey⌋.
In the morning he devours the prey,
and in the evening he divides
    the plunder."

²⁸ These are the tribes of Israel, 12 in all, and this was what their father said to them. He blessed them, and he blessed each one with a suitable blessing.

Jacob's Burial Instructions

²⁹ Then he commanded them: "I am about to be gathered to my people. Bury me with my fathers in the cave in the field of Ephron the Hittite. ³⁰ The cave is in the field of Machpelah, near Mamre, in the land of Canaan. This is the field Abraham purchased from Ephron the Hittite as a burial site. ³¹ Abraham and his wife Sarah are buried there, Isaac and his wife Rebekah are buried there, and I buried Leah there. ³² The field and the cave in it ⌊were purchased⌋ from the Hittites." ³³ When Jacob had finished instructing his sons, he drew his feet into the bed and died. He was gathered to his people.

Jacob's Embalmment

50 Then Joseph, leaning over his father's face, wept and kissed him. ² He commanded his servants who were physicians to embalm his father. So they embalmed Israel. ³ They took 40 days to complete this, for embalming takes that

---

^a**49:14** Or *sheepfolds*   ^b**49:19-20** LXX, Syr, Vg; MT reads *their heel.* ²⁰ *From Asher*   ^c**49:22** Lit *daughters*
^d**49:22,26** Hb obscure   ^e**49:24** Lit *and the hands of his*   ^f**49:24** Syr, Tg; MT reads *Jacob, from there*   ^g**49:26** Or *of the mountains*   ^h**49:26** Lit *to*

long, and the Egyptians mourned for him 70 days.

4 When the days of mourning were over, Joseph said to Pharaoh's household, "If I have found favor with you, please tell[a] Pharaoh that 5 my father made me take an oath, saying, 'I am about to die. You must bury me there in the tomb that I hewed out for myself in the land of Canaan.' Now let me go and bury my father. Then I will return."

Pharaoh Agrees to Jacob's Burial

6 So Pharaoh said, "Go and bury your father in keeping with your oath."

7 Then Joseph went to bury his father, and all Pharaoh's servants, the elders of his household, and all the elders of the land of Egypt went with him, 8 along with all Joseph's household, his brothers, and his father's household. Only their children, their sheep, and their cattle were left in the land of Goshen. 9 Horses and chariots went up with him; it was a very impressive procession. 10 When they reached the threshing floor of Atad, which is across the Jordan, they lamented and wept loudly, and Joseph mourned seven days for his father. 11 When the Canaanite inhabitants of the land saw the mourning at the threshing floor of Atad, they said, "This is a solemn mourning on the part of the Egyptians." Therefore the place is named Abel-mizraim.[b] It is across the Jordan.

12 So Jacob's sons did for him what he had commanded them. 13 They carried him to the land of Canaan and buried him in the cave at Machpelah in the field near Mamre, which Abraham had purchased as a burial site from Ephron the Hittite. 14 After Joseph buried his father, he returned to Egypt with his brothers and all who had gone with him to bury his father.

Joseph Reassures His Brothers

15 When Joseph's brothers saw that their father was dead, they said to one another, "If Joseph is holding a grudge against us, he will certainly repay us for all the wrong we caused him." 16 So they sent this message to Joseph, "Before he died your father gave a command: 17 'Say this to Joseph: Please forgive your brothers' transgression and their sin—the wrong they caused you.' Therefore, please forgive the transgression of the servants of the God of your father." Joseph wept when their message came to him. 18 Then his brothers also came to him, bowed down before him, and said, "We are your slaves!"

19 But Joseph said to them, "Don't be afraid. Am I in the place of God? 20 You planned evil against me; God planned it for good to bring about the present result—the survival of many people. 21 Therefore don't be afraid. I will take care of you and your little ones." And he comforted them and spoke kindly to them.[c]

Joseph's Death

22 Joseph and his father's household remained in Egypt. Joseph lived 110 years. 23 He saw Ephraim's sons to the third generation; the sons of Manasseh's son Machir were recognized by[d] Joseph.

24 Joseph said to his brothers, "I am about to die, but God will certainly come to your aid and bring you up from this land to the land He promised Abraham, Isaac, and Jacob." 25 So Joseph made the Israelites take an oath: "When God comes to your aid, you are to carry my bones up from here."

26 Joseph died at the age of 110. They embalmed him and placed him in a coffin in Egypt.

---

[a]50:4 Lit *please speak in the ears of*   [b]50:11 = Mourning of Egypt   [c]50:21 Lit *spoke to their hearts*   [d]50:23 Lit *were born on the knees of*; referring to a ritual of adoption or of legitimation; Gn 30:3

EXODUS

Israel Oppressed in Egypt

1 These are the names of the sons of Israel who came to Egypt with Jacob; each came with his family:

2 Reuben, Simeon, Levi, and Judah;
3 Issachar, Zebulun, and Benjamin;
4 Dan and Naphtali; Gad and Asher.

5 The total number of Jacob's descendants[a] was 70;[b] Joseph was already in Egypt.

6 Then Joseph and all his brothers and all that generation died. 7 But the Israelites were fruitful, increased rapidly, multiplied, and became extremely numerous so that the land was filled with them.

An Evil New King

8 A new king, who had not known Joseph, came to power in Egypt. 9 He said to his people, "Look, the Israelite people are more numerous and powerful than we are. 10 Let us deal shrewdly with them; otherwise they will multiply ⌊further⌋, and if war breaks out, they may join our enemies, fight against us, and leave the country." 11 So the Egyptians assigned taskmasters over the Israelites to oppress them with forced labor. They built Pithom and Rameses as supply cities for Pharaoh. 12 But the more they oppressed them, the more they multiplied and spread so that the Egyptians came to dread[c] the Israelites. 13 They worked the Israelites ruthlessly 14 and made their lives bitter with difficult labor in brick and mortar, and in all kinds of fieldwork. They ruthlessly imposed all this work on them.

King's Plan to Kill

15 Then the king of Egypt said to the Hebrew midwives, one of whom was named Shiphrah and the other Puah, 16 "When you help the Hebrew women give birth, observe them as they deliver.[d] If the child is a son, kill him, but if it's a daughter, she may live." 17 The Hebrew midwives, however, •feared God and did not do as the king of Egypt had told them; they let the boys live. 18 So the king of Egypt summoned the midwives and asked them, "Why have you done this and let the boys live?" 19 The midwives said to Pharaoh, "The Hebrew women are not like the Egyptian women, for they are vigorous and give birth before a midwife can get to them." 20 So God was good to the midwives, and the people multiplied and became very numerous. 21 Since the midwives feared God, He gave them families. 22 Pharaoh then commanded all his people: "You must throw every son born to the Hebrews[e] into the Nile, but let every daughter live."

Moses' Birth and Adoption

2 Now a man from the family of Levi married a Levite woman. 2 The woman became pregnant and gave birth to a son; when she saw that he was beautiful,[f] she hid him for three months. 3 But when she could no longer hide him, she got a papyrus basket for him and coated it with asphalt and pitch. She placed the child in it and set it among the reeds by the bank of the Nile. 4 Then his sister stood at a distance in order to see what would happen to him.

---

[a] 1:5 Lit of people issuing from Jacob's loins   [b] 1:5 LXX, DSS read 75; Gn 46:27; Ac 7:14   [c] 1:12 Or Egyptians loathed   [d] 1:16 Lit birth, look at the stones   [e] 1:22 Sam, LXX, Tg; MT omits to the Hebrews   [f] 2:2 Or healthy

⁵ Pharaoh's daughter went down to bathe at the Nile while her servant girls walked along the riverbank. Seeing the basket among the reeds, she sent her slave girl to get it. ⁶ When she opened it, she saw the child—a little boy, crying. She felt sorry for him and said, "This is one of the Hebrew boys."

⁷ Then his sister said to Pharaoh's daughter, "Should I go and call a woman from the Hebrews to nurse the boy for you?"

⁸ "Go." Pharaoh's daughter told her. So the girl went and called the boy's mother. ⁹ Then Pharaoh's daughter said to her, "Take this child and nurse him for me, and I will pay your wages." So the woman took the boy and nursed him. ¹⁰ When the child grew older, she brought him to Pharaoh's daughter, and he became her son. She named him Moses, "Because," she said, "I drew him out of the water."ᵃ

Moses Kills

¹¹ Years later,ᵇ after Moses had grown up, he went out to his own peopleᶜ and observed their forced labor. He saw an Egyptian beating a Hebrew, one of his people. ¹² Looking all around and seeing no one, he struck the Egyptian dead and hid him in the sand. ¹³ The next day he went out and saw two Hebrews fighting. He asked the one in the wrong, "Why are you attacking your neighbor?"ᵈ

¹⁴ "Who made you a leader and judge over us?" the man replied. "Are you planning to kill me as you killed the Egyptian?"

Moses Flees to Midian

Then Moses became afraid and thought: What I did is certainly known.

¹⁵ When Pharaoh heard about this, he tried to kill Moses. But Moses fled from Pharaoh and went to live in the land of Midian, and sat down by a well.

¹⁶ Now the priest of Midian had seven daughters. They came to draw water and filled the troughs to water their father's flock. ¹⁷ Then some shepherds arrived and drove them away, but Moses came to their rescue and watered their flock. ¹⁸ When they returned to their father Reuelᵉ he asked, "Why have you come back so quickly today?"

¹⁹ They answered, "An Egyptian rescued us from the shepherds. He even drew water for us and watered the flock."

²⁰ "So where is he?" he asked his daughters. "Why then did you leave the man behind? Invite him to eat dinner."

Moses Marries Zipporah

²¹ Moses agreed to stay with the man, and he gave his daughter Zipporah to Moses ιin marriageι. ²² She gave birth to a son whom he named Gershom, for he said, "I have become a stranger in a foreign land."ᶠ ²³ After a long time, the king of Egypt died. The Israelites groaned because of their difficult labor, and they cried out; and their cry for help ascended to God because of the difficult labor. ²⁴ So God heard their groaning, and He remembered His covenant with Abraham, Isaac, and Jacob. ²⁵ God saw the Israelites, and He took notice.

Moses and the Burning Bush

3 Meanwhile Moses was shepherding the flock of his father-in-law Jethro,ᵍ the priest of Midian. He led the flock to the far side of the wilderness and came to Horeb,ʰ the mountain of God. ² Then

---

ᵃ2:10 *Moses* sounds like a Hb word meaning "drawing out" and an Egyptian word meaning "born."   ᵇ2:11 Lit *And it was in those days*   ᶜ2:11 Lit *his brothers*   ᵈ2:13 Or *fellow Hebrew*   ᵉ2:18 Jethro's clan or last name was *Reuel*; Ex 3:1   ᶠ2:22 In Hb the name *Gershom* sounds like "a stranger there."   ᵍ3:1 Moses' father-in-law's first name was *Jethro*; Ex 2:18   ʰ3:1 = Desolation; another name for Mount Sinai; Dt 4:10,15; 18:16; Mal 4:4.

the Angel of the LORD appeared to him in a flame of fire within a bush. As Moses looked, he saw that the bush was on fire but was not consumed. ³ So Moses thought: I must go over and look at this remarkable sight. Why isn't the bush burning up?

⁴ When the LORD saw that he had gone over to look, God called out to him from the bush, "Moses, Moses!"

"Here I am," he answered.

⁵ "Do not come closer," He said. "Take your sandals off your feet, for the place where you are standing is holy ground." ⁶ Then He continued, "I am the God of your father,ᵃ the God of Abraham, the God of Isaac, and the God of Jacob." Moses hid his face because he was afraid to look at God.

God Calls Moses

⁷ Then the LORD said, "I have observed the misery of My people in Egypt, and have heard them crying out because of their oppressors, and I know about their sufferings. ⁸ I have come down to rescue them from the power of the Egyptians and to bring them from that land to a good and spacious land, a land flowing with milk and honey—the territory of the Canaanites, Hittites, Amorites, Perizzites, Hivites, and Jebusites. ⁹ The Israelites' cry for help has come to Me, and I have also seen the way the Egyptians are oppressing them. ¹⁰ Therefore, go. I am sending you to Pharaoh so that you may lead My people, the Israelites, out of Egypt."

Moses Protests

¹¹ But Moses asked God, "Who am I that I should go to Pharaoh and that I should bring the Israelites out of Egypt?"

¹² He answered, "I will certainly be with you, and this will be the sign to you that I have sent you: when you bring the people out of Egypt, you will all worshipᵇ God at this mountain."

¹³ Then Moses asked God, "If I go to the Israelites and say to them: The God of your fathers has sent me to you, and they ask me, 'What is His name?' what should I tell them?"

"I AM WHO I AM"

¹⁴ God replied to Moses, "I AM WHO I AM.ᶜ This is what you are to say to the Israelites: I AM has sent me to you." ¹⁵ God also said to Moses, "Say this to the Israelites: •Yahweh, the God of your fathers, the God of Abraham, the God of Isaac, and the God of Jacob, has sent me to you. This is My name forever; this is how I am to be remembered in every generation.

God's Plan for Moses

¹⁶ "Go and assemble the elders of Israel and say to them: Yahweh, the God of your fathers, the God of Abraham, Isaac, and Jacob, has appeared to me and said: I have paid close attention to you and to what has been done to you in Egypt. ¹⁷ And I have promised you that I will bring you up from the misery of Egypt to the land of the Canaanites, Hittites, Amorites, Perizzites, Hivites, and Jebusites—a land flowing with milk and honey. ¹⁸ They will listen to what you say. Then you, along with the elders of Israel, must go to the king of Egypt and say to him: The LORD, the God of the Hebrews, has met with us. Now please let us go on a three-day trip into the wilderness so that we may sacrifice to the LORD our God.

ᵃ**3:6** Sam, some LXX mss read *fathers*; Ac 7:32 ᵇ**3:12** Or *serve* ᶜ**3:14** Or *I AM BECAUSE I AM*, or *I WILL BE WHO I WILL BE*

¹⁹ "However, I know that the king of Egypt will not allow you to go, unless the is forced⌋ by a strong hand. ²⁰ I will stretch out My hand and strike Egypt with all My miracles that I will perform in it. After that, he will let you go. ²¹ And I will give this people such favor in the sight of the Egyptians that when you go, you will not go empty-handed. ²² Each woman will ask her neighbor and any woman staying in her house for silver and gold jewelry, and clothing, and you will put them on your sons and daughters. So you will plunder the Egyptians."

Miraculous Signs for Moses

4 Then Moses answered, "What if they won't believe me and will not obey me but say, 'The LORD did not appear to you'?"

² The LORD asked him, "What is that in your hand?"

"A staff," he replied.

³ Then He said, "Throw it on the ground." He threw it on the ground, and it became a snake. Moses ran from it, ⁴ but the LORD told him, "Stretch out your hand and grab it by the tail." So he stretched out his hand and caught it, and it became a staff in his hand. ⁵ "This will take place," He continued, "so they will believe that the LORD, the God of their fathers, the God of Abraham, the God of Isaac, and the God of Jacob, has appeared to you."

⁶ In addition the LORD said to him, "Put your hand inside your cloak." So he put his hand inside his cloak, and when he took it out, his hand was diseased, like snow.^a ⁷ Then He said, "Put your hand back inside your cloak." He put his hand back inside his cloak, and when he took it out,^b it had again become like the rest of his skin. ⁸ "If they will not believe you and will not respond to the evidence

of the first sign, they may believe the evidence of the second sign. ⁹ And if they don't believe even these two signs or listen to what you say, take some water from the Nile and pour it on the dry ground. The water you take from the Nile will become blood on the ground."

Moses Argues

¹⁰ But Moses replied to the LORD, "Please, Lord, I have never been eloquent—either in the past or recently or since You have been speaking to Your servant^c—because I am slow and hesitant in speech."

¹¹ The LORD said to him, "Who made the human mouth? Who makes him mute or deaf, seeing or blind? Is it not I, the LORD? ¹² Now go! I will help you speak and I will teach you what to say."

¹³ Moses said, "Please, Lord, send someone else."^d

Angry God Turns to Aaron

¹⁴ Then the LORD's anger burned against Moses, and He said, "Isn't Aaron the Levite your brother? I know that he can speak well. And also, he is on his way now to meet you. When he sees you, his heart will rejoice. ¹⁵ You will speak with him and tell him what to say. I will help^e both you and him ⌊to speak⌋, and will teach you both what to do. ¹⁶ He will speak to the people for you. He will be your spokesman, and you will serve as God to him. ¹⁷ And take this staff in your hand that you will perform the signs with."

Moses' Return to Egypt

¹⁸ Then Moses went back to his father-in-law Jethro and said to him, "Please let me return to my relatives in Egypt and see if they are still living."

Jethro said to Moses, "Go in peace."

---

^a**4:6** A reference to whiteness or flakiness of the skin ^b**4:7** Lit *out of his cloak* ^c**4:10** Moses ^d**4:13** Lit *send by the hand of whom You will send* ^e**4:15** Lit *be with*

God's Instructions

[19] Now in Midian the LORD told Moses, "Return to Egypt, for all the men who wanted to kill you are dead." [20] So Moses took his wife and sons, put them on a donkey, and set out for the land of Egypt. And Moses took God's staff in his hand.

[21] The LORD instructed Moses, "When you go back to Egypt, make sure you do in front of Pharaoh all the wonders I have put within your power. But I will harden his heart[a] so that he won't let the people go. [22] Then you will say to Pharaoh: This is what the LORD says: Israel is My firstborn son. [23] I told you: Let My son go so that he may worship Me, but you refused to let him go. Now I will kill your firstborn son!"

[24] On the trip, at an overnight campsite, it happened that the LORD confronted him and sought to put him to death. [25] So Zipporah took a flint, cut off her son's foreskin, and threw it at Moses' feet.[b] Then she said, "You are a bridegroom of blood to me!" [26] So He let him alone. At that time she said, "You are a bridegroom of blood," referring to the circumcision.[c]

Moses Meets Aaron

[27] Now the LORD had said to Aaron, "Go and meet Moses in the wilderness." So he went and met him at the mountain of God and kissed him. [28] Moses told Aaron everything the LORD had sent him to say, and about all the signs He had commanded him ιto doɩ. [29] Then Moses and Aaron went and assembled all the elders of the Israelites. [30] Aaron repeated everything the LORD had said to Moses and performed the signs before the people. [31] The people believed, and when they heard that the LORD had paid atten-tion to them and that He had seen their misery, they bowed down and wor-shiped.

Moses Confronts Pharaoh

5 Later, Moses and Aaron went in and said to Pharaoh, "This is what the LORD, the God of Israel, says: Let My people go, so that they may hold a festi-val for Me in the wilderness."

Pharaoh Refuses

[2] But Pharaoh responded, "Who is the LORD that I should obey Him by letting Israel go? I do not know the LORD, and what's more, I will not let Israel go."

[3] Then they answered, "The God of the Hebrews has met with us. Please let us go on a three-day trip into the wilder-ness so that we may sacrifice to the LORD our God, or else He may strike us with plague or sword."

[4] The king of Egypt said to them, "Moses and Aaron, why are you causing the people to neglect their work? Get to your labors!" [5] Pharaoh also said, "Look, the people of the land are so numerous, and you would stop them from work-ing."

Oppression Increases

[6] That day Pharaoh commanded the overseers of the people as well as their foremen: [7] "Don't continue to supply the people with straw for making bricks, as before. They must go and gather straw for themselves. [8] But require the same quota of bricks from them as they were making before; do not reduce it. For they are slackers—that is why they are crying out, 'Let us go and sacrifice to our God.' [9] Impose heavier work on the men. Then they will be occupied with it and not pay attention to deceptive words."

---

[a]4:21 Or will make him stubborn   [b]4:25 Lit his feet; some interpret "feet" as a euphemism for genitals   [c]4:25-26 Perhaps Zipporah appeased God on Moses' behalf by circumcising Gershom.

[10] So the overseers and foremen of the people went out and said to them, "This is what Pharaoh says: 'I am not giving you straw. [11] Go get straw yourselves wherever you can find it, but there will be no reduction at all in your workload.'" [12] So the people scattered throughout the land of Egypt to gather stubble for straw. [13] The overseers insisted, "Finish your assigned work each day, just as ⌊you did⌋ when straw was ⌊provided⌋." [14] Then the Israelite foremen, whom Pharaoh's slave drivers had set over the people, were beaten and asked, "Why haven't you finished making your prescribed number of bricks yesterday or today, as ⌊you did⌋ before?"

Israel Pleas

[15] So the Israelite foremen went in and cried for help to Pharaoh: "Why are you treating your servants this way? [16] No straw has been given to your servants, yet they say to us, 'Make bricks!' Look, your servants are being beaten, but it is your own people who are at fault."

[17] But he said, "You are slackers. Slackers! That is why you are saying, 'Let us go sacrifice to the LORD.' [18] Now get to work. No straw will be given to you, but you must produce the same quantity of bricks."

Israelites Reject Moses

[19] The Israelite foremen saw that they were in trouble when they were told, "You cannot reduce your daily quota of bricks." [20] When they left Pharaoh, they confronted Moses and Aaron, who stood ⌊waiting⌋ to meet them.

[21] "May the LORD take note of you and judge," they said to them, "because you have made us reek in front of Pharaoh and his officials—putting a sword in their hand to kill us!"

Moses Complains to God

[22] So Moses went back to the LORD and asked, "Lord, why have You caused trouble for this people? And why did You ever send me? [23] Ever since I went in to Pharaoh to speak in Your name he has caused trouble for this people, and You haven't delivered Your people at all."

6 [1] But the LORD replied to Moses, "Now you are going to see what I will do to Pharaoh: he will let them go because of My strong hand; he will drive them out of his land because of My strong hand."

God Promises Freedom

[2] Then God spoke to Moses, telling him, "I am •Yahweh. [3] I appeared to Abraham, Isaac, and Jacob as •God Almighty, but I did not make My name Yahweh known to them. [4] I also established My covenant with them to give them the land of Canaan, the land they lived in as foreigners. [5] Furthermore, I have heard the groaning of the Israelites, whom the Egyptians are forcing to work as slaves, and I have remembered My covenant.

[6] "Therefore tell the Israelites: I am Yahweh, and I will deliver you from the forced labor of the Egyptians and free you from slavery to them. I will redeem you with an outstretched arm and great acts of judgment. [7] I will take you as My people, and I will be your God. You will know that I am Yahweh your God, who delivered you from the forced labor of the Egyptians. [8] I will bring you to the land that I swore[a] to give to Abraham, Isaac, and Jacob, and I will give it to you as a possession. I am the LORD." [9] Moses told this to the Israelites, but they did not listen to him because of their broken spirit and hard labor.

[a] **6:8** Lit *raised My hand*

¹⁰ Then the LORD spoke to Moses, ¹¹ "Go and tell Pharaoh king of Egypt to let the Israelites go from his land."

Moses Objects

¹² But Moses said in the LORD's presence: "If the Israelites will not listen to me, then how will Pharaoh listen to me, since I am such a poor speaker?"ᵃ ¹³ Then the LORD spoke to Moses and Aaron and gave them commands concerning both the Israelites and Pharaoh king of Egypt to bring the Israelites out of the land of Egypt.

Family History of Moses and Aaron

¹⁴ These are the heads of their fathers' families:

The sons of Reuben, the firstborn of Israel:
Hanoch and Pallu, Hezron and Carmi.
These are the clans of Reuben.

¹⁵ The sons of Simeon:
Jemuel, Jamin, Ohad, Jachin, Zohar, and Shaul, the son of a Canaanite woman.
These are the clans of Simeon.

¹⁶ These are the names of the sons of Levi according to their genealogy:
Gershon, Kohath, and Merari.
Levi lived 137 years.

¹⁷ The sons of Gershon:
Libni and Shimei, by their clans.

¹⁸ The sons of Kohath:
Amram, Izhar, Hebron, and Uzziel.
Kohath lived 133 years.

¹⁹ The sons of Merari:
Mahli and Mushi.
These are the clans of the Levites according to their genealogy.

²⁰ Amram married his father's sister Jochebed,
and she bore him Aaron and Moses.
Amram lived 137 years.

²¹ The sons of Izhar:
Korah, Nepheg, and Zichri.

²² The sons of Uzziel:
Mishael, Elzaphan, and Sithri.

²³ Aaron married Elisheba,
daughter of Amminadab and sister of Nahshon.
She bore him Nadab and Abihu, Eleazar and Ithamar.

²⁴ The sons of Korah:
Assir, Elkanah, and Abiasaph.
These are the clans of the Korahites.

²⁵ Aaron's son Eleazar married one of the daughters of Putiel and she bore him Phinehas.
These are the heads of the Levite families by their clans.

²⁶ It was this Aaron and Moses whom the LORD told, "Bring the Israelites out of the land of Egypt according to their divisions." ²⁷ Moses and Aaron were the ones who spoke to Pharaoh king of Egypt in order to bring the Israelites out of Egypt.

Moses and Aaron before Pharaoh

²⁸ On the day the LORD spoke to Moses in the land of Egypt, ²⁹ He said to him, "I am the LORD; tell Pharaoh king of Egypt everything I am telling you."

Moses Protests Again

³⁰ But Moses replied in the LORD's presence, "Since I am such a poor speaker,ᵇ how will Pharaoh listen to me?"

7 The LORD answered Moses, "See, I have made you like God to Pharaoh,

---

ᵃ**6:12** Lit *I have uncircumcised lips*   ᵇ**6:30** Lit *I have uncircumcised lips*

and Aaron your brother will be your prophet. ² You must say whatever I command you; then Aaron your brother must declare it to Pharaoh so that he will let the Israelites go from his land. ³ But I will harden Pharaoh's heart and multiply My signs and wonders in the land of Egypt. ⁴ Pharaoh will not listen to you, but I will put My hand on Egypt and bring out the ranks of My people the Israelites, out of the land of Egypt by great acts of judgment. ⁵ The Egyptians will know that I am the LORD when I stretch out My hand against Egypt, and bring out the Israelites from among them."

Moses and Aaron Obey

⁶ So Moses and Aaron did ˌthisˌ; they did just as the LORD commanded them. ⁷ Moses was 80 years old and Aaron 83 when they spoke to Pharaoh.

Aaron's Staff

⁸ The LORD said to Moses and Aaron, ⁹ "When Pharaoh tells you: Perform a miracle, tell Aaron: Take your staff and throw it down before Pharaoh. It will become a serpent." ¹⁰ So Moses and Aaron went in to Pharaoh and did just as the LORD had commanded. Aaron threw down his staff before Pharaoh and his officials, and it became a serpent. ¹¹ But then Pharaoh called the wise men and sorcerers—the magicians of Egypt, and they also did the same thing by their occult practices. ¹² Each one threw down his staff, and it became a serpent. But Aaron's staff swallowed their staffs. ¹³ However, Pharaoh's heart hardened, and he did not listen to them, as the LORD had said.

First Plague: Water to Blood

¹⁴ Then the LORD said to Moses, "Pharaoh is unresponsive: he refuses to let the people go. ¹⁵ Go to Pharaoh in the morning. When you see him walking out to the water, stand ready to meet him by the bank of the Nile. Take in your hand the staff that turned into a snake. ¹⁶ Tell him: The LORD, the God of the Hebrews, has sent me to tell you: Let My people go, so that they may worshipª Me in the wilderness, but so far you have not listened. ¹⁷ This is what the LORD says: Here is how you will know that I am the LORD. Watch. I will strike the water in the Nile with the staff in my hand, and it will turn to blood. ¹⁸ The fish in the Nile will die, the river will stink, and the Egyptians will be unable to drink water from it."

¹⁹ So the LORD said to Moses, "Tell Aaron: Take your staff and stretch out your hand over the waters of Egypt—over their rivers, canals,ᵇ ponds, and all their water reservoirs—and they will become blood. There will be blood throughout the land of Egypt, even in wooden and stone ˌcontainersˌ."

²⁰ Moses and Aaron did just as the LORD had commanded; in the sight of Pharaoh and his officials, he raised the staff and struck the water in the Nile, and all the water in the Nile was turned to blood. ²¹ The fish in the Nile died, and the river smelled so bad the Egyptians could not drink water from it. There was blood throughout the land of Egypt.

²² But the magicians of Egypt did the same thing by their occult practices. So Pharaoh's heart hardened, and he would not listen to them, as the LORD had said. ²³ Pharaoh turned around, went into his palace, and didn't even take this to heart. ²⁴ All the Egyptians dug around the Nile for water to drink because they could not drink the water from the river. ²⁵ Seven days passed after the LORD struck the Nile.

ª7:16 Or serve; Ex 4:23   ᵇ7:19 The Hb word refers specifically to the various branches and canals of the Nile River; Ex 8:5.

Second Plague: Frogs

8 [a] Then the LORD said to Moses, "Go in to Pharaoh and tell him: This is what the LORD says: Let My people go, so that they may worship Me. [2] But if you refuse to let them go, then I will plague all your territory with frogs. [3] The Nile will swarm with frogs; they will come up and go into your palace, into your bedroom and on your bed, into the houses of your officials and your people, and into your ovens and kneading bowls. [4] The frogs will come up on you, your people, and all your officials."

[5b] The LORD then said to Moses, "Tell Aaron: Stretch out your hand with your staff over the rivers, canals, and ponds, and cause the frogs to come up onto the land of Egypt." [6] When Aaron stretched out his hand over the waters of Egypt, the frogs came up and covered the land of Egypt. [7] But the magicians did the same thing by their occult practices and brought frogs up onto the land of Egypt.

[8] Pharaoh summoned Moses and Aaron and said, "Ask the LORD that He remove the frogs from me and my people. Then I will let the people go and they can sacrifice to the LORD."

[9] Moses said to Pharaoh, "Make the choice rather than me ⌊by saying⌋ when I should ask for you, your officials, and your people, that the frogs be taken away from you and your houses, and remain only in the Nile."

[10] "Tomorrow," he answered.

Moses replied, "As you have said, so you may know there is no one like the LORD our God, [11] the frogs will go away from you, your houses, your officials, and your people. The frogs will remain only in the Nile." [12] After Moses and Aaron went out from Pharaoh, Moses cried out to the LORD for help concerning the frogs that He had brought against[c] Pharaoh. [13] The LORD did as Moses had said: the frogs in the houses, courtyards, and fields died. [14] They piled them in countless heaps, and there was a terrible odor in the land. [15] But when Pharaoh saw there was relief, he hardened his heart and would not listen to them, as the LORD had said.

Third Plague: Gnats

[16] Then the LORD said to Moses, "Tell Aaron: Stretch out your staff and strike the dust of the earth, and it will become gnats[d] throughout the land of Egypt." [17] And they did this. Aaron stretched out his hand with his staff, and when he struck the dust of the earth, gnats were on the people and animals. All the dust of the earth became gnats throughout the land of Egypt. [18] The magicians tried to produce gnats using their occult practices, but they could not. The gnats remained on the people and animals.

[19] "This is the finger of God," the magicians said to Pharaoh. But Pharaoh's heart hardened, and he would not listen to them, as the LORD had said.

Fourth Plague: Flies

[20] The LORD said to Moses, "Get up early in the morning and present yourself to Pharaoh when you see him going out to the water. Tell him: This is what the LORD says: Let My people go, so that they may worship[e] Me. [21] But if you will not let My people go, then I will send swarms of flies[f] against you, your officials, your people, and your houses. The Egyptians' houses will swarm with flies, and so will the land where they live.[g] [22] But on that day I will give special treatment to the land of Goshen, where My people are living; no flies will be there.

[a]**8:1** Ex 7:26 in Hb   [b]**8:5** Ex 8:1 in Hb   [c]**8:12** Or *frogs, as he had agreed with*   [d]**8:16** Perhaps sand fleas or mosquitoes   [e]**8:20** Or *serve*   [f]**8:21** Or *insects*   [g]**8:21** Lit *are*

This way you will know that I, the LORD, am in the land. 23 I will make a distinction[a] between My people and your people. This sign will take place tomorrow."

24 And the LORD did this. Thick swarms of flies went into Pharaoh's palace and his officials' houses. Throughout Egypt the land was ruined because of the swarms of flies. 25 Then Pharaoh summoned Moses and Aaron and said, "Go sacrifice to your God within the country."

26 But Moses said, "It would not be right[b] to do that, because what we will sacrifice to the LORD our God is detestable to the Egyptians. If we sacrifice what the Egyptians detest in front of them, won't they stone us? 27 We must go a distance of three days into the wilderness and sacrifice to the LORD our God as He instructs us."

28 Pharaoh responded, "I will let you go and sacrifice to the LORD your God in the wilderness, but don't go very far. Make an appeal for me."

29 "As soon as I leave you," Moses said, "I will appeal to the LORD, and tomorrow the swarms of flies will depart from Pharaoh, his officials, and his people. But Pharaoh must not act deceptively again by refusing to let the people go and sacrifice to the LORD." 30 Then Moses left Pharaoh's presence and appealed to the LORD. 31 The LORD did as Moses had said: He removed the swarms of flies from Pharaoh, his officials, and his people; not one was left. 32 But Pharaoh hardened his heart this time also and did not let the people go.

Fifth Plague: Death of Livestock

9 Then the LORD said to Moses, "Go in to Pharaoh and say to him: This is what the LORD, the God of the Hebrews, says: Let My people go, so that they may worship Me. 2 But if you refuse to let ⌊them⌋ go and keep holding them, 3 then the LORD's hand will bring a severe plague against your livestock in the field—the horses, donkeys, camels, herds, and flocks. 4 But the LORD will make a distinction between the livestock of Israel and the livestock of Egypt, so that nothing of all that the Israelites own will die." 5 And the LORD set a time, saying, "Tomorrow the LORD will do this thing in the land." 6 The LORD did this the next day. All the Egyptian livestock died, but none among the Israelite livestock died. 7 Pharaoh sent ⌊messengers⌋ who saw that not a single one of the Israelite livestock was dead. But Pharaoh's heart was hardened, and he did not let the people go.

Sixth Plague: Boils

8 Then the LORD said to Moses and Aaron, "Take handfuls of furnace soot, and Moses is to throw it toward heaven in the sight of Pharaoh. 9 It will become fine dust over the entire land of Egypt. It will become festering boils on people and animals throughout the land of Egypt." 10 So they took furnace soot and stood before Pharaoh. Moses threw it toward heaven, and it became festering boils on man and beast. 11 The magicians could not stand before Moses because of the boils, for the boils were on the magicians as well as on all the Egyptians. 12 But the LORD hardened Pharaoh's heart and he did not listen to them, as the LORD had told Moses.

Seventh Plague: Hail

13 Then the LORD said to Moses, "Get up early in the morning and present yourself to Pharaoh. Tell him: This is

---

[a]8:23 LXX, Syr, Vg; MT reads will place deliverance   [b]8:26 Or allowable

what the LORD, the God of the Hebrews says: Let My people go, so that they may worship Me. ¹⁴ Otherwise, I am going to send all My plagues against you, your officials, and your people. Then you will know there is no one like Me in all the earth. ¹⁵ By now I could have stretched out My hand and struck you and your people with a plague, and you would have been obliterated from the earth. ¹⁶ However, I have let you live for this purpose: to show you My power and to make My name known in all the earth. ¹⁷ You are still acting arrogantly against[a] My people by not letting them go. ¹⁸ Tomorrow at this time I will rain down the worst hail that has ever occurred in Egypt from the day it was founded until now. ¹⁹ Therefore give orders to bring your livestock and all that you have in the field into shelters. Every person and animal that is in the field and not brought inside will die when the hail falls on them." ²⁰ Those among Pharaoh's officials who •feared the word of the LORD made their servants and livestock flee to shelters, ²¹ but those who didn't take the LORD's word seriously left their servants and livestock in the field.

²² Then the LORD said to Moses, "Stretch out your hand toward heaven and let there be hail throughout the land of Egypt—on man and beast and every plant of the field in the land of Egypt." ²³ So Moses stretched out his staff toward heaven, and the LORD sent thunder and hail. Lightning struck the earth, and the LORD rained hail on the land of Egypt. ²⁴ The hail, with lightning flashing through it, was so severe that nothing like it had occurred in the land of Egypt since it had become a nation. ²⁵ Throughout the land of Egypt, the hail struck down everything in the field, both

man and beast. The hail beat down every plant of the field and shattered every tree in the field. ²⁶ The only place it didn't hail was in the land of Goshen where the Israelites were.

²⁷ Pharaoh sent for Moses and Aaron. "I have sinned this time," he said to them. "The LORD is the Righteous One, and I and my people are the guilty ones. ²⁸ Make an appeal to the LORD. There has been enough of God's thunder and hail. I will let you go; you don't need to stay any longer."

²⁹ Moses said to him, "When I have left the city, I will extend my hands to the LORD. The thunder will cease, and there will be no more hail, so that you may know the earth is the LORD's. ³⁰ But as for you and your officials, I know that you still do not fear the LORD God."

³¹ The flax and the barley were destroyed because the barley was ripe[b] and the flax was budding, ³² but the wheat and the spelt were not destroyed since they are later crops.[c]

³³ Moses went out from Pharaoh and the city, and extended his hands to the LORD. Then the thunder and hail ceased, and rain no longer poured down on the land. ³⁴ When Pharaoh saw that the rain, hail, and thunder had ceased, he sinned again and hardened his heart, he and his officials. ³⁵ So Pharaoh's heart hardened, and he did not let the Israelites go, as the LORD had said through Moses.

Eighth Plague: Locusts

10 Then the LORD said to Moses, "Go to Pharaoh, for I have hardened his heart and the hearts of his officials so that I may do these miraculous signs of Mine among them,[d] ² and so that you may tell[e] your son and grandson how severely I dealt with the Egyptians and

[a]9:17 Or still obstructing [b]9:31 Lit was ears of grain [c]9:32 Lit are late [d]10:1 Lit Mine in his midst [e]10:2 Lit tell in the ears of

performed miraculous signs among them, and you will know that I am the LORD."

3 So Moses and Aaron went in to Pharaoh and told him, "This is what the LORD, the God of the Hebrews, says: How long will you refuse to humble yourself before Me? Let My people go, that they may worship Me. 4 But if you refuse to let My people go, then tomorrow I will bring locusts into your territory. 5 They will cover the surface of the land so that no one will be able to see the land. They will eat the remainder left to you that escaped the hail; they will eat every tree you have growing in the fields. 6 They will fill your houses, all your officials' houses, and the houses of all the Egyptians—something your fathers and ancestors never saw since the time they occupied the land until today." Then he turned and left Pharaoh's presence.

7 Pharaoh's officials asked him, "How long must this man be a snare to us? Let the men go, so that they may worship the LORD their God. Don't you realize yet that Egypt is devastated?"

8 So Moses and Aaron were brought back to Pharaoh. "Go, worship the LORD your God," Pharaoh said. "But exactly who will be going?"

9 Moses replied, "We will go with our young and our old; we will go with our sons and daughters and with our flocks and herds because we must hold the LORD's festival."

10 He said to them, "May the LORD be with you if I ⌊ever⌋ let you and your families go!a Look out—you are planning evil. 11 No, only the men may go and worship the LORD, for that is what you have been asking for." And they were driven from Pharaoh's presence.

12 The LORD then said to Moses, "Stretch out your hand over the land of Egypt and the locusts will come up over it and eat every plant in the land, everything that the hail left." 13 So Moses stretched out his staff over the land of Egypt, and the LORD sent an east wind over the land all that day and through the night. By morning the east wind had brought in the locusts. 14 The locusts went up over the entire land of Egypt and settled on the whole territory of Egypt. Never before had there been such a large number of locusts, and there will never be again. 15 They covered the surface of the whole land so that the land was black, and they consumed all the plants on the ground and all the fruit on the trees that the hail had left. Nothing green was left on the trees or the plants in the field throughout the land of Egypt.

16 Pharaoh urgently sent for Moses and Aaron and said, "I have sinned against the LORD your God and against you. 17 Please forgive my sin once more and make an appeal to the LORD your God, so that He will take this death away from me." 18 Moses left Pharaoh's presence and appealed to the LORD. 19 Then the LORD changed the wind to a strong westb wind, and it carried off the locusts and blew them into the •Red Sea. Not a single locust was left in all the territory of Egypt. 20 But the LORD hardened Pharaoh's heart, and he did not let the Israelites go.

Ninth Plague: Darkness

21 Then the LORD said to Moses, "Stretch out your hand toward heaven, and there will be darkness over the land of Egypt, a darkness that can be felt." 22 So Moses stretched out his hand toward heaven, and there was thick

---

a 10:10 Pharaoh's reply is sarcastic.   b 10:19 Lit sea

darkness throughout the land of Egypt for three days. ²³ One person could not see another, and for three days they did not move from where they were. Yet all the Israelites had light where they lived.

²⁴ Pharaoh summoned Moses and said, "Go, worship the Lord. Even your families may go with you; only your flocks and your herds must stay behind."

²⁵ Moses responded, "You must also let us have[a] sacrifices and •burnt offerings to prepare for the Lord our God. ²⁶ Even our livestock must go with us; not a hoof will be left behind because we will take some of them to worship the Lord our God. We will not know what we will use to worship the Lord until we get there."

²⁷ But the Lord hardened Pharaoh's heart, and he was unwilling to let them go. ²⁸ Pharaoh said to him, "Leave me! Make sure you never see my face again, for on the day you see my face, you will die."

²⁹ "As you've said," Moses replied, "I will never see your face again."

Tenth Plague: Death of Firstborn

11 The Lord said[b] to Moses, "I will bring one more plague on Pharaoh and on Egypt. After that, he will let you go from here. When he lets ⌊you⌋ go,[c] he will drive you out of here. ² Now announce to the people that both men and women should ask their neighbors for gold and silver jewelry." ³ The Lord gave[d] the people favor in the sight of the Egyptians. And the man Moses was feared[e] in the land of Egypt, by[f] Pharaoh's officials and the people.

⁴ So Moses said, "This is what the Lord says: 'About midnight I will go throughout Egypt ⁵ and every firstborn ⌊male⌋ in the land of Egypt will die, from

the firstborn of Pharaoh who sits on his throne to the firstborn of the servant girl who is behind the millstones, as well as every firstborn of the livestock. ⁶ Then there will be a great cry of anguish through all the land of Egypt such as never was before, or ever will be again. ⁷ But against all the Israelites, whether man or beast, not ⌊even⌋ a dog will snarl,[g] so that you may know that the Lord makes a distinction between Egypt and Israel. ⁸ All these officials of yours will come down to me and bow before me, saying: Leave, you and all the people who follow you.[h] After that, I will leave.' " And he left Pharaoh's presence in fierce anger.

⁹ The Lord said to Moses, "Pharaoh will not listen to you, so that My wonders may be multiplied in the land of Egypt." ¹⁰ Moses and Aaron did all these wonders before Pharaoh, but the Lord hardened Pharaoh's heart, and he would not let the Israelites go out of his land.

Instructions for Passover

12 The Lord said to Moses and Aaron in the land of Egypt: ² "This month is to be the beginning of months for you; it is the first month of your year. ³ Tell the whole community of Israel that on the tenth day of this month they must each select an animal of the flock according to ⌊their⌋ fathers' households, one animal per household. ⁴ If the household is too small for a ⌊whole⌋ animal, that person and the neighbor nearest his house are to select one based on the combined number of people; you should apportion the animal according to what each person[i] will eat. ⁵ You must have an unblemished animal, a year-old male; you may take it from either the sheep or the

---

[a]**10:25** Lit *also give in our hand*   [b]**11:1** Or *had said*   [c]**11:1** Or *go, it will be finished—*   [d]**11:3** Or *had given*
[e]**11:3** Or *was very great*   [f]**11:3** Or *in the eyes of*   [g]**11:7** Lit *point its tongue*   [h]**11:8** Lit *people at your feet*   [i]**12:4** Or *household*

goats. [6] You are to keep it until the fourteenth day of this month; then the whole assembly of the community of Israel will slaughter the animals at twilight. [7] They must take some of the blood and put it on the two doorposts and the lintel of the houses in which they eat them. [8] They are to eat the meat that night; they should eat it, roasted over the fire along with unleavened bread and bitter herbs. [9] Do not eat any of it raw or cooked in boiling[a] water, but only roasted over fire—its head as well as its legs and inner organs. [10] Do not let any of it remain until morning; you must burn up any part of it that does remain until morning. [11] Here is how you must eat it: dressed for travel,[b] your sandals on your feet, and your staff in your hand. You are to eat it in a hurry; it is the LORD's •Passover.

[12] "I will pass through the land of Egypt on that night and strike every firstborn ⌊male⌋ in the land of Egypt, both man and beast. I am the LORD; I will execute judgments against all the gods of Egypt. [13] The blood on the houses where you are staying will be a distinguishing mark for you; when I see the blood, I will pass over you. No plague will be among you to destroy ⌊you⌋ when I strike the land of Egypt.

Passover Festival Established

[14] "This day is to be a memorial for you, and you must celebrate it as a festival to the LORD. You are to celebrate it throughout your generations as a permanent statute. [15] You must eat unleavened bread for seven days. On the first day you must remove yeast from your houses. Whoever eats what is leavened from the first day through the seventh day must be cut off from Israel. [16] You

are to hold a sacred assembly on the first day and another sacred assembly on the seventh day. No work may be done on those ⌊days⌋ except for preparing what people need to eat—you may do only that.

[17] "You are to observe the ⌊Festival of⌋ •Unleavened Bread because on this very day I brought your ranks out of the land of Egypt. You must observe this day throughout your generations as a permanent statute. [18] You are to eat unleavened bread in the first ⌊month⌋, from the evening of the fourteenth day of the month until the evening of the twenty-first day. [19] Yeast must not be found in your houses for seven days. If anyone eats something leavened, that person, whether a foreign resident or native of the land, must be cut off from the community of Israel. [20] Do not eat anything leavened; eat unleavened bread in all your homes."[c]

Israel Obeys

[21] Then Moses summoned all the elders of Israel and said to them, "Go, select an animal from the flock according to your families, and slaughter the Passover lamb. [22] Take a cluster of hyssop, dip it in the blood that is in the basin, and brush the lintel and the two doorposts with some of the blood in the basin. None of you may go out the door of his house until morning. [23] When the LORD passes through to strike Egypt and sees the blood on the lintel and the two doorposts, He will pass over the door and not let the destroyer enter your houses to strike ⌊you⌋.

[24] "Keep this command permanently as a statute for you and your descendants. [25] When you enter the land that the LORD will give you as He promised,

---

[a]12:9 Or or boiled at all in [b]12:11 Lit it: with your loins girded [c]12:20 Or settlements

you are to observe this ritual. ²⁶ When your children ask you, 'What does this ritual mean to you?' ²⁷ you are to reply, 'It is the Passover sacrifice to the LORD, for He passed over the houses of the Israelites in Egypt when He struck the Egyptians and spared our homes.'" So the people bowed down and worshiped. ²⁸ Then the Israelites went and did ⌊this⌋; they did just as the LORD had commanded Moses and Aaron.

The Exodus Begins

Firstborn Die

²⁹ Now at midnight the LORD struck every firstborn ⌊male⌋ in the land of Egypt, from the firstborn of Pharaoh who sat on his throne to the firstborn of the prisoner who was in the dungeon, and every firstborn of the livestock. ³⁰ During the night Pharaoh got up, he along with all his officials and all the Egyptians, and there was a loud wailing throughout Egypt because there wasn't a house without someone dead. ³¹ He summoned Moses and Aaron during the night and said, "Get up, leave my people, both you and the Israelites, and go, worship the LORD as you have asked. ³² Take even your flocks and your herds as you asked, and leave, and this will also be a blessing to me."

Egyptians Say Go

³³ Now the Egyptians pressured the people in order to send them quickly out of the country, for they said, "We're all going to die!" ³⁴ So the people took their dough before it was leavened, with their kneading bowls wrapped up in their clothes on their shoulders.

³⁵ The Israelites acted on Moses' word and asked the Egyptians for silver and gold jewelry and for clothing. ³⁶ And the LORD gave the people such favor in the Egyptians' sight that they gave them what they requested. In this way they plundered the Egyptians.

Israelites Flee

³⁷ The Israelites traveled from Rameses to Succoth, about 600,000 soldiers on foot, besides their families. ³⁸ An ethnically diverse crowd also went up with them, along with a huge number of livestock, both flocks and herds. ³⁹ The people baked the dough they had brought out of Egypt into unleavened loaves, since it had no yeast; for when they had been driven out of Egypt they could not delay and had not prepared any provisions for themselves.

⁴⁰ The time that the Israelites lived in Egypt[a] was 430 years. ⁴¹ At the end of 430 years, on that same day, all the divisions of the LORD went out from the land of Egypt. ⁴² It was a night of vigil in honor of the LORD, because He would bring them out of the land of Egypt. This same night is in honor of the LORD, a night vigil for all the Israelites throughout their generations.

Passover Statute

⁴³ The LORD said to Moses and Aaron, "This is the statute of the Passover: no foreigner may eat it. ⁴⁴ But any slave a man has purchased may eat it, after you have circumcised him. ⁴⁵ A temporary resident or hired hand may not eat the Passover. ⁴⁶ It is to be eaten in one house. You may not take any of the meat outside the house, and you may not break any of its bones. ⁴⁷ The whole community of Israel must celebrate[b] it. ⁴⁸ If a foreigner resides with you and wants to celebrate the LORD's Passover, every male in his household must be circumcised, and then he may participate;[c]

a**12:40** LXX, Sam add and in Canaan　b**12:47** Lit do　c**12:48** Lit may come near to do it he will become like a native of the land. But no uncircumcised person may eat it. [49] The same law will apply to both the native and the foreigner who resides among you."

[50] Then all the Israelites did ⌊this⌋; they did just as the LORD had commanded Moses and Aaron. [51] On that same day the LORD brought the Israelites out of the land of Egypt according to their military divisions.

God Commands Moses: Firstborn

13 The LORD spoke to Moses: [2] "Consecrate every firstborn male to Me, the firstborn from every womb among the Israelites, both man and animal; it is Mine."

Moses Obeys

[3] Then Moses said to the people, "Remember this day when you came out of Egypt, out of the place of slavery, for the LORD brought you out of here by the strength of ⌊His⌋ hand. Nothing leavened may be eaten. [4] Today, in the month of Abib,[a] you are leaving. [5] When the LORD brings you into the land of the Canaanites, Hittites, Amorites, Hivites, and Jebusites,[b] which He swore to your fathers that He would give you, a land flowing with milk and honey, you must carry out this ritual in this month. [6] For seven days you must eat unleavened bread, and on the seventh day there is to be a festival to the LORD. [7] Unleavened bread is to be eaten for those seven days. Nothing leavened may be found among you, and no yeast may be found among you in all your territory. [8] On that day explain to your son, 'This is because of what the LORD did for me when I came out of Egypt.' [9] Let it serve as a sign for you on your hand and as a reminder on your forehead,[c] so that the law of the LORD may be in your mouth; for the LORD brought you out of Egypt with a strong hand. [10] Keep this statute at its appointed time from year to year.

[11] "When the LORD brings you into the land of the Canaanites, as He swore to you and your fathers, and gives it to you, [12] you are to present to the LORD every firstborn male of the womb. All firstborn offspring of the livestock you own that are males will be the LORD's. [13] You must redeem every firstborn of a donkey with a flock animal, but if you do not redeem it, break its neck. However, you must redeem every firstborn among your sons.

[14] "In the future, when your son asks you, 'What does this mean?' say to him, 'By the strength of ⌊His⌋ hand the LORD brought us out of Egypt, out of the place of slavery. [15] When Pharaoh stubbornly refused to let us go, the LORD killed every firstborn ⌊male⌋ in the land of Egypt, from the firstborn of man to the firstborn of livestock. That is why I sacrifice to the LORD all the firstborn of the womb that are males, but I redeem all the firstborn of my sons.' [16] So let it be a sign on your hand and a symbol[d] on your forehead, for the LORD brought us out of Egypt by the strength of His hand."

God's Route for Exodus

[17] When Pharaoh let the people go, God did not lead them along the road to the land of the Philistines, even though it was nearby; for God said, "The people will change their minds and return to Egypt if they face war." [18] So He led the people around toward the •Red Sea along the road of the wilderness. And the Israelites left the land of Egypt in battle formation.

---

[a]**13:4** March–April; called Nisan in the post-exilic period; Neh 2:1; Est 3:7   [b]**13:5** DSS, Sam, LXX, Syr include *Girgashites* and *Perizzites*; Jos 3:10   [c]**13:9** Lit *reminder between your eyes*   [d]**13:16** Or *phylactery*

Bones of Joseph

¹⁹ Moses took the bones of Joseph with him, because Joseph had made the Israelites swear a solemn oath, saying, "God will certainly come to your aid; then you must take my bones with you from this place."

Pillars of Cloud and Fire

²⁰ They set out from Succoth and camped at Etham on the edge of the wilderness. ²¹ The LORD went ahead of them in a pillar of cloud to lead them on their way during the day and in a pillar of fire to give them light at night, so that they could travel day or night. ²² The pillar of cloud by day and the pillar of fire by night never left its place in front of the people.

14 Then the LORD spoke to Moses: ² "Tell the Israelites to turn back and camp in front of Pi-hahiroth, between Migdol and the sea; you must camp in front of Baal-zephon, facing it by the sea. ³ Pharaoh will say of the Israelites: They are wandering around the land in confusion; the wilderness has boxed them in. ⁴ I will harden Pharaoh's heart so that he will pursue them. Then I will receive glory by means of Pharaoh and all his army, and the Egyptians will know that I am the LORD." So the Israelites did this.

Egyptian Pursuit

⁵ When the king of Egypt was told that the people had fled, Pharaoh and his officials changed their minds about the people and said: "What have we done? We have released Israel from serving us." ⁶ So he got his chariot ready and took his troops[a] with him; ⁷ he took 600 of the best chariots and all the rest of the chariots of Egypt, with officers in each one.

⁸ The LORD hardened the heart of Pharaoh king of Egypt, and he pursued the Israelites, who were going out triumphantly.[b] ⁹ The Egyptians—all Pharaoh's horses and chariots, his horsemen,[c] and his army—chased after them and caught up with them as they camped by the sea beside Pi-hahiroth, in front of Baal-zephon.

Israel Terrified

¹⁰ As Pharaoh approached, the Israelites looked up and saw the Egyptians coming after them. Then the Israelites were terrified and cried out to the LORD for help. ¹¹ They said to Moses: "Is it because there are no graves in Egypt that you took us to die in the wilderness? What have you done to us by bringing us out of Egypt? ¹² Isn't this what we told you in Egypt: Leave us alone so that we may serve the Egyptians? It would have been better for us to serve the Egyptians than to die in the wilderness."

¹³ But Moses said to the people, "Don't be afraid. Stand firm and see the LORD's salvation He will provide for you today; for the Egyptians you see today, you will never see again. ¹⁴ The LORD will fight for you; you must be quiet."

Escape through the Red Sea

¹⁵ The LORD said to Moses, "Why are you crying out to Me? Tell the Israelites to break camp. ¹⁶ As for you, lift up your staff, stretch out your hand over the sea, and divide it so that the Israelites can go through the sea on dry ground. ¹⁷ I am going to harden the hearts of the Egyptians so that they will go in after them, and I will receive glory by means of Pharaoh, all his army, and his chariots and horsemen. ¹⁸ The Egyptians will know that I am the LORD when I receive glory

---

[a]**14:6** Lit *people*   [b]**14:8** Lit *with a raised hand*   [c]**14:9** Or *chariot drivers*

through Pharaoh, his chariots, and his horsemen."

[19] Then the <u>Angel of God</u>, who was going in front of the Israelite forces, moved and went behind them. The pillar of cloud moved from in front of them and stood behind them. [20] It came between the Egyptian and Israelite forces. The cloud was there ⌊in⌋ the darkness, yet it lit up the night.[a] So neither group came near the other all night long.

Walls of Water

[21] Then Moses stretched out his hand over the sea. The LORD drove the sea ⌊back⌋ with a powerful east wind all that night and turned the sea into dry land. So the waters were divided, [22] and the Israelites went through the sea on dry ground, with the waters ⌊like⌋ a wall to them on their right and their left.

[23] The Egyptians set out in pursuit—all Pharaoh's horses, his chariots, and his horsemen—and went into the sea after them. [24] Then during the morning watch, the LORD looked down on the Egyptian forces from the pillar of fire and cloud, and threw them into confusion. [25] He caused their chariot wheels to swerve[b] [c] and made them drive[d] with difficulty. "Let's get away from Israel," the Egyptians said, "because the LORD is fighting for them against Egypt!"

Egyptians Destroyed

[26] Then the LORD said to Moses, "Stretch out your hand over the sea so that the waters may come back on the Egyptians, on their chariots and horsemen." [27] So Moses stretched out his hand over the sea, and at daybreak the sea returned to its normal depth. While the Egyptians were trying to escape from it, the LORD overthrew them in the sea. [28] The waters came back and covered the chariots and horsemen, the entire army of Pharaoh, that had gone after them into the sea. None of them survived.

[29] But the Israelites had walked through the sea on dry ground, with the waters ⌊like⌋ a wall to them on their right and their left. [30] That day the LORD saved Israel from the power of the Egyptians, and Israel saw the Egyptians dead on the seashore. [31] When Israel saw the great power that the LORD used against the Egyptians, the people •feared the LORD and believed in Him and in His servant Moses.

Moses and Israel Sing

15 Then Moses and the Israelites sang this song to the LORD. They said:

I will sing to the LORD,
for He is highly exalted;
He has thrown the horse
and its rider into the sea.
[2] The LORD is my strength
    and my song;[e]
He has become my salvation.
This is my God, and I will praise
    Him,
my father's God, and I will exalt
    Him.
[3] The LORD is a warrior;
•Yahweh is His name.

[4] He threw Pharaoh's chariots
and his army into the sea;
the elite of his officers
were drowned in the •Red Sea.
[5] The floods covered them;
they sank to the depths
like a stone.
[6] LORD, Your right hand is glorious
in power.

---

[a]**14:20** Perhaps the cloud brought darkness to the Egyptians but light to the Israelites; Ex 10:22-23; Ps 105:39
[b]**14:25** Sam, LXX, Syr read *He bound their chariot wheels*   [c]**14:25** Or *fall off*   [d]**14:25** Or *and they drove them*
[e]**15:2** Or *might*

LORD, Your right hand shattered
   the enemy.
7 You overthrew Your adversaries
   by Your great majesty.
You unleashed
   Your burning wrath;
it consumed them like stubble.
8 The waters heaped up at the blast
   of Your nostrils;
the currents stood firm like a dam.
The watery depths congealed
   in the heart of the sea.
9 The enemy said:
"I will pursue, I will overtake,
I will divide the spoil.
My desire will be gratified
   at their expense.
I will draw my sword;
my hand will destroy[a] them."
10 But You blew with Your breath,
and the sea covered them.
They sank like lead
in the mighty waters.

11 LORD, who is like You
   among the gods?
Who is like You, glorious
   in holiness,
revered with praises,
   performing wonders?
12 You stretched out Your right hand,
and the earth swallowed them.
13 You will lead the people
You have redeemed
with Your faithful love;
You will guide ⌊them⌋
   to Your holy dwelling
with Your strength.
14 When the peoples hear,
   they will shudder;
anguish will seize the inhabitants
   of Philistia.
15 Then the chiefs of Edom will be
   terrified;

trembling will seize the leaders
   of Moab;
the inhabitants of Canaan
   will panic;
16 and terror and dread will fall
   on them.
They will be as still[b] as a stone
because of Your powerful arm
until Your people pass by, LORD,
until the people
   whom You purchased[c] pass by.

17 You will bring them in and plant
   them
on the mountain
   of Your possession;
LORD, You have prepared the place
for Your dwelling;
Lord,[d] Your hands have established
   the sanctuary.
18 The LORD will reign forever
   and ever!

Miriam's Song

19 When Pharaoh's horses with his chariots and horsemen went into the sea, the LORD brought the waters of the sea back over them. But the Israelites walked through the sea on dry ground. 20 Then Miriam the prophetess, Aaron's sister, took a tambourine in her hand, and all the women followed her with tambourines and dancing. 21 Miriam sang to them:

Sing to the LORD,
for He is highly exalted;
He has thrown the horse
and its rider into the sea.

Exodus into Wilderness of Shur

God Provides Water

22 Then Moses led Israel on from the Red Sea, and they went out to the Wil-

a 15:9 Or conquer   b 15:16 Or silent   c 15:16 Or created   d 15:17 Other Hb mss, DSS, Sam, Tg read LORD

derness of Shur. They journeyed for three days in the wilderness without finding water. 23 They came to Marah, but they could not drink the water at Marah because it was bitter—that is why it was named Marah.ᵃ 24 The people grumbled to Moses, "What are we going to drink?" 25 So he cried out to the LORD, and the LORD showed him a tree. When he threw it into the water, the water became drinkable.

He made a statute and ordinance for them at Marah and He tested them there. 26 He said, "If you will carefully obey the LORD your God, do what is right in His eyes, pay attention to His commands, and keep all His statutes, I will not inflict any illness on you I inflicted on the Egyptians. For I am the LORD who heals you."

27 Then they came to Elim, where there were 12 springs of water and 70 date palms, and they camped there by the waters.

Wilderness of Sin

God Provides Manna and Quail

16 The entire Israelite community departed from Elim and came to the Wilderness of Sin, which is between Elim and Sinai, on the fifteenth day of the second month after they had left the land of Egypt. 2 The entire Israelite community grumbled against Moses and Aaron in the wilderness. 3 The Israelites said to them, "If only we had died by the LORD's hand in the land of Egypt, when we sat by pots of meat and ate all the bread we wanted. Instead, you brought us into this wilderness to make this whole assembly die of hunger!"

4 Then the LORD said to Moses, "I am going to rain bread from heaven for you. The people are to go out each day and gather enough for that day. This way I will test them to see whether or not they will follow My instructions. 5 On the sixth day, when they prepare what they bring in, it will be twice as much as they gather on other days."ᵇ

6 So Moses and Aaron said to all the Israelites: "This evening you will know that it was the LORD who brought you out of the land of Egypt; 7 in the morning you will see the LORD's glory because He has heard your complaints about Him. For who are we that you complain about us?" 8 Moses continued, "The LORD will give you meat to eat this evening and abundant bread in the morning, for He has heard the complaints that you are raising against Him. Who are we? Your complaints are not against us but against the LORD."

9 Then Moses told Aaron, "Say to the entire Israelite community, 'Come before the LORD, for He has heard your complaints.'" 10 As Aaron was speaking to the entire Israelite community, they turned toward the wilderness, and there, in a cloud, the LORD's glory appeared.

11 The LORD spoke to Moses, 12 "I have heard the complaints of the Israelites. Tell them: At twilight you will eat meat, and in the morning you will eat bread until you are full. Then you will know that I am the LORD your God."

13 So at evening quail came and covered the camp. In the morning there was a layer of dew all around the camp. 14 When the layer of dew evaporated, there on the desert surface were fine flakes, as fine as frost on the ground. 15 When the Israelites saw it, they asked one another, "What is it?" because they didn't know what it was.

ᵃ15:23 = bitter, or bitterness ᵇ16:5 Lit as gathering day to day

Moses: God's Rules for Manna

Moses told them, "It is the bread the LORD has given you to eat. ¹⁶ This is what the LORD has commanded: 'Gather as much of it as each person needs to eat. You may take two quarts[a] per individual, according to the number of people each of you has in his tent.'"

Israel Disobeys

¹⁷ So the Israelites did this. Some gathered a lot, some a little. ¹⁸ When they measured it by quarts,[b] the person who gathered a lot had no surplus, and the person who gathered a little had no shortage. Each gathered as much as he needed to eat. ¹⁹ Moses said to them, "No one is to let any of it remain until morning." ²⁰ But they didn't listen to Moses; some people left part of it until morning, and it bred worms and smelled. Therefore Moses was angry with them.

²¹ They gathered it every morning. Each gathered as much as he needed to eat, but when the sun grew hot, it melted. ²² On the sixth day they gathered twice as much food, four quarts[c] apiece, and all the leaders of the community came and reported ⌊this⌋ to Moses. ²³ He told them, "This is what the LORD has said: 'Tomorrow is a day of complete rest, a holy Sabbath to the LORD. Bake what you want to bake, and boil what you want to boil, and everything left over set aside to be kept until morning.'"

²⁴ So they set it aside until morning as Moses commanded, and it didn't smell or have any maggots in it. ²⁵ "Eat it today," Moses said, "because today is a Sabbath to the LORD. Today you won't find any in the field. ²⁶ For six days you may gather it, but on the seventh day, the Sabbath, there will be none."

²⁷ Yet on the seventh day some of the people went out to gather, but they did not find any. ²⁸ Then the LORD said to Moses, "How long will you[d] refuse to keep My commands and instructions? ²⁹ Understand that the LORD has given you the Sabbath; therefore on the sixth day He will give you two days' worth of bread. Each of you stay where you are; no one is to leave his place on the seventh day." ³⁰ So the people rested on the seventh day.

Manna Memorial

³¹ The house of Israel named the substance manna.[e] It resembled coriander seed, was white, and tasted like wafers ⌊made⌋ with honey. ³² Moses said, "This is what the LORD has commanded: 'Two quarts[f] of it are to be preserved throughout your generations, so that they may see the bread I fed you in the wilderness when I brought you out of the land of Egypt.'"

³³ Moses told Aaron, "Take a container and put two quarts[g] of manna in it. Then place it before the LORD to be preserved throughout your generations." ³⁴ As the LORD commanded Moses, Aaron placed it before the •testimony to be preserved.

³⁵ The Israelites ate manna for 40 years, until they came to an inhabited land. They ate manna until they reached the border of the land of Canaan. ³⁶ (Two quarts are[h] a tenth of an ephah.)

Departure from Wilderness of Sin

Meribah: Water from a Rock

17 The entire Israelite community left the Wilderness of Sin, moving from

---

[a] **16:16** Lit *an omer* [b] **16:18** Lit *by an omer* [c] **16:22** Lit *two omers* [d] **16:28** In Hb *you* is pl, referring to the whole nation. [e] **16:31** = *What?*; Ex 16:15 [f] **16:32** Lit *A full omer* [g] **16:33** Lit *a full omer* [h] **16:36** Lit *The omer is*

one place to the next according to the LORD's command. They camped at Rephidim, but there was no water for the people to drink. ² So the people complained to Moses: "Give us water to drink."

"Why are you complaining to me?" Moses replied to them. "Why are you testing the LORD?"

³ But the people thirsted there for water, and grumbled against Moses. They said, "Why did you ever bring us out of Egypt to kill us and our children and our livestock with thirst?"

⁴ Then Moses cried out to the LORD, "What should I do with these people? In a little while they will stone me!"

⁵ The LORD answered Moses, "Go on ahead of the people and take some of the elders of Israel with you. Take the rod you struck the Nile with in your hand and go. ⁶ I am going to stand there in front of you on the rock at Horeb; when you hit the rock, water will come out of it and the people will drink." Moses did this in the sight of the elders of Israel. ⁷ He named the place Massahª and Meribahᵇ because the Israelites complained, and because they tested the LORD, saying, "Is the LORD among us or not?"

Amalekites Attack

⁸ At Rephidim, Amalekᶜ came and fought against Israel. ⁹ Moses said to Joshua, "Select some men for us, and go fight against Amalek. Tomorrow I will stand on the hilltop with God's staff in my hand."

¹⁰ Joshua did as Moses had told him, and fought against Amalek, while Moses, Aaron, and Hur went up to the top of the hill. ¹¹ While Moses held up his hand,ᵈ Israel prevailed, but whenever he put his handᵈ down, Amalek prevailed. ¹² When Moses' hands grew heavy, they took a stone and put ꞁitꞁ under him, and he sat down on it. Then Aaron and Hur supported his hands, one on one side and one on the other so that his hands remained steady until the sun went down. ¹³ So Joshua defeated Amalek and his armyᵉ with the sword.

¹⁴ The LORD then said to Moses, "Write this down on a scroll as a reminder and recite it to Joshua: I will completely blot out the memory of Amalek under heaven."

¹⁵ And Moses built an altar and named it, "The LORD Is My Banner."ᶠ ¹⁶ He said, "Indeed, ꞁmyꞁ hand is ꞁlifted upꞁ towardᵍ the LORD's throne. The LORD will be at war with Amalek from generation to generation."

Jethro's Visit

18 Moses' father-in-law Jethro, the priest of Midian, heard about everything that God had done for Moses and His people Israel, and how the LORD had brought Israel out of Egypt.

² Now Jethro, Moses' father-in-law, had taken in Zipporah, Moses' wife, after he had sent her back, ³ along with her two sons, one of whom was named Gershom (because Moses had said, "I have been a stranger in a foreign land")ʰ ⁴ and the other Eliezer (because ꞁhe had said,ꞁ "The God of my father was my helper and delivered me from Pharaoh's sword").ⁱ

⁵ Moses' father-in-law Jethro, along with Moses' wife and sons, came to him in the wilderness where he was camped at the mountain of God. ⁶ He sent word

---

ª**17:7** = testing   ᵇ**17:7** = arguing   ᶜ**17:8** A semi-nomadic people descended from Amalek, a grandson of Esau; Gn 36:12   ᵈ**17:11** Sam, LXX, Syr, Tg, Vg read *hands*   ᵉ**17:13** Or *people*   ᶠ**17:15** Or *Yahweh-nissi*   ᵍ**17:16** Or *hand was on*, or *hand was against*; Hb obscure   ʰ**18:3** The name *Gershom* sounds like Hb "a stranger there"   ⁱ**18:4** = My God Is Help

to Moses, "I, your father-in-law Jethro, am coming to you with your wife and her two sons."

⁷ So Moses went out to meet his father-in-law, bowed down, and then kissed him. They asked each other how they had been[a] and went into the tent. ⁸ Moses recounted to his father-in-law all that the LORD had done to Pharaoh and the Egyptians for Israel's sake, all the hardships that confronted them on the way, and how the LORD delivered them.

⁹ Jethro rejoiced over all the good things the LORD had done for Israel when He rescued them from the Egyptians. ¹⁰ "Blessed is the LORD," Jethro exclaimed, "who rescued you from Pharaoh and the power of the Egyptians, and snatched the people from the power of the Egyptians. ¹¹ Now I know that the LORD is greater than all gods, because He ιdid wondersι at the time the Egyptians acted arrogantly against Israel."[b]

¹² Then Jethro, Moses' father-in-law, brought a •burnt offering and sacrifices to God, and Aaron came with all the elders of Israel to eat a meal with Moses' father-in-law in God's presence.

Jethro's Management Advice

¹³ The next day Moses sat down to judge the people, and they stood around Moses from morning until evening. ¹⁴ When Moses' father-in-law saw everything he was doing for them he asked, "What is this thing you're doing for the people? Why are you alone sitting as judge, while all the people stand around you from morning until evening?" ¹⁵ Moses replied to his father-in-law, "Because the people come to me to inquire of God. ¹⁶ Whenever they have a

dispute, it comes to me, and I make a decision between one man and another. I teach ιthemι God's statutes and laws."

¹⁷ "What you're doing is not good," Moses' father-in-law said to him. ¹⁸ "You will certainly wear out both yourself and these people who are with you, because the task is too heavy for you. You can't do it alone. ¹⁹ Now listen to me; I will give you some advice, and God be with you. You be the one to represent the people before God and bring their cases to Him. ²⁰ Instruct them about the statutes and laws, and teach them the way to live and what they must do. ²¹ But you should select from all the people able men, God-fearing, trustworthy, and hating bribes. Place ιthemι over the people as officials of thousands, hundreds, fifties, and tens. ²² They should judge the people at all times. Then they can bring you every important case but judge every minor case themselves. In this way you will lighten your load,[c] and they will bear ιitι with you. ²³ If you do this, and God ιsoι directs you, you will be able to endure, and also all these people will be able to go home satisfied."[d]

Moses Obeys Jethro

²⁴ Moses listened to his father-in-law and did everything he said. ²⁵ So Moses chose able men from all Israel and made them leaders over the people ιasι officials of thousands, hundreds, fifties, and tens. ²⁶ They judged the people at all times; the hard cases they would bring to Moses, but every minor case they would judge themselves.

²⁷ Then Moses said goodbye to his father-in-law, and he journeyed to his own land.

---

[a]18:7 Lit other about well-being   [b]18:11 Hb obscure   [c]18:22 Lit lighten from on you   [d]18:23 Lit go to their place in peace

Israel at Sinai

19 In the third month, on the same day ⸤of the month⸥ that the Israelites had left the land of Egypt, <u>they entered the Wilderness of Sinai</u>. [2] After they departed from Rephidim, they entered the Wilderness of Sinai and camped in the wilderness, and Israel camped there in front of the mountain.

God Speaks to Moses on Mountain

[3] Moses went up ⸤the mountain⸥ to God, and the LORD called to him from the mountain: "This is what you must say to the house of Jacob, and explain to the Israelites: [4] You have seen what I did to the Egyptians and how I carried you on eagles' wings and brought you to Me. [5] Now <u>if you will listen to Me and carefully keep My covenant, you will be My own possession out of all the peoples, although all the earth is Mine,</u> [6] <u>and you will be My kingdom of priests and My holy nation. These are the words that you are to say to the Israelites."</u>

Moses Reports to People

[7] After Moses came back, He summoned the elders of the people, and put before them all these words that the LORD had commanded him. [8] Then all the people responded together, "We will do all that the LORD has spoken." So Moses brought the people's words back to the LORD.

God Instructs

[9] The LORD said to Moses, "I am going to come to you in a dense cloud, so that the people will hear when I speak with you and will always believe you." Then Moses reported the people's words to the LORD. [10] And the LORD told Moses, "Go to the people and purify them today and tomorrow. They must wash their clothes [11] and be prepared by the third day, for on the third day the LORD will come down on Mount Sinai in the sight of all the people. [12] Put boundaries for the people all around the ⸤mountain⸥ and say: Be careful that you don't go up on the mountain or touch its base. Anyone who touches the mountain will be put to death. [13] No hand may touch him; instead he will be stoned or shot ⸤with arrows⸥, neither animal or man will live. When the ram's horn sounds a long blast, they may go up the mountain."

[14] Then Moses came down from the mountain to the people and consecrated them, and they washed their clothes. [15] He said to the people, "Be prepared by the third day. Do not have sexual relations with women."

God on Mount Sinai

[16] On the third day, when morning came, there was thunder and lightning, a thick cloud on the mountain, and a loud trumpet sound, so that all the people in the camp shuddered. [17] Then Moses brought the people out of the camp to meet God, and they stood at the foot of the mountain. [18] Mount Sinai was completely enveloped in smoke because the LORD came down on it in fire. Its smoke went up like the smoke of a furnace, and the whole mountain shook violently. [19] As the sound of the trumpet grew louder and louder, Moses spoke and God answered him in the thunder.

God and Moses Talk

[20] The LORD came down on Mount Sinai, at the top of the mountain. Then the LORD summoned Moses to the top of the mountain, and he went up. [21] The LORD directed Moses, "Go down and warn the people not to break through to see the LORD; otherwise many of them will die. [22] Even the priests who come near the LORD must purify themselves or the

LORD will break out ⟨in anger⟩ against them."

²³ But Moses responded to the LORD, "The people cannot come up Mount Sinai, since You warned us: Put a boundary around the mountain and consider it holy." ²⁴ And the LORD replied to him, "Go down and come back with Aaron. But the priests and the people must not break through to come up to the LORD, or He will break out ⟨in anger⟩ against them." ²⁵ So Moses went down to the people and told them.

The Ten Commandments

20 Then God spoke all these words:

² I am the LORD your God, who brought you out of the land of Egypt, out of the place of slavery.

³ Do not have other gods besides Me.

⁴ Do not make an idol for yourself, whether in the shape of anything in the heavens above or on the earth below or in the waters under the earth. ⁵ You must not bow down to them or worship them; for I, the LORD your God, am a jealous God, punishing the children for the fathers' sin, to the third and fourth ⟨generations⟩ of those who hate Me, ⁶ but showing faithful love to a thousand ⟨generations⟩ of those who love Me and keep My commands.

⁷ Do not misuse the name of the LORD your God, because the LORD will punish anyone who misuses His name.

⁸ Remember to dedicate the Sabbath day: ⁹ You are to labor six days and do all your work, ¹⁰ but the seventh day is a Sabbath to the LORD your God. You must not do any work—you, your son or daughter, your male or female slave, your livestock, or the foreigner who is within your gates. ¹¹ For the LORD made the heavens and the earth, the sea, and everything in them in six days; then He rested on the seventh day. Therefore the LORD blessed the Sabbath day and declared it holy.

¹² Honor your father and your mother so that you may have a long life in the land that the LORD your God is giving you.

¹³ Do not murder.

¹⁴ Do not commit adultery.

¹⁵ Do not steal.

¹⁶ Do not give false testimony against your neighbor.

¹⁷ Do not covet your neighbor's house. Do not covet your neighbor's wife, his male or female slave, his ox or donkey, or anything that belongs to your neighbor.

The People Tremble

¹⁸ All the people witnessed[a] the thunder and lightning, the sound of the trumpet, and the mountain ⟨surrounded by⟩ smoke. When the people saw ⟨it⟩[b] they trembled and stood at a distance. ¹⁹ "You speak to us, and we will listen," they said to Moses, "but don't let God speak to us, or we will die."

²⁰ Moses responded to the people, "Don't be afraid, for God has come to test you, so that you will •fear Him and will not[c] sin." ²¹ And the people remained standing at a distance as Moses approached the thick darkness where God was.

---

[a] **20:18** Lit *saw*   [b] **20:18** Sam, LXX, Syr, Tg, Vg read *smoking; the people* (or *they*) *were afraid*   [c] **20:20** Lit *that the fear of Him may be in you, and you do not*

Divine Ordinances

God's Laws on Sacrifice

22 Then the LORD told Moses, "This is what you are to say to the Israelites: You have seen that I have spoken to you from heaven. 23 You must not make gods of silver to rival Me; you must not make ⌊gods of gold⌋ for yourselves.ᵃ

24 "You must make an earthen altar for Me and sacrifice on it your •burnt offerings and •fellowship offerings, your sheep and goats, as well as your cattle. I will come to you and bless you in every place where I cause My name to be remembered. 25 If you make a stone altar for Me, you must not build it out of cut stones. If you use your chisel on it, you will defile it. 26 You must not go up to My altar on steps, so that your nakedness is not exposed on it.

21 "These are the ordinances that you must set before them:

God's Laws on Slaves

2 "When you buy a Hebrew slave, he is to serve for six years; then in the seventh he is to leave as a free manᵇ without paying anything. 3 If he arrives alone, he is to leave alone; if he arrives withᶜ a wife, his wife is to leave with him. 4 If his master gives him a wife and she bears him sons or daughters, the wife and her children belong to her master, and the man must leave alone.

5 "But if the slave declares: 'I love my master, my wife, and my children; I do not want to leave as a free man,' 6 his master is to bring him to the judgesᵈ and then bring him to the door or doorpost. His master must pierce his ear with an awl, and he will serve his master for life.

7 "When a man sells his daughter as a slave,ᵉ she is not to leave as the male slaves do. 8 If she is displeasing to her master, who chose her for himself, then he must let her be redeemed. He has no right to sell her to foreigners because he has acted treacherously toward her. 9 Or if he chooses her for his son, he must deal with her according to the customary treatment of daughters. 10 If he takes an additional wife, he must not reduce the food, clothing, or marital rights of the first wife. 11 And if he does not do these three things for her, she may leave free of charge, without any exchange of money.ᶠ

God's Laws on Personal Injury

12 "Whoever strikes a person so that he dies must be put to death. 13 But if he didn't intend any harm,ᵍ and yet God caused it to happen by his hand, I will appoint a place for you where he may flee. 14 If a person willfullyʰ acts against his neighbor to murder him by scheming, you must take him from My altar to be put to death.

15 "Whoever strikes his father or his mother must be put to death.

16 "Whoever kidnaps a person must be put to death, whether he sells him or the person is found in his possession.

17 "Whoever curses his father or his mother must be put to death.

18 "When men quarrel and one strikes the other with a stone or fist, and the injured man does not die but is confined to bed, 19 if he can ⌊later⌋ get up and walk around outside ⌊leaning⌋ on his staff, then the one who struck ⌊him⌋ will be exempt from punishment. Nevertheless, he must pay for his lost work timeⁱ and provide for ⌊his⌋ complete recovery.

ᵃ20:23 Hb obscure   ᵇ21:2 Lit *to go forth*   ᶜ21:3 Lit *he is the husband of*   ᵈ21:6 Or *to God*; that is, to His sanctuary or court   ᵉ21:7 Or *concubine*   ᶠ21:11 Without paying a redemption price for her   ᵍ21:13 Lit *he was not lying in wait*   ʰ21:14 Or *maliciously*   ⁱ21:19 Lit *his inactivity*

[20] "When a man strikes his male or female slave with a rod, and the slave dies under his abuse,[a] the owner must be punished.[b] [21] However, if the slave can stand up after a day or two, the owner should not be punished[c] because he is his ⌊owner's⌋ property.[d]

Eye for Eye

[22] "When men get in a fight, and hit a pregnant woman so that her children are born ⌊prematurely⌋,[e] but there is no injury, the one who hit her must be fined as the woman's husband demands from him, and he must pay according to judicial assessment. [23] If there is an injury, then you must give life for life, [24] eye for eye, tooth for tooth, hand for hand, foot for foot, [25] burn for burn, bruise for bruise, wound for wound.

[26] "When a man strikes the eye of his male or female slave and destroys it, he must let the slave go free in compensation for his eye. [27] If he knocks out the tooth of his male or female slave, he must let the slave go free in compensation for his tooth.

Injuries by Animals

[28] "When an ox[f] gores a man or a woman to death, the ox must be stoned, and its meat may not be eaten, but the ox's owner is innocent. [29] However, if the ox was in the habit of goring, and its owner has been warned yet does not restrain it, and it kills a man or a woman, the ox must be stoned, and its owner must also be put to death. [30] If instead a ransom is demanded of him, he can pay a redemption price for his life in the full amount demanded from him. [31] If it gores a son or a daughter, he is to be dealt with according to this same law. [32] If the ox gores a male or female slave, he must give 30 •shekels of silver[g] to the slave's master, and the ox must be stoned.

Injuries to Animals

[33] "When a man uncovers a pit or digs a pit, and does not cover it, and an ox or a donkey falls into it, [34] the owner of the pit must give compensation; he must pay money to its owner, but the dead animal will become his.

[35] "When a man's ox injures his neighbor's ox and it dies, they must sell the live ox and divide its proceeds; they must also divide the dead animal. [36] If, however, it is known that the ox was in the habit of goring, yet its owner has not restrained it, he must compensate fully, ox for ox; the dead animal will become his.

Laws on Theft

22[h] "When a man steals an ox or a sheep[i] and butchers it or sells it, he must repay five cattle for the ox or four sheep for the sheep. [2j] If a thief is caught in the act of breaking in, and he is beaten to death, no one is guilty of bloodshed. [3] But if this happens after sunrise,[k] there is guilt of bloodshed. A thief must make full restitution. If he is unable, he is to be sold because of his theft. [4] If what was stolen—whether ox, donkey, or sheep—is actually found alive in his possession, he must repay double.

Laws Protecting Crops

[5] "When a man lets a field or vineyard be grazed in, and then allows his animals to go and graze in someone else's field, he must repay[l] with the best of his own field or vineyard.

---

[a]**21:20** Lit hand [b]**21:20** Or must suffer vengeance [c]**21:21** Or not suffer vengeance [d]**21:21** Lit money
[e]**21:22** Either a live birth or a miscarriage [f]**21:28** Or a bull, or a steer [g]**21:32** About 1 pound of silver [h]**22:1** Ex
21:37 in Hb [i]**22:1** The Hb word can refer to sheep or goats. [j]**22:2** Ex 22:1 in Hb [k]**22:3** Lit if the sun has risen over
him [l]**22:5** LXX adds from his field according to its produce. But if someone lets his animals graze an entire field, he
must repay; DSS, Sam also support this reading.

⁶ "When a fire gets out of control, spreads to thornbushes, and consumes stacks of cut grain, standing grain, or a field, the one who started the fire must make full restitution for what was burned.

Laws on Personal Property

⁷ "When a man gives his neighbor money or goods to keep, but they are stolen from that person's house, the thief, if caught, must repay double. ⁸ If the thief is not caught, the owner of the house must present himself to the judges[a] to determine[b] whether or not he has taken his neighbor's property. ⁹ In any case of wrongdoing involving an ox, a donkey, a sheep, a garment, or anything ⌊else⌋ lost, and someone claims: That's mine,[c] the case between the two parties is to come before the judges.[d] The one the judges condemn[e] must repay double to his neighbor.

¹⁰ "When a man gives his neighbor a donkey, an ox, a sheep, or any ⌊other⌋ animal to care for, but it dies, is injured, or is stolen, while no one is watching, ¹¹ there must be an oath before the LORD between the two of them to determine whether or not he has taken his neighbor's property. Its owner must accept ⌊the oath⌋, and the other man does not have to make restitution. ¹² But if, in fact, the animal was stolen from his custody, he must make restitution to its owner. ¹³ If it was actually torn apart ⌊by a wild animal⌋, he is to bring it as evidence; he does not have to make restitution for the torn carcass.

¹⁴ "When a man borrows ⌊an animal⌋ from his neighbor, and it is injured or dies while its owner is not there with it, the man must make full restitution. ¹⁵ If its owner is there with it, the man does not have to make restitution. If it was rented, the loss is covered by[f] its rental price.

Laws on Seduction

¹⁶ "When a man seduces a virgin who was not promised in marriage, and he has sexual relations with her, he must certainly pay the bridal price for her to be his wife. ¹⁷ If her father absolutely refuses to give her to him, he must pay an amount in silver equal to the bridal price for virgins.

Other Capital Offenses

¹⁸ "You must not allow a sorceress to live.

¹⁹ "Whoever has sexual intercourse with an animal must be put to death.

²⁰ "Whoever sacrifices to any gods, except the LORD alone, is to be •set apart for destruction.

Laws Protecting Foreigners, Widows, Orphans, and Debtors

²¹ "You must not exploit a foreign resident or oppress him, since you were foreigners in the land of Egypt.

²² "You must not mistreat any widow or fatherless child. ²³ If you do mistreat them, they will no doubt cry to Me, and I will certainly hear their cry. ²⁴ My anger will burn, and I will kill you with the sword; then your wives will be widows and your children fatherless.

²⁵ "If you lend money to My people— to the poor person among you, you must not be like a moneylender to him; you must not charge him interest.

²⁶ "If you ever take your neighbor's cloak as collateral, return it to him before sunset. ²⁷ For it is his only covering; it is the clothing for his body.[g] What will he sleep in? And if he cries

---

ᵃ**22:8** Or to God   ᵇ**22:8** LXX, Tg, Vg read swear   ᶜ**22:9** Lit That is it   ᵈ**22:9** Or before God   ᵉ**22:9** Or one whom God condemns   ᶠ**22:15** Lit rented, it comes with   ᵍ**22:27** Lit skin

out to Me, I will listen because I am compassionate.

Respect God

28 "You must not blaspheme God[a] or curse a leader among your people.

29 "You must not hold back ⌊offerings from⌋ your harvest or your vats. Give Me the firstborn of your sons. 30 Do the same with your cattle and your flock. Let them stay with their mothers for seven days, but on the eighth day you are to give them to Me.

31 "Be My holy people. You must not eat the meat of a mauled animal ⌊found⌋ in the field; throw it to the dogs.

Laws on Honesty and Justice

23 "You must not spread a false report. Do not join[b] the wicked to be a malicious witness.

2 "You must not follow a crowd in wrongdoing. Do not testify in a lawsuit and go along with a crowd to pervert ⌊justice⌋. 3 Do not show favoritism to a poor person in his lawsuit.

4 "If you come across your enemy's stray ox or donkey, you must return it to him.

5 "If you see the donkey of someone who hates you lying ⌊helpless⌋ under its load, and you want to refrain from helping it, you must help with it.[c]

6 "You must not deny justice to the poor among you in his lawsuit. 7 Stay far away from a false accusation. Do not kill the innocent and the just, because I will not justify the guilty. 8 You must not take a bribe, for a bribe blinds the clear-sighted and corrupts the words[d] of the righteous. 9 You must not oppress a foreign resident; you yourselves know

how it feels to be a foreigner because you were foreigners in the land of Egypt.

Observe Sabbath Years and Sabbaths

10 "Sow your land for six years and gather its produce. 11 But during the seventh year you are to let it rest and leave it uncultivated, so that the poor among your people may eat ⌊from it⌋ and the wild animals may consume what they leave. Do the same with your vineyard and your olive grove.

12 "Do your work for six days but rest on the seventh day so that your ox and your donkey may rest, and the son of your female slave as well as the foreign resident may be refreshed.

13 "Pay strict attention to everything I have said to you. You must not invoke the names of other gods; they must not be heard on your lips.[e]

Observe Three Festivals

14 "Celebrate a festival in My honor three times a year. 15 Observe the Festival of •Unleavened Bread. As I commanded you, you are to eat unleavened bread for seven days at the appointed time in the month of Abib, because you came out of Egypt in that month. No one is to appear before Me empty-handed. 16 Also ⌊observe⌋ the Festival of Harvest[f] with the •firstfruits of your produce from what you sow in the field, and ⌊observe⌋ the Festival of Ingathering[g] at the end of the year, when you gather your produce[h] from the field. 17 Three times a year all your males are to appear before the Lord GOD.

18 "You must not offer the blood of My sacrifices with anything leavened. The

a22:28 Or judges b23:1 Lit join hands with c23:5 Or load, you must refrain from leaving it to him; you must set it free with him d23:8 Or and subverts the cause e23:13 Lit mouth f23:16 The Festival of Harvest is called Festival of Weeks elsewhere in the OT; Ex 34:22. In the NT it is called Pentecost; Ac 2:1. g23:16 The Festival of Ingathering is called Festival of Booths elsewhere; Lv 23:34-36. h23:16 Lit labors

fat of My festival offering must not remain until morning.

¹⁹ "Bring the best of the firstfruits of your land to the house of the LORD your God.

"You must not boil a young goat in its mother's milk.

Israel's Guardian Angel

²⁰ "I am going to send an Angel before you to protect you on the way and bring you to the place I have prepared. ²¹ Be attentive to Him and listen to His voice. Do not defy^a Him, because He will not forgive your acts of rebellion, for My name is in Him. ²² But if you will carefully obey Him and do everything I say, then I will be an enemy to your enemies and a foe to your foes. ²³ For My Angel will go before you and bring you to ˌtheˌ land ofˌ the Amorites, Hittites, Perizzites, Canaanites, Hivites, and Jebusites, and I will wipe them out. ²⁴ You must not bow down to their gods or worship them. Do not imitate their practices. Instead, demolish them^b and smash their sacred pillars to pieces.

Obey and Be Protected

²⁵ Worship the LORD your God, and He^c will bless your bread and your water. I will take away your illnesses.^d ²⁶ No woman will miscarry or be barren in your land. I will give ˌyouˌ the full number of your days.

²⁷ "I will cause the people ahead of you to feel terror^e and throw into confusion all the nations you come to. I will make all your enemies turn their backs to you in retreat. ²⁸ I will send the hornet^f in front of you, and it will drive the Hivites, Canaanites, and Hittites away from you. ²⁹ I will not drive them out ahead of you

in a single year; otherwise, the land would become desolate, and wild animals would multiply against you. ³⁰ I will drive them out little by little ahead of you until you have become numerous^g and take possession of the land. ³¹ I will set your borders from the •Red Sea to the Mediterranean Sea,^h and from the wilderness to the Euphrates River.ⁱ For I will place the inhabitants of the land under your control, and you will drive them out ahead of you. ³² You must not make a covenant with them or their gods. ³³ They must not remain in your land, or else they will make you sin against Me. If you worship their gods, it will be a snare for you."

Blood of the Covenant

24 Then He said to Moses, "Go up to the LORD, you and Aaron, Nadab, and Abihu, and 70 of Israel's elders, and bow in worship at a distance. ² Moses alone is to approach the LORD, but the others are not to approach, and the people are not to go up with him."

³ Moses came and told the people all the commands of the LORD and all the ordinances. Then all the people responded with a single voice, "We will do everything that the LORD has commanded." ⁴ And Moses wrote down all the words of the LORD. He rose early the next morning and set up an altar and 12 pillars for the 12 tribes of Israel at the base of the mountain. ⁵ Then he sent out young Israelite men, and they offered •burnt offerings and sacrificed bulls as •fellowship offerings to the LORD. ⁶ Moses took half the blood and set it in basins; the ˌotherˌ half of the blood he sprinkled on the altar. ⁷ He then took the covenant scroll and read ˌitˌ aloud to the

---

^a**23:21** Or embitter   ^b**23:24** Probably the idols   ^c**23:25** LXX, Vg read I   ^d**23:25** Lit away illnesses from among you   ^e**23:27** Lit will send terror of Me ahead of you   ^f**23:28** Or send panic   ^g**23:30** Lit fruitful   ^h**23:31** Lit the Sea of the Philistines   ⁱ**23:31** Lit the River

people. They responded, "We will do and obey everything that the LORD has commanded."

⁸ Moses took the blood, sprinkled it on the people, and said, "This is the blood of the covenant that the LORD has made with you concerning all these words."

Moses and Leaders Meet God

⁹ Then Moses went up with Aaron, Nadab, and Abihu, and 70 of Israel's elders, ¹⁰ and they saw the God of Israel. Beneath His feet was something like a pavement made of sapphireᵃ stone, as clear as the sky itself. ¹¹ God did not harmᵇ the Israelite nobles; they saw Him, and they ate and drank.

Moses to Mount Sinai

¹² The LORD said to Moses, "Come up to Me on the mountain and stay there so that I may give you the stone tablets with the law and commands I have written for their instruction."

¹³ So Moses arose with his assistant Joshua, and went up the mountain of God. ¹⁴ He told the elders, "Wait here for us until we return to you. Aaron and Hur are here with you. Whoever has a dispute should go to them." ¹⁵ When Moses went up the mountain, the cloud covered it. ¹⁶ The glory of the LORD settled on Mount Sinai, and the cloud covered it for six days. On the seventh day He called to Moses from the cloud. ¹⁷ The appearance of the LORD's glory to the Israelites was like a consuming fire on the mountaintop. ¹⁸ Moses entered the cloud as he went up the mountain, and he remained on the mountain 40 days and 40 nights.

God Commands
Offerings for Tabernacle

25 The LORD spoke to Moses: ² "Tell the Israelites to take an offering for Me. You are to take My offering from everyone whose heart stirs him ₁to give₁. ³ This is the offering you are to receive from them: gold, silver, and bronze; ⁴ blue, purple, and scarlet yarn; fine linen and goat hair; ⁵ ram skins dyed red and manatee skins;ᶜ acacia wood; ⁶ oil for the light; spices for the anointing oil and for the fragrant incense; ⁷ and onyxᵈ along with ₁other₁ gemstones for mounting on the •ephod and breastpiece.ᵉ

⁸ "They are to make a sanctuary for Me so that I may dwell among them. ⁹ You must make ₁it₁ according to all that I show you—the design of the tabernacle as well as the design of all its furnishings."

Ark of the Covenant

¹⁰ "They are to make an ark of acacia wood, 45 inches long, 27 inches wide, and 27 inches high.ᶠ ¹¹ Overlay it with pure gold; overlay it both inside and out. Also make a gold molding all around it. ¹² Cast four gold rings for it and place ₁them₁ on its four feet, two rings on one side and two rings on the other side. ¹³ Make poles of acacia wood and overlay them with gold. ¹⁴ Insert the poles into the rings on the sides of the ark in order to carry the ark with them. ¹⁵ The poles are to remain in the rings of the ark; they must not be removed from it. ¹⁶ Put the ₁tablets of the₁ •testimony that I will give you into the ark. ¹⁷ Make a •mercy seat of pure gold, 45 inches long and 27 inches wide.ᵍ ¹⁸ Make two •cherubim of gold; make them of hammered work at

---

ᵃ**24:10** Or *lapis lazuli* ᵇ**24:11** Lit *not stretch out His hand against* ᶜ**25:5** Or *and dolphin skins*, or *and fine leather*; Hb obscure ᵈ**25:7** Or *carnelian* ᵉ**25:7** Traditionally, *breastplate* ᶠ**25:10** Lit *two and a half cubits its length, one and a half cubits its width, and one and a half cubits its height* ᵍ**25:17** Lit *two and a half cubits its length, one and a half cubits its width*

the two ends of the mercy seat. [19] Make one cherub at one end and one cherub at the other end. Make the cherubim of one piece with the mercy seat at its two ends. [20] The cherubim are to have wings spread out above, covering the mercy seat with their wings, and are to face one another. The faces of the cherubim should be toward the mercy seat. [21] Set the mercy seat on top of the ark and put the testimony that I will give you into the ark. [22] I will meet with you there above the mercy seat, between the two cherubim that are over the ark of the testimony; I will speak with you from there about all that I command you regarding the Israelites.

Tabernacle Table

[23] "You are to construct a table of acacia wood, 36 inches long, 18 inches wide, and 27 inches high.[a] [24] Overlay it with pure gold and make a gold molding all around it. [25] Make a three-inch[b] frame all around it and make a gold molding for it all around its frame. [26] Make four gold rings for it, and attach the rings to the four corners at its four legs. [27] The rings should be next to the frame as holders for the poles to carry the table. [28] Make the poles of acacia wood and overlay them with gold so that the table can be carried by them. [29] You are also to make its plates and cups, as well as its pitchers and bowls for pouring drink offerings. Make them out of pure gold. [30] Put the bread of the Presence[c] on the table before Me at all times.

The Lampstand

[31] "You are to make a lampstand out of pure, hammered gold. It is to be made of one piece: its base and shaft, its ⌐ornamental⌐ cups, and its calyxes[d] and petals. [32] Six branches are to extend from its sides, three branches of the lampstand from one side and three branches of the lampstand from the other side. [33] There are to be three cups shaped like almond blossoms, each with a calyx and petals, on the first branch, and three cups shaped like almond blossoms, each with a calyx and petals, on the next branch. It is to be this way for the six branches that extend from the lampstand. [34] There are to be four cups shaped like almond blossoms on the lampstand ⌐shaft⌐ along with its calyxes and petals. [35] For the six branches that extend from the lampstand, a calyx must be under the ⌐first⌐ pair of branches from it, a calyx under the ⌐second⌐ pair of branches from it, and a calyx under the ⌐third⌐ pair of branches from it. [36] Their calyxes and branches are to be of one piece.[e] All of it is to be a single hammered piece of pure gold.

[37] "Make seven lamps on it. Its lamps are to be set up so they illuminate the area in front of it. [38] Its snuffers and fire-pans must be of pure gold. [39] The lampstand[f] with all these utensils is to be made from 75 pounds[g] of pure gold. [40] Be careful to make ⌐everything⌐ according to the model of them you have been shown on the mountain.

Tabernacle Design

Special Curtains

26 "You are to construct the tabernacle itself with 10 curtains. You must make them of finely spun linen, and blue, purple, and scarlet yarn, with a design of •cherubim worked into them. [2] The length of each curtain should be 42 feet,[h] and the width of each curtain

---

[a] **25:23** Lit *two cubits its length, one cubit its width, and one and a half cubits its height*   [b] **25:25** Lit *Make it a handbreadth*   [c] **25:30** Or *of presentation*   [d] **25:31** The outer covering of a flower   [e] **25:36** Lit *piece with it*   [f] **25:39** Lit *It*   [g] **25:39** Lit *a talent*   [h] **26:2** Lit *28 cubits*

six feet;[a] all the curtains are to have the same measurements. [3] Five of the curtains should be joined together, and the ⌊other⌋ five curtains joined together. [4] Make loops of blue yarn on the edge of the last curtain[b] in the ⌊first⌋ set, and do the same on the edge of the outermost curtain in the second set. [5] Make 50 loops on the one curtain and make 50 loops on the edge of the curtain in the second set, so that the loops line up together. [6] Also make 50 gold clasps and join the curtains together with the clasps, so that the tabernacle may be a single unit.

[7] "You are to make curtains of goat hair for a tent over the tabernacle; make 11 of these curtains. [8] The length of each curtain should be 45 feet[c] and the width of each curtain six feet.[a] All 11 curtains are to have the same measurements. [9] Join five of the curtains by themselves, and the ⌊other⌋ six curtains by themselves. Then fold the sixth curtain double at the front of the tent. [10] Make 50 loops on the edge of the one curtain, the outermost in the ⌊first⌋ set, and make 50 loops on the edge of the ⌊corresponding⌋ curtain of the second set. [11] Make 50 bronze clasps; put the clasps through the loops and join the tent together so that it is a single unit. [12] As for the flap that is left over from the tent curtains, the leftover half curtain is to hang down over the back of the tabernacle. [13] The half yard[d] on one side and the half yard[e] on the other of what is left over along the length of the tent curtains should be hanging down over the sides of the tabernacle on either side to cover it. [14] Make a covering for the tent from ram skins dyed red, and a covering of manatee skins[f] on top of that.

Floors and Planks

[15] "You are to make upright planks[g] of acacia wood for the tabernacle. [16] The length of each plank is to be 15 feet,[h] and the width of each plank 27 inches.[i] [17] Each plank must be connected together with two tenons. Do the same for all the planks of the tabernacle. [18] Make the planks for the tabernacle as follows: 20 planks for the south side, [19] and make 40 silver bases under the 20 planks, two bases under the first plank for its two tenons, and two bases under the next plank for its two tenons; [20] 20 planks for the second side of the tabernacle, the north side, [21] along with their 40 silver bases, two bases under the first plank and two bases under each plank; [22] and make six planks for the west side of the tabernacle. [23] Make two additional planks for the two back corners of the tabernacle. [24] They are to be paired at the bottom, and joined together[j] at the[k] top in a single ring. So it should be for both of them; they will serve as the two corners. [25] There are to be eight planks with their silver bases: 16 bases; two bases under the first plank and two bases under each plank.

[26] "You are to make five crossbars of acacia wood for the planks on one side of the tabernacle, [27] five crossbars for the planks on the other side of the tabernacle, and five crossbars for the planks of the back side of the tabernacle on the west. [28] The central crossbar is to run through the middle of the planks from one end to the other. [29] Then overlay the planks with gold, and make their rings of gold as the holders for the crossbars. Also overlay the crossbars with gold. [30] You are to set up the tabernacle according to the plan for it that you have been shown on the mountain.

[a]**26:2,8** Lit *four cubits*   [b]**26:4** Lit *the one curtain on the end*   [c]**26:8** Lit *30 cubits*   [d]**26:13** Lit *The cubit*   [e]**26:13** Lit *the cubit*   [f]**26:14** Or *of dolphin skins,* or *of fine leather;* Hb obscure   [g]**26:15** Or *frames,* or *beams*   [h]**26:16** Lit *10 cubits*   [i]**26:16** Lit *a cubit and a half*   [j]**26:24** Lit *and together they are to be complete*   [k]**26:24** Lit *its*

Veil before Ark

31 "You are to make a veil of blue, purple, and scarlet yarn, and finely spun linen with a design of cherubim worked into it. 32 Hang it on four gold-plated posts of acacia wood that have gold hooks ⌊and that stand⌋ on four silver bases. 33 Hang the veil under the clasps[a] and bring the ark of the •testimony there behind the veil, so the veil will make a separation for you between the holy place and the most holy place. 34 Put the •mercy seat on the ark of the testimony in the most holy place. 35 Place the table outside the veil and the lampstand on the south side of the tabernacle, opposite the table; put the table on the north side.

Outer Screen

36 "For the entrance to the tent you are to make a screen embroidered with blue, purple, and scarlet yarn, and finely spun linen. 37 Make five posts of acacia wood for the screen and overlay them with gold; their hooks are to be gold, and you are to cast five bronze bases for them.

Altar of Burnt Offering

27 "You are to construct the altar of acacia wood. The altar must be square, seven and a half feet long, and seven and a half feet wide;[b] it must be four and a half feet high.[c] 2 Make horns for it on its four corners; the horns are to be of one piece.[d] Overlay it with bronze. 3 Make its pots for removing ashes, and its shovels, basins, meat forks, and fire-pans; make all its utensils of bronze. 4 Construct a grate for it of bronze mesh,

and make four bronze rings on the mesh at its four corners. 5 Set it below, under the altar's ledge,[e] so that the mesh comes halfway up[f] the altar. 6 Then make poles for the altar, poles of acacia wood, and overlay them with bronze. 7 The poles are to be inserted into the rings, so that the poles are on two sides of the altar when it is carried. 8 Construct the altar with boards so that it is hollow. They are to make it just as it was shown to you on the mountain.

Tabernacle Courtyard

9 "You are to make the courtyard for the tabernacle. ⌊Make the hangings⌋ on the south of the courtyard out of finely spun linen, 150 feet[g] long on that side. 10 There are to be 20 posts and 20 bronze bases. The hooks and bands[h] of the posts must be silver. 11 Then ⌊make the hangings⌋ on the north side 150 ⌊feet⌋[i] long. There are to be 20 posts and 20 bronze bases. The hooks and bands[h] of the posts must be silver. 12 ⌊Make⌋ the hangings of the courtyard on the west side 75 feet[j] long, including their 10 posts and 10 bases. 13 Make the hangings of the courtyard on the east side toward the sunrise 75 feet.[j] 14 ⌊Make⌋ the hangings on one side ⌊of the gate⌋ 22 and a half feet,[k] including their three posts and their three bases. 15 And make the hangings on the other side 22 and a half ⌊feet⌋,[l] including their three posts and their three bases. 16 The gate of the courtyard is to have a thirty-foot[m] screen embroidered with blue, purple, and scarlet yarn, and finely spun linen. It is to have four posts including their four bases.

---

a26:33 The clasps that join the 10 curtains of the tabernacle; Ex 26:6 b27:1 Lit five cubits in length and five cubits in width c27:1 Lit wide; and its height three cubits d27:2 Lit piece with it e27:5 Perhaps a ledge around the altar on which the priests could stand; Lv 9:22 f27:5 Or altar's rim, so that the grid comes halfway down g27:9 Lit 100 cubits h27:10,11 Or connecting rods i27:11 Lit 100 [cubits] j27:12,13 Lit 50 cubits k27:14 Lit 15 cubits l27:15 Lit 15 [cubits] m27:16 Lit twenty-cubit

¹⁷ "All the posts around the courtyard are to be banded with silver and have silver hooks and bronze bases. ¹⁸ The length of the courtyard is to be 150 feet, the width 75 ⌊feet⌋ at each end, and the height seven and a half feet,^a ⌊all of it made⌋ of finely spun linen. The bases of the posts must be bronze. ¹⁹ All the tools of the tabernacle for every use and all its tent pegs as well as all the tent pegs of the courtyard are to be made of bronze.

Lampstand Oil

²⁰ "You are to command the Israelites to bring you pure oil from crushed olives for the light, in order to keep the lamp burning continually. ²¹ In the tent of meeting outside the veil that is in front of the •testimony, Aaron and his sons are to tend the lamp from evening until morning before the LORD. This is to be a permanent statute for the Israelites throughout their generations.

Priestly Garments

28 "Have your brother Aaron, with his sons, come to you from the Israelites to serve Me as priest—Aaron, his sons Nadab and Abihu, Eleazar and Ithamar. ² Make holy garments for your brother Aaron, for glory and beauty. ³ You are to instruct all the skilled craftsmen,^b whom I have filled with a spirit of wisdom, to make Aaron's garments for consecrating him to serve Me as priest. ⁴ These are the garments that they must make: a breastpiece, an •ephod, a robe, a specially woven tunic,^c a turban, and a sash. They are to make holy garments for your brother Aaron and his sons so that they may serve Me as priests. ⁵ They should use^d gold; blue, purple, and scarlet yarn; and fine linen.

Priest's Ephod

⁶ "They are to make the ephod of finely spun linen embroidered with gold, and with blue, purple, and scarlet yarn. ⁷ It must have two shoulder pieces attached to its two edges so that it can be joined together. ⁸ The artistically woven waistband that is on the ephod^e must be of one piece,^f according to the same workmanship of gold, of blue, purple, and scarlet yarn, and of finely spun linen.

⁹ "Take two onyx stones and engrave on them the names of Israel's sons: ¹⁰ six of their names on the first stone and the remaining six names on the second stone, in the order of their birth. ¹¹ Engrave the two stones with the names of Israel's sons as a gem cutter engraves a seal. Mount them, surrounded with gold filigree settings. ¹² Fasten both stones on the shoulder pieces of the ephod as memorial stones for the Israelites. Aaron will carry their names on his two shoulders before the LORD as a reminder. ¹³ Fashion gold filigree settings ¹⁴ and two chains of pure gold; you will make them of braided cord work, and attach the cord chains to the settings.

Priest's Breastpiece

¹⁵ "You are to make an embroidered breastpiece for decisions.^g Make it with the same workmanship as the ephod; make it of gold, of blue, purple, and scarlet yarn, and of finely spun linen. ¹⁶ It must be square and folded double, nine inches long and nine inches wide.^h ¹⁷ Place a setting of gemstonesⁱ on it, four rows of stones:

The first row should be
a row of carnelian, topaz,
and emerald;^j

---

^a**27:18** Lit *be 100 by the cubit, and the width 50 by 50, and the height five cubits*   ^b**28:3** Lit *all wise of heart*   ^c**28:4** Hb obscure   ^d**28:5** Lit *receive*   ^e**28:8** Lit *waistband of its ephod, which is on it*   ^f**28:8** Lit *piece with the ephod*   ^g**28:15** Used for determining God's will; Nm 27:21   ^h**28:16** Lit *a span its length and a span its width*   ⁱ**28:17** Many of these stones cannot be identified with certainty.   ^j**28:17** Or *beryl*

¹⁸ the second row,
      a turquoise,^a a sapphire,^b
      and a diamond;^c
¹⁹ the third row,
      a jacinth,^d an agate,
      and an amethyst;
²⁰ and the fourth row,
      a beryl, an onyx, and a jasper.

They should be adorned with gold filigree in their settings. ²¹ The 12 stones are to correspond to the names of Israel's sons. Each stone must be engraved like a seal, with one of the names of the 12 tribes.

²² "You are to make braided chains^e of pure gold cord work for the breastpiece. ²³ Fashion two gold rings for the breastpiece and attach them to its two corners. ²⁴ Then attach the two gold cords to the two gold rings at the corners of the breastpiece. ²⁵ Attach the other ends of the two cords to the two filigree settings and in this way attach ⌊them⌋ to the ephod's shoulder pieces in the front. ²⁶ Make two ⌊other⌋ gold rings and put them at the two other corners of the breastpiece on the edge that is next to the inner border of the ephod. ²⁷ Make two ⌊more⌋ gold rings and attach them to the bottom of the ephod's two shoulder pieces on its front, close to its seam,^f and above the ephod's woven waistband. ²⁸ The craftsmen are to tie the breastpiece from its rings to the rings of the ephod with a cord of blue yarn, so that the breastpiece is above the ephod's waistband and does not come loose from the ephod.

²⁹ "Whenever he enters the sanctuary, Aaron is to carry the names of Israel's sons over his heart on the breastpiece for decisions, as a continual reminder before the LORD. ³⁰ Place the •Urim and Thummim in the breastpiece for decisions, so that they will also be over

Aaron's heart whenever he comes before the LORD. Aaron will continually carry the ⌊means of⌋ decisions for the Israelites over his heart before the LORD.

Priest's Ephod Robe

³¹ "You are to make the robe of the ephod entirely of blue yarn. ³² There should be an opening at its top in the center of it. Around the opening, there should be a woven collar with an opening like that for body armor^d so that it does not tear. ³³ Make pomegranates of blue, purple, and scarlet yarn^g on its lower hem and all around it. Put gold bells between them all the way around, ³⁴ ⌊so that⌋ gold bells and pomegranates alternate around the lower hem of the robe. ³⁵ The robe must be ⌊worn by⌋ Aaron whenever he ministers, and its sound will be heard when he enters the sanctuary before the LORD and when he exits, so that he does not die.

Priest's Turban

³⁶ "You are to make a plate^h of pure gold and engrave it, like the engraving of a seal:

> **HOLY TO THE LORD**

³⁷ Fasten it to a cord of blue yarn so it can be placed on the turban; the plate is to be on the front of the turban. ³⁸ It will be on Aaron's forehead so that Aaron may bear the guilt connected with the holy offerings that the Israelites consecrate as all their holy gifts. It is always to be on his forehead, so that they may find acceptance with the Lord.

Other Priestly Attire

³⁹ "You are to weave the tunic from fine linen, make a turban of fine linen,

^a**28:18** Or *malachite*, or *garnet*   ^b**28:18** Or *lapis lazuli*   ^c**28:18** Hb obscure; LXX, Vg read *jasper*   ^d**28:19,32** Hb obscure   ^e**28:22** The same chains mentioned in v. 14   ^f**28:27** The place where the shoulder pieces join the front of the ephod   ^g**28:33** Sam, LXX add *of finely spun linen*   ^h**28:36** Or *medallion*

and make an embroidered sash. ⁴⁰ Make tunics, sashes, and headbands for Aaron's sons to ⌊give them⌋ glory and beauty. ⁴¹ Put these on your brother Aaron and his sons; then anoint, ordain,ᵃ and consecrate them, so that they may serve Me as priests. ⁴² Make them linen undergarments to cover ⌊their⌋ naked bodies; they must extend from the waistᵇ to the thighs. ⁴³ These must be ⌊worn by⌋ Aaron and his sons whenever they enter the tent of meeting or approach the altar to minister in the sanctuary ⌊area⌋, so that they do not incur guilt and die. This is to be a permanent statute for Aaron and for his descendants after him.

Instructions on Priestly Consecration

29 "This is what you are to do for them to consecrate them to serve Me as priests. Take a young bull and two unblemished rams, ² with unleavened bread, unleavened cakes mixed with oil, and unleavened wafers coated with oil. Make them out of fine wheat flour, ³ put them in a basket, and bring them in the basket, along with the bull and two rams. ⁴ Bring Aaron and his sons to the entrance to the tent of meeting and wash them with water. ⁵ Then take the garments and clothe Aaron with the tunic, the robe for the •ephod, the ephod itself, and the breastpiece; fasten the ephod on him with its woven waistband. ⁶ Put the turban on his head and place the holy diadem on the turban. ⁷ Take the anointing oil, pour ⌊it⌋ on his head, and anoint him. ⁸ You must also bring his sons, clothe them with tunics, ⁹ fasten headbands on them, and tie sashes around both Aaron and his sons. The priesthood is to be theirs by a permanent statute. This is the way you will ordain Aaron andᶜ his sons.

Blood Ordination of Aaron and Sons

¹⁰ "You are to bring the bull to the front of the tent of meeting, and Aaron and his sons must lay their hands on the bull's head. ¹¹ Slaughter the bull before the LORD at the entrance to the tent of meeting. ¹² Take some of the bull's blood and apply ⌊it⌋ to the horns of the altar with your finger; then pour out all the ⌊rest⌋ of the blood at the base of the altar. ¹³ Take all the fat that covers the entrails, the fatty lobe of the liver, and the two kidneys with the fat on them, and burn ⌊them⌋ on the altar. ¹⁴ But burn up the bull's flesh, its hide, and its dung outside the camp; it is a •sin offering.

¹⁵ "Take one ram, and Aaron and his sons are to lay their hands on the ram's head. ¹⁶ You are to slaughter the ram, take its blood, and sprinkle ⌊it⌋ on all sides of the altar. ¹⁷ Cut the ram into pieces. Wash its entrails and shanks, and place ⌊them⌋ with its head and its pieces ⌊on the altar⌋. ¹⁸ Then burn the whole ram on the altar; it is a •burnt offering to the LORD. It is a pleasing aroma, a fire offering to the LORD.

¹⁹ "You are to take the second ram, and Aaron and his sons must lay their hands on the ram's head. ²⁰ Slaughter the ram, take some of its blood, and put it on Aaron's right earlobe, on his sons' right earlobes, on the thumbs of their right hands, and on the big toes of their right feet. Sprinkle the ⌊remaining⌋ blood on all sides of the altar. ²¹ Take some of the blood that is on the altar and some of the anointing oil, and sprinkle ⌊them⌋ on Aaron and his garments, as well as on his sons and their garments. In this way, he and his garments will become holy, as well as his sons and their garments.

²² "Take the fat from the ram, the fat tail, the fat covering the entrails, the

---

ᵃ **28:41** Lit *anoint them, fill their hand*   ᵇ **28:42** Lit *loins*   ᶜ **29:9** Lit *you will fill the hand of Aaron and the hand of*; Ex 29:23-24

fatty lobe of the liver, the two kidneys and the fat on them, and the right thigh (since this is a ram for ordinationª); ²³ take one loaf of bread, one cake of bread ⌊made⌋ with oil, and one wafer from the basket of unleavened bread that is before the LORD; ²⁴ and put all of them in the hands of Aaron and hisᵇ sons and wave them as a presentation offering before the LORD. ²⁵ Take them from their hands and burn ⌊them⌋ on the altar on top of the burnt offering, as a pleasing aroma before the LORD; it is a fire offering to the LORD.

²⁶ "Take the breast from the ram of Aaron's ordination and wave it as a presentation offering before the LORD; it is to be your portion. ²⁷ Consecrate for Aaron and his sons the breast of the presentation offering that is waved and the thigh of the contribution that is lifted up from the ram of ordination. ²⁸ This will belong to Aaron and his sons as a regular portion from the Israelites, for it is a contribution. It will be the Israelites' contribution from their •fellowship sacrifices, their contribution to the LORD.

²⁹ "The holy garments that belong to Aaron are to belong to his sons after him, so that they can be anointed and ordainedᶜ in them. ³⁰ Any priest who is one of his sons and who succeeds him and enters the tent of meeting to minister in the sanctuary must wear them for seven days.

Eating the Ram

³¹ "You are to take the ram of ordination and boil its flesh in a holy place. ³² Aaron and his sons are to eat the meat of the ram and the bread that is in the basket at the entrance to the tent of meeting. ³³ They must eat those things

by which •atonement was made at ⌊the time of⌋ their ordinationᵈ and consecration. An unauthorized person must not eat ⌊them⌋, for these things are holy. ³⁴ If any of the meat of ordination or any of the bread is left until morning, burn up what is left over. It must not be eaten because it is holy.

Holy Altar

³⁵ "This is what you are to do for Aaron and his sons based on all I have commanded you. Ordain them for seven days. ³⁶ Sacrifice a bull as a sin offering each day for atonement. Purifyᵉ the altar when you make atonement for it, and anoint it in order to consecrate it. ³⁷ For seven days you must make atonement for the altar and consecrate it. The altar will become especially holy; whatever touches the altar will become holy.

Daily Offerings

³⁸ "This is what you are to offer regularly on the altar every day: two year-old lambs. ³⁹ In the morning offer one lamb, and at twilight offer the other lamb. ⁴⁰ With the first lamb offer two quartsᶠ of fine flour mixed with one quartᵍ of crushed olive oil, and a drink offering of one quartᵍ of wine. ⁴¹ You are to offer the second lamb at twilight. Offer a •grain offering and a drink offering with it, like the one in the morning, as a pleasing aroma, a fire offering •to the LORD. ⁴² This will be a regular burnt offering throughout your generations at the entrance to the tent of meeting before the LORD, where I will meet youʰ to speak with you. ⁴³ I will also meet with the Israelites there, and that place will be consecrated by My glory. ⁴⁴ I will consecrate the tent of meeting and the altar; I will also consecrate Aaron and

---

ª**29:22** Normally the priest would receive the right thigh to be eaten, but here it is burned; Lv 7:32-34   ᵇ**29:24** Lit *in the hands of his*   ᶜ**29:29** Lit *him for anointing in them and for filling their hand*   ᵈ**29:33** Lit *made to fill their hand*   ᵉ**29:36** Or *Make a sin offering on*   ᶠ**29:40** Lit *offer a tenth*   ᵍ**29:40** Lit *a fourth of a hin*   ʰ**29:42** Moses

his sons to serve Me as priests. ⁴⁵ I will dwell among the Israelites and be their God. ⁴⁶ And they will know that I am the Lord their God, who brought them out of the land of Egypt, so that I might dwell among them. I am the Lord their God.

Design of Incense Altar

30 "You are to make an altar for the burning of incense; make it of acacia wood. ² It must be square, 18 inches long and 18 inches wide;ᵃ it must be 36 inches high.ᵇ Its horns must be of one piece.ᶜ ³ Overlay its top, all around its sides, and its horns with pure gold; make a gold molding all around it. ⁴ Make two gold rings for it under the molding on two of its sides; put these on opposite sides of it to be holders for the poles to carry it with. ⁵ Make the poles of acacia wood and overlay them with gold.

⁶ "You are to place the altar in front of the veil by the ark of the •testimony—in front of the •mercy seat that is over the testimony—where I will meet with you. ⁷ Aaron must burn fragrant incense on it; he must burn it every morning when he tends the lamps. ⁸ When Aaron sets up the lamps at twilight, he must burn incense. There is to be an incense ⌊offering⌋ before the LORD throughout your generations. ⁹ You must not offer unauthorized incense on it, or a •burnt or •grain offering; you are not to pour a drink offering on it.

Annual Sin Offering for Atonement

¹⁰ "Once a year Aaron is to perform the purification riteᵈ on the horns of the altar. Throughout your generations he is to perform the purification riteᵈ forᵉ it once a year, with the blood of the •sin offering for •atonement. The altar is especially holy to the LORD."

Atonement Money: a Ransom

¹¹ The LORD spoke to Moses: ¹² "When you take a census of the Israelites to register them, each of the men must pay a ransom for himself to the LORD as they are registered. Then no plague will come on them as they are registered. ¹³ Everyone who is registered must pay half a shekelᶠ according to the sanctuary •shekel (20 gerahs to the shekel). This half shekel is a contribution to the LORD. ¹⁴ Each man who is registered, 20 years old or more, must give this contribution to the LORD. ¹⁵ The wealthy may not give more, and the poor may not give less, than half a shekel when giving the contribution to the LORD to atone forᵍ your lives. ¹⁶ Take the atonement moneyʰ from the Israelites and use it for the service of the tent of meeting. It will serve as a reminder for the Israelites before the LORD to atone forᵍ your lives."

Bronze Basin

¹⁷ The LORD spoke to Moses: ¹⁸ "Make a bronze basin for washing and a bronze stand for it. Set it between the tent of meeting and the altar, and put water in it. ¹⁹ Aaron and his sons must wash their hands and feet from the basin. ²⁰ Whenever they enter the tent of meeting or approach the altar to minister by burning up an offering to the LORD, they must wash with water so that they will not die. ²¹ They must wash their hands and feet so that they will not die; this is to be a permanent statute for them, for Aaron and his descendants throughout their generations."

Anointing Oil

²² The LORD spoke to Moses: ²³ "Take for yourself the finest spices: 12 and a half poundsⁱ of liquid myrrh, half as much (six and a quarter poundsʲ) of fra-

---

ᵃ**30:2** Lit *one cubit its length and one cubit its width*   ᵇ**30:2** Lit *wide; and two cubits its height*   ᶜ**30:2** Lit *piece with it*   ᵈ**30:10** Or *to make atonement*   ᵉ**30:10** Or *on*   ᶠ**30:13** About ⅔ of an ounce of silver   ᵍ**30:15,16** Or *to ransom*   ʰ**30:16** Lit *the silver of the atonement*   ⁱ**30:23** Lit *500* (shekels)   ʲ**30:23** Lit *250* (shekels)

grant cinnamon, six and a quarter pounds[a] of fragrant cane, 24 12 and a half pounds[b] of cassia (by the sanctuary shekel), and one gallon[c] of olive oil. 25 Prepare from these a holy anointing oil, a scented blend, the work of a perfumer; it will be holy anointing oil.

26 "With it you are to anoint the tent of meeting, the ark of the testimony, 27 the table with all its utensils, the lampstand with its utensils, the altar of incense, 28 the altar of burnt offering with all its utensils, and the basin with its stand. 29 Consecrate them and they will be especially holy. Whatever touches them will be consecrated. 30 Anoint Aaron and his sons and consecrate them to serve Me as priests.

31 "Tell the Israelites: This will be My holy anointing oil throughout your generations. 32 It must not be used for ˌordinaryˌ anointing on a person's body, and you must not make anything like it using its formula. It is holy, and it must be holy to you. 33 Anyone who blends something like it or puts some of it on an unauthorized person must be cut off from his people."

Sacred Incense

34 The LORD said to Moses: "Take fragrant spices: stacte, onycha, and galbanum; the spices and pure frankincense are to be in equal measures. 35 Prepare expertly blended incense from these; it is to be seasoned with salt, pure and holy. 36 Grind some of it into a fine powder and put some in front of the testimony in the tent of meeting, where I will meet with you. It must be especially holy to you. 37 As for the incense you are making, you must not make ˌanyˌ for yourselves using its formula. It is to be regarded by you as sacred to the LORD. 38 Anyone who makes something like it

to smell its fragrance must be cut off from his people."

God's Spirit-filled Workers

31 The LORD also spoke to Moses: 2 "Look, I have appointed by name Bezalel son of Uri, son of Hur, of the tribe of Judah. 3 I have filled him with God's Spirit, with wisdom, understanding, and ability in every craft 4 to design artistic works in gold, silver, and bronze, 5 to cut gemstones for mounting, and to carve wood for work in every craft. 6 I have also selected Oholiab[d] son of Ahisamach, of the tribe of Dan, to be with him. I have placed wisdom within every skilled craftsman[e] in order to make all that I have commanded you: 7 the tent of meeting, the ark of the •testimony, the •mercy seat that is on top of it, and all the ˌotherˌ furnishings of the tent— 8 the table with its utensils, the pure ˌgoldˌ lampstand with all its utensils, the altar of incense, 9 the altar of •burnt offering with all its utensils, the basin with its stand— 10 the specially woven[f] garments, both the holy garments for Aaron the priest and the garments for his sons to serve as priests, 11 the anointing oil, and the fragrant incense for the sanctuary. They must make ˌthemˌ according to all that I have commanded you."

Observe My Sabbaths!

12 The LORD said to Moses: 13 "Tell the Israelites: You must observe My Sabbaths, for it is a sign between Me and you throughout your generations, so that you will know that I am the LORD who sets you apart. 14 Observe the Sabbath, for it is holy to you. Whoever profanes it must be put to death. If anyone does work on it, that person must be cut off from his people. 15 For six days work may be done, but

a**30:23** Lit *250* (shekels)   b**30:24** Lit *500* (shekels)   c**30:24** Lit *a hin*   d**31:6** LXX, Syr read *Eliab*   e**31:6** Lit *every person skilled of heart*   f**31:10** Hb obscure

on the seventh day there must be a Sabbath of complete rest, dedicated to the LORD. Anyone who does work on the Sabbath day must be put to death. ¹⁶ The Israelites must observe the Sabbath, celebrating it throughout their generations as a perpetual covenant. ¹⁷ It is a sign forever between Me and the Israelites, for in six days the LORD made the heavens and the earth, but on the seventh day He rested and was refreshed."

God's Two Stone Tablets

¹⁸ When He finished speaking with Moses on Mount Sinai, He gave him the two tablets of the testimony, stone tablets inscribed by the finger of God.

The Golden Calf

32 When the people saw that Moses delayed in coming down from the mountain, they gathered around Aaron and said to him, "Come, make us a god[a] who will go before us because this Moses, the man who brought us up from the land of Egypt—we don't know what has happened to him!"

Aaron's Sin

² Then Aaron replied to them, "Take off the gold rings that are on the ears of your wives, your sons, and your daughters and bring ⌊them⌋ to me." ³ So all the people took off the gold rings that were on their ears and brought ⌊them⌋ to Aaron. ⁴ He took ⌊the gold⌋ from their hands, fashioned it with an engraving tool, and made it into an image of a calf.

Then they said, "Israel, this is your God,[b] who brought you up from the land of Egypt!"

⁵ When Aaron saw ⌊this⌋, he built an altar before it; then he made an announcement: "There will be a festival to the LORD tomorrow." ⁶ Early the next morning they arose, offered •burnt offerings, and presented •fellowship offerings. The people sat down to eat and drink, then got up to revel.

Angry God Warns Moses

⁷ The LORD spoke to Moses: "Go down at once! For your people you brought up from the land of Egypt have acted corruptly. ⁸ They have quickly turned from the way I commanded them; they have made for themselves an image of a calf. They have bowed down to it, sacrificed to it, and said, 'Israel, this is your God,[b] who brought you up from the land of Egypt.'" ⁹ The LORD also said to Moses: "I have seen this people, and they are indeed a stiff-necked people. ¹⁰ Now leave Me alone, so that My anger can burn against them and I can destroy them. Then I will make you into a great nation."

¹¹ But Moses interceded with the LORD his God: "LORD, why does Your anger burn against Your people You brought out of the land of Egypt with great power and a strong hand? ¹² Why should the Egyptians say, 'He brought them out with an evil intent to kill them in the mountains and wipe them off the face of the earth'? Turn from Your great anger and change Your mind about this disaster ⌊planned⌋ for Your people. ¹³ Remember that You swore to Your servants Abraham, Isaac, and Israel by Yourself and declared to them, 'I will make your •offspring as numerous as the stars of the sky and will give your offspring all this land that I have promised, and they will inherit ⌊it⌋ forever.'" ¹⁴ So the LORD changed His mind about the disaster He said He would bring on His people.

Moses Returns

¹⁵ Then Moses turned and went down the mountain with the two tablets of the

---

[a]**32:1** Or us gods [b]**32:4,8** Or Israel, this is your god, or Israel, these are your gods

•testimony in his hands. They were inscribed on both sides—inscribed front and back. ¹⁶ The tablets were the work of God, and the writing was God's writing, engraved on the tablets.

¹⁷ When Joshua heard the sound of the people as they shouted, he said to Moses, "There is a sound of war in the camp."

¹⁸ But Moses replied:

It's not the sound of a victory cry
and not the sound of a cry of defeat;
I hear the sound of singing!

Moses Enraged

¹⁹ As he approached the camp and saw the calf and the dancing, Moses became enraged and threw the tablets out of his hands, smashing them at the base of the mountain. ²⁰ Then he took the calf they had made, burned ⌊it⌋ up, and ground ⌊it⌋ to powder. He scattered ⌊the powder⌋ over the surface of the water and forced the Israelites to drink ⌊the water⌋.

Aaron's Excuse

²¹ Then Moses asked Aaron, "What did this people do to you that you have led them into ⌊such⌋ a grave sin?"

²² "Don't be enraged, my lord," Aaron replied. "You yourself know that the people are ⌊intent⌋ on evil. ²³ They said to me, 'Make us a god[a] who will go before us because this Moses, the man who brought us up from the land of Egypt—we don't know what has happened to him!' ²⁴ So I said to them, 'Whoever has gold, take it off,' and they gave ⌊it⌋ to me. When I threw it into the fire, out came this calf!"

Moses Executes God's Justice

²⁵ Moses saw that the people were out of control, for Aaron had let them get out of control, so that they would be vulnera-

ble to their enemies. ²⁶ And Moses stood at the camp's entrance and said, "Whoever is for the LORD, ⌊come⌋ to me." And all the Levites gathered around him. ²⁷ He told them, "This is what the LORD, the God of Israel, says, 'Every man fasten his sword to his side; go back and forth through the camp from entrance to entrance, and each of you kill his brother, his friend, and his neighbor.'" ²⁸ The Levites did as Moses commanded, and about 3,000 men fell dead that day among the people. ²⁹ Afterwards Moses said, "Today you have been dedicated[b] to the LORD, since each man went against his son and his brother. Therefore you have brought a blessing on yourselves today."

³⁰ The following day Moses said to the people, "You have committed a great sin. Now I will go up to the LORD; perhaps I will be able to pay[c] for your sin."

Moses Pleas for People

³¹ So Moses returned to the LORD and said, "Oh, this people has committed a great sin; they have made for themselves a god of gold. ³² Now if You would only forgive their sin. But if not, please erase me from the book You have written."

³³ The LORD replied to Moses: "Whoever has sinned against Me I will erase from My book. ³⁴ Now go, lead the people to the place I told you about; see, My angel will go before you. But on the day I settle accounts, I will hold them accountable for their sin." ³⁵ And the LORD inflicted a plague on the people for what they did with the calf Aaron had made.

A Stiff-necked People

33 The LORD spoke to Moses: "Go, leave here, you and the people you brought up from the land of Egypt, to the land I promised to Abraham, Isaac, and Ja-

---

[a]**32:23** Or *us gods*   [b]**32:29** Text emended; MT reads *Today dedicate yourselves*; LXX, Vg read *Today you have dedicated yourselves*   [c]**32:30** Traditionally, *make atonement*

cob, saying: I will give it to your •offspring. [2] I will send an angel ahead of you and will drive out the Canaanites, Amorites, Hittites, Perizzites,[a] Hivites, and Jebusites. [3] ⌊Go up⌋ to a land flowing with milk and honey. But I will not go with you because you are a stiff-necked people; otherwise, I might destroy you on the way." [4] When the people heard this bad news, they mourned and didn't put on their jewelry.

[5] For the LORD said to Moses: "Tell the Israelites: You are a stiff-necked people. If I went with you for a single moment, I would destroy you. Now take off your jewelry, and I will decide what to do with you." [6] So the Israelites ⌊remained⌋ stripped of their jewelry from Mount Horeb ⌊onward⌋.

Tent of Meeting

[7] Now Moses took a tent and set it up outside the camp, far away from the camp; he called it the tent of meeting. Anyone who wanted to consult the LORD would go to the tent of meeting that was outside the camp. [8] Whenever Moses went out to the tent, all the people would stand up, each one at the door of his tent, and they would watch Moses until he entered the tent. [9] When Moses entered the tent, the pillar of cloud would come down and remain at the entrance to the tent, and ⌊the LORD⌋ would speak with Moses. [10] As all the people saw the pillar of cloud remaining at the entrance to the tent, they would stand up, then bow in worship, each one at the door of his tent. [11] The LORD spoke with Moses face to face, just as a man speaks with his friend. Then Moses would return to the camp, but his assistant, the young man Joshua son of Nun, would not leave the inside of the tent.

Moses Sees the LORD's Glory

[12] Moses said to the LORD, "Look, You have told me, 'Lead this people up,' but

You have not let me know whom You will send with me. You said, 'I know you by name, and you have also found favor in My sight.' [13] Now if I have indeed found favor in Your sight, please teach me Your ways, and I will know You and find favor in Your sight. Now consider that this nation is Your people."

[14] Then He replied, "My presence will go ⌊with you⌋, and I will give you rest."

[15] "If Your presence does not go," Moses responded to Him, "don't make us go up from here. [16] How will it be known that I and Your people have found favor in Your sight unless You go with us? I and Your people will be distinguished ⌊by this⌋ from all the other people on the face of the earth."

[17] The LORD answered Moses, "I will do this very thing you have asked, for you have found favor in My sight, and I know you by name."

[18] Then Moses said, "Please, let me see Your glory."

[19] He said, "I will cause all My goodness to pass in front of you, and I will proclaim the name •Yahweh before you. I will be gracious to whom I will be gracious, and I will have compassion on whom I will have compassion." [20] But He answered, "You cannot see My face, for no one can see Me and live." [21] The LORD said, "Here is a place near Me. You are to stand on the rock, [22] and when My glory passes by, I will put you in the crevice of the rock and cover you with My hand until I have passed by. [23] Then I will take My hand away, and you will see My back, but My face will not be seen."

New Stone Tablets

34 The LORD said to Moses, "Cut two stone tablets like the first ones, and I will write on them the words that were on the first tablets, which you

<hr>

a 33:2 Sam, LXX include *Girgashites*

broke. [2] Be prepared by morning. Come up Mount Sinai in the morning and stand before Me on the mountaintop. [3] No one may go up with you; in fact, no one must be seen anywhere on the mountain. Even the flocks and herds are not to graze in front of that mountain."

[4] Moses cut two stone tablets like the first ones. He got up early in the morning, and taking the two stone tablets in his hand, he climbed Mount Sinai, just as the LORD had commanded him.

Moses Worships Yahweh

[5] The LORD came down in a cloud, stood with him there, and proclaimed ⌊His⌋ name •Yahweh. [6] Then the LORD passed in front of him and proclaimed:

Yahweh—Yahweh is a compassionate and gracious God, slow to anger and rich in faithful love and truth, [7] maintaining faithful love to a thousand ⌊generations⌋, forgiving wrongdoing, rebellion, and sin. But He will not leave ⌊the guilty⌋ unpunished, bringing the consequences of the fathers' wrongdoing on the children and grandchildren to the third and fourth generation.

[8] Moses immediately bowed down to the ground and worshiped. [9] Then he said, "My Lord, if I have indeed found favor in Your sight, my Lord, please go with us. Even though this is a stiffnecked people, forgive our wrongdoing and sin, and accept us as Your own possession."

God Reaffirms Covenant

[10] And the LORD responded: "Look, I am making a covenant. I will perform wonders in the presence of all your people[a] that have never been done[b] in all the earth or in any nation. All the people you live among will see the LORD's work, for what I am doing with you is awe-inspiring. [11] Observe what I command you today. I am going to drive out before you the Amorites, Canaanites, Hittites, Perizzites, Hivites,[c] and Jebusites. [12] Be careful not to make a treaty with the inhabitants of the land that you are going to enter; otherwise, they will become a snare among you. [13] Instead, you must tear down their altars, smash their sacred pillars, and chop down their •Asherah poles. [14] You are to never bow down to another god because the LORD, being jealous by nature, is a jealous God.

[15] "Do not make a treaty with the inhabitants of the land, or else when they prostitute themselves with their gods and sacrifice to their gods, they will invite you, and you will eat of their sacrifice. [16] Then you will take some of their daughters ⌊as brides⌋ for your sons. Their daughters will prostitute themselves with their gods and cause your sons to prostitute themselves with their gods.

[17] "Do not make cast images of gods for yourselves.

[18] "Observe the Festival of •Unleavened Bread. You are to eat unleavened bread for seven days at the appointed time in the month of Abib as I commanded you. For you came out of Egypt in the month of Abib.

[19] "The firstborn male from every womb belongs to Me, including all your male[d] [e] livestock, the firstborn of cattle or sheep. [20] You must redeem the firstborn of a donkey with a sheep, but if you do not redeem ⌊it⌋, break its neck. You must redeem all the firstborn of your sons. No one is to appear before Me empty-handed.

[21] "You are to labor six days but you must rest on the seventh day; you must

---

[a]**34:10** Lit *in all nations* [b]**34:10** Lit *created* [c]**34:11** DSS, Sam, LXX include *Girgashites* [d]**34:19** LXX, Theod, Vg, Tg read *males* [e]**34:19** Hb obscure

even rest during plowing and harvesting times.

22 "Observe the Festival of Weeks with the •firstfruits of the wheat harvest, and the Festival of Ingathering[a] at the turn of the ⌊agricultural⌋ year. 23 Three times a year all your males are to appear before the Lord GOD, the God of Israel. 24 For I will drive out nations before you and enlarge your territory. No one will covet your land when you go up three times a year to appear before the LORD your God.

25 "Do not present[b] the blood for My sacrifice with anything leavened. The sacrifice of the •Passover Festival must not remain until morning.

26 "Bring the best firstfruits of your land to the house of the LORD your God.

"You must not boil a young goat in its mother's milk."

27 The LORD also said to Moses, "Write down these words, for I have made a covenant with you and with Israel based on these words."

28 Moses was there with the LORD 40 days and 40 nights; he did not eat bread or drink water. He wrote down on the tablets the words of the covenant—the Ten Commandments.

Moses Descends—with Radiant Face

29 As Moses descended from Mount Sinai—with the two tablets of the •testimony in his hands as he descended the mountain—he did not realize that the skin of his face shone as a result of his speaking with the LORD.[c] 30 When Aaron and all the Israelites saw Moses, the skin of his face shone! They were afraid to come near him. 31 But Moses called out to them, so Aaron and all the leaders of the community returned to him, and Moses spoke to them. 32 Afterwards all the Isra-

elites came near, and he commanded them everything the LORD had told him on Mount Sinai. 33 When Moses had finished speaking with them, he put a veil over his face. 34 But whenever Moses went before the LORD to speak with Him, he would remove the veil until he came out. After he came out, he would tell the Israelites what he had been commanded, 35 and the Israelites would see that Moses' face[d] was radiant. Then Moses would put the veil over his face again until he went to speak with the LORD.

Sabbath Command

35 Moses assembled the entire Israelite community and said to them, "These are the things that the LORD has commanded you to do: 2 For six days work is to be done, but on the seventh day you are to have a holy day, a Sabbath of complete rest to the LORD. Anyone who does work on it must be executed. 3 Do not light a fire in any of your homes on the Sabbath day."

Building the Tabernacle

4 Then Moses said to the entire Israelite community, "This is what the LORD has commanded: 5 Take up an offering for the LORD among you. Let everyone whose heart is willing bring this as the LORD's offering: gold, silver, and bronze; 6 blue, purple, and scarlet yarn; fine linen and goat hair; 7 ram skins dyed red and manatee skins;[e] acacia wood; 8 oil for the light; spices for the anointing oil and for the fragrant incense; 9 and onyx with gemstones to mount on the •ephod and breastpiece.

10 "Let all the skilled craftsmen[f] among you come and make everything that the LORD has commanded: 11 the tabernacle—its tent and covering, its clasps and

---

[a]34:22 The Festival of Ingathering is called Festival of Booths elsewhere in the OT; Lv 23:34-36 [b]34:25 Lit slaughter [c]34:29 Lit with Him [d]34:35 Lit see Moses' face, that the skin of his face [e]35:7 Or and dolphin skins, or and fine leather; Hb obscure [f]35:10 Lit the skilled of heart

planks, its crossbars, its posts and bases; [12] the ark with its poles, the •mercy seat, and the veil for the screen; [13] the table with its poles, all its utensils, and the bread of the Presence;[a] [14] the lampstand for light with its utensils and lamps as well as the oil for the light; [15] the altar of incense with its poles; the anointing oil and the fragrant incense; the entryway screen for the entrance to the tabernacle; [16] the altar of •burnt offering with its bronze grate, its poles, and all its utensils; the basin with its stand; [17] the hangings of the courtyard, its posts and bases, and the screen for the gate of the courtyard; [18] the tent pegs for the tabernacle and the tent pegs for the courtyard, along with their ropes; [19] and the specially woven[b] garments for ministering in the sanctuary—the holy garments for Aaron the priest and the garments for his sons to serve as priests."

Tabernacle Offering

[20] Then the entire Israelite community left Moses' presence. [21] Everyone whose heart was moved and whose spirit prompted him came and brought an offering to the LORD to construct the tent of meeting for every use, and ⌊to make⌋ the holy garments. [22] Both men and women came; all who had willing hearts brought brooches, earrings, rings, necklaces, and all kinds of gold jewelry—everyone who waved a presentation offering of gold to the LORD. [23] Everyone who had in his possession blue, purple, or scarlet yarn, fine linen or goat hair, ram skins dyed red or manatee skins,[c] brought ⌊them⌋. [24] Everyone who offered a contribution of silver or bronze brought it to the LORD. Everyone who possessed acacia wood useful for any task in the work brought ⌊it⌋. [25] Every skilled[d] woman spun ⌊yarn⌋

with her hands and brought it: blue, purple, and scarlet yarn, and fine linen. [26] And all the women whose hearts were moved spun the goat hair by virtue of ⌊their⌋ skill. [27] The leaders brought onyx and gemstones to mount on the ephod and breastpiece, [28] as well as the spice and oil for the light, for the anointing oil, and for the fragrant incense. [29] So the Israelites brought a freewill offering to the LORD, all the men and women whose hearts prompted them to bring ⌊something⌋ for all the work that the LORD, through Moses, had commanded to be done.

Bezalel and Oholiab:
Spirit-filled Craftsmen

[30] Moses then said to the Israelites: "Look, the Lord has appointed by name Bezalel son of Uri, son of Hur, of the tribe of Judah. [31] He has filled him with God's Spirit, with wisdom, understanding, and ability in every kind of craft [32] to design artistic works in gold, silver, and bronze, [33] to cut gemstones for mounting, and to carve wood for work in every kind of artistic craft. [34] He has also given both him and Oholiab son of Ahisamach, of the tribe of Dan, ⌊the ability⌋ to teach ⌊others⌋. [35] He has filled them with skill to do all the work of a gem cutter; a designer; an embroiderer in blue, purple, and scarlet yarn and fine linen; and a weaver. They can do every kind of craft and design artistic designs.

36 [1] Bezalel, Oholiab, and all the skilled[d] people are to work based on everything the LORD has commanded. The LORD has given them wisdom and understanding to know how to do all the work of constructing the sanctuary."

[2] So Moses summoned Bezalel, Oholiab, and every skilled[d] person in whose

---

a[35:13] Or of presentation   b[35:19] Hb obscure   c[35:23] Or or dolphin skins, or or fine leather; Hb obscure   d[35:25; 36:1,2] Lit wise of heart

heart the LORD had placed wisdom, everyone whose heart moved him, to come to the work and do it. ³ They took from Moses' presence all the contributions that the Israelites had brought for the task of making the sanctuary. Meanwhile, the people continued to bring freewill offerings morning after morning.

⁴ Then all the craftsmen who were doing all the work for the sanctuary came one by one from the work they were doing ⁵ and said to Moses, "The people are bringing more than is needed for the construction of the work the LORD commanded to be done."

Overabundant Offerings

⁶ After Moses gave an order, they sent a proclamation throughout the camp: "Let no man or woman make anything else as an offering for the sanctuary." So the people stopped. ⁷ The materials were sufficient for them to do all the work. There was more than enough.

Work Begins

⁸ All the skilled craftsmen[a] among those doing the work made the tabernacle with 10 curtains. Bezalel made them of finely spun linen, as well as blue, purple, and scarlet yarn, with a design of •cherubim worked into them. ⁹ The length of each curtain was 42 feet,[b] and the width of each curtain six feet;[c] all the curtains had the same measurements. ¹⁰ He joined five of the curtains to each other, and the ⌊other⌋ five curtains he joined to each other. ¹¹ He made loops of blue yarn on the edge of the last curtain in the first set and did the same on the edge of the outermost curtain in the second set. ¹² He made 50 loops on the one curtain and 50 loops on the edge of the curtain in the second set, so that the loops lined up with each other. ¹³ He also made 50 gold clasps and joined the curtains to each other, so that the tabernacle became a single unit.

¹⁴ He made curtains of goat hair for a tent over the tabernacle; he also made 11 of them. ¹⁵ The length of each curtain was 45 feet,[d] and the width of each curtain six feet.[c] All 11 curtains had the same measurements. ¹⁶ He joined five of the curtains together, and ⌊the other⌋ six together. ¹⁷ He made 50 loops on the edge of the outermost curtain in the ⌊first⌋ set and 50 loops on the edge of the ⌊corresponding⌋ curtain in the second set. ¹⁸ He made 50 bronze clasps to join the tent together as a single unit. ¹⁹ He also made a covering for the tent from ram skins dyed red and a covering of manatee skins[e] on top of it.

²⁰ He made upright planks[f] of acacia wood for the tabernacle. ²¹ The length of each plank was 15 feet,[g] and the width of each was 27 inches.[h] ²² There were two tenons connected to each other for each plank. He did the same for all the planks of the tabernacle. ²³ He made planks for the tabernacle as follows: 20 for the south side, ²⁴ and he made 40 silver bases to put under the 20 planks, two bases under the first plank for its two tenons, and two bases under each of the following planks for their two tenons; ²⁵ for the second side of the tabernacle, the north side, he made 20 planks, ²⁶ with their 40 silver bases, two bases under the first plank and two bases under each of the following ones; ²⁷ and for the west side of the tabernacle he made six planks. ²⁸ He also made two additional planks for the two back corners of the tabernacle. ²⁹ They were paired at the bottom and

---

[a]**36:8** Lit *the wise of heart*   [b]**36:9** Lit *28 cubits*   [c]**36:9,15** Lit *four cubits*   [d]**36:15** Lit *30 cubits*   [e]**36:19** Or *of dolphin skins, or of fine leather*; Hb obscure   [f]**36:20** Or *made frames*   [g]**36:21** Lit *10 cubits*   [h]**36:21** Lit *a cubit and a half*

joined together[a] at the[b] top in a single ring. This is what he did with both of them for the two corners. [30] So there were eight planks with their 16 silver bases, two bases under each one.

[31] He made five crossbars of acacia wood for the planks on one side of the tabernacle, [32] five crossbars for the planks on the other side of the tabernacle, and five crossbars for those at the back of the tabernacle on the west. [33] He made the central crossbar run through the middle of the planks from one end to the other. [34] He overlaid them with gold and made their rings and holders for the crossbars out of gold. He also overlaid the crossbars with gold.

[35] Then he made the veil with blue, purple, and scarlet yarn, and finely spun linen. He made it with a design of cherubim worked into it. [36] For it he made four posts of acacia wood and overlaid them with gold; their hooks were of gold. And he cast four silver bases for the posts.

[37] He made a screen embroidered with blue, purple, and scarlet yarn, and finely spun linen for the entrance to the tent, [38] together with its five posts and their hooks. He overlaid the tops of the posts and their bands with gold, but their five bases were bronze.

Bezalel Makes the Ark

37 Bezalel made the ark of acacia wood, 45 inches long, 27 inches wide, and 27 inches high.[c] [2] He overlaid it with pure gold inside and out and made a gold molding all around it. [3] He cast four gold rings for it to be on its four feet, two rings on one side and two rings on the other side. [4] He made poles of acacia wood and overlaid them with gold. [5] He inserted the poles into the rings on the sides of the ark for carrying the ark.

[6] He made a •mercy seat of pure gold, 45 inches long and 27 inches wide.[d] [7] He made two •cherubim of gold; he made them of hammered work at the two ends of the mercy seat, [8] one cherub at one end and one cherub at the other end. He made the cherubim ⌊of one piece⌋ with the mercy seat, ⌊a cherub⌋ at each end. [9] They had wings spread out, covering the mercy seat with their wings and facing each other. The faces of the cherubim were looking toward the mercy seat.

Bezalel Makes the Table

[10] He constructed the table of acacia wood, 36 inches long, 18 inches wide, and 27 inches high.[e] [11] He overlaid it with pure gold and made a gold molding all around it. [12] He made a three-inch[f] frame all around it and made a gold molding all around its frame. [13] He cast four gold rings for it and attached the rings to the four corners at its four legs. [14] The rings were next to the frame as holders for the poles to carry the table. [15] He made the poles for carrying the table from acacia wood and overlaid them with gold. [16] He also made the utensils that would be on the table out of pure gold: its plates and cups, as well as its bowls and pitchers for pouring drink offerings.

Bezalel Makes the Lampstand

[17] Then he made the lampstand out of pure hammered gold. He made it ⌊all⌋ of one piece: its base and shaft, its ⌊ornamental⌋ cups, and its calyxes[g] and petals. [18] Six branches extended from its sides,

---

[a]**36:29** Lit *and together they are to be complete*   [b]**36:29** Lit *its*   [c]**37:1** Lit *two and a half cubits its length, one and a half cubits its width, and one and a half cubits its height*   [d]**37:6** Lit *two and a half cubits its length and one and a half cubits its width*   [e]**37:10** Lit *two cubits its length, one cubit its width, and one and a half cubits its height*   [f]**37:12** Lit *a handbreadth*   [g]**37:17** = the outer covering of a flower

three branches of the lampstand from one side and three branches of the lampstand from the other side. ¹⁹ There were three cups shaped like almond blossoms, each with a calyx and petals, on the first branch, and three cups shaped like almond blossoms, each with a calyx and petals, on the next branch. It was this way for the six branches that extended from the lampstand. ²⁰ On the lampstand shaft there were four cups shaped like almond blossoms with its calyxes and petals. ²¹ For the six branches that extended from it, a calyx was under the first pair of branches from it, a calyx under the second pair of branches from it, and a calyx under the third pair of branches from it. ²² Their calyxes and branches were of one piece.ᵃ All of it was a single hammered piece of pure gold. ²³ He also made its seven lamps, snuffers, and firepans of pure gold. ²⁴ He made it and all its utensils of 75 poundsᵇ of pure gold.

Bezalel Makes Altar of Incense

²⁵ He made the altar of incense out of acacia wood. It was square, 18 inches long and 18 inches wide; it was 36 inches high.ᶜ Its horns were of one piece.ᵃ ²⁶ He overlaid it, its top, all around its sides, and its horns with pure gold. Then he made a gold molding all around it. ²⁷ He made two gold rings for it under the molding on two of its sides; ⌊he put these⌋ on opposite sides of it to be holders for the poles to carry it with. ²⁸ He made the poles of acacia wood and overlaid them with gold.

²⁹ He also made the holy anointing oil and the pure, fragrant, and expertly blended incense.

Bezalel Makes Burnt Offering Altar

38 Bezalel constructed the altar of burnt offering from acacia wood. It was square, seven and a half feet long and seven and a half feet wide,ᵈ and was four and a half feetᵉ high. ² He made horns for it on its four corners; the horns were of one piece.ᶠ Then he overlaid it with bronze.

³ He made all the altar's utensils: the pots, shovels, basins, meat forks, and firepans; he made all its utensils of bronze. ⁴ He constructed for the altar a grate of bronze mesh under its ledge,ᵍ halfway up from the bottom. ⁵ At the four corners of the bronze grate he cast four rings as holders for the poles. ⁶ He also made the poles of acacia wood and overlaid them with bronze. ⁷ Then he inserted the poles into the rings on the sides of the altar in order to carry it with them. He constructed the altar with boards so that it was hollow.

Bezalel Makes the Bronze Basin

⁸ He made the bronze basin and its stand from the ⌊bronze⌋ mirrors of the women who served at the entrance to the tent of meeting.

Bezalel Makes the Courtyard

⁹ Then he made the courtyard. The hangings on the south side of the courtyard were of finely spun linen, 150 feet in length,ʰ ¹⁰ including their 20 posts and 20 bronze bases. The hooks and bandsⁱ of the posts were silver. ¹¹ ⌊The hangings⌋ on the north side were also 150 feet in length,ʰ including their 20 posts and 20 bronze bases. The hooks and bandsⁱ of the posts were silver. ¹² The hangings on the west side were 75 feet in length,ʲ including their 10

ᵃ**37:22,25** Lit *piece with it*   ᵇ**37:24** Lit *a talent*   ᶜ**37:25** Lit *a cubit its length, a cubit its width, and two cubits its height*   ᵈ**38:1** Lit *five cubits its length and five cubits its width*   ᵉ**38:1** Lit *three cubits*   ᶠ**38:2** Lit *piece with it*   ᵍ**38:4** Or *rim*   ʰ**38:9,11** Lit *100 cubits*   ⁱ**38:10,11** Or *connecting rods*   ʲ**38:12** Lit *50 cubits*

posts and 10 bases. The hooks and bands of the posts were silver. ¹³ ⌊The hangings⌋ on the east toward the sunrise were also 75 feet in length.ᵃ ¹⁴ The hangings on one side ⌊of the gate⌋ were 22 and a half feet,ᵇ including their three posts and three bases. ¹⁵ It was the same for the other side. The hangings were 22 and a half feet,ᵇ including their three posts and three bases on both sides of the court-yard gate. ¹⁶ All the hangings around the courtyard were of finely spun linen. ¹⁷ The bases for the posts were bronze; the hooks and bandsᶜ of the posts were silver; and the plating for the tops of the posts was silver. All the posts of the courtyard were banded with silver.

¹⁸ The screen for the gate of the court-yard was embroidered with blue, purple, and scarlet yarn, and finely spun linen. It was 30 feetᵈ long, and like the hangings of the courtyard, seven and a half feetᵉ high.ᶠ ¹⁹ It had four posts, including their four bronze bases. Their hooks were sil-ver, and the bandsᶜ as well as the plating of their tops were silver. ²⁰ All the tent pegs for the tabernacle and for the sur-rounding courtyard were bronze.

Inventory of Tabernacle Materials

²¹ This is the inventory for the taberna-cle, the tabernacle of the •testimony, that was recorded at Moses' command. It was the work of the Levites under the di-rection ofᵍ Ithamar son of Aaron the priest. ²² Bezalel son of Uri, son of Hur, of the tribe of Judah, made everything that the LORD commanded Moses. ²³ With him was Oholiab son of Ahisa-mach, of the tribe of Dan, a gem cutter, a designer, and an embroiderer with blue, purple, and scarlet yarn, and fine linen.

²⁴ All the gold of the presentation offer-ing that was used for the project in all the work on the sanctuary, was 2,193 pounds,ʰ according to the sanctuary •shekel. ²⁵ The silver from those of the community who were registered was 7,544 pounds,ⁱ according to the sanctu-ary shekel— ²⁶ two-fifths of an ounceʲ per man, that is, half a shekel according to the sanctuary shekel, from everyone 20 years old or more who had crossed over to the registered group, 603,550 men. ²⁷ There were 7,500 poundsᵏ of sil-ver ⌊used⌋ to cast the bases of the sanctu-ary and the bases of the veil—100 bases from 7,500 pounds,ᵏ 75 poundsˡ for each base. ²⁸ With the ⌊remaining⌋ 44 poundsᵐ he made the hooks for the posts, over-laid their tops, and supplied bandsᶜ for them.

²⁹ The bronze of the presentation offer-ing totaled 5,310 pounds.ⁿ ³⁰ He made with it the bases for the entrance to the tent of meeting, the bronze altar and its bronze grate, all the utensils for the altar, ³¹ the bases for the surrounding court-yard, the bases for the gate of the court-yard, all the tent pegs for the tabernacle, and all the tent pegs for the surrounding courtyard.

Making the Priestly Garments

39 They made specially wovenᵒ gar-ments for ministry in the sanctu-ary, and the holy garments for Aaron from the blue, purple, and scarlet yarn, just as the LORD had commanded Moses.

Bezalel Makes the Ephod

² Bezalel made the •ephod of gold, of blue, purple, and scarlet yarn, and of finely spun linen. ³ They hammered out

---

ᵃ38:13 Lit 50 cubits   ᵇ38:14,15 Lit 15 cubits   ᶜ38:17,19,28 Or connecting rods   ᵈ38:18 Lit 20 cubits   ᵉ38:18 Lit five cubits   ᶠ38:18 Lit high in width   ᵍ38:21 Lit Levites by the hand of   ʰ38:24 Lit 29 talents and 730 shekels   ⁱ38:25 Lit 100 talents and 1,775 shekels   ʲ38:26 Lit a beka   ᵏ38:27 Lit 100 talents   ˡ38:27 Lit one talent   ᵐ38:28 Lit 1,775 (shekels)   ⁿ38:29 Lit 70 talents and 2,400 shekels   ᵒ39:1 Hb obscure

thin sheets of gold, and he[a] cut threads
[from them] to interweave with the blue,
purple, and scarlet yarn, and the fine
linen in a skillful design. [4] They made
shoulder pieces for attaching it; it was
joined together at its two edges. [5] The ar-
tistically woven waistband that was on
the ephod was of one piece with the
ephod, according to the same workman-
ship of gold, of blue, purple, and scarlet
yarn, and of finely spun linen, just as the
Lord had commanded Moses.

[6] Then they mounted the onyx stones
surrounded with gold filigree settings,
engraved with the names of Israel's sons
as a gem cutter engraves a seal. [7] He fastened them on the shoulder pieces of the
ephod as memorial stones for the Israelites, just as the Lord had commanded
Moses.

Bezalel Makes the Breastpiece

[8] He also made the embroidered
breastpiece with the same workman-
ship as the ephod of gold, of blue, purple, and scarlet yarn, and of finely spun
linen. [9] They made the breastpiece
square and folded double, nine inches
long and nine inches wide.[b] [10] They
mounted four rows of gemstones[c] on it.
The first row was a row of carnelian, topaz, and emerald;[d] [11] the second row, a
turquoise,[e] a sapphire,[f] and a diamond;[g]
[12] the third row, a jacinth,[h] an agate, and
an amethyst; [13] and the fourth row, a
beryl, an onyx, and a jasper. They were
surrounded with gold filigree in their
settings.

[14] The 12 stones corresponded to the
names of Israel's sons. Each stone was
engraved like a seal with one of the
names of the 12 tribes.

[15] They made braided chains of pure
gold cord for the breastpiece. [16] They
also fashioned two gold filigree settings
and two gold rings and attached the two
rings to its two corners. [17] Then they attached the two gold cords to the two
gold rings on the corners of the breastpiece. [18] They attached the other ends of
the two cords to the two filigree settings
and, in this way, attached [them] to the
ephod's shoulder pieces in front. [19] They
made two [other] gold rings and put
[them] at the two other corners of the
breastpiece on the edge that is next to
the inner border of the ephod. [20] They
made two [more] gold rings and attached
them to the bottom of the ephod's two
shoulder pieces on its front, close to its
seam,[i] above the ephod's woven waistband. [21] Then they tied the breastpiece
from its rings to the rings of the ephod
with a cord of blue yarn, so that the
breastpiece was above the ephod's waistband and did not come loose from the
ephod. [They did] just as the Lord had
commanded Moses.

Craftsmen Make the Robe

[22] They made the woven robe of the
ephod entirely of blue yarn. [23] There
was an opening in the center of the
robe like that for body armor[h] with a
collar around the opening so that it
would not tear. [24] They made pomegranates of finely spun blue, purple, and
scarlet yarn[j] on the lower hem of the
robe. [25] They made bells of pure gold
and attached the bells between the
pomegranates, all around the hem of
the robe between the pomegranates,
[26] a bell and a pomegranate alternating
all around the lower hem of the robe.[k]

---

[a]**39:3** Sam, Syr, Tg read *they*   [b]**39:9** Lit *a span its length and a span its width*   [c]**39:10** Many of these stones cannot
be identified with certainty.   [d]**39:10** Or *beryl*   [e]**39:11** Or *malachite,* or *garnet*   [f]**39:11** Or *lapis lazuli*   [g]**39:11** Hb
uncertain; LXX, Vg read *jasper*   [h]**39:12,23** Hb obscure   [i]**39:20** The place where the shoulder pieces join the front of
the ephod   [j]**39:24** Sam, LXX, Vg add *and linen*   [k]**39:26** Lit *bell and pomegranate, bell and pomegranate, on the hem
of the robe around*

It is to be used for ministry, just as the LORD had commanded Moses.

Other Priestly Garments

27 They made the tunics of fine woven linen for Aaron and his sons. 28 ⌊They also made⌋ the turban and the ornate headbands[a] of fine linen, the undergarments, 29 and the sash of finely spun linen of embroidered blue, purple, and scarlet yarn. ⌊They did⌋ just as the LORD had commanded Moses.

Craftsmen Make the Holy Diadem

30 They also made a plate,[b] the holy diadem, out of pure gold, and wrote on it an inscription like the engraving on a seal:

> HOLY TO THE LORD

31 Then they attached a cord of blue yarn to it in order to mount ⌊it⌋ on the turban, just as the LORD had commanded Moses.

Moses Inspects the Tabernacle

32 So all the work for the tabernacle, the tent of meeting, was finished. The Israelites did everything just as the LORD had commanded Moses. 33 Then they brought the tabernacle to Moses: the tent with all its furnishings, its clasps, its planks, its crossbars, and its posts and bases; 34 the covering of ram skins dyed red and the covering of manatee skins;[c] the veil for the screen; 35 the ark of the •testimony with its poles and the •mercy seat; 36 the table, all its utensils, and the bread of the Presence;[d] 37 the pure ⌊gold⌋ lampstand, with its lamps arranged and all its utensils, as well as the oil for the light; 38 the gold altar; the anointing oil; the fragrant incense; the screen for the entrance to the tent; 39 the bronze altar

with its bronze grate, its poles, and all its utensils; the basin with its stand; 40 the hangings of the courtyard, its posts and bases, the screen for the gate of the courtyard, its ropes and tent pegs, and all the equipment for the service of the tabernacle, the tent of meeting; 41 and the specially woven[e] garments for ministering in the sanctuary, the holy garments for Aaron the priest and the garments for his sons to serve as priests. 42 The Israelites had done all the work according to everything the LORD had commanded Moses. 43 Moses inspected all the work they had accomplished. They had done just as the LORD commanded. Then Moses blessed them.

God Orders Tabernacle Raised

40 The LORD spoke to Moses: 2 "You are to set up the tabernacle, the tent of meeting, on the first day of the first month.[f] 3 Put the ark of the •testimony there, and screen off the ark with the veil. 4 Then bring in the table and lay out its arrangement; also bring in the lampstand and set up its lamps. 5 Place the gold altar for incense in front of the ark of the testimony. Put up the screen for the entrance to the tabernacle. 6 Position the altar of burnt offering in front of the entrance to the tabernacle, the tent of meeting. 7 Place the basin between the tent of meeting and the altar, and put water in it. 8 Assemble the surrounding courtyard and hang the screen for the gate of the courtyard.

9 "Take the anointing oil, and anoint the tabernacle and everything in it; consecrate it along with all its furnishings so that it will be holy. 10 Anoint the altar of burnt offering and all its utensils; consecrate the altar so that it will be especially

---

a**39:28** Lit *and the headdresses of headbands*   b**39:30** Or *medallion*   c**39:34** Or *of dolphin skins*, or *of fine leather*; Hb obscure   d**39:36** Traditionally, *showbread*   e**39:41** Hb obscure   f**40:2** Lit *on the day of the first month, on the first of the month*

holy. [11] Anoint the basin and its stand, and consecrate it.

[12] "Then bring Aaron and his sons to the entrance to the tent of meeting and wash them with water. [13] Clothe Aaron with the holy garments, anoint him, and consecrate him, so that he can serve Me as a priest. [14] Have his sons come forward and clothe them in tunics. [15] Anoint them just as you anointed their father, so that they may also serve Me as priests. Their anointing will serve to inaugurate a permanent priesthood for them throughout their generations."

Moses Obeys

[16] Moses did everything just as the LORD had commanded him. [17] The tabernacle was set up in the first month of the second year, on the first ⌊day⌋ of the month.ª [18] Moses set up the tabernacle: he laid its bases, positioned its planks, inserted its crossbars, and set up its posts. [19] Then he spread the tent over the tabernacle and put the covering of the tent on top of it, just as the LORD had commanded Moses.

[20] Moses took the testimony and placed ⌊it⌋ in the ark, and attached the poles to the ark. He set the •mercy seat on top of the ark. [21] He brought the ark into the tabernacle, put up the veil for the screen, and screened off the ark of the testimony, just as the LORD had commanded him.

[22] Moses placed the table in the tent of meeting on the north side of the tabernacle, outside the veil. [23] He arranged the bread on it before the LORD, just as the LORD had commanded him. [24] He also put the lampstand in the tent of meeting opposite the table on the south side of the tabernacle [25] and set up the lamps before the LORD, just as the LORD had commanded him.

[26] Moses also installed the gold altar in the tent of meeting, in front of the veil, [27] and burned fragrant incense on it, just as the LORD had commanded him. [28] He put up the screen at the entrance to the tabernacle. [29] Then he placed the altar of burnt offering at the entrance to the tabernacle, the tent of meeting, and offered the •burnt offering and the •grain offering on it, just as the LORD had commanded him.

[30] He set the basin between the tent of meeting and the altar and put water in it for washing. [31] Moses, Aaron, and his sons washed their hands and feet from it. [32] They washed whenever they came to the tent of meeting and approached the altar, just as the LORD had commanded Moses.

[33] Next Moses set up the surrounding courtyard for the tabernacle and the altar and hung a screen for the gate of the courtyard. So Moses finished the work.

The LORD's Glory

[34] The cloud covered the tent of meeting, and the glory of the LORD filled the tabernacle. [35] Moses was unable to enter the tent of meeting because the cloud rested on it, and the glory of the LORD filled the tabernacle.

Cloud and Fire

[36] The Israelites set out whenever the cloud was taken up from the tabernacle throughout all the stages of their journey. [37] If the cloud was not taken up, they did not set out until the day it was taken up. [38] For the cloud of the LORD was over the tabernacle by day, and there was a fire inside the cloud by night, visible to the entire house of Israel throughout all the stages of their journey.

ª **40:17** DSS, Sam, LXX add *of their coming out of Egypt*

LEVITICUS

God Guides Moses in Speaking to Israel

Burnt Offering Rules

1 Then the LORD summoned Moses and spoke to him from the tent of meeting: ² "Speak to the Israelites and tell them: When any of you brings an offering to the LORD from the livestock, youᵃ may bring your offering from the herd or the flock.

³ "If his gift is a •burnt offering from the herd, he is to bring an unblemished male. He must bring it to the entrance to the tent of meeting so that heᵇ may be accepted by the LORD. ⁴ He is to lay his hand on the head of the burnt offering so it can be accepted on his behalf to make •atonement for him. ⁵ He is to slaughter the bull before the LORD; Aaron's sons the priests are to present the blood and sprinkle it on all sides of the altar that is at the entrance to the tent of meeting. ⁶ Then he must skin the burnt offering and cut it into pieces.ᶜ ⁷ The sons of Aaron the priest will prepare a fire on the altar and arrange wood on the fire. ⁸ Aaron's sons the priests are to arrange the pieces, the head, and the suet on top of the burning wood on the altar. ⁹ The offerer must wash its entrails and shanks with water. Then the priest will burn all of it on the altar as a burnt offering, a fire offering of a pleasing aroma to the LORD.

¹⁰ "But if his gift for a burnt offering is from the flock, from sheep or goats, he is to present an unblemished male. ¹¹ He will slaughter it on the north side of the altar before the LORD. Aaron's sons the priests will sprinkle its blood against the altar on all sides. ¹² He will cut it into piecesᶜ with its head and its suet, and the priest will arrange them on top of the burning wood on the altar. ¹³ But he is to wash the entrails and shanks with water. The priest will then present all of it and burn ⌞it⌟ on the altar; it is a burnt offering, a fire offering of a pleasing aroma to the LORD.

¹⁴ "If his gift to the LORD is a burnt offering of birds, he is to present his offering from the turtledoves or young pigeons.ᵈ ¹⁵ Then the priest must bring it to the altar, and must twist off its head and burn ⌞it⌟ on the altar; its blood should be drained at the side of the altar. ¹⁶ He will remove its digestive tract,ᵉ cutting off the tail feathers, and throw it on the east side of the altar at the place for ashes. ¹⁷ He will tear it open by its wings without dividing ⌞the bird⌟. Then the priest is to burn it on the altar on top of the burning wood. It is a burnt offering, a fire offering of a pleasing aroma to the LORD.

Grain Offering Rules

2 "When anyone presents a •grain offering as a gift to the LORD, his gift must consist of fine flour.ᶠ He is to pour olive oil on it, put frankincense on it,ᵍ ² and bring it to Aaron's sons the priests. The priest will take a handful of fine flour and oil from it, along with all its frankincense, and will burn this memorial portion of it on the altar, a fire offering of a pleasing aroma to the LORD. ³ But the rest of the grain offering will belong to Aaron and his sons, the holiest part of the fire offerings to the LORD.

ᵃ1:2 Or LORD, from the livestock you ᵇ1:3 Or it ᶜ1:6,12 Lit its pieces ᵈ1:14 Or or pigeons ᵉ1:16 Or its crop, or its crissum ᶠ2:1 Wheat flour; Ex 29:2 ᵍ2:1 DSS, Sam, LXX add it is a grain offering

4 "When you present a grain offering baked in an oven, it must be ⌊made⌋ of fine flour, either unleavened cakes mixed with oil or unleavened wafers coated with oil. 5 If your gift is a grain offering prepared on the griddle, it must be unleavened bread ⌊made⌋ of fine flour mixed with oil. 6 Break it into pieces and pour oil on it; it is a grain offering. 7 If your gift is a grain offering ⌊prepared⌋[a] in a pan, it must be made of fine flour with oil. 8 When you bring[b] to the LORD the grain offering made in any of these ways, it is to be presented to the priest, and he will take it to the altar. 9 The priest will remove the memorial portion[c] from the grain offering and burn it on the altar, a fire offering of a pleasing aroma to the LORD. 10 But the rest of the grain offering will belong to Aaron and his sons, the holiest part of the fire offerings to the LORD.

11 "No grain offering that you present to the LORD is to be made with yeast, for you are not to burn[d] any yeast or honey as a fire offering to the LORD. 12 You may present them to the LORD as an offering of •firstfruits, but they are not to be offered on the altar as a pleasing aroma. 13 You are to season each of your grain offerings with salt; you must not omit from your grain offering the salt of the covenant with your God. You are to present salt[e] with each of your offerings.

14 "If you present a grain offering of firstfruits to the LORD, you must present fresh heads of grain, crushed kernels, roasted on the fire, for your grain offering of firstfruits. 15 You are to put oil and frankincense on it; it is a grain offering. 16 The priest will then burn some of its crushed kernels and oil with all its frankincense as a fire offering to the LORD.

Fellowship Offering Rules

3 "If his offering is a •fellowship sacrifice, and he is presenting ⌊an animal⌋ from the herd, whether male or female, he must present one without blemish before the LORD. 2 He is to lay his hand on the head of his offering and slaughter it at the entrance to the tent of meeting. Then Aaron's sons the priests will sprinkle the blood on all sides of the altar. 3 He will present part of the fellowship sacrifice as a fire offering to the LORD: the fat surrounding the entrails, all the fat that is on the entrails, 4 and the two kidneys with the fat on them at the loins; he will also remove the fatty lobe of the liver with the kidneys. 5 Aaron's sons will burn it on the altar along with the •burnt offering that is on the burning wood, a fire offering of a pleasing aroma to the LORD.

6 "If his offering as a fellowship sacrifice to the LORD is from the flock, he must present a male or female without blemish. 7 If he is presenting a lamb for his offering, he is to present it before the LORD. 8 He must lay his hand on the head of his offering, then slaughter it before the tent of meeting. Aaron's sons will sprinkle its blood on all sides of the altar. 9 He will then present part of the fellowship sacrifice as a fire offering to the LORD ⌊consisting of⌋ its fat and the entire fat tail, which he is to remove close to the backbone. He will also remove the fat surrounding the entrails, all the fat on the entrails, 10 the two kidneys with the fat on them at the loins, and the fatty lobe of the liver above the kidneys. 11 Then the priest will burn it on the altar as food, a fire offering to the LORD.

12 "If his offering is a goat, he is to present it before the LORD. 13 He must lay his hand on its head and slaughter it

---

a 2:7 Or [fried]   b 2:8 DSS, LXX read When he brings   c 2:9 Lit portion of it   d 2:11 Some Hb mss, Sam, LXX, Tg read present   e 2:13 Salt, used as a preservative, is a symbol of the permanence of the covenant.

before the tent of meeting. Aaron's sons will sprinkle[a] its blood on all sides of the altar. [14] He will present part of his offering as a fire offering to the LORD: the fat surrounding the entrails, all the fat that is on the entrails, [15] and the two kidneys with the fat on them at the loins; he will also remove the fatty lobe of the liver with the kidneys. [16] Then the priest will burn them on the altar as food, a fire offering for a pleasing aroma.[b] "All fat belongs to the Lord. [17] This is a permanent statute throughout your generations, wherever you live: you must not eat any fat or any blood."

Sin Offering Rules

4 Then the LORD spoke to Moses: [2] "Tell the Israelites: When someone sins unintentionally against any of the LORD's commands and does anything prohibited by them—

[3] "If the anointed priest[c] sins, bringing guilt on the people, he is to present to the LORD a young, unblemished bull as a •sin[d] offering for the sin he has committed. [4] He must bring the bull to the entrance to the tent of meeting before the LORD, lay his hand on the bull's head, and slaughter it before the LORD. [5] The anointed priest must then take some of the bull's blood and bring it into the tent of meeting. [6] The priest is to dip his finger in the blood and sprinkle some of it seven times before the LORD in front of the veil of the sanctuary. [7] The priest must apply some of the blood to the horns of the altar of fragrant incense that is before the LORD in the tent of meeting. He must pour out the rest of the bull's blood at the base of the altar of burnt offering that is at the entrance to the tent of meeting. [8] He is to remove all the fat from the bull of the sin offering:

the fat surrounding the entrails; all the fat that is on the entrails; [9] and the two kidneys with the fat on them at the loins. He will also remove the fatty lobe of the liver with the kidneys, [10] just as the fat is removed from the ox of the •fellowship sacrifice. The priest is to burn them on the altar of burnt offering. [11] But the hide of the bull and all its flesh, with its head and shanks, and its entrails and dung— [12] all ⌊the rest⌋ of the bull—he must bring to a ceremonially clean place outside the camp to the ash heap, and must burn it on a wood fire. It is to be burned at the ash heap.

[13] "Now if the whole community of Israel errs, and the matter escapes the notice of the assembly, so that they violate any of the LORD's commands and incur guilt by doing what is prohibited, [14] then the assembly must present a young bull as a sin offering. When the sin they have committed in regard to the command becomes known, they are to bring it before the tent of meeting. [15] The elders of the assembly are to lay their hands on the bull's head before the LORD and it is to be slaughtered before the LORD. [16] The anointed priest will bring some of the bull's blood into the tent of meeting. [17] The priest is to dip his finger in the blood and sprinkle ⌊it⌋ seven times before the LORD in front of the veil. [18] He is to apply some of the blood to the horns of the altar that is before the LORD in the tent of meeting. He must pour out the rest of the blood at the base of the altar of burnt offering that is at the entrance to the tent of meeting. [19] He is to remove all the fat from it and burn it on the altar. [20] He is to offer this bull just as he did with the bull in the sin offering; he will offer it the same way. So the priest will make •atonement on their behalf, and

[a] **3:13** Or *dash*   [b] **3:16** Sam, LXX add *to the LORD*   [c] **4:3** Probably the high priest; Lv 6:22   [d] **4:3** Or *purification*

they will be forgiven. ²¹ Then he will bring the bull outside the camp and burn it just as he burned the first bull. It is the sin offering for the assembly.

²² "When a leaderᵃ sins and unintentionally violates any of the commands of the LORD his God by doing what is prohibited, and incurs guilt, ²³ or someone informs him about the sin he has committed, he is to bring an unblemished male goat as his offering. ²⁴ He is to lay his hand on the head of the goat and slaughter it at the place where the •burnt offering is slaughtered before the LORD. It is a sin offering. ²⁵ Then the priest must take some of the blood from the sin offering with his finger and apply it to the horns of the altar of burnt offering. The rest of its blood he must pour out at the base of the altar of burnt offering. ²⁶ He must burn all its fat on the altar, like the fat of the fellowship sacrifice. In this way the priest will make atonement on his behalf for that person's sin, and he will be forgiven.

²⁷ "Now if any of the common peopleᵇ sins unintentionally by violating one of the LORD's commands, does what is prohibited, and incurs guilt, ²⁸ or if someone informs him about the sin he has committed, then he is to bring an unblemished female goat as his offering for the sin that he has committed. ²⁹ He is to lay his hand on the head of the sin offering and slaughter it at the place of the burnt offering. ³⁰ Then the priest must take some of its blood with his finger and apply it to the horns of the altar of burnt offering. He must pour out the rest of its blood at the base of the altar. ³¹ He is to remove all its fat just as the fat is removed from the fellowship sacrifice. The priest is to burn ⌊it⌋ on the altar as a pleasing aroma to the LORD. In this way

the priest will make atonement on his behalf, and he will be forgiven.

³² "Or if the offering that he brings as a sin offering is a lamb, he is to bring an unblemished female. ³³ He is to lay his hand on the head of the sin offering and slaughter it as a sin offering at the place where the burnt offering is slaughtered. ³⁴ Then the priest must take some of the blood of the sin offering with his finger and apply it to the horns of the altar of burnt offering. He must pour out the rest of its blood at the base of the altar. ³⁵ He is to remove all its fat just as the fat of the lamb is removed from the fellowship sacrifice. The priest will burn it on the altar along with the fire offerings to the LORD. In this way the priest will make atonement on his behalf for the sin he has committed, and he will be forgiven.

Offerings— Sins of Omission and Uncleanness

5 "When someone sins ⌊in any of these ways⌋:

⌊If⌋ he has seen, heard, or known about something he has witnessed, and did not respond to a public call to testify, he is guilty. ² Or ⌊if⌋ someone touches anything unclean—a carcass of an unclean wild animal, or unclean livestock, or an unclean swarming creatureᶜ— without being aware of it, he is unclean and guilty. ³ Or ⌊if⌋ he touches human uncleanness—any uncleanness by which one can become defiled—without being aware of it, but ⌊later⌋ recognizes ⌊it⌋, he is guilty. ⁴ Or ⌊if⌋ someone swears rashly to do what is good or evil—concerning anything a person may speak rashly in an oath—without being aware of

---

ᵃ**4:22** Or *ruler*   ᵇ**4:27** Lit *the people of the land*   ᶜ**5:2** = a fish, insect, rodent, or reptile; Lv 11:20-23,29-31; Gn 1:20

it, but ⌊later⌋ recognizes it, he incurs guilt in such an instance.[a]

5 If someone incurs guilt in one of these cases, he is to confess he has committed that sin. 6 He must bring his restitution for the sin he has committed to the LORD: a female lamb or goat from the flock as a •sin offering. In this way the priest will make •atonement on his behalf for his sin.

Rules for the Poor

7 "But if he cannot afford an animal from the flock, then he may bring to the LORD two turtledoves or two young pigeons as restitution for his sin—one as a sin offering and the other as a •burnt offering. 8 He is to bring them to the priest, who will first present the one for the sin offering. He must twist its head at the back of the neck without severing ⌊it⌋. 9 Then he will sprinkle some of the blood of the sin offering on the side of the altar, while the rest of the blood is to be drained out at the base of the altar; it is a sin offering. 10 He must prepare the second ⌊bird⌋ as a burnt offering according to the regulation. In this way the priest will make atonement on his behalf for the sin he has committed, and he will be forgiven.

11 "But if he cannot afford[b] two turtledoves or two young pigeons, he may bring two quarts[c] of fine[d] flour[e] as an offering for his sin. He must not put olive oil or frankincense on it, for it is a sin offering. 12 He is to bring it to the priest, who will take a handful from it as its memorial portion and burn ⌊it⌋ on the altar along with the fire offerings to the LORD; it is a sin offering. 13 In this way the priest will make atonement on his behalf concerning the sin he has committed in

any of these cases, and he will be forgiven. The rest will belong to the priest, like the •grain offering."

Restitution Offering

14 Then the LORD spoke to Moses: 15 "If someone offends by sinning unintentionally in regard to any of the LORD's holy things,[f] he must bring his •restitution offering to the LORD: an unblemished ram from the flock by your valuation in silver •shekels, according to the sanctuary shekel, as a restitution offering. 16 He must make restitution for his sin regarding any holy thing, adding a fifth of its value to it, and give it to the priest. Then the priest will make atonement on his behalf with the ram of the restitution offering, and he will be forgiven.

17 "If someone sins and without knowing ⌊it⌋ violates any of the LORD's commands concerning anything prohibited, he bears the consequences of his guilt. 18 He must bring an unblemished ram from the flock according to your valuation as a restitution offering to the priest. Then the priest will make atonement on his behalf for the error he has committed unintentionally, and he will be forgiven. 19 It is a restitution offering; he is indeed guilty before the LORD."

Sins of Deceit and Fraud

6 [g] The LORD spoke to Moses: 2 "When someone sins and offends the LORD by deceiving his neighbor in regard to a deposit, a security,[h] or a robbery; or defrauds his neighbor; 3 or finds something lost and lies about it; or swears falsely about any of the sinful things a person may do— 4 once he has sinned and acknowledged ⌊his⌋ guilt—he must return what he stole or defrauded, or the

---

[a]5:4 Lit in one of such things   [b]5:11 Lit if his hand is not sufficient for   [c]5:11 Lit one-tenth of an ephah   [d]5:11 Or wheat; Ex 29:2   [e]5:11 Lit flour as a sin offering   [f]5:15 Things dedicated to the LORD such as tabernacle furnishings, priestly portions of the sacrifices, tenths, firstfruits, and firstborn livestock   [g]6:1 Lv 5:20 in Hb   [h]6:2 Or an investment

deposit entrusted to him, or the lost item he found, ⁵or anything else about which he swore falsely. He must make full restitution for it and add a fifth of its value to it. He is to pay it to its owner on the day he acknowledges ⌊his⌋ guilt. ⁶Then he must bring his •restitution offering to the LORD: an unblemished ram from the flock, according to your valuation, as a restitution offering to the priest. ⁷In this way the priest will make •atonement on his behalf before the LORD, and he will be forgiven for anything he may have done to incur guilt."

Burnt Offering Laws

⁸ᵃThe LORD spoke to Moses: ⁹"Command Aaron and his sons: This is the law of the •burnt offering; the burnt offering itself must remain on the altar's hearth all night until morning, while the fire of the altar is kept burning on it. ¹⁰The priest is to put on his linen robe and linen undergarments.ᵇ He is to remove the ashes of the burnt offering the fire has consumed on the altar, and place them beside the altar. ¹¹Then he must take off his garments, put on other clothes, and bring the ashes outside the camp to a ceremonially clean place. ¹²The fire on the altar is to be kept burning; it must not go out. Every morning the priest will burn wood on the fire. He is to arrange the burnt offering on the fire and burn the fat portions from the •fellowship offerings on it. ¹³Fire must be kept burning on the altar continually; it must not go out.

Grain Offering Laws

¹⁴"Now this is the law of the •grain offering: Aaron's sons will present it before the LORD in front of the altar. ¹⁵The priest is to remove a handful of fine flour and olive oil from the grain offering, with all the frankincense that is on the offering, and burn its memorial portion on the altar as a pleasing aroma to the LORD. ¹⁶Aaron and his sons may eat the rest of it. It is to be eaten as unleavened bread in a holy place; they are to eat it in the courtyard of the tent of meeting. ¹⁷It must not be baked with yeast; I have assigned it as their portion from My fire offerings. It is especially holy, like the •sin offering and the restitution offering. ¹⁸Any male among Aaron's descendants may eat it. It is a permanent portionᶜ throughout your generations from the fire offerings to the LORD. Anything that touches the offerings will become holy."

¹⁹The LORD spoke to Moses: ²⁰"This is the offering that Aaron and his sons must present to the LORD on the day that he is anointed: two quartsᵈ of fine flour as a regularᵉ grain offering, half of it in the morning and half in the evening. ²¹It is to be prepared with oil on a griddle; you are to bring it well-kneaded. You must present it as a grain offering of baked pieces,ᶠ a pleasing aroma to the LORD. ²²The priest, who is of Aaron's sons and will be anointed to take his place, is to prepare it. It must be completely burned as a permanent portion for the LORD. ²³Every grain offering for a priest will be a whole burnt offering; it is not to be eaten."

Sin Offering Laws

²⁴The LORD spoke to Moses: ²⁵"Tell Aaron and his sons: This is the law of the sin offering. The sin offering is most holy and must be slaughtered before the LORD at the place where the burnt offering is slaughtered. ²⁶The priest who offers it as a sin offering is to eat it. It must be eaten in a holy place, in the courtyard

---

ᵃ6:8 Lv 6:1 in Hb   ᵇ6:10 Lit undergarments on his flesh   ᶜ6:18 Or statute   ᵈ6:20 Lit a tenth of an ephah
ᵉ6:20 Daily   ᶠ6:21 Hb obscure

of the tent of meeting. [27] Anything that touches its flesh will become holy, and if any of its blood spatters on a garment, then you must wash that garment[a] in a holy place. [28] A clay pot in which the sin offering is boiled must be broken; if it is boiled in a bronze vessel, it must be scoured and rinsed with water. [29] Any male among the priests may eat it; it is especially holy. [30] But no sin offering may be eaten if its blood has been brought into the tent of meeting to make atonement in the holy place; it must be burned up.

Restitution Offering Laws

7 "Now this is the law of the •restitution offering; it is especially holy. [2] The restitution offering must be slaughtered at the place where the •burnt offering is slaughtered, and the priest is to sprinkle its blood on all sides of the altar. [3] The offerer must present all the fat from it: the fat tail, the fat surrounding the entrails,[b] [4] and the two kidneys with the fat on them at the loins; he will also remove the fatty lobe of the liver with the kidneys. [5] The priest will burn them on the altar as a fire offering to the LORD; it is a restitution offering. [6] Any male among the priests may eat it. It is to be eaten in a holy place; it is especially holy. [7] "The restitution offering is like the •sin offering; the law is the same for both. It belongs to the priest who makes •atonement with it. [8] As for the priest who presents someone's burnt offering, the hide of the burnt offering he has presented belongs to him; it is the priest's. [9] Any •grain offering that is baked in an oven, or prepared in a pan or on a griddle, belongs to the priest who presents it; it is his. [10] But any grain offering, whether dry or mixed with oil, belongs equally[c] to all of Aaron's sons.

Fellowship Sacrifice

[11] "Now this is the law of the •fellowship sacrifice that someone may present to the LORD: [12] If he presents it for thanksgiving, in addition to the thanksgiving sacrifice,[d] he is to present unleavened cakes mixed with olive oil, unleavened wafers coated with oil, and well-kneaded cakes of fine flour mixed with oil. [13] He is to present as his offering cakes of leavened bread,[e] with his thanksgiving sacrifice of fellowship. [14] From the cakes he must present one ⌐portion⌐ of each offering as a contribution to the LORD. It will belong to the priest who sprinkles the blood of the fellowship offering; it is his. [15] The meat of his thanksgiving sacrifice of fellowship must be eaten on the day he offers it; he may not leave any of it until morning.

[16] "If the sacrifice he offers is a vow[f] or a freewill offering,[g] it is to be eaten on the day he presents his sacrifice, and what is left over may be eaten on the next day. [17] But what remains of the sacrificial meat by the third day must be burned up. [18] If any of the meat of his fellowship sacrifice is eaten on the third day, it will not be accepted. It will not be credited to the one who presents it; it is repulsive. The person who eats any of it will be guilty.[h]

[19] "Meat that touches anything unclean must not be eaten; it is to be

---

[a]**6:27** Lit *wash what it spattered on*   [b]**7:3** LXX, Sam add *and all the fat that is on the entrails*; Lv 3:3,9,14; 4:8   [c]**7:10** Lit *oil, will be a man like his brother*   [d]**7:12** The *thanksgiving sacrifice* is the first of three kinds of fellowship sacrifices. It was given to express gratitude to God (Jr 33:11) in circumstances such as answered prayer (Ps 50:14-15) or safe travel (Ps 107:22-25).   [e]**7:13** Although yeast was prohibited from being burned on the altar (Lv 2:11), *leavened bread* could still be an offering (Lv 23:17-20) to be eaten by the priests and their families.   [f]**7:16** The *vow offering*, the second category of fellowship sacrifice, was brought as an expression of gratitude to fulfill a vow; Gn 28:20; 2 Sm 15:7-8; Pr 7:14.   [g]**7:16** The *freewill offering*, the third category of fellowship sacrifice, was a voluntary expression of gratitude toward God for any reason; Dt 16:10; Ps 54:6.   [h]**7:18** Or *will bear his guilt*

burned up. Everyone who is clean may eat any ⌊other⌋ meat. 20 But the one who eats meat from the LORD's fellowship sacrifice while he is unclean,ᵃ that person must be cut off from his people. 21 If someone touches anything unclean, whether human uncleanness, an unclean animal, or any unclean, detestableᵇ creature, and eats meat from the LORD's fellowship sacrifice, that person must be cut off from his people."

Fat and Blood Prohibited

22 The LORD spoke to Moses: 23 "Tell the Israelites: You are not to eat any fat of an ox, a sheep, or a goat. 24 The fat of an animal that dies naturally or is mauled by wild beastsᶜ may be used for any purpose, but you must not eat it. 25 If anyone eats animal fat from a fire offering presented to the LORD, the person who eats ⌊it⌋ must be cut off from his people. 26 Wherever you live, you must not eat the blood of any bird or animal. 27 Whoever eats any blood, that person must be cut off from his people."

Portion for the Priests

28 The LORD spoke to Moses: 29 "Tell the Israelites: The one who presents a fellowship sacrifice to the LORD must bring an offering to the LORD from his sacrifice. 30 His own hands will bring the fire offerings to the LORD. He will bring the fat together with the breast. The breast is to be waved as a presentation offering before the LORD. 31 The priest is to burn the fat on the altar, but the breast belongs to Aaron and his sons. 32 You are to give the right thigh to the priest as a contribution from your fellowship sacrifices. 33 The son of Aaron who presents the blood of the fellowship offering and the fat will have the right thigh as a portion. 34 I have taken from the Israelites the breast of the presentation offering and the thigh of the contribution from their fellowship sacrifices, and have assigned them to Aaron the priest and his sons as a permanent portionᵈ from the Israelites."

35 This is the portion from the fire offerings to the LORD for Aaron and his sons since the day they were presented to serve the LORD as priests. 36 The LORD commanded this to be given to them by the Israelites on the day He anointed them. It is a permanent portionᵈ throughout their generations.

37 This is the law for the burnt offering, the grain offering, the sin offering, the restitution offering, the ordination offering, and the fellowship sacrifice, 38 which the LORD commanded Moses on Mount Sinai on the day Heᵉ commanded the Israelites to present their offerings to the LORD in the Wilderness of Sinai.

Ordination of Aaron and His Sons

God Commands

8 The LORD spoke to Moses: 2 "Take Aaron, his sons with him, the garments, the anointing oil, the bull of the •sinᶠ offering, the two rams, and the basket of unleavened bread, 3 and assemble the whole community at the entrance to the tent of meeting." 4 So Moses did as the LORD commanded him, and the community assembled at the entrance to the tent of meeting. 5 Moses said to them, "This is what the LORD has commanded to be done."

ᵃ7:20 Lit while his uncleanness is upon him   ᵇ7:21 Some Hb mss, Sam, Syr, Tg read swarming   ᶜ7:24 Lit fat of a carcass or the fat of a mauled beast   ᵈ7:34,36 Or statute   ᵉ7:38 Or he   ᶠ8:2 Or purification

Moses Presents Aaron and Sons

⁶ Then Moses presented Aaron and his sons and washed them with water. ⁷ He put the tunic on Aaron, wrapped the sash around him, clothed him with the robe, and put the •ephod on him. He put the woven band of the ephod around him and fastened it to him. ⁸ Then he put the breastpiece on him and placed the •Urim and Thummimᵃ into the breastpiece. ⁹ He also put the turban on his head and placed the plateᵇ of gold, the holy diadem, on the front of the turban, as the LORD had commanded Moses.

¹⁰ Then Moses took the anointing oil and anointed the tabernacle and everything in it to consecrate them. ¹¹ He sprinkled some of the oil on the altar seven times, anointing the altar with all its utensils, and the basin with its stand, to consecrate them. ¹² He poured some of the anointing oil on Aaron's head and anointed and consecrated him. ¹³ Then Moses presented Aaron's sons, clothed them with tunics, wrapped sashes around them, and fastened headbands on them, as the LORD had commanded Moses.

Moses Makes Offerings

¹⁴ Then he brought the bull near for the sin offering, and Aaron and his sons laid their hands on the head of the bull for the sin offering. ¹⁵ Then Moses slaughtered ⌊it⌋,ᶜ took the blood, and applied it with his finger to the horns of the altar on all sides, purifying the altar. He poured out the blood at the base of the altar and consecrated it by making •atonement for it. ¹⁶ Moses took all the fat that was on the entrails, the fatty lobe of the liver, and the two kidneys with their fat, and he burned them on the al-

tar. ¹⁷ He burned up the bull with its hide, flesh, and dung outside the camp, as the LORD had commanded Moses.

¹⁸ Then he presented the ram for the •burnt offering, and Aaron and his sons laid their hands on the head of the ram. ¹⁹ Moses slaughtered it andᵈ sprinkled the blood on all sides of the altar. ²⁰ Moses cut the ram into pieces and burned the head, the pieces, and the suet, ²¹ but he washed the entrails and shanks with water. He then burned the entire ram on the altar. It was a burnt offering for a pleasing aroma, a fire offering to the LORD as He had commanded Moses.

²² Next he presented the second ram, the ram of ordination, and Aaron and his sons laid their hands on the head of the ram. ²³ Moses slaughtered ⌊it⌋,ᵉ took some of its blood, and put ⌊it⌋ on Aaron's right earlobe, on the thumb of his right hand, and on the big toe of his right foot. ²⁴ Moses also presented Aaron's sons and put some of the blood on their right earlobes, on the thumbs of their right hands, and on the big toes of their right feet. Then Moses sprinkled the blood on all sides of the altar. ²⁵ He took the fat— the fat tail, all the fat that was on the entrails, the fatty lobe of the liver, and the two kidneys with their fat—as well as the right thigh. ²⁶ From the basket of unleavened bread that was before the LORD he took one cake of unleavened bread, one cake of bread ⌊made⌋ with oil, and one wafer, and placed ⌊them⌋ on the fat portions and the right thigh. ²⁷ He put all ⌊these⌋ in the hands of Aaron and his sons and waved them before the LORD as a presentation offering. ²⁸ Then Moses took them from their hands and burned ⌊them⌋ on the altar with the burnt offering. This was an ordination offering for a

---

ᵃ8:8 Two objects used to determine God's will   ᵇ8:9 Or *medallion*   ᶜ8:14-15 Or *offering, and he slaughtered [it].*
¹⁵ *Then Moses*   ᵈ8:18-19 Or *ram,* ¹⁹ *and he slaughtered it. Moses*   ᵉ8:22-23 Or *ram,* ²³ *and he slaughtered [it]. Moses*

pleasing aroma, a fire offering to the LORD. [29] He also took the breast and waved it before the LORD as a presentation offering; it was Moses' portion of the ordination ram as the LORD had commanded him.

[30] Then Moses took some of the anointing oil and some of the blood that was on the altar and sprinkled ⌊them⌋ on Aaron and his garments, as well as on his sons and their garments. In this way he consecrated Aaron and his garments, as well as his sons and their garments.

[31] Moses said to Aaron and his sons, "Boil the meat at the entrance to the tent of meeting and eat it there with the bread that is in the basket for the ordination offering as I commanded:[a] Aaron and his sons are to eat it. [32] You must burn up what remains of the meat and bread. [33] You must not go outside the entrance to the tent of meeting for seven days, until the time your days of ordination are completed, because it will take seven days to ordain you.[b] [34] The LORD commanded what has been done today in order to make atonement for you. [35] You must remain at the entrance to the tent of meeting day and night for seven days and keep the LORD's charge so that you will not die, for this is what I was commanded." [36] So Aaron and his sons did everything the LORD had commanded through Moses.

The Priestly Ministry Begins

9 On the eighth day Moses summoned Aaron, his sons, and the elders of Israel. [2] He said to Aaron, "Take a young bull for a •sin[c] offering and a ram for a •burnt offering, both without blemish, and present ⌊them⌋ before the LORD. [3] And tell the Israelites:[d] 'Take a male goat for a sin offering; a calf and a lamb,

male yearlings without blemish, for a burnt offering; [4] an ox and a ram for a •fellowship offering to sacrifice before the LORD; and a •grain offering mixed with oil. For today the LORD is going to appear to you.' "

Community Witnesses

[5] They brought what Moses had commanded to the front of the tent of meeting, and the whole community came forward and stood before the LORD. [6] Moses said, "This is what the LORD commanded you to do, that the glory of the LORD may appear to you." [7] Then Moses said to Aaron, "Approach the altar and sacrifice your sin offering and your burnt offering; make •atonement for yourself and the people.[e] Sacrifice the people's offering and make atonement for them, as the LORD commanded."

Aaron Sacrifices

[8] So Aaron approached the altar and slaughtered the calf as a sin offering for himself. [9] Aaron's sons brought the blood to him, and he dipped his finger in the blood and applied it to the horns of the altar. He poured out the blood at the base of the altar. [10] He burned the fat, the kidneys, and the fatty lobe of the liver from the sin offering on the altar, as the LORD had commanded Moses. [11] He burned up the flesh and the hide outside the camp.

[12] Then he slaughtered the burnt offering. Aaron's sons brought him the blood, and he sprinkled it on all sides of the altar. [13] They brought him the burnt offering piece by piece, along with the head, and he burned ⌊them⌋ on the altar. [14] He washed the entrails and the shanks and burned them with the burnt offering on the altar.

---

[a]**8:31** LXX, Syr, Tg read *was commanded*; Ex 29:31-32   [b]**8:33** Lit *because he will fill your hands for seven days*   [c]**9:2** Or *purification*   [d]**9:3** Sam, LXX read *elders of Israel*   [e]**9:7** LXX reads *and your household*

¹⁵ Aaron presented the people's offering. He took the male goat for the people's sin offering, slaughtered it, and made a sin offering with it as he did before. ¹⁶ He presented the burnt offering and sacrificed it according to the regulation. ¹⁷ Next he presented the grain offering, took a handful of it, and burned it on the altar in addition to the morning burnt offering.

¹⁸ Finally, he slaughtered the ox and the ram as the people's fellowship sacrifice. Aaron's sons brought him the blood, and he sprinkled it on all sides of the altar. ¹⁹ They also brought the fat portions from the ox and the ram—the fat tail, the ₍fat₎ surrounding ₍the entrails₎, the kidneys, and the fatty lobe of the liver— ²⁰ and placed these on the breasts. Aaron burned the fat portions on the altar, ²¹ but he waved the breasts and the right thigh as a presentation offering before the LORD, as Moses had commanded.[a]

²² Aaron lifted up his hands toward the people and blessed them. He came down after sacrificing the sin offering, the burnt offering, and the fellowship offering. ²³ Moses and Aaron then entered the tent of meeting. When they came out, they blessed the people, and the glory of the LORD appeared to all the people. ²⁴ Fire came out from the LORD and consumed the burnt offering and the fat portions on the altar. And when all the people saw it, they shouted and fell facedown ₍on the ground₎.

Nadab and Abihu Disobey

10 Aaron's sons Nadab and Abihu each took his own firepan, put fire in it, placed incense on it, and presented unauthorized fire before the LORD, which He had not commanded them ₍to do₎. ² Then flames leaped from the LORD's presence and burned them to death before the LORD. ³ So Moses said to Aaron, "This is what the LORD meant when He said:

> I will show My holiness[b]
> to those who are near Me,
> and I will reveal My glory[c]
> before all the people."

But Aaron remained silent.

⁴ Moses summoned Mishael and Elzaphan, sons of Aaron's uncle Uzziel, and said to them, "Come here and carry your relatives away from the front of the sanctuary to ₍a place₎ outside the camp." ⁵ So they came forward and carried them in their tunics outside the camp, as Moses had said.

⁶ Then Moses said to Aaron and his sons Eleazar and Ithamar, "Do not let your hair hang loose and do not tear your garments, or else you will die, and the LORD will become angry with the whole community. However, your brothers, the whole house of Israel, may mourn over that tragedy when the LORD sent the fire. ⁷ You must not go outside the entrance to the tent of meeting or you will die, for the LORD's anointing oil is on you." So they did as Moses said.

Regulations for Priests

⁸ The LORD spoke to Aaron: ⁹ "You and your sons are not to drink wine or beer when you enter the tent of meeting, or else you will die; this is a permanent statute throughout your generations. ¹⁰ You must distinguish between the holy and the common, and the clean and the unclean, ¹¹ and teach the Israelites all the statutes that the LORD has given to them through Moses."

---

[a]**9:21** Some Hb mss, LXX, Sam read *as the LORD commanded Moses*   [b]**10:3** Or *will be treated as holy*   [c]**10:3** Or *will be glorified*

Moses Instructs Aaron and Sons

[12] Moses spoke to Aaron and his remaining sons, Eleazar and Ithamar: "Take the •grain offering that is left over from the fire offerings to the LORD, and eat it prepared without yeast beside the altar, because it is especially holy. [13] You must eat it in a holy place because it is your portion[a] and your sons' from the fire offerings to the LORD, for this is what I was commanded. [14] But you and your sons and your daughters may eat the breast of the presentation offering and the thigh of the contribution in any ceremonially clean place, because these portions have been assigned to you and your children from the Israelites' •fellowship sacrifices. [15] They are to bring the thigh of the contribution and the breast of the presentation offering, together with the offerings of fat portions made by fire, to wave as a presentation offering before the LORD. It will belong permanently to you and your children, as the LORD commanded."

[16] Later, Moses inquired about the male goat of the •sin offering, but it had already been burned up. He was angry with Eleazar and Ithamar, Aaron's surviving sons, and asked, [17] "Why didn't you eat the sin offering in the sanctuary area? For it is especially holy, and He has assigned it to you to take away the guilt of the community and make •atonement for them before the LORD. [18] Since its blood was not brought inside the sanctuary, you should have eaten it in the sanctuary ⌊area⌋, as I commanded."

[19] But Aaron replied to Moses, "See, today they presented their sin offering and their •burnt offering before the LORD. Since these things have happened to me, if I had eaten the sin offering today, would it have been acceptable in the LORD's sight?" [20] When Moses heard this, it was acceptable to him.[b]

Clean and Unclean

Land Animals

11 The LORD spoke to Moses and Aaron: [2] "Tell the Israelites: You may eat all these ⌊kinds⌋ of land animals. [3] You may eat any animal with divided hooves and that chews the cud. [4] But among the ones that chew the cud or have hooves you are not to eat ⌊these⌋:

> the camel, though it chews the cud, does not have hooves—it is unclean for you;
>
> [5] the hyrax,[c] though it chews the cud, does not have hooves—it is unclean for you;
>
> [6] the hare, though it chews the cud, does not have hooves—it is unclean for you;
>
> [7] the pig, though it has divided hooves, does not chew the cud—it is unclean for you.

[8] Do not eat any of their meat or touch their carcasses—they are unclean for you.

Aquatic Animals

[9] "This ⌊is what⌋ you may eat from all that is in the water: You may eat everything in the water that has fins and scales, whether in the seas or streams. [10] But these are to be detestable to you: everything that does not have fins and scales in the seas or streams, among all the swarming things and ⌊other⌋ living creatures in the water. [11] They are to remain detestable to you; you must not eat any of their meat, and you must detest their carcasses. [12] Everything in the water that does not have fins and scales will be detestable to you.

---

[a]**10:13** Or *statute*   [b]**10:20** Lit *acceptable in his sight*   [c]**11:5** A rabbit-like animal

Unclean Birds

13 "You are to detest these birds. They must not be eaten because they are detestable:

the eagle,[a] the bearded[b] vulture,
the black vulture,[c] 14 the kite,[d]
the various kinds of falcon,[e]
15 every kind of raven, 16 the ostrich,[f]
the short-eared owl,[g] the gull,[h]
the various kinds of hawk,
17 the little[i] owl, the cormorant,[j]
the long-eared owl,[k]
18 the white[l] owl, the desert owl,[m]
the osprey,[n] 19 the stork,[o]
the various kinds of heron,[p]
the hoopoe, and the bat.

Clean and Unclean Flying Insects

20 "All winged insects that walk on all fours are to be detestable to you. 21 But you may eat these kinds of all the winged insects that walk on all fours: those that have jointed legs above their feet for hopping on the ground. 22 You may eat these:

the various kinds of locust,
the various kinds of katydid,
the various kinds of cricket,
and the various kinds
of grasshopper.

23 All [other] winged insects that have four feet are to be detestable to you.

Purification after Touching Carcasses

24 "These will make you unclean. Whoever touches their carcasses will be unclean until evening, 25 and whoever carries any of their carcasses must wash his clothes and will be unclean until evening. 26 All animals that have hooves but do not have a divided hoof and do not chew the cud are unclean for you. Whoever touches them becomes unclean. 27 All the four-footed animals that walk on their paws are unclean for you. Whoever touches their carcasses will be unclean until evening, 28 and anyone who carries their carcasses must wash his clothes and will be unclean until evening. They are unclean for you.

29 "These creatures that swarm on the ground are unclean for you:

the weasel,[q] the mouse,
the various kinds of large lizard,[r]
30 the gecko, the monitor lizard,[s]
the common lizard,[t] the skink,[u]
and the chameleon.[v]

31 These are unclean for you among all the swarming creatures. Whoever touches them when they are dead will be unclean until evening. 32 When any one of them dies and falls on anything it becomes unclean—any item of wood, clothing, leather, •sackcloth, or any implement used for work. It is to be rinsed with water and will remain unclean until evening; then it will be clean. 33 If any of them falls into any clay pot, everything in it will become unclean; you must break it. 34 Any edible food coming into contact with [that unclean] water will become unclean, and any drinkable liquid in any container will become unclean. 35 Anything one of their carcasses falls on will become unclean. If it is an oven or stove, it must be smashed; it is unclean and will remain unclean for you.

---

[a]11:13 Or griffon-vulture   [b]11:13 Or black   [c]11:13 Or the osprey, or the bearded vulture   [d]11:14 Or hawk
[e]11:14 Or buzzards, or hawks   [f]11:16 Or eagle owl   [g]11:16 Or the night hawk, or the screech owl   [h]11:16 Or long-eared owl   [i]11:17 Or tawny   [j]11:17 Or fisher owl, or pelican   [k]11:17 Or the ibis   [l]11:18 Or little   [m]11:18 Or the pelican, or the horned owl   [n]11:18 Or Egyptian vulture   [o]11:19 Or heron   [p]11:19 Or cormorant, or hawk   [q]11:29 Or mole rat, or rat   [r]11:29 Or of thorn-tailed or dabb lizard, or of crocodile   [s]11:30 Or the spotted lizard, or the chameleon   [t]11:30 Or the gecko, or the newt, or the salamander   [u]11:30 Or sand lizard, or newt, or snail   [v]11:30 Or salamander, or mole

36 A spring or cistern containing water will remain clean, but someone who touches a carcass ⌊in it⌋ will become unclean. 37 If one of their carcasses falls on any seed that is to be sown, it is clean; 38 but if water has been put on the seed and one of their carcasses falls on it, it is unclean for you.

39 "If one of the animals that you use for food dies,a anyone who touches its carcass will be unclean until evening. 40 Anyone who eats some of its carcass must wash his clothes and will be unclean until evening. Anyone who carries its carcass must wash his clothes and will be unclean until evening.

Unclean Swarming Creatures

41 "All the creatures that swarm on the earth are detestable; they must not be eaten. 42 Do not eat any of the creatures that swarm on the earth, anything that moves on its belly or walks on all fours or on many feet,b for they are detestable. 43 Do not become contaminated by any creature that swarms; do not become unclean or defiled by them. 44 For I am the LORD your God, so you must consecrate yourselves and be holy because I am holy. You must not defile yourselves by any swarming creature that crawls on the ground. 45 For I am the LORD, who brought you up from the land of Egypt to be your God, so you must be holy because I am holy.

46 "This is the law concerning animals, birds, all living creatures that move in the water, and all creatures that swarm on the ground, 47 in order to distinguish between the unclean and the clean, between the animals that may be eaten and those that may not be eaten."

Childbirth: Purification

12 The LORD spoke to Moses: 2 "Tell the Israelites: When a woman becomes pregnant and gives birth to a male child, she will be unclean seven days, as she is during the days of her menstrual impurity. 3 The flesh of his foreskin must be circumcised on the eighth day. 4 She will continue in purification from her bleeding for 33 days. She must not touch any holy thing or go into the sanctuary until completing her days of purification. 5 But if she gives birth to a female child, she will be unclean for two weeks as ⌊she is⌋ during her ⌊menstrual⌋ impurity. She will continue in purification from her bleeding for 66 days.

Offerings after Purification

6 "When her days of purification are complete, whether for a son or daughter, she is to bring to the priest at the entrance to the tent of meeting a year-old male lamb for a •burnt offering, and a young pigeon or a turtledove for a •sinc offering. 7 He will present them before the LORD and make •atonement on her behalf; she will be clean from her discharge of blood. This is the law for a woman giving birth, whether to a male or female. 8 But if she doesn't have sufficient meansd for a sheep, she may take two turtledoves or two young pigeons, one for a burnt offering and the other for a sinc offering. Then the priest will make atonement on her behalf, and she will be clean."

Skin Diseases

Swelling, Scab, Spot

13 The LORD spoke to Moses and Aaron: 2 "When a person has a swelling,e scab,f or spot on the skin of his

---

a11:39 Dies of itself or by predators; this does not apply to animals slaughtered for food.   b11:42 Lit fours, to anything multiplying pairs of feet   c12:6,8 Or purification   d12:8 Lit if her hand cannot obtain what is sufficient   e13:2 Or discoloration   f13:2 Or rash, or eruption

body, and it becomes a disease on the skin of his body, he is to be brought to Aaron the priest or to one of his sons, the priests. ³ The priest will examine the infection on the skin of his body. If the hair in the infection has turned white and the infection appears to be deeper than the skin of his body, it is a skin disease. After the priest examines him, he must pronounce him unclean. ⁴ But if the spot on the skin of his body is white and does not appear to be deeper than the skin, and the hair in it has not turned white, the priest must quarantine the infected person for seven days. ⁵ The priest will then reexamine him on the seventh day. If the infection remains unchanged in his sight and has not spread on the skin, the priest must quarantine him for another seven days. ⁶ The priest will examine him again on the seventh day. If the infection has faded and has not spread on the skin, the priest is to pronounce him clean; it is a scab. The person is to wash his clothes and will become clean. ⁷ But if the scab spreads further on his skin after he has presented himself to the priest for his cleansing, he must present himself again to the priest. ⁸ The priest will examine him, and if the scab has spread on the skin, then the priest must pronounce him unclean; he has a skin disease.

⁹ "When a skin disease develops on a person, he is to be brought to the priest. ¹⁰ The priest will examine him. If there is a white swelling on the skin that has turned the hair white, and there is a patch of raw flesh in the swelling, ¹¹ it is a chronic disease on the skin of his body, and the priest must pronounce him unclean. He need not quarantine him, for he is unclean. ¹² But if the skin disease breaks out completely over the

skin so that it covers all the skin of the infected person from his head to his feet so far as the priest can see, ¹³ the priest will look, and if the skin disease has covered his entire body, he is to pronounce the infected person clean. Since he has turned totally white, he is clean. ¹⁴ But whenever raw flesh appears on him, he will be unclean. ¹⁵ When the priest examines the raw flesh, he must pronounce him unclean. Raw flesh is unclean; it is a skin disease. ¹⁶ But if the raw flesh changesᵃ andᵇ turns white, he must go to the priest. ¹⁷ The priest will examine him, and if the infection has turned white, the priest must pronounce the infected person clean; he is clean.

Boil

¹⁸ "When a boil appears on the skin of one's body and it heals, ¹⁹ and a white swelling or a reddish-white spot develops where the boil was, the person must present himself to the priest. ²⁰ The priest will make an examination, and if the spot seems to be beneath the skin and the hair in it has turned white, the priest must pronounce him unclean; it is a skin disease that has broken out in the boil. ²¹ But when the priest examines it, if there is no white hair in it, and it is not beneath the skin but is faded, the priest must quarantine him seven days. ²² If it spreads further on the skin, the priest must pronounce him unclean; it is an infection. ²³ But if the spot remains where it is and does not spread, it is ⌊only⌋ the scar from the boil. The priest is to pronounce him clean.

Burn

²⁴ "When there is a burn on the skin of one's body produced by fire, and the

patch made raw by the burn becomes a reddish-white or white spot, ²⁵ the priest is to examine it. If the hair in the spot has turned white and the spot appears to be deeper than the skin, it is a skin disease that has broken out in the burn. The priest must pronounce him unclean; it is a skin disease. ²⁶ But when the priest examines it, if there is no white hair in the spot and it is not beneath the skin but is faded, the priest must quarantine him seven days. ²⁷ The priest will reexamine him on the seventh day. If it has spread further on the skin, the priest must pronounce him unclean; it is a skin disease. ²⁸ But if the spot has remained where it was and has not spread on the skin but is faded, it is the swelling from the burn. The priest is to pronounce him clean, for it is ⌊only⌋ the scar from the burn.

Head Infection

²⁹ "When a man or woman has an infection on the head or chin, ³⁰ the priest must examine the infection. If it appears to be deeper than the skin, and the hair in it is yellow and sparse, the priest must pronounce the person unclean. It is a scaly outbreak,ᵃ a skin disease of the head or chin. ³¹ When the priest examines the scaly infection, if it does not appear to be deeper than the skin, and there is no black hair in it, the priest must quarantine the person with the scaly infection for seven days. ³² The priest will reexamine the infection on the seventh day. If the scaly outbreak has not spread and there is no yellow hair in it and it does not appear to be deeper than the skin, ³³ the person must shave himself but not shave the scaly area. Then the priest must quarantine the person who has the scaly outbreak

for another seven days. ³⁴ The priest will examine the scaly outbreak on the seventh day, and if it has not spread on the skin and does not appear to be deeper than the skin, the priest is to pronounce the person clean. He is to wash his clothes, and he will be clean. ³⁵ But if the scaly outbreak spreads further on the skin after his cleansing, ³⁶ the priest is to examine the person. If the scaly outbreak has spread on the skin, the priest does not need to look for yellow hair; the person is unclean. ³⁷ But if as far as he can see, the scaly outbreak remains unchanged and black hair has grown in it, then it has healed; he is clean. The priest is to pronounce the person clean.

White Spots

³⁸ "When a man or a woman has white spots on the skin of the body, ³⁹ the priest is to make an examination. If the spots on the skin of the body are dull white, it is ⌊only⌋ a rashᵇ that has broken out on the skin; the person is clean.

Baldness

⁴⁰ "If a man loses the hair of his head, he is bald, but he is clean. ⁴¹ Or if he loses the hair at his hairline, he is bald on his forehead, but he is clean. ⁴² But if there is a reddish-white infection on the bald head or forehead, it is a skin disease breaking out on his head or forehead. ⁴³ The priest is to examine him, and if the swelling of the infection on his bald head or forehead is reddish-white, like the appearance of a skin disease on his body, ⁴⁴ the man is afflicted with a skin disease; he is unclean. The priest must pronounce him unclean; the infection is on his head.

ᵃ**13:30** Or *is scall*; Hb obscure   ᵇ**13:39** Hb obscure

Rules for Warning Others

45 "The person afflicted with an infectious skin disease is to have his clothes torn and his hair hanging loose, and he must cover his mouth and cry out, 'Unclean, unclean!' 46 He will remain unclean as long as he has the infection; he is unclean. He must live alone in a place outside the camp.

Contaminated Fabric and Leather

47 "If a fabric is contaminated with mildew—in wool or linen fabric, 48 in the warp or woof of linen or wool, or in leather or anything made of leather— 49 and if the contamination is green or red in the fabric, the leather, the warp, the woof, or any leather article, it is a mildew contamination and is to be shown to the priest. 50 The priest is to examine the contamination and quarantine the contaminated fabric for seven days. 51 The priest is to reexamine the contamination on the seventh day. If it has spread in the fabric, the warp, the woof, or the leather, regardless of how it is used, the contamination is harmful mildew; it is unclean. 52 He is to burn the fabric, the warp or woof in wool or linen, or any leather article, which is contaminated. Since it is harmful mildew it must be burned up.

53 "When the priest examines ⌊it⌋, if the contamination has not spread in the fabric, the warp or woof, or any leather article, 54 the priest is to order whatever is contaminated to be washed and quarantined for another seven days. 55 After it has been washed, the priest is to reexamine the contamination. If the appearance of the contaminated article has not changed, it is unclean. Even though the contamination has not spread, you must burn up the fabric. It is a fungus[a] on the front or back ⌊of the fabric⌋.

56 "If the priest examines ⌊it⌋, and the contamination has faded after it has been washed, he must cut the contaminated section out of the fabric, the leather, or the warp or woof. 57 But if it reappears in the fabric, the warp or woof, or any leather article, it has broken out again. You must burn up whatever is contaminated. 58 But if the contamination disappears from the fabric, the warp or woof, or any leather article, which have been washed, it is to be washed again, and it will be clean.

59 "This is the law concerning a mildew contamination in wool or linen fabric, warp or woof, or any leather article, in order to pronounce it clean or unclean."

Cleansing Skin Diseases

Priest Examines

14 The LORD spoke to Moses: 2 "This is the law concerning the person afflicted with a skin disease on the day of his cleansing. He is to be brought to the priest, 3 who will go outside the camp and examine ⌊him⌋. If the skin disease has disappeared from the afflicted person,[b] 4 the priest will order that two live clean birds, cedar wood, scarlet yarn, and hyssop be brought for the one who is to be cleansed.

Priest Sacrifices

5 Then the priest will order that one of the birds be slaughtered over fresh water in a clay pot. 6 He is to take the live bird together with the cedar wood, scarlet yarn, and hyssop, and dip them all into the blood of the bird that was slaughtered over the fresh water. 7 He will then sprinkle ⌊the blood⌋ seven times on the

---

[a]13:55 Hb obscure   [b]14:3 Lit *the person afflicted with skin disease*

one who is to be cleansed from the skin disease. He is to pronounce him clean and release the live bird over the open countryside.

Wash, Shave, Sacrifice

[8] The one who is to be cleansed must wash his clothes, shave off all his hair, and bathe with water; he is clean. Afterwards he may enter the camp, but he must remain outside his tent for seven days. [9] He is to shave off all his hair ⌊again⌋ on the seventh day: his head, his beard, his eyebrows, and the rest of his hair. He is to wash his clothes and bathe himself with water; he is clean.

[10] "On the eighth day he must take two unblemished male lambs, an un-blemished year-old ewe lamb, a •grain of-fering of three quarts[a] of fine flour mixed with olive oil, and one-third of a quart[b] of olive oil. [11] The priest who performs the cleansing will place the person who is to be cleansed, together with these of-ferings, before the LORD at the entrance to the tent of meeting. [12] The priest is to take one male lamb and present it as a •restitution offering, along with the one-third quart[b] of olive oil, and he must wave them as a presentation offering be-fore the LORD. [13] He is to slaughter the male lamb at the place in the sanctuary area where the •sin offering and •burnt offering are slaughtered, for like the sin offering, the restitution offering belongs to the priest; it is especially holy. [14] The priest is to take some of the blood from the restitution offering and put ⌊it⌋ on the lobe of the right ear of the one to be cleansed, on the thumb of his right hand, and on the big toe of his right foot. [15] Then the priest will take some of the one-third of a quart[b] of olive oil and pour it into his left palm. [16] The priest will dip his right finger into the oil in his left palm and sprinkle some of the oil with his finger seven times before the LORD. [17] From the oil remaining in his palm the priest will put some on the lobe of the right ear of the one to be cleansed, on the thumb of his right hand, and on the big toe of his right foot, on top of the blood of the restitution offering. [18] What is left of the oil in the priest's palm he is to put on the head of the one to be cleansed. In this way the priest will make •atonement for him before the LORD. [19] The priest must sacrifice the sin offering and make atonement for the one to be purified from his uncleanness. Af-terwards he will slaughter the burnt of-fering. [20] The priest is to offer the burnt offering and the grain offering on the al-tar. The priest will make atonement for him, and he will be clean.

Provision for the Poor

[21] "But if he is poor and cannot afford ⌊these⌋,[c] he is to take one male lamb for a restitution offering to be waved in or-der to make atonement for him, along with two quarts[d] of fine flour mixed with olive oil for a grain offering, one-third of a quart[b] of olive oil, [22] and two turtledoves or two young pigeons, whatever he can afford,[e] one to be a sin offering and the other a burnt offering. [23] On the eighth day he is to bring these things for his cleansing to the priest at the entrance to the tent of meeting be-fore the LORD. [24] The priest will take the male lamb for the restitution offer-ing and the one-third of a quart[b] of olive oil, and wave them as a presentation of-fering before the LORD. [25] After he slaughters the male lamb for the restitu-tion offering, the priest is to take some of the blood of the restitution offering

---

[a] **14:10** Lit three-tenths; probably of an ephah   [b] **14:10,12,15,21,24** Lit one log   [c] **14:21** Lit and his hand is not
[d] **14:21** Lit him, and one-tenth; probably 1/10 of an ephah   [e] **14:22** Lit pigeons, for which his hand is sufficient

and put ⌊it⌋ on the right earlobe of the one to be cleansed, on the thumb of his right hand, and on the big toe of his right foot. ²⁶ Then the priest will pour some of the oil into his left palm. ²⁷ With his right finger the priest will sprinkle some of the oil in his left palm seven times before the LORD. ²⁸ The priest will also put some of the oil in his palm on the right earlobe of the one to be cleansed, on the thumb of his right hand, and on the big toe of his right foot, on the ⌊same⌋ place as the blood of the restitution offering. ²⁹ What is left of the oil in the priest's palm he is to put on the head of the one to be cleansed to make atonement for him before the LORD. ³⁰ He must then sacrifice one type of what he can afford,^a either the turtle-doves or young pigeons, ³¹ one as a sin offering and the other as a burnt offering, ⌊sacrificing⌋ what he can afford^b ^c together with the grain offering. In this way the priest will make atonement before the LORD for the one to be cleansed. ³² This is the law for someone who has^d a skin disease and cannot afford^e the cost of his cleansing."

Cleansing Contaminated Objects

House Mildew

³³ The LORD spoke to Moses and Aaron: ³⁴ "When you enter the land of Canaan that I am giving you as a possession, and I place a mildew contamination in a house in the land you possess,^f ³⁵ the owner of the house is to come and tell the priest: Something like mildew contamination has appeared^g in my house. ³⁶ The priest must order them to clear the house before he enters to ex-

amine the contamination, so that nothing in the house becomes unclean. Afterwards the priest will come to examine the house. ³⁷ He will examine it, and if the contamination in the walls of the house consists of green or red indentations^h that appear to be beneath the surface of the wall, ³⁸ the priest is to go outside the house to its doorway and quarantine the house for seven days. ³⁹ The priest is to return on the seventh day and examine it. If the contamination has spread on the walls of the house, ⁴⁰ the priest must order that the stones with the contamination be pulled out and thrown into an unclean place outside the city. ⁴¹ He is to have the inside of the house completely scraped, and the plasterⁱ that is scraped off must be dumped in an unclean place outside the city. ⁴² Then they must take different stones to replace the ⌊former⌋ ones and take additional plasterⁱ to re-plaster the house.

If Mildew Reappears?

⁴³ "If the contamination reappears in the house after the stones have been pulled out, and after the house has been scraped and replastered, ⁴⁴ the priest must come and examine it. If the contamination has spread in the house, it is harmful mildew; the house is unclean. ⁴⁵ It must be torn down with its stones, its beams, and all its plaster, and taken outside the city to an unclean place. ⁴⁶ Whoever enters the house during any of the days the priest quarantines it will be unclean until evening. ⁴⁷ Whoever lies down in the house is to wash his clothes, and whoever eats in it is to wash his clothes.

---

^a**14:30** Lit of that for which his hand is sufficient ^b**14:31** LXX, Syr, Vg omit what he can afford ^c**14:31** Lit [sacrificing] that for which his hand is sufficient ^d**14:32** Lit someone on whom there is ^e**14:32** Lit disease whose hand is not sufficient for ^f**14:34** Lit land of your possession ^g**14:35** Lit appeared to me ^h**14:37** Or eruptions; Hb obscure ⁱ**14:41,42** Lit dust

Clean House

48 "But when the priest comes and examines it, if the contamination has not spread in the house after it was replastered, he is to pronounce the house clean because the contamination has disappeared.[a] 49 He is to take two birds, cedar wood, scarlet yarn, and hyssop to purify the house, 50 and he is to slaughter one of the birds over a clay pot containing fresh water. 51 He will take the cedar wood, the hyssop, the scarlet yarn, and the live bird, dip them in the blood of the slaughtered bird and the fresh water, and sprinkle the house seven times. 52 He will purify the house with the blood of the bird, the fresh water, the live bird, the cedar wood, the hyssop, and the scarlet yarn. 53 Then he is to release the live bird into the open countryside outside the city. In this way he will make atonement for the house, and it will be clean.

54 "This is the law for any skin disease or mildew, for a scaly outbreak,[b] 55 for mildew in clothing or on a house, 56 and for a swelling, scab, or spot, 57 to determine when something is unclean or clean. This is the law regarding skin disease and mildew."

Bodily Discharges

15 The LORD spoke to Moses and Aaron: 2 "Speak to the Israelites and tell them: When any man has a discharge from his body, he is unclean. 3 This is uncleanness of his discharge: Whether his body secretes the discharge or retains it, he is unclean. All the days that his body secretes or retains anything because of his discharge,[c] he is unclean.[d] 4 Any bed the man with the discharge lies on will be unclean, and any furniture he sits on will be unclean.

5 Anyone who touches his bed is to wash his clothes and bathe with water, and he will remain unclean until evening. 6 Whoever sits on furniture that the man with the discharge was sitting on is to wash his clothes and bathe with water, and he will remain unclean until evening. 7 Whoever touches the body of the man with a discharge is to wash his clothes and bathe with water, and he will remain unclean until evening. 8 If the man with the discharge spits on anyone who is clean, he is to wash his clothes and bathe with water, and he will remain unclean until evening. 9 Any saddle the man with the discharge rides on will be unclean. 10 Whoever touches anything that was under him will be unclean until evening, and whoever carries such things is to wash his clothes and bathe with water, and he will remain unclean until evening. 11 If the man with the discharge touches anyone without ⌊first⌋ rinsing his hands in water, the person who was touched is to wash his clothes and bathe with water, and he will remain unclean until evening. 12 Any clay pot that the man with the discharge touches must be broken, while any wooden utensil must be rinsed with water.

Cleansing Procedure

13 "When the man with the discharge has been cured of it, he is to count seven days for his cleansing, wash his clothes, and bathe his body in fresh water; he will be clean. 14 He must take two turtledoves or two young pigeons on the eighth day, come before the LORD at the entrance to the tent of meeting, and give them to the priest. 15 The priest is to sacrifice them, one as a •sin offering and the other as a •burnt offering. In this way

---

a **14:48** Lit *healed*   b **14:54** Or *for a scall*   c **15:3** DSS, Sam, LXX; MT omits *he is unclean. All the days that his body secretes or retains anything because of his discharge*   d **15:3** A urinary tract infection

the priest will make •atonement for him before the LORD because of his discharge.

Emission of Semen

16 "When a man has an emission of semen, he is to bathe himself completely with water, and he will remain unclean until evening. 17 Any clothing or leather on which there is an emission of semen must be washed with water, and it will remain unclean until evening. 18 If a man sleeps with a woman and has an emission of semen, both of them are to bathe with water, and they will remain unclean until evening.

Female Discharge

19 "When a woman has a discharge, and it consists of blood from her body, she will be unclean because of her menstruation for seven days. Everyone who touches her will be unclean until evening. 20 Anything she lies on during her menstruation will become unclean, and anything she sits on will become unclean. 21 Everyone who touches her bed is to wash his clothes and bathe with water, and he will remain unclean until evening. 22 Everyone who touches any furniture she was sitting on is to wash his clothes and bathe with water, and he will remain unclean until evening. 23 If discharge is on the bed or the furniture she was sitting on, when he touches it he will be unclean until evening. 24 If a man sleeps with her, and ⌊blood from⌋ her menstruation gets on him, he will be unclean for seven days, and every bed he lies on will become unclean.

25 "When a woman has a discharge of her blood for many days, though it is not the time of her menstruation, or if she has a discharge beyond her period, she will be unclean all the days of her unclean discharge, as ⌊she is⌋ during the days of her menstruation. 26 Any bed she lies on during the days of her discharge will be like her bed during menstrual impurity; any furniture she sits on will be unclean as in her menstrual period. 27 Everyone who touches them will be unclean; he must wash his clothes and bathe with water, and he will remain unclean until evening. 28 When she is cured of her discharge, she is to count seven days, and after that she will be clean. 29 On the eighth day she must take two turtledoves or two young pigeons and bring them to the priest at the entrance to the tent of meeting. 30 The priest is to sacrifice one as a sin offering and the other as a burnt offering. In this way the priest will make atonement for her before the LORD because of her unclean discharge.

31 "You must keep the Israelites from their uncleanness, so that they do not die by defiling My tabernacle that is among them. 32 This is the law for someone with a discharge: a man who has an emission of semen, becoming unclean by it; 33 a woman who is in her menstrual period; anyone who has a discharge, whether male or female; and a man who sleeps with an unclean woman."

The Day of Atonement

16 The LORD spoke to Moses after the death of two of Aaron's sons when they approached the presence of[a] the LORD and died. 2 The LORD said to Moses: "Tell your brother Aaron that he may not come whenever he wants into the holy place behind the veil in front of the •mercy seat on the ark or else he will

---

[a]**16:1** LXX, Tg, Syr, Vg read *they brought strange fire before*; Nm 3:4

die, because I appear in the cloud above the mercy seat.

Restrictions on Aaron in Tabernacle

3 "Aaron is to enter the ⌊most⌋ holy place in this way: with a young bull for a •sin offering and a ram for a •burnt offering. 4 He is to wear a holy linen tunic, and linen undergarments are to be on his body. He must tie a linen sash ⌊around him⌋ and wrap his head with a linen turban. These are holy garments; he must bathe his body with water before he wears them. 5 He is to take from the Israelite community two male goats for a sin offering and one ram for a burnt offering.

Two Goats

6 "Aaron will present the bull for his sin offering and make •atonement for himself and his household. 7 Next he will take the two goats and place them before the LORD at the entrance to the tent of meeting. 8 After Aaron casts lots for the two goats, one lot for the LORD and the other for Azazel,a 9 he is to present the goat chosen by lot for the LORD and sacrifice it as a sin offering. 10 But the goat chosen by lot for Azazel is to be presented alive before the LORD to make purification with it by sending it into the wilderness for Azazel.

Sacrifice of Bull and Goat

11 "When Aaron presents the bull for his sin offering and makes atonement for himself and his household, he will slaughter the bull for his sin offering. 12 Then he must take a firepan full of fiery coals from the altar before the LORD and two handfuls of finely ground fragrant incense, and bring ⌊them⌋ inside the veil. 13 He is to put the incense on the fire before the LORD, so that the cloud of incense covers the mercy seat that is over the •testimony, or else he will die. 14 He is to take some of the bull's blood and sprinkle ⌊it⌋ with his finger against the east side of the mercy seat; then he will sprinkle some of the blood with his finger before the mercy seat seven times.

15 "When he slaughters the male goat for the people's sin offering and brings its blood inside the veil, he must do the same with its blood as he did with the bull's blood: he is to sprinkle it against the mercy seat and in front of it. 16 He will purify the ⌊most⌋ holy place in this way for all their sins because of the Israelites' impurities and rebellious acts. He will do the same for the tent of meeting that remains among them, because it is surrounded by their impurities. 17 No one may be in the tent of meeting from the time he enters to make atonement in the ⌊most⌋ holy place until he leaves after he has made atonement for himself, his household, and the whole assembly of Israel. 18 Then he will go out to the altar that is before the LORD and make atonement for it. He is to take some of the bull's blood and some of the goat's blood and put ⌊it⌋ on the horns on all sides of the altar. 19 He is to sprinkle some of the blood on it with his finger seven times to cleanse and set it apart from the Israelites' impurities.

The Scapegoat

20 "When he has finished purifying the ⌊most⌋ holy place, the tent of meeting, and the altar, he is to present the live male goat. 21 Aaron will lay both his hands on the head of the live goat and confess over it all the Israelites' wrongdoings and rebellious acts—all their sins.

---

a 16:8 *Azazel* may be the name of a demon; traditionally, *scapegoat*

He is to put them on the goat's head and send ⌞it⌟ away into the wilderness by the man appointed for the task.[a] [22] The goat will carry on it all their wrongdoings into a desolate land, and he will release it there.

Aaron Washes

[23] "Then Aaron is to enter the tent of meeting, take off the linen garments he wore when he entered the ⌞most⌟ holy place, and leave them there. [24] He will bathe his body with water in a holy place and put on his clothes. Then he must go out and sacrifice his burnt offering and the people's burnt offering; he will make atonement for himself and for the people. [25] He is to burn the fat of the sin offering on the altar. [26] The man who released the goat for Azazel is to wash his clothes and bathe his body with water; afterwards he may reenter the camp. [27] The bull for the sin offering and the goat for the sin offering, whose blood was brought into the ⌞most⌟ holy place to make atonement, must be brought outside the camp and their hide, flesh, and dung burned up. [28] The one who burns them is to wash his clothes and bathe himself with water; afterwards he may reenter the camp.

Day of Atonement:
Date and Rules Set

[29] "This is to be a permanent statute for you: In the seventh month, on the tenth ⌞day⌟ of the month you are to practice self-denial[b] and do no work, both the native and the foreigner who resides among you. [30] Atonement will be made for you on this day to cleanse you, and you will be clean from all your sins before the LORD. [31] It is a Sabbath of complete rest for you, and you must practice

self-denial; it is a permanent statute. [32] The priest who is anointed and ordained[c] to serve as ⌞high⌟ priest in place of his father will make atonement. He will put on the linen garments, the holy garments, [33] and purify the most holy place. He will purify the tent of meeting and the altar and will make atonement for the priests and all the people of the assembly. [34] This is to be a permanent statute for you, to make atonement for the Israelites once a year because of all their sins." And all this was done as the LORD commanded Moses.

Forbidden Sacrifices

Outside Camp

17 The LORD spoke to Moses: [2] "Speak to Aaron, his sons, and all the Israelites and tell them: This is what the LORD has commanded: [3] Anyone from the house of Israel who slaughters an ox, sheep, or goat in the camp, or slaughters ⌞it⌟ outside the camp, [4] instead of bringing it to the entrance to the tent of meeting to present ⌞it⌟ as an offering to the LORD before His tabernacle—that person will be charged with murder.[d] He has shed blood and must be cut off from his people. [5] This is so the Israelites will bring to the LORD the sacrifices they have been offering in the open country. They are to bring them to the priest at the entrance to the tent of meeting and offer them as •fellowship sacrifices to the LORD. [6] The priest will then sprinkle the blood on the LORD's altar at the entrance to the tent of meeting and burn the fat as a pleasing aroma to the LORD. [7] They must no longer offer their sacrifices to the goat-demons that they have prostituted themselves with. This will be a permanent statute for them throughout their generations.

---

[a]**16:21** Lit *wilderness in the hand of a ready man*   [b]**16:29** Traditionally fasting, abstinence from sex, and refraining from personal grooming   [c]**16:32** Lit *and will fill his hand*   [d]**17:4** Lit *tabernacle—murder will be charged against that person*

8 "Say to them: Anyone from the house of Israel or from the foreigners who live among them who offers a •burnt offering or a sacrifice 9 but does not bring it to the entrance to the tent of meeting to sacrifice it to the LORD, that person must be cut off from his people.

God Prohibits Eating Blood and Carcasses

10 "Anyone from the house of Israel or from the foreigners who live among them who eats any blood, I will turn[a] against that person who eats blood and cut him off from his people. 11 For the life of a creature is in the blood, and I have appointed it to you to make •atonement on the altar for[b] your lives, since it is the lifeblood that makes atonement. 12 Therefore I say to the Israelites: None of you and no foreigner who lives among you may eat blood.

13 "Any Israelite or foreigner living among them, who hunts down a wild animal or bird that may be eaten must drain its blood and cover it with dirt. 14 Since the life of every creature is its blood, I have told the Israelites: You must not eat the blood of any creature, because the life of every creature is its blood; whoever eats it must be cut off.

15 "Every person, whether the native or the foreigner, who eats an animal that died a natural death or was mauled by wild beasts is to wash his clothes and bathe with water, and he will remain unclean until evening; he will be clean. 16 But if he does not wash his clothes and bathe himself, he will bear his punishment."

God Prohibits Pagan Customs

18 The LORD spoke to Moses: 2 "Speak to the Israelites and tell them: I am the LORD your God. 3 Do not follow the practices of the land of Egypt, where you used to live, or follow the practices of the land of Canaan, where I am bringing you. You must not follow their customs. 4 You are to practice My ordinances and you are to keep My statutes by following them; I am the LORD your God. 5 Keep My statutes and ordinances; a person will live if he does them. I am the LORD.

Incest Outlawed

6 "You are not to come near any close relative[c] for sexual intercourse; I am the LORD. 7 You are not to shame your father by having sex with your mother. She is your mother; you must not have sexual intercourse with her. 8 You are not to have sex with your father's wife; it will shame your father. 9 You are not to have sexual intercourse with your sister, either your father's daughter or your mother's, whether born at home or born elsewhere. You are not to have sex with her. 10 You are not to have sexual intercourse with your son's daughter or your daughter's daughter, because it will shame your family.[d] 11 You are not to have sexual intercourse with your father's wife's daughter,[e] who is adopted by[f] your father; she is your sister. 12 You are not to have sexual intercourse with your father's sister; she is your father's close relative. 13 You are not to have sexual intercourse with your mother's sister, for she is your mother's close relative. 14 You are not to shame your father's brother by coming near his wife to have sexual intercourse; she is your aunt. 15 You are not to have sexual intercourse with your daughter-in-law. She is your son's wife; you are not to have sex with her. 16 You are not to have sexual intercourse with your brother's wife; it will

---

[a]17:10 Lit will set My face   [b]17:11 Or to ransom   [c]18:6 Lit any flesh of his flesh   [d]18:10 Lit because they are your nakedness   [e]18:11 This must refer to a daughter from a previous marriage.   [f]18:11 Lit daughter, a relative of

shame your brother. [17] You are not to have sexual intercourse with a woman and her daughter. You are not to marry her son's daughter or her daughter's daughter and have sex with her. They are close relatives; it is depraved. [18] You are not to marry a woman as a rival to her sister and have sexual intercourse with her during her ⌊sister's⌋ lifetime.

Other Sexual Sins

[19] "You are not to come near a woman during her menstrual impurity to have sexual intercourse with her. [20] You are not to have sexual intercourse with[a] your neighbor's wife, defiling yourself with her.

[21] "You are not to make any of your children pass through ⌊the fire⌋ to •Molech.[b] Do not profane the name of your God; I am the LORD. [22] You are not to sleep with a man as with a woman; it is detestable. [23] You are not to have sexual intercourse with[c] any animal, defiling yourself with it; a woman is not to present herself to an animal to mate with it; it is a perversion.

God Punishes the Defiled Land

[24] "Do not defile yourselves by any of these ⌊practices⌋, for the nations I am driving out before you have defiled themselves by all these things. [25] The land has become defiled, so I am punishing it for its sin, and the land will vomit out its inhabitants. [26] But you are to keep My statutes and ordinances. You must not commit any of these abominations—not the native or the foreigner who lives among you. [27] For the men who were in the land prior to you have committed all these abominations, and the land has become defiled. [28] If you defile the land, it will vomit you out as it has vomited out the nations that were before you. [29] Any person who does any of these abominations must be cut off from his people. [30] You must keep My instruction to not do any of the detestable customs that were practiced before you, so that you do not defile yourselves by them; I am the LORD your God."

God Says, "Be Holy"

Laws of Holiness

19 The LORD spoke to Moses: [2] "Speak to the entire Israelite community and tell them: Be holy because I, the LORD your God, am holy.

[3] "Each of you is to respect his mother and father. You are to keep My Sabbaths; I am the LORD your God. [4] Do not turn to idols or make cast images of gods for yourselves; I am the LORD your God.

[5] "When you offer a •fellowship sacrifice to the LORD, sacrifice it that you may be accepted. [6] It is to be eaten on the day you sacrifice ⌊it⌋ or on the next day, but what remains on the third day must be burned up. [7] If any is eaten on the third day, it is a repulsive thing; it will not be accepted. [8] Anyone who eats it will bear his punishment, for he has profaned what is holy to the LORD. That person must be cut off from his people.

Leave Gleanings for Poor

[9] "When you reap the harvest of your land, you are not to reap to the very edge of your field or gather ⌊the⌋ gleanings of your harvest. [10] You must not strip your vineyard bare or gather its fallen grapes. Leave them for the poor and the foreign resident; I am the LORD your God.

---

[a]**18:20** Lit *to give your emission of semen to*   [b]**18:21** An ancient Near Eastern god to whom child sacrifices were offered by fire; Lv 20:2-5; Dt 18:10; 1 Kg 11:7; 2 Kg 23:10   [c]**18:23** Lit *to give your emission to*

"You Must Not . . ."

11 "You must not steal. You must not act deceptively or lie to one another. 12 You must not swear falsely by My name, profaning the name of your God; I am the LORD. 13 "You must not oppress your neighbor or rob ⌊him⌋. The wages due a hired hand must not remain with you until morning. 14 You must not curse the deaf or put a stumbling block in front of the blind, but you are to •fear your God; I am the LORD.

15 "You must not act unjustly when rendering judgment. Do not be partial to the poor or give preference to the rich; judge your neighbor fairly. 16 You must not go about spreading slander among your people; you must not jeopardizeª your neighbor's life; I am the LORD.

17 "You must not hate your brotherᵇ in your heart. Rebuke your neighbor directly, and you will not incur guilt because of him. 18 Do not take revenge or bear a grudge against members of your community, but love your neighbor as yourself; I am the LORD.

Special Consistencies

19 "You are to keep My statutes. You must not crossbreed two different kinds of your livestock, sow your fields with two kinds of seed, or put on a garment made of two kinds of material.

Other Sexual Rules and Penalties

20 "If a man has sexual intercourse with a woman who is a slave designated for ⌊another⌋ man, but she has not been redeemed or given her freedom, there must be punishment.ᶜ They are not to be put to death, because she had not been freed. 21 However, he must bring his ram as a •restitution offering to the LORD at the entrance to the tent of meeting.

22 The priest will make •atonement on his behalf before the LORD with the ram of the restitution offering for the sin he has committed, and he will be forgiven for the sin he committed.

Forbidden Fruit

23 "When you come into the land and plant any kind of tree for food, you are to consider the fruit forbidden.ᵈ It will be forbidden to you for three years; it is not to be eaten. 24 In the fourth year all its fruit must be consecrated as a praise offering to the LORD. 25 But in the fifth year you may eat its fruit. In this way its yield will increase for you; I am the LORD your God.

Blood, Sorcery, Haircuts, Tattoos

26 "You are not to eat ⌊anything⌋ with blood ⌊in it⌋.ᵉ You are not to practice •divination or sorcery. 27 You are not to cut off the hair at the sides of your head or mar the edge of your beard. 28 You are not to make gashes on your bodies for the dead or put tattoo marks on yourselves; I am the LORD.

Don't Debase Daughters

29 "Do not debaseᶠ your daughter by making her a prostitute, or the land will be prostituted and filled with depravity. 30 You must keep My Sabbaths and revere My sanctuary; I am the LORD.

No Mediums

31 "Do not turn to mediumsᵍ or consult spiritists,ʰ or you will be defiled by them; I am the LORD your God.

Respect the Elderly

32 "You are to rise in the presence of the elderly and honor the old. Fear your God; I am the LORD.

ª19:16 Lit not stand against   ᵇ19:17 Or your fellow Israelite   ᶜ19:20 Or compensation   ᵈ19:23 Lit uncircumcised
ᵉ19:26 Or [anything] over its blood   ᶠ19:29 Lit profane   ᵍ19:31 Or spirits of the dead   ʰ19:31 Or familiar spirits

Respect Foreigners

33 "When a foreigner lives with you
in your land, you must not oppress
him. 34 You must regard the foreigner
who lives with you as the native-born
among you. You are to love him as
yourself, for you were foreigners in
the land of Egypt; I am the LORD your
God.

Honest Measurements

35 "You must not act unfairly in measurements of length, weight, or volume. 36 You are to have honest
balances, honest weights, an honest
dry measure,[a] and an honest liquid
measure;[b] I am the LORD your God,
who brought you out of the land of
Egypt. 37 You must keep all My statutes
and all My ordinances and do them; I
am the LORD."

God Prohibits and Punishes Molech Worship

20 The LORD spoke to Moses: 2 "Say
to the Israelites: Any Israelite or
foreigner living in Israel who gives any
of his children to •Molech must be put
to death; the people of the country are
to stone him. 3 I will turn[c] against that
man and cut him off from his people,
because he gave his •offspring to Molech, defiling My sanctuary and profaning My holy name. 4 But if the people
of the country look the other way
when that man[d] gives any of his children to Molech, and do not put him to
death, 5 then I will turn[c] against that
man and his family, and cut off from
their people both him and all who follow[e] him, prostituting themselves with
Molech.

God Punishes Occult

6 "Whoever turns to mediums[f] or spiritists[g] and prostitutes himself with them,
I will turn[c] against that person and cut
him off from his people. 7 Consecrate
yourselves and be holy, for I am the
LORD your God. 8 Keep My statutes and
do them; I am the LORD who sets you
apart.

God's Penalties: Family and Sexual Offenses

9 "If anyone curses his father or mother,
he must be put to death. He has cursed
his father or mother; his blood is on his
own hands.[h] 10 If a man commits adultery
with a married woman—if he commits
adultery with his neighbor's wife—both
the adulterer and the adulteress must be
put to death. 11 If a man sleeps with his father's wife, he has shamed his father.
Both of them must be put to death; their
blood is on their own hands.[i] 12 If a man
sleeps with his daughter-in-law, both of
them must be put to death. They have
acted perversely; their blood is on their
own hands.[i] 13 If a man sleeps with a man
as with a woman, they have both committed an abomination. They must be put to
death; their blood is on their own hands.[i]
14 If a man marries a woman and her
mother, it is depraved. Both he and they
must be burned with fire, so that there
will be no depravity among you. 15 If a
man has sexual intercourse with[j] an animal, he must be put to death; you are also
to kill the animal. 16 If a woman comes
near any animal and mates with it, you
are to kill the woman and the animal.
They must be put to death; their ⌊own⌋
blood is on them. 17 If a man marries his
sister, whether his father's daughter or his

[a]**19:36** Lit *honest ephah*; an *ephah* is a dry measure of grain equivalent to 22 liters. [b]**19:36** Lit *honest hin*; a *hin* is a liquid measure of about 4 liters or 1 gallon. [c]**20:3,5,6** Lit *will set My face* [d]**20:4** Lit *country ever close their eyes from that man when he* [e]**20:5** Lit *prostitute themselves with* [f]**20:6** Or *spirits of the dead* [g]**20:6** Or *familiar spirits* [h]**20:9** Lit *on him* [i]**20:11,12,13** Lit *on them* [j]**20:15** Lit *man gives his emission to*

mother's daughter, and they have sexual relations,[a] it is a disgrace. They must be cut off publicly from their people. He has had sexual intercourse with his sister; he will bear his punishment. [18] If a man sleeps with a menstruating woman and has sexual intercourse with her, he has exposed the source of her ⌊flow⌋, and she has uncovered the source of her blood. Both of them must be cut off from their people. [19] You must not have sexual intercourse with your mother's sister or your father's sister, for it is exposing one's own blood relative; both people will bear their punishment. [20] If a man sleeps with his aunt, he has shamed his uncle; they will bear their guilt and die childless. [21] If a man marries his brother's wife, it is impurity. He has shamed his brother; they will be childless.

God Demands Holiness in the Land

[22] "You are to keep all My statutes and all My ordinances, and do them, so that the land where I am bringing you to live will not vomit you out. [23] You must not follow the statutes of the nations I am driving out before you, for they did all these things, and I abhorred them. [24] And I promised you: You will inherit their land, since I will give it to you to possess, a land flowing with milk and honey. I am the LORD your God who set you apart from the peoples. [25] Therefore you must distinguish the clean animal from the unclean one, and the unclean bird from the clean one. You are not to make yourselves detestable by any land animal, bird, or whatever crawls on the ground; I have set these apart as unclean for you. [26] You are to be holy to Me because I, the LORD, am holy, and I have set you apart from the nations to be

Mine. [27] A man or a woman who is[b] a medium or a spiritist must be put to death. They are to be stoned; their blood is on their own hands."[c]

God's Special Rules for Priests

21 The LORD said to Moses: "Speak to Aaron's sons, the priests, and tell them: A priest is not to make himself ceremonially unclean for a ⌊dead⌋ person among his relatives, [2] except for his immediate family: his mother, father, son, daughter, or brother. [3] He may make himself unclean for his young unmarried sister in his immediate family. [4] He is not to make himself unclean for those related to him by marriage[d] and so defile himself.

[5] "Priests may not make bald spots on their heads, shave the edge of their beards, or make gashes on their bodies. [6] They are to be holy to their God and not profane the name of their God, because they present the fire offerings to the LORD, the food of their God. They must be holy. [7] They are not to marry a woman defiled by prostitution[e] or divorced by her husband, for the priest is holy to his God. [8] You are to consider him holy since he presents the food of your God. He will be holy to you because I, the LORD who sets you apart, am holy. [9] If a priest's daughter defiles herself by promiscuity,[f] she defiles her father; she must be burned up.

[10] "The priest who is highest among his brothers, who has had the anointing oil poured on his head and has been ordained[g] to wear the garments, must not dishevel his hair[h] or tear his garments. [11] He must not go near any dead person or make himself unclean ⌊even⌋ for his father or mother. [12] He must not leave the sanctuary

---

[a]20:17 Lit and he sees her nakedness and she sees his nakedness   [b]20:27 Lit is in them   [c]20:27 Lit on them   [d]21:4 Lit unclean a husband among his people   [e]21:7 Or a woman who has been deflowered   [f]21:9 Or prostitution   [g]21:10 Lit and one has filled his hand   [h]21:10 Or not uncover his head

or he will desecrate the sanctuary of his God, for the consecration of the anointing oil of his God is on him; I am the LORD.

Priests: Marry Virgins

13 "He is to marry a woman who is a virgin. 14 He is not to marry a widow, a divorced woman, or one defiled by prostitution. He is to marry a virgin from his own people, 15 so that he does not corrupt his bloodline[a] among his people, for I am the LORD who sets him apart."

Physical Defects and Priests

16 The LORD spoke to Moses: 17 "Tell Aaron: None of your descendants throughout your generations who has a physical defect is to come near to present the food of his God. 18 No man who has any defect is to come near: no man who is blind, lame, facially disfigured, or deformed; 19 no man who has a broken foot or hand, 20 or who is a hunchback or a dwarf,[b] or who has an eye defect, a festering rash, scabs, or a crushed testicle. 21 No descendant of Aaron the priest who has a defect is to come near to present the fire offerings to the LORD. He has a defect and is not to come near to present the food of his God. 22 He may eat the food of his God from what is especially holy as well as from what is holy. 23 But because he has a defect, he must not go near the curtain or approach the altar. He is not to desecrate My sanctuaries, for I am the LORD who sets them apart." 24 Moses said ⌊this⌋ to Aaron and his sons and to all the Israelites.

Priests, Offerings, and Food

22 The LORD spoke to Moses: 2 "Tell Aaron and his sons to deal respectfully with the holy offerings of the Israelites that they have consecrated to Me, so they do not profane My holy name; I am the LORD. 3 Say to them: If any man from any of your descendants throughout your generations is in a state of uncleanness yet approaches the holy offerings that the Israelites consecrate to the LORD, that person will be cut off from My presence; I am the LORD. 4 No man of Aaron's descendants who has a skin disease[c] or a discharge is to eat from the holy offerings until he is clean. Whoever touches anything made unclean by a dead person or by a man who has an emission of semen, 5 or whoever touches any swarming creature that makes him unclean or any person who makes him unclean—whatever his uncleanness— 6 the man who touches any of these will remain unclean until evening and is not to eat from the holy offerings unless he has bathed his body with water. 7 When the sun has set, he will become clean, and then he may eat from the holy offerings, for that is his food. 8 He must not eat an animal that died naturally or was mauled by wild beasts,[d] making himself unclean by it; I am the LORD. 9 They must keep My instruction, or they will be guilty and die because they profane it; I am the LORD who sets them apart.

Priest's Family and Guests

10 "No one outside a priest's family[e] is to eat the holy offering. A foreigner staying with a priest or a hired hand is not to eat the holy offering. 11 But if a priest purchases someone with his money, that person may eat it, and those born in his house may eat his food. 12 If the priest's daughter is married to a man outside a priest's family,[f] she is not to eat from the holy contributions.[g] 13 But if the priest's daughter becomes widowed or divorced, has no children, and returns to her

---

a21:15 Lit *not profane his seed*   b21:20 Or *or emaciated*   c22:4 Or *has leprosy or scale disease*   d22:8 Lit *eat a carcass or a mauled beast*   e22:10 Lit *No stranger*   f22:12 Lit *man, a stranger*   g22:12 Lit *the contribution of holy offerings*

father's house as in her youth, she may share her father's food. But no outsider may share it. ¹⁴ If anyone eats a holy offering in error, he must add a fifth to its value and give the holy offering to the priest. ¹⁵ The priests must not profane the holy offerings the Israelites give to the LORD ¹⁶ and have them bear the penalty of restitution if the people eat their holy offerings. For I am the LORD who sets them apart."

Special Rules for Sacrifices

¹⁷ The LORD spoke to Moses: ¹⁸ "Speak to Aaron, his sons, and all the Israelites and tell them: Any man of the house of Israel or of the foreign residents in Israel who presents his offering—whether they present freewill gifts or payment of vows to the LORD as •burnt offerings— ¹⁹ must offer an unblemished male from the cattle, sheep, or goats in order for you to be accepted. ²⁰ You are not to present anything that has a defect, because it will not be accepted on your behalf.

²¹ "When a man presents a •fellowship sacrifice to the LORD to fulfill a vow or as a freewill offering from the herd or flock, it has to be unblemished to be acceptable; there must be no defect in it. ²² You are not to present any ⌊animal⌋ to the LORD that is blind, injured, maimed, or has a running sore, festering rash, or scabs; you may not put any of them on the altar as a fire offering to the LORD. ²³ You may sacrifice as a freewill offering any animal from the herd or flock that has an elongated or stunted limb, but it is not acceptable as a vow offering. ²⁴ You are not to present to the LORD anything that has bruised, crushed, torn, or severed ⌊testicles⌋; you must not sacrifice ⌊them⌋ in your land. ²⁵ Neither you

nor[a] a foreigner are to present food to your God from any of these animals. They will not be accepted for you because they are deformed and have a defect."

²⁶ The LORD spoke to Moses: ²⁷ "When an ox, sheep, or goat is born, it must remain with[b] its mother for seven days; from the eighth day on, it will be acceptable as a gift, a fire offering to the LORD. ²⁸ But you are not to slaughter an animal from the herd or flock on the same day as its young. ²⁹ When you sacrifice a thank offering to the LORD, sacrifice it so that you may be accepted. ³⁰ It is to be eaten on the same day. Do not let any of it remain until morning; I am the LORD.

³¹ "You are to keep My commands and do them; I am the LORD. ³² You must not profane My holy name; I must be treated as holy among the Israelites. I am the LORD who sets you apart, ³³ the One who brought you out of the land of Egypt to be your God; I am the LORD."

God Sets His Holy Days

Sabbath

23 The LORD spoke to Moses: ² "Speak to the Israelites and tell them: These are My appointed times, the times of the LORD that you will proclaim as sacred assemblies.

³ "For six days work may be done, but on the seventh day there must be a Sabbath of complete rest, a sacred assembly. You are not to do any work; it is a Sabbath to the LORD wherever you live.

Passover and Unleavened Bread

⁴ "These are the LORD's appointed times, the sacred assemblies you are to proclaim at their appointed times. ⁵ The •Passover to the LORD comes in the first month, at twilight on the fourteenth day

ᵃ22:25 Lit nor from the hand of   ᵇ22:27 Lit under

of the month. ⁶ The Festival of •Unleavened Bread to the LORD is on the fifteenth day of the same month. For seven days you must eat unleavened bread. ⁷ On the first day you are to hold a sacred assembly; you are not to do any daily work. ⁸ You are to present a fire offering to the LORD for seven days. On the seventh day there will be a sacred assembly; you must not do any daily work."

⁹ The LORD spoke to Moses: ¹⁰ "Speak to the Israelites and tell them: When you enter the land I am giving you and reap its harvest,ᵃ you are to bring the first sheaf of your harvest to the priest. ¹¹ He will wave the sheaf before the LORD so that you may be accepted; the priest is to wave it on the day after the Sabbath. ¹² On the day you wave the sheaf, you are to offer a year-old male lambᵇ without blemish as a •burnt offering to the LORD. ¹³ Its •grain offering is to be four quartsᶜ of fine flour mixed with oil as a fire offering to the LORD, a pleasing aroma, and its drink offering will be one quartᵈ of wine. ¹⁴ You must not eat bread, roasted grain, or ʟanyʟ new grainᵉ until this very day, and you have brought the offering of your God. This is to be a permanent statute throughout your generations wherever you live.

Pentecost: Harvest Festival

¹⁵ "You are to count sevenᶠ complete weeksᵍ starting from the day after the Sabbath, the day you brought the sheaf of the presentation offering. ¹⁶ You are to count 50 days until the day after the seventh Sabbath and then present an offering of new grainʰ to the LORD. ¹⁷ Bring two loaves of bread from your settlements as a presentation offering, each of them made from four quartsᶜ of fine flour, baked with yeast, as •firstfruits to the LORD. ¹⁸ You are to present with the bread seven unblemished male lambs a year old, one young bull, and two rams. They will be a burnt offering to the LORD, with their grain offerings and drink offerings, a fire offering of a pleasing aroma to the LORD. ¹⁹ You are also to prepare one male goat as a •sin offering, and two male lambs a year old as a •fellowship sacrifice. ²⁰ The priest will wave the lambs with the bread of firstfruits as a presentation offering before the LORD; the bread and the two lambs will be holy to the LORD for the priest. ²¹ On that same day you are to make a proclamation and hold a sacred assembly. You are not to do any daily work. This is to be a permanent statute wherever you live throughout your generations. ²² When you reap the harvest of your land, you are not to reap all the way to the edge of your field or gather the gleanings of your harvest. Leave them for the poor and the foreign resident; I am the LORD your God."

Day of Atonement

²³ The LORD spoke to Moses: ²⁴ "Tell the Israelites: In the seventh month, on the first ʟdayʟ of the month, you are to have a day of complete rest, commemoration and jubilationⁱ—a sacred assembly. ²⁵ You must not do any daily work, but you must present a fire offering to the LORD."

²⁶ The LORD again spoke to Moses: ²⁷ "The tenth ʟdayʟ of this seventh month is the Day of •Atonement. You are to hold a sacred assembly and practice self-denial;ʲ you are to present a fire offering

ᵃ**23:10** The barley harvest   ᵇ**23:12** Or *a male lamb in its first year*   ᶜ**23:13,17** Lit *two-tenths [of an ephah]*   ᵈ**23:13** Lit *one-fourth of a hin*   ᵉ**23:14** *Grain* or bread from the *new* harvest   ᶠ**23:15** Lit *count; they will be seven*   ᵍ**23:15** Or *Sabbaths*   ʰ**23:16** From the wheat harvest; Ex 34:22   ⁱ**23:24** Lit *shout,* or *blast;* traditionally *trumpet blasts*   ʲ**23:27** Traditionally, fasting, abstinence from sex, and refraining from personal grooming

to the LORD. 28 On this particular day you are not to do any work, for it is a Day of Atonement to make atonement for yourselves before the LORD your God. 29 If any person does not practice self-denial on this particular day, he must be cut off from his people. 30 I will destroy among his people anyone who does any work on this same day. 31 You are not to do any work. This is a permanent statute throughout your generations wherever you live. 32 It will be a Sabbath of complete rest for you, and you must practice self-denial. You are to observe your Sabbath from the evening of the ninth ⌊day⌋ of the month until the ⌊following⌋ evening."

Festival of Booths

33 The LORD spoke to Moses: 34 "Tell the Israelites: The Festival of Booths[a] to the LORD begins on the fifteenth day of this seventh month and continues for seven days. 35 There is to be a sacred assembly on the first day; you are not to do any daily work. 36 You are to present a fire offering to the LORD for seven days. On the eighth day you are to hold a sacred assembly and present a fire offering to the LORD. It is a solemn gathering; you are not to do any daily work.

37 "These are the LORD's appointed times that you are to proclaim as sacred assemblies for presenting fire offerings to the LORD, burnt offerings and grain offerings, sacrifices and drink offerings, each on its ⌊designated⌋ day. 38 These are in addition to the offerings for the LORD's Sabbaths, your gifts, all your vow offerings, and all your freewill offerings that you give to the LORD.

39 "You are to celebrate the LORD's festival on the fifteenth day of the seventh month for seven days after you have gathered the produce of the land. There will be complete rest on the first day and complete rest on the eighth day. 40 On the first day you are to take the product of majestic trees—palm fronds, boughs of leafy trees, and willows of the brook—and rejoice before the LORD your God for seven days. 41 You are to celebrate it as a festival to the LORD seven days each year. This is a permanent statute for you throughout your generations; you must celebrate it in the seventh month. 42 You are to live in booths for seven days. All the native-born of Israel must live in booths, 43 so that your generations may know that I made the Israelites live in booths when I brought them out of the land of Egypt; I am the LORD your God." 44 So Moses declared the LORD's appointed times to the Israelites.

Tabernacle Oil and Bread

24 The LORD spoke to Moses: 2 "Command the Israelites to bring you pure oil of beaten olives for the light, so that the lamp will burn regularly. 3 Aaron is to tend it regularly from evening until morning before the LORD outside the veil of the •testimony in the tent of meeting. This is a permanent statute throughout your generations. 4 He must regularly tend the lamps on the pure ⌊gold⌋ lampstand in the LORD's presence.

5 "Take fine flour and bake it into 12 loaves; each loaf is to be made with four quarts.[b] 6 Arrange them in two rows, six to a row, on the pure ⌊gold⌋ table before the LORD. 7 Place pure frankincense near each row, so that it may serve as a memorial portion for the bread and a fire offering to the LORD. 8 The bread is to be set out before the LORD every Sabbath day as a perpetual covenant obligation

---

a 23:34 Or Feast of Tabernacles   b 24:5 Lit two-tenths [of an ephah]

on the part of the Israelites. ⁹ It belongs to Aaron and his sons, who are to eat it in a holy place, for it is the holiest portion for him from the fire offerings to the LORD; this is a permanent rule."

A Case of Blasphemy

¹⁰ Now the son of an Israelite mother and an Egyptian father was[a] among the Israelites. A fight broke out in the camp between the Israelite woman's son and an Israelite man. ¹¹ Her son cursed and blasphemed the Name, and they brought him to Moses. (His mother's name was Shelomith, a daughter of Dibri of the tribe of Dan.) ¹² They put him in custody until the LORD's decision could be made clear to them.

God Decrees Death

¹³ Then the LORD spoke to Moses: ¹⁴ "Bring the one who has cursed to the outside of the camp and have all who heard ⌊him⌋ lay their hands on his head; then have the whole community stone him. ¹⁵ And tell the Israelites: If anyone curses his God, he will bear the consequences of his sin. ¹⁶ Whoever blasphemes the name of the LORD is to be put to death; the whole community must stone him. If he blasphemes the Name, he is to be put to death, whether the foreign resident or the native.

God's Penalties

¹⁷ "If a man kills anyone, he must be put to death. ¹⁸ Whoever kills an animal is to make restitution for it, life for life. ¹⁹ If any man inflicts a permanent injury on his neighbor, whatever he has done is to be done to him: ²⁰ fracture for fracture, eye for eye, tooth for tooth. Whatever injury he inflicted on the person, the same is to be inflicted on him.

²¹ Whoever kills an animal is to make restitution for it, but whoever kills a person is to be put to death. ²² You are to have the same law for the foreign resident and the native, because I am the LORD your God."

Sentence: Death

²³ After Moses spoke to the Israelites, they brought the one who had cursed to the outside of the camp and stoned him. So the Israelites did as the LORD had commanded Moses.

Sabbath Years and Jubilee

25 The LORD spoke to Moses on Mount Sinai: ² "Speak to the Israelites and tell them: When you enter the land I am giving you, the land will observe a Sabbath to the LORD. ³ You may sow your field for six years, and you may prune your vineyard and gather its produce for six years. ⁴ But there will be a Sabbath of complete rest for the land in the seventh year, a Sabbath to the LORD: you are not to sow your field or prune your vineyard. ⁵ You are not to reap what grows by itself from your crop, or harvest the grapes of your untended vines. It must be a year of complete rest for the land. ⁶ ⌊Whatever⌋ the land ⌊produces during⌋ the Sabbath year can be food for you; for yourself, your male or female slave, and the hired hand or foreigner who stays with you. ⁷ All of its growth may serve as food for your livestock and the wild animals in your land.

Year of Jubilee

⁸ "You are to count seven sabbatic years, seven times seven years, so that the time period of the seven sabbatic years amounts to 49. ⁹ Then you are to sound a trumpet loudly in the seventh

---

ᵃ**24:10** Lit went out

month, on the tenth ⌊day⌋ of the month; you will sound it throughout your land on the Day of •Atonement. ¹⁰ You are to consecrate the fiftieth year and proclaim freedom in the land for all its inhabitants. It will be your Jubilee, when each of you is to return to his property and each of you to his clan. ¹¹ The fiftieth year will be your Jubilee; you are not to sow, reap what grows by itself, or harvest its untended vines. ¹² It is to be holy to you because it is the Jubilee; you may ⌊only⌋ eat its produce ⌊directly⌋ from the field.

¹³ "In this Year of Jubilee, each of you will return to his property. ¹⁴ If you make a sale to your neighbor or a purchase from him, do not cheat one another. ¹⁵ You are to make the purchase from your neighbor based on the number of years since the last Jubilee. He is to sell to you based on the number of ⌊remaining⌋ harvest years. ¹⁶ You are to increase its price in proportion to a greater amount of years, and decrease its price in proportion to a lesser amount of years, because what he is selling to you is a number of harvests. ¹⁷ You are not to cheat one another, but •fear your God, for I am the LORD your God.

Questions about Seventh Year

¹⁸ "You are to observe My statutes and ordinances and carefully observe them, so that you may live securely in the land. ¹⁹ Then the land will yield its fruit, so that you can eat, be satisfied, and live securely in the land. ²⁰ If you wonder: 'What will we eat in the seventh year if we don't sow or gather our produce?' ²¹ I will appoint My blessing for you in the sixth year, so that it will produce a crop sufficient for three years. ²² When you sow in the eighth year, you will be eating from the previous harvest. You will be eating this until the ninth year when its harvest comes in.

Jubilee: Return of Property

²³ "The land is not to be permanently sold because it is Mine, and you are only foreigners and temporary residents on My land.ᵃ ²⁴ You are to allow the redemption of any land you occupy. ²⁵ If your brother becomes destitute and sells part of his property, his nearest relative may come and redeem what his brother has sold. ²⁶ If a man has no •family redeemer, but he prospersᵇ and obtains enough to redeem his land, ²⁷ he may calculate the years since its sale, repay the balance to the man he sold it to, and return to his property. ²⁸ But if he cannot obtain enough to repay him, what he sold will remain in the possession of its purchaser until the Year of Jubilee. It is to be released at the Jubilee, so that he may return to his property.

²⁹ "If a man sells a residence in a walled city, his right of redemption will last until a year has passed after its sale; his right of redemption will last a year. ³⁰ If it is not redeemed by the end of a full year, then the house in the walled city is permanently transferred to its purchaser throughout his generations. It is not to be released on the Jubilee. ³¹ But houses in villages that have no walls around them are to be classified as open fields. The right to redeem ⌊such⌋ houses stays in effect, and they are to be released at the Jubilee.

Cities of Levites

³² "Concerning the Levitical cities, the Levites always have the right to redeem houses in the cities they possess. ³³ Whatever ⌊property⌋ one of the Levites

---

ᵃ**25:23** Lit *residents with Me*   ᵇ**25:26** Lit *but his hand reaches*

can redeema—a house sold in a city they possess—must be released at the Jubilee, because the houses in the Levitical cities are their possession among the Israelites. 34 The open pastureland around their cities may not be sold, for it is their permanent possession.

Aid to Poor

35 "If your brother becomes destitute and cannot sustain himself amongb you, you are to support him as a foreigner or temporary resident, so that he can continue to live among you. 36 Do not profit or take interest from him, but fear your God and let your brother live among you. 37 You are not to lend him your silver with interest or sell ⌊him⌋ your food for profit. 38 I am the LORD your God, who brought you out of the land of Egypt to give you the land of Canaan and to be your God.

39 "If your brother among you becomes destitute and sells himself to you, you must not force him to do slave labor. 40 Let him stay with you as a hired hand or temporary resident; he may work for you until the Year of Jubilee. 41 Then he and his children are to be released from you, and he may return to his clan and his ancestral property. 42 They are not to be sold as slaves,c because they are My slaves I brought out of the land of Egypt. 43 You are not to rule over them harshly but fear your God. 44 Your male and female slaves are to be from the nations around you; you may purchase male and female slaves. 45 You may also purchase them from the foreigners staying with you, or from their families living among you—those born in your land. These may become your property. 46 You may leave them to your sons after you to inherit as property; you can make them

slaves for life. But concerning your brothers, the Israelites, you must not rule over one another harshly.

Redemption from Foreigners

47 "If a foreigner or temporary resident ⌊living⌋ among you prospers, but your brother ⌊living⌋ near him becomes destitute and sells himself to the foreigner living among you, or to a member of the foreigner's clan, 48 he has the right of redemption after he has been sold. One of his brothers may redeem him. 49 His uncle or cousin may redeem him, or any of his close relatives from his clan may redeem him. If he prospers, he may redeem himself. 50 The one who purchased him is to calculate ⌊the time⌋ from the year he sold himself to him until the Year of Jubilee. The price of his sale will be ⌊determined⌋ by the number of years. It will be ⌊set⌋ for him like the daily wages of a hired hand. 51 If many years are still left, he must pay his redemption price in proportion to them based on his purchase price. 52 If only a few years remain until the Year of Jubilee, he will calculate and pay the price of his redemption in proportion to his ⌊remaining⌋ years. 53 He will stay with him like a man hired year by year. A foreign owner is not to rule over him harshly in your sight. 54 If he is not redeemed in any of these ⌊ways⌋, he and his children are to be released at the Year of Jubilee. 55 For the Israelites are My slaves. They are My slaves I brought out of the land of Egypt; I am the LORD your God.

God's Blessings and Discipline

26 "Do not make idols for yourselves, set up a carved image or sacred pillar for yourselves, or place a sculpted stone in your land to bow down to it, for

---

a25:33 Hb obscure   b25:35 Lit and his hand falters with   c25:42 Lit sold with a sale of a slave

I am the LORD your God. ² You must keep My Sabbaths and honor My sanctuary; I am the LORD.

Divine Promises for Obedience

³ "If you follow My statutes and faithfully observe My commands, ⁴ I will give you rain at the right time, and the land will yield its produce, and the trees of the field will bear their fruit. ⁵ Your threshing will continue until grape harvest, and the grape harvest will continue until sowing time; you will have plenty of food to eat and live securely in your land. ⁶ I will give peace to the land, and you will lie down with nothing to frighten ⸤you⸥. I will remove dangerous animals from the land, and no sword will pass through your land. ⁷ You will pursue your enemies, and they will fall before you by the sword. ⁸ Five of you will pursue 100, and 100 of you will pursue 10,000; your enemies will fall before you by the sword.

⁹ "I will turn to you, make you fruitful and multiply you, and confirm My covenant with you. ¹⁰ You will eat the old grain of the previous year and will clear out the old to make room for the new. ¹¹ I will place My residenceᵃ among you, and I will not reject you. ¹² I will walk among you and be your God, and you will be My people. ¹³ I am the LORD your God, who brought you out of the land of Egypt, so that you would no longer be their slaves. I broke the bars of your yoke and enabled you to live in freedom.ᵇ

Disobedience: Terror

¹⁴ "But if you do not obey Me and observe all these commands— ¹⁵ if you reject My statutes and despise My ordinances, and do not observe all My commands—and break My covenant, ¹⁶ then I will do this to you: I will bring terror on you—wasting disease and fever that will cause your eyes to fail and your life to ebb away. You will sow your seed in vain because your enemies will eat it. ¹⁷ I will turnᶜ against you, so that you will be defeated by your enemies. Those who hate you will rule over you, and you will flee even though no one is pursuing you.

God Will Continue to Discipline

¹⁸ "But if after these things you will not obey Me, I will proceed to discipline you seven times for your sins. ¹⁹ I will break down your strong pride. I will make your sky like iron and your land like bronze, ²⁰ and your strength will be used up for nothing. Your land will not yield its produce, and the trees of the land will not bear their fruit.

²¹ "If you act with hostility toward Me and are unwilling to obey Me, I will multiply your plagues seven times for your sins. ²² I will send wild animals against you that will deprive you of your children, ravage your livestock, and reduce your numbers until your roads are deserted.

Seven More Strikes

²³ "If in spite of these things you do not accept My discipline, but act with hostility toward Me, ²⁴ then I will act with hostility toward you; I also will strike you seven times for your sins. ²⁵ I will bring a sword against you to execute the vengeance of the covenant. Though you withdraw into your cities, I will send a pestilence among you, and you will be delivered into enemy hands. ²⁶ When I cut off your supply of bread, 10 women will bake your bread in a sin-

gle oven and ration out your bread by weight, so that you will eat but not be satisfied.

Further Disobedience, More Discipline

27 "And if in spite of this you do not obey Me but act with hostility toward Me, 28 I will act with furious hostility toward you; I will also discipline you seven times for your sins. 29 You will eat the flesh of your sons; you will eat the flesh of your daughters. 30 I will destroy your •high places, cut down your incense altars, and heap your dead bodies on the lifeless bodies of your idols; I will reject you. 31 I will reduce your cities to ruins and devastate your sanctuaries. I will not smell the pleasing aroma of your ⌊sacrifices⌋. 32 I also will devastate the land, so that your enemies who come to live there will be appalled by it. 33 But I will scatter you among the nations, and I will draw a sword ⌊to chase⌋ after you. So your land will become desolate, and your cities will become ruins.

Land Will Rest

34 "Then the land will make up for its Sabbath ⌊years⌋ during the time it lies desolate, while you are in the land of your enemies. At that time the land will rest and make up for its Sabbaths. 35 As long as it lies desolate, it will have the rest it did not have during your Sabbaths when you lived there.

God Causes Anxiety

36 "I will put anxiety in the hearts of those of you who survive in the lands of their enemies. The sound of a wind-driven leaf will put them to flight, and they will flee as one flees from a sword, and fall though no one is pursuing ⌊them⌋. 37 They will stumble over one an-

other as if ⌊fleeing⌋ from a sword though no one is pursuing ⌊them⌋. You will not be able to stand against your enemies. 38 You will perish among the nations; the land of your enemies will devour you. 39 Those[a] who survive in the lands of your enemies will waste away because of their sin; they will also waste away because of their fathers' sins along with theirs.

"But If They Will Confess . . ."

40 "But if they will confess their sin and the sin of their fathers—their unfaithfulness that they practiced against Me, and how they acted with hostility toward Me, 41 and I acted with hostility toward them and brought them into the land of their enemies—and if their uncircumcised hearts will be humbled, and if they will pay the penalty for their sin, 42 then I will remember My covenant with Jacob. I will also remember My covenant with Isaac and My covenant with Abraham, and I will remember the land. 43 For the land abandoned by them will make up for its Sabbaths by lying desolate without the people, while they pay the penalty for their sin, because they rejected My ordinances and abhorred My statutes. 44 Yet in spite of this, while they are in the land of their enemies, I will not reject or abhor them so as to destroy them and break My covenant with them, since I am the LORD their God. 45 For their sake I will remember the covenant with their fathers, whom I brought out of the land of Egypt in the sight of the nations to be their God; I am the LORD."

46 These are the statutes, ordinances, and laws the LORD established between Himself and the Israelites through Moses on Mount Sinai.

---

a **26:39** Lit *Those of you*

Funding the Sanctuary

Valuation of People

27 The LORD spoke to Moses: 2 "Speak to the Israelites and tell them: When someone makes a special vow to the LORD that involves the valuation of people, 3 if the valuation concerns a male from 20 to 60 years old, your valuation is 50 silver ·shekels ⌊measured⌋ by the standard sanctuary shekel. 4 If the person is a female, your valuation is 30 shekels. 5 If the person is from five to 20 years old, your valuation for a male is 20 shekels and for a female 10 shekels. 6 If the person is from one month to five years old, your valuation for a male is five silver shekels, and for a female your valuation is three shekels of silver. 7 If the person is 60 years or more, your valuation is 15 shekels for a male and 10 shekels for a female. 8 But if one is too poor to pay the valuation, he must present the person before the priest and the priest will set a value for him. The priest will set a value for him according to what the one making the vow can afford.

Valuation of Animals

9 "If the vow involves one of the animals that may be brought as an offering to the LORD, any of these he gives to the LORD will be holy. 10 He may not replace it or make a substitution for it, either good for bad, or bad for good. But if he does substitute one animal for another, both that animal and its substitute will be holy. 11 "If the vow involves any of the unclean animals that may not be brought as an offering to the LORD, the animal must be presented before the priest. 12 The priest will set its value, whether high or low; the price will be set as the priest makes the valuation for you. 13 If the one who brought it decides to redeem it, he must add a fifth to thea valuation.

Valuation of House

14 "When a man consecrates his house as holy to the LORD, the priest will assess its value, whether high or low. The price will stand just as the priest assesses it. 15 But if the one who consecrated his house redeems ⌊it⌋, he must add a fifth to thea valuation price, and it will be his.

Valuation of Field

16 "If a man consecrates to the LORD any part of a field that he possesses, your valuation will be proportional to the seed needed to sow it, at the rate of 50 silver shekels for ⌊every⌋ five bushelsb of barley seed.c 17 If he consecrates his field during the Year of Jubilee, the price will stand according to your valuation. 18 But if he consecrates his field after the Jubilee, the priest will calculate the price for him in proportion to the years left until the ⌊next⌋ Year of Jubilee, so that your valuation will be reduced. 19 If the one who consecrated the field decides to redeem it, he must add a fifth to thea valuation price, and the field will transfer back to him. 20 But if he does not redeem the field or if he has sold it to another man, it is no longer redeemable. 21 When the field is released in the Jubilee, it will be holy to the LORD like a field permanently set apart; it becomes the priest's property. 22 "If a person consecrates to the LORD a field he has purchased that is not part of his inherited landholding, 23 then the priest will calculate for him the amount of thea valuation up to the Year of Jubilee, and the person will pay the valua-

---

a **27:13,15,19,23** Lit *your*   b **27:16** Lit *for a homer*   c **27:16** Or *grain*

tion on that day as a holy offering to the LORD. ²⁴ In the Year of Jubilee the field will return to the one he bought it from, the original owner. ²⁵ All your valuations will be ⌊measured⌋ by the standard sanctuary shekel, 20 gerahs to the shekel.

Firstborn Livestock

²⁶ "But no one can consecrate a firstborn of the livestock, whether an animal from the herd or flock, to the LORD, because a firstborn ⌊already⌋ belongs to the LORD. ²⁷ If it is one of the unclean livestock, it must be ransomed according to your valuation by adding a fifth of its value to it. If it is not redeemed, it can be sold according to your valuation. ²⁸ "Nothing that a man permanently sets apart to the LORD from all he owns, whether a person, an animal, or his inherited landholding, can be sold or redeemed; everything set apart is especially holy to the LORD. ²⁹ No person who has been set apart ⌊for destruction⌋ is to be ransomed; he must be put to death.

Principle of Tithe

³⁰ "Every tenth of the land's produce, grain from the soil or fruit from the trees, belongs to the LORD; it is holy to the LORD. ³¹ If a man decides to redeem any part of this tenth, he must add one-fifth to its value. ³² Every tenth animal from the herd or flock, which passes under the ⌊shepherd's⌋ rod, will be holy to the LORD. ³³ He is not to inspect whether it is good or bad, and he is not to make a substitution for it. But if he does make a substitution, both the animal and its substitute will be holy; they cannot be redeemed."

³⁴ These are the commands the LORD gave Moses for the Israelites on Mount Sinai.

NUMBERS

Census of Israel

1 The LORD spoke to Moses in the tent of meeting in the Wilderness of Sinai, on the first ⌊day⌋ of the second month of the second year after Israel's departure from the land of Egypt: ² "Take a census of the entire Israelite community by their clans and their ancestral houses, counting the names of every male one by one. ³ You and Aaron are to register those who are 20 years old or more by their military divisions—everyone who can serve in Israel's army.^a ⁴ A man from each tribe is to be with you, each one the head of his ancestral house. ⁵ These are the names of the men who are to assist you:

God Picks Census Workers

Elizur son of Shedeur from Reuben;
⁶ Shelumiel son of Zurishaddai from Simeon;
⁷ Nahshon son of Amminadab from Judah;
⁸ Nethanel son of Zuar from Issachar;
⁹ Eliab son of Helon from Zebulun;
¹⁰ from the sons of Joseph:
Elishama son of Ammihud from Ephraim,
Gamaliel son of Pedahzur from Manasseh;

^a**1:3** Lit *everyone going out to war in Israel*

11 Abidan son of Gideoni
from Benjamin;
12 Ahiezer son of Ammishaddai
from Dan;
13 Pagiel son of Ochran from Asher;
14 Eliasaph son of Deuel[a] from Gad;
15 Ahira son of Enan from Naphtali.

16 These are the men called from the community; they are leaders of their ancestral tribes, the heads of Israel's clans."

Moses and Aaron Obey

17 So Moses and Aaron took these men who had been designated by name, 18 and they assembled the whole community on the first day of the second month. They recorded their ancestry by their clans and their ancestral houses, counting one by one the names of those 20 years old or more, 19 just as the LORD commanded Moses. He registered them in the Wilderness of Sinai:

20 The descendants of Reuben, the firstborn of Israel: according to their family records by their clans and their ancestral houses, counting one by one the names of every male 20 years old or more, everyone who could serve in the army, 21 those registered for the tribe of Reuben numbered 46,500.

22 The descendants of Simeon: according to their family records by their clans and their ancestral houses, those registered counting one by one the names of every male 20 years old or more, everyone who could serve in the army, 23 those registered for the tribe of Simeon numbered 59,300.

24 The descendants of Gad: according to their family records by their clans and their ancestral houses, counting the names of those 20 years old or more, everyone who could serve in the army, 25 those registered for the tribe of Gad numbered 45,650.

26 The descendants of Judah: according to their family records by their clans and their ancestral houses, counting the names of those 20 years old or more, everyone who could serve in the army, 27 those registered for the tribe of Judah numbered 74,600.

28 The descendants of Issachar: according to their family records by their clans and their ancestral houses, counting the names of those 20 years old or more, everyone who could serve in the army, 29 those registered for the tribe of Issachar numbered 54,400.

30 The descendants of Zebulun: according to their family records by their clans and their ancestral houses, counting the names of those 20 years old or more, everyone who could serve in the army, 31 those registered for the tribe of Zebulun numbered 57,400.

32 The descendants of Joseph:

The descendants of Ephraim: according to their family records by their clans and their ancestral houses, counting the names of those 20 years old or more, everyone who could serve in the army, 33 those registered for the tribe of Ephraim numbered 40,500.

34 The descendants of Manasseh: according to their family records by

their clans and their ancestral houses, counting the names of those 20 years old or more, everyone who could serve in the army, [35] those registered for the tribe of Manasseh numbered 32,200.

[36] The descendants of Benjamin: according to their family records by their clans and their ancestral houses, counting the names of those 20 years old or more, everyone who could serve in the army, [37] those registered for the tribe of Benjamin numbered 35,400.

[38] The descendants of Dan: according to their family records by their clans and their ancestral houses, counting the names of those 20 years old or more, everyone who could serve in the army, [39] those registered for the tribe of Dan numbered 62,700.

[40] The descendants of Asher: according to their family records by their clans and their ancestral houses, counting the names of those 20 years old or more, everyone who could serve in the army, [41] those registered for the tribe of Asher numbered 41,500.

[42] The descendants of Naphtali: according to their family records by their clans and their ancestral houses, counting the names of those 20 years old or more, everyone who could serve in the army, [43] those registered for the tribe of Naphtali numbered 53,400.

[44] These are the men Moses and Aaron registered, with ⌊the assistance of⌋ the 12 leaders of Israel; each represented his ancestral house. [45] So all the Israelites 20 years old or more, everyone who could serve in Israel's army, were registered by their ancestral houses. [46] All those registered numbered 603,550.

Duties of the Levites

[47] But the Levites were not registered with them by their ancestral tribe. [48] For the LORD had told Moses: [49] "Do not register or take a census of the tribe of Levi with the ⌊other⌋ Israelites. [50] Appoint the Levites over the tabernacle of the •testimony, all its furnishings, and everything in it. They are to transport the tabernacle and all its articles, take care of it, and camp around it. [51] Whenever the tabernacle is to move, the Levites are to take it down, and whenever it is to stop at a campsite, the Levites are to set it up. Any unauthorized person who comes near ⌊it⌋ must be put to death.

[52] "The Israelites are to camp by their military divisions, each man with his encampment and under his banner. [53] The Levites are to camp around the tabernacle of the testimony and watch over it, so that no wrath will fall on the Israelite community." [54] The Israelites did everything just as the LORD had commanded Moses.

Organization of the Camps

2 The LORD spoke to Moses and Aaron: [2] "The Israelites are to camp under their respective banners beside the flags of their ancestral houses. They are to camp around the tent of meeting at a distance ⌊from it⌋:

[3] Judah's military divisions will camp on the east side toward the sunrise under their banner. The leader of the descendants of Judah is Nahshon son of Amminadab. [4] His military division numbers 74,600. [5] The tribe of Issachar will camp next to it. The leader of the Issacharites is Nethanel

son of Zuar. ⁶ His military division numbers 54,400. ⁷ The tribe of Zebulun ⌊will be next⌋. The leader of the Zebulunites is Eliab son of Helon. ⁸ His military division numbers 57,400. ⁹ The total number in their military divisions who belong to Judah's encampment is 186,400; they will move out first.

¹⁰ Reuben's military divisions will camp on the south side under their banner. The leader of the Reubenites is Elizur son of Shedeur. ¹¹ His military division numbers 46,500. ¹² The tribe of Simeon will camp next to it. The leader of the Simeonites is Shelumiel son of Zurishaddai. ¹³ His military division numbers 59,300. ¹⁴ The tribe of Gad ⌊will be next⌋. The leader of the Gadites is Eliasaph son of Deuel.ᵃ ¹⁵ His military division numbers 45,650. ¹⁶ The total number in their military divisions who belong to Reuben's encampment is 151,450; they will move out second.

¹⁷ The tent of meeting is to move out with the Levites' camp, which is in the middle of the camps. They are to move out just as they camp, each in his place,ᵇ with their banners.

¹⁸ Ephraim's military divisions will camp on the west side under their banner. The leader of the Ephraimites is Elishama son of Ammihud. ¹⁹ His military division numbers 40,500. ²⁰ The tribe of Manasseh will be next to it. The leader of the Manassites is Gamaliel son of Pedahzur. ²¹ His military division numbers 32,200. ²² The tribe of Benjamin ⌊will be next⌋. The leader of the Benjaminites is Abidan son of Gideoni.

²³ His military division numbers 35,400. ²⁴ The total in their military divisions who belong to Ephraim's encampment number 108,100; they will move out third.

²⁵ Dan's military divisions will camp on the north side under their banner. The leader of the Danites is Ahiezer son of Ammishaddai. ²⁶ His military division numbers 62,700. ²⁷ The tribe of Asher will camp next to it. The leader of the Asherites is Pagiel son of Ochran. ²⁸ His military division numbers 41,500. ²⁹ The tribe of Naphtali ⌊will be next⌋. The leader of the Naphtalites is Ahira son of Enan. ³⁰ His military division numbers 53,400. ³¹ The total number who belong to Dan's encampment is 157,600; they are to move out last, with their banners."

³² These are the Israelites registered by their ancestral houses. The total number in the camps by their military divisions is 603,550. ³³ But the Levites were not registered among the Israelites, just as the LORD had commanded Moses.

Israelites Obey

³⁴ The Israelites did everything the LORD commanded Moses; they camped by their banners in this way and moved out the same way, each man by his clan and by his ancestral house.

Aaron's Sons and the Levites

3 These are the family records of Aaron and Moses at the time the LORD spoke with Moses on Mount Sinai. ² These are the names of Aaron's sons: Nadab, the firstborn, and Abihu, Eleazar, and Ithamar. ³ These are the names of

ᵃ2:14 Some Hb mss, Sam, Vg; other Hb mss read *Reuel* ᵇ2:17 Lit *each on his hand*

Aaron's sons, the anointed priests, who were ordained to serve as priests. ⁴ But Nadab and Abihu died in the LORD's presence when they presented unauthorized fire before the LORD in the Wilderness of Sinai, and they had no sons. So Eleazar and Ithamar served as priests under the direction of Aaron their father.

God's Rules on Levites

⁵ The LORD spoke to Moses: ⁶ "Bring the tribe of Levi near and present them to Aaron the priest to assist him. ⁷ They are to perform duties forª him and the entire community before the tent of meeting by attending to the service of the tabernacle. ⁸ They are to take care ofª all the furnishings of the tent of meeting and perform duties forᵇ the Israelites by attending to the service of the tabernacle. ⁹ Assign the Levites to Aaron and his sons; they have been assigned exclusively to himᶜ from the Israelites. ¹⁰ You are to appoint Aaron and his sons to carry out their priestly responsibilities, but any unauthorized person who comes near ⸤the sanctuary⸥ must be put to death."

¹¹ The LORD spoke to Moses: ¹² "See, I have taken the Levites from the Israelites in place of every firstborn Israelite from the womb. The Levites belong to Me, ¹³ because every firstborn belongs to Me. At the time I struck down every firstborn in the land of Egypt, I consecrated every firstborn in Israel to Myself, both man and animal; they are Mine; I am the LORD."

God Commands Levitical Census

¹⁴ The LORD spoke to Moses in the Wilderness of Sinai: ¹⁵ "Register the Levites by their ancestral houses and their clans. You are to register every male one month old or more." ¹⁶ So Moses registered them in obedience to the LORD as he had been commanded:

¹⁷ These were Levi's sons by name: Gershon, Kohath, and Merari. ¹⁸ These were the names of Gershon's sons by their clans: Libni and Shimei. ¹⁹ Kohath's sons by their clans were Amram, Izhar, Hebron, and Uzziel. ²⁰ Merari's sons by their clans were Mahli and Mushi. These were the Levite clans by their ancestral houses.

Gershon's Census

²¹ The Libnite clan and the Shimeite clan came from Gershon; these were the Gershonite clans. ²² Those registered, counting every male one month old or more, numbered 7,500. ²³ The Gershonite clans camped behind the tabernacle on the west side, ²⁴ and the leader of the Gershonite family was Eliasaph son of Lael. ²⁵ The Gershonites' duties at the tent of meeting involved the tabernacle, the tent, its covering, the screen for the entrance to the tent of meeting, ²⁶ the hangings of the courtyard, the screen for the entrance to the courtyard that surrounds the tabernacle and the altar, and the tent ropes—all the work relating to these.

Kohath's Census

²⁷ The Amramite clan, the Izharite clan, the Hebronite clan, and the Uzzielite clan came from Kohath; these were the Kohathites. ²⁸ Counting every male one month old or more, there were 8,600ᵈ responsible for the duties ofᵉ the sanctuary. ²⁹ The

---

ª **3:7,8** Or to guard   ᵇ **3:8** Or and guard   ᶜ **3:9** Some Hb mss, LXX, Sam read Me; Nm 8:16   ᵈ **3:28** LXX reads 8,300   ᵉ **3:28** Or for guarding

clans of the Kohathites camped on the south side of the tabernacle, [30] and the leader of the family of the Kohathite clans was Elizaphan son of Uzziel. [31] Their duties involved the ark, the table, the lampstand, the altars, the sanctuary utensils that were used with these, and the screen[a]— and all the work relating to them. [32] The chief of the Levite leaders was Eleazar son of Aaron the priest; he had oversight of those responsible for the duties of[b] the sanctuary.

Merari's Census

[33] The Mahlite clan and the Mushite clan came from Merari; these were the Merarite clans. [34] Those registered, counting every male one month old or more, numbered 6,200. [35] The leader of the family of the Merarite clans was Zuriel son of Abihail; they camped on the north side of the tabernacle. [36] The assigned duties of Merari's descendants involved the tabernacle's supports, crossbars, posts, bases, all its equipment, and all the work related to these, [37] in addition to the posts of the surrounding courtyard with their bases, tent pegs, and ropes.

Role of Moses, Aaron and His Sons

[38] Moses, Aaron, and his sons, who performed the duties of[c] the sanctuary as a service on behalf of the Israelites, camped in front of the tabernacle on the east, in front of the tent of meeting toward the sunrise. Any unauthorized person who came near ⌊it⌋ was to be put to death.

[39] The total number of all the Levite males one month old or more that Moses and Aaron[d] registered by their clans at the LORD's command was 22,000.

Levites Take Place of Firstborn

[40] The LORD told Moses: "Register every firstborn male of the Israelites one month old or more, and list their names. [41] You are to take the Levites for Me—I am the LORD—in place of every firstborn among the Israelites, and the Levites' cattle in place of every firstborn among the Israelites' cattle." [42] So Moses registered every firstborn among the Israelites, as the LORD commanded him. [43] The total number of the firstborn males one month old or more listed by name was 22,273.

[44] The LORD spoke to Moses again: [45] "Take the Levites in place of every firstborn among the Israelites, and the Levites' cattle in place of their cattle. The Levites belong to Me; I am the LORD. [46] As the redemption price for the 273 firstborn Israelites who outnumber the Levites, [47] collect five •shekels for each person, according to the standard sanctuary shekel—20 gerahs to the shekel. [48] Give the money to Aaron and his sons as the redemption price for those who are in excess among the Israelites."

[49] So Moses collected the redemption money from those in excess of the ones redeemed by the Levites. [50] He collected the money from the firstborn Israelites: 1,365 ⌊shekels[e] measured⌋ by the standard sanctuary shekel. [51] He gave the redemption money to Aaron and his sons in obedience to the LORD, just as the LORD commanded Moses.

God Fixes Duties of Kohathites

4 The LORD spoke to Moses and Aaron: [2] "Among the Levites, take a

---

[a]3:31 The *screen* between the holy of holies and the holy place; Ex 35:12   [b]3:32 Or *for guarding*   [c]3:38 Or *who guarded*   [d]3:39 Some Hb mss, Sam, Syr omit *and Aaron*   [e]3:50 Over 34 pounds of silver

census of the Kohathites by their clans and their ancestral houses, [3] men from 30 years old to 50 years old—everyone who is qualified[a] to do work at the tent of meeting.

[4] "The service of the Kohathites at the tent of meeting concerns the most holy objects. [5] Whenever the camp is about to move on, Aaron and his sons are to go in, take down the screening veil, and cover the ark of the •testimony with it. [6] They are to place over this a covering made of manatee skin,[b] spread a solid blue cloth on top, and insert its poles.

[7] "They are to spread a blue cloth over the table of the Presence and place the plates and cups on it, as well as the bowls and pitchers for the drink offering. The regular bread ⌊offering⌋ is to be on it. [8] They are to spread a scarlet cloth over them, cover them with a covering made of manatee skin,[b] and insert the poles ⌊in the table⌋.

[9] "They are to take a blue cloth and cover the lampstand used for light, with its lamps, snuffers, and firepans, as well as its jars of oil by which they service it. [10] Then they must place it with all its utensils inside a covering made of manatee skin[b] and put ⌊them⌋ on the carrying frame.

[11] "They are to spread a blue cloth over the gold altar, cover it with a covering made of manatee skin,[b] and insert its poles. [12] They are to take all the serving utensils they use in the sanctuary, place ⌊them⌋ in a blue cloth, cover them with a covering made of manatee skin,[b] and put ⌊them⌋ on a carrying frame.

[13] "They are to remove the ashes from the ⌊bronze⌋ altar, spread a purple cloth over it, [14] and place all the equipment on it that they use in serving: the firepans, meatforks, shovels, and basins—all the equipment of the altar. They are to spread a covering made of manatee skin[b] over it and insert its poles.[c]

[15] "Aaron and his sons are to finish covering the holy objects and all their equipment whenever the camp is to move on. The Kohathites will come and carry them, but they are not to touch the holy objects or they will die. These are the transportation duties of the Kohathites regarding the tent of meeting.

[16] "Eleazar, son of Aaron the priest, has oversight of the lamp oil, the fragrant incense, the daily •grain offering, and the anointing oil. ⌊He has⌋ oversight of the entire tabernacle and everything in it, the holy objects and their utensils."[d]

[17] Then the LORD spoke to Moses and Aaron: [18] "Do not allow the Kohathite tribal clans to be wiped out from the Levites. [19] Do this for them so that they may live and not die when they come near the most holy objects: Aaron and his sons are to go in and assign each man his task and transportation duty. [20] The Kohathites are not to go in and look at the holy objects, even for a moment,[e] or they will die."

God Fixes Duties of Gershonites

[21] The LORD spoke to Moses: [22] "Take a census of the Gershonites also, by their ancestral houses and their clans. [23] Register men from 30 years old to 50 years old, everyone who is qualified to perform service, to do work at the tent of meeting. [24] This is the service of the Gershonite clans regarding work and transportation duties: [25] They are to

---

[a] 4:3 Lit everyone entering the service   [b] 4:6,8,10,11,12,14 Or of dolphin skin, or of fine leather; Hb obscure
[c] 4:14 Sam, LXX add They are to take a purple cloth and cover the wash basin and its base. They are to place them in a covering made of manatee skin and put them on the carrying frame.   [d] 4:16 Or the sanctuary and its furnishings
[e] 4:20 Or at the covering of the holy objects

transport the tabernacle curtains, the tent of meeting with its covering and the covering made of manatee skin[a] on top of it, the screen for the entrance to the tent of meeting, 26 the hangings of the courtyard, the screen for the entrance at the gate of the courtyard that surrounds the tabernacle and the altar, along with their ropes and all the equipment for their service. They will carry out everything that needs to be done with these items.

27 "All the service of the Gershonites, all their transportation duties and all their ⌊other⌋ work, is to be ⌊done⌋ at the command of Aaron and his sons; you are to assign to them all that they are responsible to carry. 28 This is the service of the Gershonite clans at the tent of meeting, and their duties will be under the direction of Ithamar son of Aaron the priest.

God Fixes Duties of Merarites

29 "As for the Merarites, you are to register them by their clans and their ancestral houses. 30 Register men from 30 years old to 50 years old, everyone who is qualified to do the work of the tent of meeting. 31 This is what they are responsible to carry as the whole of their service at the tent of meeting: the supports of the tabernacle, with its crossbars, posts, and bases, 32 the posts of the surrounding courtyard with their bases, tent pegs, and ropes, including all their equipment and all the work related to them. You are to assign by name the items that they are responsible to carry. 33 This is the service of the Merarite clans regarding all their work at the tent of meeting, under the direction of Ithamar son of Aaron the priest."

Census of Levites Completed

34 So Moses, Aaron, and the leaders of the community registered the Kohathites by their clans and their ancestral houses, 35 men from 30 years old to 50 years old, everyone who was qualified for work at the tent of meeting. 36 The men registered by their clans numbered 2,750. 37 These were the registered men of the Kohathite clans, everyone who could serve at the tent of meeting. Moses and Aaron registered them at the LORD's command through Moses.

38 The Gershonites were registered by their clans and their ancestral houses, 39 men from 30 years old to 50 years old, everyone who was qualified for work at the tent of meeting. 40 The men registered by their clans and their ancestral houses numbered 2,630. 41 These were the registered men of the Gershonite clans. At the LORD's command Moses and Aaron registered everyone who could serve at the tent of meeting.

42 The men of the Merarite clans were registered by their clans and their ancestral houses, 43 those from 30 years old to 50 years old, everyone who was qualified for work at the tent of meeting. 44 The men registered by their clans numbered 3,200. 45 These were the registered men of the Merarite clans; Moses and Aaron registered them at the LORD's command through Moses.

46 Moses, Aaron, and the leaders of Israel registered all the Levites by their clans and their ancestral houses, 47 from 30 years old to 50 years old, everyone who was qualified to do the work of serving at the tent of meeting and transporting ⌊it⌋. 48 Their registered men numbered 8,580. 49 At the LORD's command they were registered under the direction of Moses, each one according to his

---

a **4:25** Or of dolphin skin, or of fine leather; Hb obscure

work and transportation duty, and his assignment was as the LORD commanded
Moses.

Isolation of Unclean

5 The LORD instructed Moses:
² "Command the Israelites to send
away anyone from the camp who is afflicted with a skin disease, anyone who
has a ⌊bodily⌋ discharge, or anyone who
is defiled because of a corpse. ³ You must
send away both male or female; send
them outside the camp, so that they will
not defile their camps where I dwell
among them." ⁴ The Israelites did this,
sending them outside the camp. The Israelites did as the LORD instructed
Moses.

Compensation for Wrongdoing

⁵ The LORD spoke to Moses: ⁶ "Tell the
Israelites: When a man or woman commits any sin against another, that person
acts unfaithfully toward the LORD and is
guilty. ⁷ The person is to confess the sin
he has committed. He is to pay full compensation, add a fifth of its value to it,
and give ⌊it⌋ to the individual he has
wronged. ⁸ But if that individual has no
relative to receive compensation,ª the
compensation goes to the LORD for the
priest, along with the •atonement ram by
which the priest will make atonement
for the ⌊guilty⌋ person. ⁹ Every holy contribution the Israelites present to the
priest will be his. ¹⁰ Each one's holy contribution is his ⌊to give⌋; what each one
gives to the priest will be his."

The Jealousy Ritual

¹¹ The LORD spoke to Moses: ¹² "Speak
to the Israelites and tell them: If any
man's wife goes astray, is unfaithful to
him, ¹³ and sleeps with another,ᵇ but it is
concealed from her husband, and she is
undetected, even though she has defiled
herself, since there is no witness against
her, and she wasn't caught ⌊in the act⌋;
¹⁴ and if a feeling of jealousy comes over
the husband and he becomes jealous because of his wife who has defiled herself—or if a feeling of jealousy comes
over him and he becomes jealous of her
though she has not defiled herself—
¹⁵ then the man is to bring his wife to
the priest. He is also to bring an offering
for her of two quartsᶜ of barley flour. He
is not to pour oil over it or put frankincense on it because it is a •grain offering
of jealousy, a grain offering for remembrance that brings sin to mind.

Bitter Water

¹⁶ "The priest is to bring her forward
and have her stand before the LORD.
¹⁷ Then the priest is to take holy water in
a clay bowl, and take some of the dust
from the tabernacle floor and put ⌊it⌋ in
the water. ¹⁸ After the priest has the
woman stand before the LORD, he is to
let down her hairᵈ and place in her
hands the grain offering for remembrance, which is the grain offering of
jealousy. The priest is to hold the bitter
water that brings a curse. ¹⁹ The priest
will require the woman to take an oath
and will say to her, 'If no man has slept
with you, if you have not gone astray and
become defiled while under your husband's authority, be unaffected by this
bitter water that brings a curse. ²⁰ But if
you have gone astray while under your
husband's authority, if you have defiled
yourself and a man other than your husband has slept with you'— ²¹ at this
point the priest must make the woman
take the oath with the sworn curse, and
he is to say to her—'May the LORD make

ª**5:8** In the case of the individual's death   ᵇ**5:13** Lit *and man lies with her [and has] an emission of semen*   ᶜ**5:15** Lit *a tenth of an ephah*   ᵈ**5:18** Or *to uncover her head*

you into an object of your people's cursing and swearing when He makes your
thigh[a] shrivel and your belly swell.[b]
²² May this water that brings a curse enter your stomach, causing ⌊your⌋ belly to
swell and ⌊your⌋ thigh to shrivel.'

"And the woman must reply, '•Amen,
Amen.'

Written Curses

²³ "Then the priest is to write these
curses on a scroll and wash ⌊them⌋ off
into the bitter water. ²⁴ He will require
the woman to drink the bitter water that
brings a curse, and it will enter her and
cause bitter suffering. ²⁵ The priest is to
take the grain offering of jealousy from
the woman's hand, wave the offering before the LORD, and bring it to the altar.
²⁶ The priest is to take a handful of the
grain offering as a memorial portion and
burn it on the altar. Then he will require
the woman to drink the water.

²⁷ "When he makes her drink the water, if she has defiled herself and been
unfaithful to her husband, the water that
brings a curse will enter her and cause
bitter suffering; her belly will swell, and
her thigh will shrivel. She will become a
curse among her people. ²⁸ But if the
woman has not defiled herself and is
pure, she will be unaffected and will be
able to conceive children.

²⁹ "This is the law regarding jealousy
when a wife goes astray and defiles herself while under her husband's authority,
³⁰ or when a feeling of jealousy comes
over a husband and he becomes jealous of
his wife. He is to have the woman stand
before the LORD, and the priest will apply
this entire ritual to her. ³¹ The husband
will be free of guilt, but that woman will
bear the consequences of her guilt."

The Nazirite Vow

6 The LORD instructed Moses: ² "Speak
to the Israelites and tell them: When
a man or woman makes a special vow, a
Nazirite vow, to consecrate himself to[c]
the LORD, ³ he is to abstain[d] from wine
and beer. He must not drink vinegar
made from wine or from beer. He must
not drink any grape juice or eat fresh
grapes or raisins. ⁴ He is not to eat anything produced by the grapevine, from
seeds to skin,[e] during his vow.

⁵ "You must not cut his hair[f] throughout the time of his vow of consecration.
He must be holy until the time is completed during which he consecrates himself to the LORD; he is to let the hair of
his head grow long. ⁶ He must not go
near a dead body during the time he consecrates himself to the LORD. ⁷ He is not
to defile himself for his father or mother,
or his brother or sister, when they die,
because the hair consecrated to his God
is on his head. ⁸ He is holy to the LORD
during the time of consecration.

Offering if Defiled

⁹ "If someone suddenly dies near him,
defiling his consecrated head of hair, he
must shave his head on the day of his
purification; he is to shave it on the seventh day. ¹⁰ On the eighth day he is to
bring two turtledoves or two young pigeons to the priest at the entrance to the
tent of meeting. ¹¹ The priest is to offer
one as a •sin offering and the other as a
•burnt offering to make •atonement on
behalf of the Nazirite, since he sinned
because of the corpse. On that day he
must consecrate[g] his head ⌊again⌋. ¹² He
is to rededicate his time of consecration
to the LORD and to bring a year-old male
lamb as a •restitution offering. But do

ᵃ**5:21-22** Possibly a euphemism for the reproductive organs   ᵇ**5:21** Or *flood*   ᶜ**6:2** Or *vow, to live as a Nazirite for*
ᵈ**6:3** The words *Nazirite, consecrate,* and *abstain* come from the same Hb word, which involves the idea of separation.
ᵉ**6:4** Or *from unripe grapes to hulls*   ᶠ**6:5** Lit *A razor is not to pass over his head*   ᵍ**6:11** Lit *set apart*

not count the previous period, because his consecrated hair became defiled.

Completion of Vow

[13] "This is the law of the Nazirite: On the day his time of consecration is completed, he must be brought to the entrance to the tent of meeting. [14] He is to present an offering to the LORD of one unblemished year-old male lamb as a burnt offering, one unblemished year-old female lamb as a sin offering, one unblemished ram as a •fellowship offering, [15] along with their •grain offerings and drink offerings, and a basket of unleavened cakes made from fine flour mixed with oil, and unleavened wafers coated with oil. [16] "The priest is to present ⌊these⌋ before the LORD and sacrifice the Nazirite's sin offering and burnt offering. [17] He will also offer the ram as a fellowship sacrifice to the LORD, together with the basket of unleavened bread. Then the priest will offer the accompanying grain offering and drink offering.

[18] "The Nazirite is to shave his consecrated head at the entrance to the tent of meeting, take the hair from his head, and put ⌊it⌋ on the fire under the fellowship sacrifice. [19] The priest is to take the boiled shoulder from the ram, one unleavened cake from the basket, and one unleavened wafer, and put ⌊them⌋ into the hands of the Nazirite after he has shaved his consecrated head. [20] The priest is to wave them as a presentation offering before the LORD. It is a holy portion for the priest, in addition to the breast of the presentation offering and the thigh of the contribution. After that, the Nazirite may drink wine.

[21] "This is the ritual of the Nazirite who vows his offering to the LORD for his consecration, in addition to whatever else he can afford; he must fulfill whatever vow he makes in keeping with the ritual for his consecration."

God Sets Priestly Blessing

[22] The LORD spoke to Moses: [23] "Tell Aaron and his sons how you are to bless the Israelites. Say to them:

[24] The LORD bless you
        and protect you;
[25] the LORD make His face shine
        on you,
        and be gracious to you;
[26] the LORD look with favor on you[a]
        and give you peace.[b]

[27] In this way they will put[c] My name on the Israelites, and I will bless them."

Offerings from the Leaders

7 On the day Moses finished setting up the tabernacle, he anointed and consecrated it and all its furnishings, along with the altar and all its utensils. After he anointed and consecrated these things, [2] the leaders of Israel, the heads of their ancestral houses, presented ⌊an offering⌋. They were the tribal leaders who supervised the registration. [3] They brought as their offering before the LORD six covered carts and 12 oxen, a cart from every two leaders and an ox from each one, and presented them in front of the tabernacle.

Lord Instructs Moses on Offerings

[4] The LORD said to Moses, [5] "Accept ⌊these⌋ from them to be used in the work of the tent of meeting, and give this offering to the Levites, to each ⌊division⌋ according to their service."

[6] So Moses took the carts and oxen and gave them to the Levites. [7] He gave the

[a]**6:26** Lit *LORD lift His face to you*   [b]**6:26** Or *prosperity*   [c]**6:27** Or *invoke*

Gershonites two carts and four oxen corresponding to their service, ⁸ and gave the Merarites four carts and eight oxen corresponding to their service, under the direction of Ithamar son of Aaron the priest. ⁹ But he did not give ⌊any⌋ to the Kohathites, since their responsibility was service related to the holy objects carried on their shoulders.

¹⁰ The leaders also presented the dedication gift for the altar when it was anointed. The leaders presented their offerings in front of the altar. ¹¹ The LORD told Moses, "Each day have one leader present his offering for the dedication of the altar."

Nahshon's Offering for Judah

¹² The one who presented his offering on the first day was Nahshon son of Amminadab from the tribe of Judah. ¹³ His offering was one silver dish weighing three and a quarter pounds[a] and one silver basin weighing one and three-quarter pounds,[b] ⌊measured⌋ by the standard sanctuary •shekel, both of them full of fine flour mixed with oil for a •grain offering; ¹⁴ one gold bowl weighing four ounces,[c] full of incense; ¹⁵ one young bull, one ram, and one male lamb a year old, for a •burnt offering; ¹⁶ one male goat for a •sin offering; ¹⁷ and two bulls, five rams, five male breeding goats, and five male lambs a year old, for the •fellowship sacrifice. This was the offering of Nahshon son of Amminadab.

Nathanel's Offering for Issachar

¹⁸ On the second day Nethanel son of Zuar, leader of Issachar, presented ⌊an offering⌋. ¹⁹ As his offering, he presented one silver dish weighing three and a quarter pounds[a] and one silver basin weighing one and three-quarter pounds,[b] ⌊measured⌋ by the standard sanctuary shekel, both of them full of fine flour mixed with oil for a grain offering; ²⁰ one gold bowl weighing four ounces,[c] full of incense; ²¹ one young bull, one ram, and one male lamb a year old, for a burnt offering; ²² one male goat for a sin offering; ²³ and two bulls, five rams, five male breeding goats, and five male lambs a year old, for the fellowship sacrifice. This was the offering of Nethanel son of Zuar.

Eliab's Offering for Zebulun

²⁴ On the third day Eliab son of Helon, leader of the Zebulunites, ⌊presented an offering⌋. ²⁵ His offering was one silver dish weighing three and a quarter pounds[a] and one silver basin weighing one and three-quarter pounds,[b] ⌊measured⌋ by the standard sanctuary shekel, both of them full of fine flour mixed with oil for a grain offering; ²⁶ one gold bowl weighing four ounces,[c] full of incense; ²⁷ one young bull, one ram, and one male lamb a year old, for a burnt offering; ²⁸ one male goat for a sin offering; ²⁹ and two bulls, five rams, five male breeding goats, and five male lambs a year old, for the fellowship sacrifice. This was the offering of Eliab son of Helon.

Elizur's Offering for Reuben

³⁰ On the fourth day Elizur son of Shedeur, leader of the Reubenites, ⌊presented an offering⌋. ³¹ His offering was one silver dish weighing

---

[a] 7:13,19,25 Lit dish, 130 its shekel-weight   [b] 7:13,19,25 Lit 70 shekels   [c] 7:14,20,26 Lit 10 (shekels)

three and a quarter pounds[a] and one silver basin weighing one and three-quarter pounds,[b] ⌊measured⌋ by the standard sanctuary shekel, both of them full of fine flour mixed with oil for a grain offering; [32] one gold bowl weighing four ounces,[c] full of incense; [33] one young bull, one ram, and one male lamb a year old, for a burnt offering; [34] one male goat for a sin offering; [35] and two bulls, five rams, five male breeding goats, and five male lambs a year old, for the fellowship sacrifice. This was the offering of Elizur son of Shedeur.

Shelumiel's Offering for Simeon

[36] On the fifth day Shelumiel son of Zurishaddai, leader of the Simeonites, ⌊presented an offering⌋. [37] His offering was one silver dish weighing three and a quarter pounds[a] and one silver basin weighing one and three-quarter pounds,[b] ⌊measured⌋ by the standard sanctuary shekel, both of them full of fine flour mixed with oil for a grain offering; [38] one gold bowl weighing four ounces,[c] full of incense; [39] one young bull, one ram, and one male lamb a year old, for a burnt offering; [40] one male goat for a sin offering; [41] and two bulls, five rams, five male breeding goats, and five male lambs a year old, for the fellowship sacrifice. This was the offering of Shelumiel son of Zurishaddai.

Eliasaph's Offering for Gad

[42] On the sixth day Eliasaph son of Deuel,[d] leader of the Gadites, ⌊presented an offering⌋. [43] His offering was one silver dish weighing three

and a quarter pounds[a] and one silver basin weighing one and three-quarter pounds,[b] ⌊measured⌋ by the standard sanctuary shekel, both of them full of fine flour mixed with oil for a grain offering; [44] one gold bowl weighing four ounces,[c] full of incense; [45] one young bull, one ram, and one male lamb a year old, for a burnt offering; [46] one male goat for a sin offering; [47] and two bulls, five rams, five male breeding goats, and five male lambs a year old, for the fellowship sacrifice. This was the offering of Eliasaph son of Deuel.[d]

Elishama's Offering for Ephraim

[48] On the seventh day Elishama son of Ammihud, leader of the Ephraimites, ⌊presented an offering⌋. [49] His offering was one silver dish weighing three and a quarter pounds[a] and one silver basin weighing one and three-quarter pounds,[b] ⌊measured⌋ by the standard sanctuary shekel, both of them full of fine flour mixed with oil for a grain offering; [50] one gold bowl weighing four ounces,[c] full of incense; [51] one young bull, one ram, and one male lamb a year old, for a burnt offering; [52] one male goat for a sin offering; [53] and two bulls, five rams, five male breeding goats, and five male lambs a year old, for the fellowship sacrifice. This was the offering of Elishama son of Ammihud.

Gamaliel's Offering for Manasseh

[54] On the eighth day Gamaliel son of Pedahzur, leader of the Manassites, ⌊presented an offering⌋. [55] His offering was one silver dish weighing

---

[a]7:31,37,43,49 Lit *dish, 130 its shekel-weight*   [b]7:31,37,43,49 Lit *70 shekels*   [c]7:32,38,44,50 Lit *10* (shekels)
[d]7:42,47 LXX, Syr read *Reuel*

three and a quarter pounds[a] and one silver basin weighing one and three-quarter pounds,[b] ⌊measured⌋ by the standard sanctuary shekel, both of them full of fine flour mixed with oil for a grain offering; [56] one gold bowl weighing four ounces,[c] full of incense; [57] one young bull, one ram, and one male lamb a year old, for a burnt offering; [58] one male goat for a sin offering; [59] and two bulls, five rams, five male breeding goats, and five male lambs a year old, for the fellowship sacrifice. This was the offering of Gamaliel son of Pedahzur.

Abidan's Offering for Benjamin

[60] On the ninth day Abidan son of Gideoni, leader of the Benjaminites, ⌊presented an offering⌋. [61] His offering was one silver dish weighing three and a quarter pounds[a] and one silver basin weighing one and three-quarter pounds,[b] ⌊measured⌋ by the standard sanctuary shekel, both of them full of fine flour mixed with oil for a grain offering; [62] one gold bowl weighing four ounces,[c] full of incense; [63] one young bull, one ram, and one male lamb a year old, for a burnt offering; [64] one male goat for a sin offering; [65] and two bulls, five rams, five male breeding goats, and five male lambs a year old, for the fellowship sacrifice. This was the offering of Abidan son of Gideoni.

Ahiezer's Offering for Dan

[66] On the tenth day Ahiezer son of Ammishaddai, leader of the Danites, ⌊presented an offering⌋. [67] His offering was one silver dish weighing three and a quarter pounds[a] and one silver basin weighing one and three-

quarter pounds,[b] ⌊measured⌋ by the standard sanctuary shekel, both of them full of fine flour mixed with oil for a grain offering; [68] one gold bowl weighing four ounces,[c] full of incense; [69] one young bull, one ram, and one male lamb a year old, for a burnt offering; [70] one male goat for a sin offering; [71] and two bulls, five rams, five male breeding goats, and five male lambs a year old, for the fellowship sacrifice. This was the offering of Ahiezer son of Ammishaddai.

Pagiel's Offering for Asher

[72] On the eleventh day Pagiel son of Ochran, leader of the Asherites, ⌊presented an offering⌋. [73] His offering was one silver dish weighing three and a quarter pounds[a] and one silver basin weighing one and three-quarter pounds,[b] ⌊measured⌋ by the standard sanctuary shekel, both of them full of fine flour mixed with oil for a grain offering; [74] one gold bowl weighing four ounces,[c] full of incense; [75] one young bull, one ram, and one male lamb a year old, for a burnt offering; [76] one male goat for a sin offering; [77] and two bulls, five rams, five male breeding goats, and five male lambs a year old, for the fellowship sacrifice. This was the offering of Pagiel son of Ochran.

Ahira's Offering for Naphtali

[78] On the twelfth day Ahira son of Enan, leader of the Naphtalites, ⌊presented an offering⌋. [79] His offering was one silver dish weighing three and a quarter pounds[a] and one silver basin weighing one and three-quarter pounds,[b] ⌊measured⌋ by the stan-

---

[a]7:55,61,67,73,79 Lit *dish, 130 its shekel-weight*   [b]7:55,61,67,73,79 Lit *70 shekels*   [c]7:56,62,68,74 Lit *10* (shekels)

dard sanctuary shekel, both of them full of fine flour mixed with oil for a grain offering; [80] one gold bowl weighing four ounces,[a] full of incense; [81] one young bull, one ram, and one male lamb a year old, for a burnt offering; [82] one male goat for a sin offering; [83] and two bulls, five rams, five male breeding goats, and five male lambs a year old, for the fellowship sacrifice. This was the offering of Ahira son of Enan.

Summary of Leaders' Gifts

[84] This was the dedication gift from the leaders of Israel for the altar when it was anointed: 12 silver dishes, 12 silver basins, and 12 gold bowls. [85] Each silver dish ⌊weighed⌋ three and a quarter pounds,[b] and each basin one and three-quarter pounds.[c] The total ⌊weight⌋ of the silver articles was 60 pounds[d] ⌊measured⌋ by the standard sanctuary shekel. [86] The 12 gold bowls full of incense each ⌊weighed⌋ four ounces[a] ⌊measured⌋ by the standard sanctuary shekel. The total ⌊weight⌋ of the gold bowls was three pounds.[e] [87] All the livestock for the burnt offering totaled 12 bulls, 12 rams, and 12 male lambs a year old, with their grain offerings, and 12 male goats for the sin offering. [88] All the livestock for the fellowship sacrifice totaled 24 bulls, 60 rams, 60 male breeding goats, and 60 male lambs a year old. This was the dedication gift for the altar after it was anointed.

Moses Hears God's Voice

[89] When Moses entered the tent of meeting to speak with the LORD, he heard the voice speaking to him from above the •mercy seat that was on the ark of the •testimony, from between the two •cherubim. He spoke to him ⌊that way⌋.

God Orders Lighting in Tabernacle

8 The LORD spoke to Moses: [2] "Speak to Aaron and tell him: When you set up the lamps, the seven lamps are to give light in front of the lampstand." [3] So Aaron did this; he set up its lamps ⌊to give light⌋ in front of the lampstand just as the LORD had commanded Moses. [4] This is the way the lampstand was made: it was a hammered work of gold, hammered from its base to its flower petals. The lampstand was made according to the pattern the LORD had shown Moses.

Consecration of Levites

God Orders Purification

[5] The LORD spoke to Moses: [6] "Take the Levites from among the Israelites and ceremonially cleanse them. [7] This is what you must do to them for their purification: Sprinkle them with the purification water. Have them shave their entire bodies and wash their clothes, and so purify themselves.

[8] "They are to take a young bull and its •grain offering of fine flour mixed with oil, and you are to take a second young bull for a •sin offering. [9] Bring the Levites before the tent of meeting and assemble the entire Israelite community. [10] Then present the Levites before the LORD, and have the Israelites lay their hands on them. [11] Aaron is to present the Levites before the LORD as a presentation offering from the Israelites, so that they may perform the LORD's work. [12] Next the Levites are to lay their hands on the heads of the bulls. Sacrifice one as

---

[a]**7:80,86** Lit 10 (shekels)   [b]**7:85** Lit 130 (shekels)   [c]**7:85** Lit 70 (shekels)   [d]**7:85** Lit 2,400 (shekels)   [e]**7:86** Lit 120 (shekels)

a sin offering and the other as a •burnt offering to the LORD, to make •atonement for the Levites.

Presentation of Levites

13 "You are to have the Levites stand before Aaron and his sons, and you are to present them before the LORD as a presentation offering. 14 In this way you are to separate the Levites from the rest of the Israelites so that the Levites will belong to Me. 15 After that the Levites may come to serve ⌊at⌋ the tent of meeting, once you have ceremonially cleansed them and presented them as a presentation offering. 16 For they have been exclusively assigned to Me from the Israelites. I have taken them for Myself in place of all who come first from the womb, every Israelite firstborn. 17 For every firstborn among the Israelites is Mine, both man and animal. I consecrated them to Myself on the day I struck down every firstborn in the land of Egypt. 18 But I have taken the Levites in place of every firstborn among the Israelites. 19 From the Israelites, I have given the Levites exclusively to Aaron and his sons to perform the work for the Israelites at the tent of meeting and to make atonement on their behalf, so that no plague will come against the Israelites when they approach the sanctuary."

Levites Go to Work

20 Moses, Aaron, and the entire Israelite community did ⌊this⌋ to the Levites. The Israelites did everything to them the LORD commanded Moses regarding the Levites. 21 The Levites purified themselves and washed their clothes; then Aaron presented[a] them before the LORD as a presentation offering. Aaron also made atonement for them to ceremoni-ally cleanse them. 22 After that, the Levites came to do their work at the tent of meeting in the presence of Aaron and his sons. So they did to them as the LORD had commanded Moses concerning the Levites.

God Fixes Levites' Term of Service

23 The LORD spoke to Moses: 24 "In regard to the Levites: From 25 years old or more, a man enters the service in the work at the tent of meeting. 25 But at 50 years old he is to retire from his service in the work and no longer serve. 26 He may assist his brothers to fulfill responsibilities[b] at the tent of meeting, but he must not do the work. This is how you are to deal with the Levites regarding their duties."

The Second Passover

Israelites Obey God

9 In the first month of the second year after their departure from the land of Egypt, the LORD told Moses in the Wilderness of Sinai: 2 "The Israelites are to observe the •Passover at its appointed time. 3 You must observe it at its appointed time on the fourteenth day of this month at twilight; you are to observe it according to all its statutes and ordinances." 4 So Moses told the Israelites to observe the Passover, 5 and they observed it in the first month on the fourteenth day at twilight in the Wilderness of Sinai. The Israelites did everything as the LORD had commanded Moses.

Unclean Men

6 But there were ⌊some⌋ men who were unclean because of a human corpse, so they could not observe the Passover on that day. These men came before Moses

---

a**8:21** Lit waved   b**8:26** Or to keep guard

and Aaron the same day [7] and said to him, "We are unclean because of a human corpse. Why should we be excluded from presenting the LORD's offering at its appointed time with the ⌊other⌋ Israelites?"

[8] Moses replied to them, "Wait here until I hear what the LORD commands for you."

God's Rules for Travelers

[9] Then the LORD spoke to Moses: [10] "Tell the Israelites: When any one of you or your descendants is unclean because of a corpse or is on a distant journey, he may still observe the Passover to the LORD. [11] Such people are to observe it in the second month, on the fourteenth day at twilight. They are to eat the animal with unleavened bread and bitter herbs; [12] they may not leave any of it until morning or break any of its bones. They must observe the Passover according to all its statutes.

God's Passover Rules for the Unclean

[13] "But the man who is ceremonially clean, is not on a journey, and yet fails to observe the Passover is to be cut off from his people, because he did not present the LORD's offering at its appointed time. That man will bear the consequences of his sin.

God's Rules for Foreigners

[14] "If a foreigner resides with you and wants to observe the Passover to the LORD, he is to do so according to the Passover statute and its ordinances. You are to apply the same statute to both the foreign resident and the native of the land."

The Cloud Guides

[15] On the day the tabernacle was set up, the cloud covered the tabernacle, the tent of the •testimony, and it appeared like fire above the tabernacle from evening until morning. [16] It remained that way continuously: the cloud would cover it,[a] appearing like fire at night. [17] Whenever the cloud was lifted up above the tent, the Israelites would set out; at the place where the cloud stopped, there the Israelites camped. [18] At the LORD's command the Israelites set out, and at the LORD's command they camped. As long as the cloud stayed over the tabernacle, they camped.

[19] Even when the cloud stayed over the tabernacle many days, the Israelites carried out the LORD's requirement and did not set out. [20] Sometimes the cloud remained over the tabernacle for ⌊only⌋ a few days. They would camp at the LORD's command and set out at the LORD's command. [21] Sometimes the cloud remained ⌊only⌋ from evening until morning; when the cloud lifted in the morning, they set out. Or if it remained a day and a night, they moved out when the cloud lifted. [22] Whether it was two days, a month, or longer,[b] the Israelites camped and did not set out as long as the cloud stayed over the tabernacle. But when it was lifted, they set out. [23] They camped at the LORD's command, and they set out at the LORD's command. They carried out the LORD's requirement according to His command through Moses.

Signals from Two Silver Trumpets

10 The LORD spoke to Moses: [2] "Make two trumpets of hammered silver to summon the community and have the camps set out. [3] When both are sounded in long blasts, the entire community is to gather before you at the entrance to the

---

tent of meeting. [4] However, if <u>one is sounded</u>, only the leaders, the heads of Israel's clans, are to gather before you.

[5] "When you sound short blasts, the camps pitched on the east are to set out. [6] When you sound short blasts a second time, the camps pitched on the south are to set out. Short blasts are to be sounded for them to set out. [7] When calling the assembly together, you are to sound long blasts, not short ones. [8] The sons of Aaron, the priests, are to sound the trumpets. Your use of these is a permanent statute throughout your generations.

[9] "When you enter into battle in your land against an adversary who is attacking you, sound short blasts on the trumpets, and you will be remembered before the LORD your God and be delivered from your enemies. [10] You are to sound the trumpets over your •burnt offerings and your •fellowship sacrifices and on your joyous occasions, your appointed festivals, and the beginning of each of your months. They will serve as a reminder for you before your God: I am the LORD your God."

On the Move: Sinai to Paran

[11] During the second year, in the second month on the twentieth ⌊day⌋ of the month, the cloud was lifted up above the tabernacle of the •testimony. [12] The Israelites traveled on from the Wilderness of Sinai, moving from one place to the next until the cloud stopped in the Wilderness of Paran. [13] They set out for the first time according to the LORD's command through Moses.

[14] The military divisions of the camp of Judah with their banner set out first, and Nahshon son of Amminadab was over Judah's divisions. [15] Nethanel son of Zuar was over the division of the Issachar tribe, [16] and Eliab son of Helon was over the division of the Zebulun tribe. [17] The tabernacle was then taken down, and the Gershonites and the Merarites set out, transporting the tabernacle.

[18] The military divisions of the camp of Reuben with their banner set out, and Elizur son of Shedeur was over Reuben's division. [19] Shelumiel son of Zurishaddai was over the division of Simeon's tribe, [20] and Eliasaph son of Deuel was over the division of the tribe of Gad. [21] The Kohathites then set out, transporting the holy objects; the tabernacle was to be set up before their arrival.

[22] Next the military divisions of the camp of Ephraim with their banner set out, and Elishama son of Ammihud was over Ephraim's division. [23] Gamaliel son of Pedahzur was over the division of the tribe of Manasseh, [24] and Abidan son of Gideoni was over the division of the tribe of Benjamin.

[25] The military divisions of the camp of Dan with their banner set out, serving as rear guard for all the camps, and Ahiezer son of Ammishaddai was over Dan's division. [26] Pagiel son of Ochran was over the division of the tribe of Asher, [27] and Ahira son of Enan was over the division of the tribe of Naphtali. [28] This was the order of march for the Israelites by their military divisions as they set out.

Moses Pleads with Brother-in-law

[29] Moses said to <u>Hobab, son of Moses' father-in-law</u>[a] Reuel[b] the Midianite: "We're setting out for the place the LORD promised: 'I will give it to you.' Come with us, and we will treat you well, for the LORD has promised good things to Israel."

---

[a]**10:29** Or *said to Hobab's brother-in-law*   [b]**10:29** Also known as Jethro; Ex 2:16-18; 3:1; 4:18

30 But he replied to him, "I don't want to go. Instead, I will go to my own land and my relatives."

31 "Please don't leave us," Moses said, "since you know where we should camp in the wilderness, and you can serve as our eyes. 32 If you come with us, whatever good the LORD does for us we will do for you."

Ark's Role in Departure

33 They set out from the mountain of the LORD on a three-day journey to seek a resting place for them, with the ark of the LORD's covenant traveling ahead of them for the three days. 34 Meanwhile, the cloud of the LORD was over them by day when they set out from the camp.

35 Whenever the ark set out, Moses would say:

Arise, LORD!
Let Your enemies be scattered,
    and those who hate You flee
        from Your presence.

36 When it came to rest, he would say:

Return, LORD,
    to the countless thousands of Israel.

People Complain

God's Fire Warning

11 Now the people began complaining openly before[a] the LORD about hardship. When the LORD heard, His anger burned, and the fire from the LORD blazed among them and consumed the outskirts of the camp. 2 Then the people cried out to Moses, and he prayed to the LORD, and the fire died down. 3 So that place was named Taberah,[b] because the LORD's fire had blazed among them.

Food Complaints

4 Contemptible people[c] among them had a strong craving ⌊for other food⌋. The Israelites cried again and said, "Who will feed us meat? 5 We remember the free fish we ate in Egypt, along with the cucumbers, melons, leeks, onions, and garlic. 6 But now our appetite is gone;[d] there's nothing to look at but this manna!"

7 The manna resembled coriander seed, and its appearance was like that of bdellium.[e] 8 The people walked around and gathered ⌊it⌋. They ground ⌊it⌋ on a pair of grinding stones or crushed ⌊it⌋ in a mortar, then boiled ⌊it⌋ in a cooking pot and shaped it into cakes. It tasted like a pastry cooked with the finest oil. 9 When the dew fell on the camp at night, the manna would fall with it.

Moses Complains to God

10 Moses heard the people, family after family, crying at the entrance of their tents. The LORD was very angry; Moses was also provoked.[f] 11 So Moses asked the LORD, "Why have You brought such trouble on Your servant? Why are You angry with me, and why do You burden me with all these people? 12 Did I conceive all these people? Did I give them birth so You should tell me, 'Carry them at your breast, as a nursing woman carries a baby,' to the land that You[g] swore to ⌊give⌋ their fathers? 13 Where can I get meat to give all these people? For they are crying to me: 'Give us meat to eat!'

14 "I can't carry all these people by myself. They are too much for me. 15 If You are going to treat me like this, please kill me right now. If You are pleased with me, don't let me see my misery ⌊any more⌋."

---

a 11:1 Lit *in the ears of*   b 11:3 = blaze   c 11:4 Or *The mixed multitude*; Hb obscure   d 11:6 Or *our lives are wasting away*, or *our throat is dry*   e 11:7 Probably a gum resin of yellowish, transparent color   f 11:10 Lit *and it was evil in the eyes of Moses*   g 11:12 One Hb ms, Sam, LXX, Syr, Tg read *I*

God's Solution:
Delegate Duties to Seventy Elders

16 The LORD answered Moses, "Bring Me 70 men from Israel known to you as elders and officers of the people. Take them to the tent of meeting and have them stand there with you. 17 Then I will come down and speak with you there. I will take some of the Spirit who is on you and put ⌊the Spirit⌋ on them. They will help you bear the burden of the people, so that you do not have to bear it by yourself.

18 "Tell the people: Purify yourselves ⌊in readiness⌋ for tomorrow, and you will eat meat because you cried before the LORD: 'Who will feed us meat? We really had it good in Egypt.' The LORD will give you meat and you will eat. 19 You will eat, not for one day, or two days, or five days, or 10 days, or 20 days, 20 but for a whole month—until it comes out of your nostrils and becomes nauseating to you—because you have rejected the LORD who is among you, and cried to Him: 'Why did we ever leave Egypt?'"

21 But Moses replied, "I'm in the middle of a people with 600,000 foot soldiers, yet You say, 'I will give them meat, and they will eat for a month.' 22 If flocks and herds were slaughtered for them, would they have enough? Or if all the fish in the sea were caught for them, would they have enough?"

23 The LORD answered Moses, "Is the LORD's power limited?[a] You will see whether or not what I have promised will happen to you."

Spirit-filled Elders

24 Moses went out and told the people the words of the LORD. He brought 70 men from the elders of the people and had them stand around the tent. 25 Then the LORD descended in the cloud and spoke to him. He took some of the Spirit that was on Moses and placed ⌊the Spirit⌋ on the 70 elders. As the Spirit rested on them, they prophesied, but they never did it again. 26 Two men had remained in the camp, one named Eldad and the other Medad; the Spirit rested on them—they were among those listed, but had not gone out to the tent—and they prophesied in the camp. 27 A young man ran and reported to Moses, "Eldad and Medad are prophesying in the camp."

Joshua's Protest

28 Joshua son of Nun, assistant to Moses since his youth,[b] responded, "Moses, my lord, stop them!"

29 But Moses asked him, "Are you jealous on my account? If only all the LORD's people were prophets, and the LORD would place His Spirit on them." 30 Then Moses returned to the camp along with the elders of Israel.

God Sends Quail

31 A wind sent by the LORD came up and blew quail in from the sea; it dropped ⌊them⌋ at the camp all around, three feet[c] off[d] the ground, about a day's journey in every direction. 32 The people were up all that day and night and all the next day gathering the quail—the one who took the least gathered 33 bushels[e]—and they spread them out all around the camp.[f]

God Sends Plague

33 While the meat was still between their teeth, before it was chewed, the LORD's anger burned against the people, and the LORD struck them with a very severe plague. 34 So they named that place

---

[a]11:23 Lit LORD's arm too short   [b]11:28 LXX, some Sam mss read Moses, from his chosen ones   [c]11:31 Lit two cubits   [d]11:31 Or on, or above   [e]11:32 Lit 10 homers   [f]11:32 To dry or cure the meat; 2 Sm 17:19; Ezk 26:5,14

Kibroth-hattaavah,[a] because there they buried the people who had craved ⌊the meat⌋.

35 From Kibroth-hattaavah the people moved on to Hazeroth[b] and remained there.

Miriam and Aaron Complain

12 Miriam and Aaron criticized Moses because of the •Cushite[c] [d] woman he married (for he had married a Cushite woman). 2 They said, "Does the LORD speak only through Moses? Does He not also speak through us?" And the LORD heard ⌊it⌋. 3 Moses was a very humble man, more so than any man on the face of the earth.

God Rebukes

4 Suddenly the LORD said to Moses, Aaron, and Miriam, "You three come out to the tent of meeting." So the three of them went out. 5 Then the LORD descended in a pillar of cloud, stood at the entrance to the tent, and summoned Aaron and Miriam. When the two of them came forward, 6 He said:

"Listen to what I say:
If there is a prophet among you
   from the LORD,
I make Myself known to him
   in a vision;
I speak with him in a dream.
7 Not so with My servant Moses;
   he is faithful in[e] all My household.
8 I speak with him directly,[f]
   openly, and not in riddles;
   he sees the form of the LORD.

So why were you not afraid to speak against My servant Moses?" 9 The LORD's anger burned against them, and He left.

Miriam's Skin

10 As the cloud moved away from the tent, Miriam's ⌊skin⌋ suddenly became diseased, as ⌊white⌋ as snow. When Aaron turned toward her, he saw that she was diseased 11 and said to Moses, "My lord, please don't hold against us this sin we have so foolishly committed. 12 Please don't let her be like a dead ⌊baby⌋ whose flesh is half eaten away when he comes out of his mother's womb."

Moses Asks Mercy

13 Then Moses cried out to the LORD, "God, please heal her!"

14 The LORD answered Moses, "If her father had merely spit in her face, wouldn't she remain in disgrace for seven days? Let her be confined outside the camp for seven days; after that she may be brought back in." 15 So Miriam was confined outside the camp for seven days, and the people did not move on until Miriam was brought back in. 16 After that, the people set out from Hazeroth and camped in the Wilderness of Paran.

Spies into Canaan

13 The LORD spoke to Moses: 2 "Send men to scout out the land of Canaan I am giving to the Israelites. Send one man who is a leader among them from each of their ancestral tribes." 3 Moses sent them from the Wilderness of Paran at the LORD's command. All the men were leaders in Israel. 4 These were their names:

Shammua son of Zaccur
   from the tribe of Reuben;
5 Shaphat son of Hori from the tribe
   of Simeon;

---

6 Caleb son of Jephunneh
    from the tribe of Judah;
7 Igal son of Joseph from the tribe
    of Issachar;
8 Hoshea son of Nun from the tribe
    of Ephraim;
9 Palti son of Raphu from the tribe
    of Benjamin;
10 Gaddiel son of Sodi from the tribe
    of Zebulun;
11 Gaddi son of Susi from the tribe
    of Manasseh (from the tribe
    of Joseph);
12 Ammiel son of Gemalli
    from the tribe of Dan;
13 Sethur son of Michael
    from the tribe of Asher;
14 Nahbi son of Vophsi from the tribe
    of Naphtali;
15 Geuel son of Machi from the tribe
    of Gad.

16 These were the names of the men Moses sent to scout out the land, and Moses renamed Hoshea son of Nun, Joshua.

Moses Instructs Spies

17 When Moses sent them to scout out the land of Canaan, he told them, "Go up this way to the •Negev, then go up into the hill country. 18 See what the land is like, and whether the people who live there are strong or weak, few or many. 19 Is the land they live in good or bad? Are the cities they live in encampments or fortifications? 20 Is the land fertile or unproductive? Are there trees in it or not? Be courageous. Bring back some fruit from the land." It was the season for the first ripe grapes.

Spies on a Mission

21 So they went up and scouted out the land from the Wilderness of Zin[a] as far as Rehob[b] near the entrance to Hamath.[c] 22 They went up through the Negev and came to Hebron, where Ahiman, Sheshai, and Talmai, the descendants of Anak, were living. Hebron was built seven years before Zoan in Egypt. 23 When they came to the Valley of Eshcol, they cut down a branch with a single cluster of grapes, which was carried on a pole by two men. ⌊They⌋ also ⌊took⌋ some pomegranates and figs. 24 That place was called the Valley of Eshcol[d] because of the cluster ⌊of grapes⌋ the Israelites cut there. 25 At the end of 40 days they returned from scouting out the land.

Spies Report

26 The men went back to Moses, Aaron, and the entire Israelite community in the Wilderness of Paran at Kadesh. They brought back a report for them and the whole community, and they showed them the fruit of the land. 27 They reported to Moses: "We went into the land where you sent us. Indeed it is flowing with milk and honey, and here is some of its fruit. 28 However, the people living in the land are strong, and the cities are large and fortified. We also saw the descendants of Anak there. 29 The Amalekites are living in the land of the Negev; the Hittites, Jebusites, and Amorites live in the hill country; and the Canaanites live by the sea and along the Jordan."

Caleb: Let's Go!

30 Then Caleb quieted the people in the presence of Moses and said, "We must go up and take possession of the land because we can certainly conquer it!"

a 13:21 Southern border of the promised land   b 13:21 Northern border of the promised land   c 13:21 Or near Lebo-hamath   d 13:24 = cluster

Other Spies: No!

31 But the men who had gone up with him responded, "We can't go up against the people because they are stronger than we are!" 32 So they gave a negative report to the Israelites about the land they had scouted: "The land we passed through to explore is one that devours its inhabitants, and all the people we saw in it are men of great size. 33 We even saw the Nephilim[a] there." (The offspring of Anak were descended from the Nephilim.) "To ourselves we seemed like grasshoppers, and we must have seemed the same to them."

Timid Israelites

14 Then the whole community broke into loud cries, and the people wept that night. 2 All the Israelites complained about Moses and Aaron, and the whole community told them, "If only we had died in the land of Egypt, or if only we had died in this wilderness! 3 Why is the LORD bringing us into this land to die by the sword? Our wives and little children will become plunder. Wouldn't it be better for us to go back to Egypt?" 4 So they said to one another, "Let's appoint a leader and go back to Egypt."

Joshua and Caleb Object

5 Then Moses and Aaron fell down with their faces ⌊to the ground⌋ in front of the whole assembly of the Israelite community. 6 Joshua son of Nun and Caleb son of Jephunneh, who were among those who scouted out the land, tore their clothes 7 and said to the entire Israelite community: "The land we passed through and explored is an extremely good land. 8 If the LORD is pleased with us, He will bring us into this land, a land flowing with milk and honey, and give it to us. 9 Only don't rebel against the LORD, and don't be afraid of the people of the land, for we will devour them. Their protection has been removed from them, and the LORD is with us. Don't be afraid of them!"

10 While the whole community threatened to stone them, the glory of the LORD appeared to all the Israelites at the tent of meeting.

God's Frustration

11 The LORD said to Moses, "How long will these people despise Me? How long will they not trust in Me despite all the signs I have performed among them? 12 I will strike them with a plague and destroy them. Then I will make you into a greater and mightier nation than they are."

Moses Reasons with God

13 But Moses replied to the LORD, "The Egyptians will hear about it, for by Your strength You brought up this people from them. 14 They will tell ⌊it to⌋ the inhabitants of this land. They have heard that You, LORD, are among these people, how You, LORD, are seen face to face, how Your cloud stands over them, and how You go before them in a pillar of cloud by day and in a pillar of fire by night. 15 If You kill this people with a single blow,[b] the nations that have heard of Your fame will declare, 16 'Since the LORD wasn't able to bring this people into the land He swore to ⌊give⌋ them, He has slaughtered them in the wilderness.'

Moses Asks Pardon

17 "So now, may My Lord's power be magnified just as You have spoken: 18 The LORD is slow to anger and rich in faithful love, forgiving wrongdoing and

---

[a]13:33 Possibly means "fallen ones"; traditionally, *giants*; Gn 6:4   [b]14:15 Lit *people as one man*

rebellion. But He will not leave ⌊the guilty⌋ unpunished, bringing the consequences of the fathers' wrongdoing on the children to the third and fourth generation. ¹⁹ Please pardon the wrongdoing of this people in keeping with the greatness of Your faithful love, just as You have forgiven them from Egypt until now."

God Pardons People—But Bars Offenders from Promised Land

²⁰ The LORD responded, "I have pardoned ⌊them⌋ as you requested. ²¹ Yet as surely as I live and as the whole earth is filled with the LORD's glory, ²² none of the men who have seen My glory and the signs I performed in Egypt and in the wilderness, and have tested Me these 10 times and did not obey Me, ²³ will ever see the land I swore to ⌊give⌋ their fathers. None of those who have despised Me will see it. ²⁴ But since My servant Caleb has a different spirit and has followed Me completely, I will bring him into the land where he has gone, and his descendants will inherit it. ²⁵ Since the Amalekites and Canaanites are living in the lowlands,^a turn back tomorrow and head for the wilderness in the direction of the •Red Sea."

²⁶ Then the LORD spoke to Moses and Aaron: ²⁷ "How long ⌊must I endure⌋ this evil community that keeps complaining about Me? I have heard the Israelites' complaints that they make against Me. ²⁸ Tell them: As surely as I live, declares the LORD, I will do to you exactly as I heard you say. ²⁹ Your corpses will fall in this wilderness—all of you who were registered ⌊in the census⌋, the entire number of you 20 years old or more—because you have complained about Me. ³⁰ I swear that none of you will enter the land I promised^b to settle you in, except Caleb son of Jephunneh and Joshua son of Nun. ³¹ I will bring your children whom you said would become plunder into the land you rejected, and they will enjoy it. ³² But as for you, your corpses will fall in this wilderness. ³³ Your children will be shepherds in the wilderness for 40 years and bear the penalty for your acts of unfaithfulness until all your corpses lie ⌊scattered⌋ in the wilderness. ³⁴ You will bear the consequences of your sins 40 years based on the number of the 40 days that you scouted the land, a year for each day.^c You will know My displeasure.^d ³⁵ I, the LORD, have spoken. I swear that I will do this to the entire evil community that has conspired against Me. They will come to an end in the wilderness, and there they will die."

God Strikes Rebel Spies

³⁶ So the men Moses sent to scout out the land, and who returned and incited the entire community to complain about him by spreading a bad report about the land— ³⁷ those men who spread the report about the land were struck down by the LORD. ³⁸ Only Joshua son of Nun and Caleb son of Jephunneh remained alive of those men who went to scout out the land.

Israel Disobeys—and is Defeated

³⁹ When Moses reported these words to all the Israelites, the people were overcome with grief. ⁴⁰ They got up early the next morning and went up the ridge of the hill country, saying, "Let's go to the place the LORD promised, for we were wrong."

⁴¹ But Moses responded, "Why are you going against the LORD's command? It won't succeed. ⁴² Don't go, because the LORD is not among you and you will be

^a**14:25** Lit *valley* ^b**14:30** Lit *I raised My hand* ^c**14:34** Lit *a day for the year, a day for the year* ^d**14:34** Or *My opposition*

defeated by your enemies. [43] The Amalekites and Canaanites are right in front of you, and you will fall by the sword. The LORD won't be with you, since you have turned from following Him."

[44] But they dared to go up the ridge of the hill country, even though the ark of the LORD's covenant and Moses did not leave the camp. [45] Then the Amalekites and Canaanites who lived in that ⌊part of the⌋ hill country came down, attacked them, and routed them as far as Hormah.

Laws on Offerings in Promised Land

15 The LORD instructed Moses: [2] "Speak to the Israelites and tell them: When you enter the land I am giving you to settle in, [3] and you make a fire offering to the LORD from the herd or flock—either a •burnt offering or a sacrifice, to fulfill a vow, or as a freewill offering, or at your appointed festivals—to produce a pleasing aroma for the LORD, [4] the one presenting his offering to the LORD must also present a •grain offering of two quarts[a] of fine flour mixed with a quart[b] of oil. [5] Prepare a quart[b] of wine as a drink offering with the burnt offering or sacrifice of each lamb.

[6] "If you prepare a grain offering with a ram, it must be four quarts[c] of fine flour mixed with a third of a gallon[d] of oil. [7] Also present a third of a gallon[d] of wine for a drink offering as a pleasing aroma to the LORD.

[8] "If you prepare a young bull as a burnt offering or as a sacrifice, to fulfill a vow, or as a •fellowship offering to the LORD, [9] a grain offering of six quarts[e] of fine flour mixed with two quarts[f] of oil must be presented with the bull. [10] Also present two quarts[f] of wine as a drink offering. It is a fire offering of pleasing aroma to the LORD. [11] This is to be done for each ox, ram, lamb, or goat. [12] This is how you must prepare each of them, no matter how many.

[13] "Every Israelite is to prepare these things in this way when he presents a fire offering as a pleasing aroma to the LORD. [14] When a foreigner resides with you or someone else is among you and wants to prepare a fire offering as a pleasing aroma to the LORD, he is to do exactly as you do throughout your generations. [15] The assembly is to have the same statute for[g] both you and the foreign resident as a permanent statute throughout your generations. You and the foreigner will be alike before the LORD. [16] The same law and the same ordinance will apply to both you and the foreigner who resides with you."

[17] The LORD instructed Moses: [18] "Speak to the Israelites and tell them: After you enter the land where I am bringing you, [19] you are to offer a contribution to the LORD when you eat from the food of the land. [20] You are to offer a loaf from your first batch of dough as a contribution; offer it just like a contribution from the threshing floor. [21] Throughout your generations, you are to give the LORD a contribution from the first batch of your dough.

Unintentional Sins

[22] "When you sin unintentionally and do not obey all these commands that the LORD spoke to Moses— [23] all that the LORD has commanded you through Moses, from the day the LORD issued the commands and onward throughout your generations— [24] and if it was done unintentionally without the community's

---

[a]**15:4** Lit *a tenth* (of an ephah)   [b]**15:4,5** Lit *a fourth hin*   [c]**15:6** Lit *two-tenths* (of an ephah)   [d]**15:6,7** Lit *a third hin*   [e]**15:9** Lit *three-tenths* (of an ephah)   [f]**15:9,10** Lit *a half hin*   [g]**15:14-15** Sam, LXX join *The assembly* to v. 14, reading LORD, the assembly must do exactly as you do. [15] The same statute will apply to

awareness, the entire community is to prepare one young bull for a burnt offering as a pleasing aroma to the LORD, with its grain offering and drink offering according to the regulation, and one male goat as a •sin offering. ²⁵ The priest must then make •atonement for the entire Israelite community so that they may be forgiven, for the sin was unintentional. They are to bring their offering, one made by fire to the LORD, and their sin offering before the LORD for their unintentional sin. ²⁶ The entire Israelite community and the foreigner who resides among them will be forgiven, since it happened to all the people unintentionally.

²⁷ "If one person sins unintentionally, he is to present a year-old female goat as a sin offering. ²⁸ The priest must then make atonement before the LORD on behalf of the person who acts in error sinning unintentionally, and when he makes atonement for him, he will be forgiven. ²⁹ You are to have the same law for the person who acts in error, whether he is an Israelite or a foreigner who lives among you.

Defiant Sins

³⁰ "But the person who acts defiantly,ᵃ whether native or foreign resident, blasphemes the LORD. That person is to be cut off from his people. ³¹ He will certainly be cut off, because he has despised the LORD's word and broken His command; his guilt remains on him."

Case of Sabbath Violation

³² While the Israelites were in the wilderness, they found a man gathering wood on the Sabbath day. ³³ Those who found him gathering wood brought him to Moses, Aaron, and the entire community. ³⁴ They placed him in custody, because it had not been decided what should be done to him. ³⁵ Then the LORD told Moses, "The man is to be put to death. The entire community is to stone him outside the camp." ³⁶ So the entire community brought him outside the camp and stoned him to death, as the LORD had commanded Moses.

Tassels: Remember Commands

³⁷ The LORD said to Moses, ³⁸ "Speak to the Israelites and tell them that throughout their generations they are to make tassels for the corners of their garments, and put a blue cord on the tassel at ⌊each⌋ corner. ³⁹ These will serve as tassels for you to look at, so that you may remember all the LORD's commands and obey them and not become unfaithful by following your own heart and your own eyes. ⁴⁰ This way you will remember and obey all My commands and be holy to your God. ⁴¹ I am the LORD your God who brought you out of the land of Egypt to be your God; I am the LORD your God."

Korah Leads Rebellion

16 Now Korah son of Izhar, son of Kohath, son of Levi, with Dathan and Abiram, sons of Eliab, and On son of Peleth, sons of Reuben, took ² 250 prominent Israelite men who were leaders of the community and representatives in the assembly, and they rebelled against Moses. ³ They came together against Moses and Aaron and told them, "You have gone too far!ᵇ Everyone in the entire community is holy, and the LORD is among them. Why then do you exalt yourselves above the LORD's assembly?"

Moses's Fire Test

⁴ When Moses heard ⌊this⌋, he fell facedown. ⁵ Then he said to Korah and all his

---

ᵃ**15:30** Lit with a high hand   ᵇ**16:3** Lit Enough of you

followers, "Tomorrow morning the LORD will reveal who belongs to Him, who is set apart, and ⌊the one⌋ He will let come near Him. He will let the one He chooses come near Him. ⁶ Korah, you and all your followers are to do this: take firepans, and tomorrow ⁷ place fire in them and put incense on them before the LORD. Then the man the LORD chooses will be the one who is set apart. It is you Levites who have gone too far!"ᵃ

Moses Rebukes Levites

⁸ Moses also told Korah, "Now listen, Levites! ⁹ Isn't it enough for you that the God of Israel has separated you from the Israelite community to bring you near to Himself, to perform the work at the LORD's tabernacle, and to stand before the community to minister to them? ¹⁰ He has brought you near, and all your fellow Levites who are with you, but you are seeking the priesthood as well. ¹¹ Therefore, it is you and all your followers who have conspired against the LORD! As for Aaron, who is heᵇ that you should complain about him?"

Moses Sends for Two Rebel Leaders

¹² Moses sent for <u>Dathan</u> and <u>Abiram</u>, the sons of Eliab, but they said, "<u>We will not come!</u> ¹³ Is it not enough that you brought us up from a land flowing with milk and honey to kill us in the wilderness? Do you also have to appoint yourself as ruler over us? ¹⁴ Furthermore, you didn't bring us to a land flowing with milk and honey or give us an inheritance of fields and vineyards. Will you gouge out the eyes of these men? We will not come!"

¹⁵ Then Moses became angry and said to the LORD, "Don't respect their offering. I have not taken one donkey from them or mistreated a single one of them." ¹⁶ So Moses told Korah, "You and all your followers are to appear before the LORD tomorrow—you, they, and Aaron. ¹⁷ Each of you is to take his firepan, place incense on it, and present his firepan before the LORD—250 firepans. You and Aaron ⌊are⌋ each ⌊to present⌋ your firepan also."

Test by Fire

¹⁸ Each man took his firepan, placed fire in it, put incense on it, and stood at the entrance to the tent of meeting along with Moses and Aaron. ¹⁹ After Korah assembled the whole community against them at the entrance to the tent of meeting, the glory of the LORD appeared to the whole community. ²⁰ The LORD spoke to Moses and Aaron, ²¹ "Separate yourselves from this community so I may consume them instantly."

Moses and Aaron Plead for Community

²² But Moses and Aaron fell facedown and said, "God, God of the spiritsᶜ of all flesh, when one man sins, will you vent Your wrath on the whole community?"

²³ The LORD replied to Moses, ²⁴ "Tell the community: Get away from the dwellings of Korah, Dathan, and Abiram."

Moses Warns Community

²⁵ Moses got up and went to Dathan and Abiram, and the elders of Israel followed him. ²⁶ He warned the community, "Get away now from the tents of these wicked men. Don't touch anything that belongs to them, or you will be swept away because of all their sins." ²⁷ So they got away from the dwellings of Korah, Dathan, and Abiram. Meanwhile,

ᵃ16:7 Lit *Enough of you, sons of Levi*   ᵇ16:11 Or *Aaron, what has he done*   ᶜ16:22 Or *breath*; Nm 27:16

Dathan and Abiram came out and stood at the entrance of their tents with their wives, children, and infants.

Moses: Earth Will Swallow Them!

[28] Then Moses said, "This is how you will know that the LORD sent me to do all these things and that it was not of my own will: [29] If these men die ⌊naturally⌋ as all people would, and suffer the fate of all, then the LORD has not sent me. [30] But if the LORD brings about something unprecedented, and the ground opens its mouth and swallows them along with all that belongs to them so that they go down alive into •Sheol, then you will know that these men have despised the LORD."

Rebels Destroyed by Earth and Fire

[31] Just as he finished speaking all these words, the ground beneath them split open. [32] The earth opened its mouth and swallowed them and their households, all Korah's people, and all ⌊their⌋ possessions. [33] They went down alive into Sheol with all that belonged to them. The earth closed over them, and they vanished from the assembly. [34] At their cries, all ⌊the people of Israel⌋ who were around them fled because they thought, "The earth may swallow us too!" [35] Fire also came out from the LORD and consumed the 250 men who were presenting the incense.

Eleazar Cleans Up

[36a] Then the LORD spoke to Moses: [37] "Tell Eleazar son of Aaron the priest to remove the firepans from the burning debris, because they are holy, and scatter the fire far away. [38] As for the firepans of those who sinned at the cost of their own lives, make them into hammered sheets as plating for the altar, for they presented them before the LORD, and the firepans are holy. They will be a sign to the Israelites."

[39] So Eleazar the priest took the bronze firepans that those who were burned had presented, and they were hammered into plating for the altar, [40] just as the LORD commanded him through Moses. It was to be a reminder for the Israelites that no unauthorized person outside the lineage of Aaron should approach to offer incense before the LORD and become like Korah and his followers.

Israel Complains Again

[41] The next day the entire Israelite community complained about Moses and Aaron, saying, "You have killed the LORD's people!" [42] When the community assembled against them, Moses and Aaron turned toward the tent of meeting, and suddenly the cloud covered it, and the LORD's glory appeared.

God: I'll Consume!

[43] Moses and Aaron went to the front of the tent of meeting, [44] and the LORD said to Moses, [45] "Get away from this community so that I may consume them instantly." But they fell facedown.

Moses' Atonement Plan

[46] Then Moses told Aaron, "Take your firepan, place fire from the altar in it, and add incense. Go quickly to the community and make •atonement for them, because wrath has come from the LORD; the plague has begun." [47] So Aaron took his firepan as Moses had ordered, ran into the middle of the assembly, and saw that the plague had begun among the people. After he added incense, he made atone-

ment for the people. [48] He stood between the dead and the living, and the plague was halted. [49] But those who died from the plague numbered 14,700, in addition to those who died because of the Korah incident. [50] Aaron then returned to Moses at the entrance to the tent of meeting, since the plague had been halted.

God's Test: Aaron's Staff

17 [a] The LORD instructed Moses: [2] "Speak to the Israelites and take one staff from them for each ancestral house, 12 staffs from all the leaders of their ancestral houses. Write each man's name on his staff. [3] Write Aaron's name on Levi's staff, because there must be one staff for the head of each ancestral house. [4] Then place them in the tent of meeting in front of the •testimony where I meet with you. [5] The staff of the man I choose will sprout, and I will rid Myself of the Israelites' complaints that they have been making about you."

[6] So Moses spoke to the Israelites, and each of their leaders gave him a staff, one for each of the leaders of their ancestral houses, 12 staffs in all. Aaron's staff was among them. [7] Moses placed the staffs before the LORD in the tent of the testimony.

Staff Blossoms: Sign for Rebels

[8] The next day Moses entered the tent of the testimony and saw that Aaron's staff, representing the house of Levi, had sprouted, formed buds, blossomed, and produced almonds! [9] Moses then brought out all the staffs from the LORD's presence to all the Israelites. They saw them, and each man took his own staff. [10] The LORD told Moses, "Put Aaron's rod back in front of the testimony to be kept as a sign for the rebels, so that you

may put an end to their complaints before Me, or else they will die." [11] So Moses did as the LORD commanded him.

[12] Then the Israelites declared to Moses, "Look, we're perishing! We're lost; we're all lost! [13] Anyone who comes near the LORD's tabernacle will die. Will we all perish?"

Duties of Priests and Levites

18 The LORD said to Aaron, "You, your sons, and your ancestral house will be responsible for sin against the sanctuary. You and your sons will be responsible for sin involving your priesthood. [2] But also bring your brothers with you from the tribe of Levi, your ancestral tribe, so they may join you and serve with you and your sons in front of the tent of the •testimony. [3] They are to perform duties for you and for the whole tent. They must not come near the sanctuary equipment or the altar; otherwise, both they and you will die. [4] They are to join you and guard the tent of meeting, doing all the work at the tent, but no unauthorized person may come near you.

[5] "You are to guard the sanctuary and the altar so that wrath may not fall on the Israelites again. [6] Look, I have selected your fellow Levites from the Israelites as a gift for you,[b] assigned by the LORD to work at the tent of meeting. [7] But you and your sons will carry out your priestly responsibilities for everything concerning the altar and for what is inside the veil, and you will do that work. I am giving you the work of the priesthood as a gift,[c] but an unauthorized person who comes near the sanctuary will be put to death."

Support for Priests and Levites

[8] Then the LORD spoke to Aaron, "Look, I have put you in charge of the

---

[a]**17:1** Nm 17:16 in Hb   [b]**18:6** LXX, Syr, Vg omit *for you*   [c]**18:7** Or *veil. So you are to perform the service; a gift of your priesthood I grant*

contributions brought to Me. As for all the holy offerings of the Israelites, I have given them to you and your sons as a portion and a perpetual statute. ⁹ A portion of the holiest offerings ⌊kept⌋ from the fire will be yours; every one of their offerings that they give Me, whether the •grain offering, •sin offering, or •restitution offering will be most holy for you and your sons. ¹⁰ You are to eat it as a most holy offering.ᵃ Every male may eat it; it is to be holy to you.

¹¹ "The contribution of their gifts also belongs to you. I have given all the Israelites' presentation offerings to you and to your sons and daughters as a perpetual statute. Every ceremonially clean person in your house may eat it. ¹² I am giving you all the best of the fresh olive oil, new wine, and grain, which the Israelites give to the LORD as their •firstfruits. ¹³ The firstfruits of all that is in their land, which they bring to the LORD, belong to you. Every clean person in your house may eat them.

¹⁴ "Everything in Israel that is permanently dedicated ⌊to the LORD⌋ belongs to you. ¹⁵ The firstborn of every living thing, man or animal, presented to the LORD belongs to you. But you must certainly redeem the firstborn of man, and redeem the firstborn of an unclean animal. ¹⁶ You will pay the redemption price for a month-old male according to your valuation: five •shekels of silver by the standard sanctuary shekel, which is 20 gerahs.

¹⁷ "However, you must not redeem the firstborn of an ox, a sheep, or a goat; they are holy. You are to sprinkle their blood on the altar and burn their fat as a fire offering for a pleasing aroma to the LORD. ¹⁸ But their meat belongs to you. It belongs to you like the breast of the presentation offering and the right thigh.

¹⁹ "I give to you and to your sons and daughters all the holy contributions that the Israelites present to the LORD as a perpetual statute. It is a perpetual covenant of salt before the LORD for you as well as your •offspring."

Lord: No Land for Priests or Levites

²⁰ The LORD told Aaron, "You will not have an inheritance in their land; there will be no portion among them for you. I am your portion and your inheritance among the Israelites.

Levites Get a Tenth

²¹ "Look, I have given the Levites every tenth in Israel as an inheritance in return for the work they do, the work of the tent of meeting. ²² The Israelites must never again come near the tent of meeting, or they will incur guilt and die. ²³ The Levites will do the work of the tent of meeting, and they will bear the ⌊consequences⌋ of their sin. The Levites will not receive an inheritance among the Israelites; this is a perpetual statute throughout your generations. ²⁴ For I have given them the tenth that the Israelites present to the LORD as a contribution for ⌊their⌋ inheritance. That is why I told them that they would not receive an inheritance among the Israelites."

God: Levites Must Tithe

²⁵ The LORD instructed Moses, ²⁶ "Speak to the Levites and tell them: When you receive from the Israelites the tenth that I have given you as your inheritance, you must present part of it as an offering to the LORD—a tenth of the tenth. ²⁷ Your offering will be credited to you as if ⌊it were your⌋ grain from the threshing floor or the full harvest from the winepress. ²⁸ You are to present an offering to the LORD from every tenth

---

ᵃ **18:10** Or *it in a most holy place*

you receive from the Israelites. Give some of it to Aaron the priest as an offering to the LORD. ²⁹ You must present the entire offering due the LORD from all your gifts. The best part of the tenth is to be consecrated.

³⁰ "Tell them further: Once you have presented the best part of the tenth, and it is credited to you Levites as the produce of the threshing floor or the winepress, ³¹ then you and your household may eat it anywhere. It is your wage in return for your work at the tent of meeting. ³² You will not incur guilt because of it once you have presented the best part of it, but you must not defile the Israelites' holy offerings, so that you will not die."

Sacrifice of Red Cow

19 The LORD spoke to Moses and Aaron, ² "This is the legal statute that the LORD has commanded: Instruct the Israelites to bring you an unblemished red cow that has no defect and has never been yoked. ³ Give it to Eleazar the priest, and he will have it brought outside the camp and slaughtered in his presence. ⁴ Eleazar the priest is to take some of its blood with his finger and sprinkle it seven times toward the front of the tent of meeting. ⁵ The cow must be burned in his sight. Its hide, flesh, and blood, are to be burned along with its dung. ⁶ The priest is to take cedar wood, hyssop, and crimson yarn, and throw ⌊them⌋ onto the fire where the cow is burning. ⁷ Then the priest must wash his clothes and bathe his body in water; after that he may enter the camp, but he will remain ceremonially unclean until evening. ⁸ The one who burned the cow must also wash his clothes and bathe his body in water, and he will remain unclean until evening.

⁹ "A man who is clean is to gather up the cow's ashes and deposit them outside the camp in a ceremonially clean place. The ashes must be kept by the Israelite community for ⌊preparing⌋ the water ⌊to remove⌋ impurity; it is a •sin offering. ¹⁰ Then the one who gathers up the cow's ashes must wash his clothes, and he will remain unclean until evening. This is a perpetual statute for the Israelites and for the foreigner who resides among them.

God: Purification and Human Corpse

¹¹ "The person who touches any human corpse will be unclean for seven days. ¹² He is to purify himself with the water[a] on the third day and the seventh day; then he will be clean. But if he does not purify himself on the third and seventh days, he will not be clean. ¹³ Anyone who touches a body of a person who has died, and does not purify himself, defiles the tabernacle of the LORD. That person will be cut off from Israel. He remains unclean because the water for impurity has not been sprinkled on him, and his uncleanness is still on him.

Death and Purification

¹⁴ "This is the law when a person dies in a tent: everyone who enters the tent and everyone who is ⌊already⌋ in the tent will be unclean for seven days, ¹⁵ and any open container without a lid tied on it is unclean. ¹⁶ Anyone in the open field who touches a person who has been killed by the sword or has died, or a human bone, or a grave, will be unclean for seven days. ¹⁷ For ⌊the purification of⌋ the unclean person, they are to take some of the ashes of the burnt sin offering, ⌊put them⌋ in a jar, and add fresh water to

^a**19:12** Or *ashes*; lit *with it*

them. ¹⁸ A person who is clean is to take hyssop, dip ⌊it⌋ in the water, and sprinkle the tent, all the furnishings, and the people who were there. He is also to sprinkle the one who touched a bone, a grave, a corpse, or a person who had been killed.

¹⁹ "The one who is clean is to sprinkle the unclean person on the third day and the seventh day. After he purifies the unclean person on the seventh day, the one being purified must wash his clothes and bathe in water, and he will be clean by evening. ²⁰ But a person who is unclean and does not purify himself, that person will be cut off from the assembly because he has defiled the sanctuary of the LORD. The water for impurity has not been sprinkled on him; he is unclean. ²¹ This is a perpetual statute for them. The person who sprinkles the water for impurity is to wash his clothes, and whoever touches the water for impurity will be unclean until evening. ²² Anything the unclean person touches will become unclean, and anyone who touches ⌊it⌋ᵃ will be unclean until evening."

Water from the Rock

Miriam Dies

20 The entire Israelite community entered the Wilderness of Zin in the first month, and theyᵇ settled in Kadesh. Miriam died and was buried there.

People Complain: No Water!

² There was no water for the community, so they assembled against Moses and Aaron. ³ The people quarreled with Moses and said, "If only we had perished when our brothers perished before the LORD. ⁴ Why have you brought the LORD's assembly into this wilderness for us and our livestock to die here? ⁵ Why have you led us up from Egypt to bring us to this evil place? It's not a place of grain, figs, vines, and pomegranates, and there is no water to drink!"

Moses and Aaron Consult God

⁶ Then Moses and Aaron went from the presence of the assembly to the doorway of the tent of meeting. They fell down with their faces ⌊to the ground⌋, and the glory of the LORD appeared to them. ⁷ The LORD spoke to Moses, ⁸ "Take the staff and assemble the community. You and your brother Aaron are to speak to the rock while they watch, and it will yield its water. You will bring out water for them from the rock and provide drink for the community and their livestock."

Moses Disobeys God

⁹ So Moses took the staff from the LORD's presence just as He had commanded him. ¹⁰ Moses and Aaron summoned the assembly in front of the rock, and Moses said to them, "Listen, you rebels! Must we bring water out of this rock for you?" ¹¹ Then Moses raised his hand and struck the rock twice with his staff, so that a great amount of water gushed out, and the community and their livestock drank.

God Punishes Moses and Aaron

¹² But the LORD said to Moses and Aaron, "Because you did not trust Me to show My holiness in the sight of the Israelites, you will not bring this assembly into the land I have given them." ¹³ These are the waters of Meribah,ᶜ where the Israelites quarreled with the LORD, and He showed His holiness to them.

ᵃ**19:22** Or [him]   ᵇ**20:1** Lit the people   ᶜ**20:13** = quarreling

Moses Asks Edom for Passage

¹⁴ Moses sent messengers from Kadesh to the king of Edom, "This is what your brother Israel says, 'You know all the hardships that have overtaken us. ¹⁵ Our fathers went down to Egypt, and we lived in Egypt many years, but the Egyptians treated us and our fathers badly. ¹⁶ When we cried out to the LORD, He heard our voice, sent an Angel,ᵃ and brought us out of Egypt. Now look, we are in Kadesh, a city on the border of your territory. ¹⁷ Please let us travel through your land. We won't travel through ⌊any⌋ field or vineyard, or drink ⌊any⌋ well water. We will travel the King's Highway; we won't turn to the right or the left until we have traveled through your territory.' "

Edom Refuses

¹⁸ But Edom answered him, "You must not travel through our land, or we will come out and confront you with the sword." ¹⁹ "We will go on the main road," the Israelites replied to them, "and if we or our herds drink your water, we will pay its price. There will be no problem; only let us travel through on foot." ²⁰ Yet Edom insisted, "You must not travel through." And they came out to confront them with a large force of heavily-armed people.ᵇ ²¹ Edom refused to allow Israel to travel through their territory, and Israel turned away from them.

Aaron's Death

²² After they set out from Kadesh, the entire Israelite community came to Mount Hor. ²³ The LORD said to Moses and Aaron at Mount Hor on the border of the land of Edom, ²⁴ "Aaron will be gathered to his people; he will not enter the land I have given the Israelites, because you both rebelled against My command at the waters of Meribah. ²⁵ Take Aaron and his son Eleazar and bring them up Mount Hor. ²⁶ Remove Aaron's garments and put them on his son Eleazar. Aaron will be gathered ⌊to his people⌋ and die there."

Eleazar Succeeds Aaron

²⁷ So Moses did as the LORD commanded, and they climbed Mount Hor in the sight of the whole community. ²⁸ After Moses removed Aaron's garments and put them on his son Eleazar, Aaron died there on top of the mountain. Then Moses and Eleazar came down from the mountain. ²⁹ When the whole community saw that Aaron had passed away, the entire house of Israel mourned for him 30 days.

Israel Defeats Canaanites

21 When the Canaanite king of Arad, who lived in the •Negev, heard that Israel was coming on the Atharim road, he fought against Israel and captured some prisoners. ² Then Israel made a vow to the LORD, "If You will deliver this people into our hands, we will •completely destroy their cities." ³ The LORD listened to Israel's request, the Canaanites were defeated, and Israel completely destroyed them and their cities. So they named the place Hormah.ᶜ

The Bronze Serpent

Israelites Grumble, God Sends Snakes

⁴ Then they set out from Mount Hor by way of the •Red Sea to bypass the land of Edom, but the peopleᵈ became impatient because of the journey. ⁵ The people

---

ᵃ**20:16** Or *a messenger*   ᵇ**20:20** Lit *with numerous people and a strong hand*   ᶜ**21:3** = destruction   ᵈ**21:4** Lit *soul of the people*

spoke against God and Moses: "Why have you led us up from Egypt to die in the wilderness? There is no bread or water, and we detest this wretched food!" [6] Then the LORD sent poisonous[a] snakes among the people, and they bit them so that many Israelites died.

People Repent

[7] The people then came to Moses and said, "We have sinned by speaking against the LORD and against you. Intercede with the LORD so that He will take the snakes away from us." And Moses interceded for the people.

God's Cure

[8] Then the LORD said to Moses, "Make a snake ˌimageˌ and mount it on a pole. When anyone who is bitten looks at it, he will recover." [9] So Moses made a bronze snake and mounted it on a pole. Whenever someone was bitten, and he looked at the bronze snake, he recovered.

Israelites Skirt Moab

[10] The Israelites set out and camped at Oboth. [11] They set out from Oboth and camped at Iye-abarim in the wilderness that borders Moab on the east. [12] From there they went and camped at Zered Valley. [13] They set out from there and camped on the other side of the Arnon ˌRiverˌ, in the wilderness that extends from the Amorite border, because the Arnon was the Moabite border between Moab and the Amorites. [14] Therefore it is stated in the Book of the LORD's Wars:

Waheb[b] in Suphah
and the ravines of the Arnon,
[15] even the slopes of the ravines
that extend to the site of Ar[c]
and lie along the border of Moab.

Israel Sings at a Well

[16] From there ˌthey wentˌ to Beer,[d] the well the LORD told Moses about, "Gather the people so I may give them water." [17] Then Israel sang this song:

Spring up, well—sing to it!
[18] The princes dug the well;
The nobles of the people
hollowed it out
with a scepter and with their staffs.

ˌThey wentˌ from the wilderness to Mattanah, [19] from Mattanah to Nahaliel, from Nahaliel to Bamoth, [20] from Bamoth to the valley in the territory of Moab near the Pisgah highlands[e] that overlook the wasteland.[f]

Israel Defeats Amorites

Israel Asks Passage

[21] Israel sent messengers to say to Sihon king of the Amorites: [22] "Let us travel through your land. We won't go into the fields or vineyards. We won't drink ˌanyˌ well water. We will travel the King's Highway until we have traveled through your territory."

King Sihon Refuses

[23] But Sihon would not let Israel travel through his territory. Instead, he gathered his whole army and went out to confront Israel in the wilderness. When he came to Jahaz, he fought against Israel. [24] Israel struck him with the sword and took possession of his land from the Arnon to the Jabbok, ˌbut only upˌ to the Ammonite border, because it was fortified.[g]

Israel Takes Amorite Cities

[25] Israel took all the cities and lived in all these Amorite cities, including Hesh-

---

[a]**21:6** Lit *burning*; LXX reads *deadly*; Syr reads *cruel*; Vg reads *fiery*   [b]**21:14** The source of the Arnon River   [c]**21:15** A city in Moab; Nm 21:28; Dt 2:9,18,29; Is 15:1   [d]**21:16** = well   [e]**21:20** Moabite mountain plateau; Nm 23:14; Dt 3:17,27; 4:49; 34:1; Jos 12:3; 13:20   [f]**21:20** Or *overlook Jeshimon*   [g]**21:24** Or *was at Az*; LXX reads *was Jazer*

bon and all its villages. ²⁶ Heshbon was the city of Sihon king of the Amorites, who had fought against the former king of Moab and had taken control of all his land as far as the Arnon. ²⁷ Therefore the poets[a] say:

Come to Heshbon, let it be rebuilt;
let the city of Sihon be restored.[b]
²⁸ For fire came out of Heshbon,
a flame from the city of Sihon.
It consumed Ar of Moab,
the lords of[c] Arnon's heights.
²⁹ Woe to you, Moab!
You have been destroyed,
people of Chemosh!
He gave up his sons as refugees,
and his daughters into captivity
to Sihon the Amorite king.
³⁰ We threw them down;
Heshbon has been destroyed
as far as Dibon.[d]
We caused desolation
as far as Nophah,
which reaches as far as Medeba.[e]

Israel Lives in Ammon

³¹ So Israel lived in the Amorites' land. ³² After Moses sent spies to Jazer, Israel captured its villages and drove out the Amorites who were there.

Israel Defeats King Og of Bashan

³³ Then they turned and went up the road to Bashan, and Og king of Bashan came out against them with his whole army to do battle at Edrei. ³⁴ But the LORD said to Moses, "Do not fear him, for I have handed him over to you along with his whole army and his land. Do to him as you did to Sihon king of the Amorites, who lived in Heshbon." ³⁵ So they struck him, his sons, and his whole army

until no one was left,[f] and they took possession of his land.

Adventures of Balaam

Moabites Fear Israelites

22 The Israelites traveled on and camped in the plains of Moab near the Jordan across from Jericho. ² Now Balak son of Zippor saw all that Israel had done to the Amorites. ³ Moab was terrified of the people because they were numerous, and dreaded the Israelites. ⁴ So the Moabites said to the elders of Midian, "This horde will devour everything around us like an ox eats up the green plants in the field."

King Balak Hires Balaam

Since Balak son of Zippor was Moab's king at that time, ⁵ he sent messengers to Balaam son of Beor at Pethor, which is by the Euphrates in the land of his people.[g] [h] Balak said to him: "Look, a people has come out of Egypt; they cover the surface of the land and are living right across from me. ⁶ Please come and put a curse on these people for me because they are more powerful than I am. I may be able to defeat them and drive them out of the land, for I know that those you bless are blessed and those you curse are cursed."

⁷ The elders of Moab and Midian departed with fees for •divination in hand. They came to Balaam and reported Balak's words to him. ⁸ He said to them, "Spend the night here, and I will give you the answer the LORD tells me." So the officials of Moab stayed with Balaam.

God Stops Balaam

⁹ Then God came to Balaam and asked, "Who are these men with you?"

10 Balaam replied to God, "Balak son of Zippor, king of Moab, sent ˌthis messageˌ to me: 11 'Look, a people has come out of Egypt, and they cover the surface of the land. Now come and put a curse on them for me. I may be able to fight against them and drive them away.'"

12 Then God said to Balaam, "You are not to go with them. You are not to curse this people, for they are blessed."

13 So Balaam got up the next morning and said to Balak's officials, "Go back to your land, because the LORD has refused to let me go with you."

14 The officials of Moab arose, returned to Balak, and reported, "Balaam refused to come with us."

King Balak Insists

15 Balak sent officials again who were more numerous and higher in rank than the others. 16 They came to Balaam and said to him, "This is what Balak son of Zippor says: 'Let nothing keep you from coming to me, 17 for I will greatly honor you and do whatever you ask me. So please come and put a curse on these people for me!'"

18 But Balaam responded to the servants of Balak, "If Balak were to give me his house full of silver and gold, I could not go against the command of the LORD my God to do ˌanythingˌ small or great. 19 Please stay here overnight as the others did, so that I may find out what else the LORD has to tell me."

God's Strategy Unfolds

20 God came to Balaam at night and said to him, "Since these men have come to summon you, get up and go with them, but you must only do what I tell you." 21 When he got up in the morning, Balaam saddled his donkey and went with the officials of Moab.

Balaam's Donkey and the Angel

22 But God was incensed that Balaam was going, and the Angel of the LORD took His stand on the path to oppose him. Balaam was riding his donkey, and his two servants were with him. 23 When the donkey saw the Angel of the LORD standing on the path with a drawn sword in His hand, she turned off the path and went into the field. So Balaam hit her to return her to the path. 24 Then the Angel of the LORD stood in a narrow passage between the vineyards, with a stone wall on either side. 25 The donkey saw the Angel of the LORD and pressed herself against the wall, squeezing Balaam's foot against it. So he hit her once again. 26 The Angel of the LORD went ahead and stood in a narrow place where there was no room to turn to the right or the left. 27 When the donkey saw the Angel of the LORD, she crouched down under Balaam. So he became furious and beat the donkey with his stick.

A Donkey Speaks

28 Then the LORD opened the donkey's mouth, and she asked Balaam, "What have I done to you that you have beaten me these three times?"

29 Balaam answered the donkey, "You made me look like a fool. If I had a sword in my hand, I'd kill you now!"

30 But the donkey said, "Am I not the donkey you've ridden all your life until today? Have I ever treated you this way before?"

"No," he replied.

Lord Opens Balaam's Eyes

31 Then the LORD opened Balaam's eyes, and he saw the Angel of the LORD standing in the path with a drawn sword in His hand. Balaam knelt and bowed with his face ˌto the groundˌ.

³² The Angel of the LORD asked him, "Why have you beaten your donkey these three times? Look, I came out to oppose you, because what you are doing is evil in My sight. ³³ The donkey saw Me and turned away from Me these three times. If she had not turned away from Me, I would have killed you by now and let her live."

Balaam Repents

³⁴ Balaam said to the Angel of the LORD, "I have sinned, for I did not know that You were standing in the path to confront me. And now, if it is evil in Your sight, I will go back."

Angel's Instructions

³⁵ Then the Angel of the LORD said to Balaam, "Go with the men, but you are to say only what I tell you." So Balaam went with Balak's officials.

³⁶ When Balak heard that Balaam was coming, he went out to meet him at the Moabite city[a] on the Arnon border at the edge of his territory. ³⁷ Balak asked Balaam, "Did I not send you an urgent summons? Why didn't you come to me? Am I really not able to reward you?"

Balaam before Barak

³⁸ Balaam said to him, "Look, I have come to you, but can I say anything I want? I must speak only the message God puts in my mouth." ³⁹ So Balaam went with Balak, and they came to Kiriath-huzoth.[b] ⁴⁰ Balak sacrificed cattle and sheep, and sent for Balaam and the officials who were with him.

⁴¹ In the morning, Balak took Balaam and brought him to Bamoth-baal.[c] From there he saw the outskirts of the people's camp.

Balaam and Balak
Prepares for God's Messages

23 Then Balaam said to Balak, "Build me seven altars here and prepare seven bulls and seven rams for me." ² So Balak did as Balaam directed, and they offered a bull and a ram on each altar. ³ Balaam said to Balak, "Stay here by your •burnt offering while I am gone. Maybe the LORD[d] will meet with me. I will tell you whatever He reveals to me." So he went to a barren hill.

⁴ God[e] met with him and Balaam said to Him, "I have arranged seven altars and offered a bull and a ram on each altar." ⁵ Then the LORD put a message in Balaam's mouth and said, "Return to Balak and say what I tell you."

⁶ So he returned to Balak, who was standing there by his burnt offering with all the officials of Moab.

Balaam's First Message

⁷ Balaam proclaimed his poem:

> Balak brought me from Aram;
> the king of Moab,
>   from the eastern mountains:
> "Come, put a curse on Jacob
>   for me;
> come, denounce Israel!"
> 8 How can I curse someone
>   God has not cursed?
> How can I denounce someone
>   the LORD has not denounced?
> 9 I see them from the top
>   of rocky cliffs,
> and I watch them from the hills.
> There is a people living alone;
>   it does not consider itself
>   among the nations.
> 10 Who has counted the dust of Jacob
>   or numbered the dust clouds[f]
>   of Israel?

---

a **22:36** Or *at Ir-moab,* or *at Ar of Moab*   b **22:39** = The City of Streets   c **22:41** = The High Places of Baal   d **23:3** DSS, LXX, Sam read *Maybe God*   e **23:4** DSS, Sam read *The Angel of God*   f **23:10** Or *numbered a fourth*

Let me die the death of the upright;
let me end of my ⌊life⌋
be like theirs.

11 "What have you done to me?" Balak asked Balaam. "I brought you to curse my enemies, but look, you have only blessed ⌊them⌋!"

12 He answered, "Shouldn't I say exactly what the LORD puts in my mouth?"

Balaam's Second Message

13 Then Balak said to him, "Please come with me to another place where you can see them. You will only see the outskirts of their camp; you won't see all of them. From there, put a curse on them for me." 14 So Balak took him to Lookout Field[a] on top of Pisgah, built seven altars, and offered a bull and a ram on each altar.

15 Balaam said to Balak, "Stay here by your burnt offering while I seek ⌊the LORD⌋ over there."

16 The LORD met with Balaam and put a message in his mouth. Then He said, "Return to Balak and say what I tell you."

17 So he returned to Balak, who was standing there by his burnt offering with the officials of Moab. Balak asked him, "What did the LORD say?"

18 Balaam proclaimed his poem:

Balak, get up and listen;
son of Zippor, pay attention to what
    I say!
19 God is not a man who lies,
or a son of man who changes
    His mind.
Does He speak and not act,
or promise and not fulfill?
20 I have indeed received ⌊a command⌋
    to bless;

since He has blessed,[b]
    I cannot change it.
21 He considers no disaster for Jacob;
He sees no trouble for Israel.[c]
The LORD their God is with them,
    and there is rejoicing over the King
    among them.
22 God brought them out of Egypt;
He is like the horns of a wild ox
    for them.[d]
23 There is no magic curse
    against Jacob
and no •divination against Israel.
It will now be said about Jacob
    and Israel,
"What ⌊great things⌋
    God has done!"
24 A people rise up like a lioness;
They rouse themselves like a lion.
They will not lie down
    until they devour the prey
    and drink the blood of the slain.

25 Then Balak told Balaam, "Don't curse them and don't bless them!"

26 But Balaam answered him, "Didn't I tell you: Whatever the LORD says, I must do?"

Balaam's Third Message

27 Again Balak said to Balaam, "Please come. I will take you to another place. Maybe it will be agreeable to God that you can put a curse on them for me there." 28 So Balak took Balaam to the top of Peor, which overlooks the wasteland.[e]

29 Balaam told Balak, "Build me seven altars here and prepare seven bulls and seven rams for me." 30 So Balak did as Balaam said and offered a bull and a ram on each altar.

24 Since Balaam saw that it pleased the LORD to bless Israel, he did not

---

a 23:14 Or to the field of Zophim   b 23:20 Sam, LXX read since I will bless   c 23:21 Or He does not observe sin in Jacob; He does not see wrongdoing in Israel, or Disaster is not observed in Jacob; trouble is not seen in Israel   d 23:22 Or Egypt; they have the horns of a wild ox   e 23:28 Or overlooks Jeshimon

go to seek omens as on previous occasions, but turned^a toward the wilderness. ² When Balaam looked up and saw Israel encamped tribe by tribe, the Spirit of God descended on him, ³ and he proclaimed his poem:

The •oracle of Balaam son of Beor,
   the oracle of the man whose eyes
     are opened,^b
⁴ the oracle of one who hears
     the sayings of God,
who sees a vision
   from the •Almighty,
who falls ˻into a trance˼
   with ˻his˼ eyes uncovered:
⁵ How beautiful are your tents, Jacob,
   your dwellings, Israel.
⁶ they stretch out like river valleys,^c
   like gardens beside a stream,
   like aloes the LORD has planted,
   like cedars beside the water.
⁷ Water will flow from his buckets,
   and his seed will be
     by abundant water.
His king be greater than Agag,^d
   and his kingdom will be exalted.
⁸ God brought him out of Egypt;
He is like^e the horns of a wild ox
   for them.
He will feed on enemy nations
   and gnaw their bones;
he will strike ˻them˼
   with his arrows.
⁹ He crouches, he lies down like a lion
or a lioness—who dares
   to rouse him?
Those who bless you will be blessed,
  and those who curse you
   will be cursed.

Balak Furious

¹⁰ Then Balak became furious with Balaam, struck his hands together, and said to him, "I summoned you to put a curse on my enemies, but instead, you have blessed ˻them these three times˼. ¹¹ Now go to your home! I said I would reward you richly, but look, the LORD has denied you a reward."

¹² Balaam answered Balak, "Didn't I previously tell the messengers you sent me: ¹³ If Balak were to give me his house full of silver and gold, I could not go against the LORD's command, to do ˻anything˼ good or bad of my own will? I will say whatever the LORD says. ¹⁴ Now I am going back to my people, but first, let me warn you what these people will do to your people in the future."

Balaam's Fourth Message

¹⁵ Then he proclaimed his poem:

The oracle of Balaam son of Beor,
   the oracle of the man whose eyes
     are opened;^b
¹⁶ the oracle of one who hears
     the sayings of God
and has knowledge
   from the •Most High,
who sees a vision
   from the Almighty,
who falls ˻into a trance˼
   with ˻his˼ eyes uncovered:
¹⁷ I see him,^f but not now;
I perceive him,^f but not near.
A star will come from Jacob,
  and a scepter will arise from Israel.
He will smash the forehead^g
   of Moab
and strike down^h all the Shethites.ⁱ
¹⁸ Edom will become a possession;
Seir will become a possession
   of its enemies,
but Israel will be triumphant.
¹⁹ One who comes from Jacob
   will rule;

^a**24:1** Lit *set his face* ^b**24:3,15** LXX reads *true*; Vg reads *closed* ^c**24:6** Or *like date palms* ^d**24:7** Sam, LXX, Sym, Theod read *Gog* ^e**24:8** Or *He has* ^f**24:17** Or *Him* ^g**24:17** Or *frontiers* ^h**24:17** Sam reads *and the skulls of*; Jr 48:45 ⁱ**24:17** Or *Sethites*

he will destroy
  the city's survivors.

²⁰ Then Balaam saw Amalek and proclaimed his poem:

Amalek was first among the nations,
  but his future is destruction.

²¹ Next he saw the Kenites and proclaimed his poem:

Your dwelling place is enduring;
  your nest is set in the cliffs.
²² Kain will be destroyed
    when Asshur takes you captive.

²³ Once more he proclaimed his poem:

Ah, who can live
  when God does this?
²⁴ Ships will come from the coast
    of Kittim;
  they will afflict Asshur and Eber,
    but they too will come to destruction.

²⁵ Balaam then arose and went back to his homeland, and Balak also went his way.

Israel Worships Baal

Israelite Leaders Sentenced to Death

25 While Israel was staying in Acacia Grove,ᵃ the people began to have sexual relations with the women of Moab. ² The women invited them to the sacrifices for their gods, and the people ate and bowed in worship to their gods. ³ So Israel aligned itself with •Baal of Peor, and the LORD's anger burned against Israel. ⁴ The LORD said to Moses, "Take all the leaders of the people and executeᵇ them in broad daylight before the LORD so that His burning anger may turn away from Israel."

⁵ So Moses told Israel's judges, "Kill each of the men who aligned themselves with Baal of Peor."

Phinehas Intervenes:
Zimri and Cozbi Executed

⁶ An Israelite man came bringing a Midianite woman to his relatives in the sight of Moses and the whole Israelite community while they were weeping at the entrance to the tent of meeting. ⁷ When Phinehas son of Eleazar, son of Aaron the priest, saw ⌊this⌋, he got up from the assembly, took a spear in his hand, ⁸ followed the Israelite man into the tent,ᶜ and drove it through both the Israelite man and the woman—through her belly. Then the plague on the Israelites was stopped, ⁹ but those who died in the plague numbered 24,000.

God Relents

¹⁰ The LORD spoke to Moses, ¹¹ "Phinehas son of Eleazar, son of Aaron the priest, has turned back My wrath from the Israelites because he was zealous among them with My zeal,ᵈ so that I did not destroy the Israelites in My zeal. ¹² Therefore declare: I grant him My covenant of peace. ¹³ It will be a covenant of perpetual priesthood for him and his descendants, because he was zealous for his God and made •atonement for the Israelites."

¹⁴ The name of the slain Israelite man, who was struck dead with the Midianite woman, was Zimri son of Salu, the leader of a Simeonite ancestral house. ¹⁵ The name of the slain Midianite woman was Cozbi, the daughter of Zur, a tribal head of an ancestral house in Midian.

Vengeance against Midianites

¹⁶ The LORD told Moses: ¹⁷ "Attack the Midianites and strike them dead. ¹⁸ For they attacked you with the treachery that they used against you in the Peor in-

ᵃ25:1 Or in Shittim ᵇ25:4 Or impale, or hang, or expose; Hb obscure ᶜ25:8 Perhaps a tent shrine or bridal tent
ᵈ25:11 Or jealousy

cident. They did the same in the case involving their sister Cozbi, daughter of the Midianite leader who was killed the day the plague came at Peor."

Second Census

26 After the plague, the LORD said to Moses and Eleazar son of Aaron the priest, 2 "Take a census of the entire Israelite community by their ancestral houses of those 20 years old or more who can serve in Israel's army."

3 So Moses and Eleazar the priest said to them in the plains of Moab by the Jordan ˻across from˼ Jericho, 4 "˻Take a census of˼ those 20 years old or more, as the LORD had commanded Moses and the Israelites who came out of the land of Egypt."

5 Reuben was the firstborn of Israel.
Reuben's descendants:
the Hanochite clan ˻from˼ Hanoch;
the Palluite clan from Pallu;
6 the Hezronite clan from Hezron;
the Carmite clan from Carmi.
7 These were the Reubenite clans, and their registered men numbered 43,730.
8 The son of Pallu was Eliab.
9 The sons of Eliab were Nemuel, Dathan, and Abiram.
(It was Dathan and Abiram, chosen by the community, who fought against Moses and Aaron; they and Korah's followers fought against the LORD. 10 The earth opened its mouth and swallowed them with Korah, when his followers died and the fire consumed 250 men. They ˻serve as˼ a warning sign. 11 The sons of Korah, however, did not die.)

12 Simeon's descendants by their clans:
the Nemuelite clan from Nemuel;[a]
the Jaminite clan from Jamin;
the Jachinite clan from Jachin;
13 the Zerahite clan from Zerah;
the Shaulite clan from Shaul.
14 These were the Simeonite clans, numbering 22,200 men.

15 Gad's descendants by their clans:
the Zephonite clan from Zephon;
the Haggite clan from Haggi;
the Shunite clan from Shuni;
16 the Oznite clan from Ozni;
the Erite clan from Eri;
17 the Arodite clan from Arod;
the Arelite clan from Areli.
18 These were the Gadite clans ˻numbered˼ by their registered men: 40,500.

19 Judah's sons included Er and Onan, but they died in the land of Canaan.
20 Judah's descendants by their clans:
the Shelanite clan from Shelah;
the Perezite clan from Perez;
the Zerahite clan from Zerah.
21 The descendants of Perez:
the Hezronite clan from Hezron;
the Hamulite clan from Hamul.
22 These were Judah's clans ˻numbered˼ by their registered men: 76,500.

23 Issachar's descendants by their clans:
the Tolaite clan from Tola;
the Punite clan from Puvah;[b]
24 the Jashubite clan from Jashub;
the Shimronite clan from Shimron.
25 These were Issachar's clans ˻numbered˼ by their registered men: 64,300.

26 Zebulun's descendants by their clans:

---

a**26:12** Syr reads *Jemuel* (Gn 46:10; Ex 6:15); 1 Ch 4:24 reads *Nemuel*   b**26:23** Sam, LXX, Vg, Syr read *Puite clan from Puah*; 1 Ch 7:1

the Seredite clan from Sered;
the Elonite clan from Elon;
the Jahleelite clan from Jahleel.

27 These were the Zebulunite clans
⌞numbered⌟
by their registered men: 60,500.

28 Joseph's descendants by their clans
⌞from⌟ Manasseh and Ephraim:

29 Manasseh's descendants:
the Machirite clan from Machir.
Machir fathered Gilead;
the Gileadite clan from Gilead.

30 These were Gilead's descendants:
the Iezerite clan ⌞from⌟ Iezer;
the Helekite clan from Helek;

31 The Asrielite clan ⌞from⌟ Asriel;
the Shechemite clan ⌞from⌟ Shechem;

32 the Shemidaite clan ⌞from⌟ Shemida;
the Hepherite clan ⌞from⌟ Hepher;

33 Zelophehad son of Hepher had no
sons—only daughters. The names
of Zelophehad's daughters were
Mahlah, Noah, Hoglah, Milcah, and
Tirzah.

34 These were Manasseh's clans,
numbered
by their registered men: 52,700.

35 These were Ephraim's descendants
by their clans:
the Shuthelahite clan
from Shuthelah;
the Becherite clan from Becher;
the Tahanite clan from Tahan.

36 These were Shuthelah's
descendants:
the Eranite clan from Eran.

37 These were the Ephraimite clans
⌞numbered⌟
by their registered men: 32,500.
These were Joseph's descendants
by their clans.

38 Benjamin's descendants
by their clans:

the Belaite clan from Bela;
the Ashbelite clan from Ashbel;
the Ahiramite clan from Ahiram;

39 the Shuphamite clan
from Shupham;[a]
the Huphamite clan from Hupham.

40 Bela's descendants ⌞from⌟ Ard
and Naaman:
the Ardite clan ⌞from⌟ Ard;
the Naamite clan from Naaman.

41 These were the Benjaminite clans
numbered
by their registered men: 45,600.

42 These were Dan's descendants
by their clans:
the Shuhamite clan from Shuham.
These were the clans of Dan
by their clans.

43 All the Shuhamite clans ⌞numbered⌟
by their registered men were
64,400.

44 Asher's descendants by their clans:
the Imnite clan from Imnah;
the Ishvite clan from Ishvi;
the Beriite clan from Beriah.

45 From Beriah's descendants:
the Heberite clan from Heber;
the Malchielite clan from Malchiel.

46 And the name of Asher's daughter
was Serah.

47 These were the Asherite clans
⌞numbered⌟
by their registered men: 53,400.

48 Naphtali's descendants
by their clans:
the Jahzeelite clan from Jahzeel;
the Gunite clan from Guni;

49 the Jezerite clan from Jezer;
the Shillemite clan from Shillem.

50 These were the Naphtali clans
numbered
by their registered men: 45,400.

---

[a] **26:39** Some Hb mss, Sam, LXX, Syr, Tg, Vg; other Hb mss read *Shephupham*

⁵¹ These registered Israelite men numbered 601,730.

God's Division of Land

⁵² The LORD spoke to Moses, ⁵³ "The land is to be divided among them as an inheritance based on the number of names. ⁵⁴ Increase the inheritance for a large ⌊tribe⌋, and decrease it for a small one. Each is to be given its inheritance according to those who were registered in it. ⁵⁵ The land must be divided by lot; they will receive an inheritance according to the names of their ancestral tribes. ⁵⁶ Each inheritance will be divided by lot among the larger and smaller ⌊tribes⌋."

Levite Clans

⁵⁷These were the Levites registered
   by their clans:
   the Gershonite clan from Gershon;
   the Kohathite clan from Kohath;
   the Merarite clan from Merari.
⁵⁸ These were the Levite family
   groups:
   the Libnite clan,
   the Hebronite clan,
   the Mahlite clan,
   the Mushite clan,
   and the Korahite clan.

Moses, Aaron, and Miriam: Family Summarized

Kohath was the ancestor of Amram. ⁵⁹ The name of Amram's wife was Jochebed, a descendant of Levi, born to Levi in Egypt. She bore to Amram: Aaron, Moses, and their sister Miriam. ⁶⁰ Nadab, Abihu, Eleazar, and Ithamar were born to Aaron, ⁶¹ but Nadab and Abihu died when they presented unauthorized fire before the LORD. ⁶² Those registered were 23,000, every male one month old or more; they were not registered among the ⌊other⌋ Israelites, because no inheri-

tance was given to them among the Israelites.

Those Barred from Promised Land

⁶³ These were the ones registered by Moses and Eleazar the priest when they registered the Israelites on the plains of Moab by the Jordan ⌊across from⌋ Jericho. ⁶⁴ But among them there was not one of those who had been registered by Moses and Aaron the priest when they registered the Israelites in the Wilderness of Sinai. ⁶⁵ For the LORD had said to them that they would all die in the wilderness. None of them was left except Caleb son of Jephunneh and Joshua son of Nun.

Daughters' Inheritance

A Practical Case

27 The daughters of Zelophehad approached; ⌊Zelophehad was the⌋ son of Hepher, son of Gilead, son of Machir, son of Manasseh from the clans of Manasseh, the son of Joseph. These were the names of his daughters: Mahlah, Noah, Hoglah, Milcah, and Tirzah. ² They stood before Moses, Eleazar the priest, the leaders, and the entire community at the entrance to the tent of meeting and said, ³ "Our father died in the wilderness, but he was not among Korah's followers, who gathered together against the LORD. Instead, he died because of his own sin, and he had no sons. ⁴ Why should the name of our father be taken away from his clan? Since he had no son, give us property among our father's brothers."

God's Law of Inheritance

⁵ Moses brought their case before the LORD, ⁶ and the LORD answered him, ⁷ "What Zelophehad's daughters say is correct. You are to give them hereditary property among their father's brothers

and transfer their father's inheritance to them. [8] Tell the Israelites: <u>When a man dies without having a son, transfer his inheritance to his daughter.</u> [9] If he has no daughter, give his inheritance to his brothers. [10] If he has no brothers, give his inheritance to his father's brothers. [11] If his father has no brothers, give his inheritance to the nearest relative of his clan, and he will take possession of it. This is to be a statutory ordinance for the Israelites as the LORD commanded Moses."

Joshua Commissioned to Succeed Moses

Moses Appeals

[12] Then the LORD said to Moses, "Go up this mountain of the Abarim ⌞range⌟[a] and see the land that I have given the Israelites. [13] After you have seen it, you will also be gathered to your people, as Aaron your brother was. [14] When the community quarreled in the Wilderness of Zin, both of you rebelled against My command to show My holiness in their sight at the waters." Those were the waters of Meribah[b] of Kadesh in the Wilderness of Zin.

[15] So Moses appealed to the LORD, [16] "May the LORD, the God of the spirits of all flesh, appoint a man over the community [17] who will go out before them and come back in before them, and who will bring them out and bring them in, so that the LORD's community won't be like sheep without a shepherd."

God Chooses Joshua

[18] The LORD replied to Moses, "Take Joshua son of Nun, a man who has the Spirit in him, and lay your hands on him. [19] Have him stand before Eleazar the priest and the whole community, and commission him in their sight. [20] Confer some of your authority on him so that the entire Israelite community will obey ⌞him⌟. [21] He will stand before Eleazar who will consult the LORD for him with the decision of the •Urim.[c] He and all the Israelites with him, even the entire community, will go out and come back in at his command."

[22] Moses did as the LORD commanded him. He took Joshua, had him stand before Eleazar the priest and the entire community, [23] laid his hands on him, and commissioned him, as the LORD had spoken through Moses.

Prescribed Offerings

28 The LORD spoke to Moses, [2] "Command the Israelites and say to them: Be sure to present to Me at its appointed time My offering and My food as My fire offering, a pleasing aroma to Me. [3] And say to them: This is the fire offering you are to present to the LORD:

Daily Offerings

"Each day ⌞present⌟ two unblemished year-old male lambs as a regular •burnt offering. [4] Offer one lamb in the morning and the other lamb at twilight, [5] along with two quarts[d] of fine flour for a •grain offering mixed with a quart[e] of beaten olive oil. [6] It is a regular burnt offering established at Mount Sinai for a pleasing aroma, a fire offering to the LORD. [7] The drink offering is to be a quart[e] with each lamb. Pour out the offering of beer to the LORD in the sanctuary area. [8] Offer the second lamb at twilight, along with the same kind of grain offering and drink offering as in the morning. It is a fire offering, a pleasing aroma to the LORD.

[a]27:12 Mount Nebo; Nm 33:47-48; Dt 32:49; Jr 22:20   [b]27:14 = quarreling   [c]27:21 The *Urim* and Thummim were 2 objects used to determine God's will; Ex 28:30.   [d]28:5 Lit *one-tenth of an ephah*   [e]28:5,7 Lit *a fourth of a hin*

Sabbath Offerings

⁹ "On the Sabbath day ⌊present⌋ two unblemished year-old male lambs, four quartsᵃ of fine flour mixed with oil as a grain offering, and its drink offering. ¹⁰ It is the burnt offering for every Sabbath, in addition to the regular burnt offering and its drink offering.

Monthly Offerings

¹¹ "At the beginning of each of your months present a burnt offering to the LORD: two young bulls, one ram, seven male lambs a year old—⌊all⌋ unblemished— ¹² with six quartsᵇ of fine flour mixed with oil as a grain offering for each bull, four quartsᵃ of fine flour mixed with oil as a grain offering for the ram, ¹³ and two quartsᶜ of fine flour mixed with oil as a grain offering for each lamb. It is a burnt offering, a pleasing aroma, a fire offering to the LORD. ¹⁴ Their drink offerings are to be two quartsᵈ of wine with each bull, one and a third quartsᵉ with the ram, and one quartᶠ with each male lamb. This is the monthly burnt offering for all the months of the year. ¹⁵ And one male goat is to be offered as a •sin offering to the LORD, in addition to the regular burnt offering with its drink offering.

Passover and Unleavened Bread Offerings

¹⁶ "The •Passover to the LORD comes in the first month, on the fourteenth day of the month. ¹⁷ On the fifteenth day of this month there will be a festival; unleavened bread is to be eaten for seven days. ¹⁸ On the first day there is to be a sacred assembly; you are not to do any daily work. ¹⁹ Present a fire offering, a burnt offering to the LORD: two young bulls, one ram, and seven male lambs a year old. Your animals are to be unblemished. ²⁰ The grain offering with them is to be of fine flour mixed with oil; offer six quartsᵇ with each bull and four quartsᵃ with the ram. ²¹ Offer two quartsᶜ with each of the seven lambs ²² and one male goat for a sin offering to make •atonement for yourselves. ²³ Offer these with the morning burnt offering that is part of the regular burnt offering. ²⁴ You are to offer the same food each day for seven days as a fire offering, a pleasing aroma to the LORD. It is to be offered with its drink offering and the regular burnt offering. ²⁵ On the seventh day you are to hold a sacred assembly; you are not to do any daily work.

Festival of Weeks Offerings

²⁶ "On the day of •firstfruits, you are to hold a sacred assembly when you present an offering of new grain to the LORD at your ⌊Festival of⌋ Weeks; you are not to do any daily work. ²⁷ Present a burnt offering for a pleasing aroma to the LORD: two young bulls, one ram, and seven male lambs a year old, ²⁸ with their grain offering of fine flour mixed with oil, six quartsᵇ with each bull, four quartsᵃ with the ram, ²⁹ and two quartsᶜ with each of the seven lambs ³⁰ and one male goat to make atonement for yourselves. ³¹ Offer ⌊them⌋ with their drink offerings in addition to the regular burnt offering and its grain offering. Your animals are to be unblemished.

New Year's Day Offerings

29 "You are to hold a sacred assembly in the seventh month, on the first ⌊day⌋ of the month, and you are not to do any daily work. This will be a day of

---

ᵃ**28:9,12,20,28** Lit *two-tenths* (of an ephah)   ᵇ**28:12,20,28** Lit *three-tenths* (of an ephah)   ᶜ**28:13,21,29** Lit *one-tenth* (of an ephah)   ᵈ**28:14** Lit *a half hin*   ᵉ**28:14** Lit *bull, a third hin*   ᶠ**28:14** Lit *a fourth hin*

jubilation[a] for you. ² Offer a •burnt offering as a pleasing aroma to the LORD: one young bull, one ram, seven male lambs a year old—ιallι unblemished— ³ with their •grain offering of fine flour mixed with oil, six quarts[b] with the bull, four quarts[c] with the ram, ⁴ and two quarts[d] with each of the seven male lambs. ⁵ Also ιofferι one male goat as a •sin offering to make •atonement for yourselves. ⁶ These are in addition to the monthly and regular burnt offerings with their grain offerings and drink offerings. They are a pleasing aroma, a fire offering to the LORD.

Day of Atonement Offerings

⁷ "You are to hold a sacred assembly on the tenth ιdayι of this seventh month and practice self-denial;[e] you must not do any work. ⁸ Present a burnt offering to the LORD, a pleasing aroma: one young bull, one ram, and seven male lambs a year old. ιAllι your animals are to be unblemished. ⁹ Their grain offering is to be of fine flour mixed with oil, six quarts[b] with the bull, four quarts[c] with the ram, ¹⁰ and two quarts[d] with each of the seven lambs. ¹¹ ιOfferι one male goat for a sin offering. The regular burnt offering with its grain offering and drink offerings are in addition to the sin offering of atonement.

Festival of Booths Offerings

¹² "You are to hold a sacred assembly on the fifteenth day of the seventh month; you must not do any daily work. You are to celebrate a seven-day festival for the LORD. ¹³ Present a burnt offering, a fire offering as a pleasing aroma to the LORD: 13 young bulls, two rams, and 14 male lambs a year old. They are to be unblemished. ¹⁴ Their grain offering is to be of fine flour mixed with oil, six quarts[b] with each of the 13 bulls, four quarts[c] with each of the two rams, ¹⁵ and two quarts[d] with each of the 14 lambs. ¹⁶ Also ιofferι one male goat as a sin offering. These are in addition to the regular burnt offering with its grain and drink offerings.

¹⁷ "On the second day ιpresentι 12 young bulls, two rams, and 14 male lambs a year old—ιallι unblemished— ¹⁸ with their grain and drink offerings for the bulls, rams, and lambs, in proportion to their number. ¹⁹ Also ιofferι one male goat as a sin offering. These are in addition to the regular burnt offering with its grain and drink[f] offerings.

²⁰ "On the third day ιpresentι 11 bulls, two rams, 14 male lambs a year old—ιallι unblemished— ²¹ with their grain and drink offerings for the bulls, rams, and lambs, in proportion to their number. ²² Also ιofferι one male goat as a sin offering. These are in addition to the regular burnt offering with its grain and drink offerings.

²³ "On the fourth day ιpresentι 10 bulls, two rams, 14 male lambs a year old—ιallι unblemished— ²⁴ with their grain and drink offerings for the bulls, rams, and lambs, in proportion to their number. ²⁵ Also ιofferι one male goat as a sin offering. These are in addition to the regular burnt offering with its grain and drink offerings.

²⁶ "On the fifth day ιpresentι nine bulls, two rams, 14 male lambs a year old—ιallι unblemished— ²⁷ with their grain and drink offerings for the bulls, rams, and lambs, in proportion to their number. ²⁸ Also ιofferι one male goat as a

ᵃ**29:1** Lit *shout,* or *blast*; traditionally, *trumpet blasts*   ᵇ**29:3,9,14** Lit *three-tenths* (of an ephah)   ᶜ**29:3,9,14** Lit *two-tenths* (of an ephah)   ᵈ**29:4,10,15** Lit *one-tenth* (of an ephah)   ᵉ**29:7** Traditionally, this involved fasting, abstinence from sex, and refraining from personal grooming   ᶠ**29:19** Some Hb mss, Syr, Vg, Sam; other Hb mss, LXX read *and their drink*

sin offering. These are in addition to the regular burnt offering with its grain and drink offerings.

29 "On the sixth day ⌐present⌐ eight bulls, two rams, 14 male lambs a year old—⌐all⌐ unblemished— 30 with their grain and drink offerings for the bulls, rams, and lambs, in proportion to their number. 31 Also ⌐offer⌐ one male goat as a sin offering. These are in addition to the regular burnt offering with its grain and drink[a] offerings.

32 "On the seventh day ⌐present⌐ seven bulls, two rams, and 14 male lambs a year old—⌐all⌐ unblemished— 33 with their grain and drink offerings for the bulls, rams, and lambs, in proportion to their number. 34 Also ⌐offer⌐ one male goat as a sin offering. These are in addition to the regular burnt offering with its grain and drink offerings.

35 "On the eighth day you are to hold a solemn assembly; you are not to do any daily work. 36 Present a burnt offering, a fire offering as a pleasing aroma to the LORD: one bull, one ram, seven male lambs a year old—⌐all⌐ unblemished— 37 with their grain and drink offerings for the bulls, rams, and lambs, in proportion to their number. 38 Also ⌐offer⌐ one male goat as a sin offering. These are in addition to the regular burnt offering with its grain and drink offerings.

39 "You must offer these to the LORD at your appointed times in addition to your vow and freewill offerings, whether burnt, grain, drink, or •fellowship offerings." 40b So Moses told the Israelites everything the LORD had commanded him.

Regulation of Vows

30 Moses told the leaders of the Israelite tribes, "This is what the LORD has commanded: 2 When a man makes a vow to the LORD or swears an oath to put himself under an obligation, he must not break his word; he must do whatever he has promised.

3 "When a woman in her father's house during her youth makes a vow to the LORD or puts ⌐herself⌐ under an obligation, 4 and her father hears about her vow or the obligation she put herself under, and he says nothing to her, all her vows and every obligation she put herself under are binding. 5 But if her father prohibits her on the day he hears ⌐about it⌐, none of her vows and none of the obligations she put herself under are binding. The LORD will absolve her because her father has prohibited her.

6 "If a woman marries while her vows or the rash commitment she herself made are binding, 7 and her husband hears ⌐about it⌐ and says nothing to her when he finds out, her vows are binding, and the obligations she put herself under are binding. 8 But if her husband prohibits her when he hears ⌐about it⌐, he will cancel her vow that is binding or the rash commitment she herself made, and the LORD will forgive her.

9 "Every vow a widow or divorcée puts herself under is binding on her.

10 "If a woman in her husband's house has made a vow or put herself under an obligation with an oath, 11 and her husband hears ⌐about it⌐, says nothing to her, and does not prohibit her, all her vows are binding, and every obligation she put herself under is binding. 12 But if her husband cancels them on the day he hears ⌐about it⌐, nothing that came from her lips, whether her vows or her obligation, is binding. Her husband has canceled them, and the LORD will absolve her. 13 Her husband may confirm or cancel any vow or any sworn obligation to

a**29:31** Some Hb mss, Syr, Tg, Vg; other Hb mss, Sam read *and their drink*   b**29:40** Nm 30:1 in Hb deny herself. [14] If her husband says nothing at all to her from day to day, he confirms all her vows and obligations, which are binding. He has confirmed them because he said nothing to her when he heard ⌊about them⌋. [15] But if he cancels them after he hears ⌊about them⌋, he will be responsible for her [a] commitment."[b]

[16] These are the statutes that the LORD commanded Moses concerning ⌊the relationship⌋ between a man and his wife, or between a father and his daughter in his house during her youth.

War with Midian

31 The LORD spoke to Moses, [2] "Execute vengeance for the Israelites against the Midianites. After that, you will be gathered to your people."

[3] So Moses spoke to the people, "Equip some of your men for war. They will go against Midian to inflict the LORD's vengeance on them. [4] Send 1,000 men to war from each Israelite tribe." [5] So 1,000 were recruited from each Israelite tribe out of the thousands[c] in Israel— 12,000 equipped for war. [6] Moses sent 1,000 from each tribe to war. They went with Phinehas son of Eleazar the priest, in whose care were the holy objects and signal trumpets.

Waging War

[7] They waged war against Midian, as the LORD had commanded Moses, and killed every male. [8] Along with the others slain by them, they killed the Midianite kings—Evi, Rekem, Zur, Hur, and Reba, the five kings of Midian. They also killed Balaam son of Beor with the sword. [9] The Israelites took the Midianite women and their children captive, and they plundered all their cattle, flocks, and property. [10] Then they burned all the cities where the Midianites lived, as well as all their encampments, [11] and took away all the spoils of war and the captives, both human and animal. [12] They brought the prisoners, animals, and spoils of war to Moses, Eleazar the priest, and the Israelite community at the camp on the plains of Moab by the Jordan ⌊across from⌋ Jericho.

[13] Moses, Eleazar the priest, and all the leaders of the community went to meet them outside the camp. [14] But Moses became furious with the officers, the commanders of thousands and commanders of hundreds, who were returning from the military campaign. [15] "Have[d] you let every female live?" he asked them. [16] "Yet they are the ones who, at Balaam's advice, incited the Israelites to unfaithfulness against the LORD in the Peor incident, so that the plague came against the LORD's community. [17] So now, kill all the male children and kill every woman who has had sexual relations with a man, [18] but keep alive for yourselves all the young females who have not had sexual relations.

[19] "You are to remain outside the camp for seven days. All of you and your prisoners who have killed a person or touched the dead are to purify yourselves on the third day and the seventh day. [20] Also purify everything: garments, leather goods, things made of goat hair, and every article of wood."

Eleazar: Purify by Fire and Water

[21] Then Eleazar the priest said to the soldiers who had gone to battle, "This is the legal statute the LORD commanded Moses: [22] Only the gold, silver, bronze, iron, tin, and lead— [23] everything that can withstand fire—put through fire, and it will be clean. It must still be puri-

---

[a]**30:15** Sam, LXX, some Syr mss read *his*   [b]**30:15** Or *will bear her guilt*   [c]**31:5** Or *clans*   [d]**31:15** Sam, LXX, Syr, Vg read *Why have*

fied with the purification water. Anything that cannot withstand fire, put through the water. ²⁴ On the seventh day wash your clothes, and you will be clean. After that you may enter the camp."

Account of Plunder

²⁵ The LORD told Moses, ²⁶ "You, Eleazar the priest, and the family leaders of the community are to take a count of what was captured, human and animal. ²⁷ Then divide the captives between the troops who went out to war and the entire community. ²⁸ Set aside a tribute for the LORD from what belongs to the fighting men who went out to war: one out of ⌊every⌋ 500 humans, cattle, donkeys, sheep, and goats. ²⁹ Take ⌊the tribute⌋ from their half and give ⌊it⌋ to Eleazar the priest as a contribution to the LORD. ³⁰ From the Israelites' half, take one out of every 50 from the people, cattle, donkeys, sheep, and goats, all the livestock, and give them to the Levites who perform the duties of[a] the LORD's tabernacle."

³¹ So Moses and Eleazar the priest did as the LORD commanded Moses. ³² The captives remaining from the plunder the army had taken totaled:

675,000 sheep and goats,
³³ 72,000 cattle,
³⁴ 61,000 donkeys,
³⁵ and 32,000 people, all the females who had not had sexual relations with a man.

³⁶ The half portion for those who went out to war numbered:

337,500 sheep and goats,
³⁷ and the tribute to the LORD
was 675
from the sheep and goats;

³⁸ from the 36,000 cattle,
the tribute to the LORD was 72;
³⁹ from the 30,500 donkeys,
the tribute to the LORD was 61;
⁴⁰ and from the 16,000 people,
the tribute to the LORD
was 32 people.

Tribute for Lord

⁴¹ Moses gave the tribute to Eleazar the priest as a contribution for the LORD, as the LORD had commanded Moses.

⁴² From the Israelites' half, which Moses separated from the men who fought, ⁴³ the community's half was:

337,500 sheep and goats,
⁴⁴ 36,000 cattle,
⁴⁵ 30,500 donkeys,
⁴⁶ and 16,000 people.

⁴⁷ Moses took one out of ⌊every⌋ 50, selected from the people and the livestock from the Israelites' half. He gave them to the Levites who perform the duties of the LORD's tabernacle, as the LORD had commanded him.

Officers: Gold for God

⁴⁸ The officers who were over the thousands of the army, the commanders of thousands and of hundreds, approached Moses ⁴⁹ and told him, "Your servants have taken a census of the fighting men under our command, and not one of us is missing. ⁵⁰ So we have presented to the LORD an offering of the gold articles each man found—armlets, bracelets, rings, earrings, and necklaces—to make •atonement for ourselves before the LORD."

⁵¹ Moses and Eleazar the priest received from them all the articles made out of gold. ⁵² All the gold of the contribution they offered to the LORD, from the commanders of thousands and of

---

ª**31:30** Or who protect

hundreds, was 420 pounds.[a] 53 Each of the soldiers had taken plunder for himself. 54 Moses and Eleazar the priest received the gold from the commanders of thousands and of hundreds and brought it into the tent of meeting as a memorial for the Israelites before the LORD.

Reuben and Gad Settle Across Jordan

They Propose

32 The Reubenites and Gadites had a very large number of livestock. When they surveyed the lands of Jazer and Gilead, they saw that the region was a ⌊good⌋ one for livestock. 2 So the Gadites and Reubenites came to Moses, Eleazar the priest, and the leaders of the community and said: 3 "⌊The territory of⌋ Ataroth, Dibon, Jazer, Nimrah, Heshbon, Elealeh, Sebam,[b] Nebo, and Beon, 4 which the LORD struck down before the community of Israel, is ⌊good⌋ land for livestock, and your servants own livestock." 5 They said, "If we have found favor in your sight, let this land be given to your servants as a possession. Don't make us cross the Jordan."

Moses Objects

6 But Moses asked the Gadites and Reubenites, "Should your brothers go to war while you stay here? 7 Why are you discouraging[c] the Israelites from crossing into the land the LORD has given them? 8 That's what your fathers did when I sent them from Kadesh-barnea to see the land. 9 After they went up as far as Eshcol Valley and saw the land, they discouraged the Israelites from entering the land the LORD had given them. 10 So the LORD's anger burned that day, and He swore an oath: 11 'Because they did not follow Me completely, none of the men

20 years old or more who came up from Egypt will see the land I swore ⌊to give⌋ Abraham, Isaac, and Jacob— 12 none except Caleb son of Jephunneh the Kenizzite and Joshua son of Nun, because they did follow the LORD completely.' 13 The LORD's anger burned against Israel, and He made them wander in the wilderness 40 years until the whole generation that had done what was evil in the LORD's sight was gone. 14 And here you, a brood of sinners, stand in your fathers' place adding even more to the LORD's burning anger against Israel. 15 If you turn back from following Him, He will once again leave this people in the wilderness, and you will destroy all of them."

A Counterproposal

16 Then they approached him and said, "We want to build sheepfolds here for our livestock and cities for our dependents. 17 But we will arm ourselves and be ready ⌊to go⌋ ahead of the Israelites until we have brought them into their place. Meanwhile, our dependents will remain in the fortified cities because of the inhabitants of the land. 18 We will not return to our homes until each of the Israelites has taken possession of his inheritance. 19 Yet we will not have an inheritance with them across the Jordan and beyond, because our inheritance will be across the Jordan to the east."

Moses Agrees

20 Moses replied to them, "If you do this—if you arm yourselves for battle before the LORD, 21 and every one of your armed men crosses the Jordan before the LORD until He has driven His enemies from His presence, 22 and the land is subdued before the LORD—afterwards you may return and be free from obligation

---

[a]31:52 Lit *16,750 shekels*   [b]32:3 Sam, LXX read *Sibmah* (as in v. 38); Syr reads *Sebah*   [c]32:7 Lit *discouraging the hearts of*

to the LORD and to Israel. And this land will belong to you as a possession before the LORD. ²³ But if you don't do this, you will certainly sin against the LORD; be sure your sin will catch up with you. ²⁴ Build cities for your dependents and folds for your flocks, but do what you have promised."

²⁵ The Gadites and Reubenites answered Moses, "Your servants will do just as my lord commands. ²⁶ Our little children, wives, livestock, and all our animals will remain here in the cities of Gilead, ²⁷ but your servants are equipped for war before the LORD and will go across to the battle as my lord orders."

Compromise Implemented

²⁸ So Moses gave orders about them to Eleazar the priest, Joshua son of Nun, and the family leaders of the Israelite tribes. ²⁹ Moses told them, "If the Gadites and Reubenites cross the Jordan with you, every man in battle formation before the LORD, and the land is subdued before you, you are to give them the land of Gilead as a possession. ³⁰ But if they don't go across with you in battle formation, they must accept land in Canaan with you."

³¹ The Gadites and Reubenites replied, "What the LORD has spoken to your servants is what we will do. ³² We will cross over in battle formation before the LORD into the land of Canaan, but we will keep our hereditary possession across the Jordan."

Deal is Sealed

³³ So Moses gave them—the Gadites, Reubenites, and half the tribe of Manasseh son of Joseph—the kingdom of Sihon king of the Amorites and the kingdom of Og king of Bashan, the land including its cities with the territories surrounding them. ³⁴ The Gadites rebuilt Dibon, Ata-

roth, Aroer, ³⁵ Atroth-shophan, Jazer, Jogbehah, ³⁶ Beth-nimrah, and Beth-haran as fortified cities, and ⌊built⌋ sheepfolds. ³⁷ The Reubenites rebuilt Heshbon, Elealeh, Kiriathaim, ³⁸ as well as Nebo and Baal-meon (whose names were changed), and Sibmah. They gave names to the cities they rebuilt.

³⁹ The descendants of Machir son of Manasseh went to Gilead, captured it, and drove out the Amorites who were there. ⁴⁰ So Moses gave Gilead to ⌊the clan of⌋ Machir son of Manasseh, and they settled in it. ⁴¹ Jair, a descendant of Manasseh, went and captured their villages, which he renamed Jair's Villages.ᵃ ⁴² Nobah went and captured Kenath with its villages and called it Nobah after his own name.

Wilderness Travels Reviewed

33 These were the stages of the Israelites' journey when they went out of the land of Egypt by their military divisions under the leadership of Moses and Aaron. ² At the LORD's command, Moses wrote down the starting points for the stages of their journey; these are the stages ⌊listed⌋ by their starting points:

³ They departed from Rameses in the first month, on the fifteenth day of the month. On the day after the •Passover the Israelites went out triumphantlyᵇ in the sight of all the Egyptians. ⁴ Meanwhile, the Egyptians were burying every firstborn male the LORD had struck down among them, for the LORD had executed judgment against their gods. ⁵ The Israelites departed from Rameses and camped at Succoth.

⁶ They departed from Succoth and camped at Etham, which is on the edge of the wilderness.

ᵃ**32:41** Or renamed Havvoth-jair ᵇ**33:3** Lit with a raised hand; Ex 14:8

7 They departed from Etham and turned back to Pi-hahiroth, which faces Baal-zephon, and they camped before Migdol.

8 They departed from Pi-hahiroth[a] and crossed through the middle of the sea into the wilderness. They took a three-day journey into the Wilderness of Etham and camped at Marah.

9 They departed from Marah and came to Elim. There were 12 springs of water and 70 date palms at Elim, so they camped there.

10 They departed from Elim and camped by the •Red Sea.

11 They departed from the Red Sea and camped in the Wilderness of Sin.

12 They departed from the Wilderness of Sin and camped in Dophkah.

13 They departed from Dophkah and camped at Alush.

14 They departed from Alush and camped at Rephidim, where there was no water for the people to drink.

15 They departed from Rephidim and camped in the Wilderness of Sinai.

16 They departed from the Wilderness of Sinai and camped at Kibroth-hattaavah.

17 They departed from Kibroth-hattaavah and camped at Hazeroth.

18 They departed from Hazeroth and camped at Rithmah.

19 They departed from Rithmah and camped at Rimmon-perez.

20 They departed from Rimmon-perez and camped at Libnah.

21 They departed from Libnah and camped at Rissah.

22 They departed from Rissah and camped at Kehelathah.

23 They departed from Kehelathah and camped at Mount Shepher.

24 They departed from Mount Shepher and camped at Haradah.

25 They departed from Haradah and camped at Makheloth.

26 They departed from Makheloth and camped at Tahath.

27 They departed from Tahath and camped at Terah.

28 They departed from Terah and camped at Mithkah.

29 They departed from Mithkah and camped at Hashmonah.

30 They departed from Hashmonah and camped at Moseroth.

31 They departed from Moseroth and camped at Bene-jaakan.

32 They departed from Bene-jaakan and camped at Hor-haggidgad.

33 They departed from Hor-haggidgad and camped at Jotbathah.

34 They departed from Jotbathah and camped at Abronah.

35 They departed from Abronah and camped at Ezion-geber.

36 They departed from Ezion-geber and camped in the Wilderness of Zin (that is, Kadesh).

37 They departed from Kadesh and camped at Mount Hor on the edge of the land of Edom. 38 At the LORD's command, Aaron the priest climbed Mount Hor and died there on the first ⌊day⌋ of the fifth month in the fortieth year after the Israelites went out of the land of Egypt. 39 Aaron was 123 years old when he died on Mount Hor. 40 At that time the Canaanite king of Arad, who lived in the •Negev in the land of Canaan, heard the Israelites were coming.

41 They departed from Mount Hor and camped at Zalmonah.

a 33:8 Some Hb mss, Sam, Syr, Vg; other Hb mss read *from before Hahiroth*

⁴²They departed from Zalmonah and camped at Punon.
⁴³They departed from Punon and camped at Oboth.
⁴⁴They departed from Oboth and camped at Iye-abarim on the border of Moab.
⁴⁵They departed from Iyimᵃ and camped at Dibon-gad.
⁴⁶They departed from Dibon-gad and camped at Almon-diblathaim.
⁴⁷They departed from Almon-diblathaim and camped in the Abarim ⌊range⌋ facing Nebo.
⁴⁸They departed from the Abarim ⌊range⌋ and camped on the plains of Moab by the Jordan ⌊across from⌋ Jericho. ⁴⁹They camped by the Jordan from Beth-jeshimoth to Acacia Meadowsᵇ on the plains of Moab.

God's Orders for Taking Canaan

Destroy Idols, Drive Out Inhabitants

⁵⁰The LORD spoke to Moses in the plains of Moab by the Jordan ⌊across from⌋ Jericho, ⁵¹"Tell the Israelites: When you cross the Jordan into the land of Canaan, ⁵²you must drive out all the inhabitants of the land before you, destroy all their stone images and cast images, and demolish all their •high places. ⁵³You are to take possession of the land and settle in it because I have given you the land to possess. ⁵⁴You are to receive the land as an inheritance by lot according to your clans. Increase the inheritance for a large clan and decrease it for a small one. Whatever place the lot indicates for someone will be his. You will receive an inheritance according to your ancestral tribes. ⁵⁵But if you don't drive out the inhabitants of the land before you, those you allow to remain will become thorns in your eyes and in your sides; they will harass you in the land where you will live. ⁵⁶And what I had planned to do to them, I will do to you."

Boundaries of Promised Land

34 The LORD spoke to Moses, ²"Command the Israelites and say to them: When you enter the land of Canaan, it will be allotted to you as an inheritanceᶜ with these borders:

³Your southern side will be from the Wilderness of Zin along the boundary of Edom. Your southern border on the east will begin at the east end of the Dead Sea. ⁴Your border will turn south of the Ascent of Akrabbim,ᵈ proceed to Zin, and end south of Kadesh-barnea. It will go to Hazar-addar and proceed to Azmon. ⁵The border will turn from Azmon to the Brook of Egypt, where it will end at the Mediterranean Sea.

⁶Your western border will be the coastline of the Mediterranean Sea; this will be your western border.

⁷This will be your northern border: From the Mediterranean Sea draw a line to Mount Hor;ᵉ ⁸from Mount Hor draw a line to the entrance of Hamath,ᶠ and the border will reach Zedad. ⁹Then the border will go to Ziphron and end at Hazar-enan. This will be your northern border.

¹⁰For your eastern border, draw a line from Hazar-enan to Shepham. ¹¹The border will go down from Shepham to Riblah east of Ain. It will continue down and reach the eastern slope of the Sea of

---

ᵃ**33:45** A contraction of *Iye-abarim*   ᵇ**33:49** Or *Abel-shittim*   ᶜ**34:2** Lit *inheritance the land of Canaan*   ᵈ**34:4** Lit *of Scorpions*; Jos 15:3; Jdg 1:36   ᵉ**34:7** In Lebanon; Nm 20:22-28; 33:37-56   ᶠ**34:8** Or *to Lebo-hamath*

Chinnereth.ᵃ ¹² Then the border will go down to the Jordan and end at the Dead Sea. This will be your land ⌊defined⌋ by its borders on all sides."

Moses Confirms Land Division

¹³ So Moses commanded the Israelites, "This is the land you are to receive by lot as an inheritance, which the LORD commanded to be given to the nine and a half tribes. ¹⁴ For the tribe of the Reubenites and the tribe of the Gadites have received ⌊their inheritance⌋ according to their ancestral houses, and half the tribe of Manasseh has received its inheritance. ¹⁵ The two and a half tribes have received their inheritance across the Jordan from Jericho, eastward toward the sunrise."

God Picks Leaders to Distribute Land

¹⁶ The LORD spoke to Moses, ¹⁷ "These are the names of the men who are to distribute the land as an inheritance for you: Eleazar the priest and Joshua son of Nun. ¹⁸ Take one leader from each tribe to distribute the land. ¹⁹ These are the names of the men:

Caleb son of Jephunneh
   from the tribe of Judah;
²⁰ Shemuel son of Ammihud
   from the tribe of Simeon;
²¹ Elidad son of Chislon from the tribe
   of Benjamin;
²² Bukki son of Jogli, a leader
   from the tribe of Dan;
²³ from the sons of Joseph:
   Hanniel son of Ephod, a leader
   from the tribe of Manasseh,
²⁴ Kemuel son of Shiphtan, a leader
   from the tribe of Ephraim;
²⁵ Eli-zaphan son of Parnach, a leader
   from the tribe of Zebulun;

²⁶ Paltiel son of Azzan, a leader
   from the tribe of Issachar;
²⁷ Ahihud son of Shelomi, a leader
   from the tribe of Asher;
²⁸ Pedahel son of Ammihud, a leader
   from the tribe of Naphtali."

²⁹ These are the ones the LORD commanded to distribute the inheritance to the Israelites in the land of Canaan.

Cities for Levites

35 The LORD again spoke to Moses in the plains of Moab by the Jordan ⌊across from⌋ Jericho: ² "Command the Israelites to give cities out of their hereditary property for the Levites to live in and pastureland around the cities. ³ The cities will be for them to live in, and their pasturelands will be for their herds, flocks, and all their ⌊other⌋ animals. ⁴ The pasturelands of the cities you are to give the Levites ⌊will extend⌋ from the city wall 500 yardsᵇ on every side. ⁵ Measure 1,000 yardsᶜ outside the city for the east side, 1,000 yardsᶜ for the south side, 1,000 yardsᶜ for the west side, and 1,000 yardsᶜ for the north side, with the city in the center. This will belong to them as pasturelands for the cities.

⁶ "The cities you give the Levites will include six cities of refuge, which you must provide so that the one who kills someone may flee there; in addition to these, give 42 ⌊other⌋ cities. ⁷ The total number of cities you give the Levites will be 48, along with their pasturelands. ⁸ Of the cities that you give from the Israelites' territory, you should take more from a larger ⌊tribe⌋ and less from a smaller one. Each ⌊tribe⌋ is to give some of its cities to the Levites in proportion to the inheritance it receives."

ᵃ**34:11** The Sea of Galilee; Jos 12:3; 13:27; Lk 5:1   ᵇ**35:4** Lit *1,000 cubits*   ᶜ**35:5** Lit *2,000 cubits*

Cities of Refuge

[9] The LORD said to Moses, [10] "Speak to the Israelites and tell them: When you cross the Jordan into the land of Canaan, [11] designate cities to serve as cities of refuge for you, so that a person who kills someone unintentionally may flee there. [12] You will have the cities as a refuge from the avenger, so that the one who kills someone will not die until he stands trial before the assembly. [13] The cities you select will be your six cities of refuge. [14] Select three cities across the Jordan and three cities in the land of Canaan to be cities of refuge. [15] These six cities will serve as a refuge for the Israelites and for the foreigner or temporary resident among them, so that anyone who kills a person unintentionally may flee there.

Crimes of Intent Excluded

[16] "If anyone strikes a person with an iron object and death results, he is a murderer; the murderer must be put to death. [17] If a man has in his hand a stone capable of causing death and strikes another man and he dies, the murderer must be put to death. [18] If a man has in his hand a wooden object capable of causing death and he dies, the murderer must be put to death. [19] The avenger of blood himself is to kill the murderer; when he finds him, he is to kill him. [20] Likewise, if anyone in hatred pushes a person or throws ⌞an object⌟ at him with malicious intent and he dies, [21] or if in hostility he strikes him with his hand and he dies, the one who struck him must be put to death; he is a murderer. The avenger of blood is to kill the murderer when he finds him.

Offenses Qualifying for Refuge

[22] "But if anyone suddenly pushes a person without hostility or throws any object at him without malicious intent [23] or drops a stone without looking that could kill a person and he dies, but he was not his enemy and wasn't trying to harm him, [24] the assembly is to judge between the slayer and the avenger of blood according to these ordinances. [25] The assembly is to protect the one who kills someone from the hand of the avenger of blood. Then the assembly will return him to the city of refuge he fled to, and he must live there until the death of the high priest who was anointed with the holy oil.

Rules for Protection

[26] "If the one who kills someone ever goes outside the border of the city of refuge he fled to, [27] and the avenger of blood finds him outside the border of his city of refuge and kills him, the avenger will not be guilty of bloodshed, [28] for the one who killed a person was supposed to live in his city of refuge until the death of the high priest. Only after the death of the high priest may the one who has killed a person return to the land he possesses. [29] These ⌞instructions⌟ will be a statutory ordinance for you throughout your generations wherever you live.

Murder Not Protected

[30] "If anyone kills a person, the murderer is to be put to death based on the word of witnesses. But no one is to be put to death based on the testimony of one witness. [31] You are not to accept a ransom for the life of a murderer who is guilty of killing someone; he must be put to death. [32] Neither should you accept a ransom for the person who flees to his city of refuge, allowing him to return and live in the land before the death of the ⌞high⌟ priest.[a]

[a] **35:32** Sam, LXX, Syr read *high priest*

³³ "Do not defile the land where you are,[a] for bloodshed defiles the land, and there can be no •atonement for the land because of the blood that is shed on it, except by the blood of the person who shed it. ³⁴ Do not make the land unclean where you live and where I reside; for I, the LORD, reside among the Israelites."

Inheritance of Zelophehad's Daughters

Issue Revisited

36 The family leaders from the clan of the descendants of Gilead—the son of Machir, son of Manasseh—one of the clans of the sons of Joseph approached and addressed Moses and the leaders who were over the Israelite families. ² They said, "The LORD commanded my lord to give the land as an inheritance by lot to the Israelites. My lord was further commanded by the LORD to give our brother Zelophehad's inheritance to his daughters. ³ If they marry any of the men from the ⌊other⌋ Israelite tribes, their inheritance will be taken away from our fathers' inheritance and added to that of the tribe into which they marry. Therefore, part of our allotted inheritance would be taken away. ⁴ When the Jubilee comes for the Israelites, their inheritance will be added to that of the tribe into which they marry, and their inheritance will be taken away from the inheritance of our ancestral tribe."

Moses Clarifies

⁵ So Moses commanded the Israelites at the word of the LORD, "What the tribe of Joseph's descendants says is right. ⁶ This is what the LORD has commanded concerning Zelophehad's daughters: They may marry anyone they like provided they marry within a clan of their ancestral tribe. ⁷ An inheritance belonging to the Israelites must not transfer from tribe to tribe, because each of the Israelites is to retain the inheritance of his ancestral tribe. ⁸ Any daughter who possesses an inheritance from an Israelite tribe must marry someone from the clan of her ancestral tribe, so that each of the Israelites will possess the inheritance of his fathers. ⁹ No inheritance is to transfer from one tribe to another, because each of the Israelite tribes is to retain its inheritance."

Daughters Obey

¹⁰ The daughters of Zelophehad did as the LORD commanded Moses. ¹¹ Mahlah, Tirzah, Hoglah, Milcah, and Noah, the daughters of Zelophehad, married cousins on their father's side. ¹² They married ⌊men⌋ from the clans of the descendants of Manasseh son of Joseph, and their inheritance remained within the tribe of their father's clan.

¹³ These are the commands and ordinances the LORD commanded the Israelites through Moses in the plains of Moab by the Jordan ⌊across from⌋ Jericho.

---

[a]**35:33** Sam, LXX, Syr, Vg, Tg read *live*

DEUTERONOMY

Introduction

1 These are the words Moses spoke to all Israel across the Jordan in the wilderness, in the •Arabah opposite Suph,ᵃ between Paran and Tophel, Laban, Hazeroth, and Di-zahab. ² It is an eleven-day journey from Horeb to Kadesh-barnea by way of Mount Seir. ³ In the fortieth year, in the eleventh month, on the first of the month, Moses told the Israelites everything the LORD had commanded him ₁to say₎ to them. ⁴ This was after he had defeated Sihon king of the Amorites, who lived in Heshbon, and Og king of Bashan, who lived in Ashtaroth, at Edrei. ⁵ Across the Jordan in the land of Moab, Moses began to explain this law, saying:

Moses Reviews Israel's Travels

Departure Mt. Horeb (Sinai)

⁶ "The LORD our God spoke to us at Horeb, 'You have stayed at this mountain long enough. ⁷ Resume your journey and go to the hill country of the Amorites and their neighbors in the Arabah, the hill country, the lowlands, the •Negev and the sea coast—to the land of the Canaanites and to Lebanon as far as the Euphrates River.ᵇ ⁸ See, I have set the land before you. Enter and take possession of the land the LORD swore to give to your fathers Abraham, Isaac, and Jacob and their descendants after them.'

He Picked Leaders for Tribes

⁹ "I said to you at that time: I can't bear ₁the responsibility for₎ you on my own. ¹⁰ The LORD your God has so multiplied you that today you are as numerous as the stars of the sky. ¹¹ May the LORD, the God of your fathers, increase you a thousand times more, and bless you as He promised you. ¹² But how can I bear your troubles, burdens, and disputes by myself? ¹³ Appoint for yourselves wise, understanding, and respected men from each of your tribes, and I will make them your leaders.

¹⁴ "You replied to me, 'What you propose to do is good.'

¹⁵ "So I took the leaders of your tribes, wise and respected men, and set them over you as leaders: officials for thousands, hundreds, fifties, and tens, and officers for your tribes. ¹⁶ I commanded your judges at that time: Hear ₁the cases₎ between your brothers, and judge rightly between a man and his brother or a foreign resident. ¹⁷ Do not show partiality when rendering judgment; listen to small and great alike. Do not be intimidated by anyone, for judgment belongs to God. Bring me any case too difficult for you, and I will hear it. ¹⁸ At that time I commanded you about all the things you were to do.

Israel Disobeyed at Kadesh-barnea

¹⁹ "We then set out from Horeb and went across all the great and terrible wilderness you saw on the way to the hill country of the Amorites, just as the LORD our God had commanded us. When we reached Kadesh-barnea, ²⁰ I said to you: You have reached the hill country of the Amorites, which the LORD our God is giving us. ²¹ See, the LORD your God has set the land before you. Go up and take possession of it as the LORD, the God of your fathers, has told you. Do not be afraid or discouraged.

ᵃ**1:1** LXX, Tg, Vg read *the Red Sea*   ᵇ**1:7** Lit *the great river, the river Euphrates*

22 "Then all of you approached me and said, 'Let's send men ahead of us, so that they may explore the land for us and bring us back a report about the route we should go up and the cities we will come to.' 23 The plan seemed good to me, so I selected 12 men from among you, one man for each tribe. 24 They left and went up into the hill country and came to the Valley of Eshcol, scouting the land. 25 They took some of the fruit from the land in their hands, carried ⌊it⌋ down to us, and brought us back a report: 'The land the LORD our God is giving us is good.'

Israel's Fear of Promised Land

26 "But you were not willing to go up, rebelling against the command of the LORD your God. 27 You grumbled in your tents and said, 'The LORD brought us out of the land of Egypt to deliver us into the hands of the Amorites so they would destroy us, because He hated us. 28 Where can we go? Our brothers have discouraged us, saying: The people are larger and taller than we are; the cities are large, fortified to the heavens. We also saw the descendants of the Anakim there.'

29 "So I said to you: Don't be terrified or afraid of them! 30 The LORD your God who goes before you will fight for you, just as you saw Him do for you in Egypt. 31 And you saw in the wilderness how the LORD your God carried you as a man carries his son all along the way you traveled until you reached this place. 32 But in spite of this you did not trust the LORD your God, 33 who went before you on the journey to seek out a place for you to camp. He went in the fire by night and in the cloud by day to guide you on the road you were to travel.

God's Punishment

34 "When the LORD heard your[a] words, He grew angry and swore an oath: 35 'None of these men in this evil generation will see the good land I swore to give your fathers, 36 except Caleb the son of Jephunneh. He will see it, and I will give him and his descendants the land on which he has set foot, because he followed the LORD completely.'

37 "The LORD was angry with me also because of you and said: 'You will not enter there either. 38 Joshua son of Nun, who attends you, will enter it. Encourage him, for he will enable Israel to inherit it. 39 Your little children whom you said would be plunder, your sons who[b] don't know good from evil, will enter there. I will give them the land, and they will take possession of it. 40 But you are to turn back and head for the wilderness by way of the •Red Sea.'

Israel Acts too Late

41 "You answered me, 'We have sinned against the LORD. We will go up and fight just as the LORD our God commanded us.' Then each of you put on his weapons of war and thought it would be easy to go up into the hill country.

42 "But the LORD said to me, 'Tell them: Don't go up and fight, for I am not with you to keep you from being defeated by your enemies.' 43 So I spoke to you, but you didn't listen. You rebelled against the LORD's command and defiantly went up into the hill country. 44 Then the Amorites who lived there came out against you and chased you like a swarm of bees. They routed you from Seir as far as Hormah. 45 When you returned, you wept before the LORD, but He didn't listen to your requests or pay attention to you. 46 For this reason you stayed in Kadesh as long as you did.[c]

---

[a]1:34 Lit the sound of your   [b]1:39 Lit who today   [c]1:46 Lit Kadesh for many days, according to the days you stayed

Israel's Journey past Seir

2 "Then we turned back and headed for the wilderness by way of the •Red Sea, as the LORD had told me, and we traveled around the hill country of Seir for many days. ² The LORD then said to me, ³ 'You've been traveling around this hill country long enough; turn north. ⁴ Command the people: You are about to travel through the territory of your brothers, the descendants of Esau, who live in Seir. They will be afraid of you, so you must be very careful. ⁵ Don't fight with them, for I will not give you any of their land, not even an inch of it,ᵃ because I have given Esau the hill country of Seir as ⌞his⌟ possession. ⁶ You may purchase food from them with silver, so that you may eat, and buy water from them to drink. ⁷ For the LORD your God has blessed you in all the work of your hands. He has watched over your journey through this immense wilderness. The LORD your God has been with you this past 40 years, and you have lacked nothing.'

Journey past Moab: Protection of Lot's Land

⁸ "So we bypassed our brothers, the descendants of Esau, who live in Seir. ⌞We turned⌟ away from the •Arabah road and from Elath and Ezion-geber. We traveled along the road to the Wilderness of Moab. ⁹ The LORD said to me, 'Show no hostility toward Moab, and do not provoke them to battle, for I will not give you any of their land as a possession, since I have given Ar as a possession to the descendants of Lot.' "

Giants in the Land

¹⁰ The Emim, a great and numerous people as tall as the Anakim, had previously lived there. ¹¹ They were also regarded as Rephaim, like the Anakim, though the Moabites called them Emim. ¹² The Horites had previously lived in Seir, but the descendants of Esau drove them out, destroying them completelyᵇ and settling in their place, just as Israel did in the land of its possession the LORD gave them.

Thirty-eight Years

¹³ "⌞The LORD said,⌟ 'Now get up and cross the Zered Valley.' So we crossed the Zered Valley. ¹⁴ The time we spent traveling from Kadesh-barnea until we crossed the Zered Valley was 38 years until the entire generation of fighting men had perished from the camp, as the LORD had sworn to them. ¹⁵ Indeed, the LORD's hand was against them, to eliminate them from the camp until they had all perished.

Journey past Ammon

¹⁶ "When all the fighting men had died among the people, ¹⁷ the LORD spoke to me, ¹⁸ 'Today you are going to cross the border of Moab at Ar. ¹⁹ When you get close to the Ammonites, don't show any hostility to them or fight with them, for I will not give you any of the Ammonites' land as a possession; I have given it as a possession to the descendants of Lot.' "

²⁰ This too used to be regarded as the land of the Rephaim. The Rephaim lived there previously, though the Ammonites called them Zamzummim, ²¹ a great and numerous people, tall as the Anakim. The LORD destroyed the Rephaim at the advance of the Ammonites, so that they drove them out and settled in their place. ²² This was just as He had done for the descendants of Esau who lived in Seir, when He destroyed the Horites

---

ᵃ**2:5** Lit *land as far as the width of a sole of a foot*   ᵇ**2:12** Lit *them before them*

before them; they drove them out and have lived in their place until now. ²³ The Caphtorim, who came from Caphtor,^a destroyed the Avvim, who lived in villages as far as Gaza, and settled in their place.

King Sihon the Amorite

²⁴ "⌊The LORD also said,⌋ 'Get up, move out, and cross the Arnon Valley. See, I have handed Sihon the Amorite, king of Heshbon, and his land over to you. Begin to take possession ⌊of it⌋; engage him in battle. ²⁵ Today I will begin to put the fear and dread of you on the peoples everywhere under heaven. They will hear the report about you, tremble, and be in anguish because of you.'

Israel Offers Peace—Sihon Refuses

²⁶ "So I sent messengers with an offer of peace to Sihon king of Heshbon from the Wilderness of Kedemoth, saying, ²⁷ 'Let us travel through your land; we will keep strictly to the highway. We will not turn to the right or the left. ²⁸ You can sell us food in exchange for silver so we may eat, and give us water for silver so we may drink. Only let us travel through on foot, ²⁹ just as the descendants of Esau who live in Seir did for us, and the Moabites who live in Ar, until we cross the Jordan into the land the LORD our God is giving us.' ³⁰ But Sihon king of Heshbon would not let us travel through his land, for the LORD your God made his spirit stubborn and his heart obstinate in order to hand him over to you, as has now taken place.

Israel Defeats Sihon

³¹ "Then the LORD said to me, 'See, I have begun to give Sihon and his land to you. Begin to take possession of it.' ³² So Sihon and his whole army came out against us for battle at Jahaz. ³³ The LORD our God handed him over to us, and we defeated him, his sons, and his whole army. ³⁴ At that time we captured all his cities and •completely destroyed the people of every city, including the women and children. We left no survivors. ³⁵ We took only the livestock and the spoil from the cities we captured as plunder for ourselves. ³⁶ There was no city that was inaccessible to^b us, from Aroer on the rim of the Arnon Valley, along with the city in the valley, even as far as Gilead. The LORD our God gave everything to us. ³⁷ But you did not go near the Ammonites' land, all along the bank of the Jabbok River and the cities of the hill country, everything that the LORD our God had commanded.

Israel Defeats King Og of Bashan

3 "Then we turned and went up the road to Bashan, and Og king of Bashan, with his whole army, came out against us for battle at Edrei. ² But the LORD said to me, 'Do not fear him, for I have handed him over to you, along with his whole army and his land. Do to him as you did to Sihon king of the Amorites, who lived in Heshbon.' ³ So the LORD our God also handed over Og king of Bashan and his whole army to us. We struck him until there was no survivor left. ⁴ We captured all his cities at that time. There wasn't a city that we didn't take from them: 60 cities, the entire region of Argob, the kingdom of Og in Bashan. ⁵ All these were fortified with high walls, gates, and bars, besides a large number of rural villages. ⁶ We •completely destroyed them, as we had done to Sihon king of Heshbon, destroying the

^a2:23 Probably Crete   ^b2:36 Or was too high for

men, women, and children of every city. [7] But we took all the livestock and the spoil from the cities as plunder for ourselves.

Tribes across Jordan

[8] "At that time we took the land from the two Amorite kings across the Jordan, from the Arnon Valley as far as Mount Hermon, [9] which the Sidonians call Sirion, but the Amorites call Senir, [10] all the cities of the plateau, Gilead, and Bashan as far as Salecah and Edrei, cities of Og's kingdom in Bashan. [11] (Only Og king of Bashan was left of the remnant of the Rephaim. His bed was made of iron.[a] Isn't it in Rabbah of the Ammonites? It is 13 feet six inches long and six feet wide by a standard measure.[b])

Land to Reuben, Gad, and Manasseh

[12] "At that time we took possession of this land. I gave to the Reubenites and Gadites ⟨the area extending⟩ from Aroer by the Arnon Valley, and half the hill country of Gilead along with its cities. [13] I gave to half the tribe of Manasseh the rest of Gilead and all Bashan, the kingdom of Og. The entire region of Argob, the whole territory of Bashan, used to be called the land of the Rephaim. [14] Jair, a descendant of Manasseh, took over the entire region of Argob as far as the border of the Geshurites and Maacathites. He called Bashan by his own name, Jair's Villages,[c] as it is today. [15] I gave Gilead to Machir, [16] and I gave to the Reubenites and Gadites ⟨the area extending⟩ from Gilead to the Arnon Valley (the middle of the valley was the border) and up to the Jabbok River, the border of the Ammonites. [17] The •Arabah and Jordan are also borders from Chinnereth[d] as far as the Sea of the Arabah, the Dead Sea, under the slopes of Pisgah on the east.

Terms for These Three Tribes

[18] "I commanded you at that time: The LORD your God has given you this land to possess. All your fighting men will cross over in battle formation ahead of your brothers the Israelites. [19] But your wives, young children, and livestock—I know that you have a lot of livestock—will remain in the cities I have given you [20] until the LORD gives rest to your brothers as He has to you, and they also take possession of the land the LORD your God is giving them across the Jordan. Then each of you may return to his possession that I have given you.

Transfer of Israel's Leadership

Moses Affirms Joshua

[21] "I commanded Joshua at that time: Your own eyes have seen everything the LORD your God has done to these two kings. The LORD will do the same to all the kingdoms you are about to enter. [22] Don't be afraid of them, for the LORD your God fights for you.

Moses Begs God

[23] "At that time I begged the LORD: [24] Lord GOD, You have begun to show Your greatness and power to Your servant, for what god is there in heaven or on earth who can perform deeds and mighty acts like Yours? [25] Please let me cross over and see the beautiful land on the other side of the Jordan, that good hill country and Lebanon.

[26] "But the LORD was angry with me on account of you and would not listen to me. The LORD said to me, 'That's enough! Do not speak to Me again about

---

[a]**3:11** Or *His sarcophagus was made of basalt* [b]**3:11** Lit *Nine cubits its length and four cubits its width, by a man's cubit* [c]**3:14** Or *Havvoth-jair* [d]**3:17** The Sea of Galilee; Jos 12:3; 13:27; Lk 5:1

this matter. [27] Go to the top of Pisgah and look to the west, north, south, and east, and see ⌊it⌋ with your own eyes, for you will not cross this Jordan. [28] But commission Joshua and encourage and strengthen him, for he will cross over ahead of the people and enable them to inherit this land that you will see.' [29] So we stayed in the valley facing Beth-peor.

Moses Calls Israel to Obey

4 "Now, Israel, listen to the statutes and ordinances I am teaching you to follow, so that you may live, enter, and take possession of the land the LORD, the God of your fathers, is giving you. [2] You must not add anything to what I command you or take anything away from it, so that you may keep the commands of the LORD your God I am giving you. [3] Your eyes have seen what the LORD did at Baal-peor, for the LORD your God destroyed every one of you who followed •Baal of Peor. [4] But you who have remained faithful[a] to the LORD your God are all alive today. [5] Look, I have taught you statutes and ordinances as the LORD my God has commanded me, so that you may follow them in the land you are entering to possess. [6] Carefully follow ⌊them⌋, for this will ⌊show⌋ your wisdom and understanding in the eyes of the peoples. When they hear about all these statutes, they will say, 'This great nation is indeed a wise and understanding people.' [7] For what great nation is there that has a god near to it as the LORD our God is ⌊to us⌋ whenever we call to Him? [8] And what great nation has righteous statutes and ordinances like this entire law I set before you today?

Obey Ten Commandments!

[9] "Only be on your guard and diligently watch yourselves, so that you don't forget the things your eyes have seen and so that they don't slip from your mind as long as you live. Teach them to your children and your grandchildren. [10] The day you stood before the LORD your God at Horeb, the LORD said to me, 'Assemble the people before Me, and I will let them hear My words, so that they may learn to •fear Me all the days they live on the earth and may instruct their children.' [11] You came near and stood at the base of the mountain, a mountain blazing with fire into the heavens and enveloped in a dense, black cloud. [12] Then the LORD spoke to you from the fire. You kept hearing the sound of the words, but didn't see a form; there was only a voice. [13] He declared His covenant to you. He commanded you to follow the Ten Commandments, which He wrote on two stone tablets. [14] At that time the LORD commanded me to teach you statutes and ordinances for you to follow in the land you are about to cross into and possess.

Worship the True God—No Idols

[15] "Be extremely careful for your own good—because you did not see any form on the day the LORD spoke to you at Horeb out of the fire— [16] not to act corruptly and make an idol for yourselves in the shape of any figure: a male or female form, [17] or the form of any beast on the earth, any winged creature that flies in the sky, [18] any creature that crawls on the ground, or any fish in the waters under the earth. [19] When you look to the heavens and see the sun, moon, and stars—all the array of heaven—do not be led astray to bow down and worship them. The LORD your God has provided them for all people everywhere under

---

[a] 4:4 Lit have held on

heaven. ²⁰ But the LORD selected you and brought you out of Egypt's iron furnace to be a people for His inheritance, as you are today.

²¹ "The LORD was angry with me on your account. He swore that I would not cross the Jordan and enter the good land the LORD your God is giving you as an inheritance. ²² I won't be crossing the Jordan because I am going to die in this land. But you are about to cross over and take possession of this good land. ²³ Be careful not to forget the covenant of the LORD your God that He made with you, and make an idol for yourselves in the shape of anything He has forbidden you. ²⁴ For the LORD your God is a consuming fire, a jealous God.

Warning: Perish and Scatter from the Land

²⁵ "When you have children and grandchildren and have been in the land a long time, and if you act corruptly, make an idol in the form of anything, and do what is evil in the sight of the LORD your God, provoking Him to anger, ²⁶ I call heaven and earth as witnesses against you today that you will quickly perish from the land you are about to cross the Jordan to possess. You will not live long there, but you will certainly be destroyed. ²⁷ The LORD will scatter you among the peoples, and you will be reduced to a few survivorsᵃ among the nations where the LORD your God will drive you. ²⁸ There you will worship man-made gods of wood and stone, which cannot see, hear, eat, or smell. ²⁹ But from there, you will search for the LORD your God, and you will find ₍Him₎ when you seek Him with all your heart and all your soul. ³⁰ When you are in distress and all these things have happened

to you, you will return to the LORD your God in later days and obey Him. ³¹ He will not leave you, destroy you, or forget the covenant with your fathers that He swore to them by oath, because the LORD your God is a compassionate God.

Exodus Unique

³² "Indeed, ask about the earlier days that preceded you, from the day God created man on the earth and from one end of the heavens to the other: Has anything like this great event ₍ever₎ happened, or has anything like it been heard of? ³³ Has a people ever heard God's voice speaking from the fire as you have, and lived? ³⁴ Or has a god ₍ever₎ attempted to go and take a nation as his own out of ₍another₎ nation, by trials, signs, wonders, and war, by a strong hand and an outstretched arm, by great terrors, as the LORD your God did for you in Egypt before your eyes? ³⁵ You were shown ₍these things₎ so that you would know that the LORD is God; there is no other besides Him. ³⁶ He let you hear His voice from heaven to instruct you. He showed you His great fire on earth, and you heard His words from the fire. ³⁷ Because He loved your fathers, He chose their descendants after them and brought you out of Egypt by His presence and great power, ³⁸ to drive out before you nations greater and stronger than you and to bring you in and give you their land as an inheritance, as is now taking place. ³⁹ Today, recognize and keep in mind that the LORD is God in heaven above and on earth below; there is no other. ⁴⁰ Keep His statutes and commands, which I am giving you today, so that you and your children after you may prosper and so that you may live long in the land the LORD your God is giving you for all time."

ᵃ4:27 Lit be left few in number

Three Cities of Refuge

⁴¹ Then Moses set apart three cities across the Jordan to the east, ⁴² where one could flee who committed manslaughter and killed his neighbor accidentally without previously hating him. He could flee to one of these cities and stay alive: ⁴³ Bezer in the wilderness on the plateau land, belonging to the Reubenites; Ramoth in Gilead, belonging to the Gadites; or Golan in Bashan, belonging to the Manassites.

Introduction to Law

⁴⁴ This is the law Moses gave the Israelites. ⁴⁵ These are the decrees, statutes, and ordinances Moses proclaimed to them after they came out of Egypt, ⁴⁶ across the Jordan in the valley facing Beth-peor in the land of Sihon king of the Amorites. He lived in Heshbon, and Moses and the Israelites defeated him after they came out of Egypt. ⁴⁷ They took possession of his land and the land of Og king of Bashan, the two Amorite kings who were across the Jordan to the east, ⁴⁸ from Aroer on the rim of the Arnon Valley as far as Mount Sion (that is, Hermon) ⁴⁹ and all the •Arabah on the east side of the Jordan as far as the Dead Sea below the slopes of Pisgah.

Ten Commandments

5 Moses summoned all Israel and said to them, "Israel, listen to the statutes and ordinances I am proclaiming as you hear them today. Learn and follow them carefully. ² The LORD our God made a covenant with us at Horeb. ³ He did not make this covenant with our fathers, but with all of us who are alive here today. ⁴ The LORD spoke to you face to face from the fire on the mountain. ⁵ At that time I was standing between the LORD

and you to report the word[a] of the LORD to you, because you were afraid of the fire and did not go up the mountain. And He said:

⁶ I am the LORD your God, who brought you out of the land of Egypt, out of the place of slavery.

⁷ Do not have other gods besides Me.

⁸ Do not make an idol for yourself in the shape of anything in the heavens above or on the earth below or in the waters under the earth. ⁹ You must not bow down to them or worship them, because I, the LORD your God, am a jealous God, punishing the children for the fathers' sin to the third and fourth ˌgenerationsˌ of those who hate Me, ¹⁰ but showing faithful love to a thousand ˌgenerationsˌ of those who love Me and keep My commands.

¹¹ Do not misuse the name of the LORD your God, because the LORD will punish anyone who misuses His name.

¹² Be careful to dedicate the Sabbath day, as the LORD your God has commanded you. ¹³ You are to labor six days and do all your work, ¹⁴ but the seventh day is a Sabbath to the LORD your God. You must not do any work—you, your son or daughter, your male or female slave, your ox or donkey, any of your livestock, or the foreigner who lives within your gates, so that your male and female slaves may rest as you do. ¹⁵ Remember that you were a slave in the land of Egypt, and the LORD your God brought you out of there with a strong hand and an outstretched

arm. That is why the LORD your God has commanded you to keep the Sabbath day.

16 Honor your father and your mother, as the LORD your God has commanded you, so that you may live long and so that you may prosper in the land the LORD your God is giving you.

17 Do not murder.

18 Do not commit adultery.

19 Do not steal.

20 Do not give dishonest testimony against your neighbor.

21 Do not desire your neighbor's wife or covet your neighbor's house, his field, his male or female slave, his ox or donkey, or anything that belongs to your neighbor.

People's Response

22 "The LORD spoke these commands in a loud voice to your entire assembly from the fire, cloud, and thick darkness on the mountain; He added nothing more. He wrote them on two stone tablets and gave them to me. 23 All of you approached me with your tribal leaders and elders when you heard the voice from the darkness and while the mountain was blazing with fire. 24 You said, 'Look, the LORD our God has shown us His glory and greatness, and we have heard His voice from the fire. Today we have seen that God speaks with a person, yet he still lives. 25 But now, why should we die? This great fire will consume us and we will die if we hear the voice of the LORD our God any longer. 26 For who out of all mankind has heard the voice of the living God speaking from the fire, as we have, and lived? 27 Go near and listen to everything the LORD our God says.

Then you can tell us everything the LORD our God tells you; we will listen and obey.'

28 "The LORD heard your[a] words when you spoke to me. He said to me, 'I have heard the words that these people have spoken to you. Everything they have said is right. 29 If only they had such a heart to •fear Me and keep all My commands, so that they and their children will prosper forever. 30 Go and tell them: Return to your tents. 31 But you stand here with Me, and I will tell you every command— the statutes and ordinances—you are to teach them, so that they may follow them in the land I am giving them to possess.'

32 "Be careful to do as the LORD your God has commanded you; you are not to turn aside to the right or the left. 33 Follow the whole instruction the LORD your God has commanded you, so that you may live, prosper, and have a long life in the land you will possess.

Greatest Commandment

6 "This is the command—the statutes and ordinances—the LORD your God has instructed me to teach you, so that you may follow them in the land you are about to enter and possess. 2 Do this so that you may •fear the LORD your God all the days of your life by keeping all His statutes and commands I am giving you, your son, and your grandson, and so that you may have a long life. 3 Listen, Israel, and be careful to follow them, so that you may prosper and multiply greatly, because the LORD, the God of your fathers, has promised you a land flowing with milk and honey.

4 "Listen, Israel: The LORD our God, the LORD is One.[b] 5 Love the LORD your God with all your heart, with all your

---

a5:28 Lit the sound of your   b6:4 Or Yahweh is our God; Yahweh is One, or The LORD is our God, the LORD alone, or The LORD our God is one LORD

soul, and with all your strength. ⁶ These words that I am giving you today are to be in your heart. ⁷ Repeat them to your children. Talk about them when you sit in your house and when you walk along the road, when you lie down and when you get up. ⁸ Bind them as a sign on your hand and let them be a symbol[a] on your forehead.[b] ⁹ Write them on the doorposts of your house and on your gates.

Don't Forget God!

¹⁰ "When the LORD your God brings you into the land He swore to your fathers Abraham, Isaac, and Jacob that He would give you—a ⌊land with⌋ large and beautiful cities that you did not build, ¹¹ houses full of every good thing that you did not fill ⌊them with⌋, wells dug that you did not dig, and vineyards and olive groves that you did not plant—and when you eat and are satisfied, ¹² be careful not to forget the LORD who brought you out of the land of Egypt, out of the place of slavery. ¹³ Fear the LORD your God, worship Him, and take ⌊your⌋ oaths in His name. ¹⁴ Do not follow other gods, the gods of the peoples around you, ¹⁵ for the LORD your God, who is among you, is a jealous God. Otherwise, the LORD your God will become angry with you and wipe you off the face of the earth. ¹⁶ Do not test the LORD your God as you tested ⌊Him⌋ at Massah. ¹⁷ Carefully observe the commands of the LORD your God, the decrees and statutes He has commanded you. ¹⁸ Do what is right and good in the LORD's sight, so that you may prosper and so that you may enter and possess the good land the LORD your God swore to ⌊give⌋ your fathers, ¹⁹ by driving out all your enemies before you, as the LORD has said.

Follow Every Commandment

²⁰ "When your son asks you in the future, 'What is the meaning of the decrees, statutes, and ordinances, which the LORD our God has commanded you?' ²¹ tell him, 'We were slaves of Pharaoh in Egypt, but the LORD brought us out of Egypt with a strong hand. ²² Before our eyes the LORD inflicted great and devastating signs and wonders on Egypt, on Pharaoh and all his household, ²³ but He brought us from there in order to lead us in and give us the land that He swore to our fathers. ²⁴ The LORD commanded us to follow all these statutes and to fear the LORD our God for our prosperity always and for our preservation, as it is today. ²⁵ Righteousness will be ours if we are careful to follow every one of these commands before the LORD our God, as He has commanded us.'

Moses on Conquering Foreign Nations

7 "When the LORD your God brings you into the land you are entering to possess, and He drives out many nations before you—the Hittites, Girgashites, Amorites, Canaanites, Perizzites, Hivites and Jebusites, seven nations more numerous and powerful than you— ² and when the LORD your God delivers them over to you and you defeat them, you must •completely destroy them. Make no treaty with them and show them no mercy. ³ Do not intermarry with them. Do not give your daughters to their sons or take their daughters for your sons, ⁴ because they will turn your sons away from Me to worship other gods. Then the LORD's anger will burn against you, and He will swiftly destroy you. ⁵ Instead, this is what you are to do to them: tear down their altars, smash their

---

[a] 6:8 Or phylactery; Mt 23:5 [b] 6:8 Lit symbol between your eyes

standing pillars, cut down their •Asherah poles, and burn up their carved images. ⁶ For you are a holy people belonging to the LORD your God. The LORD your God has chosen you to be His own possession out of all the peoples on the face of the earth.

Israel: a Chosen People

⁷ "The LORD was devoted to you and chose you, not because you were more numerous than all peoples, for you were the fewest of all peoples. ⁸ But because the LORD loved you and kept the oath He swore to your fathers, He brought you out with a strong hand and redeemed you from the place of slavery, from the power of Pharaoh king of Egypt. ⁹ Know that •Yahweh your God is God, the faithful God who keeps His gracious covenant loyalty for a thousand generations with those who love Him and keep His commands. ¹⁰ But He directly pays back[a] and destroys those who hate Him. He will not hesitate to directly pay back[b] the one who hates Him. ¹¹ So keep the command—the statutes and ordinances—that I am giving you to follow today.

Obedience Means Blessing

¹² "If you listen to and are careful to keep these ordinances, the LORD your God will keep His covenant loyalty with you, as He swore to your fathers. ¹³ He will love you, bless you, and multiply you. He will bless your descendants,[c] and the produce of your soil—your grain, new wine, and oil—the young of your herds, and the newborn of your flocks, in the land He swore to your fathers that He would give you. ¹⁴ You will be blessed above all peoples; there will be no infertile male or female among you

or your livestock. ¹⁵ The LORD will remove all sickness from you; He will not put on you all the terrible diseases of Egypt that you know about, but He will inflict them on all who hate you. ¹⁶ You must destroy all the peoples the LORD your God is delivering over to you and not look on them with pity. Do not worship their gods, for that will be a snare to you.

Don't Fear Foreign Nations

¹⁷ "If you say to yourself, 'These nations are greater than I; how can I drive them out?' ¹⁸ do not be afraid of them. Be sure to remember what the LORD your God did to Pharaoh and all Egypt: ¹⁹ the great trials that you saw, the signs and wonders, the strong hand and outstretched arm, by which the LORD your God brought you out. The LORD your God will do the same to all the peoples you fear. ²⁰ The LORD your God will also send the hornet against them until all the survivors and those hiding from you perish. ²¹ Don't be terrified of them, for the LORD your God, a great and awesome God, is among you. ²² The LORD your God will drive out these nations before you little by little. You will not be able to destroy them all at once; otherwise, the wild animals will become too numerous for you. ²³ The LORD your God will give them over to you and throw them into great confusion until they are destroyed. ²⁴ He will hand their kings over to you, and you will wipe out their names under heaven. No one will be able to stand against you; you will annihilate them. ²⁵ You must burn up the carved images of their gods. Don't covet the silver and gold on the images and take it for yourself, or else you will be ensnared by it, for it is

---

[a]7:10 Lit *He pays back to their faces*   [b]7:10 Lit *to pay back to their faces*   [c]7:13 Lit *bless the fruit of your womb*

abhorrent to the LORD your God. 26 You must not bring any abhorrent thing into your house, or you will be •set apart for destruction like it. You are to utterly detest and abhor it, because it is set apart for destruction.

Always Remember God

8 "You must carefully follow every command I am giving you today, so that you may live and increase, and may enter and take possession of the land the LORD swore to your fathers. 2 Remember that the LORD your God led you on the entire journey these 40 years in the wilderness, so that He might humble you and test you to know what was in your heart, whether or not you would keep His commands. 3 He humbled you by letting you go hungry; then He gave you manna to eat, which you and your fathers had not known, so that you might learn that man does not live on bread alone but on every word that comes from the mouth of the LORD. 4 Your clothing did not wear out, and your feet did not swell these 40 years. 5 Keep in mind that the LORD your God has been disciplining you just as a man disciplines his son. 6 So keep the commands of the LORD your God by walking in His ways and •fearing Him. 7 For the LORD your God is bringing you into a good land, a land with streams of water, springs, and deep water sources, flowing in both valleys and hills; 8 a land of wheat, barley, vines, figs, and pomegranates; a land of olive oil and honey; 9 a land where you will eat food without shortage, where you will lack nothing; a land whose rocks are iron and from whose hills you will mine copper. 10 When you eat and are full, you will praise the LORD your God for the good land He has given you.

Don't Forget in Prosperity

11 "Be careful that you don't forget the LORD your God by failing to keep His command—the ordinances and statutes—I am giving you today. 12 When you eat and are full, and build beautiful houses to live in, 13 and your herds and flocks grow large, and your silver and gold multiply, and everything else you have increases, 14 ⌊be careful⌋ that your heart doesn't become proud and you forget the LORD your God who brought you out of the land of Egypt, out of the place of slavery. 15 He led you through the great and terrible wilderness with its poisonous snakes and scorpions, a thirsty land where there was no water. He brought water out of the flintlike rock for you. 16 He fed you in the wilderness with manna that your fathers had not known, in order to humble and test you, so that in the end He might cause you to prosper. 17 You may say to yourself, 'My power and my own ability have gained this wealth for me,' 18 but remember that the LORD your God gives you the power to gain wealth, in order to confirm His covenant He swore to your fathers, as it is today. 19 If you ever forget the LORD your God and go after other gods to worship and bow down to them, I testify against you today that you will perish. 20 Like the nations the LORD is about to destroy before you, you will perish if you do not obey the LORD your God.

Moses' Warnings to Israel

You're a Stiff-Necked People!

9 "Listen, Israel: Today you are about to cross the Jordan to go and drive out nations greater and stronger than you ⌊with⌋ large cities fortified to the heavens. 2 The people are strong and tall, the descendants of the Anakim. You know about them and you have heard it said about them, 'Who can stand up to the sons of Anak?' ³ But understand that today the LORD your God will cross over ahead of you as a consuming fire; He will devastate and subdue them before you. You will drive them out and destroy them swiftly, as the LORD has told you. ⁴ When the LORD your God drives them out before you, do not say to yourself, 'The LORD brought me in to take possession of this land because of my righteousness.' Instead, the LORD will drive out these nations before you because of their wickedness. ⁵ You are not going to take possession of their land because of your righteousness or your integrity. Instead, the LORD your God will drive out these nations before you because of their wickedness, in order to keep the promise He swore to your fathers, Abraham, Isaac, and Jacob. ⁶ Understand that the LORD your God is not giving you this good land to possess because of your righteousness, for you are a stiff-necked people.

Remember Your Rebellion!

⁷ "Remember and do not forget how you provoked the LORD your God in the wilderness. You have been rebelling against the LORD from the day you left the land of Egypt until you reached this place. ⁸ You provoked the LORD at Horeb, and He was angry enough with you to destroy you. ⁹ When I went up the mountain to receive the stone tablets, the tablets of the covenant the LORD made with you, I stayed on the mountain 40 days and 40 nights. I did not eat bread or drink water. ¹⁰ On the day of the assembly the LORD gave me the two stone tablets, inscribed by God's finger. The exact words were on them, which

the LORD spoke to you from the fire on the mountain. ¹¹ The LORD gave me the two stone tablets, the tablets of the covenant, at the end of the 40 days and 40 nights.

Remember Moses' Anger!

¹² "The LORD said to me, 'Get up and go down immediately from here. For your people you brought out of Egypt have acted corruptly. They have quickly turned from the way that I commanded them; they have made a cast image for themselves.' ¹³ The LORD also said to me, 'I have seen this people, and indeed, they are a stiff-necked people. ¹⁴ Leave Me alone, and I will destroy them and blot out their name under heaven. Then I will make you into a nation stronger and more numerous than they.'

¹⁵ "So I went back down the mountain, while it was blazing with fire, and the two tablets of the covenant were in my hands. ¹⁶ I saw how you had sinned against the LORD your God; you had made a calf image for yourselves. You had quickly turned from the way the LORD had commanded for you. ¹⁷ So I took hold of the tablets and threw them from my hands, shattering them before your eyes. ¹⁸ Then I fell down like the first time in the presence of the LORD for 40 days and 40 nights; I did not eat bread or drink water because of all the sin you committed, doing what was evil in the LORD's sight and provoking Him to anger. ¹⁹ I was afraid of the fierce anger the LORD had directed against you, because He was about to destroy you. But again, the LORD listened to me on that occasion. ²⁰ The LORD was angry enough with Aaron to destroy him. But I prayed for Aaron at that time also. ²¹ I took the sinful calf you had made, burned it up, and crushed it, thoroughly grinding it to powder as fine as

dust. Then I threw it into the stream that came down from the mountain.

You Kept Provoking!

22 "You continued to provoke the LORD at Taberah, Massah, and Kibroth-hattaavah. 23 When the LORD sent you from Kadesh-barnea, He said, 'Go up and possess the land I have given you'; you rebelled against the command of the LORD your God. You did not believe or obey Him. 24 You have been rebelling against the LORD ever since I have[a] known you.

Moses Interceded in Prayer

25 "I fell down in the presence of the LORD 40 days and 40 nights because the LORD had threatened to destroy you. 26 I prayed to the LORD:

Lord GOD, do not annihilate Your people, Your inheritance, whom You redeemed through Your greatness and brought out of Egypt with a strong hand. 27 Remember Your servants Abraham, Isaac, and Jacob. Disregard this people's stubbornness, and their wickedness and sin. 28 Otherwise, those in the land you brought us from will say, 'Because the LORD wasn't able to bring them into the land He had promised them, and because He hated them, He brought them out to kill them in the wilderness.' 29 But they are Your people, Your inheritance, whom You brought out by Your great power and outstretched arm.

God Renews Covenant: New Tablets

10 "The LORD said to me at that time, 'Cut two stone tablets like the first ones and come to Me on the mountain and make a wooden ark. 2 I will write on the tablets the words that were on the first tablets you broke, and you are to place them in the ark.' 3 So I made an ark of acacia wood, cut two stone tablets like the first ones, and climbed the mountain with the two tablets in my hand. 4 Then, on the day of the assembly, the LORD wrote on the tablets what had been written previously, the Ten Commandments that He had spoken to you on the mountain from the fire. The LORD gave them to me, 5 and I went back down the mountain and placed the tablets in the ark I had made. And they have remained there, as the LORD commanded me."

Israel on the Road Again

6 The Israelites traveled from Beeroth Bene-jaakan[b] to Moserah. Aaron died and was buried there, and Eleazar his son became priest in his place. 7 They traveled from there to Gudgodah, and from Gudgodah to Jotbathah, a land with streams of water.

8 "At that time the LORD set apart the tribe of Levi to carry the ark of the LORD's covenant, to stand before the LORD to serve Him, and to bless in His name, as it is today. 9 For this reason, Levi does not have a portion or inheritance like his brothers; the LORD is his inheritance, as the LORD your God told him.

10 "I stayed on the mountain 40 days and 40 nights like the first time. The LORD also listened to me on this occasion; He agreed not to annihilate you. 11 Then the LORD said to me, 'Get up. Continue your journey ahead of the people, so that they may enter and possess the land I swore to give their fathers.'

[a] **9:24** Sam, LXX read *since He has*   [b] **10:6** Or *from the wells of Bene-jaakan*, or *from the wells of the Jaakanites*

God Requires Fear, Love, Worship

12 "And now, Israel, what does the LORD your God ask of you except to •fear the LORD your God by walking in all His ways, to love Him, and to worship the LORD your God with all your heart and all your soul? 13 Keep the LORD's commands and statutes I am giving you today, for your own good. 14 The heavens, indeed the highest heavens, belong to the LORD your God, as does the earth and everything in it. 15 Yet the LORD was devoted to your fathers and loved them. He chose their descendants after them— ⌊He chose⌋ you out of all the peoples, as it is today. 16 Therefore, circumcise your hearts and don't be stiff-necked any longer. 17 For the LORD your God is the God of gods and Lord of lords, the great, mighty, and awesome God, showing no partiality and taking no bribe. 18 He executes justice for the fatherless and the widow, and loves the foreign resident, giving him food and clothing. 19 You also must love the foreigner, since you were foreigners in the land of Egypt. 20 You are to fear the LORD your God and worship Him. Remain faithful[a] to Him and take oaths in His name. 21 He is your praise and He is your God, who has done for you these great and awesome works your eyes have seen. 22 Your fathers went down to Egypt, 70 people in all, and now the LORD your God has made you as numerous as the stars of the sky.

Love and Obey

11 "Therefore, love the LORD your God and always keep His mandate and His statutes, ordinances, and commands. 2 You must understand today that it is not your children who experienced or saw the discipline of the LORD your God:

His greatness, strong hand, and outstretched arm; 3 His signs and the works He did in Egypt to Pharaoh king of Egypt and all his land; 4 what He did to Egypt's army, its horses and chariots, when He made the waters of the •Red Sea flow over them as they pursued you, and He destroyed them completely;[b] 5 what He did to you in the wilderness until you reached this place; 6 and what He did to Dathan and Abiram, the sons of Eliab the Reubenite, when in the middle of the whole Israelite ⌊camp⌋ the earth opened its mouth and swallowed them, their households, their tents, and every living thing with them.

7 Your ⌊own⌋ eyes have seen every great work the LORD has done.

Keep Every Command

8 "Keep every command I am giving you today, so that you may have the strength to cross into and possess the land you are to inherit, 9 and so that you may live long in the land the LORD swore to your fathers to give them and their descendants, a land flowing with milk and honey. 10 For the land you are entering to possess is not like the land of Egypt, from which you have come, where you sowed your seed and irrigated by hand[c] as in a vegetable garden. 11 But the land you are entering to possess is a land of mountains and valleys, watered by rain from the sky. 12 It is a land the LORD your God cares for. He is always watching over it from the beginning to the end of the year.

If You Obey...

13 "If you carefully obey My commands I am giving you today, to love the LORD

---

a 10:20 Lit Hold on   b 11:4 Lit to this day   c 11:10 Lit foot your God and worship Him with all your heart and all your soul, [14] I[a] will provide rain for your land in season, the early and late rains, and you will harvest your grain, new wine, and oil. [15] I[a] will provide grass in your fields for your livestock. You will eat and be satisfied. [16] Be careful that you are not enticed to turn aside, worship, and bow down to other gods. [17] Then the LORD's anger will burn against you. He will close the sky, and there will be no rain; the land will not yield its produce, and you will perish quickly from the good land the LORD is giving you.

Absorb and Teach God's Words

[18] "Impress these words of Mine on your hearts and souls, bind them as a sign on your hands, and let them be a symbol[b] on your foreheads.[c] [19] Teach them to your children, talking about them when you sit in your house and when you walk along the road, when you lie down and when you get up. [20] Write them on the doorposts of your house and on your gates, [21] so that as long as the heavens are above the earth, your days and those of your children may be many in the land the LORD swore to give your fathers. [22] For if you carefully observe every one of these commands I am giving you to follow—to love the LORD your God, walk in all His ways, and remain faithful[d] to Him— [23] the LORD will drive out all these nations before you, and you will drive out nations greater and stronger than you are. [24] Every place the sole of your foot treads will be yours. Your territory will extend from the wilderness to Lebanon and from the Euphrates River[e] to the Mediterranean Sea. [25] No one will be able to stand against you; the LORD your God will put fear and dread of you in all the land where you set foot, as He has promised you.

A Blessing and a Curse

[26] "Look, today I set before you a blessing and a curse: [27] ⌊there will be⌋ a blessing, if you obey the commands of the LORD your God I am giving you today, [28] and a curse, if you do not obey the commands of the LORD your God, and you turn aside from the path I command you today by following other gods you have not known. [29] When the LORD your God brings you into the land you are entering to possess, you are to proclaim the blessing at Mount Gerizim and the curse at Mount Ebal. [30] Aren't these mountains across the Jordan, beyond the western road in the land of the Canaanites, who live in the •Arabah, opposite Gilgal, near the oaks[f] of Moreh? [31] For you are about to cross the Jordan to enter and take possession of the land the LORD your God is giving you. When you possess it and settle in it, [32] be careful to follow all the statutes and ordinances I set before you today.

God's Chosen Place of Worship
Reject Idol Sites

12 "Be careful to follow these statutes and ordinances in the land that the LORD, the God of your fathers, has given you to possess all the days you live on the earth. [2] Destroy completely all the places where the nations you are driving out worship their gods—on the high mountains, on the hills, and under every flourishing tree. [3] Tear down their altars, smash their sacred pillars, burn up their •Asherah poles, cut down the carved im-

---

[a]11:14,15 DSS, Sam, LXX read He [b]11:18 Or phylactery; Mt 23:5 [c]11:18 Lit symbol between your eyes; Dt 6:8; Ex 13:16 [d]11:22 Lit and hold on [e]11:24 Some Hb mss, LXX, Tg, Vg read the great river, the river Euphrates [f]11:30 Sam, LXX, Syr, Aq, Sym read oak; Gn 12:6

ages of their gods, and wipe out their names from every[a] place. [4] Don't worship the LORD your God this way. [5] Instead, you must go to the place the LORD your God chooses from all your tribes to put His name for His dwelling. [6] You are to bring there your •burnt offerings and sacrifices, your tenths and personal contributions,[b] your vow offerings and freewill offerings, and the firstborn of your herds and flocks. [7] You will eat there in the presence of the LORD your God and rejoice with your household in everything you do,[c] because the LORD your God has blessed you.

One Place to Sacrifice

[8] "You are not to do as we are doing here today; everyone ⌊is doing⌋ whatever seems right in his own eyes. [9] Indeed, you have not yet come into the resting place and the inheritance the LORD your God is giving you. [10] When you cross the Jordan and live in the land the LORD your God is giving you to inherit, and He gives you rest from all the enemies around you and you live in security, [11] then the LORD your God will choose the place to have His name dwell. Bring there everything I command you: your burnt offerings, sacrifices, offerings of the tenth, personal contributions,[d] and all your choice offerings you vow to the LORD. [12] You will rejoice before the LORD your God—you, your sons and daughters, your male and female slaves, and the Levite who is within your gates, since he has no portion or inheritance among you. [13] Be careful not to offer your burnt offerings in all the ⌊sacred⌋ places you see. [14] You must offer your burnt offerings only in the place the LORD chooses in one of your tribes, and there

you must do everything I command you.

Rules on Slaughtering Animals to Eat

[15] "But whenever you want, you may slaughter and eat meat within any of your gates, according to the blessing the LORD your God has given you. Those who are clean or unclean may eat it, as they would a gazelle or deer, [16] but you must not eat the blood; pour it on the ground like water. [17] Within your gates you may not eat: the tenth of your grain, new wine, or oil; the firstborn of your herd or flock; any of your vow offerings that you pledge; your freewill offerings; or your personal contributions.[e] [18] You must eat them in the presence of the LORD your God at the place the LORD your God chooses—you, your son and daughter, your male and female slave, and the Levite who is within your gates. Rejoice before the LORD your God in everything you do,[c] [19] and be careful not to neglect the Levite, as long as you live in your land.

[20] "When the LORD your God enlarges your territory as He has promised you, and you say, 'I want to eat meat' because you have a strong desire to eat meat, you may eat it whenever you want. [21] If the place where the LORD your God chooses to put His name is too far from you, you may slaughter any of your herd or flock He has given you, as I have commanded you, and you may eat it within your gates whenever you want. [22] Indeed, you may eat it as the gazelle and deer are eaten; both the clean and the unclean may eat it. [23] But don't eat the blood, since the blood is the life, and you must not eat the life with the meat. [24] Do not eat blood; pour it on the ground like

---

[a] **12:3** Lit *that*   [b] **12:6** Lit *and the contributions from your hands*   [c] **12:7,18** Lit *you put your hand to*   [d] **12:11** Lit *tenth, the contributions from your hands*   [e] **12:17** Lit *or the contributions from your hands*

water. ²⁵ Do not eat it, so that you and your children after you will prosper, because you will be doing what is right in the LORD's sight.

God's Way of Worship

Make Offerings Only at His Chosen Place

²⁶ "But you are to take the holy offerings you have and your vow offerings and go to the place the LORD chooses. ²⁷ Present the meat and blood of your burnt offerings on the altar of the LORD your God. The blood of your ⌊other⌋ sacrifices is to be poured out beside the altar of the LORD your God, but you may eat the meat. ²⁸ Be careful to obey all these things I command you, so that you and your children after you may prosper forever, because you will be doing what is good and right in the sight of the LORD your God.

Avoid Worship Habits of Pagans

²⁹ "When the LORD your God annihilates the nations before you, which you are entering to take possession of, and you drive them out and live in their land, ³⁰ be careful not to be ensnared by their ways after they have been destroyed before you. Do not inquire about their gods, asking, 'How did these nations worship their gods? I'll also do the same.' ³¹ You must not do the same to the LORD your God, because they practice for their gods every detestable thing the LORD hates. They even burn their sons and daughters in the fire to their gods. ^{32a} You must be careful to do everything I command you; do not add anything to it or take anything away from it.

Warnings on False Prophets

13 "If a prophet or someone who has dreams arises among you and pro-

claims a sign or wonder to you, ² and that sign or wonder he has promised you comes about, but he says, 'Let us follow other gods,' which you have not known, 'and let us worship them,' ³ do not listen to that prophet's words or to that dreamer. For the LORD your God is testing you to know whether you love the LORD your God with all your heart and all your soul. ⁴ You must follow the LORD your God and •fear Him. You must keep His commands and listen to His voice; you must worship Him and remain faithful^b to Him. ⁵ That prophet or dreamer must be put to death, because he has urged rebellion against the LORD your God who brought you out of the land of Egypt and redeemed you from the place of slavery, to turn you from the way the LORD your God has commanded you to walk. <u>You must purge the evil from you.</u>

Beware of Idolatry in Family

⁶ "If your brother, the son of your mother,^c or your son or daughter, or the wife you embrace, or your closest friend secretly entices you, saying, 'Let us go and worship other gods'—which neither you nor your fathers have known, ⁷ any of the gods of the peoples around you, near you or far from you, from one end of the earth to the other— ⁸ you must not yield to him or listen to him. Show him no pity,^d and do not spare ⌊him⌋ or shield him. ⁹ Instead, you must kill him. Your hand is to be the first against him to put him to death, and then the hands of all the people. ¹⁰ Stone him to death for trying to turn you away from the LORD your God who brought you out of the land of Egypt, out of the place of slavery. ¹¹ All Israel will hear and be afraid, and they will no longer do anything evil like this among you.

---

^a**12:32** Dt 13:1 in Hb   ^b**13:4** Lit *and hold on*   ^c**13:6** DSS, Sam, LXX read *If the son of your father or the son of your mother*   ^d**13:8** Lit *Your eye must not pity him*

When a City Yields to Idols

12 "If you hear it said about one of your cities the LORD your God is giving you to live in, 13 that •wicked men have sprung up among you, led the inhabitants of their city astray, and said, 'Let us go and worship other gods,' which you have not known, 14 you are to inquire, investigate, and interrogate thoroughly. If the report turns out to be true that this detestable thing has happened among you, 15 you must strike down the inhabitants of that city with the sword. •Completely destroy everyone in it as well as its livestock with the sword. 16 You are to gather all its spoil in the middle of the city square and completely burn up the city and all its spoil for the LORD your God. The city must remain a mound of ruins forever; it is not to be rebuilt. 17 Nothing •set apart for destruction is to remain in your hand, so that the LORD will turn from His burning anger and grant you mercy, show you compassion, and multiply you as He swore to your fathers. 18 This ⌊will occur⌋ if you obey the LORD your God, keeping all His commands I am giving you today, doing what is right in the sight of the LORD your God.

Forbidden Practices

14 "You are sons of the LORD your God; do not cut yourselves or make a bald spot on your head[a] on behalf of the dead, 2 for you are a holy people belonging to the LORD your God. The LORD has chosen you to be His special people out of all the peoples on the face of the earth.

Clean and Unclean Foods

3 "You must not eat any detestable thing. 4 These are the animals you may eat:

the ox, the sheep, the goat,
5 the deer, the gazelle, the roe deer,
the wild goat, the ibex,
the antelope,
and the mountain sheep.

6 You may eat any animal that has hooves divided in two and chews the cud. 7 But among the ones that chew the cud or have divided hooves, you are not to eat these:

the camel, the hare, and the hyrax,
though they chew the cud,
they do not have hooves—
they are unclean for you;
8 and the pig, though it has hooves,
it does not ⌊chew⌋ the cud—
it is unclean for you.

You must not eat their meat or touch their carcasses.

9 "You may eat everything from the water that has fins and scales, 10 but you may not eat anything that does not have fins and scales—it is unclean for you.

11 "You may eat every clean bird, 12 but these are the ones you may not eat:

the eagle, the bearded vulture,
the black vulture, 13 the kite,
the various kinds of falcon,[b]
14 every kind of raven, 15 the ostrich,
the short-eared owl, the gull,
the various kinds of hawk,
16 the little owl, the long-eared owl,
the white owl, 17 the desert owl,
the osprey, the cormorant,
18 the stork,
the various kinds of heron,
the hoopoe, and the bat.[c] 19 All
winged insects are unclean for
you; they may not be eaten. 20 But
you may eat every clean flying
creature.

a14:1 Or forehead b14:13 Some Hb mss, Sam, LXX; other Hb mss, Vg read the falcon, the various kinds of kite
c14:5-18 The identification of some of these birds or animals is uncertain.

21 "You are not to eat any carcass; you may give it to a resident alien within your gates, and he may eat it, or you may sell it to a foreigner. For you are a holy people belonging to the LORD your God. You must not boil a young goat in its mother's milk.

Devote Tenth to LORD

22 "Each year you are to set aside a tenth of all the produce grown in your fields. 23 You are to eat a tenth of your grain, new wine, and oil, and the first-born of your herd and flock, in the presence of the LORD your God at the place where He chooses to have His name dwell, so that you will always learn to •fear the LORD your God. 24 But if the distance is too great for you to carry it, since the place where the LORD your God chooses to put His name is too far away from you and since the LORD your God has blessed you, 25 then exchange it for money, take the money in your hand, and go to the place the LORD your God chooses. 26 You may spend the money on anything you want: cattle, sheep, wine, beer, or anything you desire. You are to feast there in the presence of the LORD your God and rejoice with your family. 27 Do not forget the Levite within your gates, since he has no portion or inheritance among you.

Tithe Provision for Levites

28 "At the end of ₍every₎ three years, bring a tenth of all your produce for that year and store ₍it₎ within your gates. 29 Then the Levite, who has no portion or inheritance among you, the foreign resident, fatherless, and widow within your gates may come, eat, and be satisfied. And the LORD your God will bless you in all the work of your hands that you do.

Seventh Year Rule: Cancel Debts

15 "At the end of ₍every₎ seven years you must cancel debts. 2 This is how to cancel debt: Every creditor[a] is to cancel what he has lent his neighbor. He is not to collect ₍anything₎ from his neighbor or brother, because the LORD's release of debts has been proclaimed. 3 You may collect ₍something₎ from a foreigner, but you must forgive whatever your brother owes you.

4 "There will be no poor among you, however, because the LORD is certain to bless you in the land the LORD your God is giving you to possess as an inheritance— 5 if only you obey the LORD your God and are careful to follow every one of these commands I am giving you today. 6 When the LORD your God blesses you as He has promised you, you will lend to many nations but not borrow; you will rule over many nations, but they will not rule over you.

Lend to Poor

7 "If there is a poor person among you, one of your brothers within any of your gates in the land the LORD your God is giving you, you must not be hardhearted or tightfisted toward your poor brother. 8 Instead, you are to open your hand to him and freely loan him enough for whatever need he has. 9 Be careful that there isn't this wicked thought in your heart, 'The seventh year, the year of canceling debts, is near,' and you are stingy toward your poor brother and give him ₍nothing₎. He will cry out to the LORD against you, and you will be guilty. 10 Give to him, and don't have a stingy heart[b] when you give, and because of this the LORD your God will bless you in all your work and in everything you do.[c] 11 For there will never cease to be poor

---

a15:2 Lit owner of a loan of his hand   b15:10 Lit and let not your heart be grudging   c15:10 Lit you put your hand to

people in the land; that is why I am commanding you, 'You must willingly open your hand to your afflicted and poor brother in your land.'

Seventh Year: Release Slaves

12 "If your fellow Hebrew, a man or woman, is sold to you and serves you six years, you must set him free in the seventh year. 13 When you set him free, do not send him away empty-handed. 14 Give generously to him from your flock, your threshing floor, and your winepress. You are to give him whatever the LORD your God has blessed you with. 15 Remember that you were a slave in the land of Egypt and the LORD your God redeemed you; that is why I am giving you this command today. 16 But if your slave says to you, 'I don't want to leave you,' because he loves you and your family, and is well off with you, 17 take an awl and pierce through his ear into the door, and he will become your slave for life. Also treat your female slave the same way. 18 Do not regard it as a hardship[a] when you set him free, because he worked for you six years—worth twice the wages of a hired hand. Then the LORD your God will bless you in everything you do.

Consecrate Firstborn Animals

19 "You must consecrate to the LORD your God every firstborn male produced by your herd and flock. You are not to put the firstborn of your oxen to work or shear the firstborn of your flock. 20 Each year you and your family are to eat it before the LORD your God in the place the LORD chooses. 21 But if there is a defect in the animal, if it is lame or blind or has any serious defect, you must not sacrifice it to the LORD your God. 22 Eat it within your gates; both the unclean person and the

clean ᴊmay eat itᴊ, as though it were a gazelle or deer. 23 But you must not eat its blood; pour it on the ground like water.

Law of Festivals

Passover

16 "Observe the month of Abib[b] and celebrate the •Passover to the LORD your God, because the LORD your God brought you out of Egypt by night in the month of Abib. 2 Sacrifice to the LORD your God a Passover animal from the herd or flock in the place where the LORD chooses to have His name dwell. 3 You must not eat leavened bread with it. For seven days you are to eat unleavened bread with it, the bread of hardship—because you left the land of Egypt in a hurry—so that you may remember for the rest of your life the day you left the land of Egypt. 4 No yeast is to be found anywhere in your territory for seven days, and none of the meat you sacrifice in the evening of the first day is to remain until morning. 5 You are not to sacrifice the Passover animal in any of the towns the LORD your God is giving you. 6 You must only sacrifice the Passover animal at the place where the LORD your God chooses to have His name dwell. ᴊDo thisᴊ in the evening as the sun sets at the ᴊsameᴊ time ᴊof dayᴊ you departed from Egypt. 7 You are to cook and eat ᴊitᴊ in the place the LORD your God chooses, and you are to return to your tents in the morning. 8 You must eat unleavened bread for six days. On the seventh day there is to be a solemn assembly to the LORD your God, and you must not do any work.

Festival of Weeks

9 "You are to count seven weeks, counting the weeks from the time the

---

a **15:18** Lit *Let it not be hard in your sight*   b **16:1** March–April; called Nisan in the post-exilic period; Neh 2:1; Est 3:7

sickle is first ⌊put⌋ to the standing grain. [10] You are to celebrate the Festival of Weeks to the LORD your God with a free-will offering that you give in proportion to how the LORD your God has blessed you. [11] Rejoice before the LORD your God in the place where He chooses to have His name dwell—you, your son and daughter, your male and female slave, the Levite within your gates, as well as the foreign resident, the fatherless, and the widow among you. [12] Remember that you were slaves in Egypt; carefully follow these statutes.

Festival of Booths

[13] "You are to celebrate the Festival of Booths for seven days when you have gathered in ⌊everything⌋ from your threshing floor and winepress. [14] Rejoice during your festival—you, your son and daughter, your male and female slave, as well as the Levite, the foreign resident, the fatherless, and the widow within your gates. [15] You are to hold a seven-day festival for the LORD your God in the place He chooses, because the LORD your God will bless you in all your produce and in all the work of your hands, and you will have abundant joy.

Requirement for All Males

[16] "All your males are to appear three times a year before the LORD your God in the place He chooses: at the Festival of •Unleavened Bread, the Festival of Weeks, and the Festival of Booths. No one is to appear before the LORD empty-handed. [17] Everyone ⌊must appear⌋ with a gift suited to his means, according to the blessing the LORD your God has given you.

Appointing Judges and Officials

[18] "Appoint judges and officials for your tribes in all your towns the LORD your God is giving you. They are to judge the people with righteous judgment. [19] Do not deny justice or show partiality ⌊to anyone⌋. Do not accept a bribe, for it blinds the eyes of the wise and twists the words of the righteous. [20] Pursue justice and justice alone, so that you will live and possess the land the LORD your God is giving you.

Forbidden Worship

[21] "Do not set up an •Asherah of any kind of wood next to the altar you will build for the LORD your God, [22] and do not set up a sacred pillar; the LORD your God hates them.

17 "You must not sacrifice to the LORD your God an ox or sheep with a defect or any serious flaw, for that is detestable to the LORD your God.

Judicial Procedure for Idolatry

[2] "If a man or woman among you in one of your towns that the LORD your God will give you is discovered doing evil in the sight of the LORD your God and violating His covenant [3] and has gone to worship other gods by bowing down to the sun, moon, or all the stars in the sky—which I have forbidden— [4] and if you are told or hear ⌊about it⌋, you must investigate it thoroughly. If the report turns out to be true that this detestable thing has happened in Israel, [5] you must bring out to your •gates that man or woman who has done this evil thing and stone them to death. [6] The one condemned to die is to be executed on the testimony of two or three witnesses. No one is to be executed on the testimony of a single witness. [7] The witnesses' hands are to be the first in putting him to death, and after that, the hands of all the people. You must purge the evil from you.

Hard Cases to Priests and Judges

8 "If a case is too difficult for you—concerning bloodshed, lawsuits, or assaults—cases disputed at your gates, you must go up to the place the LORD your God chooses. 9 You are to go to the Levitical priests and to the judge who presides at that time. Ask, and they will give you a verdict in the case. 10 You must abide by the verdict they give you at the place the LORD chooses. Be careful to do exactly as they instruct you. 11 You must abide by the instruction they give you and the verdict they announce to you. Do not turn to the right or the left from the decision they declare to you. 12 The person who acts arrogantly, refusing to listen either to the priest who stands there serving the LORD your God or to the judge, must die. You must purge the evil from Israel. 13 Then all the people will hear ⌊about it⌋, be afraid, and no longer behave arrogantly.

Instruction for a King

14 "When you enter the land the LORD your God is giving you, take possession of it, live in it, and say, 'We want to appoint a king over us like all the nations around us,' 15 you are to appoint over you the king the LORD your God chooses. Appoint a king from your brothers. You are not to set a foreigner over you, or one who is not of your people. 16 However, he must not acquire many horses for himself or send the people back to Egypt to acquire many horses, for the LORD has told you, 'You are never to go back that way again.' 17 He must not acquire many wives for himself so that his heart won't go astray. He must not acquire very large amounts of silver and gold for himself. 18 When he is seated on his royal throne, he is to write a copy of this instruction for himself on a scroll in the presence of the Levitical priests. 19 It is to remain with him, and he is to read from it all the days of his life, so that he may learn to •fear the LORD his God, to observe all the words of this instruction, and to do these statutes. 20 Then his heart will not be exalted above his countrymen, he will not turn from this command to the right or the left, and he and his sons will continue ruling many years[a] over Israel.

Provisions for Levites

18 "The Levitical priests, the whole tribe of Levi, will have no portion or inheritance with Israel. They will eat the LORD's fire offerings; that is their[b] [c] inheritance. 2 Although Levi has no inheritance among his brothers, the LORD is his inheritance, as He promised him. 3 This is the priests' share from the people who offer a sacrifice, whether it is an ox, a sheep, or a goat; the priests are to be given the shoulder, jaws, and stomach. 4 You are to give him the •firstfruits of your grain, new wine, and oil, and the first sheared ⌊wool⌋ of your flock. 5 For the LORD your God has chosen him and his sons from all your tribes to stand and minister in the LORD's name from now on.[d] 6 When a Levite leaves one of your towns where he lives in Israel and wants to go to the place the LORD chooses, 7 he may serve in the name of the LORD his God like all his fellow Levites who minister there in the presence of the LORD. 8 They will eat equal portions besides what he has received from the sale of the family estate.[e]

Reject Occult

9 "When you enter the land the LORD your God is giving you, do not imitate

---

[a]**17:20** Lit *will lengthen days on his kingdom*   [b]**18:1** LXX; MT reads *his*   [c]**18:1** Or *His*   [d]**18:5** Lit *name all the days*   [e]**18:8** Hb obscure

the detestable customs of those nations. [10] No one among you is to make his son or daughter pass through the fire,[a] practice •divination, tell fortunes, interpret omens, practice sorcery, [11] cast spells, consult a medium or a familiar spirit, or inquire of the dead. [12] Everyone who does these things is detestable to the LORD, and the LORD your God is driving out the nations before you because of these detestable things. [13] You must be blameless before the LORD your God. [14] Though these nations you are about to drive out listen to fortune-tellers and diviners, the LORD your God has not permitted you to do this.

True Prophets

[15] "The LORD your God will raise up for you a prophet like me from among your own brothers. You must listen to him. [16] This is what you requested from the LORD your God at Horeb on the day of the assembly when you said, 'Let us not continue to hear the voice of the LORD our God or see this great fire any longer, so that we will not die!' [17] Then the LORD said to me, 'They have spoken well. [18] I will raise up for them a prophet like you from among their brothers. I will put My words in his mouth, and he will tell them everything I command him. [19] I will hold accountable whoever does not listen to My words that he speaks in My name. [20] But the prophet who dares to speak in My name a message I have not commanded him to speak, or who speaks in the name of other gods—that prophet must die.'

Test for True Prophet

[21] You may say to yourself, 'How can we recognize a message the LORD has not spoken?' [22] When a prophet speaks in the LORD's name, and the message does not come true or is not fulfilled, that is a message the LORD has not spoken. The prophet has spoken it presumptuously. Do not be afraid of him.

Three Cities of Refuge

19 "When the LORD your God annihilates the nations whose land He is giving you, so that you drive them out and live in their cities and houses, [2] you are to set apart three cities for yourselves within the land the LORD your God is giving you to possess. [3] You are to determine the distances[b] and divide the land the LORD your God is granting you as an inheritance into three regions, so that anyone who commits manslaughter can flee to these cities.[c]

[4] "Here is the law concerning a case of someone who kills a person and flees there to save his life, having killed his neighbor accidentally without previously hating him: [5] If he goes into the forest with his neighbor to cut timber, and his hand swings the ax to chop down a tree, but the blade flies off the handle and strikes his neighbor so that he dies, that person may flee to one of these cities and live. [6] Otherwise, the avenger of blood in the heat of his anger[d] might pursue the one who committed manslaughter, overtake him because the distance is great, and strike him dead. Yet he did not deserve to die,[e] since he did not previously hate his neighbor. [7] This is why I am commanding you to set apart three cities for yourselves.

Three More Cities

[8] If the LORD your God enlarges your territory as He swore to your fathers, and gives you all the land He promised to give them— [9] provided you keep every

---

[a]**18:10** Either a Canaanite cult practice or child sacrifice   [b]**19:3** Or *to prepare the roads*   [c]**19:3** Lit *flee there*
[d]**19:6** Lit *heart*   [e]**19:6** Lit *did not have a judgment of death*

one of these commands I am giving you today and follow them, loving the LORD your God and walking in His ways at all times—you are to <u>add three more cities to these three</u>. ¹⁰ In this way, innocent blood will not be shed, and you will not become guilty of bloodshed in the land the LORD your God is giving you as an inheritance.

Premeditated Murder: No Refuge

¹¹ But if someone hates his neighbor, lies in ambush for him, attacks him, and strikes him fatally, and flees to one of these cities, ¹² the elders of his city must send ⌊for him⌋, take him from there, and hand him over to the avenger of blood and he will die. ¹³ You must not look on him with pity but purge from Israel the guilt of shedding innocent blood, and you will prosper.

Don't Move Boundary Markers!

¹⁴ "You must not move your neighbor's boundary marker, established at the start in the inheritance you will receive in the land the LORD your God is giving you to possess.

Two or More Witnesses in Court

¹⁵ "One witness cannot establish any wrongdoing or sin against a person, whatever that person has done. <u>A fact must be established by the testimony of two or three witnesses</u>. ¹⁶ "If a malicious witness testifies against someone accusing him of a crime, ¹⁷ the two people in the dispute must stand in the presence of the LORD before the priests and judges in authority at the time. ¹⁸ The judges are to make a careful investigation, and if the witness turns out to be a liar who has falsely accused his brother, ¹⁹ you must do to him as he intended to do to his brother. You

must purge the evil from you. ²⁰ Then everyone else will hear and be afraid, and they will never again do anything evil like this among you. ²¹ You must not show pity: life for life, eye for eye, tooth for tooth, hand for hand, and foot for foot.

Conduct of War

Priest Addresses Troops

20 "When you go out to war against your enemies and see horses, chariots, and an army larger than yours, do not be afraid of them, for the LORD your God, who brought you out of the land of Egypt, is with you. ² When you are about to engage in battle, the <u>priest is to come forward and address the army</u>. ³ He is to say to them: 'Listen, Israel: Today you are about to engage in battle with your enemies. Do not be fainthearted. Do not be afraid, alarmed, or terrified because of them. ⁴ For the LORD your God is the One who goes with you to fight for you against your enemies to give you victory.'

Officers Address Troops

⁵ "The <u>officers are to address the army</u>, 'Has any man built a new house and not dedicated it? Let him leave and return home. Otherwise, he may die in battle and another man dedicate it. ⁶ Has any man planted a vineyard and not begun to enjoy its fruit?ᵃ Let him leave and return home. Otherwise he may die in battle and another man enjoy its fruit.ᵇ ⁷ Has any man become •engaged to a woman and not married her? Let him leave and return home. Otherwise he may die in battle and another man marry her.' ⁸ The officers will continue to address the army and say, 'Is there any man who is afraid or fainthearted? Let him leave and

ᵃ**20:6** Lit *not put it to use*   ᵇ**20:6** Lit *man put it to use* return home, so that his brothers' hearts won't melt like his own.' [9] When the officers have finished addressing the army, they will appoint military commanders to lead it.

Rules of Military Engagement

[10] "When you approach a city to fight against it, you must make an offer of peace. [11] If it accepts your offer of peace and opens ᵢits gatesᵢ to you, all the people found in it will become forced laborers for you and serve you. [12] However, if it does not make peace with you but wages war against you, lay siege to it. [13] When the LORD your God hands it over to you, you must strike down all its males with the sword. [14] But you may take the women, children, animals, and whatever else is in the city—all its spoil—as plunder. You may enjoy the spoil of your enemies that the LORD your God has given you. [15] This is how you are to treat all the cities that are far away from you and are not among the cities of these nations. [16] However, you must not let any living thing survive among the cities of these people the LORD your God is giving you as an inheritance. [17] You must •completely destroy them—the Hittite, Amorite, Canaanite, Perizzite, Hivite, and Jebusite—as the LORD your God has commanded you, [18] so that they won't teach you to do all the detestable things they do for their gods, and you sin against the LORD your God.

Preserve Food-bearing Trees

[19] "When you lay siege to a city for a long time, fighting against it in order to capture it, you must not destroy its trees by putting an ax to them, because you can get food from them. You must not cut them down. Are trees of the field human, to come under siege by you? [20] But you may destroy the trees that you know do not produce food. You may cut them down to build siege works against the city that is waging war with you, until it falls.

Unsolved Murders

21 "If a murder victim is found lying in a field in the land the LORD your God is giving you to possess, and it is not known who killed him, [2] your elders and judges must come out and measure ᵢthe distanceᵢ from the victim to the nearby cities. [3] The elders of the city nearest to the victim are to get a cow that has not been yoked or used for work. [4] The elders of that city will bring the cow down to a continually flowing stream, to a place not tilled or sown, and they will break the cow's neck there by the stream. [5] Then the priests, the sons of Levi, will come forward, for the LORD your God has chosen them to serve Him and pronounce blessings in the LORD's name, and they are to give a ruling in[a] every dispute and ᵢcase ofᵢ assault. [6] All the elders of the city nearest to the victim will wash their hands by the stream over the heifer whose neck has been broken. [7] They will declare, 'Our hands did not shed this blood; our eyes did not see ᵢitᵢ. [8] LORD, forgive Your people Israel You redeemed, and do not hold the shedding of innocent blood against them.' Then they will be absolved of responsibility for bloodshed. [9] You must purge from yourselves the guilt of shedding innocent blood, for you will be doing what is right in the LORD's sight.

Domestic Matters

Treatment of Captured Women

[10] "When you go to war against your enemies and the LORD your God hands

---

[a] **21:5** Lit *and according to their mouth will be*

them over to you and you take some of them prisoner, and [11] if you see a beautiful woman among the captives, desire her, and want to take her as your wife, [12] you are to bring her into your house. She must shave her head, trim her nails, [13] remove the clothes she was wearing when she was taken prisoner, live in your house, and mourn for her father and mother a full month. After that, you may have sexual relations with her and be her husband, and she will be your wife. [14] Then if you are not satisfied with her, you are to let her go where she wants, but you must not sell her for money or treat her as merchandise,[a] because you have humiliated her.

Right of Firstborn

[15] "If a man has two wives, one loved and the other unloved, and both the loved and the unloved bear him sons, and if the unloved wife has the firstborn son, [16] when that man gives what he has to his sons as an inheritance, he is not to show favoritism to the son of the loved ⌊wife⌋ as his firstborn over the firstborn of the unloved wife. [17] He must acknowledge the firstborn, the son of the unloved wife, by giving him a double portion of everything that belongs to him, for he is the firstfruits of his virility; he has the rights of the firstborn.

A Rebellious Son

[18] "If a man has a stubborn and rebellious son who does not obey his father or mother and doesn't listen to them even after they discipline him, [19] his father and mother must take hold of him and bring him to the elders of his city, to the •gate of his hometown. [20] They will say to the elders of his city, 'This son of ours is stubborn and rebellious; he doesn't obey us. He's a glutton and a drunkard.'

[21] Then all the men of his city will stone him to death. You must purge the evil from you, and all Israel will hear and be afraid.

Display of the Executed

[22] "If anyone is found guilty of an offense deserving the death penalty and is executed, and you hang his body on a tree, [23] you are not to leave his corpse on the tree overnight but are to bury him that day, for anyone hung ⌊on a tree⌋ is under God's curse. You must not defile the land the LORD your God is giving you as an inheritance.

Caring for Your Brother's Property

22 "If you see your brother's ox or sheep straying, you must not ignore it; make sure you return it to your brother. [2] If your brother does not live near you or you don't know him, you are to bring the animal to your home to remain with you until your brother comes looking for it; then you can return it to him. [3] Do the same for his donkey, his garment, or anything your brother has lost and you have found. You must not ignore ⌊it⌋. [4] If you see your brother's donkey or ox fallen down on the road, you must not ignore it; you must help him lift it up.

Sexual and Miscellaneous Issues

Transvestites, Bird's Nests, Roof Railings, and Mixed Matters

[5] "A woman is not to wear male clothing, and a man is not to put on a woman's garment, for everyone who does these things is detestable to the LORD your God.

[6] "If you come across a bird's nest with chicks or eggs, either in a tree or on the

ground along the road, and the mother is sitting on the chicks or eggs, you must not take the mother along with the young. 7 You may take the young for yourself, but be sure to let the mother go free, so that you may prosper and live long. 8 If you build a new house, make a railing around your roof, so that you don't bring bloodguilt on your house if someone falls from it. 9 Do not plant your vineyard with two types of seed; otherwise, the entire harvest, both the crop you plant and the produce of the vineyard, will be defiled. 10 Do not plow with an ox and a donkey together. 11 Do not wear clothes made of both wool and linen. 12 Make tassels on the four corners of the outer garment you wear.

Rules on Virginity

13 "If a man marries a woman, has sexual relations with her, and comes to hate her, 14 and accuses ⌊her⌋ of shameful conduct, and gives her a bad name, saying, 'I married this woman and was intimate with her, but I didn't find ⌊any⌋ evidence of her virginity,' 15 the young woman's father and mother will take the evidence of her virginity and bring ⌊it⌋ to the city elders at the •gate. 16 The young woman's father will say to the elders, 'I gave my daughter to this man as a wife, but he hates her. 17 He has accused her of shameful conduct, saying: "I didn't find ⌊any⌋ evidence of your daughter's virginity, but here is the evidence of my daughter's virginity.' " They will spread out the cloth before the city elders. 18 Then the elders of that city will take the man and punish him. 19 They will also fine him 100 silver ⌊shekels⌋ and give ⌊them⌋ to the young woman's father, because that man gave an Israelite virgin a bad name. She will remain his wife; he can-

not divorce her as long as he lives. 20 But if this accusation is true and no evidence of the young woman's virginity is found, 21 they will bring the woman to the door of her father's house, and the men of her city will stone her to death. For she has committed an outrage in Israel by being promiscuous in her father's house. You must purge the evil from you.

Adultery a Capital Offense

22 "If a man is discovered having sexual relations with ⌊another⌋ man's wife, both the man who had sex with the woman and the woman must die. You must purge the evil from Israel.

Engaged Women: Premarital Sex

23 If there is a young woman who is a virgin •engaged to a man, and ⌊another⌋ man encounters her in the city and has sex with her, 24 you must take the two of them out to the gate of that city and stone them to death—the young woman because she did not cry out in the city and the man because he has violated his neighbor's fiancée. You must purge the evil from you. 25 But if the man encounters the engaged woman in the open country, and he seizes and rapes her, only the man who raped her must die. 26 Do nothing to the young woman, because she is not guilty of an offense deserving death. This case is just like one in which a man attacks his neighbor and murders him. 27 When he found her in the field, the engaged woman cried out, but there was no one to rescue her. 28 If a man encounters a young woman, a virgin who is not engaged, takes hold of her and rapes her, and they are discovered, 29 the man who raped her must give the young woman's father 50 silver ⌊shekels⌋, and

she must become his wife because he violated her. He cannot divorce her as long as he lives.

No Marriage to Father's Wife

30 "A man is not to marry his father's wife; he must not violate his father's marriage bed.[a] [b]

Exclusion and Inclusion from Assembly

23 "No man whose ⌊testicles⌋ have been crushed[c] or whose penis has been cut off may enter the LORD's assembly. 2 No one of illegitimate birth may enter the LORD's assembly; none of his descendants, even to the tenth generation, may enter the LORD's assembly. 3 No Ammonite or Moabite may enter the LORD's assembly; none of their descendants, even to the tenth generation, may ever enter the LORD's assembly. 4 This is because they did not meet you with food and water on the journey after you came out of Egypt, and because Balaam son of Beor from Pethor in Aram-naharaim was hired to curse you. 5 Yet the LORD your God would not listen to Balaam, but He turned the curse into a blessing for you because the LORD your God loves you. 6 Never seek peace or friendship with them as long as you live. 7 Do not despise an Edomite, because he is your brother. Do not despise an Egyptian, because you were a foreign resident in his land. 8 The children born to them in the third generation may enter the LORD's assembly.

Keep Military Camp Clean

9 "When you are encamped against your enemies, be careful to avoid anything offensive. 10 If there is a man among you who is unclean because of a bodily emission during the night, he must go outside the camp; he may not come anywhere inside the camp. 11 When evening approaches, he must wash with water, and when the sun sets he may come inside the camp. 12 You must have a place outside the camp and go there ⌊to relieve yourself⌋. 13 You must have a digging tool in your equipment; when you relieve yourself, dig a hole with it and cover up your excrement. 14 For the LORD your God walks throughout your camp to protect you and deliver your enemies to you; so your encampments must be holy. He must not see anything improper among you or He will turn away from you.

Protect Fugitive Slaves

15 "Do not return a slave to his master when he has escaped from his master to you. 16 Let him live among you wherever he wants within your gates. Do not mistreat him.

Cult Prostitution Forbidden

17 "No Israelite woman is to be a cult prostitute, and no Israelite man is to be a cult prostitute. 18 Do not bring a female prostitute's wages or a male prostitute's[d] earnings into the house of the LORD your God to fulfill any vow, because both are detestable to the LORD your God.

Interest on Loans

19 "Do not charge your brother interest on money, food, or anything that can earn interest. 20 You may charge a foreigner interest, but you must not charge your brother interest, so that the LORD your God may bless you in everything you do[e] in the land you are entering to possess.

Keep Your Vows!

21 "If you make a vow to the LORD your God, do not be slow to keep it, because

---

[a]22:30 Dt 23:1 in Hb   [b]22:30 Lit *not uncover the edge of his father's garment*; Ru 3:9; Ezk 16:8   [c]23:1 Lit *man bruised by crushing*   [d]23:18 Lit *a dog's*   [e]23:20 Lit *you put your hand to*

He will require it of you, and it will be counted against you as sin. ²² But if you refrain from making a vow, it will not be counted against you as sin. ²³ Be careful to do whatever comes from your lips, because you have freely vowed what you promised[a] to the LORD your God.

Eating Neighbor's Crops

²⁴ "When you enter your neighbor's vineyard, you may eat as many grapes as you want until you are full, but you must not put ᴸanyᴶ in your container. ²⁵ When you enter your neighbor's standing grain, you may pluck heads of grain with your hand, but you must not put a sickle to your neighbor's grain.

Marriage and Divorce Laws

24 "If a man marries a woman, but she becomes displeasing to him because he finds something improper about her, he may write her a divorce certificate, hand it to her, and send her away from his house. ² If after leaving his house she goes and becomes another man's wife, ³ and the second man hates her, writes her a divorce certificate, hands it to her, and sends her away from his house or if he[b] dies, ⁴ the first husband who sent her away may not marry her again after she has been defiled, because that would be detestable to the LORD. You must not bring guilt on the land the LORD your God is giving you as an inheritance.

⁵ "When a man takes a bride, he must not go out with the army or be liable for any duty. He is free ᴸto stayᴶ at home for one year, so that he can bring joy to the wife he has married.

Various Laws

⁶ "Do not take a pair of millstones or an upper millstone as security for a debt, because that is like taking a life as security.

⁷ "If a man is discovered kidnapping one of his Israelite brothers, whether he treats him as a slave or sells him, the kidnapper must die. You must purge the evil from you.

⁸ "Be careful in a case of infectious skin disease, following carefully everything the Levitical priests instruct you to do. Be careful to do as I have commanded them. ⁹ Remember what the Lord your God did to Miriam on the journey after you left Egypt.

Help the Poor

¹⁰ "When you make a loan of any kind to your neighbor, do not enter his house to collect what he offers as security. ¹¹ You must stand outside while the man you are making the loan to brings the security out to you. ¹² If he is a poor man, you must not sleep in ᴸthe garmentᴶ he has given as security. ¹³ Be sure to return it[c] to him at sunset. Then he will sleep in it and bless you, and this will be counted as righteousness to you before the LORD your God.

¹⁴ "Do not oppress a hired hand who is poor and needy, whether one of your brothers or one of the foreigners residing within a town[d] in your land. ¹⁵ You are to pay him his wages each day before the sun sets, because he is poor and depends on them. Otherwise he will cry out to the LORD against you, and you will be held guilty.

Each Punished for Own Sin

¹⁶ "Fathers are not to be put to death for ᴸtheirᴶ children or children for ᴸtheirᴶ fathers; each person will be put to death for his own sin. ¹⁷ Do not deny justice to a foreign resident ᴸorᴶ fatherless child,

a**23:23** Lit promised with your mouth   b**24:3** Lit if the second man who has taken her as his wife   c**24:13** Lit return what he has given as security   d**24:14** Lit within the gates

and do not take a widow's garment as security. ¹⁸ Remember that you were a slave in Egypt, and the LORD your God redeemed you from there. Therefore I am commanding you to do this.

Extras for Needy

¹⁹ "When you reap the harvest in your field, and you forget a sheaf in the field, do not go back to get it. It is to be left for the foreign resident, the fatherless, and the widow, so that the LORD your God may bless you in all the work of your hands. ²⁰ When you knock down the fruit from your olive tree, you must not go over the branches again. What remains will be for the foreign resident, the fatherless, and the widow. ²¹ When you gather the grapes of your vineyard, you must not glean what is left. What remains will be for the foreign resident, the fatherless, and the widow. ²² Remember that you were a slave in the land of Egypt. Therefore I am commanding you to do this.

Flogging the Guilty

25 "If there is a dispute between men, they are to go to court, and the judges will hear their case. They will clear the innocent and condemn the guilty. ² If the guilty party deserves to be flogged, the judge will make him lie down and be flogged in his presence with the number ⌊of lashes⌋ appropriate for his crime. ³ He may be flogged with 40 lashes, but no more. Otherwise, if he is flogged with more lashes than these, your brother will be degraded in your sight.

Don't Muzzle Ox

⁴ "<u>Do not muzzle an ox while it treads out grain.</u>

Preserving the Family Line

⁵ "When brothers live on the same property^a and one of them dies without a son, the wife of the dead man may not marry a stranger outside ⌊the family⌋. Her brother-in-law is to take her as his wife, have sexual relations with her, and perform the duty of a brother-in-law for her. ⁶ The first son she bears will carry on the name of the dead brother, so his name will not be blotted out from Israel. ⁷ But if the man doesn't want to marry his sister-in-law, she must go to the elders at the ⌊city⌋ •gate and say, 'My brother-in-law refuses to preserve his brother's name in Israel. He isn't willing to perform the duty of a brother-in-law for me.' ⁸ The elders of his city will summon him and speak with him. If he persists and says, 'I don't want to marry her,' ⁹ then his sister-in-law will go up to him in the sight of the elders, remove his sandal from his foot, and spit in his face. Then she will declare, 'This is what is done to a man who will not build up his brother's house.' ¹⁰ And his ⌊family⌋ name in Israel will be called 'The house of the man whose sandal was removed.'

¹¹ "If two men are fighting with each other, and the wife of one steps in to rescue her husband from the one striking him, and she puts out her hand and grabs his genitals, ¹² you are to cut off her hand. You must not show pity.

Honest Weights and Measures

¹³ "You must not have two different weights^b in your bag, one heavy and one light. ¹⁴ You must not have two differing dry measures in your house, a larger and a smaller. ¹⁵ You must have a full and honest weight, a full and honest dry measure, so that you may live long in the land the LORD your God is giving you.

---

^a**25:5** Lit *live together*   ^b**25:13** Lit *have a stone and a stone*

¹⁶ For everyone who does such things and acts unfairly is detestable to the LORD your God.

Revenge on Amalekites

¹⁷ "Remember what the Amalekites did to you on the journey after you left Egypt. ¹⁸ They met you along the way and attacked all your stragglers from behind when you were tired and weary. They did not •fear God. ¹⁹ When the LORD your God gives you rest from all the enemies around you in the land the LORD your God is giving you to possess as an inheritance, blot out the memory of Amalek from under heaven. Do not forget.

Giving Firstfruits

26 "When you enter the land the LORD your God is giving you as an inheritance, and you take possession of it and live in it, ² you must take some of the first of all the soil's produce that you harvest from the land the LORD your God is giving you and put ⌊it⌋ in a container. Then go to the place where the LORD your God chooses to have His name dwell. ³ When you come before the priest who is serving at that time, you must say to him, 'Today I acknowledge to the LORD your^a God that I have entered the land the LORD swore to our fathers to give us.'

Ritual of Giving

⁴ "Then the priest will take the container from your hand and place it before the altar of the LORD your God. ⁵ You are to respond by saying in the presence of the LORD your God:

My father was a wandering Aramean. He went down to Egypt with a few people and lived there. There he became a great, powerful, and populous nation. ⁶ But the Egyptians mistreated and afflicted us, and forced us to do hard labor. ⁷ So we called out to the LORD, the God of our fathers, and the LORD heard our cry and saw our misery, hardship, and oppression. ⁸ Then the LORD brought us out of Egypt with a strong hand and an outstretched arm, with terrifying power, and with signs and wonders. ⁹ He led us to this place and gave us this land, a land flowing with milk and honey. ¹⁰ I have now brought the first of the land's produce that You, LORD, have given me.

You will then place the container before the LORD your God and bow down to Him. ¹¹ You, the Levite, and the foreign resident among you will rejoice in all the good things the LORD your God has given you and your household.

Tenth in Third Year

¹² "When you have finished paying all the tenth of your produce in the third year, the year of the tenth, you are to give ⌊it⌋ to the Levite, the foreign resident, the fatherless, and the widow, so that they may eat in your towns and be satisfied. ¹³ Then you will say in the presence of the LORD your God:

I have taken the consecrated portion out of my house; I have also given it to the Levite, the foreign resident, the fatherless, and the widow, according to all the commands You gave me. I have not violated or forgotten Your commands. ¹⁴ I have not eaten any of it while in mourning, or removed any of it while unclean, or offered any of it for the dead. I have

^a**26:3** LXX reads *my*

obeyed the LORD my God; I have done all You commanded me. ¹⁵ Look down from Your holy dwelling, from heaven, and bless Your people Israel and the land You have given us as You swore to our fathers, a land flowing with milk and honey."

Covenant Summary

¹⁶ "The LORD your God is commanding you this day to follow these statutes and ordinances. You must be careful to follow them with all your heart and all your soul. ¹⁷ Today you have affirmed that the LORD is your God and that you will walk in His ways, keep His statutes, commands, and ordinances, and obey Him. ¹⁸ And today the LORD has affirmed that you are His special people as He promised you, that you are to keep all His commands, ¹⁹ that He will put you far above all the nations He has made in praise, fame, and glory, and that you will be a holy people to the LORD your God as He promised."

Law Written on Stones

27 Moses and the elders of Israel commanded the people, "Keep every command I am giving you today. ² At the time you cross the Jordan into the land the LORD your God is giving you, you must set up large stones and cover them with plaster. ³ Write all the words of this law on the stones after you cross to enter the land the LORD your God is giving you, a land flowing with milk and honey, as the LORD, the God of your fathers, has promised you. ⁴ When you have crossed the Jordan, you are to set up these stones on Mount Ebal, as I am commanding you today, and you are to cover them with plaster. ⁵ Build an altar of stones there to the LORD your God— you must not use any iron tool on them. ⁶ Use uncut stones to build the altar of the LORD your God and offer •burnt offerings to the LORD your God on it. ⁷ There you are to sacrifice •fellowship offerings, eat, and rejoice in the presence of the LORD your God. ⁸ Write clearly all the words of this law on the ⌊plastered⌋ stones."

Covenant Curses

⁹ Moses and the Levitical priests spoke to all Israel, "Be silent, Israel, and listen! This day you have become the people of the LORD your God. ¹⁰ Obey the LORD your God and follow His commands and statutes I am giving you today."

¹¹ On that day Moses commanded the people, ¹² "When you have crossed the Jordan, these ⌊tribes⌋ will stand on Mount Gerizim to bless the people: Simeon, Levi, Judah, Issachar, Joseph, and Benjamin. ¹³ And these ⌊tribes⌋ will stand on Mount Ebal to deliver the curse: Reuben, Gad, Asher, Zebulun, Dan, and Naphtali. ¹⁴ The Levites will proclaim in a loud voice to every Israelite:

¹⁵ 'Cursed is the person who makes
a carved idol or cast image, which
is detestable to the LORD, the work
of a craftsman, and sets ⌊it⌋ up in
secret.'
And all the people will reply,
'•Amen!'
¹⁶ 'Cursed is the one who dishonors
his father or mother.'
And all the people will say, 'Amen!'
¹⁷ 'Cursed is the one who moves his
neighbor's boundary marker.'
And all the people will say, 'Amen!'
¹⁸ 'Cursed is the one who leads a
blind person astray on the road.'
And all the people will say, 'Amen!'
¹⁹ 'Cursed is the one who denies
justice to a foreign resident, a
fatherless child, or a widow.'
And all the people will say, 'Amen!'

²⁰ 'Cursed is the one who sleeps with his father's wife, for he has violated his father's marriage bed.'ᵃ
And all the people will say, 'Amen!'
²¹ 'Cursed is the one who has sexual intercourse with any animal.'
And all the people will say, 'Amen!'
²² 'Cursed is the one who sleeps with his sister, whether his father's daughter or his mother's daughter.'
And all the people will say, 'Amen!'
²³ 'Cursed is the one who sleeps with his mother-in-law.'
And all the people will say, 'Amen!'
²⁴ 'Cursed is the one who kills his neighbor in secret.'
And all the people will say, 'Amen!'
²⁵ 'Cursed is the one who accepts a bribe to kill an innocent person.'
And all the people will say, 'Amen!'
²⁶ 'Cursed is anyone who does not put the words of this law into practice.'
And all the people will say, 'Amen!'

Blessings for Obedience

28 "Now if you faithfully obey the LORD your God and are careful to follow all His commands I am giving you today, the LORD your God will put you far above all the nations of the earth. ² All these blessings will come and overtake you, because you obey the LORD your God:

³ You will be blessed in the city
and blessed in the country.
⁴ Your descendantsᵇ will be blessed,
and your soil's produce,
and the offspring of your livestock,
including the young of your herds
and the newborn of your flocks.
⁵ Your basket and kneading bowl
will be blessed.
⁶ You will be blessed
when you come in
and blessed when you go out.

⁷ "The LORD will cause the enemies who rise up against you to be defeated before you. They will march out against you from one direction but flee from you in seven directions. ⁸ The LORD will grant you a blessing on your storehouses and on everything you do;ᶜ He will bless you in the land the LORD your God is giving you. ⁹ The LORD will establish you as His holy people, as He swore to you, if you obey the commands of the LORD your God and walk in His ways. ¹⁰ Then all the peoples of the earth will see that you are called by the LORD's name, and they will stand in awe of you. ¹¹ The LORD will make you prosper abundantly with children,ᵈ the offspring of your livestock, and your soil's produce in the land the LORD swore to your fathers to give you. ¹² The LORD will open for you His abundant storehouse, the sky, to give your land rain in its season and to bless all the work of your hands. You will lend to many nations, but you will not borrow. ¹³ The LORD will make you the head and not the tail; you will only move upward and never downward if you listen to the LORD your God's commands I am giving you today and are careful to follow [them]. ¹⁴ Do not turn aside to the right or the left from all the things I am commanding you today, and do not go after other gods to worship them.

Curses for Disobedience

¹⁵ "But if you do not obey the LORD your God by carefully following all His commands and statutes I am giving you today, all these curses will come and overtake you:

ᵃ**27:20** Lit *has uncovered the edge of his father's garment*; Ru 3:9; Ezk 16:8   ᵇ**28:4** Lit *The fruit of your womb*
ᶜ**28:8** Lit *you put your hand to*   ᵈ**28:11** Lit *abundantly in the fruit of your womb*

16 You will be cursed in the city
   and cursed in the country.
17 Your basket and kneading bowl
   will be cursed.
18 Your descendants[a] will be cursed,
   and your soil's produce,
   the young of your herds,
   and the newborn of your flocks.
19 You will be cursed when you come in
   and cursed when you go out.

20 The LORD will send against you curses, confusion, and rebuke in everything you do[b] until you are destroyed and quickly perish, because of the wickedness of your actions in abandoning Me. 21 The LORD will make pestilence cling to you until He has exterminated you from the land you are entering to possess. 22 The LORD will afflict you with wasting disease, fever, inflammation, burning heat, drought,[c] blight, and mildew; these will pursue you until you perish. 23 The sky above you will be bronze, and the earth beneath you iron. 24 The LORD will turn the rain of your land into falling[d] dust; it will descend on you from the sky until you are destroyed. 25 The LORD will cause you to be defeated before your enemies. You will march out against them from one direction but flee from them in seven directions. You will be an object of horror to all the kingdoms of the earth. 26 Your corpses will be food for all the birds of the sky and the wild animals of the land, and no one will scare them away.

Disobedience: Personal Consequences

27 "The LORD will afflict you with the boils of Egypt, tumors, a festering rash, and scabies, from which you cannot be cured. 28 The LORD will afflict you with madness, blindness, and mental confusion, 29 so that at noon you will grope as a blind man gropes in the dark. You will not be successful in anything you do. You will only be oppressed and robbed continually, and no one will help ⌊you⌋. 30 You will become •engaged to a woman, but another man will rape her. You will build a house but not live in it. You will plant a vineyard but not enjoy its fruit. 31 Your ox will be slaughtered before your eyes, but you will not eat any of it. Your donkey will be taken away from you and not returned to you. Your flock will be given to your enemies, and no one will help you. 32 Your sons and daughters will be given to another people, while your eyes grow weary looking for them every day. But you will be powerless to do anything.[e] 33 A people you don't know will eat your soil's produce and everything you have labored for. You will only be oppressed and crushed continually. 34 You will be driven mad by what you see. 35 The LORD will afflict you on your knees and thighs with painful and incurable boils from the sole of your foot to the top of your head.

National Consequences of Disobedience

36 "The LORD will bring you and your king that you have appointed to a nation neither you nor your fathers have known, and there you will worship other gods, of wood and stone. 37 You will become an object of horror, scorn, and ridicule among all the peoples where the LORD will drive you.

Disobedience: Economic Consequences

38 "You will sow much seed in the field but harvest little, because locusts will devour it. 39 You will plant and cultivate vineyards but not drink the wine or

[a]**28:18** Lit *The fruit of your womb*   [b]**28:20** Lit *you put your hand to*   [c]**28:22** Or *sword*   [d]**28:24** Lit *powder and*
[e]**28:32** Lit *day, and not for power your hand*

gather the grapes, because worms will eat them. [40] You will have olive trees throughout your territory but not anoint yourself with oil, because your olives will drop off. [41] You will father sons and daughters, but they will not remain yours, because they will be taken prisoner. [42] Whirring insects will take possession of all your trees and your land's produce. [43] The foreign resident among you will rise higher and higher above you, while you sink lower and lower. [44] He will lend to you, but you won't lend to him. He will be the head, and you will be the tail.

[45] "All these curses will come, pursue, and overtake you until you are destroyed, since you did not obey the LORD your God and keep the commands and statutes He gave you. [46] These curses will be a sign and a wonder against you and your descendants forever. [47] Because you didn't serve the LORD your God with joy and a cheerful heart, even though you had an abundance of everything, [48] you will serve your enemies the LORD will send against you, in famine, thirst, nakedness, and a lack of everything. He will place an iron yoke on your neck until He has destroyed you. [49] The LORD will bring a nation from far away, from the ends of the earth, to swoop down on you like an eagle, a nation whose language you don't understand, [50] a ruthless nation,[a] showing no respect for the old and not sparing the young. [51] They will eat the offspring of your livestock and your soil's produce until you are destroyed. They will leave you no grain, new wine, oil, young of your herds, or newborn of your flocks until they cause you to perish. [52] They will besiege you within all your gates until your high and fortified walls, that you trust in, come down throughout your land. They will besiege you within all your gates throughout the land the LORD your God has given you.

Disobedience: Cannibalism

[53] "You will eat your children,[b] the flesh of your sons and daughters the LORD your God has given you during the siege and hardship your enemy imposes on you. [54] The most sensitive and refined man among you will look grudgingly[c] at his brother, the wife he embraces,[d] and the rest of his children, [55] refusing to share with any of them his children's flesh that he will eat because he has nothing left during the siege and hardship your enemy imposes on you in all your towns. [56] The most sensitive and refined woman among you, who would not venture to set the sole of her foot on the ground because of her refinement and sensitivity, will begrudge the husband she embraces, her son, and her daughter, [57] the afterbirth that comes out from between her legs and the children she bears, because she will secretly eat them for lack of anything else during the siege and hardship your enemy imposes on you within your gates.

Disobedience: Disease Epidemics

[58] "If you are not careful to obey all the words of this law, which are written in this scroll, by •fearing this glorious and awesome name—•Yahweh, your God— [59] He will bring extraordinary plagues on you and your descendants, severe and lasting plagues, and terrible and chronic sicknesses. [60] He will afflict you again with all the diseases of Egypt, which you dreaded, and they will cling to you. [61] The LORD will also inflict you with every sickness and plague not recorded in

---

[a]28:50 Lit a nation strong of face   [b]28:53 Lit eat the fruit of your womb   [c]28:54 Lit you his eye will be evil   [d]28:54 Lit wife of his bosom

the book of this law, until you are destroyed. [62] Though you were as numerous as the stars of the sky, you will be left with only a few people, because you did not obey the LORD your God. [63] Just as the LORD was glad to cause you to prosper and to multiply you, so He will also be glad to cause you to perish and to destroy you. You will be deported from the land you are entering to possess.

Disobedience: Israel Scattered

[64] Then the LORD will scatter you among all peoples from one end of the earth to the other, and there you will worship other gods of wood and stone, which neither you nor your fathers have known. [65] You will find no peace among those nations, and there will be no resting place for the sole of your foot. There the LORD will give you a trembling heart, failing eyes, and a despondent spirit. [66] Your life will hang in doubt before you. You will be in dread night and day, never certain of survival. [67] In the morning you will say, 'If only it were evening!' and in the evening you will say, 'If only it were morning!'—because of the dread you will have in your heart and because of what you will see. [68] The LORD will take you back in ships to Egypt by a route that I said you would never see again. There you will sell yourselves to your enemies as male and female slaves, but no one will buy ₊you₊."

Moses Renews Covenant

29 [1][a] These are the words of the covenant the LORD commanded Moses to make with the Israelites in the land of Moab, in addition to the covenant He had made with them at Horeb. [2][b] Moses summoned all Israel and said to them, "You have seen with your own eyes everything the LORD did in Egypt to Pharaoh, to all his officials, and to his entire land. [3] You saw with your own eyes the great trials and those great signs and wonders. [4] Yet to this day the LORD has not given you a mind to understand, eyes to see, or ears to hear. [5] I led you 40 years in the wilderness; your clothes and the sandals on your feet did not wear out; [6] you did not eat bread or drink wine or beer—so that you might know that I am the LORD your God. [7] When you reached this place, Sihon king of Heshbon and Og king of Bashan came out against us in battle, but we defeated them. [8] We took their land and gave it as an inheritance to the Reubenites, the Gadites, and half the tribe of Manasseh. [9] Therefore, observe the words of this covenant and follow them, so that you will succeed in everything you do.

[10] "All of you are standing today before the LORD your God—your leaders, tribes, elders, officials, all the men of Israel, [11] your children, your wives, and the foreigners in your camps who cut your wood and draw your water— [12] so that you may enter into the covenant of the LORD your God, which He is making with you today, so that you may enter into His oath [13] and so that He may establish you today as His people and He may be your God as He promised you and as He swore to your fathers Abraham, Isaac, and Jacob. [14] I am making this covenant and this oath not only with you, [15] but also with those who are standing here with us today in the presence of the LORD our God and with those who are not here today.

[a]**29:1** Dt 28:69 in Hb   [b]**29:2** Dt 29:1 in Hb

Moses: Consequences
of Abandoning Covenant

16 "Indeed, you know how we lived in the land of Egypt and passed through the nations where you traveled. 17 You saw their detestable images and idols ⌊made⌋ of wood, stone, silver, and gold, which were among them. 18 Be sure there is no man, woman, clan, or tribe among you today whose heart turns away from the LORD our God to go and worship the gods of those nations. Be sure there is no root among you bearing poisonous and bitter fruit. 19 When someone hears the words of this oath, he may bless himself in his mind, thinking, 'I will have peace even though I follow my ⌊own⌋ stubborn heart.' This will lead to the destruction of the well-watered ⌊land⌋ as well as the dry ⌊land⌋. 20 The LORD will not be willing to forgive him. Instead, His anger and jealousy will burn against that person, and every curse written in this scroll will descend on him. The LORD will blot out his name under heaven, 21 and single him out for harm from all the tribes of Israel, according to all the curses of the covenant written in this book of the law.

22 "Future generations of your children who follow you and the foreigner who comes from a distant country will see the plagues of the land and the sicknesses the LORD has inflicted on it. 23 All its soil will be a burning waste of sulfur and salt, unsown, producing nothing, with no plant growing on it, just like the fall of Sodom and Gomorrah, Admah and Zeboiim, which the LORD demolished in His fierce anger. 24 All the nations will ask, 'Why has the LORD done this to this land? Why this great outburst of anger?' 25 Then people will answer, 'It is because they abandoned the covenant of the LORD, the God of their fathers, which He had made with them when He brought them out of the land of Egypt. 26 They began to worship other gods, bowing down to gods they had not known—gods that the LORD had not permitted them ⌊to worship⌋. 27 Therefore the LORD's anger burned against this land, and He brought every curse written in this book on it. 28 The LORD uprooted them from their land in ⌊His⌋ anger, fury, and great wrath, and threw them into another land where they are today.' 29 The hidden things belong to the LORD our God, but the revealed things belong to us and our children forever, so that we may follow all the words of this law.

When You Return to the LORD…

30 "When all these things happen to you—the blessings and curses I have set before you—and you come to your senses ⌊while you are⌋ in all the nations where the LORD your God has driven you, 2 and you and your children return to the LORD your God and obey Him with all your heart and all your soul by doing[a] everything I am giving you today, 3 then He will restore your fortunes,[b] have compassion on you, and gather you again from all the peoples where the LORD your God has scattered you. 4 Even if your exiles are at the ends of the earth,[c] He will gather you and bring you back from there. 5 The LORD your God will bring you into the land your fathers possessed, and you will take possession of it. He will cause you to prosper and multiply you more than ⌊He did⌋ your fathers. 6 The LORD your God will circumcise your heart and the hearts of your descendants, and you will love Him with all your heart and all your soul, so that you will live. 7 The LORD your God will put all these curses on

your enemies who hate and persecute you. [8] Then you will again obey Him and follow all His commands I am giving you today. [9] The LORD your God will make you prosper abundantly in all the work of your hands with children,[a] the offspring of your livestock, and your soil's produce. Indeed, the LORD will again delight in your prosperity, as He delighted in that of your fathers, [10] when you obey the LORD your God by keeping His commands and statutes that are written in this book of the law and return to Him with all your heart and all your soul.

Choose Life!

[11] "This command that I give you today is certainly not too difficult or beyond your reach. [12] It is not in heaven, so that you have to ask, 'Who will go up to heaven, get it for us, and proclaim it to us so that we may follow it?' [13] And it is not across the sea, so that you have to ask, 'Who will cross the sea, get it for us, and proclaim it to us so that we may follow it?' [14] But the message is very near you, in your mouth and in your heart, so that you may follow it. [15] See, today I have set before you life and prosperity, death and adversity. [16] For[b] I am commanding you today to love the LORD your God, to walk in His ways, and to keep His commands, statutes, and ordinances, so that you may live[c] and multiply, and the LORD your God may bless you in the land you are entering to possess. [17] But if your heart turns away and you do not listen and you are led astray to bow down to other gods and worship them, [18] I tell you today that you will certainly perish and will not live long in the land you are entering to possess across the Jordan. [19] I call heaven and earth as witnesses against you today that I have set before you life and death, blessing and curse. Choose life so that you and your descendants may live, [20] love the LORD your God, obey Him, and remain faithful[d] to Him. For He is your life, and He will prolong your life in the land the LORD swore to give to your fathers Abraham, Isaac, and Jacob."

Joshua Takes Moses' Place

31 Then Moses continued to speak these[e] words to all Israel, [2] saying, "I am now 120 years old; I can no longer act as your leader.[f] The LORD has told me, 'You will not cross this Jordan.' [3] The LORD your God is the One who will cross ahead of you. He will destroy these nations before you, and you will drive them out. Joshua is the one who will cross ahead of you, as the LORD has said. [4] The LORD will deal with them as He did Sihon and Og, the kings of the Amorites, and their land when He destroyed them. [5] The LORD will deliver them over to you, and you must do to them exactly as I have commanded you. [6] Be strong and courageous; don't be terrified or afraid of them. For it is the LORD your God who goes with you; He will not leave you or forsake you."

Moses Summons Joshua

[7] Moses then summoned Joshua and said to him in the sight of all Israel, "Be strong and courageous, for you will go with[g] this people into the land the LORD swore to give to their fathers. You will enable them to take possession of it. [8] The LORD is the One who will go before you. He will be with you; He will not leave you or forsake you. Do not be afraid or discouraged."

[a]**30:9** Lit *hands in the fruit of your womb*   [b]**30:16** LXX reads *If you obey the commands of the LORD your God that*   [c]**30:16** LXX reads *ordinances, then you will live*   [d]**30:20** Lit *and hold on*   [e]**31:1** Other Hb mss, DSS, LXX, Syr, Vg read *all these*   [f]**31:2** Lit *no longer go out or come in*   [g]**31:7** Other Hb mss, Sam, Syr, Vg read *you will bring*

Moses Writes Law—
and Commands Reading

⁹ Moses wrote down this law and gave it to the priests, the sons of Levi, who carried the ark of the LORD's covenant, and to all the elders of Israel. ¹⁰ Moses commanded them, "At the end of ⌊every⌋ seven years, at the appointed time in the year of debt cancellation, during the Festival of Booths, ¹¹ when all Israel assembles[a] in the presence of the LORD your God at the place He chooses, you are to read this law aloud before all Israel. ¹² Gather the people—men, women, children, and foreigners living within your gates—so that they may listen and learn to •fear the LORD your God and be careful to follow all the words of this law. ¹³ Then their children who do not know ⌊the law⌋ will listen and learn to fear the LORD your God as long as you live in the land you are crossing the Jordan to possess."

God Tells Moses to Prepare

¹⁴ The LORD said to Moses, "The time of your death is now approaching. Call Joshua and present yourselves at the tent of meeting, so that I may commission him." When Moses and Joshua went and presented themselves at the tent of meeting, ¹⁵ the LORD appeared at the tent in a pillar of cloud, and the cloud stood at the entrance to the tent.

God Foresees Israel's Disobedience

¹⁶ The LORD said to Moses, "You are about to rest with your fathers, and this people will soon commit adultery with the foreign gods of the land they are entering. They will abandon Me and break the covenant I have made with them. ¹⁷ My anger will burn against them on that day; I will abandon them and hide My face from them so that they will become easy prey.[b] Many troubles and afflictions will come to them. On that day they will say, 'Haven't these troubles come to us because our God is no longer with us?' ¹⁸ I will certainly hide My face on that day because of all the evil they have done by turning to other gods. ¹⁹ Therefore write down this song for yourselves and teach it to the Israelites; have them recite it,[c] so that this song may be a witness for Me against the Israelites. ²⁰ When I bring them into the land I swore to ⌊give⌋ their fathers, ⌊a land⌋ flowing with milk and honey, they will eat their fill and prosper.[d] They will turn to other gods and worship them, despising Me and breaking My covenant. ²¹ And when many troubles and afflictions come to them, this song will testify against them, because[e] their descendants will not have forgotten it. For I know what they are prone to do,[f] even before I bring them into the land I swore ⌊to give them⌋." ²² So Moses wrote down this song on that day and taught it to the Israelites.

God Commissions Joshua

²³ The LORD commissioned Joshua son of Nun, "Be strong and courageous, for you will bring the Israelites into the land I swore to them, and I will be with you."

Moses Warns People

²⁴ When Moses had finished writing down on a scroll every single word[g] of this law, ²⁵ he commanded the Levites who carried the ark of the LORD's covenant, ²⁶ "Take this book of the law and place it beside the ark of the covenant of the LORD your God, so that it may re-

---

a31:11 Lit comes to appear   b31:17 Lit will be for devouring   c31:19 Lit Israelites; put it in their mouths   d31:20 Lit be fat   e31:21 Lit because the mouths of   f31:21 Or know the plans they are devising   g31:24 Lit scroll the words to their completion

main there as a witness against you.
²⁷ For I know how rebellious and stiff-necked you are. If you are rebelling against the LORD now, while I am still alive, how much more ⌊will you rebel⌋ after I am dead! ²⁸ Assemble all your tribal elders and officers before me, so that I may speak these words directly to them and call heaven and earth as witnesses against them. ²⁹ For I know that after my death you will become completely corrupt and turn from the path I have commanded you. Disaster will come to you in the future, because you will do what is evil in the LORD's sight, infuriating Him with what your hands have made." ³⁰ Then Moses recited aloud every single wordᵃ of this song to the entire assembly of Israel:

Warning Song of Moses

32 Pay attention, heavens, and I
will speak;
    listen, earth, to the words
      of my mouth.
² Let my teaching fall like rain
    and my word settle like dew,
    like gentle rain on new grass
    and showers on tender plants.
³ For I will proclaim
    the LORD's name.
    Declare the greatness of our God!
⁴ The Rock—His work is perfect;
    all His ways are entirely just.
    A faithful God, without prejudice,
    He is righteous and true.

⁵ His people have acted corruptly
    toward Him;
    this is their defectᵇ—they are not
    His children
    but a devious
    and crooked generation.
⁶ Is this how you repay the LORD,

you foolish and senseless people?
    Isn't He your Father and Creator?
    Didn't He make you
      and sustain you?
⁷ Remember the days of old;
    consider the years long past.
    Ask your father,
      and he will tell you,
    your elders,
      and they will teach you.
⁸ When the •Most High gave
    the nations their inheritanceᶜ
    and divided the •human race,
    He set the boundaries
      of the peoples
    according to the number
      of the people of Israel.ᵈ
⁹ But the LORD's portion is
      His people,
    Jacob, His own inheritance.

¹⁰ He found him in a desolate land,
    in a barren, howling wilderness;
    He surrounded him, cared for him,
    and guarded him as the pupil
      of His eye.
¹¹ He watches over His nest
      like an eagle
    and hovers over His young;
    He spreads His wings, catches him,
    and lifts him up on His pinions.
¹² The LORD alone led him,
    with no help from a foreign god.ᵉ
¹³ He made him ride on the heights
      of the land
    and eat the produce of the field.
    He nourished him with honey
      from the rock
    and oil from flintlike rock,
¹⁴ cream from the herd and milk
      from the flock,
    with the fat of lambs,
    rams from Bashan, and goats,
    with the choicest grains of wheat;

ᵃ**31:30** Lit *recited the words to their completion* ᵇ**32:5** Or *Him; through their fault*; Hb obscure ᶜ**32:8** Or *Most High divided the nations* ᵈ**32:8** One DSS reads *number of the sons of God*; LXX reads *number of the angels of God* ᵉ**32:12** Lit *him, and no foreign god with Him*

you drank wine
from the finest grapes.[a]

15 Then[b] Jeshurun[c] became fat
and rebelled—
you became fat, bloated,
and gorged.
He abandoned the God
who made him
and scorned the Rock
of his salvation.
16 They provoked His jealousy
with foreign gods;
they enraged Him
with detestable practices.
17 They sacrificed to demons,
not God,
to gods they had not known,
new gods that had just arrived,
which your fathers did not fear.
18 You ignored the Rock
who gave you birth;
you forgot the God
who brought you forth.

19 When the LORD saw ⌊this⌋,
He despised ⌊them⌋,
provoked ⌊to anger⌋ by His sons
and daughters.
20 He said: "I will hide My face
from them;
I will see what will become
of them,
for they are
a perverse generation—
unfaithful children.
21 They have provoked My jealousy
with ⌊their⌋ so-called gods;[d]
they have enraged Me
with their worthless idols.
So I will provoke their jealousy
with an inferior people;[e]
I will enrage them
with a foolish nation.
22 For fire has been kindled because of
My anger
and burns to the depths of •Sheol;
it devours the land and its produce,
and scorches the foundations
of the mountains.
23 I will pile disasters on them;
I will use up My arrows
against them.
24 They will be weak from hunger,
ravaged by pestilence
and bitter plague;
I will unleash on them wild beasts
with fangs,
as well as venomous snakes
that slither in the dust.
25 Outside, the sword will take
their children,
and inside, there will be terror;
the young man and the virgin
⌊will be killed⌋,
the infant and the gray-haired man.

26 I would have said: I will cut them
to pieces[f]
and blot out the memory of them
from mankind,
27 if I had not feared insult
from the enemy,
⌊or feared⌋ that these foes
might misunderstand
and say: Our own hand
has prevailed;
it wasn't the LORD who did
all this."

28 Israel is a nation lacking sense
with no understanding at all.[g]
29 If only they were wise,
they would figure it out;
they would understand their fate.
30 How could one man pursue
a thousand,
or two put ten thousand to flight,

[a]**32:14** Lit *the blood of grapes* [b]**32:15** DSS, Sam, LXX add *Jacob ate his fill;* [c]**32:15** = Upright One, referring to Israel [d]**32:21** Lit *with no gods* [e]**32:21** Lit *with no people* [f]**32:26** LXX reads *will scatter them* [g]**32:28** Lit *understanding in them*

unless their Rock had sold them,
unless the LORD had given
  them up?
31 But their "rock" is not
  like our Rock;
even our enemies concede.
32 For their vine is from the vine
  of Sodom
and from the fields of Gomorrah.
Their grapes are poisonous;
their clusters are bitter.
33 Their wine is serpents' venom,
the deadly poison of cobras.

34 "Is it not stored up with Me,
sealed up in My vaults?
35 Vengeance[a] belongs to Me;
  I will repay.[b]
In time their foot will slip,
for their day of disaster is near,
and their doom is coming quickly."
36 The LORD will indeed vindicate
  His people
and have compassion
  on His servants
when He sees that ⌊their⌋ strength
  is gone
and no one is left—slave or free.
37 He will say: "Where are their gods,
the 'rock' they found refuge in?
38 Who ate the fat of their sacrifices
and drank the wine
  of their drink offerings?
Let them rise up and help you;
let it[c] be a shelter for you.
39 See now that I alone am He;
there is no God but Me.
I bring death and I give life;
I wound and I heal.
No one can rescue ⌊anyone⌋
  from My hand.

40 I raise My hand to heaven
  and declare:
As surely as I live forever,
41 when I sharpen
  My flashing sword,
and My hand takes hold
  of judgment,
I will take vengeance
  on My adversaries
and repay those who hate Me.
42 I will make My arrows drunk
  with blood
while My sword devours flesh—
the blood of the slain
  and the captives,
the heads of the enemy leaders."[d]

43 Rejoice, you nations,
  over His people,[e]
for He will avenge the blood
  of His servants.[f]
He will take vengeance
  on His adversaries;[g]
He will purify His land
  and His people.[h]

Follow All the Words!

44 Moses came with Joshua[i] son of Nun and recited all the words of this song in the presence of the people. 45 After Moses finished reciting all these words to all Israel, 46 he said to them, "Take to heart all these words I am giving as a warning to you today, so that you may command your children to carefully follow all the words of this law. 47 For they are not meaningless words to you but they are your life, and by them you will live long in the land you are crossing the Jordan to possess."

[a]32:35 Sam, LXX read *On a day of vengeance*   [b]32:35 LXX, Tg, Vg read *Me; and recompense I will recompense*   [c]32:38 Sam, LXX, Tg, Vg read *them*   [d]32:42 Lit *the long-haired heads of the enemy*   [e]32:43 LXX reads *Rejoice, you heavens, along with Him, and let all the sons of God worship Him; rejoice, you nations, with His People, and let all the angels of God strengthen themselves in Him*; DSS reads *Rejoice, you heavens, along with Him, and let all the angels worship Him*; Heb 1:6   [f]32:43 DSS, LXX read *sons*   [g]32:43 DSS, LXX add *and He will recompense those who hate Him*; v. 41   [h]32:43 Syr, Tg; DSS, Sam, LXX, Vg read *His people's land*   [i]32:44 LXX, Syr, Vg; MT reads *Hoshea*; Nm 13:8,16

Moses' Death

Lord's Final Instructions

48 On that same day the LORD spoke to Moses, 49 "Go up Mount Nebo in the Abarim ⌊range⌋ in the land of Moab, across from Jericho, and view the land of Canaan I am giving the Israelites as a possession. 50 Then you will die on the mountain that you go up, and you will be gathered to your people, just as your brother Aaron died on Mount Hor and was gathered to his people. 51 For ⌊both of⌋ you broke faith with Me among the Israelites at the waters of Meribath-kadesh in the Wilderness of Zin by failing to treat Me as holy in their presence. 52 Although you will view the land from a distance, which I am giving the Israelites, you will not go there."

Moses Blesses Israel

33 This is the blessing that Moses, the man of God, gave the Israelites before his death. 2 He said:

The LORD came from Sinai
and appeared to them from Seir;
He shone ⌊on them⌋
   from Mount Paran
and came with ten thousand
   holy ones,[a]
with lightning[b]
   from His right hand[c] for them.
3 Indeed He loves the people.[d]
All Your[e] holy ones[f] are
   in Your hand,
and they assemble[g] at Your feet.
Each receives Your words.
4 Moses gave us instruction,
a possession for the assembly
   of Jacob.
5 So He became King in Jeshurun[h]

when the leaders of the people
   gathered
with the tribes of Israel.

6 Let Reuben live and not die
though his people become few.

7 He said this about Judah:

LORD, hear Judah's cry
   and bring him to his people.
He fights for his cause[i]
   with his own hands,
but may You be a help
   against his foes.

8 He said about Levi:

Your Thummim and Urim[j]
   belong to Your faithful one;[k]
You tested him at Massah
and contended with him
   at the waters of Meribah.
9 He said about his father and mother,
   "I do not regard them."
He disregarded his brothers
and didn't acknowledge his sons,
for they kept Your word
and maintained Your covenant.
10 They will teach Your ordinances
   to Jacob
and Your instruction to Israel;
they will set incense before You
and whole •burnt offerings
   on Your altar.
11 LORD, bless his possessions,[l]
and accept the work of his hands.
Smash the loins of his adversaries
   and enemies,
so that they cannot rise again.

12 He said about Benjamin:

The LORD's beloved rests[m] securely
   on Him.

a33:2 LXX reads *Mount Paran with ten thousands from Kadesh*   b33:2 Or *fiery law*; Hb obscure   c32:2 Or *ones, from His southland to the mountain slopes*   d33:3 Or *peoples*   e33:3 Lit *His*, or *its*   f33:3 Either the saints of Israel or angels   g33:3 Hb obscure   h33:5 = Upright One, referring to Israel   i33:7 Or *He contends for them*   j33:8 Two objects used to determine God's will   k33:8 DSS, LXX read *Give to Levi Your Thummim, Your Urim to Your favored one*   l33:11 Or *abilities*   m33:12 Or *Let the LORD's beloved rest*

Hea shields him all day long,
and he rests on His shoulders.b

13 He said about Joseph:

May his land be blessed
  by the LORD
with the dew of heaven's bounty
and the watery depths
  that lie beneath;
14 with the bountiful harvest
    from the sun
  and the abundant yield
    of the seasons;
15 with the best products
    of the ancient mountains
  and the bounty of the eternal hills;
16 with the choice gifts of the land
  and everything in it;
  and with the favor of Him
  who appearedc in the ⌊burning⌋ bush.
  May these rest on the head
    of Joseph,
  on the crown of the prince
    of his brothers.
17 His firstborn bull hasd splendor,
  and horns likee those of a wild ox;
  he gores all the peoples with them
  to the ends of the earth.
  Such are the ten thousands
    of Ephraim,
  and such are the thousands
    of Manasseh.

18 He said about Zebulun:

Rejoice, Zebulun, in your journeys,
and Issachar, in your tents.
19 They summon the peoples
    to a mountain;
  there they offer acceptable sacrifices.
  For they draw from the wealth
    of the seas
  and the hidden treasures of the sand.

20 He said about Gad:

The one who enlarges
  Gad's ⌊territory⌋
will be blessed.
He lies down like a lion
and tears off an arm or even a head.
21 He chose the best ⌊part⌋ for himself,
  because a ruler's portion
    was assigned there for him.
  He came ⌊with⌋ the leaders
    of the people;
  he carried out the LORD's justice
  and His ordinances for Israel.

22 He said about Dan:

Dan is a young lion,
leaping out of Bashan.

23 He said about Naphtali:

Naphtali, enjoying approval,
full of the LORD's blessing,
takef possession to the west
  and the south.

24 He said about Asher:

May Asherg be the most blessed
  of the sons;
may he be the most favored
  among his brothers
and dip his foot in ⌊olive⌋ oil.h
25 May the bolts of your gate be iron
    and bronze,
  and your strength last as long as
    you live.

26 There is none like the God
    of Jeshurun,i
  who rides the heavens to your aid
  on the clouds in His majesty.
27 The God of old is
    ⌊your⌋ dwelling place,
  and underneath are
    the everlasting arms.

---

a33:12 LXX reads The Most High   b33:12 Or and He dwells among his mountain slopes   c33:16 Lit dwelt
d33:17 Some DSS, Sam, LXX, Syr, Vg read A firstborn bull—he has   e33:17 Lit and his horns are   f33:23 Sam, LXX,
Syr, Vg, Tg read he will take   g33:24 = Happy or Blessed; Gn 30:13   h33:24 A symbol for prosperity
i33:26 = Upright One, referring to Israel

He drives out the enemy
  before you,
and commands, "Destroy!"

28 So Israel dwells securely;
Jacob lives untroubled[a]
in a land of grain and new wine;
even his skies drip with dew.

29 How happy you are, Israel!
Who is like you,
a people saved by the LORD?
He is the shield that protects you,
the sword you boast in.
Your enemies will cringe
  before you,
and you will tread on their backs.[b]

Moses Dies in Moab

34 Then Moses went up from the
plains of Moab to Mount Nebo, to
the top of Pisgah, which faces Jericho,
and the LORD showed him all the land:
Gilead as far as Dan, 2 all of Naphtali, the
land of Ephraim and Manasseh, all the
land of Judah as far as the Mediterranean[c] Sea, 3 the •Negev, and the region
from the Valley of Jericho, the City of
Palms, as far as Zoar. 4 The LORD then
said to him, "This is the land I promised
Abraham, Isaac, and Jacob, 'I will give it
to your descendants.' I have let you see

it with your own eyes, but you will not
cross into it."

5 So Moses the servant of the LORD
died there in the land of Moab, as the
LORD had said. 6 He buried him[d] in the
valley in the land of Moab facing Beth-
peor, and no one to this day knows
where his grave is. 7 Moses was 120
years old when he died; his eyes were
not weak, and his vitality had not left
⌊him⌋. 8 The Israelites wept for Moses in
the plains of Moab 30 days. Then the
days of weeping and mourning for Moses
came to an end.

Joshua Takes Over

9 Joshua son of Nun was filled with the
spirit of wisdom, because Moses had laid
his hands on him. So the Israelites
obeyed him and did as the LORD had
commanded Moses. 10 No prophet has
arisen again in Israel like Moses, whom
the LORD knew face to face. 11 ⌊He was
unparalleled⌋ for all the signs and wonders the LORD sent him to do against the
land of Egypt—to Pharaoh, to all his officials, and to all his land, 12 and for all the
mighty ⌊acts of⌋ power and terrifying
deeds that Moses performed in the sight
of all Israel.

---

[a]33:28 Text emended; MT reads *Jacob's fountain is alone*   [b]33:29 Or *high places*   [c]34:2 Lit *Western*   [d]34:6 Or *He*
was buried

JOSHUA

God Encourages Joshua

1 After the death of Moses the LORD's servant, the LORD spoke to Joshua[a] son of Nun, who had served Moses: [2] "Moses My servant is dead. Now you and all the people prepare to cross over the Jordan to the land I am giving the Israelites. [3] I have given you every place where the sole of your foot treads, just as I promised Moses. [4] Your territory will be from the wilderness and Lebanon to the great Euphrates River—all the land of the Hittites—and west to the Mediterranean Sea.[b] [5] No one will be able to stand against you as long as you live. I will be with you, just as I was with Moses. I will not leave you or forsake you.

[6] "Be strong and courageous, for you will distribute the land I swore to their fathers to give them as an inheritance. [7] Above all, be strong and very courageous to carefully observe the whole instruction My servant Moses commanded you. Do not turn from it to the right or the left, so that you will have success wherever you go. [8] This book of instruction must not depart from your mouth; you are to recite it day and night, so that you may carefully observe everything written in it. For then you will prosper and succeed in whatever you do. [9] Haven't I commanded you: be strong and courageous? Do not be afraid or discouraged, for the LORD your God is with you wherever you go."

Joshua Prepares the People

[10] Then Joshua commanded the officers of the people: [11] "Go through the camp and tell the people, 'Get provisions ready for yourselves, for within three days you will be crossing the Jordan to go in and take possession of the land the LORD your God is giving you to inherit.'"

[12] Joshua said to the Reubenites, the Gadites, and half the tribe of Manasseh: [13] "Remember what Moses the LORD's servant commanded you when he said, 'The LORD your God will give you rest, and He will give you this land.' [14] Your wives, young children, and livestock may remain in the land Moses gave you on this side of the Jordan.[c] But your fighting men must cross over in battle formation[d] ahead of your brothers[e] and help them [15] until the LORD gives our brothers rest, as ᵢHe has givenᵢ you, and they too possess the land the LORD your God is giving them. You may then return to the land of your inheritance and take possession of what Moses the LORD's servant gave you on the east side of the Jordan."

People's Positive Response

[16] They answered Joshua, "Everything you have commanded us we will do, and everywhere you send us we will go. [17] We will obey you, just as we obeyed Moses in everything. And may the LORD your God be with you, as He was with Moses. [18] Anyone who rebels against your order and does not obey your words in all that you command him, will be put to death. Above all, be strong and courageous!"

Joshua Sends Spies to Jericho

2 Joshua son of Nun secretly sent two men as spies from Acacia Grove,[f]

---

[a]**1:1** = The LORD Will Save, or The LORD Is Salvation; *Joshua* is related to the name *Jesus*.   [b]**1:4** Lit *and to the Great Sea, the going down of the sun*   [c]**1:14** East of the Jordan River   [d]**1:14** Or *over armed*   [e]**1:14** Fellow Israelites   [f]**2:1** Or *from Shittim*

saying, "Go and scout the land, especially Jericho." So they left, and they came to the house of a woman, <u>a prostitute named Rahab</u>, and stayed there.

² The king of Jericho was told, "Look, some of the Israelite men have come here tonight to investigate the land." ³ Then the king of Jericho sent ⌊word⌋ to Rahab and said, "Bring out the men who came to you and entered your house, for they came to investigate the entire land."

Rahab Deceives King

⁴ But the woman had taken the two men and hidden them. So she said, "Yes, the men did come to me, but I didn't know where they were from. ⁵ At nightfall, when the gate was about to close, the men went out, and I don't know where they were going. Chase after them quickly, and you can catch up with them!" ⁶ But she had taken them up to the roof and hidden them among the stalks of flax that she had arranged on the roof. ⁷ The men pursued them along the road to the fords of the Jordan, and as soon as they left to pursue them, the gate was shut.

Rahab Seeks Protection

⁸ Before the men fell asleep, she went up on the roof ⁹ and said to them, "I know that the LORD has given you this land and that dread of you has fallen on us, and everyone who lives in the land is panicking because of you.ᵃ ¹⁰ For we have heard how the LORD dried up the waters of the •Red Sea before you when you came out of Egypt, and what you did to Sihon and Og, the two Amorite kings you •completely destroyed across the Jordan. ¹¹ When we heard this, we lost heart, and everyone's courage failedᵇ be-cause of you, for the LORD your God is God in heaven above and on earth below. ¹² Now please swear to me by the LORD that you will also show kindness to my family, because I showed kindness to you.ᶜ Give me a sure signᵈ ¹³ that you will spare the lives of my father, mother, brothers, sisters, and all who belong to them, and save us from death."

Spies Promise Reward

¹⁴ The men answered her, "⌊We will give⌋ our lives for yours. If you don't report our mission, we will show kindness and faithfulness to you when the LORD gives us the land."

¹⁵ Then she let them down by a rope through the window, since she lived in a house that was ⌊built⌋ into the wall of the city. ¹⁶ "Go to the hill country so that the men pursuing you won't find you," she said to them. "Hide yourselves there for three days until they return; afterwards, go on your way."

The Scarlet Cord

¹⁷ The men said to her, "We will be free from this oath you made us swear, ¹⁸ unless, when we enter the land, you <u>tie this scarlet cord to the window</u> through which you let us down. Bring your father, mother, brothers, and all your father's family into your house. ¹⁹ If anyone goes out the doors of your house, his blood will be on his own head, and we will be innocent. But if anyone with you in the house should be harmed,ᵉ his blood will be on our heads. ²⁰ And if you report our mission, we are free from the oath you made us swear."

²¹ "Let it be as you say," she replied, and she sent them away. After they had gone, she tied the scarlet cord to the window.

ᵃ**2:9** Or *land panics at your approach*   ᵇ**2:11** Lit *and spirit no longer remained in anyone*   ᶜ**2:12** Lit *to your father's house*   ᵈ**2:12** Or *a sign of truth*   ᵉ**2:19** Lit *if a hand should be on him*

Spies Escape

²² So the two men went into the hill country and stayed there three days until the pursuers had returned. They searched all along the way, but did not find them. ²³ Then the men returned, came down from the hill country, and crossed ⌊the Jordan⌋. They went to Joshua son of Nun and reported everything that had happened to them. ²⁴ They told Joshua, "The LORD has handed over the entire land to us. Everyone who lives in the land is also panicking because of us."ª

Israel Crosses the Jordan

Rules of the Ark

3 Joshua started early the next morning and left Acacia Groveᵇ with all the Israelites. They went as far as the Jordan and stayed there before crossing. ² After three days the officers went through the camp ³ and commanded the people: "When you see the ark of the covenant of the LORD your God carried by the Levitical priests, you must break camp and follow it. ⁴ But keep a distance of about 1,000 yardsᶜ between yourselves and the ark. Don't go near it, so that you can see the way to go, for you haven't traveled this way before."ᵈ

⁵ Joshua told the people, "Consecrate yourselves, because the LORD will do wonders among you tomorrow." ⁶ Then he said to the priests, "Take the ark of the covenant and go on ahead of the people." So they carried the ark of the covenant and went ahead of them.

God Affirms His Support

⁷ The LORD spoke to Joshua: "Today I will begin to exalt you in the sight of all Israel, so they will know that I will be with you just as I was with Moses. ⁸ Command the priests carrying the ark of the covenant: 'When you reach the edge of the waters,ᵉ stand in the Jordan.'"

⁹ Then Joshua told the Israelites, "Come closer and listen to the words of the LORD your God." ¹⁰ He said, "You will know that the living God is among you and that He will certainly dispossess before you the Canaanites, Hittites, Hivites, Perizzites, Girgashites, Amorites, and Jebusites ¹¹ when the ark of the covenant of the Lord of all the earth goes ahead of you into the Jordan. ¹² Now choose 12 men from the tribes of Israel, one man for each tribe. ¹³ When the feetᶠ of the priests who carry the ark of the LORD, the Lord of all the earth, come to rest in the Jordan's waters, its waters will be cut off. The water flowing downstream will stand up ⌊in⌋ a mass."

Crossing the Jordan

¹⁴ When the people broke camp to cross the Jordan, the priests carried the ark of the covenant ahead of the people. ¹⁵ Now the Jordan overflows its banks throughout the harvest season. But as soon as the priests carrying the ark reached the Jordan, their feet touched the water at its edge ¹⁶ and the water flowing downstream stood still, rising up ⌊in⌋ a mass that extended as far asᵍ Adam, a city next to Zarethan. The water flowing downstream into the Sea of the •Arabah (the Dead Sea) was completely cut off, and the people crossed opposite Jericho. ¹⁷ The priests carrying the ark of the LORD's covenant stood firmly on dry ground in the middle of the Jordan, while all Israel crossed on dry ground until the entire nation had finished crossing the Jordan.

ª**2:24** Or *also panics at our approach*   ᵇ**3:1** Or *left Shittim*   ᶜ**3:4** Lit *2,000 cubits*   ᵈ**3:4** Lit *yesterday and the day before*   ᵉ**3:8** Lit *waters of the Jordan*   ᶠ**3:13** Lit *soles of the feet*   ᵍ**3:16** Alt Hb tradition reads *mass at*

Twelve Memorial Stones

4 After the entire nation had finished crossing the Jordan, the LORD spoke to Joshua, ² "Choose 12 men from the people, one man for each tribe, ³ and command them, 'Take 12 stones from this place in the middle of the Jordan where the priests' feet are standing, carry them with you, and set them down at the place where you spend the night.'"

⁴ So Joshua summoned the 12 men selected from the Israelites, one man for each tribe, ⁵ and said to them, "Go across to the ark of the LORD your God in the middle of the Jordan. Each of you lift a stone onto his shoulder, one for each ͣ of the Israelite tribes, ⁶ so that this will be a sign among you. In the future, when your children ask you, 'What do these stones mean to you?' ⁷ you should tell them, 'The waters of the Jordan were cut off in front of the ark of the LORD's covenant. When it crossed the Jordan, the Jordan's waters were cut off.' Therefore these stones will always be a memorial for the Israelites."

⁸ The Israelites did just as Joshua had commanded them. The 12 men took stones from the middle of the Jordan, one for each ᵇ of the Israelite tribes, just as the LORD had told Joshua. They carried them to the camp and set them down there. ⁹ Joshua also set up 12 stones in the middle of the Jordan where the priests ͨ who carried the ark of the covenant were standing. The stones are there to this day.

¹⁰ The priests carrying the ark continued standing in the middle of the Jordan until everything was completed that the LORD had commanded Joshua to tell the people, in keeping with all that Moses had commanded Joshua. The people hurried across, ¹¹ and after everyone had finished crossing, the priests with the ark of the LORD crossed in the sight of the people. ¹² The Reubenites, Gadites, and half the tribe of Manasseh went in battle formation in front of the Israelites, as Moses had instructed them. ¹³ About 40,000 equipped for war crossed to the plains of Jericho in the LORD's presence.

Joshua's Leadership Affirmed

¹⁴ On that day the LORD exalted Joshua in the sight of all Israel, and they revered him throughout his life, as they had revered Moses. ¹⁵ The LORD told Joshua, ¹⁶ "Command the priests who carry the ark of the •testimony ͩ to come up from the Jordan."

¹⁷ So Joshua commanded the priests, "Come up from the Jordan." ¹⁸ When the priests carrying the ark of the LORD's covenant came up from the middle of the Jordan, and their feet ͤ stepped out on solid ground, the waters of the Jordan resumed their course, flowing over all the banks as before.

Entering the Promised Land

Camp at Gilgal

¹⁹ The people came up from the Jordan on the tenth day of the first month, ͟ and camped at Gilgal on the eastern limits of Jericho. ²⁰ Then Joshua set up in Gilgal the 12 stones they had taken from the Jordan, ²¹ and he said to the Israelites, "When your children ask their fathers in the future, 'What is the meaning of these stones?' ²² you should tell your children, 'Israel crossed the Jordan on dry ground.' ²³ For the LORD your God dried up the waters of the Jordan before you until you had crossed over, just as

---

ͣ**4:5** Lit *shoulder according to the number*   ᵇ**4:8** Lit *Jordan according to the number*   ͨ**4:9** Lit *feet of the priests*
ͩ**4:16** The ark of the covenant   ͤ**4:18** Lit *and the soles of the feet of the priests*   ͟**4:19** = Nisan (March–April)

the LORD your God did to the •Red Sea, which He dried up before us until we had crossed over. ²⁴ This is so that all the people of the earth may know that the LORD's hand is mighty, and so that you may always •fear the LORD your God."

God Commands Circumcision

5 When all the Amorite kings across the Jordan to the west and all the Canaanite kings near the sea heard how the LORD had dried up the waters of the Jordan before the Israelites until they had crossed over, they lost heart and their courage failed ᵃ because of the Israelites.

² At that time the LORD said to Joshua, "Make flint knives and circumcise the Israelite men again." ³ So Joshua made flint knives and circumcised the Israelite men at Gibeath-haaraloth.ᵇ ⁴ This is the reason Joshua circumcised ⌊them⌋: All the people who came out of Egypt who were males—all the men of war—had died in the wilderness along the way after they had come out of Egypt. ⁵ Though all the people who came out were circumcised, none of the people born in the wilderness along the way were circumcised after they had come out of Egypt. ⁶ For the Israelites wandered in the wilderness 40 years until all the nation's men of war who came out of Egypt had died off because they did not obey the LORD. So the LORD vowed never to let them see the land He had sworn to their fathers to give us, a land flowing with milk and honey. ⁷ Joshua raised up their sons in their place; it was these he circumcised. They were still uncircumcised, since they had not been circumcised along the way. ⁸ After the entire nation had been circumcised, they stayed where they were in the camp un-

til they recovered. ⁹ The LORD then said to Joshua, "Today I have rolled away the disgrace of Egypt from you." Therefore, that place has been called Gilgalᶜ to this day.

Manna Ceases—Food from the Land

¹⁰ While the Israelites camped at Gilgal on the plains of Jericho, they kept the •Passover on the evening of the fourteenth day of the month.ᵈ ¹¹ The day after Passover they ate unleavened bread and roasted grain from the produce of the land. ¹² And the day after they ate from the produce of the land, the manna ceased. Since there was no more manna for the Israelites, they ate from the crops of the land of Canaan that year.

Joshua Meets Commander of LORD's Army

¹³ When Joshua was near Jericho, he looked up and saw a man standing in front of him with a drawn sword in His hand. Joshua approached Him and asked, "Are You for us or for our enemies?"

¹⁴ "Neither," He replied. "I have now come as commander of the LORD's army."

Then Joshua bowed with his face to the ground in worship and asked Him, "What does my Lord want to say to His servant?"

¹⁵ The commander of the Lord's army said to Joshua, "Remove the sandals from your feet, for the place where you are standing is holy." And Joshua did so.

Conquest of Jericho
God's Battle Strategy

6 Now Jericho was strongly fortified because of the Israelites—no one leaving or entering. ² The LORD said to

---

ᵃ**5:1** Lit *and they did not have spirit in them any more*   ᵇ**5:3** Or *The Hill of Foreskins*   ᶜ**5:9** = to roll   ᵈ**5:10** = Nisan (March–April)

Joshua, "Look, I have handed Jericho, its king, and its fighting men over to you. ³ March around the city with all the men of war, circling the city one time. Do this for six days. ⁴ Have seven priests carry seven ram's-horn trumpets in front of the ark. But on the seventh day, march around the city seven times, while the priests blow the trumpets. ⁵ When there is a prolonged blast of the horn and you hear its sound, have all the people give a mighty shout. Then the city wall will collapse, and the people will advance, each man straight ahead."

Joshua Complies

⁶ So Joshua son of Nun summoned the priests and said to them, "Take up the ark of the covenant and have seven priests carry seven trumpets in front of the ark of the LORD." ⁷ He said to the people, "Move forward, march around the city, and have the armed troops go ahead of the ark of the LORD."

⁸ After Joshua had spoken to the people, seven priests carrying seven trumpets before the LORD moved forward and blew the trumpets; the ark of the LORD's covenant followed them. ⁹ While the trumpets were blowing, the armed troops went in front of the priests who blew the trumpets, and the rear guard went behind the ark. ¹⁰ But Joshua had commanded the people: "Do not shout or let your voice be heard. Don't let one word come out of your mouth until the time I say, 'Shout!' Then you are to shout." ¹¹ So the ark of the LORD was carried around the city, circling it once. They returned to the camp and spent the night there.ᵃ

¹² Joshua got up early the next morning. The priests took the ark of the LORD, ¹³ and the seven priests carrying seven trumpets marched in front of the ark of the LORD. While the trumpets were blowing, the armed troops went in front of them, and the rear guard went behind the ark of the LORD. ¹⁴ On the second day they marched around the city once and returned to the camp. They did this for six days.

Seventh Day

¹⁵ Early on the seventh day, they started at dawn and marched around the city seven times in the same way. That was the only day they marched around the city seven times. ¹⁶ After the seventh time, the priests blew the trumpets, and Joshua said to the people, "Shout! For the LORD has given you the city. ¹⁷ But the city and everything in it are •set apart to the LORD for destruction. Only Rahab the prostitute and everyone with her in the house will live, because she hid the menᵇ we sent. ¹⁸ But keep yourselves from the things set apart, or you will be set apart for destruction. If youᶜ take any of those things, you will set apart the camp of Israel for destruction and bring disaster on it. ¹⁹ For all the silver and gold, and the articles of bronze and iron, are dedicated to the LORD and must go into the LORD's treasury."

²⁰ So the people shouted, and the trumpets sounded. When they heard the blast of the trumpet, the people gave a great shout, and the wall collapsed. The people advanced into the city, each man straight ahead, and they captured the city. ²¹ They •completely destroyed everything in the city with the sword—every man and woman, both young and old, and every ox, sheep, and donkey.

ᵃ**6:11** Lit *at the camp*   ᵇ**6:17** Lit *messengers*   ᶜ**6:18** LXX reads *you covet and*; Jos 7:21

Rahab and Family Spared

22 Joshua said to the two men who had scouted the land, "Go to the prostitute's house and bring the woman out of there, and all who are with her, just as you promised her." 23 So the young men who had scouted went in and brought out Rahab and her father, mother, brothers, and all who belonged to her. They brought out her whole family and settled them outside the camp of Israel.

24 They burned up the city and everything in it, but they put the silver and gold and the articles of bronze and iron into the treasury of the LORD's house. 25 But Joshua spared Rahab the prostitute, her father's household, and all who belonged to her, because she hid the men Joshua had sent to spy on Jericho, and she lives in Israel to this day.

26 At that time Joshua imposed this curse:

Cursed before the LORD is the man who undertakes the rebuilding of this city, Jericho.
He will lay its foundation ⌊at the cost of⌋ his firstborn;
He will set up its gates ⌊at the cost of⌋ his youngest.

27 And the LORD was with Joshua, and his fame spread throughout the land.

Israel Defeated at Ai

7 The Israelites, however, were unfaithful regarding the things ⸱set apart for destruction. Achan son of Carmi, son of Zabdi, son of Zerah, of the tribe of Judah, took some of what was set apart, and the LORD's anger burned against the Israelites.

2 Joshua sent men from Jericho to Ai, which is near Beth-aven, east of Bethel, and told them, "Go up and scout the land." So the men went up and scouted Ai.

3 After returning to Joshua they reported to him, "Don't send all the people, but send about 2,000 or 3,000[a] men to attack Ai. Since the people of Ai are so few, don't wear out all our people there." 4 So about 3,000 men[b] went up there, but they fled from the men of Ai. 5 The men of Ai struck down about 36 of them and chased them from outside the gate to the quarries,[c] striking them down on the descent. As a result, the people's hearts melted and became like water.

Joshua Despairs

6 Then Joshua tore his clothes and fell before the ark of the LORD with his face to the ground until evening, as did the elders of Israel; they all put dust on their heads. 7 "Oh, Lord GOD," Joshua said, "why did You ever bring these people across the Jordan to hand us over to the Amorites for our destruction? If only we had been content to remain on the other side of the Jordan! 8 What can I say, Lord, now that Israel has turned its back ⌊and run⌋ from its enemies? 9 When the Canaanites and all who live in the land hear about this, they will surround us and wipe out our name from the earth. Then what will You do about Your great name?"

Lord Explains Remedy

10 The LORD then said to Joshua, "Stand up! Why are you on the ground?[d] 11 Israel has sinned. They have violated My covenant that I appointed for them. They have taken some of what was set apart. They have stolen, deceived, and put ⌊the things⌋ with their own belongings. 12 This is why the Israelites cannot

stand against their enemies. They will turn their backs ₍and run₎ from their enemies, because they have been set apart for destruction. I will no longer be with you unless you remove from you what is set apart.

¹³ "Go and consecrate the people. Tell them to consecrate themselves tomorrow, for this is what the LORD, the God of Israel, says, 'There are among you, Israel, things set apart. You will not be able to stand against your enemies until you remove what is set apart. ¹⁴ In the morning you must present yourselves tribe by tribe. The tribe the LORD selects is to come forward clan by clan. The clan the LORD selects is to come forward family by family. The family the LORD selects is to come forward man by man. ¹⁵ The one who is caught with the things set apart must be burned,ᵃ along with everything he has, because he has violated the LORD's covenant and committed an outrage in Israel.'"

Joshua Accuses Achan

¹⁶ Joshua got up early the next morning. He had Israel come forward tribe by tribe, and the tribe of Judah was selected. ¹⁷ He had the clans of Judah come forward, and the Zerahite clan was selected. He had the Zerahite clan come forward by heads of families,ᵇ and Zabdi was selected. ¹⁸ He then had Zabdi's family come forward man by man, and Achan son of Carmi, son of Zabdi, son of Zerah, of the tribe of Judah, was selected. ¹⁹ So Joshua said to Achan, "My son, give glory to the LORD, the God of Israel, and make a confession to Him.ᶜ I urge you, tell me what you have done. Don't hide anything from me."

Achan Confesses

²⁰ Achan replied to Joshua, "It is true. I have sinned against the LORD, the God of Israel. This is what I did: ²¹ When I saw among the spoils a beautiful cloak from Babylon,ᵈ 200 silver •shekels,ᵉ and a bar of gold weighing 50 shekels,ᶠ I coveted them and took them. You can see for yourself. They are concealed in the ground inside my tent, with the money under the cloak." ²² So Joshua sent messengers who ran to the tent, and there was the cloak, concealed in his tent, with the money underneath. ²³ They took the things from inside the tent, brought them to Joshua and all the Israelites, and spread them out in the LORD's presence.

Achan Stoned

²⁴ Then Joshua and all Israel with him took Achan son of Zerah, the silver, the cloak, and the bar of gold, his sons and daughters, his ox, donkey, and sheep, his tent, and all that he had, and brought them up to the Valley of Achor. ²⁵ Joshua said, "Why have you troubled us? Today the LORD will trouble you!" So all Israel stoned him to death. They burned their bodies,ᵍ threw stones on them, ²⁶ and raised over him a large pile of rocks that remains to this day. Then the LORD turned from His burning anger. Therefore that place has been called the Valley of Achorʰ to this day.

Israel Ambushes Ai

8 The LORD said to Joshua, "Do not be afraid or discouraged. Take the whole military force with you and go attack Ai. Look, I have handed over to you the king of Ai, his people, city, and land. ² Treat Ai and its king as you did Jericho

---

ᵃ**7:15** Lit burned with fire ᵇ**7:17** Lit forward man by man ᶜ**7:19** Or and praise Him ᵈ**7:21** Lit Shinar ᵉ**7:21** About 5 pounds of silver ᶠ**7:21** About 1 pound of gold ᵍ**7:25** Lit burned them with fire ʰ**7:26** Or of Trouble

and its king; you may plunder its spoil and livestock for yourselves. Set an ambush behind the city."

³ So Joshua and the whole military force set out to attack Ai. Joshua selected 30,000 fighting men and sent them out at night. ⁴ He commanded them: "Pay attention. Lie in ambush behind the city, not too far from it, and all of you be ready. ⁵ Then I and all the people who are with me will approach the city. When they come out against us as they did the first time, we will flee from them. ⁶ They will come after us until we have drawn them away from the city, for they will say, 'They are fleeing from us as before.' While we are fleeing from them,⁷ you are to come out of your ambush and seize the city, for the LORD your God has handed it over to you. ⁸ After taking the city, set it on fire. Follow the LORD's command—see ʟthat you doʟ as I have ordered you." ⁹ So Joshua sent them out, and they went to the ambush site and waited between Bethel and Ai, to the west of Ai. But he spent that night with the troops.

¹⁰ Joshua started early the next morning and mobilized them. Then he and the elders of Israel led the troops up to Ai. ¹¹ All thoseᵃ who were with him went up and approached the city, arriving opposite Ai, and camped to the north of it, with a valley between them and the city. ¹² Now Joshua had taken about 5,000 men and set them in ambush between Bethel and Ai, to the west of the city. ¹³ The military force was stationed in this way: the mainᵇ camp to the north of the city and its rear guard to the west of the city. And that night Joshua went into the valley.

¹⁴ When the king of Ai saw ʟthe Israelitesʟ, the men of the city hurried and went out early in the morning, so that he and all his people could engage Israel in battle at a suitable place facing the plainᶜ ʟof the Jordanʟ. But he did not know there was an ambush ʟwaitingʟ for him behind the city. ¹⁵ Joshua and all Israel pretended to be beaten back by them and fled toward the wilderness. ¹⁶ Then all the troops of Ai were summoned to pursue them, and they pursued Joshua and were drawn away from the city. ¹⁷ Not a man was left in Ai or Bethel who did not go out after Israel, leaving the city exposed while they pursued Israel.

¹⁸ Then the LORD said to Joshua, "Hold out the sword in your hand toward Ai, for I will hand the city over to you." So Joshua held out his sword toward it. ¹⁹ When he held out his hand, the men in ambush rose quickly from their position. They ran, entered the city, captured it, and immediately set it on fire.

Ai in Flames

²⁰ The men of Ai turned and looked back, and smoke from the city was rising to the sky! They could not escape in any direction, and the troops who had fled to the wilderness now became the pursuers. ²¹ When Joshua and all Israel saw that the ʟmen inʟ ambush had captured the city and that smoke was rising from it, they turned back and struck down the men of Ai. ²² The men in the ambush came out of the city against them, and the men of Ai were ʟtrappedʟ between the Israelite forces, some on one side and some on the other. They struck them down until no survivor or fugitive remained, ²³ but they captured the king of Ai alive and brought him to Joshua.

ᵃ8:11 Lit the people of war   ᵇ8:13 Lit way: all the   ᶜ8:14 Or the Arabah

Total Destruction of Ai

24 When Israel had finished killing everyone living in Ai who had pursued them into the open country, and when every last one of them had fallen by the sword, all Israel returned to Ai and struck it down with the sword. 25 The total of those who fell that day, both men and women, was 12,000—all the people of Ai. 26 Joshua did not draw back his hand that was holding the sword until all the inhabitants of Ai were •completely destroyed. 27 Israel plundered only the cattle and spoil of that city for themselves, according to the LORD's command that He had given Joshua.

28 Joshua burned Ai and left it a permanent ruin, desolate to this day. 29 He hung[a] ⌊the body of⌋ the king of Ai on a tree[b] until evening, and at sunset Joshua commanded that they take his body down from the tree. They threw it down at the entrance of the city gate and put a large pile of rocks over it, which remains to this day.

Joshua Renews Commitment to Law

30 At that time Joshua built an altar on Mount Ebal to the LORD, the God of Israel, 31 just as Moses the LORD's servant had commanded the Israelites. He built it according to what is written in the book of the law of Moses: an altar of uncut stones on which no iron tool has been used. Then they offered •burnt offerings to the LORD and sacrificed •fellowship offerings on it. 32 There on the stones, Joshua copied the law of Moses, which he had written in the presence of the Israelites. 33 All Israel, foreigner and citizen alike, with their elders, officers, and judges, stood on either side of the ark of the LORD's covenant facing the Levitical priests who carried it. As Moses the LORD's servant had commanded earlier, half of them were in front of Mount Gerizim and half in front of Mount Ebal, to bless the people of Israel.

Joshua Reads Entire Law

34 Afterwards, Joshua read aloud all the words of the law—the blessings as well as the curses—according to all that is written in the book of the law. 35 There was not a word of all that Moses had commanded that Joshua did not read before the entire assembly of Israel, including the women, little children, and foreigners who were with them.

The Gibeon Affair

Alliance Against Israel

9 When all the kings heard ⌊about Jericho and Ai⌋, those who were west of the Jordan in the hill country, in the Judean foothills,[c] and all along the coast of the Mediterranean Sea toward Lebanon—the Hittites, Amorites, Canaanites, Perizzites, Hivites, and Jebusites— 2 they formed a unified alliance to fight against Joshua and Israel.

Gibeon's Deceit

3 When the inhabitants of Gibeon heard what Joshua had done to Jericho and Ai, 4 they acted deceptively. They gathered provisions[d] and took worn-out sacks on their donkeys and old wineskins, cracked and mended. 5 ⌊They wore⌋ old, patched sandals on their feet and threadbare clothing on their bodies. Their entire provision of bread was dry and crumbly. 6 They went to Joshua in the camp at Gilgal and said to him and the men of Israel, "We have come from a distant land. Please make a treaty with us."

a8:29 Or *impaled*   b8:29 Or *wooden stake*   c9:1 Or *the Shephelah*   d9:4 Some Hb mss, LXX, Syr, Vg; MT reads *They went disguised as ambassadors*

Gibeon Negotiates

7 The men of Israel replied to the Hivites,[a] "Perhaps you live among us. How can we make a treaty with you?"

8 They said to Joshua, "We are your servants."

Then Joshua asked them, "Who are you and where do you come from?"

9 They replied to him, "Your servants have come from a far away land because of the reputation of the LORD your God. For we have heard of His fame, and all that He did in Egypt, 10 and all that He did to the two Amorite kings beyond the Jordan—Sihon king of Heshbon and Og king of Bashan, who was in Ashtaroth. 11 So our elders and all the inhabitants of our land told us, 'Take provisions with you for the journey; go and meet them and say, "We are your servants. Please make a treaty with us." ' 12 This bread of ours was warm when we took it from our houses as food on the day we left to come to you. But take a look, it is now dry and crumbly. 13 These wineskins were new when we filled them, but look, they are cracked. And these clothes and sandals of ours are worn out from the extremely long journey." 14 Then the men ⌊of Israel⌋ took some of their provisions, but did not seek the LORD's counsel. 15 So Joshua established peace with them and made a treaty to let them live, and the leaders of the community swore an oath to them.

Gibeon Unmasked

16 Three days after making the treaty with them, they heard that the Gibeonites were their neighbors, living among them. 17 So the Israelites set out and reached the Gibeonite cities on the third day. Now their cities were Gibeon, Chephirah, Beeroth, and Kiriath-jearim.

18 But the Israelites did not attack them, because the leaders of the community had sworn an oath to them by the LORD, the God of Israel. Then the whole community grumbled against the leaders.

Israel Honors Treaty

19 All the leaders answered them, "We have sworn an oath to them by the LORD, the God of Israel, and now we cannot touch them. 20 This is how we will treat them: we will let them live, so that no wrath will fall on us because of the oath we swore to them." 21 They also said, "Let them live." So the Gibeonites became woodcutters and water carriers for the whole community, as the leaders had promised them.

Joshua Issues Curse

22 Joshua summoned the Gibeonites and said to them, "Why did you deceive us by telling us you live far away from us, when in fact you live among us? 23 Therefore you are cursed and will always be slaves—woodcutters and water carriers for the house of my God."

24 The Gibeonites answered him, "It was clearly reported to your servants that the LORD your God had commanded His servant Moses to give you all the land and to destroy all the inhabitants of the land before you. We greatly feared for our lives because of you, and that is why we did this. 25 Now we are in your hands. Do to us whatever you think is right."[b] 26 This is what Joshua did to them: he delivered them from the hands of the Israelites, and they did not kill them. 27 On that day he made them woodcutters and water carriers—as they are today—for the community and for the LORD's altar at the place He would choose.

---

[a]9:7 = the men of Gibeon   [b]9:25 Lit us as is good and as is right in your eyes do

Day the Sun Stood Still

Amorite Kings Join Forces

10 Now <u>Adoni-zedek king of Jerusalem</u> heard that Joshua had captured Ai and •completely destroyed it, doing to Ai and its king as he had done to Jericho and its king, and that the inhabitants of Gibeon had made peace with Israel and were ⌞living⌟ among them. [2] So Adoni-zedek and his people were[a] greatly alarmed because Gibeon was a large city like one of the royal cities; it was larger than Ai, and all its men were warriors. [3] Therefore Adoni-zedek king of Jerusalem sent ⌞word⌟ to Hoham king of Hebron, Piram king of Jarmuth, Japhia king of Lachish, and Debir king of Eglon, saying, [4] "Come up and help me. We will attack Gibeon, because they have made peace with Joshua and the Israelites." [5] So the five Amorite kings—the kings of Jerusalem, Hebron, Jarmuth, Lachish, and Eglon—joined forces, advanced with all their armies, besieged Gibeon, and fought against it.

Gibeon's Plea

[6] Then the men of Gibeon sent ⌞word⌟ to Joshua in the camp at Gilgal: "Don't abandon[b] your servants. Come quickly and save us! Help us, for all the Amorite kings living in the hill country have joined forces against us." [7] So Joshua and his whole military force, including all the fighting men, came from Gilgal.

Lord Reassures

[8] The LORD said to Joshua, "Do not be afraid of them, for I have handed them over to you. Not one of them will be able to stand against you."

Joshua's Surprise Attack

[9] So Joshua caught them by surprise, after marching all night from Gilgal.

[10] The LORD threw them into confusion before Israel. He defeated them in a great slaughter at Gibeon, chased them through the ascent of Beth-horon, and struck them down as far as Azekah and Makkedah. [11] As they fled before Israel, the LORD threw large hailstones on them from the sky along the descent of Beth-horon all the way to Azekah, and they died. More of them died from the hail than the Israelites killed with the sword.

Joshua's Public Prayer

[12] On the day the LORD gave the Amorites over to the Israelites, Joshua spoke to the LORD in the presence of Israel:

"Sun, stand still over Gibeon,
and moon, over the valley
of Aijalon."
[13] And the sun stood still
and the moon stopped,
until the nation took vengeance
on its enemies.

Isn't this written in the Book of Jashar?[c]

So the sun stopped
in the middle of the sky
and delayed its setting
almost a full day.

[14] <u>There has been no day like it before or since, when the LORD listened to the voice of a man, because the LORD fought for Israel.</u> [15] Then Joshua and all Israel with him returned to the camp at Gilgal.

Execution of Five Kings

[16] Now the five ⌞defeated⌟ kings had fled and hidden themselves in the cave at Makkedah. [17] It was reported to Joshua: "The five kings have been found; they are hiding in the cave at Makkedah." [18] Joshua said, "Roll large stones against the mouth of the cave, and station men by it to guard the kings. [19] But

---

[a]**10:2** One Hb ms, Syr, Vg read *So he was*   [b]**10:6** Lit *Don't let your hand go from*   [c]**10:13** Or *of the Upright*

as for the rest of you, don't stay there. Pursue your enemies and attack them from behind. Don't let them enter their cities, for the LORD your God has handed them over to you." [20] So Joshua and the Israelites finished inflicting a terrible slaughter on them until they were destroyed, although a few survivors ran away to the fortified cities. [21] The people returned safely to Joshua in the camp at Makkedah. No one could say a thing[a] against the Israelites.

[22] Then Joshua said, "Open the mouth of the cave, and bring those five kings to me out of there." [23] That is what they did. They brought the five kings of Jerusalem, Hebron, Jarmuth, Lachish, and Eglon to Joshua out of the cave. [24] When they had brought the kings to him, Joshua summoned all the men of Israel and said to the military commanders who had accompanied him, "Come here and put your feet on the necks of these kings." So the commanders came forward and put their feet on their necks. [25] Joshua said to them, "Do not be afraid or discouraged. Be strong and courageous, for the LORD will do this to all the enemies you fight."

[26] After this, Joshua struck them down and executed them. He hung[b] their bodies on five trees[c] and they were there until evening. [27] At sunset Joshua commanded that they be taken down from the trees[c] and thrown into the cave where they had hidden. Then large stones were placed against the mouth of the cave, and the stones are there to this day.

Joshua Conquers Southern Cities

[28] On that day Joshua captured Makkedah and struck it down with the sword, including its king. He completely destroyed it[d] and everyone in it, leaving no survivors. So he treated the king of Makkedah as he had the king of Jericho.

[29] Joshua and all Israel with him crossed from Makkedah to Libnah and fought against Libnah. [30] The LORD also handed it and its king over to Israel. He struck it down, putting everyone in it to the sword, and left no survivors in it. He treated Libnah's king as he had the king of Jericho.

[31] From Libnah, Joshua and all Israel with him crossed to Lachish. They laid siege to it and attacked it. [32] The LORD handed Lachish over to Israel, and Joshua captured it on the second day. He struck it down, putting everyone in it to the sword, just as he had done to Libnah. [33] At that time Horam king of Gezer went to help Lachish, but Joshua struck him down along with his people, leaving no survivors in it.

[34] Then Joshua crossed from Lachish to Eglon and all Israel with him. They laid siege to it and attacked it. [35] On that day they captured it and struck it down, putting everyone in it to the sword. He completely destroyed it that day, just as he had done to Lachish.

[36] Next, Joshua and all Israel with him went up from Eglon to Hebron and attacked it. [37] They captured it and struck down its king, all its villages, and everyone in it with the sword. Just as he had done at Eglon, he left no survivors. He completely destroyed Hebron and everyone in it.

[38] Finally, Joshua turned toward Debir and attacked it. And all Israel was with him. [39] He captured it—its king and all its villages. They struck them down with the sword and completely destroyed everyone in it, leaving no survivors. He treated Debir and its king as he had treated Hebron and as he had treated Libnah and its king.

---

[a]**10:21** Lit *No one sharpened his tongue*   [b]**10:26** Or *impaled*   [c]**10:26,27** Or *wooden stakes*   [d]**10:28** Other Hb mss read *them*

⁴⁰ So Joshua conquered the whole region—the hill country, the •Negev, the Judean foothills,ᵃ and the slopes—with all their kings, leaving no survivors. He completely destroyed every living being, as the LORD, the God of Israel, had commanded. ⁴¹ Joshua conquered everyone from Kadesh-barnea to Gaza, and all the land of Goshen as far as Gibeon. ⁴² Joshua captured all these kings and their land in one campaign,ᵇ because the LORD, the God of Israel, fought for Israel. ⁴³ Then Joshua returned with all Israel to the camp at Gilgal.

Joshua Conquers Northern Cities

11 When Jabin king of Hazor heard ⌊this news⌋, he sent ⌊a message⌋ to:

Jobab king of Madon,
the kings of Shimron and Achshaph,
² and the kings of the north
in the hill country,
the plainᶜ south of Chinnereth,
the Judean foothills,ᵈ
and the Slopes of Dorᵉ to the west,
³ the Canaanites in the east and west,
the Amorites, Hittites, Perizzites,
and Jebusites in the hill country,
and the Hivites at the foot of Hermon
in the land of Mizpah.

⁴ They went out with all their armies—a multitude as numerous as the sand on the seashore—along with a vast number of horses and chariots. ⁵ All these kings joined forces; they came together and camped at the waters of Merom to attack Israel.

God: "Do not be afraid"

⁶ The LORD said to Joshua, "Do not be afraid of them, for at this time tomorrow I will hand all of them over dead to Is-

rael. You are to hamstring their horses and burn up their chariots."

Joshua Prevails

⁷ So Joshua and his whole military force surprised them at the waters of Merom and attacked them. ⁸ The LORD handed them over to Israel, and they struck them down, pursuing them as far as Great Sidon and Misrephoth-maim, and to the east as far as the valley of Mizpeh.ᶠ They struck them down, leaving no survivors. ⁹ Joshua treated them as the LORD had told him; he hamstrung their horses and burned up their chariots.

¹⁰ At that time Joshua turned back, captured Hazor, and struck down its king with the sword, because Hazor had formerly been the leader of all these kingdoms. ¹¹ They struck down everyone in it with the sword, •completely destroying them; he left no one alive. Then he burned down Hazor.

¹² Joshua captured all these kings and their cities and struck them down with the sword. He completely destroyed them, as Moses the LORD's servant had commanded. ¹³ However, Israel did not burn any of the cities that stood on their mounds except Hazor, which Joshua burned. ¹⁴ The Israelites plundered all the spoils and cattle of these cities for themselves. But they struck down every person with the sword until they had annihilated them, leaving no one alive. ¹⁵ Just as the LORD had commanded His servant Moses, Moses commanded Joshua. That is what Joshua did, leaving nothing undone of all that the LORD had commanded Moses.

Summary of Conquests

¹⁶ So Joshua took all this land—the hill country, all the •Negev, all the land of

---

ᵃ**10:40** Or *the Shephelah* ᵇ**10:42** Lit *land at one time* ᶜ**11:2** Or *the Arabah* ᵈ**11:2** Or *the Shephelah* ᵉ**11:2** Or *and in Naphoth-dor* ᶠ**11:8** = *Mizpah*; Jos 11:3; 18:26

Goshen, the Judean foothills,[a] the plain,[b] and the hill country of Israel with its Judean foothills[c]— [17] from Mount Halak, which ascends to Seir, as far as Baal-gad in the Valley of Lebanon at the foot of Mount Hermon. He captured all their kings and struck them down, putting them to death. [18] Joshua waged war with all these kings for a long time. [19] No city made peace with the Israelites except the Hivites who inhabited Gibeon; all of them were taken in battle. [20] For it was the LORD's intention to harden their hearts, so that they would engage Israel in battle, be completely destroyed without mercy, and be annihilated, just as the LORD had commanded Moses.

[21] At that time Joshua proceeded to exterminate the Anakim from the hill country—Hebron, Debir, Anab—all the hill country of Judah and of Israel. Joshua completely destroyed them with their cities. [22] No Anakim were left in the land of the Israelites, except for some remaining in Gaza, Gath, and Ashdod.

[23] So Joshua took the entire land, in keeping with all that the LORD had told Moses. Joshua then gave it as an inheritance to Israel according to their tribal allotments. After this, the land had rest from war.

Moses' Conquests East of Jordan

12 The Israelites struck down the following kings of the land and took possession of their land beyond the Jordan to the east and from the Arnon Valley to Mount Hermon, including all the •Arabah eastward:

[2] Sihon king of the Amorites lived in Heshbon. He ruled ⌊over the territory⌋ from Aroer on the rim of the Arnon Valley, along the middle of the valley, and half of Gilead up to the Jabbok River (the border of the Ammonites), [3] the Arabah east of the Sea of Chinnereth[d] to the Sea of the Arabah (that is, the Dead Sea), eastward through Beth-jeshimoth and southward[e] below the slopes of Pisgah.

[4] Og[f] king of Bashan, of the remnant of the Rephaim, lived in Ashtaroth and Edrei. [5] He ruled over Mount Hermon, Salecah, all Bashan up to the Geshurite and Maacathite border, and half of Gilead to the border of Sihon, king of Heshbon.

[6] Moses the LORD's servant and the Israelites struck them down. And Moses the LORD's servant gave their land as an inheritance to the Reubenites, Gadites, and half the tribe of Manasseh.

Joshua's Conquests West of Jordan

[7] Joshua and the Israelites struck down the following kings of the land beyond the Jordan to the west, from Baal-gad in the valley of Lebanon to Mount Halak, which ascends toward Seir (Joshua gave their land as an inheritance to the tribes of Israel according to their allotments: [8] the hill country, the Judean foothills,[a] the plain,[b] the slopes, the desert, and the •Negev of the Hittites, Amorites, Canaanites, Perizzites, Hivites, and Jebusites):

[9] the king of Jericho	one
the king of Ai, which is	
next to Bethel	one
[10] the king of Jerusalem	one
the king of Hebron	one
[11] the king of Jarmuth	one
the king of Lachish	one
[12] the king of Eglon	one

the king of Gezer	one
13 the king of Debir	one
the king of Geder	one
14 the king of Hormah	one
the king of Arad	one
15 the king of Libnah	one
the king of Adullam	one
16 the king of Makkedah	one
the king of Bethel	one
17 the king of Tappuah	one
the king of Hepher	one
18 the king of Aphek	one
the king of Lasharon	one
19 the king of Madon	one
the king of Hazor	one
20 the king of Shimron-meron	one
the king of Achshaph	one
21 the king of Taanach	one
the king of Megiddo	one
22 the king of Kedesh	one
the king of Jokneam in Carmel	one
23 the king of Dor in Naphoth-dor[a]	one
the king of Goiim in Gilgal[b]	one
24 the king of Tirzahone	
⌊the total number of⌋ all kings:	31

Unconquered Lands

13 Joshua was now old, advanced in years, and the LORD said to him, "You have become old, advanced in years, but a great deal of the land remains to be possessed. 2 This is the land that remains:

All the districts of the Philistines and the Geshurites: 3 from the Shihor east of Egypt to the border of Ekron on the north (considered to be Canaanite territory)—the five Philistine rulers of Gaza, Ashdod, Ashkelon, Gath, and Ekron, as well as the Avvites 4 in the south; all the land of the Canaanites: from Arah of the Sidonians to Aphek and as far as the border of the Amorites; 5 the land of the Gebalites; and all Lebanon east from Baal-gad below Mount Hermon to the entrance of Hamath[c]—6 all the inhabitants of the hill country from Lebanon to Misrephoth-maim, all the Sidonians.

I will drive them out before the Israelites, only distribute the land as an inheritance for Israel, as I have commanded you. 7 Therefore, divide this land as an inheritance to the nine tribes and half the tribe of Manasseh."

Inheritance East of the Jordan

8 With the other half of the tribe, the Reubenites and Gadites had received the inheritance Moses gave them beyond the Jordan to the east, just as Moses the LORD's servant had given them:

9 From Aroer on the rim of the Arnon Valley, along with the city in the middle of the valley, all the Medeba plateau as far as Dibon, 10 and all the cities of Sihon king of the Amorites, who reigned in Heshbon, to the border of the Ammonites; 11 also Gilead and the territory of the Geshurites and Maacathites, all Mount Hermon, and all Bashan to Salecah— 12 the whole kingdom of Og in Bashan, who reigned in Ashtaroth and Edrei; he was one of the remaining Rephaim.

Moses struck them down and drove them out, 13 but the Israelites did not drive out the Geshurites and Maacathites. So Geshur and Maacath live in Israel to this day.

No Land to Levi

14 He did not give any inheritance to the tribe of Levi. This was its inheri-

---

a 12:23 Or in the Slopes of Dor   b 12:23 LXX reads Galilee   c 13:5 Or to Lebo-hamath tance, just as He had promised: the offerings made by fire to the LORD, the God of Israel.

Reuben's Inheritance

15 To the tribe of the Reubenites by their clans, Moses gave 16 this as their territory:

From Aroer on the rim of the Arnon Valley, along with the city in the middle of the valley, to the whole plateau as far as[a] Medeba, 17 with Heshbon and all its cities on the plateau—Dibon, Bamoth-baal, Bethbaal-meon, 18 Jahaz, Kedemoth, Mephaath, 19 Kiriathaim, Sibmah, Zereth-shahar on the hill in the valley, 20 Beth-peor, the slopes of Pisgah, and Beth-jeshimoth— 21 all the cities of the plateau, and all the kingdom of Sihon king of the Amorites, who reigned in Heshbon. Moses had killed him and the chiefs of Midian—Evi, Rekem, Zur, Hur, and Reba—the princes of Sihon who lived in the land. 22 Along with those the Israelites put to death, they also killed the diviner, Balaam son of Beor, with the sword.

23 The border of the Reubenites was the Jordan and its plain. This was the inheritance of the Reubenites by their clans, with the cities and their villages.

Gad's Inheritance

24 To the tribe of the Gadites by their clans, Moses gave 25 this as their territory:

Jazer and all the cities of Gilead, and half the land of the Ammonites to Aroer, near Rabbah; 26 from Heshbon to Ramath-mizpeh and Betonim, and from Mahanaim to the border of Debir;[b] 27 in the valley:[c] Beth-haram, Beth-nimrah, Succoth, and Zaphon—the rest of the kingdom of Sihon king of Heshbon. ⌊Their land also included⌋ the Jordan and its territory as far as the edge of the Sea of Chinnereth[d] on the east side of the Jordan.[e]

28 This was the inheritance of the Gadites by their clans, with the cities and their villages.

"East" Manasseh's Inheritance

29 And to half the tribe of Manasseh, that is, to half the tribe of Manasseh's descendants by their clans, Moses gave 30 this as their territory:

From Mahanaim through all Bashan—all the kingdom of Og king of Bashan, including all of Jair's Villages[f] that are in Bashan—60 cities. 31 But half of Gilead, and Og's royal cities in Bashan—Ashtaroth and Edrei—are for the descendants of Machir son of Manasseh, that is, half the descendants of Machir by their clans.

32 These were the portions Moses gave ⌊them⌋ on the plains of Moab beyond the Jordan east of Jericho. 33 But Moses did not give a portion to the tribe of Levi. The LORD, the God of Israel, was their inheritance, just as He had promised them.

Israel's Inheritance in Canaan

14 The Israelites received these portions that Eleazar the priest, Joshua son of Nun, and the heads of the families of the Israelite tribes gave them in the land of Canaan. 2 Their

a13:16 Other Hb mss read plateau near　b13:26 Or Lidbir, or Lo-debar　c13:27 = the Jordan River Valley　d13:27 = the Sea of Galilee　e13:27 Lit Chinnereth beyond the Jordan to the east　f13:30 Or all of Havvoth-jair

inheritance was by lot as the LORD commanded through Moses for the nine and a half tribes, ³ because Moses had given the inheritance to the two and a half tribes beyond the Jordan.ᵃ But he gave no inheritance among them to the Levites. ⁴ The descendants of Joseph became two tribes, Manasseh and Ephraim. No portion of the land was given to the Levites except cities to live in, along with pasturelands for their cattle and livestock. ⁵ So the Israelites did as the LORD commanded Moses, and they divided the land.

Caleb's Inheritance

⁶ The descendants of Judah approached Joshua at Gilgal, and Caleb son of Jephunneh the Kenizzite said to him, "You know what the LORD promised Moses the man of God at Kadesh-barnea about you and me. ⁷ I was 40 years old when Moses the LORD's servant sent me from Kadesh-barnea to scout the land, and I brought back an honest report. ⁸ My brothers who went with me caused the people's hearts to melt with fear, but I remained loyal to the LORD my God. ⁹ On that day Moses promised me, 'The land where you have set foot will be an inheritance for you and your descendants forever, because you have remained loyal to the LORD my God.'

¹⁰ "As you see, the LORD has kept me alive ⌊these⌋ 45 years as He promised, since the LORD spoke this word to Moses while Israel was journeying in the wilderness. Here I am today, 85 years old. ¹¹ I am still as strong today as I was the day Moses sent me out. My strength for battle and for daily tasksᵇ is now as it was then. ¹² Now give me this hill country the LORD promised ⌊me⌋ on that day, because you heard then that the Anakim

are there, as well as large fortified cities. Perhaps the LORD will be with me and I will drive them out as the LORD promised."

Joshua Blesses Caleb

¹³ Then Joshua blessed Caleb son of Jephunneh and gave him Hebron as an inheritance. ¹⁴ Therefore, Hebron has belonged to Caleb son of Jephunneh the Kenizzite as an inheritance to this day, because he remained loyal to the LORD, the God of Israel. ¹⁵ Hebron's name used to be Kiriath-arba; Arba was the greatest man among the Anakim. After this, the land had rest from war.

Judah's Inheritance

15 Now the allotment for the tribe of the descendants of Judah by their clans was in the southernmost region, south of the wilderness of Zin to the border of Edom.

² Their southern border began at the tip of the Dead Sea on the south bayᶜ ³ and went south of the ascent of Akrabbim,ᵈ proceeded to Zin, ascended to the south of Kadesh-barnea, passed Hezron, ascended to Addar, and turned to Karka. ⁴ It proceeded to Azmon and to the Brook of Egypt and so the border ended at the Mediterranean Sea. This is yourᵉ southern border.

⁵ Now the eastern border was along the Dead Sea to the mouth of the Jordan.ᶠ

The border on the north side was from the bay of the sea at the mouth of the Jordan. ⁶ It ascended to Beth-hoglah, proceeded north of Beth-arabah, and ascended to the stone of Bo-

---

ᵃ**14:3** = east of the Jordan River ᵇ**14:11** Lit *for going out and coming in* ᶜ**15:2** Lit *Sea at the tongue that turns southward* ᵈ**15:3** Lit *of scorpions* ᵉ**15:4** LXX reads *their* ᶠ**15:5** The southern end of the *Jordan* River at the *Dead Sea*

han son of Reuben. ⁷ Then the border ascended to Debir from the Valley of Achor, turning north to the Gilgal that is opposite the ascent of Adummim, which is south of the ravine. The border proceeded to the waters of En-shemesh and ended at En-rogel. ⁸ From there the border ascended the Valley of Hinnom to the southern Jebusite slope (that is, Jerusalem) and ascended to the top of the hill that faces the Valley of Hinnom on the west, at the northern end of the Valley of Rephaim. ⁹ From the top of the hill the border curved to the spring of the Waters of Nephtoah, went to the cities of Mount Ephron, and then curved to Baalah (that is, Kiriath-jearim). ¹⁰ The border turned westward from Baalah to Mount Seir, went to the northern slope of Mount Jearim (that is, Chesalon), descended to Beth-shemesh, and proceeded to Timnah. ¹¹ Then the border reached to the slope north of Ekron, curved to Shikkeron, proceeded to Mount Baalah, went to Jabneel, and ended at the Mediterranean Sea.

¹² Now the western border was the coastline of the Mediterranean Sea.

This was the boundary of the descendants of Judah around their clans.

Caleb and Othniel

¹³ He gave Caleb son of Jephunneh ⌊the following⌋ portion among the descendants of Judah based on the LORD's instruction to Joshua: Kiriath-arba (that is, Hebron; Arba was the father of Anak). ¹⁴ Caleb drove out from there the three sons of Anak: Sheshai, Ahiman, and Talmai, descendants of Anak. ¹⁵ From there he marched against the inhabitants of Debir whose name used to be Kiriath-sepher, ¹⁶ and Caleb said, "I will give my daughter Achsah as a wife to the one who strikes down and captures Kiriath-sepher." ¹⁷ So Othniel son of Caleb's brother, Kenaz, captured it, and Caleb gave his daughter Achsah to him as a wife. ¹⁸ When she arrived, she persuaded Othniel to ask her father for a field. As she got off her donkey, Caleb asked her, "What do you want?" ¹⁹ She replied, "Give me a blessing. Since you have given me land in the •Negev, give me the springs of water also." So he gave her the upper and lower springs.

Judah's Cities

²⁰ This was the inheritance of the tribe of the descendants of Judah by their clans.

²¹ These were the outermost cities of the tribe of the descendants of Judah toward the border of Edom in the Negev: Kabzeel, Eder, Jagur, ²² Kinah, Dimonah, Adadah, ²³ Kedesh, Hazor, Ithnan, ²⁴ Ziph, Telem, Bealoth, ²⁵ Hazor-hadattah, Kerioth-hezron (that is, Hazor), ²⁶ Amam, Shema, Moladah, ²⁷ Hazar-gaddah, Heshmon, Beth-pelet, ²⁸ Hazar-shual, Beer-sheba, Biziothiah, ²⁹ Baalah, Iim, Ezem, ³⁰ Eltolad, Chesil, Hormah, ³¹ Ziklag, Madmannah, Sansannah, ³² Lebaoth, Shilhim, Ain, and Rimmon—29 cities in all, with their villages.

³³ In the Judean foothills:ᵃ Eshtaol, Zorah, Ashnah, ³⁴ Zanoah, En-gannim, Tappuah,ᵇ Enam, ³⁵ Jarmuth, Adullam, Socoh,ᶜ Azekah, ³⁶ Shaaraim, Adithaim, Gederah, and Gederothaim—14 cities, with their villages;

ᵃ15:33 Or the Shephelah ᵇ15:34 Or possibly 1 name: En-gannim-tappuah ᶜ15:35 Or possibly 1 name: Adullam-socoh

³⁷ Zenan, Hadashah, Migdal-gad, ³⁸ Dilan, Mizpeh, Jokthe-el, ³⁹ Lachish, Bozkath, Eglon, ⁴⁰ Cabbon, Lahmam, Chitlish, ⁴¹ Gederoth, Bethdagon, Naamah, and Makkedah—16 cities, with their villages; ⁴² Libnah, Ether, Ashan, ⁴³ Iphtah, Ashnah, Nezib, ⁴⁴ Keilah, Achzib, and Mareshah—nine cities, with their villages; ⁴⁵ Ekron, with its towns and villages; ⁴⁶ from Ekron to the sea, all the cities near Ashdod, with their villages; ⁴⁷ Ashdod, with its towns and villages; Gaza, with its towns and villages, to the Brook of Egypt and the coastline of the Mediterranean Sea.

⁴⁸ In the hill country: Shamir, Jattir, Socoh, ⁴⁹ Dannah, Kiriath-sannah (that is, Debir), ⁵⁰ Anab, Eshtemoh, Anim, ⁵¹ Goshen, Holon, and Giloh—11 cities, with their villages; ⁵² Arab, Dumah,^a Eshan, ⁵³ Janim, Beth-tappuah, Aphekah, ⁵⁴ Humtah, Kiriath-arba (that is, Hebron), and Zior—nine cities, with their villages; ⁵⁵ Maon, Carmel, Ziph, Juttah, ⁵⁶ Jezreel, Jokdeam, Zanoah, ⁵⁷ Kain, Gibeah, and Timnah—10 cities, with their villages; ⁵⁸ Halhul, Beth-zur, Gedor, ⁵⁹ Maarath, Beth-anoth, and Eltekon—six cities, with their villages;^b ⁶⁰ Kiriath-baal (that is, Kiriath-jearim), and Rabbah—two cities, with their villages.

⁶¹ In the wilderness: Beth-arabah, Middin, Secacah, ⁶² Nibshan, the City of Salt,^c and En-gedi—six cities, with their villages.

Jebusites Unconquered

⁶³ But the descendants of Judah could not drive out the Jebusites who lived in Jerusalem. So the Jebusites live in Jerusalem among the descendants of Judah to this day.

Joseph's Inheritance

16 The allotment for the descendants of Joseph^d went from the Jordan at Jericho to the waters of Jericho on the east, through the wilderness ascending from Jericho into the hill country of Bethel. ² From Bethel it went to Luz and proceeded to the border of the Archites by Ataroth. ³ It then descended westward to the border of the Japhletites as far as the border of lower Beth-horon, then to Gezer, and ended at the Mediterranean Sea. ⁴ So Ephraim and Manasseh, the sons of Joseph, received their inheritance.

Ephraim's Inheritance

⁵ This was the territory of the descendants of Ephraim by their clans:

The border of their inheritance went from Ataroth-addar on the east of Upper Beth-horon. ⁶ In the north the border went westward from Michmethath; it turned eastward from Taanath-shiloh and passed it east of Janoah. ⁷ From Janoah it descended to Ataroth and Naarah, and then reached Jericho and went to the Jordan. ⁸ From Tappuah the border^e went westward along the Brook of Kanah and ended at the Mediterranean Sea.

This was the inheritance of the tribe of the descendants of Ephraim by their clans, together with ⁹ the cities set apart for the descendants of Ephraim within the inheritance of the descendants of

^a**15:52** Other Hb mss read *Rumah*   ^b**15:59** LXX adds *Tekoa, Ephrathah (that is, Bethlehem), Peor, Etam, Culom, Tatam, Sores, Carem, Gallim, Baither, and Manach*—*11 cities, with their villages*   ^c**15:62** Or *Ir-hamelach*   ^d**16:1** The tribes of Ephraim and Manasseh   ^e**16:8** Ephraim's northern border

Manasseh—all these cities with their villages. ¹⁰ But, they did not drive out the Canaanites who lived in Gezer. So the Canaanites live in Ephraim to this day, but they are forced laborers.

"West" Manasseh's Inheritance

17 This was the allotment for the tribe of Manasseh as Joseph's firstborn. Gilead and Bashan came to Machir, the firstborn of Manasseh and the father of Gilead, who was a man of war. ² So the allotment was for the rest of Manasseh's descendants by their clans, for the sons of Abiezer, Helek, Asriel, Shechem, Hepher, and Shemida. These are the male descendants of Manasseh son of Joseph, by their clans.

³ Now Zelophehad son of Hepher, son of Gilead, son of Machir, son of Manasseh, had no sons, only daughters. These are the names of his daughters: Mahlah, Noah, Hoglah, Milcah, and Tirzah. ⁴ They came before Eleazar the priest, Joshua son of Nun, and the leaders, saying, "The LORD commanded Moses to give us an inheritance among our male relatives."ᵃ So they gave them an inheritance among their father's brothers, in keeping with the LORD's instruction. ⁵ As a result, 10 tracts fell to Manasseh, besides the land of Gilead and Bashan, which are beyond the Jordan,ᵇ ⁶ because Manasseh's daughters received an inheritance among his sons. The land of Gilead belonged to the rest of Manasseh's sons.

⁷ The border of Manasseh went from Asher to Michmethath near Shechem. It then went southward toward the inhabitants of En-tappuah. ⁸ The region of Tappuah belonged to Manasseh, but Tappuah ⌊itself⌋ on

Manasseh's border belonged to the descendants of Ephraim. ⁹ From there the border descended to the Brook of Kanah; south of the brook, cities belonged to Ephraim among Manasseh's cities. Manasseh's border was on the north side of the brook and ended at the Mediterranean Sea. ¹⁰ Ephraim's ⌊territory⌋ was to the south and Manasseh's to the north, with the Sea as its border. Theyᶜ reached Asher on the north and Issachar on the east. ¹¹ Within Issachar and Asher, Manasseh had Beth-shean with its towns, Ibleam with its towns, and the inhabitants of Dor with its towns; the inhabitants of En-dor with its towns, the inhabitants of Taanach with its towns, and the inhabitants of Megiddo with its towns—the three ⌊cities⌋ ofᵈ Naphath.

¹² The descendants of Manasseh could not possess these cities, because the Canaanites were determined to stay in this land. ¹³ However, when the Israelites grew stronger, they imposed forced labor on the Canaanites but did not drive them out completely.

Joseph's Family Asks for Extra Inheritance

¹⁴ Joseph's descendants said to Joshua: "Why did you give us only one tribal allotmentᵉ as an inheritance? We have many people, because the LORD has greatly blessed us."

¹⁵ "If you have so many people," Joshua replied to them, "go to the forest and clear ⌊an area⌋ for yourselves there in the land of the Perizzites and the Rephaim, because Ephraim's hill country is too small for you."

ᵃ**17:4** Lit *our brothers* ᵇ**17:5** East of the Jordan River ᶜ**17:10** The people of Manasseh, or Manasseh's borders
ᵈ**17:11** LXX, Vg read *the third is* ᵉ**17:14** Lit *one lot and one territory*

16 But the descendants of Joseph said, "The hill country is not enough for us, and all the Canaanites who inhabit the valley area have iron chariots, both at Beth-shean with its towns and in the Jezreel Valley."

Joshua Awards Joseph's Family More

17 So Joshua replied to Joseph's family (that is, Ephraim and Manasseh), "You have many people and great strength. You will not have just one lot, 18 because the hill country will be yours also. It is a forest; clear it and its outlying areas will be yours. You can also drive out the Canaanites, even though they have iron chariots and are strong."

Land Distribution at Shiloh

18 The entire Israelite community assembled at Shiloh where it set up the tent of meeting there; the land had been subdued by them. 2 Seven tribes among the Israelites were left who had not divided up their inheritance. 3 So Joshua said to the Israelites, "How long will you delay going out to take possession of the land that the LORD, the God of your fathers, gave you? 4 Appoint for yourselves three men from each tribe, and I will send them out. They are to go and survey the land, write a description of it for the purpose of their inheritance, and return to me. 5 Then they are to divide it into seven portions. Judah is to remain in its territory in the south, and Joseph's family in theira territory in the north. 6 When you have written a description of the seven portions of land and brought it to me, I will cast lots for you here in the presence of the LORD our God. 7 But the Levites among you do not get a portion, because their inheritance is the priesthood of the LORD. Gad, Reu-

ben, and half the tribe of Manasseh have taken their inheritance beyond the Jordan to the east, which Moses the LORD's servant gave them."

8 As the men prepared to go, Joshua commanded themb to write down a description of the land, saying, "Go and survey the land, write a description of it, and return to me. I will then cast lots for you here in Shiloh in the presence of the LORD." 9 So the men left, went through the land, and described it by towns in a document of seven sections. They returned to Joshua at the camp in Shiloh. 10 Joshua cast lots for them at Shiloh in the presence of the LORD where he distributed the land to the Israelites according to their divisions.

Benjamin's Inheritance

11 The lot came up for the tribe of Benjamin's descendants by their clans, and their allotted territory lay between Judah's descendants and Joseph's descendants.

12 Their border on the north side began at the Jordan, ascended to the slope of Jericho on the north, through the hill country westward, and ended at the wilderness of Beth-aven. 13 From there the border went toward Luz, to the southern slope of Luz (that is, Bethel); it then went down by Ataroth-addar, over the hill south of Lower Beth-horon.

14 On the west side, from the hill facing Beth-horon on the south, the border curved, turning southward, and ended at Kiriath-baal (that is, Kiriath-jearim), a city of the descendants of Judah. This was the west side ɩof their borderɩ.

15 The south side began at the edge of Kiriath-jearim, and the border ex-

---

a 18:5 = the tribes of Ephraim and Manasseh   b 18:8 Lit *the ones going around*

tended westward; it went to the spring at the Waters of Nephtoah. [16] The border descended to the foot of the hill that faces the Valley of Hinnom at the northern end of the Valley of Rephaim. It ran down the Valley of Hinnom toward the south Jebusite slope and downward to En-rogel. [17] It curved northward and went to En-shemesh and on to Geliloth, which is opposite the ascent of Adummim, and continued down to the Stone of Bohan, Reuben's son. [18] Then it went north to the slope opposite the Jordan Valley[a] [b] and proceeded into the valley.[b] [19] The border continued to the north slope of Beth-hoglah and ended at the northern bay of the Dead Sea, at the southern end of the Jordan. This was the southern border.

[20] The Jordan formed the border on the east side.

This was the inheritance of Benjamin's descendants, by their clans, according to its surrounding borders.

Benjamin's Cities

[21] These were the cities of the tribe of Benjamin's descendants by their clans:

Jericho, Beth-hoglah, Emek-keziz, [22] Beth-arabah, Zemaraim, Bethel, [23] Avvim, Parah, Ophrah, [24] Chephar-ammoni, Ophni, and Geba—12 cities, with their villages; [25] Gibeon, Ramah, Beeroth, [26] Mizpeh,[c] Chephirah, Mozah, [27] Rekem, Irpeel, Taralah, [28] Zela, Haeleph, Jebus[d] (that is, Jerusalem), Gibeah, and Kiriath[e]—14 cities, with their villages.

This was the inheritance for Benjamin's descendants by their clans.

Simeon's Inheritance

19 The second lot came out for Simeon, for the tribe of his descendants by their clans, but their inheritance was within the portion of Judah's descendants. [2] Their inheritance included:

Beer-sheba (or Sheba), Moladah, [3] Hazar-shual, Balah, Ezem, [4] Eltolad, Bethul, Hormah, [5] Ziklag, Beth-marcaboth, Hazar-susah, [6] Beth-lebaoth, and Sharuhen—13 cities, with their villages; [7] Ain, Rimmon, Ether, and Ashan—four cities, with their villages; [8] and all the villages surrounding these cities as far as Baalath-beer (Ramah of the south[f]).

This was the inheritance of the tribe of Simeon's descendants by their clans. [9] The inheritance of Simeon's descendants was within the territory of Judah's descendants, because the share for Judah's descendants was too large for them. So Simeon's descendants received an inheritance within Judah's portion.

Zebulun's Inheritance

[10] The third lot came up for Zebulun's descendants by their clans.

The territory of their inheritance stretched as far as Sarid; [11] their border went up westward to Maralah, reached Dabbesheth, and met the brook east of Jokneam. [12] From Sarid, it turned east toward the sunrise along the border of Chisloth-tabor, went to Daberath, and went up to Japhia. [13] From there, it went east toward the sunrise to Gath-hepher and to Eth-kazin; it extended to Rimmon, curving around to Neah. [14] The border then circled around Neah on

---

[a] **18:18** LXX reads *went northward to Beth-arabah*   [b] **18:18** Or *the Arabah*   [c] **18:26** Alt spelling of *Mizpah*; Jos 11:3,8   [d] **18:28** Lit *Jebusite*   [e] **18:28** LXX, Syr read *Kiriath-jearim*   [f] **19:8** Or *the Negev*

the north to Hannathon and ended at the valley of Iphtah-el, [15] along with Kattath, Nahalal, Shimron, Idalah, and Bethlehem—12 cities, with their villages.

[16] This was the inheritance of Zebulun's descendants by their clans, these cities, with their villages.

Issachar's Inheritance

[17] The fourth lot came out for the tribe of Issachar's descendants by their clans.

[18] Their territory went to Jezreel, and included Chesulloth, Shunem, [19] Hapharaim, Shion, Anaharath, [20] Rabbith, Kishion, Ebez, [21] Remeth, En-gannim, En-haddah, Beth-pazzez. [22] The border reached Tabor, Shahazumah, and Beth-shemesh, and ended at the Jordan—16 cities, with their villages.

[23] This was the inheritance of the tribe of Issachar's descendants by their clans, the cities, with their villages.

Asher's Inheritance

[24] The fifth lot came out for the tribe of Asher's descendants by their clans.

[25] Their boundary included Helkath, Hali, Beten, Achshaph, [26] Allammelech, Amad, and Mishal and reached westward to Carmel and Shihor-libnath. [27] It turned eastward to Bethdagon, passed Zebulun and the valley of Iphtah-el, north toward Bethemek and Neiel, and went north to Cabul, [28] Ebron, Rehob, Hammon, and Kanah, as far as Great Sidon. [29] The boundary then turned to Ramah as far as the fortified city of Tyre; it turned back to Hosah and ended at the sea, including Mahalab, Achzib,[a] [30] Ummah, Aphek, and Rehob—22 cities, with their villages.

[31] This was the inheritance of the tribe of Asher's descendants by their clans, these cities with their villages.

Naphtali's Inheritance

[32] The sixth lot came out for Naphtali's descendants by their clans.

[33] Their boundary went from Heleph and from the oak in Zaanannim, including Adami-nekeb and Jabneel, as far as Lakkum, and ended at the Jordan. [34] To the west, the boundary turned to Aznoth-tabor and went from there to Hukkok, reaching Zebulun on the south, Asher on the west, and Judah[b] at the Jordan on the east. [35] The fortified cities were Ziddim, Zer, Hammath, Rakkath, Chinnereth,[c] [36] Adamah, Ramah, Hazor, [37] Kedesh, Edrei, En-hazor, [38] Iron, Migdal-el, Horem, Bethanath, and Beth-shemesh—19 cities, with their villages.

[39] This was the inheritance of the tribe of Naphtali's descendants by their clans, the cities with their villages.

Dan's Inheritance

[40] The seventh lot came out for the Danite tribe by its clans.

[41] The territory of their inheritance included Zorah, Eshtaol, Ir-shemesh, [42] Shaalabbin, Aijalon, Ithlah, [43] Elon, Timnah, Ekron, [44] Eltekeh, Gibbethon, Baalath, [45] Jehud, Beneberak, Gath-rimmon, [46] Me-jarkon, and Rakkon, with the territory facing Joppa.

[47] When the territory of the Danites slipped out of their control,[d] they went

up and fought against Leshem, captured it, and struck it down with the sword. So they took possession of it, lived there, and renamed Leshem after[a] their ancestor Dan. [48] This was the inheritance of the Danite tribe by its clans, these cities with their villages.

Joshua's Inheritance

[49] When they had finished distributing the land into its territories, the Israelites gave Joshua son of Nun an inheritance among them. [50] By the LORD's command, they gave him the city Timnath-serah in the hill country of Ephraim, which he requested. He rebuilt the city and lived in it.

[51] These were the portions that Eleazar the priest, Joshua son of Nun, and the heads of the families distributed to the Israelite tribes by lot at Shiloh in the LORD's presence at the entrance to the tent of meeting. So they finished dividing up the land.

Six Cities of Refuge

20 Then the LORD spoke to Joshua, [2] "Tell the Israelites: 'Select your cities of refuge, as I instructed you through Moses, [3] so that a person who kills someone unintentionally or accidentally may flee there. These will be your refuge from the avenger of blood. [4] When someone flees to one of these cities, stands at the entrance of the city •gate, and states his case before[b] the elders of that city, they are to bring him into the city and give him a place to live among them. [5] And if the avenger of blood pursues him, they must not hand the one who committed manslaughter over to him, for he killed his neighbor accidentally and did not hate him beforehand. [6] He is to stay in that city until he

stands trial before the assembly and until the death of the high priest serving at that time. Then the one who committed manslaughter may return home to his own city from which he fled.'"

[7] So they designated Kedesh in the hill country of Naphtali in Galilee, Shechem in the hill country of Ephraim, and Kiriath-arba (that is, Hebron) in the hill country of Judah. [8] Across the Jordan east of Jericho, they selected Bezer on the wilderness plateau from Reuben's tribe, Ramoth in Gilead from Gad's tribe, and Golan in Bashan from Manasseh's tribe.

[9] These are the cities appointed for all the Israelites and foreigners among them, so that anyone who kills a person unintentionally may flee there and not die at the hand of the avenger of blood until he stands before the assembly.

Cities of the Levites

21 The heads of the Levite families approached Eleazar the priest, Joshua son of Nun, and the heads of the families of the Israelite tribes. [2] They told them at Shiloh in the land of Canaan: "The LORD commanded through Moses that we be given cities to live in, with their pasturelands for our livestock." [3] So the Israelites, by the LORD's command, gave the Levites these cities with their pasturelands from their inheritance.

[4] The lot came out for the Kohathite clans: The Levites who were the descendants of Aaron the priest received 13 cities by lot from the tribes of Judah, Simeon, and Benjamin. [5] The remaining descendants of Kohath[c] received 10 cities by lot from the clans of the tribes of Ephraim, Dan, and half the tribe of Manasseh.

---

[a] **19:47** Lit *and called Leshem, Dan, after the name of* [b] **20:4** Lit *in the ears of* [c] **21:5** = descendants not in Aaron's priestly line

⁶ Gershon's descendants received 13 cities by lot from the clans of the tribes of Issachar, Asher, Naphtali, and half the tribe of Manasseh in Bashan.

⁷ Merari's descendants received 12 cities for their clans from the tribes of Reuben, Gad, and Zebulun.

⁸ The Israelites gave these cities with their pasturelands around them to the Levites by lot, as the LORD had commanded through Moses.

Cities of Aaron's Descendants

⁹ The Israelites gave these cities by name from the tribes of the descendants of Judah and Simeon ¹⁰ to the descendants of Aaron from the Kohathite clans of the Levites, because they received the first lot. ¹¹ They gave them Kiriath-arba (that is, Hebron) with its surrounding pasturelands in the hill country of Judah. Arba was the father of Anak. ¹² But they gave the fields and villages of the city to Caleb son of Jephunneh as his possession.

¹³ They gave to the descendants of Aaron the priest:

Hebron, the city of refuge for the one who commits manslaughter, with its pasturelands, Libnah with its pasturelands, ¹⁴ Jattir with its pasturelands, Eshtemoa with its pasturelands, ¹⁵ Holon with its pasturelands, Debir with its pasturelands, ¹⁶ Ain with its pasturelands, Juttah with its pasturelands, and Beth-shemesh with its pasturelands—nine cities from these two tribes.

¹⁷ From the tribe of Benjamin ⌊they gave⌋:

Gibeon with its pasturelands, Geba with its pasturelands, ¹⁸ Anathoth with its pasturelands, and Almon with its pasturelands—four cities.

¹⁹ All 13 cities with their pasturelands were for the priests, the descendants of Aaron.

Cities of Kohath's Other Descendants

²⁰ The allotted cities to the remaining clans of Kohath's descendants, who were Levites, came from the tribe of Ephraim. ²¹ The Israelites gave them:

Shechem, the city of refuge for the one who commits manslaughter, with its pasturelands in the hill country of Ephraim, Gezer with its pasturelands, ²² Kibzaim with its pasturelands, and Beth-horon with its pasturelands—four cities.

²³ From the tribe of Dan ⌊they gave⌋:

Elteke with its pasturelands, Gibbethon with its pasturelands, ²⁴ Aijalon with its pasturelands, and Gath-rimmon with its pasturelands—four cities.

²⁵ From half the tribe of Manasseh ⌊they gave⌋:

Taanach with its pasturelands and Gath-rimmon^a with its pasturelands—two cities.

²⁶ All 10 cities with their pasturelands were for the clans of Kohath's other descendants.

Cities of Gershon's Descendants

²⁷ From half the tribe of Manasseh, ⌊they gave⌋ to the descendants of Gershon, who were one of the Levite clans:

Golan, the city of refuge for the one who commits manslaughter, with its

^a**21:25** Or *Ibleam*

pasturelands in Bashan, and Beesh-terah with its pasturelands—two cities.

28 From the tribe of Issachar ⸤they gave⸥:

Kishion with its pasturelands, Dabe-rath with its pasturelands, 29 Jarmuth with its pasturelands, and En-gan-nim with its pasturelands—four cities.

30 From the tribe of Asher ⸤they gave⸥:

Mishal with its pasturelands, Abdon with its pasturelands, 31 Helkath with its pasturelands, and Rehob with its pasturelands—four cities.

32 From the tribe of Naphtali ⸤they gave⸥:

Kedesh in Galilee, the city of refuge for the one who commits man-slaughter, with its pasturelands, Hammoth-dor with its pasturelands, and Kartan with its pasturelands—three cities.

33 All 13 cities with their pasturelands were for the Gershonites by their clans.

Cities of Merari's Descendants

34 From the tribe of Zebulun, ⸤they gave⸥ to the clans of the descendants of Merari, who were the remaining Le-vites:

Jokneam with its pasturelands, Kar-tah with its pasturelands, 35 Dimnah with its pasturelands, and Nahalal with its pasturelands—four cities.

36 From the tribe of Reuben, ⸤they gave⸥:

Bezer with its pasturelands, Jahzah[a] with its pasturelands, 37 Kedemoth with its pasturelands, and Mephaath with its pasturelands—four cities.[b]

38 From the tribe of Gad, ⸤they gave⸥:

Ramoth in Gilead, the city of refuge for the one who commits man-slaughter, with its pasturelands, Ma-hanaim with its pasturelands, 39 Heshbon with its pasturelands, and Jazer with its pasturelands—four cities in all. 40 All 12 cities were allotted to the clans of Merari's de-scendants, the remaining Levite clans.

41 Within the Israelite possession there were 48 cities in all with their pasture-lands for the Levites. 42 Each of these cit-ies had its own surrounding pasturelands; this was true for all the cit-ies.

Lord's Promises Fulfilled

43 So the LORD gave Israel all the land He had sworn to give their fathers, and they took possession of it and settled there. 44 The LORD gave them rest on ev-ery side according to all He had sworn to their fathers. None of their enemies were able to stand against them, for the LORD handed over all their enemies to them. 45 None of the good promises the LORD had made to the house of Israel failed. Everything was fulfilled.

Eastern Tribes Return Home

22 Joshua summoned the Reuben-ites, Gadites, and half the tribe of Manasseh, 2 and told them, "You have done everything Moses the LORD's ser-vant commanded you and have obeyed me in everything I commanded you. 3 You have not deserted your brothers even once this whole time but have car-ried out the requirement of the

---

a 21:36 Or Jahaz   b 21:36-37 Some Hb mss omit these vv.

command of the LORD your God. ⁴ Now that He has given your brothers rest, just as He promised them, return to your homes in your own land that Moses the LORD's servant gave you across the Jordan. ⁵ Only carefully obey the command and instruction that Moses the LORD's servant gave you: to love the LORD your God, walk in all His ways, keep His commands, remain faithfulª to Him, and serve Him with all your heart and all your soul."

⁶ Joshua blessed them and sent them on their way, and they went to their homes. ⁷ Moses had given ⌊territory⌋ to half the tribe of Manasseh in Bashan, but Joshua had given ⌊territory⌋ to the other half,ᵇ with their brothers, on the west side of the Jordan. When Joshua sent them to their homes and blessed them, ⁸ he said, "Return to your homes with great wealth: a huge number of cattle, and silver, gold, bronze, iron, and a large quantity of clothing. Share the spoil of your enemies with your brothers."

East Tribes Build Controversial Altar

⁹ The Reubenites, Gadites, and half the tribe of Manasseh left the Israelites at Shiloh in the land of Canaan to go to their own land of Gilead, which they took possession of according to the LORD's command through Moses. ¹⁰ When they came to the region ofᶜ the Jordan in the land of Canaan, the Reubenites, Gadites, and half the tribe of Manasseh built a large, impressive altar there by the Jordan.

West Tribes Threaten War

¹¹ Then the Israelites heard ⌊it⌋ said, "Look, the Reubenites, Gadites, and half the tribe of Manasseh have built an altar on the frontier of the land of Canaan at the region ofᵈ the Jordan, on the Israelite side." ¹² When the Israelites heard ⌊this⌋, the entire Israelite community assembled at Shiloh to go to war against them.

West Accuses East of Treachery

¹³ The Israelites sent Phinehas son of Eleazar the priest to the Reubenites, Gadites, and half the tribe of Manasseh, in the land of Gilead. ¹⁴ ⌊They sent⌋ 10 leaders with him—one family leader for each tribe of Israel. All of them were heads of their families among the clans of Israel. ¹⁵ They went to the Reubenites, Gadites, and half the tribe of Manasseh, in the land of Gilead, and told them, ¹⁶ "This is what the LORD's entire community says: 'What is this treachery you have committed today against the God of Israel by turning away from the LORD and building an altar for yourselves, so that you are in rebellion against the LORD today? ¹⁷ Wasn't the sin of Peor, which brought a plague on the LORD's community, enough for us, so that we have not cleansed ourselves from it even to this day, ¹⁸ and now, you would turn away from the LORD? If you rebel against the LORD today, tomorrow He will be angry with the entire community of Israel. ¹⁹ But if the land you possess is defiled, cross over to the land the LORD possesses where the LORD's tabernacle stands, and take possession ⌊of it⌋ among us. But don't rebel against the LORD or against us by building for yourselves an altar other than the altar of the LORD our God. ²⁰ Wasn't Achan son of Zerah unfaithful regarding what was •set apart for destruction, bringing wrath on the entire community of Israel? He was not the only one who perished because of his sin.'"

ª22:5 Lit commands, hold on   ᵇ22:7 Lit to his half   ᶜ22:10 Or to Geliloth by   ᵈ22:11 Or at Geliloth by

Eastern Tribes Explain

²¹ The Reubenites, Gadites, and half the tribe of Manasseh answered the leaders of the Israelite clans, ²² "The LORD is the God of gods! The LORD is the God of gods!ᵃ He knows, and may Israel also know. Do not spare us today, if ₍it was₎ in rebellion or treachery against the LORD ²³ that we have built for ourselves an altar to turn away from Him. May the LORD Himself hold us accountable if ₍we intended₎ to offer •burnt offerings and •grain offerings on it, or to sacrifice •fellowship offerings on it. ²⁴ We actually did this from a specific concern that in the future your descendants might say to our descendants, 'What relationship do you have with the LORD,ᵇ the God of Israel? ²⁵ For the LORD has made the Jordan a border between us and you descendants of Reuben and Gad. You have no share in the LORD!' So your descendants may cause our descendants to stop fearing the LORD.

²⁶ "Therefore we said: Let us take action and build an altar for ourselves, but not for burnt offering or sacrifice. ²⁷ Instead, it is to be a witness between us and you, and between the generations after us, so that we may carry out the worship of the Lord in His presence with our burnt offerings, sacrifices, and fellowship offerings. Then in the future, your descendants will not be able to say to our descendants, 'You have no share in the LORD!' ²⁸ We thought that if they said this to us or to our generations in the future, we would reply: Look at the replica of the LORD's altar that our fathers made, not for burnt offering or sacrifice, but as a witness between us and you. ²⁹ We would never rebel against the LORD or turn away from Him today by building an altar for burnt offering, grain offering, or sacrifice, other than the altar of the LORD our God, which is in front of His tabernacle."

Conflict Resolved

³⁰ When Phinehas the priest and the community leaders, the heads of Israel's clans who were with him, heard what the descendants of Reuben, Gad, and Manasseh had to say, they were pleased. ³¹ Phinehas son of Eleazar the priest said to the descendants of Reuben, Gad, and Manasseh, "Today we know that the LORD is among us, because you have not committed this treachery against Him. As a result, you have delivered the Israelites from the LORD's power."

³² Then Phinehas son of Eleazar the priest and the leaders returned from the Reubenites and Gadites in the land of Gilead to the Israelites in the land of Canaan and brought back a report to them. ³³ The Israelites were pleased with the report, and they praised God. They spoke no more about going to war against them to ravage the land where the Reubenites and Gadites lived. ³⁴ So the Reubenites and Gadites named the altar: Itᶜ is a witness between us that the LORD is God.

Joshua's Farewell Address

23 A long time after the LORD had given Israel rest from all the enemies around them, Joshua was old, getting on in years. ² So Joshua summoned all Israel, including its elders, leaders, judges, and officers, and said to them, "I am old, getting on in years, ³ and you have seen for yourselves everything the LORD your God did to all these nations on your account, because it was the LORD your God who was fighting for you.

ᵃ**22:22** Or *The Mighty One, God, the* LORD*! The Mighty One, God, the* LORD*!*, or *God, the* LORD *God! God, the* LORD *God!*   ᵇ**22:24** Lit *What to you and to the* LORD   ᶜ**22:34** Some Hb mss, Syr, Tg read *altar Witness because it*

4 See, I have allotted these remaining nations to you as an inheritance for your tribes, including all the nations I have destroyed, from the Jordan westward to the Mediterranean Sea. 5 The LORD your God will force them back on your account and drive them out before you, so that you can take possession of their land, as the LORD your God promised you.

6 "Be very strong, and continue obeying all that is written in the book of the law of Moses, so that you do not turn from it to the right or left 7 and so that you do not associate with these nations remaining among you. Do not call on the names of their gods or make an oath to them; do not worship them or bow down to them. 8 Instead, remain faithful to the LORD your God, as you have done to this day.

9 "The LORD has driven out great and powerful nations before you, and no one has been able to stand against you to this day. 10 One of you routed a thousand, because the LORD your God was fighting for you, as He promised.[a] 11 So be very diligent to love the LORD your God for your own well-being. 12 For if you turn away and cling to the rest of these nations remaining among you, and if you intermarry or associate with them and they with you, 13 know for certain that the LORD your God will not continue to drive these nations out before you. They will become a snare and a trap for you, a scourge for your sides and thorns in your eyes, until you disappear from this good land the LORD your God has given you.

14 "I am now going the way of all the earth,[b] and you know with all your heart and all your soul that none of the good promises the LORD your God made to you has failed. Everything was fulfilled for you; not one promise has failed. 15 Since every good thing the LORD your God promised you has come about, so He will bring on you every bad thing until He has annihilated you from this good land the LORD your God has given you. 16 If you break the covenant of the LORD your God, which He commanded you, and go and worship other gods, and bow down to them, the LORD's anger will burn against you, and you will quickly disappear from this good land He has given you."

Joshua Reviews Israel's History

24 Joshua assembled all the tribes of Israel at Shechem and summoned Israel's elders, leaders, judges, and officers, and they presented themselves before God. 2 Joshua said to all the people, "This is what the LORD, the God of Israel, says: 'Long ago your ancestors, including Terah, the father of Abraham and Nahor, lived beyond the Euphrates River and worshiped other gods. 3 But I took your father Abraham from the region beyond the Euphrates River, led him throughout the land of Canaan, and multiplied his descendants. I gave him Isaac, 4 and to Isaac I gave Jacob and Esau. I gave the hill country of Seir to Esau as a possession, but Jacob and his sons went down to Egypt.

5 "'Then I sent Moses and Aaron, I plagued Egypt by what I did there, and afterwards I brought you out. 6 When I brought your fathers out of Egypt and you reached the •Red Sea, the Egyptians pursued your fathers with chariots and horsemen as far as the sea. 7 Your fathers cried out to the LORD, so He put darkness between you and the Egyptians, and brought the sea over them, engulfing them. Your own eyes saw what I did

---

[a]23:10 Lit promised you   [b]23:14 = I am going to die

to Egypt. After that, you lived in the wilderness a long time.

8 " 'Later, I brought you to the land of the Amorites who lived beyond the Jordan. They fought against you, but I handed them over to you. You possessed their land, and I annihilated them before you. 9 Balak son of Zippor, king of Moab, set out to fight against Israel. He sent for Balaam son of Beor to curse you, 10 but I would not listen to Balaam. Instead, he repeatedly blessed you, and I delivered you from his hand.

11 " 'You then crossed the Jordan and came to Jericho. The people of Jericho— as well as the Amorites, Perizzites, Canaanites, Hittites, Girgashites, Hivites, and Jebusites—fought against you, but I handed them over to you. 12 I sent the hornet[a] ahead of you, and it drove out the two Amorite kings before you. It was not by your sword or bow. 13 I gave you a land you did not labor for, and cities you did not build, though you live in them; you are eating from vineyards and olive groves you did not plant.'

Joshua Calls for Covenant Renewal

14 "Therefore, •fear the LORD and worship Him in sincerity and truth. Get rid of the gods your ancestors worshiped beyond the Euphrates River and in Egypt, and worship the LORD. 15 But if it doesn't please you to worship the LORD, choose for yourselves today the one you will worship: the gods your fathers worshiped beyond the Euphrates River, or the gods of the Amorites in whose land you are living. As for me and my family, we will worship the LORD."

People Respond

16 The people replied, "We will certainly not abandon the LORD to worship other gods! 17 For the LORD our God brought us and our fathers out of the land of Egypt, the place of slavery and performed these great signs before our eyes. He also protected us all along the way we went and among all the peoples whose lands we traveled through. 18 The LORD drove out before us all the peoples, including the Amorites who lived in the land. We too will worship the LORD, because He is our God."

Joshua Warns Them

19 But Joshua told the people, "You will not be able to worship the LORD, because He is a holy God. He is a jealous God; He will not remove your transgressions and sins. 20 If you abandon the LORD and worship foreign gods, He will turn against ⌊you⌋, harm you, and completely destroy you, after He has been good to you."

21 "No!" the people answered Joshua. "We will worship the LORD."

22 Joshua then told the people, "You are witnesses against yourselves that you yourselves have chosen to worship the LORD."

"We are witnesses," they said.

23 "Then get rid of the foreign gods that are among you and offer your hearts to the LORD, the God of Israel."

24 So the people said to Joshua, "We will worship the LORD our God and obey Him."

Joshua's Memorial Stone

25 On that day Joshua made a covenant for the people at Shechem and established a statute and ordinance for them. 26 Joshua recorded these things in the book of the law of God; he also took a large stone and set it up there under the oak next to the sanctuary of the LORD.

[a]24:12 Or sent terror

27 And Joshua said to all the people, "You see this stone—it will be a witness against us, for it has heard all the words the LORD said to us, and it will be a witness against you, so that you will not deny your God." 28 Then Joshua sent the people away, each to his own inheritance.

Burial of Three Leaders
Joshua Dies

29 After these things, the LORD's servant, Joshua son of Nun, died at the age of 110. 30 They buried him in his allotted territory at Timnath-serah, in the hill country of Ephraim north of Mount Gaash. 31 Israel worshiped the LORD throughout Joshua's lifetime and during the lifetimes of the elders who outlived Joshua, and who had experienced all the works the LORD had done for Israel.

Joseph's Bones

32 Joseph's bones, which the Israelites had brought up from Egypt, were buried at Shechem in the parcel of land Jacob had purchased from the sons of Hamor, Shechem's father, for 100 qesitahs.a It was an inheritance for Joseph's descendants.

Priest Eleazar Buried

33 And Eleazar son of Aaron died, and they buried him at Gibeah,b which had been given to his son Phinehas in the hill country of Ephraim.

JUDGES

God Chooses Judah
to Attack Canaanites

1 After the death of Joshua, the Israelites inquired of the LORD, "Who will be the first to fight for us against the Canaanites?"

2 The LORD answered, "Judah is to go. I have handed the land over to him."

3 Judah said to his brother Simeon, "Come with me to my territory, and let us fight against the Canaanites. I will also go with you to your territory." So Simeon went with him.

4 When Judah attacked, the LORD handed the Canaanites and Perizzites over to them. They struck down 10,000 men in Bezek. 5 They found Adoni-bezek in Bezek, fought against him, and struck down the Canaanites and Perizzites.

6 When Adoni-bezek fled, they pursued him, seized him, and cut off his thumbs and big toes. 7 Adoni-bezek said, "Seventy kings with their thumbs and big toes cut off used to pick up ˌscrapsˌc under my table. God has repaid me for what I have done." They brought him to Jerusalem, and he died there.

Judah Captures
Jerusalem and Hebron

8 The men of Judah fought against Jerusalem and captured it. They put the city to the sword and set it on fire. 9 Afterwards, the men of Judah marched down to fight against the Canaanites who were living in the hill country, the •Negev, and the Judean foothills.d 10 Judah also marched against the Canaanites who were living in Hebron

---

a24:32 The value of this currency is unknown.   b24:33 = the Hill   c1:7 Lit toes are gathering   d1:9 Or the Shephelah

(Hebron was formerly named Kiriath-arba). They struck down Sheshai, Ahiman, and Talmai. [11] From there they marched against the residents of Debir (Debir was formerly named Kiriath-sepher).

Caleb's Deal with Othniel and Achsah

[12] Caleb said, "Whoever strikes down and captures Kiriath-sepher, I will give my daughter Achsah to him as a wife." [13] So Othniel son of Kenaz, Caleb's youngest brother, captured it, and Caleb gave his daughter Achsah to him as his wife. [14] When she arrived, she persuaded Othniel[a] to ask her father for a field. As she got off her donkey, Caleb asked her,[b] "What do you want?" [15] She answered him, "Give me a blessing. Since you have given me land in the Negev, give me springs of water also." So Caleb gave her both the upper and lower springs.[c]

Judah's Exploits

[16] The descendants of the Kenite, Moses' father-in-law, had gone up with the men of Judah from the City of Palms[d] to the Wilderness of Judah, which was in the Negev of Arad. They went to live among the people. [17] Judah went with his brother Simeon, struck the Canaanites who were living in Zephath, and •completely destroyed the town. So they named the town Hormah. [18] Judah captured Gaza and its territory, Ashkelon and its territory, and Ekron and its territory.[e] [19] The LORD was with Judah and enabled them to take possession of the hill country, but they could not drive out the people who

were living in the valley because those people had iron chariots.[f]

Caleb Gets Hebron

[20] Judah gave Hebron to Caleb, just as Moses had promised. Then Caleb drove out the three sons of Anak who lived there.[g]

Benjamin's Failure in Jerusalem

[21] At the same time the Benjaminites did not drive out the Jebusites who were living in Jerusalem. The Jebusites have lived among the Benjaminites in Jerusalem to this day.

Success of House of Joseph

[22] The house of Joseph also attacked Bethel, and the LORD was with them. [23] They sent spies to Bethel (the town was formerly named Luz). [24] The spies saw a man coming out of the town and said to him, "Please show us how to get into town, and we will treat you well." [25] When he showed them the way into the town, they put the town to the sword but released the man and his entire family. [26] Then the man went to the land of the Hittites, built a town, and named it Luz. That is its name to this day.

Failure of Other Tribes

[27] At that time Manasseh failed to take possession of Beth-shean[h] and its villages,[i] or Taanach and its villages, or the residents of Dor and its villages, or the residents of Ibleam[j] and its villages, or the residents of Megiddo and its villages. But the Canaanites refused to leave[k] this

---

[a]**1:14** LXX reads *arrived, he pressured her*   [b]**1:14** LXX reads *She grumbled while on the donkey, and she cried out from the donkey, "Into the southland you sent me out," and Caleb said*   [c]**1:15** LXX reads *me redemption of water, and Caleb gave her according to her heart the redemption of the upper and the redemption of the lower*   [d]**1:16** = Jericho; Jdg 3:13; Dt 34:3; 2 Ch 28:15   [e]**1:18** LXX reads *Judah did not inherit Gaza and its borders nor Ashkelon and its borders nor Ekron and its borders or Azotus and its surrounding lands*   [f]**1:19** LXX reads *hill country, for they were not able to drive out the residents of the valley because Rechab separated it*   [g]**1:20** LXX reads *And he inherited from there the three cities of the sons of Anak.*   [h]**1:27** LXX reads *Beth-shean, which is a Scythian city*   [i]**1:27** LXX reads *its villages nor the fields around it*   [j]**1:27** LXX reads *Balaam*   [k]**1:27** LXX reads *Canaanites began to live in*

land. [28] When Israel became stronger, they made the Canaanites serve as forced labor but never drove them out completely.

[29] At that time Ephraim failed to drive out the Canaanites who were living in Gezer, so the Canaanites have lived among them in Gezer.[a]

[30] Zebulun failed to drive out the residents of Kitron or the residents of Nahalol, so the Canaanites lived among them and served as forced labor.

[31] Asher failed to drive out the residents of Acco[b] or of Sidon, or Ahlab, Achzib, Helbah, Aphik, or Rehob. [32] The Asherites lived among the Canaanites who were living in the land, because they failed to drive them out.

[33] Naphtali did not drive out the residents of Beth-shemesh or the residents of Beth-anath. They lived among the Canaanites who were living in the land, but the residents of Beth-shemesh and Beth-anath served as their forced labor.

[34] The Amorites forced the Danites into the hill country and did not allow them to go down into the valley. [35] The Amorites refused to leave Har-heres, Aijalon, and Shaalbim. When the house of Joseph got the upper hand, the Amorites[c] were made to serve as forced labor. [36] The territory of the Amorites extended from the ascent of Akrabbim, that is from Sela upward.

Patterns of Sin and Judgment

Angel Judges at Bochim

2 The Angel of the LORD went up from Gilgal to Bochim[d] and said, "I brought you out of Egypt and led you into the land I had promised to your fa-

thers. I also said: I will never break My covenant with you. [2] You are not to make a covenant with the people who are living in this land, and you are to tear down their altars.[e] But you have not obeyed Me. What is this you have done? [3] Therefore, I now say: I will not drive out these people before you. They will be thorns[f] [g] in your sides, and their gods will be a trap to you." [4] When the Angel of the LORD had spoken these words to all the Israelites, the people wept loudly. [5] So they named that place Bochim[h] and offered sacrifices there to the LORD.

Joshua's Death

[6] Joshua sent the people away, and the Israelites went to take possession of the land, each to his own inheritance. [7] The people worshiped the LORD throughout Joshua's lifetime and during the lifetimes of the elders who outlived[i] Joshua. They had seen all the LORD's great works He had done for Israel.

[8] Joshua son of Nun, the servant of the LORD, died at the age of 110. [9] They buried him in the territory of his inheritance, in Timnath-heres, in the hill country of Ephraim, north of Mount Gaash. [10] That whole generation was also gathered to their ancestors. After them another generation rose up who did not know the LORD or the works He had done for Israel.

Israel Worships Baals and Ashtoreths

[11] The Israelites did what was evil in the LORD's sight. They worshiped the •Baals [12] and abandoned the LORD, the God of their fathers, who had brought them out of Egypt. They went after other gods from the surrounding peoples and

---

[a]**1:29** LXX reads Gezer, and became forced labor   [b]**1:31** LXX reads Acco, and they became for him forced labor and the residents of Dor   [c]**1:35** LXX reads Joseph became strong on the Amorites, they   [d]**2:1** LXX reads to the weeping place and to Bethel and to the house of Israel   [e]**2:2** LXX reads with those lying in wait in this land; neither are you to fall down in worship to their gods, but their carved images you must break to pieces and their altars you must destroy   [f]**2:3** LXX reads affliction   [g]**2:3** Lit traps   [h]**2:5** Or Weeping   [i]**2:7** Lit extended their days after

bowed down to them. They infuriated the LORD, [13] for they abandoned Him and worshiped Baal and the •Ashtoreths.

Lord's Anger and Judgment

[14] The LORD's anger burned against Israel, and He handed them over to marauders who raided them. He sold them to[a] the enemies around them, so that they could no longer resist their enemies. [15] Whenever the Israelites went out, the LORD[b] was against them and brought disaster ⌊on them⌋, just as He had promised and sworn to them. So they suffered greatly.

God Raises Judges

[16] The LORD raised up judges, who saved them from the power of their marauders, [17] but they did not listen to their judges. Instead, they prostituted themselves with other gods, bowing down to them. They quickly turned from the way of their fathers, who had walked in obedience to the LORD's commands. They did not do as their fathers did. [18] Whenever the LORD raised up a judge for the Israelites, the LORD was with him and saved the people from the power of their enemies while the judge was still alive.[c] The LORD was moved to pity whenever they groaned because of those who were oppressing and afflicting them. [19] Whenever the judge died, the Israelites would act even more corruptly than their fathers, going after other gods to worship and bow down to them. They did not turn from their ⌊evil⌋ practices or their obstinate ways.

Lord Is Angry

[20] The LORD's anger burned against Israel, and He declared, "Because this nation has violated My covenant that I made with their fathers and disobeyed Me, [21] I will no longer drive out before them any of the nations Joshua left when he died. [22] ⌊I did this⌋ to test Israel and to see whether they would keep the LORD's way by walking in it, as their fathers had." [23] The LORD left these nations and did not drive them out immediately. He did not hand them over to Joshua.

The LORD Tests Israel

3 These are the nations the LORD left in order to test Israel, since none of these Israelites had fought in[d] any of the wars with Canaan. [2] This was to teach the future generations of the Israelites ⌊how to fight in⌋ battle, especially those who had not fought before.[e] [3] ⌊These nations included:⌋ the five rulers of the Philistines and all of the Canaanites, the Sidonians, and the Hivites who lived in the Lebanese mountains[f] from Mount Baal-hermon as far as the entrance to Hamath.[g] [4] The LORD left them to test Israel, to determine if they would keep the LORD's commands He had given their fathers through[h] Moses. [5] But they settled among the Canaanites, Hittites, Amorites, Perizzites, Hivites, and Jebusites. [6] The Israelites took their daughters as wives for themselves, gave their own daughters to their sons, and worshiped their gods.

First Judge Othniel

[7] The Israelites did what was evil in the LORD's sight; they forgot the LORD their God and worshiped the •Baals and the •Asherahs. [8] The LORD's anger burned against Israel, and He sold them to[a] Cushan-rishathaim[i] king of Aram of the Two Rivers,[j] and the Israelites served him eight years.

[9] The Israelites cried out to the LORD. So the LORD raised up Othniel son of

---

[a] **2:14, 3:8** Lit *into the hand of* [b] **2:15** Lit *the hand of the LORD* [c] **2:18** Lit *enemies all the days of the judge* [d] **3:1** Lit *had known* [e] **3:2** Lit *not known it* [f] **3:3** LXX reads *in Lebanon,* without reference to mountains [g] **3:3** Or *as Lebo-hamath* [h] **3:4** Lit *by the hand of* [i] **3:8** Lit *Doubly-Evil* [j] **3:8** Or *Aram-naharaim;* = Mesopotamia

Kenaz, Caleb's youngest brother as a deliverer to save the Israelites. ¹⁰ The Spirit of the LORD was on him, and he judged Israel. Othniel went out to battle, and the LORD handed over Cushan-rishathaim king of Aram to him, so that Othniel overpowered him. ¹¹ Then the land was peaceful 40 years, and Othniel son of Kenaz died.

Judge Ehud

¹² The Israelites again did what was evil in the LORD's sight. He gave Eglon king of Moab power over Israel, because they had done what was evil in the LORD's sight. ¹³ After Eglon convinced the Ammonites and the Amalekites to join forces with him, he attacked and defeated Israel and took possession of the City of Palms.ᵃ ¹⁴ The Israelites served Eglon king of Moab 18 years.

¹⁵ Then the Israelites cried out to the LORD, and He raised up Ehud son of Gera, a left-handed Benjaminite,ᵇ as a deliverer for them. The Israelites sent him to Eglon king of Moab with tribute ⌞money⌟.

Ehud Assassinates Eglon

¹⁶ Ehud made himself a double-edged sword 18 inches long.ᶜ He strapped it to his right thigh under his clothes ¹⁷ and brought the tribute to Eglon king of Moab, who was an extremely fat man. ¹⁸ When Ehud had finished presenting the tribute, he dismissed the people who had carried it. ¹⁹ At the carved images near Gilgal he returned and said, "King ⌞Eglon⌟, I have a secret message for you." The king called for silence, and all his attendants left him. ²⁰ Then Ehud approached him while he was sitting alone in his room upstairs ⌞where it was⌟ cool. Ehud said, "I have a word from God for you," and the king stood up from his throne.ᵈ ²¹ Ehudᵉ reached with his left hand, took the sword from his right thigh, and plunged it into Eglon's belly. ²² Even the handle went in after the blade, and Eglon's fat closed in over it, so that Ehud did not withdraw the sword from his belly. And Eglon's insides came out. ²³ Ehud escaped by way of the porch, closing and locking the doors of the upstairs room behind him.

Ehud Leads Israel to Victory

²⁴ Ehud was gone when Eglon's servants came in. They looked and found the doors of the upstairs room locked and thought he was relieving himselfᶠ in the cool room. ²⁵ The servants waited until they became worried and saw that he had still not opened the doors of the upstairs room. So they took the key and opened the doors—and there was their lord lying dead on the floor!

²⁶ Ehud escaped while the servants waited. He crossed over ⌞the Jordan⌟ near the carved images and reached Seirah. ²⁷ After he arrived, he sounded the ram's horn throughout the hill country of Ephraim. The Israelites came down with him from the hill country, and he became their leader. ²⁸ He told them, "Follow me, because the LORD has handed over your enemies, the Moabites, to you." So they followed him, captured the fords of the Jordan leading to Moab, and did not allow anyone to cross over. ²⁹ At that time they struck down about 10,000 Moabites, all strong and able-bodied men. Not one of them escaped. ³⁰ Moab became subject to Is-

---

ᵃ**3:13** = Jericho; Jdg 1:16; Dt 34:3; 2 Ch 28:15   ᵇ**3:15** = son of the right hand   ᶜ**3:16** Lit *sword a gomed in length*
ᵈ**3:20** LXX reads *"A word of my God for you, O king," and Eglon rose up from the throne near him.*   ᵉ**3:21** LXX reads *It happened that when he rose up, Ehud immediately*   ᶠ**3:24** Lit *was covering his feet*

rael that day, and the land was peaceful 80 years.

Judge Shamgar

[31] After Ehud, Shamgar son of Anath ⌊became judge⌋. He delivered Israel by striking down 600 Philistines with an oxgoad.

Judge Deborah

Evil King Jabin

4 The Israelites again did what was evil in the sight of the LORD after Ehud had died. [2] So the LORD sold them into the hand of Jabin king of Canaan, who reigned in Hazor. The commander of his forces was Sisera who lived in Harosheth of the Nations.[a] [3] Then the Israelites cried out to the LORD, because Jabin had 900 iron chariots, and he harshly oppressed them 20 years.

[4] Deborah, a woman who was a prophet and the wife of Lappidoth, was judging Israel at that time. [5] It was her custom to sit under the palm tree of Deborah between Ramah and Bethel in the hill country of Ephraim, and the Israelites went up to her for judgment.

Deborah Commissions Barak

[6] She summoned Barak son of Abinoam from Kedesh in Naphtali and said to him, "Hasn't the LORD, the God of Israel, commanded ⌊you⌋: 'Go, deploy ⌊the troops⌋ on Mount Tabor, and take with you 10,000 men from the Naphtalites and Zebulunites? [7] Then I will lure Sisera commander of Jabin's forces, his chariots, and his army at the •Wadi Kishon ⌊to fight⌋ against you, and I will hand him over to you.'"

Barak's Timidity

[8] Barak said to her, "If you will go with me, I will go. But if you will not go with me, I will not go."

[9] "I will go with you," she said, "but you will receive no honor on the road you are about to take, because the LORD will sell Sisera into a woman's hand." So Deborah got up and went with Barak to Kedesh. [10] Barak summoned Zebulun and Naphtali to Kedesh; 10,000 men followed him, and Deborah also went with him.

[11] Now Heber the Kenite had moved away from the Kenites, the sons of Hobab, Moses' father-in-law, and pitched his tent beside the oak tree of Zaanannim, which was near Kedesh.

Commander Sisera Threatens

[12] It was reported to Sisera that Barak son of Abinoam had gone up Mount Tabor. [13] Sisera summoned all his 900 iron chariots and all the people who were with him from Harosheth of the Nations[a] to the Wadi Kishon. [14] Then Deborah said to Barak, "Move on, for this is the day the LORD has handed Sisera over to you. Hasn't the LORD gone before you?" So Barak came down from Mount Tabor with 10,000 men following him.

Barak Defeats Sisera's Army

[15] The LORD threw Sisera, all his charioteers, and all his army into confusion with the sword before Barak. Sisera left his chariot and fled on foot. [16] Barak pursued the chariots and the army as far as Harosheth of the Nations,[a] and the whole army of Sisera fell by the sword; not a single man was left.

Jael Assassinates Sisera

[17] Meanwhile, Sisera had fled on foot to the tent of Jael, the wife of Heber the Kenite, because there was peace between Jabin king of Hazor and the family of Heber the Kenite. [18] Jael went out to

---

[a]**4:2,13,16** Or *Harosheth-ha-goiim*

greet Sisera and said to him, "Come in, my lord. Come in with me. Don't be afraid." So he went into her tent, and she covered him with a rug. ¹⁹ He said to her, "Please give me a little water to drink for I am thirsty." She opened a container of milk, gave him a drink, and covered him ⌊again⌋. ²⁰ Then he said to her, "Stand at the entrance to the tent. If a man comes and asks you, 'Is there a man here?' say, 'No.'" ²¹ While he was sleeping from exhaustion, Heber's wife Jael took a tent peg, grabbed a hammer, and went silently to Sisera. She hammered the peg into his temple and drove it into the ground, and he died.

²² When Barak arrived in pursuit of Sisera, Jael went out to greet him and said to him, "Come and I will show you the man you are looking for." So he went in with her, and there was Sisera lying dead with a tent peg through his temple!

²³ That day God subdued Jabin king of Canaan before the Israelites. ²⁴ The power of the Israelites continued to increase against Jabin king of Canaan until they destroyed him.

Song of Deborah and Barak

5 On that day Deborah and Barak son of Abinoam sang:

² When the leaders lead^a in Israel,
when the people volunteer,
praise the LORD.
³ Listen, kings! Pay attention,
princes!
I will sing to the LORD;
I will sing praise to the LORD God
of Israel.
⁴ LORD, when You came from Seir,
when You marched from the fields
of Edom,
the earth trembled,

the heavens poured ⌊rain⌋,
the clouds poured water.
⁵ The mountains melted
before the LORD,
even Sinai^b before the LORD,
the God of Israel.

⁶ In the days of Shamgar son of Anath,
in the days of Jael,
the main ways were deserted,
because travelers kept
to the side roads.
⁷ Villages were deserted,^{c}
they were deserted in Israel,
until I,^{d} Deborah,
I^d arose, a mother in Israel.
⁸ Israel chose new gods,
then war was in the gates.
Not a shield or spear was seen
among 40,000 in Israel.
⁹ My heart is with the leaders
of Israel,
with the volunteers of the people.
Praise the LORD!
¹⁰ You who ride on white^c donkeys,
who sit on saddle blankets,
and who travel on the road,
give praise!
¹¹ Let them tell the righteous acts
of the LORD,
the righteous deeds of His warriors
in Israel,
with the voices of the singers
at the watering places.^{e}

Then the LORD's people went down
to the gates.
¹² "Awake! Awake, Deborah!
Awake! Awake, sing a song!
Arise Barak,
and take hold of your captives,
son of Abinoam!"
¹³ The survivors came down
to the nobles;

---

^{a}**5:2** Lit *the locks of hair are loose* ^{b}**5:5** Or *LORD, this [One of] Sinai* ^{c}**5:7,10** Hb obscure ^{d}**5:7** Or *you*
^{e}**5:11** Verse obscure

the LORD's people came down
to me[a] with the warriors.
14 Those with their roots in Amalek[b]
ʟcameʟ from Ephraim;
Benjamin ʟcame withʟ your people
after you.
The leaders came down
from Machir,
and those who carry
a marshal's staff ʟcameʟ
from Zebulun.
15 The princes of Issachar were
with Deborah;
Issachar was with Barak.
They set out at his heels
in the valley.
There was great searching[c] of heart
among the clans of Reuben.
16 Why did you sit
among the sheepfolds
listening to the playing of pipes
for the flocks?
There was great searching of heart
among the clans of Reuben.
17 Gilead remained
beyond the Jordan.
Dan, why did you linger
at the ships?
Asher remained at the seashore
and stayed in his harbors.
18 Zebulun was a people risking
their lives,
Naphtali also, on the heights
of the battlefield.

19 Kings came and fought.
Then the kings of Canaan fought
at Taanach by the waters
of Megiddo,
but they took no spoil of silver.
20 The stars fought from the heavens;
the stars fought with Sisera
from their courses.
21 The river Kishon swept them away,

the ancient river, the river Kishon.
March on, my soul, in strength!
22 The horses' hooves then
hammered—
the galloping, galloping
of his[d] stallions.
23 "Curse Meroz," says the Angel
of the LORD,
"Bitterly curse her inhabitants,
for they did not come to help
the LORD,
to help the LORD against
the mighty warriors."

24 Jael is most blessed of women,
the wife of Heber the Kenite;
she is most blessed among
tent-dwelling women.
25 He asked for water; she gave him
milk.
She brought him curdled milk
in a majestic bowl.
26 She reached for a tent peg,
her right hand,
for a workman's mallet.
Then she hammered Sisera—
she crushed his head;
she shattered and pierced
his temple.
27 He collapsed, he fell, he lay down
at[e] her feet;
he collapsed, he fell at her feet;
where he collapsed, there he fell—
dead.
28 Sisera's mother looked
through the window;
she ʟpeeredʟ through the lattice,
crying out:
"Why is his chariot so long
in coming?
Why don't I hear the hoofbeats
of his horses?"[f]
29 Her wisest princesses answer her;
she even answers herself:[g]

---

[a]5:13 LXX reads *down for him*   [b]5:14 LXX reads *in the valley*   [c]5:15 Some Hb mss, Syr read *There were great resolves*   [d]5:22 = Sisera's   [e]5:27 Lit *between*   [f]5:28 Lit *Why have the hoofbeats of his chariot delayed*   [g]5:29 Lit *answers her words*

30 "Are they not finding and dividing
the spoil—
a girl or two for each warrior,
the spoil of colored garments
for Sisera,
the spoil of
an embroidered garment or two
for my neck?"[a]

31 LORD, may all your enemies perish
as Sisera did.[b]
But may those who love Him
be like the rising of the sun
in its strength.

And the land was peaceful 40 years.

Midian Oppresses Israel

6 The Israelites did what was evil in the sight of the LORD. So the LORD handed them over to Midian seven years, 2 and they oppressed Israel. Because of Midian, the Israelites made hiding places for themselves in the mountains, caves, and strongholds. 3 Whenever the Israelites planted crops, the Midianites, Amalekites, and the eastern peoples came and attacked them. 4 They encamped against them and destroyed the produce of the land, even as far as Gaza. They left nothing for Israel to eat, as well as no sheep, ox or donkey. 5 For the Midianites came with their cattle and their tents like a great swarm of locusts. They and their camels were without number, and they entered the land to waste it. 6 So Israel became poverty-stricken because of Midian, and the Israelites cried out to the LORD.

God's Prophet Rebukes Israel

7 When the Israelites cried out to Him because of Midian, 8 the LORD sent a prophet to them. He said to them, "This is what the LORD God of Israel says: 'I brought you out of Egypt and out of the place of slavery. 9 I delivered you from the power of Egypt and the power of all who oppressed you. I drove them out before you and gave you their land. 10 I said to you: I am the LORD your God. Do not fear the gods of the Amorites whose land you live in. But you did not obey Me.'"

LORD Calls Gideon

11 The Angel[c] of the LORD came, and He[d] sat under the oak that was in Ophrah, which belonged to Joash, the Abiezrite. His son Gideon was threshing wheat in the wine vat in order to hide it from the Midianites. 12 Then the Angel of the LORD appeared to him and said: "The LORD is with you, mighty warrior."

Gideon's Skepticism

13 Gideon said to Him, "Please Sir,[e] if the LORD is with us, why has all this happened?[f] And where are all His wonders that our fathers told us about? They said, 'Hasn't the LORD brought us out of Egypt?' But now the LORD has abandoned us and handed us over to Midian."

God Encourages

14 The LORD[g] turned to him and said, "Go in the strength you have and deliver Israel from the power of Midian. Am I not sending you?"

Gideon Protests

15 He said to Him, "Please, Lord, how can I deliver Israel? Look, my family is the weakest in Manasseh, and I am the youngest in my father's house."

16 "But I will be with you," the LORD said to him. "You will strike Midian down ⌊as if it were⌋ one man."

ᵃ**5:30** Hb obscure   ᵇ**5:31** Lit *perish thus*   ᶜ**6:11** Or *angel*   ᵈ**6:11** Or *he* (and so throughout this chap if this angel is a divine messenger and not a theophany)   ᵉ**6:13** Lit *Please, my Lord*, or *Please, my lord*   ᶠ**6:13** Lit *this found us out*   ᵍ**6:14** LXX reads *The Angel of the LORD*

Gideon Asks for Sign

¹⁷ Then he said to Him, "If I have found favor in Your sight, give me a sign that You are speaking with me. ¹⁸ Please do not leave this place until I return to You. Let me bring my gift and set it before You."

And He said, "I will stay until you return."

¹⁹ So Gideon went and prepared a young goat and unleavened bread from a half bushel^a of flour. He placed the meat in a basket and the broth in a pot. He brought them out and offered them to Him under the oak.

²⁰ The Angel of God said to him, "Take the meat with the unleavened bread, put it on this stone, and pour the broth ₍on it₎." And he did so.

²¹ The Angel of the LORD extended the tip of the staff that was in His hand and touched the meat and the unleavened bread. Fire came up from the rock and consumed the meat and the unleavened bread. Then the Angel of the LORD vanished from his sight.

²² When Gideon realized that He was the Angel of the LORD, he said, "Oh no, Lord GOD! I have seen the Angel of the LORD face to face!"

²³ But the LORD said to him, "Peace to you. Don't be afraid, for you will not die." ²⁴ So Gideon built an altar to the LORD there and called it Yahweh Shalom.^b It is in Ophrah of the Abiezrites until today.

Lord Tells Gideon to
Replace Baal's Altar

²⁵ On that very night the LORD said to him, "Take your father's young bull and a second bull seven years old. Then tear down the altar of •Baal that belongs to your father and cut down the •Asherah pole beside it. ²⁶ Build a well-constructed altar to the LORD your God on the top of this rock. Take the second bull and offer it as a •burnt offering with the wood of the Asherah pole you cut down." ²⁷ So Gideon took 10 of his male servants and did as the LORD had told him. But because he was too afraid of his father's household and the men of the city to do it in the daytime, he did it at night.

City Accuses Gideon

²⁸ When the men of the city got up in the morning, they found Baal's altar torn down, the Asherah pole beside it cut down, and the second bull offered up on the altar that had been built. ²⁹ They said to each other, "Who did this?" After they made a thorough investigation, they said, "Gideon son of Joash did it."

³⁰ Then the men of the city said to Joash, "Bring out your son. He must die, because he tore down Baal's altar and cut down the Asherah pole beside it."

Father Joash Defends Son

³¹ But Joash said to all who stood against him, "Would you plead Baal's case for him? Would you save him? Whoever pleads his case will be put to death by morning! If he is a god, let him plead his own case, because someone tore down his altar." ³² That day, Gideon's father called him Jerubbaal, saying, "Let Baal plead his case with him," because he tore down his altar.

Gideon Begins to Lead

³³ All the Midianites, Amalekites, and Qedemites gathered together, crossed over ₍the Jordan₎, and camped in the Valley of Jezreel.

³⁴ The Spirit of the LORD enveloped Gideon, and he blew the ram's horn and the

---

^a**6:19** Lit *an ephah*   ^b**6:24** = *The LORD Is Peace*

Abiezrites rallied behind him. ³⁵ He sent messengers throughout all of Manasseh, who rallied behind him. He also sent messengers throughout Asher, Zebulun, and Naphtali, who ⌊also⌋ came to meet him.

Gideon Asks God for Sign of Fleece

³⁶ Then Gideon said to God, "If You will deliver Israel by my hand, as You said, ³⁷ I will put a fleece of wool here on the threshing floor. If dew is only on the fleece, and all the ground is dry, I will know that You will deliver Israel by my strength, as You said." ³⁸ And that is what happened. When he got up early in the morning, he squeezed the fleece and wrung dew out of it, filling a bowl with water.

Second Sign of Fleece

³⁹ Gideon then said to God, "Don't be angry with me; let me speak one more time. Please allow me to make one more test with the fleece. Let it remain dry, and the dew be all over the ground." ⁴⁰ That night God did ⌊as Gideon requested⌋: only the fleece was dry, and dew was all over the ground.

God Selects Gideon's Army

7 Jerubbaal (that is, Gideon) and everyone who was with him, got up early and camped beside the spring of Harod. The camp of Midian was north of them, below the hill of Moreh, in the valley. ² The LORD said to Gideon, "You have too many people for Me to hand the Midianites over to you,^a or else Israel might brag:^b 'I did it myself.' ³ Now announce in the presence of the people: 'Whoever is fearful and trembling may turn back and leave Mount Gilead.'" So 22,000 of the people turned back, but 10,000 remained.

God Cuts Force to 300

⁴ Then the LORD said to Gideon, "There are still too many people. Take them down to the water, and I will test them for you there. If I say to you, 'This one can go with you,' he can go. But if I say about anyone, 'This one cannot go with you,' he cannot go." ⁵ So he brought the people down to the water, and the LORD said to Gideon, "Separate everyone who laps water with his tongue like a dog. Do the same with everyone who kneels to drink." ⁶ The number of those who lapped with their hands to their mouths was 300 men, and all the rest of the people knelt to drink water. ⁷ The LORD said to Gideon, "I will deliver you with the 300 men who lapped and hand the Midianites over to you. But everyone else is to go home." ⁸ So Gideon sent all the Israelites to their tents, but kept the 300 who took^c the people's provisions and their trumpets. The camp of Midian was below him in the valley.

Gideon Spies on the Midianite Camp

⁹ That night the LORD said to him, "Get up and go into the camp, for I have given it into your hand. ¹⁰ But if you are afraid to go to the camp, go with Purah your servant. ¹¹ Listen to what they say, and then you will be strengthened to go to the camp." So he went with Purah his servant to the outpost of the troops^d who were in the camp.

The Midianite's Dream of Defeat

¹² Now the Midianites, Amalekites, and all the Qedemites had settled down in the valley like a swarm of locusts, and their camels were as innumerable as the sand on the seashore. ¹³ When Gideon arrived, there was a man telling his

---

^a7:2 Lit them   ^b7:2 Lit brag against Me   ^c7:8 Lit took in their hands   ^d7:11 Lit of those who were arranged in companies of 50

friend ⌊about⌋ a dream. He said, "Listen, I had a dream: a loaf of barley bread came tumbling into the Midianite camp, struck a tent, and it fell. The loaf turned the tent upside down so that it collapsed."

14 His friend answered: "This is nothing less than the sword of Gideon son of Joash, the Israelite. God has handed the entire Midianite camp over to him."

Gideon Defeats Midianites

15 When Gideon heard the account of the dream and its interpretation, he bowed in worship. He returned to Israel's camp and said, "Get up, for the LORD has handed the Midianite camp over to you." 16 Then he divided the 300 men into three companies and gave each of the men a trumpet in one hand and an empty pitcher with a torch inside it ⌊in the other⌋.

17 "Watch me," he said,[a] "and do the same. When I come to the outpost of the camp, do as I do. 18 When I and everyone with me blow our trumpets, you are also to blow your trumpets all around the camp. Then you will say, 'The sword of the LORD and of Gideon!'"

19 Gideon and the 100 men who were with him went to the outpost of the camp at the beginning of the middle watch after the sentries had been stationed. They blew their trumpets and broke the pitchers that were in their hands. 20 The three companies blew their trumpets and shattered their pitchers. They held their torches in their left hands, their trumpets[b] in their right hands, and shouted, "The sword of the LORD and of Gideon!" 21 Each Israelite took his position around the camp, and the entire ⌊Midianite⌋ army fled, and cried out as they ran. 22 When Gideon's

men blew their 300 trumpets, the LORD set the swords of each man in the army against each other. They fled to Beth-shittah in the direction of Zererah as far as the border of Abel-meholah near Tabbath. 23 Then the men of Israel were called from Naphtali, Asher, and Manasseh, and they pursued the Midianites.

Ephraim Joins Battle

24 Gideon sent messengers throughout the hill country of Ephraim with this message: "Come down to intercept the Midianites and take control of the watercourses ahead of them as far as Beth-barah and the Jordan." So all the men of Ephraim were called out, and they took control of the watercourses as far as Beth-barah and the Jordan. 25 They captured Oreb and Zeeb, the two princes of Midian; they killed Oreb at the rock of Oreb and Zeeb at the winepress of Zeeb, while they were pursuing the Midianites. They brought the heads of Oreb and Zeeb to Gideon across the Jordan.

8 The men of Ephraim said to him, "Why have you done this to us, not calling us when you went to fight against the Midianites?" And they argued with him violently.

Gideon Calms Angry Ephraimites

2 So he said to them, "What have I done now compared to you? Is not the gleaning of Ephraim better than the vintage of Abiezer? 3 God handed over to you Oreb and Zeeb, the two princes of Midian. What was I able to do compared to you?" When he said this, their anger against him subsided.

Gideon Pursues Kings of Midian

4 Gideon and the 300 men came to the Jordan and crossed it. They were

---

a7:17 Lit said to them   b7:20 Lit trumpets to blow

exhausted, but still in pursuit. ⁵ He said to the men of Succoth, "Please give some loaves of bread to the people who are following me,ᵃ because they are exhausted, for I am pursuing Zebah and Zalmunna, the kings of Midian."

⁶ But the princes of Succoth asked, "Areᵇ Zebah and Zalmunna now in your hands that we should give bread to your army?"

⁷ Gideon replied, "Very well, when the LORD has handed Zebah and Zalmunna over to me, I will trampleᶜ your flesh on thorns and briers from the wilderness!" ⁸ He went from there to Penuel and asked the same thing from them. The men of Penuel answered just as the men of Succoth had answered. ⁹ He also told the men of Penuel, "When I return in peace, I will tear down this tower!"

Gideon Defeats Midian Kings

¹⁰ Now Zebah and Zalmunna were in Karkor, and with them was their army of about 15,000 men, who were all those left of the entire army of the Qedemites. Those who had been killed were 120,000 warriors.ᵈ ¹¹ Gideon traveled on the caravan route,ᵉ east of Nobah and Jogbehah, and attacked their army while the army was unsuspecting. ¹² Zebah and Zalmunna fled, and he pursued them. He captured these two kings of Midian and routed the entire army.

Gideon Takes Revenge on Succoth

¹³ Gideon son of Joash returned from the battle by the ascent of Heres. ¹⁴ He captured a youth from the men of Succoth and interrogated him. The youth wrote down for him the names of the 77 princes and elders of Succoth. ¹⁵ Then he went to the men of Succoth and said, "Here are Zebah and Zal-

munna. You taunted me about them, saying, 'Areᵇ Zebah and Zalmunna now in your power that we should give bread to your exhausted men?'" ¹⁶ So he took the elders of the city, as well as some thorns and briers from the wilderness, and he disciplined the men of Succoth with them. ¹⁷ He also tore down the tower of Penuel and killed the men of the city.

Midian Kings Executed

¹⁸ He asked Zebah and Zalmunna, "What kind of men did you kill at Tabor?"

"They were like you," they said. "Each resembled the son of a king."

¹⁹ So he said, "They were my brothers, the sons of my mother! As the LORD lives, if you had let them live, I would not kill you." ²⁰ Then he said to Jether, his firstborn, "Get up and kill them." The youth did not draw his sword, because he was afraid, for he was still a youth.

²¹ Zebah and Zalmunna said, "Get up and kill us yourself, for a man is judged by his strength." So Gideon got up, killed Zebah and Zalmunna, and took the crescent ornaments that were on the necks of their camels.

Gideon's Legacy

²² Then the Israelites said to Gideon, "Rule over us, you as well as your sons and your grandsons, for you delivered us from the power of Midian."

²³ But Gideon said to them, "I will not rule over you, and my son will not rule over you; the LORD will rule over you." ²⁴ Then he said to them, "Let me make a request of you: Everyone give me an earring from his plunder." Now the enemy had gold earrings because they were Ishmaelites.

ᵃ8:5 Lit are at my feet ᵇ8:6,15 Lit Are the hands of ᶜ8:7 Or tear ᵈ8:10 Lit men who drew the sword ᵉ8:11 Lit on the route of those who live in tents

²⁵ They said, "We agree to give them." So they spread out a mantle, and everyone threw an earring from his plunder on it. ²⁶ The weight of the gold earrings he requested was about 43 pounds^a of gold, in addition to the crescent ornaments and ear pendants, the purple garments on the kings of Midian, and the chains on the necks of their camels. ²⁷ Gideon made an ephod from all this and put it in Ophrah, his hometown. Then all Israel prostituted themselves with it there, and it became a snare to Gideon and his household.

²⁸ So Midian was subdued before the Israelites, and they were no longer a threat.^b The land was peaceful 40 years during the days of Gideon. ²⁹ Jerubbaal ⌊(that is, Gideon)⌋ son of Joash went back to live at his house.

Gideon's Death

³⁰ Gideon had 70 sons, his own offspring, since he had many wives. ³¹ His concubine who was in Shechem also bore him a son, and he named him Abimelech. ³² Then Gideon son of Joash died at a ripe old age and was buried in the tomb of his father Joash in Ophrah of the Abiezrites.

After Gideon, Israel Rebels

³³ When Gideon died, the Israelites turned and prostituted themselves with the •Baals and made Baal-berith^c their god. ³⁴ The Israelites did not remember the LORD their God who had delivered them from the power of the enemies around them. ³⁵ They did not show kindness to the house of Jerubbaal (⌊that is,⌋ Gideon) for all the good he had done for Israel.

Gideon's Scheming Son Abimelech

9 Abimelech son of Jerubbaal went to his mother's brothers at Shechem and spoke to them and to all his maternal grandfather's clan, saying, ² "Please speak in the presence of all the lords of Shechem, 'Is it better for you that 70 men, all the sons of Jerubbaal, rule over you or that one man rule over you?' Remember that I am your own flesh and blood."^d

Evil King Abimelech

³ His mother's relatives spoke all these words about him in the presence of all the lords of Shechem, and they were favorable to Abimelech, for they said, "He is our brother." ⁴ So they gave him 70 pieces of silver from the temple of Baal-berith.^c Abimelech hired worthless and reckless men with this money, and they followed him.

Abimelech Murders Brothers

⁵ He went to his father's house in Ophrah and killed his 70 brothers, the sons of Jerubbaal, on top of a large stone. But Jotham, the youngest son of Jerubbaal, survived, because he hid himself. ⁶ Then all the lords of Shechem and of Beth-millo gathered together and proceeded to make Abimelech king at the oak of the pillar in Shechem.

Jotham's Prophetic Parable

⁷ When they told Jotham, he climbed to the top of Mount Gerizim, raised his voice, and called to them:

> Listen to me, lords of Shechem,
> and may God listen to you:
> ⁸ The trees set out
> to anoint a king over themselves.
> They said to the olive tree,
> "Reign over us."
> ⁹ But the olive tree said to them,
> "Should I stop giving my oil

^a**8:26** Lit *1,700 shekels* ^b**8:28** Lit *they no longer raised their head* ^c**8:33; 9:4** Lit *Baal of the Covenant,* or *Lord of the Covenant* ^d**9:2** Lit *your bone and your flesh*

that honors both God and man,
and rule[a] over the trees?"

10 Then the trees said to the fig tree,
"Come and reign over us."
11 But the fig tree said to them,
"Should I stop giving
my sweetness and my good fruit,
and rule[a] over trees?"

12 Later, the trees said
to the grapevine,
"Come and reign over us."
13 But the grapevine said to them,
"Should I stop giving my wine
that cheers both God and man,
and rule[a] over trees?"

14 Finally, all the trees said
to the bramble,
"Come and reign over us."
15 The bramble said to the trees,
"If you really are anointing me
as king over you,
come and find refuge in my shade.
But if not,
may fire come out from the bramble
and consume the cedars
of Lebanon."

Jotham's Warning

16 "Now if you have acted faithfully and honestly in making Abimelech king, if you have done well by Jerubbaal and his family, and if you have rewarded him appropriately for what he did— 17 for my father fought for you, risked his life, and delivered you from the hand of Midian, 18 and now you have attacked my father's house today, killed his 70 sons on top of a large stone, and made Abimelech, the son of his slave, king over the lords of Shechem 'because he is your brother'— 19 if then, you have acted faithfully and honestly with Jerubbaal and his house this day, rejoice in Abimelech and may he also rejoice in you. 20 But if not, may fire come from Abimelech and consume the lords of Shechem and Beth-millo, and may fire come from the lords of Shechem and Beth-millo and consume Abimelech." 21 Then Jotham fled, escaping to Beer, and lived there because of his brother Abimelech.

God's Justice for Abimelech

22 When Abimelech had ruled over Israel three years, 23 God sent an evil spirit between Abimelech and the lords of Shechem. They treated Abimelech deceitfully, 24 so that the crime against the 70 sons of Jerubbaal might come to justice and their blood would be avenged on their brother Abimelech, who killed them, and on the lords of Shechem, who had helped him kill his brothers. 25 The lords of Shechem rebelled against him by putting people on the tops of the mountains to ambush and rob everyone who passed by them on the road. So this was reported to Abimelech.

26 Gaal son of Ebed came with his brothers and crossed into Shechem, and the lords of Shechem trusted him. 27 So they went out to the countryside and harvested grapes from their vineyards. They trod the grapes and held a celebration. Then they went to the house of their god, and as they ate and drank, they cursed Abimelech. 28 Gaal son of Ebed said, "Who is Abimelech and who is Shechem that we should serve him? Isn't he the son of Jerubbaal, and isn't Zebul his officer? You are to serve the men of Hamor, the father of Shechem. Why should we serve Abimelech? 29 If only these people were in my power, I would remove Abimelech." So he said[b] to Abimelech, "Gather your army and come out."

---

[a]9:9,11,13 Lit and go to sway   [b]9:29 DSS read They said; LXX reads I would say

Abimelech's Ambush

[30] When Zebul, the ruler of the city, heard the words of Gaal son of Ebed, he was angry. [31] So he sent messengers secretly to Abimelech, saying, "Look, Gaal son of Ebed, with his brothers, have come to Shechem and are turning the city against you.[a] [32] Now tonight, you and the people with you are to come wait in ambush in the country-side. [33] Then get up early and at sun-rise, charge the city. When he and the people who are with him come out against you, do to him whatever you can."[b] [34] So Abimelech and all the peo-ple with him got up at night and waited in ambush for Shechem in four units.

[35] Gaal son of Ebed went out and stood at the entrance of the city gate. Then Abimelech and the people who were with him got up from their ambush. [36] When Gaal saw the people, he said to Zebul, "Look, people are coming down from the mountaintops!" But Zebul said to him, "The shadows of the mountains look like men to you."

[37] Then Gaal spoke again: "Look, peo-ple are coming down from the central part of the land, and one unit is coming from the direction of the Diviners' Oak." [38] Zebul replied,[c] "Where is your mouth-ing off now? You said, 'Who is Abime-lech that we should serve him?' Aren't these the people you despised? Now go and fight them!"

[39] So Gaal went out leading the lords of Shechem and fought against Abimelech, [40] but Abimelech pursued him, and Gaal fled before him. Many wounded died as far as the entrance of the gate. [41] Abimelech stayed in Arumah, and Ze-bul drove Gaal and his brothers from Shechem.

Abimelech's Second Ambush

[42] The next day when the people went into the countryside, this was reported to Abimelech. [43] He took the people, di-vided them into three companies, and waited in ambush in the countryside. He looked, and the people were coming out of the city, so he arose against them and struck them down. [44] Then Abimelech and the units that were with him rushed forward and took their stand at the en-trance of the city gate. The other two units rushed against all who were in the countryside and struck them down. [45] So Abimelech fought against the city that entire day, captured it, and killed the people who were in it. Then he tore down the city and sowed it with salt.

Massacre of Tower of Shechem

[46] When all the lords of the Tower of Shechem heard, they entered the inner chamber[d] of the temple of El-berith.[e] [47] Then it was reported to Abimelech that all the lords of the Tower of She-chem had gathered together. [48] So Abim-elech and all the people who were with him went up to Mount Zalmon. Abime-lech took his ax in his hand and cut a branch from the trees. He picked up the branch, put it on his shoulder, and said to the people who were with him, "Hurry and do what you have seen me do." [49] Each person also cut his own branch and followed Abimelech. They put the branches against the inner cham-ber and set it on fire around the people, and all the people in the Tower of She-chem died—about 1,000 men and women.

[50] Abimelech went to Thebez, camped against it, and captured it. [51] There was a strong tower inside the city, and all the men, women, and lords of the city fled

there. They locked themselves in and went up to the roof of the tower. [52] When Abimelech came to attack the tower, he approached its entrance to set it on fire.

Abimelech's Surprise Death

[53] But a woman threw the upper portion of a millstone on Abimelech's head and fractured his skull. [54] He quickly called his armor-bearer and said to him, "Draw your sword and kill me, or they'll say about me, 'A woman killed him.'" So his armor-bearer thrust him through, and he died. [55] When the Israelites saw that Abimelech was dead, they all went home.

Curse of Jotham Comes True

[56] In this way, the evil that Abimelech had done against his father, by killing his 70 brothers, God turned back on him. [57] And God also returned all the evil of the men of Shechem on their heads. So the curse of Jotham son of Jerubbaal came on them.

Judge Tola

10 After Abimelech, Tola son of Puah, son of Dodo ₍became judge₎ and began to deliver Israel. He was from Issachar and lived in Shamir in the hill country of Ephraim. [2] Tola judged Israel 23 years, and when he died, was buried in Shamir.

Judge Jair

[3] After him came Jair the Gileadite, who judged Israel 22 years. [4] He had 30 sons who rode on 30 young donkeys. They had 30 towns[a] in Gilead, which are called Jair's Villages[b] to this day. [5] When Jair died, he was buried in Kamon.

Israel Rebels Again

[6] Then the Israelites again did what was evil in the sight of the LORD. They worshiped the •Baals and the •Ashtoreths, the gods of Aram, Sidon, and Moab, and the gods of the Ammonites and the Philistines. They abandoned the LORD and did not worship Him. [7] So the LORD's anger burned against Israel, and He sold them to[c] the Philistines and the Ammonites. [8] They shattered and crushed the Israelites that year, and for 18 years ₍they did the same to₎ all the Israelites who were on the other side of the Jordan in the land of the Amorites in Gilead. [9] The Ammonites also crossed the Jordan to fight against Judah, Benjamin, and the house of Ephraim. Israel was greatly oppressed, [10] so they cried out to the LORD, saying, "We have sinned against You. We have abandoned our God and worshiped the Baals."

Lord Is Weary

[11] The LORD said to the Israelites, "When the Egyptians, Amorites, Ammonites, Philistines, [12] Sidonians, Amalekites, and Maonites[d] oppressed you, and you cried out to Me, did I not deliver you from their power? [13] But you have abandoned Me and worshiped other gods. Therefore, I will not deliver you again. [14] Go and cry out to the gods you have chosen. Let them deliver you in the time of your oppression."

[15] But the Israelites said, "We have sinned. Deal with us as You see fit;[e] only deliver us today!" [16] So they got rid of the foreign gods among them and worshiped the LORD, but He became weary of Israel's misery.

---

[a]**10:4** LXX; MT reads *donkeys*   [b]**10:4** Or *called Havvoth-jair*   [c]**10:7** Lit *into the hand of*   [d]**10:12** LXX reads
Midianites   [e]**10:15** Lit *Do to us what is good in Your eyes*

Jephthah Leads Israel

¹⁷ The Ammonites were called together, and they camped in Gilead. So the Israelites assembled and camped at Mizpah. ¹⁸ The rulers[a] of Gilead said to one another, "Which man will lead the fight against the Ammonites? He will be the leader of all the inhabitants of Gilead."

11 Jephthah the Gileadite was a great warrior, but he was the son of a prostitute, and Gilead was his father. ² Gilead's wife bore him sons, and when they grew up, they drove Jephthah out and said to him, "You will have no inheritance in our father's house, because you are the son of another woman." ³ So Jephthah fled from his brothers and lived in the land of Tob. Then some lawless men joined Jephthah and traveled with him.

Gilead Wants Jephthah

⁴ Some time later, the Ammonites fought against Israel. ⁵ When the Ammonites made war with Israel, the elders of Gilead went to get Jephthah from the land of Tob. ⁶ They said to him, "Come, be our commander, and let's fight against the Ammonites."

⁷ Jephthah replied to the elders of Gilead, "Didn't you hate me and drive me from my father's house? Why then have you come to me now when you're in trouble?"

⁸ They answered Jephthah, "Since that's true, we now turn to you. Come with us, fight the Ammonites, and you will become leader of all the inhabitants of Gilead."

⁹ So Jephthah said to them, "If you are bringing me back to fight the Ammonites and the LORD gives them to me, I will be your leader."

¹⁰ The elders of Gilead said to Jephthah, "The LORD is our witness if we don't do as you say." ¹¹ So Jephthah went with the elders of Gilead. The people put him over themselves as leader and commander, and Jephthah repeated all his terms in the presence of the LORD at Mizpah.

Jephthah Confronts Ammonites

¹² Jephthah sent messengers to the king of the Ammonites, saying, "What do you have against me that you have come to fight against me in my land?"

¹³ The king of the Ammonites said to Jephthah's messengers, "When Israel came from Egypt, they seized my land from the Arnon to the Jabbok and the Jordan. Now restore it peaceably."

Jephthah Recounts Israelite History

¹⁴ Jephthah again sent messengers to the king of the Ammonites ¹⁵ to tell him, "This is what Jephthah says: Israel did not take away the land of Moab or the land of the Ammonites. ¹⁶ But when they came from Egypt, Israel traveled through the wilderness to the •Red Sea and came to Kadesh. ¹⁷ Israel sent messengers to the king of Edom, saying, 'Please let us travel through your land,' but the king of Edom would not listen. They also sent ⌐messengers⌐ to the king of Moab, but he refused. So Israel stayed in Kadesh.

¹⁸ "Then they traveled through the wilderness and around the lands of Edom and Moab. They came to the east side of the land of Moab and camped on the other side of the Arnon but did not enter into the territory of Moab, for the Arnon was the boundary of Moab.

¹⁹ "Then Israel sent messengers to Sihon king of the Amorites, king of Heshbon. Israel said to him, 'Please let us

---

ᵃ**10:18** Lit *The people, rulers*

travel through your land to our country,' [20] but Sihon did not trust Israel.[a] Instead, Sihon gathered all his people, camped at Jahaz, and fought with Israel. [21] Then the LORD God of Israel handed over Sihon and all his people to Israel, and they defeated them. So Israel took possession of the entire land of the Amorites who lived in that country. [22] They took possession of all the territory of the Amorites from the Arnon to the Jabbok and from the wilderness to the Jordan.

Japhthah's "Challenge of the Gods"

[23] "The LORD God of Israel has now driven out the Amorites before His people Israel, but will you drive us out? [24] Isn't it true that you may possess whatever your god Chemosh drives out for you, and we may possess everything the LORD our God drives out before us? [25] Now are you any better than Balak son of Zippor, king of Moab? Did he ever contend with Israel or fight against them? [26] While Israel lived 300 years in Heshbon and its villages, in Aroer and its villages, and in all the cities that are on the banks of the Arnon, why didn't you take them back at that time? [27] I have not sinned against you, but you have wronged me by fighting against me. Let the LORD ₁who is₁ the Judge decide today between the Israelites and the Ammonites." [28] But the king of the Ammonites would not listen to Jephthah's message that he sent him.

Jephthah's Rash Vow

[29] The Spirit of the LORD came on Jephthah, who traveled through Gilead and Manasseh, and then through Mizpah of Gilead. He crossed over to the Ammonites from Mizpah of Gilead. [30] Jephthah made this vow to the LORD: "If You will

hand over the Ammonites to me, [31] whatever comes out of the doors of my house to greet me when I return in peace from the Ammonites will belong to the LORD, and I will offer it as a •burnt offering."

Jephthah Prevails

[32] Jephthah crossed over to the Ammonites to fight against them, and the LORD handed them over to him. [33] He defeated 20 of their cities with a great slaughter from Aroer all the way to the entrance of Minnith and to Abelkeramim. So the Ammonites were subdued before the Israelites.

Jephthah's Daughter

[34] When Jephthah went to his home in Mizpah, there was his daughter, coming out to meet him with tambourines and dancing! She was his only child; he had no other son or daughter besides her. [35] When he saw her, he tore his clothes and said, "No! ₁Not₁ my daughter! You have devastated me! You have brought great misery on me.[b] I have given my word to the LORD and cannot take ₁it₁ back."

[36] Then she said to him, "My father, you have given your word to the LORD. Do to me as you have said, for the LORD brought vengeance on your enemies, the Ammonites." [37] She also said to her father, "Let me do this one thing: Let me wander two months through the mountains with my friends and mourn my virginity."

Tragic Sacrifice

[38] "Go," he said. And he sent her away two months. So she left with her friends and mourned her virginity as she wandered through the mountains. [39] At the

---

[a] **11:20** Lit *Israel to travel through his territory*   [b] **11:35** Lit *have been among those who trouble me*

end of two months, she returned to her father, and he kept the vow he had made about her. And she had never been intimate with a man. Now it became a custom in Israel ⁴⁰⌊that⌋ four days each year the young women of Israel would commemorate the daughter of Jephthah the Gileadite.

Jephthah's Conflict with Ephraim

12 The men of Ephraim were called together and crossed ⌊the Jordan⌋ to Zaphon. They said to Jephthah, "Why have you crossed over to fight against the Ammonites but didn't call us to go with you? We will burn your house down with you ⌊in it⌋!"

² Then Jephthah said to them, "My people and I had a serious conflict with the Ammonites. So I called for you, but you didn't deliver me from their power. ³ When I saw that you weren't going to deliver me, I took my life in my own hands and crossed over to the Ammonites, and the LORD handed them over to me. Why then have you comeª today to fight against me?"

Civil War: Jephthah Defeats Ephraim

⁴ Then Jephthah gathered all of the men of Gilead. They fought and defeated Ephraim, because Ephraim had said, "You Gileadites are Ephraimite fugitives in ⌊the territories of⌋ Ephraim and Manasseh."

"Shibboleth"

⁵ The Gileadites captured the fords of the Jordan leading to Ephraim. Whenever a fugitive from Ephraim said, "Let me cross over," the Gileadites asked him, "Are you an Ephraimite?" If he answered, "No," ⁶ they told him, "Please say Shibboleth." If he said, "Sibboleth," because he could not pronounce it cor-

rectly, they seized him and killed him at the fords of the Jordan. At that time, 42,000 from Ephraim died.

⁷ Jephthah judged Israel six years, and when he died, he was buried in one of the cities of Gilead.ᵇ

Judge Ibzan

⁸ Ibzan, who was from Bethlehem, judged Israel after Jephthah ⁹ and had 30 sons. He gave his 30 daughters in marriage ⌊to men⌋ outside the tribe and brought back 30 wives for his sons from outside ⌊the tribe⌋. Ibzan judged Israel seven years, ¹⁰ and when he died, he was buried in Bethlehem.

Judge Elon

¹¹ Elon, who was from Zebulun, judged Israel after Ibzan. He judged Israel 10 years, ¹² and when he died, he was buried in Aijalon in the land of Zebulun.

Judge Abdon

¹³ After Elon, Abdon son of Hillel, who was from Pirathon, judged Israel. ¹⁴ He had 40 sons and 30 grandsons, who rode on 70 donkeys. Abdon judged Israel eight years, ¹⁵ and when he died, he was buried in Pirathon in the land of Ephraim, in the hill country of the Amalekites.

Samson, the Last Judge

Samson's Miraculous Birth

13 The Israelites again did what was evil in the LORD's sight, so the LORD handed them over to the Philistines 40 years. ² There was a certain man from Zorah, from the family of Dan, whose name was Manoah; his wife was barren and had no children. ³ The Angel of the LORD appeared to the woman and said to her, "It is true that you are barren

ª**12:3** Lit come to me   ᵇ**12:7** LXX reads in his city in Gilead

and have no children, but you will conceive and give birth to a son.

Angel's Rules: No Alcohol, Unclean Food, or Haircuts

4 Now please be careful not to drink wine or other alcoholic beverages, or to eat anything unclean; 5 for indeed, you will conceive and give birth to a son. You must never cut his hair,[a] because the boy will be a Nazirite to God from birth, and he will begin to save Israel from the power of the Philistines."

Manoah Double-checks with God

6 Then the woman went and told her husband, "A man of God came to me. He looked like the awe-inspiring Angel of God. I didn't ask Him where He came from, and He didn't tell me His name. 7 He said to me, 'You will conceive and give birth to a son. Therefore, do not drink wine or other alcoholic beverages, and do not eat anything unclean, because the boy will be a Nazirite to God from birth until the day of his death.'"

8 Manoah prayed to the LORD and said, "Please Lord, let the man of God you sent come again to us and teach us what we should do for the boy who will be born."

Angel's Second Appearance

9 God listened to[b] Manoah, and the Angel of God came again to the woman. She was sitting in the field, and her husband Manoah was not with her. 10 The woman ran quickly to her husband and told him, "The man who came to me today has just come back!"

11 So Manoah got up and followed his wife. When he came to the man, he asked, "Are You the man who spoke to my wife?"

"I am," He said.

12 Then Manoah asked, "When Your words come true, what will the boy's responsibilities and mission[c] be?"

13 The Angel of the LORD answered Manoah, "Your wife needs to do everything I told her. 14 She must not eat anything that comes from the grapevine or drink wine or other alcoholic beverages. And she must not eat anything unclean. Your wife must do everything I have commanded her."

Manoah's Sacrifice

15 "Please stay here," Manoah told Him, "and we will prepare a young goat for You."

16 The Angel of the LORD said to him, "If I stay, I won't eat your food. But if you want to prepare a •burnt offering, offer it to the LORD." For Manoah did not know He was the Angel of the LORD.

17 Then Manoah said to Him, "What is Your name, so that we may honor You when Your words come true?"

18 "Why do you ask My name," the Angel of the LORD asked him, "since it is wonderful."

19 Manoah took a young goat and a •grain offering and offered them on a rock to the LORD, and He did a wonderful thing[d] while Manoah and his wife were watching. 20 When the flame went up from the altar to the sky, the Angel of the LORD went up in its flame. When Manoah and his wife saw ⌊this⌋, they fell facedown on the ground. 21 The Angel of the LORD did not appear again to Manoah and his wife. Then Manoah realized that it was the Angel of the LORD.

22 "We're going to die," he said to his wife, "because we have seen God!"

23 But his wife said to him, "If the LORD had intended to kill us, He

---

a**13:5** Lit And a razor is not to go up on his head b**13:9** Lit to the voice of c**13:12** Lit work d**13:19** LXX reads to the LORD, to the One who works wonders

wouldn't have accepted the burnt offering and the grain offering from us, and He would not have shown us all these things or spoken to us now like this."

Samson's Birth

24 So the woman gave birth to a son and named him Samson. The boy grew, and the LORD blessed him. 25 Then the Spirit of the LORD began to direct him in the Camp of Dan,a between Zorah and Eshtaol.

Samson Insists on Philistine Wife

14 Samson went down to Timnah and saw a young Philistine woman there. 2 He went back and told his father and his mother: "I have seen a young Philistine woman in Timnah. Now get her for me as a wife."

3 But his father and mother said to him, "Can't you findb a young woman among your relatives or among any of our people? Must you go to the uncircumcised Philistines for a wife?"

But Samson told his father, "Get her for me, because I want her."c 4 Now his father and mother did not know this was from the LORD, who was seeking an occasion against the Philistines. At that time, the Philistines were ruling over Israel.

Samson Kills a Lion

5 Samson went down to Timnah with his father and mother and came to the vineyards of Timnah. Suddenly a young lion came roaring at him, 6 the Spirit of the LORD took control ofd him, and he tore the lion apart with his bare hands as he might have torn a young goat. But he did not tell his father or mother what he had done. 7 Then he went and spoke to

the woman, because Samson wanted her.

Honey in the Lion

8 After some time, when he returned to get her, he left ιthe roadι to see the lion's carcass, and there was a swarm of bees with honey in the carcass. 9 He scooped ισome honeyι into his hands and ate ιitι as he went along. When he returned to his father and mother, he gave ισomeι to them and they ate ιitι. But he did not tell them that he had scooped the honey from the lion's carcass.

Philistine Feast—and a Riddle

10 His father went ιto visitι the woman, and Samson prepared a feast there, as young men were accustomed to do. 11 When the Philistines saw him, they brought 30 men to accompany him. 12 "Let me tell you a riddle," Samson said to them. "If you can explain it to me during the seven days of the feast and figure it out, I will give you 30 linen garments and 30 changes of clothes. 13 But if you can't explain it to me, you must give me 30 linen garments and 30 changes of clothes."

"Tell us your riddle," they replied.e "Let's hear it."

14 So he said to them:

Out of the eater came something to eat,
and out of the strong came something sweet.

His Wife Wheedles the Answer

After three days, they were unable to explain the riddle. 15 On the fourthf day they said to Samson's wife, "Persuade your husband to explain the riddle to us, or we will burn you and your father's

a13:25 Or in Mahaneh-dan b14:3 Lit Is there not c14:3 Lit because she is right in my eyes d14:6 Lit LORD rushed on e14:13 Lit replied to him f14:15 LXX, Syr; MT reads seventh

household to death. Did you invite us here to rob us?"

¹⁶ So Samson's wife came to him, weeping, and said, "You hate me and don't love me! You told my people the riddle, but haven't explained it to me."

"Look," he said,ᵃ "I haven't even explained it to my father or mother, so ₍why₎ should I explain it to you?"

¹⁷ She wept the whole seven days of the feast, and at last, on the seventh day, he explained it to her, because she had nagged him so much. Then she explained it to her people. ¹⁸ On the seventh day before sunset, the men of the city said to him:

What is sweeter than honey?
What is stronger than a lion?

So he said to them:

If you hadn't plowed with
    my young cow,
you wouldn't know my riddle now!

Samson's Rage—and Revenge

¹⁹ The Spirit of the LORD took control of him, and he went down to Ashkelon and killed 30 of their men. He stripped them and gave their clothes to those who had explained the riddle. In a rage, Samson returned to his father's house, ²⁰ and his wife was given to one of the men who had accompanied him.

A Father-in-law's Fatal Mistake

15 Later on, during the wheat harvest, Samson ₍took₎ a young goat ₍as a gift₎ and visited his wife. "I want to go to my wife in her room," he said. But her father would not let him enter.

² "I was sure you hated her," her father said, "so I gave her to one of the men who accompanied you. Isn't her younger sister more beautiful than she is? Why not take her instead?"

Fiery Foxtails

³ Samson said to them, "This time I won't be responsible when I harm the Philistines." ⁴ So he went out and caught 300 foxes. He took torches, turned the foxes tail-to-tail, and put a torch between each pair of tails. ⁵ Then he ignited the torches and released the foxes into the standing grain of the Philistines. He burned up the piles of grain and the standing grain as well as the vineyards and olive groves.

⁶ Then the Philistines asked, "Who did this?"

They were told, "₍It was₎ Samson, the Timnite's son-in-law, because he has taken Samson's wife and given her to another man." So the Philistines went to her and her father and burned ₍them₎ to death.

Samson Takes Revenge

⁷ Then Samson told them, "Because you did this, I swear that I won't rest until I have taken vengeance on you." ⁸ He tore them limb from limbᵇ with a great slaughter, and he went down and stayed in the cave at the rock of Etam.

⁹ The Philistines went up, camped in Judah, and raided Lehi. ¹⁰ So the men of Judah said, "Why have you attacked us?"

They replied, "We have come to arrest Samson and pay him back for what he did to us."

¹¹ Then 3,000 men of Judah went to the cave at the rock of Etam, and they asked Samson, "Don't you realize that the Philistines rule over us? What have you done to us?"

"I have done to them what they did to me," he answered.ᶜ

ᵃ**14:16** Lit *said to her* ᵇ**15:8** Lit *He struck them hip on thigh* ᶜ**15:11** Lit *answered them*

¹² They said to him, "We've come to arrest you and hand you over to the Philistines."

Then Samson told them, "Swear to me that you yourselves won't kill me."

¹³ "No," they said,ᵃ "we won't kill you, but we will tie you up securely and hand you over to them." So they tied him up with two new ropes and led him away from the rock.

Lethal Weapon: Donkey's Jawbone

¹⁴ When he came to Lehi, the Philistines came to meet him shouting. The Spirit of the LORD took control ofᵇ him, and the ropes that were on his arms became like burnt flax and his bonds fell off his wrists. ¹⁵ He found a fresh jawbone of a donkey, reached out his hand, took it, and killed 1,000 men with it. ¹⁶ Then Samson said:

With the jawbone of a donkey
I have piled them in a heap.
With the jawbone of a donkey
I have killed 1,000 men.

God Sustains Samson

¹⁷ When he finished speaking, he threw away the jawbone and named that place Ramath-lehi.ᶜ ¹⁸ He became very thirsty and called out to the LORD: "You have accomplished this great victory throughᵈ Your servant. Must I now die of thirst and fall into the hands of the uncircumcised?" ¹⁹ So God split a hollow place ⌊in the ground⌋ at Lehi, and water came out of it. After Samson drank, his strength returned, and he revived. That is why he named it En-hakkore,ᵉ which is in Lehi to this day. ²⁰ And he judged Israel 20 years in the days of the Philistines.

Samson Escapes with Gaza City Doors

16 Samson went to Gaza, where he saw a prostitute and went to bed with her. ² When the Gazites ⌊heard⌋ that Samson was there, they surrounded the place and waited in ambush for him all that night at the city gate. While they were waiting quietly,ᶠ they said, "Let us wait until dawn; then we will kill him." ³ But Samson stayed in bed until midnight when he got up, took hold of the doors of the city gate along with the two gateposts, and pulled them out, bar and all. He put them on his shoulders and took them to the top of the mountain overlooking Hebron.

In Love with Delilah

⁴ Some time later, he fell in love with a woman named Delilah, who lived in the Sorek Valley. ⁵ The Philistine leaders went to her and said, "Persuade him to tell youᵍ where his great strength comes from, so we can overpower him, tie him up, and make him helpless. Each of us will then give you 1,100 pieces of silver."

⁶ So Delilah said to Samson, "Please tell me, where does your great strength ⌊come from⌋? How could ⌊someone⌋ tie you up and make you helpless?"

⁷ Samson told her, "If they tie me up with seven fresh bowstrings that have not been dried, I will become weak and be like any other man."

⁸ The Philistine leaders brought her seven fresh bowstrings that had not been dried, and she tied him up with them. ⁹ While the men in ambush were waiting in her room, she called out to him, "Samson, the Philistines are here!"ʰ But he

---

ᵃ**15:13** Lit *said to him*   ᵇ**15:14** Lit LORD *rushed on*   ᶜ**15:17** = High Place of the Jawbone   ᵈ**15:18** Lit *through the hand of*   ᵉ**15:19** = Spring of the One Who Cried Out   ᶠ**16:2** Lit *quietly all night*   ᵍ**16:5** Lit *him and see*   ʰ**16:9** Lit *are on you*

snapped the bowstrings as a strand of yarn snaps when it touches fire. ⌊The secret of⌋ his strength remained unknown.

¹⁰ Then Delilah said to Samson, "You have mocked me and told me lies! Won't you please tell me how you can be tied up?"

¹¹ He told her, "If they tie me up with new ropes that have never been used, I will become weak and be like any other man."

¹² Delilah took new ropes, tied him up with them, and shouted, "Samson, the Philistines are here!"ᵃ But while the men in ambush were waiting in her room, he snapped the ropes off his arms like a thread.

¹³ Then Delilah said to Samson, "You have mocked me all along and told me lies! Tell me how you can be tied up."

He told her, "If you weave the seven braids on my head with the web of a loom—"ᵇ

¹⁴ She fastened the braids with a pin and called to him, "Samson, the Philistines are here!"ᵃ He awoke from his sleep and pulled out the pin, with the loom and the web.

¹⁵ "How can you say, 'I love you,'" she told him, "when your heart is not with me? This is the third time you have mocked me and not told me what makes your strength so great!"

¹⁶ Because she nagged him day after day and pled with him until she wore him out,ᶜ ¹⁷ he told her the whole truth and said to her, "My hair has never been cut,ᵈ because I am a Nazirite to God from birth. If I am shaved, my strength will leave me, and I will become weak and be like any other man."

Price of a Woman's Deceit

¹⁸ When Delilah realized that he had told her the whole truth, she sent this message to the Philistine leaders: "Come one more time, for he has told me the whole truth." The Philistine leaders came to her and brought the money with them.

¹⁹ Then she let him fall asleep on her lap and called a man to shave off the seven braids on his head. In this way, she rendered him helpless,ᵉ and his strength left him. ²⁰ Then she cried, "Samson, the Philistines are here!"ᵃ When he awoke from his sleep, he said, "I will escape as I did before and shake myself free." But he did not know that the LORD had left him.

Samson's Capture and Mutilation

²¹ The Philistines seized him and gouged out his eyes. They brought him down to Gaza and bound him with bronze shackles, and he was forced to grind grain in the prison. ²² But his hair began to grow back after it had been shaved.

²³ Now the Philistine leaders gathered together to offer a great sacrifice to their god Dagon. They rejoiced and said:

> Our god has handed over
> our enemy Samson to us.

²⁴ When the people saw him, they praised their god and said:

> Our god has handed over to us
> our enemy who destroyed our land
> and who multiplied our dead.

Samson Mocked

²⁵ When they were drunk, they said, "Bring Samson here to entertain us." So

---

ᵃ**16:12,14,20** Lit are on you ᵇ**16:13-14** LXX reads loom and fasten [them] with a pin into the wall and I will become weak and be like any other man." ¹⁴ And while he was sleeping, Delilah wove the seven braids on his head into the loom. ᶜ**16:16** Lit him and he became short to death ᵈ**16:17** Lit A razor has not gone up on my head ᵉ**16:19** LXX reads way he began to weaken

they brought Samson from prison, and he entertained them. They had him stand between the pillars.

God Empowers Samson

²⁶ Samson said to the young man who was leading him by the hand, "Lead me where I can feel the pillars supporting the temple, so I can lean against them." ²⁷ The temple was full of men and women; all the leaders of the Philistines were there, and about 3,000 men and women were on the roof watching Samson entertain them. ²⁸ He called out to the LORD: "Lord GOD, please remember me. Strengthen me, God, just once more. With one act of vengeance, let me pay back the Philistines for my two eyes." ²⁹ Samson took hold of the two middle pillars supporting the temple and leaned against them, one on his right hand and the other on his left. ³⁰ Samson said, "Let me die with the Philistines."

Samson's Final Great Feat

He pushed with all his might, and the temple fell on the leaders and all the people in it. And the dead he killed at his death were more than those he had killed in his life. ³¹ Then his brothers and his father's family came down, carried him back, and buried him between Zorah and Eshtaol in the tomb of his father Manoah. So he judged Israel 20 years.

Micah's Story

Micah Confesses Theft

17 There was a man from the hill country of Ephraim named Micah. ² He said to his mother, "The 1,100 pieces of silver taken from you, and that I heard you utter a curse about—here, I have the silver with me. I took it. So now I return it to you."ᵃ

Then his mother said, "My son, you are blessed by the LORD!"

His Mother's Generosity

³ He returned the 1,100 pieces of silver to his mother, and his mother said, "I personally consecrate the silver to the LORD for my son's benefit to make a carved image overlaid with silver."ᵇ ⁴ So he returned the silver to his mother, and she took five pounds of silver and gave it to a silversmith. He made it into a carved image overlaid with silver,ᵇ and it was in Micah's house.

⁵ This man Micah had a shrine, and he made an •ephod and household idols, and installed one of his sons to be his priest. ⁶ In those days there was no king in Israel; everyone did whatever he wanted.ᶜ

Micah's Priest

⁷ There was a young man, a Levite, from Bethlehem in Judah, who resided within the clan of Judah. ⁸ The man left the town of Bethlehem in Judah to settle wherever he could find a place. On his way he came to Micah's home in the hill country of Ephraim.

⁹ "Where do you come from?" Micah asked him.

He answered him, "I am a Levite from Bethlehem in Judah, and I'm going to settle wherever I can find a place."

¹⁰ Micah replied,ᵈ "Stay with me and be my father and priest, and I will give you four ounces of silver a year, along with your clothing and provisions." So the Levite went in ¹¹ and agreed to stay with the man, and the young man became like one of his sons. ¹² Micah consecrated the Levite, and the young man

---

ᵃ**17:2** MT places this sentence at the end of v. 3.   ᵇ**17:3,4** Or *image and a cast image*   ᶜ**17:6** Lit *did what was right in his eyes*   ᵈ**17:10** Lit *replied to him*

became his priest and lived in Micah's house. [13] Then Micah said, "Now I know that the LORD will be good to me, because a Levite has become my priest."

Spies from Dan

18 In those days, there was no king in Israel, and the Danite tribe was looking for territory to occupy. Up to that time no territory had been captured ⌊by them⌋ among the tribes of Israel. [2] So the Danites sent out five brave men from all their clans, from Zorah and Eshtaol, to spy out the land and explore it. They told them, "Go and explore the land."

They came to the hill country of Ephraim as far as the home of Micah and spent the night there. [3] While they were near Micah's home, they recognized the speech of the young Levite. So they went over to him and asked, "Who brought you here? What are you doing in this place? What is keeping you here?" [4] He told them what Micah had done for him and that he had hired him as his priest.

Micah's Priest Reassures Danites

[5] Then they said to him, "Please inquire of God so we will know if we will have a successful journey."

[6] The priest told them, "Go in peace. The LORD is watching over the journey you are going on."

[7] The five men left and came to Laish. They saw that the people who were there were living securely, in the same way as the Sidonians, quiet and unsuspecting. There was nothing lacking in the land and no oppressive ruler. They were far from the Sidonians, having no alliance with anyone.[a]

Spies' Positive Report

[8] When the men went back to their clans at Zorah and Eshtaol, their people asked them, "What did you find out?"

[9] They answered, "Come on, let's go up against them, for we have seen the land, and it is very good. Why wait? Don't hesitate to go and invade and take possession of the land! [10] When you get there, you will come to an unsuspecting people and a wide-open land, for God has handed it over to you. It is a place where nothing on earth is lacking."[11] Six hundred Danites departed from Zorah and Eshtaol armed with weapons of war. [12] They went up and camped at Kiriath-jearim in Judah. This is why the place is called the Camp of Dan[b] to this day; it is west of Kiriath-jearim. [13] From there they traveled to the hill country of Ephraim and arrived at Micah's house.

Spies Return to Loot Micah's House

[14] The five men who had gone to spy out the land of Laish told their brothers, "Did you know that there are an •ephod, household gods, and a carved image overlaid with silver[c] in these houses? Now think about what you should do." [15] So they detoured there and went to the house of the young Levite at the home of Micah and greeted him. [16] The 600 Danite men were standing by the entrance of the gate, armed with their weapons of war. [17] Then the five men who had gone to spy out the land went in and took the carved image overlaid with silver,[c] the ephod, and the household idols, while the priest was standing by the entrance of the gate with the 600 men armed with weapons of war.

[18] When they entered Micah's house and took the carved image overlaid with

---

[a]**18:7** MT; some LXX mss, Sym, Lat, Syr read *Aram*   [b]**18:12** Or *called Mahaneh-dan*   [c]**18:14,17** Or *image, the cast image*   [d]**18:17** Or *image, the cast image*

silver,[a] the ephod, and the household idols, the priest said to them, "What are you doing?"

Priest Joins the Spies

[19] They told him, "Be quiet. Keep your mouth shut.[b] Come with us and be a father and a priest to us. Is it better for you to be a priest for the house of one person or for you to be a priest for a tribe and family in Israel?" [20] So the priest was pleased and took his ephod, household idols, and carved image, and went with the people. [21] They prepared to leave, putting their small children, livestock, and possessions in front of them.

Micah Confronts Danites

[22] After they were some distance from Micah's house, the men who were in the houses near it mobilized and caught up with the Danites. [23] They called to the Danites, who turned to face them, and said to Micah, "What's the matter with you that you mobilized ˌthe menˌ?"

[24] He said, "You took the gods I had made and the priest, and went away. What do I have left? How can you say to me, 'What's the matter with you?'"

Danites Intimidate Micah

[25] The Danites said to him, "Don't raise your voice against us, or angry men will attack you, and you and your family will lose your lives." [26] The Danites went on their way, and Micah turned to go back home, because he saw that they were stronger than he was.

Danites Massacre Laish

[27] After they had taken the gods Micah had made and the priest that belonged to him, they went to Laish, to a quiet and unsuspecting people. They killed them with their swords and burned down the city. [28] There was no one to save them, because it was far from Sidon and they had no alliance with anyone. It was in a valley that belonged to Beth-rehob. They rebuilt the city and lived in it. [29] They named the city Dan, after the name of their ancestor Dan, who was born to Israel. The city was formerly named Laish.

Cult of Danites Established

[30] The Danites set up the carved image for themselves. Jonathan son of Gershom, son of Moses,[c] and his sons were priests for the Danite tribe until the time of the exile from the land. [31] So they set up for themselves Micah's carved image that he had made, ˌand it was thereˌ as long as the house of God was in Shiloh.

Outrage in Benjamin

Unfaithful Concubine

19 In those days, when there was no king in Israel, a Levite living in a remote part of the hill country of Ephraim acquired a woman from Bethlehem in Judah as his concubine. [2] But she was unfaithful to[d] him and left him for her father's house in Bethlehem in Judah. She was there for a period of four months. [3] Then her husband got up and went after her to speak kindly to her[e] and bring her back. His servant and a couple of donkeys were with him. So she brought him to her father's house, and when the girl's father saw him, he gladly welcomed him. [4] His father-in-law, the girl's father, detained him, and he stayed with him for three days. They ate, drank, and spent the nights there.

---

[a]**18:18** Or *image, the cast image*   [b]**18:19** Lit *Put your hand on your mouth*   [c]**18:30** Some Hb mss, LXX, Vg; other Hb mss read *Manasseh*   [d]**19:2** LXX, Vg read *was angry with*   [e]**19:3** Lit *speak to her heart*

Delays in Bethlehem

⁵ On the fourth day, they got up early in the morning and prepared to go, but the girl's father said to his son-in-law, "Have something to eat to keep up your strength and then you can go." ⁶ So they sat down and the two of them ate and drank together. Then the girl's father said to the man, "Please agree to stay overnight and enjoy yourself." ⁷ The man got up to go, but his father-in-law persuaded him, so he stayed and spent the night there again. ⁸ He got up early in the morning of the fifth day to leave, but the girl's father said to him, "Please keep up your strength." So they waited until late afternoon and the two of them ate. ⁹ The man got up to go with his concubine and his servant, when his father-in-law, the girl's father, said to him, "Look, night is coming. Please spend the night. See, the day is almost over. Spend the night here, enjoy yourself, then you can get up early tomorrow for your journey and go home."

¹⁰ But the man was unwilling to spend the night. He got up, departed, and arrived opposite Jebus (that is, Jerusalem). The man had his two saddled donkeys and his concubine with him. ¹¹ When they were near Jebus and the day was almost gone, the servant said to his master, "Please, why notᵃ let us stop at this Jebusite city and spend the night here?"

¹² But his master replied to him, "We will not stop at a foreign city where there are no Israelites. Let's move on to Gibeah." ¹³ "Come on," he said,ᵇ "let's try to reach one of these places and spend the night in Gibeah or Ramah." ¹⁴ So they continued on their journey, and the sun set as they neared Gibeah in Benjamin. ¹⁵ They stoppedᶜ to go in and spend the night in Gibeah. The Levite went in and sat down in the city square, but no one took them into their home to spend the night.

Hospitality in Gibeah

¹⁶ In the evening, an old man came in from his work in the field. He was from the hill country of Ephraim but was residing in Gibeah, and the men of that place were Benjaminites. ¹⁷ When he looked up and saw the traveler in the city square, the old man asked, "Where are you going, and where do you come from?"

¹⁸ He answered him, "We're traveling from Bethlehem in Judah to the remote hill country of Ephraim, where I am from. I went to Bethlehem in Judah, and now I'm going to the house of the LORD.ᵈ No one has taken me into his home, ¹⁹ although we have both straw and feed for our donkeys, and bread and wine for me, your female servant, and the young man with your servant.ᵉ There is nothing we lack."

²⁰ "Peace to you," said the old man. "I'll take care of everything you need. Only don't spend the night in the square." ²¹ So he brought him to his house and fed the donkeys. Then they washed their feet and ate and drank.

A Concubine Raped and Murdered

²² While they were enjoying themselves, all of a sudden, •perverted men of the city surrounded the house and beat on the door. They said to the old man who was the owner of the house, "Bring out the man who came to your house so we can have sex with him!"

²³ The owner of the house went out and said to them, "No, don't do ˻this˼ evil, my brothers. After all, this man has

---

ᵃ**19:11** Lit *Come, please*   ᵇ**19:13** Lit *said to his servant*   ᶜ**19:15** Lit *stopped there*   ᵈ**19:18** LXX reads *to my house*
ᵉ**19:19** Some Hb mss, Syr, Tg, Vg; other Hb mss read *servants*

come into my house. Don't do this horrible thing. ²⁴ Here, let me bring out my virgin daughter and the man's concubine now. Use them and do whatever you want[a] to them. But don't do this horrible thing to this man."

²⁵ But the men would not listen to him, so the man seized his concubine and took her outside to them. They raped[b] her and abused her all night until morning. At daybreak they let her go. ²⁶ Early that morning, the woman made her way back, and as it was getting light, she collapsed at the doorway of the man's house where her master was.

²⁷ When her master got up in the morning, opened the doors of the house, and went out to leave on his journey, there was the woman, his concubine, collapsed near the doorway of the house with her hands on the threshold. ²⁸ "Get up," he told her. "Let's go." But there was no response. So the man put her on his donkey and set out for home.

Brutal Messages

²⁹ When he entered his house, he picked up a knife, took hold of his concubine, cut her into 12 pieces, limb by limb, and sent her throughout the territory of Israel. ³⁰ Everyone who saw it said, "Nothing like this has ever happened or been seen since the day the Israelites came out of the land of Egypt to this day.[c] Think it over, discuss it, and speak up!"

Israelite Outrage

20 All the Israelites from Dan to Beer-sheba and from the land of Gilead came out, and the community assembled as one body before the LORD at Mizpah. ² The leaders of all the people and of all the tribes of Israel presented themselves in the assembly of God's people: 400,000 armed foot soldiers. ³ The Benjaminites heard that the Israelites had gone up to Mizpah.

The Israelites asked, "Tell us, how did this outrage occur?"

Levite Testifies

⁴ The Levite, the husband of the murdered woman, answered: "I went to Gibeah in Benjamin with my concubine to spend the night. ⁵ Citizens of Gibeah ganged up on me and surrounded the house at night. They intended to kill me, but they raped my concubine, and she died. ⁶ Then I took my concubine and cut her in pieces, and sent her throughout Israel's territory, because they committed a horrible shame in Israel. ⁷ Look, all of you are Israelites. Give your judgment and verdict here ⌊and now⌋."

Judgment: War on Benjamin

⁸ Then all the people stood united and said, "None of us will go to his tent or return to his house. ⁹ Now this is what we will do to Gibeah: we will go against it by lot. ¹⁰ We will take 10 men out of every 100 from all the tribes of Israel, and 100 out of every 1,000, and 1,000 out of every 10,000 to get provisions for the people when they go to Gibeah in Benjamin to punish them for all the horror they did in Israel."

¹¹ So all the men of Israel gathered united against the city. ¹² Then the tribes of Israel sent men throughout the tribe of Benjamin, saying, "What is this outrage that has occurred among you? ¹³ Hand over the •perverted men in Gibeah so we can put them to death and eradicate evil from Israel." But the

---

^a**19:24** Lit *do what is good in your eyes* ^b**19:25** Lit *knew* ^c**19:30** LXX reads *day." He commanded the men he sent out, saying, "You will say this to all the men of Israel: Has anything like this happened since the day the Israelites came out of Egypt until this day?*

Benjaminites would not obey their fellow Israelites. [14] Instead, the Benjaminites gathered together from their cities to Gibeah to go out and fight against the Israelites. [15] On that day the Benjaminites rallied 26,000 armed men from their cities, besides 700 choice men rallied by the inhabitants of Gibeah. [16] There were 700 choice men who were left-handed among all these people; all could sling a stone at a hair and not miss.

[17] The Israelites, apart from Benjamin, rallied 400,000 armed men, every one an experienced warrior. [18] They set out, went to Bethel, and inquired of God. The Israelites asked, "Who is to go first to fight for us against the Benjaminites?"

God Orders Battle—Benjamin Wins

And the LORD answered, "Judah will be first."

[19] In the morning, the Israelites set out and camped near Gibeah. [20] The men of Israel went out to fight against Benjamin and took their battle positions against Gibeah. [21] The Benjaminites came out of Gibeah and slaughtered 22,000 men of Israel on the field that day. [22] But the Israelite army rallied and again took their battle positions in the same place where they positioned themselves on the first day. [23] They went up, wept before the LORD until evening, and inquired of Him: "Should we again fight against our brothers the Benjaminites?"

God Says "Fight"— Benjamin Wins Again

And the LORD answered: "Fight against them."

[24] On the second day the Israelites advanced against the Benjaminites. [25] That same day the Benjaminites came out from Gibeah to meet them and slaughtered an additional 18,000 Israelites on the field; all were armed men.

[26] The whole Israelite army went to Bethel where they wept and sat before the LORD. They fasted that day until evening and offered •burnt offerings and •fellowship offerings to the LORD. [27] Then the Israelites inquired of the LORD. In those days, the ark of the covenant of God was there, [28] and Phinehas son of Eleazar, son of Aaron, was serving before it. The Israelites asked: "Should we again fight against our brothers the Benjaminites or should we stop?"

God Says "Fight"— An Ambush Defeats Benjamin

The LORD answered: "Fight, because I will hand them over to you tomorrow." [29] So Israel set up an ambush around Gibeah. [30] On the third day the Israelites fought against the Benjaminites and took their battle positions against Gibeah as before. [31] Then the Benjaminites came out against the people and were drawn away from the city. They began to attack the people as before, killing about 30 men of Israel on the highways, one of which goes up to Bethel and the other to Gibeah through the open country. [32] The Benjaminites said, "We are defeating them as before."

But the Israelites said, "Let's flee and draw them away from the city to the highways." [33] So all the men of Israel got up from their places and took their battle positions at Baal-tamar, while the Israelites in ambush charged out of their places west of[a] Geba. [34] Then 10,000 choice men from all Israel made a frontal assault against Gibeah, and the battle was fierce, but the Benjaminites did not know that disaster was about to strike

---

[a] **20:33** LXX, Syr, Vg; MT reads *places in the plain of*, or *places in the cave of*

Philistines Defile Saul's Body

[8] The next day when the Philistines came to strip the slain, they found Saul and his three sons dead on Mount Gilboa. [9] They cut off Saul's head, stripped off his armor, and sent messengers throughout the land of the Philistines to spread the good news in the temples of their idols and among the people. [10] Then they put his armor in the temple of the •Ashtoreths and hung his body on the wall of Beth-shan.

Israelites Reclaim Saul's Remains

[11] When the residents of Jabesh-gilead heard what the Philistines had done to Saul, [12] all their brave men set out, journeyed all night, and retrieved the body of Saul and the bodies of his sons from the wall of Beth-shan. When they arrived at Jabesh, they burned the bodies there. [13] Afterwards, they took their bones and buried them under the tamarisk tree in Jabesh and fasted seven days.

2 SAMUEL

Amalekite Notifies David of Saul's Death—and Takes Credit

1 After the death of Saul, David returned from defeating the Amalekites and stayed at Ziklag two days. [2] On the third day a man with torn clothes and dust on his head came from Saul's camp. When he came to David, he fell to the ground and paid homage.

[3] David asked him, "Where have you come from?"

He replied to him, "I've escaped from the Israelite camp."

[4] "What was the outcome? Tell me," David asked him.

"The troops fled from the battle," he answered. "Many of the troops have fallen and are dead. Also, Saul and his son Jonathan are dead."

[5] David asked the young man who had brought him the report, "How do you know Saul and his son Jonathan are dead?"

[6] "I happened to be on Mount Gilboa," he replied, "and there was Saul, leaning on his spear. At that very moment the chariots and the cavalry were closing in on him. [7] When he turned around and saw me, he called out to me, so I answered: I'm at your service. [8] He asked me, 'Who are you?' I told him: I'm an Amalekite. [9] Then he begged me, 'Stand over me and kill me, for I'm mortally wounded,[a] but my life still lingers.' [10] So I stood over him and killed him because I knew that after he had fallen he couldn't survive. I took the crown that was on his head and the armband that was on his arm, and I've brought them here to my lord."

David Mourns—and Executes

[11] Then David took hold of his clothes and tore them, and all the men with him did the same. [12] They mourned, wept, and fasted until the evening for those who died by the sword—for Saul, his son Jonathan, the LORD's people, and the house of Israel.

[13] David inquired of the young man who had brought him the report, "Where are you from?"

[a]1:9 LXX reads for terrible darkness has taken hold of me

"I'm the son of a foreigner" he said. "I'm an Amalekite."

¹⁴ David questioned him, "How is it that you were not afraid to lift your hand to destroy the LORD's anointed?" ¹⁵ Then David summoned one of his servants and said, "Come here and kill him!" The servant struck him, and he died. ¹⁶ For David had said to the Amalekite, "Your blood is on your own head because your own mouth testified against you by saying, 'I killed the LORD's anointed.'"

David's Lament for Saul and Jonathan

¹⁷ David sang the following lament for Saul and his son Jonathan, ¹⁸ and he ordered that the Judahites be taught ⌊The Song of⌋ the Bow. It is written in the Book of Jashar:ᵃ

¹⁹ The splendor of Israel lies slain
　　on your heights.
　How the mighty have fallen!
²⁰ Do not tell it in Gath,
　　don't announce it in the streets
　　　of Ashkelon,
　or the daughters of the Philistines
　　will rejoice,
　and the daughters
　　of the uncircumcised will gloat.
²¹ Mountains of Gilboa,
　　let no dew or rain be on you,
　or fields of offerings,ᵇ
　for there the shield of the mighty
　　was defiled—
　the shield of Saul, no longer
　　anointed with oil.
²² Jonathan's bow never retreated,
　Saul's sword never returned
　　unstained,ᶜ
　from the blood of the slain,
　from the bodies of the mighty.
²³ Saul and Jonathan,
　loved and delightful,

they were not parted in life
　or in death.
They were swifter than eagles,
　stronger than lions.
²⁴ Daughters of Israel, weep for Saul,
　who clothed you in scarlet,
　　with luxurious things,
　who decked your garments
　　with gold ornaments.
²⁵ How the mighty have fallen
　　in the thick of battle!
Jonathan ⌊lies⌋ slain on your heights.
²⁶ I grieve for you, Jonathan
　　my brother.
You were such a friend to me.
Your love for me was
　　more wonderful
than the love of a woman ⌊for me⌋.
²⁷ How the mighty have fallen
　and the weapons of war
　　have perished!

David, King of Judah

2 Some time later, David inquired of the LORD: "Should I go to one of the towns of Judah?"

The LORD answered him, "Go."

Then David asked, "Where should I go?"

"To Hebron," the LORD replied.

² So David went there with his two wives, Ahinoam the Jezreelite and Abigail, the widow of Nabal the Carmelite. ³ In addition, David brought the men who were with him, each one with his household, and they settled in the towns near Hebron. ⁴ Then the men of Judah came, and there they anointed David king over the house of Judah. They told David: "It was the men of Jabesh-gilead who buried Saul."

⁵ David sent messengers to the men of Jabesh-gilead and said to them, "The LORD bless you, because you have shown

---

ᵃ1:18 Or of the Upright　ᵇ1:21 LXX reads firstfruits　ᶜ1:22 Lit empty

this special kindness to Saul your lord when you buried him. [6] Now, may the LORD show special kindness and faithfulness to you, and I will also show the same goodness to you because you have done this deed. [7] Therefore, be strong and courageous, for though Saul your lord is dead, the house of Judah has anointed me king over them."

Saul's Son King of Israel

[8] Abner son of Ner, commander of Saul's army, took Saul's son Ishbosheth[a] [b] and moved him to Mahanaim. [9] He made him king over Gilead, Asher, Jezreel, Ephraim, Benjamin—over all Israel. [10] Saul's son Ish-bosheth was 40 years old when he began his reign over Israel; he ruled for two years. The house of Judah, however, followed David. [11] The length of time that David was king in Hebron over the house of Judah was seven years and six months.

Abner vs. Joab

[12] Abner son of Ner and soldiers of Ishbosheth son of Saul marched out from Mahanaim to Gibeon. [13] So Joab son of Zeruiah and David's soldiers marched out and met them by the pool of Gibeon. The two groups took up positions on opposite sides of the pool.

[14] Then Abner said to Joab, "Let's have the young men get up and compete in front of us."

"Let them get up," Joab replied.

Duel of Young Men

[15] So they got up and were counted off—12 for Benjamin and Ish-bosheth son of Saul, and 12 from David's soldiers. [16] Then each man grabbed his opponent by the head and ⌊thrust⌋ his sword into his opponent's side so that

they all died together. So this place, which is in Gibeon, is named Field of Blades.[c]

David's Soldiers Defeat Abner

[17] The battle that day was extremely fierce, and Abner and the men of Israel were defeated by David's soldiers. [18] The three sons of Zeruiah were there: Joab, Abishai, and Asahel. Asahel was a fast runner, like one of the wild gazelles. [19] He chased Abner and did not turn to the right or the left in his pursuit of him. [20] Abner glanced back and said, "Is that you, Asahel?"

"Yes it is," Asahel replied.

Asahel Chases Abner

[21] Abner said to him, "Turn to your right or left, seize one of the young soldiers, and take whatever you can get from him." But Asahel would not stop chasing him. [22] Once again, Abner warned Asahel, "Stop chasing me. Why should I strike you to the ground? How could I ever look your brother Joab in the face?"

Abner Kills Asahel

[23] But Asahel refused to turn away, so Abner hit him in the stomach with the end of his spear. The spear went through his body, and he fell and died right there. When all who came to the place where Asahel had fallen and died, they stopped, [24] but Joab and Abishai pursued Abner. By sunset, they had gone as far as the hill of Ammah, which is opposite Giah on the way to the wilderness of Gibeon.

Joab Suspends Pursuit

[25] The Benjaminites rallied to Abner; they formed a single unit and took their stand on top of a hill. [26] Then Abner called

---

[a]2:8 Some LXX mss read *Ishbaal*; = Man of Baal; 1 Ch 8:33; 9:39 [b]2:8 = Man of Shame [c]2:16 Or *Helkath-hazzurim*

out to Joab: "Must the sword devour forever? Don't you realize this will only end in bitterness? How long before you tell the troops to stop pursuing their brothers?"

27 "As God lives," Joab replied, "if you had not spoken up, the troops wouldn't have stopped pursuing their brothers until morning." 28 Then Joab blew the ram's horn, and all the troops stopped; they no longer pursued Israel or continued to fight. 29 So Abner and his men marched through the •Arabah all that night. They crossed the Jordan, marched all morning,a and arrived at Mahanaim.

30 When Joab had turned back from pursuing Abner, he gathered all the troops. In addition to Asahel, 19 of David's soldiers were missing, 31 but they had killed 360 of the Benjaminites and Abner's men. 32 Afterwards, they carried Asahel to his father's tomb in Bethlehem and buried him. Then Joab and his men marched all night and reached Hebron at dawn.

Civil War: House of Saul vs. House of David

3 The war between the house of Saul and the house of David was long and drawn out, with David growing stronger and the house of Saul becoming weaker.
2 Sons were born to David in Hebron:

his firstborn was Amnon,
by Ahinoam the Jezreelite;
3 his second was Chileab,
by Abigail, the widow of Nabal
the Carmelite;
the third was Absalom,
son of Maacah the daughter
of King Talmai of Geshur;
4 the fourth was Adonijah,
son of Haggith;
the fifth was Shephatiah,
son of Abital;

5 the sixth was Ithream,
by David's wife Eglah.

These were born to David in Hebron.

Ish-bosheth Accuses Abner

6 During the war between the house of Saul and the house of David, Abner kept acquiring more power in the house of Saul. 7 Now Saul had a concubine whose name was Rizpah daughter of Aiah, and Ish-bosheth questioned Abner, "Why did you sleep with my father's concubine?"

8 Abner was very angry about Ish-bosheth's accusation. "Am I a dog's headb who belongs to Judah?" he asked. "All this time I've been loyal to the house of your father Saul, to his brothers, and to his friends and haven't handed you over to David, but now you accuse me of wrongdoing with this woman! 9 May God punish Abner and do so severely if I don't do for David what the LORD swore to him: 10 to transfer the kingdom from the house of Saul and establish the throne of David over Israel and Judah from Dan to Beer-sheba." 11 Ish-bosheth could not answer Abner because he was afraid of him.

Abner Offers Kingdom to David

12 Abner sent messengers as his representatives to say to David, "Whose land is it? Make your covenant with me, and you can be certain I am on your side to hand all Israel over to you."

13 David replied, "Good, I will make a covenant with you. However, there's one thing I require of you: Do not appear before me unless you bring Saul's daughter Michal here when you come to see me."

David Demands Return of Wife Michal

14 Then David sent messengers to say to Ish-bosheth son of Saul, "Give me back

a2:29 Or marched through the Bithron   b3:8 = a despised person

my wife, Michal. I was •engaged to her for the price of 100 Philistine foreskins."

¹⁵ So Ish-bosheth sent someone to take her away from her husband, Paltiel son of Laish. ¹⁶ Her husband followed her, weeping all the way to Bahurim. Abner said to him, "Go back." So he went back.

Abner Confers with David

¹⁷ Abner conferred with the elders of Israel: "In the past you wanted David to be king over you. ¹⁸ Now take action, because the LORD has spoken concerning David: 'Through My servant David I will save My people Israel from the power of the Philistines and the power of all Israel's enemies.'"

¹⁹ Abner also informed the Benjaminites and went to Hebron to inform David about all that was agreed on by Israel and the whole house of Benjamin. ²⁰ When Abner and 20 men came to David at Hebron, David held a banquet for him and his men.

²¹ Abner said to David, "Let me now go and I will gather all Israel to my lord the king. They will make a covenant with you, and you will rule over all you desire." So David dismissed Abner, and he went in peace.

Joab Assassinates Abner

²² Just then David's soldiers and Joab returned from a raid and brought a large amount of plundered goods with them. Abner was not with David in Hebron because David had dismissed him, and he had gone in peace. ²³ When Joab and all his army arrived, Joab was informed, "Abner son of Ner came to see the king, the king dismissed him, and he went in peace."

²⁴ Joab went to the king and said, "What have you done? Look here, Abner came to you. Why did you dismiss him? Now he's getting away. ²⁵ You know that Abner son of Ner came to deceive you and to find out about your activities and everything you're doing." ²⁶ Then Joab left David and sent messengers after Abner. They brought him back from the wellᵃ of Sirah, but David was unaware of it. ²⁷ When Abner returned to Hebron, Joab pulled him aside to the middle of the gateway, as if to speak to him privately, and there Joab stabbed him in the stomach. So Abner died in revenge for the death of Asahel,ᵇ Joab's brother.

David Reprimands Joab

²⁸ David heard ⌊about it⌋ later and said: "I and my kingdom are forever innocent before the LORD concerning the blood of Abner son of Ner. ²⁹ May it hang over Joab's head and his father's whole house, and may the house of Joab never be without someone who has an infection or leprosy or a man who can only work a spindleᶜ or someone who falls by the sword or starves." ³⁰ Joab and his brother Abishai killed Abner because he had put their brother Asahel to death in the battle at Gibeon.

³¹ David then ordered Joab and all the people who were with him, "Tear your clothes, put on •sackcloth, and mourn over Abner." And King David walked behind the funeral procession.ᵈ

³² When they buried Abner in Hebron, the king wept aloud at Abner's tomb. All the people wept, ³³ and the king sang a lament for Abner:

David's Lament for Abner

Should Abner die as a fool dies?
³⁴   Your hands were not bound,
    your feet not placed
      in bronze ⌊shackles⌋.

ᵃ**3:26** Or *cistern*   ᵇ**3:27** Lit *And he died for the blood of Asahel*   ᶜ**3:29** LXX reads *who uses a crutch*   ᵈ**3:31** Lit *the bed; or the bier*

You fell like one who falls victim
to criminals.

And all the people wept over him even
more.

35 Then they came to urge David to eat
bread while it was still day, but David
took an oath: "May God punish me and
do so severely if I taste bread or anything
else before sunset!" 36 All the people
took note of this, and it pleased them. In
fact, everything the king did pleased
them. 37 On that day all the troops and
all Israel were convinced that the king
had no part in the killing of Abner son of
Ner.

38 Then the king said to his soldiers,
"You must know that a great leader has
fallen in Israel today. 39 As for me, even
though I am the anointed king, I have little power today. These men, the sons of
Zeruiah, are too fierce for me. May the
LORD repay the evildoer according to his
evil!"

Assassination of Ish-bosheth

4 When Saul's son ⌊Ish-bosheth⌋ heard
that Abner had died in Hebron, his
courage failed, and all Israel was dismayed. 2 Saul's son had two men who
were leaders of raiding parties: one
named Baanah and the other Rechab,
sons of Rimmon the Beerothite of the
Benjaminites. Beeroth is also considered
part of Benjamin, 3 and the Beerothites
fled to Gittaim and still live there as
aliens to this very day.

4 Saul's son Jonathan had a son whose
feet were crippled. He was five years old
when the report about Saul and Jonathan
came from Jezreel. His nurse picked him
up and fled, but as she was hurrying to
flee, he fell and became lame. His name
was Mephibosheth.

5 Rechab and Baanah, the sons of Rimmon the Beerothite, set out and arrived
at Ish-bosheth's house during the heat of
the day while the king was taking his
midday nap. 6 They entered the interior
of the house as if to get wheat and
stabbed him in the stomach. Then Rechab and his brother Baanah escaped.
7 They had entered the house while Ish-
bosheth was lying on his bed in his bedroom and stabbed and killed him. Then
they beheaded him, took his head, and
traveled by way of the •Arabah all night.
8 They brought Ish-bosheth's head to
David at Hebron and said to the king,
"Here's the head of Ish-bosheth son of
Saul, your enemy who intended to take
your life. Today the LORD has granted
vengeance to my lord the king against
Saul and his offspring."

David Executes Assassins

9 But David answered Rechab and his
brother Baanah, sons of Rimmon the
Beerothite, "As surely as the LORD
lives, ⌊the One⌋ who has redeemed my
life from every distress, 10 when the
person told me, 'Look, Saul is dead,' he
thought he was a bearer of good news,
but I seized him and put him to death
at Ziklag. That was my reward to him
for his news! 11 How much more when
wicked men kill a righteous man in his
own house on his own bed! So now,
should I not require his blood from
your hands and wipe you off the
earth?"

12 So David gave orders to the young
men, and they killed Rechab and Baanah.
They cut off their hands and feet and
hung ⌊their bodies⌋ by the pool in Hebron,
but they took Ish-bosheth's head and buried it in Abner's tomb in Hebron.

David, King of Israel

5 All the tribes of Israel came to David
at Hebron and said, "Here we are,

your own flesh and blood.[a] [2] Even while Saul was king over us, you were the one who led us out ⌊to battle⌋ and brought us back. The LORD also said to you, 'You will shepherd My people Israel and be ruler over Israel.'"

[3] So all the elders of Israel came to the king at Hebron. King David made a covenant with them at Hebron in the LORD's presence, and they anointed David king over Israel.

[4] David was 30 years old when he began his reign; he reigned 40 years. [5] In Hebron he reigned over Judah seven years and six months, and in Jerusalem he reigned 33 years over all Israel and Judah.

[6] The king and his men marched to Jerusalem against the Jebusites who inhabited the land. The Jebusites had said to David: "You will never get in here. Even the blind and lame can repel you," thinking, "David can't get in here." [7] Yet David did capture the stronghold of Zion, the city of David. [8] He said that day, "Whoever attacks the Jebusites must go through the water shaft to reach the lame and the blind who are despised by David."[b] For this reason it is said, "The blind and the lame will never enter the house."[c]

[9] David took up residence in the stronghold, which he named the city of David. He built it up all the way around from the supporting terraces inward. [10] David became more and more powerful, and the LORD God of •Hosts was with him. [11] King Hiram of Tyre sent envoys to David; ⌊he also sent⌋ cedar logs, carpenters, and stonemasons, and they built a palace for David. [12] Then David knew that the LORD had established him as king over Israel and had exalted his kingdom for the sake of His people Israel.

[13] After he arrived from Hebron, David took more concubines and wives in Jerusalem, and more sons and daughters were born to him. [14] These are the names of those born to him in Jerusalem: Shammua, Shobab, Nathan, Solomon, [15] Ibhar, Elishua, Nepheg, Japhia, [16] Elishama, Eliada, and Eliphelet.

David Defeats Philistines

[17] When the Philistines heard that David had been anointed king over Israel, they all went in search of David, but he heard about it and went down to the stronghold. [18] So the Philistines came and spread out in the Valley of Rephaim.

[19] Then David inquired of the LORD: "Should I go to war against the Philistines? Will you hand them over to me?"

The LORD replied to David, "Go, for I will certainly hand the Philistines over to you."

[20] So David went to Baal-perazim and defeated them there and said, "Like a bursting flood, the LORD has burst out against my enemies before me." Therefore, he named that place the Lord Bursts Out.[d] [21] The Philistines abandoned their idols there, and David and his men carried them off.

[22] The Philistines came up again and spread out in the Valley of Rephaim. [23] So David inquired of the LORD, and He answered, "Do not make a frontal assault. Circle around behind them and attack them opposite the balsam trees. [24] When you hear the sound of marching in the tops of the balsam trees, act decisively, for then the LORD will have marched out ahead of you to attack the camp of the Philistines." [25] So David did exactly as the LORD commanded him, and he struck down the Philistines all the way from Geba to Gezer.

[a] 5:1 Lit your bone and flesh   [b] 5:8 Alt Hb tradition, LXX, Tg, Syr read who despise David   [c] 5:8 Or temple, or palace   [d] 5:20 Or Baal-perazim; 2 Sm 6:8; 1 Ch 13:11

David Moves the Ark

6 David again assembled all the choice men in Israel, 30,000. [2] He and all his troops set out to bring the ark of God from Baale-judah.[a] The ark is called by the Name, the name of the LORD of •Hosts who dwells ⌊between⌋ the •cherubim. [3] They set the ark of God on a new cart and transported it from Abinadab's house, which was on the hill. Uzzah and Ahio,[b] sons of Abinadab, were guiding the cart [4] and brought it with the ark of God from Abinadab's house on the hill. Ahio walked in front of the ark. [5] David and the whole house of Israel were celebrating before the LORD with all ⌊kinds of⌋ fir wood ⌊instruments⌋,[c] lyres, harps, tambourines, sistrums,[d] and cymbals.

Uzzah Struck Dead

[6] When they came to Nacon's threshing floor, Uzzah reached out to the ark of God and took hold of it, because the oxen had stumbled. [7] Then the LORD's anger burned against Uzzah, and God struck him dead on the spot for his irreverence, and he died there next to the ark of God. [8] David was angry because of the LORD's outburst against Uzzah, so he named that place an Outburst Against Uzzah,[e] as it is today. [9] David feared the LORD that day and said, "How can the ark of the LORD ever come to me?" [10] So he was not willing to move the ark of the LORD to the city of David; instead, he took it to the house of Obed-edom the Gittite. [11] The ark of the LORD remained in his house three months, and the LORD blessed Obed-edom and his whole family.

Ark to City of David

[12] It was reported to King David: "The LORD has blessed Obed-edom's family and all that belongs to him because of the ark of God." So David went and had the ark of God brought up from Obed-edom's house to the city of David with rejoicing. [13] When those carrying the ark of the LORD advanced six steps, he sacrificed an ox and a fattened calf. [14] David was dancing[f] with all his might before the LORD wearing a linen •ephod. [15] He and the whole house of Israel were bringing up the ark of the LORD with shouts and the sound of the ram's horn. [16] As the ark of the LORD was entering the city of David, Saul's daughter Michal looked down from the window and saw King David leaping and dancing before the LORD, and she despised him in her heart.

[17] They brought the ark of the LORD and set it in its place inside the tent David had set up for it. Then David offered •burnt offerings and •fellowship offerings in the LORD's presence. [18] When David had finished offering the burnt offering and the fellowship offerings, he blessed the people in the name of the LORD of Hosts. [19] Then he distributed a loaf of bread, a date cake, and a raisin cake to each one of the whole multitude of the people of Israel, both men and women. Then all the people left, each to his own home.

Michal Criticizes David

[20] When David returned ⌊home⌋ to bless his household, Saul's daughter Michal came out to meet him. "How the king of Israel honored himself today!" she said. "He exposed himself today in the sight of the slave girls of his subjects like a vulgar person would expose himself."

Michal's Punishment

[21] David replied to Michal, "I was dancing[g] before the LORD who chose me

---

a6:2 Alt name for Kiriath-jearim **b6:3** Or *and his brothers* **c6:5** DSS, LXX read *with tuned instruments with strength, with songs*; 1 Ch 13:8 **d6:5** = an Egyptian percussion instrument **e6:8** Or *Perez-uzzah*; 2 Sm 5:20 **f6:14** Or *whirling* **g6:21** LXX; MT omits *I was dancing*

over your father and his whole family to appoint me ruler over the LORD's people Israel. I will celebrate before the LORD, ²² and I will humble myself even more and humiliate myself.ᵃ ᵇ I will be honored by the slave girls you spoke about." ²³ And Saul's daughter Michal had no child to the day of her death.

LORD's Covenant with David

7 When the king had settled into his palace and the LORD had given him rest on every side from all his enemies, ² the king said to <u>Nathan the prophet</u>, "Look, I am living in a cedar house while the ark of God sits inside tent curtains."

³ So Nathan told the king, "Go and do all that is on your heart, for the LORD is with you."

⁴ But that night the word of the LORD came to Nathan: ⁵ "Go to My servant David and say, 'This is what the LORD says: Are you to build a house for Me to live in? ⁶ From the time I brought the Israelites out of Egypt until today I have not lived in a house; instead, I have been moving around with the tabernacle tent. ⁷ In all My journeys with all the Israelites, have I ever asked anyone among the tribes of Israel, whom I commanded to shepherd My people Israel: Why haven't you built Me a house of cedar?'

⁸ "Now this is what you are to say to My servant David: 'This is what the LORD of •Hosts says: I took you from the pasture and from following the sheep to be ruler over My people Israel. ⁹ I have been with you wherever you have gone, and I have destroyed all your enemies before you. I will make a name for you like that of the greatest in the land. ¹⁰ I will establish a place for My people Israel and plant them, so that they may live there and not be disturbed again. Evildoers will not afflict them as they have done ¹¹ ever since the day I ordered judges to be over My people Israel. I will give you rest from all your enemies.

" 'The LORD declares to you: The LORD Himself will make a house for you. ¹² When your time comes and you rest with your fathers, I will raise up after you your descendant, who will come from your body, and I will establish his kingdom. ¹³ He will build a house for My name, and I will establish the throne of his kingdom forever. ¹⁴ I will be a father to him, and he will be a son to Me. When he does wrong, I will discipline him with a human rod and with blows from others. ¹⁵ But My faithful love will never leave him as I removed it from Saul; I removed him from your way. ¹⁶ <u>Your house and kingdom will endure before Meᶜ forever, and your throne will be established forever.'"</u>

¹⁷ Nathan spoke all these words and this entire vision to David.

David's Prayer of Thanksgiving

¹⁸ Then King David went in, sat in the LORD's presence, and said, "Who am I, Lord GOD, and what is my house that You have brought me this far? ¹⁹ What You have done so farᵈ was a little thing to You, Lord GOD, for You have also spoken about Your servant's house in the distant future. And this is a revelationᵉ for mankind, Lord GOD. ²⁰ What more can David say to You? You know Your servant, Lord GOD. ²¹ Because of Your word and according to Your will, You have revealed all these great things to Your servant.

²² "This is why You are great, Lord GOD. <u>There is no one like You, and there</u>

ᵃ6:22 LXX reads more and I will be humble in your eyes ᵇ6:22 Lit more and I will be humble in my own eyes
ᶜ7:16 Some Hb mss, LXX, Syr; other Hb mss read you ᵈ7:19 Lit Yet this ᵉ7:19 Or custom, or instruction

is no God besides You, as all we have heard confirms. 23 And who is like Your people Israel? God came to one nation on earth in order to redeem a people for Himself, to make a name for Himself, and to perform for them[a] great and awesome acts, driving out nations and their gods before Your people You redeemed for Yourself from Egypt. 24 You established Your people Israel Your own people forever, and You, LORD, have become their God.

25 "Now, LORD God, fulfill the promise forever that You have made to Your servant and his house. Do as You have promised, 26 so that Your name will be exalted forever, when it is said, 'The LORD of Hosts is God over Israel.' The house of Your servant David will be established before You 27 since You, LORD of Hosts, God of Israel, have revealed this to Your servant when You said, 'I will build a house for you.' Therefore, Your servant has found the courage to pray this prayer to You. 28 Lord GOD, You are God; Your words are true, and You have promised this grace to Your servant. 29 Now, please bless Your servant's house so that it will continue before You forever. For You, Lord GOD, have spoken, and with Your blessing Your servant's house will be blessed forever."

David's Victories

8 After this, David defeated the Philistines, subdued them, and took Metheg-ammah[b] from Philistine control.[c] 2 He also defeated the Moabites, and after making them lie down on the ground, he measured them off with a cord. He measured every two cord lengths ⌊of those⌋ to be put to death and one length ⌊of those⌋ to be kept alive. So the Moabites became David's subjects and brought tribute.

3 David also defeated Hadadezer son of Rehob, king of Zobah, who went to restore his control at the Euphrates River. 4 David captured 1,700 horsemen[d] and 20,000 foot soldiers from him, and he hamstrung all the horses, and he kept 100 chariots.[e] 5 When the Arameans of Damascus came to assist King Hadadezer of Zobah, David struck down 22,000 Aramean men. 6 Then he placed garrisons in Aram of Damascus, and the Arameans became David's subjects and brought tribute. The LORD made David victorious wherever he went.

7 David took the gold shields of Hadadezer's officers and brought them to Jerusalem. 8 King David also took huge quantities of bronze from Betah[f] and Berothai, Hadadezer's cities.

9 When King Toi of Hamath heard that David had defeated the entire army of Hadadezer, 10 he sent his son Joram to King David to greet him and to congratulate him because David had fought against Hadadezer and defeated him, for Toi and Hadadezer had fought many wars. Joram had items of silver, gold, and bronze with him. 11 King David also dedicated these to the LORD, along with the silver and gold he had dedicated from all the nations he had subdued—12 from Edom,[g] Moab, the Ammonites, the Philistines, the Amalekites, and the spoil of Hadadezer son of Rehob, king of Zobah.

13 David made a reputation for himself when he returned from striking down 18,000 Edomites[h] in the Valley of Salt.[i] 14 He placed garrisons throughout Edom,

---

a7:23 Some Hb mss, Tg, Vg, Syr; other Hb mss read you b8:1 Or took control of the mother city; Hb obscure c8:1 LXX reads them, and David took tribute out of the hand of the Philistines d8:4 LXX, DSS read 1,000 chariots and 7,000 horsemen e8:4 Or chariot horses f8:8 Some LXX mss, Syr read Tebah g8:12 Some Hb mss, LXX, Syr; MT reads Aram; 1 Ch 18:11 h8:13 A few Hb mss, LXX, Syr; MT reads Arameans; 1 Ch 18:12 i8:13 = the Dead Sea region

and all the Edomites were subject to David. The LORD made David victorious wherever he went.

David's Staff

15 So David reigned over all Israel, administering justice and righteousness for all his people.

16 Joab son of Zeruiah was
over the army;
Jehoshaphat son of Ahilud was
court historian;
17 Zadok son of Ahitub
and Ahimelech son of Abiathar
were priests;
Seraiah was court secretary;
18 Benaiah son of Jehoiada ⌊was over⌋
the Cherethites and the Pelethites;
and David's sons were
chief officials.ᵃ

David's Kindness to Mephibosheth

9 David asked, "Is there anyone remaining from Saul's family I can show kindness to because of Jonathan?" 2 There was a servant of Saul's family named Ziba. They summoned him to David, and the king said to him, "Are you Ziba?"

"⌊I am⌋ your servant," he replied.

3 So the king asked, "Is there anyone left of Saul's family I can show the kindness of God to?"

Ziba said to the king, "There is still Jonathan's son who is lame in both feet."

4 The king asked him, "Where is he?"

Ziba answered the king, "You'll find him in Lo-debar at the house of Machir son of Ammiel." 5 So King David had him brought from the house of Machir son of Ammiel in Lo-debar.

6 Mephibosheth son of Jonathan son of Saul came to David, bowed down to the ground and paid homage. David said, "Mephibosheth!"

"I am your servant," he replied.

7 "Don't be afraid," David said to him, "since I intend to show you kindness because of your father Jonathan. I will restore to you all your grandfather Saul's fields, and you will always eat meals at my table."

8 Mephibosheth bowed down and said, "What is your servant that you take an interest in a dead dog like me?"

9 Then the king summoned Saul's attendant Ziba and said to him, "I have given to your master's grandson all that belonged to Saul and his family. 10 You, your sons, and your servants are to work the ground for him, and you are to bring in ⌊the crops⌋ so your master's grandson will have food to eat. But Mephibosheth, your master's grandson, is always to eat at my table." Now Ziba had 15 sons and 20 servants.

11 Ziba said to the king, "Your servant will do all my lord the king commands."

So Mephibosheth ate at David'sᵇ table just like one of the king's sons. 12 Mephibosheth had a young son whose name was Mica. All those living in Ziba's house were Mephibosheth's servants. 13 However, Mephibosheth lived in Jerusalem because he always ate at the king's table. He was lame in both feet.

War with the Ammonites

10 Some time later the king of the Ammonites died, and his son Hanun became king in his place. 2 Then David said, "I'll show kindness to Hanun son of Nahash, just as his father showed kindness to me."

Ammonites Humiliate Emissaries

So David sent his emissaries to console Hanun concerning his father. However, when they arrived in the land of the

---

ᵃ8:18 LXX; MT reads were priests; 1 Ch 18:17   ᵇ9:11 LXX; Syr reads the king's; Vg reads your; MT reads my

Ammonites, ³ the Ammonite leaders said to Hanun their lord, "Just because David has sent men with condolences for you, do you really believe he's showing respect for your father? Instead, hasn't David sent his emissaries in order to scout out the city, spy on it, and overthrow it?" ⁴ So Hanun took David's emissaries, shaved off half their beards, cut their clothes in half at the hips, and sent them away.

⁵ When this was reported to David, he sent ᴸsomeoneᴸ to meet them, since they were deeply humiliated. The king said, "Stay in Jericho until your beards grow back; then return."

⁶ When the Ammonites realized they had become repulsive to David, they hired 20,000 foot soldiers from the Arameans of Beth-rehob and Zobah, 1,000 men from the king of Maacah, and 12,000 men from Tob.

Joab's Strategy

⁷ David heard about it and sent Joab and all the fighting men. ⁸ The Ammonites marched out and lined up in battle formation at the entrance to the city gate while the Arameans of Zobah and Rehob and the men of Tob and Maacah were in the field by themselves. ⁹ When Joab saw that there was a battle line in front of him and another behind him, he chose some men out of all the elite troops of Israel and lined up in battle formation to engage the Arameans. ¹⁰ He placed the rest of the forces under the command of his brother Abishai who lined up in battle formation to engage the Ammonites.

¹¹ "If the Arameans are too strong for me," Joab said, "then you will be my help. However, if the Ammonites are too strong for you, I'll come to help you.

¹² Be strong! We must prove ourselves strong for our people and for the cities of our God. May the LORD's will be done." ª

¹³ Joab and his troops advanced to fight against the Arameans, and they fled before him. ¹⁴ When the Ammonites saw that the Arameans had fled, they too fled before Abishai and entered the city. So Joab withdrew from the attack against the Ammonites and went to Jerusalem.

Arameans Regroup

¹⁵ When the Arameans saw that they had been defeated by Israel, they regrouped. ¹⁶ Hadadezer sent ᴸmessengersᴸ to bring the Arameans who were across the Euphrates River, and they came to Helam with Shobach, commander of Hadadezer's army, leading them.

David Defeats Arameans

¹⁷ When this was reported to David, he gathered all Israel, crossed the Jordan, and went to Helam. Then the Arameans lined up in formation to engage David in battle and fought against him. ¹⁸ But the Arameans fled before Israel, and David killed 700 of their charioteers and 40,000 foot soldiers.ᵇ He also struck down Shobach commander of their army, who died there. ¹⁹ When all the kings who were Hadadezer's subjects saw that they had been defeated by Israel, they made peace with Israel and became their subjects. After this, the Arameans were afraid to ever help the Ammonites again.

David and Bathsheba

11 In the spring when kings march out ᴸto warᴸ, David sent Joab with his officers and all Israel. They destroyed the Ammonites and besieged Rabbah, but David remained in Jerusalem.

ª**10:12** Lit *the* LORD *do what is good in His eyes* ᵇ**10:18** Some LXX mss; MT reads *horsemen;* 1 Ch 19:18

2 One evening David got up from his bed and strolled around on the roof of the palace. From the roof he saw a woman bathing—a very beautiful woman. 3 So David sent someone to inquire about her, and he reported, "This is Bathsheba, daughter of Eliam and wife of Uriah the Hittite."ᵃ

Adultery

4 David sent messengers to get her, and when she came to him, he slept with her. Now she had just been purifying herself from her uncleanness. Afterwards, she returned home. 5 The woman conceived and sent word to inform David: "I am pregnant."

David's "Uriah Plan" Fails

6 David sent orders to Joab: "Send me Uriah the Hittite." So Joab sent Uriah to David. 7 When Uriah came to him, David asked how Joab and the troops were doing and how the war was going. 8 Then he said to Uriah, "Go down to your house and wash your feet." So Uriah left the palace, and a gift from the king followed him. 9 But Uriah slept at the door of the palace with all his master's servants; he did not go down to his house.

10 When it was reported to David, "Uriah didn't go home," David questioned Uriah, "Haven't you just come from a journey? Why didn't you go home?"

11 Uriah answered David, "The ark, Israel, and Judah are dwelling in tents, and my master Joab and his soldiersᵇ are camping in the open field. How can I enter my house to eat and drink and sleep with my wife? As surely as you live and by your life, I will not do this!"

12 "Stay here today also," David said to Uriah, "and tomorrow I will send you

back." So Uriah stayed in Jerusalem that day and the next. 13 Then David invited Uriah to eat and drink with him, and David got him drunk. He went out in the evening to lie down on his cot with his master's servants, but he did not go home.

David Orders Uriah's Death

14 The next morning David wrote a letter to Joab and sent it with Uriah. 15 In the letter he wrote:

> Put Uriah at the front of the fiercest fighting, then withdraw from him so that he is struck down and dies.

16 When Joab was besieging the city, he put Uriah in the place where he knew the best ⌊enemy⌋ soldiers were. 17 Then the men of the city came out and attacked Joab, and some of the men from David's soldiers fell ⌊in battle⌋; Uriah the Hittite also died.

18 Joab sent someone to report to David all the details of the battle. 19 He commanded the messenger, "When you've finished telling the king all the details of the battle— 20 if the king's anger gets stirred up and he asks you, 'Why did you get so close to the city to fight? Didn't you realize they would shoot from the top of the wall? 21 At Thebez, who struck Abimelech son of Jerubbesheth?ᶜ ᵈ Didn't a woman drop an upper millstone on him from the top of the wall so that he died? Why did you get so close to the wall?'—then say, 'Your servant Uriah the Hittite is dead also.'" 22 Then the messenger left.

Joab's Messenger

When he arrived, he reported to David all that Joab had sent him ⌊to tell⌋. 23 The messenger reported to David, "The men

---

ᵃ11:3 DSS add *Joab's armor-bearer*   ᵇ11:11 Lit *servants*   ᶜ11:21 LXX reads *Jerubbaal*   ᵈ11:21 = Gideon gained the advantage over us and came out against us in the field, but we counterattacked right up to the entrance of the gate. 24 However, the archers shot down on your soldiers from the top of the wall, and some of the king's soldiers died. Your servant Uriah the Hittite is also dead."

25 David told the messenger, "Say this to Joab: 'Don't let this matter upset you because the sword devours all alike. Intensify your fight against the city and demolish it.' Encourage him."

David Marries Bathsheba

26 When Uriah's wife heard that her husband Uriah had died, she mourned for him.[a] 27 When the time of mourning ended, David had her brought to his house. She became his wife and bore him a son. However, the LORD considered what David had done to be evil.

Nathan's Pointed Parable

12 So the LORD sent Nathan to David. When he arrived, he said to him:

There were two men in a certain city, one rich and the other poor. 2 The rich man had a large number of sheep and cattle, 3 but the poor man had nothing except one small ewe lamb that he had bought. It lived and grew up with him and his children. It shared his meager food and drank from his cup; it slept in his arms, and it was like a daughter to him. 4 Now a traveler came to the rich man, but the rich man could not bring himself to take one of his own sheep or cattle to prepare for the traveler who had come to him. Instead, he took the poor man's lamb and prepared it for his guest.[b]

5 David was infuriated with the man and said to Nathan: "As surely as the LORD lives, the man who did this deserves to die! 6 Because he has done this thing and shown no pity, he must pay four lambs for that lamb."

Nathan Accuses David

7 Nathan replied to David, "You are the man! This is what the LORD God of Israel says: 'I anointed you king over Israel, and I delivered you from the hand of Saul. 8 I gave your master's house to you and your master's wives into your arms,[c] and I gave you the house of Israel and Judah, and if that was not enough, I would have given you even more. 9 Why then have you despised the command of the LORD by doing what I consider[d] evil? You struck down Uriah the Hittite with the sword and took his wife as your own wife—you murdered him with the Ammonite's sword. 10 Now therefore, the sword will never leave your house because you despised Me and took the wife of Uriah the Hittite to be your own wife.'

11 "This is what the LORD says, 'I am going to bring disaster on you from your own family: I will take your wives and give them to another[e] before your very eyes, and he will sleep with them publicly.[f] 12 You acted in secret, but I will do this before all Israel and in broad daylight.'"[g]

David Repents—God Forgives

13 David responded to Nathan, "I have sinned against the LORD."

Then Nathan replied to David, "The LORD has taken away your sin; you will not die. 14 However, because you treated[h] the LORD with such contempt in this

---

[a] 11:26 Lit her husband   [b] 12:4 Lit for the man who had come to him   [c] 12:8 Lit bosom   [d] 12:9 Alt Hb tradition reads what He considers   [e] 12:11 Or to your neighbor   [f] 12:11 Lit in the eyes of this sun   [g] 12:12 Lit and before the sun
[h] 12:14 Alt Hb tradition, one LXX ms; MT reads treated the enemies of; DSS read treated the word of

matter, the son born to you will die."
[15] Then Nathan went home.

Death of Bathsheba's Son

The LORD struck the baby that Uriah's wife had borne to David, and he became ill. [16] David pleaded with God for the boy. He fasted, went home, and spent the night lying on the ground. [17] The elders of his house stood beside him to get him up from the ground, but he was unwilling and would not eat anything with them.

[18] On the seventh day the baby died. But David's servants were afraid to tell him the baby was dead. They said, "Look, while the baby was alive, we spoke to him, and he wouldn't listen to us. So how can we tell him the baby is dead? He may do something desperate."

[19] When David saw that his servants were whispering to each other, he guessed that the baby was dead. So he asked his servants, "Is the baby dead?"

"He is dead," they replied.

[20] Then David got up from the ground. He washed, anointed himself, changed his clothes, went to the LORD's house, and worshiped. Then he went home and requested something to eat. So they served him food, and he ate.

[21] His servants asked him, "What did you just do? While the baby was alive, you fasted and wept, but when he died, you got up and ate food."

[22] He answered, "While the baby was alive, I fasted and wept because I thought, 'Who knows? The LORD may be gracious to me and let him live.' [23] But now that he is dead, why should I fast? Can I bring him back again? I'll go to him, but he will never return to me."

Birth of Solomon

[24] Then David comforted his wife Bathsheba; he went and slept with her. She gave birth to a son and named[a] him Solomon.[b] The LORD loved him, [25] and He sent a message through Nathan the prophet, who named[c] him Jedidiah,[d] because of the LORD.

David Captures City of Rabbah

[26] Joab fought against Rabbah of the Ammonites and captured the royal fortress. [27] Then Joab sent messengers to David to say, "I have fought against Rabbah and have also captured the water supply. [28] Now therefore, assemble the rest of the troops, lay siege to the city, and capture it. Otherwise I will be the one to capture the city, and it will be named after me. [29] So David assembled all the troops and went to Rabbah; he fought against it and captured it. [30] He took the crown from the head of their king,[e] and it was placed on David's head. The crown weighed 75 pounds[f] of gold, and it had a precious stone in it. In addition, David took away a large quantity of plunder from the city. [31] He removed the people who were in the city and put them to work with saws, iron picks, and iron axes, and to labor at brickmaking. He did the same to all the Ammonite cities. Then he and all his troops returned to Jerusalem.

Amnon Rapes Tamar

13 Some time passed. David's son Absalom had a beautiful sister named Tamar, and David's son Amnon was infatuated with her. [2] Amnon was frustrated to the point of making himself sick over his sister Tamar because she was a virgin, but it seemed impossible to

---

[a]12:24 Alt Hb tradition reads he named   [b]12:24 = His Restoration, or His Peace   [c]12:25 Or prophet to name
[d]12:25 = Beloved of the LORD   [e]12:30 LXX reads of Milcom; some emend to Molech; 1 Kg 11:5,33   [f]12:30 Lit a talent

do anything to her. ³ Amnon had a friend named Jonadab, a son of David's brother Shimeah. Jonadab was a very shrewd man, ⁴ and he asked Amnon, "Why are you, the king's son, so miserable every morning? Won't you tell me?"

Amnon replied, "I'm in love with Tamar, my brother Absalom's sister."

Jonadab's Scheme

⁵ Jonadab said to him, "Lie down on your bed and pretend you're sick. When your father comes to see you, say to him, 'Please let my sister Tamar come and give me ⌊something⌋ to eat. Let her prepare food in my presence so I can watch and eat from her hand.'"

⁶ So Amnon lay down and pretended to be sick. When the king came to see him, Amnon said to him, "Please let my sister Tamar come and make a couple of cakes in my presence so I can eat from her hand."

⁷ David sent word to Tamar at the palace: "Please go to your brother Amnon's house and prepare a meal for him."

⁸ Then Tamar went to his house while Amnon was lying down. She took dough, kneaded it, made cakes in his presence, and baked them. ⁹ She brought the pan and set it down in front of him, but he refused to eat. Amnon said, "Everyone leave me!" And everyone left him. ¹⁰ "Bring the meal to the bedroom," Amnon told Tamar, "so I can eat from your hand." Tamar took the cakes she had made and went to her brother Amnon's bedroom. ¹¹ When she brought ⌊them⌋ to him to eat, he grabbed her and said,ᵃ "Come sleep with me, my sister!"

Amnon's Crime

¹² "Don't, my brother!" she cried. "Don't humiliate me, for such a thing should never be done in Israel. Don't do this horrible thing! ¹³ Where could I ever go with my disgrace? And you—you would be like one of the immoral men in Israel! Please, speak to the king, for he won't keep me from you." ¹⁴ But he refused to listen to her, and because he was stronger than she was, he raped her.

Amnon Discards Tamar

¹⁵ After this, Amnon hated Tamar with such intensity that the hatred he hated her with was greater than the love he had loved her with. "Get out of here!" he said.

¹⁶ "No," she cried,ᵇ "sending me away is much worse than the great wrong you've already done to me!" But he refused to listen to her. ¹⁷ Instead, he called to the servant who waited on him: "Throw this woman out and bolt the door behind her!" ¹⁸ Amnon's servant threw her out and bolted the door behind her. Now Tamar was wearing a long-sleevedᶜ garment, because this is what the king's virgin daughters wore. ¹⁹ Tamar put ashes on her head and tore the long-sleeved garment she was wearing. She put her hand on her head and went away weeping.

Absalom Comforts Tamar

²⁰ Her brother Absalom said to her: "Has your brother Amnon been with you? Be quiet for now, my sister. He is your brother. Don't take this thing to heart." So Tamar lived as a desolate woman in the house of her brother Absalom.

Absalom Plots Amnon's Murder

²¹ When King David heard about all these things, he was furious.ᵈ ²² Absalom didn't say anything to Amnon, either

---

ᵃ**13:11** Lit said to her   ᵇ**13:16** Lit she said to him   ᶜ**13:18** Or an ornamented; Gn 37:3   ᵈ**13:21** LXX, DSS add but he did not grieve the spirit of Amnon his son, for he loved him because he was his firstborn; 1 Kg 1:6

good or bad, because he hated Amnon since he disgraced his sister Tamar.

²³ Two years later, Absalom's sheepshearers were at Baal-hazor near Ephraim, and Absalom invited all the king's sons. ²⁴ Then he went to the king and said, "Your servant has just hired sheepshearers. Will the king and his servants please come with your servant?"

²⁵ The king replied to Absalom, "No, my son, we should not all go, or we would be a burden to you." Although Absalom urged him, he wasn't willing to go, though he did bless him.

²⁶ "If not," Absalom said, "please let my brother Amnon go with us."

The king asked him, "Why should he go with you?" ²⁷ But Absalom urged him, so he sent Amnon and all the king's sons.ᵃ

Absalom's Men Kill Amnon

²⁸ Now Absalom commanded his young men, "Watch Amnon until he is in a good mood from the wine. When I order you to strike Amnon, then kill him. Don't be afraid. Am I not the one who has commanded you? Be strong and courageous!" ²⁹ So Absalom's young men did to Amnon just as Absalom had commanded. Then all ⌊the rest of⌋ the king's sons got up, and each fled on his mule.

Conflicting Reports to David

³⁰ While they were on the way, a report reached David: "Absalom struck down all the king's sons; not even one of them survived!" ³¹ In response the king stood up, tore his clothes, and lay down on the ground, and all his servants stood by with their clothes torn.

³² But Jonadab, son of David's brother Shimeah, spoke up: "My lord must not think they have killed all the young men, the king's sons, because only Amnon is dead. In fact, Absalom has planned thisᵇ ever since the day Amnon disgraced his sister Tamar. ³³ So now, my lord the king, don't take seriously the report that says all the king's sons are dead. Only Amnon is dead."

Absalom Flees

³⁴ Meanwhile, Absalom had fled. When the young man who was standing watch looked up, there were many people coming from the road west of him from the side of the mountain.ᶜ ³⁵ Jonadab said to the king, "Look, the king's sons have come! It's exactly like your servant said." ³⁶ Just as he finished speaking, the king's sons entered and wept loudly. Then the king and all his servants also wept bitterly.

³⁷ Now Absalom fled and went to Talmai son of Ammihud, king of Geshur. And David mourned for his sonᵈ every day. ³⁸ Absalom had fled and gone to Geshur where he stayed three years. ³⁹ Then King Davidᵉ longed to go to Absalom, for David had finished grieving over Amnon's death.

Joab's Stratagem for Absalom

14 Joab son of Zeruiah observed that the king's mind was on Absalom. ² So Joab sent someone to Tekoa to bring a clever woman from there. He told her, "Pretend to be in mourning: dress in mourning clothes and don't put on any oil. Act like a woman who has been mourning for the dead for a long time. ³ Go to the king and speak these words

---

ᵃ**13:27** LXX adds *And Absalom prepared a feast like a royal feast.* ᵇ**13:32** Lit *In fact, it was established on the mouth of Absalom* ᶜ**13:34** LXX adds *And the watchman came and reported to the king saying, "I see men on the Horonaim road on the side of the mountain."* ᵈ**13:37** Probably Amnon ᵉ**13:39** DSS, LXX, Tg read *David's spirit*

to him." Then Joab told her exactly what to say.

⁴ When the woman from Tekoa came[a] to the king, she fell with her face to the ground in homage and said, "Help me, my king!"

⁵ "What's the matter?" the king asked her.

"To tell the truth, I am a widow; my husband died," she said. ⁶ "Your servant had two sons. They were fighting in the field with no one to separate them, and one struck the other and killed him. ⁷ Now the whole clan has risen up against your servant and said, 'Hand over the one who killed his brother so we may put him to death for the life of the brother he murdered. We will destroy the heir!' They would extinguish my one remaining ember by not preserving my husband's name or posterity on earth."

⁸ The king told the woman, "Go home. I will issue a command on your behalf."

⁹ Then the woman of Tekoa said to the king, "My lord the king, may any blame be on me and my father's house, and may the king and his throne be innocent."

¹⁰ "Whoever speaks to you," the king said, "bring him to me. He will not trouble you again!"

¹¹ She replied, "Please, may the king invoke the LORD your God, so that the avenger of blood will not increase the loss, and they will not eliminate my son!"

"As the LORD lives," he vowed, "not a hair of your son will fall to the ground."

¹² Then the woman said, "Please, may your servant speak a word to my lord the king?"

"Speak," he replied.

David Agrees to Absalom's Return

¹³ The woman asked, "Why have you devised something similar against the people of God? When the king spoke as he did about this matter, he has pronounced his own guilt. The king has not brought back his own banished one. ¹⁴ For we will certainly die and be like water poured out on the ground, which can't be recovered. But God would not take away a life; He would devise plans so that the one banished from Him does not remain banished.

¹⁵ "Now therefore, I've come to present this matter to my lord the king because the people have made me afraid. Your servant thought: I must speak to the king. Perhaps the king will grant his servant's request. ¹⁶ The king will surely listen in order to rescue his servant from the hand of this man who would eliminate both me and my son from God's inheritance. ¹⁷ Your servant thought: May the word of my lord the king bring relief, for my lord the king is able to discern the good and the bad like the Angel of God. May the LORD your God be with you."

¹⁸ Then the king answered the woman, "I'm going to ask you something; don't conceal it from me!"

"Let my lord the king speak," the woman replied.

¹⁹ The king asked, "Did Joab put you up to[b] all this?"

The woman answered. "As surely as you live, my lord the king, no one can turn to the right or left from all my lord the king says. Yes, your servant Joab is the one who gave orders to me; he told your servant exactly what to say. ²⁰ Joab your servant has done this to address the issue indirectly,[c] but my lord has wisdom

---

[a]14:4 Some Hb mss, LXX, Syr, Tg, Vg; other Hb mss read *spoke*   [b]14:19 Lit *Is the hand of Joab in*   [c]14:20 Lit *to go around the face of the matter*

like the wisdom of the Angel of God, knowing everything on earth."

²¹ Then the king said to Joab, "I hereby grant this request. Go, bring back the young man Absalom."

Joab Gives Thanks

²² Joab fell with his face to the ground in homage and praised the king. "Today," Joab said, "your servant knows I have found favor with you, my lord the king, because the king has granted the request of your servant."

²³ So Joab got up, went to Geshur, and brought Absalom to Jerusalem. ²⁴ However, the king added, "He may return to his house, but he may not see my face." So Absalom returned to his house, but he did not see the king.ᵃ

Absalom's Gifts

²⁵ No man in all Israel was as handsome and highly praised as Absalom. From the sole of his foot to the top of his head, he did not have a single flaw. ²⁶ When he shaved his head—he shaved ⌊it⌋ every year because ⌊his hair⌋ got so heavy for him that he had to shave it off—he would weigh the hair from his head and it would be five poundsᵇ according to the royal standard.

Absalom Forces Joab to Contact David

²⁷ Three sons were born to Absalom, and a daughter named Tamar, who was a beautiful woman. ²⁸ Absalom resided in Jerusalem two years but never saw the king. ²⁹ Then Absalom sent for Joab in order to send him to the king, but Joab was unwilling to come. So he sent again, a second time, but he still wouldn't come. ³⁰ Then Absalom said to his servants, "See, Joab has a field right next to

mine, and he has barley there. Go and set fire to it!" So Absalom's servants set the field on fire.ᶜ

³¹ Then Joab came to Absalom's house and demanded, "Why did your servants set my field on fire?"

³² "Look," Absalom explained to Joab, "I sent for you and said, 'Come here. I want to send you to the king to ask: Why have I come back from Geshur? I'd be better off if I were still there.' So now, let me see the king. If I am guilty, let him kill me."

³³ Joab went to the king and told him. So David summoned Absalom, who came to the king and bowed down with his face to the ground before the king. Then the king kissed Absalom.

Absalom's Revolt

Absalom "Steals Hearts"

15 After this, Absalom got himself a chariot, horses, and 50 men to run before him. ² He would get up early and stand beside the road leading to the city •gate. Whenever anyone had a grievance to bring before the king for settlement, Absalom called out to him and asked, "What city are you from?" If he replied, "Your servant is from one of the tribes of Israel," ³ Absalom said to him, "Look, your claims are good and right, but the king does not have anyone to listen to you." ⁴ He added, "If only someone would appoint me judge in the land. Then anyone who had a grievance or dispute could come to me, and I would make sure he received justice." ⁵ When a person approached to bow down to him, Absalom reached out his hand, took hold of him, and kissed him. ⁶ Absalom did this to all the Israelites who came to the king for a settlement.

ᵃ14:24 Lit king's face   ᵇ14:26 Lit 200 shekels   ᶜ14:30 DSS, LXX add So Joab's servants came to him with their clothes torn and said, "Absalom's servants have set the field on fire!"

So Absalom stole the hearts of the men of Israel.

Absalom Rebels in Hebron

[7] When four[a] years had passed, Absalom said to the king, "Please let me go to Hebron to fulfill a vow I made to the LORD. [8] For your servant made a vow when I lived in Geshur of Aram, saying: If the LORD really brings me back to Jerusalem, I will worship the LORD in Hebron."[b]

[9] "Go in peace," the king said to him. So he went to Hebron.

[10] Then Absalom sent messengers throughout the tribes of Israel with this message: "When you hear the sound of the ram's horn, you are to say, 'Absalom has become king in Hebron!'"

[11] Two hundred men from Jerusalem went with Absalom. They had been invited and were going innocently, for they knew nothing about the whole matter. [12] While he was offering the sacrifices, Absalom sent for David's adviser Ahithophel the Gilonite, from his city of Giloh. So the conspiracy grew strong, and the people supporting Absalom continued to increase.

[13] Then an informer came to David and reported, "The hearts of the men of Israel are with Absalom."

David Flees

[14] David said to all the servants with him in Jerusalem, "Get up. We have to flee, or we will not escape from Absalom! Leave quickly, or he will overtake us, heap disaster on us, and strike the city with the edge of the sword."

[15] The king's servants said to him, "Whatever my lord the king decides, we are your servants." [16] Then the king set out, and his entire household followed him. But he left behind 10 concubines to take care of the palace. [17] So the king set out, and all the people followed him. They stopped at the last house [18] while all his servants marched past him. Then all the Cherethites, the Pelethites, and the Gittites—600 men who came with him from Gath—marched past the king.

David's Great Heart

[19] The king said to Ittai the Gittite, "Why are you also going with us? Go back and stay with the king since you're both a foreigner and an exile from your homeland. [20] Besides, you only arrived yesterday; should I make you wander around with us today while I go wherever I can? Go back and take your brothers with you. May the LORD show you kindness and faithfulness."

[21] But in response, Ittai vowed to the king, "As surely as the LORD lives and as my lord the king lives, wherever my lord the king is, whether it means life or death, your servant will be there!"

[22] "March on," David replied to Ittai. So Ittai the Gittite marched past with all his men and the children who were with him. [23] Everyone in the countryside was weeping loudly while all the people were marching past. As the king was crossing the Kidron Valley, all the people were marching past on the road that leads to the desert.

Zadok and the Ark Return to Jerusalem

[24] Zadok was also there, and all the Levites with him were carrying the ark of the covenant of God. They set the ark of God down, and Abiathar offered ˌsacrificesˌ[c] until the people had finished marching past. [25] Then the king instructed Zadok, "Return the ark of God

[a]**15:7** Some LXX mss, Syr, Vg; other LXX mss, MT read *40* [b]**15:8** Some LXX mss; MT omits *in Hebron* [c]**15:24** Or *Abiathar went up*

to the city. If I find favor in the LORD's eyes, He will bring me back and allow me to see both it and its dwelling place. [26] However, if He should say, 'I do not delight in you,' then here I am—He can do with me whatever pleases Him."[a]

[27] The king also said to Zadok the priest, "Look,[b] return to the city in peace and your two sons with you: your son Ahimaaz and Abiathar's son Jonathan. [28] Remember, I'll wait at the fords of the wilderness until word comes from you to inform me." [29] So Zadok and Abiathar returned the ark of God to Jerusalem and stayed there.

[30] David was climbing the slope of the Mount of Olives, weeping as he ascended. His head was covered, and he was walking barefoot. Each of the people with him covered their heads and went up, weeping as they ascended.

David's Plans Against Counselor Ahithophel

[31] Then someone reported to David: "Ahithophel is among the conspirators with Absalom."

"LORD," David pleaded, "please turn the counsel of Ahithophel into foolishness!"

David Enlists Hushai as Spy

[32] When David came to the summit where he used to worship God, there to meet him was Hushai the Archite with his robe torn and dust on his head. [33] David said to him, "If you go away with me, you'll be a burden to me, [34] but if you return to the city and tell Absalom, 'I will be your servant, my king! Previously, I was your father's servant, but now I will be your servant,' then you can counteract Ahithophel's counsel for me. [35] Won't Zadok and Abiathar the priests be there with you? Report everything you hear from the king's palace to Zadok and Abiathar the priests. [36] Take note: their two sons, Zadok's son Ahimaaz and Abiathar's son Jonathan, are there with them. Send me everything you hear through them." [37] So Hushai, David's personal adviser, entered Jerusalem just as Absalom was entering the city.

Servant Ziba Helps David

16 When David had gone a little beyond the summit,[c] Ziba, Mephibosheth's servant, was right there to meet him. He had a pair of saddled donkeys loaded with 200 loaves of bread, 100 clusters of raisins, 100 ⌊bunches⌋ of summer fruit,[d] and a skin of wine. [2] The king said to Ziba, "Why do you have these?"

Ziba answered, "The donkeys are for the king's household to ride, the bread and summer fruit are for the young men to eat, and the wine is for those who become exhausted to drink in the desert."

[3] "Where is your master's son?" the king asked.

"Why, he's staying in Jerusalem," Ziba replied to the king, "for he said, 'Today, the house of Israel will restore my father's kingdom to me.'"

[4] The king said to Ziba, "All that belongs to Mephibosheth is now yours!"

"I bow ⌊before you⌋," Ziba said. "May you look favorably on me, my lord the king!"

Shimei Curses David

[5] When King David got to Bahurim, a man belonging to the family of the house of Saul was just coming out. His name was Shimei son of Gera, and he was yelling curses as he approached. [6] He threw stones at David and at all the royal[e]

---

[a]15:26 Lit me what is good in His eyes　[b]15:27 LXX; MT reads Are you a seer?　[c]16:1 = Mount of Olives
[d]16:1 Probably dates or figs　[e]16:6 Lit all King David's

servants, the people and the warriors on David's right and left. [7] Shimei said as he cursed: "Get out, get out, you worthless murderer! [8] The LORD has paid you back for all the blood of the house of Saul in whose place you rule, and the LORD has handed the kingdom over to your son Absalom. Look, you are in trouble because you're a murderer!"

[9] Then Abishai son of Zeruiah said to the king, "Why should this dead dog curse my lord the king? Let me go over and cut his head off!"

David Accepts Curses

[10] The king replied, "Sons of Zeruiah, do we agree on anything? He curses ⌊me⌋ this way because the LORD[a] told him, 'Curse David!' Therefore, who can say, 'Why did you do that?'" [11] Then David said to Abishai and all his servants, "Look, my own son, my own flesh and blood,[b] intends to take my life—how much more now this Benjaminite! Leave him alone and let him curse ⌊me⌋; the LORD has told him to. [12] Perhaps the LORD will see my affliction[c] and restore goodness to me instead of Shimei's curses today." [13] So David and his men proceeded along the road as Shimei was going along the ridge of the hill opposite him. As Shimei went, he cursed ⌊David⌋, and threw stones and dirt at him. [14] Finally, the king and all the people with him arrived[d] exhausted, so they rested there.

Ahithophel's Advice to Absalom

[15] Now Absalom and all the Israelites came to Jerusalem. Ahithophel was also with him. [16] When David's friend Hushai the Archite came to Absalom, Hushai said to Absalom, "Long live the king! Long live the king!"

[17] "Is this your loyalty to your friend?" Absalom asked Hushai. "Why didn't you go with your friend?"

[18] "Not at all," Hushai answered Absalom. "I am on the side of the one that the LORD, the people, and all the men of Israel have chosen. I will stay with him. [19] Furthermore, whom will I serve if not his son? As I served in your father's presence, I will also serve in yours."

[20] Then Absalom said to Ahithophel, "Give ⌊me⌋ your advice. What should we do?"

[21] Ahithophel replied to Absalom, "Sleep with your father's concubines he left to take care of the palace. When all Israel hears that you have become repulsive to your father, everyone with you will be encouraged." [22] So they pitched a tent for Absalom on the roof, and he slept with his father's concubines in the sight of all Israel.

[23] Now the advice Ahithophel gave in those days was like someone asking about a word from God—such was the regard that both David and Absalom had

17 for Ahithophel's advice. [1] Ahithophel said to Absalom, "Let me choose 12,000 men, and I will set out in pursuit of David tonight. [2] I will attack him while he is weak and weary, throw him into a panic, and all the people with him will scatter. I will strike down only the king [3] and bring all the people back to you. When everyone returns ⌊except⌋ the man you're seeking, all[e] the people will be at peace." [4] This proposal seemed good to Absalom and all the elders of Israel.

[5] Then Absalom said, "Summon Hushai the Archite also. Let's hear what he has to say as well."

---

[a]**16:10** Alt Hb tradition reads *If he curses, and if the LORD* [b]**16:11** Lit *son who came from my belly* [c]**16:12** Some Hb mss, LXX, Syr, Vg; other Hb mss read *iniquity* [d]**16:14** LXX adds *at the Jordan* [e]**17:3** LXX reads *to you as a bride returns to her husband. You seek the life of only one man, and all*

Hushai Counters Ahithophel

[6] So Hushai came to Absalom, and Absalom told him: "Ahithophel offered this proposal. Should we carry out his proposal? If not, what do you say?"

[7] Hushai replied to Absalom, "The advice Ahithophel has given this time is not good." [8] Hushai continued, "You know your father and his men. They are warriors and are desperate like a wild bear robbed of her cubs. Your father is an experienced soldier who won't spend the night with the people. [9] He's probably already hiding in one of the caves[a] or some other place. If some of our troops fall[b] first, someone is sure to hear and say, 'There's been a slaughter among the people who follow Absalom.' [10] Then, even a brave man with the heart of a lion will melt because all Israel knows that your father and the valiant men with him are warriors. [11] Instead, I advise that all Israel from Dan to Beer-sheba—as numerous as the sand by the sea—be gathered to you and that you personally go into battle. [12] Then we will attack David wherever we find him, and we will descend on him like dew on the ground. Not even one will be left of all the men with him. [13] If he retreats to some city, all Israel will bring ropes to that city, and we will drag its ⌊stones⌋ into the valley until not even a pebble can be found there." [14] Since the LORD had decreed that Ahithophel's good advice be undermined in order to bring about Absalom's ruin, Absalom and all the men of Israel said, "The advice of Hushai the Archite is better than Ahithophel's advice."

Spies Reach David

[15] Hushai then told the priests Zadok and Abiathar, "This is what[c] Ahithophel advised Absalom and the elders of Israel, and this is what[d] I advised. [16] Now send someone quickly and tell David, 'Don't spend the night at the wilderness ford ⌊of the Jordan⌋, but be sure to cross over, or the king and all the people with him will be destroyed.'"

[17] Jonathan and Ahimaaz were staying at En-rogel, where a servant girl would come and pass along information to them. They in turn would go and inform King David, because they dared not be seen entering the city. [18] However, a young man did see them and informed Absalom. So the two left quickly and came to the house of a man in Bahurim. He had a well in his courtyard, and they climbed down into it. [19] Then his wife took the cover, placed it over the mouth of the well, and scattered grain on it so nobody would know anything.

[20] Absalom's servants came to the woman at the house and asked, "Where are Ahimaaz and Jonathan?"

"They passed by toward the water,"[e] the woman replied to them. The men searched but did not find ⌊them⌋, so they returned to Jerusalem.

[21] After they had gone, Ahimaaz and Jonathan climbed out of the well and went and informed King David. They told him, "Get up and immediately ford the river, for Ahithophel has given this advice against you." [22] So David and all the people with him got up and crossed the Jordan. By daybreak, there was no one who had not crossed the Jordan.

Ahithophel's Suicide

[23] When Ahithophel realized that his advice had not been followed, he saddled his donkey and set out for his house in his hometown. He set his affairs in

---

a17:9 Or *pits*, or *ravines*   **b17:9** Lit *And it will be when a falling on them at*   **c17:15** Lit *Like this and like this*
d17:15 Lit *and like this and like this*   **e17:20** Or *brook*; Hb obscure

order[a] and hanged himself. So he died and was buried in his father's tomb.

David Maneuvers Against Absalom

²⁴ David had arrived at Mahanaim by the time Absalom crossed the Jordan with all the men of Israel. ²⁵ Now Absalom had appointed Amasa over the army in Joab's place. Amasa was the son of a man named Ithra[b] the Israelite;[c] Ithra had married Abigail daughter of Nahash.[d] Abigail was a sister to Zeruiah, Joab's mother. ²⁶ And Israel and Absalom camped in the land of Gilead. ²⁷ When David came to Mahanaim, Shobi son of Nahash from Rabbah of the Ammonites, Machir son of Ammiel from Lo-debar, and Barzillai the Gileadite from Rogelim ²⁸ brought beds, basins,[e] and pottery items. ⌊They also brought⌋ wheat, barley, flour, roasted grain, beans, lentils,[f] ²⁹ honey, curds, sheep, and cheese[g] from the herd for David and the people with him to eat. They had reasoned, "The people must be hungry, exhausted, and thirsty in the desert."

David Defeats Absalom's Troops

18 David reviewed his troops and appointed commanders of hundreds and of thousands over them. ² He then sent out the troops, one third under Joab, one third under Joab's brother Abishai son of Zeruiah, and one third under Ittai the Gittite. The king said to the troops, "I will also march out with you."

³ "You must not go!" the people pleaded. "If we have to flee, they will not pay any attention to us. Even if half of us die, they will not pay any attention to us because you are worth[h] 10,000 of us. Therefore, it is better if you support us from the city."

⁴ "I will do whatever you think is best," the king replied to them. So he stood beside the gate while all the troops marched out by hundreds and thousands. ⁵ The king commanded Joab, Abishai, and Ittai, "Treat the young man Absalom gently for my sake." All the people heard the king's orders to all the commanders about Absalom.

⁶ Then David's forces marched into the field to engage Israel in battle, which took place in the forest of Ephraim. ⁷ The people of Israel were defeated by David's soldiers, and the slaughter there was vast that day—20,000 ⌊casualties⌋. ⁸ The battle spread over the entire region, and that day the forest claimed more people than the sword.

Joab Kills Absalom

⁹ Absalom was riding on his mule when he happened to meet David's soldiers. When the mule went under the tangled branches of a large oak tree, Absalom's head was caught fast in the tree. The mule under him kept going, so he was suspended in midair.[i] ¹⁰ One of the men saw ⌊him⌋ and informed Joab. He said, "I just saw Absalom hanging in an oak tree!"

¹¹ "You just saw ⌊him⌋!" Joab exclaimed.[j] "Why didn't you strike him to the ground right there? I would have given you 10 silver pieces[k] and a belt!"

¹² The man replied to Joab, "Even if I had the weight of 1,000 pieces of silver[l] in my hand, I would not raise my hand against the king's son. For we heard the king command you, Abishai, and Ittai, 'Protect the young man Absalom for me.'[m] ¹³ If I had

a17:23 Lit He commanded his house   b17:25 Or Jether   c17:25 Some LXX mss read Ishmaelite   d17:25 Some LXX mss read Jesse   e17:28 LXX reads brought 10 embroidered beds with double coverings, 10 vessels   f17:28 LXX, Syr; MT adds roasted grain   g17:29 Hb obscure   h18:3 Some Hb mss, LXX, Vg; other Hb mss read because there would now be about   i18:9 Lit was between heaven and earth   j18:11 Lit Joab said to the man who told him   k18:11 c. 4 ounces   l18:12 c. 25 pounds   m18:12 Some Hb mss, LXX, Tg, Vg; other Hb mss read Protect, whoever, the young man Absalom; Hb obscure

jeopardized my own[a] life—and nothing is hidden from the king—you would have abandoned me."

[14] Joab said, "I'm not going to waste time with you!" He then took three spears in his hand and thrust them into Absalom's heart while he was still alive in the oak tree, [15] and 10 young men who were Joab's armor-bearers surrounded Absalom, struck him, and killed him.

Joab Ends the Conflict

[16] Afterwards, Joab blew the ram's horn, and the troops broke off their pursuit of Israel because Joab restrained them. [17] They took Absalom, threw him into a large pit in the forest, and piled a huge mound of stones over him. And all Israel fled, each to his tent.

[18] When he was alive, Absalom had erected for himself a pillar in the King's Valley, for he had said, "I have no son to preserve the memory of my name." So he gave the pillar his name. It is still called Absalom's Monument today.

Two Messengers to David

[19] Ahimaaz son of Zadok said, "Please let me run and tell the king the good news that the LORD has delivered him from his enemies."

[20] Joab replied to him, "You are not the man to take good news today. You may do it another day, but today you aren't taking good news, because the king's son is dead." [21] Joab then said to the •Cushite, "Go tell the king what you have seen." The Cushite bowed to Joab and took off running.

[22] However, Ahimaaz son of Zadok persisted and said to Joab, "No matter what, please let me run too behind the Cushite!"

Joab replied, "My son, why do you want to run since you won't get a reward?"

[23] "No matter what I want to run!"

"Then run!" Joab said to him. So Ahimaaz ran by way of the plain and outran the Cushite.

[24] David was sitting between the two gates when the watchman went up to the roof of the gate and over to the wall. The watchman looked out and saw a man running alone. [25] He called out and told the king.

The king said, "If he's alone, he bears good news."

As the first runner came closer, [26] the watchman saw another man running. He called out to the gatekeeper, "Look! Another man is running alone!"

"This one is also bringing good news," said the king.

[27] The watchman said, "The way the first man runs looks to me like the way Ahimaaz son of Zadok runs."

"This is a good man; he comes with good news," the king commented.

[28] Ahimaaz called out to the king, "All is well," and then bowed down to the king with his face to the ground. He continued, "May the LORD your God be praised! He delivered up the men who rebelled against my lord the king."

[29] The king asked, "Is the young man Absalom all right?"

Ahimaaz replied, "When Joab sent the king's servant and your servant, I saw a big disturbance, but I don't know what it was."

[30] The king said, "Move aside and stand here." So he stood to one side.

[31] Just then the Cushite came and said, "May my lord the king hear the good news: today the LORD has delivered you from all those rising up against you!"

---

[a] **18:13** Alt Hb tradition reads *jeopardized his*

32 The king asked the Cushite, "Is the young man Absalom all right?"

The Cushite replied, "May what has become of the young man happen to the enemies of my lord the king and to all who rise up against you with evil intent."

33a The king was deeply moved and went up to the gate chamber and wept. As he walked, he cried, "My son Absalom! My son, my son Absalom! If only I had died instead of you, Absalom, my son, my son!"

Joab Rebukes David

19 It was reported to Joab, "The king is weeping. He's mourning over Absalom." 2 That day's victory was turned into mourning for all the troops because on that day the troops heard, "The king is grieving over his son." 3 So they returned to the city quietly that day like people come in when they are humiliated after fleeing in battle. 4 But the king hid his face and cried out at the top of his voice, "My son Absalom! Absalom, my son, my son!"

5 Then Joab went into the house to the king and said, "Today you have shamed all your soldiers—those who rescued your life and the lives of your sons and daughters, your wives, and your concubines. 6 You love your enemies and hate those who love you! Today you have made it clear that the commanders and soldiers mean nothing to you. In fact, today I know that if Absalom were alive and all of us were dead, it would be fine with you!b

7 "Now get up! Go out and encouragec your soldiers, for I swear by the LORD that if you don't go out, not a man will remain with you tonight. This will be worse for you than all the trouble that has come to you from your youth until now!"

David Recalled to Kingship

8 So the king got up and sat in the •gate, and all the people were told: "Look, the king is sitting in the gate." Then they all came into the king's presence.

Meanwhile, each Israelite had fled to his tent. 9 All the people among all the tribes of Israel were arguing: "The king delivered us from the grasp of our enemies, and he rescued us from the grasp of the Philistines, but now he has fled from the land because of Absalom. 10 But Absalom, the man we anointed over us, has died in battle. So why do you say nothing about restoring the king?"

11 King David sent word to the priests, Zadok and Abiathar: "Say to the elders of Judah, 'Why should you be the last to restore the king to his palace? The talk of all Israel has reached the king at his house. 12 You are my brothers, my flesh and blood. So why should you be the last to restore the king?' 13 And tell Amasa, 'Aren't you my flesh and blood? May God punish me and do so severely if you don't become commander of the army from now on instead of Joab!' "

Return of the King

14 So he won overd all the men of Judah, and they sent word to the king: "Come back, you and all your servants." 15 Then the king returned. When he arrived at the Jordan, Judah came to Gilgal to meet the king and escort him across the Jordan.

16 Shimei son of Gera, a Benjaminite from Bahurim, hurried down with the men of Judah to meet King David. 17 There were 1,000 men from Benja-

a**18:33** 2 Sm 19:1 in Hb   b**19:6** Lit *be right in your eyes*   c**19:7** Lit *speak to the heart of*   d**19:14** Lit *he turned the heart of*

min with him. Ziba, an attendant from the house of Saul, with his 15 sons and 20 servants also rushed down to the Jordan ahead of the king. [18] They forded the Jordan to bring the king's household across and do whatever the king desired.[a]

David Forgives Shimei

When Shimei son of Gera crossed the Jordan, he fell down before the king [19] and said to him, "My lord, don't hold me guilty, and don't remember your servant's wrongdoing on the day my lord the king left Jerusalem. May the king not take it to heart. [20] For your servant knows that I have sinned. But look! Today I am the first one of the entire house of Joseph to come down to meet my lord the king."

[21] Abishai son of Zeruiah asked, "Shouldn't Shimei be put to death for this, because he ridiculed the LORD's anointed?"

[22] David answered, "Sons of Zeruiah, do we agree on anything? Have you become my adversary today? Should any man be killed in Israel today? Am I not aware that today I'm king over Israel?" [23] So the king said to Shimei, "You will not die." Then the king gave him his oath.

David Settles Mephibosheth-Ziba Issue

[24] Mephibosheth, Saul's grandson, also went down to meet the king. He had not taken care of his feet, trimmed his moustache, or washed his clothes from the day the king left until the day he returned safely. [25] When he came from Jerusalem to meet the king, the king asked him, "Mephibosheth, why didn't you come with me?"

[26] "My lord the king," he replied, "my servant ⌊Ziba⌋ betrayed me. Actually your servant said: 'I'll saddle the donkey for myself[b] so that I may ride it and go with the king'—for your servant is lame. [27] Ziba slandered your servant to my lord the king. But my lord the king is like the Angel of God, so do whatever you think best.[c] [28] For my grandfather's entire family deserves death from my lord the king, but you set your servant among those who eat at your table. So what further right do I have to keep on making appeals to the king?"

[29] The king said to him, "Why keep on speaking about ⌊these⌋ matters of yours? I hereby declare: you and Ziba are to divide the land."

[30] Mephibosheth said to the king, "Instead, since my lord the king has come to his palace safely, let Ziba take it all!"

David Blesses Barzillai—and Rewards Chimham

[31] Barzillai the Gileadite had come down from Rogelim and accompanied the king to the Jordan River to see him off at the Jordan. [32] Barzillai was a very old man—80 years old—and since he was a very wealthy man, he had provided for the needs of the king while he stayed in Mahanaim.

[33] The king said to Barzillai, "Cross over with me, and I'll provide for you[d] at my side in Jerusalem."

[34] Barzillai replied to the king, "How many years of my life are left that I should go up to Jerusalem with the king? [35] I'm now 80 years old. Can I discern what is pleasant and what is not? Can your servant taste what he eats or drinks? Can I still hear the voice of male and female singers? Why should your servant be an added burden to my lord

a**19:18** Lit *do what is good in his eyes*   b**19:26** LXX, Syr, Vg read *said to him, 'Saddle the donkey for me*   c**19:27** Lit *do what is good in your eyes*   d**19:33** LXX reads *for your old age;* Ru 4:15

the king? ³⁶ Since your servant is only going with the king a little way across the Jordan, why should the king repay me with such a reward? ³⁷ Please let your servant return so that I may die in my own city near the tomb of my father and mother. But here is your servant Chimham: let him cross over with my lord the king. Do for him what seems good to you."[a]

³⁸ The king replied, "Chimham will cross over with me, and I will do for him what seems good to you,[a] and whatever you desire from me I will do for you." ³⁹ So all the people crossed the Jordan, and then the king crossed. The king kissed Barzillai and blessed him, and Barzillai returned to his home.

Israel vs. Judah

⁴⁰ The king went on to Gilgal, and Chimham went with him. All the troops of Judah and half of Israel's escorted the king. ⁴¹ Suddenly, all the men of Israel came to the king. They asked him, "Why did our brothers, the men of Judah, take you away secretly and transport the king and his household across the Jordan, along with all of David's men?"

⁴² All the men of Judah responded to the men of Israel, "Because the king is our relative. Why does this make you angry? Have we ever eaten anything of the king's or been honored at all?"[b]

⁴³ The men of Israel answered the men of Judah: "We have 10 shares in the king, so we have a greater [claim] to David than you. Why then do you despise us? Weren't we the first to speak of restoring our king?" But the words of the men of Judah were harsher than those of the men of Israel.

Sheba's Revolt

20 Now a wicked man, a Benjaminite named Sheba son of Bichri, happened to be there. He blew the ram's horn and shouted:

We have no portion in David,
no inheritance in Jesse's son.
Each man to his tent, Israel!

² So all the men of Israel deserted David and followed Sheba son of Bichri, but the men of Judah from the Jordan all the way to Jerusalem remained loyal to their king.

³ When David came to his palace in Jerusalem, he took the 10 concubines he had left to take care of the palace and placed them under guard. He provided for them, but he was not intimate with them. They were confined until the day of their death, living as widows.

David Pursues Sheba

⁴ The king said to <u>Amasa</u>, "Summon the men of Judah to me within three days and be here yourself." ⁵ Amasa went to summon Judah, but he took longer than the time allotted him. ⁶ So David said to <u>Abishai</u>, "Sheba son of Bichri will do more harm to us than Absalom. Take your lord's soldiers and pursue him, or he will find fortified cities and elude us."[c]

Joab Assassinates Amasa

⁷ So Joab's men, the Cherethites, the Pelethites, and all the warriors marched out under Abishai's command;[d] they left Jerusalem to pursue Sheba son of Bichri. ⁸ They were at the great stone in Gibeon when Amasa joined them. Joab was wearing his uniform and over it was a belt around his waist with a sword in its sheath. As he approached, [the sword]

---

[a]**19:37,38** Lit what is good in your eyes   [b]**19:42** LXX reads king's or has he given us a gift or granted us a portion
[c]**20:6** Lit and snatch away our eyes   [d]**20:7** Lit out following him

fell out. [9] Joab asked Amasa, "Are you well, my brother?" Then with his right hand Joab grabbed Amasa by the beard to kiss him. [10] Amasa was not on guard against the sword in Joab's hand, and Joab stabbed him in the stomach with it and spilled his intestines out on the ground. Joab did not stab him again for Amasa was dead. Joab and his brother Abishai pursued Sheba son of Bichri.

[11] One of Joab's young men had stood over Amasa saying, "Whoever favors Joab and whoever is for David, follow Joab!" [12] Now Amasa was writhing in his blood in the middle of the highway, and the man had seen that all the people stopped. So he moved Amasa from the highway to the field and threw a garment over him because he realized that all those who encountered Amasa were stopping. [13] When he was removed from the highway, all the men passed by and followed Joab to pursue Sheba son of Bichri.

Joab's Siege Against Sheba

[14] Sheba passed through all the tribes of Israel to Abel of Beth-maacah. All the Berites[a] came together and followed him. [15] Joab's troops came and besieged Sheba in Abel of Beth-maacah. They built an assault ramp against the outer wall of the city. While all the troops with Joab were battering the wall to make it collapse, [16] a wise woman called out from the city, "Listen! Listen! Please tell Joab to come here and let me speak with him."

[17] When he had come near her, the woman asked, "Are you Joab?"

"I am," he replied.

"Listen to the words of your servant," she said to him.

He answered, "I'm listening."

Sheba's Head for Abel

[18] She said, "In the past they used to say, 'Seek counsel in Abel,' and that's how they settled ⌊disputes⌋. [19] I am a peaceful person, one of the faithful in Israel, but you're trying to destroy a city that is like a mother in Israel. Why would you devour the LORD's inheritance?"

[20] Joab protested: "Never! I do not want to destroy! [21] That is not ⌊my⌋ intention. There is a man named Sheba son of Bichri, from the hill country of Ephraim, who has rebelled against King David. Deliver this one man, and I will withdraw from the city."

The woman replied to Joab, "All right. His head will be thrown over the wall to you." [22] The woman went to all the people with her wise counsel, and they cut off the head of Sheba son of Bichri and threw it to Joab. So he blew the ram's horn, and they dispersed from the city, each to his own tent. Joab returned to the king in Jerusalem.

Joab Commands Army

[23] Joab commanded the whole army of Israel; Benaiah son of Jehoiada was over the Cherethites and Pelethites; [24] Adoram[b] was in charge of forced labor; Jehoshaphat son of Ahilud was court historian; [25] Sheva was court secretary; Zadok and Abiathar were priests; [26] and in addition, Ira the Jairite was David's priest.

Cause of a Famine

21 During David's reign there was a famine for three successive years, so David inquired of the LORD. The LORD answered, "It is because of the blood shed by Saul and his family when he killed the Gibeonites."

² The Gibeonites were not Israelites but rather a remnant of the Amorites. The Israelites had taken an oath concerning them, but Saul had tried to kill them in his zeal for the Israelites and Judah. So David summoned the Gibeonites and spoke to them. ³ He asked the Gibeonites, "What should I do for you? How can I wipe out this guilt so that you will bring a blessing onª the LORD's inheritance?"

⁴ The Gibeonites said to him, "We are not asking for money fromᵇ Saul or his family, and we cannot put anyone to death in Israel."

"Whatever you say, I will do for you," he said.

Justice for the Gibeonites

⁵ They replied to the king, "As for the man who annihilated us and plotted to exterminate us so we would not exist within the whole territory of Israel, ⁶ let seven of his male descendants be handed over to us so we may hangᶜ them in the presence of the LORD at Gibeah of Saul, the LORD's chosen."

The king answered, "I will hand them over."

⁷ David spared Mephibosheth, the son of Saul's son Jonathan, because of the oath of the LORD that was between David and Jonathan, Saul's son. ⁸ But the king took Armoni and Mephibosheth, who were the two sons whom Rizpah daughter of Aiah had borne to Saul, and the five sons whom Merabᵈ daughter of Saul had borne to Adriel son of Barzillai the Meholathite ⁹ and handed them over to the Gibeonites. They hangedᵉ them on the hill in the presence of the LORD; the seven of them died together. They were executed in the first days of the harvest at the beginning of the barley harvest.ᶠ

David Buries Saul, Jonathan, and Family

¹⁰ Rizpah, Aiah's daughter, took •sackcloth and spread it out for herself on the rock from the beginning of the harvest until the rain poured down from heaven on the bodies.ᵍ She kept the birds of the sky from them by day and the wild animals by night.

¹¹ When it was reported to David what Saul's concubine Rizpah, daughter of Aiah, had done, ¹² he went and got the bones of Saul and his son Jonathan from the leaders of Jabesh-gilead. They had stolen them from the public square of Beth-shan where the Philistines had hung them the day the Philistines killed Saul at Gilboa. ¹³ David had the bones brought from there. They also gathered up the bones of Saul's family who had been hung.ᵉ ¹⁴ They ˻also˼ buried the bones of Saul and his son Jonathan at Zela in the land of Benjamin in the tomb of Saul's father Kish. They did everything the king commanded. After this, God answered prayer for the land.

David's Last War: Philistine Giants

¹⁵ The Philistines again waged war against Israel. David went down with his soldiers, and they fought the Philistines, but David became exhausted. ¹⁶ Then Ishbi-benob, one of the descendants of the giant,ʰ whose bronze spear weighed about eight poundsⁱ and who wore new armor, intended to kill David. ¹⁷ But Abishai son of Zeruiah came to his aid, struck the Philistine, and killed him. Then David's men swore to him: "You must

ª21:3 Lit will bless   ᵇ21:4 Lit "Not for us silver and gold with   ᶜ21:6 Or impale, or expose   ᵈ21:8 Some Hb mss, LXX, Syr, Tg; other Hb mss read Michal   ᵉ21:9,13 Or impaled, or exposed   ᶠ21:9 = March–April   ᵍ21:10 = April to October   ʰ21:16 Or Raphah   ⁱ21:16 Lit 300 (shekels)

never again go out with us to battle. You must not extinguish the lamp of Israel."

[18] After this, there was another battle with the Philistines at Gob. At that time Sibbecai the Hushathite killed Saph, who was one of the descendants of the giant.[a]

[19] Once again there was a battle with the Philistines at Gob, and Elhanan son of Jaare-oregim the Bethlehemite killed[b] Goliath the Gittite. The shaft of his spear was like a weaver's beam.

[20] At Gath there was still another battle. A huge man was there with six fingers on each hand and six toes on each foot—24 in all. He, too, was descended from the giant.[a] [21] When he taunted Israel, Jonathan, son of David's brother Shimei, killed him.

[22] These four were descended from the giant[a] in Gath and were killed by David and his soldiers.

David's Song of Thanksgiving

22 David spoke the words of this song to the LORD on the day the LORD rescued him from the hand of all his enemies and from the hand of Saul. [2] He said:

The LORD is my rock, my fortress,
    and my deliverer,
[3] my God, my mountain[c] where
        I seek refuge.
    My shield, the •horn
        of my salvation, my stronghold,
        my refuge,
    and my Savior, You save me
        from violence.
[4] I called to the LORD, who is worthy
        of praise,
    and I was saved from my enemies.
[5] For the waves of death
        engulfed me;
    the torrents of destruction
        terrified me.

[6] The ropes of •Sheol entangled me;
    the snares of death confronted me.
[7] I called to the LORD in my distress;
    I called to my God.
    From His temple He heard
        my voice,
    and my cry for help ⌊reached⌋
        His ears.
[8] Then the earth shook and quaked;
    the foundations of the heavens[d]
        trembled;
    they shook because He burned
        with anger.
[9] Smoke rose from His nostrils,
    and consuming fire ⌊came⌋
        from His mouth;
    coals were set ablaze by it.[e]
[10] He parted the heavens
        and came down,
    a dark cloud beneath His feet.
[11] He rode on a cherub and flew,
    soaring on the wings of the wind.
[12] He made darkness a canopy
        around Him,
    a gathering[f] of water
        and thick clouds.
[13] From the radiance of His presence,
    flaming coals were ignited.
[14] The LORD thundered from heaven;
    the •Most High projected His voice.
[15] He shot arrows and scattered them;
    ⌊He hurled⌋ lightning bolts
        and routed them.
[16] The depths of the sea
        became visible,
    the foundations of the world
        were exposed
    at the rebuke of the LORD,
    at the blast of the breath
        of His nostrils.
[17] He reached down from on high
    and took hold of me;

---

[a]**21:18,20,22** Or *Raphah*   [b]**21:19** 1 Ch 20:5 adds *the brother of*   [c]**22:3** LXX; MT reads *God of my mountain*; Ps 18:2
[d]**22:8** Some Hb mss, Syr, Vg read *mountains*; Ps 18:7   [e]**22:9** Or *ablaze from Him*   [f]**22:12** Or *sieve*, or *mass*; Hb
obscure

He pulled me out of deep waters.
18 He rescued me
      from my powerful enemy
    and from those who hated me,
      for they were too strong for me.
19 They confronted me in the day
      of my distress,
    but the LORD was my support.
20 He brought me out
      to a wide-open place;
    He rescued me because
      He delighted in me.

21 The LORD rewarded me
      according to my righteousness;
    He repaid me
      according to the cleanness
      of my hands.
22 For I have kept the ways of the LORD
    and have not turned from my God
      to wickedness.
23 Indeed, I have kept
      all His ordinances in mind[a]
    and have not disregarded
      His statutes.
24 I was blameless before Him
    and kept myself from sinning.
25 So the LORD repaid me
      according to my righteousness,
      according to my cleanness[b]
      in His sight.

26 With the faithful
    You prove Yourself faithful;
    with the blameless man
    You prove Yourself blameless;
27 with the pure
    You prove Yourself pure,
    but with the crooked
    You prove Yourself shrewd.
28 You rescue an afflicted people,
    but Your eyes are set
      against the proud—

You humble them.
29 LORD, You are my lamp;
    the LORD illuminates my darkness.
30 With You I can attack a barrier,[c]
    and with my God I can leap
      over a wall.
31 God—His way is perfect;
    the word of the LORD is pure.
    He is a shield to all who take refuge
      in Him.

32 For who is God besides the LORD?
    And who is a rock? Only our God.
33 God is my strong refuge;[d]
    He makes my way perfect.[e]
34 He makes my feet like ᵢthe feet ofᵢ
      a deer
    and sets me securely
      on theᶠ heights.[g]
35 He trains my hands for war;
    my arms can bend a bow of bronze.
36 You have given me the shield
      of Your salvation;
    Your help[h] exalts me.
37 You widen ᵢa placeᵢ beneath me
      for my steps,
    and my ankles do not give way.
38 I pursue my enemies
      and destroy them;
    I do not turn back until they are
      wiped out.
39 I wipe them out and crush them,
      and they do not rise;
    they fall beneath my feet.
40 You have clothed me with strength
      for battle;
    You subdue my adversaries
      beneath me.
41 You have made my enemies retreat
      before me;[i]
    I annihilate those who hated me.
42 They look, but there is no one
      to save ᵢthemᵢ—

ᵃ22:23 Lit Indeed, all His ordinances have been in front of me   ᵇ22:25 LXX, Syr, Vg read to the cleanness of my hands;
Ps 18:24   ᶜ22:30 Or ridge   ᵈ22:33 DSS, some LXX mss, Syr, Vg read God clothes me with strength; Ps 18:32
ᵉ22:33 Some LXX mss, Syr; MT reads He sets free the blameless His way; Hb obscure   ᶠ22:34 LXX; some Hb mss
read my; other Hb mss read His   ᵍ22:34 Or on my high places   ʰ22:36 LXX reads humility; Ps 18:35   ⁱ22:41 Lit You
gave me the neck of my enemies

⌊they look⌋ to the LORD, but He does
not answer them.

43 I pulverize them like dust
of the earth;
I crush them and trample them
like mud in the streets.

44 You have freed me from the feuds
among my people;
You have appointed me the head
of nations;
a people I had not known serve me.

45 Foreigners submit to me
grudgingly;
as soon as they hear, they obey me.

46 Foreigners lose heart
and come trembling
from their fortifications.

47 The LORD lives—may my rock
be praised!
God, the rock of my salvation,
is exalted.

48 God—He gives me vengeance
and casts down peoples under me.

49 He frees me from my enemies.
You exalt me above my adversaries;
You rescue me from violent men.

50 Therefore I will praise You, LORD,
among the nations;
I will sing about Your name.

51 He is a tower of salvation
for[a] His king;
He shows loyalty to His anointed,
to David and his descendants
forever.

David's Last Words

23 These are the last words of David:

The proclamation of David
son of Jesse,
the proclamation of the man
raised on high,[b]

the one anointed by the God
of Jacob,
the favorite singer of Israel:

2 The Spirit of the LORD spoke
through me,
His word was on my tongue.

3 The God of Israel spoke;
the Rock of Israel said to me,
"The one who rules the people
with justice,
who rules in the •fear of God,

4 is like the morning light
when the sun rises
on a cloudless morning,
the glisten of rain
on sprouting grass."

5 Is it not true my house is with God?
For He has established
an everlasting covenant with me,
ordered and secured
in every ⌊detail⌋.
Will He not bring about
my whole salvation
and ⌊my⌋ every desire?

6 But all the wicked are like thorns
raked aside;
they can never be picked up
by hand.

7 The man who touches them
must be armed with iron
and the shaft of a spear.
They will be completely burned up
on the spot.

Exploits of David's Warriors

8 These are the names of David's warriors:

Josheb-basshebeth the Tahchemonite
was chief of the officers.[c] He wielded his
spear[d] against 800 ⌊men⌋ he killed at one
time.

9 After him, Eleazar son of Dodo son of
Ahohi was among the three warriors

---

with David when they defied the Philistines. The men of Israel retreated in the place they had gathered for battle, [10] but Eleazar stood ⌐his ground¬ and attacked the Philistines until his hand was tired and stuck to his sword. The LORD brought about a great victory that day. Then the troops came back to him, but only to plunder the dead.

[11] After him was Shammah son of Agee the Hararite. The Philistines had assembled ⌐in formation¬ where there was a field full of lentils. The troops fled from the Philistines, [12] but Shammah took his stand in the middle of the field, defended it, and struck down the Philistines. So the LORD brought about a great victory.

The "Water-Affair Three"

[13] Three of the 30 leading ⌐warriors¬ went down at harvest time and came to David at the cave of Adullam, while a company of Philistines was camping in the Valley of Rephaim. [14] At that time David was in the stronghold, and a Philistine garrison was at Bethlehem. [15] David was extremely thirsty[a] and said, "If only someone would bring me water to drink from the well at the city gate of Bethlehem!" [16] So three of the warriors broke through the Philistine camp and drew water from the well at the gate of Bethlehem. They brought it back to David, but he refused to drink it. Instead, he poured it out to the LORD. [17] David said, "LORD, I would never do such a thing! Is this not the blood of men who risked their lives?" So he refused to drink it. Such were the exploits of the three warriors.

Honored by the Three

[18] Abishai, Joab's brother and son of Zeruiah, was leader of the Three.[b] He raised his spear against 300 ⌐men¬ and killed them, gaining a reputation among the Three. [19] Was he not the most honored of the Three? He became their commander even though he did not become one of the Three.

[20] Benaiah son of Jehoiada was the son of a brave man from Kabzeel, a man of many exploits. Benaiah killed two sons[c] of Ariel[d] of Moab, and he went down into a pit on a snowy day and killed a lion. [21] He also killed an Egyptian, a huge man. Even though the Egyptian had a spear in his hand, Benaiah went down to him with a club, snatched the spear out of the Egyptian's hand, and then killed him with his own spear. [22] These were the exploits of Benaiah son of Jehoiada, who had a reputation among the three warriors. [23] He was the most honored of the Thirty, but he did not become one of the Three. David put him in charge of his bodyguard.

The "Thirty"

[24] Among the Thirty were:

Joab's brother Asahel,
Elhanan son of Dodo of Bethlehem,
[25] Shammah the Harodite,
Elika the Harodite,
[26] Helez the Paltite,
Ira son of Ikkesh the Tekoite,
[27] Abiezer the Anathothite,
Mebunnai the Hushathite,
[28] Zalmon the Ahohite,
Maharai the Netophathite,
[29] Heleb son of Baanah
the Netophahite,
Ittai son of Ribai from Gibeah
of the Benjaminites,
[30] Benaiah the Pirathonite,
Hiddai from the •Wadis of Gaash,[e]
[31] Abi-albon the Arbathite,

Azmaveth the Barhumite,
32 Eliahba the Shaalbonite,
the sons of Jashen,
Jonathan son of[a] 33 Shammah
the Hararite,
Ahiam son of Sharar the Hararite,
34 Eliphelet son of Ahasbai
son of the Maacathite,
Eliam son of Ahithophel
the Gilonite,
35 Hezro the Carmelite,
Paarai the Arbite,
36 Igal son of Nathan from Zobah,
Bani the Gadite,
37 Zelek the Ammonite,
Naharai the Beerothite, the armor-
bearer for Joab son of Zeruiah,
38 Ira the Ithrite,
Gareb the Ithrite,
39 and Uriah the Hittite.

There were 37 in all.

David Orders Military Census

24 The LORD's anger burned against Israel again, and it stirred up David against them to say: "Go, count ⌊the people of⌋ Israel and Judah."
2 So the king said to Joab, the commander of his army, "Go through all the tribes of Israel from Dan to Beer-sheba and register the troops so I can know their number."

Joab Protests

3 Joab replied to the king, "May the LORD your God multiply the troops 100 times more than they are—while my lord the king looks on! But why does my lord the king want to do this?"

David Overrules

4 Yet the king's order prevailed over Joab and the commanders of the army.

So Joab and the commanders of the army left the king's presence to register the troops of Israel.
5 They crossed the Jordan and camped in Aroer, south of the town in the middle of the valley, and then ⌊proceeded⌋ toward Gad and Jazer. 6 They went to Gilead and to the land of the Hittites[b] and continued on to Dan-jaan and around to Sidon. 7 They went to the fortress of Tyre and all the cities of the Hivites and Canaanites. Afterwards, they went to the •Negev of Judah at Beer-sheba.
8 When they had gone through the whole land, they returned to Jerusalem at the end of nine months and 20 days. 9 Joab gave the king the total of the registration of the troops. There were 800,000 fighting men from Israel and 500,000 men from Judah.

David Repents

10 David's conscience troubled him after he had taken a census of the troops. He said to the LORD, "I have sinned greatly in what I've done. Now, LORD, because I've been very foolish, please take away Your servant's guilt."

David's Choice of Punishment

11 When David got up in the morning, a revelation from the LORD had come to the prophet Gad, David's seer: 12 "Go and say to David, 'This is what the LORD says: I am offering you three ⌊choices⌋. Choose one of them, and I will do it to you.' "
13 So Gad went to David, told him ⌊the choices⌋, and asked him, "Do you want three[c] years of famine to come on your land, to flee from your foes three months while they pursue you, or to have a plague in your land three days? Now, think it over and decide what answer I

a23:32 Some LXX mss; MT omits son of; 1 Ch 11:34   b24:6 LXX; MT reads of Tahtim-hodshi; Hb obscure   c24:13 LXX; MT reads seven; 1 Ch 21:12

should take back to the One who sent me."

¹⁴ David answered Gad, "I have great anxiety. Please, let us fall into the LORD's hands because His mercies are great, but don't let me fall into human hands."

Lord's Plague

¹⁵ So the LORD sent a plague on Israel from that morning until the appointed time, and from Dan to Beer-sheba 70,000 men died. ¹⁶ Then the angel extended his hand toward Jerusalem to destroy it, but the LORD relented concerning the destruction and said to the angel who was destroying the people, "Enough, withdraw your hand now!" The angel of the LORD was then at the threshing floor of Araunahª the Jebusite.

¹⁷ When David saw the angel striking the people, he said to the LORD, "Look, I am the one who has sinned; I am the oneᵇ who has done wrong. But these sheep, what have they done? Please, let Your hand be against me and my father's family."

David's Altar for Plague

¹⁸ Gad came to David that day and said to him, "Go up and set up an altar to the LORD on the threshing floor of Araunah the Jebusite." ¹⁹ David went up in obedience to Gad's command, just as the LORD had commanded. ²⁰ Araunah looked down and saw the king and his servants coming toward him, so he went out and bowed to the king with his face to the ground.

²¹ Araunah said, "Why has my lord the king come to his servant?"

David replied, "To buy the threshing floor from you in order to build an altar to the LORD, so the plague on the people may be halted."

²² Araunah said to David, "My lord the king may take whatever he wantsᶜ and offer it. Here are the oxen for a •burnt offering and the threshing sledges and ox yokes for the wood. ²³ ⌊My⌋ king, Araunah gives everything here to the king." Then he said to the king, "May the LORD your God accept you."

God Ends Plague

²⁴ The king answered Araunah, "No, I insist on buying it from you for a price, for I will not offer to the LORD my God burnt offerings that cost ⌊me⌋ nothing." David bought the threshing floor and the oxen for 20 ouncesᵈ of silver. ²⁵ He built an altar to the LORD there and offered burnt offerings and •fellowship offerings. Then the LORD answered prayer on behalf of the land, and the plague on Israel ended.

ª **24:16** = *Ornan*; 1 Ch 21:15-28; 2 Ch 3:1   ᵇ**24:17** LXX reads *shepherd*   ᶜ**24:22** Lit *take what is good in his eyes*   ᵈ**24:24** Lit *50 shekels*

1 KINGS

David's Last Days

His Health Declines

1 Now King David was old and getting on in years. Although they covered him with bedclothes, he could not get warm. ² So his servants said to him: "Let us[a] search for a young virgin for my lord the king. She is to attend the king and be his caregiver. She is to lie by your side so that my lord the king will get warm." ³ They searched for a beautiful girl throughout the territory of Israel; they found Abishag the Shunammite[b] and brought her to the king. ⁴ The girl was of unsurpassed beauty, and she became the king's caregiver. She served him, but he was not intimate with[c] her.

David's Son Adonijah Bids for Power

⁵ Adonijah son of Haggith kept exalting himself, saying, "I will be king!" He also assembled chariots, cavalry, and 50 men to run ahead of him.[d] ⁶ But his father had never once reprimanded[e] him by saying, "Why do you act this way?" In addition, he was quite handsome and was born after Absalom. ⁷ He conspired[f] with Joab son of Zeruiah and with Abiathar the priest. They supported Adonijah, ⁸ but Zadok the priest, Benaiah son of Jehoiada, Nathan the prophet, Shimei, Rei, and David's warriors did not side with Adonijah.

⁹ Adonijah sacrificed sheep, oxen, and fattened cattle near the stone of Zoheleth, which is next to En-rogel. He invited all his royal brothers and all the men of Judah, the servants of the king, ¹⁰ but he did not invite Nathan the prophet, Benaiah, the warriors, or his brother Solomon.

Nathan Appeals to Bathsheba for Solomon

¹¹ Then Nathan said to Bathsheba, Solomon's mother, "Have you not heard that Adonijah son of Haggith has become king and our lord David does not know ⌊it⌋? ¹² Now please come and let me advise you. Save your life and the life of your son Solomon. ¹³ Go, approach King David and say to him, 'My lord king, did you not swear to your servant: Your son Solomon is to become king after me, and he is the one who is to sit on my throne? So why has Adonijah become king?' ¹⁴ At that moment, while you are still there speaking with the king, I'll come in after you and confirm your words."

Bathsheba Appeals to David

¹⁵ So Bathsheba went to the king in his bedroom. Since the king was very old, Abishag the Shunammite was serving him. ¹⁶ Bathsheba bowed down and paid homage to the king, and he asked, "What do you want?"

¹⁷ She replied, "My lord, you swore to your servant by the LORD your God, 'Your son Solomon is to become king after me, and he is the one who is to sit on my throne.' ¹⁸ Now look, Adonijah has become king. And,[g] my lord king, you didn't know ⌊it⌋. ¹⁹ He has lavishly sacrificed oxen, fattened cattle, and sheep. He invited all the king's sons, Abiathar the priest, and Joab the commander of the army, but he did not invite your servant Solomon. ²⁰ Now, my lord king, the

eyes of all Israel are on you to tell them who will sit on the throne of my lord the king after him. ²¹ Otherwise, when my lord the king rests with his fathers, I and my son Solomon will be regarded as criminals."

Nathan Appeals to David

²² At that moment, while she was still speaking with the king, Nathan the prophet arrived, ²³ and it was announced to the king, "Nathan the prophet is here." He came into the king's presence and bowed to him with his face to the ground.

²⁴ "My lord king," Nathan said, "did you say, 'Adonijah is to become king after me, and he is the one who is to sit on my throne'? ²⁵ For today he went down and lavishly sacrificed oxen, fattened cattle, and sheep. He invited all the sons of the king, the commanders of the army, and Abiathar the priest. And look! They're eating and drinking in his presence, and they're saying, 'Long live King Adonijah!' ²⁶ But he did not invite me— me, your servant—or Zadok the priest or Benaiah son of Jehoiada or your servant Solomon. ²⁷ I'm certain my lord the king would not have let this happen without letting your servant[a] know who will sit on my lord the king's throne after him."

David Confirms Solomon as King

²⁸ King David responded by saying, "Call in Bathsheba for me." So she came into the king's presence and stood before him. ²⁹ The king swore an oath and said, "As the LORD lives, who has redeemed my life from every difficulty, ³⁰ just as I swore to you by the LORD God of Israel: Your son Solomon is to become king after me, and he is the one who is to sit on my throne in my place, that is exactly what I will do this very day."

³¹ Bathsheba bowed with her face to the ground, paying homage to the king, and said, "May my lord King David live forever!"

³² King David then said, "Call in Zadok the priest, Nathan the prophet, and Benaiah son of Jehoiada for me." So they came into the king's presence. ³³ The king said to them, "Take my servants with you, have my son Solomon ride on my own mule, and take him down to Gihon. ³⁴ There, Zadok the priest and Nathan the prophet are to anoint him as king over Israel. You are to blow the ram's horn and say, 'Long live King Solomon!' ³⁵ You are to come up after him, and he is to come in and sit on my throne. He is the one who is to become king in my place; he is the one I have commanded to be ruler over Israel and Judah."

³⁶ "•Amen," Benaiah son of Jehoiada replied to the king. "May the LORD, the God of my lord the king, so affirm it. ³⁷ Just as the LORD was with my lord the king, so may He[b] be with Solomon and make his throne greater than the throne of my lord King David."

Solomon Anointed Publicly

³⁸ Then Zadok the priest, Nathan the prophet, Benaiah son of Jehoiada, the Cherethites, and the Pelethites went down, had Solomon ride on King David's mule, and took him to Gihon. ³⁹ Zadok the priest took the horn of oil from the tabernacle and anointed Solomon. Then they blew the ram's horn, and all the people proclaimed, "Long live King Solomon!" ⁴⁰ All the people followed him, playing flutes and rejoicing with such a great joy that the earth split open from the sound.[a]

---

[a]**1:27** Many Hb mss, LXX; alt Hb tradition reads *servants*   [b]**1:37** Alt Hb tradition reads *so He will*

Adonijah Hears of Solomon's Coronation

[41] Adonijah and all the invited guests who were with him heard ˌthe noiseˌ as they finished eating. Joab heard the sound of the ram's horn and said, "Why is the town in such an uproar?" [42] He was still speaking when Jonathan son of Abiathar the priest, suddenly arrived. Adonijah said, "Come in, for you are an excellent man, and you must be bringing good news."

[43] "Unfortunately not," Jonathan answered him. "Our lord King David has made Solomon king. [44] And with Solomon, the king has sent Zadok the priest, Nathan the prophet, Benaiah son of Jehoiada, the Cherethites, and the Pelethites, and they have had him ride on the king's mule. [45] Zadok the priest and Nathan the prophet have anointed him king in Gihon. They have gone from there rejoicing. The town has been in an uproar; that's the noise you heard. [46] Solomon has even taken his seat on the royal throne.

[47] "The king's servants have also gone to congratulate our lord King David, saying, 'May your God make the name of Solomon more famous than your name, and may He make his throne greater than your throne.' Then the king bowed in worship on his bed. [48] And the king went on to say this: 'May the LORD God of Israel be praised! Today He has provided one to sit on my throne, and I am a witness.' "[b]

Adonijah Fears Solomon

[49] Then all of Adonijah's guests got up trembling and went their separate ways. [50] Adonijah was afraid of Solomon, so he got up and went to take hold of the horns of the altar.

[51] It was reported to Solomon: "Look, Adonijah fears King Solomon, and he has taken hold of the horns of the altar, saying, 'Let King Solomon first[c] swear to me that he will not kill his servant with the sword.' "

Adonijah and Solomon Reconciled

[52] Then Solomon said, "If he is a man of character, then not a single hair of his will fall to the ground, but if evil is found in him, then he dies." [53] So King Solomon sent for him, and they took him down from the altar. He came and paid homage to King Solomon, and Solomon said to him, "Go to your home."

David's Dying Instructions to Solomon

2 As the time approached for David to die, he instructed his son Solomon, [2] "As for me, I am going the way of all of the earth. Be strong and brave, [3] and keep your obligation to the LORD your God to walk in His ways and to keep His statutes, commandments, judgments, and testimonies. This is written in the law of Moses, so that you will have success in everything you do and wherever you turn, [4] and so that the LORD will carry out His promise that He made to me: 'If your sons are careful to walk faithfully before Me with their whole mind and heart, you will never fail to have a man on the throne of Israel.'

David Warns on Joab

[5] "You also know what Joab son of Zeruiah did to me and what he did to the two commanders of Israel's army, Abner son of Ner and Amasa son of Jether. He murdered them ˌin a timeˌ of peace to avenge blood shed in war. He spilled that blood on his own waistband and on the

---

[a]**1:40** LXX reads *the land resounded with their noise*   [b]**1:48** Lit *and my eyes are seeing*   [c]**1:51** Two Hb mss, LXX, Syr, Vg read *today*

sandals of his feet.[a] [6] Act according to your wisdom, and do not let his gray head descend to •Sheol in peace.

[7] "Show loyalty to the sons of Barzillai the Gileadite and let them be among those who eat at your table because they supported me when I fled from your brother Absalom.

David Warns on Shimei

[8] "Keep an eye on Shimei son of Gera, the Benjaminite from Bahurim who is with you. He uttered malicious curses against me the day I went to Mahanaim. But he came down to meet me at the Jordan River, and I swore to him by the LORD: 'I will never kill you with the sword.' [9] So don't let him go unpunished, for you are a wise man. You know how to deal with him to bring his gray head down to Sheol with blood."

David's Death

[10] Then David rested with his fathers and was buried in the city of David. [11] The ⌊length of⌋ time David reigned over Israel was 40 years: he reigned seven years in Hebron and 33 years in Jerusalem. [12] Solomon sat on the throne of his father David, and his kingship was firmly established.

Adonijah's Foolish Request

[13] Now Adonijah son of Haggith came to Bathsheba, Solomon's mother. She asked, "Do you come peacefully?"

"Peacefully," he replied, [14] and then asked, "May I talk with you?"[b]

"Go ahead," she answered.

[15] "You know the kingship was mine," he said. "All Israel expected me to be king, but then the kingship was turned over to my brother, for the LORD gave it

to him. [16] So now I have just one request of you; don't turn me down."[c]

She said to him, "Go on."

[17] He replied, "Please speak to King Solomon since he won't turn you down. Let him give me Abishag the Shunammite as a wife."

[18] "Very well," Bathsheba replied. "I will speak to the king for you."

Bathsheba Conveys Request to Solomon

[19] So Bathsheba went to King Solomon to speak to him about Adonijah. The king stood up to greet her, bowed to her, sat down on his throne, and had a throne placed for the king's mother. So she sat down at his right hand.

[20] Then she said, "I have just one small request of you. Don't turn me down."

"⌊Go ahead and⌋ ask, mother," the king replied, "for I won't turn you down."

[21] So she said, "Let Abishag the Shunammite be given to your brother Adonijah as a wife."

Solomon Executes Adonijah

[22] King Solomon answered his mother, "Why are you requesting Abishag the Shunammite for Adonijah? Since he is my elder brother, you might as well ask the kingship for him, for Abiathar the priest, and for Joab son of Zeruiah."[d] [23] Then Solomon took an oath by the LORD: "May God punish me and do so severely if Adonijah has not made this request at the cost of his life. [24] And now, as the LORD lives, the One who established me, seated me on the throne of my father David, and made me a dynasty as He promised—I swear Adonijah will be put to death today!" [25] Then King Solomon gave the order to Benaiah son of

---

[a]2:5 LXX, Lat read on my waistband and . . . my feet; v. 31   [b]2:14 Lit then said, "I have a word for you."   [c]2:16 Lit don't make me turn my face   [d]2:22 LXX, Vg, Syr read kingship for him, and on his side are Abiathar the priest and Joab son of Zeruiah

Jehoiada, who struck down Adonijah, and he died.

The King Punishes

Solomon Banishes Abiathar

26 The king said to Abiathar the priest, "Go to your fields in Anathoth. Even though you deserve to die, I will not put you to death today, since you carried the ark of the Lord GOD in the presence of my father David and you suffered through all that my father suffered." 27 So Solomon banished Abiathar from being the LORD's priest, and it fulfilled the LORD's prophecy He had spoken at Shiloh against Eli's family.

Solomon Executes Joab

28 The news reached Joab. Since he had supported Adonijah but not Absalom, Joab fled to the LORD's tabernacle and took hold of the horns of the altar. 29 It was reported to King Solomon: "Joab has fled to the LORD's tabernacle and is now beside the altar." Then Solomon senta Benaiah son of Jehoiada and told ¡him¡, "Go and strike him down!" 30 So Benaiah went to the tabernacle and said to Joab, "This is what the king says: 'Come out!' "

But Joab said, "No, for I will die here."

So Benaiah took a message back to the king, "This is what Joab said, and this is how he answered me." 31 The king said to him, "Do just as he says. Strike him down and bury him in order to remove from me and from my father's house the blood that Joab shed without just cause. 32 The LORD will bring back his own blood on his own head because he struck down two men more righteous and better than he, without my father David's knowledge. With his sword, Joab murdered Abner son of Ner, commander of Israel's army, and Amasa son of Jether, commander of Judah's army. 33 Their blood will come back on Joab's head and on the head of his descendants forever, but for David, his descendants, his dynasty, and his throne, there will be peace from the LORD forever."

34 Benaiah son of Jehoiada went up, struck down Joab, and put him to death. He was buried at his house in the wilderness. 35 Then the king appointed Benaiah son of Jehoiada in Joab's place over the army, and he appointed Zadok the priest in Abiathar's place.

Solomon Banishes Shimei

36 Then the king summoned Shimei and said to him, "Build a house for yourself in Jerusalem and live there, but don't leave there ¡and go¡ anywhere else. 37 On the day you do leave and cross the Kidron Valley, know for sure that you will certainly die. Your blood will be on your own head."

38 Shimei said to the king, "The sentence is fair; your servant will do as my lord the king has spoken." And Shimei lived in Jerusalem for a long time.

Solomon Executes Shimei

39 But then, at the end of three years, two of Shimei's slaves ran away to Achish son of Maacah, king of Gath. Shimei was informed, "Look, your slaves are in Gath." 40 So Shimei saddled his donkey and set out to Achish at Gath to search for his slaves. He went and brought them back from Gath.

41 It was reported to Solomon that Shimei had gone from Jerusalem to Gath and had returned. 42 So the king summoned Shimei and said to him, "Didn't I

a2:29 LXX adds Joab a message: "What is the matter with you, that you have fled to the altar?" And Joab replied, "Because I feared you, I have fled to the Lord." And Solomon the king sent

make you swear by the LORD and warn you, saying, 'On the day you leave and go anywhere else, know for sure that you will certainly die'? And you said to me, 'The sentence is fair; I will obey.' 43 So why have you not kept the LORD's oath and the command that I gave you?" 44 The king also said, "You yourself know all the evil that you did to my father David. Therefore, the LORD has brought back your evil on your head, 45 but King Solomon will be blessed, and David's throne will remain established before the LORD forever."

46 Then the king commanded Benaiah son of Jehoiada, and he went out and struck Shimei down, and he died. So the kingdom was established in Solomon's hand.

LORD Appears to Solomon

3 Solomon made an alliance[a] with Pharaoh king of Egypt by marrying Pharaoh's daughter. Solomon brought her to the city of David until he finished building his palace, the LORD's temple, and the wall surrounding Jerusalem. 2 However, the people were sacrificing on the •high places, because until that time a temple for the LORD's name had not been built. 3 Solomon loved the LORD by walking in the statutes of his father David, but he also sacrificed and burned incense on the high places.

4 The king went to Gibeon to sacrifice there because it was the most famous high place. He offered 1,000 •burnt offerings on that altar. 5 At Gibeon the LORD appeared to Solomon in a dream at night. God said, "Ask. What should I give you?"

Solomon Requests Discernment

6 And Solomon replied, "You have shown great and faithful love to Your servant, my father David, because he walked before You in faithfulness, righteousness, and[b] integrity. You have continued this great and faithful love for him by giving him a son to sit on his throne, as it is today.

7 "LORD my God, You have now made Your servant king in my father David's place. Yet I am just a youth with no experience in leadership.[c] 8 Your servant is among Your people You have chosen, a[d] people too numerous to be numbered or counted. 9 So give Your servant an obedient heart to judge Your people and to discern between good and evil. For who is able to judge this great people of Yours?"

God Gives Solomon Wise Heart

10 Now it pleased the Lord that Solomon had requested this. 11 So God said to him, "Because you have requested this and did not ask for long life[e] or riches for yourself, or the death[f] of your enemies, but you asked discernment for yourself to understand justice, 12 I will therefore do what you have asked. I will give you a wise and understanding heart, so that there has never been anyone like you before and never will be again. 13 In addition, I will give you what you did not ask for: both riches and honor, so that no man in any kingdom will be your equal during your entire life. 14 If you walk in My ways and keep My statutes and commandments just as your father David did, I will give you a long life."

15 Then Solomon woke up and realized it had been a dream. He went to Jerusalem, stood before the ark of the Lord's covenant, and offered burnt offerings and •fellowship offerings. Then he held a feast for all his servants.

---

a3:1 Lit Solomon made himself a son-in-law   b3:6 Lit and with You   c3:7 Lit am a little youth and do not know to go out or come in   d3:8 Lit chosen many   e3:11 Lit for many days   f3:11 Lit life

Two Women and a Baby

¹⁶ Then two women who were prostitutes came to the king and stood before him. ¹⁷ One woman said, "Please my lord, this woman and I live in the same house, and I had a baby while she was in the house. ¹⁸ On the third day after I gave birth, she also had a baby and we were alone. No one else[a] was with us in the house; just the two of us were there. ¹⁹ During the night this woman's son died because she lay on him. ²⁰ She got up in the middle of the night and took my son from my side while your servant was asleep. She laid him at her breast, and she put her dead son in my arms. ²¹ When I got up in the morning to nurse my son, I discovered he was dead. That morning, when I looked closely at him I realized that he was not the son I gave birth to."

²² "No," the other woman said. "My son is the living one; your son is the dead one."

The first woman said, "No, your son is the dead one; my son is the living one." So they argued before the king.

Solomon's Wise Decision

²³ The king replied, "This woman says, 'This is my son who is alive, and your son is dead,' but that woman says, 'No, your son is dead, and my son is alive.'"
²⁴ The king continued, "Bring me a sword." So they brought the sword to the king. ²⁵ Solomon said, "Cut the living boy in two and give half to one and half to the other."

²⁶ The woman whose son was alive spoke to the king because she felt great compassion[b] for her son. "My lord, give her the living baby," she said, "but please don't have him killed!"

But the other one said, "He will not be mine or yours. Cut him in two!"

²⁷ The king responded, "Give the living baby to the first woman, and don't kill him. She is his mother." ²⁸ All Israel heard about the judgment the king had given, and they stood in awe of the king because they saw that God's wisdom was in him to carry out justice.

Solomon's Officials

4 King Solomon ruled over Israel, ² and these were his officials:

Azariah son of Zadok, priest;
³ Elihoreph and Ahijah the sons of Shisha, secretaries;
Jehoshaphat son of Ahilud, historian;
⁴ Benaiah son of Jehoiada, in charge of the army;
Zadok and Abiathar, priests;
⁵ Azariah son of Nathan, in charge of the deputies;
Zabud son of Nathan, a priest and adviser to the king;
⁶ Ahishar, in charge of the palace;
and Adoniram son of Abda, in charge of forced labor.

⁷ Solomon had 12 deputies for all Israel. They provided food for the king and his household; each one made provision for one month out of the year. ⁸ These were their names:

Ben-hur, in the hill country of Ephraim;
⁹ Ben-deker, in Makaz, Shaalbim, Beth-shemesh, and Elon-beth-hanan;
¹⁰ Ben-hesed, in Arubboth (he had Socoh and the whole land of Hepher);
¹¹ Ben-abinadab, in all Naphath-dor (Taphath daughter of Solomon was his wife);

---

^a3:18 Lit *No stranger*   ^b3:26 Lit *because her compassion grew hot*

¹²Baana son of Ahilud, in Taanach, Megiddo, and all Beth-shean which is beside Zarethan below Jezreel, from Beth-shean to Abel-meholah, as far as the other side of Jokmeam;

¹³Ben-geber, in Ramoth-gilead (he had the villages of Jair son of Manasseh, which are in Gilead, and he had the region of Argob, which is in Bashan, 60 great cities with walls and bronze bars);

¹⁴Ahinadab son of Iddo, ⌊in⌋ Mahanaim;

¹⁵Ahimaaz, in Naphtali (he also had married a daughter of Solomon—Basemath);

¹⁶Baana son of Hushai, in Asher and Bealoth;

¹⁷Jehoshaphat son of Paruah, in Issachar;

¹⁸Shimei son of Ela, in Benjamin;

¹⁹Geber son of Uri, in the land of Gilead, the country of Sihon king of the Amorites and of Og king of Bashan.

There was one deputy in the land of Judah.ᵃ

Solomon's Realm

²⁰Judah and Israel were as numerous as the sand by the sea; ⌊they were⌋ eating, drinking, and rejoicing. ²¹ᵇSolomon ruled over all the kingdoms from the Euphrates River to the land of the Philistines and as far as the border of Egypt. They offered tribute and served Solomon all the days of his life.

²²Solomon's provisions for one day were 150 bushelsᶜ of fine flour and 300 bushelsᵈ of meal, ²³10 fattened oxen, 20 range oxen, and 100 sheep, besides deer, gazelles, roebucks, and pen-fed poultry,ᵉ ²⁴for he had dominion over everything west of the Euphrates from Tiphsah to Gaza and over all the kings west of the Euphrates. He had peace on all his surrounding borders. ²⁵Throughout Solomon's ⌊reign⌋, Judah and Israel lived in safety from Dan to Beer-sheba, each man under his own vine and his own fig tree. ²⁶Solomon had 40,000ᶠ stalls of horses for his chariots, and 12,000 horsemen. ²⁷Each of those deputies for a month in turn provided food for King Solomon and for everyone who came to King Solomon's table. They neglected nothing. ²⁸Each man brought the barley and the straw for the chariot teams and the other horses to the required place according to his assignment.ᵍ

Solomon's Wisdom

²⁹God gave Solomon wisdom, very great insight, and understanding as ⌊vast⌋ as the sand on the seashore. ³⁰Solomon's wisdom was greater than the wisdom of all the people of the East, greater than all the wisdom of Egypt. ³¹He was wiser than anyone—wiser than Ethan the Ezrahite, and Heman, Calcol, and Darda, sons of Mahol. His reputation extended to all the surrounding nations.

Solomon's Literary Gifts

³²Solomon composed 3,000 proverbs, and his songs numbered 1,005. ³³He described trees, from the cedar in Lebanon to the hyssop growing out of the wall. He also taught about animals, birds, reptiles, and fish. ³⁴People came from everywhere, ⌊sent⌋ by every king on earth who had heard of his wisdom, to listen to Solomon's wisdom.

ᵃ**4:19** LXX; Hb omits *of Judah*   ᵇ**4:21** 1 Kg 5:1 in Hb   ᶜ**4:22** Lit *30 cors*   ᵈ**4:22** Lit *60 cors*   ᵉ**4:23** Hb obscure
ᶠ**4:26** Some LXX mss read *4,000,* as does 1 Ch 9:25; 1 Kg 10:26, 2 Ch 1:14 reads *1,400*   ᵍ**4:28** Lit *judgment*

Solomon's Temple

Hiram's Building Materials

5 a Hiram king of Tyre sent his servants to Solomon when he heard that he had been anointed king in his father's place, for Hiram had always been friends with David.

2 Solomon sent ⌊this message⌋ to Hiram: 3 "You know my father David was not able to build a temple for the name of the LORD his God. This was because of the warfare all around him until the LORD put his enemies under his feet. 4 The LORD my God has now given me rest all around; there is no enemy or crisis. 5 So I plan to build a temple for the name of the LORD my God, according to what the LORD promised my father David: 'I will put your son on your throne in your place, and he will build the temple for My name.'

6 "Therefore, command that cedars from Lebanon be cut down for me. My servants will be with your servants, and I will pay your servants' wages according to whatever you say, for you know that not a man among us knows how to cut timber like the Sidonians."

7 When Hiram heard Solomon's words, he greatly rejoiced and said, "May the LORD be praised today! He has given David a wise son to be over this great people!" 8 Then Hiram sent ⌊a reply⌋ to Solomon, saying, "I have heard your message; I will do everything you want regarding the cedar and cypress timber. 9 My servants will bring ⌊the logs⌋ down from Lebanon to the sea, and I will make them into rafts to go by sea to the place you indicate. I will break them apart there, and you can take them away. You then can meet my needs by providing my household with food."

10 So Hiram provided Solomon with all the cedar and cypress timber he wanted, 11 and Solomon provided Hiram with 100,000 bushels[b] of wheat as food for his household and 110,000 gallons[c] of beaten oil. Solomon did this for Hiram year after year.

12 The LORD gave Solomon wisdom, as He had promised him. There was peace between Hiram and Solomon, and the two of them made a treaty.

Solomon's Work Force

13 Then King Solomon drafted forced laborers from all Israel; the labor force numbered 30,000 men. 14 He sent 10,000 to Lebanon each month in shifts; one month they were in Lebanon, two months they were at home. Adoniram was in charge of the forced labor. 15 Solomon had 70,000 porters and 80,000 stonecutters in the mountains, 16 not including his 3,300[d] deputies in charge of the work. They ruled over the people doing the work. 17 The king commanded them to quarry large, costly stones to lay the foundation of the temple with dressed stones. 18 So Solomon's builders and Hiram's builders, along with the Gebalites, quarried ⌊the stone⌋ and prepared the timber and stone for the temple's construction.

Temple Building Begins

6 Solomon ⌊began to⌋ build the temple for the LORD in the four hundred eightieth year after the Israelites came out from the land of Egypt, in the fourth year of his reign over Israel, in the second month, in the month of Ziv.[e] 2 The temple that King Solomon built for the LORD was 90 feet[f] long, 30 feet[g] wide, and 45 feet[h] high. 3 The portico in front of the temple sanctuary was 30 feet[g]

---

a5:1 1 Kg 5:15 in Hb   b5:11 Lit 20,000 cors   c5:11 LXX reads 20,000 baths; MT reads 20 cors   d5:16 Some LXX mss read 3,600; 2 Ch 2:2,18   e6:1 April–May   f6:2 Lit 60 cubits   g6:2,3 Lit 20 cubits   h6:2 Lit 30 cubits

long extending across the temple's width, and 15 feet deep[a] in front of the temple. [4] He also made windows with beveled frames[b] for the temple.

[5] He then built a chambered structure[c] along the temple wall, encircling the walls of the temple, that is, the sanctuary and the inner sanctuary. And he made side chambers[d] all around. [6] The lowest chamber was seven and a half feet[e] wide, the middle was nine feet[f] wide, and the third was 10 and a half feet[g] wide. He also provided offset ledges for the temple all around the outside so that nothing would be inserted into the temple walls. [7] The temple's construction used finished stones cut at the quarry so that no hammer, chisel, or any iron tool was heard in the temple while it was being built.

[8] The door for the lowest[h] side chamber was on the right side of the temple. They went up a stairway[b] to the middle ⌊chamber⌋, and from the middle to the third. [9] When he finished building the temple, he paneled it with boards and planks of cedar. [10] He built the chambers along the entire temple, joined to the temple with cedar beams; ⌊each story was⌋ seven and a half feet[i] high.

God's Promise to Solomon

[11] The word of the LORD came to Solomon: [12] "As for this temple you are building—if you walk in My statutes, execute My ordinances, and keep all My commandments by walking in them, I will fulfill My promise to you, which I made to your father David. [13] I will live among the Israelites and not abandon My people Israel."

Solomon Finishes Temple

[14] When Solomon finished building the temple,[j] [15] he paneled the interior temple walls with cedar boards; from the temple floor to the surface of the ceiling he overlaid the interior with wood. He also overlaid the floor with cypress boards. [16] Then he lined 30 feet[k] of the rear of the temple with cedar boards from the floor to the surface of the ceiling,[l] and he built the interior as an inner sanctuary, the most holy place. [17] The temple, that is, the sanctuary in front of the most holy place,[m] was 60 feet[n] long. [18] The cedar paneling inside the temple was carved with ⌊ornamental⌋ gourds and flower blossoms. Everything was cedar; not a stone could be seen.

Inner Sanctuary

[19] He prepared the inner sanctuary inside the temple to put the ark of the LORD's covenant there. [20] The interior of the sanctuary was 30 feet[k] long, 30 feet wide, and 30 feet high; he overlaid it with pure gold. He also overlaid the cedar altar. [21] Next, Solomon overlaid the interior of the temple with pure gold, and he hung[o] gold chains across the front of the inner sanctuary and overlaid it with gold. [22] So he added the gold overlay to the entire temple until everything was completely finished, including the entire altar that belongs in the inner sanctuary.

Cherubim

[23] In the inner sanctuary he made two •cherubim 15 feet[p] high out of olive wood. [24] One wing of the ⌊first⌋ cherub was seven and a half feet long,[q] and the other wing was seven and a half feet

---

[a]6:3 Lit 10 cubits wide   [b]6:4,8 Hb obscure   [c]6:5 Lit built the house of chamber   [d]6:5 Lit made ribs or sides
[e]6:6 Lit five cubits   [f]6:6 Lit six cubits   [g]6:6 Lit seven cubits   [h]6:8 LXX, Tg; Hb reads middle   [i]6:10 Lit five cubits
[j]6:11-14 LXX omits these vv.   [k]6:16,20 Lit 20 cubits   [l]6:16 LXX; Hb omits of the ceiling; 1 Kg 6:15   [m]6:17 Hb obscure;
lit front of me   [n]6:17 Lit 40 cubits   [o]6:21 Lit he caused to pass across   [p]6:23 Lit 10 cubits   [q]6:24 Lit five cubits

long. The wingspan was 15 feet[a] from tip to tip. [25] The second cherub also was 15 feet;[a] both cherubim had the same size and shape. [26] The first cherub's height was 15 feet[a] and so was the second cherub's. [27] Then he put the cherubim inside the inner temple. Since their wings were spread out, the first one's wing touched one wall while the second cherub's wing touched the other[b] wall, and in the middle of the temple their wings were touching wing to wing. [28] He also overlaid the cherubim with gold.

Finishing Touches

[29] He carved all the surrounding temple walls with carved engravings—cherubim, palm trees and flower blossoms—in both the inner and outer sanctuaries. [30] He overlaid the temple floor with gold in both the inner and outer sanctuaries.

[31] For the entrance of the inner sanctuary, he made olive wood doors. The pillars of the doorposts were five-sided.[c] [32] The two doors were made of olive wood. He carved cherubim, palm trees and flower blossoms on them and overlaid them with gold, hammering gold over the cherubim and palm trees. [33] In the same way, he made four-sided[c] olive wood doorposts for the sanctuary entrance. [34] The two doors were made of cypress wood; the first door had two folding sides, and the second door had two folding panels. [35] He carved cherubim, palm trees and flower blossoms on them and overlaid them with gold applied evenly over the carving. [36] He built the inner courtyard with three rows of dressed stone and a row of trimmed cedar beams.

[37] The foundation of the LORD's temple was laid in ⌊Solomon's⌋ fourth year in the month of Ziv. [38] In ⌊his⌋ eleventh year in the eighth month, in the month of Bul,[d] the temple was completed in every detail and according to every specification. So he built it in seven years.

Solomon's Palace Complex

7 Solomon completed his entire palace-complex after 13 years of construction. [2] He built the House of the Forest of Lebanon. It was 150 feet[e] long, 75 feet[f] wide, and 45 feet[g] high on four rows of cedar pillars, with cedar beams on top of the pillars. [3] It was paneled above with cedar at the top of the chambers that ⌊rested⌋ on 45 pillars, fifteen per row. [4] There were three rows of window frames, facing each other[h] in three tiers.[i] [5] All the doors and doorposts had rectangular frames, the openings facing each other[j] in three tiers.[i] [6] He made the hall of pillars 75 feet[f] long and 45 feet[m] wide. A portico was in front of the pillars, and a canopy with pillars[c] was in front of them. [7] He made the Hall of the Throne where he would judge—the Hall of Judgment. It was paneled with cedar from the floor to the rafters.[n] [8] Solomon's own palace where he would live, in the other courtyard behind the hall, was of similar construction. And he made a house like this hall for Pharaoh's daughter, his wife.[o]

[9] All of these ⌊buildings⌋ were of costly stones, cut to size and sawed with saws on the inner and outer surfaces, from foundation to coping and from the outside to the great courtyard. [10] The foundation was made of large, costly stones 12 and 15 feet long.[p] [11] Above were also

costly stones, cut to size, as well as cedar wood. [12] Around the great courtyard, as well as the inner courtyard of the LORD's temple and the portico of the temple, were three rows of dressed stone and a row of trimmed cedar beams.

Hiram the Bronze Craftsman

[13] King Solomon had Hiram[a] brought from Tyre. [14] He was a widow's son from the tribe of Naphtali, and his father was a man of Tyre, a bronze craftsman. Hiram had great skill, understanding, and knowledge to do every kind of bronze work. So he came to King Solomon and carried out all his work.

Bronze Pillars

[15] He cast two ⸤hollow⸥ bronze pillars: each 27 feet[b] high and 18 feet[c] in circumference.[d] [16] He also made two capitals of cast bronze to set on top of the pillars; seven and a half feet[e] was the height of the first capital, and seven and a half feet[e] was also the height of the second capital. [17] The capitals on top of the pillars had gratings of latticework, wreaths[f] made of chainwork—seven for the first capital and seven for the second. [18] He made the pillars with two encircling rows of pomegranates on the one grating to cover the capital on top; he did the same for the second capital. [19] And the capitals on top of the pillars in the portico were shaped like lilies, six feet[g] ⸤high⸥. [20] The capitals on the two pillars were also immediately above the rounded surface next to the grating, and 200 pomegranates were in rows encircling each[h] capital. [21] He set up the pillars at the portico of the sanctuary: he set up the right pillar and named it Jachin;[i] then he set up the left pillar and named it Boaz.[j] [22] The tops of the pillars were shaped like lilies. Then the work of the pillars was completed.

Metal Reservoir

[23] He made the cast ⸤metal⸥ reservoir,[k] 15 feet[l] from brim to brim, perfectly round. It was seven and a half feet[e] high and 45 feet[m] in circumference. [24] ⸤Ornamental⸥ gourds encircled it below the brim, 10 every half yard,[n] completely encircling the reservoir. The gourds were cast in two rows when the reservoir was cast. [25] It stood on 12 oxen, three facing north, three facing west, three facing south, and three facing east. The reservoir was on top of them and all their hindquarters were toward the center. [26] The reservoir was three inches[o] thick, and its rim was fashioned like the brim of a cup or of a lily blossom. It held 11,000 gallons.[p]

Bronze Water Carts

[27] Then he made 10 bronze water carts.[q] Each water cart was six feet[g] long, six feet[g] wide, and four and a half feet[r] high. [28] This was the design of the carts: They had frames; the frames were between the cross-pieces, [29] and on the frames between the cross-pieces were lions, oxen, and •cherubim. On the cross-pieces there was a pedestal above, and below the lions and oxen were wreaths of hanging[s] work. [30] Each cart had four bronze wheels with bronze axles. Underneath the four corners of the basin were cast supports, each next to a wreath. [31] And the water cart's opening

---

inside the crown on top was 18 inches[a] wide. The opening was round, made as a pedestal 27 inches[b] wide. On it were carvings, but their frames were square, not round. [32] There were four wheels under the frames, and the wheel axles were part of the water cart; each wheel was 27 inches[c] tall. [33] The wheels' design was similar to that of chariot wheels: their axles, rims, spokes, and hubs were all of cast metal. [34] Four supports were at the four corners of each water cart; each support was one piece with the water cart. [35] At the top of the cart was a band nine inches[d] high encircling it; also, at the top of the cart, its braces and its frames were one piece with it. [36] He engraved cherubim, lions, and palm trees on the plates of its braces and on its frames, wherever each had space, with encircling wreaths. [37] In this way he made the 10 water carts using the same casting, dimensions, and shape for all of them.

Bronze Basins and Other Utensils

[38] Then he made 10 bronze basins— each basin holding 220 gallons[e] and each was six feet[f] wide—one basin for each of the 10 water carts. [39] He set five water carts on the right side of the temple and five on the left side. He put the reservoir near the right side of the temple toward the southeast. [40] Then Hiram made the basins, the shovels, and the sprinkling basins.

Hiram Completes Bronze Works

So Hiram finished all the work that he was doing for King Solomon on the LORD's temple: [41] two pillars; bowls for the capitals that were on top of the two pillars; the two gratings for covering both bowls of the capitals that were on top of the pillars; [42] the 400 pomegranates for the two gratings (two rows of pomegranates for each grating covering both capitals' bowls on top of the pillars); [43] the 10 water carts; the 10 basins on the water carts; [44] the reservoir; the 12 oxen underneath the reservoir; [45] and the pots, shovels, and sprinkling basins. All the utensils that Hiram made for King Solomon at the LORD's temple ɪwere madeɪ of burnished bronze. [46] The king had them cast in clay molds in the Jordan Valley between Succoth and Zarethan. [47] Solomon left all the utensils unweighed because there were so many; the weight of the bronze was not determined.

Completion of Temple

Gold Furnishings

[48] Solomon also made all the equipment in the LORD's temple: the gold altar; the gold table that the bread of the Presence was placed on; [49] the pure gold lampstands in front of the inner sanctuary, five on the right and five on the left; the gold flowers, lamps, and tongs; [50] the pure gold ceremonial bowls, wick trimmers, sprinkling basins, ladles,[g] and firepans; and the gold hinges for the doors of the inner temple (that is, the most holy place) and for the doors of the temple sanctuary.

[51] So all the work King Solomon did in the LORD's temple was completed. Then Solomon brought in the consecrated things of his father David—the silver, the gold, and the utensils—and put them in the treasuries of the LORD's temple.

Ark to the Temple

8 At that time Solomon assembled the elders of Israel, all the tribal heads and the ancestral leaders of the Israelites

---

[a]**7:31** Lit *a cubit*   [b]**7:31** Lit *one and a half cubits*   [c]**7:32** Lit *was one and a half cubits*   [d]**7:35** Lit *half a cubit*   [e]**7:38** Lit *40 baths*   [f]**7:38** Lit *four cubits*   [g]**7:50** Or *dishes*, or *spoons*; lit *palms*

before him at Jerusalem in order to bring the ark of the LORD's covenant from Zion, the city of David. ² So all the men of Israel were assembled in the presence of King Solomon in the seventh month, the month of Ethanim at the festival.ᵃ

³ All the elders of Israel came, and the priests picked up the ark. ⁴ The priests and the Levites brought the ark of the LORD, the tent of meeting, and the holy utensils that were in the tent. ⁵ King Solomon and the entire congregation of Israel, who had gathered around him and were with him in front of the ark, were sacrificing sheep and cattle that could not be counted or numbered, because there were so many. ⁶ The priests brought the ark of the LORD's covenant to its place, into the inner sanctuary of the temple, to the most holy place beneath the wings of the •cherubim. ⁷ For the cherubim were spreading their wings overᵇ the place of the ark, so that the cherubim covered the ark and its poles from above. ⁸ The poles were so long that their ends were seen from the holy place in front of the inner sanctuary, but they were not seen from outside the sanctuary; they are there to this day. ⁹ Nothing was in the ark except the two stone tablets that Moses had put there at Horeb,ᶜ where the LORD made a covenant with the Israelites when they came out of the land of Egypt.

God's Cloud in Temple

¹⁰ When the priests came out of the holy place, the cloud filled the LORD's temple, ¹¹ and because of the cloud, the priests were not able to continue ministering, for the glory of the LORD filled the temple.

Solomon Dedicates Temple

¹² Then Solomon said:

The LORD said that He would dwell
    in thick darkness,
¹³ but I have indeed built
    an exalted temple for You,
    a place for Your dwelling forever.

¹⁴ The king turned around and blessed the entire congregation of Israel while they were standing. ¹⁵ He said:

May the LORD God of Israel
    be praised!
He spoke directly
    to my father David,
and He has fulfilled ⸤the promise⸥
    by His power.
He said,
¹⁶ "Since the day I brought
    My people Israel out of Egypt,
I have not chosen a city to build
    a temple in
among any of the tribes of Israel,
    so that My name would be there.
But I have chosen David to rule
    My people Israel."
¹⁷ It was in the desire
    of my father David
to build a temple for the name
    of the Lord God of Israel.
¹⁸ But the Lord said
    to my father David,
"Since it was your desire to build
    a temple for My name,
you have done well to have
    this desire.
¹⁹ Yet you are not the one to build it;
    instead, your son,
    your own offspring,
will build it for My name."
²⁰ The Lord has fulfilled
    what He promised.
I have taken the place
    of my father David,
and I sit on the throne of Israel,
    as the Lord promised.

ᵃ8:2 September–October ᵇ8:7 LXX; MT reads *toward* ᶜ8:9 = Sinai

I have built the temple
 for the name of the Lord God
 of Israel.
21 I have provided a place there
 for the ark,
where the Lord's covenant is
that He made with our ancestors
when He brought them out
 of the land of Egypt.

Solomon's Prayer

22 Then Solomon stood before the altar of the LORD in front of the entire congregation of Israel and spread out his hands toward heaven. 23 He said:

LORD God of Israel,
there is no God like You
in heaven above or on earth below,
keeping the gracious covenant
with Your servants who walk
 before You
with their whole heart.
24 You have kept what You promised
to Your servant, my father David.
You spoke directly ˻to him˼
and You fulfilled ˻Your promise˼
 by Your power
as it is today.
25 Therefore, Lord God of Israel,
keep what You promised
to Your servant, my father David:
You will never fail to have a man
to sit before Me on the throne
 of Israel,
if only your sons guard their walk
 before Me
as you have walked before Me.
26 Now Lord[a] God of Israel,
please confirm what You promised
to Your servant, my father David.

27 But will God indeed live on earth?
Even heaven, the highest heaven,
 cannot contain You,

much less this temple I have built.
28 Listen[b] to Your servant's prayer
 and his petition,
Lord my God,
so that You may hear the cry
 and the prayer
that Your servant prays
 before You today,
29 so that Your eyes may watch over
 this temple night and day,
toward the place where You said:
My name will be there,
and so that You may hear the prayer
that Your servant prays
 toward this place.
30 Hear the petition of Your servant
and Your people Israel,
which they pray toward this place.
May You hear
 in Your dwelling place in heaven.
May You hear and forgive.
31 When a man sins
 against his neighbor
and is forced to take an oath,[c]
and he comes to take an oath
before Your altar in this temple,
32 may You hear in heaven and act.
May You judge Your servants,
condemning the wicked
 by bringing
what he has done on his own head
and providing justice
 for the righteous
by rewarding him according to
 his righteousness.

33 When Your people Israel
 are defeated before an enemy,
because they have sinned
 against You,
and they return to You and praise
 Your name,
and they pray and plead with You
for mercy in this temple,

---

[a]8:26 Many Hb mss, LXX, Syr, Tg ms, Vg mss, 2 Ch 6:16; MT omits LORD   [b]8:28 Lit Turn   [c]8:31 Lit and he lifts a curse against him to curse him

34 may You hear in heaven
and forgive the sin
  of Your people Israel.
May You restore them to the land
You gave their ancestors.

35 When the skies are shut
    and there is no rain,
because they have sinned
  against You,
and they pray toward this place
and praise Your name,
and they turn from their sins
because You are afflicting them,

36 may You hear in heaven
and forgive the sin of Your servants
and Your people Israel,
so that You may teach them
  the good way
they should walk in.
May You send rain on Your land
that You gave Your people
  for an inheritance.

37 When there is famine on the earth,
when there is pestilence,
when there is blight, mildew,
  locust, or grasshopper,
when their enemy besieges them
in the region
  of their fortified cities,ᵃ
ᴸwhen there isᴶ any plague
  or illness,

38 whatever prayer or petition
anyone from Your people Israel
  might have—
each man knowing
  his own afflictionsᵇ
and spreading out his hands
  toward this temple—

39 may You hear in heaven,
  Your dwelling place,
and may You forgive, act, and repay
  the man,

according to all his ways,
  since You know his heart,
for You alone know
  every human heart,

40 so that they may •fear You
all the days they live on the land
You gave our ancestors.

41 Even for the foreigner who is not
    of Your people Israel
but has come from a distant land
because of Your name—

42 for they will hear
  of Your great name,
mighty hand, and outstretched arm,
and will come and pray
  toward this temple—

43 may You hear in heaven,
  Your dwelling place,
and do according to
  all the foreigner asks You for.
Then all the people on earth
  will know Your name,
to fear You as Your people Israel do
and know that this temple
  I have built
is called by Your name.

44 When Your people go out to fight
    against their enemies,ᶜ
wherever You send them,
and they pray to the Lord
in the direction of the city
  You have chosen
and the temple I have built
  for Your name,

45 may You hear their prayer
    and petition in heaven
and uphold their cause.

46 When they sin against You—
  for there is no one
    who does not sin—
and You are angry with them
and hand them over to the enemy,

ᵃ8:37 Lit besieges him in the land of his gates   ᵇ8:38 Lit knowing in his heart of a plague   ᶜ8:44 Some Hb mss, most
ancient versions, 2 Ch 6:34; MT reads enemy

and their captors deport them
    to the enemy's country—
whether distant or nearby—
47 and when they come
    to their senses[a]
in the land where
    they were deported
and repent and petition You
    in their captors' land:
"We have sinned and done wrong;
    we have been wicked,"
48 and when they return to You
    with their whole mind and heart
in the land of their enemies
    who took them captive,
and when they pray to You
    in the direction of their land
that You gave their ancestors,
    the city You have chosen,
and the temple I have built
    for Your name,
49 may You hear in heaven,
    Your dwelling place,
their prayer and petition
    and uphold their cause.
50 May You forgive Your people
    who sinned against You
and all their rebellions[b] against You,
and may You give
    them compassion
in the eyes of their captors,
    so that they may be compassionate
    to them.
51 For they are Your people
    and Your inheritance;
You brought them out of Egypt,
    out of the middle
    of an iron furnace.
52 May Your eyes be open
    to Your servant's petition
and to the petition
    of Your people Israel,
listening to them whenever
    they call to You.

53 For You, Lord God, have set them
    apart as Your inheritance
from all the people on earth,
    as You spoke
    through Your servant Moses
when You brought their ancestors
    out of Egypt.

Solomon Blesses Congregation

54 When Solomon finished praying this entire prayer and petition to the LORD, he got up from kneeling before the altar of the LORD, with his hands spread out toward heaven, 55 and he stood and blessed the whole congregation of Israel with a loud voice: 56 "May the LORD be praised! He has given rest to His people Israel according to all He has said. Not one of all the good promises He made through His servant Moses has failed. 57 May the LORD our God be with us as He was with our ancestors. May He not abandon us or leave us. 58 May He incline our hearts toward Him to walk in all His ways and to keep His commands, ordinances, and judgments, which He commanded our ancestors. 59 May my words I have made my petition with before the LORD be near the LORD our God day and night, so that He may uphold His servant's cause and the cause of His people Israel, as each day requires, 60 and so that all the peoples of the earth may know that the LORD is God. There is no other! 61 Let your heart be completely devoted to the LORD our God to walk in His ordinances and to keep His commands, as it is today."

King and Israel Offer Sacrifices

62 The king and all Israel with him were offering sacrifices in the LORD's presence. 63 Solomon offered a sacrifice of •fellowship offerings to the LORD:

---

a8:47 Lit *they return to their heart*   b8:50 Lit *rebellions that they have rebelled*

22,000 cattle and 120,000 sheep. In this manner the king and all the Israelites dedicated the LORD's temple.

⁶⁴ On the same day, the king consecrated the middle of the courtyard that was in front of the LORD's temple because that was where he offered the •burnt offering, the •grain offering, and the fat of the fellowship offerings since the bronze altar before the LORD was too small to accommodate the burnt offerings, the grain offerings, and the fat of the fellowship offerings.

⁶⁵ Solomon and all Israel with him—a great assembly, from the entrance of Hamathª to the Brook of Egypt—observed the festival at that time in the presence of the LORD our God, seven days, and seven ⌊more⌋ days—14 days.ᵇ ⁶⁶ On the fifteenth dayᶜ he sent the people away. So they blessed the king and went home to their tents rejoicing and with joyful hearts for all the goodness that the LORD had done for His servant David and for His people Israel.

The LORD's Response

9 When Solomon finished building the temple of the LORD, the royal palace, and all that Solomon desired to do, ² the LORD appeared to Solomon a second time just as He had appeared to him at Gibeon. ³ The LORD said to him:

I have heard your prayer and petition you have made before Me. I have consecrated this temple you have built, to put My name there forever; My eyes and My heart will be there at all times.

⁴ As for you, if you walk before Me as your father David walked, with integrity of heart and uprightness,

doing everything I have commanded you, and if you keep My statutes and ordinances, ⁵ I will establish your royal throne over Israel forever, as I promised your father David: You will never fail to have a man on the throne of Israel.

⁶ If you or your sons turn away from following Me and do not keep My commands—My statutes that I have set before you—and if you go and serve other gods and worship them, ⁷ I will cut off Israel from the land I gave them, and I will rejectᵈ the temple I have sanctified for My name. Israel will become an object of scorn and ridicule among all the peoples. ⁸ Though this temple is ⌊now⌋ exalted,ᵉ every passerby will be appalled and will hiss. They will say: Why did the LORD do this to this land and this temple? ⁹ Then they will say: Because they abandoned the LORD their God who brought their ancestors out of the land of Egypt. They clung to other gods and worshiped and served them. Because of this, the LORD brought all this ruin on them.

Post-Dedication Events

King Hiram's 20 Towns

¹⁰ At the end of 20 years during which Solomon had built the two houses, the LORD's temple and the royal palace—¹¹ Hiram king of Tyre having supplied him with cedar and cypress logs and gold for his every wish—King Solomon gave Hiram 20 towns in the land of Galilee. ¹² So Hiram went out from Tyre to look over the towns that Solomon had given him, but he was not pleased with them.

ª8:65 Or from Lebo-hamath ᵇ8:65 Seven days for the dedication of the temple, and then seven days for the Festival of Tabernacles. ᶜ8:66 Lit the eighth day (after the second seven days) ᵈ9:7 Lit send from My presence
ᵉ9:8 Some ancient versions read temple will become a ruin

13 So he said, "What are these towns you've given me, my brother?" So he called them the Land of Cabul,a as they are ¡still called¡ today. 14 Now Hiram had sent the king 9,000 poundsb of gold.

Solomon's Forced Labor

15 This is the account of the forced labor that King Solomon had imposed to build the LORD's temple, his own palace, the supporting terraces, the wall of Jerusalem, and Hazor, Megiddo, and Gezer. 16 Pharaoh king of Egypt had attacked and captured Gezer. He then burned it down, killed the Canaanites who lived in the city, and gave it as a dowry to his daughter, Solomon's wife. 17 Then Solomon rebuilt Gezer, Lower Beth-horon, 18 Baalath, Tamarc in the Wilderness of Judah, 19 all the storage cities that belonged to Solomon, the chariot cities, the cavalry cities, and whatever Solomon desired to build in Jerusalem, Lebanon, or anywhere else in the land of his dominion.

20 As for all the peoples who remained of the Amorites, Hittites, Perizzites, Hivites, and Jebusites, who were not Israelites— 21 their descendants who remained in the land after them, those whom the Israelites were unable to annihilate—Solomon imposed forced labor on them; ¡it is this way¡ until today. 22 But Solomon did not consign the Israelites to slavery; they were soldiers, his servants, his commanders, his captains, and commanders of his chariots and his cavalry. 23 These were the deputies who were over Solomon's work: 550 who ruled over the people doing the work.

Pharaoh's Daughter, Offerings, and a Fleet

24 Pharaoh's daughter moved from the city of David to the house that Solomon had built for her; he then built the terraces.

25 Three times a year Solomon offered •burnt offerings and •fellowship offerings on the altar he had built for the LORD, and he burned incense with them in the LORD's presence. So he completed the temple.

26 King Solomon put together a fleet of ships at Ezion-geber, which is near Eloth on the shore of the •Red Sea in the land of Edom. 27 With the fleet, Hiram sent his servants, experienced seamen, along with Solomon's servants. 28 They went to Ophir and acquired gold there—16 tonsd—and delivered it to Solomon.

Queen of Sheba

10 The queen of Sheba heard about Solomon's fame connected with the name of the LORD and came to test him with difficult questions. 2 She came to Jerusalem with a very large retinue, with camels bearing spices, gold in great abundance, and precious stones. She came to Solomon and spoke to him about everything that was on her mind. 3 So Solomon answered all her questions; nothing was too difficult for the king to explain to her. 4 When the queen of Sheba observed all of Solomon's wisdom, the palace he had built, 5 the food at his table, his servants' residence, his attendants' service and their attire, his cupbearers, and the •burnt offerings he offered at the LORD's temple, it took her breath away.

6 She said to the king, "The report I heard in my own country about your words and about your wisdom is true. 7 But I didn't believe the reports until I came and saw with my own eyes. Indeed, I was not even told half. Your wisdom and prosperity far exceed the report

a9:13 = Like Nothing   b9:14 Lit 120 talents   c9:18 Alt Hb traditions, LXX, Syr, Tg, Vg, 2 Ch 8:4 read Tadmor. Tamar was a city in southern Judah; Ezk 47:19; 48:28.   d9:28 Lit 420 talents; about 31,500 pounds

I heard. [8] How happy are your men.[a] How happy are these servants of yours, who always stand in your presence hearing your wisdom. [9] May the LORD your God be praised! He delighted in you and put you on the throne of Israel, because of the LORD's eternal love for Israel. He has made you king to carry out justice and righteousness."

[10] Then she gave the king four and a half tons[b] of gold, a great quantity of spices, and precious stones. Never again did such a quantity of spices arrive as those the queen of Sheba gave to King Solomon.

[11] In addition, Hiram's fleet that carried gold from Ophir brought from Ophir a large quantity of almug[c] wood and precious stones. [12] The king made the almug wood into steps for the LORD's temple and the king's palace and into harps and lyres for the singers. Never ⌊before⌋ had such almug wood come, and ⌊the like⌋ has not been seen ⌊again⌋ even to this very day.

[13] King Solomon gave the queen of Sheba her every desire—whatever she asked—besides what he had given her out of his royal bounty. Then she, along with her servants, returned to her own country.

Solomon's Wealth

[14] The weight of gold that came to Solomon annually was 25 tons,[d] [15] besides what came from merchants, traders' merchandise, and all the Arabian kings and governors of the land.

[16] King Solomon made 200 large shields of hammered gold; 15 pounds[e] of gold went into each shield. [17] He made 300 small shields of hammered gold; about four pounds[f] of gold went into

each shield. The king put them in the House of the Forest of Lebanon.

[18] The king also made a large ivory throne and overlaid it with fine gold. [19] The throne had six steps; there was a rounded top at the back of the throne, armrests on either side of the seat, and two lions standing beside the armrests. [20] Twelve lions were standing there on the six steps, one at each end. Nothing like it had ever been made in any other kingdom.

[21] All of King Solomon's drinking cups were gold, and all the utensils of the House of the Forest of Lebanon were pure gold. There was no silver, since it was considered as nothing in Solomon's time, [22] for the king had ships of Tarshish at sea with Hiram's fleet, and once every three years the ships of Tarshish would arrive bearing gold, silver, ivory, apes, and peacocks.[g]

[23] King Solomon surpassed all the kings of the world in riches and in wisdom. [24] The whole world wanted an audience with Solomon to hear the wisdom that God had put in his heart. [25] Every man would bring his annual tribute: items[h] of silver and gold, clothing, weapons,[i] spices, and horses and mules.

[26] Solomon accumulated 1,400 chariots and 12,000 horsemen and stationed them in the chariot cities and with the king in Jerusalem. [27] The king made silver as common in Jerusalem as stones, and he made cedar as abundant as sycamore in the Judean foothills. [28] Solomon's horses were imported from Egypt and Kue.[j] The king's traders bought them from Kue at the going price. [29] A chariot was imported from Egypt for 15 pounds[k] ⌊of silver⌋, and a

---

[a]10:8 LXX, Syr read your wives [b]10:10 Lit 120 talents [c]10:11 Spelled algum in 2 Ch 2:8; 9:10-11 [d]10:14 Lit 666 talents [e]10:16 Lit 600 (shekels) [f]10:17 Lit three minas [g]10:22 Or baboons [h]10:25 Or vessels, or weapons [i]10:25 Or fragrant balsam [j]10:28 = Cilicia (modern Turkey) [k]10:29 Lit 600 shekels

horse for about four pounds.ᵃ In the same way, they exported them to all the kings of the Hittites and to the kings of Aram through their agents.

Solomon's Foreign Women

11 King Solomon loved many foreign women in addition to Pharaoh's daughter: Moabite, Ammonite, Edomite, Sidonian, and Hittite women ² from the nations that the LORD had told the Israelites about, "Do not intermarry with them, and they must not intermarry with you, because they will turn you away ⌊from Me⌋ to their gods." Solomon was deeply attached to these women and loved ⌊them⌋. ³ He had 700 wives who were princesses and 300 concubines, and they turned his heart away ⌊from the LORD⌋.

Solomon Seduced

⁴ When Solomon was old, his wives seduced him ⌊to follow⌋ other gods. His heart was not completely with the LORD his God, as his father David's heart had been. ⁵ Solomon followed •Ashtoreth, the goddess of the Sidonians, and •Milcom, the detestable idol of the Ammonites. ⁶ Solomon did what was evil in the LORD's sight, and unlike his father David, he did not completely follow the LORD.

⁷ At that time, Solomon built a •high place for Chemosh, the detestable idol of Moab, and for Milcom,ᵇ the detestable idol of the Ammonites on the hill across from Jerusalem. ⁸ He did the same for all his foreign wives, who were burning incense and offering sacrifices to their gods.

⁹ The LORD was angry with Solomon, because his heart had turned away from the LORD God of Israel, who had appeared to him twice. ¹⁰ He had com-

manded him about this, so that he would not follow other gods, but Solomon did not do what the LORD had commanded.

God's Judgment

¹¹ Then the LORD said to Solomon, "Since you have done thisᶜ and did not keep My covenant and My statutes, which I commanded you, I will tear the kingdom away from you and give it to your servant. ¹² However, I will not do it during your lifetime because of your father David; I will tear it out of your son's hand. ¹³ Yet, I will not tear the entire kingdom away from him. I will give one tribe to your son because of my servant David and because of Jerusalem that I chose."

Solomon's Enemies

Hadad the Edomite

¹⁴ So the LORD raised up Hadad the Edomite as an enemy against Solomon. He was of the royal family in Edom. ¹⁵ Earlier, when David was in Edom, Joab, the commander of the army, had gone to bury the dead and had struck down every male in Edom. ¹⁶ For Joab and all Israel had remained there six months, until he had killed every male in Edom. ¹⁷ Hadad fled to Egypt, along with some Edomites from his father's servants. At the time Hadad was a small boy. ¹⁸ Hadad and his men set out from Midian and went to Paran. They took men with them from Paran and went to Egypt, to Pharaoh king of Egypt, who gave Hadad a house, ordered that he ⌊be given⌋ food, and gave him land. ¹⁹ Pharaoh liked Hadad so much that he gave him a wife, the sister of his own wife, Queen Tahpenes. ²⁰ Tahpenes' sister gave birth to Hadad's son Genubath. Tahpenes ⌊herself⌋ weaned him in

---

ᵃ10:29 Lit *150 shekels*   ᵇ11:7 Lit *Molech*   ᶜ11:11 Lit *Since this was with you*

Pharaoh's palace, and Genubath ⌊lived⌋ there along with Pharaoh's sons.

21 When Hadad heard in Egypt that David rested with his fathers and that Joab, the commander of the army, was dead, Hadad said to Pharaoh, "Let me leave, so I can go to my own country." 22 But Pharaoh asked him, "What do you lack here with me for you to want to go back to your own country?"

"Nothing," he replied, "but please let me leave."

Rezon Makes Trouble

23 God raised up Rezon son of Eliada as an enemy against Solomon. Rezon had fled from his master Hadadezer king of Zobah 24 and gathered men to himself. He became captain of a raiding party when David killed the Zobaites. He[a] went to Damascus, lived there, and became king in Damascus. 25 Rezon was Israel's enemy throughout Solomon's reign, adding to the trouble Hadad ⌊had caused⌋. He ruled over Aram,[b] but he loathed Israel.

Jeroboam Rebels

26 Now Solomon's servant, Jeroboam son of Nebat, was an Ephraimite from Zeredah. His widowed mother's name was Zeruah. Jeroboam rebelled against Solomon, 27 and this is the reason he rebelled against the king: Solomon had built the supporting terraces ⌊and⌋ repaired the opening in the wall of the city of his father David. 28 Now the man Jeroboam was capable, and Solomon noticed the young man because he was getting things done. So he appointed him over the entire labor force of the house of Joseph.

Ahijah's Prophecy for Jeroboam

29 During that time, the prophet Ahijah the Shilonite met Jeroboam on the road as Jeroboam came out of Jerusalem. Now Ahijah had wrapped himself with a new cloak, and the two of them were alone in the open field. 30 Then Ahijah took hold of the new cloak he had on, tore it into 12 pieces, 31 and said to Jeroboam, "Take 10 pieces for yourself, for this is what the LORD God of Israel says: 'I am about to tear the kingdom out of Solomon's hand. I will give you 10 tribes, 32 but one tribe will remain his because of my servant David and because of Jerusalem, the city I chose out of all the tribes of Israel. 33 For they have abandoned Me; they have bowed the knee to Ashtoreth, the goddess of the Sidonians, to Chemosh, the god of Moab, and to Milcom, the god of the Ammonites. They have not walked in My ways to do right in My eyes and to carry out My statutes and My judgments as his father David did.

34 "'However, I will not take the whole kingdom from his hand but will let him be ruler all the days of his life because of My servant David, whom I chose and who kept My commandments and My statutes. 35 I will take 10 tribes of the kingdom from his son's hand and give them to you. 36 I will give one tribe to his son, so that My servant David will always have a lamp before Me in Jerusalem, the city I chose for Myself to put My name there. 37 I will appoint you, and you will reign as king over all you want, and you will be king over Israel.

38 "'After that, if you obey all I command you, walk in My ways, and do what is right in My sight in order to keep My statutes and My commandments as My servant David did, I will be with you. I will build you a lasting dynasty just as I built for David, and I will give you Israel. 39 I will humble David's

---

a**11:24** LXX; Hb reads *They*   b**11:25** Two Hb mss, LXX, Syr read *Edom* descendants, because of ⌊their unfaithfulness⌋, but not forever.' "a

40 Therefore, Solomon tried to kill Jeroboam, but he fled to Egypt, to Shishak king of Egypt, where he remained until Solomon's death.

Solomon's Death

41 The rest of the events of Solomon's ⌊reign⌋, along with all his accomplishments and his wisdom, are written about in the Book of Solomon's Events. 42 The length of Solomon's reign in Jerusalem over all Israel totaled 40 years. 43 Solomon rested with his fathers and was buried in the city of his father David. His son Rehoboam became king in his place.

Kingdom Divided

Rehoboam vs. Jeroboam

12 Then Rehoboam went to Shechem, for all Israel had gone to Shechem to make him king. 2 When Jeroboam son of Nebat heard ⌊about it⌋, for he was still in Egypt where he had fled from King Solomon's presence, Jeroboam stayed in Egypt.b 3 They summoned him, and Jeroboam and the whole assembly of Israel came and spoke to Rehoboam: 4 "Your father made our yoke harsh. You, therefore, lighten your father's harsh service and the heavy yoke he put on us, and we will serve you."

5 Rehoboam replied, "Go home for three days and then return to me." So the people left. 6 Then King Rehoboam consulted with the elders who had served his father Solomon when he was alive, asking, "How do you advise me to respond to these people?"

Advice of Elders: Rejected

7 They replied, "Today if you will be a servant to these people and serve them,

and if you respond to them by speaking kind words to them, they will be your servants forever."

8 But he rejected the advice of the elders who had advised him and consulted with the young men who had grown up with him and served him. 9 He asked them, "What message do you advise that we send back to these people who said to me, 'Lighten the yoke your father put on us'?"

Advice of Young Men: Accepted

10 Then the young men who had grown up with him told him, "This is what you should say to these people who said to you, 'Your father made our yoke heavy, but you, make it lighter on us!' This is what you should tell them: 'My little finger is thicker than my father's loins! 11 Although my father burdened you with a heavy yoke, I will add to your yoke; my father disciplined you with whips, but I will discipline you with barbed whips.' "c

King Rehoboam Threatens Jeroboam

12 So Jeroboam and all the people came to Rehoboam on the third day, as the king had ordered: "Return to me on the third day." 13 Then the king answered the people harshly. He rejected the advice the elders had given him 14 and spoke to them according to the young men's advice: "My father made your yoke heavy, but I will add to your yoke; my father disciplined you with whips, but I will discipline you with barbed whips."c

Israel Rebels

15 The king did not listen to the people, because the turn of events came from the LORD to carry out His word, which the LORD had spoken through

a**11:38-39** LXX omits *and I will give . . . but not forever*   b**12:2** LXX, Vg, 2 Ch 10:2 read *Jeroboam returned from Egypt*   c**12:11,14** Lit *with scorpions*

Ahijah the Shilonite to Jeroboam son of Nebat. [16] When all Israel saw that the king had not listened to them, the people answered him:

> What portion do we have in David?
> We have no inheritance in the son
>   of Jesse.
> Israel, return to your tents;
> David, now look
>   after your own house!

So Israel went to their tents, [17] but Rehoboam reigned over the Israelites living in the cities of Judah.

[18] Then King Rehoboam sent Adoram,[a] who was in charge of forced labor, but all Israel stoned him to death. King Rehoboam managed to get into the chariot and flee to Jerusalem. [19] Israel is in rebellion against the house of David until today.

Jeroboam, King of Israel

[20] When all Israel heard that Jeroboam had come back, they summoned him to the assembly and made him king over all Israel.

Rehoboam Prepares for War

No one followed the house of David except the tribe of Judah alone. [21] When Rehoboam arrived in Jerusalem, he mobilized 180,000 choice warriors from the entire house of Judah and the tribe of Benjamin to fight against the house of Israel to restore the kingdom to Rehoboam son of Solomon.

God Prohibits War— Rehoboam Obeys

[22] But a revelation from God came to Shemaiah, the man of God: [23] "Say to Rehoboam son of Solomon, king of Judah, to the whole house of Judah and Benjamin, and to the rest of the people, [24] 'This is what the LORD says: You are not to march up and fight against your brothers, the Israelites. Each of you must return home, for I have done this.'"

So they listened to what the LORD said and went back as He had told them.

Jeroboam Settles in Ephraim

[25] Jeroboam built Shechem in the hill country of Ephraim and lived there. From there he went out and built Penuel. [26] Jeroboam said to himself, "The way things are going⌋ now, the kingdom might return to the house of David. [27] If these people regularly go to offer sacrifices in the LORD's temple in Jerusalem, the heart of these people will return to their lord, Rehoboam king of Judah. They will murder me and go back to the king of Judah." [28] So the king sought advice.

Jeroboam's Idolatry

Then he made two gold calves, and he said to the people, "Going to Jerusalem is too difficult for you. Israel, here is your God[b] who brought you out of the land of Egypt." [29] He set up one in Bethel, and put the other in Dan. [30] This led to sin; the people walked ⌊in procession⌋ before one of the calves all the way to Dan.

[31] Jeroboam also built shrines on the •high places and set up priests from every class of people who were not Levites. [32] Jeroboam made a festival in the eighth month on the fifteenth day of the month, like the festival in Judah. He offered sacrifices on the altar; he made this offering in Bethel to sacrifice to the calves he had set up. He also stationed in Bethel the priests for the high places he had set up. [33] He offered sacrifices on[c] the altar he had set up in Bethel on the

---

[a]12:18 LXX reads *Adoniram*; 1 Kg 4:6; 5:14   [b]12:28 Or *here are your gods*   [c]12:33 Or *He went up to*

fifteenth day of the eighth month, the month he had decided on his own. He made a festival for the Israelites, offered sacrifices on the altar, and burned incense.

Man of God Warns Jeroboam

13 A man of God came from Judah to Bethel by a revelation from the LORD while Jeroboam was standing beside the altar to burn incense. ² The man of God cried out against the altar by a revelation from the LORD: "Altar, altar, this is what the LORD says, 'A son will be born to the house of David, named Josiah, and he will sacrifice on you the priests of the •high places who are burning incense on you. Human bones will be burned on you.'" ³ He gave a sign that day. He said, "This is the sign that the LORD has spoken: 'The altar will now be ripped apart, and the ashes that are on it will be spilled out.'"

Jeroboam's Withered Hand

⁴ When the king heard the word that the man of God had cried out against the altar at Bethel, Jeroboam stretched out his hand from the altar and said, "Arrest him!" But the hand he stretched out against him withered, and he could not pull it back to himself. ⁵ The altar was ripped apart, and the ashes spilled off the altar, according to the sign that the man of God had given by the word of the LORD.

Jeroboam Receives Mercy

⁶ Then the king responded to the man of God, "Please plead for the favor of the LORD your God and pray for me so that my hand may be restored to me." So the man of God pleaded for the favor of the

LORD, and the king's hand was restored to him and became as it had been at first.

⁷ Then the king declared to the man of God, "Come home with me, refresh yourself, and I'll give you a reward."

⁸ But the man of God replied, "If you were to give me half your house, I still wouldn't go with you, and I wouldn't eat bread or drink water in this place, ⁹ for this is what I was commanded by the word of the LORD: 'You must not eat bread or drink water or go back the way you came.'" ¹⁰ So he went another way; he did not go back by the way he had come to Bethel.

Old Prophet of Bethel Finds Man of God

¹¹ Now a certain old prophet was living in Bethel. His son[a] came and told him all the deeds that the man of God had done that day in Bethel. His sons also told their father the words that he had spoken to the king. ¹² Then their father said to them, "Which way did he go?" His sons had seen[b] the way taken by the man of God who had come from Judah. ¹³ Then he said to his sons, "Saddle the donkey for me." So they saddled the donkey for him, and he got on it. ¹⁴ He followed the man of God and found him sitting under an oak tree. He asked him, "Are you the man of God who came from Judah?"

"I am," he said.

¹⁵ Then he said to him, "Come home with me and eat bread."

¹⁶ But he answered, "I cannot go back with you, eat bread, or drink water with you in this place, ¹⁷ for a message came to me by the word of the LORD: 'You must not eat bread or drink water there or go back by the way you came.'"

ᵃ**13:11** Some Hb mss, LXX, Syr, Vg read *sons*   ᵇ**13:12** LXX, Syr, Tg, Vg read *sons showed him*

Old Prophet Deceives Man of God

18 He said to him, "I am also a prophet like you. An angel spoke to me by the word of the LORD: 'Bring him back with you to your house so that he may eat bread and drink water.'" The old prophet deceived him, 19 and the man of God went back with him, ate bread in his house, and drank water.

God Punishes Man of God

20 While they were sitting at the table, the word of the LORD came to the prophet who had brought him back, 21 and the prophet cried out to the man of God who had come from Judah, "This is what the LORD says: 'Because you rebelled against the command of the LORD and did not keep the commandment that the LORD your God commanded you, 22 but you went back and ate bread and drank water in the place that He said to you: Do not eat bread and do not drink water, your corpse will never reach the grave of your fathers.'"

23 So after he had eaten bread and after he had drunk, the old prophet saddled the donkey for the prophet he had brought back. 24 When he left,ᵃ a lion met him along the way and killed him. His corpse was thrown on the road, and the donkey was standing beside it; the lion was standing beside the corpse too. 25 There were men passing by who saw the corpse thrown on the road and the lion standing beside it, and they went and spoke ⌊about it⌋ in the city where the old prophet lived. 26 When the prophet who had brought him back from his way heard ⌊about it⌋, he said, "He is the man of God who disobeyed the command of the LORD. The LORD has given him to the lion, and it has mauled him and killed him, according to the word of the LORD that He spoke to him."

Old Prophet Recovers Body

27 Then the old prophet instructed his sons, "Saddle the donkey for me." They saddled it, 28 and he went and found the corpse of the man of God thrown on the road with the donkey and the lion standing beside the corpse. The lion had not eaten the corpse or mauled the donkey. 29 So the prophet lifted the corpse of the man of God and laid it on the donkey and brought it back. The old prophet came into the city to mourn and to bury him. 30 Then he laid the corpse in his own grave, and they mourned over him: "Oh, my brother!"

31 After he had buried him, he said to his sons, "When I die, you must bury me in the grave where the man of God is buried; lay my bones beside his bones, 32 for the word that he cried out by a revelation from the LORD against the altar in Bethel and against all the shrines of the high places in the cities of Samaria is certain to happen."

Jeroboam Fails to Repent

33 After all this Jeroboam did not repent of his evil way but again set up priests from every class of people for the high places. Whoever so desired it, he ordained, and they became priests of the high places. 34 For the house of Jeroboam, this was the sin that caused it to be wiped out and annihilated from the face of the earth.

Jeroboam Consults Prophet Ahijah

14 At that time Abijah son of Jeroboam became sick. 2 Jeroboam said to his wife, "Go disguise yourself, so they won't know that you're Jeroboam's wife, and go to Shiloh. Ahijah the prophet is there; it was he who told about me becoming king over this peo-

ᵃ13:23-24 LXX reads *donkey, and he turned* 24 *and left, and*

ple. [3] Take with you 10 loaves of bread, some cakes, and a jar of honey, and go to him. He will tell you what will happen to the boy."

[4] Jeroboam's wife did that: she went to Shiloh and arrived at Ahijah's house. Ahijah could not see; his gaze was fixed[a] due to his age. [5] But the LORD had said to Ahijah, "Jeroboam's wife is coming soon to ask you about her son, for he is sick. You are to say such and such to her. When she arrives, she will be disguised."

Prophet's Bad News

[6] When Ahijah heard the sound of her feet entering the door, he said, "Come in, wife of Jeroboam! Why are you disguised? I have bad news for you. [7] Go tell Jeroboam, 'This is what the LORD God of Israel says: I raised you up from among the people, appointed you ruler over My people Israel, [8] tore the kingdom away from the house of David, and gave it to you. But you were not like My servant David, who kept My commandments and followed Me with all of his heart, doing only what is right in My eyes. [9] You behaved more wickedly than all who were before you. In order to provoke Me, you have proceeded to make for yourself other gods and cast images, but you have flung Me behind your back. [10] Because of all this, I am about to bring disaster on the house of Jeroboam:

Disaster on House of Jeroboam

I will eliminate all of
   Jeroboam's males,[b]
both slave and free,[c] in Israel;
I will sweep away the house
   of Jeroboam
   as one sweeps away dung until it is
   all gone!

[11] Anyone who belongs to Jeroboam
   and dies in the city,
the dogs will eat,
and anyone who dies in the field,
the birds of the sky will eat,
for the LORD has said it!'

[12] "As for you, get up and go to your house. When your feet enter the city, the boy will die. [13] All Israel will mourn for him and bury him, for this one alone out of Jeroboam's ⌐sons⌐ will come to the grave, because in him ⌐alone⌐ out of the house of Jeroboam something was found pleasing to the LORD God of Israel. [14] The LORD will raise up for Himself a king over Israel, who will eliminate the house of Jeroboam. This is the day, yes,[c] even today! [15] For the LORD will strike Israel ⌐and the people will shake⌐ as a reed shakes in water. He will uproot Israel from this good soil that He gave to their forefathers. He will scatter them beyond the Euphrates because they made their •Asherah poles, provoking the LORD. [16] He will give up Israel, because of Jeroboam's sins that he committed and caused Israel to commit."

Jeroboam's Son Dies

[17] Then Jeroboam's wife got up and left and went to Tirzah. As she was crossing the threshold of the house, the boy died. [18] He was buried, and all Israel mourned for him, according to the word of the LORD He had spoken through His servant Ahijah the prophet.

[19] As for the rest of the events of Jeroboam's ⌐reign⌐, how he waged war and how he reigned, note that they are written about in the Historical Record of Israel's Kings. [20] The length of Jeroboam's reign was 22 years. He rested with his fathers, and his son Nadab became king in his place.

---

[a]14:4 Lit see, for his eyes stood; 1 Sm 4:15   [b]14:10 Lit eliminate Jeroboam's one who urinates against the wall
[c]14:10,14 Hb obscure

Judah's King Rehoboam

21 Now Rehoboam, Solomon's son, reigned in Judah. Rehoboam was 41 years old when he became king; he reigned 17 years in Jerusalem, the city the LORD had chosen from all the tribes of Israel to put His name. Rehoboam's mother's name was Naamah the Ammonite.

Judah Does Evil

22 Judah did what was evil in the LORD's eyes. They provoked Him to jealous anger more than all that their ancestors had done with the sins they committed. 23 They also built for themselves •high places, sacred pillars, and Asherah poles on every high hill and under every green tree; 24 there were even male shrine prostitutes in the land. They imitated all the abominations of the nations the LORD had dispossessed before the Israelites.

King Shishak of Egypt Sacks Jerusalem

25 In the fifth year of King Rehoboam, Shishak king of Egypt went to war against Jerusalem. 26 He seized the treasuries of the LORD's temple and the treasuries of the royal palace. He took everything. He took all the gold shields that Solomon had made. 27 King Rehoboam made bronze shields in their place and committed them into the care of the captains of the royal escorts[a] who guarded the entrance to the king's palace. 28 Whenever the king entered the LORD's temple, the royal escorts would carry the shields, then they would take them back to the royal escorts' armory.

29 The rest of the events of Rehoboam's ⌊reign⌋, along with all his accomplishments, are written about in the Historical Record of Judah's Kings. 30 There was war between Rehoboam and Jeroboam throughout their reigns. 31 Rehoboam rested with his fathers and was buried with his fathers in the city of David. His mother's name was Naamah the Ammonite. His son Abijam[b] became king in his place.

Judah's King Abijam Sins

15 In the eighteenth year of ⌊Israel's⌋ King Jeroboam son of Nebat, Abijam became king over Judah; 2 he reigned three years in Jerusalem. His mother's name was Maacah daughter[c] of Abishalom.

3 Abijam walked in all the sins his father had done before him, and he was not completely devoted to the LORD his God as his ancestor David had been. 4 But because of David, the LORD his God gave him a lamp in Jerusalem to raise up his son after him and to establish Jerusalem 5 because David did what was right in the LORD's eyes, and he did not turn aside from anything He had commanded him all the days of his life, except in the matter of Uriah the Hittite.

6 There had been war between Rehoboam and Jeroboam all the days of Rehoboam's life. 7 The rest of the events of Abijam's ⌊reign⌋, along with all his accomplishments, are written about in the Historical Record of Judah's Kings. There was also war between Abijam and Jeroboam. 8 Abijam rested with his fathers and was buried in the city of David. His son Asa became king in his place.

Judah's King Asa Does Right

9 In the twentieth year of Israel's King Jeroboam, Asa became king of Judah; 10 he reigned 41 years in Jerusalem. His grandmother's[d] name was Maacah daughter[c] of Abishalom.

---

a **14:27** Lit *the runners*   b **14:31** = Abijah; 2 Ch 13   c **15:2,10** Possibly *granddaughter*; 2 Ch 13:2   d **15:10** Lit *mother's*

[11] Asa did what was right in the LORD's eyes, as his ancestor David had done. [12] He banished the male shrine prostitutes from the land and removed all of the idols that his fathers had made. [13] He also removed his grandmother[a] Maacah from being queen mother because she had made an obscene image of •Asherah. Asa chopped down her obscene image and burned it in the Kidron Valley. [14] The •high places were not taken away; but Asa's heart was completely with the LORD his entire life. [15] He brought his father's consecrated gifts and his own consecrated gifts into the LORD's temple: silver, gold, and utensils.

War: Judah vs. Israel

[16] There was war between Asa and Baasha king of Israel throughout their reigns. [17] Israel's King Baasha went to war against Judah. He built Ramah in order to deny anyone access to Judah's King Asa. [18] So Asa withdrew all the silver and gold that remained in the treasuries of the LORD's temple and the treasuries of the royal palace and put it into the hands of his servants. Then King Asa sent them to Ben-hadad son of Tabrimmon son of Hezion king of Aram who lived in Damascus, saying, [19] "There is a treaty between me and you, between my father and your father. Look, I have sent you a gift of silver and gold. Go and break your treaty with Baasha king of Israel so that he will withdraw from me."

King Ben-hadad of Aram Joins King Asa and Judah

[20] Ben-hadad listened to King Asa and sent the commanders of his armies against the cities of Israel. He attacked Ijon, Dan, Abel-beth-maacah, all Chinneroth, and the whole land of Naphtali.

[21] When Baasha heard ⌊about it⌋, he quit building Ramah and stayed in Tirzah. [22] Then King Asa gave a command to everyone without exception in Judah, and they carried away the stones of Ramah and the timbers Baasha had built it with. Then King Asa built Geba of Benjamin and Mizpah with them.

[23] The rest of all the events of Asa's ⌊reign⌋, along with all his might, all his accomplishments, and the cities he built, are written about in the Historical Record of Judah's Kings. But in his old age he developed a disease in his feet. [24] Then Asa rested with his fathers and was buried in the city of his forefather David. His son Jehoshaphat became king in his place.

Israel's Evil Kings

Israel's King Nadab: Evil

[25] Nadab son of Jeroboam became king over Israel in the second year of Judah's King Asa; he reigned over Israel two years. [26] Nadab did what was evil in the LORD's sight and followed the example of his father and the sin he had caused Israel to commit.

[27] Then Baasha son of Ahijah of the house of Issachar conspired against Nadab, and Baasha struck him down at Gibbethon of the Philistines while Nadab and all Israel were besieging Gibbethon. [28] In the third year of Judah's King Asa, Baasha killed Nadab and reigned in his place.

[29] When Baasha became king, he struck down the entire house of Jeroboam. He did not leave Jeroboam anyone alive until he had destroyed his family according to the word of the LORD He had spoken through His servant Ahijah the Shilonite. [30] This was because of Jeroboam's sins he had committed and had

---

[a]**15:13** Lit *mother*

caused Israel to commit in the provocation he had provoked the LORD God of Israel with. [31] The rest of the events of Nadab's ⌊reign⌋, along with all his accomplishments, are written about in the Historical Record of Israel's Kings. [32] There was war between Asa and Baasha king of Israel throughout their reigns.

Israel's King Baasha: Evil

[33] In the third year of Judah's King Asa, Baasha son of Ahijah became king over all Israel at Tirzah; ⌊he reigned⌋ 24 years. [34] He did what was evil in the LORD's sight and followed the example of Jeroboam and the sin he had caused Israel to commit.

16 Now the word of the LORD came to Jehu son of Hanani against Baasha: [2] "Because I raised you up from the dust and made you ruler over My people Israel, but you have walked in the way of Jeroboam and have caused My people Israel to sin, provoking Me with their sins, [3] take note: I will sweep away Baasha and his house, and I will make your house like the house of Jeroboam son of Nebat:

[4]   Anyone who belongs to Baasha
    and dies in the city,
    the dogs will eat,
    and anyone who is his and dies
    in the field,
    the birds of the sky will eat.

[5] The rest of the events of Baasha's ⌊reign⌋, along with all his accomplishments and might, are written about in the Historical Record of Israel's Kings. [6] Baasha rested with his fathers and was buried in Tirzah. His son Elah became king in his place. [7] Through the prophet Jehu son of Hanani the word of the LORD also came against Baasha and against his house because of all the evil he had done in the LORD's sight, provoking Him with the work of his hands and being like the house of Jeroboam, and because Baasha had struck down the house of Jeroboam.

Israel's King Elah

[8] In the twenty-sixth year of Judah's King Asa, Elah son of Baasha became king over Israel in Tirzah; ⌊he reigned⌋ two years.

Zimri Assassinates Elah

[9] His servant Zimri, commander of half his chariots, conspired against him while Elah was in Tirzah drinking himself drunk in the house of Arza, who was in charge of the household at Tirzah. [10] In the twenty-seventh year of Judah's King Asa, Zimri went in, struck Elah down, and killed him. Then Zimri became king in his place.

King Zimri Destroys House of Baasha

[11] When he became king, as soon as he was seated on his throne, Zimri struck down the entire house of Baasha. He did not leave him a single male,[a] whether of his kinsmen or his friends. [12] So Zimri exterminated the entire house of Baasha, according to the word of the LORD He had spoken against Baasha through Jehu the prophet, [13] because of all the sins of Baasha and the sins of his son Elah, which they committed and caused Israel to commit, provoking the LORD God of Israel with their worthless idols.

[14] The rest of the events of Elah's ⌊reign⌋, along with all his accomplishments, are written about in the Historical Record of Israel's Kings.

[a]**16:11** Lit *him one who urinates against the wall*

Israel's King Zimri: Evil

15 In the twenty-seventh year of Judah's King Asa, Zimri became king for seven days in Tirzah. Now the troops were encamped against Gibbethon of the Philistines. 16 When the encamped troops heard that Zimri had not only conspired but had also struck down the king, then all Israel made Omri, the army commander, king over Israel that very day in the camp. 17 Omri along with all Israel marched up from Gibbethon and besieged Tirzah. 18 When Zimri saw that the city was captured, he entered the citadel of the royal palace and burned down the royal palace over himself. He died 19 because of his sin he committed by doing what was evil in the LORD's sight and by following the example of Jeroboam and the sin he caused Israel to commit.

20 The rest of the events of Zimri's ⌊reign⌋, along with the conspiracy that he instigated, are written about in the Historical Record of Israel's Kings. 21 At that time the people of Israel were split in half: half the people followed Tibni son of Ginath, to make him king, and half followed Omri. 22 However, the people who followed Omri proved stronger than those who followed Tibni of Ginath. So Tibni died and Omri became king.

Israel's King Omri: Evil

23 In the thirty-first year of Judah's King Asa, Omri became king over Israel; ⌊he reigned⌋ 12 years. He reigned six years in Tirzah, 24 then he bought the hill of Samaria from Shemer for 150 pounds of silver,a and he built up the hill. He named the city he built Samariab based on the name Shemer, the owner of the hill.

25 Omri did what was evil in the LORD's sight; he did more evil than all who were before him. 26 He followed the example of Jeroboam son of Nebat and the sins he caused Israel to commit, provoking the LORD God of Israel with their worthless idols. 27 The rest of the events of Omri's ⌊reign⌋, along with his accomplishments and the might he exercised, are written about in the Historical Record of Israel's Kings. 28 Omri rested with his fathers and was buried in Samaria. His son Ahab became king in his place.

Israel's King Ahab: Most Evil

29 Ahab son of Omri became king over Israel in the thirty-eighth year of Judah's King Asa; Ahab son of Omri reigned over Israel in Samaria 22 years. 30 But Ahab son of Omri did what was evil in the LORD's sight more than all who were before him. 31 Then, as if following the sin of Jeroboam son of Nebat were a trivial matter, he married Jezebel, the daughter of Ethbaal king of the Sidonians, and then proceeded to serve •Baal and worship him. 32 He set up an altar for Baal in the temple of Baal that he had built in Samaria. 33 Ahab also made an •Asherah pole. Ahab did more to provoke the LORD God of Israel than all the kings of Israel who were before him.

34 During his reign, Hiel the Bethelite built Jericho. At the cost of Abiram his firstborn, he laid its foundation, and at the cost of Segub his youngest, he set up its gates, according to the word of the LORD He had spoken through Joshua son of Nun.

Elijah the Prophet

Elijah Announces Famine

17 Now Elijah the Tishbite, from the Gilead settlers,c said to Ahab, "As the LORD God of Israel lives, I stand before Him, and there will be no dew or

---

a 16:24 Lit for two talents   b 16:24 = Belonging to Shemer's Clan   c 17:1 LXX reads from Tishbe of Gilead rain during these years except by my command!"

[2] Then a revelation from the LORD came to him: [3] "Leave here, turn eastward, and hide yourself at the •Wadi Cherith where it enters the Jordan. [4] You are to drink from the wadi. I have commanded the ravens to provide for you there."

[5] So he did what the LORD commanded. Elijah left and lived by the Wadi Cherith where it enters the Jordan. [6] The ravens kept bringing him bread and meat in the morning and in the evening, and he drank from the wadi. [7] After a while, the wadi dried up because there had been no rain in the land.

Elijah and Widow of Zarephath

[8] Then the word of the LORD came to him: [9] "Get up, go to Zarephath that belongs to Sidon, and stay there. Look, I have commanded a woman who is a widow to provide for you there." [10] So Elijah got up and went to Zarephath. When he arrived at the city gate, there was a widow woman gathering wood. Elijah called to her and said, "Please bring me a little water in a cup and let me drink." [11] As she went to get it, he called to her and said, "Please bring me a piece of bread in your hand."

[12] But she said, "As the LORD your God lives, I don't have anything baked—only a handful of flour in the jar and a bit of oil in the jug. Just now, I am gathering a couple of sticks in order to go prepare it for myself and my son so we can eat it and die."

Miracle of Oil and Flour

[13] Then Elijah said to her, "Don't be afraid; go and do as you have said. Only make me a small loaf from it and bring it

out to me. Afterwards, you may make some for yourself and your son, [14] for this is what the LORD God of Israel says: 'The flour jar will not become empty and the oil jug will not run dry until the day the LORD sends rain on the surface of the land.'"

[15] So she proceeded to do according to the word of Elijah. She and he and her household ate for many days. [16] The flour jar did not become empty, and the oil jug did not run dry, according to the word of the LORD He had spoken through[a] Elijah.

Elijah Revives Widow's Son

[17] After this, the son of the woman who owned the house became ill. His illness became very severe until no breath remained in him. [18] She said to Elijah, "Man of God, what do we have in common? Have you come to remind me of my guilt and to kill my son?"

[19] But Elijah said to her, "Give me your son." So he took him from her arms, brought him up to the upper room where he was staying, and laid him on his own bed. [20] Then he cried out to the LORD and said, "My LORD God, have You also brought tragedy on the widow I am staying with by killing her son?" [21] Then he stretched himself out over the boy three times. He cried out to the LORD and said, "My LORD God, please let this boy's life return to him!"

[22] So the LORD listened to Elijah's voice, and the boy's life returned to him, and he lived. [23] Then Elijah took the boy, brought him down from the upper room into the house, and gave him to his mother. Elijah said, "Look, your son is alive."

[24] Then the woman said to Elijah, "Now I know you are a man of God and the LORD's word in your mouth is the truth."

[a] **17:16** Lit *by the hand of*

God Sends Elijah to Ahab

18 After a long time, the word of the LORD came to Elijah in the third year: "Go and present yourself to Ahab. I will send rain on the surface of the land." ² So Elijah went to present himself to Ahab.

King Ahab and Obadiah Look for Grass

The famine was severe in Samaria. ³ Ahab called for Obadiah, who was in charge of the palace. Obadiah was a man who greatly •feared the LORD ⁴ and took 100 prophets and hid them, 50 men to a cave, and provided them with food and water when Jezebel slaughtered the LORD's prophets. ⁵ Ahab said to Obadiah, "Go throughout the land to every spring of water and to every •wadi. Perhaps we'll find grass so we can keep the horses and mules alive and not have to destroy any cattle." ⁶ They divided the land between them in order to cover it. Ahab went one way by himself, and Obadiah went the other way by himself.

Elijah Meets Obadiah

⁷ While Obadiah was ⌊walking⌋ along the road, Elijah suddenly met him. When Obadiah recognized him, he fell with his face ⌊to the ground⌋ and said, "Is it you, my lord Elijah?"

⁸ "It is I," he replied. "Go tell your lord, 'Elijah is here!'"

Obadiah's Fears

⁹ But Obadiah said, "What sin have I committed, that you are handing your servant over to Ahab to put me to death? ¹⁰ As the LORD your God lives, there is no nation or kingdom where my lord has not sent someone to search for you. When they said, 'He is not here,' he made that kingdom or nation swear they had not found you.

¹¹ "Now you say, 'Go tell your lord, "Elijah is here!"' ¹² But when I leave you, the Spirit of the LORD may carry you off to some place I don't know. Then when I go report to Ahab and he doesn't find you, he will kill me. But ⌊I⌋, your servant, have feared the LORD from my youth. ¹³ Wasn't it reported to my lord what I did when Jezebel slaughtered the LORD's prophets? I hid 100 of the prophets of the LORD, 50 men to a cave, and I provided them with food and water. ¹⁴ Now you say, 'Go tell your lord, "Elijah is here!"' He will kill me!"

¹⁵ Then Elijah said, "As the LORD of •Hosts lives, before whom I stand, today I will present myself to Ahab."

¹⁶ Obadiah went to meet Ahab and report to him. Then Ahab went to meet Elijah. ¹⁷ When Ahab saw Elijah, Ahab said to him, "Is that you, you destroyer of Israel?"

Elijah Confronts King Ahab

¹⁸ He replied, "I have not destroyed Israel, but you and your father's house have, because you have abandoned the LORD's commandments and followed the •Baals. ¹⁹ Now summon all Israel to meet me at Mount Carmel, along with the 450 prophets of Baal and the 400 prophets of •Asherah who eat at Jezebel's table."

Elijah vs. Baal Prophets: Mount Carmel

²⁰ So Ahab summoned all the Israelites and gathered the prophets at Mount Carmel. ²¹ Then Elijah approached all the people and said, "How long will you hesitate between two opinions? If •Yahweh is God, follow Him. But if Baal, follow him." But the people didn't answer him a word.

²² Then Elijah said to the people, "I am the only remaining prophet of the LORD, but Baal's prophets are 450 men. ²³ Let

two bulls be given to us. They are to choose one bull for themselves, cut it in pieces, and place it on the wood but not light the fire. I will prepare the other bull and place it on the wood but not light the fire. 24 Then you call on the name of your god, and I will call on the name of Yahweh. The God who answers with fire, He is God."

All the people answered, "That ᴸsoundsᴶ good."

25 Then Elijah said to the prophets of Baal, "Since you are so numerous, choose for yourselves one bull and prepare it first. Then call on the name of your god but don't light the fire."

26 So they took the bull that he gave them, prepared it, and called on the name of Baal from morning until noon, saying, "Baal, answer us!" But there was no sound; no one answered. Then they did their lame dance around the altar they had made.

27 At noon Elijah mocked them. He said, "Shout loudly, for he's a god! Maybe he's thinking it over; maybe he has wandered away;[a] or maybe he's on the road. Perhaps he's sleeping and will wake up!" 28 They shouted loudly, and cut themselves with knives and spears, according to their custom, until blood gushed out on them. 29 All afternoon, they kept on raving until the offering of the evening sacrifice, but there was no sound, no one answered, no one paid attention.

30 Then Elijah said to all the people, "Come near me." So all the people approached him. Then he repaired the LORD's altar that had been torn down: 31 Elijah took 12 stones—according to the number of the tribes of the sons of Jacob, to whom the word of the LORD had come, saying, "Israel will be your

name"— 32 and he built an altar with the stones in the name of Yahweh. Then he made a trench around the altar large enough to hold about four gallons.[b][c] 33 Next, he arranged the wood, cut up the bull, and placed it on the wood. He said, "Fill four water pots with water and pour it on the offering to be burned and on the wood." 34 Then he said, "A second time!" and they did it a second time. And then he said, "A third time!" and they did it a third time. 35 So the water ran all around the altar; he even filled the trench with water.

36 At the time for offering the ᴸeveningᴶ sacrifice, Elijah the prophet approached ᴸthe altarᴶ and said, "LORD God of Abraham, Isaac, and Israel, today let it be known that You are God in Israel and I am Your servant, and that at Your word I have done all these things. 37 Answer me, LORD! Answer me so that this people will know that You, Yahweh, are God and that You have turned their hearts back."

Elijah Triumphs—Baal Prophets Die

38 Then Yahweh's fire fell and consumed the •burnt offering, the wood, the stones, and the dust, and it licked up the water that was in the trench. 39 When all the people saw it, they fell facedown and said, "Yahweh, He is God! Yahweh, He is God!"

40 Then Elijah ordered them, "Seize the prophets of Baal! Do not let even one of them escape." So they seized them, and Elijah brought them down to the •Wadi Kishon and slaughtered them there. 41 Elijah said to Ahab, "Go up, eat and drink, for there is the sound of a rainstorm."

Rains Arrive

42 So Ahab went to eat and drink, but Elijah went up to the summit of Carmel. He bowed down to the ground and put

---

[a]18:27 Or has turned aside, possibly to relieve himself   [b]18:32 LXX reads trench containing two measures of seed
[c]18:32 Lit altar corresponding to a house of two seahs of seed

his face between his knees. 43 Then he said to his servant, "Go up and look toward the sea."

So he went up, looked, and said, "There's nothing."

Seven times Elijah said, "Go back." 44 On the seventh time, he reported, "There's a cloud as small as a man's hand coming from the sea."

Then Elijah said, "Go and tell Ahab, 'Get ⌞your chariot⌟ ready and go down so the rain doesn't stop you.'"

45 In a little while, the sky grew dark with clouds and wind, and there was a downpour. So Ahab got in ⌞his chariot⌟ and went to Jezreel. 46 The power of the LORD was on Elijah, and he tucked his mantle under his belt and ran ahead of Ahab to the entrance of Jezreel.

Jezebel Threatens Elijah

19 Ahab told Jezebel everything that Elijah had done and how he had killed all the prophets with the sword. 2 So Jezebel sent a messenger to Elijah, saying, "May the gods punish me and do so severely if I don't make your life like the life of one of them by this time tomorrow!"

Elijah Flees—and Despairs

3 Then Elijah became afraid[a] and immediately ran for his life. When he came to Beer-sheba that belonged to Judah, he left his servant there, 4 but he went on a day's journey into the wilderness. He sat down under a broom tree and prayed that he might die. He said, "⌞I have had⌟ enough! LORD, take my life, for I'm no better than my fathers." 5 Then he lay down and slept under the broom tree.

Touched by an Angel

Suddenly, an angel touched him. The angel told him, "Get up and eat." 6 Then he looked, and there at his head was a loaf of bread baked over hot stones and a jug of water. So he ate and drank and lay down again. 7 Then the angel of the LORD returned a second time and touched him. He said, "Get up and eat, or the journey will be too much for you." 8 So he got up, ate, and drank.

Elijah's Journey to Mt. Horeb

Then on the strength from that food, he walked 40 days and 40 nights to Horeb, the mountain of God. 9 He entered a cave there and spent the night.

Elijah Encounters God

Then the word of the LORD came to him, and He said to him, "What are you doing here, Elijah?"

10 He replied, "I have been very zealous for the LORD God of •Hosts, but the Israelites have abandoned Your covenant, torn down Your altars, and killed Your prophets with the sword. I alone am left, and they are looking for me to take my life."

11 Then He said, "Go out and stand on the mountain in the LORD's presence."

At that moment, the LORD passed by. A great and mighty wind was tearing at the mountains and was shattering cliffs before the LORD, but the LORD was not in the wind. After the wind there was an earthquake, but the LORD was not in the earthquake. 12 After the earthquake there was a fire, but the LORD was not in the fire. And after the fire there was a voice, a soft whisper. 13 When Elijah heard ⌞it⌟, he wrapped his face in his mantle and went out and stood at the entrance of the cave.

Suddenly, a voice came to him and said, "What are you doing here, Elijah?"

14 "I have been very zealous for the LORD God of Hosts," he replied, "but the

---

a 19:3 Some Hb mss, LXX, Syr, Vg; MT reads he saw

Israelites have abandoned Your covenant, torn down Your altars, and killed
Your prophets with the sword. I alone
am left, and they're looking for me to
take my life."

God's Word to Elijah

15 Then the LORD said to him, "Go and
return by the way you came to the Wilderness of Damascus. When you arrive,
you are to anoint Hazael as king over
Aram. 16 You are to anoint Jehu son of
Nimshi as king over Israel and Elisha son
of Shaphat from Abel-meholah as
prophet in your place. 17 Then Jehu will
put to death whoever escapes the sword
of Hazael, and Elisha will put to death
whoever escapes the sword of Jehu.
18 But I will leave 7,000 in Israel—every
knee that has not bowed to •Baal and every mouth that has not kissed him."

Elijah Appoints Elisha

19 Elijah left there and found Elisha son
of Shaphat as he was plowing. Twelve
teams of oxen were in front of him, and
he was with the twelfth team. Elijah
walked by him and threw his mantle
over him. 20 Elisha left the oxen, ran to
follow Elijah, and said, "Please let me
kiss my father and mother, and then I
will follow you."

"Go on back," he replied, "for what
have I done to you?"

21 So he turned back from following
him, took the team of oxen, and slaughtered them. With the oxen's wooden
yoke and plow, he cooked the meat and
gave it to the people, and they ate. Then
he left, followed Elijah, and served him.

King Ben-hadad
Challenges King Ahab

20 Now Ben-hadad king of Aram assembled his entire army. Thirty-
two kings, along with horses and chari-

otry, were with him. He marched up, besieged Samaria, and fought against it.
2 He sent messengers into the city to
Ahab king of Israel and said to him,
"This is what Ben-hadad says: 3 'Your silver and your gold are mine! And your
best wives and children are mine as
well!'"

4 Then the king of Israel answered,
"Just as you say, my lord king: I am
yours, along with all that I have."

5 The messengers then returned and
said, "This is what Ben-hadad says: 'I
have sent ⌐messengers⌐ to you, saying:
Your silver, your gold, your wives, and
your children you are to give to me. 6 But
at this time tomorrow I will send my servants to you, and they will search your
palace and your servants' houses. Whatever is precious to you, they will lay
their hands on and take away.'"

Ahab Rebuffs Ben-hadad

7 Then the king of Israel called for all
the elders of the land and said, "Think it
over and you will see that this one is
only looking for trouble, for he demanded my wives, my children, my silver, and my gold, and I didn't turn him
down."

8 All the elders and all the people said
to him, "Don't listen or agree."

9 So he said to Ben-hadad's messengers, "Say to my lord the king, 'Everything you demanded of your servant the
first time, I will do, but this thing I cannot do.'" So the messengers left and
took word back to him.

10 Then Ben-hadad sent ⌐messengers⌐ to
him and said, "May the gods punish me
and do so severely if Samaria's dust
amounts to a handful for each of the people who follow me."

11 The king of Israel answered, "Say
this: 'Let not him who puts on his armor
boast like the one who takes it off.'"

Ben-hadad Prepares for Battle

[12] When Ben-hadad heard this response, while he and the kings were drinking in the tents, he said to his servants, "Take ⌊your⌋ positions." So they took ⌊their⌋ positions against the city.

A Prophet's Word for Ahab

[13] A prophet came to Ahab king of Israel and said, "This is what the LORD says: 'Do you see this entire immense horde? Watch, I am handing it over to you today so that you may know that I am the LORD.'"

[14] Ahab asked, "By whom?"

And the prophet said, "This is what the LORD says: 'By the young men of the provincial leaders.'"

Then he asked, "Who is to start the battle?"

He said, "You."

[15] So Ahab counted the young men of the provincial leaders, and there were 232. After them he counted all the Israelite troops: 7,000. [16] They marched out at noon while Ben-hadad and the 32 kings who were helping him were getting drunk in the tents. [17] The young men of the provincial leaders marched out first. Then Ben-hadad sent out scouts, and they reported to him, saying, "Men are marching out of Samaria."

[18] So he said, "If they have marched out in peace, take them alive, and if they have marched out for battle, take them alive."

Israel Defeats Ben-hadad

[19] The young men of the provincial leaders and the army behind them marched out from the city, [20] and each one struck down his opponent. So the Arameans fled and Israel pursued them, but Ben-hadad king of Aram escaped on a horse with the cavalry. [21] Then the king of Israel marched out and attacked the cavalry and the chariotry. He inflicted a great slaughter on Aram.

[22] The prophet approached the king of Israel and said to him, "Go and strengthen yourself, then consider what you should do, for in the spring the king of Aram will march up against you."

King Ben-hadad Changes Strategy: the Plain

[23] Now the king of Aram's servants said to him, "Their gods are gods of the hill country. That's why they were stronger than we. Instead, we should fight with them on the plain; then we will certainly be stronger than they. [24] Also do this: remove each king from his position and appoint captains in their place. [25] Raise another army for yourself like the army you lost—horse for horse, chariot for chariot—and let's fight with them on the plain; and we will certainly be stronger than they." The king listened to them and did so.

[26] In the spring, Ben-hadad mobilized the Arameans and went up to Aphek to battle Israel. [27] The Israelites mobilized, gathered supplies, and went to fight them. The Israelites camped in front of them like two little flocks of goats, while the Arameans filled the landscape.

Prophet Predicts Ahab's Victory

[28] Then the man of God approached and said to the king of Israel, "This is what the LORD says: 'Because the Arameans have said: The LORD is a god of the mountains and not a god of the valleys, I will hand over this entire immense horde to you. Then you will know that I am the LORD.'"

Israel Defeats Arameans

[29] They camped opposite each other for seven days. On the seventh day, the

battle took place, and the Israelites struck down the Arameans—100,000 foot soldiers in one day. ³⁰ The ones who remained fled into the city of Aphek, and the wall fell on those 27,000 remaining men.

King Ben-hadad Flees

Ben-hadad also fled and went into an inner room in the city. ³¹ His servants said to him, "Consider this: we have heard that the kings of the house of Israel are kings ˻who show˼ special kindness. So let's put •sackcloth around our waists and ropes around our heads, and let's go out to the king of Israel. Perhaps he will spare your life."

³² So they dressed with sackcloth around their waists and ropes around their heads, went to the king of Israel, and said, "Your servant Ben-hadad says, 'Please spare my life.'"

So he said, "Is he still alive? He is my brother."

³³ Now the men were looking for a sign of hope, so they quickly latched onto the hint[a] and said, "Yes, your brother Ben-hadad."

Then he said, "Go and bring him."

Ahab Spares Ben-Hadad

So Ben-hadad came out to him, and Ahab had him come up into the chariot. ³⁴ Then Ben-hadad said to him, "The cities that my father took from your father I restore to you, and you may set up marketplaces for yourself in Damascus, like my father set up in Samaria."

˻Ahab responded˼, "On the basis of this treaty, I release you." So he made a treaty with him and released him.

God's Prophet Confronts Ahab

³⁵ One of the sons of the prophets said to his fellow prophet by the word of the LORD, "Strike me!" But the man refused to strike him.

³⁶ He told him, "Because you did not listen to the voice of the LORD, mark my words: When you leave me, a lion will kill you." When he left him, a lion found him and killed him.

³⁷ The prophet found another man and said to him, "Strike me!" So the man struck him, inflicting a wound. ³⁸ Then the prophet went and waited for the king on the road. He disguised himself with a bandage over his eyes. ³⁹ As the king was passing by, he cried out to the king and said, "Your servant marched out into the midst of the battle. Suddenly, a man turned aside and brought someone to me and said, 'Guard this man! If he is ever missing, it will be your life in place of his life, or you will weigh out 75 pounds[b] of silver.' ⁴⁰ But while your servant was busy here and there, he disappeared."

The king of Israel said to him, "That will be your sentence; you yourself have decided it."

Prophet Rebukes Ahab

⁴¹ He quickly removed the bandage from his eyes. The king of Israel recognized that he was one of the prophets. ⁴² The prophet said to him, "This is what the LORD says: 'Because you released from your hand the man I had •devoted to destruction, it will be your life in place of his life and your people in place of his people.'" ⁴³ The king of Israel left for home resentful and angry, and he entered Samaria.

Naboth Refuses to Give Vineyard to Ahab

21 Some time passed after these events. Naboth the Jezreelite had a vineyard; it was in Jezreel next to the

^a**20:33** LXX, some Hb mss, alt Hb tradition; MT reads *they hastened and caught hold; "Is this it?"*   ^b**20:39** Lit *a talent*

palace of Ahab king of Samaria. ² So Ahab spoke to Naboth, saying, "Give me your vineyard so I can have it for a vegetable garden, since it is right next to my palace. I will give you a better vineyard in its place, or if you prefer, I will give you its value in silver."

³ But Naboth said to Ahab, "I will never give my fathers' inheritance to you."

⁴ So Ahab went to his palace resentful and angry, because of what Naboth the Jezreelite had told him. He had said, "I will not give you my fathers' inheritance." He lay down on his bed, turned his face away, and didn't eat any food.

⁵ Then his wife Jezebel came to him and said to him, "Why are you so upset that you refuse to eat?"

⁶ "Because I spoke to Naboth the Jezreelite," he replied. "I told him: Give me your vineyard for silver, or if you wish, I will give you a vineyard in its place. But he said, 'I won't give you my vineyard!' "

Jezebel Kills Naboth, Takes Vineyard

⁷ Then his wife Jezebel said to him, "Now, exercise your royal power over Israel. Get up, eat some food, and be happy. ⌊For⌋ I will give you the vineyard of Naboth the Jezreelite." ⁸ So she wrote letters in Ahab's name and sealed them with his seal. She sent the letters to the elders and nobles who lived with Naboth in his city. ⁹ In the letters, she wrote:

Proclaim a fast and seat Naboth at the head of the people. ¹⁰ Then seat two •wicked men opposite him and have them testify against him, saying, "You have cursed God and king!" Then take him out and stone him to death.

¹¹ The men of his city, the elders and nobles who lived in his city, did as Jezebel had commanded them, as was written in the letters she had sent them. ¹² They proclaimed a fast and seated Naboth at the head of the people. ¹³ The two wicked men came in and sat opposite him. Then the wicked men testified against Naboth in the presence of the people, saying, "Naboth has cursed God and king!" So they took him outside the city and stoned him to death with stones. ¹⁴ Then they sent ⌊word⌋ to Jezebel, "Naboth has been stoned to death."

¹⁵ When Jezebel heard that Naboth had been stoned to death, she said to Ahab, "Get up and take possession of the vineyard of Naboth the Jezreelite who refused to give it to you for silver, since Naboth isn't alive, but dead." ¹⁶ When Ahab heard that Naboth was dead, he got up to go down to the vineyard of Naboth the Jezreelite to take possession of it.

Elijah Speaks God's Judgment on Ahab

¹⁷ Then the word of the LORD came to Elijah the Tishbite: ¹⁸ "Get up and go to meet Ahab king of Israel, who is in Samaria. You'll find him in Naboth's vineyard, where he has gone to take possession of it. ¹⁹ Tell him, 'This is what the LORD says: Have you murdered and also taken possession?' Then tell him, 'This is what the LORD says: In the place where the dogs licked Naboth's blood, the dogs will also lick your blood!' "

²⁰ Ahab said to Elijah, "So, you have caught me, my enemy."

Elijah: God's Curse on Ahab and Jezebel

He replied, "I have caught you because you devoted yourself to do what is evil in the LORD's sight. ²¹ This is what the LORD says:[a] 'I am about to bring disaster on you and will sweep away your descendants:

ᵃ**21:21** LXX; Hb omits *This is what the LORD says*

I will eliminate all of Ahab's males,[a] both slave and free, in Israel;

22 I will make your house like the house of Jeroboam son of Nebat and like the house of Baasha son of Ahijah, because you have provoked ₍My₎ anger and caused Israel to sin. 23 The LORD also speaks of Jezebel: The dogs will eat Jezebel in the plot of land[b] at Jezreel:

24 He who belongs to Ahab and dies
  in the city, the dogs will eat,
  and he who dies in the field,
  the birds of the sky will eat.'"

25 Still, there was no one like Ahab, who devoted himself to do what was evil in the LORD's sight, because his wife Jezebel incited him. 26 He committed the most detestable acts by going after idols as the Amorites had, whom the LORD had dispossessed before the Israelites.

Ahab Repents, God Lessens Punishment

27 When Ahab heard these words, he tore his clothes, put •sackcloth over his body, and fasted. He lay down in sackcloth and walked around subdued. 28 Then the word of the LORD came to Elijah the Tishbite: 29 "Have you seen how Ahab has humbled himself before Me? I will not bring the disaster during his lifetime, because he has humbled himself before Me. I will bring the disaster on his house during his son's lifetime."

King Ahab Seeks Alliance with King Jehoshaphat

22 There was a lull of three years without war between Aram and Israel. 2 However, in the third year, Jehoshaphat king of Judah went to visit the king of Israel. 3 The king of Israel had said to his servants, "Don't you know that Ramoth-gilead is ours, but we have failed to take it from the hand of the king of Aram?" 4 So he asked Jehoshaphat, "Will you go with me to fight Ramoth-gilead?"

Jehoshaphat replied to the king of Israel, "I am as you are, my people as your people, my horses as your horses." 5 But Jehoshaphat said to the king of Israel, "First, please ask what the LORD's will is."

6 So the king of Israel gathered the prophets, about 400 men, and asked them, "Should I go against Ramoth-gilead for war or should I refrain?"

They replied, "March up, and the Lord will hand it over to the king."

Jehoshaphat Asks for Prophet of Yahweh

7 But Jehoshaphat asked, "Isn't there a prophet of •Yahweh here any more? Let's ask him."

8 The king of Israel said to Jehoshaphat, "There is still one man who can ask the LORD, but I hate him because he never prophesies good about me, but only disaster. He is Micaiah son of Imlah."

"The king shouldn't say that!" Jehoshaphat replied.

9 So the king of Israel called an officer and said, "Hurry ₍and get₎ Micaiah son of Imlah!"

10 Now the king of Israel and Jehoshaphat king of Judah, clothed in royal attire, were each sitting on his own throne. They were on the threshing floor at the entrance to Samaria's •gate, and all the prophets were prophesying in front of them. 11 Then Zedekiah son of Chenaanah made iron horns and said, "This is what the LORD says: 'You will gore the

---

a21:21 Lit eliminate Ahab's one who urinates against the wall b21:23 Some Hb mss, Syr, Tg, Vg, 2 Kg 9:36; MT, LXX read the rampart

Arameans with these until they are finished off.' " [12] And all the prophets were prophesying the same: "March up to Ramoth-gilead and succeed, for the LORD will hand it over to the king."

Micaiah's Message of Defeat

[13] The messenger who went to call Micaiah instructed him, "Look, the words of the prophets are unanimously favorable for the king. So let your words be like theirs, and speak favorably."

[14] But Micaiah said, "As the LORD lives, I will say whatever the LORD says to me."

[15] So he went to the king, and the king asked him, "Micaiah, should we go to Ramoth-gilead for war, or should we refrain?"

Micaiah told him, "March up and succeed. The LORD will hand it over to the king."

[16] But the king said to him, "How many times must I make you swear not to tell me anything but the truth in the name of the LORD?"

[17] So Micaiah said:

I saw all Israel scattered on the hills
    like sheep without a shepherd.
And the Lord said,
    'They have no master;
    let everyone return home in peace.'

[18] So the king of Israel said to Jehoshaphat, "Didn't I tell you he never prophesies good about me, but only disaster?"

[19] Then Micaiah said, "Therefore, hear the word of the LORD: I saw the LORD sitting on His throne, and the whole heavenly •host was standing by Him at His right hand and at His left hand. [20] And the LORD said, 'Who will entice Ahab to march up and fall at Ramoth-gilead?' So one was saying this and another was saying that.

[21] "Then a spirit came forward, stood before the LORD, and said, 'I will entice him.'

[22] "The LORD asked him, 'How?'

"He said, 'I will go and become a lying spirit in the mouth of all his prophets.'

"Then He said, 'You will certainly entice him and prevail. Go and do that.'

[23] "You see, the LORD has put a lying spirit into the mouth of all these prophets of yours, and the LORD has pronounced disaster against you."

Micaiah Attacked

[24] Then Zedekiah son of Chenaanah came up, hit Micaiah in the face, and demanded, "Did[a] the Spirit of the LORD leave me to speak to you?"

[25] Micaiah replied, "You will soon see when you go to hide yourself in an inner chamber on that day."

[26] Then the king of Israel ordered, "Take Micaiah and return him to Amon, the governor of the city, and to Joash, the king's son, [27] and say, 'This is what the king says: Put this guy in prison and feed him only bread and water[b] until I come back safely.' "

[28] But Micaiah said, "If you ever return safely, the LORD has not spoken through me." Then he said, "Listen, all you people!"[c]

Ahab's Disguise

[29] Then the king of Israel and Judah's King Jehoshaphat went up to Ramoth-gilead. [30] But the king of Israel said to Jehoshaphat, "I will disguise myself and go into battle, but you wear your royal attire." So the king of Israel disguised himself and went into battle.

[31] Now the king of Aram had ordered his 32 chariot commanders, "Do not fight with anyone at all except the king of Israel."

---

[a]**22:24** Lit *Which way did*   [b]**22:27** Lit *him on bread of oppression and water of oppression*   [c]**22:28** LXX omits *Then he said, "Listen, all you people!"*

32 When the chariot commanders saw Jehoshaphat, they shouted, "He must be the king of Israel!" So they turned to fight against him, but Jehoshaphat cried out. 33 When the chariot commanders saw that he was not the king of Israel, they turned back from pursuing him.

A Random Arrow Kills Ahab

34 But a man drew his bow without taking special aim and struck the king of Israel through the joints of his armor. So he said to his charioteer, "Turn around and take me out of the battle,ᵃ for I am badly wounded!" 35 The battle raged throughout that day, and the king was propped up in his chariot facing the Arameans. He died that evening, and blood from his wound flowed into the bottom of the chariot. 36 Then the cry rang out in the army as the sun set, declaring:

Each man to his own city,
and each man to his own land!

Dogs Lick Ahab's Blood

37 So the king died and was brought to Samaria. They buried the king in Samaria. 38 Then someone washed the chariot at the pool of Samaria. The dogs licked up his blood, and the prostitutes bathed ⌊in it⌋, according to the word of the LORD that He had spoken. 39 The rest of the events of Ahab's ⌊reign⌋, along with all his accomplishments, the ivory palace he built, and all the cities he built, are written about in the Historical Record of Israel's Kings. 40 Ahab rested with his fathers, and his son Ahaziah became king in his place.

Judah's King Jehoshaphat

41 Jehoshaphat son of Asa became king over Judah in the fourth year of Israel's King Ahab. 42 Jehoshaphat was 35 years old when he became king; he reigned 25 years in Jerusalem. His mother's name was Azubah daughter of Shilhi. 43 He walked in all the ways of his father Asa; he did not turn away from them but did what was right in the LORD's sight. However, the •high places were not taken away;ᵇ the people still sacrificed and burned incense on the high places. 44 Jehoshaphat also made peace with the king of Israel.

45 The rest of the events of Jehoshaphat's ⌊reign⌋, along with the might he exercised and how he waged war, are written about in the Historical Record of Judah's Kings. 46 He removed from the land the rest of the male shrine prostitutes who were left from the days of his father Asa. 47 There was no king in Edom; a deputy served as king. 48 Jehoshaphat made ships of Tarshish to go to Ophir for gold, but they did not go because the ships were wrecked at Ezion-geber. 49 At that time, Ahaziah son of Ahab said to Jehoshaphat, "Let my servants go with your servants in the ships," but Jehoshaphat was not willing. 50 Jehoshaphat rested with his fathers and was buried with his fathers in the city of his forefather David. His son Jehoram became king in his place.

Israel's King Ahaziah: Evil

51 Ahaziah son of Ahab became king over Israel in Samaria in the seventeenth year of Judah's King Jehoshaphat; he reigned over Israel two years. 52 He did what was evil in the LORD's sight. He walked in the way of his father, in the way of his mother, and in the way of Jeroboam son of Nebat, who had caused Israel to sin. 53 He served •Baal and worshiped him. He provoked the LORD God of Israel just as his father had done.

2 KINGS

Ahaziah's Accident: Baal-zebub

1 After the death of Ahab, Moab rebelled against Israel. ² Ahaziah had fallen through the latticed window of his upper room in Samaria and was injured. So he sent messengers instructing them: "Go inquire of Baal-zebub,ᵃ the god of Ekron, if I will recover from this injury."

Elijah Rebukes Ahaziah

³ But the angel of the LORD said to Elijah the Tishbite, "Go and meet the messengers of the king of Samaria and ask them, 'Is it because there is no God in Israel that you are going to inquire of Baal-zebub, the god of Ekron?' ⁴ Therefore, this is what the LORD says: 'You will not get up from your sickbed—you will certainly die.'" Then Elijah left.

⁵ The messengers returned to the king, who asked them, "Why have you come back?"

⁶ They replied, "A man came to meet us and said, 'Go back to the king who sent you and declare to him: This is what the LORD says: Is it because there is no God in Israel that you're sending ⌊these men⌋ to inquire of Baal-zebub, the god of Ekron? Therefore, you will not get up from your sickbed—you will certainly die.'"

⁷ The king asked them: "What sort of man came up to meet you and spoke those words to you?"

⁸ They replied, "A hairy man with a leather belt around his waist."

He said, "It's Elijah the Tishbite."

Ahaziah Commands Elijah

⁹ So King Ahaziah sent a captain of 50 with his 50 ⌊men⌋ to Elijah. When the captain went up to him, he was sitting on top of the hill. He announced, "Man of God, the king declares, 'Come down!'"

¹⁰ Elijah responded to the captain of the 50, "If I am a man of God, may fire come down from heaven and consume you and your 50 ⌊men⌋." Then fire came down from heaven and consumed him and his 50 ⌊men⌋.

¹¹ So the king sent another captain of 50 with his 50 ⌊men⌋ to Elijah. He took in the situationᵇ and announced, "Man of God, this is what the king says: 'Come down immediately!'"

¹² Elijah responded, "If I am a man of God, may fire come down from heaven and consume you and your 50 ⌊men⌋." So a divine fireᶜ came down from heaven and consumed him and his 50 ⌊men⌋.

Ahaziah Entreats Elijah

¹³ Then the king sent a third captain of 50 with his 50 ⌊men⌋. The third captain of 50 went up and fell on his knees in front of Elijah and begged him, "Man of God, please let my life and the lives of these 50 servants of yours be precious in your sight. ¹⁴ Already fire has come down from heaven and consumed the first two captains of 50 with their fifties, but this time let my life be precious in your sight."

¹⁵ The angel of the LORD said to Elijah, "Go down with him. Don't be afraid of him." So he got up and went down with him to the king.

Elijah Rebukes Ahaziah Again

¹⁶ Then Elijah said to King Ahaziah, "This is what the LORD says: 'Because

---

ᵃ**1:2** = Lord of the Flies   ᵇ**1:11** Lit *He answered*   ᶜ**1:12** Lit *a fire of God*

you have sent messengers to inquire of Baal-zebub, the god of Ekron—is it because there is no God in Israel for you to inquire of His will? You will not get up from your sickbed; you will certainly die.'"

Death of Ahaziah

17 Ahaziah died according to the word of the LORD that Elijah had spoken. Since he had no son, Joram[a] became king in his place. ⌊This happened⌋ in the second year of Judah's King Jehoram son of Jehoshaphat.[b] 18 The rest of the events of Ahaziah's ⌊reign⌋, along with his accomplishments, are written about in the Historical Record of Israel's Kings.[c]

Elijah's Time for Heaven Approaches

2 The time had come for the LORD to take Elijah up to heaven in a whirlwind. Elijah and Elisha were traveling from Gilgal, 2 and Elijah said to Elisha, "Stay here; the LORD is sending me on to Bethel."

But Elisha replied, "As the LORD lives and as you yourself live, I will not leave you." So they went down to Bethel.

3 Then the sons of the prophets who were at Bethel came out to Elisha and said, "Do you know that today the LORD will take your master away from you?"

He said, "Yes, I know. Be quiet."

4 Elijah said to him, "Elisha, stay here; the LORD is sending me to Jericho."

But Elisha said, "As the LORD lives and as you yourself live, I will not leave you." So they went to Jericho.

5 Then the sons of the prophets who were in Jericho came up to Elisha and said, "Do you know that today the LORD will take your master away from you?"

He said, "Yes, I know. Be quiet."

6 Elijah said to him, "Stay here; the LORD is sending me to the Jordan."

But Elisha said, "As the LORD lives and as you yourself live, I will not leave you." So the two of them went on.

Elijah Parts Jordan

7 Fifty men from the sons of the prophets came and stood facing them from a distance while the two of them stood by the Jordan. 8 Elijah took his mantle, rolled it up, and struck the waters, which parted to the right and left. Then the two of them crossed over on dry ground. 9 After they had crossed over, Elijah said to Elisha, "Tell ⌊me⌋ what I can do for you before I am taken from you."

Elisha's Request

So Elisha answered, "Please, let there be a double portion of your spirit on me."

10 Elijah replied, "You have asked for something difficult. If you see me being taken from you, you will have it. If not, you won't."

Elijah's Chariot of Fire—and Whirlwind

11 As they continued walking and talking, a chariot of fire with horses of fire suddenly appeared and separated the two of them. Then Elijah went up into heaven in the whirlwind. 12 As Elisha watched, he kept crying out, "My father, my father, the chariots and horsemen of Israel!" Then he never saw Elijah again. He took hold of his own clothes and tore them into two pieces.

Elisha Succeeds Elijah

13 Elisha picked up the mantle that had fallen off Elijah and went back and stood on the bank of the Jordan. 14 Then he took the mantle Elijah had dropped and

---

a 1:17 Lit *Jehoram*; 2 Kg 8:16   b 1:17 LXX omits *in the second year* . . . *Jehoshaphat*   c 1:18 LXX adds 4 more vv. here, which essentially duplicate the information in 2 Kg 3:1-3.

struck the waters. "Where is the LORD God of Elijah?" he asked. He struck the waters himself, and they parted to the right and the left, and Elisha crossed over.

¹⁵ When the sons of the prophets from Jericho, who were facing him, saw him, they said, "The spirit of Elijah rests on Elisha." They came to meet him and bowed down to the ground in front of him.

¹⁶ Then the sons of the prophets said to Elisha, "Since there are 50 strong men here with your servants, please let them go and search for your master. Maybe the Spirit of the LORD has carried him away and put him on one of the mountains or into one of the valleys."

He answered, "Don't send ˌthemˌ."

¹⁷ However, they urged him to the point of embarrassment, so he said, "Send ˌthemˌ." They sent 50 men, who looked for three days but did not find him. ¹⁸ When they returned to him in Jericho where he was staying, he said to them, "Didn't I tell you not to go?"

Elisha's Water Miracle

¹⁹ Then the men of the city said to Elisha, "Even though our lord can see that the city's location is good, the water is bad and the land unfruitful."

²⁰ He replied, "Bring me a new bowl and put salt in it."

After they had brought him one, ²¹ Elisha went out to the spring of water, threw salt in it, and said, "This is what the LORD says: 'I have healed this water. No longer will death or unfruitfulness result from it.'" ²² Therefore, the water remains healthy to this very day according to the word that Elisha spoke.

Baldy's Curse

²³ From there Elisha went up to Bethel. As he was walking up the path, some small boys came out of the city and harassed him, chanting, "Go up, baldy! Go up, baldy!"

²⁴ He turned around, looked at them, and cursed them in the name of the LORD. Then two female bears came out of the woods and mauled 42 of the youths. ²⁵ From there Elisha went to Mount Carmel, and then he returned to Samaria.

Israel's King Joram: Evil

3 Joram son of Ahab became king over Israel in Samaria during the eighteenth year of Judah's King Jehoshaphat; he reigned 12 years. ² He did what was evil in the LORD's sight, but not like his father and mother, for he removed the sacred pillar of •Baal his father had made. ³ Nevertheless, Joram clung to the sins that Jeroboam son of Nebat had caused Israel to commit. He did not turn away from them.

Moab Rebels against Israel

⁴ King Mesha of Moab was a sheep breeder. He used to pay the king of Israel 100,000 lambs and the wool of 100,000 rams, ⁵ but when Ahab died, the king of Moab rebelled against the king of Israel. ⁶ So King Joram marched out from Samaria at that time and mobilized all Israel. ⁷ Then he sent ˌa messageˌ to King Jehoshaphat of Judah: "The king of Moab has rebelled against me. Will you go with me to fight against Moab?"

Jehoshaphat Joins Joram

Jehoshaphat said, "I will go. I am as you are, my people as your people, my horses as your horses." ⁸ Then he asked, "Which route should we take?"

Joram replied, "The route of the wilderness of Edom."

⁹ So the <u>king of Israel, the king of Judah, and the king of Edom</u> set out. After they had traveled their indirect route for

seven days, they had no water for the army or their animals.

[10] Then the king of Israel said, "Oh no, the LORD has summoned us three kings, only to hand us over to Moab."

Jehoshaphat Consults Elisha

[11] But Jehoshaphat said, "Isn't there a prophet of the LORD here? Let's inquire of the LORD through him."

One of the servants of the king of Israel answered, "Elisha son of Shaphat, who used to pour water on Elijah's hands, is here."

[12] Jehoshaphat affirmed, "The LORD's words are with him." So the king of Israel and Jehoshaphat and the king of Edom went to him.

[13] However, Elisha said to King Joram of Israel, "We have nothing in common. Go to the prophets of your father and your mother!"

But the king of Israel replied, "No, because it is the LORD who has summoned us three kings to hand us over to Moab."

Elisha's Prophecy with Music

[14] Elisha responded, "As the LORD of •Hosts lives, I stand before Him. If I did not have respect for King Jehoshaphat of Judah, I would not look at you; I wouldn't take notice of you. [15] Now, bring me a musician."

While the musician played, the LORD's hand came on Elisha. [16] Then he said, "This is what the LORD says: 'Dig ditch after ditch in this •wadi.' [17] For the LORD says, 'You will not see wind or rain, but the wadi will be filled with water, and you will drink—you and your cattle and your animals.' [18] This is easy in the LORD's sight. He will also hand Moab over to you. [19] Then you must attack every fortified city and every choice city. You must cut down every good tree and stop up every spring of water. You must

ruin every good piece of land with stones."

[20] About the time for the •grain offering the next morning, water suddenly came from the direction of Edom and filled the land.

[21] All Moab had heard that the kings had come up to fight against them. So all who could bear arms, from the youngest to the oldest, were summoned and took their stand at the border. [22] When they got up early in the morning, the sun was shining on the water, and the Moabites saw that the water across from them was red like blood. [23] "This is blood!" they exclaimed. "The kings have clashed swords and killed each other. So, to the spoil, Moab!"

Israel Attacks Moab

[24] However, when the Moabites came to Israel's camp, the Israelites attacked them, and they fled from them. So Israel went into the land and struck down the Moabites. [25] They destroyed the cities, and each of them threw stones to cover every good piece of land. They stopped up every spring of water and cut down every good tree. In the end, only the buildings of Kir-hareseth were left. Then men with slings surrounded the city and attacked it.

[26] When the king of Moab saw that the battle was too fierce for him, he took 700 swordsmen with him to try to break through to the king of Edom, but they could not do it. [27] So he took his firstborn son, who was to become king in his place, and offered him as a •burnt offering on the city wall. Great wrath was on the Israelites, and they withdrew from him and returned to their land.

Widow's Oil Jar: Elisha's Solution to Debt

4 One of the wives of the sons of the prophets cried out to Elisha, "Your servant, my husband, has died. You

know that your servant •feared the LORD. Now the creditor is coming to take my two children as his slaves."

2 Elisha asked her, "What can I do for you? Tell me, what do you have in the house?"

She said, "Your servant has nothing in the house except a jar of oil."

3 Then he said, "Go and borrow empty containers from everyone—from all your neighbors. Do not get just a few. 4 Then go in and shut the door behind you and your sons, and pour oil into all these containers. Set the full ones to one side." 5 So she left.

After she had shut the door behind her and her sons, they kept bringing her containers, and she kept pouring. 6 When they were full, she said to her son, "Bring me another container."

But he replied, "There aren't any more." Then the oil stopped.

7 She went and told the man of God, and he said, "Go sell the oil and pay your debt; you and your sons can live on the rest."

Shunammite Woman's Hospitality

8 One day Elisha went to Shunem. A prominent woman who lived there persuaded him to eat some food. So whenever he passed by, he stopped there to eat. 9 Then she said to her husband, "I know that the one who often passes by here is a holy man of God, 10 so let's make a small room upstairs and put a bed, a table, a chair, and a lamp there for him. Whenever he comes, he can stay there."

Shunammite Woman's Son

11 One day he came there and stopped and went to the room upstairs to lie down. 12 He ordered his attendant Gehazi, "Call this Shunammite woman." So he called her and she stood before him.

13 Then he said to Gehazi, "Say to her, 'Look, you've gone to all this trouble for us. What can we do for you? Can we speak on your behalf to the king or to the commander of the army?'"

She answered, "I am living among my own people."

14 So he asked, "Then what should be done for her?"

Gehazi answered, "Well, she has no son, and her husband is old."

15 "Call her," Elisha said. So Gehazi called her, and she stood in the doorway. 16 Elisha said, "At this time next year you will have a son in your arms."

Then she said, "No, my lord. Man of God, do not deceive your servant."

17 The woman conceived and gave birth to a son at the same time the following year, as Elisha had promised her.

Elisha Raises Shunammite's Son

18 The child grew and one day went out to his father and the harvesters. 19 Suddenly, he complained to his father, "My head! My head!"

His father told his servant, "Carry him to his mother." 20 So he picked him up and took him to his mother. The child sat on her lap until noon and then died. 21 Then she went up and laid him on the bed of the man of God, shut him in, and left.

22 She summoned her husband and said, "Please send me one of the servants and one of the donkeys, so I can hurry to the man of God and then come back."

23 But he said, "Why go to him today? It's neither New Moon or Sabbath."

She replied, "Everything is all right."

24 Then she saddled the donkey and said to her servant, "Hurry, don't slow the pace for me unless I tell you." 25 So she set out and went to the man of God at Mount Carmel.

When the man of God saw her at a distance, he said to his attendant Gehazi, "Look, there's the Shunammite woman. 26 Run out to meet her and ask, 'Are you all right? Is your husband all right? Is your son all right?'"

And she answered, "Everything's all right."

27 When she came up to the man of God at the mountain, she clung to his feet. Gehazi came to push her away, but the man of God said, "Leave her alone—she is in severe anguish, and the LORD has hidden it from me. He hasn't told me."

28 Then she said, "Did I ask my lord for a son? Didn't I say, 'Do not deceive me?'"

29 So Elisha said to Gehazi, "Tuck your mantle under your belt, take my staff with you, and go. If you meet anyone, don't ⌊stop to⌋ greet him, and if a man greets you, don't answer him. Then place my staff on the boy's face."

30 The boy's mother said ⌊to Elisha⌋, "As the LORD lives and as you yourself live, I will not leave you." So he got up and followed her.

31 Gehazi went ahead of them and placed the staff on the boy's face, but there was no sound or sign of life, so he went back to meet Elisha and told him, "The boy didn't wake up."

32 When Elisha got to the house, he discovered the boy lying dead on his bed. 33 So he went in, closed the door behind the two of them, and prayed to the LORD. 34 Then he went up and lay on the boy: he put mouth to mouth, eye to eye, hand to hand. While he bent down over him, the boy's flesh became warm. 35 Elisha got up, went into the house, and paced back and forth. Then he went up and bent down over him again. The boy sneezed seven times and opened his eyes.

36 Elisha called Gehazi and said, "Call the Shunammite woman." He called her and she came. Then Elisha said, "Pick up your son." 37 She came, fell at his feet, and bowed to the ground; she picked up her son and left.

Elisha "Cures" Stew

38 When Elisha returned to Gilgal, there was a famine in the land. The sons of the prophets were sitting at his feet.[a] He said to his attendant, "Put on the large pot and make stew for the sons of the prophets."

39 One went out to the field to gather herbs and found a wild vine from which he gathered as many wild gourds as his garment would hold. Then he came back and cut them up into the pot of stew, but they were unaware ⌊of what they were⌋.

40 They served some for the men to eat, but when they ate the stew they cried out, "There's death in the pot, man of God!" And they were unable to eat it.

41 Then Elisha said, "Get some meal." He threw it into the pot and said, "Serve it for the people to eat." And there was nothing bad in the pot.

Elisha Multiplies Bread

42 A man from Baal-shalishah came to the man of God with his sack full of 20 loaves of barley bread from the first bread of the harvest. Elisha said, "Give it to the people to eat."

43 But Elisha's attendant asked, "What? Am I to set 20 loaves before 100 men?"

"Give it to the people to eat," Elisha said, "for this is what the LORD says: 'They will eat, and they will have some left over.'" 44 So he gave it to them, and as the LORD had promised, they ate and had some left over.

a4:38 Lit sitting before him

Naaman's Skin Disease

5 Naaman, commander of the army for the king of Aram, was a great man in his master's sight[a] and highly regarded because through him, the LORD had given victory to Aram. The man was a brave warrior, but he had a skin disease. [2] Aram had gone on raids and brought back from the land of Israel a young girl who served Naaman's wife. [3] She said to her mistress, "If only my master would go to[b] the prophet who is in Samaria, he would cure him of his skin disease."

[4] So Naaman went and told his master what the girl from the land of Israel had said. [5] Therefore, the king of Aram said, "Go and I will send a letter ‹with you› to the king of Israel."

So he went and took with him 750 pounds[c] of silver, 150 pounds[d] of gold, and 10 changes of clothes. [6] He brought the letter to the king of Israel, and it read:

When this letter comes to you, note that I have sent you my servant Naaman for you to cure him of his skin disease.

[7] When the king of Israel read the letter, he tore his clothes and asked, "Am I God, killing and giving life that this man expects me to cure a man of his skin disease? Think it over and you will see that he is only picking a fight with[e] me."

Elisha Volunteers to Help

[8] When Elisha the man of God heard that the king of Israel tore his clothes, he sent ‹a message› to the king, "Why have you torn your clothes? Have him come to me, and he will know there is a prophet in Israel." [9] So Naaman came with his horses and chariots and stood at the door of Elisha's house.

"Wash Seven Times"

[10] Then Elisha sent him a messenger, who said, "Go wash seven times in the Jordan and your flesh will be restored and you will be clean."

[11] But Naaman got angry and left, saying, "I was telling myself: He will surely come out, stand and call on the name of •Yahweh his God, and will wave his hand over the spot and cure the skin disease. [12] Aren't Abana and Pharpar, the rivers of Damascus, better than all the waters of Israel? Could I not wash in them and be clean?" So he turned and left in a rage.

[13] But his servants approached and said to him, "My father, if the prophet had told you to do some great thing, would you not have done it? How much more ‹should you do it› when he tells you, 'Wash and be clean'?" [14] So Naaman went down and dipped himself in the Jordan seven times, according to the command of the man of God. Then his skin was restored ‹and became› like the skin of a small boy, and he was clean.

Naaman Offers Gift

[15] Then Naaman and his whole company went back to the man of God, stood before him, and declared, "I know there's no God in the whole world except in Israel. Therefore, please accept a gift from your servant."

[16] But Elisha said, "As the LORD lives, I stand before Him. I will not accept it." Naaman urged him to accept it, but he refused.

[17] Naaman responded, "If not, please let two mule-loads of dirt be given to your servant, for your servant will no longer offer a •burnt offering or a sacrifice to any other god but Yahweh. [18] However, in a particular matter may

a5:1 Lit man before his master   b5:3 Lit master was before   c5:5 Lit 10 talents   d5:5 Lit 6,000 [shekels]   e5:7 Lit only seeking an occasion against the LORD pardon your servant: When my master, ⌊the king of Aram⌋, goes into the temple of Rimmon to worship and I, as his right-hand man,[a] bow in the temple of Rimmon—when I bow[b] in the temple of Rimmon, may the LORD pardon your servant in this matter."

¹⁹ So he said to him, "Go in peace."

Gehazi's Greed

After Naaman had traveled a short distance from Elisha, ²⁰ Gehazi, the attendant of Elisha the man of God, thought: My master has let this Aramean Naaman off lightly by not accepting from him what he brought. As the LORD lives, I will run after him and get something from him.

²¹ So Gehazi pursued Naaman. When Naaman saw someone running after him, he got down from the chariot to meet him and asked, "Is everything all right?"

²² Gehazi said, "It's all right. My master has sent me to say, 'I have just now discovered that two young men from the sons of the prophets have come to me from the hill country of Ephraim. Please give them 75 pounds[c] of silver and two changes of clothes.'"

²³ But Naaman insisted, "Please, accept 150 pounds."[d] He urged Gehazi and then packed 150 pounds[d] of silver in two bags with two changes of clothes. Naaman gave them to two of his young men who carried them ahead of Gehazi. ²⁴ When Gehazi came to the hill,[e] he took the gifts from them and stored them in the house. Then he dismissed the men, and they left.

Elisha Punishes Gehazi

²⁵ Gehazi came and stood by his master. "Where did you go, Gehazi?" Elisha asked him.

"Your servant didn't go anywhere," he replied.

²⁶ But Elisha questioned him, "Wasn't my spirit there[f] when the man got down from his chariot to meet you? Is it a time to accept money and clothes, olive orchards and vineyards, sheep and oxen, and male and female slaves? ²⁷ Therefore, Naaman's skin disease will cling to you and your descendants forever." So Gehazi went out from his presence diseased—⌊white⌋ as snow.

Elisha Floats Iron Ax Head

6 The sons of the prophets said to Elisha, "Please notice that the place where we live under your supervision[g] is too small for us. ² Please let us go to the Jordan where we can each get a log and can build ourselves a place to live there."

"Go," he said.

³ Then one said, "Please come with your servants."

"I'll come," he answered.

⁴ So he went with them, and when they came to the Jordan, they cut down trees. ⁵ As one of them was cutting down a tree, the iron ⌊ax head⌋ fell into the water, and he cried out: "Oh, my master, it was borrowed!"

⁶ Then the man of God asked, "Where did it fall?"

When he showed him the place, the man of God cut a stick, threw it there, and made the iron float. ⁷ Then he said, "Pick it up." So he reached out and took it.

Aramean War

⁸ When the king of Aram was waging war against Israel, he conferred with his servants, "My camp will be at such and such a place."

---

[a]5:18 Lit worship, and he leans on my hand, and I   [b]5:18 LXX, Vg read when he bows himself   [c]5:22 Lit a talent   [d]5:23 Lit two talents   [e]5:24 Or citadel   [f]5:26 Lit "Did not my heart go   [g]6:1 Lit we are living before you

Elisha's Spiritual Eavesdropping

⁹ But the man of God sent ⌞word⌟ to the king of Israel: "Be careful passing by this place, for the Arameans are going down there." ¹⁰ Consequently, the king of Israel sent ⌞word⌟ to the place the man of God had told him about. The man of God repeatedlyᵃ warned the king, so the king would be on his guard.

¹¹ The king of Aram was enraged because of this matter, and he called his servants and demanded of them, "Tell me, which one of us is for the king of Israel?"

¹² One of his servants said, "No one, my lord the king. Elisha, the prophet in Israel, tells the king of Israel even the words you speak in your bedroom."

King of Aram Surrounds Elisha

¹³ So the king said, "Go and see where he is, so I can send ⌞men⌟ to capture him."

When he was told, "Elisha is in Dothan," ¹⁴ he sent horses, chariots, and a massive army there. They went by night and surrounded the city.

¹⁵ When the servant of the man of God got up early and went out, he discovered an army with horses and chariots surrounding the city. So he asked Elisha, "Oh, my master, what are we to do?"

God's Chariots of Fire

¹⁶ Elisha said, "Don't be afraid, for those who are with us outnumber those who are with them."

¹⁷ Then Elisha prayed, "LORD, please open his eyes and let him see." So the LORD opened the servant's eyes. He looked and saw that the mountain was covered with horses and chariots of fire all around Elisha.

Arameans Struck Blind

¹⁸ When the Arameans came against him, Elisha prayed to the LORD, "Please strike this nation with blindness." So He struck them with blindness, according to Elisha's word. ¹⁹ Then Elisha said to them, "This is not the way, and this is not the city. Follow me, and I will take you to the man you're looking for." And he led them to Samaria. ²⁰ When they entered Samaria, Elisha said, "LORD, open these men's eyes and let them see." So the LORD opened their eyes. They looked and discovered ⌞they were⌟ in Samaria.

²¹ When the king of Israel saw them, he said to Elisha, "My father, should I kill them? I will kill them."

²² Elisha replied, "Don't kill them. Do you kill those you have captured with your sword or your bow? Set food and water in front of them so they can eat and drink and go to their master."

²³ So he prepared a great feast for them. When they had eaten and drunk, he sent them away, and they went to their master. The Aramean raiders did not come into Israel's land again.

King of Aram Besieges Samaria

²⁴ Some time later, King Ben-hadad of Aram brought all his military units together and marched up to besiege Samaria. ²⁵ So there was a great famine in Samaria, and they continued the siege against it until a donkey's head ⌞sold for⌟ 80 silver ⌞•shekels⌟,ᵇ and a cupᶜ of dove's dungᵈ ⌞sold for⌟ five silver ⌞shekels⌟.ᵉ

²⁶ As the king of Israel was passing by on the wall, a woman cried out to him, "My lord the king, help!"

²⁷ He answered, "If the LORD doesn't help you, where can I get help for you?

ᵃ**6:10** Lit *not once and not twice*   ᵇ**6:25** About 2 pounds   ᶜ**6:25** Lit *a fourth of a kab*   ᵈ**6:25** Or *seedpods*, or *wild onions*   ᵉ**6:25** About 2 ounces

From the threshing floor or the wine-press?" 28 Then the king asked her, "What's the matter?"

Cannibalism in Samaria

She said, "This woman said to me, 'Give up your son, and we will eat him today. Then we will eat my son tomorrow.' 29 So we boiled my son and ate him, and I said to her the next day, 'Give up your son, and we will eat him,' but she has hidden her son."

King of Israel Threatens Elisha

30 When the king heard the woman's words, he tore his clothes. Then, as he was passing by on the wall, the people saw that there was •sackcloth under his clothes next to his skin. 31 He announced, "May God punish me and do so severely if the head of Elisha son of Shaphat remains on his shoulders today."

32 Elisha was sitting in his house, and the elders were sitting with him. The king sent a man ahead of him, but before the messenger got to him, Elisha said to the elders, "Do you see how this murderer has sent ⌊someone⌋ to cut off my head? Look, when the messenger comes, shut the door to keep him out. Isn't the sound of his master's feet behind him?"

33 While Elisha was still speaking with them, the messenger[a] came down to him. Then he said, "This disaster is from the LORD. Why should I trust the LORD any longer?"

Elisha's Prediction of Success

7 Elisha said, "Hear the word of the LORD! This is what the LORD says: 'About this time tomorrow at the gate of Samaria, six quarts[b] of fine meal ⌊will sell⌋ for a •shekel[c] and 12 quarts[d] of barley ⌊will sell⌋ for a shekel.' "[e]

2 Then the captain, the king's right-hand man, responded to the man of God, "Look, ⌊even if⌋ the LORD were to make windows in heaven, could this really happen?"

Elisha announced, "You will in fact see it with your own eyes, but you won't eat any of it."

Diseased Men Reconnoiter

3 Four men with skin diseases were at the entrance to the gate. They said to each other, "Why just sit here until we die? 4 If we say, 'Let's go into the city,' we will die there because the famine is in the city, but if we sit here, we will also die. So now, come on. Let's go to the Arameans' camp. If they let us live, we will live; if they kill us, we will die."

Aramean Camp Deserted

5 So the diseased men got up at twilight to go to the Arameans' camp. When they came to the camp's edge, they discovered that there was not a ⌊single⌋ man there, 6 for the Lord[f] had caused the Aramean camp to hear the sound of chariots, horses, and a great army. The Arameans had said to each other, "The king of Israel must have hired the kings of the Hittites and the kings of Egypt to attack us." 7 So they had gotten up and fled at twilight abandoning their tents, horses, and donkeys. The camp was intact, and they had fled for their lives.

8 When these men came to the edge of the camp, they went into a tent to eat and drink. Then they picked up the silver, gold, and clothing and went off and hid them. They came back and entered another tent, picked ⌊things⌋ up, and hid them. 9 Then they said to each other, "We're not doing what is right. Today is a day of good news. If we are silent and

---

[a]**6:33** Some emend to *king* [b]**7:1** Lit *a seah* [c]**7:1** About ½ ounce (of silver) [d]**7:1** Lit *two seahs* [e]**7:1** About ½ ounce (of silver) [f]**7:6** Many Hb mss read LORD

wait until morning light, we will be punished. Let's go tell the king's household."

Diseased Men Report

[10] The diseased men went and called to the city's gatekeepers and told them, "We went to the Aramean camp and no one was there—no human sounds. There was nothing but tethered horses and donkeys, and the tents were intact." [11] The gatekeepers called out, and ⸤the news⸥ was reported to the king's household.

[12] So the king got up in the night and said to his servants, "Let me tell you what the Arameans have done to us. They know we are starving, so they have left the camp to hide in the open country, thinking, 'When they come out of the city, we will take them alive and go into the city.'"

[13] But one of his servants responded, "Please, let ⸤messengers⸥ take five of the horses that are left in the city. ⸤The messengers⸥ are like the whole multitude of Israelites who will die,[a] so let's send them and see."

Israel Plunders Aramean Camp

[14] ⸤The messengers⸥ took two chariots with horses, and the king sent them after the Aramean army, saying, "Go and see." [15] So they followed them as far as the Jordan. They saw that the whole way was littered with clothes and equipment the Arameans had thrown off in their haste. The messengers returned and told the king. [16] Then the people went out and plundered the Aramean camp.

Elisha's Prediction Comes True

It was then that six quarts[b] of fine meal ⸤sold⸥ for a shekel[c] and 12 quarts[d] of barley ⸤sold⸥ for a shekel,[c] according to the word of the LORD. [17] The king had appointed the captain, his right-hand man, to be in charge of the gate, but the people trampled him in the gateway. He died, just as the man of God had predicted when the king came to him. [18] When the man of God had said to the king, "About this time tomorrow 12 quarts[d] of barley ⸤will sell⸥ for a shekel[c] and six quarts[b] of fine meal ⸤will sell⸥ for a shekel[c]; at the gate of Samaria," [19] this captain had answered the man of God, "Look, ⸤even if⸥ the LORD were to make windows in heaven, could this really happen?" Elisha had said, "You will in fact see it with your own eyes, but you won't eat any of it." [20] This is what happened to him: the people trampled him in the gateway, and he died.

Elisha Warns Shunammite: Famine

8 Elisha said to the woman whose son he had restored to life, "Get ready, you and your household, and go and live as a foreigner wherever you can. For the LORD has announced a seven-year famine, and it has already come to the land." [2] So the woman got ready and did what the man of God said. She and her household lived as foreigners in the land of the Philistines for seven years. [3] When the woman returned from the land of the Philistines at the end of seven years, she went to appeal to the king for her house and field.

Shunammite's Property Restored

[4] The king had been speaking to Gehazi, the servant of the man of God, saying, "Tell me all the great things Elisha has done."

---

[a]7:13 LXX, Syr, Vg, many Hb mss; MT reads *left in it. Indeed, they are like the whole multitude of Israel that are left in it; indeed, they are like the whole multitude of Israel who will die.*   [b]7:16,18 Lit *a seah*   [c]7:16,18 About ½ ounce (of silver)   [d]7:16,18 Lit *two seahs*

⁵ While he was telling the king how Elisha restored the dead ⌊son⌋ to life, the woman whose son he had restored to life came to appeal to the king for her house and field. So Gehazi said, "My lord the king, this is the woman and this is the son Elisha restored to life."

⁶ When the king asked the woman, she told him the story. So the king appointed a court official for her, saying, "Restore all that was hers, along with all the income from the field from the day she left the country until now."

Aram's King Contacts Elisha

⁷ Elisha came to Damascus while Ben-hadad king of Aram was sick, and the king was told, "The man of God has come here." ⁸ So the king said to Hazael, "Take a gift with you and go meet the man of God. Inquire of the LORD through him, 'Will I recover from this sickness?'"

⁹ Hazael went to meet Elisha, taking with him a gift: 40 camel-loads of all kinds of goods from Damascus. When he came and stood before him, he said, "Your son, Ben-hadad king of Aram, has sent me to ask you, 'Will I recover from this sickness?'"

¹⁰ Elisha told him, "Go say to him, 'You are sure toª recover.' But the LORD has shown me that he is sure to die." ¹¹ Then Elisha stared steadily at him until Hazael was ashamed.

Elisha's Prediction:
Hazael to be Cruel King

The man of God wept, ¹² and Hazael asked, "Why is my lord weeping?"

He replied, "Because I know the evil you will do to the people of Israel. You will set their fortresses on fire. You will kill their young men with the sword. You

will dash their little ones to pieces. You will rip open their pregnant women."

¹³ Hazael said, "How could your servant, a mere dog, do this monstrous thing?"

Elisha answered, "The LORD has shown me that you will be king over Aram."

¹⁴ Hazael left Elisha and went to his master, who asked him, "What did Elisha say to you?"

Hazael Kills King Ben-hadad

He responded, "He told me you are sure to recover." ¹⁵ The next day Hazael took a heavy cloth, dipped it in water, and spread it over the king's face. Ben-hadad died, and Hazael reigned instead of him.

Judah's King Jehoram: Evil

¹⁶ In the fifth year of Israel's King Joram son of Ahab, Jehoramᵇ son of Jehoshaphat became king of Judah, replacing his father.ᶜ ¹⁷ He was 32 years old when he became king; he reigned eight years in Jerusalem. ¹⁸ He walked in the way of the kings of Israel, as the house of Ahab had done, for Ahab's daughter was his wife. He did what was evil in the LORD's sight. ¹⁹ The LORD was unwilling to destroy Judah because of His servant David, since He had promised to give a lamp to David and to his sons forever.

War with Edom

²⁰ During Jehoram's reign, Edom rebelled against Judah's control and appointed their own king. ²¹ So Jehoram crossed over to Zair with all his chariots. Then at night he set out to attack the Edomites who had surrounded him and the chariot commanders, but his troops

---

ª8:10 Alt Hb tradition reads *You will not*   ᵇ8:16 = The LORD is Exalted   ᶜ8:16 Lit *Judah; Jehoshaphat had been king of Judah*

fled to their tents. ²² So Edom is still in rebellion against Judah's control today. Libnah also rebelled at that time.

²³ The rest of the events of Jehoram's ⌐reign⌐, along with all his accomplishments, are written about in the Historical Record of Israel's Kings. ²⁴ Jehoram rested with his fathers and was buried with his fathers in the city of David, and his son Ahaziah became king in his place.

Judah's King Ahaziah: Evil

²⁵ In the twelfth year of Israel's King Joram son of Ahab, Ahaziah son of Jehoram became king of Judah. ²⁶ Ahaziah was 22 years old when he became king; he reigned one year in Jerusalem. His mother's name was Athaliah, granddaughter of Israel's King Omri. ²⁷ He walked in the way of the house of Ahab and did what was evil in the LORD's sight like the house of Ahab, for he was a son-in-law to Ahab's family.

King Ahaziah Attends Wounded King Joram

²⁸ Ahaziah went with Joram son of Ahab to fight against Hazael king of Aram in Ramoth-gilead, and the Arameans wounded Joram. ²⁹ So King Joram returned to Jezreel to recover from the wounds that the Arameans had inflicted on him in Ramoth-gilead[a] when he fought against Aram's King Hazael. Then Judah's King Ahaziah son of Jehoram went down to Jezreel to visit Joram son of Ahab since Joram was ill.

Elisha's Prophet Anoints Jehu Israel's King

9 The prophet Elisha called one of the sons of the prophets and said, "Tuck your mantle under your belt, take this flask of oil with you, and go to Ramoth-gilead. ² When you get there, look for Jehu son of Jehoshaphat, son of Nimshi. Go in, get him away from his colleagues, and take him to an inner room. ³ Then, take the flask of oil, pour it on his head, and say, 'This is what the LORD says: "I anoint you king over Israel."' Open the door and escape. Don't wait." ⁴ So the young prophet went to Ramoth-gilead.

⁵ When he arrived, the army commanders were sitting there, so he said, "I have a message for you, commander."

Jehu asked, "For which one of us?"

He answered, "For you, commander."

The Prophet's Message

⁶ So Jehu got up and went into the house. The young prophet poured the oil on his head and said, "This is what the LORD God of Israel says: 'I anoint you king over the LORD's people, Israel. ⁷ You are to strike down the house of your master Ahab so that I may avenge the blood shed by the hand of Jezebel—the blood of My servants the prophets and of all the servants of the LORD. ⁸ The whole house of Ahab will perish, and I will eliminate all of Ahab's males,[b] both slave and free, in Israel. ⁹ I will make the house of Ahab like the house of Jeroboam son of Nebat and like the house of Baasha son of Ahijah. ¹⁰ The dogs will eat Jezebel in the plot of land at Jezreel—no one will bury her.'" Then the young prophet opened the door and escaped.

¹¹ When Jehu came out to his master's servants, they asked, "Is everything all right? Why did this crazy person come to you?"

Then he said to them, "You know the sort and their ranting."

¹² But they replied, "⌐That's⌐ a lie! Tell us!"

So Jehu said, "He talked to me about this and that and said, 'This is what the LORD says: I anoint you king over Israel.'"

13 Each man quickly took his garment and put it under Jehu on the bare steps.ᵃ They blew the ram's horn and proclaimed, "Jehu is king!"

Jehu Conspires Against King Joram

14 Then Jehu son of Jehoshaphat, son of Nimshi, conspired against Joram. Joram and all Israel had been at Ramoth-gilead on guard against Hazael king of Aram. 15 But King Joram had returned to Jezreel to recover from the wounds that the Arameans had inflicted on him when he fought against Aram's King Hazael. Jehu said, "If you ⌊commanders⌋ wish ⌊to make me king⌋, then don't let anyone escape from the city to go tell about it in Jezreel."

Jehu Spurns Peace from Kings Joram and Ahaziah

16 Jehu got into his chariot and went to Jezreel since Joram was laid up there and Ahaziah king of Judah had gone down to visit Joram. 17 Now the watchman was standing on the tower in Jezreel. He saw Jehu's troops approaching and shouted, "I see troops!"

Joram responded, "Choose a rider and send him to meet them and have him ask, '⌊Do you come in⌋ peace?'"

18 So a horseman went to meet Jehu and said, "This is what the king asks: '⌊Do you come in⌋ peace?'"

Jehu replied, "What do you have to do with peace?ᵇ Fall in behind me."

The watchman reported, "The messengerᵃ reached them but hasn't started back."

19 So he sent out a second horseman, who went to them and said, "This is what the king asks: '⌊Do you come in⌋ peace?'"

Jehu answered, "What do you have to do with peace?ᵇ Fall in behind me."

20 Again the watchman reported, "He reached them but hasn't started back. Also, the driving is like that of Jehu son of Nimshi—he drives like a madman."

Jehu Kills King Joram

21 "Harness!" Joram shouted, and they harnessed his chariot. Then Joram king of Israel and Ahaziah king of Judah set out, each in his own chariot, and met Jehu at the plot of land of Naboth the Jezreelite. 22 When Joram saw Jehu he asked, "⌊Do you come in⌋ peace, Jehu?"

He answered, "What peace can there be as long as there is so much prostitution and witchcraft from your mother Jezebel?"

23 Joram turned around and fled, shouting to Ahaziah, "It's treachery, Ahaziah!"

24 Then Jehu drew his bow and shot Joram between the shoulders. The arrow went through his heart, and he slumped down in his chariot. 25 Jehu said to Bidkar his aide, "Pick him up and throw him on the plot of ground belonging to Naboth the Jezreelite. For remember when you and I were riding side by side behind his father Ahab, and the LORD uttered this •oracle against him: 26 'As surely as I saw the blood of Naboth and the blood of his sons yesterday,' this is the LORD's message, 'so will I repay you on this plot of land,' this is the LORD's message. So now, according to the word of the LORD, pick him up and throw him on the plot of land."

ᵃ9:13 Lit on the bones of the steps   ᵇ9:18,19 Lit What to you and to peace

Jehu's Men Kill King Ahaziah

²⁷ When King Ahaziah of Judah saw ⌊what was happening⌋, he fled up the road toward Beth-haggan. Jehu pursued him, shouting, "Shoot him too!" So they shot him in his chariotᵃ at Gur Pass near Ibleam, but he fled to Megiddo and died there. ²⁸ Then his servants carried him to Jerusalem in a chariot and buried him in his fathers' tomb in the city of David. ²⁹ It was in the eleventh year of Joram son of Ahab that Ahaziah had become king over Judah.

Jehu to Jezebel's Eunuchs: "Throw her down!"

³⁰ When Jehu came to Jezreel, Jezebel heard about it, so she painted her eyes, adorned her head, and looked down from the window. ³¹ As Jehu entered the gate, she said, "⌊Do you come in⌋ peace, Zimri,ᵇ killer of your master?"

³² He looked up toward the window and said, "Who is on my side? Who?" Two or three eunuchs looked down at him, ³³ and he said, "Throw her down!" So they threw her down, and some of her blood splattered on the wall and on the horses, and Jehu rode over her.

³⁴ Then he went in, ate and drank, and said, "Take care of this cursed woman and bury her, since she's a king's daughter." ³⁵ But when they went out to bury her, they did not find anything but her skull, her feet, and the palms of her hands. ³⁶ So they went back and told him, and he said, "This ⌊fulfills⌋ the LORD's word that He spoke through His servant Elijah the Tishbite: 'In the plot of land at Jezreel, the <u>dogs will eat Jezebel's flesh</u>. ³⁷ Jezebel's corpse will be like manure on the surface of the field in the plot of land at Jezreel so that no one will ⌊be able⌋ to say: This is Jezebel.'"

Jehu's Challenge to House of Ahab

10 Since Ahab had 70 sons in Samaria, Jehu wrote letters and sent them to Samaria to the rulers of Jezreel, to the elders, and to the guardians of Ahab's sons,ᶜ saying:

² When this letter arrives, since your master's sons are with you and you have chariots, horses, a fortified city, and weaponry, ³ select the most qualifiedᵈ of your master's sons, set him on his father's throne, and fight for your master's house.

⁴ However, they were terrified and reasoned, "Look, two kings couldn't stand against him; how can we?"

⁵ So the overseer of the palace, the overseer of the city, the elders, and the guardians sent ⌊a message⌋ to Jehu: "We are your servants, and we will do whatever you tell us. We will not make anyone king. Do whatever you think is right."ᵉ

⁶ Then Jehu wrote them a second letter, saying:

If you are on my side, and if you will obey me, bring me the heads of your master's sons at this time tomorrow at Jezreel.

Ahab's Sons Beheaded

All 70 of the king's sons were being cared for by the city's prominent men. ⁷ When the letter came to them, they took the king's sons and slaughtered all 70, put their heads in baskets, and sent them to Jehu at Jezreel. ⁸ When the messenger came and told him, "They have brought the heads of the king's sons,"

ᵃ**9:27** LXX, Syr, some mss of Vg; Hb omits *So they shot him*   ᵇ**9:31** Zimri was another usurper; 1 Kg 16:8-20
ᶜ**10:1** LXX; MT reads *of Ahab*   ᵈ**10:3** Lit *the good and the upright*   ᵉ**10:5** Lit *Do what is good in your eyes*

the king said, "Pile them in two heaps at the entrance of the gate until morning."

Jehu Kills Rest of Ahab's House

[9] The next morning when he went out and stood ⌊at the gate⌋, he said to all the people, "You are innocent. It was I who conspired against my master and killed him. But who struck down all these? [10] Know, then, that not a word the LORD spoke against the house of Ahab will fail, for the LORD has done what He promised through His servant Elijah." [11] So Jehu killed all who remained of the house of Ahab in Jezreel—all his great men, close friends, and priests—leaving him no survivors.

[12] Then he set out and went on his way to Samaria. On the way, while he was at Beth-eked of the Shepherds, [13] Jehu met the relatives of Ahaziah king of Judah and asked, "Who are you?"

They answered, "We're Ahaziah's relatives. We've come down to greet the king's sons and the queen mother's sons."

[14] Then Jehu ordered, "Take them alive." So they took them alive and then slaughtered them at the pit of Beth-eked—42 men. He didn't spare any of them.

[15] When he left there, he found Jehonadab son of Rechab ⌊coming⌋ to meet him. He greeted him and then asked, "Is your heart one with mine?"[a]

"It is," Jehonadab replied.

Jehu said, "If it is,[b] give me your hand."

So he gave him his hand, and Jehu pulled him up into the chariot with him. [16] Then he said, "Come with me and see my zeal for the LORD!" So he let him ride with him in his chariot. [17] When Jehu came to Samaria, he struck down all who

remained from ⌊the house of⌋ Ahab in Samaria until he had annihilated his house, according to the word of the LORD spoken to Elijah.

Jehu Kills Baal Worshipers

[18] Then Jehu brought all the people together and said to them, "Ahab served •Baal a little, but Jehu will serve him a lot. [19] Now, therefore, summon to me all the prophets of Baal, all his servants, and all his priests. None must be missing, for I have a great sacrifice for Baal. Whoever is missing will not live." However, Jehu was acting deceptively in order to destroy the servants of Baal. [20] Jehu commanded, "Consecrate a solemn assembly for Baal." So they called one.

[21] Then Jehu sent ⌊messengers⌋ throughout all Israel, and all the servants of Baal[c] came; there was not a man left who did not come. They entered the temple of Baal, and it was filled from one end to the other. [22] Then he said to the custodian of the wardrobe, "Bring out the garments for all the servants of Baal." So he brought out their garments.

[23] Then Jehu and Jehonadab son of Rechab entered the temple of Baal, and Jehu said to the servants of Baal, "Look carefully to see that there are no servants of the LORD here among you—only servants of Baal." [24] Then they went in to offer sacrifices and •burnt offerings.

Now Jehu had stationed 80 men outside, and he warned ⌊them⌋, "Whoever allows any of the men I am delivering into your hands to escape ⌊will forfeit⌋ his life for theirs." [25] When he finished offering the burnt offering, Jehu said to the guards and officers, "Go in and kill them. Don't let anyone out." So they struck them down with the sword. Then the guards and officers threw ⌊the bodies⌋ out and

---

[a] **10:15** Lit *heart upright like my heart is with your heart*   [b] **10:15** LXX, Syr, Vg; Hb reads *mine?" Jehonadab said, "It is and it is*   [c] **10:21** LXX adds—*all his priests and all his prophets—*

went into the inner room of the temple of Baal. ²⁶ They brought out the pillars of the temple of Baal and burned them ²⁷ and tore down the pillar of Baal. Then they tore down the temple of Baal and made it a latrine—ˌwhich it isˌ to this day.

Jehu Evaluated: Good and Bad

²⁸ Jehu eliminated Baal ˌworshipˌ from Israel, ²⁹ but he did not turn away from the sins that Jeroboam son of Nebat had caused Israel to commit—ˌworshipingˌ the golden calves that were in Bethel and Dan. ³⁰ Nevertheless, the LORD said to Jehu, "Because you have done well in carrying out what is right in My sight and have done to the house of Ahab all that was in My heart, four generations of your sons will sit on the throne of Israel."

³¹ Yet, Jehu was not careful to follow with all his heart the law of the LORD God of Israel. He did not turn from the sins that Jeroboam had caused Israel to commit.

God Reduces Size of Israel

³² In those days the LORD began to reduce the size of Israel. Hazael defeated the Israelites throughout their territory: ³³ from the Jordan eastward, all the land of Gilead—the Gadites, the Reubenites, and the Manassites—from Aroer which is by the Arnon Valley through Gilead to Bashan.ᵃ ³⁴ Now the rest of the events of Jehu's ˌreignˌ, along with all his accomplishments and all his might, are written about in the Historical Record of Israel's Kings. ³⁵ Jehu rested with his fathers, and he was buried in Samaria. His son Jehoahaz became king in his place. ³⁶ The length of Jehu's reign over Israel in Samaria was 28 years.

Mother Athaliah Usurps the Throne of Judah

11 When Athaliah, Ahaziah's mother, saw that her son was dead, she proceeded to annihilate all the royal heirs. ² Jehosheba, ˌwho wasˌ King Jehoram's daughter and Ahaziah's sister, secretly rescued Joash son of Ahaziah from the king's sons who were being killed and ˌputˌ him and his nurse in a bedroom. So he was hidden from Athaliah and was not killed. ³ Joash was in hiding with Jehosheba in the LORD's temple six years while Athaliah ruled over the land.

Priest Jehoiada Protects Joash

⁴ Then, in the seventh year, Jehoiada sent ˌmessengersˌ and brought in the commanders of hundreds, the Carites, and the guards. He had them come to him in the LORD's temple, where he made a covenant with them and put them under oath. He showed them the king's son ⁵ and commanded them, "This is what you are to do: one third of you who come on duty on the Sabbath are to provide protection for the king's palace. ⁶ A third are to be at the Sur gate and a third at the gate behind the guards. You are to take turns providing protection for the palace.ᵇ ⁷ Your two divisions that go off duty on the Sabbath are to provide protection for the LORD's temple. ⁸ You must completely surround the king with weapons in hand. Anyone who approaches the ranks is to be put to death. You must be with the king in all his daily tasks."ᶜ

⁹ So the commanders of hundreds did everything Jehoiada the priest commanded. They each brought their men—those coming on duty on the Sabbath and those going off duty—and went to Jehoiada the priest. ¹⁰ The priest gave to

ᵃ**10:33** Lit *Arnon Valley and Gilead and Bashan*　ᵇ**11:6** Hb obscure　ᶜ**11:8** Lit *king when he goes out and when he comes in*

the commanders of hundreds King David's spears and shields that were in the LORD's temple. [11] Then the guards stood with their weapons in hand surrounding the king—from the right side of the temple to the left side, by the altar and by the temple.

Jehoiada Crowns Joash King of Judah

[12] He brought out the king's son, put the crown on him, gave him the •testimony,[a] and made him king. They anointed him and clapped their hands and cried, "Long live the king!"

Athaliah: "Treason!"

[13] When Athaliah heard the noise from the guard ˌandˌ the crowd, she went out to the people at the LORD's temple. [14] As she looked, there was the king standing by the pillar according to the custom. The commanders and the trumpeters were by the king, and all the people of the land were rejoicing and blowing trumpets. Athaliah tore her clothes and screamed "Treason! Treason!"

Jehoiada Executes Athaliah

[15] Then Jehoiada the priest ordered the commanders of hundreds in charge of the army, "Take her out between the ranks, and put anyone who follows her to death by the sword," for the priest had said, "She is not to be put to death in the LORD's temple." [16] So they arrested her, and she went out by way of the Horses' Entrance to the king's palace, where she was put to death.

Jehoiada's Reforms

[17] Then Jehoiada made a covenant between the LORD, the king, and the people that they would be the LORD's people

and ˌanother oneˌ between the king and the people.[b] [18] So all the people of the land went to the temple of •Baal and tore it down. They broke its altars and images into pieces, and they killed Mattan, the priest of Baal, at the altars.

Then ˌJehoiadaˌ the priest appointed guards for the LORD's temple. [19] He took ˌwith himˌ the commanders of hundreds, the Carites, the guards, and all the people of the land, and they brought the king from the LORD's temple. They entered the king's palace by way of the guards' gate. Then Joash sat on the throne of the kings. [20] All the people of the land rejoiced, and the city was quiet, for they had put Athaliah to death by the sword in the king's palace.

Judah's King Joash: Right with God

12 [21c] Joash[d] was seven years old when he became king. [1] In the seventh year of Jehu, Joash became king; he reigned 40 years in Jerusalem. His mother's name was Zibiah, who was from Beer-sheba. [2] Throughout the time Jehoiada the priest instructed him, Joash did what was right in the LORD's sight. [3] Yet the •high places were not taken away; the people continued sacrificing and burning incense on the high places.

Joash Commands Repair of Temple

[4] Then Joash said to the priests, "All the dedicated money brought to the LORD's temple, census money, money from vows, and all money voluntarily given for the LORD's temple, [5] each priest is to take from his assessor[e] and repair whatever damage to the temple is found.[f]

---

[a] **11:12** Or *him the copy of the covenant,* or *him a diadem,* or *him jewels*   [b] **11:17** Some Gk versions, 2 Ch 23:16 omit *and [another one] between the king and the people*   [c] **11:21** 2 Kg 12:1 in Hb   [d] **11:21** = The LORD Has Bestowed
[e] **12:5** Hb obscure   [f] **12:5** Lit *repair the breach of the house wherever there is found a breach*

⁶ But by the twenty-third year ⌊of the reign⌋ of King Joash, the priests had not repaired the damageᵃ to the temple. ⁷ So King Joash called Jehoiada the priest and the other priests and said, "Why haven't you repaired the temple's damage? Since you haven't, don't take any money from your assessors; instead, hand it over for the repair of the temple." ⁸ So the priests agreed they would not take money from the people and they would not repair the temple's damage.

Temple Collection

⁹ Then Jehoiada the priest took a chest, bored a hole in its lid, and set it beside the altar on the right side as one enters the LORD's temple; in it the priests who guarded the threshold put all the money brought into the LORD's temple. ¹⁰ Whenever they saw there was a large amount of money in the chest, the king's secretary and the high priest would go to the LORD's temple and count the money found there and tie it up in bags. ¹¹ Then they would put the counted money into the hands of those doing the work— those who oversaw the LORD's temple. They ⌊in turn⌋ would pay it out to those working on the LORD's temple—the carpenters, the builders, ¹² the masons, and the stonecutters—and ⌊would use it⌋ to buy timber and quarried stone to repair the damage to the LORD's temple and for all spending for temple repairs.

¹³ However, no silver bowls, wick trimmers, sprinkling basins, trumpets, or any articles of gold or silver were made for the LORD's temple from the money brought into the temple. ¹⁴ Instead, it was given to those doing the work, and they repaired the LORD's temple with it. ¹⁵ No accounting was required from the men who received the money to pay those doing the work, since they worked with integrity. ¹⁶ The money from the •restitution offering and the •sin offering was not brought to the LORD's temple since it belonged to the priests.

King Hazael of Aram Threatens Jerusalem

¹⁷ At that time Hazael king of Aram marched up and fought against Gath and captured it. Then he planned to attack Jerusalem.

King Joash Pays Tribute

¹⁸ So King Joash of Judah took all the consecrated items that his ancestors—Judah's kings Jehoshaphat, Jehoram, and Ahaziah—had consecrated, along with his own consecrated items and all the gold found in the treasuries of the LORD's temple and in the king's palace, and he sent ⌊them⌋ to Hazael king of Aram. Then Hazael withdrew from Jerusalem.

Servants Assassinate Joash

¹⁹ The rest of the events of Joash's ⌊reign⌋, along with all his accomplishments, are written about in the Historical Record of Judah's Kings. ²⁰ Joash's servants conspired against him and killed him at Beth-millo ⌊on the road that⌋ goes down to Silla. ²¹ His servants Jozabadᵇ son of Shimeath and Jehozabad son of Shomer struck him down, and he died. Then they buried him with his fathers in the city of David, and his son Amaziah became king in his place.

Israel's Evil King Jehoahaz

13 In the twenty-third year of Judah's King Joash son of Ahaziah, Jehoahaz son of Jehu became king over Israel in Samaria; ⌊he reigned⌋ 17 years. ² He did what was evil in the LORD's sight and

---

ᵃ**12:6** Lit *breach* in 2 Kg 12:5-12   ᵇ**12:21** Many Hb mss, LXX read *Jozacar*; 2 Ch 24:26 reads *Zabad*

followed the sins that Jeroboam son of Nebat had caused Israel to commit; he did not turn away from them. ³ So the LORD's anger burned against Israel, and He surrendered them to the power of Hazael king of Aram and his son Ben-hadad during their reigns.

God Spares Israel

⁴ Then Jehoahaz sought the LORD's favor, and the LORD heard him, for He saw the oppression the king of Aram inflicted on Israel. ⁵ Therefore, the LORD gave Israel a deliverer, and they escaped from the power of the Arameans.

Israel Sins Again

Then the people of Israel dwelt in their tents as before, ⁶ but they didn't turn away from the sins that the house of Jeroboam had caused Israel to commit. Jehoahaz walked in them, and the •Asherah pole also remained standing in Samaria. ⁷ Jehoahaz did not have an army left, except for 50 horsemen, 10 chariots, and 10,000 foot soldiers, because the king of Aram had destroyed them, making them like dust at threshing.

⁸ The rest of the events of Jehoahaz's ⌊reign⌋, along with all his accomplishments and his might, are written about in the Historical Record of Israel's Kings. ⁹ Jehoahaz rested with his fathers, and he was buried in Samaria. His son Jehoash° became king in his place.

Israel's King Jehoash: Evil

¹⁰ In the thirty-seventh year of Judah's King Joash, Jehoash son of Jehoahaz became king over Israel in Samaria; ⌊he reigned⌋ 16 years. ¹¹ He did what was evil in the LORD's sight. He did not turn away from all the sins that Jeroboam son

of Nebat had caused Israel to commit, but he walked in them.

¹² The rest of the events of Jehoash's ⌊reign⌋, along with all his accomplishments and the power he had to wage war against Judah's King Amaziah, are written about in the Historical Record of Israel's Kings. ¹³ Jehoash rested with his fathers, and Jeroboam sat on his throne. Jehoash was buried in Samaria with the kings of Israel.

Elisha's Death

¹⁴ When Elisha became sick with the illness that he died from, Jehoash king of Israel went down and wept over him and said, "My father, my father, the chariots and horsemen of Israel!"

Elisha's Prophecy of Israel over Aram

¹⁵ Elisha responded, "Take a bow and arrows." So he got a bow and arrows. ¹⁶ Then Elisha said to the king of Israel, "Put your hand on the bow." So the king put his hand on it, and Elisha put his hands on the king's hands. ¹⁷ Elisha said, "Open the east window." So he opened it. Elisha said, "Shoot!" So he shot. Then Elisha said, "The LORD's arrow of victory, yes, the arrow of victory over Aram. You are to strike down the Arameans in Aphek until you have put an end to them."

¹⁸ Then Elisha said, "Take the arrows!" So he took them, and he said to the king of Israel, "Strike the ground!" So he struck the ground three times and stopped. ¹⁹ The man of God was angry with him and said, "You should have struck the ground five or six times. Then you would have struck down Aram until you had put an end to them, but now you will only strike down Aram three times." ²⁰ Then Elisha died and was buried.

ª13:9 = Joash

Miracle from Elisha's Bones

Now marauding bands of Moabites used to come into the land in the spring of the year. ²¹ Once, as the Israelites were burying a man, suddenly they saw a marauding band, so they threw the man into Elisha's tomb. When he touched Elisha's bones, the man revived and stood up!

God's Mercy on Israel

²² Hazael king of Aram oppressed Israel throughout the reign of Jehoahaz, ²³ but the LORD was gracious to them and had compassion on them and turned toward them because of His covenant with Abraham, Isaac, and Jacob. He was not willing to destroy them. Even now He has not banished them from His presence.

²⁴ King Hazael of Aram died, and his son Ben-hadad became king in his place. ²⁵ Then Jehoash son of Jehoahaz took back from Ben-hadad son of Hazael the cities that Hazael had taken in war from Jehoash's father Jehoahaz. Jehoash defeated Ben-hadad three times and recovered the cities of Israel.

Judah's King Amaziah: Right

14 In the second year of Israel's King Jehoash[a] son of Jehoahaz,[b] Amaziah son of Joash became king of Judah. ² He was 25 years old when he became king; he reigned 29 years in Jerusalem. His mother's name was Jehoaddan[c] and was from Jerusalem. ³ He did what was right in the LORD's sight, but not like his ancestor David. He did everything his father Joash had done. ⁴ Yet, the •high places were not taken away, and the people continued sacrificing and burning incense on the high places.

⁵ As soon as the kingdom was firmly in his grasp, Amaziah killed his servants who had murdered his father the king. ⁶ However, he did not put the children of the murderers to death, as it is written in the book of the law of Moses where the LORD commanded, "Fathers must not be put to death because of children, and children must not be put to death because of fathers; instead, each one will be put to death for his own sin."

⁷ Amaziah killed 10,000 Edomites in the Valley of Salt. He took Sela in battle and called it Joktheel, ⌐which is its name⌐ to this very day. ⁸ Amaziah then sent messengers to Jehoash son of Jehoahaz, son of Jehu, king of Israel, saying, "Come, let us meet face to face."

Israel Rejects Pact with Judah

⁹ King Jehoash of Israel sent ⌐word⌐ to Amaziah king of Judah, saying, "The thistle that was in Lebanon once sent ⌐a message⌐ to the cedar that was in Lebanon, saying, 'Give your daughter to my son as a wife.' Then a wild animal that was in Lebanon passed by and trampled the thistle. ¹⁰ You have indeed defeated Edom, and you have become overconfident. Enjoy your glory and stay at home. Why should you stir up such trouble that you fall—you and Judah with you?"

Israel Defeats Judah, Sacks Temple

¹¹ But Amaziah would not listen, so King Jehoash of Israel advanced. He and King Amaziah of Judah faced off at Beth-shemesh that belongs to Judah. ¹² Judah was routed before Israel, and ⌐Judah's men⌐ fled, each to his own tent. ¹³ King Jehoash of Israel captured Judah's King Amaziah son of Joash,[d] son of Ahaziah, at Beth-shemesh. Then Jehoash went to Jerusalem and broke down 200 yards[e] of

---

[a]14:1 = Joash [b]14:1 = Joahaz [c]14:2 Alt Hb tradition, many Hb mss, Syr, Tg, Vg, 2 Ch 25:1; MT, LXX read *Jehoaddin* [d]14:13 = Jehoash [e]14:13 Lit *400 cubits*

Jerusalem's wall from the Ephraim Gate to the Corner Gate. ¹⁴ He took all the gold and silver and all the utensils found in the LORD's temple and in the treasuries of the king's palace, and the hostages. Then he returned to Samaria.

Israel's King Jehoash's Dies

¹⁵ The rest of the events of Jehoash's ⌐reign⌐, along with his accomplishments, his might, and how he waged war against Amaziah king of Judah, are written about in the Historical Record of Israel's Kings. ¹⁶ Jehoash rested with his fathers, and he was buried in Samaria with the kings of Israel. His son Jeroboam became king in his place.

Judah's King Amaziah Assassinated

¹⁷ Judah's King Amaziah son of Joash lived 15 years after the death of Israel's King Jehoash son of Jehoahaz. ¹⁸ The rest of the events of Amaziah's ⌐reign⌐ are written about in the Historical Record of Judah's Kings. ¹⁹ A conspiracy was formed against him in Jerusalem, and he fled to Lachish. However, ⌐men⌐ were sent after him to Lachish, and they put him to death there. ²⁰ They carried him back on horses, and he was buried in Jerusalem with his fathers in the city of David.

²¹ Then all the people of Judah took Azariah,[a] who was 16 years old, and made him king in place of his father Amaziah. ²² He rebuilt Elath[b] and restored it to Judah after ⌐Amaziah⌐ the king rested with his fathers.

Israel's King Jeroboam: Evil

²³ In the fifteenth year of Judah's King Amaziah son of Joash, Jeroboam son of Jehoash[c] became king of Israel in Samaria; he reigned 41 years. ²⁴ He did

what was evil in the LORD's sight. He did not turn away from all the sins Jeroboam son of Nebat had caused Israel to commit.

²⁵ It was he who restored Israel's border from Lebo-hamath as far as the Sea of the •Arabah, according to the word the LORD, the God of Israel, had spoken through His servant, the prophet Jonah son of Amittai from Gath-hepher. ²⁶ For the LORD saw that the affliction of Israel was very bitter. There was no one to help Israel, neither bond nor free. ²⁷ However, the LORD had not said He would blot out the name of Israel from under heaven, so He delivered them by the hand of Jeroboam son of Jehoash.[c]

²⁸ The rest of the events of Jeroboam's ⌐reign⌐—along with all his accomplishments and the power he had to wage war and how he recovered for Israel Damascus and Hamath, which had belonged to Judah—are written about in the Historical Record of Israel's Kings. ²⁹ Jeroboam rested with his fathers, the kings of Israel. His son Zechariah became king in his place.

Judah's King Azariah: Right

15 In the twenty-seventh year of Israel's King Jeroboam, Azariah[d] son of Amaziah became king of Judah. ² He was 16 years old when he became king; he reigned 52 years in Jerusalem. His mother's name was Jecoliah; ⌐she was⌐ from Jerusalem. ³ Azariah did what was right in the LORD's sight just as his father Amaziah had done. ⁴ Yet, the •high places were not taken away; the people continued sacrificing and burning incense on the high places.

⁵ The LORD afflicted the king, and he had a serious skin disease until the day of his death. He lived in a separate

house,[a] while Jotham, the king's son, was over the household governing the people of the land.

[6] The rest of the events of Azariah's ⌊reign⌋, along with all his accomplishments, are written about in the Historical Record of Judah's Kings. [7] Azariah rested with his fathers, and he was buried with his fathers in the city of David. His son Jotham became king in his place.

Israel's King Zechariah: Evil

[8] In the thirty-eighth year of Judah's King Azariah, Zechariah son of Jeroboam became king over Israel in Samaria for six months. [9] He did what was evil in the LORD's sight as his fathers had done. He did not turn away from the sins Jeroboam son of Nebat had caused Israel to commit.

Shallum Assassinates King Zechariah

[10] Shallum son of Jabesh conspired against Zechariah. He struck him down publicly,[b] killed him, and became king in his place. [11] As for the rest of the events of Zechariah's ⌊reign⌋, they are written about in the Historical Record of Israel's Kings. [12] The word of the LORD that He spoke to Jehu was, "Four generations of your sons will sit on the throne of Israel." And it was so.

Menahem Assassinates Israel's King Shallum

[13] In the thirty-ninth year of Judah's King Uzziah, Shallum son of Jabesh became king; he reigned in Samaria a full month. [14] Then Menahem son of Gadi came up from Tirzah to Samaria and struck down Shallum son of Jabesh there. He killed him and became king in his place. [15] As for the rest of the events of Shallum's ⌊reign⌋, along with the conspiracy that he formed, they are written about in the Historical Record of Israel's Kings.

Israel's King Menahem: Evil

[16] At that time, ⌊starting⌋ from Tirzah, Menahem attacked Tiphsah, all who were in it, and its territory. Because they wouldn't surrender, he attacked ⌊it and⌋ ripped open all the pregnant women.

[17] In the thirty-ninth year of Judah's King Azariah, Menahem son of Gadi became king over Israel; ⌊he reigned⌋ 10 years in Samaria. [18] He did what was evil in the LORD's sight. Throughout his reign, he did not turn away from the sins Jeroboam son of Nebat had caused Israel to commit.

Assyrians Invade Israel— Menahem Collaborates

[19] Pul[c] king of Assyria invaded the land, so Menahem gave Pul 75,000 pounds[d] of silver so that Pul would support him to strengthen his grip on the kingdom. [20] Then Menahem exacted 20 ounces[e] of silver from each of the wealthy men of Israel to give to the king of Assyria. So the king of Assyria withdrew and did not stay there in the land.

[21] The rest of the events of Menahem's ⌊reign⌋, along with all his accomplishments, are written about in the Historical Record of Israel's Kings. [22] Menahem rested with his fathers, and his son Pekahiah became king in his place.

Israel's King Pekahiah: Evil

[23] In the fiftieth year of Judah's King Azariah, Pekahiah son of Menahem became king over Israel in Samaria; ⌊he reigned⌋ two years. [24] He did what was

---

[a]15:5 Lit a house of freedom or of exemption   [b]15:10 Hb uncertain; some emend to at Ibleam, as some LXX mss read; Hb could mean at Kabal-am.   [c]15:19 = Tiglath-pileser   [d]15:19 Lit 1,000 talents   [e]15:20 Lit 50 shekels

evil in the LORD's sight and did not turn away from the sins Jeroboam son of Nebat had caused Israel to commit.

Pekah Assassinates King Pekahiah

25 Then his officer, Pekah son of Remaliah, conspired against him and struck him down, as well as Argob and Arieh,[a] in Samaria at the citadel of the king's palace. There were 50 Gileadite men with Pekah. He killed Pekahiah and became king in his place.

26 As for the rest of the events of Pekahiah's ⌐reign⌐, along with all his accomplishments, they are written about in the Historical Record of Israel's Kings.

Israel's King Pekah: Evil

27 In the fifty-second year of Judah's King Azariah, Pekah son of Remaliah became king over Israel in Samaria; ⌐he reigned⌐ 20 years. 28 He did what was evil in the LORD's sight. He did not turn away from the sins Jeroboam son of Nebat had caused Israel to commit.

29 In the days of Pekah king of Israel, Tiglath-pileser king of Assyria came and captured Ijon, Abel-beth-maacah, Janoah, Kedesh, Hazor, Gilead, and Galilee—all the land of Naphtali—and deported the people to Assyria.

Hoshea Assassinates Israel's King Pekah

30 Then Hoshea son of Elah organized a conspiracy against Pekah son of Remaliah. He attacked him, killed him, and became king in his place in the twentieth year of Jotham son of Uzziah.

31 As for the rest of the events of Pekah's ⌐reign⌐, along with all his accomplishments, they are written about in the Historical Record of Israel's Kings.

Judah's King Jotham: Right

32 In the second year of Israel's King Pekah son of Remaliah, Jotham son of Uzziah became king of Judah. 33 He was 25 years old when he became king; he reigned 16 years in Jerusalem. His mother's name was Jerusha daughter of Zadok. 34 He did what was right in the LORD's sight just as his father Uzziah had done. 35 Yet, the high places were not taken away; the people continued sacrificing and burning incense on the high places.

It was Jotham who built the Upper Gate of the LORD's temple. 36 The rest of the events of Jotham's ⌐reign⌐, along with all his accomplishments, are written about in the Historical Record of Judah's Kings. 37 In those days the LORD began sending Rezin king of Aram and Pekah son of Remaliah against Judah. 38 Jotham rested with his fathers, and he was buried with his fathers in the city of his ancestor David. His son Ahaz became king in his place.

Judah's King Ahaz: Evil

16 In the seventeenth year of Pekah son of Remaliah, Ahaz son of Jotham became king of Judah. 2 Ahaz was 20 years old when he became king; he reigned 16 years in Jerusalem. He did not do what was right in the sight of the LORD his God like his ancestor David 3 but walked in the way of the kings of Israel. He even made his son pass through the fire,[b] imitating the abominations of the nations the LORD had dispossessed before the Israelites. 4 He sacrificed and burned incense on the ∙high places, on the hills, and under every green tree.

5 Then Aram's King Rezin and Israel's King Pekah son of Remaliah came to

---

a**15:25** Hb obscure   b**16:3** Either a Canaanite cult practice or child sacrifice

wage war against Jerusalem. They besieged Ahaz but were not able to conquer him. [6] At that time Rezin king of Aram recovered Elath for Aram and expelled the Judahites from Elath. Then the Arameans came to Elath, and they live there until today.

Judah-Assyria Alliance

[7] So Ahaz sent messengers to Tiglath-pileser king of Assyria, saying, "I am your servant and your son. March up and save me from the power of the king of Aram and of the king of Israel, who are rising up against me." [8] Ahaz also took the silver and gold found in the LORD's temple and in the treasuries of the king's palace and sent ⌊them⌋ to the king of Assyria as a gift. [9] So the king of Assyria listened to him and marched up to Damascus and captured it. He deported its people to Kir but put Rezin to death.

Judah's King Ahaz: Idolatry

[10] King Ahaz went to Damascus to meet Tiglath-pileser king of Assyria. When he saw the altar that was in Damascus, King Ahaz sent a model of the altar and complete plans for its construction to Uriah the priest. [11] Uriah built the altar according to all ⌊the instructions⌋ King Ahaz sent from Damascus. Therefore, by the time King Ahaz came back from Damascus, Uriah the priest had made it. [12] When the king came back from Damascus, he saw the altar. Then he approached the altar and ascended it. [13] He offered his •burnt offering and his •grain offering, poured out his drink offering, and sprinkled the blood of his •fellowship offerings on the altar. [14] He took the bronze altar that was before the LORD in front of the temple between ⌊his⌋ altar and the LORD's temple, and put it on the north side of ⌊his⌋ altar.

[15] Then King Ahaz commanded Uriah the priest, "Offer on the great altar the morning burnt offering, the evening grain offering, and the king's burnt offering and his grain offering. ⌊Also offer⌋ the burnt offering of all the people of the land, their grain offering, and their drink offerings. Sprinkle on the altar all the blood of the burnt offering and all the blood of sacrifice. The bronze altar will be for me to seek guidance."[a] [16] Uriah the priest did everything King Ahaz commanded.

[17] Then King Ahaz cut off the frames of the water carts[b] and removed the bronze basin from ⌊each of⌋ them. He took the reservoir[c] from the bronze oxen that were under it and put it on a stone pavement. [18] To satisfy the king of Assyria, he removed from the LORD's temple the Sabbath canopy they had built in the palace, and ⌊he closed⌋ the outer entrance for the king.

Ahaz's Death

[19] The rest of the events of Ahaz's ⌊reign⌋, along with his accomplishments, are written about in the Historical Record of Judah's Kings. [20] Ahaz rested with his fathers and was buried with his fathers in the city of David, and his son Hezekiah became king in his place.

Israel's King Hoshea: Evil

17 In the twelfth year of Judah's King Ahaz, Hoshea son of Elah became king over Israel in Samaria; ⌊he reigned⌋ nine years. [2] He did what was evil in the LORD's sight, but not like the kings of Israel who preceded him.

---

[a]**16:15** Hb obscure   [b]**16:17** Lit *the stands*   [c]**16:17** Lit *sea*

Assyria Invades Israel

3 Shalmaneser king of Assyria attacked him, and Hoshea became his vassal and paid him tribute money. 4 But the king of Assyria discovered a conspiracy by Hoshea—he had sent envoys to So king of Egypt and had not paid tribute money to the king of Assyria as in previous years.ᵃ Therefore, the king of Assyria arrested him and put him in prison. 5 Then the king of Assyria invaded the whole land, marched up to Samaria, and besieged it for three years.

Fall of Samaria

6 In the ninth year of Hoshea, the king of Assyria captured Samaria. He deported the Israelites to Assyria and settled them in Halah and by the Habor, Gozan's river, and in the cities of the Medes.

Why Israel Fell

7 ⌊This disaster⌋ happened because the people of Israel had sinned against the LORD their God who had brought them out of the land of Egypt from the power of Pharaoh king of Egypt and because they had worshipedᵇ other gods. 8 They had lived according to the customs of the nations that the LORD had dispossessed before the Israelites and the customs the kings of Israel had introduced. 9 The Israelites secretly did what was not rightᶜ against the LORD their God. They built •high places in all their towns from watchtower to fortified city. 10 They set up for themselves sacred pillars and •Asherah poles on every high hill and under every green tree. 11 They burned incense on all the high places just like those nations that the LORD had driven out before them. They did evil things, provoking the LORD. 12 They served idols, although the

LORD had told them, "You must not do this." 13 Still, the LORD warned Israel and Judah through every prophet and every seer, saying, "Turn from your evil ways and keep My commandments and statutes according to all the law I commanded your ancestors and sent to you through My servants the prophets."

14 But they would not listen. Instead, they became obstinate likeᵈ their ancestors who did not believe the LORD their God. 15 They rejected His statutes and His covenant He had made with their ancestors and the warnings He had given them. They pursued worthless idols and became worthless themselves, following the surrounding nations the LORD had commanded them not to imitate. 16 They abandoned all the commandments of the LORD their God. They made for themselves molded images—even two calves—and an Asherah pole. They worshiped the whole heavenly •host and served •Baal. 17 They made their sons and daughters pass through the fire and practiced •divination and interpreted omens. They devoted themselves to do what was evil in the LORD's sight and provoked Him.

18 Therefore, the LORD was very angry with Israel, and He removed them from His presence. Only the tribe of Judah remained. 19 Even Judah did not keep the commandments of the LORD their God but lived according to the customs Israel had introduced. 20 So the LORD rejected all the descendants of Israel, afflicted them, and handed them over to plunderers until He had banished them from His presence.

Summary of Israel's History

21 When the LORD tore Israel from the house of David, Israel made Jeroboam

---

ᵃ17:4 Lit as year by year   ᵇ17:7 Lit feared   ᶜ17:9 Or Israelites spoke untrue words   ᵈ17:14 Lit they stiffened their neck like the neck of

son of Nebat king. Then Jeroboam led Israel away from following the LORD and caused them to commit great sin. ²² The Israelites persisted in all the sins that Jeroboam committed and did not turn away from them. ²³ Finally, the LORD removed Israel from His presence just as He had declared through all His servants the prophets. So Israel has been exiled to Assyria from their homeland until today.

Assyria: Foreign Refugees to Israel

²⁴ Then the king of Assyria brought ⌊people⌋ from Babylon, Cuthah, Avva, Hamath, and Sepharvaim and settled them in place of the Israelites in the cities of Samaria. The settlers took possession of Samaria and lived in its cities. ²⁵ When they first lived there, they did not •fear the LORD. So the LORD sent lions among them, which killed some of them. ²⁶ The settlers spoke to the king of Assyria, saying, "The nations that you have deported and placed in the cities of Samaria do not know the custom of the God of the land. Therefore, He has sent lions among them, which are killing them because the people don't know the custom of the God of the land."

King of Assyria Returns Priest of God

²⁷ Then the king of Assyria issued a command: "Send back one of the priests you deported. Have him go and live there so he can teach them the custom of the God of the land." ²⁸ So one of the priests they had deported came and lived in Bethel, and he began to teach them how they should fear the LORD.

²⁹ But ⌊the people of⌋ each nation, in the cities where they lived, were still making their own gods and putting them in the shrines of the high places that the Samaritans had made. ³⁰ The men of Babylon made Succoth-benoth, the men of Cuth made Nergal, the men of Hamath made Ashima, ³¹ the Avvites made Nibhaz and Tartak, and the Sepharvites burned their children in the fire to Adrammelech and Anammelech, the gods of the Sepharvaim. ³² So they feared the LORD, but they also appointed from their number, priests to serve them in the shrines of the high places. ³³ They feared the LORD, but they also worshiped their own gods according to the custom of the nations where they had been deported from.

³⁴ They are ⌊still⌋ practicing the former customs to this day. None of them fear the LORD or observe their statutes and ordinances, the law and commandments the LORD commanded the descendants of Jacob; He renamed him Israel. ³⁵ The LORD made a covenant with them and commanded them, "Do not fear other gods; do not bow down to them; do not serve them; do not sacrifice to them. ³⁶ Instead, fear the LORD, who brought you from the land of Egypt with great power and an outstretched arm. You are to bow down to Him, and you are to sacrifice to Him. ³⁷ You are to be careful always to observe the statutes, the ordinances, the laws, and the commandment He wrote for you; do not fear other gods. ³⁸ Do not forget the covenant that I have made with you. Do not fear other gods, ³⁹ but fear the LORD your God, and He will deliver you from the hand of all your enemies."

⁴⁰ However, they would not listen but continued practicing their former custom. ⁴¹ These nations feared the LORD but also served their idols. Their children and grandchildren continue doing as their fathers did until today.

Judah's King Hezekiah: Right

18 In the third year of Israel's King Hoshea son of Elah, Hezekiah son of Ahaz became king of Judah. [2] He was 25 years old when he became king; he reigned 29 years in Jerusalem. His mother's name was Abi[a] daughter of Zechariah. [3] He did what was right in the LORD's sight just as his ancestor David had done. [4] He removed the •high places and shattered the sacred pillars and cut down the •Asherah ⌊poles⌋. He broke into pieces the bronze snake that Moses made, for the Israelites burned incense to it up to that time. He called it Nehushtan.[b]

Hezekiah Trusts and Obeys God

[5] Hezekiah trusted in the LORD God of Israel; not one of the kings of Judah was like him, either before him or after him. [6] He held fast to the LORD and did not turn from following Him but kept the commandments the LORD had commanded Moses.

[7] The LORD was with him, and wherever he went, he prospered. He rebelled against the king of Assyria and did not serve him. [8] He defeated the Philistines as far as Gaza and its borders, from watchtower to fortified city.

Review of Israel's Fall to Assyria

[9] In the fourth year of King Hezekiah, which was the seventh year of Israel's King Hoshea son of Elah, Shalmaneser king of Assyria marched against Samaria and besieged it. [10] The Assyrians captured it at the end of three years. In the sixth year of Hezekiah, which was the ninth year of Israel's King Hoshea, Samaria was captured. [11] The king of Assyria deported the Israelites to Assyria and put them in Halah and by the Habor,

Gozan's river, and in the cities of the Medes, [12] because they did not listen to the voice of the LORD their God but violated His covenant—all He had commanded Moses the servant of the LORD. They did not listen, and they did not obey.

Sennacherib Invades Judah

[13] In the fourteenth year of King Hezekiah, Sennacherib king of Assyria attacked all the fortified cities of Judah and captured them. [14] So Hezekiah king of Judah sent word to the king of Assyria at Lachish, saying, "I have done wrong. Withdraw from me. Whatever you demand from me, I will pay."

Hezekiah Pays Tribute

The king of Assyria demanded from King Hezekiah of Judah 11 tons[c] of silver and one ton[d] of gold. [15] So Hezekiah gave ⌊him⌋ all the silver found in the LORD's temple and in the treasuries of the king's palace.

[16] At that time Hezekiah stripped ⌊the gold from⌋ the doors of the LORD's sanctuary and from the doorposts he had overlaid and gave it to the king of Assyria.

Assyria Continues Threat

[17] Then the king of Assyria sent the Tartan, the Rab-saris, and the •Rabshakeh,[e] along with a massive army, from Lachish to King Hezekiah at Jerusalem. They advanced and came to Jerusalem, and[f] they took their position by the aqueduct of the upper pool, which is by the highway to the Fuller's Field. [18] Then they called for the king, but Eliakim son of Hilkiah, who was in charge of the palace, Shebnah the court secretary, and Joah son of Asaph, the court historian, came out to them.

---

[a]**18:2** = Abijah in 2 Ch 29:1　[b]**18:4** = A bronze thing　[c]**18:14** Lit *300 talents*　[d]**18:14** Lit *30 talents*　[e]**18:17** Assyrian military titles　[f]**18:17** LXX, Syr, Vg; MT reads *and came and*

Assyrian Chief Commander's Demands

19 Then the Rabshakeh said to them, "Tell Hezekiah this is what the great king, the king of Assyria, says: 'What are you relying on?ᵃ 20 You think mere words are strategy and strength for war. What are you now relying on so that you have rebelled against me? 21 Look, you now trust in Egypt, the stalk of this splintered reed, which if a man leans on it will go into his palm and pierce it. This is how Pharaoh king of Egypt is to all who trust in him. 22 Suppose you say to me: We trust in the LORD our God. Isn't He the One whose high places and altars Hezekiah has removed, saying to Judah and to Jerusalem: You must worship at this altar in Jerusalem?'

23 "So now make a bargain with my master the king of Assyria. I'll give you 2,000 horses if you're able to supply riders for them! 24 How then can you drive back a single officer among the least of my master's servants and trust in Egypt for chariots and for horsemen? 25 Have I attacked this place to destroy it without the LORD's ⌊approval⌋? The LORD said to me, 'Attack this land and destroy it.' "

Eliakim Asks Secrecy

26 Then Eliakim son of Hilkiah, Shebnah, and Joah said to the Rabshakeh, "Please speak to your servants in Aramaic, since we understand ⌊it⌋. Don't speak with us in Hebrewᵇ within earshot of the people on the wall."

Chief Commander Appeals to People

27 But the Rabshakeh said to them, "Has my master sent me only to your master and to you to speak these words? Hasn't ⌊he⌋ also ⌊sent me⌋ to the men who sit on the wall, ⌊destined⌋ with you to eat their own excrement and drink their own urine?"

28 The Rabshakeh stood and called out loudly in Hebrew.ᵇ Then he spoke: "Hear the word of the great king, the king of Assyria. 29 This is what the king says: 'Don't let Hezekiah deceive you; he can't deliver you from my hand. 30 Don't let Hezekiah persuade you to trust in the LORD by saying: Certainly the LORD will deliver us! This city will not be handed over to the king of Assyria.'

31 "Don't listen to Hezekiah, for this is what the king of Assyria says: 'Make peaceᶜ with me and surrender to me. Then every one of you may eat from his own vine and his own fig tree, and every one may drink water from his own cistern 32 until I come and take you away to a land like your own land—a land of grain and new wine, a land of bread and vineyards, a land of olive trees and honey—so that you may live and not die. But don't listen to Hezekiah when he misleads you, saying: The LORD will deliver us. 33 Has any of the gods of the nations ever delivered his land from the power of the king of Assyria? 34 Where are the gods of Hamath and Arpad? Where are the gods of Sepharvaim, Hena, and Ivvah?ᵈ Have they delivered Samaria from my hand? 35 Who among all the gods of the lands has delivered his land from my power? So how is the LORD to deliver Jerusalem?' "

People Stay Silent

36 But the people kept silent; they answered him not a word, for the king's command was, "Don't answer him." 37 Then Eliakim son of Hilkiah, who was in charge of the palace, Shebna the court secretary, and Joah son of Asaph, the court historian, came to Hezekiah with

ᵃ18:19 Lit What is this trust which you trust   ᵇ18:26,28 Lit Judahite   ᶜ18:31 Lit a blessing   ᵈ18:34 Some LXX, Vg mss read Sepharvaim? Where are the gods of the land of Samaria?

their clothes torn and reported to him the words of the Rabshakeh.

Hezekiah Seeks Prophet Isaiah's Counsel

19 When King Hezekiah heard ⌐their report⌐, he tore his clothes, covered himself with •sackcloth, and went into the LORD's temple. ² Then he sent Eliakim, who was in charge of the palace, Shebna the court secretary, and the elders of the priests, covered with sackcloth, to the prophet Isaiah son of Amoz. ³ They said to him, "This is what Hezekiah says: 'Today is a day of distress, rebuke, and disgrace, for children have come to the point of birth, but there is no strength to deliver ⌐them⌐. ⁴ Perhaps the LORD your God will hear all the words of the •Rabshakeh, whom his master the king of Assyria sent to mock the living God, and will rebuke ⌐him for⌐ the words that the LORD your God has heard. Therefore, offer a prayer for the surviving remnant.'"

Isaiah's Answer: "Don't Be Afraid"

⁵ So the servants of King Hezekiah went to Isaiah, ⁶ who said to them, "Tell your master this, 'The LORD says: Don't be afraid because of the words you have heard, that the king of Assyria's attendants have blasphemed Me with. ⁷ I am about to put a spirit in him, and he will hear a rumor and return to his own land where I will cause him to fall by the sword.'"

King Sennacherib's Departing Threat

⁸ When the Rabshakeh heard that the king of Assyria had left Lachish, he returned and found him fighting against Libnah. ⁹ The king had heard this about Tirhakah king of •Cush:ᵃ "Look, he has set out to fight against you." So he again

sent messengers to Hezekiah, saying, ¹⁰ "Say this to Hezekiah king of Judah: 'Don't let your God, whom you trust, deceive you by promising that Jerusalem will not be handed over to the king of Assyria. ¹¹ Look, you have heard what the kings of Assyria have done to all the countries: they destroyed them completely. Will you be rescued? ¹² Did the gods of the nations that my predecessors destroyed rescue them—⌐nations such as⌐ Gozan, Haran, Rezeph, and the Edenites in Telassar? ¹³ Where is the king of Hamath, the king of Arpad, the king of the city of Sepharvaim, Hena, or Ivvah?'"

Hezekiah's Prayer

¹⁴ Hezekiah took the letter from the hand of the messengers, read it, then went up to the LORD's temple, and spread it out before the LORD. ¹⁵ Then Hezekiah prayed before the LORD: "LORD God of Israel who is enthroned ⌐above⌐ the •cherubim, You are God—You alone—of all the kingdoms of the earth. You made the heavens and the earth. ¹⁶ Listen closely, LORD, and hear; open Your eyes, LORD, and see; hear the words that Sennacherib has sent to mock the living God. ¹⁷ LORD, it is true that the kings of Assyria have devastated the nations and their lands. ¹⁸ They have thrown their gods into the fire, for they were not gods but made by human hands—wood and stone. So they have destroyed them. ¹⁹ Now, LORD our God, please save us from his hand so that all the kingdoms of the earth may know that You are the LORD God—You alone."

God's Answer through Isaiah

²⁰ Then Isaiah son of Amoz sent ⌐a message⌐ to Hezekiah: "The LORD, the God of Israel says: 'I have heard your

ᵃ**19:9** Or *Nubia*

prayer to Me about Sennacherib king of Assyria.' 21 This is the word the LORD has spoken against him:

The young woman, Daughter Zion,
despises you and scorns you:
Daughter Jerusalem
shakes ⌊her⌋ head
    behind your back.ᵃ
22 Who is it you mocked
    and blasphemed?
Against whom have you raised
    ⌊your⌋ voice
and lifted your eyes in pride?
Against the Holy One of Israel!
23 You have mocked the Lordᵇ
    throughᶜ your messengers.
You have said:

With my many chariots
I have gone up to the heights
    of the mountains,
to the far recesses of Lebanon.
I cut down its tallest cedars,
    its choice cypress trees.
I came to its farthest outpost,
    its densest forest.
24 I dug ⌊wells⌋,
and I drank foreign waters.
I dried up all the streams of Egypt
with the soles of my feet.

25 Have you not heard?
I designed it long ago;
I planned it in days gone by.
I have now brought it to pass,
and you have crushed fortified cities
    into piles of rubble.
26 Their inhabitants have
    become powerless,
dismayed, and ashamed.
They are plants of the field,
    tender grass,
grass on the rooftops,
blasted by the east wind.ᵈ

27 But I know your sitting down,ᵉ
your going out
    and your coming in,
and your raging against Me.
28 Because your raging against Me
    and your arrogance have reached
    My ears,
I will put My hook in your nose
and My bit in your mouth;
I will make you go back
the way you came.

29 This will be the sign for you: This year you will eat what grows on its own, and in the second year what grows from that. But in the third year sow and reap, plant vineyards and eat their fruit. 30 The surviving remnant of the house of Israel will again take root downward and bear fruit upward. 31 For a remnant will go out from Jerusalem, and survivors from Mount Zion. The zeal of the LORD of •Hosts will accomplish this.

32 Therefore, this is what the LORD
    says about the king of Assyria:
He will not enter this city
or shoot an arrow there
or come before it with a shield
or build up an assault ramp
    against it.
33 He will go back
on the road that he came
and he will not enter this city,
declares the LORD.
34 I will defend this city and rescue it
for My sake and for the sake
    of My servant David.

Angel of Lord
Defeats Assyrians

35 That night the angel of the LORD went out and struck down 185,000 in the camp of the Assyrians. When the people got up the ⌊next⌋ morning—there

---

ᵃ 19:21 Lit *behind you*   ᵇ 19:23 Many mss read LORD   ᶜ 19:23 Lit *by the hand of*   ᵈ 19:26 DSS; MT reads *blasted before standing grain*; Is 37:27   ᵉ 19:27 LXX; DSS read *your rising up and your sitting down*; Is 37:28

were all the dead bodies! ³⁶ So Sennacherib king of Assyria broke camp and left. He returned ⌊home⌋ and lived in Nineveh.

Sons Assassinate Sennacherib

³⁷ One day, while he was worshiping in the temple of his god Nisroch, his sons Adrammelech and Sharezer struck him down with the sword and escaped to the land of Ararat. Then his son Esarhaddon became king in his place.

Hezekiah's Terminal Illness

20 In those days Hezekiah became terminally ill. The prophet Isaiah son of Amoz came and said to him, "This is what the LORD says: 'Put your affairs in order,ᵃ for you are about to die; you will not recover.'"

Hezekiah Prays

² Then Hezekiah turned his face to the wall and prayed to the LORD, ³ "Please LORD, remember how I have walked before You faithfully and wholeheartedly and have done what is good in Your sight." And Hezekiah wept bitterly.

Isaiah: God Will Heal

⁴ Isaiah had not yet gone out of the inner courtyard when the word of the LORD came to him: ⁵ "Go back and tell Hezekiah, the leader of My people, 'This is what the LORD God of your ancestor David says: I have heard your prayer; I have seen your tears. Look, I will heal you. On the third day ⌊from now⌋ you will go up to the LORD's temple. ⁶ I will add 15 years to your life. I will deliver you and this city from the hand of the king of Assyria. I will defend this city for My sake and for the sake of My servant David.'"

Isaiah's Poultice

⁷ Then Isaiah said, "Bring a lump of pressed figs." So they brought it and applied it to his infected skin, and he recovered.

God's Sign: Sun's Shadow Reverses

⁸ Hezekiah had asked Isaiah, "What is the sign that the LORD will heal me and that I will go up to the LORD's temple on the third day?"

⁹ Isaiah said, "This is the sign to you from the LORD that He will do what He has promised: Should the shadow go ahead 10 steps or go back 10 steps?"

¹⁰ Then Hezekiah answered, "It's easy for the shadow to lengthen 10 steps. No, let the shadow go back 10 steps." ¹¹ So Isaiah the prophet called out to the LORD, and He brought the shadowᵇ back the 10 steps it had descended on Ahaz's stairway.ᶜ

Hezekiah's Folly with Babylon

¹² At that time Merodach-baladanᵈ son of Baladan, king of Babylon, sent letters and a gift to Hezekiah since he heard that Hezekiah had been sick. ¹³ Hezekiah gave them a hearing and showed them his whole treasure house—the silver, the gold, the spices, and the precious oil—and his armory, and everything that was found in his treasuries. There was nothing in his palace and in all his realm that Hezekiah did not show them.

¹⁴ Then the prophet Isaiah came to King Hezekiah and asked him, "What did these men say, and where did they come to you from?"

Hezekiah replied, "They came from a distant country, from Babylon."

¹⁵ Isaiah asked, "What have they seen in your palace?"

ᵃ**20:1** Lit *Command your house*   ᵇ**20:11** Lit *shadow on the steps*   ᶜ**20:11** Tg, Vg, DSS read *on the steps of Ahaz's roof chamber*; Is 38:8   ᵈ**20:12** A few Hb mss, LXX, Syr, Tg, some Vg mss, Is 39:1; MT reads *Berodach-baladan*

Hezekiah answered, "They have seen everything in my palace. There isn't anything in my treasuries that I didn't show them."

¹⁶ Then Isaiah said to Hezekiah, "Hear the word of the LORD: ¹⁷ 'The time will certainly come when everything in your palace and all that your fathers have stored up until this day will be carried off to Babylon; nothing will be left,' says the LORD. ¹⁸ 'Some of your descendants who come from you will be taken away, and they will become eunuchsª in the palace of the king of Babylon.'"

¹⁹ Then Hezekiah said to Isaiah, "The word of the LORD that you have spoken is good," for he thought: Why not, if there will be peace and security during my lifetime?

Hezekiah's Death

²⁰ The rest of the events of Hezekiah's ⌊reign⌋, along with all his might and how he made the pool and the tunnel and brought water into the city, are written about in the Historical Record of Judah's Kings. ²¹ Hezekiah rested with his fathers, and his son Manasseh became king in his place.

Judah's King Manasseh: Evil

21 Manasseh was 12 years old when he became king; he reigned 55 years in Jerusalem. His mother's name was Hephzibah. ² He did what was evil in the LORD's sight, imitating the abominations of the nations that the LORD had dispossessed before the Israelites.

Manasseh's Mass Idolatry

³ He rebuilt the •high places that his father Hezekiah had destroyed and reestablished the altars for •Baal. He made an •Asherah, as King Ahab of Israel had done; he also worshiped the whole heavenly •host and served them. ⁴ He would build altars in the LORD's temple, where the LORD had said, "Jerusalem is where I will put My name." ⁵ He built altars to the whole heavenly host in both courtyards of the LORD's temple. ⁶ He made his son pass through the fire, practiced witchcraft and •divination, and consulted mediums and spiritists. He did a great amount of evil in the LORD's sight, provoking ⌊Him⌋.

⁷ Manasseh set up the carved image of Asherah he made in the temple that the LORD had spoken about to David and his son Solomon, "I will establish My name forever in this temple and in Jerusalem, which I have chosen out of all the tribes of Israel. ⁸ I will never again cause the feet of the Israelites to wander from the land I gave to their ancestors if only they will be careful to do all I have commanded them—the whole law that My servant Moses commanded them." ⁹ But they did not listen; Manasseh caused them to stray so that they did greater evil than the nations the LORD had destroyed before the Israelites.

God's Judgment on Judah

¹⁰ The LORD spoke through His servants the prophets, saying, ¹¹ "Since Manasseh king of Judah has committed all these abominations—greater evil than the Amorites who preceded him had done—and by means of his idols has also caused Judah to sin, ¹² this is what the LORD God of Israel says: 'I am about to bring such disaster on Jerusalem and Judah that everyone who hears about it will shudder. ¹³ I will stretch over Jerusalem the measuring line ⌊used on⌋ Samaria and the mason's level ⌊used on⌋ the house of Ahab, and I will wipe Jerusalem

ª20:18 Or court officials

clean as one wipes a bowl—wiping it and turning it upside down. [14] I will abandon the remnant of My inheritance and hand them over to their enemies. They will become plunder and spoil to all their enemies, [15] because they have done what is evil in My sight and have provoked Me from the day their ancestors came out of Egypt until today.' "

[16] Manasseh also shed so much innocent blood that he filled Jerusalem with it from one end to another. This was in addition to his sin he caused Judah to commit so that they did what was evil in the LORD's sight.

Manasseh's Death

[17] The rest of the events of Manasseh's ⌊reign⌋, along with all his accomplishments and the sin that he committed, are written about in the Historical Record of Judah's Kings. [18] Manasseh rested with his fathers and was buried in the garden of his own house, the garden of Uzza. His son Amon became king in his place.

Judah's King Amon: Evil

[19] Amon was 22 years old when he became king; he reigned two years in Jerusalem. His mother's name was Meshullemeth daughter of Haruz; ⌊she was⌋ from Jotbah. [20] He did what was evil in the LORD's sight as his father Manasseh had done. [21] He walked in all the ways his father had walked; he served the idols his father had served, and he worshiped them. [22] He abandoned the LORD God of his ancestors and did not walk in the way of the LORD.

Servants Assassinate Amon

[23] Amon's servants conspired against the king and killed him in his own house. [24] Then the common people[a] executed all those who had conspired against King Amon and made his son Josiah king in his place.

[25] The rest of the events of Amon's ⌊reign⌋, along with his accomplishments, are written about in the Historical Record of Judah's Kings. [26] He was buried in his tomb in the garden of Uzza, and his son Josiah became king in his place.

Judah's Good King Josiah

22 Josiah was eight years old when he became king; he reigned 31 years in Jerusalem. His mother's name was Jedidah the daughter of Adaiah; ⌊she was⌋ from Bozkath. [2] He did what was right in the LORD's sight and walked in all the ways of his ancestor David; he did not turn to the right or the left.

Josiah Repairs Temple

[3] In the eighteenth year of King Josiah, the king sent the court secretary Shaphan son of Azaliah, son of Meshullam, to the LORD's temple, saying, [4] "Go up to Hilkiah the high priest so that he may total up the money brought into the LORD's temple—⌊the money⌋ the doorkeepers have collected from the people. [5] It is to be put into the hands of those doing the work—those who oversee the LORD's temple. They ⌊in turn⌋ are to give it to the workmen in the LORD's temple to repair the damage. [6] ⌊They are to give it⌋ to the carpenters, builders, and masons to buy timber and quarried stone to repair the temple. [7] But no accounting is to be required from them for the money put into their hands since they work with integrity."

a 21:24 Lit the people of the land

High Priest Hilkiah
Finds Book of Law

[8] Hilkiah the high priest told Shaphan the court secretary, "I have found the book of the law in the LORD's temple," and he gave the book to Shaphan, who read it.

[9] Then Shaphan the court secretary went to the king and reported,[a] "Your servants have emptied out the money that was found in the temple and have put it into the hand of those doing the work—those who oversee the LORD's temple." [10] Then Shaphan the court secretary told the king, "Hilkiah the priest has given me a book," and Shaphan read it in the presence of the king.

Josiah's Remorse over Law

[11] When the king heard the words of the book of the law, he tore his clothes. [12] Then he commanded Hilkiah the priest, Ahikam son of Shaphan, Achbor son of Micaiah, Shaphan the court secretary, and the king's servant Asaiah: [13] "Go and inquire of the LORD for me, the people, and all Judah about the instruction in this book that has been found. For great is the LORD's wrath that is kindled against us because our ancestors have not obeyed the words of this book in order to do everything written about us."

Prophetess Huldah
Prophesies Judgment

[14] So Hilkiah the priest, Ahikam, Achbor, Shaphan, and Asaiah went to the prophetess Huldah, wife of Shallum son of Tikvah, son of Harhas,[b] keeper of the wardrobe. She lived in Jerusalem in the Second District. They spoke with her. [15] She said to them, "This is what the LORD God of Israel says, 'Say to the man who sent you to Me: [16] This is what the LORD says: I am about to bring disaster on this place and on its inhabitants, ⌊fulfilling⌋ all the words of the book that the king of Judah has read, [17] because they have abandoned Me and burned incense to other gods in order to provoke Me with all the work of their hands. My wrath will be kindled against this place, and it will not be quenched.

Huldah: Josiah Spared

[18] Say this to the king of Judah who sent you to inquire of the LORD: This is what the LORD God of Israel says: As for the words that you heard, [19] because your heart was tender and you humbled yourself before the LORD when you heard what I spoke against this place and against its inhabitants, that they would become a desolation and a curse, and because you have torn your clothes and wept before Me, I Myself have heard you—declares the LORD. [20] Therefore, I will indeed gather you to your fathers, and you will be gathered to your grave in peace. Your eyes will not see all the disaster that I am bringing on this place.'"

Then they reported[c] to the king.

King Josiah Renews Covenant

23 So the king sent ⌊messengers⌋, and they gathered to him all the elders of Jerusalem and Judah. [2] Then the king went to the LORD's temple with all the men of Judah and all the inhabitants of Jerusalem, as well as the priests and the prophets—all the people from the youngest to the oldest. As they listened, he read all the words of the book of the covenant that had been found in the LORD's temple. [3] Next, the king stood by the pillar[d] and made a covenant in the presence of the LORD to follow the LORD and

---

[a] 22:9 Lit and returned a word to the king and said   [b] 22:14 2 Ch 34:22 reads Hasrah   [c] 22:20 Lit returned a word
[d] 23:3 2 Ch 34:31 reads platform

to keep His commandments, His decrees, and His statutes with all his mind and with all his heart, and to carry out the words of this covenant that were written in this book; all the people agreed to[a] the covenant.

Josiah Destroys Idolatry

⁴ Then the king commanded Hilkiah the high priest and the priests of the second rank and the doorkeepers to bring out of the LORD's temple all the articles made for •Baal, •Asherah, and the whole heavenly •host. He burned them outside Jerusalem in the fields of the Kidron and carried their ashes to Bethel. ⁵ Then he did away with the idolatrous priests the kings of Judah had appointed to burn incense at the •high places in the cities of Judah and in the areas surrounding Jerusalem. They had burned incense to Baal, and to the sun, moon, constellations, and the whole heavenly host. ⁶ He brought out the Asherah pole from the LORD's temple to the Kidron Valley outside Jerusalem. He burned it at the Kidron Valley, beat it to dust, and threw its dust on the graves of the common people.[b] ⁷ He also tore down the houses of the male shrine prostitutes that were in the LORD's temple, in which the women were weaving tapestries[c] for Asherah.

⁸ Then Josiah brought all the priests from the cities of Judah, and he defiled the high places from Geba to Beer-sheba, where the priests had burned incense. He tore down the high places of the gates at the entrance of the gate of Joshua the governor of the city (on the left at the city gate). ⁹ The priests of the high places, however, did not come up to the altar of the LORD in Jerusalem; instead, they ate unleavened bread with their fellow priests.

King Josiah Defiles Topheth and Molech

¹⁰ He defiled •Topheth, which is in the Valley of Hinnom, so that no one could make his son or his daughter pass through the fire to Molech. ¹¹ He did away with the horses that the kings of Judah had dedicated to the sun. ⌐They had been⌐ at the entrance of the LORD's temple in the precincts by the chamber of Nathan-melech the court official, and he burned up the chariots of the sun.

Josiah Tears Down Altars

¹² The king tore down the altars that were on the roof—Ahaz's upper chamber that the kings of Judah had made—and the altars that Manasseh had made in the two courtyards of the LORD's temple. Then he smashed them[d] there and threw their dust into the Kidron Valley. ¹³ The king also defiled the high places that were across from Jerusalem, to the south of the Mount of Destruction, which Solomon king of Israel had built for •Ashtoreth, the detestable idol of the Sidonians; for Chemosh, the detestable idol of Moab; and for •Milcom, the abomination of the Ammonites. ¹⁴ He broke the sacred pillars into pieces, cut down the Asherah poles, then filled their places with human bones.

¹⁵ He even tore down the altar at Bethel and the high place that Jeroboam son of Nebat, who caused Israel to sin, had made. Then he burned the high place, crushed it to dust, and burned the Asherah. ¹⁶ As Josiah turned, he saw the tombs there on the mountain. He sent ⌐someone⌐ to take the bones out of the tombs, and he burned them on the altar. He defiled it according to the word of the LORD proclaimed by the man of God[e]

ª**23:3** Lit *people took a stand in*   ᵇ**23:6** Lit *the sons of the people*   ᶜ**23:7** Or *clothing*   ᵈ**23:12** Text emended; MT reads *he ran from*   ᵉ**23:16** LXX adds *when Jeroboam stood by the altar of the feast. And he turned and raised his eyes to the tomb of the man of God* who proclaimed these things. ¹⁷ Then he said, "What is this monument I see?"

Josiah Spares Tomb of Prophet

The men of the city told him, "It is the tomb of the man of God who came from Judah and proclaimed these things that you have done to the altar at Bethel."

¹⁸ So he said, "Let him rest. Don't let anyone disturb his bones." So they left his bones undisturbed with the bones of the prophet who came from Samaria.

Josiah Removes Shrines in Samaria

¹⁹ Josiah also removed all the shrines of the high places that were in the cities of Samaria, which the kings of Israel had made to provoke ⌊the LORD⌋. Josiah did the same things to them that he had done at Bethel. ²⁰ He slaughtered on the altars all the priests of the high places who were there, and he burned human bones on the altars. Then he returned to Jerusalem.

King Josiah Commands Passover

²¹ The king commanded all the people, "Keep the •Passover of the LORD your God as written in the book of the covenant." ²² No such Passover had ever been kept from the time of the judges who judged Israel through the entire time of the kings of Israel and Judah. ²³ But in the eighteenth year of King Josiah, this Passover was observed to the LORD in Jerusalem.

Josiah's Zeal for the LORD

²⁴ In addition, Josiah removed the mediums, the spiritists, household idols, images, and all the detestable things that were seen in the land of Judah and in Jerusalem. He did this in order to carry out the words of the law that were written

in the book that Hilkiah the priest found in the LORD's temple. ²⁵ Before him there was no king like him who turned to the LORD with all his mind and with all his heart and with all his strength according to all the law of Moses, and no one like him arose after him.

God Rejects Judah

²⁶ In spite of all that, the LORD did not turn from the fierceness of His great wrath and anger, which burned against Judah because of all the provocations Manasseh had provoked Him with. ²⁷ For the LORD had said, "I will also remove Judah from My sight just as I have removed Israel. I will reject this city Jerusalem, that I have chosen, and the temple about which I said, 'My name will be there.'"

Egyptians Kill Josiah

²⁸ The rest of the events of Josiah's ⌊reign⌋, along with all his accomplishments, are written about in the Historical Record of Judah's Kings. ²⁹ During his reign, Pharaoh Neco king of Egypt marched up to the king of Assyria at the Euphrates river. King Josiah went to confront him, and at Megiddo when Neco saw him he killed him. ³⁰ From Megiddo his servants carried his dead body in a chariot, brought him into Jerusalem, and buried him in his own tomb. Then the common people[a] took Jehoahaz son of Josiah, anointed him, and made him king in place of his father.

Judah's King Jehoahaz: Evil

³¹ Jehoahaz was 23 years old when he became king; he reigned three months in Jerusalem. His mother's name was Hamutal daughter of Jeremiah; ⌊she was⌋ from Libnah. ³² He did what was evil in the LORD's sight just as his ancestors had done.

ᵃ**23:30** Lit *the people of the land*

Pharaoh Imprisons Jehoahaz

33 Pharaoh Neco imprisoned him at Riblah in the land of Hamath to keep him from reigning in Jerusalem, and he imposed on the land a fine of 7,500 pounds[a] of silver and 75 pounds[b] of gold.

Pharaoh Enthrones Judah's King Jehoiakim

34 Then Pharaoh Neco made Eliakim son of Josiah king in place of his father Josiah and changed Eliakim's name to Jehoiakim. But Neco took Jehoahaz and went to Egypt, and he died there. 35 So Jehoiakim gave the silver and the gold to Pharaoh, but at Pharaoh's command he taxed the land to give the money. He exacted the silver and the gold from the people of the land, each man according to his valuation, to give it to Pharaoh Neco.

36 Jehoiakim was 25 years old when he became king; he reigned 11 years in Jerusalem. His mother's name was Zebidah daughter of Pedaiah; ʋshe wasJ from Rumah. 37 He did what was evil in the LORD's sight just as his ancestors had done.

Jehoiakim Rebels Against Babylon's King Nebuchadnezzar

24 During his reign, Nebuchadnezzar king of Babylon attacked, and Jehoiakim became his vassal for three years. Then he turned and rebelled against him. 2 The LORD sent Chaldean, Aramean, Moabite, and Ammonite raiders against Jehoiakim. He sent them against Judah to destroy it, according to the word of the LORD He had spoken through His servants the prophets. 3 This happened to Judah only at the LORD's command to remove them from His sight. It was because of the sins of Manasseh, according to all he had done, 4 and also because of all the innocent

blood he had shed. He had filled Jerusalem with innocent blood, and the LORD would not forgive.

5 The rest of the events of Jehoiakim's ʋreignʁ, along with all his accomplishments, are written about in the Historical Record of Judah's Kings. 6 Jehoiakim rested with his fathers, and his son Jehoiachin became king in his place.

Babylon Replaces Egypt

7 Now the king of Egypt did not march out of his land again, for the king of Babylon took everything that belonged to the king of Egypt, from the Brook of Egypt to the Euphrates River.

Judah's King Jehoiachin: Evil

8 Jehoiachin was 18 years old when he became king; he reigned three months in Jerusalem. His mother's name was Nehushta daughter of Elnathan; ʋshe wasʁ from Jerusalem. 9 He did what was evil in the LORD's sight as his father had done.

Babylon Besieges Jerusalem

10 At that time the servants of Nebuchadnezzar king of Babylon marched up to Jerusalem, and the city came under siege. 11 Then King Nebuchadnezzar of Babylon came to the city while his servants were besieging it. 12 Jehoiachin king of Judah, along with his mother, his servants, his commanders, and his officials, surrendered to the king of Babylon.

Jerusalem Sacked

So the king of Babylon took him ʋcaptiveʁ in the eighth year of his reign. 13 He also carried off from there all the treasures of the LORD's temple and the treasures of the king's palace, and he cut into pieces all the gold articles that Solomon king of Israel had made for the LORD's

a 23:33 Lit 100 talents b 23:33 Lit one talent

sanctuary, just as God had predicted. [14] Then he deported all Jerusalem and all the commanders and all the fighting men, 10,000 captives, and all the craftsmen and metalsmiths. Except for the poorest people of the land, nobody remained.

Nebuchadnezzar Deports King Jehoiachin

[15] Nebuchadnezzar deported Jehoiachin to Babylon. Also, he took the king's mother, the king's wives, his officials, and the leading men of the land into exile from Jerusalem to Babylon. [16] The king of Babylon also brought captive into Babylon all 7,000 fighting men and 1,000 craftsmen and metalsmiths—all strong and fit for war. [17] Then the king of Babylon made Mattaniah, Jehoiachin's[a] uncle,[b] king in his place and changed his name to Zedekiah.

Judah's King Zedekiah: Evil

[18] Zedekiah was 21 years old when he became king; he reigned 11 years in Jerusalem. His mother's name was Hamutal daughter of Jeremiah; ⌊she was⌋ from Libnah. [19] Zedekiah did what was evil in the LORD's sight just as Jehoiakim had done. [20] Because of the LORD's anger, it came to the point in Jerusalem and Judah that He finally banished them from His presence. Then, Zedekiah rebelled against the king of Babylon.

Nebuchadnezzar's Siege of Jerusalem

25 In the ninth year of Zedekiah's reign, on the tenth day of the tenth month, King Nebuchadnezzar of Babylon advanced against Jerusalem with his entire army. They laid siege to the city and built a siege wall against it all around. [2] The city was under siege until King Zedekiah's eleventh year.

[3] By the ninth day of the ⌊fourth⌋ month the famine was so severe in the city that the people of the land had no food. [4] Then the city was broken into, and all the warriors ⌊fled⌋ by night by way of the gate between the two walls near the king's garden, even though the Chaldeans surrounded the city. As the king made his way along the route to the •Arabah, [5] the Chaldean army pursued him and overtook him in the plains of Jericho. Zedekiah's entire army was scattered from him. [6] The Chaldeans seized the king and brought him up to the king of Babylon at Riblah, and they passed sentence on him. [7] They slaughtered Zedekiah's sons before his eyes. Finally, the king of Babylon blinded Zedekiah, bound him in bronze ⌊chains⌋, and took him to Babylon.

Babylon Destroys Jerusalem

[8] On the seventh day of the fifth month, which was the nineteenth year of King Nebuchadnezzar, king of Babylon, Nebuzaradan, the commander of the guards, a servant of the king of Babylon, entered Jerusalem. [9] He burned the LORD's temple, the king's palace, and all the houses of Jerusalem; he burned down all the great houses. [10] The whole Chaldean army ⌊with⌋ the commander of the guards tore down the walls surrounding Jerusalem. [11] Nebuzaradan, the commander of the guards, deported the rest of the people who were left in the city, the deserters who had defected to the king of Babylon, and the rest of the population. [12] But the commander of the guards left some of the poorest of the land to be vinedressers and farmers.

[13] Now the Chaldeans broke into pieces the bronze pillars of the LORD's temple, the water carts, and the bronze reservoir, which were in the LORD's temple, and carried the bronze to Babylon. [14] They

---

[a]**24:17** Lit *his* [b]**24:17** 2 Ch 36:10 reads *brother*; Jr 37:1

also took the pots, the shovels, the wick trimmers, the dishes, and all the bronze articles used in ⌊temple⌋ service. [15] The commander of the guards took away the firepans and the sprinkling basins—whatever was gold or silver.

[16] As for the two pillars, the one reservoir, and the water carts that Solomon had made for the LORD's temple, the weight of the bronze of all these articles was beyond measure. [17] One pillar was 27 feet[a] tall and had a bronze capital on top of it. The capital, encircled by a grating and pomegranates of bronze, stood five feet[b] high. The second pillar was the same, with its own grating.

King of Babylon Executes Priests and Royal Officials

[18] The commander of the guards also took away Seraiah the chief priest, Zephaniah the priest of the second rank, and the three doorkeepers. [19] From the city he took a court official who had been appointed over the warriors; five trusted royal aides[c] found in the city; the secretary of the commander of the army, who enlisted the people of the land for military duty; and 60 men from the common people[d] who were found within the city. [20] Nebuzaradan, the commander of the guards, took them and brought them to the king of Babylon at Riblah. [21] The king of Babylon put them to death at Riblah in the land of Hamath.

Judah into Exile

So Judah went into exile from its land.

Nebuchadnezzar Appoints Gedaliah Governor of Judah

[22] Nebuchadnezzar king of Babylon appointed Gedaliah son of Ahikam, son of Shaphan, over the rest of the people he left in the land of Judah. [23] When all the commanders of the armies—they and their men—heard that the king of Babylon had appointed Gedaliah, they came to Gedaliah at Mizpah. ⌊The commanders included⌋ Ishmael son of Nethaniah, Johanan son of Kareah, Seraiah son of Tanhumeth the Netophathite, and Jaazaniah son of the Maacathite—they and their men. [24] Gedaliah swore an oath to them and their men, assuring them, "Don't be afraid of the servants of the Chaldeans. Live in the land and serve the king of Babylon, and it will go well for you."

[25] In the seventh month, however, Ishmael son of Nethaniah, son of Elishama, of the royal family, came with 10 men and struck down Gedaliah, and he died. Also, ⌊they killed⌋ the Jews and the Chaldeans who were with him at Mizpah. [26] Then all the people, from the youngest to the oldest, and the commanders of the army, left and went to Egypt, for they were afraid of the Chaldeans.

King of Babylon Pardons King Jehoiachin

[27] On the twenty-seventh day of the twelfth month of the thirty-seventh year of the exile of Judah's King Jehoiachin, Evil-merodach king of Babylon, in the year he became king, pardoned King Jehoiachin of Judah ⌊and released him⌋ from prison. [28] He spoke kindly to him and set his throne over the thrones of the kings who were with him in Babylon. [29] So Jehoiachin changed his prison clothes, and he dined regularly in the presence of the king of Babylon for the rest of his life. [30] As for his allowance, a regular allowance was given to him by the king, a portion for each day, for the rest of his life.

---

[a]**25:17** Lit *18 cubits*   [b]**25:17** Lit *three cubits*   [c]**25:19** Lit *five men who look on the king's face*   [d]**25:19** Lit *the people of the land*

1 CHRONICLES

Genealogy: Adam to Abraham

1 Adam, Seth, Enosh,
² Kenan, Mahalalel, Jared,
³ Enoch, Methuselah, Lamech,
⁴ Noah, Noah's sons:[a]
Shem, Ham, and Japheth.

⁵ Japheth's sons: Gomer, Magog,
Madai, Javan, Tubal, Meshech,
and Tiras.
⁶ Gomer's sons: Ashkenaz,
Riphath,[b] and Togarmah.
⁷ Javan's sons: Elishah, Tarshish,
Kittim, and Rodanim.[c]

⁸ Ham's sons: Cush, Mizraim,[d]
Put, and Canaan.
⁹ Cush's sons: Seba, Havilah,
Sabta, Raama, and Sabteca.
Raama's sons: Sheba and Dedan.
¹⁰ Cush fathered Nimrod, who
was the first to become a great
warrior on earth.
¹¹ Mizraim fathered Ludim,
Anamim, Lehabim, Naphtuhim,
¹² Pathrusim, Casluhim (the
Philistines came from them),
and Caphtorim.
¹³ Canaan fathered Sidon, his
firstborn, and Heth, ¹⁴ the
Jebusites, Amorites, Girgashites,
¹⁵ Hivites, Arkites, Sinites,
¹⁶ Arvadites, Zemarites,
and Hamathites.

¹⁷ Shem's sons: Elam, Asshur,
Arpachshad, Lud, Aram, Uz, Hul,
Gether, and Meshech.
¹⁸ Arpachshad fathered Shelah,
and Shelah fathered Eber. ¹⁹ Two
sons were born to Eber. One of

them was named Peleg,[e] because
the earth was divided during his
lifetime, and the name of his
brother was Joktan. ²⁰ Joktan
fathered Almodad, Sheleph,
Hazarmaveth, Jerah, ²¹ Hadoram,
Uzal, Diklah, ²² Ebal, Abimael,
Sheba, ²³ Ophir, Havilah,
and Jobab.
All of these were Joktan's sons.

²⁴ Shem, Arpachshad, Shelah,
²⁵ Eber, Peleg, Reu,
²⁶ Serug, Nahor, Terah,
²⁷ and Abram (that is, Abraham).

Abraham's Descendants

²⁸ Abraham's sons: Isaac and Ishmael.

²⁹ These are their family records:
Nebaioth, Ishmael's firstborn,
Kedar, Adbeel, Mibsam,
³⁰ Mishma, Dumah, Massa,
Hadad, Tema, ³¹ Jetur, Naphish,
and Kedemah.
These were Ishmael's sons.

³² The sons born to Keturah,
Abraham's concubine: Zimran,
Jokshan, Medan, Midian, Ishbak,
and Shuah.
Jokshan's sons: Sheba and Dedan.
³³ Midian's sons: Ephah, Epher,
Hanoch, Abida, and Eldaah.
All of these were Keturah's sons.

³⁴ Abraham fathered Isaac.
Isaac's sons: Esau and Israel.

³⁵ Esau's sons: Eliphaz, Reuel,
Jeush, Jalam, and Korah.
³⁶ Eliphaz's sons: Teman, Omar,

ª**1:4** LXX; MT omits *Noah's sons*   ᵇ**1:6** Some Hb mss, LXX, Vg, other Hb mss read *Diphath*; Gn 10:3   ᶜ**1:7** Some Hb mss, Syr read *Dodanim*; Gn 10:4   ᵈ**1:8** = Egypt   ᵉ**1:19** = Division

Zephi, Gatam, and Kenaz; and by Timna, Amalek.[a]
³⁷ Reuel's sons: Nahath, Zerah, Shammah, and Mizzah.

The Edomites

³⁸ Seir's sons: Lotan, Shobal, Zibeon, Anah, Dishon, Ezer, and Dishan.
³⁹ Lotan's sons: Hori and Homam. Timna was Lotan's sister.
⁴⁰ Shobal's sons: Alian, Manahath, Ebal, Shephi, and Onam.
Zibeon's sons: Aiah and Anah.
⁴¹ Anah's son: Dishon.
Dishon's sons: Hamran, Eshban, Ithran, and Cheran.
⁴² Ezer's sons: Bilhan, Zaavan, and Jaakan.
Dishan's sons: Uz and Aran.

⁴³ These were the kings who ruled in the land of Edom before any king ruled over the Israelites: Bela son of Beor. Bela's town was named Dinhabah. ⁴⁴ When Bela died, Jobab son of Zerah from Bozrah ruled in his place. ⁴⁵ When Jobab died, Husham from the land of the Temanites ruled in his place. ⁴⁶ When Husham died, Hadad son of Bedad, who defeated Midian in the country of Moab, ruled in his place. Hadad's town was named Avith. ⁴⁷ When Hadad died, Samlah from Masrekah ruled in his place. ⁴⁸ When Samlah died, Shaul from Rehoboth on the Euphrates River ruled in his place. ⁴⁹ When Shaul died, Baal-hanan son of Achbor ruled in his place. ⁵⁰ When Baal-hanan died, Hadad ruled in his place. Hadad's city was named Pai, and his wife's name was Mehetabel daughter of Matred, daughter of Me-zahab. ⁵¹ Then Hadad died.

Edom's chiefs: Timna, Alvah,[b] Jetheth, ⁵² Oholibamah, Elah, Pinon, ⁵³ Kenaz, Teman, Mibzar, ⁵⁴ Magdiel, and Iram. These were Edom's chiefs.

Israel's Sons

2 These were Israel's sons: Reuben, Simeon, Levi, Judah, Issachar, Zebulun, ² Dan, Joseph, Benjamin, Naphtali, Gad, and Asher.

Judah's Descendants

³ Judah's sons: Er, Onan, and Shelah. ⌊These⌋ three were born to him by Bath-shua the Canaanite woman. Er, Judah's firstborn, was evil in the LORD's sight, so He put him to death. ⁴ Judah's daughter-in-law Tamar bore him Perez and Zerah. Judah had five sons in all.

⁵ Perez's sons: Hezron and Hamul.
⁶ Zerah's sons: Zimri, Ethan, Heman, Calcol, and Dara[c]—five in all.
⁷ Carmi's son: Achar,[d] who brought trouble on Israel when he was unfaithful ⌊by taking⌋ what was •devoted to destruction.
⁸ Ethan's son: Azariah.
⁹ Hezron's sons, who were born to him: Jerahmeel, Ram, and Chelubai.[e]

¹⁰ Ram fathered Amminadab, and Amminadab fathered Nahshon, a leader of Judah's descendants.
¹¹ Nahshon fathered Salma, and Salma fathered Boaz.
¹² Boaz fathered Obed, and Obed fathered Jesse.
¹³ Jesse fathered Eliab, his firstborn; Abinadab was ⌊born⌋ second,

a1:36 LXX; MT reads *and Timna and Amalek*; Gn 36:12 **b1:51** Alt Hb tradition reads *Aliah* **c2:6** Some Hb mss, LXX, Syr, Tg, Vg read *Darda*; 1 Kg 4:31 **d2:7** = Trouble; = Achan; Jos 7:1,16-26 **e2:9** = Caleb

Shimea third, ¹⁴ Nethanel fourth, Raddai fifth, ¹⁵ Ozem sixth, and David seventh.

¹⁶ Their sisters were Zeruiah and Abigail.
Zeruiah's three sons: Abishai, Joab, and Asahel.
¹⁷ Amasa's mother was Abigail, and his father was Jether the Ishmaelite.

¹⁸ Caleb son of Hezron had children by ⌊his⌋ wife Azubah and by Jerioth. These were Azubah's sons: Jesher, Shobab, and Ardon. ¹⁹ When Azubah died, Caleb married Ephrath, and she bore him Hur. ²⁰ Hur fathered Uri, and Uri fathered Bezalel. ²¹ After this, Hezron slept with the daughter of Machir the father of Gilead. Hezron had married her when he was 60 years old, and she bore him Segub. ²² Segub fathered Jair, who possessed 23 towns in the land of Gilead. ²³ But Geshur and Aram captured^a Jair's Villages^b along with Kenath and its villages—60 towns. All these were the sons of Machir father of Gilead. ²⁴ After Hezron's death in Caleb-ephrathah, his wife Abijah bore him Ashhur the father of Tekoa.

²⁵ The sons of Jerahmeel, Hezron's firstborn: Ram, his firstborn, Bunah, Oren, Ozem, and Ahijah.
²⁶ Jerahmeel had another wife named Atarah, who was the mother of Onam.
²⁷ The sons of Ram, Jerahmeel's firstborn: Maaz, Jamin, and Eker.
²⁸ Onam's sons: Shammai and Jada.
Shammai's sons: Nadab and Abishur. ²⁹ Abishur's wife was named Abihail, who bore him Ahban and Molid.

³⁰ Nadab's sons: Seled and Appaim. Seled died without children.
³¹ Appaim's son: Ishi. Ishi's son: Sheshan. Sheshan's descendant: Ahlai.
³² The sons of Jada brother of Shammai: Jether and Jonathan. Jether died without children.
³³ Jonathan's sons: Peleth and Zaza. These were the descendants of Jerahmeel.
³⁴ Sheshan had no sons, only daughters, but he did have an Egyptian servant whose name was Jarha. ³⁵ Sheshan gave his daughter in marriage to his servant Jarha, and she bore him Attai.

³⁶ Attai fathered Nathan, and Nathan fathered Zabad.
³⁷ Zabad fathered Ephlal, and Ephlal fathered Obed.
³⁸ Obed fathered Jehu, and Jehu fathered Azariah.
³⁹ Azariah fathered Helez, and Helez fathered Eleasah.
⁴⁰ Eleasah fathered Sismai, and Sismai fathered Shallum.
⁴¹ Shallum fathered Jekamiah, and Jekamiah fathered Elishama.

⁴² The sons of Caleb brother of Jerahmeel:
Mesha, his firstborn, fathered Ziph,
and Mareshah, his second son,^c fathered Hebron.
⁴³ Hebron's sons: Korah, Tappuah, Rekem, and Shema.
⁴⁴ Shema fathered Raham, who fathered Jorkeam,
and Rekem fathered Shammai.
⁴⁵ Shammai's son was Maon,

---

^a**2:23** Lit took from them   ^b**2:23** Or captured Havvoth-jair   ^c**2:42** Lit and the sons of Mareshah

and Maon fathered Beth-zur.

⁴⁶ Caleb's concubine Ephah was the mother of Haran, Moza, and Gazez.

Haran fathered Gazez.

⁴⁷ Jahdai's sons: Regem, Jotham, Geshan, Pelet, Ephah, and Shaaph.

⁴⁸ Caleb's concubine Maacah was the mother of Sheber and Tirhanah. ⁴⁹ She was also the mother of Shaaph, Madmannah's father, and of Sheva, the father of Machbenah and Gibea. Caleb's daughter was Achsah. ⁵⁰ These were Caleb's descendants.

The sons of Hur, Ephrathah's firstborn:

Shobal fathered Kiriath-jearim;

⁵¹   Salma fathered Bethlehem, and Hareph fathered Beth-gader.

⁵² These were the descendants of Shobal the father of Kiriath-jearim: Haroeh, half of the Manahathites,ᵃ ⁵³ and the families of Kiriath-jearim—the Ithrites, Puthites, Shumathites, and Mishraites. The Zorathites and Eshtaolites descended from these.

⁵⁴ Salma's sons: Bethlehem, the Netophathites, Atroth-beth-joab, and half of the Manahathites, the Zorites, ⁵⁵ and the families of scribes who lived in Jabez—the Tirathites, Shimeathites, and Sucathites. These are the Kenites who came from Hammath, the father of Rechab's family.

David's Descendants

3 These were David's sons who were born to him in Hebron:

Amnon was the firstborn, by Ahinoam of Jezreel;

Daniel was ⌊born⌋ second, by Abigail of Carmel;

² Absalom son of Maacah, daughter of King Talmai of Geshur, was third;

Adonijah son of Haggith was fourth;

³ Shephatiah, by Abital, was fifth; and Ithream, by David's wife Eglah, was sixth.

⁴ Six sons were born to David in Hebron, where he ruled seven years and six months, and he ruled in Jerusalem 33 years.

⁵ These ⌊sons⌋ were born to him in Jerusalem:

Shimea, Shobab, Nathan, and Solomon. These four were ⌊born to him⌋ by Bath-shua daughter of Ammiel.

⁶ ⌊David's other sons⌋: Ibhar, Elishua,ᵇ Eliphelet, ⁷ Nogah, Nepheg, Japhia, ⁸ Elishama, Eliada, and Eliphelet—nine sons.

⁹ ⌊These⌋ were all David's sons, with their sister Tamar, in addition to the sons by his concubines.

Judah's Kings

¹⁰   Solomon's son was Rehoboam; his son was Abijah, his son Asa, his son Jehoshaphat, ¹¹ his son Jehoram,ᶜ ᵈ his son Ahaziah, his son Joash, ¹² his son Amaziah, his son Azariah, his son Jotham, ¹³ his son Ahaz, his son Hezekiah, his son Manasseh, ¹⁴ his son Amon, and his son Josiah.

¹⁵   Josiah's sons:

ᵃ2:52 Lit *Manuhoth*   ᵇ3:6 Lit *Elishama*; 1 Ch 14:5; 2 Sm 5:15   ᶜ3:11 Lit *Joram*   ᵈ3:11 = The LORD is Exalted

Johanan was the firstborn,
  Jehoiakim second,
Zedekiah third, and Shallum fourth.
16 Jehoiakim's sons:
his sons Jeconiah and Zedekiah.

David's Line After the Exile

17 The sons of Jeconiah the captive:
his sons Shealtiel, 18 Malchiram, Pedaiah, Shenazzar, Jekamiah, Hoshama, and Nedabiah.
19 Pedaiah's sons: Zerubbabel and Shimei.
Zerubbabel's sons: Meshullam and Hananiah, with their sister Shelomith; 20 and five others—Hashubah, Ohel, Berechiah, Hasadiah, and Jushab-hesed.
21 Hananiah's descendants: Pelatiah, Jeshaiah, and the sons of Rephaiah, Arnan, Obadiah, and Shecaniah.a
22 The sonb of Shecaniah: Shemaiah.
Shemaiah's sons: Hattush, Igal, Bariah, Neariah, and Shaphat—six.
23 Neariah's sons: Elioenai, Hizkiah, and Azrikam—three.
24 Elioenai's sons: Hodaviah, Eliashib, Pelaiah, Akkub, Johanan, Delaiah, and Anani—seven.

Judah's Descendants

4 Judah's sons: Perez, Hezron, Carmi, Hur, an Shobal.
2 Reaiah son of Shobal fathered Jahath,
and Jahath fathered Ahumai and Lahad.
These were the families of the Zorathites.

3 These were Etam's sons:c
Jezreel, Ishma, and Idbash, and their sister was named Hazzelelponi.
4 Penuel fathered Gedor, and Ezer fathered Hushah.
These were the sons of Hur, Ephrathah's firstborn and the father of Bethlehem:
5 Ashhur fathered Tekoa and had two wives, Helah and Naarah.
6 Naarah bore him Ahuzzam, Hepher, Temeni, and Haahashtari. These were Naarah's sons.
7 Helah's sons: Zereth, Zohar,d and Ethnan. 8 Koz fathered Anub, Zobebah,e and the families of Aharhel son of Harum.

Story of Jabez

9 Jabezf was more honorable than his brothers. His mother named him Jabez and said, "I gave birth to him in pain."
10 Jabez called out to the God of Israel: "If only You would bless me, extend my border, let Your hand be with me, and keep me from harm, so that I will not cause any pain."g And God granted his request.

Other Descendants of Judah

11 Chelub brother of Shuhah fathered Mehir, who was the father of Eshton. 12 Eshton fathered Beth-rapha, Paseah, and Tehinnah the father of Irnahash. These were the men of Recah.
13 Kenaz's sons: Othniel and Seraiah.
Othniel's sons: Hathath and Meonothai.h

a3:21 LXX reads Jeshaiah, his son Rephaiah, his son Arnan, his son Obadiah, and his son Shecaniah   b3:22 LXX; MT reads sons   c4:3 LXX; MT reads father   d4:7 Alt Hb tradition reads Izhar   e4:8 Or Hazzobebah   f4:9 The name Jabez sounds like Hb jazeb meaning "he causes pain."   g4:10 LXX reads and act in knowledge which doesn't hurt me   h4:13 LXX, Vg; MT omits and Meonothai

14 Meonothai fathered Ophrah, and Seraiah fathered Joab, the ancestor of ⌊those in⌋ the Valley of Craftsmen,ᵃ for they were craftsmen.

15 The sons of Caleb son of Jephunneh: Iru, Elah, and Naam. Elah's son: Kenaz.

16 Jehallelel's sons: Ziph, Ziphah, Tiria, and Asarel.

17 Ezrah's sons: Jether, Mered, Epher, and Jalon. Mered's wife Bithiahᵇ gave birth to Miriam, Shammai, and Ishbah the father of Eshtemoa. 18 These were the sons of Pharaoh's daughter Bithiah; Mered had married her. His Judean wife gave birth to Jered the father of Gedor, Heber the father of Soco, and Jekuthiel the father of Zanoah. 19 The sons of Hodiah's wife, the sister of Naham: the father of Keilah the Garmite and ⌊the father of⌋ Eshtemoa the Maacathite.

20 Shimon's sons: Amnon, Rinnah, Ben-hanan, and Tilon.

Ishi's sons: Zoheth and Ben-zoheth.

21 The sons of Shelah son of Judah: Er the father of Lecah, Laadah the father of Mareshah, the families of the guildᶜ of linen workers at Beth-ashbea, 22 Jokim, the men of Cozeba; and Joash and Saraph, who married Moabitesᵈ and returned to Lehem. These ⌊names⌋ are from ancient records. 23 They were the potters and residents of Netaim and Gederah. They lived there in the service of the king.

Simeon's Descendants

24 Simeon's sons: Nemuel, Jamin, Jarib, Zerah, and Shaul;

25 ⌊Shaul's sons:⌋ his son Shallum, his son Mibsam, and his son Mishma.

26 Mishma's sons: his son Hammuel, his son Zaccur, and his son Shimei.

27 Shimei had 16 sons and six daughters, but his brothers did not have many children, so their whole family did not become as numerous as the Judeans. 28 They lived in Beer-sheba, Moladah, Hazar-shual, 29 Bilhah, Ezem, Tolad, 30 Bethuel, Hormah, Ziklag, 31 Beth-marcaboth, Hazar-susim, Beth-biri, and Shaaraim. These were their cities until David became king. 32 Their villages were Etam, Ain, Rimmon, Tochen, and Ashan—five cities, 33 and all their surrounding villages as far as Baal. These were their settlements, and they kept a genealogical record for themselves.

34 Meshobab, Jamlech, Joshah son of Amaziah, 35 Joel, Jehu son of Joshibiah, son of Seraiah, son of Asiel, 36 Elioenai, Jaakobah, Jeshohaiah, Asaiah, Adiel, Jesimiel, Benaiah, 37 and Ziza son of Shiphi, son of Allon, son of Jedaiah, son of Shimri, son of Shemaiah—

38 these mentioned by name were leaders in their families. Their ancestral houses increased greatly. 39 They went to the entrance of Gedor, to the east side of the valley to seek pasture for their flocks. 40 They found rich, good pasture, and the land was broad, peaceful, and quiet, for some Hamites had lived there previously. 41 These who were recorded by name came in the days of King Hezekiah of Judah, attacked the Hamites' tents and the Meunim who were found there, and •set

---

ᵃ4:14 Or the Ge-harashim   ᵇ4:17 Lit She; 1 Ch 4:18   ᶜ4:21 Lit house   ᵈ4:22 Or who ruled over Moab

them apart for destruction, as they are today. Then they settled in their place because there was pasture for their flocks. [42] Now 500 men from these sons of Simeon went with Pelatiah, Neariah, Rephaiah, and Uzziel, the sons of Ishi, as their leaders to Mount Seir. [43] They struck down the remnant of the Amalekites who had escaped and still live there today.

Reuben's Descendants

5 [These were] the sons of Reuben the firstborn of Israel. He was the firstborn, but his birthright was given to the sons of Joseph son of Israel, because Reuben defiled his father's bed. He is not listed in the genealogy according to birthright. [2] Although Judah became strong among his brothers and a ruler came from him, the birthright was given to Joseph.

[3] The sons of Reuben, Israel's firstborn:
   Hanoch, Pallu, Hezron, and Carmi.
[4] Joel's sons: his son Shemaiah, his son Gog, his son Shimei,
[5] his son Micah, his son Reaiah, his son Baal, [6] and his son Beerah.

Beerah was a leader of the Reubenites, and Tiglath-pileser[a] king of Assyria took him into exile. [7] His relatives by their families as they are recorded in their genealogy: Jeiel the chief, Zechariah, [8] and Bela son of Azaz, son of Shema, son of Joel. They settled in Aroer as far as Nebo and Baal-meon. [9] They also settled in the east as far as the edge of the desert that extends to the Euphrates River, because their herds had increased in the land of Gilead. [10] During Saul's reign they waged war against the Hagrites, who were defeated by their power. And they lived in their tents throughout the region east of Gilead.

Gad's Descendants

[11] The sons of Gad lived next to them in the land of Bashan as far as Salecah:
[12] Joel the chief, Shapham the second [in command], Janai, and Shaphat in Bashan.
[13] Their relatives according to their ancestral houses: Michael, Meshullam, Sheba, Jorai, Jacan, Zia, and Eber—seven.
[14] These were the sons of Abihail son of Huri, son of Jaroah, son of Gilead, son of Michael, son of Jeshishai, son of Jahdo, son of Buz.
[15] Ahi son of Abdiel, son of Guni, was head of their ancestral houses. [16] They lived in Gilead, in Bashan and its towns, and throughout the pasturelands of Sharon. [17] All of them were registered in the genealogies during the reigns of Judah's King Jotham and Israel's King Jeroboam.

[18] The sons of Reuben and Gad and half the tribe of Manasseh had 44,760 warriors who could serve in the army—men who carried shield and sword, drew the bow, and were trained for war. [19] They waged war against the Hagrites, Jetur, Naphish, and Nodab. [20] They received help against these enemies,[b] and the Hagrites and all their allies were handed over to them, because they cried out to God in battle. He granted their request because they trusted in Him. [21] They captured the Hagrites' livestock—50,000 of their camels, 250,000 sheep, and 2,000 donkeys—as well as

100,000 people. 22 Many of the Hagrites were killed because it was God's battle. And they lived there in the Hagrites' place until the exile.

Half the Tribe of Manasseh

23 The sons of half the tribe of Manasseh settled in the land from Bashan to Baal-hermon (that is, Senir or Mount Hermon). They were numerous. 24 These were the heads of their ancestral houses: Epher, Ishi, Eliel, Azriel, Jeremiah, Hodaviah, and Jahdiel. They were brave warriors, famous men, and heads of their patriarchal families. 25 But they were unfaithful to the God of their ancestors. They prostituted themselves with the gods of the nations a God had destroyed before them. 26 So the God of Israel put it into the mind of Pul (that is, Tiglath-pileser b) king of Assyria to take the Reubenites, Gadites, and half the tribe of Manasseh into exile. He took them to Halah, Habor, Hara, and Gozan's river, ₍where they are₎ until today.

The Levites

6 c Levi's sons: Gershom, Kohath, and Merari.
2 Kohath's sons: Amram, Izhar, Hebron, and Uzziel.
3 Amram's children: Aaron, Moses, and Miriam.
Aaron's sons: Nadab, Abihu, Eleazar, and Ithamar.
4 Eleazar fathered Phinehas; Phinehas fathered Abishua;
5 Abishua fathered Bukki; Bukki fathered Uzzi;
6 Uzzi fathered Zerahiah; Zerahiah fathered Meraioth;
7 Meraioth fathered Amariah; Amariah fathered Ahitub;
8 Ahitub fathered Zadok;

Zadok fathered Ahimaaz;
9 Ahimaaz fathered Azariah; Azariah fathered Johanan;
10 Johanan fathered Azariah, who served as priest in the temple that Solomon built in Jerusalem;
11 Azariah fathered Amariah; Amariah fathered Ahitub;
12 Ahitub fathered Zadok; Zadok fathered Shallum;
13 Shallum fathered Hilkiah; Hilkiah fathered Azariah;
14 Azariah fathered Seraiah; and Seraiah fathered Jehozadak.
15 Jehozadak went into exile when the LORD sent Judah and Jerusalem into exile at the hands of Nebuchadnezzar.

16d Levi's sons: Gershom, Kohath, and Merari.
17 These are the names of Gershom's sons: Libni and Shimei.
18 Kohath's sons: Amram, Izhar, Hebron and Uzziel.
19 Merari's sons: Mahli and Mushi. These are the Levites' families according to their fathers:
20 Of Gershom: his son Libni, his son Jahath, his son Zimmah,
21 his son Joah, his son Iddo, his son Zerah, and his son Jeatherai.
22 Kohath's sons: his son Amminadab, his son Korah, his son Assir,
23 his son Elkanah, his son Ebiasaph, his son Assir, 24 his son Tahath, his son Uriel, his son Uzziah, and his son Shaul.
25 Elkanah's sons: Amasai and Ahimoth,
26 his son Elkanah, his son Zophai, his son Nahath, 27 his son Eliab,

---

a 5:25 Lit the peoples of the land   b 5:26 LXX; MT reads Tilgath-pilneser   c 6:1 1 Ch 5:27 in Hb   d 6:16 1 Ch 6:1 in Hb

his son Jeroham, and his son
Elkanah.
28 Samuel's sons: his firstborn Joel,[a]
and his second son Abijah.
29 Merari's sons: Mahli, his son Libni,
his son Shimei, his son Uzzah,
30 his son Shimea, his son Haggiah,
and his son Asaiah.

The Musicians

31 These are the men David put in
charge of the music in the LORD's temple
after the ark came to rest there. 32 They
ministered with song in front of the tabernacle, the tent of meeting, until Solomon built the LORD's temple in
Jerusalem, and they performed their task
according to the regulations ⌊given⌋ to
them. 33 These are the men who served
with their sons.

From the Kohathites:
Heman the singer,
son of Joel, son of Samuel,
34 son of Elkanah, son of Jeroham,
son of Eliel, son of Toah,
35 son of Zuph, son of Elkanah,
son of Mahath, son of Amasai,
36 son of Elkanah, son of Joel,
son of Azariah, son of Zephaniah,
37 son of Tahath, son of Assir,
son of Ebiasaph, son of Korah,
38 son of Izhar, son of Kohath,
son of Levi, son of Israel.

39 Heman's relative was •Asaph,
who stood at his right hand:
Asaph son of Berechiah,
son of Shimea,
40 son of Michael, son of Baaseiah,
son of Malchijah, 41 son of Ethni,
son of Zerah, son of Adaiah,
42 son of Ethan, son of Zimmah,
son of Shimei, 43 son of Jahath,
son of Gershom, son of Levi.

44 On the left, their relatives were
Merari's sons:
Ethan son of Kishi, son of Abdi,
son of Malluch,
45 son of Hashabiah,
son of Amaziah, son of Hilkiah,
46 son of Amzi, son of Bani,
son of Shemer, 47 son of Mahli,
son of Mushi, son of Merari,
son of Levi.

Aaron's Descendants

48 Their relatives the Levites were assigned to all the service of the tabernacle, God's temple. 49 But Aaron and his
sons did all the work of the most holy
place. They presented the offerings on
the altar of •burnt offerings and on the
altar of incense to make atonement for
Israel according to all that Moses the servant of God had commanded.

50 These are Aaron's sons: his son
Eleazar,
his son Phinehas, his son Abishua,
51 his son Bukki, his son Uzzi,
his son Zerahiah, 52 his son
Meraioth,
his son Amariah, his son Ahitub,
53 his son Zadok, and his son
Ahimaaz.

The Settlements of the Levites

54 These were the places assigned to
Aaron's sons from the Kohathite family
for their settlements in their territory,
because the ⌊first⌋ lot was for them.
55 They were given Hebron in the land of
Judah and its surrounding pasturelands,
56 but the fields and villages around the
city were given to Caleb son of Jephunneh. 57 Aaron's sons were given:

Hebron (a city of refuge), Libnah and
its pasturelands, Jattir, Eshtemoa and

---

a6:28 Some LXX mss, Syr, Arabic; other Hb mss omit *Joel*; 1 Sm 8:2

its pasturelands, [58] Hilen[a] and its pasturelands, Debir and its pasturelands, [59] Ashan and its pasturelands, and Beth-shemesh and its pasturelands. [60] From the tribe of Benjamin ⌊they were given⌋ Geba and its pasturelands, Alemeth and its pasturelands, and Anathoth and its pasturelands. They had 13 towns in all among their families.

[61] To the rest of the Kohathites, 10 towns from the half tribe of Manasseh ⌊were assigned⌋ by lot.

[62] The Gershomites ⌊were assigned⌋ 13 towns from the tribes of Issachar, Asher, Naphtali, and Manasseh in Bashan according to their families.

[63] The Merarites ⌊were assigned⌋ by lot 12 towns from the tribes of Reuben, Gad, and Zebulun according to their families. [64] So the Israelites gave these towns and their pasturelands to the Levites. [65] They assigned by lot the towns named above from the tribes of the Judahites, Simeonites, and Benjaminites.

[66] Some of the families of the Kohathites were given towns from the tribe of Ephraim for their territory:

[67] Shechem (a city of refuge) with its pasturelands in the hill country of Ephraim, Gezer and its pasturelands, [68] Jokmeam and its pasturelands, Beth-horon and its pasturelands, [69] Aijalon and its pasturelands, and Gath-rimmon and its pasturelands. [70] From half the tribe of Manasseh, Aner and its pasturelands, and Bileam and its pasturelands ⌊were given⌋ to the rest of the families of the Kohathites.

[71] The Gershomites ⌊received⌋:

Golan in Bashan and its pasturelands, and Ashtaroth and its pasturelands from the families of half the tribe of Manasseh. [72] From the tribe of Issachar ⌊they received⌋ Kedesh and its pasturelands, Daberath and its pasturelands, [73] Ramoth and its pasturelands, and Anem and its pasturelands. [74] From the tribe of Asher ⌊they received⌋ Mashal and its pasturelands, Abdon and its pasturelands, [75] Hukok and its pasturelands, and Rehob and its pasturelands. [76] From the tribe of Naphtali ⌊they received⌋ Kedesh in Galilee and its pasturelands, Hammon and its pasturelands, and Kiriathaim and its pasturelands.

[77] The rest of the Merarites ⌊received⌋:

From the tribe of Zebulun, ⌊they received⌋ Rimmono and its pasturelands and Tabor and its pasturelands. [78] From the tribe of Reuben across the Jordan at Jericho, to the east of the Jordan, ⌊they received⌋ Bezer in the desert and its pasturelands, Jahzah and its pasturelands, [79] Kedemoth and its pasturelands, and Mephaath and its pasturelands. [80] From the tribe of Gad ⌊they received⌋ Ramoth in Gilead and its pasturelands, Mahanaim and its pasturelands, [81] Heshbon and its pasturelands, and Jazer and its pasturelands.

Issachar's Descendants

7 Issachar's sons: Tola, Puah, Jashub, and Shimron—four.
[2] Tola's sons: Uzzi, Rephaiah, Jeriel, Jahmai, Ibsam, and Shemuel, the heads of their ancestral houses. During David's reign, 22,600 descendants of Tola were recorded as warriors in their genealogies.
[3] Uzzi's son: Izrahiah.
Izrahiah's sons: Michael, Obadiah,

a 6:58 Some Hb mss, LXX; other Hb mss read Hilez

Joel, Isshiah. All five of them were chiefs. [4] Along with them, they had 36,000 troops for battle according to the genealogical records of their ancestral houses, for they had many wives and children. [5] Their tribesmen who were warriors belonging to all the families of Issachar totalled 87,000 in their genealogies.

Benjamin's Descendants

[6] Three of Benjamin's ⌊sons⌋: Bela, Becher, and Jediael. [7] Bela's sons: Ezbon, Uzzi, Uzziel, Jerimoth, and Iri—five. They were warriors and heads of their ancestral houses; 22,034 were listed in their genealogies. [8] Becher's sons: Zemirah, Joash, Eliezer, Elioenai, Omri, Jeremoth, Abijah, Anathoth, and Alemeth; all these were Becher's sons. [9] Their genealogies were recorded according to the heads of their ancestral houses— 20,200 warriors. [10] Jediael's son: Bilhan. Bilhan's sons: Jeush, Benjamin, Ehud, Chenaanah, Zethan, Tarshish, and Ahishahar. [11] All these sons of Jediael listed by heads of families were warriors; there were 17,200 who could serve in the army. [12] Shuppim and Huppim were sons of Ir, and the Hushim were the sons of Aher.

Naphtali's Descendants

[13] Naphtali's sons: Jahziel, Guni, Jezer, and Shallum—Bilhah's sons.

Manasseh's Descendants

[14] Manasseh's sons through his Aramean concubine: Asriel and Machir the father of Gilead. [15] Machir took wives from Huppim and Shuppim. The name of his sister was Maacah. Another descendant was named Zelophehad, but he had only daughters. [16] Machir's wife Maacah gave birth to a son, and she named ⌊him⌋ Peresh. His brother was named Sheresh, and his sons were Ulam and Rekem. [17] Ulam's son: Bedan. These were the sons of Gilead son of Machir, son of Manasseh. [18] His sister Hammolecheth gave birth to Ishhod, Abiezer, and Mahlah. [19] Shemida's sons: Ahian, Shechem, Likhi, and Aniam.

Ephraim's Descendants

[20] Ephraim's sons: Shuthelah, and his son Bered,
his son Tahath, his son Eleadah,
his son Tahath, [21] his son Zabad,
his son Shuthelah, Ezer, and Elead.
The men of Gath who were born in the land killed Ezer and Elead because they went down to raid their cattle. [22] Their father Ephraim mourned a long time, and his relatives came to comfort him. [23] He slept with his wife, and she conceived and gave birth to a son. So he named him Beriah, because there had been misfortune in his home.[a] [24] His daughter was Sheerah, who built Lower and Upper Beth-horon and Uzzen-sheerah,
[25] his son Rephah, his son Resheph,

---

[a] 7:23 *Beriah* sounds like the Hb for "in misfortune."

his son Telah, his son Tahan,
²⁶ his son Ladan, his son
Ammihud,
his son Elishama, ²⁷ his son Nun,
and his son Joshua.

²⁸ Their holdings and settlements were Bethel and its villages; Naaran to the east, Gezer and its villages to the west, and Shechem and its villages as far as Ayyah and its villages, ²⁹ and along the borders of the sons of Manasseh, Beth-shean and its villages, Taanach and its villages, Megiddo and its villages, and Dor and its villages. The sons of Joseph son of Israel lived in these towns.

Asher's Descendants

³⁰ Asher's sons: Imnah, Ishvah, Ishvi, and Beriah, with their sister Serah.
³¹ Beriah's sons: Heber, and Malchiel, who fathered Birzaith.
³² Heber fathered Japhlet, Shomer, and Hotham, with their sister Shua.
³³ Japhlet's sons: Pasach, Bimhal, and Ashvath. These were Japhlet's sons.
³⁴ Shemer's sons: Ahi, Rohgah, Hubbah, and Aram.
³⁵ His brother Helem's sons: Zophah, Imna, Shelesh, and Amal.
³⁶ Zophah's sons: Suah, Harnepher, Shual, Beri, Imrah,
³⁷ Bezer, Hod, Shamma, Shilshah, Ithran, and Beera.
³⁸ Jether's sons: Jephunneh, Pispa, and Ara.
³⁹ Ulla's sons: Arah, Hanniel, and Rizia.
⁴⁰ All these were Asher's sons. They were the heads of their

ancestral houses, chosen men, warriors, and chiefs among the leaders. The number of men listed in their genealogies for military service was 26,000.

Benjamin's Descendants

8 Benjamin fathered Bela, his firstborn;
Ashbel was ˪born˩ second, Aharah third,
² Nohah fourth, and Rapha fifth.
³ Bela's sons: Addar, Gera, Abihud,
⁴ Abishua, Naaman, Ahoah,
⁵ Gera, Shephuphan, and Huram.
⁶ These were Ehud's sons, who were the heads of the families living in Geba and who were deported to Manahath: ⁷ Naaman, Ahijah, and Gera. Gera deported them and was the father of Uzza and Ahihud.
⁸ Shaharaim had sons in the country of Moab after he had divorced his wives Hushim and Baara. ⁹ His sons by his wife Hodesh: Jobab, Zibia, Mesha, Malcam, ¹⁰ Jeuz, Sachia, and Mirmah. These were his sons, heads of families. ¹¹ He also had sons by Hushim: Abitub and Elpaal.
¹² Elpaal's sons: Eber, Misham, and Shemed who built Ono and Lod and its villages, ¹³ Beriah and Shema, who were the heads of families of Aijalon's residents and who drove out the residents of Gath, ¹⁴ Ahio,ᵃ Shashak, and Jeremoth.
¹⁵ Zebadiah, Arad, Eder,
¹⁶ Michael, Ishpah, and Joha were Beriah's sons.

ᵃ8:13-14 LXX reads *Gath* ¹⁴ and their brother

[17] Zebadiah, Meshullam, Hizki, Heber, [18] Ishmerai, Izliah, and Jobab were Elpaal's sons. [19] Jakim, Zichri, Zabdi, [20] Elienai, Zillethai, Eliel, [21] Adaiah, Beraiah, and Shimrath were Shimei's sons. [22] Ishpan, Eber, Eliel, [23] Abdon, Zichri, Hanan, [24] Hananiah, Elam, Anthothijah, [25] Iphdeiah, and Penuel were Shashak's sons. [26] Shamsherai, Shehariah, Athaliah, [27] Jaareshiah, Elijah, and Zichri were Jeroham's sons.

[28] These were heads of families, chiefs according to their genealogies, and lived in Jerusalem.

[29] Jeiel,[a] fathered Gibeon and lived in Gibeon. His wife's name was Maacah. [30] Abdon was his firstborn son, then Zur, Kish, Baal, Nadab, [31] Gedor, Ahio, Zecher, [32] and Mikloth who fathered Shimeah. These also lived opposite their relatives in Jerusalem, with their other relatives.

[33] Ner fathered Kish, Kish fathered Saul, and Saul fathered Jonathan, Malchishua, Abinadab, and Esh-baal.[b]

[34] Jonathan's son was Merib-baal,[c] and Merib-baal fathered Micah. [35] Micah's sons: Pithon, Melech, Tarea, and Ahaz. [36] Ahaz fathered Jehoaddah, Jehoaddah fathered Alemeth, Azmaveth, and Zimri, and Zimri fathered Moza. [37] Moza fathered Binea. His son was Raphah, his son Eleasah, and his son Azel. [38] Azel had six sons, and these were their names: Azrikam, Bocheru, Ishmael, Sheariah, Obadiah, and Hanan. All these were Azel's sons.

[39] His brother Eshek's sons: Ulam was his firstborn, Jeush second, and Eliphelet third.

[40] Ulam's sons were warriors and archers. They had many sons and grandsons—150 of them.

All these were among Benjamin's sons.

After the Babylonian Exile

9 All Israel was registered in the genealogies that are written about in the Book of the Kings of Israel. But Judah was exiled to Babylon because of their unfaithfulness. [2] The first to live in their towns on their own property again were Israelites, priests, Levites, and temple servants.

[3] These people from the descendants of Judah, Benjamin, Ephraim, and Manasseh settled in Jerusalem:

[4] Uthai son of Ammihud, son of Omri,
son of Imri, son of Bani,
a descendant[d] of Perez son of Judah;

[5] from the Shilonites:
Asaiah the firstborn and his sons;

[6] and from the sons of Zerah:
Jeuel and 690 of their relatives.

[7] The Benjaminites: Sallu son of Meshullam,
son of Hodaviah, son of Hassenuah;

[8] Ibneiah son of Jeroham;
Elah son of Uzzi, son of Michri;
Meshullam son of Shephatiah,
son of Reuel, son of Ibnijah;

[9] and 956 of their relatives

according to their genealogical records. All these men were heads of their ancestral houses.

Priests and Levites

10 The priests: Jedaiah; Jehoiarib; Jachin;
11 Azariah son of Hilkiah, son of Meshullam,
son of Zadok, son of Meraioth, son of Ahitub, the chief official of God's temple;
12 Adaiah son of Jeroham, son of Pashhur,
son of Malchijah; Maasai son of Adiel,
son of Jahzerah, son of Meshullam, son of Meshillemith, son of Immer;
13 and 1,760 of their relatives, the heads of households. They were capable men employed in the ministry of God's temple.

14 The Levites: Shemaiah son of Hasshub,
son of Azrikam, son of Hashabiah of the Merarites;
15 Bakbakkar, Heresh, Galal, and Mattaniah,
son of Mica, son of Zichri, son of Asaph;
16 Obadiah son of Shemaiah, son of Galal,
son of Jeduthun; and Berechiah son of Asa,
son of Elkanah who lived in the villages of the Netophathites.

Gatekeepers

17 The gatekeepers: Shallum, Akkub, Talmon, Ahiman, and their relatives.

Shallum was their chief; 18 he was previously stationed at the King's Gate on the east side. These were the gatekeepers from the camp of the Levites.
19 Shallum son of Kore, son of Ebiasaph, son of Korah and his relatives from his household, the Korahites, were assigned to guard the thresholds of the tent.[a] Their ancestors had been assigned to the LORD's camp as guardians of the entrance. 20 In earlier times Phinehas son of Eleazar had been their leader, and the LORD was with him. 21 Zechariah son of Meshelemiah was the gatekeeper at the entrance to the tent of meeting.

22 The total number of those chosen to be gatekeepers at the thresholds was 212. They were registered by genealogy in their villages. David and Samuel the seer had appointed them to their trusted positions. 23 So they and their sons were assigned to the gates of the LORD's house, the house of the tent. 24 The gatekeepers were on the four sides: east, west, north, and south. 25 Their relatives came from their villages at fixed times to be with them seven days, 26 but the four chief gatekeepers, who were Levites, were entrusted with the rooms and the treasuries of God's temple. 27 They spent the night in the vicinity of God's temple, because they had guard duty and were in charge of opening it every morning.

Various Duties of Levites and Priests

28 Some of them were in charge of the utensils used in worship. They would count them when they brought them in and when they took them out. 29 Others

---

a 9:19 = the temple

were put in charge of the furnishings and all the utensils of the sanctuary, as well as the fine flour, wine, oil, incense, and spices. 30 But some of the priests' sons mixed the spices. 31 A Levite called Mattithiah, the firstborn of Shallum the Korahite, was entrusted with underline{baking the bread.}a 32 Some of the Kohathites' relatives were responsible for preparing the rows of the bread ⌊of the Presence⌋ every Sabbath.

33 The singers, the heads of Levite families, stayed in the ⌊temple⌋ chambers and were exempt from other tasks because they were on duty day and night. 34 These were the heads of Levite families, chiefs according to their genealogies, and lived in Jerusalem.

Saul's Family

35 Jeiel fathered Gibeon and lived in Gibeon. His wife's name was Maacah. 36 Abdon was his firstborn son, then Zur, Kish, Baal, Ner, Nadab, 37 Gedor, Ahio, Zechariah, and Mikloth. 38 Mikloth fathered Shimeam. These also lived opposite their relatives in Jerusalem with their ⌊other⌋ relatives.

39 Ner fathered Kish, Kish fathered Saul, and Saul fathered Jonathan, Malchishua, Abinadab, and Esh-baal. 40 Jonathan's son was Merib-baal, and Merib-baal fathered Micah. 41 Micah's sons: Pithon, Melech, Tahrea, and Ahaz.b 42 Ahaz fathered Jarah; Jarah fathered Alemeth, Azmaveth, and Zimri; Zimri fathered Moza. 43 Moza fathered Binea. His son was Rephaiah, his son

Eleasah, and his son Azel. 44 Azel had six sons, and these were their names: Azrikam, Bocheru, Ishmael, Sheariah, Obadiah, and Hanan. These were Azel's sons.

Deaths of Saul and Sons

10 The Philistines fought against Israel, and Israel's men fled from them and were killed on Mount Gilboa. 2 The Philistines pursued Saul and his sons and killed Saul's sons Jonathan, Abinadab, and Malchishua. 3 When the battle intensified against Saul, the archers found him and severely wounded him. 4 Then Saul said to his armor-bearer, "Draw your sword and run me through with it, or these uncircumcised men will come and torture me!" But his armor-bearer wouldn't do it because he was terrified. Then Saul took his sword and fell on it. 5 When his armor-bearer saw that Saul was dead, he also fell on his own sword and died. 6 So Saul and his three sons died—his whole house died together.

7 When all the men of Israel in the valley saw that the army had run away and that Saul and his sons were dead, they abandoned their cities and fled. So the Philistines came and settled in them. 8 The next day when the Philistines came to strip the slain, they found Saul and his sons dead on Mount Gilboa. 9 They stripped Saul, cut off his head, took his armor, and sent messengers throughout the land of the Philistines to spread the good news to their idols and their people. 10 Then they put his armor in the temple of their gods and hung his skull in the temple of Dagon. 11 When all Jabesh-gilead heard of everything the Philistines had done to

---

a**9:31** Lit *with things prepared in pans*   b**9:41** LXX, Syr, Tg, Vg, Arabic; MT omits *and Ahaz*; 1 Ch 8:35

Saul, ¹² all their brave men set out and retrieved the body of Saul and the bodies of his sons and brought them to Jabesh. They buried their bones under the oak^a in Jabesh and fasted seven days.

¹³ Saul died for his unfaithfulness to the LORD because he did not keep the LORD's word. He even consulted a medium for guidance, ¹⁴ but he did not inquire of the LORD. So the LORD put him to death and turned the kingdom over to David son of Jesse.

Israel Anoints David King

11 All Israel came together to David at Hebron and said, "Here we are, your own flesh and blood.^b ² Even when Saul was king, you led us out ⸢to battle⸣ and brought us back. The LORD your God also said to you, 'You will shepherd My people Israel and be ruler over My people Israel.'"

³ So all the elders of Israel came to the king at Hebron. David made a covenant with them at Hebron in the LORD's presence, and they anointed David king over Israel, in keeping with the LORD's word through Samuel.

David Captures Jerusalem

⁴ David and all Israel marched to Jerusalem (that is, Jebus); the Jebusites who inhabited the land were there. ⁵ The inhabitants of Jebus said to David, "You will never get in here." Yet David did capture the stronghold of Zion (that is, the city of David).

⁶ David said, "Whoever is the first to kill a Jebusite will become commander-in-chief." Joab son of Zeruiah went up first, so he became the chief.

⁷ Then David took up residence in the stronghold; therefore, it was called the city of David. ⁸ He built up the city all the way around, from the supporting terraces to the surrounding parts, and Joab restored the rest of the city. ⁹ David steadily grew more powerful, and the LORD of •Hosts was with him.

Exploits of David's Warriors

¹⁰ The following were the chiefs of David's warriors who, together with all Israel, strongly supported him in his reign to make him king according to the LORD's word about Israel. ¹¹ This is the list of David's warriors:

Jashobeam son of Hachmoni was chief of the Thirty;^c he wielded his spear against 300 and killed them at one time.

¹² After him, Eleazar son of Dodo the Ahohite was one of the three warriors. ¹³ He was with David at Pas-dammim when the Philistines had gathered there for battle. A plot of ground full of barley was there, where the troops had fled from the Philistines. ¹⁴ But Eleazar and David^d took their stand in the middle of the plot and defended it. They killed Philistines, and the LORD gave them a great victory.

¹⁵ Three of the 30 chief men went down to David, to the rock at the cave of Adullam, while the Philistine army was encamped in the Valley of Rephaim. ¹⁶ At that time David was in the stronghold, and a Philistine garrison was at Bethlehem. ¹⁷ David was extremely thirsty^e and said, "If only someone would bring me water from the well at the city gate of Bethlehem!" ¹⁸ So the Three broke through the Philistine camp and drew water from the well at the gate of Bethlehem. They brought it back to David, but he refused to drink it. Instead, he poured it out to the LORD. ¹⁹ David said, "I would never do such a thing in the presence of God! How can I drink the blood

---

^a**10:12** Or *terebinth* or *large tree*   ^b**11:1** Lit *your bone and flesh*   ^c**11:11** Alt Hb tradition reads *Three*   ^d**11:14** Lit *But they*   ^e**11:17** Lit *And David craved*

of these men who risked their lives?" For they brought it at the risk of their lives. So he would not drink it. Such were the exploits of the three warriors. ²⁰ Abishai, Joab's brother, was the leader of the Three.^a He raised his spear against 300 ⌊men⌋ and killed them, gaining a reputation among the Three. ²¹ He was the most honored of the Three and became their commander even though he did not become one of the Three.

²² Benaiah son of Jehoiada was the son of a brave man^b from Kabzeel, a man of many exploits. Benaiah killed two ⌊sons of⌋ Ariel of Moab,^c and he went down into a pit on a snowy day and killed a lion. ²³ He also killed an Egyptian who was seven and a half feet tall.^d Even though the Egyptian had a spear in his hand like a weaver's beam, Benaiah went down to him with a club, snatched the spear out of the Egyptian's hand, and then killed him with his own spear. ²⁴ These were the exploits of Benaiah son of Jehoiada, who had a reputation among the three warriors. ²⁵ He was the most honored of the Thirty, but he did not become one of the Three. David put him in charge of his bodyguard.

²⁶ The fighting men were:

Joab's brother Asahel,
Elhanan son of Dodo of Bethlehem,
²⁷ Shammoth the Harorite,
Helez the Pelonite,
²⁸ Ira son of Ikkesh the Tekoite,
Abiezer the Anathothite,
²⁹ Sibbecai the Hushathite,
Ilai the Ahohite,
³⁰ Maharai the Netophathite,
Heled son of Baanah
the Netophathite,
³¹ Ithai son of Ribai from Gibeah
of the Benjaminites,

Benaiah the Pirathonite,
³² Hurai from the •wadis of Gaash,
Abiel the Arbathite,
³³ Azmaveth the Baharumite,
Eliahba the Shaalbonite,
³⁴ the sons of^e Hashem the Gizonite,
Jonathan son of Shagee
the Hararite,
³⁵ Ahiam son of Sachar the Hararite,
Eliphal son of Ur,
³⁶ Hepher the Mecherathite,
Ahijah the Pelonite,
³⁷ Hezro the Carmelite,
Naarai son of Ezbai,
³⁸ Joel the brother of Nathan,
Mibhar son of Hagri,
³⁹ Zelek the Ammonite,
Naharai the Beerothite, the armor-
bearer for Joab son of Zeruiah,
⁴⁰ Ira the Ithrite,
Gareb the Ithrite,
⁴¹ Uriah the Hittite,
Zabad son of Ahlai,
⁴² Adina son of Shiza the Reubenite,
chief of the Reubenites, and 30
with him,
⁴³ Hanan son of Maacah,
Joshaphat the Mithnite,
⁴⁴ Uzzia the Ashterathite,
Shama and Jeiel the sons of Hotham
the Aroerite,
⁴⁵ Jediael son of Shimri
and his brother Joha the Tizite,
⁴⁶ Eliel the Mahavite,
Jeribai and Joshaviah, the sons
of Elnaam,
Ithmah the Moabite,
⁴⁷ Eliel, Obed, and Jaasiel
the Mezobaite.

David's First Supporters

12 The following were the men who came to David at Ziklag while he was still banned from the presence of

---

^a**11:20** Syr reads *Thirty*   ^b**11:22** Or *was a valiant man*   ^c**11:22** Or *He killed two Moabite warriors*   ^d**11:23** Lit *who measured five cubits*   ^e**11:34** LXX omits *the sons of*; 2 Sm 23:32

Saul son of Kish. They were among the warriors who helped him in battle. [2] They were archers who, using either their right or left hand, could ⌊throw⌋ stones ⌊with a sling⌋ or ⌊shoot⌋ arrows with a bow. They were Saul's relatives from Benjamin:

[3] Their chief was Ahiezer son of Shemaah the Gibeathite.
Then there was his brother Joash;
Jeziel and Pelet sons of Azmaveth;
Beracah, Jehu the Anathothite;
[4] Ishmaiah the Gibeonite, a warrior among the Thirty and ⌊a leader⌋ over the Thirty;
[a] Jeremiah, Jahaziel, Johanan, Jozabad the Gederathite;
[5] Eluzai, Jerimoth, Bealiah, Shemariah, Shephatiah the Haruphite;
[6] Elkanah, Isshiah, Azarel, Joezer, and Jashobeam, the Korahites;
[7] and Joelah and Zebadiah, the sons of Jeroham from Gedor.

[8] Some Gadites defected to David at his stronghold in the desert. They were fighting men, trained for battle, expert with shield and spear. Their faces were like the faces of lions, and they were as swift as gazelles on the mountains.

[9] Ezer was the chief, Obadiah second, Eliab third,
[10] Mishmannah fourth, Jeremiah fifth,
[11] Attai sixth, Eliel seventh,
[12] Johanan eighth, Elzabad ninth,
[13] Jeremiah tenth, and Machbannai eleventh.

[14] These Gadites were army commanders; the least of them was a match for a hundred, and the greatest of them for a thousand. [15] These are the men who crossed the Jordan in the first month[b] when it was overflowing all its banks, and put to flight all ⌊those in⌋ the valleys to the east and to the west.

[16] Other Benjaminites and men from Judah also went to David at the stronghold. [17] David went out to meet them and said to them, "If you have come in peace to help me, my heart will be united with you, but if you have come to betray me to my enemies even though my hands have done no wrong, may the God of our ancestors look on it and judge."

Spirit Controls Amasai

[18] Then the Spirit took control of[c] Amasai, chief of the Thirty, ⌊and he said⌋:

⌊We are⌋ yours, David,
⌊we are⌋ with you, son of Jesse!
Peace, peace to you,
and peace to him who helps you,
for your God helps you.

So David received them and made them leaders of his troops.

[19] Some Manassites defected to David when he went with the Philistines to fight against Saul. However, they did not help the Philistines because the Philistine rulers, following consultation, sent David away. They said, "It will be our heads if he defects to his master Saul." [20] When David went to Ziklag, some men from Manasseh defected to him: Adnah, Jozabad, Jediael, Michael, Jozabad, Elihu, and Zillethai, chiefs of thousands in Manasseh. [21] They helped David against the marauders, for they were all brave warriors and commanders in the army. [22] At that time, men came day after day to help David until there was a great army, like an army of God.[d]

---

[a]12:4 1 Ch 12:5 in Hb starts here, v. 5 is 1 Ch 12:6 in Hb, and so on throughout chap 12 [b]12:15 March–April [c]12:18 Lit Spirit clothed; Jdg 6:34; 2 Ch 24:20 [d]12:22 Or like the ultimate army

David's Soldiers in Hebron

23 The numbers of the armed troops who came to David at Hebron to turn Saul's kingdom over to him, according to the LORD's word, were as follows:

24 From the Judahites: 6,800 armed troops bearing shields and spears.
25 From the Simeonites: 7,100 brave warriors ready for war.
26 From the Levites: 4,600 27 in addition to Jehoiada, leader of the house of Aaron, with 3,700 men; 28 and Zadok, a young brave warrior, with 22 commanders from his own ancestral house.
29 From the Benjaminites, the relatives of Saul: 3,000 (up to that time the majority of the Benjaminites maintained their allegiance to the house of Saul).
30 From the Ephraimites: 20,800 brave warriors who were famous men in their ancestral houses.
31 From half the tribe of Manasseh: 18,000 designated by name to come and make David king.
32 From the Issacharites, who understood the times and knew what Israel should do: 200 chiefs with all their relatives under their command.
33 From Zebulun: 50,000 who could serve in the army, trained for battle with all kinds of weapons of war, with singleness of purpose to help David.a
34 From Naphtali: 1,000 commanders accompanied by 37,000 men with shield and spear.
35 From the Danites: 28,600 trained for battle.
36 From Asher: 40,000 who could serve in the army, trained for battle.
37 From across the Jordan—from the Reubenites, Gadites, and half the tribe of Manasseh: 120,000 men equipped with all the military weapons of war.

38 All these warriors, lined up in battle formation, came to Hebron with wholehearted determination to make David king over all Israel. All the rest of Israel was also of one mind to make David king. 39 They were there with David for three days, eating and drinking, for their relatives had provided for them. 40 In addition, their neighbors from as far away as Issachar, Zebulun, and Naphtali came bringing food on donkeys, camels, mules, and oxen—abundant provisions of flour, fig cakes, raisins, wine and oil, oxen, and sheep. Indeed, there was joy in Israel.

David Retrieves Ark

13 David consulted with all his leaders, the commanders of hundreds and of thousands. 2 Then he said to the whole assembly of Israel, "If it seems good to you, and if this is from the LORD our God, let us spread out and send the message to the rest of our relatives in all the districts of Israel, including the priests and Levites in their cities with pasturelands, that they should gather together with us. 3 Then let us bring back the ark of our God, for we did not inquire of Him in Saul's days." 4 Since the proposal seemed right to all the people, the whole assembly agreed to do it.

5 So David assembled all Israel, from the Shihor of Egypt to the entrance of Hamath,b to bring the ark of God from Kiriath-jearim. 6 David and all Israel went to Baalah (that is, Kiriath-jearim), which belongs to Judah, to take from there the ark of God, which is called by

a 12:33 LXX; Hb omits David   b 13:5 Or to Lebo-hamath

the name of the LORD who dwells ˌbetweenˌ the •cherubim. ⁷ At Abinadab's house, they set the ark of God on a new cart. Uzzah and Ahioª were guiding the cart.

David Celebrates, Uzzah Killed

⁸ David and all Israel were celebrating with all their might before God with songs and with lyres, harps, tambourines, cymbals, and trumpets. ⁹ When they came to Chidon's threshing floor, Uzzah reached out to hold the ark, because the oxen had stumbled. ¹⁰ Then the LORD's anger burned against Uzzah, and He struck him dead because he had reached out to the ark. So he died there in the presence of God.

David Angry—Stops Ark

¹¹ David was angry because of the LORD's outburst against Uzzah, so he named that place Outburst Against Uzzah,ᵇ as it is ˌstill namedˌ today. ¹² David feared God that day, and said, "How can I ever bring the ark of God to me?" ¹³ So David did not move the ark of God homeᶜ to the city of David; instead, he took it to the house of Obed-edom the Gittite. ¹⁴ The ark of God remained with Obed-edom's family in his house for three months, and the LORD blessed his family and all that he had.

King Hiram of Tyre Helps with Palace

14 King Hiram of Tyre sent envoys to David, along with cedar logs, stonemasons, and carpenters to build a palace for him. ² Then David knew that the LORD had established him as king over Israel and that his kingdom had been exalted for the sake of His people Israel.

David's Wives and Children

³ David took more wives in Jerusalem, and he became the father of more sons and daughters. ⁴ These are the names of the children born to him in Jerusalem: Shammua, Shobab, Nathan, Solomon, ⁵ Ibhar, Elishua, Elpelet, ⁶ Nogah, Nepheg, Japhia, ⁷ Elishama, Beeliada, and Eliphelet.

David Defeats Philistines

⁸ When the Philistines heard that David had been anointed king over all Israel, they all went in search of David; when David heard of this, he went out to face them. ⁹ Now the Philistines had come and made a raid in the Valley of Rephaim, ¹⁰ so David inquired of God, "Should I go to war against the Philistines? Will You hand them over to me?"

The LORD replied, "Go, and I will hand them over to you."

¹¹ So the Israelites went up to Baal-perazim, and David defeated the Philistines there. Then David said, "Like a bursting flood, God has used me to burst out against my enemies." Therefore, they named that place the Lord Bursts Out.ᵈ ¹² The Philistines abandoned their idols there, and David ordered that they be burned in the fire.

¹³ Once again the Philistines made a raid in the valley. ¹⁴ So David again inquired of God, and God answered him, "Do not pursue them directly. Circle down away from them and attack them opposite the balsam trees. ¹⁵ When you hear the sound of marching in the tops of the balsam trees, then march out to battle, for God will have marched out ahead of you to attack the camp of the Philistines." ¹⁶ So David did exactly as God commanded him, and they struck down the Philistine army from Gibeon to

---

ª**13:7** Or *and his brothers*   ᵇ**13:11** Or *Perez-uzzah*   ᶜ**13:13** Lit *to himself*   ᵈ**14:11** Or *Baal-perazim*

Gezer. [17] Then David's fame spread throughout the lands, and the LORD caused all the nations to be terrified of him.

Ark to Jerusalem

15 David built houses for himself in the city of David, and he prepared a place for the ark of God and pitched a tent for it. [2] Then David said, "No one but the Levites may carry the ark of God, because the LORD has chosen them to carry the ark of the LORD and to minister before Him forever."

[3] David assembled all Israel at Jerusalem to bring the ark of the LORD to the place he had prepared for it. [4] Then he gathered together the descendants of Aaron and the Levites:

[5] From the Kohathites, Uriel the leader and 120 of his relatives; [6] from the Merarites, Asaiah the leader and 220 of his relatives; [7] from the Gershomites, Joel the leader and 130 of his relatives; [8] from the Elizaphanites, Shemaiah the leader and 200 of his relatives; [9] from the Hebronites, Eliel the leader and 80 of his relatives; [10] from the Uzzielites, Amminadab the leader and 112 of his relatives.

David Orders Levites and Priests to Observe Ark Procedures

[11] David summoned the priests Zadok and Abiathar and the Levites Uriel, Asaiah, Joel, Shemaiah, Eliel, and Amminadab. [12] He said to them, "You are the heads of the Levite families. You and your relatives must consecrate yourselves so that you may bring the ark of the LORD God of Israel to ⌊the place⌋ I have prepared for it. [13] For the LORD our God burst out ⌊in anger⌋ against us because you Levites were not ⌊with⌋ us the

first time, for we didn't inquire of Him about the proper procedures." [14] So the priests and the Levites consecrated themselves to bring up the ark of the LORD God of Israel. [15] Then the Levites carried the ark of God the way Moses had commanded according to the word of the LORD: on their shoulders with the poles.

Levites Appoint Musicians

[16] Then David told the leaders of the Levites to appoint their relatives as singers and to have them raise their voices with joy accompanied by musical instruments—harps, lyres, and cymbals. [17] So the Levites appointed Heman son of Joel; from his relatives, Asaph son of Berechiah; and from their relatives the Merarites, Ethan son of Kushaiah. [18] With them were their relatives second in rank: Zechariah, Jaaziel,[a] Shemiramoth, Jehiel, Unni, Eliab, Benaiah, Maaseiah, Mattithiah, Eliphelehu, Mikneiah, and the gatekeepers Obed-edom and Jeiel. [19] The singers Heman, Asaph, and Ethan were to sound the bronze cymbals; [20] Zechariah, Aziel, Shemiramoth, Jehiel, Unni, Eliab, Maaseiah, and Benaiah were to play harps according to *Alamoth;*[b] [21] and Mattithiah, Eliphelehu, Mikneiah, Obed-edom, Jeiel, and Azaziah were to lead the music with lyres according to the •*Sheminith.* [22] Chenaniah, the leader of the Levites in music, was to direct the music because he was skillful. [23] Berechiah and Elkanah were to be gatekeepers for the ark. [24] The priests, Shebaniah, Joshaphat, Nethanel, Amasai, Zechariah, Benaiah, and Eliezer, were to blow trumpets before the ark of God. Obed-edom and Jehiah were also to be gatekeepers for the ark.

---

[a]**15:18** Some Hb mss, LXX; other Hb mss read *Zechariah son and Jaaziel*   [b]**15:20** This notation may refer to a high pitch, perhaps a tune sung by soprano voices; the Hb word means "young women."

²⁵ David, the elders of Israel, and the commanders of the thousands went with rejoicing to bring the ark of the covenant of the LORD from the house of Obed-edom. ²⁶ And because God helped the Levites who were carrying the ark of the covenant of the LORD, they sacrificed seven bulls and seven rams.

Wife Michal Despises David's Dancing

²⁷ Now David was dressed in a robe of fine linen, as were all the Levites who were carrying the ark, as well as the singers and Chenaniah, the music leader of the singers. David also wore a linen •ephod. ²⁸ So all Israel was bringing the ark of the covenant of the LORD up with shouts, the sound of the ram's horn, trumpets, and cymbals, and the playing of harps and lyres. ²⁹ As the ark of the covenant of the LORD was entering the city of David, Saul's daughter Michal looked down from the window and saw King David dancingᵃ and celebrating, and she despised him in her heart.

Ark Placed in Tent

16 They brought the ark of God and placed it inside the tent David had pitched for it. Then they offered •burnt offerings and •fellowship offerings in God's presence. ² When David had finished offering the burnt offerings and the fellowship offerings, he blessed the people in the name of the LORD. ³ Then he distributed to each and every Israelite, both men and women, a loaf of bread, a date cake, and a raisin cake.

⁴ David appointed some of the Levites to be ministers before the ark of the LORD, to celebrate the LORD God of Israel, and to give thanks and praise to Him. ⁵ •Asaph was the chief and Zecha-

riah was second to him. Jeiel, Shemiramoth, Jehiel, Mattithiah, Eliab, Benaiah, Obed-edom, and Jeiel played the harps and lyres, while Asaph ₁sounded₁ the cymbals ⁶ and the priests Benaiah and Jahaziel ₁blew₁ the trumpets regularly before the ark of the covenant of God.

David's Psalm of Thanksgiving

⁷ On that day David decreed for the first time that thanks be given to the LORD by Asaph and his relatives:

⁸ Give thanks to the LORD; call on
   His name;
proclaim His deeds among
   the peoples.
⁹ Sing to Him; sing praise to Him;
   tell about all His wonderful works!
¹⁰ Honor His holy name;
   let the hearts of those who seek
    the LORD rejoice.
¹¹ Search for the LORD and for
   His strength;
seek His face always.
¹² Remember the wonderful works
   He has done,
His wonders, and the judgments
   He has pronounced,ᵇ
¹³ you offspring of Israel His servant,
Jacob's descendants—
   His chosen ones.

¹⁴ He is the LORD our God;
His judgments ₁govern₁
   the whole earth.
¹⁵ Remember His covenant forever—
   the promise He ordained
   for a thousand generations,
¹⁶ ₁the covenant₁ He made
   with Abraham,
sworeᶜ to Isaac,
¹⁷ and confirmed to Jacob as a decree,
   and to Israel
   as an everlasting covenant:

ᵃ**15:29** Or *whirling*　ᵇ**16:12** Lit *judgments of His mouth*　ᶜ**16:16** Lit *and His oath*

18 "I will give the land of Canaan
    to you
    as your inherited portion."

19 When they[a] were few in number,
    very few indeed,
        and temporary residents
        in Canaan
20 wandering from nation to nation
    and from one kingdom to another,
21 He allowed no one to oppress
    them;
    He rebuked kings on their behalf:
22 "Do not touch My anointed ones
    or harm My prophets."

23 Sing to the LORD, all the earth.
    Proclaim His salvation from day
        to day.
24 Declare His glory
        among the nations,
    His wonderful works
        among all peoples.
25 For the LORD is great
        and is highly praised;
    He is feared above all gods.
26 For all the gods of the peoples
        are idols,
    but the LORD made the heavens.
27 Splendor and majesty are
        before Him;
    strength and joy are in His place.
28 Ascribe to the LORD, families
        of the peoples,
    ascribe to the LORD glory
        and strength.
29 Ascribe to the LORD the glory
        of His name;
    bring an offering and come
        before Him.
    Worship the LORD
        in the splendor of ⌊His⌋ holiness;
30 tremble before Him, all the earth.

The world is firmly established;

it cannot be shaken.
31 Let the heavens be glad
        and the earth rejoice,
    and let them say
        among the nations, "The LORD
        is King!"
32 Let the sea and everything in it
        resound;
    let the fields and all that is in them
        exult.
33 Then the trees of the forest
        will shout for joy before the LORD,
    for He is coming to judge the earth.

34 Give thanks to the LORD,
        for He is good;
    His faithful love endures forever.
35 And say: "Save us,
        God of our salvation;
    gather us and rescue us from
        the nations
    so that we may give thanks to
        Your holy name
    and rejoice in Your praise.
36 May the LORD, the God of Israel,
        be praised
    from everlasting to everlasting."

Then all the people said, "•Amen" and
"Praise the LORD."

David Finishes Ark Celebration

37 So David left Asaph and his relatives
there before the ark of the LORD's covenant to minister regularly before the ark
according to the daily requirements.
38 ⌊He also left⌋ Obed-edom and his[b] 68
relatives. Obed-edom son of Jeduthun
and Hosah were to be gatekeepers.
39 ⌊David left⌋ Zadok the priest and his fellow priests before the tabernacle of the
LORD at the •high place in Gibeon 40 to
offer burnt offerings regularly, morning
and evening, to the LORD on the altar of
burnt offerings and to do everything that

a16:19 One Hb ms, LXX, Vg; MT reads you   b16:38 LXX, Syr, Vg; Hb reads their

was written in the law of the LORD, which He had commanded Israel to keep. [41] With them were Heman, Jeduthun, and the rest who were chosen and designated by name to give thanks to the LORD—for His faithful love endures forever. [42] Heman and Jeduthun had with them trumpets and cymbals to play and musical instruments of God. Jeduthun's sons were at the gate.

[43] Then all the people left for their homes, and David returned ⌊home⌋ to bless his household.

David Appeals to Prophet Nathan

17 When David had settled into his palace, he said to Nathan the prophet, "Look! I am living in a cedar house while the ark of the LORD's covenant is under tent curtains."

[2] So Nathan told David, "Do all that is on your heart, for God is with you."

Word of Lord to David: No Temple

[3] But that night the word of God came to Nathan: [4] "Go to David My servant and say, 'This is what the LORD says: You are not the one to build Me a house to dwell in. [5] From the time I brought Israel out of ⌊Egypt⌋ until today I have not lived in a house; instead, I have moved from tent to tent and from tabernacle ⌊to tabernacle⌋. [6] In all My travels throughout Israel, have I ever spoken a word to even one of the judges of Israel, whom I commanded to shepherd My people, asking: Why haven't you built Me a house of cedar?'

[7] "Now this is what you will say to My servant David: 'This is what the LORD of •Hosts says: I took you from the pasture and from following the sheep, to be ruler over My people Israel. [8] I have been with you wherever you have gone, and I have destroyed all your enemies before you. I will make a name for you like that of the greatest in the land. [9] I will establish a place for My people Israel and plant them, so that they may live there and not be disturbed again. Evildoers will not continue to oppress them as they formerly have [10] ever since the day I ordered judges to be over My people Israel. I will also subdue all your enemies.

God's Promise: Eternal Kingdom

"'Furthermore, I declare to you that the LORD Himself will build a house for you. [11] When your time comes to be with your fathers, I will raise up after you your descendant,[a] who is one of your own sons, and I will establish his kingdom. [12] <u>He will build a house for Me, and I will establish his throne forever.</u> [13] I will be a father to him, and he will be a son to Me. I will not take away My faithful love from him as I took it from the one who was before you. [14] I will appoint him over My house and My kingdom forever, and his throne will be established forever.'"

[15] Nathan recounted all these words and this entire vision to David.

David's Prayer of Thanksgiving

[16] Then King David went in, sat in the LORD's presence, and said, "Who am I, LORD God, and what is my house that You have brought me this far? [17] This was a little thing to You,[b] God, for You have spoken about Your servant's house in the distant future. You regard me as a man of distinction,[c] LORD God. [18] What more can David say to You for honoring Your servant? You know Your servant. [19] LORD, You have done all this greatness,

---

[a]17:11 Lit *seed*   [b]17:17 Lit *thing in Your eyes*   [c]17:17 Hb obscure

making known all these great ⌊promises⌋ because of Your servant and according to Your will. ²⁰ LORD, there is no one like You, and there is no God besides You, as all we have heard confirms. ²¹ And who is like Your people Israel? God, You came to one nation on earth to redeem a people for Yourself, to make a name for Yourself through great and awesome deeds by driving out nations before Your people You redeemed from Egypt. ²² You made Your people Israel Your own people forever, and You, LORD, have become their God.

²³ "Now, LORD, let the word that You have spoken concerning Your servant and his house be confirmed forever, and do as You have promised. ²⁴ Let your name be confirmed and magnified forever in the saying, 'The LORD of Hosts, the God of Israel, is God over Israel.' May the house of Your servant David be established before You. ²⁵ Since You, my God, have revealed to\u1d43 Your servant that You will build him a house, Your servant has found ⌊courage⌋ to pray in Your presence. ²⁶ LORD, You indeed are God, and You have promised this good thing to Your servant. ²⁷ So now, You have been pleased to bless Your servant's house that it may continue before You forever. For You, LORD, have blessed it, and it is blessed forever."

David's Military Campaigns

18 After this, David defeated the Philistines, subdued them, and took Gath and its villages from Philistine control. ² He also defeated the Moabites, and they became David's subjects and brought tribute.

³ David also defeated King Hadadezer of Zobah at Hamath when he went to establish his control at the Euphrates River. ⁴ David captured 1,000 chariots, 7,000 horsemen, and 20,000 foot soldiers from him and hamstrung all the horses, and he kept 100 chariots.\u1d47

⁵ When the Arameans of Damascus came to assist King Hadadezer of Zobah, David struck down 22,000 Aramean men. ⁶ Then he placed garrisons\u1d9c in Aram of Damascus, and the Arameans became David's subjects and brought tribute. The LORD made David victorious wherever he went.

⁷ David took the gold shields carried by Hadadezer's officers and brought them to Jerusalem. ⁸ From Tibhath and Cun, Hadadezer's cities, David also took huge quantities of bronze, from which Solomon made the bronze reservoir, the pillars, and the bronze articles.

⁹ When King Tou of Hamath heard that David had defeated the entire army of King Hadadezer of Zobah, ¹⁰ he sent his son Hadoram to King David to greet him and to congratulate him because David had fought against Hadadezer and defeated him, for Tou and Hadadezer had fought many wars. ⌊Hadoram brought⌋ all kinds of items of gold, silver, and bronze. ¹¹ King David also dedicated these to the LORD, along with the silver and gold he had carried off from all the nations— from Edom, Moab, the Ammonites, the Philistines, and the Amalekites.

¹² Abishai son of Zeruiah struck down 18,000 Edomites in the Valley of Salt. ¹³ He put garrisons in Edom, and all the Edomites were subject to David. The LORD made David victorious wherever he went.

David's Administration

¹⁴ So David reigned over all Israel, administering justice and righteousness for all his people.

\u1d4317:25 Lit have uncovered the ear of \u1d4718:4 Or chariot horses \u1d9c18:6 Some Hb mss, LXX, Vg; other Hb mss omit garrisons; 2 Sm 8:6

¹⁵ Joab son of Zeruiah was
    over the army;
  Jehoshaphat son of Ahilud was
    court historian;
¹⁶ Zadok son of Ahitub
    and Ahimelechᵃ son of Abiathar
    were priests;
  Shavsha was court secretary;
¹⁷ Benaiah son of Jehoiada was over
    the Cherethites and the Pelethites;
  and David's sons were
    the chief officials
    at the king's side.

Ammonites Spurn David's Kindness

19 Some time later, King Nahash of the Ammonites died, and his son became king in his place. ² Then David said, "I'll show kindness to Hanun son of Nahash, because his father showed kindness to me."

So David sent messengers to console him concerning his father. However, when David's emissaries arrived in the land of the Ammonites to console him, ³ the Ammonite leaders said to Hanun, "Just because David has sent men with condolences for you, do you really believe he's showing respect for your father? Instead, hasn't David sent his emissaries in order to scout out, overthrow, and spy on the land?" ⁴ So Hanun took David's emissaries, shaved them, cut their clothes in half at the hips, and sent them away.

⁵ Someone came and reported to David about his men, so he sent ⌊someone⌋ to meet them, since the men were deeply humiliated. The king said, "Stay in Jericho until your beards grow back; then return."

Ammonites Prepare for War

⁶ When the Ammonites realized they had made themselves repulsive to David,

Hanun and the Ammonites sent 38 tonsᵇ of silver to hire chariots and horsemen from Aram-naharaim, Aram-maacah, and Zobah. ⁷ They hired 32,000 chariots and the king of Maacah with his army, who came and camped near Medeba. The Ammonites also gathered from their cities and came for the battle.

Joab vs. Ammonites and Arameans

⁸ David heard about this and sent Joab and the entire army of warriors. ⁹ The Ammonites marched out and lined up in battle formation at the entrance of the city while the kings who had come were in the field by themselves. ¹⁰ When Joab saw that there was a battle line in front of him and another behind him, he chose some men out of all the elite troopsᶜ of Israel and lined up in battle formation to engage the Arameans. ¹¹ He placed the rest of the forces under the command of his brother Abishai, and they lined up in battle formation to engage the Ammonites.

¹² "If the Arameans are too strong for me," Joab said, "then you'll be my help. However, if the Ammonites are too strong for you, I'll help you. ¹³ Be strong! We must prove ourselves strong for our people and for the cities of our God. May the LORD's will be done."ᵈ

Israel's Enemies Flee

¹⁴ Joab and the people with him approached the Arameans for battle, and they fled before him. ¹⁵ When the Ammonites saw that the Arameans had fled, they likewise fled before Joab's brother Abishai and entered the city. Then Joab went to Jerusalem.

Arameans Regroup

¹⁶ When the Arameans realized that they had been defeated by Israel, they

---

ᵃ**18:16** Some Hb mss, LXX, Syr, Vg; other Hb mss read *Abimelech*; 2 Sm 8:17   ᵇ**19:6** Lit *1,000 talents*   ᶜ**19:10** Lit *the choice ones*; 2 Sm 6:1   ᵈ**19:13** Lit *the LORD do what is good in His eyes*

sent messengers to bring out the Arameans who were across the Euphrates with Shophach, commander of Hadadezer's army, leading them.

David Defeats Arameans

[17] When this was reported to David, he gathered all Israel and crossed the Jordan. He came up to them and lined up in battle formation against them. When David lined up to engage the Arameans in battle, they fought against him. [18] But the Arameans fled before Israel, and David killed 7,000 of their charioteers and 40,000 foot soldiers. He also killed Shophach, commander of the army. [19] When Hadadezer's subjects saw that they had been defeated by Israel, they made peace with David and became his subjects. After this, the Arameans were never willing to help the Ammonites again.

Joab Captures of the City of Rabbah

20 In the spring[a] when kings march out ⌊to war⌋, Joab led the army and destroyed the Ammonites' land. He came to Rabbah and besieged it, but David remained in Jerusalem. Joab attacked Rabbah and demolished it. [2] Then David took the crown from the head of their king,[b] and it was ⌊placed⌋ on David's head. He discovered the crown weighed 75 pounds[c] of gold, and there was a precious stone in it. In addition, David took away a large quantity of plunder from the city. [3] He brought out the people who were in it and put them to work with saws,[d] iron picks, and axes.[e] David did the same to all the Ammonite cities. Then he and all his troops returned to Jerusalem.

Israel Defeats Philistine Giants

[4] After this, a war broke out with the Philistines at Gezer. At that time Sibbecai the Hushathite killed Sippai, a descendant of the giants,[f] and the Philistines were subdued.

[5] Once again there was a battle with the Philistines, and Elhanan son of Jair killed Lahmi the brother of Goliath the Gittite. The shaft of his spear was like a weaver's beam.

[6] There was still another battle at Gath where there was a man of extraordinary stature with six fingers ⌊on each hand⌋ and six toes ⌊on each foot⌋—24 in all. He, too, was descended from the giant.[g] [7] When he taunted Israel, Jonathan, son of David's brother Shimei, killed him.

[8] These were the descendants of the giant[g] in Gath killed by David and his soldiers.

David Orders Military Census

21 Satan[h] stood up against Israel and incited David to count ⌊the people of⌋ Israel. [2] So David said to Joab and the commanders of the troops, "Go and count Israel from Beer-sheba to Dan and bring ⌊a report⌋ to me so I can know their number."

Joab Objects

[3] Joab replied, "May the LORD multiply the number of His people a hundred times over! My lord the king, aren't they all my lord's servants? Why does my lord want to do this? Why should he bring guilt on Israel?"

[4] Yet the king's order prevailed over Joab. So Joab left and traveled throughout Israel and then returned to Jerusalem. [5] Joab gave David the total of the registration of the troops. In all Israel

---

[a]**20:1** Lit *At the time of the return of the year*   [b]**20:2** LXX, Vg read *of Milcom; = Molech;* 1 Kg 11:5,7   [c]**20:2** Lit *a talent*   [d]**20:3** Text emended; MT reads *and sawed them with the saw;* 2 Sm 12:31   [e]**20:3** Text emended; MT reads *saws;* 2 Sm 12:31   [f]**20:4** Or *the Rephaites*   [g]**20:6,8** Or *Raphah*   [h]**21:1** Or *An adversary;* Jb 1:6; Zch 3:1-2

there were 1,100,000 swordsmen and in Judah itself 470,000 swordsmen. ⁶ But he did not include Levi and Benjamin in the count because the king's command was detestable to him. ⁷ This command was also evil in God's sight, so He afflicted Israel.

⁸ David said to God, "I have sinned greatly because I have done this thing. Now, because I've been very foolish, please take away Your servant's guilt."

God Punishes David: a Triple Choice

⁹ Then the LORD instructed Gad, David's seer, ¹⁰ "Go and say to David, 'This is what the LORD says: I am offering you three ⸤choices⸥. Choose one of them for yourself, and I will do it to you.'"

¹¹ So Gad went to David and said to him, "This is what the LORD says: 'Take your ⸤choice⸣—¹² either three years of famine, three months of devastation by your foes with the sword of your enemy overtaking you, or three days of the sword of the LORD—a plague on the land, the angel of the LORD bringing destruction to the whole territory of Israel.' Now decide what answer I should take back to the One who sent me."

¹³ David answered Gad, "I have great anxiety. Please, let me fall into the LORD's hands because His mercies are very great, but don't let me fall into human hands."

God's Plague on Israel

¹⁴ So the LORD sent a plague on Israel, and 70,000 Israelite men died. ¹⁵ Then God sent an angel to Jerusalem to destroy it, but when the angel was about to destroy the city,ª the LORD looked, relented concerning the destruction, and said to the angel who was destroying

⸤the people⸥, "Enough, withdraw your hand now!" The angel of the LORD was then standing at the threshing floor of Ornan the Jebusite.

David Pleads for Mercy

¹⁶ When David looked up and saw the angel of the LORD standing between earth and heaven, with his drawn sword in his hand stretched out over Jerusalem, David and the elders, clothed in •sackcloth, fell down with their faces ⸤to the ground⸥. ¹⁷ David said to God, "Wasn't I the one who gave the order to count the people? I am the one who has sinned and acted very wickedly. But these sheep, what have they done? My LORD God, please let Your hand be against me and against my father's family, but don't let the plague be against Your people."

David's Altar

¹⁸ So the angel of the LORD ordered Gad to tell David to go and set up an altar to the LORD on the threshing floor of Ornan the Jebusite. ¹⁹ David went up at Gad's command spoken in the name of the LORD.

²⁰ Ornan was threshing wheat when he turned and saw the angel. His four sons, who were with him, hid themselves. ²¹ David came to Ornan, and when Ornan looked and saw David, he left the threshing floor and bowed to David with his face to the ground.

²² Then David said to Ornan, "Give me this threshing-floor plot so that I may build an altar to the LORD on it. Give it to me for the full price, so the plague on the people may be halted."

²³ Ornan said to David, "Take it! My lord the king may do whatever he wants.ᵇ See, I give the oxen for the

---

ª**21:15** Lit *but as he was destroying*   ᵇ**21:23** Lit *do what is good in his eyes*

•burnt offerings, the threshing sledges for the wood, and the wheat for the •grain offering—I give it all."

24 King David answered Ornan, "No, I insist on paying the full price, for I will not take for the LORD what belongs to you or offer burnt offerings that cost ₍me₎ nothing."

25 So David gave Ornan 15 pounds of gold[a] for the plot. 26 He built an altar to the LORD there and offered burnt offerings and •fellowship offerings. He called on the LORD, and He answered him with fire from heaven on the altar of burnt offering.

Lord Stops Plague

27 Then the LORD spoke to the angel, and he put his sword back into its sheath. 28 At that time, when David saw that the LORD answered him at the threshing floor of Ornan the Jebusite, he offered sacrifices there. 29 At that time the tabernacle of the LORD, which Moses made in the desert, and the altar of burnt offering were at the •high place in Gibeon, 30 but David could not go before it to inquire of God, because he was terrified of the sword of the LORD's 22 angel. 1 Then David said, "This is the house of the LORD God, and this is the altar of •burnt offering for Israel."

David's Preparations for the Temple

2 So David gave orders to gather the foreigners that were in the land of Israel, and he appointed stonemasons to cut finished stones for building God's house. 3 David supplied a great deal of iron to make the nails for the doors of the gateways and for the fittings, together with an immeasurable quantity of bronze, 4 and innumerable cedar logs, because the Sidonians and Tyrians had brought a large quantity of cedar logs to David. 5 David said, "My son Solomon is young and inexperienced, and the house that is to be built for the LORD must be exceedingly great and famous and glorious in all the lands. Therefore, I must make provision for it." So David made lavish preparations for it before his death.

David to Solomon: Build Temple

6 Then he summoned his son Solomon and instructed him to build a house for the LORD God of Israel. 7 "My son," David said to Solomon, "It was in my heart to build a house for the name of the LORD my God, 8 but the word of the LORD came to me: 'You have shed much blood and waged great wars. You are not to build a house for My name because you have shed so much blood on the ground before Me. 9 But a son will be born to you; he will be a man of rest. I will give him rest from all his surrounding enemies, for his name will be Solomon,[b] and I will give peace and quiet to Israel during his reign. 10 He is the one who will build a house for My name. He will be My son, and I will be his father. I will establish the throne of his kingdom over Israel forever.'

11 "Now, my son, may the LORD be with you, and may you succeed in building the house of the LORD your God, as He said about you. 12 Above all, may the LORD give you insight and understanding when He puts you in charge of Israel so that you may keep the law of the LORD your God. 13 Then you will succeed if you carefully follow the statutes and ordinances the LORD commanded Moses for Israel. Be strong and courageous. Don't be afraid or discouraged.

---

[a]21:25 Lit *600 shekels of gold by weight*   [b]22:9 The name *Solomon* sounds like Hb "peace."

¹⁴ "Notice I have taken great pains to provide for the house of the LORD— 3,775 tons of gold, 37,750 tons of silver,ᵃ and bronze and iron that can't be weighed because there is so much of it. I have also provided timber and stone, but you will need to add more to them. ¹⁵ You also have many workers: stonecutters, masons, carpenters, and people skilled in every kind of work ¹⁶ in gold, silver, bronze, and iron—beyond number. Now begin the work, and may the LORD be with you."

David to Israel: Help Solomon

¹⁷ Then David ordered all the leaders of Israel to help his son Solomon: ¹⁸ "The LORD your God is with you, isn't He? And hasn't He given you rest on every side? For He has handed the land's inhabitants over to me, and the land has been subdued before the LORD and His people. ¹⁹ Now determine in your mind and heart to seek the LORD your God. Get started building the LORD God's sanctuary so that you may bring the ark of the LORD's covenant and the holy articles of God to the temple that is to be built for the name of the LORD."

Divisions of Levites

23 When David was old and full of days, he installed his son Solomon as king over Israel. ² Then he gathered all the leaders of Israel, the priests, and the Levites. ³ The Levites 30 years old and above were counted; the total number of men was 38,000 by headcount. ⁴ "Of these," ⌊David said⌋, "24,000 are to be in charge of the work on the LORD's temple, 6,000 are to be officers and judges, ⁵ 4,000 are to be gatekeepers, and 4,000 are to praise the LORD with the instruments that I have made for worship."

⁶ Then David divided them into divisions according to Levi's sons: Gershom,ᵇ Kohath, and Merari.

⁷ The Gershomites: Ladan and Shimei.
⁸ Ladan's sons: Jehiel was the first, then Zetham, and Joel—three.
⁹ Shimei's sons: Shelomoth, Haziel, and Haran—three. Those were the heads of the families of Ladan.
¹⁰ Shimei's sons: Jahath, Zizah,ᶜ Jeush, and Beriah. Those were Shimei's sons—four. ¹¹ Jahath was the first and Zizah was the second; however, Jeush and Beriah did not have many sons, so they became an ancestral house ⌊and received⌋ a single assignment.
¹² Kohath's sons: Amram, Izhar, Hebron, and Uzziel—four.
¹³ Amram's sons: Aaron and Moses.

Aaron, along with his descendants, was set apart forever to consecrate the most holy things, to burn incense in the presence of the LORD, to minister to Him, and to pronounce blessings in His name forever. ¹⁴ As for Moses the man of God, his sons were named among the tribe of Levi.

¹⁵ Moses' sons: Gershom and Eliezer.
¹⁶ Gershom's sons: Shebuel ⌊was⌋ first.
¹⁷ Eliezer's sons were Rehabiah, first; Eliezer did not have any other sons, but Rehabiah's sons were very numerous.
¹⁸ Izhar's sons: Shelomith was first.
¹⁹ Hebron's sons: Jeriah was first, Amariah second, Jahaziel third,

---

ᵃ**22:14** Lit *100,000 talents of gold and 1,000,000 talents of silver*   ᵇ**23:6** Lit *Gershon*   ᶜ**23:10** LXX, Vg; MT reads *Zina*

and Jekameam fourth.
20 Uzziel's sons: Micah was first, and Isshiah second.
21 <u>Merari's sons</u>: Mahli and Mushi.
Mahli's sons: Eleazar and Kish.
22 Eleazar died having no sons, only daughters. Their cousins, the sons of Kish, married them.
23 Mushi's sons: Mahli, Eder, and Jeremoth—three.

David Changes Levite Duties

24 These were the sons of Levi by their ancestral houses—the heads of families, according to their registration by name in the headcount—20 years old or more, who worked in the service of the LORD's temple. 25 For David said, "The LORD God of Israel has given rest to His people, and He has come to stay in Jerusalem forever. 26 Also, the Levites no longer need to carry the tabernacle or any of the equipment for its service"— 27 for according to the last words of David, the Levites 20 years old or more were to be counted— 28 "but their duty will be to assist the sons of Aaron with the service of the LORD's temple, being responsible for the courts and the chambers, the purification of all the holy things, and the work of the service of God's temple— 29 as well as the rows ⌊of the bread of the Presence⌋, the fine flour for the •grain offering, the wafers of unleavened bread, the baking,ᵃ the mixing, and all measurements of volume and length. 30 They are also to stand every morning to give thanks and praise to the LORD, and likewise in the evening. 31 Whenever •burnt offerings are offered to the LORD on the Sabbaths, New Moons, and appointed festivals, they are to do so regularly in the LORD's presence according to the number prescribed for them. 32 They are to carry out their responsibilities to the tent of meeting, to the holy place, and to their relatives, the sons of Aaron, in the service of the LORD's temple."

Divisions of Priests

24 The divisions of the descendants of Aaron were as follows: Aaron's sons were Nadab, Abihu, Eleazar, and Ithamar. 2 But Nadab and Abihu died before their father, and they had no sons, so Eleazar and Ithamar served as priests. 3 Together with Zadok from the sons of Eleazar and Ahimelech from the sons of Ithamar, David divided them according to the assigned duties of their service. 4 Since more leaders were found among Eleazar's descendants than Ithamar's, they were divided ⌊accordingly⌋: 16 heads of ancestral houses were from Eleazar's descendants, and eight ⌊heads⌋ of ancestral houses were from Ithamar's. 5 They were divided impartially by lot, for there were officers of the sanctuary and officers of God among both Eleazar's and Ithamar's descendants. 6 The secretary, Shemaiah son of Nethanel, a Levite, recorded them in the presence of the king and the officers, Zadok the priest, Ahimelech son of Abiathar, and the heads of families of the priests and the Levites. One ancestral house was taken for Eleazar, and then one for Ithamar.

7 The first lot fell to Jehoiarib,
  the second to Jedaiah,
8 the third to Harim, the fourth
  to Seorim,
9 the fifth to Malchijah, the sixth
  to Mijamin,
10 the seventh to Hakkoz, the eighth
  to Abijah,

ᵃ23:29 Lit *the griddle*

11 the ninth to Jeshua, the tenth
    to Shecaniah,
12 the eleventh to Eliashib, the twelfth
    to Jakim,
13 the thirteenth to Huppah,
    the fourteenth to Jeshebeab,
14 the fifteenth to Bilgah,
    the sixteenth to Immer,
15 the seventeenth to Hezir,
    the eighteenth to Happizzez,
16 the nineteenth to Pethahiah,
    the twentieth to Jehezkel,
17 the twenty-first to Jachin,
    the twenty-second to Gamul,
18 the twenty-third to Delaiah,
    and the twenty-fourth to Maaziah.

19 These had their assigned duties for service when they entered the LORD's temple, according to their regulations, which they received from their ancestor Aaron, as the LORD God of Israel had commanded him.

Rest of Levites

20 As for the rest of Levi's sons:
from Amram's sons: Shubael;
from Shubael's sons: Jehdeiah.
21 From Rehabiah:
from Rehabiah's sons: Isshiah was the first.
22 From the Izharites: Shelomoth;
from Shelomoth's sons: Jahath.
23 Hebron'sᵃ sons:
Jeriah ⌊the first⌋, Amariah the second,
Jahaziel the third, and Jekameam the fourth.
24 ⌊From⌋ Uzziel's sons: Micah;
from Micah's sons: Shamir.
25 Micah's brother: Isshiah;
from Isshiah's sons: Zechariah.
26 Merari's sons: Mahli and Mushi,

⌊and from⌋ his sons, Jaaziah his son.ᵇ
27 Merari's sons, by his son Jaaziah:ᶜ
Shoham, Zaccur, and Ibri.
28 From Mahli: Eleazar, who had no sons.
29 From Kish, ⌊from⌋ Kish's sons: Jerahmeel.
30 Mushi's sons: Mahli, Eder, and Jerimoth.

Those were the sons of the Levites according to their ancestral houses. 31 They also cast lots the same way as their relatives, the sons of Aaron did in the presence of King David, Zadok, Ahimelech, and the heads of the families of the priests and Levites—the family heads and their younger brothers alike.

Levitical Musicians

25 David and the officers of the army also set apart some of the sons of •Asaph, Heman, and Jeduthun, who were to prophesy accompanied by lyres, harps, and cymbals. This is the list of the men who performed their service:

2 From Asaph's sons:
Zaccur, Joseph, Nethaniah, and Asarelah, sons of Asaph, under Asaph's authority, who prophesied under the authority of the king.
3 From Jeduthun: Jeduthun's sons:
Gedaliah, Zeri, Jeshaiah, Shimei,ᵈ Hashabiah, and Mattithiah—six— under the authority of their father Jeduthun, prophesying to the accompaniment of lyres, giving thanks and praise to the LORD.
4 From Heman: Heman's sons:
Bukkiah, Mattaniah, Uzziel, Shebuel, Jerimoth, Hananiah,

ᵃ24:23 Some Hb mss, some LXX mss; MT omits Hebron's; 1 Ch 23:19   ᵇ24:26 Or Mushi; Jaaziah's sons: Beno.
ᶜ24:27 Or sons, Jaaziah: Beno,   ᵈ25:3 One Hb ms, LXX; MT omits Shimei

Hanani, Eliathath, Giddalti, Romamti-ezer, Joshbekashah, Mallothi, Hothir, and Mahazioth. ⁵ All these sons of Heman, the king's seer, were ⌊given⌋ by the promises of God to exalt him,ᵃ for God had given Heman fourteen sons and three daughters.

Musicians' Lots

⁶ All these men were under their own fathers' authority for the music in the LORD's temple, with cymbals, harps, and lyres for the service of God's temple. Asaph, Jeduthun, and Heman were under the king's authority. ⁷ Together with their relatives who were all trained and skillful in music for the LORD, they numbered 288. ⁸ They cast lots impartially for their duties, the young and old alike, the teacher along with the pupil.

⁹ The first lot for Asaph fell
to Joseph, ⌊his sons,
and his brothers—⌋ 12⌋
⌊to⌋ Gedaliah the second: him,
his brothers, and his sons— 12
¹⁰ the third ⌊to⌋ Zaccur, his sons,
and his brothers— 12
¹¹ the fourth to Izri,ᵇ his sons,
and his brothers— 12
¹² the fifth ⌊to⌋ Nethaniah,
his sons, and his brothers— 12
¹³ the sixth ⌊to⌋ Bukkiah, his sons,
and his brothers— 12
¹⁴ the seventh ⌊to⌋ Jesarelah,
his sons, and his brothers— 12
¹⁵ the eighth ⌊to⌋ Jeshaiah,
his sons, and his brothers— 12
¹⁶ the ninth ⌊to⌋ Mattaniah,
his sons, and his brothers— 12
¹⁷ the tenth ⌊to⌋ Shimei, his sons,
and his brothers— 12
¹⁸ the eleventh ⌊to⌋ Azarel,ᶜ
his sons, and his brothers— 12

¹⁹ the twelfth to Hashabiah,
his sons, and his brothers— 12
²⁰ the thirteenth ⌊to⌋ Shubael,
his sons, and his brothers— 12
²¹ the fourteenth ⌊to⌋ Mattithiah,
his sons, and his brothers— 12
²² the fifteenth to Jeremoth,
his sons, and his brothers— 12
²³ the sixteenth to Hananiah,
his sons, and his brothers— 12
²⁴ the seventeenth
to Joshbekashah, his sons,
and his brothers— 12
²⁵ the eighteenth to Hanani,
his sons, and his brothers— 12
²⁶ the nineteenth to Mallothi,
his sons, and his brothers— 12
²⁷ the twentieth to Eliathath,
his sons, and his brothers— 12
²⁸ the twenty-first to Hothir,
his sons, and his brothers— 12
²⁹ the twenty-second to Giddalti,
his sons, and his brothers— 12
³⁰ the twenty-third to Mahazioth,
his sons, and his brothers— 12
³¹ and the twenty-fourth
to Romamti-ezer, his sons,
and his brothers— 12.

Levitical Gatekeepers

26 ⌊The following were⌋ the divisions of the gatekeepers:

From the Korahites: Meshelemiah son of Kore, one of the sons of •Asaph. ² Meshelemiah had sons: Zechariah the firstborn, Jediael the second, Zebadiah the third, Jathniel the fourth, ³ Elam the fifth, Jehohanan the sixth, and Eliehoenai the seventh. ⁴ Obed-edom also had sons:

ᵃ25:5 Or *Him*; lit *by the words of God to lift a horn* ᵇ25:11 A variant of Zeri ᶜ25:18 A variant of Uzziel

Shemaiah the firstborn, Jehozabad
the second,
Joah the third, Sachar the fourth,
Nethanel the fifth, [5] Ammiel the
sixth,
Issachar the seventh, and
Peullethai the eighth,
for God blessed him.

[6] Also, to his son Shemaiah were born sons who ruled over their ancestral houses because they were strong, capable men. [7] Shemaiah's sons: Othni, Rephael, Obed, and Elzabad; his brothers Elihu and Semachiah were also capable men. [8] All of these were among the sons of Obed-edom with their sons and brothers; they were capable men with strength for the work—62 from Obed-edom. [9] Meshelemiah also had sons and brothers who were capable men—18.

[10] Hosah, from the Merarites, also had sons: Shimri the first (although he was not the firstborn, his father had appointed him as the first), [11] Hilkiah the second, Tebaliah the third, and Zechariah the fourth. The sons and brothers of Hosah were 13 in all.

[12] These divisions of the gatekeepers, under their leading men, had duties for ministering in the LORD's temple, just as their brothers did. [13] They cast lots according to their ancestral houses, young and old alike, for each gate.

[14] The lot for the east ⌊gate⌋ fell to Shelemiah.[a] They also cast lots for his son Zechariah, an insightful counselor, and his lot came out for the north ⌊gate⌋.

[15] Obed-edom's was the south ⌊gate⌋, and his sons' ⌊lot⌋ was the storehouses; [16] for Shuppim and Hosah it was the west ⌊gate⌋ and the gate of Shallecheth on the ascending highway.

There were guards stationed at every watch. [17] There were six Levites each day[b] on the east, four each day on the north, four each day on the south, and two pair at the storehouses. [18] As for the court on the west, there were four at the highway and two at the court. [19] Those were the divisions of the gatekeepers from the sons of the Korahites and Merarites.

Levitical Treasurers and Other Officials

[20] From the Levites, Ahijah was in charge of the treasuries of God's temple and the treasuries for what had been dedicated. [21] From the sons of Ladan, who were the sons of the Gershonites through Ladan and were the heads of families belonging to Ladan the Gershonite: Jehieli. [22] The sons of Jehieli, Zetham and his brother Joel, were in charge of the treasuries of the LORD's temple.

[23] From the Amramites, the Izharites, the Hebronites, and the Uzzielites: [24] Shebuel, a descendant of Moses' son Gershom, was the officer in charge of the treasuries. [25] His relative through Eliezer: his son Rehabiah, his son Jeshaiah, his son Joram, his son Zichri, and his son Shelomith.[c] [26] This Shelomith[d] and his brothers were in charge of all the treasuries for what had been dedicated by King David, by the heads of families who were the commanders of the thousands and of the hundreds, and by the army commanders. [27] They dedicated part of the plunder from their battles for the re-

pair of the LORD's temple. [28] All that Samuel the seer, Saul son of Kish, Abner son of Ner, and Joab son of Zeruiah had dedicated, along with everything else that had been dedicated, were in the care of Shelomith[a] and his brothers.

[29] From the Izrahites: Chenaniah and his sons had the outside duties as officers and judges over Israel. [30] From the Hebronites: Hashabiah and his relatives, 1,700 capable men, had assigned duties in Israel west of the Jordan for all the work of the LORD and for the service of the king. [31] From the Hebronites: Jerijah was the head of the Hebronites, according to the genealogical records of his ancestors. In the fortieth year of David's reign a search was made, and strong, capable men were found among them at Jazer in Gilead. [32] There were among Jerijah's relatives, 2,700 capable men who were heads of families. King David appointed them over the Reubenites, the Gadites, and half the tribe of Manasseh as overseers in every matter relating to God and the king.

David's Secular Officials

27 This is the list of the Israelites, the heads of families, the commanders of thousands and the commanders of hundreds, and their officers who served the king in every matter to do with the divisions that were on rotated military duty each month throughout[b] the year. There were <u>24,000 in each division</u>:

[2] Jashobeam son of Zabdiel was in charge of the first division, for the first month; 24,000 were in his division. [3] He was a descendant of Perez and chief of all the army commanders for the first month. [4] Dodai the Ahohite was in charge

of the division for the second month, and Mikloth was the leader; 24,000 were in his division.

[5] The third army commander, as chief for the third month, was Benaiah son of Jehoiada the priest; 24,000 were in his division. [6] This Benaiah was a mighty man among the Thirty and over the Thirty, and his son Ammizabad was in charge[c] of his division.

[7] The fourth ⌊commander⌋, for the fourth month, was Joab's brother Asahel, and his son Zebadiah ⌊was commander⌋ after him; 24,000 were in his division.

[8] The fifth, for the fifth month, was the commander Shamhuth the Izrahite; 24,000 were in his division.

[9] The sixth, for the sixth month, was Ira son of Ikkesh the Tekoite; 24,000 were in his division.

[10] The seventh, for the seventh month, was Helez the Pelonite from the sons of Ephraim; 24,000 were in his division.

[11] The eighth, for the eighth month, was Sibbecai the Hushathite, a Zerahite; 24,000 were in his division.

[12] The ninth, for the ninth month, was Abiezer the Anathothite, a Benjaminite; 24,000 were in his division.

[13] The tenth, for the tenth month, was Maharai the Netophathite, a Zerahite; 24,000 were in his division.

[14] The eleventh, for the eleventh month, was Benaiah the Pirathonite from the sons of

Ephraim; 24,000 were in his division.

15 The twelfth, for the twelfth month, was Heldai the Netophathite, of Othniel's family;[a] 24,000 were in his division.

16 ⌊The following were⌋ in charge of the tribes of Israel:
For the Reubenites, Eliezer son of Zichri was the chief official; for the Simeonites, Shephatiah son of Maacah; 17 for the Levites, Hashabiah son of Kemuel; for Aaron, Zadok; 18 for Judah, Elihu, one of David's brothers; for Issachar, Omri son of Michael; 19 for Zebulun, Ishmaiah son of Obadiah;
for Naphtali, Jerimoth son of Azriel; 20 for the Ephraimites, Hoshea son of Azaziah;
for half the tribe of Manasseh, Joel son of Pedaiah; 21 for half the tribe of Manasseh in Gilead, Iddo son of Zechariah; for Benjamin, Jaasiel son of Abner; 22 for Dan, Azarel son of Jeroham.
Those were the leaders of the tribes of Israel.

23 David didn't count the men aged 20 or under, for the Lord had said He would make Israel as numerous as the stars of heaven. 24 Joab son of Zeruiah began to count them, but he didn't complete it. There was wrath against Israel because of this ⌊census⌋, and the number was not entered in the Historical Record[b] of King David.

25 Azmaveth son of Adiel was in charge of the king's storehouses. Jonathan son of Uzziah was in charge of the storehouses in the country, in the cities, in the villages, and in the fortresses. 26 Ezri son of Chelub was in charge of those who worked in the fields tilling the soil. 27 Shimei the Ramathite was in charge of the vineyards.
Zabdi the Shiphmite was in charge of the produce of the vineyards for the wine cellars. 28 Baal-hanan the Gederite was in charge of the olive and sycamore trees in the Shephelah.[c]
Joash was in charge of the stores of olive oil. 29 Shitrai the Sharonite was in charge of the herds that grazed in Sharon, while
Shaphat son of Adlai was in charge of the herds in the valleys. 30 Obil the Ishmaelite was in charge of the camels.
Jehdeiah the Meronothite was in charge of the donkeys. 31 Jaziz the Hagrite was in charge of the flocks.
All these were officials in charge of King David's property.

32 David's uncle Jonathan was a counselor; he was a man of understanding and a scribe. Jehiel son of Hachmoni attended[d] the king's sons. 33 Ahithophel was the king's counselor. Hushai the Archite was the king's friend. 34 After Ahithophel came Jehoiada son of Benaiah, then Abiathar. Joab was the commander of the king's army.

---

a27:15 Lit belonging to Othniel   b27:24 LXX; MT reads Number   c27:28 A strip of land west of the Judean mountains   d27:32 Lit was with

David's Public Commission to Solomon on Temple

28 David assembled in Jerusalem all the leaders of Israel: the leaders of the tribes, the leaders of the divisions in the king's service, the commanders of thousands and the commanders of hundreds, and the officials in charge of all the property and cattle of the king and his sons, along with the court officials, the fighting men, and all the brave warriors. ² Then King David rose to his feet and said, "Listen to me, my brothers and my people. It was in my heart to build a house as a resting place for the ark of the LORD's covenant and as a footstool for our God. I had made preparations to build, ³ but God said to me, 'You are not to build a house for My name because you are a man of war and have shed blood.'

⁴ "Yet the LORD God of Israel chose me out of all my father's household to be king over Israel forever. For He chose Judah as leader, and from the house of Judah, my father's household, and from my father's sons, He was pleased to make me king over all Israel. ⁵ And out of all my sons—for the LORD has given me many sons—He has chosen my son Solomon to sit on the throne of the LORD's kingdom over Israel. ⁶ He said to me, 'Your son Solomon is the one who is to build My house and My courts, for I have chosen him to be My son, and I will be his father. ⁷ I will establish his kingdom forever if he perseveres in keeping My commandments and My ordinances as ⌊he is⌋ today.'

⁸ "So now in the sight of all Israel, the assembly of the LORD, and in the hearing of our God, observe and seek after all the commandments of the LORD your God so that you may possess this good land and leave it as an inheritance to your descendants forever.

⁹ "As for you, Solomon my son, know the God of your father, and serve Him with a whole heart and a willing mind, for the LORD searches every heart and understands the intention of every thought. If you seek Him, He will be found by you, but if you forsake Him, He will reject you forever. ¹⁰ Realize now that the LORD has chosen you to build a house for the sanctuary. Be strong, and do it."

David Provides Written Plan

¹¹ Then David gave his son Solomon the plans for the vestibule ⌊of the temple⌋ and its buildings, treasuries, upper rooms, inner rooms, and the room for the place of •atonement. ¹² The plans contained everything he had in mind[a] for the courts of the LORD's house, all the surrounding chambers, the treasuries of God's house, and the treasuries for what is dedicated. ¹³ ⌊Also included were plans⌋ for the divisions of the priests and the Levites; all the work of service in the LORD's house; all the articles of service of the LORD's house; ¹⁴ the weight of gold for all the articles for every kind of service; the weight of all the silver articles for every kind of service; ¹⁵ the weight of the gold lampstands and their gold lamps, including the weight of each lampstand and its lamps; the weight of each silver lampstand and its lamps, according to the service of each lampstand; ¹⁶ the weight of gold for each table for the rows ⌊of the bread of the Presence⌋ and the silver for the silver tables; ¹⁷ the pure gold for the forks, sprinkling basins, and pitchers; the weight of each gold dish; the weight of each silver bowl; ¹⁸ the weight of refined gold for the altar

---

a **28:12** Or *he received from the Spirit; v. 19*

of incense; and the plans for the chariot of[a] the gold •cherubim that spread out their wings and cover the ark of the LORD's covenant.

19 David concluded, "By the LORD's hand on me, He enabled me to understand everything in writing, all the details of the plan."[b]

David Encourages Solomon

20 Then David said to his son Solomon, "Be strong and courageous, and do the work. Don't be afraid or discouraged, for the LORD God, my God, is with you. He won't leave you or forsake you until all the work for the service of the LORD's house is finished. 21 Here are the divisions of the priests and the Levites for all the service of God's house. Every willing man of any skill will be at your disposal for the work, and the leaders and all the people are at your every command."

David's Contributions to Temple

29 Then King David said to all the assembly, "My son Solomon—God has chosen him alone—is young and inexperienced. The task is great, for the temple will not be for man, but for the LORD God. 2 So to the best of my ability I've made provision for the house of my God: gold for the gold articles, silver for the silver, bronze for the bronze, iron for the iron, and wood for the wood, as well as onyx, stones for mounting,[c] antimony,[d] stones of various colors, all kinds of precious stones, and a great quantity of marble. 3 Moreover, because of my delight in the house of my God, I now give my personal treasures of gold and silver for the house of my God over and above all that I've provided for the holy house:

4 100 tons[e] of gold (gold of Ophir) and 250 tons[f] of refined silver for overlaying the walls of the buildings, 5 the gold for the gold work and the silver for the silver, for all the work to be done by the craftsmen. Now, who will volunteer to consecrate himself to the LORD today?"

Israel Contributes

6 Then the leaders of the households, the leaders of the tribes of Israel, the commanders of thousands and of hundreds, and the officials in charge of the king's work gave willingly. 7 For the service of God's house they gave 185 tons[g] of gold and 10,000 gold drachmas,[h] 375 tons[i] of silver, 675 tons[j] of bronze, and 4,000 tons[k] of iron. 8 Whoever had precious stones gave them to the treasury of the LORD's house under the care of Jehiel the Gershonite. 9 Then the people rejoiced because of their leaders'[l] willingness to give, for they had given to the LORD with a whole heart. King David also rejoiced greatly.

David's Prayer

10 Then David praised the LORD in the sight of all the assembly. David said, "May You be praised, LORD God of our father Israel, from eternity to eternity. 11 Yours, LORD, is the greatness and the power and the glory and the splendor and the majesty, for everything in the heavens and on earth belongs to You. Yours, LORD, is the kingdom, and You are exalted as head over all. 12 Riches and honor come from You, and You are the ruler of everything. In Your hand are power and might, and it is in Your hand to make great and to give strength to all. 13 Now therefore, our God, we

---

[a]**28:18** Or chariot, that is; Ps 18:10; Ezk 1:5,15 [b]**28:19** Hb obscure [c]**29:2** Or mosaic [d]**29:2** Ex 28:18 reads turquoise, which is spelled nearly the same in Hb. [e]**29:4** Lit 3,000 talents; about 113 tons [f]**29:4** Lit 7,000 talents; about 263 tons [g]**29:7** Lit 5,000 talents; about 188 tons [h]**29:7** The drachma, or daric, was a Persian gold coin, first minted by Darius I about 515 B.C.; 10,000 darics weighed about 185 pounds. [i]**29:7** Lit 10,000 talents; about 378 tons [j]**29:7** Lit 18,000 talents; about 680 tons [k]**29:7** Lit 100,000 talents; about 3,750 tons [l]**29:9** Lit because they

give You thanks and praise Your glorious name.

14 "But who am I, and who are my people, that we should be able to give as generously as this? For everything comes from You, and we have given You only what comes from Your own hand.[a] 15 For we are foreigners and sojourners in Your presence as were all our ancestors. Our days on earth are like a shadow, without hope. 16 LORD our God, all this wealth that we've provided for building You a house for Your holy name comes from Your hand; everything belongs to You. 17 I know, my God, that You test the heart and that You are pleased with uprightness. I have willingly given all these things with an upright heart, and now I have seen Your people who are present[b] here giving joyfully and[c] willingly to You. 18 LORD God of Abraham, Isaac, and Israel, our ancestors, keep this desire forever in the thoughts of the hearts of Your people, and confirm their hearts toward You. 19 Give my son Solomon a whole heart to keep and to carry out all Your commandments, Your decrees, and Your statutes, and to build the temple for which I have made provision."

People Pay Homage

20 Then David said to the whole assembly, "Praise the LORD your God." So the whole assembly praised the LORD God of their ancestors. They bowed down and paid homage to the LORD and the king.

21 The following day they offered sacrifices to the LORD and •burnt offerings to the LORD: 1,000 bulls, 1,000 rams, and 1,000 lambs, along with their drink offerings, and sacrifices in abundance for all Israel. 22 They ate and drank with great joy in the LORD's presence that day.

Enthronement of Solomon

Then, for a second time, they made David's son Solomon king; they anointed him[d] as the LORD's ruler, and Zadok as the priest. 23 Solomon sat on the LORD's throne as king in place of his father David. He prospered, and all Israel obeyed him. 24 All the leaders and the mighty men, and all of King David's sons as well, pledged their allegiance to King Solomon. 25 The LORD highly exalted Solomon in the sight of all Israel and bestowed on him such royal majesty as had not been ⌊bestowed⌋ on any king over Israel before him.

Summary of David's Life

26 David son of Jesse was king over all Israel. 27 The length of his reign over Israel was 40 years; he reigned in Hebron for seven years and in Jerusalem for 33. 28 He died at a good old age, full of days, riches, and honor, and his son Solomon became king in his place. 29 As for the events of King David's ⌊reign⌋, from beginning to end, note that they are written about in the Events of Samuel the Seer, the Events of Nathan the Prophet, and the Events of Gad the Seer, 30 along with all his reign, his might, and the incidents that affected him and Israel and all the kingdoms of the ⌊surrounding⌋ lands.

a 29:14 Lit and from Your hand we have given to You   b 29:17 Lit found   c 29:17 Or now with joy I've seen Your people who are present here giving   d 29:22 LXX, Tg, Vg; MT omits him

2 CHRONICLES

God Exalts Solomon

1 Solomon son of David strengthened his hold on his kingdom. The LORD his God was with him and highly exalted him. ² Then Solomon spoke to all Israel, to the commanders of thousands and of hundreds, to the judges, and to every leader in all Israel—the heads of the families. ³ Solomon and the whole assembly with him went to the •high place that was in Gibeon because God's tent of meeting, which the LORD's servant Moses had made in the wilderness, was there. ⁴ Now, David had brought the ark of God from Kiriath-jearim to the place[a] he had set up for it, because he had pitched a tent for it in Jerusalem, ⁵ but he put[b] the bronze altar, which Bezalel son of Uri, son of Hur, had made, in front of the LORD's tabernacle. Solomon and the assembly inquired of Him[c] ⌊there⌋. ⁶ Solomon offered sacrifices there in the LORD's presence on the bronze altar at the tent of meeting; he offered 1,000 •burnt offerings on it.

Solomon Asks for Wisdom

⁷ That night God appeared to Solomon and said to him: "Ask. What should I give you?"

⁸ And Solomon said to God: "You have shown great faithful love to my father David, and You have made me king in his place. ⁹ LORD God, let Your promise to my father David now come true. For You have made me king over a people as numerous as the dust of the earth. ¹⁰ Now, <u>grant me wisdom and knowledge so that I may lead these people</u>, for who can judge this great people of Yours?"

God Grants Wisdom

¹¹ God said to Solomon, "Because this was in your heart, and you have not requested riches, wealth, or glory, or for the life of those who hate you, and you have not even requested long life, but you have requested for yourself wisdom and knowledge that you may judge My people over whom I have made you king, ¹² wisdom and knowledge are given to you. I will also give you riches, wealth, and glory, such that it was not like this for the kings who were before you, nor will it be like this for those after you." ¹³ So Solomon went to Jerusalem from[d] the high place that was in Gibeon in front of the tent of meeting, and he reigned over Israel.

Solomon's Horses and Wealth

¹⁴ Solomon accumulated 1,400 chariots and 12,000 horsemen, which he stationed in the chariot cities and with the king in Jerusalem. ¹⁵ The king made silver and gold as common in Jerusalem as stones, and he made cedar as abundant as sycamore in the Judean foothills. ¹⁶ Solomon's horses came from Egypt and Kue.[e] The king's traders would get them from Kue at the going price. ¹⁷ A chariot could be imported from Egypt for 15 pounds[f] ⌊of silver⌋ and a horse for about four pounds.[g] In the same way, they exported them to all the kings of the Hittites and to the kings of Aram through their agents.

Solomon's Request of King Hiram of Tyre

2 ªSolomon decided to build a temple for the name of the LORD and a royal palace for himself, ²ᵇ so he assigned 70,000 men as porters, 80,000 men as stonecutters in the mountains, and 3,600 as supervisors over them. ³ Then Solomon sent ⌊word⌋ to King Hiramᶜ of Tyre:

⌊Do for me⌋ what you did for my father David. You sent him cedars to build him a house to live in. ⁴ Now I myself am building a temple for the name of the LORD my God in order to dedicate it to Him for burning sweet incense before Him, for ⌊displaying⌋ the rows ⌊of the bread of the Presence⌋ continuously, and for ⌊sacrificing⌋ •burnt offerings for the evening and the morning, the Sabbaths and the New Moons, and the appointed festivals of the LORD our God. This is ⌊ordained⌋ for Israel forever. ⁵ The temple that I am building will be great, for our God is greater than any of the gods. ⁶ But who is able to build a temple for Him, since even heaven and the highest heaven cannot contain Him? Who am I then that I should build a house for Him except as a place to burn incense before Him? ⁷ Therefore, send me a craftsman who is skilled in engraving to work with gold, silver, bronze, and iron, and with purple, crimson, and blue yarn. ⌊He will work⌋ with the craftsmen who are with me in Judah and Jerusalem, appointed by my father David. ⁸ Also, send me cedar, cypress, and algumᵈ logs from Lebanon, for I know that your servants know how to cut the trees of Lebanon. Note that my servants will be with your servants ⁹ to prepare logs for me in abundance because the temple I am building will be great and wonderful. ¹⁰ I will give your servants, the woodcutters who cut the trees, 100,000 bushelsᵉ of wheat flour, 100,000 bushelsᵉ of barley, 110,000 gallonsᶠ of wine, and 110,000 gallons of oil.ᶠ

Hiram's Reply

¹¹ Then King Hiram of Tyre wrote a letterᵍ and sent ⌊it⌋ to Solomon:

Because the LORD loves His people, He set you over them as king.

¹² Hiram also said:

May the LORD God of Israel, who made the heavens and the earth, be praised! He gave King David a wise son with insight and understanding, who will build a temple for the LORD and a royal palace for himself. ¹³ I have now sent Huram-abi,ʰ a skillful man who has understanding. ¹⁴ He is the son of a woman from the daughters of Dan. His father is a man of Tyre. He knows how to work with gold, silver, bronze, iron, stone, and wood, with purple, blue, crimson yarn, and fine linen. He knows how to do all kinds of engraving and to execute any design that may be given him. I have sent him to be with your craftsmen and the craftsmen of my lord, your father David. ¹⁵ Now, let my lord send the wheat, barley, oil, and wine to his servants as promised. ¹⁶ We will cut logs from Lebanon, as many as you need, and bring them to you as rafts by sea to Joppa. You can then take them up to Jerusalem.

ª2:1 2 Ch 1:18 in Hb   ᵇ2:2 2 Ch 2:1 in Hb   ᶜ2:3 Some Hb mss, LXX, Syr, Vg; MT reads *Huram*; 2 Sm 5:11; 1 Kg 5:1-2
ᵈ2:8 Spelled *almug* in 1 Kg 10:11-12   ᵉ2:10 Lit *20,000 cors*   ᶠ2:10 Lit *20,000 baths*   ᵍ2:11 Lit *Tyre said in writing*
ʰ2:13 Lit *Huram my father*

Solomon's Work Force

¹⁷ Solomon took a census of all the foreign men in the land of Israel, after the census that his father David had conducted, and the total was 153,600. ¹⁸ Solomon made 70,000 of them porters, 80,000 stonecutters in the mountains, and 3,600 supervisors to make the people work.

Solomon Begins Temple

3 Then Solomon began to build the LORD's temple in Jerusalem on Mount Moriah where the LORD[a] had appeared to his father David, at the site David had prepared on the threshing floor of Ornan the Jebusite. ² He began to build on the second ⌞day⌟ of the second month in the fourth year of his reign. ³ These are Solomon's foundations[b] for building God's temple: the length[c] was 90 feet,[d] and the width 30 feet.[e] ⁴ The portico, which was across the front extending across the width of the temple, was 30 feet[e] wide; its height was 30 feet;[f] [e] he overlaid its inner surface with pure gold. ⁵ The larger room[g] he paneled with cypress wood, overlaid with fine gold, and decorated with palm trees and chains. ⁶ He adorned the temple with precious stones for beauty, and the gold was the gold of Parvaim. ⁷ He overlaid the temple—the beams, the thresholds, its walls and doors—with gold, and he carved •cherubim on the walls.

Most Holy Place

⁸ Then he made the most holy place; its length corresponded to the width of the temple, 30 feet,[e] and its width was 30 feet.[e] He overlaid it with 45,000 pounds[h] of fine gold. ⁹ The weight of the nails was 20 ounces[i] of gold, and he overlaid the ceiling with gold.

¹⁰ He made <u>two cherubim</u> of sculptured work, for the most holy place, and he overlaid them with gold. ¹¹ The overall length of the wings of the cherubim was 30 feet:[e] the wing of one was seven and a half feet,[j] touching the wall of the room; its other wing was seven and a half feet,[j] touching the wing of the other cherub. ¹² The wing of the other[k] cherub was seven and a half feet,[j] touching the wall of the room; its other wing was seven and a half feet,[j] reaching the wing of the other cherub. ¹³ The wingspan of these cherubim was 30 feet.[e] They stood on their feet and faced the larger room.[l]

¹⁴ He made the veil of blue, purple, and crimson yarn and fine linen, and he wove cherubim into it.

Bronze Pillars

¹⁵ In front of the temple he made two pillars, ⌞each⌟ 27 feet[m] [n] high. The capital on top of each was seven and half feet[j] high. ¹⁶ He had made chainwork in the inner sanctuary and also put it on top of the pillars. He made 100 pomegranates and fastened them into the chainwork. ¹⁷ Then he set up the pillars in front of the sanctuary, one on the right and one on the left. He named the one on the right Jachin[o] and the one on the left Boaz.[p]

Altar, Reservoir, and Basins

4 He made a bronze altar 30 feet[e] long, 30 feet[e] wide, and 15 feet[q] high.

² Then he made the cast ⌞metal⌟ reservoir, 15 feet[q] from brim to brim, per-

fectly round. It was seven and a half feet[a] high, and 45 feet[b] in circumference. [3] The likeness of oxen[c] was below it, completely encircling it, 10 every half yard,[d] completely surrounding the reservoir. The oxen were cast in two rows when the reservoir was cast. [4] It stood on 12 oxen, three facing north, three facing west, three facing south, and three facing east. The reservoir was on top of them and all their hindquarters were toward the center. [5] The reservoir was three inches[e] thick, and its rim was fashioned like the brim of a cup or a lily blossom. It could hold 11,000 gallons.[f]

[6] He made 10 basins for washing and he put five on the right and five on the left. The parts of the •burnt offering were rinsed in them, but the reservoir was used by the priests for washing.

Lampstands, Tables, and Courts

[7] He made the 10 gold lampstands according to their specifications and put them in the sanctuary, five on the right and five on the left. [8] He made 10 tables and placed them in the sanctuary, five on the right and five on the left. He also made 100 gold bowls.

[9] He made the courtyard of the priests and the large court, and doors for the court. He overlaid the doors with bronze. [10] He put the reservoir on the right side, toward the southeast. [11] Then Huram[g] made the pots, the shovels, and the bowls.

Completion of the Bronze Furnishings

So Huram finished doing the work that he was doing for King Solomon in God's temple: [12] two pillars; the bowls and the capitals on top of the two pillars; the two gratings for covering both bowls of the capitals that were on top of the pillars; [13] the 400 pomegranates for the two gratings (two rows of pomegranates for each grating covering both capitals' bowls on top of the pillars). [14] He also made the water carts[h] and the basins on the water carts. [15] The one reservoir and the 12 oxen underneath it, [16] the pots, the shovels, the forks, and all their utensils—Huram-abi[i] made them for King Solomon for the LORD's temple. ⸢All these were made⸥ of polished bronze. [17] The king had them cast in clay molds in the Jordan Valley between Succoth and Zeredah. [18] Solomon made all these utensils in such great abundance that the weight of the bronze was not determined.

Completion of the Gold Furnishings

[19] Solomon also made all the equipment in God's temple: the gold altar; the tables on which ⸢to put⸥ the bread of the Presence; [20] the lampstands and their lamps of pure gold to burn in front of the inner sanctuary according to specifications; [21] the flowers, lamps, and gold tongs—of purest gold; [22] the wick trimmers, sprinkling basins, ladles,[j] and firepans—of purest gold; and the entryway to the temple, its inner doors to the most holy place, and the doors of the temple sanctuary—of gold.

5 So all the work Solomon did for the LORD's temple was completed. Then Solomon brought the consecrated things of his father David—the silver, the gold, and all the utensils—and put them in the treasuries of God's temple.

Ark to Most Holy Place

[2] At that time Solomon assembled at Jerusalem the elders of Israel—all the

---

[a]**4:2** Lit five cubits [b]**4:2** Lit 30 cubits [c]**4:3** 1 Kg 7:24 reads gourds [d]**4:3** Lit 10 per cubit [e]**4:5** Lit a handbreadth [f]**4:5** Emended to 2,000 baths (1 Kg 7:26); MT reads 3,000 baths [g]**4:11** Or Hiram; 1 Kg 7:13,40,45 [h]**4:14** Lit the stands [i]**4:16** Lit Huram my father [j]**4:22** Or dishes, or spoons; lit palms

tribal heads, the ancestral chiefs of the Israelites—in order to bring the ark of the covenant of the LORD up from the city of David, that is, Zion. ³ So all the men of Israel were assembled in the king's presence at the festival; this was in the seventh month.ᵃ

⁴ All the elders of Israel came, and the Levites picked up the ark. ⁵ They brought up the ark, the tent of meeting, and the holy utensils that were in the tent. The priests and the Levites brought them up. ⁶ King Solomon and the entire congregation of Israel who had gathered around him were in front of the ark sacrificing sheep and cattle that could not be counted or numbered because there were so many. ⁷ The priests brought the ark of the LORD's covenant to its place, into the inner sanctuary of the temple, to the most holy place, beneath the wings of the •cherubim. ⁸ And the cherubim spread their wings over the place of the ark so that the cherubim formed a cover above the ark and its poles. ⁹ The poles were so long that their ends were seen from the holy placeᵇ in front of the inner sanctuary, but they were not seen from outside; they are there to this very day. ¹⁰ Nothing was in the ark except the two tablets that Moses had put ˻in it˼ at Horeb,ᶜ where the LORD had made a covenant with the Israelites when they came out of Egypt.

Musicians Praise Lord

¹¹ When the priests came out of the holy place—for all the priests who were present had consecrated themselves regardless of their tour of dutyᵈ— ¹² the Levitical singers of •Asaph, of Heman, of Jeduthun, and of their sons and their relatives, dressed in fine linen, with cymbals, harps and lyres, were standing east

of the altar, and with them were 120 priests blowing trumpets. ¹³ The trumpeters and singers joined together to praise and thank the LORD with one voice. They raised ˻their˼ voices, accompanied by trumpets, cymbals, and musical instruments, in praise to the LORD:

For He is good;
His faithful love endures forever;

the temple, the LORD's temple, was filled with a cloud. ¹⁴ And because of the cloud, the priests were not able to continue ministering, for the glory of the LORD filled God's temple.

Solomon Dedicates Temple

6 Then Solomon said:

The LORD said He would dwell
    in thick darkness,
² but I have built an exalted temple
    for You,
    a place for Your residence forever.

³ Then the king turned and blessed the entire congregation of Israel while they were standing. ⁴ He said:

May the LORD God of Israel
    be praised!
He spoke directly
    to my father David,
and He has fulfilled ˻the promise˼
    by His power.
He said,
⁵ "Since the day I brought
    My people Israel
out of the land of Egypt,
I have not chosen a city to build
    a temple in
among any of the tribes of Israel,
so that My name would be there,
and I have not chosen a man
    to be ruler over My people Israel.

ᵃ5:3 = September–October   ᵇ5:9 Some Hb mss, LXX; other Hb mss read *the ark*; 1 Kg 8:8   ᶜ5:10 = Sinai   ᵈ5:11 Lit *themselves; there was no maintaining of divisions*

6 But I have chosen Jerusalem
  so that My name will be there,
  and I have chosen David
  to be over My people Israel."

7 Now it was in the heart
    of my father David
  to build a temple for the name
  of the Lord God of Israel.
8 However, the LORD said
    to my father David,
  "Since it was your desire to build
  a temple for My name,
  you have done well to have
    this desire.
9 Yet, you are not the one to build
    the temple,
  but your son, your own offspring,
  will build the temple
  for My name."
10 So the LORD has fulfilled
    what He promised.
  I have taken the place
    of my father David
  and I sit on the throne of Israel,
    as the LORD promised.
  I have built the temple
    for the name of the LORD God
    of Israel.
11 I have put the ark there,
  where the LORD's covenant is
  that He made with the Israelites.

Solomon's Prayer

12 Then Solomon stood before the altar
of the LORD in front of the entire congregation of Israel and spread out his hands.
13 For Solomon had made a bronze platform seven and a half feet[a] long, seven
and a half feet[a] wide, and four and a half
feet[b] high and put it in the court. He
stood on it, knelt down in front of the
entire congregation of Israel, and spread
out his hands toward heaven. 14 He said:

LORD God of Israel,
  there is no God like You
  in heaven or on earth,
  keeping His gracious covenant
  with Your servants who walk
    before You
  with their whole heart.
15 You have kept what You promised
  to Your servant, my father David.
  You spoke directly ιto himι,
  and You fulfilled ιYour promiseι
    by Your power,
  as it is today.
16 Therefore, LORD God of Israel,
  keep what You promised
  to Your servant, my father David:
  You will never fail to have a man
  to sit before Me on the throne
    of Israel,
  if only your sons guard their way
    to walk in My Law
  as you have walked before Me.
17 Now, LORD God of Israel,
    please confirm
  what You promised
  to Your servant David.

18 But will God indeed live on earth
    with man?
  Even heaven, the highest heaven,
    cannot contain You,
  much less this temple I have built.
19 Listen[c] to Your servant's prayer
    and his petition,
  LORD my God,
  so that You may hear the cry
    and the prayer
  that Your servant prays before You,
20 so that Your eyes watch over
    this temple
  day and night,
  toward the place where You said
  You would put Your name;
  and so that You may hear the prayer

---

[a]**6:13** Lit *five cubits*   [b]**6:13** Lit *three cubits*   [c]**6:19** Lit *Turn*

Your servant prays
   toward this place.
21 Hear the petitions of Your servant
   and Your people Israel,
   which they pray toward this place.
   May You hear
      in Your dwelling place in heaven.
   May You hear and forgive.

22 If a man sins against his neighbor
   and is forced to take an oath[a]
   and he comes to take an oath
   before Your altar in this temple,
23 may You hear in heaven and act.
   May You judge Your servants,
   condemning the wicked
      by bringing
   what he has done on his own head
   and providing justice
      for the righteous
   by rewarding him according to
      his righteousness.

24 If Your people Israel are defeated
      before an enemy,
   because they have sinned
      against You,
   and they return ⌊to You⌋ and praise
      Your name,
   and they pray and plead for mercy
   before You in this temple,
25 may You hear in heaven
   and forgive the sin
      of Your people Israel.
   May You restore them to the land
   You gave them and their ancestors.

26 When the skies are shut
      and there is no rain
   because they have sinned
      against You,
   and they pray toward this place
   and praise Your name,
   and they turn from their sins
   because You are afflicting[b] them,

27 may You hear in heaven
   and forgive the sin of Your servants
   and Your people Israel,
   so that You may teach them
      the good way
   they should walk in. May You send
      rain on Your land
   that You gave Your people
      for an inheritance.

28 When there is famine on the earth,
   when there is pestilence,
   when there is blight, mildew,
      locust, or grasshopper,
   when their enemies besiege them
   in the region of their fortified cities,[c]
   ⌊when there is⌋ any plague or illness,
29 whatever prayer or petition
   anyone from your people Israel
      might have—
   each man knowing
      his own affliction[d] and suffering,
   and spreading out his hands
      toward this temple—
30 may You hear in heaven,
      Your dwelling place,
   and may You forgive
      and repay the man
   according to all his ways,
      since You know his heart,
   for You alone know
      the human heart,
31 so that they may •fear You
   and walk in Your ways
   all the days they live on the land
   You gave our ancestors.

32 Even for the foreigner who is not
      of Your people Israel
   but has come from a distant land
   because of Your great name
   and Your mighty hand
      and outstretched arm:
   when he comes and prays
      toward this temple,

---

[a]**6:22** Lit and he lifts a curse against him to curse him   [b]**6:26** LXX, Vg; MT reads answering; 1 Kg 8:35   [c]**6:28** Lit if his
(Israel's) enemies besiege him in the land of his gates; Jos 2:7; Jdg 16:2-3   [d]**6:29** Lit plague

33 may You hear in heaven
   in Your dwelling place,
and do all the foreigner asks You for.
Then all the peoples of the earth
   will know Your name,
to fear You as Your people Israel do
and know that this temple
   I have built
   is called by Your name.

34 When Your people go out to fight
   against their enemies,
   wherever You send them,
and they pray to You
in the direction of this city
   You have chosen
and the temple that I have built
   for Your name,
35 may You hear their prayer
   and petition in heaven
and uphold their cause.

36 When they sin against You—
for there is no one
   who does not sin—
and You are angry with them
and hand them over to the enemy,
and their captors deport them
to a distant or nearby country,
37 and when they come to their senses
in the land where they
   were deported
and repent and petition You
   in their captors' land,
saying: "We have sinned
   and done wrong;
we have been wicked,"
38 and when they return to You
with their whole mind and heart
in the land of their captivity
   where they were taken captive,
and when they pray in the direction
   of their land
that You gave their ancestors,
and the city You have chosen,

and toward the temple I have built
   for Your name,
39 may You hear in heaven,
   in Your dwelling place,
their prayer and petitions
   and uphold their cause.[a]
May You forgive Your people
who sinned against You.

40 Now, my God,
please let Your eyes be open
and Your ears attentive
to the prayer of this place.
41 Now therefore:

Arise, LORD God, ⌊come⌋
   to Your resting place,
You and the ark ⌊that shows⌋
   Your strength.
May Your priests, LORD God,
   be clothed with salvation,
and may Your godly people rejoice
   in goodness.
42 LORD God, do not reject
   Your anointed one;[b]
remember the loyalty
   of Your servant David.

Dedication Ceremonies

7 When Solomon finished praying, fire descended from heaven and consumed the •burnt offering and the sacrifices, and the glory of the LORD filled the temple. 2 The priests were not able to enter the LORD's temple because the glory of the LORD filled the temple of the LORD. 3 All the Israelites were watching when the fire descended and the glory of the LORD came on the temple. They bowed down with their faces to the ground on the pavement. They worshiped and praised the LORD:

For He is good,
   for His faithful love
   endures forever.

---

a6:39 Lit and do their judgment or justice   b6:42 Some Hb mss, LXX; other Hb mss read ones; Ps 132:10

⁴ The king and all the people were offering sacrifices in the LORD's presence. ⁵ King Solomon offered a sacrifice of 22,000 cattle and 120,000 sheep. In this manner the king and all the people dedicated God's temple. ⁶ The priests were standing at their stations, as were the Levites with the musical instruments of the LORD, which King David had made to praise the LORD—"for His faithful love endures forever"—when David offered praise with them. Across from them, the priests were blowing trumpets, and all the people were standing. ⁷ Solomon consecrated the middle of the courtyard that was in front of the LORD's temple because that was where he offered the burnt offerings and the fat of the •fellowship offerings since the bronze altar that Solomon had made could not accommodate the burnt offering, the •grain offering, and the fat ιof the fellowship offeringsι.

⁸ So Solomon and all Israel with him—a very great assembly, from the entrance to Hamathª to the Brook of Egypt—observed the festival at that time for seven days. ⁹ On the eighth day they held a sacred assembly, for the dedication of the altar lasted seven days and the festival seven days. ¹⁰ On the twenty-third day of the seventh month he sent the people away to their tents, rejoicing and with happy hearts for the goodness the LORD had done for David, for Solomon, and for His people Israel.

¹¹ So Solomon finished the LORD's temple and the royal palace. Everything that had entered Solomon's heart to do for the LORD's temple and for his own palace succeeded.

The LORD's Response: Consecration

¹² Then the LORD appeared to Solomon at night and said to him:

I have heard your prayer and have chosen this place for Myself as a temple of sacrifice. ¹³ If I close the sky so there is no rain, or if I command the grasshopper to consume the land, or if I send pestilence on My people, ¹⁴ and My people who are called by My name humble themselves, pray and seek My face, and turn from their evil ways, then I will hear from heaven, forgive their sin, and heal their land. ¹⁵ My eyes will now be open and My ears attentive to prayer from this place. ¹⁶ And I have now chosen and consecrated this temple so that My name may be there forever; My eyes and My heart will be there at all times.

God's Promise and Warning

¹⁷ As for you, if you walk before Me as your father David walked, doing everything I have commanded you, and if you keep My statutes and ordinances, ¹⁸ I will establish your royal throne, as I promised your father David: You will never fail to have a man on the throne of Israel.

¹⁹ However, if you turn away and abandon My statutes and My commands that I have set before you and if you go and serve other gods and worship them, ²⁰ then I will uproot Israel from the soil that I gave them, and this temple that I have sanctified for My name I will banish from My presence; I will make it an object of scorn and ridicule among all the peoples. ²¹ As for this temple, which was exalted, every passerby will be appalled and will say: Why did the LORD do this to this land and this temple? ²² Then they will say: Be-

ª7:8 Or from Lebo-hamath

cause they abandoned the LORD God of their ancestors who brought them out of the land of Egypt. They clung to other gods and worshiped and served them. Because of this, He brought all this ruin on them.

Solomon's Later Building Projects

8 At the end of 20 years during which Solomon had built the LORD's temple and his own palace— ² Solomon having rebuilt the cities Hiram[a] gave him and having settled the Israelites there— ³ Solomon went to Hamath-zobah and seized it. ⁴ He built Tadmor in the wilderness along with all the storage cities that he built in Hamath. ⁵ He built Upper Beth-horon and Lower Beth-horon—fortified cities with walls, gates, and bars— ⁶ Baalath, all the storage cities that belonged to Solomon, all the chariot cities, the cavalry cities, and everything Solomon desired to build in Jerusalem, Lebanon, or anywhere else in the land of his dominion.

Solomon's Forced Labor

⁷ As for all the peoples who remained of the Hittites, Amorites, Perizzites, Hivites, and Jebusites, who were not from Israel— ⁸ their descendants who remained in the land after them, those whom the Israelites had not completely destroyed—Solomon imposed forced labor on them; ⌊it is this way⌋ today. ⁹ But Solomon did not consign the Israelites to be slaves for his work; they were soldiers, commanders of his captains, and commanders of his chariots and his cavalry. ¹⁰ These were King Solomon's deputies: 250 who ruled over the people.

¹¹ Solomon brought the daughter of Pharaoh from the city of David to the house he had built for her, for he said, "My wife must not live in the house[b] of David king of Israel because the places to which the ark of the LORD has come are holy."

Public Worship Established at the Temple

¹² At that time Solomon offered •burnt offerings to the LORD on the LORD's altar he had made in front of the vestibule ¹³ following the daily requirement for offerings according to the commandment of Moses for Sabbaths, New Moons, and the three annual appointed festivals: the Festival of Unleavened Bread, the Festival of Weeks, and the Festival of Booths. ¹⁴ According to the ordinances of his father David, he appointed the divisions of the priests over their service, of the Levites over their responsibilities to offer praise and to minister before the priests following the daily requirement, and of the gatekeepers by their divisions with respect to each gate, for this had been the command of David, the man of God. ¹⁵ They did not turn aside from the king's command regarding the priests and the Levites concerning any matter or concerning the treasuries. ¹⁶ All of Solomon's work was carried out from the day the foundation ⌊was laid⌋ for the LORD's temple until it was finished. So the LORD's temple was completed.

Solomon's Fleet

¹⁷ At that time Solomon went to Ezion-geber and to Eloth on the seashore in the land of Edom. ¹⁸ So through his servants, Hiram[c] sent him ships with crews of experienced seamen. They went with Solomon's servants to Ophir, took from there 17 tons[d] of gold, and delivered it to King Solomon.

---

a**8:2** = the king of Tyre   b**8:11** LXX reads *city*   c**8:18** Hb *Huram*   d**8:18** Lit *450 talents*

Queen of Sheba Visits

9 The queen of Sheba heard of Solomon's fame, so she came to test Solomon with difficult questions at Jerusalem with a very large retinue, with camels bearing spices, gold in abundance, and precious stones. She came to Solomon and spoke with him about everything that was on her mind. 2 So Solomon answered all her questions; nothing was too difficult for Solomon to explain to her. 3 When the queen of Sheba observed Solomon's wisdom, the palace he had built, 4 the food at his table, his servants' residence, his attendants' service and their attire, his cupbearers and their attire, and the •burnt offerings he offered at the LORD's temple, it took her breath away.

Queen Praises Solomon

5 She said to the king, "The report I heard in my own country about your words and about your wisdom is true. 6 But I didn't believe their reports until I came and saw with my own eyes. Indeed, I was not even told half of your great wisdom! You far exceed the report I heard. 7 How happy are your men.[a] How happy are these servants of yours, who always stand in your presence hearing your wisdom. 8 May the LORD your God be praised! He delighted in you and put you on His throne as king for the LORD your God. Because Your God loved Israel enough to establish them forever, He has set you over them as king to carry out justice and righteousness."

9 Then she gave the king four and a half tons[b] of gold, a great quantity of spices, and precious stones. There never were such spices as those the queen of Sheba gave to King Solomon. 10 In addition, Hiram's servants and Solomon's servants who brought gold from Ophir also brought algum wood and precious stones. 11 The king made the algum wood into walkways for the LORD's temple and for the king's palace and into harps and lyres for the singers. Never before had anything like them been seen in the land of Judah.

12 King Solomon gave the queen of Sheba her every desire, whatever she asked—far more than she had brought the king. Then she, along with her servants, returned to her own country.

Solomon's Great Wealth

13 The weight of gold that came to Solomon annually was 25 tons,[c] 14 besides what was brought by the merchants and traders. All the Arabian kings and governors of the land also brought gold and silver to Solomon.

15 King Solomon made 200 large shields of hammered gold; 15 pounds[d] of hammered gold went into each shield. 16 He made 300 small shields of hammered gold; about eight pounds[e] of gold went into each shield. The king put them in the House of the Forest of Lebanon. 17 The king also made a large ivory throne and overlaid it with pure gold. 18 The throne had six steps; there was a footstool covered in gold for the throne, armrests on either side of the seat, and two lions standing beside the armrests. 19 Twelve lions were standing there on the six steps, one at each end. Nothing like it had ever been made in any other kingdom.

Plenty of Gold

20 All of King Solomon's drinking cups were gold, and all the utensils of the House of the Forest of Lebanon were pure gold. There was no silver, since it was considered as nothing in Solomon's

[a]9:7 LXX, Old Lat read wives; 1 Kg 10:8   [b]9:9 Lit 120 talents   [c]9:13 Lit 666 talents   [d]9:15 Lit 600 (shekels)
[e]9:16 Lit 300 (shekels)

time, [21] for the king's ships kept going to Tarshish with Hiram's servants, and once every three years the ships of Tarshish would arrive bearing gold, silver, ivory, apes, and peacocks.[a]

[22] King Solomon surpassed all the kings of the world in riches and wisdom. [23] All the kings of the world wanted an audience with Solomon to hear the wisdom God had put in his heart. [24] Each of them would bring his own gift—items[b] of silver and gold, clothing, weapons,[c] spices, and horses and mules—as an annual tribute.

[25] Solomon had 4,000 stalls for horses and chariots, and 12,000 horsemen. He stationed them in the chariot cities and with the king in Jerusalem. [26] He ruled over all the kings from the Euphrates River to the land of the Philistines and as far as the border of Egypt. [27] The king made silver as common in Jerusalem as stones, and he made cedar as abundant as sycamore in the Judean foothills. [28] They were bringing horses for Solomon from Egypt and from all the countries.

Solomon's Death

[29] The remaining events of Solomon's ⌐reign⌐, from beginning to end, are written about in the Events of Nathan the Prophet, the Prophecy of Ahijah the Shilonite, and the Visions of Iddo the Seer concerning Jeroboam son of Nebat. [30] Solomon reigned in Jerusalem over all Israel for 40 years. [31] Solomon rested with his fathers and was buried in the city of his father David. His son Rehoboam became king in his place.

The Kingdom Divided

Jeroboam's Request

10 Then Rehoboam went to Shechem, for all Israel had gone to Shechem to make him king. [2] When Jeroboam son of Nebat heard ⌐about it⌐—for he was in Egypt where he had fled from King Solomon's presence—Jeroboam returned from Egypt. [3] So they summoned him. Then Jeroboam and all Israel came and spoke to Rehoboam: [4] "Your father made our yoke harsh. Therefore, lighten your father's harsh service and the heavy yoke he put on us, and we will serve you."

Rehoboam's Rejection

[5] Rehoboam replied, "Return to me in three days." So the people left.

[6] Then King Rehoboam consulted with the elders who had served his father Solomon when he was alive, asking, "How do you advise me to respond to this people?"

[7] They replied, "If you will be kind to these people and please them by speaking kind words to them, they will be your servants forever."

[8] But he rejected the advice of the elders who had advised him and consulted with the young men who had grown up with him, the ones serving him. [9] He asked them, "What message do you advise we send back to this people who said to me, 'Lighten the yoke your father put on us'?"

[10] Then the young men who had grown up with him told him, "This is what you should say to the people who said to you, 'Your father made our yoke heavy, but you, make it lighter on us!' This is what you should say to them: 'My little finger is thicker than my father's loins.[d] [11] Now therefore, my father burdened you with a heavy yoke, but I will add to your yoke; my father disciplined you with whips, but I, with barbed whips.'"[e]

---

[a] **9:21** Or *baboons* [b] **9:24** Or *vessels*, or *weapons* [c] **9:24** Or *fragrant balsam*; LXX reads *resin* (oil of myrrh)
[d] **10:10** Or *waist* [e] **10:11** Lit *with scorpions*

¹² So Jeroboam and all the people came to Rehoboam on the third day, just as the king had ordered, saying, "Return to me on the third day." ¹³ Then the king answered them harshly. King Rehoboam rejected the elders' advice ¹⁴ and spoke to them according to the young men's advice, saying, "My father made your yoke heavy,ᵃ but I will add to it; my father disciplined you with whips, but I, with barbed whips."ᵇ

¹⁵ The king did not listen to the people because the turn of events came from God, in order that the LORD might carry out His word that He had spoken through Ahijah the Shilonite to Jeroboam son of Nebat.

Most of Israel Rebels

¹⁶ When all Israel sawᶜ that the king had not listened to them, the people answered the king:

> What portion do we have in David?
> We have no inheritance in the son
>   of Jesse.
> Israel, each man to your tent;
> David, look after
>   your own house now!

So all Israel went to their tents.

Rehoboam Rules Judah

¹⁷ But as for the Israelites living in the cities of Judah, Rehoboam reigned over them.

¹⁸ Then King Rehoboam sent Hadoram,ᵈ who was in charge of the forced labor, but the Israelites stoned him to death. However, King Rehoboam managed to get up into the chariot to flee to Jerusalem. ¹⁹ Israel is in rebellion against the house of David until today.

Rehoboam Mobilizes Judah and Benjamin

11 When Rehoboam arrived in Jerusalem, he mobilized the house of Judah and Benjamin—180,000 choice warriors—to fight against Israel to restore the reign to Rehoboam.

God's Prophet: Don't Fight Israel

² But the word of the LORD came to Shemaiah, the man of God: ³ "Say to Rehoboam son of Solomon, king of Judah, to all Israel in Judah and Benjamin, and to the rest of the people: ⁴ 'This is what the LORD says: You are not to march up and fight against your brothers. Each of you must return home, for this incident has come from Me.'"

Rehoboam Obeys

So they listened to what the LORD said and turned back from going against Jeroboam.

Judah's King Rehoboam

⁵ Rehoboam stayed in Jerusalem, and he fortified citiesᵉ in Judah. ⁶ He built up Bethlehem, Etam, Tekoa, ⁷ Beth-zur, Soco, Adullam, ⁸ Gath, Mareshah, Ziph, ⁹ Adoraim, Lachish, Azekah, ¹⁰ Zorah, Aijalon, and Hebron, which are fortified cities in Judah and in Benjamin. ¹¹ He strengthened their fortifications and put leaders in them with supplies of food, oil, and wine. ¹² He also put large shields and spears in each and every city to make them very strong. So Judah and Benjamin were his.

ᵃ**10:14** Some Hb mss, LXX; other Hb mss read *I will make your yoke heavy*; 1 Kg 12:14   ᵇ**10:14** Lit *with scorpions*
ᶜ**10:16** Some Hb mss, LXX; other Hb mss omit *saw*; 1 Kg 12:16   ᵈ**10:18** = Adoram; 1 Kg 12:18   ᵉ**11:5** Lit *he built cities for a fortress*

Priests and Levites Side with Rehoboam

[13] The priests and Levites from all their regions throughout Israel took their stand with Rehoboam, [14] for the Levites left their pasturelands and their possessions and went to Judah and Jerusalem, because Jeroboam and his sons refused to let them serve as priests of the LORD. [15] Jeroboam appointed his own priests for the •high places, the goat-demons, and the ⌊gold⌋ calves he had made. [16] Those from every tribe of Israel who had determined in their hearts to seek the LORD their God followed the Levites to Jerusalem to sacrifice to the LORD God of their ancestors. [17] So they strengthened the kingdom of Judah and supported Rehoboam son of Solomon for three years, because they walked in the way of David and Solomon for three years.

Rehoboam's Family

[18] Rehoboam married Mahalath, daughter of David's son Jerimoth and of Abihail daughter of Jesse's son Eliab. [19] She bore him sons: Jeush, Shemariah, and Zaham. [20] After her, he married Maacah daughter[a] of Absalom. She bore him Abijah, Attai, Ziza, and Shelomith. [21] Rehoboam loved Maacah daughter[a] of Absalom more than all his wives and concubines. He acquired 18 wives and 60 concubines and was the father of 28 sons and 60 daughters.

[22] Rehoboam appointed Abijah son of Maacah as chief, leader among his brothers, intending to make him king. [23] Rehoboam also showed discernment by dispersing some of his sons to all the regions of Judah and Benjamin and to all the fortified cities. He gave them plenty of provisions and sought many wives for them.

Egyptian King Shishak Invades

12 When Rehoboam had established his sovereignty and royal power, he abandoned the law of the LORD—he and all Israel with him. [2] Because they were unfaithful to the LORD, in the fifth year of King Rehoboam, Shishak king of Egypt went to war against Jerusalem [3] with 1,200 chariots, 60,000 cavalrymen, and countless people who came with him from Egypt—Libyans, Sukkiim, and Ethiopians.[b] [4] He captured the fortified cities of Judah and came as far as Jerusalem.

Prophet Warns Rehoboam

[5] Then Shemaiah the prophet went to Rehoboam and the leaders of Judah who were gathered at Jerusalem because of Shishak. He said to them: "This is what the LORD says: 'You have abandoned Me; therefore, I have abandoned you into the hand of Shishak.'"

Rehoboam's Humility, Lord's Mercy

[6] So the leaders of Israel and the king humbled themselves and said, "The LORD is righteous."

[7] When the LORD saw that they had humbled themselves, the LORD's message came to Shemaiah: "They have humbled themselves; I will not destroy them but will grant them a little deliverance. My wrath will not be poured out on Jerusalem through Shishak. [8] However, they will become his servants so that they may recognize ⌊the difference between⌋ serving Me and serving the kingdoms of the land."

King Shishak Sacks Temple

[9] So King Shishak of Egypt went to war against Jerusalem. He seized the treasuries of the LORD's temple and the treasuries of the royal palace. He took

---

a **11:20** Possibly *granddaughter*; 2 Ch 13:2   b **12:3** Lit *Cushites*

everything. He took the gold shields that Solomon had made. ¹⁰ King Rehoboam made bronze shields in their place and committed them into the care of the captains of the royal escorts[a] who guarded the entrance to the king's palace. ¹¹ Whenever the king entered the LORD's temple, the royal escorts would carry the shields and take them back to the royal escorts' armory. ¹² When Rehoboam humbled himself, the LORD's anger turned away from him, and He did not destroy ⌊him⌋ completely. Besides that, conditions were good in Judah.

Rehoboam's Last Days

¹³ King Rehoboam established his royal power in Jerusalem. Rehoboam was 41 years old when he became king; he reigned 17 years in Jerusalem, the city the LORD had chosen from all the tribes of Israel to put His name. Rehoboam's mother's name was Naamah the Ammonite. ¹⁴ Rehoboam did what was evil, because he did not determine in his heart to seek the LORD.

¹⁵ The events of Rehoboam's ⌊reign⌋, from beginning to end, are written about in the Events of Shemaiah the Prophet and of Iddo the Seer concerning genealogies. There was war between Rehoboam and Jeroboam throughout their reigns. ¹⁶ Rehoboam rested with his fathers and was buried in the city of David. His son Abijah[b] became king in his place.

Judah's King Abijah

13 In the eighteenth year of ⌊Israel's⌋ King Jeroboam, Abijah[c] became king over Judah; ² he reigned three years in Jerusalem. His mother's name was Micaiah[d] daughter of Uriel; ⌊she was⌋ from Gibeah.

War: Abijah vs. Jeroboam

There was war between Abijah and Jeroboam. ³ Abijah set his army of warriors in order with 400,000 choice men. Jeroboam arranged his mighty army of 800,000 choice men in battle formation against him.

Abijah Challenges Jeroboam

⁴ Then Abijah stood on Mount Zemaraim, which is in the hill country of Ephraim, and said, "Jeroboam and all Israel, hear me. ⁵ Don't you know that the LORD God of Israel gave the kingship over Israel to David and his descendants forever by a covenant of salt? ⁶ But Jeroboam son of Nebat, a servant of Solomon son of David, rose up and rebelled against his lord. ⁷ Then worthless and •wicked men gathered around him to resist Rehoboam son of Solomon when Rehoboam was young, inexperienced, and unable to assert himself against them.

⁸ "And now you are saying you can assert yourselves against the LORD's kingdom in the hand of ⌊one of⌋ David's sons. You are a vast multitude and have with you the golden calves that Jeroboam made for you as gods.[e] ⁹ Didn't you banish the priests of the LORD, the descendants of Aaron and the Levites, and make your own priests like the peoples of ⌊other⌋ lands do? Whoever comes to ordain himself with a young bull and seven rams may become a priest of what are not gods.

¹⁰ "But as for us, the LORD is our God. We have not abandoned Him; the priests ministering to the LORD are descendants of Aaron, and the Levites ⌊serve⌋ at their tasks. ¹¹ They offer a •burnt offering and fragrant incense to the LORD every morning and every evening, and ⌊they set⌋ the rows of the bread ⌊of the Presence⌋ on

---

[a]**12:10** Lit *the runners*   [b]**12:16** = Abijam; 1 Kg 14:31–15:8   [c]**13:1** = Abijam; 1 Kg 14:31–15:8   [d]**13:2** LXX, Syr, Arabic read *Maacah*; 2 Ch 11:22; 1 Kg 15:2   [e]**13:8** Or *God*; 1 Kg 12:28

the ceremonially clean table. They light the lamps of the gold lampstand every evening. We are carrying out the requirements of the LORD our God, while you have abandoned Him. [12] Look, God and His priests are with us at our head. The trumpets are ready to sound the charge against you. Israelites, don't fight against the LORD God of your ancestors, for you will not succeed."

Jeroboam's Ambush

[13] Now Jeroboam had sent an ambush around to advance from behind them. So they were in front of Judah, and the ambush was behind them. [14] Judah turned and discovered that the battle was in front of them and behind them, so they cried out to the LORD. Then the priests blew the trumpets, [15] and the men of Judah raised the battle cry.

Judah and Rehoboam Defeat Israel and Jeroboam

When the men of Judah raised the battle cry, God routed Jeroboam and all Israel before Abijah and Judah. [16] So the Israelites fled before Judah, and God handed them over to them. [17] Then Abijah and his people struck them with a mighty blow, and 500,000 choice men of Israel were killed. [18] The Israelites were subdued at that time. The Judahites succeeded because they depended on the LORD, the God of their ancestors.

[19] Abijah pursued Jeroboam and captured ⌊some⌋ cities from him: Bethel and its villages, Jeshanah and its villages, and Ephron[a] and its villages. [20] Jeroboam no longer retained his power[b] during Abijah's reign; ultimately, the LORD struck him and he died.

[21] However, Abijah grew strong, acquired 14 wives, and fathered 22 sons and 16 daughters. [22] The rest of the events of Abijah's ⌊reign⌋, along with his ways and his sayings, are written about in the Writing of the Prophet Iddo.

14 [1c] Abijah rested with his fathers and was buried in the city of David. His son Asa became king in his place. During his reign the land experienced peace for 10 years.

Judah's Good King Asa

[2d] Asa did what was good and right in the sight of the LORD his God. [3] He removed the pagan altars and the •high places. He shattered their sacred pillars and chopped down their •Asherah poles. [4] He told ⌊the people of⌋ Judah to seek the LORD God of their ancestors and to carry out the instruction and the command. [5] He also removed the high places and the incense altars from all the cities of Judah, and the kingdom experienced peace under him.

King Asa's Peace

[6] Because the land experienced peace, Asa built fortified cities in Judah. No one made war with him in those days because the LORD gave him rest. [7] So he said to ⌊the people of⌋ Judah, "Let's build these cities and surround them with walls and towers, with doors and bars. The land is still ours because we sought the LORD our God. We sought Him and He gave us rest on every side." So they built and succeeded.

Ethiopians Invade

[8] Asa had an army of 300,000 from Judah bearing large shields and spears, and 280,000 from Benjamin bearing regular shields and drawing the bow. All these were brave warriors. [9] Then Zerah the •Cushite came against them with an

a **13:19** Alt Hb tradition reads *Ephrain*   b **13:20** Lit *He did not restrain the power of Jeroboam*   c **14:1** 2 Ch 13:23 in Hb   d **14:2** 2 Ch 14:1 in Hb

army of one million men and 300ª chariots. They came as far as Mareshah. ¹⁰ So Asa marched out against him and lined up in battle formation in the Valley of Zephathah at Mareshah.

King Asa Appeals to God

¹¹ Then Asa cried out to the LORD his God: "LORD, there is no one besides You to help the mighty and those without strength. Help us, LORD our God, for we depend on You, and in Your name we have come against this multitude. LORD, You are our God. Do not let a mere mortal hinder You."

God Routs Ethiopians

¹² So the LORD routed the Cushites before Asa and before Judah, and the Cushites fled. ¹³ Then Asa and the people who were with him pursued them as far as Gerar. The Cushites fell until they had no survivors, for they were crushed before the LORD and before His army. So the people of Judah carried off a great supply of loot. ¹⁴ Then they attacked all the cities around Gerar because the terror of the LORD was on them. They also plundered all the cities, since there was a great deal of plunder in them. ¹⁵ They also attacked the tents of the herdsmen and captured many sheep and camels. Then they returned to Jerusalem.

Prophecy for Judah, Benjamin, and King Asa

15 The Spirit of God came on Azariah son of Oded. ² So he went out to meet Asa and said to him, "Asa and all Judah and Benjamin, hear me. The LORD is with you when you are with Him. If you seek Him, He will be found by you, but if you abandon Him, He will abandon you. ³ For many years Israel has

been without the true God, without a teaching priest, and without law, ⁴ but when they turned to the LORD God of Israel in their distress and sought Him, He was found by them. ⁵ In those times there was no peace for those who went about their daily activities because the residents of the lands had many conflicts. ⁶ Nation was crushed by nation and city by city, for God troubled them with every possible distress. ⁷ But as for you, be strong; don't be discouraged,ᵇ for your work has a reward."

Asa Obeys, God Gives Peace

⁸ When Asa heard these words and the prophecy of ₍Azariah son of₎ Oded the prophet, he took courage and removed the detestable idols from the whole land of Judah and Benjamin and from the cities he had captured in the hill country of Ephraim. He renovated the altar of the LORD that was in front of the vestibule of the LORD's ₍temple₎. ⁹ Then he gathered all Judah and Benjamin, as well as those from ₍the tribes of₎ Ephraim, Manasseh, and Simeon who had settled among them, for they had defected to him from Israel in great numbers when they saw that the LORD his God was with him.

¹⁰ They were gathered in Jerusalem in the third month of the fifteenth year of Asa's reign. ¹¹ At that time they sacrificed to the LORD 700 cattle and 7,000 sheep from all the plunder they had brought. ¹² Then they entered into a covenant to seek the LORD God of their ancestors with all their mind and all their heart. ¹³ Whoever would not seek the LORD God of Israel would be put to death, young or old,ᶜ man or woman. ¹⁴ They took an oath to the LORD in a loud voice, with shouting, with trumpets, and with rams' horns. ¹⁵ All Judah

---

ª**14:9** Syr, Arabic read *30,000*   ᵇ**15:7** Lit *don't let your hands fail*   ᶜ**15:13** Or *insignificant or great*

rejoiced over the oath, for they had sworn it with all their mind. They had sought Him with all their heart, and He was found by them. So <u>the LORD gave them rest on every side.</u>

[16] <u>King Asa also removed Maacah, his grandmother,</u>[a] <u>from being queen mother because she had made an obscene image of •Asherah.</u> Asa chopped down her obscene image, then crushed it and burned it in the Kidron Valley. [17] The <u>•high places were not taken away from Israel;</u> nevertheless, Asa was wholehearted his entire life.[b] [18] He brought his father's consecrated gifts and his own consecrated gifts into God's temple: silver, gold, and utensils.

[19] There was no war until the thirty-fifth year of Asa's reign.

Asa's Treaty with Aram against Israel

16 In the thirty-sixth year of Asa, Israel's King Baasha went to war against Judah. He built Ramah in order to deny anyone's access—going or coming—to Judah's King Asa. [2] So Asa brought out the silver and gold from the treasuries of the LORD's temple and the royal palace and sent it to <u>Aram's King Ben-hadad,</u> who lived in Damascus, saying, [3] "There's a treaty between me and you, between my father and your father. Look, I have sent you silver and gold. Go break your treaty with Israel's King Baasha so that he will withdraw from me."

[4] Ben-hadad listened to King Asa and sent the commanders of his armies to the cities of Israel. They attacked Ijon, Dan, Abel-maim,[c] and all the storage cities[d] of Naphtali. [5] When Baasha heard ⌊about it⌋, he quit building Ramah and stopped his work. [6] Then King Asa brought all Judah, and they carried away the stones of Ramah and the timbers

Baasha had built it with. Then he built Geba and Mizpah with them.

Seer Hanani's Rebuke of Asa

[7] At that time, Hanani the seer came to King Asa of Judah and said to him, <u>"Because you depended on the king of Aram and have not depended on the LORD your God, the army of the king of Aram has escaped from your hand.</u> [8] Were not the •Cushites and Libyans a vast army with very many chariots and horsemen? When you depended on the LORD, He handed them over to you. [9] For the eyes of the LORD range throughout the earth to show Himself strong for those whose hearts are completely His. You have been foolish in this matter, for from now on, you will have wars." [10] Asa was angry with the seer and put him in prison[e] because of his anger over this. And Asa mistreated some of the people at that time.

Asa's Death

[11] Note that the events of Asa's ⌊reign⌋, from beginning to end, are written about in the Book of the Kings of Judah and Israel. [12] In the thirty-ninth year of his reign, Asa developed a disease in his feet, and his disease became increasingly severe. Yet <u>even in his disease he didn't seek the LORD but the physicians.</u> [13] Asa died in the forty-first year of his reign and rested with his fathers. [14] He was buried in his own tomb that he had hewn out for himself in the city of David. They laid him out in a coffin that was full of spices and various mixtures of prepared ointments; then they made a great fire in his honor.

Judah's Good King Jehoshaphat

17 His son Jehoshaphat became king in his place and strengthened

a**15:16** Lit mother; 2 Ch 11:22; 1 Kg 15:2   b**15:17** Lit wholehearted all his days   c**16:4** 1 Kg 15:20 reads Abel-beth-maacah   d**16:4** 1 Kg 15:20 reads all [the] Chinneroth   e**16:10** Lit the house of stocks

himself against Israel. ² He stationed troops in every fortified city of Judah and set garrisons in the land of Judah and in the cities of Ephraim that his father Asa had captured.

³ Now the LORD was with Jehoshaphat because he walked in the former ways of his father David.ª He did not seek the Baals ⁴ but sought the God of his father and walked by His commands, not according to the practices of Israel. ⁵ So the LORD established the kingdom in his hand. Then all Judah brought him tribute, and he had riches and honor in abundance. ⁶ His mind rejoiced in the LORD's ways, and he again removed the •high places and •Asherah poles from Judah.

Jehoshaphat's Educational Plan

⁷ In the third year of his reign, Jehoshaphat sent his officials—Ben-hail,ᵇ Obadiah, Zechariah, Nethanel, and Micaiah—to teach in the cities of Judah. ⁸ The Levites with them were Shemaiah, Nethaniah, Zebadiah,ᶜ Asahel, Shemiramoth, Jehonathan, Adonijah, Tobijah, and Tob-adonijah; the priests, Elishama and Jehoram, were with these Levites. ⁹ They taught throughout Judah, ιhavingι the book of the LORD's instruction with them. They went throughout the towns of Judah and taught the people.

¹⁰ The terror of the LORD was on all the kingdoms of the lands that surrounded Judah, so they didn't fight against Jehoshaphat. ¹¹ Some of the Philistines also brought gifts and silver as tribute to Jehoshaphat, and the Arabs brought him flocks: 7,700 rams and 7,700 male goats.

Jehoshaphat's Military Might

¹² Jehoshaphat grew stronger and stronger. He built fortresses and storage cities in Judah ¹³ and carried out great works in the towns of Judah. He had fighting men, brave warriors, in Jerusalem. ¹⁴ These are their numbers according to their ancestral families. For Judah, the commanders of thousands:

Adnah the commander and 300,000 brave warriors with him; ¹⁵ next to him, Jehohanan the commander and 280,000 with him; ¹⁶ next to him, Amasiah son of Zichri, the volunteer of the LORD, and 200,000 brave warriors with him; ¹⁷ from Benjamin, Eliada, a brave warrior, and 200,000 with him armed with bow and shield; ¹⁸ next to him, Jehozabad and 180,000 with him equipped for war.

¹⁹ These were the ones who served the king, besides those he stationed in the fortified cities throughout all Judah.

Jehoshaphat's Alliance with King Ahab

18 Now Jehoshaphat had riches and honor in abundance, and he made an alliance with Ahab through marriage.ᵈ ² Then after some years, he went down to visit Ahab in Samaria. Ahab sacrificed many sheep and cattle for him and for the people who were with him. Then he persuaded him to march up to Ramoth-gilead, ³ for Israel's King Ahab asked Judah's King Jehoshaphat, "Will you go with me to Ramoth-gilead?"

Jehoshaphat Asks for Yahweh's Prophet

He replied to him, "I am as you are, my people as your people; ιwe will beι with you in the battle." ⁴ But Jehosha-

---

ª**17:3** Some Hb mss, LXX omits *David*   ᵇ**17:7** = Son of Power   ᶜ**17:8** Some Hb mss, Syr, Tg, Arabic read *Zechariah*
ᵈ**18:1** Lit *made himself a son-in-law to Ahab*; 1 Kg 3:1; Ezr 9:14

phat said to the king of Israel, "First, please ask what the LORD's will is."

⁵ So the king of Israel gathered the prophets, 400 men, and asked them, "Should we go to Ramoth-gilead for war or should I refrain?"

They replied, "March up, and God will hand it over to the king."

⁶ But Jehoshaphat asked, "Isn't there a prophet of •Yahweh here any more? Let's ask him."

Prophet Micaiah

⁷ The king of Israel said to Jehoshaphat, "There is still one man who can ask the LORD, but I hate him because he never prophesies good about me, but only disaster. He is Micaiah son of Imlah."

"The king shouldn't say that," Jehoshaphat replied.

⁸ So the king of Israel called an officer and said, "Hurry ⌞and get⌟ Micaiah son of Imlah!"

⁹ Now the king of Israel and King Jehoshaphat of Judah, clothed in royal attire, were each sitting on his own throne. They were sitting on the threshing floor at the entrance to Samaria's •gate, and all the prophets were prophesying in front of them. ¹⁰ Then Zedekiah son of Chenaanah made iron horns and said, "This is what the LORD says: 'You will gore the Arameans with these until they are finished off.'" ¹¹ And all the prophets were prophesying the same, saying, "March up to Ramoth-gilead and succeed, for the LORD will hand it over to the king."

Micaiah's Message of Defeat

¹² The messenger who went to call Micaiah instructed him, "Look, the words of the prophets are unanimously favor-able for the king. So let your words be like theirs, and speak favorably."

¹³ But Micaiah said, "As the LORD lives, I will say whatever my God says."ᵃ

¹⁴ So he went to the king, and the king asked him, "Micaiah, should we go to Ramoth-gilead for war, or should Iᵇ refrain?"

Micaiah said, "March up and succeed, for they will be handed over to you."

¹⁵ But the king said to him, "How many times must I make you swear not to tell me anything but the truth in the name of the LORD?"

¹⁶ So Micaiah said:

I saw all Israel scattered on the hills
like sheep without a shepherd.
And the LORD said,
'They have no master;
let each return home in peace.'

¹⁷ So the king of Israel said to Jehoshaphat, "Didn't I tell you he never prophesies good about me, but only disaster?"

Lying Spirit Entices Ahab

¹⁸ Then Micaiah said, "Therefore, hear the word of the LORD. I saw the LORD sitting on His throne, and the whole heavenly •host was standing at His right hand and at His left hand. ¹⁹ And the LORD said, 'Who will entice Ahab king of Israel to march up and fall at Ramoth-gilead?' So one was saying this and another was saying that.

²⁰ "Then a spirit came forward, stood before the LORD, and said, 'I will entice him.'

"The LORD asked him, 'How?'

²¹ "So he said, 'I will go and become a lying spirit in the mouth of all his prophets.'

"Then He said, 'You will entice him and also prevail. Go and do that.'

ᵃ**18:13** LXX, Vg add *to me*; 1 Kg 22:14   ᵇ**18:14** LXX reads *we*; 1 Kg 22:15

²² "Now, you see, the LORD has put a lying spirit into the mouth of^a these prophets of yours, and the LORD has pronounced disaster against you."

Ahab Persecutes Micaiah

²³ Then Zedekiah son of Chenaanah came up, hit Micaiah in the face, and demanded, "Did^b the Spirit of the LORD leave me to speak to you?"

²⁴ Micaiah replied, "You will soon see when you go to hide yourself in an inner chamber on that day."

²⁵ Then the king of Israel ordered, "Take Micaiah and return him to Amon, the governor of the city, and to Joash, the king's son, ²⁶ and say, 'This is what the king says: Put this guy in prison and feed him only bread and water^c until I come back safely.'"

²⁷ But Micaiah said, "If you ever return safely, the LORD has not spoken through me." Then he said, "Listen, all you people!"

Ahab's Disguise

²⁸ Then the king of Israel and Judah's King Jehoshaphat went up to Ramoth-gilead. ²⁹ But the king of Israel said to Jehoshaphat, "I will disguise myself and go into battle, but you wear your royal attire." So the king of Israel disguised himself, and they went into battle.

³⁰ Now the king of Aram had ordered his chariot commanders, "Do not fight with anyone, small or great, except the king of Israel." ³¹ When the chariot commanders saw Jehoshaphat, they shouted, "He must be the king of Israel!" So they turned to attack him, but Jehoshaphat cried out and the LORD helped him. God drew them away from him. ³² When the chariot commanders saw that he was not the king of Israel, they turned back from pursuing him.

Ahab's Random Death

³³ But a man drew his bow without taking special aim and struck the king of Israel through the joints of his armor. So he said to the charioteer, "Turn around and take me out of the battle,^d for I am badly wounded!" ³⁴ The battle raged throughout that day, and the king of Israel propped himself up in his chariot facing the Arameans until evening. Then he died at sunset.

Jehu Rebukes Jehoshaphat

19 Jehoshaphat king of Judah returned to his home in Jerusalem in peace. ² Then Jehu son of Hanani the seer went out to confront him^e and said to King Jehoshaphat, "Do you help the wicked and love those who hate the LORD? Because of this, the LORD's wrath is on you. ³ However, some good is found in you, for you have removed the •Asherah poles from the land and have decided to seek God."

Jehoshaphat's Reforms

⁴ Jehoshaphat lived in Jerusalem, and once again he went out among the people from Beer-sheba to the hill country of Ephraim and brought them back to the LORD God of their ancestors. ⁵ He appointed judges in all the fortified cities of the land of Judah, city by city. ⁶ Then he said to the judges, "Consider what you are doing, for you do not judge for man, but for the LORD, who is with you in the matter of judgment. ⁷ And now, may the terror of the LORD be on you. Watch what you do, for there is no injustice or partiality or taking bribes with the LORD our God."

⁸ Jehoshaphat also appointed in Jerusalem some of the Levites and priests and some of the heads of the Israelite families for ⌐rendering⌐ the LORD's judgments and for ⌐settling⌐ disputes of the residents of ᵃ Jerusalem. ⁹ He commanded them, saying, "In the •fear of the LORD, with integrity, and with a whole heart, you are to do the following: ¹⁰ for every dispute that comes to you from your brothers who dwell in their cities—whether it regards differences of bloodguilt, law, commandment, statutes, or judgments—you are to warn them, so they will not incur guilt before the LORD and wrath will not come on you and your brothers. Do this, and you will not incur guilt.

¹¹ "Note that Amariah, the chief priest, is over you in all matters related to the LORD, and Zebadiah son of Ishmael, the ruler of the house of Judah, in all matters related to the king, and the Levites are officers in your presence. Be strong; may the LORD be with those who do what is good."

Jehoshaphat's War against Eastern Enemies

20 After this, the Moabites and Ammonites, together with some of the Meunites,ᵇ came ⌐to fight⌐ against Jehoshaphat. ² People came and told Jehoshaphat, "A vast multitude from beyond the Dead Sea and from Edomᶜ has come ⌐to fight⌐ against you; they are already in Hazazon-tamar" (that is, En-gedi). ³ Jehoshaphat was afraid, so he resolved to seek the LORD. So he proclaimed a fast for all Judah, ⁴ who gathered to seek the LORD. They even came from all the cities of Judah to seek Him.

Jehoshaphat's Prayer

⁵ Then Jehoshaphat stood in the assembly of Judah and Jerusalem in the LORD's temple before the new courtyard. ⁶ He said:

LORD God of our ancestors, are You not the God who is in heaven, and do You not rule over all the kingdoms of the nations? Power and might are in Your hand, and no one can stand against You. ⁷ Are You not our God who drove out the inhabitants of this land before Your people Israel and who gave it forever to the descendants of Abraham Your friend? ⁸ They have lived in the land and have built You a sanctuary in it for Your name and have said, ⁹ "If disaster comes on us—sword or judgment, pestilence or famine—we will stand before this temple and before You, for Your name is in this temple. We will cry out to You because of our distress, and You will hear and deliver."

¹⁰ Now here are the Ammonites, Moabites, and ⌐the inhabitants of⌐ Mount Seir. You did not let Israel invade them when Israel came out of the land of Egypt, but Israel turned away from them and did not destroy them. ¹¹ Look how they repay us by coming to drive us out of Your possession that You gave us as an inheritance. ¹² Our God, will You not judge them? For we are powerless before this vast multitude that comes ⌐to fight⌐ against us. We do not know what to do, but we look to You.ᵈ

God's Answer

¹³ All Judah was standing before the LORD with their infants, their wives,

---

ᵃ **19:8** LXX, Vg; MT reads *disputes and they returned to*   ᵇ **20:1** LXX; MT reads *Ammonites*; 2 Ch 26:7   ᶜ **20:2** Some Hb mss, Old Lat; other Hb mss read *Aram*   ᵈ **20:12** Lit *but on You our eyes*

and their children. ¹⁴ In the midst of the congregation, the Spirit of the LORD came on Jahaziel (son of Zechariah, son of Benaiah, son of Jeiel, son of Mattaniah, a Levite from •Asaph's descendants), ¹⁵ and he said, "Listen carefully, all Judah and you inhabitants of Jerusalem, and King Jehoshaphat. This is what the LORD says: 'Do not be afraid or discouraged because of this vast multitude, for the battle is not yours, but God's. ¹⁶ Tomorrow, go down against them. You will see them coming up the ascent of Ziz, and you will find them at the end of the valley facing the Wilderness of Jeruel. ¹⁷ You do not have to fight this ⌊battle⌋. Position yourselves, stand still, and see the salvation of the LORD. ⌊He is⌋ with you, Judah and Jerusalem. Do not be afraid or discouraged. Tomorrow, go out to face them, for the LORD is with you.'"

Jehoshaphat and Judah Praise God

¹⁸ Then Jehoshaphat bowed with his face to the ground, and all Judah and the inhabitants of Jerusalem fell down before the LORD to worship Him. ¹⁹ Then the Levites from the sons of the Kohathites and the Korahites stood up to praise the LORD God of Israel shouting in a loud voice.

Judah Praises God

²⁰ In the morning they got up early and went out to the wilderness of Tekoa. As they were about to go out, Jehoshaphat stood and said, "Hear me, Judah and you inhabitants of Jerusalem. Believe in the LORD your God, and you will be established; believe in His prophets, and you will succeed." ²¹ Then he consulted with the people and appointed some to sing for the LORD and some to praise the splendor of ⌊His⌋ holiness. When they went out in front of the armed forces, they kept singing:ᵃ

> Give thanks to the LORD,
> for His faithful love
>   endures forever.

God Gives Victory

²² The moment they began ⌊their⌋ shouts and praises, the LORD set an ambush against the Ammonites, Moabites, and ⌊the inhabitants of⌋ Mount Seir who came ⌊to fight⌋ against Judah, and they were defeated. ²³ The Ammonites and Moabites turned against the inhabitants of Mount Seir and completely annihilated them. When they had finished with the inhabitants of Seir, they helped destroy each other.

Judah's Plunder

²⁴ When Judah came to a place overlooking the wilderness, they looked toward the multitude, and there were corpses lying on the ground; nobody had escaped. ²⁵ Then Jehoshaphat and his people went to gather the plunder. They found among themᵇ an abundance of goods on the bodiesᶜ and valuable items. So they stripped them until nobody could carry any more. They were gathering the plunder for three days because there was so much. ²⁶ They assembled in the Valley of Beracahᵈ on the fourth day, for there they praised the LORD. Therefore, that place is still called the Valley of Beracah today.

²⁷ Then all the men of Judah and Jerusalem turned back with Jehoshaphat at their head, returning joyfully to Jerusalem, for the LORD enabled them to rejoice over their enemies. ²⁸ So they came into Jerusalem to the LORD's temple with harps, lyres, and trumpets.

ᵃ**20:21** Lit *saying* ᵇ**20:25** LXX reads *found cattle* ᶜ**20:25** Some Hb mss, Old Lat, Vg read *goods, garments*
ᵈ**20:26** = Blessing

²⁹ The terror of God was on all the kingdoms of the lands when they heard that the LORD had fought against the enemies of Israel. ³⁰ Then Jehoshaphat's kingdom was quiet, for his God gave him rest on every side.

Summary of Jehoshaphat's Reign

³¹ Jehoshaphat became king over Judah. He was 35 years old when he became king; he reigned 25 years in Jerusalem. His mother's name was Azubah daughter of Shilhi. ³² He walked in the way of Asa his father; he did not turn away from it but did what was right in the LORD's sight. ³³ However, the •high places were not taken away; the people had not yet determined in their hearts ⌊to worship⌋ the God of their ancestors.

³⁴ The rest of the events of Jehoshaphat's ⌊reign⌋ from beginning to end are written about in the Events of Jehu son of Hanani, which is recorded in the Book of Israel's Kings.

Jehoshaphat's Fleet of Ships

³⁵ After this, Judah's King Jehoshaphat made an alliance with Israel's King Ahaziah, who was guilty of wrongdoing. ³⁶ Jehoshaphat formed an alliance with him to make ships to go to Tarshish, and they made the ships in Ezion-geber. ³⁷ Then Eliezer son of Dodavahu of Mareshah prophesied against Jehoshaphat, saying, "Because you formed an alliance with Ahaziah, the LORD has broken up what you have made." So the ships were wrecked and were not able to go to Tarshish.

Judah's Evil King Jehoram

21 Jehoshaphat rested with his fathers and was buried with his fathers in the city of David. His son Jehoramᵃ be-

came king in his place. ² He had brothers, sons of Jehoshaphat: Azariah, Jehiel, Zechariah, Azariah, Michael, and Shephatiah; all these were the sons of Jehoshaphat, king of Judah.ᵇ ³ Their father had given them many gifts of silver, gold, and valuable things, along with fortified cities in Judah, but he gave the kingdom to Jehoram because he was the firstborn. ⁴ When Jehoram had established himself over his father's kingdom, he strengthened his position by killing with the sword all his brothers as well as some of the princes of Israel.

King Jehoram's Reign Summarized

⁵ Jehoram was 32 years old when he became king; he reigned eight years in Jerusalem. ⁶ He walked in the way of the kings of Israel, as the house of Ahab had done, for Ahab's daughter was his wife. He <u>did what was evil</u> in the LORD's sight, ⁷ but because of the covenant the LORD had made with David, He was unwilling to destroy the house of David since the LORD had promised to give a lamp to David and to his sons forever.

⁸ During Jehoram's reign, Edom rebelled against Judah's domination and appointed their own king. ⁹ So Jehoram crossed ⌊into Edom⌋ with his commanders and all his chariots. Then at night he set out to attack the Edomites who had surrounded him and the chariot commanders. ¹⁰ So Edom is still in rebellion against Judah's domination today. Libnah also rebelled at that time against his domination because he had abandoned the LORD God of his ancestors. ¹¹ Jehoram also built •high places in the hillsᶜ of Judah, and he caused the inhabitants of Jerusalem to prostitute themselves, and he led Judah astray.

ᵃ**21:1** = Joram ᵇ**21:2** Some Hb mss, LXX, Syr, Vg, Arabic; other Hb mss read *Israel* ᶜ**21:11** Some Hb mss, LXX, Vg read *cities*

Elijah's Warning Letter to Jehoram

12 Then a letter came to Jehoram from Elijah the prophet, saying:

This is what the LORD God of your ancestor David says: "Because you have not walked in the ways of your father Jehoshaphat or in the ways of Asa king of Judah 13 but have walked in the way of the kings of Israel, have caused Judah and the inhabitants of Jerusalem to prostitute themselves like the house of Ahab prostituted itself, and also have killed your brothers, your father's family, who were better than you, 14 the LORD is now about to strike your people, your sons, your wives, and all your possessions with a horrible affliction. 15 You yourself ⌊will be struck⌋ with many illnesses, including a disease of the intestines, until your intestines come out day after day because of the disease."

Jehoram's Last Days: Defeat and Disease

16 The LORD put it into the mind of the Philistines and the Arabs who live near the •Cushites to attack Jehoram. 17 So they went to war against Judah and invaded it. They carried off all the possessions found in the king's palace and also his sons and wives; not a son was left to him except Jehoahaz,[a] his youngest son.

18 After all these things, the LORD afflicted him in his intestines with an incurable disease. 19 This continued day after day until two full years passed. Then his intestines came out because of his disease, and he died from severe[b] ill-

nesses. But his people did not hold a fire in his honor like the fire in honor of his fathers.

20 Jehoram was 32 years old when he became king; he reigned eight years in Jerusalem. He died to no one's regret[c] and was buried in the city of David but not in the tombs of the kings.

Judah's Evil King Ahaziah

22 Then the inhabitants of Jerusalem made Ahaziah, his youngest son, king in his place, because the troops that had come with the Arabs to the camp had killed all the older sons.[d] So Ahaziah son of Jehoram became king of Judah. 2 Ahaziah was 22[e] years old when he became king; he reigned one year in Jerusalem. His mother's name was Athaliah, granddaughter[f] of Omri.

3 He walked in the ways of the house of Ahab, for his mother gave him evil advice. 4 So he did what was evil in the LORD's sight like the house of Ahab, for they were his advisers after the death of his father, to his destruction. 5 He also followed their advice and went with Joram[g] son of Israel's King Ahab to fight against Hazael, king of Aram, in Ramoth-gilead. The Arameans[h] wounded Joram, 6 so he returned to Jezreel to recover from the wounds they inflicted on him in Ramoth-gilead[i] when he fought against Aram's King Hazael. Then Judah's King Ahaziah[j] son of Jehoram went down to Jezreel to visit Joram son of Ahab since Joram was ill.

Jehu Kills Ahaziah

7 With his going to Joram, Ahaziah's downfall was from God, for when Ahaziah went, he went out with Joram to

---

a21:17 LXX, Syr, Tg read *Ahaziah*; = Jehoahaz b21:19 Lit *evil* c21:20 Lit *He walked in no desirability* d22:1 Lit *the former ones* e22:2 Some LXX mss, Syr; MT reads *42*; 2 Kg 8:26 f22:2 Lit *daughter* g22:5 = Jehoram (also vv. 6-7) h22:5 Lit *Rammites*; = Arameans; 2 Kg 8:28 i22:6 Lit *in Ramah* j22:6 Some Hb mss, LXX, Syr, Vg; other Hb mss read *Azariah*; 2 Kg 8:29

meet Jehu son of Nimshi, whom the LORD had anointed to destroy the house of Ahab. [8] So it happened when Jehu executed judgment on the house of Ahab, he found the rulers of Judah and the sons of Ahaziah's brothers who were serving Ahaziah, and he killed them. [9] Then Jehu looked for Ahaziah, and Jehu's soldiers captured him (he was hiding in Samaria). Then they brought him to Jehu, and they killed him. They buried him, for they said, "He is the grandson of Jehoshaphat who sought the LORD with all his heart." So the house of Ahaziah had no one to exercise power over the kingdom.

Athaliah Usurps the Throne

[10] When Athaliah, Ahaziah's mother, saw that her son was dead, she proceeded to annihilate all the royal heirs[a] of the house of Judah. [11] Jehoshabeath,[b] the king's daughter, rescued Joash son of Ahaziah from the king's sons who were being killed and put him and his nurse in a bedroom. Now Jehoshabeath was the daughter of King Jehoram and the wife of Jehoiada the priest. Since she was Ahaziah's sister, she hid Joash from Athaliah so that she did not kill him. [12] While Athaliah ruled over the land, he was hiding with them in God's temple six years.

Priest Jehoiada Overthrows Queen Athaliah

23 Then, in the seventh year, Jehoiada summoned his courage and took the commanders of hundreds into a covenant with him: Azariah son of Jeroham, Ishmael son of Jehohanan, Azariah son of Obed, Maaseiah son of Adaiah, and Elishaphat son of Zichri. [2] They made a circuit throughout Judah.

They gathered the Levites from all the cities of Judah and the heads of the families of Israel, and they came to Jerusalem.

Priest Jehoiada Protects Young King Joash

[3] Then the whole assembly made a covenant with the king in God's temple. Jehoiada said to them, "Here is the king's son! He must reign, just as the LORD promised concerning David's sons. [4] This is what you are to do: one third of you, priests and Levites who are coming on duty on the Sabbath, are to be gatekeepers. [5] A third are to be at the king's palace, and a third are to be at the Foundation Gate, and all the troops will be in the courtyards of the LORD's temple. [6] No one is to enter the LORD's temple but the priests and those Levites who serve; they may enter because they are holy, but all the people are to obey the requirement of the LORD. [7] You must completely surround the king with weapons in hand. Anyone who enters the temple is to be put to death. You must be with the king in all his daily tasks."[c]

[8] So the commanders of hundreds did everything Jehoiada the priest commanded. They each brought their men—those coming on duty on the Sabbath and those going off duty on the Sabbath—for Jehoiada the priest did not release the divisions. [9] Jehoiada the priest gave to the commanders of hundreds King David's spears, shields, and quivers[d] that were in God's temple. [10] Then he stationed all the troops with their weapons in hand surrounding the king—from the right side of the temple to the left side, by the altar and by the temple.

Joash Crowned King of Judah

¹¹ They brought out the king's son, put the crown on him, gave him the •testimony, and made him king. Jehoiada and his sons anointed him and cried, "Long live the king!"

¹² When Athaliah heard the noise from the troops, the guards, and those praising the king, she went to the troops in the LORD's temple. ¹³ As she looked, there was the king standing by his pillarᵃ at the entrance. The commanders and the trumpeters were by the king, and all the people of the land were rejoicing and blowing trumpets while the singers with musical instruments were leading the praise. Athaliah tore her clothes and screamed, "Treason, treason!"

Queen Athaliah Executed

¹⁴ Then Jehoiada the priest sent out the commanders of hundreds, those in charge of the army, saying, "Take her out between the ranks, and put anyone who follows her to death by the sword," for the priest had said, "Don't put her to death in the LORD's temple." ¹⁵ So they arrested her, and she went by the entrance of the Horses' Gate to the king's palace, where they put her to death.

Jehoiada's Spiritual Reforms

¹⁶ Then Jehoiada made a covenant between himself, the king, and the people that they would be the LORD's people. ¹⁷ So all the people went to the temple of •Baal and tore it down. They broke its altars and images into pieces and killed Mattan, the priest of Baal, at the altars. ¹⁸ Then Jehoiada put the oversight of the LORD's temple into the hands of the Levitical priests, whom David had appointed over the LORD's temple, to offer •burnt offerings to the LORD as it is writ-

ten in the law of Moses, with rejoicing and song ordained byᵇ David. ¹⁹ He stationed gatekeepers at the gates of the LORD's temple so that nothing unclean could enter for any reason. ²⁰ Then he took ⌐with him⌐ the commanders of hundreds, the nobles, the governors of the people, and all the people of the land and brought the king down from the LORD's temple. They entered the king's palace through the upper ⌐gate⌐ and seated the king on the throne of the kingdom. ²¹ All the people of the land rejoiced, and the city was quiet, for they had put Athaliah to death by the sword.

Judah's King Joash: A Mixed Reign

24 Joash was seven years old when he became king; he reigned 40 years in Jerusalem. His mother's name was Zibiah; ⌐she was⌐ from Beer-sheba. ² Throughout the time of Jehoiada the priest, Joash did what was right in the LORD's sight. ³ Jehoiada acquired two wives for him, and he was the father of sons and daughters.

Joash Repairs Temple

⁴ Afterwards, Joash took it to heart to renovate the LORD's temple. ⁵ So he gathered the priests and Levites and said, "Go out to the cities of Judah and collect money from all Israel to repair the temple of your God as needed year by year, and do it quickly."

Joash Hurries Collection

However, the Levites did not hurry. ⁶ So the king called Jehoiada the high ⌐priest⌐ and said, "Why haven't you required the Levites to bring from Judah and Jerusalem the tax ⌐imposed by⌐ the LORD's servant Moses and the assembly

ᵃ**23:13** LXX reads *post*   ᵇ**23:18** Lit *song on the hands of*

of Israel for the tent of the testimony? [7] For the sons of that wicked Athaliah broke into the LORD's temple and even used the sacred things of the LORD's temple for the •Baals."

[8] At the king's command a chest was made and placed outside the gate of the LORD's temple. [9] Then a proclamation was issued in Judah and Jerusalem that the tax God's servant Moses ⌊imposed⌋ on Israel in the wilderness be brought to the LORD. [10] All the leaders and all the people rejoiced, brought ⌊the tax⌋, and put it in the chest until it was full. [11] Whenever the chest was brought by the Levites to the king's overseers, and when they saw that there was a large amount of money, the king's secretary and the high priest's deputy came and emptied the chest, picked it up, and returned it to its place. They did this daily and gathered the money in abundance. [12] Then the king and Jehoiada gave it to those in charge of the labor on the LORD's temple, who were hiring masons and carpenters to renovate the LORD's temple, also blacksmiths and coppersmiths to repair the LORD's temple.

Temple Repairs Progress

[13] The workmen did their work, and through them the repairs progressed. They restored God's temple to its specifications and reinforced it. [14] When they finished, they presented the rest of the money to the king and Jehoiada, who made articles for the LORD's temple with it—articles for ministry and for making •burnt offerings, and ladles[a] and articles of gold and silver. They regularly offered burnt offerings in the LORD's temple throughout Jehoiada's life.

Joash's Apostasy

[15] Jehoiada died when he was old and full of days; he was 130 years old at his death. [16] He was buried in the city of David with the kings because he had done ⌊what was⌋ good in Israel with respect to God and His temple.

[17] However, after Jehoiada died, the rulers of Judah came and paid homage to the king. Then the king listened to them, [18] and they abandoned the temple of the LORD God of their ancestors and served the •Asherah poles and the idols. So there was wrath against Judah and Jerusalem for this guilt of theirs. [19] Nevertheless, He sent them prophets to bring them back to the LORD; they admonished them, but they would not listen.

Prophet Zechariah Stoned

[20] The Spirit of God took control of[b] Zechariah son of Jehoiada the priest. He stood above the people and said to them, "This is what God says: 'Why are you transgressing the LORD's commands and you do not prosper? Because you have abandoned the LORD, He has abandoned you.'" [21] But they conspired against him and stoned him at the king's command in the courtyard of the LORD's temple. [22] King Joash didn't remember the kindness that Zechariah's father Jehoiada had extended to him, but killed his son. While he was dying, he said, "May the LORD see and demand an account."

Arameans Invade Judah

[23] At the turn of the year, an Aramean army went to war against Joash. They entered Judah and Jerusalem and destroyed all the leaders of the people among them and sent all the plunder to the king of Damascus. [24] Although the

---

[a]**24:14** Or *dishes*, or *spoons*; lit *palms*   [b]**24:20** Lit *God clothed*; Jdg 6:34; 1 Ch 12:18

Aramean army came with only a few men, the LORD handed over a vast army to them because the people of Judah had abandoned the LORD God of their ancestors. So they executed judgment on Joash.

Joash Assassinated

25 When the Arameans saw that Joash had many wounds, they left him. <u>His servants conspired against him, and killed him on his bed, because he had shed the blood of the sons of Jehoiada the priest</u>. So he died, and they buried him in the city of David, but they did not bury him in the tombs of the kings. 26 Those who conspired against him were Zabad, son of the Ammonite woman Shimeath, and Jehozabad, son of the Moabite woman Shimrith.[a] 27 Concerning his sons, the many •oracles about him, and the restoration of the LORD's temple, they are recorded in the Writing of the Book of the Kings. His son Amaziah became king in his place.

Judah's King Amaziah

25 Amaziah became king ⌊when he was⌋ 25 years old; he reigned 29 years in Jerusalem. His mother's name was Jehoaddan; ⌊she was⌋ from Jerusalem. 2 <u>He did what was right in the LORD's sight but not completely.</u>
3 As soon as the kingdom was firmly in his grasp,[b] he executed his servants who had murdered his father the king. 4 However, he did not put their children to death, because—as it is written in the Law, in the book of Moses, where the LORD commanded—"Fathers must not die because of children, and children must not die because of fathers, but each one will die for his own sin."

Amaziah's Campaign against Edom

5 Then Amaziah gathered Judah and assembled them according to patriarchal family, according to commanders of thousands, and according to commanders of hundreds. He numbered those 20 years old or more for all Judah and Benjamin. He found there to be 300,000 choice men who could serve in the army, bearing spear and shield. 6 Then for 7,500 pounds[c] of silver he hired 100,000 brave warriors from Israel.

Prophet's Warning about Ephraimites

7 However, a man of God came to him and said, "King, do not let Israel's army go with you, for the LORD is not with Israel—all the Ephraimites. 8 But if you go ⌊with them⌋, do it! Be strong for battle! ⌊But⌋ God will make you stumble before the enemy, for God has the power to help or to make one stumble."
9 Then Amaziah said to the man of God, "What should I do about the 7,500 pounds[c] of silver I gave to Israel's division?"
The man of God replied, "The LORD is able to give you much more than this."
10 So Amaziah released the division that came to him from Ephraim to go home. But they got very angry with Judah and returned home in a fierce rage.

Amaziah Defeats Edomites

11 Amaziah strengthened his position and led his people to the Valley of Salt. He struck down 10,000 Seirites,[d] 12 and the Judahites captured 10,000 alive. They took them to the top of a cliff where they threw them off, and all of them were dashed to pieces.

---

[a] 24:26 = Shomer; 2 Kg 12:21   [b] 25:3 LXX, Syr; MT reads was strong on him; 1 Kg 14:4   [c] 25:6 Lit 100 talents
[d] 25:11 = Edomites

Ephraimites Raid Judah

13 As for the men of the division that Amaziah sent back so they would not go with him into battle, they raided the cities of Judah from Samaria to Beth-horon, struck down 3,000 of their people, and took a great deal of plunder.

King Amaziah Worships Edomite Gods

14 After Amaziah came from the attack on the Edomites, he brought the gods of the Seirites[a] and set them up as his gods. He worshiped before them and burned incense to them.

God's Prophet Warns Amaziah

15 So the LORD's anger was against Amaziah, and He sent a prophet to him, who said, "Why have you sought a people's gods that could not deliver their own people from your hand?"

16 While he was still speaking to him, the king asked, "Have we made you the king's counselor? Stop, why should you lose your life?"

So the prophet stopped, but he said, "I know that God intends to destroy you, because you have done this and have not listened to my advice."

Israel's King Joash Warns Amaziah

17 King Amaziah of Judah took counsel and sent ᵢwordᵢ to Jehoash[b] son of Jehoahaz, son of Jehu, king of Israel, saying, "Come, let us meet face to face."

18 King Jehoash of Israel sent ᵢwordᵢ to King Amaziah of Judah, saying, "The thistle that was in Lebanon sent ᵢa messageᵢ to the cedar that was in Lebanon, saying, 'Give your daughter to my son as a wife.' Then a wild animal that was in Lebanon passed by and trampled the thistle. 19 You have said, 'Look, I[c] have defeated Edom,' and you have become overconfident that you will get glory. Now stay at home. Why stir up such trouble so that you fall and Judah with you?"

Israel Defeats Judah

20 But Amaziah would not listen, for this ᵢturn of eventsᵢ was from God in order to hand them over to ᵢtheir enemiesᵢ because they went after the gods of Edom. 21 So King Jehoash of Israel advanced. He and King Amaziah of Judah faced off at Beth-shemesh in Judah. 22 Judah was routed before Israel, and each fled to his own tent. 23 King Jehoash of Israel captured Judah's King Amaziah son of Joash, son of Jehoahaz,[d] at Beth-shemesh. Then Jehoash took him to Jerusalem and broke down 200 yards[e] of Jerusalem's wall from the Ephraim Gate to the Corner Gate.[f] 24 He took all the gold, silver, all the utensils that were found with Obed-edom in God's temple, the treasures of the king's palace, and the hostages. Then he returned to Samaria.

Amaziah's Death

25 Judah's King Amaziah son of Joash lived 15 years after the death of Israel's King Jehoash son of Jehoahaz. 26 The rest of the events of Amaziah's ᵢreignᵢ, from beginning to end, are written about in the Book of the Kings of Judah and Israel.

27 From the time Amaziah turned from following the LORD, a conspiracy was formed against him in Jerusalem, and he fled to Lachish. However, ᵢmenᵢ were sent after him to Lachish, and they put him to death there. 28 They carried him

---

ᵃ**25:14** = Edomites   ᵇ**25:17** = Joash   ᶜ**25:19** Some LXX mss, Old Lat, Tg, Vg; MT reads *you*   ᵈ**25:23** = Ahaziah
ᵉ**25:23** Lit *400 cubits*   ᶠ**25:23** Some Hb mss; other Hb mss read *to Happoneh*; 2 Kg 14:13

back on horses and buried him with his fathers in the city of Judah.ᵃ

Judah's King Uzziah: A Good Start

26 All the people of Judah took Uzziah,ᵇ who was 16 years old, and made him king in place of his father Amaziah. ² He rebuilt Elothᶜ and restored it to Judah after ⌐Amaziah⌐ the king rested with his fathers.

³ Uzziah was 16 years old when he became king; he reigned 52 years in Jerusalem. His mother's name was Jecoliah; ⌐she was⌐ from Jerusalem. ⁴ He did what was right in the LORD's sight as his father Amaziah had done. ⁵ He sought God throughout the lifetime of Zechariah, the teacher of the •fearᵈ of God. During the time that he sought the LORD, God gave him success.

Uzziah's Victories

⁶ Uzziah went out to wage war against the Philistines, and he tore down the wall of Gath, the wall of Jabneh, and the wall of Ashdod. Then he built cities in ⌐the vicinity of⌐ Ashdod and among the Philistines. ⁷ God helped him against the Philistines, the Arabs that live in Gurbaal, and the Meunites. ⁸ The Ammonitesᵉ gave Uzziah tribute money, and his fame spread as far as the entrance of Egypt, for ⌐God⌐ made ⌐him⌐ very powerful. ⁹ Uzziah built towers in Jerusalem at the Corner Gate, the Valley Gate, and the corner buttress, and he fortified them. ¹⁰ Since he had many cattle both in the lowlands and the plain, he built towers in the desert and dug many wells. And since he was a lover of the soil, he had farmers and vinedressers in the hills and in the fertile lands.ᶠ

Uzziah's War Machine

¹¹ Uzziah had an army equipped for combat that went out to war by division according to their assignments, as recorded by Jeiel the court secretary and Maaseiah the officer under the authority of Hananiah, one of the king's commanders. ¹² The total number of heads of families was 2,600 brave warriors. ¹³ Under their authority was an army of 307,500 equipped for combat, a powerful force to help the king against the enemy. ¹⁴ Uzziah provided the entire army with shields, spears, helmets, armor, bows and slingstones. ¹⁵ He made skillfully designed devices in Jerusalem to shoot arrows and ⌐catapult⌐ large stones for use on the towers and on the corners. So his fame spread even to distant places, for he was marvelously helped until he became strong.

Uzziah Becomes Arrogant

¹⁶ But when he became strong, he grew arrogant and it led to his own destruction. He acted unfaithfully against the LORD his God by going into the LORD's sanctuary to burn incense on the incense altar. ¹⁷ Azariah the priest, along with 80 brave priests of the LORD, went in after him. ¹⁸ They took their stand against King Uzziah and said, "Uzziah, you have no right to offer incense to the LORD—only the consecrated priests, the descendants of Aaron, have the right to offer incense. Leave the sanctuary, for you have acted unfaithfully! You will not receive honor from the LORD God."

Uzziah's Skin Disease

¹⁹ Uzziah, with a censer in his hand to offer incense, was enraged. But when he became enraged with the priests, in the

ᵃ**25:28** Some Hb mss read *city of David;* 2 Kg 14:20 ᵇ**26:1** = Azariah ᶜ**26:2** LXX, Syr, Vg read *Elath;* 2 Kg 14:22 ᵈ**26:5** Some Hb mss, LXX, Syr, Tg, Arabic; other Hb mss, Vg read *visions* ᵉ**26:8** LXX reads *Meunites* ᶠ**26:10** Or *in Carmel*

presence of the priests in the LORD's temple beside the altar of incense, a skin disease broke out on his forehead. ²⁰ Then Azariah the chief priest and all the priests turned to him and saw that he was diseased on his forehead. They rushed him out of there. He himself also hurried to get out because the LORD had afflicted him. ²¹ So King Uzziah was diseased to the time of his death. He lived in quarantine[a] with a serious skin disease and was excluded from access to the LORD's temple, while his son Jotham was over the king's household governing the people of the land.

²² Now the prophet Isaiah son of Amoz wrote about the rest of the events of Uzziah's ⌊reign⌋, from beginning to end. ²³ Uzziah rested with his fathers, and he was buried with his fathers in the burial ground of the kings' cemetery, for they said, "He has a skin disease." His son Jotham became king in his place.

Judah's King Jotham

27 Jotham was 25 years old when he became king; he reigned 16 years in Jerusalem. His mother's name was Jerushah daughter of Zadok. ² He did what was right in the LORD's sight as his father Uzziah had done, except that he didn't enter the LORD's sanctuary. However, the people still behaved corruptly.

Jotham's Achievements

³ Jotham built the Upper Gate of the LORD's temple, and he built extensively on the wall of Ophel. ⁴ He also built cities in the hill country of Judah and fortresses and towers in the forests. ⁵ He waged war against the king of the Ammonites. He overpowered the Ammonites, and that year they gave him 7,500 pounds[b] of silver, 50,000 bushels[c] of wheat, and 50,000 bushels[c] of barley. They paid him the same in the second and third years. ⁶ So Jotham strengthened himself because he did not waver in obeying[d] the LORD his God.

⁷ As for the rest of the events of Jotham's ⌊reign⌋, along with all his wars and his ways, note that they are written about in the Book of the Kings of Israel and Judah. ⁸ He was 25 years old when he became king; he reigned 16 years in Jerusalem. ⁹ Jotham rested with his fathers and was buried in the city of David. His son Ahaz became king in his place.

Judah's Evil King Ahaz

28 Ahaz was 20 years old when he became king; he reigned 16 years in Jerusalem. He did not do what was right in the LORD's sight like his forefather David, ² for he walked in the ways of the kings of Israel and made cast images of the •Baals. ³ He burned incense in the Valley of Hinnom and burned his children in[e] the fire, imitating the detestable practices of the nations the LORD had dispossessed before the Israelites. ⁴ He sacrificed and burned incense on the •high places, on the hills, and under every green tree.

God Gives King Ahaz to Kings of Aram and Israel

⁵ So the LORD his God handed Ahaz over to the king of Aram. He attacked him and took many captives to Damascus.

Ahaz was also handed over to the king of Israel, who struck him with great force: ⁶ Pekah son of Remaliah killed 120,000 in Judah in one day—all brave men—because they had abandoned the LORD God of their ancestors. ⁷ An Ephraimite warrior

^a**26:21** Lit *a house of freedom* ^b**27:5** Lit *100 talents* ^c**27:5** Lit *10,000 cors* ^d**27:6** Lit *he established his ways before* ^e**28:3** LXX, Syr, Tg read *and passed his children through*; 2 Kg 16:3

named Zichri killed the king's son Maaseiah, Azrikam governor of the palace, and Elkanah who was second to the king. [8] Then the Israelites took 200,000 captives from their brothers—women, sons, and daughters. They also took a great deal of plunder from them and brought it to Samaria.

Prophet Oded to Israel: "Return the Captives"

[9] A prophet of the LORD named Oded was there. He went out to meet the army that came to Samaria and said to them, "Look, the LORD God of your ancestors handed them over to you because of His wrath against Judah, but you slaughtered them in a rage that has reached heaven. [10] Now you plan to reduce the people of Judah and Jerusalem, male and female, to slavery. Are you not also guilty before the LORD your God? [11] Listen to me and return the captives you took from your brothers, for the LORD's fierce wrath is on you."

[12] So some men who were leaders of the Ephraimites—Azariah son of Johanan, Berechiah son of Meshillemoth, Jehizkiah son of Shallum, and Amasa son of Hadlai—stood in opposition to those coming from the war. [13] They said to them, "You must not bring the captives here, for you plan to bring guilt on us from the LORD to add to our sins and our guilt. For we have much guilt, and fierce wrath is on Israel."

Israel Returns Captives

[14] The army left the captives and the plunder in the presence of the officers and the congregation. [15] Then the men who were designated by name took charge of the captives and provided clothes for their naked ones from the plunder. They clothed them, gave them sandals, food and drink, dressed their wounds, and provided donkeys for all the feeble. The Israelites brought them to Jericho, the City of Palms, among their brothers. Then they returned to Samaria.

King Ahaz Appeals to Assyria

[16] At that time King Ahaz asked the king of Assyria for help.

Edomites and Philistines Attack

[17] The Edomites came again, attacked Judah, and took captives. [18] The Philistines also raided the cities of the Judean foothills and the •Negev of Judah and captured Beth-shemesh, Aijalon, Gederoth, Soco and its villages, Timnah and its villages, Gimzo and its villages, and they lived there. [19] For the LORD humbled Judah because of King Ahaz of Judah,[a] who threw off restraint in Judah and was unfaithful to the LORD.

Even Assyria Attacks

[20] Then Tiglath-pileser[b] king of Assyria came against Ahaz; he oppressed him and did not give him support. [21] Although Ahaz plundered the LORD's temple and the palace of the king and of the rulers and gave the plunder to the king of Assyria, it did not help him.

King Ahaz Continues Idolatry

[22] At the time of his distress, King Ahaz himself became more unfaithful to the LORD. [23] He sacrificed to the gods of Damascus which had defeated him; he said, "Since the gods of the kings of Aram are helping them, I will sacrifice to them so that they will help me." But they were the downfall of him and of all Israel.

[a]**28:19** Some Hb mss; other Hb mss read *Israel* [b]**28:20** MT reads *Tilgath-pilneser*

²⁴ Then Ahaz gathered up the utensils of God's temple, cut them into pieces, shut the doors of the LORD's temple, and made himself altars on every street corner in Jerusalem. ²⁵ He made high places in every city of Judah to offer incense to other gods, and he provoked the God of his ancestors.

Ahaz's Death

²⁶ As for the rest of his deeds and all his ways, from beginning to end, they are written about in the Book of the Kings of Judah and Israel. ²⁷ Ahaz rested with his fathers and was buried in the city, in Jerusalem, and his son Hezekiah became king in his place.

Judah's Good King Hezekiah

29 Hezekiah was 25 years old when he became king; he reigned 29 years in Jerusalem. His mother's name was Abijahᵃ daughter of Zechariah. ² He did what was right in the LORD's sight just as his ancestor David had done.

Hezekiah's Temple Reforms

³ In the first year of his reign, in the first month, he opened the doors of the LORD's temple and repaired them. ⁴ Then he brought in the priests and Levites and gathered them in the eastern public square. ⁵ He said to them, "Hear me, Levites. Consecrate yourselves now and consecrate the temple of the LORD God of your ancestors. Remove everything detestable from the holy place. ⁶ For our fathers were unfaithful and did what is evil in the sight of the LORD our God. They abandoned Him, turned their faces away from the LORD's tabernacle, and turned their backs on Him.ᵇ ⁷ They also closed the doors of the vestibule, extinguished the lamps, did not burn incense, and did not offer •burnt offerings in the holy place of the God of Israel. ⁸ Therefore, the wrath of the LORD was on Judah and Jerusalem, and He made them an object of terror, horror, and hissing, as you see with your own eyes. ⁹ Our fathers fell by the sword, and our sons, our daughters, and our wives are in captivity because of this. ¹⁰ It is in my heart now to make a covenant with the LORD God of Israel so that His fierce wrath may turn away from us. ¹¹ My sons, don't be negligent now, for the LORD has chosen you to stand in His presence, to serve Him, and to be His ministers and burners of incense."

Levites Cleanse Temple

¹² Then the Levites stood up:

Mahath son of Amasai and Joel son of Azariah from the Kohathites;
Kish son of Abdi and Azariah son of Jehallelel from the Merarites;
Joah son of Zimmah and Eden son of Joah from the Gershonites;
¹³ Shimri and Jeuel from the Elizaphanites;
Zechariah and Mattaniah from the Asaphites;
¹⁴ Jehielᶜ and Shimei from the Hemanites;
Shemaiah and Uzziel from the Jeduthunites.

¹⁵ They gathered their brothers together, consecrated themselves, and went according to the king's command by the words of the LORD to cleanse the LORD's temple.

¹⁶ The priests went to the entrance of the LORD's temple to cleanse it. They took all the detestable things they found in the LORD's sanctuary to the courtyard of the LORD's temple. Then the Levites

ᵃ**29:1** = Abi; 2 Kg 18:2   ᵇ**29:6** Lit *and they gave the back of the neck*   ᶜ**29:14** Alt Hb tradition reads *Jehuel*

received them and took them outside to the Kidron Valley. [17] They began the consecration on the first day of the first month, and on the eighth day of the month they came to the vestibule of the LORD's ⌊temple⌋. They consecrated the LORD's temple for eight days, and on the sixteenth day of the first month they finished.

[18] Then they went inside to King Hezekiah and said, "We have cleansed the whole temple of the LORD, the altar of burnt offering and all its utensils, and the table for the rows ⌊of the bread of the Presence⌋ and all its utensils. [19] All the utensils that King Ahaz rejected during his reign when he became unfaithful we have set up and consecrated. They are in front of the altar of the LORD."

Renewal of Temple Worship: Sin Offering

[20] King Hezekiah got up early, gathered the city officials, and went up to the LORD's temple. [21] They brought seven bulls, seven rams, seven lambs, and seven male goats as a •sin offering for the kingdom, for the sanctuary, and for Judah. Then he told the descendants of Aaron, the priests, to offer them on the altar of the LORD. [22] So they slaughtered the bulls, and the priests received the blood and sprinkled it on the altar. They slaughtered the rams and sprinkled the blood on the altar. They slaughtered the lambs and sprinkled the blood on the altar. [23] Then they brought the sin offering goats right into the presence of the king and the congregation, who laid their hands on them. [24] The priests slaughtered the goats and put their blood on the altar for a sin offering, to make •atonement for all Israel, for the king said that the burnt offering and sin offering were for all Israel.

Temple Musicians

[25] Hezekiah stationed the Levites in the LORD's temple with cymbals, harps, and lyres according to the command of David, Gad the king's seer, and Nathan the prophet. For the command was from the LORD through His prophets. [26] The Levites stood with the instruments of David, and the priests with the trumpets.

Hezekiah Orders Burnt Offerings

[27] Then Hezekiah ordered that the burnt offering be offered on the altar. When the burnt offerings began, the song of the LORD and the trumpets began, accompanied by the instruments of David king of Israel. [28] The whole assembly was worshiping, singing the song, and blowing the trumpets—all of this ⌊continued⌋ until the burnt offering was completed. [29] When the burnt offerings were completed, the king and all those present with him bowed down and worshiped. [30] Then King Hezekiah and the officials told the Levites to sing praise to the LORD in the words of David and of •Asaph the seer. So they sang praises with rejoicing and bowed down and worshiped.

[31] Hezekiah concluded, "Now you are consecrated[a] to the LORD. Come near and bring sacrifices and thank offerings to the LORD's temple." So the congregation brought sacrifices and thank offerings, and all those with willing hearts brought burnt offerings. [32] The number of burnt offerings the congregation brought was 70 bulls, 100 rams, and 200 lambs; all these were for a burnt of-

a**29:31** Lit Now you have filled your hands

fering to the LORD. ³³ Six hundred bulls and 3,000 sheep were consecrated.

Levites Assist Priests

³⁴ However, since there were not enough priests, they weren't able to skin all the burnt offerings, so their Levite brothers helped them until the work was finished and until the priests consecrated themselves. For the Levites were more conscientious[a] to consecrate themselves than the priests were. ³⁵ Furthermore, the burnt offerings were abundant, along with the fat of the •fellowship offerings and with the •drink offerings for the burnt offering.

So the service of the LORD's temple was established. ³⁶ Then Hezekiah and all the people rejoiced over how God had prepared the people, for it had come about suddenly.

Hezekiah Schedules Passover

30 Then Hezekiah sent ⌊word⌋ throughout all Israel and Judah, and he also wrote letters to Ephraim and Manasseh to come to the LORD's temple in Jerusalem to observe the •Passover of the LORD God of Israel. ² For the king and his officials and the entire congregation in Jerusalem decided to observe the Passover of the LORD in the second month ³ because they were not able to observe it at the appropriate time, since not enough of the priests had consecrated themselves and the people hadn't been gathered together in Jerusalem. ⁴ The proposal pleased the king and the congregation, ⁵ so they affirmed the proposal and spread the message throughout all Israel, from Beer-sheba to Dan, to come to observe the Passover of the LORD God of Israel in Jerusalem, for they hadn't observed it often,[b] as prescribed.[c]

Invitation to Passover

⁶ So the couriers went throughout Israel and Judah with letters from the hand of the king and his officials, and according to the king's command, saying, "Israelites, return to the LORD God of Abraham, Isaac, and Israel so that He may return to those of you who remain, who have escaped from the grasp of the kings of Assyria. ⁷ Don't be like your fathers and your brothers who were unfaithful to the LORD God of their ancestors so that He made them an object of horror as you yourselves see. ⁸ Don't become obstinate[d] now like your fathers did. Give your allegiance[e] to the LORD, and come to His sanctuary that He has consecrated forever. Serve the LORD your God so that He may turn His fierce wrath away from you, ⁹ for when you return to the LORD, your brothers and your sons ⌊will receive⌋ mercy in the presence of their captors and will return to this land. For the LORD your God is gracious and merciful; He will not turn ⌊His⌋ face away from you if you return to Him."

Some Respond

¹⁰ The couriers traveled from city to city in the land of Ephraim and Manasseh as far as Zebulun, but the <u>inhabitants[f] laughed at them and mocked them.</u> ¹¹ But <u>some from Asher, Manasseh, and Zebulun humbled themselves and came to Jerusalem.</u> ¹² Also, the hand of God was in Judah to give them one heart to carry out the command of the king and his officials by the word of the LORD.

Passover Observed

¹³ A very large assembly of people was gathered in Jerusalem to observe the Festival of Unleavened Bread in the second month. ¹⁴ They proceeded to take

---

^a**29:34** Lit *upright of heart*; Ps 32:11; 64:10   ^b**30:5** Or *in great numbers*   ^c**30:5** Lit *often, according to what is written*   ^d**30:8** Lit *Don't stiffen your neck*   ^e**30:8** Lit *hand*   ^f**30:10** Lit *but they*

away the altars that were in Jerusalem, and they took away the incense altars and threw them into the Kidron Valley. [15] They slaughtered the Passover lamb on the fourteenth day of the second month. The priests and Levites were ashamed, and they consecrated themselves and brought •burnt offerings to the LORD's temple. [16] They stood at their prescribed posts, according to the law of Moses the man of God.

The Unclean Received

The priests sprinkled the blood ιreceivedι from the hand of the Levites, [17] for there were many in the assembly who had not consecrated themselves, and so the Levites were in charge of slaughtering the Passover ιlambsι for every unclean person to consecrate ιthe lambsι to the LORD. [18] For a large number of the people—many from Ephraim, Manasseh, Issachar, and Zebulun—were unclean, yet they had eaten the Passover contrary to what was written. But Hezekiah had interceded for them, saying, "May the good LORD provide •atonement on behalf of [19] whoever sets his whole heart on seeking God, the LORD God of his ancestors, even though not according to the purification ιrulesι of the sanctuary." [20] So the LORD heard Hezekiah and healed the people. [21] The Israelites who were present in Jerusalem observed the Festival of Unleavened Bread seven days with great joy, and the Levites and the priests praised the LORD day after day with loud instruments. [22] Then Hezekiah encouraged[a] all the Levites who performed skillfully before the LORD. They ate the appointed feast for seven days, sacrificing •fellowship offerings and giving thanks to the LORD God of their ancestors.

[23] The whole congregation decided to observe seven more days, so they observed seven days with joy, [24] for Hezekiah king of Judah contributed 1,000 bulls and 7,000 sheep for the congregation. Also, the officials contributed 1,000 bulls and 10,000 sheep for the congregation, and many priests consecrated themselves. [25] Then the whole assembly of Judah with the priests and Levites, the whole assembly that came from Israel, the foreigners who came from the land of Israel, and those who were living in Judah, rejoiced. [26] Such rejoicing had not been seen in Jerusalem since the days of Solomon son of David, the king of Israel. [27] Then the priests and the Levites stood to bless the people, and God heard their voice, and their prayer came into His holy dwelling place in heaven.

Removal of Idolatry

31 When all this was completed, all Israel who had attended went out to the cities of Judah and broke up the sacred pillars, chopped down the •Asherah poles, and tore down the •high places and altars throughout Judah and Benjamin, as well as in Ephraim and Manasseh, to the last one.[b] Then all the Israelites returned to their cities, each to his own possession.

Offerings for Levites

[2] Hezekiah reestablished the divisions of the priests and Levites for the •burnt offerings and •fellowship offerings, for ministry, for giving thanks, and for praise in the gates of the camp of the LORD, each division corresponding to his service among the priests and Levites. [3] The king contributed[c] from his own possessions for the regular morning and eve-

---

[a]**30:22** Lit *spoke to the heart of*   [b]**31:1** Lit *Manasseh, until finishing*   [c]**31:3** Lit *The king's portion*

ning burnt offerings, the burnt offerings of the Sabbaths, of the New Moons, and of the appointed feasts, as written in the law of the LORD.

Contribution to Priests and Levites

[4] He told the people who lived in Jerusalem to give a contribution for the priests and Levites so that they could devote their energy to the law of the LORD. [5] When the word spread, the Israelites gave liberally of the best of the grain, wine, oil, honey, and of all the produce of the field, and they brought an abundant tenth of everything. [6] As for the Israelites and Judahites who lived in the cities of Judah, they also ˻brought˼ a tenth of the cattle and sheep, and a tenth of the dedicated things that were consecrated to the LORD their God. They gathered ˻them˼ into large piles. [7] In the third month they began building up the piles, and they finished in the seventh month. [8] When Hezekiah and his officials came and viewed the piles, they praised the LORD and His people Israel.

Hezekiah Distributes Surplus

[9] Hezekiah asked the priests and Levites about the piles. [10] Azariah, the chief priest of the household of Zadok, answered him, "Since they began bringing the offering to the LORD's temple, we eat and are satisfied and there is plenty left over because the LORD has blessed His people; this abundance is what is left over."

[11] Hezekiah told them to prepare chambers in the LORD's temple, and they prepared ˻them˼. [12] The offering, the tenth, and the dedicated things were brought faithfully. Conaniah the Levite was the officer in charge of them, and his brother Shimei was second. [13] Jehiel, Azaziah, Nahath, Asahel, Jerimoth, Jozabad, Eliel, Ismachiah, Mahath, and Benaiah were deputies under the authority of Conaniah and his brother Shimei by appointment of King Hezekiah and of Azariah the ruler of God's temple.

[14] Kore son of Imnah the Levite, the keeper of the East Gate, was over the freewill offerings to God to distribute the contribution to the LORD and the consecrated things. [15] Eden, Miniamin, Jeshua, Shemaiah, Amariah, and Shecaniah in the cities of the priests were to faithfully distribute ˻it˼ under his authority to their brothers by divisions, whether large or small. [16] In addition, ˻they distributed it˼ to males registered by genealogy three[a] years old and above; to all who would enter the LORD's temple for their daily duty, for their service in their responsibilities according to their divisions. [17] ˻They distributed also˼ to those recorded by genealogy of the priests by their ancestral families and the Levites 20 years old and above, by their responsibilities in their divisions; [18] to those registered by genealogy—with all their infants, wives, sons, and daughters—of the whole assembly (for they had faithfully consecrated themselves as holy); [19] and to the descendants of Aaron, the priests, in the common fields of their cities, in each and every city. ˻There were˼ men who were registered by name to distribute a portion to every male among the priests and to every Levite recorded by genealogy.

[20] Hezekiah did this throughout all Judah. He did what was good and upright and true before the LORD his God. [21] He was diligent in every deed that he began in the service of God's temple, in the law and in the commandment, in order to seek his God, and he prospered.

[a] **31:16** Or *30*; 1 Ch 23:3

Assyria's
King Sennacherib Invades

32 After these faithful deeds, Sennacherib king of Assyria came and entered Judah. He laid siege to the fortified cities and intended[a] to break into them.

Hezekiah Prepares for Siege

2 Hezekiah saw that Sennacherib had come and that he planned[b] war on Jerusalem, 3 so he consulted with his officials and his warriors about stopping up the waters of the springs that were outside the city, and they helped him. 4 Many people gathered and stopped up all the springs and the stream that flowed through the land; they said, "Why should the kings of Assyria come and find plenty of water?" 5 Then Hezekiah strengthened his position by rebuilding the entire broken-down wall and heightening the towers and the other outside wall. He repaired the supporting terraces of the city of David, and made an abundance of weapons and shields.

6 He set military commanders over the people and gathered the people in the square of the city gate. Then he encouraged them,[c] saying, 7 "Be strong and courageous! Don't be afraid or discouraged before the king of Assyria or before all the multitude with him, for there are more with us than with him. 8 He has only human strength,[d] but we have the LORD our God to help us and to fight our battles." So the people relied on the words of King Hezekiah of Judah.

Servants of Sennacherib
Try Psychology

9 After this, while Sennacherib king of Assyria with all his armed forces besieged[e] Lachish, he sent his servants to Jerusalem against King Hezekiah of Judah and against all those of Judah who were in Jerusalem, saying, 10 "This is what King Sennacherib of Assyria says: 'What are you trusting in, you who remain under the siege of Jerusalem? 11 Isn't Hezekiah misleading you to give you over to death by famine and thirst when he says, "The LORD our God will deliver us from the power of the king of Assyria"? 12 Didn't Hezekiah himself remove His •high places and His altars and say to Judah and Jerusalem: "You must worship before one altar, and you must burn incense on it"?

13 " 'Don't you know what I and my fathers have done to all the peoples of the lands? Have any of the national gods of the lands been able to deliver their land from my power? 14 Who among all the gods of these nations that my fathers utterly destroyed was able to deliver his people from my power, that your God should be able to do the same for you? 15 So now, don't let Hezekiah deceive you, and don't let him mislead you like this. Don't believe him, for no god of any nation or kingdom has been able to deliver his people from my power or the power of my fathers. How much less will your gods deliver you from my power!' "

Sennacherib Mocks God

16 His servants said more against the LORD God and against His servant Hezekiah. 17 He also wrote letters to mock the LORD God of Israel, saying against Him:

Just like the national gods of the lands that did not deliver their people from my power, so Hezekiah's God will not deliver His people from my power.

---

[a]**32:1** Lit said to himself [b]**32:2** Lit that his face was for [c]**32:6** Lit he spoke to their hearts [d]**32:8** Lit With him an arm of flesh [e]**32:9** Lit with his dominion was against

¹⁸ Then they called out loudly in Hebrew[a] to the people of Jerusalem who were on the wall to frighten and discourage them in order that he might capture the city. ¹⁹ They spoke against the God of Jerusalem like they had spoken against the gods of the peoples of the land, which were made by human hands.

God Delivers Jerusalem from Sennacherib

God's Angel Defeats Assyrians

²⁰ King Hezekiah and the prophet Isaiah son of Amoz prayed about this and cried out to heaven, ²¹ and the LORD sent an angel who annihilated every brave warrior, leader, and commander in the camp of the king of Assyria. So the king of Assyria returned with shame to his land. He went to the temple of his god, and there some of his own children cut him down with the sword.

²² So the LORD saved Hezekiah and the inhabitants of Jerusalem from the power of King Sennacherib of Assyria and from the power of all others. He gave them rest[b] on every side. ²³ Many were bringing an offering to the LORD to Jerusalem and valuable gifts to King Hezekiah of Judah, and he was exalted in the eyes of all the nations after that.

Hezekiah's Illness and Pride

²⁴ In those days Hezekiah became sick to the point of death, so he prayed to the LORD, and He spoke to him and gave him a miraculous sign. ²⁵ However, because his heart was proud, Hezekiah didn't respond according to the benefit that had come to him. So there was wrath upon him, upon Judah, and upon Jerusalem. ²⁶ Then Hezekiah humbled himself for the pride of his heart—he and the inhabitants of Jerusalem—so the LORD's wrath didn't come on them during Hezekiah's lifetime.

Hezekiah's Wealth and Works

²⁷ Hezekiah had abundant riches and glory, and he made himself treasuries for silver, gold, precious stones, spices, shields, and every desirable item. ²⁸ He made warehouses for the harvest of grain, wine, and oil, and stalls for all kinds of cattle, and pens for flocks. ²⁹ He made cities for himself, and he acquired herds of sheep and cattle in abundance, for God gave him abundant possessions.

³⁰ This same Hezekiah blocked the outlet of the water of the Upper Gihon and channeled it smoothly downward and westward to the city of David. Hezekiah succeeded in everything he did. ³¹ When the ambassadors of Babylon's rulers were sent[c] to him to inquire about the miraculous sign that happened in the land, God left him to test him and discover what was in his heart.

Hezekiah's Death

³² As for the rest of the events of Hezekiah's ⌊reign⌋ and his deeds of faithful love, note that they are written about in the Visions of the Prophet Isaiah son of Amoz, and in the Book of the Kings of Judah and Israel. ³³ Hezekiah rested with his fathers and was buried on the ascent to the tombs of David's descendants. All Judah and the inhabitants of Jerusalem paid him honor at his death. His son Manasseh became king in his place.

Judah's King Manasseh

33 Manasseh was 12 years old when he became king; he reigned 55 years in Jerusalem. ² He did what was evil in the LORD's sight, imitating the detestable practices of the nations that the

---

ᵃ**32:18** Lit *Judahite*   ᵇ**32:22** Lit *He led them*; Ps 23:2   ᶜ**32:31** LXX, Tg, Vg; MT reads *of Babylon sent*

LORD had dispossessed before the Israelites. ³ He rebuilt the •high places that his father Hezekiah had torn down and reestablished the altars for the •Baals. He made •Asherah poles, and he worshiped the whole heavenly •host and served them. ⁴ He built altars in the LORD's temple, where the LORD had said: "Jerusalem is where My name will remain forever." ⁵ He built altars to the whole heavenly host in both courtyards of the LORD's temple. ⁶ He passed his sons through the fire in the Valley of Hinnom. He practiced witchcraft, •divination, and sorcery, and consulted mediums and spiritists. He did a great deal of evil in the LORD's sight, provoking Him.

⁷ Manasseh set up a carved image of the idol he had made, in God's temple, about which God had said to David and his son Solomon: "I will establish My name forever[a] in this temple and in Jerusalem, which I have chosen out of all the tribes of Israel. ⁸ I will never again remove the feet of the Israelites from upon the land where I stationed your[b] ancestors, if only they will be careful to do all that I have commanded them through Moses—all the law, statutes, and judgments." ⁹ So Manasseh caused Judah and the inhabitants of Jerusalem to stray so that they did worse evil than the nations the LORD had destroyed before the Israelites.

Assyria Attacks

¹⁰ The LORD spoke to Manasseh and his people, but they didn't listen. ¹¹ So He brought against them the military commanders of the king of Assyria.

Manasseh Captive—and Repentant

They captured Manasseh with hooks, bound him with bronze ⌊shackles⌋, and took him to Babylon. ¹² When he was in distress, he sought the favor of the LORD his God and earnestly humbled himself before the God of his ancestors. ¹³ He prayed to Him, so He heard his petition and granted his request, and brought him back to Jerusalem, to his kingdom. So Manasseh came to know that the LORD is God.

Manasseh Returns to Jerusalem—and Fortifies It

¹⁴ After this, he built the outer wall of the city of David from west of Gihon in the valley to the entrance of the Fish Gate; he brought it around the Ophel, and he heightened it considerably. He also placed military commanders in all the fortified cities of Judah.

Manasseh Removes Idolatry

¹⁵ He removed the foreign gods and the idol from the LORD's temple, along with all the altars that he had built on the mountain of the LORD's temple and in Jerusalem, and he threw them outside the city. ¹⁶ He built[c] the altar of the LORD and offered •fellowship and thank offerings on it. Then he told Judah to serve the LORD God of Israel. ¹⁷ However, the people still sacrificed at the high places, but only to the LORD their God.

Manasseh's Death

¹⁸ The rest of the events of Manasseh's ⌊reign⌋, along with his prayer to his God and the words of the seers who spoke to him in the name of the LORD God of Israel, are ⌊written about⌋ in the Events of Israel's Kings. ¹⁹ His prayer and how God granted his request, and all his sin and unfaithfulness and the sites where he built high places and set up Asherah poles and carved images before he hum-

---

ª33:7 LXX, Syr, Tg, Vg; MT reads name for Elom; 2 Kg 21:7   ᵇ33:8 LXX, Syr, Vg read land I gave to their; 2 Kg 21:8
ᶜ33:16 Some Hb mss, Syr, Tg, Arabic; other Hb mss, LXX, Vg read restored

bled himself, they are written about in the Records of Hozai. 20 Manasseh rested with his fathers, and he was buried in his own house. His son Amon became king in his place.

Judah's Evil King Amon

21 Amon was 22 years old when he became king; he reigned two years in Jerusalem. 22 He did what was evil in the LORD's sight just as his father Manasseh had done. Amon sacrificed to all the carved images that his father Manasseh had made, and he served them. 23 But he did not humble himself before the LORD like his father Manasseh humbled himself; instead, Amon increased ⌊his⌋ guilt.

24 So his servants conspired against him and put him to death in his own house. 25 Then the common people[a] executed all those who conspired against King Amon and made his son Josiah king in his place.

Judah's Good King Josiah

34 Josiah was eight years old when he became king; he reigned 31 years in Jerusalem. 2 He did what was right in the LORD's sight and walked in the ways of his ancestor David; he did not turn aside to the right or the left.

Josiah Removes Idolatry

3 In the eighth year of his reign, while he was still a youth, Josiah began to seek the God of his ancestor David, and in the twelfth year he began to cleanse Judah and Jerusalem of the •high places, the •Asherah poles, the carved images, and the cast images. 4 Then in his presence the altars of the •Baals were torn down, and the incense altars that were above them he chopped down. The Asherah poles, the carved images, and the cast images he shattered, crushed to dust,

and scattered over the graves of those who had sacrificed to them. 5 He burned the bones of the priests on their altars. So he cleansed Judah and Jerusalem. 6 ⌊He did the same⌋ in the cities of Manasseh, Ephraim, and Simeon, and as far as Naphtali ⌊and⌋ on their surrounding mountain shrines.[b] 7 He tore down the altars, and he smashed the Asherah poles and the carved images to powder. He chopped down all the incense altars throughout the land of Israel and returned to Jerusalem.

Josiah Repairs Temple

8 In the eighteenth year of his reign, in order to cleanse the land and the temple, Josiah sent Shaphan son of Azaliah, along with Maaseiah the governor of the city and the recorder Joah son of Joahaz, to repair the temple of the LORD his God.

Money for Temple

9 So they went to Hilkiah the high priest, and gave him the money brought into God's temple. The Levites and the doorkeepers had collected ⌊money⌋ from Manasseh, Ephraim, and from the entire remnant of Israel, and from all Judah, Benjamin, and the inhabitants of Jerusalem. 10 They put it into the hands of those doing the work—those who oversaw the LORD's temple. They ⌊in turn⌋ gave it to the workmen who were working in the LORD's temple, to repair and restore the temple; 11 they gave it to the carpenters and builders and ⌊also used it⌋ to buy quarried stone and timbers—for joining and to make beams—for the buildings that Judah's Kings had destroyed.

Good Workers

12 The men were doing the work with integrity. Their overseers were Jahath

---

a 33:25 Lit the people of the land   b 34:6 One Hb tradition reads Naphtali with their swords; alt Hb tradition, Syr, Vg read Naphtali, the ruins all around; Hb obscure

and Obadiah the Levites from the Merarites, and Zechariah and Meshullam from the Kohathites as supervisors. The Levites were all skilled on musical instruments. ¹³⌊They were⌋ also over the porters and were supervising all those doing the work task by task. Some of the Levites were secretaries, officers, and gatekeepers.

Recovery of Book of Law

¹⁴ When they brought out the money that had been deposited in the LORD's temple, Hilkiah the priest found the book of the law of the LORD ⌊written⌋ by the hand of Moses. ¹⁵ Consequently, Hilkiah told Shaphan the court secretary, "I have found the book of the law in the LORD's temple," and he gave the book to Shaphan.

Court Secretary Gives Law to King

¹⁶ Shaphan took the book to the king, and also reported, "Your servants are doing all that was placed in their hands. ¹⁷ They have emptied out the money that was found in the LORD's temple and have put it into the hand of the overseers and the hand of those doing the work." ¹⁸ Then Shaphan the court secretary told the king, "Hilkiah the priest gave me a book," and Shaphan read it in the presence of the king.

King Josiah Convicted

¹⁹ When the king heard the words of the law, he tore his clothes. ²⁰ Then he commanded Hilkiah, Ahikam son of Shaphan, Abdon son of Micah, Shaphan the court secretary, and the king's servant Asaiah, ²¹ "Go. Inquire of the LORD for me and for those remaining in Israel and Judah, concerning the words of the book that was found. For <u>great is the LORD's</u>

<u>wrath that is poured out on us because our fathers have not kept the word of the LORD in order to do everything written in this book.</u>"

Prophetess Huldah: Disaster

²² So Hilkiah and those the king had designated[a] went to the prophetess Huldah, the wife of Shallum son of Tokhath, son of Hasrah, keeper of the wardrobe. She lived in Jerusalem in the Second District. They spoke with her about this.

²³ She said to them, "This is what the LORD God of Israel says: Say to the man who sent you to Me, ²⁴ 'This is what the LORD says: I am about to bring disaster on this place and on its inhabitants, ⌊fulfilling⌋ all the curses written in the book that they read in the presence of the king of Judah, ²⁵ because they have abandoned Me and burned incense to other gods in order to provoke Me with all the works of their hands. My wrath will be poured out on this place, and it will not be quenched.'

Huldah: Mercy to Josiah

²⁶ Say this to the king of Judah who sent you to inquire of the LORD: 'This is what the LORD God of Israel says: As for the words that you heard, ²⁷ because your heart was tender and you humbled yourself before God when you heard His words against this place and against its inhabitants, and because you humbled yourself before Me, and you tore your clothes and wept before Me, I Myself have heard'—this is the LORD speaking. ²⁸ 'I will indeed gather you to your fathers, and you will be gathered to your grave in peace. Your eyes will not see all the disaster that I am bringing on this place and on its inhabitants.'"

Then they reported to the king.

ᵃ**34:22** LXX; MT omits *designated*

Josiah and People Affirm Covenant

29 So the king sent ⌊messengers⌋ and gathered all the elders of Judah and Jerusalem. 30 Then the king went up to the LORD's temple with all the men of Judah and the inhabitants of Jerusalem, as well as the priests and the Levites—all the people from great to small. He read in their hearing all the words of the book of the covenant that had been found in the LORD's temple. 31 Next the king stood at his post and made a covenant in the LORD's presence to follow the LORD and to keep His commandments, His decrees, and His statutes with all his heart and with all his soul in order to carry out the words of the covenant written in this book.

32 Then he had all those present in Jerusalem and Benjamin enter[a] ⌊the covenant⌋. So all the inhabitants of Jerusalem carried out the covenant of God, the God of their ancestors.

33 So Josiah removed everything that was detestable from all the lands belonging to the Israelites, and he required all who were present in Israel to serve the LORD their God. Throughout his reign they did not turn aside from following the LORD God of their ancestors.

Josiah's Passover Observance

35 Josiah observed the LORD's •Passover and slaughtered the Passover ⌊lambs⌋ on the fourteenth day of the first month. 2 He appointed the priests to their responsibilities and encouraged them to serve in the LORD's temple. 3 He said to the Levites who taught all Israel the holy things of the LORD, "Put the holy ark in the temple built by Solomon son of David king of Israel. Since you do not have to carry it on your shoulders, now serve the LORD your God and His people Israel.

4 "Organize your ancestral houses by your divisions according to the written instruction of David king of Israel and that of his son Solomon. 5 Serve in the holy place by the divisions of the ancestral houses for your brothers, the lay people,[b] and the distribution of the tribal household of the Levites. 6 Slaughter the Passover ⌊lambs⌋, consecrate yourselves, and make preparations for your brothers to carry out the word of the LORD through Moses."

Josiah and Officials' Passover Donations

7 Then Josiah donated 30,000 sheep, lambs, and kid goats, plus 3,000 bulls from his own possessions, for the Passover sacrifices for all the lay people[b] who were present.

8 His officials also donated willingly for the people, the priests, and the Levites. Hilkiah, Zechariah, and Jehiel, leaders of God's temple, gave 2,600 Passover sacrifices and 300 bulls for the priests. 9 Conaniah and his brothers Shemaiah and Nethanel, and Hashabiah, Jeiel, and Jozabad, officers of the Levites, donated 5,000 Passover sacrifices for the Levites, plus 500 bulls.

Passover Observed

10 So the service was established; the priests stood at their posts and the Levites in their divisions according to the king's command. 11 Then they slaughtered the Passover ⌊lambs⌋, and while the Levites were skinning the ⌊animals⌋, the priests sprinkled the blood[c] they had been given.[d] 12 They removed the •burnt offerings so that they might be given to the divisions of the ancestral houses of

---

[a]34:32 Lit take a stand.   [b]35:5,7 Lit the sons of the people   [c]35:11 LXX, Vg, Tg; MT omits blood   [d]35:11 Lit sprinkled from their hand

the lay people[a] to offer to the LORD, according to what is written in the book of Moses; ⌊they did⌋ the same with the bulls. 13 They roasted the Passover ⌊lambs⌋ with fire according to regulation. They boiled the holy ⌊sacrifices⌋ in pots, in kettles, and in bowls; and they quickly brought ⌊them⌋ to the lay people.[a] 14 Afterwards, they made preparations for themselves and for the priests, since the priests, the descendants of Aaron, were busy offering up burnt offerings and fat until night. So the Levites made preparations for themselves and for the priests, the descendants of Aaron.

15 The singers, the descendants of •Asaph, were at their stations according to the command of David, Asaph, Heman, and Jeduthun the king's seer. Also, the gatekeepers were at each gate. Because their Levite brothers had made preparations for them, none of them left their tasks.

16 So all the service of the LORD was established that day for observing the Passover and for offering burnt offerings on the altar of the LORD, according to the command of King Josiah. 17 The Israelites who were present ⌊in Judah⌋ also observed the Passover at that time and the Festival of Unleavened Bread for seven days. 18 No Passover had been observed like it in Israel since the days of Samuel the prophet. None of the kings of Israel ever observed a Passover like the one that Josiah observed with the priests, the Levites, all Judah, the Israelites who were present ⌊in Judah⌋, and the inhabitants of Jerusalem. 19 In the eighteenth year of Josiah's reign, this Passover was observed.

Josiah Confronts Egyptian King Neco

20 After all this that Josiah had prepared for the temple, Neco king of Egypt marched up to fight at Carchemish by the Euphrates, and Josiah went out to confront him. 21 But Neco sent messengers to him, saying, "What is ⌊the issue⌋ between you and me, king of Judah? I have not come against you today[b] but to the dynasty[c] I am fighting. God told me to hurry. Stop opposing God who is with me; don't make Him destroy you!"

Josiah's Disguise and Death

22 But Josiah did not turn away from him; instead, in order to fight with him he disguised himself.[d] He did not listen to Neco's words from the mouth of God, but went to the Valley of Megiddo to fight. 23 The archers shot King Josiah, and he said to his servants, "Take me away, for I am severely wounded!" 24 So his servants took him out of the war chariot, carried him in his second chariot, and brought him to Jerusalem. Then he died, and they buried him in the tomb of his fathers. All Judah and Jerusalem mourned for Josiah. 25 Jeremiah chanted a dirge over Josiah, and all the singing men and singing women still speak of Josiah in their dirges to this very day. They established them as a statute for Israel, and indeed they are written in the Dirges.

26 The rest of the events of Josiah's ⌊reign⌋, along with his deeds of faithful love according to what is written in the law of the LORD, 27 and his words, from beginning to end, are written about in the Book of the Kings of Israel and Judah.

Judah's King Jehoahaz

36 Then the common people[e] took Jehoahaz son of Josiah and made him king in Jerusalem in place of his father.

---

[a]35:12,13 Lit the sons of the people [b]35:21 LXX, Syr, Tg, Vg; MT reads Not against you, you today [c]35:21 Lit house [d]35:22 LXX reads he was determined [e]36:1 Lit the people of the land

[2] Jehoahaz[a] was 23 years old when he became king; he reigned three months in Jerusalem. [3] The king of Egypt deposed him in Jerusalem and fined the land 7,500 pounds[b] of silver and 75 pounds[c] of gold.

Judah's Evil King Jehoiakim

[4] Then ⌊Neco⌋ king of Egypt made Jehoahaz's brother Eliakim king over Judah and Jerusalem and changed Eliakim's name to Jehoiakim. But Neco took his brother Jehoahaz[a] and brought him to Egypt.

[5] Jehoiakim was 25 years old when he became king; he reigned 11 years in Jerusalem. He did what was evil in the sight of the LORD his God.

King Nebuchadnezzar Takes Jehoiakim to Babylon

[6] Now Nebuchadnezzar king of Babylon attacked him and bound him in bronze ⌊shackles⌋ to take him to Babylon. [7] Also Nebuchadnezzar took some of the utensils of the LORD's temple to Babylon and put them in his temple in Babylon.

[8] The rest of the deeds of Jehoiakim, the detestable things he did, and what was found against him, are written about in the Book of Israel's Kings. His son Jehoiachin became king in his place.

Judah's Evil King Jehoiachin

[9] Jehoiachin was 18[d] years old when he became king; he reigned three months and 10 days in Jerusalem. He did what was evil in the LORD's sight. [10] In the spring[e] Nebuchadnezzar sent ⌊for him⌋ and brought him to Babylon along with the valuable utensils of the LORD's temple. Then he made Jehoiachin's brother Zedekiah king over Judah and Jerusalem.

Judah's Evil King Zedekiah

[11] Zedekiah was 21 years old when he became king; he reigned 11 years in Jerusalem. [12] He did what was evil in the sight of the LORD his God and did not humble himself before Jeremiah the prophet at the LORD's command. [13] He also rebelled against King Nebuchadnezzar who had made him swear allegiance by God. He became obstinate[f] and hardened his heart against returning to the LORD God of Israel. [14] All the leaders of the priests and the people multiplied their unfaithful deeds, imitating all the detestable practices of the nations, and they defiled the LORD's temple that He had consecrated in Jerusalem.

Chaldeans Destroy Jerusalem

[15] But the LORD God of their ancestors sent word against them by the hand of his messengers, sending them time and time again, for He had compassion on His people and on His dwelling place. [16] But they kept ridiculing God's messengers, despising His words, and scoffing at His prophets, until the LORD's wrath was so stirred up against His people that there was no remedy. [17] So He brought up against them the king of the Chaldeans, who killed their choice young men with the sword in the house of their sanctuary. He had no pity on young man and virgin or elderly and aged; He handed them all over to him. [18] He took everything to Babylon—all the articles of God's temple, large and small, the treasures of the LORD's temple, and the treasures of the king and his officials. [19] Then the Chaldeans burned God's temple. They tore down Jerusalem's wall, burned down all its palaces, and destroyed all its valuable utensils.

---

[a]**36:2,4** = Joahaz   [b]**36:3** Lit *100 talents*   [c]**36:3** Lit *one talent*   [d]**36:9** Some Hb mss, LXX; other Hb mss read *eight*; 2 Kg 24:8   [e]**36:10** Lit *At the return of the year*   [f]**36:13** Lit *He stiffened his neck*

Judah to Babylon

20 Those who escaped from the sword he deported to Babylon, and they became servants to him and his sons until the rise of the Persian[a] kingdom. 21 This fulfilled the word of the LORD through Jeremiah and the land enjoyed its Sabbath rest all the days of the desolation until 70 years were fulfilled.

Decree of Persian King Cyrus: Return to Jerusalem, Rebuild Temple

22 In the first year of Cyrus king of Persia, the word of the LORD spoken through[b] Jeremiah was fulfilled. The LORD put it into the mind of King Cyrus of Persia to issue a proclamation throughout his entire kingdom and also ⌊to put it⌋ in writing:

23 This is what King Cyrus of Persia says: The LORD, the God of heaven, has given me all the kingdoms of the earth and has appointed me to build Him a temple at Jerusalem in Judah. Whoever among you of His people may go up, and may the LORD his God be with him.

EZRA

Decree of Cyrus: Jeremiah Fulfilled

1 In the first year of Cyrus king of Persia,[c] the word of the LORD spoken through Jeremiah was fulfilled. The LORD put it into the mind of King Cyrus to issue a proclamation throughout his entire kingdom and ⌊to put it⌋ in writing:

2 This is what King Cyrus of Persia says: "The LORD, the God of heaven, has given me all the kingdoms of the earth and has appointed me to build Him a house at Jerusalem in Judah. 3 Whoever is among His people, may his God be with him, and may he go to Jerusalem in Judah and build the house of the LORD, the God of Israel, the God who is in Jerusalem. 4 Let every survivor, wherever he lives, be assisted by the men of that region with silver, gold, goods, and livestock, along with a freewill offering for the house of God in Jerusalem."

Return from Exile

5 So the family leaders of Judah and Benjamin, along with the priests and Levites—everyone God had motivated[d]—prepared to go up and rebuild the LORD's house in Jerusalem. 6 All their neighbors supported them[e] with silver articles, gold, goods, livestock, and valuables, in addition to all that was given as a freewill offering. 7 King Cyrus also brought out the articles of the LORD's house that Nebuchadnezzar had taken from Jerusalem and had placed in the house of his gods. 8 King Cyrus of Persia had them brought out under the supervision of Mithredath the treasurer, who counted them out to Sheshbazzar the prince of Judah. 9 This was the inventory:

　30 gold basins, 1,000 silver basins,
　29 silver knives, 10 30 gold bowls,
　410 various[f] silver bowls,
　　and 1,000 other articles.

---

[a]**36:20** LXX reads *Median*　[b]**36:22** Lit *LORD by the mouth of*　[c]**1:1** Cyrus reigned 538–530 B.C.　[d]**1:5** Lit *everyone whose spirit God had stirred*　[e]**1:6** Lit *supported their hands*　[f]**1:10** Or *similar*

¹¹ The gold and silver articles totaled 5,400. Sheshbazzar brought all of them when the exiles went up from Babylon to Jerusalem.

Exiles Who Returned

2 These now are the people of the province who came from those captive exiles King Nebuchadnezzar of Babylonᵃ had deported to Babylon. Each of them returned to his hometown Jerusalem and Judah. ² They came with Zerubbabel, Jeshua, Nehemiah, Seraiah, Reelaiah, Mordecai, Bilshan, Mispar, Bigvai, Rehum, and Baanah.

The number of the Israelite men ⌊included⌋:ᵇ

³	Parosh's descendants	2,172
⁴	Shephatiah's descendants	372
⁵	Arah's descendants	775
⁶	Pahath-moab's descendants: Jeshua's and Joab's descendants	2,812
⁷	Elam's descendants	1,254
⁸	Zattu's descendants	945
⁹	Zaccai's descendants	760
¹⁰	Bani's descendants	642
¹¹	Bebai's descendants	623
¹²	Azgad's descendants	1,222
¹³	Adonikam's descendants	666
¹⁴	Bigvai's descendants	2,056
¹⁵	Adin's descendants	454
¹⁶	Ater's descendants: Hezekiah's	98
¹⁷	Bezai's descendants	323
¹⁸	Jorah's descendants	112
¹⁹	Hashum's descendants	223
²⁰	Gibbar's descendants	95
²¹	Bethlehem's people	123
²²	Netophah's men	56
²³	Anathoth's men	128
²⁴	Azmaveth's people	42
²⁵	Kiriatharim's, Chephirah's, and Beeroth's people	743
²⁶	Ramah's and Geba's people	621
²⁷	Michmas's men	122
²⁸	Bethel's and Ai's men	223
²⁹	Nebo's people	52
³⁰	Magbish's people	156
³¹	the other Elam's people	1,254
³²	Harim's people	320
³³	Lod's, Hadid's, and Ono's people	725
³⁴	Jericho's people	345
³⁵	Senaah's people	3,630

³⁶ The priests ⌊included⌋:

Jedaiah's descendants of the house of Jeshua	973
³⁷ Immer's descendants	1,052
³⁸ Pashhur's descendants	1,247
³⁹ and Harim's descendants	1,017

⁴⁰ The Levites ⌊included⌋:

Jeshua's and Kadmiel's descendants from Hodaviah's descendants	74

⁴¹ The singers ⌊included⌋:

•Asaph's descendants	128

⁴² The gatekeepers' descendants ⌊included⌋:

Shallum's descendants, Ater's descendants, Talmon's descendants, Akkub's descendants, Hatita's descendants, Shobai's descendants, in all	139

⁴³ The temple servants ⌊included⌋:

Ziha's descendants,
Hasupha's descendants,
Tabbaoth's descendants,
⁴⁴ Keros's descendants,
Siaha's descendants,
Padon's descendants,
⁴⁵ Lebanah's descendants,
Hagabah's descendants,

ᵃ2:1 Nebuchadnezzar reigned 605–562 B.C.   ᵇ2:2 Lit the men of the people of Israel

Akkub's descendants,
46 Hagab's descendants,
Shalmai's[a] descendants,
Hanan's descendants,
47 Giddel's descendants,
Gahar's descendants,
Reaiah's descendants,
48 Rezin's descendants,
Nekoda's descendants,
Gazzam's descendants,
49 Uzza's descendants,
Paseah's descendants,
Besai's descendants,
50 Asnah's descendants,
Meunim's[b] descendants,
Nephusim's[c] descendants,
51 Bakbuk's descendants,
Hakupha's descendants,
Harhur's descendants,
52 Bazluth's descendants,
Mehida's descendants,
Harsha's descendants,
53 Barkos's descendants,
Sisera's descendants,
Temah's descendants,
54 Neziah's descendants,
and Hatipha's descendants.

55 The descendants of Solomon's servants ⌊included⌋:

Sotai's descendants,
Hassophereth's descendants,
Peruda's descendants,
56 Jaalah's descendants,
Darkon's descendants,
Giddel's descendants,
57 Shephatiah's descendants,
Hattil's descendants,
Pochereth-hazzebaim's
descendants, and Ami's
descendants.
58 All the temple servants
and the descendants
of Solomon's servants   392

59 The following are those who came
from Tel-melah, Tel-harsha, Cherub, Ad-
dan, and Immer but were unable to
prove that their families and ancestry
were Israelite:

60 Delaiah's descendants,
Tobiah's descendants,
Nekoda's descendants   652

61 and from the descendants of the
priests: the descendants of Habaiah, the
descendants of Hakkoz, the descendants
of Barzillai— who had taken a wife from
the daughters of Barzillai the Gileadite
and was called by their name. 62 These
searched for their entries in the genealogical records, but they could not be
found, so they were disqualified from the
priesthood. 63 The governor ordered
them not to eat the most holy things until there was a priest who could consult
the Urim and Thummim.[d]

64 The whole combined assembly
numbered   42,360
65 not including their 7,337 male
and female slaves,
and their 200 male
and female singers.
66 They had 736 horses, 245 mules,
67 435 camels, and 6,720 donkeys.

Gifts for Rebuilding Temple

68 After they arrived at the LORD's
house in Jerusalem, some of the family
leaders gave freewill offerings for the
house of God in order to have it rebuilt
on its ⌊original⌋ site. 69 Based on what
they could give, they gave 61,000 gold
coins,[e] 6,250 pounds[f] of silver, and 100
priestly garments to the treasury for the
project. 70 The priests, Levites, singers,
gatekeepers, temple servants, and some
of the people settled in their towns, and

---

[a]2:46 Alt Hb tradition reads Shamlai's or Salmai's   [b]2:50 Alt Hb tradition reads Meinim's   [c]2:50 Alt Hb tradition reads
Nephisim's   [d]2:63 Two objects used to determine God's will; Ex 28:30   [e]2:69 Lit drachmas   [f]2:69 Lit 5,000 minas

⌊the rest of⌋ Israel ⌊settled⌋ in their towns.

Jeshua and Zerubbabel: Sacrifice Restored

3 By the seventh month, the Israelites had settled in their towns, and the people gathered together in Jerusalem. ² Jeshua son of Jozadak and his brothers the priests along with Zerubbabel son of Shealtiel and his brothers began to build the altar of Israel's God in order to offer •burnt offerings on it, as it is written in the law of Moses the man of God. ³ They set up the altar on its foundation and offered burnt offerings for the morning and evening on it to the LORD even though they feared the surrounding peoples. ⁴ They celebrated the Festival of Booths as prescribed, and ⌊offered⌋ burnt offerings each day, based on the number specified by ordinance for each festival day. ⁵ After that, ⌊they offered⌋ the regular burnt offering and the offerings for the beginning of each month[a] and for all the LORD's appointed holy occasions, as well as the freewill offerings brought to[b] the LORD.

⁶ On the first day of the seventh month they began to offer burnt offerings to the LORD, even though the foundation of the LORD's temple had not ⌊yet⌋ been laid. ⁷ They gave money to the stonecutters and artisans, and ⌊gave⌋ food, drink, and oil to the people of Sidon and Tyre, so they could bring cedar wood from Lebanon to Joppa by sea, according to the authorization ⌊given⌋ them by King Cyrus of Persia.

Zerubbabel and Jeshua Rebuild Temple

⁸ In the second month of the second year after they arrived at God's house in Jerusalem, Zerubbabel son of Shealtiel,

Jeshua son of Jozadak, and the rest of their brothers, including the priests, the Levites, and all who had returned to Jerusalem from the captivity, began ⌊to build⌋. They appointed the Levites who were 20 years old or more to supervise the work on the LORD's house. ⁹ Jeshua with his sons and brothers, Kadmiel with his sons, and the sons of Judah[c] and of Henadad, with their sons and brothers, the Levites, joined together to supervise those working on the house of God.

Temple Foundation Completed

¹⁰ When the builders had laid the foundation of the LORD's temple, the priests, dressed in their robes and holding trumpets, and the Levites descended from •Asaph, holding cymbals, took their positions to praise the LORD, as King David of Israel had instructed. ¹¹ They sang with praise and thanksgiving to the LORD: "For He is good; His faithful love to Israel endures forever." Then all the people gave a great shout of praise to the LORD because the foundation of the LORD's house had been laid.

¹² But many of the older priests, Levites, and family leaders, who had seen the first temple, wept loudly when they saw the foundation of this house, but many ⌊others⌋ shouted joyfully. ¹³ The people could not distinguish the sound of the joyful shouting from that of the[d] weeping, because the people were shouting so loudly. And the sound was heard far away.

Opposition to Rebuilding Temple

4 When the enemies of Judah and Benjamin heard that the returned exiles[e] were building a temple for the LORD, the God of Israel, ² they approached Zerubbabel and the leaders of

---

[a]3:5 Lit for the new moons [b]3:5 Lit well as those of everyone making a freewill offering to [c]3:9 Or Hodaviah; Ezr 2:40; Neh 7:43; 1 Esdras 5:58 [d]3:13 Lit the people [e]4:1 Lit the sons of the exile

the families and said to them, "Let us build with you, for we also worship your God and have been sacrificing to Him[a] since the time King Esar-haddon of Assyria[b] brought us here."

3 But Zerubbabel, Jeshua, and the other leaders of Israel's families answered them, "You may have no part with us in building a house for our God, since we alone must build ⌊it⌋ for the LORD, the God of Israel, as King Cyrus, the king of Persia has commanded us."

4 Then the people who were already in the land[c] discouraged[d] the people of Judah and made them afraid to build. 5 They also bribed officials ⌊to act⌋ against them to frustrate their plans throughout the reign of King Cyrus of Persia and until the reign of King Darius of Persia.[e]

Opposition to Rebuilding Jerusalem

6 At the beginning of the reign of Ahasuerus,[f] the people who were already in the land[c] wrote an accusation against the residents of Judah and Jerusalem. 7 During the time of ⌊King⌋ Artaxerxes of Persia,[g] Bishlam, Mithredath, Tabeel and the rest of his colleagues wrote to King Artaxerxes. The letter was written in Aramaic and translated.[h][i]

Opponents' Letter to Persian King Artaxerxes

8 Rehum the chief deputy and Shimshai the scribe wrote a letter to King Artaxerxes concerning Jerusalem as follows:

9 ⌊From⌋ Rehum[j] the chief deputy, Shimshai the scribe, and the rest of their colleagues—the judges and magistrates[k] from Tripolis, Persia, Erech, Babylon, Susa (that is, the people of Elam),[l] 10 and the rest of the peoples whom the great and illustrious Ashurbanipal[m] deported and settled in the cities of Samaria and the region west of the Euphrates River.

11 This is the text of the letter they sent to him:

To King Artaxerxes from your servants, the men from the region west of the Euphrates River:

12 Let it be known to the king that the Jews who came from you have returned to us at Jerusalem. They are rebuilding that rebellious and evil city, finishing its walls, and repairing its foundations. 13 Let it now be known to the king that if that city is rebuilt and its walls are finished, they will not pay tribute, duty, or land tax, and the royal revenue[n] will suffer. 14 Since we have taken an oath of loyalty to the king,[o] and it is not right for us to witness his dishonor, we have sent to inform the king 15 that a search should be made in your fathers' record books. In these record books you will discover and verify that the city is a rebellious city, harmful to kings and provinces. There have been revolts in it since ancient times. That is why this city was destroyed. 16 We advise the king that if this city is rebuilt and its walls are finished, you will not have any possession west of the Euphrates.

a4:2 Alt Hb tradition reads have not been sacrificing   b4:2 Esar-haddon reigned 681–669 B.C.; 2 Kg 19:37; Is 37:38   c4:4,6 Lit people of the land   d4:4 Lit relaxed the hands of   e4:5 Darius reigned 521–486 B.C.   f4:6 = Xerxes; he reigned 486–465 B.C.   g4:7 Artaxerxes reigned 465–425 B.C.   h4:7 Lit translated. Aramaic: i4:7 Ezr 4:8–6:18 is written in Aram.   j4:9 Lit Then Rehum   k4:9 Or ambassadors   l4:9 Aram obscure in this v.   m4:10 Lit Osnappar   n4:13 Aram obscure   o4:14 Lit have eaten the salt of the palace

Artaxerxes Supports Opponents

[17] The king sent a reply to his chief deputy Rehum, Shimshai the scribe, and the rest of their colleagues living in Samaria and elsewhere in the region west of the Euphrates River:

Greetings.

[18] The letter you sent us has been translated and read[a] in my presence. [19] I issued a decree and a search was conducted. It was discovered that this city has had uprisings against kings since ancient times, and there have been rebellions and revolts in it. [20] Powerful kings have also ruled over Jerusalem and exercised authority over the whole region, and tribute, duty, and land tax were paid to them. [21] Therefore, issue an order for these men to stop, so that this city will not be rebuilt until a ⌊further⌋ decree has been pronounced by me. [22] See that you not neglect this matter. Otherwise, the damage will increase and the royal interests[b] will suffer.

Opponents Stop Rebuilding

[23] As soon as the text of King Artaxerxes' letter was read to Rehum, Shimshai the scribe, and their colleagues, they immediately went to the Jews in Jerusalem and forcibly stopped them.

Zerubbabel and Jeshua Resume Rebuilding of Temple

[24] Now the construction of God's house in Jerusalem had stopped and remained at a standstill until the second year of the reign of King Darius of Persia.

5 [1] But when the prophets Haggai and Zechariah son of Iddo prophesied to the Jews who were in Judah and Jerusalem, in the name of the God of Israel who was over them, [2] Zerubbabel son of Shealtiel and Jeshua son of Jozadak began to rebuild God's house in Jerusalem. The prophets of God were with them, helping them.

[3] At that time Tattenai the governor of the region west of the Euphrates River, Shethar-bozenai, and their colleagues came to the Jews and asked, "Who gave you the order to rebuild this temple and finish this structure?"[c] [4] They also asked them, "What are the names of the workers[d] who are constructing this building?" [5] But God was watching[e] over the Jewish elders. These men wouldn't stop them until a report was sent to Darius, so that they could receive written instructions about this ⌊matter⌋.

Governor's Letter to Darius

[6] This is the text of the letter that Tattenai the governor of the region west of the Euphrates River, Shethar-bozenai, and their colleagues, the officials in the region, sent to King Darius. [7] They sent him a report, written as follows:

To King Darius:

All greetings.

[8] Let it be known to the king that we went to the house of the great God in the province of Judah. It is being built with cut[f] stones, and its beams are being set in the walls. This work is being done diligently and succeeding through the people's efforts. [9] So we questioned the elders and asked, "Who gave you the order to rebuild this temple and finish this structure?"[c] [10] We also asked them for their names, so that we could write

---

[a]**4:18** Or *been read clearly*   [b]**4:22** Lit *the kings*   [c]**5:3,9** Or *finish its furnishings*   [d]**5:4** One Aram ms, LXX, Syr; MT reads *Then we told them exactly what the names of the men were*   [e]**5:5** Lit *But the eye of their God was*   [f]**5:8** Or *huge*

down the names of their leaders for your information.

Jewish Elders Appeal to Decree of King Cyrus

[11] This is the reply they gave us:

We are the servants of the God of heaven and earth and are rebuilding the temple that was built many years ago, which a great king of Israel built and finished. [12] But since our fathers angered the God of heaven, He handed them over to King Nebuchadnezzar of Babylon, the Chaldean, who destroyed this temple and deported the people to Babylon. [13] However, in the first year of Cyrus king of Babylon, he issued a decree to rebuild this house of God. [14] He also took from the temple in Babylon the gold and silver articles of God's house that Nebuchadnezzar had taken from the temple in Jerusalem and carried [them] to the temple in Babylon. He released them from the temple in Babylon to a man named Sheshbazzar, the governor by the appointment of King Cyrus. [15] He told him, 'Take these articles, put them in the temple in Jerusalem, and let the house of God be rebuilt on its [original] site.' [16] Then this same Sheshbazzar came and laid the foundation of God's house in Jerusalem. It has been under construction from that time until now, yet it has not been completed.

[17] So if it pleases the king, let a search of the royal archives[a] in Babylon be conducted [to see] if it is true that a decree was issued by King Cyrus to rebuild this house of God in Jerusalem. Let the king's decision regarding [this matter] be sent to us.

Darius Finds Cyrus' Decree

6 King Darius gave the order, and they searched in the library of Babylon in the archives.[b] [2] But it was in the fortress of Ecbatana in the province of Media that a scroll was found with this record written on it:

[3] In the first year of King Cyrus, he issued a decree concerning the house of God in Jerusalem:

Let the house be rebuilt as a place for offering sacrifices, and let its [original] foundations be retained.[c] Its height is to be 90 feet[d] and its width 90 feet,[d] [4] with three layers of cut[e] stones and one of timber. The cost is to be paid from the royal treasury. [5] The gold and silver articles of God's house that Nebuchadnezzar took from the temple in Jerusalem and carried to Babylon must also be returned. They are to be brought to the temple in Jerusalem, where they belong,[f] and put into the house of God.

King Darius Affirms Cyrus

[6] Therefore, you must stay away from that place, Tattenai governor of the region west of the Euphrates River, Shethar-bozenai, and your[g] colleagues, the officials in the region. [7] Leave the construction of this house of God alone. Let the governor and elders of the Jews rebuild this house of God on its [original] site.

[8] I hereby issue a decree concerning what you must do, so that the elders

---

a**5:17** Lit treasure house   b**6:1** Lit Babylon where the treasures were stored   c**6:3** Lit be brought forth   d**6:3** Lit 60 cubits   e**6:4** Or huge   f**6:5** Lit Jerusalem, to its place,   g**6:6** Lit their

of the Jews can rebuild this house of God:

The cost is to be paid in full to these men out of the royal revenues from the taxes of the region west of the Euphrates River, so that the ⌊work⌋ will not stop. ⁹ Whatever is needed—young bulls, rams, and lambs for •burnt offerings to the God of heaven, or wheat, salt, wine, and oil, as requested by the priests in Jerusalem—let it be given to them every day without fail, ¹⁰ so that they can offer sacrifices of pleasing aroma to the God of heaven and pray for the life of the king and his sons.

Darius Warns Opponents

¹¹ I also issue a decree concerning any man who interferes with this directive:

Let a beam be torn from his house and raised up; he will be impaled on it, and his house will be made into a garbage dump because of this ⌊offense⌋. ¹² May the God who caused His name to dwell there overthrow any king or people who dares[a] to harm or interfere with this house of God in Jerusalem. I, Darius, have issued the decree. Let it be carried out diligently.

Jewish Elders Continue Rebuilding

¹³ Then Tattenai governor of the region west of the Euphrates River, Shethar-bozenai, and their colleagues diligently carried out what King Darius had decreed. ¹⁴ So the Jewish elders continued successfully with the building under the prophesying of Haggai the prophet and Zechariah son of Iddo. They finished the building according to the command of the God of Israel and the decrees of Cyrus, Darius, and King Artaxerxes of Persia. ¹⁵ This house was completed on the third day of the month of Adar[b] in the sixth year of the reign of King Darius.

Temple Dedicated

¹⁶ Then the Israelites, including the priests, the Levites, and the rest of the exiles, celebrated the dedication of this house of God with joy. ¹⁷ For the dedication of God's house they offered 100 bulls, 200 rams, and 400 lambs, as well as 12 male goats as a •sin offering for all Israel—one for each Israelite tribe. ¹⁸ They also appointed the priests by their divisions and the Levites by their groups to the service of God in Jerusalem, according to what is written in the book of Moses.

Passover Observed

¹⁹ The exiles observed the •Passover on the fourteenth day of the first month. ²⁰ All of the priests and Levites were ceremonially clean, because they had purified themselves. They killed the Passover lamb for themselves, their priestly brothers, and all the exiles. ²¹ The Israelites who had returned from exile ate ⌊it⌋, together with all who had separated themselves from the uncleanness of the Gentiles of the land[c] in order to worship the LORD, the God of Israel. ²² They observed the <u>Festival of Unleavened Bread</u> for seven days with joy, because the LORD had made them joyful, having changed the Assyrian king's attitude toward them, so that he supported them[d] in the work on the house of the God of Israel.

ᵃ**6:12** Lit who stretches out its hand   ᵇ**6:15** = February–March   ᶜ**6:21** Lit land to them   ᵈ**6:22** Lit their hands

Ezra Arrives

7 After these events, during the reign of King Artaxerxes of Persia, Ezra—

Seraiah's son, Azariah's son, Hilkiah's son, ² Shallum's son, Zadok's son, Ahitub's son, ³ Amariah's son, Azariah's son, Meraioth's son, ⁴ Zerahiah's son, Uzzi's son, Bukki's son, ⁵ Abishua's son, Phinehas's son, Eleazar's son, Aaron the chief priest's son

⁶ —came up from Babylon. He was a scribe skilled in the law of Moses, which the LORD, the God of Israel, had given. The king had granted him everything he requested because the hand of the LORD his God was on him. ⁷ Some of the Israelites, priests, Levites, singers, gatekeepers, and temple servants accompanied ⌊him⌋ to Jerusalem in the seventh year of King Artaxerxes.

⁸ Ezra^a came to Jerusalem in the fifth month, during the seventh year of the king. ⁹ He began the journey from Babylon on the first day of the first month and arrived in Jerusalem on the first day of the fifth month. The gracious hand of his God was on him, ¹⁰ because Ezra had determined in his heart to study the law of the LORD, obey ⌊it⌋, and teach ⌊its⌋ statutes and ordinances in Israel.

King Artaxerxes Commissions Ezra

¹¹ This is the text of the letter King Artaxerxes gave to Ezra the priest and scribe, an expert in matters of the LORD's commandments and statutes for Israel:^b

¹² Artaxerxes, king of kings, to Ezra the priest, an expert in the law of the God of heaven:

Greetings ⌊to you⌋.

¹³ I issue a decree that any of the Israelites in my kingdom, including their priests and Levites, who want to go to Jerusalem, may go with you. ¹⁴ You are sent by the king and his seven counselors to evaluate Judah and Jerusalem according to the law of your God, which is in your possession. ¹⁵ ⌊You are⌋ also to bring the silver and gold the king and his counselors have willingly given to the God of Israel, whose dwelling is in Jerusalem, ¹⁶ and all the silver and gold you receive throughout the province of Babylon, together with the freewill offerings given by the people and the priests to the house of their God in Jerusalem. ¹⁷ Then, you are to buy with this money as many bulls, rams, and lambs as needed, along with their •grain and drink offerings, and offer them on the altar at the house of your God in Jerusalem. ¹⁸ You may do whatever seems best to you and your brothers with the rest of the silver and gold, according to the will of your God. ¹⁹ You must deliver to the God of Jerusalem all the articles given to you for the service of the house of your God. ²⁰ You may use the royal treasury to pay for anything else you have to supply ⌊to meet⌋ the needs of the house of your God.

King Artaxerxes' Decree to Treasurers

²¹ I, King Artaxerxes, issue a decree to all the treasurers in the region west of the Euphrates River:

Whatever Ezra the priest and expert in the law of the God of heaven asks

---

^a 7:8 LXX, Syr, Vg read *They*   ^b 7:11 Ezr 7:12-26 is written in Aram.

of you must be provided promptly, [22] up to 7,500 pounds[a] of silver, 500 bushels[b] of wheat, 550 gallons[c] of wine, 550 gallons[c] of oil, and salt without limit.[d] [23] Whatever is commanded by the God of heaven must be done diligently for the house of the God of heaven, so that wrath will not fall on the realm of the king and his sons. [24] Be advised that tribute, duty, and land tax must not be imposed on any priests, Levites, singers, doorkeepers, temple servants, or ₍other₎ servants of this house of God.

Ezra's Powers

[25] And you, Ezra, according to[e] God's wisdom that you possess, appoint magistrates and judges to judge all the people in the region west of the Euphrates who know the laws of your God and to teach anyone who does not know ₍them₎. [26] Anyone who does not keep the law of your God and the law of the king, let a fair judgment be executed against him, whether death, banishment, confiscation of property, or imprisonment.

Ezra Praises Lord

[27] Praise the LORD God of our fathers, who has put it into the king's mind to glorify the house of the LORD in Jerusalem, [28] and who has shown favor to me before the king, his counselors, and all his powerful officers. So I took courage because I was strengthened by the LORD my God,[f] and I gathered Israelite leaders to return with me.

Returnees with Ezra

8 These are the family leaders and the genealogical records of those who returned with me from Babylon during the reign of King Artaxerxes:

[2] Gershom,
from Phinehas's descendants;
Daniel,
from Ithamar's descendants;
Hattush, from David's descendants,
[3] who was of
Shecaniah's descendants;
Zechariah,
from Parosh's descendants,
and 150 men with him
who were registered
by genealogy;
[4] Eliehoenai son of Zerahiah
from Pahath-moab's descendants,
and 200 men with him;
[5] Shecaniah[g] son of Jahaziel
from Zattu's descendants,
and 300 men with him;
[6] Ebed son of Jonathan
from Adin's descendants,
and 50 men with him;
[7] Jeshaiah son of Athaliah
from Elam's descendants,
and 70 men with him;
[8] Zebadiah son of Michael
from Shephatiah's descendants,
and 80 men with him;
[9] Obadiah son of Jehiel
from Joab's descendants,
and 218 men with him;
[10] Shelomith[h] son of Josiphiah
from Bani's descendants,
and 160 men with him;
[11] Zechariah son of Bebai
from Bebai's descendants,
and 28 men with him;
[12] Johanan son of Hakkatan
from Azgad's descendants,
and 110 men with him;
[13] these are the last ones,
from Adonikam's descendants,

[a]7:22 Lit 100 talents   [b]7:22 Lit 100 cors   [c]7:22 Lit 100 baths   [d]7:22 Lit without instruction   [e]7:25 Lit to your   [f]7:28 Lit because the hand of the LORD my God was on me   [g]8:5 LXX, 1 Esdras 8:32; MT reads the descendants of Shecaniah   [h]8:10 Some LXX, 1 Esdras 8:36; MT reads the descendants of Shelomith

and their names are:
Eliphelet, Jeuel, and Shemaiah,
and 60 men with them;
14 Uthai and Zaccur[a]
from Bigvai's descendants,
and 70 men with them.

Ezra Gets Organized

15 I gathered them at the river[b] that flows to Ahava, and we camped there for three days. I searched among the people and priests, but found no Levites there. 16 Then I summoned the leaders: Eliezer, Ariel, Shemaiah, Elnathan, Jarib, Elnathan, Nathan, Zechariah, and Meshullam, as well as the teachers Joiarib and Elnathan. 17 I sent them to Iddo, the leader at Casiphia, with a message for[c] him and his brothers, the temple servants at Casiphia, that they should bring us ministers for the house of our God. 18 Since the gracious hand of our God was on us, they brought us Sherebiah—a man of insight from the descendants of Mahli, a descendant of Levi son of Israel—along with his sons and brothers, 18 men, 19 plus Hashabiah, along with Jeshaiah, from the descendants of Merari, and his brothers and their sons, 20 men. 20 There were also 220 of the temple servants, who had been appointed by David and the leaders for the work of the Levites. All were identified by name.

Ezra's Spiritual Preparation—and Faith

21 I proclaimed a fast by the Ahava River,[d] so that we might humble ourselves before our God and ask Him for a safe journey for us, our children, and all our possessions. 22 I did this because I was ashamed to ask the king for infantry and cavalry to protect us from enemies during the journey, since we had told him, "The hand of our God is gracious to all who seek Him, but His great anger is against all who abandon Him." 23 So we fasted and pleaded with our God about this, and He granted our request.

Priests Carry Precious Metals

24 I selected 12 of the leading priests, along with Sherebiah, Hashabiah, and 10 of their brothers. 25 I weighed out to them the silver, the gold, and the articles—the contribution for the house of our God that the king, his counselors, his leaders, and all the Israelites who were present had offered. 26 I weighed out to them 24 tons[e] of silver, silver articles weighing 7,500 pounds,[f] 7,500 pounds[f] of gold, 27 20 gold bowls worth 1,000 gold coins,[g] and two articles of fine gleaming bronze, as valuable as gold. 28 Then I said to them, "You are holy to the LORD, and the articles are holy. The silver and gold are a freewill offering to the LORD God of your fathers. 29 Guard ˌthemˌ carefully until you weigh ˌthemˌ out in the chambers of the LORD's house before the leading priests, Levites, and heads of the Israelite families in Jerusalem." 30 So the priests and Levites took charge of the silver, the gold, and the articles that had been weighed out, to bring ˌthemˌ to the house of our God in Jerusalem.

Ezra Arrives in Jerusalem

31 We set out from the Ahava River[d] on the twelfth ˌdayˌ of the first month to go to Jerusalem. We were strengthened by our God,[h] and He protected us from the power of the enemy and from ambush along the way. 32 So we arrived at Jerusalem and rested there for three days.

[a]8:14 Alt Hb tradition, some LXX read Zabud   [b]8:15 Or canal   [c]8:17 Lit Casiphia, and I put in their mouth the words to speak to   [d]8:21 Or Canal   [e]8:26 Lit 650 talents   [f]8:26 Lit 100 talents   [g]8:27 Or 1,000 drachmas   [h]8:31 Lit The hand of our God was on us

33 On the fourth day the silver, the gold, and the articles were weighed out in the house of our God into the care of Meremoth the priest, son of Uriah. Eleazar son of Phinehas was with him. The Levites Jozabad son of Jeshua and Noadiah son of Binnui were also with them. 34 Everything was ⌊verified⌋ by number and weight, and the total weight was recorded at that time.

Offerings to God

35 The exiles who had returned from the captivity offered •burnt offerings to the God of Israel: 12 bulls for all Israel, 96 rams, and 77 lambs, along with 12 male goats as a •sin offering. All this was a burnt offering for the LORD. 36 They also delivered the king's edicts to the royal satraps and governors of the region west of the Euphrates, so that they would support the people and the house of God.

Ezra's Initial Problem: Israel's Intermarriage with Pagans

9 After these things had been done, the leaders approached me and said: "The people of Israel, the priests, and the Levites have not separated themselves from the surrounding peoples whose detestable practices are like those of the Canaanites, Hittites, Perizzites, Jebusites, Ammonites, Moabites, Egyptians, and Amorites. 2 Indeed, they have taken some of their daughters as wives for themselves and their sons, so that the holy peoplea has become mixed with the surrounding peoples. The leadersb and officials have taken the lead in this unfaithfulness!" 3 When I heard this report, I tore my tunic and robe, pulled out some of the hair from my head and beard, and sat down devastated.

Ezra Prays and Confesses for People

4 Everyone who trembled at the words of the God of Israel gathered around me, because of the unfaithfulness of the exiles, while I sat devastated until the evening offering. 5 At the evening offering, I got up from my humiliation, with my tunic and robe torn. Then I fell on my knees and spread out my hands to the LORD my God. 6 And I said:

My God, I am ashamed and embarrassed to lift my face toward You, my God, because our iniquities are higher than ⌊our⌋ heads and our guilt is as high as the heavens. 7 Our guilt has been terrible from the days of our fathers until the present. Because of our iniquities we have been handed over, along with our kings and priests, to the surrounding kings, and to the sword, captivity, plundering, and open shame, as it is today. 8 But now, for a brief moment, grace has come from the LORD our God to preserve a remnant for us and give us a stake in His holy place. Even in our slavery, God has given us new life and light to our eyes. 9 Though we are slaves, our God has not abandoned us in our slavery. He has extended grace to us in the presence of the Persian kings, giving us new life, so that we can rebuild the house of our God and repair its ruins, to give us a wall in Judah and Jerusalem.

10 Now, our God, what can we say in light ofc this? For we have abandoned the commandments 11 You gave through Your servants the prophets, saying: "The land you are entering to possess is an impure land. The surrounding peoples have

a9:2 Lit seed   b9:2 Lit hand of the leaders   c9:10 Lit say after

filled it from end to end with their uncleanness by their impurity and detestable practices. [12] So do not give your daughters to their sons in marriage or take their daughters for your sons. Never seek their peace or prosperity, so that you will be strong, eat the good things of the land, and leave ⌊it⌋ as an inheritance to your sons forever." [13] After all that has happened to us because of our evil deeds and terrible guilt—though You, our God, have punished ⌊us⌋ less than our sins ⌊deserve⌋ and have allowed us to survive[a]— [14] should we break Your commandments again and intermarry with the peoples who commit these detestable practices? Wouldn't You become ⌊so⌋ angry with us that You would destroy us, leaving no survivors? [15] LORD God of Israel, You are righteous, for we survive as a remnant today. Here we are before You with our guilt, though no one can stand in Your presence because of this.

People's Response: Send Away Foreign Wives

10 While Ezra prayed and confessed, weeping and falling facedown before the house of God, an extremely large assembly of Israelite men, women, and children gathered around him. The people also wept bitterly. [2] Then Shecaniah son of Jehiel, an Elamite, responded to Ezra: "We have been unfaithful to our God by marrying foreign women from the surrounding peoples, but there is still hope for Israel in spite of this. [3] Let us therefore make a covenant before our God to send away all the ⌊foreign⌋ wives and their children, according to the counsel of my lord and of those who

tremble at the commandment of our God. Let it be done according to the law. [4] Get up, for this matter is your responsibility, and we support you. Be strong and take action!"

Ezra Agrees—but Mourns

[5] Then Ezra got up and made the leading priests, Levites, and all Israel take an oath to do what had been said; so they took the oath. [6] Ezra then went from the house of God, walked to the chamber of Jehohanan son of Eliashib, where he spent the night.[b] He did not eat food or drink water, because he was mourning over the unfaithfulness of the exiles.

Exiles Meet

[7] They circulated a proclamation throughout Judah and Jerusalem that all the exiles should gather at Jerusalem. [8] Whoever did not come within three days would forfeit all his possessions, according to the decision of the leaders and elders, and would be excluded from the assembly of the exiles.

[9] So all the men of Judah and Benjamin gathered in Jerusalem within the three days. On the twentieth ⌊day⌋ of the ninth month, all the people sat in the square at the house of God, trembling because of this matter and because of the heavy rain. [10] Then Ezra the priest stood up and said to them, "You have been unfaithful by marrying foreign women, adding to Israel's guilt. [11] Therefore, make a confession to the LORD God of your fathers and do His will. Separate yourselves from the surrounding peoples and ⌊your⌋ foreign wives."

People's Counterproposal

[12] Then all the assembly responded with a loud voice: "Yes, we will do as

---

[a]9:13 Lit and gave us a remnant like this   [b]10:6 1 Esdras 9:2, Syr; MT, Vg read he went

you say! [13] But there are many people, and it is the rainy season. We don't have the stamina to stay out in the open. This isn't something that can be done in a day or two, for we have rebelled terribly in this matter. [14] Let our leaders represent the entire assembly. Then let all those in our towns who have married foreign women come at appointed times, together with the elders and judges of each town, in order to avert the fierce anger of our God concerning[a] this matter." [15] Only Jonathan son of Asahel and Jahzeiah son of Tikvah opposed this, with Meshullam and Shabbethai the Levite supporting them.

Ezra Consents

[16] The exiles did what had been proposed. Ezra the priest selected men[b] who were family leaders, all ⌊identified⌋ by name, to represent[c] their ancestral houses. They convened on the first day of the tenth month to investigate the matter, [17] and by the first day of the first month they had dealt with all the men who had married foreign women.

List of Those with Foreign Wives

[18] ⌊The following⌋ were found to have married foreign women from the descendants of the priests:

from the descendants of Jeshua son of Jozadak and his brothers: Maaseiah, Eliezer, Jarib, and Gedaliah. [19] They pledged[d] to send their wives away, and being guilty, ⌊they offered⌋ a ram from the flock for their guilt;

[20] Hanani and Zebadiah
from Immer's descendants;

[21] Maaseiah, Elijah, Shemaiah, Jehiel, and Uzziah
from Harim's descendants;

[22] Elioenai, Maaseiah, Ishmael, Nethanel, Jozabad,
and Elasah
from Pashhur's descendants.

[23] The Levites:

Jozabad, Shimei, Kelaiah
(that is Kelita),
Pethahiah, Judah, and Eliezer.

[24] The singers:

Eliashib.

The gatekeepers:

Shallum, Telem, and Uri.

[25] The Israelites:

Parosh's descendants: Ramiah, Izziah, Malchijah, Mijamin, Eleazar,
Malchijah,[e] and Benaiah;

[26] Elam's descendants: Mattaniah, Zechariah, Jehiel, Abdi, Jeremoth, and Elijah;

[27] Zattu's descendants: Elioenai, Eliashib, Mattaniah, Jeremoth, Zabad,
and Aziza;

[28] Bebai's descendants: Jehohanan, Hananiah, Zabbai,
and Athlai;

[29] Bani's descendants: Meshullam, Malluch, Adaiah, Jashub, Sheal, and Jeremoth;

[30] Pahath-moab's descendants: Adna, Chelal, Benaiah, Maaseiah, Mattaniah, Bezalel, Binnui, and Manasseh;

[31] Harim's descendants: Eliezer, Isshijah,
Malchijah, Shemaiah, Shimeon,

[32] Benjamin, Malluch, and Shemariah;

a10:14 Some Hb mss, LXX, Vg; other Hb mss read until.   b10:16 1 Esdras 9:16, Syr; MT, Vg read priest and men were selected   c10:16 Lit name, for   d10:19 Lit gave their hand   e10:25 Some LXX mss, 1 Esdras 9:26 read Hashabiah

33 Hashum's descendants: Mattenai,
Mattattah,
Zabad, Eliphelet, Jeremai,
Manasseh, and Shimei;
34 Bani's descendants: Maadai,
Amram, Uel,
35 Benaiah, Bedeiah, Cheluhi,
36 Vaniah, Meremoth, Eliashib,
37 Mattaniah, Mattenai, Jaasu,
38 Bani, Binnui, Shimei,
39 Shelemiah, Nathan, Adaiah,

40 Machnadebai, Shashai, Sharai,
41 Azarel, Shelemiah, Shemariah,
42 Shallum, Amariah, and Joseph;
43 Nebo's descendants: Jeiel,
Mattithiah,
Zabad, Zebina, Jaddai, Joel,
and Benaiah.

44 All of these had married foreign women, and some of the wives had borne children.

NEHEMIAH

1 The words of Nehemiah son of Hacaliah:

Bad News from Jerusalem

During the month of Chislev in the twentieth year,[a] when I was in the fortress city of Susa, 2 Hanani, one of my brothers, arrived with men from Judah, and I questioned them about Jerusalem and the Jewish remnant that had returned from exile. 3 They said to me, "The survivors in the province, who returned from the exile, are in great trouble and disgrace. Jerusalem's wall has been broken down, and its gates have been burned down."

Nehemiah's Prayer

4 When I heard these words, I sat down and wept. I mourned for a number of days, fasting and praying before the God of heaven. 5 I said,

LORD God of heaven, the great and awe-inspiring God who keeps His gracious covenant with those who love Him and keep His commands, 6 let Your eyes be open and Your ears be attentive to hear Your servant's prayer that I now pray to You day and night for Your servants, the Israelites. I confess the sins[b] we have committed against You. Both I and my father's house have sinned. 7 We have acted corruptly toward You and have not kept the commands, statutes, and ordinances You gave Your servant Moses. 8 Please remember what You commanded Your servant Moses: "ₗIfₗ you are unfaithful, I will scatter you among the peoples. 9 But if you return to Me and carefully observe My commands, even though your exiles were banished to the ends of the earth,[c] I will gather them from there and bring them to the place where I chose to have My name dwell." 10 They are Your servants and Your people. You redeemed ₗthemₗ by Your great power and strong hand. 11 Please, Lord, let Your ear be attentive to the prayer of Your servant and to that of Your servants who delight to revere Your name. Give Your servant success today, and have compassion on him in

a 1:1 The twentieth year of King Artaxerxes of Persia, November–December 446 (or 445) B.C.   b 1:6 Lit sins of the Israelites   c 1:9 Lit skies the presence of this man.ᵃ ⌊At the time,⌋ I was the king's cupbearer.

Nehemiah Meets King Artaxerxes

2 During the month of Nisan in the twentieth yearᵇ of King Artaxerxes, when wine was set before him, I took the wine and gave it to the king. I had never been sad in his presence, ² so the king said to me, "Why are youᶜ sad, when you aren't sick? This is nothing but sadness of heart."

I was overwhelmed with fear ³ and replied to the king, "May the king live forever! Why should Iᵈ not be sad when the city where my ancestors are buried lies in ruins and its gates have been destroyed by fire?"

⁴ Then the king asked me, "What is your request?"

Nehemiah Asks Permission to Rebuild

So I prayed to the God of heaven ⁵ and answered the king, "If it pleases the king, and if your servant has found favor with you, send me to Judah and to the city where my ancestors are buried,ᵉ so that I may rebuild it."

⁶ The king, with the queen seated beside him, asked me, "How long will your journey take, and when will you return?" So I gave him a definite time, and it pleased the king to send me.

⁷ I also said to the king: "If it pleases the king, let me have letters ⌊written⌋ to the governors of the region west of the Euphrates River, so that they will grant me ⌊safe⌋ passage until I reach Judah. ⁸ And ⌊let me have⌋ a letter ⌊written⌋ to •Asaph, keeper of the king's forest, so that he will give me timber to rebuild the gates of the temple's fortress, the city wall, and the home where I will live."ᶠ

King Grants Request

The king granted my ⌊requests⌋, for I was graciously strengthened by my God.ᵍ

Opposition Begins

⁹ I went to the governors of the region west of the Euphrates and gave them the king's letters. The king had also sent officers of the infantry and cavalry with me. ¹⁰ When Sanballat the Horonite and Tobiah the Ammonite official heard that someone had come to seek the well-being of the Israelites, they were greatly displeased.

Nehemiah Secret Reconnaissance

¹¹ After I arrived in Jerusalem and had been there three days, ¹² I got up at night and ⌊took⌋ a few men with me. I didn't tell anyone what my God had laid on my heart to do for Jerusalem. The only animal I tookʰ was the one I was riding. ¹³ I went out at night through the Valley Gate toward the Serpent'sⁱ Well and the Dung Gate, and I inspected the walls of Jerusalem that had been broken down and its gates that had been destroyed by fire. ¹⁴ I went on to the Fountain Gate and the King's Pool, but farther down it became too narrow for my animal to go through. ¹⁵ So I went up at night by way of the valley and inspected the wall. Then heading back, I entered through the Valley Gate and returned. ¹⁶ The officials did not know where I had gone or what I was doing, for I had not yet told the Jews, priests, nobles, officials, or the rest of those who would be doing the work. ¹⁷ So I said to them, "You see the trouble we are in. Jerusalem lies in ruins

---

ᵃ**1:11** = the king   ᵇ**2:1** March–April 445 (or 444) B.C.   ᶜ**2:2** Lit *Why is your face*   ᵈ**2:3** Lit *my face*   ᵉ**2:5** Lit *city, the house of the graves of my fathers,*   ᶠ**2:8** Lit *enter*   ᵍ**2:8** Lit *for the gracious hand of my God was on me*   ʰ**2:12** Lit *animal with me*   ⁱ**2:13** Or *Dragon's*

and its gates have been burned down. Come, let's rebuild Jerusalem's wall, so that we will no longer be a disgrace." [18] I told them how the gracious hand of my God had been on me, and what the king had said to me.

They said, "Let's start rebuilding," and they were encouraged[a] to ⌊do⌋ this good work.

Opposition Increases

[19] When Sanballat the Horonite, Tobiah the Ammonite official, and Geshem the Arab heard ⌊about this⌋, they mocked and despised us, and said, "What is this you're doing? Are you rebelling against the king?"

Nehemiah Stays Firm

[20] I gave them this reply, "The God of heaven is the One who will grant us success. We, His servants, will start building, but you have no share, right, or historic claim in Jerusalem."

Jews Rebuild Walls and Sheep Gate

3 Eliashib the high priest and his fellow priests began rebuilding the Sheep Gate. They dedicated it and installed its doors. ⌊After building the wall⌋ to the Tower of the Hundred and the Tower of Hananel, they dedicated it. [2] The men of Jericho built next to Eliashib, and next to them Zaccur son of Imri built.

Building the Fish Gate

[3] The sons of Hassenaah built the Fish Gate. They built it with beams and installed its doors, bolts, and bars. [4] Next to them Meremoth son of Uriah, son of Hakkoz, made repairs. Beside them Meshullam son of Berechiah, son of Meshezabel, made repairs. Next to them

Zadok son of Baana made repairs. [5] Beside them the Tekoites made repairs, but their nobles did not lift a finger to help[b] their supervisors.

Repairs to Old Gate, Broad Wall, and Tower of the Ovens

[6] Joiada son of Paseah and Meshullam son of Besodeiah repaired the Old[c] Gate. They built it with beams and installed its doors, bolts, and bars. [7] Next to them Melatiah the Gibeonite, Jadon the Meronothite, and the men of Gibeon and Mizpah, who were under the authority[d] of the governor of the region west of the Euphrates River. [8] After him Uzziel son of Harhaiah, the goldsmith, made repairs, and next to him Hananiah son of the perfumer made repairs. They restored Jerusalem as far as the Broad Wall.

[9] Next to them Rephaiah son of Hur, ruler over half the district of Jerusalem, made repairs. [10] After them Jedaiah son of Harumaph made repairs across from his house. Next to him Hattush the son of Hashabneiah made repairs. [11] Malchijah son of Harim and Hasshub son of Pahath-moab made repairs to another section, as well as to the Tower of the Ovens. [12] Beside him Shallum son of Hallohesh, ruler over half the district of Jerusalem, made repairs—he and his daughters.

Valley Gate, Dung Gate, and Fountain Gate

[13] Hanun and the inhabitants of Zanoah repaired the Valley Gate. They rebuilt it and installed its doors, bolts, and bars, and repaired 500 yards[e] of the wall to the Dung Gate. [14] Malchijah son of Rechab, ruler over the district of Beth-haccherem, repaired the Dung Gate. He

---

a**2:18** Lit *they put their hands* b**3:5** Lit *not bring their neck to the work of* c**3:6** Or *Jeshanah* d**3:7** Or *Mizpah, the seat*; 2 Kg 25:23; Jr 40:5-12 e**3:13** Lit *1,000 cubits*

rebuilt it and installed its doors, bolts, and bars.

15 Shallun[a] son of Col-hozeh, ruler over the district of Mizpah, repaired the Fountain Gate. He rebuilt it and roofed it. Then he installed its doors, bolts, and bars. He also made repairs to the wall of the Pool of Shelah near the king's garden, as far as the stairs that descend from the city of David.

16 After him Nehemiah son of Azbuk, ruler over half the district of Beth-zur, made repairs up to ⌊a point⌋ opposite the tombs of David, as far as the artificial pool and the House of the Warriors. 17 Next to him the Levites made repairs ⌊under⌋ Rehum son of Bani. Beside him Hashabiah, ruler over half the district of Keilah, made repairs for his district. 18 After him their fellow ⌊Levites⌋ made repairs ⌊under⌋ Binnui[b] son of Henadad, ruler over half the district of Keilah. 19 Next to him Ezer son of Jeshua, ruler over Mizpah, made repairs to another section opposite the ascent to the armory at the Angle.

The Angle, Water Gate, and Wall of Ophel

20 After him Baruch son of Zabbai[c] diligently repaired another section, from the Angle to the door of the house of Eliashib the high priest. 21 Beside him Meremoth son of Uriah, son of Hakkoz, made repairs to another section, from the door of Eliashib's house to the end of his house. 22 And next to him the priests from the surrounding area made repairs.

23 After them Benjamin and Hasshub made repairs opposite their house. Beside them Azariah son of Maaseiah, son of Ananiah, made repairs beside his house. 24 After him Binnui son of Hena-dad made repairs to another section, from the house of Azariah to the Angle and the corner. 25 Palal son of Uzai ⌊made repairs⌋ opposite the Angle and tower that juts out from the upper palace[d] of the king, by the courtyard of the guard. Beside him Pedaiah son of Parosh, 26 and the temple servants living on Ophel[e] ⌊made repairs⌋ opposite the Water Gate toward the east and the tower that juts out. 27 Next to him the Tekoites made repairs to another section from ⌊a point⌋ opposite the great tower that juts out, as far as the wall of Ophel.

Horse Gate, Inspection Gate, and Sheep Gate

28 Each of the priests made repairs above the Horse Gate, each opposite his own house. 29 After them Zadok son of Immer made repairs opposite his house. And beside him Shemaiah son of Shecaniah, guard of the East Gate, made repairs. 30 Next to him Hananiah son of Shelemiah and Hanun the sixth son of Zalaph made repairs to another section.

After them Meshullam son of Berechiah made repairs opposite his room. 31 Next to him Malchijah, one of the goldsmiths, made repairs to the house of the temple servants and the merchants, opposite the Inspection[f] Gate, and as far as the upper room of the corner. 32 The goldsmiths and merchants made repairs between the upper room of the corner and the Sheep Gate.

Sanballat and Tobiah Mock Jews

4 [g] When <u>Sanballat</u> heard that we were rebuilding the wall, he became furious. He mocked the Jews 2 before his colleagues and the powerful men[h] of Samaria, and said, "What are these

---

[a]**3:15** Some Hb mss, Syr read *Shallum*   [b]**3:18** Some Hb mss, Syr, LXX; other Hb mss, Vg read *Bavvai*; v. 24   [c]**3:20** Alt Hb tradition, Vg read *Zaccai*; Ezr 2:9   [d]**3:25** Or *and the upper tower that juts out from the palace*   [e]**3:26** = a hill in Jerusalem   [f]**3:31** Or *Muster*   [g]**4:1** Neh 3:33 in Hb   [h]**4:2** Or *the army*

pathetic Jews doing? Can they restore ⌊it⌋ by themselves? Will they offer sacrifices? Will they ever finish it? Can they bring these burnt stones back to life from the mounds of rubble?" ³ Then Tobiah the Ammonite, who was beside him, said, "Indeed, even if a fox climbed up what they are building, he would break down their stone wall!"

Nehemiah Appeals to God

⁴ Listen, our God, for we are despised. Make their insults return on their own heads and let them be taken as plunder to a land of captivity. ⁵ Do not cover their guilt or let their sin be erased from Your sight, because they have provoked^a the builders.

People Continue to Build Wall

⁶ So we rebuilt the wall until the entire wall was joined together up to half its ⌊height⌋, for the people had the will to keep working.

Opponents Conspire

^{7b} When Sanballat, Tobiah, and the Arabs, Ammonites, and Ashdodites heard that the repair to the walls of Jerusalem was progressing and that the gaps were being closed, they became furious. ⁸ They all plotted together to come and fight against Jerusalem and throw it into confusion. ⁹ So we prayed to our God and stationed a guard because of them day and night.

Threat Grows

¹⁰ In Judah, it was said:^c

The strength of the laborer fails,
since there is so much rubble.
We will never be able
to rebuild the wall.

Murder Plot

¹¹ And our enemies said, "They won't know or see anything until we're among them and can kill them and stop the work." ¹² When the Jews who lived nearby arrived, they said to us time and again,^d "Everywhere you turn, ⌊they⌋ attack^e us." ¹³ So I stationed ⌊people⌋ behind the lowest sections of the wall, at the vulnerable areas. I stationed them by families with their swords, spears, and bows.

Nehemiah Encourages

¹⁴ After I made an inspection, I stood up and said to the nobles, the officials, and the rest of the people, "Don't be afraid of them. Remember the great and awe-inspiring Lord, and fight for your countrymen, your sons and daughters, your wives and homes."

Defense: Sword and Trowel

¹⁵ When our enemies realized that we knew their scheme and that God had frustrated it, every one of us returned to his own work on the wall. ¹⁶ From that day on, half of my men did the work while the other half held spears, shields, bows, and armor. The officers supported all the people of Judah, ¹⁷ who were rebuilding the wall. The laborers who carried the loads worked with one hand and held a weapon with the other. ¹⁸ Each of the builders had his sword strapped around his waist while he was building, and the trumpeter was beside me.

Nehemiah: "God will fight for us!"

¹⁹ Then I said to the nobles, the officials, and the rest of the people: "The work is enormous and spread out, and we are separated far from one another along the

---

^a**4:5** Or *provoked [You] in front of* ^b**4:7** Neh 4:1 in Hb ^c**4:10** Lit *Judah said* ^d**4:12** Lit *us 10 times* ^e**4:12** Or *again from every place, "You must return to*

wall. 20 Wherever you hear the trumpet sound, rally to us there. Our God will fight for us!" 21 So we continued the work, while half of the men were holding spears from daybreak until the stars came out. 22 At that time, I also said to the people, "Let everyone and his servant spend the night inside Jerusalem, so that they can stand guard by night and work by day." 23 And I, my brothers, my men, and the guards with me never took off our clothes. Each carried his weapon, even when washing.ᵃ

People Complain

5 There was a widespread outcry from the people and their wives against their Jewish countrymen. 2 Some were saying, "We, our sons, and our daughters are numerous. Let us get grain so that we can eat and live." 3 Others were saying, "We are mortgaging our fields, vineyards, and homes to get grain during the famine." 4 Still others were saying, "We have borrowed money to pay the king's tax on our fields and vineyards. 5 We and our children are ⌊just⌋ like our countrymen and their children, yet we are subjecting our sons and daughters to slavery. Some of our daughters are already enslaved, but we are powerlessᵇ because our fields and vineyards belong to others."

Nehemiah Accuses Nobles

6 I became extremely angry when I heard their outcry and these complaints. 7 After seriously considering the matter, I accused the nobles and officials, saying to them, "Each of you is charging his countrymen interest." So I called a large assembly against them 8 and said, "We have done our best to buy back our Jewish countrymen who were sold to for-

eigners, but now you sell your own countrymen, and we have to buy them back." They remained silent and could not say a word. 9 Then I said, "What you are doing isn't right. Shouldn't you walk in the •fear of our God ⌊and not invite⌋ the reproach of our foreign enemies? 10 Even I, as well as my brothers and my servants, have been lending them money and grain. Please, let us stop charging this interest.ᶜ 11 Return their fields, vineyards, olive groves, and houses to them immediately, along with the percentageᵈ of the money, grain, new wine, and olive oil that you have been assessing them."

Nobles and Officials Submit

12 They responded: "We will return ⌊these things⌋ and require nothing more from them. We will do as you say."

So I summoned the priests and made everyone take an oath to do this. 13 I also shook the folds of my robe and said, "May God likewise shake from his house and property everyone who doesn't keep this promise. May he be shaken out and have nothing!"

The whole assembly said, "•Amen," and they praised the LORD. Then the people did as they had promised.

Nehemiah's Ethics

14 Furthermore, from the day King Artaxerxes appointed me to be their governor in the land of Judah—from the twentieth year until his thirty-second year, 12 years—I and my associates never ate from the food allotted to the governor. 15 The governors who preceded me had heavily burdened the people, taking food and wine from them, as well as a poundᵉ of silver. Their subordinates also oppressed the people, but I

ᵃ4:23 Lit Each his weapon the water; Hb obscure   ᵇ5:5 Lit but there is not the power in our hand   ᶜ5:10 Or us forgive these debts   ᵈ5:11 Lit hundredth   ᵉ5:15 Lit 40 shekels

didn't do this, because of the fear of God. [16] Instead, I devoted myself to the construction of the wall, and all my subordinates were gathered there for the work. We didn't buy any land.

[17] There were 150 Jews and officials, as well as guests from the surrounding nations at my table. [18] Each[a] day, one ox, six choice sheep, and some fowl were prepared for me. An abundance of all kinds of wine was ⌞provided⌟ every 10 days. But I didn't demand the food allotted to the governor, because the burden on the people was so heavy.

[19] Remember me favorably, my God, for all that I have done for this people.

Opponents Plan to Harm Nehemiah

6 When Sanballat, Tobiah, Geshem the Arab, and the rest of our enemies heard that I had rebuilt the wall and that no gap was left in it—though at that time I had not installed the doors in the gates— [2] Sanballat and Geshem sent me a message: "Come, let's meet together in the villages of[b] the Ono Valley." But they were planning to harm me.

Nehemiah: I Can't Come Down

[3] So I sent messengers to them, saying, "I am doing a great work and cannot come down. Why should the work cease while I leave it and go down to you?" [4] Four times they sent me the same proposal, and I gave them the same reply.

Sanballat Charges Rebellion

[5] Sanballat sent me this same message a fifth time by his aide, who had an open letter in his hand. [6] In it was written:

It is reported among the nations— and Geshem[c] agrees—that you and the Jews plan to rebel. This is the reason you are building the wall. According to these reports, you are to become their king [7] and have even set up the prophets in Jerusalem to proclaim on your behalf: "There is a king in Judah." These rumors will be heard by the king. So come, let's confer together.

Nehemiah Rebuts Charges

[8] Then I replied to him, "There is nothing to these rumors you are spreading; you are inventing them in your own mind." [9] For they were all trying to intimidate us, saying, "They will become discouraged[d] in the work, and it will never be finished."

But now, ⌞my God,⌟ strengthen me.[e]

Nehemiah Counters Deceitful Plan

[10] I went to the house of Shemaiah son of Delaiah, son of Mehetabel, who was restricted ⌞to his house⌟. He said:

Let us meet at the house of God inside the temple.
Let us shut the temple doors because they are coming to kill you.
They are coming to kill you tonight![f]

[11] But I said, "Should a man like me run away? How can I enter the temple and live? I will not go." [12] I realized that God had not sent him, because of the prophecy he spoke against me. Tobiah and Sanballat had hired him. [13] He was hired, so that I would be intimidated, do as he suggested, sin, and get a bad reputation, in order that they could discredit me.

Nehemiah Asks God for Justice

[14] My God, remember Tobiah and Sanballat for what they have done, and also

---

a**5:18** Lit And that which was prepared each   b**6:2** Or together at Chephirim in   c**6:6** Lit Gashmu   d**6:9** Lit saying, "Their hands will fail   e**6:9** Lit my hands   f**6:10** Or by night

Noadiah the prophetess and the other prophets who wanted to intimidate me.

The Wall Completed

15 The wall was completed in 52 days, on the twenty-fifth day of the month Elul. 16 When all our enemies heard this, all the surrounding nations were intimidated and lost their confidence,[a] for they realized that this task had been accomplished by our God.

Opponents Persist

17 During those days, the nobles of Judah sent many letters to Tobiah, and Tobiah's ⌊letters⌋ came to them. 18 For many in Judah were bound by oath to him, since he was a son-in-law of Shecaniah son of Arah, and his son Jehohanan had married the daughter of Meshullam son of Berechiah. 19 These nobles kept mentioning Tobiah's good deeds to me, and they reported my words to him. And Tobiah sent letters to intimidate me.

The Exiles Return

7 When the wall had been rebuilt and I had the doors installed, the gatekeepers, singers, and Levites were appointed. 2 Then I put my brother Hanani in charge of Jerusalem, along with Hananiah, commander of the fortress, because he was a faithful man who •feared God more than most. 3 I said to them, "Do not open the gates of Jerusalem until the sun is hot, and let the doors be shut and securely fastened while the guards are on duty. Station the citizens of Jerusalem as guards, some at their posts and some at their homes."

Nehemiah Registers by Genealogy

4 The city was large and spacious, but there were few people in it, and no houses had been built yet. 5 Then my God put it into my mind to assemble the nobles, the officials, and the people to be registered by genealogy. I found the genealogical record of those who came back first, and I found ⌊the following⌋ written in it:

6 These are the people of the province who went up from among the captive exiles deported by King Nebuchadnezzar of Babylon. Each of them returned to his own town in Jerusalem and Judah. 7 They came with Zerubbabel, Jeshua, Nehemiah, Azariah, Raamiah, Nahamani, Mordecai, Bilshan, Mispereth, Bigvai, Nehum, and Baanah.

The number of the Israelite men ⌊included⌋:

8	Parosh's descendants	2,172
9	Shephatiah's descendants	372
10	Arah's descendants	652
11	Pahath-moab's descendants: Jeshua's and Joab's descendants	2,818
12	Elam's descendants	1,254
13	Zattu's descendants	845
14	Zaccai's descendants	760
15	Binnui's descendants	648
16	Bebai's descendants	628
17	Azgad's descendants	2,322
18	Adonikam's descendants	667
19	Bigvai's descendants	2,067
20	Adin's descendants	655
21	Ater's descendants: of Hezekiah	98
22	Hashum's descendants	328
23	Bezai's descendants	324
24	Hariph's descendants	112
25	Gibeon's[b] descendants	95
26	Bethlehem's and Netophah's men	188
27	Anathoth's men	128
28	Beth-azmaveth's men	42

a6:16 Lit and fell greatly in their eyes   b7:25 Gibbar's in Ezr 2:20

29 Kiriath-jearim's, Chephirah's, and Beeroth's men   743
30 Ramah's and Geba's men   621
31 Michmas's men   122
32 Bethel's and Ai's men   123
33 the other Nebo's men   52
34 the other Elam's people   1,254
35 Harim's people   320
36 Jericho's people   345
37 Lod's, Hadid's, and Ono's people   721
38 Senaah's people   3,930

39 The priests ᵢincludedᵢ:

Jedaiah's descendants of the house of Jeshua   973
40 Immer's descendants   1,052
41 Pashhur's descendants   1,247
42 Harim's descendants   1,017

43 The Levites ᵢincludedᵢ:

Jeshua's descendants: of Kadmiel Hodevah's descendants   74

44 The singers ᵢincludedᵢ:

•Asaph's descendants   148

45 The gatekeepers ᵢincludedᵢ:

Shallum's descendants,
Ater's descendants,
Talmon's descendants,
Akkub's descendants,
Hatita's descendants,
Shobai's descendants   138

46 The temple servants ᵢincludedᵢ:

Ziha's descendants,
Hasupha's descendants,
Tabbaoth's descendants,
47 Keros's descendants,
Sia's descendants,
Padon's descendants,
48 Lebana's descendants,
Hagaba's descendants,

Shalmai's descendants,
49 Hanan's descendants,
Giddel's descendants,
Gahar's descendants,
50 Reaiah's descendants,
Rezin's descendants,
Nekoda's descendants,
51 Gazzam's descendants,
Uzza's descendants,
Paseah's descendants,
52 Besai's descendants,
Meunim's descendants,
Nephishesim's[a] descendants,
53 Bakbuk's descendants,
Hakupha's descendants,
Harhur's descendants,
54 Bazlith's descendants,
Mehida's descendants,
Harsha's descendants,
55 Barkos's descendants,
Sisera's descendants,
Temah's descendants,
56 Neziah's descendants,
Hatipha's descendants.

57 The descendants of Solomon's servants ᵢincludedᵢ:

Sotai's descendants,
Sophereth's descendants,
Perida's descendants,
58 Jaala's descendants,
Darkon's descendants,
Giddel's descendants,
59 Shephatiah's descendants,
Hattil's descendants,
Pochereth-hazzebaim's descendants,
Amon's descendants.

60 All the temple servants and the descendants of Solomon's servants   392

61 The following are those who came from Tel-melah, Tel-harsha, Cherub, Ad-

ª7:52 Alt Hb tradition reads *Nephushesim's*

don, and Immer, but were unable to prove that their families and ancestry were Israelite:

62 Delaiah's descendants,
   Tobiah's descendants,
   and Nekoda's descendants   642

63 and from the priests: the descendants of Hobaiah, the descendants of Hakkoz, and the descendants of Barzillai—who had taken a wife from the daughters of Barzillai the Gileadite and was called by their name. 64 These searched for their entries in the genealogical records, but they could not be found, so they were disqualified from the priesthood. 65 The governor ordered them not to eat the most holy things until there was a priest who could consult the Urim and Thummim.a

66 The whole combined assembly
   numbered   42,360
67 not including their 7,337 male
   and female slaves,
   as well as their 245 male
   and female singers.
68 They had 736 horses, 245 mules,b
69 435 camels, and 6,720 donkeys.

Gifts to Rebuilding Project

70 Some of the family leaders gave to the project. The governor gave 1,000 gold drachmas,c 50 bowls, and 530 priestly garments to the treasury. 71 Some of the family leaders gave 20,000 gold drachmas and 2,200 silver minasd to the treasury for the project. 72 The rest of the people gave 20,000 gold drachmas, 2,000 silver minas, and 67 priestly garments. 73 So the priests, Levites, gatekeepers, temple singers, some of the people, temple servants, and all Israel settled in their towns.

Ezra's Public Reading of Law

8 When the seventh month came and the Israelites had settled in their towns, 1 all the people gathered together at the square in front of the Water Gate. They asked Ezra the scribe to bring the book of the law of Moses that the LORD had given Israel. 2 On the first day of the seventh month, Ezra the priest brought the law before the assembly of men, women, and all who could listen with understanding. 3 While he was facing the square in front of the Water Gate, he read out of it from daybreak until noon before the men, the women, and those who could understand. All the people listened attentivelye to the book of the law. 4 Ezra the scribe stood on a high wooden platform made for this purpose. Mattithiah, Shema, Anaiah, Uriah, Hilkiah, and Maaseiah stood beside him on his right; to his left were Pedaiah, Mishael, Malchijah, Hashum, Hash-baddanah, Zechariah, and Meshullam. 5 Ezra opened the book in full view of all the people, since he was elevated above everyone. As he opened it, all the people stood up. 6 Ezra blessed the LORD, the great God, and with their hands uplifted all the people said, "•Amen, Amen!" Then they bowed down and worshiped the LORD with their faces to the ground. 7 Jeshua, Bani, Sherebiah, Jamin, Akkub, Shabbethai, Hodiah, Maaseiah, Kelita, Azariah, Jozabad, Hanan, and Pelaiah, who were Levites,f explained the law to the people as they stood in their places. 8 They read the book of the law of God, translating and giving the meaning so that the people could understand what was read. 9 Nehemiah the governor, Ezra the priest and scribe, and the Levites who were instructing the people

---

a 7:65 Two objects used to determine God's will; Ex 28:30   b 7:68 Some Hb mss, LXX; other Hb mss omit v. 68; Ezr 2:66   c 7:70 Or darics; the official Persian gold coin   d 7:71 A Babylonian coin worth 50 shekels   e 8:3 Lit The ears of all the people listened   f 8:7 Vg, 1 Esdras 9:48; MT reads Pelaiah and the Levites

said to all of them, "This day is holy to the LORD your God. Do not mourn or weep." For all the people were weeping as they heard the words of the law. [10] Then he said to them, "Go and eat what is rich, drink what is sweet, and send portions to those who have nothing prepared, since today is holy to our Lord. Do not grieve, because your strength ⌊comes from⌋ rejoicing in the LORD." [11] And the Levites quieted all the people, saying, "Be still, since today is holy. Do not grieve." [12] Then all the people began to eat and drink, send portions, and have a great celebration, because they had understood the words that were explained to them.

Family Leaders Study Law

[13] On the second day, the family leaders of all the people, along with the priests and Levites, assembled before Ezra the scribe to study the words of the law.

Reading Law Prompts Observation of Festival of Booths

[14] They found written in the law how the LORD had commanded through Moses that the Israelites should dwell in booths during the festival of the seventh month. [15] So they proclaimed and spread this news throughout all their towns and in Jerusalem, saying, "Go out to the hill country and bring back branches of olive, wild olive, myrtle, palm, and ⌊other⌋ leafy trees to make booths, just as it is written." [16] The people went out, brought back ⌊branches⌋, and made booths for themselves on each of their rooftops, and courtyards, the court of the house of God, the square by the Water Gate, and the square by the Gate of Ephraim. [17] The whole community that had returned from exile made booths and lived in them. They had not celebrated like this from the days of Joshua son of Nun until that day. And there was tremendous joy.

Ezra Continues to Read Law

[18] Ezra[a] read out of the book of the law of God every day, from the first day to the last. The Israelites celebrated the feast for seven days, and on the eighth day there was an assembly, according to the ordinance.

National Confession of Sin

9 On the twenty-fourth day of this month the Israelites assembled; they were fasting, ⌊wearing⌋ •sackcloth, ⌊and had put⌋ dust on their heads. [2] Those of Israelite descent separated themselves from all foreigners, and they stood and confessed their sins and the guilt[b] of their fathers.

People Read Law and Confess

[3] While they stood in their places, they read from the book of the law of the LORD their God for a fourth of the day and ⌊spent⌋ another fourth of the day in confession and worship of the LORD their God. [4] Jeshua, Bani, Kadmiel, Shebaniah, Bunni, Sherebiah, Bani, and Chenani stood on the raised platform ⌊built⌋ for the Levites and cried out loudly to the LORD their God.

Levites Praise and Bless Lord

[5] Then the Levites—Jeshua, Kadmiel, Bani, Hashabneiah, Sherebiah, Hodiah, Shebaniah, and Pethahiah—said:

> Stand up. Bless the LORD your God from everlasting to everlasting.
> Praise Your glorious name,

---

[a]**8:18** Other Hb mss, Syr read *They*   [b]**9:2** = liability for punishment

and may it be exalted above
   all blessing and praise.
6 You[a] alone are the LORD.
You created the heavens,
the highest heavens with all
   their host,
the earth and all that is on it,
the seas and all that is in them.
You give life to all of them,
and the heavenly host worships
   You.
7 You are the LORD God
who chose Abram
and brought him out of Ur
   of the Chaldeans,
and changed his name
   to Abraham.
8 You found his heart faithful
   in Your sight,
and made a covenant with him
to give the land of the Canaanites,
Hittites, Amorites, Perizzites,
Jebusites, and Girgashites—
to give it to his descendants.
You have kept Your promise,
for You are righteous.

9 You saw the oppression
   of our ancestors in Egypt
and heard their cry at the •Red Sea.
10 You performed signs and wonders
   against Pharaoh,
all his officials, and all the people
   of his land,
for You knew how arrogantly
   they treated our ancestors.
You made a name for Yourself
that endures to this day.
11 You divided the sea before them,
and they crossed through it
   on dry ground.
You hurled their pursuers
   into the depths
like a stone into churning waters.

12 You led them with a pillar of cloud
   by day,
and with a pillar of fire by night,
to illuminate the way
   they should go.
13 You came down on Mount Sinai,
and spoke to them from heaven.
You gave them
   impartial ordinances,
   reliable instructions,
and good decrees
   and commandments.
14 You revealed Your holy Sabbath
   to them,
and gave them commandments,
   statutes, and a law
through Your servant Moses.
15 You provided bread from heaven
   for their hunger;
You brought them water
   from the rock for their thirst.
You told them to go in and possess
   the land
You had sworn[b] to give them.

16 But our ancestors acted arrogantly;
they became stiff-necked
   and did not listen
   to Your commands.
17 They refused to listen
and did not remember
   Your wonders
You performed among them.
They became stiff-necked
   and appointed a leader
to return to their slavery in Egypt.[c]
But You are a forgiving God,
gracious and compassionate,
slow to anger and rich
   in faithful love,
and You did not abandon them.
18 Even after they had cast an image
   of a calf
for themselves and said,

[a]**9:6** LXX reads *And Ezra said: You*   [b]**9:15** Lit *lifted Your hand*   [c]**9:17** Some Hb mss, LXX; other Hb mss read *in their rebellion*

"This is your God who brought you
   out of Egypt,"
and they had committed
   terrible blasphemies,
19 You did not abandon them
   in the wilderness
because of Your great compassion.
During the day the pillar of cloud
never turned away from them,
guiding them on their journey.
And during the night the pillar
   of fire
illuminated the way they should go.
20 You sent Your good Spirit
   to instruct them.
You did not withhold Your manna
   from their mouths,
and You gave them water
   for their thirst.
21 You provided for them
   in the wilderness 40 years
and they lacked nothing.
Their clothes did not wear out,
and their feet did not swell.

22 You gave them kingdoms
   and peoples
and assigned them to be
   a boundary.
They took possession
of the land of Sihon[a]
   king of Heshbon
and of the land of Og
   king of Bashan.
23 You multiplied their descendants
   like the stars of heaven
and brought them to the land
You told their ancestors to go in
   and take possession ʟof itɹ.
24 So their descendants went in
   and possessed the land:
You subdued the Canaanites
   who inhabited the land
   before them

and handed their kings
   and the surrounding peoples
   over to them,
to do as they pleased with them.
25 They captured fortified cities
   and fertile land
and took possession of
   well-supplied houses,
rock-hewn cisterns, vineyards,
olive groves, and fruit trees
   in abundance.
They ate, were filled,
became prosperous, and delighted
   in Your great goodness.

26 But they were disobedient
   and rebelled against You.
They flung Your law
   behind their backs
and killed Your prophets
who warned them to turn them
   back to You.
They committed
   terrible blasphemies.
27 So You handed them over
   to their enemies,
who oppressed them.
In their time of distress,
   they cried out to You,
and You heard from heaven.
In Your abundant compassion
You gave them deliverers,
   who rescued them
from the power of their enemies.
28 But as soon as they had relief,
they again did what was evil
   in Your sight.
So You abandoned them
   to the power of their enemies,
who dominated them.
When they cried out to You again,
You heard from heaven and rescued
   them
many times in Your compassion.

ᵃ9:22 One Hb ms, LXX; MT, Vg read *Sihon, even the land of the*

29 You warned them to turn back
to Your law,
but they acted arrogantly
and would not obey
Your commandments.
They sinned against
Your ordinances,
by which a person will live
if he does them.
They stubbornly resisted,[a]
stiffened their necks,
and would not obey.
30 You were patient with them
for many years,
and Your Spirit warned them
through Your prophets,
but they would not listen.
Therefore, You handed them over
to the surrounding peoples.
31 However,
in Your abundant compassion,
You did not destroy them
or abandon them,
for You are a gracious
and compassionate God.
32 So now, our God—the great,
mighty,
and awe-inspiring God who keeps
His gracious covenant—
do not view lightly all the hardships
that have afflicted us,
our kings and leaders,
our priests and prophets,
our ancestors and all Your people,
from the days of the Assyrian kings
until today.
33 You are righteous concerning all
that has come on us,
because You have acted faithfully,
while we have acted wickedly.
34 Our kings, leaders, priests,
and ancestors
did not obey Your law
or listen to Your commandments

and warnings You gave them.
35 When they were in their kingdom,
with Your abundant goodness
You gave them,
and in the spacious and fertile land
You set before them,
they would not serve You or turn
from their wicked ways.
36 Here we are today,
slaves in the land You gave
our ancestors
so that they could enjoy its fruit
and its goodness.
Here we are—slaves in it!
37 Its abundant harvest goes
to the kings
You have set over us,
because of our sins.
They rule over our bodies
and our livestock as they please.
We are in great distress.

Israel's Vow of Faithfulness

38b In view of all this, we are making a binding agreement in writing on a sealed document ⌊containing the names of⌋ our leaders, Levites, and priests.

10 Those whose seals were ⌊on the document⌋ were:

Nehemiah the governor,
son of Hacaliah, and Zedekiah,
2 Seraiah, Azariah, Jeremiah,
3 Pashhur, Amariah, Malchijah,
4 Hattush, Shebaniah, Malluch,
5 Harim, Meremoth, Obadiah,
6 Daniel, Ginnethon, Baruch,
7 Meshullam, Abijah, Mijamin,
8 Maaziah, Bilgai, and Shemaiah.
These were the priests.

9 The Levites were:
Jeshua son of Azaniah,
Binnui of the sons of Henadad,
Kadmiel,

10 and their brothers
Shebaniah, Hodiah, Kelita, Pelaiah,
Hanan,
11 Mica, Rehob, Hashabiah,
12 Zaccur, Sherebiah, Shebaniah,
13 Hodiah, Bani, and Beninu.

14 The leaders of the people were:
Parosh, Pahath-moab, Elam, Zattu,
Bani,
15 Bunni, Azgad, Bebai,
16 Adonijah, Bigvai, Adin,
17 Ater, Hezekiah, Azzur,
18 Hodiah, Hashum, Bezai,
19 Hariph, Anathoth, Nebai,
20 Magpiash, Meshullam, Hezir,
21 Meshezabel, Zadok, Jaddua,
22 Pelatiah, Hanan, Anaiah,
23 Hoshea, Hananiah, Hasshub,
24 Hallohesh, Pilha, Shobek,
25 Rehum, Hashabnah, Maaseiah,
26 Ahiah, Hanan, Anan,
27 Malluch, Harim, Baanah.

28 The rest of the people—the priests, Levites, singers, gatekeepers, and temple servants, along with their wives, sons, and daughters, everyone who is able to understand and who has separated themselves from the surrounding peoples to ⌊obey⌋ the law of God— 29 join with their noble brothers and commit themselves with a sworn oath[a] to follow the law of God given through God's servant Moses and to carefully obey all the commands, ordinances, and statutes of the LORD our Lord.

Details of the Vow

30 We will not give our daughters in marriage to the surrounding peoples and will not take their daughters as wives for our sons.

31 When the surrounding peoples bring merchandise or any kind of grain to sell on the Sabbath day, we will not buy from them on the Sabbath or a holy day. We will also leave ⌊the land⌋ uncultivated in the seventh year and will cancel every debt.

32 We will impose ⌊the following⌋ commandments on ourselves:

To give an eighth of an ounce of silver[b] yearly for the service of the house of our God: 33 the bread displayed before the LORD,[c] the daily •grain offering, the regular •burnt offering, the Sabbath and New Moon offerings, the appointed festivals, the holy things, the •sin offerings to •atone for Israel, and for all the work of the house of our God.

34 We have cast lots among the priests, Levites, and people for the donation of wood by our ancestral houses at the appointed times each year. They are to bring ⌊the wood⌋ to our God's house to burn on the altar of the LORD our God, as it is written in the law.

35 ⌊We will⌋ bring the •firstfruits of our land and of every fruit tree to the LORD's house year by year. 36 ⌊We will also bring⌋ the firstborn of our sons and our livestock, as prescribed by the law, and will bring the firstborn of our herds and flocks to the house of our God, to the priests who serve in our God's house. 37 We will bring ⌊a loaf⌋ from our first batch of dough to the priests at the storerooms of the house of our God. We will also bring the firstfruits of our ⌊grain⌋ offerings, of every fruit tree, and of the new wine and oil. A tenth of our land's ⌊produce⌋ from our lands belongs to the Levites, for the Levites

---

a**10:29** Lit *and enter in a curse and in an oath*   b**10:32** Lit *give one-third of a shekel*   c**10:33** Lit *rows of bread*

are to collect the one-tenth offering in all our agricultural towns. 38 A priest of Aaronic descent must accompany the Levites when they collect the tenth, and the Levites must take a tenth of this offering to the storerooms of the treasury in the house of our God. 39 For the Israelites and the Levites are to bring the contributions of grain, new wine, and oil to the storerooms where the articles of the sanctuary are kept and where the priests, gatekeepers, and singers serve. We will not neglect the house of our God.

Lots to Resettle Jerusalem

11 Now the leaders of the people stayed in Jerusalem, and the rest of the people cast lots for one out of ten to come and live in Jerusalem, the holy city, while the other nine-tenths remained in their towns. 2 The people praised all the men who volunteered to live in Jerusalem.

3 These are the heads of the province who stayed in Jerusalem (but in the villages of Judah each lived on his own property in their towns—the Israelites, priests, Levites, temple servants, and descendants of Solomon's servants— 4 while some of the descendants of Judah and Benjamin settled in Jerusalem):

Judah's descendants:

Athaiah son of Uzziah, son of Zechariah, son of Amariah, son of Shephatiah, son of Mahalalel, of Perez's descendants; 5 and Maaseiah son of Baruch, son of Col-hozeh, son of Hazaiah, son of Adaiah, son of Joiarib, son of Zechariah, a descendant of the Shilonite. 6 The total number of Perez's descendants, who settled in Jerusalem, was 468 capable men.

7 These were Benjamin's descendants:

Sallu son of Meshullam, son of Joed, son of Pedaiah, son of Kolaiah, son of Maaseiah, son of Ithiel, son of Jeshaiah, 8 and after him Gabbai ¦and¦ Sallai: 928. 9 Joel son of Zichri was the officer over them, and Judah son of Hassenuah was second in command over the city.

10 The priests:

Jedaiah son of Joiarib, Jachin, and 11 Seraiah son of Hilkiah, son of Meshullam, son of Zadok, son of Meraioth, son of Ahitub, the chief official of God's house, 12 and their relatives who did the work at the temple: 822. Adaiah son of Jeroham, son of Pelaliah, son of Amzi, son of Zechariah, son of Pashhur, son of Malchijah 13 and his relatives, the leaders of families: 242. Amashsai son of Azarel, son of Ahzai, son of Meshillemoth, son of Immer, 14 and their relatives, capable men: 128. Zabdiel son of Haggedolim, was their chief.

15 The Levites:

Shemaiah son of Hasshub, son of Azrikam, son of Hashabiah, son of Bunni; 16 and Shabbethai and Jozabad, from the leaders of the Levites, who supervised the work outside the house of God; 17 Mattaniah son of Mica, son of Zabdi, son of •Asaph, the leader who began the thanksgiving in prayer; Bakbukiah, second among his relatives; and Abda son of Shammua, son of Galal, son of Jeduthun. 18 All the Levites in the holy city: 284.

19 The gatekeepers:

Akkub, Talmon, and their relatives, who guarded the gates: 172.

20 The rest of Israel, the priests, and the Levites were in all the villages of Judah, each on his own inherited property. 21 The temple servants lived on Ophel;[a] Ziha and Gishpa supervised the temple servants.

Levites and Priests

22 The leader of the Levites in Jerusalem was Uzzi son of Bani, son of Hashabiah, son of Mattaniah, son of Mica, of the descendants of Asaph, who were singers for the service of God's house. 23 For there was a command of the king regarding them, and an ordinance regulating[b] the singers' daily tasks. 24 Pethahiah son of Meshezabel, of the descendants of Zerah son of Judah, was the king's agent[c] in every matter concerning the people.

25 As for the farming settlements with their fields:

Some of Judah's descendants lived
in Kiriath-arba and its villages,
Dibon and its villages,
and Jekabzeel and its villages,
26 in Jeshua, Moladah, Beth-pelet,
27 Hazar-shual, and Beer-sheba
and its villages;
28 in Ziklag and Meconah
and its villages,
29 in En-rimmon, Zorah, Jarmuth, and
30 Zanoah and Adullam
with their villages;
in Lachish with its fields
and Azekah and its villages.
So they settled from Beer-sheba
to the Valley of Hinnom.

31 Benjamin's descendants:
from Geba,[d] Michmash, Aija,
and Bethel—and its villages,
32 Anathoth, Nob, Ananiah,
33 Hazor, Ramah, Gittaim,
34 Hadid, Zeboim, Neballat,
35 Lod, and Ono, the valley
of the craftsmen.
36 Some of the Judean divisions
of Levites were in Benjamin.

Priests and Levites
with Zerubbabel and Jeshua

12 These are the priests and Levites who went up with Zerubbabel son of Shealtiel and with Jeshua:

Seraiah, Jeremiah, Ezra,
2 Amariah, Malluch, Hattush,
3 Shecaniah, Rehum, Meremoth,
4 Iddo, Ginnethoi, Abijah,
5 Mijamin, Maadiah, Bilgah,
6 Shemaiah, Joiarib, Jedaiah,
7 Sallu, Amok, Hilkiah, Jedaiah.

These were the leaders of the priests and their relatives in the days of Jeshua.
8 The Levites:

Jeshua, Binnui, Kadmiel,
Sherebiah, Judah, and Mattaniah—
he and his relatives were in charge
of the praise songs.
9 Bakbukiah, Unni,[e]
and their relatives ⌊stood⌋ opposite
them in the services.
10 Jeshua fathered Joiakim,
Joiakim fathered Eliashib,
Eliashib fathered Joiada,
11 Joiada fathered Jonathan,
and Jonathan fathered Jaddua.[f]

12 In the days of Joiakim, the leaders of the priestly families were:

Meraiah	of Seraiah,
Hananiah	of Jeremiah,
13 Meshullam	of Ezra,
Jehohanan	of Amariah,
14 Jonathan	of Malluchi,
Joseph	of Shebaniah,

a11:21 A hill in Jerusalem b11:23 Lit for c11:24 Lit was at the king's hand d11:31 Or descendants from Geba [lived in]: e12:9 Alt Hb tradition reads Unno f12:10-11 These men were high priests.

15	Adna	of Harim,
	Helkai	of Meraioth,
16	Zechariah	of Iddo,
	Meshullam	of Ginnethon,
17	Zichri	of Abijah,
	Piltai	of Moadiah, of Miniamin,
18	Shammua	of Bilgah,
	Jehonathan	of Shemaiah,
19	Mattenai	of Joiarib,
	Uzzi	of Jedaiah,
20	Kallai	of Sallai,
	Eber	of Amok,
21	Hashabiah	of Hilkiah,
	and Nethanel	of Jedaiah.

More on Levites

22 In the days of Eliashib, Joiada, Johanan, and Jaddua, the leaders of the families of the Levites and priests were recorded while Darius the Persian ruled. 23 Levi's descendants, the leaders of families, were recorded in the Book of the Historical Records during the days of Johanan son of Eliashib. 24 The leaders of the Levites—Hashabiah, Sherebiah, and Jeshua son of Kadmiel, along with their relatives opposite them—gave praise and thanks, division by division, as David the man of God had prescribed. 25 ⌊This included⌋ Mattaniah, Bakbukiah, and Obadiah. Meshullam, Talmon, and Akkub were gatekeepers who guarded the storerooms at the gates. 26 These ⌊served⌋ in the days of Joiakim son of Jeshua, son of Jozadak, and in the days of Nehemiah the governor and Ezra the priest and scribe.

Dedication of the Wall

27 At the dedication of the wall of Jerusalem, they sent for the Levites wherever they lived and brought them to Jerusalem to celebrate the joyous dedication with thanksgiving and singing accompanied by cymbals, harps, and lyres.

28 The singers gathered from the region around Jerusalem, from the villages of the Netophathites, 29 from Beth-gilgal, and from the fields of Geba and Azmaveth, for they had built villages for themselves around Jerusalem. 30 After the priests and Levites had purified themselves, they purified the people, the gates, and the wall.

Nehemiah Takes Leaders to Top of Wall

31 Then I brought the leaders of Judah up on top of the wall, and I appointed two large processions that gave thanks.

First Thanksgiving Procession

One went to the right on the wall, toward the Dung Gate. 32 Hoshaiah and half the leaders of Judah followed:

33 Azariah, Ezra, Meshullam,
34 Judah, Benjamin, Shemaiah,
       and Jeremiah.

35 Some of the priests' sons had trumpets:

Zechariah son of Jonathan,
   son of Shemaiah,
son of Mattaniah,
   son of Micaiah,
son of Zaccur, son of •Asaph,
36 and his relatives:
Shemaiah, Azarel, Milalai,
Gilalai, Maai, Nethanel,
Judah, and Hanani,
with the musical instruments
   of David, the man of God.
Ezra the scribe went in front of
   them.

37 At the Fountain Gate they climbed the steps of the city of David on the ascent of the wall ⌊and went⌋ above the house of David to the Water Gate on the east.

Second Thanksgiving Procession

38 The second thanksgiving procession went to the left, and I followed it with half the people along the top of the wall, past the Tower of the Ovens to the Broad Wall, 39 above the Gate of Ephraim, and by the Old Gate, the Fish Gate, the Tower of Hananel, and the Tower of the Hundred, to the Sheep Gate. They stopped at the Gate of the Guard. 40 The two thanksgiving processions stood in the house of God. So ⌊did⌋ I and half of the officials accompanying me, as well as 41 the priests:

Eliakim, Maaseiah, Miniamin,
Micaiah, Elioenai, Zechariah,
and Hananiah, with trumpets;
42 and Maaseiah, Shemaiah, Eleazar,
Uzzi, Jehohanan, Malchijah, Elam,
and Ezer.

Then the singers sang, with Jezrahiah as the leader. 43 On that day they offered great sacrifices and rejoiced because God had given them great joy. The women and children also celebrated, and Jerusalem's rejoicing was heard far away.

Support of Levites' Ministry

44 On that same day men were placed in charge of the rooms ⌊that housed⌋ the supplies, contributions, •firstfruits, and tenths. The legally required portions for the priests and Levites were gathered from the village fields, because Judah was grateful to the priests and Levites who were serving. 45 They performed the service of their God and the service of purification, along with the singers and gatekeepers, as David and his son Solomon had prescribed. 46 For long ago, in the days of David and Asaph, there were leaders[a] of the singers and songs of praise and thanksgiving to God. 47 So in the days of Zerubbabel and Nehemiah, all Israel contributed the daily portions for the singers and gatekeepers. They also set aside daily portions for the Levites, and the Levites set aside daily portions for the descendants of Aaron.

Book of Moses Read Publicly

13 At that time the book of Moses was read publicly to[b] the people. The command was found written in it that no Ammonite or Moabite should ever enter the assembly of God, 2 because they did not meet the Israelites with food and water. Instead, they hired Balaam against them to curse them, but our God turned the curse into a blessing. 3 When they heard the law, they separated all those of mixed descent from Israel.

Priest Eliashib Favors Enemy Tobiah

4 Now before this, Eliashib the priest had been put in charge of the storerooms of the house of our God. He was a relative[c] of Tobiah 5 and had prepared a large room for him where they had previously stored the •grain offerings, the frankincense, the articles, and the tenths of grain, new wine, and oil prescribed for the Levites, singers, and gatekeepers, along with the contributions for the priests.

Nehemiah Returns and Throws Out Tobiah

6 While all this was happening, I was not in Jerusalem, because I had returned to King Artaxerxes of Babylon in the thirty-second year of his ⌊reign⌋. It was only later that I asked the king for a leave of absence 7 so I could return to Jerusalem. Then I discovered the evil that Eliashib had done on behalf of Tobiah by

[a]**12:46** Alt Hb tradition reads *there was a leader*   [b]**13:1** Lit *read in the ears of*   [c]**13:4** Or *an associate*

providing him a room in the courts of God's house. ⁸ I was greatly displeased and threw all of Tobiah's household possessions out of the room. ⁹ I ordered that the rooms be purified, and I had the articles of the house of God restored there, along with the grain offering and frankincense.

Nehemiah Corrects Neglect of Levites

¹⁰ I also found out that because the portions for the Levites had not been given, each of the Levites and the singers performing the service had gone back to his own field. ¹¹ Therefore, I rebuked the officials, saying, "Why has the house of God been neglected?" I gathered the Levites and singers together and stationed them at their posts. ¹² Then all Judah brought a tenth of the grain, new wine, and oil into the storehouses. ¹³ I appointed as treasurers over the storehouses Shelemiah the priest, Zadok the scribe, and Pedaiah of the Levites, with Hanan son of Zaccur, son of Mattaniah to assist them, because they were considered trustworthy. They were responsible for the distribution to their colleagues.

Nehemiah Prays for Himself

¹⁴ Remember me for this, my God, and don't erase the good deeds I have done for the house of my God and for its services.

Nehemiah Warns Against Selling on Sabbath

¹⁵ At that time I saw people in Judah treading wine presses on the Sabbath. They were also bringing in stores of grain and loading ⌊them⌋ on donkeys, along with wine, grapes, and figs. All kinds of goods were being brought to Jerusalem on the Sabbath day. So I warned ⌊them⌋ against selling food on that day. ¹⁶ The Tyrians living there were importing fish and all kinds of merchandise and selling them on the Sabbath to the people of Judah in Jerusalem.

¹⁷ I rebuked the nobles of Judah and said to them: "What is this evil you are doing—profaning the Sabbath day? ¹⁸ Didn't your ancestors do the same, so that our God brought all this disaster on us and on this city? And now you are rekindling ⌊His⌋ anger against Israel by profaning the Sabbath!"

Nehemiah Enforces Sabbath Rules

¹⁹ When shadows began to fall on the gates of Jerusalem just before the Sabbath, I gave orders that the gates be closed and not opened until after the Sabbath. I posted some of my men at the gates, so that no goods could enter during the Sabbath day. ²⁰ Once or twice the merchants and those who sell all kinds of goods camped outside Jerusalem, ²¹ but I warned them, "Why are you camping in front of the wall? If you do it again, I'll use forceᵃ against you." After that they did not come again on the Sabbath. ²² Then I instructed the Levites to purify themselves and guard the gates in order to keep the Sabbath day holy.

Nehemiah Prays for Himself Again

Remember me for this also, my God, and look on me with compassion in keeping with Your abundant, faithful love.

Nehemiah Curses Foreign Marriages

²³ In those days I also saw Jews who had married women from Ashdod, Ammon, and Moab. ²⁴ Half of their children spoke the language of Ashdod or of one of the other peoples but could not speak

ᵃ**13:21** Lit *again, I will send a hand*

Hebrew.[a] [25] I rebuked them, cursed them, beat some of their men, and pulled out their hair. I forced them to take an oath before God and said: "You must not give your daughters in marriage to their sons or take their daughters as wives for your sons or yourselves! [26] Didn't King Solomon of Israel sin in matters like this? There was not a king like him among many nations. He was loved by his God and God made him king over all Israel, yet foreign women drew him into sin. [27] Why then should we hear about you doing all this terrible evil and acting unfaithfully against our God by marrying foreign women?"

Nehemiah Purifies Priesthood

[28] Even one of the sons of Jehoiada, son of Eliashib the high priest, had become a son-in-law to Sanballat the Horonite. So I drove him away from me. [29] Remember them, my God, for defiling the priesthood as well as the covenant of the priesthood and the Levites. [30] So I purified them from everything foreign and assigned specific duties to each of the priests and Levites. [31] I also arranged for the donation of wood at the appointed times and for the •firstfruits.

Remember me, my God, with favor.

ESTHER

Queen Vashti Angers Persian King Ahasuerus

1 These events took place during the days of Ahasuerus,[b] who ruled 127 provinces from India to •Cush. [2] In those days King Ahasuerus reigned from his royal throne in the fortress at Susa. [3] He held a feast in the third year of his reign for all his officials and staff, the army of Persia and Media, the nobles, and the officials from the provinces. [4] He displayed the glorious wealth of his kingdom and the magnificent splendor of his greatness for a total of 180 days.

[5] At the end of this time, the king held a week-long banquet in the garden courtyard of the royal palace for all the people, from the greatest to the least, who were present in the fortress of Susa. [6] White and violet linen hangings were fastened with fine white and purple linen cords to silver rods on marble[c] columns. Gold and silver couches ʟwereʟ arrangedʟ on a mosaic pavement of red feldspar,[d] marble,[c] mother-of-pearl, and precious stones.

[7] Beverages were served in an array of gold goblets, each with a different design. Royal wine flowed freely, according to the king's bounty [8] and no restraint was placed on the drinking. The king had ordered every wine steward in his household to serve as much as each person wanted. [9] Queen Vashti also gave a feast for the women of King Ahasuerus' palace.

[10] On the seventh day, when the king was feeling good from the wine, Ahasuerus commanded Mehuman, Biztha, Harbona, Bigtha, Abagtha, Zethar, and Carkas, the seven eunuchs who personally served him, [11] to bring Queen

---

[a]**13:24** Or *Judahite*   [b]**1:1** = Xerxes   [c]**1:6** Or *alabaster*   [d]**1:6** Or *of porphyry*

Vashti before him with her royal crown. ⌊He wanted⌋ to show off her beauty to the people and the officials, because she was very beautiful. 12 But Queen Vashti refused to come at the king's command that was delivered by his eunuchs. The king became furious and his anger burned within him.

King Seeks Advice

13 The king consulted the wise men who understood the times,ᵃ for it was his normal procedure to confer with experts in law and justice. 14 The most trusted onesᵇ were Carshena, Shethar, Admatha, Tarshish, Meres, Marsena, and Memucan. They were the seven officials of Persia and Media who had personal access to the king and occupied the highest positions in the kingdom. 15 ⌊The king asked,⌋ "According to the law, what should be done with Queen Vashti, since she refused to obey King Ahasuerus' command that was delivered by the eunuchs?"

Adviser Memucan:
Replace Vashti

16 Memucan said in the presence of the king and his officials, "Queen Vashti has defied not only the king, but all the officials and the peoples who are in every one of King Ahasuerus' provinces. 17 For the queen's action will become public knowledge to all the women and cause them to despise their husbands and say, 'King Ahasuerus ordered Queen Vashti brought before him, but she did not come.' 18 ⌊Before⌋ this day ⌊is over⌋, the noble women of Persia and Media who hear about the queen's act will say ⌊the same thing⌋ to all the king's officials, resulting in more contempt and fury.

19 "If it meets the king's approval, he should personally issue a royal decree. Let it be recorded in the laws of Persia and Media, so that it cannot be revoked: Vashti is not to enter King Ahasuerus' presence, and her royal position is to be given to another woman who is more worthy than she. 20 The decree the king issues will be heard throughout his vast kingdom, so all women will honor their husbands, from the least to the greatest."

King's Decree

21 The king and his counselors approved the proposal, and he followed Memucan's advice. 22 He sent letters to all the royal provinces, to each province in its own script and to each ethnic group in its own language, that every man should be master of his own house and speak in the language of his own people.

King Begins Search for New Queen

2 Some time later, when King Ahasuerus' rage had cooled down, he remembered Vashti, what she had done, and what was decided against her. 2 The king's personal attendantsᶜ suggested, "Let a search be made for beautiful young virgins for the king. 3 Let the king appoint commissioners in each province of his kingdom, so that they may assemble all the beautiful young virgins to the harem at the fortress of Susa. ⌊Put them⌋ under the care of Hegai, the king's eunuch, who is in charge of the women, and give them the required beauty treatments. 4 Then the young woman who pleases the king will reign in place of Vashti." This suggestion pleased the king, and he did accordingly.

ᵃ1:13 Or understood propitious times   ᵇ1:14 Lit Those near him   ᶜ2:2 Lit The young men of the king who served him

Mordecai and Esther

[5] A Jewish man was in the fortress of Susa named Mordecai son of Jair, son of Shimei, son of Kish, a Benjaminite. [6] He had been taken into exile from Jerusalem with the other captives when King Nebuchadnezzar of Babylon took King Jeconiah[a] of Judah into exile. [7] Mordecai was the legal guardian of his cousin[b] Hadassah (that is, Esther), because she didn't have a father or mother. The young woman had a beautiful figure and was extremely good-looking. When her father and mother died, Mordecai had adopted her as his own daughter.

Esther Becomes
Queen Candidate

[8] When the king's command and edict became public knowledge, many young women gathered at the fortress of Susa under Hegai's care. Esther was also taken to the palace and placed under the care of Hegai, who was in charge of the women. [9] The young woman pleased him and gained his favor[c] so that he accelerated the process of the beauty treatments and the special diet that she received. He assigned seven hand-picked female servants to her from the palace and transferred her and her servants to the harem's best quarters.

Esther Hides
Jewish Identity

[10] Esther did not reveal her ethnic background or her birthplace, because Mordecai had ordered her not to. [11] Every day Mordecai took a walk in front of the harem's courtyard to learn how Esther was doing and to see what was happening to her.

Esther's Beauty Regimen

[12] During the year before each young woman's turn to go to King Ahasuerus, the harem regulation required her to receive beauty treatments with oil of myrrh for six months and then with perfumes and cosmetics for ⌊another⌋ six months. [13] When the young woman would go to the king, she was given whatever she requested to take with her from the harem to the palace. [14] She would go in the evening, and in the morning she would return to a second harem under the supervision of Shaashgaz, the king's eunuch in charge of the concubines. She never went to the king again, unless he desired her and summoned her by name.

King Chooses
Esther as Queen

[15] Esther was the daughter of Abihail, the uncle of Mordecai who had adopted ⌊her⌋ as his own daughter. When her turn came to go to the king, she did not ask for anything except what Hegai, the king's trusted official in charge of the harem, suggested. Esther won approval in the sight of everyone who saw her.

[16] Esther was taken to King Ahasuerus in the royal palace in the tenth month, the month Tebeth, in the seventh year of his reign. [17] The king loved Esther more than all the other women. She won more favor and approval from him than did any of the other virgins. He placed the royal crown on her head and made her queen in place of Vashti. [18] The king held a great banquet for all his officials and staff. It was Esther's banquet. He freed his provinces from tax payments and gave gifts worthy of the king's bounty.

---

[a]**2:6** Or *Jehoiachin*; 2 Kg 24; 25:27; 1 Ch 3:16-17 [b]**2:7** Lit *uncle's daughter* [c]**2:9** Lit *and carried faithful love before him*

¹⁹ When the young women[a] were assembled together for a second time, Mordecai was sitting at the King's Gate. ²⁰ Esther still had not revealed her birthplace or her ethnic background, as Mordecai had directed. She obeyed Mordecai's orders, as she always had while he raised her.

Mordecai Saves the King

²¹ During those days while Mordecai was sitting at the King's Gate, Bigthan and Teresh, two eunuchs who guarded the ₁king's₁ entrance, became infuriated and tried to assassinate[b] King Ahasuerus. ²² When Mordecai learned of the plot, he reported it to Queen Esther, and she told the king on Mordecai's behalf. ²³ When the report was investigated and verified, both men were hanged on the gallows. This event was recorded in the court records of daily events in the king's presence.

King Honors Haman

3 After all this took place, King Ahasuerus honored Haman, son of Hammedatha the Agagite. He promoted him in rank and gave him a higher position than all the other officials. ² The entire royal staff at the King's Gate bowed down and paid homage to Haman, because the king had commanded this to be done for him.

Mordecai Refuses to Bow to Haman

But Mordecai would not bow down or pay homage. ³ The members of the royal staff at the King's Gate asked Mordecai, "Why are you disobeying the king's command?" ⁴ When they had warned him day after day and he still would not listen to them, they told Haman to see

if Mordecai's actions would be tolerated, since he had told them he was a Jew.

Enraged Haman
Plans Death of Jews

⁵ When Haman saw that Mordecai was not bowing down or paying him homage, he was filled with rage. ⁶ And when he learned of Mordecai's ethnic identity, Haman decided not to do away with[c] Mordecai alone. He set out to destroy all of Mordecai's people, the Jews, throughout Ahasuerus' kingdom.

⁷ In the first month, the month of Nisan,[d] in King Ahasuerus' twelfth year,[e] Pur (that is, the lot) was cast before Haman for each day in each month, and it fell on the twelfth month, the month Adar.[f] ⁸ Then Haman informed King Ahasuerus, "There is one ethnic group, scattered throughout the peoples in every province of your kingdom, yet living in isolation. Their laws are different from everyone else's, so that they defy the king's laws. It is not in the king's best interest to tolerate them. ⁹ If the king approves, let an order be drawn up authorizing their destruction, and I will pay 375 tons of silver to[g] the accountants for deposit in the royal treasury."

King Approves Haman's Plan

¹⁰ The king removed his signet ring from his finger and gave it to Haman son of Hammedatha the Agagite, the enemy of the Jewish people. ¹¹ Then the king told Haman, "The money and people are given to you to do with as you see fit."

¹² The royal scribes were summoned on the thirteenth day of the first month, and the order was written exactly as

Haman commanded. ⌊It was intended for⌋ the royal satraps, the governors of each of the provinces, and the officials of each ethnic group and written for each province in its own script and to each ethnic group in its own language. It was written in the name of King Ahasuerus and sealed with the royal signet ring. ¹³ Letters were sent by couriers to each of the royal provinces ⌊telling the officials⌋ to destroy, kill, and annihilate all the Jewish people—young and old, women and children—and plunder their possessions on a single day, the thirteenth day of Adar, the twelfth month.ᵃ ¹⁴ A copy of the text, issued as law throughout every province, was distributed to all the peoples so that they might get ready for that day. ¹⁵ The couriers left, spurred on by royal command, and the law was issued in the fortress of Susa. The king and Haman sat down to drink, while the city of Susa was in confusion.

Mordecai Appeals to Esther

4 When Mordecai learned all that had occurred, he tore his clothes, put on •sackcloth and ashes, went into the middle of the city, and cried loudly and bitterly. ² He only went as far as the King's Gate, since ⌊the law⌋ prohibited anyone wearing sackcloth from entering the King's Gate. ³ There was great mourning among the Jewish people in every province where the king's command and edict came. They fasted, wept, and lamented, and many lay on sackcloth and ashes.

⁴ Esther's female servants and her eunuchs came and reported the news to her, and the queen was overcome with fear. She sent clothes for Mordecai to wear so he could take off his sackcloth,

but he did not accept ⌊them⌋. ⁵ Esther summoned Hathach, one of the king's eunuchs assigned to her, and dispatched him to Mordecai to learn what he was doing and why.ᵇ ⁶ So Hathach went out to Mordecai in the city square in front of the King's Gate. ⁷ Mordecai told him everything that had happened as well as the exact amount of money Haman had promised to pay the royal treasury for the slaughter of the Jews.

⁸ Mordecai also gave him a copy of the written decree issued in Susa ordering their destruction, so that Hathach might show it to Esther, explain it to her, and instruct her to approach the king, implore his favor, and plead with him personally for her people. ⁹ Hathach came and repeated Mordecai's response to Esther.

Esther's Caution

¹⁰ Esther spoke to Hathach and commanded him to tell Mordecai, ¹¹ "All the royal officials and the people of the royal provinces know that one law applies to every man or woman who approaches the king in the inner courtyard and who has not been summoned—⌊the⌋ death ⌊penalty⌋. Only if the king extends the golden scepter will that person live. I have not been summoned to appear before the king for the lastᶜ 30 days." ¹² Esther's response was reported to Mordecai.

Mordecai Warns Esther

¹³ Mordecai told ⌊the messenger⌋ to reply to Esther, "Don't think that you will escape the fate of all the Jews because you are in the king's palace. ¹⁴ If you keep silent at this time, liberation and deliverance will come to the Jewish people from another place, but you and

ᵃ3:13 LXX adds the text of Ahasuerus' letter here   ᵇ4:5 Lit what is this and why is this   ᶜ4:11 Lit king these

your father's house will be destroyed. Who knows, perhaps you have come to the kingdom for such a time as this."

Esther's Brave Decision

¹⁵ Esther sent this reply to Mordecai: ¹⁶ "Go and assemble all the Jews who can be found in Susa and fast for me. Don't eat or drink for three days, night and day. I and my female servants will also fast in the same way. After that, I will go to the king even if it is against the law. If I perish, I perish." ¹⁷ So Mordecai went and did everything Esther had ordered him.

Esther Approaches King

5 On the third day, Esther dressed up in her royal clothing and stood in the inner courtyard of the palace facing it. The king was sitting on his royal throne in the royal courtroom, facing its entrance. ² As soon as the king saw Queen Esther standing in the courtyard, she won his approval.[a] The king extended the golden scepter in his hand toward Esther, and she approached and touched the tip of the scepter.

King's Positive Response

³ "What is it, Queen Esther?" the king asked her. "Whatever you want, even to half the kingdom, will be given to you."

Esther's Plan: Two Banquets

⁴ "If it pleases the king," Esther replied, "may the king and Haman come today to the banquet I have prepared for them."

⁵ The king commanded, "Hurry, and get Haman so we can do as Esther has requested." So the king and Haman

went to the banquet Esther had prepared.

⁶ While drinking the[b] wine, the king asked Esther, "Whatever you ask will be given to you. Whatever you want, even to half the kingdom, will be done."

⁷ Esther answered, "This is my petition and my request: ⁸ If the king approves of me[c] and if it pleases the king to grant my petition and perform my request, may the king and Haman come to the banquet I will prepare for them. Tomorrow I will do what the king has asked."

Haman's Anger at Mordecai

⁹ That day Haman left full of joy and in good spirits.[d] But when Haman saw Mordecai at the King's Gate, and Mordecai didn't rise or tremble in fear at his presence, Haman was filled with rage toward Mordecai. ¹⁰ Yet Haman controlled himself and went home. He sent for his friends and his wife Zeresh to join him. ¹¹ Then Haman described for them his glorious wealth and his many sons. He told them all how the king had promoted him in rank and given him a high position over the other officials and the royal staff. ¹² "What's more," Haman added, "Queen Esther invited no one but me to join the king at the banquet she had prepared. I am invited again tomorrow to join her with the king. ¹³ Still, none of this satisfies me since I see Mordecai the Jew sitting at the King's Gate all the time."

Haman's Wife: Hang Mordecai

¹⁴ His wife Zeresh and all his friends told him, "Have them build a gallows

---

^a**5:2** Lit she obtained favor in his eyes; Est 2:15,17   ^b**5:6** Lit During the banquet of   ^c**5:8** Lit If I have found favor in the eyes of the king   ^d**5:9** Lit left rejoicing and good of heart

75 feet[a] high. Ask the king in the morning to hang Mordecai on it. Then go to the banquet with the king and enjoy yourself." The advice pleased Haman, so he had the gallows constructed.

King Honors Mordecai

6 That night sleep escaped the king, so he ordered the book recording daily events to be brought and read to the king. [2] They found the written report of how Mordecai had informed on Bigthana and Teresh, two eunuchs who guarded the ⌊king's⌋ entrance, when they planned to assassinate King Ahasuerus. [3] The king inquired, "What honor and special recognition have been given to Mordecai for this ⌊act⌋?"

The king's personal attendants replied, "Nothing has been done for him."

[4] The king asked, "Who's in the court?" Now Haman was just entering the outer court of the palace to ask the king to hang Mordecai on the gallows he had prepared for him.

[5] The king's attendants answered him, "See, Haman is standing in the court."

"Have him enter," the king ordered.

Haman's Unwitting Advice

[6] Haman entered, and the king asked him, "What should be done for the man the king wants to honor?"

Haman thought to himself, "Who is it the king would want to honor more than me?" [7] Haman told the king, "For the man the king wants to honor: [8] Have them bring a royal garment that the king himself has worn and a horse the king himself has ridden, which has a royal diadem on its head. [9] Put the garment and the horse under the charge of one of the king's most noble officials. Have them clothe the man the king wants to honor, parade him on the horse through the city square, and proclaim before him, 'This is what is done for the man the king wants to honor.'"

Haman Devastated

[10] The king told Haman, "Hurry, and do just as you proposed. Take a garment and a horse for Mordecai the Jew, who is sitting at the King's Gate. Do not leave out anything you have suggested." [11] So Haman took the garment and the horse. He clothed Mordecai and paraded him through the city square, crying out before him, "This is what is done for the man the king wants to honor."

[12] Then Mordecai returned to the King's Gate, but Haman, overwhelmed,[b] hurried off for home with his head covered. [13] Haman told his wife Zeresh and all his friends everything that had happened. His advisers and his wife Zeresh said to him, "If Mordecai, before whom you have begun to fall, is Jewish, you won't overcome him, because your downfall is certain." [14] While they were still speaking with him, the eunuchs of the king arrived and rushed Haman to the banquet Esther had prepared.

Esther Exposes Haman

7 The king and Haman came to feast[c] with Esther the queen. [2] Once again, on the second day while drinking wine, the king asked Esther, "Queen Esther, whatever you ask will be given to you. Whatever you seek, even to half the kingdom, will be done."

[3] Queen Esther answered, "If I have obtained your approval,[d] my king, and if

---

a**5:14** Lit *50 cubits*   b**6:12** Lit *mourning*   c**7:1** Lit *drink*   d**7:3** Lit *If I have found favor in your eyes*

the king is pleased, spare my life—ᵣthisᵢ isᵢ my request; and ᵣspareᵢ my people—ᵣthis isᵢ my desire. ⁴ For my people and I have been sold out to destruction, death, and extermination. If we had merely been sold as male and female slaves, I would have kept silent. Indeed, the trouble wouldn't be worth burdening the king."

⁵ King Ahasuerus spoke up and asked Queen Esther, "Who is this, and where is the one who would devise such a scheme?"ᵃ

⁶ Esther answered, "The adversary and enemy is this evil Haman."

Haman Judged and Executed

Haman stood terrified before the king and queen. ⁷ Angered by this, the king arose from where they were drinking wine and ᵣwent toᵢ the palace garden. Haman remained to beg Queen Esther for his life because he realized the king was planning something terrible for him. ⁸ Just as the king returned from the palace garden to the house of wine drinking, Haman was falling on the couch where Esther was reclining. The king exclaimed, "Would he actually violate the queen while I am in the palace?" As soon as the statement left the king's mouth, Haman's face was covered.

⁹ Harbona, one of the royal eunuchs, said: "There is a gallows 75 feetᵇ tall at Haman's house that he made for Mordecai, who ᵣgaveᵢ the report that savedᶜ the king."

The king commanded, "Hang him on it."

¹⁰ They hanged Haman on the gallows he had prepared for Mordecai. Then the king's anger subsided.

Mordecai Replaces Haman

8 That same day King Ahasuerus awarded Queen Esther the estate of Haman, the enemy of the Jews. Mordecai entered the king's presence because Esther had revealed her relationship to Mordecai. ² The king removed his signet ring he had recovered from Haman and gave it to Mordecai, and Esther put him in charge of Haman's estate.

Esther Intervenes for Jews

³ Then Esther addressed the king again. She fell at his feet, wept, and begged him to revoke the evil of Haman the Agagite, and his plot he had devised against the Jews. ⁴ The king extended the golden scepter toward Esther, so she got up and stood before the king.

⁵ She said, "If it pleases the king, and I have found approval before him, if the matter seems right to the king and I am pleasing in his sight, let ᵣa royal edictᵢ be written. Let it revoke the documents the scheming Haman son of Hammedatha the Agagite, wrote to destroy the Jews who ᵣresideᵢ in all the king's provinces. ⁶ For how could I bear to see the evil that would come on my people? How could I bear to see the destruction of my relatives?"

King Approves Mercy

⁷ King Ahasuerus said to Esther the Queen and to Mordecai the Jew, "Look, I have given Haman's estate to Esther, and he was hanged on the gallows because he attackedᵈ the Jews. ⁸ You may write in the king's name whatever pleases you concerning the Jews, and seal it with the royal signet ring. A

ᵃ**7:5** Lit who would fill his heart to do this   ᵇ**7:9** Lit 50 cubits   ᶜ**7:9** Lit who spoke good for   ᵈ**8:7** Lit stretched out his hand against

document written in the king's name and sealed with the royal signet ring cannot be revoked."

9 On the twenty-third day of the third month (that is, the month Sivan),[a] the royal scribes were summoned. Everything was written exactly as Mordecai ordered for the Jews, to the satraps, the governors, and the officials of the 127 provinces from India to •Cush. ⌞The edict was written⌟ for each province in its own script, for each ethnic group in its own language, and to the Jews in their own script and language.

10 Mordecai wrote in King Ahasuerus' name and sealed ⌞the edicts⌟ with the royal signet ring. He sent the documents by mounted couriers, who rode fast horses bred from the royal racing mares.

King's Edict: Jews' Right to Self-defense

11 The king's edict gave the Jews in each and every city the right to assemble and defend themselves, to destroy, kill, and annihilate every ethnic and provincial army hostile to them, including women and children, and to take their possessions as spoils of war. 12 ⌞This would take place⌟ on a single day throughout all the provinces of King Ahasuerus, on the thirteenth day of the twelfth month, the month Adar.[b]

13 A copy of the document was to be issued as law in every province. It was to be published for every ethnic group so the Jews could be ready to avenge themselves against their enemies on that day. 14 On their royal horses, the couriers rode out in haste, at the king's urgent command. The law was also issued in the fortress of Susa.

Jews Rejoice

15 Mordecai went out from the king's presence clothed in royal purple and white, with a great golden crown and a purple robe of fine linen. The city of Susa shouted and rejoiced, 16 and the Jews celebrated[c] with gladness, joy and honor. 17 In every province and every city, wherever the king's command and his law reached, rejoicing and jubilation took place among the Jews. There was a celebration and a holiday.[d] And, many of the ethnic groups of the land professed themselves to be Jews because fear of the Jews had overcome them.

Victories of the Jews

9 The king's command and law went into effect on the thirteenth day of the twelfth month, the month Adar.[b] On the day when the Jews' enemies had hoped to overpower them, just the opposite happened. The Jews overpowered those who hated them. 2 In each of King Ahasuerus' provinces the Jews assembled in their cities to attack those who intended to harm them.[e] Not a single person could withstand them; terror of them fell on every nationality.

3 All the officials of the provinces, the satraps, the governors, and the royal civil administrators[f] aided the Jews because they were afraid of Mordecai. 4 For Mordecai ⌞exercised⌟ great power in the palace, and his fame spread throughout the provinces as he became more and more powerful.

5 The Jews put all their enemies to the sword, killing and destroying them. They did what they pleased to those who hated them. 6 In the fortress of Susa the Jews killed and destroyed 500 men, 7 including Parshandatha, Dalphon, Aspatha, 8 Poratha, Adalia, Arida-

a8:9 May–June   b8:12; 9:1 February–March   c8:16 Lit had light   d8:17 Lit good day   e9:2 Lit cities to send out a hand against the seekers of their evil   f9:3 Lit and those who do the king's work; Est 3:9

tha, ⁹ Parmashta, Arisai, Aridai, and Vaizatha. ¹⁰ They killed these 10 sons of Haman son of Hammedatha, the enemy of the Jews. However, they did not seizeᵃ any plunder.

King Affirms Protection of Jews

¹¹ On that day the number of people killed in the fortress of Susa was reported to the king. ¹² The king said to Queen Esther, "In the fortress of Susa the Jews have killed and destroyed 500 men, including Haman's 10 sons. What have they done in the rest of the royal provinces? Whatever you ask will be given to you. Whatever you seek will also be done."

Esther: Kill Haman's Sons

¹³ Esther answered, "If it pleases the king, may the Jews who are in Susa also have tomorrow to carry out today's law, and may ⌊the bodies of⌋ Haman's 10 sons be hung on the gallows." ¹⁴ The king gave the orders for this to be done, so a law was announced in Susa, and they hung ⌊the bodies of⌋ Haman's 10 sons. ¹⁵ The Jews in Susa assembled again on the fourteenth day of the month of Adar and killed 300 men in Susa, but they did not seizeᵃ any plunder.

Feast of Purim

¹⁶ The rest of the Jews in the royal provinces assembled, defended themselves, and got rid ofᵇ their enemies. They killed 75,000ᶜ of those who hated them, but they did not seizeᵃ any plunder. ¹⁷ ⌊They fought⌋ on the thirteenth day of the month of Adar and rested on the fourteenth, and it became a day of feasting and rejoicing.

¹⁸ But the Jews in Susa had assembled on the thirteenth and the fourteenth days of the month. They rested on the fifteenth day of the month, and it became a day of feasting and rejoicing. ¹⁹ This explains why the rural Jews who live in villages observe the fourteenth day of the month of Adar as ⌊a time of⌋ rejoicing and feasting. It is a holiday when they send gifts to one another.

²⁰ Mordecai recorded these events and sent letters to all the Jews in all of King Ahasuerus' provinces, both near and far. ²¹ ⌊He ordered⌋ them to celebrate the fourteenth and fifteenth days of the month Adar every year ²² because during those days the Jews got rid ofᵈ their enemies. That was the month when their sorrow was turned into rejoicing and their mourning into a holiday. They were to be days of feasting, rejoicing, and of sending gifts to one another and the poor.

Meaning of Purim

²³ So the Jews agreed to continue the practice they had begun, as Mordecai had written them to do. ²⁴ For Haman son of Hammedatha the Agagite, the enemy of all the Jews, had plotted against the Jews to destroy them. He cast the Pur (that is, the lot) to crush and destroy them. ²⁵ But when the matter was brought before the king, he commanded by letter that the evil plan Haman had devised against the Jews return on his own head and that he should be hanged with his sons on the gallows. ²⁶ For this reason these days are called Purim, from the word Pur.

ᵃ**9:10,15,16** Lit *not put their hands on*   ᵇ**9:16** Lit *and gained relief from*   ᶜ**9:16** Some LXX mss read *10,107*; other LXX mss read *15,000*   ᵈ**9:22** Lit *Jews gained relief from*

Because of all the instructions in this letter as well as what they had witnessed and what had happened to them, [27] the Jews bound themselves, their descendants, and all who joined with them to a commitment that they would not fail to celebrate these two days each and every year according to the written instructions and according to the time appointed. [28] These days are remembered and celebrated by every generation, family, province, and city, so that these days of Purim will not lose their significance in Jewish life[a] and their memory will not fade from their descendants.

Esther and Mordecai Confirm Purim

[29] Queen Esther daughter of Abihail, along with Mordecai the Jew, wrote this second letter with full authority to confirm the letter about Purim. [30] He sent letters with messages of peace and faithfulness to all the Jews who were in the 127 provinces of the kingdom of Ahasuerus, [31] in order to confirm these days of Purim at their proper time just as Mordecai the Jew and Queen Esther had established them and just as they had committed themselves and their descendants to the practices of fasting and lamentation. [32] So Esther's command confirmed these customs of Purim, which were then written into the record.

Mordecai's Fame

10 King Ahasuerus imposed a tax throughout the land even to the farthest shores.[b] [2] All of his powerful and magnificent accomplishments and the detailed account of Mordecai's great rank to which the king had promoted him, have they not been written in the court record of daily events of the kings of Media and Persia? [3] Mordecai the Jew was second only to King Ahasuerus, famous among the Jews, and highly popular with many of his relatives. He continued to seek good for his people and to speak for the welfare of all his kindred.

---

a**9:28** LXX reads *will be celebrated into all times*   b**10:1** Or *imposed forced labor on the land and the coasts of the sea*

JOB

Job's Integrity and Status

1 There was a man in the country of Uz named Job. He was a man of perfect integrity, who •feared God and turned away from evil. ² He had seven sons and three daughters. ³ His estate included 7,000 sheep, 3,000 camels, 500 yoke of oxen, 500 female donkeys, and a very large number of servants. Job was the greatest man among all the people of the east.

Family Banquets— and Job's Sin Offerings

⁴ His sons used to have banquets, each at his house in turn. They would send an invitation to their three sisters to eat and drink with them. ⁵ Whenever a round of banqueting was over, Job would send ₗfor his childrenₗ and purify them, rising early in the morning to offer burnt offerings forᵃ all of them. For Job thought: Perhaps my children have sinned, having cursed God in their hearts. This was Job's regular practice.

Satan Challenges God

⁶ One day the sons of God came to present themselves before the LORD, and Satan also came with them. ⁷ The LORD asked Satan, "Where have you come from?"

"From roaming through the earth," Satan answered Him, "and walking around on it."

⁸ Then the LORD said to Satan, "Have you considered My servant Job? No one else on earth is like him, a man of perfect integrity, who fears God and turns away from evil."

⁹ Satan answered the LORD, "Does Job fear God for nothing? ¹⁰ Haven't You placed a hedge around him, his household, and everything he owns? You have blessed the work of his hands, and his possessions are spread out in the land. ¹¹ But stretch out Your hand and strike everything he owns, and he will surely curse You to Your face."

¹² "Very well," the LORD told Satan, "everything he owns is in your power. However, you must not lay a hand on Job ₗhimselfₗ." So Satan went out from the LORD's presence.

Satan's First Test of Job

¹³ One day when Job's sons and daughters were eating and drinking wine in their oldest brother's house, ¹⁴ a messenger came to Job and reported: "While the oxen were plowing and the donkeys grazing nearby, ¹⁵ the Sabeans swooped down and took them away. They struck down the servants with the sword, and I alone have escaped to tell you!"

¹⁶ He was still speaking when another ₗmessengerₗ came and reported: "A lightning storm ᵇ struck from heaven. It burned up the sheep and the servants, and devoured them, and I alone have escaped to tell you!"

¹⁷ That messenger was still speaking when ₗyetₗ another came and reported: "The Chaldeans formed three bands, made a raid on the camels, and took them away. They struck down the servants with the sword, and I alone have escaped to tell you!"

¹⁸ He was still speaking when another ₗmessengerₗ came and reported: "Your

---

ᵃ**1:5** Lit for the number of ᵇ**1:16** Lit The fire of God

sons and daughters were eating and drinking wine in their oldest brother's house. ¹⁹ Suddenly a powerful wind swept in from the desert and struck the four corners of the house. It collapsed on the young people so that they died, and I alone have escaped to tell you!"

Job's Response

²⁰ Then Job stood up, tore his robe and shaved his head.ᵃ He fell to the ground and worshiped, ²¹ saying:

> Naked I came
>   from my mother's womb,
> and naked I will leave this life.ᵇ
> The LORD gives, and the LORD
>   takes away.
> Praise the name of the LORD.

²² Throughout all this Job did not sin or blame God for anything.ᶜ

Satan's Second Challenge to God

2 One day the sons of God came again to present themselves before the LORD, and Satan also came with them to present himself before the LORD. ² The LORD asked Satan, "Where have you come from?"

"From roaming through the earth," Satan answered Him, "and walking around on it."

³ Then the LORD said to Satan, "Have you considered My servant Job? No one else on earth is like him, a man of perfect integrity, who •fears God and turns away from evil. He still retains his integrity, even though you incited Me against him, to destroy him without just cause."

⁴ "Skin for skin!" Satan answered the LORD. "A man will give up everything he owns in exchange for his life. ⁵ But stretch out Your hand and strike his flesh and bones, and he will surely curse You to Your face."

Satan's Second Test of Job

⁶ "Very well," the LORD told Satan, "he is in your power; only spare his life." ⁷ So Satan left the LORD's presence and infected Job with incurable boils from the sole of his foot to the top of his head. ⁸ Then Job took a piece of broken pottery to scrape himself while he sat among the ashes.ᵈ

⁹ His wife said to him, "Do you still retain your integrity? Curse God and die!"

Job's Accepting Response

¹⁰ "You speak as a foolish woman speaks," he told her. "Should we accept only good from God and not adversity?" Throughout all this Job did not sin in what he said.ᵉ

Job's Three Friends

¹¹ Now when Job's three friends—Eliphaz the Temanite, Bildad the Shuhite, and Zophar the Naamathite—heard about all this adversity that had happened to him, each of them came from his home. They met together to go and offer sympathy and comfort to him. ¹² When they looked from a distance, they could ⌊barely⌋ recognize him. They wept aloud, and each man tore his robe and threw dust into the air and on his head. ¹³ Then they sat on the ground with him seven days and nights, but no one spoke a word to him because they saw that his suffering was very intense.

Job's Opening Complaint

3 After this Job began to speak and cursed the day he was born. ² He said:

ᵃ**1:20** = in mourning; Gn 37:29,34; Jos 7:6   ᵇ**1:21** Lit *will return there*; Ps 139:13,15   ᶜ**1:22** Lit *or ascribe blame to God*   ᵈ**2:8** = in mourning; Jb 42:6; 2 Sm 13:19   ᵉ**2:10** Lit *sin with his lips*

³ May the day I was born perish,
and the night when they said,
"A boy is conceived."
⁴ If only that day had turned
to darkness!
May God above not care about it,
or light shine on it.
⁵ May darkness and gloom reclaim it,
and a cloud settle over it.
May an eclipse of the sunᵃ terrify it.
⁶ If only darkness had taken
that night away!
May it not appearᵇ among the days
of the year
or be listed in the calendar.ᶜ
⁷ Yes, may that night be barren;
may no joyful shout be heard in it.
⁸ Let those who curse ⌐certain⌐ days
cast a spell on it,
those who are skilled
in rousing •Leviathan.
⁹ May its morning stars grow dark.
May it wait for daylight
but have none;
may it not see the breakingᵈ
of dawn.
¹⁰ For that night did not shut
the doors of my ⌐mother's⌐ womb,
and hide sorrow from my eyes.

¹¹ Why was I not stillborn;
⌐why⌐ didn't I die as I came
from the womb?
¹² Why did the knees receive me,
and why were there breasts for me
to nurse?
¹³ For then I would have laid down
in peace;
I would be asleep.
Then I would be at rest
¹⁴ with the kings and counselors
of the earth,
who rebuilt ruined cities
for themselves,

¹⁵ or with princes who had gold,
who filled their houses with silver.
¹⁶ Or ⌐why⌐ was I not hidden
like a miscarried child,
like infants who never see daylight?
¹⁷ There the wicked cease
to make trouble,
and there the weary find rest.
¹⁸ The captives are completely at ease;
they do not hear the voice
of ⌐their⌐ oppressor.
¹⁹ Both the small and the great
are there,
and the slave is set free
from his master.

²⁰ Why is light given to one burdened
with grief,
and life to those whose existence
is bitter,
²¹ who wait for death,
but it does not come,
and search for it more than
for hidden treasure,
²² who are filled with much joy
and are glad when they reach
the grave?
²³ ⌐Why is life given⌐ to a man
whose path is hidden,
whom God has hedged in?
²⁴ I sigh when food is ⌐put⌐ before me,ᵉ
and my groans pour out like water.
²⁵ For the thing I feared has overtaken
me,
and what I dreaded has happened
to me.
²⁶ I cannot relax or be still;
I have no rest, for trouble comes.

FIRST SERIES OF SPEECHES
Eliphaz Speaks

4 Then Eliphaz the Temanite replied:
² Should anyone try to speak
with you

ᵃ**3:5** Lit *May a darkening of daylight* ᵇ**3:6** LXX, Syr, Tg, Vg; MT reads *rejoice* ᶜ**3:6** Lit *or enter the number of months* ᵈ**3:9** Lit *the eyelids* ᵉ**3:24** Or *My sighing serves as my food*

when you are exhausted?
Yet who can keep from speaking?
3 Look! You have instructed many
and have strengthened weak hands.
4 Your words have steadied the one
    who was stumbling,
and braced the knees
    that were buckling.
5 But now that this has happened
    to you,
you have become exhausted.
It strikes you, and you
    are dismayed.
6 Isn't your piety your confidence,
    and the integrity of your life[a]
    your hope?
7 Consider: who has perished
    when he was innocent?
Where have the honest
    been destroyed?
8 In my experience,
    those who plow injustice
and those who sow trouble reap
    the same.
9 They perish at a ⌊single⌋ blast
    from God
and come to an end by the breath
    of His nostrils.
10 The lion may roar
    and the fierce lion growl,
but the fangs of young lions
    are broken.
11 The strong lion dies if ⌊it catches⌋
    no prey,
and the cubs of the lioness
    are scattered.

12 A word was brought to me
    in secret;
my ears caught a whisper of it.
13 Among unsettling thoughts
    from visions in the night,
when deep sleep descends on men,
14 fear and trembling came over me

and made all my bones shake.
15 A wind[b] passed by me,
and I shuddered with fear.[c]
16 ⌊A figure⌋ stood there,
but I could not recognize
    its appearance;
a form loomed before my eyes.
I heard a quiet voice:
17 "Can a person be more righteous
    than God,
or a man more pure
    than his Maker?"
18 If God puts no trust in His servants
and He charges His angels
    with foolishness,[d]
19 how much more those who dwell
    in clay houses,
whose foundation is in the dust,
who are crushed like a moth!
20 They are smashed to pieces
    from dawn to dusk;
they perish forever while no one
    notices.
21 Are their tent cords not pulled up?
They die without wisdom.

5 Call out if you please. Will anyone
answer you?
    Which of the holy ones will you
        turn to?
2 For anger kills a fool,
    and jealousy slays the gullible.
3 I have seen a fool taking root,
    but I immediately pronounced
        a curse on his home.
4 His children are far from safety.
    They are crushed at the ⌊city⌋ •gate,
    with no one to defend ⌊them⌋.
5 The hungry consume his harvest,
    even taking it out of the thorns.[e]
    The thirsty[f] pant
        for his children's wealth.
6 For distress does not grow
    out of the soil,

and trouble does not sprout
    from the ground.
7 But <u>mankind is born for trouble</u>
    as surely as sparks fly upward.

8 However, <u>if I were you,</u>
    <u>I would appeal to God</u>
    <u>and would present my case to Him.</u>
9 He does great
    and unsearchable things,
    wonders without number.
10 He gives rain to the earth
    and sends water to the fields.
11 He sets the lowly on high,
    and mourners are lifted to safety.
12 He frustrates the schemes
    of the crafty
    so that they[a] achieve no success.
13 He traps the wise in their craftiness
    so that the plans of the deceptive
    are quickly brought to an end.
14 They encounter darkness by day,
    and they grope at noon
    as if it were night.
15 He saves the needy
    from their sharp words[b]
    and from the clutches
    of the powerful.
16 So the poor have hope,
    and injustice shuts its mouth.
17 See how happy the man is
    God corrects;
    so <u>do not reject the discipline</u>
    <u>of the •Almighty.</u>
18 For He crushes but also binds up;
    He strikes, but His hands also heal.
19 He will rescue you
    from six calamities;
    no harm will touch you in seven.
20 In famine He will redeem you
    from death,
    and in battle, from the power
    of the sword.
21 You will be safe from slander[c]

and not fear destruction
    when it comes.
22 You will laugh at destruction
    and hunger
    and not fear the animals
    of the earth.
23 For you will have a covenant
    with the stones of the field,
    and the wild animals will be
    at peace with you.
24 You will know that your tent
    is secure,
    and nothing will be missing
    when you inspect your home.
25 You will also know
    that your offspring will be many
    and your descendants like the grass
    of the earth.
26 You will approach the grave
    in full vigor,
    as a stack of sheaves is gathered
    in its season.
27 We have investigated this,
    and it is true!
    Hear it and understand ⟨it⟩
    for yourself.

Job's Despairing Reply to Eliphaz

6 Then Job answered:

2 If only my grief could be weighed
    and my devastation placed with it
    on a scale.
3 For then it would outweigh
    the sand of the seas!
    That is why my words are rash.
4 Surely the arrows of the •Almighty
    have pierced[d] me;
    my spirit drinks their poison.
    God's terrors are arrayed
    against me.
5 Does a wild donkey bray
    over fresh grass

---

or an ox low over its fodder?

6 Is bland food eaten without salt?
  Is there flavor in an egg white?[a]
7 I refuse to touch ⌊them⌋;
  they are like contaminated food.

8 If only my request
    would be granted
  and God would provide what
    I hope for:
9 that He would decide to crush me,
  to unleash His power
    and cut me off!
10 It would still bring me comfort,
   and I would leap for joy
     in unrelenting pain
   that I have not denied[b] the words
     of the Holy One.

11 What strength do I have
     that I should continue to hope?
   What is my future, that I should
     be patient?
12 Is my strength that of stone,
   or my flesh made of bronze?
13 Since I cannot help myself,
   ⌊the hope for⌋ success
     has been banished from me.

14 A despairing man should receive
     loyalty from his friends,[c]
   even if he abandons the •fear
     of the Almighty.
15 My brothers are as treacherous
     as a •wadi,
   as seasonal streams that overflow
16 and become darkened[d]
     because of ice,
   and the snow melts into them.
17 The wadis evaporate
     in warm weather;
   they disappear from their channels
     in hot weather.
18 Caravans turn away
     from their routes,

go up into the desert, and perish.
19 The caravans of Tema look
     ⌊for these streams⌋.
   The traveling merchants of Sheba
     hope for them.
20 They are ashamed because they
     had been confident
     ⌊of finding water⌋.
   When they arrive there,
     they are frustrated.
21 So ⌊this⌋ is what you have
     now become ⌊to me⌋.[e]
   When you see something dreadful,
     you are afraid.
22 Have I ever said:
     Give me ⌊something⌋
   or Pay a bribe for me
     from your wealth
23 or Deliver me
     from the enemy's power
   or Redeem me from the grasp
     of the ruthless?

24 Teach me, and I will be silent.
   Help me understand
     what I did wrong.
25 How painful honest words can be!
   But what does your rebuke prove?
26 Do you think that you can disprove
     ⌊my⌋ words
   or that a despairing man's words
     are ⌊mere⌋ wind?
27 No doubt you would cast ⌊lots⌋
     for a fatherless child
   and negotiate a price to ⌊sell⌋
     your friend.

28 But now, please look at me;
     would I lie to your face?
29 Reconsider; don't be unjust.
   Reconsider; my righteousness
     is still the issue.
30 Am I lying,
   or can I[f] not recognize lies?

---

[a]6:6 Hb obscure   [b]6:10 Lit hidden   [c]6:14 Lit To the despairing his friend loyalty, Hb obscure   [d]6:16 Or turbid
[e]6:21 Alt Hb tradition reads So you have now become nothing   [f]6:30 Lit Is there injustice on my tongue, or can my palate

Job Bemoans Human Condition

7 Isn't mankind consigned
to forced labor on earth?
Are not his days like those
of a hired hand?

2 Like a slave he longs for shade;
like a hired man he waits
for his pay.

3 So I have been made to inherit
months of futility,
and troubled nights
have been assigned to me.

4 When I lie down I think:
When will I get up?
But the evening drags on endlessly,
and I toss and turn until dawn.

5 My flesh is clothed with maggots
and encrusted with dirt.ᵃ
My skin forms scabsᵇ
and then oozes.

6 My days pass more swiftly
than a weaver's shuttle;
they come to an end without hope.

7 Remember that my life is
ₗbutₗ a breath.
My eye will never again see
anything good.

8 The eye of anyone who looks on me
will no longer see me.
Your eyes will look for me, but I
will be gone.

9 As a cloud fades away and vanishes,
so the one who goes down
to •Sheol will never rise again.

10 He will never return to his house;
his hometown will no longer
rememberᶜ him.

11 Therefore I will not restrain
my mouth.
I will speak in the anguish
of my spirit;
I will complain in the bitterness
of my soul.

12 Am I the seaᵈ or a sea monster,
that You keep me under guard?

13 When I say: My bed
will comfort me,
and my couch will ease
my complaint,

14 then You frighten me with dreams,
and terrify me with visions,

15 so that I prefer strangling,ᵉ
death rather than life in this body.ᶠ

16 I give up! I will not live forever.
Leave me alone, for my days are
a breath.ᵍ

17 What is man, that You think
so highly of him
and pay so much attention to him?

18 You inspect him every morning,
and put him to the test
every moment.

19 Will You ever look away from me,
or leave me alone until I swallow
my saliva?

Job Questions God

20 ₗIfₗ I have sinned, what have I done
to You,
Watcher of mankind?
Why have You made me
Your target,
so that I have become a burden
to You?ʰ

21 Why not forgive my sin
and pardon my transgression?
For soon I will lie down
in the grave.
You will eagerly seek me, but I
will be gone.

Bildad Rebukes Job

8 Then Bildad the Shuhite replied:
2 How long will you go on saying
these things?
Your words are a blast of wind.

ᵃ**7:5** Or *and dirty scabs*   ᵇ**7:5** Lit *skin hardens*   ᶜ**7:10** Lit *know*   ᵈ**7:12** Or *the sea god*; Jb 26:12; Ps 74:13   ᵉ**7:15** Or *suffocation*   ᶠ**7:15** Lit *than my bones*   ᵍ**7:16** Or *are futile*   ʰ**7:20** LXX, one ancient Jewish tradition; MT, Vg read *myself*

3 Does God pervert justice?
Does the •Almighty pervert
what is right?
4 Since your children sinned
against Him,
He gave them over
to their rebellion.
5 But if you earnestly seek God
and ask the Almighty for mercy,
6 if you are pure and upright,
then He will move even now
on your behalf
and restore the home where
your righteousness dwells.
7 Then, even if your beginnings
were modest,
your final days will be
full of prosperity.

8 For ask the previous generation,
and pay attention to what
their fathers discovered,
9 since we were ⌞born only⌟ yesterday
and know nothing.
Our days on earth are
but a shadow.
10 Will they not teach you
and tell you
and speak from
their understanding?
11 Does papyrus grow where there is
no marsh?
Do reeds flourish without water?
12 While still uncut shoots,
they would dry up quicker than
any ⌞other⌟ plant.
13 Such is the destiny[a] of all
who forget God;
the hope of the godless will perish.
14 His source of confidence is fragile;[b]
what he trusts in is a spider's web.
15 He leans on his web, but it doesn't
stand firm.
He grabs it, but it does not hold up.

16 He is an amply watered plant
in the sunshine;
his shoots spread out
over his garden.
17 His roots are intertwined
around a pile of rocks.
He looks for a home
among the stones.
18 If he is uprooted[c] from his place,
it will deny ⌞knowing⌟ him, saying,
"I never saw you."
19 Surely this is the joy of his way
of life;
yet others will sprout from the dust.
20 Look, God does not reject a person
of integrity,
and He will not support evildoers.
21 He will yet fill your mouth
with laughter
and your lips with a shout of joy.
22 Your enemies will be clothed
with shame;
the tent of the wicked will exist
no longer.

Job's Reply to Bildad: God's Power

9 Then Job answered:
2 Yes, I know what you've said
is true,
but how can a person be justified
before God?
3 If one wanted to take Him to court,
he could not answer God[d] once
in a thousand ⌞times⌟.
4 God is wise and all-powerful.
Who has opposed Him
and come out unharmed?
5 He removes mountains
without their knowledge,
overturning them in His anger.
6 He shakes the earth from its place
so that its pillars tremble.

---

[a]8:13 Lit Such are the ways   [b]8:14 Or cut off; Hb obscure   [c]8:18 Lit swallowed   [d]9:3 Or court, God would not answer him

7 He commands the sun not to shine
   and seals off the stars.
8 He alone stretches out the heavens
   and treads on the waves of the sea.ᵃ
9 He makes ⌊the stars⌋: the Bear,ᵇ Orion,
   the Pleiades, and the constellationsᶜ
   of the southern sky.
10 He performs great
   and unsearchable things,
   wonders without number.
11 If He passes by me,
   I wouldn't see Him;
   ⌊if⌋ He goes right by,
   I wouldn't recognize Him.
12 If He snatches ⌊something⌋,
   who can stopᵈ Him?
   Who can ask Him, "What are
   You doing?"
13 God does not hold back His anger;
   •Rahab's assistants cringe in fear
   beneath Him!

14 How then can I answer Him
   or choose my arguments
   against Him?
15 Even if I were in the right,
   I could not answer.
   I could only beg my judge
   for mercy.
16 If I summoned ⌊Him⌋
   and He answered me,
   I do not believe He would
   pay attention to what I said.
17 He batters me with a whirlwind
   and multiplies my wounds
   without cause.
18 He doesn't let me catch my breath
   but soaks me
   with bitter experiences.
19 If it is a matter of strength, look,
   He is the Mighty One!
   If it is a matter of justice, who can
   summon Him?ᵉ

20 Even if I were in the right,
   my own mouth would
   condemn me;
   if I were blameless, my mouth
   would declare me guilty.
21 Though I am blameless,
   I no longer care about myself;
   I renounce my life.
22 It is all the same. Therefore I say,
   "He destroys both the blameless
   and the wicked."
23 When disaster brings
   sudden death,
   He mocks the despair
   of the innocent.
24 The earthᶠ is handed over
   to the wicked;
   He blindfoldsᵍ its judges.
   If it isn't He, then who is it?

25 My days fly by faster
   than a runner;ʰ
   they flee without seeing any good.
26 They sweep by like boats made
   of papyrus,
   like an eagle swooping down
   on ⌊its⌋ prey.
27 If I said, "I will forget
   my complaint,
   change my expression, and smile,"
28 I would still live in terror of all
   my pains.
   I know You will not acquit me.
29 Since I will be found guilty,
   why should I labor in vain?
30 If I wash myself with snow,
   and cleanse my hands with lye,
31 then You dip me in a pit ⌊of mud⌋,
   and my own clothes despise me!
32 For He is not a man like me,
   that I can answer Him,
   that we can take each other
   to court.

ᵃ9:8 Or and walks on the back of the sea god   ᵇ9:9 Or Aldebaran   ᶜ9:9 Or chambers   ᵈ9:12 Or dissuade
ᵉ9:19 LXX; MT reads me   ᶠ9:24 Or land   ᵍ9:24 Lit covers the faces of   ʰ9:25 = a royal messenger; 2 Sm 18:19-33;
1 Kg 1:5; Est 3:13,15

33 There is no one to judge
   between us,
   to lay his hand on both of us.
34 Let Him take His rod away from me
   so His terror will no longer
   frighten me.
35 Then I would speak and not
   fear Him.
   But that is not the case; I am
   on my own.

Job's Bitterness

10 I am disgusted with my life.
   I will express my complaint
   and speak in the bitterness
   of my soul.
2 I will say to God:
   Do not declare me guilty!
   Let me know why
   You prosecute me.
3 Is it good for You to oppress,
   to reject the work of Your hands,
   and favor[a] the plans of the wicked?
4 Do You have eyes of flesh,
   or do You see as a human sees?
5 Are Your days like those
   of a human,
   or Your years like those of a man,
6 that You look for my wrongdoing
   and search for my sin,
7 even though You know that
   I am not wicked
   and that there is no one
   who can deliver from Your hand?
8 Your hands shaped me
   and formed me.
   Will You now turn around
   and destroy me?
9 Please remember that You
   formed me like clay.
   Will You now return me to dust?
10 Did You not pour me out like milk
   and curdle me like cheese?

11 You clothed me with skin and flesh,
   and wove me together with bones
   and tendons.
12 You gave me life and faithful love,
   and Your care has guarded my life.
13 Yet You concealed these ⌊thoughts⌋
   in Your heart;
   I know that this was
   Your hidden plan:[b]
14 if I sin, You would notice,[c]
   and would not acquit me
   of my wrongdoing.
15 If I am wicked, woe to me!
   And even if I am righteous, I cannot
   lift up my head.
   I am filled with shame
   and aware of my affliction.

Job Protests to God

16 If I am proud, You hunt me
   like a lion
   and again display
   Your miraculous power
   against me.
17 You produce new witnesses[d]
   against me
   and multiply Your anger
   toward me.
   Hardships assault me,
   wave after wave.[e]
18 Why did You bring me out of
   the womb?
   I should have died and never
   been seen.
19 I wish[f] I had never existed
   but had been carried
   from the womb to the grave.
20 Are my days not few? Stop ⌊it⌋[g]
   Leave me alone, so that I can smile
   a little
21 before I go to a land of darkness
   and gloom,
   never to return.

---

a **10:3** Lit *shine on*   b **10:13** Lit *was with You*   c **10:14** Lit *notice me*   d **10:17** Or *You bring fresh troops*   e **10:17** Lit *Changes and a host are with me*   f **10:19** Lit *As if*   g **10:20** Alt Hb tradition reads *Will He not leave my few days alone?*

22 ⌊It is⌋ a land of blackness
      like the deepest darkness,
    gloomy and chaotic,
      where even the light is
      like[a] the darkness.

Zophar Criticizes Job

11 Then Zophar the Naamathite replied:

2 Should this stream of words
      go unanswered
    and such a talker[b] be acquitted?
3 Should your babbling put others
      to silence,
    so that you can keep on ridiculing
    with no one to humiliate you?
4 You have said, "My teaching
      is sound,
    and I am pure in Your sight."

Zophar: God Has His Reasons

5 But if only God would speak
    and declare His case[c] against you,
6 He would show you the secrets
      of wisdom,
    for true wisdom has two sides.
    Know then that God has chosen
    to overlook some of your sin.

7 Can you fathom the depths of God
    or discover the limits
      of the •Almighty?
8 ⌊They are⌋ higher than the heavens—
      what can you do?
    ⌊They are⌋ deeper than •Sheol—
      what can you know?
9 Their measure is longer
      than the earth
    and wider than the sea.

10 If He passes by and throws
      ⌊someone⌋ in prison
    or convenes a court, who can
      stop Him?

11 Surely He knows which people
      are worthless.
    If He sees iniquity, will He not
      take note ⌊of it⌋?
12 But a stupid man
      will gain understanding
    as soon as a wild donkey is born
      a man!

Zophar's Plan for Job

13 As for you, if you redirect your heart
    and lift up your hands to Him
      ⌊in prayer⌋—
14 if there is iniquity in your hand,
      remove it,
    and don't allow injustice to dwell
      in your tents—
15 then you will hold your head high,
      free from fault.
    You will be firmly established
      and unafraid.
16 For you will forget your suffering,
    recalling ⌊it only⌋ as waters
      that have flowed by.
17 ⌊Your⌋ life will be brighter
      than noonday;
    ⌊its⌋ darkness[d] will be
      like the morning.
18 You will be confident, because
      there is hope.
    You will look carefully about
      and lie down in safety.
19 You will lie down without fear,
    and many will seek your favor.
20 But the sight of the wicked will fail.
    Their way of escape will be cut off,
    and their ⌊only⌋ hope will be to die.

Job's Reply to Zophar

12 Then Job answered:

2 No doubt you are the people,
    and wisdom will die with you!

a**10:22** Lit *chaotic, and shines as*   b**11:2** Lit *a man of lips*   c**11:5** Lit *and open His lips*   d**11:17** Text emended; MT
reads *noonday; you are dark, you*

3 But I also have a mind;
   I am not inferior to you.
   Who doesn't know the things
      you are talking about?ᵃ

4 I am a laughingstock to myᵇ friends,
   by calling on God,
      who answers me.ᶜ
   The righteous and upright man is
      a laughingstock.

5 The one who is at ease
      holds calamity in contempt
   ⌊and thinks⌋ it is prepared for those
      whose feet are slipping.

6 The tents of robbers are safe,
   and those who provoke God
      are secure;
   God's power provides this.

7 But ask the animals, and they will
      instruct you;
   ⌊ask⌋ the birds of the sky,
      and they will tell you.

8 Or speak to the earth, and it will
      instruct you;
   let the fish of the sea inform you.

9 Which of all these does not know
   that the hand of the LORD
      has done this?

10 The life of every living thing is
      in His hand,
   as well as the breath
      of all mankind.

11 Doesn't the ear test words
   as the palate tastes food?

12 Wisdom is found with the elderly,
   and understanding comes
      with long life.

13 Wisdom and strength belong
      to God;
   counsel and understanding are His.

14 Whatever He tears down cannot
      be rebuilt;
   whoever He imprisons cannot
      be released.

15 When He withholds the waters,
      everything dries up,
   and when He releases them,
      they destroy the land.

16 True wisdom and power belong
      to Him.
   The deceived and the deceiver
      are His.

17 He leads counselors away barefoot
   and makes judges go mad.

18 He releases the bondsᵈ put on
      by kings
   and ties a cloth around their waists.

19 He leads priests away barefoot
   and overthrows established leaders.

20 He deprives trusted advisers
      of speech
   and takes away the elders'
      good judgment.

21 He pours out contempt on nobles
   and disarmsᵉ the strong.

22 He reveals mysteries
      from the darkness
   and brings the deepest darkness
      into the light.

23 He makes nations great,
      then destroys them;
   He enlarges nations,
      then leads them away.

24 He deprives the world's leaders
      of reason,
   and makes them wander
      in a trackless wasteland.

25 They grope around in darkness
      without light;
   He makes them stagger
      like drunken men.

13 Look, my eyes have seen all this;
   my ears have heard
      and understood it.

ᵃ12:3 Lit With whom are not such things as these   ᵇ12:4 Lit his   ᶜ12:4 Lit him   ᵈ12:18 Text emended; MT reads discipline   ᵉ12:21 Lit and loosens the belt of

Job's Frustration with Friends

2 Everything you know, I also know;
I am not inferior to you.

3 Yet I prefer to speak
to the •Almighty
and argue my case before God.

4 But you coat ⌊the truth⌋ with lies;
you are all worthless doctors.

5 If only you would shut up
and let that be your wisdom!

6 Hear now my argument,
and listen to my defense.ᵃ

7 Would you testify unjustly
on God's behalf
or speak deceitfully for Him?

8 Would you show partiality to Him
or argue the case in His defense?

9 Would it go well
if He examined you?
Could you deceive Him
as you would deceive a man?

10 Surely He would rebuke you
if you secretly showed partiality.

11 Would God's majesty
not terrify you?
Would His dread not fall on you?

12 Your memorable sayings
are proverbs of ash;
your defenses are made of clay.

13 Be quiet,ᵇ and I will speak.
Let whatever comes happen to me.

14 Why do I put myself at riskᶜ
and take my life in my own hands?

Job's Great Resolve

15 Even if He kills me, I will hope
in Him.ᵈ
I will still defend my ways
before Him.

16 Yes, this will result
in my deliverance,
for no godless person can appear
before Him.

17 Pay close attention to my words;
let my declaration ⌊ring⌋ in your ears.

18 Now then, I have prepared
⌊my⌋ case;
I know that I am right.

19 Can anyone indict me?
If so, I will be silent and die.

Job's Appeal to God

20 Only grant ⌊these⌋ two things to me,
⌊God⌋,
so that I will not have to hide
from Your presence:

21 remove Your hand from me,
and do not let Your terror
frighten me.

22 Then call, and I will answer,
or I will speak, and You
can respond to me.

23 How many iniquities and sins
have I committed?ᵉ
Reveal to me my transgression
and sin.

24 Why do You hide Your face
and consider me Your enemy?

25 Will You frighten
a wind-driven leaf?
Will You chase after dry straw?

26 For You record bitter accusations
against me
and make me inherit the iniquities
of my youth.

27 You put my feet in the stocks
and stand watch over all my paths,
setting a limit for the solesᶠ
of my feet.

Job: Man's Condition

28 Man wears out
like something rotten,
like a moth-eaten garment.

14 Man born of woman
is short of days and full of trouble.

---

2 He blossoms like a flower,
   then withers;
he flees like a shadow
   and does not last.
3 Do You really take notice of one
   like this?
Will You bring me into judgment
   against You?ᵃ
4 Who can produce something pure
   from what is impure?
No one!
5 Since man's days are determined
and the number of his months
   depends on You,
and ₍since₎ You have setᵇ limits
   he cannot pass,
6 look away from him
   and let him rest
so that he can enjoy his day
   like a hired hand.

7 There is hope for a tree:
If it is cut down, it will
   sprout again,
and its shoots will not die.
8 If its roots grow old in the ground
and its stump starts to die
   in the soil,
9 the smell of water makes it thrive
and produce twigs like a sapling.
10 But a man dies and fades away;
he breathes his last—where is he?
11 As water disappears from the sea
and a •wadi becomes parched
   and dry,
12 so man lies down never to rise again.
They will not wake up
   until the heavens are no more;
they will not stir from their sleep.

13 If only You would hide me in •Sheol
and conceal me
   until Your anger passes,
that You would appoint a time
   for me

and then remember me.
14 When a man dies, will he
   come back to life?
₍If so,₎ I would wait all the days
   of my struggle
until my relief comes.
15 You would call, and I would
   answer You.
You would long for the work
   of Your hands.
16 For then You would count my steps
but would not take note of my sin.
17 My rebellion would be sealed up
   in a bag,
and You would cover over
   my iniquity.

18 But as a mountain collapses
   and crumbles
and a rock is dislodged
   from its place,
19 as water wears away stones
and torrents wash away the soil
   from the land,
so You destroy a man's hope.
20 You completely overpower him,
   and he passes on;
You change his appearance
   and send him away.
21 If his sons receive honor,
   he does not know it;
if they become insignificant,
   he is unaware of it.
22 He feels only the pain
   of his own body
and mourns only for himself.

SECOND SERIES OF SPEECHES
Eliphaz Censures Job

15 Then Eliphaz the Temanite replied:

2 Does a wise man answer
   with emptyᶜ counsel
or fill himselfᵈ
   with the hot east wind?

ᵃ14:3 LXX, Syr, Vg read him   ᵇ14:5 Lit set his   ᶜ15:2 Lit windy; Jb 16:3   ᵈ15:2 Lit his belly

3 Should he argue with useless talk
   or with words that serve
      no good purpose?
4 But you even undermine the •fear
   ⌊of God⌋
   and hinder meditation before Him.
5 Your iniquity teaches you
      what to say,
   and you choose the language
      of the crafty.
6 Your own mouth condemns you,
      not I;
   your own lips testify against you.

7 Were you the first person
      ever born,
   or were you brought forth
      before the hills?
8 Do you listen in on the council
      of God,
   or have a monopoly on wisdom?
9 What do you know that we don't?
   ⌊What⌋ do you understand that
      is not ⌊clear⌋ to us?
10 Both the gray-haired and the elderly
      are with us,
   men older than your father.
11 Are God's consolations not enough
      for you,
   even the words that ⌊deal⌋ gently
      with you?
12 Why has your heart misled you,
   and why do your eyes flash
13 as you turn your anger[a] against God
   and allow such words to leave
      your mouth?

14 What is man, that he
      should be pure,
   or one born of woman, that he
      should be righteous?
15 If God puts no trust
      in His holy ones
   and the heavens are not pure
      in His sight,

16 how much less one who is revolting
      and corrupt,
   who drinks injustice like water?

17 Listen to me and I will inform you.
   I will describe what I have seen,
18 what was declared by wise men
   and was not suppressed
      by their ancestors,
19 the land was given to them alone
   when no foreigner passed
      among them.

Eliphaz's View of Wicked
20 A wicked man writhes in pain
      all his days;
   few[b] years are stored up
      for the ruthless.
21 Dreadful sounds fill his ears;
   when he is at peace, a robber
      attacks him.
22 He doesn't believe he will return
      from darkness;
   he is destined for the sword.
23 He wanders about for food, ⌊saying,⌋
      "Where is it?"
   He knows the day of darkness is
      at hand.
24 Trouble and distress terrify him,
   overwhelming him like a king
      prepared for battle.
25 For he has stretched out his hand
      against God
   and has arrogantly opposed
      the •Almighty.
26 He rushes headlong at Him
   with his thick, studded shields.
27 Though his face is covered with fat[c]
   and his waistline bulges with it,
28 he will dwell in ruined cities,
   in abandoned houses destined
      to become piles of rubble.
29 He will no longer be rich;
   his wealth will not endure.

a**15:13** Or *spirit*   b**15:20** Lit *the number of*   c**15:27** Lit *with his fat*

His possessions[a] will not spread
   over the land.
30 He will not escape
   from the darkness;
 flames will wither his shoots,
 and he will depart by the breath
   of God's mouth.
31 Let him not put trust
   in worthless things, being
   led astray,
 for what he gets in exchange
   will prove worthless.
32 It will be accomplished
   before his time,
 and his branch will not flourish.
33 He will be like a vine that drops
   its unripe grapes
 and like an olive tree that sheds
   its blossoms.
34 For the company of the godless
   will be barren,
 and fire will consume the tents
   of those who offer bribes.
35 They conceive trouble
   and give birth to evil;
 their womb prepares deception.

Job Confronts Eliphaz and Friends

16 Then Job answered:
2 I have heard many things
   like these.
 You are all miserable comforters.
3 Is there ₍no₎ end
   to your empty[b] words?
 What provokes you that you
   continue testifying?
4 If you were in my place I could
   also talk like you.
 I could string words together
   against you
 and shake my head at you,
   ₍but I wouldn't₎.

5 I would encourage you
   with my mouth,
 and the consolation from my lips
   would bring relief.
6 Even if I speak, my suffering
   is not relieved,
 and if I hold back, what have I lost?

Job Links God to His Troubles

7 Surely He has now exhausted me.
 You have devastated
   my entire family.
8 You have shriveled me up[c]—
   it has become a witness;
 My frailty rises up against me
   and testifies to my face.
9 His anger tears ₍at me₎,
   and He harasses me.
 He gnashes His teeth at me.
 My enemy pierces me
   with His eyes.
10 They open their mouths against me
 and strike my cheeks
   with contempt;
 they join themselves together
   against me.
11 God hands me over to unjust men;[d]
 He throws me into the hands
   of the wicked.
12 I was at ease, but He shattered me;
 He seized ₍me₎ by the scruff
   of the neck
 and smashed me to pieces.
 He set me up as His target;
13 His archers[e] surround me.
 He pierces my kidneys
   without mercy
 and pours my bile on the ground.
14 He breaks through my defenses
   again and again;[f]
 He charges at me like a warrior.
15 I have sewn •sackcloth
   over my skin;

---

[a]15:29 Text emended; Hb uncertain   [b]16:3 Lit windy; Jb 15:2   [c]16:8 Or have seized me; Hb obscure   [d]16:11 LXX, Vg; MT reads to a boy   [e]16:13 Or arrows   [f]16:14 Lit through me, breach on breach

I have buried my strength[a]
  in the dust.
16 My face has grown red
    with weeping,
  and the shadow of death covers
    my eyes,
17 although my hands are free
    from violence
  and my prayer is pure.

18 Earth, do not cover my blood;
  may my cry for help find
    no resting place.
19 Even now my witness is in heaven,
  and my advocate is in the heights!
20 My friends scoff at me
  as I weep before God.
21 I wish that someone might arbitrate
  between a man and God
  just as a •man ⌊pleads⌋ for his friend.
22 For ⌊only⌋ a few years will pass
  before I go the way of no return.

Job: "My Spirit Is Broken"

17 My spirit is broken.
  My days are extinguished.
  A graveyard awaits me.
2 Surely mockers surround[b] me
  and my eyes must gaze
    at their rebellion.

3 Make arrangements! Put up
    security for me.[c]
  Who ⌊else⌋ will be my sponsor?[d]
4 You have closed their minds
    to understanding,
  therefore You will not honor ⌊them⌋.
5 If a man informs on his friends
    for a price,
  the eyes of his children will fail.

6 He has made me an object of scorn
    to the people;
  I have become a man people
    spit at.[e]

7 My eyes have grown dim
    from grief,
  and my whole body has become
    but a shadow.
8 The upright are appalled at this,
  and the innocent are roused
    against the godless.
9 Yet the righteous person will hold
    to his way,
  and the one whose hands are clean
    will grow stronger.
10 But come back ⌊and try⌋ again,
    all of you.[f]
  I will not find a wise man
    among you.

11 My days have slipped by;
  my plans have been ruined,
  even the things dear to my heart.
12 They turned night into day
  and ⌊made⌋ light ⌊seem⌋ near
    in the face of darkness.
13 If I await •Sheol as my home,
  spread out my bed in darkness,
14 and say to the •Pit: You are
    my father,
  and to the worm: My mother
    or my sister,
15 where then is my hope?
  Who can see ⌊any⌋ hope for me?
16 Will it go down to the gates
    of Sheol,
  or will we descend together
    to the dust?

Bildad Confronts Job

18 Then Bildad the Shuhite replied:

2 How long until you stop talking?
  Show some sense, and then
    we can talk.
3 Why are we regarded as cattle,
  as stupid in your sight?
4 You who tear yourself in anger[g]—

should the earth be abandoned
  on your account,
or a rock be removed
  from its place?

Bildad: Fate of Wicked

5 Yes, the light of the wicked
    is extinguished;
  the flame of his fire does not glow.
6 The light in his tent grows dark,
  and the lamp beside him is put out.
7 His powerful stride is shortened,
  and his own schemes trip him up.
8 For his own feet lead him
    into a net,
  and he strays into its mesh.
9 A trap catches ⌊him⌋ by the heel;
  a noose seizes him.
10 A rope lies hidden for him
    on the ground,
  and a snare ⌊waits⌋ for him
    along the path.
11 Terrors frighten him on every side
  and harass him at every step.
12 His strength is depleted;
  disaster lies ready for him
    to stumble.ᵃ
13 Parts of his skin are eaten away;
  death's firstborn consumes
    his limbs.
14 He is ripped from the security
    of his tent
  and marched away to the king
    of terrors.
15 Nothing he owned remains
    in his tent.
  Burning sulfur is scattered
    over his home.
16 His roots below dry up,
  and his branches above
    wither away.
17 ⌊All⌋ memory of him perishes
    from the earth;
  he has no name abroad.ᵇ

18 He is driven from light to darkness
  and chased
    from the inhabited world.
19 He has no children or descendants
    among his people,
  no survivor where he used to live.
20 Those in the west are appalled
    at his fate,
  while those in the east tremble
    in horror.
21 Indeed, such is the dwelling
    of the wicked,
  and this is the place of the one
    who does not know God.

Job to Bildad: Don't Torment

19 Then Job answered:
2 How long will you torment me
  and crush me with words?
3 You have humiliated me
    ten times now,
  and you mistreatᶜ me
    without shame.
4 Even if it is true that I have sinned,
  my mistake concerns onlyᵈ me.
5 If you really want to appear
    superior to me
  and would use my disgrace
    as evidence against me,
6 then understand that it is God
    who has wronged me
  and caught me in His net.

7 I cry out: Violence!
    but get no response;
  I call for help, but there is
    no justice.
8 He has blocked my way so that
    I cannot pass through;
  He has veiled my paths
    with darkness.
9 He has stripped me of my honor
  and removed the crown
    from my head.

ᵃ**18:12** Or *disaster hungers for him*   ᵇ**18:17** Or *name in the streets*   ᶜ**19:3** Hb obscure   ᵈ**19:4** Lit *mistake lives with*

10 He tears me down on every side
    so that I am ruined.ᵃ
   He uproots my hope like a tree.
11 His anger burns against me,
    and He regards me as ⌊one of⌋
    His enemies.
12 His troops advance together;
    they construct a rampᵇ against me
    and camp around my tent.

Job Lists Travails

13 He has removed my brothers
    from me;
   my acquaintances
    have abandoned me.
14 My relatives stop coming by,
    and my close friends
    have forgotten me.
15 My house guestsᶜ
    and female servants regard me
    as a stranger;
   I am a foreigner in their sight.
16 I call for my servant, but he
    does not answer,
   even if I beg him
    with my own mouth.
17 My breath is offensive to my wife,
    and my own familyᵈ
    find me repulsive.
18 Even young boys scorn me.
   When I stand up, they mock me.
19 All of my best friendsᵉ despise me,
    and those I love have turned
    against me.
20 My skin and my flesh cling
    to my bones;
   I have escaped by the skin
    of my teeth.

Job: "Have Mercy on Me"

21 Have mercy on me, my friends,
    have mercy,

   for God's hand has struck me.
22 Why do you persecute me
    as God ⌊does⌋?
   Will you never get enough
    of my flesh?
23 I wish that my words
    were written down,
   that they were recorded on a scroll
24 or were inscribed in stone forever
    by an iron stylus and lead!

Job's Hope

25 But I know my living Redeemer,ᶠ
   and He will stand on the dustᵍ
    at last.ʰ
26 Even after my skin
    has been destroyed,ⁱ
   yet I will see God inʲ my flesh.
27 I will see Him myself;
   my eyes will look at ⌊Him⌋, and not
    as a stranger.ᵏ
   My heart longsˡ within me.

28 If you say, "How will we pursue him,
   since the root of the problem lies
    with him?"ᵐ
29 be afraid of the sword,
   because wrath ⌊brings⌋ punishment
    by the sword,
   so that you may know there is
    a judgment.

Zophar Upset

20 Then Zophar the Naamathite re-
       plied:
2 This is why my unsettling thoughts
   compel me to answer,
   because I am upset!ⁿ
3 I have heard a rebuke
   that insults me,
   and my understandingᵒ
   makes me reply.

ᵃ**19:10** Lit gone   ᵇ**19:12** Lit they raise up their way   ᶜ**19:15** Or The resident aliens in my household   ᵈ**19:17** Lit and the
sons of my belly   ᵉ**19:19** Lit of the men of my council   ᶠ**19:25** Or know that my Redeemer is living   ᵍ**19:25** Or earth
ʰ**19:25** Or dust at the last, or dust as the Last One   ⁱ**19:26** Lit skin which they destroyed, or skin they destroyed in this
way   ʲ**19:26** Or apart from   ᵏ**19:27** Or not a stranger   ˡ**19:27** Lit My kidneys grow faint   ᵐ**19:28** Some Hb mss, LXX, Vg;
other Hb mss read me   ⁿ**20:2** Lit because of my feeling within me   ᵒ**20:3** Lit and a spirit from my understanding

Zophar: Destiny of Wicked

4 Don't you know that
    ever since antiquity,
from ʟthe timeʟ man was placed
    on earth,
5 the joy of the wicked has been brief
and the happiness of the godless
    has lasted only a moment?
6 Though his arrogance
    reaches heaven,
and his head touches the clouds,
7 he will vanish forever
    like his own dung.
Those who know[a] him will ask,
    "Where is he?"
8 He will fly away like a dream
    and never be found;
he will be chased away like a vision
    in the night.
9 The eye that saw him will see ʟhimʟ
    no more,
and his household will no longer
    see him.
10 His children will beg from[b] the poor,
for his own hands must give back
    his wealth.
11 His bones may be full of
    youthful vigor,
but it will lie down with him
    in the grave.

12 Though evil tastes sweet
    in his mouth
and he conceals it
    under his tongue,
13 though he cherishes it and will not
    let it go
but keeps it in his mouth,
14 yet the food in his stomach turns
    into cobras' venom inside him.
15 He swallows wealth but must
    vomit it up;
God will force it from his stomach.

16 He will suck the poison of cobras;
a viper's fangs[c] will kill him.
17 He will not enjoy the streams,
    the rivers flowing with honey
    and cream.
18 He must return the fruit of his labor
    without consuming ʟitʟ;
he doesn't enjoy the profits
    from his trading.
19 For he oppressed and abandoned
    the poor;
he seized a house he did not build.

20 Because his appetite
    is never satisfied,[d]
he does not escape his[e] desires.
21 Nothing is left for him to consume;
therefore, his prosperity
    will not last.
22 At the height of his success[f]
    distress will come to him;
the full weight of misery[g]
    will crush him.
23 When he fills his stomach,
God will send His burning anger
    against him,
raining ʟitʟ down on him
    while he is eating.[h]
24 If he flees from an iron weapon,
    ʟan arrow fromʟ a bronze bow
    will pierce him.
25 He pulls it out of his back,
    the flashing tip out of his liver.[i]
Terrors come over him.
26 Total darkness is reserved
    for his treasures.
A fire unfanned ʟby human handsʟ
    will consume him;
it will feed on what is left
    in his tent.
27 The heavens will expose his iniquity,
and the earth will rise up
    against him.

---

[a]20:7 Lit have seen [b]20:10 Or children must compensate [c]20:16 Lit tongue [d]20:20 Lit Because he does not know
ease in his stomach [e]20:20 Or satisfied he will not save what he [f]20:22 Lit In the fullness of his excess
[g]20:22 Some Hb mss, LXX, Vg; other Hb mss read the hand of everyone in misery [h]20:23 Text emended; MT reads
him, against his flesh [i]20:25 Or gallbladder

28 The possessions in his house
     will be removed,
   flowing away on the day
     of God's anger.
29 This is the wicked man's lot
     from God,
   the inheritance God ordained
     for him.

Job's Reply to Zophar

21 Then Job answered:

2 Pay close attention to my words;
   let this be the consolation
     you offer.
3 Bear with me while I speak;
   then after I have spoken, you may
     continue mocking.

4 As for me, is my complaint
     against a man?
   Then why shouldn't I
     be impatient?
5 Look at me and shudder;
   put ⌊your⌋ hand over ⌊your⌋ mouth.
6 When I think about ⌊it⌋,
   I am terrified
   and my body trembles in horror.

Job Puzzles over Prosperity of Wicked

7 Why do the wicked continue
     to live,
   growing old and becoming
     powerful?
8 Their children are established
     while they are still alive,[a]
   and their descendants,
     before their eyes.
9 Their homes are secure
     and free of fear;
   no rod from God ⌊strikes⌋ them.
10 Their bulls breed without fail;
    their cows calve
      and do not miscarry.

11 They let their little ones run
      around like lambs;
    their children skip about,
12 singing to the tambourine and lyre
    and rejoicing at the sound
      of the flute.
13 They spend[b] their days
      in prosperity
    and go down to •Sheol in peace.
14 Yet they say to God:
      "Leave us alone!
    We don't want to know Your ways.
15 Who is the •Almighty, that we
      should serve Him,
    and what will we gain by pleading
      with Him?"
16 But their prosperity is not
      of their own doing.
    The counsel of the wicked is far
      from me!

17 How often is the lamp
      of the wicked put out?
    Does disaster[c] come on them?
    Does He apportion destruction
      in His anger?
18 Are they like straw
      before the wind,
    like chaff a storm sweeps away?

Job Affirms God's Judgment

19 God reserves a person's punishment
      for his children.
    Let God repay the person himself,
      so that he may know ⌊it⌋.
20 Let his own eyes see his demise;
    let him drink from
      the Almighty's wrath!
21 For what does he care
      about his family once he is dead,
    when the number of his months
      has run out?

22 Can anyone teach God knowledge,
    since He judges the exalted ones?[d]

---

a**21:8** Lit *established before them with them*   b**21:13** Alt Hb tradition reads *fully enjoy*   c**21:17** Lit *their disaster*
d**21:22** Probably angels

23 One person dies
    in excellent health,[a]
    completely secure[b] and at ease.
24 His body is[c] well-fed,[d]
    and his bones are full
    of marrow.[e]
25 Yet another person dies
    with a bitter soul,
    having never tasted prosperity.
26 But they both lie in the dust,
    and worms cover them.

27 Look, I know your thoughts,
    the schemes you would
    wrong me with.
28 For you say, "Where now is
    the nobleman's house?"
    and "Where are the tents
    the wicked lived in?"
29 Have you never consulted
    those who travel the roads?
    Don't you accept their reports?[f]

Job:
Evil Man Spared

30 Indeed, the evil man is spared
    from the day of disaster,
    rescued from the day of wrath.
31 Who would denounce his behavior
    to his face?
    Who would repay him for what
    he has done?
32 He is carried to the grave,
    and someone keeps watch over
    ⌊his⌋ tomb.
33 The dirt on his grave is[g] sweet
    to him.
    Everyone follows behind him,
    and those who go before him are
    without number.

34 So how can you offer me
    such futile comfort?
    Your answers are deceptive.

THIRD SERIES OF SPEECHES
Eliphaz Speaks
Eliphaz Reflects on God

22 Then Eliphaz the Temanite re-
    plied:
2 Can a man be of ⌊any⌋ use to God?
    Can even a wise man be of use
    to Him?
3 Does it delight the •Almighty if you
    are righteous?
    Does He profit if you perfect
    your behavior?

4 Does He correct you and take you
    to court
    because of your piety?
5 Isn't your wickedness abundant
    and aren't your iniquities endless?
6 For you took collateral
    from your brothers without cause,
    stripping off their clothes
    and leaving them naked.
7 You gave no water to the thirsty
    and withheld food
    from the famished,
8 while the land belonged
    to a powerful man
    and an influential man lived on it.
9 You sent widows away
    empty-handed,
    and the strength of the fatherless
    was[h] crushed.
10 Therefore snares surround you,
    and sudden dread terrifies you,
11 or darkness, so you cannot see,
    and a flood of water covers you.

12 Isn't God as high as the heavens?
    And look at the highest stars—
    how lofty they are!
13 Yet you say: "What does God know?
    Can He judge
    through thick darkness?

---

[a]21:23 Lit in bone of his perfection   [b]21:23 Text emended; MT reads health, all at ease   [c]21:24 Or His sides are;
Hb obscure   [d]21:24 Lit is full of milk   [e]21:24 Lit and the marrow of his bones is watered   [f]21:29 Lit signs
[g]21:33 Lit The clods of the wadi are   [h]22:9 LXX, Syr, Vg, Tg read you have

¹⁴ Clouds veil Him so that
   He cannot see,
   as He walks on the circle
   of the sky."
¹⁵ Will you continue
   on the ancient path
   that wicked men have walked?
¹⁶ They were snatched away
   before their time,
   and their foundations
   were washed away by a river.
¹⁷ They were the ones who said
   to God, "Leave us alone!"
   and "What can the Almighty do
   to us?"ᵃ
¹⁸ But it was He who filled
   their houses with good things.
   The counsel of the wicked is
   far from me!
¹⁹ The righteous see ₗthisⱼ
   and rejoice;
   the innocent mock them, ₗsayingⱼ,
²⁰ "Surely our opponents
   are destroyed,
   and fire has consumed
   what they left behind."

Eliphaz:
Come to Terms with God

²¹ Come to terms with God and be
   at peace;
   in this wayᵇ good will come to you.
²² Receive instruction
   from His mouth,
   and place His sayings in your heart.
²³ If you return to the Almighty,
   you will be renewed.
   If you banish injustice
   from your tent
²⁴ and consign your gold to the dust,
   ₗthe gold ofⱼ Ophir to the stones
   in the •wadis,
²⁵ the Almighty will be your gold
   and your finest silver.

²⁶ Then you will delight in
   the Almighty
   and lift up your face to God.
²⁷ You will pray to Him, and He will
   hear you,
   and you will fulfill your vows.
²⁸ When you make a decision,
   it will be carried out,ᶜ
   and light will shine on your ways.
²⁹ When others are humiliated
   and you say, "Lift ₗthemⱼ up,"
   God will save the humble.ᵈ
³⁰ He will ₗevenⱼ rescue the guilty one,
   who will be rescued by the purity
   of your hands.

Job Looks for God

23 Then Job answered:
² Today also my complaint is bitter.ᵉ
   Hisᶠ hand is heavy
   despite my groaning.
³ If only I knew how to find Him,
   so that I could go to His throne.
⁴ I would plead my case before Him
   and fill my mouth with arguments.
⁵ I would learn howᵍ He would
   answer me;
   and understand what He would say
   to me.
⁶ Would He prosecute me forcefully?
   No, He will certainly pay attention
   to me.
⁷ There an upright man could reason
   with Him,
   and I would escape
   from my Judge forever.
⁸ If I go east, He is not there,
   and if I go west, I cannot
   perceive Him.
⁹ When He is at work to the north,
   I cannot see Him;
   when He turns south, I cannot
   find Him.

ᵃ22:17 LXX, Syr; MT reads him   ᵇ22:21 Lit peace; by them   ᶜ22:28 Lit out for you   ᵈ22:29 Lit bowed of eyes
ᵉ23:2 Syr, Tg, Vg; MT reads rebellion   ᶠ23:2 LXX, Syr; MT reads My   ᵍ23:5 Lit the words

10 Yet He knows the way
   I have taken;[a]
when He has tested me,
   I will emerge as pure gold.
11 My feet have followed in His tracks;
   I have kept to His way and not
      turned aside.
12 I have not departed
      from the commands of His lips;
   I have treasured[b] the words
      of His mouth
more than my daily food.

13 But He is unchangeable; who can
      oppose Him?
   He does what He desires.
14 He will certainly accomplish
      what He has decreed for me,
   and He has many more things
      like these in mind.[c]
15 Therefore I am terrified
      in His presence;
   when I consider ⌊this⌋, I am afraid
      of Him.
16 God has made my heart faint;
   the •Almighty has terrified me.
17 Yet I am not destroyed[d]
      by the darkness,
   by the thick darkness that covers
      my face.

Job: Plight of Needy

24 Why does the •Almighty
   not reserve times for judgment?
Why do those who know Him
   never see His days?
2 The wicked displace
   boundary markers.
They steal a flock and provide
   pasture for ⌊it⌋.
3 They drive away the donkeys
   ⌊owned⌋ by the fatherless
and take the widow's ox
   as collateral.

4 They push the needy off the road;
   the poor of the land are forced
      into hiding.
5 Like wild donkeys in the desert,
   the poor go out to their task
      of foraging for food;
the wilderness provides
   nourishment for their children.
6 They gather their fodder in the field
   and glean the vineyards
      of the wicked.
7 Without clothing, they spend
      the night naked,
having no covering
   against the cold.
8 Drenched by mountain rains,
   they huddle against[e] the rocks,
      shelterless.
9 The fatherless infant is snatched
      from the breast;
the nursing child of the poor
   is seized as collateral.[f]
10 Without clothing,
      they wander about naked.
They carry sheaves but go hungry.
11 They crush olives in their presses;[g]
   they tread the winepresses,
      but go thirsty.
12 From the city, men[h] groan;
   the mortally wounded cry for help,
yet God pays no attention
   to this crime.

Acts of Wicked

13 The wicked are those who rebel
      against the light.
They do not recognize its ways
   or stay on its paths.
14 The murderer rises at dawn
   to kill the poor and needy,
   and by night he becomes a thief.
15 The adulterer's eye watches
      for twilight,

---

[a]**23:10** Lit *way with me*   [b]**23:12** LXX, Vg read *treasured in my bosom*   [c]**23:14** Lit *these with Him*   [d]**23:17** Or *silenced*   [e]**24:8** Lit *they embrace*   [f]**24:9** Text emended; MT reads *breast; they seize collateral against the poor*   [g]**24:11** Lit *olives between their rows*   [h]**24:12** One Hb ms, Syr read *the dying*

thinking: No eye will see me,
he covers ⌊his⌋ face.

16 In the dark they break[a] into houses;
by day they lock themselves in,[b]
never experiencing the light.

17 For the morning is
like death's shadow to them.
Surely they are familiar
with the terrors
of death's shadow!

18 They float[c] on the surface
of the water.
Their section of the land is cursed,
so that they never go
to ⌊their⌋ vineyards.

19 As dry ground and heat
snatch away the melted snow,
so •Sheol ⌊steals⌋ those
who have sinned.

20 The womb forgets them;
worms feed on them;
they are remembered no more.
So injustice is broken like a tree.

21 They prey on[d] the barren,
childless woman
and do not deal kindly
with the widow.

Job:
Lowly End of Mighty

22 Yet God drags away[e] the mighty
by His power;
when He rises up, they have
no assurance of life.

23 He gives them a sense of security,
so they can rely ⌊on it⌋,
but His eyes ⌊watch⌋
over their ways.

24 They are exalted for a moment,
then they are gone;
they are brought low and shrivel up
like everything else.[f]
They wither like heads of grain.

25 If this is not true, then who
can prove me a liar
and show that my speech
is worthless?

Bildad: Man vs. God

25 Then Bildad the Shuhite replied:

2 Dominion and dread belong
to Him,
the One who establishes harmony
in the heavens.[g]

3 Can His troops be numbered?
Does His light not shine
on everyone?

4 How can a person be justified
before God?
How can one born of woman
be pure?

5 If even the moon does not shine
and the stars are not pure
in His sight,

6 how much less man, who is
a maggot,
and the son of man, who is a worm!

Job: God's Great Acts

26 Then Job answered:

2 How you have helped
the powerless
and delivered the arm that is weak!

3 How you have counseled
the unwise
and thoroughly explained
⌊the path to⌋ success!

4 Who did you speak these words to?
Whose breath came out of
your ⌊mouth⌋?

5 The departed spirits tremble
beneath the waters and ⌊all⌋ that
inhabit them.

6 •Sheol is naked before God,
and •Abaddon has no covering.

---

[a]24:16 Lit dig   [b]24:16 Lit they seal for themselves   [c]24:18 Lit are insignificant   [d]24:21 LXX, Tg read They harm
[e]24:22 Or God prolongs [the life of]   [f]24:24 LXX reads like a mallow plant in the heat   [g]25:2 Lit in His heights

7 He stretches the northern ⌊skies⌋
    over empty space;
  He hangs the earth on nothing.
8 He enfolds the waters
    in His clouds,
  yet the clouds do not burst
    beneath their weight.
9 He obscures the view
    of ⌊His⌋ throne,
  spreading His cloud over it.
10 He laid out the horizon
    on the surface of the waters
  at the boundary between light
    and darkness.
11 The pillars ⌊that hold up⌋
    the sky tremble,
  astounded at His rebuke.
12 By His power He stirred the sea,
  and by His understanding
    He crushed •Rahab.
13 By His breath the heavens gained
    their beauty;
  His hand pierced
    the fleeing serpent.ᵃ
14 These are but the fringes
    of His ways;
  how faint is the word we hear
    of Him!
  Who can understand
    His mighty thunder?

Job Claims Integrity and Righteousness

27 Job continued his discourse, saying:

2 As God lives, who has deprived me
    of justice,
  and the •Almighty who has
    made me bitter,
3 as long as my breath is still in me
  and the breath from God remains
    in my nostrils,
4 my lips will not speak unjustly,
  and my tongue will not utter deceit.

5 I will never affirm that you
    are right.
  I will maintain my integrityᵇ
    until I die.
6 I will cling to my righteousness
    and never let it go.
  My conscience will not accuse ⌊me⌋
    as long as I live!
7 May my enemy be like the wicked
  and my opponent like the unjust.

Job: Nothing at Death

8 For what hope does
    the godless man have when he is
    cut off,
  when God takes away his life?
9 Will God hear his cry
    when distress comes on him?
10 Will he delight in the Almighty?
  Will he call on God at all times?
11 I will teach you about God's power.
  I will not conceal
    what the Almighty has planned.ᶜ
12 All of you have seen ⌊this⌋
    for yourselves,
  why do you keep up this empty talk?
13 This is a wicked man's lot
    from God,
  the inheritance the ruthless receive
    from the Almighty.

Fleeting Wealth

14 Even if his children increase,
    they are destined for the sword;
  his descendants will never
    have enough food.
15 Those who survive him
    will be buried by the plague,
  yet their widows will not weep
    ⌊for them⌋.
16 Though he piles up silver like dust
    and heaps up a wardrobe
    like clay—

ᵃ26:13 = Leviathan; Is 27:1 ᵇ27:5 Lit will not remove my integrity from me ᶜ27:11 Lit what is with the Almighty

17 he may heap ⌞it⌟ up,
    but the righteous will wear ⌞it⌟,
    and the innocent will divide up
    his silver.
18 The house he built is
    like a moth's ⌞cocoon⌟
    or a booth set up by a watchman.
19 He lies down wealthy, but will
    do so no more;
    when he opens his eyes, it is gone.
20 Terrors overtake him like a flood;
    a storm wind sweeps him away
        at night.
21 An east wind picks him up,
    and he is gone;
    it carries him away from his place.
22 It blasts at him without mercy,
    while he flees desperately
        from its grasp.
23 It claps its hands at him
    and scorns him from its place.

Job's Hymn to Wisdom

28 Surely there is a mine for silver
    and a place where gold is refined.
2 Iron is taken from the ground,
    and copper is smelted from ore.
3 A miner puts an end
        to the darkness;
    he probes[a] the deepest recesses
    for ore in the gloomy darkness.
4 He cuts a shaft far
        from human habitation,
    ⌞in places⌟ unknown to those
        who walk above ground.[b]
    Suspended far away from people,
    the miners swing back and forth.
5 Food may come from the earth,
    but below the surface the earth
        is transformed as by fire.
6 Its rocks are a source of sapphire,[c]
    containing flecks of gold.
7 No bird of prey knows that path;

no falcon's eye has seen it.
8 Proud beasts have never walked
        on it;
    no lion has ever prowled over it.
9 The miner strikes the flint
    and transforms the mountains
        at ⌞their⌟ foundations.
10 He cuts out channels in the rocks,
    and his eyes spot every treasure.
11 He dams up the streams
        from flowing[d]
    so that he may bring to light
        what is hidden.

Job Looks for Wisdom

12 But where can wisdom be found,
    and where is understanding
        located?
13 No man can know its value,[e]
    since it cannot be found in the land
        of the living.
14 The ocean depths say, "It's not
        in me,"
    while the sea declares, "I don't
        have it."
15 Gold cannot be exchanged for it,
    and silver cannot be weighed out
        for its price.
16 Wisdom cannot be valued
        in the gold of Ophir,
    in precious onyx or sapphire.[c]
17 Gold and glass do not compare
        with it,
    and articles of fine gold
    cannot be exchanged for it.
18 Coral and quartz are not
        worth mentioning.
    The price of wisdom
        is beyond pearls.
19 Topaz from •Cush cannot compare
        with it,
    and it cannot be valued
        in pure gold.

[a]28:3 Lit probes all   [b]28:4 Lit far from with inhabitant, things forgotten by foot   [c]28:6,16 Or lapis lazuli   [d]28:11 LXX,
Vg read He explores the sources of the streams   [e]28:13 LXX reads way

20 Where then does wisdom
   come from,
and where is understanding
   located?
21 It is hidden from the eyes
   of every living thing
and concealed from the birds
   of the sky.
22 •Abaddon and Death say,
   "We have heard news of it
   with our ears."

Job: God Knows Wisdom

23 But God understands the way
   to wisdom,
and He knows its location.
24 For He looks to the ends
   of the earth
and sees everything
   under the heavens.
25 When God fixed the weight
   of the wind
and limited the water by measure,
26 when He established a limit[a]
   for the rain
and a path for the lightning,
27 He considered wisdom
   and evaluated it;
He established it and examined it.
28 He said to mankind,
   "Look! The •fear of the Lord—
   that is wisdom,
and to turn from evil
   is understanding."

Job Reflects on Contented Past

29 Job continued his discourse, saying:

2 If only I could be as in months
   gone by,
in the days when God
   watched over me,
3 when His lamp shone
   above my head,
and I walked through darkness
   by His light!
4 ⌊I would be⌋ as I was in the days
   of my youth
when God's friendship rested
   on my tent,
5 when the •Almighty was still
   with me
and my children were around me,
6 when my feet were bathed
   in cream
and the rock poured out streams
   of oil for me!

7 When I went out to the city •gate
   and took my seat
   in the town square,
8 the young men saw me
   and withdrew,
while older men stood to their feet.
9 City officials stopped talking
   and covered their mouths
   with ⌊their⌋ hands.
10 The noblemen's voices
   were hushed,
and their tongues stuck to the roof
   of their mouths.
11 When they heard me,
   they blessed me,
and when they saw me,
   they spoke well of me.[b]

Job Remembers Good Deeds

12 For I rescued the poor man
   who cried out for help,
and the fatherless child who had
   no one to support him.
13 The dying man blessed me,
and I made the widow's heart
   rejoice.
14 I clothed myself in righteousness,
   and it enveloped me;
my just decisions were like a robe
   and a turban.
15 I was eyes to the blind

---

a**28:26** Or decree b**29:11** Lit When an ear heard, it called me blessed, and when an eye saw, it testified for me

and feet to the lame.

16 I was a father to the needy,
and I examined the case
of the stranger.
17 I shattered the fangs of the unjust
and snatched the prey
from his teeth.

18 So I thought: I will die
in my own nest
and multiply ⌊my⌋ days as the sand.a
19 My roots will have access to water,
and the dew will rest
on my branches all night.
20 My strength will be refreshed
within me,
and my bow will be renewed
in my hand.

21 Men listened to me
with expectation,
waiting silently for my advice.
22 After a word from me they did not
speak again;
my speech settled on them
⌊like dew⌋.
23 They waited for me as for the rain
and opened their mouths as for
spring showers.
24 If I smiled at them, they couldn't
believe ⌊it⌋;
they were thrilled atb the light
of my countenance.
25 I directed their course and presided
as chief.
I lived as a king among his troops,
like one who comforts
those who mourn.

Job's Current Plight

30 But now they mock me,
men younger than I am,
whose fathers I would have refused
to put
with my sheep dogs.

2 What use to me was the strength
of their hands?
Their vigor had left them.
3 Emaciated from poverty
and hunger,
they gnawed the dry land,
the desolate wasteland by night.
4 They plucked mallowc
among the shrubs,
and the roots of the broom tree
were their food.
5 They were expelled
from human society;
people shouted at them
as ⌊if they were⌋ thieves.
6 They are living on the slopes
of the •wadis,
among the rocks and in holes
in the ground.
7 They bray among the shrubs;
they huddle beneath the thistles.
8 Foolish men,
without even a name!
They were forced to leave the land.

9 Now I am mocked by their songs;
I have become an object of scorn
to them.
10 They despise me and keep
their distance from me;
they do not hesitate to spit
in my face.
11 Because God has loosened
myd bowstring
and oppressed me,
they have cast off restraint
in my presence.
12 The rabblee rise up at my right;
they trapf my feet
and construct their siege rampg
against me.
13 They tear up my path;
they contribute to my destruction,
without anyone to help them.

14 They advance as through
   a gaping breach;
they keep rolling in through
   the ruins.
15 Terrors are turned loose against me;
they chase my dignity away
   like the wind,
and my prosperity has passed by
   like a cloud.

16 Now my life is poured out
   before my ⌊eyes⌋,
and days of suffering
   have seized me.
17 Night pierces my bones,
and my gnawing pains never abate.
18 My clothing is distorted
   with great force;
He chokes me by the neck
   of my garment.ᵃ
19 He throws me into the mud,
and I have become like dust
   and ashes.

Job: God Doesn't Answer

20 I cry out to You for help, but You
   do not answer me;
when I stand up, You ⌊merely⌋ look
   at me.
21 You have turned against me
   with cruelty;
You harass me
   with Your strong hand.
22 You lift me up on the wind
   and make me ride ⌊it⌋;
You scatter me in the storm.
23 Yes, I know that You will lead me
   to death—
the place appointed for all who live.

24 Yet no one would stretch out
   ⌊his⌋ hand
against a ruined manᵇ
when he cries out to him for help
because of his distress.

25 Have I not wept for those
   who have fallen on hard times?
Has my soul not grieved
   for the needy?
26 But when I hoped for good, evil came;
when I looked for light,
   darkness came.

Job's Inward Churning

27 I am churning withinᶜ
   and cannot rest;
days of suffering confront me.
28 I walk about blackened, but not
   by the sun.ᵈ
I stood in the assembly
   and cried out for help.
29 I have become a brother to jackals
and a companion of ostriches.
30 My skin blackens and flakes off,ᵉ
and my bones burn with fever.
31 My lyre is ⌊used⌋ for mourning
and my flute for the sound
   of weeping.

Job's Final Case for His Innocence

31 I have made a covenant
   with my eyes.
How then could I look
   at a young woman?ᶠ
2 For what portion ⌊would I have⌋
   from God above,
or ⌊what⌋ inheritance
   from the •Almighty on high?
3 Doesn't disaster come to the wicked
and misfortune to evildoers?
4 Does He not see my ways
and number all my steps?

5 If I have walked in falsehood
or my foot has rushed to deceit,
6 let God weigh me
   with an accurate balance,
and He will recognize my integrity.

ᵃ30:18 Hb obscure ᵇ30:24 Lit a heap of ruins ᶜ30:27 Lit My bowels boil ᵈ30:28 Or walk in sunless gloom
ᵉ30:30 Lit blackens away from me ᶠ31:1 Or a virgin

7 If my step has turned from the way,
my heart has followed my eyes,
or impurity has stained my hands,
8 let someone else eat
what I have sown,
and let my crops be uprooted.

9 If my heart has been seduced by
⌊my neighbor's⌋ wife
or I have lurked at his door,
10 let my own wife grind ⌊grain⌋
for another man,
and let other men sleep with[a] her.
11 For that would be a disgrace;
it would be a crime
deserving punishment.[b]
12 For it is a fire that consumes down
to •Abaddon;
it would destroy my entire harvest.

13 If I have dismissed the case
of my male or female servants
when they made a complaint
against me,
14 what could I do when God
stands up ⌊to judge⌋?
How should I answer Him
when He calls ⌊me⌋ to account?
15 Did not the One who made me
in the womb also make them?
Did not the same God form us both
in the womb?

16 If I have refused the wishes
of the poor
or let the widow's eyes go blind,
17 if I have eaten
my few crumbs alone
without letting the fatherless
eat any of it—
18 for from my youth, I raised him
as ⌊his⌋ father,
and since the day I was born[c]
I guided the widow—

19 if I have seen anyone dying for lack
of clothing
or a needy person without a cloak,
20 if he[d] did not bless me
while warming himself
with the fleece from my sheep,
21 if I ever cast my vote[e]
against a fatherless child
when I saw that I had support
in the ⌊city⌋ •gate,
22 then let my shoulder blade fall
from my back,
and my arm be pulled
from its socket.
23 For disaster from God terrifies me,
and because of His majesty
I could not do ⌊these things⌋.

24 If I placed my confidence in gold
or called fine gold my trust,
25 if I have rejoiced because
my wealth is great
or because my own hand
has acquired ⌊so⌋ much,
26 if I have gazed at the sun
when it was shining
or at the moon moving in splendor,
27 so that my heart
was secretly enticed
and I threw them a kiss,[f]
28 this would also be a crime
deserving punishment,
for I would have denied God above.

29 Have I rejoiced over
my enemy's distress,
or become excited when trouble
came his way?
30 I have not allowed my mouth to sin
by asking for his life with a curse.
31 Haven't the members
of my household said,
"Who is there who has not
had enough to eat at Job's table?"

---

[a]31:10 Lit men kneel down over   [b]31:11 Lit crime judges   [c]31:18 Lit and from my mother's womb   [d]31:20 Lit his
loins   [e]31:21 Lit I raise my hand   [f]31:27 Lit and my hand kissed my mouth

32 No stranger had to spend the night
    on the street,
    for I opened my door
      to the traveler.
33 Have I covered my transgressions
    as others do[a]
    by hiding my guilt in my heart,
34 because I greatly feared the crowds,
    and the contempt of the clans
      terrified me,
    so I grew silent and would not
      go outside?

35 If only I had someone to hear
    my ⌊case⌋!
    Here is my signature;
    let the Almighty answer me.
    Let my Opponent compose
    ⌊His⌋ indictment.
36 I would surely carry it
    on my shoulder
    and wear it like a crown.
37 I would give Him an account of all
    my steps;
    I would approach Him like a prince.

38 If my land cries out against me
    and its furrows join in weeping,
39 if I have consumed its produce
    without payment
    or shown contempt for its tenants,[b]
40 then let thorns grow
    instead of wheat
    and stinkweed instead of barley.
The words of Job are concluded.

Elihu Angry with Job and Friends

32 So these three men quit answering Job, because he was righteous in his own eyes. 2 Then Elihu son of Barachel the Buzite from the family of Ram became angry. He was angry at Job because he had justified himself rather than God. 3 He was also angry at Job's three friends because they had failed to refute ⌊him⌋, and yet had condemned him.

4 Now Elihu had waited to speak to Job because they were ⌊all⌋ older than he. 5 But when he saw that the three men could not answer Job, he became angry.

Young Elihu's Response

6 So Elihu son of Barachel the Buzite replied:

I am young in years,
    while you are old;
    therefore I was timid and afraid
    to tell you what I know.
7 I thought that age should speak
    and maturity should teach wisdom.
8 But it is a spirit in man[c]
    and the breath of the •Almighty
    that give him understanding.
9 It is not ⌊only⌋ the old who are wise
    or the elderly who understand
      how to judge.
10 Therefore I say, "Listen to me.
    I too will declare what I know."
11 Look, I waited for your conclusions;
    I listened to your insights
    as you sought for words.
12 I paid close attention to you.
    Yet no one proved Job wrong;
    not one of you refuted
      his arguments.
13 So do not claim,
    "We have found wisdom;
    let God deal with him, not man."
14 But Job has not directed
    his argument to me,
    and I will not respond to him
    with your arguments.

15 Job's friends are dismayed and can
    no longer answer;
    words have left them.

---

[a]31:33 Or as Adam   [b]31:39 Lit or caused the breath of its tenants to breathe out   [c]32:8 Or is the Spirit in a person

16 Should I continue to wait now that
        they are silent,
    now that they stand ⌊there⌋
        and no longer answer?
17 I too will answer;[a]
    yes, I will tell what I know.
18 For I am full of words,
    and my spirit[b] compels me
        ⌊to speak⌋.
19 My heart[c] is like unvented wine;
    it is about to burst
        like new wineskins.
20 I must speak so that
        I can find relief;
    I must open my lips and respond.
21 I will be partial to no one,
    and I will not give anyone
        an ⌊undeserved⌋ title.
22 For I do not know how to give
        ⌊such⌋ titles;
    otherwise, my Maker
        would remove me in an instant.

Elihu Confronts Job

33 But now, Job, pay attention
        to my speech,
    and listen to all my words.
2   I am going to open my mouth;
    my tongue will form words
        on my palate.
3   My words ⌊come from⌋
        my upright heart,
    and my lips speak what they know
        with sincerity.
4   The Spirit of God has made me,
    and the breath of the •Almighty
        gives me life.
5   Refute me if you can.
    Prepare your case against me;
        take your stand.
6   I am just like you before God;
    I was also pinched off
        from ⌊a piece of⌋ clay.

7   Fear of me should not terrify you;
    the pressure I exert[d] against you
        will be light.
8   Surely you have spoken
        in my hearing,
    and I have heard
        these very[e] words:
9   "I am pure, without transgression;
    I am clean and have no guilt.
10 But He finds reasons to oppose me;
    He regards me as his enemy.
11 He puts my feet in the stocks;
    He stands watch over all my paths."

Elihu: Job, You're Wrong

12 But I tell you that you are wrong
        in this ⌊matter⌋,
    since God is greater than man.
13 Why do you take Him to court
    for not answering anything
        a person asks?[f]

Elihu on God's Dealings with Humans

14 For God speaks time and again,
    but a person may not notice it.
15 In a dream, a vision in the night,
    when deep sleep falls on people
        as they slumber on ⌊their⌋ beds,
16 He uncovers their ears at that time
    and terrifies them[g] with warnings,
17 in order to turn a person
        ⌊from his⌋ actions
    and suppress his pride.[h]
18 God spares his soul from the •Pit,
    his life from crossing the river
        ⌊of death⌋.[i]
19 A person may be disciplined
        on his bed with pain
    and constant distress in his bones,
20 so that he detests bread,
    and his soul ⌊despises his⌋
        favorite food.

---

a32:17 Lit answer my part   b32:18 Lit and the spirit of my belly   c32:19 Lit belly   d33:7 Lit you; my pressure
e33:8 Lit heard a sound of   f33:13 Lit court, for he does not answer all his words   g33:16 LXX; MT reads and seals
h33:17 Lit and cover pride within a man   i33:18 Or from perishing by the sword

21 His flesh wastes away to nothing,ᵃ
   and his unseen bones stick out.
22 He draws near the Pit,
   and his life to the executioners.
23 If there is an angel on his side,
   one mediator out of a thousand,
   to tell a person what is right
      for himᵇ
24 and to be gracious to him and say,
   "Spare him from going down
      to the Pit;
   I have found a ransom,"
25 then his flesh will be healthierᶜ
      than in his youth,
   and he will return to the days
      of his youthful vigor.
26 He will pray to God, and God
      will delight in him.
   That man will behold His face
      with a shout of joy,
   and God will restore
      his righteousness to him.
27 He will look at men and say,
   "I have sinned and perverted
      what was right;
   yet I did not get what I deserved.ᵈ
28 He redeemed my soul
      from going down to the Pit,
   and I will continue to see
      the light."

How God Encourages Repentance
29 God certainly does all these things
   two or three times to a man
30 in order to turn him back
      from the Pit,
   so he may shine with the light
      of life.
31 Pay attention, Job, and listen to me.
   Be quiet, and I will speak.
32 But if you have something to say,ᵉ
   answer me;
   speak, for I would like
      to justify you.

33 If not, then listen to me;
   be quiet, and I will teach
      you wisdom.

34 Then Elihu continued,ᶠ saying:
2 Hear my words, you wise men,
   and listen to me,
      you knowledgeable ones.
3 Doesn't the ear test words
   as the palate tastes food?
4 Let us judge for ourselves
      what is right;
   let us decide together what is good.

Elihu: Job's Self-Justifications
5 For Job has declared,
   "I am righteous,
   yet God has deprived me of justice.
6 Would I lie about my case?
   My woundᵍ is incurable,
   though I am
      without transgression."
7 What man is like Job?
   He drinks derision like water.
8 He keeps company with evildoers
   and walks with wicked men.
9 For he has said,
   "A man gains nothing
   when he becomes God's friend."

Elihu: God Can't Do Wrong
10 Therefore listen to me, you men
      of understanding.
   It is impossible for God
      ⌊to do⌋ wrong,
   and ⌊for⌋ the •Almighty
      ⌊to act⌋ unjustly.
11 For He repays a person
      ⌊according to⌋ his deeds,
   and He brings his ways on him.
12 Indeed, it is true that God does not
      act wickedly
   and the Almighty does not
      pervert justice.

ᵃ33:21 Lit away from sight ᵇ33:23 Or to vouch for a person's uprightness ᶜ33:25 Hb obscure ᵈ33:27 Lit and the same was not to me ᵉ33:32 Lit If there are words ᶠ34:1 Lit answered ᵍ34:6 Lit arrow

13 Who gave Him authority
     over the earth?
   Who put Him in charge of
     the entire world?
14 If He put His mind to it
   and withdrew the spirit and breath
     He ⌊gave⌋,
15 every living thing would perish
     together
   and mankind would return
     to the dust.

16 If you ⌊have⌋ understanding,
     hear this;
   listen to what I have to say.
17 Could one who hates justice
     govern ⌊the world⌋?
   Will you condemn the mighty
     Righteous One,
18 who says to a king,
     "Worthless man!"
   and to nobles, "Wicked men!"?
19 God is not partial to princes
   and does not favor the rich
     over the poor,
   for they are all the work
     of His hands.
20 They die suddenly in the middle
     of the night;
   people shudder, then pass away.
   Even the mighty are removed
     without effort.

21 For His eyes ⌊watch⌋ over
     a man's ways,
   and He observes all his steps.

Elihu:
God's Dealings with Evildoers

22 There is no darkness,
     no deep darkness,
   where evildoers
     can hide themselves.
23 God does not ⌊need to⌋ examine
     a person further,

that one should[a] approach Him
     in court.
24 He shatters the mighty
     without an investigation
   and sets others in their place.
25 Therefore, He recognizes
     their deeds
   and overthrows ⌊them⌋ by night,
     and they are crushed.
26 In full view of the public,[b]
   He strikes them
     for their wickedness,
27 because they turned aside
     from following Him
   and did not understand any
     of His ways
28 but caused the poor to cry out
     to Him,
   and He heard the outcry
     of the afflicted.
29 But when God is silent,
     who can declare ⌊Him⌋ guilty?
   When He hides ⌊His⌋ face, who can
     see Him?
   Yet He ⌊watches⌋ over both
     individuals and nations,
30 so that godless men should not rule
   or ensnare the people.

31 Suppose someone says to God,
     "I have endured ⌊my punishment⌋;
   I will no ⌊longer⌋ act wickedly.
32 Teach me what I cannot see;
   if I have done wrong, I won't
     do it again."
33 Should God repay ⌊you⌋
     on your terms
   when you have rejected ⌊His⌋?
   You must choose, not I!
   So declare what you know.

Elihu: Job Rebels

34 Reasonable men will say to me,
   along with the wise men
     who hear me,

a34:23 Some emend to God has not appointed a time for man to   b34:26 Lit In a place of spectators

35 "Job speaks without knowledge;
   his words are without insight."
36 If only Job were tested to the limit,
   because ⌊his⌋ answers are
      ⌊like⌋ those of wicked men.
37 For he adds rebellion to his sin;
   he ⌊scornfully⌋ claps
      in our presence,
   while multiplying his words
      against God.

35 Then Elihu continued, saying:

Elihu: God and Sin

2 Do you think it is just
   when you say,
   "I am righteous before God"?
3 For you ask, "What does
   it profit You,ᵃ
   and what benefit comes to me,
   if I do not sin?"
4 I will answer you
   and your friends with you.
5 Look at the heavens and see;
   gaze at the clouds high above you.
6 If you sin, how does it affect God?
   If you multiply your transgressions,
      what does it do to Him?
7 If you are righteous, what do you
      give Him,
   or what does He receive
      from your hand?
8 Your wickedness ⌊affects⌋ a person
      like yourself,
   and your righteousness ⌊another⌋
      human being.
9 People cry out because of
      severe oppression;
   they shout for help from the arm
      of the mighty.
10 But no one asks, "Where is God
      my Maker,
   who provides ⌊us⌋ with songs
      in the night,

11 who gives us more understanding
      than the animals of the earth
   and makes us wiser than the birds
      of the sky?"
12 There they cry out,
   but He does not answer,
   because of the pride of evil men.
13 Indeed, God does not listen
      to empty ⌊cries⌋,
   and the •Almighty does not
      take note of it—
14 how much less
      whenᵇ you complainᶜ
   that you do not see Him,
   ⌊that your⌋ case is before Him
   and you are waiting for Him.
15 But now, because God's anger
      does not punish
   and He does not pay attention
      to transgression,ᵈ
16 Job opens his mouth in vain
   and multiplies words
      without knowledge.

Elihu Continues Defense of God

36 Then Elihu continued, saying:

2 Be patient with me a little longer,
      and I will inform you,
   for there is still more to be said
      on God's behalf.
3 I will get my knowledge from afar
   and ascribe righteousness
      to my Maker.
4 For my arguments are
      without flaw;ᵉ
   one who has perfect knowledge is
      with you.

5 Yes, God is mighty, but He despises
      ⌊no one⌋;
   He understands all things.ᶠ
6 He does not keep the wicked alive,
   but He gives justice to the afflicted.

ᵃ**35:3** Some emend to *me*   ᵇ**35:14** Or *How then can*   ᶜ**35:14** Lit *say*   ᵈ**35:15** LXX, Vg; MT reads *folly,* or *arrogance*;
Hb obscure   ᵉ**36:4** Lit *my words are not false*   ᶠ**36:5** Lit *He is mighty in strength of heart*

7 He does not remove His gaze
  from the righteous,
  but He seats them forever
  with enthroned kings,
  and they are exalted.

Elihu:
Obedience is Answer to Affliction

8 If people are bound with chains
  and trapped by the cords
    of affliction,
9 God tells them
  what they have done
  and how arrogantly
    they have transgressed.
10 He opens their ears to correction
  and insists they repent
    from iniquity.
11 If they serve Him obediently,
  they will end their days
    in prosperity
  and their years in happiness.
12 But if they do not obey,
  they will cross the river ⌊of death⌋ᵃ
  and die without knowledge.

13 Those who have a godless heart
    harbor anger;
  even when God binds them,
    they do not cry for help.
14 They die in their youth;
  their life ⌊ends⌋ among
    male cult prostitutes.
15 God rescues the afflicted
    by afflicting them;
  He instructs them by means of
    their torment.

16 Indeed, He lured you
  from the jawsᵇ of distress
  to a spacious
    and unconfined place.
  Your table was spread
    with choice food.

17 Yet ⌊now⌋ you are obsessed
  with the judgment due
    the wicked;
  judgment and justice
    have seized you.

Elihu: Wealth Useless in Distress

18 Be careful that no one lures you
    with riches;ᶜ
  do not let a large ransomᵈ
    lead you astray.
19 Can your wealthᵉ or all
    ⌊your⌋ physical exertion
  keep ⌊you⌋ from distress?
20 Do not long for the night
  when nations will disappear
    from their places.
21 Be careful that you do not turn
    to iniquity,
  for that is why you
  have been tested byᶠ affliction.

Elihu: Exalt and Praise God

22 Look, God shows Himself exalted
    by His power.
  Who is a teacher like Him?
23 Who has appointed His way
    for Him,
  and who has declared, "You have
    done wrong"?
24 Remember that you should praise
    His work,
  which people have sung about.
25 All mankind has seen it;
  people have looked at it
    from a distance.
26 Look, God is exalted
    beyond our knowledge;
  the number of His years
    cannot be counted.
27 For He makes waterdrops
    evaporate;ᵍ
  they distill the rain into itsʰ mist,

ᵃ**36:12** Or *will perish by the sword*   ᵇ**36:16** Lit *from a mouth of narrowness*   ᶜ**36:18** Or *you into mockery*   ᵈ**36:18** Or
bribe   ᵉ**36:19** Or *cry for help*   ᶠ**36:21** Or *for you have preferred this to*   ᵍ**36:27** Lit *He draws in waterdrops*
ʰ**36:27** Or *His*

28 which the clouds pour out
and shower abundantly
on mankind.
29 Can anyone understand
how the clouds spread out
or how the thunder roars
from God's pavilion?
30 Look, He spreads His lightning
around Him
and covers the depths of the sea.
31 For He judges the nations
with these;
He gives food in abundance.
32 He covers ⌊His⌋ hands
with lightning
and commands it to hit its mark.
33 The[a] thunder declares
His presence;[b]
the cattle also,
the approaching ⌊storm⌋.

37 My heart pounds at this
and leaps from my chest.[c]
2 Just listen to His thunderous voice
and the rumbling that comes
from His mouth.
3 He lets it loose beneath
the entire sky;
His lightning to the ends
of the earth.

Elihu: Consider God's Wonders

4 Then there comes a roaring sound;
God thunders
with His majestic voice.
He does not restrain the lightning
when His ⌊rumbling⌋ voice is heard.
5 God thunders marvelously
with His voice;
He does great things that
we cannot comprehend.
6 For He says to the snow,
"Fall to the earth,"
and the torrential rains,
His mighty torrential rains,

7 serve as His signature
to all mankind,
so that all men may know
His work.
8 The wild animals enter ⌊their⌋ lairs
and stay in their dens.
9 The windstorm comes
from its chamber,
and the cold
from the driving north winds.
10 Ice is formed by the breath of God,
and watery expanses are frozen.
11 He saturates clouds with moisture;
He scatters His lightning
through them.
12 They swirl about,
turning round and round
at His direction,
accomplishing everything
He commands them
over the surface
of the inhabited world.
13 He causes this to happen
for punishment,
for His land, or for His faithful love.

14 Listen to this, Job.
Stop and consider God's wonders.

Elihu: God Inscrutable to Man

15 Do you know how God directs
His clouds
or makes their lightning flash?
16 Do you understand
how the clouds float,
those wonderful works of Him
who has perfect knowledge?
17 You whose clothes get hot
when the south wind brings calm
to the land,
18 can you help God spread out
the skies
as hard as a cast metal mirror?
19 Teach us what we should say
to Him;

---

we cannot prepare ⌊our case⌋
because of our darkness.
20 Should He be told that I want
to speak?
Can a man speak
when he is confused?
21 Now men cannot ⌊even⌋ look
at the sun
when it is in the skies,
after a wind has swept through
and cleared them away.
22 Yet out of the north He comes,
⌊shrouded⌋ in a golden ⌊glow⌋;
awesome majesty surrounds Him.
23 The •Almighty—we cannot
reach Him—
He is exalted in power!
In His justice and righteousness,
He will not oppress.
24 Therefore, men •fear Him.
He does not look favorably on any
who are wise in heart.

The LORD Speaks

God Rebukes Job

38 Then the LORD answered Job from
the whirlwind. He said:

2 Who is this who obscures
⌊My⌋ counsel
with ignorant words?
3 Get ready to answer Me like a man;
when I question you,
you will inform Me.

God's Questions
Show Man's Limits

4 Where were you
when I established the earth?
Tell ⌊Me⌋, if you have[a]
understanding.
5 Who fixed its dimensions?
Certainly you know!
Who stretched a measuring line
across it?

6 What supports its foundations?
Or who laid its cornerstone
7 while the morning stars
sang together
and all the sons of God shouted
for joy?
8 Who enclosed the sea behind doors
when it burst from the womb,
9 when I made the clouds its garment
and thick darkness its blanket,[b]
10 when I determined its boundaries[c]
and put ⌊its⌋ bars and doors in place,
11 when I declared: "You may come
this far, but no farther;
your proud waves stop here"?

12 Have you ever in your life
commanded the morning
or assigned the dawn its place,
13 so it may seize the edges
of the earth
and shake the wicked out of it?
14 The earth is changed as clay is
by a seal;
⌊its hills⌋ stand out like ⌊the folds of⌋
a garment.
15 Light[d] is withheld from the wicked,
and the arm raised ⌊in violence⌋
is broken.

16 Have you traveled to the sources
of the sea
or walked in the depths
of the oceans?

God's Questions on Death

17 Have the gates of death
been revealed to you?
Have you seen the gates
of death's shadow?

God's Questions on Earth and Space

18 Have you comprehended the extent
of the earth?
Tell ⌊Me⌋, if you know all this.

---

[a]38:4 Lit know   [b]38:9 Lit swaddling clothes   [c]38:10 Lit I broke My statute on it   [d]38:15 Lit Their light

19 Where is the road to the home
      of light?
   ⌊Do you know⌋
      where darkness lives,
20 so you can lead it back
      to its border?
   Are you familiar with the paths
      to its home?
21 Don't you know? You were
      already born;
   you have lived so long!ᵃ
22 Have you entered the ⌊place⌋
      where the snow is stored?
   Or have you seen the storehouses
      of hail,
23 which I hold in reserve for times
      of trouble,
   for the day of warfare and battle?
24 What road leads to ⌊the place⌋
      where light is dispersed?ᵇ
   ⌊Where is the source of⌋
      the east wind that spreads
      across the earth?

25 Who cuts a channel
      for the flooding rain
   or clears the way for lightning,
26 to bring rain
      on an uninhabited land,
   ⌊on⌋ a desert with no human life,ᶜ
27 to satisfy the parched wasteland
      and cause the grass to sprout?
28 Does the rain have a father?
   Who fathered the drops of dew?
29 Whose womb did the ice
      come from?
   Who gave birth to the frost
      of heaven
30 when water becomes as hard
      as stone,ᵈ
   and the surface
      of the watery depths is frozen?

31 Can you fasten the chains
      of the Pleiades
   or loosen the belt of Orion?
32 Can you bring out
      the constellationsᵉ in their season
   and lead the Bearᶠ and her cubs?
33 Do you know the laws of heaven?
   Can you impose itsᵍ authority
      on earth?
34 Can you commandʰ the clouds
      so that a flood of water covers you?
35 Can you send out lightning bolts,
      and they go?
   Do they report to you:
      "Here we are"?

God's Questions
on Source of Wisdom

36 Who put wisdom in the heartⁱ
   or gave the mind understanding?
37 Who has the wisdom to number
      the clouds?
   Or who can tilt the water jars
      of heaven
38 when the dust hardens
      like cast metal
   and the clods ⌊of dirt⌋
      stick together?

God Probes Job's
Understanding of Animals

39 Can you hunt prey for a lioness
      or satisfy the appetite
      of young lions
40 when they crouch in their dens
      and lie in wait within their lairs?
41 Who provides the raven's food
   when its young cry out to God
   and wander about for lack of food?

39 Do you know when
      mountain goats give birth?

Have you watched the <u>deer</u>
in labor?
2 Can you count the months
they are pregnant[a]
so you can know the time
they give birth?
3 They crouch down to give birth
to their young;
they deliver their newborn.[b]
4 Their offspring are healthy
and grow up in the open field.
They leave and do not return.[c]

5 Who set the <u>wild donkey</u> free?
Who released the swift donkey
from its harness?
6 I made the wilderness its home,
and the salty wasteland
its dwelling.
7 It scoffs at the noise of the village
and never hears the shouts
of a driver.
8 It roams the mountains
for its pastureland,
searching for anything green.
9 Would the <u>wild ox</u> be willing
to serve you?
Would it spend the night
by your feeding trough?
10 Can you hold the wild ox
by its harness to the furrow?
Will it plow the valleys
behind you?
11 Can you depend on it because of
its strength?
Would you leave it to do
your hard work?
12 Can you trust the wild ox
to harvest your grain
and bring ⌊it⌋
to your threshing floor?

13 The wings of the <u>ostrich</u>
flap joyfully,

but are her feathers and plumage
like the stork's?[d]
14 She abandons her eggs
on the ground
and lets them be warmed
in the sand.
15 She forgets that a foot
may crush them
or that some wild animal
may trample them.
16 She treats her young harshly, as if
⌊they⌋ were not her own,
with no fear that her labor
may have been in vain.
17 For God has deprived her
of wisdom;
He has not endowed her
with understanding.
18 When she proudly[d] spreads
her wings,
she laughs at the horse
and its rider.

19 Do you give strength to the <u>horse</u>?
Do you adorn his neck
with a mane?[d]
20 Do you make him leap like a locust?
His proud snorting
⌊fills one with⌋ terror.
21 He paws[e] in the valley and rejoices
in his strength;
He charges into battle.[f]
22 He laughs at fear, since he is afraid
of nothing;
he does not run from the sword.
23 A quiver rattles at his side,
along with a flashing spear
and a lance.[g]
24 He charges ahead[h]
with trembling rage;
he cannot stand still
at the trumpet's sound.
25 When the trumpet blasts,
he snorts defiantly.[i]

---

[a]**39:2** Lit *months they fulfill*   [b]**39:3** Or *they send away their labor pains*   [c]**39:4** Lit *return to them*
[d]**39:13,18,19** Hb obscure   [e]**39:21** LXX, Syr; MT reads *digs*   [f]**39:21** Lit *He goes out to meet the weapon*   [g]**39:23** Or
scimitar   [h]**39:24** Lit *He swallows the ground*   [i]**39:25** Lit *he says, "Aha!"*

He smells the battle
from a distance;
he hears the officers' shouts
and the battle cry.

26 Does the <u>hawk</u> take flight
by your understanding
and spread its wings to the south?
27 Does the eagle soar
at your command
and make its nest on high?
28 It lives on a cliff where it spends
the night;
its stronghold is on a rocky crag.
29 From there it searches for prey;
its eyes penetrate the distance.
30 Its brood gulps down blood,
and wherever corpses lie,
it is there.

God Demands That Job Answer

40 The LORD answered Job:

2 Will the one who contends
with the •Almighty correct ⌊Him⌋?
Let him who argues with God
give an answer.[a]

Job Responds Humbly

3 Then Job answered the LORD:

4 I am so insignificant. How can I
answer You?
I place my hand over my mouth.
5 I have spoken once,
and I will not reply;
twice, but ⌊now⌋ I can add nothing.

God Reprimands Job

6 Then the LORD answered Job from
the whirlwind:

7 Get ready to answer Me
like a man;
When I question you, you will
inform Me.

8 Would you really challenge
My justice?
Would you declare Me guilty
to justify yourself?
9 Do you have an arm like God's?
Can you thunder with a voice
like His?

10 Adorn yourself with majesty
and splendor,
and clothe yourself with honor
and glory.
11 Unleash your raging anger;
look on every proud person
and humiliate him.
12 Look on every proud person
and humble him;
trample the wicked
where they stand.[b]
13 Hide them together in the dust;
imprison them in the grave.[c]
14 Then I will confess to you
that your own right hand
can deliver you.

God: Consider Behemoth

15 <u>Look at Behemoth</u>,
which I made along with you.
He eats grass like an ox.
16 Look at the strength of his loins
and the power in the muscles
of his belly.
17 He stiffens his tail
like a cedar tree;
the tendons of his thighs are woven
firmly together.
18 His bones are bronze tubes;
his limbs are like iron rods.
19 He is the foremost of God's works;
⌊only⌋ his Maker can draw
the sword against him.
20 The hills yield food for him,
while all ⌊sorts of⌋ wild animals
play there.

---

[a]40:2 Lit God respond to it   [b]40:12 Lit wicked in their place   [c]40:13 Lit together; bind their faces in the hidden place

21 He lies under the lotus plants,
hiding in the protection[a]
of marshy reeds.
22 Lotus plants cover him
with their shade;
the willows by the brook
surround him.
23 Though the river rages,
Behemoth is unafraid;
he remains confident, even if
the Jordan surges up to his mouth.
24 Can anyone capture him
while he looks on,[b]
or pierce his nose with snares?

God: Consider Leviathan

41[c] Can you pull in •Leviathan
with a hook
or tie his tongue down with a rope?
2 Can you put a cord[d]
through his nose
or pierce his jaw with a hook?
3 Will he beg you for mercy
or speak softly to you?
4 Will he make a covenant with you
so that you can take him as a slave
forever?
5 Can you play with him like a bird
or put him on a leash[e]
for your girls?
6 Will traders bargain for him
or divide him
among the merchants?
7 Can you fill his hide with harpoons
or his head with fishing spears?
8 Lay a[f] hand on him.
You will remember the battle
and never repeat it!
9 [g]Any hope of ⌊capturing⌋ him
proves false.
Does a person not collapse
at the very sight of him?

God Compared to Leviathan

10 No one is ferocious ⌊enough⌋
to rouse Leviathan;
who then can stand against Me?
11 Who confronted Me, that I
should repay him?
Everything under heaven belongs
to Me.

God: Leviathan's Appearance

12 I cannot be silent about his limbs,
his power,
and his graceful proportions.
13 Who can strip off
his outer covering?
Who can penetrate his double layer
of armor?[h]
14 Who can open his jaws,[i]
surrounded by
those terrifying teeth?
15 ⌊His⌋ pride is in ⌊his⌋ rows of scales,
closely sealed together.
16 One scale is so close to another[j]
that no air can pass between them.
17 They are joined to one another,
so closely connected[k] they cannot
be separated.
18 His snorting[l] flashes with light,
while his eyes are like the rays[m]
of dawn.
19 Flaming torches shoot
from his mouth;
fiery sparks fly out!
20 Smoke billows from his nostrils
as from a boiling pot
or ⌊burning⌋ reeds.
21 His breath sets coals ablaze,
and flames pour out of his mouth.
22 Strength resides in his neck,
and dismay dances before him.
23 The folds of his flesh
are joined together,

---

a 40:21 Lit plants, in the hiding place   b 40:24 Lit capture it in its eyes   c 41:1 Jb 40:25 in Hb   d 41:2 Lit reed
e 41:5 Lit or bind him   f 41:8 Lit your   g 41:9 Jb 41:1 in Hb   h 41:13 LXX; MT reads double bridle   i 41:14 Lit open the
doors of his face   j 41:16 Lit One by one they approach   k 41:17 Lit another; they cling together and   l 41:18 Or
sneezing   m 41:18 Lit eyelids

solid as metal[a] and immovable.

24 His heart is as hard as a rock,
as hard as a lower millstone!
25 When Leviathan rises, the mighty[b]
are terrified;
they withdraw because of
⌊his⌋ thrashing.
26 The sword that reaches him
will have no effect,
nor will a spear, dart, or arrow.
27 He regards iron as straw,
and bronze as rotten wood.
28 No arrow can make him flee;
slingstones become like stubble
to him.
29 A club is regarded as stubble,
and he laughs at the whirring
of a javelin.
30 His undersides are
jagged potsherds,
spreading the mud
like a threshing sledge.
31 He makes the depths seethe
like a caldron;
he makes the sea
like an ointment jar.
32 He leaves a shining wake
behind him;[c]
one would think the deep had
white hair!
33 He has no equal on earth—
a creature devoid of fear!
34 He surveys everything
that is haughty;
he is king over all
the proud beasts.[d]

Job Repents before the LORD

42 Then Job replied to the LORD:

2 I[e] know that You can do anything
and no plan of Yours
can be thwarted.

3 ⌊You asked,⌋ "Who is this
who conceals ⌊My⌋ counsel
with ignorance?"
Surely I spoke about things
I did not understand,
things too wonderful for me
to[f] know.
4 ⌊You said,⌋ "Listen now,
and I will speak.
When I question you, you will
inform Me."
5 I had heard rumors about You,
but now my eyes have seen You.
6 Therefore I take back ⌊my words⌋
and repent in dust and ashes.[g]

Lord Rebukes Eliphaz and Friends

7 After the LORD had finished speaking[h] to Job, He said to Eliphaz the Temanite: "I am angry with you and your two friends, for you have not spoken the truth about Me, as My servant Job has. 8 Now take seven bulls and seven rams, go to My servant Job, and offer a burnt offering for yourselves. Then My servant Job will pray for you. I will surely accept his ⌊prayer⌋ and not deal with you as your folly deserves. For you have not spoken the truth about Me, as My servant Job has."

Friends' Sacrifice and Job's Prayer

9 Then Eliphaz the Temanite, Bildad the Shuhite, and Zophar the Naamathite went and did as the LORD had told them, and the LORD accepted Job's ⌊prayer⌋.

God Restores Job

10 After Job had prayed for his friends, the LORD restored his prosperity and doubled his ⌊previous⌋ possessions. 11 All his brothers, sisters, and former acquain-

---

[a]41:23 Lit together, hard on him   [b]41:25 Or the divine beings   [c]41:32 Lit a path   [d]41:34 Lit the children of pride
[e]42:2 Alt Hb tradition reads You   [f]42:3 Lit me, and I did not   [g]42:6 LXX reads I despise myself and melt; I consider myself dust and ashes   [h]42:7 Lit speaking these words

tances came to his house and dined with him in his house. They offered him sympathy and comfort concerning all the adversity the LORD had brought on him. Each one gave him a *qesitah,*[a] and a gold earring.

12 So the LORD blessed the latter part of Job's life more than the earlier. He owned 14,000 sheep, 6,000 camels, 1,000 yoke of oxen, and 1,000 female donkeys. 13 He also had seven sons and three daughters. 14 He named his first ⌊daughter⌋ Jemimah, his second Keziah, and his third Keren-happuch. 15 No women as beautiful as Job's daughters could be found in all the land, and their father granted them an inheritance with their brothers.

16 Job lived 140 years after this and saw his children and their children to the fourth generation. 17 Then Job died, old and full of days.

PSALMS

BOOK I

(PSALMS 1–41)

PSALM 1

The Two Ways

1   How happy is the man
    who does not follow[b] the advice
      of the wicked,
    or take[c] the path of sinners,
    or join a group[d] of mockers!
2   Instead, his delight is in the LORD's
      instruction,
    and he meditates on it day
      and night.
3   He is like a tree planted
      beside streams of water[e] that
      bears its fruit in season[f]
    and whose leaf does not wither.
    Whatever he does prospers.

4   The wicked are not like this;
    instead, they are like chaff
      that the wind blows away.
5   Therefore the wicked
      will not survive[c] the judgment,
    and sinners will not be
      in the community
      of the righteous.

6   For the LORD watches over the way
      of the righteous,
    but the way of the wicked
      leads to ruin.

PSALM 2

Coronation of the Son

1   Why do the nations rebel[g]
    and the peoples plot in vain?
2   The kings of the earth take
      their stand
    and the rulers conspire
      together
    against the LORD
      and His Anointed One:[h]
3   "Let us tear off their chains
    and free ourselves
      from their restraints."[i]

4   The One enthroned[j] in heaven
      laughs;
    the Lord ridicules them.

a42:11 The value of the currency is unknown; Gn 33:19; Jos 24:32   b1:1 Lit *not walk in*   c1:1,5 Lit *stand in*   d1:1 Or *or sit in the seat*   e1:3 Or *beside irrigation canals*   f1:3 Lit *in its season*   g2:1 Or *conspire,* or *rage*   h2:2 Or *anointed one*   i2:3 Lit *and throw their ropes from us*   j2:4 Lit *who sits*

5 Then He speaks to them
  in His anger
and terrifies them in His wrath:
6 "I have consecrated My King[a]
  on Zion, My holy mountain."

7 I will declare the LORD's decree:
He said to Me, "You are My Son;[b]
today I have become Your[c] Father.
8 Ask of Me,
and I will make the nations
  Your[c] inheritance
and the ends of the earth
  Your[c] possession.
9 You will break[d] them with a rod
  of iron;
You[e] will shatter them
  like pottery."[f]

10 So now, kings, be wise;
receive instruction, you judges
  of the earth.
11 Serve the LORD
  with reverential awe,
and rejoice with trembling.
12 Pay homage to[g] the Son, or He[h]
  will be angry,
and you will perish
  in your rebellion,[i]
for His[j] anger may ignite
  at any moment.
All those who take refuge in Him[k]
  are happy.

PSALM 3
Confidence in Troubled Times
A psalm of David when
he fled from his son Absalom.

1 LORD, how my foes increase!
There are many who attack me.
2 Many say about me,
  "There is no help for him in God."
•Selah

3 But You, LORD, are a shield
  around me,
my glory, and the One who lifts up
  my head.
4 I cry aloud to the LORD,
and He answers me
  from His holy mountain.   Selah

5 I lie down and sleep;
I wake again because the LORD
  sustains me.
6 I am not afraid of the thousands
  of people
who have taken their stand
  against me on every side.

7 Rise up, LORD!
Save me, my God!
You strike all my enemies
  on the cheek;
You break the teeth of the wicked.
8 Salvation belongs to the LORD;
may Your blessing be
  on Your people.   Selah

PSALM 4
A Night Prayer
For the choir director:
with stringed instruments. A Davidic psalm.

1 Answer me when I call,
God, who vindicates me.[l]
You freed me from affliction;
be gracious to me and hear
  my prayer.
2 How long, exalted men,
  will my honor be insulted?
⌊How long⌋ will you love
  what is worthless
and pursue a lie?   •Selah
3 Know that the LORD has set apart
  the faithful for Himself;
the LORD will hear when I call
  to Him.

[a]2:6 Or king [b]2:7 Or me, "You are My son [c]2:7,8 Or your [d]2:9 LXX, Syr, Tg read shepherd [e]2:9 Or you [f]2:9 Lit a potter's vessel [g]2:12 Lit Kiss [h]2:12 Or son, otherwise he [i]2:12 Lit perish way [j]2:12 Or his [k]2:12 Or him [l]4:1 Or God of my righteousness

4 Be angry[a] and do not sin;
on your bed, reflect in your heart
and be still.   *Selah*
5 Offer sacrifices in righteousness[b]
and trust in the LORD.

6 Many are saying,
"Who can show us
anything good?"
Look on us with favor, LORD.

7 You have put more joy in my heart
than they have when their grain
and new wine abound.
8 I will both lie down and sleep
in peace,
for You alone, LORD, make me live
in safety.

PSALM 5
Refuge of the Righteous

For the choir director: with the flutes.
A Davidic psalm.

1 Listen to my words, LORD;
consider my sighing.
2 Pay attention to the sound
of my cry,
my King and my God,
for I pray to You.

3 At daybreak, LORD, You hear
my voice;
at daybreak I plead my case to You
and watch expectantly.

4 For You are not a God who delights
in wickedness;
evil cannot lodge with You.
5 The boastful cannot stand
in Your presence;
You hate all evildoers.
6 You destroy those who tell lies;
the LORD abhors a man
of bloodshed and treachery.

7 But I enter Your house
by the abundance
of Your faithful love;
I bow down toward
Your holy temple
in reverential awe of You.
8 LORD, lead me
in Your righteousness,
because of my adversaries;[c]
make Your way straight before me.

9 For there is nothing reliable
in what they say;[d]
destruction is within them;
their throat is an open grave;
they flatter with their tongues.
10 Punish them, God;
let them fall by their own schemes.
Drive them out because of
their many crimes,
for they rebel against You.

11 But let all who take refuge in You
rejoice;
let them shout for joy forever.
May You shelter them,
and may those who love Your name
boast about You.
12 For You, LORD, bless
the righteous one;
You surround him with favor
like a shield.

PSALM 6
A Prayer for Mercy

For the choir director:
with stringed instruments,
according to •*Sheminith*. A Davidic psalm.

1 LORD, do not rebuke me
in Your anger;
do not discipline me in Your wrath.
2 Be gracious to me, LORD,
for I am weak;[e]

---

[a]**4:4** Or *Tremble*   [b]**4:5** Or *Offer right sacrifices*; lit *Sacrifice sacrifices of righteousness*   [c]**5:8** Or *of those who lie in wait for me*   [d]**5:9** Lit *in his mouth*   [e]**6:2** Or *sick*

heal me, LORD, for my bones
   are shaking;
3 my whole being is shaken
   with terror.
And You, LORD—how long?

4 Turn, LORD! Rescue me;
save me because of
   Your faithful love.
5 For there is no remembrance of You
   in death;
who can thank You in •Sheol?

6 I am weary from my groaning;
with my tears I dampen my pillow[a]
and drench my bed every night.
7 My eyes are swollen from grief;
they[b] grow old because of all
   my enemies.

8 Depart from me, all evildoers,
for the LORD has heard the sound
   of my weeping.
9 The LORD has heard my plea
   for help;
the LORD accepts my prayer.
10 All my enemies will be ashamed
   and shake with terror;
they will turn back and suddenly
   be disgraced.

PSALM 7
Prayer for Justice

A Shiggaion[c] of David,
which he sang to the LORD concerning
the words of •Cush,[d] a Benjaminite.

1 LORD my God, I seek refuge in You;
save me from all my pursuers
   and rescue me,
2 or they[e] will tear me like a lion,
ripping me apart, with no one
   to rescue me.[f]

3 LORD my God, if I have done this,
   if there is injustice on my hands,
4 if I have done harm to one at peace
   with me
or have plundered[g] my adversary
   without cause,
5 may an enemy pursue
   and overtake me;
may he trample me to the ground
and leave my honor in the dust.
                                        •Selah

6 Rise up, LORD, in Your anger;
lift Yourself up against the fury
   of my adversaries;
awake for me;[h]
You have ordained[i] a judgment.
7 Let the assembly of peoples gather
   around You;
take Your seat[j] on high over it.
8 The LORD judges the peoples;
vindicate me, LORD,
according to my righteousness
   and my integrity.[k]

9 Let the evil of the wicked come
   to an end,
but establish the righteous.
The One who examines
   the thoughts and emotions[l]
is a righteous God.
10 My shield is with[m] God,
who saves the upright in heart.
11 God is a righteous judge,
and a God who executes justice
   every day.
12 If anyone does not repent,
God[n] will sharpen His sword;
He has strung[o] His bow
   and made it ready.
13 He has prepared
   His deadly weapons;

---

[a]6:6 Lit bed   [b]6:7 LXX, Aq, Sym, Jer read I   [c]Perhaps a passionate song with rapid changes of rhythm, or a dirge
[d]LXX, Aq, Sym, Theod, Jer read of the Cushite   [e]7:2 Lit he   [f]7:2 Lit ripping, and without a rescuer   [g]7:4 Or me and
have spared   [h]7:6 LXX reads awake, Lord my God   [i]7:6 Or me; ordain   [j]7:7 MT reads and return   [k]7:8 Lit integrity
on me   [l]7:9 Lit examines hearts and kidneys   [m]7:10 Lit on   [n]7:12 Lit He   [o]7:12 Lit bent; that is, bent the bow to
string it

He tips His arrows with fire.

14 See, he is pregnant with evil,
conceives trouble, and gives birth
to deceit.
15 He dug a pit and hollowed it out,
but fell into the hole he had made.
16 His trouble comes back
on his own head,
and his violence falls on the top
of his head.
17 I will thank the LORD
for His righteousness;
I will sing about the name
of the LORD, the •Most High.

PSALM 8
God's Glory, Man's Dignity
For the choir director: on the •*Gittith*.
A Davidic psalm.

1 LORD, our Lord,
how magnificent is Your name
throughout the earth!

You have covered the heavens
with Your majesty.[a]
2 Because of Your adversaries,
You have established
a stronghold[b]
from the mouths of children
and nursing infants,
to silence the enemy
and the avenger.

3 When I observe Your heavens,
the work of Your fingers,
the moon and the stars,
which You set in place,
4 what is man
that You remember him,
the son of man that You look
after him?
5 You made him little less than God[c] [d]

and crowned him with glory
and honor.
6 You made him lord over the works
of Your hands;
You put everything under his feet:[e]
7 all the sheep and oxen,
as well as animals in the wild,
8 birds of the sky,
and fish of the sea
passing through the currents
of the seas.

9 LORD, our Lord,
how magnificent is Your name
throughout the earth!

PSALM 9
Celebration of God's Justice
For the choir director:
according to *Muth-labben*.[f] A Davidic psalm.

1 I will thank the LORD with all
my heart;
I will declare all
Your wonderful works.
2 I will rejoice and boast about You;
I will sing about Your name,
•Most High.

3 When my enemies retreat,
they stumble and perish
before You.
4 For You have upheld my just cause;[g]
You are seated on Your throne
as a righteous judge.
5 You have rebuked the nations:
You have destroyed the wicked;
You have erased their name forever
and ever.
6 The enemy has come
to eternal ruin;
You have uprooted the cities,
and the very memory of them
has perished.

---

[a]**8:1** Lit *earth, which has set Your splendor upon the heavens*   [b]**8:2** LXX reads *established praise*   [c]**8:5** LXX reads *angels*   [d]**8:5** Or *gods*, or *a god*, or *heavenly beings*; Hb *Elohim*   [e]**8:6** Or *authority*   [f]Perhaps a musical term   [g]**9:4** Lit *my justice and my cause*

7 But the LORD sits enthroned
   forever;
 He has established His throne
   for judgment.
8 He judges the world
   with righteousness;
 He executes judgment
   on the peoples with fairness.
9 The LORD is a refuge
   for the oppressed,
 a refuge in times of trouble.
10 Those who know Your name
   trust in You
 because You have not abandoned
 those who seek You, LORD.

11 Sing to the LORD, who dwells
   in Zion;
 proclaim His deeds
 among the peoples.
12 For the One who seeks
   an accounting
 for bloodshed remembers them;
 He does not forget the cry
   of the afflicted.

13 Be gracious to me, LORD;
 consider my affliction at the hands
   of those who hate me.
 Lift me up from the gates of death,
14 so that I may declare all Your praises.
 I will rejoice in Your salvation
 within the gates of Daughter Zion.ᵃ

15 The nations have fallen into the pit
   they made;
 their foot is caught in the net
   they have concealed.
16 The LORD has revealed Himself;
 He has executed justice,
 striking downᵇ the wickedᶜ
 by the work of their hands.
                     •Higgaion.   •Selah

17 The wicked will return to •Sheol—
 all the nations that forget God.
18 For the oppressed will not always
   be forgotten;
 the hope of the afflictedᵈ
   will not perish forever.

19 Rise up, LORD! Do not
   let man prevail;
 let the nations be judged
   in Your presence.
20 Put terror in them, LORD;
 let the nations know they are
   only men.   Selah

PSALM 10
Arrogance of Wicked

1 LORD,ᵉ why do You stand
   so far away?
 Why do You hide in times
   of trouble?
2 In arrogance the wicked
   relentlessly pursue the afflicted;
 let them be caught in the schemes
   they have devised.

3 For the wicked one boasts about
   his own cravings;
 the one who is greedy cursesᶠ
   and despises the LORD.
4 In all his scheming,
 the wicked arrogantly thinks:ᵍ
 "There is no accountability,
 ⌊since⌋ God does not exist."
5 His ways are always secure;ʰ
 Your lofty judgments are beyond
   his sight;
 he scoffs at all his adversaries.
6 He says to himself, "I will never
   be moved—
 from generation to generation
 without calamity."

ᵃ9:14 Jerusalem ᵇ9:16 Or *justice, snaring* ᶜ9:16 LXX, Aq, Syr, Tg read *justice, the wicked is trapped* ᵈ9:18 Alt Hb
tradition reads *humble* ᵉ10:1 A few Hb mss and LXX connect Pss 9–10. Together these 2 psalms form a partial
•acrostic. ᶠ10:3 Or *he blesses the greedy* ᵍ10:4 Lit *wicked according to the height of his nose* ʰ10:5 Or
prosperous

7 Cursing, deceit, and violence
  fill his mouth;
trouble and malice are
  under his tongue.
8 He waits in ambush
  near the villages;
he kills the innocent
  in secret places;
his eyes are on the lookout
  for the helpless.
9 He lurks in secret like a lion
  in a thicket.
He lurks in order to seize
  the afflicted.
He seizes the afflicted
  and drags him in his net.
10 He crouches and bends down;
the helpless fall because of
  his strength.
11 He says to himself,
  "God has forgotten;
He hides His face and will
  never see."

12 Rise up, LORD God! Lift up
  Your hand.
Do not forget the afflicted.
13 Why has the wicked despised God?
He says to himself, "You will not
  demand an account."
14 But You Yourself have seen trouble
  and grief,
observing it in order to take
  the matter into Your hands.
The helpless entrusts himself to You;
You are a helper of the fatherless.
15 Break the arm of the wicked
  and evil person;
call his wickedness into account
until nothing remains of it.[a]

16 The LORD is King forever and ever;
the nations will perish
  from His land.

17 LORD, You have heard the desire
  of the humble;[b]
You will strengthen
  their hearts.
You will listen carefully,
18 doing justice for the fatherless
  and the oppressed,
so that men of the earth
  may terrify ⌊them⌋ no more.

PSALM 11
Refuge in the LORD

For the choir director. Davidic.

1 I have taken refuge
  in the LORD.
How can you say to me,
"Escape to the mountain
  like a bird!c
2 For look, the wicked string
  the bow;
they put the[d] arrow
  on the bowstring
to shoot from the shadows
  at the upright in heart.
3 When the foundations
  are destroyed,
what can the righteous do?"

4 The LORD is in His holy temple;
the LORD's throne is in heaven.
His eyes watch;
  He examines[e] •everyone.
5 The LORD examines the righteous
  and the wicked.
He hates the lover of violence.
6 He will rain burning coals
  and sulfur[f] on the wicked;
a scorching wind will be
  their portion.[g]
7 For the LORD is righteous; He loves
  righteous deeds.
The upright will see His face.

[a]10:15 Lit *account You do not find*   [b]10:17 Other Hb mss, LXX, Syr read *afflicted*   [c]11:1 LXX, Syr, Jer, Tg, MT reads *to your mountain, bird*   [d]11:2 Lit *their*   [e]11:4 Lit *His eyelids examine*   [f]11:6 Sym; MT reads *rain snares, fire*; the difference between the 2 Hb words is 1 letter   [g]11:6 Lit *be the portion of their cup*

PSALM 12

Oppression by the Wicked

For the choir director: according to •*Sheminith.*
A Davidic psalm.

1 Help, LORD, for no
  faithful one remains;
the loyal have disappeared
  from the •human race.
2 They lie to one another;
  they speak with flattering lips
  and deceptive hearts.
3 May the LORD cut off
  all flattering lips
  and the tongue that speaks boastfully.
4 They say, "Through our tongues
  we have power;[a]
  our lips are our own—who can be
  our master?"

5 "Because of the oppression
    of the afflicted
  and the groaning of the poor,
  I will now rise up," says the LORD.
  "I will put in a safe place the one
    who longs for it."

6 The words of the LORD
    are pure words,
  like silver refined
    in an earthen furnace,
  purified seven times.

7 You, LORD, will guard us;[b]
  You will protect us[c]
    from this generation forever.
8 The wicked wander[d] everywhere,
  and what is worthless is exalted
    by the human race.

PSALM 13

A Plea for Deliverance

For the choir director. A Davidic psalm.

1 LORD, how long will You continually
  forget me?

How long will You hide Your face
  from me?
2 How long will I store up
  anxious concerns[e] within me,
agony in my mind
  every day?
How long will my enemy
  dominate me?

3 Consider me and answer,
  LORD, my God.
Restore brightness
  to my eyes;
otherwise, I will sleep
  in death,
4 my enemy will say,
  "I have triumphed over him,"
and my foes will rejoice
  because I am shaken.

5 But I have trusted in
  Your faithful love;
my heart will rejoice in
  Your deliverance.
6 I will sing to the LORD
  because He has treated
  me generously.

PSALM 14

All Have Sinned

For the choir director. Davidic.

1 The fool says in his heart,
  "God does not exist."
They are corrupt; their actions
  are revolting.
There is no one who does good.
2 The LORD looks down from heaven
    on the •human race
  to see if there is one
    who is wise,
  one who seeks God.
3 All have turned away;
  all alike have
    become corrupt.

---

a**12:4** Lit *That say, "By our tongues we are strengthened*   b**12:7** Some Hb mss, LXX, Jer; other Hb mss read *them*
c**12:7** Some Hb mss, LXX; other Hb mss read *him*   d**12:8** Lit *walk about*   e**13:2** Or *up counsels*

There is no one who does good,
not even one.[a]

4 Will evildoers never understand?
They consume my people
as they consume bread;
they do not call on the LORD.

5 Then[b] they will be filled
with terror,
for God is with those
who are[c] righteous.

6 You ⌊sinners⌋ frustrate the plans
of the afflicted,
but the LORD is his refuge.

7 Oh, that Israel's deliverance
would come from Zion!
When the LORD restores
His captive people,
Jacob will rejoice; Israel will be
glad.[d]

PSALM 15
A Description of the Godly
A Davidic psalm.

1 LORD, who can dwell in Your tent?
Who can live on
Your holy mountain?

2 The one who lives honestly,
practices righteousness,
and acknowledges the truth
in his heart—
3 who does not slander
with his tongue,
who does not harm his friend
or discredit his neighbor,
4 who despises the one rejected
by the LORD,[e]
but honors those who •fear
the LORD,
who keeps his word
whatever the cost,

5 who does not lend his money
at interest
or take a bribe
against the innocent—
the one who does these things
will never be moved.

PSALM 16
Confidence in the LORD
A Davidic •Miktam.

1 Protect me, God, for I take refuge
in You.
2 I[f] said to the LORD, "You are
my Lord;
I have no good besides You."[g]
3 As for the holy people who are
in the land,
they are the noble ones in whom is
all my delight.
4 The sorrows of those who take
another ⌊god⌋
for themselves multiply;
I will not pour out
their drink offerings of blood,
and I will not speak their names
with my lips.

5 LORD, You are my portion[h]
and my cup ⌊of blessing⌋;
You hold my future.
6 The boundary lines have fallen
for me
in pleasant places;
indeed, I have
a beautiful inheritance.

7 I will praise the LORD
who counsels me—
even at night my conscience
instructs me.
8 I keep the LORD in mind[i] always.
Because He is at my right hand,
I will not be shaken.

---

[a]**14:3** Two Hb mss, some LXX mss add the material found in Rm 3:13-18   [b]**14:5** Or *There*   [c]**14:5** Lit *with the generation of the*   [d]**14:7** Or *let Jacob rejoice; let Israel be glad.*   [e]**15:4** Lit *in his eyes the rejected is despised*   [f]**16:2** Some Hb mss, LXX, Syr, Jer; other Hb mss read *You*   [g]**16:2** Or *"Lord, my good; there is none besides You."*   [h]**16:5** Or *allotted portion*   [i]**16:8** Lit *front of me*

9 Therefore my heart is glad,
　　and my spirit rejoices;
　　my body also rests securely.
10 For You will not abandon me
　　to •Sheol;
　　You will not allow
　　　Your Faithful One to see
　　　the •Pit.ᵃ
11 You reveal the path of life to me;
　　in Your presence is
　　　abundant joy;
　　in Your right hand are
　　　eternal pleasures.

PSALM 17
A Prayer for Protection
A Davidic prayer.

1 LORD, hear a just cause;
　　pay attention to my cry;
　　listen to my prayer—
　　from lips free of deceit.
2 Let my vindication
　　come from You,
　　ɪforɪ You see what is right.
3 You have tested my heart;
　　You have visited by night;
　　You have tried me and found
　　　nothing ɪevilɪ;
　　I have determined that my mouth
　　　will not sin.ᵇ
4 Concerning what people do:
　　by the word of Your lipsᶜ
　　I have avoided the ways
　　　of the violent.
5 My steps are on Your paths;
　　my feet have not slipped.

6 I call on You, God,
　　because You will answer me;
　　listen closely to me;
　　hear what I say.

7 Display the wonders
　　of Your faithful love,
　　Savior of all who seek refuge
　　from those who rebel
　　　against Your right hand.ᵈ
8 Guard me as the apple
　　of Your eye;ᵉ
　　hide me in the shadow
　　of Your wings
9 fromᶠ the wicked
　　who treat me violently,ᵍ
　　my deadly enemies
　　who surround me.
10 They have become hardened;ʰ
　　their mouths speak arrogantly.
11 They advance against me;ⁱ
　　now they surround me.
　　They are determinedʲ
　　to throw ɪmeɪ to the ground.
12 They areᵏ like a lion eager
　　to tear,
　　like a young lion lurking
　　in ambush.

13 Rise up, LORD!
　　Confront him; bring him down.
　　With Your sword, save me
　　from the wicked.
14 With Your hand, LORD, ɪsave meɪ
　　from men,
　　from men of the world,
　　whose portion is in this life:
　　You fill their bellies with what
　　　You have in store,
　　their sons are satisfied,
　　and they leave their surplus
　　　to their children.

15 But I will see Your face
　　in righteousness;
　　when I awake, I will be satisfied
　　with Your presence.ˡ

ᵃ**16:10** LXX reads *see decay*　ᵇ**17:3** Or *[evil]; my mouth will not sin*　ᶜ**17:4** God's law　ᵈ**17:7** Or *love, You who save with Your right hand those seeking refuge from adversaries*　ᵉ**17:8** Lit *as the pupil, the daughter of the eye*　ᶠ**17:9** Lit *from the presence of*　ᵍ**17:9** Or *who plunder me*　ʰ**17:10** Lit *have closed up their fat*　ⁱ**17:11**Vg; one Hb ms, LXX read *They cast me out*; MT reads *Our steps*　ʲ**17:11** Lit *They set their eyes*　ᵏ**17:12** Lit *He is*　ˡ**17:15** Lit *form*

PSALM 18
Praise for Deliverance

For the choir director.
Of the servant of the LORD, David, who spoke
the words of this song to the LORD on the day
the LORD rescued him from the hand of all his
enemies and from the hand of Saul. He said:

1 I love You, LORD, my strength.
2 The LORD is my rock,
   my fortress, and my deliverer,
   my God, my mountain
     where I seek refuge,
   my shield and the •horn
   of my salvation,
   my stronghold.
3 I called to the LORD, who is
     worthy of praise,
   and I was saved from my enemies.

4 The ropes of death were wrapped
     around me;
   the torrents of destruction
     terrified me.
5 The ropes of •Sheol entangled me;
   the snares of death confronted me.
6 I called to the LORD in my distress,
   and I cried to my God for help.
   From His temple He heard
     my voice,
   and my cry to Him
     reached His ears.

7 Then the earth shook and quaked;
   the foundations of the mountains
     trembled;
   they shook because He burned
     with anger.
8 Smoke rose from His nostrils,
   and consuming fire [came]
     from His mouth;
   coals were set ablaze by it.ᵃ
9 He parted the heavens
     and came down,
   a dark cloud beneath His feet.
10 He rode on a cherub and flew,

soaring on the wings of the wind.
11 He made darkness
     His hiding place,
   dark storm clouds His canopy
     around Him.
12 From the radiance of His presence,
   His clouds swept onward with hail
     and blazing coals.
13 The LORD thundered fromᵇ heaven;
   the •Most High projected
     His voice.ᶜ
14 He shot His arrows
     and scattered them;
   He hurledᵈ lightning bolts
     and routed them.
15 The depths of the sea
     became visible,
   the foundations of the world
     were exposed,
   at Your rebuke, LORD,
   at the blast of the breath
     of Your nostrils.

16 He reached down from on high
     and took hold of me;
   He pulled me out of deep waters.
17 He rescued me
     from my powerful enemy
   and from those who hated me,
   for they were too strong for me.
18 They confronted me in the day
     of my distress,
   but the LORD was my support.
19 He brought me out to a wide-
     open place;
   He rescued me
     because He delighted in me.

20 The LORD rewarded me
   according to my righteousness;
   He repaid me
   according to the cleanness
     of my hands.
21 For I have kept the ways
     of the LORD

ᵃ18:8 Or *ablaze from Him* ᵇ18:13 Some Hb mss, LXX, Tg, Jer; other Hb mss read *in* ᶜ18:13 Other Hb mss read *voice, with hail and fiery coals* ᵈ18:14 Or *multiplied*

and have not turned from my God
  to wickedness.
22 Indeed, I have kept all
  His ordinances in mind[a]
and have not disregarded
  His statutes.
23 I was blameless toward Him
and kept myself from sinning.
24 So the LORD repaid me
according to my righteousness,
according to the cleanness
  of my hands in His sight.

25 With the faithful
You prove Yourself faithful;
with the blameless man
You prove Yourself blameless;
26 with the pure
You prove Yourself pure,
but with the crooked
You prove Yourself shrewd.
27 For You rescue an afflicted people,
but You humble those
  with haughty eyes.
28 LORD, You light my lamp;
  my God illuminates my darkness.
29 With You I can attack a barrier,[b]
and with my God I can leap over
  a wall.

30 God—His way is perfect;
the word of the LORD is pure.
He is a shield to all who take refuge
  in Him.
31 For who is God besides the LORD?
And who is a rock? Only our God.
32 God—He clothes me with strength
and makes my way perfect.
33 He makes my feet like the feet
  of a deer
and sets me securely
  on the heights.[c]
34 He trains my hands for war;
  my arms can bend a bow of bronze.

35 You have given me the shield
  of Your salvation;
Your right hand upholds me,
and Your humility exalts me.
36 You widen ⌊a place⌋ beneath me
  for my steps,
  and my ankles do not give way.

37 I pursue my enemies
  and overtake them;
I do not turn back until they are
  wiped out.
38 I crush them, and they cannot
  get up;
they fall beneath my feet.
39 You have clothed me with strength
  for battle;
You subdue my adversaries
  beneath me.
40 You have made my enemies retreat
  before me;[d]
I annihilate those who hate me.
41 They cry for help, but there is
  no one to save ⌊them⌋—
⌊they cry⌋ to the LORD,
  but He does not answer them.
42 I pulverize them like dust
  before the wind;
I trample them[e] like mud
  in the streets.

43 You have freed me from the feuds
  among the people;
You have appointed me the head
  of nations;
a people I had not known serve me.
44 Foreigners submit to me
  grudgingly;
as soon as they hear,[f] they obey me.
45 Foreigners lose heart
and come trembling
  from their fortifications.

46 The LORD lives—may my rock
  be praised!

---

[a]18:22 Lit Indeed, all His ordinances have been in front of me   [b]18:29 Or ridge   [c]18:33 Or on my high places
[d]18:40 Or You gave me the necks of my enemies   [e]18:42 Some Hb mss, LXX, Syr, Tg; other Hb mss read I poured
them out   [f]18:44 Lit At the hearing of the ear

The God of my salvation is exalted.
47 God—He gives me vengeance
and subdues peoples under me.
48 He frees me from my enemies.
You exalt me
above my adversaries;
You rescue me from violent men.
49 Therefore I will praise You, LORD,
among the nations;
I will sing about Your name.
50 He gives great victories to His king;
He shows loyalty to His anointed,
to David
and his descendants forever.

PSALM 19
The Witness of Creation and Scripture
For the choir director. A Davidic psalm.

1 The heavens declare the glory
of God,
and the sky[a] proclaims the work
of His hands.
2 Day after day
they pour out speech;
night after night
they communicate knowledge.[b]
3 There is no speech; there are
no words;
their voice is not heard.
4 Their message[c] has gone out to all
the earth,
and their words to the ends
of the inhabited world.

In the heavens[d] He has pitched
a tent for the sun.
5 It is like a groom coming from
the[e] bridal chamber;
it rejoices like an athlete
running a course.
6 It rises from one end
of the heavens

and circles[f] to their other end;
nothing is hidden from its heat.

7 The instruction of the LORD
is perfect,
reviving the soul;
the •testimony of the LORD
is trustworthy,
making the inexperienced wise.
8 The precepts of the Lord are right,
making the heart glad;
the commandment of the LORD
is radiant,
making the eyes light up.
9 The •fear of the LORD is pure,
enduring forever;
the ordinances of the LORD
are reliable
and altogether righteous.
10 They are more desirable
than gold—
than an abundance of pure gold;
and sweeter than honey—
than honey dripping
from the comb.
11 In addition, Your servant is warned
by them;
there is great reward
in keeping them.

12 Who perceives
his unintentional sins?
Cleanse me
from my hidden faults.
13 Moreover, keep Your servant
from willful sins;
do not let them rule over me.
Then I will be innocent,
and cleansed
from blatant rebellion.
14 May the words of my mouth
and the meditation of my heart
be acceptable to You,
LORD, my rock and my Redeemer.

---

[a]**19:1** Or *expanse*   [b]**19:2** Or *Day to day pours out speech, and night to night communicates knowledge*   [c]**19:4** LXX, Sym, Syr, Vg; MT reads *line*   [d]**19:4** Lit *In them*   [e]**19:5** Lit *his*   [f]**19:6** Lit *its circuit is*

PSALM 20
Deliverance in Battle

For the choir director. A Davidic psalm.

1 May the LORD answer you in a day
   of trouble;
   may the name of Jacob's God
   protect you.
2 May He send you help
   from the sanctuary
   and sustain you from Zion.
3 May He remember
   all your offerings
   and accept your •burnt offering.
                                    •Selah

4 May He give you what
   your heart desires
   and fulfill your whole purpose.
5 Let us shout for joy
   at your victory
   and lift the banner in the name
   of our God.
   May the LORD fulfill
   all your requests.

6 Now I know that the LORD
   gives victory to His anointed;
   He will answer him
   from His holy heaven
   with mighty victories
   from[a] His right hand.
7 Some take pride in a chariot,
   and others in horses,
   but we take pride in the name
   of the LORD our God.
8 They collapse and fall,
   but we rise and stand firm.
9 LORD, give victory
   to the king!
   May He[b] answer us on the day
   that we call.

PSALM 21
The King's Victory

For the choir director. A Davidic psalm.

1 LORD, the king finds joy
   in Your strength.
   How greatly he rejoices
   in Your victory!
2 You have given him his heart's desire
   and have not denied the request
   of his lips.   •Selah
3 For You meet him with rich blessings;
   You place a crown of pure gold
   on his head.
4 He asked You for life,
   and You gave it to him—
   length of days forever and ever.
5 His glory is great
   through Your victory;
   You confer majesty and splendor
   on him.
6 You give him blessings forever;
   You cheer him with joy
   in Your presence.
7 For the king relies on the LORD;
   through the faithful love
   of the •Most High
   he is not shaken.
8 Your hand will capture
   all your enemies;
   your right hand will seize
   those who hate you.
9 You will make them ⌊burn⌋
   like a fiery furnace when you appear;
   the LORD will engulf them
   in His wrath,
   and fire will devour them.
10 You will wipe their descendants
   from the earth
   and their offspring
   from the •human race.

---

[a]20:6 Other Hb mss, Aq, Sym, Jer, Syr read *with the victorious might of*   [b]20:9 Or *LORD, save. May the king*

11 Though they intend to harm[a] you
and devise a wicked plan,
  they will not prevail.
12 Instead, you will put them to flight
when you aim your bow[b]
  at their faces.

13 Be exalted, LORD, in Your strength;
we will sing and praise Your might.

PSALM 22

From Suffering to Praise

For the choir director: according to
"The Deer of the Dawn."[c]
A Davidic psalm.

1 My God, my God, why have You
  forsaken me?
⌊Why are You⌋ so far
  from my deliverance
and from my words of groaning?[d]
2 My God, I cry by day, but You
  do not answer,
by night, yet I have no rest.
3 But You are holy,
enthroned on the praises of Israel.
4 Our fathers trusted in You;
they trusted,
  and You rescued them.
5 They cried to You and were
  set free;
they trusted in You
  and were not disgraced.

6 But I am a worm and not a man,
scorned by men and despised
  by people.
7 Everyone who sees me mocks me;
they sneer[e] and shake their heads:
8 "He relies on[f] the LORD;
let Him rescue him;
let the LORD[g] deliver him,
since He takes pleasure in him."

9 You took me from the womb,
making me secure
  while at my mother's breast.
10 I was given over to You at birth;[h]
You have been my God
  from my mother's womb.

11 Do not be far from me,
because distress is near
and there is no one to help.

12 Many bulls surround me;
strong ones of Bashan
  encircle me.
13 They open their mouths
  against me—
lions, mauling and roaring.
14 I am poured out like water,
and all my bones are disjointed;
my heart is like wax,
melting within me.
15 My strength is dried up
  like baked clay;
my tongue sticks to the roof
  of my mouth.
You put me into the dust of death.
16 For dogs have surrounded me;
a gang of evildoers has closed in
  on me;
they pierced[i] my hands
  and my feet.
17 I can count all my bones;
people[j] look and stare at me.
18 They divided my garments
  among themselves,
and they cast lots for my clothing.
19 But You, LORD, don't be far away.
My strength, come quickly
  to help me.
20 Deliver my life from the sword,
my very life[k] from the power
  of the dog.

ᵃ21:11 Lit *they stretch out evil against*   ᵇ21:12 Lit *aim with your bowstrings*   ᶜPerhaps a musical term   ᵈ22:1 Or *My words of groaning are so far from delivering me* (as a statement)   ᵉ22:7 Lit *separate with the lip*   ᶠ22:8 Or *Rely on* ᵍ22:8 Lit *let Him*   ʰ22:10 Lit *was cast on You from the womb*   ⁱ22:16 Some Hb mss, LXX, Syr; other Hb mss read *me; like a lion*   ʲ22:17 Lit *they*   ᵏ22:20 Lit *my only one*

21 Save me from the mouth
        of the lion!
    You have rescued[a] me
    from the horns of the wild oxen.

22 I will proclaim Your name
        to my brothers;
    I will praise You
        in the congregation.
23 You who •fear the LORD,
        praise Him!
    All you descendants of Jacob,
        honor Him!
    All you descendants of Israel,
        revere Him!
24 For He has not despised or detested
        the torment of the afflicted.
    He did not hide His face from him,
    but listened when he cried to Him
        for help.

25 I will give praise[b]
        in the great congregation
        because of You;
    I will fulfill my vows
        before those who fear You.[c]
26 The humble[d] will eat
        and be satisfied;
    those who seek the LORD
        will praise Him.
    May your hearts live forever!

27 All the ends of the earth
        will remember
    and turn to the LORD.
    All the families of the nations
    will bow down before You,
28 for kingship belongs to the LORD;
    He rules over the nations.
29 All who prosper on earth will eat
        and bow down;
    all those who go down to the dust
    will kneel before Him—
    even the one who cannot preserve
        his life.

30 Descendants will serve Him;
    the next generation will be told
        about the Lord.
31 They will come and tell a people
        yet to be born
    about His righteousness—
    what He has done.

PSALM 23
The Good Shepherd
A Davidic psalm.

1   The LORD is my shepherd;
    there is nothing I lack.
2   He lets me lie down
        in green pastures;
    He leads me beside quiet waters.
3   He renews my life;
    He leads me along the right paths[e]
        for His name's sake.
4   Even when I go
        through the darkest valley,[f]
    I fear no danger,
        for You are with me;
    Your rod and Your staff[g]—
        they comfort me.

5   You prepare a table before me
        in the presence of my enemies;
    You anoint my head with oil;
        my cup overflows.
6   Only goodness and faithful love
        will pursue me
    all the days of my life,
    and I will dwell in[h] the house
        of the LORD
    as long as I live.[i]

PSALM 24
The King of Glory
A Davidic psalm.

1   The earth and everything in it,
    the world and its inhabitants,

---

[a]**22:21** Lit answered [b]**22:25** Lit my praise [c]**22:25** Lit Him [d]**22:26** Or poor, or afflicted [e]**23:3** Or me in paths of righteousness [f]**23:4** Or the valley of the shadow of death [g]**23:4** A shepherd's rod and crook [h]**23:6** LXX, Sym, Syr, Tg, Vg, Jer; MT reads will return to [i]**23:6** Lit LORD for length of days; traditionally LORD forever

belong to the LORD;
2 for He laid its foundation
    on the seas
and established it on the rivers.

3 Who may ascend the mountain
    of the LORD?
Who may stand in His holy place?
4 The one who has clean hands
    and a pure heart,
who has not set his minda on
    what is false,
and who has not sworn deceitfully.
5 He will receive blessing
    from the LORD,
and righteousness from the God
    of his salvation.
6 Such is the generation of those
    who seek Him,
who seek the face of the God
    of Jacob.b   •Selah

7 Lift up your heads, you gates!
Rise up, ancient doors!
Then the King of glory
    will come in.
8 Who is this King of glory?
The LORD, strong and mighty,
the LORD, mighty in battle.
9 Lift up your heads, you gates!
Rise up, ancient doors!
Then the King of glory
    will come in.
10 Who is He, this King of glory?
The LORD of •Hosts,
He is the King of glory.   Selah

PSALM 25
Dependence on the LORD
Davidic.

1 LORD,c I turn my hope to You.d
2 My God, I trust in You.
Do not let me be disgraced;

do not let my enemies gloat
    over me.
3 Not one person who waits for You
will be disgraced;
those who act treacherously
    without cause
will be disgraced.

4 Make Your ways known to me,
    LORD;
teach me Your paths.
5 Guide me in Your truth
    and teach me,
for You are the God of my salvation;
I wait for You all day long.
6 Remember, LORD, Your compassion
and Your faithful love,
for they ⌊have existed⌋
    from antiquity.e
7 Do not remember the sins
    of my youth
or my acts of rebellion;
in keeping with Your faithful love,
    remember me
because of Your goodness, LORD.

8 The LORD is good and upright;
therefore He shows sinners
    the way.
9 He leads the humble in what
    is right
and teaches them His way.
10 All the LORD's ways ⌊show⌋
    faithful love and truth
to those who keep His covenant
    and decrees.
11 Because of Your name, LORD,
forgive my sin, for it is great.

12 Who is the person who •fears
    the LORD?
He will show him the way
    he should choose.
13 He will live a good life,

---

a24:4 Or not lifted up his soul   b24:6 Some Hb mss, LXX, Syr; other Hb mss read seek Your face, Jacob   c25:1 The lines of this poem form an •acrostic.   d25:1 Or To You, LORD, I lift up my soul   e25:6 Or everlasting

and his descendants will inherit
    the land.ᵃ
14 The secret counsel of the LORD
    is for those who fear Him,
    and He reveals His covenant
    to them.
15 My eyes are always on the LORD,
    for He will pull my feet
      out of the net.

16 Turn to me and be gracious
    to me,
    for I am alone and afflicted.
17 The distresses of my heart
    increase;ᵇ
    bring me out of my sufferings.
18 Consider my affliction
    and trouble,
    and take away all my sins.
19 Consider my enemies;
    they are numerous,
    and they hate me violently.
20 Guard me and deliver me;
    do not let me be put to shame,
    for I take refuge in You.
21 May integrity and uprightness
    keep me,
    for I wait for You.

22 God, redeem Israel, from all
    its distresses.

PSALM 26
Prayer for Vindication
Davidic.

1 Vindicate me, LORD,
    because I have lived with integrity
    and have trusted in the LORD
    without wavering.
2 Test me, LORD, and try me;
    examine my heart and mind.
3 For Your faithful love is
    before my eyes,
    and I live by Your truth.

4 I do not sit with the worthless
    or associate with hypocrites.
5 I hate a crowd of evildoers,
    and I do not sit with the wicked.
6 I wash my handsᶜ in innocence
    and go around Your altar, LORD,
7 raising my voice in thanksgiving
    and telling about
      Your wonderful works.

8 LORD, I love the house
    where You dwell,
    the place where Your glory resides.
9 Do not destroy me
    along with sinners,
    or my life along with men
    of bloodshed
10 in whose hands are evil schemes,
    and whose right hands are filled
    with bribes.

11 But I live with integrity;
    redeem me and be gracious to me.
12 My foot stands on level ground;
    I will praise the LORD
    in the assemblies.

PSALM 27
My Stronghold
Davidic.

1 The LORD is my light
    and my salvation—
    whom should I fear?
    The LORD is the stronghold
    of my life—
    of whom should I be afraid?
2 When evildoers came against me
    to devour my flesh,
    my foes and my enemies stumbled
    and fell.
3 Though an army deploy against me,
    my heart is not afraid;
    though war break out against me,
    still I am confident.

ᵃ**25:13** Or *earth* ᵇ**25:17** Or *Relieve the distresses of my heart* ᶜ**26:6** A ritual or ceremonial washing to express innocence

⁴ I have asked one thing
   from the LORD;
it is what I desire:
to dwell in the house of the LORD
all the days of my life,
gazing on the beauty of the LORD
and seeking ⌊Him⌋ in His temple.
⁵ For He will conceal me
   in His shelter
in the day of adversity;
He will hide me under the cover
   of His tent;
He will set me high on a rock.
⁶ Then my head will be high
above my enemies around me;
I will offer sacrifices in His tent
   with shouts of joy.
I will sing and make music
   to the LORD.

⁷ LORD, hear my voice when I call;
be gracious to me and answer me.
⁸ In Your behalf my heart says,
   "Seek My face."
LORD, I will seek Your face.
⁹ Do not hide Your face from me;
do not turn Your servant away
   in anger.
You have been my help;
do not leave me or abandon me,
God of my salvation.
¹⁰ Even if my father and mother
   abandon me,
the LORD cares for me.

¹¹ Because of my adversaries,
show me Your way, LORD,
and lead me on a level path.
¹² Do not give me over to the will
   of my foes,
for false witnesses rise up
   against me,
breathing violence.

¹³ I am certain that I will see
   the LORD's goodness
in the land of the living.

¹⁴ Wait for the LORD;
be courageous and let your heart
   be strong.
Wait for the LORD.

PSALM 28
My Strength
Davidic.

¹ LORD, I call to You;
my rock, do not be deaf to me.
If You remain silent to me,
I will be like those going down
   to the •Pit.
² Listen to the sound of my pleading
when I cry to You for help,
when I lift up my hands
toward Your holy sanctuary.

³ Do not drag me away
   with the wicked,
with the evildoers,
who speak in friendly ways
   with their neighbors,
while malice is in their hearts.
⁴ Repay them according to what
   they have done—
according to the evil
   of their deeds.
Repay them according to the work
   of their hands;
give them back
   what they deserve.
⁵ Because they do not consider
what the LORD has done
or the work of His hands,
He will tear them down and not
   rebuild them.

⁶ May the LORD be praised,
for He has heard the sound
   of my pleading.
⁷ The LORD is my strength
   and my shield;
my heart trusts in Him,
and I am helped.

Therefore my heart rejoices,
and I praise Him with my song.

8 The LORD is the strength
of His people;[a]
He is a stronghold of salvation
for His anointed.
9 Save Your people,
bless Your possession,
shepherd them, and carry
them forever.

PSALM 29
The Voice of the LORD
A Davidic psalm.

1 Give the LORD—
you heavenly beings[b]—
give the LORD glory and strength.
2 Give the LORD the glory due
His name;
worship the LORD
in the splendor of ⌊His⌋ holiness.[c]

3 The voice of the LORD is
above the waters.
The God of glory thunders—
the LORD, above vast waters,
4 the voice of the LORD in power,
the voice of the LORD
in splendor.
5 The voice of the LORD
breaks the cedars;
the LORD shatters the cedars
of Lebanon.
6 He makes Lebanon skip
like a calf,
and Sirion,[d] like a young wild ox.
7 The voice of the LORD flashes
flames of fire.
8 The voice of the LORD shakes
the wilderness;
the LORD shakes the wilderness
of Kadesh.

9 The voice of the LORD
makes the deer give birth[e]
and strips the woodlands bare.

In His temple all cry, "Glory!"

10 The LORD sat enthroned at the flood;
the LORD sits enthroned,
King forever.
11 The LORD gives His people strength;
the LORD blesses His people
with peace.

PSALM 30
Joy in the Morning
A psalm; a dedication song for the house.
Davidic.

1 I will exalt You, LORD,
because You have lifted me up
and have not allowed my enemies
to triumph over me.
2 LORD my God,
I cried to You for help,
and You healed me.
3 LORD, You brought me up
from •Sheol;
You spared me from among those
going down[f] to the •Pit.

4 Sing to the LORD,
you His faithful ones,
and praise His holy name.
5 For His anger lasts only a moment,
but His favor, a lifetime.
Weeping may spend the night,
but there is joy in the morning.

6 When I was secure, I said,
"I will never be shaken."
7 LORD, when You showed Your favor,
You made me stand
like a strong mountain;
when You hid Your face,
I was terrified.

---

a28:8 Some Hb mss, LXX, Syr; other Hb mss read *strength for them*   **b29:1** Or *you angels*, or *you sons of the mighty*;
lit *LORD sons of [the] gods*   **c29:2** Or *in holy attire*, or *in holy appearance*   **d29:6** Mount Hermon; Dt 3:9   **e29:9** Or *the
oaks shake*   **f30:3** Some Hb mss, LXX, Theod, Orig, Syr; other Hb mss, Aq, Sym, Tg, Jer read *from going down*

8 LORD, I called to You;
  I sought favor from my Lord:
9 "What gain is there in my death,
  in my descending to the Pit?
  Will the dust praise You?
  Will it proclaim Your truth?
10 LORD, listen and be gracious to me;
  LORD, be my helper."

11 You turned my lament
  into dancing;
  You removed my •sackcloth
  and clothed me with gladness,
12 so that I can sing to You and not
  be silent.
  LORD my God, I will praise
  You forever.

PSALM 31
A Plea for Protection

For the choir director. A Davidic psalm.

1 LORD, I seek refuge in You;
  let me never be disgraced.
  Save me by Your righteousness.
2 Listen closely to me;
  rescue me quickly.
  Be a rock of refuge for me,
  a mountain fortress to save me.
3 For You are my rock
  and my fortress;
  You lead and guide me
  because of Your name.
4 You will free me from the net
  that is secretly set for me,
  for You are my refuge.
5 Into Your hand I entrust my spirit;
  You redeem[a] me, LORD,
  God of truth.

6 I[b] hate those who are devoted
  to worthless idols,
  but I trust in the LORD.
7 I will rejoice and be glad
  in Your faithful love

because You have seen
  my affliction.
  You have known the troubles
  of my life
8 and have not handed me over
  to the enemy.
  You have set my feet
  in a spacious place.
9 Be gracious to me, LORD,
  because I am in distress;
  my eyes are worn out
  from angry sorrow—
  my whole being[c] as well.
10 Indeed, my life is consumed
  with grief,
  and my years with groaning;
  my strength has failed
  because of my sinfulness,[d]
  and my bones waste away.
11 I am ridiculed by all my adversaries
  and even by my neighbors.
  I am an object of dread
  to my acquaintances;
  those who see me in the street
  run from me.
12 I am forgotten: gone from memory
  like a dead person—
  like broken pottery.
13 I have heard the gossip of many;
  terror is on every side.
  When they conspired against me,
  they plotted to take my life.

14 But I trust in You, LORD;
  I say, "You are my God."
15 The course of my life is
  in Your power;
  deliver me from the power
  of my enemies
  and from my persecutors.
16 Show Your favor to Your servant;
  save me by Your faithful love.
17 LORD, do not let me be disgraced
  when I call on You.

---

[a]31:5 Or *You have redeemed,* or *You will redeem,* or *spirit. Redeem*   [b]31:6 One Hb ms, LXX, Syr, Vg, Jer read *You*
[c]31:9 Lit *my soul and my belly*   [d]31:10 LXX, Syr, Sym read *affliction*

Let the wicked be disgraced;
let them be silent[a][b] in •Sheol.
18 Let lying lips be quieted;
they speak arrogantly
against the righteous
with pride and contempt.

19 How great is Your goodness
that You have stored up for those
who •fear You,
and accomplished in the sight
of •everyone
for those who take refuge in You.
20 You hide them in the protection
of Your presence;
You conceal them in a shelter[c]
from the schemes of men,
from quarrelsome tongues.
21 May the LORD be praised,
for He has wonderfully shown
His faithful love to me
in a city under siege.[d]
22 In my alarm I had said,
"I am cut off from Your sight."
But You heard the sound
of my pleading
when I cried to You for help.

23 Love the LORD, all His faithful ones.
The LORD protects the loyal,
but fully repays the arrogant.
24 Be strong and courageous,
all you who put your hope
in the LORD.

PSALM 32
The Joy of Forgiveness

Davidic. A •*Maskil.*

1 How happy is the one
whose transgression is forgiven,
whose sin is covered!
2 How happy is the man
the LORD does not charge with sin,

and in whose spirit is no deceit!

3 When I kept silent,[e] my bones
became brittle
from my groaning all day long.
4 For day and night Your hand
was heavy on me;
my strength was drained[f]
as in the summer's heat.   •*Selah*
5 Then I acknowledged my sin to You
and did not conceal my iniquity.
I said,
"I will confess my transgressions
to the LORD,"
and You took away the guilt
of my sin.   *Selah*

6 Therefore let everyone
who is faithful pray to You
at a time that You may be found.[g]
When great floodwaters come,
they will not reach him.
7 You are my hiding place;
You protect me from trouble.
You surround me with joyful shouts
of deliverance.   *Selah*

8 I will instruct you and show you
the way to go;
with My eye on you,
I will give counsel.
9 Do not be like a horse or mule,
without understanding,
that must be controlled with bit
and bridle,
or else it will not come near you.

10 Many pains come to the wicked,
but the one who trusts in the LORD
will have faithful love
surrounding him.
11 Be glad in the LORD and rejoice,
you righteous ones;
shout for joy,
all you upright in heart.

---

[a]**31:17** LXX reads *brought down*   [b]**31:17** Or *them perish* or *wail*   [c]**31:20** Lit *canopy*   [d]**31:21** Or *a fortified city*
[e]**32:3** Probably a reference to a refusal to confess sin   [f]**32:4** Hb obscure   [g]**32:6** Lit *time of finding*

PSALM 33
Praise to the Creator

1 Rejoice in the LORD,
   you righteous ones;
   praise from the upright is beautiful.
2 Praise the LORD with the lyre;
   make music to Him with a ten-
   stringed harp.
3 Sing a new song to Him;
   play skillfully on the strings,
   with a joyful shout.

4 For the word of the LORD is right,
   and all His work is trustworthy.
5 He loves righteousness and justice;
   the earth is full of the LORD's
   unfailing love.

6 The heavens were made
   by the word of the LORD,
   and all the stars, by the breath
   of His mouth.
7 He gathers the waters of the sea
   into a heap;[a]
   He puts the depths
   into storehouses.
8 Let the whole earth tremble
   before the LORD;
   let all the inhabitants of the world
   stand in awe of Him.
9 For He spoke, and it came
   into being;
   He commanded, and it came
   into existence.

10 The LORD frustrates the counsel
   of the nations;
   He thwarts the plans
   of the peoples.
11 The counsel of the LORD
   stands forever,
   the plans of His heart
   from generation to generation.

12 Happy is the nation whose God is
   the LORD—
   the people He has chosen to be
   His own possession!
13 The LORD looks down from heaven;
   He observes everyone.
14 He gazes on all the inhabitants
   of the earth
   from His dwelling place.
15 He alone crafts their hearts;
   He considers all their works.
16 A king is not saved by a large army;
   a warrior will not be delivered
   by great strength.
17 The horse is a false hope for safety;
   it provides no escape by
   its great power.
18 Now the eye of the LORD is
   on those who •fear Him—
   those who depend on
   His faithful love
19 to deliver them from death
   and to keep them alive in famine.

20 We wait for the LORD;
   He is our help and shield.
21 For our hearts rejoice in Him,
   because we trust in His holy name.
22 May Your faithful love rest on us,
   LORD,
   for we put our hope in You.

PSALM 34
The LORD Delivers the Righteous

Concerning David, when he pretended
to be insane in the presence of Abimelech,[b]
who drove him out, and he departed.

1 I[c] will praise the LORD at all times;
   His praise will always be
   on my lips.
2 I will boast in the LORD;
   the humble will hear and be glad.

---

[a]33:7 LXX, Tg, Syr, Vg, Jer read *sea as in a bottle*   [b]A reference to Achish, king of Gath   [c]34:1 The lines of this poem form an •acrostic.

3 Proclaim with me
   the LORD's greatness;
   let us exalt His name together.
4 I sought the LORD,
   and He answered me
   and delivered me from all my fears.
5 Those who look to Him are[a] radiant
   with joy;
   their faces will never be ashamed.
6 This poor man cried, and the LORD
   heard ⌊him⌋
   and saved him from all his troubles.
7 The angel of the LORD encamps
   around those who •fear Him,
   and rescues them.
8 Taste and see that the LORD is good.
   How happy is the man
   who takes refuge in Him!
9 Fear the LORD, you His saints,
   for those who fear Him
   lack nothing.
10 Young lions[b] lack food
   and go hungry,
   but those who seek the LORD
   will not lack any good thing.
11 Come, children, listen to me;
   I will teach you the fear
   of the LORD.
12 Who is the man who delights
   in life,
   loving a long life to enjoy
   what is good?
13 Keep your tongue from evil
   and your lips
   from deceitful speech.
14 Turn away from evil and do
   what is good;
   seek peace and pursue it.
15 The eyes of the LORD are
   on the righteous,
   and His ears are open to their cry
   for help.

16 The face of the LORD is set
   against those who do what is evil,
   to erase all memory of them
   from the earth.
17 The righteous[c] cry out,
   and the LORD hears,
   and delivers them from all
   their troubles.
18 The LORD is near
   the brokenhearted;
   He saves those crushed in spirit.
19 Many adversities come to the one
   who is righteous,
   but the LORD delivers him
   from them all.
20 He protects all his bones;
   not one of them is broken.
21 Evil brings death to the sinner,
   and those who hate the righteous
   will be punished.
22 The LORD redeems the life
   of His servants,
   and all who take refuge in Him
   will not be punished.

PSALM 35
Prayer for Victory
Davidic.

1 Oppose my opponents, LORD;
   fight those who fight me.
2 Take Your shields—
   large and small—
   and come to my aid.
3 Draw the spear and javelin
   against my pursuers,
   and assure me: "I am
   your deliverance."

4 Let those who seek to kill me
   be disgraced and humiliated;
   let those who plan to harm me
   be turned back and ashamed.
5 Let them be like husks in the wind,

with the angel of the L<small>ORD</small>
driving them away.
6 Let their way be dark and slippery,
with the angel of the L<small>ORD</small>
pursuing them.
7 They hid their net for me
without cause;
they dug a pit for me
without cause.
8 Let ruin come
on him unexpectedly,
and let the net that he hid
ensnare him;
let him fall into it—to his ruin.
9 Then I will rejoice in the L<small>ORD</small>;
I will delight in His deliverance.
10 My very bones will say,
"L<small>ORD</small>, who is like You,
rescuing the poor from one
too strong for him,
the poor or the needy from one
who robs him?"

11 Malicious witnesses come forward;
they question me about things
I do not know.
12 They repay me evil for good,
making me desolate.
13 Yet when they were sick,
my clothing was •sackcloth;
I humbled myself with fasting,
and my prayer was genuine.ᵃ
14 I went about ⌊grieving⌋ as if
for my friend or brother;
I was bowed down with grief,
like one mourning a mother.
15 But when I stumbled, they gathered
in glee;
they gathered against me.
Assailants I did not know
tore at me and did not stop.
16 With godless mockeryᵇ
they gnashed their teeth at me.

17 Lord, how long will You look on?
Rescue my life from their ravages,
my very lifeᶜ from the young lions.
18 I will praise You
in the great congregation;
I will exalt You
among many people.
19 Do not let my deceitful enemies
rejoice over me;
do not let those who hate me
without cause
look at me maliciously.
20 For they do not speak
in friendly ways,
but contrive deceitful schemesᵈ
against those who live peacefully
in the land.
21 They open their mouths wide
against me and say,
"Aha, aha! We saw it!"ᵉ
22 You saw it, L<small>ORD</small>; do not be silent.
Lord, do not be far from me.
23 Wake up and rise to my defense,
to my cause, my God and my L<small>ORD</small>!
24 Vindicate me, L<small>ORD</small>, my God,
in keeping with Your righteousness,
and do not let them rejoice
over me.
25 Do not let them say in their hearts,
"Aha! Just what we wanted."
Do not let them say,
"We have swallowed him up!"
26 Let those who rejoice
at my misfortune
be disgraced and humiliated;
let those who exalt themselves
over me
be clothed with shame
and reproach.

27 Let those who want my vindication
shout for joy and be glad;
let them continually say,

ᵃ**35:13** Lit *prayer returned to my chest*   ᵇ**35:16** Hb obscure   ᶜ**35:17** Lit *my only one*   ᵈ**35:20** Lit *but devise deceitful words*   ᵉ**35:21** Lit *Our eyes saw!*

"The LORD be exalted,
who wants His servant's well-
being."
28 And my tongue will proclaim
Your righteousness,
Your praise all day long.

PSALM 36
Human Wickedness and God's Love

For the choir director. ⌊A psalm⌋ of David,
the LORD's servant.

1 An oracle within my heart
concerning the transgression
of the wicked:
There is no dread of God
before his eyes,
2 for in his own eyes
he flatters himself ⌊too much⌋
to discover and hate his sin.
3 The words of his mouth
are malicious and deceptive;
he has stopped acting wisely
and doing good.
4 Even on his bed he makes
malicious plans.
He sets himself on a path
that is not good
and does not reject evil.

5 LORD, Your faithful love ⌊reaches⌋
to heaven,
Your faithfulness to the skies.
6 Your righteousness is
like the highest mountain;
Your judgments,
like the deepest sea.
LORD, You preserve man and beast.
7 God, Your faithful love
is so valuable
that •people take refuge
in the shadow of Your wings.
8 They are filled from the abundance
of Your house;

You let them drink
from Your refreshing stream,
9 for with You is life's fountain.
In Your light we will see light.
10 Spread Your faithful love over those
who know You,
and Your righteousness
over the upright in heart.
11 Do not let the foot of the arrogant
come near me
or the hand of the wicked
drive me away.
12 There the evildoers fall;
they have been thrown down
and cannot rise.

PSALM 37
Instruction in Wisdom

Davidic.

1 Do[a] not be agitated by evildoers;
do not envy those who do wrong.
2 For they wither quickly like grass
and wilt like tender green plants.

3 Trust in the LORD and do
what is good;
dwell in the land
and live securely.[b]
4 Take delight in the LORD,
and He will give you
your heart's desires.

5 Commit your way to the LORD;
trust in Him, and He will act,
6 making your righteousness shine
like the dawn,
your justice like the noonday.

7 Be silent before the LORD and wait
expectantly for Him;
do not be agitated by one
who prospers in his way,
by the man who carries out
evil plans.

---

[a]37:1 The lines of this poem form an •acrostic. [b]37:3 Or *and cultivate faithfulness*

8 Refrain from anger and give up
  ⌜your⌝ rage;
  do not be agitated—it can only
  bring harm.
9 For evildoers will be destroyed,
  but those who put their hope
  in the LORD
  will inherit the land.ᵃ

10 A little while, and the wicked
  will be no more;
  though you look for him,
  he will not be there.
11 But the humble will inherit
  the landᵃ
  and will enjoy abundant prosperity.

12 The wicked schemes
  against the righteous
  and gnashes his teeth at him.
13 The Lord laughs at him
  because He sees that his day
  is coming.
14 The wicked have drawn the sword
  and strung theᵇ bow
  to bring down the afflicted
  and needy
  and to slaughter those whose way
  is upright.
15 Their swords will enter
  their own hearts,
  and their bows will be broken.

16 Better the little
  that the righteous man has
  than the abundance
  of many wicked people.
17 For the armsᶜ of the wicked
  will be broken,
  but the LORD supports
  the righteous.
18 The LORD watches over
  the blameless all their days,

and their inheritance
  will last forever.
19 They will not be disgraced in times
  of adversity;
  they will be satisfied in days
  of hunger.

20 But the wicked will perish;
  the LORD's enemies, like the glory
  of the pastures,
  will fade away—
  they will fade away like smoke.

21 The wicked borrows
  and does not repay,
  but the righteous is gracious
  and giving.
22 Those who are blessed by Him
  will inherit the land,ᵃ
  but those cursed by Him
  will be destroyed.

23 A man's steps are established
  by the LORD,
  and He takes pleasure in his way.
24 Though he falls, he will not
  be overwhelmed,
  because the LORD holds his hand.ᵈ

25 I have been young and now
  I am old,
  yet I have not seen
  the righteous abandoned
  or his children begging bread.
26 He is always generous,
  always lending,
  and his children are a blessing.

27 Turn away from evil and do
  what is good,
  and dwell thereᵉ forever.
28 For the LORD loves justice
  and will not abandon
  His faithful ones.
  They are kept safe forever,

ᵃ37:9,11,22 Or earth   ᵇ37:14 Lit their   ᶜ37:17 Or power   ᵈ37:24 Or LORD supports with His hand   ᵉ37:27 Dwell in
the land

but the children of the wicked
   will be destroyed.
29 The righteous will inherit the land[a]
   and dwell in it permanently.

30 The mouth of the righteous
     utters wisdom;
   his tongue speaks what is just.
31 The instruction of his God is
     in his heart;
   his steps do not falter.

32 The wicked lies in wait
     for the righteous
   and seeks to kill him;
33 the LORD will not leave him
     in his hand[b]
   or allow him to be condemned
     when he is judged.

34 Wait for the LORD and keep His way,
   and He will exalt you to inherit
     the land.
   You will watch when the wicked
     are destroyed.

35 I have seen a wicked, violent man
   well-rooted[c] like
     a flourishing native tree.
36 Then I passed by and[d] noticed
     he was gone;
   I searched for him, but he could not
     be found.

37 Watch the blameless and observe
     the upright,
   for the man of peace will have
     a future.[e]
38 But transgressors will all
     be eliminated;
   the future[e] of the wicked
     will be destroyed.

39 The salvation of the righteous is
     from the LORD,
   their refuge in a time of distress.

40 The LORD helps and delivers them;
   He will deliver them
     from the wicked
   and will save them
   because they take refuge in Him.

PSALM 38
Prayer of a Suffering Sinner
A Davidic psalm for remembrance.

1 LORD, do not punish me
     in Your anger
   or discipline me in Your wrath.
2 For Your arrows have sunk into me,
   and Your hand has pressed down
     on me.

3 There is no soundness in my body
   because of Your indignation;
   there is no health in my bones
     because of my sin.
4 For my sins have flooded
     over my head;
   they are a burden too heavy for me
     to bear.
5 My wounds are foul and festering
   because of my foolishness.
6 I am bent over and brought low;
   all day long I go around
     in mourning.
7 For my loins are full of
     burning pain,
   and there is no health in my body.
8 I am faint and severely crushed;
   I groan because of the anguish
     of my heart.

9 Lord, my every desire is known
     to[f] You;
   my sighing is not hidden from You.
10 My heart races, my strength
     leaves me,
   and even the light of my eyes
     has faded.[g]

---

[a]37:29 Or *earth*   [b]37:33 Or *power*   [c]37:35 Hb obscure   [d]37:36 DSS, LXX, Syr, Vg, Jer; MT reads *Then he passed away, and I*   [e]37:37 Or *posterity*   [f]38:9 Lit *is in front of*   [g]38:10 Or *and the light of my eyes—even that is not with me*

11 My loved ones and friends
    stand back from my affliction,
and my relatives stand
    at a distance.
12 Those who seek my life set traps,
and those who want to harm me
    threaten to destroy me;
they plot treachery all day long.

13 I am like a deaf person;
    I do not hear.
I am like a speechless person
who does not open his mouth.
14 I am like a man who does not hear
and has no arguments in his mouth.

Hope and Confession

15 I put my hope in You, LORD;
You will answer, Lord my God.
16 For I said, "Don't let them rejoice
    over me—
those who are arrogant toward me
when I stumble."
17 For I am about to fall,
and my pain is constantly with me.
18 So I confess my guilt;
I am anxious because of my sin.
19 But my enemies are vigorous
    and powerful;[a]
many hate me for no reason.
20 Those who repay evil for good
attack me for pursuing good.

21 LORD, do not abandon me;
my God, do not be far from me.
22 Hurry to help me,
Lord, my Savior.

PSALM 39

The Fleeting Nature of Life

For the choir director, for Jeduthun.
A Davidic psalm.

1 I said, "I will guard my ways
so that I may not sin
    with my tongue;
I will guard my mouth
    with a muzzle
as long as the wicked are
    in my presence."
2 I was speechless and quiet;
I kept silent, even from
    ⌊speaking⌋ good,
and my pain intensified.
3 My heart grew hot within me;
as I mused, a fire burned.
I spoke with my tongue:

4 "LORD, reveal to me the end
    of my life
and the number of my days.
Let me know how transitory I am.
5 You, indeed, have made my days
    short in length,
and my life span as nothing
    in Your sight.
Yes, every mortal man is
    only a vapor. •*Selah*
6 Certainly, man walks about
    like a mere shadow.
Indeed, they frantically rush around
    in vain,
gathering possessions
without knowing who will get them.

7 "Now, Lord, what do I wait for?
My hope is in You.
8 Deliver me from all
    my transgressions;
do not make me the taunt of fools.
9 I am speechless; I do not open
    my mouth
because of what You have done.
10 Remove Your torment from me;
I fade away because of the force
    of Your hand.
11 You discipline a man
    with punishment for sin,
consuming like a moth
    what is precious to him;
every man is a mere vapor. *Selah*

a**38:19** Or *numerous*

12 "Hear my prayer, LORD,
    and listen to my cry for help;
    do not be silent at my tears.
    For I am a foreigner residing
        with You,
    a sojourner like all my fathers.
13 Turn Your angry gaze from me
    so that I may be cheered up
    before I die and am gone."

PSALM 40
Thanksgiving and a Cry for Help
For the choir director. A Davidic psalm.

1 I waited patiently for the LORD,
    and He turned to me and heard
    my cry for help.
2 He brought me up
    from a desolate[a] pit,
    out of the muddy clay,
    and set my feet on a rock,
    making my steps secure.
3 He put a new song
    in my mouth,
    a hymn of praise to our God.
    Many will see and fear,
    and put their trust in the LORD.

4 How happy is the man
    who has put his trust in the LORD
    and has not turned to the proud
    or to those who run after lies!
5 LORD my God, You have done
    many things—
    Your wonderful works
        and Your plans for us;
    none can compare with You.
    If I were to report and speak
    ⌊of them⌋,
    they are more than can be told.

6 You do not delight in sacrifice
    and offering;
    You open my ears to listen.[b]

You do not ask for
    a whole •burnt offering
    or a •sin offering.
7 Then I said, "See, I have come;
    it is written about me
    in the volume of the scroll.
8 I delight to do Your will, my God;
    Your instruction resides
        within me."[c]

9 I proclaim righteousness
    in the great assembly;
    see, I do not keep
    my mouth closed[d]
    —as You know, LORD.
10 I did not hide Your righteousness
    in my heart;
    I spoke about Your faithfulness
    and salvation;
    I did not conceal Your constant love
    and truth
    from the great assembly.

11 LORD, do not withhold
    Your compassion from me;
    Your constant love and truth
    will always guard me.
12 For troubles without number
    have surrounded me;
    my sins have overtaken me;
    I am unable to see.
    They are more than the hairs
    of my head,
    and my courage leaves me.
13 LORD, be pleased to deliver me;
    hurry to help me, LORD.

14 Let those who seek to take my life
    be disgraced and confounded.
    Let those who wish me harm
    be driven back and humiliated.
15 Let those who say to me,
    "Aha, aha!"
    be horrified because of their shame.

---

a 40:2 Or watery   b 40:6 Lit You hollow out ears for me   c 40:8 Lit instruction within my inner being   d 40:9 Lit not
restrain my lips

¹⁶ Let all who seek You rejoice
    and be glad in You;
let those who love Your salvation
    continually say,
    "The LORD is great!"
¹⁷ I am afflicted and needy;
    the Lord thinks of me.
You are my help and my deliverer;
    my God, do not delay.

PSALM 41
Victory in Spite of Betrayal
For the choir director. A Davidic psalm.

Caring for Poor

¹ Happy is one who cares
    for the poor;
the LORD will save him in a day
    of adversity.
² The LORD will keep him
    and preserve him;
he will be blessed in the land.
You will not give him over
    to the desire of his enemies.
³ The LORD will sustain him
    on his sickbed;
You will heal him on the bed
    where he lies.

Confession

⁴ I said, "LORD, be gracious to me;
heal me, for I have sinned
    against You."

Victory despite Betrayal

⁵ My enemies speak maliciously
    about me:
"When will he die and be forgotten?"
⁶ When one ⌊of them⌋ comes to visit,
    he speaks deceitfully;
he stores up evil in his heart;
he goes out and talks.
⁷ All who hate me whisper together
    about me;

they plan to harm me.
⁸ "Lethal poison has been poured
    into him,
and he won't rise again from where
    he lies!"
⁹ Even my friend^a in whom
    I trusted,
one who ate my bread,
has lifted up his heel against me.

¹⁰ But You, LORD, be gracious to me
    and raise me up;
then I will repay them.
¹¹ By this I know that You delight
    in me:
my enemy does not shout
    in triumph over me.
¹² You supported me because of
    my integrity
and set me
    in Your presence forever.
¹³ May the LORD, the God of Israel,
    be praised
from everlasting to everlasting.
•Amen and amen.

BOOK II

(PSALMS 42–72)
PSALM 42
Longing for God
For the choir director.
A •*Maskil* of the sons of Korah.

¹ As a deer longs for streams
    of water,
so I long for You, God.
² I thirst for God, the living God.
When can I come and appear
    before God?
³ My tears have been my food
    day and night,
while all day long people say to me,
    "Where is your God?"

^a**41:9** Lit *Even a man of my peace*

4 I remember this as I pour out
    my heart:
how I walked with many,
leading the festive procession
    to the house of God,
with joyful and thankful shouts.

Response to Depression

5 Why am I so depressed?
Why this turmoil within me?
Put your hope in God, for I will
    still praise Him,
my Savior and my God.
6 I[a] am deeply depressed;
therefore I remember You
    from the land of Jordan
and the peaks of Hermon,
    from Mount Mizar.
7 Deep calls to deep in the roar
    of Your waterfalls;
all Your breakers and Your billows
    have swept over me.
8 The LORD will send His faithful love
    by day;
His song will be with me
    in the night—
a prayer to the God of my life.

9 I will say to God, my rock,
"Why have You forgotten me?
Why must I go about in sorrow
because of
    the enemy's oppression?"
10 My adversaries taunt me,
    as if crushing my bones,
while all day long they say
    to me,
"Where is your God?"
11 Why am I so depressed?
Why this turmoil within me?
Put your hope in God, for I will
    still praise Him,
my Savior and my God.

PSALM 43[b]
Rescue Me

1 Vindicate me, God, and defend
    my cause
against an ungodly nation;
rescue me from the deceitful
    and unjust man.
2 For You are the God of my refuge.
Why have You rejected me?
Why must I go about in sorrow
because of the enemy's oppression?

3 Send Your light and Your truth;
    let them lead me.
Let them bring me
    to Your holy mountain,
to Your dwelling place.
4 Then I will come to the altar
    of God,
to God, my greatest joy.
I will praise You with the lyre,
God, my God.

5 Why am I so depressed?
Why this turmoil within me?
Put your hope in God, for I will
    still praise Him,
my Savior and my God.

PSALM 44
Israel's Complaint

For the choir director.
A •Maskil of the sons of Korah.

1 God, we have heard with our ears—
our forefathers have told us—
the work You accomplished
    in their days,
in days long ago:
2 to plant them,
You drove out the nations
    with Your hand;
to settle them,
You crushed the peoples.

---

[a] **42:5-6** Some Hb mss, LXX, Syr; other Hb mss read *Him, the salvation of His presence.* [b] *My God, I*   [b] **Ps 43** Many Hb mss connect Pss 42–43

3 For they did not take the land
    by their sword—
their arm did not
    bring them victory—
but by Your right hand, Your arm,
and the light of Your face,
for You were pleased with them.

4 You are my King, my God,
    who ordains[a] victories for Jacob.
5 Through You we drive back
    our foes;
through Your name we trample
    our enemies.
6 For I do not trust in my bow,
    and my sword does not
    bring me victory.
7 But You give us victory
    over our foes
and let those who hate us
    be disgraced.
8 We boast in God all day long;
we will praise Your name forever.
                                            •Selah

9 But You have rejected
    and humiliated us;
You do not march out
    with our armies.
10 You make us retreat from the foe,
and those who hate us
    have taken plunder for themselves.
11 You hand us over to be eaten
    like sheep
and scatter us among the nations.
12 You sell Your people for nothing;
You make no profit
    from selling them.
13 You make us an object of reproach
    to our neighbors,
a source of mockery and ridicule
    to those around us.
14 You make us a joke
    among the nations,

a laughingstock[b]
    among the peoples.
15 My disgrace is before me
    all day long,
and shame has covered my face,
16 because of the voice of the scorner
    and reviler,
because of the enemy and avenger.

17 All this has happened to us,
    but we have not forgotten You
    or betrayed Your covenant.
18 Our hearts have not turned back;
our steps have not strayed
    from Your path.
19 But You have crushed us in a haunt
    of jackals
and have covered us
    with deepest darkness.
20 If we had forgotten the name
    of our God
and spread out our hands
    to a foreign god,
21 wouldn't God have found this out,
since He knows the secrets
    of the heart?

            "Wake up, Lord!"

22 Because of You we are slain
    all day long;
we are counted as sheep
    to be slaughtered.

23 Wake up, LORD!
    Why are You sleeping?
Get up! Don't reject us forever!
24 Why do You hide Yourself
and forget our affliction
    and oppression?
25 For we have sunk down to the dust;
our bodies cling to the ground.
26 Rise up! Help us!
    Redeem us because of
        Your faithful love.

---

[a]**44:4** LXX, Syr, Aq; MT reads *King, God; ordain*   [b]**44:14** Lit *shaking of the head*

PSALM 45
A Royal Wedding Song

For the choir director:
according to "The Lilies."[a]
A •Maskil of the sons of Korah. A love song.

1 My heart is moved
by a noble theme
as I recite my verses to the king;
my tongue is the pen
of a skillful writer.
2 You are the most handsome
of •men;
grace flows from your lips.
Therefore God
has blessed you forever.

3 Mighty warrior, strap your sword
at your side.
In your majesty and splendor—
4 in your splendor ride triumphantly
in the cause of truth, humility,
and justice.
May your right hand show
your awe-inspiring deeds.
5 Your arrows pierce the hearts
of the king's enemies;
the peoples fall under you.

6 Your throne, God, is[b] forever
and ever;
the scepter of Your[c] kingdom is
a scepter of justice.
7 You love righteousness
and hate wickedness;
therefore God, your God,
has anointed you,
more than your companions,
with the oil of joy.
8 Myrrh, aloes, and cassia ⌊perfume⌋
all your garments;
from ivory palaces harps
bring you joy.
9 Kings' daughters are
among your honored women;
the queen, adorned with gold
from Ophir,
stands at your right hand.

10 Listen, daughter, pay attention
and consider:
forget your people
and your father's house,
11 and the king will desire your beauty.
Bow down to him,
for he is your lord.
12 The daughter of Tyre,
the wealthy people,
will seek your favor with gifts.
13 In ⌊her chamber⌋, the royal daughter
is all glorious,
her clothing embroidered with gold.
14 In colorful garments she is led
to the king;
after her, the virgins,
her companions, are brought
to you.
15 They are led in with gladness
and rejoicing;
they enter the king's palace.

16 Your sons will succeed
your ancestors;
you will make them princes
throughout the land.
17 I will cause your name
to be remembered
for all generations;
therefore the peoples
will praise you forever and ever.

PSALM 46
God Our Refuge

For the choir director. A song of the sons
of Korah. According to Alamoth.[d]

1 God is our refuge and strength,
a helper who is always found
in times of trouble.

---

[a]Apparently a hymn tune; compare Pss 60; 69; 80   [b]45:6 Or Your divine throne is, or Your throne is God's   [c]45:6 Or your   [d]This notation may refer to a high pitch, perhaps a tune sung by soprano voices; the Hb word means "young women."

2 Therefore we will not be afraid,
   though the earth trembles
   and the mountains topple
   into the depths of the seas,
3 though its waters roar and foam
   and the mountains quake
      with its turmoil.   •Selah

4 ⌊There is⌋ a river—
   its streams delight the city of God,
   the holy dwelling place
      of the •Most High.
5 God is within her;
      she will not be toppled.
   God will help her
      when the morning dawns.
6 Nations rage, kingdoms topple;
   the earth melts when He lifts
      His voice.
7 The LORD of •Hosts is with us;
   the God of Jacob is our stronghold.
                              Selah

8 Come, see the works of the LORD,
   who brings devastation
      on the earth.
9 He makes wars cease
      throughout the earth.
   He shatters bows and cuts spears
      to pieces;
   He burns up the chariots.[a]
10 "Stop ⌊your fighting⌋—and know
      that I am God,
   exalted among the nations,
   exalted on the earth."
11 The LORD of Hosts is with us;
   the God of Jacob is our stronghold.
                              Selah

PSALM 47
God Our King

For the choir director. A psalm of the sons
of Korah.

1 Clap your hands, all you peoples;
   shout to God with a jubilant cry.

2 For the LORD •Most High is awe-
      inspiring,
   a great King over all the earth.
3 He subdues peoples under us
   and nations under our feet.
4 He chooses for us
      our inheritance—
   the pride of Jacob, whom He loves.
                              •Selah

5 God ascends amid shouts of joy,
   the LORD, amid the sound
      of trumpets.
6 Sing praise to God, sing praise;
   sing praise to our King, sing praise!
7 Sing a song of instruction,[b]
   for God is King of all the earth.

8 God reigns over the nations;
   God is seated on His holy throne.
9 The nobles of the peoples
      have assembled
   ⌊with⌋ the people of the God
      of Abraham.
   For the leaders[c] of the earth
      belong to God;
   He is greatly exalted.

PSALM 48
Zion Exalted

A song. A psalm of the sons of Korah.

1 The LORD is great and is
      highly praised
   in the city of our God.
   His holy mountain,
    2 rising splendidly,
   is the joy of the whole earth.
   Mount Zion on the slopes
      of the north
   is the city of the great King.
3 God is known as a stronghold
   in its citadels.

4 Look! The kings assembled;
   they advanced together.

[a]46:9 Lit chariots with fire   [b]47:7 Hb a Maskil   [c]47:9 Lit shields

5 They looked, and froze with fear;
   they fled in terror.
6 Trembling seized them there,
   agony like that of a woman in labor,
7 as You wrecked the ships
      of Tarshish
   with the east wind.

8 Just as we heard, so we have seen
   in the city of the LORD of •Hosts,
   in the city of our God;
   God will establish it forever.   •Selah

9 God, within Your temple,
   we contemplate Your faithful love.
10 Your name, God, like Your praise,
   reaches to the ends of the earth;
   Your right hand is filled
      with justice.
11 Mount Zion is glad.
   The towns[a] of Judah rejoice
   because of Your judgments.

12 Go around Zion, encircle it;
   count its towers,
13 note its ramparts; tour its citadels
   so that you can tell
      a future generation:
14 "This God, our God
   forever and ever—
   He will lead us eternally."[b]

PSALM 49
Misplaced Trust in Wealth
For the choir director.
A psalm of the sons of Korah.

1 Hear this, all you peoples;
   listen, all who inhabit the world,
2 both low and high,[c]
   rich and poor together.
3 My mouth speaks wisdom;
   my heart's meditation
   ⌊brings⌋ understanding.

4 I turn my ear to a proverb;
   I explain my riddle with a lyre.
5 Why should I fear in times
      of trouble?
   The iniquity of my foes
      surrounds me.
6 They trust in their wealth
   and boast of their abundant riches.
7 Yet these cannot redeem a person[d]
   or pay his ransom to God—
8 since the price of redeeming him is
      too costly,
   one should forever stop trying[e]—
9 so that he may live forever
   and not see the •Pit.

10 For one can see that wise men die;
   the foolish and the senseless also
      pass away.
   Then they leave their wealth
      to others.
11 Their graves are
      their eternal homes,[f]
   their homes from generation
      to generation,
   though they have named estates
      after themselves.
12 But despite ⌊his⌋ assets,[g]
   man will not last;
   he is like the animals that perish.

13 This is the way of those
      who are arrogant,
   and of their followers,
   who approve of their words.[h]
                                    •Selah
14 Like sheep they are headed
      for •Sheol;
   Death will shepherd them.
   The upright will rule over them
      in the morning,
   and their form will waste away
      in Sheol,

---

[a]48:11 Lit *daughters*   [b]48:14 Some Hb mss, LXX; other Hb mss read *over death*   [c]49:2 Lit *both sons of Adam and sons of man*   [d]49:7 Or *Certainly he cannot redeem himself,* or *Yet he cannot redeem a brother*   [e]49:8 Or *costly, it will cease forever*   [f]49:11 LXX, Syr, Tg; MT reads *Their inner thought is that their houses are eternal*   [g]49:12 Or *honor*   [h]49:13 Lit *and after them with their mouth they were pleased*

far from their lofty abode.

15 But God will redeem my life
   from the power of Sheol,
   for He will take me.   *Selah*

16 Do not be afraid when a man
      gets rich,
   when the wealth[a]
      of his house increases.
17 For when he dies, he will take
      nothing at all;
   his wealth[a] will not follow
      him down.
18 Though he praises himself
      during his lifetime—
   and people praise you
      when you do well for yourself—
19 he will go to the generation
      of his fathers;
   they will never see the light.
20 A man with valuable possessions[b]
   but without understanding
   is like the animals that perish.

PSALM 50
God as Judge
A psalm of •Asaph.

1 God, the LORD God[c] speaks;
   He summons the earth from east
      to west.[d]
2 From Zion, the perfection of beauty,
   God appears in radiance.[e]
3 Our God is coming; He will not
      be silent!
   Devouring fire precedes Him,
   and a storm rages around Him.
4 On high, He summons heaven
      and earth
   in order to judge His people.
5 "Gather My faithful ones to Me,
   those who made a covenant
      with Me by sacrifice."

6 The heavens proclaim
      His righteousness,
   for God is the judge.   •*Selah*

7 "Listen, My people,
      and I will speak;
   I will testify against you, Israel.
   I am God, your God.
8 I do not rebuke you
      for your sacrifices
   or for your •burnt offerings,
   which are continually before Me.
9 I will not accept a bull
      from your household
   or male goats from your pens,
10 for every animal of the forest
      is Mine,
   the cattle on a thousand hills.
11 I know every bird
      of the mountains,[f]
   and the creatures of the field
   are Mine.
12 If I were hungry, I would not
      tell you,
   for the world and everything in it
      is Mine.
13 Do I eat the flesh of bulls
   or drink the blood of goats?
14 Sacrifice a thank offering to God,
   and pay your vows
      to the •Most High.
15 Call on Me in a day of trouble;
   I will rescue you,
      and you will honor Me."

God's Words to Wicked

16 But God says to the wicked:
   "What right do you have to recite
      My statutes
   and to take My covenant
      on your lips?
17 You hate instruction
   and turn your back on My words.[g]

---

[a]49:16,17 Or glory   [b]49:20 Or with honor   [c]50:1 Or The Mighty One, God, the LORD, or The God of gods, the LORD
[d]50:1 Lit from the rising of the sun to its setting   [e]50:2 Or God shines forth   [f]50:11 LXX, Syr, Tg read heavens
[g]50:17 Or and cast My words behind you

18 When you see a thief,
you make friends with him,
and you associate with adulterers.
19 You unleash your mouth for evil
and harness your tongue for deceit.
20 You sit, maligning your brother,
slandering your mother's son.
21 You have done these things,
and I kept silent;
you thought I was just like you.
But I will rebuke you
and lay out the case before you.ª

Salvation for Wicked

22 "Understand this,
you who forget God,
or I will tear you apart,
and there will be no rescuer.
23 Whoever sacrifices a thank offering
honors Me,
and whoever orders his conduct,
I will show him the salvation of God."

PSALM 51
Prayer for Restoration

For the choir director.
A Davidic psalm, when Nathan the prophet
came to him after he had gone to Bathsheba.

1 Be gracious to me, God,
according to Your faithful love;
according to Your abundant
compassion,
blot out my rebellion.
2 Wash away my guilt,
and cleanse me from my sin.
3 For I am conscious of my rebellion,
and my sin is always before me.
4 Against You—You alone—
I have sinned
and done this evil in Your sight.
So You are right
when You pass sentence;
You are blameless when You judge.

Sinful from Birth

5 Indeed, I was guilty
⌊when I⌋ was born;
I was sinful when my mother
conceived me.
6 Surely You desire integrity
in the inner self,
and You teach me wisdom
deep within.
7 Purify me with hyssop,
and I will be clean;
wash me, and I will be
whiter than snow.
8 Let me hear joy and gladness;
let the bones You have crushed
rejoice.
9 Turn Your face awayᵇ from my sins
and blot out all my guilt.

Plea for Clean Heart

10 God, create a clean heart for me
and renew a steadfastᶜ spirit
within me.
11 Do not banish me
from Your presence
or take Your Holy Spirit from me.
12 Restore the joy of Your salvation
to me,
and give me a willing spirit.ᵈ
13 Then I will teach the rebellious
Your ways,
and sinners will return to You.
14 Save me from the guilt
of bloodshed, God,
the God of my salvation,
and my tongue will sing
of Your righteousness.
15 Lord, open my lips,
and my mouth will declare
Your praise.
16 You do not want a sacrifice,
or I would give it;

ª**50:21** Lit *out before your eyes*   ᵇ**51:9** Lit *Hide Your face*   ᶜ**51:10** Or *right*   ᵈ**51:12** Or *and sustain me with a noble spirit*

You are not pleased
with a •burnt offering.
17 The sacrifice pleasing to God is[a]
a broken spirit.
God, You will not despise a broken
and humbled heart.

18 In Your good pleasure, cause Zion
to prosper;
build[b] the walls of Jerusalem.
19 Then You will delight
in righteous sacrifices,
whole burnt offerings;
then bulls will be offered
on Your altar.

PSALM 52
God Judges Proud

For the choir director. A Davidic •Maskil. When
Doeg the Edomite went and reported to Saul,
telling him, "David went to Ahimelech's house."

1 Why brag about evil, you hero!
God's faithful love is constant.
2 Like a sharpened razor,
your tongue devises destruction,
working treachery.
3 You love evil instead of good,
lying instead of speaking truthfully.
•Selah
4 You love any words that destroy,
you treacherous tongue!

5 This is why God will bring
you down forever.
He will take you, ripping you out of
your tent;
He will uproot you from the land
of the living.   Selah
6 The righteous will look on with awe
and will ridicule him:
7 "Here is the man
who would not make God his refuge,
but trusted in the abundance
of his riches,

taking refuge
in his destructive behavior."[c]

8 But I am like a flourishing olive tree
in the house of God;
I trust in God's faithful love
forever and ever.
9 I will praise You forever for what
You have done.
In the presence
of Your faithful people,
I will put my hope in Your name,
for it is good.

PSALM 53
A Portrait of Sinners

For the choir director: on Mahalath.[d]
A Davidic •Maskil.

Atheist as Fool

1 The fool says in his heart,
"God does not exist."
They are corrupt, and they do
vile deeds.
There is no one who does good.
2 God looks down from heaven
on the •human race
to see if there is one who is wise
and who seeks God.

All Sin

3 Everyone has turned aside;
they have all become corrupt.
There is no one who does good,
not even one.

4 Will evildoers never understand?
They consume My people
as they consume bread;
they do not call on God.
5 Then they will be filled
with terror—
terror like no other—
because God will scatter

---

[a]**51:17** Lit *The sacrifices of God are*   [b]**51:18** Or *rebuild*   [c]**52:7** Or *riches, and grew strong in his evil desire*; lit *his destruction*   [d]Perhaps a song tune, a musical instrument, or a dance; may be related to Hb for "sickness"

the bones of those
  who besiege you.
You will put them to shame,
  for God has rejected them.

6 Oh, that Israel's deliverance
    would come from Zion!
  When God restores
    His captive people,
  Jacob will rejoice;
    Israel will be glad.

PSALM 54
Prayer for Deliverance

For the choir director:
with stringed instruments.
A Davidic •Maskil. When the Ziphites went and
said to Saul, "Is David not hiding among us?"

1 God, save me by Your name,
    and vindicate me by Your might!
2 God, hear my prayer;
    listen to the words of my mouth.
3 For strangers rise up against me,
    and violent men seek my life.
  They have no regard for God.[a]
                                    •Selah

4 God is my helper;
    the Lord is the sustainer
    of my life.[b]
5 He will repay my adversaries
    for ⌊their⌋ evil.
  Because of Your faithfulness,
    annihilate them.

6 I will sacrifice a freewill offering
    to You.
  I will praise Your name, LORD,
    because it is good.
7 For He has delivered me
    from every trouble,
  and my eye has looked down on
    my enemies.

PSALM 55
Betrayal by a Friend

For the choir director:
with stringed instruments. A Davidic •Maskil.

Answer Me!

1 God, listen to my prayer
    and do not ignore[c] my plea for help.
2 Pay attention to me and answer me.
  I am restless and in turmoil
    with my complaint,
3 because of the enemy's voice,
  because of the pressure[d]
    of the wicked.
  For they bring down disaster on me[e]
  and harass me in anger.

4 My heart shudders within me;
    terrors of death sweep over me.
5 Fear and trembling grip me;
    horror has overwhelmed me.

Wings of a Dove

6 I said, "If only I had[f] wings
    like a dove!
  I would fly away and find rest.
7 How far away I would flee;
    I would stay in the wilderness.
                                    •Selah
8 I would hurry to my shelter
    from the raging wind
    and the storm."

9 Lord, confuse[g] and confound
    their speech,[h]
  for I see violence and strife
    in the city;
10 day and night they make the rounds
    on its walls.
  Crime and trouble are within it;
11 destruction is inside it;
  oppression and deceit never leave
    its marketplace.

---

[a]54:3 Lit They do not set God before them   [b]54:4 Or is with those who sustain my life   [c]55:1 Lit hide Yourself from
[d]55:3 Or threat, or oppression   [e]55:3 LXX, Syr, Sym; MT reads they cause me to totter   [f]55:6 Lit "Who will give to
me . . . dove? (as a question)   [g]55:9 Or destroy   [h]55:9 Lit and divide their tongue

Betrayed by a Friend

12 Now, it is not an enemy
     who insults me—
otherwise I could bear it;
it is not a foe who rises up
     against me—
otherwise I could hide from him.
13 But it is you, a man who is my peer,
     my companion and good friend!
14 We used to have close fellowship;
     we walked with the crowd
          into the house of God.

15 Let death take them by surprise;
     let them go down to •Sheol alive,
because evil is in their homes
     and within them.
16 But I call to God,
     and the LORD will save me.
17 I complain and groan morning,
     noon, and night,
and He hears my voice.
18 Though many are against me,
     He will redeem me
          from my battle unharmed.
19 God, the One enthroned
     from long ago,
will hear, and will humiliate them
                                   Selah
because they do not change
and do not •fear God.

20 He^a acts violently
against those at peace with him;
he violates his covenant.
21 His buttery words are smooth,^b
but war is in his heart.
His words are softer than oil,
but they are drawn swords.

22 Cast your burden on the LORD,
and He will support you;
He will never allow the righteous
to be shaken.

23 You, God, will bring them down
     to the pit of destruction;
men of bloodshed and treachery
will not live out half their days.
But I will trust in You.

PSALM 56
Call for God's Protection

For the choir director: according to
"A Silent Dove Far Away."^c A Davidic •*Miktam*.
When the Philistines seized him in Gath.

1 Be gracious to me, God,
     for man tramples me;
he fights and oppresses me all day
     long.
2 My adversaries trample me all day,
for many arrogantly fight
     against me.^d

3 When I am afraid,
I will trust in You.
4 In God, whose word I praise,
in God I trust; I will not fear.
What can man do to me?

5 They twist my words all day long;
all their thoughts are against me
     for evil.
6 They stir up strife,^e they lurk;
they watch my steps
while they wait to take my life.
7 Will they escape in spite of
     such sin?
God, bring down the nations
     in wrath.

8 You Yourself have recorded
     my wanderings.^f
Put my tears in Your bottle.
Are they not in Your records?
9 Then my enemies will retreat
     on the day when I call.
This I know: God is for me.

---

^a**55:20** The evil man   ^b**55:21** Other Hb mss, Sym, Syr, Tg, Jer read *His speech is smoother than butter*   ^cPossibly a song tune   ^d**56:2** Or *many fight against me, O exalted One*, or *many fight against me from the heights*   ^e**56:6** Or *They attack*   ^f**56:8** Or *misery*

10 In God, whose word I praise,
　　in the LORD, whose word I praise,
11 in God I trust; I will not fear.
　　What can man do to me?

12 I am obligated by vows[a]
　　to You, God;
　　I will make my thank offerings
　　to You.
13 For You delivered me from death,
　　even my feet from stumbling,
　　to walk before God in the light
　　of life.

PSALM 57
Praise for God's Protection

For the choir director: "Do Not Destroy." [b]
A Davidic •Miktam. When he fled before Saul
into the cave.

1 Be gracious to me, God, be gracious
　　to me,
　　for I take refuge in You.
　　I will seek refuge in the shadow
　　of Your wings
　　until danger passes.
2 I call to God •Most High,
　　to God who fulfills ⌊His purpose⌋
　　for me.[c]
3 He reaches down from heaven
　　and saves me,
　　challenging the one
　　who tramples me. •Selah
　　God sends His faithful love
　　and truth.
4 I am in the midst of lions;
　　I lie down with those
　　who devour •men.
　　Their teeth are spears and arrows;
　　their tongues are sharp swords.
5 God, be exalted above the heavens;
　　let Your glory be above
　　the whole earth.
6 They prepared a net for my steps;
　　I was downcast.

They dug a pit ahead of me,
　　but they fell into it! *Selah*
7 My heart is confident, God,
　　my heart is confident.
　　I will sing; I will sing praises.
8 Wake up, my soul![d]
　　Wake up, harp and lyre!
　　I will wake up the dawn.
9 I will praise You, Lord,
　　among the peoples;
　　I will sing praises to You
　　among the nations.
10 For Your faithful love is as high as
　　the heavens;
　　Your faithfulness reaches
　　to the clouds.
11 God, be exalted above the heavens;
　　let Your glory be
　　over the whole earth.

PSALM 58
Cry against Injustice

For the choir director: "Do Not Destroy."[b]
A Davidic •Miktam.

1 Do you really speak righteously,
　　you mighty ones?[e]
　　Do you judge •people fairly?
2 No, you practice injustice
　　in your hearts;
　　with your hands
　　you weigh out violence
　　in the land.

3 The wicked go astray
　　from the womb;
　　liars err from birth.
4 They have venom like the venom
　　of a snake,
　　like the deaf cobra that stops up
　　its ears,
5 that does not listen to the sound
　　of the charmers
　　who skillfully weave spells.

---

⁶ God, knock the teeth
    out of their mouths;
LORD, tear out
    the young lions' fangs.
⁷ They will vanish like water
    that flows by;
they will aim
    their useless arrows.ᵃ ᵇ
⁸ Like a slug that moves along
    in slime,
like a woman's miscarried ⌊child⌋,
    they will not see the sun.
⁹ Before your pots can feel the heat
    of the thorns—
whether green or burning—
He will sweep them away.ᶜ
¹⁰ The righteous will rejoice
    when he sees the retribution;
he will wash his feet in the blood
    of the wicked.
¹¹ Then people will say,
    "Yes, there is a reward
    for the righteous!
There is a God who judges
    on earth!"

PSALM 59
God Our Stronghold

For the choir director: "Do Not Destroy."ᵈ
A Davidic •*Miktam*. When Saul sent ⌊agents⌋ to
watch the house and kill him.

¹ Deliver me from my enemies,
    my God;
protect me from those who rise up
    against me.
² Deliver me from those
    who practice sin,
and save me from men
    of bloodshed.
³ LORD, look! They set an ambush
    for me.

Powerful men attack me,
    but not because of any sin
    or rebellion of mine.
⁴ For no fault of mine,
    they run and take up a position.
Awake to help me, and take notice.
⁵ You, LORD God of •Hosts,
    God of Israel,
rise up to punish all the nations;
do not show grace
    to any wicked traitors.   •*Selah*

⁶ They return at evening,
    snarling like dogs
and prowling around the city.
⁷ Look, they spew
    from their mouths—
sharp words fromᵉ their lips.
"For who," ⌊they say,⌋ "will hear?"
⁸ But You laugh at them, LORD;
    You ridicule all the nations.
⁹ I will keep watch for You,
    myᶠ strength,
because God is my stronghold.
¹⁰ My faithful Godᵍ will come
    to meet me;
God will let me look down on
    my adversaries.

¹¹ Do not kill them; otherwise,
    my people will forget.
By Your power, make them
    homeless wanderers
and bring them down,
    Lord, our shield.
¹² The sin of their mouths is the word
    of their lips,
so let them be caught
    in their pride.
They utter curses and lies.
¹³ Consume ⌊them⌋ in rage;
    consume ⌊them⌋ until
    they are gone.

ᵃ**58:7** Or *their arrows as if they were circumcised*; Hb obscure   ᵇ**58:7** Or *they wither like trampled grass*   ᶜ**58:9** Or
thorns, He will sweep it away, whether raw or cooking, or *thorns, He will sweep him away alive in fury*   ᵈPossibly a
song tune   ᵉ**59:7** Lit *swords are on*   ᶠ**59:9** Some Hb mss, LXX, Vg, Tg; other Hb mss read *his*   ᵍ**59:10** Alt Hb
traditions read *God in His faithful love*, or *My God, His faithful love*

Then they will know to the ends
  of the earth
that God rules over Jacob.   *Selah*

14 And they return at evening,
  snarling like dogs
and prowling around the city.
15 They scavenge for food;
  they growl if they are not satisfied.

16 But I will sing of Your strength
  and will joyfully proclaim
  Your faithful love in the morning.
For You have been a stronghold
  for me,
a refuge in my day of trouble.
17 To You, my strength, I sing praises,
because God is my stronghold—
  my faithful God.

PSALM 60
Prayer in Difficult Times

For the choir director: according to
"The Lily of Testimony."[a]
A Davidic •*Miktam* for teaching.
When he fought with Aram-naharaim and
Aram-zobah, and Joab returned and struck
Edom in the Valley of Salt, [killing] 12,000.

1 God, You have rejected us;
  You have broken out[b] against us;
  You have been angry. Restore us![c]
2 You have shaken the land
  and split it open.
Heal its fissures, for it shudders.
3 You have made Your people
  suffer hardship;
You have given us a wine to drink
  that made us stagger.
4 You have given a signal flag to those
  who •fear You,
so that they can flee
  before the archers.[d]   •*Selah*
5 Save with Your right hand,
  and answer me,

so that those You love
  may be rescued.

6 God has spoken in His sanctuary:[e]
  "I will triumph!
  I will divide up Shechem.
I will apportion the Valley
  of Succoth.
7 Gilead is Mine, Manasseh is Mine,
  and Ephraim is My helmet;
  Judah is My scepter.
8 Moab is My washbasin;
on Edom I throw My sandal.
Over Philistia I shout in triumph."

9 Who will bring me
  to the fortified city?
Who will lead me to Edom?
10 Is it not You, God, who have
  rejected us?
God, You do not march out
  with our armies.
11 Give us aid against the foe,
for human help is worthless.
12 With God
  we will perform valiantly;
He will trample our foes.

PSALM 61
Security in God

For the choir director: on stringed instruments.
Davidic.

1 God, hear my cry;
  pay attention to my prayer.
2 I call to You from the ends
  of the earth
when my heart is without strength.
Lead me to a rock that is
  high above me,
3 for You have been a refuge for me,
a strong tower in the face
  of the enemy.
4 I will live in Your tent forever

---

a Possibly a song tune b **60:1** Lit *have burst through* c **60:1** Or *Turn back to us* d **60:4** Or *can rally before the archers,*
or *can rally because of the truth* e **60:6** Or *has promised by His holy nature*

and take refuge under the shelter
  of Your wings.   •*Selah*

5 God, You have heard my vows;
You have given a heritage
  to those who fear Your name.
6 Add days to the king's life;
may his years span
  many generations.
7 May he sit enthroned
  before God forever;
appoint faithful love and truth
  to guard him.
8 Then I will continually sing
  of Your name,
fulfilling my vows day by day.

PSALM 62
Trust in God Alone

For the choir director: according to Jeduthun.
A Davidic psalm.

1 I am at rest in God alone;
my salvation comes from Him.
2 He alone is my rock
  and my salvation,
my stronghold;
  I will never be shaken.

3 How long will you
  threaten a man?
Will all of you attack[a]
as if he were a leaning wall
or a tottering stone fence?
4 They only plan to bring him down
from his high position.
They take pleasure in lying;
they bless with their mouths,
but they curse inwardly. •*Selah*

5 Rest in God alone, my soul,
for my hope comes from Him.
6 He alone is my rock
  and my salvation,
my stronghold; I will not
  be shaken.

7 My salvation and glory
  depend on God;
my strong rock, my refuge,
  is in God.
8 Trust in Him at all times,
  you people;
pour out your hearts before Him.
God is our refuge.   *Selah*

9 •Men are only a vapor;
exalted men, an illusion.
On a balance scale, they go up;
together they ⌊weigh⌋ less than
  a vapor.
10 Place no trust in oppression,
or false hope in robbery.
If wealth increases,
pay no attention to it.[b]

11 God has spoken once;
I have heard this twice:
strength belongs to God,
12 and faithful love belongs
  to You, LORD.
For You repay each according to
  his works.

PSALM 63
Praise God Who Satisfies

A Davidic psalm. When he was
in the Wilderness of Judah.

1 God, You are my God;
  I eagerly seek You.
I thirst for You;
my body faints for You
in a land that is dry, desolate,
  and without water.
2 So I gaze on You in the sanctuary
to see Your strength and Your glory.

3 My lips will glorify You
because Your faithful love is better
  than life.
4 So I will praise You as long as
  I live;

[a]**62:3** Other Hb mss read *you be struck down* [b]**62:10** Lit *increases, do not set heart*

at Your name, I will lift up
my hands.
5 You satisfy me as with rich food;[a]
my mouth will praise You
with joyful lips.

Meditate on God at Night

6 When, on my bed, I think of You,
I meditate on You
during the night watches
7 because You are my help;
I will rejoice in the shadow
of Your wings.
8 I follow close to You;
Your right hand holds on to me.

9 But those who seek to destroy
my life
will go into the depths of the earth.
10 They will be given over
to the power of the sword;
they will become the jackals' prey.
11 But the king will rejoice in God;
all who swear by Him[b] will boast,
for the mouths of liars will be shut.

PSALM 64
Protection from Evildoers
For the choir director. A Davidic psalm.

1 God, hear my voice
when I complain.
Protect my life from the terror
of the enemy.
2 Hide me from the scheming
of the wicked,
from the mob of evildoers,
3 who sharpen their tongues
like swords
and aim bitter words like arrows,
4 shooting from concealed places
at the innocent.

They shoot at him suddenly
and are not afraid.
5 They encourage each other
in an evil plan;[c] [d]
they talk about hiding traps and say,
"Who will see them?"[e]
6 They devise crimes [and say,]
"We have perfected a secret plan."
The inner man and the heart
are mysterious.

7 But God will shoot them
with arrows;
suddenly, they will be wounded.
8 They will be made to stumble;
their own tongues work
against them.
All who see them will shake
their heads.
9 Then everyone will fear
and will tell about God's work,
for they will understand
what He has done.

10 The righteous rejoice in the LORD
and take refuge in Him;
all the upright in heart offer praise.

PSALM 65
God's Care for the Earth
For the choir director. A Davidic psalm. A song.

1 Praise is rightfully Yours,[f]
God, in Zion;[g]
vows to You will be fulfilled.
2 All humanity will come to You,
the One who hears prayer.
3 Iniquities overwhelm me;
only You can •atone for[h]
our rebellions.
4 How happy is the one You choose
and bring near to live
in Your courts!

We will be satisfied
  with the goodness of Your house,
  the holiness of Your temple.ᵃ

5 You answer us in righteousness,
  with awe-inspiring works,
  God of our salvation,
  the hope of all the ends
    of the earth
  and of the distant seas;
6 You establish the mountains
    by Yourᵇ power,
  robed with strength;
7 You silence the roar of the seas,
  the roar of their waves,
  and the tumult of the nations.
8 Those who live far away are awed
    by Your signs;
  You make east and west
    shout for joy.

9 You visit the earth
    and water it abundantly,
  enriching it greatly.
  God's stream is filled
    with water,
  for You prepare the earthᶜ
    in this way,
  providing ⌊people⌋ with grain.
10 You soften it with showers
    and bless its growth,
  soaking its furrows and leveling
    its ridges.
11 You crown the year
    with Your goodness;
  Your ways overflow with plenty.ᵈ
12 The wilderness pastures overflow,
  and the hills are robed with joy.
13 The pastures are clothed
    with flocks,
  and the valleys covered
    with grain.
  They shout in triumph; indeed,
    they sing.

PSALM 66
Praise for God's Mighty Acts
For the choir director. A song. A psalm.

1 Shout joyfully to God, all the earth!
2 Sing the glory of His name;
  make His praise glorious.
3 Say to God, "How awe-inspiring
    are Your works!
  Your enemies will cringe
    before You
  because of Your great strength.
4 All the earth will worship You
  and sing praise to You.
  They will sing praise
    to Your name."   •Selah

5 Come and see the works of God;
  His acts toward •mankind are awe-
    inspiring.
6 He turned the sea into dry land,
  and they crossed the river on foot.
  There we rejoiced in Him.
7 He rules forever by His might;
  He keeps His eye on the nations.
  The rebellious should not
    exalt themselves.   Selah
8 Praise our God, you peoples;
  let the sound of His praise
    be heard.
9 He keeps us aliveᵉ
  and does not allow our feet to slip.
10 For You, God, tested us;
  You refined us as silver is refined.
11 You lured us into a trap;
  You placed burdens on our backs.
12 You let men ride over our heads;
  we went through fire and water,
  but You brought us out
    to abundance.ᶠ

13 I will enter Your house
    with •burnt offerings;
  I will pay You my vows

ᵃ65:4 Or house, Your holy temple ᵇ65:6 Some LXX mss, Vg; MT reads His ᶜ65:9 Lit prepare it ᵈ65:11 Lit ways
drip with fat ᵉ66:9 Lit He sets our soul in life ᶠ66:12 Or a place of satisfaction

14 that my lips promised
and my mouth spoke
    during my distress.
15 I will offer You fattened sheep
    as burnt offerings,
with the fragrant smoke of rams;
I will sacrifice oxen with goats.
                                    Selah

16 Come and listen, all who •fear God,
and I will tell what He has done
    for me.
17 I cried out to Him with my mouth,
and praise was on my tongue.
18 If I had been aware of malice
    in my heart,
the Lord would not have listened.

"God Has Listened"

19 However, God has listened;
He has paid attention to the sound
    of my prayer.
20 May God be praised!
He has not turned away my prayer
or turned His faithful love from me.

PSALM 67
Let All Praise God

For the choir director:
with stringed instruments. A psalm. A song.

1 May God be gracious to us
    and bless us;
look on us with favor   •*Selah*
2 so that Your way may be known
    on earth,
Your salvation among all nations.

3 Let the peoples praise You, God;
let all the peoples praise You.
4 Let the nations rejoice and shout
    for joy,
for You judge the peoples
    with fairness
and lead the nations on earth. *Selah*

5 Let the peoples praise You, God,
let all the peoples praise You.

6 The earth has produced its harvest;
God, our God, blesses us.
7 God will bless us,
and all the ends of the earth
    will •fear Him.

PSALM 68
God's Majestic Power

For the choir director. A Davidic psalm. A song.

1 God arises. His enemies scatter,
and those who hate Him flee
    from His presence.
2 As smoke is blown away,
so You blow ⌊them⌋ away.
As wax melts before the fire,
so the wicked are destroyed
    before God.
3 But the righteous are glad;
they rejoice before God
    and celebrate with joy.

4 Sing to God! Sing praises
    to His name.
Exalt Him who rides
    on the clouds ᵃ—
His name is •Yahwehᵇ—and rejoice
    before Him.
5 A father of the fatherless
and a champion of widows
is God in His holy dwelling.
6 God provides homes for those
    who are deserted.
He leads out the prisoners
    to prosperity,ᶜ
but the rebellious live
    in a scorched land.

7 God, when You went out
    before Your people,
when You marched
    through the desert,   •*Selah*

ᵃ**68:4** Or *rides through the desert*   ᵇ**68:4** Lit *Yah*   ᶜ**68:6** Or *prisoners with joyous music*; Hb uncertain

⁸ the earth trembled, and the skies
    poured down ⌊rain⌋
before God, the God of Sinai,ᵃ
before God, the God of Israel.
⁹ You, God, showered abundant rain;
You revived Your inheritance
    when it languished.
¹⁰ Your people settled in it;
by Your goodness You provided
    for the poor, God.

¹¹ The Lord gave the command;
a great company of women brought
    the good news:
¹² "The kings of the armies flee—
    they flee!"
She who stays at home divides
    the spoil.
¹³ Whileᵇ you lie
    among the sheepfolds,ᶜ
the wings of a dove are covered
    with silver,
and its feathers
    with glistening gold.
¹⁴ When the •Almighty scattered kings
    in the land,
it snowed on Zalmon.ᵈ

¹⁵ Mount Bashan is
    God's towering mountain;
Mount Bashan is a mountain
    of many peaks.
¹⁶ Why gaze with envy,
    you mountain peaks,
at the mountainᵉ God desired
    for His dwelling?
The LORD will live ⌊there⌋ forever!
¹⁷ God's chariots are tens
    of thousands,
thousands and thousands;
the Lord is among them
    in the sanctuaryᶠ
as He was at Sinai.

¹⁸ You ascended to the heights,
    taking away captives;
You received gifts fromᵍ people,
    even from the rebellious,
so that the LORD God
    might live ⌊there⌋.ʰ

¹⁹ May the Lord be praised!
Day after day He bears our burdens;
God is our salvation.   *Selah*
²⁰ Our God is a God of salvation,
and escape from death belongs
    to the Lord GOD.
²¹ Surely God crushes the heads
    of His enemies,
the hairy head of one who goes on
    in his guilty acts.
²² The Lord said,
    "I will bring ⌊them⌋ back
    from Bashan;
I will bring ⌊them⌋ back
    from the depths of the sea
²³ so that your foot may wadeⁱ
    in blood
and your dogs' tongues may have
    their share
from the enemies."
²⁴ People have seen
    Your procession, God,
the procession of my God,
    my King, in the sanctuary.ʲ
²⁵ Singersᵏ lead the way,
with musicians following;
among them are young women
    playing tambourines.
²⁶ Praise God in the assemblies;
⌊praise⌋ the LORD from the fountain
    of Israel.
²⁷ There is Benjamin, the youngest,
    leading them,
the rulers of Judah
    in their assembly,ˡ

ᵃ**68:8** Lit *God, this Sinai*   ᵇ**68:13** Or *If*   ᶜ**68:13** Or *campfires, or saddlebags*; Hb obscure   ᵈ**68:14** Or *Black Mountain*   ᵉ**68:16** Mount Zion   ᶠ**68:17** Or *in holiness*   ᵍ**68:18** Lit *among*   ʰ**68:18** Or *even those rebelling against the LORD God's living there*, or *even rebels are living with the LORD God*; Hb obscure   ⁱ**68:23** LXX, Syr read *dip*   ʲ**68:24** Or *in holiness*   ᵏ**68:25** Some Hb mss, LXX, Syr read *Officials*   ˡ**68:27** Hb obscure

the rulers of Zebulun, the rulers
of Naphtali.

28 Your God has decreed
your strength.
Show Your strength, God,
You who have acted on our behalf.
29 Because of Your temple
at Jerusalem,
kings will bring tribute to You.
30 Rebuke the beast[a] in the reeds,
the herd of bulls with the calves
of the peoples.
Trample underfoot those with bars
of silver.[b]
Scatter the peoples
who take pleasure in war.
31 Ambassadors will come[c]
from Egypt;
•Cush[d] will stretch out its hands[e]
to God.
32 Sing to God, you kingdoms
of the earth;
sing praise to the Lord,   Selah
33 to Him who rides in the ancient,
highest heavens.
Look, He thunders
with His powerful voice!
34 Ascribe power to God.
His majesty is over Israel,
His power among the clouds.
35 God, You are awe-inspiring
in Your sanctuaries.
The God of Israel gives power
and strength to His people.
May God be praised!

PSALM 69
Plea for Rescue

For the choir director: according to
"The Lilies."[f] Davidic.

1 Save me, God,
for the water has risen to my neck.

2 I have sunk in deep mud,
and there is no footing;
I have come into deep waters,
and a flood sweeps over me.
3 I am weary from my crying;
my throat is parched.
My eyes fail, looking for my God.
4 Those who hate me without cause
are more numerous than the hairs
of my head;
my deceitful enemies, who would
destroy me,
are powerful.
Though I did not steal,
I must repay.
5 God, You know my foolishness,
and my guilty acts are not hidden
from You.
6 Do not let those who put their hope
in You
be disgraced because of me,
Lord God of •Hosts;
do not let those who seek You
be humiliated because of me,
God of Israel.
7 For I have endured insults
because of You,
and shame has covered my face.
8 I have become a stranger
to my brothers
and a foreigner
to my mother's sons
9 because zeal for Your house
has consumed me,
and the insults of those
who insult You
have fallen on me.
10 I mourned and fasted,
but it brought me insults.
11 I wore •sackcloth as my clothing,
and I was a joke to them.
12 Those who sit at the city •gate
talk about me,

---

a**68:30** Probably Egypt   b**68:30** Or *peoples, trampling on those who take pleasure in silver,* or *peoples, trampling on the bars of silver,* or *peoples, who trample each other for bars of silver*   c**68:31** Or *They bring red cloth,* or *They bring bronze*   d**68:31** Modern Sudan   e**68:31** Probably with tribute or in submission   f Apparently a hymn tune; compare Pss 45; 60; 80

and drunkards make up songs
about me.

13 But as for me, LORD,
my prayer to You is for a time
of favor.
In Your abundant,
faithful love, God,
answer me with
Your sure salvation.
14 Rescue me from the miry mud;
don't let me sink.
Let me be rescued from those
who hate me,
and from the deep waters.
15 Don't let the floodwaters
sweep over me
or the deep swallow me up;
don't let the •Pit close its mouth
over me.
16 Answer me, LORD,
for Your faithful love is good;
in keeping with
Your great compassion,
turn to me.
17 Don't hide Your face
from Your servant,
for I am in distress.
Answer me quickly!
18 Draw near to me and redeem me;
ransom me because of my enemies.

19 You know the insults I endure—
my shame and disgrace.
You are aware of
all my adversaries.
20 Insults have broken my heart,
and I am in despair.
I waited for sympathy,
but there was none;
for comforters, but found no one.
21 Instead, they gave me gall[a]
for my food,
and for my thirst
they gave me vinegar to drink.

22 Let their table set before them be
a snare,
and let it be a trap for ⌊their⌋ allies.
23 Let their eyes grow too dim to see,
and let their loins
continually shake.
24 Pour out Your rage on them,
and let Your burning anger
overtake them.
25 Make their fortification desolate;
may no one live in their tents.
26 For they persecute the one
You struck
and talk about the pain of those
You wounded.
27 Add guilt to their guilt;
do not let them share
in Your righteousness.
28 Let them be erased from the book
of life
and not be recorded
with the righteous.

29 But as for me—poor and in pain—
let Your salvation protect me, God.
30 I will praise God's name with song
and exalt Him with thanksgiving.
31 That will please the LORD
more than an ox,
more than a bull with horns
and hooves.
32 The humble will see it and rejoice.
You who seek God, take heart!
33 For the LORD listens to the needy
and does not despise
His own who are prisoners.

34 Let heaven and earth praise Him,
the seas and everything that moves
in them,
35 for God will save Zion
and build up[b] the cities of Judah.
They will live there and possess it.
36 The descendants of His servants
will inherit it,

a**69:21** A bitter substance   b**69:35** Or *and rebuild*

and those who love His name
will live in it.

PSALM 70
A Call for Deliverance

For the choir director. Davidic.
To bring remembrance.

"Hurry ... Lord!"

1 God, deliver me.
Hurry to help me, LORD!

2 Let those who seek my life
be disgraced and confounded;
let those who wish me harm
be driven back and humiliated.

3 Let those who say, "Aha, aha!"
retreat because of their shame.

4 Let all who seek You rejoice
and be glad in You;
let those who love Your salvation
continually say, "God is great!"

5 I am afflicted and needy;
hurry to me, God.
You are my help and my deliverer;
LORD, do not delay.

PSALM 71
God's Help in Old Age

1 LORD, I seek refuge in You;
never let me be disgraced.

2 In Your justice, rescue
and deliver me;
listen closely to me and save me.

3 Be a rock of refuge for me,
where I can always go.
Give the command to save me,
for You are my rock and fortress.

4 Deliver me, my God, from the hand
of the wicked,
from the grasp of the unjust
and oppressive.

5 For You are my hope, Lord GOD,
my confidence from my youth.

6 I have leaned on You from birth;
You took me from
my mother's womb.
My praise is always about You.

7 I have become an ominous sign
to many,
but You are my strong refuge.

8 My mouth is full of praise
and honor to You all day long.

9 Don't discard me in my old age;
as my strength fails,
do not abandon me.

10 For my enemies talk about me,
and those who spy on me
plot together,

11 saying, "God has abandoned him;
chase him and catch him,
for there is no one to rescue ⌊him⌋."

12 God, do not be far from me;
my God, hurry to help me.

13 May my adversaries be disgraced
and confounded;
may those who seek my harm
be covered with disgrace
and humiliation.

14 But I will hope continually
and will praise You more and more.

15 My mouth will tell
about Your righteousness
and Your salvation all day long,
though I cannot sum them up.

16 I come because of the mighty acts
of the Lord GOD;
I will proclaim Your righteousness,
Yours alone.

17 God, You have taught me
from my youth,
and I still proclaim
Your wonderful works.

18 Even when I am old and gray,
God, do not abandon me.
Then I will[a] proclaim Your power
to ⌊another⌋ generation,

[a] 71:18 Lit me until I

Your strength to all who are
to come.

19 Your righteousness
reaches heaven, God,
You who have done great things;
God, who is like You?

20 You caused me to experience
many troubles and misfortunes,
but You will revive me again.
You will bring me up again,
even from the depths of the earth.

21 You will increase my honor
and comfort me once again.

22 Therefore, with a lute
I will praise You
for Your faithfulness, my God;
I will sing to You with a harp,
Holy One of Israel.

23 My lips will shout for joy
when I sing praise to You,
because You have redeemed me.

24 Therefore, my tongue will proclaim
Your righteousness all day long,
for those who seek my harm
will be disgraced and confounded.

PSALM 72
Prayer for the King
Solomonic.

1 God, give Your justice to the king
and Your righteousness
to the king's son.

2 He will judge Your people
with righteousness
and Your afflicted ones with justice.

3 May the mountains
bring prosperity[a] to the people,
and the hills, righteousness.

4 May he vindicate the afflicted
among the people,
help the poor,
and crush the oppressor.

5 May he continue[b]
while the sun endures,
and as long as the moon,
throughout all generations.

6 May he be like rain that falls
on the cut grass,
like spring showers that water
the earth.

7 May the righteous[c] flourish
in his days,
and prosperity[a] abound
until the moon is no more.

8 And may he rule from sea to sea
and from the Euphrates
to the ends of the earth.

9 May desert tribes kneel before him
and his enemies lick the dust.

10 May the kings of Tarshish
and the coasts and islands
bring tribute,
the kings of Sheba and Seba
offer gifts.

11 And let all kings bow down to him,
all nations serve him.

12 For he will rescue the poor
who cry out
and the afflicted who have
no helper.

13 He will have pity on the poor
and helpless
and save the lives of the poor.

14 He will redeem them
from oppression and violence,
for their lives are precious[d]
in his sight.

15 May he live long!
May gold from Sheba be given
to him.
May prayer be offered
for him continually,
and may he be blessed all day long.

---

a72:3,7 Or *peace*   b72:5 LXX; MT reads *May they fear you*   c72:7 Some Hb mss, LXX, Syr, Jer read *May righteousness*   d72:14 Or *valuable*

16 May there be plenty of grain
  in the land;
may it wave on the tops
  of the mountains.
May its crops be like Lebanon.
May people flourish in the cities
like the grass of the field.
17 May his name endure forever;
  as long as the sun shines,
may his fame increase.
May all nations be blessed by him
and call him blessed.

18 May the LORD God, the God
  of Israel, be praised,
who alone does wonders.
19 May His glorious name
  be praised forever;
the whole earth is filled
  with His glory.
•Amen and amen.
20 The prayers of David son of Jesse
  are concluded.

BOOK III

(PSALMS 73–89)

PSALM 73

God's Ways Vindicated

A psalm of •Asaph.

Slipping Feet

1 God is indeed good to Israel,
to the pure in heart.
2 But as for me, my feet
  almost slipped;
my steps nearly went astray.

Prosperity of Wicked

3 For I envied the arrogant;
I saw the prosperity of the wicked.

4 They have an easy time
  until they die,[a]

and their bodies are well-fed.[b]
5 They are not in trouble like others;
they are not afflicted
  like most people.
6 Therefore, pride is their necklace,
and violence covers them
  like a garment.
7 Their eyes bulge out from fatness;
the imaginations of their hearts
  run wild.
8 They mock,
  and they speak maliciously;
they arrogantly
  threaten oppression.
9 They set their mouths
  against heaven,
and their tongues strut
  across the earth.
10 Therefore His people turn to them[c]
and drink in their
  overflowing waters.[d]
11 They say, "How can God know?
Does the •Most High
  know everything?"
12 Look at them—the wicked!
They are always at ease,
and they increase their wealth.

Personal Comparison with Wicked

13 Did I purify my heart
and wash my hands in innocence
  for nothing?
14 For I am afflicted all day long,
and punished every morning.
15 If I had decided to say
  these things ⌊aloud⌋,
I would have betrayed
  Your people.[e]

Understanding the Wicked

16 When I tried to understand all this,
it seemed hopeless[f]
17 until I entered God's sanctuary.
Then I understood their destiny.

---

[a]73:4 Lit *For there are no pangs to their death* [b]73:4 Lit *fat* [c]73:10 Lit *turn here* [d]73:10 Lit *and waters of fullness are drained by them* [e]73:15 Lit *betrayed the generation of Your sons* [f]73:16 Lit *it was trouble in my eyes*

18 Indeed You put them
      in slippery places;
   You make them fall into ruin.
19 How suddenly they become
      a desolation!
   They come to an end, swept away
      by terrors.
20 Like one waking from a dream,
   Lord, when arising,
      You will despise their image.

21 When I became embittered
   and my innermost being[a]
      was wounded,
22 <u>I was a fool and didn't understand;</u>
   <u>I was an unthinking animal</u>
      <u>toward You.</u>
23 Yet I am always with You;
   You hold my right hand.
24 You guide me with Your counsel,
   and afterwards You will take me up
      in glory.[b]
25 Whom do I have in heaven but You?
   And I desire nothing on earth but You.
26 My flesh and my heart may fail,
   but God is the strength[c] of my heart,
   my portion forever.
27 Those far from You
      will certainly perish;
   You destroy all who are
      unfaithful to You.
28 But as for me, <u>God's presence is</u>
      <u>my good.</u>
   <u>I have made the Lord GOD my refuge,</u>
   <u>so I can tell about all You do.</u>

PSALM 74
Prayer for Israel
A •*Maskil* of •Asaph.

Have You Rejected Us?

1 Why have You
      rejected ⌊us⌋ forever, God?

Why does Your anger burn
   against the sheep of Your pasture?
2 Remember Your congregation,
   which You purchased long ago
   and redeemed as the tribe
      for Your own possession.
   ⌊Remember⌋ Mount Zion
      where You dwell.
3 Make Your way[d]
      to the everlasting ruins,
   to all that the enemy has destroyed
      in the sanctuary.
4 Your adversaries roared
      in the meeting place
   where You met with us.[e]
   They set up their emblems as signs.
5 It was like men in a thicket of trees,
   wielding axes,
6 then smashing all the carvings
   with hatchets and picks.
7 They set Your sanctuary on fire;
   they utterly[f] desecrated
   the dwelling place of Your name.
8 They said in their hearts,
   "Let us oppress them relentlessly."
   They burned down every place
      throughout the land
   where God met with us.[g]
9 <u>We don't see any signs for us.</u>
   <u>There is no longer a prophet.</u>
   <u>And none of us knows how long</u>
      <u>this will last.</u>
10 God, how long will the foe mock?
   Will the enemy insult
      Your name forever?

Prayer for God's Hand

11 Why do You hold back Your hand?
   Stretch out[h] Your right hand
      and destroy ⌊them⌋!

12 God my king is from ancient times,
   performing saving acts
      on the earth.

[a]**73:21** Lit *my kidneys*   [b]**73:24** Or *will receive me with honor*   [c]**73:26** Lit *rock*   [d]**74:3** Lit *Lift up Your steps*   [e]**74:4** Lit *in Your meeting place*   [f]**74:7** Lit *they to the ground*   [g]**74:8** Lit *every meeting place of God in the land*   [h]**74:11** Lit *From Your bosom*

13 You divided the sea
     with Your strength;
   You smashed the heads
     of the sea monsters
   in the waters;
14 You crushed the heads
     of •Leviathan;
   You fed him to the creatures
     of the desert.
15 You opened up springs
     and streams;
   You dried up ever-flowing rivers.
16 The day is Yours, also the night;
   You established the moon
     and the sun.
17 You set all the boundaries
     of the earth;
   You made summer and winter.

18 Remember this: the enemy
     has mocked the LORD,
   and a foolish people has insulted
     Your name.
19 Do not give the life of Your dove
     to beasts;[a]
   do not forget the lives
     of Your poor people forever.
20 Consider the covenant,
   for the dark places of the land
     are full of violence.
21 Do not let the oppressed turn away
     in shame;
   let the poor and needy
     praise Your name.
22 Arise, God, defend
     Your cause!
   Remember the insults
     that fools bring against You
     all day long.
23 Do not forget the clamor
     of Your adversaries,
   the tumult of Your opponents
     that goes up constantly.

PSALM 75
God Judges the Wicked

For the choir director: "Do Not Destroy."[b]
A psalm of •Asaph. A song.

1 We give thanks to You, God;
   we give thanks to You,
     for Your name is near.
   People tell about
     Your wonderful works.

2 "When I choose a time,
   I will judge fairly.
3 When the earth and all
     its inhabitants shake,
   I am the One who steadies
     its pillars.   •Selah
4 I say to the boastful, 'Do not boast,'
   and to the wicked, 'Do not lift up
     your •horn.
5 Do not lift up your horn
     against heaven
   or speak arrogantly.'"

6 Exaltation does not come
   from the east, the west,
     or the desert,
7 for God is the judge:
   He brings down one
     and exalts another.
8 For there is a cup
     in the LORD's hand,
   full of wine blended with spices,
     and He pours from it.
   All the wicked of the earth
     will drink,
   draining it to the dregs.

9 As for me, I will tell
     about Him forever;
   I will sing praise to the God
     of Jacob.

10 "I will cut off all the horns
     of the wicked,

---

[a]**74:19** One Hb ms, LXX, Syr read *Do not hand over to beasts a soul that praises You*   [b]Apparently a tune for the psalm

but the horns of the righteous
will be lifted up."

PSALM 76
God, the Powerful Judge

For the choir director:
with stringed instruments.
A psalm of •Asaph. A song.

¹ God is known in Judah;
His name is great in Israel.
² His tent is in Salem,ᵃ
His dwelling place in Zion.
³ There He shatters the bow's
flaming arrows,
the shield, the sword,
and the weapons of war.   •Selah

⁴ You are resplendent and majestic
⌊coming down⌋ from the mountains
of prey.
⁵ The brave-hearted
have been plundered;
they have slipped
into their ⌊final⌋ sleep.
None of the warriors was able to lift
a hand.
⁶ At Your rebuke, God of Jacob,
both chariot and horse lay still.

⁷ And You—You are to be •feared.ᵇ
When You are angry,
who can stand before You?
⁸ From heaven
You pronounced judgment.
The earth feared and grew quiet
⁹ when God rose up to judge
and to save all the lowly
of the earth.   Selah
¹⁰ Even human wrath
will praise You;
You will clothe Yourself
with their remaining wrath.ᶜ

¹¹ Make and keep your vows
to the LORD your God;

let all who are around Him
bring tribute
to the awe-inspiring One.ᵈ
¹² He humbles the spirit of leaders;
He is feared by the kings of the earth.

PSALM 77
Confidence in Time of Crisis

For the choir director: according to Jeduthun.
Of •Asaph. A psalm.

¹ I cry aloud to God,
aloud to God, and He will hear me.
² In my day of trouble I sought
the Lord.
My hands were lifted up
all night long;
I refused to be comforted.

Types of Meditation

³ I think of God; I groan;
I meditate; my spirit
becomes weak.   •Selah

⁴ You have kept me from closing
my eyes;
I am troubled and cannot speak.
⁵ I consider days of old,
years long past.
⁶ At night I remember my music;
I meditate in my heart,
and my spirit ponders.

⁷ "Will the Lord reject forever
and never again show favor?
⁸ Has His faithful love
ceased forever?
Is ⌊His⌋ promise at an end
for all generations?
⁹ Has God forgotten to be gracious?
Has He in anger
withheld His compassion?" Selah

¹⁰ So I say, "It is my sorrowᵉ
that the right hand
of the •Most High has changed."

ᵃ**76:2** Jerusalem   ᵇ**76:7** Or *are awe-inspiring*   ᶜ**76:10** Hb obscure   ᵈ**76:11** Or *tribute with awe*   ᵉ**77:10** Lit *"My piercing*

11 I will remember the LORD's works;
yes, I will remember
Your ancient wonders.
12 I will reflect on all You have done
and meditate on Your actions.

13 God, Your way is holy.
What god is great like God?
14 You are the God
who works wonders;
You revealed Your strength
among the peoples.
15 With power You redeemed
Your people,
the descendants of Jacob
and Joseph. *Selah*

16 The waters saw You, God.
The waters saw You;
they trembled.
Even the depths shook.
17 The clouds poured down water.
The storm clouds thundered;
Your arrows flashed back and forth.
18 The sound of Your thunder was
in the whirlwind;
lightning lit up the world.
The earth shook and quaked.
19 Your way went through the sea,
and Your path through
the great waters,
but Your footprints were unseen.
20 You led Your people like a flock
by the hand of Moses and Aaron.

PSALM 78
Lessons from Israel's Past

A •*Maskil* of •Asaph.

1 My people, hear my instruction;
listen to what I say.
2 I will declare wise sayings;
I will speak mysteries
from the past—
3 things we have heard and known
and that our fathers
have passed down to us.

4 We must not hide them
from their children,
but must tell a future generation
the praises of the LORD,
His might,
and the wonderful works
He has performed.
5 He established a •testimony
in Jacob
and set up a law in Israel,
which He commanded our fathers
to teach to their children
6 so that a future generation—
children yet to be born—
might know.
They were to rise and tell
their children
7 so that they might
put their confidence in God
and not forget God's works,
but keep His commandments.
8 Then they would not be
like their fathers,
a stubborn and rebellious generation,
a generation whose heart
was not loyal
and whose spirit was not faithful
to God.

9 The Ephraimite archers turned back
on the day of battle.
10 They did not keep God's covenant
and refused to live by His law.
11 They forgot what He had done,
the wonderful works
He had shown them.
12 He worked wonders in the sight
of their fathers,
in the land of Egypt, the region
of Zoan.
13 He split the sea
and brought them across;
the water stood firm like a wall.
14 He led them with a cloud by day
and with a fiery light
throughout the night.

15 He split rocks in the wilderness
   and gave them drink as abundant
      as the depths.
16 He brought streams out of the stone
   and made water flow down
      like rivers.

17 But they continued to sin
      against Him,
   rebelling in the desert
      against the •Most High.
18 They deliberately[a] tested God,
   demanding the food they craved.
19 They spoke against God, saying,
   "Is God able to provide food
      in the wilderness?
20 Look! He struck the rock and water
      gushed out;
   torrents overflowed.
   But can He also provide bread
   or furnish meat for His people?"

God's Anger

21 Therefore, the LORD heard
      and became furious;
   then fire broke out against Jacob,
   and anger flared up against Israel
22 because they did not believe God
   or rely on His salvation.
23 He gave a command
      to the clouds above
   and opened the doors of heaven.
24 He rained manna for them to eat;
   He gave them grain from heaven.
25 People[b] ate the bread of angels.[c]
   He sent them an abundant supply
      of food.
26 He made the east wind blow
      in the skies
   and drove the south wind
      by His might.
27 He rained meat on them like dust,
   and winged birds like the sand
      of the seas.

28 He made ⌊them⌋ fall in His camp,
   all around His tent.[d] [e]
29 They ate and were
      completely satisfied,
   for He gave them what they craved.
30 Before they had satisfied
      their desire,
   while the food was still
      in their mouths,
31 God's anger flared up against them,
   and He killed
      some of their best men.
   He struck down Israel's choice
      young men.

32 Despite all this, they kept sinning
   and did not believe
      His wonderful works.
33 He made their days end in futility,
   their years in sudden disaster.
34 When He killed ⌊some of⌋ them,
   ⌊the rest⌋ began to seek Him;
   they repented
      and searched for God.
35 They remembered that God was
      their rock,
   the Most High God,
      their Redeemer.
36 But they deceived Him
      with their mouths,
   they lied to Him with their tongues,
37 their hearts were insincere
      toward Him,
   and they were unfaithful
      to His covenant.
38 Yet He was compassionate;
   He •atoned for[f] ⌊their⌋ guilt
   and did not destroy ⌊them⌋.
   He often turned His anger aside
   and did not unleash[g] all His wrath.
39 He remembered that they were
      ⌊only⌋ flesh,
   a wind that passes
      and does not return.

---

a**78:18** Lit in their heart   b**78:25** Lit Man   c**78:25** Lit mighty ones   d**78:28** LXX, Syr read in their camp . . . their tents
e**78:28** Or in its camp, all around its tents   f**78:38** Or He wiped out, or He forgave   g**78:38** Or stir up

40 How often they rebelled
   against Him
in the wilderness
and grieved Him in the desert.
41 They constantly tested God
and provoked the Holy One
   of Israel.
42 They did not remember
   His power ⌊shown⌋
on the day He redeemed them
   from the foe,
43 when He performed
   His miraculous signs in Egypt
and His marvels in the region
   of Zoan.
44 He turned their rivers into blood,
and they could not drink
   from their streams.
45 He sent among them swarms
   of flies,
which fed on them,
and frogs, which devastated them.
46 He gave their crops
   to the caterpillar
and the fruit of their labor
   to the locust.
47 He killed their vines with hail
and their sycamore-fig trees
   with a flood.
48 He handed over their livestock
   to hail
and their cattle to lightning bolts.
49 He sent His burning anger
   against them:
fury, indignation, and calamity—
a band of deadly messengers.[a]
50 He cleared a path for His anger.
He did not spare them from death,
but delivered their lives
   to the plague.
51 He struck all the firstborn in Egypt,
the first progeny of the tents
   of Ham.[b]

52 He led His people out like sheep
and guided them like a flock
   in the wilderness.
53 He led them safely,
   and they were not afraid;
but the sea covered their enemies.
54 He brought them to His holy land,
to the mountain
   His right hand acquired.
55 He drove out nations before them.
He apportioned their inheritance
   by lot
and settled the tribes of Israel
   in their tents.

56 But they rebelliously tested
   the Most High God,
for they did not keep His decrees.
57 They treacherously turned away
   like their fathers;
they became warped
   like a faulty bow.
58 They enraged Him
   with their •high places
and provoked His jealousy
   with their carved images.
59 God heard and became furious;
He completely rejected Israel.
60 He abandoned the tabernacle
   at Shiloh,
the tent where He resided
   among men.[c]
61 He gave up His strength[d]
   to captivity
and His splendor to the hand of a foe.
62 He surrendered His people
   to the sword
because He was enraged
   with His heritage.
63 Fire consumed
   His chosen young men,
and His young women
   had no wedding songs.[e]

---

[a]78:49 Or *angels*   [b]78:51 Ham's descendants who settled in Egypt; Ps 105:23,27   [c]78:60 Hb *adam*   [d]78:61 See Ps 132:8 where the ark of the covenant is the *ark of His strength.*   [e]78:63 Lit *virgins were not praised*

64 His priests fell by the sword,
but the[a] widows could not lament.[b]

65 Then the Lord awoke as if
from sleep,
like a warrior from the effects
of wine.
66 He beat back His foes;
He gave them lasting shame.
67 He rejected the tent of Joseph
and did not choose the tribe
of Ephraim.
68 He chose instead the tribe of Judah,
Mount Zion, which He loved.
69 He built His sanctuary
like the heights,[c]
like the earth that
He established forever.
70 He chose David His servant
and took him from the sheepfolds;
71 He brought him from tending ewes
to be shepherd
over His people Jacob—
over Israel, His inheritance.
72 He shepherded them
with a pure heart
and guided them
with his skillful hands.

PSALM 79
Faith amid Confusion

A psalm of •Asaph.

1 God, the nations have invaded
Your inheritance,
desecrated Your holy temple,
and turned Jerusalem into ruins.
2 They gave the corpses
of Your servants
to the birds of the sky for food,
the flesh of Your godly ones
to the beasts of the earth.
3 They poured out their blood
like water all around Jerusalem,
and there was no one
to bury ⌊them⌋.
4 We have become an object
of reproach
to our neighbors,
a source of mockery and ridicule
to those around us.

5 How long, LORD? Will You
be angry forever?
Will Your jealousy keep burning
like fire?
6 Pour out Your wrath on the nations
that don't acknowledge You,
on the kingdoms that don't call on
Your name,
7 for they have devoured Jacob
and devastated his homeland.
8 Do not hold past sins[d] against us;
let Your compassion come
to us quickly,
for we have become weak.
9 God of our salvation, help us—
for the glory of Your name.
Deliver us and •atone for[e] our sins,
because of Your name.
10 Why should the nations ask,
"Where is their God?"
Before our eyes,
let vengeance for the shed blood
of Your servants
be known among the nations.
11 Let the groans of the prisoners
reach You;
according to Your great power,
preserve those condemned to die.

12 Pay back sevenfold
to our neighbors
the reproach they have hurled
at You, Lord.
13 Then we, Your people, the sheep
of Your pasture,
will thank You forever;

a**78:64** Lit *His*   b**78:64** War probably prevented customary funerals.   c**78:69** Either the heights of heaven or the
mountain heights   d**79:8** Or *hold the sins of past generations*   e**79:9** Or *and wipe out*, or *and forgive*

we will declare Your praise
to generation after generation.

PSALM 80
Prayer for Restoration

For the choir director: according to
"The Lilies."[a] A testimony of •Asaph. A psalm.

1 Listen, Shepherd of Israel,
who guides Joseph like a flock;
You who sit enthroned
⌊on⌋ the •cherubim,
rise up
2 at the head of Ephraim,
Benjamin, and Manasseh.[b]
Rally Your power and come
to save us.
3 Restore us, God;
look ⌊on us⌋ with favor,
and we will be saved.

4 LORD God of •Hosts,
how long will You be angry
with Your people's prayers?
5 You fed them the bread of tears
and gave them a full measure[c]
of tears to drink.
6 You set us at strife with our neighbors;
our enemies make fun of us.
7 Restore us, God of Hosts;
look ⌊on us⌋ with favor, and we
will be saved.

8 You uprooted a vine from Egypt;
You drove out the nations
and planted it.
9 You cleared ⌊a place⌋ for it;
it took root and filled the land.
10 The mountains were covered
by its shade,
and the mighty cedars[d]
with its branches.
11 It sent out sprouts toward the Sea[e]
and shoots toward the River.[f]

12 Why have You broken down
its walls
so that all who pass by
pick its fruit?
13 The boar from the forest
gnaws at it,
and creatures of the field
feed on it.
14 Return, God of Hosts.
Look down from heaven and see;
take care of this vine,
15 the root[g] Your right hand
has planted,
the shoot[h] that You made strong
for Yourself.
16 It was cut down and burned up;[i]
they[j] perish at the rebuke
of Your countenance.
17 Let Your hand be with the man
at Your right hand,
with the son of man
You have made strong for Yourself.
18 Then we will not turn away
from You;
revive us, and we will call
on Your name.
19 Restore us, LORD God of Hosts;
look ⌊on us⌋ with favor, and we will
be saved.

PSALM 81
Call to Obedience

For the choir director: on the •Gittith.
Of •Asaph.

1 Sing for joy to God our strength;
shout in triumph to the God
of Jacob.
2 Lift up a song—
play the tambourine,
the melodious lyre, and the harp.
3 Blow the horn
during the new moon

---

[a]Possibly a hymn tune; compare Pss 45; 60; 69   [b]**80:2** See Nm 2:17-24 for the order of these names in the marching order of the camp of Israel.   [c]**80:5** Lit *a one-third measure*   [d]**80:10** Lit *the cedars of God*   [e]**80:11** The Mediterranean   [f]**80:11** The Euphrates   [g]**80:15** Hb obscure   [h]**80:15** Or *son*   [i]**80:16** Lit *burned with fire*   [j]**80:16** Or *may they*

and during the full moon,
on the day of our feast.[a]
4 For this is a statute for Israel,
a judgment of the God of Jacob.
5 He set it up as an ordinance
for Joseph
when He went throughout[b]
the land of Egypt.

I heard an unfamiliar language:
6 "I relieved his shoulder
from the burden;
his hands were freed from ⌊carrying⌋
the basket.
7 You called out in distress,
and I rescued you;
I answered you
from the thundercloud.
I tested you at the waters
of Meribah.   •Selah
8 Listen, My people, and I will
admonish you.
Israel, if you would only listen to Me!
9 There must not be a strange god
among you;
you must not bow down
to a foreign god.
10 I am •Yahweh your God,
who brought you up from the land
of Egypt.
Open your mouth wide, and I will
fill it.

11 "But My people did not listen to Me;
Israel did not obey Me.
12 So I gave them over
to their stubborn hearts
to follow their own plans.
13 If only My people would listen
to Me
and Israel would follow My ways,
14 I would quickly subdue
their enemies
and turn My hand
against their foes."

15 Those who hate the LORD
would pretend submission to Him;
their doom would last forever.
16 But He would feed Israel[c]
with the best wheat.
"I would satisfy you with honey
from the rock."

PSALM 82
Plea for Righteous Judgment
A psalm of •Asaph.

1 God has taken His place
in the divine assembly;
He judges among the gods:[d]
2 "How long will you judge unjustly
and show partiality to the wicked?
•Selah
3 Provide justice for the needy
and the fatherless;
uphold the rights of the oppressed
and the destitute.
4 Rescue the poor and needy;
save them from the hand
of the wicked."

5 They do not know or understand;
they wander in darkness.
All the foundations of the earth
are shaken.

6 I said, "You are gods;
you are all sons of the •Most High.
7 However, you will die like men
and fall like any other ruler."

8 Rise up, God, judge the earth,
for all the nations belong to You.

PSALM 83
Prayer against Enemies
A song. A psalm of •Asaph.

1 God, do not keep silent.
Do not be deaf, God; do not be idle.

2 See how Your enemies
   make an uproar;
those who hate You
   have acted arrogantly.ᵃ
3 They devise clever schemes
   against Your people;
they conspire against
   Your treasured ones.
4 They say, "Come, let us
   wipe them out as a nation
so that Israel's name will no longer
   be remembered."
5 For they have conspired
   with one mind;
they form an allianceᵇ against You—
6 the tents of Edom
   and the Ishmaelites,
Moab and the Hagrites,
7 Gebal, Ammon, and Amalek,
Philistia with the inhabitants
   of Tyre.
8 Even Assyria has joined them;
they lend supportᶜ to the sons
   of Lot.ᵈ   •Selah

9 Deal with them as ⌊You did⌋
   with Midian,
as ⌊You did⌋ with Sisera
and Jabin at the Kishon River.
10 They were destroyed at En-dor;
they became manure
   for the ground.
11 Make their nobles like Oreb
   and Zeeb,
and all their tribal leaders
   like Zebah and Zalmunna,
12 who said, "Let us seize
   God's pastures for ourselves."

13 Make them like tumbleweed,
   my God,
like straw before the wind.
14 As fire burns a forest,
as a flame blazes
   through mountains,

15 so pursue them with Your tempest
and terrify them with Your storm.
16 Cover their faces with shame
so that they will seek
   Your name, LORD.
17 Let them be put to shame
   and terrified forever;
let them perish in disgrace.
18 May they know that You alone—
whose name is •Yahweh—
are the •Most High
   over all the earth.

PSALM 84
Longing for God's House
For the choir director: on the •*Gittith*.
A psalm of the sons of Korah.

1 How lovely is Your dwelling place,
LORD of •Hosts.
2 I long and yearn
for the courts of the LORD;
my heart and flesh cry out
   forᵉ the living God.

3 Even a sparrow finds a home,
and a swallow, a nest for herself
where she places her young—
near Your altars, LORD of Hosts,
my King and my God.
4 How happy are those who reside
   in Your house,
who praise You continually.   •Selah

5 Happy are the people
   whose strength is in You,
whose hearts are set on pilgrimage.
6 As they pass through the Valley
   of Baca,ᶠ
they make it a source
   of springwater;
even the autumn rain will cover it
   with blessings.ᵍ
7 They go from strength to strength;
each appears before God in Zion.

ᵃ**83:2** Lit *have lifted their head*   ᵇ**83:5** Lit *they cut a covenant*   ᶜ**83:8** Lit *they are an arm*   ᵈ**83:8** Moab and Edom
ᵉ**84:2** Or *flesh shout for joy to*   ᶠ**84:6** Or *Valley of Tears*   ᵍ**84:6** Or *pools*

8 LORD God of Hosts, hear my prayer;
listen, God of Jacob. *Selah*
9 Consider our shield,[a] God;
look on the face
of Your anointed one.

10 Better a day in Your courts
than a thousand ⟨anywhere else⟩.
I would rather be at the door
of the house of my God
than to live in the tents
of the wicked.
11 For the LORD God is a sun and shield.
The LORD gives grace and glory;
He does not withhold the good
from those who live with integrity.
12 LORD of Hosts,
happy is the person who trusts
in You!

PSALM 85
Restoration of Favor
For the choir director.
A psalm of the sons of Korah.

1 LORD, You showed favor
to Your land;
You restored Jacob's prosperity.[b]
2 You took away Your people's guilt;
You covered all their sin. •*Selah*
3 You withdrew all Your fury;
You turned from Your burning anger.

4 Return to us, God of our salvation,
and abandon Your displeasure with us.
5 Will You be angry with us forever?
Will You prolong Your anger for all
generations?
6 Will You not revive us again
so that Your people may rejoice
in You?
7 Show us Your faithful love, LORD,
and give us Your salvation.

8 I will listen to what God will say;
surely the LORD will declare peace

to His people, His godly ones,
and not let them go back
to foolish ways.
9 His salvation is very near
those who fear Him,
so that glory may dwell in our land.
10 Faithful love and truth
will join together;
righteousness and peace
will embrace.
11 Truth will spring up from the earth,
and righteousness will look
down from heaven.
12 Also, the LORD will provide
what is good,
and our land will yield its crops.
13 Righteousness will go before Him
to prepare the way for His steps.

PSALM 86
Lament and Petition
A Davidic prayer.

1 Listen, LORD, and answer me,
for I am poor and needy.
2 Protect my life, for I am faithful.
You are my God; save Your servant
who trusts in You.
3 Be gracious to me, Lord,
for I call to You all day long.
4 Bring joy to Your servant's life,
since I set my hope on You, Lord.
5 For You, Lord, are kind and ready
to forgive,
abundant in faithful love to all
who call on You.
6 LORD, hear my prayer;
listen to my plea for mercy.
7 I call on You in the day of my distress,
for You will answer me.

8 Lord, there is no one like You
among the gods,
and there are no works like Yours.

a**84:9** The king   b**85:1** Or *restored Jacob from captivity*

9 All the nations You have made
   will come and bow down
      before You, Lord,
   and will honor Your name.
10 For You are great
      and perform wonders;
   You alone are God.

11 Teach me Your way, LORD,
   and I will live by Your truth.
   Give me an undivided mind to fear
   Your name.
12 I will praise You with all my heart,
   Lord my God,
   and will honor Your name forever.
13 For Your faithful love for me
   is great,
   and You deliver my life
   from the depths of •Sheol.

14 God, arrogant people
   have attacked me;
   a gang of ruthless men seeks
   my life.
   They have no regard for You.
15 But You, Lord, are a compassionate
   and gracious God,
   slow to anger and abundant
   in faithful love and truth.
16 Turn to me and be gracious to me.
   Give Your strength to Your servant;
   save the son of Your female servant.
17 Show me a sign of Your goodness;
   my enemies will see and be put
   to shame
   because You, LORD, have helped
   and comforted me.

PSALM 87
Zion, the City of God

A psalm of the sons of Korah. A song.

1 His foundation is
   on the holy mountains.
2 The LORD loves the gates of Zion

more than all the dwellings
   of Jacob.[a]
3 Glorious things are said about you,
   city of God.   •Selah

4 "I will mention those
   who know Me:
   •Rahab, Babylon, Philistia, Tyre,
   and •Cush[b]—
   each one was born there."
5 And it will be said of Zion,
   "This one and that one were born
   in her."
   The •Most High Himself
   will establish her.
6 When He registers the peoples,
   the LORD will record,
   "This one was born there."   Selah
7 Singers and dancers alike ⌊will say⌋,
   "All my springs are in you."

PSALM 88
Cry of Desperation

A song. A psalm of the sons of Korah.
For the choir director: according to Mahalath
Leannoth. A •Maskil of Heman the Ezrahite.

1 LORD, God of my salvation,
   I cry out before You day and night.
2 May my prayer reach Your presence;
   listen to my cry.

3 For I have had enough troubles,
   and my life is near •Sheol.
4 I am counted among those
      going down to the •Pit.
   I am like a man without strength,
5 abandoned[c] among the dead.
   I am like the slain lying
      in the grave,
   whom You no longer remember,
   and who are cut off
      from Your care.[d]

6 You have put me in the lowest part
   of the Pit,

---

a87:2 Places in Israel   b87:4 Modern Sudan   c88:5 Or set free   d88:5 Or hand

in the darkest places, in the depths.
7 Your wrath weighs heavily on me;
You have overwhelmed me with all
Your waves. •Selah
8 You have distanced my friends
from me;
You have made me repulsive
to them.
I am shut in and cannot go out.
9 My eyes are worn out from crying.
LORD, I cry out to You all day long;
I spread out my hands to You.

10 Do You work wonders for the dead?
Do departed spirits rise up
to praise You? Selah
11 Will Your faithful love be declared
in the grave,
Your faithfulness in •Abaddon?
12 Will Your wonders be known
in the darkness,
or Your righteousness in the land
of oblivion?

13 But I call to You for help, LORD;
in the morning my prayer
meets You.
14 LORD, why do You reject me?
Why do You hide Your face
from me?
15 From my youth,
I have been afflicted and near
death.
I suffer Your horrors;
I am desperate.
16 Your wrath sweeps over me;
Your terrors destroy me.
17 They surround me like water
all day long;
they close in on me
from every side.
18 You have distanced loved one
and neighbor from me;
darkness is my ⌊only⌋ friend.ᵃ

PSALM 89

God's Power and Promises

A •*Maskil* of Ethan the Ezrahite.

1 I will sing about the LORD's
faithful love forever;
with my mouth
I will proclaim Your faithfulness
to all generations.
2 For I will declare,
"Faithful love is built up forever;
You establish Your faithfulness
in the heavens."

3 ⌊The LORD said,⌋
"I have made a covenant
with My chosen one;
I have sworn an oath to David
My servant:
4 'I will establish
your offspring forever
and build up your throne
for all generations.'" •*Selah*

5 LORD, the heavens praise
Your wonders—
Your faithfulness also—
in the assembly of the holy ones.
6 For who in the skies can compare
with the LORD?
Who among the heavenly beingsᵇ is
like the LORD?
7 God is greatly feared in the council
of the holy ones,
more awe-inspiring thanᶜ
all who surround Him.
8 LORD God of •Hosts,
who is strong like You, LORD?
Your faithfulness surrounds You.
9 You rule the raging sea;
when its waves surge,
You still them.
10 You crushed •Rahab like one
who is slain;

ᵃ**88:18** Or *from me, my friends. Oh darkness!* ᵇ**89:6** Or *the angels,* or *the sons of the mighty* ᶜ**89:7** Or *ones, revered by*

You scattered Your enemies
with Your powerful arm.
11 The heavens are Yours; the earth
also is Yours.
The world and everything in it—
You founded them.
12 North and south—
You created them.
Tabor and Hermon shout for joy
at Your name.
13 You have a mighty arm;
Your hand is powerful;
Your right hand is lifted high.
14 Righteousness and justice are
the foundation
of Your throne;
faithful love and truth
go before You.
15 Happy are the people who know
the joyful shout;
LORD, they walk in the light
of Your presence.
16 They rejoice in Your name
all day long,
and they are exalted
by Your righteousness.
17 For You are
their magnificent strength;
by Your favor our •horn is exalted.
18 Surely our shield[a]
belongs to the LORD,
our king to the Holy One of Israel.

19 You once spoke in a vision
to Your loyal ones
and said: "I have granted help
to a warrior;
I have exalted one chosen[b]
from the people.
20 I have found David My servant;
I have anointed him
with My sacred oil.
21 My hand will always be with him,
and My arm will strengthen him.

22 The enemy will not afflict[c] him;
no wicked man will oppress him.
23 I will crush his foes before him
and strike those who hate him.
24 My faithfulness and love will be
with him,
and through My name
his horn will be exalted.
25 I will extend his power
to the sea
and his right hand to the rivers.
26 He will call to Me, 'You are
my Father,
my God, the rock of my salvation.'
27 I will also make him My firstborn,
greatest of the kings of the earth.
28 I will always preserve
My faithful love for him,
and My covenant with him
will endure.
29 I will establish his line forever,
his throne as long as heaven lasts.[d]
30 If his sons forsake My instruction
and do not live by My ordinances,
31 if they dishonor My statutes
and do not keep
My commandments,
32 then I will call their rebellion
to account with the rod,
their sin with blows.
33 But I will not withdraw
My faithful love from him
or betray My faithfulness.
34 I will not violate My covenant
or change what My lips have said.
35 Once and for all
I have sworn an oath
by My holiness;
I will not lie to David.
36 His offspring will continue forever,
his throne like the sun before Me,
37 like the moon, established forever,
a faithful witness in the sky." *Selah*

---

a 89:18 The king   b 89:19 Or *exalted a young man*   c 89:22 Or *not exact tribute from*   d 89:29 Lit *as days of heaven*

Perplexity about God's Promises

38 But You have spurned
     and rejected him;
   You have become enraged
     with Your anointed.
39 You have repudiated the covenant
     with Your servant;
   You have completely dishonored
     his crown.ᵃ
40 You have broken down
     all his walls;
   You have reduced his fortified cities
     to ruins.
41 All who pass by plunder him;
   he has become a joke
     to his neighbors.
42 You have lifted high the right hand
     of his foes;
   You have made all
     his enemies rejoice.
43 You have also turned back
     his sharp sword
   and have not let him stand
     in battle.
44 You have made his splendorᵇ cease
   and have overturned his throne.
45 You have shortened the days
     of his youth;
   You have covered him with shame.

                                    Selah

46 How long, LORD? Will You hide
     Yourself forever?
   Will Your anger keep burning
     like fire?
47 Remember how short my life is.
   Have You created •everyone
     for nothing?
48 What man can live
     and never see death?
   Who can save himself
     from the power of •Sheol?   *Selah*
49 Lord, where are the former acts
   of Your faithful love

that You swore to David
   in Your faithfulness?
50 Remember, Lord, the ridicule
     against Your servants—
   in my heart I carry ⌊abuse⌋ from all
     the peoples—
51 how Your enemies
     have ridiculed, LORD,
   how they have ridiculed every step
     of Your anointed.

52 May the LORD be praised forever.
   •Amen and amen.

BOOK IV

(PSALMS 90–106)

PSALM 90

Eternal God and Mortal Man

A prayer of Moses the man of God.

1 Lord, You have been our refugeᶜ
     in every generation.
2 Before the mountains were born,
   before You gave birth to the earth
     and the world,
   from eternity to eternity,
     You are God.
3 You return mankind to the dust,
   saying, "Return,
     descendants of Adam."
4 For in Your sight a thousand years
   are like yesterday that passes by,
   like a few hours of the night.
5 You end their life;ᵈ they sleep.
   They are like grass that grows
     in the morning—
6 in the morning it sprouts
     and grows;
   by evening it withers and dries up.

7 For we are consumed
     by Your anger;
   we are terrified by Your wrath.

ᵃ**89:39** Lit *have dishonored his crown to the ground*   ᵇ**89:44** Hb obscure   ᶜ**90:1** A few Hb mss, LXX; MT reads *dwelling place*   ᵈ**90:5** Or *You overwhelm them*; Hb uncertain

8   You have set our unjust ways
        before You,
    our secret sins in the light
        of Your presence.
9   For all our days ebb away
        under Your wrath;
    we end our years like a sigh.
10 Our lives last[a] seventy years
    or, if we are strong,
        eighty years.
    Even the best of them are[b] struggle
        and sorrow;
    indeed, they pass quickly and we
        fly away.
11 Who understands the power
        of Your anger?
    Your wrath matches the fear
        that is due You.
12 Teach us to number
        our days carefully
    so that we may develop wisdom
        in our hearts.[c]

13 LORD—how long?
    Turn and have compassion
        on Your servants.
14 Satisfy us in the morning
        with Your faithful love
    so that we may shout with joy
        and be glad all our days.
15 Make us rejoice for as many days
        as You have humbled us,
    for as many years as
        we have seen adversity.
16 Let Your work be seen
        by Your servants,
    and Your splendor
        by their children.
17 Let the favor of the Lord our God
        be on us;
    establish for us the work
        of our hands—
    establish the work
        of our hands!

PSALM 91

Protection of the Most High

1   The one who lives
        under the protection
        of the •Most High
    dwells in the shadow
        of the •Almighty.
2   I will say[d] to the LORD, "My refuge
        and my fortress,
    my God, in whom I trust."
3   He Himself will deliver you
        from the hunter's net,
    from the destructive plague.
4   He will cover you with His feathers;
    you will take refuge
        under His wings.
    His faithfulness will be
        a protective shield.
5   You will not fear the terror
        of the night,
    the arrow that flies by day,
6   the plague that stalks in darkness,
    or the pestilence that ravages
        at noon.
7   Though a thousand fall at your side
    and ten thousand
        at your right hand,
    the pestilence will not reach you.
8   You will only see it with your eyes
    and witness the punishment
        of the wicked.

9   Because you have made the LORD—
        my refuge,
    the Most High—
        your dwelling place,
10 no harm will come to you;
    no plague will come near your tent.

Angels' Protection

11 For He will give His angels orders
    concerning you,

---

[a]**90:10** Lit *The days of our years in them*   [b]**90:10** LXX, Tg, Syr, Vg read *Even their span is*; Hb obscure   [c]**90:12** Or *develop a heart of wisdom*   [d]**91:1-2** LXX, Syr, Jer read *Almighty, saying,* or *Almighty, he will say*

to protect you in all your ways.

12 They will support you
    with their hands
    so that you will not strike your foot
    against a stone.

13 You will tread on the lion
    and the cobra;
    you will trample the young lion
    and the serpent.

14 Because he is lovingly devoted
    to Me,
    I will deliver him;
    I will exalt him because he knows
    My name.

15 When he calls out to Me,
    I will answer him;
    I will be with him in trouble.
    I will rescue him
    and give him honor.

16 I will satisfy him with a long life
    and show him My salvation.

PSALM 92
God's Love and Faithfulness

A psalm. A song for the Sabbath day.

1 It is good to praise the LORD,
    to sing praise to Your name,
    •Most High,

2 to declare Your faithful love
    in the morning
    and Your faithfulness at night,

3 with a ten-stringed harp
    and the music of a lyre.

4 For You have made me rejoice, LORD,
    by what You have done;
    I will shout for joy
    because of the works of Your hands.

5 How magnificent are Your works,
    LORD,
    how profound Your thoughts!

6 A stupid person does not know,
    a fool does not understand this:

7 though the wicked sprout like grass
    and all evildoers flourish,
    they will be eternally destroyed.

8 But You, LORD, are exalted forever.

9 For indeed, LORD, Your enemies—
    indeed, Your enemies will perish;
    all evildoers will be scattered.

10 You have lifted up my •horn
    like that of a wild ox;
    I have been anointed[a] with oil.

11 My eyes look down on my enemies;
    my ears hear evildoers
        when they attack me.

12 The righteous thrive
        like a palm tree
    and grow like a cedar tree
        in Lebanon.

13 Planted in the house of the LORD,
    they thrive in the courtyards
        of our God.

14 They will still bear fruit in old age,
    healthy and green,

15 to declare: "The LORD is just;
    He is my rock,
    and there is no unrighteousness
        in Him."

PSALM 93
God's Eternal Reign

1 The LORD reigns! He is robed
        in majesty;
    The LORD is robed,
        enveloped in strength.
    The world is firmly established;
    it cannot be shaken.

2 Your throne has been established
    from the beginning;[b]
    You are from eternity.

3 The floods have lifted up, LORD,
    the floods have lifted up their voice;
    the floods lift up
        their pounding waves.

---

^a**92:10** Syr reads *You have anointed me*   ^b**93:2** Lit *from then*

⁴ Greater than the roar
   of many waters—
the mighty breakers of the sea—
the LORD on high is majestic.

⁵ LORD, Your testimonies
   are completely reliable;
holiness is the beauty
   ofᵃ Your house
for all the days to come.

PSALM 94
The Just Judge

¹ LORD, God of vengeance—
God of vengeance, appear.
² Rise up, Judge of the earth;
repay the proud what they deserve.
³ LORD, how long will the wicked—
how long will the wicked gloat?

⁴ They pour out arrogant words;
all the evildoers boast.
⁵ LORD, they crush Your people;
they afflict Your heritage.
⁶ They kill the widow
   and the foreigner
and murder the fatherless.
⁷ They say, "The LORD doesn't see it.
The God of Jacob
   doesn't pay attention."

⁸ Pay attention, you stupid people!
Fools, when will you be wise?
⁹ Can the One who shaped the ear
   not hear,
the One who formed the eye
   not see?
¹⁰ The One who instructs nations,
the One who teaches
   man knowledge—
does He not discipline?
¹¹ The LORD knows man's thoughts;
they are meaningless.ᵇ

¹² LORD, happy is the man
   You discipline

and teach from Your law
¹³ to give him relief
   from troubled times
until a pit is dug for the wicked.
¹⁴ The LORD will not forsake
   His people
or abandon His heritage,
¹⁵ for justice will again be righteous,
and all the upright in heart
   will followᶜ it.

¹⁶ Who stands up for me
   against the wicked?
Who takes a stand for me
   against evildoers?
¹⁷ If the LORD had not been my help,
I would soon rest in the silence
  ⌊of death⌋.
¹⁸ If I say, "My foot is slipping,"
Your faithful love
   will support me, LORD.
¹⁹ When I am filled with cares,
Your comfort brings me joy.

²⁰ Can a corrupt throne—
one that creates trouble by law—
become Your ally?
²¹ They band together against the life
   of the righteous
and condemn the innocent
   to death.
²² But the LORD is my refuge;
my God is the rock
   of my protection.
²³ He will pay them back for their sins
and destroy them for their evil.
The LORD our God
   will destroy them.

PSALM 95
Worship and Warning

¹ Come, let us shout joyfully
   to the LORD,
shout triumphantly to the rock
   of our salvation!

ᵃ**93:5** Or *holiness characterizes* ᵇ**94:11** Or *futile* ᶜ**94:15** Or *heart will support;* lit *heart after*

2 Let us enter His presence
   with thanksgiving;
   let us shout triumphantly to Him
   in song.

3 For the LORD is a great God,
   a great King above all gods.
4 The depths of the earth are
   in His hand,
   and the mountain peaks are His.
5 The sea is His; He made it.
   His hands formed the dry land.

6 Come, let us worship
   and bow down;
   let us kneel before the LORD
   our Maker.
7 For He is our God,
   and we are the people
   of His pasture,
   the sheep under His care.[a]

Today, if you hear His voice:
8 "Do not harden your hearts
   as at Meribah,
   as on that day at Massah
   in the wilderness
9 where your fathers tested Me;
   they tried Me, though
   they had seen what I did.
10 For 40 years I was disgusted
   with that generation;
   I said, 'They are a people
   whose hearts go astray;
   they do not know My ways.'
11 So I swore in My anger,
   'They will not enter My rest.'"

PSALM 96
King of the Earth

1 Sing a new song to the LORD;
   sing to the LORD, all the earth.
2 Sing to the LORD, praise His name;
   proclaim His salvation from day
   to day.

3 Declare His glory
   among the nations,
   His wonderful works
   among all peoples.

4 For the LORD is great and is
   highly praised;
   He is feared above all gods.
5 For all the gods of the peoples
   are idols,
   but the LORD made the heavens.
6 Splendor and majesty are
   before Him;
   strength and beauty are
   in His sanctuary.

7 Ascribe to the LORD, you families
   of the peoples,
   ascribe to the LORD glory
   and strength.
8 Ascribe to the LORD the glory
   of His name;
   bring an offering and enter
   His courts.
9 Worship the LORD in the splendor
   of ₌His₌ holiness;
   tremble before Him, all the earth.

10 Say among the nations:
   "The LORD reigns.
   The world is firmly established;
   it cannot be shaken.
   He judges the peoples fairly."
11 Let the heavens be glad
   and the earth rejoice;
   let the sea and all
   that fills it resound.
12 Let the fields and everything
   in them exult.
   Then all the trees of the forest
   will shout for joy
13 before the LORD,
   for He is coming—
   for He is coming to judge the earth.
   He will judge the world
   with righteousness

[a] 95:7 Lit sheep of His hand

and the peoples
with His faithfulness.

PSALM 97
The Majestic King

1 The LORD reigns! Let
the earth rejoice;
let the many coasts and islands
be glad.

2 Clouds and thick darkness surround
Him;
righteousness and justice are
the foundation of His throne.
3 Fire goes before Him
and burns up His foes
on every side.
4 His lightning lights up the world;
the earth sees and trembles.
5 The mountains melt like wax
at the presence of the LORD—
at the presence of the Lord of all
the earth.
6 The heavens proclaim
His righteousness;
all the peoples see His glory.

7 All who serve carved images,
those who boast in idols, will be
put to shame.
All the gods[a] must worship Him.

8 Zion hears and is glad,
and the towns[b] of Judah rejoice
because of Your judgments, LORD.
9 For You, LORD,
are the •Most High over
all the earth;
You are exalted above all the gods.

10 You who love the LORD, hate evil!
He protects the lives
of His godly ones;

He rescues them from the hand
of the wicked.
11 Light dawns[c] [d] for the righteous,
gladness for the upright in heart.
12 Be glad in the LORD,
you righteous ones,
and praise His holy name.[e]

PSALM 98
Praise the King
A psalm.

1 Sing a new song to the LORD,
for He has performed wonders;
His right hand and holy arm
have won Him victory.
2 The LORD has made His victory
known;
He has revealed His righteousness
in the sight of the nations.
3 He has remembered His love
and faithfulness to the house
of Israel;
all the ends of the earth
have seen our God's victory.

4 Shout to the LORD, all the earth;
be jubilant, shout for joy, and sing.
5 Sing to the LORD with the lyre,
with the lyre and melodious song.
6 With trumpets and the blast
of the ram's horn
shout triumphantly
in the presence of the LORD,
our King.

7 Let the sea and all that fills it,
the world and those who live in it,
resound.
8 Let the rivers clap their hands;
let the mountains shout together
for joy
9 before the LORD,
for He is coming to judge the earth.

[a]97:7 LXX, Syr read *All His angels*; Heb 1:6 [b]97:8 Lit *daughters* [c]97:11 One Hb ms, LXX, other versions read *rises to shine*; Ps 112:4 [d]97:11 Lit *Light is sown* [e]97:12 Lit *praise the mention*, or *memory, of His holiness*

He will judge the world righteously
and the peoples fairly.

PSALM 99
The King Is Holy

1 The LORD reigns! Let
  the peoples tremble.
  He is enthroned
  above the •cherubim.
  Let the earth quake.
2 The LORD is great in Zion;
  He is exalted above
  all the peoples.
3 Let them praise Your great
  and awe-inspiring name.
  He is holy.

4 The mighty King loves justice.
  You have established fairness;
  You have administered justice
  and righteousness in Jacob.
5 Exalt the LORD our God;
  bow in worship at His footstool.
  He is holy.

6 Moses and Aaron were
    among His priests;
  Samuel also was among
    those calling on His name.
  They called to the LORD,
    and He answered them.
7 He spoke to them in a pillar
    of cloud;
  they kept His decrees
    and the statutes He gave them.
8 LORD our God,
    You answered them.
  You were a God
    who forgave them,
  but punished[a] their misdeeds.[b]

9 Exalt the LORD our God;
  bow in worship
    at His holy mountain,
  for the LORD our God is holy.

PSALM 100
Be Thankful
A psalm of thanksgiving.

1 Shout triumphantly to the LORD,
  all the earth.
2 Serve the LORD with gladness;
  come before Him with joyful songs.
3 Acknowledge that the LORD is God.
  He made us, and we are His[c]—
  His people, the sheep
  of His pasture.
4 Enter His gates with thanksgiving
  and His courts with praise.
  Give thanks to Him and praise
  His name.
5 For the LORD is good, and His love
  is eternal;
  His faithfulness endures
  through all generations.

PSALM 101
A Vow of Integrity
A Davidic psalm.

1 I will sing of faithful love
  and justice;
  I will sing praise to You, LORD.
2 I will pay attention to the way
  of integrity.
  When will You come to me?
  I will live with integrity of heart
  in my house.

No Godless Eyes

3 I will not set anything godless
  before my eyes.
  I hate the doing of transgression;
  it will not cling to me.
4 A devious heart will be far
  from me;
  I will not be involved with[d] evil.
5 I will destroy anyone
  who secretly slanders his neighbor;

[a]**99:8** Lit *avenged*   [b]**99:8** Or *but avenged misdeeds done against them*   [c]**100:3** Alt Hb tradition, other Hb mss, LXX, Syr, Vg read *and not we ourselves*   [d]**101:4** Lit *not know*

I cannot tolerate anyone
with haughty eyes
  or an arrogant heart.
6 My eyes ⌊favor⌋ the faithful
  of the land
so that they may sit down with me.
The one who follows the way
  of integrity
may serve me.
7 No one who acts deceitfully
will live in my palace;
no one who tells lies
will remain in my presence.[a]
8 Every morning I will destroy
all the wicked of the land,
eliminating all evildoers
  from the LORD's city.

PSALM 102
Prayer in Affliction

A prayer of an afflicted person who is weak
and pours out his lament before the LORD.

1 LORD, hear my prayer;
let my cry for help come
  before You.
2 Do not hide Your face from me
in my day of trouble.
Listen closely to me;
answer me quickly when I call.

3 For my days vanish like smoke,
and my bones burn like a furnace.
4 My heart is afflicted,
  withered like grass;
I even forget to eat my food.
5 Because of the sound
  of my groaning,
my flesh sticks to my bones.
6 I am like a desert owl,[b]
like an owl among the ruins.
7 I stay awake;
I am like a solitary bird on a roof.
8 My enemies taunt me all day long;
they ridicule and curse me.

9 I eat ashes like bread
and mingle my drinks with tears
10 because of Your indignation
  and wrath;
for You have picked me up
  and thrown me aside.
11 My days are like
a lengthening shadow,
and I wither away like grass.

Praise Eternal God

12 But You, LORD,
  are enthroned forever;
Your fame ⌊endures⌋
  to all generations.
13 You will arise and have compassion
  on Zion,
for it is time to show favor to her—
the appointed time has come.
14 For Your servants take delight
  in its stones
and favor its dust.

15 Then the nations will fear the name
  of the LORD,
and all the kings of the earth
  Your glory,
16 for the LORD will rebuild Zion;
He will appear in His glory.
17 He will pay attention to the prayer
  of the destitute
and will not despise their prayer.

18 This will be written
  for a later generation,
and a newly created people
  will praise the LORD:
19 He looked down from
  His holy heights—
the LORD gazed out from heaven
  to earth—
20 to hear a prisoner's groaning,
to set free those condemned to die,[c]
21 so that they might declare
the name of the LORD in Zion

---

a**101:7** Lit *in front of my eyes* b**102:6** Or *a pelican of the desert* c**102:20** Lit *free sons of death*

and His praise in Jerusalem,

22 when peoples and kingdoms
are assembled
to serve the LORD.

23 He has broken my[a] strength
in midcourse;
He has shortened my days.

24 I say: "My God, do not take me
in the middle of my life![b]
Your years continue
through all generations.

25 Long ago You established the earth,
and the heavens are the work
of Your hands.

26 They will perish, but You
will endure;
all of them will wear out
like clothing.
You will change them
like a garment,
and they will pass away.

27 But You are the same,
and Your years will never end.

28 Your servants' children
will dwell ⌊securely⌋,
and their offspring will be
established before You."

PSALM 103
The Forgiving God
Davidic.

1 My soul, praise the LORD,
and all that is within me, praise
His holy name.

2 My soul, praise the LORD,
and do not forget all His benefits.

3 He forgives all your sin;
He heals all your diseases.

4 He redeems your life from the •Pit;
He crowns you with faithful love
and compassion.

5 He satisfies you[c] with goodness;

your youth is renewed
like the eagle.

6 The LORD executes acts
of righteousness
and justice for all the oppressed.

7 He revealed His ways to Moses,
His deeds to the people of Israel.

8 The LORD is compassionate
and gracious,
slow to anger and full
of faithful love.

9 He will not always accuse ⌊us⌋
or be angry forever.

10 He has not dealt with us as
our sins deserve
or repaid us according to
our offenses.

11 For as high as the heavens
are above the earth,
so great is His faithful love
toward those who fear Him.

12 As far as the east is from the west,
so far has He removed
our transgressions from us.

13 As a father has compassion
on his children,
so the LORD has compassion
on those who fear Him.

14 For He knows what we are
made of,
remembering that we are dust.

15 As for man, his days are
like grass—
he blooms like a flower of the field;

16 when the wind passes over it,
it vanishes,
and its place is no longer known.[d]

17 But from eternity to eternity
the LORD's faithful love is toward
those who fear Him,
and His righteousness
toward the grandchildren

---

[a]**102:23** Other Hb mss, LXX read *His*   [b]**102:24** Lit *my days*   [c]**103:5** Lit *satisfies your ornament*; Hb obscure
[d]**103:16** Lit *place no longer knows it*

18 of those who keep His covenant,
who remember to observe
His instructions.

19 The LORD has established
His throne in heaven,
and His kingdom rules over all.

20 Praise the LORD,
ₗallₗ His angels of great strength,
who do His word,
obedient to His command.

21 Praise the LORD, all His armies,
His servants who do His will.

22 Praise the LORD, all His works
in all the places where He rules.
My soul, praise the LORD!

PSALM 104
God the Creator

1 My soul, praise the LORD!
LORD my God, You are very great;
You are clothed with majesty
and splendor.

2 He wraps Himself in light as if
it were a robe,
spreading out the sky like a canopy,

3 laying the beams of His palace
on the waters ₗaboveₗ,
making the clouds His chariot,
walking on the wings of the wind,

4 and making the winds
His messengers,[a]
flames of fire His servants.

5 He established the earth
on its foundations;
it will never be shaken.

6 You covered it with the deep
as if it were a garment;
the waters stood
above the mountains.

7 At Your rebuke the waters fled;
at the sound of Your thunder
they hurried away—

8 mountains rose and valleys sank[b]—
to the place You established
for them.

9 You set a boundary
they cannot cross;
they will never cover
the earth again.

10 He causes the springs to gush
into the valleys;
they flow between the mountains.

11 They supply water
for every wild beast;
the wild donkeys quench
their thirst.

12 The birds of the sky live
beside ₗthe springsₗ;
they sing among the foliage.

13 He waters the mountains
from His palace;
the earth is satisfied by the fruit
of Your labor.

14 He causes grass to grow
for the livestock
and ₗprovidesₗ crops for man
to cultivate,
producing food from the earth,

15 wine that makes
man's heart glad—
making his face shine with oil—
and bread that sustains man's heart.

16 The trees of the LORD flourish,[c]
the cedars of Lebanon
that He planted.

17 There the birds make their nests;
the stork makes its home
in the pine trees.

18 The high mountains are
for the wild goats;
the cliffs are a refuge for hyraxes.

19 He made the moon to mark
the[d] seasons;
the sun knows when to set.

---

[a]**104:4** Or angels   [b]**104:7-8** Or away. They flowed over the mountains and went down valleys   [c]**104:16** Lit are satisfied   [d]**104:19** Lit moon for

20 You bring darkness,
   and it becomes night,
   when all the forest animals stir.
21 The young lions roar for their prey
   and seek their food from God.
22 The sun rises; they go back
   and lie down in their dens.
23 Man goes out to his work
   and to his labor until evening.

24 How countless are
   Your works, LORD!
   In wisdom You have made them all;
   the earth is full of Your creatures.ᵃ
25 Here is the sea, vast and wide,
   teeming with creatures
   beyond number—
   living things both large and small.
26 There the ships move about,
   and •Leviathan, which You formed
   to play there.
27 All of them wait for You
   to give them their food
   at the right time.
28 When You give it to them,
   they gather it;
   when You open Your hand,
   they are satisfied with good things.
29 When You hide Your face,
   they are terrified;
   when You take away their breath,
   they die and return to the dust.
30 When You send Your breath,ᵇ
   they are created,
   and You renew the face
   of the earth.

31 May the glory of the LORD
   endure forever;
   may the LORD rejoice in His works.
32 He looks at the earth,
   and it trembles;
   He touches the mountains,
   and they pour out smoke.
33 I will sing to the LORD all my life;

I will sing praise to my God
   while I live.
34 May my meditation be pleasing
   to Him;
   I will rejoice in the LORD.
35 May sinners vanish from the earth
   and the wicked be no more.
   My soul, praise the LORD!
   •Hallelujah!

PSALM 105
God's Faithfulness to His People

1 Give thanks to the LORD, call on
   His name;
   proclaim His deeds
   among the peoples.
2 Sing to Him, sing praise to Him;
   tell about all His wonderful works!
3 Honor His holy name;
   let the hearts of those who seek
   the LORD rejoice.
4 Search for the LORD and for
   His strength;
   seek His face always.
5 Remember the wonderful works
   He has done,
   His wonders,
   and the judgments He has pronou
   nced,ᶜ
6 you offspring of Abraham
   His servant,
   Jacob's descendants—
   His chosen ones.
7 He is the LORD our God;
   His judgments ⌊govern⌋
   the whole earth.
8 He forever remembers
   His covenant,
   the promise He ordained
   for a thousand generations—
9 ⌊the covenant⌋ He made
   with Abraham,
   sworeᵈ to Isaac,

ᵃ104:24 Lit possessions ᵇ104:30 Or Spirit ᶜ105:5 Lit judgments of His mouth ᵈ105:9 Lit and His oath

10 and confirmed to Jacob as a decree
   and to Israel
       as an everlasting covenant:
11 "I will give the land of Canaan
       to you
   as your inherited portion."

12 When they were few in number,
   very few indeed,
   and temporary residents in Canaan,
13 wandering from nation to nation
   and from one kingdom to another,
14 He allowed no one
       to oppress them;
   He rebuked kings on their behalf:
15 "Do not touch My anointed ones,
   or harm My prophets."

16 He called down famine
       against the land
   and destroyed
       the entire food supply.
17 He had sent a man ahead of them—
   Joseph, who was sold as a slave.
18 They hurt his feet with shackles;
   his neck was put in an iron collar.
19 Until the time his prediction
       came true,
   the word of the LORD tested him.
20 The king sent ˻for him˼
       and released him;
   the ruler of peoples set him free.
21 He made him master
       of his household,
   ruler over all his possessions—
22 binding[a] his officials at will
   and instructing his elders.

23 Then Israel went to Egypt;
   Jacob lived as a foreigner
       in the land of Ham.[b]
24 The LORD[c] made His people
       very fruitful;
   He made them more numerous
       than their foes,

25 whose hearts He turned to hate
       His people
   and to deal deceptively
       with His servants.
26 He sent Moses His servant,
   and Aaron, whom He had chosen.
27 They performed
       His miraculous signs
       among them,
   and wonders in the land of Ham.[b]
28 He sent darkness,
       and it became dark—
   for did they[d] not defy
       His commands?
29 He turned their waters into blood
   and caused their fish to die.
30 Their land was overrun with frogs,
   even in their kings' chambers.
31 He spoke, and insects came—
   gnats throughout their country.
32 He gave them hail for rain,
   and lightning throughout
       their land.
33 He struck their vines and fig trees
   and shattered the trees
       of their territory.
34 He spoke and locusts came—
   young locusts without number.
35 They devoured all the vegetation
       in their land
   and consumed the produce
       of their soil.
36 He struck all the firstborn
       in their land,
   all their first progeny.

37 Then He brought Israel out
       with silver and gold,
   and no one among
       His tribes stumbled.
38 Egypt was glad when they left,
   for dread of Israel[e] had fallen
       on them.
39 He spread a cloud as a covering

---

a**105:22** LXX, Syr, Vg read *teaching*   b**105:23,27** Egypt   c**105:24** Lit *He*   d**105:28** LXX, Syr read *for they did . . .* (as a statement)   e**105:38** Lit *them*

and ⌊gave⌋ a fire to light up
the night.

40 They asked, and He brought quail
and satisfied them with bread
from heaven.

41 He opened a rock, and water
gushed out;
it flowed like a stream
in the desert.

42 For He remembered
His holy promise
to Abraham His servant.

43 He brought His people out
with rejoicing,
His chosen ones with shouts of joy.

44 He gave them the lands
of the nations,
and they inherited
what other peoples had worked for.

45 ⌊All this happened⌋
so that they might keep His statutes
and obey His laws.
•Hallelujah!

PSALM 106
Israel's Unfaithfulness to God

1 •Hallelujah!
Give thanks to the LORD,
for He is good;
His faithful love endures forever.

2 Who can declare
the LORD's mighty acts
or proclaim all the praise
due Him?

3 How happy are those
who uphold justice,
who practice righteousness
at all times.

4 Remember me, LORD,
when You show favor
to Your people.
Come to me with Your salvation

5 so that I may enjoy the prosperity
of Your chosen ones,

rejoice in the joy of Your nation,
and boast about Your heritage.

6 Both we and our fathers
have sinned;
we have gone astray
and have acted wickedly.

7 Our fathers in Egypt did not grasp
⌊the significance of⌋
Your wonderful works
or remember Your many acts
of faithful love;
instead, they rebelled by the sea—
the •Red Sea.

8 Yet He saved them
because of His name,
to make His power known.

9 He rebuked the Red Sea,
and it dried up;
He led them through the depths
as through a desert.

10 He saved them from the hand
of the adversary;
He redeemed them from the hand
of the enemy.

11 Water covered their foes;
not one of them remained.

12 Then they believed His promises
and sang His praise.

13 They soon forgot His works
and would not wait for His counsel.

14 They were seized with craving
in the wilderness
and tested God in the desert.

15 He gave them what they asked for,
but sent a wasting disease
among them.

16 In the camp they were envious
of Moses
and of Aaron, the LORD's holy one.

17 The earth opened up
and swallowed Dathan;
it covered the assembly of Abiram.

18 Fire blazed throughout
their assembly;
flames consumed the wicked.

¹⁹ At Horeb they made a calf
and worshiped
the cast metal image.
²⁰ They exchanged their glory[a]
for the image of a grass-eating ox.
²¹ They forgot God their Savior,
who did great things in Egypt,
²² wonderful works in the land
of Ham,[b]
awe-inspiring deeds at the Red Sea.
²³ So He said
He would have destroyed them—
if Moses His chosen one
had not stood before Him
in the breach
to turn His wrath away
from destroying ⌊them⌋.
²⁴ They despised the pleasant land
and did not believe His promise.
²⁵ They grumbled in their tents
and did not listen
to the LORD's voice.
²⁶ So He raised His hand against them
⌊with an oath⌋
that He would make them fall
in the desert
²⁷ and would disperse
their descendants[c]
among the nations,
scattering them
throughout the lands.

²⁸ They aligned themselves with •Baal
of Peor
and ate sacrifices offered
to lifeless gods.[d]
²⁹ They provoked the LORD
with their deeds,
and a plague broke out
against them.
³⁰ But Phinehas stood up
and intervened,
and the plague was stopped.

³¹ It was credited to him
as righteousness
throughout all generations to come.

Moses' Sin

³² They angered ⌊the LORD⌋
at the waters of Meribah,
and Moses suffered[e]
because of them;
³³ for they embittered his spirit,[f]
and he spoke rashly with his lips.

Israel's Sins

³⁴ They did not destroy the peoples
as the LORD had commanded them,
³⁵ but mingled with the nations
and adopted their ways.
³⁶ They served their idols,
which became a snare to them.
³⁷ They sacrificed their sons
and daughters to demons.
³⁸ They shed innocent blood—
the blood of their sons
and daughters
whom they sacrificed to the idols
of Canaan;
so the land became polluted
with blood.
³⁹ They defiled themselves
by their actions
and prostituted themselves
by their deeds.

God's Response

⁴⁰ Therefore the LORD's anger burned
against His people,
and He abhorred
His own inheritance.
⁴¹ He handed them over
to the nations;
those who hated them ruled them.
⁴² Their enemies oppressed them,

---

[a]**106:20** = God   [b]**106:22** Egypt   [c]**106:27** Syr; MT reads *would make their descendants fall*   [d]**106:28** Lit *sacrifices for dead ones*   [e]**106:32** Lit *and it was evil for Moses*   [f]**106:33** Some Hb mss, LXX, Syr, Jer; other Hb mss read *they rebelled against His Spirit*

and they were subdued
  under their power.
43 He rescued them many times,
  but they continued
    to rebel deliberately
  and were beaten down by their sin.

44 When He heard their cry,
  He took note of their distress,
45 remembered His covenant
    with them,
  and relented according to
    the abundance
  of His faithful love.
46 He caused them to be pitied
  before all their captors.

47 Save us, LORD our God,
  and gather us from the nations,
  so that we may give thanks
    to Your holy name
  and rejoice in Your praise.

48 May the LORD, the God of Israel,
    be praised
from everlasting to everlasting.
Let all the people say, "•Amen!"
Hallelujah!

BOOK V

(PSALMS 107–150)

PSALM 107

Thanksgiving for God's Deliverance

1 Give thanks to the LORD,
  for He is good;
His faithful love endures forever.
2 Let the redeemed
  of the LORD proclaim
that He has redeemed them
  from the hand of the foe
3 and has gathered them
  from the lands—

from the east and the west,
from the north and the south.

4 Some[a] wandered
  in the desolate wilderness,
finding no way to a city
  where they could live.
5 They were hungry and thirsty;
  their spirits failed[b] within them.
6 Then they cried out to the LORD
  in their trouble;
He rescued them
  from their distress.
7 He led them by the right path
to go to a city where
  they could live.
8 Let them give thanks to the LORD
for His faithful love
and His wonderful works
  for the •human race.
9 For He has satisfied the thirsty
and filled the hungry
  with good things.

10 Others[a] sat in darkness
  and gloom[c]—
prisoners in cruel chains—
11 because they rebelled
  against God's commands
and despised the counsel
  of the •Most High.
12 He broke their spirits[d]
  with hard labor;
they stumbled, and there was
  no one to help.
13 Then they cried out to the LORD
  in their trouble;
He saved them from their distress.
14 He brought them out of darkness
  and gloom[c]
and broke their chains apart.
15 Let them give thanks to the LORD
for His faithful love
and His wonderful works
  for the human race.

---

a**107:4,10** Lit *They* b**107:5** Lit *their soul fainted* c**107:10,14** Or *the shadow of death* d**107:12** Lit *hearts*

16 For He has broken down
   the bronze gates
   and cut through the iron bars.

17 Fools suffered affliction
   because of their rebellious ways
   and their sins.
18 They loathed all food
   and came near the gates of death.
19 Then they cried out to the LORD
   in their trouble;
   He saved them from their distress.
20 He sent His word and healed them;
   He rescued them from the •Pit.
21 Let them give thanks to the LORD
   for His faithful love
   and His wonderful works
   for the human race.
22 Let them offer sacrifices
   of thanksgiving
   and announce His works
   with shouts of joy.

To Sea in Ships

23 Others[a] went to sea in ships,
   conducting trade
   on the vast waters.
24 They saw the LORD's works,
   His wonderful works in the deep.
25 He spoke and raised a tempest
   that stirred up the waves
   of the sea.[b]
26 Rising up to the sky, sinking down
   to the depths,
   their courage[c] melting away
   in anguish,
27 they reeled and staggered
   like drunken men,
   and all their skill was useless.
28 Then they cried out to the LORD
   in their trouble,
   and He brought them
   out of their distress.
29 He stilled the storm to a murmur,

and the waves of the sea[d]
were hushed.
30 They rejoiced when the waves[e]
   grew quiet.
   Then He guided them to the harbor
   they longed for.
31 Let them give thanks to the LORD
   for His faithful love
   and His wonderful works
   for the human race.
32 Let them exalt Him in the assembly
   of the people
   and praise Him in the council
   of the elders.

33 He turns rivers into desert,
   springs of water
   into thirsty ground,
34 and fruitful land
   into salty wasteland,
   because of the wickedness
   of its inhabitants.
35 He turns a desert into a pool
   of water,
   dry land into springs of water.
36 He causes the hungry
   to settle there,
   and they establish a city
   where they can live.
37 They sow fields
   and plant vineyards
   that yield a fruitful harvest.
38 He blesses them,
   and they multiply greatly;
   He does not let
   their livestock decrease.
39 When they are diminished
   and are humbled
   by cruel oppression and sorrow,
40 He pours contempt on nobles
   and makes them wander
   in trackless wastelands.
41 But He lifts the needy out of
   their suffering

---

a**107:23** Lit *They*   b**107:25** Lit *of it*   c**107:26** Lit *souls*   d**107:29** Lit *of them*   e**107:30** Lit *when they*

and makes their families ⌊multiply⌋
like flocks.
42 The upright see it and rejoice,
and all injustice shuts its mouth.

43 Let whoever is wise pay attention
to these things
and consider[a] the LORD's acts
of faithful love.

PSALM 108
A Plea for Victory

A song. A Davidic psalm.

1 My heart is confident, God;[b]
I will sing; I will sing praises
with the whole of my being.[c]
2 Wake up, harp and lyre!
I will wake up the dawn.
3 I will praise You, LORD,
among the peoples;
I will sing praises to You
among the nations.
4 For Your faithful love is higher
than the heavens;
Your faithfulness reaches
the clouds.
5 God, be exalted
above the heavens;
let Your glory be over
the whole earth.
6 Save with Your right hand
and answer me
so that those You love
may be rescued.

7 God has spoken in His sanctuary:[d]
"I will triumph!
I will divide up Shechem.
I will apportion the Valley
of Succoth.
8 Gilead is Mine, Manasseh is Mine,
and Ephraim is My helmet;
Judah is My scepter.

9 Moab is My washbasin;
on Edom I throw My sandal.
Over Philistia I shout in triumph."
10 Who will bring me
to the fortified city?
Who will lead me to Edom?
11 Have You not rejected us, God?
God, You do not march out
with our armies.
12 Give us aid against the foe,
for human help is worthless.
13 With God we will perform valiantly;
He will trample our foes.

PSALM 109
Prayer against an Enemy

For the choir director. A Davidic psalm.

1 God of my praise, do not be silent.

2 For wicked and deceitful mouths
open against me;
they speak against me
with lying tongues.
3 They surround me
with hateful words
and attack me without cause.
4 In return for my love
they accuse me,
but I continue to pray.[e]
5 They repay me evil for good,
and hatred for my love.

6 Set a wicked person over him;
let an accuser[f] stand
at his right hand.
7 When he is judged, let him
be found guilty,
and let his prayer be counted as sin.
8 Let his days be few;
let another take over his position.
9 Let his children be fatherless
and his wife a widow.

---

[a]**107:43** Lit *and let them consider*   [b]**108:1** Some Hb mss, LXX, Syr add *my heart is confident*; Ps 57:7   [c]**108:1** Lit *praises, even my glory*   [d]**108:7** Or *has promised by His holy nature*   [e]**109:4** Lit *but I, prayer*   [f]**109:6** Or *adversary*

10 Let his children wander as beggars,
   searching ⌊for food⌋ far[a]
     from their demolished homes.
11 Let a creditor seize all he has;
   let strangers plunder what he has
     worked for.
12 Let no one show him kindness,
   and let no one be gracious
     to his fatherless children.
13 Let the line of his descendants
     be cut off;
   let their name be blotted out
     in the next generation.
14 Let his forefathers' guilt
   be remembered before the LORD,
   and do not let his mother's sin
     be blotted out.
15 Let their sins[b] always remain
     before the LORD,
   and let Him cut off ⌊all⌋ memory
     of them from the earth.

16 For he did not think to show kindness,
   but pursued the wretched poor
     and the brokenhearted
   in order to put them to death.
17 He loved cursing—let it fall on him;
   he took no delight in blessing—
     let it be far from him.
18 He wore cursing like his coat—
   let it enter his body like water
   and go into his bones like oil.
19 Let it be like a robe he wraps
     around himself,
   like a belt he always wears.
20 Let this be the LORD's payment
     to my accusers,
   to those who speak evil against me.

Prayer for Deliverance

21 But You, GOD my Lord,
   deal ⌊kindly⌋ with me
     because of Your name;
   deliver me because of the goodness
   of Your faithful love.

Physical and Emotional Pain

22 For I am poor and needy;
   my heart is wounded within me.
23 I fade away
     like a lengthening shadow;
   I am shaken off like a locust.
24 My knees are weak from fasting,
   and my body is emaciated.[c]
25 I have become an object of ridicule
     to my accusers;[d]
   when they see me, they shake
     their heads ⌊in scorn⌋.

26 Help me, LORD my God;
   save me according to
     Your faithful love
27 so they may know that this is
     Your hand
   and that You, LORD, have done it.
28 Though they curse, You will bless.
   When they rise up, they will be
     put to shame,
   but Your servant will rejoice.
29 My accusers will be clothed
     with disgrace;
   they will wear their shame
     like a cloak.

Thanks and Praise

30 I will fervently thank the LORD
     with my mouth;
   I will praise Him in the presence
     of many.
31 For He stands at the right hand
     of the needy,
   to save him
     from those who would condemn
     him.

PSALM 110
Priestly King
A Davidic psalm.

1 The LORD declared to my Lord:
   "Sit at My right hand

---

[a]**109:10** LXX reads *beggars, driven far*   [b]**109:15** Lit *Let them*   [c]**109:24** Lit *denied from fat*   [d]**109:25** Lit *to them*

until I make Your enemies
   Your footstool.”
2 The LORD will extend
   Your mighty scepter from Zion.
   Rule^a over
   Your surrounding^b enemies.
3 Your people will volunteer
   on Your day of battle.^c
   In holy splendor, from the womb
      of the dawn,
   the dew
      of Your youth belongs to You.^d
4 The LORD has sworn an oath
   and will not take it back:
   “Forever, You are a priest
   like Melchizedek.”

5 The Lord is at Your right hand;
   He will crush kings on the day
   of His anger.
6 He will judge the nations,
   heaping up corpses;
   He will crush leaders
   over the entire world.
7 He will drink from the brook
   by the road;
   therefore, He will lift up His head.

PSALM 111
Praise for the LORD's Works

1 •Hallelujah!^e
   I will praise the LORD with all
      my heart
   in the assembly of the upright
      and in the congregation.
2 The LORD's works are great,
   studied by all who delight in them.
3 All that He does is splendid
      and majestic;
   His righteousness endures forever.
4 He has caused His wonderful works
      to be remembered.

The LORD is gracious
   and compassionate.
5 He has provided food for those
   who fear Him;
   He remembers
   His covenant forever.
6 He has shown His people
   the power of His works
   by giving them the inheritance
   of the nations.
7 The works of His hands are truth
   and justice;
   all His instructions are trustworthy.
8 They are established forever
   and ever,
   enacted in truth and uprightness.
9 He has sent redemption
   to His people.
   He has ordained
   His covenant forever.
   His name is holy and awe-inspiring.
10 The •fear of the LORD is
   the beginning of wisdom;
   all who follow His instructions^f
   have good insight.
   His praise endures forever.

PSALM 112
Traits of the Righteous

1 •Hallelujah!^g
   Happy is the man who •fears
      the LORD,
   taking great delight
   in His commandments.

2 His descendants will be powerful
   in the land;
   the generation of the upright
   will be blessed.
3 Wealth and riches are in his house,
   and his righteousness
      endures forever.

---

^a**110:2** One Hb ms, LXX, Tg read *You will rule*   ^b**110:2** Lit *Rule in the midst of Your*   ^c**110:3** Lit *power*
^d**110:3** Hb obscure   ^e**111:1** The lines of this poem form an •acrostic.   ^f**111:10** Lit *follow them*   ^g**112:1** The lines of
this poem form an •acrostic.

4 Light shines in the darkness
    for the upright.
  He is gracious, compassionate,
    and righteous.
5 Good will come to a man
    who lends generously
  and conducts his business fairly.
6 He will never be shaken.
  The righteous will be
    remembered forever.
7 He will not fear bad news;
  his heart is confident,
    trusting in the LORD.
8 His heart is assured; he will not fear.
  In the end he will look in triumph
    on his foes.
9 He distributes freely to the poor;
  his righteousness endures forever.
  His •horn will be exalted in honor.

10 The wicked man will see ⌊it⌋
    and be angry;
  he will gnash his teeth in despair.
  The desire of the wicked will come
    to nothing.

PSALM 113
Praise to Merciful God

1 •Hallelujah!
  Give praise, servants of the LORD;
  praise the name of the LORD.
2 Let the name of the LORD
    be praised
  both now and forever.
3 From the rising of the sun
    to its setting,
  let the name of the LORD
    be praised.

4 The LORD is exalted above
    all the nations,
  His glory above the heavens.
5 Who is like the LORD our God—
  the One enthroned on high,
6 who stoops down to look
  on the heavens and the earth?

7 He raises the poor from the dust
  and lifts the needy
    from the garbage pile
8 in order to seat them
    with nobles—
  with the nobles of His people.
9 He gives the childless woman
    a household,
  ⌊making her⌋ the joyful mother
    of children.
  Hallelujah!

PSALM 114
God's Deliverance of Israel

1 When Israel came out of Egypt—
  the house of Jacob from a people
  who spoke a foreign language—
2 Judah became His sanctuary,
  Israel, His dominion.

3 The sea looked and fled;
  the Jordan turned back.
4 The mountains skipped like rams,
  the hills, like lambs.
5 Why was it, sea, that you fled?
  Jordan, that you turned back?
6 Mountains, that you skipped
    like rams?
  Hills, like lambs?

7 Tremble, earth, at the presence
    of the Lord,
  at the presence of the God of Jacob,
8 who turned the rock into a pool
    of water,
  the flint into a spring of water.

PSALM 115
Glory to God Alone

1 Not to us, LORD, not to us,
  but to Your name give glory
  because of Your faithful love,
    because of Your truth.
2 Why should the nations say,
  "Where is their God?"

3 Our God is in heaven
and does whatever He pleases.

4 Their idols are silver and gold,
made by human hands.
5 They have mouths,
but cannot speak,
eyes, but cannot see.
6 They have ears, but cannot hear,
noses, but cannot smell.
7 They have hands, but cannot feel,
feet, but cannot walk.
They cannot make a sound
with their throats.
8 Those who make them are[a] just
like them,
as are all who trust in them.

9 Israel,[b] trust in the LORD!
He is their help and shield.
10 House of Aaron, trust in the LORD!
He is their help and shield.
11 You who •fear the LORD,
trust in the LORD!
He is their help and shield.
12 The LORD remembers us
and will bless ⌊us⌋.
He will bless the house of Israel;
He will bless the house of Aaron;
13 He will bless those who fear
the LORD—
small and great alike.
14 May the LORD add to
⌊your numbers⌋,
both yours and your children's.
15 May you be blessed by the LORD,
the Maker of heaven and earth.
16 The heavens are the LORD's,[c]
but the earth He has given
to the •human race.
17 It is not the dead who praise
the LORD,
nor any of those descending
into the silence ⌊of death⌋.

18 But we will praise the LORD,
both now and forever.
•Hallelujah!

PSALM 116
Thanks to God for Deliverance

1 I love the LORD
because He has heard
my appeal for mercy.
2 Because He has turned His ear
to me,
I will call ⌊out to Him⌋ as long as
I live.

3 The ropes of death were wrapped
around me,
and the torments of •Sheol
overcame me;
I encountered trouble and sorrow.
4 Then I called on the name
of the LORD:
"LORD, save me!"

5 The LORD is gracious and righteous;
our God is compassionate.

Lord Guards Inexperienced

6 The LORD guards the inexperienced;
I was helpless, and He saved me.
7 Return to your rest, my soul,
for the LORD has been good to you.
8 For You, ⌊LORD,⌋ rescued me
from death,
my eyes from tears,
my feet from stumbling.
9 I will walk before the LORD
in the land of the living.
10 I believed, even when I said,
"I am severely afflicted."
11 In my alarm I said,
"Everyone is a liar."

12 How can I repay the LORD
all the good He has done for me?

---

a**115:8** Or *May those who make them become*   b**115:9** Other Hb mss, LXX, Syr read *House of Israel*   c**115:16** Lit
LORD's heavens

13 I will take the cup of salvation
   and worship[a] the LORD.
14 I will fulfill my vows to the LORD
   in the presence of all His people.

15 The death of His faithful ones
   is valuable in the LORD's sight.
16 LORD, I am indeed Your servant;
   I am Your servant, the son
     of Your female servant.
   You have loosened my bonds.

17 I will offer You a sacrifice
     of thanksgiving
   and will worship[a] the LORD.
18 I will fulfill my vows to the LORD,
   in the very presence of all
     His people,
19 in the courts
     of the LORD's house—
   within you, Jerusalem.
   •Hallelujah!

PSALM 117
Universal Call to Praise

1 Praise the LORD, all nations!
  Glorify Him, all peoples!
2 For great is His faithful love to us;
  the LORD's faithfulness
    endures forever.
  •Hallelujah!

PSALM 118
Thanksgiving for Victory

1 Give thanks to the LORD,
    for He is good;
  His faithful love endures forever.
2 Let Israel say,
  "His faithful love endures forever."
3 Let the house of Aaron say,
  "His faithful love endures forever."
4 Let those who fear the LORD say,
  "His faithful love endures forever."

5 I called to the LORD in distress;
  the LORD answered me
  ⌊and put me⌋ in a spacious place.[b]
6 The LORD is for me;
    I will not be afraid.
  What can man do to me?
7 With the LORD for me as my helper,
  I will look in triumph on those
    who hate me.

Bible's Middle Verse: Psalm 118:8

8 It is better to take refuge
    in the LORD
  than to trust in man.
9 It is better to take refuge
    in the LORD
  than to trust in nobles.

10 All the nations surrounded me;
   in the name of the LORD
     I destroyed them.
11 They surrounded me, yes,
     they surrounded me;
   in the name of the LORD
     I destroyed them.
12 They surrounded me like bees;
   they were extinguished like a fire
     among thorns;
   in the name of the LORD
     I destroyed them.
13 You[c] pushed me[d] hard
     to make me fall,
   but the LORD helped me.
14 The LORD is my strength
     and my song;
   He has become my salvation.

15 There are shouts of joy and victory
   in the tents of the righteous:
   "The LORD's right hand strikes
     with power!
16 The LORD's right hand is raised!
   The LORD's right hand strikes
     with power!"

---

a 116:13,17 Or proclaim or invoke the name of; lit call on the name of   b 118:5 Or answered me with freedom
c 118:13 Perhaps the enemy   d 118:13 LXX, Syr, Jer read I was pushed

¹⁷ I will not die, but I will live
and proclaim what the LORD
has done.
¹⁸ The LORD disciplined me severely
but did not give me over to death.
¹⁹ Open the gates of righteousness
for me;
I will enter through them
and give thanks to the LORD.
²⁰ This is the gate of the LORD;
the righteous will enter
through it.
²¹ I will give thanks to You
because You have answered me
and have become my salvation.

Rejected Stone: Cornerstone

²² The stone that
the builders rejected
has become the cornerstone.
²³ This came from the LORD;
it is wonderful in our eyes.

Day the Lord Has Made

²⁴ This is the day the LORD has made;
let us rejoice and be glad in it.

²⁵ LORD, save us!
LORD, please grant us success!
²⁶ Blessed is he who comes
in the name of the LORD.
From the house of the LORD
we bless you.
²⁷ The LORD is God and has given us
light.
Bind the festival sacrifice
with cords
to the horns of the altar.
²⁸ You are my God, and I will give
You thanks.
⟨You are⟩ my God; I will exalt You.
²⁹ Give thanks to the LORD,
for He is good;
His faithful love endures forever.

PSALM 119
Delight in God's Word

א *Alef*

¹ How^a happy are those whose way
is blameless,
who live according to the law
of the LORD!
² Happy are those who keep
His decrees
and seek Him with all their heart.
³ They do nothing wrong;
they follow His ways.
⁴ You have commanded
that Your precepts
be diligently kept.
⁵ If only my ways were committed
to keeping Your statutes!
⁶ Then I would not be ashamed
when I think about
all Your commands.
⁷ I will praise You
with a sincere heart
when I learn
Your righteous judgments.
⁸ I will keep Your statutes;
never abandon me.

ב *Bet*

Bible Memory

⁹ How can a young man keep his way
pure?
By keeping Your^b word.
¹⁰ I have sought You with all my heart;
don't let me wander
from Your commands.
¹¹ I have treasured Your word
in my heart
so that I may not sin against You.
¹² LORD, may You be praised;
teach me Your statutes.
¹³ With my lips I proclaim
all the judgments from Your mouth.

---

^a**119:1** The stanzas of this poem form an •acrostic.   ^b**119:9** Or *keeping it according to Your*

14 I rejoice in the way ⌊revealed by⌋
   Your decrees
   as much as in all riches.

Guidelines on Meditation

15 I will meditate on Your precepts
   and think about Your ways.
16 I will delight in Your statutes;
   I will not forget Your word.

ג Gimel

17 Deal generously with Your servant
   so that I might live;
   then I will keep Your word.
18 Open my eyes so that I may see
   wonderful things in Your law.
19 I am a stranger on earth;
   do not hide Your commands
      from me.
20 I am continually overcome
   by longing for Your judgments.
21 You rebuke the proud, the accursed,
   who wander from Your commands.
22 Take insult and contempt away
      from me,
   for I have kept Your decrees.
23 Though princes sit together
      speaking against me,
   Your servant will think
      about Your statutes;
24 Your decrees are my delight
   and my counselors.

ד Dalet

25 My life is down in the dust;
   give me life through Your word.
26 I told You about my life,
   and You listened to me;
   teach me Your statutes.
27 Help me understand
   the meaning of Your precepts
   so that I can meditate on
      Your wonders.

28 I am weary[a] from grief;
   strengthen me through Your word.
29 Keep me from the way of deceit,
   and graciously give me
      Your instruction.
30 I have chosen the way of truth;
   I have set Your ordinances
      ⌊before me⌋.
31 I cling to Your decrees;
   LORD, do not put me to shame.
32 I pursue the way of Your commands,
   for You broaden
      my understanding.[b]

ה He

33 Teach me, LORD, the meaning
   of Your statutes,
   and I will always keep them.[c]
34 Help me understand
   Your instruction,
   and I will obey it
   and follow it with all my heart.
35 Help me stay on the path
   of Your commands,
   for I take pleasure in it.
36 Turn my heart to Your decrees
   and not to material gain.
37 Turn my eyes
   from looking at what is worthless;
   give me life in Your ways.[d]
38 Confirm what You said
      to Your servant,
   for it produces reverence for You.
39 Turn away the disgrace I dread;
   indeed, Your judgments are good.
40 How I long for Your precepts!
   Give me life through
      Your righteousness.

ו Vav

41 Let Your faithful love
      come to me, LORD,
   Your salvation, as You promised.

---

[a] 119:28 Or My soul weeps [b] 119:32 Lit You enlarge my heart [c] 119:33 Or will keep it as my reward [d] 119:37 Other Hb mss, Tg read word

42 Then I can answer the one
      who taunts me,
   for I trust in Your word.
43 Never take the word of truth
      from my mouth,
   for I hope in Your judgments.
44 I will always keep Your law,
   forever and ever.
45 I will walk freely in an open place
   because I seek Your precepts.
46 I will speak of Your decrees
      before kings
   and not be ashamed.
47 I delight in Your commands,
   which I love.
48 I will lift up my hands
      to Your commands,
   which I love,
   and will meditate on Your statutes.

ז Zayin

49 Remember ⸤Your⸥ word
      to Your servant;
   You have given me hope through it.
50 This is my comfort in my affliction:
   Your promise has given me life.
51 The arrogant constantly
      ridicule me,
   but I do not turn away
      from Your instruction.
52 LORD, I remember Your judgments
      from long ago
   and find comfort.
53 Rage seizes me because of
      the wicked
   who reject Your instruction.
54 Your statutes are ⸤the theme of⸥
      my song
   during my earthly life.[a]

Lord's Name in Night

55 I remember Your name
      in the night, LORD,
   and I keep Your law.

Obedience to God's Precepts

56 This is my ⸤practice⸥:
   I obey Your precepts.

ח Khet

57 The LORD is my portion;[b]
   I have promised to keep
      Your words.
58 I have sought Your favor with all
      my heart;
   be gracious to me according to
      Your promise.
59 I thought about my ways
   and turned my steps back
      to Your decrees.
60 I hurried, not hesitating
   to keep Your commands.
61 Though the ropes of the wicked
   were wrapped around me,
   I did not forget Your law.

Thanks at Midnight

62 I rise at midnight to thank You
   for Your righteous judgments.
63 I am a friend to all who •fear You,
   to those who keep Your precepts.
64 LORD, the earth is filled with
      Your faithful love;
   teach me Your statutes.

ט Tet

65 LORD, You have treated
      Your servant well,
   just as You promised.
66 Teach me good judgment
      and discernment,
   for I rely on Your commands.
67 Before I was afflicted
      I went astray,
   but now I keep Your word.
68 You are good, and You do
      what is good;
   teach me Your statutes.

---

[a]119:54 Lit song in the house of my sojourning [b]119:57 Lit You are my portion, LORD

69 The arrogant have smeared me
     with lies,
   but I obey Your precepts with all
     my heart.
70 Their hearts are hard
     and insensitive,
   but I delight in Your instruction.
71 It was good for me to be afflicted
   so that I could learn Your statutes.
72 Instruction from Your lips is better
     for me
   than thousands of gold
     and silver pieces.

* י Yod*

73 Your hands made me
     and formed me;
   give me understanding
   so that I can learn Your commands.
74 Those who fear You will see me
     and rejoice,
   for I put my hope in Your word.
75 I know, LORD, that Your judgments
     are just
   and that You have afflicted me fairly.
76 May Your faithful love comfort me,
   as You promised Your servant.
77 May Your compassion come to me
   so that I may live,
   for Your instruction is my delight.

Meditate on Precepts

78 Let the arrogant be put to shame
   for slandering me with lies;
   I will meditate on Your precepts.
79 Let those who fear You,
   those who know Your decrees,
     turn to me.
80 May my heart be blameless
     regarding Your statutes
   so that I will not be put to shame.

כ Kaf

81 I long for Your salvation;
   I put my hope in Your word.

82 My eyes grow weary
     ⌊looking⌋ for what
       You have promised;
   I ask, "When will You comfort me?"
83 Though I have become
     like a wineskin ⌊dried⌋ by smoke,
   I do not forget Your statutes.
84 How many days ⌊must⌋
     Your servant ⌊wait⌋?
   When will You execute judgment
     on my persecutors?
85 The arrogant have dug pits for me;
   they violate Your instruction.
86 All Your commands are true;
   people persecute me with lies—
     help me!
87 They almost ended my life
     on earth,
   but I did not abandon
     Your precepts.
88 Give me life in accordance with
     Your faithful love,
   and I will obey the decree
     You have spoken.

ל Lamed

Lord's Word Forever

89 LORD, Your word is forever;
   it is firmly fixed in heaven.
90 Your faithfulness is
     for all generations;
   You established the earth,
     and it stands firm.
91 They stand today
     in accordance with
       Your judgments,
   for all things are Your servants.
92 If Your instruction had not been
     my delight,
   I would have died in my affliction.
93 I will never forget Your precepts,
   for You have given me life
     through them.
94 I am Yours; save me,
   for I have sought Your precepts.

Contemplate God's Decrees

95 The wicked hope to destroy me,
    but I contemplate Your decrees.
96 I have seen a limit to all perfection,
    but Your command is without limit.

ב *Mem*

Meditate on God's Teaching

97 How I love Your teaching!
    It is my meditation all day long.
98 Your command makes me wiser
        than my enemies,
    for it is always with me.
99 I have more insight than
        all my teachers
    because Your decrees are
        my meditation.
100 I understand more than the elders
    because I obey Your precepts.
101 I have kept my feet
        from every evil path
    to follow Your word.
102 I have not turned from
        Your judgments,
    for You Yourself have
        instructed me.

God's Sweet-tasting Words

103 How sweet Your word is
        to my taste—
    ⌊sweeter⌋ than honey to my mouth.
104 I gain understanding
        from Your precepts;
    therefore I hate every false way.

נ *Nun*

God's Word: Lamp and Light

105 Your word is a lamp for my feet
    and a light on my path.
106 I have solemnly sworn
        to keep Your righteous judgments.
107 I am severely afflicted;

LORD, give me life
    through Your word.
108 LORD, please accept
        my willing offerings of praise,
    and teach me Your judgments.
109 My life is constantly in danger,[a]
    yet I do not forget Your instruction.
110 The wicked have set a trap for me,
    but I have not wandered
        from Your precepts.
111 I have Your decrees
        as a heritage forever;
    indeed, they are the joy of my heart.
112 I am resolved to obey Your statutes
    to the very end.[b]

ס *Samek*

113 I hate the double-minded,
    but I love Your instruction.
114 You are my shelter and my shield;
    I put my hope in Your word.
115 Depart from me, you evil ones,
    so that I may obey
        my God's commands.
116 Sustain me as You promised,
        and I will live;
    do not let me be ashamed
        of my hope.
117 Sustain me so that I can be safe
    and be concerned with
        Your statutes continually.
118 You reject all who stray
        from Your statutes,
    for their deceit is a lie.
119 You remove all the wicked on earth
    as if they were[c] dross;
    therefore, I love Your decrees.
120 I tremble[d] in awe of You;
    I fear Your judgments.

ע *Ayin*

121 I have done what is just and right;
    do not leave me to my oppressors.

---

[a] **119:109** Lit *in my hand*   [b] **119:112** Or *statutes; the reward is eternal*   [c] **119:119** Other Hb mss, DSS, LXX, Aq, Sym, Jer read *All the wicked of the earth You count as*   [d] **119:120** Lit *My flesh shudders*

122 Guarantee Your servant's well-
    being;
  do not let the arrogant oppress me.
123 My eyes grow weary ⌊looking for⌋
    Your salvation
  and for Your righteous promise.
124 Deal with Your servant based on
    Your faithful love;
  teach me Your statutes.
125 I am Your servant;
    give me understanding
  so that I may know Your decrees.
126 It is time for the LORD to act,
  ⌊for⌋ they have broken Your law.
127 Since I love Your commandments
  more than gold,
    even the purest gold,
128 I carefully follow[a] all Your precepts
  and hate every false way.

פ Pe

129 Your decrees are wonderful;
  therefore I obey them.
130 The revelation of Your words
    brings light
  and gives understanding
    to the inexperienced.
131 I pant with open mouth
  because I long
    for Your commands.
132 Turn to me and be gracious to me,
  as is ⌊Your⌋ practice toward those
    who love Your name.
133 Make my steps steady
    through Your promise;
  don't let sin dominate me.
134 Redeem me
    from human oppression,
  and I will keep Your precepts.
135 Show favor to Your servant,
  and teach me Your statutes.
136 My eyes pour out streams of tears
  because people do not follow
    Your instruction.

צ Tsade

137 You are righteous, LORD,
  and Your judgments are just.
138 The decrees You issue are righteous
  and altogether trustworthy.
139 My anger overwhelms me
  because my foes forget Your words.

God's Word is Pure

140 Your word is completely pure,
  and Your servant loves it.
141 I am insignificant and despised,
  but I do not forget Your precepts.
142 Your righteousness is
    an everlasting righteousness,
  and Your instruction is true.
143 Trouble and distress
    have overtaken me,
  but Your commands are my delight.
144 Your decrees are righteous forever.
  Give me understanding,
    and I will live.

ק Qof

145 I call with all my heart;
    answer me, LORD.
  I will obey Your statutes.
146 I call to You; save me,
  and I will keep Your decrees.

Prayer and Meditation at Night

147 I rise before dawn and cry out
    for help;
  I put my hope in Your word.
148 I am awake through each watch
    of the night
  to meditate on Your promise.
149 In keeping with Your faithful love,
    hear my voice.
  LORD, give me life, in keeping with
    Your justice.
150 Those who pursue evil plans[b]
    come near;
  they are far from Your instruction.

[a]**119:128** Lit *I therefore follow carefully*   [b]**119:150** Some Hb mss, LXX, Sym, Jer read *who maliciously persecute me*

151 You are near, LORD,
and all Your commands are true.
152 Long ago I learned from Your decrees
that You have established
them forever.

ר Resh

153 Consider my affliction
and rescue me,
for I have not forgotten
Your instruction.
154 Defend my cause, and redeem me;
give me life, as You promised.
155 Salvation is far from the wicked
because they do not seek
Your statutes.
156 Your compassions are many, LORD;
give me life, according to
Your judgments.
157 My persecutors and foes are many.
I have not turned
from Your decrees.
158 I have seen the disloyal
and feel disgust
because they do not keep Your word.
159 Consider how I love Your precepts;
LORD, give me life, according to
Your faithful love.
160 The entirety of Your word is truth,
and all Your righteous judgments
endure forever.

ש Sin/ ש Shin

161 Princes have persecuted me
without cause,
but my heart fears ⌊only⌋
Your word.
162 I rejoice over Your promise
like one who finds vast treasure.
163 I hate and abhor falsehood,
⌊but⌋ I love Your instruction.

Praise Seven Times a Day

164 I praise You seven times a day
for Your righteous judgments.

165 Abundant peace belongs to those
who love Your instruction;
nothing makes them stumble.
166 LORD, I hope for Your salvation
and carry out Your commands.
167 I obey Your decrees
and love them greatly.
168 I obey Your precepts and decrees,
for all my ways are before You.

ת Tav

God Teaches

169 Let my cry reach You, LORD;
give me understanding according to
Your word.
170 Let my plea reach You;
rescue me according to
Your promise.
171 My lips pour out praise,
for You teach me Your statutes.
172 My tongue sings
about Your promise,
for all Your commandments
are righteous.
173 May Your hand be ready
to help me,
for I have chosen Your precepts.
174 I long for Your salvation, LORD,
and Your instruction is
my delight.
175 Let me live, and I will praise You;
may Your judgments help me.
176 I wander like a lost sheep;
seek Your servant,
for I do not forget
Your commands.

PSALM 120
Cry for Truth and Peace

A •song of ascents.

1 In my distress I called to the LORD,
and He answered me:
2 "LORD, deliver me from lying lips
and a deceitful tongue."

3 What will He give you,
  and what will He do to you,
  you deceitful tongue?
4 A warrior's sharp arrows,
  with burning charcoal!ᵃ

5 What misery that I have stayed
    in Meshech,
  that I have lived among the tents
    of Kedar!ᵇ
6 I have lived too long
  with those who hate peace.
7 I am for peace; but when I speak,
  they are for war.

PSALM 121
The LORD Our Protector

A •song of ascents.

"Raise My Eyes"

1 I raise my eyes
    toward the mountains.
  Where will my help come from?
2 My help comes from the LORD,
  the Maker of heaven and earth.

3 He will not allow your foot
    to slip;
  your Protector will not
    slumber.
4 Indeed, the Protector of Israel
  does not slumber or sleep.

5 The LORD protects you;
  the LORD is a shelter right
    by your side.ᶜ
6 The sun will not strike you
    by day,
  or the moon by night.

7 The LORD will protect you
    from all harm;
  He will protect your life.
8 The LORD will protect your coming
    and going
  both now and forever.

PSALM 122
A Prayer for Jerusalem

A Davidic •song of ascents.

House of the Lord

1 I rejoiced with those who said
    to me,
  "Let us go to the house of the LORD."
2 Our feet are standing
  within your gates, Jerusalem—

3 Jerusalem, built as a city
    ⌊should be⌋,
  solidly joined together,
4 where the tribes, the tribes
    of the LORD, go up
  to give thanks to the name
    of the LORD.
  (This is an ordinance for Israel.)
5 There, thrones for judgment
    are placed,
  thrones of the house of David.

Pray for Peace of Jerusalem

6 Pray for the peace of Jerusalem:
  "May those who love
    you prosper;
7 may there be peace
    within your walls,
  prosperity within your fortresses."
8 Because of my brothers and friends,
  I will say, "Peace be with you."
9 Because of the house of the LORD
    our God,
  I will seek your good.

PSALM 123
Looking for God's Favor

A •song of ascents.

1 I lift my eyes to You,
  the One enthroned in heaven.
2 Like a servant's eyes
    on His master's hand,

ᵃ**120:4** Lit *with coals of the broom bush*   ᵇ**120:5** *Meshech*: a people far to the north of Palestine; *Kedar*: a nomadic people of the desert to the southeast   ᶜ**121:5** Lit *is your shelter at your right hand*

like a servant girl's eyes
  on her mistress's hand,
so our eyes are on the LORD
  our God
until He shows us favor.

3 Show us favor, LORD, show us
    favor,
  for we've had more than enough
    contempt.
4 We've had more than enough
    scorn from the arrogant
  ⌊and⌋ contempt from the proud.

PSALM 124
LORD Is on Our Side

A Davidic •song of ascents.

1 If the LORD had not been
    on our side—
  let Israel say—
2 If the LORD had not been
    on our side
  when men attacked us,
3 then they would have
    swallowed us alive
  in their burning anger
    against us.
4 Then the waters would have
    engulfed us;
  the torrent would have swept
    over us;
5 the raging waters would have swept
    over us.

6 Praise the LORD,
  who has not let us be ripped apart
    by their teeth.
7 We have escaped like a bird
    from the hunter's net;
  the net is torn,
    and we have escaped.
8 Our help is in the name
    of the LORD,
  the Maker of heaven and earth.

PSALM 125
Israel's Stability

A •song of ascents.

1 Those who trust in the LORD are
    like Mount Zion.
  It cannot be shaken;
    it remains forever.
2 Jerusalem—the mountains
    surround her.
  And the LORD surrounds
    His people,
  both now and forever.

3 The scepter of the wicked
    will not remain
  over the land allotted
    to the righteous,
  so that the righteous will not apply
    their hands to injustice.
4 Do what is good, LORD, to the good,
  to those whose hearts are upright.
5 But as for those who turn aside
    to crooked ways,
  the LORD will banish them
    with the evildoers.

Peace be with Israel.

PSALM 126
Zion's Restoration

A •song of ascents.

1 When the LORD restored
    the fortunes of Zion,ᵃ
  we were like those who dream.
2 Our mouths were filled
    with laughter then,
  and our tongues with shouts of joy.
  Then they said among the nations,
  "The LORD has done great things
    for them."
3 The LORD had done great things
    for us;
  we were joyful.

ᵃ**126:1** Or *LORD returned those of Zion who had been captives*

4 Restore our fortunes,[a] LORD,
like watercourses in the •Negev.[b]

Sow in Tears, Reap with Joy

5 Those who sow in tears
will reap with shouts of joy.
6 Though one goes along weeping,
carrying the bag of seed,
he will surely come back
with shouts of joy,
carrying his sheaves.

PSALM 127
The Blessing of the LORD

A Solomonic •song of ascents.

Lord Builds House

1 Unless the LORD builds a house,
its builders labor over it in vain;
unless the LORD watches over
a city,
the watchman stays alert in vain.

God Gives Sleep

2 In vain you get up early
and stay up late,
eating food earned by hard work;
certainly He gives sleep to the one
He loves.[c]

Sons a Heritage

3 Sons are indeed a heritage
from the LORD,
children, a reward.
4 Like arrows in the hand of a warrior
are the sons born in one's youth.
5 Happy is the man who has filled
his quiver with them.
Such men will never be put
to shame
when they speak
with ⌊their⌋ enemies
at the city •gate.

PSALM 128
Blessings for Those
Who Fear God

A •song of ascents.

1 How happy is everyone who •fears
the LORD,
who walks in His ways!
2 You will surely eat
what your hands have worked for.
You will be happy,
and it will go well for you.
3 Your wife will be like a fruitful vine
within your house,
your sons, like young olive trees
around your table.
4 In this very way
the man who fears the LORD
will be blessed.

5 May the LORD bless you from Zion,
so that you will see the prosperity
of Jerusalem
all the days of your life,
6 and will see your children's
children!

Peace be with Israel.

PSALM 129
Protection of Oppressed

A •song of ascents.

1 Since my youth they have often
attacked me—
let Israel say—
2 Since my youth they have often
attacked me,
but they have not prevailed
against me.
3 Plowmen plowed over my back;
they made their furrows long.
4 The LORD is righteous;
He has cut the ropes
of the wicked.

---

[a]126:4 Or Return our captives   [b]126:4 Seasonal streams in the arid south country   [c]127:2 Or work; He gives such things to His loved ones while [they] sleep

5 Let all who hate Zion
   be driven back in disgrace.
6 Let them be like grass
      on the rooftops,
   which withers before it grows up[a]
7 and can't even fill the hands
      of the reaper
   or the arms of the one
      who binds sheaves.
8 Then none who pass by will say,
   "May the LORD's blessing be
      on you."

We bless you in the name
   of the LORD.

PSALM 130
Calling to Lord
A •song of ascents.

1 Out of the depths I call
   to You, LORD!
2 Lord, listen to my voice;
   let Your ears be attentive
   to my cry for help.

3 LORD, if You considered sins,
   Lord, who could stand?
4 But with You there is forgiveness,
   so that You may be revered.

Wait for Lord

5 I wait for the LORD; I wait,
   and put my hope in His word.
6 I ⌊wait⌋ for the Lord
   more than watchmen
      for the morning—
   more than watchmen
      for the morning.

7 Israel, put your hope in the LORD.
   For there is faithful love
      with the LORD,
   and with Him is redemption
      in abundance.

8 And He will redeem Israel
   from all its sins.

PSALM 131
Childlike Spirit
A Davidic •song of ascents.

1 LORD, my heart is not proud;
   my eyes are not haughty.
   I do not get involved with things
   too great or too difficult for me.
2 Instead, I have calmed
      and quieted myself
   like a little weaned child
      with its mother;
   I am like a little child.

3 Israel, put your hope in the LORD,
   both now and forever.

PSALM 132
David and Zion Chosen
A •song of ascents.

1 LORD, remember David
   and all the hardships he endured,
2 and how he swore an oath
      to the LORD,
   making a vow to the Mighty One
      of Jacob:
3 "I will not enter my house[b]
   or get into my bed,[c]
4 I will not allow my eyes to sleep
   or my eyelids to slumber
5 until I find a place for the LORD,
   a dwelling for the Mighty One
      of Jacob."

6 We heard of ⌊the ark⌋
      in Ephrathah;[d]
   we found it in the fields of Jaar.[e]
7 Let us go to His dwelling place;
   let us worship at His footstool.
8 Arise, LORD, come to
   Your resting place,

[a]129:6 Or it can be pulled out   [b]132:3 Lit enter the tent of my house   [c]132:3 Lit into the couch of my bed
[d]132:6 Bethlehem or the district around it; Gn 35:19   [e]132:6 Kiriath-jearim; 1 Sm 7:1-2

You and the ark ⌊that shows⌋
  Your strength.
9 May Your priests be clothed
    with righteousness,
  and may Your godly people shout
    for joy.
10 Because of Your servant David,
    do not reject Your anointed one.[a]

God's Promise to David

11 The LORD swore an oath to David,
   a promise He will not abandon:
   "I will set one of your descendants[b]
   on your throne.
12 If your sons keep My covenant
   and My decrees
     that I will teach them,
   their sons will also sit
     on your throne, forever."

13 For the LORD has chosen Zion;
   He has desired it for His home:
14 "This is My resting place forever;
   I will make My home here
   because I have desired it.
15 I will abundantly bless its food;
   I will satisfy its needy with bread.
16 I will clothe its priests with salvation,
   and its godly people will shout for joy.
17 There I will make a •horn grow
     for David;
   I have prepared a lamp for
     My anointed one.
18 I will clothe his enemies
     with shame,
   but the crown he wears[c]
     will be glorious."

PSALM 133
Living in Harmony
A Davidic •song of ascents.

1 How good and pleasant it is
   when brothers can live together!

2 It is like fine oil on the head,
   running down on the beard,
   running down Aaron's beard,
   on his robes.
3 It is like the dew of Hermon[d]
   falling on the mountains of Zion.
   For there the LORD has appointed
     the blessing—
   life forevermore.

PSALM 134
Call to Evening Worship
A •song of ascents.

1 Now praise the LORD,
   all you servants of the LORD
   who stand in the LORD's house
     at night!
2 Lift up your hands
     in the holy place,
   and praise the LORD!

3 May the LORD,
   Maker of heaven and earth,
   bless you from Zion.

PSALM 135
LORD Is Great

1 •Hallelujah!
   Praise the name of the LORD.
   Give praise, you servants
     of the LORD
2 who stand in the house
     of the LORD,
   in the courts of the house
     of our God.
3 Praise the LORD, for the LORD
     is good;
   sing praise to His name,
     for it is delightful.
4 For the LORD has chosen Jacob
     for Himself,
   Israel as His treasured possession.

---

[a]**132:10** The king [b]**132:11** Lit *set the fruit of your womb* [c]**132:18** Lit *but on him his crown* [d]**133:3** The tallest
mountain in the region, noted for its abundant precipitation

5 For I know that the LORD is great;
   our Lord is greater than all gods.
6 The LORD does whatever He pleases
   in heaven and on earth,
   in the seas and all the depths.
7 He causes the clouds to rise
      from the ends of the earth.
   He makes lightning for the rain
   and brings the wind
      from His storehouses.

8 He struck down the firstborn
      of Egypt,
   both people and animals.
9 He sent signs and wonders
      against you, Egypt,
   against Pharaoh and all his officials.
10 He struck down many nations
   and slaughtered mighty kings:
11 Sihon king of the Amorites,
   Og king of Bashan,
   and all the kings of Canaan.
12 He gave their land as an inheritance,
   an inheritance to His people Israel.

13 LORD, Your name ⌊endures⌋ forever,
   Your reputation, LORD,
   through all generations.
14 For the LORD will judge His people
   and have compassion
      on His servants.

15 The idols of the nations are of silver
      and gold,
   made by human hands.
16 They have mouths,
      but cannot speak,
   eyes, but cannot see.
17 They have ears, but cannot hear;
   indeed, there is no breath
      in their mouths.
18 Those who make them are just
      like them,
   as are all who trust in them.

19 House of Israel, praise the LORD!
   House of Aaron, praise the LORD!

20 House of Levi, praise the LORD!
   You who revere the LORD,
      praise the LORD!
21 May the LORD be praised from Zion;
   He dwells in Jerusalem.
   Hallelujah!

PSALM 136
"His Love Is Eternal"

1 Give thanks to the LORD,
   for He is good.
      His love is eternal.
2 Give thanks to the God of gods.
      His love is eternal.
3 Give thanks to the Lord of lords.
      His love is eternal.
4 He alone does great wonders.
      His love is eternal.
5 He made the heavens skillfully.
      His love is eternal.
6 He spread the land on the waters.
      His love is eternal.
7 He made the great lights:
      His love is eternal.
8 the sun to rule by day,
      His love is eternal.
9 the moon and stars to rule by night.
      His love is eternal.
10 He struck the firstborn
      of the Egyptians
      His love is eternal.
11 and brought Israel out from among
   them
      His love is eternal.
12 with a strong hand
   and outstretched arm.
      His love is eternal.
13 He divided the •Red Sea
      His love is eternal.
14 and led Israel through,
      His love is eternal.
15 but hurled Pharaoh and his army
   into the Red Sea.
      His love is eternal.

16 He led His people
   in the wilderness.
      His love is eternal.
17 He struck down great kings
      His love is eternal.
18 and slaughtered famous kings—
      His love is eternal.
19 Sihon king of the Amorites
      His love is eternal.
20 and Og king of Bashan—
      His love is eternal.
21 and gave their land as
   an inheritance,
      His love is eternal.
22 an inheritance to Israel His servant.
      His love is eternal.
23 He remembered us
   in our humiliation
      His love is eternal.
24 and rescued us from our foes.
      His love is eternal.
25 He gives food to every creature.
      His love is eternal.
26 Give thanks to the God of heaven!
      His love is eternal.

PSALM 137
Lament of the Exiles

1 By the rivers of Babylon—
   there we sat down and wept
   when we remembered Zion.
2 There we hung up our lyres
   on the poplar trees,
3 for our captors there asked us
      for songs,
   and our tormentors, for rejoicing:
   "Sing us one of the songs of Zion."
4 How can we sing the LORD's song
   on foreign soil?
5 If I forget you, Jerusalem,
   may my right hand forget
   ⌊its skill⌋.

6 May my tongue stick to the roof
      of my mouth
   if I do not remember you,
   if I do not exalt Jerusalem
      as my greatest joy!
7 Remember, LORD,
   ⌊what⌋ the Edomites said
   that day[a] at Jerusalem:
   "Destroy it! Destroy it
   down to its foundations!"
8 Daughter Babylon,
      doomed to destruction,
   happy is the one who pays you back
   what you have done to us.
9 Happy is he who takes
   your little ones
   and dashes them against the rocks.

PSALM 138
A Thankful Heart
Davidic.

1 I will give You thanks
   with all my heart;
   I will sing Your praise
   before the heavenly beings.[b]
2 I will bow down
   toward Your holy temple
   and give thanks to Your name
   for Your constant love
      and faithfulness.
   You have exalted Your name
   and Your promise above
      everything else.
3 On the day I called,
   You answered me;
   You increased strength within me.[c]

4 All the kings on earth
   will give You thanks, LORD,
   when they hear
   what You have promised.[d]
5 They will sing of the LORD's ways,
   for the LORD's glory is great.

---

[a]**137:7** The day Jerusalem fell to the Babylonians in 586 B.C.   [b]**138:1** Or *the gods* (Jb 1:6; 2:1), or *before judges* or *kings* (Ps 82:1,6-7; Ex 21:6; 22:7-8); Hb *Elohim*   [c]**138:3** Hb obscure   [d]**138:4** Lit *hear the words of Your mouth*

⁶ Though the LORD is exalted,
   He takes note of the humble;
   but He knows the haughty
      from afar.
⁷ If I walk in the thick of danger,
   You will preserve my life
   from the anger of my enemies.
   You will extend Your hand;
   Your right hand will save me.
⁸ The LORD will fulfill ⌊His purpose⌋
      for me.
   LORD, Your love is eternal;
   do not abandon the work
      of Your hands.

PSALM 139
All-Knowing, Ever-Present God
For the choir director. A Davidic psalm.

¹ LORD, You have searched me
      and known me.
² You know when I sit down
      and when I stand up;
   You understand my thoughts
      from far away.
³ You observe my travels
      and my rest;
   You are aware of all my ways.
⁴ Before a word is on my tongue,
   You know all about it, LORD.
⁵ You have encircled me;
   You have placed Your hand
      on me.
⁶ ⌊This⌋ extraordinary knowledge is
      beyond me.
   It is lofty; I am unable to ⌊reach⌋ it.

⁷ Where can I go to escape
      Your Spirit?
   Where can I flee
      from Your presence?
⁸ If I go up to heaven, You are there;
   if I make my bed in •Sheol,
      You are there.

⁹ If I live at the eastern horizon
   ⌊or⌋ settle at the western limits,[a]
¹⁰ even there Your hand will lead me;
   Your right hand will hold on to me.
¹¹ If I say, "Surely the darkness
      will hide me,
   and the light around me
      will become night"—
¹² even the darkness is not dark
      to You.
   The night shines like the day;
   darkness and light are alike to You.

¹³ For it was You who created
      my inward parts;[b]
   You knit me together
      in my mother's womb.
¹⁴ I will praise You,
   because I have been remarkably
      and wonderfully made.[c] [d]
   Your works are wonderful,
   and I know ⌊this⌋ very well.
¹⁵ My bones were not hidden
      from You
   when I was made in secret,
   when I was formed in the depths
      of the earth.
¹⁶ Your eyes saw me when
      I was formless;
   all ⌊my⌋ days were written
      in Your book and planned
   before a single one of them began.

¹⁷ God, how difficult[e]
      Your thoughts are
   for me ⌊to comprehend⌋;
   how vast their sum is!
¹⁸ If I counted them,
   they would outnumber the grains
      of sand;
   when I wake up,[f] I am still
      with You.

¹⁹ God, if only You would kill
      the wicked—

---

[a]**139:9** Lit *I take up the wings of the dawn; I dwell at the end of the sea*   [b]**139:13** Lit *my kidneys*   [c]**139:14** DSS, some LXX mss, Syr, Jer read *because You are remarkable and wonderful*   [d]**139:14** Hb obscure   [e]**139:17** Or *precious*
[f]**139:18** Other Hb mss read *I come to an end*

you bloodthirsty men, stay away
  from me—

20 who invoke You deceitfully.
Your enemies swear ⌊by You⌋ falsely.

21 LORD, don't I hate those
  who hate You,
and detest those who rebel
  against You?

22 I hate them with extreme hatred;
I consider them my enemies.

23 Search me, God, and know
  my heart;
test me and know my concerns.

24 See if there is any offensive[a] way
  in me;
lead me in the everlasting way.

PSALM 140
Prayer for Rescue
For the choir director. A Davidic psalm.

1 Rescue me, LORD, from evil men.
Keep me safe from violent men

2 who plan evil in their hearts.
They stir up wars all day long.

3 They make their tongues
as sharp as a snake's bite;
viper's venom is under their lips.
                              •Selah

4 Protect me, LORD,
from the clutches of the wicked.
Keep me safe from violent men
who plan to make me stumble.[b]

5 The proud hide a trap with ropes
  for me;
they spread a net along the path
and set snares for me.   Selah

6 I say to the LORD,
"You are my God."
Listen, LORD, to my cry for help.

7 Lord GOD, my strong Savior,
You shield my head on the day
  of battle.

8 LORD, do not grant the desires
  of the wicked;
do not let them achieve their goals.
⌊Otherwise,⌋ they will become
  proud.   Selah

9 As for the heads of those
  who surround me,
let the trouble their lips cause
overwhelm ⌊them⌋.

10 Let hot coals fall on them.
Let them be thrown into the fire,
into the abyss, never again to rise.

11 Do not let a slanderer stay
  in the land.
Let evil relentlessly[c] hunt down
  a violent man.

12 I[d] know that the LORD upholds
the just cause of the poor,
justice for the needy.

13 Surely the righteous will praise
  Your name;
the upright will live in
  Your presence.

PSALM 141
Protection from Sin and Sinners
A Davidic psalm.

1 LORD, I call on You; hurry
to ⌊help⌋ me.
Listen to my voice when I call
on You.

2 May my prayer be set before You
  as incense,
the raising of my hands
as the evening offering.

3 LORD, set up a guard for my mouth;
keep watch at the door
  of my lips.

4 Do not let my heart turn
to any evil thing
or wickedly perform reckless acts
with men who commit sin.

a139:24 Or *idolatrous* b140:4 Lit *to trip up my steps* c140:11 Hb obscure d140:12 Alt Hb tradition reads *You*

Do not let me feast
  on their delicacies.
5 Let the righteous one strike me—
  it is ⌊an act of⌋ faithful love;
  let him rebuke me—
  it is oil for my head;
  let me[a] not refuse it.
  Even now my prayer is against
  the evil acts of the wicked.[b]
6 When their rulers[c]
    will be thrown off
  the sides of a cliff,
  the people[d] will listen to my words,
  for they are pleasing.

7 As when one plows and breaks up
    the soil,
  ⌊turning up rocks⌋,
  so our[e] bones have been scattered
  at the mouth of •Sheol.

8 But my eyes ⌊look⌋ to You, Lord God.
  I seek refuge in You; do not
    let me die.[f]
9 Protect me from[g] the trap
    they have set for me,
  and from the snares of evildoers.
10 Let the wicked fall
    into their own nets,
  while I pass ⌊safely⌋ by.

PSALM 142
Cry of Distress

A Davidic •Maskil. When he was in the cave.
A prayer.

1 I cry aloud to the LORD;
  I plead aloud to the LORD for mercy.
2 I pour out my complaint
    before Him;
  I reveal my trouble to Him.
3 Although my spirit is weak
    within me,
  You know my way.

Along this path I travel
  they have hidden a trap
    for me.
4 Look to the right and see:[h]
  no one stands up for me;
  there is no refuge for me;
  no one cares about me.

5 I cry to You, LORD;
  I say, "You are my shelter,
  my portion in the land
    of the living."
6 Listen to my cry,
  for I am very weak.
  Rescue me from those
    who pursue me,
  for they are too strong for me.
7 Free me from prison
  so that I can praise Your name.
  The righteous will gather
    around me
  because You deal generously
    with me.

PSALM 143
Cry for Help

A Davidic psalm.

1 LORD, hear my prayer.
  In Your faithfulness
    listen to my plea,
  and in Your righteousness
    answer me.
2 Do not bring Your servant
    into judgment,
  for no one alive is righteous
    in Your sight.

3 For the enemy has pursued me,
  crushing me to the ground,
  making me live in darkness
  like those long dead.
4 My spirit is weak within me;
  my heart is overcome with dismay.

Meditate on Memories

5 I remember the days of old;
<u>I meditate on all You have done;</u>
I reflect on the work of Your hands.
6 I spread out my hands to You;
I am like parched land before You.
•Selah

7 Answer me quickly, LORD;
my spirit fails.
Don't hide Your face from me,
or I will be like those
going down to the •Pit.
8 Let me experience
Your faithful love in the morning,
for I trust in You.
Reveal to me the way I should go,
because I long for You.
9 Rescue me from my enemies,
LORD;
I come to You for protection.[a]

Teach Me Your Will

10 <u>Teach me to do Your will,</u>
<u>for You are my God.</u>
May Your gracious Spirit
lead me on level ground.

11 Because of Your name, •Yahweh,
let me live.
In Your righteousness deliver me
from trouble,
12 and in Your faithful love
destroy my enemies.
Wipe out all those who attack me,
for I am Your servant.

PSALM 144
A King's Prayer

Davidic.

1 <u>May the LORD my rock be praised,</u>
<u>who trains my hands for battle</u>
<u>and my fingers for warfare.</u>

2 He is my faithful love
and my fortress,
my stronghold and my deliverer.
He is my shield, and I take refuge
in Him;
He subdues my people[b] under me.

3 <u>LORD, what is man,</u>
<u>that You care for him,</u>
<u>the son of man, that You think</u>
<u>of him?</u>
4 <u>Man is like a breath;</u>
<u>his days are like a passing shadow.</u>

5 LORD, part Your heavens
and come down.
Touch the mountains,
and they will smoke.
6 Flash ⌈Your⌉ lightning and scatter
the foe;[c]
shoot Your arrows and rout them.
7 Reach down[d] from on high;
rescue me from deep water,
and set me free
from the grasp of foreigners
8 whose mouths speak lies,
whose right hands are deceptive.

9 God, I will sing a new song to You;
I will play on a ten-stringed harp
for You—
10 the One who gives victory to kings,
who frees His servant David
from the deadly sword.
11 Set me free and rescue me
from the grasp of foreigners
whose mouths speak lies,
whose right hands are deceptive.

12 Then our sons will be like plants
nurtured in their youth,
our daughters, like corner pillars
that are carved in the palace style.
13 Our storehouses will be full,
supplying all kinds of produce;

---

[a]**143:9** One Hb ms, LXX; MT reads *I cover myself to You* [b]**144:2** Other Hb mss, DSS, Aq, Syr, Tg, Jer read *subdues peoples*; Ps 18:47; 2 Sm 22:48 [c]**144:6** Lit *scatter them* [d]**144:7** Lit *down Your hands*

our flocks will increase
by thousands
and tens of thousands in
our open fields.
14 Our cattle will be well fed.[a]
There will be no breach
ⸯin the wallsⸯ,
no going ⸯinto captivityⸯ,[b]
and no cry of lament in
our public squares.
15 Happy are the people with
such ⸯblessingsⸯ.
Happy are the people whose God is
the LORD.

PSALM 145
Praising God's Greatness

A Davidic hymn.

1 I[c] exalt You, my God the King,
and praise Your name
forever and ever.
2 I will praise You every day;
I will honor Your name
forever and ever.

3 •Yahweh is great
and is highly praised;
His greatness is unsearchable.
4 One generation will declare
Your works to the next
and will proclaim
Your mighty acts.
5 I[d] will speak of
Your glorious splendor
and[e] Your wonderful works.
6 They will proclaim the power
of Your awe-inspiring works,
and I will declare Your greatness.[f]
7 They will give a testimony
of Your great goodness
and will joyfully sing
of Your righteousness.

8 The LORD is gracious
and compassionate,
slow to anger and great
in faithful love.
9 The LORD is good to everyone;
His compassion ⸯrestsⸯ
on all He has made.
10 All You have made
will praise You, LORD;
the[g] godly will bless You.
11 They will speak of the glory
of Your kingdom
and will declare Your might,
12 informing ⸯallⸯ people[h]
of Your mighty acts
and of the glorious splendor
of Your[i] kingdom.
13 Your kingdom is
an everlasting kingdom;
Your rule is for all generations.
The LORD is faithful in all
His words
and gracious in all His actions.[j]
14 The LORD helps all who fall;
He raises up all
who are oppressed.[k]
15 All eyes look to You,
and You give them their food
in due time.
16 You open Your hand
and satisfy the desire
of every living thing.
17 The LORD is righteous
in all His ways
and gracious in all His acts.
18 The LORD is near all who call out
to Him,
all who call out to Him
with integrity.
19 He fulfills the desires of those
who •fear Him;

---

[a]**144:14** Or *will bear heavy loads*, or *will be pregnant*   [b]**144:14** Or *be no plague, no miscarriage*   [c]**145:1** The lines of this poem form an •acrostic.   [d]**145:5** LXX, Syr read *They*   [e]**145:5** LXX, Syr read *and they will tell of*   [f]**145:6** Alt Hb tradition, Jer read *great deeds*   [g]**145:10** Lit *Your*   [h]**145:12** Lit *informing the sons of man*   [i]**145:12** LXX, Syr, Jer; MT reads *His*   [j]**145:13** One Hb ms, DSS, LXX, Syr; most Hb mss omit *The LORD is faithful in all His words and gracious in all His actions.*   [k]**145:14** Lit *bowed down*

He hears their cry for help
    and saves them.
20 The LORD guards all those
    who love Him,
but He destroys all the wicked.
21 My mouth will declare
    the LORD's praise;
let every living thing
praise His holy name forever
    and ever.

PSALM 146
God of Compassion

1 •Hallelujah!
My soul, praise the LORD.
2 I will praise the LORD all my life;
I will sing to the LORD as long as
    I live.

3 Do not trust in nobles,
in man, who cannot save.
4 When his breath[a] leaves him,
he returns to the ground;
on that day his plans die.

5 Happy is the one whose help is
    the God of Jacob,
whose hope is in the LORD his God,
6 the Maker of heaven and earth,
the sea and everything in them.
He remains faithful forever,
7 executing justice for the exploited
and giving food to the hungry.
The LORD frees prisoners.
8 The LORD opens ⌊the eyes of⌋
    the blind.
The LORD raises up those
    who are oppressed.[b]
The LORD loves the righteous.
9 The LORD protects foreigners
and helps the fatherless
    and the widow,
but He frustrates the ways
    of the wicked.

10 The LORD reigns forever;
Zion, your God ⌊reigns⌋
    for all generations.
Hallelujah!

PSALM 147
God Restores Jerusalem

1 •Hallelujah!
How good it is to sing to our God,
for praise is pleasant and lovely.

2 The LORD rebuilds Jerusalem;
He gathers Israel's exiled people.
3 He heals the brokenhearted
and binds up their wounds.
4 He counts the number of the stars;
He gives names to all of them.
5 Our Lord is great, vast in power;
His understanding is infinite.[c]
6 The LORD helps the afflicted
but brings the wicked
    to the ground.

7 Sing to the LORD with thanksgiving;
play the lyre to our God,
8 who covers the sky with clouds,
prepares rain for the earth,
and causes grass to grow
    on the hills.
9 He provides the animals
    with their food,
and the young ravens,
    what they cry for.

10 He is not impressed by the strength
    of a horse;
He does not value the power[d]
    of a man.
11 The LORD values
    those who fear Him,
those who put their hope
    in His faithful love.

12 Exalt the LORD, Jerusalem;
praise your God, Zion!

---

a146:4 Or spirit b146:8 Lit bowed down c147:5 Lit understanding has no number d147:10 Lit legs

13 For He strengthens the bars
   of your gates
and blesses your children
   within you.
14 He endows your territory
   with prosperity;[a]
He satisfies you
   with the finest wheat.

His Word Runs Swiftly

15 He sends His command
   throughout the earth;
His word runs swiftly.

God of Winter

16 He spreads snow like wool;
He scatters frost like ashes;
17 He throws His hailstones
   like crumbs.
Who can withstand His cold?
18 He sends His word and melts them;
He unleashes His winds,[b]
   and the waters flow.

19 He declares His word to Jacob,
His statutes and judgments
   to Israel.
20 He has not done this for any nation;
they do not know[c] ⌊His⌋ judgments.
Hallelujah!

PSALM 148
Creation's Praise of the LORD

1 •Hallelujah!
Praise the LORD from the heavens;
praise Him in the heights.
2 Praise Him, all His angels;
praise Him, all His •hosts.
3 Praise Him, sun and moon;
praise Him, all you shining stars.
4 Praise Him, highest heavens,
and you waters above the heavens.
5 Let them praise the name
   of the LORD,

for He commanded,
   and they were created.
6 He set them in position
   forever and ever;
He gave an order that will never
   pass away.

7 Praise the LORD from the earth,
all sea monsters and ocean depths,
8 lightning[d] and hail,
   snow and cloud,
powerful wind that executes
   His command,
9 mountains and all hills,
fruit trees and all cedars,
10 wild animals and all cattle,
creatures that crawl
   and flying birds,
11 kings of the earth and all peoples,
princes and all judges of the earth,
12 young men as well as
   young women,
old and young together.
13 Let them praise the name
   of the LORD,
for His name alone is exalted.
His majesty covers
   heaven and earth.
14 He has raised up a •horn
   for His people,
praise from all His godly ones,
from the Israelites, the people
   close to Him.
Hallelujah!

PSALM 149
Praise for God's Triumph

1 •Hallelujah!
Sing to the LORD a new song,
His praise in the assembly
   of the godly.
2 Let Israel celebrate its Maker;
let the children of Zion rejoice
   in their King.

---

[a]147:14 Or peace   [b]147:18 Or breath   [c]147:20 DSS, LXX, Syr, Tg read He has not made known to them
[d]148:8 Or fire

3 Let them praise His name
  with dancing
and make music to Him
  with tambourine and lyre.
4 For the LORD takes pleasure
  in His people;
He adorns the humble
  with salvation.
5 Let the godly celebrate
  in triumphal glory;
let them shout for joy
  on their beds.

6 Let the exaltation of God be
  in their mouths[a]
and a two-edged sword
  in their hands,
7 inflicting vengeance on the nations
and punishment
  on the peoples,
8 binding their kings
  with chains
and their dignitaries
  with iron shackles,
9 carrying out the judgment
  decreed against them.

This honor is for
  all His godly people.
Hallelujah!

PSALM 150

Praise the LORD

1 •Hallelujah!
Praise God in His sanctuary.
Praise Him in His mighty heavens.
2 Praise Him for His powerful acts;
praise Him
  for His abundant greatness.

3 Praise Him with trumpet blast;
praise Him with harp and lyre.
4 Praise Him with tambourine
  and dance;
praise Him with flute and strings.
5 Praise Him
  with resounding cymbals;
praise Him with clashing cymbals.

6 Let everything that breathes
  praise the LORD.
Hallelujah!

---

a **149:6** Lit throat

PROVERBS

Purpose of Proverbs

1 The proverbs of Solomon
son of David, king of Israel:

2 For gaining wisdom
and being instructed;
for understanding insightful sayings;

3 for receiving wise instruction
⌊in⌋ righteousness, justice,
and integrity;

4 for teaching shrewdness
to the inexperienced,[a]
knowledge and discretion
to a young man—

5 a wise man will listen and increase
his learning,
and a discerning man
will obtain guidance—

6 for understanding a proverb
or a parable,[b]
the words of the wise,
and their riddles.

7 The •fear of the LORD
is the beginning of knowledge;
fools despise wisdom
and instruction.[c]

Avoid Path of Violent

8 Listen, my son,
to your father's instruction,
and don't reject
your mother's teaching,

9 for they will be a garland of grace
on your head
and a ⌊gold⌋ chain around your neck.

10 My son, if sinners entice you,
don't be persuaded.

11 If they say—"Come with us!
Let's set an ambush
and kill someone.[d]

Let's attack some innocent person
just for fun![e]

12 Let's swallow them alive,
like •Sheol,
still healthy as they go down
to the •Pit.

13 We'll find all kinds
of valuable property
and fill our houses with plunder.

14 Throw in your lot with us,
and we'll all share our money"[f]—

15 my son, don't travel that road
with them
or set foot on their path,

16 because their feet run
toward trouble
and they hurry to commit murder.[g]

17 It is foolish to spread a net
where any bird can see it,

18 but they set an ambush
to kill themselves;[h]
they attack their own lives.

19 Such are the paths of all
who pursue gain dishonestly;
it takes the lives of those who profit
from it.[i]

Wisdom's Plea

20 Wisdom calls out in the street;
she raises her voice
in the public squares.

21 She cries out above[j]
the commotion;
she speaks at the entrance
of the city •gates:

22 "How long, foolish ones, will you
love ignorance?
⌊How long⌋ will ⌊you⌋ mockers
enjoy mocking
and ⌊you⌋ fools hate knowledge?

---

a**1:4** Or *simple,* or *gullible*   b**1:6** Or *an enigma*   c**1:7** This verse states the theme of Pr.   d**1:11** Lit *Let's ambush for blood*   e**1:11** Lit *person for no reason*   f**1:14** Lit *us; one bag will be for all of us*   g**1:16** Lit *to shed blood*   h**1:18** Lit *they ambush for their blood*   i**1:19** Lit *takes the life of its masters*   j**1:21** Lit *at the head of*

23 If you turn to my discipline,[a]
    then I will pour out my spirit
        on you
    and teach you my words.
24 Since I called out and you refused,
    extended my hand and no one
        paid attention,
25 since you neglected all my counsel
    and did not accept my correction,
26 I, in turn, will laugh at
        your calamity.
    I will mock when terror strikes you,
27 when terror strikes you like a storm
    and your calamity comes
        like a whirlwind,
    when trouble and stress
        overcome you.
28 Then they will call me,
        but I won't answer;
    they will search for me, but won't
        find me.
29 Because they hated knowledge,
    didn't choose to fear the LORD,
30 were not interested in my counsel,
    and rejected all my correction,
31 they will eat the fruit of their way
    and be glutted with
        their own schemes.
32 For the waywardness
        of the inexperienced
        will kill them,
    and the complacency of fools
        will destroy them.
33 But whoever listens to me
        will live securely
    and be free from the fear
        of danger."

Wisdom's Worth

2 My son, if you accept my words
    and store up my commands
        within you,
2 listening closely[b] to wisdom

and directing your heart
    to understanding;
3 furthermore, if you call out
        to insight
    and lift your voice
        to understanding,
4 if you seek it like silver
    and search for it
        like hidden treasure,
5 then you will understand the •fear
        of the LORD
    and discover the knowledge of God.
6 For the LORD gives wisdom;
    from His mouth come knowledge
        and understanding.
7 He stores up success[c]
        for the upright;
    He is a shield for those who live
        with integrity
8 so that He may guard the paths
        of justice
    and protect the way
        of His loyal followers.
9 Then you will understand
        righteousness, justice,
    and integrity—every good path.
10 For wisdom will enter your mind,
    and knowledge will delight
        your heart.
11 Discretion will watch over you,
    and understanding will guard you,
12 rescuing you from the way of evil—
    from the one who says
        perverse things,
13 ⌊from⌋ those who abandon
        the right paths
    to walk in ways of darkness,
14 ⌊from⌋ those who enjoy doing evil
    and celebrate perversity,
15 whose paths are crooked,
    and whose ways are devious.
16 It will rescue you
        from a forbidden woman,

---

a 1:23 Lit *back to my reprimands*   b 2:2 Lit *you, stretching out your ear*   c 2:7 Or *resourcefulness*

from a stranger[a]
with her flattering talk,

17 who abandons the companion
of her youth
and forgets the covenant
of her God;

18 for her house sinks down to death
and her ways to the land
of the departed spirits.

19 None return who go to her;
none reach the paths of life.

20 So follow the way of good people,
and keep to the paths
of the righteous.

21 For the upright will inhabit
the land,
and those of integrity will remain
in it;

22 but the wicked will be cut off
from the land,
and the treacherous uprooted
from it.

Trust the LORD

3 My son, don't forget my teaching,
but let your heart keep
my commands;

2 for they will bring you
many days, a full life,[b] and well-
being.

3 Never let loyalty and faithfulness
leave you.
Tie them around your neck;
write them on the tablet
of your heart.

4 Then you will find favor
and high regard
in the sight of God and man.

5 Trust in the LORD with all
your heart,
and do not rely on
your own understanding;

6 think about Him in all your ways,

and He will guide you
on the right paths.

7 Don't consider yourself to be wise;
•fear the LORD and turn away
from evil.

8 This will be healing for your body[c]
and strengthening for your bones.

First Produce

9 Honor the LORD
with your possessions
and with the first produce
of your entire harvest;

10 then your barns will be
completely filled,
and your vats will overflow
with new wine.

11 Do not despise
the LORD's instruction, my son,
and do not loathe His discipline;

12 for the LORD disciplines the one
He loves,
just as a father, the son
he delights in.

Wisdom Brings Happiness

13 Happy is a man who finds wisdom
and who acquires understanding,

14 for she is more profitable than silver,
and her revenue is better than gold.

15 She is more precious than jewels;
nothing you desire compares
with her.

16 Long life[d] is in her right hand;
in her left, riches and honor.

17 Her ways are pleasant,
and all her paths, peaceful.

18 She is a tree of life to those
who embrace her,
and those who hold on to her
are happy.

19 The LORD founded the earth
by wisdom

---

[a]**2:16** Or *foreign woman*   [b]**3:2** Lit *days, years of life*   [c]**3:8** Lit *navel*   [d]**3:16** Lit *Length of days*

and established the heavens
   by understanding.
20 By His knowledge
   the watery depths broke open,
   and the clouds dripped with dew.

21 Maintain ˻your˼ competence
   and discretion.
   My son, don't lose sight of them.
22 They will be life for you[a]
   and adornment[b] for your neck.
23 Then you will go safely
   on your way;
   your foot will not stumble.
24 When you lie[c] down, you will not
      be afraid;
   you will lie down, and your sleep
      will be pleasant.
25 Don't fear sudden danger
   or the ruin of the wicked
      when it comes,
26 for the LORD will be
   your confidence[d]
   and will keep your foot
      from a snare.

Treat Others Fairly

27 When it is in your power,[e]
   don't withhold good from the one
      to whom it is due.
28 Don't say to your neighbor,
   "Go away! Come back later.
   I'll give it tomorrow"—
      when it is there with you.
29 Don't plan any harm
   against your neighbor,
   for he trusts you and lives near you.
30 Don't accuse anyone without cause,
   when he has done you no harm.
31 Don't envy a violent man
   or choose any of his ways;
32 for the devious are detestable
      to the LORD,
   but He is a friend[f] to the upright.

33 The LORD's curse is
   on the household of the wicked,
   but He blesses the home
      of the righteous;
34 He mocks those who mock,
   but gives grace to the humble.
35 The wise will inherit honor,
   but He holds fools up to dishonor.[g]

A Father's Example

4 Listen, ˻my˼ sons,
   to a father's discipline,
   and pay attention so that
      you may gain understanding,
2 for I am giving you
   good instruction.
   Don't abandon my teaching.
3 When I was a son with my father,
   tender and precious to my mother,
4 he taught me and said:
   "Your heart must hold on
      to my words.
   Keep my commands and live.
5 Get wisdom, get understanding;
   don't forget or turn away
      from the words of my mouth.
6 Don't abandon wisdom,
   and she will watch over you;
   love her, and she will guard you.
7 Wisdom is supreme—
   so get wisdom.
   And whatever else you get,
      get understanding.
8 Cherish her, and she will exalt you;
   if you embrace her, she will
      honor you.
9 She will place a garland of grace
   on your head;
   she will give you a crown of beauty."

Two Ways of Life

10 Listen, my son. Accept my words,
   and you will live many years.

---

[a]3:22 Or be your throat; Hb nephesh can mean throat, soul, or life.   [b]3:22 Or grace   [c]3:24 LXX reads sit   [d]3:26 Or be at your side   [e]3:27 Lit in the power of your hands   [f]3:32 Or confidential counsel   [g]3:35 Or but haughty fools dishonor, or but fools exalt dishonor

11 I am teaching you the way
    of wisdom;
I am guiding you on straight paths.
12 When you walk, your steps will not
    be hindered;
when you run,
    you will not stumble.
13 Hold on to instruction; don't let go.
Guard it, for it is your life.
14 Don't set foot on the path
    of the wicked;
don't proceed in the way
    of evil ones.
15 Avoid it; don't travel on it.
Turn away from it, and pass it by.
16 For they can't sleep
unless they have done what is evil;
they are robbed of sleep
    unless they make
    someone stumble.
17 They eat the bread of wickedness
and drink the wine of violence.
18 The path of the righteous is
    like the light of dawn,
shining brighter and brighter
    until midday.
19 But the way of the wicked is
    like the darkest gloom;
they don't know what makes
    them stumble.

The Straight Path

20 My son, pay attention to my words;
listen closely to my sayings.
21 Don't lose sight of them;
keep them within your heart.
22 For they are life to those
    who find them,
and health to one's whole body.
23 Guard your heart above all else,[a]
for it is the source of life.
24 Don't let your mouth
    speak dishonestly,

and don't let your lips
    talk deviously.
25 Let your eyes look forward;
fix your gaze[b] straight ahead.
26 Carefully consider the path[c]
    for your feet,
and all your ways
    will be established.
27 Don't turn to the right
    or to the left;
keep your feet away from evil.

Avoid Seduction

5 My son, pay attention
    to my wisdom;
listen closely[d] to my understanding
2 so that ⌊you⌋ may maintain
    discretion
and your lips safeguard knowledge.
3 Though the lips
    of the forbidden woman
    drip honey
and her words are[e]
    smoother than oil,
4 in the end she's as bitter
    as •wormwood
and as sharp as a double-
    edged sword.
5 Her feet go down to death;
her steps head straight for •Sheol.
6 She doesn't consider the path
    of life;
she doesn't know that her ways
    are unstable.

7 So now, ⌊my⌋ sons, listen to me,
and don't turn away from the words
    of my mouth.
8 Keep your way far from her.
Don't go near the door
    of her house.
9 Otherwise, you will give up
    your vitality to others
and your years to someone cruel;

---

a 4:23 Or heart with all diligence   b 4:25 Lit eyelids   c 4:26 Or Clear a path   d 5:1 Lit wisdom; stretch out your ear
e 5:3 Lit her palate is

10 strangers will drain your resources,
    and your earnings will end up
        in a foreigner's house.
11 At the end of your life,
    you will lament
    when your physical body
        has been consumed,
12 and you will say,
    "How I hated discipline,
    and how my heart
        despised correction.
13 I didn't obey my teachers
    or listen closely[a] to my mentors.
14 I was on the verge of complete ruin
    before the entire community."

Enjoy Marriage

15 Drink water from your own cistern,
    water flowing from your own well.
16 Should your springs flow
        in the streets,
    streams of water
        in the public squares?
17 They should be for you alone
    and not for you ⌊to share⌋
        with strangers.
18 Let your fountain be blessed,
    and take pleasure in the wife
        of your youth.
19 A loving doe, a graceful fawn—
    let her breasts always satisfy you;
    be lost in her love forever.
20 Why, my son, would you
        be infatuated
    with a forbidden woman
    or embrace the breast of a stranger?
21 For a man's ways are
        before the LORD's eyes,
    and He considers all his paths.
22 A wicked man's iniquities
        entrap him;
    he is entangled in the ropes
        of his own sin.

23 He will die because there is
        no instruction,
    and be lost because of
        his great stupidity.

Financial Entanglements

6 My son, if you have put up security
    for your neighbor[b]
    or entered into an agreement
        with[c] a stranger,[d]
2 you have been trapped
        by the words of your lips[e]—
    ensnared by the words
        of your mouth.
3 Do this, then, my son,
        and free yourself,
    for you have put yourself
        in your neighbor's power:
    Go, humble yourself, and plead
        with your neighbor.
4 Don't give sleep to your eyes
    or slumber to your eyelids.
5 Escape like a gazelle
        from a hunter,[f]
    like a bird from a fowler's trap.[f]

Laziness

6 Go to the ant, you slacker!
    Observe its ways and become wise.
7 Without leader, administrator,
        or ruler,
8 it prepares its provisions
        in summer;
    it gathers its food during harvest.
9 How long will you stay in bed,
        you slacker?
    When will you get up
        from your sleep?
10 A little sleep, a little slumber,
    a little folding of the arms to rest,
11 and your poverty will come like
        a robber,
    your need, like a bandit.

---

a**5:13** Lit *or turn my ear*   b**6:1** Or *friend*   c**6:1** Lit *or shaken hands for* or *with*   d**6:1** The Hb word for *stranger* can refer
to a foreigner, an Israelite outside one's family, or simply to another person.   e**6:2** Lit *mouth*   f**6:5** Lit *hand*

The Malicious Man

12 A worthless person, a wicked man,
   who goes around
     speaking dishonestly,
13 who winks his eyes, signals
     with his feet,
  and gestures with his fingers,
14 who plots evil with perversity
     in his heart—
  he stirs up trouble constantly.
15 Therefore calamity
     will strike him suddenly;
  he will be shattered instantly—
     beyond recovery.

What the LORD Hates

16 Six things the LORD hates;
  in fact, seven are detestable
     to Him:
17 arrogant eyes, a lying tongue,
  hands that shed innocent blood,
18 a heart that plots wicked schemes,
  feet eager to run to evil,
19 a lying witness who gives
     false testimony,
  and one who stirs up trouble
     among brothers.

Warning against Adultery

20 My son, keep
     your father's command,
  and don't reject
     your mother's teaching.
21 Always bind them to your heart;
  tie them around your neck.
22 When you walk here and there,
     they will guide you;
  when you lie down, they will
     watch over you;
  when you wake up, they will
     talk to you.
23 For a commandment is a lamp,
     teaching is a light,
and corrective instructions are
     the way to life.
24 They will protect you
     from an evil woman,[a]
  from the flattering[b] tongue
     of a stranger.
25 Don't lust in your heart
     for her beauty
  or let her captivate you
     with her eyelashes.
26 For a prostitute's fee is only a loaf
     of bread,[c]
  but an adulteress[d] goes
     after ⌊your⌋ very life.
27 Can a man embrace fire[e]
  and his clothes not be burned?
28 Can a man walk on coals
  without scorching his feet?
29 So it is with the one
     who sleeps with
  another man's wife;
     no one who touches her
     will go unpunished.
30 People don't despise the thief
     if he steals
  to satisfy himself
     when he is hungry.
31 Still, if caught, he must pay
     seven times as much;
  he must give up all the wealth
     in his house.
32 The one who commits adultery[f]
     lacks sense;
  whoever does so destroys himself.
33 He will get a beating[g] and dishonor,
  and his disgrace will
     never be removed.
34 For jealousy enrages a husband,
  and he will show no mercy
     when he takes revenge.
35 He will not be appeased
     by anything
  or be persuaded by lavish gifts.

---

[a]6:24 LXX reads *from a married woman* [b]6:24 Lit *smooth* [c]6:26 Or *On account of a prostitute,*
[one is left with] only a loaf of bread [d]6:26 Lit *but a wife of a man* [e]6:27 Lit *man take fire to his bosom* [f]6:32 Lit
commits adultery with a woman [g]6:33 Or *plague*

7

My son, obey my words,
and treasure my commands.
2 Keep my commands and live;
protect my teachings
as you would the pupil of your eye.
3 Tie them to your fingers;
write them on the tablet
of your heart.
4 Say to wisdom, "You are my sister,"
and call understanding
⌊your⌋ relative.
5 She will keep you
from a forbidden woman,
a stranger with her flattering talk.

A Story of Seduction

6 At the window of my house
I looked through my lattice.
7 I saw among the inexperienced,ᵃ
I noticed among the youths,
a young man lacking sense.
8 Crossing the street near her corner,
he strolled down the road
to her house
9 at twilight, in the evening,
in the dark of the night.
10 A woman came to meet him,
dressed like a prostitute,
having a hidden agenda.ᵇ
11 She is loud and defiant;
her feet do not stay at home.
12 Now in the street,
now in the squares,
she lurks at every corner.
13 She grabs him and kisses him;
she brazenly saysᶜ to him,
14 "I've made •fellowship offerings;ᵈ
today I've fulfilled my vows.
15 So I came out to meet you,
to search for you,
and I've found you.
16 I've spread coverings on my bed—
richly colored linen from Egypt.

17 I've perfumed my bed
with myrrh, aloes, and cinnamon.
18 Come, let's drink deeply
of lovemaking until morning.
Let's feast on each other's love!
19 My husband isn't home;
he went on a long journey.
20 He took a bag of money with him
and will come home at the time
of the full moon."
21 She seduces him
with her persistent pleading;
she lures with her flatteringᵉ talk.
22 He follows her impulsively
like an ox going to the slaughter,
like a deer bounding
toward a trapᶠ
23 until an arrow pierces itsᵍ liver,
like a bird darting into a snare—
he doesn't know it will cost him
his life.

24 Now, ⌊my⌋ sons, listen to me,
and pay attention to the words
of my mouth.
25 Don't let your heart turn aside
to her ways;
don't stray onto her paths.
26 For she has brought many
down to death;
her victims are countless.ʰ
27 Her house is the road to •Sheol,
descending to the chambers
of death.

Wisdom's Appeal

8

Doesn't Wisdom call out?
Doesn't Understanding make
her voice heard?
2 At the heights overlooking
the road,
at the crossroads, she takes
her stand.

ᵃ**7:7** Or *simple,* or *gullible,* or *naive*   ᵇ**7:10** Or *prostitute, with a guarded heart*   ᶜ**7:13** Lit *she makes her face strong and says*   ᵈ**7:14** Meat from a fellowship offering had to be eaten on the day it was offered; therefore she is inviting him to a feast at her house.   ᵉ**7:21** Lit *smooth*   ᶠ**7:22** Text emended; lit *like shackles for the discipline of a fool;* Hb obscure   ᵍ**7:23** Or *his*   ʰ**7:26** Or *and powerful men are all her victims*

3 Beside the gates at the entry
 to[a] the city,
at the main entrance, she cries out:
4 "People, I call out to you;
 my cry is to mankind.
5 Learn to be shrewd,
 you who are inexperienced;
develop common sense,
 you who are foolish.
6 Listen, for I speak of noble things,
 and what my lips say is right.
7 For my mouth tells the truth,
 and wickedness is detestable
 to my lips.
8 All the words of my mouth
 are righteous;
none of them are deceptive
 or perverse.
9 All of them are clear
 to the perceptive,
and right to those
 who discover knowledge.
10 Accept my instruction
 instead of silver,
and knowledge rather
 than pure gold.
11 For wisdom is better
 than precious stones,
and nothing desirable can compare
 with it.
12 I, Wisdom, share a home
 with shrewdness
and have knowledge and discretion.
13 To •fear the LORD is to hate evil.
I hate arrogant pride, evil conduct,
and perverse speech.
14 I possess good advice
 and competence;[b]
I have understanding and strength.
15 It is by me that kings reign
 and rulers enact just law;
16 by me, princes lead,
 as do nobles
 ⌊and⌋ all righteous judges.[c]

17 I love those who love me,
and those who search for me
 find me.
18 With me are riches and honor,
lasting wealth and righteousness.
19 My fruit is better than solid gold,
and my harvest than pure silver.
20 I walk in the way of righteousness,
along the paths of justice,
21 giving wealth as an inheritance
 to those who love me,
and filling their treasuries.

22 The LORD made[d] me
at the beginning of His creation,[e]
before His works of long ago.
23 I was formed before ancient times,
from the beginning,
 before the earth began.
24 I was brought forth
when there were
 no watery depths
and no springs filled with water.
25 I was brought forth
before the mountains and hills
 were established,
26 before He made the land, the fields,
or the first soil on earth.
27 I was there when He established
 the heavens,
when He laid out the horizon
 on the surface of the ocean,
28 when He placed the skies above,
when the fountains of the ocean
 gushed forth,
29 when He set a limit for the sea
so that the waters would not violate
 His command,
when He laid out the foundations
 of the earth.
30 I was a skilled craftsman[f]
 beside Him.
I was His[g] delight every day,
always rejoicing before Him.

a8:3 Lit the mouth of b8:14 Or resourcefulness c8:16 Some Hb mss, LXX read nobles who judge the earth
d8:22 Or possessed, or begot e8:22 Lit way f8:30 Or a confidante, or a child g8:30 LXX; Hb omits His

31 I was rejoicing in
   His inhabited world,
   delighting in the •human race.

32 And now, ₍my₎ sons, listen to me;
   those who keep my ways
      are happy.
33 Listen to instruction and be wise;
   don't ignore it.
34 Anyone who listens to me is happy,
   watching at my doors every day,
   waiting by the posts of my doorway.
35 For the one who finds me finds life
   and obtains favor from the LORD,
36 but the one who sins against me
      harms himself;
   all who hate me love death."

Wisdom versus Foolishness

9 Wisdom has built her house;
   she has carved out
      her seven pillars.
2 She has prepared her meat;
   she has mixed her wine;
   she has also set her table.
3 She has sent out her servants;
   she calls out from
      the highest points of the city:
4 "Whoever is inexperienced,
      enter here!"
   To the one who lacks sense,
      she says,
5 "Come, eat my bread,
   and drink the wine I have mixed.
6 Leave inexperience behind,
   and you will live;
   pursue the way of understanding.
7 The one who corrects a mocker
   will bring dishonor on himself;
   the one who rebukes a wicked man
      will get hurt.ᵃ
8 Don't rebuke a mocker, or he will
      hate you;
   rebuke a wise man, and he will
      love you.

9 Instruct a wise man, and he will be
      wiser still;
   teach a righteous man, and he will
      learn more.
10 The •fear of the LORD is
   the beginning of wisdom,
   and the knowledge of the Holy One
   is understanding.
11 For by Wisdom your days
      will be many,
   and years will be added to your life.
12 If you are wise, you are wise
      for your own benefit;
   if you mock, you alone will bear
      ₍the consequences₎."

Woman Folly

13 The woman Folly is rowdy;
   she is gullible and knows nothing.
14 She sits by the doorway
      of her house,
   on a seat at the highest point
      of the city,
15 calling to those who pass by,
   who go straight ahead
      on their paths:
16 "Whoever is inexperienced,
      enter here!"
   To the one who lacks sense,
      she says,
17 "Stolen water is sweet,
   and bread ₍eaten₎ secretly is tasty!"
18 But he doesn't know
      that the departed spirits are there,
   that her guests are in the depths
   of •Sheol.

Collection of Solomon's Proverbs

10 Solomon's proverbs:

   A wise son brings joy to his father,
   but a foolish son, heartache
      to his mother.

ᵃ9:7 Lit man his blemish

Honest Diligence

2 Ill-gotten gains do not profit
     anyone,
  but righteousness rescues
     from death.

3 The LORD will not let the righteous
     go hungry,
  but He denies the wicked
     what they crave.

4 Idle hands make one poor,
  but diligent hands bring riches.

5 The son who gathers
     during summer is prudent;
  the son who sleeps during harvest
     is disgraceful.

6 Blessings are on the head
     of the righteous,
  but the mouth of the wicked
     conceals violence.

7 The remembrance of the righteous
     is a blessing,
  but the name of the wicked
     will rot.

8 A wise heart accepts commands,
  but foolish lips will be destroyed.

9 The one who lives with integrity
     lives securely,
  but whoever perverts his ways
     will be found out.

10 A sly wink of the eye
      causes grief,
   and foolish lips will be destroyed.

11 The mouth of the righteous is
      a fountain of life,
   but the mouth of the wicked
      conceals violence.

12 Hatred stirs up conflicts,
   but love covers all offenses.

13 Wisdom is found on the lips
      of the discerning,
   but a rod is for the back of the one
      who lacks sense.

14 The wise store up knowledge,
   but the mouth of the fool
      hastens destruction.

15 A rich man's wealth is
      his fortified city;
   the poverty of the poor is
      their destruction.

16 The labor of the righteous leads
      to life;
   the activity of the wicked leads
      to sin.

17 The one who follows instruction is
      on the path to life,
   but the one who rejects correction
      goes astray.

Wise, Honest Lips

18 The one who conceals hatred has
      lying lips,
   and whoever spreads slander is
      a fool.

19 When there are many words,
      sin is unavoidable,
   but the one who controls his lips
      is wise.

20 The tongue of the righteous is
      pure silver;
   the heart of the wicked is
      of little value.

21 The lips of the righteous feed many,
   but fools die for lack of sense.

22 The LORD's blessing enriches,
   and struggle adds nothing to it.ᵃ

23 As shameful conduct is pleasure
      for a fool,

ᵃ10:22 Or and He adds no trouble to it

so wisdom is for a man
of understanding.

24 What the wicked dreads will come
to him,
but what the righteous desires
will be given to him.

25 When the whirlwind passes,
the wicked are no more,
but the righteous
are secure forever.

26 Like vinegar to the teeth and smoke
to the eyes,
so the slacker is to the one
who sends him ⌊on an errand⌋.

27 The •fear of the LORD
prolongs life,ᵃ
but the years of the wicked
are cut short.

28 The hope of the righteous is joy,
but the expectation of the wicked
comes to nothing.

29 The way of the LORD is a stronghold
for the honorable,
but destruction awaits
the malicious.

30 The righteous will never be shaken,
but the wicked will not remain
on the earth.

31 The mouth of the righteous
produces wisdom,
but a perverse tongue will be
cut out.

32 The lips of the righteous know
what is appropriate,
but the mouth of the wicked,
⌊only⌋ what is perverse.

Honesty, Righteousness

11 Dishonest scales are detestable
to the LORD,

but an accurate weight is
His delight.

2 When pride comes,
disgrace follows,
but with humility comes wisdom.

3 The integrity of the upright
guides them,
but the perversity
of the treacherous destroys them.

4 Wealth is not profitable on a day
of wrath,
but righteousness rescues
from death.

5 The righteousness of the blameless
clears his path,
but the wicked person will fall
because of his wickedness.

6 The righteousness of the upright
rescues them,
but the treacherous are trapped
by their own desires.

7 When the wicked dies,
his expectation comes to nothing,
and hope placed in wealthᵇ ᶜ
vanishes.

8 The righteous is rescued
from trouble;
in his place, the wicked goes in.

9 With his mouth the ungodly
destroys his neighbor,
but through knowledge
the righteous are rescued.

10 When the righteous thrive,
a city rejoices,
and when the wicked die, there is
joyful shouting.

Fate of Cities

11 A city is built up by the blessing
of the upright,

ᵃ**10:27** Lit LORD adds to days   ᵇ**11:7** LXX reads hope of the ungodly   ᶜ**11:7** Or strength

but it is torn down by the mouth
of the wicked.

Silence

12 Whoever shows contempt
for his neighbor lacks sense,
but a man with understanding
keeps silent.

13 A gossip goes around revealing
a secret,
but the trustworthy keeps
a confidence.

Many Counselors

14 Without guidance, people fall,
but with many counselors
there is deliverance.

15 If someone puts up security
for a stranger,
he will suffer for it,
but the one who hates
such agreements is protected.

16 A gracious woman gains honor,
but violent[a] men gain ⌊only⌋ riches.

17 A kind man benefits himself,
but a cruel man brings disaster
on himself.

18 The wicked man earns
an empty wage,
but the one who sows righteousness,
a true reward.

19 Genuine righteousness ⌊leads⌋
to life,
but pursuing evil ⌊leads⌋ to death.

20 Those with twisted minds
are detestable to the LORD,
but those with blameless conduct
are His delight.

21 Be assured[b] that the wicked
will not go unpunished,

but the offspring of the righteous
will escape.

22 A beautiful woman who rejects
good sense
is like a gold ring in a pig's snout.

23 The desire of the righteous
⌊turns out⌋ well,
but the hope of the wicked
⌊leads to⌋ wrath.

Give and Receive

24 One person gives freely,
yet gains more;
another withholds what is right,
only to become poor.

25 A generous person
will be enriched,
and the one who gives a drink of
water
will receive water.

26 People will curse anyone
who hoards grain,
but a blessing will come to the one
who sells it.

27 The one who searches
for what is good finds favor,
but if someone looks for trouble,
it will come to him.

28 Anyone trusting in his riches
will fall,
but the righteous will flourish
like foliage.

29 The one who brings ruin
on his household
will inherit the wind,
and a fool will be a slave
to someone whose heart is wise.

30 The fruit of the righteous is a tree
of life,
but violence[c] takes lives.

[a]11:16 Or ruthless   [b]11:21 Lit Hand to hand   [c]11:30 LXX, Syr; MT reads but a wise one

31 If the righteous will be repaid
      on earth,
   how much more the wicked
      and sinful.

Accept Correction and Counsel

12 Whoever loves instruction
      loves knowledge,
   but one who hates correction
      is stupid.

2 The good obtain favor
      from the LORD,
   but He condemns a man
      who schemes.

3 Man cannot be made secure
      by wickedness,
   but the root of the righteous
      is immovable.

4 A capable wife[a] is
      her husband's crown,
   but a wife who causes shame
      is like rottenness in his bones.

5 The thoughts of the righteous
      ⌊are⌋ just,
   but guidance from the wicked
      ⌊leads to⌋ deceit.

6 The words of the wicked are
      a deadly ambush,
   but the speech of the upright
      rescues them.

7 The wicked are overthrown
      and perish,
   but the house of the righteous
      will stand.

8 A man is praised for his insight,
   but a twisted mind is despised.

9 Better to be dishonored, yet have
      a servant,
   than to act important but have
      no food.

Animal's Health

10 A righteous man cares about
      his animal's health,
   but ⌊even⌋ the merciful acts
      of the wicked are cruel.

Hard Work

11 The one who works his land
      will have plenty of food,
   but whoever chases fantasies
      lacks sense.

12 The wicked desire
      what evil men have,[b]
   but the root of the righteous
      produces ⌊fruit⌋.

13 An evil man is trapped
      by ⌊his⌋ rebellious speech,
   but the righteous escapes
      from trouble.

14 A man will be satisfied with good
      by the words of his mouth,
   and the work of a man's hands
      will reward him.

Wise Counsel and Speech

15 A fool's way is right
      in his own eyes,
   but whoever listens to counsel
      is wise.

16 A fool's displeasure is known
      at once,
   but whoever ignores an insult
      is sensible.

17 Whoever speaks the truth declares
      what is right,
   but a false witness, deceit.

18 There is one who speaks rashly,
      like a piercing sword;
   but the tongue of the wise
      ⌊brings⌋ healing.

[a]12:4 Or A wife of quality, or A wife of good character   [b]12:12 Or desire a stronghold of evil

Truth and Lies

19 Truthful lips endure forever,
   but a lying tongue, only a moment.

20 Deceit is in the hearts of those
      who plot evil,
   but those who promote peace
      have joy.

21 No disaster ⌞overcomes⌟
      the righteous,
   but the wicked are full of misery.

22 Lying lips are detestable
      to the LORD,
   but faithful people are His delight.

23 A shrewd person
      conceals knowledge,
   but a foolish heart
      publicizes stupidity.

24 The diligent hand will rule,
   but laziness will lead to forced labor.

Anxious Heart

25 Anxiety in a man's heart
      weighs it down,
   but a good word cheers it up.

26 A righteous man is careful
      in dealing with his neighbor,[a]
   but the ways of wicked men
      lead them astray.

27 A lazy man doesn't roast his game,
   but to a diligent man, his wealth
      is precious.

28 There is life in the path
      of righteousness,
   but another path leads to death.[b]

13 A wise son ⌞hears his⌟
      father's instruction,
   but a mocker doesn't listen
      to rebuke.

2 From the words of his mouth,
   a man will enjoy good things,
   but treacherous people have
      an appetite for violence.

3 The one who guards his mouth
      protects his life;
   the one who opens his lips invites
      his own ruin.

On Wealth

4 The slacker craves,
      yet has nothing,
   but the diligent is fully satisfied.

5 The righteous hate lying,
   but the wicked act disgustingly
      and disgracefully.

6 Righteousness guards people
      of integrity,[c]
   but wickedness undermines
      the sinner.

7 One man pretends to be rich
      but has nothing;
   another pretends to be poor but has
      great wealth.

8 Riches are a ransom
      for a man's life,
   but a poor man hears no threat.

9 The light of the righteous
      shines brightly,
   but the lamp of the wicked
      is extinguished.

10 Arrogance leads to nothing
      but strife,
   but wisdom is gained by those
      who take advice.

11 Wealth obtained by fraud
      will dwindle,
   but whoever earns it through labor[d]
      will multiply it.

---

a**12:26** Or man guides his neighbor   b**12:28** Or righteousness, and in its path there is no death   c**13:6** Lit guards integrity of way   d**13:11** Lit whoever gathers upon (his) hand

Health and Hope

12 Delayed hope makes
   the heart sick,
   but fulfilled desire is a tree of life.

13 The one who has contempt
   for instruction will pay
   the penalty,
   but the one who respects
   a command will be rewarded.

14 A wise man's instruction is
   a fountain of life,
   turning people away
   from the snares of death.

15 Good sense wins favor,
   but the way of the treacherous
   never changes.ᵃ

16 Every sensible person
   acts knowledgeably,
   but a fool displays his stupidity.

17 A wicked messenger falls
   into trouble,
   but a trustworthy courier
   ⌊brings⌋ healing.

18 Poverty and disgrace
   ⌊come to⌋ those
   who ignore instruction,
   but the one who accepts rebuke
   will be honored.

19 Desire fulfilled is sweet to the taste,
   but fools hate to turn from evil.

Walk with Wise

20 The one who walks with the wise
   will become wise,
   but a companion of fools
   will suffer harm.

21 Disaster pursues sinners,
   but good rewards the righteous.

22 A good man leaves an inheritance
   to hisᵇ grandchildren,
   but the sinner's wealth is stored up
   for the righteous.

23 The field of the poor yields
   abundant food,
   but without justice, it is
   swept away.

24 The one who will not use the rod
   hates his son,
   but the one who loves him
   disciplines him diligently.

25 A righteous man eats
   until he is satisfied,
   but the stomach of the wicked
   is empty.

Wise and Foolish

14 Every wise woman builds
   her house,
   but a foolish one tears it down
   with her own hands.

2 Whoever lives with integrity
   •fears the LORD,
   but the one who is devious
   in his ways despises Him.

3 The proud speech of a fool ⌊brings⌋
   a rod ⌊of discipline⌋,ᶜ
   but the lips of the wise
   protect them.

4 Where there are no oxen,
   the feeding-trough is empty,ᵈ
   but an abundant harvest ⌊comes⌋
   through the strength of an ox.

5 An honest witness
   does not deceive,
   but a dishonest witness utters lies.

6 A mocker seeks wisdom
   and doesn't find it,

ᵃ13:15 LXX, Syr, Tg read treacherous will perish   ᵇ13:22 Or inheritance: his   ᶜ14:3 Or In the mouth of a fool is a rod for his back, if text is emended   ᵈ14:4 Or clean

but knowledge ⌜comes⌝ easily
    to the perceptive.

7 Stay away from a foolish man;
    you will gain no knowledge
      from his speech.

8 The sensible man's wisdom is
    to consider his way,
  but the stupidity of fools
    deceives ⌜them⌝.

9 Fools mock at making restitution,[a]
  but there is goodwill
    among the upright.

10 The heart knows its own bitterness,
  and no outsider shares in its joy.

11 The house of the wicked
    will be destroyed,
  but the tent of the upright
    will stand.[b]

12 There is a way that seems right
    to a man,
  but its end is the way[c] to death.

13 Even in laughter a heart
    may be sad,
  and joy may end in grief.

14 The disloyal will get
    what their conduct deserves,
  and a good man,
    what his ⌜deeds deserve⌝.

15 The inexperienced believe
    anything,
  but the sensible watch[d] their steps.

16 A wise man is cautious and turns
    from evil,
  but a fool is easily angered
    and is careless.[e]

17 A quick-tempered man
    acts foolishly,
  and a man who schemes is hated.

18 The gullible inherit foolishness,
  but the sensible are crowned
    with knowledge.

19 The evil bow before those
    who are good,
  the wicked, at the gates
    of the righteous.

Wealth and Hard Work

20 A poor man is hated even
    by his neighbor,
  but there are many who love
    the rich.

21 The one who despises
    his neighbor sins,
  but whoever shows kindness
    to the poor will be happy.

22 Don't those who plan evil
    go astray?
  But those who plan good
    find loyalty and faithfulness.

23 There is profit in all hard work,
  but endless talk[f] leads only
    to poverty.

24 The crown of the wise is
    their wealth,
  but the foolishness of fools
    produces foolishness.

25 A truthful witness rescues lives,
  but one who utters lies is deceitful.

26 In the fear of the LORD one has
    strong confidence
  and his children have a refuge.

27 The fear of the LORD is a fountain
    of life,
  turning people from the snares
    of death.

28 A large population is
    a king's splendor,

---

[a] **14:9** Or at guilt offerings   [b] **14:11** Lit flourish   [c] **14:12** Lit ways   [d] **14:15** Lit the prudent understand   [e] **14:16** Or and falls   [f] **14:23** Lit but word of lips

but a shortage of people is
a ruler's devastation.

29 A patient person ⌞shows⌟ great
understanding,
but a quick-tempered one
promotes foolishness.

Health and Tranquil Heart

30 A tranquil heart is life to the body,
but jealousy is rottenness
to the bones.

31 The one who oppresses the poor
insults their Maker,
but one who is kind to the needy
honors Him.

32 The wicked are thrown down
by their own sin,
but the righteous have a refuge
when they die.

33 Wisdom resides in the heart
of the discerning;
she is known[a] even among fools.

Nation's Righteousness

34 Righteousness exalts a nation,
but sin is a disgrace to any people.

35 A king favors a wise servant,
but his anger falls on
a disgraceful one.

Gentle Answer and Wrath

15 A gentle answer turns away anger,
but a harsh word stirs up wrath.

2 The tongue of the wise
makes knowledge attractive,
but the mouth of fools
blurts out foolishness.

Eyes of LORD

3 The eyes of the LORD are
everywhere,
observing the wicked and the good.

4 The tongue that heals is a tree
of life,
but a devious tongue[b]
breaks the spirit.

Discipline and Correction

5 A fool despises
his father's instruction,
but a person who heeds correction
is sensible.

6 The house of the righteous
has great wealth,
but trouble accompanies
the income of the wicked.

7 The lips of the wise
broadcast knowledge,
but not so the heart of fools.

8 The sacrifice of the wicked
is detestable to the LORD,
but the prayer of the upright is
His delight.

9 The LORD detests the way
of the wicked,
but He loves the one
who pursues righteousness.

10 Discipline is harsh for the one
who leaves the path;
the one who hates correction
will die.

11 •Sheol and •Abaddon lie open
before the LORD—
how much more, human hearts.

12 A mocker doesn't love one
who corrects him;
he will not consult the wise.

Joyful Heart and Health

13 A joyful heart makes
a face cheerful,

---

[a] **14:33** LXX reads *unknown*   [b] **15:4** Lit *but crookedness in it*

but a sad heart produces
  a broken spirit.

14 A discerning mind
  seeks knowledge,
but the mouth of fools feeds
  on foolishness.

15 All the days of the oppressed
  are miserable,
but a cheerful heart has
  a continual feast.

Wealth Problems

16 Better a little with the •fear
  of the LORD
than great treasure with turmoil.

17 Better a meal of vegetables
  where there is love
than a fattened calf with hatred.

18 A hot-tempered man
  stirs up conflict,
but a man slow to anger
  calms strife.

19 A slacker's way is like
  a thorny hedge,
but the path of the upright is
  a highway.

20 A wise son brings joy to his father,
but a foolish one despises
  his mother.

21 Foolishness brings joy to one
  without sense,
but a man with understanding
  walks a straight path.

Plans and Counsel

22 Plans fail when there is no counsel,
but with many advisers
  they succeed.

23 A man takes joy in giving
  an answer;[a]

and a timely word—how good
  that is!

24 For the discerning the path of life
  leads upward,
so that he may avoid going down
  to Sheol.

25 The LORD destroys the house
  of the proud,
but He protects
  the widow's territory.

26 The LORD detests the plans
  of an evil man,
but pleasant words are pure.

27 The one who profits dishonestly
  troubles his household,
but the one who hates bribes
  will live.

Think before Answering

28 The mind of the righteous person
  thinks before answering,
but the mouth of the wicked
  blurts out evil things.

29 The LORD is far
  from the wicked,
but He hears the prayer
  of the righteous.

Good News and Health

30 Bright eyes cheer the heart;
good news strengthens[b]
  the bones.

31 An ear that listens to life-
  giving rebukes
will be at home among the wise.

Secrets to Success

32 Anyone who ignores instruction
  despises himself,
but whoever listens to correction
  acquires good sense.[c]

[a]15:23 Lit in an answer of his mouth   [b]15:30 Lit makes fat   [c]15:32 Lit acquires a heart

33 The fear of the LORD is
    wisdom's instruction,
    and humility comes before honor.

16 The reflections of the heart
    belong to man,
    but the answer of the tongue is
      from the LORD.

2 All a man's ways seem right
    in his own eyes,
    but the LORD weighs the motives.ª

3 <u>Commit your activities to the LORD
    and your plans will be achieved</u>.

4 The LORD has prepared everything
    for His purpose—
    even the wicked for the day
      of disaster.

5 Everyone with a proud heart is
    detestable to the LORD;
    be assured,ᵇ he will not
      go unpunished.

6 Wickedness is •atoned for by loyalty
    and faithfulness,
    and one turns from evil by the •fear
      of the LORD.

7 When a man's ways please
      the LORD,
    Heᶜ makes even his enemies to be
      at peace with him.

8 Better a little with righteousness
    than great income with injustice.

9 <u>A man's heart plans his way,
    but the Lord determines his steps</u>.

God and Kings

10 God's verdict is on the lips
      of a king;ᵈ
    his mouth should not err
      in judgment.

11 Honest balances and scales are
      the LORD's;
    all the weights in the bagᵉ are
      His concern.

12 Wicked behaviorᶠ is detestable
      to kings,
    since a throne is established
      through righteousness.

13 Righteous lips are a king's delight,
    and he loves one
      who speaks honestly.

14 A king's fury is a messenger
      of death,
    but a wise man appeases it.

15 When a king's face lights up,
      there is life;
    his favor is like a cloud
      with spring rain.

16 Acquire wisdom—
    how much better it is than gold!
    And acquire understanding—
    it is preferable to silver.

17 The highway of the upright
      avoids evil;
    the one who guards his way
      protects his life.

Pride before Destruction

18 <u>Pride comes before destruction,
    and an arrogant spirit before a fall</u>.

19 Better to be lowly of spirit
      with the humbleᵍ
    than to divide plunder
      with the proud.

20 The one who understands a matter
      finds success,
    and the one who trusts in the LORD
      will be happy.

ª**16:2** Lit *weighs spirits*   ᵇ**16:5** Lit *hand to hand*   ᶜ**16:7** Or *he*   ᵈ**16:10** Or *A divination is on the lips of a king*
ᵉ**16:11** Merchants kept the stones for their balance scales in a bag.   ᶠ**16:12** Whether the wicked behavior is on the
part of the king or someone else is ambiguous in Hb.   ᵍ**16:19** Alt Hb tradition reads *afflicted*

21 Anyone with a wise heart
    is called discerning,
  and pleasant speech[a]
    increases learning.

22 Insight is a fountain of life
    for its possessor,
  but folly is the instruction of fools.

23 A wise heart instructs its mouth
  and increases learning
    with its speech.[b]

Pleasant Words and Health

24 Pleasant words are a honeycomb:
  sweet to the taste[c] and health
    to the body.[d]

25 There is a way that seems right
    to a man,
  but in the end it is the way
    of death.

26 A worker's appetite works for him
  because his hunger[e] urges him on.

Peace, Age, and Patience

27 A worthless man digs up evil,
  and his speech is like
    a scorching fire.

28 A contrary man spreads conflict,
  and a gossip separates friends.

29 A violent man lures his neighbor,
  leading him in a way that is
    not good.

30 The one who narrows his eyes
    is planning deceptions;
  the one who compresses his lips
    brings about evil.

31 Gray hair is a glorious crown;
  it is found in the way
    of righteousness.

32 Patience is better than power,
  and controlling one's temper,[f]
    than capturing a city.

33 The lot is cast into the lap,
  but its every decision is
    from the LORD.

17 Better a dry crust with peace
  than a house full of feasting
    with strife.

2 A wise servant will rule over
    a disgraceful son
  and share an inheritance
    among brothers.

3 A crucible is for silver and a smelter
    for gold,
  but the LORD is a tester of hearts.

Wise and Malicious Talk

4 A wicked person listens to
    malicious talk;[g]
  a liar pays attention to
    a destructive tongue.

5 The one who mocks the poor
    insults his Maker,
  and one who rejoices over
    disaster
  will not go unpunished.

6 Grandchildren are the crown
    of the elderly,
  and the pride of sons is
    their fathers.

7 Excessive speech is not appropriate
    on a fool's lips;
  how much worse are lies
    for a ruler.

8 A bribe seems like a magic stone
    to its owner;
  wherever he turns, he succeeds.

---

a **16:21** Lit *and sweetness of lips*   b **16:23** Lit *learning upon his lips*   c **16:24** Lit *throat*   d **16:24** Lit *bones*   e **16:26** Lit
mouth   f **16:32** Lit *and ruling over one's spirit*   g **17:4** Lit *to lips of iniquity*

9 Whoever conceals an offense
   promotes love,
but whoever gossips about it
   separates friends.

10 A rebuke cuts into
   a perceptive person
more than a hundred lashes
   into a fool.

11 An evil man seeks only rebellion;
   a cruel messenger[a] will be sent
   against him.

12 Better for a man to meet a bear
   robbed of her cubs
than a fool in his foolishness.

13 If anyone returns evil for good,
   evil will never depart
   from his house.

14 To start a conflict is to release
   a flood;
stop the dispute before
   it breaks out.

15 Acquitting the guilty
   and condemning the just—
both are detestable to the LORD.

Financial Wisdom

16 Why does a fool have money
   in his hand
with no intention
   of buying wisdom?

17 A friend loves at all times,
and a brother is born for
   a difficult time.

18 One without sense enters
   an agreement[b]
and puts up security
   for his friend.

19 One who loves to offend
   loves strife;
one who builds a high threshold
   invites injury.

20 One with a twisted mind
   will not succeed,
and one with deceitful speech
   will fall into ruin.

21 A man fathers a fool
   to his own sorrow;
the father of a fool has no joy.

Joyful Heart: Good Medicine

22 A joyful heart is good medicine,
but a broken spirit dries up
   the bones.

23 A wicked man secretly takes a bribe
   to subvert the course of justice.

24 Wisdom is the focus
   of the perceptive,
but a fool's eyes roam to the ends
   of the earth.

25 A foolish son is grief to his father
and bitterness to the one
   who bore him.

26 It is certainly not good to fine
   an innocent person,
or to beat a noble for his honesty.[c]

Verbal Restraint

27 The intelligent person restrains
   his words,
and one who keeps a cool head[d]
is a man of understanding.

28 Even a fool is considered wise
   when he keeps silent,
discerning, when he seals his lips.

18 One who isolates himself pursues
   ⌞selfish⌟ desires;
he rebels against
   all sound judgment.

---

2 A fool does not delight
      in understanding,
   but only wants to show off
      his opinions.ᵃ

3 When a wicked man comes,
      shame does also,
   and along with dishonor, disgrace.

4 The words of a man's mouth
      are deep waters,
   a flowing river, a fountain
      of wisdom.

5 It is not good to show partiality
      to the guilty
   by perverting the justice
      due the innocent.

6 A fool's lips lead to strife,
   and his mouth provokes a beating.

7 A fool's mouth is his devastation,
   and his lips are a trap for his life.

8 A gossip's words are
      like choice food
   that goes down
      to one's innermost being.ᵇ

Laziness and Wealth

9 The one who is truly lazy
      in his work
   is brother to a vandal.ᶜ

10 The name of the LORD is
      a strong tower;
   the righteous run to it
      and are protected.ᵈ

11 A rich man's wealth is
      his fortified city;
   in his imagination it is
      like a high wall.

12 Before his downfall a man's heart
      is proud,
   but before honor comes humility.

13 The one who gives an answer
      before he listens—
   this is foolishness and disgrace
      for him.

14 A man's spirit can
      endure sickness,
   but who can survive
      a broken spirit?

15 The mind of the discerning
      acquires knowledge,
   and the ear of the wise seeks it.

16 A gift opens doorsᵉ for a man
   and brings him before the great.

Advice on Words

17 The first to state his case
      seems right
   until another comes and cross-
      examines him.

18 ₍Casting₎ the lot ends quarrels
   and separates powerful opponents.

19 An offended brother is
      ₍harder to reach₎ᶠ
   than a fortified city,
   and quarrels are like the bars
      of a fortress.

20 From the fruit of his mouth
      a man's stomach is satisfied;
   he is filled with the product
      of his lips.

21 Life and death are in the power
      of the tongue,
   and those who love it will eat
      its fruit.

22 A man who finds a wife finds
      a good thing
   and obtains favor from the LORD.

23 The poor man pleads,
   but the rich one answers roughly.

ᵃ18:2 Lit to uncover his heart   ᵇ18:8 Lit to the chambers of the belly   ᶜ18:9 Lit master of destruction   ᵈ18:10 Lit raised high   ᵉ18:16 Lit gift makes room   ᶠ18:19 LXX, Syr, Tg, Vg read is stronger

24 A man with many friends
    may be harmed,[a]
 but there is a friend
    who stays closer than a brother.

Poverty and Riches

19 Better a poor man who walks
    in integrity
 than someone who has
    deceitful lips and is a fool.

2 Even zeal is not good
    without knowledge,
 and the one who acts hastily[b] sins.

3 A man's own foolishness leads
    him astray,
 yet his heart rages
    against the LORD.

4 Wealth attracts many friends,
 but a poor man is separated
    from his friend.

Lies and Laziness

5 A false witness will not
    go unpunished,
 and one who utters lies
    will not escape.

6 Many seek the favor of a ruler,
 and everyone is a friend of one
    who gives gifts.

7 All the brothers of a poor man
    hate him;
 how much more do his friends
    keep their distance from him!
 He may pursue ⌊them with⌋ words,
 ⌊but⌋ they are not ⌊there⌋.[c]

8 The one who acquires good sense[d]
    loves himself;
 one who safeguards understanding
    finds success.

9 A false witness will not
    go unpunished,
 and one who utters lies perishes.

10 Luxury is not appropriate
    for a fool—
 how much less for a slave to rule
    over princes!

11 A person's insight gives
    him patience,
 and his virtue is to overlook
    an offense.

12 A king's rage is like a lion's roar,
 but his favor is like dew
    on the grass.

Fathers, Sons, and Wives

13 A foolish son is his father's ruin,
 and a wife's nagging is
    an endless dripping.

14 A house and wealth are inherited
    from fathers,
 but a sensible wife is
    from the LORD.

15 Laziness induces deep sleep,
 and a lazy person will go hungry.

16 The one who keeps commands
    preserves himself;
 one who disregards[e] his ways
    will die.

17 Kindness to the poor is a loan
    to the LORD,
 and He will give a reward
    to the lender.[f]

18 Discipline your son
    while there is hope;
 don't be intent on killing him.[g]

19 A person with great anger bears
    the penalty;

a 18:24 Some LXX mss, Syr, Tg, Vg read *friends must be friendly*   b 19:2 Lit *who is hasty with feet*   c 19:7 Hb uncertain in this line   d 19:8 Lit *acquires a heart*   e 19:16 Or *despises*, or *treats lightly*   f 19:17 Lit *to him*   g 19:18 Lit *don't lift up your soul to his death*

if you rescue him, you'll have
to do it again.

20 Listen to counsel
and receive instruction
so that you may be wise
in later life.ᵃ

Man's Plans, Lord's Decree

21 Many plans are in a man's heart,
but the LORD's decree will prevail.

22 A man's desire should be loyalty
to the covenant;
better to be a poor man
than a perjurer.

23 The •fear of the LORD leads to life;
one will sleep at nightᵇ
without danger.

Slackers, Mockers, and Fools

24 The slacker buries his hand
in the bowl;
he doesn't even bring it back
to his mouth.

25 Strike a mocker, and the
inexperienced learn a lesson;
rebuke the discerning,
and he gains knowledge.

26 The one who assaults his father
and evicts his mother
is a disgraceful and shameful son.

27 If you stop listening to instruction,
my son,
you will stray from the words
of knowledge.

28 A worthless witness mocks justice,
and a wicked mouth
swallows iniquity.

29 Judgments are prepared for mockers,
and beatings for the backs of fools.

20 Wine is a mocker, beer is
a brawler,
and whoever staggers
because of them is not wise.

2 A king's terrible wrath is
like the roaring of a lion;
anyone who provokes him
endangers himself.

3 It is honorable for a man to resolve
a dispute,
but any fool can get himself
into a quarrel.

4 The slacker does not plow
during planting season;ᶜ
at harvest time he looks,ᵈ
and there is nothing.

Guidelines for Success

5 Counsel in a man's heart is
deep water;
but a man of understanding
draws it up.

6 Many a man proclaims
his own loyalty,
but who can find
a trustworthy man?

7 The one who lives with integrity
is righteous;
his childrenᵉ who come after him
will be happy.

8 A king sitting on a throne
to judge
sifts out all evil with his eyes.

9 Who can say, "I have kept
my heart pure;
I am cleansed from my sin"?

10 Differing weights
and varying measuresᶠ—
both are detestable to the LORD.

ᵃ**19:20** Lit *in your end*   ᵇ**19:23** Lit *will spend the night satisfied*   ᶜ**20:4** Lit *plow in winter*   ᵈ**20:4** Lit *inquires*
ᵉ**20:7** Lit *sons*   ᶠ**20:10** Lit *Stone and stone, measure and measure*

¹¹ Even a young man is known
    by his actions—
by whether his behavior is pure
    and upright.

¹² The hearing ear
    and the seeing eye—
the LORD made them both.

¹³ Don't love sleep, or you will
    become poor;
open your eyes, and you'll have
    enough to eat.

¹⁴ "It's worthless, it's worthless!"
    the buyer says,
but after he is on his way, he gloats.

¹⁵ There is gold and a multitude
    of jewels,
but knowledgeable lips are
    a rare treasure.

¹⁶ Take his garment,^a
for he has put up security
    for a stranger;
get collateral if it is for foreigners.

¹⁷ Food gained by fraud is sweet
    to a man,
but afterwards his mouth is full
    of gravel.

Good Counsel

¹⁸ Finalize plans through counsel,
and wage war with sound guidance.

¹⁹ The one who reveals secrets is
    a constant gossip;
avoid someone with a big mouth.

²⁰ Whoever curses his father
    or mother—
his lamp will go out
    in deep darkness.

²¹ An inheritance gained prematurely
will not be blessed ultimately.

²² Don't say, "I will avenge this evil!"
Wait on the LORD, and He will
    rescue you.

²³ Differing weights^b are detestable
    to the LORD,
and dishonest scales are unfair.

²⁴ A man's steps are determined
    by the LORD,
so how can anyone understand
    his own way?

²⁵ It is a trap for anyone to dedicate
    something rashly
and later to reconsider his vows.

²⁶ A wise king separates out the wicked
and drives the threshing wheel
    over them.

Lamp of Lord

²⁷ A person's breath is the lamp
    of the LORD,
searching the innermost parts.^c

²⁸ Loyalty and faithfulness deliver a king;
through loyalty he maintains
    his throne.

²⁹ The glory of young men is
    their strength,
and the splendor of old men is
    gray hair.

³⁰ Lashes and wounds purge away evil,
and beatings cleanse
    the innermost parts.^d

God and Kings

21 A king's heart is a water channel
    in the LORD's hand:
He directs it wherever He chooses.

² All the ways of a man seem right
    to him,
but the LORD evaluates the motives.

---

^a**20:16** A debtor's outer garment held as collateral; Dt 24:12-13,17; Jb 22:6   ^b**20:23** Lit *A stone and a stone*
^c**20:27** Lit *the chambers of the belly*   ^d**20:30** Lit *beatings the chambers of the belly*

3 Doing what is righteous and just
is more acceptable to the LORD
than sacrifice.

4 The lamp[a] that guides the wicked—
haughty eyes and an arrogant heart—
is sin.

The Diligent and Reckless

5 The plans of the diligent
certainly lead to profit,
but anyone who is reckless
only becomes poor.

6 Making a fortune
through a lying tongue
is a vanishing mist,[b] a pursuit
of death.[c] [d]

7 The violence of the wicked
sweeps them away
because they refuse to act justly.

8 A guilty man's conduct is crooked,
but the behavior of the innocent
is upright.

Nagging Wife

9 Better to live on the corner of a roof
than to share a house
with a nagging wife.

10 A wicked person desires evil;
he has no consideration[e]
for his neighbor.

11 When a mocker is punished,
the inexperienced become wiser;
when one teaches a wise man,
he acquires knowledge.

12 The Righteous One considers
the house of the wicked;
He brings the wicked to ruin.

13 The one who shuts his ears
to the cry of the poor

will himself also call out
and not be answered.

14 A secret gift soothes anger,
and a covert bribe,[f] fierce rage.

15 Justice executed is a joy
to the righteous
but a terror to those
who practice iniquity.

16 The man who strays from the way
of wisdom
will come to rest
in the assembly
of the departed spirits.

Wine and Oil

17 The one who loves pleasure
will become a poor man;
whoever loves wine and oil will not
get rich.

18 The wicked are a ransom
for the righteous,
and the treacherous,
for[g] the upright.

19 Better to live in a wilderness
than with a nagging and hot-
tempered wife.

20 Precious treasure and oil are
in the dwelling of the wise,
but a foolish man consumes them.[h]

21 The one who pursues righteousness
and faithful love
will find life, righteousness,
and honor.

22 The wise conquer a city
of warriors
and bring down its mighty fortress.

23 The one who guards his mouth
and tongue
keeps himself out of trouble.

---

[a]21:4 Some Hb mss, ancient versions read *tillage*   [b]21:6 Or *a breath blown away*   [c]21:6 Some Hb mss, LXX, Vg read
a snare of death   [d]21:6 Lit *is vanity, ones seeking death*   [e]21:10 Or *favor*   [f]21:14 Lit *a bribe in the bosom*
[g]21:18 Or *in place of*   [h]21:20 Lit *it*

24 The proud and arrogant person,
    named "Mocker,"
  acts with excessive pride.

25 A slacker's craving will kill him
  because his hands refuse to work.
26 He is filled with craving[a] all day long,
  but the righteous give and don't
    hold back.

27 The sacrifice of a wicked person
    is detestable—
  how much more so
    when he brings it
      with ulterior motives!

28 A lying witness will perish,
  but the one who listens
    will speak successfully.

29 A wicked man puts on a bold face,
  but the upright man considers
    his way.

30 No wisdom, no understanding,
    and no counsel
  ⌊will prevail⌋ against the LORD.

31 A horse is prepared for the day
    of battle,
  but victory comes from the LORD.

Good Name

22 A good name is to be chosen
    over great wealth;
  favor is better than silver and gold.

2 The rich and the poor have this
    in common:[b]
  the LORD made them both.[c]

3 A sensible person sees danger
    and takes cover,
  but the inexperienced keep going
    and are punished.

4 The result of humility is •fear
    of the LORD,
  along with wealth, honor, and life.

5 There are thorns and snares
    on the path of the crooked;
  the one who guards himself stays
    far from them.

"Teach a Youth"

6 Teach a youth about the way
    he should go;
  even when he is old
    he will not depart from it.

Borrower and Lender

7 The rich rule over the poor,
  and the borrower is a slave
    to the lender.
8 The one who sows injustice
    will reap disaster,
  and the rod of his fury
    will be destroyed.

9 A generous person[d]
    will be blessed,
  for he shares his food
    with the poor.

10 Drive out a mocker, and conflict
    goes too;
  then lawsuits and dishonor
    will cease.

11 The one who loves a pure heart
  and gracious lips—the king is
    his friend.

12 The LORD's eyes keep watch
    over knowledge,
  but He overthrows the words
    of the treacherous.

13 The slacker says,
    "There's a lion outside!
  I'll be killed in the streets!"

14 The mouth of the forbidden woman
    is a deep pit;
  a man cursed by the LORD will fall
    into it.

[a]21:26 Lit *He craves a craving* [b]22:2 Lit *poor meet* [c]22:2 Lit *all* [d]22:9 Lit *Good of eye*

¹⁵ Foolishness is tangled up
   in the heart of a youth;
the rod of discipline will drive it
   away from him.

¹⁶ Oppressing the poor
   to enrich oneself,
and giving to the rich—both lead
   only to poverty.

Words of the Wise

¹⁷ Listen closely,^a pay attention
   to the words of the wise,
and apply your mind
   to my knowledge.
¹⁸ For it is pleasing if you keep them
   within you
and if^b they are constantly
   on your lips.
¹⁹ I have instructed you today—
   even you—
so that your confidence may be
   in the LORD.
²⁰ Haven't I written for you thirty
   sayings^c
about counsel and knowledge,
²¹ in order to teach you true
   and reliable words,
so that you may give
   a dependable report^d
to those who sent you?

²² Don't rob a poor man
   because he is poor,
and don't crush the oppressed
   at the •gate,
²³ for the LORD will take up their case
   and will plunder those
   who plunder them.

²⁴ Don't make friends
   with an angry man,^e
and don't be a companion of a hot-
   tempered man,

²⁵ or you will learn his ways
   and entangle yourself in a snare.

No Security for Loans

²⁶ Don't be one of those
   who enter agreements,^f
who put up security for loans.
²⁷ If you have no money to pay,
   even your bed will be taken
   from under you.

²⁸ Don't move an ancient property line
   that your fathers set up.

Skilled Man

²⁹ Do you see a man skilled
   in his work?
He will stand in the presence
   of kings.
He will not stand in the presence
   of unknown men.

Rules with Rulers

23 When you sit down to dine
   with a ruler,
consider carefully what^g is
   before you,
² and stick a knife in your throat
   if you have a big^h appetite;
³ don't desire his choice food,
   for that food is deceptive.

⁴ Don't wear yourself out to get rich;
   stop giving your attention to it.
⁵ As soon as your eyes fly to it,
   it disappears,
for it makes wings for itself
   and flies like an eagle to the sky.

⁶ Don't eat a stingy person's bread,ⁱ
   and don't desire his choice food,
⁷ for as he thinks within himself,
   so he is.
"Eat and drink," he says to you,

---

^a**22:17** Lit *Stretch out your ear*   ^b**22:18** Or *you; let them be,* or *you, so that*   ^c**22:20** Text emended; one Hb tradition reads *you previously;* alt Hb tradition reads *you excellent things;* LXX, Syr, Vg read *you three times*   ^d**22:21** Lit *give dependable words*   ^e**22:24** Lit *with a master of anger*   ^f**22:26** Lit *who shakes hands*   ^g**23:1** Or *who*   ^h**23:2** Lit *you are the master of an*   ⁱ**23:6** Lit *eat bread of an evil eye*

but his heart is not with you.
8 You will vomit the little
    you've eaten
  and waste your pleasant words.

9 Don't speak to[a] a fool,
  for he will despise the insight
    of your words.
10 Don't move
    an ancient property line,
  and don't encroach on the fields
    of the fatherless,
11 for their Redeemer is strong,
  and He will take up their case
    against you.

Youths and Child-rearing

12 Apply yourself to instruction
  and listen to words of knowledge.
13 Don't withhold correction
    from a youth;
  if you beat him with a rod,
    he will not die.
14 Strike him with a rod,
  and you will rescue his life
    from •Sheol.

15 My son, if your heart is wise,
  my heart will indeed rejoice.
16 My innermost being will cheer
  when your lips say what is right.

17 Don't be jealous of sinners;
  instead, always •fear the LORD.
18 For then you will have a future,
  and your hope will never fade.

19 Listen, my son, and be wise;
  keep your mind
    on the right course.
20 Don't associate with those
    who drink too much wine,
  or with those
    who gorge themselves on meat.

21 For the drunkard and the glutton
    will become poor,
  and grogginess will clothe ⌊them⌋
    in rags.

22 Listen to your father who gave
    you life,
  and don't despise your mother
    when[b] she is old.
23 Buy—and do not sell—truth,
  wisdom, instruction,
    and understanding.
24 The father of a righteous son
    will rejoice greatly,
  and one who fathers a wise son
    will delight in him.
25 Let your father and mother have joy,
  and let her who gave birth to you
    rejoice.

Prostitutes and Wine

26 My son, give me your heart,
  and let your eyes observe my ways.
27 For a prostitute is a deep pit,
  and a forbidden woman is
    a narrow well;
28 indeed, she sets an ambush
    like a robber
  and increases those among men
    who are unfaithful.

29 Who has woe? Who has sorrow?
  Who has conflicts?
    Who has complaints?
  Who has wounds for no reason?
  Who has red eyes?
30 Those who linger over wine,
  those who go looking
    for mixed wine.
31 Don't gaze at wine when it is red,
  when it gleams in the cup
  and goes down smoothly.
32 In the end it bites like a snake
  and stings like a viper.

a 23:9 Lit in the ears of   b 23:22 Or because

33 Your eyes will see strange things,
    and you will say absurd things.ᵃ
34 You'll be like someone sleeping
      out at sea
    or lying down on the top
      of a ship's mast.
35 "They struck me, butᵇ I feel
      no pain!
    They beat me, but I didn't know it!
    When will I wake up?
    I'll look for another ⌊drink⌋."

Don't Envy the Evil

24 Don't envy evil men
     or desire to be with them,
2 for their hearts plan violence,
    and their words stir up trouble.

3 A house is built by wisdom,
    and it is established
      by understanding;
4 by knowledge the rooms are filled
    with every precious
      and beautiful treasure.

5 A wise warrior is better
      than a strong one,
    and a man of knowledge than one
      of strength;
6 for you should wage war
      with sound guidance—
    victory comes
      with many counselors.

7 Wisdom is inaccessible toᶜ a fool;
    he does not open his mouth
      at the •gate.
8 The one who plots evil
    will be called a schemer.
9 A foolish scheme is sin,
    and a mocker is detestable
      to people.

10 If you do nothing in a difficult time,
    your strength is limited.

11 Rescue those being taken off
      to death,
    and save those stumbling
      toward slaughter.
12 If you say, "But we didn't know
      about this,"
    won't He who weighs hearts
      consider it?
    Won't He who protects
      your life know?
    Won't He repay a person
      according to his work?

13 Eat honey, my son, for it is good,
    and the honeycomb is sweet
      to your palate;
14 realize that wisdom is the same
      for you.
    If you find it, you will have a future,
    and your hope will never fade.

15 Don't set an ambush, wicked man,
    at the campᵈ of the righteous man;
    don't destroy his dwelling.

Resilience of Righteous

16 Though a righteous man falls
      seven times,
    he will get up,
    but the wicked will stumble into ruin.

17 Don't gloat when your enemy falls,
    and don't let your heart rejoice
      when he stumbles,
18 or the LORD will see, be displeased,
    and turn His wrath away from him.

19 Don't worry because of evildoers,
    and don't envy the wicked.
20 For the evil have no future;
    the lamp of the wicked will be
      put out.

21 My son, •fear the LORD, as well as
      the king,
    and don't associate with rebels,ᵉ

---

22 for their destruction
    will come suddenly;
who knows what disaster these two
    can bring?

23 These ⌊sayings⌋ also
    belong to the wise:

It is not good to show partiality
    in judgment.
24 Whoever says to the guilty,
    "You are innocent"—
people will curse him, and tribes
    will denounce him;
25 but it will go well with those
    who convict the guilty,
and a generous blessing will come
    to them.

26 He who gives an honest answer
gives a kiss on the lips.

27 Complete your outdoor work,
    and prepare your field;
afterwards, build your house.

28 Don't testify against your neighbor
    without cause.
Don't deceive with your lips.
29 Don't say, "I'll do to him
    what he did to me;
I'll repay the man for what
    he has done."

Fruits of Slacker

30 I went by the field of a slacker
and by the vineyard of a man
    lacking sense.
31 Thistles had come up everywhere,
    weeds covered the ground,
and the stone wall was ruined.
32 I saw, and took it to heart;
I looked, and received instruction:
33 a little sleep, a little slumber,
a little folding of the arms to rest,

34 and your poverty will come
    like a robber,
your need, like a bandit.

Hezekiah's Collection

25 These too are proverbs
    of Solomon,
which the men of Hezekiah,
    king of Judah, copied.

2 It is the glory of God to conceal
    a matter
and the glory of kings to investigate
    a matter.
3 As the heaven is high and the earth
    is deep,
so the hearts of kings cannot
    be investigated.

4 Remove impurities from silver,
and a vessel will be produced[a]
    for a silversmith.
5 Remove the wicked
    from the king's presence,
and his throne will be established
    in righteousness.

Don't Brag

6 Don't brag about yourself
    before the king,
and don't stand in the place
    of the great;
7 for it is better for him to say to you,
    "Come up here!"
than to demote you in plain view
    of a noble.[b]

Beware of Lawsuits

8 Don't take a matter to court hastily.
Otherwise, what will
    you do afterwards
if your opponent[c] humiliates you?
9 Make your case
    with your opponent[c]
without revealing another's secret;

---

[a]**25:4** Lit *will come out*; Ex 32:24   [b]**25:7** Lit *you before a noble whom your eyes see*   [c]**25:8** Or *neighbor*

10 otherwise, the one who hears
　　will disgrace you,
　and you'll never live it down.ᵃ

Apt Words

11 A word spoken at the right time
　is like golden apples
　　on a silver tray.ᵇ
12 A wise correction to a receptive ear
　is like a gold ring or an ornament
　　of gold.
13 To those who send him,
　　a trustworthy messenger
　is like the coolness of snow
　　on a harvest day;
　he refreshes the life of his masters.
14 The man who boasts about a gift
　　that does not exist
　is like clouds and wind
　　without rain.
15 A ruler can be persuaded
　　through patience,
　and a gentle tongue can break
　　a bone.
16 If you find honey, eat only
　　what you need;
　otherwise, you'll get sick from it
　　and vomit.

Visits to Neighbors

17 Seldom set foot
　　in your neighbor's house;
　otherwise, he'll get sick of you
　　and hate you.

18 A man giving false testimony
　　against his neighbor
　is like a club, a sword,
　　or a sharp arrow.
19 Trusting an unreliable person
　　in a time of trouble
　is like a rotten tooth
　　or a faltering foot.

20 Singing songs to a troubled heart
　is like taking off clothing
　　on a cold day,
　or like ₍pouring₎ vinegar on soda.ᶜ

Feed Your Enemy

21 If your enemy is hungry, give him
　　food to eat,
　and if he is thirsty, give him water
　　to drink;
22 for you will heap coals on his head,
　and the Lᴏʀᴅ will reward you.

23 The north wind produces rain,
　and a backbiting tongue,
　　angry looks.
24 Better to live on the corner of a roof
　than in a house shared
　　with a nagging wife.
25 Good news from a distant land
　is like cold water
　　to a parched throat.ᵈ
26 A righteous person who yields
　　to the wicked
　is like a muddied spring
　　or a polluted well.
27 It is not good to eat
　　too much honey,
　or to seek glory after glory.

Temper Control

28 A man who does not control
　　his temper
　is like a city whose wall
　　is broken down.

Fool Problems

26 Like snow in summer and rain
　at harvest,
　honor is inappropriate for a fool.
2 Like a flitting sparrow
　　or a fluttering swallow,
　an undeserved curse
　　goes nowhere.

ᵃ**25:10** Lit *and your evil report will not turn back*　ᵇ**25:11** Or *like apples of gold in settings of silver*　ᶜ**25:20** Lit *natron, or sodium carbonate*　ᵈ**25:25** Or *a weary person*

3 A whip for the horse, a bridle
    for the donkey,
and a rod for the backs of fools.
4 Don't answer a fool according to
    his foolishness,
or you'll be like him yourself.
5 Answer a fool according to
    his foolishness,
or he'll become wise
    in his own eyes.
6 The one who sends a message
    by a fool's hand
cuts off his own feet
    and drinks violence.
7 A proverb in the mouth of a fool
is like lame legs that hang limp.
8 Giving honor to a fool
is like binding a stone in a sling.ᵃ
9 A proverb in the mouth of a fool
is like a stick with thorns,
brandished byᵇ the hand
    of a drunkard.
10 The one who hires a fool,
    or who hires those passing by,
is like an archer
    who wounds everyone.
11 As a dog returns to its vomit,
so a fool repeats his foolishness.
12 Do you see a man who is wise
    in his own eyes?
There is more hope for a fool
    than for him.

Slackers Stumble

13 The slacker says, "There's a lion
    in the road—
a lion in the public square!"
14 A door turns on its hinge,
and a slacker, on his bed.
15 The slacker buries his hand
    in the bowl;
he is too weary to bring it
    to his mouth.

16 In his own eyes, a slacker is wiser
than seven men
    who can answer sensibly.

Meddlers, Bad Jokers, Gossips

17 A passerby who meddles
    in a quarrel that's not his
is like one who grabs a dog
    by the ears.
18 Like a madman who throws
    flaming darts and deadly arrows,
19 so is the man who deceives
    his neighbor
and says, "I was only joking!"

20 Without wood, fire goes out;
without a gossip,
    conflict dies down.
21 As charcoal for embers and wood
    for fire,
so is a quarrelsome man
    for kindling strife.
22 A gossip's words are
    like choice food
that goes down to
    one's innermost being.ᶜ

Evil Hearts

23 Smoothᵈ lips with an evil heart
are like glaze on an earthen vessel.
24 A hateful person disguises himself
    with his speech
and harbors deceit within.
25 When he speaks graciously,
    don't believe him,
for there are seven abominations
    in his heart.
26 Though his hatred is concealed
    by deception,
his evil will be revealed
    in the assembly.
27 The one who digs a pit will fall
    into it,
and whoever rolls a stone—

ᵃ**26:8** A stone bound in a sling would not release and could harm the person using the sling. A modern equivalent is jamming a cork in a gun barrel.   ᵇ**26:9** Lit *thorn that goes up into*   ᶜ**26:22** Lit *to the chambers of the belly*
ᵈ**26:23** LXX; MT reads *Burning*

it will come back on him.

28 A lying tongue hates
      those it crushes,
   and a flattering mouth causes ruin.

27 Don't boast about tomorrow,
      for you don't know what a day
      might bring.

True Friends

2 Let another praise you, and not
      your own mouth—
   a stranger, and not your own lips.

3 A stone is heavy and sand,
      a burden,
   but aggravation from a fool
      outweighs them both.

4 Fury is cruel, and anger is a flood,
   but who can withstand jealousy?

5 Better an open reprimand
   than concealed love.

6 The wounds of a friend
      are trustworthy,
   but the kisses of an enemy
      are excessive.

7 A person who is full tramples
      on a honeycomb,
   but to a hungry person,
      any bitter thing is sweet.

8 A man wandering from his home
   is like a bird wandering
      from its nest.

9 Oil and incense bring joy
      to the heart,
   and the sweetness of a friend
      is better than self-counsel.ᵃ

10 Don't abandon your friend
       or your father's friend,
    and don't go
       to your brother's house

in your time of calamity;
   better a neighbor nearby
      than a brother far away.

11 Be wise, my son, and bring
       my heart joy,
    so that I can answer anyone
       who taunts me.

12 The sensible see danger
       and take cover;
    the foolish keep going
       and are punished.

13 Take his garment,ᵇ
    for he has put up security
       for a stranger;
    get collateral if it is for foreigners.ᶜ

14 If one blesses his neighbor
    with a loud voice early
       in the morning,
    it will be counted as a curse to him.

15 An endless dripping on a rainy day
    and a nagging wife are alike.
16 The one who controls her controls
       the wind
    and grasps oil with his right hand.

17 Iron sharpens iron,
    and one man sharpens another.ᵈ

18 Whoever tends a fig tree will eat
       its fruit,
    and whoever looks after his master
       will be honored.

19 As the water reflects the face,
    so the heart reflects the person.

20 •Sheol and •Abaddon are
       never satisfied,
    and people's eyes are
       never satisfied.

21 Silver is ⌊tested⌋ in a crucible,
       gold in a smelter,

ᵃ27:9 LXX reads *heart, but the soul is torn up by affliction*   ᵇ27:13 A debtor's outer garment held as collateral;
Dt 24:12-13; Am 2:8   ᶜ27:13 Lit *a foreign woman*   ᵈ27:17 Lit *and a man sharpens his friend's face*

and a man, by the praise
he receives.[a]

22 Though you grind a fool
in a mortar with a pestle
along with grain,
you will not separate his foolishness
from him.

Financial Preparation

23 Know well the condition
of your flock,
and pay attention to your herds,
24 for wealth is not forever;
not even a crown lasts
for all time.
25 When hay is removed
and new growth appears
and the grain from the hills
is gathered in,
26 lambs will provide
your clothing,
and goats, the price of a field;
27 there will be enough goat's milk
for your food—
food for your household
and nourishment
for your servants.

Results of Lawlessness

28 The wicked flee when no one
is pursuing ⌊them⌋,
but the righteous are as bold
as a lion.

2 When a land is in rebellion, it has
many rulers,
but with a discerning
and knowledgeable person,
it endures.
3 A destitute leader[b] who oppresses
the poor
is like a driving rain that leaves
no food.

4 Those who reject the law
praise the wicked,
but those who keep the law battle
against them.
5 Evil men do not understand justice,
but those who seek the LORD
understand everything.
6 Better a poor man who lives
with integrity
than a rich man who distorts right
and wrong.[c]
7 A discerning son keeps the law,
but a companion of gluttons
humiliates his father.
8 Whoever increases his wealth
through excessive interest
collects it for one who is kind
to the poor.

Impediment to Prayer

9 Anyone who turns his ear
away from hearing the law—
even his prayer is detestable.
10 The one who leads the upright
into an evil way
will fall into his own pit,
but the blameless will inherit
what is good.
11 A rich man is wise in his own eyes,
but a poor man
who has discernment
sees through him.
12 When the righteous triumph,
there is great rejoicing,[d]
but when the wicked come to power,
people hide themselves.

Confession and Prosperity

13 The one who conceals his sins
will not prosper,

[a]27:21 Lit The crucible for silver and the smelter for gold, and a man for a mouth of praise.   [b]28:3 LXX reads
A wicked man   [c]28:6 Lit who twists two ways   [d]28:12 Lit glory

but whoever confesses
and renounces them
will find mercy.

¹⁴ Happy is the one who is always
reverent,
but one who hardens his heart falls
into trouble.

¹⁵ A wicked ruler over
a helpless people
is like a roaring lion
or a charging bear.

¹⁶ A leader who lacks understanding
is very oppressive,
but one who hates unjust gain
prolongs his life.

¹⁷ A man burdened by bloodguilt[a]
will be a fugitive until death.
Let no one help him.

¹⁸ The one who lives with integrity
will be helped,
but one who distorts right
and wrong[b]
will suddenly fall.

¹⁹ The one who works his land
will have plenty of food,
but whoever chases fantasies
will have his fill of poverty.

²⁰ A faithful man will have
many blessings,
but one in a hurry to get rich
will not go unpunished.

²¹ It is not good to show partiality—
yet a man may sin for a piece
of bread.

²² A greedy man[c] is in a hurry
for wealth;
he doesn't know that poverty
will come to him.

²³ One who rebukes a person
will later find more favor
than one who flatters[d]
with his tongue.

Sin without Standards

²⁴ The one who robs his father
or mother
and says, "That's no sin,"
is a companion to a man
who destroys.

²⁵ A greedy person provokes conflict,
but whoever trusts in the LORD
will prosper.

²⁶ The one who trusts in himself[e] is
a fool,
but one who walks in wisdom
will be safe.

Give and Receive

²⁷ The one who gives to the poor
will not be in need,
but one who turns his eyes away[f]
will receive many curses.

²⁸ When the wicked come to power,
people hide,
but when they are destroyed,
the righteous flourish.

Rules for Relationships

29 One who becomes stiff-necked,
after many reprimands
will be broken suddenly—
and without a remedy.

² When the righteous flourish,
the people rejoice,
but when the wicked rule,
people groan.

³ A man who loves wisdom brings joy
to his father,

---

[a] **28:17** Lit *the blood of a person*   [b] **28:18** Lit *who is twisted regarding two ways*   [c] **28:22** Lit *A man with an evil eye*
[d] **28:23** Lit *is smooth*   [e] **28:26** Lit *his heart*   [f] **28:27** Lit *who shuts his eyes*

but one who consorts
   with prostitutes destroys
   his wealth.

4 By justice a king brings stability
   to a land,
but a man ⌊who demands⌋
   "contributions"[a]
demolishes it.

5 A man who flatters[b] his neighbor
spreads a net for his feet.

6 An evil man is caught by sin,
but the righteous one sings
   and rejoices.

7 The righteous person knows
   the rights[c] of the poor,
but the wicked one does not
   understand these concerns.

8 Mockers inflame a city,
but the wise turn away anger.

9 If a wise man goes to court
   with a fool,
there will be ranting and raving
   but no resolution.[d]

10 Bloodthirsty men hate
   an honest person,
but the upright care about him.[e]

11 A fool gives full vent to his anger,[f]
but a wise man holds it in check.

12 If a ruler listens to lies,
all his servants will be wicked.

13 The poor and the oppressor
   have this in common:[g]
the LORD gives light to the eyes
   of both.

14 A king who judges the poor
   with fairness—
his throne will be established forever.

Correct Sons

15 A rod of correction
   imparts wisdom,
but a youth left to himself[h]
is a disgrace to his mother.

16 When the wicked increase,
   rebellion increases,
but the righteous will see
   their downfall.

17 Discipline your son,
   and he will give you comfort;
he will also give you delight.

Personal Flaws

18 Without revelation[i] people
   run wild,
but one who keeps the law
   will be happy.

19 A servant cannot be disciplined
   by words;
though he understands,
   he doesn't respond.

20 Do you see a man who speaks
   too soon?
There is more hope for a fool
   than for him.

21 A slave pampered from his youth
will become arrogant[j] later on.

22 An angry man stirs up conflict,
and a hot-tempered man[k]
   increases rebellion.

23 A person's pride will humble him,
but a humble spirit
   will gain honor.

24 To be a thief's partner is
   to hate oneself;
he hears the curse but
   will not testify.[l]

---

[a]**29:4** The Hb word usually refers to offerings in worship.　[b]**29:5** Lit *is smooth on*　[c]**29:7** Lit *justice*　[d]**29:9** Lit *rest*　[e]**29:10** Or *person, and seek the life of the upright*　[f]**29:11** Lit *spirit*　[g]**29:13** Lit *oppressor meet*　[h]**29:15** Lit *youth sent away*; Jb 39:5; Is 16:2　[i]**29:18** Lit *vision*　[j]**29:21** Hb obscure　[k]**29:22** Lit *a master of rage*　[l]**29:24** When a call for witnesses was made public, anyone with information who did not submit his testimony was under a curse; Lv 5:1.

25 The fear of man is a snare,
   but the one who trusts in the LORD
      is protected.[a]

26 Many seek a ruler's favor,
   but a man receives justice
      from the LORD.

27 An unjust man is detestable
      to the righteous,
   and one whose way is upright
   is detestable to the wicked.

Words of Agur

30 The words of Agur son of Jakeh.
         The oracle.[b]

The man's oration to Ithiel, to Ithiel
and Ucal:[c]

2 I am the least intelligent of men,[d]
   and I lack man's ability
      to understand.

God's Son

3 I have not gained wisdom,
   and I have no knowledge
      of the Holy One.
4 Who has gone up to heaven
      and come down?
   Who has gathered the wind
      in His hands?
   Who has bound up the waters
      in a cloak?
   Who has established all the ends
      of the earth?
   What is His name,
   and what is the name of His Son—
   if you know?

God's Pure, Complete Word

5 Every word of God is pure;[e]
   He is a shield to those
      who take refuge in Him.

6 Don't add to His words,
   or He will rebuke you,
      and you will be proved a liar.

7 Two things I ask of You;
   don't deny them to me
      before I die:
8 Keep falsehood and deceitful words
      far from me.
   Give me neither poverty
      nor wealth;
   feed me with the food I need.
9 Otherwise, I might have too much
   and deny You, saying,
   "Who is the LORD?"
   or I might have nothing and steal,
   profaning[f] the name of my God.

10 Don't slander a servant
      to his master,
    or he will curse you, and you will
       become guilty.

Evil Generation

11 There is a generation that curses
       its father
    and does not bless its mother.
12 There is a generation that is pure
       in its own eyes,
    yet is not washed from its filth.
13 There is a generation—
       how haughty its eyes
    and pretentious its looks.[g]
14 There is a generation whose teeth
       are swords,
    whose fangs are knives,
    devouring the oppressed
       from the land
    and the needy from among
       mankind.

15 The leech has two daughters:
       Give, Give.
    Three things are never satisfied;

---

a**29:25** Lit *raised high*   b**30:1** Or *The burden*, or *Jakeh from Massa*; Pr 31:1   c**30:1** Hb uncertain. Sometimes read with
different word division as *oration: I am weary, God, I am weary, God, and I am exhausted*, or *oration: I am not God, I am
not God, that I should prevail*. LXX reads *My son, fear my words and when you have received them repent. The man
says these things to the believers in God, and I pause*.   d**30:2** Lit *I am more stupid than a man*   e**30:5** Lit *refined*, like
metal   f**30:9** Lit *grabbing*   g**30:13** Lit *and its eyelids lifted up*

four never say, "Enough!":
16 •Sheol; a barren womb;
earth, which is never satisfied
    with water;
and fire, which never says,
    "Enough!"

17 As for the eye that ridicules a father
and despises obedience
    to a mother,
may ravens of the valley
    pluck it out
and young vultures eat it.

18 Three things are beyond me;
four I can't understand:
19 the way of an eagle in the sky,
the way of a snake on a rock,
the way of a ship at sea,
and the way of a man
    with a young woman.

Adulteress with No Values

20 This is the way of an adulteress:
she eats and wipes her mouth
and says, "I've done
    nothing wrong."

21 The earth trembles
    under three things;
it cannot bear up under four:
22 a servant when he becomes king,
a fool when he is stuffed with food,
23 an unloved woman
    when she marries,
and a serving girl when she ousts
    her lady.

Humans and Animals

24 Four things on earth are small,
yet they are extremely wise:
25 the ants are not a strong people,
yet they store up their food
    in the summer;
26 hyraxes are not a mighty people,

yet they make their homes
    in the cliffs;
27 locusts have no king,
yet all of them march in ranks;
28 a lizardᵃ can be caught
    in your hands,
yet it lives in kings' palaces.

29 Three things are stately
    in their stride,
even four are stately in their walk:
30 a lion, which is mightiest
    among beasts
and doesn't retreat before anything,
31 a strutting rooster,ᵇ a goat,
and a king at the head of his army.ᶜ

32 If you have been foolish
    by exalting yourself,
or if you've been scheming,
put your hand over your mouth.
33 For the churning of milk
    produces butter,
and twisting a nose draws blood,
and stirring up anger
    produces strife.

Words of Lemuel

31 The words of King Lemuel,
    an oracleᵈ that his mother
    taught him:

2 What ⌊should I say⌋, my son?
What, son of my womb?
What, son of my vows?
3 Don't spend your energy on women
or your efforts on those
    who destroy kings.
4 It is not for kings, Lemuel,
it is not for kings to drink wine
or for rulers ⌊to desire⌋ beer.
5 Otherwise, theyᵉ will drink,
forget what is decreed,
and pervert justice for all
    the oppressed.ᶠ

ᵃ**30:28** Or *spider*   ᵇ**30:31** Or *a greyhound*   ᶜ**30:31** LXX reads *king haranguing his people*   ᵈ**31:1** Or *of Lemuel, king of Massa*   ᵉ**31:5** Lit *he*   ᶠ**31:5** Lit *sons of affliction*

6 Give beer to one who is dying,
and wine to one whose life is bitter.
7 Let him drink so that he can forget
his poverty
and remember his trouble no more.
8 Speak up[a] for those who have
no voice,[b]
for the justice of all
who are dispossessed.[c]
9 Speak up,[a] judge righteously,
and defend the cause of[d]
the oppressed and needy.

Praise of Capable Wife

10 Who can find a capable wife?[e]
She is far more precious
than jewels.[f]
11 The heart of her husband trusts
in her,
and he will not lack anything good.
12 She rewards him with good,
not evil,
all the days of her life.
13 She selects wool and flax[g]
and works with willing hands.
14 She is like the merchant ships,
bringing her food from far away.
15 She rises while it is still night
and provides food
for her household
and portions[h] for her servants.
16 She evaluates a field and buys it;
she plants a vineyard
with her earnings.[i]
17 She draws on her strength[j]
and reveals that her arms are strong.
18 She sees that her profits are good,
and her lamp never goes out at night.
19 She extends her hands
to the spinning staff,
and her hands hold the spindle.
20 Her hands reach[k] out to the poor,
and she extends her hands
to the needy.
21 She is not afraid for her household
when it snows,
for all in her household
are doubly clothed.[l]
22 She makes her own bed coverings;
her clothing is fine linen
and purple.
23 Her husband is known
at the city •gates,
where he sits among the elders
of the land.
24 She makes and sells
linen garments;
she delivers belts[m]
to the merchants.
25 Strength and honor are
her clothing,
and she can laugh at the time
to come.
26 She opens her mouth
with wisdom,
and loving instruction[n] is
on her tongue.
27 She watches over the activities
of her household
and is never idle.[o]
28 Her sons rise up
and call her blessed.
Her husband also praises her:
29 "Many women[p] are capable,
but you surpass them all!"
30 Charm is deceptive and beauty
is fleeting,
but a woman who •fears the LORD
will be praised.
31 Give her the reward of her labor,[q]
and let her works praise her
at the city gates.

[a]**31:8,9** Lit *Open your mouth* [b]**31:8** Lit *who are mute* [c]**31:8** Lit *all the sons of passing away* [d]**31:9** Lit *and justice for* [e]**31:10** Or *a wife of quality*, or *a wife of good character*; Ru 2:1; 3:11 [f]**31:10** Vv. 10-31 form an •acrostic in Hb. [g]**31:13** Plant from which linen is made [h]**31:15** Or *tasks* [i]**31:16** Or *vineyard by her own labors* [j]**31:17** Lit *She wraps strength around her like a belt* [k]**31:20** Lit *Her hand reaches* [l]**31:21** LXX, Vg; MT reads *are dressed in scarlet* [m]**31:24** Or *sashes* [n]**31:26** Or *and the teaching of kindness* [o]**31:27** Lit *and does not eat the bread of idleness* [p]**31:29** Lit *daughters* [q]**31:31** Lit *the fruit of her hands*

ECCLESIASTES

Everything is Futile

1 The words of the Teacher,[a] son of David, king in Jerusalem.

2 "Absolute futility,"
   says the Teacher.
  "Absolute futility. Everything
   is futile."

3 What does a man gain for all
   his efforts
  he labors at under the sun?

4 A generation goes and a generation
   comes,
  but the earth remains forever.

5 The sun rises and the sun sets;
  panting, ⌊it returns⌋ to its place
   where it rises.

6 Gusting to the south,
  turning to the north,
  turning, turning, goes the wind,
  and the wind returns in its cycles.

7 All the streams flow to the sea,
   yet the sea is never full.
  The streams are flowing to the place,
   and they flow there again.

8 All things[b] are wearisome;
   man is unable to speak.
  The eye is not satisfied by seeing
   or the ear filled with hearing.

Nothing New

9 What has been is what will be,
  and what has been done is
   what will be done;
  there is nothing new
   under the sun.

10 Can one say about anything,
   "Look, this is new"?
  It has already existed in the ages
   before us.

11 There is no memory of those
   who[c] came before;
  and of those who[c] will come after
  there will also be no memory
   among those who follow ⌊them⌋.

Limits of Wisdom

12 I, the Teacher, have been[d] king over Israel in Jerusalem. 13 I applied my mind to seek and explore through wisdom all that is done under heaven. God has given •people this miserable task to keep them occupied. 14 I have seen all the things that are done under the sun and have found everything to be futile, a pursuit of the wind.[e] 15What is crooked cannot be straightened; what is lacking cannot be counted.

16 I said to myself,[f] "Look, I have amassed wisdom far beyond all those who were over Jerusalem before me, and my mind has thoroughly grasped[g] wisdom and knowledge." 17 I applied my mind to know wisdom and knowledge, madness and folly; I learned that this too is a pursuit of the wind.[e]

18 For with much wisdom is
   much sorrow;
  as knowledge increases,
   grief increases.

Emptiness of Pleasure

2 I said to myself, "Go ahead, I will test you with pleasure and enjoy what is good." But it turned out to be futile. 2 I said about laughter, "It is madness," and about pleasure, "What does this accomplish?" 3 I explored with my mind how to let my body enjoy life[h] with

a1:1 Or of Qoheleth, or of the Leader of the Assembly b1:8 Or words c1:11 Or of the things that d1:12 Or Teacher, was e1:14,17 Or a feeding on wind, or an affliction of spirit f1:16 Lit said with my heart g1:16 Or discerned h2:3 Lit to pull my body

wine and how to grasp folly—my mind still guiding me with wisdom—until I could see what is good for •people to do under heaven[a] during the few days of their lives.

Emptiness of Possessions

[4] I increased my achievements. I built houses and planted vineyards for myself. [5] I made gardens and parks for myself and planted every kind of fruit tree in them. [6] I constructed reservoirs of water for myself from which to irrigate a grove of flourishing trees. [7] I acquired male and female servants and had slaves who were born in my house. I also owned many herds of cattle and flocks, more than all who were before me in Jerusalem. [8] I also amassed silver and gold for myself, and the treasure of kings and provinces. I gathered male and female singers for myself, and many concubines, the delights of men.[b] [9] Thus, I became great and surpassed all who were before me in Jerusalem; my wisdom also remained with me. [10] All that my eyes desired, I did not deny them. I did not refuse myself any pleasure, for I took pleasure in all my struggles. This was my reward for all my struggles. [11] When I considered all that I had accomplished[c] and what I had labored to achieve, I found everything to be futile and a pursuit of the wind. There was nothing to be gained under the sun.

Wisdom, Madness, and Folly

[12] Then I turned to consider wisdom, madness, and folly, for what will the man be like who comes after the king? He[d] will do what has already been done. [13] And I realized that there is an advantage to wisdom over folly, like the advantage of light over darkness.

[14] The wise man has eyes in his head,
      but the fool walks in darkness.

Yet I also knew that one fate comes to them both. [15] So I said to myself, "What happens to the fool will also happen to me. Why then have I been overly wise?" And I said to myself that this is also futile. [16] For, just like the fool, there is no lasting remembrance of the wise man, since in the days to come both will be forgotten. How is it that the wise man dies just like the fool? [17] Therefore, I hated life because the work that was done under the sun was distressing to me. For everything is futile and a pursuit of the wind.

Emptiness of Work

[18] I hated all my work at which I labored under the sun because I must leave it to the man who comes after me. [19] And who knows whether he will be a wise man or a fool? Yet he will take over all my work that I labored at skillfully under the sun. This too is futile. [20] So I began to give myself over[e] to despair concerning all my work I had labored at under the sun. [21] For there is a man whose work was done with wisdom, knowledge, and skill, but he must give his portion to a man who has not worked for it. This too is futile and a great wrong. [22] For what does a man get with all his work and all his efforts that he labors with under the sun? [23] For all his days are filled with grief, and his occupation is sorrowful; even at night, his mind does not rest. This too is futile.

---

[a]**2:3** Two Hb mss, LXX, Syr read *the sun*   [b]**2:8** LXX, Theod, Syr read *and male cupbearers and female cupbearers*; Aq, Tg, Vg read *a cup and cups*; Hb obscure   [c]**2:11** Lit *all my works that my hands had done*   [d]**2:12** Other Hb mss read *They*   [e]**2:20** Lit *And I turned to cause my heart*

Eat, Drink, Enjoy

24 There is nothing better for man than to eat, drink, and to enjoy[a][b] his work. I have seen that even this is from God's hand. 25 For who can eat and who can enjoy life[c] apart from Him?[d] 26 For to the man who is pleasing in His sight, He gives wisdom, knowledge, and joy, but to the sinner He gives the task of gathering and accumulating in order to give to the one who is pleasing in God's sight. This too is futile and a pursuit of the wind.

Mystery of Time

3 There is an occasion
    for everything,
  and a time for every activity
  under heaven:
2 a time to give birth and a time
     to die;
   a time to plant and a time
     to uproot;[e]
3 a time to kill and a time to heal;
   a time to tear down and a time
     to build;
4 a time to weep and a time to laugh;
   a time to mourn and a time
     to dance;
5 a time to throw stones and a time
     to gather stones;
   a time to embrace and a time
     to avoid embracing;
6 a time to search and a time to count
     as lost;
   a time to keep and a time
     to throw away;
7 a time to tear and a time to sew;
   a time to be silent and a time
     to speak;
8 a time to love and a time to hate;
   a time for war and a time
     for peace.

Eternity in Heart

9 What does the worker gain from his struggles? 10 I have seen the task that God has given •people to keep them occupied. 11 He has made everything appropriate[f] in its time. He has also put eternity in their hearts,[g] but man cannot discover the work God has done from beginning to end. 12 I know that there is nothing better for them than to rejoice and enjoy the[h] good life. 13 It is also the gift of God whenever anyone eats, drinks, and enjoys all his efforts. 14 I know that all God does will last forever; there is no adding to it or taking from it. God works so that people will be in awe of Him. 15 Whatever is, has already been, and whatever will be, already is. God repeats what has passed.[i]

Mystery of Injustice and Death

16 I also observed under the sun: there is wickedness at the place of judgment and there is wickedness at the place of righteousness. 17 I said to myself, "God will judge the righteous and the wicked, since there is a time for every activity and every work." 18 I said to myself, "This happens concerning people, so that God may test them and they may see for themselves that they are like animals." 19 For the fate of people and the fate of animals is the same. As one dies, so dies the other; they all have the same breath. People have no advantage over animals, for everything is futile. 20 All are going to the same place; all come from dust, and all return to dust. 21 Who knows if the spirit of people rises upward and the spirit of animals goes downward to the earth? 22 I have seen that there is nothing better than for a

---

a2:24 Syr, Tg; MT reads *There is no good in man who eats and drinks and enjoys*   b2:24 Lit *and his soul sees good*   c2:25 LXX, Theod, Syr read *can drink*   d2:25 Other Hb mss, LXX, Syr read *me*   e3:2 Lit *uproot what is planted*   f3:11 Or *beautiful*   g3:11 Or *has put a sense of past and future into their minds*, or *has placed ignorance in their hearts*   h3:12 Lit *his*   i3:15 Lit *God seeks [the] pursued*; or *God calls the past to account*, or *God seeks what is past*, or *God seeks the persecuted*

person to enjoy his activities, because that is his reward. For who can enable him to see what will happen after he dies?[a]

4 Again, I observed all the acts of oppression being done under the sun. Look at the tears of those who are oppressed; they have no one to comfort them. Power is with those who oppress them; they have no one to comfort them. [2] So I admired the dead, who have already died, more than the living, who are still alive. [3] But better than either of them is the one who has not yet existed, who has not seen the evil activity that is done under the sun.

Loneliness of Wealth

[4] I saw that all labor and all skillful work is due to a man's jealousy of his friend. This too is futile and a pursuit of the wind.

[5] The fool folds his arms
and consumes his own flesh.
[6] Better one handful with rest,
than two handfuls with effort
and pursuit of the wind.

[7] Again, I saw futility under the sun: [8] There is a person without a companion,[b] without even a son or brother, and though there is no end to all his struggles, his eyes are still not content with riches. "So who am I struggling for," he asks, "and depriving myself from good?" This too is futile and a miserable task.

Two Better than One

[9] Two are better than one because they have a good reward for their efforts. [10] For if either falls, his companion can lift him up; but pity the one who falls without another to lift him up. [11] Also, if two lie down together, they can keep warm; but how can one person alone keep warm? [12] And if somebody overpowers one person, two can resist him. A cord of three strands is not easily broken.

[13] Better is a poor but wise youth than an old but foolish king who no longer pays attention to warnings. [14] For he came from prison to be king, even though he was born poor in his kingdom. [15] I saw all the living who move about under the sun follow[c] a second youth who succeeds him. [16] There is no limit to all the •people who were before them, yet those who come later will not rejoice in him. This too is futile and a pursuit of the wind.

Caution in God's Presence

5 [d] Guard your step when you go to the house of God. Better to draw near in obedience than to offer the sacrifice as fools do, for they are ignorant and do wrong. [2e] Do not be hasty to speak, and do not be impulsive to make a speech before God. God is in heaven and you are on earth, so let your words be few. [3] For dreams result from much work and a fool's voice from many words. [4] When you make a vow to God, don't delay fulfilling it, because He does not delight in fools. Fulfill what you vow. [5] Better that you do not vow than that you vow and not fulfill it. [6] Do not let your mouth bring guilt on you, and do not say in the presence of the messenger that it was a mistake. Why should God be angry with your words and destroy the work of your hands? [7] For many dreams bring futility, also many words. So, •fear God.

---

[a]**3:22** Lit *after him* [b]**4:8** Lit *person, but there is not a second,* [c]**4:15** Lit *with* [d]**5:1** Ec 4:17 in Hb [e]**5:2** Ec 5:1 in Hb

Realities of Wealth

[8] If you see oppression of the poor and perversion of justice and righteousness in the province, don't be astonished at the situation, because one official protects another official, and higher officials ⌊protect⌋ them. [9] The profit from the land is taken by all; the king is served by the field.[a]

[10] The one who loves money is never satisfied with money, and whoever loves wealth ⌊is⌋ never ⌊satisfied⌋ with income. This too is futile. [11] When good things increase, the ones who consume them multiply; what, then, is the profit to the owner, except to gaze at them with his eyes? [12] The sleep of the worker is sweet, whether he eats little or much; but the abundance of the rich permits him no sleep.

[13] There is a sickening tragedy I have seen under the sun: wealth kept by its owner to his harm. [14] That wealth was lost in a bad venture, so when he fathered a son, he was empty-handed. [15] As he came from his mother's womb, so he will go again, naked as he came; he will take nothing for his efforts that he can carry in his hands. [16] This too is a sickening tragedy: exactly as he comes, so he will go. What does he gain who struggles for the wind? [17] What is more, he eats in darkness all his days, with much sorrow, sickness, and anger.

Enjoy Labor: Gift of God

[18] Here is what I have seen to be good: it is appropriate to eat, drink, and experience good in all the labor one does under the sun during the few days of his life God has given him, because that is his reward. [19] God has also given riches and wealth to every man, and He has allowed him to enjoy them, take his reward, and rejoice in his labor. This is a gift of God, [20] for he does not often consider the days of his life because God keeps him occupied with the joy of his heart.

Tragedy: No Enjoyment of Riches

6 Here is a tragedy I have observed under the sun, and it weighs heavily on humanity:[b] [2] God gives a man riches, wealth, and honor so that he lacks nothing of all he desires for himself, but God does not allow him to enjoy them. Instead, a stranger will enjoy them. This is futile and a sickening tragedy. [3] A man may father a hundred children and live many years. No matter how long he lives,[c] if he is not satisfied by good things and does not even have a proper burial, I say that a stillborn child is better off than he. [4] For he comes in futility and he goes in darkness, and his name is shrouded in darkness. [5] Though a stillborn child does not see the sun and is not conscious, it has more rest than he. [6] And if he lives a thousand years twice, but does not experience happiness, do not both go to the same place?

Appetite Never Satisfied

[7] All man's labor is for his stomach,[d] yet the appetite is never satisfied.

[8] What advantage then does the wise man have over the fool? What ⌊advantage⌋ is there for the poor person who knows how to conduct himself before others? [9] Better what the eyes see than wandering desire. This too is futile and a pursuit of the wind.

[10] Whatever exists was given its name long ago,[e] and who man is, is known. But he is not able to contend with the

[a]5:9 Or An advantage for the land in every respect is a king for a cultivated field; Hb obscure   [b]6:1 Or it is common among men   [c]6:3 Lit how many years   [d]6:7 Lit mouth   [e]6:10 Lit name already

One stronger than he. ¹¹ For when there are many words, they increase futility. What is the advantage for man? ¹² For who knows what is good for man in life, in the few days of his futile life that he spends like a shadow? Who can tell man what will happen after him under the sun?

Wise Sayings

7 A good name is better than
  fine perfume,
and the day of one's death than
  the day of one's birth.
² It is better to go to a house
  of mourning
than to go to a house of feasting,
since that is the end of all mankind,
and the living should take it
  to heart.
³ Grief is better than laughter,
for when a face is sad, a heart
  may be glad.
⁴ The heart of the wise is in a house
  of mourning,
but the heart of fools is in a house
  of pleasure.
⁵ It is better to listen to rebuke
  from a wise person
than to listen to the song of fools.
⁶ For like the crackling
  of ⌊burning⌋ thorns under the pot,
so is the laughter of the fool.
This too is futile.
⁷ Surely, the practice of extortion
  turns a wise person into a fool,
and a bribe destroys the mind.
⁸ The end of a matter is better
  than its beginning;
a patient spirit is better
  than a proud spirit.
⁹ Don't let your spirit rush
  to be angry,

for anger abides in the heart
  of fools.
¹⁰ Don't say, "Why were
  the former days better
  than these?"
For it is not wise of you to ask this.
¹¹ Wisdom is as good
  as an inheritance,
and an advantage to those who see
  the sun.

Wisdom Protects

¹² For wisdom is protection as money
  is protection,
and the advantage of knowledge is
  that wisdom preserves the life
  of its owner.
¹³ Consider the work of God;
for who can straighten out what
  He has made crooked?

¹⁴ In the day of prosperity be joyful, but in the day of adversity, consider: without question, God has made the one as well as the other, so that man cannot discover anything that will come after him.

Avoiding Extremes

¹⁵ In my futile lifeᵃ I have seen everything: there is a righteous man who perishes in spite of his righteousness, and there is a wicked man who lives long in spite of his evil. ¹⁶ Don't be excessively righteous, and don't be overly wise. Why should you destroy yourself? ¹⁷ Don't be excessively wicked, and don't be foolish. Why should you die before your time?

Fear God, Be Wise

¹⁸ It is good that you grasp the one and do not let the other slip from your hand. For the one who •fears God will end up with both of them.

¹⁹ Wisdom makes the wise man
    stronger
  than ten rulers of a city.

All Sin

²⁰ There is certainly no righteous man
    on the earth
  who does good and never sins.

Ignore Offense

²¹ Don't pay attention^a to everything
•people say, or you may hear your ser-
vant cursing you; ²² for you know that
many times you yourself have cursed
others.

What the Teacher Found

²³ I have tested all this by wisdom. I re-
solved, "I will be wise," but it was beyond me. ²⁴ What exists is beyond ⌊reach⌋
and very deep. Who can discover it? ²⁵ I
turned my thoughts to know, explore,
and seek wisdom and an explanation ⌊for
things⌋, and to know that wickedness is
stupidity and folly is madness. ²⁶ And I
find more bitter than death the woman
who is a trap, her heart a net, and her
hands chains. The one who pleases God
will escape her, but the sinner will be
captured by her. ²⁷ "Look," says the
Teacher, "this I have discovered, by adding one thing to another to find out the
explanation, ²⁸ which my soul continually searches for but does not find:
among a thousand ⌊people⌋ I have found
one ⌊true⌋ man, but among all these I
have not found a true woman. ²⁹ Only
see this: I have discovered that God
made people upright, but they pursued
many schemes."

Wisdom, Authorities, and Inequities

8 Who is like the wise person, and
who knows the interpretation of a

matter? A man's wisdom brightens his
face, and the sternness of his face is
changed.

² Keep^b the king's command. Concern-
ing an oath by God, ³ do not be in a
hurry. Leave his presence, and don't persist in a bad cause, since he will do
whatever he wants. ⁴ For the king's word
is authoritative, and who can say to him,
"What are you doing?"

Right Timing

⁵ The one who keeps a command will
not experience anything harmful, and a
wise heart knows the right time and procedure. ⁶ For every activity there is a
right time and procedure, even though
man's troubles are heavy on him. ⁷ Yet
no one knows what will happen, be-
cause who can tell him what will happen? ⁸ No one has authority over the
wind^c to restrain it, and there is no authority over the day of death; there is no
furlough in battle, and wickedness will
not allow those who practice it to es-
cape. ⁹ All this I have seen, applying my
mind to all the work that is done under
the sun, at a time when one man has authority over another to his harm.

¹⁰ In such circumstances, I saw the
wicked buried. They came and went
from the holy place, and they were
praised^d in the city where they did so.
This too is futile.

Reason for No Criminal Deterrence

¹¹ Because the sentence against a crimi-
nal act is not carried out quickly, therefore the heart of •people is filled ⌊with
the desire⌋ to commit crime. ¹² Although
a sinner commits crime a hundred times
and prolongs his life, yet I also know that
it will go well with God-fearing people,
for they are reverent before Him.

---

^a**7:21** Lit *Don't give your heart*   ^b**8:2** Some Hb mss, LXX, Vg, Tg, Syr; other Hb mss read *I, keep*   ^c**8:8** Or *life-
breath*   ^d**8:10** Some Hb mss, LXX, Aq, Theod, Sym; other Hb mss read *forgotten*

[13] However, it will not go well with the wicked, and they will not lengthen their days like a shadow, for they are not reverent before God.

[14] There is a futility that is done on the earth: there are righteous people who get what the actions of the wicked deserve, and there are wicked people who get what the actions of the righteous deserve. I say that this too is futile. [15] So I commended enjoyment, because there is nothing better for man under the sun except to eat, drink, and enjoy himself, for this will accompany him in his labor during the years of his days that God gives him under the sun.

Limits to Human Intellect

[16] When I applied my mind to know wisdom and to observe the activity that is done on the earth (even though one's eyes do not close in sleep day or night), [17] I observed all the work of God ⌊and concluded⌋ that man is unable to discover the work that is done under the sun. Even though a man labors hard to explore it, he cannot find it; even if the wise man claims to know it, he is unable to discover it.

Enjoy Life Despite Death

9 Indeed, I took all this to heart and explained it all: the righteous, the wise, and their works are in God's hands. •People don't know whether ⌊to expect⌋ love or hate. Everything lies ahead of them. [2] Everything is the same for everyone: there is one fate for the righteous and the wicked, for the good and the bad,[a] for the clean and the unclean, for the one who sacrifices and the one who does not sacrifice. As it is for the good, so it is for the sinner, as for the one who takes an oath, so for the one who fears an oath. [3] This is an evil in all that is done under the sun: there is one fate for everyone. In addition, the hearts of people are full of evil, and madness is in their hearts while they live—after that they go to the dead. [4] But there is hope for whoever is joined[b] with all the living, since a live dog is better than a dead lion. [5] For the living know that they will die, but the dead don't know anything. There is no longer a reward for them because the memory of them is forgotten. [6] Their love, their hate, and their envy have already disappeared, and there is no longer a portion for them in all that is done under the sun.

[7] Go, eat your bread with pleasure, and drink your wine with a cheerful heart, for God has already accepted your works. [8] Let your clothes be white all the time, and never let oil be lacking on your head. [9] Enjoy life with the wife you love all the days of your fleeting[c] life, which has been given to you under the sun, all your fleeting days. For that is your portion in life and in your struggle under the sun. [10] Whatever your hands find to do, do with ⌊all⌋ your strength, because there is no work, planning, knowledge, or wisdom in •Sheol where you are going.

Race Not to Swift

[11] Again I saw under the sun that the race is not to the swift, or the battle to the strong, or bread to the wise, or riches to the discerning, or favor to the skillful; rather, time and chance happen to all of them. [12] For man certainly does not know his time: like fish caught in a cruel net, or like birds caught in a trap, so people are trapped in an evil time, as it suddenly falls on them.

---

[a]**9:2** LXX, Aq, Syr, Vg; MT omits *and the bad*   [b]**9:4** Alt Hb tradition reads *chosen*   [c]**9:9** Or *futile*

Short Story: Wise Man and City

¹³ I have observed that this also is wisdom under the sun, and it is significant to me: ¹⁴ There was a small city with few men in it. A great king came against it, surrounded it, and built large siege works against it. ¹⁵ Now a poor wise man was found in the city, and he delivered the city by his wisdom. Yet no one remembered that poor man. ¹⁶ And I said, "Wisdom is better than strength, but the wisdom of the poor man is despised, and his words are not heeded."

¹⁷ The calm words of the wise
   are heeded
   more than the shouts of a ruler
   over fools.
¹⁸ Wisdom is better than weapons
   of war,
   but one sinner can destroy
   much good.

Burden of Folly

10 Dead flies make a perfumer's oil
   ferment and stink;
   so a little folly outweighs wisdom
   and honor.
² A wise man's heart ⌊goes⌋
   to theᵃ right,
   but a fool's heart to theᵃ left.
³ Even when the fool walks
   along the road, his heart
   lacks sense,
   and he shows everyone he is a fool.

Be Stalwart!

⁴ If the ruler's anger rises against you,
   don't leave your place,
   for calmness puts great offenses
   to rest.

⁵ There is an evil I have seen under the sun, an error proceeding from the presence of the ruler:

⁶ The fool is appointed
   to great heights,
but the rich remain
   in lowly positions.
⁷ I have seen slaves on horses,
but princes walking on the ground
   like slaves.

Take Care!

⁸ The one who digs a pit may fall
   into it,
and the one who breaks
   through a wall may be bitten
   by a snake.
⁹ The one who quarries stones
   may be hurt by them;
the one who splits trees
   may be endangered by them.
¹⁰ If the ax is dull, and one does not
   sharpen its edge,
then one must exert
   more strength;
however, the advantage of wisdom
   is that it brings success.
¹¹ If the snake bites before
   it is charmed,
then there is no advantage
   for the charmer.ᵇ
¹² The words from the mouth
   of a wise man are gracious,
but the lips of a fool
   consume him.
¹³ The beginning of the words
   of his mouth is folly,
but the end of his speaking
   is evil madness.
¹⁴ Yet the fool multiplies words.
No one knows what will happen,
and who can tell anyone
   what will happen after him?
¹⁵ The struggles of fools
   weary them,
for they don't know how to go
   to the city.

ᵃ**10:2** Lit *his* ᵇ**10:11** Lit *master of the tongue*

Real Estate

16 Woe to you, land, when your king
is a household servant,
and your princes feast
in the morning.
17 Blessed are you, land,
when your king is a son
of nobles
and your princes feast
at the proper time—
for strength and not
for drunkenness.
18 Because of laziness the roof
caves in,
and because of negligent hands
the house leaks.
19 A feast is prepared for laughter,
and wine makes life happy,
and money is the answer
for everything.

Guard Lips!

20 Do not curse the king
even in your thoughts,
and do not curse a rich person
even in your bedroom,
for a bird of the sky may carry
the message,
and a winged creature may report
the matter.

Invest in Life

11 Send your bread on the surface
of the waters,
for after many days you may find it.
2 Give a portion to seven or even
to eight,
for you don't know what disaster
may happen on earth.
3 If the clouds are full,
they will pour out rain
on the earth;
whether a tree falls to the south
or the north,

the place where the tree falls,
there it will lie.
4 One who watches the wind
will not sow,
and the one who looks at the clouds
will not reap.

Mystery of God's Creation

5 Just as you don't know the path
of the wind,
or how bones ⌊develop⌋
in[a] the womb
of a pregnant woman,
so you don't know the work of God
who makes everything.
6 In the morning sow your seed,
and at evening do not let
your hand rest,
because you don't know
which will succeed,
whether one or the other,
or if both of them will be
equally good.
7 Light is sweet,
and it is pleasing for the eyes to see
the sun.
8 For if a man should live many years,
let him rejoice in them all,
and let him remember the days
of darkness, since they
will be many.
All that comes is futile.
9 Rejoice, young man,
while you are young,
and let your heart be glad
in the days of your youth.
And walk in the ways of your heart
and in the sights of your eyes;
but know that for all of these things
God will bring you to judgment.
10 Remove sorrow from your heart,
and put away pain from your flesh,
because youth and the prime of life
are fleeting.

[a]11:5 Or *know how the life-breath comes to the bones in*

Twilight of Life

12 So <u>remember your Creator in the days of your youth:</u>

Before the days of adversity come,
and the years approach
when you will say,
"I have no delight in them";
2 before the sun and the light
are darkened,
and the moon and the stars,
and the clouds return
after[a] the rain;
3 on the day when the guardians
of the house tremble,
and the strong men stoop,
the women who grind cease
because they are few,
and the ones who watch
through the windows see dimly,
4 and the doors at the street are shut
while the sound of the mill fades;
when one rises at the sound
of a bird,
and all the daughters of song
grow faint.
5 Also, they are afraid of heights
and dangers on the road;
the almond tree blossoms,
the grasshopper loses its spring,[b]
and the caper berry has no effect;
for man is headed
to his eternal home,
and mourners will walk around
in the street;
6 before the silver cord is snapped,[c]
and the golden bowl is broken,
and the jar is shattered
at the spring,

and the wheel is broken
into the well;
7 and the dust returns to the earth
as it once was,
and the spirit returns to God
who gave it.

8 "Absolute futility," says the Teacher. "Everything is futile."

Teacher's Objectives

9 In addition to the Teacher being a wise man, he constantly taught the •people knowledge; he weighed, explored, and arranged many proverbs. 10 The Teacher sought to find delightful sayings and to accurately write words of truth.

One Shepherd

11 The sayings of the wise are like goads, and those from masters of collections are like firmly embedded nails. <u>The sayings are given by one Shepherd.</u>[d]

Warning: Study and Books

12 But beyond these, my son, be warned: <u>there is no end to the making of many books, and much study wearies the body.</u>

Fear and Obey God

13 When all has been heard, the conclusion of the matter is: •<u>fear God and keep His commands, because this ⌊is for⌋ all humanity.</u> 14 For God will bring every act to judgment, including every hidden thing, whether good or evil.

---

a**12:2** Or *with*   b**12:5** Or *grasshopper is weighed down,* or *grasshopper drags itself along*   c**12:6** Alt Hb tradition reads *removed*   d**12:11** Or *by a shepherd*

SONG OF SONGS

1 Solomon's Finest Song[a]

The Bride (W) and
Young Women of Jerusalem (Y)

W[b]
² Oh, that he would kiss me
with the kisses of his mouth!
For your[c] love is[d] more delightful
than wine.
³ The fragrance of your perfume
is intoxicating;
your name is perfume poured out.
No wonder young women[e] adore
you.
⁴ Take me with you—let us hurry.
Oh, that the king would bring[f] me
to his chambers.

Y We will rejoice and be glad for you;
we will praise your love
more than wine.

W It is only right that they adore you.
⁵ Daughters of Jerusalem,
I am dark like the tents of Kedar,
yet lovely like the curtains
of Solomon.
⁶ Do not stare at me because
I am dark,
for the sun has gazed on me.
My mother's sons were angry
with me;
they made me a keeper
of the vineyards.
I have not kept my own vineyard.[g]

⁷ Tell me, you, the one I love:

Where do you pasture your sheep?
Where do you let them rest
at noon?
Why should I be like one who veils
herself[h] [i]
beside the flocks
of your companions?

Bridegroom (M)

M[j] ⁸ If you do not know,
most beautiful of women,
follow[k] the tracks of the flock,
and pasture your young goats
near the shepherds' tents.

⁹ I compare you, my darling,
to a[l] mare
among Pharaoh's chariots.[m]
¹⁰ Your cheeks are beautiful
with jewelry,
your neck with its necklace.
¹¹ We will make gold jewelry for you,
accented with silver.

W
¹² While the king is on his couch,[n]
my perfume[o] releases its fragrance.
¹³ My love is a sachet of myrrh to me,
spending the night
between my breasts.
¹⁴My love is a cluster
of henna blossoms to me,
in the vineyards of En-gedi.[p]

M
¹⁵ How beautiful you are, my darling.
How very beautiful!
Your eyes are doves.

---

a1:1 Or *The Song of Songs, which is Solomon's* **b1:2** The **W**, **M**, **Y**, **N**, and **B** indicate the editors' opinions of the changes of speakers: **W** = Woman, **M** = Man, **Y** = Young women of Jerusalem, **N** = Narrator, **B** = Brothers. If a letter is in parenthesis **(W)**, there is a question about the identity of the speaker. **c1:2** Unexpected change of grammatical persons, here from *he* and *his* to *your*, is a Hb poetic device. **d1:2** Or *your caresses are*, or *your lovemaking is* **e1:3** Or *wonder virgins* **f1:4** Or *The king has brought* **g1:6** Lit *my vineyard, which is mine*; Sg 8:12 **h1:7** Or *who wanders* **i1:7** To express shame or grief, or to conceal identity as a prostitute would; Gn 38:14-15 **j1:8** Some understand the young women to be the speakers in this verse. **k1:8** Lit *go out for yourself into* **l1:9** Lit *my* **m1:9** Pharaoh's chariot horses were stallions. **n1:12** Or *is at his table* **o1:12** Lit *nard* **p1:14** = Wellspring of the Young Goat; Sg 1:8

W

16 How handsome you are, my love.
   How delightful!
   Our bed is lush with foliage;
17 the beams of our house are cedars,
   and our rafters are cypresses.ᵃ

2 I am a roseᵇ of Sharon,
   a lilyᶜ of the valleys.
M² Like a lily among thorns,
   so is my darling
      among the young women.

W³ Like an apricotᵈ tree
      among the trees of the forest,
   so is my love
      among the young men.
   I delight to sit in his shade,
   and his fruit is sweet to my taste.
4 He brought me
      to the banquet hall,ᵉ
   and he looked on me with love.ᶠ
5 Sustain me with raisins;
   refresh me with apricots,ᵍ
   for I am lovesick.
6 His left hand is under my head,
   and his right hand embraces me.ʰ
7 Young women of Jerusalem,
      I charge you,
   by the gazelles and the wild does
      of the field:
   do not stir up or awaken love
   until the appropriate time.ⁱ

8 Listen! My love ⌊is approaching⌋.
   Look! Here he comes,
   leaping over the mountains,
   bounding over the hills.
9 My love is like a gazelle
   or a young stag.
   Look, he is standing
      behind our wall,
   gazing through the windows,

peering through the lattice.
10 My love calls to me:
M Arise, my darling.
   Come away, my beautiful one.
11 For now the winter is past;
   the rain has ended and gone away.
12 The blossoms appear
      in the countryside.
   The time of singingʲ has come,
   and the turtledove's cooing is heard
      in our land.
13 The fig tree ripens its figs;
   the blossoming vines give off
      their fragrance.
   Arise, my darling.
   Come away, my beautiful one.

14 My dove, in the clefts of the rock,
   in the crevices of the cliff,
   let me see your face,ᵏ
   let me hear your voice;
   for your voice is sweet,
   and your face is lovely.

(W)
15 Catch the foxes for us—
   the little foxes that ruin
      the vineyards—
   for our vineyards are in bloom.

W
16 My love is mine and I am his;
   he feeds among the lilies.
17 Before the day breaksˡ
   and the shadows flee,
   turn ⌊to me⌋, my love, and be
      like a gazelle
   or a young stag
      on the divided mountains.

3 In my bed at nightᵐ
   I sought the one I love;
   I sought him, but did not find him.ⁿ
2 I will arise now and go
      about the city,

ᵃ**1:17** Or firs, or pines ᵇ**2:1** Not the modern flower, but a common wildflower in northern Israel; perhaps a meadow saffron ᶜ**2:1** Or lotus ᵈ**2:3** Or apple ᵉ**2:4** Lit the house of wine ᶠ**2:4** Or and his banner over me is love ᵍ**2:5** Or apples ʰ**2:6** Or Let his left hand be under . . . , and his right hand embrace me ⁱ**2:7** Lit until it pleases ʲ**2:12** Or pruning ᵏ**2:14** Or form ˡ**2:17** Lit breathes ᵐ**3:1** Or bed night after night ⁿ**3:1** LXX adds I called him, but he did not answer me

through the streets and the plazas.
I will seek the one I love.
I sought him, but did not find him.
3 The guards who go about the city
    found me.
"Have you seen the one I love?"
ˌI asked themˌ.
4 I had just passed them
when I found the one I love.
I held on to him and would not
    let him go
until I brought him
    to my mother's house—
to the chamber of the one
who conceived me.
5 Young women of Jerusalem,
    I charge you,
by the gazelles and the wild does
    of the field:
do not stir up or awaken love
until the appropriate time.[a]

The Narrator Comments

N 6 What is this coming up
    from the wilderness
like columns of smoke,
scented with myrrh
    and frankincense
from every fragrant powder
    of the merchant?
7 It is Solomon's royal litter[b]
surrounded by 60 warriors
from the mighty of Israel.
8 All of them are skilled with swords
and trained in warfare.
Each has his sword at his side
ˌto guardˌ against the terror
    of the night.[c]

9 King Solomon made a sedan chair[d]
    for himself
with wood from Lebanon.

10 He made its posts of silver,
its back[e] of gold,
and its seat of purple.
Its interior is inlaid with love[f]
by the young women of Jerusalem.
11 Come out, young women of Zion,
and gaze at King Solomon,
wearing the crown
    his mother placed on him
the day of his wedding—
the day of his heart's rejoicing.

M
4 How beautiful you are, my darling.
How very beautiful!
Behind your veil,
your eyes are doves.
Your hair is like a flock of goats
streaming down Mount Gilead.
2 Your teeth are like a flock
    of newly shorn ˌsheepˌ
coming up from washing,
each one having a twin,
and not one missing.[g]
3 Your lips are like a scarlet cord,
and your mouth[h] is lovely.
Behind your veil,
your brow[i] is like a slice
    of pomegranate.
4 Your neck is like the tower
    of David,
constructed in layers.
A thousand bucklers are hung
    on it—
all of them shields of warriors.[j]
5 Your breasts are like two fawns,
twins of a gazelle, that feed
    among the lilies.
6 Before the day breaks[k]
and the shadows flee,
I will make my way
    to the mountain of myrrh
and the hill of frankincense.

---

[a]3:5 Lit *until it pleases*   [b]3:7 A conveyance carried on the shoulders of servants   [c]3:8 *Of the night* is the same Hb word translated *at night* in Sg 3:1.   [d]3:9 Perhaps a synonym for the Hb word translated *litter* in Sg 3:7; also called a *palanquin*   [e]3:10 Or *base*, or *canopy*   [f]3:10 Or *leather*   [g]4:2 Lit *and no one bereaved among them*   [h]4:3 Or *speech*   [i]4:3 Or *temple*, or *cheek*, or *lips*   [j]4:4 The imagery in this v. may have been suggested by the woman's necklace.   [k]4:6 Lit *breathes*

⁷ You are absolutely beautiful,
　　my darling,
　with no imperfection in you.

⁸ Come with me from Lebanon,^a
　　my bride—
　with me from Lebanon!
　Descend from the peak of Amana,
　from the summit of Senir
　　and Hermon,
　from the dens of the lions,
　from the mountains of the leopards.

⁹ You have captured my heart,
　　my sister,^b my bride.
　You have captured my heart
　　with one glance of your eyes,
　with one jewel of your necklace.

¹⁰ How delightful your love is,
　　my sister, my bride.
　Your love is much better than wine,
　and the fragrance of your perfume
　　than any balsam.

¹¹ Your lips drip ⌊sweetness like⌋
　　the honeycomb, my bride.
　Honey and milk are
　　under your tongue.
　The fragrance of your garments is
　　like the fragrance of Lebanon.

¹² My sister, my bride, ⌊you are⌋
　　a locked garden—
　a locked garden^c and a sealed spring.

¹³ Your branches are a paradise^d
　　of pomegranates
　with choicest fruits,
　henna with nard—

¹⁴ nard and saffron, calamus
　　and cinnamon,
　with all the trees of frankincense,
　myrrh and aloes,
　with all the best spices.

¹⁵ ⌊You are⌋ a garden spring,
　a well of flowing water
　streaming from Lebanon.

W

¹⁶ Awaken, north wind—
　come, south wind.
　Blow on my garden,
　and spread the fragrance
　　of its spices.
　Let my love come to his garden
　and eat its choicest fruits.

M

5

I have come to my garden—
　my sister, my bride.
I gather^e my myrrh with my spices.
I eat my honeycomb
　with my honey.
I drink my wine with my milk.

N　Eat, friends!
　Drink, be intoxicated with love!^f

W

² I sleep, but my heart is awake.
　A sound! My love is knocking!

M　Open to me, my sister, my darling,
　my dove, my perfect one.
　For my head is drenched with dew,
　my hair with droplets of the night.

W

³ I have taken off my clothing.
　How can I put it back on?
　I have washed my feet.
　How can I get them dirty?

⁴ My love thrust his hand
　　through the opening,
　and my feelings were stirred
　　for him.

⁵ I rose to open for my love.
　My hands dripped with myrrh,
　my fingers with flowing myrrh
　on the handles of the bolt.

⁶ I opened to my love,
　but my love had turned
　　and gone away.
　I was crushed^g that he had left.^h

---

^a**4:8** The Hb word for *Lebanon* is similar to the word for *frankincense*; Sg 4:6,14,15.　^b**4:9** A term of endearment;
Pr 7:4　^c**4:12** Other Hb mss read *locked fountain*　^d**4:13** Or *park*, or *orchard*　^e**5:1** Lit *pluck*　^f**5:1** Or *Drink your fill*,
lovers　^g**5:6** Lit *My soul went out*　^h**5:6** Or *spoken*

I sought him, but did not find him.
I called him, but he did not answer.
7 The guards who go about the city
found me.
They beat and wounded me;
they took my cloak[a] from me—
the guardians of the walls.
8 Young women of Jerusalem,
I charge you:
if you find my love,
tell him that I am lovesick.

Y 9 What makes the one you love
better than another,
most beautiful of women?
What makes him better than
another,
that you would give us this charge?

W
10 My love is fit and strong,[b]
notable among ten thousand.
11 His head is purest gold.
His hair is wavy[c]
and black as a raven.
12 His eyes are like doves
beside streams of water,
washed in milk
and set like jewels.[d]
13 His cheeks are like beds of spice,
towers of[e] perfume.
His lips are lilies,
dripping with flowing myrrh.
14 His arms[f] are rods of gold
set[g] with topaz.[h]
His body[i] is an ivory panel
covered with sapphires.
15 His legs are alabaster pillars
set on pedestals of pure gold.
His presence[j] is like Lebanon,
as majestic as the cedars.
16 His mouth is sweetness.
He is absolutely desirable.

This is my love, and this is
my friend,
young women of Jerusalem.

Y
6 Where has your love gone,
most beautiful of women?
Which way has he[k] turned?
We will seek him with you.
W 2 My love has gone down
to his garden,
to beds of spice,
to feed in the gardens
and gather lilies.
3 I am my love's and my love is mine;
he feeds among the lilies.

M
4 You are as beautiful as Tirzah,[l]
my darling,
lovely as Jerusalem,
awe-inspiring as an army
with banners.
5 Turn your eyes away from me,
for they captivate me.
Your hair is like a flock of goats
streaming down from Gilead.
6 Your teeth are like a flock of ewes
coming up from washing,
each one having a twin,
and not one missing.[m]
7 Behind your veil,
your brow[n] is like a slice
of pomegranate.
8 There are 60 queens
and 80 concubines
and young women[o]
without number.
9 But my dove, my virtuous one,
is unique;
she is the favorite of her mother,
perfect to the one who gave
her birth.

---

a5:7 Or veil, or shawl b5:10 Or is radiant and ruddy c5:11 Or is [like] palm leaves; Hb obscure d5:12 Lit milk sitting
in fullness e5:13 LXX, Vg read spice, yielding f5:14 Lit hands g5:14 Lit filled; Sg 5:2,12 h5:14 Probably yellow
topaz i5:14 Lit abdomen j5:15 The total effect of his appearance k6:1 Lit your love l6:4 = a mountain city in
Manasseh m6:6 Lit and no one bereaved among them n6:7 Or temple, or cheek, or lips o6:8 Or and virgins; Sg 1:3

Women see her and declare
her fortunate;
queens and concubines also,
and they sing her praises:

Y[a]

10 Who is this[b] who shines
like the dawn—
as beautiful as the moon,
bright as the sun,
awe-inspiring as an army
with banners?

W

11 I came down to the walnut grove
to see the blossoms of the valley,
to see if the vines were budding
and the pomegranates blooming.
12 Before I knew it,
my desire put me
⌊among⌋ the chariots
of my noble people.[c]

Y

13d Come back, come back,
Shulammite![e]
Come back, come back, that
we may look at you!

M Why are you looking
at the Shulammite,
as you ⌊look⌋ at the dance
of the two camps?[f]

7 How beautiful are
your sandaled feet, princess![g]
The curves of your thighs are
like jewelry,
the handiwork of a master.
2 Your navel is a rounded bowl;
it never lacks mixed wine.
Your waist[h] is a mound of wheat
surrounded by lilies.
3 Your breasts are like two fawns,
twins of a gazelle.

4 Your neck is like a tower of ivory,
your eyes like pools in Heshbon
by the gate of Bath-rabbim.
Your nose is like the tower
of Lebanon
looking toward Damascus.
5 Your head crowns you[i]
like Mount Carmel,
the hair of your head
like purple cloth—
a king could be held captive
in your tresses.
6 How beautiful you are
and how pleasant,
⌊my⌋ love, with such delights!
7 Your stature is like a palm tree;
your breasts are clusters ⌊of fruit⌋.
8 I said, "I will climb the palm tree
and take hold of its fruit."
May your breasts be like clusters
of grapes,
and the fragrance of your breath
like apricots.
9 Your mouth[j] is like fine wine—

W flowing smoothly for my love
gliding past my lips and teeth![k]
10 I belong to my love,
and his desire is for me.
11 Come, my love,
let's go to the field;
let's spend the night
among the henna blossoms.[l]
12 Let's go early to the vineyards;
let's see if the vine has budded,
if the blossom has opened,
if the pomegranates are in bloom.
There I will give you my love.
13 The mandrakes give off
a fragrance,
and at our doors is every delicacy—
new as well as old.

a6:10 Some see v. 10 as spoken by **M**   b6:10 The pronoun *this* is feminine in Hb.   c6:12 Or *of Amminadib*, or *of my people of a prince*; Hb obscure   d6:13 Sg 7:1 in Hb   e6:13 Perhaps an inhabitant of the town of Shunem, or "the peaceable one," or a feminine form of Solomon's name   f6:13 Or *dance of Mahanaim*; Gn 32:2   g7:1 Lit *daughter of a nobleman* or *prince*   h7:2 Or *belly*   i7:5 Lit *head upon you is*   j7:9 Lit *palate*   k7:9 LXX, Syr, Vg; MT reads *past lips of sleepers*   l7:11 Or *the villages*

I have treasured them up for you,
  my love.

8 If only I could treat you
  like my brother,[a]
one who nursed
  at my mother's breasts,
I would find you in public
  and kiss you,
and no one would scorn me.
² I would lead you, I would take you,
  to the house of my mother
  who taught me.[b]
I would give you spiced wine
  to drink
from my pomegranate juice.
³ His left hand is under my head,
  and his right hand embraces me.
⁴ Young women of Jerusalem,
  I charge you:
do not stir up or awaken love
until the appropriate time.

Y ⁵ Who is this coming up
  from the wilderness,
leaning on the one she loves?

W

I awakened you under
  the apricot tree.
There your mother conceived you;
there she conceived and gave you
  birth.
⁶ Set me as a seal on your heart,
  as a seal on your arm.
For love is as strong as death;
ardent love is as unrelenting
  as •Sheol.
Love's flames are fiery flames—
the fiercest of all.[c]
⁷ Mighty waters cannot extinguish
  love;

rivers cannot sweep it away.
If a man were to give all his wealth[d]
  for love,
it would be utterly scorned.

Brothers Intervene

B ⁸ Our sister is young;
she has no breasts.
What will we do for our sister
on the day she is spoken for?
⁹ If she is a wall,
we will build a silver parapet on it.
If she is a door,
we will enclose it with cedar planks.[e]

W
¹⁰ I am[f] a wall
and my breasts like towers.
So in his eyes I have become
like one who finds peace.[g]

¹¹ Solomon owned a vineyard in Baal-
  hamon.
He leased the vineyard to tenants.
Each was to bring for his fruit
1,000 pieces of silver.
¹² I have my own vineyard.[h]
The 1,000 are for you, Solomon,
but 200 for those who guard
  its fruits.

M
¹³ You[i] who dwell in the gardens—
companions are listening
  for your voice—
let me hear you!

W
¹⁴ Hurry ⌊to me⌋, my love,
and be like a gazelle
or a young stag
on the mountains of spices.

ᵃ**8:1** Lit *Would that you were like a brother to me*   ᵇ**8:2** LXX adds *and into the chamber of the one who bore me*
ᶜ**8:6** Or *the blaze of the LORD*   ᵈ**8:7** Lit *all the wealth of his house*   ᵉ**8:8-9** Vv. 8-9 may record what the girl's brothers
(Sg 1:6) used to say; Gn 24:29; 34:6-18.   ᶠ**8:10** Or *was*   ᵍ**8:10** *Shalom*, the Hb word for *peace*, sounds similar to
Solomon and *Shulammite* in Hb.   ʰ**8:12** Lit *My vineyard, which is mine, is before me*; Sg 1:6   ⁱ**8:13** *You* is feminine in
Hb.

ISAIAH

1 The vision concerning Judah and Jerusalem that Isaiah son of Amoz saw during the reigns[a][b] of Uzziah, Jotham, Ahaz, and Hezekiah, kings of Judah.

Judah on Trial

2 Listen, heavens,
   and pay attention, earth,
for the LORD has spoken:
"I have raised children[c]
   and brought them up,
but they have rebelled against Me.
3 The ox knows its owner,
and the donkey
   its master's feeding-trough,
⌊but⌋ Israel does not know;
My people do not understand."

4 Oh—sinful nation,
people weighed down
   with iniquity,
brood of evildoers,
depraved children![c]
They have abandoned the LORD;
they have despised the Holy One
   of Israel;
they have turned their backs
   ⌊on Him⌋.

5 Why do you want more beatings?
Why do you keep on rebelling?
The whole head is hurt,
and the whole heart is sick.
6 From the sole of the foot
   even to the head,
no spot is uninjured—
wounds, welts, and festering sores
not cleansed, bandaged,
or soothed with oil.

7 Your land is desolate,
   your cities burned with fire;
before your very eyes
foreigners devour your fields—
a desolation overthrown
   by foreigners.
8 Daughter Zion is abandoned
like a shelter in a vineyard,
like a shack in a cucumber field,
like a besieged city.
9 If the LORD of •Hosts
had not left us a few survivors,
we would be like Sodom,
we would resemble Gomorrah.

10 Hear the word of the LORD,
you rulers of Sodom!
Listen to the instruction
   of our God,
you people of Gomorrah!
11 "What are all your sacrifices
   to Me?"
asks the LORD.
"I have had enough
   of •burnt offerings and rams
and the fat of well-fed cattle;
I have no desire for the blood
   of bulls,
lambs, or male goats.
12 When you come to appear
   before Me,
who requires this from you—
⌊this⌋ trampling of My courts?
13 Stop bringing useless offerings.
I despise ⌊your⌋ incense.
New Moons and Sabbaths,
and the calling
   of solemn assemblies—
I cannot stand iniquity
   with a festival.
14 I hate your New Moons
   and prescribed festivals.
They have become a burden
   to Me;
I am tired of putting up with ⌊them⌋.

[a]**1:1** Lit *saw in the days* [b]**1:1** c. 792–686 B.C. [c]**1:2,4** Or *sons*

¹⁵ When you lift up your hands
⌊in prayer⌋,
I will refuse to look at you;
even if you offer countless prayers,
I will not listen.
Your hands are covered with blood.

Purification of Jerusalem

¹⁶ "Wash yourselves.
   Cleanse yourselves.
Remove your evil deeds
   from My sight.
Stop doing evil.
¹⁷ Learn to do what is good.
Seek justice.
Correct the oppressor.[a]
Defend the rights of the fatherless.
Plead the widow's cause.

¹⁸ "Come, let us discuss this,"
says the LORD.
"Though your sins are like scarlet,
they will be as white as snow;
though they are as red as crimson,
they will be like wool.
¹⁹ If you are willing and obedient,
you will eat the good things
   of the land.
²⁰ But if you refuse and rebel,
you will be devoured
   by the sword."
For the mouth of the LORD
   has spoken.

²¹ The faithful city—
what an adulteress she has become!
She was once full of justice.
Righteousness once dwelt in her—
but now, murderers!
²² Your silver has become dross,[b]
your beer[c] is diluted with water.
²³ Your rulers are rebels,
friends of thieves.
They all love graft
and chase after bribes.

They do not defend the rights
   of the fatherless,
and the widow's case never comes
   before them."

²⁴ Therefore the Lord GOD of Hosts,
the Mighty One
   of Israel, declares:
"Ah, I will gain satisfaction
   against My foes;
I will take revenge
   against My enemies.
²⁵ I will turn My hand against you
and will burn away
   your dross[b] completely;[d]
I will remove all your impurities.
²⁶ I will restore your judges to what
   they once were,[e]
and your advisers
   to their former state.[f]
Afterwards you will be called
   the Righteous City,
a Faithful City."

²⁷ Zion will be redeemed by justice,
her repentant ones
   by righteousness.
²⁸ But both rebels and sinners
   will be destroyed,
and those who abandon the LORD
   will perish.
²⁹ Indeed, they[g] will be ashamed
   of the sacred trees
you desired,
and you will be embarrassed
   because of the gardens
you have chosen.
³⁰ For you will become like an oak
whose leaves are withered,
and like a garden without water.
³¹ The strong one will become tinder,
and his work a spark;
both will burn together,
with no one to quench
   ⌊the flames⌋.

---

[a]**1:17** Or *Aid the oppressed*   [b]**1:22,25** Or *burnished lead*; = lead oxide   [c]**1:22** Or *wine*   [d]**1:25** Lit *dross as with lye*
[e]**1:26** Lit *judges as at the first*   [f]**1:26** Lit *advisers as at the beginning*   [g]**1:29** Some Hb mss; other Hb mss, Tg read *you*

City of Peace

2 The <u>vision that Isaiah son of Amoz</u>
<u>saw concerning Judah and Jerusalem:</u>

² In the last days
the mountain of the LORD's house
  will be established
at the top of the mountains
and will be raised above the hills.
All nations will stream to it,
³ and many peoples will come
  and say,
"Come, let us go up
  to the mountain of the LORD,
to the house of the God of Jacob.
He will teach us about His ways
so that we may walk in His paths."
For instruction will go out of Zion
and the word of the LORD
  from Jerusalem.
⁴ He will settle disputes
  among the nations
and provide arbitration
  for many peoples.
<u>They will turn their swords</u>
  <u>into plows</u>
<u>and their spears</u>
  <u>into pruning knives.</u>
<u>Nations will not take up the sword</u>
  <u>against ⌊other⌋ nations,</u>
<u>and they will never again train</u>
  <u>for war.</u>

Day of the LORD

⁵ House of Jacob,
come and let us walk
  in the LORD's light.
⁶ For You have abandoned
  Your people,
the house of Jacob,
because they are full of ⌊•divination⌋
  <u>from the East</u>
and of <u>fortune-tellers</u>
  <u>like the Philistines.</u>
They are in league[a] with foreigners.

⁷ Their[b] land is full of silver and gold,
  and there is no limit
    to their treasures;
their land is full of horses,
  and there is no limit
    to their chariots.
⁸ <u>Their land is full of idols;</u>
  they bow down to the work
    of their hands,
  to what their fingers have made.
⁹ So humanity is brought low,
  and man is humbled.
  Do not forgive them!
¹⁰ Go into the rocks
  and hide in the dust
  from the terror of the LORD
  and from His majestic splendor.
¹¹ Human pride[c] will be humbled,
  and the loftiness of men
    will be brought low;
  the LORD alone will be exalted
    on that day.

¹² For a day belonging to the LORD
    of •Hosts is ⌊coming⌋
  against all that is proud and lofty,
  against all that is lifted up—it will
    be humbled—
¹³ against all the cedars of Lebanon,
  lofty and lifted up,
  against all the oaks of Bashan,
¹⁴ against all the high mountains,
  against all the lofty hills,
¹⁵ against every high tower,
  against every fortified wall,
¹⁶ against every ship of Tarshish,
  and against every splendid
    sea vessel.
¹⁷ So human pride will be
    brought low,
  and the loftiness of men
    will be humbled;
  <u>the LORD alone will be exalted</u>
    <u>on that day.</u>
¹⁸ The idols will vanish completely.

---

[a]2:6 Or *They teem*, or *They partner*; Hb obscure   [b]2:7 Lit *Its*; = the house of Jacob   [c]2:11 Lit *Mankind's proud eyes*

¹⁹ People will go into caves
   in the rocks
and holes in the ground,
away from the terror of the LORD
and from His majestic splendor,
when He rises to terrify the earth.
²⁰ On that day people will throw
   their silver and gold idols,
which they made to worship,
to the moles and the bats.
²¹ They will go into the caves
   of the rocks
and the crevices in the cliffs,
away from the terror of the LORD
and from His majestic splendor,
when He rises to terrify the earth.
²² Put no more trust in man,
   who has only the breath
   in his nostrils.
What is he really worth?

Judah's Leaders Judged

3 Observe this: The Lord GOD
   of •Hosts
is about to remove from Jerusalem
   and from Judah
every kind of security:
   the entire supply of bread
   and water,
² the hero and warrior,
   the judge and prophet,
   the fortune-teller and elder,
³ the commander of 50
   and the dignitary,
the counselor, cunning magician,^a
   and necromancer.^b
⁴ "I will make youths their leaders,
and the unstable^c
   will govern them."
⁵ The people will oppress
   one another,
man against man, neighbor
   against neighbor;

the youth will act arrogantly
   toward the elder,
and the worthless
   toward the honorable.
⁶ A man will even seize his brother
in his father's house, ⌊saying:⌋
"You have a cloak—you be
   our leader!
This heap of rubble will be
   under your control."
⁷ On that day he will cry out, saying:
"I'm not a healer.
I don't even have food or clothing
   in my house.
Don't make me the leader
   of the people!"
⁸ For Jerusalem has stumbled
and Judah has fallen
because they have spoken
   and acted against the LORD,
defying His glorious presence.

Flaunted Sin

⁹ The look on their faces testifies
   against them,
and like Sodom, they flaunt
   their sin.
They do not conceal it.
Woe to them!
For they have brought evil
   on themselves.
¹⁰ Tell the righteous that
   it will go well ⌊for them⌋,
for they will eat the fruit
   of their deeds.
¹¹ Woe to the wicked—
   ⌊it will go⌋ badly ⌊for them⌋,
for what they have done
   will be done to them.
¹² Youths oppress My people,
   and women rule over them.
My people, your leaders
   mislead you;

---

^a**3:3** Or *skilled craftsman*   ^b**3:3** Or *medium*   ^c**3:4** Or *mischief-makers*

they confuse the direction
  of your paths.

13 The LORD rises to argue the case
  and stands to judge the people.
14 The LORD brings ⌊this⌋ charge
  against the elders and leaders
    of His people:
  "You have devastated the vineyard.
  The plunder from the poor is
    in your houses.
15 Why do you crush My people
  and grind the faces of the poor?"
  says the Lord GOD of Hosts.

Jerusalem's Women Judged

16 The LORD also says:

Because the daughters of Zion
    are haughty,
  walking with heads held high
  and seductive eyes,
  going along with prancing steps,
  jingling their ankle bracelets,
17 the Lord will put scabs
    on the heads
  of the daughters of Zion,
  and the LORD will shave
    their foreheads bare.

18 On that day the Lord will strip their finery: ankle bracelets, headbands, crescents, 19 pendants, bracelets, veils, 20 headdresses, ankle jewelry, sashes, perfume bottles, amulets, 21 signet rings, nose rings, 22 festive robes, capes, cloaks, purses, 23 garments, linen clothes, turbans, and veils.

24 Instead of perfume there will be
    a stench;
  instead of a belt, a rope;
  instead of
    beautifully styled hair, baldness;
  instead of fine clothes, •sackcloth;
  instead of beauty, branding.ᵃ

25 Your men will fall by the sword,
  your warriors in battle.
26 Then her gates will lament
    and mourn;
  deserted, she will sit on the ground.

4 On that day seven women
  will seize one man, saying,
  "We will eat our own bread
  and provide our own clothing.
  Just let us be called by your name.
  Take away our disgrace."

Zion's Future Glory

2 On that day the branch of the LORD will be beautiful and glorious, and the fruit of the land will be the pride and glory of Israel's survivors. 3 Whoever remains in Zion and whoever is left in Jerusalem will be called holy—all in Jerusalem who are destined to live— 4 when the Lord has washed away the filth of the daughters of Zion and cleansed the bloodguilt from the heart of Jerusalem by a spirit of judgment and a spirit of burning. 5 Then the LORD will create a cloud of smoke by day and a glowing flame of fire by night over the entire site of Mount Zion and over its assemblies. For there will be a canopy over all the glory,ᵇ 6 and there will be a booth for shade from heat by day, and a refuge and shelter from storm and rain.

Song of the Vineyard

5 I will sing about the one I love,
  a song about my loved one's vineyard:
  The one I love had a vineyard
  on a very fertile hill.
2 He broke up the soil, cleared it
    of stones,
  and planted it with the finest vines.
  He built a tower in the middle of it
  and even hewed
    out a winepress there.

ᵃ**3:24** DSS read *shame*   ᵇ**4:5** Or *For glory will be a canopy over all*

He expected it to yield
 good grapes,
but it yielded worthless grapes.
³ So now, residents of Jerusalem
 and men of Judah,
please judge between Me
 and My vineyard.
⁴ What more could I have done
 for My vineyard
than I did?
Why, when I expected a yield
 of good grapes,
did it yield worthless grapes?
⁵ Now I will tell you
what I am about to do
 to My vineyard:
I will remove its hedge,
and it will be consumed;
I will tear down its wall,
and it will be trampled.
⁶ I will make it a wasteland.
It will not be pruned or weeded;
thorns and briers will grow up.
I will also give orders to the clouds
that rain should not fall on it.

Vineyard: House of Israel

⁷ For the vineyard of the LORD
 of •Hosts
is the house of Israel,
and the men^a of Judah,
the plant He delighted in.
He looked for justice
but saw injustice,
for righteousness,
but heard cries of wretchedness.

Judah's Sins Denounced

⁸ Woe to those who add house
 to house
and join field to field
until there is no more room
and you alone are left in the land.

⁹ In my hearing the LORD of Hosts ⌊has
taken an oath⌋:

Indeed, many houses
 will become desolate,
grand and lovely ones
 without inhabitants.
¹⁰ For a ten-acre^b vineyard will yield
only six gallons,^c
and 10 bushels^d of seed will yield
only ⌊one⌋ bushel.^e
¹¹ Woe to those who rise early
 in the morning
in pursuit of beer,
who linger into the evening,
inflamed by wine.
¹² At their feasts they have lyre, harp,
tambourine, flute, and wine.
They do not perceive
 the LORD's actions,
and they do not see the work
 of His hands.
¹³ Therefore My people go into exile
because they lack knowledge;
the^f dignitaries are starving,
and the^f masses are parched with thirst.
¹⁴ Therefore •Sheol enlarges its throat
and opens wide its enormous jaws,
and down go Zion's dignitaries,
 her masses,
her crowds, and those who carouse
 in her!
¹⁵ Humanity is brought low,
 man is humbled,
and haughty eyes are humbled.
¹⁶ But the LORD of Hosts is exalted
 by His justice,
and the holy God is distinguished
 by righteousness.
¹⁷ Lambs will graze
 as ⌊if in⌋^g their own pastures,
and strangers^h will eat
 ⌊among⌋ the ruins of the rich.

---

^a5:7 Lit man   ^b5:10 Lit ten-yoke   ^c5:10 Lit one bath   ^d5:10 Lit one homer   ^e5:10 Lit [one] ephah   ^f5:13 Lit its
^g5:17 Syr reads graze in   ^h5:17 LXX reads sheep

18 Woe to those who drag wickedness
with cords of deceit
and ⌊pull⌋ sin along with cart ropes,
19 to those who say:
"Let Him hurry up and do
His work quickly
so that we can see it!
Let the plan of the Holy One
of Israel take place
so that we can know it!"

Woe to Those without Standards

20 Woe to those who call evil good
and good evil,
who substitute darkness for light
and light for darkness,
who substitute bitter for sweet
and sweet for bitter.
21 Woe to those who are wise
in their own opinion
and clever in their own sight.[a]
22 Woe to those who are heroes
at drinking wine,
who are fearless at mixing beer,
23 who acquit the guilty for a bribe
and deprive the innocent of justice.

24 Therefore, as a tongue of fire
consumes straw
and as dry grass shrivels
in the flame,
so their roots will become
like something rotten
and their blossoms will blow away
like dust,
for they have rejected
the instruction of the LORD
of Hosts,
and they have despised
the word of the Holy One of Israel.
25 Therefore the LORD's anger burns
against His people.
He raised His hand against them
and struck them;
the mountains quaked,

and their corpses were like garbage
in the streets.
In all this, His anger is
not removed,
and His hand is still raised
⌊to strike⌋.

26 He raises a signal flag
for the distant nations
and whistles for them
from the ends of the earth.
Look—how quickly and swiftly
they come!
27 None of them grows weary
or stumbles;
no one slumbers or sleeps.
No belt is loose,
and no sandal strap broken.
28 Their arrows are sharpened,
and all their bows strung.
Their horses' hooves are like flint;
their ⌊chariot⌋ wheels are
like a whirlwind.
29 Their roaring is like a lion's;
they roar like young lions;
they growl and seize their prey
and carry ⌊it⌋ off,
and no one can rescue ⌊it⌋.
30 On that day they will roar over it,
like the roaring of the sea.
When one looks at the land,
there will be darkness
and distress;
light will be obscured by clouds.[b]

Isaiah's Vision, Call and Mission

6 In the year that King Uzziah died, I saw the Lord seated on a high and lofty throne, and His robe[c] filled the temple. [2] Seraphim[d] were standing above Him; each one had six wings: with two he covered his face, with two he covered his feet, and with two he flew. [3] And one called to another:

---

[a]**5:21** Lit *clever before their face* [b]**5:30** Lit *its clouds* [c]**6:1** Lit *seam* [d]**6:2** = heavenly beings

Holy, holy, holy is the LORD
of •Hosts;
His glory fills the whole earth.

4 The foundations of the doorways shook at the sound of their voices, and the temple was filled with smoke. 5 Then I said:

Woe is me, for I am ruined,
because I am a man
of unclean lips
and live among a people
of unclean lips,
⌊and⌋ because my eyes have seen
the King,
the LORD of Hosts.

Angel's Touch

6 Then one of the seraphim flew to me, and in his hand was a glowing coal that he had taken from the altar with tongs. 7 He touched my mouth ⌊with it⌋ and said:

Now that this has touched
your lips,
your wickedness is removed,
and your sin is atoned for.

8 Then I heard the voice of the Lord saying:

Who should I send?
Who will go for Us?

I said:

Here I am. Send me.

9 And He replied:

Go! Say to these people:
Keep listening,
but do not understand;
keep looking, but do not perceive.
10 Dull the minds of these people's;[a]
deafen their ears and blind
their eyes;

otherwise they might see
with their eyes
and hear with their ears,
understand with their minds,
turn back, and be healed.

11 Then I said, "Until when, Lord?"
And He replied:

Until cities lie in ruins
without inhabitants,
houses are without people,
the land is ruined and desolate,
12 and the LORD drives the people
far away,
leaving great emptiness in the land.
13 Though a tenth will remain
in the land,
it will be burned again.
Like the terebinth or the oak,
which leaves a stump when felled,
the holy •seed is the stump.

Message to Ahaz

7 This took place during the reign of Ahaz, son of Jotham, son of Uzziah king of Judah: Rezin king of Aram, along with Pekah, son of Remaliah, king of Israel, waged war against Jerusalem, but he could not succeed. 2 When it became known to the house of David that Aram had occupied Ephraim, the heart of Ahaz[b] and the hearts of his people trembled like trees of a forest shaking in a wind.

3 Then the LORD said to Isaiah, "Go out with your son Shear-jashub to meet Ahaz at the end of the conduit of the upper pool, by the road to the Fuller's Field. 4 Say to him: Calm down and be quiet. Don't be afraid or fainthearted because of these two smoldering stubs of firebrands, Rezin of Aram, and the son of Remaliah. 5 For Aram, along with Ephraim and the son of Remaliah, has

a6:10 Lit heart   b7:2 Lit Aram has rested upon Ephraim, his heart plotted harm against you. They say: ⁶ Let us go up against Judah, terrorize it, and conquer it for ourselves. Then we can install Tabeel's son as king in it."

⁷ This is what the Lord GOD says:

It will not happen; it will not occur.
⁸ Theᵃ head of Aram is Damascus,
the head of Damascus is Rezin
(within 65 years
Ephraim will be too shattered to be a people),
⁹ the head of Ephraim is Samaria,
and the head of Samaria is the son of Remaliah.
If you do not stand firm in your faith,
then you will not stand at all.

Immanuel Prophecy

¹⁰ Then the LORD spoke again to Ahaz: ¹¹ "Ask for a sign from the LORD your God—from the depths of •Sheol to the heights of heaven."

¹² But Ahaz replied, "I will not ask. I will not test the LORD."

¹³ Isaiah said, "Listen, house of David! Is it not enough for you to try the patience of men? Will you also try the patience of my God? ¹⁴ Therefore, the Lord Himself will give youᵇ a sign: The virgin will conceive,ᶜ have a son, and name him Immanuel.ᵈ ¹⁵ By the time he learns to reject what is bad and choose what is good, he will be eating butterᵉ and honey. ¹⁶ For before the boy knows to reject what is bad and choose what is good, the land of the two kings you dread will be abandoned. ¹⁷ The LORD will bring on you, your people, and the house of your father, such a time as has never been since Ephraim separated from Judah—the king of Assyria ⌊is coming⌋.

¹⁸ On that day
the LORD will whistle to the fly

that is at the farthest streams
of the Nile
and to the bee that is in the land
of Assyria.
¹⁹ All of them will come and settle
in the steep ravines, in the clefts
of the rocks,
in all the thornbushes, and in all
the water holes.

²⁰ On that day the Lord will use a razor hired from beyond the Euphrates River—the king of Assyria—to shave the head, the hair on the legs, and to remove the beard as well.

²¹ On that day
a man will raise a young cow
and two sheep,
²² and from the abundant milk
they give
he will eat butter,
for every survivor in the land
will eat butter and honey.

²³ And on that day
every place where there were
1,000 vines,
worth 1,000 pieces of silver,
will become thorns and briers.
²⁴ A man will go there with bow
and arrows
because the whole land
will be thorns and briers.
²⁵ You will not go to all the hills
that were once tilled with a hoe,
for fear of the thorns and briers.
⌊Those hills⌋ will be places for oxen
to graze
and for sheep to trample.

Coming Assyrian Invasion

8 Then the LORD said to me, "Take a large piece of parchmentᶠ and write on it with an ordinary pen:ᵍ Maher-

---

ᵃ**7:8** Lit *For the* ᵇ**7:14** The pronoun *you* is pl ᶜ**7:14** Or *virgin is pregnant, will* ᵈ**7:14** = God With Us; Is 8:10 ᵉ**7:15** Or *sour milk* ᶠ**8:1** Hb obscure ᵍ**8:1** Lit *with the pen of a man*

shalal-hash-baz.[a] [2] I have appointed[b] trustworthy witnesses—Uriah the priest and Zechariah son of Jeberechiah."

Isaiah's Son: Tie-in to Prophecy

[3] I was then intimate with the prophetess, and she conceived and gave birth to a son. The LORD said to me, "Name him Maher-shalal-hash-baz, [4] for before the boy knows how to call out father or mother, the wealth of Damascus and the spoils of Samaria will be carried off to the king of Assyria."

[5] The LORD spoke to me again:

[6] Because these people rejected
the slowly flowing waters of Shiloah
and rejoiced with[c] Rezin
and the son of Remaliah,
[7] the Lord will certainly bring
against them
the mighty rushing waters
of the Euphrates River—
the king of Assyria and all his glory.
It will overflow its channels
and spill over all its banks.
[8] It will pour into Judah,
flood over it, and sweep through,
reaching up to the neck;
and its spreading streams[d]
will fill your entire land, Immanuel!

[9] Band together, peoples, and be broken;
pay attention, all you distant lands;
prepare for war, and be broken;
prepare for war, and be broken.
[10] Devise a plan; it will fail.
Make a prediction; it will not happen.
For God is with us.[e]

LORD of Hosts, the Only Refuge

[11] For this is what the LORD said to me with great power, to keep[f] me from going the way of this people:

[12] Do not call everything an alliance
these people say is an alliance.
Do not fear what they fear;
do not be terrified.
[13] You are to regard only the LORD
of •Hosts as holy.
Only He should be •feared;
only He should be held in awe.
[14] He will be a sanctuary;
but for the two houses of Israel,
He will be a stone to stumble over
and a rock to trip over,
and a trap and a snare
to the inhabitants of Jerusalem.
[15] Many will stumble over these;
they will fall and be broken;
they will be snared and captured.

[16] Bind up the •testimony.
Seal up the instruction
among my disciples.
[17] I will wait for the LORD,
who is hiding His face
from the house of Jacob.
I will wait for Him.

Don't Consult Dead

[18] Here I am with the children the LORD has given me to be signs and wonders in Israel from the LORD of Hosts who dwells on Mount Zion. [19] When they say to you, "Consult the spirits of the dead and the spiritists who chirp and mutter," shouldn't a people consult their God?[g] ⌊Should they consult⌋ the dead on behalf of the living? [20] To the law and to the testimony! If they do not speak according to this word, there will be no dawn for them.

[21] They will wander through the land, dejected and hungry. When they are famished, they will become enraged, and, looking upward, will curse their king and their God. [22] They will look

---

[a]**8:1** Or *Speeding to the Plunder, Hurrying to the Spoil* [b]**8:2** Vg; MT, one DSS ms read *I will appoint*; one DSS ms, LXX, Syr, Tg read *Appoint* [c]**8:6** Or *and rejoiced over* [d]**8:8** Or *wings* [e]**8:10** Or *For Immanuel*; Is 7:14; 8:8 [f]**8:11** Or *instruct* [g]**8:19** Or *gods*

toward the earth and see only distress, darkness, and the gloom of affliction, and they will be driven into thick darkness.

Birth of the Prince of Peace

9 ^a Nevertheless, the gloom of the distressed land will not be like that of the former times when He humbled the land of Zebulun and the land of Naphtali. But in the future He will bring honor to the Way of the Sea, to the land east of the Jordan, and to Galilee of the nations.

2b The people walking in darkness
have seen a great light;
on those living in the land
of darkness,
a light has dawned.
3 You have enlarged the nation
and increased its joy.ᶜ
ʟThe peopleʲ have rejoiced
before You
as they rejoice at harvest time
and as they rejoice
when dividing spoils.
4 For You have shattered
their burdensome yoke
and the rod on their shoulders,
the staff of their oppressor,
just as ʟYou didʲ on the day
of Midian.
5 For the trampling boot of battle
and the bloodied garments of war
will be burned as fuel for the fire.

Wonderful Counselor

6 For a child will be born for us,
a son will be given to us,
and the government will be
on His shoulders.
He will be named
Wonderful Counselor, Mighty God,
Eternal Father, Prince of Peace.
7 The dominion will be vast,

and its prosperity will never end.
He will reign on the throne
of David
and over his kingdom,
to establish and sustain it
with justice and righteousness
from now on and forever.
The zeal of the LORD of •Hosts
will accomplish this.

Hand Raised against Israel

8 The Lord sent a message
against Jacob;
it came against Israel.
9 All the people—
Ephraim and the inhabitants
of Samaria—will know it.
They will say with pride
and arrogance:
10 "The bricks have fallen,
but we will rebuild
with cut stones;
the sycamores have been cut down,
but we will replace them
with cedars."
11 The LORD has raised up
Rezin's adversaries against him
and stirred up his enemies.
12 Aram from the east and Philistia
from the west
have consumed Israel
with open mouths.
In all this, His anger
is not removed,
and His hand is still raised
ʟto strikeʲ.

People Disobey, God Cuts Off

13 The people did not turn to Him
who struck them;
they did not seek the LORD
of Hosts.
14 So the LORD cut off Israel's head
and tail,

palm branch and reed
in a single day.

15 The head is the elder,
the honored one;
the tail is the prophet,
the lying teacher.

16 The leaders of the people
mislead ⌞them⌟,
and those they mislead
are swallowed up.[a]

17 Therefore the Lord does not
rejoice over[b]
Israel's[c] young men
and has no compassion
on its fatherless and widows,
for everyone is a godless evildoer,
and every mouth speaks folly.
In all this, His anger
is not removed,
and His hand is still raised
⌞to strike⌟.

18 For wickedness burns like a fire
that consumes thorns and briers
and kindles the forest thickets
so that they go up in a column
of smoke.

19 The land is scorched
by the wrath of the LORD of Hosts,
and the people are like fuel
for the fire.
No one has compassion
on his brother.

20 They carve ⌞meat⌟ on the right,
but they are ⌞still⌟ hungry;
they have eaten on the left,
but they are ⌞still⌟ not satisfied.
Each one eats the flesh
of his own arm.

21 Manasseh is with Ephraim,
and Ephraim with Manasseh;
together, both are against Judah.
In all this, His anger is
not removed,

and His hand is still raised
⌞to strike⌟.

Woe to Oppressive Law-Makers

10 Woe to those enacting
crooked statutes
and writing oppressive laws

2 to keep the poor from getting
a fair trial
and to deprive the afflicted
among my people of justice,
so that widows can be their spoil
and they can plunder the fatherless.

3 What will you do on the day
of punishment
when devastation comes
from far away?
Who will you run to for help?
Where will you leave your wealth?

4 ⌞There will be nothing to do⌟
except crouch among the prisoners
or fall among the slain.
In all this, His anger is not removed,
and His hand is still raised ⌞to strike⌟.

Assyria,
God's Instrument of Wrath

5 Woe to Assyria, the rod
of My anger—
the staff in their hands is My wrath.

6 I will send him against
a godless nation;
I will command him ⌞to go⌟
against a people destined
for My rage,
to take spoils, to plunder,
and to trample them down like clay
in the streets.

7 But this is not what he intends;
this is not what he plans.
It is his intent to destroy
and to cut off many nations.

8 For he says:
Aren't all my commanders kings?

---

⁹ Isn't Calno like Carchemish?
Isn't Hamath like Arpad?
Isn't Samaria like Damascus?ᵃ

¹⁰ As my hand seized
the idolatrous kingdoms,
whose idols exceeded
those of Jerusalem and Samaria,

¹¹ and as I did to Samaria and its idols
will I not also do to Jerusalem
and its idols?

Judgment on Assyria

¹² But when the Lord finishes all His work against Mount Zion and Jerusalem, ⌊He will say,⌋ "Iᵇ will punish the king of Assyria for his arrogant acts and the proud look in his eyes." ¹³ For he said:

I have done ⌊this⌋
by my own strength
and wisdom, for I am clever.
I abolished the borders of nations
and plundered their treasures;
like a mighty warrior, I subjugated
the inhabitants.ᶜ

¹⁴ My hand has reached out, as if
into a nest,
to seize the wealth of the nations.
Like one gathering
abandoned eggs,
I gathered the whole earth.
No wing fluttered;
no beak opened or chirped.

¹⁵ Does an ax exalt itself
above the one who chops with it?
Does a saw magnify itself
above the one who saws with it?
As if a staff could wave
those who liftᵈ it!
As if a rod could lift
what isn't wood!ᵉ

¹⁶ Therefore the Lord GOD of •Hosts
will inflict an emaciating disease
on the well-fed of Assyria,

and He will kindle a burning fire
under its glory.

¹⁷ Israel's Light will become a fire,
and its Holy One, a flame.
In one day it will burn up
Assyria's thorns and thistles.

¹⁸ He will completely destroy
the glory of its forests and orchards
as a sickness consumes a person.

¹⁹ The remaining trees of its forest
will be so few in number
that a child could count them.

Israel's Remnant Will Return

²⁰ On that day the remnant of Israel and the survivors of the house of Jacob will no longer depend on the one who struck them, but they will faithfully depend on the LORD, the Holy One of Israel.

²¹ The remnant will return,
the remnant of Jacob,
to the Mighty God.

²² Israel, even if your people were
as numerous
as the sand of the sea,
⌊only⌋ a remnant of them will return.
Destruction has been decreed;
justice overflows.

²³ For throughout the land
the Lord GOD of Hosts
is carrying out a destruction
that was decreed.

²⁴ Therefore, the Lord GOD of Hosts says this: "My people who dwell in Zion, do not fear Assyria, though he strikes you with a rod and raises his staff over you as the Egyptians did. ²⁵ In just a little while My wrath will be spent and My anger will turn to their destruction." ²⁶ And the LORD of Hosts will brandish a whip against him as ⌊He did when He⌋ struck Midian at the rock of Oreb; and

ᵃ**10:9** Cities conquered by Assyria　　ᵇ**10:12** LXX reads *Jerusalem, He*　　ᶜ**10:13** Or *I brought down their kings*
ᵈ**10:15** Some Hb mss, Syr, Vg read *wave he who lifts*　　ᵉ**10:15** A human being

He will raise His staff over the sea as ⌞He did⌟ in Egypt.

God Will Judge Assyria

27 On that day
his burden will fall
  from your shoulders,
and his yoke from your neck.
The yoke will be broken because of
  ⌞his⌟ fatness.[a]

28 Assyria has come to Aiath
and has gone through Migron,
storing his equipment
  at Michmash.

29 They crossed over
  at the ford, saying,
"We will spend the night at Geba."
The people of Ramah are trembling;
those at Gibeah of Saul have fled.

30 Cry aloud, daughter of Gallim!
Listen, Laishah!
Anathoth is miserable.

31 Madmenah has fled.
The inhabitants of Gebim
  have sought refuge.

32 Today he will stand at Nob,
shaking his fist at the mountain
  of Daughter Zion,
the hill of Jerusalem.

33 Look, the Lord GOD of Hosts
will chop off the branches
  with terrifying power,
and the tall ⌞trees⌟ will be cut down,
the high ⌞trees⌟ felled.

34 He is clearing the thickets
  of the forest with an ax,
and Lebanon with its majesty
  will fall.

Reign of Davidic King

11 Then a shoot will grow
from the stump of Jesse,
and a branch from his roots
  will bear fruit.

2 The Spirit of the LORD will rest
  on Him—
a Spirit of wisdom
  and understanding,
a Spirit of counsel and strength,
a Spirit of knowledge
  and of the •fear of the LORD.

3 His delight will be in the fear
  of the LORD.
He will not judge
by what He sees with His eyes,
He will not execute justice
by what He hears with His ears,

4 but He will judge
  the poor righteously
and execute justice
  for the oppressed of the land.
He will strike the land
with discipline[b] from His mouth,
and He will kill the wicked
with a command[c] from His lips.

5 Righteousness and faithfulness
will be a belt around His waist.

6 The wolf will live
  with the lamb,
and the leopard will lie down
  with the goat.
The calf, the young lion,
  and the fatling will be together,
and a child will lead them.

7 The cow and the bear will graze,
their young ones
  will lie down together,
and the lion will eat straw
  like an ox.

8 An infant will play
  beside the cobra's pit,
and a toddler will put his hand
  into a snake's den.

9 No one will harm or destroy
on My entire holy mountain,
for the land will be as full
of the knowledge of the LORD
as the sea is filled with water.

---

a**10:27** Hb obscure   b**11:4** Lit *the rod*   c**11:4** Lit *with the breath*

Israel Regathered

10 On that day the root of Jesse
  will stand as a banner
    for the peoples.
The nations will seek Him,
  and His resting place
    will be glorious.

11 On that day the Lord will ⌞extend⌟
His hand a second time to recover—
from Assyria, Egypt, Pathros, •Cush,
Elam, •Shinar, Hamath, and the coasts
and islands of the west—the remnant of
His people who survive.

12 He will lift up a banner
    for the nations
  and gather the dispersed of Israel;
  He will collect the scattered
    of Judah
  from the four corners of the earth.
13 Ephraim's envy will cease;
  Judah's harassment will end.
Ephraim will no longer be envious
    of Judah,
  and Judah will not harass Ephraim.
14 But they will swoop down
  on the Philistine flank to the west.
Together they will plunder
  the people of the east.
They will extend their power
  over Edom and Moab,
and the Ammonites will be
  their subjects.
15 The LORD will divide[a] the Gulf
    of Suez.[b]
He will wave His hand
  over the Euphrates
with His mighty wind
and will split it into seven streams,
letting people walk through on foot.
16 There will be a highway
  for the remnant of His people
who will survive from Assyria,
  as there was for Israel

when they came up from the land
  of Egypt.

Song of Praise

12 On that day you will say:
"I will praise You, LORD,
although You were angry with me.
Your anger has turned away,
and You have had compassion on me.
2 Indeed, God is my salvation.
I will trust ⌞Him⌟ and not be afraid.
Because •Yah, the LORD,
is my strength and my song,
He has become my salvation."
3 You will joyfully draw water
from the springs of salvation,
4 and on that day you will say:
"Give thanks to the LORD;
  proclaim His name!
Celebrate His deeds
  among the peoples.
Declare that His name is exalted.
5 Sing to the LORD, for He has done
  glorious things.
Let this be known
  throughout the earth.
6 Cry out and sing, citizen of Zion,
for the Holy One of Israel is
  among you
in ⌞His⌟ greatness."

Oracle against Babylon

13 An •oracle against Babylon that Isaiah son of Amoz saw:

2 Lift up a banner
  on a barren mountain.
Call out to them.
Wave your hand, and they will go
through the gates of the nobles.
3 I have commanded
  My chosen ones;
I have also called My warriors,
who exult in My triumph,
to execute My wrath.

---

[a] 11:15 Or *destroy*, or *dry up* (text emended)   [b] 11:15 Lit *the Sea of Egypt*

4 Listen, a tumult
   on the mountains,
like that of a mighty people!
Listen, an uproar
   among the kingdoms,
like nations being
   gathered together!
The LORD of •Hosts is mobilizing
   an army for war.
5 They are coming from a far land,
from the distant horizon—
the LORD and the weapons
   of His wrath—
to destroy the whole country.[a]

6 Wail! For the day of the LORD
   is near.
It will come like destruction
   from the •Almighty.
7 Therefore everyone's hands
   will become weak,
and every man's heart will melt.
8 They will be horrified;
   pain and agony will seize ⌊them⌋;
they will be in anguish
   like a woman in labor.
They will look at each other,
   their faces flushed with fear.

Day of the Lord

9 Look, the day of the LORD
   is coming—
cruel, with rage
   and burning anger—
to make the earth a desolation
and to destroy the sinners on it.
10 Indeed, the stars of the sky
   and its constellations[b]
will not give their light.
The sun will be dark when it rises,
and the moon will not shine.
11 I will bring disaster on the world,
   and their ⌊own⌋ iniquity,
   on the wicked.

I will put an end to the pride
   of the arrogant
and humiliate the insolence
   of tyrants.
12 I will make man scarcer than gold,
   and mankind more rare
   than the gold of Ophir.
13 Therefore I will make
   the heavens tremble,
and the earth will shake
   from its foundations
at the wrath of the LORD of Hosts,
   on the day of His burning anger.
14 Like wandering gazelles
   and like sheep without a shepherd,
each one will turn
   to his own people,
each one will flee to his own land.
15 Whoever is found will be stabbed,
   and whoever is caught will die
   by the sword.
16 Their children will be smashed
   ⌊to death⌋ before their eyes;
   their houses will be looted,
   and their wives raped.
17 Look! I am stirring up the Medes
   against them,
who cannot be bought off
   with[c] silver
and who have no desire for gold.
18 ⌊Their⌋ bows will cut young men
   to pieces.
They will have no compassion
   on little ones;
   they will not look with pity
   on children.

End of Babylon

19 And Babylon, the jewel
   of the kingdoms,
the glory of the pride
   of the Chaldeans,
will be like Sodom and Gomorrah
when God overthrew them.

---

a **13:5** Or earth   b **13:10** Or Orions   c **13:17** Lit who have no regard for

20 It will never be inhabited
   or lived in from generation
      to generation;
   a nomad will not pitch
      his tent there,
   and shepherds will not let
      ⌊their flocks⌋ rest there.
21 But wild animals
      will lie down there,
   and owls will fill the houses.
   Ostriches will dwell there,
   and wild goats will leap about.
22 Hyenas will howl in the fortresses,
      and jackals,
      in the luxurious palaces.
   Babylon's time is almost up;
      her days are almost over.

Israel's Return

14 For the LORD will have compassion
on Jacob and will choose Israel
again. He will settle them on their own
land. The foreigner will join them and be
united with the house of Jacob. 2 The nations will escort Israel and bring it to its
homeland. Then the house of Israel will
possess them as male and female slaves
in the LORD's land. They will make captives of their captors and will rule over
their oppressors.

Downfall of King of Babylon

3 When the LORD gives you rest from
your pain, torment, and the hard labor
you were forced to do, 4 you will sing
this song ⌊of contempt⌋ about the king of
Babylon and say:

   How the oppressor
      has quieted down,
   and how the raging[a]
      has become quiet!
5 The LORD has broken the staff
      of the wicked,
   the scepter of the rulers.

6 It struck the peoples in anger
   with unceasing blows.
   It subdued the nations in rage
   with relentless persecution.
7 All the earth is calm and at rest;
   people shout with a ringing cry.
8 Even the cypresses and the cedars
      of Lebanon
   rejoice over you:
   "Since you have been laid low,
   no woodcutter has come
      against us."
9 •Sheol below is eager to greet
      your coming.
   He stirs up the spirits
      of the departed for you—
   all the rulers[b] of the earth.
   He makes all the kings
      of the nations
   rise from their thrones.
10 They all respond to you, saying:
   "You too have become as weak
      as we are;
   you have become like us!
11 Your splendor has been
      brought down to •Sheol,
   ⌊along with⌋ the music
      of your harps.
   Maggots are spread out under you,
   and worms cover you."

Shining Morning Star

12 Shining morning star,[c]
   how you have fallen
      from the heavens!
   You destroyer of nations,
   you have been cut down
      to the ground.
13 You said to yourself:
   "I will ascend to the heavens;
   I will set up my throne
   above the stars of God.
   I will sit on the mount
      of the ⌊gods'⌋ assembly,

[a]**14:4** DSS; MT obscure [b]**14:9** Lit rams [c]**14:12** Or Day Star, son of the dawn

in the remotest parts of the North.ᵃ

¹⁴ I will ascend above
the highest clouds;
I will make myself
like the •Most High.”

¹⁵ But you will be brought down
to Sheol
into the deepest regions of the •Pit.

¹⁶ Those who see you will stare
at you;
they will look closely at you:
“Is this the man who caused
the earth to tremble,
who shook the kingdoms,

¹⁷ who turned the world
into a wilderness,
who trampled its cities
and would not release the prisoners
to return home?”

¹⁸ All the kings of the nations
lie in splendor,
each in his own tomb.

¹⁹ But you are thrown out
without a grave,
like a worthless branch,
covered by those slain
with the sword
and dumped into a rocky pit
like a trampled corpse.

²⁰ You will not join them in burial,
because you destroyed your land
and slaughtered your own people.
The offspring of evildoers
will never be remembered.

²¹ Prepare a place of slaughter
for his sons,
because of the iniquity
of their fathers.
They never rise up to possess a land
or fill the surface of the earth
with cities.

²² “I will rise up against them”—the
declaration of the LORD of •Hosts—“and

I will cut off from Babylon her reputation, remnant, offspring, and posterity”—the LORD’s declaration. ²³ “I will
make her a swampland and a region for
wild animals,ᵇ and I will sweep her away
with a broom of destruction.”

⌊This is⌋ the declaration
of the LORD of Hosts.

Assyria to Be Destroyed

²⁴ The LORD of Hosts has sworn:

As I have planned, so it will be;
as I have purposed it,
so it will happen.

²⁵ I will break Assyria in My land;
I will tread him down
on My mountain.
Then his yoke will be taken
from them,
and his burden will be removed
from their shoulders.

²⁶ This is the plan prepared
for the whole earth,
and this is the hand stretched out
against all the nations.

²⁷ The LORD of Hosts Himself
has planned it;
therefore, who can stand
in its way?
It is His hand that is outstretched,
so who can turn it back?

Oracle against Philistia

²⁸ In the year that King Ahaz died, this
•oracle came:

²⁹ Don’t rejoice, all of you
⌊in⌋ Philistia,
because the rod of the one
who struck you is broken.
For a viper will come out
of the rootᶜ of a snake,
and from its egg comes
a flying serpent.

ᵃ14:13 Or of Zaphon   ᵇ14:23 Hb obscure   ᶜ14:29 Or stock

³⁰ Then the firstborn of the poor
will be well fed,
and the impoverished will lie down
in safety,
but I will kill your root with hunger,
and your remnant will be slain.^a
³¹ Wail, you gates! Cry out, city!
Tremble with fear, all Philistia!
For a cloud of dust is coming
from the north,
and there is no one missing from
⌊the invader's⌋ ranks.
³² What answer will be given
to the messengers
from that nation?
The LORD has founded Zion,
and His afflicted people find refuge
in her.

Oracle against Moab

15 An •oracle against Moab:

Ar in Moab is devastated,
destroyed in a night.
Kir in Moab is devastated,
destroyed in a night.
² Dibon went up to its temple
to weep at its •high places.
Moab wails on Nebo
and at^b Medeba.
Every head is shaved;
every beard is cut off.
³ In its streets they wear •sackcloth;
on its rooftops
and in its public squares
everyone wails,
falling down and weeping.
⁴ Heshbon and Elealeh cry out;
their voices are heard as far away
as Jahaz.
Therefore the soldiers of Moab
cry out,
and they tremble.^c
⁵ My heart cries out over Moab,

whose fugitives ⌊flee⌋ as far as Zoar,
to Eglath-shelishiyah;
they go up the slope
of Luhith weeping;
they raise a cry of destruction
on the road to Horonaim.
⁶ The waters of Nimrim are desolate;
the grass is withered, the foliage
is gone,
and the vegetation has vanished.
⁷ So they carry their wealth
and belongings
over the •Wadi of the Willows.
⁸ For their cry echoes
throughout the territory of Moab.
Their wailing reaches Eglaim;
their wailing reaches Beer-elim.
⁹ The waters of Dibon^d are full
of blood,
but I will bring on Dibon^d
even more ⌊than this⌋—
a lion for those who escape
from Moab,
and for the survivors in the land.

16 Send lambs to the ruler
of the land,
from Sela in the desert
to the mountain of Daughter Zion.
² Like a bird fleeing,
forced from the nest,
the daughters of Moab
will be at the fords of the Arnon.

³ Give us counsel and make
a decision.
⌊Shelter us⌋ at noonday
with shade that is as dark as night.
Hide the refugee;
do not betray the one who flees.
⁴ Let my refugees stay with you;
be a refuge for Moab^e
from the aggressor.

When the oppressor has gone,

---

^a**14:30** DSS, Syr, Tg; MT reads *and he will kill*   ^b**15:2** Or *wails over Nebo and over*   ^c**15:4** Lit *out, he trembles within himself*   ^d**15:9** DSS, some LXX mss, Vg; MT reads *Dimon*   ^e**16:4** Or *you; Moab—be a refuge for him*

destruction has ended,
and marauders have vanished
  from the land.
5 Then in the tent of David
  a throne will be established
    by faithful love.
  A judge who seeks what is right
  and is quick to execute justice
  will sit on the throne forever.

6 We have heard of Moab's pride—
  how very proud he is—
  his haughtiness, his pride,
    his arrogance,
  and his empty boasting.
7 Therefore let Moab wail;
  let every one of them wail for Moab.
  Mourn, you who are
    completely devastated,
  for the raisin cakes of Kir-hareseth.
8 For Heshbon's terraced vineyards
  and the grapevines of Sibmah
    have withered.
  The rulers of the nations
  have trampled its choice vines
  that reached as far as Jazer
  and spread to the desert.
  Their shoots spread out
  and reached the Dead Sea.
9 So I join with Jazer
  to weep for the vines of Sibmah;
  I drench Heshbon and Elealeh
    with my tears.
  Triumphant shouts
    have fallen silent[a]
  over your summer ⌊fruit⌋
    and your harvest.
10 Joy and rejoicing
    have been removed
    from the orchard;
  no one is singing or shouting for joy
    in the vineyards.
  No one tramples grapes[b]
    in the winepresses.

I have put an end to the shouting.
11 Therefore I moan like ⌊the sound of⌋
    a lyre for Moab,
    ⌊as does⌋ my innermost being
    for Kir-heres.
12 When Moab appears
    on the •high place,
  when he tires[c] himself out
  and comes to his sanctuary to pray,
  it will do him no good.

13 This is the message that the LORD
previously announced about Moab.
14 And now the LORD says, "In three
years, as a hired worker counts years,
Moab's splendor will become an object
of contempt, in spite of a very large population. And those who are left will be
few and weak."

Oracle against Damascus

17 An •oracle against Damascus:

  Look, Damascus is no longer a city.
  It has become a ruined heap.
2 The cities of Aroer are forsaken;
  they will be ⌊places⌋ for flocks.
  They will lie down without fear.
3 The fortress disappears
    from Ephraim,
  and a kingdom from Damascus.
  The remnant of Aram will be
  like the splendor of the Israelites.
      ⌊This is⌋ the declaration
        of the LORD of •Hosts.

Judgment against Israel

4 On that day
  the splendor of Jacob will fade,
  and his healthy body[d]
    will become emaciated.
5 It will be as if a reaper had gathered
    standing grain—
  his arm harvesting the heads
    of grain—

and as if one had gleaned heads
of grain
in the valley of Rephaim.
⁶ Only gleanings will be left in Israel,
as if an olive tree
had been beaten—
two or three berries at the very top
of the tree,
four or five on its fruitful branches.
⌊This is⌋ the declaration
of the LORD, the God of Israel.

⁷ On that day people will look to their Maker and will turn their eyes to the Holy One of Israel. ⁸ They will not look to the altars they made with their hands or to the •Asherahs and incense altars they made with their fingers.

⁹ On that day their strong cities
will be
like the abandoned woods
and mountaintopsᵃ
that were abandoned because of
the Israelites;
there will be desolation.
¹⁰ For you have forgotten the God
of your salvation,
and you have failed to remember
the rock of your strength;
therefore you will plant
beautiful plants
and set out cuttings
from exotic vines.
¹¹ On the day that you plant,
you will help them to grow,
and in the morning
you will help your seed to sprout,
⌊but⌋ the harvest will vanish
on the day of disease
and incurable pain.

Judgment against the Nations

¹² Ah! The roar of many peoples—
they roar like the roaring
of the seas.
The raging of the nations—
they rage like the raging
of mighty waters.
¹³ The nations rage like the raging
of many waters.
He rebukes them, and they flee
far away,
driven before the wind like chaff
on the hills
and like dead thistles before a gale.
¹⁴ In the evening—sudden terror!
Before morning—it is gone!
This is the fate of those
who plunder us
and the lot of those who ravage us.

Envoys by Sea

18 Ah! The land
of buzzing insect wingsᵇ
beyond the rivers of •Cush
² sends envoys by sea,
in reed vessels on the waters.

Go, swift messengers,
to a nation tall and smooth-skinned,
to a people feared near and far,
a powerful nation
with a strange language,ᶜ
whose land is divided by rivers.
³ All you inhabitants of the world
and you who live on the earth,
when a banner is raised
on the mountains, look!
When a trumpet sounds, listen!

⁴ For, the LORD said to me:
I will quietly look out
from My place,
like shimmering heat in sunshine,
like a rain cloud in harvest heat.
⁵ For before the harvest,
when the blossoming is over

ᵃ**17:9** LXX reads *like the Amorites and the Hivites*; some Hb mss read *like the Horesh and the Amir*   ᵇ**18:1** Or *of sailing ships*   ᶜ**18:2** Hb obscure

and the blossom becomes
　a ripening grape,
He will cut off the shoots
　with a pruning knife,
and tear away and remove
　the branches.
⁶ They will all be left for the birds
　of prey on the hills
and for the wild animals
　of the land.
The birds will spend the summer
　on them,
and all the animals, the winter
　on them.

⁷ At that time a gift will be brought to the LORD of •Hosts from[a] a people tall and smooth-skinned, a people feared near and far, a powerful nation with a strange language, whose land is divided by rivers—to Mount Zion, the place of the name of the LORD of Hosts.

Oracle against Egypt

19 An •oracle against Egypt:

Look, the LORD rides
　on a swift cloud
and is coming to Egypt.
Egypt's idols will tremble
　before Him,
and Egypt's heart will melt
　within it.
² I will provoke Egypt against Egypt;
each will fight against his brother
　and each against his friend,
city against city,
　kingdom against kingdom.
³ Egypt's spirit will be disturbed
　within it,
and I will frustrate its plans.
Then they will seek idols, ghosts,
spirits of the dead, and spiritists.
⁴ I will deliver Egypt into the hands
　of harsh masters,

and a strong king will rule it.
　⌊This is⌋ the declaration
　of the Lord GOD of •Hosts.

⁵ The waters of the sea will dry up,
and the river will be parched
　and dry.
⁶ The channels will stink;
they will dwindle,
　and Egypt's canals
　will be parched.
Reed and rush will die.[b]
⁷ The reeds by the Nile,
　by the mouth of the river,
and all the cultivated areas
　of the Nile
will wither, blow away, and vanish.
⁸ Then the fishermen will mourn.
All those who cast hooks
　into the Nile will lament,
and those who spread nets
　on the water will shrivel up.
⁹ Those who work with flax
　will be dismayed;
the combers and weavers
　will turn pale.[c]
¹⁰ ⌊Egypt's⌋ weavers[d] will be dejected;
all her wage earners
　will be demoralized.

¹¹ The princes of Zoan
　are complete fools;
Pharaoh's wisest advisers
　give stupid advice!
How can you say to Pharaoh,
"I am one[e] of the wise,
　a student of eastern[f] kings."
¹² Where then are your wise men?
Let them tell you and reveal
what the LORD of Hosts has planned
　against Egypt.
¹³ The princes of Zoan
　have been fools;
the princes of Memphis
　are deceived.

Her tribal chieftains have led
Egypt astray.
14 The LORD has mixed within her
a spirit of confusion.
ιThe leadersι have made Egypt
stagger in all she does,
as a drunkard staggers in his vomit.
15 No head or tail, palm or reed,
will be able to do anything
for Egypt.

Egypt Will Know the LORD

16 On that day Egypt will be like women. She will tremble with fear because of the threatening hand of the LORD of Hosts when He raises it against her. 17 The land of Judah will terrify Egypt; whenever Judah is mentioned, Egypt will tremble because of what the LORD of Hosts has planned against it.

18 On that day five cities in the land of Egypt will speak the language of Canaan and swear loyalty to the LORD of Hosts. One of the cities will be called the City of the Sun.ª b

19 On that day there will be an altar to the LORD in the center of the land of Egypt and a pillar to the LORD near her border. 20 It will be a sign and witness to the LORD of Hosts in the land of Egypt. When they cry out to the LORD because of their oppressors, He will send them a savior and leader, and he will rescue them. 21 The LORD will make Himself known to Egypt, and Egypt will know the LORD on that day. They will offer sacrifices and offerings; they will make vows to the LORD and fulfill them. 22 The LORD will strike Egypt, striking and healing. Then they will return to the LORD and He will hear their prayers and heal them.

23 On that day there will be a highway from Egypt to Assyria. Assyria will go to Egypt, Egypt to Assyria, and Egypt will worship with Assyria.

24 On that day Israel will form a triple ιallianceι with Egypt and Assyria—a blessing within the land. 25 The LORD of Hosts will bless them, saying, "Blessed be Egypt My people, Assyria My handiwork, and Israel My inheritance."

Naked Isaiah

20 In the year that the commander-in-chief, sent by Sargon king of Assyria, came to Ashdod and attacked and captured it— 2 during that time the LORD had spoken through Isaiah son of Amoz, saying, "Go, take off your •sackclothᶜ and remove the sandals from your feet," and he did so, going naked and barefoot— 3 the LORD said, "As My servant Isaiah has gone naked and barefoot three years as a sign and omen against Egypt and •Cush, 4 so the king of Assyria will lead the captives of Egypt and the exiles of Cush, young and old alike, naked and barefoot, with bared buttocks, to Egypt's shame.

No Help from Cush or Egypt

5 Those who made Cush their hope and Egypt their boast will be dismayed and ashamed. 6 And the inhabitants of this coastland will say on that day: Look, this is what has happened to those we relied on and fled to for help to rescue ιusι from the king of Assyria! Now, how will we escape?"

Judgment on Babylon

21 An •oracle against the desert by the sea:

Like storms that pass
over the •Negev,
it comes from the desert,
from the land of terror.

ª19:18 Some Hb mss, DSS, Sym, Tg, Vg, Arabic; other Hb mss read of Destruction; LXX reads of Righteousness
ᵇ19:18 The ancient Egyptian city Heliopolis ᶜ20:2 Lit off the sackcloth from your loins

2 A troubling vision is declared
   to me:
"The treacherous one
   acts treacherously,
and the destroyer destroys.
Advance, Elam! Lay siege,
   you Medes!
I will put an end to all
   her groaning."

3 Therefore I am[a] filled with anguish.
Pain grips me, like the pain
   of a woman in labor.
I am too perplexed to hear,
too dismayed to see.
4 My heart staggers;
horror terrifies me.
He has turned my last glimmer
   of hope[b]
into sheer terror.
5 Prepare a table, and spread out
   a carpet!
Eat and drink!
Rise up, you princes, and oil
   the shields!

6 For the Lord has said to me,
"Go, post a lookout;
let him report what he sees.
7 When he sees riders—
pairs of horsemen,
riders on donkeys,
riders on camels—
pay close attention."
8 Then the lookout[c] reported,
"Lord, I stand on the watchtower
   all day,
and I stay at my post all night.
9 Look, riders come—
horsemen in pairs."
And he answered, saying,
"Babylon has fallen, has fallen.
All the idols of her gods

have been shattered
   on the ground."

10 My downtrodden
   and threshed people,
I have declared to you
what I have heard from the LORD
   of •Hosts,
the God of Israel.

Oracle against Dumah

11 An oracle against Dumah:[d]

One calls to me from Seir,
"Watchman, what is ⌊left⌋
   of the night?
Watchman, what is ⌊left⌋
   of the night?"
12 The watchman said,
"Morning has come, and also night.
If you want to ask, ask!
Come back again."

Oracle against Arabia

13 An oracle against Arabia:

You will camp for the night
   in the scrublands of the desert,[e]
you caravans of Dedanites.
14 Bring water for the thirsty.
The inhabitants of the land
   of Tema
meet[f] the refugees with food.
15 For they have fled from swords,
from the drawn sword,
and from the bent bow,
from the stress of battle.

16 For the Lord said this to me:
"Within one year, as a hired worker
counts years, all the glory of Kedar will
be gone. 17 The remaining Kedarite archers will be few in number." For the
LORD, the God of Israel, has spoken.

a 21:3 Lit Therefore my loins are   b 21:4 Lit my twilight   c 21:8 DSS, Syr; MT reads Then a lion   d 21:11 Some Hb mss,
LXX read Edom   e 21:13 LXX, Syr, Tg, Vg read scrublands at evening   f 21:14 LXX, Syr, Tg, Vg read meet as a
command

Oracle against Jerusalem

22 An •oracle against the Valley of Vision:

What's the matter with you?
Why have all of you gone up
to the rooftops?
2 The noisy city, the jubilant town,
is filled with revelry.
Your dead did not die by the sword;
they were not killed in battle.
3 All your rulers have fled together,
captured without a bow.
All your fugitives
were captured together;
they had fled far away.
4 Therefore I said,
"Look away from me!
Let me weep bitterly!
Do not try to comfort me
about the destruction
of my dearª people."
5 For the Lord GOD of •Hosts
had a day of tumult, trampling,
and bewilderment
in the Valley of Vision—
people shoutingᵇ and crying
to the mountains;
6 Elam took up a quiver
with chariots and horsemen,ᶜ
and Kir uncovered the shield.
7 Your best valleys were full
of chariots,
and horsemen were positioned
at the gates.
8 He removed the defenses of Judah.

On that day you looked to the weapons in the House of the Forest. 9 You saw that there were many breaches in ⌊the walls of⌋ the city of David. You collected water from the lower pool. 10 You counted the houses of Jerusalem so that you could tear them down to fortify the wall. 11 You made a reservoir between the walls for the waters of the ancient pool, but you did not look to the One who made it, or consider the One who created it long ago.

12 On that day the Lord GOD of Hosts
called for weeping, for wailing,
for shaven heads,
and for the wearing of •sackcloth.
13 But look: joy and gladness,
butchering of cattle,
slaughtering of sheep,
eating of meat, and drinking
of wine—
"Let us eat and drink, for tomorrow
we die!"
14 The LORD of Hosts has revealed
⌊this⌋ in my hearing:
"This sin of yours will neverᵈ be
wiped out."
The Lord GOD of Hosts has spoken.

Oracle against Shebna, the Steward

15 The Lord GOD of Hosts said: "Go to Shebna, that steward who is in charge of the palace, ⌊and say to him:⌋ 16 What are you doing here? Who authorized you to carve out a tomb for yourself here, carving your tomb on the height and cutting a crypt for yourself out of rock? 17 Look, young man! The LORD is about to shake you violently. He will take hold of you, 18 wind you up into a ball, and sling you into a wide land.ᵉ There you will die, and there your glorious chariots will be—a disgrace to the house of your lord. 19 I will remove you from your office; you will be ousted from your position.

20 "On that day I will call for my servant, Eliakim son of Hilkiah. 21 I will clothe him with your robe and tie your sash around him. I will put your authority into his hand, and he will be like a father to the inhabitants of Jerusalem and to the House of Judah. 22 I will place the

---

ª**22:4** Lit *of the daughter of my*   ᵇ**22:5** Or *Vision—a tearing down of a wall*, or *Vision—Kir raged*; Hb obscure
ᶜ**22:6** Lit *chariots of man*   ᵈ**22:14** Lit *will not until you die*   ᵉ**22:17-18** Hb obscure

key of the House of David on his shoulder; what he opens, no one can close; what he closes, no one can open. 23 I will drive him, like a peg, into a firm place. He will be a throne of honor for his father's house. 24 They will hang on him the whole burden of his father's house: the descendants and the offshoots—all the small vessels, from bowls to every kind of jar. 25 On that day"—the declaration of the LORD of Hosts—"the peg that was driven into a firm place will give way, be cut off, and fall, and the load on it will be destroyed." Indeed, the LORD has spoken.

Oracle against Tyre

23 An •oracle against Tyre:

Wail, ships of Tarshish,
for your haven has been destroyed.
Word has reached them
from the land of Cyprus.ª
2 Mourn, inhabitants
of the coastland,
you merchants of Sidon;
your agentsᵇ have crossed the sea
3 on many waters.
Tyre's revenue was the grain
from Shihor—
the harvest of the Nile.
She was the merchant
among the nations.
4 Be ashamed Sidon, the stronghold
of the sea,
for the sea has spoken:
"I have not been in labor
or given birth.
I have not raised young men
ᴸorᴶ brought up young women."
5 When the news reaches Egypt,
they will be in anguish
over the news about Tyre.
6 Cross over to Tarshish;

wail, inhabitants of the coastland!
7 Is this your jubilant ᴸcityᴶ,
whose origin was in ancient times,
whose feet have taken her
to settle far away?
8 Who planned this against Tyre,
the bestower of crowns,
whose traders are princes,
whose merchants are
the honored ones of the earth?
9 The LORD of •Hosts planned it,
to desecrate all ᴸitsᴶ glorious beauty,
to disgrace all the honored ones
of the earth.
10 Overflowᶜ your land like the Nile,
daughter of Tarshish;
there is no longer anything
to restrain ᴸyouᴶ.ᵈ
11 He stretched out His hand
over the sea;
He made kingdoms tremble.
The LORD has commanded
that the Canaanite fortresses
be destroyed.
12 He said,
"You will not rejoice any more,
ravished young woman,
daughter of Sidon.
Get up and cross over to Cyprus—
even there you will have no rest!"
13 Look at the land of Chaldeans—
a people who no longer exist.
Assyria destined it for wild beasts.
They set up their siege towers
and stripped its palaces.
They made it a ruin.

"Tyre Will Be Forgotten"

14 Wail, ships of Tarshish,
because your fortress is destroyed!

15 On that day Tyre will be forgotten for 70 years—the life span of one king. At the end of 70 years, what the song

---

ª**23:1** Hb *Kittim*   ᵇ**23:2** DSS; MT reads *Sidon, whom the seafarers have filled*   ᶜ**23:10** DSS, LXX read *Work*
ᵈ**23:10** Or *longer any harbor*

ₗsaysₗ about the prostitute will happen to Tyre:

16 Pick up ₗyourₗ harp,
　　stroll through the city,
　　prostitute forgotten ₗby menₗ.
　　Play skillfully,
　　sing many a song,
　　and you will be thought of again.

17 And at the end of the 70 years, the LORD will restore Tyre and she will go back into business, prostituting herself with all the kingdoms of the world on the face of the earth. 18 But her profits and wages will be dedicated to the LORD. They will not be stored or saved, for her profit will go to those who live in the LORD's presence, to provide them with ample food and sacred clothing.

The Earth Judged

24 Look, the LORD is stripping
　　the earth bare
　　and making it desolate.
　　He will twist its surface and scatter
　　　its inhabitants:
2　people and priest alike,
　　servant and master,
　　female servant and mistress,
　　buyer and seller,
　　lender and borrower,
　　creditor and debtor.
3　The earth will be stripped
　　　completely bare
　　and will be totally plundered,
　　for the LORD has spoken
　　　this message.

4　The earth mourns and withers;
　　the world wastes away and withers;
　　the exalted people of the earth
　　　waste away.
5　The earth is polluted
　　by its inhabitants,

for they have transgressed
　teachings,
overstepped decrees,
and broken
　the everlasting covenant.
6　Therefore a curse has consumed
　　the earth,
　and its inhabitants
　　have become guilty;
　the earth's inhabitants
　　have been burned,
　and only a few survive.
7　The new wine mourns;
　the vine withers.
　All the carousers now groan.
8　The joyful tambourines
　　have ceased.
　The noise of the jubilant
　　has stopped.
　The joyful lyre has ceased.
9　They no longer sing
　　and drink wine;
　beer is bitter to those who drink it.
10　The city of chaos is shattered;
　every house is closed to entry.
11　In the streets they cryᵃ for wine.
　All joy grows dark;
　earth's rejoicing goes into exile.
12　Only desolation remains in the city;
　its gate has collapsed in ruins.
13　For this is how it will be on earth
　among the nations:
　like a harvested olive tree,
　like a gleaning after a grape harvest.

14　They raise their voices,
　　they sing out;
　they proclaim in the west
　the majesty of the LORD.
15　Therefore in the east honor
　　the LORD!
　In the islands of the west ₗhonorₗ
　the name of the LORD, the God
　　of Israel.

ᵃ**24:11** Lit *streets she* (the city) *cries*

¹⁶ From the ends of the earth
we hear songs:
The Splendor of the Righteous One.

But I said, "I waste away!
I waste away!^a
Woe is me."
The treacherous act treacherously;
the treacherous deal
very treacherously.

¹⁷ Terror, pit, and snare ⌊await⌋ you
who dwell on the earth.
¹⁸ Whoever flees at the sound
of terror
will fall into a pit,
and whoever escapes from the pit
will be caught in a snare.
For the windows are opened
from above,
and the foundations of the earth
are shaken.
¹⁹ The earth is completely devastated;
the earth is split open;
the earth is violently shaken.
²⁰ The earth staggers like a drunkard
and sways like a hut.
Earth's rebellion weighs it down,
and it falls, never to rise again.

²¹ On that day the LORD will punish
the host of heaven above
and kings of the earth below.
²² They will be gathered together
like prisoners in a pit.
They will be confined to a dungeon;
after many days
they will be punished.
²³ The moon will be put to shame
and the sun disgraced,
because the LORD of •Hosts
will reign as king
on Mount Zion in Jerusalem,
and He will ⌊display His⌋ glory
in the presence of His elders.

Salvation and Judgment on That Day

25 LORD, You are my God;
I will exalt You. I will praise
Your name,
for You have accomplished
wonders,
plans ⌊formed⌋ long ago,
with perfect faithfulness.
² For You have turned the city
into a pile of rubble,
a fortified city, into a ruin;
the fortress of barbarians is
no longer a city;
it will never be rebuilt.
³ Therefore, a strong people
will honor You.
A city of violent people^b
will •fear You.
⁴ For You have been a stronghold
for the poor,
a stronghold for the humble person
in his distress,
a refuge from the rain, a shade
from the heat.
When the breath of the violent
is like rain ⌊against⌋ a wall,
⁵ like heat in a dry land,
You subdue the uproar
of barbarians.
As^c the shade of a cloud ⌊cools⌋
the heat of the day,
⌊so⌋ He stills the song of the violent.

⁶ The LORD of •Hosts will prepare
a feast
for all the peoples
on this mountain^d—
a feast of aged wine, choice meat,^e
finely aged wine.
⁷ On this mountain
⌊He⌋ will destroy the ⌊burial⌋ shroud,
the shroud over all the peoples,
the sheet covering all the nations;

---

^a**24:16** Hb obscure   ^b**25:3** Lit *nations*   ^c**25:5** Lit *In*   ^d**25:6** Mount Zion; Is 2:2-4; 24:23   ^e**25:6** Lit *wine, fat full of marrow*

Destroy Death Forever

8 He will destroy death forever.
The Lord GOD will wipe away
the tears
from every face
and remove His people's disgrace
from the whole earth,
for the LORD has spoken.

9 On that day it will be said,
"Look, this is our God;
we have waited for Him,
and He has saved us.
This is the LORD; we have waited
for Him.
Let us rejoice and be glad
in His salvation."

10 For the LORD's power will rest
on this mountain.

But Moab will be trampled
in his place[a]
as straw is trampled in a dung pile.
11 He will spread out his arms
in the middle of it,
as a swimmer spreads out ˻his arms˼
to swim.
His pride will be brought low,
along with the trickery
of his hands.
12 The high-walled fortress
will be brought down,
thrown to the ground, to the dust.

Song of Judah

26 On that day this song will be sung
in the land of Judah:

We have a strong city.
Salvation is established as walls
and ramparts.
2 Open the gates
so a righteous nation can come in—
one that remains faithful.
3 You will keep in perfect peace
the mind ˻that is˼ dependent ˻on You˼,

for it is trusting in You.
4 Trust in the LORD forever,
because in •Yah, the LORD, is
an everlasting rock!
5 For He has humbled those who live
in lofty places—
an inaccessible city.
He brings it down;
He brings it down to the ground;
He throws it to the dust.
6 Feet trample it,
the feet of the humble,
the steps of the poor.

God's People Vindicated

7 The path of the righteous is level;
You clear a straight path
for the righteous.
8 Yes, LORD, we wait for You
in the path of Your judgments.
Our desire is for Your name
and renown.
9 I long for You in the night;
yes, my spirit within me
diligently seeks You,
for when Your judgments are
˻in˼ the land,
the inhabitants of the world
will learn righteousness.
10 ˻But if˼ the wicked is shown favor,
he does not learn righteousness.
In a righteous land he acts unjustly
and does not see the majesty
of the LORD.
11 LORD, Your hand is lifted up
˻to take action˼,
but they do not see it.
They will see ˻Your˼ zeal
for ˻Your˼ people,
and they will be put to shame.
The fire for Your adversaries
will consume them!
12 LORD, You will establish peace
for us,

a **25:10** Or trampled under Him

for You have also done all our work
  for us.
13 LORD, our God, other lords
  than You have ruled over us,
but we remember Your name alone.

14 The dead do not live;
  departed spirits do not rise up.
Indeed, You have visited
  and destroyed them;
You have wiped out all memory
  of them.
15 You have added
  to the nation, LORD.
You have added to the nation;
  You are honored.
You have expanded all the borders
  of the land.
16 LORD, they went to You
  in their distress;
they poured out whispered ⸤prayers
because⸥ Your discipline ⸤fell⸥
  on them.ᵃ
17 As a pregnant woman
  about to give birth
writhes and cries out in her pains,
so we were before You, LORD.
18 We became pregnant, we writhed
  in pain;
we gave birth to wind.
We have won no victories on earth,
and the earth's inhabitants
  have not fallen.

"Your Dead Will Live"

19 Your dead will live; their bodiesᵇ
  will rise.
Awake and sing, you who dwell
  in the dust!
For you will be covered
  with the morning dew,ᶜ
and the earth will bring forth
  the departed spirits.

20 Go, my people, enter your rooms

and close your doors behind you.
Hide for a little while
  until the wrath has passed.
21 For look, the LORD is coming
  from His place
to punish the inhabitants
  of the earth for their iniquity.
The earth will reveal the blood
  shed on it
and will no longer conceal
  her slain.

Leviathan Slain

27 On that day the LORD with His harsh, great, and strong sword, will bring judgment on •Leviathan, the fleeing serpent—Leviathan, the twisting serpent. He will slay the monster that is in the sea.

The LORD's Vineyard

2 On that day
  sing about a desirable vineyard:
3 I, the LORD, watch over it;
  I water it regularly.
I guard it night and day
  so that no one disturbs it.
4 I am not angry,
  but if it produces thorns and briers
    for Me,
I will fight against it, trample it,
  and burn it to the ground.
5 Or let it take hold of My strength;
  let it make peace with Me—
  make peace with Me.

"Israel Will Blossom"

6 In days to come,
  Jacob will take root.
Israel will blossom and bloom
  and fill the whole world with fruit.
7 Did the LORD strike Israel
  as He struck the one
  who struck Israel?

ᵃ26:16 Hb obscure ᵇ26:19 Lit *live; my body they* ᶜ26:19 Lit *For your dew is a dew of lights*

Was he killed like those killed
　by Him?
8 You disputed with her
　by banishing and driving her away.[a]
He removed ⌊her⌋
　with His severe storm
on the day of the east wind.
9 Therefore Jacob's iniquity
　will be purged in this way,
and the result of the removal
　of his sin will be this:
when he makes all the altar stones
like crushed bits of chalk,
no •Asherah poles or incense altars
　will remain standing.
10 For the fortified city
　will be deserted,
pastures abandoned and forsaken
　like a wilderness.
Calves will graze there,
and there they will spread out
　and strip its branches.
11 When its branches dry out,
　they will be broken off.
Women will come and make fires
　with them,
for they are not a people
　with understanding.
Therefore their Maker will not
　have compassion on them,
and their Creator will not
　be gracious to them.
12 On that day
the LORD will thresh grain
　from the Euphrates River
as far as the •Wadi of Egypt,
and you Israelites will be gathered
　one by one.
13 On that day
a great trumpet will be blown,
and those lost in the land of Assyria
　will come,
as well as those dispersed
　in the land of Egypt;

and they will worship the LORD
　at Jerusalem on the holy mountain.

Woe to Samaria

28 Woe to the majestic crown
　of Ephraim's drunkards,
and to the fading flower
　of its beautiful splendor,
which is on the summit above
　the rich valley.
⌊Woe⌋ to those overcome with wine.
2 Look, the Lord has a strong
　and mighty one—
like a devastating hail storm,
like a storm with strong
　flooding waters.
He will bring it across the land
　with ⌊His⌋ hand.
3 The majestic crown
　of Ephraim's drunkards
will be trampled underfoot.
4 The fading flower
　of his beautiful splendor,
which is on the summit
　above the rich valley,
will be like a ripe fig
　before the summer harvest.
Whoever sees it will swallow it
while it is still in his hand.
5 On that day
the LORD of •Hosts will become
　a crown of beauty
and a diadem of splendor
　to the remnant of His people,
6 a spirit of justice
　to the one who sits in judgment,
and strength
　to those who turn back the battle
　　at the gate.

Drunken Prophets and Priests

7 These also stagger because of wine
　and stumble under the influence
　of beer:

priest and prophet stagger
  because of beer,
they are confused by wine.
They stumble because of beer,
they are muddled in ⌊their⌋ visions,
they stumble in ⌊their⌋ judgments.
8 Indeed, all their tables are covered
    with vomit;
  there is no place without a stench.
9 Who is he[a] trying to teach?
  Who is he[a] trying to instruct?
  Infants[b] ⌊just⌋ weaned from milk?
  Babies[b] removed from the breast?
10 For ⌊he says⌋: "Law after law,
    law after law,
  line after line, line after line,
  a little here, a little there."[c]
11 So He will speak to this people
  with stammering speech
  and in a foreign language.
12 He had said to them:
  "This is the place of rest,
  let the weary rest;
  this is the place of repose."
  But they would not listen.

13 Then the word of the LORD came
    to them:
  "Law after law, law after law,
  line after line, line after line,
  a little here, a little there,"[d]
  so they go stumbling backwards,
  to be broken, trapped,
    and captured.

A Deal with Death

14 Therefore hear the word
    of the LORD, you mockers
  who rule this people in Jerusalem.
15 For you said, "We have cut a deal
    with Death,
  and we have made an agreement
    with •Sheol;

when the overwhelming scourge
    passes through,
  it will not touch us,
  because we have made falsehood
    our refuge
  and have hidden behind treachery."

Cornerstone in Zion

16 Therefore the Lord GOD said:
  "Look, I have laid a stone in Zion,
  a tested stone,
  a precious cornerstone,
    a sure foundation;
  the one who believes
    will be unshakable.[e]
17 And I will make justice
    the measuring line
  and righteousness
    the mason's level."
  Hail will sweep away
    the false refuge,
  and water will flood
    your hiding place.
18 Your deal with Death
    will be dissolved,
  and your agreement with Sheol
    will not last.
  When the overwhelming scourge
    passes through,
  you will be trampled.
19 Every time it passes through,
  it will carry you away;
  it will pass through
    every morning—
  every day and every night.
  Only terror will cause you
  to understand the message.[f]
20 Indeed, the bed is too short
    to stretch out on,
  and its cover too small
    to wrap up in.
21 For the LORD will rise up as ⌊He did⌋
    at Mount Perazim.

[a]28:9 Or He [b]28:9 Lit Those [c]28:10 Hb obscure; perhaps the mockers of v. 9 are mimicking the prophet's words as baby talk. [d]28:13 Hb obscure; the LORD quotes the mockers' words in v. 10 to represent the unintelligible language of the Assyrian invaders. [e]28:16 Lit will not hurry [f]28:19 Or The understanding of the message will cause sheer terror

He will rise in wrath,
 as at the valley of Gibeon,
to do His work, His strange work,
and to perform His task,
 His disturbing task.
22 So now, do not mock,
or your shackles
 will become stronger.
Indeed, I have heard
 from the Lord GOD of Hosts
a decree of destruction
 for the whole land.

God's Wonderful Advice

23 Listen and hear my voice.
Pay attention and hear what I say.
24 Does the plowman plow every day
 to plant seed?
Does he ⌊continuously⌋ break up
 and cultivate the soil?
25 When he has leveled its surface,
does he not then scatter cumin
 and sow black cumin?
He plants wheat in rows and barley
 in plots,
with spelt as their border.
26 His God teaches him order;
He instructs him.
27 Certainly black cumin is not threshed
with a threshing board,
and a cart wheel is not rolled
 over the cumin.
But black cumin is beaten out
 with a stick,
and cumin with a rod.
28 Bread grain is crushed,
but is not threshed endlessly.
Though the wheel
 of ⌊the farmer's⌋ cart rumbles,
his horses do not crush it.
29 This also comes from the LORD
 of Hosts.
He gives wonderful advice;
He gives great wisdom.

Woe to Jerusalem

29 Woe to Ariel,[a] Ariel,
 the city where David camped!
Continue year after year;
let the festivals recur.
2 I will oppress Ariel,
and there will be mourning
 and crying,
and she will be to Me
 like an Ariel.[a]
3 I will camp in a circle around you;
I will besiege you with earth ramps,
and I will set up my siege towers
 against you.
4 You will be brought down;
you will speak from the ground,
and your words will come from low
 in the dust.
Your voice will be like that
 of a spirit from the ground;
your speech will whisper
 from the dust.

5 The multitude of your foes[b] will be
 like fine dust,
and the multitude of the ruthless,
 like blowing chaff.
Then suddenly, in an instant,
6 you will be visited by the LORD
 of •Hosts
with thunder, earthquake,
 and loud noise,
storm, tempest, and a flame
 of consuming fire.
7 The multitude of all the nations
going out to battle against Ariel—
all the attackers, the siege-works
 against her,
and those who oppress her—
will then be like a dream, a vision
 in the night.
8 It will be like a hungry one
 who dreams he is eating,
then wakes and is still hungry;

---

a**29:1,2** Hb obscure; perhaps = "altar hearth" or "lion of God" b**29:5** Lit *foreigners*

and like a thirsty one who dreams
   he is drinking,
then wakes and is still thirsty,
   longing for water.
So will be the multitude
   of all the nations
who go to battle
   against Mount Zion.

9 Stop and be astonished;
   blind yourselves and be blind!
They are drunk,ᵃ but not
   with wine;
they stagger,ᵇ but not with beer.
10 For the LORD has poured out on you
an overwhelming urge toᶜ sleep;
He has shut your eyes—
   the prophets,
and covered your heads—the seers.

11 For you the entire vision will be like the words of a sealed document. If it is given to one who can read and he is asked to read it,ᵈ he will say, "I can't read it, because it is sealed." 12 And if the document is given to one who cannot read and he is asked to read it,ᵉ he will say, "I can't read."

Results of Lip-service

13 The Lord said:

Because these people approach Me
   with their mouths
to honor Me with lip-serviceᶠ—
yet their hearts are far from Me,
and their worship ₍consists of₎
   man-made rules
learned ₍by rote₎—
14 therefore I will again confound
   these people
with wonder after wonder.
The wisdom of their wise men
   will vanish,

and the understanding
   of the perceptive will be hidden.

Potter and Clay

15 Woe to those who go
   to great lengths
to hide their plans from the LORD.
₍They do₎ their works in darkness,
and say, "Who sees us?
   Who knows us?"
16 You have turned things around,
as if the potter were the same
   as the clay.
How can what is made say
   about its maker,
"He didn't make me"?
How can what is formed
say about the one who formed it,
"He doesn't understand
   ₍what he's doing₎"?

Joy in the Lord

17 Isn't ₍it true that₎ in just
   a little while
Lebanon will become an orchard,
and the orchard will seem
   like a forest?
18 On that day the deaf will hear
the words of a document,
and out of a deep darkness
the eyes of the blind will see.
19 The humble will have joy
after joy in the LORD,
and the poor people will rejoice
in the Holy One of Israel.
20 For the ruthless one will vanish,
the scorner will disappear,
and all those who lie in wait
   with evil intent
will be killed—
21 those who, with ₍their₎ speech,
accuse a person of wrongdoing,

ᵃ**29:9** LXX, Tg, Vg read *Be drunk* ᵇ**29:9** Tg, Vg read *wine; stagger* ᶜ**29:10** Lit *you a spirit of* ᵈ**29:11** Lit *If one gives it to one who knows the document, saying, "Read this, please"* ᵉ**29:12** Lit *who does not know the document, saying, "Read this, please"* ᶠ**29:13** Lit *their mouth and honor Me with its lips*

who set a trap at the •gate
for the mediator,
and without cause deprive
the righteous of justice.

22 Therefore, the LORD who redeemed
Abraham says this about the house of Jacob:

Jacob will no longer be ashamed
and his face will no longer be pale.
23 For when he sees his children,
the work of My hands
within his ˻nation˼,
they will honor My name,
they will honor the Holy One
of Jacob
and stand in awe of the God
of Israel.
24 Those who are confused
will gain understanding
and those who grumble
will accept instruction.

Condemnation
of Egyptian Alliance

30 Woe to the rebellious children!
˻This is˼ the LORD's declaration.
They carry out a plan,
but not Mine,
They make an alliance,
but against My will,
piling sin on top of sin.
2 They set out to go down to Egypt
without asking My advice,
in order to seek shelter
under Pharaoh's protection
and take refuge in Egypt's shadow.
3 But Pharaoh's protection
will become your shame,
and refuge in Egypt's shadow
your disgrace.
4 For though hisᵃ princes are at Zoan
and his messengers reach
as far as Hanes,

5 everyone will be ashamed
because of a people who can't help.
They are of no benefit, they are
no help;
they are good for nothing
but shame and reproach.

6 An •oracle about the animals of the
•Negev:ᵇ

Through a land of trouble
and distress,
of lioness and lion,
of viper and flying serpent,
they carry their wealth
on the backs of donkeys
and their treasures on the humps
of camels,
to a people who will not help them.
7 Egypt's help is
completely worthless;
therefore, I call her:
•Rahab Who Just Sits.

Rebellious Israel

8 Go now, write it on a tablet
in their presence
and inscribe it on a scroll;
it will be for the future,
forever and ever.
9 They are a rebellious people,
deceptive children,
children who do not obey
the LORD's instruction.
10 They say to the seers,
"Do not see,"
and to the prophets,
"Do not prophesy the truth to us.
Tell us flattering things.
Prophesy illusions.
11 Get out of the way!
Leave the pathway.
Rid us of the Holy One of Israel."
12 Therefore the Holy One
of Israel says:

ᵃ**30:4** Or *Judah's* ᵇ**30:6** Or *Southland*

"Because you have rejected
   this message
and have trusted in oppression
   and deceit,
and have depended on them,
13 this iniquity of yours will be
   like a spreading breach,
   a bulge in a high wall
   whose collapse will come
      very suddenly.
14 Its collapse will be
   like the shattering
of a potter's jar, crushed to pieces,
so that not even a fragment
   of pottery
will be found among
   its shattered remains—
no fragment large enough
   to take fire from a hearth
or scoop water from a cistern."
15 For the Lord GOD, the Holy One
   of Israel, has said:
"You will be delivered by returning
   and resting;
your strength will lie
   in quiet confidence.
But you are not willing."
16 You say, "No!
We will escape on horses"—
therefore you will escape!—
and, "We will ride on fast horses"—
but those who pursue you
   will be faster.
17 One thousand ⌊will flee⌋
   at the threat of one,
at the threat of five you will flee,
until you alone remain
like a ⌊solitary⌋ pole
   on a mountaintop
or a banner on a hill.

LORD's Mercy to Israel

18 Therefore the LORD is waiting
   to show you mercy,

and is rising up
   to show you compassion,
for the LORD is a just God.
Happy are all who wait patiently
   for Him.

19 For you people will live on Zion in
Jerusalem and will never cry again. He
will show favor to you at the sound of
your cry; when He hears, He will answer
you. 20 The Lord will give you meager
bread and water during oppression, but
your Teacher[a] will not hide Himself[b] any
longer. Your eyes will see your Teacher,[a]
21and whenever you turn to the right or
to the left, your ears will hear this command behind you: "This is the way. Walk
in it." 22 Then you will defile your silver-
plated idols and your gold-plated images.
You will throw them away like menstrual cloths, and call them filth.

23 Then He will send rain for your seed
that you have sown in the ground, and
the food, the produce of the ground, will
be rich and plentiful. On that day your
cattle will graze in open pastures. 24 The
oxen and donkeys that work the ground
will eat salted fodder scattered with winnowing shovel and fork. 25 Streams and
watercourses will be on every high
mountain and every raised hill on the
day of great slaughter when the towers
fall. 26 The moonlight will be as bright as
the sunlight, and the sunlight will be
seven times brighter—like the light of
seven days—on the day that the LORD
bandages His people's injuries and heals
the wounds He inflicted.

Annihilation of Assyrians

27 Look, •Yahweh[c] comes
   from far away,
His anger burning and heavy
   with smoke.[d]
His lips are full of fury,

---

[a]30:20 Or teachers   [b]30:20 Or themselves   [c]30:27 Lit the name Yahweh   [d]30:27 Hb obscure

and His tongue is
   like a consuming fire.
28 His breath is like
      an overflowing torrent
   that rises to the neck.
   ⌊He comes⌋ to sift the nations
      in a sieve of destruction
   and to put a bridle on the jaws
      of the peoples
   to lead ⌊them⌋ astray.
29 Your singing will be like that
   on the night of a holy festival,
   And ⌊your⌋ heart will rejoice
   like one who walks ⌊to the music⌋
      of a flute,
   going up to the mountain
      of the LORD,
   to the Rock of Israel.
30 And the LORD will make
      the splendor of His voice heard
   and reveal His arm striking
   in angry wrath and a flame
      of consuming fire,
   in driving rain, a torrent,
      and hailstones.
31 Assyria will be shattered
      by the voice of the LORD.
   He will strike with a rod.
32 And every stroke
      of the appointed[a] staff
   that the LORD brings down
      on him
   will be ⌊to the sound⌋
      of tambourines and lyres;
   He will fight against him
      with brandished weapons.
33 Indeed! •Topheth has been ready
   for the king for a long time now.
   His funeral pyre is deep
      and wide,
   with plenty of fire and wood.
   The breath of the LORD,
      like a torrent of brimstone,
   kindles it.

The LORD, the Only Help

31 Woe to those who go down
      to Egypt for help
   and who depend on horses!
   They trust in the number
      of chariots
   and in the great strength
      of charioteers.
   They do not look to the Holy One
      of Israel
   and they do not seek
      the LORD's help.
2 But He also is wise
      and brings disaster.
   He does not go back on what
      He says;
   He will rise up against the house
      of wicked men
   and against the allies of evildoers.
3 Egyptians are men, not God;
   their horses are flesh, not spirit.
   When the LORD raises His hand
      ⌊to strike⌋,
   the helper will stumble
      and the helped will fall;
   both will perish together.

4 For this is what the LORD said to me:

   As a lion or young lion growls
      over its prey
   when a band of shepherds
      is called out against it,
   and is not terrified
      by their shouting
   or subdued by their noise,
   so the LORD of •Hosts
      will come down
   to fight on Mount Zion
   and on its hill.

5 Like hovering birds,
   so the LORD of Hosts
      will protect Jerusalem—
   by protecting ⌊it⌋, He will rescue ⌊it⌋,
   by sparing ⌊it⌋, He will deliver ⌊it⌋.

a **30:32** Some Hb mss read *punishing*

⁶ Return to the One the Israelites have greatly rebelled against. ⁷ For on that day, each one will reject the silver and gold idols that your own hands have sinfully made.

Fall of Assyria

⁸ Then Assyria will fall,
but not by human sword;
a sword will devour him,
but not one made by man.
He will flee from the sword,
his young men will be put
to forced labor.
⁹ His rockᵃ will pass away
because of fear,
and his officers will be afraid
because of the signal flag.

ₗThis isₗ the LORD's declaration—whose fire is in Zion and whose furnace is in Jerusalem.

Righteous Kingdom Announced

32 Indeed, a king
will reign righteously,
and rulers will rule justly.
² Each will be like a shelter
from the wind,
a refuge from the rain,
like streams of water in a dry land
and the shade of a massive rock
in an arid land.
³ Then the eyes of those who see
will not be closed,
and the ears of those who hear
will listen.
⁴ The reckless mind
will gain knowledge,
and the stammering tongue
will speak clearly and fluently.
⁵ A fool will no longer be called
a noble,
nor a scoundrel said
to be important.

⁶ For a fool speaks foolishness
and his mind plots iniquity.
He lives in a godless way
and speaks falsely about the LORD.
He leaves the hungry empty
and deprives the thirsty of drink.
⁷ The scoundrel's weapons
are destructive;
he hatches plots to destroy
the needy with lies,
and by charging the poor
during a judgment.
⁸ But a noble person plans
noble things;
he stands up for noble causes.

Warnings on Judgment

⁹ Stand up, you complacent women;
listen to me.
Pay attention to what I say,
you overconfident daughters.
¹⁰ In a little more than a year
you overconfident ones
will shudder,
for the vintage will fail
and the harvest will not come.
¹¹ Shudder, you complacent ones;
tremble, you overconfident ones!
Strip yourselves bare
and put ₗ•sacklothₗ
about your waists.
¹² Beat your breasts ₗin mourningₗ
for the delightful fields
and the fruitful vines,
¹³ for the ground of my people
growing thorns and briers,
indeed, for every joyous house
in the joyful city.
¹⁴ For the palace will be forsaken,
the busy city abandoned.
The hill and the watchtower
will become
barren places forever,
the joy of wild asses,

and a pasture for flocks,
15 until the Spirit from heaven
     is poured out on us.
Then the desert will become
     an orchard,
and the orchard will seem
     like a forest.

Results of Righteousness

16 Then justice will inhabit
     the wilderness,
and righteousness will dwell
     in the orchard.
17 The result of righteousness
     will be peace;
the effect of righteousness
will be quiet confidence forever.
18 Then my people will dwell
     in a peaceful place,
and in safe and restful dwellings.
19 But hail will level the forest,[a]
and the city will sink
     into the depths.
20 Happy are you who sow seed
beside abundant waters,
who let ox and donkey range freely.

Praises to the LORD

33 Woe, you destroyer
       never destroyed,
you traitor never betrayed!
When you have finished destroying,
you will be destroyed.
When you have finished betraying,
they will betray you.

2   LORD, be gracious to us! We wait
    for You.
    Be our strength every morning,
    and our salvation in time of trouble.
3   The peoples flee
       at the thunderous noise;
    the nations scatter when You rise
       in Your majesty.

4   Your spoil will be gathered
       as locusts are gathered;
    people will swarm over it
       like an infestation of locusts.
5   The LORD is exalted, for He dwells
       on high;
    He has filled Zion with justice
       and righteousness.
6   There will be times of security
       for you—
    a storehouse of salvation, wisdom,
       and knowledge.
    The •fear of the LORD is
       Zion's treasure.

7   Listen! Their warriors cry loudly
       in the streets;
    the messengers of peace
       weep bitterly.
8   The highways are deserted;
    travel has ceased.
    An agreement has been broken,
    cities[b] despised,
    and human life disregarded.
9   The land mourns and withers;
    Lebanon is ashamed and decayed.
    Sharon is like a desert;
    Bashan and Carmel shake off
       ⌊their⌋ leaves.

Lord Rises Up

10 "Now I will rise up," says the LORD.
    "Now I will lift Myself up.
    Now I will be exalted.
11 You will conceive chaff;
    you will give birth to stubble.
    Your breath is fire that will
       consume you.
12 The peoples will be burned
       to ashes,
    like thorns cut down and burned
       in a fire.
13 You who are far off, hear what
       I have done;

you who are near,
know My strength."

14 The sinners in Zion are afraid;
trembling seizes the ungodly:
"Who among us can dwell
with a consuming fire?
Who among us can dwell
with ever-burning flames?"

Benefits of Living Righteously

15 The one who lives righteously
and speaks rightly,
who refuses gain from extortion,
whose hand never takes a bribe,
who stops his ears from listening
to murderous plots[a]
and shuts his eyes to avoid
endorsing evil[b]—
16 he will dwell on the heights;
his refuge will be
the rocky fortresses,
his food provided,
his water assured.

17 Your eyes will see the king
in his beauty;
you will see a vast land.
18 Your mind will meditate
on the ⌊past⌋ terror:
"Where is the accountant?[c]
Where is the tribute collector?[d]
Where is the one who spied out
our defenses?"[e]
19 You will no longer see
the barbarians,
a people whose speech is difficult
to comprehend—
who stammer in a language that is
not understood.
20 Look at Zion, the city
of our festival times.
Your eyes will see Jerusalem,
a peaceful pasture, a tent
that does not wander;

its tent pegs will not be pulled up
nor will any of its cords
be loosened.
21 For there the majestic One,
the LORD, will be for us,
a place of rivers and broad streams,
where ships that are rowed
will not go,
and majestic vessels will not pass.
22 For the LORD is our Judge,
the LORD is our lawgiver,
the LORD is our King.
He will save us.
23 Your ropes are slack;
they cannot hold the base
of the mast
or spread out the flag.
Then abundant spoil
will be divided,
the lame will plunder it,
24 and none there will say,
"I am sick."
The people who dwell there
will be forgiven ⌊their⌋ iniquity.

Judgment of the Nations

34 You nations, come here
and listen;
you peoples, pay attention!
Let the earth hear, and all
that fills it,
the world and all that comes
from it.
2 The LORD is angry with all
the nations—
furious with all their armies.
He will set them apart
for destruction,
giving them over to slaughter.
3 Their slain will be thrown out,
and the stench of their corpses
will rise;
the mountains flow[f]
with their blood.

a**33:15** Lit to bloods   b**33:15** Lit eyes from seeing evil   c**33:18** Lit counter   d**33:18** Lit weigher   e**33:18** Lit who counts towers   f**34:3** Or melt, or dissolve

⁴ All^a the heavenly bodies
    will dissolve.
The skies will roll up like a scroll,
and their stars will all wither
as leaves wither on the vine,
and foliage on the fig tree.

Judgment of Edom

⁵ When My sword has drunk its fill^b
    in the heavens
it will then come down on Edom
and on the people I have •set apart
    for destruction.
⁶ The LORD's sword is covered
    with blood.
It drips with fat,
with the blood of lambs and goats,
with the fat of the kidneys of rams.
For the LORD has a sacrifice
    in Bozrah,
a great slaughter in the land
    of Edom.
⁷ The wild oxen will be struck^c down
    with them,
and young bulls
    with the mighty bulls.
Their land will be soaked
    with^d blood,
and their soil will be saturated
    with fat.

⁸ For the LORD has a day
    of vengeance,
a time of paying back ⌊Edom⌋
for its hostility against Zion.
⁹ ⌊Edom's⌋ streams will be turned
    into pitch,
her soil into sulfur;
her land will become burning pitch.
¹⁰ It will never go out—day or night.
Its smoke will go up forever.
It will be desolate, from generation
    to generation;

no one will pass through it forever
    and ever.
¹¹ The desert owl^e and the hedgehog^f
    will possess it,
and the great owl and the raven
    will dwell there.
⌊The LORD⌋ will stretch out
    a measuring line
and a plumb line over her
for ⌊her⌋ destruction and chaos.
¹² No nobles will be left to proclaim
    a king,
and all her princes will come
    to nothing.
¹³ Her palaces will be overgrown
    with thorns;
her fortified cities, with thistles
    and briers.
She will become a dwelling
    for jackals,
an abode^g for ostriches.
¹⁴ The wild beasts will meet hyenas,
and one wild goat will call
    to another.
Indeed, the screech owl
    will stay there
and will find a resting place
    for herself.
¹⁵ The sand partridge^h will make
    her nest there;
she will lay and hatch her eggs
and will gather ⌊her brood⌋
    under her shadow.
Indeed, the birds of prey
    will gather there,
each with its mate.
¹⁶ Search and read the scroll
    of the LORD:
Not one of them will be missing,
none will be lacking its mate,
because He has ordered it
    by myⁱ mouth,

^a**34:4** DSS read *And the valleys will be split, and all*   ^b**34:5** DSS read *sword will appear*   ^c**34:7** Or *will go*   ^d**34:7** Or *will drink its fill of*   ^e**34:11** Or *The pelican*   ^f**34:11** Or *owl*   ^g**34:13** DSS, LXX, Syr, Tg; MT reads *jackals, grass*   ^h**34:15** Or *The arrow snake,* or *The owl*   ⁱ**34:16** Some Hb mss; other Hb mss, DSS, Syr, Tg read *His*

ISAIAH 36:4

and He will gather them
by His Spirit.

17 He has ordained a lot for them;
His hand allotted their portion
with a measuring line.
They will possess it forever;
they will dwell in it
from generation to generation.

God's Ransomed People Return to Zion

35 The wilderness and the dry land
will be glad;
the desert will rejoice and blossom
like a rose.[a]

2 It will blossom abundantly
and will also rejoice with joy
and singing.
The glory of Lebanon will be given
to it,
the splendor of Carmel and Sharon.
They will see the glory of the LORD,
the splendor of our God.

3 Strengthen the weak hands,
steady the shaking knees!

4 Say to the faint-hearted:
"Be strong; do not fear!
Here is your God;
vengeance is coming.
God's retribution is coming; He will
save you."

5 Then the eyes of the blind
will be opened,
and the ears of the deaf unstopped.

6 Then the lame will leap like a deer,
and the tongue of the mute
will sing for joy,
for water will gush
in the wilderness,
and streams in the desert;

7 the parched ground will become
a pool of water,
and the thirsty land springs
of water.

In the haunt of jackals,
in their lairs,
there will be grass, reeds,
and papyrus.

8 A road will be there and a way;
it will be called the Holy Way.
The unclean will not travel on it,
but it will be for him who walks
the path.
Even the fool will not go astray.

9 There will be no lion there,
and no vicious beast will go up
on it;
they will not be found there.
But the redeemed will walk ⌊on it⌋,

10 and the ransomed of the LORD
will return
and come to Zion with singing,
crowned with unending joy.
Joy and gladness
will overtake ⌊them⌋,
and sorrow and sighing will flee.

Sennacherib Threatens Hezekiah

36 In the fourteenth year of King
Hezekiah, Sennacherib king of Assyria advanced against all the fortified
cities of Judah and captured them.
2 Then the king of Assyria sent the •Rab-
shakeh, along with a massive army, from
Lachish to King Hezekiah at Jerusalem.
The Assyrian stood near the conduit of
the upper pool, by the road to the
Fuller's Field. 3 Eliakim son of Hilkiah,
who was in charge of the palace, Shebna
the scribe, and Joah son of Asaph, the
record keeper, came out to him.

Assyrians Mock God

4 The Rabshakeh said to them, "Tell
Hezekiah:

The great king, the king of Assyria,
says this: 'What are you basing your

35:1 Or meadow saffron

confidence on?[a] [5] I[b] say that your plans and military preparedness are mere words. Now who are you trusting in that you have rebelled against me? [6] Look, you are trusting in Egypt, that splintered reed of a staff, which will enter and pierce the hand of anyone who leans on it. This is how Pharaoh king of Egypt is to all who trust in him. [7] Suppose you say to me: We trust in the LORD our God. Isn't He the One whose •high places and altars Hezekiah has removed, saying to Judah and Jerusalem: You are to worship at this altar?

[8] Now make a deal with my master, the king of Assyria. I'll give you 2,000 horses if you can put riders on them! [9] How then can you repel ⌊the attack[c] of even⌋ the weakest of my master's officers, and trust in Egypt for chariots and horsemen? [10] Have I attacked this land to destroy it without the LORD's ⌊approval⌋? The LORD said to me, 'Attack this land and destroy it.'"

[11] Then Eliakim, Shebna, and Joah said to the Rabshakeh, "Please speak to your servants in Aramaic, for we understand ⌊it⌋; don't speak to us in Hebrew[d] within earshot of the people who are on the wall."

Assyrians Mock Hezekiah

[12] But the Rabshakeh replied, "Has my master sent me to speak these words to your master and to you, and not to the men who sit on the wall, ⌊who are destined⌋ with you to eat their excrement and drink their urine?"

[13] Then the Rabshakeh stood and called out loudly in Hebrew:[d]

Listen to the words of the great king, the king of Assyria! [14] The king says: "Don't let Hezekiah deceive you, for he cannot deliver you. [15] Don't let Hezekiah persuade you to trust the LORD, saying, 'The LORD will surely deliver us. This city will not be handed over to the king of Assyria.'"

[16] Don't listen to Hezekiah. For the king of Assyria says: "Make peace[e] with me and surrender to me; then every one of you will eat from his own vine and his own fig tree and drink water from his own cistern [17] until I come and take you away to a land like your land, a land of grain and new wine, a land of bread and vineyards. [18] ⌊Beware⌋ that Hezekiah does not mislead you by saying, 'The LORD will deliver us.' Has any one of the gods of the nations delivered his land from the hand of the king of Assyria? [19] Where are the gods of Hamath and Arpad? Where are the gods of Sepharvaim? Have they delivered Samaria from my hand? [20] Who of all the gods of these lands ⌊ever⌋ delivered his land from my hand, that the LORD should deliver Jerusalem?"

[21] But they were silent and did not answer him at all, for the king's command was, "Don't answer him." [22] Then Eliakim son of Hilkiah, who was in charge of the palace, Shebna the scribe, and Joah son of Asaph, the record keeper, came to Hezekiah with their clothes torn, and they reported to him the words of the Rabshakeh.

---

[a]**36:4** Lit *What is this trust that you trust* [b]**36:5** DSS read *You;* 2 Kg 18:20 [c]**36:9** Or *you refuse [a request]*
[d]**36:11,13** Or *the Judean language* [e]**36:16** Lit *a blessing*

Hezekiah Seeks Isaiah's Counsel

37 When King Hezekiah heard ⌊their report⌋, he tore his clothes, put on •sackcloth, and went to the house of the LORD. ² Then he sent Eliakim, who was in charge of the palace, Shebna the scribe, and the older priests, wearing sackcloth, to the prophet Isaiah son of Amoz. ³ They said to him, "Hezekiah says: 'Today is a day of distress, rebuke, and disgrace, ⌊as⌋ when children come to the point of birth, and there is no strength to deliver them. ⁴ Perhaps the LORD your God will hear the words of the •Rabshakeh, whom his master, the king of Assyria, sent to mock the living God, and will rebuke ⌊him for⌋ the words that the LORD your God has heard. Therefore offer a prayer for the surviving remnant.'"

Isaiah Reassures

⁵ When King Hezekiah's servants came to Isaiah, ⁶ Isaiah said to them, "Say this to your master, 'The LORD says: Don't be afraid because of the words you have heard, which the king of Assyria's attendants have blasphemed Me with. ⁷ Look! I am putting a spirit in him and he will hear a rumor and return to his own land, where I will cause him to fall by the sword.'"

Sennacherib's Letter against God

⁸ When the Rabshakeh heard that the king had left Lachish, he returned and discovered that the king of Assyria was fighting against Libnah. ⁹ The king had heard this about Tirhakah, king of •Cush:[a] "He has set out to fight against you." So when he heard this, he sent messengers to Hezekiah, saying, ¹⁰ "Say this to Hezekiah king of Judah: 'Don't let your God, whom you trust, deceive you by saying that Jerusalem won't be handed over to the king of Assyria. ¹¹ Look, you have heard what the kings of Assyria have done to all the countries; they destroyed them completely. Will you be rescued? ¹² Did the gods of the nations that my predecessors[b] destroyed rescue them—Gozan, Haran, Rezeph, and the Edenites in Telassar? ¹³ Where is the king of Hamath, the king of Arpad, the king of the city of Sepharvaim, Hena, or Ivvah?'"

Hezekiah's Prayer

¹⁴ Hezekiah took the letter from[c] the messengers, read it, then went up to the LORD's house and spread it out before the LORD. ¹⁵ Hezekiah prayed to the LORD: ¹⁶ "LORD of •Hosts, God of Israel, who is enthroned above the •cherubim, You are God—You alone—of all the kingdoms of the earth. You made the heavens and the earth. ¹⁷ Listen closely, LORD, and hear; open Your eyes, LORD, and see; hear all the words that Sennacherib has sent to mock the living God. ¹⁸ LORD, it is true that the kings of Assyria have devastated all these countries and their lands ¹⁹ and have thrown their gods into the fire; for they were not gods but made by human hands—wood and stone. So they have destroyed them. ²⁰ Now, LORD our God, save us from his hand so that all the kingdoms of the earth may know that You are the LORD—You alone."

Isaiah's Answer to Hezekiah

²¹ Then Isaiah son of Amoz sent ⌊a message⌋ to Hezekiah: "The LORD, the God of Israel, says: 'Because you prayed to Me about Sennacherib king of Assyria, ²² this is the word the LORD has spoken against him:

ᵃ**37:9** Or *Nubia*   ᵇ**37:12** Lit *fathers*   ᶜ**37:14** Lit *from the hand of*

God's Words against Sennacherib

The young woman, Daughter Zion,
despises you and scorns you:
Daughter Jerusalem
shakes ιherι head
behind your back.ª

23 Who is it you have mocked
and blasphemed?
Who have you raised
ιyourι voice against
and lifted your eyes in pride?
Against the Holy One of Israel!

24 You have mocked the LORD
throughᵇ your servants.
You have said: With my
many chariots
I have gone up to the heights
of the mountains,
to the far recesses of Lebanon.
I cut down its tallest cedars,
its choice cypress trees.
I came to its remotest heights,
its densest forest.

25 I dug ιwellsιᶜ and drank water.
I dried up all the streams of Egypt
with the soles of my feet.

26 Have you not heard?
I designed it long ago;
I planned it in days gone by.
I have now brought it to pass,
and you have crushed
fortified cities
into piles of rubble.

27 Their inhabitants have
become powerless,
dismayed, and ashamed.
They are plants of the field,
tender grass,
grass on the rooftops,
blasted by the east wind.ᵈ

28 But I knowᵉ your sitting down,
your going out and your coming in,
and your raging against Me.

29 Because your raging against Me
and your arrogance has reached
My ears,
I will put My hook in your nose
and My bit in your mouth;
I will make you go back
the way you came.

God's Words for Judah

30 "'This will be the sign for you: This year you will eat what grows on its own, and in the second year what grows from that. But in the third year sow and reap, plant vineyards and eat their fruit. 31 The surviving remnant of the house of Judah will again take root downward and bear fruit upward. 32 For a remnant will go out from Jerusalem, and survivors from Mount Zion. The zeal of the LORD of Hosts will accomplish this.'

God's Plan to Defend Jerusalem

33 "'Therefore, this is what the LORD says about the king of Assyria:

He will not enter this city
or shoot an arrow there
or come before it with a shield
or build up an assault ramp
against it.

34 He will go back
on the road that he came
and he will not enter this city.
ιThis isι the LORD's declaration.

35 I will defend this city and rescue it,
because of Me
and because of My servant David.'"

Sennacherib's Defeat and Death

36 Then the angel of the LORD went out and struck down 185,000 in the camp of the Assyrians. When the people got up the ιnextι morning—there were all the dead bodies! 37 So Sennach-

ª**37:22** Lit behind you   ᵇ**37:24** Lit by the hand of   ᶜ**37:25** DSS add in foreign lands; 2 Kg 19:24   ᵈ**37:27** DSS; MT reads rooftops, field before standing grain   ᵉ**37:28** DSS read know your rising up and

erib king of Assyria broke camp and left. He returned ⌊home⌋ and lived in Nineveh.

38 One day, while he was worshiping in the temple of his god Nisroch, his sons Adrammelech and Sharezer struck him down with the sword and escaped to the land of Ararat. Then his son Esarhaddon became king in his place.

Hezekiah's Illness and Recovery

38 In those days Hezekiah became terminally ill. The prophet Isaiah son of Amoz came and said to him, "This is what the LORD says: 'Put your affairs in order,ᵃ for you are about to die; you will not recover.'"ᵇ

Hezekiah Prays

2 Then Hezekiah turned his face to the wall and prayed to the LORD. 3 He said, "Please, LORD, remember how I have walked before You faithfully and wholeheartedly, and have done what is good in Your sight." And Hezekiah wept bitterly.

God's Answer

4 Then the word of the LORD came to Isaiah: 5 "Go and tell Hezekiah that this is what the LORD God of your ancestor David says: I have heard your prayer; I have seen your tears. Look, I am going to add 15 years to your life.ᶜ 6 And I will deliver you and this city from the hand of the king of Assyria; I will defend this city. 7 This is the sign to you from the LORD that the LORD will do whatᵈ He has promised:ᵉ 8 I am going to make the sun's shadow that goes down on Ahaz's stairway return by 10 steps." So the sun's shadowᶠ went back the 10 steps it had descended.

Hezekiah's Poem

9 A poem by Hezekiah king of Judah after he had been sick and had recovered from his illness:

10 I said: In the primeᵍ of my lifeᶜ
     I must go to the gates of •Sheol;
     I am deprived of the rest
        of my years.
11 I said: I will never see the LORD,
     the LORD in the land of the living;
     I will not look on humanity
        any longer
     with the inhabitants of what is
        passing away.ʰ
12 My dwelling is plucked up
        and removed from me
     like a shepherd's tent.
     I have rolled up my life
        like a weaver;
     He cuts me off from the loom.ⁱ
     You make an end of me from day
        until night.
13 I thought until the morning:
     He will break all my bones
        like a lion;
     You make an end of me
        day and night.
14 I chirp like a swallow ⌊or⌋ a crane;
     I moan like a dove.
     My eyes grow weak looking upward.
     Lord, I am oppressed; support me.
15 What can I say?
     He has spoken to me,
     and He Himself has done it.
     I walk along slowly all my years
     because of the bitterness
        of my soul,
16 Lord, because of these ⌊promises⌋
        people live,
     and in all of them is the life
        of my spirit as well;
     You have restored me to health
     and let me live.

ᵃ38:1 Lit Command your house   ᵇ38:1 Lit live   ᶜ38:5,10 Lit days   ᵈ38:7 Lit this thing   ᵉ38:7 Lit said   ᶠ38:8 Lit And the sun   ᵍ38:10 Lit quiet   ʰ38:11 Some Hb mss, Tg read of the world   ⁱ38:12 Lit thrum

^{17} Indeed, it was for ⌊my own⌋ welfare
that I had such great bitterness;
but Your love ⌊has delivered⌋ me
from the •Pit of destruction,
for You have thrown all my sins
    behind Your back.
^{18} For Sheol cannot thank You;
Death cannot praise You.
Those who go down to the Pit
cannot hope for Your faithfulness.
^{19} The living, only the living
    can thank You,
as I do today;
a father will make Your faithfulness
    known to children
^{20} The LORD will^a save me;
we will play stringed instruments
all the days of our lives
at the house of the LORD.

Isaiah's Poultice

^{21} Now Isaiah had said, "Let them take a lump of figs and apply it to his infected skin, so that he may recover." ^{22} And Hezekiah had asked, "What is the sign that I will go up to the LORD's temple?"

Hezekiah's Folly

39 At that time Merodach-baladan son of Baladan, king of Babylon, sent letters and a gift to Hezekiah since he heard that he had been sick and had recovered. ^{2} Hezekiah was pleased with them, and showed them his treasure house—the silver, the gold, the spices, and the precious oil—and all his armory, and everything that was found in his treasuries. There was nothing in his palace and in all his realm that Hezekiah did not show them.

Isaiah's Warning

^{3} Then Isaiah the prophet came to King Hezekiah and asked him, "What did these men say? The men who came to you—where were they from?"

Hezekiah replied, "They came to me from a distant country, from Babylon."

^{4} And he asked, "What have they seen in your palace?"

Hezekiah answered, "They have seen everything in my palace. There isn't anything in my storehouses that I didn't show them."

^{5} Then Isaiah said to Hezekiah, "Hear the word of the LORD of •Hosts: ^{6} 'The time will certainly come when everything in your palace and all that your fathers have stored up until this day will be carried off to Babylon; nothing will be left,' says the LORD. ^{7} 'Some of your descendants who come from you will be taken away, and they will be eunuchs in the palace of the king of Babylon.' "

^{8} Then Hezekiah said to Isaiah, "The word of the LORD that you have spoken is good." For he thought: There will be peace and security during my lifetime.

God's People Comforted

40 "Comfort, comfort My people," says your God.
^{2} Speak tenderly to^b Jerusalem,
and announce to her
that her time of servitude is over,
her iniquity has been pardoned,
and she has received
    from the LORD's hand
    double for all her sins.

^{3} A voice of one crying out:

Prepare the way of the LORD
    in the wilderness;
make a straight highway
    for our God in the desert.
^{4} Every valley will be lifted up,
and every mountain and hill
    will be leveled;

---

^{a}**38:20** Lit to ^{b}**40:2** Lit Speak to the heart of

the uneven ground
will become smooth,
and the rough places a plain.
5 And the glory of the LORD
will appear,
and all humanity[a]
will see ⌊it⌋ together,
for the mouth of the LORD
has spoken.

6 A voice was saying, "Cry out!"
Another[b] said,
"What should I cry out?"
"All humanity is grass,
and all its goodness is
like the flower of the field.
7 The grass withers, the flowers fade
when the breath[c] of the LORD blows
on them;[d]
indeed, the people are grass.
8 The grass withers, the flowers fade,
but the word of our God
remains forever."

9 Zion, herald of good news,
go up on a high mountain.
Jerusalem, herald of good news,
raise your voice loudly.
Raise it, do not be afraid!
Say to the cities of Judah,
"Here is your God!"
10 See, the Lord GOD comes
with strength,
and His power establishes His rule.
His reward is with Him,
and His gifts accompany Him.
11 He protects His flock
like a shepherd;
He gathers the lambs in His arms
and carries ⌊them⌋ in the fold
of His ⌊garment⌋.
He gently leads those
that are nursing.

12 Who has measured the waters
in the hollow of his hand
or marked off the heavens
with the span ⌊of his hand⌋?
Who has gathered the dust
of the earth in a measure
or weighed the mountains
in a balance
and the hills in scales?
13 Who has directed[e] the Spirit
of the LORD,
or who gave Him His counsel?
14 Who did He consult with?
Who gave Him understanding
and taught Him the paths of justice?
Who taught Him knowledge
and showed Him the way
of understanding?

Lord of Nations

15 Look, the nations are like a drop
in a bucket;
they are considered as a speck
of dust on the scales;
He lifts up the islands like fine dust.
16 Lebanon is not enough for fuel,
or its animals enough
for a •burnt offering.
17 All the nations are as nothing
before Him;
they are considered by Him
as nothingness and emptiness.

18 Who will you compare God with?
What likeness will you
compare Him to?
19 To an idol?—⌊something that⌋
a smelter casts,
and a metalworker plates with gold
and makes silver welds ⌊for it⌋?
20 To one who shapes a pedestal,
choosing wood that does not rot?[f]
He looks for a skilled craftsman

---

[a]**40:5** Lit *flesh* [b]**40:6** DSS, LXX, Vg read *I* [c]**40:7** Or *wind*, or *Spirit* [d]**40:7** Lit *it* [e]**40:13** Or *measured*, or *comprehended* [f]**40:20** Or *who is too poor for such an offering*, or *who chooses mulberry wood as a votive gift*; Hb obscure

to set up an idol that will not
fall over.

Lord of Universe

21 Do you not know?
Have you not heard?
Has it not been declared to you
from the beginning?
Have you not considered
the foundations of the earth?

22 God is enthroned above the circle
of the earth;
its inhabitants are
like grasshoppers.
He stretches out the heavens
like thin cloth
and spreads them out like a tent
to live in.

23 He reduces princes to nothing
and makes the judges of the earth
to be irrational.

24 They are barely planted,
barely sown,
their stem hardly takes root
in the ground
when He blows on them
and they wither,
and a whirlwind carries them away
like stubble.

25 "Who will you compare Me to,
or who is My equal?"
asks the Holy One.

26 Look up[a] and see:
who created these?
He brings out the starry host
by number;
He calls all of them by name.
Because of His great power
and strength,
not one of them is missing.

27 Jacob, why do you say,
and Israel, why do you assert:
"My way is hidden from the LORD,

and my claim is ignored
by my God"?

28 Do you not know?
Have you not heard?
•Yahweh is the everlasting God,
the Creator of the whole earth.
He never grows faint or weary;
there is no limit
to His understanding.

29 He gives strength to the weary
and strengthens the powerless.

30 Youths may faint and grow weary,
and young men stumble and fall,

31 but those who trust in the LORD
will renew their strength;
they will soar on wings like eagles;
they will run and not grow weary;
they will walk and not faint.

LORD vs. Nations

41 "Be silent before Me, islands!
And let peoples renew
their strength.
Let them approach,
then let them testify;
let us come together for the trial.

2 Who has stirred him up
from the east?
He calls righteousness to his feet.[b]
The LORD[c] hands nations over
to him,
and he subdues kings.
He makes ⌊them⌋ like dust
⌊with⌋ his sword,
like wind-driven stubble
⌊with⌋ his bow.

3 He pursues them, going on safely,
hardly touching the path
with his feet.

Lord: First and Last

4 Who has performed and done ⌊this⌋,
calling the generations
from the beginning?

---

[a]**40:26** Lit *Lift up your eyes on high*   [b]**41:2** Hb obscure   [c]**41:2** Lit *He*

I, the LORD, am the first,
and with the last—I am He."

5 The islands see and are afraid,
the ends of the earth tremble.
They approach and arrive.
6 Each one helps the other,
and says to another,
"Take courage!"
7 The craftsman encourages
the metalworker;
the one who flattens
with the hammer
ʟsupportsʟ the one who strikes
the anvil,
saying of the soldering, "It is good."
He fastens it with nails so that
it will not fall over.

God of Israel

8 But you, Israel, My servant,
Jacob, whom I have chosen,
descendant of Abraham,
My friend—
9 I brought^a you from the ends
of the earth
and called you
from its farthest corners.
I said to you: You are My servant;
I have chosen you and not
rejected you.
10 Do not fear, for I am with you;
do not be afraid, for I am your God.
I will strengthen you; I will
help you;
I will hold on to you
with My righteous right hand.

11 Be sure that all who are enraged
against you
will be ashamed and disgraced;
those who contend with you
will become as nothing
and will perish.

12 You will look for those who contend
with you,
but you will not find them.
Those who war against you
will become absolutely nothing.
13 For I, the LORD your God,
hold your right hand
and say to you: Do not fear,
I will help you.
14 Do not fear, you worm Jacob,
you men^b of Israel:
I will help you—
the LORD's declaration.
Your Redeemer is the Holy One
of Israel.
15 See, I will make you
into a sharp threshing board,
new, with many teeth.
You will thresh mountains
and pulverize ʟthemʟ,
and make hills like chaff.
16 You will winnow them
and a wind will carry them away,
and a gale will scatter them.
But you will rejoice in the LORD;
you will boast in the Holy One
of Israel.

17 The poor and the needy seek water,
but there is none;
their tongues are parched
with thirst.
I, the LORD, will answer them;
I, the God of Israel, do not
forsake them.
18 I will open rivers
on the barren heights,
and springs in the middle
of the plains.
I will turn the desert into a pool
of water
and dry land into springs of water.
19 I will plant cedars in the desert,
acacias, myrtles, and olive trees.

---

^a41:9 Or *seized*   ^b41:14 MT; LXX reads *small number*; DSS read *dead ones*

I will put cypress trees
　　in the desert,
　　elms and box trees together,
20 so that all may see and know,
　　consider and understand,
　　that the hand of the LORD
　　　has done this,
　　the Holy One of Israel
　　　has created it.

God Challenges False Gods

21 "Submit your case," says the LORD.
"Present your arguments,"
　　says Jacob's King.
22 "Let them come and tell us
　　what will happen.
　　Tell us the past events,
　　so that we may reflect on it
　　and know the outcome.
　　Or tell us the future.
23 Tell us the coming events,
　　then we will know
　　　that you are gods.
　　Indeed, do ⌊something⌋ good or bad,
　　then we will be in awe[a]
　　　and perceive.
24 Look, you are nothing
　　and your work is worthless.
　　Anyone who chooses you
　　　is detestable.

25 "I have raised up one
　　　from the north, and he has come,
　　one from the east who invokes
　　　My[b] name.
　　He will march over rulers as if
　　　they were mud,
　　like a potter who treads the clay.
26 Who told about this
　　　from the beginning,
　　so that we might know,
　　and from times past,
　　so that we might say: He is right?
　　No one announced it,

no one told it,
　　no one heard your words.
27 I was the first to say to Zion:[c]
Look! Here they are!
　　and I gave a herald of good news
　　　to Jerusalem.
28 When I look, there is no one;
　　there is no counselor among them;
　　when I ask them, they have
　　　nothing to say.
29 Look, all of them are a delusion;[d]
　　their works are nonexistent;
　　their images are wind
　　and emptiness.

Servant's Mission

42 "This is My Servant;
　　　I strengthen Him,
　　⌊this is⌋ My Chosen One; I delight
　　　in Him.
　　I have put My Spirit on Him;
　　He will bring justice[e] to the nations.
2 He will not cry out or shout
　　or make His voice heard
　　　in the streets.
3 He will not break a bruised reed,
　　and He will not put out
　　　a smoldering wick;
　　He will faithfully bring justice.
4 He will not grow weak
　　　or be discouraged
　　until He has established justice
　　on earth.
　　The islands will wait
　　　for His instruction."

5 This is what God the LORD says—
　　who created the heavens
　　　and stretched them out,
　　who spread out the earth
　　　and what comes from it,
　　who gives breath to the people
　　　on it
　　and life[f] to those who walk on it—

a 41:23 DSS read we may hear   b 41:25 DSS read his   c 41:27 Lit First to Zion   d 41:29 DSS, Syr read are nothing
e 42:1 DSS read His justice   f 42:5 Lit spirit

6 "I, the LORD, have called you
for a righteous ⌞purpose⌟,[a]
and I will hold you by your hand.
I will keep you, and I make you
a covenant for the people
⌞and⌟ a light to the nations,
7 in order to open blind eyes,
    to bring out prisoners
        from the dungeon,
⌞and⌟ those sitting in darkness
    from the prison house.

"I am Yahweh"

8 I am •Yahweh, that is My name;
I will not give My glory to another,
or My praise to idols.
9 The past events
    have indeed happened.
Now I declare new events;
I announce them to you
    before they occur."

Song of Praise

10 Sing a new song to the LORD;
⌞sing⌟ His praise from the ends
    of the earth,
you who go down to the sea
    with all that fills it,
you islands with your[b] inhabitants.
11 Let the desert and its cities shout,
the settlements where Kedar dwells
    ⌞cry aloud⌟.
Let the inhabitants of Sela
    sing for joy;
let them cry out
    from the mountaintops.
12 Let them give glory to the LORD,
and declare His praise
    in the islands.
13 The LORD advances like a warrior;
He stirs up His zeal like a soldier.
He shouts, He roars aloud,
He prevails over His enemies.

14 "I have kept silent from ages past;
I have been quiet
    and restrained Myself.
⌞But now,⌟ I will groan like a woman
    in labor,
gasping breathlessly.
15 I will lay waste mountains and hills,
and dry up all their vegetation.
I will turn rivers into islands,
and dry up marshes.
16 I will lead the blind by a way
    they did not know;
I will guide them on paths
    they have not known.
I will turn darkness to light in front
    of them,
and rough places into level ground.
This is what I will do for them,
and I will not forsake them.
17 They will be turned back
    ⌞and⌟ utterly ashamed—
those who trust in idols
and say to metal-plated images:
You are our gods!

Israel's Blindness and Deafness

18 "Listen, you deaf!
Look, you blind, so that
    you may see.
19 Who is blind but My servant,
or deaf like My messenger
    I am sending?
Who is blind
    like ⌞My⌟ dedicated one,[c]
or blind like the servant
    of the LORD?
20 Though seeing many things,[d]
    you do not obey.
Though ⌞his⌟ ears are open,
    he does not listen."

21 The LORD was pleased, because of
    His righteousness,

---

[a]42:6 Or you by [My] righteousness; lit you in righteousness   [b]42:10 Lit their   [c]42:19 Hb obscure   [d]42:20 Alt Hb
tradition reads You see many things;

to magnify ⌊His⌋ instruction
and make it glorious.

Plight of Israel

22 But this is a people plundered
and looted,
all of them trapped in holes
or imprisoned in dungeons.
They have become plunder,
with no one to rescue them,
and loot, with no one saying
"Give ⌊it⌋ back!"
23 Who among you will pay attention
to this?
Let him listen and obey
in the future.
24 Who gave Jacob to the robber,[a]
and Israel to the plunderers?
Was it not the LORD?
Have we not sinned against Him?
They were not willing to walk
in His ways,
and they would not listen
to His instruction.
25 So He poured out on Jacob
His furious anger
and the power of war.
It surrounded him with fire,
but he did not know ⌊it⌋;
it burned him, but he paid
no attention.[b]

Restoration of Israel

43 Now this is what the LORD says—
the One who created you, Jacob,
and the One who formed
you, Israel—
"Do not fear, for I have
redeemed you;
I have called you by your name;
you are Mine.
2 I will be with you
when you pass
through the waters,

and ⌊when you pass⌋
through the rivers,
they will not overwhelm you.
You will not be scorched
when you walk through the fire,
and the flame will not burn you.
3 For I the LORD your God,
the Holy One of Israel,
and your Savior,
give Egypt as a ransom for you,
•Cush and Seba in your place.
4 Because you are precious
in My sight
and honored, and I love you,
I will give human beings
in your place,
and peoples in place of your life.
5 Do not fear, for I am with you;
I will bring your descendants
from the east,
and gather you from the west.
6 I will say to the north:
Give ⌊them⌋ up!
and to the south:
Do not hold ⌊them⌋ back!
Bring My sons from far away,
and My daughters from the ends
of the earth—
7 everyone called by My name
and created for My glory.
I have formed him;
indeed, I have made him."

8 Bring out a people who are blind,
yet have eyes,
and are deaf, yet have ears.
9 All the nations
are gathered together,
and the peoples are assembled.
Who among them can declare this,
and tell us the former things?
Let them present their witnesses
to vindicate ⌊themselves⌋,
so that people may hear and say,
"It is true."

a**42:24** Lit to loot   b**42:25** Lit he did not put on heart

10 "You are My witnesses"—
            the LORD's declaration—
"and My servant
    whom I have chosen,
so that you may know
    and believe Me
and understand that I am He.
No god was formed before Me,
and there will be none after Me.
11 I, I am the LORD,
    and there is no other Savior
        but Me.
12 I alone declared, saved,
        and proclaimed—
    and not some foreign god[a]
        among you.
    So you are My witnesses"—
            the LORD's declaration—
    "and[b] I am God.
13 Also, from today on I am He ⌊alone⌋,
    and no one can take ⌊anything⌋
        from My hand.
    I act, and who can reverse it?"

God's Deliverance
of Rebellious Israel

14 This is what the LORD, your Redeemer, the Holy One of Israel says:

    Because of you, I will send
        to Babylon
    and bring all of them as fugitives,[c]
    even the Chaldeans in the ships
        in which they rejoice.[d]
15 I am the LORD, your Holy One,
    the Creator of Israel, your King.

16 This is what the LORD says—
    who makes a way in the sea,
    and a path through surging waters,
17 who brings out the chariot
        and horse,
    the army
        and the mighty one together

(they lie down, they do not
    rise again;
they are extinguished,
    quenched like a wick)—
18 "Do not remember the past events,
    pay no attention to things of old.
19 Look, I am about to do
    something new;
    even now it is coming.
        Do you not see it?
    Indeed, I will make a way
        in the wilderness,
    rivers[e] in the desert.
20 The animals of the field
        will honor Me,
    jackals and ostriches,
    because I provide water
        in the wilderness,
    and rivers in the desert,
    to give drink to My chosen people.
21 The people I formed for Myself
    will declare My praise.

Israel Sins

22 "But Jacob, you have not called
        on Me,
    because, Israel, you have
        become weary of Me.
23 You have not brought Me
        your sheep for •burnt offerings
    or honored Me
        with your sacrifices.
    I have not burdened you
        with offerings
    or wearied you with incense.[f]
24 You have not bought Me
        aromatic cane with silver,
    or satisfied Me with the fat
        of your sacrifices.
    But you have burdened Me
        with your sins;
    you have wearied Me
        with your iniquities.

a43:12 Lit not a foreigner   b43:12 Or that   c43:14 Or will break down all their bars   d43:14 Hb obscure   e43:19
DSS read paths   f43:23 With demands for offerings and incense

25 "It is I who sweep away
    your transgressions
  for My own sake
  and remember your sins
    no more.
26 Take Me to court; let us argue
    our case together.
  State your ⌊case⌋, so that you may
    be vindicated.
27 Your first father sinned,
  and your mediators have rebelled
    against Me.
28 So I defiled the officers
    of the sanctuary,
  and gave Jacob over
    to total destruction
  and Israel to abuse.

Spiritual Blessing

44 "And now listen,
        Jacob My servant,
    Israel whom I have chosen.
2 This is the word of the LORD
    your Maker who shaped you
      from birth;
  He[a] will help you:
  Do not fear; Jacob is My servant;
  I have chosen Jeshurun.
3 For I will pour water
    on the thirsty land,
  and streams on the dry ground;
  I will pour out My Spirit
    on your descendants
  and My blessing on your offspring.
4 They will sprout
    among[b] the grass
  like poplars by the streambeds.
5 This one will say: I am the LORD's;
  another will call ⌊himself⌋
    by the name of Jacob;
  still another will write on his hand:
    The LORD's,
  and name ⌊himself⌋ by the name
    of Israel."

No God Other Than Yahweh

6 This is what the LORD, the King of Israel and its Redeemer, the LORD of
•Hosts, says:

  I am the first and I am the last.
  There is no God but Me.
7 Who, like Me, can announce
    ⌊the future⌋?
  Let him say so and make a case
    before Me,
  since I have established
    an ancient people.
  Let these gods declare[c]
    the coming things,
  and what will take place.
8 Do not be startled or afraid.
  Have I not told you and declared it
    long ago?
  You are my witnesses!
  Is there any God but Me?
  There is no ⌊other⌋ Rock;
    I do not know any.

Idols Condemned

9 All who make idols are nothing,
  and what they treasure
    does not profit.
  Their witnesses do not see
    or know ⌊anything⌋,
  so they will be put to shame.
10 Who makes a god or casts
    a metal image
  for no profit?
11 Look, all its worshipers will be
    put to shame,
  and the craftsmen are humans.
  They all will assemble and stand;
  they all will be startled
    and put to shame.

12 The ironworker labors
    over the coals,
  shapes the idol with hammers,

---

a 44:2 Lit *from the womb, and He*   b 44:4 DSS, LXX, a few Hb mss read *as among*   c 44:7 Lit *declare them—*

and works it with his strong arm.
Also he grows hungry
  and his strength fails;
he doesn't drink water and is faint.

13 The woodworker stretches out
    a measuring line,
he outlines it with a stylus;
he shapes it with chisels
and outlines it with a compass.
He makes it according to
    a human likeness,
like a beautiful person,
to dwell in a temple.

14 He cuts down[a] cedars for his use,
or he takes a cypress[b] or an oak.
He lets it grow strong
    among the trees of the forest.
He plants a laurel, and the rain
    makes it grow.

15 It serves as fuel for man.
He takes some of it
    and warms himself;
also he kindles a fire
    and bakes bread;
he even makes it into a god
    and worships it;
he makes it an idol and bows down
    to it.

16 He burns half of it in a fire,
and he roasts meat on that half.
He eats the roast and is satisfied.
He warms himself and says, "Ah!
I am warm, I see the blaze."

17 He makes a god or his idol
    with the rest of it.
He bows down to it and worships;
He prays to it, "Save me, for you are
    my god."

18 Such people[c] do not comprehend
and cannot understand,
for He has shut their eyes[d]
    so they cannot see,
and their minds
    so they cannot understand.

19 No one reflects,
no one has the perception
    or insight to say,
"I burned half of it in the fire,
I also baked bread on its coals,
I roasted meat and ate.
I will make something detestable
    with the rest of it,
and I will bow down to a block
    of wood."

20 He feeds on[e] ashes.
⌊His⌋ deceived mind
    has led him astray,
and he cannot deliver himself,
or say, "Isn't there a lie
    in my right hand?"

God Calls to Israel

21 Remember these things, Jacob,
and Israel, for you are My servant;
I formed you, you are My servant;
Israel, you will never be forgotten
    by Me.[f]

22 I have swept away
    your transgressions like a cloud,
and your sins like a mist.
Return to Me,
for I have redeemed you.

23 Rejoice, heavens, for the LORD
    has acted;
shout, depths of the earth.
Break out into singing, mountains,
forest, and every tree in it.
For the LORD has redeemed Jacob,
and glorifies Himself through Israel.

Restoration of Israel
through Cyrus

24 This is what the LORD, your Redeemer who formed you from the
womb, says:

I am the LORD,
who made everything;

---

[a] **44:14** Lit *To cut down for himself*   [b] **44:14** Exact type of tree uncertain   [c] **44:18** Lit *They*   [d] **44:18** Or *for their eyes are shut*   [e] **44:20** Or *He shepherds*   [f] **44:21** DSS, LXX, Tg read *Israel, do not forget Me*

who stretched out the heavens
　　by Myself;
who alone spread out the earth;
25 who destroys the omens
　　of the false prophets
and makes fools of diviners;
who confounds the wise
and makes
　　their knowledge foolishness;
26 who confirms the message
　　of His servant
and fulfills the counsel
　　of His messengers;
who says to Jerusalem: She will
　　be inhabited,
and to the cities of Judah: They will
　　be rebuilt,
and I will restore her ruins;
27 who says to the depths of the sea:
　　Be dry,
and I will dry up your rivers;
28 who says to Cyrus: My shepherd,
he will fulfill all My pleasure
and say to Jerusalem: She will
　　be rebuilt,
and of the temple: Its foundation
　　will be laid.

Cyrus, God's Anointed

45 The LORD says this to Cyrus,
　　His anointed,
whose right hand I have grasped
to subdue nations before him,
to unloose the loins[a] of kings,
to open the doors before him
and the gates will not be shut:
2 "I will go before you
and level the uneven places;[b]
I will shatter the bronze doors
and cut the iron bars in two.
3 I will give you the treasures
　　of darkness
and riches from secret places,

so that you may know that I,
　　the LORD,
the God of Israel call you
　　by your name.
4 I call you by your name,
because of Jacob My servant
and Israel My chosen one.
I give a name to you,
though you do not know Me.
5 I am the LORD, and there is
　　no other;
there is no God but Me.
I will strengthen[c] you,
though you do not know Me,
6 so that all may know
　　from the rising of the sun
　　to its setting
that there is no one but Me.
I am the LORD, and there is
　　no other.
7 I form light and create darkness,
I make success and create disaster;
I, the LORD, do all these things.

8 "Heavens, sprinkle from above,
and let the skies
　　shower righteousness.
Let the earth open up
that salvation sprout
and righteousness spring up with it.
I, the LORD, have created it.

Clay and Potter

9 "Woe to the one who argues
　　with his Maker—
one clay pot among many.[d]
Does clay say to the one forming it:
What are you making?
Or does your work ˻say˼:
He has no hands?[e]
10 How absurd is the one who says
　　to ˻his˼ father:
What are you fathering?
or to ˻his˼ mother:

---

a45:1 To gird *the loins* is to prepare for battle (2 Sm 20:8), so to *unloose* them is to surrender.　b45:2 DSS, LXX read *the mountains*　c45:5 Lit *gird*　d45:9 Lit *a clay pot with clay pots of the ground*　e45:9 Or *. . . making? Your work has no hands* (or *handles*).

What are you giving birth to?"

11 This is what the LORD,
　　the Holy One of Israel
　　　and its Maker, says:
　　"Ask Me what is to happen
　　　to[a] My sons,
　　and instruct Me about the work
　　　of My hands.
12 I made the earth,
　　and created man on it.
　　It was My hands that stretched out
　　　the heavens,
　　and I commanded all their host.
13 I have raised him up in righteousness,
　　and will level all roads for him.
　　He will rebuild My city,
　　and set My exiles free,
　　not for a price or a bribe,"
　　says the LORD of •Hosts.

God Alone is the Savior

14 This is what the LORD says:

The products of Egypt
　　and the merchandise of •Cush
and the Sabeans, men of stature,
will come over to you
and will be yours;
they will follow you,
they will come over in chains;
and bow down to you.
They will confess[b] to you:
God is indeed with you,
　　and there is no other;
there is no other God.
15 Yes, You are a God
　　who hides Himself,
　　God of Israel, Savior.
16 All of them are put to shame,
　　even humiliated;
　　the makers of idols
　　go in humiliation together.
17 Israel will be saved by the LORD
with an everlasting salvation;

you will not be put to shame
　　or humiliated
for all eternity.

18 For this is what the LORD says—
　　God is the Creator of the heavens.
　　He formed the earth and made it;
　　He established it;
　　He did not create it to be empty,
　　⌊but⌋ formed it to be inhabited—
　　"I am the LORD,
　　and there is no other.
19 I have not spoken in secret,
　　somewhere in a land of darkness.
　　I did not say to the descendants
　　　of Jacob:
　　Seek Me in a wasteland.
　　I, the LORD, speak truthfully;
　　I say what is right.

20 "Come, gather together,
　　and draw near, you fugitives
　　　of the nations.
　　Those who carry their wooden idols,
　　and pray to a god who cannot save,
　　have no knowledge.
21 Speak up and present ⌊your case⌋[c]—
　　yes, let them take counsel together.
　　Who predicted this long ago?
　　Who announced it
　　　from ancient times?
　　Was it not I, the LORD?
　　There is no other God but Me,
　　a righteous God and Savior;
　　there is no one except Me.
22 Turn to Me and be saved,
　　all the ends of the earth.
　　For I am God,
　　and there is no other.
23 By Myself I have sworn;[d]
　　Truth has gone from My mouth,
　　a word that will not be revoked:
　　Every knee will bow to Me,
　　every tongue will swear allegiance.

---

[a] **45:11** Or *Me the coming things about*　[b] **45:14** Lit *pray*　[c] **45:21** Lit *and approach*　[d] **45:23** God takes an oath based on His own character.

24 It will be said to Me:
   Only in the LORD
   is righteousness and strength.”
   All who are incensed against Him
   will come to Him and be
      put to shame.
25 All the descendants of Israel
   will be justified and find glory
      through the LORD.

False Gods Cower

46 Bel crouches; Nebo cowers.
   Their idols are consigned
   to beasts and cattle.
   The ⌊images⌋ you carry are loaded,
   as a burden for the weary ⌊animal⌋.

2 The gods cower;
   they crouch together;
   they are not able to rescue
      the burden,
   but they themselves go
      into captivity.

3 “Listen to Me, house of Jacob,
   all the remnant of the house
      of Israel,
   who have been sustained
      from the womb,
   carried along since birth.
4 I will be the same
      until ⌊your⌋ old age,
   and I will bear ⌊you⌋ up when you
      turn gray.
   I have made ⌊you⌋,
      and I will carry ⌊you⌋;
   I will bear and save ⌊you⌋.

5 “Who will you compare Me
      or make Me equal to?
   Who will you measure Me with,
   so that we should be
      like each other?
6 Those who pour out their bags
      of gold
   and weigh out silver on scales—

they hire a goldsmith
   and he makes it into a god.
   Then they kneel and bow down
      to it.
7 They lift it to their shoulder
      and bear it along;
   they set it in its place, and there
      it stands;
   it does not budge from its place.
   They cry out to it
      but it doesn’t answer;
   it saves no one from his trouble.

No One Like God

8 “Remember this and be brave;[a]
   take it to heart, you transgressors!
9 Remember what happened
      long ago,
   for I am God, and there is no other;
   ⌊I am⌋ God, and no one is like Me.
10 I declare the end
      from the beginning,
   and from long ago what is
      not yet done,
   saying: My plan will take place,
   and I will do all My will.
11 I call a bird of prey[b] from the east,
   a man for My purpose
      from a far country.
   Yes, I have spoken; so I will also
      bring it about.
   I have planned it; I will also do it.
12 Listen to me, you hardhearted,
   far removed from justice:
13 I am bringing My justice near;
   it is not far away,
   and My salvation will not delay.
   I will put salvation in Zion,
   My splendor in Israel.

Fall of Babylon

47 “Go down and sit in the dust,
   Virgin Daughter Babylon.
   Sit on the ground without a throne,

---

[a]**46:8** Hb obscure   [b]**46:11** = Cyrus; Is 41:2-3; 44:28–45:1

Daughter Chaldea!
For you will no longer be called
    pampered and spoiled.
2 Take millstones and grind meal;
remove your veil,
strip off ⌜your⌝ skirt,
    bare your thigh,
wade through the streams.
3 Your nakedness will be uncovered,
and your shame will be exposed.
I will take vengeance;
I will spare no one.[a]
4 The Holy One of Israel is
    our Redeemer;
the LORD of •Hosts is His name.

5 "Daughter Chaldea,
sit in silence and go into darkness.
For you will no longer be called
    mistress of kingdoms.
6 I was angry with My people;
I profaned My possession,
and I placed them
    under your control.
You showed them no mercy;
you made your yoke very heavy
    on the elderly.

No Hope for Wicked Babylon

7 You said: I will be
    the mistress forever.
You did not take these things
    to heart
or think about their outcome.

8 "So now hear this, lover of luxury,
who sits securely,
who says to herself:
I, and no one else,
will never be a widow
or know the loss of children.
9 These two things will happen
    to you
suddenly, in one day:
loss of children and widowhood.

They will happen to you
    in their entirety,
in spite of your many sorceries
and the potency of your spells.
10 You were secure
    in your wickedness;
you said: No one sees me.
Your wisdom and knowledge
led you astray.
You said to yourself:
I, and no one else.
11 But disaster will happen to you;
you will not know how to avert it.
And it will fall on you,
but you will be unable to ward
    it off.[b]
Devastation will happen
    to you suddenly
and unexpectedly.

Babylon's Occult Culture Condemned

12 So take your stand with your spells
    and your many sorceries,
which you have
    wearied yourself with
    from your youth.
Perhaps you will be able
    to succeed;
perhaps you will inspire terror!
13 You are worn out
    with your many consultations.
So let them stand and save you—
the astrologers,[c] who observe
    the stars,
who predict monthly
what will happen to you.
14 Look, they are like stubble;
fire burns them up.
They cannot deliver themselves
from the power[d] of the flame.
This is not a coal
    for warming themselves,
or a fire to sit beside!
15 This is what they are to you—

---

[a]**47:3** Hb obscure   [b]**47:11** Or *to atone for it*   [c]**47:13** Lit *dividers of the heavens*   [d]**47:14** Lit *hand*

those who have wearied you
and have traded with you
   from your youth—
each wanders on his own way;
no one can save you.

Israel: Leave Babylon!

48 "Listen to this, house of Jacob—
   those who are called
   by the name Israel
and have descended from[a] Judah,
who swear by the name
   of the LORD
and declare the God of Israel,
⌊but⌋ not in truth or righteousness.
2 For they are named
   after the Holy City,
and lean on the God of Israel;
His name is •Yahweh of •Hosts.
3 I declared the past events long ago;
they came out of My mouth;
   I proclaimed them.
Suddenly I acted,
   and they occurred.
4 Because I know
   that you are stubborn,
and your neck is iron[b]
and your forehead bronze,
5 therefore I declared to you
   long ago;
I announced it to you
   before it occurred,
so you could not claim: My idol
   caused them;
my carved image and cast idol
   control them.
6 You have heard it. Observe it all.
Will you not acknowledge it?
From now on I will announce
   new things to you,
hidden things that
   you have not known.
7 They have been created now,
   and not long ago;

you have not heard of them
   before today,
so you could not claim, "I already
   knew them!"
8 You have never heard; you have
   never known;
For a long time your ears have not
   been open.
For I knew that you
   were very treacherous,
and were known as a rebel
   from birth.
9 I will delay My anger for the honor
   of My name,
and I will restrain Myself
   for your benefit
   and ⌊for⌋ My praise,
so that you will not be destroyed.

God Refines Israel

10 Look, I have refined you, but not
   as silver;
I have tested[c] you in the furnace
   of affliction.
11 I will act for My own sake,
   indeed, My own,
for how can I[d] be defiled?
I will not give My glory to another.

12 "Listen to Me, Jacob,
and Israel, the one called by Me:
I am He; I am the first,
I am also the last.
13 My own hand founded the earth,
and My right hand spread out
   the heavens;
when I summoned them,
they stood up together.

Listen, Israel!

14 All of you, assemble and listen!
Who among the idols[e] has declared
   these things?
The LORD loves him;[f]

a**48:1** Lit *have come from the waters of*   b**48:4** Lit *is an iron sinew*   c**48:10** Or *chosen*   d**48:11** DSS, Syr; MT reads
it   e**48:14** Lit *among them*   f**48:14** Cyrus

he will accomplish His will
  against Babylon,
and His arm ⌊will be against⌋
  the Chaldeans.
15 I—I have spoken;
  yes, I have called him;
I have brought him,
  and he will succeed in his mission.
16 Approach Me and listen to this.
From the beginning I have not
  spoken in secret;
from the time anything existed,
  I was there."
And now the Lord GOD
  has sent me and His Spirit.

17 This is what the LORD, your Redeemer, the Holy One of Israel says:

I am the LORD your God,
who teaches you for ⌊your⌋ benefit,
who leads you in the way
  you should go.
18 If only you had paid attention
  to My commands.
Then your peace would have been
  like a river,
and your righteousness
  like the waves of the sea.
19 Your descendants would have been
  as ⌊countless⌋ as the sand,
and the offspring of your body
  like its grains;
their name would not be cut off
  or eliminated from My presence.

20 Leave Babylon,
flee from the Chaldeans!
Declare with a shout of joy,
  proclaim this,
  let it go out to the end of the earth;
announce,
  "The LORD has redeemed
  His servant Jacob!"
21 They did not thirst

when He led them
  through the deserts;
He made water flow for them
  from the rock;
He split the rock, and water
  gushed out.
22 "There is no peace," says the LORD,
  "for the wicked."

God's Servant Brings Salvation

49 Coastlands,[a] listen to me;
  distant peoples, pay attention.
The LORD called me
  before I was born.
He named me while I was
  in my mother's womb.
2 He made my words
  like a sharp sword;
He hid me in the shadow
  of His hand.
He made me
  like a sharpened arrow;
He hid me in His quiver.
3 He said to me, "You are
  My servant, Israel;
I will be glorified in him."
4 But I myself said: I have labored
  in vain,
I have spent my strength
  for nothing and futility;
yet my vindication is
  with the LORD,
and my reward is with my God.
5 And now, says the LORD,
who formed me from the womb
  to be His servant,
to bring Jacob back to Him
so that Israel might be gathered
  to Him;
for I am honored in the sight
  of the LORD,
and my God is my strength—

a 49:1 Or Islands

6 He says,
"It is not enough for you to be
My servant
raising up the tribes of Jacob
and restoring the protected ones
of Israel.
I will also make you a light
for the nations,
to be My salvation to the ends
of the earth."

7 This is what the LORD,
the Redeemer of Israel,
his Holy One says
to one who is despised,
to one abhorred by people,[a]
to a servant of rulers:
"Kings will see and stand up,
and princes[b] will bow down,
because of the LORD,
who is faithful,
the Holy One of Israel—
and He has chosen you."

8 This is what the LORD says:

I will answer you in a time of favor,
and I will help you in the day
of salvation.
I will keep you,
and I will appoint you
to be a covenant for the people,
to restore the land,
to make them possess
the desolate inheritances,
9 saying to the prisoners: Come out,
and to those who are in darkness:
Show yourselves.
They will feed along the pathways,
and their pastures will be on all
the barren heights.
10 They will not hunger or thirst,
the scorching heat or sun will not
strike them;
for their compassionate One
will guide them,
and lead them to springs of water.
11 I will make all My mountains
into a road,
and My highways will be raised up.
12 See, these will come from far away,
from the north and from the west,[c]
and from the land of Sinim.[d]

13 Shout for joy, you heavens!
Earth, rejoice!
Mountains break
into joyful shouts!
For the LORD has comforted
His people,
and will have compassion
on His afflicted ones.

Zion Remembered

14 Zion says, "The LORD
has abandoned me;
The Lord has forgotten me!"
15 "Can a woman forget
her nursing child,
or lack compassion for the child
of her womb?
Even if these forget,
yet I will not forget you.
16 Look, I have inscribed you
on the palms of My hands;
your walls are continually
before Me.
17 Your builders[e] hurry;
those who destroy
and devastate you will leave you.
18 Look up, and look around.
They all gather together; they come
to you.
As I live"—
the LORD's declaration—
"you will wear all your children[f]
as jewelry,
and put them on as a bride does.
19 For your waste and desolate places
and your land marked by ruins—

---

a 49:7 Or by [the] nation   b 49:7 Lit princes and they   c 49:12 Lit sea   d 49:12 MT; DSS read of the Syenites; perhaps
modern Aswan in southern Egypt   e 49:17 DSS, Aq, Theod, Vg; MT, Syr, Sym read sons   f 49:18 Lit all of them

will now be indeed too small
for the inhabitants,
and those who swallowed you up
will be far away.
20 The children that you have been
deprived of
will yet say in your hearing:
This place is too small for me;
make room for me so that
I may settle.
21 Then you will say within yourself:
Who fathered these for me?
I was deprived of my children
and barren,
exiled and wandering—
but who brought them up?
See, I was left by myself—
but these, where did
they come from?"a

22 This is what the Lord GOD says:

Look, I will lift up My hand
to the nations,
and raise My banner
to the peoples.
They will bring your sons
in their arms,
and your daughters will be carried
on their shoulders.
23 Kings will be your foster fathers,
and their queensb
your nursing mothers.
They will bow down to you
with their faces to the ground,
and lick the dust at your feet.
Then you will know that I am
the LORD;
those who put their hope in Me
will not be put to shame.

24 Can the prey be taken
from the mighty,
or the captives of the righteousc
be delivered?
25 For this is what the LORD says:

"Even the captives of a mighty man
will be taken,
and the prey of a tyrant
will be delivered;
I will contend with the one
who contends with you,
and I will save your children.
26 I will make your oppressors eat
their own flesh,
and they will be drunk
with their own blood
as with sweet wine.
Then all flesh will know
that I, the LORD, am your Savior,
and your Redeemer,
the Mighty One of Jacob."

50 This is what the LORD says:

Where is
your mother's divorce certificate
that I used to send her away?
Or who were My creditors
that I sold you to?
Look, you were sold
for your iniquities,
and your mother was put away
because of your transgressions.
2 Why was no one there
when I came?
Why was there no one to answer
when I called?
Is My hand too short to redeem?
Or do I have no power to deliver?
Look, I dry up the sea
by My rebuke;
I turn the rivers into a wilderness;
their fish rot because of lack of water
and die of thirst.
3 I dress the heavens in black
and make •sackcloth
their clothing.

God's Obedient Servant

4 The Lord GOD has given Me

the tongue of those
  who are instructed
to know how to sustain the weary
  with a word.
He awakens ⌊Me⌋ each morning;
He awakens My ear to listen
  like those being instructed.
5 The Lord GOD has opened My ear,
  and I was not rebellious;
  I did not turn back.
6 I gave My back to those
  who beat Me,
and My cheeks to those
  who tore out My beard.
I did not hide My face from scorn
  and spitting.
7 The Lord GOD will help Me;
therefore I have not
  been humiliated;
therefore I have set My face
  like flint,
and I know I will not
  be put to shame.
8 The One who justifies Me is near;
who will contend with Me?
Let us confront each other.ᵃ
Who has a case against Me?ᵇ
Let him come near Me!
9 In truth, the Lord GOD
  will help Me;
who is he who will condemn Me?
Indeed, all of them will wear out
  like a garment;
a moth will devour them.
10 Who among you •fears the LORD,
listening to the voice
  of His servant?
Who ⌊among you⌋ walks
  in darkness,
and has no light?
Let him trust in the name
  of the LORD;
let him lean on his God.
11 Look, all you who kindle a fire,

who encircle yourselves
  withᶜ firebrands;
walk in the light of your fire
and in the firebrands you have lit!
This is what you'll get
  from My hand:
you will lie down in a place
  of torment.

Salvation for Zion

51 Listen to Me, you
  who pursue righteousness,
you who seek the LORD:
Look to the rock from which
  you were cut,
and to the quarry from which
  you were dug.
2 Look to Abraham your father,
and to Sarah who gave birth to you
  in pain.
When I called him, he was
  only one;
I blessed him and made him many.
3 For the LORD will comfort Zion;
He will comfort
  all her waste places,
and He will make her wilderness
  like Eden,
and her desert like the garden
  of the LORD.
Joy and gladness will be found
  in her,
thanksgiving and melodious song.

4 Pay attention to Me, My people,
and listen to Me, My nation;
for instruction will come from Me,
and My justice for a light
  to the nations.
I will bring it about quickly.
5 My righteousness is near,
My salvation appears,
and My arms will bring justice
  to the nations.

ᵃ**50:8** Lit *us stand*   ᵇ**50:8** Lit *Who is lord of My judgment*   ᶜ**50:11** Syr reads *who set ablaze*

The coastlands[a] will put their hope
   in Me,
and they will look to My strength.[b]
6 Look up to the heavens,
   and look at the earth beneath;
for the heavens will vanish
   like smoke,
the earth will wear out
   like a garment,
and its inhabitants will die
   in like manner.[c]
But My salvation will last forever,
and My righteousness will never
   be shattered.

7 Listen to Me, you who
   know righteousness,
the people in whose heart is
   My instruction:
do not fear disgrace by men,
and do not be shattered
   by their taunts.
8 For the moth will devour them
   like a garment,
and the worm will eat them
   like wool.
But My righteousness
   will last forever,
and My salvation
   for all generations.

Wake Up!

9 Wake up, wake up!
Put on the strength
   of the LORD's power.
Wake up as in days past,
   as in generations of long ago.
Wasn't it You who hacked •Rahab
   to pieces,
who pierced the sea monster?
10 Wasn't it You who dried up the sea,
   the waters of the great deep,
who made the sea-bed into a road
for the redeemed to pass over?

God's Ransomed Return

11 And the ransomed of the LORD
   will return
and come to Zion with singing,
   crowned with unending joy.
Joy and gladness
   will overtake ⌊them⌋,
and sorrow and sighing will flee.

12 I—I am the One who comforts you.
Who are you that you should
   fear man who dies,
or a son of man who is given up
   like grass?
13 But you have forgotten the LORD,
   your Maker,
who stretched out the heavens
and laid the foundations
   of the earth.
You are in constant dread
   all day long
because of the fury
   of the oppressor,
who has set himself to destroy.
But where is the fury
   of the oppressor?
14 The prisoner[d] is soon to be set free;
he will not die ⌊and go⌋ to the •Pit,
and his food will not be lacking.
15 For I am the LORD your God
who stirs up the sea so that
   its waves roar—
His name is •Yahweh of •Hosts.
16 I have put My words
   in your mouth,
and covered you in the shadow
   of My hand,
in order to plant[e] the heavens,
to found the earth,
and to say to Zion, "You are
   My people."

17 Wake yourself, wake yourself up!
Stand up, Jerusalem,

---

a51:5 Or *islands*   b51:5 Lit *arm*   c51:6 Some DSS read *die like gnats*   d51:14 Hb obscure   e51:16 Syr reads *to stretch out*

you who have drunk the cup
  of His fury
from the hand of the LORD;
you who have drunk the goblet
  to the dregs—
the cup that ⌊causes people⌋
  to stagger.
18 There is no one to guide her
   among all the children
     she has raised;
   there is no one to take hold
     of her hand
   among all the offspring
     she has brought up.
19 These two things have happened
   to you:
   devastation and destruction,
   famine and sword.
   Who will grieve for you?
   How can I[a] comfort you?
20 Your children have fainted;
   they lie at the head of every street
   like an antelope in a net.
   They are full of the LORD's fury,
   the rebuke of your God.

21 So listen to this, afflicted
   and drunken one—but not
     with wine.
22 This is what your Lord says—
   Yahweh, even your God,
   who defends His people—
   "Look, I have removed
   the cup of staggering
     from your hand;
   that goblet, the cup of My fury.
   You will never drink it again.
23 I will put it into the hands
     of your tormenters,
   who said to you:
   Lie down, so we can walk
     over you.
   You made your back
     like the ground,

and like a street for those who walk
  on it.

Jerusalem Saved

52 "Wake up, wake up;
   put on your strength, Zion!
Put on your beautiful garments,
Jerusalem, the Holy City!
For the uncircumcised
  and the unclean
will no longer enter you.
2 Stand up, shake the dust
   off yourself!
Take your seat, Jerusalem.
Remove the bonds[b] from your neck,
captive Daughter Zion."
3 For this is what the LORD says:
"You were sold for nothing,
and you will be redeemed
  without silver."
4 For this is what the Lord GOD says:
"At first My people went down
  to Egypt to live there,
then Assyria oppressed them
  without cause.[c]
5 So now what have I here"—
        the LORD's declaration—
"that My people are taken away
  for nothing?
Its rulers wail"—
        the LORD's declaration—
"and My name is continually
  blasphemed all day long.
6 Therefore My people will know
   My name;
therefore ⌊they will know⌋
  on that day
that I am He who says:
Here I am."

7 How beautiful on the mountains
are the feet of the herald,
who proclaims peace,
who brings news of good things,

---

a51:19 MT, Tg; DSS, LXX, Syr, Vg read you? Who can   b52:2 Alt Hb tradition reads The bonds are removed
c52:4 Or them at last, or them for nothing

who proclaims salvation,
who says to Zion,
  "Your God reigns!"
8 The voices of your watchmen—
they lift up their voices,
shouting for joy together;
for every eye will see
when the LORD returns to Zion.
9 Be joyful, rejoice together,
you ruins of Jerusalem!
For the LORD has comforted
  His people;
He has redeemed Jerusalem.
10 The LORD has displayed
  His holy arm
in the sight of all the nations;
all the ends of the earth will see
the salvation of our God.

11 Leave, leave, go out from there!
Do not touch anything unclean;
go out from her, purify yourselves,
you who carry the vessels
  of the LORD.
12 For you will not leave in a hurry,
and you will not have to take flight;
because the LORD is going
  before you,
and the God of Israel is
  your rear guard.

Success of God's Servant

13 See, My servant[a] will act wisely;[b]
He will be raised and lifted up
and greatly exalted.
14 Just as many were appalled
  at You[c]—
His appearance was so disfigured
that He did not look like a man,
and His form did not resemble
  a human being—
15 so He will sprinkle[d] many nations.[e]
Kings will shut their mouths
because of Him,

For they will see
  what had not been told them,
and they will understand
  what they had not heard.

Man of Suffering

53 Who has believed
  what we have heard?[f]
And who has the arm of the LORD
  been revealed to?
2 He grew up before Him
  like a young plant
and like a root out of dry ground.
He had no form or splendor
  that we should look at Him,
no appearance that we should
  desire Him.
3 He was despised and rejected
  by men,
a man of suffering who knew
  what sickness was.
He was like one
  people turned away from;[g]
He was despised, and we didn't
  value Him.

"He Carried Our Pains"

4 Yet He Himself bore our sicknesses,
and He carried our pains;
but we in turn regarded Him stricken,
struck down by God, and afflicted.
5 But He was pierced because of
  our transgressions,
crushed because of our iniquities;
punishment for our peace was
  on Him,
and we are healed by His wounds.

"For the Iniquity of Us All"

6 We all went astray like sheep;
we all have turned to our own way;
and the LORD has punished Him
for[h] the iniquity of us all.

a52:13 Tg adds the Messiah   b52:13 Or will be successful   c52:14 Some Hb mss, Syr, Tg read Him   d52:15 As the blood of a sacrifice is sprinkled on the altar on behalf of the people   e52:15 LXX reads so many nations will marvel at Him   f53:1 Or believed our report   g53:3 Lit And like a hiding of faces from Him   h53:6 Lit with; or has placed on Him

7 He was oppressed and afflicted,
  yet He did not open His mouth.
  Like a lamb led to the slaughter
  and like a sheep silent
    before her shearers,
  He did not open His mouth.
8 He was taken away because of
    oppression and judgment;
  and who considered His fate?[a]
  For He was cut off from the land
    of the living;
  He was struck because of
  My people's rebellion.
9 They[b] made His grave
    with the wicked,
  and with a rich man at His death,
  although He had done
    no violence
  and had not spoken deceitfully.

"The Lord Was
Pleased to Crush Him"

10 Yet the LORD was pleased
    to crush Him,
  and He made Him sick.
  When[c] You make Him
    a •restitution offering,
  He will see ⌊His⌋ •seed,
    He will prolong His days,
  and the will of the LORD
    will succeed by His hand.
11 He will see ⌊it⌋[d] out of His anguish,
  and He will be satisfied
    with His knowledge.
  My righteous servant
    will justify many,
  and He will carry their iniquities.
12 Therefore I will give Him[e] the many
    as a portion,
  and He will receive[f] the mighty
    as spoil,
  because He submitted Himself
    to death,
  and was counted among the rebels;

yet He bore the sin of many
and interceded for the rebels.

Future Glory for Israel

54 "Rejoice, barren one, who did not
    give birth;
  burst into song and shout,
  you who have not been in labor!
  For the children of the forsaken one
    will be more
  than the children
    of the married woman,"
  says the LORD.
2 "Enlarge the site of your tent,
  and let your tent curtains
    be stretched out;
  do not hold back;
  lengthen your ropes,
  and drive your pegs deep.
3 For you will spread out to the right
    and to the left,
  and your descendants
    will dispossess nations
  and inhabit the desolate cities.

4 "Do not be afraid, for you will not
    be put to shame;
  don't be humiliated,
    for you will not be disgraced.
  For you will forget the shame
    of your youth,
  and you will no longer remember
  the disgrace of your widowhood.
5 For your husband is your Maker—
  His name is •Yahweh of •Hosts—
  and the Holy One of Israel is
    your Redeemer;
  He is called the God of all the earth.
6 For the LORD has called you,
  like a wife deserted and wounded
    in spirit,
  a wife of one's youth
    when she is rejected,"
  says your God.

---

[a]**53:8** Or *and as for His generation, who considered [Him]?* [b]**53:9** DSS; MT reads *He* [c]**53:10** Or *If* [d]**53:11** DSS,
LXX read *see light* [e]**53:12** Or *Him with* [f]**53:12** Or *receive with*

7 "I deserted you for a brief moment,
but I will take you back
   with great compassion.
8 In a surge of anger
I hid My face from you
   for a moment,
but I will have compassion on you
with everlasting love,"
says the LORD your Redeemer.
9 "For this is like the days[a] of Noah
   to Me:
when I swore that the waters
   of Noah
would never flood the earth again,
so I have sworn that I will not
   be angry with you
or rebuke you.
10 Though the mountains move
and the hills shake,
My love will not be removed
   from you
and My covenant of peace will not
   be shaken,"
says your compassionate LORD.

11 "Poor ⌊Jerusalem⌋, storm-tossed,
   and not comforted,
I will set your stones
   in black mortar,[b]
and lay your foundations
   in sapphires.[c]
12 I will make your battlements[d]
   of rubies,
your gates of sparkling stones,
and all your walls
   of precious stones.
13 Then all your children
   will be taught by the LORD,
their prosperity will be great,
14 and you will be established
on ⌊a foundation of⌋ righteousness.
You will be far from oppression,
you will certainly not be afraid;
you will be far from terror,

it will certainly not come near you.
15 If anyone attacks you,
it is not from Me;
whoever attacks you
will fall before you.
16 Look, I have created the craftsman
who blows on the charcoal fire
and produces a weapon suitable
   for its task;
and I have created the destroyer
   to work havoc.
17 No weapon formed against you
   will succeed,
and you will refute any accusation[e]
raised against you in court.
This is the heritage
   of the LORD's servants,
and their righteousness is
   from Me."
      ⌊This is⌋ the LORD's declaration.

Come to the LORD

55 "Come, everyone who is thirsty,
   come to the waters;
and you without money,
come, buy, and eat!
Come, buy wine and milk
without money and without cost!
2 Why do you spend money on what
   is not food,
and your wages on what
   does not satisfy?
Listen carefully to Me, and eat
   what is good,
and you will enjoy the choicest
   of foods.[f]
3 Pay attention and come to Me;
listen, so that you will live.
I will make an everlasting covenant
   with you,
the promises assured to David.
4 Since I have made him a witness
   to the peoples,

a 54:9 DSS, Cairo Geniza; MT, LXX read waters b 54:11 Lit in antimony c 54:11 Or lapis lazuli d 54:12 Lit suns;
perhaps shields; Ps 84:11 e 54:17 Lit refute every tongue f 55:2 Lit enjoy fatness

a leader and commander
 for the peoples,
5 so you will summon a nation
   you do not know,
 and nations who do not know you
   will run to you.
 For the LORD your God,
 even the Holy One of Israel,
 has glorified you."

6 Seek the LORD
   while He may be found;
 call to Him while He is near.
7 Let the wicked one abandon
   his way,
 and the sinful one his thoughts;
 let him return to the LORD,
 so He may have compassion
   on him,
 and to our God, for He will
   freely forgive.

"My Thoughts Are Not Your Thoughts"

8 "For My thoughts are not
   your thoughts,
 and your ways are not My ways."
   ⌊This is⌋ the LORD's declaration.
9 "For as heaven is higher than earth,
 so My ways are higher
   than your ways,
 and My thoughts
   than your thoughts.
10 For just as rain and snow fall
   from heaven,
 and do not return there
 without saturating the earth,
 and making it germinate
   and sprout,
 and providing seed to sow
   and food to eat,
11 so My word that comes
   from My mouth
 will not return to Me empty,
 but it will accomplish what I please,
 and will prosper in what I send it
   ⌊to do⌋."

12 You will indeed go out with joy
 and be peacefully guided;
 the mountains and the hills
   will break into singing
   before you,
 and all the trees of the field
   will clap ⌊their⌋ hands.
13 Instead of the thornbush, a cypress
   will come up,
 and instead of the brier, a myrtle
   will come up;
 it will make a name for the LORD
 as an everlasting sign that will not
   be destroyed.

A House of Prayer for All

56 This is what the LORD says:
Preserve justice and do
   what is right,
 for My salvation is coming soon,
 and My righteousness
   will be revealed.
2 Happy is the man who does this,
 anyone who maintains this,
 who keeps the Sabbath
   without desecrating it,
 and keeps his hand from doing
   any evil.

3 No foreigner who has converted
   to the LORD
 should say,
 "The LORD will exclude me
   from His people";
 and the eunuch should not say,
 "Look, I am a dried-up tree."
4 For the LORD says this:
 "For the eunuchs who keep
   My Sabbaths,
 and choose what pleases Me,
 and hold firmly to My covenant,
5 I will give them, in My house
   and within My walls,
 a memorial and a name
 better than sons and daughters.

I will give each ⌞of them⌟
an everlasting name
that will never be cut off.
6 And the foreigners who convert
to the LORD,
minister to Him,
love the LORD's name,
and are His servants,
all who keep the Sabbath
without desecrating it,
and who hold firmly
to My covenant—
7 I will bring them
to My holy mountain
and let them rejoice in My house
of prayer.
Their •burnt offerings
and sacrifices
will be acceptable on My altar,
for My house will be called a house
of prayer for all nations."
        8 ⌞This is⌟ the declaration
                of the Lord GOD,
        who gathers the dispersed
                of Israel:

"I will gather to them still others
besides those already gathered."

Unrighteous Leaders Condemned

9 All you animals of the field
and forest,
come and eat!
10 Israel's[a] watchmen are blind,
all of them,
they know nothing;
all of them are mute dogs,
they cannot bark;
they dream, lie down,
and love to sleep.
11 These dogs have fierce appetites;
they never have enough.
And they are shepherds
who have no discernment;
all of them turn to their own way,
every last one for his own gain.
12 "Come, let me get ⌞some⌟ wine,
let's guzzle ⌞some⌟ beer;
and tomorrow will be like today,
only far better!"

57
The righteous one perishes,
and no one takes it to heart;
faithful men are swept away,
with no one realizing
that the righteous one
is swept away
from the presence[b] of evil.
2 He will enter into peace—
they will rest on their beds[c]—
everyone who lives uprightly.

Pagan Religion Denounced

3 But come here,
you sons of a sorceress,
offspring of an adulterer
and a prostitute![d]
4 Who is it you are mocking?
Who is it you are opening
your mouth
and sticking out your tongue at?
Isn't it you, you rebellious children,
you race of liars,
5 who burn with lust
among the oaks,
under every flourishing tree,
who slaughter children
in the •wadis
below the clefts of the rocks?
6 Your portion is
among the smooth ⌞stones⌟
of the wadi;
indeed, they are your lot.
You have even poured out
a drink offering to them;
you have offered a •grain offering;
should I be satisfied with these?

---

[a]56:10 Or *His*, or *Its*   [b]57:1 Or *away because*   [c]57:2 Either their deathbed or their grave   [d]57:3 Lit *and she acted as a harlot*

7 You have placed your bed
 on a high and lofty mountain;
 you also went up there
  to offer sacrifice.
8 You have set up your memorial
 behind the door and doorpost.
 For away from Me, you stripped,
 went up, and made
  your bed wide,
 and you have made a bargain[a]
  for yourself with them.
 You have loved their bed;
 you have gazed on their genitals.[b]
9 You went to the king with oil
 and multiplied your perfumes;
 you sent your envoys far away
 and sent ⌊them⌋ down
  even to •Sheol.
10 You became weary
  on your many journeys,
 ⌊but⌋ you did not say, "I give up!"
 You found a renewal
  of your strength;[c]
 therefore you did not grow weak.
11 Who was it you dreaded
  and feared,
 so that you lied and didn't
  remember Me
 or take it to heart?
 Have I not kept silent for such
  a long time[d]
 and you do not •fear Me?
12 I will expose your righteousness,
 and your works—they will not
  profit you.
13 When you cry out,
 let your collection ⌊of idols⌋
  deliver you!
 The wind will carry all of them off,
 a breath will take them away.
 But whoever takes refuge in Me
 will inherit the land
 and possess My holy mountain.

Healing and Peace

14 He said,
 "Build it up, build it up,
  prepare the way,
 remove ⌊every⌋ obstacle
  from My people's way."
15 For the High and Exalted One
 who lives forever, whose name
  is Holy says this:
 "I live in a high and holy place,
 and with the oppressed and lowly
  of spirit,
 to revive the spirit of the lowly
 and revive the heart
  of the oppressed.
16 For I will not accuse ⌊you⌋ forever,
 and I will not always be angry;
 for then the spirit would grow weak
  before Me,
 even the breath ⌊of man⌋,
  which I have made.
17 Because of his sinful greed
  I was angry,
 so I struck him; I was angry
  and hid;[e]
 but he went on turning back
  to the desires of his heart.
18 I have seen his ways,
  but I will heal him;
 I will lead him and comfort him
  and his mourners,
19 creating words of praise."[f]
 The LORD says,
 "Peace, peace to the one who is far
  or near,
 and I will heal him.
20 But the wicked are
  like the storm-tossed sea,
 for it cannot be still,
 and its waters churn up mire
  and muck.
21 There is no peace for the wicked,"
 says my God.

---

[a]57:8 Lit you cut [b]57:8 Lit hand; probably a euphemism for the male organ [c]57:10 Lit found life of your hand
[d]57:11 MT, DSS; LXX reads And I, when I see you, I pass by [e]57:17 Lit him; hiding and I am angry [f]57:19 Lit
creating fruit of the lips

False Fasting

58 "Cry out loudly,[a] don't hold back!
Raise your voice like a trumpet.
Tell My people their transgression,
and the house of Jacob their sins.

2 They seek Me day after day
and delight to know My ways,
like a nation that does what is right
and does not abandon the justice
of their God.
They ask Me
for righteous judgments;
they delight in the nearness
of God."

3 "Why have we fasted,
but You have not seen?
We have denied ourselves,
but You haven't noticed!"[b]
"Look, you do as you please
on the day of your fast,
and oppress all your workers.

4 You fast ⌊with⌋ contention and strife
to strike viciously with ⌊your⌋ fist.
You cannot fast as ⌊you do⌋ today,
⌊hoping⌋ to make your voice heard
on high.

5 Will the fast I choose be like this:
A day for a person to deny himself,
to bow his head like a reed,
and to spread out •sackcloth
and ashes?
Will you call this a fast
and a day acceptable to the LORD?

God's True Fasting

6 Isn't the fast I choose:
To break the chains of wickedness,
to untie the ropes of the yoke,
to set the oppressed free,
and to tear off every yoke?

7 Is it not to share your bread
with the hungry,
to bring the poor and homeless
into your house,
to clothe the naked
when you see him,
and to not ignore[c] your own flesh
⌊and blood⌋?

8 Then your light will appear
like the dawn,
and your recovery
will come quickly.
Your righteousness will go
before you,
and the LORD's glory will be
your rear guard.

9 At that time, when you call,
the LORD will answer;
when you cry out, He will say:
Here I am.
If you get rid of the yoke from those
around you,[d]
the finger-pointing
and malicious speaking,

10 and if you offer yourself[e]
to the hungry,
and satisfy the afflicted one,
then your light will shine
in the darkness,
and your night will be like noonday.

11 The LORD will always lead you,
satisfy you in a parched land,
and strengthen your bones.
You will be like a watered garden
and like a spring whose waters
never run dry.

12 Some of you will rebuild
the ancient ruins;
you will restore
the foundations laid long ago;[f]
you will be called the repairer
of broken walls,
the restorer of streets
where people live.

a**58:1** Lit *with throat*   b**58:3** *"Why have we . . . but you haven't noticed!"* are Israel's words to God.   c**58:7** Lit *not hide yourself from*   d**58:9** Lit *from your midst*   e**58:10** Some Hb mss, LXX, Syr read *offer your bread*   f**58:12** Lit *foundations generation and generation*

Honor Sabbath

13 "If you keep from desecrating[a]
    the Sabbath,
from doing whatever you want
    on My holy day;
if you call the Sabbath a delight,
and the holy ⌊day⌋
    of the LORD honorable;
if you honor it, not going
    your own ways,
seeking your own pleasure,
    or talking too much;[b]
14 then you will delight yourself
    in the LORD,
and I will make you ride
    over the heights of the land,
and let you enjoy the heritage
    of your father Jacob."
For the mouth of the LORD
    has spoken.

Pervasive Sin

59 Indeed, the LORD's hand is not
      too short to save,
    and His ear is not too deaf to hear.
2 But your iniquities
    have built barriers
between you and your God,
and your sins have made Him
    hide ⌊His⌋ face from you
so that He does not listen.
3 For your hands are defiled
    with blood,
and your fingers with iniquity;
your lips have spoken lies,
and you mutter injustice.
4 No one makes claims justly;
no one pleads honestly.
They trust in empty
    and worthless words;
they conceive trouble
    and give birth to iniquity.
5 They hatch viper's eggs
and weave spider's webs.

Whoever eats their eggs will die;
crack one open, and a viper
    is hatched.
6 Their webs cannot
    become clothing,
and they cannot cover themselves
    with their works.
Their works are sinful works,
and violent acts are in their hands.
7 Their feet run after evil,
and they rush to shed
    innocent blood.
Their thoughts are sinful thoughts;
ruin and wretchedness are
    in their paths.
8 They have not known the path
    of peace,
and there is no justice
    in their ways.
They have made
    their roads crooked;
no one who walks on them
    will know peace.
9 Therefore justice is far from us,
and righteousness does not
    reach us.
We hope for light,
    but there is darkness;
for brightness, but we live
    in the night.
10 We grope along a wall
    like the blind;
we grope like those without eyes.
We stumble at noon as though
    it were twilight;
⌊we are⌋ like the dead among those
    who are healthy.
11 We all growl like bears
and moan like doves.
We hope for justice,
    but there is none;
for salvation, ⌊but⌋ it is far from us.
12 For our transgressions
    have multiplied before You,

ᵃ58:13 Lit keep your foot from   ᵇ58:13 Lit or speak a word

and our sins testify against us.
For our transgressions are with us,
and we know our iniquities:

13 transgression and deception
    against the LORD,
turning away from following
    our God,
speaking oppression and revolt,
conceiving and uttering lying words
    from the heart.

14 Justice is turned back,
and righteousness stands far off.
For truth has stumbled
    in the public square,
and honesty cannot enter.

15 Truth is missing,
and whoever turns from evil
    is plundered.

The LORD saw that there was
    no justice,
and He was offended.

16 He saw that there was no man—
He was amazed that there was
    no one interceding;
so His own arm
    brought salvation,
and His own righteousness
    supported Him.

17 He put on righteousness
    like a breastplate,
and a helmet of salvation
    on His head;
He put on garments of vengeance
    for clothing,
and He wrapped Himself in zeal
    as in a cloak.

18 Thus He will repay according to
    ⌊their⌋ deeds:
fury to His enemies,
retribution to His foes,
and He will repay the coastlands.

19 They will •fear the name
    of the LORD in the west,
and His glory in the east;

for He will come
    like a rushing stream
driven by the wind of the LORD.

20 The Redeemer will come to Zion,
and to those in Jacob who turn
    from transgression.
        ⌊This is⌋ the LORD's declaration.

21 "As for Me, this is My covenant
with them," says the LORD: "My Spirit
who is on you, and My words that I have
put in your mouth, will not depart from
your mouth, or from the mouth of your
children, or from the mouth of your children's children, from now on and forever," says the LORD.

LORD's Glory in Zion

60 Arise, shine, for your light
    has come,
and the glory of the Lord shines
    over you.[a]

2 For look, darkness covers the earth,
and total darkness the peoples;
but the LORD will shine over you,
and His glory will appear over you.

3 Nations will come to your light,
and kings to the brightness
    of your radiance.

4 Raise your eyes and look around:
they all gather and come to you;
your sons will come from far away,
and your daughters will be carried
    on the hip.

5 Then you will see and be radiant,
and your heart will tremble
    and rejoice,[b]
because the riches of the sea
    will become yours,
and the wealth of the nations
    will come to you.

6 Caravans of camels will cover
    your land[c]—
young camels of Midian
    and Ephah—

---

[a]**60:1** *You* refers to Jerusalem.   [b]**60:5** Lit *expand*   [c]**60:6** Lit *cover you*

all of them will come from Sheba.
They will carry gold
  and frankincense
and proclaim the praises
  of the LORD.
7 All the flocks of Kedar
  will be gathered to you;
the rams of Nebaioth will serve you
and go up on My altar
  as an acceptable ⌊sacrifice⌋.
I will glorify My beautiful house.
8 Who are these who fly like a cloud,
like doves to their shelters?
9 Yes, the islands will wait for Me
with the ships of Tarshish
  in the lead,
to bring your children
  from far away,
their silver and gold with them,
for the honor of the LORD your God,
the Holy One of Israel,
who has glorified you.
10 Foreigners will build up your walls,
and their kings will serve you.
Although I struck you in My wrath,
yet I will show mercy to you
  with My favor.
11 Your gates will always be open;
they will never be shut day or night
so that the wealth of the nations
may be brought into you,
with their kings being led
  ⌊in procession⌋.
12 For the nation and the kingdom
that will not serve you will perish;
those nations will be annihilated.
13 The glory of Lebanon will come
  to you—
⌊its⌋ pine, fir, and cypress together—
to beautify the place
  of My sanctuary,
and I will glorify
  My dwelling place.[a]
14 The sons of your oppressors

will come and bow down to you;
all who reviled you
will fall down on their faces
  at your feet.
They will call you the City
  of the LORD,
Zion of the Holy One of Israel.
15 Instead of your being deserted
  and hated,
with no one passing through,
I will make you an object
  of eternal pride,
a joy from age to age.
16 You will nurse on the milk
  of nations,
and nurse at the breast of kings;
you will know that I, the LORD,
  am your Savior
and Redeemer, the Mighty One
  of Jacob.
17 I will bring gold instead of bronze;
I will bring silver instead of iron,
bronze instead of wood,
and iron instead of stones.
I will appoint peace as your guard
and righteousness as your ruler.
18 Violence will never again
  be heard of in your land;
devastation and destruction
⌊will be gone from⌋ your borders.
But you will name
  your walls salvation,
and your gates praise.
19 The sun will no longer be your light
  by day,
and the brightness of the moon
  will not shine on you;
but the LORD will be
  your everlasting light,
and your God will be your splendor.
20 Your sun will no longer set,
and your moon will not fade;
for the LORD will be
  your everlasting light,

and the days of your sorrow
  will be over.
21 Then all your people
      will be righteous;
  they will possess the land forever;
  they are the branch I planted,
  the work of My[a] hands,
  so that I may be glorified.
22 The least will become a thousand,
  the smallest a mighty nation.
  I am the LORD;
  I will accomplish it quickly
      in its time.

Messiah's Jubilee

61 The Spirit of the Lord GOD is
      on Me,
because the Lord has anointed Me
to bring good news to the poor.
He has sent Me to heal[b]
  the brokenhearted,
to proclaim liberty to the captives,
and freedom to the prisoners;
2 to proclaim the year
      of the LORD's favor,
  and the day
      of our God's vengeance;
  to comfort all who mourn,
3 to provide for those who mourn
      in Zion;
  to give them a crown of beauty
      instead of ashes,
  festive oil instead of mourning,
  and splendid clothes
      instead of despair.[c]
  And they will be called
      righteous trees,
  planted by the LORD,
  to glorify Him.

4 They will rebuild the ancient ruins;
  they will restore
      the former devastations;
  they will renew the ruined cities,

the devastations
  of many generations.
5 Strangers will stand and feed
      your flocks,
  and foreigners will be
      your plowmen and vinedressers.
6 But you will be called
      the LORD's priests;
  they will speak of you as ministers
      of our God;
  you will eat the wealth
      of the nations,
  and you will boast in their riches.
7 Because your shame was double,
  and they cried out,
      "Disgrace is their portion,"
  therefore, they will possess double
      in their land,
  and eternal joy will be theirs.

8 For I the LORD love justice;
  I hate robbery and injustice;[d]
  I will faithfully reward them
  and make an everlasting covenant
      with them.
9 Their descendants will be known
      among the nations,
  and their posterity
      among the peoples.
  All who see them will recognize
  that they are a people the LORD
      has blessed.

10 I greatly rejoice in the LORD,
  I exult in my God;
  for He has clothed me
      with the garments of salvation
  and wrapped me in a robe
      of righteousness,
  as a bridegroom wears a turban
  and as a bride adorns herself
      with her jewels.
11 For as the earth brings forth
      its growth,

---

a **60:21** LXX, DSS read *His*   b **61:1** Lit *bind up*   c **61:3** Lit *a dim spirit*   d **61:8** Some Hb mss, DSS, LXX, Syr, Tg, Vg;
other Hb mss read *robbery with a burnt offering*

and as a garden enables
what is sown to spring up,
so the Lord GOD
will cause righteousness
and praise
to spring up before all the nations.

Zion's Restoration

62 I will not keep silent
because of Zion,
and I will not keep still
because of Jerusalem
until her righteousness shines
like a bright light,
and her salvation
like a flaming torch.
2 Nations will see
your righteousness,
and all kings your glory.
You will be called by a new name
that the LORD's mouth
will announce.
3 You will be a glorious crown
in the LORD's hand,
and a royal diadem in the palm
of your God.
4 You will no longer
be called Deserted,
and your land will not
be called Desolate;
instead, you will be called
My Delight is in Her,[a]
and your land Married;[b]
for the LORD delights in you,
and your land will be married.
5 For as a young man marries a virgin,
so your sons will marry you;
and as a bridegroom rejoices[c]
over ⌊his⌋ bride,
so your God will rejoice over you.
6 Jerusalem,
I have appointed watchmen
on your walls;

they will never be silent,
day or night.
You, who remind the LORD,
no rest for you!
7 Do not give Him rest
until He establishes
and makes her Jerusalem
the praise of the earth.

8 The LORD has sworn
with His right hand
and His strong arm:
I will no longer give your grain
to your enemies for food,
and foreigners will not drink
your new wine
you have labored for.
9 For those who gather grain
will eat it
and praise the LORD,
and those who harvest the grapes
will drink ⌊the wine⌋
in My holy courts.

10 Go out, go out
through the gates;
prepare a way for the people!
Build it up, build up the highway;
clear away the stones!
Raise a banner for the peoples.

"Your Salvation Is Coming"

11 Look, the LORD has proclaimed
to the end of the earth,
"Say to Daughter Zion:
Look, your salvation is coming,
His reward is with Him,
and His recompense is
before Him."
12 And they will be called[d]
the Holy People,
the LORD's Redeemed;
and you will be called Cared For,
A City Not Deserted.

---

a**62:4** Hb *Hephzibah*   b**62:4** Hb *Beulah*   c**62:5** Lit *and the rejoicing of the bridegroom*   d**62:12** Lit *will call them*

LORD's Day of Vengeance

63 Who is this coming from Edom
in crimson-stained garments
from Bozrah—
this One who is splendid
in His apparel,
rising up proudly[a]
in His great might?

It is I, proclaiming vindication,[b]
powerful to save.

2 Why is Your clothing red,
and Your garments like one
who treads a winepress?

3 I trampled the winepress alone,
and no one from the nations was
with Me.
I trampled them in My anger
and ground them underfoot
in My fury;
their blood spattered
My garments,
and all My clothes were stained.

4 For I planned the day
of vengeance,[c]
and the year
of My redemption[d] came.

5 I looked, but there was no one
to help,
and I was amazed
that no one assisted;
so My arm accomplished victory
for Me,
and My wrath assisted Me.

6 I crushed nations in My anger;
I made them drunk with My wrath
and poured out their blood
on the ground.

Remembrance of Grace

7 I will make known
the LORD's faithful love
⌊and⌋ the LORD's praiseworthy acts,
because of all the LORD has done
for us—
even the many good things
⌊He has done⌋ for the house
of Israel
and has done for them based on
His compassions
and the abundance of
His faithful love.

8 He said, "They are indeed
My people,
children who will not be disloyal,"
and He became their Savior.

9 In all their suffering, He suffered,[e]
and the Angel of His Presence
saved them.
He redeemed them
because of His love
and compassion;
He lifted them up and carried them
all the days of the past.

10 But they rebelled,
and grieved His Holy Spirit.
So He became their enemy
⌊and⌋ fought against them.

11 Then He[f] remembered the days
of the past,
⌊the days⌋ of Moses ⌊and⌋ his people.
Where is He who brought them up
out of the sea
with the shepherds[g] of His flock?
Where is He who put
His Holy Spirit among the flock?

12 He sent His glorious arm
at Moses' right hand,
divided the waters before them
to obtain eternal fame for Himself,

13 and led them through the depths
like a horse in the wilderness,
so that they did not stumble.

14 Like cattle that go down
into the valley,

---

a**63:1** Syr, Vg read *apparel, striding forward*   b**63:1** Or *righteousness*   c**63:4** Lit *For day of vengeance in My heart*
d**63:4** Or *blood revenge*   e**63:9** Alt Hb tradition reads *did not suffer*   f**63:11** Or *he*, or *they*   g**63:11** LXX, Tg, Syr read
shepherd

the Spirit of the LORD
   gave them[a] rest.
You led Your people this way
to make a glorious name
   for Yourself.

Israel's Prayer

15 Look down from heaven and see
from Your lofty home—
   holy and beautiful.
Where is Your zeal
   and Your might?
Your yearning[b]
   and Your compassion
are withheld from me.
16 Yet You are our Father,
even though Abraham does not
   know us
and Israel doesn't recognize us.
You, LORD, are our Father;
from ancient times,
Your name is our Redeemer.
17 Why, LORD, do You make us stray
   from Your ways?
You harden our hearts so we do not
  •fear[c] You.
Return, because of Your servants,
the tribes of Your heritage.
18 Your holy people had a possession[d]
for a little while,
⌊but⌋ our enemies
   have trampled down
Your sanctuary.
19 We have become like those
   You never ruled over,
like those not called by Your name.

64 [e] If only You would tear
   the heavens open
⌊and⌋ come down,
so that mountains would quake
   at Your presence—
2[f] as fire kindles the brushwood,
and fire causes water to boil—

to make Your name known
   to Your enemies,
so that nations will tremble
   at Your presence!
3 When You did awesome deeds
that we did not expect,
You came down,
and the mountains quaked
   at Your presence.
4 From ancient times no one
   has heard,
no one has listened,
no eye has seen any God
   except You,
who acts on behalf of the one
   who waits for Him.
5 You welcome the one who joyfully
   does what is right;
they remember You in Your ways.
But we have sinned, and You
   were angry;
we will remain in Your ways[g]
   and be saved.
6 All of us have become
   like something unclean,
and all our righteous acts are
   like a polluted[h] garment;
all of us wither like a leaf,
and our iniquities carry us away
   like the wind.
7 No one calls on Your name,
striving to take hold of You.
For You have hidden Your face
   from us
and made us melt
   because of[i] [j] our iniquity.

Work of Your Hands

8 Yet LORD, You are our Father;
we are the clay, and You are
   our potter;
we all are the work of Your hands.
9 LORD, do not be terribly angry

---

[a]63:14 Lit him [b]63:15 Lit The agitation of Your inward parts [c]63:17 Lit our heart from fearing [d]63:18 Or Your people possessed Your holy place [e]64:1 Is 63:19b in Hb [f]64:2 Is 64:1 in Hb [g]64:5 Lit in them [h]64:6 Lit menstrual [i]64:7 LXX, Syr, Vg, Tg read and delivered us into the hand of [j]64:7 Lit melt by the hand

or remember ⌊our⌋ iniquity forever.
Please look—all of us are
  Your people!
10 Your holy cities have become
  a wilderness;
Zion has become a wilderness,
Jerusalem a desolation.
11 Our holy and beautiful[a] temple,
where our fathers praised You,
  has been burned with fire,
and all that was dear to us lies
  in ruins.
12 LORD, after all this, will You
  restrain Yourself?
Will You keep silent
and afflict severely?

LORD's Response

65 "I was sought by those
      who did not ask;[b]
I was found by those
  who did not seek Me.
I said: Here I am, here I am,
to a nation that was not called
  by[c] My name.
2 I spread out My hands all day long
to a rebellious people
who walk in the wrong path,
following their own thoughts.
3 These people
  continually provoke Me
to My face,
sacrificing in gardens,
burning incense on bricks,
4 sitting among the graves,
spending nights in secret places,
eating swine's flesh,
and putting polluted broth
  in their bowls.[d]
5 They say: Keep to yourself,
don't come near me,
  for I am too holy for you!

These practices are smoke
  in My nostrils,
a fire that burns all day long.
6 It is written before Me:
I will not keep silent,
  but I will repay;
I will repay them fully[e]
7 ⌊for⌋ your iniquities
  and the iniquities
of your[f] fathers together,"
says the LORD.
"Because they burned incense
  on the mountains
and reproached Me on the hills,
I will reward them fully[g]
for their former deeds."

God Saves Remnant

8 The LORD says this:

As the new wine is found
  in a bunch of grapes,
and one says: Don't destroy it,
for there's some good[h] in it,
so I will act because of
  My servants
and not destroy them all.
9 I will produce descendants
  from Jacob,
and heirs to My mountains
  from Judah;
My chosen ones will possess it,
and My servants will dwell there.
10 Sharon will be a pasture for flocks,
and the Valley of Achor a place
  for cattle to lie down,
for My people
  who have sought Me.
11 But you who abandon the LORD,
who forget My holy mountain,
who prepare a table for Fortune[i]
and fill bowls of mixed wine
  for Destiny,

a64:11 Or glorious; Is 60:7   b65:1 LXX, Syr, DSS, Tg read ask for Me   c65:1 LXX, Syr, DSS, Tg, Vg read that did not
call on   d65:3-4 These vv. catalog pagan worship.   e65:6 Lit repay into their lap   f65:7 LXX, Syr read [for] their
iniquities and the iniquities of their   g65:7 Lit reward into their lap   h65:8 Or there's a blessing   i65:11 A pagan god

12 I will destine you for the sword,
and all of you will kneel down
   to be slaughtered,
because I called
   and you did not answer,
I spoke and you did not hear;
you did what was evil in My sight
and chose what I did not delight in.

13 Therefore, this is what the Lord GOD
says:

My servants will eat,
but you will be hungry;
My servants will drink,
but you will be thirsty;
My servants will rejoice,
but you will be put to shame.
14 My servants will shout for joy
   from a glad heart,
but you will cry out
   from an anguished heart,
and you will lament out of
   a broken spirit.
15 You will leave your name behind
as a curse for My chosen ones,
and the Lord GOD will kill you;
but He will give His servants
   another name.
16 Whoever is blessed in the land
will be blessed by the God of truth,
and whoever swears in the land
will swear by the God of truth.
For the former troubles
   will be forgotten
and hidden from My sight.

A New Creation

17 "For I will create a new heaven
   and a new earth;
the past events will not
   be remembered or come to mind.
18 Then be glad and rejoice forever
in what I am creating;

for I will create Jerusalem to be
   a joy,
and its people to be a delight.
19 I will rejoice in Jerusalem
and be glad in My people.
The sound of weeping and crying
will no longer be heard in her.
20 In her, a nursing infant
   will no longer live
only a few days,a
or an old man not live out his days.
Indeed, the youth will die
   at a hundred years,
and the one who misses
   a hundred years will be cursed.
21 People will build houses and live
   ⌊in them⌋;
they will plant vineyards and eat
   their fruit.
22 They will not build and others live
   ⌊in them⌋;
they will not plant and others eat.
For My people's lives will be
like the lifetime of a tree.
My chosen ones will fully enjoy
the work of their hands.
23 They will not labor without success
or bear children ⌊destined⌋
   for disaster,
for they will be a people blessed
   by the LORD
along with their descendants.
24 Even before they call, I will answer;
while they are still speaking,
   I will hear.
25 The wolf and the lamb
   will feed together,b
and the lion will eat straw like the ox,
but the serpent's food will be dust!
They will not do what is evil
   or destroy
on My entire holy mountain,"
says the LORD.

a65:20 Lit her, no longer infant of days   b65:25 Lit as one

Final Judgment and Joyous Restoration

66 This is what the LORD says:
Heaven is My throne,
and earth is My footstool.
What house could you
 possibly build for Me?
And what place could be My home?
² My hand made all these things,
and so they all came into being.
  ⌊This is⌋ the LORD's declaration.

Test for God's Favor

I will look favorably on this kind
 of person:
one who is humble,
 submissive[a] in spirit,
and who trembles at My word.
³ One slaughters an ox, one kills
 a man;
one sacrifices a lamb, one breaks
 a dog's neck;
one offers a •grain offering,
 one offers swine's blood;
one offers incense, one praises
 an idol—
all these have chosen their ways
and delight in their abominations.
⁴ So I will choose their punishment,
and I will bring on them
 what they dread,
because I called
 and no one answered;
I spoke and they didn't hear;
they did what was evil in My sight
and chose what I didn't delight in.

⁵ You who tremble at His word,
hear the word of the LORD:
"Your brothers who hate
 and exclude you
because of Me have said:
Let the LORD be glorified,
so that we can see your joy!

But they will be put to shame."

⁶ A sound of uproar from the city!
A voice from the temple—
the voice of the LORD,
paying back His enemies
 what they deserve!

⁷ Before Zion was in labor,
 she gave birth;
before she was in pain,
 she delivered a boy.
⁸ Who has heard of
 such a thing?
Who has seen such things?
Can a land be born in one day,
or a nation be delivered
 in an instant?
Yet as soon as Zion was
 in labor,
she gave birth to her sons.
⁹ "Will I bring a baby to the point
 of birth
and not deliver ⌊it⌋?"
says the LORD;
"or will I who deliver,
 close ⌊the womb⌋?"
says your God.
¹⁰ Be glad for Jerusalem and rejoice
 over her,
all who love her.
Rejoice greatly with her,
all who mourn over her—
¹¹ so that you may nurse
 and be satisfied
from her comforting breast
and drink deeply
 and delight yourselves
from her glorious breasts.

Peace like a River

¹² For this is what the LORD says:

I will make peace flow to her
 like a river,

ᵃ**66:2** Lit *broken*

and the wealth^a of nations
  like a flood;
you will nurse and be carried
  on ⌊her⌋ hip,
and bounced on ⌊her⌋ lap.

"As a Mother Comforts Her Son…"

13 As a mother comforts her son,
  so I will comfort you,
and you will be comforted
  in Jerusalem.

14 You will see, you will rejoice,
  and you^b will flourish like grass;
then the LORD's power
  will be revealed to His servants,
but He will show His wrath
  against His enemies.

"Lord will come with fire…"

15 Look, the LORD will come
  with fire—
His chariots are
  like the whirlwind—
to execute His anger with fury,
  and His rebuke with flames of fire.
16 For the LORD
  will execute judgment
on all flesh with His fiery sword,
  and many will be slain by the LORD.

17 "Those who dedicate and purify
themselves to ⌊enter⌋ the groves following their leader,^c eating meat from pigs,
vermin, and rats, will perish together."
    ⌊This is⌋ the LORD's declaration.
18 "Knowing^d their works and their
thoughts, I have come to gather all nations and languages; they will come and
see My glory. 19 I will establish a sign
among them, and I will send survivors
from them to the nations—to Tarshish,
Put,^e Lud (who are archers), Tubal, Javan, and the islands far away—who
have not heard of My fame or seen My
glory. And they will proclaim My glory
among the nations. 20 They will bring all
your brothers from all the nations as a
gift to the LORD on horses and chariots,
in litters, and on mules and camels, to
My holy mountain Jerusalem, says the
LORD, just as the Israelites bring an offering in a clean vessel to the house of
the LORD. 21 I will also take some of
them as priests and Levites," says the
LORD.

22 "For just as the new heavens
    and the new earth,
  which I will make,
  will endure before Me"—
        the LORD's declaration—
"so will your offspring
  and your name endure.

"All Mankind Will … Worship Me"

23 All mankind will come
  to worship Me,
  from one New Moon to another,
  and from one Sabbath to another,"
says the LORD.

24 "As they leave, they will see the
dead bodies of the men who have rebelled against Me; for their maggots will
never die, their fire will never go out,
and they will be a horror to all mankind."

---

^a66:12 Or *glory*   ^b66:14 Lit *your bones*   ^c66:17 Hb obscure   ^d66:18 LXX, Syr; MT omits *Knowing*   ^e66:19 LXX; MT
reads *Pul*; Jr 46:9

JEREMIAH

1

¹ The words of Jeremiah, the son of Hilkiah, one of the priests living in Anathoth in the territory of Benjamin. ² The word of the LORD came to him in the thirteenth year of the reign of Josiah son of Amon, king of Judah. ³ It also came throughout the days of Jehoiakim son of Josiah, king of Judah, until the fifth month of the eleventh year of Zedekiah son of Josiah, king of Judah, when the people of Jerusalem went into exile.

God Calls Jeremiah

⁴ The word of the LORD came to me:

⁵ I chose you before I formed you
　　in the womb;
I set you apart
　　before you were born.
I appointed you a prophet
　　to the nations.

⁶ But I protested, "Oh no, Lord GOD! Look, I don't know how to speak since I am ⌊only⌋ a youth."

⁷ Then the LORD said to me:

Do not say: I am ⌊only⌋ a youth,
for you will go to everyone
　　I send you to
and speak whatever I tell you.
⁸ Do not be afraid of anyone,
for I will be with you
　　to deliver you.

⌊This is⌋ the LORD's declaration.

⁹ Then the LORD reached out His hand, touched my mouth, and told me:

Look, I have filled your mouth
　　with My words.
¹⁰ See, today I have set you
　　over nations and kingdoms
to uproot and tear down,

to destroy and demolish,
to build and plant.

Two Visions

¹¹ Then the word of the LORD came to me, asking, "What do you see, Jeremiah?"

I replied, "I see a branch of an almond tree."

¹² The LORD said to me, "You have seen correctly, for I watch over My word to accomplish it." ¹³ Again the word of the LORD came to me inquiring, "What do you see?"

And I replied, "I see a boiling pot, its mouth tilted from the north ⌊to the south⌋."

¹⁴ Then the LORD said to me, "Disaster will be poured out[a] from the north on all who live in the land. ¹⁵ Indeed, I am about to summon all the clans and kingdoms of the north."

⌊This is⌋ the LORD's declaration.

They will come, and each ⌊king⌋
　　will set up his throne
at the entrance to Jerusalem's gates.
They will attack
　　all her surrounding walls
and all the other cities of Judah.

¹⁶ "I will pronounce My judgments against them for all the evil they did when they abandoned Me to burn incense to other gods and to worship the works of their own hands. ¹⁷ "Now, get ready. Stand up and tell them everything that I command you. Do not be intimidated by them or I will cause you to cower before them. ¹⁸ Today, I am the One who has made you a fortified city, an iron pillar, and

ᵃ1:14 LXX reads *will boil*

bronze walls against the whole land—
against the kings of Judah, its officials, its
priests, and the population. ¹⁹ They will
fight against you but never prevail over
you, since I am with you to rescue you."
⌐This is⌐ the LORD's declaration.

God, through Jeremiah, Accuses Israel of Apostasy

2 The word of the LORD came to me:
² "Go and announce directly to Jerusalem that this is what the LORD says:

I remember the loyalty
    of your youth,
your love as a bride—
how you followed Me
    in the wilderness,
in a land not sown.
³ Israel was holy to the LORD,
    the •firstfruits of His harvest.
All who ate of it found
    themselves guilty;
disaster came on them."
        ⌐This is⌐ the LORD's declaration.

⁴ Hear the word of the LORD,
    house of Jacob
and all families of the house
    of Israel.
⁵ Here is what the LORD says:

What fault did your fathers find
    in Me
that they went so far from Me,
followed worthless idols,
and became worthless themselves?
⁶ They stopped asking: Where is
    the LORD
who brought us from the land
    of Egypt,
who led us through the wilderness,
through a land of deserts
    and ravines,
through a land of drought
    and darkness,ᵃ

a land no one traveled through
and where no one lived?
⁷ I brought you to a fertile land
to eat its fruit and bounty,
but after you entered, you defiled
    My land;
you made My inheritance detestable.

Israel Turns to Idols

⁸ The priests quit asking: Where is
    the LORD?
The experts in the law no longer
    knew Me,
and the rulers rebelled against Me.
The prophets prophesied by •Baal
and followed useless idols.

⁹ Therefore, I will bring a case
    against you again.
        ⌐This is⌐ the LORD's declaration.
I will bring a case
    against your children's children.
¹⁰ Cross over to Cyprusᵇ and take
    a look.
Send ⌐someone⌐ to Kedar
    and consider carefully;
see if there has ever been
    anything like this:
¹¹ Has a nation ⌐ever⌐ exchanged
    its gods?
(but they were not gods!)
Yet My people have exchanged
    theirᶜ Glory
for useless idols.
¹² Be horrified at this, heavens;
be shocked and utterly appalled.
        ⌐This is⌐ the LORD's declaration.

¹³ For My people have committed
    a double evil:
They have abandoned Me,
the fountain of living water,
and dug cisterns for themselves,
cracked cisterns that cannot
    hold water.

ᵃ**2:6** Or *shadow of death*   ᵇ**2:10** Lit *to the islands of Kittim*   ᶜ**2:11** Alt Hb tradition reads *My.*

Consequences of Apostasy

14 Is Israel a slave?
Was he born into slavery?[a]
Why else has he become a prey?
15 The young lions have roared
    at him;
they have roared loudly.
They have laid waste his land.
His cities are in ruins,
    without inhabitants.
16 The men of Memphis
    and Tahpanhes
have also broken your skull.
17 Have you not brought this
    on yourself
by abandoning the LORD your God
while He was leading you
    along the way?
18 Now what will you gain
by traveling along the way to Egypt
to drink the waters of the Nile?[b]
What will you gain
by traveling along the way
    to Assyria
to drink the waters
    of the Euphrates?
19 Your own evil will discipline you;
your own apostasies
    will reprimand you.
Think it over and see how evil
    and bitter it is
for you to abandon the LORD
    your God
and to have no •fear of Me.
                ⌊This is⌋ the declaration
                of the Lord GOD of •Hosts.

Lord Accuses Israel

20 For long ago I[c] broke your yoke;
I[c] tore off your fetters.
You insisted: I will not serve!
On every high hill
and under every leafy tree
you lie down ⌊like⌋ a prostitute.

21 I planted you, a choice vine
from the very best seed.
How then could you turn into
a degenerate, foreign vine?
22 Even if you wash with lye
and use a great amount of soap,
the stain of your guilt is still
    in front of Me.
                ⌊This is⌋ the
                Lord GOD's declaration.
23 How can you protest:
    I am not defiled;
I have not followed the Baals?
Look at your behavior in the valley;
acknowledge what you have done.
⌊You are⌋ a swift young camel
twisting and turning on her way,
24 a wild donkey at home[d]
    in the wilderness.
She sniffs the wind in the heat
    of her desire.
Who can control her passion?
All who look for her will not
    become tired;
they will find her
    in her mating season.[e]
25 Keep your feet from going bare
and your throat from thirst.
But you say: It's hopeless;
I love strangers,
and I will continue to follow them.

26 Like the shame of a thief
    when he is caught,
so the house of Israel has been
    put to shame.
They, their kings, their officials,
    their priests, and their prophets
27 say to a tree: You are my father,
and to a stone: You gave birth
    to me.
For they have turned their back
    to Me
and not their face,

---

[a]2:14 Lit born of a house   [b]2:18 Lit of Shichor   [c]2:20 LXX reads you   [d]2:24 Lit donkey taught   [e]2:24 Lit her month

but in their time of disaster
  they beg:
Rise up and save us!
28 But where are your gods you made
    for yourself?
Let them rise up and save you
in your time of disaster if they can,
for your gods are as numerous
    as your cities, Judah.

God's Judgment Deserved

29 Why do you bring a case
     against Me?
All of you have rebelled against Me.
       ⌊This is⌋ the LORD's declaration.
30 I have struck down your children
     in vain;
they would not accept discipline.
Your own sword has devoured
     your prophets
like a ravaging lion.
31 ⌊Evil⌋ generation,
    pay attention to the word
    of the LORD!
Have I been a wilderness to Israel
or a land of dense darkness?
Why do My people claim:
We will go where we want;ᵃ
we will no longer come to You?
32 Can a young woman forget
     her jewelry
or a bride her wedding sash?
Yet My people have forgotten Me
for countless days.
33 How skillfully you pursue love;
    you also teach evil women
    your ways.
34 Moreover, your skirts are stained
    with the blood
    of the innocent poor.
You did not catch them breaking
    and entering.
But in spite of all these things
35 you claim: I am innocent.

His anger is sure to turn away
    from me.
But I will certainly judge you
because you have said: I have
    not sinned.
36 How unstable you are,
    constantly changing your way!
You will be put to shame by Egypt
just as you were put to shame
    by Assyria.
37 Moreover, you will be led out
    from here
with your hands on your head
since the LORD has rejected
    those you trust;
you will not succeed even with
    their help.ᵇ

Israel a Prostitute

3 Ifᶜ a man divorces his wife
and she leaves him
    to marry another,
can he ever return to her?
Wouldn't such a landᵈ become
    totally defiled?
But you!
You have played the prostitute
    with many partners—
can you return to Me?
       ⌊This is⌋ the LORD's declaration.
2 Look to the barren heights and see.
Where have you not been immoral?
You sat waiting for them
    beside the highways
like a nomad in the desert.
You have defiled the land
with your prostitution
    and wickedness.
3 This is why the showers
    haven't come—
why there has been no spring rain.
You have the brazen look
    of a prostituteᵉ
and refuse to be ashamed.

ᵃ2:31 Or We have taken control, or We can roam   ᵇ2:37 Lit with them   ᶜ3:1 One Hb ms, LXX, Syr; other Hb mss read
Saying: If   ᵈ3:1 LXX reads woman   ᵉ3:3 Lit have a prostitute's forehead

⁴ Have you not lately called Me:
  My Father,
  my youthful companion?
⁵ Will He bear a grudge forever?
  Will He be endlessly infuriated?
  This is what you have spoken
    and done,
  the evil you are capable of.

Unfaithful Israel, Treacherous Judah

⁶ In the days of King Josiah the LORD asked me, "Have you seen what unfaithful Israel has done? She has ascended every high hill and gone under every green tree to prostitute herself there. ⁷ I thought: After she has done all these things, she will return to Me. But she didn't return, and her treacherous sister Judah saw it. ⁸ I[a] observed that it was because unfaithful Israel had committed adultery that I had sent her away and had given her a certificate of divorce. Nevertheless, her treacherous sister Judah was not afraid but also went and prostituted herself. ⁹ Indifferent to[b] her prostitution, she defiled the land and committed adultery with stone and tree. ¹⁰ Yet in spite of all this, her treacherous sister Judah didn't return to Me with all her heart—only in pretense."

⌊This is⌋ the LORD's declaration.

"Return, Unfaithful Israel"

¹¹ The LORD announced to me, "Unfaithful Israel has shown herself more righteous than treacherous Judah. ¹² Go, proclaim these words to the north, and say:

Return, unfaithful Israel.
⌊This is⌋ the LORD's declaration.

God Offers Forgiveness

I will not look on you with anger,[c]
for I am unfailing in My love.
⌊This is⌋ the LORD's declaration.
I will not be angry forever.
¹³ Only acknowledge your guilt—
you have rebelled against the LORD
  your God.
You have scattered your favors
  to strangers
under every green tree
and have not obeyed My voice.
⌊This is⌋ the LORD's declaration.

¹⁴ "Return, you faithless children"—⌊this is⌋ the LORD's declaration—"for I am your master, and I will take you, one from a city and two from a family, and I will bring you to Zion. ¹⁵ I will give you shepherds who are loyal to Me,[d] and they will shepherd you with knowledge and skill. ¹⁶ When you multiply and increase in the land, in those days"—the LORD's declaration—"no one will say any longer: The ark of the LORD's covenant. It will never come to mind, and no one will remember or miss it. It will never again be made. ¹⁷ At that time Jerusalem will be called, The LORD's Throne, and all the nations will be gathered to it, to the name of the LORD in Jerusalem. They will cease to follow the stubbornness of their evil hearts. ¹⁸ In those days the house of Judah will join with the house of Israel, and they will come together from the land of the north to the land I have given your ancestors to inherit."

True Repentance

¹⁹ I thought: How I long to make you
  ⌊My⌋ sons
and give you a desirable land,
  the most beautiful inheritance of all
    the nations.
I thought: You will call Me,
  my Father,

ᵃ3:8 One Hb ms, Syr read *She*   ᵇ3:9 Lit *From the lightness of*   ᶜ3:12 Lit *not cause My face to fall on you*   ᵈ3:15 Lit *shepherds according to My heart*

and never turn away from Me.

20 However, as a woman may betray
     her lover,[a]
so you have betrayed Me,
     house of Israel.
     ⌊This is⌋ the LORD's declaration.

21 A sound is heard
     on the barren heights,
the children of Israel weeping
     and begging for mercy,
for they have perverted their way;
they have forgotten the LORD
     their God.

22 Return, you faithless children.
I will heal your unfaithfulness.

A Model Confession

"Here we are, coming to You,
     for You are the LORD our God.

23 Surely, falsehood comes
     from the hills,
commotion from the mountains,
but the salvation of Israel
is only in the LORD our God.

24 From the time of our youth
the shameful one[b] has consumed
what our fathers have worked for—
     their flocks and their herds,
     their sons and their daughters.

25 Let us lie down in our shame;
let our disgrace cover us.
We have sinned against the LORD
     our God,
both we and our fathers,
from the time of our youth
     even to this day.
We have not obeyed the voice
of the LORD our God."

Blessing from Repentance

4 If you return,[c] Israel—
     ⌊this is⌋ the LORD's declaration—
⌊if⌋ you return to Me,
if you remove your detestable idols

from My presence
and do not waver,

2 if you swear, As the LORD lives,
     in truth, in justice,
     and in righteousness,
then the nations will be blessed[d]
     by Him
and will pride themselves in Him.

3 For this is what the LORD says to the
men of Judah and Jerusalem:

Break up the unplowed ground;
do not sow among the thorns.

4 Circumcise yourselves to the LORD;
remove the foreskin of your hearts,
men of Judah and residents
     of Jerusalem.
Otherwise, My wrath
     will break out like fire
and burn with no one
     to extinguish ⌊it⌋
because of your evil deeds.

Judgment from the North

5 Declare in Judah, proclaim in Jerusalem, and say:

Blow the ram's horn
     throughout the land.
Cry out loudly and say:
Assemble yourselves,
and let's flee to the fortified cities.

6 Lift up a signal flag toward Zion.
Run for cover! Don't stand still!
For I am bringing disaster
     from the north—
a great destruction.

7 A lion has gone up from his thicket;
a destroyer of nations has set out.
He has left his lair
to make your land a waste.
Your cities will be reduced
     to uninhabited ruins.

8 Because of this, put on •sackcloth;
mourn and wail,

---

a3:20 Lit friend   b3:24 = a euphemism for Baal   c4:1 Or Repent   d4:2 Or will bless themselves

for the LORD's burning anger
has not turned away from us.

Fear and Trembling on "That Day"

⁹ "On that day"—⌐this is⌐ the LORD's
declaration—"the king and the officials
will lose their courage. The priests will
tremble in fear, and the prophets will be
scared speechless."

¹⁰ I said, "Oh no, Lord GOD, You have
certainly deceived this people and Jerusalem, by announcing, 'You will have
peace,' while a sword is atᵃ our throats."

¹¹ At that time it will be said to this
people and to Jerusalem, "A searing
wind ⌐blows⌐ from the barren heights in
the wilderness on the way to My dearᵇ
people. ⌐It comes⌐ not to winnow or to
sift; ¹² a wind too strong for this comes at
My call.ᶜ Now I will also pronounce judgments against them."

13   Look, he advances like clouds;
     his chariots are like a storm.
     His horses are swifter than eagles.
     Woe to us, for we are ruined!
14   Wash the evil
       from your heart, Jerusalem,
     so that you will be delivered.
     How long will you harbor
     malicious thoughts within you?
15   For a voice announces from Dan,
     proclaiming malice
       from Mount Ephraim.
16   Warn the nations: Look!
     Proclaim to Jerusalem:
     Those who besiege are coming
     from a distant land;
     they raise their voices
     against the cities of Judah.
17   They have her surrounded
     like those who guard a field,
     because she has rebelled
       against Me.

⌐This is⌐ the LORD's declaration.
18   Your way of life and your actions
     have brought this on you.
     This is your punishment. It is
     very bitter,
     because it has reached your heart!

Jeremiah's Lament
for His People

19   My anguish, my anguish!ᵈ I writhe
       in agony!
     Oh, the pain inᵉ my heart!
     My heart pounds;
     I cannot be silent.
     For you, my soul,
     have heard the sound
       of the ram's horn—
     the shout of battle.
20   Disaster after disaster is reported,
     for the whole land is destroyed.
     Suddenly my tents are destroyed,
     my tent curtains, in a moment.
21   How long must I see the signal flag
     and hear the sound
       of the ram's horn?

A People Skilled in Evil

22   For My people are fools;
     they do not know Me.
     They are foolish children,
     without understanding.
     They are skilled in doing what is evil,
     but they do not know how to do
       what is good.

A Devastated Earth

23   I looked at the earth,
     and it was formless and empty.
     ⌐I looked⌐ to the heavens,
     and their light was gone.
24   I looked at the mountains,
     and they were quaking;
     all the hills shook.

ᵃ4:10 Lit sword touches   ᵇ4:11 Lit to the daughter of My   ᶜ4:12 Lit comes for Me   ᵈ4:19 Lit My inner parts, my inner
parts   ᵉ4:19 Lit the walls of

25 I looked, and no man was left;
   all the birds of the sky had fled.
26 I looked, and the fertile field was
      a wilderness.
   All its cities were torn down
   because of the LORD
   and His burning anger.

27 For this is what the LORD says:

   The whole land will be a desolation,
   but I will not finish it off.
28 Because of this, the earth will mourn;
   the skies above will grow dark.
   I have spoken; I have planned,
   and I will not relent or turn back
      from it.

29 Every city flees
   at the sound of the horseman
      and the archer.
   They enter the thickets
   and climb among the rocks.
   Every city is abandoned;
   no inhabitant is left.
30 And you devastated one, what are
      you doing
   that you dress yourself in scarlet,
   that you adorn yourself
      with gold jewelry,
   that you enlarge your eyes
      with paint?
   You beautify yourself for nothing.
   Your lovers reject you;
   they want to take your life.
31 I hear a cry like a woman in labor,
   ₍a cry of₎ anguish like one bearing
      her first child.
   The cry of Daughter Zion
      gasping for breath,
   stretching out her hands:
   Woe is me, for my life is weary
   because of the murderers!

Depravity of Jerusalem

5 Roam through the streets
   of Jerusalem.

   Look and take note;
   search in her squares.
   If you find a single person,
   anyone who acts justly,
   who seeks to be faithful,
   then I will forgive her.
2 When they say,
   "As the LORD lives,"
   they are swearing falsely.
3 LORD, don't Your eyes
   ₍look for₎ faithfulness?
   You have struck them, but they felt
      no pain.
   You finished them off,
   but they refused
      to accept discipline.
   They made their faces harder
      than rock,
   and they refused to return.

When Powerful People Sin

4 Then I thought:

   They are just the poor;
   they have played the fool.
   For they don't understand the way
      of the LORD,
   the justice of their God.
5 I will go to the powerful
   and speak to them.
   Surely they know the way
      of the LORD,
   the justice of their God.
   However, these also had broken
      the yoke
   and torn off the fetters.

Results of Disobedience

6 Therefore, a lion from the forest
      will strike them down.
   A wolf from an arid plain
      will ravage them.
   A leopard keeps watch over
      their cities.
   Anyone who leaves them
      will be torn to pieces

because their rebellious acts
are many,
their unfaithful deeds numerous.

7 Why should I forgive you?
Your children have abandoned Me
and sworn by those who are
not gods.
I satisfied their needs, yet they
committed adultery;
they gashed themselves
at the prostitute's house.
8 They are well-fed,[a] eager[b] stallions,
each neighing after
someone else's wife.
9 Should I not punish them
for these things?
⌊This is⌋ the LORD's declaration.
Should I not avenge Myself
on such a nation as this?

10 Go up among her vineyard terraces
and destroy them,
but do not finish them off.
Prune away her shoots,
for they do not belong to the LORD.
11 They, the house of Israel
and the house of Judah,
have dealt very treacherously
with Me.
⌊This is⌋ the LORD's declaration.
12 They have contradicted the LORD
and insisted, "It won't happen.[c]
Harm won't come to us;
we won't see sword or famine."
13 The prophets become ⌊only⌋ wind,
for the ⌊LORD's⌋ word is not in them.
This will in fact happen to them.

Coming Judgment

14 Therefore, this is what the Lord GOD
of •Hosts says:

Because you have spoken
this word,
I am going to make My words

become fire in your mouth.
These people are the wood,
and the fire will consume them.

A Nation Far Away

15 I am about to bring a nation
from far away against you,
house of Israel.
⌊This is⌋ the LORD's declaration.
It is an established nation,
an ancient nation,
a nation whose language
you do not know
and whose speech
you do not understand.
16 Their quiver is like an open grave;
they are all mighty warriors.
17 They will consume your harvest
and your food.
They will consume your sons
and your daughters.
They will consume your flocks
and your herds.
They will consume your vines
and your fig trees.
They will destroy with the sword
your fortified cities in which
you trust.

18 "But even in those days"—⌊this is⌋
the LORD's declaration—"I will not finish
you off. 19 When people ask: For what offense has the LORD our God done all
these things to us? You will respond to
them: Just as you abandoned Me and
served foreign gods in your land, so will
you serve strangers in a land that is not
yours.

Warning to Judah

20 "Declare this in the house of Jacob;
proclaim it in Judah, saying:

21 Hear this,
you foolish and senseless[d] people.

---

a 5:8 Lit well-equipped; Hb obscure   b 5:8 Lit early-rising; Hb obscure   c 5:12 Lit He does not exist   d 5:21 Lit without heart

<u>They have eyes, but they don't see.</u>
<u>They have ears, but they don't hear.</u>
22 Do you not •fear Me?
⌊This is⌋ the LORD's declaration.
Do you not tremble before Me,
the One who set the sand
    as the boundary of the sea,
an enduring barrier that
    it cannot cross?
The waves surge, but they
    cannot prevail.
They roar but cannot pass over it.
23 But these people have stubborn
    and rebellious hearts.
They have turned aside
    and have gone away.
24 They have not said to themselves:
Let's fear the LORD our God,
who gives the rain, both early
    and late, in its season,
who guarantees to us
    the fixed weeks of the harvest.
25 Your guilty acts have diverted
    these things ⌊from you⌋.
Your sins have withheld
    ⌊My⌋ bounty from you,
26 for wicked men live
    among My people.
They watch like fowlers
    lying in wait.ᵃ
They set a trap;
    they catch men.
27 Like a cage full of birds,
so their houses are full of deceit.
Therefore they have
    grown powerful and rich.
28 They have become fat and sleek.
They have also excelled
    in evil matters.
They have not taken up cases,
such as the case of orphans,
    so they might prosper,
and they have not defended
    the rights of the needy.

29 Should I not punish them
    for these things?
        ⌊This is⌋ the LORD's declaration.
Should I not avenge Myself
on such a nation as this?
30 A horrible, terrible thing
has taken place in the land.
31 The prophets prophesy falsely,
and the priests rule
    by their own authority.
My people love it like this.
But what will you do at the end
    of it?

Threatened Siege of Jerusalem

6 Run for cover, Benjaminites,
out of Jerusalem!
Sound the ram's horn in Tekoa;
raise a smoke signal over Beth-
    haccherem,ᵇ
for disaster threatens
    from the north,
even great destruction.
2 ⌊Though she is⌋ beautiful
    and delicate,
I will destroyᶜ Daughter Zion.
3 Shepherds and their flocks
    will come against her;
they will pitch ⌊their⌋ tents
    all around her.
Each will pasture his own portion.
4 Set ⌊them⌋ apart for war against her;
rise up, let's attack at noon.
Woe to us, for the day is passing;
the evening shadows grow long.
5 Rise up, let's attack by night.
Let us destroy her fortresses."

6 For this is what the LORD of •Hosts
says:

Cut down the trees;
raise a siege ramp
    against Jerusalem.
This city must be punished.

ᵃ5:26 Hb obscure   ᵇ6:1 Or House of the Vineyard; Neh 3:14   ᶜ6:2 Or silence

There is nothing but oppression
  within her.
7 As a well gushes out its water,
  so she pours forth her evil.[a]
Violence and destruction resound
  in her.
Sickness and wounds keep coming
  to My attention.
8 Be warned, Jerusalem,
  or I will be torn away from you;
I will make you a desolation,
  a land devoid of inhabitant.

Wrath on Israel

9 This is what the LORD of Hosts says:

Glean as thoroughly as a vine
  the remnant of Israel.
Pass your hand once more
  like a grape gatherer
  over the branches.
10 Who can I speak to and give
  such a warning[b]
that they will listen?
Look, their ear is uncircumcised,[c]
  so they cannot pay attention.
See, the word of the LORD
  has become contemptible
  to them—
they find no pleasure in it.
11 But I am full of the LORD's wrath;
  I am tired of holding it back.
Pour ⌊it⌋ out on the children
  in the street,
on the gang of young men as well.
For both husband and wife
  will be captured,
the old with the very old.[d]
12 Their houses will be turned over
  to others,
⌊their⌋ fields and wives as well,
for I will stretch out My hand
  against the residents of the land.
  ⌊This is⌋ the LORD's declaration.

13 For from the least to the greatest
  of them,
everyone is gaining profit unjustly.
From prophet to priest,
  everyone deals falsely.
14 They have treated My people's
  brokenness superficially,
claiming: Peace, peace,
when there is no peace.
15 Were they ashamed
  when they acted so abhorrently?
They weren't at all ashamed.
They can no longer
  feel humiliation.
Therefore, they will fall
  among the fallen.
When I punish them,
  they will collapse,
says the LORD.

Disaster Because of Disobedience

16 This is what the LORD says:

Stand by the roadways and look.
Ask about the ancient paths:
Which is the way to what is good?
Then take it
and find rest for yourselves.
But they protested: We won't!
17 I appointed watchmen over you
⌊and said:⌋ Listen for the sound
  of the ram's horn.
But they protested:
  We won't listen!
18 Therefore listen, you nations
and you witnesses,
learn what ⌊the charge⌋ is
  against them.
19 Listen, earth!
I am about to bring disaster
  on these people,
the fruit of their own plotting,
for they have paid no attention
  to My word.

---

[a]**6:7** Or *well keeps its water fresh, so she keeps her evil fresh* [b]**6:10** Or *and bear witness* [c]**6:10** = unresponsive to God [d]**6:11** Lit *with fullness of days*

They have rejected My law.

20 What use to Me is frankincense
from Sheba
or sweet cane from a distant land?
Your •burnt offerings
are not acceptable;
your sacrifices do not please Me.

21 Therefore, this is what the LORD says:
I am going to place
stumbling blocks
before these people;
fathers and sons together
will stumble over them;
friends and neighbors
will ₍also₎ perish.

A Cruel Nation from the North

22 This is what the LORD says:

Look, an army is coming
from a northern land;
a great nation will be awakened
from the remote regions
of the earth.

23 They grasp bow and javelin.
They are cruel and show no mercy.
Their voice roars like the sea,
and they ride on horses,
lined up like men in battle formation
against you, Daughter Zion.

24 We have heard about it,
and we are discouraged.ᵃ
Distress has seized us—
pain like a woman in labor.

Terror on Every Side

25 Don't go out to the fields;
don't walk on the road.
For the enemy has a sword;
terror is on every side.

26 My dearᵇ people, dress yourselves
in •sackcloth
and roll in the dust.

Mourn ₍as you would for₎
an only son,
a bitter lament,
for suddenly the destroyer
will come on us.

God Appoints Jeremiah as Examiner

27 I have appointed you to be
an assayer among My people—
a refinerᶜ—
so you may know and assay
their way of life.

28 All are stubborn rebels
spreading slander.
₍They are₎ bronze and iron;
all of them are corrupt.

29 The bellows blow,
blasting the lead with fire.
The refining is completely in vain;
the evil ones are not separated out.

30 They are called rejected silver,
for the LORD has rejected them.

False Trust in the Temple

7 ₍This is₎ the word that came to Jeremiah from the LORD: ² "Stand in the gate of the house of the LORD and there call out this word: Hear the word of the LORD, all ₍you people₎ of Judah who enter through these gates to worship the LORD.

³ "This is what the LORD of •Hosts, the God of Israel, says: Correct your ways and your deeds, and I will allow you to live in this place. ⁴ Do not trust deceitful words, chanting: This is the temple of the LORD, the temple of the LORD, the temple of the LORD. ⁵ Instead, if you really change your ways and your actions, if you act justly toward one another,ᵈ ⁶ if you no longer oppress the alien, the fatherless, and the widow and no longer shed innocent blood in this

---

ᵃ6:24 Lit and our hands fail   ᵇ6:26 Lit Daughter of My   ᶜ6:27 Text emended; MT reads fortress   ᵈ7:5 Lit justly between a man and his neighbor

place or follow other gods, bringing harm on yourselves, ⁷ I will allow you to live in this place, the land I gave to your ancestors forever and ever. ⁸⌊But⌋ look, you keep trusting in deceitful words that cannot help.

⁹ "Do you steal, murder, commit adultery, swear falsely, burn incense to •Baal, and follow other gods that you have not known? ¹⁰ Then do you come and stand before Me in this house called by My name and insist: We are safe? As a result, you are free to continue doing all these detestable acts! ¹¹ Has this house, which is called by My name, become a den of robbers in your view? Yes, I too have seen ⌊it⌋."

⌊This is⌋ the LORD's declaration.

Shiloh as a Warning

¹² "But return to My place that was at Shiloh, where I made My name dwell at first. See what I did to it because of the evil of My people Israel. ¹³ Now, because you have done all these things"—⌊this is⌋ the LORD's declaration—"and because I have spoken to you time and time again[a] but you wouldn't listen, and I have called to you, but you wouldn't answer, ¹⁴ what I did to Shiloh I will do to the house that is called by My name—the house in which you trust—the place that I gave you and your ancestors. ¹⁵ I will drive you from My presence, just as I drove out all of your brothers, all the descendants of Ephraim.

Do Not Pray for Judah

¹⁶ "As for you, do not pray for these people. Do not offer a cry or a prayer on their behalf, and do not beg Me, for I will not listen to you. ¹⁷ Don't you see how they behave in the cities of Judah and in the streets of Jerusalem? ¹⁸ The sons gather wood, the fathers light the fire, and the women knead dough to make cakes for the queen of heaven,[b] and they pour out drink offerings to other gods so that they provoke Me to anger. ¹⁹ But are they really provoking Me?" ⌊This is⌋ the LORD's declaration. "Isn't it they themselves ⌊being provoked⌋ to disgrace?"

²⁰ Therefore, this is what the Lord GOD says: "Look, My anger—My burning wrath—is about to be poured out on this place, on man and beast, on the tree of the field, and on the fruit of the ground. My wrath will burn and not be quenched."

Obedience over Sacrifice

²¹ This is what the LORD of Hosts, the God of Israel, says: "Add your •burnt offerings to your other sacrifices, and eat the meat yourselves, ²² for when I brought your ancestors out of the land of Egypt, I did not speak with them or command them concerning burnt offering and sacrifice. ²³ However, I did give them this command: Obey Me, and then I will be your God, and you will be My people. You must walk in every way I command you so that it may go well with you." ²⁴ Yet they didn't listen or pay attention but walked according to their own advice and according to their own stubborn, evil heart. They went backward and not forward. ²⁵ Since the day your ancestors came out of the land of Egypt until this day, I have sent all My servants the prophets to you time and time again.[c] ²⁶ However, they wouldn't listen to Me or pay attention but became obstinate;[d] they did more evil than their ancestors.

Lament for Disobedient Judah

²⁷ "When you speak all these things to them, they will not listen to you. When

---

^a**7:13** Lit *you rising early and speaking*   ^b**7:18** = a pagan goddess   ^c**7:25** Lit *you, each day rising early and sending*   ^d**7:26** Lit *but stiffened their neck*

you call to them, they will not answer you. 28 You must therefore declare to them: This is the nation that would not listen to the voice of the LORD their God and would not accept discipline. Truth[a] has perished—it has disappeared from their mouths. 29 Cut off the hair of your sacred vow[b] and throw it away. Raise up a dirge on the barren heights, for the LORD has rejected and abandoned the generation under His wrath.

30 "For the Judeans have done what is evil in My sight." ⌊This is⌋ the LORD's declaration. "They have set up their detestable things in the house that is called by My name and defiled it. 31 They have built the •high places of Topheth[c] in the Valley of Hinnom[d] in order to burn their sons and daughters in the fire, a thing I did not command; I never entertained the thought.[e]

Valley of Slaughter

32 "Therefore, take note! Days are coming"—the LORD's declaration—"when ⌊this place⌋ will no longer be called Topheth and the Valley of Hinnom, but the Valley of Slaughter. Topheth will become a cemetery,[f] because there will be no other burial place. 33 The corpses of these people will become food for the birds of the sky and for the wild animals of the land, with no one to scare them off. 34 I will remove from the cities of Judah and the streets of Jerusalem the sound of joy and gladness and the voices of the bridegroom and the bride, for the land will become a desolate waste.

Bones of Judah's Leaders

8 "At that time"—⌊this is⌋ the LORD's declaration—"the bones of the kings of Judah, the bones of her officials, the bones of the priests, the bones of the prophets, and the bones of the residents of Jerusalem will be brought out of their graves. 2 They will be exposed to the sun, the moon, and the whole heavenly •host, which they have loved, served, followed, pursued, and worshiped. ⌊Their bones⌋ will not be collected and buried but will become like manure on the surface of the soil. 3 Death will be chosen over life by all the survivors of this evil family, those who remain wherever I have banished them." ⌊This is⌋ the declaration of the LORD of Hosts.

4 You are to say to them: This is what the LORD says:

Do ⌊people⌋ fall and not
   get up again?
If they turn away, do they
   not return?
5 Why have these people
   turned away?
Why is Jerusalem always
   turning away?
They take hold of deceit;
they refuse to return.
6 I have paid careful attention.
They do not speak what is right.
No one regrets his evil,
asking: What have I done?
Everyone has stayed his course
like a horse rushing into battle.
7 Even the stork in the sky
knows her seasons.
The turtledove, swallow, and crane[g]
are aware of their migration,
but My people do not know
the requirements of the LORD.

Punishment for Judah's Leaders

8 How can you claim: We are wise;
the law of the LORD is with us?
In fact, the lying pen of scribes

---

[a]7:28 Or *Faithfulness*   [b]7:29 Lit *off your consecration*   [c]7:31 Lit *of the fireplace*   [d]7:31 A valley south of Jerusalem   [e]7:31 Lit *command, and it did not arise on My heart*   [f]7:32 Lit *They will bury in Topheth*   [g]8:7 Hb obscure

has produced falsehood.
⁹ The wise will be put to shame;
they will be dismayed and snared.
They have rejected the word
of the LORD,
so what wisdom do they
really have?
¹⁰ Therefore, I will give their wives
to other men,
their fields to new occupants,
for from the least to the greatest,
everyone is gaining profit unjustly.
From prophet to priest,
everyone deals falsely.
¹¹ They have treated superficially
the brokenness
of My dearᵃ people,
claiming: Peace, peace,
when there is no peace.

No Shame

¹² Were they ashamed
when they acted so abhorrently?
They weren't at all ashamed.
They can no longer
feel humiliation.
Therefore, they will fall
among the fallen.
When I punish them,
they will collapse,
says the LORD.

¹³ I will gather them and bring them
to an end.ᵇ
ₗThis isₗ the LORD's declaration.
There will be no grapes
on the vine,
no figs on the fig tree,
and even the leaf will wither.
Whatever I have given them
will be lost to them.

God's People Unrepentant

¹⁴ Why are we just sitting here?

Gather together; let us enter
the fortified cities
and there suffer our fate,ᶜ
for the LORD our God
has condemnedᵈ us.
He has given us poisoned water
to drink,
because we have sinned
against the LORD.

No Peace, Only Terror

¹⁵ We hoped for peace, but there was
nothing good;
for a time of healing, but there was
only terror.

¹⁶ From Dan is heard
the snorting of horses.
At the sound of the neighing
of mighty steeds,
the whole land quakes.
They come to devour the land
and everything in it,
the city and all its residents.
¹⁷ Indeed, I am about to send snakes
among you,
poisonous vipers that cannot
be charmed.
They will bite you.
ₗThis isₗ the LORD's declaration.

Lament over Judah

¹⁸ My joy has flown away;
grief has settled on me.
My heart is sick.
¹⁹ Listen—the cry of my dearᵉ people
from a far away land:
Is the LORD no longer in Zion,
her King not in her midst?
Why have they provoked Me
to anger
with their graven images,
with their worthless
foreign idols?

20 Harvest has passed,
   summer has ended,
but we have not been saved.
21 I am broken by the brokenness
   of my dear[a] people.
I mourn; horror has taken hold
   of me.
22 <u>Is there no balm[b] in Gilead?</u>
<u>Is there no physician there?</u>
So why has the healing
   of my dear[a] people
not come about?

9[c] If my head were water,
   my eyes a fountain of tears,
I would weep day and night
over the slain
   of my dear[d] people.
2[e] If only I had a traveler's
   lodging place
in the wilderness,
I would abandon my people
and depart from them,
for they are all adulterers,
a solemn assembly
   of treacherous people.

3 They bent their tongues
  ⌊like⌋ their bows;
lies and not faithfulness prevail
   in the land,
for they proceed from one evil
   to another,
and they do not take Me
   into account.
      ⌊This is⌋ the LORD's declaration.

Deceit and Betrayal

4 Everyone has to be on guard
   against his friend.
Don't trust any brother,
for every brother will
   certainly deceive,
and every friend spread slander.

5 Each one betrays his friend;
no one tells the truth.
They have taught their tongues
   to speak lies;
they wear themselves out
   doing wrong.
6 You live in ⌊a world⌋ of deception.[f]
In ⌊their⌋ deception they refuse
   to know Me.
      ⌊This is⌋ the LORD's declaration.

God's Pending Test

7 Therefore, this is what the LORD of
•Hosts says:

I am about to refine them
   and test them,
for what else can I do
because of My dear[g] people?[h]
8 Their tongues are deadly arrows—
they speak deception.
With his mouth
a man speaks peaceably
   with his friend,
but inwardly he sets up
   an ambush.
9 Should I not punish them
   for these things?
      ⌊This is⌋ the LORD's declaration.
Should I not take My revenge[i]
against a nation such as this?

10 I will raise weeping and a lament
over the mountains,
a dirge over the wilderness
   grazing land,
for they have been so scorched
that no one passes through.
The sound of cattle is
   no longer heard.
From the birds of the sky
   to the animals,
⌊everything⌋ has fled—they have
   gone away.

Coming Destruction of Jerusalem and Judah

11 I will make Jerusalem a heap
   of rubble,
   a jackals' den.
   I will make the cities of Judah
   a desolation,
   an uninhabited place.

12 Who is the man wise enough to understand this? Who has the LORD spoken to, that he may explain it? Why is the land destroyed and scorched like a wilderness, so no one can pass through?

Coming Exile

13 The LORD said, "It is because they abandoned My law I set in front of them and did not obey My voice or walk according to it. 14 Instead, they followed the stubbornness of their hearts and the •Baals, as their fathers taught them." 15 Therefore, this is what the LORD of Hosts, the God of Israel, says: "I am about to feed this people •wormwood and give them poisonous waters to drink. 16 I will scatter them among nations that they and their fathers have not known. I will send a sword after them until I have finished them off."

Women Mourn over Judah

17 This is what the LORD of Hosts says:

Consider, and summon the women
   who mourn;
   send for the skillful women.
18 Let them come quickly to raise
   a lament over us
   so that our eyes may overflow
   with tears,
   our eyelids soaked with weeping.
19 For a sound of lamentation is heard
   from Zion:
   How devastated we are.

We are greatly ashamed,
   for we have abandoned the land;
   our dwellings have been
   torn down.
20 Now hear the word of the LORD,
   you women.
   Pay attention toª the word
   of His mouth.
   Teach your daughters a lament
   and one another a dirge,
21 for Death has climbed
   through our windows;
   it has entered our fortresses,
   cutting off children
   from the streets,
   young men from the squares.

22 Speak as follows:
This is what the LORD says:

Human corpses will fall
   like manure on the surface
   of the field,
   like newly cut grain after the reaper
   with no one to gather ᵢitᵢ.

Boast in the LORD

23 This is what the LORD says:

The wise must not boast
   in his wisdom;
   the mighty must not boast
   in his might;
   the rich must not boast
   in his riches.
24 But the one who boasts
   should boast in this,
   that he understands
   and knows Me—
   that I am the LORD,
   showing faithful love,
   justice, and righteousness
   on the earth,
   for I delight in these things.
      ᵢThis isᵢ the LORD's declaration.

ª9:20 Lit Your ears must receive

25 "The days are coming"—the LORD's declaration—"when I will punish all the circumcised yet uncircumcised: 26 Egypt, Judah, Edom, the Ammonites, Moab, all those who clip the hair on their temples[a] and reside in the wilderness. All these nations are uncircumcised, and the whole house of Israel is uncircumcised in heart."

False Gods vs. Creator

10 Hear the word that the LORD has spoken to[b] you, house of Israel. 2 This is what the LORD says:

Do not learn the way of the nations
or be terrified by signs
  in the heavens,
although the nations are terrified
  by them,
3 for the customs of the peoples
  are worthless.
Someone cuts down a tree
  from the forest;
ᵢit isᵢ worked by the hands
  of a craftsman with a chisel.
4 He decorates it with silver
  and gold.
It is fastened with hammer
  and nails,
so it won't totter.
5 Like scarecrows
  in a cucumber patch,
their idols cannot speak.
They must be carried because
  they cannot walk.
Do not fear them for they can do
  no harm—
and they cannot do any good.

6 LORD, there is no one like You.
You are great;
Your name is great in power.
7 Who should not •fear You,
King of the nations?

It is what You deserve.
For among all the wise people
  of the nations
and among all their kingdoms,
there is no one like You.
8 They are both senseless and foolish,
instructed by worthless idols
ᵢmade ofᵢ wood!
9 Beaten silver is brought
  from Tarshish,
and gold from Uphaz[c]
from the hands of a goldsmith,
the work of a craftsman.
Their clothing is blue and purple,
all the work of skilled artisans.
10 But the LORD is the true God;
He is the living God
  and eternal King.
The earth quakes at His wrath,
and the nations cannot endure
  His rage.

Great Power of the Lord

11 You are to say this to them: The gods that did not make the heavens and the earth will perish from the earth and from under these heavens.[d]

12 He made the earth by His power,
established the world
  by His wisdom,
and spread out the heavens
  by His understanding.
13 When He thunders,[e]
the waters in the heavens
  are in turmoil,
and He causes the clouds to rise
from the ends of the earth.
He makes lightning for the rain
and brings the wind
  from His storehouses.

14 Everyone is stupid and ignorant.
Every goldsmith is put to shame
by ᵢhisᵢ carved image,

---

[a]9:26 Or who live in distant places; Jr 25:23; 49:32; Lv 19:27   [b]10:1 Or against   [c]10:9 Or Ophir   [d]10:11 This is the only Aram v. in Jr.   [e]10:13 Lit At His giving of the voice

for his cast images are a lie;
there is no breath in them.
15 They are worthless, a work
to be mocked.
At the time of their punishment
they will be destroyed.
16 Jacob's Portion[a] is not like these
because He is the One who formed
all things.
Israel is the tribe of His inheritance;
the LORD of •Hosts is His name.

Exile After the Siege

17 Gather up your belongings[b]
from the ground,
you who live under siege.

18 For this is what the LORD says:

Look, I am slinging out
the land's residents at this time
and bringing them such distress
that they will feel it.

Jeremiah Grieves

19 Woe to me because of
my brokenness—
I am severely wounded!
I exclaimed, "This is
my intense suffering,
but I must bear it."
20 My tent is destroyed;
all my tent cords are snapped.
My sons have departed from me
and are no more.
ˌI haveˌ no one to pitch
my tent again
or to hang up my curtains.
21 For the shepherds are stupid:
they don't seek the LORD.
Therefore they have not prospered,
and their whole flock is scattered.
22 Listen! A noise—it is coming—
a great commotion from the land
to the north.

The cities of Judah will be
made desolate,
a jackals' den.

A Man's Way ... Is Not His Own

23 I know, LORD,
that a man's way of life is not
his own;
no one who walks determines
his own steps.
24 Discipline me, LORD,
but with justice—
not in Your anger,
or You will reduce me to nothing.
25 Pour out Your wrath
on the nations
that don't recognize You
and on the families
that don't call on Your name,
for they have consumed Jacob;
they have consumed him
and finished him off
and made his homeland desolate.

God Reminds
Judah of the Covenant

11 ˌThis isˌ the word that came to Jeremiah from the LORD: 2 "Listen to the words of this covenant, and tell them to the men of Judah and the residents of Jerusalem. 3 You must tell them: This is what the LORD, the God of Israel, says: Let a curse be on the man who does not obey the words of this covenant, 4 which I commanded your ancestors when I brought them out of the land of Egypt, out of the iron furnace. I declared: 'Obey Me, and do everything that I command you, and you will be My people, and I will be your God,' 5 in order to establish the oath I swore to your ancestors, to give ˌthemˌ a land flowing with milk and honey, as it is today."

I answered, "•Amen, LORD."

ᵃ**10:16** = the LORD   ᵇ**10:17** Lit *bundle*

Curses for Disobedience

⁶ The LORD said to me, "Proclaim all these words in the cities of Judah and in the streets of Jerusalem: Obey the words of this covenant and carry them out. ⁷ For I strongly warned your ancestors when I brought them out of the land of Egypt until today, warning them time and time again:ᵃ Obey My voice. ⁸ Yet they would not obey or pay attention; each one followed the stubbornness of his evil heart. So I brought on them all the curses of this covenant, because they had not done what I commanded ⌊them⌋ to do."

Disaster Awaits

⁹ The LORD said to me, "A conspiracy has been discovered among the men of Judah and the residents of Jerusalem. ¹⁰ They have returned to the sins of their ancestors who refused to obey My words and have followed other gods to worship them. The house of Israel and the house of Judah broke My covenant I made with their ancestors.

¹¹ "Therefore, this is what the LORD says: I am about to bring on them disaster that they cannot escape. They will cry out to Me, but I will not hear them. ¹² Then the cities of Judah and the residents of Jerusalem will go and cry out to the gods they have been burning incense to, but they certainly will not save them in their time of disaster. ¹³ Your gods are indeed as numerous as your cities, Judah, and the altars you have set up to Shameᵇ—altars to burn incense to •Baal—as numerous as the streets of Jerusalem.

"Do Not Pray"

¹⁴ "As for you, do not pray for these people. Do not raise up a cry or a prayer on their behalf, for I will not be listening when they call out to Me at the time of their disaster.

¹⁵ What ⌊right⌋ does
  My beloved have
to be in My house,
having carried out so many
  evil schemes?
Can holy meatᶜ prevent
  your disasterᵈ
so you can rejoice?
¹⁶ The LORD named you
a flourishing olive tree,
beautiful with well-formed fruit.
He has set fire to it,
and its branches are consumedᵉ
with a great roaring sound.

¹⁷ "The LORD of •Hosts who planted you has decreed disaster against you, because of the harm the house of Israel and the house of Judah brought on themselves, provoking Me to anger by burning incense to Baal."

¹⁸ The LORD informed me, so I knew.
  Then You helped me to see
    their deeds,
¹⁹ for I was like a docileᶠ lamb led
  to slaughter.
I didn't know that they had
  devised plots against me:
"Let's destroy the tree
  with its fruit;ᵍ
let's cut him off from the land
  of the living
so that his name will no longer
  be remembered."
²⁰ But, LORD of Hosts,
  who judges righteously,
who tests heartʰ and mind,
let me see Your vengeance
  on them,
for I have presented my case
  to You.

ᵃ11:7 Lit today, rising early and warning ᵇ11:13 = Baal ᶜ11:15 = sacrifices ᵈ11:15 LXX; MT reads meat pass from you ᵉ11:16 Vg; MT reads broken ᶠ11:19 Or pet ᵍ11:19 Lit bread ʰ11:20 Lit kidneys

²¹ Therefore, here is what the LORD says concerning the people of Anathoth who want to take your life. They warn, "You must not prophesy in the name of the LORD, or you will certainly die at our hand." ²² Therefore, this is what the LORD of Hosts says: "I am about to punish them. The young men will die by the sword; their sons and daughters will die by famine. ²³ They will have no remnant, for I will bring disaster on the people of Anathoth ⌊in⌋ the year of their punishment."

Jeremiah Complains to God

12 You will be righteous, LORD,
     even if I bring a case against You.
   Yet, I wish to contend with You:
   Why does the way of the wicked
     prosper?
   ⌊Why⌋ do the treacherous live
     at ease?
² You planted them, and they
     have taken root.
   They have grown
     and produced fruit.
   You are ever on their lips,ᵃ
   but far from their conscience.ᵇ
³ As for You, You know me, LORD;
     You see me.
   You test whether my heart is
     with You.
   Drag the wicked away like sheep
     to slaughter,
   and set them apart for the day
     of killing.
⁴ How long will the land mourn
   and the grass of every field
     wither?
   Because of the evil of its residents,
   animals and birds have been
     swept away,
   for ⌊the people⌋ have said,
   "He cannot see what our end
     will be."ᶜ

The LORD's Response

⁵ If you have raced with runners
   and they have worn you out,
   how can you compete with horses?
   If you stumble in a peaceful land,
   what will you do in the thickets
     of the Jordan?
⁶ Even your brothers—
     your own father's household—
   even they were treacherous to you;
   even they have cried out loudly
     after you.
   Do not have confidence in them,
   though they speak well of you.

⁷ I have abandoned My house;
   I have deserted My inheritance.
   I have given the love of My life
   into the hand of her enemies.
⁸ My inheritance has acted
     toward Me
   like a lion in the forest.
   She has roared against Me.
   Therefore, I hate her.
⁹ Is My inheritance like a hyenaᵈ
     to Me?
   Are birds of prey circling her?
   Go, gather all the wild animals;
   bring them to devour ⌊her⌋.
¹⁰ Many shepherds have destroyed
     My vineyard;
   they have trampled My plot of land.
   They have turned My desirable plot
   into a desolate wasteland.
¹¹ They have made it a desolation.
   It mourns, desolate, before Me.
   All the land is desolate,
   but no one takes it to heart.
¹² Over all the barren heights
     in the wilderness
   the destroyers have come,
   for the LORD has a sword
     that devours
   from one end of the earth
     to the other.

ᵃ**12:2** Lit *are near in their mouth*   ᵇ**12:2** Lit *kidneys*   ᶜ**12:4** LXX reads *see our ways*   ᵈ**12:9** Hb obscure

No one has peace.

13 They have sown wheat
    but harvested thorns.
   They have exhausted themselves
    but have no profit.
   Be put to shame by your harvests
   because of the LORD's
    burning anger.

God's Plans for Evil Neighbors

14 This is what the LORD says: "Concerning all My evil neighbors who attack the inheritance that I bequeathed to My people, Israel, I am about to uproot them from their land, and I will uproot the house of Judah from among them. 15 After I have uprooted them, I will once again have compassion on them and return each one to his inheritance and to his land. 16 If they will diligently learn the ways of My people—to swear by My name, 'As the LORD lives,' just as they taught My people to swear by •Baal—they will be built up among My people. 17 However, if they will not obey, then I will uproot and destroy that nation."

⌐This is⌐ the LORD's declaration.

God: Buy Linen Underwear

13 This is what the LORD said to me: "Go and buy yourself linen underwear and put it on,[a] but don't get it wet." 2 So I bought underwear as the LORD instructed me and put it on.

3 Then the word of the LORD came to me a second time: 4 "Take the underwear that you bought and are wearing,[b] and go at once to the Euphrates River and hide it in a rocky crevice." 5 So I went and hid it by the Euphrates, as the LORD commanded me.

6 A long time later the LORD said to me, "Go at once to the Euphrates and get the underwear that I commanded you to hide there." 7 So I went to the Euphrates and dug up the underwear and got it from the place where I had hidden it, but it was ruined—of no use whatsoever.

Judah Like Underwear

8 Then the word of the LORD came to me: 9 "This is what the LORD says: Just like this I will ruin the great pride of both Judah and Jerusalem. 10 These evil people, who refuse to listen to Me, who walk in the stubbornness of their own hearts, and who have followed other gods to serve and worship—they will be like this underwear, of no use whatsoever. 11 Just as underwear clings to one's waist, so I fastened the whole house of Israel and of Judah to Me"—⌐this is the LORD's declaration⌐—"so that they might be My people for My fame, praise, and glory, but they would not obey.

Wine Jars: Drunkenness

12 "Say this to them: This is what the LORD, the God of Israel, says: Every jar should be filled with wine. Then they will respond to you: Don't we know that every jar should be filled with wine? 13 And you will say to them, This is what the LORD says: I am about to fill all who live in this land—the kings who reign for David on his throne, the priests, the prophets and all the residents of Jerusalem—with drunkenness. 14 I will smash them against each other, fathers and sons alike"—the LORD's declaration. "I will allow no mercy, pity, or compassion ⌐to keep Me⌐ from destroying them."

LORD's Warning

15 Listen and pay attention.
   Do not be proud,
   for the LORD has spoken.

---

a**13:1** Lit *around your waist*   b**13:4** Lit *wearing around your waist*

16 Give glory to the LORD your God
   before He brings darkness,
   before your feet stumble
   on the mountains at dusk.
   You wait for light,
   but He brings darkest gloom[a]
   and makes thick darkness.
17 But if you will not listen,
   my innermost being will weep
      in secret
   because of your pride.
   My eyes will overflow with tears,
   for the LORD's flock has been
      taken captive.
18 Say to the king
      and the queen mother:
   Take a humble seat,
   for your glorious crowns
   have fallen from your heads.
19 The cities of the •Negev are
      under siege;
   no one can help ⌐them⌐.
   All of Judah has been taken
      into exile,
   taken completely into exile.
20 Look up and see
   those coming from the north.
   Where is the flock entrusted to you,
   the sheep ⌐that were⌐ your pride?

Destiny of Jerusalem

21 What will you say when He appoints
   close friends as leaders over you,
   ones you yourself trained?
   Won't labor pains seize you,
   as ⌐they do⌐ a woman in labor?
22 And when you ask yourself:
   Why have these things happened
      to me?—
   it is because of your great guilt
   that your skirts have been
      stripped off,
   your body ravished.[b]

23 Can the •Cushite change his skin,
   or a leopard his spots?
   If so, you might be able to do
      what is good,
   you who are instructed in evil.
24 I will scatter you[c]
   like drifting chaff
   before the desert wind.
25 This is your lot,
   what I have decreed for you—
      ⌐this is⌐ the LORD's declaration—
   because you have forgotten Me
   and trusted in Falsehood.[d]
26 I will pull your skirts up
      over your face
   so that your shame might be seen.
27 Your adulteries
      and your ⌐lustful⌐ neighings,
   your heinous prostitution
   on the hills, in the fields—
   I have seen your detestable acts.
   Woe to you, Jerusalem!
   You are unclean—
   for how long yet?

The Drought

14 The word of the LORD that came to
   Jeremiah concerning the drought:

2 Judah mourns;
   her gates languish.
   ⌐Her people⌐ are on the ground
      in mourning;
   Jerusalem's cry rises up.
3 Their nobles send their servants[e]
      for water.
   They go to the cisterns;
   they find no water;
   their containers return empty.
   They are ashamed and humiliated;
   they cover their heads.
4 The ground is cracked
   since no rain ⌐has fallen⌐
      on the land.

a13:16 Or brings a shadow of death   b13:22 Lit your heels have suffered violence   c13:24 Lit them   d13:25 = Baal
e14:3 Lit little ones

The farmers are ashamed;
they cover their heads.
5 Even the doe in the field
gives birth and abandons ⌊her fawn⌋
since there is no grass.
6 Wild donkeys stand
   on the barren heights
panting for air like jackals.
Their eyes fail
because there are no green plants.
7 Though our guilt testifies
   against us,
Lord, act for Your name's sake.
Indeed, our rebellions are many;
we have sinned against You.
8 Hope of Israel,
its Savior in time of distress,
why are You like an alien
   in the land,
like a traveler stopping only
   for the night?
9 Why are You like a helpless man,
like a warrior unable to save?
Yet You are among us, Lord,
and we are called by Your name.
Don't leave us!

10 This is what the Lord says concerning these people:

Truly they love to wander;
they never rest their feet.
So the Lord does not accept them.
Now He will remember their guilt
and punish their sins.

False Prophets to be Punished

11 Then the Lord said to me, "Do not pray for the well-being of these people. 12 If they fast, I will not hear their cry of despair. If they offer •burnt offering and •grain offering, I will not accept them. Rather, I will finish them off by sword, famine, and plague."

13 And I replied, "Oh no, Lord God! The prophets are telling them, 'You won't see sword or suffer famine. I will

certainly give you true peace in this place.'"

14 But the Lord said to me, "These prophets are prophesying a lie in My name. I did not send them, nor did I command them or speak to them. They are prophesying to you a false vision, worthless •divination, the deceit of their own minds.

Sword and Famine

15 "Therefore, this is what the Lord says concerning the prophets who prophesy in My name, though I did not send them, and who say: There will never be sword or famine in this land: By sword and famine these prophets will meet their end. 16 The people they are prophesying to will be thrown into the streets of Jerusalem because of the famine and the sword. There will be no one to bury them—they, their wives, their sons, and their daughters. I will pour out their own evil on them."

Jeremiah's Plea to God

17 You are to speak this word to them:
Let my eyes overflow with tears;
day and night may ⌊they⌋ not stop,
for the virgin daughter
   of my people
has been destroyed
   by a great disaster,
an extremely severe wound.
18 If I go out to the field,
look—those slain by the sword!
If I enter the city,
look—those ill from famine!
For both prophet and priest
travel to a land they do not know.

19 Have You completely
   rejected Judah?
Do You detest Zion?
Why do You strike us
with no hope of healing for us?
We hoped for peace,

but there was nothing good;
for a time of healing,
but there was only terror.

Confession of Guilt for Judah

20 We acknowledge
   our wickedness, LORD,
the guilt of our fathers;
indeed, we have sinned
   against You.
21 Because of Your name,
   don't despise ⌊us⌋.
Don't disdain Your glorious throne.
Remember Your covenant with us;
do not break it.
22 Can any of the worthless idols
   of the nations bring rain?
Or can the skies alone
   give showers?
Are You not the LORD our God?
We therefore put our hope in You,
for You have done all these things.

The LORD Rejects Plea

15 Then the LORD said to me: "Even if Moses and Samuel should stand before Me, My compassions would not ⌊reach out⌋ to these people. Send them from My presence, and let them go. ² If they ask you: Where will we go? you must tell them: This is what the LORD says:

Those ⌊destined⌋ for death, to death;
those ⌊destined⌋ for the sword,
   to the sword.
Those ⌊destined⌋ for famine,
   to famine;
those ⌊destined⌋ for captivity,
   to captivity.

Four Judgments

³ "I will ordain four kinds[a] ⌊of judgment⌋ for them"—⌊this is⌋ the LORD's declaration—"the sword to kill, the dogs to drag away, and the birds of the sky and the wild animals of the land to devour and destroy. ⁴ I will make them a horror to all the kingdoms of the earth because of Manasseh son of Hezekiah, the king of Judah, for what he did in Jerusalem.

5 Who will have pity on you,
   Jerusalem?
Who will show sympathy
   toward you?
Who will turn aside
to ask about your welfare?
6 You have left Me.
   ⌊This is⌋ the LORD's declaration.
You have turned your back,
so I have stretched out My hand
   against you
and destroyed you.
I am tired of showing compassion.
7 I scattered them
   with a winnowing fork
at the gates of the land.
I made ⌊them⌋ childless; I destroyed
   My people.
They would not turn from their ways.
8 I made their widows more numerous
than the sand of the seas.
I brought against the mother
   of young men
a destroyer at noon.
I suddenly released on her
agitation and terrors.
9 The mother of seven grew faint;
she breathed her ⌊last⌋ breath.
Her sun set while it was still day;
she was ashamed and humiliated.
The rest of them I will give over
   to the sword
in the presence of their enemies."
   ⌊This is⌋ the LORD's declaration.

Jeremiah Complains Again

10 Woe is me, my mother,
   that you gave birth to me,

ᵃ**15:3** Lit *families*

a man who incites dispute
　and conflict
　in all the land.
I did not lend or borrow,
　yet everyone curses me.

The LORD's Response

¹¹ The LORD said:

Assuredly, I will set you free
　and care for you.ᵃ
Assuredly, I will intercede for you
　in a time of trouble,
　in your time of distress,
　　with the enemy.
¹² Can anyone smash iron,
　iron from the north, or bronze?
¹³ Your wealth and your treasures
I will give as plunder, without cost,
　for all your sins,
　and within all your borders.
¹⁴ Then I will make you serve
　　your enemiesᵇ
　in a land you do not know,
　for My anger will kindle a fire
　that will burn against you.

Jeremiah's Prayer for Vengeance

¹⁵ You know, LORD;
　remember me and take note of me.
Avenge me against my persecutors.
In Your patience,ᶜ
　don't take me away.
Know that I suffer disgrace
　for Your honor.
¹⁶ Your words were found,
　and I ate them.
Your words became a delight to me
　and the joy of my heart,
　for I am called by Your name,
LORD God of •Hosts.
¹⁷ I never sat with the band
　of revelers,
　and I did not celebrate ⌊with them⌋.

Because Your hand was ⌊on me⌋,
　I sat alone,
　for You filled me with indignation.
¹⁸ Why has my pain
　become unending,
my wound incurable,
　refusing to be healed?
You truly have become
　like a mirage to me—
water that is not reliable.

God Tells Jeremiah to Repent

¹⁹ Therefore, this is what the LORD says:

If you return, I will restore you;
　you will stand in My presence.
And if you speak noble ⌊words⌋,
　rather than worthless ones,
you will be My spokesman.
It is they who must return to you;
　you must not return to them.
²⁰ Then I will make you
　a fortified wall of bronze
to this people.
They will fight against you
　but will not overcome you,
for I am with you
　to save you and deliver you.
　　⌊This is⌋ the LORD's declaration.
²¹ I will deliver you from the power
　of evil people
and redeem you from the control
　of the ruthless.

No Marriage for Jeremiah

16 The word of the LORD came to me: ² "You must not marry or have sons or daughters in this place. ³ For this is what the LORD says concerning sons and daughters born in this place as well as concerning the mothers who bear them and the fathers who father them in this land: ⁴ They will die from deadly dis-

---

ᵃ**15:11** Lit *free for good*　ᵇ**15:14** Some Hb mss, LXX, Syr, Tg; other Hb mss read *you pass through*　ᶜ**15:15** Lit *In the slowness of Your anger*

eases. They will not be mourned or buried but will be like manure on the face of the earth. They will be finished off by sword and famine. Their corpses will become food for the birds of the sky and for the wild animals of the land.

A People without Peace

5 "For this is what the LORD says: Don't enter a house where a mourning feast is taking place.ᵃ Don't go to lament or sympathize with them, for I have removed My peace from these people"— ⌊this is⌋ the LORD's declaration—"⌊as well as My⌋ faithful love and compassion. 6 Both great and small will die in this land without burial. No lament will be made for them, nor will anyone cut himself or shave his head for them.ᵇ 7 Food won't be provided for the mourner to comfort him because of the dead. A cup of consolation won't be given him because of ⌊the loss of⌋ his father or mother. 8 You must not enter the house where feasting is taking place to sit with them to eat and drink. 9 For this is what the LORD of •Hosts, the God of Israel, says: I am about to eliminate from this place, before your very eyes and in your time, the sound of joy and gladness, the voice of the bridegroom and the bride.

Abandoning the LORD and His Law

10 "When you tell these people all these things, they will say to you: Why has the LORD declared all this great disaster against us? What is our guilt? What is our sin that we have committed against the LORD our God? 11 Then you will answer them: Because your fathers abandoned Me"—the LORD's declaration— "and followed other gods, served them, and worshiped them. Indeed, they abandoned Me and did not keep My law.

12 You did more evil than your fathers. Look, each one of you was following the stubbornness of his evil heart, not obeying Me. 13 So I will hurl you from this land into a land that you and your fathers are not familiar with. There you will worship other gods both day and night, for I will not grant you grace.ᶜ

14 "However, take note! The days are coming"—the LORD's declaration— "when it will no longer be said: As the LORD lives who brought the Israelites from the land of Egypt, 15 but rather: As the LORD lives who brought the Israelites from the land of the north and from all the other lands where He had banished them. For I will return them to their land that I gave to their ancestors.

Punishment of Exile

16 "I am about to send for many fishermen"—the LORD's declaration—"and they will fish for them. Then I will send for many hunters, and they will hunt them down on every mountain and hill and out of the clefts of the rocks, 17 for My gaze takes in all their ways. They are not concealed from Me, and their guilt is not hidden from My sight. 18 I will first repay them double for their guilt and sin because they have polluted My land. They have filled My inheritance with the lifelessness of their detestable and abhorrent idols."

19 LORD, my strength
  and my stronghold,
 my refuge in a time of distress,
 the nations will come to You
 from the ends of the earth,
  and they will say,
 "Our fathers inherited only lies,
 worthless idols of no benefit at all."
20 Can one make gods for himself?

ᵃ16:5 Lit house of mourning ᵇ16:6 Cutting and shaving were pagan mourning rituals; Jr 41:5; 47:5; Dt 14:1. ᶜ16:13 Or compassion

But they are not gods.

21 "Therefore, I am about
  to inform them,
  and this time I will
  make them know
My power and My might;
then they will know that My name
  is •Yahweh."

Persistent Sin of Judah

17 The sin of Judah is written
  with an iron stylus.
With a diamond point
it is engraved on the tablet
  of their hearts
and on the horns of their[a] altars,
2 while their children remember
    their altars
  and their •Asherah poles,
    by the green trees
  on the high hills—
3 My mountains in the countryside.
Your wealth and all your treasures
I will give up as plunder
because of the sin
  of your •high places[b]
within all your borders.
4 You will, of yourself, relinquish
    your inheritance
  that I gave you.
I will make you serve
  your enemies
in a land you do not know,
for you have set My anger on fire;
it will burn forever.

Curse and Blessing

5 This is what the LORD says:

Cursed is the man who trusts
  in mankind,
who makes ⌊human⌋ flesh
  his strength
and turns his heart from the LORD.

6 He will be like a juniper
    in the •Arabah;
  he cannot see when good comes
  but dwells in the parched places
    in the wilderness,
  in a salt land where no one lives.
7 Blessed is the man who trusts
    in the LORD,
  whose confidence indeed is
    the LORD.
8 He will be like a tree planted
    by water:
  it sends its roots out
    toward a stream,
  it doesn't fear when heat comes,
  and its foliage remains green.
  It will not worry in a year
    of drought
  or cease producing fruit.

Deceitful Heart

9 The heart is more deceitful
    than anything else
  and desperately sick—
    who can understand it?
10 I, the Lord, examine the mind,
  I test the heart[c]
  to give to each according to
    his way,
  according to what
    his actions deserve.
11 He who makes a fortune unjustly
  is ⌊like⌋ a partridge that hatches eggs
    it didn't lay.
  In the middle of his days
  ⌊his riches⌋ will abandon him,
  so in the end he will be a fool.

12 A throne of glory
    on high from the beginning
  is the place of our sanctuary,
13 LORD, the hope of Israel,
    all who abandon You
  will be put to shame.

---

[a]**17:1** Some Hb mss, Syr, Vg; other Hb mss read *your* [b]**17:3** Lit *plunder, your high places because of sin* [c]**17:10** Lit *kidneys*

All who turn away from Me
will be written in the dirt,
for they have abandoned
the fountain of living water,
the LORD.

Jeremiah's Plea for Protection

14 Heal me, LORD,
and I will be healed;
save me, and I will be saved,
for You are my praise.
15 Hear how they keep
challenging me,
"Where is the word of the LORD?
Let it come!"
16 But I have not run away from being
Your shepherd,
and I have not longed for
the fatal day.
You know my words were spoken
in Your presence.
17 Don't become a terror to me.
You are my refuge in the day
of disaster.
18 Let my persecutors be
put to shame,
but don't let me be put to shame.
Let them be terrified, but don't
let me be terrified.
Bring on them the day of disaster;
shatter them
with total[a] destruction.

Lord: Observe the Sabbath

19 This is what the LORD said to me,
"Go and stand in the People's Gate,
through which the kings of Judah enter
and leave, and in all the gates of Jerusalem. 20 Announce to them: Hear the
word of the LORD, kings of Judah, all Judah, and all the residents of Jerusalem
who enter through these gates. 21 This is
what the LORD says: Watch yourselves;
do not pick up a load and bring it in
through the gates of Jerusalem on the
Sabbath day. 22 You must not carry a load
out of your houses on the Sabbath day or
do any work, but you must consecrate
the Sabbath day, just as I commanded
your ancestors. 23 They wouldn't listen
or pay attention but became obstinate,
not listening or accepting discipline.

24 "However, if you listen to Me, says
the LORD, and do not bring loads through
the gates of this city on the Sabbath day
and consecrate the Sabbath day and do
no work on it, 25 kings and princes will
enter through the gates of this city. They
will sit on the throne of David, riding in
chariots and on horses with their officials, the men of Judah, and the residents
of Jerusalem. This city will be inhabited
forever. 26 Then ⌊people⌋ will come from
the cities of Judah and from the area
around Jerusalem, from the land of Benjamin and from the Judean foothills, from
the hill country and from the •Negev
bringing •burnt offerings and sacrifice,
•grain offerings and frankincense, and
thank offerings to the house of the LORD.
27 If you do not listen to Me to consecrate
the Sabbath day by not carrying a load
while entering the gates of Jerusalem on
the Sabbath day, I will set fire to its gates,
and it will consume the citadels of Jerusalem and not be extinguished."

The Potter Illustration

18 ⌊This is⌋ the word that came to Jeremiah from the LORD: 2 "Go down at
once to the potter's house; there I will
reveal My words to you." 3 So I went
down to the potter's house, and there he
was, working away at the wheel.[b] 4 But
the jar that he was making from the clay
became flawed in the potter's hand, so
he made it into another jar, as it seemed
right for him to do.

a17:18 Lit double   b18:3 Lit pair of stones

⁵ The word of the LORD came to me: ⁶ "House of Israel, can I not treat you as this potter ⌐treats his clay⌐?"—⌐this is⌐ the LORD's declaration. "Just like clay in the potter's hand, so are you in My hand, house of Israel. ⁷ At one moment I might announce concerning a nation or a kingdom that I will uproot, tear down, and destroy ⌐it⌐. ⁸ However, if that nation I have made an announcement about, turns from its evil, I will not bring the disaster on it I had planned. ⁹ At ⌐another⌐ time I announce that I will build and plant a nation or a kingdom. ¹⁰ However, if it does what is evil in My sight by not listening to My voice, I will not bring the good I had said I would do to it. ¹¹ So now, say to the men of Judah and to the residents of Jerusalem: This is what the LORD says: I am about to bring harm to you and make plans against you. Turn now, each from your evil way, and correct your ways and your deeds. ¹² But they will say: It's hopeless. We will continue to follow our plans, and each of us will continue to act according to the stubbornness of his evil heart."

Deluded Israel

¹³ Therefore, this is what the LORD says:

Ask among the nations,
Who has heard ⌐things⌐ like these?
Virgin Israel has done
a most terrible thing.
¹⁴ Does the snow of Lebanon
ever leave the highland crags?
Or does cold water flowing
from a distance ever fail?
¹⁵ Yet My people have forgotten Me.
They burn incense to false ⌐idols⌐
that make them stumble
in their ways—

in the ancient roads—
to walk on ⌐new⌐ paths,
not the highway.
¹⁶ They have made their land
a horror,
a perpetual object of scorn;[a]
everyone who passes by it
will be horrified
and shake his head.
¹⁷ I will scatter them
before the enemy
like the east wind.
I will show them[b] ⌐My⌐ back and not
⌐My⌐ face
on the day of their calamity.

Plot against Jeremiah

¹⁸ Then certain ones said, "Come, let's make plans against Jeremiah, for the law will never be lost from the priest, or counsel from the wise, or an oracle from the prophet. Come, let's denounce him[c] and pay no attention to all his words."

¹⁹ Pay attention to me, LORD.
Hear what my opponents
are saying!
²⁰ Should good be repaid with evil?
Yet they have dug a pit for me.
Remember how I stood before You
to speak good on their behalf,
to turn Your anger from them.
²¹ Therefore, hand their children
over to famine,
and pour the sword's power
on them.
Let their wives become childless
and widowed,
their husbands slain
by deadly disease,[d]
their young men struck down
by the sword in battle.
²² Let a cry be heard
from their houses

ª**18:16** Lit *hissing*   ᵇ**18:17** LXX, Lat, Syr, Tg; MT reads *will look at them*   ᶜ**18:18** Lit *let's strike him with the tongue*
ᵈ**18:21** Lit *by death*

when You suddenly bring raiders
  against them,
for they have dug a pit
  to capture me
and have hidden snares for my feet.
23 But You, LORD, know
  all their deadly plots against me.
Do not wipe out their guilt;
  do not blot out their sin before You.
Let them be forced to stumble
  before You;
deal with them in the time
  of Your anger.

The Clay Jug

19 This is what the LORD says: "Go, buy a potter's clay jug. Take[a] some of the elders of the people and some of the elders of the priests 2 and go out to the Valley of Hinnom near the entrance of the Potsherd Gate. Proclaim there the words I speak to you. 3 Say: Hear the word of the LORD, kings of Judah and residents of Jerusalem. This is what the LORD of •Hosts, the God of Israel, says: I am going to bring such disaster on this place that everyone who hears about it will shudder[b] 4 because they have abandoned Me and made this a foreign place. They have burned incense in it to other gods that they, their fathers, and the kings of Judah have never known. They have filled this place with the blood of the innocent. 5 They have built •high places to •Baal on which to burn their children in the fire as burnt offerings to Baal, something I have never commanded or mentioned; I never entertained the thought.[c]

6 "Therefore, take note! The days are coming"—⌊this is⌋ the LORD's declaration—"when this place will no longer be called Topheth and the Valley of Hinnom, but the Valley of Slaughter. 7 I will spoil the plans of Judah and Jerusalem in this place. I will make them fall by the sword before their enemies, by the hand of those who want to take their life. I will provide their corpses as food for the birds of the sky and for the wild animals of the land. 8 I will make this city desolate, an object of scorn. Everyone who passes by it will be horrified and scoff because of all its wounds. 9 I will make them eat the flesh of their sons and their daughters, and they will eat each other's flesh in the siege and distress that their enemies, those who want to take their life, inflict on them.

"Shatter the Jug"

10 "Then you are to shatter the jug in the presence of the people traveling with you, 11 and you are to proclaim to them: This is what the LORD of Hosts says: I will shatter these people and this city, like one shatters a potter's jar that can never again be mended. They will bury in Topheth until there is no place left to bury. 12 I will do so to this place"—⌊this is⌋ the declaration of the LORD—"and to its residents, making this city like Topheth. 13 The houses of Jerusalem and the houses of the kings of Judah will become impure like that place Topheth—all the houses on whose rooftops they have burned incense to the whole heavenly host and poured out drink offerings to other gods."

14 Jeremiah came back from Topheth, where the LORD had sent him to prophesy, stood in the courtyard of the LORD's temple, and proclaimed to all the people, 15 "This is what the LORD of Hosts, the God of Israel, says: 'I am about to bring on this city—and on all its ⌊dependent⌋ villages—all the disaster that I spoke against it, for they have become obstinate, not obeying My words.' "

---

a**19:1** Syr, Tg; MT omits *Take*   b**19:3** Lit *shudder their ears*; 1 Sm 3:11; 2 Kg 21:12   c**19:5** Lit *mentioned, and it did not arise on My heart*

Priest Pashur Beats Jeremiah

20 Pashhur the priest, the son of Immer and chief officer in the house of the LORD, heard Jeremiah prophesying these things. ² So Pashhur had Jeremiah the prophet beaten and put him in the stocks at the Upper Benjamin Gate in the LORD's temple. ³ The next day, when Pashhur released Jeremiah from the stocks, Jeremiah said to him, "The LORD does not call you Pashhur, but Magor-missabib,ᵃ ⁴ for this is what the LORD says, 'I am about to make you a terror to both yourself and those you love. They will fall by the sword of their enemies before your very eyes. I will hand Judah over to the king of Babylon, and he will deport them to Babylon and put them to the sword. ⁵ I will give away all the wealth of this city, all its products and valuables. Indeed, I will hand all the treasures of the kings of Judah over to their enemies. They will plunder them, seize them, and carry them off to Babylon. ⁶ As for you, Pashhur, and all who live in your house, you will go into captivity. You will go to Babylon. There you will die, and there you will be buried, you and all your friends that you prophesied falsely to.'"

Jeremiah Complains to God

⁷ You deceived me, LORD,
    and I was deceived.
  You seized me and prevailed.
  I am a laughingstock all the time;
    everyone ridicules me.
⁸ For whenever I speak, I cry out—
  I proclaim: Violence
    and destruction!
  because the word of the LORD
    has become for me
    constant disgrace and derision.
⁹ If I say: I won't mention Him
  or speak any longer in His name,
  His message becomes a fire burning
    in my heart,
  shut up in my bones.
  I become tired of holding it in,
    and I cannot prevail.
¹⁰ For I have heard the gossip
    of the multitudes,
  "Terror is on every side!ᵇ
  Report him; let's report him!"
  Everyone I trustedᶜ watches
    for my fall.
  "Perhaps he will be deceived
  so that we might prevail against him
  and take our vengeance on him."

Jeremiah's Faith

¹¹ But the LORD is with me
  like a violent warrior.
  Therefore, my persecutors
    will stumble and not prevail.
  Since they have not succeeded,
    they will be utterly shamed,
  an everlasting humiliation that will
    never be forgotten.
¹² LORD of •Hosts, testing
    the righteous
  and seeing the heartᵈ and mind,
  let me see Your vengeance
    on them,
  for I have presented my case to You.
¹³ Sing to the LORD!
  Praise the LORD,
  for He rescues the life of the needy
  from the hand of evil people.

Jeremiah's Depression

¹⁴ Cursed be the day
  on which I was born.
  The day my mother bore me—
  let it never be blessed.
¹⁵ Cursed be the man
  who brought the news
    to my father, saying,

ᵃ**20:3** = Terror Is on Every Side; Jr 6:25; 20:10; 46:5 ᵇ**20:10** Hb *Magor-missabib*; Jr 20:3 ᶜ**20:10** Lit *Every man of my peace*; Ps 41:9 ᵈ**20:12** Lit *kidneys*

"A male child is born to you,"
    bringing him great joy.
16 Let that man be like the cities
    the LORD overthrew
        without compassion.
    Let him hear an outcry
        in the morning
    and a war cry at noontime
17 because he didn't kill me
        in the womb
    so that my mother might have been
        my grave,
    her womb eternally pregnant.
18 Why did I come out of the womb
    to see ⌊only⌋ struggle and sorrow,
    to end my life in shame?

King Zedekiah
Pleads with Jeremiah

21 ⌊This is⌋ the word that came to Jeremiah from the LORD when King Zedekiah sent Pashhur son of Malchijah and the priest Zephaniah son of Maaseiah to Jeremiah, asking, 2 "Ask the LORD on our behalf, since Nebuchadnezzar[a] king of Babylon is making war against us. Perhaps the LORD will perform for us something like all His ⌊past⌋ wonderful works so that ⌊Nebuchadnezzar⌋ will withdraw from us."

Jeremiah: Lord Will Fight You

3 But Jeremiah answered, "This is what you are to say to Zedekiah: 4 'This is what the LORD, the God of Israel, says: I will repel the weapons of war in your hands, those you are using to fight the king of Babylon and the Chaldeans[b] who are besieging you outside the wall, and I will bring them into the center of this city. 5 I will fight against you with an outstretched hand and a mighty arm, with anger, rage, and great wrath. 6 I will strike the residents of this city, both man and beast. They will die in a great plague. 7 Afterwards' "—⌐this is⌐ the LORD's declaration—" 'King Zedekiah of Judah, his officers, and the people—those in this city who survive the plague, the sword, and the famine—I will hand over to King Nebuchadnezzar of Babylon, to their enemies, yes, to those who want to take their lives. He will put them to the sword; he won't spare them or show pity or compassion.'

Warning to People: Surrender

8 "But you must say to this people, 'This is what the LORD says: Look, I am presenting to you the way of life and the way of death. 9 Whoever stays in this city will die by the sword, famine, and plague, but whoever goes out and surrenders to the Chaldeans who are besieging you will live and will retain his life like the spoils ⌊of war⌋. 10 For I have turned[c] against this city to ⌊bring⌋ disaster and not good'"—⌐this is⌐ the LORD's declaration. "'It will be handed over to the king of Babylon, who will burn it down.'

Warning to King: Be Just

11 "And to the house of the king of Judah ⌊say this⌋: 'Hear the word of the LORD! 12 House of David, this is what the LORD says:

Administer justice every morning,
    and rescue the victim of robbery
    from the hand of his oppressor,
    or My anger will flare up like fire
    and burn unquenchably
    because of their evil deeds.
13 Beware! I am against you,
    you who sit above the valley,
    ⌊you atop⌋ the rocky plateau—
        ⌐this is⌐ the LORD's declaration—

---

a 21:2 Lit *Nebuchadrezzar*   b 21:4 = Babylonians   c 21:10 Lit *set My face*

you who say: Who can come down
  against us?
Who can enter our hiding places?
14 I will punish you according to
  what you have done—
    ⌊this is⌋ the LORD's declaration.
  I will kindle a fire in its forest
  that will consume everything
  around it.' "

Judgment against Sinful Kings

22 This is what the LORD says: "Go
down to the palace of the king of
Judah and announce this word there.
2 You are to say: Hear the word of the
LORD, king of Judah, you who sit on the
throne of David—you, your officers, and
your people who enter these gates.
3 This is what the LORD says: Administer
justice and righteousness. Rescue the
victim of robbery from the hand of his
oppressor. Don't exploit or brutalize the
alien, the fatherless, or the widow. Don't
shed innocent blood in this place. 4 For if
you conscientiously carry out this word,
then kings sitting on David's throne will
enter through the gates of this palace
riding on chariots and horses—they,
their officers, and their people. 5 But if
you do not obey these words, then I
swear by Myself"—⌊this is⌋ the LORD's
declaration—"that this house will become a ruin."
6 For this is what the LORD says concerning the house of the king of Judah:

You are like Gilead to Me,
  ⌊or⌋ the summit of Lebanon,
but I will certainly turn you
  into a wilderness,
  uninhabited cities.
7 I will appoint destroyers
  against you,
  each with his weapons.

They will cut down the choicest
  of your cedars
  and throw them into the fire.

8 "Many nations will pass by this city
and ask one another: Why did the LORD
do such a thing to this great city? 9 They
will answer: Because they abandoned
the covenant of the LORD their God and
worshiped and served other gods."

Message Concerning King Shallum

10   Do not weep for the dead;
  do not mourn for him.ᵃ
Weep bitterly for the one
  who has gone away,
for he will never return again
  and see his native land.

11 For this is what the LORD says concerning Shallum son of Josiah, king of Judah, who succeeded Josiah his father as
king: "He has left this place—he will
never return here again, 12 but he will
die in the place where they deported
him, never seeing this land again."

Message: Jehoiakim

13   Woe for the one who builds
  his palace
  through unrighteousness,
  his upper rooms through injustice,
  who makes his fellow man serve
  without pay
  and will not give him his wages,
14   who says: I will build myself
  a massive palace,
  with spacious upper rooms.
  He will cut windowsᵇ in it,
  and it will be paneled with cedar
  and painted with vermilion.
15   Are you a king because you excel
  in cedar?
  Your own father, did he not
  eat and drink?

ᵃ22:10 The person referred to in this v. is the Shallum of v.11   ᵇ22:14 Lit My windows

He administered justice
and righteousness,
then it went well with him.
16 He took up the case of the poor
and needy,
then it went well.
Is this not what it means
to know Me?
⌊This is⌋ the LORD's declaration.
17 But you have eyes and heart
for nothing
except your own unjust gain,
shedding innocent blood
and committing extortion
and oppression.

18 Therefore, this is what the LORD
says concerning Jehoiakim son of Josiah,
king of Judah:

They will not mourn
for him, ⌊saying,⌋
Woe, my brother! or Woe,
⌊my⌋ sister!
They will not mourn
for him, saying,
Woe, lord! Woe, his majesty!
19 He will be buried ⌊like⌋ a donkey,
dragged off and thrown
outside the gates of Jerusalem.
20 Go up to Lebanon and cry out;
raise your voice in Bashan;
cry out from Abarim,
for all your lovers^a
have been crushed.
21 I spoke to you when
you were secure.
You said: I will not listen.
This has been your way
since youth;
indeed, you have never listened
to Me.
22 The wind will take charge of^b all
your shepherds,

and your lovers^a will go
into captivity.
Then you will be ashamed
and humiliated
because of all your evil.
23 You residents of Lebanon,
nestled among the cedars,
how you will groan^c
when labor pains come on you,
agony like a woman in labor.

Message: Coniah

24 "As I live," says the LORD, "though
you, Coniah^d son of Jehoiakim, the king
of Judah, were a signet ring on My right
hand, I would tear you from it. 25 In fact,
I will hand you over to those you dread,
who want to take your life, to Nebuchadnezzar king of Babylon and the Chaldeans. 26 I will hurl you and the mother
who gave birth to you into another land,
where neither of you were born, and
there you will both die. 27 They will
never return to the land they long to return to."

28 Is this man Coniah
a despised, shattered pot,
a jar no one wants?
Why are he and his descendants
hurled out
and cast into a land
they have not known?
29 Earth, earth, earth,
hear the word of the LORD!

30 This is what the LORD says:

Record this man as childless,
a man who will not be successful
in his lifetime.
None of his descendants
will succeed
in sitting on the throne of David
or ruling again in Judah.

---

^a 22:20,22 Or friends, or allies   ^b 22:22 Lit will shepherd   ^c 22:23 LXX, Syr, Vg; MT reads will be pitied
^d 22:24 = Jehoiachin

Lord and His Sheep

23 "Woe to the shepherds who destroy and scatter the sheep of My pasture!" ⌊This is⌋ the LORD's declaration. ² "Therefore, this is what the LORD, the God of Israel, says about the shepherds who shepherd My people: You have scattered My flock, banished them, and have not attended to them. I will attend to you because of your evil acts"—the LORD's declaration. ³ "I will gather the remnant of My flock from all the lands where I have banished them, and I will return them to their grazing land. They will become fruitful and numerous. ⁴ I will raise up shepherds over them who will shepherd them. They will no longer be afraid or dismayed, nor will any be missing." ⌊This is⌋ the LORD's declaration.

Righteous Branch of David

⁵ "The days are coming"—⌊this is⌋ the LORD's declaration—"when I will raise up a righteous Branch of David. He will reign wisely as king and administer justice and righteousness in the land. ⁶ In His days Judah will be saved, and Israel will dwell securely. This is what He will be named: The LORD Is Our Righteousness. ⁷ The days are coming"—the LORD's declaration—"when it will no longer be said: As the LORD lives who brought the Israelites from the land of Egypt, ⁸ but: As the LORD lives, who brought and led the descendants of the house of Israel from the land of the north and from all the other countries where Iᵃ had banished them. They will dwell once more in their own land."

God Condemns False Prophets

⁹ Concerning the prophets:

My heart is broken within me,
and all my bones tremble.

I have become like a drunkard,
like a man overcome by wine,
because of the LORD,
because of His holy words.
¹⁰ For the land is full of adulterers;
the land mourns because
of the curse,
and the grazing lands
in the wilderness have dried up.
Their way of lifeᵇ has become evil,
and their power is not rightly used
¹¹ because both prophet and priest
are ungodly,
even in My house I have found
their evil.
⌊This is⌋ the LORD's declaration.
¹² Therefore, their way will be to them
like slippery paths in the gloom.
They will be driven away
and fall down there,
for I will bring disaster on them,
the year of their punishment.
⌊This is⌋ the LORD's declaration.

Disgusting, Horrible Prophets of Samaria and Jerusalem

¹³ Among the prophets of Samaria
I saw something disgusting:
They prophesied by •Baal
and led My people Israel astray.
¹⁴ Among the prophets of Jerusalem also
I saw a horrible thing:
They commit adultery and walk
in lies.
They strengthen the hands
of evildoers,
and none turns his back on evil.
They are all like Sodom to Me;
Jerusalem's residents are
like Gomorrah.

¹⁵ Therefore, this is what the LORD of
•Hosts says concerning the prophets:

I am about to feed them •wormwood

and give them poisoned water
    to drink,
for from the prophets of Jerusalem
    ungodliness[a] has spread
    throughout the land.

Don't Listen to Prophets

16 This is what the LORD of Hosts says:
"Do not listen to the words of the prophets who prophesy to you. They are making
you worthless. They speak visions from
their own minds, not from the LORD's
mouth. 17 They keep on saying to those
who despise Me: The LORD has said: You
will have peace. To everyone who walks
in the stubbornness of his heart they have
said, No harm will come to you."

18 For who has stood in the council
        of the LORD
    to see and hear His word?
    Who has paid attention to His word
        and obeyed?
19 Look, a storm from the LORD!
    Wrath has gone forth,
    a whirling storm.
    It will whirl about the head
        of the wicked.
20 The LORD's anger will not turn back
    until He has completely fulfilled
        the purposes of His heart.
    In time to come you will
        understand it clearly.

21 I did not send these prophets,
    yet they ran ⌊with a message⌋.
    I did not speak to them,
    yet they prophesied.
22 If they had really stood
        in My council,
    they would have enabled
        My people to hear My words
    and would have turned them back
        from their evil ways
    and their evil deeds.

A God Who is Near and Far Away

23 "Am I a God who is only near"—
⌊this is⌋ the LORD's declaration—"and not
a God who is far away? 24 Can a man
hide himself in secret places where I
cannot see him?"—the LORD's declaration. "Do I not fill the heavens and the
earth?"—the LORD's declaration.

Prophets' Dreams

25 "I have heard what the prophets who
prophesy a lie in My name have said: I
had a dream! I had a dream! 26 How long
will this continue in the minds of the
prophets prophesying lies, prophets of the
deceit of their own minds? 27 Through
their dreams that they tell one another,
they make plans to cause My people to
forget My name as their fathers forgot My
name through Baal worship. 28 The
prophet who has ⌊only⌋ a dream should re-
count the dream, but the one who has My
word should speak My word truthfully, for
what is straw ⌊compared⌋ to grain?"—the
LORD's declaration. 29 "Is not My word like
fire"—the LORD's declaration—"and like a
sledgehammer that pulverizes rock?
30 Therefore, take note! I am against the
prophets"—the   LORD's   declaration—
"who steal My words from each other. 31 I
am against the prophets"—the LORD's
declaration—"who use their own tongues
to deliver an oracle. 32 I am against those
who prophesy false dreams"—the LORD's
declaration—"telling them and leading
My people astray with their falsehoods
and their boasting. It was not I who sent
or commanded them, and they are of no
benefit at all to these people"—⌊this is⌋ the
LORD's declaration.

Burden of the LORD

33 "Now when these people or a
prophet or a priest asks you: What is the

a23:15 Or pollution

burden of the LORD? you will respond to them: What is the burden? I will throw you away"—⌐this is⌐ the LORD's declaration. ³⁴ "As for the prophet, priest, or people who say: The burden of the LORD, I will punish that man and his household. ³⁵ This is what each man is to say to his friend and to his brother: What has the LORD answered? or What has the LORD spoken? ³⁶ But no longer refer toᵃ the burden of the LORD, for each man's word becomes his burden and you pervert the words of the living God, the LORD of Hosts, our God. ³⁷ You must say to the prophet: What has the LORD answered you? and What has the LORD spoken? ³⁸ But if you say: The burden of the LORD, then this is what the LORD says: Because you have said, The burden of the LORD, and I specifically told you not to say, The burden of the LORD, ³⁹ I will surely forget youᵇ and throw away from My presence both you and the city that I gave you and your fathers. ⁴⁰ I will bring on you everlasting shame and humiliation that will never be forgotten."

Good and Bad Figs

24 After Nebuchadnezzar king of Babylon had deported Jeconiahᶜ son of Jehoiakim king of Judah, the officials of Judah, and the craftsmen and metalsmiths from Jerusalem and had brought them to Babylon, the LORD showed me two baskets of figs placed before the temple of the LORD. ² One basket ⌐contained⌐ very good figs, like early figs, but the other basket contained very bad figs, so bad they were inedible. ³ The LORD said to me, "What do you see, Jeremiah?" I said, "Figs! The good figs are very good, but the bad figs are extremely bad, so bad they are inedible."

⁴ The word of the LORD came to me: ⁵ "This is what the LORD, the God of Israel, says: Like these good figs, so I regard as good the exiles from Judah I sent away from this place to the land of the Chaldeans. ⁶ I will keep My eyes on them for their good and will return them to this land. I will build them up and not demolish them; I will plant them and not uproot them. ⁷ I will give them a heart to know Me, that I am the LORD. They will be My people, and I will be their God because they will return to Me with all their heart.

⁸ "But as for the bad figs, so bad they are inedible, this is what the LORD says: in this way I will deal with Zedekiah king of Judah, his officials, and the remnant of Jerusalem—those remaining in this land and those living in the land of Egypt. ⁹ I will make them an object of horror and disaster to all the kingdoms of the earth, a disgrace, an object of scorn, ridicule, and cursing, wherever I have banished them. ¹⁰ I will send the sword, famine, and plague against them until they have perished from the land I gave to them and their ancestors."

Seventy-Year Exile

25 ⌐This is⌐ the word that came to Jeremiah concerning all the people of Judah in the fourth year of Jehoiakim son of Josiah, king of Judah (which was the first year of Nebuchadnezzar king of Babylon). ² The prophet Jeremiah spoke concerning all the people of Judah and all the residents of Jerusalem as follows: ³ "From the thirteenth year of Josiah son of Amon, king of Judah, until this very day—23 years—the word of the LORD has come to me, and I have spoken to you time and time again,ᵈ but you have not obeyed. ⁴ The LORD sent all His ser-

---

ᵃ**23:36** Or *longer remember*   ᵇ**23:39** Some Hb mss; other Hb mss, LXX, Syr, Vg read *surely lift you up*   ᶜ**24:1** = Jehoiachin; Jr 52:31-34; 2 Kg 24:6-15; 25:27-30   ᵈ**25:3** Lit *you; rising early and speaking*

vants the prophets to you time and time again,[a] but you have not obeyed or even paid attention.[b] [5] He announced, 'Turn, each of you, from your[c] evil way of life and from your evil deeds. Live in the land the LORD gave to you and your ancestors forever and ever. [6] Do not follow other gods to serve them and to worship them, and do not provoke Me to anger by the work of your hands. Then I will do you no harm.

[7] "'But you would not obey Me'—⌐this is⌐ the LORD's declaration—'in order that you might provoke Me to anger by the work of your hands and bring disaster on yourselves.'

[8] "Therefore, this is what the LORD of •Hosts says: 'Because you have not obeyed My words, [9] I am going to send for all the families of the north'—⌐this is⌐ the LORD's declaration—'and ⌐send for⌐ My servant Nebuchadnezzar king of Babylon, and I will bring them against this land, against its residents, and against all these surrounding nations, and I will •completely destroy them and make them a desolation, a derision, and ruins forever. [10] I will eliminate the sound of joy and gladness from them—the voice of the bridegroom and the bride, the sound of the millstones and the light of the lamp. [11] This whole land will become a desolate ruin, and these nations will serve the king of Babylon for 70 years. [12] When the 70 years are completed, I will punish the king of Babylon and that nation'—⌐this is⌐ the LORD's declaration—'the land of the Chaldeans, for their guilt, and I will make it a ruin forever. [13] I will bring on that land all My words I have spoken against it, all that is written in this book that Jeremiah prophesied against all the nations. [14] For many nations and great kings will en-

slave them, and I will repay them according to their deeds and the work of their hands.'"

Cup of God's Wrath

[15] This is what the LORD, the God of Israel, said to me: "Take this cup of the wine of wrath from My hand and make all the nations I am sending you to drink from it. [16] They will drink, stagger,[d] and go out of their minds because of the sword I am sending among them."

[17] So I took the cup from the LORD's hand and made all the nations drink ⌐from it⌐, everyone the LORD sent me to. [18] ⌐These included:⌐

Jerusalem and the ⌐other⌐ cities of Judah, its kings and its officials, to make them a desolate ruin, an object of scorn and cursing—as it is today;
[19] Pharaoh king of Egypt, his officers, his leaders, all his people,
[20] and all the mixed peoples;
all the kings of the land of Uz;
all the kings of the land of the Philistines—Ashkelon, Gaza, Ekron, and the remnant of Ashdod;
[21] Edom, Moab, and the Ammonites;
[22] all the kings of Tyre,
all the kings of Sidon,
and the kings of the coastlands across the sea;
[23] Dedan, Tema, Buz, and all those who shave their temples;[e]
[24] all the kings of Arabia,
and all the kings of the mixed peoples who have settled in the desert;
[25] all the kings of Zimri,
all the kings of Elam,
and all the kings of Media;

---

[a] **25:4** Lit *prophets, rising early and sending* [b] **25:4** Lit *even inclined your ears* [c] **25:5** Lit *his* [d] **25:16** Or *vomit*
[e] **25:23** Or *who live in distant places*; Jr 9:26; 49:32; Lv 19:27

26 all the kings of the north, both near and far from one another; that is, all the kingdoms of the world which are on the face of the earth. Finally, the king of Sheshacha will drink after them.

27 "Then you are to say to them: This is what the LORD of Hosts, the God of Israel, says: Drink, get drunk, and vomit. Fall down and never get up again, as a result of the sword I am sending among you. 28 Ifb they refuse to take the cup from you and drink, you are to say to them: This is what the LORD of Hosts says: You must drink! 29 For I am already bringing disaster on the city that bears My name, so how could you possibly go unpunished? You will not go unpunished, for I am summoning a sword against all the inhabitants of the earth"—ᵢthis isᵢ the declaration of the LORD of Hosts.

Judgment on the Whole World

30 "As for you, you are to prophesy all these things to them, and say to them:

The LORD roars from on high;
He raises His voice
 from His holy dwelling.
He roars loudly
 over His grazing land;
He calls out with a shout, like those
 who tread ᵢgrapesᵢ,
against all the inhabitants
 of the earth.
31 The tumult reaches to the ends
 of the earth
because the LORD brings a case
 against the nations.
He enters into judgment
 with all flesh.

As for the wicked,
He hands them over
 to the sword—
 ᵢThis isᵢ the LORD's declaration.

32 "This is what the LORD of Hosts says:

Pay attention! Disaster goes forth
from nation to nation.
A great storm is stirred up
from the ends of the earth."

33 Those slain by the LORD on that day will be ᵢspreadᵢ from one end of the earth to the other. They will not be mourned, gathered, or buried. They will be like manure on the surface of the ground.

34 Wail, you shepherds, and cry out.
 Roll ᵢin the dustᵢ,c you leaders
  of the flock.
 Because the days of your slaughter
  have come,
 you will fall and become shattered
  like a precious vase.
35 Flight will be impossible
  for the shepherds,
 and escape, for the leaders
  of the flock.
36 ᵢHearᵢ the sound
  of the shepherds' cry,
 the wail of the leaders of the flock,
 for the LORD is destroying
  their pasture.
37 Peaceful grazing land
  will become lifeless
 because of
  the LORD's burning anger.
38 He has left His den like a lion,
 for their land has become
  a desolation
 because of the swordd
  of the oppressor,
 because of His burning anger.

a25:26 Probably a code name for Babylon   b25:28 Or When   c25:34 = a mourning custom   d25:38 Some Hb mss, LXX, Tg; other Hb mss read burning; Jr 46:16

Jeremiah's Speech in the Temple

26 At the beginning of the reign of Jehoiakim son of Josiah, king of Judah, this word came from the LORD: ² "This is what the LORD says: Stand in the courtyard of the LORD's temple and speak all the words I have commanded you to speak to all Judah's cities that are coming to worship there. Do not hold back a word. ³ Perhaps they will listen and return—each from his evil way of life—so that I might relent concerning the disaster that I plan to do to them because of the evil of their deeds. ⁴ You are to say to them: This is what the LORD says: If you do not listen to Me by living according to My law that I set before you ⁵ and by listening to the words of My servants the prophets I have been sending you time and time again,ᵃ though you did not listen, ⁶ I will make this temple like Shiloh. I will make this city an object of cursing for all the nations of the earth."

Jeremiah Seized

⁷ The priests, the prophets, and all the people heard Jeremiah speaking these words in the temple of the LORD. ⁸ He finished the address the LORD had commanded him to deliver to all the people. Then the priests, the prophets, and all the people took hold of him, yelling, "You must surely die! ⁹ How dare you prophesy in the name of the LORD, 'This temple will become like Shiloh and this city will become an uninhabited ruin'!" Then all the people assembled against Jeremiah at the LORD's temple.

¹⁰ When the officials of Judah heard these things, they went up from the king's palace to the LORD's temple and sat at the entrance of the New Gate.ᵇ ¹¹ Then the priests and prophets said to the officials and all the people, "This man deserves the death sentence because he has prophesied against this city, as you have heard with your own ears."

Jeremiah's Defense

¹² Then Jeremiah said to all the officials and the people, "The LORD sent me to prophesy all the words that you have heard against this temple and city. ¹³ So now, correct your ways and deeds and obey the voice of the LORD your God so that He might relent concerning the disaster that He warned about. ¹⁴ As for me, here I am in your hands; do to me what you think is good and right. ¹⁵ But know for certain that if you put me to death, you will bring innocent blood on yourselves, on this city, and on its residents, for it is certain the LORD has sent me to speak all these things directly to you."

Jeremiah Released

¹⁶ Then the officials and all the people told the priests and prophets, "This man doesn't deserve the death sentence, for he has spoken to us in the name of the LORD our God!"

¹⁷ Some of the elders of the land stood up and said to all the assembled people, ¹⁸ "Micah the Moreshite prophesied in the days of Hezekiah king of Judah and said to all the people of Judah, 'This is what the LORD of •Hosts says:

Zion will be plowed like a field,
Jerusalem will become ruins,
and the temple mount
a forested hill.'

¹⁹ Did Hezekiah king of Judah and all ⌊the people of⌋ Judah put him to death? Did he not •fear the LORD and plead for the

---

ᵃ**26:5** Lit *you, rising early and sending*   ᵇ**26:10** Some Hb mss, Syr, Tg, Vg add *of the house*

LORD's favor,[a] and did not the LORD relent concerning the disaster He had pronounced against them? We are about to bring great harm on ourselves!"

Prophet Uriah Executed

20 Another man was also prophesying in the name of the LORD—Uriah son of Shemaiah from Kiriath-jearim. He prophesied against this city and against this land in words like all those of Jeremiah. 21 King Jehoiakim, all his warriors, and all the officials heard his words, and the king tried to put him to death. When Uriah heard, he fled in fear and went to Egypt. 22 But King Jehoiakim sent men to Egypt: Elnathan son of Achbor and ˌcertain otherˌ men with him ˌwentˌ to Egypt. 23 They brought Uriah out of Egypt and took him to King Jehoiakim, who executed him with the sword and threw his corpse into the burial place of the common people.[b]

24 But Ahikam son of Shaphan supported Jeremiah, so he was not handed over to the people to be put to death.

Jeremiah: Yoke of Babylon

27 At the beginning of the reign of Zedekiah[c] son of Josiah, king of Judah, this word came to Jeremiah from the LORD:[d] 2 "This is what the LORD said to me: Make fetters and yoke bars for yourself and put them on your neck. 3 Send ˌwordˌ to the king of Edom, the king of Moab, the king of the Ammonites, the king of Tyre, and the king of Sidon through messengers who are coming to Zedekiah king of Judah in Jerusalem. 4 Command them ˌto goˌ to their masters, saying: This is what the LORD of •Hosts, the God of Israel, says: This is what you must say to your masters: 5 By My great strength and out-stretched arm, I made the earth, and the people, and animals on the face of the earth. I give it to anyone I please.[e] 6 So now I have placed all these lands under the authority of My servant Nebuchadnezzar, king of Babylon. I have even given him the wild animals to serve him. 7 All nations will serve him, his son, and his grandson until the time for his own land comes, and then many nations and great kings will enslave him.

8 "As for the nation or kingdom that does not serve Nebuchadnezzar king of Babylon and does not place its neck under the yoke of the king of Babylon, that nation I will punish by sword, famine, and plague"—ˌthis isˌ the LORD's declaration—"until through him I have destroyed it. 9 But as for you, do not listen to your prophets, your diviners, your dreamers, your fortune-tellers, or your sorcerers who say to you: Don't serve the king of Babylon! 10 for they prophesy a lie to you so that you will be removed from your land. I will banish you, and you will perish. 11 But as for the nation that will put its neck under the yoke of the king of Babylon and serve him, I will leave it in its own land, and that nation will till[f] it and reside in it." ˌThis isˌ the LORD's declaration.

Jeremiah Warns Zedekiah

12 I spoke to Zedekiah king of Judah in the same way: "Put your necks under the yoke of the king of Babylon, serve him and his people, and live! 13 Why should you and your people die by the sword, famine, or plague as the LORD has threatened against any nation that does not serve the king of Babylon? 14 Do not listen to the words of the prophets who are telling you, 'You must not serve the king of Babylon,' for they are prophesy-

ing a lie to you. [15] 'I have not sent them'—this is the LORD's declaration— 'and they are prophesying falsely in My name; therefore, I will banish you, and you will perish—you and the prophets who are prophesying to you.'"

Jeremiah Warns Priests and People

[16] Then I spoke to the priests and all these people, saying, "This is what the LORD says, 'Do not listen to the words of your prophets. They are prophesying to you, claiming: Look, very soon now the articles of the LORD's temple will be brought back from Babylon. They are prophesying a lie to you. [17] Do not listen to them. Serve the king of Babylon and live! Why should this city become a ruin? [18] If they are indeed prophets and if the word of the LORD is with them, let them intercede with the LORD of Hosts not to let the articles that remain in the LORD's temple, in the palace of the king of Judah, and in Jerusalem go to Babylon.' [19] For this is what the LORD of Hosts says about the pillars, the sea, the water carts, and the rest of the articles that still remain in this city, [20] those Nebuchadnezzar king of Babylon did not take when he deported Jeconiah[a] son of Jehoiakim, king of Judah, from Jerusalem to Babylon along with all the nobles of Judah and Jerusalem. [21] Yes, this is what the LORD of Hosts, the God of Israel, says about the articles that remain in the temple of the LORD, in the palace of the king of Judah, and in Jerusalem: [22] 'They will be brought to Babylon and will remain there until I attend to them again.' This is the LORD's declaration. 'Then I will bring them up and restore them to this place.'"

Hananiah's False Prophecy

28 n that same year, at the beginning of the reign of Zedekiah king of Ju-

dah, in the fifth month of the fourth year, the prophet Hananiah son of Azzur from Gibeon said to me in the temple of the LORD in the presence of the priests and all the people, [2] "This is what the LORD of •Hosts, the God of Israel, says: 'I have broken the yoke of the king of Babylon. [3] Within two years I will restore to this place all the articles of the LORD's temple that Nebuchadnezzar king of Babylon took from here and transported to Babylon. [4] And I will restore to this place Jeconiah[b] son of Jehoiakim, king of Judah, and all the exiles from Judah who went to Babylon'—this is the LORD's declaration—'for I will break the yoke of the king of Babylon.'"

Jeremiah's Response to Hananiah

[5] The prophet Jeremiah replied to the prophet Hananiah in the presence of the priests and all the people who were standing in the temple of the LORD. [6] The prophet Jeremiah said, "•Amen! May the LORD do so. May the LORD make the words you have prophesied come true and may He restore the articles of the LORD's temple and all the exiles from Babylon to this place! [7] Only listen to this message I am speaking in your hearing and in the hearing of all the people. [8] The prophets who preceded you and me from ancient times prophesied war, disaster,[c] and plague against many lands and great kingdoms. [9] As for the prophet who prophesies peace—only when the word of the prophet comes true will the prophet be recognized as one whom the LORD has truly sent."

Hananiah Breaks Jeremiah's Yoke

[10] The prophet Hananiah then took the yoke bar from the neck of Jeremiah the prophet and broke it. [11] In the presence of all the people Hananiah proclaimed,

---

[a] **27:20** = Jehoiachin   [b] **28:4** = Jehoiachin   [c] **28:8** Some Hb mss, Vg read *famine*

"This is what the LORD says: 'In this way, within two years I will break the yoke of Nebuchadnezzar, king of Babylon, from the neck of all the nations.'" Jeremiah the prophet then went on his way.

LORD's Word against Hananiah

12 The word of the LORD came to Jeremiah after Hananiah the prophet had broken the yoke bar from the neck of Jeremiah the prophet: 13 "Go say to Hananiah: This is what the LORD says: You broke a wooden yoke bar, but in its place you will make an iron yoke bar. 14 For this is what the LORD of Hosts, the God of Israel, says: I have put an iron yoke on the neck of all these nations that they might serve Nebuchadnezzar king of Babylon, and they will serve him. I have also put the wild animals under him."

Jeremiah Rebukes, Hananiah Dies

15 The prophet Jeremiah said to the prophet Hananiah, "Listen, Hananiah! The LORD did not send you, but you have led these people to trust in a lie. 16 Therefore, this is what the LORD says: 'I am about to send you off the face of the earth. You will die this year because you have spoken rebellion against the LORD.'" 17 And the prophet Hananiah died that year in the seventh month.

Jeremiah's Letter to the Exiles

29 This is the text of the letter that Jeremiah the prophet sent from Jerusalem to the rest of the elders of the exiles, the priests, the prophets, and all the people Nebuchadnezzar had deported from Jerusalem to Babylon. 2 ⌊This was⌋ after King Jeconiah,ᵃ the queen mother, the court officials, the officials of Judah and Jerusalem, the craftsmen, and the metalsmiths had left Jerusalem.

3 ⌊The letter was sent⌋ by Elasah son of Shaphan and Gemariah son of Hilkiah whom Zedekiah king of Judah had sent to Babylon to Nebuchadnezzar king of Babylon. ⌊The letter⌋ stated:

4 This is what the LORD of •Hosts, the God of Israel, says to all the exiles I deported from Jerusalem to Babylon: 5 "Build houses and live ⌊in them⌋. Plant gardens and eat their produce. 6 Take wives and have sons and daughters. Take wives for your sons and give your daughters to men ⌊in marriage⌋ so that they may bear sons and daughters. Multiply there; do not decrease. 7 Seek the welfare of the city I have deported you to. Pray to the LORD on its behalf, for when it has prosperity, you will prosper."

8 For this is what the LORD of Hosts, the God of Israel, says: "Don't let your prophets who are among you and your diviners deceive you, and don't listen to the dreams you elicit from them, 9 for they are prophesying falsely to you in My name. I have not sent them." ⌊This is⌋ the LORD's declaration.

10 For this is what the LORD says: "When 70 years for Babylon are complete, I will attend to you and will confirm My promise concerning you to restore you to this place. 11 For I know the plans I have for you"—⌊this is⌋ the LORD's declaration—"plans for ⌊your⌋ welfare, not for disaster, to give you a future and a hope. 12 You will call to Me and come and pray to Me, and I will listen to you. 13 You will seek Me and find Me when you search for Me with all your heart. 14 I will be found

---

ᵃ**29:2** = Jehoiachin

by you"—the LORD's declaration—"and I will restore your fortunes[a] and gather you from all the nations and places where I banished you"—the LORD's declaration. "I will restore you to the place I deported you from."

15 You have said, "The LORD has raised up prophets for us in Babylon!" 16 But this is what the LORD says concerning the king sitting on David's throne and concerning all the people living in this city—that is, concerning your brothers who did not go with you into exile. 17 This is what the LORD of Hosts says: "I am about to send against them sword, famine, and plague and will make them like rotten figs that are inedible because they are so bad. 18 I will pursue them with sword, famine, and plague. I will make them a horror to all the kingdoms of the earth—a curse and a desolation, an object of scorn and a disgrace among all the nations where I will have banished them. 19 ⌊I will do this⌋ because they have not listened to My words"—⌊this is⌋ the LORD's declaration—"that I sent to them with My servants the prophets time and time again.[b] And you too have not listened." ⌊This is⌋ the LORD's declaration.

20 Hear the word of the LORD, all you exiles I have sent from Jerusalem to Babylon. 21 This is what the LORD of Hosts, the God of Israel, says to Ahab son of Kolaiah and to Zedekiah son of Maaseiah, the ones prophesying a lie to you in My name: "I am about to hand them over to Nebuchadnezzar king of Babylon, and he will kill them before your very eyes. 22 Based on ⌊what happens to⌋ them, all the exiles of Judah who are in Babylon will create a curse that says: May the LORD make you like Zedekiah and Ahab, whom the king of Babylon roasted in the fire! 23 because they have committed an outrage in Israel by committing adultery with their neighbors' wives and have spoken a lie in My name, which I did not command them. I am He who knows, and I am a witness." ⌊This is⌋ the LORD's declaration.

24 To Shemaiah the Nehelamite you are to say, 25 "This is what the LORD of Hosts, the God of Israel, says: You[c] in your own name have sent out letters to all the people of Jerusalem, to the priest Zephaniah son of Maaseiah, and to all the priests, saying: 26 The LORD has appointed you priest in place of Jehoiada the priest to be the chief officer in the temple of the LORD, responsible for every madman who acts like a prophet. You must confine him in stocks and an iron collar. 27 So now, why have you not rebuked Jeremiah of Anathoth who has been acting like a prophet among you? 28 For he has sent ⌊word⌋ to us in Babylon, claiming: The exile will be long. Build houses and settle down. Plant gardens and eat their produce."

29 Zephaniah the priest read this letter in the hearing of Jeremiah the prophet.

Message about Shemaiah

30 Then the word of the LORD came to Jeremiah: 31 "Send ⌊a message⌋ to all the exiles, saying: This is what the LORD says

---

a29:14 Or will end your captivity   b29:19 Lit prophets, rising up early and sending   c29:25 Lit Because you concerning Shemaiah the Nehelamite. Because Shemaiah prophesied to you, though I did not send him, and made you trust a lie, 32 this is what the LORD says: I am about to punish Shemaiah the Nehelamite and his descendants. There will not be even one of his ⌊descendants⌋ living among these people, nor will any ever see the good that I will bring to My people"—⌊this is⌋ the LORD's declaration—"for he has preached rebellion against the LORD."

Restoration from Captivity

30 ⌊This is⌋ the word that came to Jeremiah from the LORD. 2 This is what the LORD, the God of Israel, says: "Write down on a scroll all the words that I have spoken to you, 3 for the days are certainly coming"—⌊this is⌋ the LORD's declaration—"when I will restore the fortunesª of My people Israel and Judah"—the LORD's declaration. "I will restore them to the land I gave to their ancestors and they will possess it."

4 These are the words the LORD spoke to Israel and Judah. 5 Yes, this is what the LORD says:

We have heard a cry of terror,
    of dread—there is no peace.
6   Ask and see
    whether a male can give birth.
    Why then do I see every man
    with his hands on his stomach
        like a woman in labor
    and every face turned pale?
7   How awful that day will be!
    There will be none like it!
    It will be a time of trouble
        for Jacob,
    but he will be delivered out of it.

8 "On that day"—⌊this is⌋ the declaration of the LORD of •Hosts—"I will break his yoke from your neck and snap your fetters so strangers will never again enslave him. 9 They will serve the LORD their God and I will raise up David their king for them."

10 As for you, My servant Jacob,
        do not be afraid—
        ⌊this is⌋ the LORD's declaration—
    and do not be dismayed, Israel,
    for I will without fail save you
        from far away,
    your descendants, from the land
        of their captivity!
    Jacob will return and have calm
        and quiet
    with no one to frighten him.
11 For I will be with you—
        ⌊this is⌋ the LORD's declaration—
        to save you!
    I will bring destruction
        on all the nations
    where I have scattered you;
    however, I will not
        bring destruction on you.
    I will discipline you justly,
    but I will by no means
        leave you unpunished.

Healing Zion's Wounds

12 For this is what the LORD says:

    Your injury is incurable;
        your wound most severe.
13 No one takes up the case
        for your sores.
    You have nothing that can heal you.
14 All your lovers have forgotten you;
        they no longer look for you,
    for I have struck you
        like an enemy would,
    with the discipline
        of someone cruel,
    because of your enormous guilt
    and your innumerable sins.

ª**30:3** Or will end the captivity

Guilt and Sin Cause Misfortune

15 Why do you cry out
      about your injury?
   Your pain has no cure!
   I have done these things to you
   because of your enormous guilt
   and your innumerable sins.
16 Nevertheless, all who devoured you
      will be devoured,
   and all your adversaries—
      all of them—
   will go off into exile.
   Your despoilers will become spoil,
   and all who plunder you
      will be plundered.
17 But I will bring you health
   and will heal you of your wounds—
      ⌊this is⌋ the LORD's declaration—
   for they call you The Outcast,
   that Zion no one cares about.

Restoration of the Land

18 This is what the LORD says:

   I will certainly restore the fortunesᵃ
      of Jacob's tents
   and show compassion
      on his dwellings.
   Every city will be rebuilt
      on its mound;
   every citadel will stand
      on its proper site.
19 Thanksgiving will come
      out of them,
   a sound of celebration.
   I will multiply them,
      and they will not decrease;
   I will honor them, and they will not
      be insignificant.
20 His children will be as in past days;
   his congregation will be established
      in My presence.
   I will punish all his oppressors.
21 Jacob's leader will be one of them;
   his ruler will issue from him.

I will invite him to Me, and he will
      approach Me,
   for who would otherwise
      risk his life to approach Me?
         ⌊This is⌋ the LORD's declaration.
22 You will be My people,
   and I will be your God.

Wrath of God

23 Look, a storm from the LORD!
   Wrath has gone forth.
   A churning storm,
   it will whirl about the head
      of the wicked.
24 The LORD's burning anger will not
      turn back
   until He has completely fulfilled
      the purposes of His heart.
   In time to come you will
      understand it.

God's Faithful Love
for His People

31 "At that time"—⌊this is⌋ the LORD's
declaration—"I will be God of all
the families of Israel, and they will be
My people."
   2 This is what the LORD says:

   They found favor
      in the wilderness—
   the people who survived the sword.
   ⌊When⌋ Israel went to find rest,
3   the LORD appeared to himᵇ
      from far away.
   I have loved you
      with an everlasting love;
   therefore, I have continued
      to extend faithful love to you.
4 Again I will build you so that
      you will be rebuilt,
   Virgin Israel.
   You will take up
      your tambourines again
   and go forth in joyful dancing.

ᵃ**30:18** Or *certainly end the captivity*   ᵇ**31:3** LXX; MT reads *me*

5 You will plant vineyards again
   on the mountains of Samaria;
   the planters will plant
      and will enjoy ⌊the fruit⌋.
6 For there will be a day
      when watchmen will call out
   in the hill country of Ephraim:
   Get up, let's go up to Zion,
   to the LORD our God!

God Returns People Home

7 For this is what the LORD says:

   Sing with joy for Jacob;
   shout for the chief of the nations!
   Proclaim, praise, and say:
   LORD, save Your people,
      the remnant of Israel!
8 Watch! I am going to bring them
      from the northern land.
   I will gather them
      from remote regions
         of the earth—
   the blind and the lame will be
      with them,
   along with those who are pregnant
      and those about to give birth.
   They will return here
      as a great assembly!
9 They will come weeping,
   but I will bring them back
      with consolation.[a]
   I will lead them to •wadis ⌊filled⌋
      with water
   by a smooth way where
      they will not stumble,
   for I am Israel's Father,
   and Ephraim is My firstborn.
10 Nations, hear the word of the LORD,
    and tell it among the
       far off coastlands!
    Say: The One who scattered Israel
       will gather him.
    He will watch over him
       as a shepherd ⌊guards⌋ his flock,

11 for the LORD has ransomed Jacob
    and redeemed him from the power
       of one stronger than he.
12 They will come and shout for joy
       on the heights of Zion;
    they will be radiant with joy
    because of the LORD's goodness,
    because of the grain, the new wine,
       the fresh oil,
    and because of the young
       of the flocks and herds.
    Their life will be
       like an irrigated garden,
    and they will no longer grow weak
       ⌊from hunger⌋.
13 Then the virgin will rejoice
       with dancing,
    while young and old men
       ⌊rejoice⌋ together.
    I will turn their mourning
       into joy,
    give them consolation,
    and ⌊bring⌋ happiness out of grief.
14 I will give the priests their fill
       with abundance,[b]
    and My people will be satisfied
       with My goodness.
          ⌊This is⌋ the LORD's declaration.

Lament Turned to Joy

15 This is what the LORD says:

    A voice was heard in Ramah,
    a lament with bitter weeping—
    Rachel weeping for her children,
    refusing to be comforted
       for her children
    because they are no more.

16 This is what the LORD says:

    Keep your voice from weeping
    and your eyes from tears,
    for the reward for your work
       will come—
          ⌊this is⌋ the LORD's declaration—

---

[a]31:9 LXX; MT reads *supplications*   [b]31:14 Lit *fatness*

and your children will return
   from the enemy's land.
17 There is hope for your future—
      ⌐this is⌐ the LORD's declaration—
   and your children will return
      to their own territory.
18 I have heard Ephraim moaning:
   You disciplined me,
      and I have been disciplined
   like an untrained calf.
   Restore me, and I will return,
   for you, LORD, are my God.
19 After I returned, I repented;
   After I was instructed, I struck
      my thigh ⌐in grief⌐.
   I was ashamed and humiliated
   because I bore the disgrace
      of my youth.
20 Isn't Ephraim a precious son to Me,
      a delightful child?
   Whenever I speak against him,
   I certainly still think about him.
   Therefore, My inner being yearns
      for him;
   I will truly have compassion
      on him.
         ⌐This is⌐ the LORD's declaration.

Repentance and Restoration

21 Set up road markers for yourself;
   establish signposts!
   Keep the highway in mind,
   the way you have traveled.
   Return, Virgin Israel!
   Return to these cities of yours.
22 How long will you turn
      here and there,
   faithless daughter?
   For the LORD creates
      something new in the land[a]—
   a female[b] will shelter[c] a man.

23 This is what the LORD of •Hosts, the
God of Israel, says: "When I restore their

fortunes,[d] they will once again speak this
word in the land of Judah and in its cities: May the LORD bless you, righteous
settlement, holy mountain. 24 Judah and
all its cities will live in it together—also
farmers and those who move[e] with the
flocks— 25 for I satisfy the thirsty person
and feed all those who are weak."

26 At this I awoke and looked around.
My sleep had been most pleasant to me.

27 "The days are coming"—⌐this is⌐ the
LORD's declaration—"when I will sow
the house of Israel and the house of Judah with the seed of man and the seed of
beast. 28 Just as I watched over them to
uproot and to tear them down, to demolish and to destroy, and to cause disaster,
so will I be attentive to build and to
plant them," says the LORD. 29 "In those
days, it will never again be said:

   The fathers have eaten sour grapes,
      and the children's teeth are set
         on edge.

30 Rather, each will die for his own
wrongdoing. Anyone who eats sour
grapes—his own teeth will be set on
edge.

New Covenant

31 "Look, the days are coming"—⌐this
is⌐ the LORD's declaration—"when I will
make a new covenant with the house of
Israel and with the house of Judah.
32 ⌐This one will⌐ not be like the covenant I made with their ancestors when
I took them by the hand to bring them
out of the land of Egypt— a covenant
they broke even though I had married
them"— the LORD's declaration.
33 "Instead, this is the covenant I will
make with the house of Israel after
those days"— the LORD's declaration. "I
will place My law[f] within them and

---

[a]31:22 Or *new on earth*   [b]31:22 Or *woman*   [c]31:22 Or *female surrounds* (Dt 32:10; Ps 32:7,10), or *female courts*; Hb
obscure   [d]31:23 Or *I end their captivity*   [e]31:24 Tg, Vg, Aq, Sym; MT reads *and they will move*   [f]31:33 Or
instruction

write it on their hearts. I will be their God, and they will be My people. ³⁴ No longer will one teach his neighbor or his brother, saying: Know the LORD, for they will all know Me, from the least to the greatest of them"—the LORD's declaration. "For I will forgive their wrongdoing and never again remember their sin."

³⁵ This is what the LORD says:

The One who gives the sun for light
  by day,
the fixed order of moon and stars
  for light by night,
who stirs up the sea and makes
  its waves roar—
the LORD of Hosts is His name:
³⁶ If this fixed order departs
  from My presence—
    ⌐this is⌐ the LORD's declaration—
then also Israel's descendants
  will cease
to be a nation before Me forever.

³⁷ This is what the LORD says:

If the heavens above
  can be measured
and the foundations
  of the earth below explored,
I will reject all of
  Israel's descendants
because of all they have done—
    ⌐this is⌐ the LORD's declaration.

³⁸ "Look, the days are coming"—the LORD's declaration—"when the city^a from the Tower of Hananel to the Corner Gate will be rebuilt for the LORD. ³⁹ A measuring line will once again stretch out straight to the hill of Gareb and then turn toward Goah. ⁴⁰ The whole valley—the corpses, the ashes, and all the fields as far as the Kidron Valley to the corner of the Horse Gate to the east—will be holy to the LORD. It will never be uprooted or demolished again."

Jeremiah in Jail

32 ⌐This is⌐ the word that came to Jeremiah from the LORD in the tenth year of Zedekiah king of Judah, which was the eighteenth year of Nebuchadnezzar. ² At that time, the army of the king of Babylon was besieging Jerusalem, and Jeremiah the prophet was imprisoned in the guard's courtyard in the palace of the king of Judah. ³ Zedekiah king of Judah had imprisoned him, saying: "Why are you prophesying, 'This is what the LORD says: Look, I am about to hand this city over to Babylon's king, and he will capture it. ⁴ Zedekiah king of Judah will not escape from the Chaldeans; indeed, he will certainly be handed over to Babylon's king. They will speak face to face^b and meet eye to eye. ⁵ He will take Zedekiah to Babylon where he will stay until I attend to him'—⌐this is⌐ the LORD's declaration. 'You will fight the Chaldeans, but you will not succeed'?"

God Tells Jeremiah to Buy Land

⁶ Jeremiah replied, "The word of the LORD came to me: ⁷ 'Watch! Hanamel, the son of your uncle Shallum, is coming to you to say: Buy my field in Anathoth for yourself, for you own the right of redemption to buy it.'

⁸ "Then my cousin Hanamel ⌐came⌐ to the guard's courtyard as the LORD had said and urged me, 'Please buy my field in Anathoth in the land of Benjamin, for you own the right of inheritance and redemption. Buy it for yourself.' Then I knew that this was the word of the LORD. ⁹ So I bought the field in Anathoth from my cousin Hanamel, and I weighed out to him the money—17 •shekels^c of

---

^a**31:38** = Jerusalem   ^b**32:4** Lit *His mouth will speak with his mouth*   ^c**32:9** About 7 ounces

silver. [10] I recorded it on a scroll, sealed it, called in witnesses, and weighed out the silver on a scale. [11] I took the purchase agreement—the sealed copy with its terms and conditions and the open copy— [12] and gave the purchase agreement to Baruch son of Neriah, son of Mahseiah. ⌊I did this⌋ in the sight of my cousin[a] Hanamel, the witnesses who were signing the purchase agreement, and all the Judeans sitting in the guard's courtyard.

Jeremiah Instructs
Baruch on Purchase

[13] "I instructed Baruch in their sight, [14] 'This is what the LORD of •Hosts, the God of Israel, says: Take these scrolls— this purchase agreement with the sealed copy and this open copy—and put them in an earthen storage jar so they will last a long time. [15] For this is what the LORD of Hosts, the God of Israel, says: Houses, fields, and vineyards will again be bought in this land.'

Jeremiah Prays for Land Deal

[16] "After I had given the purchase agreement to Baruch, son of Neriah, I prayed to the LORD: [17] Ah, Lord GOD! You Yourself made the heavens and earth by Your great power and with Your outstretched arm. Nothing is too difficult for You! [18] You show faithful love to thousands but lay the fathers' sins on their sons' laps after them, great and mighty God whose name is the LORD of Hosts, [19] the One great in counsel and mighty in deed, whose eyes are on all the ways of the sons of men in order to give to each person according to his ways and the result of his deeds. [20] You performed signs and wonders in the land of Egypt and do so to this very day both in Israel and among mankind. You made a name for Yourself, as ⌊is the case⌋ today. [21] You brought Your people Israel out of Egypt with signs and wonders, with a strong hand and an outstretched arm, and with great terror. [22] You gave them this land You swore ⌊to give⌋ to their ancestors, a land flowing with milk and honey. [23] They entered and possessed it, but they did not obey Your voice or live according to Your law. They failed to perform all You commanded them to do, and so You have brought all this disaster on them. [24] Look! Siege ramps have come against the city to capture it, and the city, as a result of the sword, famine, and plague, has been handed over to the Chaldeans who are fighting against it. What You have spoken has happened. Look, You can see it! [25] Yet You, Lord GOD, have said to me: Buy the field with silver and call in witnesses—even though the city has been handed over to the Chaldeans!"

God Assures Jeremiah

[26] Then the word of the LORD came to Jeremiah: [27] "Look, I am the LORD, the God of all flesh. Is anything too difficult for Me? [28] Therefore, this is what the LORD says: I am about to hand this city over to the Chaldeans, to Babylon's king Nebuchadnezzar, and he will capture it. [29] The Chaldeans who are going to fight against this city will come, set this city on fire, and burn it along with the houses where incense has been burned to •Baal on their rooftops and where drink offerings have been poured out to other gods to provoke Me to anger. [30] From their youth, the Israelites and Judeans have done nothing but what is evil in My sight! They have done nothing but provoke Me to anger by the work

[a]**32:12** Some Hb mss, LXX, Syr; other Hb mss read *uncle*

of their hands"—⌞this is⌟ the LORD's declaration— ³¹ "for this city has been up
against My wrath and fury from the day
it was built until now. I will therefore remove it from My presence, ³² because of
all the evil the Israelites and Judeans
have done to provoke Me to anger—
they, their kings, their officials, their
priests, and their prophets, the men of
Judah, and the residents of Jerusalem.
³³ They have turned their backs to Me
and not their faces. Though I taught
them time and time again,ᵇ they do not
listen and receive discipline. ³⁴ They
have placed their detestable things in
the house that is called by My name and
have defiled it. ³⁵ They have built the
•high places of Baal in the Valley of Hinnom to make their sons and daughters
pass through ⌞the fire⌟ to •Molech—
something I had not commanded them. I
had never entertained the thoughtᶜ that
they do this detestable act causing Judah
to sin!

God Will Return His People to Safety

³⁶ "Now therefore, this is what the
LORD, the God of Israel, says to this city
about which you said: It has been
handed over to Babylon's king through
sword, famine, and plague: ³⁷ I am about
to gather them from all the lands where I
have banished them in My wrath, rage,
and great fury, and I will return them to
this place and make them live in safety.
³⁸ They will be My people, and I will be
their God. ³⁹ I will give them one heart
and one way so that for their good and
for ⌞the good of⌟ their descendants after
them, they will •fear Me always.
⁴⁰ "I will make with them an everlasting covenant: I will never turn away
from doing good to them, and I will put
fear of Me in their hearts so they will

never again turn away from Me. ⁴¹ I will
rejoice over them to do what is good to
them, and I will plant them faithfully in
this land with all My mind and heart.
⁴² "For this is what the LORD says: Just
as I have brought all this great disaster
on these people, so am I about to bring
on them all the good I am promising
them. ⁴³ Fields will be bought in this
land about which you are saying: It's a
desolation without man or beast; it has
been handed over to the Chaldeans!
⁴⁴ Fields will be purchased with silver,
the transaction written on a scroll and
sealed, and witnesses will be called on in
the land of Benjamin, in the areas surrounding Jerusalem, and in Judah's cities—the cities of the hill country, the
cities of the Judean foothills, and the cities of the •Negev—because I will restore
their fortunes."ᵈ

⌞This is⌟ the LORD's declaration.

God Reassures Jeremiah

33 While he was still confined in the
guard's courtyard, the word of the
LORD came to Jeremiah a second time:
² "The LORD who made the earth,ᵉ the
LORD who forms it to establish it, the
LORD is His name, says this: ³ Call to Me
and I will answer you and tell you great
and wondrous things you do not know.
⁴ For this is what the LORD, the God of Israel, says concerning the houses of this
city and the palaces of Judah's kings, the
ones torn down ⌞for defense⌟ against the
siege ramps and the sword: ⁵ The people
coming to fight the Chaldeans will fill the
houses with the corpses of ⌞their own⌟
men I strike down in My wrath and rage.
I have hidden My face from this city because of all their evil. ⁶ Yet I will certainly bring health and healing to it and
will indeed heal them. I will let them ex-

ᵇ**32:33** Lit them, rising up early and teaching   ᶜ**32:35** Lit them, and it did not arise on My heart   ᵈ**32:44** Or will end
their captivity   ᵉ**33:2** LXX; MT reads made it

perience the abundance[a] of peace and truth. [7] I will restore the fortunes[b] of Judah and of Israel and will rebuild them as in former times. [8] I will purify them from all the wrongs they have committed against Me, and I will forgive all the wrongs they have committed against Me, rebelling against Me. [9] This city will bear on My behalf a name of joy, praise, and glory before all the nations of the earth, who will hear of all the good I will do for them. They will tremble with awe because of all the good and all the peace I will bring about for them.

God Promises Israel's Restoration

[10] "This is what the LORD says: In this place which you say is a ruin, without man or beast—that is, in Judah's cities and Jerusalem's streets that are a desolation without man, without inhabitant, and without beast—there will be heard again [11] a sound of joy and gladness, the voice of the bridegroom and the bride, and the voice of those saying,

Praise the LORD of •Hosts,
for the LORD is good;
His faithful love endures forever

as they bring thank offerings to the temple of the LORD. For I will restore the fortunes[b] of the land as in former times, says the LORD.

[12] "This is what the LORD of Hosts says: In this desolate place—without man or beast—and in all its cities there will once more be a grazing land where shepherds may rest flocks. [13] The flocks will again pass under the hands of the one who counts them in the cities of the hill country, the cities of the Judean foothills, the cities of the •Negev, the land of Benjamin—the cities surrounding Jerusalem and Judah's cities, says the LORD.

God Reaffirms Covenant with David

[14] "Look, the days are coming"—this is⌋ the LORD's declaration—"when I will fulfill the good promises that I have spoken concerning the house of Israel and the house of Judah. [15] In those days and at that time I will cause a Branch of righteousness to sprout up for David, and He will administer justice and righteousness in the land. [16] In those days Judah will be saved, and Jerusalem will dwell securely, and this is what she will be named: The LORD Is Our Righteousness. [17] For this is what the LORD says: David will never fail to have a man sitting on the throne of the house of Israel. [18] The Levitical priests will never fail to have a man always before Me to offer •burnt offerings, to burn •grain offerings, and to make sacrifices."

Coming of David's Son

[19] The word of the LORD came to Jeremiah: [20] "This is what the LORD says: If you can break My covenant with the day and My covenant with the night so that day and night cease to come at their regular time, [21] then also My covenant with My servant David may be broken so that he will not have a son reigning on his throne, and the Levitical priests will not be My ministers. [22] The hosts of heaven cannot be counted; the sand of the sea cannot be measured. So, too, I will make the descendants of My servant David and the Levites who minister to Me innumerable."

[23] The word of the LORD came to Jeremiah: [24] "Have you not noticed what these people have said? They say: The LORD has rejected the two families He had chosen. My people are treated with contempt and no longer regarded as a

---

[a]**33:6** Or *fragrance*; Hb obscure   [b]**33:7,11** Or *will end the captivity*

nation among them. ²⁵ This is what the LORD says: If I do not ⌊keep⌋ My covenant with the day and with the night and fail to establish the fixed order of heaven and earth, ²⁶ then I might also reject the •seed of Jacob and of My servant David—not taking from his descendants rulers over the descendants of Abraham, Isaac, and Jacob. Instead, I will restore their fortunes[a] and have compassion on them."

Jeremiah's Prediction of King Zedekiah's Defeat

34 ⌊This is⌋ the word that came to Jeremiah from the LORD when Nebuchadnezzar, king of Babylon, all his army, all the earthly kingdoms under his control, and all other nations were fighting against Jerusalem and all its surrounding cities: ² "This is what the LORD, the God of Israel, says: Go, speak to Zedekiah, king of Judah, and tell him: This is what the LORD says: I am about to hand this city over to the king of Babylon, and he will burn it down. ³ As for you, you will not escape from his hand but are certain to be captured and handed over to him. You will meet the king of Babylon eye to eye and speak face to face;[b] you will go to Babylon.

⁴ "Yet hear the LORD's word, Zedekiah, king of Judah. This is what the LORD says concerning you: You will not die by the sword; ⁵ you will die peacefully. There will be a burning ceremony for you just like the burning ceremonies for your fathers, the former kings who preceded you. Alas, lord! will be the lament for you, for I have spoken ⌊this⌋ word." ⌊This is⌋ the LORD's declaration.

⁶ So Jeremiah the prophet related all these words to Zedekiah king of Judah in Jerusalem ⁷ while the king of Babylon's army was attacking Jerusalem and all of Judah's remaining cities—against Lachish and Azekah, for only they were left among Judah's fortified cities.

People Double-cross Slaves

⁸ ⌊This is⌋ the word that came to Jeremiah from the LORD after King Zedekiah made a covenant with all the people who were in Jerusalem to proclaim freedom to them, ⁹ so each man would free his male and female Hebrew slaves and no one enslave his Judean brother. ¹⁰ All the officials and people who entered into covenant to free their male and female slaves—in order not to enslave them any longer—obeyed and freed them. ¹¹ Afterwards, however, they changed their minds and took back their male and female slaves they had freed and forced them to become slaves ⌊again⌋.

God Punishes the People

¹² Then the word of the LORD came to Jeremiah from the LORD: ¹³ "This is what the LORD, the God of Israel, says: I made a covenant with your ancestors when I brought them out of the land of Egypt, out of the place of slavery, saying: ¹⁴ At the end of seven years, each of you must free his Hebrew brother who sold himself[c] to you. He may serve you six years, but then you must send him out free from you. But your ancestors did not obey Me or pay any attention. ¹⁵ Today you repented and did what pleased Me, each of you proclaiming freedom for his neighbor. You made a covenant before Me at the temple called by My name. ¹⁶ But you have changed your minds and profaned My name. Each has taken back his male and female slaves who had been freed ⌊to go⌋ wherever they wanted, and you have ⌊again⌋ subjugated them to be your slaves.

---

[a]33:26 Or *instead end their captivity*   [b]34:3 Lit *and his mouth will speak to your mouth*   [c]34:14 Or *who was sold*

[17] "Therefore, this is what the LORD says: You have not obeyed Me by proclaiming freedom, each man for his brother and for his neighbor. I hereby proclaim freedom for you"—ˌthis isˌ the LORD's declaration—"to the sword, to plague, and to famine! I will make you a horror to all the earth's kingdoms. [18] As for those who disobeyed My covenant, not keeping the terms of the covenant they made before Me, I will treat them like the calf they cut in two in order to pass between its pieces. [19] The officials of Judah and Jerusalem, the court officials, the priests, and all the people of the land who passed between the pieces of the calf [20] will be handed over to their enemies, to those who want to take their life. Their corpses will become food for the birds of the sky and for the wild animals of the land. [21] I will hand Zedekiah king of Judah and his officials over to their enemies, to those who want to take their life, to the king of Babylon's army that is withdrawing. [22] I am about to give the command"—ˌthis isˌ the LORD's declaration—"and I will bring them back to this city. They will fight against it, capture it, and burn it down. I will make Judah's cities a desolation, without inhabitant."

Rechabites' Obedient Example

35 ˌThis isˌ the word that came to Jeremiah from the LORD in the days of Jehoiakim son of Josiah, king of Judah: [2] "Go to the house of the Rechabites, speak to them, and bring them to one of the chambers of the temple of the LORD to offer them a drink of wine."

[3] So I took Jaazaniah son of Jeremiah, son of Habazziniah, and his brothers and all his sons—the entire house of the Rechabites— [4] and I brought them into the temple of the LORD to a chamber ˌoccupied byˌ the sons of Hanan son of Igdaliah, a man of God, who had a chamber near the officials' chamber, which was above the chamber of Maaseiah son of Shallum the doorkeeper. [5] I set jars filled with wine and some cups before the sons of the house of the Rechabites and said to them, "Drink wine!"

Rechabites Refuse Wine

[6] But they replied, "We do not drink wine, for Jonadab, son of our ancestor Rechab, commanded: 'You and your sons must never drink wine. [7] You must not build a house or sow seed or plant a vineyard. ˌThose thingsˌ are not for you. Rather, you must live in tents your whole life, so you may live a long time on the soil where you stay as a resident alien.' [8] We have obeyed the voice of Jonadab, son of our ancestor Rechab, in all he commanded us. So we haven't drunk wine our whole life—we, our wives, our sons, and our daughters. [9] We also have not built houses to live in and do not have vineyard, field, or seed. [10] But we have lived in tents and have obeyed and done as our ancestor Jonadab commanded us. [11] However, when Nebuchadnezzar king of Babylon marched into the land, we said: Come, let's go into Jerusalem to get away from the Chaldean and Aramean armies. So we have been living in Jerusalem."

Lord Punishes Disobedience

[12] Then the word of the LORD came to Jeremiah: [13] "This is what the LORD of •Hosts, the God of Israel, says: Go, say to the men of Judah and the residents of Jerusalem: Will you not accept discipline by listening to My words?"—ˌthis isˌ the LORD's declaration. [14] "The words of Jonadab, son of Rechab, have been carried out. He commanded his sons not to

drink wine, and they have not drunk to this very day because they have obeyed their ancestor's command. But I have spoken to you time and time again,[a] and you have not obeyed Me! [15] Time and time again[b] I have sent you all My servants the prophets, proclaiming: Turn, each one from his evil way of life, and correct your actions. Stop following other gods to serve them. Live in the land that I gave you and your ancestors. But you would not pay attention or obey Me. [16] Yes, the sons of Jonadab son of Rechab carried out their ancestor's command he gave them, but these people have not obeyed Me. [17] Therefore, this is what the LORD, the God of Hosts, the God of Israel, says: I will certainly bring to Judah and to all the residents of Jerusalem all the disaster I have pronounced against them because I have spoken to them, but they have not obeyed, and I have called to them, but they would not answer."

Rechabites Rewarded for Obedience

[18] Jeremiah said to the house of the Rechabites: "This is what the LORD of Hosts, the God of Israel, says: 'Because you have obeyed the command of your ancestor Jonadab and have kept all his commands and have done all that he commanded you, [19] this is what the LORD of Hosts, the God of Israel, says: Jonadab son of Rechab will never fail to have a man to always stand before Me.'"

God Orders Scroll

36 In the fourth year of Jehoiakim son of Josiah, king of Judah, this word came to Jeremiah from the LORD: [2] "Take a scroll, and write on it all the words I have spoken to you concerning Israel, Judah, and all the nations from the time I ⌊first⌋ spoke to you during Josiah's reign until today. [3] Perhaps, when the house of Judah hears about all the disaster I am planning to bring on them, each one of them will turn from his evil way. Then I will forgive their wrongdoing and sin."

Jeremiah Dictates Scroll to Baruch

[4] So Jeremiah summoned Baruch son of Neriah. At Jeremiah's dictation,[c] Baruch wrote on a scroll all the words the LORD had spoken to Jeremiah. [5] Then Jeremiah commanded Baruch, "I am restricted; I cannot enter the temple of the LORD, [6] so you must go and read from the scroll—which you wrote at my dictation[d]—the words of the LORD in the hearing of the people at the temple of the LORD on a day of fasting. You must also read them in the hearing of all the Judeans who are coming from their cities. [7] Perhaps their petition will come before the LORD, and each one will turn from his evil way, for the anger and fury that the LORD has pronounced against this people are great." [8] So Baruch son of Neriah did everything Jeremiah the prophet had commanded him. At the LORD's temple he read the LORD's words from the scroll.

Baruch Reads Scroll

[9] In the fifth year of Jehoiakim son of Josiah, king of Judah, in the ninth month, all the people of Jerusalem and all those coming in from Judah's cities into Jerusalem proclaimed a fast before the LORD. [10] Then at the LORD's temple, in the chamber of Gemariah son of Shaphan the scribe, in the upper courtyard at the opening of the New Gate of the LORD's temple, in the hearing of all the

---

[a]**35:14** Lit you, rising up early and speaking   [b]**35:15** Lit Rising up early and sending   [c]**36:4** Lit From Jeremiah's mouth   [d]**36:6** Lit wrote from my mouth

people, Baruch read Jeremiah's words from the scroll.

11 When Micaiah son of Gemariah, son of Shaphan, heard all the words of the LORD from the scroll, 12 he went down to the scribe's chamber in the king's palace. All the officials were sitting there—Elishama the scribe, Delaiah son of Shemaiah, Elnathan son of Achbor, Gemariah son of Shaphan, Zedekiah son of Hananiah, and all the other officials. 13 Micaiah reported to them all the words he had heard when Baruch read from the scroll in the hearing of the people. 14 Then all the officials sent ⌊word⌋ to Baruch through Jehudi son of Nethaniah, son of Shelemiah, son of Cushi, saying, "Bring the scroll that you read in the hearing of the people, and come." So Baruch son of Neriah took the scroll and went to them. 15 They said to him, "Sit down and read ⌊it⌋ in our hearing." So Baruch read ⌊it⌋ in their hearing.

Officials Fear Words

16 When they had heard all the words, they turned to each other in fear and said to Baruch, "We must surely tell the king all these things." 17 Then they asked Baruch, "Tell us—how did you write all these words? At his dictation?"a 18 Baruch said to them, "At his dictation.a He recited all these words to me while I was writing on the scroll in ink."

Jehoiakim Burns Scroll

19 The officials said to Baruch, "You and Jeremiah must hide yourselves and tell no one where you are." 20 Then they came to the king at the courtyard, having deposited the scroll in the chamber of Elishama the scribe, and reported everything in the hearing of the king.

21 The king sent Jehudi to get the scroll, and he took it from the chamber of Elishama the scribe. Jehudi then read it in the hearing of the king and all the officials who were standing by the king. 22 Since it was the ninth month, the king was sitting in his winter quarters with a fire burning in front of him. 23 As soon as Jehudi would read three or four columns, Jehoiakim would cut the scrollb with a scribe's knife and throw the columns into the blazing fire until the entire scroll was consumed by the fire in the brazier. 24 As they heard all these words, the king and all of his servants did not become terrified or tear their garments. 25 Even though Elnathan, Delaiah, and Gemariah had urged the king not to burn the scroll, he would not listen to them.

Baruch and Jeremiah Hide

26 Then the king commanded Jerahmeel the king's son, Seraiah son of Azriel, and Shelemiah son of Abdeel to seize Baruch the scribe and Jeremiah the prophet, but the LORD had hidden them.

Jeremiah Dictates Another Scroll

27 After the king had burned the scroll with the words Baruch had written at Jeremiah's dictation,c the word of the LORD came to Jeremiah: 28 "Take another scroll, and once again write on it the very words that were on the original scroll that Jehoiakim king of Judah burned. 29 You are to proclaim concerning Jehoiakim king of Judah: This is what the LORD says: You have burned the scroll, saying: Why have you written on it: The king of Babylon will certainly come and destroy this land and cause it to be without man or beast?

---

a36:17,18 Lit From his mouth   b36:23 Lit columns, he would tear it   c36:27 Lit written from Jeremiah's mouth

Prediction against King Jehoiakim

30 Therefore, this is what the LORD says concerning Jehoiakim king of Judah: He will have no one to sit on David's throne, and his corpse will be thrown out ⌊to be exposed⌋ to the heat of day and the frost of night. 31 I will punish him, his descendants, and his officers for their wrongdoing. I will bring on them, on the residents of Jerusalem, and on the men of Judah all the disaster, which I warned them about but they did not listen."

32 Then Jeremiah took another scroll and gave it to Baruch son of Neriah, the scribe, and he wrote on it at Jeremiah's dictation[a] all the words of the scroll that Jehoiakim, Judah's king, had burned in the fire. And many other words like them were added.

Jerusalem's Last Days

37 Zedekiah son of Josiah reigned as king in the land of Judah in place of Jehoiachin[b] son of Jehoiakim, for Nebuchadnezzar king of Babylon made him king. 2 He and his officers and the people of the land did not obey the words of the LORD that He spoke through Jeremiah the prophet.

King Zedekiah Inquires of Jeremiah

3 Nevertheless, King Zedekiah sent Jehucal son of Shelemiah and Zephaniah son of Maaseiah, the priest, to Jeremiah the prophet, requesting, "Please pray to the LORD our God for us!" 4 Jeremiah was going about his daily tasks[c] among the people, for they had not ⌊yet⌋ put him into the prison. 5 Pharaoh's army had left Egypt, and when the Chaldeans, who were besieging Jerusalem, heard the report, they withdrew from Jerusalem.

God's Reply to Zedekiah

6 The word of the LORD came to Jeremiah the prophet: 7 "This is what the LORD, the God of Israel, says: This is what you will say to Judah's king, who is sending you to inquire of Me: Watch: Pharaoh's army, which has come out to help you, is going to return to its own land of Egypt. 8 The Chaldeans will then return and fight against this city. They will capture it and burn it down. 9 This is what the LORD says: Don't deceive yourselves by saying: The Chaldeans will leave us for good, for they will not leave. 10 Indeed, if you were to strike down the entire Chaldean army that is fighting with you, and there remained among them only the badly wounded[d] men, each in his tent, they would get up and burn this city down."

Jeremiah's Imprisonment

11 When the Chaldean army withdrew from Jerusalem because of Pharaoh's army, 12 Jeremiah ⌊started to⌋ leave Jerusalem to go to the land of Benjamin to claim his portion there among the people. 13 But when he was at the Benjamin Gate, an officer of the guard was there, whose name was Irijah son of Shelemiah, son of Hananiah, and he apprehended Jeremiah the prophet, saying, "You are deserting to the Chaldeans."

14 "⌊That's⌋ a lie," Jeremiah replied. "I am not deserting to the Chaldeans!" Irijah would not listen to him but apprehended Jeremiah and took him to the officials. 15 The officials were angry at Jeremiah and beat him and placed him in jail in the house of Jonathan the scribe, for it had been made into a prison. 16 So Jeremiah went into a cell in the dungeon and stayed there many days.

---

[a]36:32 Lit it from Jeremiah's mouth   [b]37:1 = Coniah   [c]37:4 Lit was coming in and going out   [d]37:10 Lit the pierced

Zedekiah Summons Jeremiah

[17] King Zedekiah later sent ⌊for him⌋ and received him, and in his house privately asked him, "Is there a word from the LORD?"

"There is," Jeremiah responded, and he continued, "You will be handed over to the king of Babylon." [18] Then Jeremiah said to King Zedekiah, "How have I sinned against you or your servants or these people that you have put me in prison? [19] Where are your prophets who prophesied to you, claiming, 'The king of Babylon will not come against you and this land'? [20] So now please listen, my lord the king. May my petition come before you. Don't send me back to the house of Jonathan the scribe, or I will die there."

[21] So King Zedekiah gave orders, and Jeremiah was placed in the guard's courtyard. He was given a loaf of bread each day from the baker's street until all the bread was gone from the city. So Jeremiah remained in the guard's courtyard.

Jeremiah Thrown into a Cistern

38 Now Shephatiah son of Mattan, Gedaliah son of Pashhur, Jucal[a] son of Shelemiah, and Pashhur son of Malchijah heard the words Jeremiah was speaking to all the people: [2] "This is what the LORD says: 'Whoever stays in this city will die by the sword, famine, and plague, but whoever surrenders to the Chaldeans will live. He will keep his life like the spoils ⌊of war⌋ and will live.' [3] This is what the LORD says: 'This city will most certainly be handed over to the king of Babylon's army, and he will capture it.' "

[4] The officials then said to the king, "This man ought to die, because he is weakening the morale of the warriors who remain in this city and of all the people by speaking to them in this way. This man is not seeking the well-being of this people, but disaster."

[5] King Zedekiah said, "Here he is; he's in your hands since the king can't do anything against you." [6] So they took Jeremiah and dropped him into the cistern of Malchiah the king's son, which was in the guard's courtyard, lowering Jeremiah with ropes. There was no water in the cistern, only mud, and Jeremiah sank in the mud.

Jeremiah Rescued

[7] But Ebed-melech, a •Cushite court official employed in the king's palace, heard Jeremiah had been put into the cistern. While the king was sitting at the Benjamin Gate, [8] Ebed-melech went from the king's palace and spoke to the king: [9] "My lord king, these men have been evil in all they have done to Jeremiah the prophet. They have dropped him into the cistern where he will die from hunger, because there is no more bread in the city."

[10] So the king commanded Ebed-melech, the Cushite, "Take from here 30 men under your authority and pull Jeremiah the prophet up from the cistern before he dies."

[11] So Ebed-melech took the men under his authority and went to the king's palace to a place below the storehouse.[b] From there he took old rags and worn-out clothes and lowered them by ropes to Jeremiah in the cistern. [12] Ebed-melech the Cushite cried out to Jeremiah, "Place these old rags and clothes between your armpits and the ropes." Jeremiah did so, [13] and they pulled him up with the ropes and lifted him out of the cistern, but he continued to stay in the guard's courtyard.

a**38:1** = Jehucal; Jr 37:3   b**38:11** Or treasury

Zedekiah's Final Meeting with Jeremiah

¹⁴ King Zedekiah sent for Jeremiah the prophet and received him at the third entrance of the LORD's temple. The king said to Jeremiah, "I am going to ask you something; don't hide anything from me."

¹⁵ Jeremiah replied to Zedekiah, "If I tell you, you will kill me, won't you? Besides, if I give you advice, you won't listen to me anyway."

¹⁶ King Zedekiah swore to Jeremiah in private, "As the LORD lives, who has given us this life, I will not kill you or hand you over to these men who want to take your life."

God's Word for Zedekiah

¹⁷ Jeremiah therefore said to Zedekiah, "This is what the LORD, the God of •Hosts, the God of Israel, says: 'If indeed you surrender to the officials of the king of Babylon, then you will live, this city will not be burned down, and you and your household will survive. ¹⁸ But if you do not surrender to the officials of the king of Babylon, then this city will be handed over to the Chaldeans. They will burn it down, and you yourself will not escape from them.'"

¹⁹ But King Zedekiah said to Jeremiah, "I am worried about the Judeans who have deserted to the Chaldeans. They may hand me over to them to abuse me."

Jeremiah Warns King

²⁰ "They will not hand you over," Jeremiah replied. "Obey the voice of the LORD in what I am telling you, so it may go well for you and you can live. ²¹ But if you refuse to surrender, this is the verdictᵃ that the LORD has shown me: ²² 'All

the womenᵇ who remain in the palace of Judah's king will be brought out to the officials of the king of Babylon and will say:

> Your trusted friendsᶜ misledᵈ you
> and overcame you.
> Your feet sank into the mire,
> and they deserted you.

²³ All your wives and sons will be brought out to the Chaldeans. You yourself will not escape from them, for you will be seized by the king of Babylon and this city will burn down.'"

King Warns Prophet

²⁴ Then Zedekiah warned Jeremiah, "Don't let anyone know about these things or you will die. ²⁵ If the officials hear that I have spoken with you and come and demand of you, 'Tell us what you said to the king; don't hide anything from us and we won't kill you. Also, what did the king say to you?' ²⁶ then you will tell them, 'I was bringing before the king my petition that he not return me to the house of Jonathan to die there.'" ²⁷ When all the officials came to Jeremiah and questioned him, he reported the exact words to them the king had commanded, and they quit speaking with him because nothing had been heard. ²⁸ Jeremiah remained in the guard's courtyard until the day Jerusalem was captured, and he was ⌊there⌋ when it happened.ᵉ

Fall of Jerusalem to Babylon

39 In the ninth year of Zedekiah king of Judah, in the tenth month, King Nebuchadnezzar of Babylon advanced against Jerusalem with his entire army and laid siege to it. ² In the fourth month

---

ᵃ**38:21** Or promise; lit word ᵇ**38:22** Or wives ᶜ**38:22** Lit The men of your peace ᵈ**38:22** Or incited ᵉ**38:28** Or captured. This is what happened when Jerusalem was captured:

of Zedekiah's eleventh year, on the ninth day of the month, the city was broken into. ³ All the officials of the king of Babylon entered and sat at the Middle Gate: Nergal-sharezer, Samgar-nebo, Sarsechim the Rab-saris, Nergal-sharezer the Rab-mag, and all the rest of the officials of Babylon's king.

King and Soldiers Flee

⁴ When he saw them, Zedekiah king of Judah and all the soldiers fled. They left the city at night by way of the king's garden through the gate between the two walls. They left along the route to the •Arabah. ⁵ However, the Chaldean army pursued them and overtook Zedekiah in the plainsᵃ of Jericho, arrested him, and brought him to Nebuchadnezzar, Babylon's king, at Riblah in the land of Hamath. The king passed sentence on him ⌊there⌋.

Zedekiah Punished

⁶ At Riblah the king of Babylon slaughtered Zedekiah's sons before his eyes, and he ⌊also⌋ slaughtered all Judah's nobles. ⁷ Then he blinded Zedekiah and put him in bronze chains to take him to Babylon. ⁸ The Chaldeans next burned down the king's palace and the people's houses and tore down the walls of Jerusalem. ⁹ Nebuzaradan, the commander of the guards, deported to Babylon the rest of the people—those who had remained in the city and those deserters who had defected to him along with the rest of the people who had remained. ¹⁰ ⌊However,⌋ Nebuzaradan, the commander of the guards, left in the land of Judah some of the poor people who owned nothing, and he gave them vineyards and fields at that time.

Nebuchadnezzar Frees Jeremiah

¹¹ ⌊Speaking⌋ through Nebuzaradan, captain of the guard, King Nebuchadnezzar of Babylon gave orders concerning Jeremiah, saying: ¹² "Take him, look after him, and don't let any harm come to him; do for him whatever he says." ¹³ Nebuzaradan, captain of the guard, Nebushazban the Rab-saris, Nergal-sharezer the Rab-mag, and all the captains of the king of Babylon ¹⁴ had Jeremiah brought from the guard's courtyard and turned him over to Gedaliah son of Ahikam, son of Shaphan, to take him home. So he settled among ⌊his own⌋ people.

Jeremiah's Jerusalem Prophecy Fulfilled

¹⁵ Now the word of the LORD had come to Jeremiah when he was confined in the guard's courtyard: ¹⁶ "Go tell Ebed-melech the •Cushite: This is what the LORD of •Hosts, the God of Israel, says: I am about to fulfill My words for harm and not for good against this city. They will take place before your eyes on that day. ¹⁷ But I will rescue you on that day"—⌊this is⌋ the LORD's declaration— "and you will not be handed over to the men you fear. ¹⁸ Indeed, I will certainly deliver you so that you do not fall by the sword. Because you have trusted in Me, you will keep your life like the spoils ⌊of war⌋." ⌊This is⌋ the LORD's declaration.

Jeremiah Stays in Judah

40 ⌊This is⌋ the word that came to Jeremiah from the LORD after Nebuzaradan, captain of the guard, released him at Ramah when he had been bound in chains with all the exiles of Jerusalem and Judah who were being exiled to Babylon. ² The captain of the guard took

---

ᵃ **39:5** Lit *Arabah*

Jeremiah and said to him, "The LORD your God decreed this disaster on this place, ³ and the LORD has fulfilled ⌊it⌋. He has done just what He decreed. Because you ⌊people⌋ have sinned against the LORD and have not obeyed Him, this thing has happened. ⁴ Now pay attention ⌊to what I say⌋. Today I am setting you free from the chains that were on your hands. If it pleases you to come with me to Babylon, come, and I will take care of you. But if it seems wrong to you to come with me to Babylon, go no farther.ᵃ Look—the whole land is in front of you. Wherever it seems good and right for you to go, go there."

Gedaliah Appointed over Judah

⁵ When Jeremiah had not yet turned ⌊to go, Nebuzaradan said to him:⌋ "Returnᵇ to Gedaliah son of Ahikam, son of Shaphan, whom the king of Babylon has appointed over the cities of Judah, and stay with him among the people or go wherever you want to go." So the captain of the guard gave him a ration and a gift and released him. ⁶ Jeremiah therefore went to Gedaliah son of Ahikam at Mizpah, and he stayed with him among the people who remained in the land.

Gedaliah Advises Peace

⁷ When all the commanders of the armies in the field—they and their men—heard that the king of Babylon had appointed Gedaliah son of Ahikam over the land and that he had put him in charge of the men, women, and children, the poorest of the land who had not been deported to Babylon, ⁸ they came to Gedaliah at Mizpah. ⌊The commanders included⌋ Ishmael son of Nethaniah, Johanan and Jonathan the sons of Kareah, Seraiah son of Tanhumeth, the sons of Ephai the Netophathite, and Jezaniah son of the Maacathite—they and their men.

⁹ Gedaliah son of Ahikam, son of Shaphan, swore an oath to them and their men, assuring them, "Don't be afraid to serve the Chaldeans. Live in the land and serve the king of Babylon, and it will go well for you. ¹⁰ As for me, I am going to live in Mizpah to representᶜ ⌊you⌋ before the Chaldeans who come to us. As for you, gather wine, summer fruit, and oil, place them in your ⌊storage⌋ jars, and live in the cities you have captured."

¹¹ When all the Judeans in Moab and among the Ammonites and in Edom and in all the other lands also heard that the king of Babylon had left a remnant in Judah and had appointed Gedaliah son of Ahikam, son of Shaphan, over them, ¹² they all returned from all the places where they had been banished and came to the land of Judah, to Gedaliah at Mizpah, and harvested a great amount of wine and summer fruit.

Gedaliah Ignores Warning about Ishmael

¹³ Meanwhile, Johanan son of Kareah and all the commanders of the armies in the field came to Gedaliah at Mizpah ¹⁴ and warned him, "Don't you realize that Baalis, king of the Ammonites, has sent Ishmael son of Nethaniah to strike you down?" But Gedaliah son of Ahikam would not believe them. ¹⁵ Then Johanan son of Kareah suggested to Gedaliah in private at Mizpah, "Let me go kill Ishmael son of Nethaniah. No one will know it. Why should he strike you down and scatter all of Judah that has gathered to you so that the remnant of Judah would perish?"

ᵃ**40:4** Lit *Babylon, stop*   ᵇ**40:5** LXX reads *But if not, run, return*; Hb obscure   ᶜ**40:10** Lit *to stand*

[16] But Gedaliah son of Ahikam responded to Johanan son of Kareah, "Don't do that! What you're saying about Ishmael is a lie."

Ishmael Assassinates Gedaliah

41 In the seventh month, Ishmael son of Nethaniah, son of Elishama, of the royal family and one of the king's chief officers, came with 10 men to Gedaliah son of Ahikam at Mizpah. They ate a meal together there in Mizpah, [2] but then Ishmael son of Nethaniah and the 10 men who were with him got up and struck down Gedaliah son of Ahikam, son of Shaphan, with the sword; he killed the one the king of Babylon had appointed in the land. [3] Ishmael also struck down all the Judeans who were with Gedaliah at Mizpah, as well as the Chaldean soldiers who were there.

Ishmael Slaughters Many More

[4] On the second day after he had killed Gedaliah, when no one knew ⌊yet⌋, [5] 80 men came from Shechem, Shiloh, and Samaria who had shaved their beards, torn their garments, and gashed themselves, and who were carrying •grain and incense offerings to bring to the temple of the LORD. [6] Ishmael son of Nethaniah came out of Mizpah to meet them, weeping as he came. When he encountered them, he said: "Come to Gedaliah son of Ahikam!" [7] But when they came into the city, Ishmael son of Nethaniah and the men with him slaughtered them and threw them into[a] a cistern.

[8] However, there were 10 men among them who said to Ishmael, "Don't kill us, for we have hidden treasure in the field—wheat, barley, oil, and honey!" So he stopped and did not kill them along with their companions. [9] Now the cistern where Ishmael had thrown all the corpses of the men he had struck down was a large one[b] that King Asa had made in the encounter with Baasha king of Israel. Ishmael son of Nethaniah filled ⌊it⌋ with the slain.

Ishmael Takes Captives

[10] Then Ishmael took captive all the remnant of the people of Mizpah including the daughters of the king—all those who remained in Mizpah over whom Nebuzaradan, captain of the guard, had appointed Gedaliah son of Ahikam. Ishmael son of Nethaniah took them captive and set off to cross over to the Ammonites.

Johanan Rescues Captives

[11] When Johanan son of Kareah and all the commanders of the armies with him heard of all the evil that Ishmael son of Nethaniah had done, [12] they took all their men and went to fight with Ishmael son of Nethaniah and found him by the great pool in Gibeon. [13] When all the people with Ishmael saw Johanan son of Kareah and all the commanders of the army with him, they rejoiced, [14] and all the people whom Ishmael had taken captive from Mizpah turned around and rejoined Johanan son of Kareah.

Ishmael Escapes

[15] But Ishmael son of Nethaniah escaped from Johanan with eight men and went to the Ammonites. [16] Johanan son of Kareah and all the commanders of the armies with him then took from Mizpah all the remnant of the people whom he had recovered from Ishmael son of Nethaniah after Ishmael had killed Gedaliah son of Ahikam—men, soldiers, women, children, and court officials whom he

---

[a]41:7 Syr; MT reads *slaughtered them in*   [b]41:9 LXX; MT reads *down by the hand of Gedaliah*

brought back from Gibeon. [17] They left, stopping in Geruth Chimham, which is near Bethlehem, in order to make their way into Egypt [18] away from the Chaldeans. For they feared them because Ishmael son of Nethaniah had struck down Gedaliah son of Ahikam, whom the king of Babylon had appointed in the land.

People Seek Jeremiah's Counsel

42 Then all the commanders of the armies, along with Johanan son of Kareah, Jazaniah son of Hoshaiah, and all the people from the least to the greatest, approached [2] Jeremiah the prophet and said, "May our petition come before you; pray to the LORD your God on our behalf, on behalf of this entire remnant (for few of us remain out of the many, as you can see with your own eyes), [3] that the LORD your God may tell us the way we should walk and the thing we should do."

[4] So Jeremiah the prophet said to them, "I have heard. I will now pray to the LORD your God according to your words, and every word that the LORD answers you I will tell you; I won't withhold a word from you."

[5] And they said to Jeremiah, "As for every word the LORD your God sends you to ⌊tell⌋ us, if we don't act accordingly, may the LORD be a true and faithful witness against us. [6] Whether it is pleasant or unpleasant, we will obey the voice of the LORD our God to whom we are sending you so that it may go well with us. We will certainly obey the voice of the LORD our God!"

Jeremiah's Advice to Stay

[7] Now at the end of 10 days, the word of the LORD came to Jeremiah, [8] and he summoned Johanan son of Kareah, all the commanders of the armies who were with him, and all the people from the least to the greatest.

[9] He said to them, "This is what the LORD says, the God of Israel to whom you sent me to bring your petition before Him: [10] 'If you will indeed stay in this land, then I will rebuild and not demolish you, and I will plant and not uproot you, because I relent concerning the disaster that I have brought on you. [11] Don't be afraid of the king of Babylon whom you now fear; don't be afraid of him'—⌊this is⌋ the LORD's declaration— 'because I am with you to save you and deliver you from him. [12] I will grant you compassion, and he[a] will have compassion on you and allow you to return to your own soil.

Don't Go to Egypt!

[13] But if you say: We will not stay in this land, so as not to obey the voice of the LORD your God, [14] and if you say: No, instead we'll go to the land of Egypt where we will not see war or hear the sound of the ram's horn or hunger for food, and we'll live there, [15] then hear the word of the LORD, remnant of Judah! This is what the LORD of •Hosts, the God of Israel, says: If you are firmly resolved to go to Egypt and live there for a while, [16] then the sword you fear will overtake you there in the land of Egypt, and the famine you are worried about will follow on your heels[b] there to Egypt, and you will die there. [17] All who resolve to go to Egypt to live there for a while will die by the sword, famine, and plague. They will have no survivor or escapee from the disaster I will bring on them.'

[18] "For this is what the LORD of Hosts, the God of Israel, says: 'Just as My anger and fury were poured out on Jerusalem's residents, so will My fury pour out on

---

[a]**42:12** LXX reads I [b]**42:16** Lit will cling after you

you if you go to Egypt. You will become an object of execration, scorn, cursing, and disgrace, and you will never see this place again.' ¹⁹ The LORD has spoken concerning you, remnant of Judah: 'Don't go to Egypt.' Know for certain that I have warned you today! ²⁰ You have led your own selves astray because you are the ones who sent me to the LORD your God, saying, 'Pray to the LORD our God on our behalf, and as for all that the LORD our God says, tell it to us, and we'll act accordingly.' ²¹ For I have told you today, but you have not obeyed the voice of the LORD your God in everything He has sent me to ˌtellˌ you. ²² Now therefore, know for certain that by the sword, famine, and plague you will die in the place where you desired to go to live for a while."

Jeremiah's Counsel Rejected

43 When Jeremiah had finished speaking to all the people all the words of the LORD their God—all these words the LORD their God had sent him to give them— ² then Azariah son of Hoshaiah, Johanan son of Kareah, and all the other arrogant men responded to Jeremiah, "You are speaking a lie! The LORD our God has not sent you to say, 'You must not go to Egypt to live there for a while!' ³ Rather, Baruch son of Neriah is inciting you against us to hand us over to the Chaldeans to put us to death or to deport us to Babylon!"

⁴ So Johanan son of Kareah and all the commanders of the armies did not obey the voice of the LORD to stay in the land of Judah. ⁵ Instead, Johanan son of Kareah and all the commanders of the armies took the whole remnant of Judah, those who had returned from all the nations where they had been banished to

live in the land of Judah for a while— ⁶ the men, women, children, king's daughters, and everyone whom Nebuzaradan, captain of the guard, had allowed to remain with Gedaliah son of Ahikam son of Shaphan, along with Jeremiah the prophet and Baruch son of Neriah— ⁷ and they went to the land of Egypt because they did not obey the voice of the LORD. They went as far as Tahpanhes.

God's Sign to People in Egypt

⁸ Then the word of the LORD came to Jeremiah at Tahpanhes: ⁹ "Pick up some large stones and set them in the mortar of the brick pavement that is at the opening of Pharaoh's palace at Tahpanhes. ˌDo thisˌ in the sight of the Judean men ¹⁰ and tell them: This is what the LORD of •Hosts, the God of Israel, says: I will send for My servant Nebuchadnezzar king of Babylon, and I will place his throne on these stones that I have embedded, and he will pitch his pavilion over them. ¹¹ He will come and strike down the land of Egypt—those ˌdestinedˌ for death, to death; those ˌdestinedˌ for captivity, to captivity; and those ˌdestinedˌ for the sword, to the sword. ¹² Iᵃ will kindle a fire in the temples of Egypt's gods, and he will burn them and take them prisoner. He will clean the land of Egypt as a shepherd picks lice offᵇ his garment, and he will leave there unscathed. ¹³ He will smash the sacred pillars of the sun templeᶜ in the land of Egypt and burn down the temples of the Egyptian gods."

God's Judges His People in Egypt

44 ˌThis isˌ the word that came to Jeremiah for all the Jews living in the land of Egypt—at Migdol, Tahpanhes,

---

ᵃ**43:12** LXX, Syr, Vg read *He*　ᵇ**43:12** Or *will wrap himself in the land of Egypt as a shepherd wraps himself in*
ᶜ**43:13** = *of Heliopolis*; Hb *Beth-shemesh*

Memphis, and in the land of Pathros: ² "This is what the LORD of •Hosts, the God of Israel, says: You have seen all the disaster I brought against Jerusalem and all Judah's cities; look, they are a ruin today without an inhabitant in them ³ because of their evil ways that provoked Me to anger, going and burning incense to serve other gods they, you, and your fathers did not know. ⁴ So I sent you all My servants the prophets time and time again,ᵃ saying, Don't do this detestable thing that I hate. ⁵ But they did not listen or pay attention; they did not turn from their evil or stop burning incense to other gods. ⁶ So My fierce wrath poured forth and burned in Judah's cities and Jerusalem's streets so that they became the desolate ruin they are today.

⁷ "So now, this is what the LORD, the God of Hosts, the God of Israel, says: Why are you doing such great harm to yourselves? You are cutting off man and woman, child and infant from Judah, leaving yourselves without a remnant. ⁸ You are provoking Me to anger by the work of your hands. You are burning incense to other gods in the land of Egypt where you have gone to live for a while. As a result, you will be cut off and become an object of cursing and insult among all the nations of earth. ⁹ Have you forgotten the evils of your fathers, the evils of Judah's kings, the evils of their wives, your own evils, and the evils of your wives that were committed in the land of Judah and in the streets of Jerusalem? ¹⁰ They have not become humble to this day, and they have not •feared or walked by My law or My statutes that I set before you and your ancestors.

¹¹ "Therefore, this is what the LORD of Hosts, the God of Israel, says: I am about to turn against you to ⌊bring⌋ disaster, to cut off all Judah. ¹² And I will take away the remnant of Judah, those who have resolved to go to the land of Egypt to live there for a while; they will meet their end. All of them in the land of Egypt will fall by the sword; they will meet their end by famine. From the least to the greatest, they will die by the sword and by famine. Then they will become an object of execration, of scorn, of cursing, and of disgrace. ¹³ I will punish those living in the land of Egypt just as I punished Jerusalem by sword, famine, and plague. ¹⁴ Then the remnant of Judah— those going to live for a while there in the land of Egypt—will have no fugitive or survivor to return to the land of Judah where they are longingᵇ to return to live, for they will not return except ⌊for a few⌋ fugitives."

People's Stubborn Response

¹⁵ However, all the men who knew that their wives were burning incense to other gods, all the women standing by— a great assembly—and all the people who were living in the land of Egypt at Pathros answered Jeremiah, ¹⁶ "As for the word you spoke to us in the name of the LORD, we are not going to listen to you! ¹⁷ Instead, we will do everything we said we would: burn incense to the queen of heavenᶜ and offer drink offerings to her just as we, our fathers, our kings, and our officials did in Judah's cities and in Jerusalem's streets. Then we had enough food and good things and saw no disaster, ¹⁸ but from the time we ceased to burn incense to the queen of heaven and to offer her drink offerings, we have lacked everything, and through sword and famine we have met our end."

ᵃ**44:4** Lit *prophets, rising up early and sending*   ᵇ**44:14** Lit *lifting up their soul*   ᶜ**44:17** =Ashtoreth, or Astarte

Women Worship
Queen of Heaven

19 And the women said,a "When we burned incense to the queen of heaven and poured out drink offerings to her, was it apart from our husbands' knowledge that we made sacrificial cakes in her image and poured out drink offerings to her?"

Jeremiah Warns Them

20 But Jeremiah responded to all the people—the men, women, and all the people who were answering him—saying, 21 "As for the incense you burned in Judah's cities and in Jerusalem's streets—you, your fathers, your kings, your officials, and the people of the land—did the LORD not remember them? He brought this to mind. 22 The LORD can no longer bear your evil deeds and the detestable acts you have committed, so your land has become a waste, a desolation, and an object of cursing, without inhabitant, as ⌊you see⌋ today. 23 Because you burned incense and sinned against the LORD and didn't obey the LORD's voice and didn't walk in His law, His statutes, and His testimonies, this disaster has come to you, as ⌊you see⌋ today."

24 Then Jeremiah said to all the people, including all the women, "Hear the word of the LORD, all Judah who are in the land of Egypt. 25 This is what the LORD of Hosts, the God of Israel, says: 'As for you and your wives, you women have spoken with your mouths, and you men fulfilled it by your deeds, saying: We will keep our vows we have made to burn incense to the queen of heaven and to pour out drink offerings for her. ⌊Go ahead,⌋ confirm your vows! Pay your vows!'

Disaster for Judah
Remnant in Egypt

26 "Therefore, hear the word of the LORD, all you Judeans who live in the land of Egypt: 'I have sworn by My great name, says the LORD, that My name will never again be invoked by anyone of Judah in all the land of Egypt, saying, As the Lord GOD lives. 27 I am watching over them for disaster and not for good, and every man of Judah who is in the land of Egypt will meet his end by sword or famine until they are finished off. 28 Those who escape the sword will return from the land of Egypt to the land of Judah only few in number, and the whole remnant of Judah, the ones going to the land of Egypt to live there for a while, will know whose word stands, Mine or theirs! 29 This will be a sign to you'—⌊this is⌋ the LORD's declaration—'that I am about to punish you in this place, so you may know that My words of disaster concerning you will certainly come to pass. 30 This is what the LORD says: I am about to hand over Pharaoh Hophra, Egypt's king, to his enemies, to those who want to take his life, just as I handed over Judah's King Zedekiah to Babylon's King Nebuchadnezzar, who was his enemy, the one who wanted to take his life.'"

LORD's Message to Baruch

45 ⌊This is⌋ the word that Jeremiah the prophet spoke to Baruch son of Neriah when he wrote these words on a scroll at Jeremiah's dictationb in the fourth year of Jehoiakim son of Josiah, king of Judah: 2 "This is what the LORD, the God of Israel, says to you, Baruch: 3 'You have said, Woe is me, because the LORD has added misery to my pain! I am worn out withc groaning and have found no rest.

---

a44:19 LXX, Syr; MT omits *And the women said*   b45:1 Lit *scroll from Jeremiah's mouth*   c45:3 Lit *I labored in my*

4 " 'This is what you are to say to him: This is what the LORD says: What I have built I am about to demolish, and what I have planted I am about to uproot—the whole land! 5 But as for you, do you seek great things for yourself? Stop seeking! For I am about to bring disaster on every living creature'—ᴊthis isᴊ the LORD's declaration—'but I will grant you your life like the spoils ᴊof warᴊ wherever you go.' "

PROPHECIES AGAINST
THE NATIONS

46 The word of the LORD that came to Jeremiah the prophet about the nations:

Prophecies against Egypt

2 About Egypt and the army of Pharaoh Neco, Egypt's king, which was defeated at Carchemish on the Euphrates River by Nebuchadnezzar king of Babylon in the fourth year of Judah's King Jehoiakim son of Josiah:

3   Deploy small shields and large;
      draw near for battle!
4   Harness the horses;
      mount the steeds;ᵃ
      take your positions with helmets on!
      Polish the lances;
      put on armor!
5   Why have I seen ᴊthisᴊ?
      They are terrified,
      they are retreating,
      their warriors are crushed,
      they flee headlong,
      they never look back,
      terror is on every side!
      ᴊThis isᴊ the LORD's declaration.
6   The swift cannot flee,
      and the warrior cannot escape!
      In the north by the bank
      of the Euphrates River,
      they stumble and fall.

7   Who is this, rising like the Nile,
      like rivers whose waters churn?
8   Egypt rises like the Nile,
      and its waters churn like rivers.
      He boasts: I will go up, I will cover
        the earth;
      I will destroy cities
        with their residents.
9   Rise up, you cavalry!
      Race furiously, you chariots!
      Let the warriors go forth—
      •Cush and Put,
      who are able to handle shields,
      and the Ludim,
      who are able to handle and string
        the bow.
10 That day belongs to the Lord,
        the GOD of •Hosts,
      a day of vengeance
        to avenge Himself
      against His adversaries.
      The sword will devour
        and be satisfied;
      it will drink its fill of their blood,
      because it will be a sacrifice
        to the Lord, the GOD of Hosts,
      in the northern land
        by the Euphrates River.

11 Go up to Gilead and get balm,
      Virgin Daughter Egypt!
      You have multiplied remedies
        in vain;
      there is no healing for you.
12 The nations have heard
        of your dishonor,
      and your outcry fills the earth,
      because warrior stumbles
        against warrior
      and together both of them
        have fallen.

Nebuchadnezzar Will Defeat Egypt

13 ᴊThis isᴊ the word the LORD spoke to Jeremiah the prophet about the coming

ᵃ46:4 Or *mount up, riders*

of Nebuchadnezzar king of Babylon to
defeat the land of Egypt:

14 Announce it in Egypt,
    and proclaim it in Migdol!
  Proclaim it in Memphis
    and in Tahpanhes!
  Say: Take positions!
    Prepare yourself,
  for the sword devours
    all around you.
15 Why have your strong ones
    been swept away?
  Each has not stood,
  for the LORD has thrust him down.
16 He continues to stumble.
  Indeed, each falls over the other.
  They say: Get up! Let's return
    to our people
  and to the land of our birth,
  away from the sword
    that oppresses.
17 There they will cry out:
  Pharaoh king of Egypt was all noise;
  he let the opportune moment pass.

18 As I live—
    ⌊this is⌋ the King's declaration;
    the LORD of Hosts is His name.

  He will come like Tabor
    among the mountains
  and like Carmel by the sea.
19 Pack your bags for exile,
  inhabitant of Daughter Egypt!
  For Memphis will become
    a desolation,
  uninhabited ruins.

20 Egypt is a beautiful young cow,
  but a horsefly from the north
    is coming against her.ᵃ
21 Even her mercenaries among her
  are like stall-fed calves.
  They too will turn back;
  together they will flee;

  they will not take their stand,
  for the day of their calamity
    is coming on them,
  the time of their punishment.
22 Egypt will hiss
    like a slithering snake,ᵇ
  for ⌊the enemy⌋ will come
    with an army;
  with axes they will come
    against her
  like those who cut trees.
23 They will cut down her forest—
    ⌊this is⌋ the LORD's declaration—
  though it is dense,
  for they are more numerous
    than locusts;
  they cannot be counted.
24 Daughter Egypt will be
    put to shame,
  handed over to a northern people.

25 The LORD of Hosts, the God of Israel, says: "I am about to punish Amon, ⌊god⌋ of Thebes, along with Pharaoh, Egypt, her gods, and her kings—Pharaoh and those trusting in him. 26 I will hand them over to those who want to take their lives—to Nebuchadnezzar king of Babylon and his officers. But after this, it will be inhabited again as in ancient times."

    ⌊This is⌋ the LORD's declaration.

God Reassures Israel

27 But you, My servant Jacob,
  do not be afraid,
  and do not be discouraged, Israel,
  for without fail I will save you
    from far away
  and your descendants,
    from the land of their captivity!
  Jacob will return and have calm
    and quiet
  with no one to frighten him.

ᵃ**46:20** Some Hb mss, LXX, Syr; other Hb mss read *is coming, coming* ᵇ**46:22** Lit *Her sound, she will go like a snake*

28 And you, My servant Jacob,
   do not be afraid—
      ⌊this is⌋ the LORD's declaration—
  for I will be with you.
  I will bring destruction
   on all the nations
  where I have banished you,
  but I will not bring destruction
   on you.
  I will discipline you with justice,
  but I will by no means
   leave you unpunished.

Prophecies against the Philistines

47 ⌊This is⌋ the word of the LORD that came to Jeremiah the prophet about the Philistines before Pharaoh defeated Gaza. 2 This is what the LORD says:

Look, waters are rising
  from the north
and becoming
  an overflowing •wadi.
They will overflow the land
  and everything in it,
the cities and their inhabitants.
The people will cry out,
and every inhabitant of the land
  will wail.
3 At the sound
  of the stomping hooves
  of his stallions,
the rumbling of his chariots,
and the clatter of their wheels,
fathers will not turn back
  for their sons,
because they will be
  utterly helplessª
4 on account of the day
  that is coming
to destroy all the Philistines,
to cut off from Tyre and Sidon

every remaining ally.
Indeed, the LORD is
  about to destroy the Philistines,
the remnant of the islands
  of Caphtor.ᵇ
5 Baldness is coming to Gaza.
Ashkelon will become silent,
a remnant of their valley.
How long will you gash yourself?

6 Ah, sword of the LORD!
How long will you be restless?
Go back to your scabbard;
  be still; be silent!
7 How can itᶜ rest
when the LORD has given it
  a command?
He has assigned it
against Ashkelon and the shore
  of the sea.

Prophecies against Moab

48 About Moab, this is what the LORD of •Hosts, the God of Israel, says:

Woe to Nebo, because it is
  about to be destroyed;
Kiriathaim will be put to shame;
  it will be taken captive.
The fortress will be put to shame
  and dismayed!
2 There is no longer praise for Moab;
they plan harm against her
  in Heshbon:
Come, let's cut her off
  from nationhood.
You madmen will also be silenced;
the sword will pursue you.
3 A voice cries out from Horonaim:
devastation and great disaster!
4 Moab will be shattered;
her little ones will cry out.
5 For on the ascent to Luhith
they will be weeping continually,ᵈ

ª**47:3** Lit because of laziness of hands   ᵇ**47:4** Probably Crete; Gn 10:14; Dt 2:23; Am 9:7   ᶜ**47:7** LXX, Vg; MT reads you   ᵈ**48:5** Lit Luhith, weeping goes up with weeping

and on the descent to Horonaim
will be heard cries of distress
over the destruction:

6 Flee! Save your lives!
Be like a juniper
bush[a] in the wilderness.

False God Chemosh into Exile

7 Because you trust in your works[b]
and treasures,
you will be captured also.
Chemosh will go into exile
with his priests and officials.

8 The destroyer will move
against every town;
not one town will escape.
The valley will perish,
and the plain will be annihilated,
as the LORD has said.

9 Make Moab a salt marsh,[c] [d]
for she will run away;[e]
her towns will become a desolation,
without inhabitant.

10 Cursed is the one
who does
the LORD's business deceitfully,[f]
and cursed is the one
who withholds his sword
from bloodshed.

11 Moab has been left quiet
since his youth,
settled ⌊like wine⌋ on its dregs.
He hasn't been poured
from one container to another
or gone into exile.
So his taste has remained the same,
and his aroma hasn't changed.

12 Therefore look, the days
are coming—
⌊this is⌋ the LORD's declaration—
when I will send those to him,
who will pour him out.

They will empty his containers
and smash his jars.

13 Moab will be put to shame
because of Chemosh,
just as the house of Israel was
put to shame
because of Bethel
that they trusted in.

14 How can you say,
We are warriors—
mighty men ⌊ready⌋ for battle?

15 The destroyer of Moab
and its towns
has come up,[g]
and the best of its young men
have gone down to slaughter.
⌊This is⌋ the King's declaration;
the LORD of Hosts is His name.

Moab to Shame

16 Moab's calamity is near at hand;
his disaster is rushing swiftly.

17 Mourn for him,
all you surrounding ⌊nations⌋,
everyone who knows his name.
Say: How the mighty scepter
is shattered,
the glorious staff!

18 Come down from glory;
sit on parched ground,
resident of the daughter of Dibon,
for the destroyer of Moab has come
against you;
he has destroyed your fortresses.

19 Stand by the highway and look,
resident of Aroer!
Ask him who is fleeing or her
who is escaping,
What happened?

20 Moab is put to shame,
indeed dismayed.
Wail and cry out!

---

a48:6 Or like Aroer; Jr 48:19; Is 17:2 b48:7 LXX reads strongholds c48:9 LXX reads a sign; Vg reads a flower; Syr,
Tg read a crown; others read Moab fly away d48:9 = to make a conquered city uninhabitable; Jdg 9:45 e48:9 Hb
obscure f48:10 Or negligently g48:15 Or Moab is destroyed; he has come up against its city

Declare by the Arnon
that Moab is destroyed.

21 "Judgment has come to the land of the plateau—to Holon, Jahzah, Mephaath, 22 Dibon, Nebo, Beth-diblathaim, 23 Kiriathaim, Beth-gamul, Beth-meon, 24 Kerioth, Bozrah, and all the towns of the land of Moab, those far and near. 25 Moab's •horn is chopped off; his arm is shattered."

ιThis isι the LORD's declaration.

Moab a Laughingstock

26 "Make him drunk, because he has exalted himself against the LORD. Moab will wallow in his own vomit, and he will also become a laughingstock. 27 Wasn't Israel a laughingstock to you? Was he ever found among thieves? For whenever you speak of him you shake ιyour headι."

28   Abandon the towns!
       Live in the cliffs,
     residents of Moab!
       Be like a dove
     that nests inside the mouth
       of a cave.

29   We have heard of Moab's pride,
       great pride, indeed—
     his insolence, arrogance, pride,
       and haughty heart.
30   I know his outburst.
           ιThis isι the LORD's declaration.
       It is empty.
       His boast is empty.
31   Therefore, I will wail over Moab.
     I will cry out for Moab, all of it;
       he will moan for the men
         of Kir-heres.
32   I will weep for you, vine of Sibmah,
       with more than the weeping
         for Jazer.

Your tendrils have extended
  to the sea;
they have reached to the sea
  ιand toι Jazer.a
The destroyer has fallen
  on your summer fruit
  and grape harvest.
33 Joy and celebration are taken
      from the fertile field
    and from the land of Moab.
    I have stopped the flow of wine
      from the winepresses;
    no one will tread with shouts of joy.
    The shouting is not a shout of joy.

Mourning in Moab

34 "There is a cry from Heshbon to Elealeh; they raise their voices as far as Jahaz—from Zoar to Horonaim ιandι Eglath-shelishiyah—because even the waters of Nimrim have become desolate. 35 In Moab, I will stop"—ιthis isι the LORD's declaration—"the one who offers sacrifices on the •high place and burns incense to his gods. 36 Therefore, My heart moans like flutes for Moab, and My heart moans like flutes for the people of Kir-heres. And therefore, the wealth he has gained has perished. 37 Indeed, every head is bald and every beard clipped; on every hand is a gash and •sackcloth around the waist. 38 On all the rooftops of Moab and in her public squares, everyone is mourning because I have shattered Moab like a jar no one wants." ιThis isι the LORD's declaration. 39 "How broken it is! They wail! How Moab has turned his back! He is ashamed. Moab will become a laughingstock and a shock to all those around him."

40 For this is what the LORD says:

He will swoop down like an eagle
and spread his wings against Moab.

a48:32 Some Hb mss read reached as far as Jazer; Is 16:8

41 The towns have[a] been captured,
   and the strongholds seized.
   In that day the heart
      of Moab's warriors
   will be like the heart of a woman
      with contractions.
42 Moab will be destroyed as a people
   because he has exalted himself
      against the LORD.
43 Panic, pit, and trap
   await you, resident of Moab.
      ⌊This is⌋ the LORD's declaration.
44 He who flees from the panic
      will fall in the pit,
   and he who climbs from the pit
   will be captured in the trap,
   for I will bring against Moab
   the year of their punishment.
      ⌊This is⌋ the LORD's declaration.

45 Those who flee will stand exhausted
      in Heshbon's shadow
   because fire has come out
      from Heshbon
   and a flame from within Sihon.
   It will devour Moab's forehead
   and the skull of the noisemakers.
46 Woe to you, Moab!
   The people of Chemosh
      have perished
   because your sons have been
      taken captive
   and your daughters have gone
      into captivity.

Restoration of Moab

47 Yet, I will restore the fortunes[b]
      of Moab in the last days.
      ⌊This is⌋ the LORD's declaration.
   The judgment on Moab ends here.

Prophecies against Ammon

49 About the Ammonites, this is
   what the LORD says:

Does Israel have no sons?
Is he without an heir?
Why then has
   •Milcom[c] [d] dispossessed Gad
and his people settled
   in their cities?
2 Therefore look, the days
   are coming—
      ⌊this is⌋ the LORD's declaration—
   when I will make the shout
      of battle heard
   against Rabbah of the Ammonites.
   It will become a desolate mound,
   and its villages will be burned down.
   Israel will dispossess
      their dispossessors,
   says the LORD.
3 Wail, Heshbon, for Ai is devastated;
   cry out, daughters of Rabbah!
   Clothe yourselves with •sackcloth,
      and lament;
   run back and forth
      within your walls,[e]
   because Milcom will go into exile
   together with his priests
      and officials.
4 Why do you brag
      about your valleys,
   your flowing valley,[f]
   you faithless daughter?
   You who trust in your treasures
   ⌊and boast⌋: Who can attack me?
5 Look, I am about to bring terror
      on you—
      ⌊this is⌋ the declaration of the Lord,
         the GOD of •Hosts—
   from all those around you.
   You will be banished,
      each man headlong,
   with no one to gather up
      the fugitives.
6 But after that, I will restore
   the fortunes[g] of the Ammonites.
      ⌊This is⌋ the LORD's declaration.

---

[a]48:41 Or Kerioth has   [b]48:47 Or will end the captivity   [c]49:1 LXX, Syr, Vg; MT reads Malkam   [d]49:1 = Molech; 1 Kg
11:5   [e]49:3 Or sheep pens   [f]49:4 Or about your strength, your ebbing strength   [g]49:6 Or will end the captivity

Prophecies against Edom

⁷ About Edom, this is what the LORD of Hosts says:

> Is there no longer wisdom
>   in Teman?ᵃ
> Has counsel perished
>   from the prudent?
> Has their wisdom rotted away?

⁸ Run! Turn back! Lie low,
>   residents of Dedan,
> for I will bring Esau's calamity
>   on him
> at the time I punish him.

⁹ If grape harvesters came to you,
>   wouldn't they leave
>   some gleanings?
> Were thieves to come in the night,
> they would destroy only
>   what they wanted.

¹⁰ But I will strip Esau bare;
> I will uncover his secret places.
> He will try to hide himself,
>   but he will be unable.
> His descendants will be destroyed
>   along with his relatives
>   and neighbors.
> He will exist no longer.

¹¹ Abandon your orphans;
>   I will preserve them;
> let your widows trust in Me.

¹² "For this is what the LORD says: If those who do not deserve to drink the cup must drink it, can you possibly remain unpunished? You will not remain unpunished, for you must drink ⌊it⌋ too. ¹³ For by Myself I have sworn"—the LORD's declaration—"Bozrahᵇ will become a desolation, a disgrace, a ruin, and a curse, and all her cities will become ruins forever."

¹⁴ I have heard a message
>   from the LORD;

> an envoy has been sent
>   among the nations:
> Assemble yourselves to come
>   against her.
> Rise up for war!

¹⁵ Look, I will certainly make you
>   insignificant among the nations,
> despised among humanity.

¹⁶ As to the terror you cause,ᶜ
> your presumptuous heart
>   has deceived you.
> You who live in the clefts
>   of the rock,ᵈ
> you who occupy
>   the mountain summit,
> though you elevate your nest
>   like the eagle,
> even from there I will bring
>   you down.
>   ⌊This is⌋ the LORD's declaration.

¹⁷ "Edom will become a desolation. Everyone who passes by her will be horrified and scoff because of all her wounds. ¹⁸ As when Sodom and Gomorrah were overthrown along with their neighbors," says the LORD, "no one will live there; no human being will even stay in it as a resident alien.

¹⁹ "Look, it will be like a lion coming up from the thicketsᵉ of the Jordan to the perennially watered grazing land. Indeed, I will chase Edom away from her ⌊land⌋ in a flash. I will appoint whoever is chosen for her. For who is like Me? Who will summon Me? Who is the shepherd who can stand against Me?"

²⁰ Therefore, hear the plans that the LORD has drawn up against Edom and the strategies He has devised against the people of Teman: The flock's little lambs will certainly be dragged away, and their grazing land will be made desolate because of them. ²¹ At the sound of their

---

ᵃ49:7 = southern Edom, or Edom; Ezk 25:13; Ob 9   ᵇ49:13 = Edom's capital; Am 1:12   ᶜ49:16 Lit *Your horror*
ᵈ49:16 = Petra; Jdg 1:36; 2 Kg 14:7; Is 16:1   ᵉ49:19 Lit *pride*; Jr 12:5; 50:44; Zch 11:3

fall the earth will quake; the sound of her cry will be heard at the •Red Sea. ²² Look! It will be like an eagle soaring upward, then swooping down and spreading its wings over Bozrah. In that day the hearts of Edom's warriors will be like the heart of a woman with contractions.

Prophecies against Damascus

²³ About Damascus:

Hamath and Arpad are
    put to shame,
for they have heard a bad report
    and are agitated;
in the sea there is anxiety
    that cannot be calmed.
²⁴ Damascus has become weak;
she has turned to run;
panic has gripped her.
Distress and labor pains
    have seized her
like a woman in labor.
²⁵ How can the city of praise
    not be abandoned,
the town that brings Me joy?
²⁶ Therefore, her young men will fall
    in her public squares;
all the warriors will be silenced
    in that day.
        ₍This is₎ the declaration of
            the LORD of Hosts.

²⁷ I will set fire to the wall
    of Damascus;
it will devour Ben-hadad's citadels.

Prophecies against Kedar and Hazor

²⁸ About Kedar and the kingdoms of Hazor, which Nebuchadnezzar, Babylon's king, defeated, this is what the LORD says:

Rise up, go against Kedar,
    and destroy the people of the east!

²⁹ They will take their tents
    and their flocks
along with their tent curtains
    and all their equipment.
They will take their camels
    for themselves.
They will call out to them:
    Terror is on every side!
³⁰ Run! Escape quickly! Lie low,
    residents of Hazor—
        ₍this is₎ the LORD's declaration—
for Nebuchadnezzar
    king of Babylon
has drawn up a plan against you;
he has devised a strategy
    against you.
³¹ Rise up, go up against a nation
    at ease,
one living in security.
        ₍This is₎ the LORD's declaration.
They have no doors, not even
    a gate bar;
they live alone.
³² Their camels will become plunder,
and their massive herds of cattle
    will become spoil.
I will scatter them to the wind
    in every direction,
those who shave their temples;
I will bring calamity on them
    across all their borders.
        ₍This is₎ the LORD's declaration.
³³ Hazor will become a jackals' den,
    a desolation forever.
No one will live there;
no human being will even stay in it
    as a resident alien.

Prophecies against Elam

³⁴ ₍This is₎ the word of the LORD that came to Jeremiah the prophet about Elam[a] at the beginning of the reign of Zedekiah king of Judah. ³⁵ This is what the LORD of Hosts says:

I am about to shatter Elam's bow,
the source[a] of their might.
36 I will bring the four winds
against Elam
from the four corners
of the heavens,
and I will scatter them
to all these winds.
There will not be a nation
to which Elam's banished ones
will not go.
37 I will devastate Elam
before their enemies,
before those who want to take
their lives.
I will bring disaster on them,
My burning anger.
⌊This is⌋ the LORD's declaration.
I will send the sword after them
until I finish them off.
38 I will set My throne in Elam,
and I will destroy the king
and officials from there.
⌊This is⌋ the LORD's declaration.

39 In the last days,
I will restore the fortunes[b] of Elam.
⌊This is⌋ the LORD's declaration.

Prophecies against Babylon

50 The word the LORD spoke about
Babylon, the land of the Chaldeans, through Jeremiah the prophet:

2 Announce to the nations;
proclaim and raise up a signal flag;
proclaim, and hide nothing.
Say: Babylon is captured;
Bel is put to shame;
Marduk is devastated;
her idols are put to shame;
her false gods, devastated.
3 For a nation from the north
will come against her;
it will make her land desolate.

No one will be living in it—
both man and beast will escape.[c]

Awakening and Escape of Israel

4 In those days and at that time—
⌊this is⌋ the LORD's declaration—
the Israelites and Judeans
will come together,
weeping as they come,
and will seek the LORD their God.
5 They will ask about Zion,
⌊turning⌋ their faces to this road.
They will come
and join themselves[d] to the LORD
in an everlasting covenant that will
never be forgotten.

6 My people are lost sheep;
their shepherds have
led them astray,
guiding them the wrong way
in the mountains.
They have wandered
from mountain to hill;
they have forgotten
their resting place.
7 All who found them
devoured them.
Their adversaries said:
We're not guilty;
instead, they have sinned
against the LORD,
their righteous grazing land,
the hope of their ancestors,
the LORD.

8 Escape from Babylon;
depart from the Chaldeans' land.
Be like the rams that lead the flock.
9 For I will soon stir up and bring
against Babylon
an assembly of great nations
from the north country.
They will line up
in battle formation against her;

---

[a] **49:35** Lit *first*   [b] **49:39** Or *will end the captivity*   [c] **50:3** Lit *escape; they will walk*   [d] **50:5** LXX; MT reads *Come and join yourselves*

from there she will be captured.
Their arrows will be like those
    of a skilled[a] warrior
who does not return empty-handed.

Fall of Babylon

10 The Chaldeans will
        become plunder;
    all her plunderers will be
        fully satisfied.
            ⌊This is⌋ the LORD's declaration.
11 Because you rejoice,
    because you sing in triumph—
    you who plundered
        My inheritance—
    because you frolic like a young cow
        treading grain
    and neigh like stallions,
12 your mother will be
        utterly humiliated;
    she who bore you will be
        put to shame.
    Look! She will lag behind
        all[b] the nations—
    a dry land, a wilderness,
        an •Arabah.
13 Because of the LORD's wrath,
    she will not be inhabited;
    she will become a desolation,
        every bit of her.
    Everyone who passes
        through Babylon
    will be horrified
    and scoff because of all her wounds.
14 Line up in battle formation
        around Babylon,
    all you archers!
    Shoot at her! Do not spare
        an arrow,
    for she has sinned against the LORD.
15 Raise a war cry against her
        on every side!
    She has thrown up her hands
        ⌊in surrender⌋;

her defense towers have fallen;
her walls are demolished.
Since this is
    the LORD's vengeance,
take out your vengeance on her;
as she has done, do the same
    to her.
16 Cut off the sower from Babylon
    as well as him who wields
        the sickle at harvest time.
    Because of the oppressor's sword,
    each will turn to his own people,
    each will flee to his own land.

Return of God's People

17 Israel is a stray lamb,
        chased by lions.
    The first who devoured him was
        the king of Assyria;
    this last who has crunched
        his bones
    was Nebuchadnezzar
        king of Babylon.

18 Therefore, this is what the LORD of
•Hosts, the God of Israel, says: "I am
about to punish the king of Babylon and
his land just as I punished the king of Assyria.

19 I will return Israel
        to his grazing land,
    and he will feed on Carmel
        and Bashan;
    he will be satisfied
    in the hill country of Ephraim
        and of Gilead.
20 In those days and at that time—
        ⌊this is⌋ the LORD's declaration—
    one will search for Israel's guilt,
    but there will be none,
    and for Judah's sins,
    but they will not be found,
    for I will forgive those I leave
        as a remnant.

---

[a]50:9 Some Hb mss, LXX, Syr; other Hb mss read *bereaving*   [b]50:12 Lit *Look! The last of*

Invasion of Babylon

21 Go against the land of Merathaim,
and against those living in Pekod.
Put them to the sword;
•completely destroy them—
ᴛthis isᴊ the LORD's declaration—
do everything I have
commanded you.

22 The sound of war is in the land—
a great destruction.

23 How the hammer
of the whole earth
is cut down and smashed!
What a horror Babylon has become
among the nations!

24 Babylon, I laid a trap for you,
and you were caught,
but you did not even know it.
You were found and captured
because you fought
against the LORD.

25 The LORD opened His armory
and brought out His weapons
of wrath,
because it is a task of the Lord GOD
of Hosts
in the land of the Chaldeans.

26 Come against her
from the most distant places.ᵃ
Open her granaries;
pile her up like mounds of grain
and completely destroy her.
Leave her no survivors.

27 Put all her young bulls
to the sword;
let them go down to the slaughter.
Woe to them, because their day
has come,
the time of their punishment.

Humiliation of Babylon

28 ᴛThere isᴊ a voice of fugitives
and escapees
from the land of Babylon
announcing in Zion the vengeance
of the LORD our God,
the vengeance for His temple.

29 Summon the archers to Babylon,
all who string the bow;
camp all around her;
let none escape.
Repay her according to her deeds;
just as she has done, do the same
to her,
for she has acted arrogantly
against the LORD,
against the Holy One of Israel.

30 Therefore, her young men will fall
in her public squares;
all the warriors will be silenced
in that day.
ᴛThis isᴊ the LORD's declaration.

31 Look, I am against you,
you arrogant one—
ᴛthis isᴊ the declaration of
the Lord GOD of Hosts—
because your day has come,
the time when I will punish you.

32 The arrogant will stumble and fall
with no one to pick him up.
I will set fire to his cities,
and it will consume everything
around him."

Desolation of Babylon

33 This is what the LORD of Hosts
says:

Israelites and Judeans alike
have been oppressed.
All their captors hold them fast;
they refuse to release them.

34 Their Redeemer is strong;
the LORD of Hosts is His name.
He will fervently plead their case
so that He might bring rest
to the earth
but turmoil to those who live
in Babylon.

ᵃ50:26 Lit from the end

35 A sword is over the Chaldeans—
    ⌊this is⌋ the LORD's declaration—
against those who live in Babylon,
against her officials, and against
    her sages.
36 A sword is against the diviners,
and they will act foolishly.
A sword is
    against her heroic warriors,
and they will be terrified.
37 A sword is against his horses
    and chariots
and against all the foreigners
    among them,
and they will be like women.
A sword is against her treasuries,
and they will be plundered.
38 A drought will come on her waters,
and they will be dried up.
For it is a land of carved images,
and they go mad because of
    terrifying things.ᵃ

39 Therefore, desert creaturesᵇ
    will live with jackals,
and ostriches will also live in her.
It will never again be inhabited
or lived in through all generations.
40 Just as when God overthrew Sodom
    and Gomorrah
and their neighboring towns—
    ⌊this is⌋ the LORD's declaration—
so no one will live there;
no human being will even stay
    in it
as a resident alien.

Conquest of Babylon

41 Look! A people comes
    from the north.
A great nation and many kings
    will be stirred up
from the remote regions
    of the earth.

42 They grasp bow and javelin.
They are cruel and show no mercy.
Their voice roars like the sea,
and they ride on horses,
lined up like men
    in battle formation
against you, Daughter of Babylon.
43 The king of Babylon has heard
    reports about them,
and his hands fall helpless.
Distress has seized him—
    pain, like a woman in labor.

God: Who is like Me?

44 "Look, it will be like a lion coming
up from the thicketsᶜ of the Jordan to the
perennially watered grazing land. Indeed, I will chase Babylonᵈ away from
her ⌊land⌋ in a flash. I will appoint whoever is chosen for her. For who is like
Me? Who will summon Me? Who is the
shepherd who can stand against Me?"
45 Therefore, hear the plans that the
LORD has drawn up against Babylon and
the strategies He has devised against the
land of the Chaldeans: Certainly the
flock's little lambs will be dragged away;
certainly the grazing land will be made
desolate because of them. 46 At the
sound of Babylon's conquest the earth
will quake; a cry will be heard among
the nations.

God Judges Babylon

51 This is what the LORD says:

I am about to stir up
    a destructive windᵉ
against Babylon
and against the population
    of Leb-qamai.ᶠ
2 I will send strangers to Babylon
who will scatter her and strip
    her land bare,

ᵃ50:38 Or of dreaded gods   ᵇ50:39 Or desert demons; Rv 18:2   ᶜ50:44 Lit pride; Jr 12:5; 50:44; Zch 11:3
ᵈ50:44 Lit them   ᵉ51:1 Or stir up the spirit of a destroyer   ᶠ51:1 = a name for Chaldeans

for they will come against her
from every side in the day
    of disaster.
3 Don't let the archer string
    his bow;
don't let him put on[a] his armor.
Don't spare her young men;
•completely destroy
    her entire army!
4 Those who were slain will fall
    in the land of the Chaldeans,
those who were pierced through,
    in her streets.
5 For Israel and Judah are not
    left widowed
by their God, the LORD of •Hosts,
though their land is full of guilt
against the Holy One of Israel.

6 Leave Babylon;
save your lives, each of you!
Don't be silenced by her guilt.
For this is the time
    of the LORD's vengeance—
He will pay her what she deserves.
7 Babylon was a golden cup
    in the LORD's hand
making the whole earth drunk.
The nations drank her wine;
therefore, the nations go mad.
8 Suddenly Babylon fell
    and was shattered.
Wail for her;
get balm for her wound—
perhaps she can be healed.

9 We tried to heal Babylon,
but she could not be healed.
Abandon her!
Let each of us go to his own land,
for her judgment extends to the sky
and reaches as far as the clouds.

10 The LORD has brought about
    our vindication;
come, let's tell in Zion

what the LORD our God
    has accomplished.
11 Sharpen the arrows!
Fill the quivers!
The LORD has put it into the mind
of the kings of the Medes
because His plan is aimed
    at Babylon
to destroy her,
for it is the LORD's vengeance,
vengeance for His temple.
12 Raise up a signal flag
against the walls of Babylon;
fortify the watch post;
set the watchmen in place;
prepare the ambush.
For the LORD has both planned
    and accomplished
what He has threatened
against those who live in Babylon.
13 You who reside by many waters,
rich in treasures,
your end has come,
your life thread is cut.

Praise to God

14 The LORD of Hosts has sworn by
Himself:

I will fill you up with men
    as with locusts,
and they will sing the victory song
    over you.

15 He made the earth by His power,
established the world
    by His wisdom,
and spread out the heavens
    by His understanding.
16 When He thunders,[b]
the waters in the heavens are
    in turmoil,
and He causes the clouds
to rise from the ends of the earth.
He makes lightning for the rain

and brings the wind
   from His storehouses.

17 Everyone is stupid and ignorant.
   Every goldsmith is put to shame
      by ⌊his⌋ carved image,
   for his cast images are a lie;
   there is no breath in them.
18 They are worthless, a work
      to be mocked.
   At the time of their punishment
   they will be destroyed.
19 Jacob's Portion[a] is not like these
   because He is the One who formed
      all things.
   ⌊Israel is⌋ the tribe
      of His inheritance;
   the LORD of Hosts is His name.

"You Are My Battle Club"

20 You are My battle club,
   My weapons of war.
   With you I will smash nations;
   with you I will bring kingdoms
      to ruin.
21 With you I will smash the horse
      and its rider;
   with you I will smash the chariot
      and its rider.
22 With you I will smash man
      and woman;
   with you I will smash the old man
      and the youth;
   with you I will smash
      the young man and the virgin.
23 With you I will smash the shepherd
      and his flock;
   with you I will smash the farmer
      and his ox-team.[b]
   With you I will smash governors
      and officials.

Babylon Repaid

24 "I will repay Babylon and all the residents of Chaldea for all their evil they have done in Zion before your very eyes."
      ⌊This is⌋ the LORD's declaration.

25 Look, I am against you,
      devastating mountain—
      ⌊this is⌋ the LORD's declaration—
   you devastate the whole earth.
   I will stretch out My hand
      against you,
   roll you down from the cliffs,
   and turn you into
      a burned-out mountain.
26 No one will be able to retrieve
      a cornerstone
   or a foundation stone from you,
   because you will become
      desolate forever.
      ⌊This is⌋ the LORD's declaration.

27 Raise a signal flag in the land;
   blow a ram's horn
      among the nations;
   set apart the nations against her.
   Summon kingdoms against her—
   Ararat, Minni, and Ashkenaz.
   Appoint a marshal against her;
   bring up horses like a swarm[c]
      of locusts.
28 Set apart the nations for battle
      against her—
   the kings of Media,
   her governors and all her officials,
   and all the lands they rule.
29 The earth quakes and trembles,
   because the LORD's purposes
      against Babylon stand:
   to make the land of Babylon
      an uninhabited desolation.
30 Babylon's warriors have
      stopped fighting;
   they sit in their strongholds.
   Their might is exhausted;
   they have become like women.
   Babylon's homes have been
      set ablaze,

---

[a]51:19 = the LORD   [b]51:23 Lit yoke   [c]51:27 Hb obscure

her gate bars are shattered.
³¹ Messenger races
      to meet messenger,
and herald to meet herald,
to announce to the king of Babylon
that his city has been captured
from end ⌊to end⌋.
³² The fords have been seized,
the marshes set on fire,
and the soldiers are terrified.

³³ For this is what the LORD of Hosts,
the God of Israel, says:

The daughter of Babylon is
      like a threshing floor
at the time it is trampled.
In just a little while
      her harvest time will come.

³⁴ "Nebuchadnezzar of Babylon
      has devoured me;
he has crushed me.
He has set me aside
      like an empty dish;
he has swallowed me
      like a sea monster;
he filled his belly
      with my delicacies;
he has vomited me out,"^a
³⁵ says the inhabitant of Zion;
"Let the violence ⌊done⌋ to me
      and my family ⌊be done⌋
      to Babylon.
Let my blood be on the inhabitants
      of Chaldea,"
says Jerusalem.

Lord's Vengeance for Israel

³⁶ Therefore, this is what the LORD
says:

I am about to plead your case
and take vengeance on your behalf;
I will dry up her sea
and make her fountain run dry.

³⁷ Babylon will become a heap
      of rubble,
a jackals' den,
a desolation and an object of scorn,
without inhabitant.
³⁸ They will roar together
      like young lions;
they will growl like lion cubs.
³⁹ While they are flushed with heat,
      I will serve them a feast,
and I will make them drunk so that
      they revel.^b
Then they will fall asleep forever
and never wake up.
            ⌊This is⌋ the LORD's declaration.
⁴⁰ I will bring them down like lambs
      to the slaughter,
like rams together with male goats.

⁴¹ How Sheshach has been captured,
the praise
      of the whole earth seized.
What a horror Babylon has become
among the nations!
⁴² The sea has risen over Babylon;
she is covered
      with its turbulent waves.
⁴³ Her cities have become
      a desolation,
a dry and arid land,
a land where no one lives,
where no human being
      passes through.

God Punishes Bel and Idols

⁴⁴ I will punish Bel in Babylon.
I will make him vomit
      what he swallowed.
The nations will no longer stream
      to him;
even Babylon's wall will fall.

⁴⁵ Come out from among her,
      My people!
Save your lives, each of you,

---

^a**51:34** Lit *has rinsed me off*   ^b**51:39** LXX reads *pass out*

from the LORD's burning anger.
⁴⁶ May you not become faint-hearted
    and fearful
when the report is proclaimed
    in the land,
for the report will come one year,
and then another the next year.
There will be violence in the land
with ruler against ruler.
⁴⁷ Therefore, look, the days
    are coming
when I will punish
    Babylon's carved images.
Her entire land will suffer shame,
and all her slain will lie fallen
    within her.
⁴⁸ Heaven and earth and everything
    in them
will shout for joy over Babylon
because the destroyers
    from the north
will come against her.
    ⌊This is⌋ the LORD's declaration.

Israel and Babylon

⁴⁹ Babylon must fall ⌊because of⌋
    the slain of Israel,
even as the slain of all the earth fell
because of Babylon.
⁵⁰ You who have escaped the sword,
go and do not stand still!
Remember the LORD from far away,
and let Jerusalem come
    to your mind.

⁵¹ We are ashamed
because we have heard insults.
Humiliation covers our faces
because foreigners have entered
the holy places
    of the LORD's temple.

⁵² Therefore, look, the days
    are coming—
    ⌊this is⌋ the LORD's declaration—
when I will punish
    her carved images,

and the wounded will groan
throughout her land.
⁵³ Even if Babylon should ascend
    to the heavens
and fortify her tall fortresses,
destroyers will come against her
    from Me.
    ⌊This is⌋ the LORD's declaration.

Devastation of Babylon

⁵⁴ The sound of a cry from Babylon!
The sound of great destruction
from the land of the Chaldeans!
⁵⁵ For the LORD is going
    to devastate Babylon;
He will silence her mighty voice.
Their waves roar
    like abundant waters;
the tumult of their voice resounds,
⁵⁶ for a destroyer is coming
    against her,
against Babylon.
Her warriors will be captured,
their bows shattered,
for the LORD is a God
    of retribution;
He will certainly repay.
⁵⁷ I will make her princes
    and sages drunk,
along with her governors, officials,
    and warriors.
Then they will fall asleep forever
and never wake up.
    ⌊This is⌋ the King's declaration;
    the LORD of Hosts is His name.

⁵⁸ This is what the LORD of Hosts says:

Babylon's thick walls will be
    totally demolished,
and her high gates consumed
    by fire.
The peoples will have labored
    for nothing;
the nations will exhaust themselves
    ⌊only to feed⌋ the fire.

Jeremiah's Command to Seraiah about Babylon's Disaster

59 ⌊This is⌋ what Jeremiah the prophet commanded Seraiah son of Neriah son of Mahseiah, the quartermaster, when he went to Babylon with Zedekiah king of Judah in the fourth year of Zedekiah's reign. 60 Jeremiah wrote on one scroll about all the disaster that would come to Babylon; all these words were written against Babylon.

61 Jeremiah told Seraiah, "When you get to Babylon, see that you read all these words aloud. 62 You must say, 'LORD, You have threatened to cut off this place so that no one will live in it— man or beast. Indeed, it will remain desolate forever.' 63 When you have finished reading this scroll, tie a stone to it and throw it into the middle of the Euphrates River. 64 Then say, 'In the same way, Babylon will sink and never rise again because of the disaster I am bringing on her. They will grow weary.'"

The words of Jeremiah end here.

Fall of Jerusalem

52 Zedekiah was 21 years old when he became king; he reigned 11 years in Jerusalem. His mother's name was Hamutal daughter of Jeremiah; ⌊she was⌋ from Libnah. 2 Zedekiah did what was evil in the LORD's sight just as Jehoiakim had done. 3 Because of the LORD's anger, it came to the point in Jerusalem and Judah that He finally banished them from His presence. Nevertheless, Zedekiah rebelled against the king of Babylon.

4 In the ninth year of Zedekiah's reign, on the tenth day of the tenth month, King Nebuchadnezzar of Babylon advanced against Jerusalem with his entire army. They laid siege to the city and built a siege wall all around it. 5 The city was under siege until King Zedekiah's eleventh year.

6 By the ninth day of the fourth month the famine was so severe in the city that the people of the land had no food. 7 Then the city was broken into, and all the warriors fled. They left the city by night by way of the gate between the two walls near the king's garden, though the Chaldeans surrounded the city. They made their way along the route to the •Arabah. 8 The Chaldean army pursued the king and overtook Zedekiah in the plains of Jericho. Zedekiah's entire army was scattered from him. 9 The Chaldeans seized the king and brought him to the king of Babylon at Riblah in the land of Hamath, and he passed sentence on him.

10 At Riblah the king of Babylon slaughtered Zedekiah's sons before his eyes and also slaughtered the Judean commanders. 11 Then he blinded Zedekiah and bound him with bronze chains. The king of Babylon brought Zedekiah to Babylon, where he kept him in custody[a] until his dying day.

Babylon Commander Burns Jerusalem Temple

12 On the tenth day of the fifth month—which was the nineteenth year of King Nebuchadnezzar, king of Babylon—Nebuzaradan, the commander of the guards, entered Jerusalem as the representative of[b] the king of Babylon. 13 He burned the LORD's temple, the king's palace, all the houses of Jerusalem, and all the houses of the nobles. 14 The whole Chaldean army with the commander of the guards tore down all the walls surrounding Jerusalem. 15 Nebuzaradan, the commander of the guards, deported some of the poorest of the people, as

---

a 52:11 Lit in a house of guards   b 52:12 Lit Jerusalem; he stood before

well as the rest of the people who were left in the city, the deserters who had defected to the king of Babylon, and the rest of the craftsmen. ¹⁶ But some of the poor people of the land Nebuzaradan, the commander of the guards, left to be vinedressers and farmers.

Chaldeans Plunder Precious Metals

¹⁷ Now the Chaldeans broke into pieces the bronze pillars for the LORD's temple and the water carts and the bronze reservoir that were in the LORD's temple, and carried all the bronze to Babylon. ¹⁸ They took the pots, the shovels, the wick trimmers, the sprinkling basins, the dishes, and all the bronze articles used in ⌊temple⌋ service. ¹⁹ The commander of the guards took away the bowls, the firepans, the sprinkling basins, the pots, the lampstands, the pans, and the drink offering bowls—whatever was gold or silver.

²⁰ As for the two pillars, the one reservoir, and the 12 bronze bulls under the water carts that King Solomon had made for the LORD's temple, the weight of the bronze of all these articles was beyond measure. ²¹ One pillar was 27 feet[a] tall, had a circumference of 18 feet,[b] was hollow—four fingers thick—²² and had a bronze capital on top of it. One capital, encircled by bronze latticework and pomegranates, stood seven and a half feet[c] high. The second pillar was the same, with pomegranates. ²³ ⌊Each capital had⌋ 96 pomegranates all around it. All the pomegranates around the latticework numbered 100.

Commander Nebuzaradan Takes Captives

²⁴ The commander of the guards also took away Seraiah the chief priest, Zephaniah the priest of the second rank, and the three doorkeepers. ²⁵ From the city he took a court official who had been appointed over the warriors; seven trusted royal aides[d] found in the city; the secretary of the commander of the army, who enlisted the people of the land for military duty; and 60 men from the common people who were found within the city. ²⁶ Nebuzaradan, the commander of the guards, took them and brought them to the king of Babylon at Riblah. ²⁷ The king of Babylon put them to death at Riblah in the land of Hamath. Thus Judah went into exile from its land.

Judah into Exile

²⁸ These are the people Nebuchadnezzar deported: in the seventh year, 3,023 Jews; ²⁹ in his eighteenth year,[e] 832 people from Jerusalem; ³⁰ in Nebuchadnezzar's twenty-third year, Nebuzaradan, the commander of the guards, deported 745 Jews. All together 4,600 people ⌊were deported⌋.

King of Babylon Pardons Judah's King Jehoiachin

³¹ On the twenty-fifth day of the twelfth month of the thirty-seventh year of the exile of Judah's King Jehoiachin, Evil-merodach king of Babylon, in the ⌊first⌋ year of his reign, pardoned King Jehoiachin of Judah and released him from the prison. ³² He spoke kindly to him and set his throne above the thrones of the kings who were with him in Babylon. ³³ So Jehoiachin changed his prison clothes, and he dined regularly in the presence of the king of Babylon for the rest of his life. ³⁴ As for his allowance, a regular allowance was given to him by the king of Babylon, a portion for each day until the day of his death, for the rest of his life.

---

[a]**52:21** Lit *18 cubits*   [b]**52:21** Lit *12 cubits*   [c]**52:22** Lit *five cubits*   [d]**52:25** Lit *seven men who look on the king's face*
[e]**52:29** Some Hb mss, Syr add *he deported*

LAMENTATIONS

Lament over Jerusalem

א Alef

1 How[a] she sits alone,
  the city ⌊once⌋ crowded
    with people!
She who was great
    among the nations
has become like a widow.
The princess among
    the provinces
has become a slave.

ב Bet

2 She weeps aloud
    during the night,
with tears on her cheeks.
There is no one to offer
    her comfort,
⌊not one⌋ from all her lovers.[b]
All her friends
    have betrayed her;
they have become her enemies.

ג Gimel

3 Judah has gone into exile
following[c] affliction
    and harsh slavery;
she lives among the nations
but finds no place to rest.
All her pursuers
    have overtaken her
in narrow places.

ד Dalet

4 The roads to Zion mourn,
for no one comes
    to the appointed festivals.
All her gates are deserted;
her priests groan,
her young women grieve,
and she herself is bitter.

ה He

5 Her adversaries have become
    ⌊her⌋ masters;
her enemies are at ease,
for the LORD has made her suffer
because of her many transgressions.
Her children have gone away
as captives before the adversary.

ו Vav

6 All her splendor has vanished
from Daughter Zion.
Her leaders are like stags
that find no pasture;
they walk away exhausted
before the hunter.

ז Zayin

7 During the days of her affliction
    and homelessness
Jerusalem remembers all
    her precious belongings
that were ⌊hers⌋ in days of old.
When her people fell
    into the adversary's hand,
she had no one to help.
The adversaries looked at her,
laughing over her downfall.

ח Khet

Sins of Jerusalem

8 <u>Jerusalem has sinned grievously;</u>
<u>therefore, she has become an object</u>
    <u>of scorn.</u>[d]
All who honored her
    ⌊now⌋ despise her,
for they have seen her nakedness.
She herself groans and turns away.

ט Tet

9 Her uncleanness ⌊stains⌋ her skirts.
She never considered her end.

---

a 1:1 The stanzas in Lm 1–4 form an •acrostic.   b 1:2 = Jerusalem's political allies; Jr 22:20-22; Ezk 23   c 1:3 Or because of   d 1:8 Or become impure

Her downfall was astonishing;
there was no one to comfort her.
LORD, look on my affliction,
for the enemy triumphs!

' Yod

10 The adversary has seized
all her precious belongings.
She has even seen the nations
enter her sanctuary—
those You had forbidden
to enter Your assembly.

כ Kaf

Jerusalem's People Groan

11 All her people groan
while they search for bread.
They have traded
  their precious belongings for food
in order to stay alive.
LORD, look and see
how I have become despised.

ל Lamed

12 Is this nothing to you, all you
  who pass by?
Look and see!
Is there any pain like mine,
which was dealt out to me,
which the LORD made ⌊me⌋ suffer
on the day of His burning anger?

מ Mem

13 He sent fire from on high
  into my bones;
He made it descend.ᵃ
He spread a net for my feet
and turned me back.
He made me desolate,
sick all day long.

נ Nun

Jerusalem Recognizes Sins

14 My transgressions
  have been formed into a yoke,ᵇ ᶜ

fastened together by His hand;
they have been placed on my neck,
and the Lord has broken
  my strength.
He has handed me over
to those I cannot withstand.

ס Samek

15 The Lord has rejected
all the mighty men within me.
He has summoned an armyᵈ
  against me
to crush my young warriors.
The Lord has trampled
  Virgin Daughter Judah
⌊like grapes⌋ in a winepress.

ע Ayin

Jerusalem Weeps

16 I weep because of these things;
my eyes flowᵉ with tears.
For there is no one nearby
  to comfort ⌊me⌋,
no one to keep me alive.
My children are desolate
because the enemy has prevailed.

פ Pe

17 Zion stretches out her hands;
there is no one to comfort her.
The LORD has issued a decree
  against Jacob
that his neighbors should be
  his adversaries.
Jerusalem has become
something impure among them.

צ Tsade

Confession of Sin

18 The LORD is in the right,
for I have rebelled
  against His command.
Listen, all you people;
look at my pain.

ᵃ1:13 DSS, LXX; MT reads *bones, and it prevailed against them*   ᵇ1:14 Some Hb mss, LXX read *He kept watch over my transgressions*   ᶜ1:14 Or *The yoke of my transgressions is bound*; Hb obscure   ᵈ1:15 Or *has announced an appointed time*   ᵉ1:16 Lit *my eye, my eye flows*

My young men and women
have gone into captivity.

ק Qof

19 I called to my lovers,
but they betrayed me.
My priests and elders
perished in the city
while searching for food
to keep themselves alive.

ר Resh

20 LORD, see how I am in distress.
I am churning within;
my heart is broken,[a]
for I have been very rebellious.
Outside, the sword takes
the children;
inside, there is death.

שׁ Shin

21 People have heard me groaning,
but there is no one to comfort me.
All my enemies have heard
of my misfortune;
they are glad that
You have caused ⌊it⌋.
Bring on the day
You have announced,
so that they may become like me.

ת Tav

22 Let all their wickedness come
before You,
and deal with them
as You have dealt with me
because of all my transgressions.
For my groans are many,
and I am sick at heart.

God's Judgment on Jerusalem

א Alef

2 How the Lord has overshadowed
Daughter Zion with His anger!
He has thrown down Israel's glory

from heaven to earth.
He has abandoned His footstool[b]
in the day of His anger.

ב Bet

Wrath of God

2 Without compassion the Lord
has swallowed up
all the dwellings of Jacob.
In His wrath He has demolished
the fortified cities
of Daughter Judah.
He brought ⌊them⌋ to the ground
and defiled the kingdom
and its leaders.

ג Gimel

3 He has cut off every •horn
of Israel
in His burning anger
and withdrawn His right hand
in the presence of the enemy.
He has blazed against Jacob
like a flaming fire
that consumes everything
⌊in its path⌋.

ד Dalet

4 Like an enemy He has bent
His bow;
His right hand is positioned
like an adversary.
He has killed everyone
who was loved,[c]
pouring out His wrath like fire
on the tent of Daughter Zion.

ה He

5 The Lord is like an enemy;
He has swallowed up Israel.
He swallowed up all its palaces
and destroyed its fortified cities.
He has multiplied mourning
and lamentation
within Daughter Judah.

---

a **1:20** Lit *is turned within me*   b **2:1** Either the ark of the covenant or the temple   c **2:4** Lit *killed all the delights of the eye*; Ezk 24:16

ו *Vav*

Lord Rejects Temple

6 He has done violence
   to His temple[a]
as if ⌊it were⌋ a garden ⌊booth⌋,
destroying His place of meeting.
The LORD has abolished
appointed festivals and Sabbaths
   in Zion.
He has despised king and priest
in His fierce anger.

ז *Zayin*

7 The Lord has rejected His altar,
repudiated His sanctuary;
He has handed the walls
   of her palaces
over to the enemy.
They have raised a shout
   in the house of the LORD
as on the day
   of an appointed festival.

ח *Khet*

God Destroys Wall of Zion

8 The LORD determined to destroy
the wall of Daughter Zion.
He stretched out a measuring line
and did not restrain Himself
   from destroying.
He made the ramparts
   and walls grieve;
together they waste away.

ט *Tet*

9 Zion's gates have fallen
   to the ground;
He has destroyed and shattered
   the bars on her ⌊gates⌋.
Her king and her leaders ⌊live⌋
   among the nations,
instruction[b] is no more,
and even her prophets receive
no vision from the LORD.

י *Yod*

Zion's Women Mourn

10 The elders of Daughter Zion
sit on the ground in silence.
They have thrown dust
   on their heads
and put on •sackcloth.
The young women of Jerusalem
have bowed their heads
   to the ground.

כ *Kaf*

11 My eyes are worn out
   from weeping;
I am churning within.
My heart is poured out in grief[c]
because of the destruction
   of my dear people,
because children and infants faint
in the streets of the city.

ל *Lamed*

12 They cry out to their mothers:
Where is the grain and wine?
as they faint like the wounded
in the streets of the city,
as their lives fade away
in the arms of their mothers.

מ *Mem*

"Who Can Heal You?"

13 What can I say on your behalf?
To what can I compare you,
   Daughter Jerusalem?
What can I liken you to,
so that I may console you,
   Virgin Daughter Zion?
For your ruin is as vast as the sea.
Who can heal you?

נ *Nun*

14 Your prophets saw visions for you
that were empty and deceptive;
they did not reveal your guilt
and so restore your fortunes.

---

[a] **2:6** Lit *booth*   [b] **2:9** Or *the law*   [c] **2:11** Lit *My liver is poured out on the ground*

They saw •oracles for you
that were empty and misleading.

ס Samek
Scorn of Observers

15 All who pass by
ᴌscornfullyᴊ clap their hands at you.
They hiss and shake their heads
at Daughter Jerusalem:
Is this the city that was called
the perfection of beauty,
the joy of the whole earth?

פ Pe

16 All your enemies
open their mouths against you.
They hiss and gnash ᴌtheirᴊ teeth,
saying, "We have swallowed
ᴌherᴊ up.
This is the day we have waited for!
We have lived to see ᴌitᴊ."

ע Ayin

17 The LORD has done
what He planned;
He has accomplished His decree,
which He ordained in days of old.
He has demolished
without compassion,
letting the enemy gloat over you
and exalting the horn
of your adversaries.

צ Tsade
Crying Hearts

18 The hearts of the people cry out
to the Lord.
Wall of Daughter Zion,
let ᴌyourᴊ tears run down like a river
day and night.
Give yourself no relief
and your[a] eyes no rest.

ק Qof

19 Arise, cry out in the night,
from the first watch of the night.
Pour out your heart like water
before the Lord's presence.
Lift up your hands to Him
for the lives of your children
who are fainting from hunger
on the corner of every street.

ר Resh

20 LORD, look and consider
who You have done this to.
Should women eat
their own children,
the infants they have nurtured?[b]
Should priests and prophets
be killed in the Lord's sanctuary?

ש Shin

21 ᴌBothᴊ young and old
are lying on the ground
in the streets.
My young men and women
have fallen by the sword.
You have killed ᴌthemᴊ in the day
of Your anger,
slaughtering without compassion.

ת Tav

22 You summoned my attackers[c]
on every side,
as if ᴌforᴊ an appointed festival day;
on the day of the LORD's anger
no one escaped or survived.
My enemy has destroyed
those I nurtured[d] and reared.

Author's Personal Testimony
א Alef

3 I am the man
who has seen affliction
under the rod of God's wrath.
2 He has driven me away
and forced ᴌmeᴊ to walk
in darkness instead of light.
3 Yes, He repeatedly turns His hand
against me all day long.

a2:18 Lit and the daughter of your   b2:20 Or infants in a healthy condition; Hb obscure   c2:22 Or terrors   d2:22 Or I
bore healthy; Hb obscure

‎בּ Bet

4 He has worn away my flesh
   and skin;
   He has shattered my bones.
5 He has laid siege against me,
   encircling me with bitterness
      and hardship.
6 He has made me dwell in darkness
   like those who have been dead
      for ages.

‎גּ Gimel

7 He has walled me in
   so I cannot escape;
   He has weighed me down
      with chains.
8 Even when I cry out and plead
      for help,
   He rejects my prayer.
9 He has walled in my ways
      with cut stones;
   He has made my paths crooked.

‎דּ Dalet

10 He is[a] a bear waiting in ambush,
   a lion in hiding;
11 He forced me off my way
      and tore me to pieces;
   He left me desolate.
12 He bent His bow
   and set me as the target
      for His arrow.

‎הּ He

13 He pierced my kidneys
   with His arrows.
14 I am a laughingstock
      to all my people,[b]
   mocked by their songs all day long.
15 He filled me with bitterness,
   sated me with •wormwood.

‎וּ Vav

16 He ground my teeth on gravel
   and made me cower[c] in the dust.

17 My soul has been deprived[d]
      of peace;
   I have forgotten what happiness is.
18 Then I thought: My future[e] is lost,
   as well as my hope from the Lᴏʀᴅ.

‎זּ Zayin

19 Remember[f] my affliction
      and my homelessness,
   the wormwood and the poison.
20 I continually remember ⌊them⌋
   and have become depressed.[g]

A Source of Hope

21 Yet I call this to mind,
   and therefore I have hope:

‎חּ Khet

22 ⌊Because of⌋ the Lᴏʀᴅ's faithful love
   we do not perish,[h]
   for His mercies never end.
23 They are new every morning;
   great is Your faithfulness!
24 I say: The Lᴏʀᴅ is my portion,
   therefore I will put my hope in Him.

‎טּ Tet

Wait Quietly

25 The Lᴏʀᴅ is good to those who wait
      for Him,
   to the person who seeks Him.
26 It is good to wait quietly
   for deliverance from the Lᴏʀᴅ.
27 It is good for a man to bear the yoke
   while he is ⌊still⌋ young.

‎יּ Yod

28 Let him sit alone and be silent,
   for God has disciplined him.
29 Let him put his mouth
      in the dust—
   perhaps there is ⌊still⌋ hope.
30 Let him offer ⌊his⌋ cheek
   to the one who would strike him;
   let him be filled with shame.

---

[a]3:10 Lit *is to me*   [b]3:14 Some Hb mss, LXX, Vg; other Hb mss, Syr read *all peoples*   [c]3:16 Or *and trampled me*   [d]3:17 Syr, Vg; MT reads *You deprived my soul*   [e]3:18 Or *splendor*   [f]3:19 Or *I remember*   [g]3:20 Alt Hb tradition reads *and You cause me to collapse*   [h]3:22 One Hb mss, Syr, Tg read *The Lᴏʀᴅ's faithful love, indeed, does not perish*

כ *Kaf*

Lord Will Not Reject Forever

31 For the Lord
    will not reject ⌊us⌋ forever.
32 Even if He causes suffering,
    He will show compassion
    according to His abundant,
        faithful love.
33 For He does not enjoy
    bringing affliction
    or suffering on •mankind.

ל *Lamed*

Lord's against Injustice

34 Crushing all the prisoners
    of the land[a]
    beneath one's feet,
35 denying justice to a man
    in the presence of the •Most High,
36 or suppressing a person's lawsuit—
    the Lord does not approve
    ⌊of these things⌋.

מ *Mem*

Lord Ordains All

37 Who is there who speaks
    and it happens,
    unless the Lord has ordained ⌊it⌋?
38 Do not both adversity and good
    come from the mouth
    of the Most High?
39 Why should ⌊any⌋ living
    person complain,
    ⌊any⌋ man, because
    of the punishment for his sins?

נ *Nun*

Call to Repentance

40 Let us search out and examine
    our ways,
    and turn back to the LORD.
41 Let us lift up our hearts
    and ⌊our⌋ hands
    to God in heaven:

42 We have sinned and rebelled;
    You have not forgiven.

ס *Samek*

43 You have covered Yourself in anger
    and pursued us;
    You have killed
    without compassion.
44 You have covered Yourself
    with a cloud
    so that no prayer can pass through.
45 You have made us disgusting filth
    among the peoples.

פ *Pe*

46 All our enemies
    open their mouths against us.
47 We have experienced panic
    and pitfall,
    devastation and destruction.
48 My eyes flow with streams of tears
    because of the destruction
    of my dear people.

ע *Ayin*

49 My eyes overflow unceasingly,
    without end,
50 until the LORD looks down
    from heaven and sees.
51 My eyes bring me grief
    because of ⌊the fate of⌋
    all the women in my city.

צ *Tsade*

Jeremiah Recalls Pit

52 For no ⌊apparent⌋ reason,
    my enemies[b]
    hunted me like a bird.
53 They dropped me alive into[c] a pit
    and threw stones at me.
54 Water flooded over my head,
    and I thought: I'm going to die!

ק *Qof*

55 I called on Your name, •Yahweh,
    from the depths of the •Pit.

ᵃ**3:34** Or *earth*   ᵇ**3:52** Or *Those who were my enemies for no reason*   ᶜ**3:53** Or *They ended my life in*; Hb obscure

⁵⁶ You hear my plea:
Do not ignore my cry for relief.
⁵⁷ You come near when I call on You;
You say: "Do not be afraid."

ר Resh

Jeremiah's Faith in God

⁵⁸ You defend my cause, Lord;
You redeem my life.
⁵⁹ LORD, You see the wrong
done to me;
judge my case.
⁶⁰ You see all their malice,
all their plots against me.

שׁ Sin/ שׁ Shin

⁶¹ LORD, You hear their insults,
all their plots against me.
⁶² The slanderª and murmuring
of my opponents
attack me all day long.
⁶³ When they sit and when
they rise, look,
I am mocked by their songs.

ת Tav

⁶⁴ You will pay them back
what they deserve, LORD,
according to the work
of their hands.
⁶⁵ You will give them a heart
filled with anguish.ᵇ
May Your curse be on them!
⁶⁶ You will pursue ₍them₎ in anger
and destroy them
under Your heavens.ᶜ ᵈ

Terrors of the Besieged Jerusalem

א Alef

4 How the gold
has become tarnished,
the fine gold become dull!

The stones of the templeᵉ
lie scattered
at the corner of every street.

ב Bet

² Zion's precious people—
₍once₎ worth their weight
in pure gold—
how they are regarded as clay jars,
the work of a potter's hands!

ג Gimel

³ Even jackals offer ₍their₎ breasts
to nurse their young,
but my dear people
have become cruel
like ostriches in the wilderness.

ד Dalet

⁴ The nursing infant's tongue
clings to the roof of his mouth
from thirst.
Little children beg for bread,
but no one gives them ₍any₎.

ה He

⁵ Those who used to eat delicacies
are destitute in the streets;
those who were reared
in purple ₍garments₎
huddle in garbage heaps.

ו Vav

⁶ The punishment of my dear people
is greater than that of Sodom,
which was overthrown
in an instant
without a hand laid on it.

ז Zayin

⁷ Her dignitaries were brighter
than snow,
whiter than milk;
₍their₎ bodiesᶠ were more ruddy
than coral,
their appearance ₍like₎ sapphire.ᵍ

ª**3:62** Lit *lips*   ᵇ**3:65** Or *them an obstinate heart*; Hb obscure   ᶜ**3:66** LXX, Syr, Vg read *heavens, LORD*   ᵈ**3:66** Lit *under the LORD's heavens*   ᵉ**4:1** Or *The sacred gems*   ᶠ**4:7** Lit *bones*   ᵍ**4:7** Or *lapis lazuli*

ה Khet

8 ⌊Now⌋ they appear darker than soot;
   they are not recognized
      in the streets.
   Their skin has shriveled
      on their bones;
   it has become dry like wood.

ט Tet

9 Those slain by the sword are
      better off
   than those slain by hunger,
   who waste away,
      pierced ⌊with pain⌋
   because the fields lack produce.

י Yod

10 The hands of compassionate women
   have cooked their own children;
   they became their food
   during the destruction
      of my dear people.

כ Kaf

11 The LORD has exhausted His wrath,
   poured out His burning anger;
   He has ignited a fire in Zion,
   and it has consumed
      her foundations.

ל Lamed

Reason for Disaster:
Sins of Prophets and Priests

12 The kings of the earth
   and all the world's inhabitants
      did not believe
   that an enemy or adversary
   could enter Jerusalem's gates.

מ Mem

13 ⌊Yet it happened⌋ because of the sins
      of her prophets
   and the guilt of her priests,
   who shed the blood
      of the righteous
   within her.

נ Nun

14 Blind, they stumbled in the streets,
   defiled by this blood,
   so that no one dared
   to touch their garments.

ס Samek

15 "Stay away! Unclean!"
      people shouted at them.
   "Away, away! Don't touch ⌊us⌋!"
   So they wandered aimlessly.
   It was said among the nations,
   "They can stay here no longer."

פ Pe

16 The LORD Himself
      has scattered them;
   He regards them no more.
   The priests are not respected;
   the elders find no favor.

ע Ayin

17 All the while our eyes were failing
   ⌊as we looked⌋ in vain for assistance;
   we watched from our towers
   for a nation[a] that refused to help.

צ Tsade

18 Our steps were closely followed,
   so that we could not walk
      in our streets.
   Our end drew near; our time
      ran out.
   Our end had come!

ק Qof

19 Those who chased us were swifter
   than eagles in the sky;
   they relentlessly pursued us
      over the mountains
   and ambushed us in the wilderness.

ר Resh

20 The LORD's anointed,[b] the breath
      of our life,[c]
   was captured in their traps;
   we had said about him:

---

a 4:17 Probably Egypt   b 4:20 = King Zedekiah; 2 Kg 25:7   c 4:20 Lit nostrils

We will live under his protection
among the nations.

שׂ Sin

21 So rejoice and be glad,
Daughter Edom,
you resident of the land of Uz!
Yet the cup will pass to you as well;
you will get drunk
and expose yourself.

ת Tav

Zion's Punishment Complete

22 Daughter Zion, your punishment
is complete;
He will not lengthen your exile.ᵃ
But He will punish your iniquity,
Daughter Edom,
and will expose your sins.

Prayer for Restoration

5 •Yahweh, remember
what has happened to us.
Look, and see our disgrace!
2 Our inheritance
has been turned over to strangers,
our houses to foreigners.
3 We have become
orphans, fatherless;
our mothers are widows.
4 We must pay for the water
we drink;
our wood comes at a price.
5 We are closely pursued;
we are tired, and no one
offers us rest.
6 We made a treaty withᵇ Egypt
and with Assyria,
to get enough food.
7 Our fathers sinned;
they no longer exist,
but we bear their punishment.

8 Slaves rule over us;
no one rescues ⌊us⌋
from their hands.
9 We secure our food at the risk
of our lives
because of the sword
in the wilderness.
10 Our skin is as hotᶜ as an oven
from the ravages of hunger.
11 Women are raped in Zion,
virgins in the cities of Judah.
12 Princes are hung up by their hands;
elders are shown no respect.
13 Young men labor at millstones;
boys stumble under ⌊loads of⌋ wood.
14 The elders have left the city •gate,
the young men, their music.
15 Joy has left our hearts;
our dancing has turned
to mourning.

"We Have Sinned"

16 The crown has fallen
from our head.
Woe to us, for we have sinned.
17 Because of this, our heart is sick;
because of these, our eyes
grow dim:
18 because of Mount Zion,
which lies desolate
⌊and has⌋ jackals prowling in it.
19 You, LORD, are enthroned forever;
Your throne endures
from generation to generation.
20 Why have You forgotten us forever,
abandoned us for ⌊our⌋ entire lives?
21 LORD, restore us to Yourself, so we
may return;
renew our days as in former times,
22 unless You have completely
rejected us
and are intensely angry with us.

ᵃ**4:22** Or *not deport you again*   ᵇ**5:6** Lit *We gave the hand to*   ᶜ**5:10** Or *black*; Hb obscure

EZEKIEL

Time and Place of First Vision

1 In the thirtieth year, in the fourth ⌊month⌋, on the fifth ⌊day⌋ of the month, while I was among the exiles by the Chebar Canal, the heavens opened and I saw visions of God. ² On the fifth ⌊day⌋ of the month—it was the fifth year of King Jehoiachin's exile— ³ the word of the LORD came directly to Ezekiel the priest, the son of Buzi, in the land of the Chaldeans by the Chebar Canal. And the LORD's hand was on him there.

Four-faced Creatures

⁴ I looked and there was a whirlwind coming from the north, a great cloud with fire flashing back and forth and brilliant light all around it. In the center of the fire, there was a gleam like amber. ⁵ The form of four living creatures came from it. And this was their appearance: They had human form, ⁶ but each of them had four faces and four wings. ⁷ Their legs were straight, and the soles of their feet were like the hooves of a calf, sparkling like the gleam of polished bronze. ⁸ ⌊They had⌋ human hands under their wings on their four sides. All four of them had faces and wings. ⁹ Their wings were touching. The creatures did not turn as they moved; each one went straight ahead. ¹⁰ The form of ⌊each of⌋ their faces was that of a man, and each of the four had the face of a lion on the right, the face of an ox on the left, and the face of an eagle. ¹¹ ⌊That is what⌋ their faces ⌊were like⌋. Their wings were spread upward; each had two ⌊wings⌋ touching that of another and two wings covering its body. ¹² Each creature went straight ahead. Wherever the Spirit[a] wanted to go, they went without turning as they moved.

¹³ The form of the living creatures was like the appearance of burning coals of fire and torches. Fire was moving back and forth between the living creatures; it was bright, with lightning coming out of it. ¹⁴ The creatures were darting back and forth like flashes of lightning.

Wheels of Creatures

¹⁵ When I looked at the living creatures, there was one wheel on the ground beside each creature that had four faces. ¹⁶ The appearance of the wheels and their craftsmanship was like the gleam of beryl, and all four had the same form. Their appearance and craftsmanship was like a wheel within a wheel. ¹⁷ When they moved, they went in any of the four directions, without pivoting as they moved. ¹⁸ Their rims were large and frightening. Each of their four rims were full of eyes all around. ¹⁹ So when the living creatures moved, the wheels moved beside them, and when the creatures rose from the earth, the wheels also rose. ²⁰ Wherever the Spirit[a] wanted to go, the creatures went in the direction the Spirit was moving. The wheels rose alongside them, for the spirit of the living creatures was in the wheels. ²¹ When the creatures moved, the wheels moved; when the creatures stood still, the wheels stood still; and when the creatures rose from the earth, the wheels rose alongside them, for the spirit of the living creatures was in the wheels.

---

a **1:12,20** Or *spirit*

²² The shape of an expanse, with a gleam like awe-inspiring crystal, was spread out over the heads of the living creatures. ²³ And under the expanse their wings extended one toward another. Each of them also had two wings covering their bodies. ²⁴ When they moved, I heard the sound of their wings like the roar of mighty waters, like the voice of the •Almighty, and a sound of commotion like the noise of an army. When they stood still, they lowered their wings.

Voice, Throne, and God's Glory

²⁵ A voice came from above the expanse over their heads; when they stood still, they lowered their wings. ²⁶ The shape of a throne with the appearance of sapphire^a stone was above the expanse.^b There was a form with the appearance of a human on the throne high above. ²⁷ From what seemed to be His waist up, I saw a gleam like amber, with what looked like fire enclosing it all around. From what seemed to be His waist down, I also saw what looked like fire. There was a brilliant light all around Him. ²⁸ The appearance of the brilliant light all around was like that of a rainbow in a cloud on a rainy day. This was the appearance of the form of the LORD's glory. When I saw ⌊it⌋, I fell facedown and heard a voice speaking.

Voice Commands Ezekiel

2 He said to me, "Son of man, stand up on your feet and I will speak with you." ² As He spoke to me, the Spirit entered me and set me on my feet, and I listened to the One who was speaking to me. ³ He said to me: "Son of man, I am sending you to the Israelites ⌊and⌋ to the rebellious nations^c who have rebelled against Me. The Israelites and their ancestors have transgressed against Me to this day. ⁴ The children are obstinate^d and hardhearted. I am sending you to them, and you must say to them: This is what the Lord GOD says. ⁵ Whether they listen or refuse ⌊to listen⌋—for they are a rebellious house—they will know that a prophet has been among them.

Son of Man, Do Not Fear

⁶ "But you, son of man, do not be afraid of them or their words, though briers and thorns are beside you and you live among scorpions. Don't be afraid of their words or be discouraged by ⌊the look on⌋ their faces, for they are a rebellious house. ⁷ But speak My words to them whether they listen or refuse ⌊to listen⌋, for they are rebellious.

"Eat This Scroll"

⁸ "And you, son of man, listen to what I tell you: Do not be rebellious like that rebellious house. Open your mouth and eat what I am giving you." ⁹ So I looked and saw a hand reaching out to me, and there was a written scroll in it. ¹⁰ When He unrolled it before me, it was written on the front and back; ⌊words of⌋ lamentation, mourning, and woe were written on it.

3 He said to me: "Son of man, eat what you find ⌊here⌋. Eat this scroll, then go and speak to the house of Israel." ² So I opened my mouth, and He fed me the scroll. ³ "Son of man," he said to me, "eat^e and fill your stomach with this scroll I am giving you." So I ate ⌊it⌋, and it was as sweet as honey in my mouth.

⁴ Then He said to me: "Son of man, go to the house of Israel and speak My words to them. ⁵ For you are not being sent to a people of unintelligible speech

---

^a**1:26** Or *lapis lazuli*   ^b**1:26** Lit *expanse that was over their head*   ^c**2:3** LXX omits *to the rebellious nations*   ^d**2:4** Lit *hard of face*   ^e**3:3** Lit *feed your belly*

or difficult language but to the house of Israel. ⁶ ⌊You are⌋ not ⌊being sent⌋ to many peoples of unintelligible speech or difficult language, whose words you cannot understand. No doubt, if I sent you to them, they would listen to you. ⁷ But the house of Israel will not want to listen to you because they do not want to listen to Me. For the whole house of Israel is hardheaded and hardhearted. ⁸ Look, I have made your face as hard as their faces and your forehead as hard as their foreheads. ⁹ I have made your forehead like a diamond, harder than flint. Don't be afraid of them or discouraged by ⌊the look on⌋ their faces, even though they are a rebellious house."

¹⁰ Next He said to me: "Son of man, listen carefully to all My words that I speak to you and take ⌊them⌋ to heart. ¹¹ Go to your people, the exiles, and speak to them. Tell them: This is what the Lord GOD says, whether they listen or refuse ⌊to listen⌋."

Spirit Lifts Ezekiel

¹² The Spirit then lifted me up, and I heard a great rumbling sound behind me—praise the glory of the LORD in His place!— ¹³ with theᵃ sound of the living creatures' wings brushing against each other and the sound of the wheels beside them, a great rumbling sound. ¹⁴ So the Spirit lifted me up and took me away. I left in bitterness and in an angry spirit, and the LORD's hand was on me powerfully. ¹⁵ I came to the exiles at Tel-abib, who were living by the Chebar Canal, and I sat there stunned for seven days.

Ezekiel as Watchman

¹⁶ Now at the end of seven days the word of the LORD came to me: ¹⁷ "Son of man, I have made you a watchman over the house of Israel. When you hear a word from My mouth, give them a warning from Me.

Ezekiel's Heavy Responsibility

¹⁸ If I say to the wicked person: You will surely die, but you do not warn him— you don't speak out to warn him about his wicked way in order to save his life—that wicked person will die for his iniquity. Yet I will hold you responsible for his blood. ¹⁹ But if you warn a wicked person and he does not turn from his wickedness or his wicked way, he will die for his iniquity, but you will have saved your life. ²⁰ Now if a righteous person turns from his righteousness and practices iniquity, and I put a stumbling block in front of him, he will die. If you did not warn him, he will die because of his sin and the righteous acts he did will not be remembered. Yet I will hold you responsible for his blood. ²¹ But if you warn the righteous person that he should not sin, and he does not sin, he will indeed live because he listened to ⌊your⌋ warning, and you will have saved your life."

Spirit Moves Ezekiel

²² Then the hand of the LORD was on me there, and He said to me, "Get up, go out to the plain, and I will speak with you there." ²³ So I got up and went out to the plain. The LORD's glory was present there, like the glory I had seen by the Chebar Canal, and I fell facedown. ²⁴ The Spirit entered me and set me on my feet. He spoke with me and said: "Go, shut yourself inside your house. ²⁵ And you, son of man, they will put ropes on you and bind you with them so you cannot go out among them. ²⁶ I will make your tongue stick to the roof of your mouth, and you will be mute and unable to rebuke them, for they are

ᵃ**3:12-13** Some emend to *behind me as the glory of the LORD rose from His place:* ¹³ *the*

a rebellious house. ²⁷ But when I speak with you, I will open your mouth, and you will say to them: This is what the Lord God says. Let the one who listens, listen, and let the one who refuses, refuse—for they are a rebellious house.

Jerusalem's Siege Dramatized: the Brick

4 "Now you, son of man, take a brick, set it in front of you, and draw the city of Jerusalem on it. ² Then lay siege against it: construct a siege wall, build a ramp, pitch military camps, and place battering rams against it on all sides. ³ Take an iron plate and set it up as an iron wall between yourself and the city. Turn your face toward it so that it is under siege, and besiege it. This will be a sign for the house of Israel.

Ezekiel's Left and Right Sides

⁴ "Then lie down on your left side and place the iniquityᵃ of the house of Israel on it. You will bear their iniquity for the number of days you lie on your side. ⁵ For I have assigned you the years of their iniquity according to the number of days ⌊you lie down⌋, 390 days; so you will bear the iniquity of the house of Israel. ⁶ When you have completed these days, lie down again, but on your right side, and bear the iniquity of the house of Judah. I have assigned you 40 days, a day for each year. ⁷ You must turn your face toward the siege of Jerusalem with your arm bared, and prophesy against it. ⁸ Be aware that I will put cords on you so you cannot turn from side to side until you have finished the days of your siege.

Sign of the Unclean Bread

⁹ "Also take wheat, barley, beans, lentils, millet, and spelt. Put them in a single container and make them into bread for yourself. You are to eat it during the number of days you lie on your side, 390 days. ¹⁰ The food you eat each day will be eight ouncesᵇ by weight; you will eat it from time to time.ᶜ ¹¹ You are also to drink water by measure, one-sixth of a gallon,ᵈ ⌊which⌋ you will drink from time to time. ¹² You will eat it as ⌊you would⌋ a barley cake and bake it over dried human excrement in their sight." ¹³ The Lord said, "This is how the Israelites will eat their bread—ceremonially unclean—among the nations where I will banish them."

¹⁴ But I said, "Ah, Lord God, I have never been defiled. From my youth until now I have not eaten anything that died naturally or was mauled by wild beasts. And impure meat has never entered my mouth."

¹⁵ He replied to me, "Look, I will let you ⌊use⌋ cow dung instead of human excrement, and you can make your bread over that." ¹⁶ Then He said to me, "Son of man, I am going to cut off the supply of bread in Jerusalem. They will anxiously eat bread ⌊rationed⌋ by weight and in dread drink water by measure. ¹⁷ So they will lack bread and water; everyone will be devastated and waste away because of their iniquity.

Sign of the Sword and Shave

5 "Now you, son of man, take a sharp sword, use it as you would a barber's razor, and shave your head and beard. Then take a pair of scales and divide the hair. ² You are to burn up one third ⌊of it⌋ in the city when the days of the siege have ended; you are to take one third and slash ⌊it⌋ with the sword all around the city; and you are to scatter one third to the wind, for I will draw a sword ⌊to chase⌋ after them. ³ But you are to take a few strands from the hair and secure

---

ᵃ4:4 Or punishment ᵇ4:10 Lit 20 shekels ᶜ4:10 Or it at set times ᵈ4:11 Lit hin

them in the folds of your ⌊robe⌋. ⁴ Take some more of them, throw them into the fire, and burn them in it. A fire will spread from it to the whole house of Israel.

God Explains Dramas

⁵ "This is what the Lord GOD says: I have set this Jerusalem in the center of the nations, with countries all around her. ⁶ But she has rebelled against My ordinances with more wickedness than the nations, and against My statutes more than the countries that surround her. For her people have rejected My ordinances and have not walked in My statutes.

Results of Jerusalem's Rebellion

⁷ "Therefore, this is what the Lord GOD says: Because you have been more insubordinate than the nations around you—you have not walked in My statutes or kept My ordinances; you have not even kept the ordinances of the nations around you—⁸ therefore, this is what the Lord GOD says: See, I am against you, ⌊Jerusalem⌋, and I will execute judgments within you in the sight of the nations. ⁹ Because of all your abominations, I will do to you what I have never done before and what I will never do again. ¹⁰ As a result, fathers will eat ⌊their⌋ sons within Jerusalem,ᵃ and sons will eat their fathers. I will execute judgments against you and scatter all your survivors to every direction of the wind.

¹¹ "Therefore, as I live"—⌊this is⌋ the declaration of the Lord GOD—"I am going to cut ⌊you⌋ off and show ⌊you⌋ no pity, because you have defiled My sanctuary with all your detestable practices and abominations. Yes, I will not spare ⌊you⌋. ¹² One third of your people will die by plague and be consumed by famine within you; one third will fall by the sword all around you; and I will scatter one third to every direction of the wind, and I will draw a sword ⌊to chase⌋ after them. ¹³ When My anger is spent and I have vented My wrath on them, I will be appeased. Then, after I have spent My wrath on them, they will know that I, the LORD, have spoken in My jealousy.

¹⁴ "I will make you a ruin and a disgrace among the nations around you, in the sight of everyone who passes by. ¹⁵ So youᵇ will be a disgrace and a taunt, a warning and a horror, to the nations around you when I execute judgments against you in anger, wrath, and furious rebukes. I, the LORD, have spoken. ¹⁶ When I shoot deadly arrows of famine at them, arrows for destruction that I will send to destroy you, ⌊inhabitants of Jerusalem⌋, I will intensify the famine against you and cut off your supply of bread. ¹⁷ I will send famine and dangerous animals against you. They will leave you childless, ⌊Jerusalem⌋. Plague and bloodshed will sweep through you, and I will bring a sword against you. I, the LORD, have spoken."

Prophecy against Israel's Idolatry

6 The word of the LORD came to me: ² "Son of man, turn your face toward the mountains of Israel and prophesy against them. ³ You are to say: Mountains of Israel, hear the word of the Lord GOD! This is what the Lord GOD says to the mountains and the hills, to the ravines and the valleys: I am about to bring a sword against you, and I will destroy your •high places. ⁴ Your altars will be desolated and your incense altars smashed. I will throw down your slain in front of your idols. ⁵ I will lay the corpses of the Israelites in front of their idols and

ᵃ**5:10** Lit *you*   ᵇ**5:15** DSS, LXX, Syr, Tg, Vg; MT reads *she* scatter your bones around your altars. [6] Wherever you live the cities will be in ruins and the high places will be desolate, so that your altars will lie in ruins and be desecrated,[a] your idols smashed and obliterated, your incense altars cut down, and your works wiped out. [7] The slain will fall among you, and you will know that I am the LORD.

God Saves Remnant

[8] "Yet I will leave a remnant when you are scattered among the nations, for throughout the countries there will be some of you who will escape the sword. [9] Then your survivors will remember Me among the nations where they are taken captive, how I was crushed by their promiscuous hearts that turned away from Me and by their eyes that lusted after their idols. They will loathe themselves because of the evil things they did, their abominations of every kind. [10] And they will know that I am the LORD; I did not threaten to bring this disaster on them without a reason.

Lament over Fall of Jerusalem

[11] "This is what the Lord GOD says: Clap your hands, stamp your feet, and cry out over all the evil abominations of the house of Israel, who will fall by the sword, famine, and plague. [12] The one who is far off will die by plague; the one who is near will fall by the sword; and the one who remains and is spared[b] will die of famine. In this way I will exhaust My wrath on them. [13] You will ⌊all⌋ know that I am the LORD when their slain lie among their idols around their altars, on every high hill, on all the mountaintops, and under every green tree and every leafy oak—the places where they offered pleasing aromas to all their idols. [14] I will

stretch out My hand against them, and wherever they live I will make the land a desolate waste, from the wilderness to Diblah.[c] Then they will know that I am •Yahweh."

Announcement of the End

7 And the word of the LORD came to me: [2] "Son of man, this is what the Lord GOD says to the land of Israel:

An end! The end has come
on the four corners of the land.
[3] The end is now on you;
I will send My anger against you
and judge you according to
your ways.
I will punish you for all
your abominations.
[4] I will not look on you with pity
or spare ⌊you⌋,
but I will punish you for your ways
and for your abominations
within you.
Then you will know that I am
the LORD."

[5] This is what the Lord GOD says:

Look, one disaster after another
is coming!
[6] An end has come; the end has come!
It has awakened against you.
Look, it is coming!
[7] Doom[a] has come on you,
inhabitants of the land.
The time has come; the day is near.
There will be panic
on the mountains
and not celebration.
[8] I will pour out My wrath on you
very soon;
I will exhaust My anger against you
and judge you
according to your ways.

I will punish you for all
   your abominations.
9 I will not look on ⌊you⌋ with pity
   or spare ⌊you⌋.
I will punish you for your ways
and for your abominations
   within you.
Then you will know
that it is I, the LORD, who strikes.

10 Look, the day is coming!
Doom has gone out.
The rod has blossomed;
arrogance has bloomed.
11 Violence has grown into a rod
   of wickedness;
none of them ⌊will remain⌋:
none of their multitude,
none of their wealth,
and none of the eminent[a]
   among them.

12 The time has come; the day
   has arrived.
Let the buyer not rejoice
and the seller not mourn,
for wrath is on all her multitude.
13 The seller will certainly not return
to what was sold
as long as he and the buyer
   remain alive.[b]
For the vision concerning
   all its people
will not be revoked,
and none of them will preserve
his life because of his iniquity.

14 They have blown the trumpet
and prepared everything,
but no one goes to war,
for My wrath is on all her multitude.
15 The sword is on the outside;
   plague and famine are
      on the inside.
Whoever is in the field will die
   by the sword,

and famine and plague will devour
whoever is in the city.

Plight of Survivors

16 The survivors among them
      will escape
and live on the mountains
like doves of the valley,
all of them moaning,
each over his own iniquity.
17 All their hands will become weak,
and all ⌊their⌋ knees will turn
      to water.
18 They will put on •sackcloth,
and horror will overwhelm them.
Shame will cover all ⌊their⌋ faces,
and all their heads will be bald.
19 They will throw their silver
      into the streets,
and their gold will seem like
      something filthy.
Their silver and gold will be unable
      to save them
in the day of the LORD's wrath.
They will not satisfy their appetites
or fill their stomachs,
for these were the stumbling blocks
that brought about their iniquity.

20 He appointed
      His beautiful ornaments
      for majesty,
but[c] they made
      their abhorrent images
      from them,
their detestable things.
Therefore, I have made these
into something filthy for them.
21 I will hand these things over
to foreigners as plunder
and to the wicked of the earth
      as spoil,
and they will profane them.
22 I will turn My face from the wicked

---

a7:11 Some Hb mss, Syr, Vg read and no rest   b7:13 Lit sold, while still in life is their life   c7:20 Or They turned their
beautiful ornaments into objects of pride, and

as they profane My treasured place.
Violent men will enter it
  and profane it.

23 Forge the chain,
  for the land is filled with crimes
    of bloodshed,
  and the city is filled with violence.
24 So I will bring the most evil
  of nations
  to take possession of their houses.
I will put an end to the pride
  of the strong,
and their sacred places
  will be profaned.
25 Anguish is coming!
They will seek peace,
  but there will be none.
26 Disaster after disaster will come,
and there will be rumor
  after rumor.
Then they will seek a vision
  from a prophet,
but instruction will perish
  from the priests
and counsel from the elders.
27 The king will mourn;
the prince will be clothed in grief;
and the hands of the people
  of the land will tremble.
I will deal with them according to
  their own conduct,
and I will judge them
  by their own standards.
Then they will know that I am
  the LORD.

Ezekiel's Visionary Journey to Jerusalem

8 In the sixth year, in the sixth ⌊month⌋, on the fifth ⌊day⌋ of the month, I was sitting in my house and the elders of Judah were sitting in front of me, and there the hand of the Lord GOD came down on me. ² I looked, and there was a form that had the appearance of a man.ᵃ From what seemed to be His waist down was fire, and from His waist up was something that looked bright, like the gleam of amber. ³ He stretched out what appeared to be a hand and took me by the hair of my head. Then the Spirit lifted me up between earth and heaven and carried me in visions of God to Jerusalem, to the entrance of the inner gate that faces north, where the offensive statue that provokes jealousy was located. ⁴ I saw the glory of the God of Israel there, like the vision I had seen in the plain.

God Reveals Abominations in Temple

⁵ The LORD said to me, "Son of man, look toward the north." I looked to the north, and there was this offensive statue north of the altar gate, at the entrance. ⁶ He said to me, "Son of man, do you see what they are doing, the great abominations that the house of Israel is committing here, so that I must depart from My sanctuary? You will see even greater abominations."

⁷ Then He brought me to the entrance of the court, and when I looked there was a hole in the wall. ⁸ He said to me, "Son of man, dig through the wall." So I dug through the wall, and there was a doorway. ⁹ He said to me, "Go in and see the terrible abominations they are committing here." ¹⁰ I went in and looked, and there engraved all around the wall was every form of detestable thing, crawling creatures and beasts, as well as all the idols of the house of Israel.

¹¹ Seventy elders from the house of Israel were standing before them, with Jaazaniah son of Shaphan standing among them. Each had an incense burner in his hand, and a fragrant cloud of incense

---

ᵃ**8:2** LXX; MT, Vg read *of fire*

was rising up. 12 Then He said to me, "Son of man, do you see what the elders of the house of Israel are doing in the darkness, each at the shrine of his idol? For they are saying: The LORD does not see us. The LORD has abandoned the land." 13 Again He said to me, "You will see even greater abominations, which they are committing."

Ezekiel Sees Weeping for Pagan God Tammuz

14 So He brought me to the entrance of the north gate of the LORD's house, and I saw women sitting there weeping for Tammuz. 15 And He said to me, "Do you see ⌊this⌋, son of man? You will see even greater abominations than these."

Ezekiel Sees Sun Worship

16 So He brought me to the inner court of the LORD's house, and there were about 25 men at the entrance of the LORD's temple, between the portico and the altar, with their backs to the LORD's temple and their faces ⌊turned⌋ to the east. They were bowing to the east in worship of the sun. 17 And He said to me, "Do you see ⌊this⌋, son of man? Is it not enough for the house of Judah to commit the abominations they are practicing here, that they must also fill the land with violence and repeatedly provoke Me to anger, even putting the branch to their nose?a 18 Therefore I will respond with wrath. I will not show pity or spare ⌊them⌋. Though they cry out in My ears with a loud voice, I will not listen to them."

Ezekiel's Vision of Slaughter in Jerusalem

9 Then He called to me directly with a loud voice, "Come near, execution-

ers of the city, each ⌊of you⌋ with a destructive weapon in his hand." 2 And I saw six men coming from the direction of the Upper Gate, which faces north, each with a war club in his hand. There was another man among them, clothed in linen, with writing equipment at his side. They came and stood beside the bronze altar.

3 Then the glory of the God of Israel rose from above the •cherubim where it had been, to the threshold of the temple. He called to the man clothed in linen with the writing equipment at his side. 4 "Pass throughout the city of Jerusalem," the LORD said to him, "and put a mark on the foreheads of the men who sigh and groan over all the abominations committed in it."

5 To the others He said in my hearing, "Pass through the city after him and start killing; do not show pity or spare ⌊them⌋! 6 Slaughter the old men, the young men and women, as well as the ⌊older⌋ women and little children, but do not come near anyone who has the mark. Now begin at My sanctuary." So they began with the elders who were in front of the temple. 7 Then He said to them, "Defile the temple and fill the courts with the slain. Go!" So they went out killing ⌊people⌋ in the city.

Killing and Man in Linen

8 While they were killing, I was left alone. And I fell facedown and cried out, "Ah, Lord GOD! Are You going to destroy the entire remnant of Israel when You pour out Your wrath on Jerusalem?"

9 He answered me: "The iniquity of the house of Israel and Judah is extremely great; the land is full of bloodshed, and the city full of perversity. For they say: The LORD has abandoned the

---

a8:17 Possibly a pagan ritual or a euphemism for offensive behavior

land; He does not see. ¹⁰ But as for Me, I will not show pity or spare ⌊them⌋. I will bring their actions down on their own heads." ¹¹ Then the man clothed in linen with the writing equipment at his side reported back, "I have done as You commanded me."

God's Glory Leaves the Temple

10 Then I looked, and there above the expanse over the heads of the •cherubim was something like sapphireᵃ stone resembling the shape of a throne that appeared above them. ² The LORD spoke to the man clothed in linen and said, "Go inside the wheelwork beneath the cherubim. Fill your hands with hot coals from among the cherubim and scatter ⌊them⌋ over the city." So he went in as I watched.

Work of Cherubim

³ Now the cherubim were standing to the south of the temple when the man went in, and the cloud filled the inner court. ⁴ Then the glory of the LORD rose from above the cherubim to the threshold of the temple. The temple was filled with the cloud, and the court was filled with the brightness of the LORD's glory. ⁵ The sound of the cherubim's wings could be heard as far as the outer court; it was like the voice of •God Almighty when He speaks.

⁶ After the LORD commanded the man clothed in linen, saying, "Take fire from inside the wheelwork, from among the cherubim," the man went in and stood beside a wheel. ⁷ Then one of the cherubim reached out his hand to the fire that was among them. He took ⌊some⌋, and put ⌊it⌋ into the hands of the man clothed in linen, who took it and went out. ⁸ The cherubim appeared to have the form of human hands under their wings.

⁹ I looked, and there were four wheels beside the cherubim, one wheel beside each cherub. The luster of the wheels was like the gleam of beryl. ¹⁰ In appearance, all four had the same form, like a wheel within a wheel. ¹¹ When they moved, they would go in any of the four directions, without pivoting as they moved. But wherever the head faced, they would go in that direction,ᵇ without pivoting as they went. ¹² Their entire bodies, including their backs, hands, wings, and the wheels that the four of them had, were full of eyes all around. ¹³ As I listened the wheels were called "the wheelwork." ¹⁴ Each one had four faces: the first face was that of a cherub, the second that of a man, the third that of a lion, and the fourth that of an eagle.

¹⁵ The cherubim ascended; these were the living creatures I had seen by the Chebar Canal. ¹⁶ When the cherubim moved, the wheels moved beside them, and when they lifted their wings to rise from the earth, even then the wheels did not veer away from them. ¹⁷ When the cherubim stood still, the wheels stood still, and when they ascended, the wheels ascended with them, for the spirit of the living creatures was in them.

¹⁸ Then the glory of the LORD moved away from the threshold of the temple and stood above the cherubim. ¹⁹ The cherubim lifted their wings and ascended from the earth right before my eyes; the wheels were beside them as they went. The glory of the God of Israel was above them, and it stood at the entrance to the eastern gate of the LORD's house.

²⁰ These were the living creatures I had seen beneath the God of Israel by the Chebar Canal, and I recognized that they were cherubim. ²¹ Each had four

---

ᵃ**10:1** Or *lapis lazuli*   ᵇ**10:11** Lit *go after it*

faces and each had four wings, with the form of human hands under their wings. 22 Their faces looked like the same faces I had seen by the Chebar Canal. Each creature went straight ahead.

Vision of Israel's 25 Corrupt Leaders

11 The Spirit then lifted me up and brought me to the eastern gate of the LORD's house, which faces east, and at the gate's entrance were 25 men. Among them I saw Jaazaniah son of Azzur, and Pelatiah son of Benaiah, leaders of the people. 2 The LORD said to me, "Son of man, these are the men who plan evil and give wicked advice in this city. 3 They are saying: Isn't the time near to build houses?ª The city is the pot, and we are the meat. 4 Therefore, prophesy against them. Prophesy, son of man!"

Spirit on Elijah

5 Then the Spirit of the LORD came on me, and He told me, "You are to say: This is what the LORD says: That is what you are thinking, house of Israel; and I know the thoughts that arise in your mind. 6 You have multiplied your slain in this city, filling its streets with the dead.

7 "Therefore, this is what the Lord GOD says: The slain you have put within it are the meat, and the city is the pot, but Iᵇ will remove you from it. 8 You fear the sword, so I will bring the sword against you." ⌊This is⌋ the declaration of the Lord GOD. 9 "I will bring you out of the city and hand you over to foreigners; I will execute judgments against you. 10 You will fall by the sword, and I will judge you at the border of Israel. Then you will know that I am the LORD. 11 The city will not be a pot for you, and you will not be the meat within it. I will

judge you at the border of Israel, 12 so you will know that I am the LORD, whose statutes you have not followed and whose ordinances you have not practiced. Instead, you have acted according to the ordinances of the nations around you."

13 Now while I was prophesying, Pelatiah son of Benaiah died. Then I fell facedown and cried out with a loud voice: "Ah, Lord GOD! Will You bring to an end the remnant of Israel?"

God Promises Israel's Restoration

14 The word of the LORD came to me again: 15 "Son of man, your own relatives, those who have the right to redeem you,ᶜ ᵈ and the entire house of Israel, all of them, are those the residents of Jerusalem have said this to: Stay away from the LORD; this land has been given to us as a possession.

16 "Therefore say: This is what the Lord GOD says: Though I sent them far away among the nations and scattered them among the countries, yet for a little while I have been a sanctuary for them in the countries where they have gone.

17 "Therefore say: This is what the Lord GOD says: I will gather you from the peoples and assemble you from the countries where you have been scattered, and I will give you the land of Israel.

18 "When they arrive there, they will remove all its detestable things and all its abominations from it. 19 And I will give them one heart and put a new spirit within them; I will remove their heart of stone from their bodiesᵉ and give them a heart of flesh, 20 so they may follow My statutes, keep My ordinances, and practice them. Then they will be My people, and I will be their God. 21 But as for

---

ª**11:3** Or *The time is not near to build houses.*   ᵇ**11:7** Some Hb mss, LXX, Syr, Tg, Vg; other Hb mss read *He*
ᶜ**11:15** LXX, Syr read *your relatives, your fellow exiles*   ᵈ**11:15** Or *own brothers, your relatives*   ᵉ**11:19** Lit *flesh*

those whose hearts pursue their desire for detestable things and abominations, I will bring their actions down on their own heads." ⌊This is⌋ the declaration of the Lord GOD.

God's Glory Leaves Jerusalem

²² Then the •cherubim, with the wheels beside them, lifted their wings, and the glory of the God of Israel was above them. ²³ The glory of the LORD rose up from within the city and stood on the mountain east of the city.ᵃ ²⁴ The Spirit lifted me up and brought me to Chaldea and to the exiles in a vision from the Spirit of God. After the vision I had seen left me, ²⁵ I spoke to the exiles about all the things the LORD had shown me.

Ezekiel "Goes into Exile"

12 The word of the LORD came to me: ² "Son of man, you are living among a rebellious house. They have eyes to see but do not see, and ears to hear but do not hear, for they are a rebellious house.

³ "Son of man, pack your bags for exile and go into exile in their sight during the day. You will go into exile from your place to another place while they watch; perhaps they will understand, though they are a rebellious house. ⁴ During the day, bring out your bags like an exile's bags while they look on. Then in the evening go out in their sight like those going into exile. ⁵ As they watch, dig through the wall and take the ⌊bags⌋ out through it. ⁶ And while they look on, lift ⌊the bags⌋ to ⌊your⌋ shoulder and take ⌊them⌋ out in the dark; cover your face so that you cannot see the land. For I have made you a sign to the house of Israel."

⁷ So I did just as I was commanded. I brought out my bags like an exile's bags in the daytime. In the evening I dug through the wall by hand; I took ⌊them⌋ out in the dark, carrying ⌊them⌋ on my shoulder in their sight.

"I Am a Sign"

⁸ Then the word of the LORD came to me in the morning: ⁹ "Son of man, hasn't the house of Israel, that rebellious house, asked you: What are you doing? ¹⁰ Say to them: This is what the Lord GOD says: This •oracle is about the princeᵇ in Jerusalem and all the house of Israel who are living there.ᶜ ¹¹ You are to say: I am a sign for you. Just as I have done, so it will be done to them; they will go into exile, into captivity. ¹² The prince who is among them will lift ⌊his bags⌋ to his shoulder in the dark and go out. Theyᵈ will dig through the wall to bring ⌊him⌋ out through it. He will cover his face so he cannot see the land with his eyes. ¹³ But I will spread My net over him, and he will be caught in My snare. I will bring him to Babylon, the land of the Chaldeans, yet he will not see it, and he will die there. ¹⁴ I will also scatter all the attendants who surround him and all his troops to every direction of the wind, and I will draw a sword ⌊to chase⌋ after them. ¹⁵ They will know that I am the LORD when I disperse them among the nations and scatter them among the countries. ¹⁶ But I will spare a few of them from the sword, famine, and plague so they can tell about all their abominations among the nations where they go. Then they will know that I am the LORD."

Ezekiel Dramatizes Israel's Anxiety

¹⁷ The word of the LORD came to me: ¹⁸ "Son of man, eat your bread with trembling and drink your water with shaking and anxiety. ¹⁹ Then say to the

---

ᵃ**11:23** = the Mount of Olives   ᵇ**12:10** = King Zedekiah   ᶜ**12:10** Lit *are among them*   ᵈ**12:12** LXX, Syr read *He*

people of the land: This is what the Lord GOD says about the residents of Jerusalem in the land of Israel: They will eat their bread with anxiety and drink their water in dread, for their[a] land will be stripped of everything in it because of the violence of all who live there. 20 The inhabited cities will be destroyed, and the land will become a desolation. Then you will know that I am the LORD."

God Stops a Deceptive Proverb

21 Again the word of the LORD came to me: 22 "Son of man, what is this proverb you ⌊people⌋ have about the land of Israel, which goes:

The days keep passing by,
and every vision fails?

23 Therefore say to them: This is what the Lord GOD says: I will put a stop to this proverb, and they will not use it again in Israel. But say to them: The days draw near, as well as the fulfillment of every vision. 24 For there will no longer be any false vision or flattering •divination within the house of Israel. 25 But I, the LORD, will speak whatever message I will speak, and it will be done. It will no longer be delayed. For in your days, rebellious house, I will speak a message and bring it to pass." ⌊This is⌋ the declaration of the Lord GOD.

26 The word of the LORD came to me: 27 "Son of man, notice that the house of Israel is saying: The vision that he sees concerns many years ⌊from now⌋; he prophesies about distant times. 28 Therefore say to them: This is what the Lord GOD says: None of My words will be delayed any longer. The message I speak will be fulfilled." ⌊This is⌋ the declaration of the Lord GOD.

God Condemns False Prophets

13 The word of the LORD came to me: 2 "Son of man, prophesy against the prophets of Israel who are prophesying. Say to those who prophesy out of their own imagination: Hear the word of the LORD! 3 This is what the Lord GOD says: Woe to the foolish prophets who follow their own spirit and have seen nothing. 4 Your prophets, Israel, are like jackals among ruins. 5 You did not go up to the gaps or restore the wall around the house of Israel so that it might stand in battle on the day of the LORD. 6 They see false visions and speak lying •divinations. They claim: ⌊This is⌋ the LORD's declaration, when the LORD did not send them, yet they wait for the fulfillment of ⌊their⌋ message. 7 Didn't you see a false vision and speak a lying divination when you proclaimed: ⌊This is⌋ the LORD's declaration, even though I had not spoken?

8 "Therefore, this is what the Lord GOD says: I am against you because you have spoken falsely and had lying visions." ⌊This is⌋ the declaration of the Lord GOD. 9 "My hand will be against the prophets who see false visions and speak lying divinations. They will not be present in the fellowship of My people or be recorded in the register of the house of Israel, and they will not enter the land of Israel. Then you will know that I am the Lord GOD.

"Peace, When there Is No Peace"

10 "Since they have led My people astray saying: Peace, when there is no peace, for when someone builds a wall they plaster it with whitewash, 11 therefore, tell those who plaster ⌊it⌋ that it will fall. Torrential rain will come, and I will send hailstones plunging[b] down, and a windstorm will be released.

---

a 12:19 Lit *its*; = Jerusalem's   b 13:11 One Hb ms, LXX, Vg; MT reads *and you, hailstones, will plunge*

¹² Now when the wall has fallen, will you not be asked: Where is the coat of whitewash that you put on ⌊it⌋?

¹³ "So this is what the Lord GOD says: I will release a windstorm in My wrath. Torrential rain will come in My anger, and hailstones ⌊will fall⌋ in destructive fury. ¹⁴ I will tear down the wall you plastered with whitewash and knock it to the ground so that its foundation is exposed. The city will fall, and you will be destroyed within it. Then you will know that I am the LORD. ¹⁵ After I exhaust My wrath against the wall and against those who plaster it with whitewash, I will say to you: The wall is no more and neither are those who plastered it— ¹⁶ those prophets of Israel who prophesied to Jerusalem and saw a vision of peace for her when there was no peace." ⌊This is⌋ the declaration of the Lord GOD.

False Female Prophets

¹⁷ "Now, son of man, turnª toward the women of your people who prophesy out of their own imagination. Prophesy against them ¹⁸ and say: This is what the Lord GOD says: Woe to the women who sew ⌊magic⌋ bands on the wrist of every hand and who make veils for the heads of people of every height in order to ensnare lives. Will you ensnare the lives of My people but preserve your own? ¹⁹ You profane Me in front of My people for handfuls of barley and scraps of bread; you kill those who should not die and spare those who should not live, when you lie to My people, who listen to lies.

²⁰ "Therefore, this is what the Lord GOD says: I am against your ⌊magic⌋ bands that you ensnare people with like birds, and I will tear them from your arms. I will free the people you have ensnared like birds. ²¹ I will also tear off your veils and deliver My people from your hands, so that they will no longer be prey in your hands. Then you will know that I am the LORD. ²² Because you have disheartened the righteous person with lies, even though I have not caused him grief, and because you have encouraged the wicked person not to turn from his evil way to save his life, ²³ therefore you will no longer see false visions or practice divination. I will deliver My people from your hands. Then you will know that I am the LORD."

Idolatrous Elders Punished

14 Some of the elders of Israel came to me and sat down in front of me. ² Then the word of the LORD came to me: ³ "Son of man, these men have set up idols in their hearts and have put sinful stumbling blocks before their faces. Should I be consulted by them at all?

⁴ "Therefore, speak to them and tell them: This is what the Lord GOD says: When anyone from the house of Israel sets up idols in his heart, puts a sinful stumbling block before his face, and then comes to the prophet, I, the LORD, will answer him appropriately.ᵇ ⌊I will answer him⌋ according to his many idols, ⁵ so that I may take hold of the house of Israel by their hearts, because they are all estranged from Me by their idols.

⁶ "Therefore, say to the house of Israel: This is what the Lord GOD says: Repent and turn away from your idols; turn your faces away from all your abominations. ⁷ For when anyone from the house of Israel or from the foreigners who reside in Israel separates himself from Me, setting up idols in his heart and putting a sinful stumbling block before his face, and then comes to the prophet to inquire of Me,ᶜ I, the LORD, will answer him Myself. ⁸ I will turn against that one and

---

ª**13:17** Lit *set your face*   ᵇ**14:4** Alt Hb tradition reads *him who comes*   ᶜ**14:7** Lit *Me for himself*

make him a sign and a proverb; I will cut him off from among My people. Then you will know that I am the LORD.

God Will Destroy False Prophets

⁹ "But if the prophet is deceived and speaks a message, it was I, the LORD, who deceived that prophet. I will stretch out My hand against him and destroy him from among My people Israel. ¹⁰ They will bear their punishment—the punishment of the one who inquires will be the same as that of the prophet— ¹¹ in order that the house of Israel may no longer stray from following Me and no longer defile themselves with all their transgressions. Then they will be My people and I will be their God." ⌊This is⌋ the declaration of the Lord GOD.

Four Devastating Judgments

¹² The word of the LORD came to me: ¹³ "Son of man, if a land sins against Me by acting faithlessly, and I stretch out My hand against it to cut off its supply of bread, to send famine through it, and to wipe out ⌊both⌋ man and animal from it, ¹⁴ even ⌊if⌋ these three men—Noah, Daniel, and Job—were in it, they would deliver ⌊only⌋ themselves by their righteousness." ⌊This is⌋ the declaration of the Lord GOD.

¹⁵ "If I allow dangerous animals to pass through the land and depopulate it so that it becomes desolate, with no one passing through ⌊it⌋ for ⌊fear of⌋ the animals, ¹⁶ even ⌊if⌋ these three men were in it, as I live"—the declaration of the Lord GOD—"they could not deliver ⌊their⌋ sons or daughters. They alone would be delivered, but the land would be desolate.

¹⁷ "Or if I bring a sword against that land and say: Let a sword pass through it, so that I wipe out ⌊both⌋ man and animal from it, ¹⁸ even ⌊if⌋ these three men were in it, as I live"—the declaration of the Lord GOD—"they could not deliver ⌊their⌋ sons or daughters, but they alone would be delivered.

¹⁹ "Or if I send a plague into that land and pour out My wrath on it with bloodshed to wipe out ⌊both⌋ man and animal from it, ²⁰ even ⌊if⌋ Noah, Daniel, and Job were in it, as I live"—the declaration of the Lord GOD—"they could not deliver ⌊their⌋ son or daughter. They would deliver ⌊only⌋ themselves by their righteousness.

²¹ "For this is what the Lord GOD says: How much worse will it be when I send My four devastating judgments against Jerusalem—sword, famine, dangerous animals, and plague—in order to wipe out ⌊both⌋ man and animal from it! ²² Even so, there will be survivors left in it, sons and daughters who will be brought out. Indeed, they will come out to you, and you will observe their conduct and actions. Then you will be consoled about the devastation I have brought on Jerusalem, about all I have brought on it. ²³ They will bring you consolation when you see their conduct and actions, and you will know that it was not without cause that I have done what I did to it." ⌊This is⌋ the declaration of the Lord GOD.

Parable of the Useless Vine

15 Then the word of the LORD came to me: ² "Son of man, how does the wood of the vine, that branch among the trees of the forest, compare to any other wood? ³ Can wood be taken from it to make something useful? Or can anyone make a peg from it to hang things on? ⁴ In fact, it is put into the fire as fuel. The fire devours both of its ends, and the middle is charred. Can it be useful for anything? ⁵ Even when it was whole it could not be made into a useful object.

How much less can it ever be made into anything useful when the fire has devoured it and it is charred!

⁶ "Therefore, this is what the Lord GOD says: Like the wood of the vine among the trees of the forest, which I have given to the fire as fuel, so I will give up the residents of Jerusalem. ⁷ I will turn against them. They may have escaped from the fire, but it will ₍still₎ consume them. And you will know that I am the LORD when I turn against them. ⁸ I will make the land desolate because they have acted unfaithfully." ₍This is₎ the declaration of the Lord GOD.

Parable of God's Adulterous Wife

16 The word of the LORD came to me again: ² "Son of man, explain Jerusalem's abominations to her. ³ You are to say: This is what the Lord GOD says to Jerusalem: Your origin and your birth were in the land of the Canaanites. Your father was an Amorite and your mother a Hittite. ⁴ As for your birth, your umbilical cord wasn't cut on the day you were born, and you weren't washed clean[a] with water. You were not rubbed with salt or wrapped in cloths. ⁵ No one cared ₍enough₎ about you to do even one of these things out of compassion for you. But you were thrown out into the open field because you were despised on the day you were born.

⁶ "I passed by you and saw you lying in your blood, and I said to you ₍as you lay₎ in your blood: Live! Yes, I said to you ₍as you lay₎ in your blood: Live![b] ⁷ I made you thrive[a] like plants of the field. You grew up and matured and became very beautiful.[b] Your breasts were formed and your hair grew, but you were stark naked.

⁸ "Then I passed by you and saw you, and you were indeed at the age for love. So I spread the edge of My garment over you and covered your nakedness. I pledged Myself to you, entered into a covenant with you, and you became Mine." ₍This is₎ the declaration of the Lord GOD. ⁹ "I washed you with water, rinsed off your blood, and anointed you with oil. ¹⁰ I clothed you in embroidered cloth and provided you with leather sandals. I also wrapped you in fine linen and covered you with silk. ¹¹ I adorned you with jewelry, putting bracelets on your wrists and a chain around your neck. ¹² I put a ring in your nose, earrings on your ears, and a beautiful tiara on your head. ¹³ So you were adorned with gold and silver, and your clothing was ₍made₎ of fine linen, silk, and embroidered cloth. You ate fine flour, honey, and oil. You became extremely beautiful and attained royalty. ¹⁴ Your fame spread among the nations because of your beauty, for it was perfect through My splendor, which I had bestowed on you." ₍This is₎ the declaration of the Lord GOD.

"But ... You Acted Like a Prostitute"

¹⁵ "But you were confident in your beauty and acted like a prostitute because of your fame. You lavished your sexual favors on everyone who passed by. Your beauty became his.[a] ¹⁶ You took some of your garments and made colorful •high places for yourself, and you engaged in prostitution on them. These places should not have been built, and this should never have happened![a] ¹⁷ You also took your beautiful jewelry made from the gold and silver I had given you, and you made male images so that you could engage in prostitution with them. ¹⁸ Then you took your embroidered

---

ᵃ**16:4,15,16** Hb obscure   ᵇ**16:6** Some Hb mss, LXX, Syr omit *Yes, I said to you [as you lay] in your blood: Live!*
ᵃ**16:7** LXX reads *Thrive; I made you*   ᵇ**16:7** Or *matured and developed the loveliest of ornaments*

garments to cover them, and set My oil and incense before them. ¹⁹ You also set before them as a pleasing aroma the food I gave you—the fine flour, oil, and honey that I fed you. That is what happened." ⌊This is⌋ the declaration of the Lord GOD.

Even Child Sacrifice

²⁰ "You even took your sons and daughters you bore to Me and sacrificed them to these images as food. Wasn't your prostitution enough? ²¹ You slaughtered My children and gave them up when you passed them through ⌊the fire⌋ to the images. ²² In all your abominations and acts of prostitution, you did not remember the days of your youth when you were stark naked and lying in your blood.

²³ "Then after all your evil—Woe, woe to you!"—the declaration of the Lord GOD— ²⁴ "you built yourself a mound and made yourself an elevated place in every square. ²⁵ You built your elevated place at the head of every street and turned your beauty into an abomination. You spread your legs to everyone who passed by and increased your prostitution. ²⁶ You engaged in promiscuous acts with Egyptian men, your well-endowed neighbors, and increased your prostitution to provoke Me to anger.

Hearts Inflamed with Lust

²⁷ "Therefore, I stretched out My hand against you and reduced your provisions. I gave you over to the desire of those who hate you, the Philistine women, who were embarrassed by your indecent behavior. ²⁸ Then you engaged in prostitution with the Assyrian men because you were not satisfied. Even though you did this with them, you were still not satisfied. ²⁹ So you extended your prostitution to Chaldea, the land of merchants, but you were not even satisfied with this!

³⁰ "How your heart was inflamed ⌊with lust⌋"—the declaration of the Lord GOD—"when you did all these things, the acts of a brazen prostitute, ³¹ building your mound at the head of every street and making your elevated place in every square. But you were unlike a prostitute because you scorned payment. ³² You adulterous wife, who receives strangers instead of her husband! ³³ Men give gifts to all prostitutes, but you gave gifts to all your lovers. You bribed them to come to you from all around for your sexual favors. ³⁴ So you were the opposite of other women in your acts of prostitution; no one solicited you. When you paid a fee instead of one being paid to you, you were the opposite.

Fate of Prostitute

³⁵ "Therefore, you prostitute, hear the word of the LORD! ³⁶ This is what the Lord GOD says: Because your lust was poured out and your nakedness exposed by your acts of prostitution with your lovers, and because of all your detestable idols and the blood of your children that you gave to them, ³⁷ I am therefore going to gather all the lovers you pleased—all those you loved as well as all those you hated. I will gather them against you from all around and expose your nakedness to them so they see you completely naked. ³⁸ I will judge you the way adulteresses and those who shed blood are judged. Then I will bring about your bloodshed in wrath and jealousy. ³⁹ I will hand you over to them, and they will level your mounds and tear down your elevated places. They will strip off your clothes, take your beautiful jewelry, and leave you stark naked. ⁴⁰ They will bring a mob against you to stone you and cut you to pieces with their swords. ⁴¹ Then they will burn down your houses and ex-

ecute judgments against you in the sight of many women. I will stop you from being a prostitute, and you will never again pay fees for lovers. ⁴² So I will satisfy My wrath against you, and My jealousy will turn away from you. Then I will be silent and no longer angry. ⁴³ Because you did not remember the days of your youth but enraged Me with all these things, I will also bring your actions down on your own head." ⌞This is⌟ the declaration of the Lord GOD. "Haven't you committed immoral acts in addition to all your abominations?

"Like Mother, Like Daughter"

⁴⁴ "Look, everyone who uses proverbs will say this proverb about you:

Like mother, like daughter.

⁴⁵ You are the daughter of your mother, who despised her husband and children. You are the sister of your sisters, who despised their husbands and children. Your mother was a Hittite and your father an Amorite. ⁴⁶ Your older sister was Samaria, who lived with her daughters to the north of you, and your younger sister was Sodom, who lived with her daughters to the south of you. ⁴⁷ Didn't you walk in their ways and practice their abominations? It was only a short time before you behaved more corruptly than they did.ᵃ

Jerusalem Worse than Sisters

⁴⁸ "As I live"—the declaration of the Lord GOD—"your sister Sodom and her daughters have not behaved as you and your daughters have. ⁴⁹ Now this was the iniquity of your sister Sodom: she and her daughters had pride, plenty of food, and comfortable security, but didn't support the poor and needy.

⁵⁰ They were haughty and did detestable things before Me, so I removed them when I saw ⌞this⌟.ᵇ ⁵¹ But Samaria did not commit ⌞even⌟ half your sins. You have multiplied your abominations beyond theirs and made your sisters appear righteous by all the abominations you have committed. ⁵² You must also bear your disgrace, since you have been an advocate for your sisters. For they appear more righteous than you because of your sins, which you committed more abhorrently than they ⌞did⌟. So you also, be ashamed and bear your disgrace, since you have made your sisters appear righteous.

⁵³ "I will restore their fortunes, the fortunes of Sodom and her daughters and those of Samaria and her daughters. I will also restoreᶜ your fortunes among them, ⁵⁴ so you will bear your disgrace and be ashamed of all you did when you comforted them. ⁵⁵ As for your sisters, Sodom and her daughters and Samaria and her daughters will return to their former state. You and your daughters will also return to your former state. ⁵⁶ Didn't you treat your sister Sodom as an object of scorn when you were proud, ⁵⁷ before your wickedness was exposed? It was like the time you were scorned by the daughters of Aramᵈ and all those around her, and by the daughters of the Philistines—those who treated you with contempt from every side. ⁵⁸ You yourself must bear the consequences of your indecency and abominations"—the LORD's declaration.

⁵⁹ "For this is what the Lord GOD says: I will deal with you according to what you have done, since you have despised the oath by breaking the covenant. ⁶⁰ But I will remember the covenant I made with you in the days of your youth, and I

ᵃ**16:47** Lit *they in all your ways*   ᵇ**16:50** Or *them as you have seen*   ᶜ**16:53** LXX, Vg; MT reads *Samaria and her daughters and the fortunes of*   ᵈ**16:57** Other Hb mss, Syr read *Edom*

will establish an everlasting covenant with you. 61 Then you will remember your ways and be ashamed when you[a] receive your older and younger sisters. I will give them to you as daughters, but not because of your covenant. 62 I will establish My covenant with you, and you will know that I am the LORD, 63 so that when I make •atonement for all you have done, you will remember and be ashamed, and never open your mouth again because of your disgrace." ⌊This is⌋ the declaration of the Lord GOD.

Parable of the Eagles

17 The word of the LORD came to me: 2 "Son of man, pose a riddle and speak a parable to the house of Israel. 3 You are to say: This is what the Lord GOD says:

A great eagle with great wings,
　long pinions,
and full plumage of many colors
came to Lebanon and took the top
　of the cedar.
4　He plucked off its topmost shoot,
　brought it to the land of merchants,
　and set it in a city of traders.
5　Then he took some
　of the land's seed
　and put it in a fertile field;
　he set it ⌊like⌋ a willow,
　a plant[b] by abundant waters.
6　It sprouted and became
　a spreading vine,
　low in height with its branches
　　turned toward him,
　yet its roots stayed under it.
　So it became a vine,
　produced branches,
　and sent forth shoots.

7　But there was <u>another great eagle</u>
　with great wings and thick plumage.

And this vine bent its roots
　toward him!
It stretched out its branches to him
　from its planting bed,
　so that he might water it.
8　It had been planted
　in a good field by abundant waters
　in order to produce branches,
　bear fruit, and become
　a splendid vine.

9 You are to say: This is what the Lord GOD says:

Will it flourish?
Will he not tear out its roots
　and strip off its fruit
　so that it shrivels?
All its fresh leaves will wither!
Great strength and many people
　will not be needed to pull it
　　from its roots.
10　Even though it is planted,
　will it flourish?
Won't it completely wither
　when the east wind strikes it?
　<u>It will wither on the bed</u>
　<u>where it sprouted</u>."

Meaning of Parable

11 The word of the LORD came to me: 12 "Now say to that rebellious house: Don't you know what these things mean? Tell ⌊them⌋: The king of Babylon came to Jerusalem, took its king and officials, and brought them back with him to Babylon. 13 He took one of the royal family and made a covenant with him, putting him under oath. Then he took away the leading men of the land, 14 so the kingdom might be humble and not exalt itself but might keep his covenant in order to endure. 15 However, this king revolted against him by sending his ambassadors to Egypt so they might give

[a]16:61 Some LXX, Syr read I / [b]17:5 Hb obscure

him horses and a large army. Will he flourish? Will the one who does such things escape? Can he break a covenant and ⌊still⌋ escape?

Revolting King Will Not Escape

16 "As I live"—⌊this is⌋ the declaration of the Lord GOD—"he will die in Babylon, in the land of the king who put him on the throne, whose oath he despised and whose covenant he broke. 17 Pharaoh will not help him with ⌊his⌋ great army and vast horde in battle, when ramps are built and siege walls constructed to destroy many lives. 18 He despised the oath by breaking the covenant. He did all these things even though he gave his hand ⌊in pledge⌋. He will not escape!"

19 Therefore, this is what the Lord GOD says: "As I live, I will bring down on his head My oath that he despised and My covenant that he broke. 20 I will spread My net over him, and he will be captured in My snare. I will bring him to Babylon and execute judgment on him there for the treachery he committed against Me. 21 All the fugitives[a] among his troops will fall by the sword, and those who survive will be scattered to every direction of the wind. Then you will know that I, •Yahweh, have spoken."

God's Sprig of Hope

22 This is what the Lord GOD says:

I will take ⌊a sprig⌋
from the lofty top of the cedar
and plant ⌊it⌋.
I will pluck a tender sprig
from its topmost shoots,
and I will plant ⌊it⌋
on a high towering mountain.
23 I will plant it on Israel's
high mountain

so that it may bear branches,
produce fruit,
and become a majestic cedar.
Birds of every kind will nest
under it,
taking shelter in the shade
of its branches.
24 Then all the trees of the field
will know
that I am the LORD.
I bring down the tall tree,
and make the low tree tall.
I cause the green tree to wither
and make the withered tree thrive.
I, Yahweh, have spoken
and I will do ⌊it⌋.

Personal Responsibility for Sin

18 The word of the LORD came to me: 2 "What do you mean by using this proverb concerning the land of Israel:

The fathers eat sour grapes,
and the children's teeth are set
on edge?

3 As I live"—⌊this is⌋ the declaration of the Lord GOD—"you will no longer use this proverb in Israel. 4 Look, every life belongs to Me. The life of the father is like the life of the son—both belong to Me. The person who sins is the one who will die.

The Righteous Father

5 "Now suppose a man is righteous and does what is just and right: 6 He does not eat at the mountain ⌊shrines⌋ or raise his eyes to the idols of the house of Israel. He does not defile his neighbor's wife or come near a woman during her menstrual impurity. 7 He doesn't oppress anyone but returns his collateral to the debtor. He does not commit robbery, but gives his bread to the hungry and covers

---

a **17:21** Some Hb mss, LXX, Syr, Tg read *choice men*

the naked with clothing. [8] He doesn't lend at interest or for profit but keeps his hand from wrongdoing and carries out true justice between men. [9] He follows My statutes and keeps My ordinances, acting faithfully. Such a person is righteous; he will certainly live." ⌊This is⌋ the declaration of the Lord GOD.

The Violent Son

[10] "Now suppose the man has a violent son, who sheds blood and does any of these ⌊things⌋, [11] though the father has done none of them. Indeed, when the son eats at the mountain ⌊shrines⌋ and defiles his neighbor's wife, [12] and ⌊when⌋ he oppresses the poor and needy, commits robbery, and does not return collateral, and ⌊when⌋ he raises his eyes to the idols, commits abominations, [13] and lends at interest or for profit, will he live? He will not live! Since he has committed all these abominations, he will certainly die. His blood will be on him.

The Good Son

[14] "Now suppose he has a son who sees all the sins his father has committed, and though he sees them, he does not do likewise. [15] He does not eat at the mountain ⌊shrines⌋ or raise his eyes to the idols of the house of Israel. He does not defile his neighbor's wife. [16] He doesn't oppress anyone, hold collateral, or commit robbery. He gives his bread to the hungry and covers the naked with clothing. [17] He keeps his hand from ⌊harming⌋ the poor, not taking interest or profit ⌊on a loan⌋. He practices My ordinances and follows My statutes. Such a person will not die for his father's iniquity. He will certainly live.

Good Son Escapes Bad Father's Sin

[18] "As for his father, he will die for his own iniquity because he practiced fraud, robbed ⌊his⌋ brother, and did what was wrong among his people. [19] But you may ask: Why doesn't the son suffer punishment for the father's iniquity? Since the son has done what is just and right, carefully observing all My statutes, he will certainly live. [20] The person who sins is the one who will die. A son won't suffer punishment for the father's iniquity, and a father won't suffer punishment for the son's iniquity. The righteousness of the righteous person will be on him, and the wickedness of the wicked person will be on him.

Power of Repentance

[21] "Now if the wicked person turns from all the sins he has committed, keeps all My statutes, and does what is just and right, he will certainly live; he will not die. [22] None of the transgressions he has committed will be held against him. He will live because of the righteousness he has practiced. [23] Do I take any pleasure in the death of the wicked?" ⌊This is⌋ the declaration of the Lord GOD. "Instead, don't I ⌊take pleasure⌋ when he turns from his ways and lives? [24] But when a righteous person turns from his righteousness and practices iniquity, committing the same abominations that the wicked do, will he live? None of the righteous acts he did will be remembered. He will die because of the treachery he has engaged in and the sin he has committed.

Who Is Unfair?

[25] "But you say: The Lord's way isn't fair. Now listen, house of Israel: Is it My way that is unfair? Instead, isn't it your ways that are unfair? [26] When a righteous person turns from his righteousness and practices iniquity, he will die for this. He will die because of the iniquity he has practiced. [27] But if a wicked

person turns from the wickedness he has committed and does what is just and right, he will preserve his life. ²⁸ He will certainly live because he thought it over and turned from all the transgressions he had committed; he will not die. ²⁹ But the house of Israel says: The Lord's way isn't fair. Is it My ways that are unfair, house of Israel? Instead, isn't it your ways that are unfair?

³⁰ "Therefore, house of Israel, I will judge each one of you according to his ways." ⌊This is⌋ the declaration of the LORD God. "Repent and turn from all your transgressions, so they will not be a stumbling block that causes your punishment. ³¹ Throw off all the transgressions you have committed, and make yourselves a new heart and a new spirit. Why should you die, house of Israel? ³² For I take no pleasure in anyone's death." ⌊This is⌋ the declaration of the Lord GOD. "So repent and live!

A Lament for Israel's Princes

19 "Now, lament for the princes of Israel ² and say:

What was your mother? A lioness!
She lay down among the lions;
she reared her cubs
   among the young lions.
³ She brought up one of her cubs,
and he became a young lion.
After he learned to tear prey,
he devoured people.
⁴ When the nations heard about him,
he was caught in their pit.
Then they led him away with hooks
to the land of Egypt.

⁵ When she saw that she waited
   ⌊in vain⌋,
that her hope was lost,
she took another of her cubs

and made him a young lion.
⁶ He prowled among the lions,
and he became a young lion.
After he learned to tear prey,
he devoured people.
⁷ He devastatedᵃ their strongholds
and destroyed their cities.
The land and everything
   in it shuddered
at the sound of his roaring.

Nations Enslaved the Lion

⁸ Then the nations from
   the surrounding provinces
set out against him.
They spread their net over him;
he was caught in their pit.
⁹ They put a wooden yoke on himᵇ
   with hooks
and led him away to the king
   of Babylon.
They brought him into the
   fortresses
so his roar could no longer be heard
on the mountains of Israel.

Your Mother Was a Vine

¹⁰ Your mother was like a vine
   in your vineyard,ᶜ
planted by the water;
it was fruitful and full of branches
because of plentiful waters.
¹¹ It had strong branches, ⌊fit⌋ for
   the scepters of rulers;
its height towered
   among the clouds.ᵈ
So it was conspicuous for its height
as well as its many branches.
¹² But it was uprooted in fury,
thrown to the ground,
and the east wind dried up its fruit.
Its strong branches were torn off
   and dried up;
fire consumed them.

ᵃ**19:7** Tg, Aq; LXX reads *fed on*; MT reads *knew*   ᵇ**19:9** Or *put him in a cage*   ᶜ**19:10** Some Hb mss; other Hb mss read *blood*   ᵈ**19:11** Or *thick foliage*

13 Now it is planted in the wilderness,
in a dry and thirsty land.
14 Fire has gone out from its
main brancha
and has devoured its fruit,
so that it no longer has
a strong branch,
a scepter for ruling.

This is a lament and should be used as a lament."

God to Ezekiel: Explain to Elders the Abominations

20 In the seventh year, in the fifth ⌊month⌋, on the tenth ⌊day⌋ of the month, some of Israel's elders came to consult the LORD, and they sat down in front of me. 2 Then the word of the LORD came to me: 3 "Son of man, speak with the elders of Israel and tell them: This is what the Lord GOD says: Are you coming to consult Me? As I live, I will not be consulted by you." ⌊This is⌋ the declaration of the Lord GOD.

4 "Will you pass judgment against them, will you pass judgment, son of man? Explain to them the abominations of their fathers. 5 Say to them: This is what the Lord GOD says: On the day I chose Israel, I swore an oathb to the descendants of Jacob's house and made Myself known to them in the land of Egypt. I swore to them, saying: I am the LORD your God. 6 On that day I sworec to them that I would bring them out of the land of Egypt into a land I had searched out for them, ⌊a land⌋ flowing with milk and honey, the most beautiful of all lands. 7 I also said to them: Each of you must throw away the detestable things that are before your eyes and not defile yourselves with the idols of Egypt. I am the LORD your God.

"They Rebelled against Me"

8 "But they rebelled against Me and were unwilling to listen to Me. None of them threw away the detestable things that were before their eyes, and they did not forsake the idols of Egypt. So I considered pouring out My wrath on them, exhausting My anger against them within the land of Egypt. 9 But I acted for the sake of My name, so that it would not be profaned in the eyes of the nations they were living among, in whose sight I had made Myself known to Israel by bringing them out of Egypt.

10 "So I brought them out of the land of Egypt and led them into the wilderness. 11 Then I gave them My statutes and explained My ordinances to them—the person who does them will live by them. 12 I also gave them My Sabbaths to serve as a sign between Me and them, so they will know that I am the LORD who sets them apart as holy.

13 "But the house of Israel rebelled against Me in the wilderness. They did not follow My statutes and they rejected My ordinances—the person who does them will live by them. They also completely profaned My Sabbaths. So I considered pouring out My wrath on them in the wilderness to put an end to them. 14 But I acted because of My name, so that it would not be profaned in the eyes of the nations in whose sight I had brought them out. 15 However, I sworec to them in the wilderness that I would not bring them into the land I had given ⌊them⌋—the most beautiful of all lands, flowing with milk and honey— 16 because they rejected My ordinances, profaned My Sabbaths, and did not follow My statutes. For their hearts went after their idols. 17 But I spared them

---

a19:14 Lit from the branch of its parts   b20:5 Lit I lifted My hand   c20:6,15 Lit lifted My hand

from destruction and did not bring them to an end in the wilderness.

18 "Then I said to their children in the wilderness: Don't follow the statutes of your fathers, defile yourselves with their idols, or keep their ordinances. 19 I am the LORD your God. Follow My statutes, keep My ordinances, and practice them. 20 Keep My Sabbaths holy, and they will be a sign between Me and you, so you may know that I am the LORD your God.

21 "But the children rebelled against Me. They did not follow My statutes or carefully keep My ordinances—the person who does them will live by them. They also profaned My Sabbaths. So I considered pouring out My wrath on them and exhausting My anger against them in the wilderness. 22 But I withheld My hand and acted because of My name, so that it would not be profaned in the eyes of the nations in whose sight I brought them out. 23 However, I swore[a] to them in the wilderness that I would disperse them among the nations and scatter them among the countries. 24 For they did not practice My ordinances but rejected My statutes and profaned My Sabbaths, and their eyes were fixed on their fathers' idols. 25 I also gave them statutes that were not good and ordinances that did not bring them life. 26 When they made every firstborn pass through ⌊the fire⌋, I defiled them through their gifts in order to devastate them so they would know that I am the LORD.

27 "Therefore, son of man, speak to the house of Israel, and tell them: This is what the Lord GOD says: In this way also your fathers blasphemed Me by committing treachery against Me: 28 When I brought them into the land that I swore[a] to give them and they saw any high hill or leafy tree, they offered their sacrifices and presented their offensive offerings there. They also sent up their pleasing aromas and poured out their drink offerings there. 29 So I asked them: What is this •high place you are going to? And it is called High Place to this day.

30 "Therefore say to the house of Israel: This is what the Lord GOD says: Are you defiling yourselves the way your fathers did, and prostituting yourselves with their detestable things? 31 When you offer your gifts, making your children pass through the fire, you continue to defile yourselves with all your idols to this day. So should I be consulted by you, house of Israel? As I live"—⌊this is⌋ the declaration of the Lord GOD—"I will not be consulted by you!

Israel's Restoration

32 "When you say: Let us be like the nations, like the peoples of ⌊other⌋ countries, worshiping wood and stone, what you have in mind will never happen. 33 As I live"—the declaration of the Lord GOD—"I will rule over you with a strong hand, an outstretched arm, and outpoured wrath. 34 I will bring you from the peoples and gather you from the countries where you were scattered, with a strong hand, an outstretched arm, and outpoured wrath. 35 I will lead you into the wilderness of the peoples and enter into judgment with you there face to face. 36 Just as I entered into judgment with your fathers in the wilderness of the land of Egypt, so I will enter into judgment with you." ⌊This is⌋ the declaration of the Lord GOD. 37 "I will make you pass under the rod and will bring you into the bond of the covenant. 38 And I will also purge you of those who rebel and transgress against Me. I will bring them out of the land where they live as

a **20:23,28** Lit lifted My hand

foreign residents, but they will not enter the land of Israel. Then you will know that I am the LORD.

Holy Offerings

39 "As for you, house of Israel, this is what the Lord GOD says: Go and serve your idols, each of you. But afterwards you will surely listen to Me, and you will no longer defile My holy name with your gifts and idols. 40 For on My holy mountain, Israel's high mountain"—the declaration of the Lord GOD—"there the entire house of Israel, all of them, will serve Me in the land. There I will accept them and will require your contributions and choicest gifts, all your holy offerings. 41 When I bring you from the peoples and gather you from the countries where you have been scattered, I will accept you as a pleasing aroma. And I will demonstrate My holiness through you in the sight of the nations. 42 When I lead you into the land of Israel, the land I swore[a] to give your fathers, you will know that I am the LORD. 43 There you will remember your ways and all your deeds you have defiled yourselves with, and you will loathe yourselves for all the evil things you have done. 44 You will know that I am the LORD, house of Israel, when I have dealt with you because of My name rather than according to your evil ways and corrupt acts." ⌊This is⌋ the declaration of the Lord GOD.

Fire in the South

45b The word of the LORD came to me: 46 "Son of man, face the south and preach against it. Prophesy against the forest land in the •Negev, 47 and say to the forest there: Hear the word of the LORD! This is what the Lord GOD says: I am about to ignite a fire in you, and it will devour every green tree and every dry tree in you. The blazing flame will not be extinguished, and every face from the south to the north will be scorched by it. 48 Then all people will see that I, •Yahweh, have kindled it. It will not be extinguished."

49 Then I said, "Ah, Lord GOD, they are saying of me: Isn't he ⌊just⌋ posing riddles?"

God's Sword of Judgment

21[c] The word of the LORD came to me again: 2 "Son of man, turn your face toward Jerusalem and preach against the sanctuaries. Prophesy against the land of Israel, 3 and say to it: This is what the LORD says: I am against you. I will draw My sword from its sheath and cut off both the righteous and the wicked from you. 4 Since I will cut off[d] ⌊both⌋ the righteous and the wicked, My sword will therefore come out of its sheath against everyone from the south to the north. 5 So all the people will know that I, the LORD, have taken My sword from its sheath—it will not be sheathed again.

6 "But you, son of man, groan! Groan bitterly with a broken heart[e] right before their eyes. 7 And when they ask you: Why are you groaning? then say: Because of the news that is coming. Every heart will melt, and every hand will become weak. Every spirit will be discouraged, and every knee will turn to water. Yes, it is coming and it will happen." ⌊This is⌋ the declaration of the Lord GOD.

8 The word of the LORD came to me: 9 "Son of man, prophesy: This is what the Lord says! You are to proclaim:

A sword! A sword is sharpened
and also polished.
10   It is sharpened for slaughter,

---

a**20:42** Lit lifted My hand   b**20:45** Ezk 21:1 in Hb   c**21:1** Ezk 21:6 in Hb   d**21:4** Lit off from you   e**21:6** Lit with broken loins

polished to flash like lightning!
Should we rejoice?
The scepter of My son,
the sword despises every tree.[a]
11 The sword is given to be polished,
to be grasped in the hand.
It is sharpened, and it is polished,
to be put in the hand of the slayer.
12 Cry out and wail, son of man,
for it is against My people.
It is against all the princes
of Israel!
They are given over to the sword
with My people.
Therefore strike ⌞your⌟ thigh
⌞in grief⌟.
13 Surely it will be a trial!
And what if the sword despises
even the scepter?
The scepter will not continue.[a]
⌞This is⌟ the declaration
of the Lord GOD.

14 Therefore, son of man, prophesy
and clap ⌞your⌟ hands together.
Let the sword strike two times,
even three.
It is a sword for massacre,
a sword for great massacre—
it surrounds[b] them!
15 I have appointed a sword
for slaughter[a]
at all their gates,
so that their hearts may melt
and many may stumble.
Alas! It is ready to flash
like lightning;
it is drawn[a] for slaughter.
16 Slash to the right;
turn to the left—
wherever your blade is directed.
17 I also will clap My hands together,
and I will satisfy My wrath.
I, the LORD, have spoken."

Two Roads for Sword: Rabbah and Judah

18 Then the word of the LORD came to me: 19 "Now you, son of man, mark out two roads that the sword of Babylon's king can take. Both of them should originate from the same land. And make a signpost at the fork in the road to ⌞each⌟ city. 20 Mark out a road that the sword can take to Rabbah of the Ammonites and to Judah into fortified Jerusalem.

King of Babylon: Divination

21 For the king of Babylon stands at the split in the road, at the fork of the two roads, to practice •divination: he shakes the arrows, consults the idols, and observes the liver. 22 The answer marked[c] Jerusalem appears in his right hand, ⌞indicating⌟ that he should set up battering rams, give the order to[d] slaughter, raise a battle cry, set battering rams against the gates, build a ramp, and construct a siege wall. 23 It will seem like false divination in the eyes of those who have sworn an oath to the Babylonians, but it will draw attention to ⌞their⌟ guilt so that they will be captured.

24 "Therefore, this is what the Lord GOD says: Because you have drawn attention to your guilt, exposing your transgressions, so that your sins are revealed in all your actions, since you have done this, you will be captured by them.

Wicked Prince of Israel

25   And you, profane
and wicked prince of Israel,[e]
the day has come
for your punishment."[f]

26 This is what the Lord GOD says:

---

[a]21:10,13,15 Hb obscure   [b]21:14 Or penetrates   [c]21:22 Lit The divination for   [d]21:22 Lit rams, open the mouth in
[e]21:25 = King Zedekiah   [f]21:25 Lit come in the time of the punishment of the end

Remove the turban, and take off
the crown.
Things will not remain
as they are;[a]
exalt the lowly and bring down
the exalted.
27 A ruin, a ruin,
I will make it a ruin!
Yet this will not happen
until He comes;
I have given the judgment to Him.[b]

Fate of Ammonites

28 "Now prophesy, son of man, and
say: This is what the Lord GOD says concerning the Ammonites and their contempt. You are to proclaim:

Sword, sword!
⌊You are⌋ drawn for slaughter,
polished to consume, to flash
like lightning.
29 While they offer false visions
and lying divinations about you,
⌊the time⌋ has come to put you
to the necks of the profane
wicked ones;
the day has come
for your punishment.[c]
30 Return ⌊it⌋ to its sheath!

I will judge you[d]
in the place where you were created,
in the land of your origin.
31 I will pour out My indignation
on you;
I will blow the fire of My fury
on you.
I will hand you over to brutal men,
skilled at destruction.
32 You will be fuel for the fire.
Your blood will be ⌊spilled⌋
in the land.
You will not be remembered,
for I, the LORD, have spoken."

Indictment of Sinful Jerusalem

22 The word of the LORD came to me:
2 "Now, son of man, will you pass
judgment? Will you pass judgment
against the city of blood? Then explain
all her abominations to her. 3 You are to
say: This is what the Lord GOD says: A
city that sheds blood within her ⌊walls⌋
so that her time of judgment has come
and who makes idols for herself so that
she is defiled! 4 You are guilty of the
blood you have shed, and you are defiled
from the idols you have made. You have
brought your ⌊judgment⌋ days near and
have come to your years ⌊of punishment⌋.
Therefore, I have made you a disgrace to
the nations and a mockery to all the
lands. 5 Those who are near and those
far away from you will mock you, you infamous one full of turmoil.

Evil Princes of Israel

6 "Look, every prince of Israel within
you has used his strength to shed blood.
7 Father and mother are treated with
contempt, and the foreign resident is exploited within you. The fatherless and
widow are oppressed in you. 8 You despise My holy things and profane My
Sabbaths. 9 There are men within you
who slander in order to shed blood. People who ⌊live⌋ in you eat at the mountain
⌊shrines⌋; they commit immoral acts
within you. 10 Men within you have sexual intercourse with ⌊their⌋ father's wife,
and violate women during their menstrual impurity. 11 One man within you
commits an abomination with his neighbor's wife; another wickedly defiles his
daughter-in-law; and ⌊yet⌋ another violates his sister, his father's daughter.
12 People who ⌊live⌋ in you accept bribes
in order to shed blood. You take interest
and profit ⌊on a loan⌋ and brutally extort

a21:26 Lit This not this   b21:27 Or comes to whom it rightfully belongs, and I will give it to Him; Gn 49:10   c21:29 Lit
come in the time of the punishment of the end   d21:30 = the Ammonites

your neighbors. You have forgotten Me." ⌊This is⌋ the declaration of the Lord GOD. ¹³ "Now look, I clap My hands together against the unjust gain you have made and against the blood shed among you. ¹⁴ Will your courage endure or your hands be strong in the days when I deal with you? I, the LORD, have spoken, and I will act. ¹⁵ I will disperse you among the nations and scatter you among the countries; I will purge your uncleanness. ¹⁶ Youᵃ will be profaned in the sight of the nations. Then you will know that I am the LORD."

Jerusalem: God's Furnace

¹⁷ The word of the LORD came to me: ¹⁸ "Son of man, the house of Israel has become dross to Me. All of them are copper, tin, iron, and lead inside the furnace; they are the dross of silver. ¹⁹ Therefore, this is what the Lord GOD says: Because all of you have become dross, I am about to gather you into Jerusalem. ²⁰ Just as one gathers silver, copper, iron, lead, and tin into the furnace to blow fire on them and melt them, so I will gather ⌊you⌋ in My anger and wrath, put you ⌊inside⌋, and melt you. ²¹ Yes, I will gather you together and blow on you with the fire of My fury, and you will be melted within the city. ²² As silver is melted inside a furnace, so you will be melted inside the city. Then you will know that I, the LORD, have poured out My wrath on you."

Indictment of a Sinful Land

²³ The word of the LORD came to me: ²⁴ "Son of man, say to her: You are a land that has not been cleansed, that has not received rain in the day of indignation. ²⁵ The conspiracy of her prophets within her isᵇ like a roaring lion tearing ⌊its⌋

prey: they devour people, seize wealth and valuables, and multiply the widows within her. ²⁶ Her priests do violence to My law and profane My holy things. They make no distinction between the holy and the common, and they do not explain the difference between the clean and the unclean. They disregardᶜ My Sabbaths, and I am profaned among them.

²⁷ "Her officials within her are like wolves tearing ⌊their⌋ prey, shedding blood, and destroying lives in order to get unjust gain. ²⁸ Her prophets plaster with whitewash for them by seeing false visions and lying •divinations, and they say: This is what the Lord GOD says, when the LORD has not spoken. ²⁹ The people of the land have practiced extortion and committed robbery. They have oppressed the poor and needy and unlawfully exploited the foreign resident. ³⁰ I searched for a man among them who would repair the wall and stand in the gap before Me on behalf of the land so that I might not destroy it, but I found no one. ³¹ So I have poured out My indignation on them and consumed them with the fire of My fury. I have brought their actions down on their own heads." ⌊This is⌋ the declaration of the Lord GOD.

Two Immoral Sisters: Samaria and Jerusalem

23 The word of the LORD came to me again: ² "Son of man, there were two women, daughters of the same mother, ³ who acted like prostitutes in Egypt, behaving promiscuously in their youth. Their breasts were fondled there, and their virgin nipples caressed. ⁴ The older one was named Oholah,ᵈ and her sister was Oholibah.ᵉ They became Mine and gave birth to sons and daughters. As

---

ᵃ**22:16** One Hb ms, LXX, Syr, Vg read *I*   ᵇ**22:24-25** LXX reads *indignation,* 25 *whose princes within her are*   ᶜ**22:26** Lit *close their eyes from*   ᵈ**23:4** = Her Tent   ᵉ**23:4** = My Tent Is in Her

for their names, <u>Oholah represents Samaria and Oholibah represents Jerusalem</u>.

Sins of Samaria

⁵ "Oholah acted like a prostitute even though she was Mine. She lusted after her lovers, the Assyrians: warriors ⁶ dressed in blue, governors and prefects, all of them desirable young men, horsemen riding on steeds. ⁷ She offered her sexual favors to them; all of them were the elite of Assyria. She defiled herself with all those she lusted after and with all their idols. ⁸ She didn't give up her promiscuity that began in Egypt, when men slept with her in her youth, caressed her virgin nipples, and poured out their lust on her. ⁹ Therefore, I handed her over to her lovers, the Assyrians she lusted for. ¹⁰ They exposed her nakedness, seized her sons and daughters, and killed her with the sword. Since they executed judgment against her, she became notorious among women.

Jerusalem More Depraved than Samaria

¹¹ "Now her sister Oholibah saw ⌊this⌋, but she was ⌊even⌋ more depraved in her lust than Oholah, and made her promiscuous acts worse than those of her sister. ¹² She lusted after the Assyrians: governors and prefects, warriors splendidly dressed, horsemen riding on steeds, all of them desirable young men. ¹³ And I saw that she had defiled herself; both of them ⌊had taken⌋ the same path. ¹⁴ But she increased her promiscuity when she saw male figures carved on the wall, images of the Chaldeans, engraved in vermilion, ¹⁵ wearing belts on their waists and flowing turbans on their heads; all of them looked like officers, a depiction of the Babylonians in Chaldea, the land of their birth. ¹⁶ At the sight of them[a] she lusted after them and sent messengers to them in Chaldea. ¹⁷ Then the Babylonians came to her, to the bed of love, and defiled her with their lust. But after she was defiled by them, she turned away from them in disgust. ¹⁸ When she flaunted her promiscuity and exposed her nakedness, I turned away from her in disgust just as I turned away from her sister. ¹⁹ Yet she multiplied her acts of promiscuity, remembering the days of her youth when she acted like a prostitute in the land of Egypt ²⁰ and lusted after their lovers, whose sexual members were like those of donkeys and whose emission was like that of stallions. ²¹ So you revisited the indecency of your youth, when the Egyptians caressed your nipples to enjoy your youthful breasts.

Fate of Jerusalem

²² "Therefore Oholibah, this is what the Lord GOD says: I am going to incite your lovers against you, those you turned away from in disgust. I will bring them against you from every side: ²³ the Babylonians and all the Chaldeans; Pekod, Shoa, and Koa; and all the Assyrians with them—desirable young men, all of them governors and prefects, officers and administrators, all of them riding on horses. ²⁴ They will come against you with an alliance of nations and with weapons, chariots, and[b] wagons. They will set themselves against you on every side with shields, bucklers, and helmets. I will delegate judgment to them, and they will judge you by their own standards. ²⁵ When I vent My jealous rage on you, they will deal with you in wrath. They will cut off your nose and ears, and

---

ᵃ**23:16** Lit *of her eyes*   ᵇ**23:24** LXX reads *nations, from the north, chariots and*; Hb obscure

your descendants will fall by the sword. They will seize your sons and daughters, and your descendants will be consumed by fire. ²⁶ They will strip off your clothes and take your beautiful jewelry. ²⁷ So I will put an end to your indecency and sexual immorality, which began in the land of Egypt, and you will not look longingly at them or remember Egypt any more.

²⁸ "For this is what the Lord GOD says: I am going to hand you over to those you hate, to those you turned away from in disgust. ²⁹ They will treat you with hatred, take all you have worked for, and leave you stark naked, so that the shame of your debauchery will be exposed, both your indecency and promiscuity. ³⁰ These things will be done to you because you acted like a prostitute with the nations, defiling yourself with their idols. ³¹ You have followed the path of your sister, so I will put her cup in your hand."

³² This is what the Lord GOD says:

You will drink your sister's cup,
   which is deep and wide.
You will be an object ofᵃ ridicule
      and scorn,
   for it holds ⌊so⌋ much.
³³ You will be filled with drunkenness
      and grief,
   with a cup of devastation
      and desolation,
   the cup of your sister Samaria.
³⁴ You will drink it and drain ⌊it⌋;
   then you will gnaw
      its broken pieces,
   and tear your breasts.
For I have spoken.
            ⌊This is⌋ the declaration
                  of the Lord GOD.

³⁵ Therefore, this is what the Lord GOD says: "Because you have forgotten Me and cast Me behind your back, you must bear the consequences of your indecency and promiscuity."

Lord: Ezekiel Will Pass Judgment on Sisters

³⁶ Then the LORD said to me: "Son of man, will you pass judgment against Oholah and Oholibah? Then declare their abominations to them. ³⁷ For they have committed adultery, and blood is on their hands; they have committed adultery with their idols. They have even made the children they bore to Me pass through ⌊the fire⌋ as food for the idols. ³⁸ They also did this to Me: they defiled My sanctuary on that same day and profaned My Sabbaths. ³⁹ On the same day they slaughtered their children for their idols, they entered My sanctuary to profane it. Yes, that is what they did inside My house.

⁴⁰ "In addition, they sent for men who came from far away when a messenger was dispatched to them. And look how they came! You bathed, painted your eyes, and adorned yourself with jewelry for them. ⁴¹ You sat on a luxurious couch with a table spread before it, on which you had set My incense and oil. ⁴² The sound of a carefree crowd was there. Drunkardsᵇ from the desert were brought in, along with common men. They put bracelets on the women's hands and beautiful crowns on their heads. ⁴³ Then I said concerning this woman worn out by adultery: Will they now have illicit sex with her, even her? ⁴⁴ Yet they had sex with her as one does with a prostitute. This is how they had sex with Oholah and Oholibah, those obscene women. ⁴⁵ But righteous men will judge them the way adulteresses and those who shed blood are judged, for

ᵃ**23:32** Or *It will bring*   ᵇ**23:42** Or *Sabeans*

they are adulteresses and blood is on their hands.

"Consign Them to Terror and Plunder"

⁴⁶ "This is what the Lord GOD says: Summonᵃ an assembly against them and consign them to terror and plunder. ⁴⁷ The assembly will stone them and cut them down with their swords. They will kill their sons and daughters and burn their houses with fire. ⁴⁸ So I will put an end to indecency in the land, and all the women will be admonished not to imitate your indecent behavior. ⁴⁹ They will repay you for your indecency, and you will bear the consequences for your sins of idolatry. Then you will know that I am the Lord GOD."

Parable of the Boiling Pot

24 The word of the LORD came to me in the ninth year, in the tenth month, on the tenth ⌞day⌟ of the month: ² "Son of man, write down today's date, this very day. The king of Babylon has laid siege to Jerusalem this very day. ³ Now speak a parable to the rebellious house. Tell them: This is what the Lord GOD says:

Put the pot on ⌞the fire⌟—
put ⌞it⌟ on,
and then pour water into it!
⁴ Place the pieces of meat in it,
every good piece—
thigh and shoulder.
Fill it with choice bones.
⁵ Take the choicest of the flock
and also pile up the fuelᵇ under it.
Bring it to a boil
and cook the bones in it."

⁶ Therefore, this is what the Lord GOD says:

Woe to the city of bloodshed,
the pot that has rust inside it,
and whose rust will not come off!
Empty it piece by piece;
lots should not be cast
for its contents.
⁷ For the blood she shedᶜ is
in her midst.
She put it out on the bare rock;
she didn't pour it on the ground
to cover it with dust.
⁸ In order to stir up wrath
and take vengeance,
I have put her blood
on the bare rock,
so that it would not be covered.

⁹ Therefore, this is what the Lord GOD says:

Woe to the city of bloodshed!
I Myself will make the pile
of kindling large.
¹⁰ Pile on the logs and kindle the fire!
Cook the meat well
and mix in the spices!ᵈ ᵉ
Let the bones be burned!
¹¹ Set the empty pot on its coals
so that it becomes hot
and its copper glows.
Then its impurity will melt
inside it;
its rust will be consumed.
¹² It has frustrated every effort;ᶠ
its thick rust will not come off.
Into the fire with its rust!
¹³ Because of the indecency
of your uncleanness—
since I tried to purify you,
but you would not be purified
from your uncleanness—
you will not be pure again
until I have satisfied My wrath
on you.

ᵃ**23:46** Or *I will summon*   ᵇ**24:5** Lit *bones*   ᶜ**24:7** Lit *For her blood*   ᵈ**24:10** Some Hb mss read *well; remove the broth*; LXX reads *fire so that the meat may be cooked and the broth may be reduced*   ᵉ**24:10** Or *and stir the broth*
ᶠ**24:12** Hb obscure

¹⁴ I, the LORD, have spoken.
It is coming, and I will do it!
I will not refrain, I will not show pity,
and I will not relent.
Iᵃ will judge you
according to your ways and deeds.
⌊This is⌋ the declaration
of the Lord GOD.

Death of Ezekiel's Wife: A Sign

¹⁵ Then the word of the LORD came to me: ¹⁶ "Son of man, I am about to take the delight of your eyes away from you with a fatal blow. But you must not lament or weep or let your tears flow. ¹⁷ Groan quietly; do not observe mourning rites for the dead. Put on your turban and strap your sandals on your feet; do not cover ⌊your⌋ mustache or eat the bread of mourners."ᵇ

¹⁸ I spoke to the people in the morning, and my wife died in the evening. The next morning I did just as I was commanded. ¹⁹ Then the people asked me, "Won't you tell us what these things you are doing mean for us?"

Meaning of Wife's Death

²⁰ So I answered them: "The word of the LORD came to me: ²¹ 'Say to the house of Israel: This is what the Lord GOD says: I am about to desecrate My sanctuary, the pride of your power, the delight of your eyes, and the desire of your heart. Also, the sons and daughters you left behind will fall by the sword. ²² Then you will do just as I have done: You will not cover ⌊your⌋ mustache or eat the bread of mourners.ᵇ ²³ Your turbans will remain on your heads and your sandals on your feet. You will not lament or weep but will waste away because of your sins and will groan to one another. ²⁴ Now Ezekiel will be a sign for you. You will do everything

that he has done. When this happens, you will know that I am the Lord GOD.

²⁵ " 'Son of man, know that on the day I take their stronghold from them, their pride and joy, the delight of their eyes and the longing of their hearts, ⌊as well as⌋ their sons and daughters, ²⁶ on that day a fugitive will come to you and report the news. ²⁷ On that day your mouth will be opened ⌊to talk⌋ with him; you will speak and no longer be mute. So you will be a sign for them, and they will know that I am the LORD.' "

PROPHECIES AGAINST THE NATIONS

Judgment against Ammon

25 Then the word of the LORD came to me: ² "Son of man, turn your face toward the Ammonites and prophesy against them. ³ Say to the Ammonites: Hear the word of the Lord GOD: This is what the Lord GOD says: Because you said: Good! about My sanctuary when it was desecrated, about the land of Israel when it was laid waste, and about the house of Judah when they went into exile, ⁴ therefore I am about to give you to the people of the east as a possession. They will set up their encampments and pitch their tents among you. They will eat your fruit and drink your milk. ⁵ I will make Rabbah a pasture for camels and Ammon a sheepfold. Then you will know that I am the LORD."

⁶ For this is what the Lord GOD says: "Because you clapped ⌊your⌋ hands, stamped ⌊your⌋ feet, and rejoiced over the land of Israel with wholehearted contempt, ⁷ therefore I am about to stretch out My hand against you and give you as plunder to the nations. I will cut you off from the peoples and eliminate you from the countries. I will destroy

ᵃ**24:14** Some Hb mss, LXX, Syr, Tg, Vg; other Hb mss read *They*   ᵇ**24:17,22** Lit *men*

you, and you will know that I am the LORD."

Judgment against Moab

8 This is what the Lord GOD says: "Because Moab and Seir said: Look, the house of Judah is like all the ⌊other⌋ nations, 9 therefore I am about to expose Moab's flank beginning with its[a] frontier cities, the pride of the land: Beth-jeshimoth, Baal-meon, and Kiriathaim. 10 I will give it along with Ammon to the people of the east as a possession, so that Ammon will not be remembered among the nations. 11 So I will execute judgments against Moab, and they will know that I am the LORD."

Judgment against Edom

12 This is what the Lord GOD says: "Because Edom acted vengefully against the house of Judah and incurred grievous guilt by taking revenge on them, 13 therefore this is what the Lord GOD says: I will stretch out My hand against Edom and cut off both man and animal from it. I will make it a wasteland; they will fall by the sword from Teman to Dedan. 14 I will take My vengeance on Edom through My people Israel, and they will deal with Edom according to My anger and wrath. So they will know My vengeance." ⌊This is⌋ the declaration of the Lord GOD.

Judgment against Philistia

15 This is what the Lord GOD says: "Because the Philistines acted in vengeance and took revenge with deep contempt, destroying ⌊because of their⌋ ancient hatred, 16 therefore this is what the Lord GOD says: I am about to stretch out My hand against the Philistines, cutting off the Cherethites and wiping out what re-

mains of the coastal peoples.[b] 17 I will execute great vengeance against them with furious rebukes. They will know that I am the LORD when I take My vengeance on them."

Downfall of Tyre

26 In the eleventh year, on the first ⌊day⌋ of the month, the word of the LORD came to me: 2 "Son of man, because Tyre said about Jerusalem: Good! The gateway to the peoples is shattered. She has been turned over to me. I will be filled ⌊now that⌋ she lies in ruins, 3 therefore this is what the Lord GOD says: See, I am against you, Tyre! I will raise up many nations against you, just as the sea raises its waves. 4 They will destroy the walls of Tyre and demolish her towers. I will scrape the soil from her and turn her into a bare rock. 5 She will become a place in the sea to spread nets, for I have spoken." ⌊This is⌋ the declaration of the Lord GOD. "She will become plunder for the nations, 6 and her villages on the mainland will be slaughtered by the sword. Then they will know that I am the LORD."

King Nebuchadnezzar against Tyre

7 For this is what the Lord GOD says: "See, I am about to bring King Nebuchadnezzar of Babylon, king of kings, against Tyre from the north with horses, chariots, cavalry, and a vast company of troops. 8 He will slaughter your villages on the mainland with the sword. He will set up siege works against you, and will build a ramp[c] and raise a wall of shields against you. 9 He will direct the blows of his battering rams against your walls and tear down your towers with his iron tools. 10 His horses will be so numerous that their dust will cover you. When he

---

a25:9 Lit with the cities, with its   b25:16 Lit the seacoast   c26:8 Lit ramp against you

enters your gates as ⌊an army⌋ entering a breached city, your walls will shake from the noise of cavalry, wagons, and chariots. ¹¹ He will trample all your streets with the hooves of his horses. He will slaughter your people with the sword, and your mighty pillars will fall to the ground. ¹² They will take your wealth as spoil and plunder your merchandise. They will also demolish your walls and tear down your beautiful homes. Then they will throw your stones, timber, and soil into the water. ¹³ I will put an end to the noise of your songs, and the sound of your lyres will no longer be heard. ¹⁴ I will turn you into a bare rock, and you will be a place to spread nets. You will never be rebuilt, for I, the LORD, have spoken." ⌊This is⌋ the declaration of the Lord GOD.

¹⁵ This is what the Lord GOD says to Tyre: "Won't the coasts and islands quake at the sound of your downfall, when the wounded groan and slaughter occurs within you? ¹⁶ All the princes of the sea will descend from their thrones, remove their robes, and strip off their embroidered garments. They will clothe themselves with trembling; they will sit on the ground, tremble continually, and be appalled at you. ¹⁷ Then they will lament for you and say of you:

How you have perished,
 city of renown,
you who were populated
 from the seas!ᵃ
She who was powerful on the sea,
she and all of her inhabitants
inflicted their terror.ᵇ
¹⁸ Now the coastlands tremble
on the day of your downfall;
the islands in the sea
are alarmed by your demise."

¹⁹ For this is what the Lord GOD says: "When I make you a ruined city like ⌊other⌋ deserted cities, when I raise up the deep against you so that the mighty waters cover you, ²⁰ then I will bring you down ⌊to be⌋ with those who descend to the •Pit, to the people of antiquity. I will make you dwell in the underworldᶜ likeᵈ the ancient ruins, with those who descend to the Pit, so that you will no longer be inhabited or display ⌊your⌋ splendorᵉ in the land of the living. ²¹ I will make you an object of horror, and you will no longer exist. You will be sought but will never be found again." ⌊This is⌋ the declaration of the Lord GOD.

Sinking of Tyre

27 The word of the LORD came to me: ² "Now, son of man, lament for Tyre. ³ Say to Tyre, who is located at the entrance of the sea, merchant of the peoples to many coasts and islands: This is what the Lord GOD says:

Tyre, you declared:
 I am perfect in beauty.
⁴ Your realm was in the heart
 of the sea;
your builders perfected your beauty.
⁵ They constructed all your planking
 with pine trees from Senir.ᶠ
They took a cedar from Lebanon
 to make a mast for you.
⁶ They made your oars of oaks
 from Bashan.
They made your deck
 of cypress wood
from the coasts of Cyprus,
 ⌊inlaid⌋ with ivory.
⁷ Your sail was ⌊made of⌋
fine embroidered linen from Egypt,
and served as your banner.

ᵃ**26:17** Some LXX mss read *How you were destroyed from the seas, city of renown!* ᵇ**26:17** Lit *and all her inhabitants who put their terror on all her inhabitants*; Hb obscure ᶜ**26:20** Lit *the lower parts of the earth* ᵈ**26:20** Some Hb mss, LXX; other Hb mss, Syr read *in* ᵉ**26:20** LXX reads *or appear* ᶠ**27:5** = Mount Hermon

Your awning was of blue
  and purple fabric
from the coasts of Elishah.
8 The inhabitants of Sidon and Arvad
  were your rowers.
Your wise men were
  within you, Tyre;
they were your helmsmen.
9 The elders of Gebal and its
  wise men
were within you,
  repairing your leaks.

All the ships of the sea
  and their sailors
came to[a] you to barter
  for your goods.
10 ⌊Men of⌋ Persia, Lud, and Put
  were in your army, ⌊serving⌋
  as your warriors.
They hung shields and helmets
  in you;
they gave you splendor.
11 Men of Arvad and Helech
  were ⌊stationed⌋ on your walls
  all around,
and Gamadites were
  in your towers.
They hung their shields[b] all around
  your walls;
they perfected your beauty.

12 "Tarshish was your trading partner because of ⌊your⌋ great wealth of every kind. They exchanged silver, iron, tin, and lead for your merchandise. 13 Javan, Tubal, and Meshech were your merchants. They exchanged slaves[c] and bronze utensils for your goods. 14 Those from Beth-togarmah exchanged horses, war horses, and mules for your merchandise. 15 Men of Dedan[d] were also your merchants; many coasts and islands were your regular markets. They brought back ivory tusks and ebony as your payment. 16 Aram[e][f] was your trading partner because of your numerous products. They exchanged turquoise,[g] purple and embroidered cloth, fine linen, coral,[h] and rubies[i] for your merchandise. 17 Judah and the land of Israel were your merchants. They exchanged wheat from Minnith, meal,[j] honey, oil, and balm for your goods. 18 Damascus was also your trading partner because of your numerous products and your great wealth of every kind, ⌊trading⌋ in wine from Helbon and white wool.[k] 19 Vedan[l] and Javan from Uzal[m] dealt in your merchandise; wrought iron, cassia, and aromatic cane were ⌊exchanged⌋ for your goods. 20 Dedan was your merchant in saddlecloths for riding. 21 Arabia and all the princes of Kedar were your business[n] partners, trading with you in lambs, rams, and goats. 22 The merchants of Sheba and Raamah traded with you. They exchanged gold, the best of all spices, and all kinds of precious stones for your merchandise. 23 Haran, Canneh, Eden, the merchants of Sheba, Asshur, and Chilmad traded with you. 24 They were your merchants in choice garments, cloaks of blue and embroidered materials, and multicolored carpets,[m] which were bound and secured with cords in your marketplace. 25 Ships of Tarshish were the carriers for your goods.

So you became full
  and heavily loaded[o]
  in the heart of the sea.
26 Your rowers have brought you
  onto the high seas,
but the east wind has shattered you
  in the heart of the sea.

[a]27:9 Lit sailors were with   [b]27:11 Or quivers; Hb obscure   [c]27:13 Lit souls of men   [d]27:15 LXX reads Rhodes   [e]27:16 Some Hb mss, Aq, Syr read Edom   [f]27:16 = Syria   [g]27:16 Hb obscure; Ezk 28:13; Ex 28:18; 39:11   [h]27:16 Hb obscure; Jb 28:18   [i]27:16 Hb obscure; Is 54:12   [j]27:17 Or resin; Hb obscure   [k]27:18 Or and wool from Zahar   [l]27:19 Or Dan   [m]27:19,24 Hb obscure   [n]27:21 Lit trading   [o]27:25 Or and very glorious

Tyre Pulls Down Others

27 Your wealth, merchandise,
   and goods,
your sailors and helmsmen,
those who repair your leaks,
those who barter for your goods,
and all the warriors within you,
with all the other people on board,[a]
sink into the heart of the sea
on the day of your downfall.

28 The countryside shakes
at the sound of your sailors' cries.
29 All those who handle an oar
disembark from their ships.
The sailors and all the helmsmen
   of the sea
stand on the shore.
30 They raise their voices over you
and cry out bitterly.
They throw dust on their heads;
they roll in ashes.
31 They shave their heads
   because of you
and wrap themselves in •sackcloth.
They weep over you
with deep anguish
   and bitter mourning.

32 In their wailing they lament
   for you,
mourning over you:
Who was like Tyre,
silenced[b] in the middle of the sea?
33 When your merchandise
   was unloaded from the seas,
you satisfied many peoples.
You enriched the kings of the earth
with your abundant wealth
   and goods.
34 Now you are shattered by the sea
in the depths of the waters;
your goods and the people
   within you
have gone down.

35 All the inhabitants of the coasts
   and islands
are appalled at you.
Their kings shudder with fear;
ʟtheirʟ faces are contorted.
36 Those who trade
   among the peoples
hiss at you;
you have become an object
   of horror
and will never exist again."

Fall of Tyre's Ruler

28 The word of the LORD came to me:
2 "Son of man, say to the ruler of
Tyre: This is what the Lord GOD says:

Your[c] heart is proud,
and you have said: I am a god;
I sit in the seat of gods
in the heart of the sea.
Yet you are a man and not a god,
though you have regarded
   your heart
as that of a god.
3 Yes, you are wiser than Daniel;
no secret is hidden from you!
4 By your wisdom and understanding
you have acquired wealth
   for yourself.
You have acquired gold and silver
for your treasuries.
5 By your great skill in trading
you have increased your wealth,
but your heart has become proud
because of your wealth."

6 Therefore this is what the Lord GOD
says:

Because you regard your heart
   as that of a god,
7 I am about to bring strangers
   against you,
ruthless men from the nations.
They will draw their swords

---

[a]27:27 Lit *with all your assembly among you*   [b]27:32 Hb obscure   [c]28:2 Lit *Because your*

against your magnificent wisdom
and will defile your splendor.
8 They will bring you down
   to the •Pit,
and you will die a violent death
in the heart of the sea.
9 Will you still say: I am a god,
in the presence of those
   who kill[a] you?
Yet you will be ⌊shown to be⌋ a man,
   not a god,
in the hands of those who kill you.
10 You will die the death
of the uncircumcised
at the hands of strangers.
For I have spoken.
       ⌊This is⌋ the declaration
          of the Lord GOD.

Lament for Tyre's King

11 The word of the LORD came to me:
12 "Son of man, lament for the king of
Tyre and say to him: This is what the
Lord GOD says:

You were the seal[b] of perfection,[c]
full of wisdom and perfect
   in beauty.
13 You were in Eden, the garden
   of God.
Every kind of precious stone
   covered you:
carnelian, topaz, and diamond,[c]
beryl, onyx, and jasper,
sapphire,[d] turquoise[e] and emerald.[f]
Your mountings and settings
   were crafted in gold;
they were prepared on the day
   you were created.
14 You were an anointed
   guardian cherub,
for[g] I had appointed you.
You were on the holy mountain
   of God;

you walked among the fiery stones.
15 From the day you were created
you were blameless in your ways
until wickedness was found in you.
16 Through the abundance
   of your trade,
you were filled with violence,
   and you sinned.
So I expelled you in disgrace
from the mountain of God,
and banished you,
   guardian cherub,[h]
from among the fiery stones.
17 Your heart became proud
   because of your beauty;
For the sake of your splendor
you corrupted your wisdom.
So I threw you down to the earth;
I made a spectacle of you
   before kings.
18 You profaned your sanctuaries
by the magnitude of your iniquities
in your dishonest trade.
So I sent out fire from within you,
and it consumed you.
I reduced you to ashes
   on the ground
in the sight of everyone
   watching you.
19 All those who know you
   among the nations
are appalled at you.
You have become an object of horror
and will never exist again."

A Prophecy against Sidon

20 The word of the LORD came to me:
21 "Son of man, turn your face toward Sidon and prophesy against it. 22 You are to
say: This is what the Lord GOD says:

Look! I am against you, Sidon,
and I will display My glory
   within you.

They will know that I am the LORD
when I execute judgments
    against her
and demonstrate My holiness
    through her.
23 I will send a plague against her
and bloodshed in her streets;
the slain will fall within her,
while the sword is against her[a]
    on every side.
Then they will know that
    I am the LORD.

24 "The house of Israel will no longer be hurt by[b] prickling briers or painful thorns from all their neighbors who treat them with contempt. Then they will know that I am the Lord GOD.

25 "This is what the Lord GOD says: When I gather the house of Israel from the peoples where they are scattered and demonstrate My holiness through them in the sight of the nations, then they will live in their own land, which I gave to My servant Jacob. 26 They will live there securely, build houses, and plant vineyards. They will live securely when I execute judgments against all their neighbors who treat them with contempt. Then they will know that I am the LORD their God."

Prophecy of Egypt's Ruin

29 In the tenth year, in the tenth ⌊month⌋ on the twelfth ⌊day⌋ of the month, the word of the LORD came to me: 2 "Son of man, turn your face toward Pharaoh king of Egypt and prophesy against him and against all of Egypt. 3 Speak ⌊to him⌋ and say: This is what the Lord GOD says:

Look, I am against you, Pharaoh
    king of Egypt,
the great monster[c] lying
    in the middle of his Nile,

who says: My Nile is my own;
    I made ⌊it⌋ for myself.
4 I will put hooks in your jaws
and make the fish of your streams
    cling to your scales.
I will haul you up
from the middle of your Nile,
and all the fish of your streams
    will cling to your scales.
5 I will leave you in the desert,
you and all the fish of your streams.
You will fall on the open ground
and will not be taken away
    or gathered ⌊for burial⌋.
I have given you
to the beasts of the earth
and the birds of the sky as food.
6 Then all the inhabitants of Egypt
    will know that I am the LORD,
for they[d] have been a staff
    ⌊made⌋ of reed
    to the house of Israel.
7 When Israel grasped you
    by the hand,
you splintered, tearing all
    their shoulders;
when they leaned on you,
you shattered and made all
    their hips unsteady.[e]

8 "Therefore this is what the Lord GOD says: I am going to bring a sword against you and wipe out man and animal from you. 9 The land of Egypt will be a desolate ruin. Then they will know that I am the LORD. Because you[f] said: The Nile is my own; I made ⌊it⌋, 10 therefore, I am against you and your Nile. I will turn the land of Egypt into ruins, a desolate waste from Migdol to Syene, as far as the border of •Cush. 11 No human foot will pass through it, and no animal foot will pass through it. It will be uninhabited for 40 years. 12 I will make the land of Egypt a

desolation among[a] desolate lands, and its cities will be a desolation among[b] ruined cities for 40 years. I will disperse the Egyptians among the nations and scatter them across the countries.

Egypt a Lowly Kingdom

[13] "For this is what the Lord GOD says: At the end of 40 years I will gather the Egyptians from the nations where they were dispersed. [14] I will restore the fortunes of Egypt and bring them back to the land of Pathros, the land of their origin. There they will be a lowly kingdom. [15] Egypt will be the lowliest of kingdoms and will never again exalt itself over the nations. I will make them so small they cannot rule over the nations. [16] It will never again be an object of trust for the house of Israel, drawing attention to their sin of turning to the Egyptians. Then they will know that I am the Lord GOD."

God Gives Egypt to Babylon

[17] In the twenty-seventh year in the first ⌐month⌐, on the first ⌐day⌐ of the month, the word of the LORD came to me: [18] "Son of man, Nebuchadnezzar king of Babylon made his army labor strenuously against Tyre. Every head was made bald and every shoulder chafed, but he and his army received no compensation from Tyre for the labor he expended against it. [19] Therefore this is what the Lord GOD says: I am going to give the land of Egypt to Nebuchadnezzar king of Babylon, who will carry off its wealth, seizing its spoil and taking its plunder. This will be his army's compensation. [20] I have given him the land of Egypt as the pay he labored for, since they worked for Me." ⌐This is⌐ the declaration of the Lord GOD. [21] "In that day I will cause a •horn to sprout for the house

of Israel, and I will enable you to speak out among them. Then they will know that I am the LORD."

Egypt's Doom

30 The word of the LORD came to me: [2] "Son of man, prophesy and say: This is what the Lord GOD says:

Wail: Alas for the day!
[3] For a day is near;
a day belonging to the LORD is near.
It will be a day of clouds,
a time ⌐of doom⌐ for the nations.
[4] A sword will come against Egypt,
and there will be anguish in •Cush
when the slain fall in Egypt,
and its wealth is taken away,
and its foundations are torn down.
[5] Cush, Put, and Lud,
and all the various foreign troops,[c]
plus Libya[d] and the men
of the covenant land[e]
will fall by the sword
along with them.
[6] This is what the LORD says:
Those who support Egypt will fall,
and its proud strength will collapse.
From Migdol to Syene
they will fall within it by the sword.
⌐This is⌐ the declaration
of the Lord GOD.
[7] They will be desolate
among[f] desolate lands,
and their cities will lie
among ruined[g] cities.
[8] They will know that I am the LORD
when I set fire to Egypt
and all its allies are shattered.

[9] On that day, messengers will go out from Me in ships to terrify confident Cush. Anguish will come over them on the day of Egypt's ⌐doom⌐. For indeed it is coming."

---

[a]**29:12** Or *Egypt the most desolate of*   [b]**29:12** Or *be the most desolate of*   [c]**30:5** Or *all Arabia*   [d]**30:5** Lit *Cub*; Hb obscure   [e]**30:5** Probably = Israel   [f]**30:7** Or *be the most desolate of*   [g]**30:7** Or *will be the most ruined of*

¹⁰ This is what the Lord G<small>OD</small> says:

I will put an end to the hordes^a
  of Egypt
by the hand of Nebuchadnezzar
  king of Babylon.
¹¹ He along with his people,
  ruthless men from the nations,
will be brought in to destroy
  the land.
They will draw their swords
  against Egypt
and fill the land with the slain.
¹² I will make the streams dry
and sell the land into the hands
  of evil men.
I will bring desolation
on the land and everything in it
by the hands of foreigners.
I, the L<small>ORD</small>, have spoken.

¹³ This is what the Lord G<small>OD</small> says:

I will destroy the idols and put
  an end
to the false gods in Memphis.
There will no longer be
  a prince from the land of Egypt.
So I will instill fear in that land.
¹⁴ I will make Pathros desolate,
  set fire to Zoan,
and execute judgments
  on Thebes.
¹⁵ I will pour out My wrath
  on Pelusium,
the stronghold of Egypt,
and will wipe out the crowds^a
  of Thebes.
¹⁶ I will set fire to Egypt;
Pelusium will writhe in anguish,
Thebes will be breached,
and Memphis will face foes
  in broad daylight.^b
¹⁷ The young men of On^c
  and Pi-beseth
will fall by the sword,

and those cities^d will go
  into captivity.
¹⁸ The day will be dark^e
  in Tehaphnehes,
when I break the yoke
  of Egypt there
and its proud strength
comes to an end in the city.
A cloud will cover Tehaphnehes,^f
and its villages will go
  into captivity.
¹⁹ So I will execute judgments
  against Egypt,
and they will know that
  I am the L<small>ORD</small>.

Pharaoh's Power Broken

²⁰ In the eleventh year, in the first ⌊month⌋, on the seventh ⌊day⌋ of the month, the word of the L<small>ORD</small> came to me: ²¹ "Son of man, I have broken the arm of Pharaoh king of Egypt. Look, it has not been bandaged—⌊no⌋ medicine has been applied and no splint put on to bandage it so that it can grow strong ⌊enough⌋ to handle a sword. ²² Therefore this is what the Lord G<small>OD</small> says: Look! I am against Pharaoh king of Egypt. I will break his arms, both the strong one and the one ⌊already⌋ broken, and will make the sword fall from his hand. ²³ I will disperse the Egyptians among the nations and scatter them among the countries. ²⁴ I will strengthen the arms of Babylon's king and place My sword in his hand. But I will break the arms of Pharaoh, and he will groan before him as a mortally wounded man. ²⁵ I will strengthen the arms of Babylon's king, but Pharaoh's arms will fall. They will know that I am the L<small>ORD</small> when I place My sword in the hand of Babylon's king and he wields it against the land of Egypt. ²⁶ When I disperse the Egyptians among the

---

^a**30:10,15** Or *pomp,* or *wealth* ^b**30:16** Or *foes daily* ^c**30:17** LXX, Vg; MT reads *iniquity* ^d**30:17** Or *and the women;* lit *and they* ^e**30:18** Some Hb mss, LXX, Syr, Tg, Vg; MT reads *will withhold* ^f**30:18** Or *Egypt;* lit *it*

nations and scatter them among the countries, they will know that I am the LORD."

Downfall of Egypt and Assyria

31 In the eleventh year, in the third ⌞month⌟, on the first ⌞day⌟ of the month, the word of the LORD came to me: ² "Son of man, say to Pharaoh king of Egypt and to his hordes:

> Who are you like
>   in your greatness?
> ³ Think of Assyria, a cedar
>   in Lebanon,
> with beautiful branches
>   and shady foliage,
> and of lofty height.
> Its top was among the clouds.ᵃ
> ⁴ The waters caused it to grow;
>   the underground springs
>   made it tall,
> directing their rivers all around
> the place where the tree
>   was planted
> and sending their channels
> to all the trees of the field.
> ⁵ Therefore the cedar became greater
>   in height
> than all the trees of the field.
> Its branches multiplied,
> and its boughs grew long
> as it spread ⌞them⌟ out
> because of the plentiful water.
> ⁶ All the birds of the sky
> nested in its branches,
> and all the animals of the field
> gave birth beneath its boughs;
> all the great nations lived
>   in its shade.
> ⁷ It was beautiful in its greatness,
>   in the length of its limbs,
> for its roots extended
>   to abundant water.

> ⁸ The cedars in God's garden
>   could not rival it;
> the pine trees couldn't compare
>   with its branches,
> nor could the plane trees match
>   its boughs.
> No tree in the garden of God
> could compare with it in beauty.
> ⁹ I made it beautiful with its
>   many limbs,
> and all the trees of Eden,
> which were in God's garden,
>   envied it.

¹⁰ "Therefore this is what the Lord GOD says: Since itᵇ became great in height and set its top among the clouds,ᵃ and itᶜ grew proud on account of its height, ¹¹ I determined to hand it over to a ruler of nations; he would surely deal with it. I banished it because of its wickedness. ¹² Foreigners, ruthless men from the nations, cut it down and left it lying. Its limbs fell on the mountains and in every valley; its boughs lay broken in all the earth's ravines. All the peoples of the earth left its shade and abandoned it. ¹³ All the birds of the sky nested on its fallen trunk, and all the animals of the field were among its boughs. ¹⁴ ⌞This happened⌟ so that no trees ⌞planted⌟ beside water would become great in height and set their tops among the clouds,ᵃ and so that no ⌞other⌟ well-watered trees would reach them in height. For they have all been consigned to death, to the underworld, among the •people who descend to the •Pit.

¹⁵ "This is what the Lord GOD says: I caused grieving on the day the cedar went down to •Sheol. I closed off the underground deep because of it:ᵈ I held back the rivers of the deep, and ⌞its⌟ abundant waters were restrained. I

ᵃ31:3,10,14 Or *thick foliage*   ᵇ31:10 Syr, Vg; MT, LXX read *you*   ᶜ31:10 Lit *its heart*   ᵈ31:15 Or *I covered it with the underground deep*

made Lebanon mourn on account of it, and all the trees of the field fainted because of it. ¹⁶ I made the nations quake at the sound of its downfall, when I threw it down to Sheol ⌞to be⌟ with those who descend to the Pit. Then all the trees of Eden, all the well-watered trees, the choice and best of Lebanon, were comforted in the underworld. ¹⁷ They too descended with it to Sheol, to those slain by the sword. As its allies[a] [b] they had lived in its shade among the nations.

¹⁸ "Who then are you like in glory and greatness among Eden's trees? You also will be brought down to the underworld ⌞to be⌟ with the trees of Eden. You will lie among the uncircumcised with those slain by the sword. This is Pharaoh and all his hordes"—the declaration of the Lord GOD.

A Lament for Pharaoh

32 In the twelfth year, in the twelfth month, on the first ⌞day⌟ of the month, the word of the LORD came to me: ² "Son of man, lament for Pharaoh king of Egypt and say to him:

You compare yourself to a lion
of the nations,
but[c] you are like a monster
in the seas.
You thrash about in your rivers,
churn up the waters with your feet,
and muddy the[d] rivers."

³ This is what the Lord GOD says:

I will spread My net over you
with an assembly of many peoples,
and they[e] will haul you up
in My net.
⁴ I will abandon you on the land
and hurl you on the open field.
I will cause all the birds of the sky

to settle on you
and let the beasts
of the entire earth
eat their fill of you.
⁵ I will put your flesh
on the mountains
and fill the valleys
with your carcass.

Blood in Egypt

⁶ I will drench the land
with the flow of your blood,
⌞even⌟ to the mountains;
the ravines will be filled
with your ⌞gore⌟.

⁷ When I snuff you out,
I will cover the heavens
and darken their stars.
I will cover the sun with a cloud,
and the moon will not give
its light.
⁸ I will darken all the shining lights
in the heavens over you,
and will bring darkness
on your land.
⌞This is⌟ the declaration
of the Lord GOD.

⁹ I will trouble the hearts
of many peoples,
when I bring about
your destruction
among the nations,
in countries you do not know.
¹⁰ I will cause many nations
to be appalled at you,
and their kings will shudder
with fear because of you
when I brandish My sword
in front of them.
On the day of your downfall
each of them will tremble
every moment for his life.

a **31:17** LXX, Syr read *offspring*   b **31:17** Lit *arm*   c **32:2** Or *Lion of the nations, you are destroyed;*   d **32:2** Lit *their*
e **32:3** LXX, Vg read *I*

Sword of Babylon against Egypt

¹¹ For this is what the Lord GOD says:

The sword of Babylon's king
will come against you!
¹² I will make your hordes fall
by the swords of warriors,
all of them ruthless men
   from the nations.
They will ravage Egypt's pride,
and all its hordes will be destroyed.
¹³ I will slaughter all its cattle
that are beside many waters.
No human foot
   will churn them again,
and no cattle hooves
   will disturb them.
¹⁴ Then I will let their waters settle
and will make their rivers flow
   like oil.
                         ⌊This is⌋ the declaration
                              of the Lord GOD.
¹⁵ When I make the land of Egypt
   a desolation,
so that it is emptied of everything
   in it,
when I strike down all
   who live there,
then they will know that
   I am the LORD.

¹⁶ "This is a lament that will be chanted; the women of the nations will chant it. They will chant it over Egypt and all its hordes." ⌊This is⌋ the declaration of the Lord GOD.

Egypt in Sheol

¹⁷ In the twelfth year,^a on the fifteenth ⌊day⌋ of the month, the word of the LORD came to me: ¹⁸ "Son of man, wail over the hordes of Egypt and <u>bring Egypt and the daughters of mighty nations down to the underworld,</u>^b ⌊to be⌋ with those who descend to the •Pit:

¹⁹ Whom do you surpass in loveliness?
Go down and be laid to rest
   with the uncircumcised!
²⁰ They will fall among those slain
   by the sword.
A sword is appointed!
They drag her and all
   her hordes away.
²¹ Warrior leaders will speak
   from the middle of •Sheol
about him^c and his allies:
They have come down;
   the uncircumcised lie
   slain by the sword.

²² <u>Assyria</u> is there with all
   her company;
her graves are all around her.
All of them are slain, fallen
   by the sword.
²³ Her graves are set
   in the deepest regions of the Pit,
and her company is all around
   her burial place.
All of them are slain, fallen
   by the sword—
they who ⌊once⌋ spread terror
   in the land of the living.

²⁴ <u>Elam</u> is there
with all her hordes
   around her grave.
All of them are slain, fallen
   by the sword—
they who went down
   to the underworld^b
   uncircumcised,
who ⌊once⌋ spread their terror
   in the land of the living.
They bear their disgrace
   with those who descend to the Pit.
²⁵ Among the slain
they prepare a resting place
   for Elam
   with all her hordes.

Her graves are all around her.
All of them are uncircumcised,
slain by the sword,
although their terror
     was ⌊once⌋ spread
in the land of the living.
They bear their disgrace
with those who descend to the Pit.
They are placed among the slain.

26 Meshech and Tubal[a] are there,
with all their hordes.
Their graves are all around them.
All of them are uncircumcised,
     slain by the sword,
although their terror was
     ⌊once⌋ spread
in the land of the living.
27 They do[b] not lie down
with the fallen warriors
     of the uncircumcised,[c]
who went down to Sheol
with their weapons of war,
whose swords were placed
     under their heads.
The punishment for their sins
rested on their bones,
although the terror
     of ⌊these⌋ warriors
was ⌊once⌋ in the land of the living.
28 But you will be shattered
and will lie down
     among the uncircumcised,
with those slain by the sword.

29 Edom is there, her kings and all
     her princes,
who, despite their strength,
     have been placed
among those slain by the sword.
They lie down
     with the uncircumcised,
with those who descend to the Pit.

30 All the leaders of the north
and all the Sidonians are there.

They went down in shame
     with the slain,
despite the terror
     their strength inspired.
They lie down uncircumcised
with those slain by the sword.
They bear their disgrace
with those who descend to the Pit.

31 Pharaoh will see them
and be comforted over all
     his hordes—
Pharaoh and all his army,
slain by the sword.
          ⌊This is⌋ the declaration
               of the Lord GOD.

32 For I will spread My[d] terror
     in the land of the living,
so Pharaoh and all his hordes
will be laid to rest
     among the uncircumcised,
with those slain by the sword."
          ⌊This is⌋ the declaration
               of the Lord GOD.

Ezekiel as Israel's Watchman

33 The word of the LORD came to me:
² "Son of man, speak to your people and tell them: Suppose I bring the
sword against a land, and the people of
that land select a man from among them,
appointing him as their watchman, ³ and
he sees the sword coming against the
land and blows his trumpet to warn the
people. ⁴ Then, if anyone hears the
sound of the trumpet but ignores the
warning, and the sword comes and takes
him away, his blood will be on his own
head. ⁵ ⌊Since⌋ he heard the sound of the
trumpet but ignored the warning, his
blood is on his own hands.[e] If he had
taken warning, he would have saved his
life. ⁶ However, if the watchman sees the
sword coming but doesn't blow the

ᵃ**32:26** Lit *Meshech-tubal*   ᵇ**32:27** Or *Do they . . . ?*   ᶜ**32:27** LXX reads *of antiquity*   ᵈ**32:32** Alt Hb tradition, LXX, Syr
read *his*   ᵉ**33:5** Lit *on him*

trumpet, so that the people aren't warned, and the sword comes and takes away their lives, then they have been taken away because of their iniquity, but I will hold the watchman accountable for their blood.

Duties of Watchman

7 "As for you, son of man, I have made you a watchman for the house of Israel. When you hear a word from My mouth, give them a warning from Me. 8 If I say to the wicked: Wicked one, you will surely die, but you do not speak out to warn him about his way, that wicked person will die for his iniquity, yet I will hold you responsible for his blood. 9 But if you warn a wicked person to turn from his way and he doesn't turn from it, he will die for his iniquity, but you will have saved your life.

10 "Now as for you, son of man, say to the house of Israel: You have said this: Our transgressions and our sins are ⌊heavy⌋ on us, and we are wasting away because of them! How then can we survive? 11 Tell them: As I live"—the declaration of the Lord GOD—"I take no pleasure in the death of the wicked, but rather that the wicked person should turn from his way and live. Repent, repent of your evil ways! Why will you die, house of Israel?

12 "Now, son of man, say to your people: The righteousness of the righteous person will not save him on the day of his transgression; neither will the wickedness of the wicked person cause him to stumble on the day he turns from his wickedness. The righteous person won't be able to survive by his righteousness on the day he sins. 13 When I tell the righteous person that he will surely live, but he trusts in his righteousness and commits iniquity, then none of his righteousness will be remembered, and he will die because of the iniquity he has committed.

Repentance Means Life

14 "So when I tell the wicked person: You will surely die, but he repents of his sin and does what is just and right— 15 he returns collateral, makes restitution for what he has stolen, and walks in the statutes of life without practicing iniquity—he will certainly live; he will not die. 16 None of the sins he committed will be held against him. He has done what is just and right; he will certainly live.

17 "But your people say: The Lord's way isn't fair, even though it is their own way that isn't fair. 18 When a righteous person turns from his righteousness and commits iniquity, he will die on account of this. 19 But when a wicked person turns from his wickedness and does what is just and right, he will live because of this. 20 Yet you say: The Lord's way isn't fair. I will judge each of you according to his ways, house of Israel."

News of Jerusalem's Fall

21 In the twelfth year of our exile, in the tenth ⌊month⌋, on the fifth ⌊day⌋ of the month, a fugitive from Jerusalem came to me and reported, "The city has been taken!" 22 Now the hand of the LORD had been on me the evening before the fugitive arrived, and He opened my mouth before the man came to me in the morning. So my mouth was opened and I was no longer mute.

Israel's Continued Rebellion

23 Then the word of the LORD came to me: 24 "Son of man, those who live in thea

a33:24 Lit these

ruins in the land of Israel are saying: Abraham was only one person, yet he received possession of the land. But we are many; the land has been given to us as a possession. ²⁵ Therefore say to them: This is what the Lord GOD says: You eat ⌊meat⌋ with blood ⌊in it⌋, raise your eyes to your idols, and shed blood. Should you then receive possession of the land? ²⁶ You have relied on your swords, you have committed abominations, and each of you has defiled his neighbor's wife. Should you then receive possession of the land?

Punishment for Rebellion

²⁷ "Tell them this: This is what the Lord GOD says: As surely as I live, those who are in the ruins will fall by the sword, those in the open field I have given to wild animals to be devoured, and those in the strongholds and caves will die by plague. ²⁸ I will make the land a desolate waste, and its proud strength will come to an end. The mountains of Israel will become desolate, with no one passing through. ²⁹ They will know that I am the LORD when I make the land a desolate waste because of all the abominations they have committed.

³⁰ "Now, son of man, your people are talking about you near the ⌊city⌋ walls and in the doorways of their houses. One person speaks to another, each saying to his brother: Come and hear what the message is that comes from the LORD! ³¹ So My people come to you in crowds,[a] sit in front of you, and hear your words, but they don't obey them. Although they express love with their mouths, their hearts pursue unjust gain. ³² Yes, to them you are like a singer of love songs who has a beautiful voice and plays skillfully on an instrument. They hear your words, but they don't obey

them. ³³ Yet when it comes—and it will definitely come—then they will know that a prophet has been among them."

Shepherds and God's Flock

34 The word of the LORD came to me: ² "Son of man, prophesy against the shepherds of Israel. Prophesy, and say to them: This is what the Lord GOD says to the shepherds: <u>Woe to the shepherds of Israel</u>, who have been feeding themselves! Shouldn't the shepherds feed their flock? ³ You eat the fat, wear the wool, and butcher the fatlings, but you do not tend the flock. ⁴ You have not strengthened the weak, healed the sick, bandaged the injured, brought back the strays, or sought the lost. Instead, you have ruled them with violence and cruelty. ⁵ They were scattered for lack of a shepherd; they became food for all the wild animals when they were scattered. ⁶ My flock went astray on all the mountains and every high hill. They were scattered over the whole face of the earth, and there was no one searching or seeking ⌊for them⌋.

Fate of Evil Shepherds

⁷ "Therefore, you shepherds, hear the word of the LORD. ⁸ As I live"—the declaration of the Lord GOD—"because My flock has become ⌊prey and⌋ food for every wild animal since ⌊they⌋ lack a shepherd, for My shepherds do not search for My flock, and ⌊because⌋ the shepherds feed themselves rather than My flock, ⁹ therefore, you shepherds, hear the word of the LORD!

¹⁰ "This is what the Lord GOD says: Look, I am against the shepherds. I will demand My flock from them[b] and prevent them from shepherding the flock. The shepherds will no longer feed

^a**33:31** Lit *you like the coming of a people*   ^b**34:10** Lit *their hand*

themselves, for I will rescue My flock from their mouths so that they will not be food for them.

The Lord Is Their Shepherd

¹¹ "For this is what the Lord GOD says: See, I Myself will search for My flock and look for them. ¹² As a shepherd looks for his sheep on the day he is among his scattered flock, so I will look for My flock. I will rescue them from all the places where they have been scattered on a cloudy and dark day. ¹³ I will bring them out from the peoples, gather them from the countries, and bring them into their own land. I will shepherd them on the mountains of Israel, in the ravines, and in all the inhabited places of the land. ¹⁴ I will tend them with good pasture, and their grazing place will be on Israel's lofty mountains. There they will lie down in a good grazing place; they will feed in rich pasture on the mountains of Israel. ¹⁵ I will tend My flock and let them lie down." ˌThis isˌ the declaration of the Lord GOD. ¹⁶ "I will seek the lost, bring back the strays, bandage the injured, and strengthen the weak, but I will destroyᵃ the fat and the strong. I will shepherd them with justice.

God Judges Flock

¹⁷ "The Lord GOD says to you, My flock: I am going to judge between one sheep and another, between the rams and male goats. ¹⁸ Isn't it enough for you to feed on the good pasture? Must you also trample the rest of the pasture with your feet? Or ˌisn't it enoughˌ that you drink the clear water? Must you also muddy the rest with your feet? ¹⁹ Yet My flock has to feed on what your feet have trampled, and drink what your feet have muddied.

²⁰ "Therefore, this is what the Lord GOD says to them: See, I Myself will judge between the fat sheep and the lean sheep. ²¹ Since you have pushed with flank and shoulder and butted all the weak ones with your horns until you scattered them all over, ²² I will save My flock, and they will no longer be prey for you. I will judge between one sheep and another. ²³ I will appoint over them a single shepherd, My servant David, and he will shepherd them. He will tend them himself and will be their shepherd. ²⁴ I, the LORD, will be their God, and My servant David will be a prince among them. I, the LORD, have spoken.

²⁵ "I will make a covenant of peace with them and eliminate dangerous animals in the land, so that they may live securely in the wilderness and sleep in the forest. ²⁶ I will make them and the area around My hill a blessing: I will send down showers in their season— showersᵇ of blessing. ²⁷ The trees of the field will give their fruit, and the land will yield its produce; My flock will be secure in their land. They will know that I am the LORD when I break the bars of their yoke and rescue them from the hands of those who enslave them. ²⁸ They will no longer be prey for the nations, and the wild animals of the land will not consume them. They will live securely, and no one will frighten ˌthemˌ. ²⁹ I will establish for them a place renowned for ˌitsˌ agriculture,ᶜ and they will no longer be victims of famine in the land. They will no longer endure the insults of the nations. ³⁰ Then they will know that I, the LORD their God, am with them, and that they, the house of Israel, are My people." ˌThis isˌ the declaration of the Lord GOD. ³¹ "You are My flock, the human flock of My pasture,

---

ᵃ**34:16** Some Hb mss, LXX, Syr, Vg read *watch over*   ᵇ**34:26** Lit *season; they will be showers*   ᶜ**34:29** LXX, Syr read *a plant of peace*

and I am your God." ⌊This is⌋ the declaration of the Lord GOD.

A Prophecy against Edom

35 The word of the LORD came to me: 2 "Son of man, turn your face toward Mount Seir and prophesy against it. 3 Say to it: This is what the Lord GOD says:

Look! I am against you, Mount Seir.
I will stretch out My hand
     against you
and make you a desolate waste.
4 I will turn your cities into ruins,
     and you will become a desolation.
Then you will know that
     I am the LORD.

5 "Because you maintained an ancient hatred and handed over the Israelites to the power of the sword in the time of their disaster, the time of final punishment, 6 therefore, as I live"—⌊this is⌋ the declaration of the Lord GOD—"I will destine you for bloodshed, and it will pursue you. Since you did not hate bloodshed, it will pursue you. 7 I will make Mount Seir a desolate waste and will cut off from it those who come and go. 8 I will fill its mountains with the slain; those slain by the sword will fall on your hills, in your valleys, and in all your ravines. 9 I will make you a perpetual desolation; your cities will not be inhabited. Then you will know that I am the LORD.

10 "Because you said: These two nations and two lands will be mine, and we will possess them—though the LORD was there— 11 therefore, as I live"—the declaration of the Lord GOD—"I will treat ⌊you⌋ according to the anger and jealousy you showed in your hatred of them. I will make Myself known among them[a] when I judge you. 12 Then you will know that I, the LORD, have heard all the blasphemies you uttered against the

mountains of Israel, saying: They are desolate. They have been given to us to devour! 13 You boasted against Me with your mouth, and spoke many words against Me. I heard ⌊it⌋ Myself!

14 "This is what the Lord GOD says: While the whole world rejoices, I will make you a desolation. 15 Just as you rejoiced over the inheritance of the house of Israel because it became a desolation, so I will deal with you: you will become a desolation, Mount Seir, and ⌊so will⌋ all Edom in its entirety. Then they will know that I am the LORD.

Restoration of Israel's Mountains

36 "Son of man, prophesy to the mountains of Israel and say: Mountains of Israel, hear the word of the LORD. 2 This is what the Lord GOD says: Because the enemy has said about you, 'Good! The ancient heights have become our possession,' 3 therefore, prophesy and say: This is what the Lord GOD says: Because they have made you desolate and have trampled you from every side, so that you became a possession for the rest of the nations and an object of people's gossip and slander, 4 therefore, mountains of Israel, hear the word of the Lord GOD. This is what the Lord GOD says to the mountains and hills, to the ravines and valleys, to the desolate ruins and abandoned cities, which have become plunder and a mockery to the rest of the nations all around.

5 "This is what the Lord GOD says: Certainly in My burning zeal I speak against the rest of the nations and all of Edom, who took[b] My land as their own possession with wholehearted rejoicing and utter contempt, so that its pastureland became[c] plunder. 6 Therefore, prophesy concerning the land of Israel and say to

a 35:11 LXX reads you   b 36:5 Lit gave   c 36:5 Or contempt, to empty it of; Hb obscure

the mountains and hills, to the ravines and valleys: This is what the Lord GOD says: Look, I speak in My burning zeal because you have endured the insults of the nations. [7] Therefore this is what the Lord GOD says: I swear[a] that the nations all around you will endure their own insults.

Fruit for Israel

[8] "You, mountains of Israel, will put forth your branches and bear your fruit for My people Israel, since their arrival is near. [9] Look! I am on your side; I will turn toward you, and you will be tilled and sown. [10] I will fill you with people, with the whole house of Israel in its entirety. The cities will be inhabited and the ruins rebuilt. [11] I will fill you with people and animals, and they will increase and be fruitful. I will make you inhabited as you once were and make ⌊you⌋ better off than you were before. Then you will know that I am the LORD. [12] I will cause people, My people Israel, to walk on you; they will possess you, and you will be their inheritance. You will no longer deprive them of ⌊their⌋ children.

[13] "This is what the Lord GOD says: Because people are saying to you: You devour men and deprive your nation of children, [14] therefore, you will no longer devour men and deprive your nation of children."[b] ⌊This is⌋ the declaration of the Lord GOD. [15] "I will no longer allow the insults of the nations to be heard against you, and you will not have to endure the reproach of the peoples any more; you will no longer cause your nation to stumble."[c] ⌊This is⌋ the declaration of the Lord GOD.

Restoration of Israel's People

[16] The word of the LORD came to me: [17] "Son of man, while the house of Israel lived in their land, they defiled it with their conduct and actions. Their behavior before Me was like menstrual impurity. [18] So I poured out My wrath on them because of the blood they had shed on the land, and because they had defiled it with their idols. [19] I dispersed them among the nations, and they were scattered among the countries. I judged them according to their conduct and actions. [20] When they came to the nations where they went, they profaned My holy name, because it was said about them: These are the people of the LORD, yet they had to leave His land ⌊in exile⌋. [21] Then I had concern for My holy name, which the house of Israel profaned among the nations where they went.

[22] "Therefore, say to the house of Israel: This is what the Lord GOD says: It is not for your sake that I will act, house of Israel, but for My holy name, which you profaned among the nations where you went. [23] I will honor the holiness of My great name, which has been profaned among the nations—the name you have profaned among them. The nations will know that I am •Yahweh"—the declaration of the Lord GOD—"when I demonstrate My holiness through you in their sight.

Cleansing of Israel

[24] "For I will take you from the nations and gather you from all the countries, and will bring you into your own land. [25] I will also sprinkle clean water on you, and you will be clean. I will cleanse you from all your impurities and all your idols. [26] I will give you a new heart and put a new spirit within you; I will remove your heart of stone[d] and give you a heart of flesh. [27] I will place My Spirit within you and cause you to follow My

---

[a]**36:7** Lit *lift up My hand*   [b]**36:14** Alt Hb tradition reads *and cause your nation to stumble*   [c]**36:15** Some Hb mss, Tg read *no longer bereave your nation of children*   [d]**36:26** Lit *stone from your flesh*

statutes and carefully observe My ordinances. 28 Then you will live in the land that I gave your fathers; you will be My people, and I will be your God. 29 I will save you from all your uncleanness. I will summon the grain and make it plentiful, and will not bring famine on you. 30 I will also make the fruit of the trees and the produce of the field plentiful, so that you will no longer experience reproach among the nations on account of famine.

31 "Then you will remember your evil ways and your deeds that were not good, and you will loathe yourselves for your iniquities and abominations. 32 It is not for your sake that I will act"—the declaration of the Lord GOD—"let this be known to you. Be ashamed and humiliated because of your ways, house of Israel!

33 "This is what the Lord GOD says: On the day I cleanse you from all your iniquities, I will cause the cities to be inhabited, and the ruins will be rebuilt. 34 The desolate land will be cultivated instead of lying desolate in the sight of everyone who passes by. 35 Then they will say: This land that was desolate has become like the garden of Eden. The cities that were once ruined, desolate, and destroyed are ⌊now⌋ fortified and inhabited. 36 Then the nations that remain around you will know that I, the LORD, have rebuilt what was destroyed and have replanted what was desolate. I, the LORD, have spoken and I will do ⌊it⌋.

37 "This is what the Lord GOD says: I will respond to the house of Israel and do this for them: I will multiply them in number like a flock.a 38 So the ruined cities will be filled with a flock of people, just as the flock of sheep for sacrifice is filledb in Jerusalem during its appointed festivals. Then they will know that I am the LORD."

Valley of Dry Bones

37 The hand of the LORD was on me, and He brought me out by His Spirit and set me down in the middle of the valley; it was full of bones. 2 He led me all around them. There were a great many of them on the surface of the valley, and they were very dry. 3 Then He said to me, "Son of man, can these bones live?"

I replied, "Lord GOD, ⌊only⌋ You know."

4 He said to me, "Prophesy concerning these bones and say to them: Dry bones, hear the word of the LORD! 5 This is what the Lord GOD says to these bones: I will cause breath to enter you, and you will live. 6 I will put tendons on you, make flesh grow on you, and cover you with skin. I will put breath in you so that you come to life. Then you will know that I am the LORD."

Ezekiel Prophesies on Bones

7 So I prophesied as I had been commanded. While I was prophesying, there was a noise, a rattling sound, and the bones came together, bone to bone. 8 As I looked, tendons appeared on them, flesh grew, and skin covered them, but there was no breath in them. 9 He said to me, "Prophesy to the breath,c prophesy, son of man. Say to it: This is what the Lord GOD says: Breath, come from the four winds and breathe into these slain so that they may live!" 10 So I prophesied as He commanded me; the breathc entered them, and they came to life and stood on their feet, a vast army.

11 Then He said to me, "Son of man, these bones are the whole house of

---

a 36:37 Lit flock of people   b 36:38 Lit the flock of consecrated things, as the flock   c 37:9,10 Or wind, or spirit

Israel. Look how they say: Our bones are dried up, and our hope has perished; we are cut off. ¹² Therefore, prophesy and say to them: This is what the Lord GOD says: I am going to open your graves and bring you up from them, My people, and lead you into the land of Israel. ¹³ You will know that I am the LORD, My people, when I open your graves and bring you up from them. ¹⁴ I will put My Spirit in you, and you will live, and I will settle you in your own land. Then you will know that I am the LORD. I have spoken, and I will do ⌊it⌋." ⌊This is⌋ the declaration of the LORD.

Reunification of Israel: Two Sticks

¹⁵ The word of the LORD came to me: ¹⁶ "Son of man, take a single stick and write on it: Belonging to Judah and the Israelites associated with him. Then take another stick and write on it: Belonging to Joseph—the stick of Ephraim—and all the house of Israel associated with him. ¹⁷ Then join them together into a single stick so that they become one in your hand. ¹⁸ When your people ask you: Won't you explain to us what you mean by these things?— ¹⁹ tell them: This is what the Lord GOD says: I am going to take the stick of Joseph—which is in the hand of Ephraim—and the tribes of Israel associated with him, and put them together with the stick of Judah. I will make them into a single stick so that they become one in My hand. ²⁰ "When the sticks you have written on are in your hand and in full view of the people, ²¹ tell them: This is what the Lord GOD says: I am going to take the Israelites out of the nations where they have gone. I will gather them from all around and bring them into their own land. ²² I will make them one nation in the land, on the mountains of Israel, and one king will rule over all of them. They will no longer be two nations and will no longer be divided into two kingdoms. ²³ They will not defile themselves any more with their idols, their detestable things, and all their transgressions. I will save them from all their apostasies by whichª they sinned, and I will cleanse them. Then they will be My people, and I will be their God. ²⁴ My servant David will be king over them, and there will be one shepherd for all of them. They will follow My ordinances, and keep My statutes and obey them.

A Future, Everlasting Kingdom

²⁵ "They will live in the land that I gave to My servant Jacob, where your fathers lived. They will live in it forever with their children and grandchildren, and My servant David will be their prince forever. ²⁶ I will make a covenant of peace with them; it will be an everlasting covenant with them. I will establish and multiply them, and will set My sanctuary among them forever. ²⁷ My dwelling place will be with them; I will be their God, and they will be My people. ²⁸ When My sanctuary is among them forever, the nations will know that I, the LORD, sanctify Israel."

God against Gog

38 The word of the LORD came to me: ² "Son of man, turn your face toward Gog, of the land of Magog, the chief prince ofᵇ Meshech and Tubal. Prophesy against him ³ and say: This is what the Lord GOD says: Look, I am against you, Gog, chief prince of Meshech and Tubal. ⁴ I will turn you around, put hooks in your jaws, and

---

ª**37:23** Some Hb mss, LXX, Sym; other Hb mss read *their settlements where*; Ezk 6:6,13-14   ᵇ**38:2** Or *the prince of Rosh,*

bring you out with all your army, including horses and riders, who are all splendidly dressed, a huge company armed with shields and bucklers, all of them brandishing swords. ⁵ Persia, •Cush, and Put are with them, all of them with shields and helmets; ⁶ Gomer with all its troops; and Beth-togarmah from the remotest parts of the north along with all its troops—many peoples are with you.

⁷ "Be prepared and get yourself ready, you and all your company who have been mobilized around you; you will be their guard. ⁸ After a long time you will be summoned. In the last years you will enter a land that has been restored from warᵃ and regathered from many peoples to the mountains of Israel, which had long been a ruin. They were brought out from the peoples, and all of them ⌊now⌋ live securely. ⁹ You, all of your troops, and many peoples with you will advance, coming like a thunderstorm; you will be like a cloud covering the land.

An Evil Plan

¹⁰ "This is what the Lord GOD says: On that day, thoughts will arise in your mind, and you will devise an evil plan. ¹¹ You will say: I will go up against a land of open villages; I will come against a tranquil people who are living securely, all of them living without walls and without bars or gates— ¹² in order to seize spoil and carry off plunder, to turn your hand against ruins now inhabited and against a people gathered from the nations, who have been acquiring cattle and possessions and who live at the center of the world. ¹³ Sheba and Dedan and the merchants of Tarshish with all its rulersᵇ will ask you: Have you come to seize spoil? Have you assembled your hordes to carry off plunder, to make off with sil-

ver and gold, to take cattle and possessions, to seize great spoil?

¹⁴ "Therefore prophesy, son of man, and say to Gog: This is what the Lord GOD says: On that day when My people Israel are dwelling securely, will you not know ⌊this⌋ ¹⁵ and come from your place in the remotest parts of the north—you and many peoples with you, who are all riding horses—a mighty horde, a huge army? ¹⁶ You will advance against My people Israel like a cloud covering the land. It will happen in the last days, Gog, that I will bring you against My land so that the nations may know Me, when I show Myself holy through you in their sight.

Israel's Battle with Gog

¹⁷ "This is what the Lord GOD says: Are you the one I spoke about in former times through My servants, the prophets of Israel, who for years prophesied in those times that I would bring you against them? ¹⁸ Now on that day, the day when Gog comes against the land of Israel"—⌊this is⌋ the declaration of the Lord GOD—"My wrath will flare up.ᶜ ¹⁹ I swear in My zeal and fiery rage: On that day there will be a great earthquake in the land of Israel. ²⁰ The fish of the sea, the birds of the sky, the animals of the field, every creature that crawls on the ground, and every human being on the face of the earth will tremble before Me. The mountains will be thrown down, the cliffs will collapse, and every wall will fall to the ground. ²¹ I will call for a sword against him on all My mountains"—the declaration of the Lord GOD—"and every man's sword will be against his brother. ²² I will execute judgment on him with plague and bloodshed. I will pour out torrential rain, hailstones,

---

ᵃ**38:8** Lit *from the sword*   ᵇ**38:13** Lit *young lions,* or *villages*   ᶜ**38:18** Lit *up in My anger*

fire, and brimstone on him, as well as his troops and the many peoples who are with him. ²³ I will display My greatness and holiness, and will reveal Myself in the sight of many nations. Then they will know that I am the LORD.

Disposal of Gog

39 "As for you, son of man, prophesy against Gog and say: This is what the Lord GOD says: Look, I am against you, Gog, chief prince of ᵃ Meshech and Tubal. ² I will turn you around, drive you on, and lead you up from the remotest parts of the north. I will bring you against the mountains of Israel. ³ Then I will knock your bow from your left hand and make your arrows drop from your right hand. ⁴ You, all your troops, and the peoples who are with you will fall on the mountains of Israel. I will give you as food to every kind of predatory bird and to the wild animals. ⁵ You will fall on the open field, for I have spoken." ⌊This is⌋ the declaration of the Lord GOD.

Fire against Magog

⁶ "I will send fire against Magog and those who live securely on the coasts and islands. Then they will know that I am the LORD. ⁷ So I will make My holy name known among My people Israel and will no longer allow it to be profaned. Then the nations will know that I am the LORD, the Holy One in Israel. ⁸ Yes, it is coming, and it will happen." ⌊This is⌋ the declaration of the Lord GOD. "This is the day I have spoken about.

⁹ "Then the inhabitants of Israel's cities will go out, kindle fires, and burn the weapons—the bucklers and shields, the bows and arrows, the clubs and spears. For seven years they will use them to make fires. ¹⁰ They will not gather wood

from the countryside or cut ⌊it⌋ down from the forests, for they will use the weapons to make fires. They will take the loot from those who looted them and plunder those who plundered them." ⌊This is⌋ the declaration of the Lord GOD.

Israel Buries Gog

¹¹ "Now on that day I will give Gog a burial place there in Israel—the Valley of the Travelersᵇ east of the Sea. It will block those who travel through, for Gog and all his hordes will be buried there. So ⌊it⌋ will be called the Valley of Hamon-gog.ᶜ ¹² The house of Israel will spend seven months burying them in order to cleanse the land. ¹³ All the people of the land will bury ⌊them⌋ and their fame will spread on the day I display My glory." ⌊This is⌋ the declaration of the Lord GOD.

¹⁴ "They will appoint men on a full-time basis to pass through the land and bury the invadersᵈ who remain on the surface of the ground, in order to cleanse it. They will make ⌊their⌋ search at the end of the seven months. ¹⁵ When they pass through the land and one of them sees a human bone, he will erect ⌊a⌋ marker next to it until the buriers have buried it in the Valley of Hamon-gog. ¹⁶ There will even be a city named Hamonahᵉ ⌊there⌋. So they will cleanse the land.

Feast of Birds and Wild Animals

¹⁷ "Son of man, this is what the Lord GOD says: Tell every kind of bird and all the wild animals: Assemble and come! Gather from all around to My sacrificial feast that I am slaughtering for you, a great feast on the mountains of Israel; you will eat flesh and drink blood. ¹⁸ You will eat the flesh of mighty men and drink the blood of the earth's princes:

ᵃ39:1 Or Gog, prince of Rosh,   ᵇ39:11 Hb obscure   ᶜ39:11 = Hordes of Gog   ᵈ39:14 Or basis, some to pass through the land, and with them some to bury those   ᵉ39:16 Hamonah is related to the Hb word for "horde."

rams, lambs, male goats, and bulls, all of them fatlings of Bashan. ¹⁹ You will eat fat until you are satisfied and drink blood until you are drunk, at My sacrificial feast that I have prepared for you. ²⁰ At My table you will eat your fill of horses and riders, of mighty men and all the warriors." ⌊This is⌋ the declaration of the Lord GOD.

Israel's Restoration to God

²¹ "I will display My glory among the nations, and all the nations will see the judgment I have executed and the hand I have laid on them. ²² From that day forward the house of Israel will know that I am the LORD their God. ²³ And the nations will know that the house of Israel went into exile on account of their iniquity, because they dealt unfaithfully with Me. Therefore, I hid My face from them and handed them over to their enemies, so that they all fell by the sword. ²⁴ I dealt with them according to their uncleanness and transgressions, and I hid My face from them.

Restoration of Israel

²⁵ "So this is what the Lord GOD says: Now I will restore the fortunes of Jacob and have compassion on the whole house of Israel, and I will be jealous for My holy name. ²⁶ They will feel remorse for[a] [b] their disgrace and all the unfaithfulness they committed against Me, when they live securely in their land with no one to frighten ⌊them⌋. ²⁷ When I bring them back from the peoples and gather them from the countries of their enemies, I will demonstrate My holiness through them in the sight of many nations. ²⁸ They will know that I am the LORD their God when I regather them to their own land after having exiled them among the nations. I will leave none of them behind.[c] ²⁹ I will no longer hide My face from them, for I will pour out My Spirit on the house of Israel." ⌊This is⌋ the declaration of the Lord GOD.

The New Temple

40 In the twenty-fifth year of our exile, at the beginning of the year, on the tenth day of the month in the fourteenth year after Jerusalem had been captured, on that very day the LORD's hand was on me, and He brought me there. ² In visions of God He took me to the land of Israel and set me down on a very high mountain. On its southern ⌊slope⌋ was a structure resembling a city. ³ He brought me there, and I saw a man whose appearance was like bronze, with a linen cord and a measuring rod in his hand. He was standing by the gate. ⁴ He spoke to me: "Son of man, look with your eyes, listen with your ears, and pay attention to everything I am going to show you, for you have been brought here so that I might show ⌊it⌋ to you. Report everything you see to the house of Israel."

The Wall and Outer Gates

⁵ Now there was a wall surrounding the outside of the temple. The measuring rod in the man's hand was six units of 21 inches;[d] each unit was the standard length plus three inches.[e] He measured the thickness of the ⌊wall⌋ structure; it was about 10 feet,[f] and its height was the same.[f] ⁶ Then he came to the gate that faced east and climbed its steps. He measured the threshold of the gate; it was 10 feet deep—the first threshold was 10 feet deep. ⁷ Each

---

ᵃ **39:26** Some emend to *will forget* ᵇ **39:26** Lit *will bear* ᶜ **39:28** Lit *behind there any longer* ᵈ **40:5** This unit of measure approximately = a long cubit (perhaps 20 ½ inches) ᵉ **40:5** Lit *six cubits by the cubit and a handbreadth* ᶠ **40:5** Lit *was one rod*

recess was about 10 feet[a] long and 10 feet[b] deep, and there was ⌐a space of⌐ eight and three-quarter feet[c] between the recesses. The ⌐inner⌐ threshold of the gate on the temple side next to the gate's portico was about 10 feet.[a] [8] Next he measured the portico of the gate; [9] it[d] was 14 feet,[e] and its pilasters were three and a half feet.[f] The portico of the gate was on the temple side.

[10] There were three recesses on each side of the east gate, each with the same measurements, and the pilasters on either side also had the same measurements. [11] Then he measured the width of the gate's entrance; it was 17 and a half feet,[g] while the width[h] of the gateway was 22 and three-quarter feet.[i] [12] There was a barrier of 21 inches[j] in front of the recesses on both sides, and the recesses on each side were 10 and a half feet[k] square. [13] Then he measured the gateway from the roof of one recess to the roof of the ⌐opposite⌐ one; the distance was 43 and three-quarter feet.[l] The openings of the recesses faced each other. [14] Next, he measured the pilasters—105 feet.[m] The gate extended around to the pilaster of the court.[n] [15] ⌐The distance⌐ from the front of the gate at the entrance to the front of the gate's portico on the inside was 87 and a half feet.[o] [16] The recesses and their pilasters had beveled windows all around the inside of the gateway. The porticos also had windows all around on the inside. Each pilaster was decorated with palm trees.

[17] Then he brought me into the outer court, and there were chambers and a paved surface laid out all around the court. Thirty chambers faced the pave-

ment, [18] which flanked the gates and corresponded to the length of the gates; ⌐this⌐ was the lower pavement. [19] Then he measured the distance from the front of the lower gate to the exterior front of the inner court; it was 175 feet.[p] ⌐This⌐ was the east; next the north ⌐is described⌐.

[20] He measured the gate of the outer court facing north, ⌐both⌐ its length and width. [21] Its three recesses on each side, its pilasters, and its portico had the same measurements as the first gate: 87 and a half feet[o] long and 43 and three-quarter feet[l] wide. [22] Its windows, portico, and palm trees had the same measurements as those of the gate that faced east. Seven steps led up to the gate, and its portico was ahead of them. [23] The inner court had a gate facing the north gate, like the one on the east. He measured the distance from gate to gate; it was 175 feet.[p]

[24] He brought me to the south side, and there was also a gate on the south. He measured its pilasters and portico; they had the same measurements as the others. [25] Both the gate and its portico had windows all around, like the other windows. It was 87 and a half feet[o] long and 43 and three-quarter feet[l] wide. [26] Its stairway had seven steps, and its portico was ahead of them. It had palm trees on its pilasters, one on each side. [27] The inner court had a gate on the south. He measured from gate to gate on the south; it was 175 feet.[p]

The Inner Gates

[28] Then he brought me to the inner court through the south gate. When he measured the south gate, it had the same

[a]**40:7** Lit was one rod   [b]**40:7** Lit and one rod   [c]**40:7** Lit five cubits   [d]**40:8-9** Some Hb mss, Syr, Vg; other Hb mss read gate facing the temple side; it was one rod. [9] Then he measured the portico of the gate; it   [e]**40:9** Lit eight cubits   [f]**40:9** Lit two cubits   [g]**40:11** Lit 10 cubits   [h]**40:11** Lit length   [i]**40:11** Lit 13 cubits   [j]**40:12** Lit one cubit   [k]**40:12** Lit six cubits   [l]**40:13,21,25** Lit 25 cubits   [m]**40:14** Lit 60 cubits   [n]**40:14** Hb obscure   [o]**40:15,21,25** Lit 50 cubits   [p]**40:19,23,27** Lit 100 cubits

measurements as the others. [29] Its recesses, pilasters, and portico had the same measurements as the others. Both it and its portico had windows all around. It was 87 and a half feet[a] long and 43 and three-quarter feet[b] wide. [30] (There were porticoes all around, 43 and three-quarter feet long and eight and three-quarter feet[c] wide.[d]) [31] Its portico faced the outer court, and its pilasters were decorated with palm trees. Its stairway had eight steps.

[32] Then he brought me to the inner court on the east side. When he measured the gate, it had the same measurements as the others. [33] Its recesses, pilasters, and portico had the same measurements as the others. Both it and its portico had windows all around. It was 87 and a half feet[a] long and 43 and three-quarter feet[b] wide. [34] Its portico faced the outer court, and its pilasters were decorated with palm trees on each side. Its stairway had eight steps.

[35] Then he brought me to the north gate. When he measured ⌊it⌋, it had the same measurements as the others, [36] ⌊as did⌋ its recesses, pilasters, and portico. It also had windows all around. It was 87 and a half feet[a] long and 43 and three-quarter feet[b] wide. [37] Its portico[e] faced the outer court, and its pilasters were decorated with palm trees on each side. Its stairway had eight steps.

Rooms for Preparing Sacrifices

[38] There was a chamber whose door ⌊opened⌋ into the portico of the gate.[f] The •burnt offering was to be washed there. [39] Inside the portico of the gate there were two tables on each side, on which to slaughter the burnt offering, •sin offering, and •restitution offering. [40] Outside, as one approaches the entrance of the north gate, there were two tables on one side and two ⌊more⌋ tables on the other side of the gate's portico. [41] So there were four tables inside the gate and four outside, eight tables ⌊in all⌋ on which the slaughtering was to be done. [42] There were also four tables of cut stone for the burnt offering, ⌊each⌋ 31 and a half inches[g] long, 31 and a half inches wide, and 21 inches[h] high. The utensils used to slaughter the burnt offerings and ⌊other⌋ sacrifices were placed on them. [43] There were three-inch[i] hooks[j] fastened all around the inside of the room, and the flesh of the offering was to be laid on the tables.

Rooms for Singers and Priests

[44] Outside the inner gate, within the inner court, there were chambers for the singers:[k] one[l] beside the north gate, facing south, and another beside the south[m] gate, facing north. [45] Then the man said to me: "This chamber that faces south is for the priests who keep charge of the temple. [46] The chamber that faces north is for the priests who keep charge of the altar. These are the sons of Zadok, the ones from the sons of Levi who may approach the LORD to serve Him." [47] Next he measured the court. It was square, 175 feet[n] long and 175 feet wide. The altar was in front of the temple.

[48] Then he brought me to the portico of the temple and measured the pilasters of the portico; they were eight and three-quarter feet[c] ⌊thick⌋ on each side. The width of the gateway was 24 and a half feet,[o] and the sidewalls of the gate were[p] five and a quarter feet[q] ⌊wide⌋ on

a 40:29,33,39 Lit 50 cubits   b 40:29,33,36 Lit 25 cubits   c 40:30,48 Lit five cubits   d 40:30 Some Hb mss, LXX omit v. 30   e 40:37 LXX; MT reads pilasters   f 40:38 Text emended; MT reads door was by the pilasters, at the gates   g 40:42 Lit one and a half cubits   h 40:42 Lit one cubit   i 40:43 Lit one-handbreadth   j 40:43 Or ledges   k 40:44 LXX reads were two chambers   l 40:44 LXX; MT reads singers, which was   m 40:44 LXX; MT reads east   n 40:47 Lit 100 cubits   o 40:48 Lit 14 cubits   p 40:48 LXX; MT omits 24 and a half feet, and the sidewalls of the gate were   q 40:48 Lit three cubits each side. [49] The portico was 35 feet[a] across and 21[b] feet[c] deep, and 10 steps led[d] up to it. There were pillars by the pilasters, one on each side.

Inside the Temple

41 Next he brought me into the great hall and measured the pilasters; on each side the width of the pilaster was 10 and a half feet.[e][f] [2] The width of the entrance was 17 and a half feet,[g] and the sidewalls of the entrance were eight and three-quarter feet[h] ⌊wide⌋ on each side. He also measured the length of the great hall, 70 feet,[i] and the width, 35 feet.[a] [3] He went inside ⌊the next room⌋ and measured the pilasters at the entrance; they were three and a half feet[j] ⌊wide⌋. The entrance was 10 and a half feet[f] ⌊wide⌋, and the width of the entrance's sidewalls on each side[k] was 12 and a quarter feet.[l] [4] He then measured the length of the room adjacent to the great hall, 35 feet,[a] and the width, 35 feet. And he said to me, "This is the most holy place."

Outside the Temple

[5] Then he measured the wall of the temple; it was 10 and a half feet[f] ⌊thick⌋. The width of the side rooms all around the temple was seven feet.[m] [6] The side rooms were arranged one above another in three stories of 30 rooms each.[n] There were ledges on the wall of the temple all around to serve as supports for the side rooms, so that the supports would not be in the temple wall ⌊itself⌋. [7] The side rooms surrounding ⌊the temple⌋ widened at each successive story, for the structure surrounding the temple ⌊went up⌋ by

stages. This was the reason for the temple's broadness as it rose. And so, one would go up from the lowest story to the highest by means of the middle one.[o] [8] I saw that the temple had a raised platform surrounding ⌊it⌋; this foundation for the side rooms was 10 and a half feet high.[p] [9] The thickness of the outer wall of the side rooms was eight and three-quarter feet.[h] The free space between the side rooms of the temple [10] and the ⌊outer⌋ chambers was 35 feet[a] wide all around the temple. [11] The side rooms opened into the free space, one entrance toward the north and another to the south. The area of free space was eight and three-quarter feet[h] wide all around.

[12] Now the building that faced the temple yard toward the west was 122 and a half feet[q] wide. The wall of the building was eight and three-quarter feet[h] thick on all sides, and the building's length was 157 and a half feet.[r]

[13] Then the man measured the temple; it was 175 feet[s] long. In addition, the temple yard and the building, including its walls, were 175 feet long. [14] The width of the front of the temple along with the temple yard to the east was 175 feet. [15] Next he measured the length of the building facing the temple yard to the west, with its galleries[t] on each side; it was 175 feet.

Interior Wooden Structures

The interior of the great hall and the porticoes of the court— [16] the thresholds, the beveled windows, and the balconies all around with their three levels opposite the threshold—were overlaid with wood on all sides. ⌊They were paneled⌋ from the

---

[a]**40:49; 41:2,4,10** Lit *20 cubits* [b]**40:49** LXX; MT reads *19 and a quarter* [c]**40:49** Lit *12 cubits* [d]**40:49** MT reads *and it was on steps that they would go* [e]**41:1** LXX; MT reads *pilasters; they were 10 and a half feet wide on each side—the width of the tabernacle* [f]**41:1,3,5** Lit *six cubits* [g]**41:2** Lit *10 cubits* [h]**41:2,9,11,12** Lit *five cubits* [i]**41:2** Lit *40 cubits* [j]**41:3** Lit *two cubits* [k]**41:3** LXX; MT reads *width of the entrance* [l]**41:3** Lit *seven cubits* [m]**41:5** Lit *four cubits* [n]**41:6** Lit *another three and 30 times* [o]**41:7** Hb obscure [p]**41:8** Lit *a full rod of six cubits of a joint*; Hb obscure [q]**41:12** Lit *70 cubits* [r]**41:12** Lit *90 cubits* [s]**41:13** Lit *100 cubits* [t]**41:15** Or *ledges*

ground to the windows (but the windows were covered), [17] reaching to the top of the entrance, and as far as the inner temple and on the outside. On every wall all around, on the inside and outside, was a pattern [18] carved with •cherubim and palm trees. There was a palm tree between each pair of cherubim. Each cherub had two faces: [19] a human face turned toward the palm tree on one side, and a lion's face turned toward it on the other. They were carved throughout the temple on all sides. [20] Cherubim and palm trees were carved from the ground to the top of the entrance and on the wall of the great hall.

[21] The doorposts of the great hall were square, and the front of the sanctuary had the same appearance. [22] The altar was[a] made of wood, five and a quarter feet[b] high and three and a half feet[c] long.[d] It had corners, and its length[e] and sides were of wood. The man told me, "This is the table that stands before the LORD."

[23] The great hall and the sanctuary each had a double door, [24] and each of the doors had two swinging panels. There were two panels for one door and two for the other. [25] Cherubim and palm trees were carved on the doors of the great hall like those carved on the walls. There was a wooden canopy[f] outside, in front of the portico. [26] There were beveled windows and palm trees on both sides, on the sidewalls of the portico, the side rooms of the temple, and the canopies.[f]

The Priests' Chambers

42 Then the man led me out by way of the north gate into the outer court. He brought me to the group of chambers opposite the temple yard and opposite the building to the north. [2] Along the length ⌊of the chambers⌋, which was 175 feet,[g] there was an entrance on the north; the width was 87 and a half feet.[h] [3] Opposite the 35 ⌊foot space⌋[i] belonging to the inner court and opposite the paved surface belonging to the outer court, ⌊the structure rose⌋ gallery by gallery in three tiers. [4] In front of the chambers was a walkway toward the inside, 17 and a half feet[j] wide and 175 feet[g] long,[k] and their entrances were on the north. [5] The upper chambers were narrower because the galleries took away more space from them than from the lower and middle stories of the building. [6] For they were arranged in three stories and had no pillars like the pillars of the courts; therefore the upper chambers were set back from the ground more than the lower and middle stories. [7] A wall on the outside ran in front of the chambers, parallel to them, toward the outer court; it was 87 and a half feet[h] long. [8] For the chambers on the outer court were 87 and a half feet long, while those facing the great hall were 175 feet[g] ⌊long⌋. [9] At the base of these chambers there was an entryway on the east side as one enters them from the outer court.

[10] In the thickness of the wall of the court toward the south,[l] there were chambers facing the temple yard and the ⌊western⌋ building, [11] with a passageway in front of them, just like the chambers that faced north. Their length and width, as well as all their exits, measurements, and entrances, were identical. [12] The entrance at the beginning of the passageway, the way in front of the

---

[a] **41:21-22** Or *and in front of the sanctuary was something that looked like* [22] *an altar*　[b] **41:22** Lit *three cubits*　[c] **41:22** Lit *two cubits*　[d] **41:22** LXX reads *long and three and a half feet wide*　[e] **41:22** LXX reads *base*　[f] **41:25,26** Hb obscure　[g] **42:2,4,8** Lit *100 cubits*　[h] **42:2,7** Lit *50 cubits*　[i] **42:3** Lit *20 [cubits]*　[j] **42:4** Lit *10 cubits*　[k] **42:4** LXX, Syr; MT reads *wide, a way of one cubit*　[l] **42:10** LXX; MT reads *east*

corresponding[a] wall as one enters on the east side, was similar to the entrances of the chambers that were on the south side.

[13] Then the man said to me, "The northern and southern chambers that face the temple yard are the holy chambers where the priests who approach the LORD will eat the most holy offerings. There they will deposit the most holy offerings—the •grain offerings, •sin offerings, and •restitution offerings—for the place is holy. [14] Once the priests have entered, they must not go out from the holy area to the outer court until they have removed the clothes they minister in, for these are holy. They are to put on other clothes before they approach the public area."

Outside Dimensions of the Temple Complex

[15] When he finished measuring inside the temple complex, he led me out by way of the gate that faced east and measured all around the complex.

[16] He measured the east side with a measuring rod;
it was 875 feet[b] by the measuring rod.[c]
[17] He[d] measured the north side;
it was 875 feet by the measuring rod.[c]
[18] He[e] measured the south side;
it was 875 feet by the measuring rod.
[19] Then he turned to the west side and measured 875 feet by the measuring rod.

[20] He measured the temple complex on all four sides. It had a wall all around [it], 875 [feet] long and 875 [feet] wide, to separate the holy from the common.

Return of the LORD's Glory

43 He led me to the gate, the one that faces east, [2] and I saw the glory of the God of Israel coming from the east. His voice sounded like the roar of mighty waters, and the earth shone with His glory. [3] The vision I saw was like the one I had seen when He[f] came to destroy the city, and like the ones I had seen by the Chebar Canal. I fell facedown. [4] The glory of the LORD entered the temple by way of the gate that faced east. [5] Then the Spirit lifted me up and brought me to the inner court, and the glory of the LORD filled the temple.

"The Place of My Throne"

[6] While the man was standing beside me, I heard someone speaking to me from the temple. [7] He said to me: "Son of man, this is the place of My throne and the place for the soles of My feet, where I will dwell among the Israelites forever. [The house of] Israel and their kings will no longer defile My holy name by their [religious] prostitution and by the corpses[g] of their kings at their •high places.[h] [8] Whenever they placed their threshold next to My threshold and their doorposts beside My doorposts, with [only] a wall between Me and them, they were defiling My holy name by the abominations they committed. So I destroyed them in My anger. [9] Now let them remove their prostitution and the corpses[g] of their kings far from Me, and I will dwell among them forever.

"Describe the Temple"

[10] "As for you, son of man, describe the temple to the house of Israel, so that they may be ashamed of their iniquities.

a**42:12** Or *protective;* Hb obscure   b**42:16** Lit *500 in rods;* also in vv. 17-20   c**42:16,17** Lit *rod all around*
d**42:17** LXX reads *Then he turned to the north and*   e**42:18** LXX reads *Then he turned to the south and*   f**43:3** Some
Hb mss, Theod, Vg; other Hb mss, LXX, Syr read *I*   g**43:7,9** Or *monuments*   h**43:7** Some Hb mss, Theod, Tg read
their death

Let them measure ⌊its⌋ pattern, [11] and they will be ashamed of all that they have done. Reveal[a] the design of the temple to them—its layout with its exits and entrances—its complete design along with all its statutes, design specifications, and laws. Write it down in their sight so that they may observe its complete design and all its statutes and may carry them out. [12] This is the law of the temple: all its surrounding territory on top of the mountain will be especially holy. Yes, this is the law of the temple.

The Altar

[13] "These are the measurements of the altar in units of length (each unit being the standard length plus three inches):[b] the gutter is 21 inches[c] ⌊deep⌋ and 21 inches wide, with a rim of nine inches[d] around its edge. This is the base[e] of the altar. [14] ⌊The distance⌋ from the gutter on the ground to the lower ledge is three and a half feet,[f] and the width ⌊of the ledge⌋ is 21 inches.[c] There are seven feet [g] from the small ledge to the large ledge, ⌊whose⌋ width is also 21 inches. [15] The altar hearth[h] is seven feet[g] ⌊high⌋, and four horns project upward from the hearth. [16] The hearth is square, 21 feet[i] long by 21 feet wide. [17] The ledge is 24 and a half feet[j] long by 24 and a half feet wide, with four equal sides. The rim all around it is 10 and a half inches,[k] and its gutter is 21 inches[c] all around it. The altar's steps face east."

Burnt Offerings and Blood

[18] Then He said to me: "Son of man, this is what the Lord GOD says: These are the statutes for the altar on the day it is constructed, so that •burnt offerings

may be sacrificed on it and blood may be sprinkled on it: [19] You are to give a bull from the herd as a •sin offering to the Levitical priests who are from the offspring of Zadok, who approach Me in order to serve Me." ⌊This is⌋ the declaration of the Lord GOD. [20] "You must take some of its blood and apply ⌊it⌋ to the four horns of the altar, the four corners of the ledge, and all around the rim. In this way you will purify the altar and make •atonement for it. [21] Then you must take away the bull for the sin offering, and it must be burned outside the sanctuary in the place appointed for the temple.

[22] "On the second day you are to present an unblemished male goat as a sin offering. They will purify the altar just as they did with the bull. [23] When you have finished the purification, you are to present a young, unblemished bull and an unblemished ram from the flock. [24] You must present them before the LORD; the priests will throw salt on them and sacrifice them as a burnt offering to the LORD. [25] You will offer a goat for a sin offering each day for seven days. A young bull and a ram from the flock, both unblemished, must also be offered. [26] For seven days the priests are to make atonement for the altar and cleanse it. In this way they will consecrate it[l] [27] and complete the days ⌊of purification⌋. Then on the eighth day and afterwards, the priests will offer your burnt offerings and •fellowship offerings on the altar, and I will accept you." ⌊This is⌋ the declaration of the Lord GOD.

The Prince's Privilege

44 The man then brought me back toward the sanctuary's outer gate

[a]43:10-11 LXX, Vg; MT reads pattern. [11] And if they are ashamed . . . done, reveal   [b]43:13 Lit in cubits (a cubit being a cubit plus a handbreadth)   [c]43:13,14,17 Lit one cubit   [d]43:13 Lit one span   [e]43:13 LXX reads height   [f]43:14 Lit two cubits   [g]43:14,15 Lit four cubits   [h]43:15 Hb obscure   [i]43:16 Lit 12 cubits   [j]43:17 Lit 14 cubits   [k]43:17 Lit one-half cubit   [l]43:26 Lit will fill its hands

that faced east, and it was closed. ² The LORD said to me: "This gate will remain closed. It will not be opened, and no one will enter through it, because the LORD, the God of Israel, has entered through it. Therefore it will remain closed. ³ The prince himself will sit in the gateway to eat a meal before the LORD. He must enter by way of the portico of the gate and go out the same way."

Ezekiel Sees Glory of Lord

⁴ Then the man brought me by way of the north gate to the front of the temple. I looked, and the glory of the LORD filled His temple. And I fell facedown. ⁵ The LORD said to me: "Son of man, pay attention; look with your eyes and listen with your ears to everything I tell you about all the statutes and laws of the LORD's temple. Take careful note of the entrance of the temple along with all the exits of the sanctuary.

Levites' Duties and Privileges

⁶ "Say to the rebellious people, the house of Israel: This is what the Lord GOD says: ⌐I have had⌐ enough of all your abominations, house of Israel. ⁷ When you brought in foreigners, uncircumcised in both heart and flesh, to occupy My sanctuary, you defiled My temple while you offered My food—the fat and the blood. Youᵃ broke My covenant with all your abominations. ⁸ You have not kept charge of My holy things but have appointed ⌐others⌐ to keep charge of My sanctuary for you.

⁹ "This is what the Lord GOD says: No foreigner, uncircumcised in heart and flesh, may enter My sanctuary, not even a foreigner who is among the Israelites. ¹⁰ Surely the Levites who wandered

away from Me when Israel went astray, and who strayed from Me after their idols, will bear the consequences of their sin. ¹¹ Yet they will occupy My sanctuary, serving as guards at the temple gates and ministering at the temple. They will slaughter the •burnt offerings and ⌐other⌐ sacrifices for the people and will stand before them to serve them. ¹² Because they ministered to the house of Israel before their idols and became a sinful stumbling block to them, therefore I swore an oathᵇ against them"—⌐this is⌐ the declaration of the Lord GOD—"that they would bear the consequences of their sin. ¹³ They must not approach Me to serve Me as priests or come near any of My holy things or the most holy things. They will bear their disgrace and the consequences of the abominations they committed. ¹⁴ Yet I will make them responsible for the duties of the temple—for all its work and everything done in it.

Priests' Duties and Privileges

¹⁵ "But the Levitical priests descended from Zadok, who kept charge of My sanctuary when the Israelites went astray from Me, will approach Me to serve Me. They will stand before Me to offer Me fat and blood." ⌐This is⌐ the declaration of the Lord GOD. ¹⁶ "They are the ones who may enter My sanctuary and draw near to My table to serve Me. They will keep My mandate. ¹⁷ When they enter the gates of the inner court they must wear linen garments; they must not have on them anything made of wool when they minister at the gates of the inner court and within ⌐it⌐. ¹⁸ They must wear linen turbans on their heads and linen undergar-

---

ᵃ**44:7** LXX, Syr, Vg; MT reads *They* ᵇ**44:12** Lit *I lifted My hand*

ments around their waists. They are not to put on ⌊anything that makes them⌋ sweat. [19] Before they go out to the outer court,[a] to the people, they must take off the clothes they have been ministering in, leave them in the holy chambers, and dress in other clothes so that they do not transmit holiness to the people through their clothes.

Personal and Marriage Rules for Priests

[20] "They may not shave their heads or let their hair grow long, but must carefully trim their hair. [21] No priest may drink wine before he enters the inner court. [22] He is not to marry a widow or a divorced woman, but must marry a virgin from the offspring of the house of Israel, or a widow who is the widow of a priest. [23] They must teach My people the difference between the holy and the common, and explain to them the difference between the clean and the unclean.

Ritual Cleansing

[24] "In a dispute, they will officiate as judges and decide the case according to My ordinances. They must observe My laws and statutes regarding all My appointed festivals, and keep My Sabbaths holy. [25] A priest may not come ⌊near⌋ a dead person so that he becomes defiled. However, he may defile himself for a father, a mother, a son, a daughter, a brother, or an unmarried sister. [26] After he is cleansed, he is to count off seven days for himself. [27] On the day he goes into the sanctuary, into the inner court to minister in the sanctuary, he must present his •sin offering." ⌊This is⌋ the declaration of the Lord GOD.

Priests and Property

[28] "This will be their inheritance: I am their inheritance. You are to give them no possession in Israel: I am their possession. [29] They will eat the •grain offering, the sin offering, and the •restitution offering. Everything in Israel that is permanently dedicated ⌊to the LORD⌋ will belong to them. [30] The best of all the •firstfruits of every kind and contribution of every kind from all your gifts will belong to the priests. You are to give your first batch of dough to the priest so that a blessing may rest on your homes. [31] The priests may not eat any bird or animal that died naturally or was mauled by wild beasts.

The Sacred Portion of the Land

45 "When you divide the land by lot as an inheritance, you must set aside a donation to the LORD, a holy portion of the land, eight and one-third ⌊miles⌋[b] long and six and two-thirds ⌊miles⌋ [c] wide. This entire tract of land will be holy. [2] In this area there will be a square ⌊section⌋[d] for the sanctuary, 875 by 875 ⌊feet⌋,[e] with 87 and a half feet[f] of open space all around it. [3] From this holy portion,[g] you will measure off an area eight and one-third ⌊miles⌋[b] long and three and one-third ⌊miles⌋[h] wide, in which the sanctuary, the most holy place, will stand.[i] [4] It will be a holy area of the land to be used by the priests who minister in the sanctuary, who draw near to serve the LORD. It will be a place for their houses, as well as a holy area for the sanctuary. [5] There will be ⌊another area⌋ eight and one-third ⌊miles⌋[b] long and three and one-third ⌊miles⌋[h] wide for the Levites who minister in the temple; it will be their possession for towns to live in.[j]

[a]44:19 Some Hb mss, LXX, Syr, Vg; other Hb mss read *court, to the outer court*   [b]45:1,3,5,6 Lit *25,000 [cubits]*   [c]45:1 LXX = *20,000 [cubits]*; MT reads *10,000 [cubits]*, or *four and one-third [miles]*   [d]45:2 Lit *square all around*   [e]45:2 Lit *500 by 500 [cubits]*   [f]45:2 Lit *50 cubits*   [g]45:3 Lit *this measured [portion]*   [h]45:3,5 Lit *10,000 [cubits]*   [i]45:3 Lit *be*   [j]45:5 LXX; MT, Syr, Tg, Vg read *possession—20 chambers*

City Property

6 "As the property of the city, you must set aside an area one and two-thirds [of a mile][a] wide and eight and one-third [miles] [b] long, adjacent to the holy donation [of land]. It will be for the whole house of Israel. 7 And the prince will have the area on each side of the holy donation [of land] and the city's property, adjacent to the holy donation and the city's property, stretching to the west on the west side and to the east on the east side. [Its] length will correspond to one of the [tribal] portions from the western boundary to the eastern boundary. 8 This will be his land as a possession in Israel. My princes will no longer oppress My people but give the [rest of the] land to the house of Israel according to their tribes.

9 "This is what the Lord GOD says: You have gone too far,[c] princes of Israel! Put away violence and oppression and do what is just and right. Put an end to your evictions of My people." [This is] the declaration of the Lord GOD. 10 "You must have honest balances, an honest dry measure,[d] and an honest liquid measure.[e] 11 The dry measure[f] and the liquid measure[g] will be uniform, with the liquid measure containing five and a half gallons[h] and the dry measure [holding] half a bushel.[h] Their measurement will be one-tenth of the standard larger capacity measure.[i] 12 The •shekel will weigh 20 gerahs. Your mina will equal 60 shekels.

Contribution to the Sacrifices

13 "This is the contribution you are to offer: Three quarts[j] from five bushels[k] of wheat and[l] three quarts from five bush-els of barley. 14 The quota of oil in liquid measures[m] will be one percent of every[n] cor. [The cor equals] 10 liquid measures [or] one standard larger capacity measure,[o] since 10 liquid measures equal one standard larger capacity measure. 15 And [the quota] from the flock is one animal out of every 200 from the well-watered pastures of Israel. [These are] for the •grain offerings, •burnt offerings, and •fellowship offerings, to make •atonement for the people." [This is] the declaration of the Lord GOD. 16 "All the people of the land must take part in this contribution for the prince in Israel. 17 Then the burnt offerings, grain offerings, and drink offerings for the festivals, New Moons, and Sabbaths—for all the appointed times of the house of Israel—will be the prince's responsibility. He will provide the •sin offerings, grain offerings, burnt offerings, and fellowship offerings to make atonement on behalf of the house of Israel.

18 "This is what the Lord GOD says: In the first [month], on the first [day] of the month, you are to take a young, unblemished bull and purify the sanctuary. 19 The priest must take some of the blood from the sin offering and apply [it] to the temple doorposts, the four corners of the altar's ledge, and the doorposts of the gate to the inner court. 20 You must do the same thing on the seventh [day] of the month for everyone who sins unintentionally or through ignorance. In this way you will make atonement for the temple.

Passover Observance

21 "In the first [month], on the fourteenth day of the month, you are to cele-

---

a45:6 Lit 5,000 [cubits]   b45:6 Lit 25,000 [cubits]   c45:9 Lit Enough of you.   d45:10 Lit an honest ephah   e45:10 Lit and an honest bath   f45:11 Lit the ephah   g45:11 Lit the bath   h45:11 Lit one-tenth of a homer   i45:13 Lit be [based] on the homer   i45:13 Lit One-sixth of an ephah   k45:13 Lit a homer   l45:13 LXX, Vg; MT reads and you are to give   m45:14 Lit oil, the bath, the oil   n45:14 Lit be one-tenth of the bath from the   o45:14 Lit 10 baths, a homer

brate the •Passover, a festival of seven days ⌞during which⌟ unleavened bread will be eaten. 22 On that day the prince will provide a bull as a sin offering on behalf of himself and all the people of the land. 23 During the seven days of the festival, he will provide seven bulls and seven rams without blemish as a burnt offering to the LORD on each of the seven days, along with a male goat each day for a sin offering. 24 He will also provide a grain offering of half a bushel[a] per bull and half a bushel per ram, along with a gallon[b] of oil for every half bushel. 25 At the festival ⌞that begins⌟ on the fifteenth day of the seventh month,[c] he will provide the same things for seven days—the same sin offerings, burnt offerings, grain offerings, and oil.

Sacrifices at Appointed Times

46 "This is what the Lord GOD says: The gate of the inner court that faces east must be closed during the six days of work, but it will be opened on the Sabbath day and opened on the day of the New Moon. 2 The prince should enter from the outside by way of the gate's portico and stand at the doorpost of the gate while the priests sacrifice his •burnt offerings and •fellowship offerings. He will bow in worship at the threshold of the gate and then depart, but the gate must not be closed until evening. 3 The people of the land will also bow in worship before the LORD at the entrance of that gate on the Sabbaths and New Moons.

4 "The burnt offering that the prince presents to the LORD on the Sabbath day is to be six unblemished lambs and an unblemished ram. 5 The •grain offering will be half a bushel[d] with the ram, and the grain offering with the lambs will be

whatever he wants to give, as well as a gallon[b] of oil for every half bushel. 6 On the day of the New Moon, ⌞the burnt offering⌟ is to be a young, unblemished bull, as well as six lambs and a ram without blemish. 7 He will provide a grain offering of half a bushel[d] with the bull, half a bushel with the ram, and whatever he can afford with the lambs, together with a gallon[b] of oil for every half bushel. 8 When the prince enters, he must go in by way of the gate's portico and go out the same way.

9 "When the people of the land come before the LORD at the appointed times,[e] whoever enters by way of the north gate to worship must go out by way of the south gate, and whoever enters by way of the south gate must go out by way of the north gate. No one must return through the gate by which he entered, but must go out by the opposite gate. 10 When the people enter, the prince will enter with them, and when they leave, he will leave. 11 At the festivals and appointed times, the grain offering will be half a bushel[d] with the bull, half a bushel with the ram, and whatever he wants to give with the lambs, along with a gallon[b] of oil for every half bushel.

12 "When the prince makes a freewill offering, whether a burnt offering or a fellowship offering as a freewill offering to the LORD, the gate that faces east must be opened for him. He is to offer his burnt offering or fellowship offering just as he does on the Sabbath day. Then he will go out, and the gate must be closed after he leaves.

13 "You must offer an unblemished year-old male lamb as a daily burnt offering to the LORD; you will offer it every morning. 14 You must also prepare a grain offering every morning along with

---

[a]**45:24** Lit *an ephah*   [b]**45:24; 46:5,7,11** Lit *a hin*   [c]**45:25** = the Festival of Booths; Lv 23:33-43; Dt 16:13-15
[d]**46:5,7,11** Lit *an ephah*   [e]**46:9** Or *the festivals*

it: three quarts,[a] with one-third of a gallon[b] of oil to moisten the fine flour—a grain offering to the LORD. ⌊This is⌋ a permanent statute ⌊to be observed⌋ regularly. [15] They will offer the lamb, the grain offering, and the oil every morning as a regular burnt offering.

Transfer of Royal Lands

[16] "This is what the Lord GOD says: If the prince gives a gift to each of his sons as their inheritance, it will belong to his sons. It will become their property by inheritance. [17] But if he gives a gift from his inheritance to one of his servants, it will belong to that servant until the year of freedom, when it will revert to the prince. His inheritance belongs only to his sons; it is theirs. [18] The prince must not take any of the people's inheritance, evicting them from their property. He is to provide an inheritance for his sons from his own property, so that none of My people will be displaced from his own property."

Temple Kitchens

[19] Then he brought me through the entrance that was at the side of the gate, into the priests' holy chambers, which faced north. I saw a place there at the far western end. [20] He said to me, "This is the place where the priests will boil the •restitution offering and the •sin offering, and where they will bake the grain offering, so that they do not bring ⌊them⌋ into the outer court and transmit holiness to the people." [21] Next he brought me into the outer court and led me past its four corners. There was a ⌊separate⌋ court in each of its corners. [22] In the four corners of the ⌊outer⌋ court there were enclosed[c] courts, 70 ⌊feet⌋[d] long by 52

and a half ⌊feet⌋[e] wide. All four corner areas had the same dimensions. [23] There was a ⌊stone⌋ wall[f] around the inside of them, around the four of them, with ovens built at the base of the walls on all sides. [24] He said to me: "These are the kitchens where those who minister at the temple will cook the people's sacrifices."

Life-Giving River

47 Then he brought me back to the entrance of the temple and there was water flowing from under the threshold of the temple toward the east, for the temple faced east. The water was coming down from under the south side ⌊of the threshold⌋ of the temple, south of the altar. [2] Next he brought me out by way of the north gate and led me around the outside to the outer gate that faced east; there the water was trickling from the south side. [3] As the man went out east with a measuring line in his hand, he measured off a third of a mile[g] and led me through the water. It came up to ⌊my⌋ ankles. [4] Then he measured off a third ⌊of a mile⌋ and led me through the water. It came up to ⌊my⌋ knees. He measured off another third ⌊of a mile⌋ and led me through ⌊the water⌋. It came up to ⌊my⌋ waist. [5] Again he measured off a third of a ⌊mile⌋, and it was a river that I could not cross ⌊on foot⌋. For the water had risen; it was deep enough to swim in, a river that could not be crossed ⌊on foot⌋.

[6] He asked me, "Do you see ⌊this⌋, son of man?" Then he led me back to the bank of the river. [7] When I had returned, I saw a very large number of trees along both sides of the riverbank. [8] He said to me, "This water flows out to the eastern region and goes down to the •Arabah.

---

[a]**46:14** Lit one-sixth of an ephah   [b]**46:14** Lit one-third of a hin   [c]**46:22** Hb obscure   [d]**46:22** Lit 40 [cubits]   [e]**46:22** Lit 30 [cubits]   [f]**46:23** Or a row   [g]**47:3** Lit 1,000 cubits; also in vv. 4-5

When it enters the sea, the sea of foul water,[a] [b] the water ⌊of the sea⌋ becomes fresh. [9] Every ⌊kind of⌋ living creature that swarms will live wherever the river flows,[c] and there will be a huge number of fish because this water goes there. Since the water will become fresh, there will be life everywhere the river goes. [10] Fishermen will stand beside it from En-gedi to En-eglaim.[d] These will become places where nets are spread out to dry. Their fish will consist of many different kinds, like the fish of the Mediterranean Sea. [11] Yet its swamps and marshes will not be healed; they will be left for salt. [12] All ⌊kinds of⌋ trees providing food will grow along both banks of the river. Their leaves will not wither, and their fruit will not fail. Each month they will bear fresh fruit because the water ⌊comes⌋ from the sanctuary. Their fruit will be used for food and their leaves for medicine."

Borders of the Land

[13] This is what the Lord GOD says: "This is[e] the border you will ⌊use to⌋ divide the land as an inheritance for the 12 tribes of Israel. Joseph will receive two shares. [14] You will inherit it in equal portions, since I swore[f] to give it to your ancestors. So this land will fall to you as an inheritance.

[15] "This is to be the border of the land:

On the north side it will extend from the Mediterranean Sea by way of Hethlon and Lebo-hamath to Zedad,[g] [16] Berothah, and Sibraim (which is between the border of Damascus and the border of Hamath), ⌊as far as⌋ Hazer-hatticon, which is on the border of Hauran. [17] So the border will run from the sea to Hazar-enon at the border of Damascus, with the territory of Hamath to the north. This will be the northern side.

[18] On the east side it will run between Hauran and Damascus, along the Jordan between Gilead and the land of Israel; you will measure from the ⌊northern⌋ border to the eastern sea.[b] This will be the eastern side.

[19] On the south side it will run from Tamar to the waters of Meribath-kadesh,[h] and on to the Brook ⌊of Egypt⌋ as far as the Mediterranean Sea. This will be the southern side.

[20] On the west side the Mediterranean Sea will be the border, from the ⌊southern⌋ border up to a point opposite Lebo-hamath. This will be the western side.

[21] "You are to divide this land among yourselves according to the tribes of Israel. [22] You will allot it as an inheritance for yourselves and for the foreigners living among you, who have fathered children among you. You will treat them[i] like native-born Israelites; along with you, they will be allotted an inheritance among the tribes of Israel. [23] In whatever tribe the foreigner lives, you will assign his inheritance there." ⌊This is⌋ the declaration of the Lord GOD.

Tribal Allotments

48 "Now these are the names of the tribes:

From the northern end, along the road of Hethlon, to Lebo-hamath as far as Hazar-enon, at the

---

[a]**47:8** Or *enters the sea, being brought out to the sea*; Hb obscure   [b]**47:8,18** = the Dead Sea   [c]**47:9** LXX, Vg; MT reads *the two rivers flow*   [d]**47:10** Two springs near the Dead Sea   [e]**47:13** Tg, Vg; Syr reads *The valley of*   [f]**47:14** Lit *lifted My hand*   [g]**47:15** LXX; MT reads *[and] Lebo to Zedad, Hamath*; Ezk 48:1   [h]**47:19** = Kadesh-barnea   [i]**47:22** Lit *They will be to you*

northern border of Damascus, alongside Hamath and extending from the eastern side to the sea, will be <u>Dan</u>—one portion.

2 Next to the territory of Dan, from the east side to the west, will be <u>Asher</u>—one ⌊portion⌋.

3 Next to the territory of Asher, from the east side to the west, will be <u>Naphtali</u>—one ⌊portion⌋.

4 Next to the territory of Naphtali, from the east side to the west, will be <u>Manasseh</u>—one ⌊portion⌋.

5 Next to the territory of Manasseh, from the east side to the west, will be <u>Ephraim</u>—one ⌊portion⌋.

6 Next to the territory of Ephraim, from the east side to the west, will be <u>Reuben</u>—one ⌊portion⌋.

7 Next to the territory of Reuben, from the east side to the west, will be <u>Judah</u>—one ⌊portion⌋.

8 "Next to the territory of Judah, from the east side to the west, will be <u>the portion you donate</u> ⌊to the LORD⌋, eight and one-third ⌊miles⌋[a] wide, and as long as one of the ⌊tribal⌋ portions from the east side to the west. The sanctuary will be in the middle of it.

9 "The ⌊special⌋ portion you donate to the LORD will be eight and one-third ⌊miles⌋[a] long and three and one-third ⌊miles⌋[b] wide. 10 This holy donation will be set apart for the <u>priests ⌊alone⌋</u>. It will be eight and one-third ⌊miles long⌋[a] on the northern side, three and one-third ⌊miles⌋[b] wide on the western side, three and one-third ⌊miles⌋ wide on the eastern side, and eight and one-third ⌊miles⌋[a] long on the southern side. The LORD's sanctuary will be in the middle of it. 11 It is for the consecrated priests, the sons of Zadok, who kept My charge and did not go astray as the Levites did when the Israelites went astray. 12 It will be a special donation for them out of the ⌊holy⌋ donation of the land, a most holy place adjacent to the territory of the Levites.

13 "Next to the territory of the priests, the <u>Levites</u> ⌊will have an area⌋ eight and one-third ⌊miles⌋[a] long and three and one-third ⌊miles⌋[b] wide. The total length will be eight and one-third ⌊miles⌋[a] and the width three and one-third ⌊miles⌋.[b] 14 They must not sell or exchange any of it, and they must not transfer this choice ⌊part⌋ of the land, for it is holy to the LORD.

15 "The remaining ⌊area⌋, one and two-thirds ⌊of a mile⌋[c] wide and eight and one-third ⌊miles long⌋,[a] will be for <u>common use by the city, for ⌊both⌋ residential and open space</u>. The city will be in the middle of it. 16 These are the city's measurements:

one and a half ⌊miles⌋[d] on the north side;
one and a half ⌊miles⌋ on the south side;
one and a half ⌊miles⌋ on the east side;
and one and a half ⌊miles⌋ on the west side.

17 The city's open space will extend:

425 ⌊feet⌋[e] to the north,
425 ⌊feet⌋ to the south,
425 ⌊feet⌋ to the east,
and 425 ⌊feet⌋ to the west.

18 "The remainder of the length alongside the holy donation will be three and one-third ⌊miles⌋[b] to the east and three and one-third ⌊miles⌋ to the west. It will run alongside the holy donation. Its pro-

a48:8,9,10,13,15, Lit 25,000 [cubits]   b48:9,10,13,18 Lit 10,000 [cubits]   c48:15 Lit 5,000 [cubits]   d48:16 Lit 4,500 [cubits]   e48:17 Lit 250 [cubits]

duce will be <u>food for the workers</u> of the city. ¹⁹ The city's workers from all the tribes of Israel will cultivate it. ²⁰ The entire donation will be eight and one-third ˌmilesˌᵃ by eight and one-third ˌmilesˌ; you are to set apart the holy donation along with the city property as a square ˌareaˌ.

²¹ "The remaining ˌareaˌ on both sides of the holy donation and the city property will belong to <u>the prince</u>. He will own ˌthe landˌ adjacent to the ˌtribalˌ portions, next to the eight and one-third ˌmilesˌᵃ of the donation as far as the eastern border andᵇ next to the eight and one-third ˌmiles of the donationˌᵃ as far as the western border. The holy donation and the sanctuary of the temple will be in the middle of it. ²² Except for the Levitical property and the city property in the middle of the area belonging to the prince, the area between the territory of Judah and that of Benjamin will belong to the prince.

²³ "As for the rest of the tribes:

From the east side to the west, will be <u>Benjamin</u>—one ˌportionˌ.
²⁴ Next to the territory of Benjamin, from the east side to the west, will be <u>Simeon</u>—one ˌportionˌ.
²⁵ Next to the territory of Simeon, from the east side to the west, will be <u>Issachar</u>—one ˌportionˌ.
²⁶ Next to the territory of Issachar, from the east side to the west, will be <u>Zebulun</u>—one ˌportionˌ.
²⁷ Next to the territory of Zebulun, from the east side to the west, will be <u>Gad</u>—one ˌportionˌ.

²⁸ Next to the territory of Gad toward the south side, the border will run from Tamar to the waters of Meribath-kadesh, to the Brook ˌof Egyptˌ, and out to the Mediterranean Sea. ²⁹ This is the land you are to allot as an inheritance to Israel's tribes, and these will be their portions." ˌThis isˌ the declaration of the Lord GOD.

The New City

³⁰ "These are the exits of the city:

On the north side, which measures one and a half ˌmilesˌ,ᶜ ³¹ there will be three gates facing north, the gates of the city being named for the tribes of Israel: one, the gate of Reuben; one, the gate of Judah; and one, the gate of Levi.
³² On the east side, which is one and a half ˌmilesˌ,ᵈ there will be three gates: one, the gate of Joseph; one, the gate of Benjamin; and one, the gate of Dan.
³³ On the south side, which measures one and a half ˌmilesˌ, there will be three gates: one, the gate of Simeon; one, the gate of Issachar; and one, the gate of Zebulun.
³⁴ On the west side, which is one and a half ˌmilesˌ, there will be three gates: one, the gate of Gad; one, the gate of Asher; and one, the gate of Naphtali.

³⁵ The perimeter ˌof the cityˌ will be six ˌmilesˌ,ᵉ and <u>the name of the city from that day on will be: •Yahweh Is There.</u>"

ᵃ**48:20,21** Lit *25,000 [cubits]*   ᵇ**48:21** Lit *border, and to the west,*   ᶜ**48:30** Lit *4,500 [cubits]*   ᵈ**48:32** Lit *4,500 [cubits]; also in vv. 33-34*   ᵉ**48:35** Lit *18,000 [cubits]*

DANIEL

Daniel's Captivity in Babylon

1 In the third year of the reign of Jehoi-akim king of Judah, Nebuchadnezzar[a] king of Babylon came to Jerusalem and laid siege to it. [2] The Lord handed Jehoia-kim king of Judah over to him, along with some of the vessels from the house of God. Nebuchadnezzar carried them to the land of Babylon,[b] to the house of his god,[c] and put the vessels in the treasury of his god.

King Chooses Elite Young Israeli Men

[3] The king ordered Ashpenaz, the chief of his court officials,[d] to bring some of the Israelites from the royal family and from the nobility— [4] young men without any physical defect, good-looking, suit-able for instruction in all wisdom, knowledgeable, perceptive, and capable of serving in the king's palace—and to teach them the Chaldean language and literature. [5] The king assigned them daily provisions from the royal food and from the wine that he drank. They were to be trained for three years, and at the end of that time they were to serve in the king's court.[e] [6] Among them, from the descendants of Judah, were Daniel, Han-aniah, Mishael, and Azariah. [7] The chief official gave them ⌞different⌟ names: to Daniel, he gave the name Belteshazzar; to Hananiah, Shadrach; to Mishael, Me-shach; and to Azariah, Abednego.

Daniel's Faithfulness in Babylon

[8] Daniel determined that he would not defile himself with the king's food or with the wine he drank. So he asked per-mission from the chief official not to de-file himself. [9] God had granted Daniel favor and compassion from the chief offi-cial, [10] yet he said to Daniel, "My lord the king assigned your food and drink. I'm afraid ⌞of what would happen⌟ if he saw your faces looking thinner than those of the other young men your age. You would endanger my life[f] with the king."

Dietary Test

[11] So Daniel said to the guard whom the chief official had assigned to Daniel, Han-aniah, Mishael, and Azariah, [12] "Please test your servants for 10 days. Let us be given vegetables to eat and water to drink. [13] Then examine our appearance and the appearance of the young men who are eating the king's food, and deal with your servants based on what you see." [14] He agreed with them in this mat-ter and tested them for 10 days. [15] At the end of 10 days they looked better and healthier[g] than all the young men who were eating the king's food. [16] So the guard continued to remove their food and the wine they were to drink and gave them vegetables.

Faithfulness Rewarded

[17] God gave these four young men knowledge and understanding in every kind of literature and wisdom. Daniel also understood visions and dreams of every kind. [18] At the end of the time that the king had said to present them, the chief official presented them to Nebu-chadnezzar. [19] The king interviewed them, and among all of them, no one was found equal to Daniel, Hananiah,

a1:1 Or Nebuchadrezzar   b1:2 Lit Shinar; Gn 10:10; 11:2; 14:1,9   c1:2 Or gods   d1:3 Or his eunuchs   e1:5 Lit to stand before the king   f1:10 Lit would make my head guilty   g1:15 Lit fatter of flesh

Mishael, and Azariah. So they began to serve in the king's court. [20] In every matter of wisdom and understanding that the king consulted them about, he found them 10 times[a] better than all the diviner-priests and mediums in his entire kingdom. [21] Daniel remained there until the first year of King Cyrus.

Nebuchadnezzar's Dream

2 In the second year of his reign, Nebuchadnezzar had dreams that troubled him, and sleep deserted him. [2] So the king gave orders to summon the diviner-priests, mediums, sorcerers, and Chaldeans[b] to tell the king his dreams. When they came and stood before the king, [3] he said to them, "I have had a dream and am anxious to understand it."

[4] The Chaldeans spoke to the king (Aramaic[c] begins here): "May the king live forever. Tell your servants the dream, and we will give the interpretation."

King's Hard Demand

[5] The king replied to the Chaldeans, "My word is final: If you don't tell me the dream and its interpretation, you will be torn limb from limb,[d] and your houses will be made a garbage dump. [6] But if you make the dream and its interpretation known to me, you'll receive gifts, a reward, and great honor from me. So make the dream and its interpretation known to me."

[7] They answered a second time, "May the king tell the dream to his servants, and we will give the interpretation."

[8] The king replied, "I know for certain you are trying to gain some time, because you see that my word is final. [9] If you don't tell me the dream, there is one decree for you. You have conspired to tell me something false or fraudulent until the situation changes. So tell me the dream and I will know you can give me its interpretation."

King Orders Death of Wise Men

[10] The Chaldeans answered the king, "No one on earth can make known what the king requests. Consequently, no king, however great and powerful, has ever asked anything like this of any diviner-priest, medium, or Chaldean. [11] What the king is asking is so difficult that no one can make it known to him except the gods, whose dwelling is not with mortals." [12] Because of this, the king became violently angry and gave orders to destroy all the wise men of Babylon. [13] The decree was issued that the wise men were to be executed, and they searched for Daniel and his friends, to execute them.

Daniel Intervenes

[14] Then Daniel responded with tact and discretion to Arioch, the commander of the king's guard,[e] who had gone out to execute the wise men of Babylon. [15] He asked Arioch, the king's officer, "Why is the decree from the king so harsh?"[f] Then Arioch explained the situation to Daniel. [16] So Daniel went and asked the king to give him some time, so that he could give the king the interpretation.

Daniel Asks for Prayer

[17] Then Daniel went to his house and told his friends Hananiah, Mishael, and Azariah about the matter, [18] urging them to ask the God of heaven for mercy concerning this mystery, so Daniel and his friends would not be killed with the rest of Babylon's wise men.

---

[a]**1:20** Lit *hands*   [b]**2:2** In this chap *Chaldeans* = influential Babylonian wise men   [c]**2:4** The text from here through chap 7 is written in *Aramaic.*   [d]**2:5** Lit *be made into limbs*   [e]**2:14** Or *executioners*   [f]**2:15** Or *urgent*

Mystery Revealed—
Daniel Praises God

¹⁹ The mystery was then revealed to Daniel in a vision at night, and Daniel praised the God of heaven ²⁰ and declared:

> May the name of God
> be praised forever and ever,
> for wisdom and power belong
>   to Him.
> ²¹ He changes the times and seasons;
> He removes kings
>   and establishes kings.
> He gives wisdom to the wise
> and knowledge to those
> who have understanding.
> ²² He reveals the deep
>   and hidden things;
> He knows what is in the darkness,
> and light dwells with Him.
> ²³ I offer thanks and praise to You,
> God of my fathers,
> because You have given me
> wisdom and power.
> And now You have let me know
> what we asked of You,
> for You have let us know
> the king's mystery.ᵃ

Daniel Takes Answer to King

²⁴ Therefore Daniel went to Arioch, whom the king had assigned to destroy the wise men of Babylon. He came and said to him, "Don't kill the wise men of Babylon! Bring me before the king, and I will give him the interpretation."

²⁵ Then Arioch quickly brought Daniel before the king and said to him, "I have found a man among the Judean exiles who can let the king know the interpretation."

²⁶ The king said in reply to Daniel, whose name was Belteshazzar, "Are you able to tell me the dream I had and its interpretation?"

Daniel Credits God

²⁷ Daniel answered the king: "No wise man, medium, diviner-priest, or astrologer is able to make known to the king the mystery he asked about. ²⁸ But there is a God in heaven who reveals mysteries, and He has let King Nebuchadnezzar know what will happen in the last days.

Daniel Describes Dream

Your dream and the visions ₍that came into₎ your mind ₍as you lay₎ in bed were these: ²⁹ Your Majesty, while you were in your bed, thoughts came ₍to your mind₎ about what will happen in the future.ᵇ The revealer of mysteries has let you know what will happen. ³⁰ As for me, this mystery has been revealed to me, not because I have more wisdom than anyone living, but in order that the interpretation might be made known to the king, and that you may understand the thoughts of your mind.

³¹ "My king, as you were watching, a colossal statue appeared. That statue, tall and dazzling, was standing in front of you, and its appearance was terrifying. ³² The head of the statue was pure gold, its chest and arms were silver, its stomach and thighs were bronze, ³³ its legs were iron, and its feet were partly iron and partly fired clay. ³⁴ As you were watching, a stone broke off without a hand touching it,ᶜ struck the statue on its feet of iron and fired clay, and crushed them. ³⁵ Then the iron, the fired clay, the bronze, the silver, and the gold were shattered and became like chaff from the summer threshing floors. The wind carried them away, and not a trace of them could be found. But the stone that struck

ᵃ**2:23** Lit *matter*   ᵇ**2:29** Lit *happen after this*   ᶜ**2:34** Lit *off not by hands* the statue became a great mountain and filled the whole earth.

Daniel Interprets Dream

36 "This was the dream; now we will tell the king its interpretation. 37 Your Majesty, you are king of kings. The God of heaven has given you sovereignty, power, strength, and glory. 38 Wherever people live—or wild animals, or birds of the air—He has handed them over to you and made you ruler over them all. You are the head of gold.

39 "After you, there will arise another kingdom, inferior to yours, and then another, a third kingdom, of bronze, which will rule the whole earth. 40 A fourth kingdom will be as strong as iron; for iron crushes and shatters everything, and like iron that smashes, it will crush and smash all the others.ᵃ 41 You saw the feet and toes, partly of a potter's fired clay and partly of iron—it will be a divided kingdom, though some of the strength of iron will be in it. You saw the iron mixed with clay, 42 and that the toes of the feet were part iron and part fired clay—part of the kingdom will be strong, and part will be brittle. 43 You saw the iron mixed with clay—the peoples will mix with one anotherᵇ but will not hold together, just as iron does not mix with fired clay.

Eternal Kingdom

44 "In the days of those kings, the God of heaven will set up a kingdom that will never be destroyed, and this kingdom will not be left to another people. It will crush all these kingdoms and bring them to an end, but will itself endure forever. 45 You saw a stone break off from the mountain without a hand touching it,ᶜ and it crushed the iron, bronze, fired clay, silver, and gold. The great God has told the king what will happen in the future.ᵈ The dream is true, and its interpretation certain."

Nebuchadnezzar's Response

46 Then King Nebuchadnezzar fell down, paid homage to Daniel, and gave orders to present an offering and incense to him. 47 The king said to Daniel, "Your God is indeed God of gods, Lord of kings, and a revealer of mysteries, since you were able to reveal this mystery." 48 Then the king promoted Daniel and gave him many generous gifts. He made him ruler over the entire province of Babylon and chief governor over all the wise men of Babylon. 49 At Daniel's request, the king appointed Shadrach, Meshach, and Abednego to manage the province of Babylon. But Daniel remained at the king's court.

Nebuchadnezzar's Gold Statue

3 King Nebuchadnezzar made a gold statue, 90 feet high and nine feet wide.ᵉ He set it up on the plain of Dura in the province of Babylon. 2 King Nebuchadnezzar sent word to assemble the satraps, prefects, governors, advisers, treasurers, judges, magistrates, and all the rulers of the provinces to attend the dedication of the statue King Nebuchadnezzar had set up. 3 So the satraps, prefects, governors, advisers, treasurers, judges, magistrates, and all the rulers of the provinces assembled for the dedication of the statue the king had set up. Then they stood before the statue Nebuchadnezzar had set up.

"Worship the Gold Statue"

4 A herald loudly proclaimed, "People of every nation and language, you are

ᵃ2:40 Lit all these ᵇ2:43 Lit another in the seed of men ᶜ2:45 Lit mountain, not by hands ᵈ2:45 Lit happen after this ᵉ3:1 Lit statue, its height 60 cubits, its width six cubits

commanded: [5] When you hear the sound of the horn, flute, zither,[a] lyre,[b] harp, drum,[c] and every kind of music, you are to fall down and worship the gold statue that King Nebuchadnezzar has set up. [6] But whoever does not fall down and worship will immediately be thrown into a furnace of blazing fire."

[7] Therefore, when all the people heard the sound of the horn, flute, zither, lyre, harp, and every kind of music, people of every nation and language fell down and worshiped the gold statue that King Nebuchadnezzar had set up.

Shadrach, Meshach, and Abednego Accused

[8] Some Chaldeans took this occasion to come forward and maliciously accuse[d] the Jews. [9] They said to King Nebuchadnezzar, "May the king live forever. [10] You as king have issued a decree that everyone who hears the sound of the horn, flute, zither, lyre, harp, drum, and every kind of music must fall down and worship the gold statue. [11] Whoever does not fall down and worship will be thrown into a furnace of blazing fire. [12] There are some Jews you have appointed to manage the province of Babylon: Shadrach, Meshach, and Abednego. These men have ignored you, the king; they do not serve your gods or worship the gold statue you have set up."

Fury of King

[13] Then in a furious rage Nebuchadnezzar gave orders to bring in Shadrach, Meshach, and Abednego. So these men were brought before the king. [14] Nebuchadnezzar asked them, "Shadrach, Meshach, and Abednego, is it true that you don't serve my gods or worship the gold statue I have set up? [15] Now if you're ready, when you hear the sound of the horn, flute, zither, lyre, harp, drum, and every kind of music, fall down and worship the statue I made. But if you don't worship it, you will immediately be thrown into a furnace of blazing fire—and who is the god who can rescue you from my power?"

[16] Shadrach, Meshach, and Abednego replied to the king, "Nebuchadnezzar, we don't need to give you an answer to this question. [17] If the God we serve exists, then He can rescue us from the furnace of blazing fire, and He can rescue us from the power of you, the king. [18] But even if He does not rescue us,[e] we want you as king to know that we will not serve your gods or worship the gold statue you set up."

Furnace of Blazing Fire

[19] Then Nebuchadnezzar was filled with rage, and the expression on his face changed toward Shadrach, Meshach, and Abednego. He gave orders to heat the furnace seven times more than was customary, [20] and he commanded some of the strongest soldiers in his army to tie up Shadrach, Meshach, and Abednego and throw them into the furnace of blazing fire. [21] So these men, in their trousers, robes, head coverings,[f] and other clothes, were tied up and thrown into the furnace of blazing fire. [22] Since the king's command was so urgent[g] and the furnace extremely hot, the raging flames[h] killed those men who carried Shadrach, Meshach, and Abednego up. [23] And these three men, Shadrach, Meshach, and Abednego fell, bound, into the furnace of blazing fire.

---

[a]**3:5** Or *lyre* [b]**3:5** Or *sambuke*; a type of triangular harp with 4 or more strings [c]**3:5** Or *pipe*; the identity of these instruments is uncertain. [d]**3:8** Lit *and eat the pieces of* [e]**3:18** Lit *But if not* [f]**3:21** The identity of these articles of clothing is uncertain. [g]**3:22** Or *harsh* [h]**3:22** Lit *the flame of the fire*

Four Men in Fire

²⁴ Then King Nebuchadnezzar jumped up in alarm. He said to his advisers, "Didn't we throw three men, bound, into the fire?"

"Yes, of course, Your Majesty," they replied to the king.

²⁵ He exclaimed, "Look! I see four men, not tied, walking around in the fire unharmed; and the fourth looks like a son of the gods."ᵃ

The Three Emerge

²⁶ Nebuchadnezzar then approached the door of the furnace of blazing fire and called: "Shadrach, Meshach, and Abednego, you servants of the •Most High God—come out!" So Shadrach, Meshach, and Abednego came out of the fire. ²⁷ When the satraps, prefects, governors, and the king's advisers gathered around, they saw that the fire had no effect onᵇ the bodies of these men: not a hair of their heads was singed, their robes were unaffected, and there was no smell of fire on them. ²⁸ Nebuchadnezzar exclaimed, "Praise to the God of Shadrach, Meshach, and Abednego! He sent His angelᶜ and rescued His servants who trusted in Him. They violated the king's command and risked their lives rather than serve or worship any god except their own God. ²⁹ Therefore I issue a decree that anyone of any people, nation, or language who says anything offensive against the God of Shadrach, Meshach, and Abednego will be torn limb from limb and his house made a garbage dump. For there is no other god who is able to deliver like this." ³⁰ Then the king rewarded Shadrach, Meshach, and Abednego in the province of Babylon.

Nebuchadnezzar's Proclamation

4ᵈ King Nebuchadnezzar,

To those of every people, nation, and language, who live in all the earth:

May your prosperity increase. ² I am pleased to tell you about the miracles and wonders the •Most High God has done for me.

³ How great are His miracles,
and how mighty His wonders!
His kingdom is an eternal kingdom,
and His dominion is
from generation to generation.

Nebuchadnezzar's Second Dream

⁴ᵉ I, Nebuchadnezzar, was at ease in my house and flourishing in my palace. ⁵ I had a dream, and it frightened me; while in my bed, the images and visions in my mind alarmed me. ⁶ So I issued a decree to bring all the wise men of Babylon to me in order that they might make the dream's interpretation known to me. ⁷ When the diviner-priests, mediums, Chaldeans, and astrologers came in, I told them the dream, but they could not make its interpretation known to me.

⁸ Finally Daniel, named Belteshazzar after the name of my god—and the spirit of the holy gods is in him—came before me. I told him the dream: ⁹ Belteshazzar, head of the diviners, because I know that you have a spirit of the holy gods and that no mystery puzzles you, explain to me the visions of my dream that I saw, and its interpretation. ¹⁰ In the visions of my mind as I was lying in bed, I saw this:

ᵃ**3:25** Or of a divine being ᵇ**3:27** Lit fire had not overcome ᶜ**3:28** Or messenger ᵈ**4:1** Dn 3:31 in Hb ᵉ**4:4** Dn 4:1 in Hb

There was a tree in the middle
  of the earth,
and its height was great.
11 The tree grew large and strong;
  its top reached to the sky,
and it was visible to the ends
  of the[a] earth.
12 Its leaves were beautiful, its fruit
    was abundant,
and on it was food for all.
Wild animals found shelter
    under it,
the birds of the air lived
  in its branches,
and every creature was fed from it.

13 As I was lying in my bed, I also saw in the visions of my mind an observer, a holy one,[b] coming down from heaven. 14 He called out loudly:

Cut down the tree and chop off
    its branches;
strip off its leaves and scatter
    its fruit.
Let the animals flee from under it,
and the birds from its branches.
15 But leave the stump with its roots
    in the ground,
and with a band of iron and bronze
    around it,
in the tender grass of the field.
Let him be drenched with dew
    from the sky
and share the plants of the earth
  with the animals.
16 Let his mind be changed from that
    of a man,
and let him be given the mind
    of an animal
for seven periods of time.[c] [d]
17 This word is by decree
  of the observers;
the matter is a command
  from the holy ones.

This is so the living will know
  that the Most High is ruler
  over the kingdom of men.
He gives it to anyone He wants
  and sets over it the lowliest of men.

18 This is the dream that I, King Nebuchadnezzar, had. Now, Belteshazzar, tell me the interpretation, because none of the wise men of my kingdom can make the interpretation known to me. But you can, because you have the spirit of the holy gods.

Daniel Interprets Second Dream

19 Then Daniel, whose name is Belteshazzar, was stunned for a moment, and his thoughts alarmed him. The king said, "Belteshazzar, don't let the dream or its interpretation alarm you."

Belteshazzar answered, "My lord, may the dream apply to those who hate you, and its interpretation to your enemies! 20 The tree you saw, which grew large and strong, whose top reached to the sky and was visible to all the earth, 21 whose leaves were beautiful and its fruit abundant—and on it was food for all, under it the wild animals lived, and in its branches the birds of the air lived— 22 that tree is you, the king. For you have become great and strong: your greatness has grown and even reaches the sky, and your dominion ⌊extends⌋ to the ends of the earth.

23 "The king saw an observer, a holy one, coming down from heaven and saying, 'Cut down the tree and destroy it, but leave the stump with its roots in the ground and with a band of iron and bronze around it, in the tender grass of the field. Let him be drenched with dew from the sky, and share ⌊food⌋ with the wild animals for seven periods of time.' 24 This is the interpretation, Your Maj-

---

a 4:11 Lit of all the   b 4:13 = an angel   c 4:16 Lit animal as seven times pass over him   d 4:16 Perhaps = 7 years esty, and this is the sentence of the Most High that has been passed against my lord the king: [25] You will be driven away from people to live with the wild animals. You will feed on grass like cattle and be drenched with dew from the sky for seven periods of time, until you acknowledge that the Most High is ruler over the kingdom of men, and He gives it to anyone He wants. [26] As for the command to leave the tree's stump with its roots, your kingdom will be restored[a] to you as soon as you acknowledge that Heaven[b] rules. [27] Therefore, may my advice seem good to you my king. Separate yourself from your sins by doing what is right, and from your injustices by showing mercy to the needy. Perhaps there will be an extension of your prosperity."

Sentence against Nebuchadnezzar Executed

[28] All this happened to King Nebuchadnezzar. [29] At the end of 12 months, as he was walking on the roof of the royal palace in Babylon, [30] the king exclaimed, "Is this not Babylon the Great that I have built by my vast power to be a royal residence and to display my majestic glory?"

[31] While the words were still in the king's mouth, a voice came from heaven: "King Nebuchadnezzar, to you it is declared that the kingdom has departed from you. [32] You will be driven away from people to live with the wild animals, and you will feed on grass like cattle for seven periods of time, until you acknowledge that the Most High is ruler over the kingdom of men, and He gives it to anyone He wants."

[33] At that moment the sentence against Nebuchadnezzar was executed. He was driven away from people. He ate grass like cattle, and his body was drenched with dew from the sky, until his hair grew like eagles' ₁feathers₁ and his nails like birds' ₁claws₁.

Nebuchadnezzar's Praise

[34] But at the end of those days, I, Nebuchadnezzar, looked up to heaven, and my sanity returned to me. Then I praised the Most High and honored and glorified Him who lives forever:

> For His dominion is
>   an everlasting dominion,
> and His kingdom is from generation
>   to generation.
> [35] All the inhabitants of the earth
>   are counted as nothing,
> and He does what He wants
>   with the army of heaven
> and the inhabitants of the earth.
> There is no one who can hold back
>   His hand
> or say to Him,
>   "What have You done?"

[36] At that time my sanity returned to me, and my majesty and splendor returned to me for the glory of my kingdom. My advisers and my nobles sought me out, I was reestablished over my kingdom, and even more greatness came to me. [37] Now I, Nebuchadnezzar, praise, exalt, and glorify the King of heaven, because all His works are true and His ways are just. And He is able to humble those who walk in pride.

Belshazzar's Feast

5 King Belshazzar held a great feast for 1,000 of his nobles and drank wine in their presence. [2] Under the influence of[c] the wine, Belshazzar gave orders to bring in the gold and silver vessels that his predecessor[d] Nebuchadnezzar had

---

[a]**4:26** Lit *enduring*   [b]**4:26** = God   [c]**5:2** Or *When he tasted*   [d]**5:2** Or *father,* or *grandfather*

taken from the temple in Jerusalem, so that the king and his nobles, wives, and concubines could drink from them. ³ So they brought in the gold[a] vessels that had been taken from the temple, the house of God in Jerusalem, and the king and his nobles, wives, and concubines drank from them. ⁴ They drank the wine and praised their gods made of gold and silver, bronze, iron, wood, and stone.

Handwriting on the Wall

⁵ At that moment the fingers of a man's hand appeared and began writing on the plaster of the king's palace wall next to the lampstand. As the king watched the hand[b] that was writing, ⁶ his face turned pale,[c] and his thoughts so terrified him that his hip joints shook and his knees knocked together. ⁷ The king called out to bring in the mediums, Chaldeans, and astrologers. He said to these wise men of Babylon, "Whoever reads this inscription and gives me its interpretation will be clothed in purple, have a gold chain around his neck, and have the third highest position in the kingdom." ⁸ So all the king's wise men came in, but none could read the inscription or make known its interpretation to him. ⁹ Then King Belshazzar became even more terrified, his face turned pale,[d] and his nobles were bewildered.

Queen Recommends Daniel

¹⁰ Because of the outcry of the king and his nobles, the queen[e] came to the banquet hall. "May the king live forever," she said. "Don't let your thoughts terrify you or your face be pale.[f] ¹¹ There is a man in your kingdom who has the spirit of the holy gods in him. In the days of your predecessor he was found to

have insight, intelligence, and wisdom like the wisdom of the gods. Your predecessor, King Nebuchadnezzar, appointed him chief of the diviners, mediums, Chaldeans, and astrologers. Your own predecessor, the king, ¹²⌐did this⌐ because Daniel, the one the king named Belteshazzar, was found to have an extraordinary spirit, knowledge and perception, and the ability to interpret dreams, explain riddles, and solve problems. Therefore, summon Daniel, and he will give the interpretation."

Daniel before King Belshazzar

¹³ Then Daniel was brought before the king. The king said to him, "Are you Daniel, one of the Judean exiles that my predecessor the king brought from Judah? ¹⁴ I've heard that you have the spirit of the gods in you, and that you have insight, intelligence, and extraordinary wisdom. ¹⁵ Now the wise men and mediums were brought before me to read this inscription and make its interpretation known to me, but they could not give its interpretation. ¹⁶ However, I have heard about you that you can give interpretations and solve problems. Therefore, if you can read this inscription and give me its interpretation, you will be clothed in purple, have a gold chain around your neck, and have the third highest position in the kingdom."

Daniel Responds

¹⁷ Then Daniel answered the king, "You may keep your gifts, and give your rewards to someone else; however, I will read the inscription for the king and make the interpretation known to him. ¹⁸ Your Majesty, the •Most High God gave sovereignty, greatness, glory, and majesty to your predecessor Nebuchad-

---

[a]5:3 Theod, Vg add and silver   [b]5:5 Lit part of the hand   [c]5:5-6 Lit writing, ⁶ the king's brightness changed   [d]5:9 Lit his brightness changed on him   [e]5:10 Perhaps the queen mother   [f]5:10 Lit your brightness change

nezzar. ¹⁹ Because of the greatness He gave him, all peoples, nations, and languages were terrified and fearful of him. He killed anyone he wanted and kept alive anyone he wanted; he exalted anyone he wanted and humbled anyone he wanted. ²⁰ But when his heart was exalted and his spirit became arrogant, he was deposed from his royal throne and his glory was taken from him. ²¹ He was driven away from people, his mind was like an animal's, he lived with the wild donkeys, he was fed grass like cattle, and his body was drenched with dew from the sky until he acknowledged that the Most High God is ruler over the kingdom of men and sets anyone He wants over it.

Daniel Rebukes Belshazzar

²² "But you his successor, Belshazzar, have not humbled your heart, even though you knew all this. ²³ Instead, you have exalted yourself against the Lord of heaven. The vessels from His house[a] were brought to you, and as you and your nobles, wives, and concubines drank wine from them, you praised the gods made of silver and gold, bronze, iron, wood, and stone, which do not see or hear or understand. But you have not glorified the God who holds your life-breath in His hand and who controls the whole course of your life.[b] ²⁴ Therefore, He sent the hand, and this writing was inscribed.

Daniel Interprets Inscription

²⁵ "This is the writing that was inscribed:

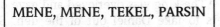

MENE, MENE, TEKEL, PARSIN

²⁶ This is the interpretation of the message:

MENE[c] ⌊means that⌋ God has numbered ⌊the days of⌋ your kingdom and brought it to an end. ²⁷ TEKEL[d] ⌊means that⌋ you have been weighed in the balance and found deficient. ²⁸ PERES[e] ⌊means that⌋ your kingdom has been divided and given to the Medes and Persians."

King Rewards Daniel

²⁹ Then Belshazzar gave an order, and they clothed Daniel in purple, ⌊placed⌋ a gold chain around his neck, and issued a proclamation concerning him that he should be the third ruler in the kingdom.

Darius Succeeds Belshazzar

³⁰ That very night Belshazzar the king of the Chaldeans was killed, ³¹f and Darius the Mede received the kingdom at the age of 62.

Plot against Daniel

6 Darius decided[g] to appoint 120 satraps over the kingdom, stationed throughout the realm, ² and over them three administrators, including Daniel. These satraps would be accountable to them so that the king would not be defrauded. ³ Daniel[h] distinguished himself above the administrators and satraps because he had an extraordinary spirit, so the king planned to set him over the whole realm. ⁴ The administrators and satraps, therefore, kept trying to find a charge against Daniel regarding the kingdom. But they could find no charge or corruption, for he was trustworthy, and no negligence or corruption was found in him. ⁵ Then these men said, "We will

---

[a]**5:23** = God's temple   [b]**5:23** Lit *and all your ways belong to Him*   [c]**5:26** Or *numbered*, or *a mina*; = a weight of 500 to 600 grams   [d]**5:27** Or *weighed*, or *a shekel*; = a weight of 10 grams   [e]**5:28** Or *divided*, or *half a shekel*; sg form of *PARSIN* in v. 25   [f]**5:31** Dn 6:1 in Hb   [g]**6:1** Lit *It was pleasing before Darius*   [h]**6:3** Lit *Now this Daniel*

never find any charge against this Daniel unless we find something against him concerning the law of his God."

[6] So the administrators and satraps went together to the king and said to him, "May King Darius live forever. [7] All the administrators of the kingdom, the prefects, satraps, advisers, and governors have agreed that the king should establish an ordinance and enforce an edict that for 30 days, <u>anyone who petitions any god or man except you, the king, will be thrown into the lions' den.</u> [8] Therefore, Your Majesty, establish the edict and sign the document so that, as a law of the Medes and Persians, it is irrevocable and cannot be changed." [9] So King Darius signed the document.

Daniel's Defiant Prayers

[10] When Daniel learned that the document had been signed, he went into his house. The windows in its upper room opened toward Jerusalem, and three times a day he got down on his knees, prayed, and gave thanks to his God, just as he had done before. [11] Then these men went as a group and found Daniel petitioning and imploring his God. [12] So they approached the king and asked about his edict: "Didn't you sign an edict that for 30 days any man who petitions any god or man except you, the king, will be thrown into the lions' den?"

The king answered, "As a law of the Medes and Persians, the order stands and is irrevocable."

[13] Then they replied to the king, "Daniel, one of the Judean exiles, has ignored you, the king, and the edict you signed, for he prays three times a day." [14] As soon as the king heard this, he was very displeased; he set his mind on rescuing

Daniel and made every effort until sundown to deliver him.

[15] Then these men went to the king and said to him, "You as king know it is a law of the Medes and Persians that no edict or ordinance the king establishes can be changed."

Daniel in Lions' Den

[16] So the king gave the order, and they brought Daniel and threw him into the lions' den. The king said to Daniel, "May your God, whom you serve continually, rescue you!" [17] A stone was brought and placed over the mouth of the den. The king sealed it with his own signet ring and with the signet rings of his nobles, so that nothing in regard to Daniel could be changed. [18] Then the king went to his palace and spent the night fasting. No diversions[a] were brought to him, and he could not sleep.

God's Angel Rescues Daniel

[19] At the first light of dawn the king got up and hurried to the lions' den. [20] When he reached the den, he cried out in anguish to Daniel. "Daniel, servant of the living God," the king said,[b] "has your God whom you serve continually been able to rescue you from the lions?"

[21] Then Daniel spoke with the king: "May the king live forever. [22] My God sent His angel and shut the lions' mouths. They haven't hurt me, for I was found innocent before Him. Also, I have not committed a crime against you my king."

Daniel's Accusers Executed

[23] The king was overjoyed and gave orders to take Daniel out of the den. So Daniel was taken out of the den, unin-

---

jured, for he trusted in his God. 24 The king then gave the command, and those men who had maliciously accused Daniel[a] were brought and thrown into the lions' den—they, their children, and their wives. They had not reached the bottom of the den before the lions overpowered them and crushed all their bones.

King Darius Honors God

25 Then King Darius wrote to those of every people, nation, and language who live in all the earth: "May your prosperity abound. 26 I issue a decree that in all my royal dominion, people must tremble in fear before the God of Daniel:

For He is the living God,
    and He endures forever;
His kingdom will never
    be destroyed,
    and His dominion has no end.
27 He rescues and delivers;
He performs signs and wonders
    in the heavens and on the earth,
    for He has rescued Daniel
    from the power of the lions."

28 So Daniel prospered during the reign of Darius and[b] the reign of Cyrus the Persian.

Daniel's Vision of Four Beasts

7 In the first year of Belshazzar king of Babylon, Daniel had a dream with visions in his mind as he was lying in his bed. He wrote down the dream, and here is the summary[c] of his account. 2 Daniel said, "In my vision at night I was watching, and suddenly the four winds of heaven stirred up the great sea. 3 Four huge beasts came up from the sea, each different from the other.

4 "The first was like a lion but had eagle's wings. I continued watching until its wings were torn off. It was lifted up from the ground, set on its feet like a man, and given a human mind.

5 "Suddenly, another beast appeared, a second one, that looked like a bear. It was raised up on one side, with three ribs in its mouth between its teeth. It was told, 'Get up! Gorge yourself on flesh.'

6 "While I was watching, another beast appeared. It was like a leopard with four wings of a bird on its back. It had four heads and was given authority to rule.

7 "While I was watching in the night visions, a fourth beast appeared, frightening and dreadful, and incredibly strong, with large iron teeth. It devoured and crushed, and it trampled with its feet whatever was left. It was different from all the beasts before it, and it had 10 horns.

8 "While I was considering the horns, suddenly another horn, a little one, came up among them, and three of the first horns were uprooted before it. There were eyes in this horn like a man's, and it had a mouth that spoke arrogantly.

Ancient of Days and Son of Man

9 "As I kept watching,

thrones were set in place,
    and the Ancient of Days
    took His seat.
His clothing was white like snow,
    and the hair of His head
    like whitest wool.
His throne was flaming fire;
    its wheels were blazing fire.
10   A river of fire was flowing,
    coming out from His presence.

---

a6:24 Lit had eaten his pieces   b6:28 Or Darius, even   c7:1 Lit beginning

Thousands upon thousands
  served Him;
ten thousand times ten thousand
  stood before Him.
The court was convened,
  and the books were opened.

¹¹ "I watched, then, because of the sound of the arrogant words the horn was speaking. As I continued watching, the beast was killed and its body destroyed and given over to the burning fire. ¹² As for the rest of the beasts, their authority to rule was removed, but an extension of life was granted to them for a certain period of time. ¹³ I continued watching in the night visions,

and I saw One like a son of man
coming with the clouds of heaven.
He approached the Ancient
  of Days
and was escorted before Him.
¹⁴ He was given authority to rule,
  and glory, and a kingdom;
so that those of every people,
nation, and language
should serve Him.
His dominion is
  an everlasting dominion
that will not pass away,
and His kingdom is one
that will not be destroyed.

Interpretation of Vision

¹⁵ "As for me, Daniel, my spirit was deeply distressed within me,ᵃ and the visions in my mind terrified me. ¹⁶ I approached one of those who were standing by and asked him the true meaning of all this. So he let me know the interpretation of these things: ¹⁷ 'These huge beasts, four in number, are four kings who will rise from the earth. ¹⁸ But the holy ones of the •Most High will receive the kingdom and possess it forever, yes, forever and ever.'

¹⁹ "Then I wanted to know the true meaning of the fourth beast, the one different from all the others, extremely terrifying, with iron teeth and bronze claws, devouring, crushing, and trampling with its feet whatever was left. ²⁰ ⌊I also wanted to know⌋ about the 10 horns on its head and about the other horn that came up, before which three fell— the horn that had eyes, and a mouth that spoke arrogantly, and that was more visible than the others. ²¹ As I was watching, this horn made war with the holy ones and was prevailing over them ²² until the Ancient of Days arrived and a judgment was given in favor of the holy ones of the Most High, for the time had come, and the holy ones took possession of the kingdom.

²³ "This is what he said: 'The fourth beast will be a fourth kingdom on the earth, different from all the other kingdoms. It will devour the whole earth, trample it down, and crush it. ²⁴ The 10 horns are 10 kings who will rise from this kingdom. Another, different from the previous ones, will rise after them and subdue three kings. ²⁵ He will speak words against the Most High and oppressᵇ the holy ones of the Most High. He will intend to change religious festivalsᶜ and laws, and the holy ones will be handed over to him for a time, times, and half a time.ᵈ ²⁶ But the court will convene, and his dominion will be taken away, to be completely destroyed forever. ²⁷ The kingdom, dominion, and greatness of the kingdoms under all of heaven will be given to the people, the holy ones of the Most High. His kingdom will be an everlasting kingdom, and all rulers will serve and obey Him.'

ᵃ7:15 Lit *was distressed in the middle of its sheath*   ᵇ7:25 Lit *wear out*   ᶜ7:25 Lit *change times*   ᵈ7:25 Or *for three and a half years*

²⁸ "This is the end of the interpretation. As for me, Daniel, my thoughts terrified me greatly, and my face turned pale,ᵃ but I kept the matter to myself."

Vision of a Ram and a Goat

8 In the third year of King Belshazzar's reign, a vision appeared to me, Daniel, after the one that had appeared to me earlier. ² I saw the vision, and as I watched, I was in the fortress city of Susa, in the province of Elam. I saw in the vision that I was beside the Ulai Canal. ³ I looked up,ᵇ and there was a ram standing beside the canal. He had two horns. The two horns were long, but one was longer than the other, and the longer one came up last. ⁴ I saw the ram charging to the west, the north, and the south. No animal could stand against him, and there was no rescue from his power. He did whatever he wanted and became great.

⁵ As I was observing, a male goat appeared, coming from the west across the surface of the entire earth without touching the ground. The goat had a conspicuous hornᶜ between his eyes. ⁶ He came toward the two-horned ram I had seen standing beside the canal and rushed at him with savage fury. ⁷ I saw him approaching the ram, and infuriated with him, he struck the ram, shattering his two horns, and the ram was not strong enough to stand against him. The goat threw him to the ground and trampled him, and there was no one to rescue the ram from his power. ⁸ Then the male goat became very great, but when he became powerful, the large horn was shattered. Four conspicuous horns came up in its place, ⌊pointing⌋ toward the four winds of heaven.

The Little Horn

⁹ From one of them a little horn emerged and grew extensively toward the south and the east and toward the beautiful land.ᵈ ¹⁰ It grew as high as the heavenly •host, made some of the stars and some of the host fall to the earth, and trampled them. ¹¹ It made itself great, even up to the Prince of the host; it removed His daily sacrifice and overthrew the place of His sanctuary. ¹² Because of rebellion, a host, together with the daily sacrifice, will be given over. The horn will throw truth to the ground and will be successful in whatever it does.

¹³ Then I heard a holy one speaking, and another holy one said to the speaker, "How long will ⌊the events of⌋ this vision last—the daily sacrifice, the rebellion that makes desolate, and the giving over of the sanctuary and of the host to be trampled?"

¹⁴ He said to me,ᵉ "For 2,300 evenings and mornings; then the sanctuary will be restored."

Interpretation of the Vision

¹⁵ While I, Daniel, was watching the vision and trying to understand it, there stood before me someone who appeared to be a man. ¹⁶ I heard a human voice calling from the middle of the Ulai: "Gabriel, explain the vision to this man."

¹⁷ So he approached where I was standing; when he came near, I was terrified and fell facedown. "Son of man," he said to me, "understand that the vision refers to the time of the end."

¹⁸ While he was speaking to me, I fell into a deep sleep, with my face ⌊to the ground⌋. Then he touched me, made me stand up, ¹⁹ and said, "I am here to tell you what will happen at the conclusion

of the time of wrath, because it refers to the appointed time of the end. ²⁰ The two-horned ram that you saw represents the kings of Media and Persia. ²¹ The shaggy goat represents the king of Greece, and the large horn between his eyes represents the first king.ᵃ ²² The four horns that took the place of the shattered horn represent four kingdoms. They will rise from that nation, but without its power.

²³ Near the end of their kingdoms,
   when the rebels have reached
   the full measure of their sin,ᵇ
   an insolent king, skilled
      in intrigue,ᶜ
   will come to the throne.
²⁴ His power will be great,
   but it will not be his own.
   He will cause terrible destruction
   and succeed in whatever he does.
   He will destroy the powerful
   along with the holy people.
²⁵ He will cause deceit to prosper
   through his cunning
      and by his influence,
   and in his own mind he will
      make himself great.
   In ₍a time of₎ peace,
      he will destroy many;
   he will even stand
      against the Prince of princes.
   But he will be shattered,
      not by human hands.
²⁶ The vision of the evenings
      and the mornings
   that has been told is true.
   Now you must seal up the vision
   because it refers to many days
   ₍in the future₎."

²⁷ I, Daniel, was overcome and lay sick for days. Then I got up and went about the king's business. I was greatly dis-turbed by the vision and could not un-derstand it.

Daniel's Prayer

9 In the first year of Darius, who was the son of Ahasuerus, was a Mede by birth, and was ruler over the kingdom of the Chaldeans— ² in the first year of his reign, I, Daniel, understood from the books according to the word of the LORD to Jeremiah the prophet that the number of years for the desolation of Jerusalem would be 70. ³ So I turned my attention to the Lord God to seek Him by prayer and petitions, with fasting, •sackcloth, and ashes.

Daniel's Confession for Israel

⁴ I prayed to the LORD my God and confessed:

Ah, Lord—the great and awe-inspir-ing God who keeps His gracious cov-enant with those who love Him and keep His commandments— ⁵ we have sinned, done wrong, acted wickedly, rebelled, and turned away from Your commandments and ordi-nances. ⁶ We have not listened to Your servants the prophets, who spoke in Your name to our kings, leaders, fathers, and all the people of the land.

⁷ Lord, righteousness belongs to You, but this day public shame belongs to us: the men of Judah, the residents of Jerusalem, and all Israel—those who are near and those who are far, in all the countries where You have dispersed them because of the dis-loyalty they have shown toward You. ⁸ LORD, public shame belongs to us, our kings, our leaders, and our fa-thers, because we have sinned

---

ᵃ8:21 = Alexander the Great ᵇ8:23 Lit *have become complete* ᶜ8:23 Lit *king, and understanding riddles*

against You. ⁹ Compassion and forgiveness belong to the Lord our God, though we have rebelled against Him ¹⁰ and have not obeyed the voice of the LORD our God by following His instructions that He set before us through His servants the prophets.

¹¹ All Israel has broken Your law and turned away, refusing to obey You. The promised curseª written in the law of Moses, the servant of God, has been poured out on us because we have sinned against Him. ¹² He has carried out His words that He spoke against us and against our rulersᵇ by bringing on us so great a disaster that nothing like what has been done to Jerusalem has ever been done under all of heaven. ¹³ Just as it is written in the law of Moses, all this disaster has come on us, yet we have not appeased the LORD our God by turning from our injustice and paying attention to Your truth. ¹⁴ So the LORD kept the disaster in mind and brought it on us, for the LORD our God is righteous in all He has done. But we have not obeyed Him.

Daniel Prays for Jerusalem

¹⁵ Now, Lord our God, who brought Your people out of the land of Egypt with a mighty hand and made Your name ⌊renowned⌋ as it is this day, we have sinned, we have acted wickedly. ¹⁶ Lord, in keeping with all Your righteous acts, may Your anger and wrath turn away from Your city Jerusalem, Your holy mountain; for because of our sins and the injustices of our fathers, Jerusalem and Your people have become an object of ridicule to all those around us.

¹⁷ Therefore, our God, hear the prayer and the petitions of Your servant. Show Your favor to Your desolate sanctuary for the Lord's sake. ¹⁸ Listen,ᶜ my God, and hear. Open Your eyes and see our desolations and the city called by Your name. For we are not presenting our petitions before You based on our righteous acts, but based on Your abundant compassion. ¹⁹ Lord, hear! Lord, forgive! Lord, listen and act! My God, for Your own sake, do not delay, because Your city and Your people are called by Your name.

70 Weeks of Years

²⁰ While I was speaking, praying, confessing my sin and the sin of my people Israel, and presenting my petition before •Yahweh my God concerning the holy mountain of my God— ²¹ while I was praying, Gabriel, the man I had seen in the first vision, came to me in my extreme weariness, about the time of the evening offering. ²² He gave me this explanation: "Daniel, I've come now to give you understanding. ²³ At the beginning of your petitions an answer went out, and I have come to give it, for you are treasured ⌊by God⌋. So consider the message and understand the vision:

²⁴ Seventy weeksᵈ are decreed
  about your people
    and your holy city—
  to bring the rebellion to an end,
  to put a stop to sin,
  to wipe away injustice,
  to bring in
    everlasting righteousness,
  to seal up vision and prophecy,

ª9:11 Lit *The curse and the oath* ᵇ9:12 Lit *against rulers who ruled us* ᶜ9:18 Lit *Stretch out Your ear* ᵈ9:24 = 490 years; 2 Ch 36:21; Jr 25:11-12; 29:10

and to anoint the most holy place.

²⁵ Know and understand this:

From the issuing of the decree
to restore and rebuild Jerusalem
until •Messiah the Prince[a]
will be seven weeks
  and 62 weeks.[b]
It will be rebuilt with a plaza
  and a moat,
but in difficult times.

²⁶ After those 62 weeks[c]
the Messiah will be cut off
and will have nothing.
The people of the coming prince
will destroy the city
  and the sanctuary.
The[d] end will come with a flood,
and until the end
  there will be[e] war;
desolations are decreed.

²⁷ He will make a firm covenant[f]
with many for one week,[g]
but in the middle of the week
he will put a stop to sacrifice
  and offering.
And the abomination of desolation
will be on a wing of the temple[h i]
until the decreed destruction
is poured out on the desolator."

Vision of a Glorious One

10 In the third year of Cyrus king of Persia, a message was revealed to Daniel, who was named Belteshazzar. The message was true and was about a great conflict. He understood the message and had understanding of the vision.

² In those days I, Daniel, was mourning for three full weeks. ³ I didn't eat any rich food, no meat or wine entered my mouth, and I didn't put any oil ʟon my body ʟ until the three weeks were over. ⁴ On the twenty-fourth day of the first month,[j] as I was standing on the bank of the great river, the Tigris, ⁵ I looked up, and there was a man dressed in linen, with a belt of gold from Uphaz[k] around his waist. ⁶ His body was like topaz,[l] his face like the brilliance of lightning, his eyes like flaming torches, his arms and feet like the gleam of polished bronze, and the sound of his words like the sound of a multitude.

⁷ Only I, Daniel, saw the vision. The men who were with me did not see it, but a great terror fell on them, and they ran and hid. ⁸ I was left alone, looking at this great vision. No strength was left in me; my face grew deathly pale,[m] and I was powerless. ⁹ I heard the words he said, and when I heard them I fell into a deep sleep,[n] with my face to the ground.

Angelic Conflict

¹⁰ Suddenly, a hand touched me and raised me to my hands and knees. ¹¹ He said to me, "Daniel, you are a man treasured ʟby Godʟ. Understand the words that I'm saying to you. Stand on your feet, for I have now been sent to you." After he said this to me, I stood trembling.

¹² "Don't be afraid, Daniel," he said to me, "for from the first day that you purposed to understand and to humble yourself before your God, your prayers were heard. I have come because of your prayers. ¹³ But the prince of the kingdom of Persia opposed me for 21 days. Then Michael, one of the chief princes, came to help me after I had been left there with the kings of Persia. ¹⁴ Now I have come to help you under-

---

ᵃ9:25 Or *until an anointed one, a prince* ᵇ9:25 = 49 years and 434 years ᶜ9:26 = 434 years ᵈ9:26 Lit *Its,* or *His*
ᵉ9:26 Or *end of a* ᶠ9:27 Or *will enforce a covenant* ᵍ9:27 = 7 years ʰ9:27 LXX; MT reads *of abominations*
ⁱ9:27 Or *And the desolator will be on the wing of abominations,* or *And the desolator will come on the wings of monsters* (or *of horror*); Hb obscure ʲ10:4 Nisan (March–April) ᵏ10:5 Some Hb mss read *Ophir* ˡ10:6 The identity of this stone is uncertain. ᵐ10:8 Lit *my splendor was turned on me to ruin* ⁿ10:9 Lit *a sleep on my face*

stand what will happen to your people in the last days, for the vision refers to those days."

[15] While he was saying these words to me, I turned my face toward the ground and was speechless. [16] Suddenly one with human likeness touched my lips. I opened my mouth and said to the one standing in front of me, "My lord, because of the vision, I am overwhelmed and powerless. [17] How can someone like me, your servant,[a] speak with someone like you, my lord? Now I have no strength, and there is no breath in me." [18] Then the one with human likeness touched me again and strengthened me. [19] He said, "Don't be afraid, you who are[b] treasured ⌊by God⌋. Peace to you; be very strong!"

As he spoke to me, I was strengthened and said, "Let my lord speak, for you have strengthened me."

[20] He said, "Do you know why I've come to you? I must return at once to fight against the prince of Persia, and when I leave, the prince of Greece will come. [21] No one has the courage to support me against them except Michael, your prince. However, I will tell you what is recorded in the book of truth.

11 [1] In the first year of Darius the Mede, I stood up to strengthen and protect him. [2] Now I will tell you the truth.

Prophecies about Persia and Greece

"Three more kings will arise in Persia, and the fourth will be far richer than the others. By the power he gains through his riches, he will stir up everyone against the kingdom of Greece. [3] Then a warrior king will arise; he will rule a vast realm and do whatever he wants. [4] But as soon as he is established, his kingdom will be broken up and divided to the four winds of heaven, but not to his descendants; it will not be the same kingdom that he ruled, because his kingdom will be uprooted and will go to others besides them.

Kings of South and North

[5] "The king of the South will grow powerful, but one of his commanders will grow more powerful and will rule a kingdom greater than his. [6] After some years they will form an alliance, and the daughter of the king of the South will go to the king of the North to seal the agreement. She will not retain power, and his strength will not endure. She will be given up, together with her entourage, her father,[c] and the one who supported her during those times. [7] In the place of the king of the South, one from her family[d] will rise up, come against the army, and enter the fortress of the king of the North. He will take action against them and triumph. [8] He will take even their gods captive to Egypt, with their metal images and their precious articles of silver and gold. For some years he will stay away from the king of the North, [9] who will enter the kingdom of the king of the South and then return to his own land.

Infuriated King of South

[10] "His sons will mobilize for war and assemble a large number of armed forces. They will advance, sweeping through like a flood,[e] and will again wage war as far as his fortress. [11] Infuriated, the king of the South will march out to fight with the king of the North, who will raise a great multitude, but the multitude will be handed over to

[a]**10:17** Lit *Can I, a servant of my lord*   [b]**10:19** Lit *afraid, man*   [c]**11:6** One Hb ms, Theod read *child*; Vg, Syr read *children*   [d]**11:7** Lit *from the shoot of her roots*   [e]**11:10** Lit *advance and overflow and pass through*

his enemy. [12] When the multitude is carried off, he will become arrogant and cause tens of thousands to fall, but he will not triumph. [13] The king of the North will again raise a multitude larger than the first. After some years[a] he will advance with a great army and many supplies.

Enemies of King of South

[14] "In those times many will rise up against the king of the South. Violent ones among your own people will assert themselves to fulfill a vision, but they will fail. [15] Then the king of the North will come, build up an assault ramp, and capture a well-fortified city. The forces of the South will not stand; even their select troops will not be able to resist. [16] The king of the North who comes against him will do whatever he wants, and no one can oppose him. He will establish himself in the beautiful land[b] with total destruction in his hand. [17] He will resolve to come with the force of his whole kingdom and will reach an agreement with him.[c] He will give him a daughter in marriage[d] to destroy it,[e] but she will not stand with him or support him. [18] Then he will turn his attention to the coasts and islands[f] and capture many. But a commander will put an end to his taunting; instead, he will turn his taunts against him. [19] He will turn his attention back to the fortresses of his own land, but he will stumble, fall, and be no more.

[20] "In his place one will arise who will send out a tax collector for the glory of the kingdom; but within a few days he will be shattered, though not in anger[g] or in battle.

Kingdom Seized by Intrigue

[21] "In his place a despised person will arise; royal honors will not be given to him, but he will come during a time of peace[h] and seize the kingdom by intrigue. [22] A flood of forces will be swept away before him; they will be shattered, as well as the covenant prince. [23] After an alliance is made with him, he will act deceitfully. He will rise to power with a small nation.[i] [24] During a time of peace,[j] he will come into the richest parts of the province and do what his fathers and predecessors never did. He will lavish plunder, loot, and wealth on his followers, and he will make plans against fortified cities, but only for a time.

[25] "With a large army he will stir up his power and his courage against the king of the South. The king of the South will prepare for battle with an extremely large and powerful army, but he will not succeed, because plots will be made against him. [26] Those who eat his provisions will destroy him; his army will be swept away, and many will fall slain. [27] The two kings, whose hearts are bent on evil, will speak lies at the same table but to no avail, for still the end will come at the appointed time. [28] The king of the North will return to his land with great wealth, but his heart will be set against the holy covenant;[k] he will take action, then return to his own land.

Abomination of Desolation Set Up

[29] "At the appointed time he will come again to the South, but this time[l] will not be like the first. [30] Ships of Kittim[m] will come against him, and be-

ing intimidated, he will withdraw. Then he will rage against the holy covenant and take action. On his return, he will favor those who abandon the holy covenant. [31] His forces will rise up and desecrate the temple fortress. They will abolish the daily sacrifice and set up the <u>abomination of desolation</u>. [32] With flattery he will corrupt those who act wickedly toward the covenant, but the people who know their God will be strong and take action. [33] Those who are wise among the people will give understanding to many, yet they will die by sword and flame, and be captured and plundered for a time. [34] When defeated, they will be helped by some, but many others will join them insincerely. [35] Some of the wise will fall so that they may be refined, purified, and cleansed until the time of the end, for it will still come at the appointed time.

Blasphemy of King

[36] "Then the king will do whatever he wants. He will exalt and magnify himself above every god, and he will say outrageous things against the God of gods. He will be successful until the time of wrath is completed, because what has been decreed will be accomplished. [37] He will not show regard for the gods[a] of his fathers, the god longed for by women, or for any other god, because he will magnify himself above all. [38] Instead, he will honor a god of fortresses—a god his fathers did not know—with gold, silver, precious stones, and riches. [39] He will deal with the strongest fortresses with ⌞the help of⌟ a foreign god. He will greatly honor those who acknowledge him,[b] making them rulers over many and distributing land as a reward.

Battle at End Time

[40] "At the time of the end, the king of the South will engage him in battle, but the king of the North will storm against him with chariots, horsemen, and many ships. He will invade countries and sweep through them like a flood. [41] He will also invade the beautiful land, and many will fall. But these will escape from his power: Edom, Moab, and the prominent people[c] of the Ammonites. [42] He will extend his power against the countries, and not even the land of Egypt will escape. [43] He will get control over the hidden treasures of gold and silver and over all the riches of Egypt. The Libyans and •Cushites will also be in submission.[d] [44] But reports from the east and the north will terrify him, and he will go out with great fury to destroy and annihilate many. [45] He will pitch his royal tents between the sea and[e] the beautiful holy mountain, but he will meet his end with no one to help him.

Michael Rises Up

12 At that time
   Michael the great prince
   who stands watch over your people
      will rise up.
   There will be a time of distress
   such as never has occurred
   since nations came into being
      until that time.
   But at that time all your people
   who are found written in the book
      will escape.

Resurrection of Just and Unjust

[2] Many of those who sleep in the dust
      of the earth will awake,
      some to eternal life,

---

a **11:37** Or God   b **11:39** Or those he acknowledges   c **11:41** Lit the first   d **11:43** Lit Cushites at his steps   e **11:45** Or the seas at

and some to shame
  and eternal contempt.
³ Those who are wise will shine
  like the bright expanse
  ⌊of the heavens⌋,
  and those who lead many
  to righteousness,
  like the stars forever and ever.

Divine Instructions to Daniel

⁴ "But you, Daniel, keep these words secret and seal the book until the time of the end. Many will roam about, and knowledge will increase."ᵃ
⁵ Then I, Daniel, looked, and two others were standing there, one on this bank of the river and one on the other. ⁶ One said to the man dressed in linen, who was above the waters of the river, "How long until the end of these extraordinary things?" ⁷ Then I heard the man dressed in linen, who was above the waters of the river. He raised both his handsᵇ toward heaven and swore by

Him who lives eternally that it would be for a time, times, and half ⌊a time⌋. When the power of the holy people is shattered, all these things will be completed.

Secret Sealed until End

⁸ I heard but did not understand. So I asked, "My lord, what will be the outcome of these things?"
⁹ He said, "Go on your way, Daniel, for the words are secret and sealed until the time of the end. ¹⁰ Many will be purified, cleansed, and refined, but the wicked will act wickedly; none of the wicked will understand, but the wise will understand. ¹¹ From the time the daily sacrifice is abolished and the abomination of desolation is set up, there will be 1,290 days. ¹² Blessed is the one who waits for and reaches 1,335 days. ¹³ But as for you, go on your way to the end;ᶜ you will rest, then rise to your destiny at the end of the days."

ᵃ**12:4** LXX reads *and the earth will be filled with unrighteousness* ᵇ**12:7** Lit *raised his right and his left* ᶜ**12:13** LXX omits *to the end*

HOSEA

1 The word of the LORD that came to Hosea son of Beeri during the reigns of Uzziah, Jotham, Ahaz, and Hezekiah, kings of Judah, and of Jeroboam son of Joash, king of Israel.

Hosea's Marriage and Children

² When the LORD first spoke to Hosea, He said this to him:

> Go and marry a promiscuous wife
> and ⌊have⌋ children of promiscuity,
> for the whole land
>   has been promiscuous
> by abandoning the LORD.

³ So he went and married Gomer daughter of Diblaim, and she conceived and bore him a son. ⁴ Then the LORD said to him:

> Name him Jezreel,
>   for in a little while
> I will avenge the bloodshed
>   of Jezreel
> on the house of Jehu
> and put an end to the kingdom
>   of the house of Israel.
> ⁵ On that day I will break the bow
>   of Israel
> in the valley of Jezreel.ᵃ

⁶ She conceived again and gave birth to a daughter, and the LORD said to him:

> Name her No Compassion,ᵇ for I
>   will no longer have compassion
> on the house of Israel.
> I will certainly take them away.
> ⁷ But I will have compassion
>   on the house of Judah,
> and I will deliver them by
>   the LORD their God.

> I will not deliver them
>   by bow, sword, or war,
> or by horses and cavalry.

⁸ After Gomer had weaned No Compassion, she conceived and gave birth to a son. ⁹ Then the LORD said:

> Name him Not My People,ᶜ
> for you are not My people,
> and I will not be your God.ᵈ
> ¹⁰ᵉ Yet the number of the Israelites
> will be like the sand of the sea,
> which cannot be measured
>   or counted.
> And in the place where
>   they were told:
> You are not My people,
> they will be called:
> Sons of the living God.
> ¹¹ And the Judeans and the Israelites
> will be gathered together.
> They will appoint for themselves
>   a single ruler,
> and go up fromᶠ the land.
> For the day of Jezreel will be great.

2ᵍ Callʰ your brothers: My People
>   and your sisters: Compassion.

Israel's Adultery Rebuked

> ² Rebuke your mother; rebuke ⌊her⌋.
> For she is not My wife and I am not
>   her husband.
> Let her remove
>   the promiscuous look
>   from her face
> and her adultery
>   from between her breasts.
> ³ Otherwise, I will strip her naked
> and expose her as she was
>   on the day of her birth.
> I will make her like a desert

ᵃ**1:5** = God sows ᵇ**1:6** Hb *Lo-ruhamah* ᶜ**1:9** Hb *Lo-ammi* ᵈ**1:9** Lit *not be yours* ᵉ**1:10** Hs 2:1 in Hb ᶠ**1:11** Or *and flourish in*; Hb obscure ᵍ**2:1** Hs 2:3 in Hb ʰ**2:1** Lit *Say to*

and like a parched land,
and I will let her die of thirst.
⁴ I will have no compassion
on her children
because they are the children
of promiscuity.
⁵ For their mother is promiscuous;
she conceived them
and acted shamefully.
For she thought: I will go
after my lovers,
the men who give me my food
and water,
my wool and flax, my oil and drink.

God Judges Israel

⁶ Therefore, this is what I will do:
I will block her^a way with thorns;
I will enclose her with a wall,
so that she cannot find her paths.
⁷ She will pursue her lovers
but not catch them;
she will seek them
but not find ⌊them⌋.
Then she will think:
I will go back
to my former husband,
for then it was better for me
than now.
⁸ She does not recognize
that it is I who gave her the grain,
the new wine, and the oil.
I lavished silver and gold on her,
which they used for •Baal.
⁹ Therefore, I will take back My grain
in its time
and My new wine in its season;
I will take away My wool and linen,
which were to cover
her nakedness.
¹⁰ Now I will expose her shame
in the sight of her lovers,
and no one will rescue her
from My hands.

¹¹ I will put an end to all
her celebrations:
her feasts, New Moons,
and Sabbaths—
all her festivals.
¹² I will devastate her vines
and fig trees.
She thinks that these are
her wages
that her lovers have given her.
I will turn them into a thicket,
and the wild animals will eat them.
¹³ And I will punish her for the days
of the Baals
when she burned incense to them,
put on her rings and jewelry,
and went after her lovers,
but forgot Me.
⌊This is⌋ the LORD's declaration.

Israel's Adultery Forgiven

¹⁴ Therefore, I am going
to persuade her,
lead her to the wilderness,
and speak tenderly to her.^b
¹⁵ There I will give her vineyards
back to her
and make the Valley of Achor^c
into a gateway of hope.
There she will respond as ⌊she did⌋
in the days of her youth,
as in the day she came out
of the land of Egypt.
¹⁶ In that day—
the LORD's declaration—
you will call ⌊Me⌋: My husband,
and no longer call Me: My Baal.^d
¹⁷ For I will remove the names
of the Baals
from her mouth;
they will no longer be remembered
by their names.
¹⁸ On that day I will make a covenant
for them

with the wild animals, the birds
   of the sky,
and the creatures that crawl
   on the ground.
I will shatter bow, sword,
and weapons of war in the land[a]
and will enable the people
   to rest securely.
19 I will take you to be
   My wife forever.
I will take you to be My wife
   in righteousness,
justice, love, and compassion.
20 I will take you to be My wife
   in faithfulness,
and you will know the LORD.
21 On that day I will respond—
       the LORD's declaration.
I will respond to the sky,
and it will respond to the earth.
22 The earth will respond to the grain,
the new wine, and the oil,
and they will respond to Jezreel.
23 I will sow her[b] in the land
   for Myself,
and I will have compassion
   on No Compassion;
I will say to Not My People:
You are My people,
and he will say: ₍You are₎ My God.

Restoration of Israel

3 Then the LORD said to me, "Go
again; show love to a woman who is
loved by another man and is an adulteress, just as the LORD loves the Israelites
though they turn to other gods and love
raisin cakes."

2 So I bought her for 15 •shekels of silver and five bushels of barley.[c] [d] 3 I said
to her, "You must live with me many
days. Don't be promiscuous or belong to
any man, and I will act the same way toward you."

4 For the Israelites must live many days
without king or prince, without sacrifice
or sacred pillar, and without •ephod or
household idols. 5 Afterwards, the people of Israel will return and seek the
LORD their God and David their king.
They will come with awe to the LORD
and to His goodness in the last days.

God's Case against Israel

4 Hear the word of the LORD,
   people of Israel,
for the LORD has a case
   against the inhabitants of the land:
There is no truth, no faithful love,
and no knowledge of God
   in the land!
2 Cursing, lying, murder, stealing,
   and adultery are rampant;
one act of bloodshed
   follows another.
3 For this reason the land mourns,
and everyone who lives
   in it languishes,
along with the wild animals
   and the birds of the sky;
even the fish of the sea disappear.

God Accuses Priests

4 But let no one dispute;
   let no one argue,
for My case is against you priests.[e] [f]
5 You will stumble by day;
the prophet will also stumble
   with you by night.
And I will destroy your mother.
6 My people are destroyed for lack
   of knowledge.
Because you have
   rejected knowledge,

---

[a]2:18 Or war on the earth   [b]2:23 = Israel   [c]3:2 LXX reads barley and a measure of wine   [d]3:2 Lit silver, a homer of
barley, and a lethek of barley   [e]4:4 Text emended; MT reads argue, and your people are like those contending with a
priest   [f]4:4 Hb obscure

I will reject you from serving
as My priest.
Since you have forgotten the law
of your God,
I will also forget your sons.

7 The more they multiplied,
the more they sinned against Me.
I[a] will change their honor
into disgrace.
8 They feed on the sin[b] of My people;
they have an appetite
for their transgressions.
9 ⌊The same judgment⌋ will happen
to both people and priests.
I will punish them for their ways
and repay them for their deeds.
10 They will eat but not be satisfied;
they will be promiscuous
but not multiply;
for they have abandoned
their devotion to the LORD.
11 Promiscuity, wine, and new wine
take away ⌊one's⌋ understanding.

God Condemns Idolatry

12 My people consult
their wooden ⌊idols⌋,
and their divining rods
inform them.
For a spirit of promiscuity
leads them astray;
they act promiscuously
in disobedience to[c] their God.
13 They sacrifice on the mountaintops,
and they burn offerings on the hills,
and under oaks, poplars,
and terebinths,
because their shade is pleasant.
And so your daughters
act promiscuously
and your daughters-in-law
commit adultery.
14 I will not punish your daughters

when they act promiscuously
or your daughters-in-law
when they commit adultery,
for the men themselves go off
with prostitutes
and make sacrifices
with cult prostitutes.
People without discernment
are doomed.

Warnings for Israel and Judah

15 Israel, if you act promiscuously,
don't let Judah become guilty!
Do not go to Gilgal
or make a pilgrimage to Beth-aven,[d]
and do not swear an oath:
As the LORD lives!
16 For Israel is as obstinate
as a stubborn cow.
Can the LORD now shepherd them
like a lamb in an open meadow?
17 Ephraim is attached to idols;
leave him alone!
18 When their drinking is over,
they turn to promiscuity.
Israel's leaders[e] fervently
love disgrace.[f]
19 A wind with its wings will
carry them off,[g]
and they will be ashamed
of their sacrifices.

Scope of God's Judgment

5 Hear this, priests!
Pay attention, house of Israel!
Listen, royal house!
For the judgment applies to you
because you have been a snare
at Mizpah
and a net spread out on Tabor.
2 Rebels are deeply involved
in slaughter;
I will be a punishment
for all of them.[f]

3 I know Ephraim,
  and Israel is not hidden from Me.
  For now, Ephraim,
  you have acted promiscuously;
  Israel is defiled.

"A Spirit of Promiscuity"

4 Their actions do not allow ⌊them⌋
  to return to their God,
  for a spirit of promiscuity
    is among them,
  and they do not know the LORD.
5 Israel's arrogance testifies
    against them.ᵃ
  Both Israel and Ephraim stumble
  because of their wickedness;
  even Judah will stumble with them.
6 They go with their flocks and herds
  to seek the LORD
  but do not find ⌊Him⌋;
  He has withdrawn from them.
7 They betrayed the LORD;
  indeed, they gave birth
    to illegitimate children.
  Now the New Moon
    will devour them
  along with their fields.

8 Blow the horn in Gibeah,
  the trumpet in Ramah;
  raise the war cry in Beth-aven:
  After you, Benjamin!
9 Ephraim will become a desolation
  on the day of punishment;
  I announce what is certain
  among the tribes of Israel.
10 The princes of Judah are like those
  who move boundary markers;
  I will pour out My fury on them
  like water.
11 Ephraim is oppressed,
    crushed in judgment,
  for he is determined to follow
  what is worthless.ᵇ
12 So I am like rot to Ephraim

and like decay to the house
  of Judah.
13 When Ephraim saw his sickness
  and Judah his wound,
  Ephraim went to Assyria
  and sent ⌊a delegation⌋
    to the great king.ᶜ
  But he cannot cure you or heal
  your wound.
14 For I am like a lion to Ephraim
  and like a young lion to the house
  of Judah.
  Yes, I will tear ⌊them⌋ to pieces
    and depart.
  I will carry ⌊them⌋ off,
  and no one can rescue ⌊them⌋.
15 I will depart and return to My place
  until they recognize their guilt
    and seek My face;
  they will search for Me
    in their distress.

Call to Repentance

6 Come, let us return to the LORD.
  For He has torn ⌊us⌋,
  and He will heal us;
  He has wounded ⌊us⌋,
  and He will bind up our wounds.
2 He will revive us after two days,
  and on the third day
    He will raise us up
  so we can live in His presence.
3 Let us strive to know the LORD.
  His appearance is as sure as
    the dawn.
  He will come to us like the rain,
  like the spring showers that water
    the land.

LORD's First Lament

4 What am I going to do
    with you, Ephraim?
  What am I going to do
    with you, Judah?

ᵃ5:5 Lit against his face ᵇ5:11 Or follow a command; Hb obscure ᶜ5:13 Or to King Yareb

Your loyalty is like
   the morning mist
and like the early dew
   that vanishes.
⁵ This is why I have used
   the prophets
to cut them down;ᵃ
I have killed them with the words
   of My mouth.
My judgment strikes
   like lightning.ᵇ

Loyalty, Not Sacrifice

⁶ For I desire loyalty
   and not sacrifice,
the knowledge of God rather than
   •burnt offerings.

⁷ But they, like Adam,ᶜ have violated
   the covenant;
there they have betrayed Me.
⁸ Gilead is a city of evildoers,
   tracked with bloody footprints.
⁹ Like robbers who wait in ambush
   for someone,
a band of priests murders
   on the road to Shechem.
They commit atrocities.
¹⁰ I have seen something horrible
   in the house of Israel:
Ephraim's promiscuity is there;
   Israel is defiled.
¹¹ A harvest is also appointed
   for you, Judah.

When Iᵈ return My people
   from captivity,

7 ¹ when I heal Israel,
the sins of Ephraim and the crimes
   of Samaria
will be exposed.
For they practice fraud;
a thief breaks in;
a gang pillages outside.

² But they never consider
   that I remember all their evil.
Now their sins are all around them;
   they are right in front of My face.

Israel's Corruption

³ They please the king
   with their evil,
the princes with their lies.
⁴ All of them commit adultery;
⌞they are⌟ like an oven heated
   by a baker
who stops stirring ⌞the fire⌟
from the kneading of the dough
   until it is leavened.
⁵ On the day of our king,
the princes are sick with the heat
   of wine—
there is a conspiracy with traitors.ᵉ
⁶ For they—their hearts
   like an oven—
draw him into their oven.
Their anger smolders all night;
in the morning it blazes
   like a flaming fire.
⁷ All of them are as hot as an oven,
   and they consume their rulers.
All their kings fall;
not one of them calls on Me.ᶠ

⁸ Ephraim has allowed himself
   to get mixed up with the nations.
Ephraim is unturned bread,
   baked on a griddle.
⁹ Foreigners consume his strength,
   but he does not notice.
Even his hair is streaked with gray,
   but he does not notice.
¹⁰ Israel's arrogance testifies
   against them,ᵍ
yet they do not return to the LORD
   their God,
and for all this, they do not
   seek Him.

ᵃ**6:5** Or *have cut down the prophets*   ᵇ**6:5** LXX, Syr, Tg; MT reads *Your judgments go out as light*   ᶜ**6:7** Or *they, as at Adam,* or *they, like men,*   ᵈ**6:11** Or *you, Judah, when I*   ᵉ**7:5** Lit *wine—he stretches out his hand to scorners*; Hb obscure   ᶠ**7:3-7** These vv. may refer to a king's assassination; Hb obscure.   ᵍ**7:10** Lit *against his face*

¹¹ So Ephraim has become like a silly,
   senseless dove;
they call to Egypt, and they go
   to Assyria.

"I Will Spread My Net"

¹² As they are going, I will spread
   My net over them;
I will bring them down like birds
   of the sky.
I will discipline them
   in accordance
with the news that
   reaches^a their assembly.

LORD's Second Lament

¹³ Woe to them, for they fled
   from Me;
destruction to them,
   for they rebelled against Me!
Though I want to redeem ⌊them⌋,
   they speak lies against Me.
¹⁴ They do not cry to Me
   from their hearts;
rather, they wail on their beds.
They slash themselves^b for grain
   and wine;
they turn away from Me.
¹⁵ I trained and strengthened
   their arms,
but they plot evil against Me.
¹⁶ They turn, but not to what
   is above;^c
they are like a faulty bow.
Their leaders will fall by the sword
because of the cursing
   of their tongue.
They will be ridiculed for this
   in the land of Egypt.

Israel's False Hopes

8 ⌊Put⌋ the horn to your mouth!
   One like an eagle comes
against the house of the LORD,
because they transgress
   My covenant
and rebel against My law.
² Israel cries out to Me:
My God, we know You!
³ Israel has rejected what is good;
an enemy will pursue him.

Israel's Idols

⁴ They have installed kings,
but not through Me.
They have appointed leaders,
but without My approval.
They make their silver and gold
into idols for themselves
for their own destruction.^d
⁵ Your calf-idol^e is rejected, Samaria.
My anger burns against them.
How long will they be incapable
   of innocence?
⁶ For this thing is from Israel—
a craftsman made it,
   and it is not God.
The calf of Samaria will be smashed
   to bits!

⁷ Indeed, <u>they sow the wind
and reap the whirlwind</u>.
There is no standing grain;
what sprouts fails to yield flour.
Even if they did,
foreigners would swallow it up.
⁸ Israel is swallowed up!
Now they are among the nations
like discarded pottery.
⁹ For they have gone up to Assyria
⌊like⌋ a wild donkey going off
   on its own.
Ephraim has paid for love.
¹⁰ Even though they hire ⌊lovers⌋
   among the nations,
I will now round them up,
and they will begin to decrease
   in number

under the burden of the king
and leaders.

11 When Ephraim multiplied his altars
for sin,
they became his altars for sinning.
12 Though I were to write out for him
ten thousand points of My law,
they would be[a] regarded
as something alien.
13 Though they offer sacrificial gifts[b]
and eat the flesh,
the LORD does not accept them.
Now He will remember their guilt
and punish their sins;
they will return to Egypt.
14 Israel has forgotten his Maker
and built palaces;
Judah has also multiplied
fortified cities.
I will send fire on their cities,
and it will consume their citadels.

The Coming Exile

9 Israel, do not rejoice jubilantly
as the nations do,
for you have acted promiscuously,
leaving your God.
You have loved the wages
of a prostitute
on every grain-threshing floor.
2 Threshing floor and wine vat
will not sustain them,
and the new wine will fail them.
3 They will not stay in the land
of the LORD.
Instead, Ephraim will return
to Egypt,
and they will eat unclean food
in Assyria.
4 They will not pour out
their wine offerings to the LORD,
and their sacrifices
will not please Him.

Their ⌊food⌋ will be like the bread
of mourners;
all who eat it become defiled.
For their bread will be
for their appetites ⌊alone⌋;
it will not enter the house
of the LORD.
5 What will you do on a festival day,
on the day of the LORD's feast?
6 For even if they flee
from devastation,
Egypt will gather them,
and Memphis will bury them.
Thistles will take possession
of their precious silver;
thorns will invade their tents.

Days of Punishment
and Retribution

7 The days of punishment have come;
the days of retribution have come.
Let Israel recognize it!
The prophet is a fool,
and the inspired man is insane,
because of the magnitude
of your guilt and hostility.
8 Ephraim's watchman is
with my God.
The prophet ⌊encounters⌋
a fowler's snare
on all his ways.
Hostility is in the house of his God!
9 They have deeply
corrupted themselves
as in the days of Gibeah.
He will remember their guilt;
He will punish their sins.

Israel's Shame

10 I discovered Israel
like grapes in the wilderness.
I saw your fathers
like the first fruit of the fig tree
in its first season.

---

[a]8:12 Or Though I wrote out . . . law, they are   [b]8:13 Hb obscure

But they went to Baal-peor,
consecrated themselves
  to Shame,[a]
and became detestable,
like the thing they loved.

Ephraim's Barrenness

11 Ephraim's glory will fly away
     like a bird:
   no birth, no gestation,
     no conception.
12 Even if they raise children,
   I will bereave them of each one.
   Yes, woe to them when I depart
     from them!
13 I have seen Ephraim like Tyre,
     planted in a meadow,
   so Ephraim will bring out
     his children
   to the executioner.
14 Give them, LORD—
   What should You give?
   Give them a womb
     that miscarries
   and breasts that are dry!

15 All their evil appears at Gilgal,
   for there I came to hate them.
   I will drive them from My house
   because of their evil,
     wicked actions.
   I will no longer love them;
   all their leaders are rebellious.
16 Ephraim is blighted;
   their roots are withered;
   they cannot bear fruit.
   Even if they bear children,
   I will kill the precious offspring
     of their wombs.
17 My God will reject them
   because they have not listened
     to Him;
   they will become wanderers
     among the nations.

Vine and Calf

10 Israel is a lush[b] vine;
     it yields fruit for itself.
   The more his fruit increased,
   the more he increased the altars.
   The better his land produced,
   the better they made
     the sacred pillars.

Devious Hearts

2 Their hearts are devious;[c]
  now they must bear their guilt.
  The LORD will break down
    their altars
  and demolish their sacred pillars.
3 In fact, they are now saying:
  "We have no king!
  For we do not •fear the LORD.
  What can a king do for us?"
4 They speak ⌊mere⌋ words,
  taking false oaths
    while making covenants.
  So lawsuits break out
  like poisonous weeds
    in the furrows of a field.

Samaria's Calf Idol

5 The residents of Samaria
    will have anxiety
  over the calf of Beth-aven.
  Indeed, its idolatrous priests
    rejoiced over it;
  the people will mourn over it,
  over its glory.
  It will certainly depart from them.
6 The calf itself will be taken
    to Assyria
  as an offering to the great king.[d]
  Ephraim will experience shame;
  Israel will be ashamed
    of its counsel.
7 Samaria's king will disappear[e]
  like foam[f] on the surface
    of the water.

---

[a]9:10 = a Hb term of derision for *Baal*   [b]10:1 Or *ravaged*   [c]10:2 Or *divided*   [d]10:6 Or *to King Yareb*   [e]10:7 Or *will be cut off*   [f]10:7 Or *a stick*

8 The •high places of Aven,
  the sin of Israel,
will be destroyed;
thorns and thistles will grow
  over their altars.
They will say to the mountains,
  "Cover us!"
and to the hills, "Fall on us!"

Sin Defeats Israel

9 Israel, you have sinned
  since the days of Gibeah;
they have taken their stand there.
Will not war against the unjust
  overtake them in Gibeah?
10 I will discipline them
  at my discretion;
nations will be gathered
  against them
to put them in bondage[a]
for their two crimes.

11 Ephraim is a well-trained
  young cow
that loves to thresh,
but I will place a yoke on[b] her
  fine neck.
I will harness Ephraim;
Judah will plow;
Jacob will do the final plowing.
12 Sow righteousness
  for yourselves
and reap faithful love;
break up your untilled ground.
It is time to seek the LORD
until He comes
  and sends righteousness
on you like the rain.

13 You have plowed wickedness
  and reaped injustice;
you have eaten the fruit of lies.
Because you have trusted
  in your own way[c]

and in your large number
  of soldiers,
14 the roar of battle will rise
  against your people,
and all your fortifications
  will be demolished
in a day of war,
like Shalman's destruction
  of Beth-arbel.
Mothers will be dashed to pieces
along with ⌊their⌋ children.
15 So it will be done to you, Bethel,
because of your extreme evil.
At dawn the king of Israel will be
  totally destroyed.

LORD's Love for Israel

11 When Israel was a child,
I loved him,
and out of Egypt I called My son.
2 ⌊The more⌋ they[d] called them,[e]
⌊the more⌋ they[e] departed from Me.[f]
They kept sacrificing to the •Baals
and burning offerings to idols.
3 It was I who taught Ephraim
  to walk,
taking them[g] in My arms,
but they never knew
  that I healed them.
4 I led them with human cords,
  with ropes of kindness.
To them I was like one
who eases the yoke from their jaws;
I bent down to give them food.
5 Israel will not return to the land
  of Egypt
and Assyria will be his king,
because they refused to repent.
6 A sword will whirl
  through his cities;
it will destroy and devour the bars
  of his gates,[h]
because of their schemes.

---

[a]**10:10** LXX, Syr, Vg read *against them when they are disciplined* [b]**10:11** Lit *will pass over* [c]**10:13** LXX reads *your chariots* [d]**11:2** Perhaps *the prophets* [e]**11:2** = Israel [f]**11:2** LXX; MT reads *them* [g]**11:3** LXX, Syr, Vg; MT reads *him* [h]**11:6** Or *devour his empty talkers,* or *devour his limbs*; Hb obscure

7 My people are bent on turning
   from Me.
Though they call to Him on high,
He will not exalt them at all.

God's Anguish for His People

8 How can I give you up, Ephraim?
How can I surrender you, Israel?
How can I make you like Admah?
How can I treat you like Zeboiim?
I have had a change of heart;
My compassion is stirred!
9 I will not vent the full fury
   of My anger;
I will not turn back
   to destroy Ephraim.
For I am God and not man,
the Holy One among you;
I will not come in rage.ᵃ
10 They will follow the LORD;
He will roar like a lion.
When He roars,
His children will come trembling
   from the west.
11 They will be roused like birds
   from Egypt
and like doves from the land
   of Assyria.
Then I will settle them
   in their homes.
          ⌊This is⌋ the LORD's declaration.

12b Ephraim surrounds me with lies,
the house of Israel, with deceit.
Judah still wanders with Elᶜ
and is faithful to holy ones.ᵈ ᵉ

God's Case against
Jacob's Heirs

12 Ephraim chasesᶠ the wind
   and pursues the east wind.
He continually multiplies lies
   and violence.

He makes a covenant with Assyria,
and olive oil is carried to Egypt.
2 The LORD also has a dispute
   with Judah.
He is about to punish Jacob
   according to his ways;
He will repay him based on
   his actions.
3 In the womb he grasped
   his brother's heel,
and as an adult he wrestled
   with God.
4 Jacob struggled with the Angel
   and prevailed;
he wept and sought His favor.
He found himᵍ at Bethel,
and there He spoke with him.ʰ
5 •Yahweh is the God of •Hosts;
Yahweh is His name.

You Must Return to God

6 But you must return to your God.
Maintain love and justice,
and always put your hope in God.

7 A merchant loves to extort
with dishonest scales in his hands.
8 But Ephraim says:
"How rich I have become;
I made it all myself.
In all my earnings,
no one can find any crime in me
that I can be punished for!"ⁱ

Judgment on
Apostate Israel

9 I have been the LORD your God
ever sinceʲ the land of Egypt.
I will make you live in tents again,
as in the festival days.
10 I spoke through the prophets
and granted many visions;

ᵃ**11:9** Or *come into any city*; Hb obscure   ᵇ**11:12** Hs 12:1 in Hb   ᶜ**11:12** Or *God*   ᵈ**11:12** Or *Judah walks with God and is faithful to the Holy One*; Hb obscure   ᵉ**11:12** Possibly angels, or less likely, pagan gods or idols   ᶠ**12:1** Or *feeds on*, or *tends*   ᵍ**12:4** Or *Him*   ʰ**12:4** LXX, Syr; MT reads *us*   ⁱ**12:8** Lit *crime which is sin*   ʲ**12:9** LXX reads *God who brought you out of*

I gave parables
    through the prophets.
[11] Since Gilead is full of evil,
    they will certainly come to nothing.
They sacrifice bulls in Gilgal;
    even their altars will be like heaps
      of rocks
    on the furrows of a field.

Further Indictment
of Jacob's Heirs

[12] Jacob fled to the land of Aram.
Israel worked to earn a wife;
    he tended flocks for a wife.
[13] The LORD brought Israel from Egypt
    by a prophet,
and Israel was tended by a prophet.

[14] Ephraim has provoked bitter anger,
so his Lord will leave his bloodguilt
    on him
and repay him for his contempt.

13 When Ephraim spoke,
    there was trembling;
he was exalted in Israel.
But he incurred guilt through •Baal
    and died.

[2] Now they continue to sin
and make themselves a cast image,
idols skillfully made
    from their silver,
all of them the work of craftsmen.
People say about them,
    "Let the men who sacrifice[a] kiss
      the calves."
[3] Therefore, they will be
    like the morning mist,
like the early dew that vanishes,
like chaff blown
    from a threshing floor,
or like smoke from a window.

Death and Resurrection

[4] I have been the LORD your God
    ever since[b] the land of Egypt;
you know no God but Me,
and no Savior exists besides Me.
[5] I knew[c] you in the wilderness,
    in the land of drought.
[6] When they had pasture,
    they became satisfied;
they were satisfied,
and their hearts became proud.
    Therefore they forgot Me.
[7] So I will be like a lion to them;
    I will lurk like a leopard
      on the path.
[8] I will attack them
like a bear robbed of her cubs
and tear open the rib cage
    over their hearts.
I will devour them there
    like a lioness,
like a wild beast that would rip
    them open.
[9] I will destroy you, Israel;
    you have no help but Me.[d]

[10] Where now is your king,[e]
that he may save you in all
    your cities,
and the[f] rulers[g] you
    demanded, saying:
Give me a king and leaders?
[11] I give you a king in My anger
and take away ⌊a king⌋ in My wrath.
[12] Ephraim's guilt is preserved;
    his sin is stored up.
[13] Labor pains come on him.
He is not a wise son;
when the time comes,
he will not be born.[h]

[14] I will[i] <u>ransom them from the power
of •Sheol.</u>

---

[a]**13:2** Or *Those who make human sacrifices*; 2 Kg 17:16-17 [b]**13:4** DSS, LXX read *God who brought you out of*
[c]**13:5** LXX, Syr read *fed* [d]**13:9** LXX reads *At your destruction, Israel, who will help you?* [e]**13:10** LXX, Syr, Vg; MT
reads *I will be your king* [f]**13:10** Lit *your* [g]**13:10** Or *judges* [h]**13:13** Lit *he will not present himself at the opening of the
womb for sons* [i]**13:14** Or *Should I . . . ?*

I will[a] redeem them from death.
Death, where are your barbs?
Sheol, where is your sting?
Compassion is hidden
from My eyes.

Coming Judgment

15 Although he flourishes
among [his] brothers,[b]
an east wind will come,
a wind from the LORD rising up
from the desert.
His water source will fail,
and his spring will run dry.
The wind[c] will plunder the treasury
of every precious item.

16d Samaria will bear her guilt
because she has rebelled
against her God.
They will fall by the sword;
their little ones will be dashed
to pieces,
and their pregnant women
ripped open.

A Plea to Repent

14 Israel, return to the LORD
your God,
for you have stumbled in your sin.
2 Take words [of repentance] with you
and return to the LORD.
Say to Him: "Forgive all [our] sin
and accept what is good,
so that we may repay You
with praise[e] from our[f] lips.
3 Assyria will not save us,
we will not ride on horses,
and we will no longer proclaim:
Our gods!

to the work of our hands.
For the fatherless
receives compassion in You."

Promise of Restoration

4 I will heal their apostasy;
I will freely love them,
for My anger will have turned
from him.
5 I will be like the dew to Israel;
he will blossom like the lily
and take root like
[the cedars of] Lebanon.
6 His new branches will spread,
and his splendor will be
like the olive tree,
his fragrance, like
[the forest of] Lebanon.
7 The people will return and live
beneath his shade.
They will grow grain
and blossom like the vine.
His renown will be like the wine
of Lebanon.

8 Ephraim, why should I[g] have
anything more
to do with idols?
It is I who answer and watch
over him.
I am like a flourishing pine tree;
your fruit comes from Me.

9 Let whoever is wise understand
these things,
and whoever is insightful
recognize them.
For the ways of the LORD are right,
and the righteous walk in them,
but the rebellious stumble in them.

JOEL

1

The word of the LORD that came to Joel son of Pethuel:

Plague of Locusts

2 Hear this, you elders;
listen, all you inhabitants
   of the land.
Has anything like this
   ever happened in your days
or in the days of your ancestors?
3 Tell your children about it,
and let your children
   tell their children,
and their children
   the next generation.
4 What the devouring locust has left,
the swarming locust has eaten;
what the swarming locust has left,
the young locust has eaten;
and what the young locust has left,
the destroying locust has eaten.

5 Wake up, you drunkards, and weep;
wail, all you wine drinkers,
because of the sweet wine,
for it has been taken
   from your mouth.
6 For a nation has invaded My land,
powerful and without number;
its teeth are the teeth of a lion,
and it has the fangs of a lioness.
7 It has devastated My grapevine
and splintered My fig tree.
It has stripped off its bark
   and thrown it away;
its branches have turned white.
8 Grieve like a young woman dressed
   in •sackcloth,
⌊mourning⌋ for the husband
   of her youth.
9 •Grain and drink offerings
have been cut off

from the house of the LORD;
the priests, who are ministers
   of the LORD, mourn.
10 The fields are destroyed;
the land grieves;
indeed, the grain is destroyed;
the new wine is dried up;
and the olive oil fails.
11 Be ashamed, you farmers,
wail, you vinedressers,[a]
over the wheat and the barley,
because the harvest of the field
   has perished.
12 The grapevine is dried up,
and the fig tree is withered;
the pomegranate, the date palm,
   and the apple—
all the trees of the orchard—
   have withered.
Indeed, human joy has dried up.

"Lament, You Priests"

13 Dress ⌊in sackcloth⌋ and lament,
   you priests;
wail, you ministers of the altar.
Come and spend the night
   in sackcloth,
you ministers of my God,
because grain and drink offerings
are withheld from the house
   of your God.
14 Announce a sacred fast;
proclaim an assembly!
Gather the elders
and all the residents of the land
at the house of the LORD your God,
and cry out to the LORD.

Day of the LORD is Near

15 Woe because of that day!
For the Day of the LORD is near

<hr>

a **1:11** Or *The farmers are dismayed, the vinedressers wail*

and will come as devastation
  from the •Almighty.
16 Hasn't the food been cut off
  before our eyes,
  joy and gladness
  from the house of our God?
17 The seeds lie shriveled
  in their casings.ᵃ
The storehouses are in ruin,
and the granaries are broken down,
because the grain has withered away.
18 How the animals groan!
The herds of cattle wander
  in confusion
since they have no pasture.
Even the flocks of sheep
  suffer punishment.
19 I call to You, LORD,
for fire has consumed
the pastures of the wilderness,
and flames have devoured
all the trees of the countryside.
20 Even the wild animals cry out
  toᵇ You,
for the river beds are dried up,
and fire has consumed
the pastures of the wilderness.

A Day of Darkness

2 Blow the horn in Zion;
sound the alarm
  on My holy mountain!
Let all the residents
  of the land tremble,
for the Day of the LORD is coming;
in fact, it is near—
2 a day of darkness and gloom,
a day of clouds and dense overcast,
like the dawn spreading
  over the mountains;
a great and strong people ⌊appears⌋,
such as never existed in ages past
and never will again
in all the generations to come.

3 A fire destroysᶜ in front of them,
and behind them a flame devours.
The land in front of them
is like the Garden of Eden,
but behind them,
it is like a desert wasteland;
there is no escape from them.
4 Their appearance is like that
  of horses,
and they gallop like war horses.
5 They bound on the tops
  of the mountains.
Their sound is like the sound
  of chariots,
like the sound of fiery flames
  consuming stubble,
like a mighty army deployed
  for war.

Nations Writhe

6 Nations writhe in horror
  before them;
all faces turn pale.
7 They attack as warriors ⌊attack⌋;
they scale walls as men
  of war ⌊do⌋.
Each goes on his own path,
and they do not change
  their course.
8 They do not push each other;
each man proceeds
  on his own path.
They dodge the missiles,
  never stopping.
9 They storm the city;
they run on the wall;
they climb into the houses;
they enter through the windows
  like thieves.
10 The earth quakes before them;
the sky shakes.
The sun and moon grow dark,
and the stars cease their shining.

ᵃ1:17 Or clods; Hb obscure ᵇ1:20 Or animals pant for; Hb obscure ᶜ2:3 Lit consumes

Voice of the Lord

11 The LORD raises His voice
in the presence of His army.
His camp is very large;
Those who carry out His command
   are powerful.
Indeed, the Day of the LORD
   is terrible and dreadful—
who can endure it?

God's Call for Repentance

12 Even now—
      ⌊this is⌋ the LORD's declaration—
turn to Me with all your heart,
with fasting, weeping,
   and mourning.
13 Tear your hearts,
   not just your clothes,
and return to the LORD your God.
For He is gracious
   and compassionate,
slow to anger, rich in faithful love,
and He relents
   from sending disaster.
14 Who knows? He may turn and relent
and leave a blessing behind Him,
⌊so you can⌋ offer grain and wine
to the LORD your God.

15 Blow the horn in Zion!
Announce a sacred fast;
proclaim an assembly.
16 Gather the people;
sanctify the congregation;
assemble the aged;[a]
gather the children,
even those nursing at the breast.
Let the bridegroom
   leave his bedroom,
and the bride
   her honeymoon chamber.
17 Let the priests, the LORD's ministers,
weep between the portico[b]
   and the altar.
Let them say:

"Have pity on Your people, LORD,
and do not make Your inheritance
   a disgrace,
an object of scorn
   among the nations.
Why should it be said
   among the peoples,
'Where is their God?'"

God's Response to His People

18 Then the LORD became jealous for
His land and spared His people. 19 The
LORD answered His people:

Look, I am about to send you
grain, new wine, and olive oil.
You will be satiated with them,
and I will no longer make you
a disgrace among the nations.

20 I will drive the northerner
   far from you
and banish him to a dry
   and desolate land,
his front ranks into the Dead Sea,
and his rear guard
   into the Mediterranean Sea.
His stench will rise;
yes, his rotten smell will rise,
for he has done catastrophic things.

"Don't Be Afraid, Land"

21 Don't be afraid, land;
rejoice and be glad,
for the LORD has done great things.
22 Don't be afraid, wild animals,
for the wilderness pastures
   have turned green,
the trees bear their fruit,
and the fig tree and grapevine yield
   their riches.

"Children of Zion, Rejoice"

23 Children of Zion, rejoice
   and be glad

---

a 2:16 Or *elders*   b 2:17 = the temple porch; 1 Kg 6:3; 7:6-21

in the LORD your God,
because He gives you
  the autumn rain
for your vindication.[a]
He sends showers for you,
both autumn and spring rain
  as before.
24 The threshing floors will be full
  of grain,
and the vats will overflow
with new wine and olive oil.

25 I will repay you for the years
that the swarming locust ate,
the young locust,
  the destroying locust,
and the devouring locust—
My great army that I sent
  against you.
26 You will have plenty to eat
  and be satisfied.
You will praise the name
  of •Yahweh your God,
who has dealt wondrously
  with you.
My people will never again be put
  to shame.
27 You will know that I am present
  in Israel
and that I am the LORD your God,
and there is no other.
My people will never again be put
  to shame.

God's Promise of His Spirit

28b After this
I will pour out My Spirit
  on all humanity;
then your sons and your daughters
  will prophesy,
your old men will have dreams,
and your young men
  will see visions.
29 I will even pour out My Spirit

on the male and female slaves
  in those days.
30 I will display wonders
in the heavens and on the earth:
blood, fire, and columns of smoke.
31 The sun will be turned to darkness
and the moon to blood
before the great and awe-inspiring
Day of the LORD comes.

Everyone Who Calls on Yahweh Is Saved

32 Then everyone who calls
on the name of Yahweh
  will be saved,
for there will be an escape
for those on Mount Zion
  and in Jerusalem,
as the LORD promised,
among the survivors the LORD calls.

Judgment of the Nations

3[c] Yes, in those days and at that time,
when I restore the fortunes
  of Judah and Jerusalem,
2 I will gather all the nations
and take them to the Valley
  of Jehoshaphat.[d] I will enter
into judgment with them there
because of My people,
  My inheritance Israel.
The nations have scattered
  the Israelites
in foreign countries
and divided up My land.

God Condemns Child Prostitution

3 They cast lots for My people;
they bartered a boy for a prostitute
and sold a girl for wine to drink.

God's Retribution on Nations

4 And also: Tyre, Sidon, and all the territories of Philistia—what are you to

---

[a]**2:23** Or *righteousness*   [b]**2:28** Jl 3:1 in Hb   [c]**3:1** Jl 4:1 in Hb   [d]**3:2** = The LORD Will Judge

Me? Are you paying Me back or trying to get even with Me? I will quickly bring retribution on your heads. ⁵ For you took My silver and gold and carried My finest treasures to your temples. ⁶ You sold the people of Judah and Jerusalem to the Greeks to remove them far from their own territory. ⁷ Look, I am about to rouse them up from the place where you sold them; I will bring retribution on your heads. ⁸ I will sell your sons and daughters into the hands of the people of Judah, and they will sell them to the Sabeans,ᵃ to a distant nation, for the LORD has spoken.

9 Proclaim this among the nations:
Prepare for holy war;
rouse the warriors;
let all the men of war advance
and attack!
10 Hammer your plowshares
into swords
and your pruning knives
into spears.
Let even the weakling say: I am
a warrior.
11 Come quickly,ᵇ all
you surrounding nations;
gather yourselves.
Bring down
Your warriors there, LORD.

12 Let the nations be roused
and come to the Valley
of Jehoshaphat,
for there I will sit down
to judge all the surrounding nations.
13 Swing the sickle
because the harvest is ripe.
Come and trample ⌊the grapes⌋
because the winepress is full;
the wine vats overflow
because the wickedness
of the nations is great.

14 Multitudes, multitudes
in the valley of decision!
For the Day of the LORD is near
in the valley of decision.
15 The sun and moon will grow dark,
and the stars will cease
their shining.
16 The LORD will roar from Zion
and raise His voice
from Jerusalem;
heaven and earth will shake.
But the LORD will be a refuge
for His people,
a stronghold for the Israelites.

Israel Blessed

17 Then you will know
that I am the LORD your God,
who dwells in Zion,
My holy mountain.
Jerusalem will be holy,
and foreigners will never
overrun it again.
18 In that day
the mountains will drip
with sweet wine,
and the hills will flow with milk.
All the streams of Judah will flow
with water,
and a spring will issue
from the LORD's house,
watering the Valley of Acacias.ᶜ
19 Egypt will become desolate,
and Edom a desert wasteland,
because of the violence ⌊done⌋
to the people of Judah
in whose land they shed
innocent blood.
20 But Judah will be inhabited forever,
and Jerusalem from generation
to generation.
21 I will pardon their bloodguilt,ᵈ
⌊which⌋ I have not pardoned,
for the LORD dwells in Zion.

ᵃ3:8 Probably = the south Arabian kingdom of Sheba (modern Yemen)   ᵇ3:11 LXX, Syr, Tg read *Gather yourselves and come*; Hb obscure   ᶜ3:18 Or *Shittim*   ᵈ3:21 LXX, Syr read *I will avenge their blood*

AMOS

A Sheep Breeder Prophesies

1 The words of Amos, who was one of the sheep breeders[a] from Tekoa— what he saw regarding Israel in the days of Uzziah, king of Judah, and Jeroboam son of Joash, king of Israel, two years before the earthquake. ² He said:

> The LORD roars from Zion
> and raises His voice
>   from Jerusalem;
> the pastures
>   of the shepherds mourn,[b]
> and the summit of Carmel withers.

Judgment on Israel's Neighbors

³ The LORD says:

> I will not relent
>   from punishing Damascus
> for three crimes, even four,
> because they threshed Gilead
>   with iron sledges.
> ⁴ Therefore, I will send fire
>   against Hazael's palace,
> and it will consume
>   Ben-hadad's citadels.
> ⁵ I will break down the gates[c]
>   of Damascus.
> I will cut off the ruler
>   from the Valley of Aven,
> and the one who wields the scepter
>   from Beth-eden.
> The people of Aram will be exiled
>   to Kir.
> The LORD has spoken.

⁶ The LORD says:

> I will not relent
>   from punishing Gaza

for three crimes, even four,
> because they exiled
>   a whole community,
> handing them over to Edom.
> ⁷ Therefore, I will send fire
>   against the walls of Gaza,
> and it will consume its citadels.
> ⁸ I will cut off the ruler from Ashdod,
> and the one who wields the scepter
>   from Ashkelon.
> I will also turn My hand
>   against Ekron,
> and the remainder of the Philistines
>   will perish.
> The Lord GOD has spoken.

⁹ The LORD says:

> I will not relent
>   from punishing Tyre
> for three crimes, even four,
> because they handed over
>   a whole community of exiles
>   to Edom
> and broke[d] a treaty of brotherhood.
> ¹⁰ Therefore, I will send fire
>   against the walls of Tyre,
> and it will consume its citadels.

¹¹ The LORD says:

> I will not relent
>   from punishing Edom
> for three crimes, even four,
> because he pursued his brother
>   with the sword.
> He stifled his compassion,
> his anger tore ⌊at them⌋ continually,
> and he harbored
>   his rage incessantly.
> ¹² Therefore, I will send fire
>   against Teman,

ᵃ**1:1** Or *the shepherds* ᵇ**1:2** Or *dry up* ᶜ**1:5** Lit *gate bars* ᵈ**1:9** Lit *and did not remember*

and it will consume the citadels
of Bozrah.

13 The LORD says:

I will not relent from punishing
the Ammonites
for three crimes, even four,
because they ripped open
the pregnant women of Gilead
in order to enlarge their territory.
14 Therefore, I will set fire to the walls
of Rabbah,
and it will consume its citadels.
There will be shouting on the day
of battle
and a violent wind on the day
of the storm.
15 Their king and his princes
will go into exile together.
The LORD has spoken.

God Judges Moab

2 The LORD says:

I will not relent
from punishing Moab
for three crimes, even four,
because he burned to lime
the bones of the king of Edom.
2 Therefore, I will send fire
against Moab,
and it will consume the citadels
of Kerioth.
Moab will die with a tumult,
with shouting and the sound
of the ram's horn.
3 I will cut off the judge
from the land
and kill all its officials with him.
The LORD has spoken.

God Judges Judah

4 The LORD says:

I will not relent
from punishing Judah

for three crimes, even four,
because they have rejected the law
of the LORD
and have not kept His statutes.
The lies that
their ancestors followed
have led them astray.
5 Therefore, I will send fire
against Judah,
and it will consume the citadels
of Jerusalem.

God Judges Israel

6 The LORD says:

I will not relent
from punishing Israel
for three crimes, even four,
because they sell a righteous person
for silver
and a needy person for a pair
of sandals.
7 They trample the heads of the poor
on the dust of the ground
and block the path of the needy.
A man and his father
have sexual relations
with the same girl,
profaning My holy name.
8 They stretch out beside every altar
on garments taken as collateral,
and they drink in the house
of their God
wine obtained through fines.

9 Yet I destroyed the Amorite
as Israel advanced;
his height was like the cedars,
and he was as sturdy
as the oaks;
I destroyed his fruit above
and his roots beneath.
10 And I brought you from the land
of Egypt
and led you 40 years
in the wilderness

in order to possess the land
of the Amorite.

11 I raised up some of your sons
as prophets
and some of your young men
as Nazirites.
Is this not the case, Israelites?
⌊This is⌋ the LORD's declaration.

12 But you made the Nazirites
drink wine
and commanded the prophets:
Do not prophesy.

13 Look, I am about to crushª ⌊you⌋
in your place
as a wagon full of sheaves
crushes ⌊grain⌋.

14 Escape will fail the swift,
the strong one will not prevail
by his strength,
and the brave will not save his life.

15 The archer will not stand
⌊his ground⌋,
the ⌊one who is⌋ swift of foot
will not save himself,
and the one riding a horse
will not save his life.

16 Even the most courageous
of the warriors
will flee naked on that day—
the LORD's declaration.

God's Disappointment with Israel

3 Listen to this message that the LORD
has spoken against you, Israelites,
against the entire clan that I brought
from the land of Egypt:

2 I have known only you
out of all the clans of the earth;
therefore, I will punish you for all
your iniquities.

3 Can two walk together
without agreeing to meet?ᵇ

4 Does a lion roar in the forest

when it has no prey?
Does a young lion growl
from its lair
unless it has captured ⌊something⌋?

5 Does a bird land in a trap
on the ground
if there is no bait for it?
Does a trap spring from the ground
when it has caught nothing?

6 If a ram's horn is blown in a city,
aren't people afraid?
If a disaster occurs in a city,
hasn't the LORD done it?

7 Indeed, the Lord GOD does nothing
without revealing His counsel
to His servants the prophets.

8 A lion has roared;
who will not fear?
The Lord GOD has spoken;
who will not prophesy?

9 Proclaim on the citadels in Ashdod
and on the citadels in the land
of Egypt:
Assemble on the mountains
of Samaria
and see the great turmoil in the city
and the acts of oppression within it.

10 The people are incapable
of doing right—
the LORD's declaration—
those who store up violence
and destruction
in their citadels.

Israel's Punishment Certain

11 Therefore, the Lord GOD says:

An enemy will surround the land;
he will destroy your strongholds
and plunder your citadels.

12 The LORD says:

As the shepherd snatches two legs
or a piece of an ear

<hr>

ª2:13 Or *hinder*; Hb obscure   ᵇ3:3 LXX reads *without meeting*

from the lion's mouth,
so the Israelites who live in Samaria
will be rescued
with ⌊only⌋ the corner of a bed
or the[a] cushion[b] of a couch.[c]

13 Listen and testify against the house
of Jacob—
⌊this is⌋ the declaration
of the Lord GOD,
the God of •Hosts.

14 I will punish the altars of Bethel
on the day I punish Israel
for its crimes;
the horns of the altar will be cut off
and fall to the ground.

15 I will demolish the winter house
and the summer house;
the houses ⌊inlaid with⌋ ivory
will be destroyed,
and the great houses will come
to an end—
the LORD's declaration.

Israel's Social and Spiritual Corruption

4 Listen to this message, you cows
of Bashan
who are on the hill of Samaria,
women who oppress the poor
and crush the needy,
who say to their husbands,
"Bring us something to drink."

2 The Lord GOD has sworn by His holiness:

Look, the days are coming[d]
when you will be taken away
with hooks,
every last ⌊one⌋ of you
with fishhooks.

3 You will go through breaches
in the wall,
each woman straight ahead,

and you will be driven along
toward Harmon.
⌊This is⌋ the LORD's declaration.

4 Come to Bethel and rebel;
rebel even more at Gilgal!
Bring your sacrifices
every morning,
your tenths every three days.

5 Offer leavened bread as
a thank offering,
and loudly proclaim
your freewill offerings,
for that is what you Israelites
love ⌊to do⌋!
⌊This is⌋ the LORD's declaration.

God's Discipline Failed

6 I gave you absolutely nothing to eat[e]
in all your cities,
a shortage of food in all
your communities,
yet you did not return to Me—
the LORD's declaration.

7 I also withheld the rain from you
while there were still three months
until harvest.
I sent rain on one city
but no rain on another.
One field received rain
while a field with no rain withered.

8 Two or three cities staggered
to another city to drink water
but were not satisfied,
yet you did not return to Me—
the LORD's declaration.

9 I struck you with blight
and mildew;
the locust devoured
your many gardens and vineyards,
your fig trees and olive trees,
yet you did not return to Me—
the LORD's declaration.

---

a**3:12** Or Israelites will be rescued, those who sit in Samaria on a corner of a bed or a   b**3:12** Hb obscure
c**3:12** LXX, Aq, Sym, Theod, Syr, Tg, Vg read or in Damascus   d**4:2** Lit coming on you   e**4:6** Lit you cleanness of teeth

¹⁰ I sent plagues like those of Egypt;
I killed your young men
with the sword,
along with your captured horses.
I caused the stench of your camp
to fill your nostrils,
yet you did not return to Me—
the LORD's declaration.

¹¹ I overthrew some of you
as Iᵃ overthrew Sodom
and Gomorrah,
and you were like a burning stick
snatched from a fire,
yet you did not return to Me—
the LORD's declaration.

Prepare to Meet Your God!

¹² Therefore, Israel, that is what
I will do to you,
and since I will do that to you,
Israel, prepare to meet your God!
¹³ He is here:
the One who forms the mountains,
creates the wind,
and reveals Hisᵇ thoughts to man,
the One who makes the dawn
out of darkness
and strides on the heights
of the earth.
•Yahweh, the God of •Hosts,
is His name.

Lamentation for Israel

5 Listen to this message that I am singing for you, a lament, house of Israel:

² She has fallen;
Virgin Israel will never rise again.
She lies abandoned on her land,
with no one to raise her up.

³ For the Lord GOD says:

The city that marches out
a thousand ⌊strong⌋

will have ⌊only⌋ a hundred left,
and the one that marches out
a hundred ⌊strong⌋
will have ⌊only⌋ ten left in the house
of Israel.

Seek God and Live

⁴ For the LORD says to the house of Israel:

Seek Me and live!
⁵ Do not seek Bethel
or go to Gilgal
or journey to Beer-sheba,
for Gilgal will certainly go
into exile,
and Bethel will come to nothing.
⁶ Seek •Yahweh and live,
or He will spread like fire
⌊throughout⌋ the house of Joseph;
it will consume ⌊everything,⌋
with no one at Bethel
to extinguish it.
⁷ Those who turn justice
into •wormwood
throw righteousness to the ground.
⁸ The One who made the Pleiades
and Orion,
who turns darknessᶜ into dawn
and darkens day into night,
who summons the waters of the sea
and pours them out over the face
of the earth—
Yahweh is His name.
⁹ He brings destructionᵈ on the strong,ᵉ
and it falls on the stronghold.
¹⁰ They hate the one who convicts
⌊the guilty⌋
at the city •gate
and despise the one who speaks
with integrity.
¹¹ Therefore, because you trample on
the poor
and exact a grain tax from him,

ᵃ**4:11** Lit *God*   ᵇ**4:13** Or *his*   ᶜ**5:8** Or *turns the shadow of death*   ᵈ**5:9** Hb obscure   ᵉ**5:9** Or *stronghold*

you will never live in the houses
  of cut stone
you have built;
you will never drink the wine
from the lush vineyards
you have planted.

"Your Crimes Are Many"

12 For I know your crimes are many
and your sins innumerable.
They oppress the righteous,
  take a bribe,
and deprive the poor of justice
  at the gates.

Seek Good, Not Evil

13 Therefore, the wise person
  will keep silent
at such a time,
for the days are evil.

14 Seek good and not evil
so that you may live,
and the LORD, the God of •Hosts,
will be with you,
as you have claimed.

15 Hate evil and love good;
establish justice in the gate.
Perhaps the LORD, the God
  of Hosts, will be gracious
to the remnant of Joseph.

16 Therefore Yahweh, the God of Hosts,
the Lord, says:

There will be wailing in all
  the public squares;
they will cry out in anguish[a] in all
  the streets.
The farmer will be called on to mourn,
and professional mourners[b] to wail.

17 There will be wailing in all
  the vineyards,
for I will pass among you.
The LORD has spoken.

Day of the LORD

18 Woe to you who long for the Day
  of the LORD!
What will the Day of the LORD
  be for you?
It will be darkness and not light.

19 It will be like a man who flees
  from a lion
only to have a bear confront him.
He goes home and rests his hand
  against the wall
only to have a snake bite him.

20 Won't the Day of the LORD
be darkness rather than light,
even gloom without any brightness
  in it?

21 I hate, I despise your feasts!
I can't stand the stench
of your solemn assemblies.

22 Even if you offer Me
your •burnt offerings
  and •grain offerings,
I will not accept ⌊them⌋;
I will have no regard
for your •fellowship offerings
  of fattened cattle.

23 Take away from Me the noise
  of your songs!
I will not listen to the music
  of your harps.

24 But let justice flow like water,
and righteousness,
  like an unfailing stream.

Israel Follows False Gods

25 "House of Israel, was it sacrifices and grain offerings that you presented to Me during the 40 years in the wilderness? 26 But you have taken up[c] Sakkuth[d] [e] your king[f] and Kaiwan[g] [h] your star god, images you have made for yourselves. 27 So I will send you into exile be-

a 5:16 Lit *will say, "Alas! Alas!"*   b 5:16 Lit *and those skilled in lamentation*   c 5:26 Or *you will lift up*   d 5:26 LXX, Sym, Syr, Vg read *the tent*; Ac 7:43   e 5:26 Lit *Sikkuth*; probably a Mesopotamian war god also called Adar or Ninurta   f 5:26 LXX, Vg read *up the tent of Molech*; Ac 7:43   g 5:26 LXX reads *Rephan*; Ac 7:43   h 5:26 Lit *Kiyyun*; probably a Mesopotamian god identified with Saturn

yond Damascus." Yahweh, the God of Hosts, is His name. He has spoken.

Woe to the Complacent

6 Woe to those who are at ease in Zion
and to those who feel secure
    on the hill of Samaria—
the notable people in this first
    of the nations,
those the house of Israel comes to.
2 Cross over to Calneh and see;
    go from there to great Hamath;
then go down to Gath
    of the Philistines.
Are you better than these kingdoms?
Is their territory larger than yours?
3 You dismiss any thought
    of the evil day
and bring in a reign of violence.

4 They lie on beds ⌊inlaid with⌋ ivory,
    sprawled out on their couches,
and dine on lambs from the flock
    and calves from the stall.
5 They improvise songsa to the sound
    of the harp
and inventb their own
    musical instruments like David.
6 They drink wine by the bowlful
    and anoint themselves
        with the finest oils
but do not grieve over the ruin
    of Joseph.
7 Therefore, they will now go
    into exile
as the first of the captives,
    and the feasting of those
        who sprawl out
will come to an end.

God Judges Israel's Pride

8 The Lord GOD has sworn by Him-self—the declaration of •Yahweh, the God of •Hosts:

I loathe Jacob's pride
    and hate his citadels,
so I will hand over the city
    and everything in it.

9 And if there are 10 men left in one house, they will die. 10 A close relativec and a burner,d will remove his corpsee from the house. He will call to someone in the inner recesses of the house, "Any more with you?"
That person will reply, "None."
Then he will say, "Silence, because Yahweh's name must not be invoked."
11 For the LORD commands:

The large house will be smashed
    to pieces,
and the small house to rubble.

12 Do horses run on rock,
    or does someone plow ⌊it⌋
        with oxen?f
Yet you have turned justice
    into poison
and the fruit of righteousness
    into •wormwood—
13 you who rejoice over Lo-debar
    and say, "Didn't we
        capture Karnaim
for ourselves by our own strength?"
14 But look, I am raising up a nation
    against you, house of Israel—
        ⌊this is⌋ the declaration
            of the Lord,
                the GOD of Hosts—
and they will oppress you
    from the entrance of Hamathg
to the Brook of the •Arabah.h

Amos' First Vision: Locusts

7 The Lord GOD showed me this: He was forming a swarm of locusts at the time the spring crop first began to sprout—after the cutting of the king's

---

a6:5 Hb obscure   b6:5 Or *compose on*   c6:10 Lit *His uncle*   d6:10 Or *burner of incense*, or *burner of a memorial fire*, or *burner of a body*; Hb obscure   e6:10 Lit *remove bones*   f6:12 Others emend to *plow the sea*   g6:14 Or *from Lebo-hamath*; 2 Kg 14:25,28   h6:14 Probably the Valley of Zared at the southeast end of the Dead Sea

hay. ² When the locusts finished eating the vegetation of the land, I said, "Lord GOD, please forgive! How will Jacob survive since he is so small?"

³ The LORD relented concerning this. "It will not happen," He said.

Second Vision: Fire

⁴ The Lord GOD showed me this: The Lord GOD was calling for a judgment by fire. It consumed the great deep and devoured the land. ⁵ Then I said, "Lord GOD, please stop! How will Jacob survive since he is so small?"

⁶ The LORD relented concerning this. "This will not happen either," said the Lord GOD.

Third Vision:
A Plumb Line

⁷ He showed me this: The Lord was standing there by a vertical wall with a plumb line in His hand. ⁸ The LORD asked me, "What do you see, Amos?"

I replied, "A plumb line."

Then the Lord said, "I am setting a plumb line among My people Israel; I will no longer spare them:

⁹   Isaac's •high places will be deserted,
     and Israel's sanctuaries
        will be in ruins;
     I will rise up against the house
        of Jeroboam
     with a sword."

Priest Amaziah's Opposition

¹⁰ Amaziah the priest of Bethel sent ⌞word⌟ to Jeroboam king of Israel, saying, "Amos has conspired against you ⌞right here⌟ in the house of Israel. The land cannot endure all his words, ¹¹ for Amos has said this: 'Jeroboam will die by the sword, and Israel will certainly go into exile from its homeland.' "

¹² Then Amaziah said to Amos, "Go away, you seer! Flee to the land of Judah. Earn your living[a] and give ⌞your⌟ prophecies there, ¹³ but don't ever prophesy at Bethel again, for it is the king's sanctuary and a royal temple."

Amos Answers Amaziah

¹⁴ So Amos answered Amaziah, "I was[b] not a prophet or the son of a prophet;[c] rather, I was[b] a herdsman, and I took care of sycamore figs. ¹⁵ But the LORD took me from following the flock and said to me, 'Go, prophesy to My people Israel.' "

¹⁶ Now hear the word of the LORD. You say:

Do not prophesy against Israel;
   do not preach against the house
      of Isaac.

¹⁷ Therefore, this is what the LORD says:

Your wife will be a prostitute
   in the city,
your sons and daughters will fall
   by the sword,
and your land will be divided up
   with a measuring line.
You yourself will die on pagan[d] soil,
and Israel will certainly go into exile
   from its homeland.

Fourth Vision:
A Basket of Summer Fruit

8 The Lord GOD showed me this: A basket of summer fruit. ² He asked me, "What do you see, Amos?"

I replied, "A basket of summer fruit."

The LORD said to me, "The end has come for My people Israel; I will no longer spare them. ³ In that day the temple[e] songs will become wailing"—the Lord GOD's declaration. "Many dead bodies, thrown everywhere! Silence!"

---

^a**7:12** Lit *Eat bread*   ^b**7:14** Or *am*   ^c**7:14** = a prophet's disciple or a member of a prophetic guild; 2 Kg 2:3-15; 4:38; 9:1   ^d**7:17** Lit *unclean*   ^e**8:3** Or *palace*

Punishment for Trampling the Needy

4 Hear this, you who trample
  on the needy
and do away with the poor of the land,
5 asking, "When will the New Moon
  be over
so we may sell grain,
and the Sabbath,
so we may market wheat?
We can reduce the measure
while increasing the price[a]
and cheat with dishonest scales.
6 We can buy the poor with silver
and the needy for a pair of sandals
and even sell the wheat husks!"

7 The LORD has sworn by the Pride of
Jacob:[b]

I will never forget all their deeds.
8 Because of this,
  won't the land quake
and all who dwell in it mourn?
All of it will rise like the Nile;
it will surge and then subside
like the Nile in Egypt.

9 And in that day—
                ⌊this is⌋ the declaration
                of the Lord GOD—

Darkness at Noon

I will make the sun go down
  at noon;
I will darken the land
  in the daytime.
10 I will turn your feasts
  into mourning
and all your songs into lamentation;
I will cause everyone[c]
  to wear •sackcloth
and every head to be shaved.
I will make that grief
like mourning for an only son
and its outcome like a bitter day.

Famine and Drought

11 Hear this! The days are coming—
                ⌊this is⌋ the declaration
                of the Lord GOD—
when I will send a famine
  through the land:
not a famine of bread or a thirst
  for water,
but of hearing the words of the LORD.
12 People will stagger from sea to sea
and roam from north to east,
seeking the word of the LORD,
but they will not find it.
13 In that day
  the beautiful young women,
the young men also, will faint
  from thirst.
14 Those who swear by the guilt
  of Samaria
and say, "As your god lives, Dan,"
or "As the
  way[d] [e] of Beer-sheba lives"—
they will fall, never to rise again.

Fifth Vision: LORD beside Altar

9 I saw the LORD standing beside the
altar, and He said:

  Strike the capitals of the pillars
  so that the thresholds shake;
  knock them down on the heads
    of all the people.
  Then I will kill the rest of them
    with the sword.
  None of those who flee will get away;
  none of their fugitives will escape.
2 If they dig down to •Sheol,
  from there My hand will take them;
  if they climb up to heaven,
  from there I will bring them down.
3 If they hide themselves
  on the top of Carmel,
  from there I will track them down
  and seize them;

---

if they conceal themselves
from My sight on the sea floor,
from there I will command
the ⌊sea⌋ serpent to bite them.
4 And if they are driven
by their enemies into captivity,
from there I will command
the sword to kill them.
I will fix My eyes on them
for harm and not for good.

5 The Lord, the GOD of •Hosts—
He touches the earth;
it melts, and all who dwell
on it mourn;
all of it rises like the Nile
and subsides like the Nile of Egypt.
6 He builds His upper chambers
in the heavens
and lays the foundation of His vault
on the earth.
He summons the waters of the sea
and pours them out on the face
of the earth.
•Yahweh is His name.

God Announces Judgment

7 Israelites, are you not
like the •Cushites to Me?
⌊This is⌋ the LORD's declaration.
Didn't I bring Israel from the land
of Egypt,
the Philistines from Caphtor,[a]
and the Arameans from Kir?
8 Look, the eyes of the Lord GOD
are on the sinful kingdom,
and I will destroy it
from the face of the earth.
However, I will not totally destroy
the house of Jacob—
the LORD's declaration—

9 for I am about to give the command,
and I will shake the house of Israel
among all the nations,

as one shakes a sieve,
but not a pebble will fall
to the ground.
10 All the sinners among My people,
who say:
Disaster will never overtake[b]
or confront us,
will die by the sword.

God Announces Restoration

11 In that day
I will restore the fallen booth
of David:
I will repair its gaps,
restore its ruins,
and rebuild it as in the days of old,
12 so that they may possess
the remnant of Edom
and all the nations
that are called by My name[c]—
⌊this is⌋ the LORD's declaration—
He will do this.

13 Hear this! The days are coming—
the LORD's declaration—
when the plowman will overtake
the reaper
and the one who treads grapes,
the sower of seed.
The mountains will drip
with sweet wine,
and all the hills will flow ⌊with it⌋.
14 I will restore the fortunes
of My people Israel.[d]
They will rebuild and occupy
ruined cities,
plant vineyards and drink
their wine,
make gardens and eat their produce.
15 I will plant them on their land,
and they will never again
be uprooted
from the land I have given them.
Yahweh your God has spoken.

---

[a]9:7 = Crete; Dt 2:23; Jr 47:4   [b]9:10 Or You will not let disaster come near   [c]9:12 LXX reads so that the remnant of man and all the nations . . . may seek [Me]; Ac 15:17   [d]9:14 Or restore My people Israel from captivity

OBADIAH

The vision of Obadiah.

Edom's Certain Judgment

This is what the Lord GOD has said about Edom:

> We have heard a message
> from the LORD;
> an envoy has been sent
> among the nations:
> Rise up, and let us go to war
> against her.[a]
> 2 Look, I will make you insignificant
> among the nations;
> you will be deeply despised.
> 3 Your presumptuous heart
> has deceived you,
> you who live in clefts of the rock[b]
> in your home on the heights,
> who say to yourself:
> Who can bring me down
> to the ground?
> 4 Though you seem to soar[c]
> like an eagle
> and make your nest
> among the stars,
> even from there I will
> bring you down.
> ⌊This is⌋ the LORD's declaration.
>
> 5 If thieves came to you,
> if marauders by night—
> how ravaged you will be!—
> wouldn't they steal only
> what they wanted?
> If grape pickers came to you,
> wouldn't they leave some grapes?
> 6 How Esau will be pillaged,
> his hidden treasures searched out!
> 7 Everyone who has a treaty with you
> will drive you to the border;
> everyone at peace with you
> will deceive and conquer you.
> Those who eat your bread
> will set[d] a trap for you.
> He will be unaware of it.
> 8 In that day—
> the LORD's declaration—
> will I not eliminate the wise ones
> of Edom
> and those who understand
> from the hill country of Esau?
> 9 Teman,[e] your warriors
> will be terrified
> so that everyone
> from the hill country of Esau
> will be destroyed by slaughter.

Edom's Sins against Judah

> 10 You will be covered with shame
> and destroyed forever
> because of violence done
> to your brother Jacob.
> 11 On the day you stood aloof,
> on the day strangers captured
> his wealth,[f]
> while foreigners entered his •gate
> and cast lots for Jerusalem,
> you were just like one of them.

"Do Not Gloat"

> 12 Do not gloat[g] over your brother
> in the day of his calamity;
> do not rejoice over the people
> of Judah
> in the day of their destruction;
> do not boastfully mock[h]
> in the day of distress.

---

[a]1 = Edom   [b]3 Or *in Sela*; probably = Petra; Jdg 1:36; 2 Kg 14:7; Is 16:1   [c]4 Or *to build high*   [d]7 Some LXX mss, Sym, Tg, Vg; MT reads *They will set your bread as*   [e]9 = a region or city in Edom   [f]11 Or *forces*   [g]12-14 Or *You should not have gloated . . .* (using the same form *You should not have . . .* in each of the following 8 commands)   [h]12 Lit *not make your mouth big*

13 Do not enter the gate of My people
   in the day of their disaster.
   Yes, you—do not gloat
     over their misery
   in the day of their disaster
   and do not appropriate
     their possessions
   in the day of their disaster.
14 Do not stand at the crossroads[a]
   to cut off their fugitives,
   and do not hand over
     their survivors
   in the day of distress.

Judgment of Nations

15 For the Day of the LORD is near,
   against all the nations.
   As you have done, so it will be
     done to you;
   what you deserve will return
     on your own head.
16 For as you have drunk
     on My holy mountain,
   so all the nations will
     drink[b] continually.
   They will drink and gulp down
   and be as though they had
     never been.
17 But there will be a deliverance
     on Mount Zion,
   and it will be holy;
   the house of Jacob will dispossess
   those who dispossessed them.[c]
18 Then the house of Jacob will be
   a ˌblazingˌ fire,

and the house of Joseph
  a ˌburningˌ flame,
but the house of Esau
  will be stubble;
they[d] will set them on fire
  and consume them.[e]
Therefore no survivor will remain
of the house of Esau,
for the LORD has spoken.

Future Blessing for Israel

19 ˌPeople fromˌ the •Negev
     will possess
   the hill country of Esau;
   ˌthose fromˌ the Judean foothills
     will possess
   ˌthe land ofˌ the Philistines.
   They[d] will possess
   the territories of Ephraim
     and Samaria,
   while Benjamin
     will possess Gilead.
20 The exiles of the Israelites who are
     in Halah[f]
   who are among the Canaanites
     as far as Zarephath
   and the exiles of Jerusalem who are
     in Sepharad
   will possess the cities
     of the Negev.
21 Saviors[g] will ascend Mount Zion
   to rule over the hill country
     of Esau,
   but the kingdom will be the LORD's.

---

[a]14 Hb obscure   [b]16 = drink a cup of judgment   [c]17 DSS, LXX, Syr, Vg, Tg; MT reads *Jacob will possess its inheritance*   [d]18,19 = the house of Jacob   [e]18 = Edom   [f]20 Or *of this host of the Israelites*; Hb obscure   [g]21 Or *Those who have been delivered*

JONAH

Jonah's Flight

1 The word of the LORD came to Jonah son of Amittai: ² "Get up! Go to the great city of Nineveh and preach against it, because their wickedness has confronted Me." ³ However, Jonah got up to flee to Tarshish from the LORD's presence. He went down to Joppa and found a ship going to Tarshish. He paid the fare and went down into it to go with them to Tarshish, from the LORD's presence.

The Violent Storm

⁴ Then the LORD hurled a violent wind on the sea, and such a violent storm arose on the sea that the ship threatened to break apart. ⁵ The sailors were afraid, and each cried out to his god. They threw the ship's cargo into the sea to lighten the load. Meanwhile, Jonah had gone down to the lowest part of the vessel and had stretched out and fallen into a deep sleep.

⁶ The captain approached him and said, "What are you doing sound asleep? Get up! Call to your god.ᵃ Maybe this god will consider us, and we won't perish."

⁷ "Come on!" the sailors said to each other. "Let's cast lots. Then we will know who is to blame for this trouble we're in." So they cast lots, and the lot singled out Jonah. ⁸ Then they said to him, "Tell us who is to blame for this trouble we're in. What is your business and where are you from? What is your country and what people are you from?"

⁹ He answered them, "I am a Hebrew. I worshipᵇ •Yahweh, the God of the heavens, who made the sea and the dry land."

Jonah: "Throw Me into the Sea"

¹⁰ Then the men were even more afraid and said to him, "What is this you've done?" For the men knew he was fleeing from the LORD's presence, because he had told them. ¹¹ So they said to him, "What should we do to you to calm this sea that's against us?" For the sea was getting worse and worse.

¹² He answered them, "Pick me up and throw me into the seaᶜ so it may quiet down for you, for I know that I'm to blame for this violent storm that is against you." ¹³ Nevertheless, the men rowed hard to get back to dry land, but they could not because the sea was raging against them more and more.

The Great Fish

¹⁴ So they called out to the LORD: "Please, Yahweh, don't let us perish because of this man's life, and don't charge us with innocent blood! For You, Yahweh, have done just as You pleased." ¹⁵ Then they picked up Jonah and threw him into the sea, and the sea stopped its raging. ¹⁶ The men •feared the LORD even more, and they offered a sacrifice to the LORD and made vows. ¹⁷ᵈ Then the LORD appointed a great fish to swallow Jonah, and Jonah was inᵉ the fish three days and three nights.

Jonah's Prayer

2 Jonah prayed to the LORD his God from insideᶠ the fish:

²   I called to the LORD in my distress,
    and He answered me.

ᵃ**1:6** Or *God* ᵇ**1:9** Or *fear* ᶜ**1:12** Lit *sea that's against you* ᵈ**1:17** Jnh 2:1 in Hb ᵉ**1:17** Lit *in the belly of* ᶠ**2:1** Lit *from the belly of*

I cried out for help in the belly
   of •Sheol;
You heard my voice.
3 You threw me into the depths,
   into the heart of the seas,
   and the current[a] overcame me.
All Your breakers and Your billows
   swept over me.
4 But I said: I have been banished
   from Your sight,
   yet I will look once more[b]
   toward Your holy temple.
5 The waters engulfed me up
    to the neck;[c]
   the watery depths overcame me;
seaweed was wrapped
   around my head.
6 I sank to the foundations
   of the mountains;
   the earth with its prison bars closed
   behind me forever!
But You raised my life from the •Pit,
   LORD my God!
7 As my life was fading away,
   I remembered the LORD.
My prayer came to You,
   to Your holy temple.
8 Those who cling to worthless idols
   forsake faithful love,
9 but as for me, I will sacrifice to You
   with a voice of thanksgiving.
I will fulfill what I have vowed.
Salvation[d] is from the LORD!

10 Then the LORD commanded the fish, and it vomited Jonah onto dry land.

Jonah Obeys God

3 Then the word of the LORD came to Jonah a second time: 2 "Get up! Go to the great city of Nineveh and preach the message that I tell you." 3 So Jonah got up and went to Nineveh according to the LORD's command.

Jonah Preaches in Nineveh

Now Nineveh was an extremely large city,[e] a three-day walk.[f] 4 Jonah set out on the first day of his walk in the city and proclaimed, "In 40 days Nineveh will be overthrown!" 5 The men of Nineveh believed in God.[g] They proclaimed a fast and dressed in •sackcloth—from the greatest of them to the least.

The King Believes

6 When word reached the king of Nineveh, he got up from his throne, took off his royal robe, put on sackcloth, and sat in ashes. 7 Then he issued a decree in Nineveh:

By order of the king and his nobles: No man or beast, herd or flock, is to taste anything at all. They must not eat or drink water. 8 Furthermore, both man and beast must be covered with sackcloth, and everyone must call out earnestly to God. Each must turn from his evil ways and from the violence[h] he is doing.[i] 9 Who knows? God may turn and relent; He may turn from His burning anger so that we will not perish.

God Relents

10 Then God saw their actions—that they had turned from their evil ways—so God relented from the disaster He had threatened to do to them. And He did not do it.

Jonah's Anger

4 But Jonah was greatly displeased and became furious. 2 He prayed to the LORD: "Please, LORD, isn't this what I said while I was still in my own country? That's why I fled toward Tarshish in the first place. I knew that You are a merciful and compassionate God, slow to become angry, rich in faithful love, and One who relents from ⌐sending¬ disaster. ³ And now, LORD, please take my life from me, for it is better for me to die than to live."

⁴ The LORD asked, "Is it right for you to be angry?"

Worm and Plant

⁵ Jonah left the city and sat down east of it. He made himself a shelter there and sat in its shade to see what would happen to the city. ⁶ Then the LORD God appointed a plant,ᵃ and it grew up to provide shade over Jonah's head to ease his discomfort.ᵇ Jonah was greatly pleased with the plant. ⁷ When dawn came the next day, God appointed a worm that attacked the plant, and it withered.

⁸ As the sun was rising, God appointed a scorching east wind. The sun beat down on Jonah's head so that he almost fainted, and he wanted to die. He said, "It's better for me to die than to live."

Merciful God Rebukes Jonah

⁹ Then God asked Jonah, "Is it right for you to be angry about the plant?"

"⌐Yes,¬" he replied. "It is right. I'm angry enough to die!"

¹⁰ So the LORD said, "You cared about the plant, which you did not labor over and did not grow. It appeared in a night and perished in a night. ¹¹ Should I not care about the great city of Nineveh, which has more than 120,000 peopleᶜ who cannot distinguish between their right and their left, as well as many animals?"

MICAH

1 The word of the LORD that came to Micah the Moreshite—what he saw regarding Samaria and Jerusalem in the days of Jotham, Ahaz, and Hezekiah, kings of Judah.

Coming Judgment on Israel

² Listen, all you peoples;
pay attention, earthᵈ and everyone
in it!
The Lord GOD will be a witness
against you,
the Lord, from His holy temple.
³ Look, the LORD is leaving His place
and coming down to trample
the heightsᵉ of the earth.
⁴ The mountains will melt
beneath Him,
and the valleys will split apart,

like wax near a fire,
like water cascading down
a mountainside.
⁵ All this will happen because of
Jacob's rebellion
and the sins of the house of Israel.
What is the rebellion of Jacob?
Isn't it Samaria?
And what is the •high place
of Judah?
Isn't it Jerusalem?
⁶ Therefore, I will make Samaria
a heap of ruins in the countryside,
a planting area for a vineyard.
I will roll her stones
into the valley
and expose her foundations.
⁷ All her carved images
will be smashed to pieces,

ᵃ**4:6** = either a castor-oil plant or a climbing gourd   ᵇ**4:6** Lit *to deliver him from his evil*   ᶜ**4:11** Or *men*   ᵈ**1:2** Or *land*   ᵉ**1:3** Or *high places*

all her wages will be burned
in the fire,
and I will destroy all her idols.
Since she collected the wages
of a prostitute,
they will be used again
for a prostitute.

Micah's Lament

8 Because of this I will lament
and wail;
I will walk barefoot and naked.
I will howl like the jackals
and mourn like ostriches.[a]
9 For her wound is incurable
and has reached even Judah;
it has approached the gate
of my people,
as far as Jerusalem.

10 Don't announce it in Gath,
don't weep at all.
In Beth-leaphrah roll in the dust.
11 Depart in shameful nakedness,
you residents of Shaphir;
the residents of Zaanan will not
come out.
Beth-ezel is lamenting;
its support[b] is taken from you.
12 Though the residents of Maroth
anxiously wait for something good,
calamity has come from the LORD
to the gate of Jerusalem.
13 Harness the horses to the chariot,
you residents of Lachish.
This was the beginning of sin
for Daughter Zion,
because Israel's acts of rebellion
can be traced to you.
14 Therefore, send farewell gifts
to Moresheth-gath;
the houses of Achzib are
a deception
to the kings of Israel.

15 I will again bring a conqueror
against you who live in Mareshah.
The nobility[c] of Israel will come
to Adullam.
16 Shave yourselves bald and cut off
your hair
in sorrow for your
precious children;
make yourselves as bald as an eagle,
for they have been taken from you
into exile.

God Judges Oppressors

2 Woe to those who dream
up wickedness
and prepare evil ⌊plans⌋
on their beds!
At morning light they
accomplish it
because the power is
in their hands.
2 They covet fields and seize them;
they also take houses.
They deprive a man of his home,
a person of his inheritance.

3 Therefore, the LORD says:

I am now planning a disaster
against this nation;
you cannot free your necks from it.
Then you will not walk so proudly
because it will be an evil time.
4 In that day one will take up a taunt
against you,
and lament mournfully, saying:
We are totally ruined!
He measures out the allotted land
of my people.
How He removes ⌊it⌋ from me!
He allots our fields to traitors.
5 Therefore, there will be no one
in the assembly of the LORD
to divide the land by casting lots.[d]

---

a1:8 Or *eagle owls*; lit *daughters of the desert*   b1:11 Lit *its standing place*; Hb obscure   c1:15 Lit *glory*   d2:5 Lit
LORD *stretching the measuring line by lot*

God's Word Rejected

6 "Stop your preaching,"
   they[a] preach.
"They should not preach
   these things;
shame will not overtake us."[b]
7 House of Jacob, should it be asked:
"Is the Spirit
   of the LORD impatient?
Are these the things He does?"
Don't My words bring good
   to the one who walks uprightly?
8 But recently My people have risen up
   like an enemy:
You strip off the splendid robe
   from those who are
     passing through confidently,
like those returning from war.
9 You force the women of My people
   out of their comfortable homes,
and you take My blessing[c]
   from their children forever.
10 Get up and leave,
   for this is not your place of rest,
because defilement
   brings destruction—
     a grievous destruction!
11 If a man of spirit[d] comes
   and invents lies:
"I will preach to you about wine
   and beer,"
he would be just the preacher
   for this people!

Remnant Regathered

12 I will indeed gather all
   of you, Jacob;
I will collect the remnant of Israel.
I will bring them together
   like sheep in a pen,
like a flock in the middle of its fold.
It will be noisy with people.
13 One who breaks open ⌊the way⌋
   will advance before them;

they will break out, pass
   through the gate,
and leave by it.
Their King will pass through
   before them,
the LORD as their leader.

God Judges Unjust Leaders

3 Then I said: "Now listen,
   leaders of Jacob,
you rulers of the house of Israel.
Aren't you supposed to know
   what is just?
2 You hate good and love evil.
You tear off the skin of people
  and ⌊strip⌋ their flesh
   from their bones.
3 You eat the flesh of my people
after you strip their skin from them
and break their bones.
You chop them up
   like flesh for the cooking pot,
like meat in a caldron."
4 Then they will cry out to the LORD,
   but He will not answer them.
He will hide His face from them
   at that time
because of the crimes
   they have committed.

False Prophets Judged

5 This is what the LORD says
   concerning the prophets
who lead my people astray,
who proclaim peace
   when they have ⌊food⌋ to sink
     their teeth into
but declare war against the one
who puts nothing in their mouths.
6 Therefore, it will be night for you—
   without visions;
it will grow dark for you—
   without •divination.
The sun will set on these prophets,

---

[a] **2:6** = the prophets   [b] **2:6** Text emended; MT reads *things. Shame will not depart.*   [c] **2:9** Perhaps = land   [d] **2:11** Lit wind

and the daylight will turn black
  over them.
7 Then the seers will be ashamed
  and the diviners disappointed.
  They will all cover their mouths[a]
  because there will be no answer
  from God.

8 But as for me, I am filled
  with power
  by the Spirit of the LORD,
  with justice and courage,
  to proclaim to Jacob his rebellion
  and to Israel his sin.

Zion's Destruction

9 Listen to this, leaders of the house
  of Jacob,
  you rulers of the house of Israel,
  who abhor justice
  and pervert everything that is right,
10 who build Zion with bloodshed
  and Jerusalem with injustice.
11 Her leaders issue rulings
    for a bribe,
  her priests teach for payment,
  and her prophets
    practice divination for money.
  Yet they lean on the LORD, saying,
  "Isn't the LORD among us?
  No calamity will overtake us."
12 Therefore, because of you,
  Zion will be plowed like a field,
  Jerusalem will become ruins,
  and the hill of the temple mount
  will be a thicket.

Last Days:
Mountain of Lord's House

4 In the last days
  the mountain of the LORD's house
  will be established
  at the top of the mountains
  and will be raised above the hills.
  Peoples will stream to it,

2 and many nations will come
  and say,
  "Come, let us go up
    to the mountain of the LORD,
  to the house of the God of Jacob.

LORD's Rule from
Restored Zion

He will teach us about His ways
  so we may walk in His paths."
For instruction will go out of Zion
  and the word of the LORD
    from Jerusalem.
3 He will settle disputes
    among many peoples
  and provide arbitration
    for strong nations
  that are far away.
  They will beat their swords
    into plows,
  and their spears
    into pruning knives.
  Nation will not take up the sword
    against nation,
  and they will never again train
    for war.
4 But each man will sit
    under his grapevine
  and under his fig tree
  with no one to frighten ⌊him⌋.
  For the mouth of the LORD of •Hosts
  has promised ⌊this⌋.
5 Though all the peoples each walk
  in the name of their gods,
  we will walk in the name
    of •Yahweh our God
  forever and ever.

6 On that day—
    ⌊this is⌋ the LORD's declaration—

The Lame into a Remnant

I will assemble the lame
  and gather the scattered,
  those I have injured.

---

a 3:7 Lit mustache

7 I will make the lame
   into a remnant,
those far removed
   into a strong nation.
Then the LORD will rule over them
   in Mount Zion
from this time on and forever.
8 And you, watchtower for the flock,
   fortified hill[a] of Daughter Zion,
the former rule will come to you,
sovereignty will come
   to Daughter Jerusalem.

From Exile to Victory

9 Now, why are you shouting loudly?
Is there no king with you?
Has your counselor perished,
so that anguish grips you
   like a woman in labor?
10 Writhe and cry out,[b]
   Daughter Zion,
like a woman in labor.
For now you will leave the city
and camp in the open fields.
You will go to Babylon;
there you will be rescued;
there the LORD will redeem you
from the power of your enemies!
11 Many nations have now assembled
   against you;
they say, "Let her be defiled,
and let us feast our eyes on Zion."
12 But they do not know
   the LORD's intentions
or understand His plan,
that He has gathered them
like sheaves to the threshing floor.
13 Rise and thresh, Daughter Zion,
for I will make your horns iron
and your hooves bronze,
so you can crush many peoples.
Then you[c] will devote
what they plundered to the LORD,

their wealth to the Lord of all
   the earth.

From Defeated Ruler
to Conquering King

5 [d] Now daughter ⌊who is⌋
   under attack,
you slash yourself ⌊in grief⌋;
a siege is set against us!
They are striking the judge of Israel
on the cheek with a rod.

From Bethlehem, a Ruler

2 [e] Bethlehem Ephrathah,
you are small among the clans
   of Judah;
One will come from you
to be ruler over Israel for Me.
His origin[f] is from antiquity,
from eternity.[g]
3 Therefore, He will abandon them
   until the time
when she who is in labor
   has given birth;
then the rest of His brothers
   will return
to the people of Israel.
4 He will stand and shepherd ⌊them⌋
in the strength of •Yahweh,
in the majestic name of Yahweh
   His God.
They will live securely,
for then His greatness will extend
to the ends of the earth.
5 There[h] will be peace.
When Assyria invades our land,
when it marches
   against our fortresses,
we will raise against it
   seven shepherds,
even eight leaders of men.
6 They will shepherd the land
   of Assyria with the sword,

the land of Nimrod
  with a drawn blade.[a]
So He will rescue us from Assyria
  when it invades our land,
  when it marches
    against our territory.

Lion-like Remnant

7 Then the remnant of Jacob
will be among many peoples
like dew from the LORD,
like showers on the grass,
which do not wait for anyone
or linger for •mankind.
8 Then the remnant of Jacob
will be among the nations,
  among many peoples,
like a lion among animals
  of the forest,
like a young lion among flocks
  of sheep,
which tramples and tears
  as it passes through,
and there is no one
  to rescue them.
9 Your hand will be lifted up
  against your adversaries,
and all your enemies
  will be destroyed.
10 In that day—
        the LORD's declaration—

End of Idolatry

I will remove your horses from you
and wreck your chariots.
11 I will remove the cities
  of your land
and tear down all your fortresses.
12 I will remove sorceries
  from your hands,
and you will not have
  any more fortune-tellers.
13 I will remove your carved images
and sacred pillars from you,

so that you will not bow
  down again
to the work of your hands.
14 I will pull up the •Asherah poles
  from among you
and demolish your cities.[b]
15 I will take vengeance in anger
  and wrath
against the nations that have not
  obeyed Me.

God's Case against Judah

6 Now listen to what the LORD is saying:

Rise, plead your case
  before the mountains,
and let the hills hear your voice.
2 Listen to the LORD's lawsuit,
you mountains
  and enduring foundations
  of the earth,
because the LORD has a case
  against His people,
and He will argue it against Israel.
3 My people, what have I done
  to you,
or how have I wearied you?
Testify against Me!
4 Indeed, I brought you up
  from the land of Egypt
and redeemed you from that place
  of slavery.
I sent Moses, Aaron, and Miriam
  ahead of you.

Remember Balak and Balaam

5 My people,
  remember what Balak
    king of Moab proposed,
  what Balaam son of Beor
    answered him,
  and what happened
    from Acacia Grove[c] to Gilgal,

---

[a] 5:6 Aq, Vg; MT, Sym read Nimrod at its gateways   [b] 5:14 Or shrines   [c] 6:5 Or Shittim

so that you may acknowledge
the LORD's righteous acts.

Micah Questions God

6 What should I bring
  before the LORD
when I come to bow before God
  on high?
Should I come before Him
  with •burnt offerings,
with year-old calves?
7 Would the LORD be pleased
  with thousands of rams,
or with ten thousand streams of oil?
Should I give my firstborn
  for my transgression,
the child of my body
  for my own sin?

8 He has told you men what is good
and what it is the LORD requires
  of you:
Only to act justly,
to love faithfulness,
and to walk humbly with your God.

God's Verdict
on Jerusalem

9 The voice of the LORD calls out
  to the city[a]
(and it is wise to •fear Your name):
"Pay attention to the rod
and the One who ordained it.[b]
10 Are there still[c] the treasures
  of wickedness
and the accursed short measure
in the house of the wicked?
11 Can I excuse wicked scales
or bags of deceptive weights?
12 For the wealthy of the city are full
  of violence,
and its residents speak lies;
the tongues in their mouths
  are deceitful.

13 "As a result, I have begun to strike
  you severely,[d]
bringing desolation because of
  your sins.
14 You will eat but not be satisfied,
for there will be hunger within you.
What you acquire, you cannot save,
and what you do save,
I will give to the sword.[c]
15 You will sow but not reap;
you will press olives
but not anoint yourself with oil;
and ⌊you will tread⌋ grapes
but not drink the wine.
16 The statutes of Omri
and all the practices
  of Ahab's house
have been observed;
you have followed their policies.
Therefore, I will make you
  a desolate place
and the city's[e] residents an object
  of contempt;[f]
you will bear the scorn
  of My people."[g]

Micah's Sadness:
Israel's Moral Decline

7 How sad for me!
For I am like one who—
when the summer fruit
  has been gathered
after the gleaning
  of the grape harvest—
⌊finds⌋ no grape cluster to eat,
no early fig, which I crave.
2 Godly people have vanished
  from the land;
there is no one upright
  among the people.
All of them wait in ambush
  to shed blood;
they hunt each other with a net.

a6:9 = Jerusalem   b6:9 Or *attention, you tribe. Who has ordained it?*; Hb obscure   c6:10 Hb obscure   d6:13 LXX, Aq, Theod, Syr, Vg; MT reads *I have made [you] sick by striking you down*   e6:16 Lit *and its*   f6:16 Lit *residents a hissing*   g6:16 LXX reads *of the peoples*

3 Both hands are good
    at accomplishing evil:
the official and the judge demand
    a bribe;
when the powerful man
    communicates his evil desire,
they plot it together.
4 The best of them is like a brier;
the most upright is worse
    than a hedge of thorns.
The day of your watchmen,
⌊the day of⌋ your punishment,
    is coming;
at this time their panic is here.

Prevalence of Distrust

5 Do not rely on a friend;
don't trust in a close companion.
Seal your mouth
from the woman who lies
    in your arms.
6 For a son considers his father a fool,
a daughter opposes her mother,
and a daughter-in-law is
    against her mother-in-law;
a person's enemies are the people
    in his own home.
7 But as for me, I will look
    to the LORD;
I will wait for the God
    of my salvation.
My God will hear me.

Zion's Vindication

8 Do not rejoice over me, my enemy!
Though I have fallen,
    I will stand up;
though I sit in darkness,
the LORD will be my light.
9 Because I have sinned against Him,
I must endure the LORD's rage
until He argues my case
and establishes justice for me.
He will bring me into the light;

I will see His salvation.[a]
10 Then my enemy will see,
and she will be covered
    with shame,
the one who said to me,
"Where is the LORD your God?"
My eyes will look at her in triumph;
at that time she will be trampled
like mud in the streets.
11 A day will come for rebuilding
    your walls;
on that day ⌊your⌋ boundary
    will be extended.
12 On that day people will come
    to you
from Assyria and the cities of Egypt,
even from Egypt
    to the Euphrates River
and from sea to sea
and mountain to mountain.
13 Then the earth will become
    a wasteland
because of its inhabitants,
and as a result of their actions.

Micah's Prayer Answered

14 Shepherd Your people
    with Your staff,
the flock that is Your possession.
They live alone in a scrubland,
surrounded by pastures.
Let them graze in Bashan
    and Gilead
as in ancient times.
15 I will show them[b] wondrous deeds
as in the days of your exodus
from the land of Egypt.
16 Nations will see and be ashamed
of[c] all their power.
They will put ⌊their⌋ hands
    over ⌊their⌋ mouths,
and their ears will become deaf.
17 They will lick the dust like a snake;

they will come trembling out of
  their hiding places
like reptiles slithering
  on the ground.
They will tremble before the LORD
  our God;
they will stand in awe of You.

God's Faithful Love

18 Who is a God like You,
  removing iniquity and passing
    over rebellion
for the remnant of His inheritance?

He does not hold on
  to His anger forever,
because He delights
  in faithful love.
19 He will again have compassion
  on us;
He will vanquish our iniquities.
You will cast all our[a] sins
  into the depths of the sea.
20 You will show loyalty to Jacob
  and faithful love to Abraham,
as You swore to our fathers
  from days long ago.

NAHUM

1 The •oracle concerning Nineveh. The
  book of the vision of Nahum the El-
koshite.

God's Vengeance

2 The LORD is a jealous
    and avenging God;
  the LORD takes vengeance
    and is fierce in[b] wrath.
  The LORD takes vengeance
    against His foes;
  He is furious with His enemies.
3 The LORD is slow to anger but great
    in power;
  the LORD will never leave
    ⌊the guilty⌋ unpunished.
  His path is in the whirlwind
    and storm,
  and clouds are the dust
    beneath His feet.
4 He rebukes the sea so that
    it dries up,
  and He makes all the rivers run dry.
  Bashan and Carmel wither;
  even the flower
    of Lebanon withers.

5 The mountains quake before Him,
  and the hills melt;
the earth
    trembles[c] [d] at His presence—
the world and all who live in it.
6 Who can withstand
    His indignation?
Who can endure
    His burning anger?
His wrath is poured out like fire,
even rocks are shattered
    before Him.

Destruction of Nineveh

7 The LORD is good,
    a stronghold in a day of distress;
  He cares for those who take refuge
    in Him.
8 But He will completely
    destroy Nineveh[e]
  with an overwhelming flood,
  and He will chase His enemies
    into darkness.

9 Whatever you[f] plot
    against the LORD,

a7:19 Some Hb mss, LXX, Syr, Vg; other Hb mss read *their*   b1:2 Lit *is a master of*   c1:5 Some emend to *is laid waste*   d1:5 Lit *lifts*   e1:8 Lit *her place*   f1:9 = Nineveh

He will bring ⌊it⌋
  to complete destruction;
oppression will not rise up
  a second time.
10 For they will be consumed
  like entangled thorns,
like a drunkard's drink,
  and like straw that is fully dry.[a]
11 One has gone out from Nineveh,[b]
  who plots evil against the LORD,
  and is a wicked counselor.

Promise of Judah's Deliverance

12 This is what the LORD says:

Though they are strong[c]
  and numerous,
they will still be mowed down,
  and he[d] will pass away.
Though I have afflicted you,[e]
  I will afflict you no longer.
13 For I will now break off his[f] yoke
    from you
  and tear off your shackles.

Assyrian King's Demise

14 The LORD has issued an order concerning you:[f]

There will be no offspring
  to carry on your name.[g]
I will eliminate the carved idol
  and cast image
from the house of your gods;
I will prepare your grave,
  for you are contemptible.

15h Look to the mountains—
  the feet of one bringing good news
  and proclaiming peace!
Celebrate your festivals, Judah;
  fulfill your vows.
For the wicked one will never again

march through you;
  he will be entirely wiped out.

Attack against Nineveh

2 One who scatters is coming up
    against you.
Man the fortifications!
Watch the road!
Brace[i] yourself!
Summon all your strength!

2 For the LORD will restore
    the majesty of Jacob,
yes,[j] the majesty of Israel,
  though ravagers have ravaged them
  and ruined their vine branches.

3 The shields of his[k] warriors
    are dyed red;
the valiant men are dressed
    in scarlet.
The fittings of the chariot flash
    like fire
on the day
    of its ⌊battle⌋ preparations,
  and the spears are brandished.

4 The chariots dash madly
    through the streets;
they rush around in the plazas.
They look like torches;
they dart back and forth
    like lightning.

5 He gives orders to his officers;
they stumble as they advance.
They race to its wall;
  the protective shield is set in place.

6 The river gates are opened,
  and the palace erodes away.

Desolation and Plunder

7 Beauty[l] is stripped,[m]
  she is carried away;
  her ladies-in-waiting moan

a1:10 Hb obscure   b1:11 Lit from you   c1:12 Lit intact   d1:12 = either the king of Assyria or his army   e 1:12 =
Judah   f1:13,14 Probably = the king of Assyria   g1:14 Lit It will not be sown from your name any longer   h1:15 Nah
2:1 in Hb   i2:1 Lit Strengthen   j2:2 Or like   k2:3 = the army commander attacking Nineveh   l2:7 Text emended; MT
reads Huzzab   m2:7 Hb obscure

like the sound of doves,
and beat their breasts.

8 Nineveh has been like a pool
of water
from her ˌfirstˌ days,ᵃ
but they are fleeing.
"Stop! Stop!" ˌthey cry,ˌ
but no one turns back.

9 "Plunder the silver!
Plunder the gold!"
There is no end to the treasure,
an abundance
of every precious thing.

10 Desolation, decimation,
devastation!
Hearts melt,
knees tremble,
loins shake,
every face grows pale!

11 Where is the lions' lair,
or the feeding ground
of the young lions,
where the lion
and lioness prowled,
and the lion's cub,
with nothing to frighten
them away?

12 The lion mauled whatever
its cubs needed
and strangled ˌpreyˌ
for its lionesses.
It filled up its dens with the kill,
and its lairs with mauled prey.

13 Beware, I am against you—
the declaration
of the Lord of •Hosts.
I will make your chariots go up
in smokeᵇ
and the sword will devour
your young lions.
I will cut off your prey
from the earth,
and the sound of your messengers
will never be heard again.

Nineveh's Downfall

3 Woe to the city of blood,
totally deceitful,
full of plunder,
never without prey.

2 The crack of the whip
and rumble of the wheel,
galloping horse
and jolting chariot!

3 Charging horseman,
flashing sword,
shining spear;
heaps of slain,
mounds of corpses,
dead bodies without end—
they stumble over their dead.

Nineveh's Sins

4 Because of the
continual prostitution
of the prostitute,
the attractive mistress
of sorcery,
who betrays nations
by her prostitution
and clans by her witchcraft,

5 I am against you—
the declaration
of the Lord of •Hosts.
I will lift your skirts
over your face
and display your nakedness
to nations,
your shame to kingdoms.

6 I will throw filth on you
and treat you with contempt;
I will make a spectacle of you.

7 Then all who see you will recoil
from you, saying:
Nineveh is devastated;
who will show sympathy
to her?
Where can I find anyone
to comfort you?

ᵃ **2:8** Hb obscure   ᵇ**2:13** Lit *will burn her chariots in smoke*

Nineveh and Thebes Compared

8 Are you better than Thebes[a]
    that sat along the Nile
with water surrounding her,
    whose rampart was the sea,
    the river[b][c] her wall?
9 •Cush and Egypt were
    her endless source of strength;
Put and Libya were
    among her[d] allies.
10 Yet she became an exile;
    she went into captivity.
Her children were also dashed
    to pieces
    at the head of every street.
They cast lots for her dignitaries,
    and all her nobles were bound
    in chains.

Weakness and Cowardice

11 You[e] also will become drunk;
    you will hide yourself.[f]
You also will seek refuge
    from the enemy.

12 All your fortresses are fig trees
    with figs that ripened first;
when shaken, they fall—
    right into the mouth of the eater!

13 Look, your troops are women
    among you;
the gates of your land
    are wide open to your enemies.
Fire will devour the bars
    ⌊of your gates⌋.

14 Draw water for the siege;
    strengthen your fortresses.

Step into the clay and tread
    the mortar;
take hold of the brick-mold!
15 The fire will devour you there;
    the sword will cut you down.
It will devour you
    like the young locust.
Multiply yourselves
    like the young locust,
multiply like the swarming locust!

Nineveh's Weak Leaders

16 You have made your merchants
    more numerous than the stars
    of the sky.
The young locust strips[g] ⌊the land⌋
    and flies away.
17 Your court officials are
    like the swarming locust,
and your scribes like clouds
    of locusts,
which settle on the walls
    on a cold day;
when the sun rises, they take off,
    and no one knows where they are.

18 King of Assyria,
    your shepherds slumber;
your officers sleep.[h]
Your people are scattered
    across the mountains
with no one to gather
    ⌊them⌋ together.
19 There is no remedy for your injury;
    your wound is severe.
All who hear the news about you
    will clap their hands
    because of you,
for who has not experienced
    your constant cruelty?

---

[a] **3:8** Lit *No-amon* [b] **3:8** LXX, Syr, Vg read *water* [c] **3:8** Lit *sea from sea* [d] **3:9** Lit *your*; = Thebes [e] **3:11** = Nineveh
[f] **3:11** Or *will be overcome* [g] **3:16** Or *sheds [its skin]* [h] **3:18** Probably = sleep in death

HABAKKUK

1 The •oracle that Habakkuk the prophet saw.

Habakkuk's First Prayer

2 How long, LORD, must I call
  for help
and You do not listen,
or cry out to You about violence
and You do not save?
3 Why do You force me to look
  at injustice?
Why do You tolerate[a] wrongdoing?
Oppression and violence are right
  in front of me.
Strife is ongoing,
  and conflict escalates.
4 This is why the law is ineffective
and justice never emerges.
For the wicked restrict
  the righteous;
therefore, justice
  comes out perverted.

God's First Answer

5 Look at the nations[b]
  and observe—
be utterly astounded!
For something is taking place
  in your days
that you will not believe
when you hear about it.

I Am Raising Up Chaldeans

6 Look! I am raising up
  the Chaldeans,[c]
that bitter, impetuous nation
that marches across
  the earth's open spaces
to seize territories not its own.
7 They are fierce and terrifying;

their views of justice
  and sovereignty
stem from themselves.
8 Their horses are swifter
  than leopards
and more fierce[d] than wolves
  of the night.
Their horsemen charge ahead;
their horsemen come
  from distant ⌊lands⌋.
They fly like an eagle,
  swooping to devour.
9 All of them come to do violence;
their faces are set
  in determination.[e]
They gather prisoners like sand.
10 They mock kings,
and rulers are a joke to them.
They laugh at every fortress
and build siege ramps to capture it.
11 Then they sweep by like the wind
and pass through.
They are guilty,[f] their strength
  is their god.

Habakkuk's Second Prayer

12 Are You not from eternity,
  •Yahweh my God?
My Holy One, You[g] will not die.
LORD, You appointed them
  to execute judgment;
⌊my⌋ Rock, You destined them
  to punish ⌊us⌋.
13 ⌊Your⌋ eyes are too pure to look
  on evil,
and You cannot
  tolerate wrongdoing.
So why do You tolerate those
  who are treacherous?
Why are You silent

---

while one[a] who is wicked
  swallows up
one[b] who is more righteous
  than himself?

14 You have made mankind
  like the fish of the sea,
  like marine creatures that have
    no ruler.
15 The Chaldeans pull them all up
  with a hook,
  catch them in their dragnet,
  and gather them
    in their fishing net;
  that is why they are glad
  and rejoice.
16 That is why they sacrifice
  to their dragnet
  and burn incense
  to their fishing net,
  for by these things their portion
    is rich
  and their food plentiful.
17 Will they therefore empty their net[c]
  and continually slaughter nations
    without mercy?

Habakkuk Waits for God's Response

2 I will stand at my guard post
  and station myself
    on the lookout tower.
I will watch to see what He will say
  to me
and what I should[d] reply
  about my complaint.

God's Second Answer

2 The LORD answered me:

Write down this vision;
clearly inscribe it on tablets
so one may easily read it.[e]
3 For the vision is yet
  for the appointed time;

it testifies about the end
  and will not lie.
Though it delays, wait for it,
since it will certainly come and not
  be late.

Righteous Will Live by Faith

4 Look, his ego is inflated;[f]
  he is without integrity.
But the righteous one will live
  by his faith.[g]
5 Moreover, wine[h] betrays;
  an arrogant man is never at rest.[i]
He enlarges his appetite
  like •Sheol,
and like Death he is never satisfied.
He gathers all the nations
  to himself;
he collects all the peoples
  for himself.

The Woe Oracles

6 Won't all of these take up a taunt
  against him,
with mockery and riddles
  about him?
They will say:

Woe to him who amasses
  what is not his—
how much longer?—
and loads himself with goods
  taken in pledge.
7 Won't your creditors
  suddenly arise,
and those who disturb you
  wake up?
Then you will become spoil
  for them.
8 Since you have plundered
  many nations,
all the peoples who remain
  will plunder you—
because of human bloodshed

---

[a] 1:13 = Babylon; perhaps personified in its king   [b] 1:13 = Judah   [c] 1:17 DSS read *sword*   [d] 2:1 Syr reads *what He will*   [e] 2:2 Lit *one who reads in it may run*   [f] 2:4 Hb obscure   [g] 2:4 Or *faithfulness*   [h] 2:5 DSS read *wealth*   [i] 2:5 Or *man does not endure;* Hb obscure

and violence against lands, cities,
and all who live in them.

9 Woe to him who unjustly gains
wealth for his house[a]
to place his nest on high,
to escape from the reach
of disaster!
10 You have planned shame
for your house
by wiping out many peoples
and sinning against your own self.
11 For the stones will cry out
from the wall,
and the rafters will answer them
from the woodwork.

12 Woe to him who builds a city
with bloodshed
and founds a town with injustice!
13 Is it not from the LORD of •Hosts,
that the peoples labor ⌊only⌋ to fuel
the fire
and countries exhaust themselves
for nothing?
14 For the earth will be filled
with the knowledge
of the LORD's glory,
as the waters cover the sea.

15 Woe to him who gives
his neighbors drink,
pouring out your wrath[b]
and even making them drunk,
in order to look at their nakedness!
16 You will be filled with disgrace
instead of glory.
You also—drink,
and expose your uncircumcision![c]
The cup in the LORD's right hand
will come around to you,
and utter disgrace will cover
your glory.
17 For ⌊your⌋ violence against Lebanon
will overwhelm you;

the destruction of animals
will terrify you,[d]
because of ⌊your⌋ human bloodshed
and violence
against lands, cities, and all
who live in them.

Foolishness of Idols

18 What use is a carved idol
after its craftsman carves it?
It is ⌊only⌋ a cast image, a teacher
of lies.
For the one who crafts its shape
trusts in it
and makes idols that cannot speak.
19 Woe to him who says to wood:
Wake up!
or to mute stone: Come alive!
Can it teach?
Look! It may be plated with gold
and silver,
yet there is no breath in it at all.

20 But the LORD is
in His holy temple;
let everyone on earth
be silent in His presence.

Habakkuk's Third Prayer

3 A prayer of Habakkuk the prophet.
According to *Shigionoth*.[e]

2 LORD, I have heard the report
about You;
LORD, I stand in awe of Your deeds.
Revive ⌊Your work⌋ in these years;
make ⌊it⌋ known in these years.
In ⌊Your⌋ wrath remember mercy!

God's Splendor

3 God comes from Teman,
the Holy One from Mount Paran.
                              •Selah
His splendor covers the heavens,
and the earth is full of His praise.

---

[a]2:9 Or *dynasty*   [b]2:15 Or *venom*   [c]2:16 DSS, LXX, Aq, Syr, Vg read *and stagger*   [d]2:17 DSS, LXX, Aq, Syr, Tg, Vg;
MT reads *them*   [e]3:1 Perhaps a passionate song with rapid changes of rhythm, or a dirge   [f]3:6 Or *surveys*

4 ⌊His⌋ brilliance is like light;
rays are flashing from His hand.
This is where His power is hidden.

God's Power

5 Plague goes before Him,
and pestilence follows in His steps.
6 He stands and shakes[f] the earth;
He looks and startles the nations.
The age-old mountains break apart;
the ancient hills sink down.
His pathways are ancient.
7 I see the tents of Cushan[g]
in distress;
the tent curtains of the land
of Midian tremble.

God's Anger

8 Are You angry at the rivers, LORD?
Is Your wrath against the rivers?
Or is Your rage against the sea
when You ride on Your horses,
Your victorious chariot?
9 You took the sheath from Your bow;
the arrows are ready[h] to be used
with an oath.[i]   Selah
You split the earth with rivers.
10 The mountains see You
and shudder;
a downpour of water sweeps by.
The deep roars with its voice
and lifts its waves[j] high.
11 Sun and moon stand still
in ⌊their⌋ lofty residence,
at the flash of Your flying arrows,
at the brightness
of Your shining spear.
12 You march across the earth
with indignation;
You trample down the nations
in wrath.

13 You come out to save Your people,
to save Your anointed.[k]
You crush the leader of the house
of the wicked
and strip ⌊him⌋ from foot[l] to neck.
                              Selah
14 You pierce his head
with his own spears;
his warriors storm out to scatter us,
gloating as if ready
to secretly devour the weak.
15 You tread the sea with Your horses,
stirring up the great waters.

Habakkuk's
Confidence in God

16 I heard, and I trembled within;
my lips quivered at the sound.
Rottenness entered my bones;
I trembled where I stood.
Now I must quietly wait for the day
of distress
to come against the people
invading us.
17 Though the fig tree does not bud
and there is no fruit on the vines,
though the olive crop fails
and the fields produce no food,
though there are no sheep
in the pen
and no cattle in the stalls,
18 yet I will triumph in the LORD;
I will rejoice in the God
of my salvation!
19 •Yahweh my Lord is my strength;
He makes my feet like those
of a deer
and enables me to walk
on mountain heights!
For the choir director: on[m] stringed instruments.

---

g **3:7** = Midian   h **3:9** Or set   i **3:9** Hb obscure   j **3:10** Lit hands   k **3:13** = the Davidic king or the nation of Israel
l **3:13** Lit foundation   m **3:19** Lit on my

ZEPHANIAH

1 The word of the LORD that came to Zephaniah son of Cushi, son of Gedaliah, son of Amariah, son of Hezekiah, in the days of Josiah son of Amon, king of Judah.

Great Day of the LORD

2 I will completely
sweep away everything
from the face of the earth—
ɪthis isɪ the LORD's declaration.
3 I will sweep away man and animal;
I will sweep away the birds of the sky
and the fish of the sea,
and the ruins[a] along with the wicked.
I will cut off mankind
from the face of the earth—
the LORD's declaration.

4 I will stretch out My hand
against Judah
and against all the residents
of Jerusalem.
I will cut off from this place
every vestige of •Baal,
the names of the pagan priests
along with the priests;
5 those who bow in worship
on the rooftops
to the heavenly host;
those who bow and pledge loyalty
to the LORD
but also pledge loyalty to •Milcom;[b]
6 and those who turn back
from following the LORD,
who do not seek the LORD
or inquire of Him.
7 Be silent in the presence
of the Lord GOD,
for the Day of the LORD is near.
Indeed, the LORD has prepared
a sacrifice;

He has consecrated His guests.
8 On the day of the LORD's sacrifice
I will punish the officials,
the king's sons,
and all who are dressed
in foreign clothing.
9 On that day I will punish
all who skip over the threshold,[c]
who fill their master's house
with violence and deceit.
10 On that day—
the LORD's declaration—
there will be an outcry
from the Fish Gate,
a wailing from the Second District,
and a loud crashing from the hills.
11 Wail, you residents of the Hollow,[d]
for all the merchants[e]
will be silenced;
all those loaded with silver will be
cut off.
12 And at that time I will
search Jerusalem with lamps
and punish the men
who settle down comfortably,[f]
who say to themselves:
The LORD will not do good or evil.
13 Their wealth will become plunder
and their houses a ruin.
They will build houses
but never live ɪin themɪ,
plant vineyards but never drink
their wine.

Day of Lord Is Near

14 The great Day of the LORD is near,
near and rapidly approaching.
Listen, the Day of the LORD—
there the warrior's cry is bitter.

---

[a]**1:3** Perhaps objects connected with idolatry [b]**1:5** Some LXX mss, Syr, Vg; MT, other LXX mss read *their king*
[c]**1:9** Hb obscure [d]**1:11** Or *the market district* [e]**1:11** Or *Canaanites* [f]**1:12** Lit *who thicken on their dregs*

15 That day is a day of wrath,
    a day of trouble and distress,
    a day of destruction and desolation,
    a day of darkness and gloom,
    a day of clouds and blackness,
16 a day of trumpet ⸢blast⸣ and battle cry
    against the fortified cities,
    and against the high corner towers.
17 I will bring distress on mankind,
    and they will walk like the blind
    because they have sinned
        against the LORD.
    Their blood will be poured out
        like dust
    and their flesh like dung.
18 Their silver and their gold
    will not be able to rescue them
    on the day of the LORD's wrath.
    The whole earth will be consumed
    by the fire of His jealousy.
    For He will make a complete,
    yes, a horrifying end
    of all the inhabitants of the earth.

Call to Repentance

2 Gather yourselves together;
    gather together,
        undesirable[a] nation,
2   before the decree takes effect
    and the day passes like chaff,
    before the burning
        of the LORD's anger overtakes you,
    before the day of the LORD's anger
        overtakes you.
3   Seek the LORD, all you humble
        of the earth,
    who carry out what He commands.
    Seek righteousness, seek humility;
    perhaps you will be concealed
    on the day of the LORD's anger.

Judgment against Nations

4   For Gaza will be abandoned,
    and Ashkelon will become a ruin.

Ashdod will be driven out at noon,
    and Ekron will be uprooted.
5   Woe, inhabitants of the seacoast,
    nation of the Cherethites![b]
    The word of the LORD is
        against you,
    Canaan, land of the Philistines:
    I will destroy you until there is
        no one left.
6   The seacoast will
        become pasturelands
    with caves for shepherds and folds
        for sheep.
7   The coastland will belong
    to the remnant of the house
        of Judah;
    they will find pasture there.
    They will lie down in the evening
    among the houses of Ashkelon,
    for the LORD their God will return
        to them
    and restore their fortunes.

8   I have heard the taunting of Moab
    and the insults of the Ammonites,
    who have taunted My people
    and threatened their territory.
9   Therefore, as I live—
                    the declaration
        of the LORD of •Hosts,
            the God of Israel—
    Moab will be like Sodom
    and the Ammonites
        like Gomorrah—
    a place overgrown with weeds,
    a salt pit,
        and a perpetual wasteland.
    The remnant of My people
        will plunder them;
    the remainder of My nation
        will dispossess them.
10 This is what they get
        for their pride,
    because they have taunted
        and acted arrogantly

against the people of the LORD
   of Hosts.
11 The LORD will be terrifying to them
   when He starves all the gods
     of the earth.
Then all the distant coastlands
   of the nations
will bow in worship to Him,
   each in its own place.

12 You •Cushites will also be slain
   by My sword.

13 He will also stretch out His hand
   against the north
and destroy Assyria;
He will make Nineveh a desolate ruin,
   dry as the desert.
14 Herds will lie down in the middle
   of it,
   every kind of wild animal.a
Both the desert owlb
   and the screech owlc
will roost in the capitals of its pillars.
⌊Their⌋ calls will soundd
   from the window,
but devastatione will be
   on the threshold,
for He will expose the cedar work.f
15 This is the self-assured city
that lives in security,
that thinks to herself:
I am, and there is no one besides me.
What a desolation she has become,
a place for wild animals to lie down!
Everyone who passes by her
   jeersg and shakes his fist.

Woe to Oppressive Jerusalem

3 Woe to the city that is rebellioush
   and defiled,
   the oppressive city!
2 She has not obeyed;
   she has not accepted discipline.

She has not trusted in the LORD;
   she has not drawn near to her God.
3 Thei princes within her are
   roaring lions;
her judges are wolves of the night,
   which leave nothing
     forj the morning.
4 Her prophets are reckless—
   treacherous men.
Her priests profane the sanctuary;
   they do violence to instruction.
5 The righteous LORD is in her;
   He does no wrong.
He applies His justice morning
   by morning;
He does not fail at dawn,
yet the one who does wrong
   knows no shame.

6 I have cut off nations;
   their corner towers are destroyed.
I have laid waste their streets,
   with no one to pass through.
Their cities lie devastated,
   without a person,
   without an inhabitant.
7 I thought: You
   will certainly •fear Me
and accept correction.
Then her dwelling placek
would not be cut off
⌊based on⌋ all that I had allocated
   to her.
However, they became
   more corrupt
in all their actions.
8 Therefore, wait for Me—
     the LORD's declaration—
until the day I rise up for plunder.l
For My decision is
   to gather nations,
to assemble kingdoms,
in order to pour out My indignation
   on them,

---

a2:14 Lit every wild animal of a nation; Pr 30:25   b2:14 Or the pelican; Hb obscure   c2:14 Or the hedgehog; Hb obscure   d2:14 Lit sing   e2:14 LXX, Vg read ravens   f2:14 Hb obscure   g2:15 Or hisses   h3:1 Or filthy   i3:3 Lit Her   j3:3 Or that had nothing to gnaw in   k3:7 LXX, Syr read her eyes   l3:8 LXX, Syr read for a witness; Vg reads up forever

all My burning anger;
for the whole earth will be consumed
by the fire of My jealousy.

God Promises Final
Restoration of Jerusalem

9 For I will then restore
pure speech to the peoples
so that all of them may call
on the name of •Yahweh
and serve Him
with a single purpose.[a]

10 From beyond the rivers of •Cush
My supplicants, My dispersed people,
will bring an offering to Me.

11 On that day you[b] will not be put
to shame
because of everything
you have done
in rebelling against Me.
For then I will remove
your boastful braggarts
from among you,
and you will never again be haughty
on My holy mountain.

12 I will leave
a meek and humble people
among you,
and they will trust in the name
of Yahweh.

13 The remnant of Israel will no longer
do wrong or tell lies;
a deceitful tongue will not be found
in their mouths.
But they will pasture and lie down,
with nothing to make ⌊them⌋ afraid.

"Sing for Joy"

14 Sing for joy, Daughter Zion;
shout loudly, Israel!
Be glad and rejoice with all
⌊your⌋ heart,
Daughter Jerusalem!

King of Israel Is among You

15 The LORD has removed
your punishment;
He has turned back your enemy.
The King of Israel, the LORD,
is among you;
you need no longer fear harm.

16 On that day it will be said
to Jerusalem:
"Do not fear;
Zion, do not let your hands
grow weak.

17 The LORD your God is among you,
a warrior who saves.
He will rejoice over you
with gladness.
He will bring ⌊you⌋ quietness[c]
with His love.
He will delight in you with shouts
of joy."

"Yahweh Has Spoken"

18 I will gather those
who have been driven
from the appointed festivals;
⌊They will be⌋ a tribute from you,[d]
and reproach ⌊on her⌋.[e]

19 Yes, at that time
I will deal with all who afflict you.
I will save the lame and gather
the scattered;
I will make those
who were disgraced
throughout the earth
receive praise and fame.

20 At that time I will bring you[f] back,
yes, at the time I will gather you.
I will make you famous
and praiseworthy
among all the peoples of the earth,
when I restore your fortunes
before your eyes.
Yahweh has spoken.

---

a**3:9** Lit *with one shoulder*   b**3:11** = Israel   c**3:17** LXX, Syr read *He will renew you*   d**3:18** = Jerusalem   e**3:18** Hb obscure   f**3:20** = people of Israel

HAGGAI

God's Command to Rebuild the Temple

1 In the second year of King Darius,[a] on the first day of the sixth month, the word of the LORD came through Haggai the prophet to Zerubbabel son of Shealtiel, the governor of Judah, and to Joshua son of Jehozadak, the high priest:

2 "The LORD of •Hosts says this: These people say: The time has not come for the house of the LORD to be rebuilt."

3 The word of the LORD came through Haggai the prophet: 4 "Is it a time for you yourselves to live in your paneled houses, while this house[b] lies in ruins?" 5 Now, the LORD of Hosts says this: "Think carefully about[c] your ways:

Lord's Message to People

6 You have planted much
but harvested little.
You eat
but never have enough
to be satisfied.
You drink
but never have enough
to become drunk. You put on clothes
but never have enough
to get warm.
The wage earner ⌊puts his⌋ wages
into a bag with a hole in it."

Results of Not Rebuilding Temple

7 The LORD of Hosts says this: "Think carefully about[c] your ways. 8 Go up into the hills, bring down lumber, and build the house. Then I will be pleased with it and be glorified," says the LORD. 9 "You expected much, but then it amounted to little. When you brought ⌊the harvest⌋ to your house, I ruined[d] it. Why?" ⌊This is⌋ the declaration of the LORD of Hosts. "Because My house still lies in ruins, while each of you is busy with his own house.

10 So on your account,[e]
the skies have withheld the dew
and the land its crops.
11 I have summoned a drought
on the fields and the hills,
on the grain, new wine, olive oil,
and whatever the ground yields,
on the people and animals,
and on all that
your hands produce."

People's Response

12 Then Zerubbabel son of Shealtiel, the high priest Joshua son of Jehozadak, and the entire remnant of the people obeyed the voice of the LORD their God and the words of the prophet Haggai, because the LORD their God had sent him. So the people •feared the LORD.

13 Haggai, the LORD's messenger, delivered the LORD's message to the people, "I am with you"—the LORD's declaration. 14 The LORD stirred up the spirit of Zerubbabel son of Shealtiel, governor of Judah, the spirit of the high priest Joshua son of Jehozadak, and the spirit of all the remnant of the people. They began work on the house of •Yahweh of Hosts, their God, 15 on the twenty-fourth day of the sixth month, in the second year of King Darius.

God's Encouragement and Promise

2 On the twenty-first day of the seventh month, the word of the LORD came through Haggai the prophet: 2 "Speak to

a**1:1** King of Persia 522–486 B.C.   b**1:4** = the temple   c**1:5,7** Lit *Place your heart on*   d**1:9** Lit *blew on*   e**1:10** Or *So above you*

Zerubbabel son of Shealtiel, governor of Judah, to the high priest Joshua son of Jehozadak, and to the remnant of the people: ³ Who is left among you who saw this house in its former glory? How does it look to you now? Doesn't it seem like nothing to you?ᵃ ⁴ Even so, be strong, Zerubbabel"—the LORD's declaration. "Be strong, Joshua son of Jehozadak, high priest. Be strong, all you people of the land"—the LORD's declaration. "Work! For I am with you"—the declaration of the LORD of •Hosts. ⁵ "ₗThis isₗ the promise I made to you when you came out of Egypt, and My Spirit is present among you; don't be afraid."

⁶ For the LORD of Hosts says this: "Once more, in a little while, I am going to shake the heavens and the earth, the sea and the dry land. ⁷ I will shake all the nations so that the treasures of all the nations will come, and I will fill this house with glory," says the LORD of Hosts. ⁸ "The silver and gold belong to Me"—the declaration of the LORD of Hosts. ⁹ "The final glory of this houseᵇ will be greater than the first," says the LORD of Hosts. "I will provide peace in this place"—the declaration of the LORD of Hosts.

From Deprivation to Blessing

¹⁰ On the twenty-fourth day of the ninth ₗmonthₗ, in the second year of Darius, the word of the LORD came to Haggai the prophet: ¹¹ "This is what the LORD of Hosts says: Ask the priests for a ruling. ¹² If a man is carrying consecrated meat in the fold of his garment, and with his fold touches bread, stew, wine, oil, or any other food, does it become holy?" The priests answered, "No."

¹³ Then Haggai asked, "If someone defiled by ₗcontact withₗ a corpse touches any of these, does it become defiled?"

The priests answered, "It becomes defiled."

A People Defiled

¹⁴ Then Haggai replied, "So is this people, and so is this nation before Me"— the LORD's declaration. "And so is every work of their hands; even what they offer there is defiled.

¹⁵ "Now, reflect back from this day: Before one stone was placed on another in the LORD's temple, ¹⁶ what state were you in?ᶜ When someone came to a ₗgrainₗ heap of 20 measures, it ₗonlyₗ amounted to 10; when one came to the winepress to dip 50 measures from the vat, it ₗonlyₗ amounted to 20. ¹⁷ I struck you—all the work of your hands—with blight, mildew, and hail, but you didn't turn to Me"—the LORD's declaration. ¹⁸ "Consider carefully from this day forward; from the twenty-fourth day of the ninth month, from the day the foundation of the LORD's temple was laid; consider it carefully. ¹⁹ Is there still seed left in the granary? The vine, the fig, the pomegranate, and the olive tree have not yet produced. But from this day on I will bless you."

God's Promise to Zerubbabel

²⁰ The word of the LORD came to Haggai a second time on the twenty-fourth day of the month: ²¹ "Speak to Zerubbabel, governor of Judah: I am going to shake the heavens and the earth. ²² I will overturn royal thrones and destroy the power of the Gentile kingdoms. I will overturn chariots and their riders. Horses and their riders will fall, each by his brother's sword. ²³ On that day"—the declaration of the LORD of Hosts—"I will take you, Zerubbabel son of Shealtiel, My servant"—the LORD's declaration—"and make you like My signet ring, for I have chosen you." ₗThis isₗ the declaration of the LORD of Hosts.

ᵃ2:3 Lit *Is it not in your eyes?*   ᵇ2:9 Or *The glory of this latter house*   ᶜ2:16 Hb obscure

ZECHARIAH

Plea for Repentance

1 In the eighth month, in the second year of Darius, the word of the LORD came to the prophet Zechariah son of Berechiah, son of Iddo: ² "The LORD was extremely angry with your ancestors. ³ So tell the people: This is what the Lord of •Hosts says: Return to Me"—this is the declaration of the Lord of Hosts—"and I will return to you, says the LORD of Hosts. ⁴ Do not be like your ancestors; the earlier prophets proclaimed to them: This is what the LORD of Hosts says: Turn from your evil ways and your evil deeds. But they did not listen or pay attention to Me"—the LORD's declaration. ⁵ "Where are your ancestors now? And do the prophets live forever? ⁶ But didn't My words and My statutes that I commanded My servants the prophets overtake your ancestors? They repented and said: As the LORD of Hosts purposed to deal with us for our ways and deeds, so He has dealt with us."

THE NIGHT VISIONS

⁷ On the twenty-fourth day of the eleventh month, which is the month of Shebat, in the second year of Darius, the word of the LORD came to the prophet Zechariah son of Berechiah, son of Iddo:

First Vision: Horsemen

⁸ I looked out in the night and saw a man riding on a red horse. He was standing among the myrtle trees in the valley. Behind him were red, sorrel, and white horses. ⁹ I asked, "What are these, my lord?"

The angel who was talking to me replied, "I will show you what they are."

¹⁰ Then the man standing among the myrtle trees explained, "They are the ones the LORD has sent to patrol the earth."

¹¹ They reported to the Angel of the LORD standing among the myrtle trees, "We have patrolled the earth, and right now the whole earth is calm and quiet."

¹² Then the Angel of the LORD responded, "How long, LORD of Hosts, will You withhold mercy from Jerusalem and the cities of Judah that You have been angry with these 70 years?" ¹³ The LORD replied with kind and comforting words to the angel who was speaking with me.

¹⁴ So the angel who was speaking with me said, "Proclaim: The LORD of Hosts says: I am extremely jealous for Jerusalem and Zion. ¹⁵ I am fiercely angry with the nations that are at ease, for I was a little angry, but they made it worse. ¹⁶ Therefore, this is what the LORD says: I have graciously returned to Jerusalem; My house will be rebuilt within it"—the declaration of the LORD of Hosts—"and a measuring line will be stretched out over Jerusalem.

¹⁷ "Proclaim further: This is what the LORD of Hosts says: My cities will again overflow with prosperity; the LORD will once more comfort Zion and again choose Jerusalem."

Second Vision: Four Horns and Craftsmen

¹⁸ᵃ Then I looked up and saw four •horns. ¹⁹ So I asked the angel who was speaking with me, "What are these?"

And he said to me, "These are the horns that scattered Judah, Israel, and Jerusalem."

ᵃ**1:18** Zch 2:1 in Hb

20 Then the LORD showed me four craftsmen. 21 I asked, "What are they coming to do?"

He replied, "These are the horns that scattered Judah so no one could raise his head. These ⌊craftsmen⌋ have come to terrify them, to cut off the horns of the nations that raised ⌊their⌋ horns against the land of Judah to scatter it."

Third Vision: Surveyor

2 a I looked up and saw a man with a measuring line in his hand. 2 I asked, "Where are you going?"

He answered me, "To measure Jerusalem to determine its width and length."

3 Then the angel who was speaking with me went out, and another angel went out to meet him. 4 He said to him, "Run and tell this young man: Jerusalem will be inhabited without walls because of the number of people and livestock in it." 5 The declaration of the LORD: "I will be a wall of fire around it, and I will be the glory within it."

6 "Get up! Leave the land of the north"—the LORD's declaration—"for I have scattered you like the four winds of heaven"—the LORD's declaration. 7 "Go, Zion! Escape, you who are living with Daughter Babylon." 8 For the LORD of •Hosts says this: "He has sent Meb for ⌊His⌋ glory against the nations who are plundering you, for anyone who touches you touches the pupilc of Hisd eye. 9 I will move against them with Mye power, and they will become plunder for their own servants. Then you will know that the LORD of Hosts has sent Me.b

10 "Daughter Zion, shout for joy and be glad, for I am coming to dwell among you"—the LORD's declaration. 11 "Many nations will join themselves to the LORD on that day and become Myf people. I will dwell among you, and you will know that the LORD of Hosts has sent Meb to you. 12 The LORD will take possession of Judah as His portion in the Holy Land, and He will once again choose Jerusalem. 13 Let all people be silent before the LORD, for He is coming from His holy dwelling."

Fourth Vision: High Priest and Branch

3 Then he showed me Joshua the high priest standing before the Angel of the LORD, with Satang standing at his right side to accuse him. 2 The LORDh said to Satan: "The LORD rebuke you, Satan! May the LORD who has chosen Jerusalem rebuke you! Isn't this man a burning stick snatched from the fire?"

3 Now Joshua was dressed with filthyi clothes as he stood before the Angel. 4 So Hej spoke to thosek standing before Him, "Take off his filthy clothes!" Then He said to him, "See, I have removed your guilt from you, and I will clothe you with splendid robes."

5 Then I said, "Let them put a clean turban on his head." So a clean turban was placed on his head, and they clothed him in garments while the Angel of the LORD was standing nearby.

6 Then the Angel of the LORD charged Joshua: 7 "This is what the LORD of •Hosts says: If you walk in My ways and keep My instructions, you will both rule My house and take care of My courts; I will also grant you access among these who are standing here.

"My Servant, the Branch"

8 "Listen, Joshua the high priest, you and your colleagues sitting before you; indeed, these men are a sign that I am

---

a2:1 Zch 2:5 in Hb   b2:8,9,11 Or me   c2:8 Or apple   d2:8 Alt Hb tradition reads My   e2:9 Or my   f2:11 LXX, Syr read His   g3:1 Or the Adversary   h3:2 Syr reads The Angel of the LORD   i3:3 Probably = human excrement   j3:4 = the Angel of the LORD   k3:4 = the angels

about to bring <u>My servant, the Branch</u>. ⁹ Notice <u>the stone</u> I have set before Joshua; on ⌊that⌋ one stone are seven eyes. I will engrave an inscription on it"—the declaration of the LORD of Hosts—"and I will take away the guilt of this land in a single day. ¹⁰ On that day, each of you will invite his neighbor to ⌊sit⌋ under ⌊his⌋ vine and fig tree." ⌊This is⌋ the declaration of the LORD of Hosts.

Fifth Vision: Gold Lampstand

4 The angel who was speaking with me then returned and roused me as one awakened out of sleep. ² He asked me, "What do you see?"

I replied, "I see a solid gold lampstand there with a bowl on its top. It has seven lamps on it and seven channels for each of ᵃ the lamps on its top. ³ There are also two olive trees beside it, one on the right of the bowl and the other on its left."

⁴ Then I asked the angel who was speaking with me, "What are these, my lord?"

⁵ "Don't you know what they are?" replied the angel who was speaking with me.

I said, "No, my lord."

⁶ So he answered me, "This is the word of the LORD to Zerubbabel: 'Not by strength or by might, but by My Spirit,' says the LORD of •Hosts. ⁷ 'What are you, great mountain? Before Zerubbabel you will become a plain. And he will bring out the capstone accompanied by shouts of: Grace, grace to it!'"

⁸ Then the word of the LORD came to me: ⁹ "Zerubbabel's hands have laid the foundation of this house, and his hands will complete it. Then you will know that the LORD of Hosts has sent me to you. ¹⁰ For who scorns the day of small things? These seven eyes of the LORD, which scan throughout the whole earth, will rejoice when they see the plumb lineᵇ in Zerubbabel's hand."

¹¹ I asked him, "What are the two olive trees on the right and left of the lampstand?" ¹² And I questioned him further, "What are the two olive branches beside the two gold conduits, from which golden ⌊oil⌋ pours out?"

¹³ Then he inquired of me, "Don't you know what these are?"

"No, my lord," I replied.

¹⁴ "These are the two anointed ones,"ᶜ he said, "who stand by the Lord of the whole earth."

Sixth Vision: Flying Scroll

5 I looked up again and saw a flying scroll. ² "What do you see?" he asked me.

"I see a flying scroll," I replied, "30 feetᵈ long and 15 feetᵉ wide."

³ Then he said to me, "This is <u>the curse</u> that is going out over the whole land, for every thief will be removed according to what is written on one side, and everyone who swears ⌊falsely⌋ will be removed according to what is written on the other side. ⁴ I will send it out,"—the declaration of the LORD of •Hosts—"and it will enter the house of the thief and the house of the one who swears falsely by My name. It will stay inside his house and destroy it along with its timbers and stones."

Seventh Vision: Woman in the Basket

⁵ Then the angel who was speaking with me came forward and told me, "Look up and see what this is that is approaching."

⁶ So I asked, "What is it?"

He responded, "It's a measuring basketᶠ that is approaching." And he

---

ᵃ**4:2** Or *seven lips to;* each lip would hold a wick for the lamp.   ᵇ**4:10** Lit *the tin stone*   ᶜ**4:14** = Joshua and Zerubbabel   ᵈ**5:2** Lit *20 cubits*   ᵉ**5:2** Lit *10 cubits*   ᶠ**5:6** Lit *It's an ephah*

continued, "This is their iniquity[a] in all the land." [7] Then a lead cover was lifted, and there was a woman sitting inside the basket. [8] "This is Wickedness," he said. He shoved her down into the basket and pushed the lead weight over its opening. [9] Then I looked up and saw two women approaching with the wind in their wings. Their wings were like those of a stork, and they lifted up the basket between earth and sky.

[10] So I asked the angel who was speaking with me, "Where are they taking the basket?"

[11] "To build a shrine for it in the land of •Shinar,"[b] he told me. "When that is ready, ⌊the basket⌋ will be placed there on its pedestal."

Eighth Vision: Four Chariots

6 Then I looked up again and saw four chariots coming from between two mountains. And the mountains were made of bronze. [2] The first chariot had red horses, the second chariot black horses, [3] the third chariot white horses, and the fourth chariot dappled horses— ⌊all⌋ strong horses. [4] So I inquired of the angel who was speaking with me, "What are these, my lord?"

[5] The angel told me, "These are the four spirits[c] of heaven going out after presenting themselves to the Lord of the whole earth. [6] The one with the black horses is going to the land of the north, the white horses are going after them, but the dappled horses are going to the land of the south." [7] As the strong horses went out, they wanted to go patrol the earth, and the LORD said, "Go, patrol the earth." So they patrolled the earth. [8] Then He summoned me saying, "See, those going to the land of the north have pacified My Spirit in the northern land."

Crowning of the Branch

[9] The word of the LORD came to me: [10] "Take ⌊an offering⌋ from the exiles, from Heldai, Tobijah, and Jedaiah, who have arrived from Babylon, and go that same day to the house of Josiah son of Zephaniah. [11] Take silver and gold, make crowns and place them on the head of Joshua son of Jehozadak, the high priest. [12] You are to tell him: This is what the LORD of •Hosts says: Here is a man whose name is Branch; He will branch out from His place and build the LORD's temple. [13] Yes, He will build the LORD's temple; He will be clothed in splendor and will sit on His throne and rule. There will also be a priest on His throne, and there will be peaceful counsel between the two of them. [14] The crown will reside in the LORD's temple as a memorial to Heldai, Tobijah, Jedaiah, and Hen[d] son of Zephaniah. [15] People who are far off will come and build the LORD's temple, and you will know that the LORD of Hosts has sent Me to you. This will happen when you fully obey the LORD your God."

Disobedience and Fasting

7 In the fourth year of King Darius, the word of the LORD came to Zechariah on the fourth day of the ninth month, which is Chislev. [2] Now ⌊the people of⌋ Bethel had sent Sharezer, Regem-melech, and their men to plead for the LORD's favor [3] by asking the priests who were at the house of the LORD of •Hosts as well as the prophets, "Should we mourn and fast in the fifth month as we have done these many years?"

[4] Then the word of the LORD of Hosts came to me: [5] "Ask all the people of the land and the priests: When you fasted and lamented in the fifth and in the sev-

[a]**5:6** One Hb ms, LXX, Syr; MT reads *eye* [b]**5:11** = Babylon; Gn 10:10 [c]**6:5** Or *winds* [d]**6:14** Probably = Josiah; Zch 6:10; in Hb *Hen* = favor

enth ⌊months⌋ for these 70 years, <u>did you really fast for Me?</u> ⁶ When you eat and drink, don't you eat and drink ⌊simply⌋ for yourselves? ⁷ Aren't ⌊these⌋ the words that the Lᴏʀᴅ proclaimed through the earlier prophets when Jerusalem was inhabited and secure,ª along with its surrounding cities, and when the southern region and the Judean foothills were inhabited?"

⁸ The word of the Lᴏʀᴅ came to Zechariah: ⁹ "The Lᴏʀᴅ of Hosts says this: Render true justice. Show faithful love and compassion to one another. ¹⁰ Do not oppress the widow or the fatherless, the stranger or the poor, and do not plot evil in your hearts against one another. ¹¹ But they refused to pay attention and turned a stubborn shoulder; they closed their ears so they could not hear. ¹² They made their hearts like a rock so as not to obey the law or the words that the Lᴏʀᴅ of Hosts had sent by His Spirit through the earlier prophets. Therefore great anger came from the Lᴏʀᴅ of Hosts. ¹³ Just as He had called, and they would not listen, so when they called, I would not listen," says the Lᴏʀᴅ of Hosts. ¹⁴ "I scattered them with a windstorm over all the nations that had not known them, and the land was left desolate behind them, with no one coming or going. They turned a pleasant land into a desolation."

God: "I Am Extremely Jealous"

8 The word of the Lᴏʀᴅ of •Hosts came: ² "The Lᴏʀᴅ of Hosts says this: I am extremely jealous for Zion; I am jealous for her with great wrath."

Return of God to Zion

³ The Lᴏʀᴅ says this: "I will return to Zion and live in Jerusalem. Then Jerusalem will be called the Faithful City, the mountain of the Lᴏʀᴅ of Hosts, and the Holy Mountain." ⁴ The Lᴏʀᴅ of Hosts says this: "Old men and women will again sit along the streets of Jerusalem, each with a staff in hand because of advanced age. ⁵ The streets of the city will be filled with boys and girls playing in them." ⁶ The Lᴏʀᴅ of Hosts says this: "Though it may seem incredible to the remnant of this people in those days, should it also seem incredible to Me?"—the declaration of the Lᴏʀᴅ of Hosts. ⁷ The Lᴏʀᴅ of Hosts says this: "I will save My people from the land of the east and the land of the west. ⁸ I will bring them ⌊back⌋ to live in Jerusalem. They will be My people, and I will be their faithful and righteous God."

God's Promise for His People

⁹ The Lᴏʀᴅ of Hosts says this: "Let your hands be strong, you who now hear these words that the prophets spoke when the foundations were laid for the rebuilding of the temple, the house of the Lᴏʀᴅ of Hosts. ¹⁰ For prior to those days neither man nor beast had wages. There was no safety from the enemy for anyone who came or went, for I turned everyone against his neighbor. ¹¹ But now, I will not treat the remnant of this people as in the former days"—the declaration of the Lᴏʀᴅ of Hosts. ¹² "For they will sow in peace: the vine will yield its fruit, the land will yield its produce, and the skies will yield their dew. I will give the remnant of this people all these things as an inheritance. ¹³ As you have been a curse among the nations, house of Judah and house of Israel, so I will save you, and you will be a blessing. Don't be afraid; let your hands be strong." ¹⁴ For the Lᴏʀᴅ of Hosts says this: "As I resolved to treat you badly when your fathers provoked Me to

ª **7:7** Or *prosperous*

anger, and would not relent," says the LORD of Hosts, [15] "so I have resolved again in these days to do what is good to Jerusalem and the house of Judah. Don't be afraid. [16] These are the things you must do: Speak truth to one another; render honest and peaceful judgments in your •gates. [17] Do not plot evil in your hearts against your neighbor, and do not love perjury, for I hate all this"—the LORD's declaration.

Feasting and Pleading

[18] Then the word of the LORD of Hosts came to me: [19] "The LORD of Hosts says this: The fast of the fourth ⌊month⌋, the fast of the fifth, the fast of the seventh, and the fast of the tenth will become times of joy, gladness, and cheerful festivals for the house of Judah. Therefore, love truth and peace." [20] The LORD of Hosts says this: "Peoples will yet come, the residents of many cities; [21] the residents of one city will go to another, saying: Let's go at once to plead for the LORD's favor and to seek the LORD of Hosts. I am also going. [22] Many peoples and strong nations will come to seek the LORD of Hosts in Jerusalem and to plead for the LORD's favor." [23] The LORD of Hosts says this: "In those days, 10 men from nations of every language will grab the robe of a Jewish man tightly, urging: Let us go with you, for we have heard that God is with you."

Judgment of Zion's Enemies

9 An •Oracle

The word of the LORD
is against the land of Hadrach,
and Damascus is its resting place—
for the eyes of men
and all the tribes of Israel
are on the LORD[a]—

[2] and also against Hamath,
which borders it,
as well as Tyre and Sidon,
though they are very shrewd.
[3] Tyre has built herself a fortress;
she has heaped up silver like dust
and gold like the dirt of the streets.
[4] Listen! The Lord will
impoverish her
and cast her wealth into the sea;
she herself will be consumed by fire.
[5] Ashkelon will see it and be afraid;
Gaza too, and will writhe
in great pain,
as will Ekron, for her hope will fail.
There will cease to be a king
in Gaza,
and Ashkelon will
become uninhabited.
[6] A mongrel people will live
in Ashdod,
and I will destroy the pride
of the Philistines.
[7] I will remove the blood
from their mouths
and the detestable things
from between their teeth.
Then they too will become
a remnant for our God;
they will become like a clan in Judah
and Ekron like the Jebusites.
[8] I will set up camp at My house
against an army,[b]
against those who march
back and forth,
and no oppressor will march
against them again,
for now I have seen
with My own eyes.

Coming of Zion's King

[9] Rejoice greatly, Daughter Zion!
Shout in triumph,
Daughter Jerusalem!

See, your King is coming to you;
He is righteous and victorious,[a]
humble and riding on a donkey,
on a colt, the foal of a donkey.

Changes by God

10 I will cut off the chariot
from Ephraim
and the horse from Jerusalem.
The bow of war will be removed,
and He will proclaim peace
to the nations.
His dominion will extend from sea
to sea,
from the Euphrates River
to the ends of the earth.

11 As for you,
because of the blood
of your covenant,
I will release your prisoners
from the waterless cistern.

12 Return to a stronghold,
you prisoners who have hope;
today I declare that I will restore
double to you.

13 For I will bend Judah ⌊as My bow⌋;
I will fill that bow with Ephraim.
I will rouse your sons, Zion,
against your sons, Greece.[b]
I will make you
like a warrior's sword.

14 Then the LORD will appear
over them,
and His arrow will fly like lightning.
The Lord GOD will sound
the trumpet
and advance
with the southern storms.

15 The LORD of •Hosts will defend them.
They will consume and conquer
with slingstones;
they will drink and be rowdy as if
with wine.
They will be as full as
the sprinkling basin,

like ⌊those⌋ at the corners
of the altar.

16 The LORD their God will save them
on that day
as the flock of His people;
for they are like jewels in a crown,
sparkling over His land.

17 How lovely and beautiful
they will be!
Grain will make
the young men flourish,
and new wine, the young women.

LORD Restores His People

10 Ask the LORD for rain
in the season of spring rain.
The LORD makes the rain clouds,
and He will give them showers
of rain
and crops in the field for everyone.

2 For the idols speak falsehood,
and the diviners see illusions;
they relate empty dreams
and offer empty comfort.
Therefore ⌊the people⌋ wander
like sheep;
they suffer affliction because
there is no shepherd.

Cornerstone from Judah

3 My anger burns
against the shepherds,
so I will punish the leaders.[c]
For the LORD of •Hosts has tended
His flock,
the house of Judah;
He will make them
like His majestic steed in battle.

4 From them[d] will come
the cornerstone,
from them the tent peg,
from them the battle bow,
from them every ruler.
Together 5 they will be like warriors
in battle

trampling down the mud
of the streets.
They will fight because the LORD is
with them,
and they will put horsemen
to shame.
6 I will strengthen the house of Judah
and deliver the house of Joseph.ª
I will restoreᵇ them
because I have compassion on them,
and they will be
as though I had never rejected them.
For I am the LORD their God,
and I will answer them.
7 Ephraim will be like a warrior,
and their hearts will be glad as if
with wine.
Their children will see it and be glad;
their hearts will rejoice in the LORD.

8 I will whistle and gather them
because I have redeemed them;
they will be as numerous as
they once were.
9 Though I sow them
among the nations,
they will remember Me
in the distant lands;
they and their children will live
and return.
10 I will bring them back
from the land of Egypt
and gather them from Assyria.
I will bring them to the land
of Gilead
and to Lebanon,
but it will not be enough for them.
11 Heᶜ will pass through the sea
of distress
and strike the waves of the sea;
all the depths of the Nile
will dry up.
The pride of Assyria will be
brought down,

and the scepter of Egypt will come
to an end.
12 I will strengthen them in the LORD,
and they will march in His name—
⌞this is⌟ •Yahweh's declaration.

Israel's Shepherds: Good and Bad

11 Open your gates, Lebanon,
and fire will consume your cedars.
2 Wail, cypress, for the cedar
has fallen;
the glorious ⌞trees⌟ are destroyed!
Wail, oaks of Bashan,
for the stately forest has fallen!
3 Listen to the wail of the shepherds,
for their glory is destroyed.
Listen to the roar of young lions,
for the thickets of the Jordan
areᵈ destroyed.

God: Shepherd the Flock

4 The LORD my God says this: "Shepherd the flock intended for slaughter. 5 Those who buy them slaughter them but are not punished. Those who sell them say: Praise the LORD because I have become rich! Even their own shepherds have no compassion for them. 6 Indeed, I will no longer have compassion on the inhabitants of the land"—the LORD's declaration. "Instead, I will turn everyone over to his neighbor and his king. They will devastate the land, and I will not deliver ⌞it⌟ from them."

Shepherding the Flock

7 So I shepherded the flock intended for slaughter, the afflicted of the flock.ᵉ I took two staffs, calling one Favor and the other Union, and I shepherded the flock. 8 In one month I got rid of three shepherds. I became impatient with them, and they also detested me. 9 Then I said,

---

ª**10:6** = the northern kingdom ᵇ**10:6** Other Hb mss, LXX read *settle* ᶜ**10:11** = the LORD ᵈ**11:3** Lit *for the majesty of the Jordan is* ᵉ**11:7** LXX reads *slaughter that belonged to the sheep merchants*

"I will no longer shepherd you. Let what is dying die, and let what is going astray go astray; let the rest devour each other's flesh." ¹⁰ Next I took my staff called Favor and cut it in two, annulling the covenant I had made with all the peoples. ¹¹ It was annulled on that day, and so the afflicted of the flockᵃ who were watching me knew that it was the word of the LORD. ¹² Then I said to them, "If it seems right to you, give me my wages; but if not, keep ⌊them⌋." So they weighed my wages, 30 pieces of silver.

¹³ "Throw it to the potter,"ᵇ the LORD said to me—this magnificent price I was valued by them. So I took the 30 pieces of silver and threw it into the house of the LORD, to the potter.ᶜ ¹⁴ Then I cut in two my second staff, Union, annulling the brotherhood between Judah and Israel.

¹⁵ The LORD also said to me: "Take the equipment of a foolish shepherd. ¹⁶ I am about to raise up a shepherd in the land who will not care for those who are going astray, and he will not seek the lostᵈ or heal the broken. He will not sustain the healthy,ᵉ but he will devour the flesh of the fat ⌊sheep⌋ and tear off their hooves.

¹⁷ Woe to the worthless shepherd
who deserts the flock!
May a sword strikeᶠ his arm
and his right eye!
May his arm wither away
and his right eye go
completely blind!"

Judah's Security

An •Oracle

The word of the LORD
concerning Israel.
A declaration of the LORD,
who stretched out the heavens,

laid the foundation of the earth,
and formed the spirit of man
within him.

² "Look, I will make Jerusalem a cup that causes staggering for the peoples who surround the city. The siege against Jerusalem will also involve Judah. ³ On that day I will make Jerusalem a heavy stone for all the peoples; all who try to lift it will injure themselves severely when all the nations of the earth gather against her. ⁴ On that day"—the LORD's declaration—"I will strike every horse with panic and its rider with madness. I will keep a watchful eye on the house of Judah but strike all the horses of the nations with blindness. ⁵ Then ⌊each of⌋ the leaders of Judah will think to himself: The residents of Jerusalem are my strength through the LORD of •Hosts, their God. ⁶ On that day I will make the leaders of Judah like a firepot in a woodpile, like a flaming torch among sheaves; they will consume all the peoples around them on the right and the left, while Jerusalem continues to be inhabited on its site, in Jerusalem. ⁷ The LORD will save the tents of Judah first, so that the glory of David's house and the glory of Jerusalem's residents may not be greater than that of Judah. ⁸ On that day the LORD will defend the inhabitants of Jerusalem, so that the one who is weakest among them will be like David on that day, and the house of David will be like God, like the Angel of the LORD, before them. ⁹ On that day I will set out to destroy all the nations that come against Jerusalem.

Mourning for the Pierced One

¹⁰ "Then I will pour out a spiritᵍ of grace and prayer on the house of David and the residents of Jerusalem, and they

ᵃ11:11 LXX reads and the sheep merchants ᵇ11:13 Syr reads treasury; Mt 27:5 ᶜ11:13 One Hb ms, Syr read treasury ᵈ11:16 Lit young ᵉ11:16 Or exhausted ᶠ11:17 Lit be against ᵍ12:10 Or out the Spirit

will look at[a] Me whom they pierced. They will mourn for Him as one mourns for an only child and weep bitterly for Him as one weeps for a firstborn. [11] On that day the mourning in Jerusalem will be as great as the mourning of Hadad-rimmon in the plain of Megiddo. [12] The land will mourn, every family by itself: the family of David's house by itself and their women by themselves; the family of Nathan's[b] house by itself and their women by themselves; [13] the family of Levi's house by itself and their women by themselves; the family of Shimei[c] by itself and their women by themselves; [14] all the remaining families, every family by itself, and their women by themselves.

God's People Cleansed

13 "On that day a fountain will be opened for the house of David and for the residents of Jerusalem, ˩to wash away˩ sin and impurity. [2] On that day"—the declaration of the LORD of •Hosts—"I will erase the names of the idols from the land, and they will no longer be remembered. I will remove the prophets[d] and the unclean spirit from the land. [3] If a man still prophesies, his father and his mother who bore him will say to him: You cannot remain alive because you have spoken falsely in the name of the LORD. When he prophesies, his father and his mother who bore him will pierce him through. [4] On that day every prophet will be ashamed of his vision when he prophesies; they will not put on a hairy cloak in order to deceive. [5] He will say: I am not a prophet; I am a tiller of the soil, for a man purchased[e] me as a servant since my youth. [6] If someone asks him: What are these wounds on your chest?[f]—then he will answer: The wounds I received in the house of my friends.

[7] Sword, awake
 against My shepherd,
 against the man who is
 My associate—
                    the declaration
         of the LORD of Hosts.
 Strike the shepherd, and the sheep
   will be scattered;
 I will also turn My hand
   against the little ones.
[8] In the whole land—
         the LORD's declaration—
 two-thirds[g] will be cut off and die,
 but a third will be left in it.
[9] I will put this third through the fire;
 I will refine them as silver is refined
 and test them as gold is tested.
 They will call on My name,
 and I will answer them.
 I will say: They are My people,
 and they will say: The LORD is
   our God."

LORD's Triumph and Reign

14 A day of the LORD is coming when your plunder will be divided in your presence. [2] I will gather all the nations against Jerusalem for battle. The city will be captured, the houses looted, and the women raped. Half the city will go into exile, but the rest of the people will not be removed from the city.

Lord Stands
on Mount of Olives

[3] Then the LORD will go out to fight against those nations as He fights on a day of battle. [4] On that day His feet will stand on the •Mount of Olives, which faces Jerusalem on the east. The Mount of Olives will be split in half from east to

---

[a]**12:10** Or to   [b]**12:12** = a son of David; 2 Sm 5:14; Lk 3:31   [c]**12:13** = a descendant of Levi; Ex 6:16-17; Nm 3:18; 1 Ch 6:17   [d]**13:2** = false prophets   [e]**13:5** Or sold   [f]**13:6** Lit wounds between my hands   [g]**13:8** Lit two-thirds in it

west, forming a huge valley, so that half the mountain will move to the north and half to the south. ⁵ You will flee by My mountain valley,ᵃ for the valley of the mountains will extend to Azal. You will flee as you fledᵇ from the earthquake in the days of Uzziah king of Judah. Then the LORD my God will come and all the holy ones with Him.ᶜ

⁶ On that day there will be no light; the sunlight and moonlightᵈ will diminish.ᵉ ⁷ It will be a day known ⌊only⌋ to •Yahweh, without day or night, but there will be light at evening.

⁸ On that day living water will flow out from Jerusalem, half of it toward the eastern seaᶠ and the other half toward the western sea,ᵍ in summer and winter alike. ⁹ On that day Yahweh will become king over all the earth—Yahweh alone, and His name alone. ¹⁰ All the land from Geba to Rimmon south of Jerusalem will be changed into a plain. But ⌊Jerusalem⌋ will be raised up and will remainʰ on its site from the Benjamin Gate to the place of the First Gate,ⁱ to the Corner Gate, and from the Tower of Hananel to the royal winepresses. ¹¹ People will live there, and never again will there be a curse of destruction. So Jerusalem will dwell in security.

Plague of the Lord

¹² This will be the plague the LORD strikes all the peoples with, who have warred against Jerusalem: their flesh will rot while they stand on their feet, their eyes will rot in their sockets, and their tongues will rot in their mouths. ¹³ On that day a great panic from the LORD will be among them, so that each will seize the hand of another, and the hand of one will rise against the other. ¹⁴ Judah will also fight at Jerusalem, and the wealth of all the surrounding nations will be collected: gold, silver, and clothing in great abundance. ¹⁵ The same plague as the previous one will strikeʲ the horses, mules, camels, donkeys, and all the animals that are in those camps.

¹⁶ Then all the survivors from the nations that came against Jerusalem will go up year after year to worship the King, the LORD of •Hosts, and to celebrate the Festival of Booths. ¹⁷ Should any of the families of the earth not go up to Jerusalem to worship the King, the LORD of Hosts, rain will not fall on them. ¹⁸ And if the peopleᵏ of Egypt will not go up and enter, then rain will not fall on them; thisˡ will be the plague the LORD inflicts on the nations who do not go up to celebrate the Festival of Booths. ¹⁹ This will be the punishment of Egypt and all the nations that do not go up to celebrate the Festival of Booths.

²⁰ On that day, ⌊the words⌋

$$\boxed{\text{HOLY TO THE LORD}}$$

will be on the bells of the horses. The pots in the house of the LORD will be like the sprinkling basins before the altar. ²¹ Every pot in Jerusalem and in Judah will be holy to the LORD of Hosts. Everyone who sacrifices will come and take some of the pots to cook in. And on that day there will no longer be a Canaaniteᵐ in the house of the LORD of Hosts.

ᵃ**14:5** Some Hb mss, LXX, Sym, Tg read *You will be blocked—the valley of My mountains—* ᵇ**14:5** LXX reads *It will be blocked as it was blocked* ᶜ**14:5** Some Hb mss, LXX, Vg, Tg, Syr; other Hb mss read *you* ᵈ**14:6** Lit *light; the precious things* ᵉ**14:6** LXX, Sym, Syr, Tg, Vg read *no light or cold or ice* ᶠ**14:8** = the Dead Sea ᵍ**14:8** = the Mediterranean Sea ʰ**14:10** Or *will be inhabited* ⁱ**14:10** Or *the former gate* ʲ**14:15** Lit *be on* ᵏ**14:18** Lit *family* ˡ**14:18** Lit *it* ᵐ**14:21** Or *merchant*

MALACHI

LORD's Love for Israel

1 An •oracle: The word of the LORD to Israel through Malachi.[a2] "I have loved you," says the LORD.

But you ask: "How have You loved us?"

Jacob Loved, Esau Hated

"Wasn't Esau Jacob's brother?" ⌊This is⌋ the LORD's declaration. "Even so, I loved Jacob, 3 but I hated Esau. I turned his mountains into a wasteland, and ⌊gave⌋ his inheritance to the desert jackals."

4 Though Edom says: "We have been devastated, but we will rebuild[b] the ruins," the LORD of •Hosts says this: "They may build, but I will demolish. They will be called a wicked country and the people the LORD has cursed[c] forever. 5 Your own eyes will see this, and you yourselves will say: The LORD is great, ⌊even⌋ beyond[d] the borders of Israel.

Disobedience of Priests

6 "A son honors ⌊his⌋ father, and a servant his master. But if I am a father, where is My honor? And if I am a master, where is ⌊your⌋ •fear of Me? says the LORD of Hosts to you priests, who despise My name."

Yet you ask: "How have we despised Your name?"

7 "By presenting defiled food on My altar."

You ask: "How have we defiled You?"

When you say: "The LORD's table is contemptible."

8 "When you present a blind ⌊animal⌋ for sacrifice, is it not wrong? And when you present a lame or sick ⌊animal⌋, is it not wrong? Bring it to your governor! Would he be pleased with you or show you favor?" asks the LORD of Hosts. 9 "And now ask for God's favor. Will He be gracious to us? ⌊Since⌋ this has come from your hands, will He show any of you favor?" asks the LORD of Hosts. 10 "I wish one of you would shut the ⌊temple⌋ doors, so you would no longer kindle a useless ⌊fire on⌋ My altar! I am not pleased with you," says the LORD of Hosts, "and I will accept no offering from your hands.

"My Name Will Be Great"

11 "For My name will be great among the nations, from the rising of the sun to its setting. Incense[e] and pure offerings will be presented in My name in every place because My name will be great among the nations,"[f] says the LORD of Hosts.

12 But you are profaning it[g] when you say: "The Lord's table is defiled, and its product, its food, is contemptible." 13 You also say: "Look, what a nuisance!" "And you scorn[h] it," says the LORD of Hosts. "You bring stolen,[i] lame, or sick animals. You bring this as an offering! Am I to accept that from your hands?" asks the LORD.

14 "The deceiver is cursed who has an ⌊acceptable⌋ male in his flock and makes a vow but sacrifices a defective ⌊animal⌋ to the Lord. For I am a great King," says the LORD of Hosts, "and My name[j] will be feared among the nations.

---

a**1:1** = My Messenger   b**1:4** Or *will return and build*   c**1:4** Or *LORD is angry with*   d**1:5** Or *great over*   e**1:11** Or *Burnt offerings*   f**1:11** Many translations supply present tense verbs in this v. rather than future tense.   g**1:12** = the LORD's name   h**1:13** Lit *blow at*   i**1:13** Or *injured*   j**1:14** Or *Because I am . . . LORD of Hosts, My name*

Warning to Priests

2 "Therefore, this decree is for you priests: [2] If you don't listen, and if you don't take it to heart to honor My name," says the LORD of •Hosts, "I will send a curse among you, and I will curse your blessings. In fact, I have already begun to curse them because you are not taking it to heart.

Recall Covenant with Levi

[3] "Look, I am going to rebuke your descendants, and I will spread animal waste[a] over your faces, the waste from your festival sacrifices, and you will be taken away with it. [4] Then you will know that I sent you this decree so My covenant with Levi may continue," says the LORD of Hosts. [5] "My covenant with him was one of life and peace, and I gave these to him; it called for reverence, and he revered Me and stood in awe of My name. [6] True instruction was in his mouth, and nothing wrong was found on his lips. He walked with Me in peace and fairness and turned many from sin. [7] For the lips of a priest should guard knowledge, and people should seek instruction from his mouth, because he is the messenger of the LORD of Hosts.

You Have Violated Levi's Covenant

[8] "You, on the other hand, have turned from the way. You have caused many to stumble by your instruction. You have violated[b] the covenant of Levi," says the LORD of Hosts. [9] "So I in turn have made you despised and humiliated before all the people because you are not keeping My ways but are showing partiality in ⌞your⌟ instruction."

Judah's Marital Unfaithfulness

[10] Don't all of us have one Father? Didn't one God create us? Why then do we act treacherously against one another, profaning the covenant of our fathers? [11] Judah has acted treacherously, and a detestable thing has been done in Israel and in Jerusalem. For Judah has profaned the LORD's sanctuary,[c] which He loves, and has married the daughter of a foreign god.[d] [12] To the man who does this, may the LORD cut off any descendants[e] [f] from the tents of Jacob, even if they present an offering to the LORD of Hosts.

False Spirituality

[13] And this is another thing you do: you cover the LORD's altar with tears, with weeping and groaning, because He no longer respects your offerings or receives ⌞them⌟ gladly from your hands. [14] Yet you ask, "For what reason?" Because the LORD has been a witness between you and the wife of your youth. You have acted treacherously against her, though she was your marriage partner and your wife by covenant. [15] Didn't the one ⌞God⌟ make ⌞us⌟ with a remnant of His life-breath? And what does the One seek?[g] A godly •offspring. So watch yourselves carefully,[h] and do not act treacherously against the wife of your youth.

[16] "If he hates and divorces ⌞his wife⌟," says the LORD God of Israel, "he[i] covers his garment with injustice," says the LORD of Hosts. Therefore, watch yourselves carefully,[j] and do not act treacherously.

---

[a]**2:3** = dung or entrails   [b]**2:8** Lit *corrupted*   [c]**2:11** Or *profaned what is holy to the LORD*   [d]**2:11** = a woman who worshiped a foreign god; Nm 21:29   [e]**2:12** One Hb ms, LXX, DSS read *off one witnessing or answering*   [f]**2:12** Lit *off one waking or answering*; Hb obscure   [g]**2:15** Or *Did the One not make them? So their flesh and spirit belong to Him*, or *No one who does this even has a remnant of the Spirit in him*; Hb obscure   [h]**2:15** Lit *So guard yourselves in your spirit*   [i]**2:16** Or *The LORD God of Israel says that He hates divorce and the one who*   [j]**2:16** Lit *Therefore, guard yourselves in your spirit*

"You Have Wearied the Lord"

17 You have wearied the LORD with your words.

Yet you ask, "How have we wearied ⌊Him⌋?"

When you say, "Everyone who does evil is good in the LORD's sight, and He is pleased with them," or "Where is the God of justice?"

Coming Messenger of Covenant

3 "See, I am going to send My messenger, and he will clear the way before Me. Then the Lord you seek will suddenly come to His temple, the Messenger of the covenant you desire—see, He is coming," says the LORD of •Hosts. 2 But who can endure the day of His coming? And who will be able to stand when He appears? For He will be like a refiner's fire and like cleansing lye. 3 He will be like a refiner and purifier of silver; He will purify the sons of Levi and refine them like gold and silver. Then they will present offerings to the LORD in righteousness. 4 And the offerings of Judah and Jerusalem will please the LORD as in days of old and years gone by.

5 "I will come to you in judgment, and I will be ready to witness against sorcerers and adulterers; against those who swear falsely; against those who oppress the widow and the fatherless, and cheat the wage earner; and against those who deny ⌊justice to⌋ the foreigner. They do not •fear Me," says the LORD of Hosts. 6 "Because I, •Yahweh, have not changed, you descendants of Jacob have not been destroyed.

You Are Robbing Me!

7 "Since the days of your fathers, you have turned from My statutes; you have not kept ⌊them⌋. Return to Me, and I will return to you," says the LORD of Hosts.

But you ask: "How can we return?"

8 "Will a man rob God? Yet you are robbing Me!"

You ask: "How do we rob You?"

Test of the Tithe

"⌊By not making the payments⌋ of 10 percent and the contributions. 9 You are suffering under a curse, yet you—the whole nation—are ⌊still⌋ robbing Me. 10 Bring the full 10 percent into the storehouse so that there may be food in My house. Test Me in this way," says the LORD of Hosts. "See if I will not open the floodgates of heaven and pour out a blessing for you without measure. 11 I will rebuke the devourer[a] for you, so that it will not ruin the produce of your ground, and your vine in your field will not be barren," says the LORD of Hosts. 12 "Then all the nations will consider you fortunate, for you will be a delightful land," says the LORD of Hosts.

The Righteous and Wicked

13 "Your words against Me are harsh," says the LORD.

Yet you ask: "What have we spoken against You?"

14 You have said: "It is useless to serve God. What have we gained by keeping His requirements and walking mournfully before the LORD of Hosts? 15 So now we consider the arrogant to be fortunate. Not only do those who commit wickedness prosper, they even test God and escape."

16 At that time those who feared the LORD spoke to one another. The LORD took notice and listened. So a book of remembrance was written before Him for those who feared Yahweh and had high

---

a**3:11** Perhaps = locusts; Jl 1:4; 2:25

regard for His name. [17] "They will be Mine," says the LORD of Hosts, "a special possession on the day I am preparing. I will have compassion on them as a man has compassion on his son who serves him. [18] So you will again see the difference between the righteous and the wicked, between one who serves God and one who does not serve Him.

Day of the LORD

4 [a] "For indeed, the day is coming, burning like a furnace, when all the arrogant and everyone who commits wickedness will become stubble. The coming day will consume them," says the LORD of •Hosts, "not leaving them root or branches. [2] But for you who •fear My name, the sun of righteousness will rise with healing in its wings, and you will go out and playfully jump like calves from the stall.[b] [3] You will trample the wicked, for they will be ashes under the soles of your feet on the day I am preparing," says the LORD of Hosts.

Final Warning: Coming of Elijah

[4] "Remember the instruction of Moses My servant, the statutes and ordinances I commanded him at Horeb for all Israel. [5] Look, I am going to send you Elijah the prophet before the great and awesome Day of the LORD comes. [6c] And he will turn the hearts of fathers to ⌞their⌟ children and the hearts of children to their fathers. Otherwise, I will come and strike the land[d] with a curse."

---

[a]**4:1** Mal 3:19 in Hb   [b]**4:2** Or *like stall-fed calves*   [c]**4:6** Mal 3:24 in Hb   [d]**4:6** Or *earth*

THE
NEW TESTAMENT

MATTHEW

The Genealogy of Jesus Christ

1 The historical record[a] of Jesus Christ, the Son of David, the Son of Abraham:

From Abraham to David

2 Abraham fathered[b] Isaac,
Isaac fathered Jacob,
Jacob fathered Judah
and his brothers,
3 Judah fathered Perez and Zerah
by Tamar,
Perez fathered Hezron,
Hezron fathered Aram,
4 Aram fathered Aminadab,
Aminadab fathered Nahshon,
Nahshon fathered Salmon,
5 Salmon fathered Boaz by Rahab,
Boaz fathered Obed by Ruth,
Obed fathered Jesse,
6 and Jesse fathered King David.

From David to the Babylonian Exile

Then[c] David fathered Solomon
by Uriah's wife,
7 Solomon fathered Rehoboam,
Rehoboam fathered Abijah,
Abijah fathered Asa,[d]
8 Asa[d] fathered Jehoshaphat,
Jehoshaphat fathered Joram,
Joram fathered Uzziah,
9 Uzziah fathered Jotham,
Jotham fathered Ahaz,
Ahaz fathered Hezekiah,
10 Hezekiah fathered Manasseh,
Manasseh fathered Amon,[e]
Amon[e] fathered Josiah,
11 and Josiah fathered Jechoniah
and his brothers
at the time of the exile to Babylon.

From the Exile to the Messiah

12 Then after the exile to Babylon
Jechoniah fathered Salathiel,
Salathiel fathered Zerubbabel,
13 Zerubbabel fathered Abiud,
Abiud fathered Eliakim,
Eliakim fathered Azor,
14 Azor fathered Zadok,
Zadok fathered Achim,
Achim fathered Eliud,
15 Eliud fathered Eleazar,
Eleazar fathered Matthan,
Matthan fathered Jacob,
16 and Jacob fathered Joseph
the husband of Mary,
who gave birth to[f] Jesus
who is called the •Messiah.

17 So all the generations from Abraham to David were 14 generations; and from David until the exile to Babylon, 14 generations; and from the exile to Babylon until the Messiah, 14 generations.

Nativity of the Messiah

18 The birth of Jesus Christ came about this way: After His mother Mary had been •engaged to Joseph, it was discovered before they came together that she was pregnant by the Holy Spirit. 19 So her husband Joseph, being a righteous man, and not wanting to disgrace her publicly, decided to divorce her secretly.

20 But after he had considered these things, an angel of the Lord suddenly appeared to him in a dream, saying, "Joseph, son of David, don't be afraid to take Mary as your wife, because what

---

a**1:1** Or *The book of the genealogy* b**1:2** In vv. 2-16 either a son, as here, or a later descendant, as in v. 8 c**1:6** Other mss add *King* d**1:7,8** Other mss read *Asaph* e**1:10** Other mss read *Amos* f**1:16** Lit *Mary, from whom was born*

has been conceived in her is by the Holy Spirit. 21 She will give birth to a son, and you are to name Him Jesus,ᵃ because He will save His people from their sins."

22 Now all this took place to fulfill what was spoken by the Lord through the prophet:

23   See, the virgin will
         become pregnant
      and give birth to a son,
      and they will name Him
         Immanuel,ᵇ

which is translated "God is with us."
24 When Joseph got up from sleeping, he did as the Lord's angel had commanded him. He married her 25 but did not know her intimately until she gave birth to a son.ᶜ And he named Him Jesus.

Wise Men Seek the King

2 After Jesus was born in Bethlehem of Judea in the days of King •Herod, •wise men from the east arrived unexpectedly in Jerusalem, 2 saying, "Where is He who has been born King of the Jews? For we saw His star in the eastᵈ and have come to worship Him."ᵉ

Herod's Plot

3 When King Herod heard this, he was deeply disturbed, and all Jerusalem with him. 4 So he assembled all the •chief priests and •scribes of the people and asked them where the •Messiah would be born.
5 "In Bethlehem of Judea," they told him, "because this is what was written by the prophet:

6   And you, Bethlehem, in the land
         of Judah,

are by no means least
   among the leaders of Judah:
because out of you will come
   a leader
who will shepherd My people
   Israel."ᶠ

7 Then Herod secretly summoned the wise men and asked them the exact time the star appeared. 8 He sent them to Bethlehem and said, "Go and search carefully for the child. When you find Him, report back to me so that I too can go and worship Him."ᵍ
9 After hearing the king, they went on their way. And there it was—the star they had seen in the east!ʰ It led them until it came and stopped above the place where the child was. 10 When they saw the star, they were overjoyed beyond measure. 11 Entering the house, they saw the child with Mary His mother, and falling to their knees, they worshiped Him.ⁱ Then they opened their treasures and presented Him with gifts: gold, frankincense, and myrrh. 12 And being warned in a dream not to go back to Herod, they returned to their own country by another route.

Flight into Egypt

13 After they were gone, an angel of the Lord suddenly appeared to Joseph in a dream, saying, "Get up! Take the child and His mother, flee to Egypt, and stay there until I tell you. For Herod is about to search for the child to destroy Him." 14 So he got up, took the child and His mother during the night, and escaped to Egypt. 15 He stayed there until Herod's death, so that what was spoken by the Lord through the prophet might be fulfilled: Out of Egypt I called My Son.ʲ

Herod Massacres the Innocents

[16] Then Herod, when he saw that he had been outwitted by the wise men, flew into a rage. He gave orders to massacre all the male children in and around Bethlehem who were two years[a] old and under, in keeping with the time he had learned from the wise men. [17] Then what was spoken through Jeremiah the prophet was fulfilled:

[18]
A voice was heard in Ramah,
weeping,[b] and great mourning,
Rachel weeping for her children;
and she refused to be consoled,
because they were no more.[c]

Holy Family in Nazareth

[19] After Herod died, an angel of the Lord suddenly appeared in a dream to Joseph in Egypt, [20] saying, "Get up! Take the child and His mother and go to the land of Israel, because those who sought the child's life are dead." [21] So he got up, took the child and His mother, and entered the land of Israel. [22] But when he heard that Archelaus[d] was ruling over Judea in place of his father Herod, he was afraid to go there. And being warned in a dream, he withdrew to the region of Galilee. [23] Then he went and settled in a town called Nazareth to fulfill what was spoken through the prophets, that He will be called a •Nazarene.

John the Baptist: Messiah's Herald

3 In those days John the Baptist came, preaching in the Wilderness of Judea [2] and saying, "Repent, because the kingdom of heaven has come near!" [3] For he is the one spoken of through the prophet Isaiah, who said:

A voice of one crying out
in the wilderness:
"Prepare the way for the Lord;
make His paths straight!"[e]

[4] John himself had a camel-hair garment with a leather belt around his waist, and his food was locusts and wild honey. [5] Then ⌊people from⌋ Jerusalem, all Judea, and all the vicinity of the Jordan were flocking to him, [6] and they were baptized by him in the Jordan River as they confessed their sins.

[7] When he saw many of the •Pharisees and •Sadducees coming to the place of his baptism,[f] he said to them, "Brood of vipers! Who warned you to flee from the coming wrath? [8] Therefore produce fruit consistent with[g] repentance. [9] And don't presume to say to yourselves, 'We have Abraham as our father.' For I tell you that God is able to raise up children for Abraham from these stones! [10] Even now the ax is ready to strike the root of the trees! Therefore every tree that doesn't produce good fruit will be cut down and thrown into the fire.

Baptisms of Repentance and Fire

[11] "I baptize you with[h] water for repentance,[i] but the One who is coming after me is more powerful than I. I am not worthy to take off[j] His sandals. He Himself will baptize you with[h] the Holy Spirit and fire. [12] His winnowing shovel[k] is in His hand, and He will clear His threshing floor and gather His wheat into the barn. But the chaff He will burn up with fire that never goes out."

Baptism of Jesus

13 Then Jesus came from Galilee to John at the Jordan, to be baptized by him. 14 But John tried to stop Him, saying, "I need to be baptized by You, and yet You come to me?"

15 Jesus answered him, "Allow it for now, because this is the way for us to fulfill all righteousness." Then he allowed Him ⌊to be baptized⌋.

16 After Jesus was baptized, He went up immediately from the water. The heavens suddenly opened for Him,ª and He saw the Spirit of God descending like a dove and coming down on Him. 17 And there came a voice from heaven:

This is My beloved Son.
I take delight in Him!

Devil Tempts Jesus

4 Then Jesus was led up by the Spirit into the wilderness to be tempted by the Devil. 2 After He had fasted 40 days and 40 nights, He was hungry. 3 Then the tempter approached Him and said, "If You are the Son of God, tell these stones to become bread."

4 But He answered, "It is written:

Man must not live on bread alone
but on every word that comes
from the mouth of God."ᵇ

5 Then the Devil took Him to the holy city,ᶜ had Him stand on the pinnacle of the temple, 6 and said to Him, "If You are the Son of God, throw Yourself down. For it is written:

He will give His angels orders
concerning you, and
they will support you
with their hands
so that you will not strike
your foot against a stone."ᵈ

7 Jesus told him, "It is also written: Do not test the Lord your God."ᵉ

8 Again, the Devil took Him to a very high mountain and showed Him all the kingdoms of the world and their splendor. 9 And he said to Him, "I will give You all these things if You will fall down and worship me."ᶠ

10 Then Jesus told him, "Go away,ᵍ Satan! For it is written:

Worship the Lord your God,
and serve only Him."ʰ

11 Then the Devil left Him, and immediately angels came and began to serve Him.

Jesus' Ministry in Galilee

12 When He heard that John had been arrested, He withdrew into Galilee. 13 He left Nazareth behind and went to live in Capernaum by the sea, in the region of Zebulun and Naphtali. 14 This was to fulfill what was spoken through the prophet Isaiah:

15 Land of Zebulun and land
of Naphtali,
along the sea road,
beyond the Jordan,
Galilee of the Gentiles!
16 The people who live in darkness
have seen a great light,
and for those living
in the shadowland of death,
light has dawned.ⁱ ʲ

17 From then on Jesus began to preach, "Repent, because the kingdom of heaven has come near!"

Jesus Calls Peter and Andrew

18 As He was walking along the Sea of Galilee, He saw two brothers, Simon, who was called Peter, and his brother An-

ª3:16 Other mss omit for Him ᵇ4:4 Dt 8:3 ᶜ4:5 Jerusalem ᵈ4:6 Ps 91:11-12 ᵉ4:7 Dt 6:16 ᶠ4:9 Or and pay me homage ᵍ4:10 Other mss read Get behind Me ʰ4:10 Dt 6:13 ⁱ4:16 Lit dawned on them ʲ4:15-16 Is 9:1-2

drew. They were casting a net into the sea, since they were fishermen. ¹⁹ "Follow Me," He told them, "and I will make you fish for[a] people!" ²⁰ Immediately they left their nets and followed Him.

Jesus Calls James and John Zebedee

²¹ Going on from there, He saw two other brothers, James the son of Zebedee, and his brother John. They were in a boat with Zebedee their father, mending their nets, and He called them. ²² Immediately they left the boat and their father and followed Him.

Teaching, Preaching, Healing

²³ Jesus was going all over Galilee, teaching in their •synagogues, preaching the good news of the kingdom, and healing every[b] disease and sickness among the people. ²⁴ Then the news about Him spread throughout Syria. So they brought to Him all those who were afflicted, those suffering from various diseases and intense pains, the demon-possessed, the epileptics, and the paralytics. And He healed them. ²⁵ Large crowds followed Him from Galilee, •Decapolis, Jerusalem, Judea, and beyond the Jordan.

SERMON ON THE MOUNT

5 When He saw the crowds, He went up on the mountain, and after He sat down, His disciples came to Him. ² Then[c] He began to teach them, saying:

Beatitudes: "Blessed Are..."

³ "Blessed are the poor in spirit,
  because the kingdom of heaven
  is theirs.
⁴ Blessed are those who mourn,
  because they will be comforted.
⁵ Blessed are the gentle,
  because they will inherit the earth.

⁶ Blessed are those who hunger
  and thirst for righteousness,
  because they will be filled.
⁷ Blessed are the merciful,
  because they will be shown mercy.
⁸ Blessed are the pure in heart,
  because they will see God.
⁹ Blessed are the peacemakers,
  because they will be called
  sons of God.
¹⁰ Blessed are those
  who are persecuted
  for righteousness,
  because the kingdom of heaven
  is theirs.

¹¹ "Blessed are you when they insult you and persecute you and falsely say every kind of evil against you because of Me. ¹² Be glad and rejoice, because your reward is great in heaven. For that is how they persecuted the prophets who were before you.

Believers Are Salt and Light

¹³ "You are the salt of the earth. But if the salt should lose its taste, how can it be made salty? It's no longer good for anything but to be thrown out and trampled on by men.

¹⁴ "You are the light of the world. A city situated on a hill cannot be hidden. ¹⁵ No one lights a lamp and puts it under a basket,[d] but rather on a lampstand, and it gives light for all who are in the house. ¹⁶ In the same way, let your light shine[e] before men, so that they may see your good works and give glory to your Father in heaven.

Christ Fulfills the Law

¹⁷ "Don't assume that I came to destroy the Law or the Prophets. I did not come to destroy but to fulfill. ¹⁸ For •I assure you: Until heaven and earth pass

---

ᵃ**4:19** Lit *you fishers of*   ᵇ**4:23** Or *every kind of*   ᶜ**5:2** Lit *Then opening His mouth*   ᵈ**5:15** A large basket used to measure grain   ᵉ**5:16** Or *way, your light must shine*

away, not the smallest letter[a] or one stroke of a letter will pass from the law until all things are accomplished. [19] Therefore, whoever breaks one of the least of these commandments and teaches people to do so will be called least in the kingdom of heaven. But whoever practices and teaches ⌊these commandments⌋ will be called great in the kingdom of heaven. [20] For I tell you, unless your righteousness surpasses that of the •scribes and •Pharisees, you will never enter the kingdom of heaven.

Murder Begins in the Heart

[21] "You have heard that it was said to our ancestors,[b] Do not murder,[c] and whoever murders will be subject to judgment. [22] But I tell you, everyone who is angry with his brother[d] will be subject to judgment. And whoever says to his brother, 'Fool!'[e] will be subject to the •Sanhedrin. But whoever says, 'You moron!' will be subject to •hellfire.[f] [23] So if you are offering your gift on the altar, and there you remember that your brother has something against you, [24] leave your gift there in front of the altar. First go and be reconciled with your brother, and then come and offer your gift. [25] Reach a settlement quickly with your adversary while you're on the way with him, or your adversary will hand you over to the judge, the judge to[g] the officer, and you will be thrown into prison. [26] I assure you: You will never get out of there until you have paid the last penny![h]

Adultery in the Heart

[27] "You have heard that it was said, Do not commit adultery.[i] [28] But I tell you, everyone who looks at a woman to lust for her has already committed adultery with her in his heart. [29] If your right eye •causes you to sin, gouge it out and throw it away. For it is better that you lose one of the parts of your body than for your whole body to be thrown into hell. [30] And if your right hand causes you to sin, cut it off and throw it away. For it is better that you lose one of the parts of your body than for your whole body to go into hell!

Jesus Censures Divorce Practices

[31] "It was also said, Whoever divorces his wife must give her a written notice of divorce.[j] [32] But I tell you, everyone who divorces his wife, except in a case of sexual immorality,[k] causes her to commit adultery. And whoever marries a divorced woman commits adultery.

Take No Oaths!

[33] "Again, you have heard that it was said to our ancestors,[b] You must not break your oath, but you must keep your oaths to the Lord.[l] [34] But I tell you, don't take an oath at all: either by heaven, because it is God's throne; [35] or by the earth, because it is His footstool; or by Jerusalem, because it is the city of the great King. [36] Neither should you swear by your head, because you cannot make a single hair white or black. [37] But let your word 'yes' be 'yes,' and your 'no' be 'no.'[m] Anything more than this is from the evil one.

Go the Second Mile

[38] "You have heard that it was said, An eye for an eye and a tooth for a tooth.[n]

---

[a]**5:18** Or *not one iota; iota* is the *smallest letter* of the Gk alphabet.   [b]**5:21,33** Lit *to the ancients*   [c]**5:21** Ex 20:13; Dt 5:17   [d]**5:22** Other mss add *without a cause*   [e]**5:22** Lit *Raca*, an Aram term of abuse similar to "airhead"   [f]**5:22** Lit *the gehenna of fire*   [g]**5:25** Other mss read *judge will hand you over to*   [h]**5:26** Lit *quadrans*, the smallest and least valuable Roman coin, worth ⅟₆₄ of a daily wage   [i]**5:27** Ex 20:14; Dt 5:18   [j]**5:31** Dt 24:1   [k]**5:32** Gk *porneia* = fornication, or possibly a violation of Jewish marriage laws   [l]**5:33** Lv 19:12; Nm 30:2; Dt 23:21   [m]**5:37** Say what you mean and mean what you say   [n]**5:38** Ex 21:24; Lv 24:20; Dt 19:21

39 But I tell you, don't resist[a] an evildoer. On the contrary, if anyone slaps you on your right cheek, turn the other to him also. 40 As for the one who wants to sue you and take away your shirt,[b] let him have your coat[c] as well. 41 And if anyone forces[d] you to go one mile, go with him two. 42 Give to the one who asks you, and don't turn away from the one who wants to borrow from you.

Love Your Enemies

43 "You have heard that it was said, Love your neighbor[e] and hate your enemy. 44 But I tell you, love your enemies[f] and pray for those who[g] persecute you, 45 so that you may be[h] sons of your Father in heaven. For He causes His sun to rise on the evil and the good, and sends rain on the righteous and the unrighteous. 46 For if you love those who love you, what reward will you have? Don't even the tax collectors do the same? 47 And if you greet only your brothers, what are you doing out of the ordinary?[i] Don't even the Gentiles[j] do the same? 48 Be perfect, therefore, as your heavenly Father is perfect.

How to Give

6 "Be careful not to practice your righteousness[k] in front of people, to be seen by them. Otherwise, you will have no reward from your Father in heaven. 2 So whenever you give to the poor, don't sound a trumpet before you, as the hypocrites do in the •synagogues and on the streets, to be applauded by people. •I assure you: They've got their reward! 3 But when you give to the poor, don't let your left hand know what your right hand is doing, 4 so that your giving may be in secret. And your Father who sees in secret will reward you.[l]

How to Pray

5 "Whenever you pray, you must not be like the hypocrites, because they love to pray standing in the synagogues and on the street corners to be seen by people. I assure you: They've got their reward! 6 But when you pray, go into your private room, shut your door, and pray to your Father who is in secret. And your Father who sees in secret will reward you.[m] 7 When you pray, don't babble like the idolaters,[n] since they imagine they'll be heard for their many words. 8 Don't be like them, because your Father knows the things you need before you ask Him.

The Model Prayer

9 "Therefore, you should pray like this:

Our Father in heaven,
Your name be honored as holy.
10   Your kingdom come.
Your will be done
on earth as it is in heaven.
11   Give us today our daily bread.[o]
12   And forgive us our debts,
as we also have forgiven
our debtors.
13   And do not bring us
into[p] temptation,
but deliver us from the evil one.[q]
[For Yours is the kingdom
and the power
and the glory forever. •Amen.][r]

---

[a]5:39 Or don't set yourself against, or don't retaliate against   [b]5:40 Lit tunic = inner garment   [c]5:40 Lit robe, or garment = outer garment   [d]5:41 Roman soldiers could require people to carry loads for them.   [e]5:43 Lv 19:18   [f]5:44 Other mss add bless those who curse you, do good to those who hate you,   [g]5:44 Other mss add mistreat you and   [h]5:45 Or may become, or may show yourselves to be   [i]5:47 Lit doing more, or doing that is superior   [j]5:47 Other mss read tax collectors   [k]6:1 Other mss read charitable giving   [l]6:4 Other mss read will Himself reward you openly   [m]6:6 Other mss add openly   [n]6:7 Or Gentiles, or nations, or heathen, or pagans   [o]6:11 Or our necessary bread, or our bread for tomorrow   [p]6:13 Or do not cause us to come into   [q]6:13 Or from evil   [r]6:13 Other mss omit bracketed text

Forgive!

14 "For if you forgive people their wrongdoing,[a] your heavenly Father will forgive you as well. 15 But if you don't forgive people,[b] your Father will not forgive your wrongdoing.[a]

How to Fast

16 "Whenever you fast, don't be sad-faced like the hypocrites. For they make their faces unattractive[c] so their fasting is obvious to people. I assure you: They've got their reward! 17 But when you fast, put oil on your head, and wash your face, 18 so that you don't show your fasting to people but to your Father who is in secret. And your Father who sees in secret will reward you.[d]

God and Possessions

19 "Don't collect for yourselves treasures[e] on earth, where moth and rust destroy and where thieves break in and steal. 20 But collect for yourselves treasures in heaven, where neither moth nor rust destroys, and where thieves don't break in and steal. 21 For where your treasure is, there your heart will be also.

22 "The eye is the lamp of the body. If your eye is good, your whole body will be full of light. 23 But if your eye is bad, your whole body will be full of darkness. So if the light within you is darkness—how deep is that darkness!

24 "No one can be a slave of two masters, since either he will hate one and love the other, or be devoted to one and despise the other. You cannot be slaves of God and of money.

Cure for Anxiety

25 "This is why I tell you: Don't worry about your life, what you will eat or what you will drink; or about your body, what you will wear. Isn't life more than food and the body more than clothing? 26 Look at the birds of the sky: they don't sow or reap or gather into barns, yet your heavenly Father feeds them. Aren't you worth more than they? 27 Can any of you add a single •cubit to his height[f] by worrying? 28 And why do you worry about clothes? Learn how the wildflowers of the field grow: they don't labor or spin thread. 29 Yet I tell you that not even Solomon in all his splendor was adorned like one of these! 30 If that's how God clothes the grass of the field, which is here today and thrown into the furnace tomorrow, won't He do much more for you—you of little faith? 31 So don't worry, saying, 'What will we eat?' or 'What will we drink?' or 'What will we wear?' 32 For the idolaters[g] eagerly seek all these things, and your heavenly Father knows that you need them. 33 But seek first the kingdom of God[h] and His righteousness, and all these things will be provided for you. 34 Therefore don't worry about tomorrow, because tomorrow will worry about itself. Each day has enough trouble of its own.

Do Not Judge

7 "Do not judge, so that you won't be judged. 2 For with the judgment you use,[i] you will be judged, and with the measure you use,[j] it will be measured to you. 3 Why do you look at the speck in your brother's eye but don't notice the log in your own eye? 4 Or how can you say to your brother, 'Let me take the speck out of your eye,' and look, there's a log in your eye? 5 Hypocrite! First take the log out of your eye, and then you will see clearly to take the speck out of your brother's eye. 6 Don't give what is holy

to dogs or toss your pearls before pigs, or they will trample them with their feet, turn, and tear you to pieces.

Keep Asking, Searching, Knocking

[7] "Keep asking,[a] and it will be given to you. Keep searching,[b] and you will find. Keep knocking,[c] and the door[d] will be opened to you. [8] For everyone who asks receives, and the one who searches finds, and to the one who knocks, the door[e] will be opened. [9] What man among you, if his son asks him for bread, will give him a stone? [10] Or if he asks for a fish, will give him a snake? [11] If you then, who are evil, know how to give good gifts to your children, how much more will your Father in heaven give good things to those who ask Him!

Golden Rule

[12] Therefore, whatever you want others to do for you, do also the same for them—this is the Law and the Prophets.[f]

Entering the Kingdom

[13] "Enter through the narrow gate. For the gate is wide and the road is broad that leads to destruction, and there are many who go through it. [14] How narrow is the gate and difficult the road that leads to life, and few find it.

False Prophets

[15] "Beware of false prophets who come to you in sheep's clothing but inwardly are ravaging wolves. [16] You'll recognize them by their fruit. Are grapes gathered from thornbushes or figs from thistles? [17] In the same way, every good tree produces good fruit, but a bad tree produces bad fruit. [18] A good tree can't produce bad fruit; nei-

ther can a bad tree produce good fruit. [19] Every tree that doesn't produce good fruit is cut down and thrown into the fire. [20] So you'll recognize them by their fruit.

[21] "Not everyone who says to Me, 'Lord, Lord!' will enter the kingdom of heaven, but ⌊only⌋ the one who does the will of My Father in heaven. [22] On that day many will say to Me, 'Lord, Lord, didn't we prophesy in Your name, drive out demons in Your name, and do many miracles in Your name?' [23] Then I will announce to them, 'I never knew you! Depart from Me, you lawbreakers!'[g] [h]

Two Foundations: Rock and Sand

[24] "Therefore, everyone who hears these words of Mine and acts on them will be like a sensible man who built his house on the rock. [25] The rain fell, the rivers rose, and the winds blew and pounded that house. Yet it didn't collapse, because its foundation was on the rock. [26] But everyone who hears these words of Mine and doesn't act on them will be like a foolish man who built his house on the sand. [27] The rain fell, the rivers rose, the winds blew and pounded that house, and it collapsed. And its collapse was great!"

[28] When Jesus had finished this sermon,[i] the crowds were astonished at His teaching, [29] because He was teaching them like one who had authority, and not like their •scribes.

Jesus Cleanses a Leper

8 When He came down from the mountain, large crowds followed Him. [2] Right away a man with a serious skin disease came up and knelt before Him, saying, "Lord, if You are willing, You can make me clean."[j]

---

[a]**7:7** Or *Ask* [b]**7:7** Or *Search* [c]**7:7** Or *Knock* [d]**7:7** Lit *and it* [e]**7:8** Lit *knocks, it* [f]**7:12** When capitalized, *the Law and the Prophets* = the OT [g]**7:23** Lit *you who work lawlessness* [h]**7:23** Ps 6:8 [i]**7:28** Lit *had ended these words*
[j]**8:2** In these vv. 2-3, *clean* includes healing, ceremonial purification, return to fellowship with people, and worship in the temple; Lv 14:1-32.

³ Reaching out His hand He touched him, saying, "I am willing; be made clean." Immediately his disease was healed.ᵃ ⁴ Then Jesus told him, "See that you don't tell anyone; but go, show yourself to the priest, and offer the gift that Moses prescribed, as a testimony to them."

Capernaum: A Centurion's Faith

⁵ When He entered Capernaum, a •centurion came to Him, pleading with Him, ⁶ "Lord, my servant is lying at home paralyzed, in terrible agony!"

⁷ "I will come and heal him," He told him.

⁸ "Lord," the centurion replied, "I am not worthy to have You come under my roof. But only say the word, and my servant will be cured. ⁹ For I too am a man under authority, having soldiers under my command.ᵇ I say to this one, 'Go!' and he goes; and to another, 'Come!' and he comes; and to my slave, 'Do this!' and he does it."

¹⁰ Hearing this, Jesus was amazed and said to those following Him, "•I assure you: I have not found anyone in Israel with so great a faith! ¹¹ I tell you that many will come from east and west, and recline at the table with Abraham, Isaac, and Jacob in the kingdom of heaven. ¹² But the sons of the kingdom will be thrown into the outer darkness. In that place there will be weeping and gnashing of teeth." ¹³ Then Jesus told the centurion, "Go. As you have believed, let it be done for you." And his servant was cured that very moment.ᶜ

Jesus Heals Peter's Mother-in-law

¹⁴ When Jesus went into Peter's house, He saw his mother-in-law lying in bed with a fever. ¹⁵ So He touched her hand, and the fever left her. Then she got up and began to serve Him.

Jesus Drives Out Demons and Heals Sick

¹⁶ When evening came, they brought to Him many who were demon-possessed. He drove out the spirits with a word and healed all who were sick, ¹⁷ so that what was spoken through the prophet Isaiah might be fulfilled:

He Himself took our weaknesses and carried our diseases.ᵈ

Crowds Follow Jesus

¹⁸ When Jesus saw large crowdsᵉ around Him, He gave the order to go to the other side ιof the seaι.ᶠ ¹⁹ A •scribe approached Him and said, "Teacher, I will follow You wherever You go!"

²⁰ Jesus told him, "Foxes have dens and birds of the sky have nests, but the Son of Man has no place to lay His head."

²¹ "Lord," another of His disciples said, "first let me go bury my father."ᵍ

²² But Jesus told him, "Follow Me, and let the dead bury their own dead."

Wind and Wave Obey Christ

²³ As He got into theʰ boat, His disciples followed Him. ²⁴ Suddenly, a violent storm arose on the sea, so that the boat was being swamped by the waves. But He was sleeping. ²⁵ So the disciples came and woke Him up, saying, "Lord, save ιusι! We're going to die!"

²⁶ But He said to them, "Why are you fearful, you of little faith?" Then He got up and rebuked the winds and the sea. And there was a great calm.

ᵃ8:3 Lit cleansed ᵇ8:9 Lit under me ᶜ8:13 Or that hour; lit very hour ᵈ8:17 Is 53:4 ᵉ8:18 Other mss read saw a crowd ᶠ8:18 Sea of Galilee ᵍ8:21 Not necessarily meaning his father was already dead ʰ8:23 Other mss read to a

27 The men were amazed and asked, "What kind of man is this?—even the winds and the sea obey Him!"

Jesus Drives Demons Out—and into Pigs

28 When He had come to the other side, to the region of the Gadarenes,[a] two demon-possessed men met Him as they came out of the tombs. They were so violent that no one could pass that way. 29 Suddenly they shouted, "What do You have to do with us,[b c] Son of God? Have You come here to torment us before the time?"

30 Now a long way off from them, a large herd of pigs was feeding. 31 "If You drive us out," the demons begged Him, "send us into the herd of pigs."

32 "Go!" He told them. So when they had come out, they entered the pigs. And suddenly the whole herd rushed down the steep bank into the sea and perished in the water. 33 Then the men who tended them fled. They went into the city and reported everything—especially what had happened to those who were demon-possessed. 34 At that, the whole town went out to meet Jesus. When they saw Him, they begged Him to leave their region.

Son of Man Forgives and Heals

9 So He got into a boat, crossed over, and came to His own town. 2 Just then some men[d] brought to Him a paralytic lying on a stretcher. Seeing their faith, Jesus told the paralytic, "Have courage, son, your sins are forgiven."

3 At this, some of the •scribes said among themselves, "He's blaspheming!"

4 But perceiving their thoughts, Jesus said, "Why are you thinking evil things in your hearts?[e] 5 For which is easier: to say, 'Your sins are forgiven,' or to say, 'Get up and walk'? 6 But so you may know that the •Son of Man has authority on earth to forgive sins"—then He told the paralytic, "Get up, pick up your stretcher, and go home." 7 And he got up and went home. 8 When the crowds saw this, they were awestruck[f g] and gave glory to God who had given such authority to men.

Call of Matthew

9 As Jesus went on from there, He saw a man named Matthew sitting at the tax office, and He said to him, "Follow Me!" So he got up and followed Him.

10 While He was reclining at the table in the house, many tax collectors and sinners came as guests to eat[h] with Jesus and His disciples. 11 When the •Pharisees saw this, they asked His disciples, "Why does your Teacher eat with tax collectors and sinners?"

12 But when He heard this, He said, "Those who are well don't need a doctor, but the sick do. 13 Go and learn what this means: **I desire mercy and not sacrifice.**[i] For I didn't come to call the righteous, but sinners."[j]

John's Disciples: Question about Fasting

14 Then John's disciples came to Him, saying, "Why do we and the Pharisees fast often, but Your disciples do not fast?"

15 Jesus said to them, "Can the wedding guests[k] be sad while the groom is with them? The days will come when

a8:28 Other mss read Gergesenes b8:29 Other mss add Jesus c8:29 Lit What to us and to You d9:2 Lit then they e9:4 Or minds f9:8 Other mss read amazed g9:8 Lit afraid h9:10 Lit came, they were reclining (at the table); at important meals the custom was to recline on a mat at a low table and lean on the left elbow. i9:13 Hs 6:6 j9:13 Other mss add to repentance k9:15 Lit the sons of the bridal chamber

the groom will be taken away from them, and then they will fast. [16] No one patches an old garment with unshrunk cloth, because the patch pulls away from the garment and makes the tear worse. [17] And no one puts[a] new wine into old wineskins. Otherwise, the skins burst, the wine spills out, and the skins are ruined. But they put new wine into fresh wineskins, and both are preserved."

A Girl Restored and a Woman Healed

[18] As He was telling them these things, suddenly one of the leaders[b] came and knelt down before Him, saying, "My daughter is near death,[c] but come and lay Your hand on her, and she will live." [19] So Jesus and His disciples got up and followed him.

[20] Just then, a woman who had suffered from bleeding for 12 years approached from behind and touched the •tassel on His robe, [21] for she said to herself, "If I can just touch His robe, I'll be made well!"[d]

[22] But Jesus turned and saw her. "Have courage, daughter," He said. "Your faith has made you well."[e] And the woman was made well from that moment.[f]

[23] When Jesus came to the leader's house, He saw the flute players and a crowd lamenting loudly. [24] "Leave," He said, "because the girl isn't dead, but sleeping." And they started laughing at Him. [25] But when the crowd had been put outside, He went in and took her by the hand, and the girl got up. [26] And this news spread throughout that whole area.

Jesus Heals the Blind

[27] As Jesus went on from there, two blind men followed Him, shouting, "Have mercy on us, Son of David!"

[28] When He entered the house, the blind men approached Him, and Jesus said to them, "Do you believe that I can do this?"

"Yes, Lord," they answered Him.

[29] Then He touched their eyes, saying, "Let it be done for you according to your faith!" [30] And their eyes were opened. Then Jesus warned them sternly, "Be sure that no one finds out!"[g] [31] But they went out and spread the news about Him throughout that whole area.

Jesus Drives Out a Demon of Speech

[32] Just as they were going out, a demon-possessed man who was unable to speak was brought to Him. [33] When the demon had been driven out, the man[h] spoke. And the crowds were amazed, saying, "Nothing like this has ever been seen in Israel!"

[34] But the Pharisees said, "He drives out demons by the ruler of the demons!"

Lord of the Harvest

[35] Then Jesus went to all the towns and villages, teaching in their •synagogues, preaching the good news of the kingdom, and healing every[i] disease and every sickness.[j] [36] When He saw the crowds, He felt compassion for them, because they were weary and worn out, like sheep without a shepherd. [37] Then He said to His disciples, "The harvest is abundant, but the workers are few. [38] Therefore, pray to the Lord of the harvest to send out workers into His harvest."

Jesus Commissions the Twelve

10 Summoning His 12 disciples, He gave them authority over unclean[k] spirits, to drive them out and to heal every[a] disease and sickness. [2] These are the names of the 12 apostles:

> First, Simon, who is called Peter,
> and Andrew his brother;
> James the son of Zebedee,
> and John his brother;
> [3] Philip and Bartholomew;[b]
> Thomas and Matthew
>   the tax collector;
> James the son of Alphaeus,
>   and Thaddaeus;[c]
> [4] Simon the Zealot,[d]
>   and Judas Iscariot,[e]
> who also betrayed Him.

Jesus Instructs and Sends the Twelve

[5] Jesus sent out these 12 after giving them instructions: "Don't take the road leading to other nations, and don't enter any •Samaritan town. [6] Instead, go to the lost sheep of the house of Israel. [7] As you go, announce this: 'The kingdom of heaven has come near.' [8] Heal the sick, raise the dead, cleanse those with skin diseases, drive out demons. You have received free of charge; give free of charge. [9] Don't take along gold, silver, or copper for your money-belts. [10] Don't take a traveling bag for the road, or an extra shirt, sandals, or a walking stick, for the worker is worthy of his food.

[11] "When you enter any town or village, find out who is worthy, and stay there until you leave. [12] Greet a household when you enter it, [13] and if the household is worthy, let your peace be on it. But if it is unworthy, let your peace return to you. [14] If anyone will not welcome you or listen to your words, shake the dust off your feet when you leave that house or town. [15] •I assure you: It will be more tolerable on the day of judgment for the land of Sodom and Gomorrah than for that town.

Jesus Predicts Persecutions

[16] "Look, I'm sending you out like sheep among wolves. Therefore be as shrewd as serpents and as harmless as doves. [17] Because people will hand you over to sanhedrins[f] and flog you in their •synagogues, beware of them. [18] You will even be brought before governors and kings because of Me, to bear witness to them and to the nations. [19] But when they hand you over, don't worry about how or what you should speak. For you will be given what to say at that hour, [20] because you are not speaking, but the Spirit of your Father is speaking through you.

[21] "Brother will betray brother to death, and a father his child. Children will even rise up against their parents and have them put to death. [22] You will be hated by everyone because of My name. But the one who endures to the end will be delivered.[g] [23] When they persecute you in one town, escape to another. For I assure you: You will not have covered the towns of Israel before the •Son of Man comes. [24] A disciple[h] is not above his teacher, or a slave above his master. [25] It is enough for a disciple to become like his teacher and a slave like his master. If they called the head of the house '•Beelzebul,' how much more the members of his household!

Fear God

[26] "Therefore, don't be afraid of them, since there is nothing covered that won't be uncovered, and nothing hidden that won't be made known. [27] What I tell you in the dark, speak in the light. What

you hear in a whisper,ª proclaim on the housetops. ²⁸ Don't fear those who kill the body but are not able to kill the soul; rather, fear Him who is able to destroy both soul and body in •hell. ²⁹ Aren't two sparrows sold for a penny?ᵇ Yet not one of them falls to the ground without your Father's consent.ᶜ ³⁰ But even the hairs of your head have all been counted. ³¹ Don't be afraid therefore; you are worth more than many sparrows.

"Acknowledge Me Before Men"

³² "Therefore, everyone who will acknowledge Me before men, I will also acknowledge him before My Father in heaven. ³³ But whoever denies Me before men, I will also deny him before My Father in heaven. ³⁴ Don't assume that I came to bring peace on the earth. I did not come to bring peace, but a sword. ³⁵ For I came to turn

> a man against his father,
> a daughter against her mother,
> a daughter-in-law against
>   her mother-in-law;
> ³⁶ and a man's enemies will be
>   the members of his household.ᵈ

³⁷ The person who loves father or mother more than Me is not worthy of Me; the person who loves son or daughter more than Me is not worthy of Me. ³⁸ And whoever doesn't take up his cross and followᵉ Me is not worthy of Me. ³⁹ Anyone findingᶠ his life will lose it, and anyone losingᵍ his life because of Me will find it.

A Cup of Cold Water

⁴⁰ "The one who welcomes you welcomes Me, and the one who welcomes Me welcomes Him who sent Me. ⁴¹ Anyone whoʰ welcomes a prophet because he is a prophetⁱ will receive a prophet's reward. And anyone whoʲ welcomes a righteous person because he's righteousᵏ will receive a righteous person's reward. ⁴² And whoever gives just a cup of cold water to one of these little ones because he is a discipleˡ—I assure you: He will never lose his reward!"

John the Baptist Questions Jesus

11 When Jesus had finished giving orders to His 12 disciples, He moved on from there to teach and preach in their towns. ² When John heard in prison what the •Messiah was doing, he sent ɪa messageɪ by his disciples ³ and asked Him, "Are You the One who is to come, or should we expect someone else?"

⁴ Jesus replied to them, "Go and report to John what you hear and see: ⁵ the blind see, the lame walk, those with skin diseases are healed,ᵐ the deaf hear, the dead are raised, and the poor are told the good news. ⁶ And if anyone is not offended because of Me, he is blessed."

Jesus Praises John the Baptist

⁷ As these men went away, Jesus began to speak to the crowds about John: "What did you go out into the wilderness to see? A reed swaying in the wind? ⁸ What then did you go out to see? A man dressed in soft clothes? Look, those who wear soft clothes are in kings' palaces. ⁹ But what did you go out to see? A prophet? Yes, I tell you, and far more than a prophet. ¹⁰ This is the one it is written about:

ª**10:27** Lit *in the ear*   ᵇ**10:29** Gk *assarion, a small copper coin*   ᶜ**10:29** Lit *ground apart from your Father*   ᵈ**10:35-36** Mc 7:6   ᵉ**10:38** Lit *follow after*   ᶠ**10:39** Or *The one who finds*   ᵍ**10:39** Or *and the one who loses*   ʰ**10:41** Or *The one who*   ⁱ**10:41** Lit *prophet in the name of a prophet*   ʲ**10:41** Or *And the one who*   ᵏ**10:41** Lit *person in the name of a righteous person*   ˡ**10:42** Lit *little ones in the name of a disciple*   ᵐ**11:5** Lit *cleansed*

> Look, I am sending My messenger
> ahead of You;[a]
> he will prepare Your way
> before You.[b]

[11] "•I assure you: Among those born of women no one greater than John the Baptist has appeared,[c] but the least in the kingdom of heaven is greater than he. [12] From the days of John the Baptist until now, the kingdom of heaven has been suffering violence,[d] and the violent have been seizing it by force. [13] For all the prophets and the law prophesied until John; [14] if you're willing to accept it, he is the Elijah who is to come. [15] Anyone who has ears[e] should listen!

Jesus Criticizes an Unresponsive Generation

[16] "To what should I compare this generation? It's like children sitting in the marketplaces who call out to each other:

> [17] We played the flute for you,
> but you didn't dance;
> we sang a lament,
> but you didn't mourn![f]

[18] For John did not come eating or drinking, and they say, 'He has a demon!' [19] The •Son of Man came eating and drinking, and they say, 'Look, a glutton and a drunkard, a friend of tax collectors and sinners!' Yet wisdom is vindicated[g] by her deeds."[h]

[20] Then He proceeded to denounce the towns where most of His miracles were done, because they did not repent: [21] "Woe to you, Chorazin! Woe to you, Bethsaida! For if the miracles that were done in you had been done in Tyre and Sidon, they would have repented in sackcloth and ashes long ago! [22] But I tell you, it will be more tolerable for Tyre and Sidon on the day of judgment than for you. [23] And you, Capernaum, will you be exalted to heaven? You will go down to •Hades. For if the miracles that were done in you had been done in Sodom, it would have remained until today. [24] But I tell you, it will be more tolerable for the land of Sodom on the day of judgment than for you."

The Son Praises the Father

[25] At that time Jesus said, "I praise[i] You, Father, Lord of heaven and earth, because You have hidden these things from the wise and learned and revealed them to infants. [26] Yes, Father, because this was Your good pleasure.[j] [27] All things have been entrusted to Me by My Father. No one knows[k] the Son except the Father, and no one knows the Father except the Son and anyone to whom the Son desires[l] to reveal Him.

The Easy Yoke

[28] "Come to Me, all of you who are weary and burdened, and I will give you rest. [29] All of you, take up My yoke and learn from Me, because I am gentle and humble in heart, and you will find rest for yourselves. [30] For My yoke is easy and My burden is light."

Jesus Is Lord of the Sabbath

12 At that time Jesus passed through the grainfields on the Sabbath. His disciples were hungry and began to pick and eat some heads of grain. [2] But when the •Pharisees saw it, they said to Him, "Look, Your disciples are doing what is not lawful to do on the Sabbath!"

---

[a]**11:10** Lit messenger before Your face   [b]**11:10** Mal 3:1   [c]**11:11** Lit arisen   [d]**11:12** Or has been forcefully advancing   [e]**11:15** Other mss add to hear   [f]**11:17** Or beat your breasts   [g]**11:19** Or declared right   [h]**11:19** Other mss read children   [i]**11:25** Or thank   [j]**11:26** Lit was well-pleasing in Your sight   [k]**11:27** Or knows exactly   [l]**11:27** Or wills, or chooses

³ He said to them, "Haven't you read what David did when he and those who were with him were hungry— ⁴ how he entered the house of God, and they ateᵃ the •sacred bread, which is not lawful for him or for those with him to eat, but only for the priests? ⁵ Or haven't you read in the Lawᵇ that on Sabbath days the priests in the temple violate the Sabbath and are innocent? ⁶ But I tell you that something greater than the temple is here! ⁷ If you had known what this means: **I desire mercy and not sacrifice,**ᶜ you would not have condemned the innocent. ⁸ For the •Son of Man is Lord of the Sabbath."

Jesus Heals Paralyzed Hand on Sabbath

⁹ Moving on from there, He entered their •synagogue. ¹⁰ There He saw a man who had a paralyzed hand. And in order to accuse Him they asked Him, "Is it lawful to heal on the Sabbath?"

¹¹ But He said to them, "What man among you, if he had a sheepᵈ that fell into a pit on the Sabbath, wouldn't take hold of it and lift it out? ¹² A man is worth far more than a sheep, so it is lawful to do good on the Sabbath."

¹³ Then He told the man, "Stretch out your hand." So he stretched it out, and it was restored, as good as the other. ¹⁴ But the Pharisees went out and plotted against Him, how they might destroy Him.

Isaiah Fulfilled: Servant of the Lord

¹⁵ When Jesus became aware of this, He withdrew from there. Huge crowdsᵉ followed Him, and He healed them all. ¹⁶ He warned them not to make Him known, ¹⁷ so that what was spoken through the prophet Isaiah might be fulfilled:

¹⁸ Here is My Servant
  whom I have chosen,
My beloved in whom
  My soul delights;
I will put My Spirit on Him,
and He will proclaim justice
  to the nations.
¹⁹ He will not argue or shout,
and no one will hear His voice
  in the streets.
²⁰ He will not break a bruised reed,
and He will not put out
  a smoldering wick,
until He has led justice to victory.ᶠ
²¹ The nations will put their hope
  in His name.ᵍ

A House Divided

²² Then a demon-possessed man who was blind and unable to speak was brought to Him. He healed him, so that the manʰ could both speak and see. ²³ And all the crowds were astounded and said, "Perhaps this is the Son of David!"

²⁴ When the Pharisees heard this, they said, "The man drives out demons only by •Beelzebul, the ruler of the demons."

²⁵ Knowing their thoughts, He told them: "Every kingdom divided against itself is headed for destruction, and no city or house divided against itself will stand. ²⁶ If Satan drives out Satan, he is divided against himself. How then will his kingdom stand? ²⁷ And if I drive out demons by Beelzebul, who is it your sons drive them out by? For this reason they will be your judges. ²⁸ If I drive out demons by the Spirit of God, then the kingdom of God has come to you. ²⁹ How can someone enter a strong

ᵃ**12:4** Other mss read *he ate*   ᵇ**12:5** The Torah (the Pentateuch)   ᶜ**12:7** Hs 6:6   ᵈ**12:11** Or *had one sheep*   ᵉ**12:15** Other mss read *Many*   ᶠ**12:20** Or *until He has successfully put forth justice*   ᵍ**12:18-21** Is 42:1-4   ʰ**12:22** Lit *mute*

man's house and steal his possessions unless he first ties up the strong man? Then he can rob his house. ³⁰ Anyone who is not with Me is against Me, and anyone who does not gather with Me scatters. ³¹ Because of this, I tell you, people will be forgiven every sin and blasphemy, but the blasphemy against[a] the Spirit will not be forgiven.[b] ³² Whoever speaks a word against the Son of Man, it will be forgiven him. But whoever speaks against the Holy Spirit, it will not be forgiven him, either in this age or in the one to come.

A Tree and Its Fruit

³³ "Either make the tree good and its fruit good, or make the tree bad[c] and its fruit bad; for a tree is known by its fruit. ³⁴ Brood of vipers! How can you speak good things when you are evil? For the mouth speaks from the overflow of the heart. ³⁵ A good man produces good things from his storeroom of good,[d] and an evil man produces evil things from his storeroom of evil. ³⁶ I tell you that on the day of judgment people will have to account for every careless word they speak.[e] ³⁷ For by your words you will be acquitted, and by your words you will be condemned."

Sign of Jonah

³⁸ Then some of the •scribes and Pharisees said to Him, "Teacher, we want to see a sign from You." ³⁹ But He answered them, "An evil and adulterous generation demands a sign, but no sign will be given to it except the sign of the prophet Jonah. ⁴⁰ For as Jonah was in the belly of the great fish three days and three nights, so the Son of Man will be in the heart of the earth three days and three

nights. ⁴¹ The men of Nineveh will stand up at the judgment with this generation and condemn it, because they repented at Jonah's proclamation; and look—something greater than Jonah is here! ⁴² The queen of the south will rise up at the judgment with this generation and condemn it, because she came from the ends of the earth to hear the wisdom of Solomon; and look—something greater than Solomon is here!

Unclean Spirit's Return

⁴³ "When an unclean[f] spirit comes out of a man, it roams through waterless places looking for rest but doesn't find any. ⁴⁴ Then it says, 'I'll go back to my house that I came from.' And when it arrives, it finds ⌊the house⌋ vacant, swept, and put in order. ⁴⁵ Then off it goes and brings with it seven other spirits more evil than itself, and they enter and settle down there. As a result, that man's last condition is worse than the first. That's how it will also be with this evil generation."

Jesus' Mother and Brothers: Teaching on True Relationships

⁴⁶ He was still speaking to the crowds when suddenly His mother and brothers were standing outside wanting to speak to Him. ⁴⁷ Someone told Him, "Look, Your mother and Your brothers are standing outside, wanting to speak to You."[g] ⁴⁸ But He replied to the one who told Him, "Who is My mother and who are My brothers?" ⁴⁹ And stretching out His hand toward His disciples, He said, "Here are My mother and My brothers! ⁵⁰ For whoever does the will of My Father in heaven, that person is My brother and sister and mother."

Parable of the Sower

13 On that day Jesus went out of the house and was sitting by the sea. ² Such large crowds gathered around Him that He got into a boat and sat down, while the whole crowd stood on the shore.

³ Then He told them many things in parables, saying: "Consider the sower who went out to sow. ⁴ As he was sowing, some seeds fell along the path, and the birds came and ate them up. ⁵ Others fell on rocky ground, where there wasn't much soil, and they sprang up quickly since the soil wasn't deep. ⁶ But when the sun came up they were scorched, and since they had no root, they withered. ⁷ Others fell among thorns, and the thorns came up and choked them. ⁸ Still others fell on good ground, and produced a crop: some 100, some 60, and some 30 times ⌞what was sown⌟. ⁹ Anyone who has ears[a] should listen!"

Why Jesus Used Parables

¹⁰ Then the disciples came up and asked Him, "Why do You speak to them in parables?"

¹¹ He answered them, "Because the secrets[b] of the kingdom of heaven have been given for you to know, but it has not been given to them. ¹² For whoever has, ⌞more⌟ will be given to him, and he will have more than enough. But whoever does not have, even what he has will be taken away from him. ¹³ For this reason I speak to them in parables, because looking they do not see, and hearing they do not listen or understand. ¹⁴ Isaiah's prophecy is fulfilled in them, which says:

You will listen and listen,
    yet never understand;
and you will look and look,
    yet never perceive.
¹⁵ For this people's heart
    has grown callous;
their ears are hard of hearing,
    and they have shut their eyes;
otherwise they might see
    with their eyes
and hear with their ears,
    understand with their hearts
and turn back—
    and I would cure them.[c]

¹⁶ "But your eyes are blessed because they do see, and your ears because they do hear! ¹⁷ For •I assure you: Many prophets and righteous people longed to see the things you see yet didn't see them; to hear the things you hear yet didn't hear them.

Parable of Sower Explained

¹⁸ "You, then, listen to the parable of the sower: ¹⁹ When anyone hears the word[d] about the kingdom and doesn't understand it, the evil one comes and snatches away what was sown in his heart. This is the one <u>sown along the path</u>. ²⁰ And the one <u>sown on rocky ground</u>—this is one who hears the word and immediately receives it with joy. ²¹ Yet he has no root in himself, but is short-lived. When pressure or persecution comes because of the word, immediately he stumbles. ²² Now the one <u>sown among the thorns</u>—this is one who hears the word, but the worries of this age and the seduction[e] of wealth choke the word, and it becomes unfruitful. ²³ But the one <u>sown on the good ground</u>—this is one who hears and understands the word, who does bear fruit

---

a13:9 Other mss add *to hear*   **b13:11** The Gk word *mysteria* does not mean "mysteries" in the Eng sense; it means what we can know only by divine revelation.   **c13:14-15** Is 6:9-10   **d13:19** Gk *logos = word*, or *message*, or *saying*, or *thing*   **e13:22** Or *pleasure*, or *deceitfulness*

and yields: some 100, some 60, some 30 times ⌊what was sown⌋."

Parable of Wheat and Weeds

²⁴ He presented another parable to them: "The kingdom of heaven may be compared to a man who sowed good seed in his field. ²⁵ But while people were sleeping, his enemy came, sowed weeds[a] among the wheat, and left. ²⁶ When the plants sprouted and produced grain, then the weeds also appeared. ²⁷ The landowner's slaves came to him and said, 'Master, didn't you sow good seed in your field? Then where did the weeds come from?'

²⁸ " 'An enemy did this!' he told them.

" 'So, do you want us to go and gather them up?' the slaves asked him.

²⁹ " 'No,' he said. 'When you gather up the weeds, you might also uproot the wheat with them. ³⁰ Let both grow together until the harvest. At harvest time I'll tell the reapers: Gather the weeds first and tie them in bundles to burn them, but store the wheat in my barn.' "

Parables of Mustard Seed and of Yeast

³¹ He presented another parable to them: "The kingdom of heaven is like a mustard seed that a man took and sowed in his field. ³² It's the smallest of all the seeds, but when grown, it's taller than the vegetables and becomes a tree, so that the birds of the sky come and nest in its branches."

³³ He told them another parable: "The kingdom of heaven is like yeast that a woman took and mixed into 50 pounds[b] of flour until it spread through all of it."[c]

Using Parables Fulfills Prophecy

³⁴ Jesus told the crowds all these things in parables, and He would not speak anything to them without a parable, ³⁵ so that what was spoken through the prophet might be fulfilled:

**I will open My mouth in parables;
I will declare things kept secret
from the foundation of the world.**[d]

Jesus Interprets Wheat and Weeds

³⁶ Then He dismissed the crowds and went into the house. His disciples approached Him and said, "Explain the parable of the weeds in the field to us."

³⁷ He replied: "The One who sows the good seed is the •Son of Man; ³⁸ the field is the world; and the good seed—these are the sons of the kingdom. The weeds are the sons of the evil one, and ³⁹ the enemy who sowed them is the Devil. The harvest is the end of the age, and the harvesters are angels. ⁴⁰ Therefore just as the weeds are gathered and burned in the fire, so it will be at the end of the age. ⁴¹ The Son of Man will send out His angels, and they will gather from His kingdom everything that causes sin[e] and those guilty of lawlessness.[f] ⁴² They will throw them into the blazing furnace where there will be weeping and gnashing of teeth. ⁴³ Then the righteous will shine like the sun in their Father's kingdom. Anyone who has ears[g] should listen!

Parables of Hidden Treasure and Priceless Pearl

⁴⁴ "The kingdom of heaven is like treasure, buried in a field, that a man found and reburied. Then in his joy he goes

---

[a]**13:25** Or *darnel*, a weed similar in appearance to wheat in the early stages   [b]**13:33** Lit *3 sata*; about 40 quarts
[c]**13:33** Or *until all of it was leavened*   [d]**13:35** Ps 78:2   [e]**13:41** Or *stumbling*   [f]**13:41** Or *those who do lawlessness*
[g]**13:43** Other mss add *to hear*

and sells everything he has and buys that field.

45 "Again, the kingdom of heaven is like a merchant in search of fine pearls. 46 When he found one priceless[a] pearl, he went and sold everything he had, and bought it.

Parable of the Net

47 "Again, the kingdom of heaven is like a large net thrown into the sea. It collected every kind of fish, 48 and when it was full, they dragged it ashore, sat down, and gathered the good fish into containers, but threw out the worthless ones. 49 So it will be at the end of the age. The angels will go out, separate the evil people from the righteous, 50 and throw them into the blazing furnace. In that place there will be weeping and gnashing of teeth.

Storehouse of Truth

51 "Have you understood all these things?"[b]

"Yes," they told Him.

52 "Therefore," He said to them, "every student of Scripture[c] instructed in the kingdom of heaven is like a landowner who brings out of his storeroom what is new and what is old." 53 When Jesus had finished these parables, He left there.

Nazareth Rejects Jesus

54 He went to His hometown and began to teach them in their •synagogue, so that they were astonished and said, "How did this wisdom and these miracles come to Him? 55 Isn't this the carpenter's son? Isn't His mother called Mary, and His brothers James, Joseph,[d] Simon, and Judas? 56 And His sisters, aren't they all with us? So where does He get all these things?" 57 And they were offended by Him.

But Jesus said to them, "A prophet is not without honor except in his hometown and in his household." 58 And He did not do many miracles there because of their unbelief.

Herod the Tetrarch Arrests John the Baptist

14 At that time •Herod the tetrarch heard the report about Jesus. 2 "This is John the Baptist!" he told his servants. "He has been raised from the dead, and that's why supernatural powers are at work in him."

3 For Herod had arrested John, chained[e] him, and put him in prison on account of Herodias, his brother Philip's wife, 4 since John had been telling him, "It's not lawful for you to have her!" 5 Though he wanted to kill him, he feared the crowd, since they regarded him as a prophet.

Herod's Birthday Party

6 But when Herod's birthday celebration came, Herodias' daughter danced before them[f] and pleased Herod. 7 So he promised with an oath to give her whatever she might ask. 8 And prompted by her mother, she answered, "Give me John the Baptist's head here on a platter!" 9 Although the king regretted it, he commanded that it be granted because of his oaths and his guests.

Herod Beheads John the Baptist

10 So he sent orders and had John beheaded in the prison. 11 His head was brought on a platter and given to the girl, who carried it to her mother. 12 Then his disciples came, removed the

---

a**13:46** Or *very precious*   b**13:51** Other mss add *Jesus asked them*   c**13:52** Or *every scribe*   d**13:55** Other mss read *Joses*; Mk 6:3   e**14:3** Or *bound*   f**14:6** Lit *danced in the middle*

corpse,[a] buried it, and went and reported to Jesus.

Jesus Feeds 5,000

[13] When Jesus heard about it, He withdrew from there by boat to a remote place to be alone. When the crowds heard this, they followed Him on foot from the towns. [14] As He stepped ashore,[b] He saw a huge crowd, felt compassion for them, and healed their sick.

[15] When evening came, the disciples approached Him and said, "This place is a wilderness, and it is already late.[c] Send the crowds away so they can go into the villages and buy food for themselves."

[16] "They don't need to go away," Jesus told them. "You give them something to eat."

[17] "But we only have five loaves and two fish here," they said to Him.

[18] "Bring them here to Me," He said. [19] Then He commanded the crowds to sit down[d] on the grass. He took the five loaves and the two fish, and looking up to heaven, He blessed them. He broke the loaves and gave them to the disciples, and the disciples ⌊gave them⌋ to the crowds. [20] Everyone ate and was filled. Then they picked up 12 baskets full of leftover pieces! [21] Now those who ate were about 5,000 men, besides women and children.

Jesus Walks on Water

[22] Immediately He[e] made the disciples get into the boat and go ahead of Him to the other side, while He dismissed the crowds. [23] After dismissing the crowds, He went up on the mountain by Himself to pray. When evening came, He was there alone. [24] But the boat was already over a mile[f] from land,[g] battered by the waves, because the wind was against them. [25] Around three in the morning,[h] He came toward them walking on the sea. [26] When the disciples saw Him walking on the sea, they were terrified. "It's a ghost!" they said, and cried out in fear.

[27] Immediately Jesus spoke to them. "Have courage! It is I. Don't be afraid."

Peter Tries to Walk on Water

[28] "Lord, if it's You," Peter answered Him, "command me to come to You on the water."

[29] "Come!" He said.

And climbing out of the boat, Peter started walking on the water and came toward Jesus. [30] But when he saw the strength of the wind,[i] he was afraid. And beginning to sink he cried out, "Lord, save me!"

[31] Immediately Jesus reached out His hand, caught hold of him, and said to him, "You of little faith, why did you doubt?" [32] When they got into the boat, the wind ceased. [33] Then those in the boat worshiped Him and said, "Truly You are the Son of God!"

Miraculous Healings: Touching the Tassel

[34] Once they crossed over, they came to land at Gennesaret. [35] When the men of that place recognized Him, they alerted[j] the whole vicinity and brought to Him all who were sick. [36] They were begging Him that they might only touch the •tassel on His robe. And as many as touched it were made perfectly well.

---

[a]**14:12** Other mss read *body*   [b]**14:14** Lit *Coming out* (of the boat)   [c]**14:15** Lit *and the time* (for the evening meal) *has already passed*   [d]**14:19** Lit *to recline*   [e]**14:22** Other mss read *Jesus*   [f]**14:24** Lit *already many stadia; 1 stadion* = 600 feet   [g]**14:24** Other mss read *already in the middle of the sea*   [h]**14:25** Lit *fourth watch of the night* = 3 to 6 a.m.   [i]**14:30** Other mss read *saw the wind*   [j]**14:35** Lit *sent into*

Pharisees and Scribes: Tradition of the Elders

15 Then •Pharisees and •scribes came from Jerusalem to Jesus and asked, [2] "Why do Your disciples break the tradition of the elders? For they don't wash their hands when they eat!"[a]

[3] He answered them, "And why do you break God's commandment because of your tradition? [4] For God said:[b]

Honor your father
and your mother;[c] and,
The one who speaks evil of father
or mother
must be put to death.[d]

[5] But you say, 'Whoever tells his father or mother, "Whatever benefit you might have received from me is a gift [committed to the temple]"— [6] he does not have to honor his father.'[e] In this way, you have revoked God's word[f] because of your tradition. [7] Hypocrites! Isaiah prophesied correctly about you when he said:

[8] These people[g] honor Me
with their lips,
but their heart is far from Me.
[9] They worship Me in vain,
teaching as doctrines
the commands of men."[h]

Jesus: Defilement from Within

[10] Summoning the crowd, He told them, "Listen and understand: [11] It's not what goes into the mouth that defiles a man, but what comes out of the mouth, this defiles a man."

[12] Then the disciples came up and told Him, "Do You know that the Pharisees took offense when they heard this statement?"

Blind Guides

[13] He replied, "Every plant that My heavenly Father didn't plant will be uprooted. [14] Leave them alone! They are blind guides.[i] And if the blind guide the blind, both will fall into a pit."

Jesus Explains Defilement of Heart

[15] Then Peter replied to Him, "Explain this parable to us."

[16] "Are even you still lacking in understanding?" He[j] asked. [17] "Don't you realize[k] that whatever goes into the mouth passes into the stomach and is eliminated?[l] [18] But what comes out of the mouth comes from the heart, and this defiles a man. [19] For from the heart come evil thoughts, murders, adulteries, sexual immoralities, thefts, false testimonies, blasphemies. [20] These are the things that defile a man, but eating with unwashed hands does not defile a man."

A Gentile Mother's Faith

[21] When Jesus left there, He withdrew to the area of Tyre and Sidon. [22] Just then a Canaanite woman from that region came and kept crying out,[m] "Have mercy on me, Lord, Son of David! My daughter is cruelly tormented by a demon."

[23] Yet He did not say a word to her. So His disciples approached Him and urged Him, "Send her away because she cries out after us."[n]

[24] He replied, "I was sent only to the lost sheep of the house of Israel."

[25] But she came, knelt before Him, and said, "Lord, help me!"

---

[a]**15:2** Lit *eat bread* = eat a meal   [b]**15:4** Other mss read *commanded, saying*   [c]**15:4** Ex 20:12; Dt 5:16   [d]**15:4** Ex 21:17; Lv 20:9   [e]**15:6** Other mss read *then he does not have to honor his father or mother*   [f]**15:6** Other mss read *commandment*   [g]**15:8** Other mss add *draws near to Me with their mouths, and*   [h]**15:8-9** Is 29:13 LXX   [i]**15:14** Other mss add *for the blind*   [j]**15:16** Other mss read *Jesus*   [k]**15:17** Other mss add *yet*   [l]**15:17** Lit *and goes out into the toilet*   [m]**15:22** Other mss read *and cried out to Him*   [n]**15:23** Lit *she is yelling behind us* or *after us*

26 He answered, "It isn't right to take the children's bread and throw it to their dogs."

27 "Yes, Lord," she said, "yet even the dogs eat the crumbs that fall from their masters' table!"

28 Then Jesus replied to her, "Woman, your faith is great. Let it be done for you as you want." And from that moment[a] her daughter was cured.

Jesus Heals Many on a Mountain

29 Moving on from there, Jesus passed along the Sea of Galilee. He went up on a mountain and sat there, 30 and large crowds came to Him, having with them the lame, the blind, the deformed, those unable to speak, and many others. They put them at His feet, and He healed them. 31 So the crowd was amazed when they saw those unable to speak talking, the deformed restored, the lame walking, and the blind seeing. And they gave glory to the God of Israel.

Jesus Feeds 4,000

32 Now Jesus summoned His disciples and said, "I have compassion on the crowd, because they've already stayed with Me three days and have nothing to eat. I don't want to send them away hungry; otherwise they might collapse on the way."

33 The disciples said to Him, "Where could we get enough bread in this desolate place to fill such a crowd?"

34 "How many loaves do you have?" Jesus asked them.

"Seven," they said, "and a few small fish."

35 After commanding the crowd to sit down on the ground, 36 He took the seven loaves and the fish, and He gave thanks, broke them, and kept on giving them to the disciples, and the disciples ⌊gave them⌋ to the crowds. 37 They all ate and were filled. Then they collected the leftover pieces—seven large baskets full. 38 Now those who ate were 4,000 men, besides women and children. 39 After dismissing the crowds, He got into the boat and went to the region of Magadan.[b]

Religious Leaders Ask for Sign

16 The •Pharisees and •Sadducees approached, and as a test, asked Him to show them a sign from heaven.

2 He answered them: "When evening comes you say, 'It will be good weather because the sky is red.' 3 And in the morning, 'Today will be stormy because the sky is red and threatening.' You[c] know how to read the appearance of the sky, but you can't read the signs of the times.[d] 4 An evil and adulterous generation wants a sign, but no sign will be given to it except the sign of[e] Jonah." Then He left them and went away.

Yeast of Pharisees and Sadducees

5 The disciples reached the other shore,[f] and they had forgotten to take bread.

6 Then Jesus told them, "Watch out and beware of the yeast[g] of the Pharisees and Sadducees."

7 And they discussed among themselves, "We didn't bring any bread."

8 Aware of this, Jesus said, "You of little faith! Why are you discussing among yourselves that you do not have bread? 9 Don't you understand yet? Don't you remember the five loaves for the 5,000 and how many baskets you collected? 10 Or the seven loaves for the 4,000 and

---

[a]15:28 Lit hour   [b]15:39 Other mss read Magdala   [c]16:3 Other mss read Hypocrites! You   [d]16:2-3 Other mss omit When (v. 2) through end of v. 3   [e]16:4 Other mss add the prophet   [f]16:5 Lit disciples went to the other side
[g]16:6 Or leaven

how many large baskets you collected? [11] Why is it you don't understand that when I told you, 'Beware of the yeast of the Pharisees and Sadducees,' it wasn't about bread?" [12] Then they understood that He did not tell them to beware of the yeast in bread, but of the teaching of the Pharisees and Sadducees.

Peter's Confession of the Messiah

[13] When Jesus came to the region of Caesarea Philippi,[a] He asked His disciples, "Who do people say that the •Son of Man is?"[b] [14] And they said, "Some say John the Baptist; others, Elijah; still others, Jeremiah or one of the prophets." [15] "But you," He asked them, "who do you say that I am?" [16] Simon Peter answered, "You are the •Messiah, the Son of the living God!" [17] And Jesus responded, "Simon son of Jonah,[c] you are blessed because flesh and blood did not reveal this to you, but My Father in heaven. [18] And I also say to you that you are Peter,[d] and on this rock[e] I will build My church, and the forces[f] of •Hades will not overpower it. [19] I will give you the keys of the kingdom of heaven, and whatever you bind on earth is already bound[g] in heaven, and whatever you loose on earth is already loosed[h] in heaven."

Jesus' Orders to Keep Quiet

[20] And He gave the disciples orders to tell no one that He was[i] the Messiah.

Jesus Predicts His Death and Resurrection

[21] From then on Jesus began to point out to His disciples that He must go to Jerusalem and suffer many things from the elders, •chief priests, and •scribes, be killed, and be raised the third day. [22] Then Peter took Him aside and began to rebuke Him, "Oh no,[j] Lord! This will never happen to You!"

"Get Behind Me, Satan!"

[23] But He turned and told Peter, "Get behind Me, Satan! You are an offense to Me because you're not thinking about God's concerns,[k] but man's."

Take Up Your Cross

[24] Then Jesus said to His disciples, "If anyone wants to come with Me, he must deny himself, take up his cross, and follow Me. [25] For whoever wants to save his •life will lose it, but whoever loses his life because of Me will find it. [26] What will it benefit a man if he gains the whole world yet loses his life? Or what will a man give in exchange for his life? [27] For the Son of Man is going to come with His angels in the glory of His Father, and then He will reward each according to what he has done. [28] •I assure you: There are some standing here who will not taste death until they see the Son of Man coming in His kingdom."

The Transfiguration

17 After six days Jesus took Peter, James, and his brother John, and led them up on a high mountain by themselves. [2] He was transformed[l] in front of them, and His face shone like the sun. Even His clothes became as white as the light. [3] Suddenly, Moses and Elijah appeared to them, talking with Him.

---

[a]**16:13** A town north of Galilee at the base of Mount Hermon   [b]**16:13** Other mss read *that I, the Son of Man, am*   [c]**16:17** Or *son of John*   [d]**16:18** *Peter* (Gk *Petros*) = a specific stone or rock   [e]**16:18** *Rock* (Gk *petra*) = a rocky crag or bedrock   [f]**16:18** Lit *gates*   [g]**16:19** Or *earth will be bound*   [h]**16:19** Or *earth will be loosed*   [i]**16:20** Other mss add *Jesus*   [j]**16:22** Lit *Mercy to You = May God have mercy on You*   [k]**16:23** Lit *about the things of God*   [l]**17:2** Or *transfigured*

4 Then Peter said to Jesus, "Lord, it's good for us to be here! If You want, I will make[a] three •tabernacles here: one for You, one for Moses, and one for Elijah." 5 While he was still speaking, suddenly a bright cloud covered[b] them, and a voice from the cloud said:

> This is My beloved Son.
> I take delight in Him.
> Listen to Him!

6 When the disciples heard it, they fell facedown and were terrified. 7 Then Jesus came up, touched them, and said, "Get up; don't be afraid." 8 When they looked up they saw no one except Him[c]—Jesus alone. 9 As they were coming down from the mountain, Jesus commanded them, "Don't tell anyone about the vision until the •Son of Man is raised[d] from the dead."

10 So the disciples questioned Him, "Why then do the •scribes say that Elijah must come first?"

11 "Elijah is coming[e] and will restore everything," He replied.[f] 12 "But I tell you: Elijah has already come, and they didn't recognize him. On the contrary, they did whatever they pleased to him. In the same way the Son of Man is going to suffer at their hands."[g] 13 Then the disciples understood that He spoke to them about John the Baptist.

Power of Faith over a Demon

14 When they reached the crowd, a man approached and knelt down before Him. 15 "Lord," he said, "have mercy on my son, because he has seizures[h] and suffers severely. He often falls into the fire and often into the water. 16 I brought him to Your disciples, but they couldn't heal him."

17 Jesus replied, "You unbelieving and rebellious[i] generation! How long will I be with you? How long must I put up with you? Bring him here to Me." 18 Then Jesus rebuked the demon,[j] and it[k] came out of him, and from that moment[l] the boy was healed.

19 Then the disciples approached Jesus privately and said, "Why couldn't we drive it out?"

20 "Because of your little faith," He[m] told them. "For •I assure you: If you have faith the size of[n] a mustard seed, you will tell this mountain, 'Move from here to there,' and it will move. Nothing will be impossible for you. [21 However, this kind does not come out except by prayer and fasting.]"[o]

Jesus' Second Prediction of His Death

22 As they were meeting[p] in Galilee, Jesus told them, "The Son of Man is about to be betrayed into the hands of men. 23 They will kill Him, and on the third day He will be raised up." And they were deeply distressed.

Jesus Pays the Temple Tax

24 When they came to Capernaum, those who collected the double-drachma tax[q] approached Peter and said, "Doesn't your Teacher pay the double-drachma tax?"

25 "Yes," he said.

When he went into the house, Jesus spoke to him first,[r] "What do you think, Simon? Who do earthly kings collect

---

a17:4 Other mss read wish, let's make   b17:5 Or enveloped; Ex 40:34-35   c17:8 Other mss omit Him   d17:9 Other mss read Man has risen   e17:11 Other mss add first   f17:11 Other mss read Jesus said to them   g17:12 Lit suffer by them   h17:15 Lit he is moonstruck; thought to be a form of epilepsy   i17:17 Or corrupt, or perverted, or twisted; Dt 32:5   j17:18 Lit rebuked him or it   k17:18 Lit the demon   l17:18 Lit hour   m17:20 Other mss read your unbelief," Jesus   n17:20 Lit faith like   o17:21 Other mss omit bracketed text; Mk 9:29   p17:22 Other mss read were staying   q17:24 Jewish men paid this tax to support the temple; Ex 30:11-16. A double-drachma could purchase 2 sheep.   r17:25 Lit Jesus anticipated him by saying

tariffs or taxes from? From their sons or from strangers?"[a]

26 "From strangers," he said.[b] "Then the sons are free," Jesus told him. 27 "But, so we won't offend them, go to the sea, cast in a fishhook, and catch the first fish that comes up. When you open its mouth you'll find a coin.[c] Take it and give it to them for Me and you."

Who Is Greatest?

18 At that time[d] the disciples came to Jesus and said, "Who is greatest in the kingdom of heaven?"

2 Then He called a child to Him and had him stand among them. 3 "•I assure you," He said, "unless you are converted[e] and become like children, you will never enter the kingdom of heaven. 4 Therefore, whoever humbles himself like this child—this one is the greatest in the kingdom of heaven. 5 And whoever welcomes[f] one child like this in My name welcomes Me.

Jesus Warns about "Little Ones"

6 "But whoever •causes the downfall of one of these little ones who believe in Me—it would be better for him if a heavy millstone[g] were hung around his neck and he were drowned in the depths of the sea! 7 Woe to the world because of offenses.[h] For offenses must come, but woe to that man by whom the offense comes. 8 If your hand or your foot causes your downfall, cut it off and throw it away. It is better for you to enter life maimed or lame, than to have two hands or two feet and be thrown into the eternal fire. 9 And if your eye causes your downfall, gouge it out and throw it away. It is better for you to enter life with one eye, rather than to have two eyes and be thrown into •hellfire![i]

Parable of Lost Sheep

10 "See that you don't look down on one of these little ones, because I tell you that in heaven their angels continually view the face of My Father in heaven. [11 For the •Son of Man has come to save the lost.][j] 12 What do you think? If a man has 100 sheep, and one of them goes astray, won't he leave the 99 on the hillside and go and search for the stray? 13 And if he finds it, I assure you: He rejoices over that sheep[k] more than over the 99 that did not go astray. 14 In the same way, it is not the will of your Father in heaven that one of these little ones perish.

Restoring a Brother

15 "If your brother sins against you,[l] go and rebuke him in private.[m] If he listens to you, you have won your brother. 16 But if he won't listen, take one or two more with you, so that **by the testimony[n] of two or three witnesses every fact may be established.**[o] 17 If he pays no attention to them, tell the church.[p] But if he doesn't pay attention even to the church, let him be like an unbeliever[q] and a tax collector to you. 18 I assure you: Whatever you bind on earth is already bound[r] in heaven, and whatever you loose on earth is already loosed[s] in heaven. 19 Again, I assure you: If two of you on earth agree about any matter that you[t] pray for, it will be done for you[u] by My Father in heaven. 20 For where two

---

a**17:25** Or foreigners   b**17:26** Other mss read Peter said to Him   c**17:27** Gk stater, worth 2 double-drachmas   d**18:1** Lit hour   e**18:3** Or are turned around   f**18:5** Or receives   g**18:6** A millstone turned by a donkey   h**18:7** Or causes of stumbling   i**18:9** Lit gehenna of fire   j**18:11** Other mss omit bracketed text   k**18:13** Lit over it   l**18:15** Other mss omit against you   m**18:15** Lit him between you and him alone   n**18:16** Lit mouth   o**18:16** Dt 19:15   p**18:17** Or congregation   q**18:17** Or like a Gentile   r**18:18** Or earth will be bound   s**18:18** Or earth will be loosed   t**18:19** Lit they   u**18:19** Lit for them

or three are gathered together in My name, I am there among them."

Parable of Unforgiving Slave

²¹ Then Peter came to Him and said, "Lord, how many times could my brother sin against me and I forgive him? As many as seven times?"

²² "I tell you, not as many as seven," Jesus said to him, "but 70 times seven.ᵃ ²³ For this reason, the kingdom of heaven can be compared to a king who wanted to settle accounts with his •slaves. ²⁴ When he began to settle accounts, one who owed 10,000 talentsᵇ was brought before him. ²⁵ Since he had no way to pay it back, his master commanded that he, his wife, his children, and everything he had be sold to pay the debt.

²⁶ "At this, the •slave fell facedown before him and said, 'Be patient with me, and I will pay you everything!' ²⁷ Then the master of that •slave had compassion, released him, and forgave him the loan.

²⁸ "But that •slave went out and found one of his fellow slaves who owed him 100 •denarii.ᶜ He grabbed him, started choking him, and said, 'Pay what you owe!'

²⁹ "At this, his fellow •slave fell downᵈ and began begging him, 'Be patient with me, and I will pay you back.' ³⁰ But he wasn't willing. On the contrary, he went and threw him into prison until he could pay what was owed. ³¹ When the other slaves saw what had taken place, they were deeply distressed and went and reported to their master everything that had happened.

³² "Then, after he had summoned him, his master said to him, 'You wicked •slave! I forgave you all that debt because you begged me. ³³ Shouldn't you also have had mercy on your fellow slave, as I had mercy on you?' ³⁴ And his master got angry and handed him over to the jailersᵉ until he could pay everything that was owed. ³⁵ So My heavenly Father will also do to you if each of you does not forgive his brotherᶠ from hisᵍ heart."

Question of Divorce

19 When Jesus had finished this instruction, He departed from Galilee and went to the region of Judea across the Jordan. ² Large crowds followed Him, and He healed them there. ³ Some •Pharisees approached Him to test Him. They asked, "Is it lawful for a man to divorce his wife on any grounds?"

⁴ "Haven't you read," He replied, "that He who createdʰ them in the beginning **made them male and female,ⁱ** ⁵ and He also said:

> **For this reason a man will leave**
> **his father and mother**
> **and be joined to his wife,**
> **and the two will become**
> **one flesh?ʲ**

⁶ So they are no longer two, but one flesh. Therefore what God has joined together, man must not separate."

⁷ "Why then," they asked Him, "did Moses command ⌊us⌋ to give divorce papers and to send her away?"

⁸ He told them, "Moses permitted you to divorce your wives because of the hardness of your hearts. But it was not like that from the beginning. ⁹ And I tell you, whoever divorces his wife, except for sexual immorality, and marries another, commits adultery."ᵏ

ᵃ**18:22** Or *but 77 times*   ᵇ**18:24** A huge sum of money that could never be repaid by a slave; a talent = 6,000 denarii   ᶜ**18:28** A small sum compared to 10,000 talents   ᵈ**18:29** Other mss add *at his feet*   ᵉ**18:34** Or *torturers*   ᶠ**18:35** Other mss add *his trespasses*   ᵍ**18:35** Lit *your*   ʰ**19:4** Other mss read *made*   ⁱ**19:4** Gn 1:27; 5:2   ʲ**19:5** Gn 2:24   ᵏ**19:9** Other mss add *Also whoever marries a divorced woman commits adultery*; Mt 5:32

¹⁰ His disciples said to Him, "If the relationship of a man with his wife is like this, it's better not to marry!"

¹¹ But He told them, "Not everyone can accept this saying, but only those it has been given to. ¹² For there are eunuchs who were born that way from their mother's womb, there are eunuchs who were made by men, and there are eunuchs who have made themselves that way because of the kingdom of heaven. Let anyone accept this who can."

Jesus Blesses Children

¹³ Then children were brought to Him so He might put His hands on them and pray. But the disciples rebuked them. ¹⁴ Then Jesus said, "Leave the children alone, and don't try to keep them from coming to Me, because the kingdom of heaven is made up of people like this."ᵃ ¹⁵ After putting His hands on them, He went on from there.

The Rich Young Man

¹⁶ Just then someone came up and asked Him, "Teacher, what good must I do to have eternal life?"

¹⁷ "Why do you ask Me about what is good?"ᵇ He said to him. "There is only One who is good.ᶜ If you want to enter into life, keep the commandments."

¹⁸ "Which ones?" he asked Him.

Jesus answered,

> Do not murder;
> do not commit adultery;
> do not steal;
> do not bear false witness;
> ¹⁹ honor your father
>   and your mother;
> and love your neighbor
>   as yourself.ᵈ

²⁰ "I have kept all these,"ᵉ the young man told Him. "What do I still lack?"

²¹ "If you want to be perfect,"ᶠ Jesus said to him, "go, sell your belongings and give to the poor, and you will have treasure in heaven. Then come, follow Me."

²² When the young man heard that command, he went away grieving, because he had many possessions.

Eye of a Needle

²³ Then Jesus said to His disciples, "•I assure you: It will be hard for a rich person to enter the kingdom of heaven! ²⁴ Again I tell you, it is easier for a camel to go through the eye of a needle than for a rich person to enter the kingdom of God."

²⁵ When the disciples heard this, they were utterly astonished and asked, "Then who can be saved?"

²⁶ But Jesus looked at them and said, "With men this is impossible, but with God all things are possible."

²⁷ Then Peter responded to Him, "Look, we have left everything and followed You. So what will there be for us?"

²⁸ Jesus said to them, "I assure you: In the Messianic Age,ᵍ when the •Son of Man sits on His glorious throne, you who have followed Me will also sit on 12 thrones, judging the 12 tribes of Israel. ²⁹ And everyone who has left houses, brothers or sisters, father or mother,ʰ children, or fields because of My name will receive 100 times more and will inherit eternal life. ³⁰ But many who are first will be last, and the last first.

ᵃ**19:14** Lit *heaven is of such ones*   ᵇ**19:17** Other mss read *Why do you call Me good?*   ᶜ**19:17** Other mss read *No one is good but One—God*   ᵈ**19:18-19** Ex 20:12-16; Dt 5:16-20; Lv 19:18   ᵉ**19:20** Other mss add *from my youth*   ᶠ**19:21** Or *complete*   ᵍ**19:28** Lit *the regeneration*   ʰ**19:29** Other mss add *or wife*

Parable of the Vineyard Workers

20 "For the kingdom of heaven is like a landowner who went out early in the morning to hire workers for his vineyard. ² After agreeing with the workers on one •denarius for the day, he sent them into his vineyard. ³ When he went out about nine in the morning,ᵃ he saw others standing in the marketplace doing nothing. ⁴ To those men he said, 'You also go to my vineyard, and I'll give you whatever is right.' So off they went. ⁵ About noon and at three,ᵇ he went out again and did the same thing. ⁶ Then about fiveᶜ he went and found others standing around,ᵈ and said to them, 'Why have you been standing here all day doing nothing?'

⁷ " 'Because no one hired us,' they said to him.

" 'You also go to my vineyard,' he told them.ᵉ ⁸ When evening came, the owner of the vineyard told his foreman, 'Call the workers and give them their pay, starting with the last and ending with the first.'ᶠ

⁹ "When those who were hired about fiveᶜ came, they each received one denarius. ¹⁰ So when the first ones came, they assumed they would get more, but they also received a denarius each. ¹¹ When they received it, they began to complain to the landowner: ¹² 'These last men put in one hour, and you made them equal to us who bore the burden of the day and the burning heat!'

¹³ "He replied to one of them, 'Friend, I'm doing you no wrong. Didn't you agree with me on a denarius? ¹⁴ Take what's yours and go. I want to give this last man the same as I gave you. ¹⁵ Don't I have the right to do what I want with my business?ᵍ Are you jealousʰ because I'm generous?'ⁱ

¹⁶ "So the last will be first, and the first last."ʲ

Jesus' Third Prediction of His Death

¹⁷ While going up to Jerusalem, Jesus took the 12 disciples aside privately and said to them on the way: ¹⁸ "Listen! We are going up to Jerusalem. The •Son of Man will be handed over to the •chief priests and •scribes, and they will condemn Him to death. ¹⁹ Then they will hand Him over to the Gentiles to be mocked, flogged,ᵏ and crucified, and He will be resurrectedˡ on the third day."

A Mother's Request

²⁰ Then the mother of Zebedee's sons approached Him with her sons. She knelt down to ask Him for something. ²¹ "What do you want?" He asked her.

"Promise,"ᵐ she said to Him, "that these two sons of mine may sit, one on Your right and the other on Your left, in Your kingdom."

²² But Jesus answered, "You don't know what you're asking. Are you able to drink the cupⁿ that I am about to drink?"ᵒ

"We are able," they said to Him.

²³ He told them, "You will indeed drink My cup.ᵖ But to sit at My right and left is not Mine to give; instead, it belongs to those for whom it has been prepared by My Father." ²⁴ When the 10

ᵃ**20:3** Lit *about the third hour*   ᵇ**20:5** Lit *about the sixth hour and the ninth hour*   ᶜ**20:6,9** Lit *about the eleventh hour*
ᵈ**20:6** Other mss add *doing nothing*   ᵉ**20:7** Other mss add *'and you'll get whatever is right.'*   ᶠ**20:8** Lit *starting from the last until the first*   ᵍ**20:15** Lit *with what is mine*   ʰ**20:15** Lit *Is your eye evil*, an idiom for jealousy or stinginess
ⁱ**20:15** Lit *good*   ʲ**20:16** Other mss add *For many are called, but few are chosen.*   ᵏ**20:19** Or *scourged*   ˡ**20:19** Other mss read *will rise again*   ᵐ**20:21** Lit *Say*   ⁿ**20:22** Figurative language referring to His coming suffering; Mt 26:39; Jn 18:11   ᵒ**20:22** Other mss add *and (or) to be baptized with the baptism that I am baptized with*   ᵖ**20:23** Other mss add *and be baptized with the baptism that I am baptized with*

ₗdisciplesⱼ heard this, they became indignant with the two brothers. 25 But Jesus called them over and said, "You know that the rulers of the Gentiles dominate them, and the men of high position exercise power over them. 26 It must not be like that among you. On the contrary, whoever wants to become great among you must be your servant, 27 and whoever wants to be first among you must be your slave; 28 just as the Son of Man did not come to be served, but to serve, and to give His life—a ransom for many."

Two Blind Men Healed

29 As they were leaving Jericho, a large crowd followed Him. 30 There were two blind men sitting by the road. When they heard that Jesus was passing by, they cried out, "Lord, have mercy on us, Son of David!" 31 The crowd told them to keep quiet, but they cried out all the more, "Lord, have mercy on us, Son of David!"

32 Jesus stopped, called them, and said, "What do you want Me to do for you?"

33 "Lord," they said to Him, "open our eyes!" 34 Moved with compassion, Jesus touched their eyes. Immediately they could see, and they followed Him.

Triumphal Entry

21 When they approached Jerusalem and came to Bethphage at the •Mount of Olives, Jesus then sent two disciples, 2 telling them, "Go into the village ahead of you. At once you will find a donkey tied there, and a colt with her. Untie them and bring them to Me. 3 If anyone says anything to you, you should say that the Lord needs them, and immediately he will send them."

4 This took place so that what was spoken through the prophet might be fulfilled:

5 •Tell Daughter Zion,
"See, your King is coming to you,
gentle, and mounted on a donkey,
even on a colt,
the foal of a beast of burden."[a]

6 The disciples went and did just as Jesus directed them. 7 They brought the donkey and the colt; then they laid their robes on them, and He sat on them. 8 A very large crowd spread their robes on the road; others were cutting branches from the trees and spreading them on the road. 9 Then the crowds who went ahead of Him and those who followed kept shouting:

•*Hosanna* to the Son of David!
Blessed is He who comes
in the name of the Lord![b]
Hosanna in the highest heaven!

10 When He entered Jerusalem, the whole city was shaken, saying, "Who is this?" 11 And the crowds kept saying, "This is the prophet Jesus from Nazareth in Galilee!"

Jesus Cleanses the Temple Complex

12 Jesus went into the •temple complex[c] and drove out all those buying and selling in the temple. He overturned the money changers' tables and the chairs of those selling doves. 13 And He said to them, "It is written, **My house will be called a house of prayer.**[d] But you are making it **a den of thieves!**"[e]

Children Cheer Jesus

14 The blind and the lame came to Him in the temple complex, and He healed them. 15 When the •chief priests and the

---

a 21:5 Is 62:11; Zch 9:9   b 21:9 Ps 118:25-26   c 21:12 Other mss add of God   d 21:13 Is 56:7   e 21:13 Jr 7:11

•scribes saw the wonders that He did and the children in the temple complex cheering, "Hosanna to the Son of David!" they were indignant ¹⁶ and said to Him, "Do You hear what these ⌐children⌐ are saying?"

"Yes," Jesus told them. "Have you never read:

> **You have prepared**ᵃ **praise**
> **from the mouths of children**
> **and nursing infants**"?ᵇ

¹⁷ Then He left them, went out of the city to Bethany, and spent the night there.

Barren Fig Tree

¹⁸ Early in the morning, as He was returning to the city, He was hungry. ¹⁹ Seeing a lone fig tree by the road, He went up to it and found nothing on it except leaves. And He said to it, "May no fruit ever come from you again!" At once the fig tree withered.

²⁰ When the disciples saw it, they were amazed and said, "How did the fig tree wither so quickly?"

²¹ Jesus answered them, "•I assure you: If you have faith and do not doubt, you will not only do what was done to the fig tree, but even if you tell this mountain, 'Be lifted up and thrown into the sea,' it will be done. ²² And if you believe, you will receive whatever you ask for in prayer."

Chief Priests and Elders Challenge Messiah's Authority

²³ When He entered the temple complex, the chief priests and the elders of the people came up to Him as He was teaching and said, "By what authority are You doing these things? Who gave You this authority?"

Jesus Responds

²⁴ Jesus answered them, "I will also ask you one question, and if you answer it for Me, then I will tell you by what authority I do these things. ²⁵ Where did John's baptism come from? From heaven or from men?"

They began to argue among themselves, "If we say, 'From heaven,' He will say to us, 'Then why didn't you believe him?' ²⁶ But if we say, 'From men,' we're afraid of the crowd, because everyone thought John was a prophet." ²⁷ So they answered Jesus, "We don't know."

And He said to them, "Neither will I tell you by what authority I do these things.

Parable of Two Sons

²⁸ "But what do you think? A man had two sons. He went to the first and said, 'My son, go, work in the vineyard today.'

²⁹ "He answered, 'I don't want to!' Yet later he changed his mind and went. ³⁰ Then the man went to the other and said the same thing.

" 'I will, sir,' he answered. But he didn't go.

³¹ "Which of the two did his father's will?"

"The first," they said.

Jesus said to them, "I assure you: Tax collectors and prostitutes are entering the kingdom of God before you! ³² For John came to you in the way of righteousness,ᶜ and you didn't believe him. Tax collectors and prostitutes did believe him, but you, when you saw it, didn't even change your minds then and believe him.

Parable of Vineyard Owner

³³ "Listen to another parable: There was a man, a landowner, who planted a

---

ᵃ**21:16** Or *restored*   ᵇ**21:16** Ps 8:3 LXX   ᶜ**21:32** John came preaching and practicing righteousness

vineyard, put a fence around it, dug a winepress in it, and built a watchtower. He leased it to tenant farmers and went away. 34 When the grape harvest[a] drew near, he sent his slaves to the farmers to collect his fruit. 35 But the farmers took his slaves, beat one, killed another, and stoned a third. 36 Again, he sent other slaves, more than the first group, and they did the same to them. 37 Finally, he sent his son to them. 'They will respect my son,' he said.

38 "But when the tenant farmers saw the son, they said among themselves, 'This is the heir. Come, let's kill him and take his inheritance!' 39 So they seized him and threw him out of the vineyard, and killed him. 40 Therefore, when the owner of the vineyard comes, what will he do to those farmers?"

41 "He will completely destroy those terrible men," they told Him, "and lease his vineyard to other farmers who will give him his produce at the harvest."[b]

42 Jesus said to them, "Have you never read in the Scriptures:

The stone that
  the builders rejected
has become the cornerstone.[c]
This came from the Lord
  and is wonderful in our eyes?[d]

43 Therefore I tell you, the kingdom of God will be taken away from you and given to a nation producing its[e] fruit. [44 Whoever falls on this stone will be broken to pieces; but on whomever it falls, it will grind him to powder!"][f]

45 When the chief priests and the •Pharisees heard His parables, they knew He was speaking about them. 46 Although they were looking for a way to arrest Him, they feared the crowds, because they[g] regarded Him as a prophet.

Parable of the Wedding Banquet

22 Once more Jesus spoke to them in parables: 2 "The kingdom of heaven may be compared to a king who gave a wedding banquet for his son. 3 He sent out his •slaves to summon those invited to the banquet, but they didn't want to come. 4 Again, he sent out other slaves, and said, 'Tell those who are invited: Look, I've prepared my dinner; my oxen and fattened cattle have been slaughtered, and everything is ready. Come to the wedding banquet.'

5 "But they paid no attention and went away, one to his own farm, another to his business. 6 And the others seized his •slaves, treated them outrageously and killed them. 7 The king[h] was enraged, so he sent out his troops, destroyed those murderers, and burned down their city.

8 "Then he told his •slaves, 'The banquet is ready, but those who were invited were not worthy. 9 Therefore, go to where the roads exit the city and invite everyone you find to the banquet.' 10 So those slaves went out on the roads and gathered everyone they found, both evil and good. The wedding banquet was filled with guests.[i] 11 But when the king came in to view the guests, he saw a man there who was not dressed for a wedding. 12 So he said to him, 'Friend, how did you get in here without wedding clothes?' The man was speechless.

13 "Then the king told the attendants, 'Tie him up hand and foot,[j] and throw him into the outer darkness, where there will be weeping and gnashing of teeth.'

---

a21:34 Lit the season of fruits   b21:41 Lit him the fruits in their seasons   c21:42 Lit the head of the corner   d21:42 Ps 118:22-23   e21:43 The word its refers back to kingdom.   f21:44 Other mss omit this v.   g21:46 The crowds h22:7 Other mss read But when the (that) king heard about it he   i22:10 Lit those reclining (to eat)   j22:13 Other mss add take him away

[14] "For many are invited, but few are chosen."

God and Caesar

[15] Then the •Pharisees went and plotted how to trap Him by what He said.[a] [16] They sent their disciples to Him, with the •Herodians. "Teacher," they said, "we know that You are truthful and teach truthfully the way of God. You defer to no one, for You don't show partiality.[b] [17] Tell us, therefore, what You think. Is it lawful to pay taxes to Caesar or not?"

[18] But perceiving their malice, Jesus said, "Why are you testing Me, hypocrites? [19] Show Me the coin used for the tax." So they brought Him a •denarius. [20] "Whose image and inscription is this?" He asked them.

[21] "Caesar's," they said to Him.

Then He said to them, "Therefore, give back to Caesar the things that are Caesar's, and to God the things that are God's." [22] When they heard this, they were amazed. So they left Him and went away.

Sadducees and Resurrection

[23] The same day some •Sadducees, who say there is no resurrection, came up to Him and questioned Him: [24] "Teacher, Moses said, **if a man dies, having no children, his brother is to marry his wife and raise up offspring for his brother.**[c] [25] Now there were seven brothers among us. The first got married and died. Having no offspring, he left his wife to his brother. [26] The same happened to the second also, and the third, and so to all seven.[d] [27] Then last of all the woman died. [28] Therefore,

in the resurrection, whose wife will she be of the seven? For they all had married her."[e]

[29] Jesus answered them, "You are deceived, because you don't know the Scriptures or the power of God. [30] For in the resurrection they neither marry nor are given in marriage but are like[f] angels in heaven. [31] Now concerning the resurrection of the dead, haven't you read what was spoken to you by God: [32] **I am the God of Abraham and the God of Isaac and the God of Jacob**?[g] He[h] is not the God of the dead, but of the living."

[33] And when the crowds heard this, they were astonished at His teaching.

Primary Commandments

[34] When the Pharisees heard that He had silenced the Sadducees, they came together in the same place. [35] And one of them, an expert in the law, asked a question to test Him: [36] "Teacher, which commandment in the law is the greatest?"[i]

[37] He said to him, "**Love the Lord your God with all your heart, with all your soul, and with all your mind.**[j] [38] This is the greatest and most important[k] commandment. [39] The second is like it: **Love your neighbor as yourself.**[l] [40] All the Law and the Prophets depend[m] on these two commandments."

The Question about the Messiah

[41] While the Pharisees were together, Jesus questioned them, [42] "What do you think about the •Messiah? Whose Son is He?"

"David's," they told Him.

[43] He asked them, "How is it then that David, inspired by the Spirit,[n] calls Him 'Lord':

[a]**22:15** Lit *trap Him in [a] word*   [b]**22:16** Lit *don't look on the face of men*; that is, on the outward appearance
[c]**22:24** Dt 25:5   [d]**22:26** Lit *so until the seven*   [e]**22:28** Lit *all had her*   [f]**22:30** Other mss add *God's*   [g]**22:32** Ex 3:6,15-16   [h]**22:32** Other mss read *God*   [i]**22:36** Lit *is great*   [j]**22:37** Dt 6:5   [k]**22:38** Lit *and first*   [l]**22:39** Lv 19:18   [m]**22:40** Or *hang*   [n]**22:43** Lit *David in Spirit*

44 The Lord declared to my Lord,
    'Sit at My right hand
    until I put Your enemies
    under Your feet'?[a] [b]

45 "If David calls Him 'Lord,' how then can the Messiah be his Son?" 46 No one was able to answer Him at all,[c] and from that day no one dared to question Him any more.

Jesus Denounces Religious Hypocrites

23 Then Jesus spoke to the crowds and to His disciples: 2 "The •scribes and the •Pharisees are seated in the chair of Moses.[d] 3 Therefore do whatever they tell you and observe ⌊it⌋. But don't do what they do,[e] because they don't practice what they teach. 4 They tie up heavy loads that are hard to carry[f] and put them on people's shoulders, but they themselves aren't willing to lift a finger[g] to move them. 5 They do everything[h] to be observed by others: They enlarge their phylacteries[i] and lengthen their •tassels.[j] 6 They love the place of honor at banquets, the front seats in the •synagogues, 7 greetings in the marketplaces, and to be called '•Rabbi' by people.

8 "But as for you, do not be called 'Rabbi,' because you have one Teacher,[k] and you are all brothers. 9 Do not call anyone on earth your father, because you have one Father, who is in heaven. 10 And do not be called masters either, because you have one Master,[l] the •Messiah. 11 The greatest among you will be your servant. 12 Whoever exalts himself will be humbled, and whoever humbles himself will be exalted.

Woe to You, Scribes and Pharisees

13 "But woe to you, scribes and Pharisees, hypocrites! You lock up the kingdom of heaven from people. For you don't go in, and you don't allow those entering to go in.

[14 "Woe to you, scribes and Pharisees, hypocrites! You devour widows' houses and make long prayers just for show.[m] This is why you will receive a harsher punishment.][n]

15 "Woe to you, scribes and Pharisees, hypocrites! You travel over land and sea to make one •proselyte, and when he becomes one, you make him twice as fit for •hell[o] as you are!

16 "Woe to you, blind guides, who say, 'Whoever takes an oath by the sanctuary, it means nothing. But whoever takes an oath by the gold of the sanctuary is bound by his oath.'[p] 17 Blind fools![q] For which is greater, the gold or the sanctuary that sanctified the gold? 18 Also, 'Whoever takes an oath by the altar, it means nothing. But whoever takes an oath by the gift that is on it is bound by his oath.'[p] 19 Blind people![r] For which is greater, the gift or the altar that sanctifies the gift? 20 Therefore the one who takes an oath by the altar takes an oath by it and by everything on it. 21 The one who takes an oath by the sanctuary takes an oath by it and by Him who dwells in it. 22 And the one who takes an oath by heaven takes an oath by God's throne and by Him who sits on it.

23 "Woe to you, scribes and Pharisees, hypocrites! You pay a tenth of[s] mint, dill, and cumin,[t] yet you have neglected the more important matters of the law—jus-

a22:44 Other mss read until I make Your enemies Your footstool   b22:44 Ps 110:1   c22:46 Lit answer Him a word
d23:2 Perhaps a special chair for teaching in synagogues, or a metaphorical phrase for teaching with Moses' authority
e23:3 Lit do according to their works   f23:4 Other mss omit that are hard to carry   g23:4 Lit lift with their finger
h23:5 Lit do all their works   i23:5 Small leather boxes containing OT texts, worn by Jews on their arms and foreheads
j23:5 Other mss add on their robes   k23:8 Other mss add the Messiah   l23:10 Or Teacher   m23:14 Or prayers with
false motivation   n23:14 Other mss omit bracketed text   o23:15 Lit twice the son of gehenna   p23:16,18 Lit is
obligated   q23:17 Lit Fools and blind   r23:19 Other mss read Fools and blind   s23:23 Or You tithe   t23:23 A plant
whose seeds are used as a seasoning

tice, mercy, and faith. These things should have been done without neglecting the others. ²⁴ Blind guides! You strain out a gnat, yet gulp down a camel!

²⁵ "Woe to you, scribes and Pharisees, hypocrites! You clean the outside of the cup and dish, but inside they are full of greed[a] and self-indulgence! ²⁶ Blind Pharisee! First clean the inside of the cup,[b] so the outside of it[c] may also become clean.

²⁷ "Woe to you, scribes and Pharisees, hypocrites! You are like whitewashed tombs, which appear beautiful on the outside, but inside are full of dead men's bones and every impurity. ²⁸ In the same way, on the outside you seem righteous to people, but inside you are full of hypocrisy and lawlessness.

²⁹ "Woe to you, scribes and Pharisees, hypocrites! You build the tombs of the prophets and decorate the monuments of the righteous, ³⁰ and you say, 'If we had lived in the days of our fathers, we wouldn't have taken part with them in shedding the prophets' blood.'[d] ³¹ You therefore testify against yourselves that you are sons of those who murdered the prophets. ³² Fill up, then, the measure of your fathers' sins![e]

³³ "Snakes! Brood of vipers! How can you escape being condemned to hell?[f] ³⁴ This is why I am sending you prophets, sages, and scribes. Some of them you will kill and crucify, and some of them you will flog in your synagogues and hound from town to town. ³⁵ So all the righteous blood shed on the earth will be charged to you,[g] from the blood of righteous Abel to the blood of Zechariah, son of Berechiah, whom you murdered between the sanctuary and the altar. ³⁶ •I assure you: All these things will come on this generation!

Jesus Laments over Jerusalem

³⁷ "Jerusalem, Jerusalem! The city who kills the prophets and stones those who are sent to her. How often I wanted to gather your children together, as a hen gathers her chicks[h] under her wings, yet you were not willing! ³⁸ See, your house is left to you desolate. ³⁹ For I tell you, you will never see Me again until you say, **Blessed is He who comes in the name of the Lord!**"[i]

Jesus Predicts Destruction of Temple

24 As Jesus left and was going out of the •temple complex, His disciples came up and called His attention to the temple buildings. ² Then He replied to them, "Don't you see all these things? •I assure you: Not one stone will be left here on another that will not be thrown down!"

Signs of End of the Age

³ While He was sitting on the •Mount of Olives, the disciples approached Him privately and said, "Tell us, when will these things happen? And what is the sign of Your coming and of the end of the age?"

⁴ Then Jesus replied to them: "Watch out that no one deceives you. ⁵ For many will come in My name, saying, 'I am the •Messiah,' and they will deceive many. ⁶ You are going to hear of wars and rumors of wars. See that you are not alarmed, because these •things must take place, but the end is not yet. ⁷ For nation will rise up against nation, and kingdom against kingdom. There will be famines[j] and earthquakes in various places. ⁸ All these events are the beginning of birth pains.

---

[a]**23:25** Or *full of violence* [b]**23:26** Other mss add *and dish* [c]**23:26** Other mss read *of them* [d]**23:30** Lit *have been partakers with them in the blood of the prophets* [e]**23:32** Lit *the measure of your fathers* [f]**23:33** Lit *escape from the judgment of gehenna* [g]**23:35** Lit *will come on you* [h]**23:37** Or *as a mother bird gathers her young* [i]**23:39** Ps 118:26 [j]**24:7** Other mss add *epidemics*

Jesus Predicts Persecutions— and Other Signs

9 "Then they will hand you over for persecution,[a] and they will kill you. You will be hated by all nations because of My name. 10 Then many will take offense, betray one another and hate one another. 11 Many false prophets will rise up and deceive many. 12 Because lawlessness will multiply, the love of many will grow cold. 13 But the one who endures to the end will be delivered.[b] 14 This good news of the kingdom will be proclaimed in all the world[c] as a testimony to all nations. And then the end will come.

The Great Tribulation

15 "So when you see **the abomination that causes desolation,**[d] [e] spoken of by the prophet Daniel, standing in the holy place" (let the reader understand[f]), 16 "then those in Judea must flee to the mountains! 17 A man on the housetop[g] must not come down to get things out of his house. 18 And a man in the field must not go back to get his clothes. 19 Woe to pregnant women and nursing mothers in those days! 20 Pray that your escape may not be in winter or on a Sabbath. 21 For at that time there will be great tribulation, the kind that hasn't taken place from the beginning of the world until now and never will again! 22 Unless those days were limited, no one would[h] survive.[i] But those days will be limited because of the elect.

23 "If anyone tells you then, 'Look, here is the Messiah!' or, 'Over here!' do not believe it! 24 False messiahs[j] and false prophets will arise and perform great signs and wonders to lead astray, if possible, even the elect. 25 Take note: I have told you in advance. 26 So if they tell you, 'Look, he's in the wilderness!' don't go out; 'Look, he's in the inner rooms!' do not believe it. 27 For as the lightning comes from the east and flashes as far as the west, so will be the coming of the •Son of Man. 28 Wherever the carcass is, there the vultures[k] will gather.

The Coming of the Son of Man

29 "Immediately after the tribulation of those days:

The sun will be darkened,
  and the moon will not shed
    its light;
  the stars will fall from the sky,
  and the celestial powers
    will be shaken.

30 "Then the sign of the Son of Man will appear in the sky, and then all the peoples of the earth[l] will mourn;[m] and they will see the Son of Man coming on the clouds of heaven with power and great glory. 31 He will send out His angels with a loud trumpet, and they will gather His elect from the four winds, from one end of the sky to the other.

Parable of the Fig Tree

32 "Now learn this parable from the fig tree: As soon as its branch becomes tender and sprouts leaves, you know that summer is near. 33 In the same way, when you see all these things, recognize[n] that He[o] is near—at the door! 34 I assure you: This generation will certainly not pass away until all these things take place. 35 Heaven and earth will pass away, but My words will never pass away.

---

[a]**24:9** Or *tribulation,* or *distress*   [b]**24:13** Or *be saved*   [c]**24:14** Or *in all the inhabited earth*   [d]**24:15** Or *abomination of desolation,* or *desolating sacrilege*   [e]**24:15** Dn 9:27   [f]**24:15** These are, most likely, Matthew's words to his readers.   [g]**24:17** Or *roof*   [h]**24:22** Lit *short, all flesh would not*   [i]**24:22** Or *be saved* or *delivered*   [j]**24:24** Or *False christs*   [k]**24:28** Or *eagles*   [l]**24:30** Or *all the tribes of the land*   [m]**24:30** Lit *will beat;* = *beat their breasts*   [n]**24:33** Or *things, you know*   [o]**24:33** Or *it;* = *summer*

No One Knows the Day or Hour

36 "Now concerning that day and hour no one knows—neither the angels in heaven, nor the Son[a]—except the Father only. 37 As the days of Noah were, so the coming of the Son of Man will be. 38 For in those days before the flood they were eating and drinking, marrying and giving in marriage, until the day Noah boarded the ark. 39 They didn't know[b] until the flood came and swept them all away. So this is the way the coming of the Son of Man will be: 40 Then two men will be in the field: one will be taken and one left. 41 Two women will be grinding at the mill: one will be taken and one left. 42 Therefore be alert, since you don't know what day[c] your Lord is coming. 43 But know this: If the homeowner had known what time[d] the thief was coming, he would have stayed alert and not let his house be broken into. 44 This is why you also must be ready, because the Son of Man is coming at an hour you do not expect.

Faithful Service to the Messiah

45 "Who then is a faithful and sensible slave, whom his master has put in charge of his household, to give them food at the proper time? 46 That slave whose master finds him working when he comes will be rewarded. 47 I assure you: He will put him in charge of all his possessions. 48 But if that wicked slave says in his heart, 'My master is delayed,' 49 and starts to beat his fellow slaves, and eats and drinks with drunkards, 50 that slave's master will come on a day he does not expect and at an hour he does not know. 51 He will cut him to pieces[e] and assign him a place with the hypo-crites. In that place there will be weeping and gnashing of teeth.

Parable of the 10 Virgins

25 "Then the kingdom of heaven will be like 10 virgins[f] who took their lamps and went out to meet the groom. 2 Five of them were foolish and five were sensible. 3 When the foolish took their lamps, they didn't take oil with them. 4 But the sensible ones took oil in their flasks with their lamps. 5 Since the groom was delayed, they all became drowsy and fell asleep.

6 "In the middle of the night there was a shout: 'Here's the groom! Come out to meet him.'

7 "Then all those virgins got up and trimmed their lamps. 8 But the foolish ones said to the sensible ones, 'Give us some of your oil, because our lamps are going out.'

9 "The sensible ones answered, 'No, there won't be enough for us and for you. Go instead to those who sell, and buy oil for yourselves.'

10 "When they had gone to buy some, the groom arrived. Then those who were ready went in with him to the wedding banquet, and the door was shut.

11 "Later the rest of the virgins also came and said, 'Master, master, open up for us!'

12 "But he replied, '•I assure you: I do not know you!'

13 "Therefore be alert, because you don't know either the day or the hour.[g]

Parable of the Talents

14 "For it is just like a man going on a journey. He called his own •slaves and turned over his possessions to them. 15 To one he gave five talents;[h] to

a24:36 Other mss omit *nor the Son* b24:39 *They didn't know* the day and hour of the coming judgment
c24:42 Other mss read *hour*; = time d24:43 Lit *watch*; a division of the night in ancient times e24:51 Lit *him in two*
f25:1 Or *bridesmaids* g25:13 Other mss add *in which the Son of Man is coming.* h25:15 Worth a very large sum of money; a talent = 6,000 •denarii

another, two; and to another, one—to each according to his own ability. Then he went on a journey. Immediately [16] the man who had received five talents went, put them to work, and earned five more. [17] In the same way the man with two earned two more. [18] But the man who had received one talent went off, dug a hole in the ground, and hid his master's money.

[19] "After a long time the master of those •slaves came and settled accounts with them. [20] The man who had received five talents approached, presented five more talents, and said, 'Master, you gave me five talents. Look, I've earned five more talents.'

[21] "His master said to him, 'Well done, good and faithful •slave! You were faithful over a few things; I will put you in charge of many things. Share your master's joy!'

[22] "Then the man with two talents also approached. He said, 'Master, you gave me two talents. Look, I've earned two more talents.'

[23] "His master said to him, 'Well done, good and faithful •slave! You were faithful over a few things; I will put you in charge of many things. Share your master's joy!'

[24] "Then the man who had received one talent also approached and said, 'Master, I know you. You're a difficult man, reaping where you haven't sown and gathering where you haven't scattered seed. [25] So I was afraid and went off and hid your talent in the ground. Look, you have what is yours.'

[26] "But his master replied to him, 'You evil, lazy •slave! If you knew that I reap where I haven't sown and gather where I haven't scattered, [27] then[a] you should have deposited my money with the bankers. And when I returned I would have received my money[b] back with interest.

[28] " 'So take the talent from him and give it to the one who has 10 talents. [29] For to everyone who has, more will be given, and he will have more than enough. But from the one who does not have, even what he has will be taken away from him. [30] And throw this good-for-nothing •slave into the outer darkness. In that place there will be weeping and gnashing of teeth.'

Sheep and the Goats

[31] "When the •Son of Man comes in His glory, and all the angels[c] with Him, then He will sit on the throne of His glory. [32] All the nations[d] will be gathered before Him, and He will separate them one from another, just as a shepherd separates the sheep from the goats. [33] He will put the sheep on His right, and the goats on the left. [34] Then the King will say to those on His right, 'Come, you who are blessed by My Father, inherit the kingdom prepared for you from the foundation of the world.

35   For I was hungry
     and you gave Me something to eat;
     I was thirsty
     and you gave Me something
       to drink;
     I was a stranger
       and you took Me in;
36   I was naked and you clothed Me;
     I was sick and you took care of Me;
     I was in prison and you visited Me.'

[37] "Then the righteous will answer Him, 'Lord, when did we see You hungry and feed You, or thirsty and give You something to drink? [38] When did we see You a stranger and take You in, or with-

a25:26-27 Or So you knew . . . scattered? Then (as a question)   b25:27 Lit received what is mine   c25:31 Other mss read holy angels   d25:32 Or the Gentiles

out clothes and clothe You? [39] When did we see You sick, or in prison, and visit You?'

[40] "And the King will answer them, 'I assure you: Whatever you did for one of the least of these brothers of Mine, you did for Me.' [41] Then He will also say to those on the left, 'Depart from Me, you who are cursed, into the eternal fire prepared for the Devil and his angels!

[42] For I was hungry
and you gave Me nothing to eat;
I was thirsty
and you gave Me nothing to drink;
[43] I was a stranger
and you didn't take Me in;
I was naked
and you didn't clothe Me,
sick and in prison
and you didn't take care of Me.'

[44] "Then they too will answer, 'Lord, when did we see You hungry, or thirsty, or a stranger, or without clothes, or sick, or in prison, and not help You?'

[45] "Then He will answer them, 'I assure you: Whatever you did not do for one of the least of these, you did not do for Me either.'

[46] "And they will go away into eternal punishment, but the righteous into eternal life."

Plot to Kill Jesus

26 When Jesus had finished saying all this, He told His disciples, [2] "You know[a] that the •Passover takes place after two days, and the •Son of Man will be handed over to be crucified."

[3] Then the •chief priests[b] and the elders of the people assembled in the palace of the high priest, who was called Caiaphas, [4] and they conspired to arrest Jesus in a treacherous way and kill Him.

[5] "Not during the festival," they said, "so there won't be rioting among the people."

Jesus Anointed at Bethany

[6] While Jesus was in Bethany at the house of Simon, a man who had a serious skin disease, [7] a woman approached Him with an alabaster jar of very expensive fragrant oil. She poured it on His head as He was reclining at the table. [8] When the disciples saw it, they were indignant. "Why this waste?" they asked. [9] "This might have been sold for a great deal and given to the poor."

[10] But Jesus, aware of this, said to them, "Why are you bothering this woman? She has done a noble thing for Me. [11] You always have the poor with you, but you do not always have Me. [12] By pouring this fragrant oil on My body, she has prepared Me for burial. [13] •I assure you: Wherever this gospel is proclaimed in the whole world, what this woman has done will also be told in memory of her."

Judas Iscariot Betrays Jesus

[14] Then one of the Twelve—the man called Judas Iscariot—went to the chief priests [15] and said, "What are you willing to give me if I hand Him over to you?" So they weighed out 30 pieces of silver for him. [16] And from that time he started looking for a good opportunity to betray Him.

Preparations for Last Passover

[17] On the first day of •Unleavened Bread the disciples came to Jesus and asked, "Where do You want us to prepare the Passover so You may eat it?"

[18] "Go into the city to a certain man," He said, "and tell him, 'The Teacher

says: My time is near; I am celebrating the Passover at your place[a] with My disciples.'" ¹⁹ So the disciples did as Jesus had directed them and prepared the Passover. ²⁰ When evening came, He was reclining at the table with the Twelve. ²¹ While they were eating, He said, "I assure you: One of you will betray Me."

Judas Identified as Betrayer

²² Deeply distressed, each one began to say to Him, "Surely not I, Lord?"

²³ He replied, "The one who dipped his hand with Me in the bowl—he will betray Me. ²⁴ The Son of Man will go just as it is written about Him, but woe to that man by whom the Son of Man is betrayed! It would have been better for that man if he had not been born."

²⁵ Then Judas, His betrayer, replied, "Surely not I, •Rabbi?"

"You have said it," He told him.

The First Lord's Supper

²⁶ As they were eating, Jesus took bread, blessed and broke it, gave it to the disciples, and said, "Take and eat it; this is My body." ²⁷ Then He took a cup, and after giving thanks, He gave it to them and said, "Drink from it, all of you. ²⁸ For this is My blood ⌊that establishes⌋ the covenant;[b] it is shed for many for the forgiveness of sins. ²⁹ But I tell you, from this moment I will not drink of this fruit of the vine until that day when I drink it in a new way[c] in My Father's kingdom with you." ³⁰ After singing psalms,[d] they went out to the •Mount of Olives.

Jesus Predicts Peter's Denial

³¹ Then Jesus said to them, "Tonight all of you will run away[e] because of Me, for it is written:

**I will strike the shepherd,
and the sheep of the flock
will be scattered.**[f]

³² But after I have been resurrected, I will go ahead of you to Galilee."

³³ Peter told Him, "Even if everyone runs away because of You, I will never run away!"

³⁴ "I assure you," Jesus said to him, "tonight—before the rooster crows, you will deny Me three times!"

³⁵ "Even if I have to die with You," Peter told Him, "I will never deny You!" And all the disciples said the same thing.

Prayer in Garden of Gethsemane

³⁶ Then Jesus came with them to a place called Gethsemane,[g] and He told the disciples, "Sit here while I go over there and pray." ³⁷ Taking along Peter and the two sons of Zebedee, He began to be sorrowful and deeply distressed. ³⁸ Then He said to them, "My soul is swallowed up in sorrow[h]—to the point of death.[i] Remain here and stay awake with Me." ³⁹ Going a little farther,[j] He fell facedown and prayed, "My Father! If it is possible, let this cup pass from Me. Yet not as I will, but as You will."

⁴⁰ Then He came to the disciples and found them sleeping. He asked Peter, "So, couldn't you[k] stay awake with Me one hour? ⁴¹ Stay awake and pray, so that you won't enter into temptation. The spirit is willing, but the flesh is weak."

ᵃ**26:18** Lit *Passover with you*   ᵇ**26:28** Other mss read *new covenant*   ᶜ**26:29** Or *drink new wine*; lit *drink it new*   ᵈ**26:30** Pss 113–118 were sung during and after the Passover meal.   ᵉ**26:31** Or •*stumble*   ᶠ**26:31** Zch 13:7   ᵍ**26:36** A garden east of Jerusalem at the base of the Mount of Olives; *Gethsemane* = olive oil press   ʰ**26:38** Or *I am deeply grieved*, or *I am overwhelmed by sorrow*; Ps 42:6,11; 43:5   ⁱ**26:38** Lit *unto death*   ʲ**26:39** Other mss read *Drawing nearer*   ᵏ**26:40** *You* = all 3 disciples because the verb in Gk is pl

"Your Will Be Done"

42 Again, a second time, He went away and prayed, "My Father, if this[a] cannot pass[b] unless I drink it, Your will be done." 43 And He came again and found them sleeping, because they could not keep their eyes open.[c]

44 After leaving them, He went away again and prayed a third time, saying the same thing once more. 45 Then He came to the disciples and said to them, "Are you still sleeping and resting?[d] Look, the time is near. The Son of Man is being betrayed into the hands of sinners. 46 Get up; let's go! See—My betrayer is near."

The Judas Kiss

47 While He was still speaking, Judas, one of the Twelve, suddenly arrived. A large mob, with swords and clubs, was with him from the chief priests and elders of the people. 48 His betrayer had given them a sign: "The One I kiss, He's the One; arrest Him!" 49 So he went right up to Jesus and said, "Greetings, Rabbi!"—and kissed Him.

50 "Friend," Jesus asked him, "why have you come?"[e]

Perish by a Sword

Then they came up, took hold of Jesus, and arrested Him. 51 At that moment one of those with Jesus reached out his hand and drew his sword. He struck the high priest's slave and cut off his ear.

52 Then Jesus told him, "Put your sword back in place because all who take up a sword will perish by a sword. 53 Or do you think that I cannot call on My Father, and He will provide Me at once with more than 12 legions[f] of angels? 54 How,

then, would the Scriptures be fulfilled that say it must happen this way?"

55 At that time Jesus said to the crowds, "Have you come out with swords and clubs, as if I were a criminal,[g] to capture Me? Every day I used to sit, teaching in the •temple complex, and you didn't arrest Me. 56 But all this has happened so that the prophetic Scriptures[h] would be fulfilled." Then all the disciples deserted Him and ran away.

Jesus Faces Sanhedrin

57 Those who had arrested Jesus led Him away to Caiaphas the high priest, where the •scribes and the elders had convened. 58 Meanwhile, Peter was following Him at a distance right to the high priest's courtyard.[i] He went in and was sitting with the temple police[j] to see the outcome.[k]

Two False Witnesses

59 The chief priests and the whole •Sanhedrin were looking for false testimony against Jesus so they could put Him to death. 60 But they could not find any, even though many false witnesses came forward.[l] Finally, two[m] who came forward 61 stated, "This man said, 'I can demolish God's sanctuary and rebuild it in three days.'"

62 The high priest then stood up and said to Him, "Don't You have an answer to what these men are testifying against You?" 63 But Jesus kept silent. Then the high priest said to Him, "By the living God I place You under oath: tell us if You are the •Messiah, the Son of God!"

Jesus Affirms His Status

64 "You have said it,"[n] Jesus told him. "But I tell you, in the future[o] you will see **the Son of Man seated at the right**

---

[a]**26:42** Other mss add *cup* [b]**26:42** Other mss add *from Me* [c]**26:43** Lit *because their eyes were weighed down* [d]**26:45** Or *Sleep on now and take your rest.* [e]**26:50** Or *Jesus told him, "do what you have come for."* (as a statement) [f]**26:53** A Roman legion contained up to 6,000 soldiers. [g]**26:55** Lit *as against a criminal* [h]**26:56** Or *the Scriptures of the prophets* [i]**26:58** Or *high priest's palace* [j]**26:58** Or *the officers, or the servants* [k]**26:58** Lit *end* [l]**26:60** Other mss add *they found none* [m]**26:60** Other mss add *false witnesses* [n]**26:64** Or *That is true*, an affirmative oath; Mt 27:11; Mk 15:2 [o]**26:64** Lit *you, from now*

hand of the Power and **coming on the clouds of heaven.**"ᵃ

Charge of Blasphemy

⁶⁵ Then the high priest tore his robes and said, "He has blasphemed! Why do we still need witnesses? Look, now you've heard the blasphemy! ⁶⁶ What is your decision?"ᵇ

They answered, "He deserves death!" ⁶⁷ Then they spit in His face and beat Him; others slapped Him ⁶⁸ and said, "Prophesy to us, Messiah! Who hit You?"

Peter Denies His Lord

⁶⁹ Now Peter was sitting outside in the courtyard. A servant approached him and she said, "You were with Jesus the Galilean too."

⁷⁰ But he denied it in front of everyone: "I don't know what you're talking about!"

⁷¹ When he had gone out to the gateway, another woman saw him and told those who were there, "This man was with Jesus the •Nazarene!"

⁷² And again he denied it with an oath, "I don't know the man!"

⁷³ After a little while those standing there approached and said to Peter, "You certainly are one of them, since even your accentᶜ gives you away."

⁷⁴ Then he started to curseᵈ and to swear with an oath, "I do not know the man!" Immediately a rooster crowed, ⁷⁵ and Peter remembered the words Jesus had spoken, "Before the rooster crows, you will deny Me three times." And he went outside and wept bitterly.

Chief Priests and Elders Hand Jesus Over to Pilate

27 When daybreak came, all the •chief priests and the elders of the people plotted against Jesus to put Him to death. ² After tying Him up, they led Him away and handed Him over to •Pilate,ᵉ the governor.

Judas Hangs Himself

³ Then Judas, His betrayer, seeing that He had been condemned, was full of remorse and returned the 30 pieces of silver to the chief priests and elders. ⁴ "I have sinned by betraying innocent blood," he said.

"What's that to us?" they said. "See to it yourself!"

⁵ So he threw the silver into the sanctuary and departed. Then he went and hanged himself.

⁶ The chief priests took the silver and said, "It's not lawful to put it into the temple treasury,ᶠ since it is blood money."ᵍ ⁷ So they conferred together and bought the potter's field with it as a burial place for foreigners. ⁸ Therefore that field has been called "Blood Field" to this day. ⁹ Then what was spoken through the prophet Jeremiah was fulfilled:

They took the 30 pieces of silver, the price of Him whose price was set by the sons of Israel, ¹⁰ and they gave them for the potter's field, as the Lord directed me.ʰ

Jesus Faces Governor Pilate

¹¹ Now Jesus stood before the governor. "Are You the King of the Jews?" the governor asked Him.

Jesus answered, "You have said it."ⁱ ¹² And while He was being accused by the chief priests and elders, He didn't answer.

ᵃ**26:64** Ps 110:1; Dn 7:13 ᵇ**26:66** Lit *What does it seem to you?* ᶜ**26:73** Or *speech* ᵈ**26:74** To call down curses on himself if what he said weren't true ᵉ**27:2** Other mss read *Pontius Pilate* ᶠ**27:6** See Mk 7:11 where the same Gk word used here (*Corban*) means a gift (pledged to the temple). ᵍ**27:6** Lit *the price of blood* ʰ**27:9-10** Jr 32:6-9; Zch 11:12-13 ⁱ**27:11** Or *That is true,* an affirmative oath; Mt 26:64; Mk 15:2

[13] Then Pilate said to Him, "Don't You hear how much they are testifying against You?" [14] But He didn't answer him on even one charge, so that the governor was greatly amazed.

Pilate: Jesus or Barabbas?

[15] At the festival the governor's custom was to release to the crowd a prisoner they wanted. [16] At that time they had a notorious prisoner called Barabbas.[a] [17] So when they had gathered together, Pilate said to them, "Who is it you want me to release for you—Barabbas,[a] or Jesus who is called •Messiah?" [18] For he knew they had handed Him over because of envy.

Pilate's Wife Pleads for Jesus

[19] While he was sitting on the judge's bench, his wife sent word to him, "Have nothing to do with that righteous man, for today I've suffered terribly in a dream because of Him!"

Chief Priests and Elders Sway Crowds

[20] The chief priests and the elders, however, persuaded the crowds to ask for Barabbas and to execute Jesus. [21] The governor asked them, "Which of the two do you want me to release for you?"

"Barabbas!" they answered.

[22] Pilate asked them, "What should I do then with Jesus, who is called Messiah?"

They all answered, "Crucify Him!"[b]

[23] Then he said, "Why? What has He done wrong?"

But they kept shouting, "Crucify Him!" all the more.

[24] When Pilate saw that he was getting nowhere,[c] but that a riot was starting instead, he took some water, washed his hands in front of the crowd, and said, "I am innocent of this man's blood.[d] See to it yourselves!"

[25] All the people answered, "His blood be on us and on our children!" [26] Then he released Barabbas to them. But after having Jesus flogged,[e] he handed Him over to be crucified.

Mocked by the Military

[27] Then the governor's soldiers took Jesus into •headquarters and gathered the whole •company around Him. [28] They stripped Him and dressed Him in a scarlet robe. [29] They twisted together a crown of thorns, put it on His head, and placed a reed in His right hand. And they knelt down before Him and mocked Him: "Hail, King of the Jews!" [30] Then they spit at Him, took the reed, and kept hitting Him on the head. [31] When they had mocked Him, they stripped Him of the robe, put His clothes on Him, and led Him away to crucify Him.

Crucified Between Two Criminals

[32] As they were going out, they found a Cyrenian man named Simon. They forced this man to carry His cross. [33] When they came to a place called *Golgotha* (which means Skull Place), [34] they gave Him wine[f] mixed with gall to drink. But when He tasted it, He would not drink it. [35] After crucifying Him they divided His clothes by casting lots.[g] [36] Then they sat down and were guarding Him there. [37] Above His head they put up the charge against Him in writing:

> **THIS IS JESUS
> THE KING OF THE JEWS**

---

[a]**27:16,17** Other mss read *Jesus Barabbas* [b]**27:22** Lit *"Him—be crucified!"* [c]**27:24** Lit *that it availed nothing*
[d]**27:24** Other mss read *this righteous man's blood* [e]**27:26** Roman flogging was done with a whip made of leather strips embedded with pieces of bone or metal that brutally tore the flesh. [f]**27:34** Other mss read *sour wine*
[g]**27:35** Other mss add *that what was spoken by the prophet might be fulfilled: "They divided My clothes among them, and for My clothing they cast lots."*

38 Then two criminals[a] were crucified with Him, one on the right and one on the left. 39 Those who passed by were yelling insults at[b] Him, shaking their heads 40 and saying, "The One who would demolish the sanctuary and rebuild it in three days, save Yourself! If You are the Son of God, come down from the cross!" 41 In the same way the chief priests, with the •scribes and elders,[c] mocked Him and said, 42 "He saved others, but He cannot save Himself! He is the King of Israel! Let Him[d] come down now from the cross, and we will believe in Him. 43 He has put His trust in God; let God rescue Him now—if He wants Him![e] For He said, 'I am God's Son.'" 44 In the same way even the criminals who were crucified with Him kept taunting Him.

"My God, My God"

45 From noon until three in the afternoon[f] darkness came over the whole land.[g] 46 At about three in the afternoon Jesus cried out with a loud voice, "*Elí, Elí, lemá sabachtháni?*" that is, "**My God, My God, why have You forsaken**[h] **Me?**"[i] 47 When some of those standing there heard this, they said, "He's calling for Elijah!" 48 Immediately one of them ran and got a sponge, filled it with sour wine, fixed it on a reed, and offered Him a drink. 49 But the rest said, "Let's see if Elijah comes to save Him!"

Death of Jesus

50 Jesus shouted again with a loud voice and gave up His spirit. 51 Suddenly, the curtain of the sanctuary[j] was split in two from top to bottom; the earth quaked and the rocks were split. 52 The tombs also were opened and many bodies of the saints who had gone to their rest[k] were raised. 53 And they came out of the tombs after His resurrection, entered the holy city, and appeared to many.

54 When the •centurion and those with him, who were guarding Jesus, saw the earthquake and the things that had happened, they were terrified and said, "This man really was God's Son!"[l]

Jesus' Female Followers

55 Many women who had followed Jesus from Galilee and ministered to Him were there, looking on from a distance. 56 Among them were •Mary Magdalene, Mary the mother of James and Joseph, and the mother of Zebedee's sons.

Burial of Jesus

57 When it was evening, a rich man from Arimathea named Joseph came, who himself had also become a disciple of Jesus. 58 He approached Pilate and asked for Jesus' body. Then Pilate ordered that it[m] be released. 59 So Joseph took the body, wrapped it in clean, fine linen, 60 and placed it in his new tomb, which he had cut into the rock. He left after rolling a great stone against the entrance of the tomb. 61 Mary Magdalene and the other Mary were seated there, facing the tomb.

Religious Leaders and Pilate: A Closely Guarded Tomb

62 The next day, which followed the preparation day, the chief priests and the

---

a**27:38** Or *revolutionaries*   b**27:39** Lit *passed by blasphemed* or *were blaspheming*   c**27:41** Other mss add *and Pharisees*   d**27:42** Other mss read *If He . . . Israel, let Him*   e**27:43** Or *if He takes pleasure in Him*; Ps 22:8   f**27:45** Lit *From the sixth hour to the ninth hour*   g**27:45** Or *whole earth*   h**27:46** Or *abandoned*   i**27:46** Ps 22:1   j**27:51** A heavy curtain separated the inner room of the temple from the outer.   k**27:52** Lit *saints having fallen asleep*; that is, they had died   l**27:54** Or *the Son of God*   m**27:58** Other mss read *that the body*

•Pharisees gathered before Pilate [63] and said, "Sir, we remember that while this deceiver was still alive, He said, 'After three days I will rise again.' [64] Therefore give orders that the tomb be made secure until the third day. Otherwise, His disciples may come, steal Him, and tell the people, 'He has been raised from the dead.' Then the last deception will be worse than the first."

[65] "You have[a] a guard ⌊of soldiers⌋,"[b] Pilate told them. "Go and make it as secure as you know how." [66] Then they went and made the tomb secure by sealing the stone and setting the guard.[c]

Resurrection Morning

28 After the Sabbath, as the first day of the week was dawning, •Mary Magdalene and the other Mary went to view the tomb. [2] Suddenly there was a violent earthquake, because an angel of the Lord descended from heaven and approached ⌊the tomb⌋. He rolled back the stone and was sitting on it. [3] His appearance was like lightning, and his robe was as white as snow. [4] The guards were so shaken from fear of him that they became like dead men.

[5] But the angel told the women, "Don't be afraid, because I know you are looking for Jesus who was crucified. [6] He is not here! For He has been resurrected, just as He said. Come and see the place where He lay. [7] Then go quickly and tell His disciples, 'He has been raised from the dead. In fact, He is going ahead of you to Galilee; you will see Him there.' Listen, I have told you."

Jesus Meets Women

[8] So, departing quickly from the tomb with fear and great joy, they ran to tell His disciples the news. [9] Just then[d] Jesus met them and said, "Good morning!" They came up, took hold of His feet, and worshiped Him. [10] Then Jesus told them, "Do not be afraid. Go and tell My brothers to leave for Galilee, and they will see Me there."

Chief Priests and Elders Bribe Soldiers to Lie

[11] As they were on their way, some of the guard came into the city and reported to the •chief priests everything that had happened. [12] After the priests[e] had assembled with the elders and agreed on a plan, they gave the soldiers a large sum of money [13] and told them, "Say this, 'His disciples came during the night and stole Him while we were sleeping.' [14] If this reaches the governor's ears,[f] we will deal with[g] him and keep you out of trouble." [15] So they took the money and did as they were instructed. And this story has been spread among Jewish people to this day.

The Great Commission

[16] The 11 disciples traveled to Galilee, to the mountain where Jesus had directed them. [17] When they saw Him, they worshiped,[h] but some doubted. [18] Then Jesus came near and said to them, "All authority has been given to Me in heaven and on earth. [19] Go, therefore, and make disciples of[i] all nations, baptizing them in the name of the Father and of the Son and of the Holy Spirit, [20] teaching them to observe everything I have commanded you. And remember,[j] I am with you always,[k] to the end of the age."

[a]**27:65** Or "Take   [b]**27:65** It is uncertain whether this guard consisted of temple police or Roman soldiers.   [c]**27:66** Lit stone with the guard   [d]**28:9** Other mss add as they were on their way to tell the news to His disciples   [e]**28:12** Lit After they   [f]**28:14** Lit this is heard by the governor   [g]**28:14** Lit will persuade   [h]**28:17** Other mss add Him   [i]**28:19** Lit and instruct, or and disciple (as a verb)   [j]**28:20** Lit look   [k]**28:20** Lit all the days

MARK

Messiah's Herald

1 The beginning of the gospel of Jesus Christ, the Son of God. ² As it is written in Isaiah the prophet:ª

> Look, I am sending My messenger
>   ahead of You,
> who will prepare Your way.ᵇ
> ³ A voice of one crying out
>   in the wilderness:
> "Prepare the way for the Lord;
>   make His paths straight!"ᶜ

Ministry of John the Baptist

⁴ John came baptizingᵈ in the wilderness and preaching a baptism of repentanceᵉ for the forgiveness of sins. ⁵ The whole Judean countryside and all the people of Jerusalem were flocking to him, and they were baptized by him in the Jordan River as they confessed their sins. ⁶ John wore a camel-hair garment with a leather belt around his waist and ate locusts and wild honey. ⁷ He was preaching: "Someone more powerful than I will come after me. I am not worthy to stoop down and untie the strap of His sandals. ⁸ I have baptized you withᶠ water, but He will baptize you withᶠ the Holy Spirit."

Baptism of Jesus

⁹ In those days Jesus came from Nazareth in Galilee and was baptized in the Jordan by John. ¹⁰ As soon as He came up out of the water, He saw the heavens being torn open and the Spirit descending to Him like a dove. ¹¹ And a voice came from heaven:

> You are My beloved Son;
>   I take delight in You!ᵍ

Temptation of Jesus

¹² Immediately the Spirit drove Him into the wilderness. ¹³ He was in the wilderness 40 days, being tempted by Satan. He was with the wild animals, and the angels began to serve Him.

Jesus' Ministry in Galilee

¹⁴ After John was arrested, Jesus went to Galilee, preaching the good newsʰ ⁱ of God:ʲ ¹⁵ "The time is fulfilled, and the kingdom of God has come near. Repent and believe in the good news!"

Two Disciples: Simon and Andrew

¹⁶ As He was passing along by the Sea of Galilee, He saw Simon and Andrew, Simon's brother. They were casting a net into the sea, since they were fishermen. ¹⁷ "Follow Me," Jesus told them, "and I will make you fish forᵏ people!"

Two More: James and John

¹⁸ Immediately they left their nets and followed Him. ¹⁹ Going on a little farther, He saw James the son of Zebedee and his brother John. They were in their boat mending their nets. ²⁰ Immediately He called them, and they left their father Zebedee in the boat with the hired men and followed Him.

Jesus Drives Out Unclean Spirit

²¹ Then they went into Capernaum, and right away He entered the •syna-

---

ª1:2 Other mss read *in the prophets* ᵇ1:2 Other mss add *before You* ᶜ1:2-3 Mal 3:1; Is 40:3 ᵈ1:4 Or *John the Baptist came,* or *John the Baptizer came* ᵉ1:4 Or *a baptism based on repentance* ᶠ1:8 Or *in* ᵍ1:11 Or *In You I am well pleased* ʰ1:14 Other mss add *of the kingdom* ⁱ1:14 Or *gospel* ʲ1:14 Either *from God* or *about God* ᵏ1:17 Lit *you to become fishers of*

gogue on the Sabbath and began to teach. 22 They were astonished at His teaching because, unlike the •scribes, He was teaching them as one having authority.

23 Just then a man with an unclean spirit was in their synagogue. He cried out,a 24 "What do You have to do with us,b Jesus—Nazarene? Have You come to destroy us? I know who You are—the Holy One of God!"

25 But Jesus rebuked him and said, "Be quiet,c and come out of him!" 26 And the unclean spirit convulsed him, shouted with a loud voice, and came out of him.

27 Then they were all amazed, so they began to argue with one another, saying, "What is this? A new teaching with authority!d He commands even the unclean spirits, and they obey Him." 28 His fame then spread throughout the entire vicinity of Galilee.

Healings at Capernaum: Simon Peter's Mother-in-Law

29 As soon as they left the synagogue, they went into Simon and Andrew's house with James and John. 30 Simon's mother-in-law was lying in bed with a fever, and they told Him about her at once. 31 So He went to her, took her by the hand, and raised her up. The fever left her,e and she began to serve them.

32 When evening came, after the sun had set, they began bringing to Him all those who were sick and those who were demon-possessed. 33 The whole town was assembled at the door, 34 and He healed many who were sick with various diseases and drove out many demons. But He would not permit the demons to speak, because they knew Him.

Jesus Prays Early in Morning

35 Very early in the morning, while it was still dark, He got up, went out, and made His way to a deserted place. And He was praying there. 36 Simon and his companions went searching for Him. 37 They found Him and said, "Everyone's looking for You!"

Jesus Preaches in Galilee

38 And He said to them, "Let's go on to the neighboring villages so that I may preach there too. This is why I have come." 39 So He went into all of Galilee, preaching in their synagogues and driving out demons.

Jesus Cleanses a Leper

40 Then a man with a serious skin disease came to Him and, on his knees,f begged Him: "If You are willing, You can make me clean."g

41 Moved with compassion, Jesus reached out His hand and touched him. "I am willing," He told him. "Be made clean." 42 Immediately the disease left him, and he was healed.h 43 Then He sternly warned him and sent him away at once, 44 telling him, "See that you say nothing to anyone; but go and show yourself to the priest, and offer what Moses prescribed for your cleansing, as a testimony to them." 45 Yet he went out and began to proclaim it widely and to spread the news, with the result that Jesus could no longer enter a town openly. But He was out in deserted places, and they would come to Him from everywhere.

---

a1:23 Other mss add to the beginning of v. 24: "Leave us alone. b1:24 Lit What to us and to You c1:25 Or Be muzzled d1:27 Other mss read What is this? What is this new teaching? For with authority e1:31 Other mss add at once f1:40 Other mss omit on his knees g1:40 In these vv., clean includes healing, ceremonial purification, return to fellowship with people, and worship in the temple; Lv 14:1-32. h1:42 Lit made clean

Son of Man Forgives
and Heals a Paralytic

2 When He entered Capernaum again after some days, it was reported that He was at home. ² So many people gathered together that there was no more room, not even in the doorway, and He was speaking the message to them. ³ Then they came to Him bringing a paralytic, carried by four men. ⁴ Since they were not able to bring him to[a] Jesus because of the crowd, they removed the roof above where He was. And when they had broken through, they lowered the stretcher on which the paralytic was lying.

⁵ Seeing their faith, Jesus told the paralytic, "Son, your sins are forgiven."

⁶ But some of the •scribes were sitting there, thinking to themselves:[b] ⁷ "Why does He speak like this? He's blaspheming! Who can forgive sins but God alone?"

⁸ Right away Jesus understood in His spirit that they were reasoning like this within themselves and said to them, "Why are you reasoning these things in your hearts?[c] ⁹ Which is easier: to say to the paralytic, 'Your sins are forgiven,' or to say, 'Get up, pick up your stretcher, and walk'? ¹⁰ But so you may know that the •Son of Man has authority on earth to forgive sins," He told the paralytic, ¹¹ "I tell you: get up, pick up your stretcher, and go home."

¹² Immediately he got up, picked up the stretcher, and went out in front of everyone. As a result, they were all astounded and gave glory to God, saying, "We have never seen anything like this!"

Call of Levi (Matthew)

¹³ Then Jesus went out again beside the sea. The whole crowd was coming to Him, and He taught them. ¹⁴ Then, moving on, He saw Levi the son of Alphaeus sitting at the tax office, and He said to him, "Follow Me!" So he got up and followed Him.

Jesus Dines with Sinners

¹⁵ While He was reclining at the table in Levi's house, many tax collectors and sinners were also guests[d] with Jesus and His disciples, because there were many who were following Him. ¹⁶ When the scribes of the •Pharisees[e] saw that He was eating with sinners and tax collectors, they asked His disciples, "Why does He eat[f] with tax collectors and sinners?"

¹⁷ When Jesus heard this, He told them, "Those who are well don't need a doctor, but the sick ⌊do need one⌋. I didn't come to call the righteous, but sinners."

A Question about Fasting

¹⁸ Now John's disciples and the Pharisees[g] were fasting. People came and asked Him, "Why do John's disciples and the Pharisees' disciples fast, but Your disciples do not fast?"

¹⁹ Jesus said to them, "The wedding guests[h] cannot fast while the groom is with them, can they? As long as they have the groom with them, they cannot fast. ²⁰ But the time[i] will come when the groom is taken away from them, and then they will fast in that day. ²¹ No one sews a patch of unshrunk cloth on an old garment. Otherwise, the new patch pulls away from the old cloth, and a worse tear is made. ²² And no one puts new wine into old wineskins. Otherwise, the wine will burst the skins, and the wine is lost as well as the skins.[j] But new wine is for fresh wineskins."

a2:4 Other mss read *able to get near*   b2:6 Or *there, reasoning in their hearts*   c2:8 Or *minds*   d2:15 Lit *reclining* (at the table); at important meals the custom was to recline on a mat at a low table and lean on the left elbow.   e2:16 Other mss read *scribes and Pharisees*   f2:16 Other mss add *and drink*   g2:18 Other mss read *the disciples of John and of the Pharisees*   h2:19 Lit *The sons of the bridal chamber*   i2:20 Lit *the days*   j2:22 Other mss read *the wine spills out and the skins will be ruined*

Jesus: Lord of the Sabbath

23 On the Sabbath He was going through the grainfields, and His disciples began to make their way picking some heads of grain. 24 The Pharisees said to Him, "Look, why are they doing what is not lawful on the Sabbath?"

25 He said to them, "Have you never read what David and those who were with him did when he was in need and hungry— 26 how he entered the house of God in the time of Abiathar the high priest and ate the •sacred bread—which is not lawful for anyone to eat except the priests—and also gave some to his companions?" 27 Then He told them, "The Sabbath was made fora man and not man fora the Sabbath. 28 Therefore the Son of Man is Lord even of the Sabbath."

Man with Paralyzed Hand

3 Now He entered the •synagogue again, and a man was there who had a paralyzed hand. 2 In order to accuse Him, they were watching Him closely to see whether He would heal him on the Sabbath. 3 He told the man with the paralyzed hand, "Stand before us."b 4 Then He said to them, "Is it lawful on the Sabbath to do good or to do evil, to save life or to kill?" But they were silent. 5 After looking around at them with anger and sorrow at the hardness of their hearts, He told the man, "Stretch out your hand." So he stretched it out, and his hand was restored.

Plot to Kill Jesus

6 Immediately the •Pharisees went out and started plotting with the •Herodians against Him, how they might destroy Him.

Jesus Ministers to Multitude

7 Jesus departed with His disciples to the sea, and a great multitude followed from Galilee, Judea, 8 Jerusalem, Idumea, beyond the Jordan, and around Tyre and Sidon. The great multitude came to Him because they heard about everything He was doing. 9 Then He told His disciples to have a small boat ready for Him, so the crowd would not crush Him. 10 Since He had healed many, all who had diseases were pressing toward Him to touch Him. 11 Whenever the unclean spirits saw Him, those possessed fell down before Him and cried out, "You are the Son of God!" 12 And He would strongly warn them not to make Him known.

Jesus Appoints 12 Apostles

13 Then He went up the mountain and summoned those He wanted, and they came to Him. 14 He also appointed 12— He also named them apostlesc—to be with Him, to send them out to preach, 15 and to have authority tod drive out demons.

16 He appointed the Twelve:e

To Simon, He gave the name Peter;
17   and to James the son of Zebedee, and to his brother John, He gave the name "Boanerges" (that is, "Sons of Thunder");
18   Andrew; Philip and Bartholomew; Matthew and Thomas; James the son of Alphaeus, and Thaddaeus; Simon the Zealot,f
19   and Judas Iscariot,g who also betrayed Him.

a2:27 Or because of b3:3 Lit Rise up in the middle c3:14 Other mss omit He also named them apostles
d3:15 Other mss add heal diseases, and to e3:16 Other mss omit He appointed the Twelve f3:18 Lit the
Cananaean g3:19 Iscariot probably = "a man of Kerioth," a town in Judea.

A House Divided

20 Then He went home, and the crowd gathered again so that they were not even able to eat.ᵃ 21 When His family heard this, they set out to restrain Him, because they said, "He's out of His mind."

22 The •scribes who had come down from Jerusalem said, "He has •Beelzebul in Him!" and, "He drives out demons by the ruler of the demons!"

23 So He summoned them and spoke to them in parables: "How can Satan drive out Satan? 24 If a kingdom is divided against itself, that kingdom cannot stand. 25 If a house is divided against itself, that house cannot stand. 26 And if Satan rebels against himself and is divided, he cannot stand but is finished!ᵇ

27 "On the other hand, no one can enter a strong man's house and rob his possessions unless he first ties up the strong man. Then he will rob his house. 28 •I assure you: People will be forgiven for all sinsᶜ and whatever blasphemies they may blaspheme. 29 But whoever blasphemes against the Holy Spirit never has forgiveness, but is guilty of an eternal sin"ᵈ— 30 because they were saying, "He has an unclean spirit."

Jesus on Mother, Brothers, and Sisters

31 Then His mother and His brothers came, and standing outside, they sent ⌊word⌋ to Him and called Him. 32 A crowd was sitting around Him and told Him, "Look, Your mother, Your brothers, and Your sistersᵉ are outside asking for You."

33 He replied to them, "Who are My mother and My brothers?" 34 And looking about at those who were sitting in a circle around Him, He said, "Here are My mother and My brothers! 35 Whoever does the will of God is My brother and sister and mother."

Parable of Sower

4 Again He began to teach by the sea, and a very large crowd gathered around Him. So He got into a boat on the sea and sat down, while the whole crowd was on the shore facing the sea. 2 He taught them many things in parables, and in His teaching He said to them: 3 "Listen! Consider the sower who went out to sow. 4 As he sowed, this occurred: Some seed fell along the path, and the birds came and ate it up. 5 Other seed fell on rocky ground where it didn't have much soil, and it sprang up right away, since it didn't have deep soil. 6 When the sun came up, it was scorched, and since it didn't have a root, it withered. 7 Other seed fell among thorns, and the thorns came up and choked it, and it didn't produce a crop. 8 Still others fell on good ground and produced a crop that increased 30, 60, and 100 times ⌊what was sown⌋." 9 Then He said, "Anyone who has ears to hear should listen!"

Why Jesus Used Parables

10 When He was alone with the Twelve, those who were around Him asked Him about the parables. 11 He answered them, "The secretᶠ of the kingdom of God has been granted to you, but to those outside, everything comes in parables 12 so that

**they may look and look,
yet not perceive;
they may listen and listen,
yet not understand;**

ᵃ**3:20** Lit *eat bread,* or *eat a meal*   ᵇ**3:26** Lit *but he has an end*   ᶜ**3:28** Lit *All things will be forgiven the sons of men*
ᵈ**3:29** Other mss read *is subject to eternal judgment*   ᵉ**3:32** Other mss omit *and Your sisters*   ᶠ**4:11** The Gk word
mysterion does not mean "mystery" in the Eng sense; it means what we can know only by divine revelation.

otherwise, they might
  turn back—
and be forgiven."ᵃ ᵇ

Parable of Sower Explained

¹³ Then He said to them: "Do you not understand this parable? How then will you understand any of the parables? ¹⁴ The sower sows the word. ¹⁵ Theseᶜ are the ones along the path where the word is sown: when they hear, immediately Satan comes and takes away the word sown in them.ᵈ ¹⁶ And these areᵉ the ones sown on rocky ground: when they hear the word, immediately they receive it with joy. ¹⁷ But they have no root in themselves; they are short-lived. When affliction or persecution comes because of the word, they immediately stumble. ¹⁸ Others are sown among thorns; these are the ones who hear the word, ¹⁹ but the worries of this age, the seductionᶠ of wealth, and the desires for other things enter in and choke the word, and it becomes unfruitful. ²⁰ But the ones sown on good ground are those who hear the word, welcome it, and produce a crop: 30, 60, and 100 times ⌊what was sown⌋."

Nothing Concealed

²¹ He also said to them, "Is a lamp brought in to be put under a basket or under a bed? Isn't it to be put on a lampstand? ²² For nothing is concealed except to be revealed, and nothing hidden except to come to light. ²³ If anyone has ears to hear, he should listen!" ²⁴ Then He said to them, "Pay attention to what you hear. By the measure you use,ᵍ it will be measured and added to you. ²⁵ For to the one who has, it will be given, and from the one who does not have, even what he has will be taken away."

Parable of Growing Grain

²⁶ "The kingdom of God is like this," He said. "A man scatters seed on the ground; ²⁷ he sleeps and rises—night and day, and the seed sprouts and grows—he doesn't know how. ²⁸ The soil produces a crop by itself—first the blade, then the head, and then the ripe grain on the head. ²⁹ But as soon as the crop is ready, he sends for the sickle, because harvest has come."

Parable of Mustard Seed

³⁰ And He said: "How can we illustrate the kingdom of God, or what parable can we use to describe it? ³¹ It's like a mustard seed that, when sown in the soil, is smaller than all the seeds on the ground. ³² And when sown, it comes up and grows taller than all the vegetables, and produces large branches, so that the birds of the sky can nest in its shade."

Jesus' Use of Parables

³³ He would speak the word to them with many parables like these, as they were able to understand. ³⁴ And He did not speak to them without a parable. Privately, however, He would explain everything to His own disciples.

Wind and Sea Obey the Master

³⁵ On that day, when evening had come, He told them, "Let's cross over to the other side ⌊of the lake⌋." ³⁶ So they left the crowd and took Him along since He was ⌊already⌋ in the boat. And other boats were with Him. ³⁷ A fierce windstorm arose, and the waves were breaking over the boat, so that the boat was already being swamped. ³⁸ But He was in the stern, sleeping on the cushion. So they woke Him up and said to Him,

ᵃ**4:12** Other mss read *and their sins be forgiven them* ᵇ**4:12** Is 6:9-10 ᶜ**4:15** Some people ᵈ**4:15** Other mss read *in their hearts* ᵉ**4:16** Other mss read *are like* ᶠ**4:19** Or *pleasure, or deceitfulness* ᵍ**4:24** Lit *you measure*

"Teacher! Don't you care that we're going to die?"

³⁹ He got up, rebuked the wind, and said to the sea, "Silence! Be still!" The wind ceased, and there was a great calm. ⁴⁰ Then He said to them, "Why are you fearful? Do you still have no faith?"

⁴¹ And they were terrified and asked one another, "Who then is this? Even the wind and the sea obey Him!"

Jesus Drives out Legion

5 Then they came to the other side of the sea, to the region of the Gerasenes.ᵃ ² As soon as He got out of the boat, a man with an unclean spirit came out of the tombs and met Him. ³ He lived in the tombs. No one was able to restrain him any more—even with chains— ⁴ because he often had been bound with shackles and chains, but had snapped off the chains and smashed the shackles. No one was strong enough to subdue him. ⁵ And always, night and day, he was crying out among the tombs and in the mountains and cutting himself with stones.

⁶ When he saw Jesus from a distance, he ran and knelt down before Him. ⁷ And he cried out with a loud voice, "What do You have to do with me,ᵇ Jesus, Son of the Most High God? I begᶜ You before God, don't torment me!" ⁸ For He had told him, "Come out of the man, you unclean spirit!"

⁹ "What is your name?" He asked him.

"My name is Legion,"ᵈ he answered Him, "because we are many." ¹⁰ And he kept begging Him not to send them out of the region.

Demons Enter Pigs

¹¹ Now a large herd of pigs was there, feeding on the hillside. ¹² The demonsᵉ begged Him, "Send us to the pigs, so we may enter them." ¹³ And He gave them permission. Then the unclean spirits came out and entered the pigs, and the herd of about 2,000 rushed down the steep bank into the sea and drowned there. ¹⁴ The men who tended themᶠ ran off and reported it in the town and the countryside, and people went to see what had happened. ¹⁵ They came to Jesus and saw the man who had been demon-possessed by the legion, sitting there, dressed and in his right mind; and they were afraid. ¹⁶ The eyewitnesses described to them what had happened to the demon-possessed man and ₜtoldₗ about the pigs. ¹⁷ Then they began to beg Him to leave their region.

Mission of Man Who Was Demon-Possessed

¹⁸ As He was getting into the boat, the man who had been demon-possessed kept begging Him to be with Him. ¹⁹ But He would not let him; instead, He told him, "Go back home to your own people, and report to them how much the Lord has done for you and how He has had mercy on you." ²⁰ So he went out and began to proclaim in the •Decapolis how much Jesus had done for him, and they were all amazed.

Jairus Appeals for Daughter

²¹ When Jesus had crossed over again by boat to the other side, a large crowd gathered around Him while He was by the sea. ²² One of the •synagogue leaders, named Jairus, came, and when he saw Jesus, he fell at His feet ²³ and kept begging Him, "My little daughter is at death's door.ᵍ Come and lay Your hands on her so she can get well and live."

ᵃ5:1 Other mss read *Gadarenes*; other mss read *Gergesenes* ᵇ5:7 Lit *What to me and to You* ᶜ5:7 Or *adjure*
ᵈ5:9 A Roman legion contained up to 6,000 soldiers; here *legion* indicates a large number. ᵉ5:12 Other mss read *All the demons* ᶠ5:14 Other mss read *tended the pigs* ᵍ5:23 Lit *My little daughter has it finally*; = to be at the end of life

Woman with Issue of Blood Intervenes

²⁴ So Jesus went with him, and a large crowd was following and pressing against Him. ²⁵ A woman suffering from bleeding for 12 years ²⁶ had endured much under many doctors. She had spent everything she had and was not helped at all. On the contrary, she became worse. ²⁷ Having heard about Jesus, she came behind Him in the crowd and touched His robe. ²⁸ For she said, "If I can just touch His robes, I'll be made well!" ²⁹ Instantly her flow of blood ceased, and she sensed in her body that she was cured of her affliction.

³⁰ At once Jesus realized in Himself that power had gone out from Him. He turned around in the crowd and said, "Who touched My robes?"

³¹ His disciples said to Him, "You see the crowd pressing against You, and You say, 'Who touched Me?' "

³² So He was looking around to see who had done this. ³³ Then the woman, knowing what had happened to her, came with fear and trembling, fell down before Him, and told Him the whole truth. ³⁴ "Daughter," He said to her, "your faith has made you well.ᵃ Go in peace and be freeᵇ from your affliction."

Report of Death of Jairus' Daughter

³⁵ While He was still speaking, people came from the synagogue leader's house and said, "Your daughter is dead. Why bother the Teacher any more?"

³⁶ But when Jesus overheard what was said, He told the synagogue leader, "Don't be afraid. Only believe." ³⁷ He did not let anyone accompany Him except Peter, James, and John, James' brother. ³⁸ They came to the leader's house, and He saw a commotion—people weeping and wailing loudly. ³⁹ He went in and said to them, "Why are you making a commotion and weeping? The child is not dead but •asleep."

The Daughter Restored

⁴⁰ They started laughing at Him, but He put them all outside. He took the child's father, mother, and those who were with Him, and entered the place where the child was. ⁴¹ Then He took the child by the hand and said to her, *"Talitha koum!"* ᶜ (which is translated, "Little girl, I say to you, get up!"). ⁴² Immediately the girl got up and began to walk. (She was 12 years old.) At this they were utterly astounded. ⁴³ Then He gave them strict orders that no one should know about this and said that she should be given something to eat.

Jesus Rejected at Nazareth

6 He went away from there and came to His hometown, and His disciples followed Him. ² When the Sabbath came, He began to teach in the •synagogue, and many who heard Him were astonished. "Where did this man get these things?" they said. "What is this wisdom given to Him, and how are these miracles performed by His hands? ³ Isn't this the carpenter, the son of Mary, and the brother of James, Joses, Judas, and Simon? And aren't His sisters here with us?" So they were offended by Him.

A Prophet Is Not without Honor

⁴ Then Jesus said to them, "A prophet is not without honor except in his hometown, among his relatives, and in his household." ⁵ So He was not able to do any miraclesᵈ there, except that He laid His hands on a few sick people and

---

ᵃ5:34 Or *has saved you*   ᵇ5:34 Lit *healthy*   ᶜ5:41 An Aram expression   ᵈ6:5 Lit *miracle*

healed them. ⁶ And He was amazed at their unbelief.

Jesus Commissions the 12

Now He was going around the villages in a circuit, teaching. ⁷ He summoned the Twelve and began to send them out in pairs and gave them authority over unclean spirits. ⁸ He instructed them to take nothing for the road except a walking stick: no bread, no traveling bag, no money in their belts. ⁹ They were to wear sandals, but not put on an extra shirt. ¹⁰ Then He said to them, "Whenever you enter a house, stay there until you leave that place. ¹¹ If any place does not welcome you and people refuse to listen to you, when you leave there, shake the dust off your feet as a testimony against them."[a]

¹² So they went out and preached that people should repent. ¹³ And they were driving out many demons, anointing many sick people with oil, and healing.

Herod and John the Baptist

¹⁴ King •Herod heard of this, because Jesus' name had become well known. Some[b] said, "John the Baptist has been raised from the dead, and that's why supernatural powers are at work in him." ¹⁵ But others said, "He's Elijah." Still others said, "He's a prophet[c]—like one of the prophets."

¹⁶ When Herod heard of it, he said, "John, the one I beheaded, has been raised!" ¹⁷ For Herod himself had given orders to arrest John and to chain him in prison on account of Herodias, his brother Philip's wife, whom he had married. ¹⁸ John had been telling Herod, "It is not lawful for you to have your brother's wife!" ¹⁹ So Herodias held a grudge against him and wanted to kill him. But she could not, ²⁰ because Herod was in awe of[d] John and was protecting him, knowing he was a righteous and holy man. When Herod heard him he would be very disturbed,[e] yet would hear him gladly.

²¹ Now an opportune time came on his birthday, when Herod gave a banquet for his nobles, military commanders, and the leading men of Galilee. ²² When Herodias' own daughter[f] came in and danced, she pleased Herod and his guests. The king said to the girl, "Ask me whatever you want, and I'll give it to you." ²³ So he swore oaths to her: "Whatever you ask me I will give you, up to half my kingdom."

²⁴ Then she went out and said to her mother, "What should I ask for?"

"John the Baptist's head!" she said.

²⁵ Immediately she hurried to the king and said, "I want you to give me John the Baptist's head on a platter—right now!"

Herod Beheads John the Baptist

²⁶ Though the king was deeply distressed, because of his oaths and the guests[g] he did not want to refuse her. ²⁷ The king immediately sent for an executioner and commanded him to bring John's head. So he went and beheaded him in prison, ²⁸ brought his head on a platter, and gave it to the girl. Then the girl gave it to her mother. ²⁹ When his disciples[h] heard about it, they came and removed his corpse and placed it in a tomb.

Jesus Feeds 5,000

³⁰ The apostles gathered around Jesus and reported to Him all that they had

---

[a]**6:11** Other mss add *I assure you, it will be more tolerable for Sodom or Gomorrah on judgment day than for that town.* [b]**6:14** Other mss read *He* [c]**6:15** Lit *Others said, "A prophet* [d]**6:20** Or *Herod feared* [e]**6:20** Other mss read *When he heard him, he did many things* [f]**6:22** Other mss read *When his daughter Herodias* [g]**6:26** Lit *and those reclining at the table* [h]**6:29** John's disciples

done and taught. ³¹ He said to them, "Come away by yourselves to a remote place and rest a while." For many people were coming and going, and they did not even have time to eat. ³² So they went away in the boat by themselves to a remote place, ³³ but many saw them leaving and recognized them. People ran there by land from all the towns and arrived ahead of them.ᵃ ³⁴ So as He stepped ashore, He saw a huge crowd and had compassion on them, because they were like sheep without a shepherd. Then He began to teach them many things.

³⁵ When it was already late, His disciples approached Him and said, "This place is a wilderness, and it is already late! ³⁶ Send them away, so they can go into the surrounding countryside and villages to buy themselves something to eat."

³⁷ "You give them something to eat," He responded.

They said to Him, "Should we go and buy 200 •denarii worth of bread and give them something to eat?"

³⁸ And He asked them, "How many loaves do you have? Go look."

When they found out they said, "Five, and two fish."

³⁹ Then He instructed them to have all the people sit downᵇ in groups on the green grass. ⁴⁰ So they sat down in ranks of hundreds and fifties. ⁴¹ Then He took the five loaves and the two fish, and looking up to heaven, He blessed and broke the loaves. He kept giving them to His disciples to set before the people. He also divided the two fish among them all. ⁴² Everyone ate and was filled. ⁴³ Then they picked up 12 baskets full of pieces of bread and fish. ⁴⁴ Now those who ate the loaves were 5,000 men.

Jesus Walks on Water

⁴⁵ Immediately He made His disciples get into the boat and go ahead of Him to the other side, to Bethsaida, while He dismissed the crowd. ⁴⁶ After He said good-bye to them, He went away to the mountain to pray. ⁴⁷ When evening came, the boat was in the middle of the sea, and He was alone on the land. ⁴⁸ He saw them being battered as they rowed,ᶜ because the wind was against them. Around three in the morningᵈ He came toward them walking on the sea and wanted to pass by them. ⁴⁹ When they saw Him walking on the sea, they thought it was a ghost and cried out; ⁵⁰ for they all saw Him and were terrified. Immediately He spoke with them and said, "Have courage! It is I. Don't be afraid." ⁵¹ Then He got into the boat with them, and the wind ceased. They were completely astounded,ᵉ ⁵² because they had not understood about the loaves. Instead, their hearts were hardened.

Other Miraculous Healings

⁵³ When they had crossed over, they came to land at Gennesaret and beached the boat. ⁵⁴ As they got out of the boat, people immediately recognized Him. ⁵⁵ They hurried throughout that vicinity and began to carry the sick on stretchers to wherever they heard He was. ⁵⁶ Wherever He would go, into villages, towns, or the country, they laid the sick in the marketplaces and begged Him that they might touch just the •tassel of His robe. And everyone who touched it was made well.

ᵃ6:33 Other mss add and gathered around Him   ᵇ6:39 Lit people recline   ᶜ6:48 Or them struggling as they rowed   ᵈ6:48 Lit Around the fourth watch of the night = 3 to 6 a.m.   ᵉ6:51 Lit were astounded in themselves

Pharisees and Scribes Challenge Disciples' Unclean Hands

7 The •Pharisees and some of the •scribes who had come from Jerusalem gathered around Him. ² They observed that some of His disciples were eating their bread with unclean—that is, unwashed—hands. ³ (For the Pharisees, in fact all the Jews, will not eat unless they wash their hands ritually, keeping the tradition of the elders. ⁴ When they come from the marketplace, they do not eat unless they have washed. And there are many other customs they have received and keep, like the washing of cups, jugs, copper utensils, and dining couches.ᵃ) ⁵ Then the Pharisees and the scribes asked Him, "Why don't Your disciples live according to the tradition of the elders, instead of eating bread with ritually uncleanᵇ hands?"

Jesus Calls Them Hypocrites

⁶ He answered them, "Isaiah prophesied correctly about you hypocrites, as it is written:

These people honor Me
  with their lips,
but their heart is far from Me.
⁷ They worship Me in vain,
  teaching as doctrines
  the commands of men.ᶜ

⁸ Disregarding the command of God, you keep the tradition of men."ᵈ ⁹ He also said to them, "You completely invalidate God's command in order to maintainᵉ your tradition! ¹⁰ For Moses said:

Honor your father
  and your mother;ᶠ and,

Whoever speaks evil of father
  or mother
must be put to death.ᵍ

¹¹ But you say, 'If a man tells his father or mother: Whatever benefit you might have received from me is Corban'" (that is, a gift ⌊committed to the temple⌋), ¹² "you no longer let him do anything for his father or mother. ¹³ You revoke God's word by your tradition that you have handed down. And you do many other similar things." ¹⁴ Summoning the crowd again, He told them, "Listen to Me, all of you, and understand: ¹⁵ Nothing that goes into a person from outside can defile him, but the things that come out of a person are what defile him. ¹⁶ If anyone has ears to hear, he should listen!"ʰ

Jesus Explains Defilement Parable

¹⁷ When He went into the house away from the crowd, the disciples asked Him about the parable. ¹⁸ And He said to them, "Are you also as lacking in understanding? Don't you realize that nothing going into a man from the outside can defile him? ¹⁹ For it doesn't go into his heart but into the stomach and is eliminated."ⁱ (As a result, He made all foods clean.ʲ) ²⁰ Then He said, "What comes out of a person—that defiles him. ²¹ For from within, out of people's hearts, come evil thoughts, sexual immoralities, thefts, murders, ²² adulteries, greed, evil actions, deceit, lewdness, stinginess,ᵏ blasphemy, pride, and foolishness. ²³ All these evil things come from within and defile a person."

A Greek Mother's Faith

²⁴ He got up and departed from there to the region of Tyre and Sidon.ˡ He en-

---

ᵃ7:4 Other mss omit *and dining couches* ᵇ7:5 Other mss read *with unwashed* ᶜ7:6-7 Is 29:13 ᵈ7:8 Other mss add *The washing of jugs, and cups, and many other similar things you practice.* ᵉ7:9 Other mss read *to establish*
ᶠ7:10 Ex 20:12; Dt 5:16 ᵍ7:10 Ex 21:17; Lv 20:9 ʰ7:16 Other mss omit this verse ⁱ7:19 Lit *goes out into the toilet*
ʲ7:19 Other mss read *is eliminated, making all foods clean."* ᵏ7:22 Lit *evil eye* ˡ7:24 Other mss omit *and Sidon*

tered a house and did not want anyone to know it, but He could not escape notice. ²⁵ Instead, immediately after hearing about Him, a woman whose little daughter had an unclean spirit came and fell at His feet. ²⁶ Now the woman was Greek, a Syrophoenician by birth, and she kept asking Him to drive the demon out of her daughter. ²⁷ He said to her, "Allow the children to be satisfied first, because it isn't right to take the children's bread and throw it to the dogs."

²⁸ But she replied to Him, "Lord, even the dogs under the table eat the children's crumbs."

²⁹ Then He told her, "Because of this reply, you may go. The demon has gone out of your daughter." ³⁰ When she went back to her home, she found her child lying on the bed, and the demon was gone.

Jesus Heals Deaf Man

³¹ Again, leaving the region of Tyre, He went by way of Sidon to the Sea of Galilee, through^a the region of the •Decapolis. ³² They brought to Him a deaf man who also had a speech difficulty, and begged Jesus to lay His hand on him. ³³ So He took him away from the crowd privately. After putting His fingers in the man's ears and spitting, He touched his tongue. ³⁴ Then, looking up to heaven, He sighed deeply and said to him, *"Ephphatha!"* ^b (that is, "Be opened!"). ³⁵ Immediately his ears were opened, his speech difficulty was removed,^c and he began to speak clearly. ³⁶ Then He ordered them to tell no one, but the more He would order them, the more they would proclaim it.

"He Has Done Everything Well!"

³⁷ They were extremely astonished and said, "He has done everything well!

He even makes deaf people hear, and people unable to speak, talk!"

Jesus Feeds 4,000

8 In those days there was again a large crowd, and they had nothing to eat. He summoned the disciples and said to them, ² "I have compassion on the crowd, because they've already stayed with Me three days and have nothing to eat. ³ If I send them home famished,^d they will collapse on the way, and some of them have come a long distance."

⁴ His disciples answered Him, "Where can anyone get enough bread here in this desolate place to fill these people?"

⁵ "How many loaves do you have?" He asked them.

"Seven," they said. ⁶ Then He commanded the crowd to sit down on the ground. Taking the seven loaves, He gave thanks, broke the ⌊loaves⌋, and kept on giving ⌊them⌋ to His disciples to set before ⌊the people⌋. So they served the ⌊loaves⌋ to the crowd. ⁷ They also had a few small fish, and when He had blessed them, He said these were to be served as well. ⁸ They ate and were filled. Then they collected seven large baskets of leftover pieces. ⁹ About 4,000 ⌊men⌋ were there. He dismissed them ¹⁰ and immediately got into the boat with His disciples and went to the district of Dalmanutha.^e

Yeast of Pharisees and Herod

¹¹ The •Pharisees came out and began to argue with Him, demanding of Him a sign from heaven to test Him. ¹² But sighing deeply in His spirit, He said, "Why does this generation demand a sign? •I assure you: No sign will be given to this generation!" ¹³ Then He left them, got on board ⌊the boat⌋ again, and went to the other side.

---

^a**7:31** Or *into*   ^b**7:34** An Aram expression   ^c**7:35** Lit *opened, the bond of his tongue was untied*   ^d**8:3** Or *fasting*
^e**8:10** Probably on the western shore of the Sea of Galilee

14 They had forgotten to take bread and had only one loaf with them in the boat. 15 Then He commanded them: "Watch out! Beware of the yeast of the Pharisees and the yeast of •Herod."

Jesus' Plea for Understanding

16 They were discussing among themselves that they did not have any bread. 17 Aware of this, He said to them, "Why are you discussing that you do not have any bread? Do you not yet understand or comprehend? Is your heart hardened? 18 **Do you have eyes, and not see, and do you have ears, and not hear?**ᵃ And do you not remember? 19 When I broke the five loaves for the 5,000, how many baskets full of pieces of bread did you collect?"

"Twelve," they told Him.

20 "When I broke the seven loaves for the 4,000, how many large baskets full of pieces of bread did you collect?"

"Seven," they said.

21 And He said to them, "Don't you understand yet?"

Jesus Heals Blind Man

22 Then they came to Bethsaida. They brought a blind man to Him and begged Him to touch him. 23 He took the blind man by the hand and brought him out of the village. Spitting on his eyes and laying His hands on him, He asked him, "Do you see anything?"

24 He looked up and said, "I see people—they look to me like trees walking."

25 Again Jesus placed His hands on the man's eyes, and he saw distinctly. He was cured and could see everything clearly. 26 Then He sent him home, saying, "Don't even go into the village."ᵇ

Peter's Confession of the Messiah

27 Jesus went out with His disciples to the villages of Caesarea Philippi. And on the road He asked His disciples, "Who do people say that I am?"

28 They answered Him, "John the Baptist; others, Elijah; still others, one of the prophets."

29 "But you," He asked them again, "who do you say that I am?"

Peter answered Him, "You are the •Messiah!"

30 And He strictly warned them to tell no one about Him.

Jesus Predicts His Death and Resurrection

31 Then He began to teach them that the •Son of Man must suffer many things, and be rejected by the elders, the •chief priests, and the •scribes, be killed, and rise after three days. 32 He was openly talking about this. So Peter took Him aside and began to rebuke Him.

Jesus Rebukes Peter

33 But turning around and looking at His disciples, He rebuked Peter and said, "Get behind Me, Satan, because you're not thinking about God's concerns,ᶜ but man's!"

"Take Up His Cross"

34 Summoning the crowd along with His disciples, He said to them, "If anyone wants to be My follower, he must deny himself, take up his cross, and follow Me. 35 For whoever wants to save his •life will lose it, but whoever loses his life because of Me and the gospel will save it. 36 For what does it benefit a man to gain the whole world yet lose his life? 37 What can a man give in exchange for his life? 38 For

ᵃ8:18 Jr 5:21; Ezk 12:2 ᵇ8:26 Other mss add or tell anyone in the village ᶜ8:33 Lit about the things of God

whoever is ashamed of Me and of My words in this adulterous and sinful generation, the Son of Man will also be ashamed of him when He comes in the glory of His Father with the holy angels."

9 Then He said to them, "•I assure you: There are some standing here who will not taste death until they see the kingdom of God come in power."

The Transfiguration

2 After six days Jesus took Peter, James, and John and led them up on a high mountain by themselves to be alone. He was transformed[a] in front of them, 3 and His clothes became dazzling—extremely white as no launderer on earth could whiten them. 4 Elijah appeared to them with Moses, and they were talking with Jesus.

5 Then Peter said to Jesus, "•Rabbi, it is good for us to be here! Let us make three •tabernacles: one for You, one for Moses, and one for Elijah"— 6 because he did not know what he should say, since they were terrified.

7 A cloud appeared, overshadowing them, and a voice came from the cloud:

This is My beloved Son;
listen to Him!

8 Then suddenly, looking around, they no longer saw anyone with them except Jesus alone.

9 As they were coming down from the mountain, He ordered them to tell no one what they had seen until the •Son of Man had risen from the dead. 10 They kept this word to themselves, discussing what "rising from the dead" meant.

Elijah First

11 Then they began to question Him, "Why do the •scribes say that Elijah must come first?"

12 "Elijah does come first and restores everything," He replied. "How then is it written about the Son of Man that He must suffer many things and be treated with contempt? 13 But I tell you that Elijah really has come, and they did to him whatever they wanted, just as it is written about him."

Power of Faith over a Demon

14 When they came to the disciples, they saw a large crowd around them and scribes disputing with them. 15 All of a sudden, when the whole crowd saw Him, they were amazed[b] and ran to greet Him. 16 Then He asked them, "What are you arguing with them about?"

17 Out of the crowd, one man answered Him, "Teacher, I brought my son to You. He has a spirit that makes him unable to speak. 18 Wherever it seizes him, it throws him down, and he foams at the mouth, grinds his teeth, and becomes rigid. So I asked Your disciples to drive it out, but they couldn't."

19 He replied to them, "You unbelieving generation! How long will I be with you? How long must I put up with you? Bring him to Me." 20 So they brought him to Him. When the spirit saw Him, it immediately convulsed the boy. He fell to the ground and rolled around, foaming at the mouth. 21 "How long has this been happening to him?" Jesus asked his father.

"From childhood," he said. 22 "And many times it has thrown him into fire or water to destroy him. But if You can do anything, have compassion on us and help us."

23 Then Jesus said to him, " 'If You can?'[c] [d] Everything is possible to the one who believes."

---

[a]9:2 Or transfigured   [b]9:15 Or surprised   [c]9:23 Other mss add believe   [d]9:23 Jesus appears to quote the father's words in v. 22 and then comment on them.

²⁴ Immediately the father of the boy cried out, "I do believe! Help my unbelief."

²⁵ When Jesus saw that a crowd was rapidly coming together, He rebuked the unclean spirit, saying to it, "You mute and deaf spirit,ᵃ I command you: come out of him and never enter him again!"

²⁶ Then it came out, shrieking and convulsing himᵇ violently. The boy became like a corpse, so that many said, "He's dead." ²⁷ But Jesus, taking him by the hand, raised him, and he stood up.

²⁸ After He went into a house, His disciples asked Him privately, "Why couldn't we drive it out?"

²⁹ And He told them, "This kind can come out by nothing but prayer [and fasting]."ᶜ

Jesus' Second Prediction of His Death

³⁰ Then they left that place and made their way through Galilee, but He did not want anyone to know it. ³¹ For He was teaching His disciples and telling them, "The Son of Man is being betrayedᵈ into the hands of men. They will kill Him, and after He is killed, He will rise three days later." ³² But they did not understand this statement, and they were afraid to ask Him.

Who is the Greatest?

³³ Then they came to Capernaum. When He was in the house, He asked them, "What were you arguing about on the way?" ³⁴ But they were silent, because on the way they had been arguing with one another about who was the greatest. ³⁵ Sitting down, He called the Twelve and said to them, "If anyone wants to be first, he must be last of all and servant of all." ³⁶ Then He took a child, had him stand among them, and taking him in His arms, He said to them, ³⁷ "Whoever welcomesᵉ one little child such as this in My name welcomes Me. And whoever welcomes Me does not welcome Me, but Him who sent Me."

In Jesus' Name

³⁸ John said to Him, "Teacher, we saw someoneᶠ driving out demons in Your name, and we tried to stop him because he wasn't following us."

³⁹ "Don't stop him," said Jesus, "because there is no one who will perform a miracle in My name who can soon afterwards speak evil of Me. ⁴⁰ For whoever is not against us is for us. ⁴¹ And whoever gives you a cup of water to drink because of My name,ᵍ since you belong to the •Messiah—I assure you: He will never lose his reward.

Warnings from Jesus

⁴² "But whoever •causes the downfall of one of these little ones who believe in Me—it would be better for him if a heavy millstoneʰ were hung around his neck and he were thrown into the sea. ⁴³ And if your hand causes your downfall, cut it off. It is better for you to enter life maimed than to have two hands and go to •hell—the unquenchable fire, [⁴⁴ where

> Their worm does not die,
> and the fire is not quenched.]ᶜ ⁱ

⁴⁵ And if your foot causes your downfall, cut it off. It is better for you to enter life lame than to have two feet and be thrown into hell— [the unquenchable fire, ⁴⁶ where

> Their worm does not die,
> and the fire is not quenched.]ᶜ ⁱ

ᵃ9:25 A spirit that caused the boy to be deaf and unable to speak   ᵇ9:26 Other mss omit *him*   ᶜ9:29,44,46 Other mss omit bracketed text   ᵈ9:31 Or *handed over*   ᵉ9:37 Or *Whoever receives*   ᶠ9:38 Other mss add *who didn't go along with us*   ᵍ9:41 Lit *drink in the name*; = Messiah   ʰ9:42 A millstone turned by a donkey   ⁱ9:44,46 Is 66:24

[47] And if your eye causes your downfall, gouge it out. It is better for you to enter the kingdom of God with one eye than to have two eyes and be thrown into hell, [48] where

> Their worm does not die,
> and the fire is not quenched.[a]

[49] For everyone will be salted with fire.[b] [c] [50] Salt is good, but if the salt should lose its flavor, how can you make it salty? Have salt among yourselves and be at peace with one another."

Pharisees: Question of Divorce

10 He set out from there and went to the region of Judea and across the Jordan. Then crowds converged on Him again and, as He usually did, He began teaching them once more. [2] Some •Pharisees approached Him to test Him. They asked, "Is it lawful for a man to divorce ⌊his⌋ wife?"

[3] He replied to them, "What did Moses command you?"

[4] They said, "Moses permitted us to write divorce papers and send her away."

[5] But Jesus told them, "He wrote this commandment for you because of the hardness of your hearts. [6] But from the beginning of creation God[d] **made them male and female.**[e]

> [7] **For this reason a man will leave his father and mother [and be joined to his wife,]**[f]
> [8] **and the two will become one flesh.**[g]

So they are no longer two, but one flesh. [9] Therefore what God has joined together, man must not separate."

[10] Now in the house the disciples questioned Him again about this matter. [11] And He said to them, "Whoever divorces his wife and marries another commits adultery against her. [12] Also, if she divorces her husband and marries another, she commits adultery."

Jesus Blesses Children

[13] Some people were bringing little children to Him so He might touch them, but His disciples rebuked them. [14] When Jesus saw it, He was indignant and said to them, "Let the little children come to Me. Don't stop them, for the kingdom of God belongs to such as these. [15] •I assure you: Whoever does not welcome[h] the kingdom of God like a little child will never enter it." [16] After taking them in His arms, He laid His hands on them and blessed them.

The Rich Man

[17] As He was setting out on a journey, a man ran up, knelt down before Him, and asked Him, "Good Teacher, what must I do to inherit eternal life?"

[18] "Why do you call Me good?" Jesus asked him. "No one is good but One—God. [19] You know the commandments:

> Do not murder;
> do not commit adultery;
> do not steal;
> do not bear false witness;
> do not defraud;
> honor your father and mother."[i]

[20] He said to Him, "Teacher, I have kept all these from my youth."

[21] Then, looking at him, Jesus loved him and said to him, "You lack one thing: Go, sell all you have and give to the poor, and you will have treasure in

[a]**9:48** Is 66:24   [b]**9:49** Other mss add *and every sacrifice will be salted with salt*   [c]**9:49** Lv 2:16; Ezk 43:24
[d]**10:6** Other mss omit *God*   [e]**10:6** Gn 1:27; 5:2   [f]**10:7** Other mss omit bracketed text   [g]**10:7-8** Gn 2:24
[h]**10:15** Or *not receive*   [i]**10:19** Ex 20:12-16; Dt 5:16-20

heaven. Then come,[a] follow Me." 22 But he was stunned[b] at this demand, and he went away grieving, because he had many possessions.

Possessions and the Kingdom

23 Jesus looked around and said to His disciples, "How hard it is for those who have wealth to enter the kingdom of God!" 24 But the disciples were astonished at His words. Again Jesus said to them, "Children, how hard it is[c] to enter the kingdom of God! 25 It is easier for a camel to go through the eye of a needle than for a rich person to enter the kingdom of God."

26 So they were even more astonished, saying to one another, "Then who can be saved?"

27 Looking at them, Jesus said, "With men it is impossible, but not with God, because all things are possible with God."

Peter: We've Left Everything

28 Peter began to tell Him, "Look, we have left everything and followed You."

29 "I assure you," Jesus said, "there is no one who has left house, brothers or sisters, mother or father,[d] children, or fields because of Me and the gospel, 30 who will not receive 100 times more, now at this time—houses, brothers and sisters, mothers and children, and fields, with persecutions—and eternal life in the age to come. 31 But many who are first will be last, and the last first."

Jesus' Third Prediction of His Death

32 They were on the road, going up to Jerusalem, and Jesus was walking ahead of them. They were astonished, but those who followed Him were afraid. Taking the Twelve aside again, He began to tell them the things that would happen to Him.

33 "Listen! We are going up to Jerusalem. The •Son of Man will be handed over to the •chief priests and the •scribes, and they will condemn Him to death. Then they will hand Him over to the Gentiles, 34 and they will mock Him, spit on Him, flog[e] Him, and kill Him, and He will rise after three days."

James and John:
Right and Left Hand

35 Then James and John, the sons of Zebedee, approached Him and said, "Teacher, we want You to do something for us if we ask You."

36 "What do you want Me to do for you?" He asked them.

37 They answered Him, "Allow us to sit at Your right and at Your left in Your glory."

38 But Jesus said to them, "You don't know what you're asking. Are you able to drink the cup I drink or to be baptized with the baptism I am baptized with?"

39 "We are able," they told Him.

Jesus said to them, "You will drink the cup I drink, and you will be baptized with the baptism I am baptized with. 40 But to sit at My right or left is not Mine to give; instead, it is for those it has been prepared for." 41 When the [other] 10 [disciples] heard this, they began to be indignant with James and John.

42 Jesus called them over and said to them, "You know that those who are regarded as rulers of the Gentiles dominate them, and their men of high positions exercise power over them. 43 But it must not be like that among you. On the contrary, whoever wants to become great among you must be your

---

a**10:21** Other mss add *taking up the cross, and*   b**10:22** Or *he became gloomy*   c**10:24** Other mss add *for those trusting in wealth*   d**10:29** Other mss add *or wife*   e**10:34** Or *scourge*

servant, [44] and whoever wants to be first among you must be a •slave to all. [45] For even the Son of Man did not come to be served, but to serve, and to give His life—a ransom for many."[a]

Blind Bartimaeus Healed

[46] They came to Jericho. And as He was leaving Jericho with His disciples and a large crowd, Bartimaeus (the son of Timaeus), a blind beggar, was sitting by the road. [47] When he heard that it was Jesus the •Nazarene, he began to cry out, "Son of David, Jesus, have mercy on me!" [48] Many people told him to keep quiet, but he was crying out all the more, "Have mercy on me, Son of David!"

[49] Jesus stopped and said, "Call him."

So they called the blind man and said to him, "Have courage! Get up; He's calling for you." [50] He threw off his coat, jumped up, and came to Jesus.

[51] Then Jesus answered him, "What do you want Me to do for you?"

"Rabbouni," [b] the blind man told Him, "I want to see!"

[52] "Go your way," Jesus told him. "Your faith has healed you." Immediately he could see and began to follow Him on the road.

The Triumphal Entry

11 When they approached Jerusalem, at Bethphage and Bethany near the •Mount of Olives, He sent two of His disciples [2] and told them, "Go into the village ahead of you. As soon as you enter it, you will find a young donkey tied there, on which no one has ever sat. Untie it and bring it here. [3] If anyone says to you, 'Why are you doing this?' say, 'The Lord needs it and will send it back here right away.'"

[4] So they went and found a young donkey outside in the street, tied by a door. They untied it, [5] and some of those standing there said to them, "What are you doing, untying the donkey?" [6] They answered them just as Jesus had said, so they let them go. [7] Then they brought the donkey to Jesus and threw their robes on it, and He sat on it.

[8] Many people spread their robes on the road, and others spread leafy branches cut from the fields.[c] [9] Then those who went ahead and those who followed kept shouting:

•Hosanna!
Blessed is He who comes
in the name of the Lord![d]
[10] Blessed is the coming kingdom of our father David!
Hosanna **in the highest heaven!**

[11] And He went into Jerusalem and into the •temple complex. After looking around at everything, since it was already late, He went out to Bethany with the Twelve.

Jesus Curses Barren Fig Tree

[12] The next day when they came out from Bethany, He was hungry. [13] After seeing in the distance a fig tree with leaves, He went to find out if there was anything on it. When He came to it, He found nothing but leaves, because it was not the season for figs. [14] He said to it, "May no one ever eat fruit from you again!" And His disciples heard it.

Jesus Cleanses Temple Complex

[15] They came to Jerusalem, and He went into the temple complex and began to throw out those buying and selling in the temple. He overturned the money changers' tables and the chairs of those

---

[a]**10:45** Or *in the place of many*; Is 53:10-12   [b]**10:51** Hb for *my teacher*; Jn 20:16   [c]**11:8** Other mss read *others were cutting leafy branches from the trees and spreading them on the road*   [d]**11:9** Ps 118:26

selling doves, ¹⁶ and would not permit anyone to carry goods through the temple complex.

¹⁷ Then He began to teach them: "Is it not written, **My house will be called a house of prayer for all nations**?ᵃ But you have made it **a den of thieves!**"ᵇ ¹⁸ Then the •chief priests and the •scribes heard it and started looking for a way to destroy Him. For they were afraid of Him, because the whole crowd was astonished by His teaching.

¹⁹ And whenever evening came, they would go out of the city.

Barren Fig Tree Is Withered

²⁰ Early in the morning, as they were passing by, they saw the fig tree withered from the roots up. ²¹ Then Peter remembered and said to Him, "•Rabbi, look! The fig tree that You cursed is withered."

²² Jesus replied to them, "Have faith in God. ²³ •I assure you: If anyone says to this mountain, 'Be lifted up and thrown into the sea,' and does not doubt in his heart, but believes that what he says will happen, it will be done for him. ²⁴ Therefore, I tell you, all the things you pray and ask for—believe that you have receivedᶜ them, and you will have them. ²⁵ And whenever you stand praying, if you have anything against anyone, forgive him, so that your Father in heaven will also forgive you your wrongdoing.ᵈ [²⁶ But if you don't forgive, neither will your Father in heaven forgive your wrongdoing."]ᵉ

Religious Leaders Challenge Messiah's Authority

²⁷ They came again to Jerusalem. As He was walking in the temple complex, the chief priests, the scribes, and the elders came and asked Him, ²⁸ "By what authority are You doing these things? Who gave You this authority to do these things?"

Jesus' Astute Answer

²⁹ Jesus said to them, "I will ask you one question; then answer Me, and I will tell you by what authority I am doing these things. ³⁰ Was John's baptism from heaven or from men? Answer Me." ³¹ They began to argue among themselves: "If we say, 'From heaven,' He will say, 'Then why didn't you believe him?' ³² But if we say, 'From men' "— they were afraid of the crowd, because everyone thought that John was a genuine prophet. ³³ So they answered Jesus, "We don't know."

And Jesus said to them, "Neither will I tell you by what authority I do these things."

Parable of Vineyard Owner

12 Then He began to speak to them in parables: "A man planted a vineyard, put a fence around it, dug out a pit for a winepress, and built a watchtower. Then he leased it to tenant farmers and went away. ² At harvest time he sent a •slave to the farmers to collect some of the fruit of the vineyard from the farmers. ³ But they took him, beat him, and sent him away empty-handed. ⁴ Again he sent another slave to them, and theyᶠ hit him on the head and treated him shamefully.ᵍ ⁵ Then he sent another, and they killed that one. ⌊He⌋ also ⌊sent⌋ many others; they beat some and they killed some.

⁶ "He still had one to send, a beloved son. Finally he sent him to them, saying, 'They will respect my son.'

ᵃ**11:17** Is 56:7   ᵇ**11:17** Jr 7:11   ᶜ**11:24** Other mss read *you receive*; other mss read *you will receive*   ᵈ**11:25** These are the only uses of this word in Mk. It means "the violation of the Law" or "stepping over a boundary" or "departing from the path" or "trespass."   ᵉ**11:26** Other mss omit bracketed text   ᶠ**12:4** Other mss add *threw stones and*   ᵍ**12:4** Other mss add *and sent him off*

7 "But those tenant farmers said among themselves, 'This is the heir. Come, let's kill him, and the inheritance will be ours!' 8 So they seized him, killed him, and threw him out of the vineyard.

9 "Therefore, what will the owner[a] of the vineyard do? He will come and destroy the farmers and give the vineyard to others. 10 Haven't you read this Scripture:

> The stone that the builders
>   rejected
>   has become the cornerstone.[b]
> 11 This came from the Lord
>   and is wonderful in our eyes?"[c]

12 Because they knew He had said this parable against them, they were looking for a way to arrest Him, but they were afraid of the crowd. So they left Him and went away.

God and Caesar

13 Then they sent some of the •Pharisees and the •Herodians to Him to trap Him by what He said.[d] 14 When they came, they said to Him, "Teacher, we know You are truthful and defer to no one, for You don't show partiality[e] but teach truthfully the way of God. Is it lawful to pay taxes to Caesar or not? 15 Should we pay, or should we not pay?"

But knowing their hypocrisy, He said to them, "Why are you testing Me? Bring Me a •denarius to look at." 16 So they brought one. "Whose image and inscription is this?" He asked them.

"Caesar's," they said.

17 Then Jesus told them, "Give back to Caesar the things that are Caesar's, and to God the things that are God's." And they were amazed at Him.

Sadducees' Challenge on Resurrection

18 Some •Sadducees, who say there is no resurrection, came to Him and questioned Him: 19 "Teacher, Moses wrote for us that **if a man's brother dies, leaves his wife behind, and leaves no child, his brother should take the wife and produce •offspring for his brother.**[f] 20 There were seven brothers. The first took a wife, and dying, left no offspring. 21 The second also took her, and he died, leaving no offspring. And the third likewise. 22 The seven also[g] left no offspring. Last of all, the woman died too. 23 In the resurrection, when they rise,[h] whose wife will she be, since the seven had married her?"[i]

Jesus' Comeback

24 Jesus told them, "Are you not deceived because you don't know the Scriptures or the power of God? 25 For when they rise from the dead, they neither marry nor are given in marriage but are like angels in heaven. 26 Now concerning the dead being raised—haven't you read in the book of Moses, in the passage about the burning bush, how God spoke to him: **I am the God of Abraham and the God of Isaac and the God of Jacob?**[j] 27 He is not God of the dead but of the living. You are badly deceived."

Two Main Commandments

28 One of the •scribes approached. When he heard them debating and saw that Jesus answered them well, he asked Him, "Which commandment is the most important of all?"[k]

---

[a]**12:9** Or *lord* [b]**12:10** Lit *the head of the corner* [c]**12:10-11** Ps 118:22-23 [d]**12:13** Lit *trap Him in (a) word*
[e]**12:14** Lit *don't look on the face of men*; that is, on the outward appearance [f]**12:19** Gn 38:8; Dt 25:5 [g]**12:22** Other mss add *had taken her and* [h]**12:23** Other mss omit *when they rise* [i]**12:23** Lit *the seven had her as a wife*
[j]**12:26** Ex 3:6,15-16 [k]**12:28** Lit *Which commandment is first of all?*

29 "This is the most important,"ª Jesus answered:

Listen, Israel! The Lord our God, the Lord is One.ᵇ 30 Love the Lord your God with all your heart, with all your soul, with all your mind, and with all your strength.ᶜ ᵈ

31 "The second is: Love your neighbor as yourself.ᵉ There is no other commandment greater than these."

The Perceptive Scribe

32 Then the scribe said to Him, "You are right, Teacher! You have correctly said that He is One, and there is no one else except Him. 33 And to love Him with all your heart, with all your understanding,ᶠ and with all your strength, and to love your neighbor as yourself, is far more ⌊important⌋ than all the burnt offerings and sacrifices."

34 When Jesus saw that he answered intelligently, He said to him, "You are not far from the kingdom of God." And no one dared to question Him any longer.

Jesus' Question about Messiah

35 So Jesus asked this question as He taught in the •temple complex, "How can the scribes say that the •Messiah is the Son of David? 36 David himself says by the Holy Spirit:

The Lord declared to my Lord,
'Sit at My right hand
until I put Your enemies
under Your feet.'ᵍ

37 David himself calls Him 'Lord'; how then can the Messiah be his Son?" And the large crowd was listening to Him with delight.

Jesus Warns against the Scribes

38 He also said in His teaching, "Beware of the scribes, who want to go around in long robes, and who want greetings in the marketplaces, 39 the front seats in the •synagogues, and the places of honor at banquets. 40 They devour widows' houses and say long prayers just for show. These will receive harsher punishment."

The Widow's Gift

41 Sitting across from the temple treasury, He watched how the crowd dropped money into the treasury. Many rich people were putting in large sums. 42 And a poor widow came and dropped in two tiny coins worth very little.ʰ 43 Summoning His disciples, He said to them, "•I assure you: This poor widow has put in more than all those giving to the temple treasury. 44 For they all gave out of their surplus, but she out of her poverty has put in everything she possessed—all she had to live on."

Jesus Predicts Destruction of Temple

13 As He was going out of the •temple complex, one of His disciples said to Him, "Teacher, look! What massive stones! What impressive buildings!"

2 Jesus said to him, "Do you see these great buildings? Not one stone will be left here on another that will not be thrown down!"

Jesus Lists Signs of End of Age

3 While He was sitting on the •Mount of Olives across from the temple complex, Peter, James, John, and Andrew asked Him privately, 4 "Tell us, when

ª12:29 Other mss add of all the commandments   ᵇ12:29 Or The Lord our God is one Lord.   ᶜ12:30 Dt 6:4-5; Jos 22:5   ᵈ12:30 Other mss add This is the first commandment.   ᵉ12:31 Lv 19:18   ᶠ12:33 Other mss add with all your soul   ᵍ12:36 Ps 110:1   ʰ12:42 Lit dropped in two lepta, which is a quadrans; the lepton was the smallest and least valuable Gk coin in use. The quadrans, 1⁄64 of a daily wage, was the smallest Roman coin.

will these things happen? And what will be the sign when all these things are about to take place?"

⁵ Then Jesus began by telling them: "Watch out that no one deceives you. ⁶ Many will come in My name, saying, 'I am He,' and they will deceive many. ⁷ When you hear of wars and rumors of wars, don't be alarmed; these things must take place, but the end is not yet. ⁸ For nation will rise up against nation, and kingdom against kingdom. There will be earthquakes in various places, and famines.ᵃ These are the beginning of birth pains.

Jesus Predicts Persecutions

⁹ "But you, be on your guard! They will hand you over to sanhedrins,ᵇ and you will be flogged in the •synagogues. You will stand before governors and kings because of Me, as a witness to them. ¹⁰ And the good newsᶜ must first be proclaimed to all nations. ¹¹ So when they arrest you and hand you over, don't worry beforehand what you will say. On the contrary, whatever is given to you in that hour—say it. For it isn't you speaking, but the Holy Spirit. ¹² Then brother will betray brother to death, and a father his child. Children will rise up against parents and put them to death. ¹³ And you will be hated by everyone because of My name. But the one who endures to the end will be delivered.ᵈ

Great Tribulation

¹⁴ "When you see the **abomination that causes desolation**ᵉ standing where it should not" (let the reader understand),ᶠ "then those in Judea must flee to the mountains! ¹⁵ A man on the housetop must not come down or go in to get anything out of his house. ¹⁶ And a man in the field must not go back to get his clothes. ¹⁷ Woe to pregnant women and nursing mothers in those days! ¹⁸ Pray itᵍ won't happen in winter. ¹⁹ For those will be days of tribulation, the kind that hasn't been from the beginning of the world,ʰ which God created, until now and never will be again! ²⁰ Unless the Lord limited those days, no one would survive.ⁱ But He limited those days because of the elect, whom He chose.

²¹ "Then if anyone tells you, 'Look, here is the •Messiah! Look—there!' do not believe it! ²² For false messiahsʲ and false prophets will rise up and will perform signs and wonders to lead astray, if possible, the elect. ²³ And you must watch! I have told you everything in advance.

Coming of Son of Man

²⁴ "But in those days, after that tribulation:

> The sun will be darkened,
> and the moon will not shed
>   its light;
> ²⁵ the stars will be falling
>   from the sky,
> and the celestial powers
>   will be shaken.

²⁶ Then they will see the •Son of Man coming in clouds with great power and glory. ²⁷ He will send out the angels and gather His elect from the four winds, from the end of the earth to the end of the sky.

Parable of Fig Tree

²⁸ "Learn this parable from the fig tree: As soon as its branch becomes tender and sprouts leaves, you know that

---

ᵃ**13:8** Other mss add *and disturbances*   ᵇ**13:9** Local Jewish courts or local councils   ᶜ**13:10** Or *the gospel*
ᵈ**13:13** Or *saved*   ᵉ**13:14** Dn 9:27   ᶠ**13:14** These are, most likely, Mark's words to his readers.   ᵍ**13:18** Other mss read *pray that your escape*   ʰ**13:19** Lit *creation*   ⁱ**13:20** Lit *days, all flesh would not survive*   ʲ**13:22** Or *false christs*

summer is near. ²⁹ In the same way, when you see these things happening, know^a that He^b is near—at the door! ³⁰ •I assure you: This generation will certainly not pass away until all these things take place. ³¹ Heaven and earth will pass away, but My words will never pass away.

No One Knows the Day or Hour

³² "Now <u>concerning that day or hour no one knows—neither the angels in heaven nor the Son—except the Father.</u> ³³ Watch! Be alert!^c For you don't know when the time is ⌐coming⌐. ³⁴ It is like a man on a journey, who left his house, gave authority to his •slaves, gave each one his work, and commanded the doorkeeper to be alert. ³⁵ Therefore be alert, since you don't know when the master of the house is coming—whether in the evening or at midnight or at the crowing of the rooster or early in the morning. ³⁶ Otherwise, he might come suddenly and find you sleeping. ³⁷ And what I say to you, I say to everyone: Be alert!"

Again, a Plot to Kill Jesus

14 After two days it was the •Passover and the Festival of •Unleavened Bread. The •chief priests and the •scribes were looking for a treacherous way to arrest and kill Him. ² "Not during the festival," they said, "or there may be rioting among the people."

Woman Anoints Jesus at Bethany

³ While He was in Bethany at the house of Simon who had a serious skin disease, as He was reclining at the table, a woman came with an alabaster jar of pure and expensive fragrant oil of nard. She broke the jar and poured it on His head. ⁴ But some were expressing indignation to one another: "Why has this fragrant oil been wasted? ⁵ For this oil might have been sold for more than 300 •denarii and given to the poor." And they began to scold her.

Jesus Defends Woman

⁶ Then Jesus said, "Leave her alone. Why are you bothering her? She has done a noble thing for Me. ⁷ You always have the poor with you, and you can do good for them whenever you want, but you do not always have Me. ⁸ She has done what she could; she has anointed My body in advance for burial. ⁹ •I assure you: Wherever the gospel is proclaimed in the whole world, what this woman has done will also be told in memory of her."

Judas Arranges Betrayal

¹⁰ Then Judas Iscariot, one of the Twelve, went to the chief priests to hand Him over to them. ¹¹ And when they heard this, they were glad and promised to give him silver.^d So he started looking for a good opportunity to betray Him.

Preparation for Last Passover

¹² On the first day of Unleavened Bread, when they sacrifice the Passover lamb, His disciples asked Him, "Where do You want us to go and prepare the Passover so You may eat it?"

¹³ So He sent two of His disciples and told them, "Go into the city, and a man carrying a water jug will meet you. Follow him. ¹⁴ Wherever he enters, tell the owner of the house, 'The Teacher says, "Where is the guest room for Me to eat the Passover with My disciples?"' ¹⁵ He will show you a large room upstairs, furnished and ready. Make the preparations

for us there." ¹⁶ So the disciples went out, entered the city, and found it just as He had told them, and they prepared the Passover.

Jesus Announces Betrayal

¹⁷ When evening came, He arrived with the Twelve. ¹⁸ While they were reclining and eating, Jesus said, "I assure you: One of you will betray Me—one who is eating with Me!"

¹⁹ They began to be distressed and to say to Him one by one, "Surely not I?" ²⁰ He said to them, "ⱼIt isⱼ one of the Twelve—the one who is dipping ⱼbreadⱼ with Me in the bowl. ²¹ For the •Son of Man will go just as it is written about Him, but woe to that man by whom the Son of Man is betrayed! It would have been better for that man if he had not been born."

First Lord's Supper

²² As they were eating, He took bread, blessed and broke it, gave it to them, and said, "Take ⱼitⱼ;ᵃ this is My body."

²³ Then He took a cup, and after giving thanks, He gave it to them, and so they all drank from it. ²⁴ He said to them, "This is My blood ⱼthat establishesⱼ the covenant;ᵇ it is shed for many. ²⁵ I assure you: I will no longer drink of the fruit of the vine until that day when I drink it in a new wayᶜ in the kingdom of God." ²⁶ After singing psalms,ᵈ they went out to the •Mount of Olives.

Jesus Predicts Peter's Denial

²⁷ Then Jesus said to them, "All of you will run away,ᵉ ᶠ because it is written:

I will strike the shepherd,
and the sheep will be scattered.ᵍ

²⁸ But after I have been resurrected, I will go ahead of you to Galilee."

²⁹ Peter told Him, "Even if everyone runs away, I will certainly not!"

³⁰ "I assure you," Jesus said to him, "today, this very night, before the rooster crows twice, you will deny Me three times!"

³¹ But he kept insisting, "If I have to die with You, I will never deny You!" And they all said the same thing.

Prayer in Garden of Gethsemane

³² Then they came to a place named Gethsemane, and He told His disciples, "Sit here while I pray." ³³ He took Peter, James, and John with Him, and He began to be deeply distressed and horrified. ³⁴ Then He said to them, "My soul is swallowed up in sorrowʰ—to the point of death. Remain here and stay awake." ³⁵ Then He went a little farther, fell to the ground, and began to pray that if it were possible, the hour might pass from Him. ³⁶ And He said, "•Abba, Father! All things are possible for You. Take this cup away from Me. Nevertheless, not what I will, but what You will."

³⁷ Then He came and found them sleeping. "Simon, are you sleeping?" He asked Peter. "Couldn't you stay awake one hour? ³⁸ Stay awake and pray so that you won't enter into temptation. The spirit is willing, but the flesh is weak."

³⁹ Once again He went away and prayed, saying the same thing. ⁴⁰ And He came again and found them sleeping, because they could not keep their eyes open.ⁱ They did not know what to say to Him. ⁴¹ Then He came a third time and said to them, "Are you still sleeping and resting? Enough! The time has come.

ᵃ14:22 Other mss add *eat;* ᵇ14:24 Other mss read *the new covenant* ᶜ14:25 Or *drink new wine*; lit *drink it new* ᵈ14:26 Pss 113–118 were sung during and after the Passover meal. ᵉ14:27 Other mss add *because of Me this night* ᶠ14:27 Or •*stumble* ᵍ14:27 Zch 13:7 ʰ14:34 Or *I am deeply grieved* ⁱ14:40 Lit *because their eyes were weighed down*

Look, the Son of Man is being betrayed into the hands of sinners. ⁴² Get up; let's go! See—My betrayer is near."

The Judas Kiss

⁴³ While He was still speaking, Judas, one of the Twelve, suddenly arrived. With him was a mob, with swords and clubs, from the chief priests, the scribes, and the elders. ⁴⁴ His betrayer had given them a signal. "The One I kiss," he said, "He's the One; arrest Him and take Him away under guard." ⁴⁵ So when he came, he went right up to Him and said, "•Rabbi!"—and kissed Him. ⁴⁶ Then they took hold of Him and arrested Him. ⁴⁷ And one of those who stood by drew his sword, struck the high priest's •slave, and cut off his ear.

⁴⁸ But Jesus said to them, "Have you come out with swords and clubs, as though I were a criminal,ᵃ to capture Me? ⁴⁹ Every day I was among you, teaching in the •temple complex, and you didn't arrest Me. But the Scriptures must be fulfilled." ⁵⁰ Then they all deserted Him and ran away.

A Young Man Flees

⁵¹ Now a certain young man,ᵇ having a linen cloth wrapped around his naked body, was following Him. They caught hold of him, ⁵² but he left the linen cloth behind and ran away naked.

Jesus Faces Sanhedrin

⁵³ They led Jesus away to the high priest, and all the chief priests, the elders, and the scribes convened. ⁵⁴ Peter followed Him at a distance, right into the high priest's courtyard. He was sitting with the temple police,ᶜ warming himself by the fire.ᵈ

⁵⁵ The chief priests and the whole •Sanhedrin were looking for testimony against Jesus to put Him to death, but they could find none. ⁵⁶ For many were giving false testimony against Him, but the testimonies did not agree. ⁵⁷ Some stood up and were giving false testimony against Him, stating, ⁵⁸ "We heard Him say, 'I will demolish this sanctuary made by ⌊human⌋ hands, and in three days I will build another not made by hands.'" ⁵⁹ Yet their testimony did not agree even on this.

⁶⁰ Then the high priest stood up before them all and questioned Jesus, "Don't You have an answer to what these men are testifying against You?" ⁶¹ But He kept silent and did not answer anything. Again the high priest questioned Him, "Are You the •Messiah, the Son of the Blessed One?"

Jesus Confesses He Is Messiah

⁶² "I am," said Jesus, "and all of youᵉ will see **the Son of Man seated at the right hand** of the Power and **coming with the clouds of heaven.**"ᶠ

High Priest Charges Blasphemy

⁶³ Then the high priest tore his robes and said, "Why do we still need witnesses? ⁶⁴ You have heard the blasphemy! What is your decision?"ᵍ

And they all condemned Him to be deserving of death. ⁶⁵ Then some began to spit on Him, to blindfold Him, and to beat Him, saying, "Prophesy!" Even the temple police took Him and slapped Him.

Peter Denies His Lord

⁶⁶ While Peter was in the courtyard below, one of the high priest's servants

---

ᵃ**14:48** Lit *as against a criminal* ᵇ**14:51** Perhaps John Mark who later wrote this Gospel ᶜ**14:54** Or *the officers*; lit *the servants* ᵈ**14:54** Lit *light* ᵉ**14:62** Lit *and you* (pl in Gk) ᶠ**14:62** Ps 110:1; Dn 7:13 ᵍ**14:64** Lit *How does it appear to you?*

came. [67] When she saw Peter warming himself, she looked at him and said, "You also were with that •Nazarene, Jesus."

[68] But he denied it: "I don't know or understand what you're talking about!" Then he went out to the entryway, and a rooster crowed.[a]

[69] When the servant saw him again she began to tell those standing nearby, "This man is one of them!"

[70] But again he denied it. After a little while those standing there said to Peter again, "You certainly are one of them, since you're also a Galilean!"[b]

[71] Then he started to curse[c] and to swear with an oath, "I don't know this man you're talking about!"

[72] Immediately a rooster crowed a second time, and Peter remembered when Jesus had spoken the word to him, "Before the rooster crows twice, you will deny Me three times." When he thought about it, he began to weep.[d]

Jesus Faces Pilate

15 As soon as it was morning, the •chief priests had a meeting with the elders, •scribes, and the whole •Sanhedrin. After tying Jesus up, they led Him away and handed Him over to •Pilate.

[2] So Pilate asked Him, "Are You the King of the Jews?"

He answered him, "You have said it."[e]

[3] And the chief priests began to accuse Him of many things. [4] Then Pilate questioned Him again, "Are You not answering anything? Look how many things they are accusing You of!" [5] But Jesus still did not answer anything, so Pilate was amazed.

Pilate: Jesus or Barabbas?

[6] At the festival it was Pilate's custom to release for the people a prisoner they requested. [7] There was one named Barabbas, who was in prison with rebels who had committed murder during the rebellion. [8] The crowd came up and began to ask ⌊Pilate⌋ to do for them as was his custom. [9] So Pilate answered them, "Do you want me to release the King of the Jews for you?" [10] For he knew it was because of envy that the chief priests had handed Him over. [11] But the chief priests stirred up the crowd so that he would release Barabbas to them instead.

[12] Pilate asked them again, "Then what do you want me to do with the One you call the King of the Jews?"

[13] Again they shouted, "Crucify Him!"

[14] Then Pilate said to them, "Why? What has He done wrong?"

But they shouted, "Crucify Him!" all the more.

[15] Then, willing to gratify the crowd, Pilate released Barabbas to them. And after having Jesus flogged,[f] he handed Him over to be crucified.

Jesus Mocked by Military

[16] Then the soldiers led Him away into the courtyard (that is, •headquarters) and called the whole •company together. [17] They dressed Him in a purple robe, twisted together a crown of thorns, and put it on Him. [18] And they began to salute Him, "Hail, King of the Jews!" [19] They kept hitting Him on the head with a reed and spitting on Him. Getting down on their knees, they were paying Him homage. [20] When they had mocked Him, they stripped Him of the purple robe, put His clothes on Him, and led Him out to crucify Him.

---

[a]**14:68** Other mss omit *and a rooster crowed*   [b]**14:70** Other mss add *and your speech shows it*   [c]**14:71** To call down curses on himself if what he said weren't true   [d]**14:72** Or *he burst into tears*, or *he broke down*   [e]**15:2** Or *That is true*, an affirmative oath; Mt 26:64; 27:11   [f]**15:15** Roman flogging was done with a whip made of leather strips embedded with pieces of bone or metal that brutally tore the flesh.

Jesus Crucified between Two Criminals

21 They forced a man coming in from the country, who was passing by, to carry Jesus' cross. He was Simon, a Cyrenian, the father of Alexander and Rufus. 22 And they brought Jesus to the place called Golgotha (which means Skull Place). 23 They tried to give Him wine mixed with myrrh, but He did not take it. 24 Then they crucified Him and divided His clothes, casting lots for them to decide what each would get. 25 Now it was nine in the morning[a] when they crucified Him. 26 The inscription of the charge written against Him was

---

THE KING OF THE JEWS

---

27 They crucified two criminals[b] with Him, one on His right and one on His left. [28 So the Scripture was fulfilled that says: **And He was counted among outlaws.**][c][d] 29 Those who passed by were yelling insults at[e] Him, shaking their heads, and saying, "Ha! The One who would demolish the sanctuary and build it in three days, 30 save Yourself by coming down from the cross!" 31 In the same way, the chief priests with the scribes were mocking Him to one another and saying, "He saved others; He cannot save Himself! 32 Let the •Messiah, the King of Israel, come down now from the cross, so that we may see and believe." Even those who were crucified with Him were taunting Him.

Darkness at Noon

33 When it was noon,[f] darkness came over the whole land[g] until three in the afternoon.[h] 34 And at three[h] Jesus cried out with a loud voice, *"Eloi, Eloi, lemá[i] sabachtháni?"* which is translated, "My God, My God, why have You forsaken Me?"[j] 35 When some of those standing there heard this, they said, "Look, He's calling for Elijah!" 36 Someone ran and filled a sponge with sour wine, fixed it on a reed, offered Him a drink, and said, "Let's see if Elijah comes to take Him down!"

Death of Jesus

37 But Jesus let out a loud cry and breathed His last. 38 Then the curtain of the sanctuary[k] was split in two from top to bottom. 39 When the •centurion, who was standing opposite Him, saw the way He[l] breathed His last, he said, "This man really was God's Son!"[m]

Three Woman Onlookers

40 There were also women looking on from a distance. Among them were •Mary Magdalene, Mary the mother of James the younger and of Joses, and Salome. 41 When He was in Galilee, they would follow Him and help Him. Many other women had come up with Him to Jerusalem.

Burial of Jesus

42 When it was already evening, because it was preparation day (that is, the day before the Sabbath), 43 Joseph of Arimathea, a prominent member of the Sanhedrin who was himself looking forward to the kingdom of God, came and boldly went in to Pilate and asked for Jesus' body. 44 Pilate was surprised that He was already dead. Summoning the centurion,

---

a**15:25** Lit *was the third hour* b**15:27** Or *revolutionaries* c**15:28** Other mss omit bracketed text d**15:28** Is 53:12 e**15:29** Lit *passed by blasphemed* f**15:33** Lit *the sixth hour* g**15:33** Or *whole earth* h**15:33,34** Lit *the ninth hour* i**15:34** Other mss read *lama*; other mss read *lima* j**15:34** Ps 22:1 k**15:38** A heavy curtain separated the inner room of the temple from the outer. l**15:39** Other mss read *saw that He cried out like this and* m**15:39** Or *the Son of God;* Mk 1:1

he asked him whether He had already died. ⁴⁵ When he found out from the centurion, he gave the corpse to Joseph. ⁴⁶ After he bought some fine linen, he took Him down and wrapped Him in the linen. Then he placed Him in a tomb cut out of the rock, and rolled a stone against the entrance to the tomb. ⁴⁷ Now Mary Magdalene and Mary the mother of Joses were watching where He was placed.

Resurrection Morning

16 When the Sabbath was over, •Mary Magdalene, Mary the mother of James, and Salome bought spices, so they could go and anoint Him. ² Very early in the morning, on the first day of the week, they went to the tomb at sunrise. ³ They were saying to one another, "Who will roll away the stone from the entrance to the tomb for us?" ⁴ Looking up, they observed that the stone—which was very large—had been rolled away. ⁵ When they entered the tomb, they saw a young manᵃ dressed in a long white robe sitting on the right side; they were amazed and alarmed.ᵇ

⁶ "Don't be alarmed," he told them. "You are looking for Jesus the •Nazarene, who was crucified. He has been resurrected! He is not here! See the place where they put Him. ⁷ But go, tell His disciples and Peter, 'He is going ahead of you to Galilee; you will see Him there just as He told you.'"

⁸ So they went out and started running from the tomb, because trembling and astonishment overwhelmed them. And they said nothing to anyone, since they were afraid.

Appearances of the Risen Lord

[⁹ Early on the first day of the week, after He had risen, He appeared first to Mary Magdalene, out of whom He had driven seven demons. ¹⁰ She went and reported to those who had been with Him, as they were mourning and weeping. ¹¹ Yet, when they heard that He was alive and had been seen by her, they did not believe it. ¹² Then after this, He appeared in a different form to two of them walking on their way into the country. ¹³ And they went and reported it to the rest, who did not believe them either.

Great Commission

¹⁴ Later, He appeared to the Eleven themselves as they were reclining at the table. He rebuked their unbelief and hardness of heart, because they did not believe those who saw Him after He had been resurrected. ¹⁵ Then He said to them, "Go into all the world and preach the gospel to the whole creation. ¹⁶ Whoever believes and is baptized will be saved, but whoever does not believe will be condemned. ¹⁷ And these signs will accompany those who believe: In My name they will drive out demons; they will speak in new languages; ¹⁸ they will pick up snakes;ᶜ if they should drink anything deadly, it will never harm them; they will lay hands on the sick, and they will get well."

The Ascension

¹⁹ Then after speaking to them, the Lord Jesus was taken up into heaven and sat down at the right hand of God. ²⁰ And they went out and preached everywhere, the Lord working with them and confirming the word by the accompanying signs.]ᵈ

ᵃ**16:5** In Mt 28:2, the young man = an angel   ᵇ**16:5** *Amazed and alarmed* translate the idea of one Gk word.
ᶜ**16:18** Other mss add *with their hands*   ᵈ**16:9-20** Other mss omit bracketed text

LUKE

Luke's Methodology and Purpose

1 Many have undertaken to compile a narrative about the events that have been fulfilled[a] among us, [2] just as the original eyewitnesses and servants of the word handed them down to us. [3] It also seemed good to me, since I have carefully investigated everything from the very first, to write to you in orderly sequence, most honorable Theophilus, [4] so that you may know the certainty of the things about which you have been instructed.[b]

Zechariah and Elizabeth

[5] In the days of King •Herod of Judea, there was a priest of Abijah's division[c] named Zechariah. His wife was from the daughters of Aaron, and her name was Elizabeth. [6] Both were righteous in God's sight, living without blame according to all the commandments and requirements of the Lord. [7] But they had no children[d] because Elizabeth could not conceive,[e] and both of them were well along in years.[f]

Zechariah Burns Incense

[8] When his division was on duty and he was serving as priest before God, [9] it happened that he was chosen by lot, according to the custom of the priesthood, to enter the sanctuary of the Lord and burn incense. [10] At the hour of incense the whole assembly of the people was praying outside.

Gabriel Predicts Birth of John the Baptist

[11] An angel of the Lord appeared to him, standing to the right of the altar of incense. [12] When Zechariah saw him, he was startled and overcome with fear.[g] [13] But the angel said to him:

Do not be afraid, Zechariah,
because your prayer
has been heard.
Your wife Elizabeth will bear you
a son,
and you will name him John.
[14] There will be joy and delight
for you,
and many will rejoice at his birth.
[15] For he will be great in the sight
of the Lord
and will never drink wine or beer.
He will be filled
with the Holy Spirit
while still in his mother's womb.
[16] He will turn many
of the sons of Israel
to the Lord their God.
[17] And he will go before Him
in the spirit and power of Elijah,
to turn the hearts of fathers
to their children,
and the disobedient
to the understanding
of the righteous,
to make ready for the Lord
a prepared people.

Zechariah Questions Gabriel

[18] "How can I know this?" Zechariah asked the angel. "For I am an old man, and my wife is well along in years."[h]

Gabriel Rebukes

19 The angel answered him, "I am Gabriel, who stands in the presence of God, and I was sent to speak to you and tell you this good news. 20 Now listen! You will become silent and unable to speak until the day these things take place, because you did not believe my words, which will be fulfilled in their proper time."

21 Meanwhile, the people were waiting for Zechariah, amazed that he stayed so long in the sanctuary. 22 When he did come out, he could not speak to them. Then they realized that he had seen a vision in the sanctuary. He kept making signs to them and remained speechless. 23 When the days of his ministry were completed, he went back home.

John Conceived

24 After these days his wife Elizabeth conceived and kept herself in seclusion for five months. She said, 25 "The Lord has done this for me. He has looked with favor in these days to take away my disgrace among the people."

Gabriel Appears to Mary

26 In the sixth month, the angel Gabriel was sent by God to a town in Galilee called Nazareth, 27 to a virgin •engaged to a man named Joseph, of the house of David. The virgin's name was Mary. 28 And ⌊the angel⌋ came to her and said, "Rejoice, favored woman! The Lord is with you."a 29 But she was deeply troubled by this statement, wondering what kind of greeting this could be.

Gabriel Announces Jesus' Birth

30 Then the angel told her:

Do not be afraid, Mary,
   for you have found favor with God.

31 Now listen:
You will conceive and give birth to
   a son,
   and you will call His name JESUS.
32 He will be great
   and will be called
   the Son of the Most High,
   and the Lord God will give Him
   the throne of His father David.
33 He will reign over the house
   of Jacob forever,
   and His kingdom will have no end.

Virgin Mary Questions

34 Mary asked the angel, "How can this be, since I have not been intimate with a man?"b

Gabriel Explains

35 The angel replied to her:

The Holy Spirit will come
   upon you,
   and the power of the Most High
   will overshadow you.
Therefore the holy One to be born
   will be called the Son of God.

36 And consider your relative Elizabeth—even she has conceived a son in her old age, and this is the sixth month for her who was called barren. 37 For nothing will be impossible with God."

"I Am the Lord's Slave"

38 "I am the Lord's •slave,"c said Mary. "May it be done to me according to your word." Then the angel left her.

Mary Visits Elizabeth

39 In those days Mary set out and hurried to a town in the hill country of Judah 40 where she entered Zechariah's house and greeted Elizabeth. 41 When Elizabeth heard Mary's greeting, the

a1:28 Other mss add *blessed are you among women*   b1:34 Lit *since I do not know a man*   c1:38 Lit *Look, the Lord's slave* baby leaped inside her,^a and Elizabeth was filled with the Holy Spirit. ⁴² Then she exclaimed with a loud cry:

> You are the most blessed of women,
> and your child will be blessed!^b

⁴³ How could this happen to me, that the mother of my Lord should come to me? ⁴⁴ For you see, when the sound of your greeting reached my ears, the baby leaped for joy inside me!^c ⁴⁵ She who has believed is blessed because what was spoken to her by the Lord will be fulfilled!"

Mary's Song of Praise

⁴⁶ And Mary said:

> My soul proclaims the greatness
> of^d the Lord,
> ⁴⁷ and my spirit has rejoiced in God
> my Savior,
> ⁴⁸ because He has looked with favor
> on the humble condition
> of His •slave.
> Surely, from now on all generations
> will call me blessed,
> ⁴⁹ because the Mighty One
> has done great things for me,
> and His name is holy.
> ⁵⁰ His mercy is from generation
> to generation
> on those who fear Him.
> ⁵¹ He has done a mighty deed
> with His arm;
> He has scattered the proud
> because of the thoughts
> of their hearts;
> ⁵² He has toppled the mighty
> from their thrones
> and exalted the lowly.
> ⁵³ He has satisfied the hungry
> with good things
> and sent the rich away empty.

> ⁵⁴ He has helped His servant Israel,
> mindful of His mercy,^e
> ⁵⁵ just as He spoke to our ancestors,
> to Abraham and his
> descendants^f forever.

⁵⁶ And Mary stayed with her about three months; then she returned to her home.

Birth and Naming of John

⁵⁷ Now the time had come for Elizabeth to give birth, and she had a son. ⁵⁸ Then her neighbors and relatives heard that the Lord had shown her His great mercy,^g and they rejoiced with her. ⁵⁹ When they came to circumcise the child on the eighth day, they were going to name him Zechariah, after his father. ⁶⁰ But his mother responded, "No! He will be called John."

⁶¹ Then they said to her, "None of your relatives has that name." ⁶² So they motioned to his father to find out what he wanted him to be called. ⁶³ He asked for a writing tablet and wrote:

> HIS NAME IS JOHN

And they were all amazed. ⁶⁴ Immediately his mouth was opened and his tongue ⌊set free⌋, and he began to speak, praising God. ⁶⁵ Fear came on all those who lived around them, and all these things were being talked about throughout the hill country of Judea. ⁶⁶ All who heard about ⌊him⌋ took ⌊it⌋ to heart, saying, "What then will this child become?" For, indeed, the Lord's hand was with him.

Zechariah's Prophecy

⁶⁷ Then his father Zechariah was filled with the Holy Spirit and prophesied:

^a**1:41** Lit *leaped in her abdomen* or *womb*   ^b**1:42** Lit *and the fruit of your abdomen* (or *womb*) *is blessed*   ^c**1:44** Lit *in my abdomen* or *womb*   ^d**1:46** Or *soul magnifies*   ^e**1:54** Because He remembered His mercy; see Ps 98:3   ^f**1:55** Or *offspring*; lit *seed*   ^g**1:58** Lit *the Lord magnified His mercy with her*

68 Praise the Lord, the God of Israel,
   because He has visited
   and provided redemption
      for His people.
69 He has raised up a •horn
   of salvation[a] for us
   in the house of His servant David,
70 just as He spoke by the mouth
   of His holy prophets
   in ancient times;
71 salvation from our enemies
   and from the clutches[b] of those
      who hate us.
72 He has dealt mercifully
   with our fathers
   and remembered
      His holy covenant—
73 the oath that He swore to our father
   Abraham.
   He has given us the privilege,
74 since we have been rescued
   from our enemies' clutches,[c]
   to serve Him without fear
75 in holiness and righteousness
   in His presence all our days.
76 And child, you will be called
   a prophet of the Most High,
   for you will go before the Lord
   to prepare His ways,
77 to give His people knowledge
      of salvation
   through the forgiveness
      of their sins.
78 Because of our God's merciful
      compassion,
   the Dawn from on high will visit
      us
79 to shine on those who live
      in darkness
   and the shadow of death,
   to guide our feet into the way
      of peace.

John Grows up Strong

80 The child grew up and became spiritually strong, and he was in the wilderness until the day of his public appearance to Israel.

Birth of Jesus

2 In those days a decree went out from Caesar Augustus[d] that the whole empire[e] should be registered. 2 This first registration took place while[f] Quirinius was governing Syria. 3 So everyone went to be registered, each to his own town.

4 And Joseph also went up from the town of Nazareth in Galilee, to Judea, to the city of David, which is called Bethlehem, because he was of the house and family line of David, 5 to be registered along with Mary, who was •engaged to him[g] and was pregnant. 6 While they were there, the time came for her to give birth. 7 Then she gave birth to her firstborn Son, and she wrapped Him snugly in cloth and laid Him in a feeding trough—because there was no room for them at the inn.

Shepherds and Angels

8 In the same region, shepherds were staying out in the fields and keeping watch at night over their flock. 9 Then an angel of the Lord stood before[h] them, and the glory of the Lord shone around them, and they were terrified.[i] 10 But the angel said to them, "Don't be afraid, for look, I proclaim to you good news of great joy that will be for all the people: 11 today a Savior, who is •Messiah the Lord, was born for you in the city of David. 12 This will be the sign for you: you will find a baby wrapped snugly in cloth and lying in a feeding trough."

¹³ Suddenly there was a multitude of the heavenly host with the angel, praising God and saying:

¹⁴   Glory to God in the highest heaven,
        and peace on earth to people
           He favors!ᵃ ᵇ

¹⁵ When the angels had left them and returned to heaven, the shepherds said to one another, "Let's go straight to Bethlehem and see what has happened, which the Lord has made known to us."

¹⁶ They hurried off and found both Mary and Joseph, and the baby who was lying in the feeding trough. ¹⁷ After seeing ⌊them⌋, they reported the message they were told about this child, ¹⁸ and all who heard it were amazed at what the shepherds said to them. ¹⁹ But Mary was treasuring up all these thingsᶜ in her heart and meditating on them. ²⁰ The shepherds returned, glorifying and praising God for all they had seen and heard, just as they had been told.

Circumcision and Presentation of Jesus

²¹ When the eight days were completed for His circumcision, He was named JESUS—the name given by the angel before He was conceived.ᵈ ²² And when the days of their purification according to the law of Moses were finished, they brought Him up to Jerusalem to present Him to the Lord ²³ (just as it is written in the law of the Lord: **Every firstborn maleᵉ will be dedicatedᶠ to the Lordᵍ**) ²⁴ and to offer a sacrifice (according to what is stated in the law of the Lord: **a pair of turtledoves or two young pigeonsʰ**).

Simeon's Prophetic Praise

²⁵ There was a man in Jerusalem whose name was Simeon. This man was righteous and devout, looking forward to Israel's consolation,ⁱ and the Holy Spirit was on him. ²⁶ It had been revealed to him by the Holy Spirit that he would not see death before he saw the Lord's Messiah. ²⁷ Guided by the Spirit, he enteredʲ the •temple complex. When the parents brought in the child Jesus to perform for Him what was customary under the law, ²⁸ Simeon took Him up in his arms, praised God, and said:

²⁹   Now, Master,
        You can dismiss Your •slave
           in peace,
        according to Your word.
³⁰   For my eyes have seen
        Your salvation.
³¹   You have prepared ⌊it⌋
        in the presence of all peoples—
³²   a light for revelation
        to the Gentilesᵏ
        and glory to Your people Israel.

³³ His father and motherˡ were amazed at what was being said about Him. ³⁴ Then Simeon blessed them and told His mother Mary: "Indeed, this child is destined to cause the fall and rise of many in Israel and to be a sign that will be opposedᵐ— ³⁵ and a sword will pierce your own soul—that the thoughtsⁿ of many hearts may be revealed."

Anna's Testimony

³⁶ There was also a prophetess, Anna, a daughter of Phanuel, of the tribe of Asher. She was well along in years,ᵒ having lived with her husband seven years after her marriage,ᵖ ³⁷ and was a widow

---

ᵃ**2:14** Other mss read *earth good will to people*   ᵇ**2:14** Or *earth to men of good will*   ᶜ**2:19** Lit *these words*   ᵈ**2:21** Or *conceived in the womb*   ᵉ**2:23** Lit *"Every male that opens a womb*   ᶠ**2:23** Lit *be called holy*   ᵍ**2:23** Ex 13:2,12
ʰ**2:24** Lv 5:11; 12:8   ⁱ**2:25** The coming of the Messiah with His salvation for the nation; Lk 2:26,30; Is 40:1; 61:2
ʲ**2:27** Lit *And in the Spirit, he came into the*   ᵏ**2:32** Or *the nations*   ˡ**2:33** Other mss read *But Joseph and His mother*
ᵐ**2:34** Or *spoken against*   ⁿ**2:35** Or *schemes*   ᵒ**2:36** Lit *in many days*   ᵖ**2:36** Lit *years from her virginity*

for 84 years.[a] She did not leave the temple complex, serving God night and day with fastings and prayers. 38 At that very moment,[b] she came up and began to thank God and to speak about Him to all who were looking forward to the redemption of Jerusalem.[c]

Family's Return to Nazareth

39 When they had completed everything according to the law of the Lord, they returned to Galilee, to their own town of Nazareth. 40 The boy grew up and became strong, filled with wisdom, and God's grace was on Him.

In His Father's House

41 Every year His parents traveled to Jerusalem for the •Passover Festival. 42 When He was 12 years old, they went up according to the custom of the festival. 43 After those days were over, as they were returning, the boy Jesus stayed behind in Jerusalem, but His parents[d] did not know it. 44 Assuming He was in the traveling party, they went a day's journey. Then they began looking for Him among their relatives and friends. 45 When they did not find Him, they returned to Jerusalem to search for Him. 46 After three days, they found Him in the temple complex sitting among the teachers, listening to them and asking them questions. 47 And all those who heard Him were astounded at His understanding and His answers. 48 When His parents saw Him, they were astonished, and His mother said to Him, "Son, why have You treated us like this? Your father and I have been anxiously searching for You."

49 "Why were you searching for Me?" He asked them. "Didn't you know that I had to be in My Father's house?"[e] 50 But they did not understand what He said to them.

In Favor with God and People

51 Then He went down with them and came to Nazareth and was obedient to them. His mother kept all these things in her heart. 52 And Jesus increased in wisdom and stature, and in favor with God and with people.

John the Baptist: Messiah's Herald

3 In the fifteenth year of the reign of Tiberius Caesar,[f] while Pontius •Pilate was governor of Judea, •Herod was tetrarch[g] of Galilee, his brother Philip tetrarch of the region of Iturea[h] and Trachonitis,[h] and Lysanias tetrarch of Abilene,[i] 2 during the high priesthood of Annas and Caiaphas, God's word came to John the son of Zechariah in the wilderness. 3 He went into all the vicinity of the Jordan, preaching a baptism of repentance[j] for the forgiveness of sins, 4 as it is written in the book of the words of the prophet Isaiah:

> A voice of one crying out
>   in the wilderness:
> "Prepare the way
>   for the Lord;
> make His paths straight!
> 5 Every valley will be filled,
> and every mountain and hill
>   will be made low;[k]
> the crooked will become
>   straight,
> the rough ways smooth,
> 6 and everyone[l] will see
>   the salvation of God."[m]

[a]2:37 Or *she was a widow until the age of 84*   [b]2:38 Lit *very hour*   [c]2:38 Other mss read *in Jerusalem*   [d]2:43 Other mss read *but Joseph and His mother*   [e]2:49 Or *be involved in My Father's interests* (or *things*), or *be among My Father's people*   [f]3:1 Emperor who ruled the Roman Empire A.D. 14–37   [g]3:1 Or *ruler*   [h]3:1 A small province northeast of Galilee   [i]3:1 A small Syrian province   [j]3:3 Or *baptism based on repentance*   [k]3:5 Lit *be humbled*   [l]3:6 Lit *all flesh*   [m]3:4-6 Is 40:3-5

John's Strong Preaching

[7] He then said to the crowds who came out to be baptized by him, "Brood of vipers! Who warned you to flee from the coming wrath? [8] Therefore produce fruit consistent with repentance. And don't start saying to yourselves, 'We have Abraham as our father,' for I tell you that God is able to raise up children for Abraham from these stones! [9] Even now the ax is ready to strike[a] the root of the trees! Therefore every tree that doesn't produce good fruit will be cut down and thrown into the fire."

[10] "What then should we do?" the crowds were asking him.

[11] He replied to them, "The one who has two shirts[b] must share with someone who has none, and the one who has food must do the same."

John Warns
Tax Collectors and Soldiers

[12] Tax collectors also came to be baptized, and they asked him, "Teacher, what should we do?"

[13] He told them, "Don't collect any more than what you have been authorized."

[14] Some soldiers also questioned him: "What should we do?"

He said to them, "Don't take money from anyone by force or false accusation; be satisfied with your wages."

John Looks for Messiah

[15] Now the people were waiting expectantly, and all of them were debating in their minds[c] whether John might be the •Messiah. [16] John answered them all, "I baptize you with[d] water, but One is coming who is more powerful than I. I am not worthy to untie the strap of His sandals. He will baptize you with[d] the Holy Spirit and fire. [17] His winnowing shovel[e] is in His hand to clear His threshing floor and gather the wheat into His barn, but the chaff He will burn up with a fire that never goes out." [18] Then, along with many other exhortations, he proclaimed good news to the people. [19] But Herod the tetrarch, being rebuked by him about Herodias, his brother's wife, and about all the evil things Herod had done, [20] added this to everything else—he locked John up in prison.

Baptism of Jesus

[21] When all the people were baptized, Jesus also was baptized. As He was praying, heaven opened, [22] and the Holy Spirit descended on Him in a physical appearance like a dove. And a voice came from heaven:

> You are My beloved Son.
> I take delight in You!

Luke's Genealogy
of Jesus Christ

[23] As He began ⌊His ministry⌋, Jesus was about 30 years old and was thought to be[f] the

son of Joseph, ⌊son⌋[g] of Heli,
[24] ⌊son⌋ of Matthat, ⌊son⌋ of Levi,
⌊son⌋ of Melchi, ⌊son⌋ of Jannai,
⌊son⌋ of Joseph,
[25] ⌊son⌋ of Mattathias,
⌊son⌋ of Amos, ⌊son⌋ of Nahum,
⌊son⌋ of Esli, ⌊son⌋ of Naggai,
[26] ⌊son⌋ of Maath, ⌊son⌋ of Mattathias,
⌊son⌋ of Semein, ⌊son⌋ of Josech,
⌊son⌋ of Joda, [27] ⌊son⌋ of Joanan,
⌊son⌋ of Rhesa, ⌊son⌋ of Zerubbabel,

⌊son⌋ of Shealtiel, ⌊son⌋ of Neri,
28 ⌊son⌋ of Melchi, ⌊son⌋ of Addi,
⌊son⌋ of Cosam, ⌊son⌋ of Elmadam,
⌊son⌋ of Er, 29 ⌊son⌋ of Joshua,
⌊son⌋ of Eliezer, ⌊son⌋ of Jorim,
⌊son⌋ of Matthat, ⌊son⌋ of Levi,
30 ⌊son⌋ of Simeon, ⌊son⌋ of Judah,
⌊son⌋ of Joseph, ⌊son⌋ of Jonam,
⌊son⌋ of Eliakim, 31 ⌊son⌋ of Melea,
⌊son⌋ of Menna, ⌊son⌋ of Mattatha,
⌊son⌋ of Nathan, ⌊son⌋ of David,
32 ⌊son⌋ of Jesse, ⌊son⌋ of Obed,
⌊son⌋ of Boaz, ⌊son⌋ of Salmon,ᵃ
⌊son⌋ of Nahshon,
33 ⌊son⌋ of Amminadab,
⌊son⌋ of Ram,ᵇ ⌊son⌋ of Hezron,
⌊son⌋ of Perez, ⌊son⌋ of Judah,
34 ⌊son⌋ of Jacob, ⌊son⌋ of Isaac,
⌊son⌋ of Abraham, ⌊son⌋ of Terah,
⌊son⌋ of Nahor, 35 ⌊son⌋ of Serug,
⌊son⌋ of Reu, ⌊son⌋ of Peleg,
⌊son⌋ of Eber, ⌊son⌋ of Shelah,
36 ⌊son⌋ of Cainan, ⌊son⌋ of Arphaxad,
⌊son⌋ of Shem, ⌊son⌋ of Noah,
⌊son⌋ of Lamech,
37 ⌊son⌋ of Methuselah,
⌊son⌋ of Enoch, ⌊son⌋ of Jared,
⌊son⌋ of Mahalaleel,
⌊son⌋ of Cainan,
38 ⌊son⌋ of Enos, ⌊son⌋ of Seth,
⌊son⌋ of Adam, ⌊son⌋ of God.

Temptation of Jesus

4 Then Jesus returned from the Jordan, full of the Holy Spirit, and was led by the Spirit in the wilderness ² for 40 days to be tempted by the Devil. He ate nothing during those days, and when they were over,ᶜ He was hungry. ³ The Devil said to Him, "If You are the Son of God, tell this stone to become bread."

⁴ But Jesus answered him, "It is written: **Man must not live on bread alone.**"ᵈ ᵉ

⁵ So he took Him upᶠ and showed Him all the kingdoms of the world in a moment of time. ⁶ The Devil said to Him, "I will give You their splendor and all this authority, because it has been given over to me, and I can give it to anyone I want. ⁷ If You, then, will worship me,ᵍ all will be Yours."

⁸ And Jesus answered him,ʰ "It is written:

**Worship the Lord your God,
and serve Him only.**"ⁱ

⁹ So he took Him to Jerusalem, had Him stand on the pinnacle of the temple, and said to Him, "If You are the Son of God, throw Yourself down from here. ¹⁰ For it is written:

**He will give His angels orders
concerning you,
to protect you,ʲ ¹¹ and
they will support you
with their hands,
so that you will not strike
your foot against a stone.**"ᵏ

¹² And Jesus answered him, "It is said: **Do not test the Lord your God.**"ˡ

¹³ After the Devil had finished every temptation, he departed from Him for a time.

Jesus' Ministry in Galilee

¹⁴ Then Jesus returned to Galilee in the power of the Spirit, and news about Him spread throughout the entire vicinity. ¹⁵ He was teaching in their •synagogues, being acclaimedᵐ by everyone.

ᵃ**3:32** Other mss read *Sala* ᵇ**3:33** Other mss read *Amminadab, son of Aram, son of Joram*; other mss read *Amminadab, son of Admin, son of Arni* ᶜ**4:2** Lit *were completed* ᵈ**4:4** Other mss add *but on every word of God* ᵉ**4:4** Dt 8:3 ᶠ**4:5** Other mss read *So the Devil took Him up on a high mountain* ᵍ**4:7** Lit *will fall down before me* ʰ**4:8** Other mss add *"Get behind Me, Satan!* ⁱ**4:8** Dt 6:13 ʲ**4:10** Ps 91:11 ᵏ**4:11** Ps 91:12 ˡ**4:12** Dt 6:16 ᵐ**4:15** Or *glorified*

Jesus Reads Isaiah
at Nazareth Synagogue

16 He came to Nazareth, where He had been brought up. As usual, He entered the synagogue on the Sabbath day and stood up to read. 17 The scroll of the prophet Isaiah was given to Him, and unrolling the scroll, He found the place where it was written:

18 **The Spirit of the Lord is on Me,**
because He has anointed Me
to preach good news to the poor.
He has sent Me[a]
to proclaim freedom[b]
  to the captives
and recovery of sight to the blind,
to set free the oppressed,
19 **to proclaim the year**
  of the Lord's favor.[c] [d]

20 He then rolled up the scroll, gave it back to the attendant, and sat down. And the eyes of everyone in the synagogue were fixed on Him. 21 He began by saying to them, "Today as you listen, this Scripture has been fulfilled."

Jesus Issues Challenge

22 They were all speaking well of Him[e] and were amazed by the gracious words that came from His mouth, yet they said, "Isn't this Joseph's son?"

23 Then He said to them, "No doubt you will quote this proverb[f] to Me: 'Doctor, heal yourself.' 'All we've heard that took place in Capernaum, do here in Your hometown also.'"

24 He also said, "•I assure you: No prophet is accepted in his hometown. 25 But I say to you, there were certainly many widows in Israel in Elijah's days, when the sky was shut up for three years and six months while a great famine came over all the land. 26 Yet Elijah was not sent to any of them—but to a widow at Zarephath in Sidon. 27 And in the prophet Elisha's time, there were many in Israel who had serious skin diseases, yet not one of them was healed[g]—only Naaman the Syrian."

His Listeners are Enraged

28 When they heard this, everyone in the synagogue was enraged. 29 They got up, drove Him out of town, and brought Him to the edge[h] of the hill their town was built on, intending to hurl Him over the cliff. 30 But He passed right through the crowd and went on His way.

Capernaum:
Jesus Drives Out Unclean Spirit

31 Then He went down to Capernaum, a town in Galilee, and was teaching them on the Sabbath. 32 They were astonished at His teaching because His message had authority. 33 In the synagogue there was a man with an unclean demonic spirit who cried out with a loud voice, 34 "Leave us alone![i] What do You have to do with us,[j] Jesus—•Nazarene? Have You come to destroy us? I know who You are—the Holy One of God!"

35 But Jesus rebuked him and said, "Be quiet and come out of him!"

And throwing him down before them, the demon came out of him without hurting him at all. 36 They were all struck with amazement and kept saying to one another, "What is this message? For He commands the unclean spirits with authority and power, and they come out!" 37 And news about Him began to go out to every place in the vicinity.

---

a**4:18** Other mss add to heal the brokenhearted,   b**4:18** Or release, or forgiveness   c**4:19** The time of messianic grace   d**4:18-19** Is 61:1-2   e**4:22** Or They were testifying against Him   f**4:23** Or parable   g**4:27** Lit cleansed   h**4:29** Lit brow   i**4:34** Or Ha!, or Ah!   j**4:34** Lit What to us and to You

Jesus Heals Simon's Mother-in-law

38 After He left the synagogue, He entered Simon's house. Simon's mother-in-law was suffering from a high fever, and they asked Him about her. 39 So He stood over her and rebuked the fever, and it left her. She got up immediately and began to serve them.

More Healing and Rebuking in Capernaum

40 When the sun was setting, all those who had anyone sick with various diseases brought them to Him. As He laid His hands on each one of them, He would heal them. 41 Also, demons were coming out of many, shouting and saying, "You are the Son of God!" But He rebuked them and would not allow them to speak, because they knew He was the •Messiah.

Jesus Preaches in Galilee

42 When it was day, He went out and made His way to a deserted place. But the crowds were searching for Him. They came to Him and tried to keep Him from leaving them. 43 But He said to them, "I must proclaim the good news about the kingdom of God to the other towns also, because I was sent for this purpose." 44 And He was preaching in the synagogues of Galilee.a

Jesus Calls Simon Peter

5 As the crowd was pressing in on Jesus to hear God's word, He was standing by Lake Gennesaret.b 2 He saw two boats at the edge of the lake;c the fishermen had left them and were washing their nets. 3 He got into one of the boats, which belonged to Simon, and

asked him to put out a little from the land. Then He sat down and was teaching the crowds from the boat.

4 When He had finished speaking, He said to Simon, "Put out into deep water and let downd your nets for a catch."

5 "Master," Simon replied, "we've worked hard all night long and caught nothing! But at Your word, I'll let down the nets."e

6 When they did this, they caught a great number of fish, and their netse began to tear. 7 So they signaled to their partners in the other boat to come and help them; they came and filled both boats so full that they began to sink.

8 When Simon Peter saw this, he fell at Jesus' knees and said, "Go away from me, because I'm a sinful man, Lord!" 9 For he and all those with him were amazedf at the catch of fish they took, 10 and so were James and John, Zebedee's sons, who were Simon's partners.

New Disciples Follow Him

"Don't be afraid," Jesus told Simon. "From now on you will be catching people!" 11 Then they brought the boats to land, left everything, and followed Him.

Jesus Cleanses a Leper

12 While He was in one of the towns, a man was there who had a serious skin disease all over him. He saw Jesus, fell facedown, and begged Him: "Lord, if You are willing, You can make me clean."g

13 Reaching out His hand, He touched him, saying, "I am willing; be made clean," and immediately the disease left him. 14 Then He ordered him to tell no one: "But go and show yourself to the priest, and offer what Moses prescribed

---

a4:44 Other mss read *Judea* b5:1 = Sea of Galilee c5:2 Lit *boats standing by the lake* d5:4 Lit *and you* (Gk pl) *let down* e5:5,6 Other mss read *net* (Gk sg) f5:9 Or *For amazement had seized him and all those with him* g5:12 In these verses, *clean* includes healing, ceremonial purification, return to fellowship with people, and worship in the temple; Lv 14:1-32.

for your cleansing as a testimony to them."

15 But the news[a] about Him spread even more, and large crowds would come together to hear Him and to be healed of their sicknesses. 16 Yet He often withdrew to deserted places and prayed.

Son of Man Forgives and Heals Paralyzed Man

17 On one of those days while He was teaching, •Pharisees and teachers of the law were sitting there who had come from every village of Galilee and Judea, and also from Jerusalem. And the Lord's power to heal was in Him. 18 Just then some men came, carrying on a stretcher a man who was paralyzed. They tried to bring him in and set him down before Him. 19 Since they could not find a way to bring him in because of the crowd, they went up on the roof and lowered him on the stretcher through the roof tiles into the middle of the crowd before Jesus.

20 Seeing their faith He said, "Friend,[b] your sins are forgiven you."

21 Then the •scribes and the Pharisees began to reason: "Who is this man who speaks blasphemies? Who can forgive sins but God alone?"

22 But perceiving their thoughts, Jesus replied to them, "Why are you reasoning this in your hearts?[c] 23 Which is easier: to say, 'Your sins are forgiven you,' or to say, 'Get up and walk'? 24 But so you may know that the •Son of Man has authority on earth to forgive sins"—He told the paralyzed man, "I tell you: get up, pick up your stretcher, and go home."

25 Immediately he got up before them, picked up what he had been lying on,

and went home glorifying God. 26 Then everyone was astounded, and they were giving glory to God. And they were filled with awe and said, "We have seen incredible things today!"

Call of Levi

27 After this, Jesus went out and saw a tax collector named Levi sitting at the tax office, and He said to him, "Follow Me!" 28 So, leaving everything behind, he got up and began to follow Him.

Jesus Dines with Tax Collectors and Sinners

29 Then Levi hosted a grand banquet for Him at his house. Now there was a large crowd of tax collectors and others who were guests[d] with them. 30 But the Pharisees and their scribes were complaining to His disciples, "Why do you eat and drink with tax collectors and sinners?"

31 Jesus replied to them, "The healthy don't need a doctor, but the sick do. 32 I have not come to call the righteous, but sinners to repentance."

Question about Fasting

33 Then they said to Him, "John's disciples fast often and say prayers, and those of the Pharisees do the same, but Yours eat and drink."[e]

34 Jesus said to them, "You can't make the wedding guests[f] fast while the groom is with them, can you? 35 But the days will come when the groom will be taken away from them—then they will fast in those days."

Parable of New Wineskins

36 He also told them a parable: "No one tears a patch from a new garment

a5:15 Lit the word   b5:20 Lit Man   c5:22 Or minds   d5:29 Lit were reclining (at the table); at important meals the custom was to recline on a mat at a low table and lean on the left elbow.   e5:33 Other mss read "Why do John's . . . drink?" (as a question)   f5:34 Or the friends of the groom; lit sons of the bridal chamber

and puts it on an old garment. Otherwise, not only will he tear the new, but also the piece from the new garment will not match the old. ³⁷ And no one puts new wine into old wineskins. Otherwise, the new wine will burst the skins, it will spill, and the skins will be ruined. ³⁸ But new wine should be put into fresh wineskins.ᵃ ³⁹ And no one, after drinking old wine, wants new, because he says, 'The old is better.' "ᵇ

Disciples Pick in Grainfields on Sabbath

6 On a Sabbath,ᶜ He passed through the grainfields. His disciples were picking heads of grain, rubbing them in their hands, and eating them. ² But some of the •Pharisees said, "Why are you doing what is not lawful on the Sabbath?" ³ Jesus answered them, "Haven't you read what David and those who were with him did when he was hungry— ⁴ how he entered the house of God, and took and ate the •sacred bread, which is not lawful for any but the priests to eat? He even gave some to those who were with him." ⁵ Then He told them, "The •Son of Man is Lord of the Sabbath."

Man with Paralyzed Hand: Sabbath Healing

⁶ On another Sabbath He entered the •synagogue and was teaching. A man was there whose right hand was paralyzed. ⁷ The •scribes and Pharisees were watching Him closely, to see if He would heal on the Sabbath, so that they could find a charge against Him. ⁸ But He knew their thoughts and told the man with the paralyzed hand, "Get up and stand here."ᵈ So he got up and stood there. ⁹ Then Jesus said to them, "I ask you: is

it lawful on the Sabbath to do good or to do evil, to save life or to destroy it?" ¹⁰ After looking around at them all, He told him, "Stretch out your hand." He did so, and his hand was restored.ᵉ ¹¹ They, however, were filled with rage and started discussing with one another what they might do to Jesus.

The 12 Apostles

¹² During those days He went out to the mountain to pray and spent all night in prayer to God. ¹³ When daylight came, He summoned His disciples, and He chose 12 of them—He also named them apostles:

¹⁴   Simon, whom He also named Peter,
       and Andrew his brother;
       James and John;
       Philip and Bartholomew;
¹⁵   Matthew and Thomas;
       James the son of Alphaeus,
       and Simon called the Zealot;
¹⁶   Judas the son of James,
       and Judas Iscariot, who became
       a traitor.

Jesus Teaches on Level Place

¹⁷ After coming down with them, He stood on a level place with a large crowd of His disciples and a great multitude of people from all Judea and Jerusalem and from the seacoast of Tyre and Sidon. ¹⁸ They came to hear Him and to be healed of their diseases; and those tormented by unclean spirits were made well. ¹⁹ The whole crowd was trying to touch Him, because power was coming out from Him and healing them all.

The Beatitudes

²⁰ Then looking up atᶠ His disciples, He said:

ᵃ**5:38** Other mss add *And so both are preserved.*   ᵇ**5:39** Other mss read *is good*   ᶜ**6:1** Other mss read *a second-first Sabbath;* perhaps a special Sabbath   ᵈ**6:8** Lit *stand in the middle*   ᵉ**6:10** Other mss add *as sound as the other*
ᶠ**6:20** Lit *Then lifting up His eyes to*

Blessed are you who are poor,
because the kingdom of God
is yours.
21 Blessed are you
who are hungry now,
because you will be filled.
Blessed are you who weep now,
because you will laugh.
22 Blessed are you when people
hate you,
when they exclude you, insult you,
and slander your name as evil,
because of the Son of Man.

23 "Rejoice in that day and leap for joy! Take note—your reward is great in heaven, because this is the way their ancestors used to treat the prophets.

Woe to the Self-Satisfied

24 But woe to you who are rich,
because you have received
your comfort.
25 Woe to you who are full now,
because you will be hungry.
Woe to youᵃ who are laughing now,
because you will mourn and weep.
26 Woe to youᵃ
when all people speak well of you,
because this is the way
their ancestors
used to treat the false prophets.

Love Your Enemies

27 "But I say to you who listen: Love your enemies, do good to those who hate you, 28 bless those who curse you, pray for those who mistreat you. 29 If anyone hits you on the cheek, offer the other also. And if anyone takes away your coat, don't hold back your shirt either. 30 Give to everyone who asks from you, and from one who takes away your things, don't ask for them back. 31 Just as you want others to do for you, do the same for them. 32 If you love those who love you, what credit is that to you? Even sinners love those who love them. 33 If you do ⌐what is⌐ good to those who are good to you, what credit is that to you? Even sinners do that. 34 And if you lend to those from whom you expect to receive, what credit is that to you? Even sinners lend to sinners to be repaid in full. 35 But love your enemies, do ⌐what is⌐ good, and lend, expecting nothing in return. Then your reward will be great, and you will be sons of the Most High. For He is gracious to the ungrateful and evil. 36 Be merciful, just as your Father also is merciful.

Do Not Judge

37 "Do not judge, and you will not be judged. Do not condemn, and you will not be condemned. Forgive, and you will be forgiven. 38 Give, and it will be given to you; a good measure—pressed down, shaken together, and running over—will be poured into your lap. For with the measure you use,ᵇ it will be measured back to you."

39 He also told them a parable: "Can the blind guide the blind? Won't they both fall into a pit? 40 A disciple is not above his teacher, but everyone who is fully trained will be like his teacher.

41 "Why do you look at the speck in your brother's eye, but don't notice the log in your own eye? 42 Or how can you say to your brother, 'Brother, let me take out the speck that is in your eye,' when you yourself don't see the log in your eye? Hypocrite! First take the log out of your eye, and then you will see clearly to take out the speck in your brother's eye.

A Tree and Its Fruit

43 "A good tree doesn't produce bad fruit; on the other hand, a bad tree

ᵃ**6:25,26** Other mss omit *to you*   ᵇ**6:38** Lit *you measure* doesn't produce good fruit. ⁴⁴ For each tree is known by its own fruit. Figs aren't gathered from thornbushes, or grapes picked from a bramble bush. ⁴⁵ A good man produces good out of the good storeroom of his heart. An evil man produces evil out of the evil storeroom, for his mouth speaks from the overflow of the heart.

Two
Foundations

⁴⁶ "Why do you call Me 'Lord, Lord,' and don't do the things I say? ⁴⁷ I will show you what someone is like who comes to Me, hears My words, and acts on them: ⁴⁸ He is like a man building a house, who dug deepᵃ and laid the foundation on the rock. When the flood came, the river crashed against that house and couldn't shake it, because it was well built. ⁴⁹ But the one who hears and does not act is like a man who built a house on the ground without a foundation. The river crashed against it, and immediately it collapsed. And the destruction of that house was great!"

A Centurion's Faith:
Healing of Slave

7 When He had concluded all His sayings in the hearing of the people, He entered Capernaum. ² A •centurion's •slave, who was highly valued by him, was sick and about to die. ³ When the centurion heard about Jesus, he sent some Jewish elders to Him, requesting Him to come and save the life of his slave. ⁴ When they reached Jesus, they pleaded with Him earnestly, saying, "He is worthy for You to grant this, ⁵ because he loves our nation and has built us a •synagogue." ⁶ Jesus went with them, and when He was not far fromᵇ the house, the centurion sent friends to tell Him, "Lord, don't trouble Yourself, since I am not worthy to have You come under my roof. ⁷ That is why I didn't even consider myself worthy to come to You. But say the word, and my servant will be cured.ᶜ ⁸ For I too am a man placed under authority, having soldiers under my command.ᵈ I say to this one, 'Go!' and he goes; and to another, 'Come!' and he comes; and to my slave, 'Do this!' and he does it."

⁹ Jesus heard this and was amazed at him, and turning to the crowd following Him, He said, "I tell you, I have not found so great a faith even in Israel!" ¹⁰ When those who had been sent returned to the house, they found the •slave in good health.

Son of Widow
of Nain Raised to Life

¹¹ Soon afterwards He was on His way to a town called Nain. His disciples and a large crowd were traveling with Him. ¹² Just as He neared the gate of the town, a dead man was being carried out. He was his mother's only son, and she was a widow. A large crowd from the city was also with her. ¹³ When the Lord saw her, He had compassion on her and said, "Don't cry." ¹⁴ Then He came up and touched the open coffin,ᵉ and the pallbearers stopped. And He said, "Young man, I tell you, get up!"

¹⁵ The dead man sat up and began to speak, and Jesus gave him to his mother. ¹⁶ Then fearᶠ came over everyone, and they glorified God, saying, "A great prophet has risen among us," and "God has visitedᵍ His people." ¹⁷ This report about Him went throughout Judea and all the vicinity.

ᵃ6:48 Lit dug and went deep ᵇ7:6 Lit and He already was not far from ᶜ7:7 Other mss read and let my servant be cured ᵈ7:8 Lit under me ᵉ7:14 Or the bier ᶠ7:16 Or awe ᵍ7:16 Or come to help

John the Baptist
Questions Jesus

¹⁸ Then John's disciples told him about all these things. So John summoned two of his disciples ¹⁹ and sent them to the Lord, asking, "Are You the One who is to come, or should we look for someone else?"

²⁰ When the men reached Him, they said, "John the Baptist sent us to ask You, 'Are You the One who is to come, or should we look for someone else?'"

Jesus Answers

²¹ At that time Jesus healed many people of diseases, plagues, and evil spirits, and He granted sight to many blind people. ²² He replied to them, "Go and report to John the things you have seen and heard: The blind receive their sight, the lame walk, those with skin diseases are healed,ᵃ the deaf hear, the dead are raised, and the poor have the good news preached to them. ²³ And anyone who is not offended because of Me is blessed."

Jesus Praises
John the Baptist

²⁴ After John's messengers left, He began to speak to the crowds about John: "What did you go out into the wilderness to see? A reed swaying in the wind? ²⁵ What then did you go out to see? A man dressed in soft robes? Look, those who are splendidly dressedᵇ and live in luxury are in royal palaces. ²⁶ What then did you go out to see? A prophet? Yes, I tell you, and far more than a prophet. ²⁷ This is the one it is written about:

Look, I am sending My messenger
    ahead of You;ᶜ
he will prepare Your way
    before You.ᵈ

²⁸ I tell you, among those born of women no one is greater than John,ᵉ but the least in the kingdom of God is greater than he."

²⁹ (And when all the people, including the tax collectors, heard this, they acknowledged God's way of righteousness,ᶠ because they had been baptized with John's baptism. ³⁰ But since the •Pharisees and experts in the law had not been baptized by him, they rejected the plan of God for themselves.)

An Unresponsive Generation

³¹ "To what then should I compare the people of this generation, and what are they like? ³² They are like children sitting in the marketplace and calling to each other:

We played the flute for you,
    but you didn't dance;
we sang a lament,
    but you didn't weep!

³³ For John the Baptist did not come eating bread or drinking wine, and you say, 'He has a demon!' ³⁴ The •Son of Man has come eating and drinking, and you say, 'Look, a glutton and a drunkard, a friend of tax collectors and sinners!' ³⁵ Yet wisdom is vindicatedᵍ by all her children."

Jesus Eats
with Simon the Pharisee

³⁶ Then one of the Pharisees invited Him to eat with him. He entered the Pharisee's house and reclined at the table.

Female Sinner Anoints His Feet

³⁷ And a woman in the town who was a sinner found out that Jesus was reclining at the table in the Pharisee's house. She

---

ᵃ7:22 Lit cleansed ᵇ7:25 Or who have glorious robes ᶜ7:27 Lit messenger before Your face ᵈ7:27 Mal 3:1
ᵉ7:28 Other mss read women is not a greater prophet than John the Baptist ᶠ7:29 Lit they justified God ᵍ7:35 Or wisdom is declared right

brought an alabaster flask of fragrant oil
[38] and stood behind Him at His feet,
weeping, and began to wash His feet
with her tears. She wiped His feet with
the hair of her head, kissing them and
anointing them with the fragrant oil.

Simon's Critical Attitude

[39] When the Pharisee who had invited
Him saw this, he said to himself, "This
man, if He were a prophet, would know
who and what kind of woman this is
who is touching Him—she's a sinner!"

Jesus Replies with Story

[40] Jesus replied to him, "Simon, I have
something to say to you."

"Teacher," he said, "say it."

[41] "A creditor had two debtors. One
owed 500 •denarii, and the other 50.
[42] Since they could not pay it back, he
graciously forgave them both. So, which
of them will love him more?"

[43] Simon answered, "I suppose the one
he forgave more."

Lesson:
Much Forgiveness, Much Love

"You have judged correctly," He told
him. [44] Turning to the woman, He said
to Simon, "Do you see this woman? I
entered your house; you gave Me no
water for My feet, but she, with her
tears, has washed My feet and wiped
them with her hair. [45] You gave Me no
kiss, but she hasn't stopped kissing My
feet since I came in. [46] You didn't anoint
My head with oil, but she has anointed
My feet with fragrant oil. [47] Therefore I
tell you, her many sins have been forgiven; that's why[a] she loved much. But
the one who is forgiven little, loves little." [48] Then He said to her, "Your sins
are forgiven."

Pharisees' Criticism, Woman's Faith

[49] Those who were at the table with
Him began to say among themselves,
"Who is this man who even forgives
sins?"

[50] And He said to the woman, "Your
faith has saved you. Go in peace."

Many Women
Support Christ's Work

8 Soon afterwards He was traveling
from one town and village to another, preaching and telling the good
news of the kingdom of God. The
Twelve were with Him, [2] and also some
women who had been healed of evil
spirits and sicknesses: Mary, called
•Magdalene (seven demons had come
out of her); [3] Joanna the wife of Chuza,
•Herod's steward; Susanna; and many
others who were supporting them from
their possessions.

Parable of the Sower

[4] As a large crowd was gathering, and
people were flocking to Him from every
town, He said in a parable: [5] "A sower
went out to sow his seed. As he was
sowing, some fell along the path; it was
trampled on, and the birds of the sky ate
it up. [6] Other seed fell on the rock; when
it sprang up, it withered, since it lacked
moisture. [7] Other seed fell among
thorns; the thorns sprang up with it and
choked it. [8] Still other seed fell on good
ground; when it sprang up, it produced a
crop: 100 times ⌊what was sown⌋." As He
said this, He called out, "Anyone who
has ears to hear should listen!"

Why Jesus Used Parables

[9] Then His disciples asked Him, "What
does this parable mean?" [10] So He said,
"The secrets[b] of the kingdom of God

have been given for you to know, but to the rest it is in parables, so that

**Looking they may not see,
and hearing they may not
understand.**ᵃ

Jesus Explains
Parable of Sower

¹¹ "This is the meaning of the parable:ᵇ The seed is the word of God. ¹² The seeds along the path are those who have heard. Then the Devil comes and takes away the word from their hearts, so that they may not believe and be saved. ¹³ And the seeds on the rock are those who, when they hear, welcome the word with joy. Having no root, these believe for a while and depart in a time of testing. ¹⁴ As for the seed that fell among thorns, these are the ones who, when they have heard, go on their way and are choked with worries, riches, and pleasures of life, and produce no mature fruit. ¹⁵ But the seed in the good ground—these are the ones who,ᶜ having heard the word with an honest and good heart, hold on to it and by enduring, bear fruit.

Lamp on
a Lampstand

¹⁶ "No one, after lighting a lamp, covers it with a basket or puts it under a bed, but puts it on a lampstand so that those who come in may see the light. ¹⁷ For nothing is concealed that won't be revealed, and nothing hidden that won't be made known and come to light. ¹⁸ Therefore, take care how you listen. For whoever has, more will be given to him; and whoever does not have, even what he thinks he has will be taken away from him."

Spiritual and Blood
Relationships

¹⁹ Then His mother and brothers came to Him, but they could not meet with Him because of the crowd. ²⁰ He was told, "Your mother and Your brothers are standing outside, wanting to see You."
²¹ But He replied to them, "My mother and My brothers are those who hear and do the word of God."

Wind and Wave Obey Jesus

²² One day He and His disciples got into a boat, and He told them, "Let's cross over to the other side of the lake." So they set out, ²³ and as they were sailing He fell asleep. Then a fierce windstorm came down on the lake; they were being swamped and were in danger. ²⁴ They came and woke Him up, saying, "Master, Master, we're going to die!" Then He got up and rebuked the wind and the raging waves. So they ceased, and there was a calm. ²⁵ He said to them, "Where is your faith?"

They were fearful and amazed, asking one another, "Who can this be?ᵈ He commands even the winds and the waves, and they obey Him!"

Demons Driven
Out by the Master

²⁶ Then they sailed to the region of the Gerasenes,ᵉ which is opposite Galilee. ²⁷ When He got out on land, a demon-possessed man from the town met Him. For a long time he had worn no clothes and did not stay in a house but in the tombs. ²⁸ When he saw Jesus, he cried out, fell down before Him, and said in a loud voice, "What do You have to do with me,ᶠ Jesus, You Son of the Most High God? I beg You, don't torment me!"

ᵃ**8:10** Is 6:9   ᵇ**8:11** Lit *But this is the parable:*   ᶜ**8:15** Or *these are the kind who*   ᵈ**8:25** Lit *Who then is this?*
ᵉ**8:26** Other mss read *the Gadarenes*   ᶠ**8:28** Lit *What to me and to You*

29 For He had commanded the unclean spirit to come out of the man. Many times it had seized him, and although he was guarded, bound by chains and shackles, he would snap the restraints and be driven by the demon into deserted places.

30 "What is your name?" Jesus asked him.

"Legion," he said—because many demons had entered him. 31 And they begged Him not to banish them to the •abyss.

Into the Herd of Pigs

32 A large herd of pigs was there, feeding on the hillside. The demons begged Him to permit them to enter the pigs, and He gave them permission. 33 The demons came out of the man and entered the pigs, and the herd rushed down the steep bank into the lake and drowned. 34 When the men who tended them saw what had happened, they ran off and reported it in the town and in the countryside. 35 Then people went out to see what had happened. They came to Jesus and found the man the demons had departed from, sitting at Jesus' feet, dressed and in his right mind. And they were afraid. 36 Meanwhile the eyewitnesses reported to them how the demon-possessed man was delivered. 37 Then all the people of the Gerasene region[a] asked Him to leave them, because they were gripped by great fear. So getting into the boat, He returned.

Healed Demoniac on a Mission

38 The man from whom the demons had departed kept begging Him to be with Him. But He sent him away and said, 39 "Go back to your home, and tell all that God has done for you." And off he went, proclaiming throughout the town all that Jesus had done for him.

Jairus' Daughter at Death's Door

40 When Jesus returned, the crowd welcomed Him, for they were all expecting Him. 41 Just then, a man named Jairus came. He was a leader of the •synagogue. He fell down at Jesus' feet and pleaded with Him to come to his house, 42 because he had an only daughter about 12 years old, and she was at death's door.[b]

Jesus Touched by Ill Woman

While He was going, the crowds were nearly crushing Him. 43 A woman suffering from bleeding for 12 years, who had spent all she had on doctors[c] yet could not be healed by any, 44 approached from behind and touched the •tassel of His robe. Instantly her bleeding stopped.

45 "Who touched Me?" Jesus asked.

When they all denied it, Peter[d] said, "Master, the crowds are hemming You in and pressing against You."[e]

46 "Somebody did touch Me," said Jesus. "I know that power has gone out from Me." 47 When the woman saw that she was discovered,[f] she came trembling and fell down before Him. In the presence of all the people, she declared the reason she had touched Him and how she was instantly cured. 48 "Daughter," He said to her, "your faith has made you well.[g] Go in peace."

Jesus Raises Jairus' Daughter

49 While He was still speaking, someone came from the synagogue leader's ⌊house⌋, saying, "Your daughter is dead. Don't bother the Teacher anymore."

---

[a]8:37 Other mss read the Gadarenes [b]8:42 Lit she was dying [c]8:43 Other mss omit who had spent all she had on doctors [d]8:45 Other mss add and those with him [e]8:45 Other mss add and You say, 'Who touched Me?' [f]8:47 Lit she had not escaped notice [g]8:48 Or has saved you

50 When Jesus heard it, He answered him, "Don't be afraid. Only believe, and she will be made well." 51 After He came to the house, He let no one enter with Him except Peter, John, James, and the child's father and mother. 52 Everyone was crying and mourning for her. But He said, "Stop crying, for she is not dead but asleep."

53 They started laughing at Him, because they knew she was dead. 54 So He[a] took her by the hand and called out, "Child, get up!" 55 Her spirit returned, and she got up at once. Then He gave orders that she be given something to eat. 56 Her parents were astounded, but He instructed them to tell no one what had happened.

Jesus Commissions the Twelve

9 Summoning the Twelve, He gave them power and authority over all the demons, and ⌊power⌋ to heal[b] diseases. 2 Then He sent them to proclaim the kingdom of God and to heal the sick. 3 "Take nothing for the road," He told them, "no walking stick, no traveling bag, no bread, no money; and don't take an extra shirt. 4 Whatever house you enter, stay there and leave from there. 5 If they do not welcome you, when you leave that town, shake off the dust from your feet as a testimony against them." 6 So they went out and traveled from village to village, proclaiming the good news and healing everywhere.

Herod's Desire to See Jesus

7 •Herod the tetrarch heard about everything that was going on. He was perplexed, because some said that John had been raised from the dead, 8 some that Elijah had appeared, and others that one of the ancient prophets had risen. 9 "I beheaded John," Herod said, "but who is this I hear such things about?" And he wanted to see Him.

Jesus Feeds 5,000

10 When the apostles returned, they reported to Jesus all that they had done. He took them along and withdrew privately to a[c] town called Bethsaida. 11 When the crowds found out, they followed Him. He welcomed them, spoke to them about the kingdom of God, and cured[d] those who needed healing.

12 Late in the day,[e] the Twelve approached and said to Him, "Send the crowd away, so they can go into the surrounding villages and countryside to find food and lodging, because we are in a deserted place here."

13 "You give them something to eat," He told them.

"We have no more than five loaves and two fish," they said, "unless we go and buy food for all these people." 14 (For about 5,000 men were there.)

Then He told His disciples, "Have them sit down[f] in groups of about 50 each." 15 They did so, and had them all sit down. 16 Then He took the five loaves and the two fish, and looking up to heaven, He blessed and broke them. He kept giving them to the disciples to set before the crowd. 17 Everyone ate and was filled. Then they picked up[g] 12 baskets of leftover pieces.

---

a**8:54** Other mss add *having put them all outside*   b**9:1** In this passage, different Gk words are translated as *heal*. In Eng, "to heal" or "to cure" are synonyms with little distinction in meaning. Technically, we do not heal or cure diseases. People are healed or cured from diseases.   c**9:10** Other mss add *deserted place near a*   d**9:11** Or *healed*; in this passage, different Gk words are translated as *heal*. In Eng, "to heal" or "to cure" are synonyms with little distinction in meaning. Technically, we do not heal or cure diseases. People are healed or cured from diseases.   e**9:12** Lit *When the day began to decline*   f**9:14** Lit *them recline*   g**9:17** Lit *Then were picked up by them*

Peter's Confession of the Messiah

18 While He was praying in private and His disciples were with Him, He asked them, "Who do the crowds say that I am?"

19 They answered, "John the Baptist; others, Elijah; still others, that one of the ancient prophets has come back."a

20 "But you," He asked them, "who do you say that I am?"

Peter answered, "God's •Messiah!"

Jesus Predicts His Death and Resurrection

21 But He strictly warned and instructed them to tell this to no one, 22 saying, "The •Son of Man must suffer many things and be rejected by the elders, •chief priests, and •scribes, be killed, and be raised the third day."

Take Up Your Cross

23 Then He said to ⌊them⌋ all, "If anyone wants to come withb Me, he must deny himself, take up his cross daily,c and follow Me. 24 For whoever wants to save his •life will lose it, but whoever loses his life because of Me will save it. 25 What is a man benefited if he gains the whole world, yet loses or forfeits himself? 26 For whoever is ashamed of Me and My words, the Son of Man will be ashamed of him when He comes in His glory and that of the Father and the holy angels. 27 I tell you the truth: there are some standing here who will not taste death until they see the kingdom of God."

The Transfiguration

28 About eight days after these words, He took along Peter, John, and James, and went up on the mountain to pray. 29 As He was praying, the appearance of His face changed, and His clothes became dazzling white. 30 Suddenly, two men were talking with Him—Moses and Elijah. 31 They appeared in glory and were speaking of His death,d which He was about to accomplish in Jerusalem.

32 Peter and those with him were in a deep sleep,e and when they became fully awake, they saw His glory and the two men who were standing with Him. 33 As the two men were departing from Him, Peter said to Jesus, "Master, it's good for us to be here! Let us make three •tabernacles: one for You, one for Moses, and one for Elijah"—not knowing what he said.

34 While he was saying this, a cloud appeared and overshadowed them. They became afraid as they entered the cloud. 35 Then a voice came from the cloud, saying:

This is My Son, the Chosen One;f listen to Him!

36 After the voice had spoken, only Jesus was found. They kept silent, and in those days told no one what they had seen.

Power of Faith over a Demon

37 The next day, when they came down from the mountain, a large crowd met Him. 38 Just then a man from the crowd cried out, "Teacher, I beg You to look at my son, because he's my only ⌊child⌋. 39 Often a spirit seizes him; suddenly he shrieks, and it throws him into convulsions until he foams at the mouth;g woundingh him, it hardly ever leaves him. 40 I begged Your disciples to drive it out, but they couldn't."

---

a9:19 Lit *has risen*   b9:23 Lit *come after*   c9:23 Other mss omit *daily*   d9:31 Or *departure*; Gk *exodus*   e9:32 Lit *were weighed down with sleep*   f9:35 Other mss read *the Beloved*   g9:39 Lit *convulsions with foam*   h9:39 Or *bruising*, or *mauling*

⁴¹ Jesus replied, "You unbelieving and rebellious^a generation! How long will I be with you and put up with you? Bring your son here."

⁴² As the boy was still approaching, the demon knocked him down and threw him into severe convulsions. But Jesus rebuked the unclean spirit, cured the boy, and gave him back to his father. ⁴³ And they were all astonished at the greatness of God.

Jesus' Second Prediction of His Death

While everyone was amazed at all the things He was doing, He told His disciples, ⁴⁴ "Let these words sink in:^b the Son of Man is about to be betrayed into the hands of men."

⁴⁵ But they did not understand this statement; it was concealed from them so that they could not grasp it, and they were afraid to ask Him about it.^c

Who Is the Greatest?

⁴⁶ Then an argument started among them about who would be the greatest of them. ⁴⁷ But Jesus, knowing the thoughts of their hearts, took a little child and had him stand next to Him. ⁴⁸ He told them, "Whoever welcomes^d this little child in My name welcomes Me. And whoever welcomes Me welcomes Him who sent Me. For whoever is least among you— this one is great."

Another Drives Out Demons In His Name

⁴⁹ John responded, "Master, we saw someone driving out demons in Your name, and we tried to stop him because he does not follow us."

⁵⁰ "Don't stop him," Jesus told him, "because whoever is not against you is for you."^e

The Journey to Jerusalem

⁵¹ When the days were coming to a close for Him to be taken up,^f He determined^g to journey to Jerusalem. ⁵² He sent messengers ahead of Him, and on the way they entered a village of the •Samaritans to make preparations for Him.

Jesus Rejects a Violent Solution

⁵³ But they did not welcome Him, because He determined to journey to Jerusalem. ⁵⁴ When the disciples James and John saw this, they said, "Lord, do You want us to call down fire from heaven to consume them?"^h

⁵⁵ But He turned and rebuked them,^i ⁵⁶ and they went to another village.

Cost of Following Jesus

⁵⁷ As they were traveling on the road someone said to Him, "I will follow You wherever You go!"

⁵⁸ Jesus told him, "Foxes have dens, and birds of the sky^j have nests, but the Son of Man has no place to lay His head." ⁵⁹ Then He said to another, "Follow Me."

"Lord," he said, "first let me go bury my father."^k

⁶⁰ But He told him, "Let the dead bury their own dead, but you go and spread the news of the kingdom of God."

⁶¹ Another also said, "I will follow You, Lord, but first let me go and say good-bye to those at my house."

⁶² But Jesus said to him, "No one who puts his hand to the plow and looks back is fit for the kingdom of God."

---

^a **9:41** Or *corrupt*, or *perverted*, or *twisted*; Dt 32:5   ^b **9:44** Lit *Put these words in your ears*   ^c **9:45** Lit *about this statement*   ^d **9:48** Or *receives* throughout the verse   ^e **9:50** Other mss read *against us is for us*   ^f **9:51** His ascension   ^g **9:51** Lit *He stiffened His face to go*; Is 50:7   ^h **9:54** Other mss add *as Elijah also did*   ^i **9:55-56** Other mss add *and said, "You don't know what kind of spirit you belong to. 56 For the Son of Man did not come to destroy people's lives but to save them."*   ^j **9:58** Wild birds, as opposed to domestic birds   ^k **9:59** Not necessarily meaning his father was already dead

Jesus Sends Out Seventy

10 After this, the Lord appointed 70[a] others, and He sent them ahead of Him in pairs to every town and place where He Himself was about to go. ² He told them: "The harvest is abundant, but the workers are few. Therefore, pray to the Lord of the harvest to send out workers into His harvest. ³ Now go; I'm sending you out like lambs among wolves. ⁴ Don't carry a money-bag, traveling bag, or sandals; don't greet anyone along the road. ⁵ Whatever house you enter, first say, 'Peace to this household.' ⁶ If a son of peace[b] is there, your peace will rest on him; but if not, it will return to you. ⁷ Remain in the same house, eating and drinking what they offer, for the worker is worthy of his wages. Don't be moving from house to house. ⁸ When you enter any town, and they welcome you, eat the things set before you. ⁹ Heal the sick who are there, and tell them, 'The kingdom of God has come near you.' ¹⁰ When you enter any town, and they don't welcome you, go out into its streets and say, ¹¹ 'We are wiping off ⎣as a witness⎦ against you even the dust of your town that clings to our feet. Know this for certain: the kingdom of God has come near.' ¹² I tell you, on that day it will be more tolerable for Sodom than for that town.

Woe to Unrepentant Towns

¹³ "Woe to you, Chorazin! Woe to you, Bethsaida! For if the miracles that were done in you had been done in Tyre and Sidon, they would have repented long ago, sitting in sackcloth and ashes! ¹⁴ But it will be more tolerable for Tyre and Sidon at the judgment than for you. ¹⁵ And you, Capernaum, will you be exalted to heaven? No, you will go down to •Hades! ¹⁶ Whoever listens to you listens to Me. Whoever rejects you rejects Me. And whoever rejects Me rejects the One who sent Me."

Joyful Return of the Seventy

¹⁷ The Seventy[c] returned with joy, saying, "Lord, even the demons submit to us in Your name."

"I Watched Satan Fall"

¹⁸ He said to them, "I watched Satan fall from heaven like a lightning flash. ¹⁹ Look, I have given you the authority to trample on snakes and scorpions and over all the power of the enemy; nothing will ever harm you. ²⁰ However, don't rejoice that[d] the spirits submit to you, but rejoice that your names are written in heaven."

Son Reveals the Father

²¹ In that same hour He[e] rejoiced in the Holy[f] Spirit and said, "I praise[g] You, Father, Lord of heaven and earth, because You have hidden these things from the wise and the learned and have revealed them to infants. Yes, Father, because this was Your good pleasure.[h] ²² All things have[i] been entrusted to Me by My Father. No one knows who the Son is except the Father, and who the Father is except the Son, and anyone to whom the Son desires[j] to reveal Him."

²³ Then turning to His disciples He said privately, "The eyes that see the things you see are blessed! ²⁴ For I tell you that many prophets and kings wanted to see the things you see yet didn't see them; to hear the things you hear yet didn't hear them."

ᵃ**10:1** Other mss read *72*   ᵇ**10:6** A peaceful person; one open to the message of the kingdom   ᶜ**10:17** Other mss read *The Seventy-two*   ᵈ**10:20** Lit *don't rejoice in this, that*   ᵉ**10:21** Other mss read *Jesus*   ᶠ**10:21** Other mss omit *Holy*   ᵍ**10:21** Or *thank*, or *confess*   ʰ**10:21** Lit *was well-pleasing in Your sight*   ⁱ**10:22** Other mss read *And turning to the disciples, He said, "Everything has*   ʲ**10:22** Or *wills*, or *chooses*

Question on Eternal Life

25 Just then an expert in the law stood up to test Him, saying, "Teacher, what must I do to inherit eternal life?"

26 "What is written in the law?" He asked him. "How do you read it?"

27 He answered:

Love the Lord your God with all your heart, with all your soul, with all your strength, and with all your mind; and **your neighbor as yourself.**a

28 "You've answered correctly," He told him. "Do this and you will live."

29 But wanting to justify himself, he asked Jesus, "And who is my neighbor?"

Parable of Good Samaritan

30 Jesus took up ⌊the question⌋ and said: "A man was going down from Jerusalem to Jericho and fell into the hands of robbers. They stripped him, beat him up, and fled, leaving him half dead. 31 A priest happened to be going down that road. When he saw him, he passed by on the other side. 32 In the same way, a Levite, when he arrived at the place and saw him, passed by on the other side. 33 But a •Samaritan on his journey came up to him, and when he saw ⌊the man⌋, he had compassion. 34 He went over to him and bandaged his wounds, pouring on oil and wine. Then he put him on his own animal, brought him to an inn, and took care of him. 35 The next dayb he took out two •denarii, gave them to the innkeeper, and said, 'Take care of him. When I come back I'll reimburse you for whatever extra you spend.'

Which Was a Neighbor?

36 "Which of these three do you think proved to be a neighbor to the man who fell into the hands of the robbers?"

37 "The one who showed mercy to him," he said.

Then Jesus told him, "Go and do the same."

Martha and Mary Welcome Jesus

38 While they were traveling, He entered a village, and a woman named Martha welcomed Him into her home.c 39 She had a sister named Mary, who also sat at the Lord'sd feet and was listening to what He said.e 40 But Martha was distracted by her many tasks, and she came up and asked, "Lord, don't You care that my sister has left me to serve alone? So tell her to give me a hand."f

41 The Lordg answered her, "Martha, Martha, you are worried and upset about many things, 42 but one thing is necessary. Mary has made the right choice,h and it will not be taken away from her."

The Model Prayer

11 He was praying in a certain place, and when He finished, one of His disciples said to Him, "Lord, teach us to pray, just as John also taught his disciples."

2 He said to them, "Whenever you pray, say:

Father,i
Your name be honored as holy.
Your kingdom come.j
3 Give us each day our daily bread.k
4 And forgive us our sins,
   for we ourselves also
   forgive everyone

---

a**10:27** Dt 6:5; Lv 19:18   b**10:35** Other mss add *as he was leaving*   c**10:38** Other mss omit *into her home*
d**10:39** Other mss read *at Jesus'*   e**10:39** Lit *to His word* or *message*   f**10:40** Or *tell her to help me*   g**10:41** Other mss read *Jesus*   h**10:42** Lit *has chosen the good part*   i**11:2** Other mss read *Our Father in heaven*   j**11:2** Other mss add *Your will be done on earth as it is in heaven*   k**11:3** Or *our bread for tomorrow*

in debt[a] to us.
And do not bring us
  into temptation."[b]

Friend at Midnight

[5] He also said to them: "Suppose one of you[c] has a friend and goes to him at midnight and says to him, 'Friend, lend me three loaves of bread, [6] because a friend of mine on a journey has come to me, and I don't have anything to offer him.'[d] [7] Then he will answer from inside and say, 'Don't bother me! The door is already locked, and my children and I have gone to bed. I can't get up to give you anything.' [8] I tell you, even though he won't get up and give him anything because he is his friend, yet because of his persistence,[e] he will get up and give him as much as he needs.

Keep Asking, Searching, Knocking

[9] "So I say to you, keep asking,[f] and it will be given to you. Keep searching,[g] and you will find. Keep knocking,[h] and the door will be opened to you. [10] For everyone who asks receives, and the one who searches finds, and to the one who knocks, the door will be opened. [11] What father among you, if his son[i] asks for a fish, will give him a snake instead of a fish? [12] Or if he asks for an egg, will give him a scorpion? [13] If you then, who are evil, know how to give good gifts to your children, how much more will the heavenly Father give[j] the Holy Spirit to those who ask Him?"

Skepticism about Jesus' Power over Demons

[14] Now He was driving out a demon that was mute.[k] When the demon came out, the man who had been mute, spoke, and the crowds were amazed. [15] But some of them said, "He drives out demons by •Beelzebul, the ruler of the demons!" [16] And others, as a test, were demanding of Him a sign from heaven.

His Response: A House Divided

[17] Knowing their thoughts, He told them: "Every kingdom divided against itself is headed for destruction, and a house divided against itself falls. [18] If Satan also is divided against himself, how will his kingdom stand? For you say I drive out demons by Beelzebul. [19] And if I drive out demons by Beelzebul, who is it your sons[l] drive them out by? For this reason they will be your judges. [20] If I drive out demons by the finger of God, then the kingdom of God has come to you. [21] When a strong man, fully armed, guards his estate, his possessions are secure.[m] [22] But when one stronger than he attacks and overpowers him, he takes from him all his weapons[n] he trusted in, and divides up his plunder. [23] Anyone who is not with Me is against Me, and anyone who does not gather with Me scatters.

An Unclean Spirit Returns

[24] "When an unclean spirit comes out of a man, it roams through waterless places looking for rest, and not finding rest, it then[o] says, 'I'll go back to my house where I came from.' [25] And returning, it finds ⌊the house⌋ swept and put in order. [26] Then it goes and brings seven other spirits more evil than itself, and they enter and settle down there. As a result, that man's last condition is worse than the first."

---

[a]11:4 Or *everyone who wrongs us* [b]11:4 Other mss add *But deliver us from the evil one* [c]11:5 Lit *Who of you*
[d]11:6 Lit *I have nothing to set before him* [e]11:8 Or *annoying persistence,* or *shamelessness* [f]11:9 Or *you, ask*
[g]11:9 Or *Search* [h]11:9 Or *Knock* [i]11:11 Other mss read *son asks for bread, would give him a stone? Or if he*
[j]11:13 Lit *the Father from heaven will give* [k]11:14 A demon that caused the man to be mute [l]11:19 Your exorcists
[m]11:21 Lit *his possessions are in peace* [n]11:22 Gk *panoplia,* the armor and weapons of a foot soldier; Eph 6:11,13
[o]11:24 Other mss omit *then*

Test of True Blessedness

²⁷ As He was saying these things, a woman from the crowd raised her voice and said to Him, "The womb that bore You and the one who nursed You are blessed!"

²⁸ He said, "Even more, those who hear the word of God and keep it are blessed!"

Sign of Jonah

²⁹ As the crowds were increasing, He began saying: "This generation is an evil generation. It demands a sign, but no sign will be given to it except the sign of Jonah.ᵃ ³⁰ For just as Jonah became a sign to the people of Nineveh, so also the •Son of Man will be to this generation. ³¹ The queen of the south will rise up at the judgment with the men of this generation and condemn them, because she came from the ends of the earth to hear the wisdom of Solomon, and look— something greater than Solomon is here! ³² The men of Nineveh will rise up at the judgment with this generation and condemn it, because they repented at Jonah's proclamation, and look—something greater than Jonah is here!

Lamp of the Body

³³ "No one lights a lamp and puts it in the cellar or under a basket,ᵇ but on a lampstand, so that those who come in may see its light. ³⁴ Your eye is the lamp of the body. When your eye is good, your whole body is also full of light. But when it is bad, your body is also full of darkness. ³⁵ Take care then, that the light in you is not darkness. ³⁶ If therefore your whole body is full of light, with no part of it in darkness, the whole body will be full of light, as when a lamp shines its light on you."ᶜ

Jesus Dines with a Pharisee

³⁷ As He was speaking, a •Pharisee asked Him to dine with him. So He went in and reclined at the table. ³⁸ When the Pharisee saw this, he was amazed that He did not first perform the ritual wash-ingᵈ before dinner. ³⁹ But the Lord said to him: "Now you Pharisees clean the outside of the cup and dish, but inside you are full of greed and evil. ⁴⁰ Fools! Didn't He who made the outside make the inside too? ⁴¹ But give to charity what is within,ᵉ and then everything is clean for you.

Jesus Denounces Religious Hypocrisy

⁴² "But woe to you Pharisees! You give a tenthᶠ of mint, rue, and every kind of herb, and you bypassᵍ justice and love for God.ʰ These things you should have done without neglecting the others.

⁴³ "Woe to you Pharisees! You love the front seat in the •synagogues and greetings in the marketplaces.

⁴⁴ "Woe to you!ⁱ You are like unmarked graves; the people who walk over them don't know it."

Jesus Denounces Experts in Religious Law

⁴⁵ One of the experts in the law answered Him, "Teacher, when You say these things You insult us too."

⁴⁶ Then He said: "Woe also to you experts in the law! You load people with burdens that are hard to carry, yet you yourselves don't touch these burdens with one of your fingers.

⁴⁷ "Woe to you! You build monumentsʲ to the prophets, and your fathers killed them. ⁴⁸ Therefore you are witnesses that you approveᵏ the deeds of your fa-

---

ᵃ**11:29** Other mss add *the prophet*   ᵇ**11:33** Other mss omit *or under a basket*   ᶜ**11:36** Or *shines on you with its rays*   ᵈ**11:38** Lit *He did not first wash*   ᵉ**11:41** Or *But donate from the heart as charity*   ᶠ**11:42** Or *a tithe*   ᵍ**11:42** Or *neglect*   ʰ**11:42** Lit *the justice and the love of God*   ⁱ**11:44** Other mss read *you scribes and Pharisees, hypocrites!*   ʲ**11:47** Or *graves*   ᵏ**11:48** Lit *witnesses and approve*

thers, for they killed them, and you build their monuments.[a] 49 Because of this, the wisdom of God said, 'I will send them prophets and apostles, and some of them they will kill and persecute,' 50 so that this generation may be held responsible for the blood of all the prophets shed since the foundation of the world[b]— 51 from the blood of Abel to the blood of Zechariah, who perished between the altar and the sanctuary.

"Yes, I tell you, this generation will be held responsible.[c]

52 "Woe to you experts in the law! You have taken away the key of knowledge! You didn't go in yourselves, and you hindered those who were going in."

Scribes and Pharisees Plot against Him

53 When He left there,[d] the •scribes and the Pharisees began to oppose Him fiercely and to cross-examine Him about many things; 54 they were lying in wait for Him to trap Him in something He said.[e]

Guard Against Yeast of Pharisees—Hypocrisy

12 In these circumstances,[f] a crowd of many thousands came together, so that they were trampling on one another. He began to say to His disciples first: "Be on your guard against the yeast[g] of the •Pharisees, which is hypocrisy. 2 There is nothing covered that won't be uncovered, nothing hidden that won't be made known. 3 Therefore whatever you have said in the dark will be heard in the light, and what you have whispered in an ear in private rooms will be proclaimed on the housetops.

Fear God

4 "And I say to you, My friends, don't fear those who kill the body, and after that can do nothing more. 5 But I will show you the One to fear: Fear Him who has authority to throw ⌊people⌋ into •hell after death. Yes, I say to you, this is the One to fear! 6 Aren't five sparrows sold for two pennies?[h] Yet not one of them is forgotten in God's sight. 7 Indeed, the hairs of your head are all counted. Don't be afraid; you are worth more than many sparrows!

Acknowledge Christ

8 "And I say to you, anyone who acknowledges Me before men, the •Son of Man will also acknowledge him before the angels of God, 9 but whoever denies Me before men will be denied before the angels of God. 10 Anyone who speaks a word against the Son of Man will be forgiven, but the one who blasphemes against the Holy Spirit will not be forgiven. 11 Whenever they bring you before •synagogues and rulers and authorities, don't worry about how you should defend yourselves or what you should say. 12 For the Holy Spirit will teach you at that very hour what must be said."

Jesus Not a Judge Over Possessions

13 Someone from the crowd said to Him, "Teacher, tell my brother to divide the inheritance with me."

14 "Friend,"[i] He said to him, "who appointed Me a judge or arbitrator over you?" 15 He then told them, "Watch out and be on guard against all greed because one's life is not in the abundance of his possessions."

---

[a]11:48 Other mss omit *their monuments*   [b]11:50 Lit *so that the blood of all . . . world may be required of this generation,*   [c]11:51 Lit *you, it will be required of this generation*   [d]11:53 Other mss read *And as He was saying these things to them*   [e]11:54 Other mss add *so that they might bring charges against Him*   [f]12:1 Or *Meanwhile,* or *At this time,* or *During this period*   [g]12:1 Or *leaven*   [h]12:6 Lit *two assaria; the assarion* (sg) was a small copper coin   [i]12:14 Lit *Man*

Parable of Rich Fool

16 Then He told them a parable: "A rich man's land was very productive. 17 He thought to himself, 'What should I do, since I don't have anywhere to store my crops? 18 I will do this,' he said. 'I'll tear down my barns and build bigger ones and store all my grain and my goods there. 19 Then I'll say to myself, "You[a] have many goods stored up for many years. Take it easy; eat, drink, and enjoy yourself."'

20 "But God said to him, 'You fool! This very night your •life is demanded of you. And the things you have prepared— whose will they be?'

21 "That's how it is with the one who stores up treasure for himself and is not rich toward God."

Jesus' Cure for Anxiety

22 Then He said to His disciples: "Therefore I tell you, don't worry about your life, what you will eat; or about the body, what you will wear. 23 For life is more than food and the body more than clothing. 24 Consider the ravens: they don't sow or reap; they don't have a storeroom or a barn; yet God feeds them. Aren't you worth much more than the birds? 25 Can any of you add a •cubit to his height[b] by worrying? 26 If then you're not able to do even a little thing, why worry about the rest?

27 "Consider how the wildflowers grow: they don't labor or spin thread. Yet I tell you, not even Solomon in all his splendor was adorned like one of these! 28 If that's how God clothes the grass, which is in the field today and is thrown into the furnace tomorrow, how much more will He do for you—

you of little faith? 29 Don't keep striving for what you should eat and what you should drink, and don't be anxious. 30 For the Gentile world eagerly seeks all these things, and your Father knows that you need them.

Seek His Kingdom

31 "But seek His kingdom, and these things will be provided for you. 32 Don't be afraid, little flock, because your Father delights to give you the kingdom. 33 Sell your possessions and give to the poor. Make money-bags for yourselves that won't grow old, an inexhaustible treasure in heaven, where no thief comes near and no moth destroys. 34 For where your treasure is, there your heart will be also.

Be Ready for Master's Return

35 "Be ready for service[c] and have your lamps lit. 36 You must be like people waiting for their master to return[d] from the wedding banquet so that when he comes and knocks, they can open ⌊the door⌋ for him at once. 37 Those •slaves the master will find alert when he comes will be blessed. •I assure you: He will get ready,[e] have them recline at the table, then come and serve them. 38 If he comes in the middle of the night, or even near dawn,[f] and finds them alert, those slaves are blessed. 39 But know this: if the homeowner had known at what hour the thief was coming, he would not have let his house be broken into. 40 You also be ready, because the Son of Man is coming at an hour that you do not expect."

---

a12:19 Lit say to my soul, "Soul, you   b12:25 Or add one moment to his life-span   c12:35 Lit Let your loins be girded; an idiom for tying up loose outer clothing in preparation for action; Ex 12:11   d12:36 Lit master, when he should return   e12:37 Lit will gird himself   f12:38 Lit even in the second or third watch

Importance of Preparation for Return of Master

⁴¹ "Lord," Peter asked, "are You telling this parable to us or to everyone?"

⁴² The Lord said: "Who then is the faithful and sensible manager his master will put in charge of his household servants to give them their allotted food at the proper time? ⁴³ That •slave whose master finds him working when he comes will be rewarded. ⁴⁴ I tell you the truth: he will put him in charge of all his possessions. ⁴⁵ But if that slave says in his heart, 'My master is delaying his coming,' and starts to beat the male and female slaves, and to eat and drink and get drunk, ⁴⁶ that slave's master will come on a day he does not expect him and at an hour he does not know. He will cut him to pieces[a] and assign him a place with the unbelievers.[b] ⁴⁷ And that slave who knew his master's will and didn't prepare himself or do it[c] will be severely beaten. ⁴⁸ But the one who did not know and did things deserving of blows will be beaten lightly. Much will be required of everyone who has been given much. And even more will be expected of the one who has been entrusted with more.[d]

Jesus Brings Not Peace but Division

⁴⁹ "I came to bring fire on the earth, and how I wish it were already set ablaze! ⁵⁰ But I have a baptism to be baptized with, and how it consumes Me until it is finished! ⁵¹ Do you think that I came here to give peace to the earth? No, I tell you, but rather division! ⁵² From now on, five in one household will be divided: three against two, and two against three.

⁵³ They will be divided,
   father against son,
   son against father,
   mother against daughter,
   daughter against mother,
   mother-in-law against
      her daughter-in-law,
   and daughter-in-law against
      mother-in-law."[e]

Learning to Interpret the Time

⁵⁴ He also said to the crowds: "When you see a cloud rising in the west, right away you say, 'A storm is coming,' and so it does. ⁵⁵ And when the south wind is blowing, you say, 'It's going to be a scorcher!' and it is. ⁵⁶ Hypocrites! You know how to interpret the appearance of the earth and the sky, but why don't you know how to interpret this time?

Settle before Prison!

⁵⁷ "Why don't you judge for yourselves what is right? ⁵⁸ As you are going with your adversary to the ruler, make an effort to settle with him on the way. Then he won't drag you before the judge, the judge hand you over to the bailiff, and the bailiff throw you into prison. ⁵⁹ I tell you, you will never get out of there until you have paid the last cent."[f]

Repent or Perish

13 At that time, some people came and reported to Him about the Galileans whose blood •Pilate had mixed with their sacrifices. ² And He[g] responded to them, "Do you think that these Galileans were more sinful than all Galileans because they suffered these things? ³ No, I tell you; but unless you repent, you will all perish as well! ⁴ Or those 18 that the tower in Siloam fell on and killed—do you think they were

---

[a]**12:46** Lit *him in two* [b]**12:46** Or *unfaithful,* or *untrustworthy* [c]**12:47** Lit *or do toward his will* [d]**12:48** Or *much*
[e]**12:53** Mc 7:6 [f]**12:59** Gk *lepton,* the smallest and least valuable copper coin in use [g]**13:2** Other mss read *Jesus*

more sinful than all the people who live in Jerusalem? [5] No, I tell you; but unless you repent, you will all perish as well!"

Parable of the Barren Fig Tree

[6] And He told this parable: "A man had a fig tree that was planted in his vineyard. He came looking for fruit on it and found none. [7] He told the vineyard worker, 'Listen, for three years I have come looking for fruit on this fig tree and haven't found any. Cut it down! Why should it even waste the soil?'

[8] "But he replied to him, 'Sir,[a] leave it this year also, until I dig around it and fertilize it. [9] Perhaps it will bear fruit next year, but if not, you can cut it down.'"

Another Sabbath: Jesus Heals a Daughter of Abraham

[10] As He was teaching in one of the •synagogues on the Sabbath, [11] a woman was there who had been disabled by a spirit[b] for over 18 years. She was bent over and could not straighten up at all.[c] [12] When Jesus saw her, He called out to her,[d] "Woman, you are free of your disability." [13] Then He laid His hands on her, and instantly she was restored and began to glorify God.

[14] But the leader of the synagogue, indignant because Jesus had healed on the Sabbath, responded by telling the crowd, "There are six days when work should be done; therefore come on those days and be healed and not on the Sabbath day."

[15] But the Lord answered him and said, "Hypocrites! Doesn't each one of you untie his ox or donkey from the feeding trough on the Sabbath and lead it to water? [16] Satan has bound this woman, a daughter of Abraham, for 18 years—shouldn't she be untied from this bondage on the Sabbath day?"

[17] When He had said these things, all His adversaries were humiliated, but the whole crowd was rejoicing over all the glorious things He was doing.

Parables of Mustard Seed and Yeast

[18] He said therefore, "What is the kingdom of God like, and what can I compare it to? [19] It's like a mustard seed that a man took and sowed in his garden. It grew and became a tree, and the birds of the sky nested in its branches."

[20] Again He said, "What can I compare the kingdom of God to? [21] It's like yeast that a woman took and mixed into 50 pounds[e] of flour until it spread through the entire mixture."[f]

Enter the Narrow Door

[22] He went through one town and village after another, teaching and making His way to Jerusalem. [23] "Lord," someone asked Him, "are there few being saved?"[g]

He said to them, [24] "Make every effort to enter through the narrow door, because I tell you, many will try to enter and won't be able [25] once the homeowner gets up and shuts the door. Then you will stand[h] outside and knock on the door, saying, 'Lord, open up for us!' He will answer you, 'I don't know you or where you're from.' [26] Then you will say,[i] 'We ate and drank in Your presence, and You taught in our streets!' [27] But He will say, 'I tell you, I don't know you or where you're from. Get away from Me, all you workers of unrighteousness!' [28] There will be weeping and gnashing of teeth in that place, when you see Abra-

---

[a]**13:8** Or Lord   [b]**13:11** Lit had a spirit of disability   [c]**13:11** Or straighten up completely   [d]**13:12** Or He summoned her   [e]**13:21** Lit 3 sata; about 40 quarts   [f]**13:21** Or until all of it was leavened   [g]**13:23** Or are the saved few? (in number); lit are those being saved few?   [h]**13:25** Lit you will begin to stand   [i]**13:26** Lit you will begin to say

ham, Isaac, Jacob, and all the prophets in the kingdom of God but yourselves thrown out. ²⁹ They will come from east and west, from north and south, and recline at the table in the kingdom of God. ³⁰ Note this: <u>some are last who will be first, and some are first who will be last.</u>"

Jesus Clashes with Herod Antipas (the Tetrarch)

³¹ At that time some •Pharisees came and told Him, "Go, get out of here! •Herod wants to kill You!"

³² He said to them, "Go tell that fox, 'Look! I'm driving out demons and performing healings today and tomorrow, and on the third day^a I will complete My work.'^{b} ³³ Yet I must travel today, tomorrow, and the next day, because it is not possible for a prophet to perish outside of Jerusalem!

Jesus Laments over Jerusalem

³⁴ "Jerusalem, Jerusalem! The city who kills the prophets and stones those who are sent to her. How often I wanted to gather your children together, as a hen gathers her chicks under her wings, but you were not willing! ³⁵ See, your house^c is abandoned to you. And I tell you, you will not see Me until the time comes when you say, **Blessed is He who comes in the name of the Lord!**"^{d}

Jesus Eats with Pharisee: a Sabbath Controversy

14 One Sabbath, when He went to eat^e at the house of one of the leading •Pharisees, they were watching Him closely. ² There in front of Him was a man whose body was swollen with fluid.^{f} ³ In response, Jesus asked the law experts and the Pharisees, "Is it lawful

to heal on the Sabbath or not?" ⁴ But they kept silent. He took the man, healed him, and sent him away. ⁵ And to them, He said, "Which of you whose son or ox falls into a well, will not immediately pull him out on the Sabbath day?" ⁶ To this they could find no answer.

Jesus on Humility: a Wedding Banquet

⁷ He told a parable to those who were invited, when He noticed how they would choose the best places for themselves: ⁸ "When you are invited by someone to a wedding banquet, don't recline at the best place, because a more distinguished person than you may have been invited by your host.^{g} ⁹ The one who invited both of you may come and say to you, 'Give your place to this man,' and then in humiliation, you will proceed to take the lowest place.

¹⁰ "But when you are invited, go and recline in the lowest place, so that when the one who invited you comes, he will say to you, 'Friend, move up higher.' You will then be honored in the presence of all the other guests. ¹¹ <u>For everyone who exalts himself will be humbled, and the one who humbles himself will be exalted.</u>"

¹² He also said to the one who had invited Him, "When you give a lunch or a dinner, don't invite your friends, your brothers, your relatives, or your rich neighbors, because they might invite you back, and you would be repaid. ¹³ On the contrary, when you host a banquet, invite those who are poor, maimed, lame, or blind. ¹⁴ And you will be blessed, because they cannot repay you; for you will be repaid at the resurrection of the righteous."

^{a}**13:32** Very shortly ^{b}**13:32** Lit *I will be finished* ^{c}**13:35** Probably the temple; Jr 12:7; 22:5 ^{d}**13:35** Ps 118:26 ^{e}**14:1** Lit *eat bread*; = eat a meal ^{f}**14:2** Afflicted with dropsy or edema ^{g}**14:8** Lit *by him*

Parable of the Large Banquet

¹⁵ When one of those who reclined at the table with Him heard these things, he said to Him, "The one who will eat bread in the kingdom of God is blessed!"

¹⁶ Then He told him: "A man was giving a large banquet and invited many. ¹⁷ At the time of the banquet, he sent his slave to tell those who were invited, 'Come, because everything is now ready.'

¹⁸ "But without exceptionᵃ they all began to make excuses. The first one said to him, 'I have bought a field, and I must go out and see it. I ask you to excuse me.'

¹⁹ "Another said, 'I have bought five yoke of oxen, and I'm going to try them out. I ask you to excuse me.'

²⁰ "And another said, 'I just got married,ᵇ and therefore I'm unable to come.'

²¹ "So the slave came back and reported these things to his master. Then in anger, the master of the house told his slave, 'Go out quickly into the streets and alleys of the city, and bring in here the poor, maimed, blind, and lame!'

²² " 'Master,' the slave said, 'what you ordered has been done, and there's still room.'

²³ "Then the master told the slave, 'Go out into the highways and lanes and make them come in, so that my house may be filled. ²⁴ For I tell you, not one of those men who were invited will enjoy my banquet!' "

Cost of Following Jesus

²⁵ Now great crowds were traveling with Him. So He turned and said to them: ²⁶ "If anyone comes to Me and does not hate his own father and mother, wife and children, brothers and sisters—yes, and even his own life—he cannot be My disciple. ²⁷ Whoever does not bear his own cross and come after Me cannot be My disciple.

Calculating the Cost: a Tower and a War

²⁸ "For which of you, wanting to build a tower, doesn't first sit down and calculate the cost to see if he has enough to complete it? ²⁹ Otherwise, after he has laid the foundation and cannot finish it, all the onlookers will begin to make fun of him, ³⁰ saying, 'This man started to build and wasn't able to finish.'

³¹ "Or what king, going to war against another king, will not first sit down and decide if he is able with 10,000 to oppose the one who comes against him with 20,000? ³² If not, while the other is still far off, he sends a delegation and asks for terms of peace. ³³ In the same way, therefore, every one of you who does not say good-bye toᶜ all his possessions cannot be My disciple.

Tasty Salt

³⁴ "Now, salt is good, but if salt should lose its taste, how will it be made salty? ³⁵ It isn't fit for the soil or for the manure pile; they throw it out. Anyone who has ears to hear should listen!"

Pharisees and Scribes Complain

15 All the tax collectors and sinners were approaching to listen to Him. ² And the •Pharisees and •scribes were complaining, "This man welcomes sinners and eats with them!"

Jesus Answers: Parable of Lost Sheep

³ So He told them this parable: ⁴ "What man among you, who has 100 sheep and loses one of them, does not leave the 99 in the open fieldᵈ and go after the lost

---

ᵃ**14:18** Lit And from one (voice)　　ᵇ**14:20** Lit I have married a woman　　ᶜ**14:33** Or does not renounce or leave
ᵈ**15:4** Or the wilderness

one until he finds it? ⁵ When he has found it, he joyfully puts it on his shoulders, ⁶ and coming home, he calls his friends and neighbors together, saying to them, 'Rejoice with me, because I have found my lost sheep!' ⁷ I tell you, in the same way, there will be more joy in heaven over one sinner who repents than over 99 righteous people who don't need repentance.

Parable of Lost Coin

⁸ "Or what woman who has 10 silver coins,ᵃ if she loses one coin, does not light a lamp, sweep the house, and search carefully until she finds it? ⁹ When she finds it, she calls her women friends and neighbors together, saying, 'Rejoice with me, because I have found the silver coin I lost!' ¹⁰ I tell you, in the same way, there is joy in the presence of God's angels over one sinner who repents."

Parable of Lost Son

Foolish Younger Son

¹¹ He also said: "A man had two sons. ¹² The younger of them said to his father, 'Father, give me the share of the estate I have coming to me.' So he distributed the assetsᵇ to them. ¹³ Not many days later, the younger son gathered together all he had and traveled to a distant country, where he squandered his estate in foolish living. ¹⁴ After he had spent everything, a severe famine struck that country, and he had nothing.ᶜ ¹⁵ Then he went to work forᵈ one of the citizens of that country, who sent him into his fields to feed pigs. ¹⁶ He longed to eat his fill fromᵉ the carob podsᶠ the pigs were eating, but no one would give him any.

¹⁷ When he came to his senses,ᵍ he said, 'How many of my father's hired hands have more than enough food, and here I am dyingʰ of hunger!ⁱ ¹⁸ I'll get up, go to my father, and say to him, Father, I have sinned against heaven and in your sight. ¹⁹ I'm no longer worthy to be called your son. Make me like one of your hired hands.' ²⁰ So he got up and went to his father. But while the son was still a long way off, his father saw him and was filled with compassion. He ran, threw his arms around his neck,ʲ and kissed him. ²¹ The son said to him, 'Father, I have sinned against heaven and in your sight. I'm no longer worthy to be called your son.'

Father's Celebration

²² "But the father told his •slaves, 'Quick! Bring out the best robe and put it on him; put a ring on his fingerᵏ and sandals on his feet. ²³ Then bring the fattened calf and slaughter it, and let's celebrate with a feast, ²⁴ because this son of mine was dead and is alive again; he was lost and is found!' So they began to celebrate.

Older Son's Anger

²⁵ "Now his older son was in the field; as he came near the house, he heard music and dancing. ²⁶ So he summoned one of the servants and asked what these things meant. ²⁷ 'Your brother is here,' he told him, 'and your father has slaughtered the fattened calf because he has him back safe and sound.'ˡ

²⁸ "Then he became angry and didn't want to go in. So his father came out and pleaded with him. ²⁹ But he replied to his father, 'Look, I have been slaving

---

ᵃ**15:8** Gk *10 drachmas*; a *drachma* was a silver coin = a •*denarius*.   ᵇ**15:12** Lit *livelihood, or living*   ᶜ**15:14** Lit *and he began to be in need*   ᵈ**15:15** Lit *went and joined with*   ᵉ**15:16** Other mss read *to fill his stomach with*   ᶠ**15:16** Seed casings of a tree used as food for cattle, pigs, and sometimes the poor   ᵍ**15:17** Lit *to himself*   ʰ**15:17** The word *dying* is translated *lost* in vv. 4-9 and vv. 24,32.   ⁱ**15:17** Or *dying in the famine*; v. 14   ʲ**15:20** Lit *He ran, fell on his neck*   ᵏ**15:22** Lit *hand*   ˡ**15:27** Lit *him back healthy*

many years for you, and I have never disobeyed your orders, yet you never gave me a young goat so I could celebrate with my friends. [30] But when this son of yours came, who has devoured your assets[a] with prostitutes, you slaughtered the fattened calf for him.'

Father's Wise Insight

[31] "'Son,'[b] he said to him, 'you are always with me, and everything I have is yours. [32] But we had to celebrate and rejoice, because this brother of yours was dead and is alive again; he was lost and is found.'"

Parable of
Dishonest Manager

16 He also said to the disciples: "There was a rich man who received an accusation that his manager was squandering his possessions. [2] So he called the manager in and asked, 'What is this I hear about you? Give an account of your management, because you can no longer be [my] manager.'

[3] "Then the manager said to himself, 'What should I do, since my master is taking the management away from me? I'm not strong enough to dig; I'm ashamed to beg. [4] I know what I'll do so that when I'm removed from management, people will welcome me into their homes.'

[5] "So he summoned each one of his master's debtors. 'How much do you owe my master?' he asked the first one.

[6] "'A hundred measures of oil,' he said.

"'Take your invoice,' he told him, 'sit down quickly, and write 50.'

[7] "Next he asked another, 'How much do you owe?'

"'A hundred measures of wheat,' he said.

"'Take your invoice,' he told him, 'and write 80.'

[8] "The master praised the unrighteous manager because he had acted astutely. For the sons of this age are more astute than the sons of light [in dealing] with their own people.[c] [9] And I tell you, make friends for yourselves by means of the unrighteous money so that when it fails,[d] they may welcome you into eternal dwellings. [10] Whoever is faithful in very little is also faithful in much, and whoever is unrighteous in very little is also unrighteous in much. [11] So if you have not been faithful with the unrighteous money, who will trust you with what is genuine? [12] And if you have not been faithful with what belongs to someone else, who will give you what is your own? [13] No household slave can be the •slave of two masters, since either he will hate one and love the other, or he will be devoted to one and despise the other. You can't be slaves to both God and money."

Law, Prophets,
and Kingdom of God

[14] The •Pharisees, who were lovers of money, were listening to all these things and scoffing at Him. [15] And He told them: "You are the ones who justify yourselves in the sight of others, but God knows your hearts. For what is highly admired by people is revolting in God's sight.

[16] "The Law and the Prophets were[e] until John; since then, the good news of the kingdom of God has been proclaimed, and everyone is strongly urged to enter it.[f] [17] But it is easier for

---

'.it *livelihood,* or *living* [b]**15:31** Or *Child* [c]**16:8** Lit *own generation* [d]**16:9** Other mss read *when you fail* or vay [e]**16:16** Perhaps *were proclaimed,* or *were in effect* [f]**16:16** Or *everyone is forcing his way into it*

heaven and earth to pass away than for one stroke of a letter in the law to drop out.

Divorce and Adultery

18 "Everyone who divorces his wife and marries another woman commits adultery, and everyone who marries a woman divorced from her husband commits adultery.

Rich Man and Lazarus

19 "There was a rich man who would dress in purple and fine linen, feasting lavishly every day. 20 But a poor man named Lazarus, covered with sores, was left at his gate. 21 He longed to be filled with what fell from the rich man's table, but instead the dogs would come and lick his sores. 22 One day the poor man died and was carried away by the angels to Abraham's side.ª The rich man also died and was buried. 23 And being in torment in •Hades, he looked up and saw Abraham a long way off, with Lazarus at his side. 24 'Father Abraham!' he called out, 'Have mercy on me and send Lazarus to dip the tip of his finger in water and cool my tongue, because I am in agony in this flame!'

25 " 'Son,'ᵇ Abraham said, 'remember that during your life you received your good things, just as Lazarus received bad things, but now he is comforted here, while you are in agony. 26 Besides all this, a great chasm has been fixed between us and you, so that those who want to pass over from here to you cannot; neither can those from there cross over to us.'

27 " 'Father,' he said, 'then I beg you to send him to my father's house— 28 because I have five brothers—to warn

them, so they won't also come to this place of torment.'

29 "But Abraham said, 'They have Moses and the prophets; they should listen to them.'

30 " 'No, father Abraham,' he said. 'But if someone from the dead goes to them, they will repent.'

31 "But he told him, 'If they don't listen to Moses and the prophets, they will not be persuaded if someone rises from the dead.' "

Jesus Warns about "Little Ones"

17 He said to His disciples, "Offensesᶜ will certainly come,ᵈ but woe to the one they come through! 2 It would be better for him if a millstoneᵉ were hung around his neck and he were thrown into the sea than for him to cause one of these little ones to •stumble. 3 Be on your guard.

Dealing with Sinful Brother

If your brother sins,ᶠ rebuke him, and if he repents, forgive him. 4 And if he sins against you seven times in a day, and comes back to you seven times, saying, 'I repent,' you must forgive him."

"Increase Our Faith"

5 The apostles said to the Lord, "Increase our faith."

6 "If you have faith the size ofᵍ a mustard seed," the Lord said, "you can say to this mulberry tree, 'Be uprooted and planted in the sea,' and it will obey you.

7 "Which one of you having a slave plowing or tending sheep, will say to him when he comes in from the field, 'Come at once and sit down to eat'? 8 Instead, will he not tell him, 'Prepare something for me to eat, get ready,ʰ and

---

ª**16:22** Lit to the fold of Abraham's robe, or to Abraham's bosom; see Jn 13:23   ᵇ**16:25** Lit Child   ᶜ**17:1** Or Traps, or Bait-sticks, or Causes of stumbling, or Causes of sin   ᵈ**17:1** Lit It is impossible for offenses not to come   ᵉ**17:2** Large stone used for grinding grains into flour   ᶠ**17:3** Other mss add against you   ᵍ**17:6** Lit faith like   ʰ**17:8** Lit eat, tuck in your robe, or eat, gird yourself

serve me while I eat and drink; later you can eat and drink'? ⁹ Does he thank that slave because he did what was commanded?ᵃ ¹⁰ In the same way, when you have done all that you were commanded, you should say, 'We are good-for-nothing slaves; we've only done our duty.' "

Ten Lepers Healed

¹¹ While traveling to Jerusalem, He passed betweenᵇ Samaria and Galilee. ¹² As He entered a village, 10 men with serious skin diseases met Him. They stood at a distance ¹³ and raised their voices, saying, "Jesus, Master, have mercy on us!"

¹⁴ When He saw them, He told them, "Go and show yourselves to the priests." And while they were going, they were healed.ᶜ

One Grateful Leper

¹⁵ But one of them, seeing that he was healed, returned and, with a loud voice, gave glory to God. ¹⁶ He fell facedown at His feet, thanking Him. And he was a •Samaritan.

¹⁷ Then Jesus said, "Were not 10 cleansed? Where are the nine? ¹⁸ Didn't any returnᵈ to give glory to God except this foreigner?" ¹⁹ And He told him, "Get up and go on your way. Your faith has made you well."ᵉ

Coming of the Kingdom

²⁰ Being asked by the •Pharisees when the kingdom of God will come, He answered them, "The kingdom of God is not coming with something observable; ²¹ no one will say,ᶠ 'Look here!' or 'There!' For you see, the kingdom of God is among you."

²² Then He told the disciples: "The days are coming when you will long to see one of the days of the •Son of Man, but you won't see it. ²³ They will say to you, 'Look there!' or 'Look here!' Don't follow or run after them. ²⁴ For as the lightning flashes from horizon to horizon and lights up the sky, so the Son of Man will be in His day. ²⁵ But first He must suffer many things and be rejected by this generation.

²⁶ "Just as it was in the days of Noah, so it will be in the days of the Son of Man: ²⁷ people went on eating, drinking, marrying and giving in marriage until the day Noah boarded the ark, and the flood came and destroyed them all. ²⁸ It will be the same as it was in the days of Lot: people went on eating, drinking, buying, selling, planting, building. ²⁹ But on the day Lot left Sodom, fire and sulfur rained from heaven and destroyed them all. ³⁰ It will be like that on the day the Son of Man is revealed. ³¹ On that day, a man on the housetop, whose belongings are in the house, must not come down to get them. Likewise the man who is in the field must not turn back. ³² Remember Lot's wife! ³³ Whoever tries to make his •life secureᵍ ʰ will lose it, and whoever loses his life will preserve it. ³⁴ I tell you, on that night two will be in one bed: one will be taken and the other will be left. ³⁵ Two women will be grinding grain together: one will be taken and the other left. [³⁶ Two will be in a field: one will be taken, and the other will be left."]ⁱ

³⁷ "Where, Lord?" they asked Him.

He said to them, "Where the corpse is, there also the vultures will be gathered."

ᵃ17:9 Other mss add *I don't think so*   ᵇ17:11 Or *through the middle of*   ᶜ17:14 Lit *cleansed*   ᵈ17:18 Lit *Were they not found returning*   ᵉ17:19 Or *faith has saved you*   ᶠ17:21 Lit *they will not say*   ᵍ17:33 Other mss read *to save his life*   ʰ17:33 Or *tries to retain his life*   ⁱ17:36 Other mss omit bracketed text

Parable of the Persistent Widow

18 He then told them a parable on the need for them to pray always and not become discouraged: ² "There was a judge in one town who didn't fear God or respect man. ³ And a widow in that town kept coming to him, saying, 'Give me justice against my adversary.'

⁴ "For a while he was unwilling, but later he said to himself, 'Even though I don't fear God or respect man, ⁵ yet because this widow keeps pestering me,ᵃ I will give her justice, so she doesn't wear me outᵇ by her persistent coming.'"

⁶ Then the Lord said, "Listen to what the unjust judge says. ⁷ Will not God grant justice to His elect who cry out to Him day and night? Will He delay ⸤to help⸥ them?ᶜ ⁸ I tell you that He will swiftly grant them justice. Nevertheless, when the •Son of Man comes, will He find that faithᵈ on earth?"

Parable of Pharisee and the Tax Collector

⁹ He also told this parable to some who trusted in themselves that they were righteous and looked down on everyone else: ¹⁰ "Two men went up to the •temple complex to pray, one a •Pharisee and the other a tax collector. ¹¹ The Pharisee took his standᵉ and was praying like this: 'God, I thank You that I'm not like other peopleᶠ—greedy, unrighteous, adulterers, or even like this tax collector. ¹² I fast twice a week; I give a tenthᵍ of everything I get.'

¹³ "But the tax collector, standing far off, would not even raise his eyes to heaven but kept striking his chestʰ and saying, 'God, turn Your wrath from

meⁱ—a sinner!' ¹⁴ I tell you, this one went down to his house justified rather than the other; because everyone who exalts himself will be humbled, but the one who humbles himself will be exalted."

Jesus Blesses the Children

¹⁵ Some people were even bringing infants to Him so He might touch them, but when the disciples saw it, they rebuked them. ¹⁶ Jesus, however, invited them: "Let the little children come to Me, and don't stop them, because the kingdom of God belongs to such as these. ¹⁷ •I assure you: Whoever does not welcome the kingdom of God like a little child will never enter it."

Rich Ruler and Eternal Life

¹⁸ A ruler asked Him, "Good Teacher, what must I do to inherit eternal life?"

¹⁹ "Why do you call Me good?" Jesus asked him. "No one is good but One— God. ²⁰ You know the commandments:

> **Do not commit adultery;**
> **do not murder;**
> **do not steal;**
> **do not bear false witness;**
> **honor your father and mother.**"ʲ

²¹ "I have kept all these from my youth," he said.

²² When Jesus heard this, He told him, "You still lack one thing: sell all that you have and distribute it to the poor, and you will have treasure in heaven. Then come, follow Me."

²³ After he heard this, he became extremely sad, because he was very rich.

Possessions and the Kingdom

[24] Seeing that he became sad,[a] Jesus said, "How hard it is for those who have wealth to enter the kingdom of God! [25] For it is easier for a camel to go through the eye of a needle than for a rich person to enter the kingdom of God."

[26] Those who heard this asked, "Then who can be saved?"

[27] He replied, "What is impossible with men is possible with God."

[28] Then Peter said, "Look, we have left what we had and followed You."

[29] So He said to them, "I assure you: There is no one who has left a house, wife or brothers, parents or children because of the kingdom of God, [30] who will not receive many times more at this time, and eternal life in the age to come."

Jesus' Third Prediction of His Death

[31] Then He took the Twelve aside and told them, "Listen! We are going up to Jerusalem. Everything that is written through the prophets about the Son of Man will be accomplished. [32] For He will be handed over to the Gentiles, and He will be mocked, insulted, spit on; [33] and after they flog Him, they will kill Him, and He will rise on the third day."

[34] They understood none of these things. This saying[b] was hidden from them, and they did not grasp what was said.

Jesus in Jericho

Blind Man Receives Sight

[35] As He drew near Jericho, a blind man was sitting by the road begging. [36] Hearing a crowd passing by, he inquired what this meant. [37] "Jesus the •Nazarene is passing by," they told him.

[38] So he called out, "Jesus, Son of David, have mercy on me!" [39] Then those in front told him to keep quiet,[c] but he kept crying out all the more, "Son of David, have mercy on me!"

[40] Jesus stopped and commanded that he be brought to Him. When he drew near, He asked him, [41] "What do you want Me to do for you?"

"Lord," he said, "I want to see!"

[42] "Receive your sight!" Jesus told him. "Your faith has healed you."[d] [43] Instantly he could see, and he began to follow Him, glorifying God. All the people, when they saw it, gave praise to God.

Jesus Visits Zacchaeus

19 He entered Jericho and was passing through. [2] There was a man named Zacchaeus who was a chief tax collector, and he was rich. [3] He was trying to see who Jesus was, but he was not able because of the crowd, since he was a short man. [4] So running ahead, he climbed up a sycamore tree to see Jesus, since He was about to pass that way. [5] When Jesus came to the place, He looked up and said to him, "Zacchaeus, hurry and come down, because today I must stay at your house."

[6] So he quickly came down and welcomed Him joyfully. [7] All who saw it began to complain, "He's gone to lodge with a sinful man!"

Zacchaeus' Restitution

[8] But Zacchaeus stood there and said to the Lord, "Look, I'll give[e] half of my possessions to the poor, Lord! And if I have extorted anything from anyone, I'll pay[f] back four times as much!"

[a]**18:24** Other mss omit *he became sad*   [b]**18:34** The meaning of the saying   [c]**18:39** Or *those in front rebuked him*   [d]**18:42** Or *has saved you*   [e]**19:8** Or *I give*   [f]**19:8** Or *I pay*

9 "Today salvation has come to this house," Jesus told him, "because he too is a son of Abraham. 10 For the •Son of Man has come to seek and to save the lost."ᵃ

Parable of the Nobleman and 10 Minas

11 As they were listening to this, He went on to tell a parable because He was near Jerusalem, and they thought the kingdom of God was going to appear right away.

12 Therefore He said: "A nobleman traveled to a far country to receive for himself authority to be kingᵇ and then return. 13 He called 10 of his •slaves, gave them 10 minas,ᶜ and told them, 'Engage in business until I come back.'

His Rebellious Subjects

14 "But his subjects hated him and sent a delegation after him, saying, 'We don't want this man to rule over us!'

Work of His Slaves Evaluated

15 "At his return, having received the authority to be king,ᵇ he summoned those •slaves he had given the money to so he could find out how much they had made in business. 16 The first came forward and said, 'Master, your mina has earned 10 more minas.'

17 "'Well done, goodᵈ •slave!' he told him. 'Because you have been faithful in a very small matter, have authority over 10 towns.'

18 "The second came and said, 'Master, your mina has made five minas.'

19 "So he said to him, 'You will be over five towns.'

20 "And another came and said, 'Master, here is your mina. I have kept it hidden away in a cloth 21 because I was

afraid of you, for you're a tough man: you collect what you didn't deposit and reap what you didn't sow.'

Judgment Rendered

22 "He told him, 'I will judge you by what you have said,ᵉ you evil •slave! If you knew I was a tough man, collecting what I didn't deposit and reaping what I didn't sow, 23 why didn't you put my money in the bank? And when I returned, I would have collected it with interest!' 24 So he said to those standing there, 'Take the mina away from him and give it to the one who has 10 minas.'

25 "But they said to him, 'Master, he has 10 minas.'

26 "'I tell you, that to everyone who has, more will be given; and from the one who does not have, even what he does have will be taken away. 27 But bring here these enemies of mine, who did not want me to rule over them, and slaughterᶠ them in my presence.'"

Jesus' Triumphal Entry

28 When He had said these things, He went on ahead, going up to Jerusalem. 29 As He approached Bethphage and Bethany, at the place called the •Mount of Olives, He sent two of the disciples 30 and said, "Go into the village ahead of you. As you enter it, you will find a young donkey tied there, on which no one has ever sat. Untie it and bring it here. 31 If anyone asks you, 'Why are you untying it?' say this: 'The Lord needs it.'"

32 So those who were sent left and found it just as He had told them. 33 As they were untying the young donkey, its owners said to them, "Why are you untying the donkey?"

ᵃ19:10 Or save what was lost   ᵇ19:12,15 Lit to receive for himself a kingdom or sovereignty   ᶜ19:13 = Gk coin worth 100 drachmas or about 100 days' wages   ᵈ19:17 Or capable   ᵉ19:22 Lit you out of your mouth   ᶠ19:27 Or execute

³⁴ "The Lord needs it," they said. ³⁵ Then they brought it to Jesus, and after throwing their robes on the donkey, they helped Jesus get on it. ³⁶ As He was going along, they were spreading their robes on the road. ³⁷ Now He came near the path down the Mount of Olives, and the whole crowd of the disciples began to praise God joyfully with a loud voice for all the miracles they had seen:

³⁸ Blessed is the King
who comes in the name
of the Lord.ᵃ ᵇ
Peace in heaven
and glory in the highest heaven!

Jesus Rebuffs Pharisees

³⁹ Some of the •Pharisees from the crowd told Him, "Teacher, rebuke Your disciples."

⁴⁰ He answered, "I tell you, if they were to keep silent, the stones would cry out!"

Jesus' Love for Jerusalem

⁴¹ As He approached and saw the city, He wept over it, ⁴² saying, "If you knew this day what ⌊would bring⌋ peace—but now it is hidden from your eyes. ⁴³ For the days will come on you when your enemies will build an embankment against you, surround you, and hem you in on every side. ⁴⁴ They will crush you and your children within you to the ground, and they will not leave one stone on another in you, because you did not recognize the time of your visitation."

Jesus Cleanses Temple Complex

⁴⁵ He went into the •temple complex and began to throw out those who were selling,ᶜ ⁴⁶ and He said, "It is written,

My house will be a house of prayer, but you have made it a den of thieves!"ᵈ

⁴⁷ Every day He was teaching in the temple complex. The •chief priests, the •scribes, and the leaders of the people were looking for a way to destroy Him, ⁴⁸ but they could not find a way to do it, because all the people were captivated by what they heard.ᵉ

Religious Leaders Challenge Authority of Jesus

20 One dayᶠ as He was teaching the people in the •temple complex and proclaiming the good news, the •chief priests and the •scribes, with the elders, came up ² and said to Him: "Tell us, by what authority are You doing these things? Who is it who gave You this authority?"

Jesus Replies with a Question

³ He answered them, "I will also ask you a question. Tell Me, ⁴ was the baptism of John from heaven or from men?"

⁵ They discussed it among themselves: "If we say, 'From heaven,' He will say, 'Why didn't you believe him?' ⁶ But if we say, 'From men,' all the people will stone us, because they are convinced that John was a prophet."

⁷ So they answered that they did not know its origin.ᵍ

⁸ And Jesus said to them, "Neither will I tell you by what authority I do these things."

Parable of Vineyard Owner

⁹ Then He began to tell the people this parable: "A man planted a vineyard, leased it to tenant farmers, and went away for a long time. ¹⁰ At harvest time he sent a •slave to the farmers so that

ᵃ**19:38** The words *the King* are substituted for *He* in Ps 118:26.   ᵇ**19:38** Ps 118:26   ᶜ**19:45** Other mss add *and buying in it*   ᵈ**19:46** Is 56:7; Jr 7:11   ᵉ**19:48** Lit *people hung on what they heard*   ᶠ**20:1** Lit *It happened on one of the days*
ᵍ**20:7** Or *know where it was from*

they might give him some fruit from the vineyard. But the farmers beat him and sent him away empty-handed. [11] He sent yet another slave, but they beat that one too, treated him shamefully, and sent him away empty-handed. [12] And he sent yet a third, but they wounded this one too and threw him out.

[13] "Then the owner of the vineyard said, 'What should I do? I will send my beloved son. Perhaps[a] they will respect him.'

[14] "But when the tenant farmers saw him, they discussed it among themselves and said, 'This is the heir. Let's kill him, so the inheritance will be ours!' [15] So they threw him out of the vineyard and killed him.

"Therefore, what will the owner of the vineyard do to them? [16] He will come and destroy those farmers and give the vineyard to others."

But when they heard this they said, "No—never!"

[17] But He looked at them and said, "Then what is the meaning of this Scripture:[b]

**The stone that the builders rejected—
this has become
the cornerstone?[c] [d]**

[18] Everyone who falls on that stone will be broken to pieces, and if it falls on anyone, it will grind him to powder!"

Religious Leaders Want "To Get Their Hands on Him"

[19] Then the scribes and the chief priests looked for a way to get their hands on Him that very hour, because they knew He had told this parable against them, but they feared the people.

Giving to God and Caesar

[20] They[e] watched closely and sent spies who pretended to be righteous,[f] so they could catch Him in what He said,[g] to hand Him over to the governor's rule and authority. [21] They questioned Him, "Teacher, we know that You speak and teach correctly, and You don't show partiality,[h] but teach truthfully the way of God. [22] Is it lawful for us to pay taxes to Caesar or not?"

[23] But detecting their craftiness, He said to them,[i] [24] "Show Me a •denarius. Whose image and inscription does it have?"

"Caesar's," they said.

[25] "Well then," He told them, "give back to Caesar the things that are Caesar's and to God the things that are God's."

[26] They were not able to catch Him in what He said[g] in public,[j] and being amazed at His answer, they became silent.

Sadducees and the Resurrection: the Seven Brothers

[27] Some of the •Sadducees, who say there is no resurrection, came up and questioned Him: [28] "Teacher, Moses wrote for us that **if a man's brother** has a wife, and **dies childless, his brother should take the wife and produce •offspring for his brother.**[k] [29] Now there were seven brothers. The first took a wife and died without children. [30] Also the second[l] [31] and the third took her. In the same way, all seven died and left no children. [32] Finally, the woman died too. [33] Therefore, in the resurrection, whose wife will the woman be? For all seven had married her."[m]

---

a**20:13** Other mss add *when they see him*   b**20:17** Lit *What then is this that is written*   c**20:17** Lit *the head of the corner*   d**20:17** Ps 118:22   e**20:20** The scribes and chief priests of v. 19   f**20:20** Or *upright*; that is, loyal to God's law   g**20:20,26** Lit *catch Him in [a] word*   h**20:21** Lit *You don't receive a face*   i**20:23** Other mss add *"Why are you testing Me?*   j**20:26** Lit *in front of the people*   k**20:28** Dt 25:5   l**20:30** Other mss add *took her as wife, and he died without children*   m**20:33** Lit *had her as wife*

Jesus' Response

³⁴ Jesus told them, "The sons of this age marry and are given in marriage. ³⁵ But those who are counted worthy to take part in that age and in the resurrection from the dead neither marry nor are given in marriage. ³⁶ For they cannot die anymore, because they are like angels and are sons of God, since they are sons of the resurrection. ³⁷ Moses even indicated ⌊in the passage⌋ about the burning bush that the dead are raised, where he calls the Lord **the God of Abraham and the God of Isaac and the God of Jacob.**ᵃ ³⁸ He is not God of the dead but of the living, because all are living toᵇ Him."

³⁹ Some of the scribes answered, "Teacher, You have spoken well." ⁴⁰ And they no longer dared to ask Him anything.

Jesus Poses Question about the Messiah

⁴¹ Then He said to them, "How can they say that the •Messiah is the Son of David? ⁴² For David himself says in the Book of Psalms:

The Lord declared to my Lord,
'Sit at My right hand
⁴³   **until I make Your enemies**
        Your footstool.'ᶜ

⁴⁴ David calls Him 'Lord'; how then can the Messiah be his Son?"

Jesus Warns against Scribes

⁴⁵ While all the people were listening, He said to His disciples, ⁴⁶ "Beware of the scribes, who want to go around in long robes and who love greetings in the marketplaces, the front seats in the •synagogues, and the places of honor at banquets. ⁴⁷ They devour widows' houses and say long prayers just for show. These will receive greater punishment."ᵈ

Poor Widow's Gift

21 He looked up and saw the rich dropping their offerings into the temple treasury. ² He also saw a poor widow dropping in two tiny coins.ᵉ ³ "I tell you the truth," He said. "This poor widow has put in more than all of them. ⁴ For all these people have put in gifts out of their surplus, but she out of her poverty has put in all she had to live on."

Jesus Predicts Destruction of Temple

⁵ As some were talking about the •temple complex, how it was adorned with beautiful stones and gifts dedicated to God,ᶠ He said, ⁶ "These things that you see—the days will come when not one stone will be left on another that will not be thrown down!"

Jesus on Signs of End of Age

⁷ "Teacher," they asked Him, "so when will these things be? And what will be the sign when these things are about to take place?"

⁸ Then He said, "Watch out that you are not deceived. For many will come in My name, saying, 'I am He,' and, 'The time is near.' Don't follow them. ⁹ When you hear of wars and rebellions,ᵍ don't be alarmed. Indeed, these things must take place first, but the end won't come right away."

¹⁰ Then He told them: "Nation will be raised up against nation, and kingdom against kingdom. ¹¹ There will be violent earthquakes, and famines and plagues in various places, and there will be terrifying sights and great signs from

---

ᵃ**20:37** Ex 3:6,15   ᵇ**20:38** Or *with*   ᶜ**20:42-43** Ps 110:1   ᵈ**20:47** Or *judgment*   ᵉ**21:2** Lit *two lepta*; the *lepton* was the smallest and least valuable Gk coin in use.   ᶠ**21:5** Gifts given to the temple in fulfillment of vows to God   ᵍ**21:9** Or *insurrections*, or *revolutions*

heaven. ¹² But before all these things, they will lay their hands on you and persecute you. They will hand you over to the •synagogues and prisons, and you will be brought before kings and governors because of My name. ¹³ It will lead to an opportunity for you to witness.ᵃ ¹⁴ Therefore make up your mindsᵇ not to prepare your defense ahead of time, ¹⁵ for I will give you such wordsᶜ and a wisdom that none of your adversaries will be able to resist or contradict. ¹⁶ You will even be betrayed by parents, brothers, relatives, and friends. They will kill some of you. ¹⁷ You will be hated by everyone because of My name, ¹⁸ but not a hair of your head will be lost. ¹⁹ By your endurance gainᵈ your •lives.

Destruction of Jerusalem

²⁰ "When you see Jerusalem surrounded by armies, then recognize that its desolation has come near. ²¹ Then those in Judea must flee to the mountains! Those inside the cityᵉ must leave it, and those who are in the country must not enter it, ²² because these are days of vengeance to fulfill all the things that are written. ²³ Woe to pregnant women and nursing mothers in those days, for there will be great distress in the landᶠ and wrath against this people. ²⁴ They will fall by the edge of the sword and be led captive into all the nations, and Jerusalem will be trampled by the Gentilesᵍ until the times of the Gentiles are fulfilled.

Coming of the Son of Man

²⁵ "Then there will be signs in the sun, moon, and stars; and there will be an-guish on the earth among nations bewildered by the roaring sea and waves. ²⁶ People will faint from fear and expectation of the things that are coming on the world, because the celestial powers will be shaken. ²⁷ Then they will see the •Son of Man coming in a cloud with power and great glory. ²⁸ But when these things begin to take place, stand up and lift up your heads, because your redemption is near!"

Parable of the Fig Tree

²⁹ Then He told them a parable: "Look at the fig tree, and all the trees. ³⁰ As soon as they put out ⌊leaves⌋ you can see for yourselves and recognize that summer is already near. ³¹ In the same way, when you see these things happening, recognizeʰ that the kingdom of God is near. ³² •I assure you: This generation will certainly not pass away until all things take place. ³³ Heaven and earth will pass away, but My words will never pass away.

Need for Watchfulness

³⁴ "Be on your guard, so that your minds are not dulledⁱ from carousing,ʲ drunkenness, and worries of life, or that day will come on you unexpectedly ³⁵ like a trap. For it will come on all who live on the face of the whole earth. ³⁶ But be alert at all times, praying that you may have strengthᵏ to escape all these things that are going to take place and to stand before the Son of Man."

³⁷ During the day, He was teaching in the temple complex, but in the evening He would go out and spend the night on what is called the •Mount of Olives. ³⁸ Then all the people would come early

---

ᵃ**21:13** Lit lead to a testimony for you   ᵇ**21:14** Lit Therefore place (determine) in your hearts   ᶜ**21:15** Lit you a mouth   ᵈ**21:19** Other mss read endurance you will gain   ᵉ**21:21** Lit inside her   ᶠ**21:23** Or the earth   ᵍ**21:24** Or nations   ʰ**21:31** Or you know   ⁱ**21:34** Lit your hearts are not weighed down   ʲ**21:34** Or hangovers   ᵏ**21:36** Other mss read you may be counted worthy

in the morning to hear Him in the temple complex.

Plot to Kill Jesus

22 The Festival of •Unleavened Bread, which is called •Passover, was drawing near. ² The •chief priests and the •scribes were looking for a way to put Him to death, because they were afraid of the people.

Satan Enters Judas

³ Then Satan entered Judas, called Iscariot, who was numbered among the Twelve. ⁴ He went away and discussed with the chief priests and temple police how he could hand Him over to them. ⁵ They were glad and agreed to give him silver.ᵃ ⁶ So he accepted ⌐the offer⌐ and started looking for a good opportunity to betray Him to them when the crowd was not present.

Preparation for Passover

⁷ Then the Day of Unleavened Bread came when the Passover lamb had to be sacrificed. ⁸ Jesus sent Peter and John, saying, "Go and prepare the Passover meal for us, so we can eat it."

⁹ "Where do You want us to prepare it?" they asked Him.

¹⁰ "Listen," He said to them, "when you've entered the city, a man carrying a water jug will meet you. Follow him into the house he enters. ¹¹ Tell the owner of the house, 'The Teacher asks you, "Where is the guest room where I can eat the Passover with My disciples?"' ¹² Then he will show you a large, furnished room upstairs. Make the preparations there."

¹³ So they went and found it just as He had told them, and they prepared the Passover.

The First Lord's Supper

¹⁴ When the hour came, He reclined at the table, and the apostles with Him. ¹⁵ Then He said to them, "I have fervently desired to eat this Passover with you before I suffer. ¹⁶ For I tell you, I will not eat it againᵇ until it is fulfilled in the kingdom of God." ¹⁷ Then He took a cup, and after giving thanks, He said, "Take this and share it among yourselves. ¹⁸ For I tell you, from now on I will not drink of the fruit of the vine until the kingdom of God comes."

¹⁹ And He took bread, gave thanks, broke it, gave it to them, and said, "This is My body, which is given for you. Do this in remembrance of Me."

²⁰ In the same way He also took the cup after supper and said, "This cup is the new covenant ⌐established by⌐ My blood; it is shed for you.ᶜ ²¹ But look, the hand of the one betraying Me is at the table with Me! ²² For the •Son of Man will go away as it has been determined, but woe to that man by whom He is betrayed!"

²³ So they began to argue among themselves which of them it could be who was going to do this thing.

Disciples Dispute over Greatness

²⁴ Then a dispute also arose among them about who should be considered the greatest. ²⁵ But He said to them, "The kings of the Gentiles dominate them, and those who have authority over them are calledᵈ 'Benefactors.'ᵉ ²⁶ But it must not be like that among you. On the contrary, whoever is greatest among you must become like the youngest, and whoever leads, like the one serving. ²⁷ For who is greater, the one at the table or the one serving? Isn't

---

ᵃ**22:5** Or *money*; Mt 26:15 specifies 30 pieces of silver; Zch 11:12-13　ᵇ**22:16** Other mss omit *again*
ᶜ**22:19-20** Other mss omit *which is given for you* (v. 19) through the end of v. 20　ᵈ**22:25** Or *them call themselves*
ᵉ**22:25** Title of honor given to those who benefited the public good

it the one at the table? But I am among you as the One who serves. [28] You are the ones who stood by Me in My trials. [29] I bestow on you a kingdom, just as My Father bestowed one on Me, [30] so that you may eat and drink at My table in My kingdom. And you will sit on thrones judging the 12 tribes of Israel.

Peter's Denial Predicted

[31] "Simon, Simon,[a] look out! Satan has asked to sift you[b] like wheat. [32] But I have prayed for you[c] that your faith may not fail. And you, when you have turned back, strengthen your brothers."

[33] "Lord," he told Him, "I'm ready to go with You both to prison and to death!"

[34] "I tell you, Peter," He said, "the rooster will not crow today until[d] you deny three times that you know Me!"

Money-Bag, Suitcase, and Sword

[35] He also said to them, "When I sent you out without money-bag, traveling bag, or sandals, did you lack anything?"

"Not a thing," they said.

[36] Then He said to them, "But now, whoever has a money-bag should take it, and also a traveling bag. And whoever doesn't have a sword should sell his robe and buy one. [37] For I tell you, what is written must be fulfilled in Me: **And He was counted among the outlaws.**[e] Yes, what is written about Me is coming to its fulfillment."

[38] "Lord," they said, "look, here are two swords."

"Enough of that!"[f] He told them.

Prayer in the Garden

[39] He went out and made His way as usual to the •Mount of Olives, and the disciples followed Him. [40] When He reached the place, He told them, "Pray that you may not enter into temptation." [41] Then He withdrew from them about a stone's throw, knelt down, and began to pray, [42] "Father, if You are willing, take this cup away from Me—nevertheless, not My will, but Yours, be done."

[[43] Then an angel from heaven appeared to Him, strengthening Him. [44] Being in anguish, He prayed more fervently, and His sweat became like drops of blood falling to the ground.][g] [45] When He got up from prayer and came to the disciples, He found them sleeping, exhausted from their grief.[h] [46] "Why are you sleeping?" He asked them. "Get up and pray, so that you won't enter into temptation."

Judas Kisses Jesus

[47] While He was still speaking, suddenly a mob was there, and one of the Twelve named Judas was leading them. He came near Jesus to kiss Him, [48] but Jesus said to him, "Judas, are you betraying the Son of Man with a kiss?"

[49] When those around Him saw what was going to happen, they asked, "Lord, should we strike with the sword?" [50] Then one of them struck the high priest's slave and cut off his right ear.

[51] But Jesus responded, "No more of this!"[i] And touching his ear, He healed him. [52] Then Jesus said to the chief priests, temple police, and the elders who had come for Him, "Have you come out with swords and clubs as if I were a criminal?[j] [53] Every day while I was with you in the •temple complex, you never laid a hand on Me. But this is your hour—and the dominion of darkness."

---

[a]**22:31** Other mss read *Then the Lord said, "Simon, Simon*   [b]**22:31** *you* (pl in Gk)   [c]**22:32** *you* (sg in Gk)
[d]**22:34** Other mss read *before*   [e]**22:37** Is 53:12   [f]**22:38** Or *It is enough!*   [g]**22:43-44** Other mss omit bracketed text
[h]**22:45** Lit *sleeping from grief*   [i]**22:51** Lit *Permit as far as this*   [j]**22:52** Lit *as against a criminal*

Peter Denies His Lord

⁵⁴ They seized Him, led Him away, and brought Him into the high priest's house. Meanwhile Peter was following at a distance. ⁵⁵ They lit a fire in the middle of the courtyard and sat down together, and Peter sat among them. ⁵⁶ When a servant saw him sitting in the firelight, and looked closely at him, she said, "This man was with Him too."

⁵⁷ But he denied it: "Woman, I don't know Him!"

⁵⁸ After a little while, someone else saw him and said, "You're one of them too!"

"Man, I am not!" Peter said.

⁵⁹ About an hour later, another kept insisting, "This man was certainly with Him, since he's also a Galilean."

⁶⁰ But Peter said, "Man, I don't know what you're talking about!" Immediately, while he was still speaking, a rooster crowed. ⁶¹ Then the Lord turned and looked at Peter. So Peter remembered the word of the Lord, how He had said to him, "Before the rooster crows today, you will deny Me three times." ⁶² And he went outside and wept bitterly.

Jesus Mocked and Beaten

⁶³ The men who were holding Jesus started mocking and beating Him. ⁶⁴ After blindfolding Him, they kept[a] asking, "Prophesy! Who hit You?" ⁶⁵ And they were saying many other blasphemous things against Him.

Jesus Faces the Sanhedrin

⁶⁶ When daylight came, the elders[b] of the people, both the chief priests and the scribes, convened and brought Him before their •Sanhedrin. ⁶⁷ They said, "If You are the •Messiah, tell us."

But He said to them, "If I do tell you, you will not believe. ⁶⁸ And if I ask you, you will not answer. ⁶⁹ But from now on, the Son of Man will be seated at the right hand of the Power of God."

⁷⁰ They all asked, "Are You, then, the Son of God?"

And He said to them, "You say that I am."

⁷¹ "Why do we need any more testimony," they said, "since we've heard it ourselves from His mouth?"

Jesus Faces Pilate

23 Then their whole assembly rose up and brought Him before •Pilate. ² They began to accuse Him, saying, "We found this man subverting our nation, opposing payment of taxes to Caesar, and saying that He Himself is the •Messiah, a King."

³ So Pilate asked Him, "Are You the King of the Jews?"

He answered him, "You have said it."[c]

⁴ Pilate then told the •chief priests and the crowds, "I find no grounds for charging this man."

⁵ But they kept insisting, "He stirs up the people, teaching throughout all Judea, from Galilee where He started even to here."

Pilate Sends Jesus to Herod Antipas

⁶ When Pilate heard this,[d] he asked if the man was a Galilean. ⁷ Finding that He was under •Herod's jurisdiction, he sent Him to Herod, who was also in Jerusalem during those days. ⁸ Herod was very glad to see Jesus; for a long time he had wanted to see Him, because he had heard about Him and was hoping to see some miracle[e] performed by Him. ⁹ So he kept asking Him questions, but Jesus did not answer him.

ᵃ**22:64** Other mss add *striking Him on the face and*   ᵇ**22:66** Or *council of elders*   ᶜ**23:3** Or *That is true;* an affirmative oath   ᵈ**23:6** Other mss read *heard "Galilee"*   ᵉ**23:8** Or *sign*

¹⁰ The chief priests and the •scribes stood by, vehemently accusing Him. ¹¹ Then Herod, with his soldiers, treated Him with contempt, mocked Him, dressed Him in a brilliant robe, and sent Him back to Pilate. ¹² That very day Herod and Pilate became friends.^a Previously, they had been hostile toward each other.

Jesus' Second Appearance before Pilate

¹³ Pilate called together the chief priests, the leaders, and the people, ¹⁴ and said to them, "You have brought me this man as one who subverts the people. But in fact, after examining Him in your presence, I have found no grounds to charge this man with those things you accuse Him of. ¹⁵ Neither has Herod, because he sent Him back to us. Clearly, He has done nothing to deserve death. ¹⁶ Therefore I will have Him whipped^b and ⌊then⌋ release Him." [¹⁷ For according to the festival he had to release someone to them.]^c

Release Barabbas!

¹⁸ Then they all cried out together, "Take this man away! Release Barabbas to us!" ¹⁹ (He had been thrown into prison for a rebellion that had taken place in the city, and for murder.)

Crucify Him!

²⁰ Pilate, wanting to release Jesus, addressed them again, ²¹ but they kept shouting, "Crucify! Crucify Him!"

²² A third time he said to them, "Why? What has this man done wrong? I have found in Him no grounds for the death penalty. Therefore I will have Him whipped and ⌊then⌋ release Him."

Pilate Releases Barabbas and Hands over Jesus

²³ But they kept up the pressure, demanding with loud voices that He be crucified. And their voices^d won out. ²⁴ So Pilate decided to grant their demand ²⁵ and released the one they were asking for, who had been thrown into prison for rebellion and murder. But he handed Jesus over to their will.

Way to the Cross

²⁶ As they led Him away, they seized Simon, a Cyrenian, who was coming in from the country, and laid the cross on him to carry behind Jesus. ²⁷ A great multitude of the people followed Him, including women who were mourning and lamenting Him. ²⁸ But turning to them, Jesus said, "Daughters of Jerusalem, do not weep for Me, but weep for yourselves and your children. ²⁹ Look, the days are coming when they will say, 'Blessed are the barren, the wombs that never bore, and the breasts that never nursed!' ³⁰ Then they will begin to say to the mountains, 'Fall on us!' and to the hills, 'Cover us!'^e ³¹ For if they do these things when the wood is green, what will happen when it is dry?"

Jesus Crucified between Two Criminals

³² Two others—criminals—were also led away to be executed with Him. ³³ When they arrived at the place called The Skull, they crucified Him there, along with the criminals, one on the right and one on the left. [³⁴ Then Jesus said, "Father, forgive them, because they do not know what they are doing."]^c And they divided His clothes and cast lots.

---

^a**23:12** Lit *friends with one another*   ^b**23:16** Gk *paideuo;* to discipline or "teach a lesson"; 1 Kg 12:11,14 LXX; 2 Ch 10:11,14; perhaps a way of referring to the Roman scourging; Lat *flagellatio*   ^c**23:17,34** Other mss omit bracketed text   ^d**23:23** Other mss add *and those of the chief priests*   ^e**23:30** Hs 10:8

³⁵ The people stood watching, and even the leaders kept scoffing: "He saved others; let Him save Himself if this is God's Messiah, the Chosen One!" ³⁶ The soldiers also mocked Him. They came offering Him sour wine ³⁷ and said, "If You are the King of the Jews, save Yourself!"

³⁸ An inscription was above Him:^a

> **THIS IS**
> **THE KING OF THE JEWS**

³⁹ Then one of the criminals hanging there began to yell insults at^b Him: "Aren't You the Messiah? Save Yourself and us!"

The Repentant Criminal

⁴⁰ But the other answered, rebuking him: "Don't you even fear God, since you are undergoing the same punishment? ⁴¹ We are punished justly, because we're getting back what we deserve for the things we did, but this man has done nothing wrong." ⁴² Then he said, "Jesus, remember me^c when You come into Your kingdom!"

⁴³ And He said to him, "•I assure you: Today you will be with Me in paradise."

Darkness at Noon: Death of Jesus

⁴⁴ It was now about noon,^d and darkness came over the whole land^e until three,^f ⁴⁵ because the sun's light failed.^g The curtain of the sanctuary was split down the middle. ⁴⁶ And Jesus called out with a loud voice, "Father, **into Your hands I entrust My spirit.**"^h Saying this, He breathed His last.

⁴⁷ When the •centurion saw what happened, he began to glorify God, saying, "This man really was righteous!" ⁴⁸ All the crowds that had gathered for this spectacle, when they saw what had taken place, went home, striking their chests.ⁱ ⁴⁹ But all who knew Him, including the women who had followed Him from Galilee, stood at a distance, watching these things.

Burial of Jesus

⁵⁰ There was a good and righteous man named Joseph, a member of the •Sanhedrin, ⁵¹ who had not agreed with their plan and action. He was from Arimathea, a Judean town, and was looking forward to the kingdom of God. ⁵² He approached Pilate and asked for Jesus' body. ⁵³ Taking it down, he wrapped it in fine linen and placed it in a tomb cut into the rock, where no one had ever been placed.^j ⁵⁴ It was preparation day, and the Sabbath was about to begin.^k ⁵⁵ The women who had come with Him from Galilee followed along and observed the tomb and how His body was placed. ⁵⁶ Then they returned and prepared spices and perfumes. And they rested on the Sabbath according to the commandment.

Resurrection Morning

24 On the first day of the week, very early in the morning, they^l came to the tomb, bringing the spices they had prepared. ² They found the stone rolled away from the tomb. ³ They went in but did not find the body of the Lord Jesus. ⁴ While they were perplexed about this, suddenly two men stood by them in dazzling clothes. ⁵ So the women were terrified and bowed down to the ground.^m

"Why are you looking for the living among the dead?" asked the men. ⁶ "He is not here, but He has been resurrected!

^a**23:38** Other mss add *written in Greek, Latin, and Hebrew letters*   ^b**23:39** Or *began to blaspheme*   ^c**23:42** Other mss add *Lord*   ^d**23:44** Lit *about the sixth hour*   ^e**23:44** Or *whole earth*   ^f**23:44** Lit *the ninth hour*   ^g**23:45** Other mss read *three, and the sun was darkened*   ^h**23:46** Ps 31:5   ⁱ**23:48** *Mourning*   ^j**23:53** Or *interred,* or *laid*   ^k**23:54** Lit *was dawning;* not in the morning but at sundown Friday   ^l**24:1** Other mss add *and other women with them*   ^m**24:5** Lit *and inclined their faces to the ground*

Remember how He spoke to you when He was still in Galilee, [7] saying, 'The •Son of Man must be betrayed into the hands of sinful men, be crucified, and rise on the third day'?" [8] And they remembered His words.

Women Report
to Skeptical Disciples

[9] Returning from the tomb, they reported all these things to the Eleven and to all the rest. [10] •Mary Magdalene, Joanna, Mary the mother of James, and the other women with them were telling the apostles these things. [11] But these words seemed like nonsense to them, and they did not believe the women. [12] Peter, however, got up and ran to the tomb. When he stooped to look in, he saw only the linen cloths.[a] So he went home, amazed at what had happened.

Risen Jesus
and Emmaus Disciples

[13] Now that same day two of them were on their way to a village called[b] Emmaus, which was about seven miles[c] from Jerusalem. [14] Together they were discussing everything that had taken place. [15] And while they were discussing and arguing, Jesus Himself came near and began to walk along with them. [16] But they[d] were prevented from recognizing Him. [17] Then He asked them, "What is this dispute that you're having[e] with each other as you are walking?" And they stopped ⌊walking and looked⌋ discouraged.

[18] The one named Cleopas answered Him, "Are You the only visitor in Jerusalem who doesn't know the things that happened there in these days?"

[19] "What things?" He asked them.

So they said to Him, "The things concerning Jesus the •Nazarene, who was a Prophet powerful in action and speech before God and all the people, [20] and how our •chief priests and leaders handed Him over to be sentenced to death, and they crucified Him. [21] But we were hoping that He was the One who was about to redeem Israel. Besides all this, it's the third day since these things happened. [22] Moreover, some women from our group astounded us. They arrived early at the tomb, [23] and when they didn't find His body, they came and reported that they had seen a vision of angels who said He was alive. [24] Some of those who were with us went to the tomb and found it just as the women had said, but they didn't see Him."

Jesus Rebukes
and Teaches Them

[25] He said to them, "How unwise and slow you are to believe in your hearts all that the prophets have spoken! [26] Didn't the •Messiah have to suffer these things and enter into His glory?" [27] Then beginning with Moses and all the Prophets, He interpreted for them the things concerning Himself in all the Scriptures.

[28] They came near the village where they were going, and He gave the impression that He was going farther. [29] But they urged Him: "Stay with us, because it's almost evening, and now the day is almost over." So He went in to stay with them.

Jesus Recognized

[30] It was as He reclined at the table with them that He took the bread, blessed and broke it, and gave it to them. [31] Then their eyes were opened, and they recognized Him, but He

---

[a]**24:12** Other mss add *lying there*   [b]**24:13** Lit *village, which name is*   [c]**24:13** Lit *about 60 stadia*; 1 *stadion* = 600 feet   [d]**24:16** Lit *their eyes*   [e]**24:17** Lit *What are these words that you are exchanging*

disappeared from their sight. ³²So they said to each other, "Weren't our hearts ablaze within us while He was talking with us on the road and explaining the Scriptures to us?"

The Two Report

³³That very hour they got up and returned to Jerusalem. They found the Eleven and those with them gathered together, ³⁴who said,ᵃ "The Lord has certainly been raised, and has appeared to Simon!" ³⁵Then they began to describe what had happened on the road and how He was made known to them in the breaking of the bread.

Jesus Appears to Eleven and Others

³⁶And as they were saying these things, He Himself stood among them. He said to them, "Peace to you!" ³⁷But they were startled and terrified and thought they were seeing a ghost. ³⁸"Why are you troubled?" He asked them. "And why do doubts arise in your hearts? ³⁹Look at My hands and My feet, that it is I Myself! Touch Me and see, because a ghost does not have flesh and bones as you can see I have." ⁴⁰Having said this, He showed them His hands and feet. ⁴¹But while they still could not believeᵇ because of ⌊their⌋ joy and were amazed, He asked them,

"Do you have anything here to eat?" ⁴²So they gave Him a piece of a broiled fish,ᶜ ⁴³and He took it and ate in their presence.

Jesus Teaches from Scriptures

⁴⁴Then He told them, "These are My words that I spoke to you while I was still with you—that everything written about Me in the Law of Moses, the Prophets, and the Psalms must be fulfilled." ⁴⁵Then He opened their minds to understand the Scriptures. ⁴⁶He also said to them, "This is what is written:ᵈ the Messiah would suffer and rise from the dead the third day, ⁴⁷and repentance forᵉ forgiveness of sins would be proclaimed in His name to all the nations, beginning at Jerusalem. ⁴⁸You are witnesses of these things. ⁴⁹And look, I am sending youᶠ what My Father promised. As for you, stay in the cityᵍ until you are empoweredʰ from on high."

Ascension of Jesus

⁵⁰Then He led them out as far as Bethany, and lifting up His hands He blessed them. ⁵¹And while He was blessing them, He left them and was carried up into heaven. ⁵²After worshiping Him, they returned to Jerusalem with great joy. ⁵³And they were continually in the •temple complex blessing God.ⁱ

ᵃ**24:34** Gk is specific that this refers to the Eleven and those with them.   ᵇ**24:41** Or *they still disbelieved*
ᶜ**24:42** Other mss add *and some honeycomb*   ᵈ**24:46** Other mss add *and thus it was necessary that*   ᵉ**24:47** Other mss read *repentance and*   ᶠ**24:49** Lit *upon you*   ᵍ**24:49** Other mss add *of Jerusalem*   ʰ**24:49** Lit *clothed with power*   ⁱ**24:53** Other mss read *praising and blessing God. Amen.*

JOHN

In the Beginning, the Word

1 In the beginning was the Word,[a]
and the Word was with God,
and the Word was God.

2 He was with God in the beginning.

3 All things were created
through Him,
and apart from Him not one thing
was created
that has been created.

4 Life was in Him,[b]
and that life was
the light of men.

5 That light shines in the darkness,
yet the darkness did not
overcome[c] it.

Mission of John the Baptist

6 There was a man named John
who was sent from God.

7 He came as a witness
to testify about the light,
so that all might believe
through him.[d]

8 He was not the light,
but he came to testify
about the light.

9 The true light, who gives light
to everyone,
was coming into the world.[e]

Christ in the World

10 He was in the world,

and the world was created
through Him,
yet the world did not recognize
Him.

11 He came to His own,[f]
and His own people[f]
did not receive Him.

12 But to all who did receive Him,
He gave them the right to be[g]
children of God,
to those who believe in His name,

13 who were born,
not of blood,[h]
or of the will of the flesh,
or of the will of man,[i]
but of God.

14 The Word became flesh[j]
and took up residence[k] among us.
We observed His glory,
the glory as the •One and Only Son[l]
from the Father,
full of grace and truth.

15 (John testified concerning Him
and exclaimed,
"This was the One of whom I said,
'The One coming after me
has surpassed me,
because He existed before me.'")

16 Indeed, we have all received grace
after grace
from His fullness,

17 for although the law was given
through Moses,

---

^a**1:1** The *Word* (Gk *Logos*) is a title for Jesus as the communication and the revealer of God the Father; Jn 1:14,18; Rv 19:13.   ^b**1:3-4** Other punctuation is possible: . . . *not one thing was created. What was created in Him was life*   ^c**1:5** Or *grasp,* or *comprehend,* or *overtake;* Jn 12:35   ^d**1:7** Or *through it* (the light)   ^e**1:9** Or *The true light who comes into the world gives light to everyone,* or *The true light enlightens everyone coming into the world.*   ^f**1:11** The same Gk adjective is used twice in this verse: the first refers to all that Jesus owned as Creator (*to His own*); the second refers to the Jews (*His own people*).   ^g**1:12** Or *become*   ^h**1:13** Lit *bloods;* the pl form of *blood* occurs only here in the NT. It may refer either to lineal descent (that is, blood from one's father and mother) or to the OT sacrificial system (that is, the various blood sacrifices). Neither is the basis for birth into the family of God.   ⁱ**1:13** Or *not of human lineage, or of human capacity, or of human volition*   ^j**1:14** The eternally existent Word (vv. 1-2) took on full humanity, but without sin; Heb 4:15.   ^k**1:14** Lit *and tabernacled,* or *and dwelt in a tent;* this word occurs only here in John. A related word, referring to the Festival of Tabernacles, occurs only in 7:2; Ex 40:34-38.   ^l**1:14** *Son* is implied from the reference to the Father and from Gk usage.

grace and truth came
    through Jesus Christ.
¹⁸ No one has ever seen God.^a
The One and Only Son^b—
    the One who is
      at the Father's side^c—
He has revealed Him.

John the Baptist's Testimony

¹⁹ This is John's testimony when the
•Jews from Jerusalem sent priests and
Levites to ask him, "Who are you?"

²⁰ He did not refuse to answer, but he
declared: "I am not the •Messiah."

²¹ "What then?" they asked him. "Are
you Elijah?"

"I am not," he said.

"Are you the Prophet?"^d

"No," he answered.

²² "Who are you, then?" they asked.
"We need to give an answer to those
who sent us. What can you tell us about
yourself?"

²³ He said, "I am a **voice of one crying
out in the wilderness: Make straight
the way of the Lord**^e—just as Isaiah the
prophet said."

²⁴ Now they had been sent from the
•Pharisees. ²⁵ So they asked him, "Why
then do you baptize if you aren't the
Messiah, or Elijah, or the Prophet?"

²⁶ "I baptize with^f water," John an-
swered them. "Someone stands among
you, but you don't know ⌊Him⌋. ²⁷ He is
the One coming after me,^g whose sandal
strap I'm not worthy to untie."

²⁸ All this happened in Bethany^h across
the Jordan,ⁱ where John was baptizing.

John: "The Lamb of God"

²⁹ The next day John saw Jesus coming
toward him and said, "Here is the Lamb
of God, who takes away the sin of the
world! ³⁰ This is the One I told you
about: 'After me comes a man who has
surpassed me, because He existed before
me.' ³¹ I didn't know Him, but I came
baptizing with^f water so He might be revealed to Israel."

³² And John testified, "I watched the
Spirit descending from heaven like a
dove, and He rested on Him. ³³ I didn't
know Him, but He^j who sent me to
baptize with^f water told me, 'The One
you see the Spirit descending and resting on—He is the One who baptizes
with^f the Holy Spirit.' ³⁴ I have seen
and testified that He is the Son of
God!"^k

John's Two Disciples: Andrew and Another

³⁵ Again the next day, John was stand-
ing with two of his disciples. ³⁶ When he
saw Jesus passing by, he said, "Look! The
Lamb of God!"

³⁷ The two disciples heard him say this
and followed Jesus. ³⁸ When Jesus turned
and noticed them following Him, He
asked them, "What are you looking for?"

They said to Him, "•Rabbi" (which
means "Teacher"), "where are You staying?"

³⁹ "Come and you'll see," He replied.
So they went and saw where He was
staying, and they stayed with Him that
day. It was about 10 in the morning.^l

---

^a**1:18** Since God is an infinite being, no one can see Him in His absolute essential nature; Ex 33:18-23.   ^b**1:18** Other
mss read *God*   ^c**1:18** Lit *is in the bosom of the Father*   ^d**1:21** Probably = the Prophet in Dt 18:15   ^e**1:23** Is 40:3
^f**1:26,31,33** Or *in*   ^g**1:27** Other mss add *who came before me*   ^h**1:28** Other mss read *in Bethabara*   ⁱ**1:28** Another
Bethany, near Jerusalem, was the home of Lazarus, Martha, and Mary; Jn 11:1.   ^j**1:33** *He* refers to God the Father,
who gave John a sign to help him identify the Messiah. Vv. 32-34 indicate that John did not know that Jesus was the
Messiah until the Spirit descended upon Him at His baptism.   ^k**1:34** Other mss read *is the Chosen One of God*
^l**1:39** Lit *about the tenth hour.* Various methods of reckoning time were used in the ancient world. John probably used a
different method from the other 3 Gospels. If John used the same method of time reckoning as the other 3 Gospels, the
translation would be: *It was about four in the afternoon.*

Andrew Brings Simon Peter

⁴⁰ Andrew, Simon Peter's brother, was one of the two who heard John and followed Him. ⁴¹ He first found his own brother Simon and told him, "We have found the Messiah!"ᵃ (which means "Anointed One"), ⁴² and he brought ⌊Simon⌋ to Jesus.

When Jesus saw him, He said, "You are Simon, son of John.ᵇ You will be called •Cephas" (which means "Rock").

Jesus Calls Philip

⁴³ The next day Heᶜ decided to leave for Galilee. Jesus found Philip and told him, "Follow Me!"

Philip Brings Nathanael

⁴⁴ Now Philip was from Bethsaida, the hometown of Andrew and Peter. ⁴⁵ Philip found Nathanaelᵈ and told him, "We have found the One Moses wrote about in the Law (and so did the prophets): Jesus the son of Joseph, from Nazareth!"

⁴⁶ "Can anything good come out of Nazareth?" Nathanael asked him.

"Come and see," Philip answered.

⁴⁷ Then Jesus saw Nathanael coming toward Him and said about him, "Here is a true Israelite; no deceit is in him."

⁴⁸ "How do you know me?" Nathanael asked.

"Before Philip called you, when you were under the fig tree, I saw you," Jesus answered.

⁴⁹ "Rabbi," Nathanael replied, "You are the Son of God! You are the King of Israel!"

⁵⁰ Jesus responded to him, "Do you believe ⌊only⌋ because I told you I saw you under the fig tree? Youᵉ will see greater things than this." ⁵¹ Then He said, "•I assure you: Youᶠ will see heaven opened and the angels of God ascending and descending on the •Son of Man."

First Sign: Turning Water into Wine

2 On the third day a wedding took place in Cana of Galilee. Jesus' mother was there, and ² Jesus and His disciples were invited to the wedding as well. ³ When the wine ran out, Jesus' mother told Him, "They don't have any wine."

⁴ "What has this concern of yours to do with Me,ᵍ •woman?" Jesus asked. "My hourʰ has not yet come."

⁵ "Do whatever He tells you," His mother told the servants.

⁶ Now six stone water jars had been set there for Jewish purification. Each contained 20 or 30 gallons.ⁱ

⁷ "Fill the jars with water," Jesus told them. So they filled them to the brim. ⁸ Then He said to them, "Now draw some out and take it to the chief servant."ʲ And they did.

⁹ When the chief servant tasted the water (after it had become wine), he did not know where it came from—though the servants who had drawn the water knew. He called the groom ¹⁰ and told him, "Everybody sets out the fine wine first, then, after people have drunk freely, the inferior. But you have kept the fine wine until now."

ᵃ**1:41** In the NT, the word Messiah translates the Gk word *Christos* ("Anointed One"), except here and in Jn 4:25 where it translates *Messias*.   ᵇ**1:42** Other mss read *Simon, son of Jonah*   ᶜ**1:43** Or *he*, referring either to Peter (v. 42) or Andrew (vv. 40-41)   ᵈ**1:45** Probably the Bartholomew of the other Gospels and Acts   ᵉ**1:50** *You* (sg in Gk) refers to Nathanael.   ᶠ**1:51** *You* is pl in Gk and refers to Nathanael and the other disciples.   ᵍ**2:4** Or *You and I see things differently*; lit *What to Me and to you*; Mt 8:29; Mk 1:24; 5:7; Lk 8:28   ʰ**2:4** The time of His sacrificial death and exaltation; Jn 7:30; 8:20; 12:23,27; 13:1; 17:1   ⁱ**2:6** Lit *2 or 3 measures*   ʲ**2:8** Lit *ruler of the table*; perhaps *master of the feast*, or *headwaiter*

[11] Jesus performed this first sign[a] in Cana of Galilee. He displayed His glory, and His disciples believed in Him.

[12] After this, He went down to Capernaum, together with His mother, His brothers, and His disciples, and they stayed there only a few days.

Jesus Cleanses the Temple Complex

[13] The Jewish •Passover was near, so Jesus went up to Jerusalem. [14] In the •temple complex He found people selling oxen, sheep, and doves, and ⌊He also found⌋ the money changers sitting there. [15] After making a whip out of cords, He drove everyone out of the temple complex with their sheep and oxen. He also poured out the money changers' coins and overturned the tables. [16] He told those who were selling doves, "Get these things out of here! Stop turning My Father's house into a marketplace!"[b]

[17] And His disciples remembered that it is written: **Zeal for Your house will consume Me.**[c]

Jesus Predicts His Resurrection

[18] So the Jews replied to Him, "What sign ⌊of authority⌋ will You show us for doing these things?"

[19] Jesus answered, "Destroy this sanctuary, and I will raise it up in three days."

[20] Therefore the Jews said, "This sanctuary took 46 years to build, and will You raise it up in three days?"

[21] But He was speaking about the sanctuary of His body. [22] So when He was raised from the dead, His disciples remembered that He had said this. And they believed the Scripture and the statement Jesus had made.

[23] While He was in Jerusalem at the Passover Festival, many trusted in His name when they saw the signs He was doing. [24] Jesus, however, would not entrust Himself to them, since He knew them all [25] and because He did not need anyone to testify about man; for He Himself knew what was in man.

Jesus and Nicodemus

3 There was a man from the •Pharisees named Nicodemus, a ruler of the Jews. [2] This man came to Him at night and said, "•Rabbi, we know that You have come from God as a teacher, for no one could perform these signs You do unless God were with him."

[3] Jesus replied, "•I assure you: Unless someone is born again,[d] he cannot see the kingdom of God."

[4] "But how can anyone be born when he is old?" Nicodemus asked Him. "Can he enter his mother's womb a second time and be born?"

[5] Jesus answered, "I assure you: Unless someone is born of water and the Spirit,[e] he cannot enter the kingdom of God. [6] Whatever is born of the flesh is flesh, and whatever is born of the Spirit is spirit. [7] Do not be amazed that I told you that you[f] must be born again. [8] The wind[g] blows where it pleases, and you hear its sound, but you don't know where it comes from or where it is going. So it is with everyone born of the Spirit."

[9] "How can these things be?" asked Nicodemus.

[10] "Are you a teacher[h] of Israel and don't know these things?" Jesus replied.

---

[a]**2:11** Lit *this beginning of the signs*; Jn 4:54; 20:30. Seven miraculous signs occur in John's Gospel and are so noted in the headings. [b]**2:16** Lit *a house of business* [c]**2:17** Ps 69:9 [d]**3:3** The same Gk word can mean *again* or *from above* (also in v. 7). [e]**3:5** Or *spirit, or wind*; the Gk word *pneuma* can mean *wind, spirit,* or *Spirit,* each of which occurs in this context. [f]**3:7** The pronoun is pl in Gk. [g]**3:8** The Gk word *pneuma* can mean *wind, spirit,* or *Spirit,* each of which occurs in this context. [h]**3:10** Or *the teacher*

[11] "I assure you: We speak what We know and We testify to what We have seen, but you[a] do not accept Our testimony.[b] [12] If I have told you about things that happen on earth and you don't believe, how will you believe if I tell you about things of heaven? [13] No one has ascended into heaven except the One who descended from heaven—the •Son of Man.[c] [14] Just as Moses lifted up the snake in the wilderness, so the Son of Man must be lifted up, [15] so that everyone who believes in Him will[d] have eternal life.

[16] "For God loved the world in this way: He gave His •One and Only Son, so that everyone who believes in Him will not perish but have eternal life. [17] For God did not send His Son into the world that He might condemn the world, but that the world might be saved through Him. [18] Anyone who believes in Him is not condemned, but anyone who does not believe is already condemned, because he has not believed in the name of the One and Only Son of God.

[19] "This, then, is the judgment: the light has come into the world, and people loved darkness rather than the light because their deeds were evil. [20] For everyone who practices wicked things hates the light and avoids it,[e] so that his deeds may not be exposed. [21] But anyone who lives by[f] the truth comes to the light, so that his works may be shown to be accomplished by God."[g]

Jesus and John the Baptist

[22] After this, Jesus and His disciples went to the Judean countryside, where He spent time with them and baptized.

[23] John also was baptizing in Aenon near Salim, because there was plenty of water there. People were coming and being baptized, [24] since John had not yet been thrown into prison.

[25] Then a dispute arose between John's disciples and a •Jew[h] about purification. [26] So they came to John and told him, "Rabbi, the One you testified about, and who was with you across the Jordan, is baptizing—and everyone is flocking to Him."

[27] John responded, "No one can receive a single thing unless it's given to him from heaven. [28] You yourselves can testify that I said, 'I am not the •Messiah, but I've been sent ahead of Him.' [29] He who has the bride is the groom. But the groom's friend, who stands by and listens for him, rejoices greatly[i] at the groom's voice. So this joy of mine is complete. [30] He must increase, but I must decrease."

The One from Heaven

[31] The One who comes from above is above all. The one who is from the earth is earthly and speaks in earthly terms.[j] The One who comes from heaven is above all. [32] He testifies to what He has seen and heard, yet no one accepts His testimony. [33] The one who has accepted His testimony has affirmed that God is true. [34] For God sent Him, and He speaks God's words, since He[k] gives the Spirit without measure. [35] The Father loves the Son and has given all things into His hands. [36] The one who believes in the Son has eternal life, but the one who refuses to believe in the Son will not see life; instead, the wrath of God remains on him.

---

[a]3:11 The word you in Gk is pl here and throughout v. 12.   [b]3:11 The pl forms (We, Our) refer to Jesus and His authority to speak for the Father.   [c]3:13 Other mss add who is in heaven   [d]3:15 Other mss add not perish, but   [e]3:20 Lit and does not come to the light   [f]3:21 Lit who does   [g]3:21 It is possible that Jesus' words end at v. 15. Ancient Gk did not have quotation marks.   [h]3:25 Other mss read and the Jews   [i]3:29 Lit with joy rejoices   [j]3:31 Or of earthly things   [k]3:34 Other mss read since God

Jesus and
the Samaritan Woman

4 When Jesus[a] knew that the •Pharisees heard He was making and baptizing more disciples than John [2] (though Jesus Himself was not baptizing, but His disciples were), [3] He left Judea and went again to Galilee. [4] He had to travel through Samaria, [5] so He came to a town of Samaria called Sychar near the property[b] that Jacob had given his son Joseph. [6] Jacob's well was there, and Jesus, worn out from His journey, sat down at the well. It was about six in the evening.[c]

[7] A woman of Samaria came to draw water.

"Give Me a drink," Jesus said to her, [8] for His disciples had gone into town to buy food.

[9] "How is it that You, a Jew, ask for a drink from me, a •Samaritan woman?" she asked Him. For Jews do not associate with[d] Samaritans.[e]

[10] Jesus answered, "If you knew the gift of God, and who is saying to you, 'Give Me a drink,' you would ask Him, and He would give you living water."

[11] "Sir," said the woman, "You don't even have a bucket, and the well is deep. So where do you get this 'living water'? [12] You aren't greater than our father Jacob, are you? He gave us the well and drank from it himself, as did his sons and livestock."

[13] Jesus said, "Everyone who drinks from this water will get thirsty again. [14] But whoever drinks from the water that I will give him will never get thirsty again—ever! In fact, the water I will give him will become a well[f] of water springing up within him for eternal life."

[15] "Sir," the woman said to Him, "give me this water so I won't get thirsty and come here to draw water."

[16] "Go call your husband," He told her, "and come back here."

[17] "I don't have a husband," she answered.

"You have correctly said, 'I don't have a husband,'" Jesus said. [18] "For you've had five husbands, and the man you now have is not your husband. What you have said is true."

[19] "Sir," the woman replied, "I see that You are a prophet. [20] Our fathers worshiped on this mountain,[g] yet you ⌊Jews⌋ say that the place to worship is in Jerusalem."

[21] Jesus told her, "Believe Me, •woman, an hour is coming when you will worship the Father neither on this mountain nor in Jerusalem. [22] You Samaritans[h] worship what you do not know. We worship what we do know, because salvation is from the Jews. [23] But an hour is coming, and is now here, when the true worshipers will worship the Father in spirit and truth. Yes, the Father wants such people to worship Him. [24] God is spirit, and those who worship Him must worship in spirit and truth."

[25] The woman said to Him, "I know that •Messiah[i] is coming" (who is called Christ). "When He comes, He will explain everything to us."

[26] "I am ⌊He⌋," Jesus told her, "the One speaking to you."

Jesus' Special Food—
and a Ripened Harvest

[27] Just then His disciples arrived, and they were amazed that He was talking

---

[a]4:1 Other mss read *the Lord*   [b]4:5 Lit *piece of land*   [c]4:6 Lit *the sixth hour*; see note at Jn 1:39; an alternate time reckoning would be *noon*   [d]4:9 Or *do not share vessels with*   [e]4:9 Other mss omit *For Jews do not associate with Samaritans.*   [f]4:14 Or *spring*   [g]4:20 Mount Gerizim, where there had been a Samaritan temple that rivaled Jerusalem's   [h]4:22 *Samaritans* is implied since the Gk verb and pronoun are pl.   [i]4:25 In the NT, the word *Messiah* translates the Gk word *Christos* ("Anointed One"), except here and in Jn 1:41 where it translates *Messias*.

with a woman. Yet no one said, "What do You want?" or "Why are You talking with her?"

²⁸ Then the woman left her water jar, went into town, and told the men, ²⁹ "Come, see a man who told me everything I ever did! Could this be the Messiah?" ³⁰ They left the town and made their way to Him.

³¹ In the meantime the disciples kept urging Him, "•Rabbi, eat something."

³² But He said, "I have food to eat that you don't know about."

³³ The disciples said to one another, "Could someone have brought Him something to eat?"

³⁴ "My food is to do the will of Him who sent Me and to finish His work," Jesus told them. ³⁵ "Don't you say, 'There are still four more months, then comes the harvest'? Listen ₍to what₎ I'm telling you: Openᵃ your eyes and look at the fields, for they are readyᵇ for harvest. ³⁶ The reaper is already receiving pay and gathering fruit for eternal life, so the sower and reaper can rejoice together. ³⁷ For in this case the saying is true: 'One sows and another reaps.' ³⁸ I sent you to reap what you didn't labor for; others have labored, and you have benefited fromᶜ their labor."

Savior of the World

³⁹ Now many Samaritans from that town believed in Him because of what the woman saidᵈ when she testified, "He told me everything I ever did." ⁴⁰ Therefore, when the Samaritans came to Him, they asked Him to stay with them, and He stayed there two days. ⁴¹ Many more believed because of what He said.ᵉ ⁴² And they told the woman, "We no longer believe because of what you said,

for we have heard for ourselves and know that this really is the Savior of the world."ᶠ

A Galilean Welcome

⁴³ After two days He left there for Galilee. ⁴⁴ Jesus Himself testified that a prophet has no honor in his own country. ⁴⁵ When they entered Galilee, the Galileans welcomed Him because they had seen everything He did in Jerusalem during the festival. For they also had gone to the festival.

Second Sign: Healing an Official's Son

⁴⁶ Then He went again to Cana of Galilee, where He had turned the water into wine. There was a certain royal official whose son was ill at Capernaum. ⁴⁷ When this man heard that Jesus had come from Judea into Galilee, he went to Him and pleaded with Him to come down and heal his son, for he was about to die.

⁴⁸ Jesus told him, "Unless you ₍people₎ see signs and wonders, you will not believe."

⁴⁹ "Sir," the official said to Him, "come down before my boy dies!"

⁵⁰ "Go," Jesus told him, "your son will live." The man believed whatᵍ Jesus said to him and departed.

⁵¹ While he was still going down, his •slaves met him saying that his boy was alive. ⁵² He asked them at what time he got better. "Yesterday at seven in the morningʰ the fever left him," they answered. ⁵³ The father realized this was the very hour at which Jesus had told him, "Your son will live." Then he himself believed, along with his whole household.

ᵃ**4:35** Lit *Raise*   ᵇ**4:35** Lit *white*   ᶜ**4:38** Lit *you have entered into*   ᵈ**4:39** Lit *because of the woman's word*   ᵉ**4:41** Lit *because of His word*   ᶠ**4:42** Other mss add *the Messiah*   ᵍ**4:50** Lit *the word*   ʰ**4:52** Or *seven in the evening*; lit *at the seventh hour*; see note at Jn 1:39; an alternate time reckoning would be *at one in the afternoon*

54 This therefore was the second sign Jesus performed after He came from Judea to Galilee.

Third Sign: Jesus Heals Sick

5 After this, a Jewish festival took place, and Jesus went up to Jerusalem. 2 By the Sheep Gate in Jerusalem there is a pool, called Bethesda[a] in Hebrew, which has five colonnades.[b] 3 Within these lay a multitude of the sick—blind, lame, and paralyzed [—waiting for the moving of the water, 4 because an angel would go down into the pool from time to time and stir up the water. Then the first one who got in after the water was stirred up recovered from whatever ailment he had].[c]

Man Sick 38 Years

5 One man was there who had been sick for 38 years. 6 When Jesus saw him lying there and knew he had already been there a long time, He said to him, "Do you want to get well?"

7 "Sir," the sick man answered, "I don't have a man to put me into the pool when the water is stirred up, but while I'm coming, someone goes down ahead of me."

8 "Get up," Jesus told him, "pick up your bedroll and walk!" 9 Instantly the man got well, picked up his bedroll, and started to walk.

Now that day was the Sabbath, 10 so the •Jews said to the man who had been healed, "This is the Sabbath! It's illegal for you to pick up your bedroll."

11 He replied, "The man who made me well told me, 'Pick up your bedroll and walk.' "

12 "Who is this man who told you, 'Pick up ∟your bedroll⌟ and walk?' " they asked. 13 But the man who was cured did not know who it was, because Jesus had slipped away into the crowd that was there.[d]

14 After this, Jesus found him in the •temple complex and said to him, "See, you are well. Do not sin any more, so that something worse doesn't happen to you." 15 The man went and reported to the Jews that it was Jesus who had made him well.

The Son Acknowledges His Father

16 Therefore, the Jews began persecuting Jesus[e] because He was doing these things on the Sabbath. 17 But Jesus responded to them, "My Father is still working, and I am working also." 18 This is why the Jews began trying all the more to kill Him: not only was He breaking the Sabbath, but He was even calling God His own Father, making Himself equal with God.

Relationship between Father and Son

19 Then Jesus replied, "•I assure you: The Son is not able to do anything on His own, but only what He sees the Father doing. For whatever the Father[f] does, the Son also does these things in the same way. 20 For the Father loves the Son and shows Him everything He is doing, and He will show Him greater works than these so that you will be amazed. 21 And just as the Father raises the dead and gives them life, so the Son also gives life to anyone He wants to. 22 The Father, in fact, judges no one but has given all judgment to the Son, 23 so that all people will honor the Son just as they honor the Father. Anyone who does not honor the Son does not honor the Father who sent Him.

a 5:2 Other mss read Bethzatha; other mss read Bethsaida   b 5:2 Rows of columns supporting a roof   c 5:3-4 Other mss omit bracketed text   d 5:13 Lit slipped away, there being a crowd in that place   e 5:16 Other mss add and trying to kill Him   f 5:19 Lit whatever that One

Life and Judgment

24 "I assure you: Anyone who hears My word and believes Him who sent Me has eternal life and will not come under judgment but has passed from death to life.

25 "I assure you: An hour is coming, and is now here, when the dead will hear the voice of the Son of God, and those who hear will live. 26 For just as the Father has life in Himself, so also He has granted to the Son to have life in Himself. 27 And He has granted Him the right to pass judgment, because He is the •Son of Man. 28 Do not be amazed at this, because a time is coming when all who are in the graves will hear His voice 29 and come out—those who have done good things, to the resurrection of life, but those who have done wicked things, to the resurrection of judgment.

30 "I can do nothing on My own. I judge only as I hear, and My judgment is righteous, because I do not seek My own will, but the will of Him who sent Me.

Four Witnesses to Jesus

31 "If I testify about Myself, My testimony is not valid.ª 32 There is Another who testifies about Me, and I know that the testimony He gives about Me is valid.ᵇ 33 You have sent ⌐messengers⌐ to John, and he has testified to the truth. 34 I don't receive man's testimony, but I say these things so that you may be saved. 35 Johnᶜ was a burning and shining lamp, and for a time you were willing to enjoy his light.

36 "But I have a greater testimony than John's because of the works that the Father has given Me to accomplish. These very works I am doing testify about Me that the Father has sent Me. 37 The Father who sent Me has Himself testified about Me. You have not heard His voice at any time, and you haven't seen His form. 38 You don't have His word living in you, because you don't believe the One He sent. 39 You pore overᵈ the Scriptures because you think you have eternal life in them, yet they testify about Me. 40 And you are not willing to come to Me that you may have life.

41 "I do not accept glory from men, 42 but I know you—that you have no love for God within you. 43 I have come in My Father's name, yet you don't accept Me. If someone else comes in his own name, you will accept him. 44 How can you believe? While accepting glory from one another, you don't seek the glory that comes from the only God. 45 Do not think that I will accuse you to the Father. Your accuser is Moses, on whom you have set your hope. 46 For if you believed Moses, you would believe Me, because he wrote about Me. 47 But if you don't believe his writings, how will you believe My words?"

Fourth Sign: Feeding 5,000

6 After this, Jesus crossed the Sea of Galilee (or Tiberias). 2 And a huge crowd was following Him because they saw the signs that He was performing on the sick. 3 So Jesus went up a mountain and sat down there with His disciples.

Question for Philip

4 Now the •Passover, a Jewish festival, was near. 5 Therefore, when Jesus looked up and noticed a huge crowd coming toward Him, He asked Philip, "Where will we buy bread so these people can eat?" 6 He asked this to test him, for He Himself knew what He was going to do.

7 Philip answered, "Two hundred •denarii worth of bread wouldn't be enough for each of them to have a little."

ª5:31 Or *not true*　ᵇ5:32 Or *true*　ᶜ5:35 Lit *That man*　ᵈ5:39 In Gk this could be a command: *Pore over . . .*

Andrew's Idea

[8] One of His disciples, Andrew, Simon Peter's brother, said to Him, [9] "There's a boy here who has five barley loaves and two fish—but what are they for so many?" [10] Then Jesus said, "Have the people sit down."

There was plenty of grass in that place, so they sat down. The men numbered about 5,000. [11] Then Jesus took the loaves, and after giving thanks He distributed them to those who were seated—so also with the fish, as much as they wanted.

[12] When they were full, He told His disciples, "Collect the leftovers so that nothing is wasted." [13] So they collected them and filled 12 baskets with the pieces from the five barley loaves that were left over by those who had eaten.

[14] When the people saw the sign[a] He had done, they said, "This really is the Prophet who was to come into the world!" [15] Therefore, when Jesus knew that they were about to come and take Him by force to make Him king, He withdrew again[b] to the mountain by Himself.

Fifth Sign: Walking on Water

[16] When evening came, His disciples went down to the sea, [17] got into a boat, and started across the sea to Capernaum. Darkness had already set in, but Jesus had not yet come to them. [18] Then a high wind arose, and the sea began to churn. [19] After they had rowed about three or four miles,[c] they saw Jesus walking on the sea. He was coming near the boat, and they were afraid.

[20] But He said to them, "It is I.[d] Don't be afraid!" [21] Then they were willing to take Him on board, and at once the boat was at the shore where they were heading.

Bread of Life

[22] The next day, the crowd that had stayed on the other side of the sea knew there had been only one boat.[e] ⌊They also knew⌋ that Jesus had not boarded the boat with His disciples, but that His disciples had gone off alone. [23] Some boats from Tiberias came near the place where they ate the bread after the Lord gave thanks. [24] When the crowd saw that neither Jesus nor His disciples were there, they got into the boats and went to Capernaum looking for Jesus.

[25] When they found Him on the other side of the sea, they said to Him, "•Rabbi, when did You get here?"

[26] Jesus answered, "•I assure you: You are looking for Me, not because you saw the signs, but because you ate the loaves and were filled. [27] Don't work for the food that perishes but for the food that lasts for eternal life, which the •Son of Man will give you, because God the Father has set His seal of approval on Him."

[28] "What can we do to perform the works of God?" they asked.

[29] Jesus replied, "This is the work of God: that you believe in the One He has sent."

[30] "What sign then are You going to do so we may see and believe You?" they asked. "What are You going to perform? [31] Our fathers ate the manna in the wilderness, just as it is written: **He gave them bread from heaven to eat.**"[f] [g]

[32] Jesus said to them, "I assure you: Moses didn't give you the bread from heaven, but My Father gives you the real bread from heaven. [33] For the bread of God is the One who comes down from heaven and gives life to the world."

---

[a]**6:14** Other mss read *signs* [b]**6:15** A previous withdrawal is mentioned in Mk 6:31-32, an event that occurred just before the feeding of the 5,000. [c]**6:19** Lit *25 or 30 stadia*; 1 *stadion* = 600 feet [d]**6:20** Lit *I am* [e]**6:22** Other mss add *into which His disciples had entered* [f]**6:31** Bread miraculously provided by God for the Israelites [g]**6:31** Ex 16:4; Ps 78:24

³⁴ Then they said, "Sir, give us this bread always!"

³⁵ "I am the bread of life," Jesus told them. "No one who comes to Me will ever be hungry, and no one who believes in Me will ever be thirsty again. ³⁶ But as I told you, you've seen Me,ª and yet you do not believe. ³⁷ Everyone the Father gives Me will come to Me, and the one who comes to Me I will never cast out. ³⁸ For I have come down from heaven, not to do My will, but the will of Him who sent Me. ³⁹ This is the will of Him who sent Me: that I should lose none of those He has given Me but should raise them up on the last day. ⁴⁰ For this is the will of My Father: that everyone who sees the Son and believes in Him may have eternal life, and I will raise him up on the last day."

⁴¹ Therefore the Jews started complaining about Him, because He said, "I am the bread that came down from heaven." ⁴² They were saying, "Isn't this Jesus the son of Joseph, whose father and mother we know? How can He now say, 'I have come down from heaven'?"

⁴³ Jesus answered them, "Stop complaining among yourselves. ⁴⁴ No one can come to Me unless the Father who sent Me drawsᵇ him, and I will raise him up on the last day. ⁴⁵ It is written in the Prophets: **And they will all be taught by God.**ᶜ Everyone who has listened to and learned from the Father comes to Me— ⁴⁶ not that anyone has seen the Father except the One who is from God. He has seen the Father.

⁴⁷ "I assure you: Anyone who believesᵈ has eternal life. ⁴⁸ I am the bread of life. ⁴⁹ Your fathers ate the manna in the wilderness, and they died. ⁵⁰ This is the bread that comes down from heaven so that anyone may eat of it and not die. ⁵¹ I am the living bread that came down from heaven. If anyone eats of this bread he will live forever. The bread that I will give for the life of the world is My flesh."

⁵² At that, the Jews argued among themselves, "How can this man give us His flesh to eat?"

⁵³ So Jesus said to them, "I assure you: Unless you eat the flesh of the Son of Man and drink His blood, you do not have life in yourselves. ⁵⁴ Anyone who eats My flesh and drinks My blood has eternal life, and I will raise him up on the last day, ⁵⁵ because My flesh is real food and My blood is real drink. ⁵⁶ The one who eats My flesh and drinks My blood lives in Me, and I in him. ⁵⁷ Just as the living Father sent Me and I live because of the Father, so the one who feeds on Me will live because of Me. ⁵⁸ This is the bread that came down from heaven; it is not like the mannaᵉ your fathers ate—and they died. The one who eats this bread will live forever."

⁵⁹ He said these things while teaching in the •synagogue in Capernaum.

Many Disciples Desert Jesus

⁶⁰ Therefore, when many of His disciples heard this, they said, "This teaching is hard! Who can acceptᶠ it?"

⁶¹ Jesus, knowing in Himself that His disciples were complaining about this, asked them, "Does this offend you? ⁶² Then what if you were to observe the Son of Man ascending to where He was before? ⁶³ The Spirit is the One who gives life. The flesh doesn't help at all. The words that I have spoken to you are spirit and are life. ⁶⁴ But there are some among you who don't believe." (For Jesus knew from the beginning those who would notᵍ believe and the one

ª**6:36** Other mss omit *Me*   ᵇ**6:44** Or *brings*, or *leads*; see the use of this Gk verb in Jn 12:32; 21:6; Ac 16:19; Jms 2:6.
ᶜ**6:45** Is 54:13   ᵈ**6:47** Other mss add *in Me*   ᵉ**6:58** Other mss omit *the manna*   ᶠ**6:60** Lit *hear*   ᵍ**6:64** Other mss omit *not*

who would betray Him.) [65] He said, "This is why I told you that no one can come to Me unless it is granted to him by the Father."

Jesus Challenges the 12

[66] From that moment many of His disciples turned back and no longer accompanied Him. [67] Therefore Jesus said to the Twelve, "You don't want to go away too, do you?"

[68] Simon Peter answered, "Lord, who will we go to? You have the words of eternal life. [69] We have come to believe and know that You are the Holy One of God!"[a]

[70] Jesus replied to them, "Didn't I choose you, the Twelve? Yet one of you is the Devil!" [71] He was referring to Judas, Simon Iscariot's son,[b c] one of the Twelve, because he was going to betray Him.

Unbelief of Jesus' Brothers

7 After this, Jesus traveled in Galilee, since He did not want to travel in Judea because the •Jews were trying to kill Him. [2] The Jewish Festival of Tabernacles[d e] was near, [3] so His brothers said to Him, "Leave here and go to Judea so Your disciples can see Your works that You are doing. [4] For no one does anything in secret while he's seeking public recognition. If You do these things, show Yourself to the world." [5] (For not even His brothers believed in Him.)

[6] Jesus told them, "My time has not yet arrived, but your time is always at hand. [7] The world cannot hate you, but it does hate Me because I testify about it—that its deeds are evil. [8] Go up to the festival yourselves. I'm not going up to the festival yet,[f] because My time has not yet

fully come." [9] After He had said these things, He stayed in Galilee.

Jesus at the Festival of Tabernacles

[10] After His brothers had gone up to the festival, then He also went up, not openly but secretly. [11] The Jews were looking for Him at the festival and saying, "Where is He?" [12] And there was a lot of discussion about Him among the crowds. Some were saying, "He's a good man." Others were saying, "No, on the contrary, He's deceiving the people." [13] Still, nobody was talking publicly about Him because they feared the Jews.

[14] When the festival was already half over, Jesus went up into the •temple complex and began to teach. [15] Then the Jews were amazed and said, "How does He know the Scriptures, since He hasn't been trained?"

Jesus Explains His Teaching

[16] Jesus answered them, "My teaching isn't Mine but is from the One who sent Me. [17] If anyone wants to do His will, he will understand whether the teaching is from God or if I am speaking on My own. [18] The one who speaks for himself seeks his own glory. But He who seeks the glory of the One who sent Him is true, and there is no unrighteousness in Him. [19] Didn't Moses give you the law? Yet none of you keeps the law! Why do you want to kill Me?"

[20] "You have a demon!" the crowd responded. "Who wants to kill You?"

[21] "I did one work, and you are all amazed," Jesus answered. [22] "Consider this: Moses has given you circumcision—not that it comes from Moses but from the fathers—and you circumcise a

---

[a]**6:69** Other mss read *You are the Messiah, the Son of the Living God* [b]**6:71** Other mss read *Judas Iscariot, Simon's son* [c]**6:71** Lit *Judas, of Simon Iscariot* [d]**7:2** Or *Booths* [e]**7:2** One of 3 great Jewish religious festivals, along with Passover and Pentecost; Ex 23:14; Dt 16:16 [f]**7:8** Other mss omit *yet*

man on the Sabbath. ²³ If a man receives circumcision on the Sabbath so that the law of Moses won't be broken, are you angry at Me because I made a man entirely well on the Sabbath? ²⁴ Stop judging according to outward appearances; rather judge according to righteous judgment."

Identity of the Messiah

²⁵ Some of the people of Jerusalem were saying, "Isn't this the man they want to kill? ²⁶ Yet, look! He's speaking publicly and they're saying nothing to Him. Can it be true that the authorities know He is the •Messiah? ²⁷ But we know where this man is from. When the Messiah comes, nobody will know where He is from."

²⁸ As He was teaching in the temple complex, Jesus cried out, "You know Me and you know where I am from. Yet I have not come on My own, but the One who sent Me is true. You don't know Him; ²⁹ I know Him because I am from Him, and He sent Me."

³⁰ Then they tried to seize Him. Yet no one laid a hand on Him because His hourᵃ had not yet come. ³¹ However, many from the crowd believed in Him and said, "When the Messiah comes, He won't perform more signs than this man has done, will He?"

³² The •Pharisees heard the crowd muttering these things about Him, so the •chief priests and the Pharisees sent temple police to arrest Him.

³³ Then Jesus said, "I am only with you for a short time. Then I'm going to the One who sent Me. ³⁴ You will look for Me, but you will not find Me; and where I am, you cannot come."

³⁵ Then the Jews said to one another, "Where does He intend to go so we won't find Him? He doesn't intend to go to the Dispersionᵇ among the Greeks and teach the Greeks, does He? ³⁶ What is this remark He made: 'You will look for Me, and you will not find Me; and where I am, you cannot come'?"

Promise of the Spirit

³⁷ On the last and most important day of the festival, Jesus stood up and cried out, "If anyone is thirsty, he should come to Meᶜ and drink! ³⁸ The one who believes in Me, as the Scripture has said,ᵈ will have streams of living water flow from deep within him." ³⁹ He said this about the Spirit, whom those who believed in Him were going to receive, for the Spiritᵉ had not yet been received,ᶠ ᵍ because Jesus had not yet been glorified.

People Divided over Jesus

⁴⁰ When some from the crowd heard these words, they said, "This really is the Prophet!"ʰ ⁴¹ Others said, "This is the Messiah!" But some said, "Surely the Messiah doesn't come from Galilee, does He? ⁴² Doesn't the Scripture say that the Messiah comes from David's offspringⁱ and from the town of Bethlehem, where David once lived?" ⁴³ So a division occurred among the crowd because of Him. ⁴⁴ Some of them wanted to seize Him, but no one laid hands on Him.

Temple Police and Pharisees Debate over Jesus

⁴⁵ Then the temple police came to the chief priests and Pharisees, who asked them, "Why haven't you brought Him?"

ᵃ**7:30** The time of His sacrificial death and exaltation; Jn 2:4; 8:20; 12:23,27; 13:1; 17:1   ᵇ**7:35** Jewish people scattered throughout Gentile lands who spoke Gk and were influenced by Gk culture   ᶜ**7:37** Other mss omit *to Me* ᵈ**7:38** Jesus may have had several OT passages in mind; Is 58:11; Ezk 47:1-12; Zch 14:8   ᵉ**7:39** Other mss read *Holy Spirit*   ᶠ**7:39** Other mss read *had not yet been given*   ᵍ**7:39** Lit *the Spirit was not yet*; the word *received* is implied from the previous clause.   ʰ**7:40** Probably = the Prophet in Dt 18:15   ⁱ**7:42** Lit *seed*

46 The police answered, "No man ever spoke like this!"ᵃ

47 Then the Pharisees responded to them: "Are you fooled too? 48 Have any of the rulers believed in Him? Or any of the Pharisees? 49 But this crowd, which doesn't know the law, is accursed!"

Nicodemus Defends Jesus

50 Nicodemus—the one who came to Him previously, being one of them—said to them, 51 "Our law doesn't judge a man before it hears from him and knows what he's doing, does it?"

52 "You aren't from Galilee too, are you?" they replied. "Investigate and you will see that no prophet arises from Galilee."ᵇ

[53 So each one went to his house.

8 1 But Jesus went to the •Mount of Olives.

An Adulteress Forgiven

2 At dawn He went to the •temple complex again, and all the people were coming to Him. He sat down and began to teach them.

3 Then the •scribes and the •Pharisees brought a woman caught in adultery, making her stand in the center. 4 "Teacher," they said to Him, "this woman was caught in the act of committing adultery. 5 In the law Moses commanded us to stone such women. So what do You say?" 6 They asked this to trap Him, in order that they might have evidence to accuse Him.

Jesus stooped down and started writing on the ground with His finger. 7 When they persisted in questioning Him, He stood up and said to them, "The one without sin among you should be the first to throw a stone at her."

8 Then He stooped down again and continued writing on the ground. 9 When they heard this, they left one by one, starting with the older men. Only He was left, with the woman in the center. 10 When Jesus stood up, He said to her, "•Woman, where are they? Has no one condemned you?"

11 "No one, Lord,"ᶜ she answered.

"Neither do I condemn you," said Jesus. "Go, and from now on do not sin any more."]ᵈ

12 Then Jesus spoke to them again: "I am the light of the world. Anyone who follows Me will never walk in the darkness but will have the light of life."

Pharisees Challenge Jesus' Self-Witness

13 So the Pharisees said to Him, "You are testifying about Yourself. Your testimony is not valid."ᵉ

14 "Even if I testify about Myself," Jesus replied, "My testimony is valid,ᶠ because I know where I came from and where I'm going. But you don't know where I come from or where I'm going. 15 You judge by human standards.ᵍ I judge no one. 16 And if I do judge, My judgment is true, because I am not alone, but I and the Father who sent Me ⌊judge together⌋. 17 Even in your law it is written that the witness of two men is valid. 18 I am the One who testifies about Myself, and the Father who sent Me testifies about Me."

19 Then they asked Him, "Where is Your Father?"

"You know neither Me nor My Father," Jesus answered. "If you knew Me, you would also know My Father." 20 He spoke these words by the trea-

ᵃ7:46 Other mss read *like this man*   ᵇ7:52 Jonah and probably other prophets did come from Galilee; 2 Kgs 14:25
ᶜ8:11 Or *Sir*; Jn 4:15,49; 5:7; 6:34; 9:36   ᵈ8:11 Other mss omit bracketed text   ᵉ8:13 The law of Moses required at least 2 witnesses to make a claim legally valid (v. 17).   ᶠ8:14 Or *true*   ᵍ8:15 Lit *You judge according to the flesh*

sury,[a] while teaching in the temple complex. But no one seized Him, because His hour[b] had not come.

Jesus Predicts His Departure

²¹ Then He said to them again, "I'm going away; you will look for Me, and you will die in your sin. Where I'm going, you cannot come."

²² So the Jews said again, "He won't kill Himself, will He, since He says, 'Where I'm going, you cannot come'?"

²³ "You are from below," He told them, "I am from above. You are of this world; I am not of this world. ²⁴ Therefore I told you that you will die in your sins. For if you do not believe that I am ⌊He⌋,[c] you will die in your sins."

²⁵ "Who are You?" they questioned.

"Precisely what I've been telling you from the very beginning," Jesus told them. ²⁶ "I have many things to say and to judge about you, but the One who sent Me is true, and what I have heard from Him—these things I tell the world."

²⁷ They did not know He was speaking to them about the Father. ²⁸ So Jesus said to them, "When you lift up the •Son of Man, then you will know that I am ⌊He⌋, and that I do nothing on My own. But just as the Father taught Me, I say these things. ²⁹ The One who sent Me is with Me. He has not left Me alone, because I always do what pleases Him."

"The Truth Will Set You Free"

³⁰ As He was saying these things, many believed in Him. ³¹ So Jesus said to the Jews who had believed Him, "If you continue in My word,[d] you really are My disciples. ³² You will know the truth, and the truth will set you free."

³³ "We are descendants[e] of Abraham," they answered Him, "and we have never been enslaved to anyone. How can You say, 'You will become free'?"

Slave of Sin

³⁴ Jesus responded, "•I assure you: Everyone who commits sin is a slave of sin. ³⁵ A slave does not remain in the household forever, but a son does remain forever. ³⁶ Therefore if the Son sets you free, you really will be free. ³⁷ I know you are descendants[e] of Abraham, but you are trying to kill Me because My word[d] is not welcome among you. ³⁸ I speak what I have seen in the presence of the Father,[f] and therefore you do what you have heard from your father."

Abraham's Children

³⁹ "Our father is Abraham!" they replied.

"If you were Abraham's children," Jesus told them, "you would do what Abraham did. ⁴⁰ But now you are trying to kill Me, a man who has told you the truth that I heard from God. Abraham did not do this! ⁴¹ You're doing what your father does."

"We weren't born of sexual immorality," they said. "We have one Father—God."

⁴² Jesus said to them, "If God were your Father, you would love Me, because I came from God and I am here. For I didn't come on My own, but He sent Me. ⁴³ Why don't you understand what I say? Because you cannot listen to[g] My word. ⁴⁴ You are of your father the Devil, and you want to carry out your father's desires. He was a murderer from the beginning and has not

---

ᵃ8:20 A place for offerings to be given, perhaps in the court of women   ᵇ8:20 The time of His sacrificial death and exaltation; Jn 2:4; 7:30; 12:23,27; 13:1; 17:1   ᶜ8:24 Jesus claimed to be deity, but the Pharisees didn't understand His meaning.   ᵈ8:31,37 Or My teaching, or My message   ᵉ8:33,37 Or offspring; lit seed; Jn 7:42   ᶠ8:38 Other mss read of My Father   ᵍ8:43 Or cannot hear

stood in the truth, because there is no truth in him. When he tells a lie, he speaks from his own nature,[a] because he is a liar and the father of liars.[b] 45 Yet because I tell the truth, you do not believe Me. 46 Who among you can convict Me of sin? If I tell the truth, why don't you believe Me? 47 The one who is from God listens to God's words. This is why you don't listen, because you are not from God."

Jesus and Abraham

48 The Jews responded to Him, "Aren't we right in saying that You're a •Samaritan and have a demon?"

49 "I do not have a demon," Jesus answered. "On the contrary, I honor My Father and you dishonor Me. 50 I do not seek My glory; the One who seeks it also judges. 51 I assure you: If anyone keeps My word, he will never see death—ever!"

52 Then the Jews said, "Now we know You have a demon. Abraham died and so did the prophets. You say, 'If anyone keeps My word, he will never taste death—ever!' 53 Are You greater than our father Abraham who died? Even the prophets died. Who do You pretend to be?"[c]

54 "If I glorify Myself," Jesus answered, "My glory is nothing. My Father—you say about Him, 'He is our God'—He is the One who glorifies Me. 55 You've never known Him, but I know Him. If I were to say I don't know Him, I would be a liar like you. But I do know Him, and I keep His word. 56 Your father Abraham was overjoyed that he would see My day; he saw it and rejoiced."

"I Am"

57 The Jews replied, "You aren't 50 years old yet, and You've seen Abraham?"[d]

58 Jesus said to them, "I assure you: Before Abraham was, I am."[e]

59 At that, they picked up stones to throw at Him. But Jesus was hidden[f] and went out of the temple complex.[g]

Sixth Sign: Healing a Man Born Blind

9 As He was passing by, He saw a man blind from birth. 2 His disciples questioned Him: "•Rabbi, who sinned, this man or his parents, that he was born blind?"

3 "Neither this man nor his parents sinned," Jesus answered. "⌊This came about⌋ so that God's works might be displayed in him. 4 We[h] must do the works of Him who sent Me[i] while it is day. Night is coming when no one can work. 5 As long as I am in the world, I am the light of the world."

6 After He said these things He spit on the ground, made some mud from the saliva, and spread the mud on his eyes. 7 "Go," He told him, "wash in the pool of Siloam" (which means "Sent"). So he left, washed, and came back seeing.

8 His neighbors and those who formerly had seen him as a beggar said, "Isn't this the man who sat begging?" 9 Some said, "He's the one." "No," others were saying, "but he looks like him."

He kept saying, "I'm the one!"

10 Therefore they asked him, "Then how were your eyes opened?"

11 He answered, "The man called Jesus made mud, spread it on my eyes, and told me, 'Go to Siloam and wash.' So

---

[a]8:44 Lit *from his own things*   [b]8:44 Lit *of it*   [c]8:53 Lit *Who do You make Yourself?*   [d]8:57 Other mss read *and Abraham has seen You?*   [e]8:58 *I AM* is the name God gave Himself at the burning bush; Ex 3:13-14; see note at Jn 8:24.   [f]8:59 Or *Jesus hid Himself*   [g]8:59 Other mss add *and having gone through their midst, He passed by*   [h]9:4 Other mss read *I*   [i]9:4 Other mss read *sent us*

when I went and washed I received my sight."

12 "Where is He?" they asked.

"I don't know," he said.

Healed Man's Testimony

13 They brought the man who used to be blind to the •Pharisees. 14 The day that Jesus made the mud and opened his eyes was a Sabbath. 15 So again the Pharisees asked him how he received his sight.

"He put mud on my eyes," he told them. "I washed and I can see."

16 Therefore some of the Pharisees said, "This man is not from God, for He doesn't keep the Sabbath!" But others were saying, "How can a sinful man perform such signs?" And there was a division among them.

17 Again they asked the blind man,[a] "What do you say about Him, since He opened your eyes?"

"He's a prophet," he said.

18 The Jews did not believe this about him—that he was blind and received sight—until they summoned the parents of the one who had received his sight. 19 They asked them, "Is this your son, ⌊the one⌋ you say was born blind? How then does he now see?"

20 "We know this is our son and that he was born blind," his parents answered. 21 "But we don't know how he now sees, and we don't know who opened his eyes. Ask him; he's of age. He will speak for himself." 22 His parents said these things because they were afraid of the Jews, since the Jews had already agreed that if anyone confessed Him as •Messiah, he would be banned from the •synagogue. 23 This is why his parents said, "He's of age; ask him."

24 So a second time they summoned the man who had been blind and told him, "Give glory to God.[b] We know that this man is a sinner!"

25 He answered, "Whether or not He's a sinner, I don't know. One thing I do know: I was blind, and now I can see!"

26 Then they asked him, "What did He do to you? How did He open your eyes?"

27 "I already told you," he said, "and you didn't listen. Why do you want to hear it again? You don't want to become His disciples too, do you?"

28 They ridiculed him: "You're that man's disciple, but we're Moses' disciples. 29 We know that God has spoken to Moses. But this man—we don't know where He's from!"

30 "This is an amazing thing," the man told them. "You don't know where He is from, yet He opened my eyes! 31 We know that God doesn't listen to sinners, but if anyone is God-fearing and does His will, He listens to him. 32 Throughout history[c] no one has ever heard of someone opening the eyes of a person born blind. 33 If this man were not from God, He wouldn't be able to do anything."

34 "You were born entirely in sin," they replied, "and are you trying to teach us?" Then they threw him out.[d]

Jesus: Blind Man's Sight, Pharisees' Blindness

35 When Jesus heard that they had thrown the man out, He found him and asked, "Do you believe in the •Son of Man?"[e]

36 "Who is He, Sir, that I may believe in Him?" he asked.

37 Jesus answered, "You have seen Him; in fact, He is the One speaking with you."

---

[a]9:17 = the man who had been blind   [b]9:24 *Give glory to God* was a solemn charge to tell the truth; Jos 7:19.
[c]9:32 Lit *From the age*   [d]9:34 = they banned him from the synagogue; v. 22   [e]9:35 Other mss read *the Son of God*

[38] "I believe, Lord!" he said, and he worshiped Him.

[39] Jesus said, "I came into this world for judgment, in order that those who do not see will see and those who do see will become blind."

[40] Some of the Pharisees who were with Him heard these things and asked Him, "We aren't blind too, are we?"

[41] "If you were blind," Jesus told them, "you wouldn't have sin.[a] But now that you say, 'We see'—your sin remains.

Shepherd's Voice

10 "•I assure you: Anyone who doesn't enter the sheep pen by the door but climbs in some other way, is a thief and a robber. [2] The one who enters by the door is the shepherd of the sheep. [3] The door-keeper opens it for him, and the sheep hear his voice. He calls his own sheep by name and leads them out. [4] When he has brought all his own outside, he goes ahead of them. The sheep follow him because they recognize his voice. [5] They will never follow a stranger; instead they will run away from him, because they don't recognize the voice of strangers."

[6] Jesus gave them this illustration, but they did not understand what He was telling them.

The Good Shepherd

[7] So Jesus said again, "I assure you: I am the door of the sheep. [8] All who came before Me[b] are thieves and robbers, but the sheep didn't listen to them. [9] I am the door. If anyone enters by Me, he will be saved and will come in and go out and find pasture. [10] A thief comes only to steal and to kill and to destroy. I have come that they may have life and have it in abundance.

[11] "I am the good shepherd. The good shepherd lays down his life for the sheep. [12] The hired man, since he is not the shepherd and doesn't own the sheep, leaves them[c] and runs away when he sees a wolf coming. The wolf then snatches and scatters them. [13] ⌊This happens⌋ because he is a hired man and doesn't care about the sheep.

[14] "I am the good shepherd. I know My own sheep, and they know Me, [15] as the Father knows Me, and I know the Father. I lay down My life for the sheep. [16] But I have other sheep that are not of this fold; I must bring them also, and they will listen to My voice. Then there will be one flock, one shepherd. [17] This is why the Father loves Me, because I am laying down My life so I may take it up again. [18] No one takes it from Me, but I lay it down on My own. I have the right to lay it down, and I have the right to take it up again. I have received this command from My Father."

[19] Again a division took place among the Jews because of these words. [20] Many of them were saying, "He has a demon and He's crazy! Why do you listen to Him?" [21] Others were saying, "These aren't the words of someone demon-possessed. Can a demon open the eyes of the blind?"

Jesus at Festival of Dedication

[22] Then the Festival of Dedication[d] took place in Jerusalem, and it was winter. [23] Jesus was walking in the •temple complex in Solomon's Colonnade.[e] [24] Then the Jews surrounded Him and asked, "How long are You going to keep us in suspense?[f] If You are the •Messiah, tell us plainly."[g]

[a]**9:41** To *have sin* is an idiom that refers to guilt caused by sin.   [b]**10:8** Other mss omit *before Me*   [c]**10:12** Lit *leaves the sheep*   [d]**10:22** Or *Hanukkah*, also called *the Feast of Lights*; this festival commemorated the rededication of the temple in 164 B.C.   [e]**10:23** Rows of columns supporting a roof   [f]**10:24** Lit *How long are you taking away our life?*   [g]**10:24** Or *openly*, or *publicly*

25 "I did tell you and you don't believe," Jesus answered them. "The works that I do in My Father's name testify about Me. 26 But you don't believe because you are not My sheep.ᵃ 27 My sheep hear My voice, I know them, and they follow Me. 28 I give them eternal life, and they will never perish—ever! No one will snatch them out of My hand. 29 My Father, who has given them to Me, is greater than all. No one is able to snatch them out of the Father's hand. 30 The Father and I are one."ᵇ

Threat to Stone Jesus

31 Again the Jews picked up rocks to stone Him.

32 Jesus replied, "I have shown you many good works from the Father. Which of these works are you stoning Me for?"

33 "We aren't stoning You for a good work," the Jews answered, "but for blasphemy, because You—being a man—make Yourself God."

34 Jesus answered them, "Isn't it written in your law,ᶜ I said, you are gods?ᵈ 35 If He called those whom the word of God came to 'gods'—and the Scripture cannot be broken— 36 do you say, 'You are blaspheming' to the One the Father set apart and sent into the world, because I said: I am the Son of God? 37 If I am not doing My Father's works, don't believe Me. 38 But if I am doing them and you don't believe Me, believe the works. This way you will know and understandᵉ that the Father is in Me and I in the Father." 39 Then they were trying again to seize Him, yet He eluded their grasp.

Many beyond the Jordan Believe

40 So He departed again across the Jordan to the place where John had been baptizing earlier, and He remained there. 41 Many came to Him and said, "John never did a sign, but everything John said about this man was true." 42 And many believed in Him there.

Lazarus Dies at Bethany

11 Now a man was sick, Lazarus, from Bethany, the village of Mary and her sister Martha. 2 Mary was the one who anointed the Lord with fragrant oil and wiped His feet with her hair, and it was her brother Lazarus who was sick. 3 So the sisters sent a message to Him: "Lord, the one You love is sick."

4 When Jesus heard it, He said, "This sickness will not end in death but is for the glory of God, so that the Son of God may be glorified through it." 5 (Jesus loved Martha, her sister, and Lazarus.) 6 So when He heard that he was sick, He stayed two more days in the place where He was. 7 Then after that, He said to the disciples, "Let's go to Judea again."

8 "•Rabbi," the disciples told Him, "just now the Jews tried to stone You, and You're going there again?"

9 "Aren't there 12 hours in a day?" Jesus answered. "If anyone walks during the day, he doesn't stumble, because he sees the light of this world. 10 If anyone walks during the night, he does stumble, because the light is not in him." 11 He said this, and then He told them, "Our friend Lazarus has fallen •asleep, but I'm on My way to wake him up."

12 Then the disciples said to Him, "Lord, if he has fallen asleep, he will get well."

13 Jesus, however, was speaking about his death, but they thought He was speaking about natural sleep. 14 So Jesus then told them plainly, "Lazarus has died. 15 I'm glad for you that I wasn't

---

ᵃ10:26 Other mss add just as I told you ᵇ10:30 Lit I and the Father—We are one. ᶜ10:34 Other mss read in the law ᵈ10:34 Ps 82:6 ᵉ10:38 Other mss read know and believe

there so that you may believe. But let's go to him."

Thomas' Boldness

¹⁶ Then Thomas (called "Twin") said to his fellow disciples, "Let's go so that we may die with Him."

The Resurrection
and the Life

¹⁷ When Jesus arrived, He found that Lazarus had already been in the tomb four days. ¹⁸ Bethany was near Jerusalem (about two miles[a] away). ¹⁹ Many of the Jews had come to Martha and Mary to comfort them about their brother. ²⁰ As soon as Martha heard that Jesus was coming, she went to meet Him. But Mary remained seated in the house.

²¹ Then Martha said to Jesus, "Lord, if You had been here, my brother wouldn't have died. ²² Yet even now I know that whatever You ask from God, God will give You."

²³ "Your brother will rise again," Jesus told her.

²⁴ Martha said, "I know that he will rise again in the resurrection at the last day."

²⁵ Jesus said to her, "I am the resurrection and the life. The one who believes in Me, even if he dies, will live. ²⁶ Everyone who lives and believes in Me will never die—ever. Do you believe this?"

²⁷ "Yes, Lord," she told Him, "I believe You are the •Messiah, the Son of God, who was to come into the world."

Jesus Shares Sorrow of Death

²⁸ Having said this, she went back and called her sister Mary, saying in private, "The Teacher is here and is calling for you."

²⁹ As soon as she heard this, she got up quickly and went to Him. ³⁰ Jesus had not yet come into the village but was still in the place where Martha had met Him. ³¹ The Jews who were with her in the house consoling her saw that Mary got up quickly and went out. So they followed her, supposing that she was going to the tomb to cry there.

³² When Mary came to where Jesus was and saw Him, she fell at His feet and told Him, "Lord, if You had been here, my brother would not have died!"

³³ When Jesus saw her crying, and the Jews who had come with her crying, He was angry[b] in His spirit and deeply moved. ³⁴ "Where have you put him?" He asked.

"Lord," they told Him, "come and see."

³⁵ Jesus wept.

³⁶ So the Jews said, "See how He loved him!" ³⁷ But some of them said, "Couldn't He who opened the blind man's eyes also have kept this man from dying?"

Seventh Sign: Jesus Raises Lazarus from Dead

³⁸ Then Jesus, angry in Himself again, came to the tomb. It was a cave, and a stone was lying against it. ³⁹ "Remove the stone," Jesus said.

Martha, the dead man's sister, told Him, "Lord, he already stinks. It's been four days."

⁴⁰ Jesus said to her, "Didn't I tell you that if you believed you would see the glory of God?"

⁴¹ So they removed the stone. Then Jesus raised His eyes and said, "Father, I thank You that You heard Me. ⁴² I know that You always hear Me, but because of the crowd standing here I said this, so

---

[a]11:18 Lit 15 stadia; 1 stadion = 600 feet   [b]11:33 The Gk word is very strong and probably indicates Jesus' anger against sin's tyranny and death.

they may believe You sent Me." 43 After He said this, He shouted with a loud voice, "Lazarus, come out!" 44 The dead man came out bound hand and foot with linen strips and with his face wrapped in a cloth. Jesus said to them, "Loose him and let him go."

Plot to Kill Jesus

45 Therefore many of the Jews who came to Mary and saw what He did believed in Him. 46 But some of them went to the •Pharisees and told them what Jesus had done.

47 So the •chief priests and the Pharisees convened the •Sanhedrin and said, "What are we going to do since this man does many signs? 48 If we let Him continue in this way, everybody will believe in Him! Then the Romans will come and remove both our place and our nation."

49 One of them, Caiaphas, who was high priest that year, said to them, "You know nothing at all! 50 You're not considering that it is to your[b] advantage that one man should die for the people rather than the whole nation perish." 51 He did not say this on his own, but being high priest that year he prophesied that Jesus was going to die for the nation, 52 and not for the nation only, but also to unite the scattered children of God. 53 So from that day on they plotted to kill Him. 54 Therefore Jesus no longer walked openly among the Jews but departed from there to the countryside near the wilderness, to a town called Ephraim. And He stayed there with the disciples.

55 The Jewish •Passover was near, and many went up to Jerusalem from the country to purify[c] themselves before the Passover. 56 They were looking for Jesus and asking one another as they stood in the •temple complex: "What do you think? He won't come to the festival, will He?" 57 The chief priests and the Pharisees had given orders that if anyone knew where He was, he should report it so they could arrest Him.

Anointing at Bethany

12 Six days before the •Passover, Jesus came to Bethany where Lazarus[d] was, the one Jesus had raised from the dead. 2 So they gave a dinner for Him there; Martha was serving them, and Lazarus was one of those reclining at the table with Him. 3 Then Mary took a pound of fragrant oil—pure and expensive nard—anointed Jesus' feet, and wiped His feet with her hair. So the house was filled with the fragrance of the oil.

Judas Iscariot Objects

4 Then one of His disciples, Judas Iscariot (who was about to betray Him), said, 5 "Why wasn't this fragrant oil sold for 300 •denarii[e] and given to the poor?" 6 He didn't say this because he cared about the poor but because he was a thief. He was in charge of the money-bag and would steal part of what was put in it.

7 Jesus answered, "Leave her alone; she has kept it for the day of My burial. 8 For you always have the poor with you, but you do not always have Me."

Decision to Kill Lazarus

9 Then a large crowd of the Jews learned He was there. They came not only because of Jesus, but also to see Lazarus the one He had raised from the

a11:48 The temple or possibly all of Jerusalem   b11:50 Other mss read to our   c11:55 The law of Moses required God's people to purify or cleanse themselves so they could celebrate the Passover. Jews often came to Jerusalem a week early to do this; Nm 9:4-11.   d12:1 Other mss read Lazarus who died   e12:5 This amount was about a year's wages for a common worker.

dead. ¹⁰ Therefore the •chief priests decided to also kill Lazarus, ¹¹ because he was the reason many of the Jews were deserting them[a] and believing in Jesus.

Triumphal Entry

¹² The next day, when the large crowd that had come to the festival heard that Jesus was coming to Jerusalem, ¹³ they took palm branches and went out to meet Him. They kept shouting: "•Hosanna! Blessed is He who comes in the name of the Lord[b]—the King of Israel!"

¹⁴ Jesus found a young donkey and sat on it, just as it is written: ¹⁵ **Fear no more, Daughter Zion; look! your King is coming, sitting on a donkey's colt.**[c]

¹⁶ His disciples did not understand these things at first. However, when Jesus was glorified, then they remembered that these things had been written about Him and that they had done these things to Him. ¹⁷ Meanwhile the crowd, which had been with Him when He called Lazarus out of the tomb and raised him from the dead, continued to testify.[d] ¹⁸ This is also why the crowd met Him, because they heard He had done this sign.

¹⁹ Then the •Pharisees said to one another, "You see? You've accomplished nothing. Look—the world has gone after Him!"

Philip Brings Greeks to Andrew and Jesus

²⁰ Now some Greeks were among those who went up to worship at the festival. ²¹ So they came to Philip, who was from Bethsaida in Galilee, and requested of him, "Sir, we want to see Jesus." ²² Philip went and told Andrew; then Andrew and Philip went and told Jesus.

²³ Jesus replied to them, "The hour has come for the •Son of Man to be glorified.

Jesus Predicts His Crucifixion

²⁴ "•I assure you: Unless a grain of wheat falls into the ground and dies, it remains by itself. But if it dies, it produces a large crop.[e] ²⁵ The one who loves his life will lose it, and the one who hates his life in this world will keep it for eternal life. ²⁶ If anyone serves Me, he must follow Me. Where I am, there My servant also will be. If anyone serves Me, the Father will honor him.

²⁷ "Now My soul is troubled. What should I say—Father, save Me from this hour? But that is why I came to this hour. ²⁸ Father, glorify Your name!"[f]

Then a voice came from heaven: "I have glorified it, and I will glorify it again!"

²⁹ The crowd standing there heard it and said it was thunder. Others said, "An angel has spoken to Him!"

³⁰ Jesus responded, "This voice came, not for Me, but for you. ³¹ Now is the judgment of this world. Now the ruler of this world will be cast out. ³² As for Me, if I am lifted up[g] from the earth I will draw all ⌊people⌋ to Myself." ³³ He said this to signify what kind of death He was about to die.

³⁴ Then the crowd replied to Him, "We have heard from the law that the •Messiah will remain forever. So how can You say, 'The Son of Man must be lifted up'?[g] Who is this Son of Man?"

³⁵ Jesus answered, "The light will be with you only a little longer. Walk while you have the light so that darkness doesn't overtake you. The one who walks in darkness doesn't know where he's going. ³⁶ While you have the light,

---

[a]**12:11** Lit *going away*   [b]**12:13** Ps 118:25-26   [c]**12:15** Zch 9:9   [d]**12:17** Other mss read *Meanwhile the crowd, which had been with Him, continued to testify that He had called Lazarus out of the tomb and raised him from the dead.*
[e]**12:24** Lit *produces much fruit*   [f]**12:28** Other mss read *Your Son*   [g]**12:32,34** Or *exalted*

believe in the light so that you may become sons of light." Jesus said this, then went away and hid from them.

Isaiah's Prophecies Fulfilled

³⁷ Even though He had performed so many signs in their presence, they did not believe in Him. ³⁸ But this was to fulfill the word of Isaiah the prophet, who said:ᵃ

> Lord, who has believed
> our message?
> And who has the arm of the Lord
> been revealed to?ᵇ

³⁹ This is why they were unable to believe, because Isaiah also said:

> ⁴⁰ He has blinded their eyes
> and hardened their hearts,
> so that they would not see
> with their eyes
> or understand with their hearts,
> and be converted,
> and I would heal them.ᶜ

⁴¹ Isaiah said these things becauseᵈ he saw His glory and spoke about Him. ⁴² Nevertheless, many did believe in Him even among the rulers, but because of the Pharisees they did not confess Him, so they would not be banned from the •synagogue. ⁴³ For they loved praise from men more than praise from God.ᵉ

Summary of Jesus' Mission

⁴⁴ Then Jesus cried out, "The one who believes in Me believes not in Me, but in Him who sent Me. ⁴⁵ And the one who sees Me sees Him who sent Me. ⁴⁶ I have come as a light into the world, so that everyone who believes in Me would not remain in darkness. ⁴⁷ If anyone hears My words and doesn't keep them, I do not judge him; for I did not come to judge the world but to save the world. ⁴⁸ The one who rejects Me and doesn't accept My sayings has this as his judge:ᶠ the word I have spoken will judge him on the last day. ⁴⁹ For I have not spoken on My own, but the Father Himself who sent Me has given Me a command as to what I should say and what I should speak. ⁵⁰ I know that His command is eternal life. So the things that I speak, I speak just as the Father has told Me."

Jesus Washes His Disciples' Feet

13 Before the •Passover Festival, Jesus knew that His hour had come to depart from this world to the Father. Having loved His own who were in the world, He loved them to the end.ᵍ

² Now by the time of supper, the Devil had already put it into the heart of Judas, Simon Iscariot's son, to betray Him. ³ Jesus knew that the Father had given everything into His hands, that He had come from God, and that He was going back to God. ⁴ So He got up from supper, laid aside His robe, took a towel, and tied it around Himself. ⁵ Next, He poured water into a basin and began to wash His disciples' feet and to dry them with the towel tied around Him.

⁶ He came to Simon Peter, who asked Him, "Lord, are You going to wash my feet?"

⁷ Jesus answered him, "What I'm doing you don't understand now, but afterwards you will know."

⁸ "You will never wash my feet—ever!" Peter said.

Jesus replied, "If I don't wash you, you have no part with Me."

ᵃ**12:38** Lit *which he said*   ᵇ**12:38** Is 53:1   ᶜ**12:40** Is 6:10   ᵈ**12:41** Other mss read *when*   ᵉ**12:43** Lit *loved glory of men more than glory of God*; v. 41; Jn 5:41   ᶠ**12:48** Lit *has the one judging him*   ᵍ**13:1** *to the end* = *completely* or *always*

⁹ Simon Peter said to Him, "Lord, not only my feet, but also my hands and my head."

¹⁰ "One who has bathed," Jesus told him, "doesn't need to wash anything except his feet, but he is completely clean. You are clean, but not all of you." ¹¹ For He knew who would betray Him. This is why He said, "You are not all clean."

Meaning of Footwashing

¹² When Jesus had washed their feet and put on His robe, He reclined[a] again and said to them, "Do you know what I have done for you? ¹³ You call Me Teacher and Lord. This is well said, for I am. ¹⁴ So if I, your Lord and Teacher, have washed your feet, you also ought to wash one another's feet. ¹⁵ For I have given you an example that you also should do just as I have done for you.

¹⁶ "•I assure you: A slave is not greater than his master,[b] and a messenger is not greater than the one who sent him. ¹⁷ If you know these things, you are blessed if you do them. ¹⁸ I'm not speaking about all of you; I know those I have chosen. But the Scripture must be fulfilled: **The one who eats My bread[c] has raised his heel against Me.**[d]

¹⁹ "I am telling you now before it happens, so that when it does happen you will believe that I am [He]. ²⁰ I assure you: The one who receives whomever I send receives Me, and the one who receives Me receives Him who sent Me."

Judas' Betrayal Predicted

²¹ When Jesus had said this, He was troubled in His spirit and testified, "I assure you: One of you will betray Me!"

²² The disciples started looking at one another—uncertain which one He was speaking about. ²³ One of His disciples, the one Jesus loved, was reclining close beside Jesus.[e] ²⁴ Simon Peter motioned to him to find out who it was He was talking about. ²⁵ So he leaned back against Jesus and asked Him, "Lord, who is it?"

²⁶ Jesus replied, "He's the one I give the piece of bread to after I have dipped it." When He had dipped the bread, He gave it to Judas, Simon Iscariot's son.[f] ²⁷ After [Judas ate] the piece of bread, Satan entered him. Therefore Jesus told him, "What you're doing, do quickly."

²⁸ None of those reclining at the table knew why He told him this. ²⁹ Since Judas kept the money-bag, some thought that Jesus was telling him, "Buy what we need for the festival," or that he should give something to the poor. ³⁰ After receiving the piece of bread, he went out immediately. And it was night.

The New Commandment

³¹ When he had gone out, Jesus said, "Now the •Son of Man is glorified, and God is glorified in Him. ³² If God is glorified in Him,[g] God will also glorify Him in Himself and will glorify Him at once.

³³ "Children, I am with you a little while longer. You will look for Me, and just as I told the Jews, 'Where I am going you cannot come,' so now I tell you.

³⁴ "I give you a new commandment: love one another. Just as I have loved you, you must also love one another. ³⁵ By this all people will know that you are My disciples, if you have love for one another."

Jesus Predicts Peter's Denials

³⁶ "Lord," Simon Peter said to Him, "where are You going?"

---

[a]**13:12** At important meals the custom was to recline on a mat at a low table and lean on the left elbow.   [b]**13:16** Or lord   [c]**13:18** Other mss read *eats bread with Me*   [d]**13:18** Ps 41:9   [e]**13:23** Lit *reclining at Jesus' breast*; that is, on His right; Jn 1:18   [f]**13:26** Other mss read *Judas Iscariot, Simon's son*   [g]**13:32** Other mss omit *If God is glorified in Him*

Jesus answered, "Where I am going you cannot follow Me now, but you will follow later."

[37] "Lord," Peter asked, "why can't I follow You now? I will lay down my life for You!"

[38] Jesus replied, "Will you lay down your life for Me? I assure you: A rooster will not crow until you have denied Me three times.

Way to the Father

14 "Your heart must not be troubled. Believe[a] in God; believe also in Me. [2] In My Father's house are many dwelling places;[b] if not, I would have told you. I am going away to prepare a place for you. [3] If I go away and prepare a place for you, I will come back and receive you to Myself, so that where I am you may be also. [4] You know the way where I am going."[c]

Thomas Questions

[5] "Lord," Thomas said, "we don't know where You're going. How can we know the way?"

[6] Jesus told him, "I am the way, the truth, and the life. No one comes to the Father except through Me.

[7] "If you know Me, you will also know[d] My Father. From now on you do know Him and have seen Him."

Philip: "Show Us the Father"

[8] "Lord," said Philip, "show us the Father, and that's enough for us."

[9] Jesus said to him, "Have I been among you all this time without your knowing Me, Philip? The one who has seen Me has seen the Father. How can you say, 'Show us the Father'? [10] Don't

you believe that I am in the Father and the Father is in Me? The words I speak to you I do not speak on My own. The Father who lives in Me does His works. [11] Believe Me that I am in the Father and the Father is in Me. Otherwise, believe[e] because of the works themselves.

Praying in Jesus' Name

[12] "•I assure you: The one who believes in Me will also do the works that I do. And he will do even greater works than these, because I am going to the Father. [13] Whatever you ask in My name, I will do it so that the Father may be glorified in the Son. [14] If you ask Me[f] anything in My name, I will do it.[g]

Another Counselor Promised

[15] "If you love Me, you will keep[h] My commandments. [16] And I will ask the Father, and He will give you another •Counselor to be with you forever. [17] He is the Spirit of truth. The world is unable to receive Him because it doesn't see Him or know Him. But you do know Him, because He remains with you and will be[i] in you. [18] I will not leave you as orphans; I am coming to you.

Unity of Father, Son, and Believers

[19] "In a little while the world will see Me no longer, but you will see Me. Because I live, you will live too. [20] In that day you will know that I am in My Father, you are in Me, and I am in you. [21] The one who has My commands and keeps them is the one who loves Me. And the one who loves Me will be loved by My Father. I also will love him and will reveal Myself to him."

---

[a]**14:1** Or *You believe*   [b]**14:2** The Vg used the Lat term *mansio*, a traveler's resting place. The Gk word is related to the verb *meno*, meaning *remain* or *stay*, which occurs 40 times in John.   [c]**14:4** Other mss read this verse: *And you know where I am going, and you know the way*   [d]**14:7** Other mss read *If you had known Me, you would have known*
[e]**14:11** Other mss read *believe Me*   [f]**14:14** Other mss omit *Me*   [g]**14:14** Other mss omit all of v. 14   [h]**14:15** Other mss read *If you love Me, keep* (as a command)   [i]**14:17** Other mss read *and is*

Another Judas Questions Jesus

²² Judas (not Iscariot) said to Him, "Lord, how is it You're going to reveal Yourself to us and not to the world?"

²³ Jesus answered, "If anyone loves Me, he will keep My word. My Father will love him, and We will come to him and make Our home with him. ²⁴ The one who doesn't love Me will not keep My words. The word that you hear is not Mine but is from the Father who sent Me.

Father, Son, and Holy Spirit

²⁵ "I have spoken these things to you while I remain with you. ²⁶ But the Counselor, the Holy Spirit—the Father will send Him in My name—will teach you all things and remind you of everything I have told you.

Jesus' Gift of Peace

²⁷ "Peace I leave with you. <u>My peace I give to you</u>. I do not give to you as the world gives. Your heart must not be troubled or fearful. ²⁸ You have heard Me tell you, 'I am going away and I am coming to you.' If you loved Me, you would have rejoiced that I am going to the Father, because the Father is greater than I. ²⁹ I have told you now before it happens so that when it does happen you may believe. ³⁰ I will not talk with you much longer, because the ruler of the world is coming. He has no power over Me.ᵃ ³¹ On the contrary, ⸤I am going away⸥ᵇ so that the world may know that I love the Father. Just as the Father commanded Me, so I do.

"Get up; let's leave this place.

Vine and Branches

15 "<u>I am the true vine, and My Father is the vineyard keeper.</u> ² Every branch in Me that does not produce fruit He removes, and He prunes every branch that produces fruit so that it will produce more fruit. ³ You are already clean because of the word I have spoken to you. ⁴ Remain in Me, and I in you. Just as a branch is unable to produce fruit by itself unless it remains on the vine, so neither can you unless you remain in Me.

⁵ "<u>I am the vine; you are the branches.</u> The one who remains in Me and I in him produces much fruit, because you can do nothing without Me. ⁶ If anyone does not remain in Me, he is thrown aside like a branch and he withers. They gather them, throw them into the fire, and they are burned. ⁷ <u>If you remain in Me and My words remain in you, ask whatever you want and it will be done for you.</u> ⁸ My Father is glorified by this: that you produce much fruit and prove to beᶜ My disciples.

Christlike Love

⁹ "As the Father has loved Me, I have also loved you. <u>Remain in My love.</u> ¹⁰ If you keep My commands you will remain in My love, just as I have kept My Father's commands and remain in His love. ¹¹ "I have spoken these things to you so that My joy may be in you and your joy may be complete. ¹² This is My command: <u>love one another as I have loved you.</u> ¹³ No one has greater love than this, that someone would lay down his life for his friends. ¹⁴ You are My friends if you do what I command you. ¹⁵ I do not call you slaves anymore, because a slave doesn't know what his masterᵈ is doing. I have called you friends, because I have made known to you everything I have heard from My Father. ¹⁶ You did not choose Me, but I chose you. I appointed

---

ᵃ**14:30** Lit *He has nothing in Me*   ᵇ**14:31** Probably refers to the cross   ᶜ**15:8** Or *and become*   ᵈ**15:15** Or *lord*

you that you should go out and produce fruit and that your fruit should remain, so that whatever you ask the Father in My name, He will give you. 17 This is what I command you: love one another.

Jesus Predicts
Persecutions of Disciples

18 "If the world hates you, understand that it hated Me before it hated you. 19 If you were of the world, the world would love ⌊you as⌋ its own. However, because you are not of the world, but I have chosen you out of it, the world hates you. 20 Remember the word I spoke to you: 'A slave is not greater than his master.' If they persecuted Me, they will also persecute you. If they kept My word, they will also keep yours. 21 But they will do all these things to you on account of My name, because they don't know the One who sent Me. 22 If I had not come and spoken to them, they would not have sin.ᵃ Now they have no excuse for their sin. 23 The one who hates Me also hates My Father. 24 If I had not done the works among them that no one else has done, they would not have sin. Now they have seen and hated both Me and My Father. 25 But ⌊this happened⌋ so that the statement written in their law might be fulfilled: **They hated Me for no reason.**ᵇ

The Counselor is Coming

26 "When the •Counselor comes, the One I will send to you from the Father— the Spirit of truth who proceeds from the Father—He will testify about Me. 27 You also will testify, because you have been with Me from the beginning.

16 "I have told you these things to keep you from stumbling. 2 They will ban you from the •synagogues. In fact, a time is coming when anyone who kills you will think he is offering service to God. 3 They will do these things because they haven't known the Father or Me. 4 But I have told you these things so that when their timeᶜ comes you may remember I told them to you. I didn't tell you these things from the beginning, because I was with you.

Counselor's Ministry

5 "But now I am going away to Him who sent Me, and not one of you asks Me, 'Where are You going?' 6 Yet, because I have spoken these things to you, sorrow has filled your heart. 7 Nevertheless, I am telling you the truth. It is for your benefit that I go away, because if I don't go away the •Counselor will not come to you. If I go, I will send Him to you. 8 When He comes, He will convict the world about sin, righteousness, and judgment: 9 about sin, because they do not believe in Me; 10 about righteousness, because I am going to the Father and you will no longer see Me; 11 and about judgment, because the ruler of this world has been judged.

12 "I still have many things to tell you, but you can't bear them now. 13 When the Spirit of truth comes, He will guide you into all the truth. For He will not speak on His own, but He will speak whatever He hears. He will also declare to you what is to come. 14 He will glorify Me, because He will take from what is Mine and declare it to you. 15 Everything the Father has is Mine. This is why I told you that He takes from what is Mine and will declare it to you.

Disciples Confused

16 "A little while and you will no longer see Me; again a little while and you will see Me."ᵈ

ᵃ**15:22** To *have sin* is an idiom that refers to guilt caused by sin.   ᵇ**15:25** Ps 69:4   ᶜ**16:4** Other mss read *when the time*   ᵈ**16:16** Other mss add *because I am going to the Father*

[17] Therefore some of His disciples said to one another, "What is this He tells us: 'A little while and you will not see Me; again a little while and you will see Me'; and, 'because I am going to the Father'?" [18] They said, "What is this He is saying,[a] 'A little while'? We don't know what He's talking about!"

Jesus: Sorrow Turned to Joy

[19] Jesus knew they wanted to question Him, so He said to them, "Are you asking one another about what I said, 'A little while and you will not see Me; again a little while and you will see Me'?

[20] "•I assure you: You will weep and wail, but the world will rejoice. You will become sorrowful, but your sorrow will turn to joy. [21] When a woman is in labor she has pain because her time has come. But when she has given birth to a child, she no longer remembers the suffering because of the joy that a person has been born into the world. [22] So you also have sorrow[b] now. But I will see you again. Your hearts will rejoice, and no one will rob you of your joy. [23] In that day you will not ask Me anything.

Ask and You'll Receive

"I assure you: Anything you ask the Father in My name, He will give you. [24] Until now you have asked for nothing in My name. Ask and you will receive, that your joy may be complete.

From Suffering to Victory

[25] "I have spoken these things to you in figures of speech. A time is coming when I will no longer speak to you in figures, but I will tell you plainly about the Father. [26] In that day you will ask in My name. I am not telling you that I will make requests to the Father on your behalf. [27] For the Father Himself loves you, because you have loved Me and have believed that I came from God.[c] [28] I came from the Father and have come into the world. Again, I am leaving the world and going to the Father."

[29] "Ah!" His disciples said. "Now You're speaking plainly and not using any figurative language. [30] Now we know that You know everything and don't need anyone to question You. By this we believe that You came from God."

[31] Jesus responded to them, "Do you now believe? [32] Look: An hour is coming, and has come, when each of you will be scattered to his own home, and you will leave Me alone. Yet I am not alone, because the Father is with Me. [33] I have told you these things so that in Me you may have peace. You will have suffering in this world. Be courageous! I have conquered the world."

Jesus' Priestly Prayer

Jesus Prays for Himself

17 Jesus spoke these things, looked up to heaven, and said:

Father,
the hour has come.
Glorify Your Son
so that the Son may glorify You,
[2] for You gave Him authority
over all flesh;[d]
so He may give eternal life
to all You have given Him.
[3] This is eternal life:
that they may know You,
the only true God,
and the One You have sent—
Jesus Christ.
[4] I have glorified You on the earth
by completing the work
You gave Me to do.

[a]16:18 Other mss omit *He is saying*   [b]16:22 Other mss read *will have sorrow*   [c]16:27 Other mss read *from the Father*   [d]17:2 Or *people*

⁵ Now, Father, glorify Me
  in Your presence
with that glory I had with You
  before the world existed.

Jesus Prays for His Disciples

⁶ I have revealed Your name
  to the men You gave Me
  from the world.
They were Yours, You gave them
  to Me,
and they have kept Your word.
⁷ Now they know that all things
You have given to Me are from You,
⁸ because the words that You
  gave Me,
I have given them.
They have received them
and have known for certain
that I came from You.
They have believed
  that You sent Me.
⁹ I pray[a] for them.
I am not praying for the world
but for those You have given Me,
because they are Yours.
¹⁰ All My things are Yours,
and Yours are Mine,
and I have been glorified in them.
¹¹ I am no longer in the world,
but they are in the world,
and I am coming to You.
Holy Father,
protect[b] them by Your name
that You have given Me,
so that they may be one
  as We are one.
¹² While I was with them,
I was protecting them
  by Your name
that You have given Me.
I guarded them and not one
of them is lost,
except the son of destruction,[c]

so that the Scripture may be
  fulfilled.
¹³ Now I am coming to You,
and I speak these things
  in the world
so that they may have My joy
  completed in them.
¹⁴ I have given them Your word.
The world hated them
because they are not of the world,
as I am not of the world.
¹⁵ I am not praying
that You take them out of the world
but that You protect them
  from the evil one.
¹⁶ They are not of the world,
as I am not of the world.
¹⁷ Sanctify[d] them by the truth;
Your word is truth.
¹⁸ As You sent Me into the world,
I also have sent them
  into the world.
¹⁹ I sanctify Myself for them,
so they also may be sanctified
  by the truth.

Jesus Prays for All Believers

²⁰ I pray not only for these,
but also for those who believe
  in Me
through their message.
²¹ May they all be one,
as You, Father, are in Me and I am
  in You.
May they also be one[e] in Us,
so the world may believe
  You sent Me.
²² I have given them the glory
You have given Me.
May they be one as We are one.
²³ I am in them and You are in Me.
May they be made completely one,
so the world may know You have
  sent Me

ᵃ**17:9** Lit *ask* (throughout this passage)   ᵇ**17:11** Lit *keep* (throughout this passage)   ᶜ**17:12** The one destined for destruction, loss, or perdition   ᵈ**17:17** Set apart for special use   ᵉ**17:21** Other mss omit *one*

and have loved them as
    You have loved Me.
24 Father,
    I desire those You have given Me
    to be with Me where I am.
    Then they will see My glory,
    which You have given Me
    because You loved Me
    before the world's foundation.
25 Righteous Father!
    The world has not known You.
    However, I have known You,
    and these have known
    that You sent Me.
26 I made Your name known to them
    and will make it known,
    so the love You have loved Me with
    may be in them and I may be
    in them.

Jesus Betrayed in Garden

18 After Jesus had said these things, He went out with His disciples across the Kidron Valley, where there was a garden, and He and His disciples went into it. 2 Judas, who betrayed Him, also knew the place, because Jesus often met there with His disciples. 3 So Judas took a •company of soldiers and some temple police from the •chief priests and the •Pharisees and came there with lanterns, torches, and weapons.

4 Then Jesus, knowing everything that was about to happen to Him, went out and said to them, "Who is it you're looking for?"

5 "Jesus the •Nazarene," they answered.

"I am He,"a Jesus told them.

Judas, who betrayed Him, was also standing with them. 6 When He told them, "I am He," they stepped back and fell to the ground.

7 Then He asked them again, "Who is it you're looking for?"

"Jesus the Nazarene," they said.

8 "I told you I am ⌊He⌋," Jesus replied. "So if you're looking for Me, let these men go." 9 This was to fulfill the words He had said: "I have not lost one of those You have given Me."

Simon Peter Wields Sword

10 Then Simon Peter, who had a sword, drew it, struck the high priest's slave, and cut off his right ear. (The slave's name was Malchus.)

11 At that, Jesus said to Peter, "Sheathe your sword! Am I not to drink the cup the Father has given Me?"

Jesus Arrested and Taken to Annas

12 Then the company of soldiers, the commander, and the Jewish temple police arrested Jesus and tied Him up. 13 First they led Him to Annas, for he was the father-in-law of Caiaphas, who was high priest that year. 14 Caiaphas was the one who had advised the Jews that it was advantageous that one man should die for the people.

Peter Denies Jesus Once

15 Meanwhile Simon Peter was following Jesus, as was another disciple. That disciple was an acquaintance of the high priest; so he went with Jesus into the high priest's courtyard. 16 But Peter remained standing outside by the door. So the other disciple, the one known to the high priest, went out and spoke to the girl who was the doorkeeper and brought Peter in.

17 Then the slave girl who was the doorkeeper said to Peter, "You aren't one of this man's disciples too, are you?"

"I am not!" he said. 18 Now the slaves and the temple police had made a char-

a**18:5** Lit *I am*; see note at Jn 8:58

coal fire, because it was cold. They were standing there warming themselves, and Peter was standing with them, warming himself.

Jesus before Annas

¹⁹ The high priest questioned Jesus about His disciples and about His teaching.

²⁰ "I have spoken openly to the world," Jesus answered him. "I have always taught in the •synagogue and in the •temple complex, where all the Jews congregate, and I haven't spoken anything in secret. ²¹ Why do you question Me? Question those who heard what I told them. Look, they know what I said."

²² When He had said these things, one of the temple police standing by slapped Jesus, saying, "Is this the way you answer the high priest?"

²³ "If I have spoken wrongly," Jesus answered him, "give evidenceᵃ about the wrong; but if rightly, why do you hit Me?"

²⁴ Then Annas sent Him bound to Caiaphas the high priest.

Peter Denies Jesus Twice More

²⁵ Now Simon Peter was standing and warming himself. They said to him, "You aren't one of His disciples too, are you?"

He denied it and said, "I am not!"

²⁶ One of the high priest's slaves, a relative of the man whose ear Peter had cut off, said, "Didn't I see you with Him in the garden?"

²⁷ Peter then denied it again. Immediately a rooster crowed.

Jesus before Pilate

²⁸ Then they took Jesus from Caiaphas to the governor's •headquarters. It was early morning. They did not enter the headquarters themselves; otherwise they would be defiled and unable to eat the •Passover.

²⁹ Then •Pilate came out to them and said, "What charge do you bring against this man?"

³⁰ They answered him, "If this man weren't a criminal,ᵇ we wouldn't have handed Him over to you."

³¹ So Pilate told them, "Take Him yourselves and judge Him according to your law."

"It's not legalᶜ for us to put anyone to death," the Jews declared. ³² They said this so that Jesus' words might be fulfilled signifying what sort of death He was going to die.

Pilate Questions Jesus Privately

³³ Then Pilate went back into the headquarters, summoned Jesus, and said to Him, "Are You the King of the Jews?"

³⁴ Jesus answered, "Are you asking this on your own, or have others told you about Me?"

³⁵ "I'm not a Jew, am I?" Pilate replied. "Your own nation and the chief priests handed You over to me. What have You done?"

³⁶ "My kingdom is not of this world," said Jesus. "If My kingdom were of this world, My servantsᵈ would fight, so that I wouldn't be handed over to the Jews. As it is, My kingdom does not have its origin here."ᵉ

³⁷ "You are a king then?" Pilate asked.

"You say that I'm a king," Jesus replied. "I was born for this, and I have come into the world for this: to testify to the truth. Everyone who is of the truth listens to My voice."

³⁸ "What is truth?" said Pilate.

Pilate: Release Jesus?

After he had said this, he went out to the Jews again and told them, "I find no grounds for charging Him. ³⁹ You have a

---

ᵃ**18:23** Or *him, testify* ᵇ**18:30** Lit *an evil doer* ᶜ**18:31** According to Roman law ᵈ**18:36** Or *attendants,* or *helpers*
ᵉ**18:36** Lit *My kingdom is not from here*

custom that I release one ⌜prisoner⌝ to you at the Passover. So, do you want me to release to you the King of the Jews?"

⁴⁰ They shouted back, "Not this man, but Barabbas!" Now Barabbas was a revolutionary.ᵃ

Pilate Orders Jesus Flogged

19 Then •Pilate took Jesus and had Him flogged. ² The soldiers also twisted together a crown of thorns, put it on His head, and threw a purple robe around Him. ³ And they repeatedly came up to Him and said, "Hail, King of the Jews!" and were slapping His face.

⁴ Pilate went outside again and said to them, "Look, I'm bringing Him outside to you to let you know I find no grounds for charging Him."

Pilate Argues
with Religious Authorities

⁵ Then Jesus came out wearing the crown of thorns and the purple robe. Pilate said to them, "Here is the man!"

⁶ When the •chief priests and the temple police saw Him, they shouted, "Crucify! Crucify!"

Pilate responded, "Take Him and crucify Him yourselves, for I find no grounds for charging Him."

⁷ "We have a law," the Jews replied to him, "and according to that law He must die, because He made Himselfᵇ the Son of God."

Pilate Questions
Jesus Further

⁸ When Pilate heard this statement, he was more afraid than ever. ⁹ He went back into the •headquarters and asked Jesus, "Where are You from?" But Jesus did not give him an answer. ¹⁰ So Pilate

said to Him, "You're not talking to me? Don't You know that I have the authority to release You and the authority to crucify You?"

¹¹ "You would have no authority over Me at all," Jesus answered him, "if it hadn't been given you from above. This is why the one who handed Me over to you has the greater sin."ᶜ

Pilate Tries to Release Jesus

¹² From that moment Pilate made every effortᵈ to release Him. But the Jews shouted, "If you release this man, you are not Caesar's friend. Anyone who makes himself a king opposes Caesar!"

¹³ When Pilate heard these words, he brought Jesus outside. He sat down on the judge's bench in a place called the Stone Pavement (but in Hebrew *Gabbatha*). ¹⁴ It was the preparation day for the •Passover, and it was about six in the morning.ᵉ Then he told the Jews, "Here is your king!"

Pilate Consents to Crucifixion

¹⁵ But they shouted, "Take Him away! Take Him away! Crucify Him!"

Pilate said to them, "Should I crucify your king?"

"We have no king but Caesar!" the chief priests answered.

¹⁶ So then, because of them, he handed Him over to be crucified.

The Crucifixion

Therefore they took Jesus away.ᶠ ¹⁷ Carrying His own cross, He went out to what is called Skull Place, which in Hebrew is called *Golgotha*. ¹⁸ There they crucified Him and two others with Him, one on either side, with Jesus in the middle. ¹⁹ Pilate also had a sign lettered

---

ᵃ**18:40** Or *robber*; see Jn 10:1,8 for the same Gk word used here   ᵇ**19:7** He claimed to be   ᶜ**19:11** To *have sin* is an idiom that refers to guilt caused by sin.   ᵈ**19:12** Lit *Pilate was trying*   ᵉ**19:14** Lit *the sixth hour*; see note at Jn 1:39; an alternate time reckoning would be *about noon*   ᶠ**19:16** Other mss add *and led Him out*

and put on the cross. The inscription was:

JESUS THE NAZARENE THE KING OF THE JEWS

---

20 Many of the Jews read this sign, because the place where Jesus was crucified was near the city, and it was <u>written in Hebrew,</u>[a] <u>Latin, and Greek</u>. 21 So the chief priests of the Jews said to Pilate, "Don't write, 'The King of the Jews,' but that He said, 'I am the King of the Jews.'"

22 Pilate replied, "What I have written, I have written."

23 When the soldiers crucified Jesus, they took His clothes and divided them into four parts, a part for each soldier. They also took the tunic, which was seamless, woven in one piece from the top. 24 So they said to one another, "Let's not tear it, but toss for it, to see who gets it." ⌊They did this⌋ to fulfill the Scripture that says: **They divided My clothes among themselves, and they cast lots for My clothing.**[b] And this is what the soldiers did.

Jesus' Provision for His Mother

25 Standing by the cross of Jesus were His mother, His mother's sister, Mary the wife of Clopas, and •Mary Magdalene. 26 When Jesus saw His mother and the disciple He loved standing there, He said to His mother, "•Woman, here is your son." 27 Then He said to the disciple, "Here is your mother." And from that hour the disciple took her into his home.

Finished Work of Jesus

28 After this, when Jesus knew that everything was now accomplished that the Scripture might be fulfilled, He said,

"I'm thirsty!" 29 A jar full of sour wine was sitting there; so they fixed a sponge full of sour wine on hyssop[c] and held it up to His mouth.

30 When Jesus had received the sour wine, He said, "It is finished!" Then bowing His head, He gave up His spirit.

Soldier Pierces Jesus' Side

31 Since it was the preparation day, the Jews did not want the bodies to remain on the cross on the Sabbath (for that Sabbath was a special[d] day). They requested that Pilate have the men's legs broken and that ⌊their bodies⌋ be taken away. 32 So the soldiers came and broke the legs of the first man and of the other one who had been crucified with Him. 33 When they came to Jesus, they did not break His legs since they saw that He was already dead. 34 But one of the soldiers pierced His side with a spear, and at once blood and water came out. 35 He who saw this has testified so that you also may believe. His testimony is true, and he knows he is telling the truth. 36 For these things happened so that the Scripture would be fulfilled: **Not one of His bones will be broken.**[e] 37 Also, another Scripture says: **They will look at the One they pierced.**[f]

Jesus' Burial

38 After this, <u>Joseph of Arimathea</u>, who was a disciple of Jesus—but secretly because of his fear of the Jews—asked Pilate that he might remove Jesus' body. Pilate gave him permission, so he came and took His body away. 39 <u>Nicodemus</u> (who had previously come to Him at night) also came, bringing a mixture of about 75 pounds[g] of myrrh and aloes. 40 Then they took Jesus' body and wrapped it in linen cloths with the aromatic spices, according

---

[a]19:20 Or *Aramaic*   [b]19:24 Ps 22:18   [c]19:29 Or *with hyssop*   [d]19:31 Lit *great*   [e]19:36 Ex 12:46; Nm 9:12; Ps 34:20   [f]19:37 Zch 12:10   [g]19:39 Lit *100 litrai*; a Roman *litrai* = 12 ounces

to the burial custom of the Jews. ⁴¹ There was a garden in the place where He was crucified. A new tomb was in the garden; no one had yet been placed in it. ⁴² They placed Jesus there because of the Jewish preparation and since the tomb was nearby.

Resurrection

Empty Tomb

20 On the first day of the week •Mary Magdalene came to the tomb early, while it was still dark. She saw that the stone had been removedᵃ from the tomb. ² So she ran to Simon Peter and to the other disciple, the one Jesus loved, and said to them, "They have taken the Lord out of the tomb, and we don't know where they have put Him!"

³ At that, Peter and the other disciple went out, heading for the tomb. ⁴ The two were running together, but the other disciple outran Peter and got to the tomb first. ⁵ Stooping down, he saw the linen cloths lying there, yet he did not go in. ⁶ Then, following him, Simon Peter came also. He entered the tomb and saw the linen cloths lying there. ⁷ The wrapping that had been on His head was not lying with the linen cloths but was folded up in a separate place by itself. ⁸ The other disciple, who had reached the tomb first, then entered the tomb, saw, and believed. ⁹ For they still did not understand the Scripture that He must rise from the dead. ¹⁰ Then the disciples went home again.

Mary Magdalene Sees Risen Lord

¹¹ But Mary stood outside facing the tomb, crying. As she was crying, she stooped to look into the tomb. ¹² She saw two angels in white sitting there, one at the head and one at the feet, where Jesus' body had been lying. ¹³ They said to her, "•Woman, why are you crying?"

"Because they've taken away my Lord," she told them, "and I don't know where they've put Him." ¹⁴ Having said this, she turned around and saw Jesus standing there, though she did not know it was Jesus.

¹⁵ "Woman," Jesus said to her, "why are you crying? Who is it you are looking for?"

Supposing He was the gardener, she replied, "Sir, if you've removed Him, tell me where you've put Him, and I will take Him away."

¹⁶ Jesus said, "Mary."

Turning around, she said to Him in Hebrew, *"Rabbouni!"*ᵇ—which means "Teacher."

¹⁷ "Don't cling to Me," Jesus told her, "for I have not yet ascended to the Father. But go to My brothers and tell them that I am ascending to My Father and your Father—to My God and your God."

¹⁸ Mary Magdalene went and announced to the disciples, "I have seen the Lord!" And she told them whatᶜ He had said to her.

Disciples Commissioned

¹⁹ In the evening of that first day of the week, the disciples were ⌐gathered together⌐ with the doors locked because of their fear of the Jews. Then Jesus came, stood among them, and said to them, "Peace to you!"

²⁰ Having said this, He showed them His hands and His side. So the disciples rejoiced when they saw the Lord.

²¹ Jesus said to them again, "Peace to you! As the Father has sent Me, I also send you." ²² After saying this, He breathed on them and said,ᵈ "Receive

---

ᵃ**20:1** Lit *She saw the stone removed*   ᵇ**20:16** *Rabbouni* is also used in Mk 10:51   ᶜ**20:18** Lit *these things*   ᵈ**20:22** Lit *He breathed and said to them*

the Holy Spirit. 23 If you forgive the sins of any, they are forgiven them; if you retain ⸤the sins of⸥ any, they are retained."

Thomas Doubts

24 But one of the Twelve, Thomas (called "Twin"), was not with them when Jesus came. 25 So the other disciples kept telling him, "We have seen the Lord!"

But he said to them, "If I don't see the mark of the nails in His hands, put my finger into the mark of the nails, and put my hand into His side, I will never believe!"

26 After eight days His disciples were indoors again, and Thomas was with them. Even though the doors were locked, Jesus came and stood among them. He said, "Peace to you!"

Thomas Sees and Believes

27 Then He said to Thomas, "Put your finger here and observe My hands. Reach out your hand and put it into My side. Don't be an unbeliever, but a believer."

28 Thomas responded to Him, "My Lord and my God!"

29 Jesus said, "Because you have seen Me, you have believed.ᵃ Those who believe without seeing are blessed."

Purpose of This Gospel

30 Jesus performed many other signs in the presence of His disciples that are not written in this book. 31 But these are written so that you may believe Jesus is the •Messiah, the Son of God,ᵇ and by believing you may have life in His name.

Jesus' Third Appearance to the Disciples

21 After this, Jesus revealed Himself again to His disciples by the Sea of Tiberias.ᶜ He revealed Himself in this way:

A Fishing Trip in Galilee

2 Simon Peter, Thomas (called "Twin"), Nathanael from Cana of Galilee, Zebedee's sons, and two others of His disciples were together.

3 "I'm going fishing," Simon Peter said to them.

"We're coming with you," they told him. They went out and got into the boat, but that night they caught nothing.

Jesus on the Shore

4 When daybreak came, Jesus stood on the shore. However, the disciples did not know it was Jesus.

5 "Men,"ᵈ Jesus called to them, "you don't have any fish, do you?"

"No," they answered.

6 "Cast the net on the right side of the boat," He told them, "and you'll find some." So they did,ᵉ and they were unable to haul it in because of the large number of fish. 7 Therefore the disciple, the one Jesus loved, said to Peter, "It is the Lord!"

When Simon Peter heard that it was the Lord, he tied his outer garment around himᶠ (for he was stripped) and plunged into the sea. 8 But since they were not far from land (about 100 yardsᵍ away), the other disciples came in the boat, dragging the net full of fish. 9 When they got out on land, they saw a charcoal fire there, with fish lying on it, and bread.

ᵃ20:29 Or have you believed? (as a question)   ᵇ20:31 Or that the Messiah, the Son of God, is Jesus   ᶜ21:1 The Sea of Galilee; Sea of Tiberias is used only in John; Jn 6:1,23   ᵈ21:5 Lit Children   ᵉ21:6 Lit they cast   ᶠ21:7 Lit he girded his garment   ᵍ21:8 Lit about 200 cubits

[10] "Bring some of the fish you've just caught," Jesus told them. [11] So Simon Peter got up and hauled the net ashore, full of large fish—153 of them. Even though there were so many, the net was not torn.

[12] "Come and have breakfast," Jesus told them. None of the disciples dared ask Him, "Who are You?" because they knew it was the Lord. [13] Jesus came, took the bread, and gave it to them. He did the same with the fish.

[14] This was now the third time[a] Jesus appeared[b] to the disciples after He was raised from the dead.

Jesus' Threefold Restoration of Peter

[15] When they had eaten breakfast, Jesus asked Simon Peter, "Simon, son of John,[c] do you love[d] Me more than these?"

"Yes, Lord," he said to Him, "You know that I love You."

"Feed My lambs," He told him.

[16] A second time He asked him, "Simon, son of John, do you love Me?"

"Yes, Lord," he said to Him, "You know that I love You."

"Shepherd My sheep," He told him.

[17] He asked him the third time, "Simon, son of John, do you love Me?"

Peter was grieved that He asked him the third time, "Do you love Me?" He said, "Lord, You know everything! You know that I love You."

"Feed My sheep," Jesus said. [18] "•I assure you: When you were young, you would tie your belt and walk wherever you wanted. But when you grow old, you will stretch out your hands and someone else will tie you and carry you where you don't want to go." [19] He said this to signify by what kind of death he would glorify God.[e] After saying this, He told him, "Follow Me!"

Jesus Corrected False Report

[20] So Peter turned around and saw the disciple Jesus loved following them. ⌊That disciple⌋ was the one who had leaned back against Jesus at the supper and asked, "Lord, who is the one that's going to betray You?" [21] When Peter saw him, he said to Jesus, "Lord—what about him?"

[22] "If I want him to remain until I come," Jesus answered, "what is that to you? As for you, follow Me."

[23] So this report[f] spread to the brothers[g] that this disciple would not die. Yet Jesus did not tell him that he would not die, but, "If I want him to remain until I come, what is that to you?"

Epilogue

[24] This is the disciple who testifies to these things and who wrote them down. We know that his testimony is true.

[25] And there are also many other things that Jesus did, which, if they were written one by one, I suppose not even the world itself could contain the books[h] that would be written.

---

[a]21:14 The other two are in Jn 20:19-29.   [b]21:14 Lit *was revealed* (see v. 1)   [c]21:15-17 Other mss read *Simon, son of Jonah*; Jn 1:42; Mt 16:17   [d]21:15-17 Two synonyms are translated *love* in this conversation: *agapao*, the first 2 times by Jesus (vv. 15-16); and *phileo*, the last time by Jesus (v. 17) and all 3 times by Peter (vv. 15-17). Peter's threefold confession of love for Jesus corresponds to his earlier threefold denial of Jesus; Jn 18:15-18,25-27.   [e]21:19 Jesus predicts that Peter would be martyred. Church tradition says that Peter was crucified upside down.   [f]21:23 Lit *this word*   [g]21:23 The word *brothers* refers to the whole Christian community.   [h]21:25 Lit *scroll*

ACTS

Prologue

1 I wrote the first narrative, Theophilus, about all that Jesus began to do and teach [2] until the day He was taken up, after He had given orders through the Holy Spirit to the apostles whom He had chosen. [3] After He had suffered, He also presented Himself alive to them by many convincing proofs, appearing to them during 40 days and speaking about the kingdom of God.

Jesus Promises Holy Spirit

[4] While He was together with them,[a] He commanded them not to leave Jerusalem, but to wait for the Father's promise. "This," ⌊He said, "is what⌋ you heard from Me; [5] for John baptized with water, but you will be baptized with the Holy Spirit not many days from now."

[6] So when they had come together, they asked Him, "Lord, at this time are You restoring the kingdom to Israel?"

[7] He said to them, "It is not for you to know times or periods that the Father has set by His own authority. [8] But you will receive power when the Holy Spirit has come upon you, and you will be My witnesses in Jerusalem, in all Judea and Samaria, and to the ends[b] of the earth."

The Ascension

[9] After He had said this, He was taken up as they were watching, and a cloud received Him out of their sight. [10] While He was going, they were gazing into heaven, and suddenly two men in white clothes stood by them. [11] They said, "Men of Galilee, why do you stand looking up into heaven? This Jesus, who has been taken from you into heaven, will come in the same way that you have seen Him going into heaven."

United in Prayer

[12] Then they returned to Jerusalem from the mount called Olive Grove, which is near Jerusalem—a Sabbath day's journey away. [13] When they arrived, they went to the room upstairs where they were staying:

> Peter, John,
> James, Andrew,
> Philip, Thomas,
> Bartholomew, Matthew,
> James the son of Alphaeus,
> Simon the Zealot, and Judas
> the son of James.

[14] All these were continually united in prayer,[c] along with the women, including Mary[d] the mother of Jesus, and His brothers.

Peter Discusses Judas Iscariot

[15] During these days Peter stood up among the brothers[e]—the number of people who were together was about 120—and said: [16] "Brothers, the Scripture had to be fulfilled that the Holy Spirit through the mouth of David spoke in advance about Judas, who became a guide to those who arrested Jesus. [17] For he was one of our number and was allotted a share in this ministry." [18] Now this man acquired a field with his unrighteous wages; and falling headfirst, he burst open in the middle, and all his insides spilled out. [19] This became known to all the residents of Jerusalem, so that

---

in their own language that field is called *Hakeldama,* that is, Field of Blood. [20] "For it is written in the Book of Psalms:

> Let his dwelling become desolate;
> let no one live in it;[a] and
> Let someone else take
>   his position.[b]

Matthias Chosen
to Replace Betrayer

[21] "Therefore, from among the men who have accompanied us during the whole time the Lord Jesus went in and out among us— [22] beginning from the baptism of John until the day He was taken up from us—from among these, it is necessary that one become a witness with us of His resurrection."

[23] So they proposed two: Joseph, called Barsabbas, who was also known as Justus, and Matthias. [24] Then they prayed, "You, Lord, know the hearts of all; show which of these two You have chosen [25] to take the place[c] in this apostolic service that Judas left to go to his own place." [26] Then they cast lots for them, and the lot fell to Matthias. So he was numbered with the 11 apostles.

Pentecost

2 When the day of Pentecost had arrived, they were all together in one place. [2] Suddenly a sound like that of a violent rushing wind came from heaven, and it filled the whole house where they were staying. [3] And tongues, like flames of fire that were divided, appeared to them and rested on each one of them. [4] Then they were all filled with the Holy Spirit and began to speak in different languages, as the Spirit gave them ability for speech.

Foreign Jews Amazed

[5] There were Jews living in Jerusalem, devout men from every nation under heaven. [6] When this sound occurred, the multitude came together and was confused because each one heard them speaking in his own language. [7] And they were astounded and amazed, saying,[d] "Look, aren't all these who are speaking Galileans? [8] How is it that we hear, each of us, in our own native language? [9] Parthians, Medes, Elamites; those who live in Mesopotamia, in Judea and Cappadocia, Pontus and Asia, [10] Phrygia and Pamphylia, Egypt and the parts of Libya near Cyrene; visitors from Rome, both Jews and •proselytes, [11] Cretans and Arabs—we hear them speaking in our own languages the magnificent acts of God." [12] And they were all astounded and perplexed, saying to one another, "What could this be?" [13] But some sneered and said, "They're full of new wine!"

Peter's Pentecost Sermon

[14] But Peter stood up with the Eleven, raised his voice, and proclaimed to them: "Jewish men and all you residents of Jerusalem, let this be known to you and pay attention to my words. [15] For these people are not drunk, as you suppose, since it's only nine in the morning.[e] [16] On the contrary, this is what was spoken through the prophet Joel:

Joel's Prophecy

[17] **And it will be** in the last days,
> says God,
> that **I will pour out My Spirit**
>   **on all humanity;**
> **then your sons**
>   **and your daughters**
>   **will prophesy,**

---

a1:20 Ps 69:25   **b1:20** Ps 109:8   **c1:25** Other mss read *to share*   **d2:7** Other mss add *to one another*   **e2:15** Lit *it's the third hour of the day*

your young men will see visions,
and your old men will dream
dreams.
18 I will even pour out My Spirit
on My male and female slaves
in those days,
and they will prophesy.
19 I will display wonders
in the heaven above
and signs on the earth below:
blood and fire and a cloud of smoke.
20 The sun will be turned to darkness,
and the moon to blood,
before the great and remarkable
day of the Lord comes;
21 then whoever calls on the name
of the Lord will be saved.ª

Peter Preaches Christ Crucified

22 "Men of Israel, listen to these words: This Jesus the •Nazarene was a man pointed out to you by God with miracles, wonders, and signs that God did among you through Him, just as you yourselves know. 23 Though He was delivered up according to God's determined plan and foreknowledge, youᵇ usedᵇ lawless peopleᶜ to nail Him to a cross and kill Him. 24 God raised Him up, ending the pains of death, because it was not possible for Him to be held by it. 25 For David says of Him:

I saw the Lord ever before me;
because He is at my right hand,
I will not be shaken.
26 Therefore my heart was glad,
and my tongue rejoiced.
Moreover my flesh will rest
in hope,
27 because You will not leave
my soul in •Hades,
or allow Your Holy One
to see decay.

28 You have revealed the paths of life
to me;
You will fill me with gladness
in Your presence.ᵈ

29 "Brothers, I can confidently speak to you about the patriarch David: he is both dead and buried, and his tomb is with us to this day. 30 Since he was a prophet, he knew that God had sworn an oath to him to seat one of his descendantsᵉ ᶠ on his throne. 31 Seeing this in advance, he spoke concerning the resurrection of the •Messiah:

Heᵍ was not left in Hades,
and His flesh did not experience
decay.ʰ

Peter Preaches Resurrection

32 "God has resurrected this Jesus. We are all witnesses of this. 33 Therefore, since He has been exalted to the right hand of God and has received from the Father the promised Holy Spirit, He has poured out what you both see and hear. 34 For it was not David who ascended into the heavens, but he himself says:

The Lord said to my Lord,
'Sit at My right hand
35 until I make Your enemies
Your footstool.'ⁱ

36 "Therefore let all the house of Israel know with certainty that God has made this Jesus, whom you crucified, both Lord and Messiah!"

Listeners "Pierced to the Heart"

37 When they heard this, they were pierced to the heart and said to Peter and the rest of the apostles: "Brothers, what must we do?"

ª2:17-21 Jl 2:28-32   ᵇ2:23 Other mss read you have taken   ᶜ2:23 Or used the hand of lawless ones   ᵈ2:25-28 Ps 16:8-11   ᵉ2:30 Other mss add according to the flesh to raise up the Messiah   ᶠ2:30 Lit one from the fruit of his loin   ᵍ2:31 Other mss read His soul   ʰ2:31 Ps 16:10   ⁱ2:34-35 Ps 110:1

Peter: Repent and Be Baptized

[38] "Repent," Peter said to them, "and be baptized, each of you, in the name of Jesus the Messiah for the forgiveness of your sins, and you will receive the gift of the Holy Spirit. [39] For the promise is for you and for your children, and for all who are far off,[a] as many as the Lord our God will call." [40] And with many other words he testified and strongly urged them, saying, "Be saved from this corrupt[b] generation!"

3000 Receive Christ

[41] So those who accepted his message were baptized, and that day about 3,000 people were added to them. [42] And they devoted themselves to the apostles' teaching, to fellowship, to the breaking of bread, and to prayers.

Sharing, Praising, Evangelizing

[43] Then fear came over everyone, and many wonders and signs were being performed through the apostles. [44] Now all the believers were together and had everything in common. [45] So they sold their possessions and property and distributed the proceeds to all, as anyone had a need.[c] [46] And every day they devoted themselves ⌊to meeting⌋ together in the •temple complex, and broke bread from house to house. They ate their food with gladness and simplicity of heart, [47] praising God and having favor with all the people. And every day the Lord added to them[d] those who were being saved.

Peter Heals a Lame Man

3 Now Peter and John were going up together to the •temple complex at the hour of prayer at three in the after-

noon.[e] [2] And a man who was lame from his mother's womb was carried there and placed every day at the temple gate called Beautiful, so he could beg from those entering the temple complex. [3] When he saw Peter and John about to enter the temple complex, he asked for help. [4] Peter, along with John, looked at him intently and said, "Look at us." [5] So he turned to them,[f] expecting to get something from them. [6] But Peter said, "I have neither silver nor gold, but what I have, I give to you: In the name of Jesus Christ the •Nazarene, get up and walk!" [7] Then, taking him by the right hand he raised him up, and at once his feet and ankles became strong. [8] So he jumped up, stood, and started to walk, and he entered the temple complex with them—walking, leaping, and praising God. [9] All the people saw him walking and praising God, [10] and they recognized that he was the one who used to sit and beg at the Beautiful Gate of the temple complex. So they were filled with awe and astonishment at what had happened to him.

Peter Preaches in Solomon's Colonnade

[11] While he[g] was holding on to Peter and John, all the people, greatly amazed, ran toward them in what is called Solomon's Colonnade. [12] When Peter saw this, he addressed the people: "Men of Israel, why are you amazed at this? Or why do you stare at us, as though by our own power or godliness we had made him walk? [13] The God of Abraham, Isaac, and Jacob, the God of our fathers, has glorified His Servant Jesus, whom you handed over and denied in the presence of •Pilate, when he had decided to re-

---

[a]**2:39** Remote in time or space   [b]**2:40** Or *crooked*, or *twisted*   [c]**2:45** Or *to all, according to one's needs*   [d]**2:47** Other mss read *to the church*   [e]**3:1** Lit *at the ninth hour*   [f]**3:5** Or *he paid attention to them*   [g]**3:11** Other mss read *the lame man who was healed*

lease Him. ¹⁴ But you denied the Holy and Righteous One, and asked to have a murderer given to you. ¹⁵ And you killed the source^a of life, whom God raised from the dead; we are witnesses of this. ¹⁶ By faith in His name, His name has made this man strong, whom you see and know. So the faith that comes through Him has given him this perfect health in front of all of you.

¹⁷ "And now, brothers, I know that you did it in ignorance, just as your leaders also did. ¹⁸ But what God predicted through the mouth of all the prophets— that His •Messiah would suffer—He has fulfilled in this way. ¹⁹ Therefore repent and turn back, that your sins may be wiped out so that seasons of refreshing may come from the presence of the Lord, ²⁰ and He may send Jesus, who has been appointed Messiah for you. ²¹ Heaven must welcome^b Him until the times of the restoration of all things, which God spoke about by the mouth of His holy prophets from the beginning. ²² Moses said:^c

The Lord your God will raise up for you a Prophet like me from among your brothers. You must listen to Him in everything He will say to you. ²³ And it will be that everyone who will not listen to that Prophet will be completely cut off from the people.^d

²⁴ "In addition, all the prophets who have spoken, from Samuel and those after him, have also announced these days. ²⁵ You are the sons of the prophets and of the covenant that God made with your forefathers, saying to Abraham, **And in your seed all the families of the earth will be blessed.**^e ²⁶ God raised up

His Servant^f and sent Him first to you to bless you by turning each of you from your evil ways."

Peter and John Arrested

4 Now as they were speaking to the people, the priests, the commander of the temple guard, and the •Sadducees confronted them, ² because they were provoked that they were teaching the people and proclaiming in the person of Jesus^g the resurrection from the dead. ³ So they seized them and put them in custody until the next day, since it was already evening. ⁴ But many of those who heard the message believed, and the number of the men came to about 5,000.

Peter and John Face Jewish Leaders

⁵ The next day, their rulers, elders, and •scribes assembled in Jerusalem ⁶ with Annas the high priest, Caiaphas, John and Alexander, and all the members of the high-priestly family.^h ⁷ After they had Peter and John standⁱ before them, they asked the question: "By what power or in what name have you done this?"

⁸ Then Peter was filled with the Holy Spirit and said to them, "Rulers of the people and elders:^j ⁹ If we are being examined today about a good deed done to a disabled man—by what means he was healed— ¹⁰ let it be known to all of you and to all the people of Israel, that by the name of Jesus Christ the •Nazarene— whom you crucified and whom God raised from the dead—by Him this man is standing here before you healthy. ¹¹ This ⌊Jesus⌋ is

The stone despised by you builders, who has become the cornerstone.^k

^a**3:15** Or *the Prince,* or *the Ruler*   ^b**3:21** Or *receive,* or *retain*   ^c**3:22** Other mss add *to the fathers*   ^d**3:22-23** Dt 18:15-19   ^e**3:25** Gn 12:3; 18:18; 22:18; 26:4   ^f**3:26** Other mss add *Jesus*   ^g**4:2** Lit *proclaiming in Jesus*   ^h**4:6** Or *high-priestly class,* or *high-priestly clan*   ⁱ**4:7** Lit *had placed them*   ^j**4:8** Other mss add *of Israel*   ^k**4:11** Ps 118:22

¹² There is salvation in no one else, for there is no other name under heaven given to people by which we must be saved."

Religious Leaders: Don't Preach or Teach in Name of Jesus

¹³ When they observed the boldness of Peter and John and realized that they were uneducated and untrained men, they were amazed and knew that they had been with Jesus. ¹⁴ And since they saw the man who had been healed standing with them, they had nothing to say in response. ¹⁵ After they had ordered them to leave the •Sanhedrin, they conferred among themselves, ¹⁶ saying, "What should we do with these men? For an obvious sign, evident to all who live in Jerusalem, has been done through them, and we cannot deny it! ¹⁷ But so this does not spread any further among the people, let's threaten them against speaking to anyone in this name again." ¹⁸ So they called for them and ordered them not to preach or teach at all in the name of Jesus.

Peter and John: Can't Stop Speaking

¹⁹ But Peter and John answered them, "Whether it's right in the sight of God ⌞for us⌟ to listen to you rather than to God, you decide; ²⁰ for we are unable to stop speaking about what we have seen and heard."

Peter and John Released

²¹ After threatening them further, they released them. They found no way to punish them, because the people were all giving glory to God over what had been done; ²² for the man was over 40 years old on whom this sign of healing had been performed.

Believers Pray for Boldness

²³ After they were released, they went to their own fellowshipᵃ and reported all that the •chief priests and the elders had said to them. ²⁴ When they heard this, they raised their voices to God unanimously and said, "Master, You are the One who made the heaven, the earth, and the sea, and everything in them. ²⁵ You said through the Holy Spirit, by the mouth of our father David Your servant:ᵇ

> Why did the Gentiles rage,
>   and the peoples plot futile things?
> ²⁶ The kings of the earth
>   took their stand,
>   and the rulers assembled together
> against the Lord and
>   against His •Messiah.ᶜ

²⁷ "For, in fact, in this city both •Herod and Pontius •Pilate, with the Gentiles and the peoples of Israel, assembled together against Your holy Servant Jesus, whom You anointed, ²⁸ to do whatever Your hand and Your plan had predestined to take place. ²⁹ And now, Lord, consider their threats, and grant that Your slaves may speak Your message with complete boldness, ³⁰ while You stretch out Your hand for healing, signs, and wonders to be performed through the name of Your holy Servant Jesus."

Results of Believers' Prayer

³¹ When they had prayed, the place where they were assembled was shaken, and they were all filled with the Holy Spirit and began to speak God's message with boldness.

Believers Share

³² Now the multitude of those who believed were of one heart and soul, and

---

no one said that any of his possessions was his own, but instead they held everything in common. ³³ And with great power the apostles were giving testimony to the resurrection of the Lord Jesus, and great grace was on all of them. ³⁴ For there was not a needy person among them, because all those who owned lands or houses sold them, brought the proceeds of the things that were sold, ³⁵ and laid them at the apostles' feet. This was then distributed to each person as anyone had a need.

Enter Barnabas

³⁶ Joseph, a Levite and a Cypriot by birth, whom the apostles named Barnabas, which is translated Son of Encouragement, ³⁷ sold a field he owned, brought the money, and laid it at the apostles' feet.

Ananias and Sapphira Lie to Holy Spirit

5 But a man named Ananias, with Sapphira his wife, sold a piece of property. ² However, he kept back part of the proceeds with his wife's knowledge, and brought a portion of it and laid it at the apostles' feet.

Peter Challenges Ananias

³ Then Peter said, "Ananias, why has Satan filled your heart to lie to the Holy Spirit and keep back part of the proceeds from the field? ⁴ Wasn't it yours while you possessed it? And after it was sold, wasn't it at your disposal? Why is it that you planned this thing in your heart? You have not lied to men but to God!" ⁵ When he heard these words, Ananias dropped dead, and a great fear came on all who heard. ⁶ The young men got up, wrapped ⸤his body⸥, carried him out, and buried him.

Peter Challenges Sapphira

⁷ There was an interval of about three hours; then his wife came in, not knowing what had happened. ⁸ "Tell me," Peter asked her, "did you sell the field for this price?"

"Yes," she said, "for that price."

⁹ Then Peter said to her, "Why did you agree to test the Spirit of the Lord? Look! The feet of those who have buried your husband are at the door, and they will carry you out!"

¹⁰ Instantly she dropped dead at his feet. When the young men came in, they found her dead, carried her out, and buried her beside her husband. ¹¹ Then great fear came on the whole church and on all who heard these things.

Apostles Do Signs and Wonders

¹² Many signs and wonders were being done among the people through the hands of the apostles. By common consent they would all meet in Solomon's Colonnade. ¹³ None of the rest dared to join them, but the people praised them highly. ¹⁴ Believers were added to the Lord in increasing numbers—crowds of both men and women. ¹⁵ As a result, they would carry the sick out into the streets and lay them on beds and pallets so that when Peter came by, at least his shadow might fall on some of them. ¹⁶ In addition, a multitude came together from the towns surrounding Jerusalem, bringing sick people and those who were tormented by unclean spirits, and they were all healed.

Religious Leaders Arrest Apostles

¹⁷ Then the high priest took action. He and all his colleagues, those who belonged to the party of the •Sadducees, were filled with jealousy. ¹⁸ So they

arrested[a] the apostles and put them in the city jail.

Angel Rescues Them

[19] But an angel of the Lord opened the doors of the jail during the night, brought them out, and said, [20] "Go and stand in the •temple complex, and tell the people all about this life." [21] In obedience to this, they entered the temple complex at daybreak and began to teach.

Religious Leaders Arrest Apostles Again

When the high priest and those who were with him arrived, they convened the •Sanhedrin—the full Senate of the sons of Israel—and sent ⌊orders⌋ to the jail to have them brought. [22] But when the temple police got there, they did not find them in the jail, so they returned and reported, [23] "We found the jail securely locked, with the guards standing in front of the doors; but when we opened them, we found no one inside!" [24] As[b] the captain of the temple police and the •chief priests heard these things, they were baffled about them, as to what could come of this.

[25] Someone came and reported to them, "Look! The men you put in jail are standing in the temple complex and teaching the people." [26] Then the captain went with the temple police and brought them in without force, because they were afraid the people might stone them. [27] When they had brought them in, they had them stand before the Sanhedrin, and the high priest asked, [28] "Didn't we strictly order you not to teach in this name? And look, you have filled Jerusalem with your teaching and are determined to bring this man's blood on us!"

"We Must Obey God Rather Than Men"

[29] But Peter and the apostles replied, "We must obey God rather than men. [30] The God of our fathers raised up Jesus, whom you had murdered by hanging Him on a tree. [31] God exalted this man to His right hand as ruler and Savior, to grant repentance to Israel, and forgiveness of sins. [32] We are witnesses of these things, and so is the Holy Spirit whom God has given to those who obey Him."

Gamaliel Cautions Sanhedrin

[33] When they heard this, they were enraged and wanted to kill them. [34] A •Pharisee named Gamaliel, a teacher of the law who was respected by all the people, stood up in the Sanhedrin and ordered the men[c] to be taken outside for a little while. [35] He said to them, "Men of Israel, be careful about what you're going to do to these men. [36] Not long ago Theudas rose up, claiming to be somebody, and a group of about 400 men rallied to him. He was killed, and all his partisans were dispersed and came to nothing. [37] After this man, Judas the Galilean rose up in the days of the census and attracted a following.[d] That man also perished, and all his partisans were scattered. [38] And now, I tell you, stay away from these men and leave them alone. For if this plan or this work is of men, it will be overthrown; [39] but if it is of God, you will not be able to overthrow them. You may even be found fighting against God." So they were persuaded by him. [40] After they called in the apostles and had them flogged, they ordered them not to speak in the name of Jesus and released them. [41] Then they went out from the presence of the Sanhedrin, rejoicing that they were counted

---

[a]**5:18** Lit *laid hands on*   [b]**5:24** Other mss add *the high priest and*   [c]**5:34** Other mss read *apostles*   [d]**5:37** Lit *and drew people after him*

worthy to be dishonored on behalf of the name.[a] [42] Every day in the temple complex, and in various homes, they continued teaching and proclaiming the good news that the •Messiah is Jesus.[b]

Seven Chosen to Serve

6 In those days, as the number of the disciples was multiplying, there arose a complaint by the Hellenistic Jews[c] against the Hebraic Jews[d] that their widows were being overlooked in the daily distribution. [2] Then the Twelve summoned the whole company of the disciples and said, "It would not be right for us to give up preaching about God to wait on tables. [3] Therefore, brothers, select from among you seven men of good reputation, full of the Spirit and wisdom, whom we can appoint to this duty. [4] But we will devote ourselves to prayer and to the preaching ministry." [5] The proposal pleased the whole company. So they chose Stephen, a man full of faith and the Holy Spirit, and Philip, Prochorus, Nicanor, Timon, Parmenas, and Nicolaus, a •proselyte from Antioch. [6] They had them stand before the apostles, who prayed and laid their hands on them.[e]

[7] So the preaching about God flourished, the number of the disciples in Jerusalem multiplied greatly, and a large group of priests became obedient to the faith.

Stephen Accused of Blasphemy

[8] Stephen, full of grace and power, was performing great wonders and signs among the people. [9] Then some from what is called the Freedmen's •Synagogue, composed of both Cyrenians and Alexandrians, and some from Cilicia and Asia, came forward and disputed with Stephen. [10] But they were unable to stand up against the wisdom and the Spirit by whom he spoke.

False Witnesses

[11] Then they induced men to say, "We heard him speaking blasphemous words against Moses and God!" [12] They stirred up the people, the elders, and the •scribes; so they came up, dragged him off, and took him to the •Sanhedrin. [13] They also presented false witnesses who said, "This man does not stop speaking blasphemous words against this holy place and the law. [14] For we heard him say that Jesus, this •Nazarene, will destroy this place and change the customs that Moses handed down to us." [15] And all who were sitting in the Sanhedrin looked intently at him and saw that his face was like the face of an angel.

Stephen Begins Address

7 "Is this true?"[f] the high priest asked. [2] "Brothers and fathers," he said, "listen: The God of glory appeared to our father Abraham when he was in Mesopotamia, before he settled in Haran, [3] and said to him:

> **Get out of your country
> and away from your relatives,
> and come to the land
> that I will show you.**[g]

[4] "Then he came out of the land of the Chaldeans and settled in Haran. And from there, after his father died, God had him move to this land in which you now live. [5] He didn't give him an inheritance in it, not even a foot of ground, but He promised to give it to him as a possession, and to his descendants after him, even though he was childless. [6] God spoke in this way:

---

[a]**5:41** Other mss add *of Jesus*, or *of Christ*   [b]**5:42** Or *that Jesus is the Messiah*   [c]**6:1** Jews of Gk language and culture   [d]**6:1** Jews of Aram or Hb language and culture   [e]**6:6** The laying on of hands signified the prayer of blessing for the beginning of a new ministry.   [f]**7:1** Lit *"Are these things so?"*   [g]**7:3** Gn 12:1

His descendants would be
　　strangers in a foreign country,
　and they would enslave
　　and oppress them for 400 years.
7　I will judge the nation
　　that they will serve as slaves,
　　God said.
　After this, they will come out
　　and worship Me in this place.[a]

[8] Then He gave him the covenant of circumcision. This being so, he fathered Isaac and circumcised him on the eighth day; Isaac did the same with Jacob, and Jacob with the 12 patriarchs.

Stephen: Patriarchs in Egypt

[9] "The patriarchs became jealous of Joseph and sold him into Egypt, but God was with him [10] and rescued him out of all his troubles. He gave him favor and wisdom in the sight of Pharaoh, king of Egypt, who appointed him governor over Egypt and over his whole household. [11] Then a famine came over all of Egypt and Canaan, with great suffering, and our forefathers could find no food. [12] When Jacob heard there was grain in Egypt, he sent our forefathers the first time. [13] The second time, Joseph was revealed to his brothers, and Joseph's family became known to Pharaoh. [14] Joseph then invited his father Jacob and all his relatives, 75 people in all, [15] and Jacob went down to Egypt. He and our forefathers died there, [16] were carried back to Shechem, and were placed in the tomb that Abraham had bought for a sum of silver from the sons of Hamor in Shechem.

Stephen: Moses, a Rejected Savior

[17] "As the time was drawing near to fulfill the promise that God had made to Abraham, the people flourished and multiplied in Egypt [18] until a different king ruled over Egypt[b] who did not know Joseph. [19] He dealt deceitfully with our race and oppressed our forefathers by making them leave their infants outside so they wouldn't survive.[c] [20] At this time Moses was born, and he was beautiful before God. He was nursed in his father's home three months, [21] and when he was left outside, Pharaoh's daughter adopted and raised him as her own son. [22] So Moses was educated in all the wisdom of the Egyptians, and was powerful in his speech and actions.

[23] "As he was approaching the age of 40, he decided[d] to visit his brothers, the sons of Israel. [24] When he saw one of them being mistreated, he came to his rescue and avenged the oppressed man by striking down the Egyptian. [25] He assumed his brothers would understand that God would give them deliverance through him, but they did not understand. [26] The next day he showed up while they were fighting and tried to reconcile them peacefully, saying, 'Men, you are brothers. Why are you mistreating each other?'

[27] "But the one who was mistreating his neighbor pushed him[e] away, saying:

Who appointed you a ruler and a judge over us? [28] Do you want to kill me, the same way you killed the Egyptian yesterday?[f]

Stephen: God Calls Moses

[29] "At this disclosure, Moses fled and became an exile in the land of Midian, where he fathered two sons. [30] After 40 years had passed, an angel[g] appeared to him in the desert of Mount Sinai, in the flame of a burning bush. [31] When Moses saw it, he was amazed at the sight. As he

[a]7:6-7 Gn 15:13-14　[b]7:18 Other mss omit *over Egypt*　[c]7:19 A common pagan practice of population control by leaving infants outside to die　[d]7:23 Lit *40, it came into his heart*　[e]7:27 Moses　[f]7:27-28 Ex 2:14　[g]7:30 Other mss add *of the Lord*

was approaching to look at it, the voice of the Lord came: ³² **I am the God of your forefathers—the God of Abraham, of Isaac, and of Jacob.**ᵃ So Moses began to tremble and did not dare to look.

³³ "Then the Lord said to him:

Take the sandals off your feet, because the place where you are standing is holy ground. ³⁴ **I have certainly seen the oppression of My people in Egypt; I have heard their groaning and have come down to rescue them. And now, come, I will send you to Egypt.**ᵇ

³⁵ "This Moses, whom they rejected when they said, **Who appointed you a ruler and a judge?**ᶜ—this one God sent as a ruler and a redeemer by means of the angel who appeared to him in the bush. ³⁶ This man led them out and performed wonders and signs in the land of Egypt, at the Red Sea, and in the desert for 40 years.

Stephen: Israel's Rebellion against God

³⁷ "This is the Moses who said to the sons of Israel, **God**ᵈ **will raise up for you a Prophet like me from among your brothers.**ᵉ ³⁸ He is the one who was in the congregation in the desert together with the angel who spoke to him on Mount Sinai, and with our forefathers. He received living oracles to give to us. ³⁹ Our forefathers were unwilling to obey him, but pushed him away, and in their hearts turned back to Egypt. ⁴⁰ They told Aaron:

Make us gods who will go before us. As for this Moses who brought us out of the land of Egypt, we don't know what's become of him.ᶠ

⁴¹ They even made a calf in those days, offered sacrifice to the idol, and were celebrating what their hands had made. ⁴² Then God turned away and gave them up to worship the host of heaven, as it is written in the book of the prophets:

Did you bring Me offerings
  and sacrifices
for 40 years in the desert,
  O house of Israel?
⁴³ No, you took up
  the tent of Molochᵍ
and the star of
  your god Rephan,ʰ
the images that you made
  to worship.
So I will deport you
  beyond Babylon!ⁱ

Stephen: God's Real Tabernacle

⁴⁴ "Our forefathers had the tabernacle of the testimony in the desert, just as He who spoke to Moses commanded him to make it according to the pattern he had seen. ⁴⁵ Our forefathers in turn received it and with Joshua brought it in when they dispossessed the nations that God drove out before our fathers, until the days of David. ⁴⁶ He found favor in God's sight and asked that he might provide a dwelling place for the Godʲ of Jacob. ⁴⁷ But it was Solomon who built Him a house. ⁴⁸ However, the Most High does not dwell in sanctuaries made with hands, as the prophet says:

⁴⁹ Heaven is My throne,
  and earth My footstool.
What sort of house will you build
  for Me? says the Lord,
  or what is My resting place?
⁵⁰ Did not My hand make all
  these things?ᵏ

ᵃ**7:32** Ex 3:6,15   ᵇ**7:33-34** Ex 3:5,7-8,10   ᶜ**7:35** Ex 2:14   ᵈ**7:37** Other mss read *'The Lord your God*   ᵉ**7:37** Dt 18:15   ᶠ**7:40** Ex 32:1,23   ᵍ**7:43** Canaanite or Phoenician sky or sun god   ʰ**7:43** Perhaps an Assyrian star god—the planet Saturn   ⁱ**7:42-43** Am 5:25-27   ʲ**7:46** Other mss read *house*   ᵏ**7:49-50** Is 66:1-2

Stephen's Accusation: Resisting the Holy Spirit

51 "You stiff-necked people with uncircumcised hearts and ears! You are always resisting the Holy Spirit; as your forefathers did, so do you. 52 Which of the prophets did your fathers not persecute? They even killed those who announced beforehand the coming of the Righteous One, whose betrayers and murderers you have now become. 53 You received the law under the direction of angels and yet have not kept it."

Stephen Stoned: First Christian Martyr

54 When they heard these things, they were enraged in their hearts[a] and gnashed their teeth at him. 55 But Stephen, filled by the Holy Spirit, gazed into heaven. He saw God's glory, with[b] Jesus standing at the right hand of God, and he said, 56 "Look! I see the heavens opened and the •Son of Man standing at the right hand of God!"

57 Then they screamed at the top of their voices, stopped their ears, and rushed together against him. 58 They threw him out of the city and began to stone him.

Role of Saul

And the witnesses laid their robes at the feet of a young man named Saul. 59 They were stoning Stephen as he called out: "Lord Jesus, receive my spirit!" 60 Then he knelt down and cried out with a loud voice, "Lord, do not charge them with this sin!" And saying this, he fell •asleep.[c]

Saul the Persecutor

8 Saul agreed with putting him to death.

On that day a severe persecution broke out against the church in Jerusalem, and all except the apostles were scattered throughout the land of Judea and Samaria. 2 But devout men buried Stephen and mourned deeply over him. 3 Saul, however, was ravaging the church, and he would enter house after house, drag off men and women, and put them in prison.

Philip to Samaria

4 So those who were scattered went on their way proclaiming the message of good news. 5 Philip went down to a[d] city in Samaria and preached the •Messiah to them. 6 The crowds paid attention with one mind to what Philip said, as they heard and saw the signs he was performing. 7 For unclean spirits, crying out with a loud voice, came out of many who were possessed, and many who were paralyzed and lame were healed. 8 So there was great joy in that city.

Sorcerer Simon Responds to Philip

9 A man named Simon had previously practiced sorcery in that city and astounded the •Samaritan people, while claiming to be somebody great. 10 They all paid attention to him, from the least of them to the greatest, and they said, "This man is called the Great Power of God!"[e] 11 They were attentive to him because he had astounded them with his sorceries for a long time. 12 But when they believed Philip, as he proclaimed the good news about the kingdom of God and the name of Jesus Christ, both men and women were baptized. 13 Then even Simon himself believed. And after he was baptized, he went around constantly with[f] Philip and was astounded as

---

a7:54 Or were cut to the quick   b7:55 Lit and   c7:60 He died; see Jn 11:11; 1 Co 11:30; 1 Th 4:13-15   d8:5 Other mss read the   e8:10 Or This is the power of God called Great   f8:13 Or he kept close company with

he observed the signs and great miracles that were being performed.

Peter and John: Holy Spirit to Samaria

14 When the apostles who were at Jerusalem heard that Samaria had welcomed God's message, they sent Peter and John to them. 15 After they went down there, they prayed for them, that they might receive the Holy Spirit. 16 For He had not yet come down on[a] any of them; they had only been baptized in the name of the Lord Jesus. 17 Then Peter and John laid their hands on them, and they received the Holy Spirit.

Simon Sins

18 When Simon saw that the Holy[b] Spirit was given through the laying on of the apostles' hands, he offered them money, 19 saying, "Give me this power too, so that anyone I lay hands on may receive the Holy Spirit."

Peter Rebukes Simon

20 But Peter told him, "May your silver be destroyed with you, because you thought the gift of God could be obtained with money! 21 You have no part or share in this matter, because your heart is not right before God. 22 Therefore repent of this wickedness of yours, and pray to the Lord that the intent of your heart may be forgiven you. 23 For I see you are poisoned by bitterness and bound by iniquity."

24 "Please pray[c] to the Lord for me," Simon replied, "so that nothing you[c] have said may happen to me."

25 Then, after they had testified and spoken the message of the Lord, they traveled back to Jerusalem, evangelizing many villages of the •Samaritans.

Philip: Conversion of Ethiopian Official

26 An angel of the Lord spoke to Philip: "Get up and go south to the road that goes down from Jerusalem to desert Gaza."[d] 27 So he got up and went. There was an Ethiopian man, a eunuch and high official of Candace, queen of the Ethiopians, who was in charge of her entire treasury. He had come to worship in Jerusalem 28 and was sitting in his chariot on his way home, reading the prophet Isaiah aloud.

29 The Spirit told Philip, "Go and join that chariot."

30 When Philip ran up to it, he heard him reading the prophet Isaiah, and said, "Do you understand what you're reading?"

31 "How can I," he said, "unless someone guides me?" So he invited Philip to come up and sit with him. 32 Now the Scripture passage he was reading was this:

Ethiopian Reads Isaiah 53

He was led like a sheep
    to the slaughter,
and as a lamb is silent
    before its shearer,
so He does not open His mouth.
33 In His humiliation justice
    was denied Him.
Who will describe
    His generation?
For His life is taken
    from the earth.[e]

Philip Shares Good News

34 The eunuch replied to Philip, "I ask you, who is the prophet saying this about—himself or another person?" 35 So Philip proceeded[f] to tell him the good news about Jesus, beginning from that Scripture.

---

a8:16 Or yet fallen on   b8:18 Other mss omit Holy   c8:24 Gk words you and pray are plural   d8:26 Perhaps old Gaza or the road near the desert   e8:32-33 Is 53:7-8   f8:35 Lit Philip opened his mouth

36 As they were traveling down the road, they came to some water. The eunuch said, "Look, there's water! What would keep me from being baptized?" [37 And Philip said, "If you believe with all your heart you may." And he replied, "I believe that Jesus Christ is the Son of God."]a 38 Then he ordered the chariot to stop, and both Philip and the eunuch went down into the water, and he baptized him. 39 When they came up out of the water, the Spirit of the Lord carried Philip away, and the eunuch did not see him any longer. But he went on his way rejoicing. 40 Philip appeared inb Azotus,c and passing through, he was evangelizing all the towns until he came to Caesarea.

Paul on Damascus Road

9 Meanwhile Saul, still breathing threats and murder against the disciples of the Lord, went to the high priest 2 and requested letters from him to the •synagogues in Damascus, so that if he found any who belonged to the Way, either men or women, he might bring them as prisoners to Jerusalem. 3 As he traveled and was nearing Damascus, a light from heaven suddenly flashed around him. 4 Falling to the ground, he heard a voice saying to him, "Saul, Saul, why are you persecuting Me?"

"I Am Jesus"

5 "Who are You, Lord?" he said.

"I am Jesus, whom you are persecuting," He replied. 6 "But get up and go into the city, and you will be told what you must do."

7 The men who were traveling with him stood speechless, hearing the sound but seeing no one. 8 Then Saul got up from the ground, and though his eyes were open, he could see nothing. So they took him by the hand and led him into Damascus. 9 He was unable to see for three days, and did not eat or drink.

Saul Receives Sight

10 Now in Damascus there was a disciple named Ananias. And the Lord said to him in a vision, "Ananias!"

"Here I am, Lord!" he said.

11 "Get up and go to the street called Straight," the Lord said to him, "to the house of Judas, and ask for a man from Tarsus named Saul, since he is praying there. 12 In a visiond he has seen a man named Ananias coming in and placing his hands on him so he may regain his sight."

13 "Lord," Ananias answered, "I have heard from many people about this man, how much harm he has done to Your saints in Jerusalem. 14 And he has authority here from the •chief priests to arrest all who call on Your name."

15 But the Lord said to him, "Go! For this man is My chosen instrument to carry My name before Gentiles, kings, and the sons of Israel. 16 I will certainly show him how much he must suffer for My name!"

17 So Ananias left and entered the house. Then he placed his hands on him and said, "Brother Saul, the Lord Jesus, who appeared to you on the road you were traveling, has sent me so you may regain your sight and be filled with the Holy Spirit."

Saul Baptized

18 At once something like scales fell from his eyes, and he regained his sight. Then he got up and was baptized. 19 And after taking some food, he regained his strength.

a8:37 Other mss omit bracketed text   b8:40 Or Philip was found at, or Philip found himself in   c8:40 Or Ashdod
d9:12 Other mss omit In a vision

Saul Proclaims the Messiah

Saul[a] was with the disciples in Damascus for some days. [20] Immediately he began proclaiming Jesus in the synagogues: "He is the Son of God."

[21] But all who heard him were astounded and said, "Isn't this the man who, in Jerusalem, was destroying those who called on this name, and then came here for the purpose of taking them as prisoners to the chief priests?" [22] But Saul grew more capable, and kept confounding the Jews who lived in Damascus by proving that this One is the •Messiah.

Murder Plot—and Escape

[23] After many days had passed, the Jews conspired to kill him, [24] but their plot became known to Saul. So they were watching the gates day and night intending to kill him, [25] but his disciples took him by night and lowered him in a large basket through ⌊an opening in⌋ the wall.

Saul to Jerusalem, Then Tarsus

[26] When he arrived in Jerusalem, he tried to associate with the disciples, but they were all afraid of him, since they did not believe he was a disciple. [27] Barnabas, however, took him and brought him to the apostles and explained to them how, on the road, Saul[b] had seen the Lord, and that He had talked to him, and how in Damascus he had spoken boldly in the name of Jesus. [28] Saul[b] was coming and going with them in Jerusalem, speaking boldly in the name of the Lord. [29] He conversed and debated with the Hellenistic Jews,[c] but they attempted to kill him. [30] When the brothers found out, they took him down to Caesarea and sent him off to Tarsus.

[31] So the church throughout all Judea, Galilee, and Samaria had peace, being built up and walking in the fear of the Lord and in the encouragement of the Holy Spirit, and it increased in numbers.

Peter Heals Aeneas

[32] As Peter was traveling from place to place,[d] he also came down to the saints[e] who lived in Lydda. [33] There he found a man named Aeneas, who was paralyzed and had been bedridden for eight years. [34] Peter said to him, "Aeneas, Jesus Christ heals you. Get up and make your own bed,"[f] and immediately he got up. [35] So all who lived in Lydda and Sharon saw him and turned to the Lord.

Peter Restores Dorcas to Life

[36] In Joppa there was a disciple named Tabitha, which is translated Dorcas.[g] She was always doing good works and acts of charity. [37] In those days she became sick and died. After washing her, they placed her in a room upstairs. [38] Since Lydda was near Joppa, the disciples heard that Peter was there and sent two men to him who begged him, "Don't delay in coming with us." [39] So Peter got up and went with them. When he arrived, they led him to the room upstairs. And all the widows approached him, weeping and showing him the robes and clothes that Dorcas had made while she was with them. [40] Then Peter sent them all out of the room. He knelt down, prayed, and turning toward the body said, "Tabitha, get up!" She opened her eyes, saw Peter, and sat up. [41] He gave her his hand and helped her stand up. Then he called the saints and widows and presented her alive. [42] This became known throughout all Joppa, and many

a**9:19** Lit He   b**9:27,28** Lit he   c**9:29** Lit Hellenists; that is, Gk-speaking Jews   d**9:32** Lit Peter was passing through all   e**9:32** The believers   f**9:34** Or and get ready to eat   g**9:36** Dorcas = Gazelle

believed in the Lord. [43] And Peter[a] stayed on many days in Joppa with Simon, a leather tanner.[b]

Gentile Pentecost

Centurion Cornelius' Vision

10 There was a man in Caesarea named Cornelius, a •centurion of what was called the Italian •Regiment. [2] He was a devout man and feared God along with his whole household. He did many charitable deeds for the Jewish people and always prayed to God. [3] At about three in the afternoon[c] he distinctly saw in a vision an angel of God who came in and said to him, "Cornelius!"

[4] Looking intently at him, he became afraid and said, "What is it, Lord?"

And he told him, "Your prayers and your acts of charity have come up as a memorial offering before God. [5] Now send men to Joppa and call for Simon, who is also named Peter. [6] He is lodging with Simon, a tanner, whose house is by the sea."

[7] When the angel who spoke to him had gone, he called two of his household slaves and a devout soldier, who was one of those who attended him. [8] After explaining everything to them, he sent them to Joppa.

Peter's Vision

[9] The next day, as they were traveling and nearing the city, Peter went up to pray on the housetop at about noon.[d] [10] Then he became hungry and wanted to eat, but while they were preparing something he went into a visionary state. [11] He saw heaven opened and an object coming down that resembled a large sheet being lowered to the earth by its four corners. [12] In it were all the four-footed animals and reptiles of the earth, and the birds of the sky. [13] Then a voice said to him, "Get up, Peter; kill and eat!"

[14] "No, Lord!" Peter said. "For I have never eaten anything common[e] and unclean!"

[15] Again, a second time, a voice said to him, "What God has made clean, you must not call common." [16] This happened three times, and then the object was taken up into heaven.

Peter Visits Cornelius

[17] While Peter was deeply perplexed about what the vision he had seen might mean, the men who had been sent by Cornelius, having asked directions to Simon's house, stood at the gate. [18] They called out, asking if Simon, who was also named Peter, was lodging there.

[19] While Peter was thinking about the vision, the Spirit told him, "Three men are here looking for you. [20] Get up, go downstairs, and accompany them with no doubts at all, because I have sent them."

[21] Then Peter went down to the men and said, "Here I am, the one you're looking for. What is the reason you're here?"

[22] They said, "Cornelius, a centurion, an upright and God-fearing man, who has a good reputation with the whole Jewish nation, was divinely directed by a holy angel to call you to his house and to hear a message from you." [23] Peter[f] then invited them in and gave them lodging.

The next day he got up and set out with them, and some of the brothers from Joppa went with him. [24] The following day he entered Caesarea. Now Cornelius was expecting them and had

[a]9:43 Lit he   [b]9:43 Tanners were considered ritually unclean because of their occupation.   [c]10:3 Lit about the ninth hour   [d]10:9 Lit about the sixth hour   [e]10:14 Perhaps profane, or non-sacred; Jews ate distinctive food according to OT law and their traditions, similar to modern kosher or non-kosher foods.   [f]10:23 Lit He

called together his relatives and close friends. ²⁵ When Peter entered, Cornelius met him, fell at his feet, and worshiped him.

²⁶ But Peter helped him up and said, "Stand up! I myself am also a man." ²⁷ While talking with him, he went on in and found that many had come together there. ²⁸ Peterᵃ said to them, "You know it's forbidden for a Jewish man to associate with or visit a foreigner. But God has shown me that I must not call any person common or unclean. ²⁹ That's why I came without any objection when I was sent for. So I ask, 'Why did you send for me?' "

³⁰ Cornelius replied, "Four days ago at this hour, at three in the afternoon,ᵇ I wasᶜ praying in my house. Just then a man in a dazzling robe stood before me ³¹ and said, 'Cornelius, your prayer has been heard, and your acts of charity have been remembered in God's sight. ³² Therefore send someone to Joppa and invite Simon here, who is also named Peter. He is lodging in Simon the tanner's house by the sea.'ᵈ ³³ Therefore I immediately sent for you, and you did the right thing in coming. So we are all present before God, to hear everything you have been commanded by the Lord."

Peter's Good News for Gentiles

³⁴ Then Peter began to speak: "In truth, I understand that God doesn't show favoritism, ³⁵ but in every nation the person who fears Him and does righteousness is acceptable to Him. ³⁶ He sent the message to the sons of Israel, proclaiming the good news of peace through Jesus Christ—He is Lord of all. ³⁷ You know the eventsᵉ that took place throughout all Judea, beginning from Galilee after the baptism that John preached: ³⁸ how God anointed Jesus of Nazareth with the Holy Spirit and with power, and how He went about doing good and curing all who were under the tyranny of the Devil, because God was with Him. ³⁹ We ourselves are witnesses of everything He did in both the Judean country and in Jerusalem; yet they killed Him by hanging Him on a tree. ⁴⁰ God raised up this man on the third day and permitted Him to be seen, ⁴¹ not by all the people, but by us, witnesses appointed beforehand by God, who ate and drank with Him after He rose from the dead. ⁴² He commanded us to preach to the people, and to solemnly testify that He is the One appointed by God to be the Judge of the living and the dead. ⁴³ All the prophets testify about Him that through His name everyone who believes in Him will receive forgiveness of sins."

Holy Spirit for Gentiles

⁴⁴ While Peter was still speaking these words, the Holy Spirit came down on all those who heard the message. ⁴⁵ The circumcised believersᶠ who had come with Peter were astounded, because the gift of the Holy Spirit had been poured out on the Gentiles also. ⁴⁶ For they heard them speaking in ⌊other⌋ languages and declaring the greatness ofᵍ God.

Gentiles Baptized

Then Peter responded, ⁴⁷ "Can anyone withhold water and prevent these from being baptized, who have received the Holy Spirit just as we have?" ⁴⁸ And he commanded them to be baptized in the name of Jesus Christ. Then they asked him to stay for a few days.

ᵃ**10:28** Lit He   ᵇ**10:30** Lit at the ninth hour   ᶜ**10:30** Other mss add fasting and   ᵈ**10:32** Other mss add When he arrives, he will speak to you.   ᵉ**10:37** Lit thing, or word   ᶠ**10:45** Jewish Christians who stressed circumcision; Ac 11:2; 15:5; Gl 2:12; Col 4:11; Ti 1:10   ᵍ**10:46** Or and magnifying

Peter Defends
Gentile Salvation in Jerusalem

11 The apostles and the brothers who were throughout Judea heard that the Gentiles had welcomed God's message also. ² When Peter went up to Jerusalem, those who stressed circumcision[a] argued with him, ³ saying, "You visited uncircumcised men and ate with them!"

⁴ Peter began to explain to them in an orderly sequence, saying: ⁵ "I was in the town of Joppa praying, and I saw, in a visionary state, an object coming down that resembled a large sheet being lowered from heaven by its four corners, and it came to me. ⁶ When I looked closely and considered it, I saw the four-footed animals of the earth, the wild beasts, the reptiles, and the birds of the sky. ⁷ Then I also heard a voice telling me, 'Get up, Peter; kill and eat!'

⁸ " 'No, Lord!' I said. 'For nothing common or unclean has ever entered my mouth!' ⁹ But a voice answered from heaven a second time, 'What God has made clean, you must not call common.'

¹⁰ "Now this happened three times, and then everything was drawn up again into heaven. ¹¹ At that very moment, three men who had been sent to me from Caesarea arrived at the house where we were. ¹² Then the Spirit told me to go with them with no doubts at all. These six brothers accompanied me, and we went into the man's house. ¹³ He reported to us how he had seen the angel standing in his house and saying, 'Send[b] to Joppa, and call for Simon, who is also named Peter. ¹⁴ He will speak words[c] to you by which you and all your household will be saved.'

¹⁵ "As I began to speak, the Holy Spirit came down on them, just as on us at the beginning. ¹⁶ Then I remembered the word of the Lord, how He said, 'John baptized with water, but you will be baptized with the Holy Spirit.' ¹⁷ Therefore, if God gave them the same gift that He also gave to us when we believed on the Lord Jesus Christ, how could I possibly hinder God?"

¹⁸ When they heard this they became silent. Then they glorified God, saying, "So God has granted repentance resulting in life[d] to even the Gentiles!"

Church in Antioch

¹⁹ Those who had been scattered as a result of the persecution that started because of Stephen made their way as far as Phoenicia, Cyprus, and Antioch, speaking the message to no one except Jews. ²⁰ But there were some of them, Cypriot and Cyrenian men, who came to Antioch and began speaking to the Hellenists,[e] [f] proclaiming the good news about the Lord Jesus. ²¹ The Lord's hand was with them, and a large number who believed turned to the Lord.

Barnabas to Antioch

²² Then the report about them reached the ears of the church in Jerusalem, and they sent out Barnabas to travel[g] as far as Antioch. ²³ When he arrived and saw the grace of God, he was glad, and he encouraged all of them to remain true to the Lord with a firm resolve of the heart— ²⁴ for he was a good man, full of the Holy Spirit and of faith—and large numbers of people were added to the Lord.

Barnabas Brings Saul to Antioch

²⁵ Then he[h] went to Tarsus to search for Saul, ²⁶ and when he found him he

---

ᵃ**11:2** Lit *those of the circumcision*   ᵇ**11:13** Other mss add *men*   ᶜ**11:14** Or *speak a message*   ᵈ**11:18** Or *repentance to life*   ᵉ**11:20** Other mss read *Greeks*   ᶠ**11:20** In this context, a non-Jewish person who spoke Gk   ᵍ**11:22** Other mss omit *to travel*   ʰ**11:25** Other mss read *Barnabas*

brought him to Antioch. For a whole year they met with the church and taught large numbers, and the disciples were first called Christians in Antioch.

Prophet Agabus Predicts Famine

27 In those days some prophets came down from Jerusalem to Antioch. 28 Then one of them, named Agabus, stood up and predicted by the Spirit that there would be a severe famine throughout the Roman world.[a] This took place during the time of Claudius.[b]

Relief Provided by Barnabas and Saul

29 So each of the disciples, according to his ability, determined to send relief to the brothers who lived in Judea. 30 This they did, sending it to the elders by means of Barnabas and Saul.

James Martyred by Herod Agrippa I

12 About that time King •Herod cruelly attacked some who belonged to the church, 2 and he killed James, John's brother, with the sword.

Herod Arrests Peter

3 When he saw that it pleased the Jews, he proceeded to arrest Peter too, during the days of •Unleavened Bread. 4 After the arrest, he put him in prison and assigned four squads of four soldiers each to guard him, intending to bring him out to the people after the •Passover. 5 So Peter was kept in prison, but prayer was being made earnestly to God for him by the church.

Angel Rescues Peter

6 On the night before Herod was to bring him out ⌊for execution⌋, Peter was sleeping between two soldiers, bound with two chains, while the sentries in front of the door guarded the prison. 7 Suddenly an angel of the Lord appeared, and a light shone in the cell. Striking Peter on the side, he woke him up and said, "Quick, get up!" Then the chains fell off his wrists. 8 "Get dressed," the angel told him, "and put on your sandals." And he did so. "Wrap your cloak around you," he told him, "and follow me." 9 So he went out and followed, and he did not know that what took place through the angel was real, but thought he was seeing a vision. 10 After they passed the first and second guard posts, they came to the iron gate that leads into the city, which opened to them by itself. They went outside and passed one street, and immediately the angel left him.

Peter to Mary's House

11 Then Peter came to himself and said, "Now I know for certain that the Lord has sent His angel and rescued me from Herod's grasp and from all that the Jewish people expected." 12 When he realized this, he went to the house of Mary, the mother of John Mark,[c] where many had assembled and were praying. 13 He knocked at the door in the gateway, and a servant named Rhoda came to answer. 14 She recognized Peter's voice, and because of her joy she did not open the gate, but ran in and announced that Peter was standing at the gateway.

15 "You're crazy!" they told her. But she kept insisting that it was true. Then they said, "It's his angel!" 16 Peter, however, kept on knocking, and when they opened the door and saw him, they were astounded.

17 Motioning to them with his hand to be silent, he explained to them how the

---

[a]11:28 Or the whole world   [b]11:28 Emperor A.D. 41–54; there was a famine A.D. 47–48.   [c]12:12 Lit John who was called Mark

Lord had brought him out of the prison. "Report these things to James[a] and the brothers," he said. Then he departed and went to a different place.

[18] At daylight, there was a great commotion[b] among the soldiers as to what could have become of Peter. [19] After Herod had searched and did not find him, he interrogated the guards and ordered their execution. Then Herod went down from Judea to Caesarea and stayed there.

King Herod's Death

[20] He had been very angry with the Tyrians and Sidonians.[c] Together they presented themselves before him, and having won over Blastus, who was in charge of the king's bedroom, they asked for peace, because their country was supplied with food from the king's country. [21] So on an appointed day, dressed in royal robes and seated on the throne, Herod delivered a public address to them. [22] The populace began to shout, "It's the voice of a god and not of a man!" [23] At once an angel of the Lord struck him because he did not give the glory to God, and he became infected with worms and died. [24] Then God's message flourished and multiplied. [25] And Barnabas and Saul returned to[d] Jerusalem after they had completed their relief mission, on which they took John Mark.[e]

Paul's First Missionary Journey

Barnabas and Saul Prepare for Mission Field

13 In the local church at Antioch there were prophets and teachers: Barnabas, Simeon who was called Niger, Lucius the Cyrenian, Manaen, a close friend of •Herod the tetrarch, and Saul.

[2] As they were ministering to[f] the Lord and fasting, the Holy Spirit said, "Set apart for Me Barnabas and Saul for the work that I have called them to." [3] Then, after they had fasted, prayed, and laid hands on them,[g] they sent them off.

Mission to Cyprus

[4] Being sent out by the Holy Spirit, they came down to Seleucia, and from there they sailed to Cyprus. [5] Arriving in Salamis, they proclaimed God's message in the Jewish •synagogues. They also had John as their assistant. [6] When they had gone through the whole island as far as Paphos, they came across a sorcerer, a Jewish false prophet named Bar-Jesus. [7] He was with the •proconsul, Sergius Paulus, an intelligent man. This man summoned Barnabas and Saul and desired to hear God's message. [8] But Elymas, the sorcerer, which is how his name is translated, opposed them and tried to turn the proconsul away from the faith.

Saul Called Paul

[9] Then Saul—also called Paul—filled with the Holy Spirit, stared straight at the sorcerer[h] [10] and said, "You son of the Devil, full of all deceit and all fraud, enemy of all righteousness! Won't you ever stop perverting the straight paths of the Lord? [11] Now, look! The Lord's hand is against you: you are going to be blind, and will not see the sun for a time." Suddenly a mist and darkness fell on him, and he went around seeking someone to lead him by the hand.

[12] Then the proconsul, seeing what happened, believed and was astonished at the teaching about the Lord.

---

a**12:17** This was James, the Lord's brother; see Mk 6:3. This was not James the apostle; see Ac 12:2.   b**12:18** Or was no small disturbance   c**12:20** The people of the area of modern Lebanon   d**12:25** Other mss read from   e**12:25** Lit John who was called Mark   f**13:2** Or were worshiping   g**13:3** See note at Ac 6:6   h**13:9** Lit at him

Paul's Sermon in Antioch of Pisidia

13 Paul and his companions set sail from Paphos and came to Perga in Pamphylia. John, however, left them and went back to Jerusalem. 14 They continued their journey from Perga and reached Antioch in Pisidia. On the Sabbath day they went into the synagogue and sat down. 15 After the reading of the Law and the Prophets, the leaders of the synagogue sent ₍word₎ to them, saying, "Brothers, if you have any message of encouragement for the people, you can speak."

Paul Preaches in Antioch

16 Then standing up, Paul motioned with his hand and spoke: "Men of Israel, and you who fear God, listen! 17 The God of this people Israel chose our forefathers, exalted the people during their stay in the land of Egypt, and led them out of it with a mighty[a] arm. 18 And for about 40 years He put up with them[b] in the desert; 19 then after destroying seven nations in the land of Canaan, He gave their land to them as an inheritance. 20 This all took about 450 years. After this, He gave them judges until Samuel the prophet. 21 Then they asked for a king, so God gave them Saul the son of Kish, a man of the tribe of Benjamin, for 40 years. 22 After removing him, He raised up David as their king, of whom He testified: 'I have found David the son of Jesse, a man after My heart,[c] who will carry out all My will.'

23 "From this man's descendants, according to the promise, God brought the Savior, Jesus,[d] to Israel. 24 Before He came to public attention,[e] John had previously proclaimed a baptism of repentance to all the people of Israel. 25 Then as John was completing his life work, he said, 'Who do you think I am? I am not the One. But look! Someone is coming after me, and I am not worthy to untie the sandals on His feet.'

26 "Brothers, sons of Abraham's race, and those among you who fear God, the message of this salvation has been sent to us. 27 For the residents of Jerusalem and their rulers, since they did not recognize Him or the voices of the prophets that are read every Sabbath, have fulfilled their words[f] by condemning Him. 28 Though they found no grounds for the death penalty, they asked •Pilate to have Him killed. 29 When they had fulfilled all that had been written about Him, they took Him down from the tree and put Him in a tomb. 30 But God raised Him from the dead, 31 and He appeared for many days to those who came up with Him from Galilee to Jerusalem, who are now His witnesses to the people. 32 And we ourselves proclaim to you the good news of the promise that was made to our forefathers. 33 God has fulfilled this to us their children by raising up Jesus, as it is written in the second Psalm:

> You are My Son;
> today I have become
> Your Father.[g] [h]

34 Since He raised Him from the dead, never to return to decay, He has spoken in this way, **I will grant you the faithful covenant blessings[i] made to David.[j]** 35 Therefore He also says in another passage, **You will not allow Your Holy One to see decay.[k]** 36 For David, after serving his own generation in God's plan, fell •asleep, was buried with his fathers, and decayed. 37 But the One whom God raised up did not decay. 38 Therefore, let

a13:17 Lit with an uplifted b13:18 Other mss read He cared for them c13:22 1 Sm 13:14; Ps 89:20 d13:23 Other mss read brought salvation e13:24 Lit Before the face of His entrance f13:27 Lit fulfilled them g13:33 Or I have begotten You h13:33 Ps 2:7 i13:34 Lit faithful holy things j13:34 Is 55:3 k13:35 Ps 16:10

it be known to you, brothers, that through this man forgiveness of sins is being proclaimed to you, [39] and everyone who believes in Him is justified from everything, which you could not be justified from through the law of Moses. [40] So beware that what is said in the prophets does not happen to you:

[41] Look, you scoffers,
      marvel and vanish away,
      because I am doing a work
        in your days,
      a work that you will
        never believe,
      even if someone were
        to explain it to you."[a]

Paul and Barnabas Evangelize

[42] As they[b] were leaving, they[c] [d] begged that these matters be presented to them the following Sabbath. [43] After the synagogue had been dismissed, many of the Jews and devout •proselytes followed Paul and Barnabas, who were speaking with them and persuading them to continue in the grace of God.

Jewish Opposition in Antioch

[44] The following Sabbath almost the whole town assembled to hear the message of the Lord.[e] [45] But when the Jews saw the crowds, they were filled with jealousy and began to oppose what Paul was saying by insulting him.

Paul and Barnabas Turn to Gentiles

[46] Then Paul and Barnabas boldly said: "It was necessary that God's message be spoken to you first. But since you reject it, and consider yourselves unworthy of eternal life, we now turn to the Gentiles! [47] For this is what the Lord has commanded us:

  I have appointed you as a light
    for the Gentiles,
  to bring salvation to the ends[f]
    of the earth."[g]

[48] When the Gentiles heard this, they rejoiced and glorified the message of the Lord, and all who had been appointed to eternal life believed. [49] So the message of the Lord spread through the whole region. [50] But the Jews incited the religious women of high standing and the leading men of the city. They stirred up persecution against Paul and Barnabas and expelled them from their district. [51] But shaking the dust off their feet against them, they proceeded to Iconium. [52] And the disciples were filled with joy and the Holy Spirit.

Paul and Barnabas to Iconium

14 The same thing happened in Iconium; they entered the Jewish •synagogue and spoke in such a way that a great number of both Jews and Greeks believed. [2] But the Jews who refused to believe stirred up and poisoned the minds[h] of the Gentiles against the brothers. [3] So they stayed there for some time and spoke boldly, in reliance on the Lord, who testified to the message of His grace by granting that signs and wonders be performed through them. [4] But the people of the city were divided, some siding with the Jews and some with the apostles.

Persecution by Gentiles and Jews

[5] When an attempt was made by both the Gentiles and Jews, with their rulers, to assault and stone them, [6] they found out about it and fled to the Lycaonian towns called Lystra and Derbe, and to

---

[a]13:41 Hab 1:5   [b]13:42 Paul and Barnabas   [c]13:42 Other mss read *they were leaving the synagogue of the Jews, the Gentiles*   [d]13:42 The people   [e]13:44 Other mss read *of God*   [f]13:47 Lit *the end*   [g]13:47 Is 49:6   [h]14:2 Lit *and harmed the souls*

the surrounding countryside. ⁷ And there they kept evangelizing.

Lystra: Paul Heals Lame Man

⁸ In Lystra a man without strength in his feet, lame from birth,ᵃ and who had never walked, sat ⁹ and heard Paul speaking. After observing him closely and seeing that he had faith to be healed, ¹⁰⌊Paul⌋ said in a loud voice, "Stand up straight on your feet!" And he jumped up and started to walk around.

Missionaries Mistaken for Gods

¹¹ When the crowds saw what Paul had done, they raised their voices, saying in the Lycaonian language, "The gods have come down to us in the form of men!" ¹² And they started to call Barnabas, Zeus, and Paul, Hermes, because he was the main speaker. ¹³ Then the priest of Zeus, whose temple was just outside the town, brought oxen and garlands to the gates. He, with the crowds, intended to offer sacrifice.

Paul and Barnabas Protest

¹⁴ The apostles Barnabas and Paul tore their robes when they heard this and rushed into the crowd, shouting: ¹⁵ "Men! Why are you doing these things? We are men also, with the same nature as you, and we are proclaiming good news to you, that you should turn from these worthless things to the living God, **who made the heaven, the earth, the sea, and everything in them.**ᵇ ¹⁶ In past generations He allowed all the nations to go their own way, ¹⁷ although He did not leave Himself without a witness, since He did good: giving you rain from heaven and fruitful seasons, and satisfying yourᶜ hearts with food and happiness."

¹⁸ Even though they said these things, they barely stopped the crowds from sacrificing to them.

Further Persecution

¹⁹ Then some Jews came from Antioch and Iconium, and when they had won over the crowds and stoned Paul, they dragged him out of the city, thinking he was dead. ²⁰ After the disciples surrounded him, he got up and went into the town. The next day he left with Barnabas for Derbe.

Paul and Barnabas Strengthen Churches

²¹ After they had evangelized that town and made many disciples, they returned to Lystra, to Iconium, and to Antioch, ²² strengthening the heartsᵈ of the disciples by encouraging them to continue in the faith, and by telling them, "It is necessary to pass through many troubles on our way into the kingdom of God."

²³ When they had appointed elders in every church and prayed with fasting, they committed them to the Lord in whom they had believed. ²⁴ Then they passed through Pisidia and came to Pamphylia. ²⁵ After they spoke the message in Perga, they went down to Attalia.

End of First Journey

²⁶ From there they sailed back to Antioch where they had been entrusted to the grace of God for the work they had completed. ²⁷ After they arrived and gathered the church together, they reported everything God had done with them, and that He had opened the door of faith to the Gentiles. ²⁸ And they spent a considerable timeᵉ with the disciples.

ᵃ**14:8** Lit *from his mother's womb*   ᵇ**14:15** Ex 20:11; Ps 146:6   ᶜ**14:17** Other mss read *our*   ᵈ**14:22** Lit *souls*
ᵉ**14:28** Or *spent no little time*

Theological Dispute in Antioch

15 Some men came down from Judea and began to teach the brothers: "Unless you are circumcised according to the custom prescribed by Moses, you cannot be saved!" [2] But after Paul and Barnabas had engaged them in serious argument and debate, they arranged for Paul and Barnabas and some others of them to go up to the apostles and elders in Jerusalem concerning this controversy. [3] When they had been sent on their way by the church, they passed through both Phoenicia and Samaria, explaining in detail the conversion of the Gentiles, and they created great joy among all the brothers.

[4] When they arrived at Jerusalem, they were welcomed by the church, the apostles, and the elders, and they reported all that God had done with them. [5] But some of the believers from the party of the •Pharisees stood up and said, "It is necessary to circumcise them and to command them to keep the law of Moses!"

The Jerusalem Council

[6] Then the apostles and the elders assembled to consider this matter. [7] After there had been much debate, Peter stood up and said to them: "Brothers, you are aware that in the early days God made a choice among you,[a] that by my mouth the Gentiles would hear the gospel message and believe. [8] And God, who knows the heart, testified to them by giving[b] the Holy Spirit, just as He also did to us. [9] He made no distinction between us and them, cleansing their hearts by faith. [10] Why, then, are you now testing God by putting on the disciples' necks a yoke that neither our forefathers nor we have been able to bear?

[11] On the contrary, we believe we are saved through the grace of the Lord Jesus, in the same way they are."

[12] Then the whole assembly fell silent and listened to Barnabas and Paul describing all the signs and wonders God had done through them among the Gentiles. [13] After they stopped speaking, James responded: "Brothers, listen to me! [14] Simeon[c] has reported how God first intervened to take from the Gentiles a people for His name. [15] And the words of the prophets agree with this, as it is written:

[16] **After these things I will return**
and will rebuild David's tent,
  which has fallen down.
I will rebuild its ruins
  and will set it up again,
[17] **so that those who are left**
  of mankind
  may seek the Lord—
even all the Gentiles
  who are called by My name,
says the Lord who does
  these things,
[18] **which have been known**
  from long ago.[d] [e]

[19] Therefore, in my judgment, we should not cause difficulties for those who turn to God from among the Gentiles, [20] but instead we should write to them to abstain from things polluted by idols, from sexual immorality, from eating anything that has been strangled, and from blood. [21] For since ancient times, Moses has had in every city those who proclaim him, and he is read aloud in the •synagogues every Sabbath day."

Letter to Gentile Believers

[22] Then the apostles and the elders, with the whole church, decided to select

a15:7 Other mss read *us*   **b15:8** Other mss add *them*   **c15:14** Simon (Peter)   **d15:17-18** Other mss read *says the Lord who does all these things. Known to God from long ago are all His works.*   **e15:16-18** Am 9:11-12; Is 45:21

men from among them and to send them to Antioch with Paul and Barnabas: Judas, called Barsabbas, and Silas, both leading men among the brothers. 23 They wrote this letter to be delivered by them:[a]

From the apostles and the elders, your brothers,
To the brothers from among the Gentiles in Antioch, Syria, and Cilicia: Greetings.
24 Because we have heard that some to whom we gave no authorization went out from us and troubled you with their words and unsettled your hearts,[b] 25 we have unanimously decided to select men and send them to you along with our beloved Barnabas and Paul, 26 who have risked their lives for the name of our Lord Jesus Christ. 27 Therefore we have sent Judas and Silas, who will personally report the same things by word of mouth.[c] 28 For it was the Holy Spirit's decision—and ours—to put no greater burden on you than these necessary things: 29 that you abstain from food offered to idols, from blood, from eating anything that has been strangled, and from sexual immorality. If you keep yourselves from these things, you will do well.
Farewell.

Outcome of Jerusalem Letter

30 Then, being sent off, they went down to Antioch, and after gathering the assembly, they delivered the letter. 31 When they read it, they rejoiced because of its encouragement. 32 Both Judas and Silas, who were also prophets themselves, encouraged the brothers and strengthened them with a long message. 33 After spending some time there, they were sent back in peace by the brothers to those who had sent them.[d] [e] 35 But Paul and Barnabas, along with many others, remained in Antioch teaching and proclaiming the message of the Lord.

Paul and Barnabas: Dispute and Split

36 After some time had passed, Paul said to Barnabas, "Let's go back and visit the brothers in every town where we have preached the message of the Lord, and see how they're doing." 37 Barnabas wanted to take along John Mark.[f] 38 But Paul did not think it appropriate to take along this man who had deserted them in Pamphylia and had not gone on with them to the work. 39 There was such a sharp disagreement that they parted company, and Barnabas took Mark with him and sailed off to Cyprus.

Paul's Second Missionary Journey

Paul Chooses Silas

40 Then Paul chose Silas and departed, after being commended to the grace of the Lord by the brothers. 41 He traveled through Syria and Cilicia, strengthening the churches.

Paul Selects Timothy

16 Then he went on to Derbe and Lystra, where there was a disciple named Timothy, the son of a believing Jewish woman, but his father was a Greek. 2 The brothers at Lystra and Iconium spoke highly of him. 3 Paul wanted Timothy[g] to go with him, so he took him and circumcised him because of the Jews

who were in those places, since they all knew that his father was a Greek. ⁴ As they traveled through the towns, they delivered the decisions reached by the apostles and elders at Jerusalem for them to observe. ⁵ So the churches were strengthened in the faith and were increased in number daily.

Paul Begins His Evangelization of Europe

⁶ They went through the region of Phrygia and Galatia and were prevented by the Holy Spirit from speaking the message in the province of Asia. ⁷ When they came to Mysia, they tried to go into Bithynia, but the Spirit of Jesus did not allow them. ⁸ So, bypassing Mysia, they came down to Troas. ⁹ During the night a vision appeared to Paul: a Macedonian man was standing and pleading with him, "Cross over to Macedonia and help us!" ¹⁰ After he had seen the vision, weᵃ immediately made efforts to set out for Macedonia, concluding that God had called us to evangelize them.

Philippi: Lydia's Conversion

¹¹ Then, setting sail from Troas, we ran a straight course to Samothrace, the next day to Neapolis, ¹² and from there to Philippi, a Roman colony, which is a leading city of that district of Macedonia. We stayed in that city for a number of days. ¹³ On the Sabbath day we went outside the city gate by the river, where we thought there was a place of prayer. We sat down and spoke to the women gathered there. ¹⁴ A woman named Lydia, a dealer in purple cloth from the city of Thyatira, who worshiped God, was listening. The Lord opened her heart to pay attention to what was spo-

ken by Paul. ¹⁵ After she and her household were baptized, she urged us, "If you consider me a believer in the Lord, come and stay at my house." And she persuaded us.

Paul and Silas Counter Spirit of Divination

¹⁶ Once, as we were on our way to prayer, a slave girl met us who had a spirit of predictionᵇ and made a large profit for her owners by fortune-telling. ¹⁷ As she followed Paul and us she cried out, "These men are the slaves of the •Most High God, who are proclaiming to youᶜ the way of salvation." ¹⁸ And she did this for many days.

But Paul was greatly aggravated, and turning to the spirit, said, "I command you in the name of Jesus Christ to come out of her!" And it came out right away.ᵈ

Paul and Silas into Prison

¹⁹ When her owners saw that their hope of profit was gone, they seized Paul and Silas and dragged them into the marketplace to the authorities. ²⁰ And bringing them before the chief magistrates, they said, "These men are seriously disturbing our city. They are Jews, ²¹ and are promoting customs that are not legal for us as Romans to adopt or practice."

²² Then the mob joined in the attack against them, and the chief magistrates stripped off their clothes and ordered them to be beaten with rods. ²³ After they had inflicted many blows on them, they threw them in jail, ordering the jailer to keep them securely guarded. ²⁴ Receiving such an order, he put them into the inner prison and secured their feet in the stocks.

ᵃ**16:10** The use of *we* in this passage probably indicates that the author Luke is joining Paul's missionary team here. ᵇ**16:16** Or *a spirit by which she predicted the future* ᶜ**16:17** Other mss read *us* ᵈ**16:18** Lit *out this hour*

Prayer, Singing, and a Midnight Earthquake

25 About midnight Paul and Silas were praying and singing hymns to God, and the prisoners were listening to them. 26 Suddenly there was such a violent earthquake that the foundations of the jail were shaken, and immediately all the doors were opened, and everyone's chains came loose. 27 When the jailer woke up and saw the doors of the prison open, he drew his sword and was going to kill himself, since he thought the prisoners had escaped.

28 But Paul called out in a loud voice, "Don't harm yourself, because all of us are here!"

29 Then the jailer[a] called for lights, rushed in, and fell down trembling before Paul and Silas. 30 Then he escorted them out and said, "Sirs, what must I do to be saved?"

"Believe on the Lord Jesus"

31 So they said, "Believe on the Lord Jesus, and you will be saved—you and your household." 32 Then they spoke the message of the Lord to him along with everyone in his house. 33 He took them the same hour of the night and washed their wounds. Right away he and all his family were baptized. 34 He brought them up into his house, set a meal before them, and rejoiced because he had believed God with his entire household.

"We Are Roman Citizens"

35 When daylight came, the chief magistrates sent the police to say, "Release those men!"

36 The jailer reported these words to Paul: "The magistrates have sent orders for you to be released. So come out now and go in peace."

37 But Paul said to them, "They beat us in public without a trial, although we are Roman citizens, and threw us in jail. And now are they going to smuggle us out secretly? Certainly not! On the contrary, let them come themselves and escort us out!"

An Official Apology

38 Then the police reported these words to the magistrates. And they were afraid when they heard that Paul and Silas[b] were Roman citizens. 39 So they came and apologized to them, and escorting them out, they urged them to leave town. 40 After leaving the jail, they came to Lydia's house where they saw and encouraged the brothers, and departed.

Short Ministry in Thessalonica

17 Then they traveled through Amphipolis and Apollonia and came to Thessalonica, where there was a Jewish •synagogue. 2 As usual, Paul went to them, and on three Sabbath days reasoned with them from the Scriptures, 3 explaining and showing that the •Messiah had to suffer and rise from the dead, and saying: "This is the Messiah, Jesus, whom I am proclaiming to you." 4 Then some of them were persuaded and joined Paul and Silas, including a great number of God-fearing Greeks, as well as a number[c] of the leading women.

Attack on Jason's House

5 But the Jews became jealous, and when they had brought together some scoundrels from the marketplace and formed a mob, they set the city in an uproar. Attacking Jason's house, they searched for them to bring them out to the public assembly. 6 When they did not

a16:29 Lit Then he   b16:38 Lit heard they   c17:4 Lit as well as not a few

find them, they dragged Jason and some of the brothers before the city officials, shouting, "These men who have turned the world upside down have come here too, ⁷ and Jason has received them as guests! They are all acting contrary to Caesar's decrees, saying that there is another king—Jesus!" ⁸ The Jewsª stirred up the crowd and the city officials who heard these things. ⁹ So taking a security bond from Jason and the others, they released them.

Beroeans Search Scriptures

¹⁰ As soon as it was night, the brothers sent Paul and Silas off to Beroea. On arrival, they went into the synagogue of the Jews. ¹¹ The people here were more open-minded than those in Thessalonica, since they welcomed the message with eagerness and examined the Scriptures daily to see if these things were so. ¹² Consequently, many of them believed, including a number of the prominent Greek women as well as men. ¹³ But when the Jews from Thessalonica found out that God's message had been proclaimed by Paul at Beroea, they came there too, agitating and disturbingᵇ the crowds. ¹⁴ Then the brothers immediately sent Paul away to go to the sea, but Silas and Timothy stayed on there. ¹⁵ Those who escorted Paul brought him as far as Athens, and after receiving instructions for Silas and Timothy to come to him as quickly as possible, they departed.

Paul in Athens

¹⁶ While Paul was waiting for them in Athens, his spirit was troubled within him when he saw that the city was full of idols. ¹⁷ So he reasoned in the synagogue with the Jews and with those who worshiped God, and in the marketplace every day with those who happened to be there. ¹⁸ Then also, some of the Epicurean and Stoic philosophers argued with him. Some said, "What is this pseudo-intellectualᶜ trying to say?"

Others replied, "He seems to be a preacher of foreign deities"—because he was telling the good news about Jesus and the resurrection. ¹⁹ They took him and brought him to the Areopagus,ᵈ and said, "May we learn about this new teaching you're speaking of? ²⁰ For what you say sounds strange to us, and we want to know what these ideas mean." ²¹ Now all the Athenians and the foreigners residing there spent their time on nothing else but telling or hearing something new.

Paul's Areopagus Address

²² Then Paul stood in the middle of the Areopagus and said: "Men of Athens! I see that you are extremely religious in every respect. ²³ For as I was passing through and observing the objects of your worship, I even found an altar on which was inscribed:

> ## TO AN UNKNOWN GOD

Therefore, what you worship in ignorance, this I proclaim to you. ²⁴ The God who made the world and everything in it—He is Lord of heaven and earth and does not live in shrines made by hands. ²⁵ Neither is He served by human hands, as though He needed anything, since He Himself gives everyone life and breath and all things. ²⁶ From one manᵉ He has made every nation of men to live all over the earth and has determined their

---

ª**17:8** Lit *They*   ᵇ**17:13** Other mss omit *and disturbing*   ᶜ**17:18** Lit *this seed picker*; that is, one who picks up scraps   ᵈ**17:19** Or *Mars Hill*, the oldest and most famous court in Athens with jurisdiction in moral, religious, and civil matters   ᵉ**17:26** Other mss read *one blood*

appointed times and the boundaries of where they live, ²⁷ so that they might seek God, and perhaps they might reach out and find Him, though He is not far from each one of us. ²⁸ For in Him we live and move and exist, as even some of your own poets have said, 'For we are also His offspring.'ᵃ ²⁹ Being God's offspring, then, we shouldn't think that the divine nature is like gold or silver or stone, an image fashioned by human art and imagination.

³⁰ "Therefore, having overlooked the times of ignorance, God now commands all people everywhere to repent, ³¹ because He has set a day on which He is going to judge the world in righteousness by the Man He has appointed. He has provided proof of this to everyone by raising Him from the dead."

³² When they heard about resurrection of the dead, some began to ridicule him. But others said, "We will hear you about this again." ³³ So Paul went out from their presence. ³⁴ However, some men joined him and believed, among whom were Dionysius the Areopagite, a woman named Damaris, and others with them.

Paul with Aquila and Priscilla in Corinth

18 After this, heᵇ left from Athens and went to Corinth, ² where he found a Jewish man named Aquila, a native of Pontus, who had recently come from Italy with his wife Priscilla because Claudiusᶜ had ordered all the Jews to leave Rome. Pauldᵈ came to them, ³ and being of the same occupation, stayed with them and worked, for they were tentmakers by trade. ⁴ He reasoned in the •synagogue every Sabbath and tried to persuade both Jews and Greeks.

Silas and Timothy Join Paul

⁵ When Silas and Timothy came down from Macedonia, Paul was occupied with preaching the messageᵉ and solemnly testified to the Jews that the •Messiah is Jesus. ⁶ But when they resisted and blasphemed, he shook out his clothesᶠ and told them, "Your blood is on your own heads! I am clean. From now on I will go to the Gentiles."

Paul Turns to Gentiles

⁷ So he left there and went to the house of a man named Titius Justus, a worshiper of God, whose house was next door to the synagogue. ⁸ Crispus, the leader of the synagogue, believed the Lord, along with his whole household; and many of the Corinthians, when they heard, believed and were baptized.

⁹ Then the Lord said to Paul in a night vision, "Don't be afraid, but keep on speaking and don't be silent. ¹⁰ For I am with you, and no one will lay a hand on you to hurt you, because I have many people in this city." ¹¹ And he stayed there a year and six months, teaching the word of God among them.

Jewish Opponents Charge Paul

¹² While Gallio was •proconsul of Achaia, the Jews made a united attack against Paul and brought him to the judge's bench. ¹³ "This man," they said, "persuades people to worship God contrary to the law!"

¹⁴ And as Paul was about to open his mouth, Gallio said to the Jews, "If it were a matter of a crime or of moral evil, it would be reasonable for me to put up with you Jews. ¹⁵ But if these are questions about words, names, and your own law, see to it yourselves. I don't want to

---

ᵃ**17:28** This citation is from Aratus, a third-century B.C. Gk poet.   ᵇ**18:1** Other mss read *Paul*   ᶜ**18:2** Roman emperor A.D. 41–54; he expelled all Jews from Rome in A.D. 49.   ᵈ**18:2** Lit *He*   ᵉ**18:5** Other mss read *was urged by the Spirit*   ᶠ**18:6** A symbolic display of protest; see Ac 13:51; Mt 10:14

be a judge of such things." [16] So he drove them from the judge's bench. [17] Then they all[a] seized Sosthenes, the leader of the synagogue, and beat him in front of the judge's bench. But none of these things concerned Gallio.

Paul Returns to Jerusalem

[18] So Paul, having stayed on for many days, said good-bye to the brothers and sailed away to Syria. Priscilla and Aquila were with him. He shaved his head at Cenchreae, because he had taken a vow. [19] When they reached Ephesus he left them there, but he himself entered the synagogue and engaged in discussion with[b] the Jews. [20] And though they asked him to stay for a longer time, he declined, [21] but said good-bye and stated,[c] "I'll come back to you again, if God wills." Then he set sail from Ephesus.

[22] On landing at Caesarea, he went up and greeted the church,[d] and went down to Antioch.

Paul's Third Missionary Journey

[23] He set out, traveling through one place after another in the Galatian territory and Phrygia, strengthening all the disciples.

Eloquent Apollos in Ephesus

[24] A Jew named Apollos, a native Alexandrian, an eloquent man who was powerful in the Scriptures, arrived in Ephesus. [25] This man had been instructed in the way of the Lord; and being fervent in spirit,[e] he spoke and taught the things about Jesus accurately, although he knew only John's baptism. [26] He began to speak boldly in the synagogue.

Priscilla and Aquila Instruct Apollos

After Priscilla and Aquila heard him, they took him home[f] and explained the way of God to him more accurately. [27] When he wanted to cross over to Achaia, the brothers wrote to the disciples urging them to welcome him. After he arrived, he greatly helped those who had believed through grace. [28] For he vigorously refuted the Jews in public, demonstrating through the Scriptures that Jesus is the Messiah.

Paul in Ephesus: 12 Disciples of John the Baptist

19 While Apollos was in Corinth, Paul traveled through the interior regions and came to Ephesus. He found some disciples [2] and asked them, "Did you receive the Holy Spirit when you believed?"

"No," they told him, "we haven't even heard that there is a Holy Spirit."

[3] "Then with what ⌊baptism⌋ were you baptized?" he asked them.

"With John's baptism," they replied.

[4] Paul said, "John baptized with a baptism of repentance, telling the people that they should believe in the One who would come after him, that is, in Jesus."

[5] On hearing this, they were baptized in the name of the Lord Jesus. [6] And when Paul had laid his hands on them, the Holy Spirit came on them, and they began to speak with ⌊other⌋ languages and to prophesy. [7] Now there were about 12 men in all.

Lecture Hall of Tyrannus

[8] Then he entered the •synagogue and spoke boldly over a period of three months, engaging in discussion and trying to persuade them about the things

---

[a]**18:17** Other mss read *Then all the Greeks* [b]**18:19** Or *and addressed* [c]**18:21** Other mss add *"By all means it is necessary to keep the coming festival in Jerusalem. But* [d]**18:22** The church in Jerusalem [e]**18:25** Or *in the Spirit* [f]**18:26** Lit *they received him*

related to the kingdom of God. ⁹ But when some became hardened and would not believe, slandering the Way in front of the crowd, he withdrew from them and met separately with the disciples, conducting discussions every day in the lecture hall of Tyrannus. ¹⁰ And this went on for two years, so that all the inhabitants of the province of Asia, both Jews and Greeks, heard the word of the Lord.

Paul Heals at Ephesus

¹¹ God was performing extraordinary miracles by Paul's hands, ¹² so that even facecloths or work aprons[a] that had touched his skin were brought to the sick, and the diseases left them, and the evil spirits came out of them.

Seven Sons of Sceva:
Evil Spirit

¹³ Then some of the itinerant Jewish exorcists attempted to pronounce the name of the Lord Jesus over those who had evil spirits, saying, "I command you by the Jesus whom Paul preaches!" ¹⁴ Seven sons of Sceva, a Jewish •chief priest, were doing this. ¹⁵ The evil spirit answered them, "Jesus I know, and Paul I recognize—but who are you?" ¹⁶ Then the man who had the evil spirit leaped on them, overpowered them all, and prevailed against them, so that they ran out of that house naked and wounded. ¹⁷ This became known to everyone who lived in Ephesus, both Jews and Greeks. Then fear fell on all of them, and the name of the Lord Jesus was magnified.

Books of Magic Burned

¹⁸ And many who had become believers came confessing and disclosing their practices, ¹⁹ while many of those who had practiced magic collected their books and burned them in front of everyone. So they calculated their value, and found it to be 50,000 pieces of silver. ²⁰ In this way the Lord's message flourished and prevailed.

Paul Decides to Go to Jerusalem

²¹ When these events were over, Paul resolved in the Spirit to pass through Macedonia and Achaia and go to Jerusalem. "After I've been there," he said, "I must see Rome as well!" ²² So after sending two of those who assisted him, Timothy and Erastus, to Macedonia, he himself stayed in the province of Asia for a while.

Demetrius the Silversmith:
Riot in Ephesus

²³ During that time there was a major[b] disturbance about the Way. ²⁴ For a person named Demetrius, a silversmith who made silver shrines of Artemis,[c] provided a great deal of[d] business for the craftsmen. ²⁵ When he had assembled them, as well as the workers engaged in this type of business, he said: "Men, you know that our prosperity is derived from this business. ²⁶ You both see and hear that not only in Ephesus, but in almost the whole province of Asia, this man Paul has persuaded and misled a considerable number of people by saying that gods made by hand are not gods! ²⁷ So not only do we run a risk that our business may be discredited, but also that the temple of the great goddess Artemis may be despised and her magnificence come to the verge of ruin—the very one whom the whole province of Asia and the world adore."

---

[a]19:12 Or *that also sweatbands and sweatcloths* or *handkerchiefs*   [b]19:23 Lit *was not a little*   [c]19:24 Artemis was the ancient Gk mother goddess believed to control all fertility.   [d]19:24 Lit *provided not a little*

Great Is Artemis!

²⁸ When they had heard this, they were filled with rage and began to cry out, "Great is Artemis of the Ephesians!" ²⁹ So the city was filled with confusion; and they rushed all together into the amphitheater, dragging along Gaius and Aristarchus, Macedonians who were Paul's traveling companions. ³⁰ Though Paul wanted to go in before the people, the disciples did not let him. ³¹ Even some of the provincial officials of Asia, who were his friends, sent word to him, pleading with him not to take a chance by going^a into the amphitheater. ³² Meanwhile, some were shouting one thing and some another, because the assembly was in confusion, and most of them did not know why they had come together. ³³ Then some of the crowd gave Alexander advice when the Jews pushed him to the front. So motioning with his hand, Alexander wanted to make his defense to the people. ³⁴ But when they recognized that he was a Jew, a united cry went up from all of them for about two hours: "Great is Artemis of the Ephesians!"

City Clerk Calms Crowd

³⁵ However, when the city clerk had calmed the crowd down, he said, "Men of Ephesus! What man is there who doesn't know that the city of the Ephesians is the temple guardian of the great^b Artemis, and of the image that fell from heaven? ³⁶ Therefore, since these things are undeniable, you must keep calm and not do anything rash. ³⁷ For you have brought these men here who are not temple robbers or blasphemers of our^c goddess. ³⁸ So if Demetrius and the craftsmen who are with him have a case against anyone, the courts are in session, and there are •proconsuls. Let them bring charges against one another. ³⁹ But if you want something else, it must be decided in a legal assembly. ⁴⁰ In fact, we run a risk of being charged with rioting for what happened today, since there is no justification that we can give as a reason for this disorderly gathering." ⁴¹ After saying this, he dismissed the assembly.

Paul to Macedonia

20 After the uproar was over, Paul sent for the disciples, encouraged them, and after saying good-bye, departed to go to Macedonia. ² And when he had passed through those areas and exhorted them at length, he came to Greece ³ and stayed three months.

Plot against Paul

When he was about to set sail for Syria, a plot was devised against him by the Jews, so a decision was made to go back through Macedonia. ⁴ He was accompanied^d by Sopater, son of Pyrrhus,^e from Beroea, Aristarchus and Secundus from Thessalonica, Gaius from Derbe, Timothy, and Tychicus and Trophimus from Asia. ⁵ These men went on ahead and waited for us in Troas, ⁶ but we sailed away from Philippi after the days of •Unleavened Bread. In five days we reached them at Troas, where we spent seven days.

Paul Revives Eutychus at Troas

⁷ On the first day of the week,^f we^g assembled to break bread. Paul spoke to them, and since he was about to depart the next day, he extended his message until midnight. ⁸ There were many

---

^a**19:31** Lit *not to give himself*   ^b**19:35** Other mss add *goddess*   ^c**19:37** Other mss read *your*   ^d**20:4** Other mss add *to Asia*   ^e**20:4** Other mss omit *son of Pyrrhus*   ^f**20:7** Lit *On one between the Sabbaths*; that is, Sunday   ^g**20:7** Other mss read *the disciples*

lamps in the room upstairs where we were assembled, ⁹ and a young man named Eutychus was sitting on a window sill and sank into a deep sleep as Paul kept on speaking. When he was overcome by sleep he fell down from the third story, and was picked up dead. ¹⁰ But Paul went down, threw himself on him, embraced him, and said, "Don't be alarmed, for his •life is in him!" ¹¹ After going upstairs, breaking the bread, and eating, he conversed a considerable time until dawn. Then he left. ¹² They brought the boy home alive and were greatly comforted.

Paul by Land: Troas to Miletus

¹³ Then we went on ahead to the ship and sailed for Assos, from there intending to take Paul on board. For these were his instructions, since he himself was going by land. ¹⁴ When he met us at Assos, we took him on board and came to Mitylene. ¹⁵ Sailing from there, the next day we arrived off Chios. The following day we crossed over to Samos, andᵃ the day after, we came to Miletus. ¹⁶ For Paul had decided to sail past Ephesus so he would not have to spend time in the province of Asia, because he was hurrying to be in Jerusalem, if possible, for the day of Pentecost.

Paul's Farewell Address to Ephesian Elders

¹⁷ Now from Miletus, he sent to Ephesus and called for the elders of the church. ¹⁸ And when they came to him, he said to them: "You know, from the first day I set foot in Asia, how I was with you the whole time— ¹⁹ serving the Lord with all humility, with tears, and with the trials that came to me through the plots of the Jews— ²⁰ and that I did not shrink back from proclaiming to you anything that was profitable, or from teaching it to you in public and from house to house. ²¹ I testified to both Jews and Greeks about repentance toward God and faith in our Lord Jesus.

²² "And now I am on my way to Jerusalem, bound in my spirit, not knowing what I will encounter there, ²³ except that in town after town the Holy Spirit testifies to me that chains and afflictions are waiting for me. ²⁴ But I count my life of no value to myself, so that I may finish my courseᵇ and the ministry I received from the Lord Jesus, to testify to the gospel of God's grace.

²⁵ "And now I know that none of you, among whom I went about preaching the kingdom, will ever see my face again. ²⁶ Therefore I testify to you this day that I am innocentᶜ of everyone's blood, ²⁷ for I did not shrink back from declaring to you the whole plan of God. ²⁸ Be on guard for yourselves and for all the flock, among whom the Holy Spirit has appointed you as •overseers, to shepherd the church of God,ᵈ which He purchased with His own blood. ²⁹ I know that after my departure savage wolves will come in among you, not sparing the flock. ³⁰ And men from among yourselves will rise up with deviant doctrines to lure the disciples into following them. ³¹ Therefore be on the alert, remembering that night and day for three years I did not stop warning each one of you with tears.

³² "And nowᵉ I commit you to God and to the message of His grace, which is able to build you up and to give you an inheritance among all who are sanctified. ³³ I have not coveted anyone's silver or gold or clothing. ³⁴ You yourselves know that these hands have provided for

ᵃ**20:15** Other mss add *after staying at Trogyllium*   ᵇ**20:24** Other mss add *with joy*   ᶜ**20:26** Lit *clean*   ᵈ**20:28** Other mss read *church of the Lord*; other mss read *church of the Lord and God*   ᵉ**20:32** Other mss add *brothers,*

my needs, and for those who were with me. [35] In every way I've shown you that by laboring like this, it is necessary to help the weak and to keep in mind the words of the Lord Jesus, for He said, 'It is more blessed to give than to receive.'"

[36] After he said this, he knelt down and prayed with all of them. [37] There was a great deal of weeping by everyone. And embracing Paul, they kissed him, [38] grieving most of all over his statement that they would never see his face again. Then they escorted him to the ship.

Paul and Company to Syria

21 After we tore ourselves away from them and set sail, we came by a direct route to Cos, the next day to Rhodes, and from there to Patara. [2] Finding a ship crossing over to Phoenicia, we boarded and set sail. [3] After we sighted Cyprus, leaving it on the left, we sailed on to Syria and arrived at Tyre, because the ship was to unload its cargo there.

Disciples at Tyre Warn Paul

[4] So we found some disciples and stayed there seven days. They said to Paul through the Spirit not to go to Jerusalem. [5] When our days there were over, we left to continue our journey, while all of them, with their wives and children, escorted us out of the city. After kneeling down on the beach to pray, [6] we said good-bye to one another. Then we boarded the ship, and they returned home.

At Caesarea with Philip the Evangelist

[7] When we completed our voyage from Tyre, we reached Ptolemais, where we greeted the brothers and stayed with them one day. [8] The next day we left and came to Caesarea, where we entered the house of Philip the evangelist, who was one of the Seven, and stayed with him. [9] This man had four virgin daughters who prophesied.

Prophet Agabus Warns Paul

[10] While we were staying there many days, a prophet named Agabus came down from Judea. [11] He came to us, took Paul's belt, tied his own feet and hands, and said, "This is what the Holy Spirit says: 'In this way the Jews in Jerusalem will bind the man who owns this belt, and deliver him into Gentile hands.'" [12] When we heard this, both we and the local people begged him not to go up to Jerusalem.

Paul: Ready to Be Bound and Die

[13] Then Paul replied, "What are you doing, weeping and breaking my heart? For I am ready not only to be bound, but also to die in Jerusalem for the name of the Lord Jesus." [14] Since he would not be persuaded, we stopped talking and simply said, "The Lord's will be done!"

Paul and Company Arrive at Jerusalem

[15] After these days we got ready and went up to Jerusalem. [16] Some of the disciples from Caesarea also went with us and brought us to Mnason, a Cypriot and an early disciple, with whom we were to stay.

Paul Reports to James and Elders

[17] When we reached Jerusalem, the brothers welcomed us gladly. [18] The following day Paul went in with us to James, and all the elders were present. [19] After greeting them, he related one by one what God did among the Gentiles through his ministry.

[20] When they heard it, they glorified God and said, "You see, brother, how

many thousands of Jews there are who have believed, and they are all zealous for the law. [21] But they have been told about you that you teach all the Jews who are among the Gentiles to abandon Moses, by telling them not to circumcise their children or to walk in our customs. [22] So what is to be done?[a] They will certainly hear that you've come.

Elders' Plan for Paul

[23] Therefore do what we tell you: We have four men who have obligated themselves with a vow. [24] Take these men, purify yourself along with them, and pay for them to get their heads shaved. Then everyone will know that what they were told about you amounts to nothing, but that you yourself are also careful about observing the law. [25] With regard to the Gentiles who have believed, we have written a letter containing our decision that[b] they should keep themselves from food sacrificed to idols, from blood, from what is strangled, and from sexual immorality."

Paul Triggers Riot in Temple Complex

[26] Then the next day, Paul took the men, having purified himself along with them, and entered the temple, announcing the completion of the purification days when the offering for each of them would be made. [27] As the seven days were about to end, the Jews from the province of Asia saw him in the •temple complex, stirred up the whole crowd, and seized him, [28] shouting, "Men of Israel, help! This is the man who teaches everyone everywhere against our people, our law, and this place. What's more, he also brought Greeks into the temple and has profaned this holy place." [29] For they had previously seen Trophimus the Ephesian in the city with him, and they supposed that Paul had brought him into the temple complex.[c]

Soldiers Intervene

[30] The whole city was stirred up, and the people rushed together. They seized Paul, dragged him out of the temple complex, and at once the gates were shut. [31] As they were trying to kill him, word went up to the commander of the •regiment that all Jerusalem was in chaos. [32] Taking along soldiers and •centurions, he immediately ran down to them. Seeing the commander and the soldiers, they stopped beating Paul. [33] Then the commander came up, took him into custody, and ordered him to be bound with two chains. He asked who he was and what he had done. [34] Some in the mob were shouting one thing and some another. Since he was not able to get reliable information because of the uproar, he ordered him to be taken into the barracks. [35] When Paul[d] got to the steps, he had to be carried by the soldiers because of the mob's violence, [36] for the mass of people were following and yelling, "Kill him!"

Paul's Defense before Jerusalem Mob

[37] As he was about to be brought into the barracks, Paul said to the commander, "Am I allowed to say something to you?"

He replied, "Do you know Greek? [38] Aren't you the Egyptian who raised a rebellion some time ago and led 4,000 Assassins[e] into the desert?"

[39] Paul said, "I am a Jewish man from Tarsus of Cilicia, a citizen of an

important city.ᵃ Now I ask you, let me speak to the people."

⁴⁰ After he had given permission, Paul stood on the steps and motioned with his hand to the people. When there was a great hush, he addressed them in the Hebrew language: ¹ "Brothers and fathers, listen now to my defense before you."

Paul Relates
His Background

² When they heard that he was addressing them in the Hebrew language, they became even quieter. ³ He continued, "I am a Jewish man, born in Tarsus of Cilicia, but brought up in this cityᵇ at the feet of Gamaliel, and educated according to the strict view of our patriarchal law. Being zealous for God, just as all of you are today, ⁴ I persecuted this Way to the death, binding and putting both men and women in jail, ⁵ as both the high priest and the whole council of elders can testify about me. Having received letters from them to the brothers, I was traveling to Damascus to bring those who were prisoners there to be punished in Jerusalem.

Paul Testifies to His
Conversion and Calling

⁶ "As I was traveling and near Damascus, about noon an intense light from heaven suddenly flashed around me. ⁷ I fell to the ground and heard a voice saying to me, 'Saul, Saul, why are you persecuting Me?'

⁸ "I answered, 'Who are You, Lord?'

"He said to me, 'I am Jesus the •Nazarene, whom you are persecuting!' ⁹ Now those who were with me saw the light,ᶜ but they did not hear the voice of the One who was speaking to me.

¹⁰ "Then I said, 'What should I do, Lord?'

"And the Lord told me, 'Get up and go into Damascus, and there you will be told about everything that is assigned for you to do.'

¹¹ "Since I couldn't see because of the brightness of that light, I was led by the hand by those who were with me, and came into Damascus. ¹² Someone named Ananias, a devout man according to the law, having a good reputation with all the Jews residing there, ¹³ came to me, stood by me, and said, 'Brother Saul, regain your sight.' And in that very hour I looked up and saw him. ¹⁴ Then he said, 'The God of our fathers has appointed you to know His will, to see the Righteous One, and to hear the sound of His voice.ᵈ ¹⁵ For you will be a witness for Him to all people of what you have seen and heard. ¹⁶ And now, why delay? Get up and be baptized, and wash away your sins by calling on His name.'

¹⁷ "After I came back to Jerusalem and was praying in the •temple complex, I went into a visionary state ¹⁸ and saw Him telling me, 'Hurry and get out of Jerusalem quickly, because they will not accept your testimony about Me!'

¹⁹ "But I said, 'Lord, they know that in •synagogue after synagogue I had those who believed in You imprisoned and beaten. ²⁰ And when the blood of Your witness Stephen was being shed, I myself was standing by and approving,ᵉ and I guarded the clothes of those who killed him.'

²¹ "Then He said to me, 'Go, because I will send you far away to the Gentiles.'"

Crowd Rejects Paul

²² They listened to him up to this word. Then they raised their voices,

---

ᵃ**21:39** Lit *of no insignificant city*   ᵇ**22:3** Probably Jerusalem, but others think Tarsus   ᶜ**22:9** Other mss add *and were afraid*   ᵈ**22:14** Lit *to hear a voice from His mouth*   ᵉ**22:20** Other mss add *of his murder*

shouting, "Wipe this person off the earth—it's a disgrace for him to live!"

Roman Commander
Orders Scourge

²³ As they were yelling and flinging aside their robes and throwing dust into the air, ²⁴ the commander ordered him to be brought into the barracks, directing that he be examined with the scourge, so he could discover the reason they were shouting against him like this.

Paul Pleads Roman Citizenship

²⁵ As they stretched him out for the lash, Paul said to the •centurion standing by, "Is it legal for you to scourge a man who is a Roman citizen and is uncondemned?"

²⁶ When the centurion heard this, he went and reported to the commander, saying, "What are you going to do? For this man is a Roman citizen."

²⁷ The commander came and said to him, "Tell me—are you a Roman citizen?"

"Yes," he said.

²⁸ The commander replied, "I bought this citizenship for a large amount of money."

"But I myself was born a citizen," Paul said.

²⁹ Therefore, those who were about to examine him withdrew from him at once. The commander too was alarmed when he realized Paul was a Roman citizen and he had bound him.

Roman Commander
Puts Paul before Sanhedrin

³⁰ The next day, since he wanted to find out exactly why Paul was being accused by the Jews, he released him[a] and instructed the •chief priests and all the •Sanhedrin to convene. Then he brought Paul down and placed him before them.

23 ¹ Paul looked intently at the •Sanhedrin and said, "Brothers, I have lived my life before God in all good conscience until this day." ² But the high priest Ananias ordered those who were standing next to him to strike him on the mouth. ³ Then Paul said to him, "God is going to strike you, you whitewashed wall! You are sitting there judging me according to the law, and in violation of the law are you ordering me to be struck?"

⁴ And those standing nearby said, "Do you dare revile God's high priest?"

Paul Pits Sadducees
against Pharisees

⁵ "I did not know, brothers," Paul said, "that it was the high priest. For it is written, **You must not speak evil of a ruler of your people.**"[b] ⁶ When Paul realized that one part of them were •Sadducees and the other part were •Pharisees, he cried out in the Sanhedrin, "Brothers, I am a Pharisee, a son of Pharisees! I am being judged because of the hope of the resurrection of the dead!"

Paul's Words Spark Dispute

⁷ When he said this, a dispute broke out between the Pharisees and the Sadducees, and the assembly was divided. ⁸ For the Sadducees say there is no resurrection, and no angel or spirit, but the Pharisees affirm them all.

⁹ The shouting grew loud, and some of the •scribes of the Pharisees' party got up and argued vehemently: "We find nothing evil in this man. What if a spirit or an angel has spoken to him?"[c] ¹⁰ When the dispute became violent, the commander feared that Paul might be

---

ᵃ**22:30** Other mss add *from his chains*   ᵇ**23:5** Ex 22:28   ᶜ**23:9** Other mss add *Let us not fight God.*

torn apart by them and ordered the troops to go down, rescue him from them, and bring him into the barracks.

Plot against Paul

[11] The following night, the Lord stood by him and said, "Have courage! For as you have testified about Me in Jerusalem, so you must also testify in Rome."

[12] When it was day, the Jews formed a conspiracy and bound themselves under a curse: neither to eat nor to drink until they had killed Paul. [13] There were more than 40 who had formed this plot. [14] These men went to the •chief priests and elders and said, "We have bound ourselves under a solemn curse that we won't eat anything until we have killed Paul. [15] So now you, along with the Sanhedrin, make a request to the commander that he bring him down to you[a] as if you were going to investigate his case more thoroughly. However, before he gets near, we are ready to kill him."

Warning from Paul's Nephew

[16] But the son of Paul's sister, hearing about their ambush, came and entered the barracks and reported it to Paul. [17] Then Paul called one of the •centurions and said, "Take this young man to the commander, because he has something to report to him."

[18] So he took him, brought him to the commander, and said, "The prisoner Paul called me and asked me to bring this young man to you, because he has something to tell you."

[19] Then the commander took him by the hand, led him aside, and inquired privately, "What is it you have to report to me?"

[20] "The Jews," he said, "have agreed to ask you to bring Paul down to the Sanhedrin tomorrow, as though they are going to hold a somewhat more careful inquiry about him. [21] Don't let them persuade you, because there are more than 40 of them arranging to ambush him, men who have bound themselves under a curse not to eat or drink until they kill him. Now they are ready, waiting for a commitment from you."

[22] So the commander dismissed the young man and instructed him, "Don't tell anyone that you have informed me about this."

Paul To Caesarea by Night

[23] He summoned two of his centurions and said, "Get 200 soldiers ready with 70 cavalry and 200 spearmen to go to Caesarea at nine tonight.[b] [24] Also provide mounts so they can put Paul on them and bring him safely to Felix the governor."

[25] He wrote a letter of this kind:

[26] Claudius Lysias,

To the most excellent governor Felix:

Greetings.

[27] When this man had been seized by the Jews and was about to be killed by them, I arrived with my troops and rescued him because I learned that he is a Roman citizen. [28] Wanting to know the charge for which they were accusing him, I brought him down before their Sanhedrin. [29] I found out that the accusations were about disputed matters in their law, and that there was no charge that merited death or chains. [30] When I was informed that there was a plot against the man,[c] I sent him to you right away. I also ordered

his accusers to state their case against him in your presence.[a]

31 Therefore, during the night, the soldiers took Paul and brought him to Antipatris as they were ordered. 32 The next day, they returned to the barracks, allowing the cavalry to go on with him. 33 When these men entered Caesarea and delivered the letter to the governor, they also presented Paul to him. 34 After he[b] read it, he asked what province he was from. So when he learned he was from Cilicia, 35 he said, "I will give you a hearing whenever your accusers get here too." And he ordered that he be kept under guard in •Herod's palace.[c]

High Priest and Elders Accuse Paul

24 After five days Ananias the high priest came down with some elders and a lawyer[d] named Tertullus. These men presented their case against Paul to the governor. 2 When he was called in, Tertullus began to accuse him and said: "Since we enjoy great peace because of you, and reforms are taking place for the benefit of this nation by your foresight, 3 we gratefully receive them always and in all places, most excellent Felix, with all thankfulness. 4 However, so that I will not burden you any further, I beg you in your graciousness to give us a brief hearing. 5 For we have found this man to be a plague, an agitator among all the Jews throughout the Roman world, and a ringleader of the sect of the •Nazarenes! 6 He even tried to desecrate the temple, so we apprehended him [and wanted to judge him according to our law. 7 But Lysias the commander came and took him from our

hands, commanding his accusers to come to you.][e] 8 By examining him yourself you will be able to discern all these things of which we accuse him." 9 The Jews also joined in the attack, alleging that these things were so.

Paul's Defense before Governor Felix

10 When the governor motioned to him to speak, Paul replied: "Because I know you have been a judge of this nation for many years, I am glad to offer my defense in what concerns me. 11 You are able to determine that it is no more than 12 days since I went up to worship in Jerusalem. 12 And they didn't find me disputing with anyone or causing a disturbance among the crowd, either in the temple complex or in the •synagogues, or anywhere in the city. 13 Neither can they provide evidence to you of what they now bring against me. 14 But I confess this to you: that according to the Way, which they call a sect, so I worship my fathers' God, believing all the things that are written in the Law and in the Prophets. 15 And I have a hope in God, which these men themselves also accept, that there is going to be a resurrection,[f] both of the righteous and the unrighteous. 16 I always do my best to have a clear conscience toward God and men. 17 After many years, I came to bring charitable gifts and offerings to my nation, 18 and while I was doing this, some Jews from the province of Asia found me ritually purified in the temple, without a crowd and without any uproar. 19 It is they who ought to be here before you to bring charges, if they have anything against me. 20 Either let

---

[a]23:30 Other mss add Farewell [b]23:34 Other mss read the governor [c]23:35 Lit praetorium, a Lat word that can also refer to a military headquarters, to the governor's palace, or to the emperor's imperial guard [d]24:1 Gk rhetor; compare the Eng "rhetoric," "rhetorician"—an orator skilled in public speaking. In this situation, skill in the Gk language was needed. [e]24:6-7 Other mss omit bracketed text [f]24:15 Other mss add of the dead

these men here state what wrongdoing they found in me when I stood before the •Sanhedrin, ²¹ or about this one statement I cried out while standing among them, 'Today I am being judged before you concerning the resurrection of the dead.' "

Felix Postpones Verdict

²² Since Felix was accurately informed about the Way, he adjourned the hearing, saying, "When Lysias the commander comes down, I will decide your case." ²³ He ordered that the •centurion keep Paul[a] under guard, though he could have some freedom, and that he should not prevent any of his friends from serving[b] him.

Felix and Drusilla Question Paul

²⁴ After some days, when Felix came with his wife Drusilla, who was Jewish, he sent for Paul and listened to him on the subject of faith in Christ Jesus. ²⁵ Now as he spoke about righteousness, self-control, and the judgment to come, Felix became afraid and replied, "Leave for now, but when I find time I'll call for you." ²⁶ At the same time he was also hoping that money would be given to him by Paul.[c] For this reason he sent for him quite often and conversed with him.

Festus Succeeds Felix

²⁷ After two years had passed, Felix received a successor, Porcius Festus, and because he wished to do a favor for the Jews, Felix left Paul in prison.

Festus Confers with Jewish Leaders

25 Three days after Festus arrived in the province, he went up to Jerusalem from Caesarea. ² Then the •chief priests and the leaders of the Jews pre-sented their case against Paul to him; and they appealed, ³ asking him to do them a favor against Paul,[d] that he might summon him to Jerusalem. They were preparing an ambush along the road to kill him. ⁴ However, Festus answered that Paul should be kept at Caesarea, and that he himself was about to go there shortly. ⁵ "Therefore," he said, "let the men of authority among you go down with me and accuse him, if there is any wrong in this man."

Paul Appears before Festus

⁶ When he had spent not more than eight or 10 days among them, he went down to Caesarea. The next day, seated at the judge's bench, he commanded Paul to be brought in. ⁷ When he arrived, the Jews who had come down from Jerusalem stood around him and brought many serious charges that they were not able to prove, ⁸ while Paul made the defense that, "Neither against the Jewish law, nor against the temple, nor against Caesar have I sinned at all."

⁹ Then Festus, wanting to do a favor for the Jews, replied to Paul, "Are you willing to go up to Jerusalem, there to be tried before me on these charges?"

Paul Appeals to Caesar

¹⁰ But Paul said: "I am standing at Caesar's tribunal, where I ought to be tried. I have done no wrong to the Jews, as even you can see very well. ¹¹ If then I am doing wrong, or have done anything deserving of death, I do not refuse to die, but if there is nothing to what these men accuse me of, no one can give me up to them. I appeal to Caesar!"

¹² After Festus conferred with his council, he replied, "You have appealed to Caesar; to Caesar you will go!"

^a**24:23** Lit *him*   ^b**24:23** Other mss add *or visiting*   ^c**24:26** Other mss add *so that he might release him*   ^d**25:3** Lit *asking a favor against him*

King Herod Agrippa II and Bernice Visit Festus

¹³ After some days had passed, King Agrippa[a] and Bernice arrived in Caesarea and paid a courtesy call on Festus. ¹⁴ Since they stayed there many days, Festus presented Paul's case to the king, saying, "There's a man who was left as a prisoner by Felix. ¹⁵ When I was in Jerusalem, the chief priests and the elders of the Jews presented their case and asked for a judgment against him. ¹⁶ I answered them that it's not the Romans' custom to give any man up[b] before the accused confronts the accusers face to face and has an opportunity to give a defense concerning the charge. ¹⁷ Therefore, when they had assembled here, I did not delay. The next day I sat at the judge's bench and ordered the man to be brought in. ¹⁸ Concerning him, the accusers stood up and brought no charge of the sort I was expecting. ¹⁹ Instead they had some disagreements with him about their own religion and about a certain Jesus, a dead man whom Paul claimed to be alive. ²⁰ Since I was at a loss in a dispute over such things, I asked him if he wished to go to Jerusalem and be tried there concerning these matters. ²¹ But when Paul appealed to be held for trial by the Emperor, I ordered him to be kept in custody until I could send him to Caesar."

²² Then Agrippa said to Festus, "I would like to hear the man myself."

"Tomorrow," he said, "you will hear him."

Paul before Agrippa

²³ So the next day, Agrippa and Bernice came with great pomp and entered the auditorium with the commanders and prominent men of the city. When Festus gave the command, Paul was brought in. ²⁴ Then Festus said: "King Agrippa and all men present with us, you see this man about whom the whole Jewish community has appealed to me, both in Jerusalem and here, shouting that he should not live any longer. ²⁵ Now I realized that he had not done anything deserving of death, but when he himself appealed to the Emperor, I decided to send him. ²⁶ I have nothing definite to write to the Emperor about him. Therefore, I have brought him before all of you, and especially before you, King Agrippa, so that after this examination is over, I may have something to write. ²⁷ For it seems unreasonable to me to send a prisoner and not to indicate the charges against him."

Paul's Defense before Agrippa

26 Agrippa said to Paul, "It is permitted for you to speak for yourself."

Then Paul stretched out his hand and began his defense: ² "I consider myself fortunate, King Agrippa, that today I am going to make a defense before you about everything I am accused of by the Jews, ³ especially since you are an expert in all the Jewish customs and controversies. Therefore I beg you to listen to me patiently.

⁴ "All the Jews know my way of life from my youth, which was spent from the beginning among my own nation and in Jerusalem. ⁵ They had previously known me for quite some time, if they were willing to testify, that according to the strictest party of our religion I lived as a •Pharisee. ⁶ And now I stand on trial for the hope of the promise made by God to our fathers, ⁷ ⌊the promise⌋ our 12 tribes hope to attain as they earnestly serve Him night and day. Because of this

hope I am being accused by the Jews, O king! [8] Why is it considered incredible by any of you that God raises the dead? [9] In fact, I myself supposed it was necessary to do many things in opposition to the name of Jesus the •Nazarene. [10] This I actually did in Jerusalem, and I locked up many of the saints in prison, since I had received authority for that from the •chief priests. When they were put to death, I cast my vote against them. [11] In all the •synagogues I often tried to make them blaspheme by punishing them. Being greatly enraged at them, I even pursued them to foreign cities.

Paul: On His Conversion and Commission

[12] "Under these circumstances I was traveling to Damascus with authority and a commission from the chief priests. [13] At midday, while on the road, O king, I saw a light from heaven brighter than the sun, shining around me and those traveling with me. [14] When we had all fallen to the ground, I heard a voice speaking to me in the Hebrew language, 'Saul, Saul, why are you persecuting Me? It is hard for you to kick against the goads.'[a]

[15] "But I said, 'Who are You, Lord?'

"And the Lord replied: 'I am Jesus, whom you are persecuting. [16] But get up and stand on your feet. For I have appeared to you for this purpose, to appoint you as a servant and a witness of things you have seen,[b] and of things in which I will appear to you. [17] I will rescue you from the people and from the Gentiles, to whom I now send you, [18] to open their eyes that they may turn from darkness to light and from the power of Satan to God, that they may receive forgiveness of sins and a share among those who are sanctified by faith in Me.'

[19] "Therefore, King Agrippa, I was not disobedient to the heavenly vision. [20] Instead, I preached to those in Damascus first, and to those in Jerusalem and in all the region of Judea, and to the Gentiles, that they should repent and turn to God, and do works worthy of repentance. [21] For this reason the Jews seized me in the •temple complex and were trying to kill me. [22] Since I have obtained help that comes from God, to this day I stand and testify to both small and great, saying nothing else than what the prophets and Moses said would take place— [23] that the •Messiah must suffer, and that as the first to rise from the dead, He would proclaim light to our people and to the Gentiles."

"Out of Your Mind, Paul!"

[24] As he was making his defense this way, Festus exclaimed in a loud voice, "You're out of your mind, Paul! Too much study is driving you mad!"

[25] But Paul replied, "I'm not out of my mind, most excellent Festus. On the contrary, I'm speaking words of truth and good judgment. [26] For the king knows about these matters. It is to him I am actually speaking boldly. For I'm not convinced that any of these things escapes his notice, since this was not done in a corner! [27] King Agrippa, do you believe the prophets? I know you believe."

"Except for These Chains"

[28] Then Agrippa said to Paul, "Are you going to persuade me to become a Christian so easily?"

[29] "I wish before God," replied Paul, "that whether easily or with difficulty,

---

[a]**26:14** Sharp sticks used to prod animals, such as oxen in plowing   [b]**26:16** Other mss read *things in which you have seen Me*

not only you but all who listen to me today might become as I am—except for these chains."

[30] So the king, the governor, Bernice, and those sitting with them got up, [31] and when they had left they talked with each other and said, "This man is doing nothing that deserves death or chains."

[32] Then Agrippa said to Festus, "This man could have been released if he had not appealed to Caesar."

Paul and Company Sail for Rome

27 When it was decided that we were to sail to Italy, they handed over Paul and some other prisoners to a •centurion named Julius, of the Imperial •Regiment. [2] So when we had boarded a ship of Adramyttium, we put to sea, intending to sail to ports along the coast of the province of Asia. Aristarchus, a Macedonian of Thessalonica, was with us. [3] The next day we put in at Sidon, and Julius treated Paul kindly and allowed him to go to his friends to receive their care. [4] When we had put out to sea from there, we sailed along the northern coast[a] of Cyprus because the winds were against us. [5] After sailing through the open sea off Cilicia and Pamphylia, we reached Myra in Lycia. [6] There the centurion found an Alexandrian ship sailing for Italy and put us on board. [7] Sailing slowly for many days, we came with difficulty as far as Cnidus. But since the wind did not allow us to approach it, we sailed along the south side[a] of Crete off Salmone. [8] With yet more difficulty we sailed along the coast, and came to a place called Fair Havens near the city of Lasea.

Centurion and Captain Ignore Paul's Advice

[9] By now much time had passed, and the voyage was already dangerous. Since the Fast[b] was already over, Paul gave his advice [10] and told them, "Men, I can see that this voyage is headed toward damage and heavy loss, not only of the cargo and the ship, but also of our lives." [11] But the centurion paid attention to the captain and the owner of the ship rather than to what Paul said. [12] Since the harbor was unsuitable to winter in, the majority decided to set sail from there, hoping somehow to reach Phoenix, a harbor on Crete open to the southwest and northwest, and to winter there.

Fierce Northeaster

[13] When a gentle south wind sprang up, they thought they had achieved their purpose; they weighed anchor and sailed along the shore of Crete. [14] But not long afterwards, a fierce wind called the "northeaster"[c] rushed down from the island.[d] [15] Since the ship was caught and was unable to head into the wind, we gave way to it and were driven along. [16] After running under the shelter of a little island called Cauda,[e] we were barely able to get control of the skiff. [17] After hoisting it up, they used ropes and tackle and girded the ship. Then, fearing they would run aground on the Syrtis,[f] they lowered the drift-anchor, and in this way they were driven along. [18] Because we were being severely battered by the storm, they began to jettison the cargo the next day. [19] On the third day, they threw the ship's gear overboard with their own hands.

---

[a]27:4,7 Lit sailed under the lee   [b]27:9 The Day of Atonement   [c]27:14 Lit Euraquilo, a violent northeast wind   [d]27:14 Lit from her   [e]27:16 Or Clauda   [f]27:17 Syrtis = sand banks or bars near North Africa

Paul Reassures

20 For many days neither sun nor stars appeared, and the severe storm kept raging; finally all hope that we would be saved was disappearing. 21 Since many were going without food, Paul stood up among them and said, "You men should have followed my advice not to sail from Crete and sustain this damage and loss. 22 Now I urge you to take courage, because there will be no loss of any of your lives, but only of the ship. 23 For this night an angel of the God I belong to and serve stood by me, 24 saying, 'Don't be afraid, Paul. You must stand before Caesar. And, look! God has graciously given you all those who are sailing with you.' 25 Therefore, take courage, men, because I believe God that it will be just the way it was told to me. 26 However, we must run aground on a certain island."

27 When the fourteenth night came, we were drifting in the Adriatic Sea,ᵃ and in the middle of the night the sailors thought they were approaching land.ᵇ 28 They took a sounding and found it to be 120 feetᶜ deep; when they had sailed a little farther and sounded again, they found it to be 90 feetᵈ deep. 29 Then, fearing we might run aground in some rocky place, they dropped four anchors from the stern and prayed for daylight to come.

Paul Takes Charge in Disaster

30 Some sailors tried to escape from the ship; they had let down the skiff into the sea, pretending that they were going to put out anchors from the bow. 31 Paul said to the centurion and the soldiers, "Unless these men stay in the ship, you cannot be saved." 32 Then the soldiers cut the ropes holding the skiff and let it drop away.

33 When it was just about daylight, Paul urged them all to take food, saying, "Today is the fourteenth day that you have been waiting and going without food, having eaten nothing. 34 Therefore I urge you to take some food. For this has to do with your survival, since not a hair will be lost from the head of any of you." 35 After he said these things and had taken some bread, he gave thanks to God in the presence of them all, and when he had broken it, he began to eat. 36 They all became encouraged and took food themselves. 37 In all there were 276 of us on the ship. 38 And having eaten enough food, they began to lighten the ship by throwing the grain overboard into the sea.

Shipwreck

39 When daylight came, they did not recognize the land, but sighted a bay with a beach. They planned to run the ship ashore if they could. 40 After casting off the anchors, they left them in the sea, at the same time loosening the ropes that held the rudders. Then they hoisted the foresail to the wind and headed for the beach. 41 But they struck a sandbar and ran the ship aground. The bow jammed fast and remained immovable, but the stern began to break up with the pounding of the waves.

42 The soldiers' plan was to kill the prisoners so that no one could swim off and escape. 43 But the centurion kept them from carrying out their plan because he wanted to save Paul, so he ordered those who could swim to jump overboard first and get to land. 44 The rest were to follow, some on planks and some on debris from the ship. In this way, all got safely to land.

ᵃ27:27 Part of the northern Mediterranean Sea; not the modern Adriatic Sea east of Italy ᵇ27:27 Lit thought there was land approaching them ᶜ27:28 Lit 20 fathoms ᵈ27:28 Lit 15 fathoms

Hospitality on Malta

28 Safely ashore, we then learned that the island was called Malta. [2] The local people showed us extraordinary kindness, for they lit a fire and took us all in, since rain was falling and it was cold. [3] As Paul gathered a bundle of brushwood and put it on the fire, a viper came out because of the heat and fastened itself to his hand. [4] When the local people saw the creature hanging from his hand, they said to one another, "This man is probably a murderer, and though he has escaped the sea, Justice[a] does not allow him to live!" [5] However, he shook the creature off into the fire and suffered no harm. [6] They expected that he would swell up or suddenly drop dead. But after they waited a long time and saw nothing unusual happen to him, they changed their minds and said he was a god.

Paul's Ministry in Malta

[7] Now in the area around that place was an estate belonging to the leading man of the island, named Publius, who welcomed us and entertained us hospitably for three days. [8] It happened that Publius' father was in bed suffering from fever and dysentery. Paul went to him, and praying and laying his hands on him, he healed him. [9] After this, the rest of those on the island who had diseases also came and were cured. [10] So they heaped many honors on us, and when we sailed, they gave us what we needed.

Rome at Last

[11] After three months we set sail in an Alexandrian ship that had wintered at the island, with the Twin Brothers[b] as its figurehead. [12] Putting in at Syracuse, we stayed three days. [13] From there, after making a circuit along the coast,[c] we reached Rhegium. After one day a south wind sprang up, and the second day we came to Puteoli. [14] There we found believers[d] and were invited to stay with them for seven days.

And so we came to Rome. [15] Now the believers[d] from there had heard the news about us and had come to meet us as far as Forum of Appius and Three Taverns. When Paul saw them, he thanked God and took courage. [16] And when we entered Rome,[e] Paul was permitted to stay by himself with the soldier who guarded him.

Paul's First Interview with Roman Jews

[17] After three days he called together the leaders of the Jews. And when they had gathered he said to them: "Brothers, although I have done nothing against our people or the customs of our forefathers, I was delivered as a prisoner from Jerusalem into the hands of the Romans [18] who, after examining me, wanted to release me, since I had not committed a capital offense. [19] Because the Jews objected, I was compelled to appeal to Caesar; it was not as though I had any accusation against my nation. [20] So, for this reason I've asked to see you and speak to you. In fact, it is for the hope of Israel that I'm wearing this chain."

[21] And they said to him, "We haven't received any letters about you from Judea; none of the brothers has come and reported or spoken anything evil about you. [22] But we consider it suitable to hear from you what you think. For concerning this sect, we are aware that it is spoken against everywhere."

---

[a]**28:4** Gk *Dike*, a goddess of justice   [b]**28:11** Gk *Dioscuri*, twin sons of Zeus   [c]**28:13** Other mss read *From there, casting off*,   [d]**28:14,15** Lit *brothers*   [e]**28:16** Other mss add *the centurion turned the prisoners over to the military commander; but*

Response to Paul's Message

23 After arranging a day with him, many came to him at his lodging. From dawn to dusk he expounded and witnessed about the kingdom of God. He persuaded them concerning Jesus from both the Law of Moses and the Prophets. 24 Some were persuaded by what he said, but others did not believe.

25 Disagreeing among themselves, they began to leave after Paul made one statement: "The Holy Spirit correctly spoke through the prophet Isaiah to your[a] forefathers 26 when He said,

Go to this people
  and say:
'You will listen and listen,
  yet never understand;
and you will look and look,
  yet never perceive.
27 For this people's heart
  has grown callous,
  their ears are hard of hearing,

and they have shut their eyes;
  otherwise
they might see with their eyes
and hear with their ears,
understand with their heart,
and be converted—
and I would heal them.'[b]

28 Therefore, let it be known to you that this saving work of God has been sent to the Gentiles; they will listen!" [29 After he said these things, the Jews departed, while engaging in a prolonged debate among themselves.][c]

Paul's Two-Year Ministry in Rome

30 Then he stayed two whole years in his own rented house. And he welcomed all who visited him, 31 proclaiming the kingdom of God and teaching the things concerning the Lord Jesus Christ with full boldness and without hindrance.

a28:25 Other mss read *our*   b28:26-27 Is 6:9-10   c28:29 Other mss omit bracketed text

ROMANS

God's Good News for Rome

1 Paul, a slave of Christ Jesus, called as an apostle[a] and singled out for God's good news— [2] which He promised long ago through His prophets in the Holy Scriptures— [3] concerning His Son, Jesus Christ our Lord, who was a descendant of David[b] according to the flesh [4] and was established as the powerful Son of God by the resurrection from the dead according to the Spirit of holiness.[c] [5] We have received grace and apostleship through Him to bring about[d] the obedience of faith[e] among all the nations,[f] on behalf of His name, [6] including yourselves who are also Jesus Christ's by calling:

[7] To all who are in Rome, loved by God, called as saints.

Grace to you and peace from God our Father and the Lord Jesus Christ.

Paul's Desire to Visit Rome

[8] First, I thank my God through Jesus Christ for all of you because the news of your faith[g] is being reported in all the world. [9] For God, whom I serve with my spirit in ⌊telling⌋ the good news about His Son, is my witness that I constantly mention you, [10] always asking in my prayers that if it is somehow in God's will, I may now at last succeed in coming to you. [11] For I want very much to see you, that I may impart to you some spiritual gift to strengthen you, [12] that is, to be mutually encouraged by each other's faith, both yours and mine.

[13] Now I want you to know,[h] brothers, that I often planned to come to you (but was prevented until now) in order that I might have a fruitful ministry[i] among you, just as among the rest of the Gentiles. [14] I am obligated both to Greeks and barbarians,[j] both to the wise and the foolish. [15] So I am eager to preach the good news to you also who are in Rome.

Righteous Will Live by Faith

[16] For I am not ashamed of the gospel,[k] because it is God's power for salvation to everyone who believes, first to the Jew, and also to the Greek. [17] For in it God's righteousness is revealed from faith to faith,[l] just as it is written: **The righteous will live by faith.**[m] [n]

Guilt of Gentile World

[18] For God's wrath is revealed from heaven against all godlessness and unrighteousness of people who by their unrighteousness suppress the truth, [19] since what can be known[o] about God is evident among them, because God has shown it to them. [20] From the creation of the world His invisible attributes, that is, His eternal power and divine nature, have been clearly seen, being understood through what He has made. As a result, people[p] are without excuse. [21] For though they knew God, they did not glorify Him as God or show gratitude. Instead, their thinking became nonsense, and their senseless minds[q] were darkened.

---

a**1:1** Or *Jesus, a called apostle* b**1:3** Lit *was of the seed of David* c**1:4** Or *the spirit of holiness,* or *the Holy Spirit*
d**1:5** Lit *Him into,* or *Him for* e**1:5** Or *the obedience that is faith,* or *the faithful obedience,* or *the obedience that comes from faith* f**1:5** Or *Gentiles* g**1:8** Or *because your faith* h**1:13** Lit *I don't want you to be unaware* i**1:13** Lit *have some fruit* j**1:14** Or *non-Greeks* k**1:16** Other mss add *of Christ* l**1:17** Or *revealed out of faith into faith* m**1:17** Or *The one who is righteous by faith will live* n**1:17** Hab 2:4 o**1:19** Or *what is known* p**1:20** Lit *they* q**1:21** Lit *hearts*

Trap of Idolatry

[22] Claiming to be wise, they became fools [23] and exchanged the glory of the immortal God for images resembling mortal man, birds, four-footed animals, and reptiles.

[24] Therefore God delivered them over in the cravings of their hearts to sexual impurity, so that their bodies were degraded among themselves. [25] They exchanged the truth of God for a lie, and worshiped and served something created instead of the Creator, who is blessed forever. •Amen.

From Idolatry to Sexual Depravity

[26] This is why God delivered them over to degrading passions. For even their females exchanged natural sexual intercourse[a] for what is unnatural. [27] The males in the same way also left natural sexual intercourse[a] with females and were inflamed in their lust for one another. Males committed shameless acts with males and received in their own persons[b] the appropriate penalty for their perversion.[c]

Nature of Gentile Evil

[28] And because they did not think it worthwhile to have God in their knowledge, God delivered them over to a worthless mind to do what is morally wrong. [29] They are filled with all unrighteousness,[d] evil, greed, and wickedness. They are full of envy, murder, disputes, deceit, and malice. They are gossips, [30] slanderers, God-haters, arrogant, proud, boastful, inventors of evil, disobedient to parents, [31] undiscerning, untrustworthy, unloving,[e] and unmerciful. [32] Although they know full well God's just sentence—that those who practice such things deserve to die[f]—they not only do them, but even applaud[g] others who practice them.

God's Righteous Judgment

2 Therefore, anyone of you[h] who judges is without excuse. For when you judge another, you condemn yourself, since you, the judge, do the same things. [2] We know that God's judgment on those who do such things is based on the truth. [3] Do you really think—anyone of you who judges those who do such things yet do the same—that you will escape God's judgment? [4] Or do you despise the riches of His kindness, restraint, and patience, not recognizing[i] that God's kindness is intended to lead you to repentance? [5] But because of your hardness and unrepentant heart you are storing up wrath for yourself in the day of wrath, when God's righteous judgment is revealed. [6] He **will repay each one according to his works:**[j] [7] eternal life to those who by patiently doing good seek for glory, honor, and immortality; [8] but wrath and indignation to those who are self-seeking and disobey the truth, but are obeying unrighteousness; [9] affliction and distress for every human being who does evil, first to the Jew, and also to the Greek; [10] but glory, honor, and peace for everyone who does good, first to the Jew, and also to the Greek. [11] There is no favoritism with God.

Gentiles a Law to Themselves

[12] All those who sinned without the law will also perish without the law, and all those who sinned under the law will be judged by the law. [13] For the hearers of the law are not righteous before God, but the doers of the law will be declared

---

[a]**1:26,27** Lit natural use   [b]**1:27** Or in themselves   [c]**1:27** Or error   [d]**1:29** Other mss add sexual immorality   [e]**1:31** Other mss add unforgiving   [f]**1:32** Lit things are worthy of death   [g]**1:32** Lit even take pleasure in   [h]**2:1** Lit Therefore, O man, every one   [i]**2:4** Or patience, because you do not recognize   [j]**2:6** Ps 62:12; Pr 24:12

righteous.[a] [14] So, when Gentiles, who do not have the law, instinctively do what the law demands, they are a law to themselves even though they do not have the law. [15] They show that the work of the law[b] is written on their hearts. Their consciences testify in support of this, and their competing thoughts either accuse or excuse them[c] [16] on the day when God judges what people have kept secret, according to my gospel through Christ Jesus.

Jewish Violation of the Law

[17] Now if[d] you call yourself a Jew, and rest in the law, and boast in God, [18] and know His will, and approve the things that are superior, being instructed from the law, [19] and are convinced that you are a guide for the blind, a light to those in darkness, [20] an instructor of the ignorant, a teacher of the immature, having in the law the full expression[e] of knowledge and truth— [21] you then, who teach another, do you not teach yourself? You who preach, "You must not steal"—do you steal? [22] You who say, "You must not commit adultery"—do you commit adultery? You who detest idols, do you rob their temples? [23] You who boast in the law, do you dishonor God by breaking the law? [24] For, as it is written: **The name of God is blasphemed among the Gentiles because of you.**[f]

Circumcision of the Heart

[25] For circumcision benefits you if you observe the law, but if you are a lawbreaker, your circumcision has become uncircumcision. [26] Therefore if an uncircumcised man keeps the law's requirements, will his uncircumcision not be counted as circumcision? [27] A man who is physically uncircumcised, but who fulfills the law, will judge you who are a lawbreaker in spite of having the letter ⌊of the law⌋ and circumcision. [28] For a person is not a Jew who is one outwardly, and ⌊true⌋ circumcision is not something visible in the flesh. [29] On the contrary, a person is a Jew who is one inwardly, and circumcision is of the heart—by the Spirit, not the letter.[g] His praise[h] is not from men but from God.

Advantage of the Jews

3 So what advantage does the Jew have? Or what is the benefit of circumcision? [2] Considerable in every way. First, they were entrusted with the spoken words of God. [3] What then? If some did not believe, will their unbelief cancel God's faithfulness? [4] Absolutely not! God must be true, but everyone is a liar, as it is written:

> **That You may be justified**
> **in Your words**
> **and triumph when You judge.**[i]

"Is God Unrighteous to Inflict Wrath?"

[5] But if our unrighteousness highlights[j] God's righteousness, what are we to say? I use a human argument:[k] Is God unrighteous to inflict wrath? [6] Absolutely not! Otherwise, how will God judge the world? [7] But if by my lie God's truth is amplified to His glory, why am I also still judged as a sinner? [8] And why not say, just as some people slanderously claim we say, "Let us do evil so that good may come"? Their condemnation is deserved!

---

[a]**2:13** Or *will be justified* or *acquitted*   [b]**2:15** The code of conduct required by the law   [c]**2:15** Internal debate, either in a person or among the pagan moralists   [d]**2:17** Other mss read *Look*—   [e]**2:20** Or *the embodiment*   [f]**2:24** Is 52:5   [g]**2:29** Or *heart—spiritually, not literally*   [h]**2:29** In Hb, the words *Jew, Judah,* and *praise* are related.   [i]**3:4** Ps 51:4   [j]**3:5** Or *shows,* or *demonstrates*   [k]**3:5** Lit *I speak as a man*

Whole World Guilty before God

9 What then? Are we any better?[a] Not
at all! For we have previously charged
that both Jews and Gentiles[b] are all under sin,[c] 10 as it is written:[d]

There is no one righteous,
not even one;
11 **there is no one who understands,**
there is no one who seeks God.
12 **All have turned away,**
together they have become
useless;
there is no one who does good,
there is not even one.[e]
13 **Their throat is an open grave;**
they deceive with their tongues.[f]
Vipers' venom is
under their lips.[g]
14 **Their mouth is full of cursing**
and bitterness.[h]
15 **Their feet are swift**
to shed blood;
16 **ruin and wretchedness are**
in their paths,
17 **and the path of peace**
they have not known.[i]
18 **There is no fear of God**
before their eyes.[j]

No One Justified by Law

19 Now we know that whatever the
law says speaks to those who are subject
to the law,[k] so that every mouth may be
shut and the whole world may become
subject to God's judgment.[l] 20 For no
flesh will be justified[m] in His sight by the
works of the law, for through the law
⌊comes⌋ the knowledge of sin.

Justified by His Grace—through Faith

21 But now, apart from the law, God's
righteousness has been revealed—at-
tested by the Law and the Prophets[n] 22—
that is, God's righteousness through faith
in Jesus Christ,[o] to all who believe, since
there is no distinction. 23 For all have
sinned and fall short of the[p] glory of God.
24 They are justified freely by His grace
through the redemption that is in Christ
Jesus. 25 God presented Him as a propitiation[q] through faith in His blood, to demonstrate His righteousness, because in
His restraint God passed over the sins
previously committed. 26 He presented
Him to demonstrate His righteousness at
the present time, so that He would be
righteous and declare righteous[r] the one
who has faith in Jesus.

Human Boasting Excluded—by Law of Faith

27 Where then is boasting? It is excluded. By what kind of law?[s] By one of
works? No, on the contrary, by a law[t] of
faith. 28 For we conclude that a man is
justified by faith apart from works of law.
29 Or is God for Jews only? Is He not also
for Gentiles? Yes, for Gentiles too,
30 since there is one God who will justify
the circumcised by faith and the uncircumcised through faith. 31 Do we then
cancel the law through faith? Absolutely
not! On the contrary, we uphold the law.

Abraham Justified by Faith

4 What then can we say that Abraham, our forefather according to the

[a] **3:9** Are we Jews any better than the Gentiles? [b] **3:9** Lit *Greeks* [c] **3:9** Under sin's power or dominion [d] **3:10** Paul constructs this charge from a chain of OT quotations, mainly from the Psalms. [e] **3:10-12** Ps 14:1-3; 53:1-3; see Ec 7:20 [f] **3:13** Ps 5:9 [g] **3:13** Ps 140:3 [h] **3:14** Ps 10:7 [i] **3:15-17** Is 59:7-8 [j] **3:18** Ps 36:1 [k] **3:19** Lit *those in the law* [l] **3:19** Or *become guilty before God*, or *may be accountable to God* [m] **3:20** Or *will be declared righteous*, or *will be acquitted* [n] **3:21** When capitalized, *the Law and the Prophets* = OT [o] **3:22** Or *through the faithfulness of Jesus Christ* [p] **3:23** Or *and lack the* [q] **3:25** Or *as a propitiatory sacrifice*, or *as an offering of atonement*, or *as a mercy seat*; see Heb 9:5. The word *propitiation* has to do with the removal of divine wrath. Jesus' death is the means that turns God's wrath from the sinner; see 2 Co 5:21. [r] **3:26** Or *and justify*, or *and acquit* [s] **3:27** Or *what principle?* [t] **3:27** Or *a principle*

flesh, has found? [2] If Abraham was justified[a] by works, then he has something to brag about—but not before God.[b] [3] For what does the Scripture say?

> Abraham believed God,
> and it was credited to him
> for righteousness.[c]

[4] Now to the one who works, pay is not considered as a gift, but as something owed. [5] But to the one who does not work, but believes on Him who declares righteous[d] the ungodly, his faith is credited for righteousness.

David Celebrated Righteousness apart from Works

[6] Likewise, David also speaks of the blessing of the man to whom God credits righteousness apart from works:

> [7] How happy those whose lawless
>   acts are forgiven
>   and whose sins are covered!
> [8] How happy the man whom
>   the Lord will never charge
>   with sin![e]

God Justified Abraham before Circumcision

[9] Is this blessing only for the circumcised, then? Or is it also for the uncircumcised? For we say, **Faith was credited to Abraham for righteousness.**[c] [10] How then was it credited—while he was circumcised, or uncircumcised? Not while he was circumcised, but uncircumcised. [11] And he received the sign of circumcision as a seal of the righteousness that he had by faith[f] while still uncircumcised. This was to make him the father of all who believe but are not circumcised, so that righteousness may be credited to them also. [12] And he became the father of the circumcised, not only to those who are circumcised, but also to those who follow in the footsteps of the faith our father Abraham had while still uncircumcised.

God's Promise to Abraham Granted through Faith

[13] For the promise to Abraham or to his descendants that he would inherit the world was not through the law, but through the righteousness that comes by faith.[f] [14] If those who are of the law are heirs, faith is made empty and the promise is canceled. [15] For the law produces wrath; but where there is no law, there is no transgression.

[16] This is why the promise is by faith, so that it may be according to grace, to guarantee it to all the descendants—not only to those who are of the law,[g] but also to those who are of Abraham's faith. He is the father of us all [17] in God's sight. As it is written: **I have made you the father of many nations.**[h] He believed in God, who gives life to the dead and calls things into existence that do not exist. [18] Against hope, with hope he believed, so that he became **the father of many nations,**[h] according to what had been spoken: **So will your descendants be.**[i] [19] He considered[j] his own body to be already dead (since he was about a hundred years old), and the deadness of Sarah's womb, without weakening in the faith. [20] He did not waver in unbelief at God's promise, but was strengthened in his faith and gave glory to God, [21] because he was fully convinced that what He had promised He was also able to perform. [22] Therefore, **it was credited to him for**

---

[a]**4:2** Or *was declared righteous,* or *was acquitted*   [b]**4:2** He has no reason for boasting in God's presence   [c]**4:3,9** Gn 15:6   [d]**4:5** Or *who acquits,* or *who justifies*   [e]**4:7-8** Ps 32:1-2   [f]**4:11,13** Lit *righteousness of faith*   [g]**4:16** Or *not to those who are of the law only*   [h]**4:17,18** Gn 17:5   [i]**4:18** Gn 15:5   [j]**4:19** Other mss read *He did not consider*

righteousness.ª ²³ Now it was credited to him was not written for Abraham alone, ²⁴ but also for us. It will be credited to us who believe in Him who raised Jesus our Lord from the dead. ²⁵ He was delivered up for ᵇ our trespasses and raised for ᵇ our justification.ᶜ

Wonderful Results of Faith

5 Therefore, since we have been declared righteous by faith, we have peaceᵈ with God through our Lord Jesus Christ. ² Also through Him, we have obtained access by faithᵉ into this grace in which we stand, and we rejoice in the hope of the glory of God. ³ And not only that, but we also rejoice in our afflictions, because we know that affliction produces endurance, ⁴ endurance produces proven character, and proven character produces hope. ⁵ This hope does not disappoint, because God's love has been poured out in our hearts through the Holy Spirit who was given to us.

Those Declared Righteous Are Reconciled and Saved

⁶ For while we were still helpless, at the appointed moment, Christ died for the ungodly. ⁷ For rarely will someone die for a just person—though for a good person perhaps someone might even dare to die. ⁸ But God proves His own love for us in that while we were still sinners Christ died for us! ⁹ Much more then, since we have now been declared righteous by His blood, we will be saved through Him from wrath. ¹⁰ For if, while we were enemies, we were reconciled to God through the death of His Son, ⌊then how⌋ much more, having been reconciled, will we be saved by His life!

¹¹ And not only that, but we also rejoice in God through our Lord Jesus Christ, through whom we have now received reconciliation.

Death through Adam and Life through Christ

¹² Therefore, just as sin entered the world through one man, and death through sin, in this way death spread to all men, because all sinned.ᶠ ¹³ In fact, sin was in the world before the law, but sin is not charged to one's account when there is no law. ¹⁴ Nevertheless, death reigned from Adam to Moses, even over those who did not sin in the likeness of Adam's transgression. He is a prototype of the Coming One.

¹⁵ But the gift is not like the trespass. For if by the one man's trespass the many died, how much more have the grace of God and the gift overflowed to the many by the grace of the one man, Jesus Christ. ¹⁶ And the gift is not like the one man's sin, because from one sin came the judgment, resulting in condemnation, but from many trespasses came the gift, resulting in justification.ᶜ ¹⁷ Since by the one man's trespass, death reigned through that one man, how much more will those who receive the overflow of grace and the gift of righteousness reign in life through the one man, Jesus Christ.

¹⁸ So then, as through one trespass there is condemnation for everyone, so also through one righteous act there is life-giving justificationᵍ for everyone. ¹⁹ For just as through one man's disobedience the many were made sinners, so also through the one man's obedience the many will be made righteous. ²⁰ The law came along to multiply the trespass.

ª**4:22** Gn 15:6   ᵇ**4:25** Or *because of*   ᶜ**4:25; 5:16**Or *acquittal*   ᵈ**5:1** Other mss read *faith, let us have peace,* which can also be translated *faith, let us grasp the fact that we have peace*   ᵉ**5:2** Other mss omit *by faith*   ᶠ**5:12** Or *have sinned*   ᵍ**5:18** Lit *is justification of life*

But where sin multiplied, grace multiplied even more, [21] so that, just as sin reigned in death, so also grace will reign through righteousness, resulting in eternal life through Jesus Christ our Lord.

New Life in Christ

6 What should we say then? Should we continue in sin in order that grace may multiply? [2] Absolutely not! How can we who died to sin still live in it? [3] Or are you unaware that all of us who were baptized into Christ Jesus were baptized into His death? [4] Therefore we were buried with Him by baptism into death, in order that, just as Christ was raised from the dead by the glory of the Father, so we too may •walk in a new way[a] of life. [5] For if we have been joined with Him in the likeness of His death, we will certainly also be[b] in the likeness of His resurrection. [6] For we know that our old self[c] was crucified with Him in order that sin's dominion over the body[d] may be abolished, so that we may no longer be enslaved to sin, [7] since a person who has died is freed[e] from sin's claims.[f] [8] Now if we died with Christ, we believe that we will also live with Him, [9] because we know that Christ, having been raised from the dead, no longer dies. Death no longer rules over Him. [10] For in that He died, He died to sin once for all; but in that He lives, He lives to God. [11] So, you too consider yourselves dead to sin, but alive to God in Christ Jesus.[g]

Offer All Parts of Yourself to God

[12] Therefore do not let sin reign in your mortal body, so that you obey[h] its desires. [13] And do not offer any parts[i] of it to sin as weapons for unrighteousness.

But as those who are alive from the dead, offer yourselves to God, and all the parts[i] of yourselves to God as weapons for righteousness. [14] For sin will not rule over you, because you are not under law but under grace.

From Slaves of Sin to Slaves of God

[15] What then? Should we sin because we are not under law but under grace? Absolutely not! [16] Do you not know that if you offer yourselves to someone[j] as obedient slaves, you are slaves of that one you obey—either of sin leading to death or of obedience leading to righteousness? [17] But thank God that, although you used to be slaves of sin, you obeyed from the heart that pattern of teaching you were entrusted to, [18] and having been liberated from sin, you became enslaved to righteousness. [19] I am using a human analogy[k] because of the weakness of your flesh.[l] For just as you offered the parts[i] of yourselves as slaves to moral impurity, and to greater and greater lawlessness, so now offer them as slaves to righteousness, which results in sanctification.

The Path to Sanctification (Holiness)

[20] For when you were slaves of sin, you were free from allegiance to righteousness.[m] [21] And what fruit was produced[n] then from the things you are now ashamed of? For the end of those things is death. [22] But now, since you have been liberated from sin and become enslaved to God, you have your fruit, which results in sanctification[o]—and the end is eternal life! [23] For the wages of sin is death, but the gift of God is eternal life in Christ Jesus our Lord.

---

[a]6:4 Or in newness   [b]6:5 Be joined with Him   [c]6:6 Lit man; that is, the person that one was in Adam   [d]6:6 Lit that the body of sin   [e]6:7 Lit acquitted, or justified   [f]6:7 Lit from sin   [g]6:11 Other mss add our Lord   [h]6:12 Other mss add sin (lit it) in   [i]6:13,19 Or members   [j]6:16 Lit that to whom you offer yourselves   [k]6:19 Lit I speak humanly; Paul is personifying sin and righteousness as slave masters.   [l]6:19 Or your human nature   [m]6:20 Lit free to righteousness   [n]6:21 Lit what fruit do you have   [o]6:22 Or holiness

Illustration from Marriage

7 Since I am speaking to those who understand law, brothers, are you unaware that the law has authority over someone as long as he lives? [2] For example, a married woman is legally bound to her husband while he lives. But if her husband dies, she is released from the law regarding the husband. [3] So then, if she gives herself to another man while her husband is living, she will be called an adulteress. But if her husband dies, she is free from that law. Then, if she gives herself to another man, she is not an adulteress.

[4] Therefore, my brothers, you also were put to death in relation to the law through the ⌊crucified⌋ body of the •Messiah, so that you may belong to another—to Him who was raised from the dead—that we may bear fruit for God. [5] For when we were in the flesh,[a] the sinful passions operated through the law in every part of us[b] and bore fruit for death. [6] But now we have been released from the law, since we have died to what held us, so that we may serve in the new way[c] of the Spirit and not in the old letter of the law.

Sin Springs to Life in the Law

[7] What should we say then? Is the law sin? Absolutely not! On the contrary, I would not have known sin if it were not for the law. For example, I would not have known what it is to covet if the law had not said, **Do not covet.**[d] [8] And sin, seizing an opportunity through the commandment, produced in me coveting of every kind. For apart from the law sin is dead. [9] Once I was alive apart from the law, but when the commandment came, sin sprang to life [10] and I died. The commandment that was meant for life resulted in death for me. [11] For sin, seizing an opportunity through the commandment, deceived me, and through it killed me. [12] So then, the law is holy, and the commandment is holy and just and good.

Paul's Dilemma with Sin

[13] Therefore, did what is good cause my death?[e] Absolutely not! On the contrary, sin, in order to be recognized as sin, was producing death in me through what is good, so that through the commandment sin might become sinful beyond measure. [14] For we know that the law is spiritual; but I am made out of flesh,[f] sold into sin's power. [15] For I do not understand what I am doing, because I do not practice what I want to do, but I do what I hate. [16] And if I do what I do not want to do, I agree with the law that it is good. [17] So now I am no longer the one doing it, but it is sin living in me. [18] For I know that nothing good lives in me, that is, in my flesh. For the desire to do what is good is with me, but there is no ability to do it. [19] For I do not do the good that I want to do, but I practice the evil that I do not want to do. [20] Now if I do what I do not want, I am no longer the one doing it, but it is the sin that lives in me. [21] So I discover this principle:[g] when I want to do good, evil is with me. [22] For in my inner self[h] I joyfully agree with God's law. [23] But I see a different law in the parts of my body,[i] waging war against the law of my mind and taking me prisoner to the law of sin in the parts of my body.[i] [24] What a wretched man I am! Who will rescue me from this body of death? [25] I thank God through Jesus Christ our Lord![j] So then, with my mind I myself am a slave to the law of God, but with my flesh, to the law of sin.

[a]**7:5** *in the flesh* = a person's life before accepting Christ [b]**7:5** Lit *of our members* [c]**7:6** Lit *in newness* [d]**7:7** Ex 20:17 [e]**7:13** Lit *good become death to me?* [f]**7:14** Other mss read *I am carnal* [g]**7:21** Or *law* [h]**7:22** Lit *inner man* [i]**7:23** Lit *my members* [j]**7:25** Or *Thanks be to God—(it is done) through Jesus Christ our Lord!*

Answer to the Dilemma: Christ and God's Life-Giving Spirit

8 Therefore, no condemnation now exists for those in Christ Jesus,[a] [2] because the Spirit's law of life in Christ Jesus has set you[b] free from the law of sin and of death. [3] What the law could not do since it was limited[c] by the flesh, God did. He condemned sin in the flesh by sending His own Son in flesh like ours under sin's domain,[d] and as a sin offering, [4] in order that the law's requirement would be accomplished in us who do not •walk according to the flesh but according to the Spirit. [5] For those whose lives are[e] according to the flesh think about the things of the flesh, but those whose lives are[e] according to the Spirit, about the things of the Spirit. [6] For the mind-set of the flesh is death, but the mind-set of the Spirit is life and peace. [7] For the mind-set of the flesh is hostile to God because it does not submit itself to God's law, for it is unable to do so. [8] Those whose lives are[f] in the flesh are unable to please God. [9] You, however, are not in the flesh, but in the Spirit, since[g] the Spirit of God lives in you. But if anyone does not have the Spirit of Christ, he does not belong to Him. [10] Now if Christ is in you, the body is dead[h] because of sin, but the Spirit[i] is life because of righteousness. [11] And if the Spirit of Him who raised Jesus from the dead lives in you, then He who raised Christ from the dead will also bring your mortal bodies to life through[j] His Spirit who lives in you.

Holy Spirit's Ministries

[12] So then, brothers, we are not obligated to the flesh to live according to the flesh, [13] for if you live according to the flesh, you are going to die. But if by the Spirit you put to death the deeds of the body, you will live. [14] All those led by God's Spirit are God's sons. [15] For you did not receive a spirit of slavery to fall back into fear, but you received the Spirit of adoption, by whom we cry out, "•Abba, Father!" [16] The Spirit Himself testifies together with our spirit that we are God's children, [17] and if children, also heirs—heirs of God and co-heirs with Christ—seeing that[g] we suffer with Him so that we may also be glorified with Him.

The Creation Groans

[18] For I consider that the sufferings of this present time are not worth comparing with the glory that is going to be revealed to us. [19] For the creation eagerly waits with anticipation for God's sons to be revealed. [20] For the creation was subjected to futility—not willingly, but because of Him who subjected it—in the hope [21] that the creation itself will also be set free from the bondage of corruption into the glorious freedom of God's children. [22] For we know that the whole creation has been groaning together with labor pains until now. [23] And not only that, but we ourselves who have the Spirit as the •firstfruits—we also groan within ourselves, eagerly waiting for adoption, the redemption of our bodies. [24] Now in this hope we were saved, yet hope that is seen is not hope, because who hopes for what he sees? [25] But if we hope for what we do not see, we eagerly wait for it with patience.

Spirit's Unspoken Groanings

[26] In the same way the Spirit also joins to help in our weakness, because we do

not know what to pray for as we should, but the Spirit Himself intercedes for us[a] with unspoken groanings. ²⁷ And He who searches the hearts knows the Spirit's mind-set, because He intercedes for the saints according to the will of God.

All Things Word Together for the Good

²⁸ We know that all things work together[b] for the good[c] of those who love God: those who are called according to His purpose. ²⁹ For those He foreknew[d] He also predestined to be conformed to the image of His Son, so that He would be the firstborn among many brothers. ³⁰ And those He predestined, He also called; and those He called, He also justified; and those He justified, He also glorified.

Believers' Triumph

31 What then are we to say
      about these things?
    If God is for us, who is against us?
32 He did not even spare His own Son,
      but offered Him up for us all;
    how will He not also with Him
      grant us everything?
33 Who can bring an accusation
      against God's elect?
    God is the One who justifies.
34 Who is the one who condemns?
    Christ Jesus is the One who died,
      but even more, has been raised;
    He also is at the right hand of God
      and intercedes for us.
35 Who can separate us
      from the love of Christ?
    Can affliction or anguish
      or persecution

or famine or nakedness or danger
      or sword?
36 As it is written:
    Because of You we are being
      put to death all day long;
    we are counted as sheep
      to be slaughtered.[e]
37 No, in all these things we are
      more than victorious
    through Him who loved us.
38 For I am persuaded that
      neither death nor life,
    nor angels nor rulers,
    nor things present,
      nor things to come, nor powers,
39 nor height, nor depth, nor
      any other created thing
    will have the power to separate us
    from the love of God that is
    in Christ Jesus our Lord!

Paul's Sorrow at Israel's Rejection of Christ

9 I speak the truth in Christ—I am not lying; my conscience is testifying to me with the Holy Spirit[f]— ² that I have intense sorrow and continual anguish in my heart. ³ For I could wish that I myself were cursed and cut off[g] from the •Messiah for the benefit of my brothers, my countrymen by physical descent.[h] ⁴ They are Israelites, and to them belong the adoption, the glory, the covenants, the giving of the law, the temple service, and the promises. ⁵ The forefathers are theirs, and from them, by physical descent,[i] came the Messiah, who is God over all, blessed forever.[j] •Amen.

True Israel: Children of Promise

⁶ But it is not as though the word of God has failed. For not all who are descended

^a**8:26** Some mss omit *for us*   ^b**8:28** Other mss read *that God works together in all things*   ^c**8:28** The ultimate good   ^d**8:29** From eternity God knew His people and entered into a personal relationship with them   ^e**8:36** Ps 44:22; see Is 53:7; Zch 11:4,7   ^f**9:1** Or *testifying with me by the Holy Spirit*   ^g**9:3** Lit *were anathema*   ^h**9:3** Lit *countrymen according to the flesh*   ⁱ**9:5** Lit *them, according to the flesh*   ^j**9:5** Or *the Messiah, the One who is over all, the God who is blessed forever,* or *Messiah. God, who is over all, be blessed forever*

from Israel are Israel. [7] Neither are they all children because they are Abraham's descendants.[a] On the contrary, **in Isaac your seed will be called.**[b] [8] That is, it is not the children by physical descent[c] who are God's children, but the children of the promise are considered seed. [9] For this is the statement of the promise: **At this time I will come, and Sarah will have a son.**[d] [10] And not only that, but also when Rebekah became pregnant[e] by Isaac our forefather [11] (for though they had not been born yet or done anything good or bad, so that God's purpose according to election might stand, [12] not from works but from the One who calls) she was told: **The older will serve the younger.**[f] [13] As it is written: **Jacob I have loved, but Esau I have hated.**[g]

God's Sovereign Selection Is Just

[14] What should we say then? Is there injustice with God? Absolutely not! [15] For He tells Moses:

> I will show mercy to whom
> I show mercy,
> and I will have compassion
> on whom I have compassion.[h]

Operation of God's Mercy

[16] So then it does not depend on human will or effort,[i] but on God who shows mercy. [17] For the Scripture tells Pharaoh:

> For this reason I raised you up:
> so that I may display
> My power in you,
> and that My name
> may be proclaimed
> in all the earth.[j]

[18] So then, He shows mercy to whom He wills, and He hardens whom He wills.

[19] You will say to me, therefore, "Why then does He still find fault? For who can resist His will?" [20] But who are you—anyone[k] who talks back to God? Will what is formed say to the one who formed it, "Why did you make me like this?" [21] Or has the potter no right over His clay, to make from the same lump one piece of pottery for honor and another for dishonor? [22] And what if God, desiring to display His wrath and to make His power known, endured with much patience objects of wrath ready for destruction? [23] And ⌊what if⌋ He did this to make known the riches of His glory on objects of mercy that He prepared beforehand for glory— [24] on us whom He also called, not only from the Jews but also from the Gentiles? [25] As He also says in Hosea:

> I will call "Not-My-People,"
> "My-People,"
> and she who is "Unloved,"
> "Beloved."[l]

> [26] And it will be in the place where
>   they were told,
>   you are not My people,
>   there they will be called
>   sons of the living God.[m]

[27] But Isaiah cries out concerning Israel:

> Though the number
>   of Israel's sons is like
>   the sand of the sea,
>   only the remnant will be saved;
> [28] for the Lord will execute
>   His sentence
>   completely and decisively
>   on the earth.[n] [o]

[29] And just as Isaiah predicted:

> If the Lord of Hosts[p] had not left
>   us a seed,

---

[a]**9:7** Lit seed   [b]**9:7** Gn 21:12   [c]**9:8** Lit *children of the flesh*   [d]**9:9** Gn 18:10,14   [e]**9:10** Or *Rebekah conceived by the one act of sexual intercourse*   [f]**9:12** Gn 25:23   [g]**9:13** Mal 1:2-3   [h]**9:15** Ex 33:19   [i]**9:16** Lit *on the one willing*, or *on the one running*   [j]**9:17** Ex 9:16   [k]**9:20** Lit *you, O man*   [l]**9:25** Hs 2:23   [m]**9:26** Hs 1:10   [n]**9:28** Or *land*   [o]**9:27-28** Is 10:22-23; 28:22; Hs 1:10   [p]**9:29** Gk *Sabaoth*; this word is a transliteration of the Hb word for *Hosts*, or *Armies*.

we would have become
like Sodom,
and we would have been made
like Gomorrah.[a]

Israel's Present Lack of Faith

30 What should we say then? Gentiles, who did not pursue righteousness, have obtained righteousness—namely the righteousness that comes from faith. 31 But Israel, pursuing the law for righteousness, has not achieved the law.[b] 32 Why is that? Because they did not pursue it by faith, but as if it were by works.[c] They stumbled over the stumbling stone. 33 As it is written:

Look! I am putting a stone in Zion
to stumble over,
and a rock to trip over,
yet the one who believes on Him
will not be put to shame.[d]

God's Righteousness by Belief in Christ

10 Brothers, my heart's desire and prayer to God concerning them[e] is for their salvation! 2 I can testify about them that they have zeal for God, but not according to knowledge. 3 Because they disregarded the righteousness from God and attempted to establish their own righteousness, they have not submitted to God's righteousness. 4 For Christ is the end[f] of the law for righteousness to everyone who believes. 5 For Moses writes about the righteousness that is from the law: **The one who does these things will live by them.**[g] 6 But the righteousness that comes from faith speaks like this: **Do not say in your heart, "Who will go up to heaven?"**[h] that is, to bring Christ down 7 or, **"Who will go down into the •abyss?"**[i] that is, to bring Christ up from the dead. 8 On the contrary, what does it say? **The message is near you, in your mouth and in your heart.**[j] This is the message of faith that we proclaim: 9 if you confess with your mouth, "Jesus is Lord," and believe in your heart that God raised Him from the dead, you will be saved. 10 With the heart one believes, resulting in righteousness, and with the mouth one confesses, resulting in salvation. 11 Now the Scripture says, **No one who believes on Him will be put to shame,**[k] 12 for there is no distinction between Jew and Greek, since the same Lord of all is rich to all who call on Him. 13 For **everyone who calls on the name of the Lord will be saved.**[l]

Israel's Rejection of the Message

14 But how can they call on Him in whom they have not believed? And how can they believe without hearing about Him? And how can they hear without a preacher? 15 And how can they preach unless they are sent? As it is written: **How welcome**[m] **are the feet of those**[n] **who announce the gospel of good things!**[o] 16 But all did not obey the gospel. For Isaiah says, **Lord, who has believed our message?**[p] 17 So faith comes from what is heard, and what is heard comes through the message about Christ.[q] 18 But I ask, "Did they not hear?" Yes, they did:

Their voice has gone out
to all the earth,
and their words to the ends
of the inhabited world.[r]

[a] **9:29** Is 1:9 [b] **9:31** Other mss read *the law for righteousness* [c] **9:32** Other mss add *of the law* [d] **9:33** Is 8:14; 28:16 [e] **10:1** Other mss read *God for Israel* [f] **10:4** Or *goal* [g] **10:5** Lv 18:5 [h] **10:6** Dt 9:4; 30:12 [i] **10:7** Dt 30:13 [j] **10:8** Dt 30:14 [k] **10:11** Is 28:16 [l] **10:13** Jl 2:32 [m] **10:15** Or *timely*, or *beautiful* [n] **10:15** Other mss read *feet of those who announce the gospel of peace, of those* [o] **10:15** Is 52:7; Nah 1:15 [p] **10:16** Is 53:1 [q] **10:17** Other mss read *God* [r] **10:18** Ps 19:4

[19] But I ask, "Did Israel not understand?" First, Moses said:

> I will make you jealous of those
>   who are not a nation;
> I will make you angry by a nation
>   that lacks understanding.[a]

[20] And Isaiah says boldly:

> I was found by those
>   who were not looking for Me;
> I revealed Myself to those
>   who were not asking for Me.[b]

[21] But to Israel he says: **All day long I have spread out My hands to a disobedient and defiant people.**[c]

God Has Not Rejected His People!

11 I ask, then, has God rejected His people? Absolutely not! For I too am an Israelite, a descendant of Abraham, from the tribe of Benjamin. [2] God has not rejected His people whom He foreknew. Or do you not know what the Scripture says in the Elijah section— how he pleads with God against Israel?

> [3] **Lord, they have killed**
> **Your prophets, torn down**
> **Your altars;**
> **and I am the only one left,**
> **and they are trying to take**
> **my life!**[d]

The Remnant Chosen by Grace

[4] But what was God's reply to him? **I have left 7,000 men for Myself who have not bowed down to Baal.**[e] [5] In the same way, then, there is also at the present time a remnant chosen by grace. [6] Now if by grace, then it is not by works; otherwise grace ceases to be grace.[f]

[7] What then? Israel did not find what it was looking for, but the elect did find it. The rest were hardened, [8] as it is written:

> God gave them a spirit of stupor,
>   eyes that cannot see and ears
>   that cannot hear, to this day.[g]

[9] And David says:

> Let their feasting[h] become a snare
>   and a trap,
>   a pitfall and a retribution to them.
> [10] Let their eyes be darkened
>   so they cannot see,
> and their backs be bent
>   continually.[i]

Israel's Stumbling Helps Gentiles

[11] I ask, then, have they stumbled so as to fall? Absolutely not! On the contrary, by their stumbling,[j] salvation has come to the Gentiles to make Israel[k] jealous. [12] Now if their stumbling[j] brings riches for the world, and their failure riches for the Gentiles, how much more will their full number bring!

Israel's Jealousy Leads to Salvation

[13] Now I am speaking to you Gentiles. In view of the fact that I am an apostle to the Gentiles, I magnify my ministry, [14] if I can somehow make my own people[l] jealous and save some of them. [15] For if their being rejected is world reconciliation, what will their acceptance mean but life from the dead? [16] Now if the •firstfruits offered up are holy, so is the whole batch. And if the root is holy, so are the branches.

Root and Branches

[17] Now if some of the branches were broken off, and you, though a wild olive branch, were grafted in among them, and have come to share in the rich

root[a] of the cultivated olive tree, [18] do not brag that you are better than those branches. But if you do brag—you do not sustain the root, but the root sustains you. [19] Then you will say, "Branches were broken off so that I might be grafted in." [20] True enough; they were broken off by unbelief, but you stand by faith. Do not be arrogant, but be afraid. [21] For if God did not spare the natural branches, He will not spare you either. [22] Therefore, consider God's kindness and severity: severity toward those who have fallen, but God's kindness toward you—if you remain in His kindness. Otherwise you too will be cut off. [23] And even they, if they do not remain in unbelief, will be grafted in, because God has the power to graft them in again. [24] For if you were cut off from your native wild olive, and against nature were grafted into a cultivated olive tree, how much more will these—the natural branches—be grafted into their own olive tree?

Secret of Israel's Salvation

[25] So that you will not be conceited, brothers, I do not want you to be unaware of this •mystery: a partial hardening has come to Israel until the full number of the Gentiles has come in. [26] And in this way all[b] Israel will be saved, as it is written:

The Liberator will come
from Zion;
He will turn away godlessness
from Jacob.
[27] And this will be My covenant
with them,[c]
when I take away their sins.[d]

[28] Regarding the gospel, they are enemies for your advantage, but regarding

election, they are loved because of their forefathers, [29] since God's gracious gifts and calling are irrevocable.[e] [30] As you once disobeyed God, but now have received mercy through their disobedience, [31] so they too have now disobeyed, ⌊resulting⌋ in mercy to you, so that they also now[f] may receive mercy. [32] For God has imprisoned all in disobedience, so that He may have mercy on all.

Paul's Hymn of Praise

[33] Oh, the depth of the riches
both of the wisdom
and the knowledge of God!
How unsearchable His judgments
and untraceable His ways!
[34] **For who has known the mind**
of the Lord?
Or who has been His counselor?
[35] **Or who has ever first given**
to Him,
and has to be repaid?[g]
[36] For from Him and through Him
and to Him are all things.
To Him be the glory forever.
•Amen.

Your Bodies a Living Sacrifice

12 Therefore, brothers, by the mercies of God, I urge you to present your bodies as a living sacrifice, holy and pleasing to God; this is your spiritual worship.[h] [2] Do not be conformed to this age, but be transformed by the renewing of your mind, so that you may discern what is the good, pleasing, and perfect will of God.

Many Spiritual Gifts but One Body

[3] For by the grace given to me, I tell everyone among you not to think of himself more highly than he should think.

a**11:17** Other mss read *the root and the richness*   b**11:26** Or *And then all*   c**11:26-27** Is 59:20-21
d**11:27** Jr 31:31-34   e**11:29** Or *are not taken back*   f**11:31** Other mss omit *now*   g**11:34-35** Is 40:13; Jb 41:11;
Jr 23:18   h**12:1** Or *your reasonable service*

Instead, think sensibly, as <u>God has distributed a measure of faith to each one</u>. [4] Now as we have many parts in one body, and all the parts do not have the same function, [5] in the same way we who are many are one body in Christ and individually members of one another. [6] According to the grace given to us, we have different gifts:

If <u>prophecy</u>, use it according to the standard of faith;
[7] if <u>service</u>, in service; if <u>teaching</u>, in teaching;
[8] if <u>exhorting</u>, in exhortation; giving, with generosity;
<u>leading</u>, with diligence;
<u>showing mercy</u>,
with cheerfulness.

Christian Ethics

[9] Love must be without hypocrisy. Detest evil; cling to what is good. [10] Show family affection to one another with brotherly love. Outdo one another in showing honor. [11] Do not lack diligence; be fervent in spirit; serve the Lord. [12] Rejoice in hope; be patient in affliction; be persistent in prayer. [13] Share with the saints in their needs; pursue hospitality. [14] Bless those who persecute you; bless and do not curse. [15] Rejoice with those who rejoice; weep with those who weep. [16] Be in agreement with one another. Do not be proud; instead, associate with the humble. Do not be wise in your own estimation. [17] Do not repay anyone evil for evil. Try to do what is honorable in everyone's eyes. [18] If possible, on your part, live at peace with everyone. [19] Friends, do not avenge yourselves; instead, leave room for His[a] wrath. For it is written: **Vengeance be-**

longs to Me; I will repay,[b] says the Lord. [20] But

> **If your enemy is hungry, feed him.**
> **If he is thirsty, give him something to drink.**
> **For in so doing you will be heaping fiery coals on his head.**[c]

[21] Do not be conquered by evil, but conquer evil with good.

Christian's Duties to the State

13 Everyone must submit to the governing authorities, for there is no authority except from God, and those that exist are instituted by God. [2] So then, the one who resists the authority is opposing God's command, and those who oppose it will bring judgment on themselves. [3] For rulers are not a terror to good conduct, but to bad. Do you want to be unafraid of the authority? Do good and you will have its approval. [4] For government is God's servant to you for good. But if you do wrong, be afraid, because it does not carry the sword for no reason. For government is God's servant, an avenger that brings wrath on the one who does wrong. [5] Therefore, you must submit, not only because of wrath, but also because of your conscience. [6] And for this reason you pay taxes, since the ⌊authorities⌋ are God's public servants, continually attending to these tasks.[d] [7] Pay your obligations to everyone: taxes to those you owe taxes, tolls to those you owe tolls, respect to those you owe respect, and honor to those you owe honor.

Love Our Primary Duty

[8] Do not owe anyone anything,[e] except to love one another, for the one who

loves another has fulfilled the law. ⁹ The commandments:

> **Do not commit adultery,**
> **do not murder,**
> **do not steal,**ᵃ
> **do not covet,**ᵇ

and if there is any other commandment—all are summed up by this: **Love your neighbor as yourself.**ᶜ

¹⁰ Love does no wrong to a neighbor. Love, therefore, is the fulfillment of the law.

Put On Christ

¹¹ Besides this, knowing the time, it is already the hour for youᵈ to wake up from sleep, for now our salvation is nearer than when we first believed. ¹² The night is nearly over, and the daylight is near, so let us discard the deeds of darkness and put on the armor of light. ¹³ Let us •walk with decency, as in the daylight: not in carousing and drunkenness; not in sexual impurity and promiscuity; not in quarreling and jealousy. ¹⁴ But put on the Lord Jesus Christ, and make no plans to satisfy the fleshly desires.

Law of Liberty

14 Accept anyone who is weak in faith,ᵉ but don't argue about doubtful issues. ² One person believes he may eat anything, but one who is weak eats only vegetables. ³ One who eats must not look down on one who does not eat; and one who does not eat must not criticize one who does, because God has accepted him. ⁴ Who are you to criticize another's household slave? Before his own Lord he stands or falls. And stand he will! For the Lord is ableᶠ to make him stand.

⁵ One person considers one day to be above another day. Someone else considers every day to be the same. Each one must be fully convinced in his own mind. ⁶ Whoever observes the day, observes it to the Lord.ᵍ Whoever eats, eats to the Lord, since he gives thanks to God; and whoever does not eat, it is to the Lord that he does not eat, yet he thanks God. ⁷ For none of us lives to himself, and no one dies to himself. ⁸ If we live, we live to the Lord; and if we die, we die to the Lord. Therefore, whether we live or die, we belong to the Lord. ⁹ Christ died and came to life for this: that He might rule over both the dead and the living. ¹⁰ But you, why do you criticize your brother? Or you, why do you look down on your brother? For we will all stand before the judgment seat of God.ʰ ¹¹ For it is written:

> **As I live, says the Lord,**
> **every knee will bow to Me,**
> **and every tongue will give praise to God.**ⁱ

¹² So then, each of us will give an account of himself to God.

Law of Love

¹³ Therefore, let us no longer criticize one another, but instead decide not to put a stumbling block or pitfall in your brother's way. ¹⁴ (I know and am persuaded by the Lord Jesus that nothing is unclean in itself. Still, to someone who considers a thing to be unclean, to that one it is unclean.) ¹⁵ For if your brother is hurt by what you eat, you are no longer •walking according to love. By

---

ᵃ**13:9** Other mss add *you shall not bear false witness*　ᵇ**13:9** Ex 20:13-17; Dt 5:17-21　ᶜ**13:9** Lv 19:18　ᵈ**13:11** Other mss read *for us*　ᵉ**14:1** Or *weak in the Faith*　ᶠ**14:4** Other mss read *For God has the power*　ᵍ**14:6** Other mss add *but whoever does not observe the day, it is to the Lord that he does not observe it*　ʰ**14:10** Other mss read *of Christ*　ⁱ**14:11** Is 45:23; 49:18

what you eat, do not destroy that one for whom Christ died. [16] Therefore, do not let your good be slandered, [17] for the kingdom of God is not eating and drinking, but righteousness, peace, and joy in the Holy Spirit. [18] Whoever serves the •Messiah in this way is acceptable to God and approved by men.

Don't Make Brother Stumble

[19] So then, we must pursue what promotes peace and what builds up one another. [20] Do not tear down God's work because of food. Everything is clean, but it is wrong for a man to cause stumbling by what he eats. [21] It is a noble thing not to eat meat, or drink wine, or do anything that makes your brother stumble.[a] [22] Do you have faith? Keep it to yourself before God. Blessed is the man who does not condemn himself by what he approves. [23] But whoever doubts stands condemned if he eats, because his eating is not from faith, and everything that is not from faith is sin.

Bear Neighbor's Weaknesses

15 Now we who are strong have an obligation to bear the weaknesses of those without strength, and not to please ourselves. [2] Each one of us must please his neighbor for his good, in order to build him up. [3] For even the •Messiah did not please Himself. On the contrary, as it is written, **The insults of those who insult You have fallen on Me.**[b] [4] For whatever was written before was written for our instruction, so that through our endurance and through the encouragement of the Scriptures we may have hope. [5] Now may the God of endurance and encouragement grant you agreement with one another, according to Christ Jesus, [6] so that you may glorify the God and Father of our Lord Jesus Christ with a united mind and voice.

Gentiles and Jews— Glorify God Together

[7] Therefore accept one another, just as the Messiah also accepted you, to the glory of God. [8] Now I say that Christ has become a servant of the circumcised[c] on behalf of the truth of God, to confirm the promises to the fathers, [9] and so that Gentiles may glorify God for His mercy. As it is written:

> **Therefore I will praise You among the Gentiles, and I will sing psalms to Your name.**[d]

[10] Again it says: **Rejoice, you Gentiles, with His people!**[e] [11] And again:

> **Praise the Lord, all you Gentiles; all the peoples should praise Him!**[f]

[12] And again, Isaiah says:

> **The root of Jesse will appear, the One who rises to rule the Gentiles; in Him the Gentiles will hope.**[g]

[13] Now may the God of hope fill you with all joy and peace in believing, so that you may overflow with hope by the power of the Holy Spirit.

Paul Has Proclaimed Gospel from Jerusalem to Illyricum

[14] Now, my brothers, I myself am convinced about you that you also are full of goodness, filled with all knowledge, and able to instruct one another. [15] Nevertheless, to remind you, I have written to you more boldly on some points[h] because of the grace given me by God [16] to

---

[a]**14:21** Other mss add *or offended or weakened*   [b]**15:3** Ps 69:9   [c]**15:8** The Jews   [d]**15:9** 2 Sm 22:50; Ps 18:49   [e]**15:10** Dt 32:43   [f]**15:11** Ps 117:1   [g]**15:12** Is 11:10   [h]**15:15** Other mss add *brothers*

be a minister of Christ Jesus to the Gentiles, serving as a priest of God's good news. My purpose is that the offering of the Gentiles may be acceptable, sanctified by the Holy Spirit. ¹⁷ Therefore I have reason to boast in Christ Jesus regarding what pertains to God. ¹⁸ For I would not dare say anything except what Christ has accomplished through me to make the Gentiles obedient by word and deed, ¹⁹ by the power of miraculous signs and wonders, and by the power of God's Spirit. As a result, I have fully proclaimed the good news about the Messiah from Jerusalem all the way around to Illyricum.ª ²⁰ So my aim is to evangelize where Christ has not been named, in order that I will not be building on someone else's foundation, ²¹ but, as it is written:

> Those who had no report of Him
> will see,
> and those who have not heard
> will understand.ᵇ

Paul's Travel Plans

²² That is why I have been prevented many times from coming to you. ²³ But now I no longer have any work to do in these provinces,ᶜ and I have strongly desired for many years to come to you ²⁴ whenever I travel to Spain.ᵈ For I do hope to see you when I pass through, and to be sent on my way there by you, once I have first enjoyed your company for a while. ²⁵ Now, however, I am traveling to Jerusalem to serve the saints; ²⁶ for Macedonia and Achaiaᵉ were pleased to make a contribution to the poor among the saints in Jerusalem. ²⁷ Yes, they were pleased, and they are indebted to them. For if the Gentiles have shared in their spiritual benefits, then they are obligated to minister to Jewsᶠ in material needs.

Paul Looks toward Spain

²⁸ So when I have finished this and safely delivered the fundsᵍ to them, I will go by way of you to Spain. ²⁹ But I know that when I come to you, I will come in the fullness of the blessingʰ of Christ.

Paul Pleads for Prayers

³⁰ Now I implore you, brothers, through the Lord Jesus Christ and through the love of the Spirit, to agonize together with me in your prayers to God on my behalf: ³¹ that I may be rescued from the unbelievers in Judea, that my service for Jerusalem may be acceptable to the saints, ³² and that, by God's will, I may come to you with joy and be refreshed together with you.

³³ The God of peace be with all of you. •Amen.

Paul's Commendation of Phoebe

16 I commend to you our sister Phoebe, who is a servantⁱ of the church in Cenchreae. ² So you should welcome her in the Lord in a manner worthy of the saints, and assist her in whatever matter she may require your help. For indeed she has been a benefactor of many—and of me also.

Paul Greets Roman Christians

³ Give my greetings to Priscaʲ and Aquila, my co-workers in Christ Jesus, ⁴ who risked their own necks for my life. Not only do I thank them, but so do all the Gentile churches.

ª**15:19** A Roman province northwest of Greece on the eastern shore of the Adriatic Sea   ᵇ**15:21** Is 52:15   ᶜ**15:23** Lit *now, having no longer a place in these parts*   ᵈ**15:24** Other mss add *I will come to you.*   ᵉ**15:26** The churches of these provinces   ᶠ**15:27** Lit *to them*   ᵍ**15:28** Lit *delivered this fruit*   ʰ**15:29** Other mss add *of the gospel* ⁱ**16:1** Others interpret this term in a technical sense: *deacon*, or *deaconess*, or *minister*   ʲ**16:3** Traditionally, *Priscilla*, as in Ac 18:2,18,26

5 Greet also the church that meets in their home.

Greet my dear friend Epaenetus, who is the first convert[a] to Christ from Asia.[b]

6 Greet Mary,[c] who has worked very hard for you.[d]

7 Greet Andronicus and Junia,[e] my fellow countrymen and fellow prisoners. They are outstanding among the apostles, and they were also in Christ before me.

8 Greet Ampliatus, my dear friend in the Lord.

9 Greet Urbanus, our co-worker in Christ, and my dear friend Stachys.

10 Greet Apelles, who is approved in Christ.

Greet those who belong to the household of Aristobulus.

11 Greet Herodion, my fellow countryman.

Greet those who belong to the household of Narcissus who are in the Lord.

12 Greet Tryphaena and Tryphosa, who have worked hard in the Lord.

Greet my dear friend Persis, who has worked very hard in the Lord.

13 Greet Rufus, chosen in the Lord; also his mother—and mine.

14 Greet Asyncritus, Phlegon, Hermes, Patrobas, Hermas, and the brothers who are with them.

15 Greet Philologus and Julia, Nereus and his sister, and Olympas, and all the saints who are with them.

16 Greet one another with a holy kiss. All the churches of Christ send you greetings.

Paul Warns against Divisive People

17 Now I implore you, brothers, watch out for those who cause dissensions and pitfalls contrary to the doctrine you have learned. Avoid them; 18 for such people do not serve our Lord Christ but their own appetites,[f] and by smooth talk and flattering words they deceive the hearts of the unsuspecting.

Paul's Confident Conclusion

19 The report of your obedience has reached everyone. Therefore I rejoice over you. But I want you to be wise about what is good, yet innocent about what is evil. 20 The God of peace will soon crush Satan under your feet. The grace of our Lord Jesus be with you.

21 Timothy, my co-worker, and Lucius, Jason, and Sosipater, my fellow countrymen, greet you.

22 I Tertius, who penned this epistle in the Lord, greet you.

23 Gaius, who is host to me and to the whole church, greets you. Erastus, the city treasurer, and our brother Quartus greet you.

[24 The grace of our Lord Jesus Christ be with you all.][g]

To Him Be the Glory Forever!

25 Now to Him who has power to strengthen you according to my gospel and the proclamation of Jesus Christ, according to the revelation of the sacred secret kept silent for long ages, 26 but now revealed and made known through the prophetic Scriptures, according to the command of the eternal God, to advance the obedience of faith among all nations— 27 to the only wise God, through Jesus Christ—to Him be the glory forever![h] •Amen.

---

[a]16:5 Lit the firstfruits   [b]16:5 Other mss read Achaia   [c]16:6 Or Maria   [d]16:6 Other mss read us   [e]16:7 Either a feminine name or Junias, a masculine name   [f]16:18 Lit belly   [g]16:24 Other mss omit bracketed text; see v. 20
[h]16:25-27 Other mss have these vv. at the end of chap 14 or 15.

1 CORINTHIANS

Paul's Greeting—with Sosthenes

1 Paul, called as an apostle of Christ Jesus by God's will, and our brother Sosthenes:

2 To God's church at Corinth, to those who are sanctified in Christ Jesus and called as saints, with all those in every place who call on the name of Jesus Christ our Lord—theirs and ours.

3 Grace to you and peace from God our Father and the Lord Jesus Christ.

Paul's Thanksgiving

4 I always thank my God for you because of God's grace given to you in Christ Jesus, 5 that by Him you were made rich in everything—in all speaking and all knowledge— 6 as the testimony about Christ was confirmed among you, 7 so that you do not lack any spiritual gift as you eagerly wait for the revelation of our Lord Jesus Christ. 8 He will also confirm you to the end, blameless in the day of our Lord Jesus Christ. 9 God is faithful; by Him you were called into fellowship with His Son, Jesus Christ our Lord.

Spiritual Divisions at Corinth

10 Now I urge you, brothers, in the name of our Lord Jesus Christ, that you all say the same thing, that there be no divisions among you, and that you be united with the same understanding and the same conviction. 11 For it has been reported to me about you, my brothers, by members of Chloe's household, that there are quarrels among you. 12 What I am saying is this: each of you says, "I'm with Paul," or "I'm with Apollos," or "I'm with •Cephas," or "I'm with

Christ." 13 Is Christ divided? Was it Paul who was crucified for you? Or were you baptized in Paul's name? 14 I thank God[a] [b] that I baptized none of you except Crispus and Gaius, 15 so that no one can say you had been baptized in my name. 16 I did, in fact, baptize the household of Stephanas; beyond that, I don't know if I baptized anyone else. 17 For Christ did not send me to baptize, but to preach the gospel—not with clever words, so that the cross of Christ will not be emptied ⌊of its effect⌋.

We Preach Christ Crucified

18 For to those who are perishing the message of the cross is foolishness, but to us who are being saved it is God's power. 19 For it is written:

> I will destroy the wisdom
>   of the wise,
> and I will set aside
>   the understanding
>   of the experts.[c]

20 Where is the philosopher?[d] Where is the scholar? Where is the debater of this age? Hasn't God made the world's wisdom foolish? 21 For since, in God's wisdom, the world did not know God through wisdom, God was pleased to save those who believe through the foolishness of the message preached. 22 For the Jews ask for signs and the Greeks seek wisdom, 23 but we preach Christ crucified, a stumbling block to the Jews and foolishness to the Gentiles.[e] 24 Yet to those who are called, both Jews and Greeks, Christ is God's power and God's wisdom, 25 because God's foolishness is wiser than human wisdom, and God's

a1:14 Other mss omit God b1:14 Or I am thankful c1:19 Is 29:14 d1:20 Or wise e1:23 Other mss read Greeks

weakness is stronger than human strength.

Boast Only in the Lord

[26] Brothers, consider your calling: not many are wise from a human perspective,[a] not many powerful, not many of noble birth. [27] Instead, God has chosen the world's foolish things to shame the wise, and God has chosen the world's weak things to shame the strong. [28] God has chosen the world's insignificant and despised things—the things viewed as nothing—so He might bring to nothing the things that are viewed as something, [29] so that no one[b] can boast in His presence. [30] But from Him you are in Christ Jesus, who for us became wisdom from God, as well as righteousness, sanctification, and redemption, [31] in order that, as it is written: **The one who boasts must boast in the Lord.**[c]

Paul's Powerful Proclamation

2 When I came to you, brothers, announcing the testimony[d] of God to you, I did not come with brilliance of speech or wisdom. [2] For I determined to know nothing among you except Jesus Christ and Him crucified. [3] And I was with you in weakness, in fear, and in much trembling. [4] My speech and my proclamation were not with persuasive words of wisdom,[e] but with a demonstration of the Spirit and power, [5] so that your faith might not be based on men's wisdom but on God's power.

God's Spiritual Wisdom

[6] However, among the mature we do speak a wisdom, but not a wisdom of this age, or of the rulers of this age, who are coming to nothing. [7] On the contrary, we speak God's hidden wisdom in a •mystery, which God predestined before the ages for our glory. [8] None of the rulers of this age knew it, for if they had known it, they would not have crucified the Lord of glory. [9] But as it is written:

> What no eye has seen and no ear has heard,
> and what has never come into a man's heart,
> is what God has prepared for those who love Him.[f]

[10] Now God has revealed them to us by the Spirit, for the Spirit searches everything, even the deep things of God. [11] For who among men knows the concerns[g] of a man except the spirit of the man that is in him? In the same way, no one knows the concerns[g] of God except the Spirit of God. [12] Now we have not received the spirit of the world, but the Spirit who is from God, in order to know what has been freely given to us by God. [13] We also speak these things, not in words taught by human wisdom, but in those taught by the Spirit, explaining spiritual things to spiritual people.[h] [14] But the natural man does not welcome what comes from God's Spirit, because it is foolishness to him; he is not able to know it since it is evaluated[i] spiritually. [15] The spiritual person, however, can evaluate[j] everything, yet he himself cannot be evaluated[i] by anyone. [16] For:

> who has known the Lord's mind,
> that he may instruct Him?[k]

But we have the mind of Christ.

Problem of Spiritual Immaturity

3 Brothers, I was not able to speak to you as spiritual people but as people

---

[a]**1:26** Lit *wise according to the flesh*   [b]**1:29** Lit *that not all flesh*   [c]**1:31** Jr 9:24   [d]**2:1** Other mss read *mystery*
[e]**2:4** Other mss read *human wisdom*   [f]**2:9** Is 52:15; 64:4   [g]**2:11** Lit *things*   [h]**2:13** Or *things with spiritual words*
[i]**2:14,15** Or *judged*, or *discerned*   [j]**2:15** Or *judge*, or *discern*   [k]**2:16** Is 40:13

of the flesh, as babies in Christ. [2] I fed you milk, not solid food, because you were not yet able to receive it. In fact, you are still not able, [3] because you are still fleshly. For since there is envy and strife[a] among you, are you not fleshly and living like ordinary people?[b] [4] For whenever someone says, "I'm with Paul," and another, "I'm with Apollos," are you not ⌊typical⌋ men?[c]

Different Roles of God's Servants

[5] So, what is Apollos? And what is Paul? They are servants through whom you believed, and each has the role the Lord has given. [6] I planted, Apollos watered, but God gave the growth. [7] So then neither the one who plants nor the one who waters is anything, but only God who gives the growth. [8] Now the one who plants and the one who waters are equal, and each will receive his own reward according to his own labor. [9] For we are God's co-workers. You are God's field, God's building.

Christ is Foundation

[10] According to God's grace that was given to me, as a skilled master builder I have laid a foundation, and another builds on it. But each one must be careful how he builds on it, [11] because no one can lay any other foundation than what has been laid—that is, Jesus Christ. [12] If anyone builds on the foundation with gold, silver, costly stones, wood, hay, or straw, [13] each one's work will become obvious, for the day[d] will disclose it, because it will be revealed by fire; the fire will test the quality of each one's work. [14] If anyone's work that he has built survives, he will receive a reward. [15] If anyone's work is burned up, it will

be lost, but he will be saved; yet it will be like an escape through fire.[e]

[16] Don't you know that you are God's sanctuary and that the Spirit of God lives in you? [17] If anyone ruins God's sanctuary, God will ruin him; for God's sanctuary is holy, and that is what you are.

Folly of Human Wisdom

[18] No one should deceive himself. If anyone among you thinks he is wise in this age, he must become foolish so that he can become wise. [19] For the wisdom of this world is foolishness with God, since it is written: **He catches the wise in their craftiness**[f]— [20] and again, **The Lord knows the reasonings of the wise, that they are futile.**[g] [21] So no one should boast in men, for all things are yours: [22] whether Paul or Apollos or •Cephas or the world or life or death or things present or things to come—all are yours, [23] and you belong to Christ, and Christ to God.

God's Faithful Managers

4 A person should consider us in this way: as servants of Christ and managers of God's •mysteries. [2] In this regard, it is expected of managers that each one be found faithful. [3] It is of little importance that I should be evaluated by you or by a human court.[h] In fact, I don't even evaluate myself. [4] For I am not conscious of anything against myself, but I am not justified by this. The One who evaluates me is the Lord. [5] Therefore don't judge anything prematurely, before the Lord comes, who will both bring to light what is hidden in darkness and reveal the intentions of the hearts. And then praise will come to each one from God.

---

a**3:3** Other mss add *and divisions*   b**3:3** Lit *and walking according to man*   c**3:4** Other mss read *are you not carnal*
d**3:13** The Day of Christ's judgment of believers   e**3:15** Lit *yet so as through fire*   f**3:19** Jb 5:13   g**3:20** Ps 94:11
h**4:3** Lit *a human day*

Apostles' Example of Humility

[6] Now, brothers, I have applied these things to myself and Apollos for your benefit, so that you may learn from us the saying: "Nothing beyond what is written."[a] The purpose is that none of you will be inflated with pride in favor of one person over another. [7] For who makes you so superior? What do you have that you didn't receive? If, in fact, you did receive it, why do you boast as if you hadn't received it? [8] Already you are full! Already you are rich! You have begun to reign as kings without us—and I wish you did reign, so that we also could reign with you! [9] For I think God has displayed us, the apostles, in last place, like men condemned to die: we have become a spectacle to the world and to angels and to men. [10] We are fools for Christ, but you are wise in Christ! We are weak, but you are strong! You are distinguished, but we are dishonored! [11] Up to the present hour we are both hungry and thirsty; we are poorly clothed, roughly treated, homeless; [12] we labor, working with our own hands. When we are reviled, we bless; when we are persecuted, we endure it; [13] when we are slandered, we entreat. We are, even now, like the world's garbage, like the filth of all things.

Paul's Fatherly Care

[14] I'm not writing this to shame you, but to warn you as my dear children. [15] For you can have 10,000 instructors in Christ, but you can't have many fathers. Now I have fathered you in Christ Jesus through the gospel. [16] Therefore I urge you, be imitators of me. [17] This is why I have sent to you Timothy, who is my beloved and faithful child in the Lord. He will remind you about my ways in Christ Jesus, just as I teach everywhere in every church. [18] Now some are inflated with pride, as though I were not coming to you. [19] But I will come to you soon, if the Lord wills, and I will know not the talk but the power of those who are inflated with pride. [20] For the kingdom of God is not in talk but in power. [21] What do you want? Should I come to you with a rod, or in love and a spirit of gentleness?

Immoral Church Members

5 It is widely reported that there is sexual immorality among you, and the kind of sexual immorality that is not even condoned[b] among the Gentiles—a man is living with his father's wife. [2] And you are inflated with pride, instead of filled with grief so that he who has committed this act might be removed from among you. [3] For though absent in body but present in spirit, I have already decided about him who has done this thing as though I were present. [4] In the name of our Lord Jesus, when you are assembled, along with my spirit and with the power of our Lord Jesus, [5] turn that one over to Satan for the destruction of the flesh, so that his spirit may be saved in the Day of the Lord.

Evil Yeast

[6] Your boasting is not good. Don't you know that a little yeast permeates the whole batch of dough? [7] Clean out the old yeast so that you may be a new batch, since you are unleavened. For Christ our •Passover has been sacrificed.[c] [8] Therefore, let us observe the feast, not with old yeast, or with the yeast of malice and evil, but with the unleavened bread of sincerity and truth.

---

[a] **4:6** The words in quotation marks could refer to the OT, a Jewish maxim, or a popular proverb. [b] **5:1** Other mss read *named* [c] **5:7** Other mss add *for us*

Apply Church Discipline!

⁹ I wrote to you in a letter not to associate with sexually immoral people— ¹⁰ by no means referring to this world's immoral people, or to the greedy and swindlers, or to idolaters; otherwise you would have to leave the world. ¹¹ But now I am writing[a] you not to associate with anyone who bears the name of brother who is sexually immoral or greedy, an idolater or a reviler, a drunkard or a swindler. Do not even eat with such a person. ¹² For what is it to me to judge outsiders? Do you not judge those who are inside? ¹³ But God judges outsiders. **Put away the evil person from among yourselves.**[b]

No Lawsuits among Believers

6 Does any of you who has a complaint against someone dare go to law before the unrighteous,[c] and not before the saints? ² Or do you not know that the saints will judge the world? And if the world is judged by you, are you unworthy to judge the smallest cases? ³ Do you not know that we will judge angels—not to speak of things pertaining to this life? ⁴ So if you have cases pertaining to this life, do you select those[d] who have no standing in the church to judge? ⁵ I say this to your shame! Can it be that there is not one wise person among you who will be able to arbitrate between his brothers? ⁶ Instead, brother goes to law against brother, and that before unbelievers!

⁷ Therefore, it is already a total defeat for you that you have lawsuits against one another. Why not rather put up with injustice? Why not rather be cheated? ⁸ Instead, you act unjustly and cheat—and this to brothers!

Those Who Won't Inherit Kingdom

⁹ Do you not know that the unjust will not inherit God's kingdom? Do not be deceived: no sexually immoral people, idolaters, adulterers, male prostitutes, homosexuals, ¹⁰ thieves, greedy people, drunkards, revilers, or swindlers will inherit God's kingdom. ¹¹ Some of you were like this; but you were washed, you were sanctified, you were justified in the name of the Lord Jesus Christ and by the Spirit of our God.

Glorify God in Body and Spirit

¹² "Everything is permissible for me,"[e] but not everything is helpful. "Everything is permissible for me,"[e] but I will not be brought under the control of anything. ¹³ "Foods for the stomach and the stomach for foods,"[e] but God will do away with both of them.[f] The body is not for sexual immorality but for the Lord, and the Lord for the body. ¹⁴ God raised up the Lord and will also raise us up by His power. ¹⁵ Do you not know that your bodies are the members of Christ? So should I take the members of Christ and make them members of a prostitute? Absolutely not! ¹⁶ Do you not know that anyone joined to a prostitute is one body with her? For it says, **The two will become one flesh.**[g] ¹⁷ But anyone joined to the Lord is one spirit with Him.

Flee Sexual Immorality!

¹⁸ Flee from sexual immorality! "Every sin a person can commit is outside the body,"[h] but the person who is sexually immoral sins against his own body. ¹⁹ Do you not know that your body is a sanctuary of the Holy Spirit who is in you,

a5:11 Or now I wrote   b5:13 Dt 17:7   c6:1 Unbelievers; see v. 6   d6:4 Or life, appoint those (as a command)   e6:12,13 The words in quotation marks are most likely slogans used by some Corinthian Christians. Paul evaluates and corrects these slogans.   f6:13 Lit both it and them   g6:16 Gn 2:24   h6:18 See note at 1 Co 6:12

whom you have from God? You are not your own, [20] for you were bought at a price; therefore glorify God in your body.[a]

Principles of Marriage

7 About the things you wrote:[b] "It is good for a man not to have relations with[c] a woman."[d] [2] But because of sexual immorality,[e] each man should have his own wife, and each woman should have her own husband. [3] A husband should fulfill his marital duty to his wife, and likewise a wife to her husband. [4] A wife does not have authority over her own body, but her husband does. Equally, a husband does not have authority over his own body, but his wife does. [5] Do not deprive one another—except when you agree, for a time, to devote yourselves to[f] prayer. Then come together again; otherwise, Satan may tempt you because of your lack of self-control. [6] I say this as a concession, not as a command. [7] I wish that all people were just like me. But each has his own gift from God, one this and another that.

Advice to the Unmarried

[8] I say to the unmarried and to widows: It is good for them if they remain as I am. [9] But if they do not have self-control, they should marry, for it is better to marry than to burn with desire.

Advice to Married People

[10] I command the married—not I, but the Lord—a wife is not to leave[g] her husband. [11] But if she does leave, she must remain unmarried or be reconciled to her husband—and a husband is not to leave his wife. [12] But to the rest I, not the Lord, say: If any brother has an unbe-

lieving wife, and she is willing to live with him, he must not leave her. [13] Also, if any woman has an unbelieving husband, and he is willing to live with her, she must not leave her husband. [14] For the unbelieving husband is sanctified by the wife, and the unbelieving wife is sanctified by the Christian husband. Otherwise your children would be unclean, but now they are holy. [15] But if the unbeliever leaves, let him leave.[g] A brother or a sister is not bound in such cases. God has called you[h] to peace. [16] For you, wife, how do you know whether you will save your husband? Or you, husband, how do you know whether you will save your wife?

Live as You Were Called

[17] However, each one must live his life in the situation the Lord assigned when God called him.[i] This is what I command in all the churches. [18] Was anyone already circumcised when he was called? He should not undo his circumcision. Was anyone called while uncircumcised? He should not get circumcised. [19] Circumcision does not matter and uncircumcision does not matter, but keeping God's commandments does. [20] Each person should remain in the life situation[j] in which he was called. [21] Were you called while a slave? It should not be a concern to you. But if you can become free, by all means take the opportunity.[k] [22] For he who is called by the Lord as a slave is the Lord's freedman.[l] Likewise he who is called as a free man[m] is Christ's slave. [23] You were bought at a price; do not become slaves of men. [24] Brothers, each person should remain with God in whatever situation he was called.

Counsel for Unmarried and Widows

²⁵ About virgins: I have no command from the Lord, but I do give an opinion as one who by the Lord's mercy is trustworthy. ²⁶ Therefore I consider this to be good because of the present distress: it is fine for a man to stay as he is. ²⁷ Are you bound to a wife? Do not seek to be loosed. Are you loosed from a wife? Do not seek a wife. ²⁸ However, if you do get married, you have not sinned, and if a virgin marries, she has not sinned. But such people will have trouble in this life,ᵃ and I am trying to spare you. ²⁹ And I say this, brothers: the time is limited, so from now on those who have wives should be as though they had none, ³⁰ those who weep as though they did not weep, those who rejoice as though they did not rejoice, those who buy as though they did not possess, ³¹ and those who use the world as though they did not make full use of it. For this world in its current form is passing away.

³² I want you to be without concerns. An unmarried man is concerned about the things of the Lord—how he may please the Lord. ³³ But a married man is concerned about the things of the world—how he may please his wife— ³⁴ and he is divided. An unmarried woman or a virgin is concerned about the things of the Lord, so that she may be holy both in body and in spirit. But a married woman is concerned about the things of the world—how she may please her husband. ³⁵ Now I am saying this for your own benefit, not to put a restraint on you, but because of what is proper, and so that you may be devoted to the Lord without distraction.

³⁶ But if any man thinks he is acting improperly toward his virgin,ᵇ if she is past marriageable age,ᶜ and so it must

be, he can do what he wants. He is not sinning; they can get married. ³⁷ But he who stands firm in his heart (who is under no compulsion, but has control over his own will) and has decided in his heart to keep his own virgin, will do well. ³⁸ So then he who marriesᵈ his virgin does well, but he who does not marryᵉ will do better.

³⁹ A wife is boundᶠ as long as her husband is living. But if her husband dies, she is free to be married to anyone she wants—only in the Lord.ᵍ ⁴⁰ But she is happier if she remains as she is, in my opinion. And I think that I also have the Spirit of God.

Food Offered to Idols

8 About food offered to idols: We know that "we all have knowledge."ʰ Knowledge inflates with pride, but love builds up. ² If anyone thinks he knows anything, he does not yet know it as he ought to know it. ³ But if anyone loves God, he is known by Him.

⁴ About eating food offered to idols, then, we know that "an idol is nothing in the world,"ʰ and that "there is no God but one."ʰ ⁵ For even if there are so-called gods, whether in heaven or on earth—as there are many "gods" and many "lords"—

⁶ yet for us there is one God,
the Father,
from whom are all things, and we
for Him;
and one Lord, Jesus Christ,
through whom are all things,
and we through Him.

Don't Be Stumbling Block

⁷ However, not everyone has this knowledge. In fact, some have been so

---

ᵃ**7:28** Lit *in the flesh*   ᵇ**7:36** (1) a man's fiancée, or (2) his daughter, or (3) his Levirate wife, or (4) a celibate companion   ᶜ**7:36** Or *virgin, if his passions are strong,*   ᵈ**7:38** Or *marries off*   ᵉ**7:38** Or *marry her off*   ᶠ**7:39** Other mss add *by law*   ᵍ**7:39** Only a believer   ʰ**8:1,4** See note at 1 Co 6:12

used to idolatry up until now, that when they eat food offered to an idol, their conscience, being weak, is defiled. [8] Food will not make us acceptable to God. We are not inferior if we don't eat, and we are not better if we do eat. [9] But be careful that this right of yours in no way becomes a stumbling block to the weak. [10] For if somebody sees you, the one who has this knowledge, dining in an idol's temple, won't his weak conscience be encouraged to eat food offered to idols? [11] Then the weak person, the brother for whom Christ died, is ruined by your knowledge. [12] Now when you sin like this against the brothers and wound their weak conscience, you are sinning against Christ. [13] Therefore, if food causes my brother to fall, I will never again eat meat, so that I won't cause my brother to fall.

Paul's Example as an Apostle

9 Am I not free? Am I not an apostle? Have I not seen Jesus our Lord? Are you not my work in the Lord? [2] If I am not an apostle to others, at least I am to you, for you are the seal of my apostleship in the Lord. [3] My defense to those who examine me is this: [4] Don't we have the right to eat and drink? [5] Don't we have the right to be accompanied by a Christian wife, like the other apostles, the Lord's brothers, and •Cephas? [6] Or is it only Barnabas and I who have no right to refrain from working? [7] Who ever goes to war at his own expense? Who plants a vineyard and does not eat its fruit? Or who shepherds a flock and does not drink the milk from the flock? [8] Am I saying this from a human perspective? Doesn't the law also say the same thing? [9] For it is written in the law of Moses, **Do not muzzle an ox while it treads out the grain.**[a] Is God really concerned with oxen? [10] Or

isn't He really saying it for us? Yes, this is written for us, because he who plows ought to plow in hope, and he who threshes should do so in hope of sharing the crop. [11] If we have sown spiritual things for you, is it too much if we reap material things from you? [12] If others share this authority over you, don't we even more?

Paul Preaches without Payment

However, we have not used this authority; instead we endure everything so that we will not hinder the gospel of Christ. [13] Do you not know that those who perform the temple services eat the food from the temple, and those who serve at the altar share in the offerings of the altar? [14] In the same way, the Lord has commanded that those who preach the gospel should earn their living by the gospel.

[15] But I have used none of these rights, and I have not written this to make it happen that way for me. For it would be better for me to die than for anyone to deprive me of my boast! [16] For if I preach the gospel, I have no reason to boast, because an obligation is placed on me. And woe to me if I do not preach the gospel! [17] For if I do this willingly, I have a reward; but if unwillingly, I am entrusted with a stewardship. [18] What then is my reward? To preach the gospel and offer it free of charge, and not make full use of my authority in the gospel.

"All Things to All People"

[19] For although I am free from all people, I have made myself a slave to all, in order to win more people. [20] To the Jews I became like a Jew, to win Jews; to those under the law, like one under the law— though I myself am not under the law[b]— to win those under the law. [21] To those

---

a **9:9** Dt 25:4   b **9:20** Other mss omit *though I myself am not under law*

who are outside the law, like one outside the law—not being outside God's law, but under the law of Christ—to win those outside the law. 22 To the weak I became weak, in order to win the weak. I have become all things to all people, so that I may by all means save some. 23 Now I do all this because of the gospel, that I may become a partner in its benefits.ᵃ

Run to Win

24 Do you not know that the runners in a stadium all race, but only one receives the prize? Run in such a way that you may win. 25 Now everyone who competes exercises self-control in everything. However, they do it to receive a perishable crown, but we an imperishable one. 26 Therefore I do not run like one who runs aimlessly, or box like one who beats the air. 27 Instead, I discipline my body and bring it under strict control, so that after preaching to others, I myself will not be disqualified.

Paul's Warnings from Israel's Past

10 Now I want you to know, brothers, that our fathers were all under the cloud, all passed through the sea, 2 and all were baptized into Moses in the cloud and in the sea. 3 They all ate the same spiritual food, 4 and all drank the same spiritual drink. For they drank from a spiritual rock that followed them, and that rock was Christ. 5 But God was not pleased with most of them, for they were struck down in the desert.

6 Now these things became examples for us, so that we will not desire evil as they did.ᵇ 7 Don't become idolaters as some of them were; as it is written, **The people sat down to eat and drink, and**

got up to play.ᶜ ᵈ 8 Let us not commit sexual immorality as some of them did,ᵉ and in a single day 23,000 people fell dead. 9 Let us not tempt Christ as some of them did,ᶠ and were destroyed by snakes. 10 Nor should we complain as some of them did,ᵍ and were killed by the destroyer.ʰ 11 Now these things happened to them as examples, and they were written as a warning to us, on whom the ends of the ages have come. 12 Therefore, whoever thinks he stands must be careful not to fall! 13 No temptation has overtaken you except what is common to humanity. God is faithful and He will not allow you to be tempted beyond what you are able, but with the temptation He will also provide a way of escape, so that you are able to bear it.

Paul Warns against Idolatry

14 Therefore, my dear friends, flee from idolatry. 15 I am speaking as to wise people. Judge for yourselves what I say. 16 The cup of blessing that we bless, is it not a sharing in the blood of Christ? The bread that we break, is it not a sharing in the body of Christ? 17 Because there is one bread, we who are many are one body, for all of us share that one bread. 18 Look at the people of Israel.ⁱ Are not those who eat the sacrifices partners in the altar? 19 What am I saying then? That food offered to idols is anything, or that an idol is anything? 20 No, but I do say that what theyʲ sacrifice, they sacrifice to demons and not to God. I do not want you to be partners with demons! 21 You cannot drink the cup of the Lord and the cup of demons. You cannot share in the Lord's table and the table of demons. 22 Or are we provoking the Lord to jealousy? Are we stronger than He?

ᵃ**9:23** Lit partner of it ᵇ**10:6** Lit they desired ᶜ**10:7** Or to dance ᵈ**10:7** Ex 32:6 ᵉ**10:8** Lit them committed sexual immorality ᶠ**10:9** Lit them tempted ᵍ**10:10** Lit them complained ʰ**10:10** Or the destroying angel ⁱ**10:18** Lit Look at Israel according to the flesh ʲ**10:20** Other mss read Gentiles

Christian Liberty

23 "Everything is permissible,"ᵃ ᵇ but not everything is helpful. "Everything is permissible,"ᵃ ᵇ but not everything builds up. 24 No one should seek his own ⌊good⌋, but ⌊the good⌋ of the other person.

25 Eat everything that is sold in the meat market, asking no questions for conscience' sake, for 26 **the earth is the Lord's, and all that is in it.**ᶜ 27 If one of the unbelievers invites you over and you want to go, eat everything that is set before you, without raising questions of conscience. 28 But if someone says to you, "This is food offered to an idol," do not eat it, out of consideration for the one who told you, and for conscience' sake.ᵈ 29 I do not mean your own conscience, but the other person's. For why is my freedom judged by another person's conscience? 30 If I partake with thanks, why am I slandered because of something for which I give thanks?

31 Therefore, whether you eat or drink, or whatever you do, do everything for God's glory. 32 Give no offense to the Jews or the Greeks or the church of God, 33 just as I also try to please all people in all things, not seeking my own profit, but the profit of many, that they may be saved.

11 1 Be imitators of me, as I also am of Christ.

Instructions about Head Coverings

2 Now I praise youᵉ because you remember me in all things and keep the traditions just as I delivered them to you. 3 But I want you to know that Christ is the head of every man, and the man is the head of the woman,ᶠ and God is the head of Christ. 4 Every man who prays or prophesies with some-thing on his head dishonors his head. 5 But every woman who prays or prophesies with her head uncovered dishonors her head, since that is one and the same as having her head shaved. 6 So if a woman's headᵍ is not covered, her hair should be cut off. But if it is disgraceful for a woman to have her hair cut off or her head shaved, she should be covered.

7 A man, in fact, should not cover his head, because he is God's image and glory, but woman is man's glory. 8 For man did not come from woman, but woman came from man; 9 and man was not created for woman, but woman for man. 10 This is why a woman should have ⌊a symbol of⌋ authority on her head: because of the angels. 11 However, in the Lord, woman is not independent of man, and man is not independent of woman. 12 For just as woman came from man, so man comes through woman, and all things come from God.

13 Judge for yourselves: Is it proper for a woman to pray to God with her head uncovered? 14 Does not even nature itself teach you that if a man has long hair it is a disgrace to him, 15 but that if a woman has long hair, it is her glory? For her hair is given to herʰ as a covering. 16 But if anyone wants to argue about this, we have no otherⁱ custom, nor do the churches of God.

The Lord's Supper

17 Now in giving the following instruction I do not praise you, since you come together not for the better but for the worse. 18 For, to begin with, I hear that when you come together as a church there are divisions among you, and in part I believe it. 19 There must, indeed, be

---

ᵃ**10:23** Other mss add *for me*   ᵇ**10:23** See note at 1 Co 6:12   ᶜ**10:26** Ps 24:1   ᵈ**10:28** Other mss add *"For the earth is the Lord's and all that is in it."*   ᵉ**11:2** Other mss add *brothers,*   ᶠ**11:3** Or *the husband is the head of the wife*   ᵍ**11:6** Lit *a woman*   ʰ**11:15** Other mss omit *to her*   ⁱ**11:16** Or *no such*

factions among you, so that the approved among you may be recognized. 20 Therefore when you come together in one place, it is not really to eat the Lord's Supper. 21 For in eating, each one takes his own supper ahead of others, and one person is hungry while another is drunk! 22 Don't you have houses to eat and drink in? Or do you look down on the church of God and embarrass those who have nothing? What should I say to you? Should I praise you? I do not praise you for this!

23 For I received from the Lord what I also passed on to you: on the night when He was betrayed, the Lord Jesus took bread, 24 gave thanks, broke it, and said,a "This is My body, which isb for you. Do this in remembrance of Me."

25 In the same way ⌊He⌋ also ⌊took⌋ the cup, after supper, and said, "This cup is the new covenant in My blood. Do this, as often as you drink it, in remembrance of Me." 26 For as often as you eat this bread and drink the cup, you proclaim the Lord's death until He comes.

Perform Self-Examination

27 Therefore, whoever eats the bread or drinks the cup of the Lord in an unworthy way will be guilty of sin against the bodyc and blood of the Lord. 28 So a man should examine himself; in this way he should eat of the bread and drink of the cup. 29 For whoever eats and drinks without recognizing the body,d eats and drinks judgment on himself. 30 This is why many are sick and ill among you, and many have fallen •asleep. 31 If we were properly evaluating ourselves, we would not be judged, 32 but when we are judged, we are disciplined by the Lord, so that we may not be condemned with the world. 33 Therefore, my brothers, when you come together to eat, wait for one an-

other. 34 If anyone is hungry, he should eat at home, so that you can come together and not cause judgment. And I will give instructions about the other matters whenever I come.

Diversity of Spiritual Gifts

12 About matters of the spirit:e brothers, I do not want you to be unaware. 2 You know how, when you were pagans, you were led to dumb idols—being led astray. 3 Therefore I am informing you that no one speaking by the Spirit of God says, "Jesus is cursed," and no one can say, "Jesus is Lord," except by the Holy Spirit.

4 Now there are different gifts, but the same Spirit. 5 There are different ministries, but the same Lord. 6 And there are different activities, but the same God is active in everyone and everything.f 7 A manifestation of the Spirit is given to each person to produce what is beneficial:

8   to one is given a message
       of wisdom through the Spirit,
     to another, a message
       of knowledge
       by the same Spirit,
9   to another, faith by the same Spirit,
     to another, gifts of healing
       by the one Spirit,
10 to another, the performing
       of miracles,
     to another, prophecy,
     to another, distinguishing
       between spirits,
     to another, different kinds
       of languages,
     to another, interpretation
       of languages.

11 But one and the same Spirit is active in all these, distributing to each one as He wills.

a11:24 Other mss add "Take, eat. b11:24 Other mss add broken c11:27 Lit be guilty of the body d11:29 Other mss read drinks unworthily, not discerning the Lord's body e12:1 Lit About things spiritual f12:6 Lit God acts all things in all

Unity Yet Diversity in the Body

[12] For as the body is one and has many parts, and all the parts of that body, though many, are one body—so also is Christ. [13] For we were all baptized by one Spirit into one body—whether Jews or Greeks, whether slaves or free—and we were all made to drink of one Spirit. [14] So the body is not one part but many. [15] If the foot should say, "Because I'm not a hand, I don't belong to the body," in spite of this it still belongs to the body. [16] And if the ear should say, "Because I'm not an eye, I don't belong to the body," in spite of this it still belongs to the body. [17] If the whole body were an eye, where would the hearing be? If the whole were an ear, where would be the sense of smell? [18] But now God has placed the parts, each one of them, in the body just as He wanted. [19] And if they were all the same part, where would the body be? [20] Now there are many parts, yet one body.

[21] So the eye cannot say to the hand, "I don't need you!" nor again the head to the feet, "I don't need you!" [22] On the contrary, all the more, those parts of the body that seem to be weaker are necessary. [23] And those parts of the body that we think to be less honorable, we clothe these with greater honor, and our unpresentable parts have a better presentation. [24] But our presentable parts have no need ᴸof clothingᴶ. Instead, God has put the body together, giving greater honor to the less honorable, [25] so that there would be no division in the body, but that the members would have the same concern for each other. [26] So if one member suffers, all the members suffer with it; if one member is honored, all the members rejoice with it.

Roles in Church

[27] Now you are the body of Christ, and individual members of it. [28] And God has placed these in the church:

> first apostles, second prophets,
>> third teachers, next, miracles,
> then gifts of healing, helping,
>> managing, various kinds
>> of languages.
>
> [29] Are all apostles? Are all prophets?
> Are all teachers?
>> Do all do miracles?
> [30] Do all have gifts of healing?
>> Do all speak in languages?
> Do all interpret?

[31] But desire the greater gifts. And I will show you an even better way.

Love: The Superior Way

13 If I speak the languages of men
> and of angels,
> but do not have love,
> I am a sounding gong
> or a clanging cymbal.
> [2] If I have ᴸthe gift ofᴶ prophecy,
> and understand all •mysteries
> and all knowledge,
> and if I have all faith,
> so that I can move mountains,
> but do not have love,
> I am nothing.
> [3] And if I donate all my goods to feed
> the poor,
> and if I give my body
> to be burned,ᵃ
> but do not have love,
> I gain nothing.
> [4] Love is patient; love is kind.
> Love does not envy;
> is not boastful; is not conceited;
> [5] does not act improperly;
> is not selfish;
> is not provoked; does not keep
> a record of wrongs;

ᵃ**13:3** Other mss read *to boast*

⁶ finds no joy in unrighteousness,
　　but rejoices in the truth;
⁷ bears all things, believes all things,
　　hopes all things, endures all things.
⁸ Love never ends.
　But as for prophecies,
　　they will come to an end;
　as for languages, they will cease;
　as for knowledge, it will come
　　to an end.
⁹ For we know in part,
　　and we prophesy in part.
¹⁰ But when the perfect comes,
　　the partial will come to an end.
¹¹ When I was a child, I spoke
　　like a child,
　I thought like a child,
　　I reasoned like a child.
　When I became a man, I put aside
　　childish things.
¹² For now we see indistinctly,
　　as in a mirror, but then
　　face to face.
　Now I know in part, but then
　I will know fully,
　　as I am fully known.
¹³ Now these three remain:
　　faith, hope, and love.
　But the greatest of these is love.

Prophecy: A Superior Gift

14 Pursue love and desire spiritual gifts, and above all that you may prophesy. ² For the person who speaks in ⌊another⌋ language is not speaking to men but to God, since no one understands him; however, he speaks •mysteries in the Spirit.ᵃ ³ But the person who prophesies speaks to people for edification, encouragement, and consolation. ⁴ The person who speaks in ⌊another⌋ language builds himself up, but he who prophesies builds up the church. ⁵ I wish all of you

spoke in other languages, but even more that you prophesied. The person who prophesies is greater than the person who speaks in languages, unless he interprets so that the church may be built up.

Speaking in Other Languages

⁶ But now, brothers, if I come to you speaking in ⌊other⌋ languages, how will I benefit you unless I speak to you with a revelation or knowledge or prophecy or teaching? ⁷ Even inanimate things producing sounds—whether flute or harp—if they don't make a distinction in the notes, how will what is played on the flute or harp be recognized? ⁸ In fact, if the trumpet makes an unclear sound, who will prepare for battle? ⁹ In the same way, unless you use your tongue for intelligible speech, how will what is spoken be known? For you will be speaking into the air. ¹⁰ There are doubtless many different kinds of languages in the world, and all have meaning.ᵇ ¹¹ Therefore, if I do not know the meaning of the language, I will be a foreignerᶜ to the speaker, and the speaker will be a foreigner to me. ¹² So also you—since you are zealous in matters of the spirit,ᵈ seek to excel in building up the church.

¹³ Therefore the person who speaks in ⌊another⌋ language should pray that he can interpret. ¹⁴ For if I pray in ⌊another⌋ language, my spirit prays, but my understanding is unfruitful. ¹⁵ What then? I will pray with the spirit, and I will also pray with my understanding. I will sing with the spirit, and I will also sing with my understanding. ¹⁶ Otherwise, if you bless with the spirit, how will the uninformed personᵉ say "•Amen" at your giving of thanks, since he does not know what you are saying? ¹⁷ For you may very

---

ᵃ**14:2** Or *in spirit*, or *in his spirit*　ᵇ**14:10** Lit *and none is without a sound*　ᶜ**14:11** Gk *barbaros* = in Eng *a barbarian.* To a Gk, a *barbaros* was anyone who did not speak Gk.　ᵈ**14:12** Lit *zealous of spirits; spirits* = human spirits, spiritual gifts or powers, or the Holy Spirit　ᵉ**14:16** Lit *the one filling the place of the uninformed*

well be giving thanks, but the other person is not being built up. ¹⁸ I thank God that I speak in ⌞other⌟ languages more than all of you; ¹⁹ yet in the church I would rather speak five words with my understanding, in order to teach others also, than 10,000 words in ⌞another⌟ language.

²⁰ Brothers, don't be childish in your thinking, but be infants in evil and adult in your thinking. ²¹ It is written in the law:

By people of other languages
and by the lips of foreigners,
I will speak to this people;
and even then, they will not listen
to Me,ᵃ

says the Lord. ²² It follows that speaking in other languages is intended as a sign,ᵇ not to believers but to unbelievers. But prophecy is not for unbelievers but for believers. ²³ Therefore if the whole church assembles together, and all are speaking in ⌞other⌟ languages, and people who are uninformed or unbelievers come in, will they not say that you are out of your minds? ²⁴ But if all are prophesying, and some unbeliever or uninformed person comes in, he is convicted by all and is judged by all. ²⁵ The secrets of his heart will be revealed, and as a result he will fall down on his face and worship God, proclaiming, "God is really among you."

Order in Church Meetings

²⁶ How is it then, brothers? Whenever you come together, each oneᶜ has a psalm, a teaching, a revelation, ⌞another⌟ language, or an interpretation. All things must be done for edification. ²⁷ If any person speaks in ⌞another⌟ language, there should be only two, or at the most three, each in turn, and someone must interpret. ²⁸ But if there is no interpreter, that person should keep silent in the church and speak to himself and to God. ²⁹ Two or three prophets should speak, and the others should evaluate. ³⁰ But if something has been revealed to another person sitting there, the first prophet should be silent. ³¹ For you can all prophesy one by one, so that everyone may learn and everyone may be encouraged. ³² And the prophets' spirits are under the control of the prophets, ³³ since God is not a God of disorder but of peace.

As in all the churches of the saints, ³⁴ the womenᵈ should be silent in the churches, for they are not permitted to speak, but should be submissive, as the law also says. ³⁵ And if they want to learn something, they should ask their own husbands at home, for it is disgraceful for a woman to speak in the church meeting. ³⁶ Did the word of God originate from you, or did it come to you only?

³⁷ If anyone thinks he is a prophet or spiritual, he should recognize that what I write to you is the Lord's command. ³⁸ But if anyone ignores this, he will be ignored.ᵉ ³⁹ Therefore, my brothers, be eager to prophesy, and do not forbid speaking in ⌞other⌟ languages. ⁴⁰ But everything must be done decently and in order.

Resurrection Essential to the Gospel

15 Now brothers, I want to clarifyᶠ for you the gospel I proclaimed to you; you received it and have taken your stand on it. ² You are also saved by it, if you hold to the message I proclaimed to you—unless you believed to no purpose.ᵍ ³ For I passed on to you as most important what I also received:

that Christ died for our sins
according to the Scriptures,
⁴ that He was buried,
that He was raised on the third day
according to the Scriptures,

Christ's Resurrection Appearances

⁵ and that He appeared to •Cephas,
then to the Twelve.
⁶ Then He appeared to
over 500 brothers at one time,
most of whom remain
to the present,
but some have fallen •asleep.
⁷ Then He appeared to James,
then to all the apostles.
⁸ Last of all, as to one
abnormally born,
He also appeared to me.

⁹ For I am the least of the apostles, unworthy to be called an apostle, because I persecuted the church of God. ¹⁰ But by God's grace I am what I am, and His grace toward me was not ineffective. However, I worked more than any of them, yet not I, but God's grace that was with me. ¹¹ Therefore, whether it is I or they, so we preach and so you have believed.

If Christ Not Raised, Your Faith Is Worthless

¹² Now if Christ is preached as raised from the dead, how can some of you say, "There is no resurrection of the dead"? ¹³ But if there is no resurrection of the dead, then Christ has not been raised; ¹⁴ and if Christ has not been raised, then our preaching is without foundation, and so is your faith.ᵃ ¹⁵ In addition, we are found to be false witnesses about God, because we have testified about God that He raised up Christ—whom He did not raise up if in fact the dead are not raised. ¹⁶ For if the dead are not raised, Christ has not

been raised. ¹⁷ And if Christ has not been raised, your faith is worthless; you are still in your sins. ¹⁸ Therefore those who have fallen asleep in Christ have also perished. ¹⁹ If we have placed our hope in Christ for this life only, we should be pitied more than anyone.

Christ's Resurrection Guarantees Ours

²⁰ But now Christ has been raised from the dead, the •firstfruits of those who have fallen asleep. ²¹ For since death came through a man, the resurrection of the dead also comes through a man. ²² For just as in Adam all die, so also in Christ all will be made alive. ²³ But each in his own order: Christ, the firstfruits; afterward, at His coming, the people of Christ. ²⁴ Then comes the end, when He hands over the kingdom to God the Father, when He abolishes all rule and all authority and power. ²⁵ For He must reign until He puts all His enemies under His feet. ²⁶ The last enemy to be abolished is death. ²⁷ For **He has put everything under His feet.**ᵇ But when it says "everything" is put under Him, it is obvious that He who puts everything under Him is the exception. ²⁸ And when everything is subject to Him, then the Son Himself will also be subject to Him who subjected everything to Him, so that God may be all in all.

Resurrection Affirmed by Christian Experience

²⁹ Otherwise what will they do who are being baptized for the dead? If the dead are not raised at all, then why are peopleᶜ baptized for them?ᵈ ³⁰ Why are we in danger every hour? ³¹ I affirm by the pride in you that I have in Christ Jesus our Lord: I die every day! ³² If I fought wild animals

ᵃ**15:14** Or *preaching is useless, and your faith also is useless*, or *preaching is empty, and your faith also is empty*
ᵇ**15:27** Ps 8:6   ᶜ**15:29** Lit *they*   ᵈ**15:29** Other mss read *for the dead*

in Ephesus with only human hope,[a] what good does that do me?[b] If the dead are not raised, **Let us eat and drink, for tomorrow we die.**[c] [33] Do not be deceived: "Bad company corrupts good morals."[d] [34] Become right-minded[e] and stop sinning, because some people are ignorant about God. I say this to your shame.

Nature of Resurrection Body

[35] But someone will say, "How are the dead raised? What kind of body will they have when they come?" [36] Foolish one! What you sow does not come to life unless it dies. [37] And as for what you sow— you are not sowing the future body, but only a seed,[f] perhaps of wheat or another grain. [38] But God gives it a body as He wants, and to each of the seeds its own body. [39] Not all flesh is the same flesh; there is one flesh for humans, another for animals, another for birds, and another for fish. [40] There are heavenly bodies and earthly bodies, but the splendor of the heavenly bodies is different from that of the earthly ones. [41] There is a splendor of the sun, another of the moon, and another of the stars; for star differs from star in splendor. [42] So it is with the resurrection of the dead:

Sown in corruption,
　　raised in incorruption;
[43] sown in dishonor, raised in glory;
　　sown in weakness, raised in power;
[44] sown a natural body,
　　raised a spiritual body.

If there is a natural body, there is also a spiritual body. [45] So it is written: **The first man Adam became a living being;**[g] the last Adam became a life-giving Spirit. [46] However, the spiritual is not first, but the natural; then the spiritual.

[47] The first man was from the earth
　　and made of dust;
　　the second man is[h] from heaven.
[48] Like the man made of dust,
　　so are those who are made of dust;
　　like the heavenly man, so are those
　　who are heavenly.
[49] And just as we have borne
　　the image of the man
　　made of dust,
we will also bear the image
　　of the heavenly man.

We Will All Be Changed

[50] Brothers, I tell you this: flesh and blood cannot inherit the kingdom of God, and corruption cannot inherit incorruption. [51] Listen! I am telling you a •mystery:

We will not all fall asleep,
　　but we will all be changed,
[52] in a moment, in the twinkling
　　of an eye, at the last trumpet.
For the trumpet will sound,
　　and the dead will be raised
　　incorruptible,
and we will be changed.
[53] Because this corruptible
　　must be clothed
　　with incorruptibility,
and this mortal must be clothed
　　with immortality.

Victory over Death

[54] Now when this corruptible
　　is clothed with incorruptibility,
and this mortal is clothed
　　with immortality,
then the saying that is written
　　will take place:
**Death has been swallowed up
　　in victory.**[i]
[55] **O Death, where is your victory?**

a**15:32** Lit *Ephesus according to man*   b**15:32** Lit *what to me the profit?*   c**15:32** Is 22:13   d**15:33** A quotation from the poet Menander, *Thais*, 218   e**15:34** Lit *Sober up righteously*   f**15:37** Lit *but a naked seed*   g**15:45** Gn 2:7   h**15:47** Other mss add *the Lord*   i**15:54** Is 25:8

O Death, where is your sting?[a]

56 Now the sting of death is sin, and
the power of sin is the law.
57 But thanks be to God, who gives us
the victory
through our Lord Jesus Christ!

58 Therefore, my dear brothers, be steadfast, immovable, always excelling in the
Lord's work, knowing that your labor in
the Lord is not in vain.

Collection for the Jerusalem Church

16 Now about the collection for the
saints: you should do the same as I
instructed the Galatian churches. 2 On
the first day of the week, each of you is
to set something aside and save to the
extent that he prospers, so that no collections will need to be made when I
come. 3 And when I arrive, I will send
those whom you recommend by letter to
carry your gracious gift to Jerusalem. 4 If
it is also suitable for me to go, they will
travel with me.

Paul's Travel Plans

5 I will come to you after I pass through
Macedonia—for I will be traveling
through Macedonia— 6 and perhaps I will
remain with you, or even spend the winter, that you may send me on my way
wherever I go. 7 I don't want to see you
now just in passing, for I hope to spend
some time with you, if the Lord allows.
8 But I will stay in Ephesus until Pentecost, 9 because a wide door for effective
ministry has opened for me[b]—yet many
oppose me. 10 If Timothy comes, see that
he has nothing to fear from you, because

he is doing the Lord's work, just as I am.
11 Therefore no one should look down on
him; but you should send him on his way
in peace so he can come to me, for I am
expecting him with the brothers.[c]
12 About our brother Apollos: I
strongly urged him to come to you with
the brothers, but he was not at all willing to come now. However, when he has
time, he will come.

Final Exhortation

13 Be alert, stand firm in the faith, be
brave and strong. 14 Your every ⌊action⌋
must be done with love.

15 Brothers, you know the household of
Stephanas: they are the •firstfruits of
Achaia and have devoted themselves to
serving the saints. I urge you 16 also to
submit to such people, and to everyone
who works and labors with them. 17 I am
delighted over the presence of Stephanas,
Fortunatus, and Achaicus, because these
men have made up for your absence.
18 For they have refreshed my spirit and
yours. Therefore recognize such people.

Paul Concludes

19 The churches of the Asian province
greet you. Aquila and Priscilla greet you
heartily in the Lord, along with the
church that meets in their home. 20 All
the brothers greet you. Greet one another with a holy kiss.
21 This greeting is in my own hand[d]—
Paul. 22 If anyone does not love the Lord,
a curse be on him. *Maranatha!*[e] 23 The
grace of our Lord Jesus be with you.
24 My love be with all of you in Christ
Jesus.

a15:55 Hs 13:14   **b16:9** Lit *for a door has opened to me, great and effective*   **c16:11** *With the brothers* may connect with
Paul or Timothy.   **d16:21** Paul normally dictated his letters to a secretary, but signed the end of each letter himself; see Rm
16:22; Gl 6:11; Col 4:18; 2 Th 3:17.   **e16:22** Aram expression meaning *Our Lord come!*, or *Our Lord has come!*

2 CORINTHIANS

Greeting—from Paul and Timothy

1 Paul, an apostle of Christ Jesus by God's will, and Timothy our[a] brother:

To God's church at Corinth, with all the saints who are throughout Achaia.

² Grace to you and peace from God our Father and the Lord Jesus Christ.

God of Comfort

³ Blessed be the God and Father of our Lord Jesus Christ, the Father of mercies and the God of all comfort. ⁴ He comforts us in all our affliction,[b] so that we may be able to comfort those who are in any kind of affliction, through the comfort we ourselves receive from God. ⁵ For as the sufferings of Christ overflow to us, so our comfort overflows through Christ. ⁶ If we are afflicted, it is for your comfort and salvation; if we are comforted, it is for your comfort, which is experienced in the endurance of the same sufferings that we suffer. ⁷ And our hope for you is firm, because we know that as you share in the sufferings, so you will share in the comfort.

Paul Describes His Affliction

⁸ For we don't want you to be unaware, brothers, of our affliction that took place in the province of Asia: we were completely overwhelmed—beyond our strength—so that we even despaired of life. ⁹ However, we personally had a death sentence within ourselves so that we would not trust in ourselves, but in God who raises the dead. ¹⁰ He has delivered us from such a terrible death, and He will deliver us; we have placed our hope in Him that He will deliver us again. ¹¹ And you can join in helping with prayer for us, so that thanks may be given by many[c] on our[d] behalf for the gift that came to us through the prayers of many.

Paul's Clear Conscience

¹² For our boast is this: the testimony of our conscience that we have conducted ourselves in the world, and especially toward you, with God-given sincerity and purity, not by fleshly[e] wisdom but by God's grace. ¹³ Now we are writing you nothing other than what you can read and also understand. I hope you will understand completely— ¹⁴ as you have partially understood us—that we are your reason for pride, as you are ours, in the day of our[f] Lord Jesus.

Paul's Postponed Visit

¹⁵ In this confidence, I planned to come to you first, so you could have a double benefit,[g] ¹⁶ and to go on to Macedonia with your help, then come to you again from Macedonia and be given a start by you on my journey to Judea. ¹⁷ So when I planned this, was I irresponsible? Or what I plan, do I plan in a purely human[h] way so that I say "Yes, yes" and "No, no" simultaneously? ¹⁸ As God is faithful, our message to you is not "Yes and no." ¹⁹ For the Son of God, Jesus Christ, who was preached among you by us—by me and Silvanus[i]

ᵃ**1:1** Lit *the*   ᵇ**1:4** Or *trouble*, or *tribulation*, or *trials*, or *oppression*; the Gk word has a lit meaning of being under pressure.   ᶜ**1:11** Lit *by many faces*   ᵈ**1:11** Other mss read *your*   ᵉ**1:12** The word *fleshly* (characterized by flesh) indicates that the wisdom is natural rather than spiritual.   ᶠ**1:14** Other mss omit *our*   ᵍ**1:15** Other mss read *a second joy*   ʰ**1:17** Or *a worldly*, or *a fleshly*, or *a selfish*   ⁱ**1:19** Or *Silas*; see Ac 15:22-32; 16:19-40; 17:1-16

and Timothy—did not become "Yes and no"; on the contrary, "Yes" has come about in Him. 20 For every one of God's promises is "Yes" in Him. Therefore the "•Amen" is also through Him for God's glory through us. 21 Now the One who confirms us with you in Christ, and has anointed us, is God; 22 He has also sealed us and given us the Spirit as a down payment in our hearts.

23 I call on God as a witness against me:a it was to spare you that I did not come to Corinth. 24 Not that we have control ofb your faith, but we are workers with you for your joy, because you stand by faith. 1 In fact, I made up my mind about this:c not to come to you on another painful visit.d 2 For if I cause you pain, then who will cheer me other than the one hurt?e 3 I wrote this very thing so that when I came I wouldn't have pain from those who ought to give me joy, because I am confident about all of you that my joy is yours.f 4 For out of an extremely troubled and anguished heart I wrote to you with many tears— not that you should be hurt, but that you should know the abundant love I have for you.

Paul Urges Forgiveness of a Sinner

5 If anyone has caused pain, he has not caused pain to me, but in some degree— not to exaggerate—to all of you. 6 The punishment by the majority is sufficient for such a person, 7 so now you should forgive and comfort him instead; otherwise, this one may be overwhelmed by excessive grief. 8 Therefore I urge you to confirm your love to him. 9 It was for this purpose I wrote: so I may know your proven character, if you are obedient in everything. 10 Now to whom you forgive anything, I do too. For what I have forgiven, if I have forgiven anything, it is for you in the presence of Christ, 11 so that we may not be taken advantage of by Satan; for we are not ignorant of his intentions.g

Paul's Trip to Macedonia— and Anxiety for Titus

12 When I came to Troas for the gospel of Christ, a door was opened to me by the Lord. 13 I had no rest in my spirit because I did not find my brother Titus, but I said good-bye to them and left for Macedonia.

Paul's Ministry of Life or Death

14 But thanks be to God, who always puts us on displayh in Christ,i and spreads through us in every place the scent of knowing Him. 15 For to God we are the fragrance of Christ among those who are being saved and among those who are perishing. 16 To some we are a scent of death leading to death, but to others, a scent of life leading to life. And who is competent for this? 17 For we are not like the manyj who make a trade in God's message ⌊for profit⌋, but as those with sincerity, we speak in Christ, as from God and before God.

"You Are Christ's Letter"

3 Are we beginning to commend ourselves again? Or like some, do we need letters of recommendation to you or from you? 2 You yourselves are our letter, written on our hearts, recognized and read by everyone, 3 since it is plain that you are Christ's letter, producedk by us, not written with ink but with the

---

a1:23 Lit against my soul b1:24 Or we lord it over, or we rule over c2:1 Lit I decided this for myself d2:1 Lit not again in sorrow to come to you e2:2 Lit the one pained f2:3 Lit is of you all g2:11 Or thoughts h2:14 Or always leads us in a triumphal procession, or less likely, always causes us to triumph i2:14 Lit in the Christ, or in the Messiah; see 1 Co 15:22; Eph 1:10,12,20; 3:11 j2:17 Other mss read the rest k3:3 Lit ministered to

Spirit of the living God; not on stone tablets but on tablets that are hearts of flesh.

Paul's Competence from God

4 We have this kind of confidence toward God through Christ: 5 not that we are competent in[a] ourselves to consider anything as coming from ourselves, but our competence is from God. 6 He has made us competent to be ministers of a new covenant, not of the letter, but of the Spirit; for the letter kills, but the Spirit produces life.

New Ministry of Spirit

7 Now if the ministry of death, chiseled in letters on stones, came with glory, so that the sons of Israel were not able to look directly at Moses' face because of the glory from his face—a fading ⌊glory⌋— 8 how will the ministry of the Spirit not be more glorious? 9 For if the ministry of condemnation had glory, the ministry of righteousness overflows with even more glory. 10 In fact, what had been glorious is not glorious in this case because of the glory that surpasses it. 11 For if what was fading away was glorious, what endures will be even more glorious.

12 Therefore having such a hope, we use great boldness— 13 not like Moses, who used to put a veil over his face so that the sons of Israel could not look at the end of what was fading away. 14 But their minds were closed.[b] For to this day, at the reading of the old covenant, the same veil remains; it is not lifted, because it is set aside ⌊only⌋ in Christ. 15 However, to this day, whenever Moses is read, a veil lies over their hearts, 16 but whenever a person turns to the Lord, the veil is removed. 17 Now the Lord is the Spirit; and where the Spirit of the Lord is, there is freedom. 18 We all, with unveiled faces, are reflecting[c] the glory of the Lord and are being transformed into the same image from glory to glory;[d] this is from the Lord who is the Spirit.[e]

The Light of the Gospel

4 Therefore, since we have this ministry, as we have received mercy, we do not give up. 2 Instead, we have renounced shameful secret things, not •walking in deceit or distorting God's message, but in God's sight we commend ourselves to every person's conscience by an open display of the truth. 3 But if, in fact, our gospel is veiled, it is veiled to those who are perishing. 4 Regarding them: the god of this age has blinded the minds of the unbelievers so they cannot see the light of the gospel of the glory of Christ,[f] who is the image of God. 5 For we are not proclaiming ourselves but Jesus Christ as Lord, and ourselves as your slaves because of Jesus. 6 For God, who said, "Light shall shine out of darkness"—He has shone in our hearts to give the light of the knowledge of God's glory in the face of Jesus Christ.

Treasure in Clay Jars

7 Now we have this treasure in clay jars, so that this extraordinary power may be from God and not from us. 8 We are pressured in every way but not crushed; we are perplexed but not in despair; 9 we are persecuted but not abandoned; we are struck down but not destroyed. 10 We always carry the death of Jesus in our body, so that the life of Jesus may also be revealed in our body. 11 For we who live

---

a**3:5** Lit *from*　　b**3:14** Lit *their thoughts were hardened*　　c**3:18** Or *are looking as in a mirror at*　　d**3:18** Progressive glorification or sanctification　　e**3:18** Or *from the Spirit of the Lord,* or *from the Lord, the Spirit*　　f**4:4** Or *the gospel of the glorious Christ,* or *the glorious gospel of Christ*

are always given over to death because of Jesus, so that Jesus' life may also be revealed in our mortal flesh. [12] So death works in us, but life in you. [13] And since we have the same spirit of faith in accordance with what is written, **I believed, therefore I spoke,**[a] we also believe, and therefore speak, [14] knowing that the One who raised the Lord Jesus will raise us also with Jesus, and present us with you. [15] For all this is because of you, so that grace, extended through more and more people, may cause thanksgiving to overflow to God's glory.

Inner and Outer Person

[16] Therefore we do not give up; even though our outer person is being destroyed, our inner person is being renewed day by day. [17] For our momentary light affliction[b] is producing for us an absolutely incomparable eternal weight of glory. [18] So we do not focus on what is seen, but on what is unseen; for what is seen is temporary, but what is unseen is eternal.

Our Future after Death

5 For we know that if our earthly house, a tent,[c] is destroyed, we have a building from God, a house[d] not made with hands, eternal in the heavens. [2] And, in fact, we groan in this one, longing to put on our house from heaven, [3] since, when we are clothed,[e] we will not be found naked. [4] Indeed, we who are in this tent groan, burdened as we are, because we do not want to be unclothed but clothed, so that mortality may be swallowed up by life. [5] And the One who prepared us for this very thing is God, who gave us the Spirit as a down payment.

We Walk by Faith, Not by Sight

[6] Therefore, though we are always confident and know that while we are at home in the body we are away from the Lord— [7] for we •walk by faith, not by sight— [8] yet we are confident and satisfied to be out of the body and at home with the Lord. [9] Therefore, whether we are at home or away, we make it our aim to be pleasing to Him. [10] For we must all appear before the judgment seat of Christ, so that each may be repaid for what he has done in the body, whether good or bad.

[11] Knowing, then, the fear of the Lord, we persuade people. We are completely open before God, and I hope we are completely open to your consciences as well. [12] We are not commending ourselves to you again, but giving you an opportunity to be proud of us, so that you may have a reply for those who take pride in the outward appearance[f] rather than in the heart. [13] For if we are out of our mind, it is for God; if we have a sound mind, it is for you. [14] For Christ's love compels[g] us, since we have reached this conclusion: if One died for all, then all died. [15] And He died for all so that those who live should no longer live for themselves, but for the One who died for them and was raised.

Ambassadors for Christ: Ministry of Reconciliation

[16] From now on, then, we do not know[h] anyone in a purely human way.[i] Even if we have known[j] Christ in a purely human way,[k] yet now we no longer know[h] Him like that. [17] Therefore if anyone is in Christ, there is a new creation; old things have passed away, and

---

[a]**4:13** Ps 116:10 LXX [b]**4:17** See note at 2 Co 1:4 [c]**5:1** Our present physical body [d]**5:1** *a building . . . a house* = our future body [e]**5:3** Other mss read *stripped* [f]**5:12** Lit *in face* [g]**5:14** Or *For the love of Christ impels,* or *For the love of Christ controls* [h]**5:16** Or *regard* [i]**5:16** Lit *anyone according to the flesh* [j]**5:16** Or *have regarded* [k]**5:16** Lit *Christ according to the flesh*

look, new things[a] have come. [18] Now everything is from God, who reconciled us to Himself through Christ and gave us the ministry of reconciliation: [19] that is, in Christ, God was reconciling the world to Himself, not counting their trespasses against them, and He has committed the message of reconciliation to us. [20] Therefore, we are ambassadors for Christ; certain that God is appealing through us, we plead on Christ's behalf, "Be reconciled to God." [21] He made the One who did not know sin to be sin for us, so that we might become the righteousness of God in Him.

6 Working together[b] with Him, we also appeal to you: "Don't receive God's grace in vain." [2] For He says:

> In an acceptable time, I heard you,
> and in the day of salvation,
> I helped you.[c]

Look, now is the acceptable time; look, now is the day of salvation.

Stresses of Paul's Ministry

[3] We give no opportunity for stumbling to anyone, so that the ministry will not be blamed. [4] But in everything, as God's ministers, we commend ourselves:

> by great endurance, by afflictions,
> by hardship, by pressures,
> [5] by beatings, by imprisonments,
> by riots, by labors,
> by sleepless nights,
> by times of hunger,
> [6] by purity, by knowledge,
> by patience, by kindness,
> by the Holy Spirit, by sincere love,
> [7] by the message of truth,
> by the power of God;
> through weapons of righteousness
> on the right hand and the left,

> [8] through glory and dishonor,
> through slander and good report;
> as deceivers yet true;
> [9] as unknown yet recognized;
> as dying and look—we live;
> as being chastened yet not killed;
> [10] as grieving yet always rejoicing;
> as poor yet enriching many;
> as having nothing
> yet possessing everything.

[11] We have spoken openly[d] to you, Corinthians; our heart has been opened wide. [12] You are not limited by us, but you are limited by your own affections. [13] Now in like response—I speak as to children—you also should be open to us.

Separation for God

[14] Do not be mismatched with unbelievers. For what partnership is there between righteousness and lawlessness? Or what fellowship does light have with darkness? [15] What agreement does Christ have with Belial?[e] Or what does a believer have in common with an unbeliever? [16] And what agreement does God's sanctuary have with idols? For we[f] are the sanctuary of the living God, as God said:

> I will dwell among them and walk
> among them,
> and I will be their God,
> and they will be My people.[g]
> [17] Therefore, come out
> from among them
> and be separate, says the Lord;
> do not touch any unclean thing,
> and I will welcome you.[h]
> [18] I will be a Father to you,
> and you will be sons
> and daughters to Me,
> says the Lord Almighty.[i]

---

[a]5:17 Other mss read *look, all new things*   [b]6:1 Or *As we work together*   [c]6:2 Is 49:8   [d]6:11 Lit *Our mouths have been open*   [e]6:15 Or *Beliar,* a name for the Devil or antichrist in extra-biblical Jewish writings   [f]6:16 Other mss read *you*   [g]6:16 Lv 26:12; Jr 31:33; 32:38; Ezk 37:26   [h]6:17 Is 52:11   [i]6:18 2 Sm 7:14; Is 43:6; 49:22; 60:4; Hs 1:10

7 Therefore dear friends, since we have such promises, we should wash ourselves clean from every impurity of the flesh and spirit, making our sanctification complete[a] in the fear of God.

Paul's Joy in Afflictions

² Take us into your hearts.[b] We have wronged no one, corrupted no one, defrauded no one. ³ I don't say this to condemn you, for I have already said that you are in our hearts, to die together and to live together. ⁴ I have great confidence in you; I have great pride in you. I am filled with encouragement; I am overcome with joy in all our afflictions.

Paul's Anxiety— and Comfort—over Titus

⁵ In fact, when we came into Macedonia, we[c] had no rest. Instead, we were afflicted in every way: struggles on the outside, fears inside. ⁶ But God, who comforts the humble, comforted us by the coming of Titus, ⁷ and not only by his coming, but also by the comfort he received from you. He announced to us your deep longing, your sorrow,[d] your zeal for me, so that I rejoiced even more. ⁸ For although I grieved you with my letter, I do not regret it—even though I did regret it since I saw that the letter grieved you, though only for a little while. ⁹ Now I am rejoicing, not because you were grieved, but because your grief led to repentance. For you were grieved as God willed, so that you didn't experience any loss from us.

Godly Grief and Worldly Grief: Repentance vs. Death

¹⁰ For godly grief produces a repentance not to be regretted and leading to salvation, but worldly grief produces death.

¹¹ For consider how much diligence this very thing—this grieving as God wills—has produced in you: what a desire to clear yourselves, what indignation, what fear, what deep longing, what zeal, what justice! In every way you have commended yourselves to be pure in this matter. ¹² So even though I wrote to you, it was not because of the one who did wrong, or because of the one who was wronged, but in order that your diligence for us might be made plain to you in the sight of God. ¹³ For this reason we have been comforted.

Paul's Joy over Titus

In addition to our comfort, we were made to rejoice even more over the joy Titus had,[e] because his spirit was refreshed by all of you. ¹⁴ For if I have made any boast to him about you, I have not been embarrassed; but as I have spoken everything to you in truth, so our boasting to Titus has also turned out to be the truth. ¹⁵ And his affection toward you is even greater as he remembers the obedience of all of you, and how you received him with fear and trembling. ¹⁶ I rejoice that I have complete confidence in you.

Paul Commends Macedonia Churches for Generosity

8 We want you to know, brothers, about the grace of God granted to the churches of Macedonia: ² during a severe testing by affliction, their abundance of joy and their deep poverty overflowed into the wealth of their generosity. ³ I testify that, on their own, according to their ability and beyond their ability, ⁴ they begged us insistently for the privilege of sharing in the ministry to the saints, ⁵ and not just as we had hoped. Instead, they gave them-

---

[a]7:1 Or spirit, perfecting holiness   [b]7:2 Lit Make room for us.   [c]7:5 Lit our flesh   [d]7:7 Or lamentation, or mourning
[e]7:13 Lit the joy of Titus

selves especially to the Lord, then to us by God's will. [6] So we urged Titus that, just as he had begun, so he should also complete this grace to you. [7] Now as you excel in everything—in faith, in speech, in knowledge, in all diligence, and in your love for us[a]—excel also in this grace.

Paul Appeals to Corinth for Gifts— and Equality

[8] I am not saying this as a command. Rather, by means of the diligence of others, I am testing the genuineness of your love. [9] For you know the grace of our Lord Jesus Christ: although He was rich, for your sake He became poor, so that by His poverty you might become rich. [10] Now I am giving an opinion on this because it is profitable for you, who a year ago began not only to do something but also to desire it.[b] [11] But now finish the task[c] as well, that just as there was eagerness to desire it, so there may also be a completion from what you have. [12] For if the eagerness is there, it is acceptable according to what one has, not according to what he does not have. [13] It is not that there may be relief for others and hardship for you, but it is a question of equality[d]— [14] at the present time your surplus is ⌊available⌋ for their need, so that their abundance may also become ⌊available⌋ for your need, that there may be equality. [15] As it has been written:

**The person who gathered much
did not have too much,
and the person who gathered
little did not have too little.[e]**

Administration of the Collection

[16] Thanks be to God who put the same diligence for you into the heart of Titus.

[17] For he accepted our urging and, being very diligent, went out to you by his own choice. [18] With him we have sent the brother who is praised throughout the churches for his gospel ministry.[f] [19] And not only that, but he was also appointed by the churches to accompany us with this gift[g] that is being administered by us for the glory of the Lord Himself and to show our eagerness ⌊to help⌋. [20] We are taking this precaution so no one can find fault with us concerning this large sum administered by us. [21] For we are making provision for what is honorable, not only before the Lord but also before men. [22] We have also sent with them our brother whom we have often tested, in many circumstances, and found diligent—and now even more diligent because of his great confidence in you. [23] As for Titus, he is my partner and co-worker serving you; as for our brothers, they are the messengers of the churches, the glory of Christ. [24] Therefore, before the churches, show them the proof of your love and of our boasting about you.

Motivations for Giving

9 Now concerning the ministry to the saints, it is unnecessary for me to write to you. [2] For I know your eagerness, and I brag about you to the Macedonians:[h] "Achaia[i] has been prepared since last year," and your zeal has stirred up most of them. [3] But I sent the brothers so our boasting about you in the matter would not prove empty, and so you would be prepared just as I said. [4] For if any Macedonians should come with me and find you unprepared, we, not to mention you, would be embarrassed in that situation.[j] [5] Therefore I considered it necessary to urge the brothers to go on ahead to you and arrange in advance the generous gift you promised, so that it will be ready as a gift and not an extortion.

Sowing and Reaping Generously

6 Remember this:a the person who sows sparingly will also reap sparingly, and the person who sows generously will also reap generously. 7 Each person should do as he has decided in his heart—not out of regret or out of necessity, for God loves a cheerful giver. 8 And God is able to make every grace overflow to you, so that in every way, always having everything you need, you may excel in every good work. 9 As it is written:

> He has scattered;
> He has given to the poor;
> His righteousness endures
>   forever.b

10 Now the One who provides seed for the sower and bread for food will provide and multiply your seed and increase the harvest of your righteousness, 11 as you are enriched in every way for all generosity, which produces thanksgiving to God through us. 12 For the ministry of this service is not only supplying the needs of the saints, but is also overflowing in many acts of thanksgiving to God. 13 Through the proof of this service, they will glorify God for your obedience to the confession ofc the gospel of Christ, and for your generosity in sharing with them and with others. 14 And in their prayers for you they will have deep affection ford you because of the surpassing grace of God on you. 15 Thanks be to God for His indescribable gift.

Paul's Apostolic Authority

10 Now I, Paul, make a personal appeal to you by the gentleness and graciousness of Christ—I who am humble among you in person, but bold toward you when absent. 2 I beg you that when I am present I will not need to be bold with the confidence by which I plan to challenge certain people who think we are •walking in a fleshly way.e 3 For although we are walking in the flesh, we do not wage war in a fleshly way,f 4 since the weapons of our warfare are not fleshly, but are powerful through God for the demolition of strongholds. We demolish arguments 5 and every high-minded thing that is raised up against the knowledge of God, taking every thought captive to the obedience of Christ. 6 And we are ready to punish any disobedience, once your obedience is complete.

7 Look at what is obvious.g If anyone is confident that he belongs to Christ, he should remind himself of this: just as he belongs to Christ, so do we. 8 For if I boast some more about our authority, which the Lord gave for building you up and not for tearing you down, I am not ashamed. 9 I don't want to seem as though I am trying to terrify you with my letters. 10 For it is said, "His letters are weighty and powerful, but his physical presence is weak, and his public speaking is despicable." 11 Such a person should consider this: what we are in the words of our letters when absent, we will be in actions when present.

"Boast in the Lord"

12 For we don't dare classify or compare ourselves with some who commend themselves. But in measuring themselves by themselves and comparing

a9:6 Lit And this   b9:9 Ps 112:9   c9:13 Or your obedient confession to   d9:14 Or will long for   e10:2 Lit walking according to flesh   f10:3 Lit war according to flesh   g10:7 Or You are looking at things outwardly

themselves to themselves, they lack understanding. ¹³ We, however, will not boast beyond measure, but according to the measure of the area ⌊of ministry⌋ that God has assigned to us, ⌊which⌋ reaches even to you. ¹⁴ For we are not overextending ourselves, as if we had not reached you, since we have come to you with the gospel of Christ. ¹⁵ We are not bragging beyond measure about other people's labors. But we have the hope that as your faith increases, our area ⌊of ministry⌋ will be greatly enlarged, ¹⁶ so that we may preach the gospel to the regions beyond you, not boasting about what has already been done in someone else's area ⌊of ministry⌋. ¹⁷ So **the one who boasts must boast in the Lord.**ᵃ ¹⁸ For it is not the one commending himself who is approved, but the one the Lord commends.

Paul and False Apostles

11 I wish you would put up with a little foolishness from me. Yes, do put up with me.ᵇ ² For I am jealous over you with a godly jealousy, because I have promised you in marriage to one husband—to present a pure virgin to Christ. ³ But I fear that, as the serpent deceived Eve by his cunning, your minds may be corrupted from a complete and pureᶜ devotion to Christ. ⁴ For if a person comes and preaches another Jesus, whom we did not preach, or you receive a different spirit, which you had not received, or a different gospel, which you had not accepted, you put up with it splendidly!

⁵ Now I consider myself in no way inferior to the "super-apostles." ⁶ Though untrained in public speaking, I am certainly not ⌊untrained⌋ in knowledge. Indeed, we have always made that clear to you in everything. ⁷ Or did I commit a

sin by humbling myself so that you might be exalted, because I preached the gospel of God to you free of charge? ⁸ I robbed other churches by taking pay ⌊from them⌋ to minister to you. ⁹ When I was present with you and in need, I did not burden anyone, for the brothers who came from Macedonia supplied my needs. I have kept myself, and will keep myself, from burdening you in any way. ¹⁰ As the truth of Christ is in me, this boasting of mine will not be stoppedᵈ in the regions of Achaia. ¹¹ Why? Because I don't love you? God knows I do!

¹² But I will continue to do what I am doing, in order to cut off the opportunity of those who want an opportunity to be regarded just as we are in what they are boasting about. ¹³ For such people are false apostles, deceitful workers, disguising themselves as apostles of Christ. ¹⁴ And no wonder! For Satan himself is disguised as an angel of light. ¹⁵ So it is no great thing if his servants also disguise themselves as servants of righteousness. Their destinyᵉ will be according to their works.

Paul's Physical Sufferings for Christ

¹⁶ I repeat: no one should consider me a fool. But if ⌊you do⌋, at least accept me as a fool, so I too may boast a little. ¹⁷ What I say in this matterᶠ of boasting, I don't speak as the Lord would, but foolishly. ¹⁸ Since many boast from a human perspective,ᵍ I will also boast. ¹⁹ For you gladly put up with fools since you are so smart!ʰ ²⁰ In fact, you put up with it if someone enslaves you, if someone devours you, if someone captures you, if someone dominates you, or if someone hits you in the face. ²¹ I say this to ⌊our⌋ shame: we have been weak.

ᵃ**10:17** Jr 9:24   ᵇ**11:1** Or *Yes, you are putting up with me*   ᶜ**11:3** Other mss omit *and pure*   ᵈ**11:10** Or *silenced*
ᵉ**11:15** Lit *end*   ᶠ**11:17** Or *business, or confidence*   ᵍ**11:18** Lit *boast according to the flesh*   ʰ**11:19** Or *are wise*

But in whatever anyone dares to boast—I am talking foolishly—I also dare:

22 Are they Hebrews? So am I.
Are they Israelites? So am I.
Are they the seed of Abraham?
So am I.
23 Are they servants of Christ?
I'm talking like a madman—
I'm a better one:
with far more labors,
many more imprisonments,
far worse beatings, near death[a]
many times.
24 Five times I received from the Jews
40 lashes minus one.
25 Three times I was beaten
with rods.[b]
Once I was stoned.[c]
Three times I was shipwrecked.
I have spent a night and a day
in the depths of the sea.
26 On frequent journeys, I faced
dangers from rivers,
dangers from robbers,
dangers from my own people,
dangers from the Gentiles,
dangers in the city,
dangers in the open country,
dangers on the sea, and dangers
among false brothers;
27 labor and hardship,
many sleepless nights,
hunger and thirst,
often without food, cold,
and lacking clothing.

Paul's Emotional Suffering

28 Not to mention[d] other things, there is the daily pressure on me: my care for all the churches. 29 Who is weak, and I am not weak? Who is made to stumble, and I do not burn with indignation? 30 If boasting is necessary, I will boast about my weaknesses. 31 The eternally blessed One, the God and Father of the Lord Jesus, knows I am not lying. 32 In Damascus, the governor under King Aretas[e] guarded the city of the Damascenes in order to arrest me, 33 so I was let down in a basket through a window in the wall and escaped his hands.

Visit to the Third Heaven

12 It is necessary to boast; it is not helpful, but I will move on to visions and revelations of the Lord. 2 I know a man in Christ who was caught up into the third heaven 14 years ago. Whether he was in the body or out of the body, I don't know; God knows. 3 I know that this man—whether in the body or out of the body I do not know, God knows— 4 was caught up into paradise. He heard inexpressible words, which a man is not allowed to speak. 5 I will boast about this person, but not about myself, except of my weaknesses. 6 For if I want to boast, I will not be a fool, because I will be telling the truth. But I will spare you, so that no one can credit me with something beyond what he sees in me or hears from me, 7 especially because of the extraordinary revelations.

Paul's Thorn in the Flesh

Therefore, so that I would not exalt myself, a thorn in the flesh was given to me, a messenger[f] of Satan to torment me so I would not exalt myself. 8 Concerning this, I pleaded with the Lord three times to take it away from me. 9 But He said to me, "My grace is sufficient for you, for power[g] is perfected in weakness." Therefore, I will most

a11:23 Lit and in deaths   b11:25 A specifically Roman punishment; see Ac 16:22   c11:25 A common Jewish method of capital punishment; see Ac 14:5   d11:28 Lit Apart from   e11:32 Aretus IV (9 B.C.–A.D. 40), a Nabatean Arab king   f12:7 Or angel   g12:9 Other mss read My power

gladly boast all the more about my weaknesses, so that Christ's power may reside in me. ¹⁰ So because of Christ, I am pleased in weaknesses, in insults, in catastrophes, in persecutions, and in pressures. For when I am weak, then I am strong.

Signs of an Apostle

¹¹ I have become a fool; you forced it on me. I ought to have been recommended by you, since I am in no way inferior to the "super-apostles," even though I am nothing. ¹² The signs of an apostle were performed among you in all endurance—not only signs but also wonders and miracles. ¹³ So in what way were you treated worse than the other churches, except that I personally did not burden you? Forgive me this wrong!

Paul's Concern for Corinthians

¹⁴ Look! I am ready to come to you this third time. I will not burden you, for I am not seeking what is yours, but you. For children are not obligated to save up for their parents, but parents for their children. ¹⁵ I will most gladly spend and be spent for you.ᵃ If I love you more, am I to be loved less? ¹⁶ Now granted, I have not burdened you; yet sly as I am, I took you in by deceit! ¹⁷ Did I take advantage of you by anyone I sent you? ¹⁸ I urged Titus ⌊to come⌋, and I sent the brother with him. Did Titus take advantage of you? Didn't we •walk in the same spirit and in the same footsteps?

¹⁹ You have thought all along that we were defending ourselves to you.ᵇ ⌊No⌋, in the sight of God we are speaking in Christ, and everything, dear friends, is for building you up. ²⁰ For I fear that perhaps when I come I will not find you to

be what I want, and I may not be found by you to be what you want;ᶜ there may be quarreling, jealousy, outbursts of anger, selfish ambitions, slander, gossip, arrogance, and disorder. ²¹ I fear that when I come my God will againᵈ humiliate me in your presence, and I will grieve for many who sinned before and have not repented of the uncleanness, sexual immorality, and promiscuity they practiced.

Paul Warns About His Third Visit

13 This is the third time I am coming to you. **On the testimonyᵉ of two or three witnesses every word will be confirmed.**ᶠ ² I gave warning, and I give warning—as when I was present the second time, so now while I am absent—to those who sinned before and to all the rest: if I come again, I will not be lenient, ³ since you seek proof of Christ speaking in me. He is not weak toward you, but powerful among you. ⁴ In fact, He was crucified in weakness, but He lives by God's power. For we also are weak in Him, yet toward you we will live with Him by God's power.

"Test Yourselves"

⁵ Test yourselves ⌊to see⌋ if you are in the faith. Examine yourselves. Or do you not recognize for yourselves that Jesus Christ is in you?—unless you fail the test.ᵍ ⁶ And I hope you will recognize that we are not failing the test. ⁷ Now we pray to God that you do nothing wrong, not that we may appear to pass the test, but that you may do what is right, even though we ⌊may appear⌋ to fail. ⁸ For we are not able to do anything against the truth, but only for the truth. ⁹ In fact, we rejoice when we are weak and you are strong. We also pray for this: your maturity.ʰ ¹⁰ This is why I am

---

ᵃ**12:15** Lit *for your souls,* or *for your lives*   ᵇ**12:19** Or *Have you thought . . . to you?*   ᶜ**12:20** Lit *be as you want*
ᵈ**12:21** Or *come again my God will*   ᵉ**13:1** Lit *mouth*   ᶠ**13:1** Dt 17:6; 19:15   ᵍ**13:5** Or *you are disqualified,* or *you are counterfeit*   ʰ**13:9** Or *completion,* or *restoration*

writing these things while absent, that when I am there I will not use severity, in keeping with the authority the Lord gave me for building up and not for tearing down.

Paul's Uplifting Finale

[11] Finally, brothers, rejoice. Be restored, be encouraged, be of the same mind, be at peace, and the God of love and peace will be with you. [12] Greet one another with a holy kiss. All the saints greet you.

[13] The grace of the Lord Jesus Christ, and the love of God, and the fellowship of the Holy Spirit be with all of you.[a]

GALATIANS

Greeting—from Paul and Brothers

1 Paul, an apostle—not from men or by man, but by Jesus Christ and God the Father who raised Him from the dead— [2] and all the brothers who are with me:

To the churches of Galatia.[b]

[3] Grace to you and peace from God the Father and our Lord[c] Jesus Christ, [4] who gave Himself for our sins to rescue us from this present evil age, according to the will of our God and Father, [5] to whom be the glory forever and ever. •Amen.

Paul: No Other Gospel

[6] I am amazed that you are so quickly turning away from Him who called you by the grace of Christ, ⌊and are turning⌋ to a different gospel— [7] not that there is another ⌊gospel⌋, but there are some who are troubling you and want to change the gospel of Christ. [8] But even if we or an angel from heaven should preach to you a gospel other than what we have preached to you, a curse be on him![d] [9] As we have said before, I now say again: if anyone preaches to you a gospel contrary to what you received, a curse be on him![e]

[10] For am I now trying to win the favor of people, or God? Or am I striving to please people? If I were still trying to please people, I would not be a slave of Christ.

Paul Defends His Apostleship

[11] Now I want you to know, brothers, that the gospel preached by me is not based on a human point of view.[f] [12] For I did not receive it from a human source and I was not taught it, but it came by a revelation from Jesus Christ.

Paul's Early Spiritual History

[13] For you have heard about my former way of life in Judaism: I persecuted God's church to an extreme degree and tried to destroy it; [14] and I advanced in Judaism beyond many contemporaries among my people, because I was extremely zealous for the traditions of my ancestors. [15] But when God, who from my mother's womb set me apart and called me by His grace, was pleased [16] to reveal His Son in me, so

---

[a] **13:12-13** Some translations divide these 2 vv. into 3 vv. so that v. 13 begins with *All the saints* . . . and v. 14 begins with *The grace of* . . . [b] **1:2** A Roman province in what is now Turkey [c] **1:3** Other mss read *God our Father and the Lord* [d] **1:8** Or *you, let him be condemned*, or *you, let him be condemned to hell*; Gk *anathema* [e] **1:9** Or *received, let him be condemned*, or *received, let him be condemned to hell*; Gk *anathema* [f] **1:11** Lit *not according to man*

that I could preach Him among the Gentiles, I did not immediately consult with anyone.[a] [17] I did not go up to Jerusalem to those who had become apostles before me; instead I went to Arabia and came back to Damascus.

[18] Then after three years I did go up to Jerusalem to get to know •Cephas,[b] and I stayed with him 15 days. [19] But I didn't see any of the other apostles except James, the Lord's brother. [20] Now in what I write to you, I'm not lying. God is my witness.[c]

[21] Afterwards, I went to the regions of Syria and Cilicia. [22] I remained personally unknown to the Judean churches in Christ; [23] they simply kept hearing: "He who formerly persecuted us now preaches the faith he once tried to destroy." [24] And they glorified God because of me.

Paul Defends His Gospel at Jerusalem

2 Then after 14 years I went up again to Jerusalem with Barnabas, taking Titus along also. [2] I went up because of a revelation and presented to them the gospel I preach among the Gentiles—but privately to those recognized ⌊as leaders⌋—so that I might not be running, or have run, in vain. [3] But not even Titus who was with me, though he was a Greek, was compelled to be circumcised. [4] ⌊This issue arose⌋ because of false brothers smuggled in, who came in secretly to spy on our freedom that we have in Christ Jesus, in order to enslave us. [5] But we did not yield in submission to these people for even an hour, so that the truth of the gospel would remain for you.

Paul and Peter: Different Apostolic Missions

[6] But from those recognized as important (what they really were makes no difference to me; God does not show favoritism[d])—those recognized as important added nothing to me. [7] On the contrary, they saw that I had been entrusted with the gospel for the uncircumcised, just as Peter was for the circumcised. [8] For He who was at work with Peter in the apostleship to the circumcised was also at work with me among the Gentiles. [9] When James, •Cephas, and John, recognized as pillars, acknowledged the grace that had been given to me, they gave the right hand of fellowship to me and Barnabas, ⌊agreeing⌋ that we should go to the Gentiles and they to the circumcised. [10] ⌊They asked⌋ only that we would remember the poor, which I made every effort to do.

Paul Opposes Peter

[11] But when Cephas[b] came to Antioch, I opposed him to his face because he stood condemned.[e] [12] For he used to eat with the Gentiles before certain men came from James. However, when they came, he withdrew and separated himself, because he feared those from the circumcision party. [13] Then the rest of the Jews joined his hypocrisy, so that even Barnabas was carried away by their hypocrisy. [14] But when I saw that they were deviating from the truth of the gospel, I told Cephas[b] in front of everyone, "If you, who are a Jew, live like a Gentile and not like a Jew, how can you compel Gentiles to live like Jews?"[f]

Paul Affirms Justification by Faith

[15] We are Jews by birth and not "Gentile sinners"; [16] yet we know that no one is justified by the works of the law but by faith in Jesus Christ.[g] And we have believed in Christ Jesus, so that we might

---

[a]1:16 Lit *flesh and blood*　[b]1:18; 2:11,14 Other mss read *Peter*　[c]1:20 Lit *Behold, before God*　[d]2:6 Or *God is not a respecter of persons;* lit *God does not receive the face of man*　[e]2:11 Or *he was in the wrong*　[f]2:14 Some translations continue the quotation through v. 16 or v. 21.　[g]2:16 Or *by the faithfulness of Jesus Christ*

be justified by faith in Christ[a] and not by the works of the law, because by the works of the law no human being will[b] be justified. [17] But if, while seeking to be justified by Christ, we ourselves are also found to be sinners, is Christ then a promoter[c] of sin? Absolutely not! [18] If I rebuild those things that I tore down, I show myself to be a lawbreaker. [19] For through the law I have died to the law, that I might live to God. I have been crucified with Christ; [20] and I no longer live, but Christ lives in me. The life I now live in the flesh,[d] I live by faith in the Son of God, who loved me and gave Himself for me. [21] I do not set aside the grace of God; for if righteousness comes through the law, then Christ died for nothing.

"You Foolish Galatians!"

3 You foolish Galatians! Who has hypnotized you,[e] before whose eyes Jesus Christ was vividly portrayed[f] as crucified? [2] I only want to learn this from you: Did you receive the Spirit by the works of the law or by hearing with faith?[g] [3] Are you so foolish? After beginning with the Spirit, are you now going to be made complete by the flesh?[h] [4] Did you suffer so much for nothing—if in fact it was for nothing? [5] So then, does God[i] supply you with the Spirit and work miracles among you by the works of the law or by hearing with faith?[g]

[6] Just as Abraham **believed God, and it was credited to him for righteousness,**[j] [7] so understand that those who have faith are Abraham's sons. [8] Now the Scripture foresaw that God would justify the Gentiles by faith and foretold the good news to Abraham, saying, **All the nations will be blessed in you.**[k] [9] So those who have faith are blessed with Abraham, who had faith.[l]

Limits of the Law

[10] For all who ⌊rely on⌋ the works of the law are under a curse, because it is written: **Cursed is everyone who does not continue doing everything written in the book of the law.**[m] [11] Now it is clear that no one is justified before God by the law, because **the righteous will live by faith.**[n] [12] But the law is not based on faith; instead, **the one who does these things will live by them.**[o] [13] Christ has redeemed us from the curse of the law by becoming a curse for us, because it is written: **Cursed is everyone who is hung on a tree.**[p] [14] The purpose was that the blessing of Abraham would come to the Gentiles in Christ Jesus, so that we could receive the promise of the Spirit through faith.

[15] Brothers, I'm using a human illustration.[q] No one sets aside even a human covenant that has been ratified, or makes additions to it. [16] Now the promises were spoken to Abraham and to his seed. He does not say "and to seeds," as though referring to many, but **and to your seed,**[r] referring to one, who is Christ. [17] And I say this: the law, which came 430 years later, does not revoke a covenant that was previously ratified by God,[s] so as to cancel the promise. [18] For if the inheritance is from the law, it is no longer from the promise; but God granted it to Abraham through the promise.

Purpose of the Law

[19] Why the law then? It was added because of transgressions until the Seed to whom the promise was made would

---

[a]**2:16** Or *by the faithfulness of Christ* [b]**2:16** Lit *law all flesh will not* [c]**2:17** Or *servant* [d]**2:20** The physical body [e]**3:1** Other mss add *not to obey the truth* [f]**3:1** Other mss add *among you* [g]**3:2,5** Lit *by law works or faith hearing* or *hearing the message* [h]**3:3** By human effort [i]**3:5** Lit *He* [j]**3:6** Gn 15:6 [k]**3:8** Gn 12:3; 18:18 [l]**3:9** Or *with believing Abraham* [m]**3:10** Dt 27:26 [n]**3:11** Hab 2:4 [o]**3:12** Lv 18:5 [p]**3:13** Dt 21:23 [q]**3:15** Lit *I speak according to man* [r]**3:16** Gn 12:7; 13:15; 17:8; 24:7 [s]**3:17** Other mss add *in Christ*

come. ⌊The law⌋ was ordered through angels by means of a mediator. ²⁰ Now a mediator is not for just one person, but God is one. ²¹ Is the law therefore contrary to God's promises? Absolutely not! For if a law had been given that was able to give life, then righteousness would certainly be by the law. ²² But the Scripture has imprisoned everything under sin's power,ᵃ so that the promise by faith in Jesus Christ might be given to those who believe. ²³ Before this faith came, we were confined under the law, imprisoned until the coming faith was revealed. ²⁴ The law, then, was our guardianᵇ until Christ, so that we could be justified by faith. ²⁵ But since that faith has come, we are no longer under a guardian,ᵇ ²⁶ for you are all sons of God through faith in Christ Jesus.

All One in Christ Jesus

²⁷ For as many of you as have been baptized into Christ have put on Christ. ²⁸ There is no Jew or Greek, slave or free, male or female; for you are all one in Christ Jesus. ²⁹ And if you are Christ's, then you are Abraham's seed, heirs according to the promise. ¹ Now I say that as long as the heir is a child, he differs in no way from a slave, though he is the owner of everything. ² Instead, he is under guardians and stewards until the time set by his father. ³ In the same way we also, when we were children, were in slavery under the elemental forces of the world. ⁴ But when the completion of the time came, God sent His Son, born of a woman, born under the law, ⁵ to redeem those under the law, so that we might receive adoption as sons. ⁶ And because you are sons, God has

sent the Spirit of His Son into ourᶜ hearts, crying, "•*Abba*, Father!" ⁷ So you are no longer a slave, but a son; and if a son, then an heir through God.

Paul's Concern: Elemental Forces and Special Days

⁸ But in the past, when you didn't know God, you were enslaved to thingsᵈ that by nature are not gods. ⁹ But now, since you know God, or rather have become known by God, how can you turn back again to the weak and bankrupt elemental forces? Do you want to be enslaved to them all over again? ¹⁰ You observe ⌊special⌋ days, months, seasons, and years. ¹¹ I am fearful for you, that perhaps my labor for you has been wasted.

Paul's Physical Weakness—and Galatians' Compassion

¹² I beg you, brothers: become like me, for I also became like you. You have not wronged me; ¹³ you know that previously I preached the gospel to you in physical weakness, ¹⁴ and though my physical condition was a trial for you,ᵉ you did not despise or reject me. On the contrary, you received me as an angel of God, as Christ Jesus ⌊Himself⌋.

Paul Must Tell Truth

¹⁵ What happened to this blessedness of yours? For I testify to you that, if possible, you would have torn out your eyes and given them to me. ¹⁶ Have I now become your enemy by telling you the truth? ¹⁷ Theyᶠ are enthusiastic about you, but not for any good. Instead, they want to isolate you so you will be enthusiastic about them. ¹⁸ Now it is always good to be enthusiastic about good—and

---

ᵃ**3:22** Lit *under sin*   ᵇ**3:24,25** The word translated *guardian* in vv. 24-25 is different from the word in Gl 4:2. In our culture, we do not have a slave who takes a child to and from school, protecting the child from harm or corruption. In Gk the word *paidogogos* described such a slave. This slave was not a teacher.   ᶜ**4:6** Other mss read *your*   ᵈ**4:8** Or *beings*   ᵉ**4:14** Other mss read *me*   ᶠ**4:17** The false teachers

not just when I am with you. ¹⁹ My children, again I am in the pains of childbirth for you until Christ is formed in you. ²⁰ I'd like to be with you right now and change my tone of voice, because I don't know what to do about you.

Sarah and Hagar: Two Covenants

²¹ Tell me, you who want to be under the law, don't you hear the law? ²² For it is written that Abraham had two sons, one by a slave and the other by a free woman. ²³ But the one by the slave was born according to the flesh, while the one by the free woman was born as the result of a promise. ²⁴ These things are illustrations,ᵃ for the women represent the two covenants. One is from Mount Sinai and bears children into slavery—this is Hagar. ²⁵ Now Hagar is Mount Sinai in Arabia and corresponds to the present Jerusalem, for she is in slavery with her children. ²⁶ But the Jerusalem above is free, and she is our mother. ²⁷ For it is written:

Rejoice, O barren woman
who does not give birth.
Break forth and shout,
you who are not in labor,
for the children of the desolate
     are many,
more numerous than those
of the woman
     who has a husband.ᵇ

²⁸ Now you, brothers, like Isaac, are children of promise. ²⁹ But just as then the child born according to the flesh persecuted the one born according to the Spirit, so also now. ³⁰ But what does the Scripture say?

Throw out the slave and her son,
for the son of the slave will never
inherit with the son of the free
woman.ᶜ

³¹ Therefore, brothers, we are not children of the slave but of the free woman.

Christian Freedom

5 Christ has liberated us into freedom. Therefore stand firm and don't submit again to a yoke of slavery. ² Take note! I, Paul, tell you that if you get circumcised, Christ will not benefit you at all. ³ Again I testify to every man who gets circumcised that he is obligated to keep the entire law. ⁴ You who are trying to be justified by the law are alienated from Christ; you have fallen from grace! ⁵ For by the Spirit we eagerly wait for the hope of righteousness from faith. ⁶ For in Christ Jesus neither circumcision nor uncircumcision accomplishes anything; what matters is faith working through love.

⁷ You were running well. Who prevented you from obeying the truth? ⁸ This persuasion did not come from Him who called you. ⁹ A little yeast leavens the whole lump of dough. ¹⁰ In the Lord I have confidence in you that you will not accept any other view. But whoever it is who is troubling you will pay the penalty. ¹¹ Now brothers, if I still preach circumcision, why am I still persecuted? In that case the offense of the cross has been abolished. ¹² I wish those who are disturbing you might also get themselves castrated!

¹³ For you are called to freedom, brothers; only don't use this freedom as an opportunity for the flesh, but serve one another through love. ¹⁴ For the entire law is fulfilled in one statement: **Love your neighbor as yourself.**ᵈ ¹⁵ But if you bite and devour one another, watch out, or you will be consumed by one another.

Spirit vs. Flesh

¹⁶ I say then, •walk by the Spirit and you will not carry out the desire of the

ᵃ**4:24** Typology or allegory   ᵇ**4:27** Is 54:1   ᶜ**4:30** Gn 21:10   ᵈ**5:14** Lv 19:18

flesh. [17] For the flesh desires what is against the Spirit, and the Spirit desires what is against the flesh; these are opposed to each other, so that you don't do what you want. [18] But if you are led by the Spirit, you are not under the law.

Works of Flesh

[19] Now the works of the flesh are obvious:[a][b] sexual immorality, moral impurity, promiscuity, [20] idolatry, sorcery, hatreds, strife, jealousy, outbursts of anger, selfish ambitions, dissensions, factions, [21] envy,[c] drunkenness, carousing, and anything similar, about which I tell you in advance—as I told you before—that those who practice such things will not inherit the kingdom of God.

Fruit of Spirit

[22] But the fruit of the Spirit is love, joy, peace, patience, kindness, goodness, faith,[d] [23] gentleness, self-control. Against such things there is no law. [24] Now those who belong to Christ Jesus have crucified the flesh with its passions and desires. [25] If we live by the Spirit, we must also follow the Spirit. [26] We must not become conceited, provoking one another, envying one another.

Carry One Another's Burdens

6 Brothers, if someone is caught in any wrongdoing, you who are spiritual should restore such a person with a gentle spirit, watching out for yourselves so you won't be tempted also. [2] Carry one another's burdens; in this way you will fulfill the law of Christ. [3] For if anyone considers himself to be something when he is nothing, he is deceiving himself. [4] But each person should examine his own work, and then he will have a reason for boasting in himself alone, and not in respect to someone else. [5] For each person will have to carry his own load.

[6] The one who is taught the message must share his goods with the teacher. [7] Don't be deceived: God is not mocked. For whatever a man sows he will also reap, [8] because the one who sows to his flesh will reap corruption from the flesh, but the one who sows to the Spirit will reap eternal life from the Spirit. [9] So we must not get tired of doing good, for we will reap at the proper time if we don't give up. [10] Therefore, as we have opportunity, we must work for the good of all, especially for those who belong to the household of faith.

Paul's Concluding Exhortation

[11] Look at what large letters I have written to you in my own handwriting. [12] Those who want to make a good showing in the flesh are the ones who would compel you to be circumcised—but only to avoid being persecuted for the cross of Christ. [13] For even the circumcised don't keep the law themselves; however, they want you to be circumcised in order to boast about your flesh. [14] But as for me, I will never boast about anything except the cross of our Lord Jesus Christ, through whom[e] the world has been crucified to me, and I to the world. [15] For[f] both circumcision and uncircumcision mean nothing; ⌊what matters⌋ instead is a new creation. [16] May peace be on all those who follow this standard, and mercy also be on the Israel of God!

[17] From now on, let no one cause me trouble, because I carry the marks of Jesus on my body. [18] Brothers, the grace of our Lord Jesus Christ be with your spirit. •Amen.

a**5:19** Other mss add *adultery* b**5:19** Lit *obvious, which are:* c**5:21** Other mss add *murders* d**5:22** Or *faithfulness*
e**6:14** Or *which* f**6:15** Other mss add *in Christ Jesus*

EPHESIANS

Greeting

1 Paul, an apostle of Christ Jesus by God's will:

To the saints and believers in Christ Jesus at Ephesus.[a]

[2] Grace to you and peace from God our Father and the Lord Jesus Christ.

God Has Chosen Us

[3] Blessed be the God and Father of our Lord Jesus Christ, who has blessed us with every spiritual blessing in the heavens, in Christ; [4] for He chose us in Him, before the foundation of the world, to be holy and blameless in His sight.[b] In love[c] [5] He predestined us to be adopted through Jesus Christ for Himself, according to His favor and will, [6] to the praise of His glorious grace that He favored us with in the Beloved.

Redemption through His Blood

[7] In Him we have redemption through His blood, the forgiveness of our trespasses, according to the riches of His grace [8] that He lavished on us with all wisdom and understanding. [9] He made known to us the •mystery of His will, according to His good pleasure that He planned in Him [10] for the administration[d] of the days of fulfillment[e]—to bring everything together in the •Messiah, both things in heaven and things on earth in Him.

[11] In Him we were also made His inheritance,[f] predestined according to the purpose of the One who works out everything in agreement with the decision of His will, [12] so that we who had already put our hope in the Messiah might bring praise to His glory.

[13] In Him you also, when you heard the word of truth, the gospel of your salvation—in Him when you believed—were sealed with the promised Holy Spirit. [14] He is the down payment of our inheritance, for the redemption of the possession,[g] to the praise of His glory.

Paul's Gives Thanks—and Prays for Their Spiritual Insight

[15] This is why, since I heard about your faith in the Lord Jesus and your love for all the saints, [16] I never stop giving thanks for you as I remember you in my prayers. [17] ⌊I pray⌋ that the God of our Lord Jesus Christ, the glorious Father,[h] would give you a spirit of wisdom and revelation in the knowledge of Him. [18] ⌊I pray⌋ that the eyes of your heart may be enlightened so you may know what is the hope of His calling, what are the glorious riches of His inheritance among the saints, [19] and what is the immeasurable greatness of His power to us who believe, according to the working of His vast strength.

God Shows His Power in Christ

[20] He demonstrated ⌊this power⌋ in the Messiah by raising Him from the dead and seating Him at His right hand in the heavens— [21] far above every ruler and authority, power and dominion, and every title given,[i] not only in this age but also in the one to come. [22] And **He put everything under His feet**[j] and appointed Him as head over everything for

the church, 23 which is His body, the fullness of the One who fills all things in every way.

Ephesians Go from Death to Life

2 And you were dead in your trespasses and sins 2 in which you previously •walked according to this worldly age, according to the ruler of the atmospheric domain,[a] the spirit now working in the disobedient.[b] 3 We too all previously lived among them in our fleshly desires, carrying out the inclinations of our flesh and thoughts, and by nature we were children under wrath, as the others were also. 4 But God, who is abundant in mercy, because of His great love that He had for us,[c] 5 made us alive with the •Messiah even though we were dead in trespasses. By grace you are saved! 6 He also raised us up with Him and seated us with Him in the heavens, in Christ Jesus, 7 so that in the coming ages He might display the immeasurable riches of His grace in ⌊His⌋ kindness to us in Christ Jesus. 8 For by grace you are saved through faith, and this is not from yourselves; it is God's gift— 9 not from works, so that no one can boast. 10 For we are His creation—created in Christ Jesus for good works, which God prepared ahead of time so that we should walk in them.

Gentile and Jewish Unity in Christ

11 So then, remember that at one time you were Gentiles in the flesh—called "the uncircumcised" by those called "the circumcised," done by hand in the flesh. 12 At that time you were without the Messiah, excluded from the citizenship of Israel, and foreigners to the covenants of the promise, with no hope and without God in the world. 13 But now in Christ Jesus, you who were far away have been brought near by the blood of the Messiah. 14 For He is our peace, who made both groups one and tore down the dividing wall of hostility. In His flesh, 15 He did away with the law of the commandments in regulations, so that He might create in Himself one new man from the two, resulting in peace. 16 ⌊He did this so⌋ that He might reconcile both to God in one body through the cross and put the hostility to death by it.[d] 17 When ⌊Christ⌋ came, He proclaimed the good news of peace to you who were far away and peace to those who were near. 18 For through Him we both have access by one Spirit to the Father. 19 So then you are no longer foreigners and strangers, but fellow citizens with the saints, and members of God's household, 20 built on the foundation of the apostles and prophets, with Christ Jesus Himself as the cornerstone. 21 The whole building is being fitted together in Him and is growing into a holy sanctuary in the Lord, 22 in whom you also are being built together for God's dwelling in the Spirit.

Paul's "Mystery of the Messiah": Gentiles Co-heirs

3 For this reason, I, Paul, the prisoner of Christ Jesus on behalf of you Gentiles— 2 you have heard, haven't you, about the administration of God's grace that He gave to me for you? 3 The •mystery was made known to me by revelation, as I have briefly written above. 4 By reading this you are able to understand my insight about the mystery of the •Messiah. 5 This was not made known to people[e] in other generations as it is now revealed to His holy apostles and prophets by the Spirit: 6 the Gentiles are co-heirs, members of the same body, and

partners of the promise in Christ Jesus through the gospel. ⁷ I was made a servant of this ⌊gospel⌋ by the gift of God's grace that was given to me by the working of His power.

⁸ This grace was given to me—the least of all the saints!—to proclaim to the Gentiles the incalculable riches of the Messiah, ⁹ and to shed light for all about the administration of the mystery hidden for ages in God who created all things. ¹⁰ This is so that God's multi-faceted wisdom may now be made known through the church to the rulers and authorities in the heavens. ¹¹ This is according to the purpose of the ages, which He made in the Messiah, Jesus our Lord, ¹² in whom we have boldness, access, and confidence through faith in Him.ᵃ ¹³ So then I ask you not to be discouraged over my afflictions on your behalf, for they are your glory.

Paul Prays for Their Spiritual Power

¹⁴ For this reason I bow my knees before the Fatherᵇ ¹⁵ from whom every family in heaven and on earth is named. ¹⁶ ⌊I pray⌋ that He may grant you, according to the riches of His glory, to be strengthened with power through His Spirit in the inner man, ¹⁷ and that the Messiah may dwell in your hearts through faith. ⌊I pray that⌋ you, being rooted and firmly established in love, ¹⁸ may be able to comprehend with all the saints what is the length and width, height and depth ⌊of God's love⌋, ¹⁹ and to know the Messiah's love that surpasses knowledge, so you may be filled with all the fullness of God.

²⁰ Now to Him who is able to do above and beyond all that we ask or think—according to the power that works in you— ²¹ to Him be glory in the church and in Christ Jesus to all generations, forever and ever. •Amen.

Unity in Body of Christ

4 I, therefore, the prisoner in the Lord, urge you to •walk worthy of the calling you have received, ² with all humility and gentleness, with patience, acceptingᶜ one another in love, ³ diligently keeping the unity of the Spirit with the peace that binds ⌊us⌋. ⁴ There is one body and one Spirit, just as you were called to one hopeᵈ at your calling; ⁵ one Lord, one faith, one baptism, ⁶ one God and Father of all, who is above all and through all and in all.

⁷ Now grace was given to each one of us according to the measure of the •Messiah's gift. ⁸ For it says:

> When He ascended on high,
>   He took prisoners
>   into captivity;ᵉ
> He gave gifts to people.ᶠ

⁹ But what does "He ascended" mean except that Heᵍ descended to the lower parts of the earth?ʰ ¹⁰ The One who descended is the same as the One who ascended far above all the heavens, that He might fillⁱ all things.

Diversity of Spiritual Gifts

¹¹ And He personally gave some to be apostles, some prophets, some evangelists, some pastors and teachers, ¹² for the training of the saints in the work of ministry, to build up the body of Christ, ¹³ until we all reach unity in the faith and in the knowledge of God's Son, ⌊growing⌋ into a mature man with a stature measured by Christ's fullness. ¹⁴ Then we will no longer be little chil-

---

ᵃ**3:12** Or *through His faithfulness* ᵇ**3:14** Other mss add *of our Lord Jesus Christ* ᶜ**4:2** Or *tolerating* ᵈ**4:4** Lit *called in one hope* ᵉ**4:8** Or *He led the captives* ᶠ**4:8** Ps 68:18 ᵍ**4:9** Other mss add *first* ʰ**4:9** Or *the lower parts, namely, the earth* ⁱ**4:10** Or *fulfill*; see Eph 1:23

dren, tossed by the waves and blown around by every wind of teaching, by human cunning with cleverness in the techniques of deceit. [15] But speaking the truth in love, let us grow in every way into Him who is the head—Christ. [16] From Him the whole body, fitted and knit together by every supporting ligament, promotes the growth of the body for building up itself in love by the proper working of each individual part.

"Put on the New Man"

[17] Therefore, I say this and testify in the Lord: You should no longer walk as the Gentiles walk, in the futility of their thoughts. [18] They are darkened in their understanding, excluded from the life of God, because of the ignorance that is in them and because of the hardness of their hearts. [19] They became callous and gave themselves over to promiscuity for the practice of every kind of impurity with a desire for more and more.[a]

[20] But that is not how you learned about the Messiah, [21] assuming you heard Him and were taught by Him, because the truth is in Jesus: [22] you took off[b] your former way of life, the old man that is corrupted by deceitful desires; [23] you are being renewed[c] in the spirit of your minds; [24] you put on[d] the new man, the one created according to God's ⌐likeness⌐ in righteousness and purity of the truth.

Truth, Anger, Honesty, Rotten Talk

[25] Since you put away lying, **Speak the truth, each one to his neighbor,**[e] because we are members of one another. [26] **Be angry and do not sin.**[f] Don't let the sun go down on your anger, [27] and don't give the Devil an opportunity. [28] The thief must no longer steal. Instead, he must do honest work with his own hands, so that he has something to share with anyone in need. [29] No rotten talk should come from your mouth, but only what is good for the building up of someone in need,[g] in order to give grace to those who hear. [30] And don't grieve God's Holy Spirit, who sealed you[h] for the day of redemption. [31] All bitterness, anger and wrath, insult and slander must be removed from you, along with all wickedness. [32] And be kind and compassionate to one another, forgiving one another, just as God also forgave you[i] in Christ.

No Coarse Talking or Immorality

5 Therefore, be imitators of God, as dearly loved children. [2] And •walk in love, as the •Messiah also loved us and gave Himself for us, a sacrificial and fragrant offering to God. [3] But sexual immorality and any impurity or greed should not even be heard of[j] among you, as is proper for saints. [4] And coarse and foolish talking or crude joking are not suitable, but rather giving thanks. [5] For know and recognize this: no sexually immoral or impure or greedy person, who is an idolater, has an inheritance in the kingdom of the Messiah and of God.

"Walk as Children of Light"

[6] Let no one deceive you with empty arguments, for because of these things God's wrath is coming on the disobedient.[k] [7] Therefore, do not become their partners. [8] For you were once darkness, but now ⌐you are⌐ light in the Lord. Walk as children of light— [9] for the fruit of the

---

[a]**4:19** Lit *with greediness* [b]**4:21-22** Or *Jesus. This means: take off* (as a command) [c]**4:22-23** Or *desires; renew* (as a command) [d]**4:23-24** Or *minds; and put on* (as a command) [e]**4:25** Zch 8:16 [f]**4:26** Ps 4:4 [g]**4:29** Lit *for the building up of the need* [h]**4:30** Or *Spirit, by whom you were sealed* [i]**4:32** Other mss read *us* [j]**5:3** Or *be named* [k]**5:6** Lit *sons of disobedience*

light[a] ⌞results⌟ in all goodness, righteousness, and truth— [10] discerning what is pleasing to the Lord.

Expose Darkness

[11] Don't participate in the fruitless works of darkness, but instead, expose them. [12] For it is shameful even to mention what is done by them in secret. [13] Everything exposed by the light is made clear, [14] for what makes everything clear is light. Therefore it is said:

Get up, sleeper, and rise up
    from the dead,
and the Messiah will shine on you.[b]

Walk Wisely

[15] Pay careful attention, then, to how you walk—not as unwise people but as wise— [16] making the most of the time,[c] because the days are evil. [17] So don't be foolish, but understand what the Lord's will is. [18] And don't get drunk with wine, which ⌞leads to⌟ reckless actions, but be filled with the Spirit:

[19]   speaking to one another in psalms,
    hymns, and spiritual songs,
    singing and making music
    to the Lord in your heart,
[20]   giving thanks always for everything
    to God the Father in the name
    of our Lord Jesus Christ,

Mutual Submission

[21]   submitting to one another
    in the fear of Christ.

Wives and Husbands

[22] Wives, submit[d] to your own husbands as to the Lord, [23] for the husband is head of the wife as also Christ is head of the church. He is the Savior of the body.

[24] Now as the church submits to Christ, so wives should ⌞submit⌟ to their husbands in everything. [25] Husbands, love your wives, just as also Christ loved the church and gave Himself for her, [26] to make her holy, cleansing[e] her in the washing of water by the word. [27] He did this to present the church to Himself in splendor, without spot or wrinkle or any such thing, but holy and blameless. [28] In the same way, husbands should love their wives as their own bodies. He who loves his wife loves himself. [29] For no one ever hates his own flesh, but provides and cares for it, just as Christ does for the church, [30] since we are members of His body.[f]

[31]   **For this reason a man**
    will leave his father and mother
    and be joined to his wife,
    and the two will become
    one flesh.[g]

[32] This •mystery is profound, but I am talking about Christ and the church. [33] To sum up, each one of you is to love his wife as himself, and the wife is to respect her husband.

Children and Parents

6 Children, obey your parents in the Lord, because this is right. [2] **Honor your father and mother**—which is the first commandment[h] with a promise— [3] **that it may go well with you and that you may have a long life in the land.**[i] [j] [4] And fathers, don't stir up anger in your children, but bring them up in the training and instruction of the Lord.

Slaves and Masters

[5] Slaves, obey your human[k] masters with fear and trembling, in the sincerity of your heart, as to Christ. [6] Don't ⌞work only⌟

a**5:9** Other mss read *fruit of the Spirit*; see Gl 5:22, but compare Eph 5:11-14   b**5:14** This poem may have been an early Christian hymn based on several passages in Isaiah; see Is 9:2; 26:19; 40:1; 51:17; 52:1; 60:1.   c**5:16** Lit *buying back the time*   d**5:22** Other mss omit *submit*   e**5:26** Or *having cleansed*   f**5:30** Other mss add *and of His flesh and of His bones*   g**5:31** Gn 2:24   h**6:2** Or *is a preeminent commandment*   i**6:3** Or *life on the earth*   j**6:2-3** Ex 20:12   k**6:5** Lit *according to the flesh*

while being watched, in order to please men, but as slaves of Christ, do God's will from your heart.[a] [7] Render service with a good attitude, as to the Lord and not to men, [8] knowing that whatever good each one does, slave or free, he will receive this back from the Lord. [9] And masters, treat them the same way, without threatening them, because you know that both their and your Master is in heaven, and there is no favoritism with Him.

Spiritual Warfare

[10] Finally, be strengthened by the Lord and by His vast strength. [11] Put on the full armor of God so that you can stand against the tactics[b] of the Devil. [12] For our battle is not against flesh and blood, but against the rulers, against the authorities, against the world powers of this darkness, against the spiritual forces of evil in the heavens.

Full Armor of God

[13] This is why you must take up the full armor of God, so that you may be able to resist in the evil day, and having prepared everything, to take your stand. [14] Stand, therefore,

> with truth like a belt
> around your waist,
> righteousness like armor
> on your chest,
> [15] and your feet sandaled
> with readiness for the gospel
> of peace.[c]

[16] In every situation take the shield
> of faith,
> and with it you will be able
> to extinguish
> the flaming arrows
> of the evil one.
[17] Take the helmet of salvation,
> and the sword
> of the Spirit,
> which is God's word.

Paul's Prayer Requests

[18] With every prayer and request, pray at all times in the Spirit, and stay alert in this, with all perseverance and intercession for all the saints. [19] Pray also for me, that the message may be given to me when I open my mouth to make known with boldness the •mystery of the gospel. [20] For this I am an ambassador in chains. Pray that I might be bold enough in Him to speak as I should.

Paul's Farewell

[21] Tychicus, our dearly loved brother and faithful servant[d] in the Lord, will tell you everything so that you also may know how I am and what I'm doing. [22] I am sending him to you for this very reason, to let you know how we are and to encourage your hearts.

[23] Peace to the brothers, and love with faith, from God the Father and the Lord Jesus Christ. [24] Grace be with all who have undying love for our Lord Jesus Christ.[e] [f]

---

[a] 6:6 Lit from soul   [b] 6:11 Or schemes, or tricks   [c] 6:15 Ready to go tell others about the gospel   [d] 6:21 Or deacon
[e] 6:24 Other mss add Amen.   [f] 6:24 Lit all who love our Lord Jesus Christ in incorruption

PHILIPPIANS

Greeting — from Paul and Timothy

1 Paul and Timothy, slaves of Christ Jesus:

To all the saints in Christ Jesus who are in Philippi, including the •overseers and deacons.

 ² Grace to you and peace from God our Father and the Lord Jesus Christ.

Paul's Thanksgiving and Prayer for Philippians

³ I give thanks to my God for every remembrance of you,ᵃ ⁴ always praying with joy for all of you in my every prayer, ⁵ because of your partnership in the gospel from the first day until now. ⁶ I am sure of this, that He who started a good work in youᵇ will carry it on to completion until the day of Christ Jesus. ⁷ It is right for me to think this way about all of you, because I have you in my heart,ᶜ and you are all partners with me in grace, both in my imprisonment and in the defense and establishment of the gospel. ⁸ For God is my witness, how I deeply miss all of you with the affection of Christ Jesus. ⁹ And I pray this: that your love will keep on growing in knowledge and every kind of discernment, ¹⁰ so that you can determine what really matters and can be pure and blameless inᵈ the day of Christ, ¹¹ filled with the fruit of righteousness that ⌊comes⌋ through Jesus Christ, to the glory and praise of God.

Paul's News about Spread of Gospel

¹² Now I want you to know, brothers, that what has happened to me has actually resulted in the advancement of the gospel, ¹³ so that it has become known throughout the whole imperial guard,ᵉ and to everyone else, that my imprisonment is for Christ.ᶠ ¹⁴ Most of the brothers in the Lord have gained confidence from my imprisonment and dare even more to speak the messageᵍ fearlessly. ¹⁵ Some, to be sure, preach Christ out of envy and strife, but others out of good will.ʰ ¹⁶ These do so out of love, knowing that I am appointed for the defense of the gospel; ¹⁷ the others proclaim Christ out of rivalry, not sincerely, seeking to cause ⌊me⌋ trouble in my imprisonment.ⁱ ¹⁸ What does it matter? Just that in every way, whether out of false motives or true, Christ is proclaimed. And in this I rejoice. Yes, and I will rejoice ¹⁹ because I know this will lead to my deliveranceʲ through your prayers and help from the Spirit of Jesus Christ. ²⁰ My eager expectation and hope is that I will not be ashamed about anything, but that now as always, with all boldness, Christ will be highly honored in my body, whether by life or by death.

"Living Is Christ"

²¹ For me, living is Christ and dying is gain. ²² Now if I live on in the flesh, this means fruitful work for me; and I don't know which one I should choose. ²³ I am pressured by both. I have the desire to depart and be with Christ—which is far better— ²⁴ but to remain in the flesh is more necessary for you. ²⁵ Since I am persuaded of this, I know that I will remain and continue with all of you for

---

ᵃ**1:3** Or *for your every remembrance of me*   ᵇ**1:6** Or *work among you*   ᶜ**1:7** Or *because you have me in your heart*
ᵈ**1:10** Or *until*   ᵉ**1:13** Lit *praetorium*, a Lat word that can also refer to a military headquarters, to the governor's palace, or to Herod's palace   ᶠ**1:13** Lit *in Christ*   ᵍ**1:14** Other mss add *of God*   ʰ**1:15** The good will of men, or God's good will or favor   ⁱ**1:17** Lit *sincerely, intending to raise tribulation to my bonds*   ʲ**1:19** Or *salvation*, or *vindication*

your advancement and joy in the faith, [26] so that, because of me, your confidence may grow in Christ Jesus when I come to you again.

Stand Firm

[27] Just one thing: live your life in a manner worthy of the gospel of Christ. Then, whether I come and see you or am absent, I will hear about you that you are standing firm in one spirit, with one mind,[a] working side by side for the faith of the gospel, [28] not being frightened in any way by your opponents. This is evidence of their destruction, but of your deliverance—and this is from God. [29] For it has been given to you on Christ's behalf not only to believe in Him, but also to suffer for Him, [30] having the same struggle that you saw I had and now hear about me.

Be Humble

2 If then there is any encouragement in Christ, if any consolation of love, if any fellowship with the Spirit, if any affection and mercy, [2] fulfill my joy by thinking the same way, having the same love, sharing the same feelings, focusing on one goal. [3] Do nothing out of rivalry or conceit, but in humility consider others as more important than yourselves. [4] Everyone should look out not ʟonlyʜ for his own interests, but also for the interests of others.

Christ's Humility, Self-emptying, and Exaltation

[5] Make your own attitude that of Christ Jesus,

[6] who, existing in the form of God,
  did not consider
   equality with God
  as something to be used
   for His own advantage.[b]

[7] Instead He emptied Himself
  by assuming the form of a slave,
  taking on the likeness of men.
  And when He had come as a man
   in His external form,
[8] He humbled Himself
  by becoming obedient
  to the point of death—
   even to death on a cross.
[9] For this reason God also
   highly exalted Him
  and gave Him the name that is
   above every name,
[10] so that at the name of Jesus
   every knee should bow—
  of those who are in heaven
   and on earth
   and under the earth—
[11] and every tongue should confess
   that Jesus Christ is Lord,
  to the glory of God the Father.

"Work Out Your Own Salvation"

[12] So then, my dear friends, just as you have always obeyed, not only in my presence, but now even more in my absence, work out your own salvation with fear and trembling. [13] For it is God who is working in you, ʟenabling youʜ both to will and to act for His good purpose. [14] Do everything without grumbling and arguing, [15] so that you may be blameless and pure, children of God who are faultless in a crooked and perverted generation, among whom you shine like stars in the world. [16] Hold firmly[c] the message of life. Then I can boast in the day of Christ that I didn't run in vain or labor for nothing. [17] But even if I am poured out as a drink offering on the sacrifice and service of your faith, I am glad and rejoice with all of you. [18] In the same way you also should rejoice and share your joy with me.

---

[a]**1:27** Lit *soul* [b]**2:6** Or *to be grasped,* or *to be held on to* [c]**2:16** Or *Offer,* or *Hold out*

Paul Will Send Timothy

[19] Now I hope in the Lord Jesus to send Timothy to you soon so that I also may be encouraged when I hear news about you. [20] For I have no one else like-minded who will genuinely care about your interests; [21] all seek their own interests, not those of Jesus Christ. [22] But you know his proven character, because he has served with me in the gospel ministry like a son with a father. [23] Therefore, I hope to send him as soon as I see how things go with me. [24] And I am convinced in the Lord that I myself will also come quickly.

Paul Also Sends Epaphroditus

[25] But I considered it necessary to send you Epaphroditus—my brother, co-worker, and fellow soldier, as well as your messenger and minister to my need— [26] since he has been longing for all of you and was distressed because you heard that he was sick. [27] Indeed, he was so sick that he nearly died. However, God had mercy on him, and not only on him but also on me, so that I would not have one grief on top of another. [28] For this reason, I am very eager to send him so that you may rejoice when you see him again and I may be less anxious. [29] Therefore, welcome him in the Lord with all joy and hold men like him in honor, [30] because he came close to death for the work of Christ, risking his life to make up what was lacking in your ministry to me.

Paul's Warnings

3 Finally, my brothers, rejoice in the Lord. To write to you again about this is no trouble for me and is a protection for you.

[2] Watch out for "dogs,"[a] watch out for evil workers, watch out for those who mutilate the flesh. [3] For we are the circumcision, the ones who serve by the Spirit of God, boast in Christ Jesus, and do not put confidence in the flesh— [4] although I once had confidence in the flesh too.

Paul's Hebrew Pedigree

If anyone else thinks he has grounds for confidence in the flesh, I have more: [5] circumcised the eighth day; of the nation of Israel, of the tribe of Benjamin, a Hebrew born of Hebrews; as to the law, a •Pharisee; [6] as to zeal, persecuting the church; as to the righteousness that is in the law, blameless.

Priority of Christ for Paul

[7] But everything that was a gain to me, I have considered to be a loss because of Christ. [8] More than that, I also consider everything to be a loss in view of the surpassing value of knowing Christ Jesus my Lord. Because of Him I have suffered the loss of all things and consider them filth, so that I may gain Christ [9] and be found in Him, not having a righteousness of my own from the law, but one that is through faith in Christ[b]—the righteousness from God based on faith. [10] ⌊My goal⌋ is to know Him and the power of His resurrection and the fellowship of His sufferings, being conformed to His death, [11] assuming that I will somehow reach the resurrection from among the dead.

Paul Reaches for God's Goal

[12] Not that I have already reached ⌊the goal⌋ or am already fully mature, but I make every effort to take hold of it because I also have been taken hold of by Christ Jesus. [13] Brothers, I do not[c] consider myself to have taken hold of it. But

one thing I do: forgetting what is behind and reaching forward to what is ahead, [14] I pursue as my goal the prize promised by God's heavenly[a] call in Christ Jesus. [15] Therefore, all who are mature should think this way. And if you think differently about anything, God will reveal this to you also. [16] In any case, we should live up to whatever ⌊truth⌋ we have attained. [17] Join in imitating me, brothers, and observe those who live according to the example you have in us. [18] For I have often told you, and now say again with tears, that many live as enemies of the cross of Christ. [19] Their end is destruction; their god is their stomach; their glory is in their shame. They are focused on earthly things, [20] but <u>our citizenship is in heaven</u>, from which we also eagerly wait for a Savior, the Lord Jesus Christ. [21] He will transform the body of our humble condition into the likeness of His glorious body, by the power that enables Him to subject everything to Himself.

Paul's Answer to Anxiety

4 So then, in this way, my dearly loved brothers, my joy and crown, stand firm in the Lord, dear friends. [2] I urge Euodia and I urge Syntyche to agree in the Lord. [3] Yes, I also ask you, true partner,[b] to help these women who have contended for the gospel at my side, along with Clement and the rest of my co-workers whose names are in the book of life. [4] Rejoice in the Lord always. I will say it again: Rejoice! [5] Let your graciousness be known to everyone. The Lord is near. [6] Don't worry about anything, but in everything, through prayer and petition with thanksgiving, let your requests be made known to God. [7] And the peace of God, which surpasses every thought,

will guard your hearts and your minds in Christ Jesus.

Topics for Meditation

[8] Finally brothers, whatever is true, whatever is honorable, whatever is just, whatever is pure, whatever is lovely, whatever is commendable—if there is any moral excellence and if there is any praise—dwell on these things. [9] Do what you have learned and received and heard and seen in me, and the God of peace will be with you.

Paul's Secret to Contentment in All Circumstances

[10] I rejoiced in the Lord greatly that now at last you have renewed your care for me. You were, in fact, concerned about me, but lacked the opportunity ⌊to show it⌋. [11] I don't say this out of need, for I have learned to be content in whatever circumstances I am. [12] I know both how to have a little, and I know how to have a lot. In any and all circumstances I have learned the secret ⌊of being content⌋—whether well-fed or hungry, whether in abundance or in need. [13] <u>I am able to do all things through Him[c] who strengthens me</u>. [14] Still, you did well by sharing with me in my hardship.

Paul's Appreciation of Philippian Support

[15] And you, Philippians, know that in the early days of the gospel, when I left Macedonia, no church shared with me in the matter of giving and receiving except you alone. [16] For even in Thessalonica you sent ⌊gifts⌋ for my need several times. [17] Not that I seek the gift, but I seek the fruit that is increasing to your account. [18] But I have received everything in full, and I have an abundance. I am fully

---

supplied, having received from Epaphroditus what you provided—a fragrant offering, a welcome sacrifice, pleasing to God. [19] And my God will supply all your needs according to His riches in glory in Christ Jesus. [20] Now to our God and Father be glory forever and ever. •Amen.

Final Greetings

[21] Greet every saint in Christ Jesus. Those brothers who are with me greet you. [22] All the saints greet you, but especially those from Caesar's household. [23] The grace of the Lord Jesus Christ be with your spirit.[a]

COLOSSIANS

Greeting—from Paul and Timothy

1 Paul, an apostle of Christ Jesus by God's will, and Timothy our[b] brother: [2] To the saints and faithful brothers in Christ in Colossae.

Grace to you and peace from God our Father.[c]

Paul's Thanksgiving

[3] We always thank God, the Father of our Lord Jesus Christ, when we pray for you, [4] for we have heard of your faith in Christ Jesus and of the love you have for all the saints [5] because of the hope reserved for you in heaven. You have already heard about ⌊this hope⌋ in the message of truth, the gospel [6] that has come to you. It is bearing fruit and growing all over the world, just as it has among you since the day you heard it and recognized God's grace in the truth.[d] [7] You learned this from Epaphras, our much loved fellow slave. He is a faithful minister of the •Messiah on your[e] behalf, [8] and he has told us about your love in the Spirit.

Paul Prays for Their Spiritual Growth

[9] For this reason also, since the day we heard this, we haven't stopped praying for you. We are asking that you may be filled with the knowledge of His will in all wisdom and spiritual understanding, [10] so that you may •walk worthy of the Lord, fully pleasing ⌊to Him⌋, bearing fruit in every good work and growing in the knowledge of God. [11] May you be strengthened with all power, according to His glorious might, for all endurance and patience, with joy [12] giving thanks to the Father, who has enabled you[f] to share in the saints'[g] inheritance in the light.

Power and Centrality of Christ

[13] He has rescued us from the domain of darkness and transferred us into the kingdom of the Son He loves, [14] in whom we have redemption,[h] the forgiveness of sins.

[15] He is the image of the invisible God,
      the firstborn over all creation;[i]
[16] because by Him everything
      was created,
   in heaven and on earth, the visible
      and the invisible,
   whether thrones or dominions
      or rulers or authorities—
   all things have been created
      through Him and for Him.
[17] He is before all things, and by Him
      all things hold together.

a4:23 Other mss add *Amen.*   b1:1 Lit *the*   c1:2 Other mss add *and the Lord Jesus Christ*   d1:6 Or *and truly recognized God's grace*   e1:7 Other mss read *our*   f1:12 Other mss read *us*   g1:12 Or *holy ones'*   h1:14 Other mss add *through His blood*   i1:15 The One who is preeminent over all creation

18 He is also the head of the body,
   the church;
He is the beginning, the firstborn
   from the dead,
so that He might come to have
   first place in everything.
19 For God was pleased to have
   all His fullness dwell in Him,
20 and through Him to reconcile
   everything to Himself
by making peace through the blood
   of His crossa—
whether things on earth or things
   in heaven.

"He Has Reconciled You"

21 And you were once alienated and hostile in mind because of your evil actions. 22 But now He has reconciled you by His physical bodyb through His death, to present you holy, faultless, and blameless before Him— 23 if indeed you remain grounded and steadfast in the faith, and are not shifted away from the hope of the gospel that you heard. This gospel has been proclaimed in all creation under heaven, and I, Paul, have become a minister of it.

Paul's Ministry to the Gentiles

24 Now I rejoice in my sufferings for you, and I am completing in my flesh what is lacking in Christ's afflictions for His body, that is, the church. 25 I have become its minister, according to God's administration that was given to me for you, to make God's message fully known, 26 the •mystery hidden for ages and generations but now revealed to His saints. 27 God wanted to make known to those among the Gentiles the glorious wealth of this mystery, which is Christ in you, the hope of glory. 28 We proclaim Him, warning and teaching everyone

with all wisdom, so that we may present everyone mature in Christ. 29 I labor for this, striving with His strength that works powerfully in me.

2 For I want you to know how great a struggle I have for you, for those in Laodicea, and for all who have not seen me in person. 2 I want their hearts to be encouraged and joined together in love, so that they may have all the riches of assured understanding, and have the knowledge of God's •mystery—Christ.c 3 In Him all the treasures of wisdom and knowledge are hidden.

Paul: Beware of Spiritual Deceit

4 I am saying this so that no one will deceive you with persuasive arguments. 5 For I may be absent in body, but I am with you in spirit, rejoicing to see your good order and the strength of your faith in Christ.

6 Therefore as you have received Christ Jesus the Lord, •walk in Him, 7 rooted and built up in Him and established in the faith, just as you were taught, and overflowing with thankfulness.

8 Be careful that no one takes you captive through philosophy and empty deceit based on human tradition, based on the elemental forces of the world, and not based on Christ. 9 For in Him the entire fullness of God's natured dwells bodily,e 10 and you have been filled by Him, who is the head over every ruler and authority. 11 In Him you were also circumcised with a circumcision not done with hands, by putting off the body of flesh, in the circumcision of the •Messiah. 12 Having been buried with Him in baptism, you were also raised with Him through faith in the working of God, who raised Him from the dead. 13 And when you were dead in trespasses and in

a1:20 Other mss add through Him   b1:22 His body of flesh on the cross   c2:2 Other mss read mystery of God, both of the Father and of Christ; other ms variations exist on this v.   d2:9 Or the deity   e2:9 Or nature lives in a human body

the uncircumcision of your flesh, He made you alive with Him and forgave us all our trespasses. [14] He erased the certificate of debt, with its obligations, that was against us and opposed to us, and has taken it out of the way by nailing it to the cross. [15] He disarmed the rulers and authorities and disgraced them publicly; He triumphed over them by Him.[a]

Don't Be Judged by Food, Drink, or Sabbaths

[16] Therefore don't let anyone judge you in regard to food and drink or in the matter of a festival or a new moon or a sabbath day.[b] [17] These are a shadow of what was to come; the substance is[c] the Messiah. [18] Let no one disqualify you,[d] insisting on ascetic practices and the worship of angels, claiming access to a visionary realm and inflated without cause by his fleshly mind. [19] He doesn't hold on to the head, from whom the whole body, nourished and held together by its ligaments and tendons, develops with growth from God.

Exercise Freedom

[20] If you died with Christ to the elemental forces of this world, why do you live as if you still belonged to the world? Why do you submit to regulations: [21] "Don't handle, don't taste, don't touch"? [22] All these ⌊regulations⌋ refer to what is destroyed by being used up; they are human commands and doctrines. [23] Although these have a reputation of wisdom by promoting ascetic practices, humility, and severe treatment of the body, they are not of any value against fleshly indulgence.

Life of the New Believer

3 So if you have been raised with the •Messiah, seek what is above, where the Messiah is, seated at the right hand of God. [2] Set your minds on what is above, not on what is on the earth. [3] For you have died, and your life is hidden with the Messiah in God. [4] When the Messiah, who is your[e] life, is revealed, then you also will be revealed with Him in glory.

[5] Therefore, put to death whatever in you is worldly:[f] sexual immorality, impurity, lust, evil desire, and greed, which is idolatry. [6] Because of these, God's wrath comes on the disobedient,[g] [7] and you once •walked in these things when you were living in them. [8] But now you must also put away all the following: anger, wrath, malice, slander, and filthy language from your mouth. [9] Do not lie to one another, since you have put off the old man with his practices [10] and have put on the new man, who is being renewed in knowledge according to the image of his Creator. [11] Here there is not Greek and Jew, circumcision and uncircumcision, barbarian, Scythian,[h] slave and free; but Christ is all and in all.

Signs of the True Christian Life

[12] Therefore, God's chosen ones, holy and loved, put on heartfelt compassion, kindness, humility, gentleness, and patience, [13] accepting one another and forgiving one another if anyone has a complaint against another. Just as the Lord has forgiven you, so also you must ⌊forgive⌋. [14] Above all, ⌊put on⌋ love—the perfect bond of unity. [15] And let the peace of the Messiah, to which you were also called in one body, control your hearts. Be thankful. [16] Let the message about the Messiah dwell richly among you, teaching and admonishing one another in all wisdom, and singing psalms, hymns, and spiritual songs, with gratitude in your

---

[a]**2:15** Or *them through it; that is, through the cross*   [b]**2:16** Or *or sabbaths*   [c]**2:17** Or *substance belongs to*   [d]**2:18** Or *no one cheat us out of your prize*   [e]**3:4** Other mss read *our*   [f]**3:5** Lit *death, the members on the earth*   [g]**3:6** Other mss omit *on the disobedient*   [h]**3:11** A term for a savage

hearts to God. [17] And whatever you do, in word or in deed, do everything in the name of the Lord Jesus, giving thanks to God the Father through Him.

Christ in Your Home

[18] Wives, be submissive to your husbands, as is fitting in the Lord.
[19] Husbands, love your wives and don't become bitter against them.
[20] Children, obey your parents in everything, for this is pleasing in the Lord.
[21] Fathers, do not exasperate your children, so they won't become discouraged.
[22] Slaves, obey your human masters in everything; don't work only while being watched, in order to please men, but ⌊work⌋ wholeheartedly, fearing the Lord.
[23] Whatever you do, do it enthusiastically,[a] as something done for the Lord and not for men, [24] knowing that you will receive the reward of an inheritance from the Lord—you serve the Lord Christ. [25] For the wrongdoer will be paid back for whatever wrong he has done, and there is no favoritism.

4 Masters, supply your slaves with what is right and fair, since you know that you too have a Master in heaven.

Devotion to Prayer

[2] Devote yourselves to prayer; stay alert in it with thanksgiving. [3] At the same time, pray also for us that God may open a door to us for the message, to speak the •mystery of the •Messiah—for which I am in prison— [4] so that I may reveal it as I am required to speak. Walk in Wisdom

[5] •Walk in wisdom toward outsiders, making the most of the time. [6] Your speech should always be gracious, seasoned with salt, so that you may know how you should answer each person.

Paul's Specific Greetings

[7] Tychicus, a loved brother, a faithful servant, and a fellow slave in the Lord, will tell you all the news about me. [8] I have sent him to you for this very purpose, so that you may know how we are,[b] and so that he may encourage your hearts. [9] He is with Onesimus, a faithful and loved brother, who is one of you. They will tell you about everything here.

[10] Aristarchus, my fellow prisoner, greets you, as does Mark, Barnabas' cousin (concerning whom you have received instructions: if he comes to you, welcome him), [11] and so does Jesus who is called Justus. These alone of the circumcision are my co-workers for the kingdom of God, and they have been a comfort to me. [12] Epaphras, who is one of you, a slave of Christ Jesus, greets you. He is always contending for you in his prayers, so that you can stand mature and fully assured[c] in everything God wills. [13] For I testify about him that he works hard[d] for you, for those in Laodicea, and for those in Hierapolis. [14] Luke, the loved physician, and Demas greet you. [15] Give my greetings to the brothers in Laodicea, and to Nympha and the church in her house. [16] And when this letter has been read among you, have it read also in the church of the Laodiceans; and see that you also read the letter from Laodicea. [17] And tell Archippus, "Pay attention to the ministry you have received in the Lord, so that you can accomplish it."

[18] This greeting is in my own hand—Paul. Remember my imprisonment. Grace be with you.[e]

---

[a]**3:23** Lit *do it from the soul*   [b]**4:8** Other mss read *that he may know how you are*   [c]**4:12** Other mss read *and complete*   [d]**4:13** Other mss read *he has a great zeal*   [e]**4:18** Other mss add *Amen*.

1 THESSALONIANS

Greeting—from Paul, Silvanus, and Timothy

1 Paul, Silvanus,[a] and Timothy:
To the church of the Thessalonians in God the Father and the Lord Jesus Christ.
Grace to you and peace.[b]

Paul Gives Thanks

2 We always thank God for all of you, remembering you constantly in our prayers. 3 We recall, in the presence of our God and Father, your work of faith, labor of love, and endurance of hope in our Lord Jesus Christ, 4 knowing your election, brothers loved by God. 5 For our gospel did not come to you in word only, but also in power, in the Holy Spirit, and with much assurance. You know what kind of men we were among you for your benefit, 6 and you became imitators of us and of the Lord when, in spite of severe persecution, you welcomed the message with the joy from the Holy Spirit.

Thessalonians an Example

7 As a result, you became an example to all the believers in Macedonia and Achaia. 8 For the Lord's message rang out from you, not only in Macedonia and Achaia, but in every place that your faith[c] in God has gone out, so we don't need to say anything. 9 For they themselves report about us what kind of reception we had from you: how you turned to God from idols to serve the living and true God, 10 and to wait for His Son from heaven, whom He raised from the dead—Jesus, who rescues us from the coming wrath.

Paul's Bold Speech and Good Conduct

2 For you yourselves know, brothers, that our visit with you was not without result. 2 On the contrary, after we had previously suffered and been outrageously treated in Philippi, as you know, we were emboldened by our God to speak the gospel of God to you in spite of great opposition. 3 For our exhortation didn't come from error or impurity or an intent to deceive. 4 Instead, just as we have been approved by God to be entrusted with the gospel, so we speak, not to please men, but rather God, who examines our hearts. 5 For we never used flattering speech, as you know, or had greedy motives—God is our witness— 6 and we didn't seek glory from people, either from you or from others. 7 Although we could have been a burden as Christ's apostles, instead we were gentle[d] among you, as a nursing mother nurtures her own children. 8 We cared so much for you that we were pleased to share with you not only the gospel of God but also our own lives, because you had become dear to us. 9 For you remember our labor and hardship, brothers. Working night and day so that we would not burden any of you, we preached God's gospel to you. 10 You are witnesses, and so is God, of how devoutly, righteously, and blamelessly we conducted ourselves with you believers. 11 As you know, like a father with his own children, 12 we encouraged, comforted, and implored each one of you to •walk worthy of God, who calls you into His own kingdom and glory.

a1:1 Or Silas; see Ac 15:22-32; 16:19-40; 17:1-16 b1:1 Other mss add from God our Father and the Lord Jesus Christ c1:8 Or in every place news of your faith d2:7 Other mss read infants

Positive Reception of Paul's Message

13 Also, this is why we constantly thank God, because when you received the message about God that you heard from us, you welcomed it not as a human message, but as it truly is, the message of God, which also works effectively in you believers.

Opposition to Gospel

14 For you, brothers, became imitators of God's churches in Christ Jesus that are in Judea, since you have also suffered the same things from people of your own country, just as they did from the Jews. 15 They killed both the Lord Jesus and the prophets, and persecuted us; they displease God, and are hostile to everyone, 16 hindering us from speaking to the Gentiles so that they may be saved. As a result, they are always adding to the number of their sins, and wrath has overtaken them completely.a

Paul's Desire to See Thessalonians

17 But as for us, brothers, after we were forced to leave you for a short time (in person, not in heart), we greatly desired and made every effort to return and see you face to face. 18 So we wanted to come to you—even I, Paul, time and again—but Satan hindered us. 19 For who is our hope, or joy, or crown of boasting in the presence of our Lord Jesus at His coming? Is it not you? 20 For you are our glory and joy!

Paul's Anxiety—and Efforts to Strengthen Persecuted Believers

3 Therefore, when we could no longer stand it, we thought it was better to be left alone in Athens. 2 And we sent Timothy, our brother and God's co-worker b in the gospel of Christ, to strengthen and encourage you concerning your faith, 3 so that no one will be shaken by these persecutions. For you yourselves know that we are appointed to c this. 4 In fact, when we were with you, we told you previously that we were going to suffer persecution, and as you know, it happened. 5 For this reason, when I could no longer stand it, I also sent to find out about your faith, fearing that the tempter had tempted you and that our labor might be for nothing.

Paul Encouraged by Timothy

6 But now Timothy has come to us from you and brought us good news about your faith and love, and that you always have good memories of us, wanting to see us, as we also want to see you. 7 Therefore, brothers, in all our distress and persecution, we were encouraged about you through your faith. 8 For now we live, if you stand firm in the Lord. 9 How can we thank God for you in return for all the joy we experience because of you before our God, 10 as we pray earnestly night and day to see you face to face and to complete what is lacking in your faith?

Paul Prays for Church

11 Now may our God and Father Himself, and our Lord Jesus, direct our way to you. 12 And may the Lord cause you to increase and overflow with love for one another and for everyone, just as we also do for you. 13 May He make your hearts blameless in holiness before our God and Father at the coming of our Lord Jesus with all His saints. •Amen.d

Paul Calls for Sanctification

4 Finally then, brothers, we ask and encourage you in the Lord Jesus,

---

a2:16 Or to the end   b3:2 Other mss read servant   c3:3 Or we are destined for   d3:13 Other mss omit Amen.

that as you have received from us how you must •walk and please God—as you are doing[a]—do so even more. ² For you know what commands we gave you through the Lord Jesus.

³ For this is God's will, your sanctification: that you abstain from sexual immorality, ⁴ so that each of you knows how to possess his own vessel[b] in sanctification and honor, ⁵ not with lustful desires, like the Gentiles who don't know God. ⁶ This means one must not transgress against and defraud his brother in this matter, because the Lord is an avenger of all these offenses,[c] as we also previously told and warned you. ⁷ For God has not called us to impurity, but to sanctification. ⁸ Therefore, the person who rejects this does not reject man, but God, who also gives you His Holy Spirit.

Love More! Be Financially Independent!

⁹ About brotherly love: you don't need me to write you because you yourselves are taught by God to love one another. ¹⁰ In fact, you are doing this toward all the brothers in the entire region of Macedonia. But we encourage you, brothers, to do so even more, ¹¹ to seek to lead a quiet life, to mind your own business,[d] and to work with your own hands, as we commanded you, ¹² so that you may walk properly[e] in the presence of outsiders[f] and not be dependent on anyone.[g]

Details of Christ's Second Coming

¹³ We do not want you to be uninformed, brothers, concerning those who are •asleep, so that you will not grieve like the rest, who have no hope. ¹⁴ Since we believe that Jesus died and rose again, in the same way God will bring with Him those who have fallen asleep through[h] Jesus.[i] ¹⁵ For we say this to you by a revelation from the Lord:[j] We who are still alive at the Lord's coming will certainly have no advantage over[k] those who have fallen asleep. ¹⁶ For the Lord Himself will descend from heaven with a shout,[l] with the archangel's voice, and with the trumpet of God, and the dead in Christ will rise first. ¹⁷ Then we who are still alive will be caught up together with them in the clouds to meet the Lord in the air; and so we will always be with the Lord. ¹⁸ Therefore encourage[m] one another with these words.

Day of the Lord

5 About the times and the seasons: brothers, you do not need anything to be written to you. ² For you yourselves know very well that the Day of the Lord will come just like a thief in the night. ³ When they say, "Peace and security," then sudden destruction comes on them, like labor pains on a pregnant woman, and they will not escape. ⁴ But you, brothers, are not in the dark, so that this day would overtake you like a thief. ⁵ For you are all sons of light and sons of the day. We're not of the night or of darkness. ⁶ So then, we must not sleep, like the rest, but we must stay awake and be sober. ⁷ For those who sleep, sleep at night, and those who get drunk are drunk at night. ⁸ But since we are of the day, we must be sober and put the armor of faith and love on our chests, and put on a helmet of the hope of salvation. ⁹ For God did not appoint us to wrath, but to obtain salvation through our Lord Jesus Christ, ¹⁰ who died for us, so that whether we are awake or •asleep, we

---

[a]4:1 Lit walking [b]4:4 Or to control his own body, or to acquire his own wife [c]4:6 Lit things [d]4:11 Lit to practice one's own things [e]4:12 Or may live respectably [f]4:12 Non-Christians [g]4:12 Or not need anything, or not be in need [h]4:14 Or asleep in [i]4:14 those who have fallen asleep through Jesus = Christians who have died [j]4:15 Or a word of the Lord [k]4:15 Or certainly not precede [l]4:16 Or command [m]4:18 Or comfort

will live together with Him. [11] Therefore encourage one another and build each other up as you are already doing.

Paul's Final Exhortations

[12] Now we ask you, brothers, to give recognition to those who labor among you and lead you in the Lord and admonish you, [13] and to esteem them very highly in love because of their work. Be at peace among yourselves. [14] And we exhort you, brothers: warn those who are lazy,[a] comfort the discouraged, help the weak, be patient with everyone. [15] See to it that no one repays evil for evil to anyone, but always pursue what is good for one another and for all.

[16] Rejoice always!
[17] Pray constantly.
[18] Give thanks in everything,

for this is God's will for you in Christ Jesus.
[19] Don't stifle the Spirit.
[20] Don't despise prophecies,
[21] but test all things. Hold on to what is good.
[22] Stay away from every form of evil.

Paul's Final Blessings

[23] Now may the God of peace Himself sanctify you completely. And may your spirit, soul, and body be kept sound and blameless for the coming of our Lord Jesus Christ. [24] He who calls you is faithful, who also will do it. [25] Brothers, pray for us also. [26] Greet all the brothers with a holy kiss. [27] I charge you by the Lord that this letter be read to all the brothers. [28] May the grace of our Lord Jesus Christ be with you!

2 THESSALONIANS

Greeting—from Paul, Silvanus, and Timothy

1 Paul, Silvanus,[b] and Timothy:
To the church of the Thessalonians in God our Father and the Lord Jesus Christ.
[2] Grace to you and peace from God our Father and the Lord Jesus Christ.

God's Judgment and Glory

[3] We must always thank God for you, brothers, which is fitting, since your faith is flourishing, and the love of every one of you for one another is increasing. [4] Therefore we ourselves boast about you among God's churches—about your endurance and faith in all the persecutions and afflictions you endure. [5] It is a clear

evidence of God's righteous judgment that you will be counted worthy of God's kingdom, for which you also are suffering, [6] since it is righteous for God to repay with affliction those who afflict you, [7] and ⌊to reward⌋ with rest you who are afflicted, along with us. ⌊This will take place⌋ at the revelation of the Lord Jesus from heaven with His powerful angels, [8] taking vengeance with flaming fire on those who don't know God and on those who don't obey the gospel of our Lord Jesus. [9] These will pay the penalty of everlasting destruction, away from the Lord's presence and from His glorious strength, [10] in that day when He comes to be glorified by His saints and to be admired by all those who have believed,

a5:14 Or who are disorderly, or who are undisciplined   b1:1 Or Silas; see Ac 15:22-32; 16:19-40; 17:1-16 because our testimony among you was believed. [11] And in view of this, we always pray for you that our God will consider you worthy of His calling, and will, by His power, fulfill every desire for goodness and the work of faith, [12] so that the name of our Lord Jesus will be glorified by you, and you by Him, according to the grace of our God and the Lord Jesus Christ.

Day of the Lord: "Man of Lawlessness" Appears First

2 Now concerning the coming of our Lord Jesus Christ and our being gathered to Him: we ask you, brothers, [2] not to be easily upset in mind or troubled, either by a spirit or by a message or by a letter as if from us, alleging that the Day of the Lord[a] has come. [3] Don't let anyone deceive you in any way. For ˻that day˼ will not come unless the apostasy[b] comes first and the man of lawlessness[c] is revealed, the son of destruction. [4] He opposes and exalts himself above every so-called god or object of worship, so that he sits[d] in God's sanctuary,[e] publicizing that he himself is God.

Lord Jesus Will Destroy Lawless One

[5] Don't you remember that when I was still with you I told you about this? [6] And you know what currently restrains ˻him˼, so that he will be revealed in his time. [7] For the •mystery of lawlessness is already at work; but the one now restraining will do so until he is out of the way, [8] and then the lawless one will be revealed. The Lord Jesus will destroy him with the breath of His mouth and will bring him to nothing with the brightness of His coming. [9] The coming ˻of the lawless one˼ is based on Satan's working, with all kinds of false miracles, signs, and wonders, [10] and with every unrighteous deception among those who are perishing. ˻They perish˼ because they did not accept the love of the truth in order to be saved. [11] For this reason God sends them a strong delusion so that they will believe what is false, [12] so that all will be condemned—those who did not believe the truth but enjoyed unrighteousness.

Stand Firm

[13] But we must always thank God for you, brothers loved by the Lord, because from the beginning[f] God has chosen you for salvation through sanctification by the Spirit and through belief in the truth. [14] He called you to this through our gospel, so that you might obtain the glory of our Lord Jesus Christ. [15] Therefore, brothers, stand firm and hold to the traditions you were taught, either by our message or by our letter.

[16] May our Lord Jesus Christ Himself and God our Father, who has loved us and given us eternal encouragement and good hope by grace, [17] encourage your hearts and strengthen you in every good work and word.

Pray for Us

3 Finally, pray for us, brothers, that the Lord's message may spread rapidly and be honored, just as it was with you, [2] and that we may be delivered from wicked and evil men, for not all have faith. [3] But the Lord is faithful; He will strengthen and guard you from the evil one. [4] We have confidence in the Lord about you, that you are doing and will do what we command. [5] May the Lord direct your hearts to God's love and Christ's endurance.

[a]2:2 Other mss read *Christ*   [b]2:3 Or *rebellion*   [c]2:3 Other mss read *man of sin*   [d]2:4 Other mss add *as God*
[e]2:4 Or *temple*   [f]2:13 Other mss read *because as a firstfruit*

Paul Warns against Irresponsible Behavior

⁶ Now we command you, brothers, in the name of our Lord Jesus Christ, to keep away from every brother who •walks irresponsibly and not according to the tradition received from us. ⁷ For you yourselves know how you must imitate us: we were not irresponsible among you; ⁸ we did not eat anyone's bread free of charge; instead, we labored and toiled, working night and day, so that we would not be a burden to any of you. ⁹ It is not that we don't have the right ⌊to support⌋, but we did it to make ourselves an example to you so that you would imitate us. ¹⁰ In fact, when we were with you, this is what we commanded you: "If anyone isn't willing to work, he should not eat." ¹¹ For we hear that there are some among you who walk irresponsibly, not working at all, but interfering with the work ⌊of others⌋. ¹² Now we command and exhort such people, by the Lord Jesus Christ, that quietly working, they may eat their own bread.ᵃ ¹³ Brothers, do not grow weary in doing good.

¹⁴ And if anyone does not obey our instruction in this letter, take note of that person; don't associate with him, so that he may be ashamed. ¹⁵ Yet don't treat him as an enemy, but warn him as a brother.

Final Greetings

¹⁶ May the Lord of peace Himself give you peace always in every way. The Lord be with all of you. ¹⁷ This greeting is in my own hand—Paul. This is a sign in every letter; this is how I write. ¹⁸ The grace of our Lord Jesus Christ be with all of you.

1 TIMOTHY

Greeting

1 Paul, an apostle of Christ Jesus according to the command of God our Savior and of Christ Jesus, our hope:

² To Timothy, my true child in the faith.

Grace, mercy, and peace from God theᵇ Father and Christ Jesus our Lord.

Fight False Teachers

³ As I urged you when I went to Macedonia, remain in Ephesus so that you may command certain people not to teach other doctrine ⁴ or to pay attention to myths and endless genealogies. These promote empty speculations rather than God's plan, which operates by faith.

⁵ Now the goal of our instruction is love from a pure heart, a good conscience, and a sincere faith. ⁶ Some have deviated from these and turned aside to fruitless discussion. ⁷ They want to be teachers of the law, although they don't understand what they are saying or what they are insisting on. ⁸ Now we know that the law is good, provided one uses it legitimately. ⁹ We know that the law is not meant for a righteous person, but for the lawless and rebellious, for the ungodly and sinful, for the unholy and irreverent, for those who kill their fathers and mothers, for murderers, ¹⁰ for the sexually immoral and homosexuals, for kidnappers, liars, perjurers, and for

ᵃ**3:12** Or *food*   ᵇ**1:2** Other mss read *our*

whatever else is contrary to the sound teaching [11] based on the glorious gospel of the blessed God that was entrusted to me.

Paul's Personal Testimony

[12] I give thanks to Christ Jesus our Lord, who has strengthened me, because He considered me faithful, appointing me to the ministry— [13] one who was formerly a blasphemer, a persecutor, and an arrogant man. Since it was out of ignorance that I had acted in unbelief, I received mercy, [14] and the grace of our Lord overflowed, along with the faith and love that are in Christ Jesus. [15] This saying is trustworthy and deserving of full acceptance: "Christ Jesus came into the world to save sinners"—and I am the worst of them. [16] But I received mercy because of this, so that in me, the worst ˪of them˩, Christ Jesus might demonstrate the utmost patience as an example to those who would believe in Him for eternal life. [17] Now to the King eternal, immortal, invisible, the only[a] God, be honor and glory forever and ever. •Amen.

Engage in Spiritual Battle

[18] Timothy, my child, I am giving you this instruction in keeping with the prophecies previously made about you, so that by them you may strongly engage in battle, [19] having faith and a good conscience. Some have rejected these and have suffered the shipwreck of their faith. [20] Hymenaeus and Alexander are among them, and I have delivered them to Satan, so that they may be taught not to blaspheme.

Paul's Instructions on Prayer

2 First of all, then, I urge that petitions, prayers, intercessions, and thanksgivings be made for everyone, [2] for kings and all those who are in authority, so that we may lead a tranquil and quiet life in all godliness and dignity.

Christ a Ransom for All

[3] This is good, and it pleases God our Savior, [4] who wants everyone to be saved and to come to the knowledge of the truth.

[5] For there is one God
   and one mediator between God
      and man,
   a man, Christ Jesus,
[6] who gave Himself—a ransom
      for all,
   a testimony at the proper time.

[7] For this I was appointed a herald, an apostle (I am telling the truth;[b] I am not lying), and a teacher of the Gentiles in faith and truth.

Paul's Instructions for Men and Women

[8] Therefore I want the men in every place to pray, lifting up holy hands without anger or argument. [9] Also, the women are to dress themselves in modest clothing, with decency and good sense; not with elaborate hairstyles, gold, pearls, or expensive apparel, [10] but with good works, as is proper for women who affirm that they worship God. [11] A woman should learn in silence with full submission. [12] I do not allow a woman to teach or to have authority over a man; instead, she is to be silent. [13] For Adam was created first, then Eve. [14] And Adam was not deceived, but the woman was deceived and transgressed. [15] But she will be saved through childbearing, if she continues[c] in faith, love, and holiness, with good sense.

---

[a]**1:17** Other mss add *wise*   [b]**2:7** Other mss add *in Christ*   [c]**2:15** Lit *if they continue*

Qualifications of Overseers

3 This saying is trustworthy:[a] "If any-one aspires to be an •overseer, he de-sires a noble work." [2] An overseer, therefore, must be above reproach, the husband of one wife, self-controlled, sen-sible, respectable, hospitable, an able teacher,[b] [3] not addicted to wine, not a bully but gentle, not quarrelsome, not greedy— [4] one who manages his own household competently, having his chil-dren under control with all dignity. [5] (If anyone does not know how to manage his own household, how will he take care of God's church?) [6] He must not be a new convert, or he might become con-ceited and fall into the condemnation of the Devil. [7] Furthermore, he must have a good reputation among outsiders, so that he does not fall into disgrace and the Devil's trap.

Qualifications of Deacons

[8] <u>Deacons</u>, likewise, should be worthy of respect, not hypocritical, not drinking a lot of wine, not greedy for money, [9] holding the •mystery of the faith with a clear conscience. [10] And they must also be tested first; if they prove blameless, then they can serve as deacons. [11] Wives, too, must be worthy of respect, not slanderers, self-controlled, faithful in everything. [12] Deacons must be hus-bands of one wife, managing their chil-dren and their own households competently. [13] For those who have served well as deacons acquire a good standing for themselves, and great bold-ness in the faith that is in Christ Jesus.

Mystery of Godliness

[14] I write these things to you, hoping to come to you soon. [15] But if I should be delayed, ⌊I have written⌋ so that you will know how people ought to act in God's household, which is the church of the living God, the pillar and foundation of the truth. [16] And most certainly, the mys-tery of godliness is great:

> He[c] was manifested in the flesh,
> justified in the Spirit,
> seen by angels,
> preached among the Gentiles,
> believed on in the world,
> taken up in glory.

Latter Times: Demonic Influence

4 Now the Spirit explicitly says that in the latter times some will depart from the faith, paying attention to de-ceitful spirits and the teachings of de-mons, [2] through the hypocrisy of liars whose consciences are seared. [3] They forbid marriage and demand abstinence from foods that God created to be re-ceived with gratitude by those who be-lieve and know the truth.

God's "Good" Creation

[4] <u>For everything created by God is good, and nothing should be rejected if it is re-ceived with thanksgiving,</u> [5] <u>since it is sanctified by the word of God and by prayer.</u>

Training in Godliness

[6] If you point these things out to the brothers, you will be a good servant of Christ Jesus, nourished by the words of the faith and of the good teaching that you have followed. [7] But have nothing to do with irreverent and silly myths. Rather, train yourself in godliness, [8] for,

> the training of the body has
> a limited benefit,
> but godliness is beneficial
> in every way,

---

[a]**3:1** *This saying is trustworthy* could refer to 1 Tm 2:15.   [b]**3:2** Or *hospitable, skillful in teaching*   [c]**3:16** Other mss read *God*

since it holds promise
for the present life
and also for the life to come.

⁹ This saying is trustworthy and deserves full acceptance. ¹⁰ In fact, we labor and strive[a] for this, because we have put our hope in the living God, who is the Savior of everyone, especially of those who believe.

Paul Advises Timothy on Ministry

¹¹ Command and teach these things. ¹² No one should despise your youth; instead, you should be an example to the believers in speech, in conduct, in love,[b] in faith, in purity. ¹³ Until I come, give your attention to public reading, exhortation, and teaching. ¹⁴ Do not neglect the gift that is in you; it was given to you through prophecy, with the laying on of hands by the council of elders. ¹⁵ Practice these things; be committed to them, so that your progress may be evident to all. ¹⁶ Be conscientious about yourself and your teaching; persevere in these things, for by doing this you will save both yourself and your hearers.

5 Do not rebuke an older man, but exhort him as a father, younger men as brothers, ² older women as mothers, and with all propriety, the younger women as sisters.

Support of Widows

³ Support[c] widows who are genuinely widows. ⁴ But if any widow has children or grandchildren, they should learn to practice their religion toward their own family first and to repay their parents, for this pleases God. ⁵ The real widow, left all alone, has put her hope in God and continues night and day in her petitions

and prayers; ⁶ however, she who is self-indulgent is dead even while she lives. ⁷ Command this, so that they won't be blamed. ⁸ Now if anyone does not provide for his own relatives, and especially for his household, he has denied the faith and is worse than an unbeliever.

⁹ No widow should be placed on the official support list[d] unless she is at least 60 years old, has been the wife of one husband, ¹⁰ and is well known for good works—that is, if she has brought up children, shown hospitality, washed the saints' feet, helped the afflicted, and devoted herself to every good work. ¹¹ But refuse to enroll younger widows; for when they are drawn away from Christ by desire, they want to marry, ¹² and will therefore receive condemnation because they have renounced their original pledge. ¹³ At the same time, they also learn to be idle, going from house to house; they are not only idle, but are also gossips and busybodies, saying things they shouldn't say. ¹⁴ Therefore, I want younger women to marry, have children, manage their households, and give the adversary no opportunity to accuse us. ¹⁵ For some have already turned away to follow Satan. ¹⁶ If any[e] believing woman has widows, she should help them, and the church should not be burdened, so that it can help those who are genuinely widows.

Honor Elders, Preachers, and Teachers

¹⁷ The elders who are good leaders should be considered worthy of an ample honorarium,[f] especially those who work hard at preaching and teaching. ¹⁸ For the Scripture says:

**You must not muzzle an ox
that is threshing grain,**[g] and,

**The laborer is worthy
of his wages.**

Rules for Church Discipline
and Practice

¹⁹ Don't accept an accusation against an elder unless it is supported by two or three witnesses. ²⁰ Publicly rebuke[a] those who sin, so that the rest will also be afraid. ²¹ I solemnly charge you, before God and Christ Jesus and the elect angels, to observe these things without prejudice, doing nothing out of favoritism. ²² Don't be too quick to lay hands on[b] anyone, and don't share in the sins of others. Keep yourself pure.

Paul's Health Advice

²³ Don't continue drinking only water, but use a little wine because of your stomach and your frequent illnesses. ²⁴ Some people's sins are evident, going before them to judgment, but ⌊the sins⌋ of others follow them. ²⁵ Likewise, good works are obvious, and those that are not ⌊obvious⌋ cannot remain hidden.

Slaves Honor Masters

6 All who are under the yoke as slaves must regard their own masters to be worthy of all respect, so that God's name and His teaching will not be blasphemed. ² And those who have believing masters should not be disrespectful to them because they are brothers, but should serve them better, since those who benefit from their service are believers and dearly loved.

Warnings on False Doctrine and
Human Greed

Teach and encourage these things. ³ If anyone teaches other doctrine and does not agree with the sound teaching of our Lord Jesus Christ and with the teaching that promotes godliness, ⁴ he is conceited, understanding nothing, but having a sick interest in disputes and arguments over words. From these come envy, quarreling, slanders, evil suspicions, ⁵ and constant disagreement among men whose minds are depraved and deprived of the truth, who imagine that godliness[c] is a way to material gain.[d] ⁶ But godliness with contentment is a great gain.

⁷ For we brought nothing
    into the world, and[e] we can take
    nothing out.
⁸ But if we have food and clothing,[f]
    we will be content with these.

⁹ But those who want to be rich fall into temptation, a trap, and many foolish and harmful desires, which plunge people into ruin and destruction. ¹⁰ For the love of money is a root[g] of all kinds of evil, and by craving it, some have wandered away from the faith and pierced themselves with many pains.

Good Fight for Faith

¹¹ Now you, man of God, run
     from these things;
    but pursue righteousness,
     godliness, faith,
    love, endurance, and gentleness.
¹² Fight the good fight for the faith;
    take hold of eternal life,
    to which you were called
    and have made a good confession
    before many witnesses.

¹³ In the presence of God, who gives life to all, and before Christ Jesus, who gave a good confession before Pontius •Pilate, I charge you ¹⁴ to keep the

---

commandment without spot or blame until the appearing of our Lord Jesus Christ, [15] which God[a] will bring about in His own time. ⌊He is⌋

the blessed and only Sovereign,
the King of kings,
and the Lord of lords,
[16] the only One who has immortality,
dwelling in unapproachable light,
whom none of mankind has seen
    or can see,
to whom be honor
    and eternal might.
•Amen.

Instructions to the Rich

[17] Instruct those who are rich in the present age not to be arrogant or to set their hope on the uncertainty of wealth, but on God,[b] who richly provides us with all things to enjoy. [18] ⌊Instruct them⌋ to do good, to be rich in good works, to be generous, willing to share, [19] storing up for themselves a good foundation for the age to come, so that they may take hold of life that is real.

Guard the Heritage

[20] Timothy, guard what has been entrusted to you, avoiding irreverent, empty speech and contradictions from the "knowledge" that falsely bears that name. [21] By professing it, some people have deviated from the faith.

Grace be with all of you.

2 TIMOTHY

Greeting

1 Paul, an apostle of Christ Jesus by God's will, for the promise of life in Christ Jesus:

[2] To Timothy, my dearly loved child.

Grace, mercy, and peace from God the Father and Christ Jesus our Lord.

Paul Prays for Timothy—and Recalls His "Family Faith"

[3] I thank God, whom I serve with a clear conscience as my forefathers did, when I constantly remember you in my prayers night and day. [4] Remembering your tears, I long to see you so that I may be filled with joy, [5] clearly recalling your sincere faith that first lived in your grandmother Lois, then in your mother Eunice, and that I am convinced is in you also.

Not a Spirit of Fearfulness

[6] Therefore, I remind you to keep ablaze the gift of God that is in you through the laying on of my hands. [7] For God has not given us a spirit[c] of fearfulness, but one of power, love, and sound judgment.

Not Ashamed of the Gospel

[8] So don't be ashamed of the testimony about our Lord, or of me His prisoner. Instead, share in suffering for the gospel, relying on the power of God,

[9] who has saved us and called us
with a holy calling,
not according to our works,
but according to His own purpose
    and grace,

---

which was given to us
 in Christ Jesus before time began.
10 This has now been made evident
 through the appearing of our Savior
 Christ Jesus,
 who has abolished death
and has brought life
 and immortality to light
 through the gospel.

11 For this ⌊gospel⌋ I was appointed a herald, apostle, and teacher,[a] 12 and that is why I suffer these things. But I am not ashamed, because I know whom I have believed and am persuaded that He is able to guard what has been entrusted to me[b] until that day.

Hold to Sound Teaching

13 Hold on to the pattern of sound teaching that you have heard from me, in the faith and love that are in Christ Jesus. 14 Guard, through the Holy Spirit who lives in us, that good thing entrusted to you. 15 This you know: all those in Asia have turned away from me, including Phygelus and Hermogenes. 16 May the Lord grant mercy to the household of Onesiphorus, because he often refreshed me and was not ashamed of my chains. 17 On the contrary, when he was in Rome, he diligently searched for me and found me. 18 May the Lord grant that he obtain mercy from the Lord on that day. And you know how much he ministered at Ephesus.

Be Strong in Grace

2 You, therefore, my child, be strong in the grace that is in Christ Jesus. 2 And what you have heard from me in the presence of many witnesses, commit to faithful men who will be able to teach others also.

A Good Soldier of Christ

3 Share in suffering as a good soldier of Christ Jesus. 4 To please the recruiter, no one serving as a soldier gets entangled in the concerns of everyday life. 5 Also, if anyone competes as an athlete, he is not crowned unless he competes according to the rules. 6 It is the hardworking farmer who ought to be the first to get a share of the crops. 7 Consider what I say, for the Lord will give you understanding in everything.

8 Keep in mind Jesus Christ, risen from the dead, descended from David, according to my gospel. 9 For this I suffer, to the point of being bound like a criminal; but God's message is not bound. 10 This is why I endure all things for the elect: so that they also may obtain salvation, which is in Christ Jesus, with eternal glory. 11 This saying is trustworthy:

For if we have died with Him,
 we will also live with Him;
12 if we endure,
 we will also reign with Him;
 if we deny Him,
 He will also deny us;
13 if we are faithless,
 He remains faithful,
 for He cannot deny Himself.

Be an Approved Worker

14 Remind them of these things, charging them before God[c] not to fight about words; this is in no way profitable and leads to the ruin of the hearers. 15 Be diligent to present yourself approved to God, a worker who doesn't need to be ashamed, correctly teaching the word of truth. 16 But avoid irreverent, empty speech, for this will produce an even greater measure of godlessness. 17 And their word will spread like gangrene,

---

[a] **1:11** Other mss add *of the Gentiles*　[b] **1:12** Or *guard what I have entrusted to Him,* or *guard my deposit*
[c] **2:14** Other mss read *before the Lord*

among whom are Hymenaeus and Phile-tus. ¹⁸ They have deviated from the truth, saying that the resurrection has already taken place, and are overturning the faith of some. ¹⁹ Nevertheless, God's solid foundation stands firm, having this inscription:

> The Lord knows those
>   who are His,ᵃ and
> Everyone who names the name
>   of the Lord
> **must turn away**
>   **from unrighteousness.**

²⁰ Now in a large house there are not only gold and silver bowls, but also those of wood and earthenware, some for specialᵇ use, some for ordinary. ²¹ So if anyone purifies himself from these things, he will be a specialᶜ instrument, set apart, useful to the Master, prepared for every good work.

²² Flee from youthful passions, and pursue righteousness, faith, love, and peace, along with those who call on the Lord from a pure heart. ²³ But reject foolish and ignorant disputes, knowing that they breed quarrels. ²⁴ The Lord's slave must not quarrel, but must be gentle to everyone, able to teach,ᵈ and patient, ²⁵ instructing his opponents with gentleness. Perhaps God will grant them repentance to know the truth. ²⁶ Then they may come to their senses and escape the Devil's trap, having been captured by him to do his will.

Difficult Times and Disobedient People

3 But know this: difficult times will come in the last days. ² For people will be lovers of self, lovers of money, boastful, proud, blasphemers, disobedi-

ent to parents, ungrateful, unholy, ³ unloving, irreconcilable, slanderers, without self-control, brutal, without love for what is good, ⁴ traitors, reckless, conceited, lovers of pleasure rather than lovers of God, ⁵ holding to the form of religion but denying its power. Avoid these people!

⁶ For among them are those who worm their way into households and capture idle women burdened down with sins, led along by a variety of passions, ⁷ always learning and never able to come to a knowledge of the truth. ⁸ Just as Jannes and Jambres resisted Moses, so these also resist the truth, men who are corrupt in mind, worthless in regard to the faith. ⁹ But they will not make further progress, for their lack of understanding will be clear to all, as theirsᵉ was also.

The Sacred Scriptures

¹⁰ But you have followed my teaching, conduct, purpose, faith, patience, love, and endurance, ¹¹ along with the persecutions and sufferings that came to me in Antioch, Iconium, and Lystra. What persecutions I endured! Yet the Lord rescued me from them all. ¹² In fact, all those who want to live a godly life in Christ Jesus will be persecuted. ¹³ Evil people and imposters will become worse, deceiving and being deceived. ¹⁴ But as for you, continue in what you have learned and firmly believed, knowing those from whom you learned, ¹⁵ and that from childhood you have known the sacred Scriptures, which are able to instruct you for salvation through faith in Christ Jesus. ¹⁶ All Scripture is inspired by Godᶠ and is profitable for teaching, for rebuking, for correcting, for training in righteousness, ¹⁷ so that the man of God

ᵃ2:19 Nm 16:5   ᵇ2:20 Or honorable   ᶜ2:21 Or an honorable   ᵈ2:24 Or everyone, skillful in teaching   ᵉ3:9 Referring to Jannes and Jambres   ᶠ3:16 Lit breathed out by God; the Scripture is the product of God's Spirit working through men; see 2 Pt 1:20-21.

may be complete, equipped for every good work.

Rebuke, Correct, Encourage

4 Before God and Christ Jesus, who is going to judge the living and the dead, and by His appearing and His kingdom, I solemnly charge you: 2 proclaim the message; persist in it whether convenient or not; rebuke, correct, and encourage with great patience and teaching.

Beware of "Itch" for the New

3 For the time will come when they will not tolerate sound doctrine, but according to their own desires, will accumulate teachers for themselves because they have an itch to hear something new.[a] 4 They will turn away from hearing the truth and will turn aside to myths. 5 But as for you, keep a clear head about everything, endure hardship, do the work of an evangelist, fulfill your ministry.

6 For I am already being poured out as a drink offering, and the time for my departure is close. 7 I have fought the good fight, I have finished the race, I have kept the faith. 8 In the future, there is reserved for me the crown of righteousness, which the Lord, the righteous Judge, will give me on that day, and not only to me, but to all those who have loved His appearing.

Notes on Personalities

9 Make every effort to come to me soon, 10 for Demas has deserted me, because he loved this present world, and has gone to Thessalonica. Crescens has gone to Galatia, Titus to Dalmatia. 11 Only Luke is with me. Bring Mark with you, for he is useful to me in the ministry. 12 I have sent Tychicus to Ephesus. 13 When you come, bring the cloak I left in Troas with Carpus, as well as the scrolls, especially the parchments. 14 Alexander the coppersmith did great harm to me. The Lord will repay him according to his works. 15 Watch out for him yourself, because he strongly opposed our words.

Paul Deserted at First Defense

16 At my first defense, no one came to my assistance, but everyone deserted me. May it not be counted against them. 17 But the Lord stood with me and strengthened me, so that the proclamation might be fully made through me, and all the Gentiles might hear. So I was rescued from the lion's mouth. 18 The Lord will rescue me from every evil work and will bring me safely into His heavenly kingdom. To Him be the glory forever and ever! •Amen.

Benediction

19 Greet Prisca and Aquila, and the household of Onesiphorus. 20 Erastus has remained at Corinth; Trophimus I left sick at Miletus. 21 Make every effort to come before winter. Eubulus greets you, as do Pudens, Linus, Claudia, and all the brothers.

22 The Lord be with your spirit. Grace be with you!

a 4:3 Or to hear what they want to hear; lit themselves, itching in the hearing

TITUS

Greeting

1 Paul, a slave of God, and an apostle of Jesus Christ for the faith of God's elect and the knowledge of the truth that leads[a] to godliness, [2] in the hope of eternal life that God, who cannot lie, promised before time began, [3] and has in His own time revealed His message in the proclamation that I was entrusted with by the command of God our Savior:

[4] To Titus, my true child in our common faith.

Grace and peace from God the Father and Christ Jesus our Savior.

Rules for Titus' Appointment of Elders and Overseers in Crete

[5] The reason I left you in Crete was to set right what was left undone and, as I directed you, to appoint elders in every town: [6] someone who is blameless, the husband of one wife, having faithful[b] children not accused of wildness or rebellion. [7] For an •overseer, as God's manager, must be blameless, not arrogant, not quick tempered, not addicted to wine, not a bully, not greedy for money, [8] but hospitable, loving what is good, sensible, righteous, holy, self-controlled, [9] holding to the faithful message as taught, so that he will be able both to encourage with sound teaching and to refute those who contradict it.

Silence Spiritual Rebels

[10] For there are also many rebellious people, idle talkers and deceivers, especially those from Judaism.[c] [11] It is necessary to silence them; they overthrow whole households by teaching for dishonest gain what they should not. [12] One of their very own prophets said,

> Cretans are always liars, evil beasts,
> lazy gluttons.[d]

[13] This testimony is true. So, rebuke them sharply, that they may be sound in the faith [14] and may not pay attention to Jewish myths and the commandments of men who reject the truth. [15] To the pure, everything is pure, but to those who are defiled and unbelieving nothing is pure; in fact, both their mind and conscience are defiled. [16] They profess to know God, but they deny Him by their works. They are detestable, disobedient, and disqualified for any good work.

Pursue Sound Teaching

2 But you must speak what is consistent with sound teaching. [2] Older men are to be self-controlled, worthy of respect, sensible, and sound in faith, love, and endurance. [3] In the same way, older women are to be reverent in behavior, not slanderers, not addicted to much wine. ⌊They are⌋ to teach what is good, [4] so that they may encourage the young women to love their husbands and children, [5] to be sensible, pure, good homemakers, and submissive to their husbands, so that God's message will not be slandered.

[6] Likewise, encourage the young men to be sensible [7] about everything. Set an example of good works yourself, with integrity and dignity[e] in your teaching. [8] Your message is to be sound beyond reproach, so that the opponent will be

---

[a]**1:1** Or *corresponds*   [b]**1:6** Or *believing*   [c]**1:10** Lit *the circumcision*   [d]**1:12** This saying is from the Cretan poet Epimenides (6th century B.C.).   [e]**2:7** Other mss add *incorruptibility*

ashamed, having nothing bad to say about us.

⁹ Slaves are to be submissive to their masters in everything, and to be well-pleasing, not talking back ¹⁰ or stealing, but demonstrating utter faithfulness, so that they may adorn the teaching of God our Savior in everything.

¹¹ For the grace of God has appeared, with salvationᵃ for all people, ¹² instructing us to deny godlessness and worldly lusts and to live in a sensible, righteous, and godly way in the present age, ¹³ while we wait for the blessed hope and the appearing of the glory of our great God and Savior, Jesus Christ. ¹⁴ He gave Himself for us to redeem us from all lawlessness and to cleanse for Himself a special people, eager to do good works.

¹⁵ Say these things, and encourage and rebuke with all authority. Let no one disregardᵇ you.

Importance of Good Works

3 Remind them to be submissive to rulers and authorities, to obey, to be ready for every good work, ² to slander no one, to avoid fighting, and to be kind, always showing gentleness to all people. ³ For we too were once foolish, disobedient, deceived, captives of various passions and pleasures, living in malice and envy, hateful, detesting one another.

⁴ But when the goodness and love
    for man
appeared from God our Savior,
⁵ He saved us—
    not by works of righteousness
    that we had done,
but according to His mercy,

through the washing
    of regeneration
and renewal by the Holy Spirit.
⁶ This ⌊Spirit⌋ He poured out on us
    abundantly
through Jesus Christ our Savior,
⁷ so that having been justified
    by His grace,
we may become heirs
    with the hope of eternal life.

⁸ This saying is trustworthy. I want you to insist on these things, so that those who have believed God might be careful to devote themselves to good works. These are good and profitable for everyone.

Avoid Foolish Debates and Divisions

⁹ But avoid foolish debates, genealogies, quarrels, and disputes about the law, for they are unprofitable and worthless. ¹⁰ Reject a divisive person after a first and second warning, ¹¹ knowing that such a person is perverted and sins, being self-condemned.

Final Instructions and Closing

¹² When I send Artemas to you, or Tychicus, make every effort to come to me in Nicopolis, for I have decided to spend the winter there. ¹³ Diligently help Zenas the lawyer and Apollos on their journey, so that they will lack nothing. ¹⁴ And our people must also learn to devote themselves to good works for cases of urgent need, so that they will not be unfruitful. ¹⁵ All those who are with me greet you. Greet those who love us in the faith. Grace be with all of you.

ᵃ**2:11** Or *appeared, bringing salvation* ᵇ**2:15** Or *despise*

PHILEMON

Greeting—from Paul and Timothy

Paul, a prisoner of Christ Jesus, and Timothy, our brother:

To Philemon, our dear friend and co-worker, [2] to Apphia our sister,[a] to Archippus our fellow soldier, and to the church that meets in your house.

[3] Grace to you and peace from God our Father and the Lord Jesus Christ.

Philemon's Love and Faith

[4] I always thank my God when I mention you in my prayers, [5] because I hear of your love and faith toward[b] the Lord Jesus and for all the saints. [6] ⌊I pray⌋ that your participation in the faith may become effective through knowing every good thing that is in us[c] for ⌊the glory of⌋ Christ. [7] For I have great joy and encouragement from your love, because the hearts of the saints have been refreshed through you, brother.

Appeal for Slave Onesimus

[8] For this reason, although I have great boldness in Christ to command you to do what is right, [9] I appeal, instead, on the basis of love. I, Paul, as an elderly man[d] and now also as a prisoner of Christ Jesus, [10] appeal to you for my child, whom I fathered[e] while in chains— Onesimus.[f] [11] Once he was useless to you, but now he is useful to both you and me. [12] I am sending him—a part of myself[g]—back to you.[h] [13] I wanted to keep him with me, so that in my imprisonment for the gospel he might serve me in your place. [14] But I didn't want to do anything without your consent, so that your good deed might not be out of obligation, but of your own free will. [15] For perhaps this is why he was separated ⌊from you⌋ for a brief time, so that you might get him back permanently, [16] no longer as a slave, but more than a slave—as a dearly loved brother. This is especially so to me, but even more to you, both in the flesh and in the Lord.[i]

Charge His Wrongs to My Account

[17] So if you consider me a partner, accept him as you would me. [18] And if he has wronged you in any way, or owes you anything, charge that to my account. [19] I, Paul, write this with my own hand: I will repay it—not to mention to you that you owe me even your own self. [20] Yes, brother, may I have joy from you in the Lord; refresh my heart in Christ. [21] Since I am confident of your obedience, I am writing to you, knowing that you will do even more than I say. [22] But meanwhile, also prepare a guest room for me, for I hope that through your prayers I will be restored to you.

Final Greetings

[23] Epaphras, my fellow prisoner in Christ Jesus, greets you, and so do [24] Mark, Aristarchus, Demas, and Luke, my co-workers.

[25] The grace of the Lord[j] Jesus Christ be with your spirit.

---

[a]**2** Other mss read *our beloved* [b]**5** Lit *faith that you have toward* [c]**6** Other mss read *in you* [d]**9** Or *an ambassador*
[e]**10** Referring to the fact that Paul led him to Christ; see 1 Co 4:15 [f]**10** The name *Onesimus* in Gk means "useful."
[g]**12** Lit *him—that is, my inward parts* [h]**12** Other mss read *him back. Receive him as a part of myself.* [i]**16** Both physically and spiritually [j]**25** Other mss read *our Lord*

HEBREWS

Divine Nature of the Son

1 Long ago God spoke to the fathers by the prophets at different times and in different ways. [2] In these last days, He has spoken to us by ⌊His⌋ Son, whom He has appointed heir of all things and through whom He made the universe.[a] [3] He is the radiance[b] of His glory, the exact expression[c] of His nature, and He sustains all things by His powerful word. After making purification for sins,[d] He sat down at the right hand of the Majesty on high.[e]

Son Superior to Angels

[4] So He became higher in rank than the angels, just as the name He inherited is superior to theirs.

The Son Superior to Angels

[5] For to which of the angels did He ever say, **You are My Son; today I have become Your Father,**[f g] or again, **I will be His Father, and He will be My Son?**[h] [6] When He again brings His firstborn into the world,[i] He says, **And all God's angels must worship Him.**[j] [7] And about the angels He says:

> **He makes His angels winds,**[k] **and His servants**[l] **a fiery flame;**[m]

[8] but about the Son:

> **Your throne, O God, is forever and ever,**
> **and the scepter of Your kingdom is a scepter of justice.**

> [9] **You have loved righteousness and hated lawlessness;**
> **this is why God, Your God, has anointed You,**
> **rather than Your companions,**[n o]
> **with the oil of joy.**

[10] And:

> **In the beginning, Lord, You established the earth,**
> **and the heavens are the works of Your hands;**
> [11] **they will perish, but You remain. They will all wear out like clothing;**
> [12] **You will roll them up like a cloak,**[p]
> **and they will be changed like a robe.**
> **But You are the same, and Your years will never end.**[q]

[13] Now to which of the angels has He ever said:

> **Sit at My right hand until I make Your enemies Your footstool?**[r s]

[14] Are they not all ministering spirits sent out to serve those who are going to inherit salvation?

Author Warns against Neglect of Salvation

2 We must therefore pay even more attention to what we have heard, so that we will not drift away. [2] For if the message spoken through angels was legally binding,[t] and every transgression

---

[a]1:2 Lit *ages* [b]1:3 Or *reflection* [c]1:3 Or *representation*, or *copy*, or *reproduction* [d]1:3 Other mss read *for our sins by Himself* [e]1:3 Or *He sat down on high at the right hand of the Majesty* [f]1:5 Or *have begotten You* [g]1:5 Ps 2:7 [h]1:5 2 Sm 7:14; 1 Ch 17:13 [i]1:6 Or *And again, when He brings His firstborn into the world* [j]1:6 Dt 32:43 LXX; Ps 97:7 [k]1:7 Or *spirits* [l]1:7 Or *ministers* [m]1:7 Ps 104:4 [n]1:9 Or *associates* [o]1:8-9 Ps 45:6-7 [p]1:12 Other mss omit *like a cloak* [q]1:10-12 Ps 102:25-27 [r]1:13 Or *enemies a footstool for Your feet* [s]1:13 Ps 110:1 [t]2:2 Or *valid*, or *reliable*

and disobedience received a just punishment, ³ how will we escape if we neglect such a great salvation? It was first spoken by the Lord and was confirmed to us by those who heard Him. ⁴ At the same time, God also testified by signs and wonders, various miracles, and distributions ⌊of gifts⌋ from the Holy Spirit according to His will.

Jesus Lower than Angels—for a Time

⁵ For He has not subjected to angels the world to come that we are talking about. ⁶ But one has somewhere testified:

What is man,
  that You remember him,
or the son of man,
  that You care for him?
⁷ You made him lower
  than the angels for a short time;
You crowned him with glory
  and honor^a
⁸ and subjected everything
  under his feet.^b

For in **subjecting everything** to him, He left nothing not subject to him. As it is, we do not yet see **everything subjected** to him. ⁹ But we do see Jesus—**made lower than the angels for a short time** so that by God's grace He might taste death for everyone—crowned with glory and honor because of the suffering of death.

Jesus, Our Brother

¹⁰ For it was fitting, in bringing many sons to glory, that He, for whom and through whom all things exist, should make the source^c of their salvation perfect through sufferings. ¹¹ For the One who sanctifies and those who are sanctified all have one Father.^d That is why He is not ashamed to call them brothers, ¹² saying:

I will proclaim Your name
  to My brothers;
I will sing hymns to You
  in the congregation.^e

¹³ Again, I will trust in Him.^f And again, Here I am with the children God gave Me.^g

Jesus' Death Destroys Devil

¹⁴ Now since the children have flesh and blood in common, He also shared in these, so that through His death He might destroy the one holding the power of death—that is, the Devil— ¹⁵ and free those who were held in slavery all their lives by the fear of death. ¹⁶ For it is clear that He does not reach out to help angels, but to help Abraham's offspring.

Jesus a Merciful High Priest

¹⁷ Therefore He had to be like His brothers in every way, so that He could become a merciful and faithful high priest in service^h to God, to make propitiationⁱ for the sins of the people. ¹⁸ For since He Himself was tested and has suffered, He is able to help those who are tested.

Jesus Greater than Moses

3 Therefore, holy brothers and companions in a heavenly calling, consider Jesus, the apostle and high priest of our confession; ² He was faithful to the One who appointed Him, just as Moses was in all God's^j household. ³ For Jesus^k is considered worthy of more glory than Moses, just as the builder has more

^a**2:7** Other mss add *and set him over the works of your hands* ^b**2:6-8** Ps 8:5-7 LXX ^c**2:10** Or *pioneer*, or *leader* ^d**2:11** Or *father*, or *origin*, or *all are of one* ^e**2:12** Ps 22:22 ^f**2:13** Is 8:17 LXX; 12:2 LXX; 2 Sm 22:3 LXX ^g**2:13** Is 8:18 LXX ^h**2:17** Lit *things* ⁱ**2:17** The word *propitiation* has to do with the removal of divine wrath. Jesus' death is the means that turns God's wrath from the sinner; see 2 Co 5:21. ^j**3:2** Lit *His* ^k**3:3** Lit *He*

honor than the house. ⁴ Now every house is built by someone, but the One who built everything is God. ⁵ Moses was faithful as a servant in all God'sᵃ household, as a testimony to what would be said ⌊in the future⌋. ⁶ But Christ was faithful as a Son over His household, whose household we are if we hold on to the courage and the confidence of our hope.ᵇ

Author Warns against Unbelief

⁷ Therefore, as the Holy Spirit says:

> Today, if you hear His voice,
> ⁸ do not harden your hearts
>   as in the rebellion,
>   on the day of testing in the desert,
> ⁹ where your fathers tested Me,
>   tried ⌊Me⌋,
>   and saw My works ¹⁰ for 40 years.
> Therefore I was provoked
>   with this generation
>   and said, "They always go astray
>   in their hearts,
>   and they have not known
>   My ways."
> ¹¹ So I swore in My anger,
>   "They will not enter My rest."ᶜ

¹² Watch out, brothers, so that there won't be in any of you an evil, unbelieving heart that departs from the living God. ¹³ But encourage each other daily, while it is still called **today**, so that none of you is hardened by sin's deception. ¹⁴ For we have become companions of the •Messiah if we hold firmly until the end the realityᵈ that we had at the start. ¹⁵ As it is said:

> Today, if you hear His voice,
>   do not harden your hearts
>   as in the rebellion.ᵉ

¹⁶ For who heard and rebelled? Wasn't it really all who came out of Egypt under Moses? ¹⁷ And with whom was He "provoked for 40 years"? Was it not with those who sinned, whose bodies fell in the desert? ¹⁸ And to whom did He "swear that they would not enter His rest," if not those who disobeyed? ¹⁹ So we see that they were unable to enter because of unbelief.

God's Promised "Rest"

4 Therefore, while the promise remains of entering His rest, let us fear so that none of you should miss it.ᶠ ² For we also have received the good news just as they did; but the message they heard did not benefit them, since they were not united with those who heard it in faithᵍ ³ (for we who have believed enter the rest), in keeping with whatʰ He has said:

> So I swore in My anger,
>   they will not enter My rest.ⁱ

God's Seventh Day of Rest

And yet His works have been finished since the foundation of the world, ⁴ for somewhere He has spoken about the seventh day in this way:

> And on the seventh day
> God rested from all His works.ʲ

Disobedience Bars
Entry into God's Rest

⁵ Again, in that passage ⌊He says⌋, **They will never enter My rest.**ⁱ ⁶ Since it remains for some to enter it, and those who formerly received the good news did not enter because of disobedience, ⁷ again, He specifies a certain day—

ᵃ**3:5** Lit *His*   ᵇ**3:6** Other mss add *firm to the end*   ᶜ**3:7-11** Ps 95:7-11   ᵈ**3:14** Or *confidence*   ᵉ**3:15** Ps 95:7-8   ᶠ**4:1** Or *should seem to miss it*   ᵍ**4:2** Other mss read *since it was not united by faith in those who heard*   ʰ**4:3** Or *rest), just as*   ⁱ**4:3,5** Ps 95:11   ʲ**4:4** Gn 2:2

today—speaking through David after such a long time, as previously stated:

> Today if you hear His voice,
> do not harden your hearts.[a]

[8] For if Joshua had given them rest, He would not have spoken later about another day.

"A Sabbath Rest Remains"

[9] A Sabbath rest remains, therefore, for God's people. [10] For the person who has entered His rest has rested from his own works, just as God did from His. [11] Let us then make every effort to enter that rest, so that no one will fall into the same pattern of disobedience.

[12] For the word of God is living and effective and sharper than any two-edged sword, penetrating as far as to divide soul, spirit, joints, and marrow; it is a judge of the ideas and thoughts of the heart. [13] No creature is hidden from Him, but all things are naked and exposed to the eyes of Him to whom we must give an account.

Jesus Our Great High Priest

[14] Therefore since we have a great high priest who has passed through the heavens—Jesus the Son of God—let us hold fast to the confession.

Jesus Tested as We Are— without Sin

[15] For we do not have a high priest who is unable to sympathize with our weaknesses, but One who has been tested in every way as we are, yet without sin. [16] Therefore let us approach the throne of grace with boldness, so that we may receive mercy and find grace to help us at the proper time.

Messiah, a Priest of Melchizedek

5 For every high priest taken from men is appointed in service[b] to God for the people, to offer both gifts and sacrifices for sins. [2] He is able to deal gently with those who are ignorant and are going astray, since he himself is also subject to weakness. [3] Because of this, he must make a sin offering for himself as well as for the people. [4] No one takes this honor on himself; instead, a person is called by God, just as Aaron was. [5] In the same way, the •Messiah did not exalt Himself to become a high priest, but the One who said to Him, **You are My Son; today I have become Your Father,**[c] [6] also said in another passage, **You are a priest forever in the order of Melchizedek.**[d]

[7] During His earthly life,[e] He offered prayers and appeals, with loud cries and tears, to the One who was able to save Him from death, and He was heard because of His reverence. [8] Though a Son, He learned obedience through what He suffered. [9] After He was perfected, He became the source of eternal salvation to all who obey Him, [10] and He was declared by God a high priest "in the order of Melchizedek."

Problem of Immaturity

[11] We have a great deal to say about this, and it's difficult to explain, since you have become slow to understand. [12] For though by this time you ought to be teachers, you need someone to teach you again the basic principles of God's revelation. You need milk, not solid food. [13] Now everyone who lives on milk is inexperienced with the message about righteousness, because he is an infant. [14] But solid food is for the mature—for

those whose senses have been trained to distinguish between good and evil.

"Let Us Go On To Maturity"

6 Therefore, leaving the elementary message about the •Messiah, let us go on to maturity, not laying again the foundation of repentance from dead works, faith in God, [2] teaching about ritual washings,[a] laying on of hands, the resurrection of the dead, and eternal judgment. [3] And we will do this if God permits.

Author Warns against Falling Away

[4] For it is impossible to renew to repentance those who were once enlightened, who tasted the heavenly gift, became companions with the Holy Spirit, [5] tasted God's good word and the powers of the coming age, [6] and who have fallen away, because,[b] to their own harm, they are recrucifying the Son of God and holding Him up to contempt. [7] For ground that has drunk the rain that has often fallen on it, and that produces vegetation useful to those it is cultivated for, receives a blessing from God. [8] But if it produces thorns and thistles, it is worthless and about to be cursed, and will be burned at the end.

Author Confident of Their Salvation

[9] Even though we are speaking this way, dear friends, in your case we are confident of the better things connected with salvation. [10] For God is not unjust; He will not forget your work and the love[c] you showed for His name when you served the saints—and you continue to serve them. [11] Now we want each of you to demonstrate the same diligence for the final realization of your hope,

[12] so that you won't become lazy, but imitators of those who inherit the promises through faith and perseverance.

Heirs of the Promise

[13] For when God made a promise to Abraham, since He had no one greater to swear by, He swore by Himself:

[14] **I will most certainly bless you,
and I will greatly multiply you.[d]**

[15] And so, after waiting patiently, Abraham[e] obtained the promise. [16] For men swear by something greater than themselves, and for them a confirming oath ends every dispute. [17] Because God wanted to show His unchangeable purpose even more clearly to the heirs of the promise, He guaranteed it with an oath, [18] so that through two unchangeable things, in which it is impossible for God to lie, we who have fled for refuge might have strong encouragement to seize the hope set before us. [19] We have this hope—like a sure and firm anchor of the soul—that enters the inner sanctuary behind the curtain. [20] Jesus has entered there on our behalf as a forerunner, because He has become a "high priest forever in the order of Melchizedek."

Greatness of Melchizedek

7 For this Melchizedek—

King of Salem, priest of the Most
    High God,
who met Abraham and blessed him
    as he returned from defeating
    the kings,
[2] and Abraham gave him a tenth
    of everything;
first, his name means
    "king of righteousness,"

---

[a]**6:2** Or *about baptisms*   [b]**6:6** Or *while*   [c]**6:10** Other mss read *labor of love*   [d]**6:14** Gn 22:17   [e]**6:15** Lit *he*

then also, "king of Salem,"
  meaning "king of peace";
³ without father, mother,
  or genealogy,
having neither beginning of days
  nor end of life,
but resembling the Son of God—

remains a priest forever.

Tithes Confirm Melchizedek

⁴ Now consider how great this man was, to whom even Abraham the patriarch gave a tenth of the plunder! ⁵ The sons of Levi who receive the priestly office have a commandment according to the law to collect a tenth from the people—that is, from their brothers—though they have ⌊also⌋ descended from Abraham.ᵃ ⁶ But one without thisᵇ lineage collected tithes from Abraham and blessed the one who had the promises. ⁷ Without a doubt,ᶜ the inferior is blessed by the superior. ⁸ In the one case, men who will die receive tithes; but in the other case, ⌊Scripture⌋ testifies that he lives. ⁹ And in a sense Levi himself, who receives tithes, has paid tithes through Abraham, ¹⁰ for he was still within his forefatherᵈ when Melchizedek met him.

Melchizedek's Superior Priesthood

¹¹ If, then, perfection came through the Levitical priesthood (for under it the people received the law), what further need was there for another priest to arise in the order of Melchizedek, and not to be described as being in the order of Aaron? ¹² For when there is a change of the priesthood, there must be a change of law as well. ¹³ For the One about whom these things are said belonged to a different tribe, from which no one has served at the altar. ¹⁴ Now it

is evident that our Lord came from Judah, and about that tribe Moses said nothing concerning priests.

¹⁵ And this becomes clearer if another priest like Melchizedek arises, ¹⁶ who doesn't become a ⌊priest⌋ based on a legal command concerning physicalᵉ descent but based on the power of an indestructible life. ¹⁷ For it has been testified:

You are a priest forever
  in the order of Melchizedek.ᶠ

¹⁸ So the previous commandment is annulled because it was weak and unprofitable ¹⁹ (for the law perfected nothing), but a better hope is introduced, through which we draw near to God.

Jesus the Guarantee

²⁰ None of this ⌊happened⌋ without an oath. For others became priests without an oath, ²¹ but He with an oath made by the One who said to Him:

The Lord has sworn,
  and He will not change
  His mind,
  You are a priest forever.ᶠ

²² So Jesus has also become the guarantee of a better covenant.

²³ Now many have become ⌊Levitical⌋ priests, since they are prevented by death from remaining in office. ²⁴ But because He remains forever, He holds His priesthood permanently. ²⁵ Therefore He is always able to saveᵍ those who come to God through Him, since He always lives to intercede for them.

²⁶ For this is the kind of high priest we need: holy, innocent, undefiled, separated from sinners, and exalted above the heavens. ²⁷ He doesn't need to offer sacrifices every day, as high priests do—first for their own sins, then for those of

---

ᵃ**7:5** Lit *have come out of Abraham's loins* ᵇ**7:6** Lit *their* ᶜ**7:7** Or *Beyond any dispute* ᵈ**7:10** Lit *still in his father's loins* ᵉ**7:16** Or *fleshly* ᶠ**7:17,21** Ps 110:4 ᵍ**7:25** Or *He is able to save completely*

the people. He did this once for all when He offered Himself. ²⁸ For the law appoints as high priests men who are weak, but the promise of the oath, which came after the law, ⌊appoints⌋ a Son, who has been perfected forever.

Jesus' Heavenly Priesthood

8 Now the main point of what is being said is this: we have this kind of high priest, who sat down at the right hand of the throne of the Majesty in the heavens, ² a minister of the sanctuary and the true tabernacle, which the Lord set up, and not man. ³ For every high priest is appointed to offer gifts and sacrifices; therefore it was necessary for this ⌊priest⌋ also to have something to offer. ⁴ Now if He were on earth, He wouldn't be a priest, since there are thoseᵃ offering the gifts prescribed by the law. ⁵ These serve as a copy and shadow of the heavenly things, as Moses was warned when he was about to complete the tabernacle. For He said, **Be careful that you make everything according to the pattern that was shown to you on the mountain.**ᵇ ⁶ But Jesusᶜ has now obtained a superior ministry, and to that degree He is the mediator of a better covenant, which has been legally enacted on better promises.

God's New Covenant— Announced by Jeremiah

⁷ For if that first ⌊covenant⌋ had been faultless, no opportunity would have been sought for a second one. ⁸ But finding fault with His people,ᵈ He says:ᵉ

"Look, the days are coming,"
  says the Lord,
"when I will make
  a new covenant
with the house of Israel
and with the house of Judah—
⁹ not like the covenant
  that I made with their fathers
  on the day I took them
    by their hand
  to lead them out of the land
    of Egypt.
Because they did not continue
  in My covenant,
I disregarded them,"
  says the Lord.
¹⁰ "But this is the covenant
  that I will make with the house
    of Israel
after those days," says the Lord:
"I will put My laws
  into their minds,
and I will write them
  on their hearts,
and I will be their God,
and they will be My people.
¹¹ And each person will not teach
  his fellow citizen,ᶠ
and each his brother, saying,
  'Know the Lord,'
because they will all know Me,
  from the least to the greatest
    of them.
¹² For I will be merciful
  to their wrongdoing,
and I will never again remember
  their sins."ᵍ ʰ

¹³ By saying, a new ⌊covenant⌋, He has declared that the first is old. And what is old and aging is about to disappear.

Old Covenant Tabernacle Ministry

9 Now the first ⌊covenant⌋ also had regulations for ministry and an earthly sanctuary. ² For a tabernacle was set up; and in the first room, which is called "the holy place," were the lampstand,

---

ᵃ**8:4** Other mss read *priests* ᵇ**8:5** Ex 25:40 ᶜ**8:6** Lit *He* ᵈ**8:8** Lit *with them* ᵉ**8:8** Other mss read *finding fault, He says to them* ᶠ**8:11** Other mss read *neighbor* ᵍ**8:12** Other mss add *and their lawless deeds* ʰ**8:8-12** Jr 31:31-34

the table, and the presentation loaves. ³ Behind the second curtain, the tabernacle was called "the holy of holies." ⁴ It contained the gold altar of incense and the ark of the covenant, covered with gold on all sides, in which there was a gold jar containing the manna, Aaron's rod that budded, and the tablets of the covenant. ⁵ The cherubim of glory were above it overshadowing the mercy seat. It is not possible to speak about these things in detail right now.

⁶ These things having been set up this way, the priests enter the first room repeatedly, performing their ministry. ⁷ But the high priest alone enters the second room, and that only once a year, and never without blood, which he offers for himself and for the sins of the people committed in ignorance. ⁸ The Holy Spirit was making it clear that the way into the holy of holies had not yet been disclosed while the first tabernacle was still standing. ⁹ This is a symbol for the present time, during which gifts and sacrifices are offered that cannot perfect the worshiper's conscience. ¹⁰ They are physical regulations and only deal with food, drink, and various washings imposed until the time of restoration.

New Covenant Ministry

¹¹ Now the •Messiah has appeared, high priest of the good things that have come.ᵃ In the greater and more perfect tabernacle not made with hands (that is, not of this creation), ¹² He entered the holy of holies once for all, not by the blood of goats and calves, but by His own blood, having obtained eternal redemption. ¹³ For if the blood of goats and bulls and the ashes of a heifer sprinkling those who are defiled, sanctify for the purification of the flesh, ¹⁴ how much more will the blood of the Messiah, who through the eternal Spirit offered Himself without blemish to God, cleanse ourᵇ consciences from dead works to serve the living God?

Jesus, Mediator of New Covenant

¹⁵ Therefore He is the mediator of a new covenant,ᶜ so that those who are called might receive the promise of the eternal inheritance, because a death has taken place for redemption from the transgressions ⌐committed⌐ under the first covenant. ¹⁶ Where a will exists, the death of the testator must be established. ¹⁷ For a will is valid only when people die, since it is never in force while the testator is living.

Blood Necessary for Purification

¹⁸ That is why even the first covenant was inaugurated with blood. ¹⁹ For when every commandment had been proclaimed by Moses to all the people according to the law, he took the blood of calves and goats, along with water, scarlet wool, and hyssop, and sprinkled the scroll itself and all the people, ²⁰ saying, **This is the blood of the covenant that God has commanded for you.**ᵈ ²¹ In the same way, he sprinkled the tabernacle and all the vessels of worship with blood. ²² According to the law almost everything is purified with blood, and without the shedding of blood there is no forgiveness.

²³ Therefore it was necessary for the copies of the things in the heavens to be purified with these ⌐sacrifices⌐, but the heavenly things themselves ⌐to be purified⌐ with better sacrifices than these. ²⁴ For the Messiah did not enter a sanctuary made with hands (only a modelᵉ of the true one) but into heaven itself, that

---

ᵃ**9:11** Other mss read *that are to come* ᵇ**9:14** Other mss read *your* ᶜ**9:15** The Gk word used here and in vv. 15-18 can be translated *covenant, will,* or *testament.* ᵈ**9:20** Ex 24:8 ᵉ**9:24** Or *antitype,* or *figure*

He might now appear in the presence of God for us. ²⁵ He did not do this to offer Himself many times, as the high priest enters the sanctuary yearly with the blood of another. ²⁶ Otherwise, He would have had to suffer many times since the foundation of the world. But now He has appeared one time, at the end of the ages, for the removal of sin by the sacrifice of Himself. ²⁷ And just as it is appointed for people to die once—and after this, judgment— ²⁸ so also the Messiah, having been offered once to bear the sins of many, will appear a second time, not to bear sin, but ᵃ to bring salvation to those who are waiting for Him.

Jesus, Perfect Sacrifice

10 Since the law has ⌊only⌋ a shadow of the good things to come, and not the actual form of those realities, it can never perfect the worshipers by the same sacrifices they continually offer year after year. ² Otherwise, wouldn't they have stopped being offered, since the worshipers, once purified, would no longer have any consciousness of sins? ³ But in the sacrifices ᵇ there is a reminder of sins every year. ⁴ For it is impossible for the blood of bulls and goats to take away sins.

⁵ Therefore, as He was coming into the world, He said:

> You did not want sacrifice
>   and offering,
> but You prepared a body for Me.
> ⁶ You did not delight
>   in whole burnt offerings
>   and sin offerings.
> ⁷ Then I said, "See, I have come—
>   it is written about Me
>   in the volume of the scroll—
>   to do Your will, O God!" ᶜ

⁸ After He says above, **You did not desire or delight in sacrifices and offerings, whole burnt offerings and sin offerings,** (which are offered according to the law), ⁹ He then says, **See, I have come to do Your will.** ᵈ He takes away the first to establish the second. ¹⁰ By this will, we have been sanctified through the offering of the body of Jesus Christ once and for all.

Jesus' One Offering

¹¹ Now every priest stands day after day ministering and offering time after time the same sacrifices, which can never take away sins. ¹² But this man, after offering one sacrifice for sins forever, sat down at the right hand of God. ¹³ He is now waiting until His enemies are made His footstool. ¹⁴ For by one offering He has perfected forever those who are sanctified. ¹⁵ The Holy Spirit also testifies to us about this. For after He had said:

> ¹⁶ **This is the covenant
>   that I will make with them
>   after those days, says the Lord:
>   I will put My laws on their hearts,
>   and I will write them
>   on their minds,**

¹⁷ ⌊He adds⌋:

> **I will never again remember
>   their sins and their lawless acts.** ᵉ

¹⁸ Now where there is forgiveness of these, there is no longer an offering for sin.

Boldness through Christ's Blood

¹⁹ Therefore, brothers, since we have boldness to enter the sanctuary through the blood of Jesus, ²⁰ by the new and living way that He has inaugurated for us,

---

ᵃ **9:28** Lit *time, apart from sin,*   ᵇ **10:3** Lit *in them*   ᶜ **10:5-7** Ps 40:6-8   ᵈ **10:9** Other mss add *O God*   ᵉ **10:16-17** Jr 31:33-34

through the curtain (that is, His flesh); [21] and since we have a great high priest over the house of God, [22] let us draw near with a true heart in full assurance of faith, our hearts sprinkled ⌊clean⌋ from an evil conscience and our bodies washed in pure water. [23] Let us hold on to the confession of our hope without wavering, for He who promised is faithful. [24] And let us be concerned about one another in order to promote love and good works, [25] not staying away from our meetings, as some habitually do, but encouraging each other, and all the more as you see the day drawing near.

Warning against Willful Sin

[26] For if we deliberately sin after receiving the knowledge of the truth, there no longer remains a sacrifice for sins, [27] but a terrifying expectation of judgment, and the fury of a fire about to consume the adversaries. [28] If anyone disregards Moses' law, he dies without mercy, based on the testimony of two or three witnesses. [29] How much worse punishment, do you think one will deserve who has trampled on the Son of God, regarded as profane[a] the blood of the covenant by which he was sanctified, and insulted the Spirit of grace? [30] For we know the One who has said, **Vengeance belongs to Me, I will repay,**[b][c] and again, **The Lord will judge His people.**[d] [31] It is a terrifying thing to fall into the hands of the living God!

[32] Remember the earlier days when, after you had been enlightened, you endured a hard struggle with sufferings. [33] Sometimes you were publicly exposed to taunts and afflictions, and at other times you were companions of those who were treated that way. [34] For you sympathized with the prisoners[e] and accepted with joy the confiscation of your possessions, knowing that you yourselves have a better and enduring possession.[f] [35] So don't throw away your confidence, which has a great reward. [36] For you need endurance, so that after you have done God's will, you may receive what was promised.

[37] For in yet **a very little while,**
the Coming One will come
and not delay.
[38] **But My righteous one**[g] **will live**
by faith;
and if he draws back,
My soul has no pleasure in him.[h]

[39] But we are not those who draw back and are destroyed, but those who have faith and obtain life.

Definition of Faith

11 Now faith is the reality[i] of what is hoped for, the proof[j] of what is not seen. [2] For by it our ancestors were approved.

[3] By faith we understand that the universe was[k] created by the word[l] of God, so that what is seen has been made from things that are not visible.

Heroes of Faith

[4] By faith Abel offered to God a better sacrifice than Cain ⌊did⌋. By this he was approved as a righteous man, because God approved his gifts, and even though he is dead, he still speaks through this.

[5] By faith, Enoch was taken away so that he did not experience death, and **he was not to be found because God took him away.**[m] For prior to his

---

[a]**10:29** Or *ordinary*   [b]**10:30** Other mss add *says the Lord*   [c]**10:30** Dt 32:35   [d]**10:30** Dt 32:36   [e]**10:34** Other mss read *sympathized with my imprisonment*   [f]**10:34** Other mss add *in heaven*   [g]**10:38** Other mss read *the righteous one*   [h]**10:37-38** Is 26:20 LXX; Hab 2:3-4   [i]**11:1** Or *assurance*   [j]**11:1** Or *conviction*   [k]**11:3** Or *the worlds were,* or *the ages were*   [l]**11:3** Or *voice,* or *utterance*   [m]**11:5** Gn 5:21-24

transformation he was approved, having pleased God. 6 Now without faith it is impossible to please God, for the one who draws near to Him must believe that He exists and rewards those who seek Him.

7 By faith Noah, after being warned about what was not yet seen, in reverence built an ark to deliver his family. By this he condemned the world and became an heir of the righteousness that comes by faith.

8 By faith Abraham, when he was called, obeyed and went out to a place he was going to receive as an inheritance; he went out, not knowing where he was going. 9 By faith he stayed as a foreigner in the land of promise, living in tents with Isaac and Jacob, co-heirs of the same promise. 10 For he was looking forward to the city that has foundations, whose architect and builder is God.

11 By faith even Sarah herself, when she was barren, received power to conceive offspring, even though she was past the age, since she[a] considered that the One who had promised was faithful. 12 And therefore from one man—in fact, from one as good as dead—came offspring as numerous as the stars of heaven and as innumerable as the grains of sand by the seashore.

13 These all died in faith without having received the promises, but they saw them from a distance, greeted them, and confessed that they were foreigners and temporary residents on the earth. 14 Now those who say such things make it clear that they are seeking a homeland. 15 If they had been remembering that land they came from, they would have had opportunity to return. 16 But they now aspire to a better land—a heavenly one. Therefore God is not ashamed to be called their God, for He has prepared a city for them.

17 By faith Abraham, when he was tested, offered up Isaac; he who had received the promises was offering up his unique son, 18 about whom it had been said, **In Isaac your seed will be called.**[b] 19 He considered God to be able even to raise someone from the dead, from which he also got him back as an illustration.[c]

20 By faith Isaac blessed Jacob and Esau concerning things to come. 21 By faith Jacob, when he was dying, blessed each of the sons of Joseph, and, **he worshiped, leaning on the top of his staff.**[d] 22 By faith Joseph, as he was nearing the end of his life, mentioned the exodus of the sons of Israel and gave instructions concerning his bones.

23 By faith Moses, after he was born, was hidden by his parents for three months, because they saw that the child was beautiful, and they didn't fear the king's edict. 24 By faith Moses, when he had grown up, refused to be called the son of Pharaoh's daughter 25 and chose to suffer with the people of God rather than to enjoy the short-lived pleasure of sin. 26 For he considered reproach for the sake of the •Messiah to be greater wealth than the treasures of Egypt, since his attention was on the reward.

27 By faith he left Egypt behind, not being afraid of the king's anger, for he persevered, as one who sees Him who is invisible. 28 By faith he instituted the •Passover and the sprinkling of the blood, so that the destroyer of the firstborn might not touch them. 29 By faith they crossed the Red Sea as though they were on dry land. When the Egyptians attempted to do this, they were drowned.

---

a**11:11** Or By faith Abraham, even though he was past age—and Sarah herself was barren—received the ability to procreate since he   b**11:18** Gn 21:12   c**11:19** Or foreshadowing, or parable, or type   d**11:21** Gn 47:31

³⁰ By faith the walls of Jericho fell down after being encircled for seven days. ³¹ By faith <u>Rahab</u> the prostitute received the spies in peace and didn't perish with those who disobeyed.

³² And what more can I say? Time is too short for me to tell about <u>Gideon, Barak, Samson, Jephthah, of David and Samuel and the prophets,</u> ³³ who by faith conquered kingdoms, administered justice, obtained promises, shut the mouths of lions, ³⁴ quenched the raging of fire, escaped the edge of the sword, gained strength after being weak, became mighty in battle, and put foreign armies to flight. ³⁵ Women received their dead raised to life again. Some men were tortured, not accepting release, so that they might gain a better resurrection, ³⁶ and others experienced mockings and scourgings, as well as bonds and imprisonment. ³⁷ They were stoned,^a they were sawed in two, they died by the sword, they wandered about in sheepskins, in goatskins, destitute, afflicted, and mistreated. ³⁸ The world was not worthy of them. They wandered in deserts, mountains, caves, and holes in the ground.

³⁹ All these were approved through their faith, but they did not receive what was promised, ⁴⁰ since God had provided something better for us, so that they would not be made perfect without us.

Call to Endurance

12 Therefore since we also have such a large cloud of witnesses surrounding us, let us lay aside every weight and the sin that so easily ensnares us, and run with endurance the race that lies before us, ² keeping our eyes on Jesus,^b the source and perfecter^c

of our faith, who for the joy that lay before Him^d endured a cross and despised the shame, and has sat down at the right hand of God's throne.

Discipline of the Lord

³ For consider Him who endured such hostility from sinners against Himself, so that you won't grow weary and lose heart. ⁴ In struggling against sin, you have not yet resisted to the point of shedding your blood. ⁵ And you have forgotten the exhortation that addresses you as sons:

My son, do not take
  the Lord's discipline lightly,
or faint when you are reproved
  by Him;
⁶ for the Lord disciplines the one
  He loves,
and punishes every son
  whom He receives.^e

God's Discipline Compared with That of Human Father

⁷ Endure it as discipline: God is dealing with you as sons. For what son is there whom a father does not discipline? ⁸ But if you are without discipline—which all^f receive^g—then you are illegitimate children and not sons. ⁹ Furthermore, we had natural fathers discipline us, and we respected them. Shouldn't we submit even more to the Father of spirits and live? ¹⁰ For they disciplined us for a short time based on what seemed good to them, but He does it for our benefit, so that we can share His holiness. ¹¹ No discipline seems enjoyable at the time, but painful. Later on, however, it yields the fruit of peace and righteousness to those who have been trained by it.

^a**11:37** Other mss add *they were tempted*   ^b**12:2** Or *looking to Jesus*   ^c**12:2** Or *the founder and completer*   ^d**12:2** Or *who instead of the joy lying before Him; that is, the joy of heaven*   ^e**12:6** Pr 3:11-12   ^f**12:8** In context *all* refers to Christians.   ^g**12:8** Lit *discipline, of which all have become participants*

[12] Therefore strengthen your tired hands and weakened knees, [13] and make straight paths for your feet, so that what is lame may not be dislocated,[a] but healed instead.

Warning: Don't Fall Short of God's Grace

[14] Pursue peace with everyone, and holiness—without it no one will see the Lord. [15] See to it that no one falls short of the grace of God and that no root of bitterness springs up, causing trouble and by it, defiling many.

Warning against Sin of Esau

[16] And see that there isn't any immoral or irreverent person like Esau, who sold his birthright in exchange for one meal. [17] For you know that later, when he wanted to inherit the blessing, he was rejected because he didn't find any opportunity for repentance, though he sought it with tears.

"You Have Come to Mount Zion"

[18] For you have not come to what could be touched, to a blazing fire, to darkness, gloom, and storm, [19] to the blast of a trumpet, and the sound of words. (Those who heard it begged that not another word be spoken to them, [20] for they could not bear what was commanded: **And if even an animal touches the mountain, it must be stoned!**[b] [21] And the appearance was so terrifying that Moses said, **I am terrified and trembling.**[c]) [22] Instead, you have come to Mount Zion, to the city of the living God (the heavenly Jerusalem), to myriads of angels in festive gathering, [23] to the assembly of the firstborn whose names have been written[d] in heaven, to God who is the judge of all, to the spirits of righteous people made perfect, [24] to Jesus (mediator of a new covenant), and to the sprinkled blood, which says better things than the ⌊blood⌋ of Abel.

Don't Reject or Turn Away

[25] See that you do not reject the One who speaks; for if they did not escape when they rejected Him who warned them on earth, even less will we if we turn away from Him who warns us from heaven. [26] His voice shook the earth at that time, but now He has promised, **Yet once more I will shake not only the earth but also heaven.**[e] [27] Now this expression, "Yet once more," indicates the removal of what can be shaken—that is, created things—so that what is not shaken might remain. [28] Therefore, since we are receiving a kingdom that cannot be shaken, let us hold on to grace.[f] By it, we may serve God acceptably, with reverence and awe; [29] for our God is a consuming fire.

Final Exhortations

13 Let brotherly love continue. [2] Don't neglect to show hospitality, for by doing this some have welcomed angels as guests without knowing it. [3] Remember the prisoners, as though you were in prison with them, and the mistreated, as though you yourselves were suffering bodily.[g] [4] Marriage must be respected by all, and the marriage bed kept undefiled, because God will judge immoral people and adulterers. [5] Your life should be free from the love of money. Be satisfied with what you have, for He Himself has said, **I will never leave you or forsake you.**[h] [6] Therefore, we may boldly say:

---

[a]**12:13** Or *so that the lame will not be turned aside*   [b]**12:20** Ex 19:12   [c]**12:21** Dt 9:19   [d]**12:23** Or *registered*
[e]**12:26** Hg 2:6   [f]**12:28** Or *let us give thanks,* or *let us have grace*   [g]**13:3** Or *mistreated, since you are also in a body*
[h]**13:5** Dt 31:6

The Lord is my helper;
I will not be afraid.
What can man do to me?[a]

[7] Remember your leaders who have spoken God's word to you. As you carefully observe the outcome of their lives, imitate their faith. [8] Jesus Christ is the same yesterday, today, and forever. [9] Don't be led astray by various kinds of strange teachings; for it is good for the heart to be established by grace and not by foods, since those involved in them have not benefited. [10] We have an altar from which those who serve the tabernacle do not have a right to eat. [11] For the bodies of those animals whose blood is brought into the holy of holies by the high priest as a sin offering are burned outside the camp. [12] Therefore Jesus also suffered outside the gate, so that He might sanctify[b] the people by His own blood. [13] Let us then go to Him outside the camp, bearing His disgrace. [14] For here we do not have an enduring city; instead, we seek the one to come. [15] Therefore, through Him let us continually offer up to God a sacrifice of praise, that is, the fruit of our lips that confess His name. [16] Don't neglect to do good and to share, for God is pleased with such sacrifices. [17] Obey your leaders[c] and submit to them, for they keep watch over your souls as those who will give an account, so that they can do this with joy and not with grief, for that would be unprofitable for you. [18] Pray for us; for we are convinced that we have a clear conscience, wanting to conduct ourselves honorably in everything. [19] And I especially urge you to pray[d] that I may be restored to you very soon.

Benediction and Farewell

[20] Now may the God of peace, who brought up from the dead our Lord Jesus—the great Shepherd of the sheep—with the blood of the everlasting covenant, [21] equip[e] you with all that is good to do His will, working in us what is pleasing in His sight, through Jesus Christ, to whom be glory forever and ever.[f] •Amen.

[22] Brothers, I urge you to receive this word of exhortation, for I have written to you in few words. [23] Be aware that our brother Timothy has been released. If he comes soon enough, he will be with me when I see you. [24] Greet all your leaders and all the saints. Those who are from Italy greet you. [25] Grace be with all of you.

---

[a]**13:6** Ps 118:6   [b]**13:12** Or *set apart,* or *consecrate*   [c]**13:17** Or *rulers*   [d]**13:19** Lit *to do this*   [e]**13:21** Or *perfect*
[f]**13:21** Other mss omit *and ever*

JAMES

Greeting

1 James, a slave of God and of the Lord Jesus Christ:

To the 12 tribes in the Dispersion.

Greetings.

Testing Produces Endurance and Maturity

² Consider it a great joy, my brothers, whenever you experience various trials, ³ knowing that the <u>testing of your faith produces endurance</u>. ⁴ But endurance must do its complete work, so that you may be mature and complete, lacking nothing.

Ask in Faith for Wisdom

⁵ Now if any of you lacks wisdom, he should ask God, who gives to all generously and without criticizing, and it will be given to him. ⁶ But let him ask in faith without doubting. For the doubter is like the surging sea, driven and tossed by the wind. ⁷ That person should not expect to receive anything from the Lord. ⁸ An indecisive man is unstable in all his ways.

Humble and Rich

⁹ The brother of humble circumstances should boast in his exaltation; ¹⁰ but the one who is rich ⌊should boast⌋ in his humiliation, because he will pass away like a flower of the field. ¹¹ For the sun rises with its scorching heat and dries up the grass; its flower falls off, and its beautiful appearance is destroyed. In the same way, the rich man will wither away while pursuing his activities.

How Trials and Temptations Work

¹² Blessed is a man who endures trials,ᵃ because when he passes the test he will receive the crown of life that Heᵇ has promised to those who love Him.

¹³ No one undergoing a trial should say, "I am being tempted by God." For God is not tempted by evil,ᶜ and He Himself doesn't tempt anyone. ¹⁴ But each person is tempted when he is drawn away and enticed by his own evil desires. ¹⁵ Then after desire has conceived, it gives birth to sin, and when sin is fully grown, it gives birth to death.

¹⁶ Don't be deceived, my dearly loved brothers. ¹⁷ Every generous act and every perfect gift is from above, coming down from the Father of lights; with Him there is no variation or shadow cast by turning. ¹⁸ By His own choice, He gave us a new birth by the message of truthᵈ so that we would be the •firstfruits of His creatures.

Be Slow to Anger

¹⁹ My dearly loved brothers, understand this: everyone must be quick to hear, slow to speak, and slow to anger, ²⁰ for man's anger does not accomplish God's righteousness. ²¹ Therefore, ridding yourselves of all moral filth and evil excess, humbly receive the implanted word, which is able to save you.ᵉ

Be Doers of the Word

²² But be doers of the word and not hearers only, deceiving yourselves. ²³ Because if anyone is a hearer of the word and not a doer, he is like a man

---

ᵃ**1:12** Lit *trial*, used as a collective   ᵇ**1:12** Other mss read *that the Lord*   ᶜ**1:13** Or *evil persons*, or *evil things*
ᵈ**1:18** *message of truth* = the gospel   ᵉ**1:21** Lit *save your souls*

looking at his own face[a] in a mirror; [24] for he looks at himself, goes away, and right away forgets what kind of man he was. [25] But the one who looks intently into the perfect law of freedom and perseveres in it, and is not a forgetful hearer but a doer who acts—this person will be blessed in what he does.

Pure Religion Defined

[26] If anyone[b] thinks he is religious, without controlling his tongue but deceiving his heart, his religion is useless. [27] Pure and undefiled religion before our[c] God and Father is this: to look after orphans and widows in their distress and to keep oneself unstained by the world.

Sin of Favoritism

2 My brothers, hold your faith in our glorious Lord Jesus Christ without showing favoritism. [2] For suppose a man comes into your meeting wearing a gold ring, dressed in fine clothes, and a poor man dressed in dirty clothes also comes in. [3] If you look with favor on the man wearing the fine clothes so that you say, "Sit here in a good place," and yet you say to the poor man, "Stand over there," or, "Sit here on the floor by my footstool," [4] haven't you discriminated among yourselves and become judges with evil thoughts?

God Has Chosen the Poor

[5] Listen, my dear brothers: Didn't God choose the poor in this world to be rich in faith and heirs of the kingdom that He has promised to those who love Him? [6] Yet you dishonored that poor man. Don't the rich oppress you and drag you into the courts? [7] Don't they blaspheme the noble name that you bear?

[8] If you really carry out the royal law prescribed in Scripture, **Love your neighbor as yourself,**[d] you are doing well. [9] But if you show favoritism, you commit sin and are convicted by the law as transgressors. [10] For whoever keeps the entire law, yet fails in one point, is guilty of ⌊breaking it⌋ all. [11] For He who said, **Do not commit adultery,**[e] also said, **Do not murder.**[f] So if you do not commit adultery, but you do murder, you are a lawbreaker.

[12] Speak and act as those who will be judged by the law of freedom. [13] For judgment is without mercy to the one who hasn't shown mercy. Mercy triumphs over judgment.

Faith without Works is Dead

[14] What good is it, my brothers, if someone says he has faith, but does not have works? Can his faith[g] save him? [15] If a brother or sister is without clothes and lacks daily food, [16] and one of you says to them, "Go in peace, keep warm, and eat well," but you don't give them what the body needs, what good is it? [17] In the same way faith, if it doesn't have works, is dead by itself. [18] But someone will say, "You have faith, and I have works."[h] Show me your faith without works, and I will show you faith from my works.[i] [19] You believe that God is one; you do well. The demons also believe—and they shudder.

Justified by Works

[20] Foolish man! Are you willing to learn that faith without works is useless? [21] Wasn't Abraham our father justified by works when he offered Isaac his son on the altar? [22] You see that faith was active together with his works, and by works,

---

[a]**1:23** Lit *at the face of his birth*   [b]**1:26** Other mss add *among you*   [c]**1:27** Or *before the*   [d]**2:8** Lv 19:18   [e]**2:11** Ex 20:14; Dt 5:18   [f]**2:11** Ex 20:13; Dt 5:17   [g]**2:14** Or *Can faith*, or *Can that faith*, or *Can such faith*   [h]**2:18** The quotation may end here or after v. 18b or v. 19.   [i]**2:18** Other mss read *Show me your faith from your works, and from my works I will show you my faith.*

faith was perfected. [23] So the Scripture was fulfilled that says, **Abraham believed God, and it was credited to him for righteousness,**[a] and he was called God's friend. [24] You see that a man is justified by works and not by faith alone. [25] And in the same way, wasn't Rahab the prostitute also justified by works when she received the messengers and sent them out by a different route? [26] For just as the body without the spirit is dead, so also <u>faith without works is dead.</u>

Control Your Tongue

3 Not many should become teachers, my brothers, knowing that we will receive a stricter judgment; [2] for we all stumble in many ways. If anyone does not stumble in what he says,[b] he is a mature man who is also able to control his whole body.[c]

[3] Now when we put bits into the mouths of horses to make them obey us, we also guide the whole animal.[d] [4] And consider ships: though very large and driven by fierce winds, they are guided by a very small rudder wherever the will of the pilot directs. [5] So too, though the tongue is a small part ⸤of the body⸥, it boasts great things. Consider how large a forest a small fire ignites. [6] And <u>the tongue is a fire.</u> The tongue, a world of unrighteousness, is placed among the parts of our ⸤bodies⸥; it pollutes the whole body, sets the course of life on fire, and is set on fire by •hell.

[7] For every creature—animal or bird, reptile or fish—is tamed and has been tamed by man, [8] but no man can tame the tongue. It is a restless evil, full of deadly poison. [9] With it we bless our[e] Lord and Father, and with it we curse men who are made in God's likeness.

[10] Out of the same mouth come blessing and cursing. My brothers, these things should not be this way. [11] Does a spring pour out sweet and bitter water from the same opening? [12] Can a fig tree produce olives, my brothers, or a grapevine ⸤produce⸥ figs? Neither can a saltwater spring yield fresh water.

Wisdom from Above

[13] Who is wise and understanding among you? He should show his works by good conduct with wisdom's gentleness. [14] But if you have bitter envy and selfish ambition in your heart, don't brag and lie in defiance of the truth. [15] Such wisdom does not come down from above, but is earthly, sensual, demonic. [16] For where envy and selfish ambition exist, there is disorder and every kind of evil. [17] But <u>the wisdom from above is first pure, then peace-loving, gentle, compliant, full of mercy and good fruits, without favoritism and hypocrisy.</u> [18] And the fruit of righteousness is sown in peace by those who make peace.

Source of Wars and Fighting

4 What is the source of the wars and the fights among you? Don't they come from the cravings that are at war within you?[f] [2] You desire and do not have. You murder and covet and cannot obtain. You fight and war. <u>You do not have because you do not ask.</u> [3] <u>You ask and don't receive because you ask wrongly, so that you may spend it on your desires for pleasure.</u>

World's Friend, God's Enemy

[4] Adulteresses![g] Do you not know that friendship with the world is hostility toward God? So whoever wants to be the world's friend becomes God's enemy.

---

[a]**2:23** Gn 15:6 [b]**3:2** Lit *in word* [c]**3:2** Lit *to bridle the whole body* [d]**3:3** Lit *whole body* [e]**3:9** Or *bless the* [f]**4:1** Lit *war in your members* [g]**4:4** Other mss read *Adulterers and adulteresses*

⁵ Or do you think it's without reason the Scripture says that the Spirit He has caused to live in us yearns jealously?ᵃ

⁶ But He gives greater grace. Therefore He says:

**God resists the proud,
but gives grace to the humble.**ᵇ

Submit to God, Resist the Devil

⁷ Therefore, submit to God. But resist the Devil, and he will flee from you. ⁸ Draw near to God, and He will draw near to you. Cleanse your hands, sinners, and purify your hearts, double-minded people! ⁹ Be miserable and mourn and weep. Your laughter must change to mourning and your joy to sorrow. ¹⁰ Humble yourselves before the Lord, and He will exalt you.

¹¹ Don't criticize one another, brothers. He who criticizes a brother or judges his brother criticizes the law and judges the law. But if you judge the law, you are not a doer of the law but a judge. ¹² There is one lawgiver and judgeᶜ who is able to save and to destroy. But who are you to judge your neighbor?

Our Will and His Will

¹³ Come now, you who say, "Today or tomorrow we will travel to such and such a city and spend a year there and do business and make a profit." ¹⁴ You don't even know what tomorrow will bring—what your life will be! For you are a bit of smoke that appears for a little while, then vanishes.

¹⁵ Instead, you should say, "If the Lord wills, we will live and do this or that." ¹⁶ But as it is, you boast in your arrogance. All such boasting is evil. ¹⁷ So, for the person who knows to do good and doesn't do it, it is a sin.

James Warns the Rich

5 Come now, you rich people! Weep and wail over the miseries that are coming on you. ² Your wealth is ruined: your clothes are moth-eaten; ³ your silver and gold are corroded, and their corrosion will be a witness against you and will eat your flesh like fire. You stored up treasure in the last days! ⁴ Look! The pay that you withheld from the workers who reaped your fields cries out, and the outcry of the harvesters has reached the ears of the Lord of •Hosts.ᵈ ⁵ You have lived luxuriously on the land and have indulged yourselves. You have fattened your hearts forᵉ the day of slaughter. ⁶ You have condemned—you have murdered—the righteous man; he does not resist you.

Be Patient until Lord's Coming

⁷ Therefore, brothers, be patient until the Lord's coming. See how the farmer waits for the precious fruit of the earth and is patient with it until it receives the early and the late rains. ⁸ You also must be patient. Strengthen your hearts, because the Lord's coming is near.

⁹ Brothers, do not complain about one another, so that you will not be judged. Look, the judge stands at the door! ¹⁰ Brothers, take the prophets who spoke in the Lord's name as an example of suffering and patience. ¹¹ See, we count as blessed those who have endured.ᶠ You have heard of Job's endurance and have seen the outcome from the Lord: the Lord is very compassionate and merciful.

ᵃ**4:5** Or *He who caused the Spirit to live in us yearns jealously,* or *the spirit He caused to live in us yearns jealously,* or *He jealously yearns for the Spirit He made to live in us* ᵇ**4:6** Pr 3:34 ᶜ**4:12** Other mss omit *and judge* ᵈ**5:4** Gk *Sabaoth;* this word is a transliteration of the Hb word for *Hosts,* or *Armies.* ᵉ**5:5** Or *hearts in* ᶠ**5:11** Or *have persevered*

No Swearing

¹² Now above all, my brothers, do not swear, either by heaven or by earth or with any other oath. Your "yes" must be "yes," and your "no" must be "no," so that you won't fall under judgment.ᵃ

Secrets of Effective Prayer

¹³ Is anyone among you suffering? He should pray. Is anyone cheerful? He should sing praises. ¹⁴ Is anyone among you sick? He should call for the elders of the church, and they should pray over him after anointing him with olive oil in the name of the Lord. ¹⁵ The prayer of faith will save the sick person, and the Lord will raise him up; and if he has committed sins, he will be forgiven.

¹⁶ Therefore, confess your sins to one another and pray for one another, so that you may be healed. The intense prayer of the righteous is very powerful. ¹⁷ Elijah was a man with a nature like ours; yet he prayed earnestly that it would not rain, and for three years and six months it did not rain on the land. ¹⁸ Then he prayed again, and the sky gave rain and the land produced its fruit.

Turn Back Sinners

¹⁹ My brothers, if any among you strays from the truth, and someone turns him back, ²⁰ he should know that whoever turns a sinner from the error of his way will save his •life from death and cover a multitude of sins.

1 PETER

Greeting to Dispersion

1 Peter, an apostle of Jesus Christ:
To the temporary residents of the Dispersion in the provinces of Pontus, Galatia, Cappadocia, Asia, and Bithynia, chosen ² according to the foreknowledge of God the Father and set apart by the Spirit for obedience and ⌊for the⌋ sprinkling with the blood of Jesus Christ.

May grace and peace be multiplied to you.

New Birth into a Living Hope

³ Blessed be the God and Father of our Lord Jesus Christ. According to His great mercy, He has given us a new birth into a living hope through the resurrection of Jesus Christ from the dead, ⁴ and into an inheritance that is imperishable, uncorrupted, and unfading, kept in heaven for you, ⁵ who are being protected by God's power through faith for a salvation that is ready to be revealed in the last time. ⁶ You rejoice in this,ᵇ though now for a short time you have had to be distressed by various trials ⁷ so that the genuineness of your faith—more valuable than gold, which perishes though refined by fire—may result inᶜ praise, glory, and honor at the revelation of Jesus Christ. ⁸ You love Him, though you have not seen Him. And though not seeing Him now, you believe in Him and rejoice with inexpressible and glorious joy, ⁹ because you are receiving the goal of yourᵈ faith, the salvation of your souls.ᵉ

Prophets and Salvation

¹⁰ Concerning this salvation, the prophets who prophesied about the

ᵃ**5:12** Other mss read *fall into hypocrisy*   ᵇ**1:6** Or *In this (fact) rejoice*   ᶜ**1:7** Lit *may be found for*   ᵈ**1:9** Other mss read *our*, or they omit the possessive pronoun   ᵉ**1:9** Or *your lives*

grace that would come to you searched and carefully investigated. [11] They inquired into what time or what circumstances[a] the Spirit of Christ within them was indicating when He testified in advance to the messianic sufferings[b] and the glories that would follow.[c] [12] It was revealed to them that they were not serving themselves but you concerning things that have now been announced to you through those who preached the gospel to you by the Holy Spirit sent from heaven. Angels desire to look into these things.

Peter Calls for Holy Living

[13] Therefore, get your minds ready for action,[d] being self-disciplined, and set your hope completely on the grace to be brought to you at the revelation of Jesus Christ. [14] As obedient children, do not be conformed to the desires of your former ignorance [15] but, as the One who called you is holy, you also are to be holy in all your conduct; [16] for it is written, **Be holy, because I am holy.**[e]

Redeemed by the Blood

[17] And if you address as Father the One who judges impartially based on each one's work, you are to conduct yourselves in reverence during this time of temporary residence. [18] For you know that you were redeemed from your empty way of life inherited from the fathers, not with perishable things, like silver or gold, [19] but with the precious blood of Christ, like that of a lamb without defect or blemish. [20] He was destined[f] before the foundation of the world, but was revealed at the end of the times for you [21] who through Him are

believers in God, who raised Him from the dead and gave Him glory, so that your faith and hope are in God.

[22] By obedience to the truth,[g] having purified yourselves[h] for sincere love of the brothers, love one another earnestly from a pure[i] heart, [23] since you have been born again—not of perishable seed but of imperishable—through the living and enduring word of God. [24] For

> All flesh is like grass,
>   and all its glory like a flower
>   of the grass.
> The grass withers, and the flower
>   drops off,
> [25] but the word of the Lord
>   endures forever.[j]

And this is the word that was preached as the gospel to you.

Living Stone and Holy Priesthood

2 So rid yourselves of all wickedness, all deceit, hypocrisy, envy, and all slander. [2] Like newborn infants, desire the unadulterated spiritual milk, so that you may grow by it in ⌊your⌋ salvation,[k] [3] since **you have tasted that the Lord is good.**[l] [4] Coming to Him, a living stone— rejected by men but chosen and valuable to God— [5] you yourselves, as living stones, are being built into a spiritual house for a holy priesthood to offer spiritual sacrifices acceptable to God through Jesus Christ. [6] For it stands in Scripture:

> **Look! I lay a stone in Zion,**
>   **a chosen and valuable**
>   **cornerstone,**
>   **and the one who believes in Him**
>   **will never be put to shame!**[m] [n]

[a]1:11 Or *inquired about the person or time*   [b]1:11 Or *the sufferings of Christ*   [c]1:11 Lit *the glories after that*   [d]1:13 Lit *Therefore, gird the loins of your minds*   [e]1:16 Lv 11:44-45; 19:2; 20:7   [f]1:20 Or *was chosen, or was known*   [g]1:22 Other mss add *through the Spirit*   [h]1:22 Or *purified your souls*   [i]1:22 Other mss omit *pure*   [j]1:24-25 Is 40:6-8   [k]2:2 Other mss omit *in your salvation*   [l]2:3 Ps 34:8   [m]2:6 Or *be disappointed*   [n]2:6 Is 28:16 LXX

[7] So the honor is for you who believe; but for the unbelieving,

> The stone that the builders
> rejected—
> this One has become
> the cornerstone,[a]

and

[8] A stone that causes men
> to stumble,[b]
> and a rock that trips them up.[c] [d]

They stumble by disobeying the message; they were destined for this.

[9] But you are **a chosen race,**[e] [f]
> **a royal priesthood,**[g]
> **a holy nation,**[h] **a people**
> **for His possession,**[i]
> **so that you may proclaim**
> **the praises**[j] [k]
> of the One who called you
> out of darkness
> into His marvelous light.
[10] Once you were not a people,
> but now you are God's people;
> you had not received mercy,
> but now you have received mercy.

Peter's Call to Good Works

[11] Dear friends, I urge you as aliens and temporary residents to abstain from fleshly desires that war against you.[l] [12] Conduct yourselves honorably among the Gentiles,[m] so that in a case where they speak against you as those who do evil, they may, by observing your good works, glorify God in a day of visitation.[n]

Submit to Human Institutions

[13] Submit to every human institution because of the Lord, whether to the Emperor[o] as the supreme authority, [14] or to governors as those sent out by him to punish those who do evil and to praise those who do good. [15] For it is God's will that you, by doing good, silence the ignorance of foolish people. [16] As God's slaves, ⌊live⌋ as free people, but don't use your freedom as a way to conceal evil. [17] Honor everyone. Love the brotherhood. Fear God. Honor the Emperor.[o]

Submission of Slaves to Masters

[18] Household slaves, submit yourselves to your masters with all respect, not only to the good and gentle but also to the cruel.[p] [19] For it ⌊brings⌋ favor[q] if, because of conscience toward God,[r] someone endures grief from suffering unjustly. [20] For what credit is there if you endure when you sin and are beaten? But when you do good and suffer, if you endure, it brings favor with God.

Rationale for Submission: Example of Christ

[21] For you were called to this,
> because Christ also suffered
> for you,
> leaving you an example,
> so that you should follow
> in His steps.
[22] He **did not commit sin,**
> **and no deceit was found**
> **in His mouth;**[s]
[23] when reviled, He did not revile
> in return;
> when suffering,
> He did not threaten,
> but committed Himself to the One
> who judges justly.
[24] He Himself bore our sins
> in His body on the tree,

[a]**2:7** Ps 118:22   [b]**2:8** Or *a stone causing stumbling*   [c]**2:8** Or *a rock to trip over*   [d]**2:8** Is 8:14   [e]**2:9** Or *chosen generation,* or *chosen nation*   [f]**2:9** Is 43:20 LXX; Dt 7:6; 10:15   [g]**2:9** Ex 19:6; 23:22 LXX; Is 61:6   [h]**2:9** Ex 19:6; 23:22 LXX   [i]**2:9** Ex 19:5; 23:22 LXX; Dt 4:20; 7:6; Is 43:21 LXX   [j]**2:9** Or *the mighty deeds*   [k]**2:9** Is 42:12; 43:21   [l]**2:11** Lit *against the soul*   [m]**2:12** Or *among the nations,* or *among the pagans*   [n]**2:12** A day when God intervenes in human history, either in grace or in judgment   [o]**2:13,17** Lit *king*   [p]**2:18** Lit *crooked,* or *unscrupulous*   [q]**2:19** Other mss add *with God*   [r]**2:19** Other mss read *because of a good conscience*   [s]**2:22** Is 53:9

so that, having died to sins,
we might live for righteousness;
by **His wounding**
you have been healed.[a]

25 For you **were like sheep**
going astray,[b]
but you have now returned
to the shepherd and guardian[c]
of your souls.

Wives and Husbands

3 Wives, in the same way, submit yourselves to your own husbands so that,
even if some disobey the ⌊Christian⌋ message, they may be won over[d] without a
message by the way their wives live,
2 when they observe your pure, reverent
lives. 3 Your beauty should not consist of
outward things ⌊like⌋ elaborate hairstyles
and the wearing of gold ornaments[e] or
fine clothes; 4 instead, ⌊it should consist of⌋
the hidden person of the heart with the
imperishable quality of a gentle and quiet
spirit, which is very valuable in God's
eyes. 5 For in the past, the holy women
who hoped in God also beautified themselves in this way, submitting to their
own husbands, 6 just as Sarah obeyed
Abraham, calling him lord. You have become her children when you do good and
aren't frightened by anything alarming.

7 Husbands, in the same way, live
with your wives with understanding of
their weaker nature[f] yet showing them
honor as co-heirs of the grace of life, so
that your prayers will not be hindered.

Do No Evil

8 Now finally, all of you should be like-
minded and sympathetic, should love believers,[g] and be compassionate and humble,[h] 9 not paying back evil for evil or
insult for insult but, on the contrary, giving a blessing, since you were called for
this, so that you can inherit a blessing.

10 For **the one who wants to love life**
and to see good days
must keep his tongue from evil
and his lips from speaking deceit,
11 **and he must turn away from evil**
and do good.
He must seek peace
and pursue it,
12 **because the eyes of the Lord**
are on the righteous
and His ears are open
to their request.
But the face of the Lord is
against those who do evil.[i]

Suffer for Good, Not Evil

13 And who will harm[j] you if you are
passionate for what is good?[k] 14 But even
if you should suffer for righteousness, you
are blessed. **Do not fear what they fear**
or be disturbed,[l] 15 but set apart the
•Messiah[m] as Lord in your hearts, and always be ready to give a defense to anyone
who asks you for a reason[n] for the hope
that is in you. 16 However, do this with
gentleness and respect, keeping your conscience clear,[o] so that when you are accused,[p] those who denounce your
Christian life will be put to shame. 17 For
it is better to suffer for doing good, if that
should be God's will,[q] than for doing evil.

Christ's Example of Suffering

18 For Christ also suffered for sins
once for all,[r]
the righteous for the unrighteous,[s]

[a]2:24 Is 53:5 [b]2:25 Is 53:6 [c]2:25 Or overseer [d]3:1 Lit may be gained [e]3:3 Lit and of putting around of gold items
[f]3:7 Lit understanding as the weaker vessel [g]3:8 Lit brotherly-loving [h]3:8 Other mss read courteous [i]3:10-12 Ps 34:12-
16 [j]3:13 Or will mistreat, or will do evil to [k]3:13 Lit you are zealots, or you are partisans for the good, or you are eager
to do good [l]3:14 Is 8:12 [m]3:15 Other mss read set God [n]3:15 Or who demands of you an accounting [o]3:16 Lit
good; or keeping a clear conscience [p]3:16 Other mss read when they speak against you as evildoers [q]3:17 Lit if the
will of God should will [r]3:18 Other mss read died for sins on our behalf; other mss read died for our sins; other mss read
died for sins on your behalf [s]3:18 Or the Righteous One in the place of the unrighteous many

that He might bring you[a] to God,
after being put to death
   in the fleshly realm[b]
but made alive
   in the spiritual realm.[c]

[19] In that state[d] He also went and made a proclamation to the spirits in prison[e] [20] who in the past were disobedient, when God patiently waited in the days of Noah while an ark was being prepared; in it, a few—that is, eight people[f]—were saved through water. [21] Baptism, which corresponds to this, now saves you (not the removal of the filth of the flesh, but the pledge[g] of a good conscience toward God) through the resurrection of Jesus Christ. [22] Now that He has gone into heaven, He is at God's right hand, with angels, authorities, and powers subjected to Him.

Have Christ's Resolve

4 Therefore, since Christ suffered[h] in the flesh,[i] arm yourselves also with the same resolve[j]—because the One who suffered in the flesh[i] has finished with sin[k]— [2] in order to live the remaining time in the flesh,[i] no longer for human desires,[l] but for God's will. [3] For there has already been enough time spent in doing the will of the pagans:[m] carrying on in unrestrained behavior, evil desires, drunkenness, orgies, carousing, and lawless idolatry. [4] In regard to this, they are surprised that you don't plunge with them into the same flood[n] of dissipation—and they slander you. [5] They will give an account to the One who stands ready to judge the living and the dead. [6] For this reason the gospel was also preached to ⌊those who are now⌋ dead, so that, although they might be judged by men in the fleshly realm,[b] they might live by God in the spiritual realm.[o]

End-Time Conduct

[7] Now the end of all things is near; therefore, be clear-headed and disciplined for prayer. [8] Above all, keep your love for one another at full strength, since **love covers a multitude of sins.**[p] [9] Be hospitable to one another without complaining. [10] Based on the gift they have received, everyone should use it to serve others, as good managers of the varied grace of God. [11] If anyone speaks, ⌊his speech should be⌋ like the oracles of God; if anyone serves, ⌊his service should be⌋ from the strength God provides, so that in everything God may be glorified through Jesus Christ. To Him belong the glory and the power forever and ever. •Amen.

Joy and Blessing in Christian Suffering

[12] Dear friends, when the fiery ordeal[q] arises among you to test you, don't be surprised by it, as if something unusual were happening to you. [13] Instead, as you share in the sufferings of the •Messiah rejoice, so that you may also rejoice with great joy at the revelation of His glory. [14] If you are ridiculed for the name of Christ, you are blessed, because the Spirit of glory and of God rests on you.[r] [15] None of you, however, should suffer as a murderer, a thief, an evildoer, or as a meddler.[s] [16] But if ⌊anyone suffers⌋ as a

[a]**3:18** Other mss read *us* [b]**3:18; 4:6** Or *in the flesh* [c]**3:18** Or *in the spirit,* or *in the Spirit* [d]**3:19** Or *In whom,* or *At that time,* or *In which* [e]**3:19** The *spirits in prison* are most likely fallen supernatural beings or angels; see 2 Pt 2:4; Jd 6. [f]**3:20** Lit *souls* [g]**3:21** Or *the appeal* [h]**4:1** Other mss read *suffered for us* [i]**4:1,2** *In the flesh* probably means "in human existence"; see 1 Pt 3:18. [j]**4:1** Or *perspective,* or *attitude* [k]**4:1** Or *the one who has suffered in the flesh has ceased from sin* [l]**4:2** Lit *for desires of human beings* [m]**4:3** Or *Gentiles* [n]**4:4** Lit *you don't run with them into the same pouring out* [o]**4:6** Or *in the spirit* [p]**4:8** Pr 10:12 [q]**4:12** Lit *the burning* [r]**4:14** Other mss add *He is blasphemed because of them, but He is glorified because of you.* [s]**4:15** Or *as one who defrauds others*

Christian, he should not be ashamed, but should glorify God with that name. [17] For the time has come for judgment to begin with God's household; and if it begins with us, what will the outcome be for those who disobey the gospel of God?

> [18] And if the righteous is saved
>   with difficulty,
>   what will become of the ungodly
>   and the sinner?[a]

[19] So those who suffer according to God's will should, in doing good, entrust themselves to a faithful Creator.

Exhortation to Elders

5 Therefore, as a fellow elder and witness to the sufferings of the •Messiah, and also a participant in the glory about to be revealed, I exhort the elders among you: [2] shepherd God's flock among you, not overseeing[b] out of compulsion but freely, according to God's ⌊will⌋;[c] not for the money but eagerly; [3] not lording it over those entrusted to you, but being examples to the flock. [4] And when the chief Shepherd appears, you will receive the unfading crown of glory.

Advice to Young Men

[5] Likewise, you younger men, be subject to the elders. And all of you clothe yourselves with[d] humility toward one another, because

> God resists the proud,
>   but gives grace to the humble.[e]

"Casting All Your Care Upon Him"

[6] Humble yourselves therefore under the mighty hand of God, so that He may exalt you in due time,[f] [7] casting all your care upon Him, because He cares about you.

"Be on the Alert!"

[8] Be sober! Be on the alert! Your adversary the Devil is prowling around like a roaring lion, looking for anyone he can devour. [9] Resist him, firm in the faith, knowing that the same sufferings are being experienced by your brothers in the world.

[10] Now the God of all grace, who called you to His eternal glory in Christ Jesus, will personally[g] restore, establish, strengthen, and support you after you have suffered a little.[h] [11] To Him be the dominion[i] forever.[j] •Amen.

Peter's Helpers and Companions

[12] Through Silvanus,[k] whom I consider a faithful brother, I have written briefly, encouraging you and testifying that this is the true grace of God. Take your stand in it! [13] She who is in Babylon, also chosen, sends you greetings, as does Mark, my son. [14] Greet one another with a kiss of love. Peace to all of you who are in Christ.[l]

---

[a]**4:18** Pr 11:31 LXX   [b]**5:2** Other mss omit *overseeing*   [c]**5:2** Other mss omit *according to God's will*   [d]**5:5** Lit *you tie around yourselves*   [e]**5:5** Pr 3:34 LXX   [f]**5:6** Lit *in time*   [g]**5:10** Lit *Himself*   [h]**5:10** Or *a little while, or to a small extent*   [i]**5:11** Other mss read *dominion and glory*; other mss read *glory and dominion*   [j]**5:11** Other mss read *forever and ever*   [k]**5:12** Or *Silas*; Ac 15:22-32; 16:19-40; 17:1-16   [l]**5:14** Other mss read *Christ Jesus. Amen.*

2 PETER

Greeting

1 Simeon[a] Peter, a slave and an apostle of Jesus Christ:

To those who have obtained a faith of equal privilege with ours[b] through the righteousness of our God and Savior Jesus Christ.

² May grace and peace be multiplied to you through the knowledge of God and of Jesus our Lord.

Fruitful Spiritual Qualities

³ For His[c] divine power has given us everything required for life and godliness, through the knowledge of Him who called us by[d] His own glory and goodness. ⁴ By these He has given us very great and precious promises, so that through them you may share in the divine nature, escaping the corruption that is in the world because of evil desires. ⁵ For this very reason, make every effort to supplement your faith with goodness, goodness with knowledge, ⁶ knowledge with self-control, self-control with endurance, endurance with godliness, ⁷ godliness with brotherly affection, and brotherly affection with love. ⁸ For if these qualities are yours and are increasing, they will keep you from being useless or unfruitful in the knowledge of our Lord Jesus Christ. ⁹ The person who lacks these things is blind and shortsighted, and has forgotten the cleansing from his past sins. ¹⁰ Therefore, brothers, make every effort to confirm your calling and election, because if you do these things you will never stumble. ¹¹ For in this way, entry into the eternal kingdom of our Lord and Savior Jesus Christ will be richly supplied to you.

Peter Will Remind

¹² Therefore I will always remind you about these things, even though you know them and are established in the truth you have. ¹³ I consider it right, as long as I am in this tent,[e] to wake you up with a reminder, ¹⁴ knowing that I will soon lay aside my tent, as our Lord Jesus Christ has also shown me. ¹⁵ And I will also make every effort that after my departure[f] you may be able to recall these things at any time.

Peter Recalls Transfiguration

¹⁶ For we did not follow cleverly contrived myths when we made known to you the power and coming of our Lord Jesus Christ; instead, we were eyewitnesses of His majesty. ¹⁷ For when He received honor and glory from God the Father, a voice came to Him from the Majestic Glory:

This is My beloved Son.[g]
I take delight in Him![h]

¹⁸ And we heard this voice when it came from heaven while we were with Him on the holy mountain.

Prophetic Word Confirmed

¹⁹ So we have the prophetic word strongly confirmed. You will do well to pay attention to it, as to a lamp shining in a dismal place, until the day dawns and the morning star arises in your hearts. ²⁰ First of all, you should know this: no prophecy of Scripture comes from one's own interpretation, ²¹ because no prophecy ever came by the will of man; instead, moved by the Holy Spirit, men spoke from God.

---

a 1:1 Simeon **b** 1:1 Or *obtained a faith of the same kind as ours* **c** 1:3 Lit *As His* **d** 1:3 Or *to* **e** 1:13 A euphemism for Peter's body **f** 1:15 Or *my death* **g** 1:17 Other mss read *My Son, My Beloved* **h** 1:17 A reference to the transfiguration; see Mt 17:5

God's Judgment
on False Prophets and Teachers

2 But there were also false prophets among the people, just as there will be false teachers among you. They will secretly bring in destructive heresies, even denying the Master who bought them, and will bring swift destruction on themselves. ² Many will follow their unrestrained ways, and because of them the way of truth will be blasphemed. ³ In their greed they will exploit you with deceptive words. Their condemnation, ₍pronounced₎ long ago, is not idle, and their destruction does not sleep.

God's Dealings
with Godly and Ungodly

⁴ For if God didn't spare the angels who sinned, but threw them down into Tartarusᵃ and delivered them to be kept in chainsᵇ of darkness until judgment; ⁵ and if He didn't spare the ancient world, but protected Noah, a preacher of righteousness, and seven others,ᶜ when He brought a flood on the world of the ungodly; ⁶ and if He reduced the cities of Sodom and Gomorrah to ashes and condemned them to ruin,ᵈ making them an example to those who were going to be ungodly;ᵉ ⁷ and if He rescued righteous Lot, distressed by the unrestrained behavior of the immoral ⁸ (for as he lived among them, that righteous man tormented himself day by day with the lawless deeds he saw and heard)— ⁹ then the Lord knows how to rescue the godly from trials and to keep the unrighteous under punishment until the day of judgment, ¹⁰ especially those who follow the polluting desires of the flesh and despise authority.

Peter Condemns
Blasphemy and Immorality

Bold, arrogant people! They do not tremble when they blaspheme the glorious ones; ¹¹ however, angels, who are greater in might and power, do not bring a slanderous charge against them before the Lord.ᶠ ¹² But these people, like irrational animals—creatures of instinct born to be caught and destroyed—speak blasphemies about things they don't understand, and in their destruction they too will be destroyed, ¹³ suffering harm as the payment for unrighteousness. They consider it a pleasure to carouse in the daytime. They are blots and blemishes, delighting in their deceptionsᵍ as they feast with you, ¹⁴ having eyes full of adultery and always looking for sin, seducing unstable people, and with hearts trained in greed. Accursed children! ¹⁵ By abandoning the straight path, they have gone astray and have followed the path of Balaam, the son of Bosor,ʰ who loved the wages of unrighteousness, ¹⁶ but received a rebuke for his transgression: a speechless donkey spoke with a human voice and restrained the prophet's madness.

End for Those Who Fall Away

¹⁷ These people are springs without water, mists driven by a whirlwind. The gloom of darkness has been reserved for them. ¹⁸ For uttering bombastic, empty words, they seduce, by fleshly desires and debauchery, people who have barely escapedⁱ from those who live in error. ¹⁹ They promise them freedom, but they themselves are slaves of corruption, since people are enslaved to whatever defeats them. ²⁰ For if, having escaped

---

ᵃ2:4 *Tartarus* is a Gk name for a subterranean place of divine punishment lower than Hades.   ᵇ2:4 Other mss read *in pits*   ᶜ2:5 Lit *righteousness, as the eighth*   ᵈ2:6 Other mss omit *to ruin*   ᵉ2:6 Other mss read *an example of what is going to happen to the ungodly*   ᶠ2:11 Other mss read *them from the Lord*   ᵍ2:13 Other mss read *delighting in the love feasts*   ʰ2:15 Other mss read *Beor*   ⁱ2:18 Or *people who are barely escaping*

the world's impurity through the knowledge of our Lord and Savior Jesus Christ, they are again entangled in these things and defeated, the last state is worse for them than the first. ²¹ For it would have been better for them not to have known the way of righteousness than, after knowing it, to turn back from the holy commandment delivered to them. ²² It has happened to them according to the true proverb: **A dog returns to its own vomit,**ᵃ and, "a sow, after washing itself, wallows in the mud."

Day of the Lord

3 Dear friends, this is now the second letter I've written you; in both, I awaken your pure understanding with a reminder, ² so that you can remember the words previously spoken by the holy prophets, and the commandment of our Lord and Savior ⌊given⌋ through your apostles. ³ First, be aware of this: scoffers will come in the last days to scoff, following their own lusts, ⁴ saying, "Where is the promise of His coming? For ever since the fathers fell •asleep, all things continue as they have been since the beginning of creation." ⁵ They willfully ignore this: long ago the heavens and the earth existed out of water and through water by the word of God. ⁶ Through these the world of that time perished when it was flooded by water. ⁷ But by the same word the present heavens and earth are held in store for fire, being kept until the day of judgment and destruction of ungodly men.

1000 Years with the Lord

⁸ Dear friends, don't let this one thing escape you: with the Lord one day is like 1,000 years, and 1,000 years like one day. ⁹ The Lord does not delay His prom-

ise, as some understand delay, but is patient with you, not wanting any to perish, but all to come to repentance. ¹⁰ But the Day of the Lord will come like a thief;ᵇ on that ⌊day⌋ the heavens will pass away with a loud noise, the elements will burn and be dissolved, and the earth and the works on it will be disclosed.ᶜ ¹¹ Since all these things are to be destroyed in this way, ⌊it is clear⌋ what sort of people you should be in holy conduct and godliness ¹² as you wait for and earnestly desire the coming of the day of God, because of which the heavens will be on fire and be dissolved, and the elements will melt with the heat. ¹³ But based on His promise, we wait for new heavens and a new earth, where righteousness will dwell.

Paul's Letters: Like Rest of Scripture

¹⁴ Therefore, dear friends, while you wait for these things, make every effort to be found in peace without spot or blemish before Him. ¹⁵ Also, regard the patience of our Lord as ⌊an opportunity for⌋ salvation, just as our dear brother Paul, according to the wisdom given to him, has written to you. ¹⁶ He speaks about these things in all his letters, in which there are some matters that are hard to understand. The untaught and unstable twist them to their own destruction, as they also do with the rest of the Scriptures.

¹⁷ Therefore, dear friends, since you have been forewarned, be on your guard, so that you are not led away by the error of the immoral and fall from your own stability. ¹⁸ But grow in the grace and knowledge of our Lord and Savior Jesus Christ. To Him be the glory both now and to the day of eternity.ᵈ •Amen.ᵉ

ᵃ**2:22** Pr 26:11 ᵇ**3:10** Other mss add *in the night* ᶜ**3:10** Other mss read *will be burned up* ᵈ**3:18** Or *now and forever* ᵉ**3:18** Other mss omit *Amen.*

1 JOHN

Prologue

1 What was from the beginning,
what we have heard,
what we have seen with our eyes,
what we have observed,
and have touched with our hands,
concerning the Word of life—
2 that life was revealed,
and we have seen it
and we testify and declare to you
the eternal life that was
with the Father
and was revealed to us—
3 what we have seen and heard
we also declare to you,
so that you may have fellowship
along with us;
and indeed our fellowship is
with the Father
and with His Son Jesus Christ.
4 We are writing these things[a]
so that our[b] joy may be complete.

Fellowship with God

5 Now this is the message we have heard from Him and declare to you: God is light, and there is absolutely no darkness in Him. 6 If we say, "We have fellowship with Him," and •walk in darkness, we are lying and are not practicing[c] the truth. 7 But if we walk in the light as He Himself is in the light, we have fellowship with one another, and the blood of Jesus His Son cleanses us from all sin. 8 If we say, "We have no sin," we are deceiving ourselves, and the truth is not in us. 9 If we confess our sins, He is faithful and righteous to forgive us our sins and to cleanse us from all unrighteousness. 10 If we say, "We have not sinned," we make Him a liar, and His word is not in us.

Jesus is Propitiation for Sins of Whole World

2 My little children, I am writing you these things so that you may not sin. But if anyone does sin, we have an •advocate with the Father—Jesus Christ the righteous One. 2 He Himself is the propitiation[d] for our sins, and not only for ours, but also for those of the whole world.

Test of Knowing God

3 This is how we are sure that we have come to know Him: by keeping His commands. 4 The one who says, "I have come to know Him," without keeping His commands, is a liar, and the truth is not in him. 5 But whoever keeps His word, truly in him the love of God is perfected.[e] This is how we know we are in Him: 6 the one who says he remains in Him should •walk just as He walked.

7 Dear friends, I am not writing you a new command, but an old command that you have had from the beginning. The old command is the message you have heard. 8 Yet I am writing you a new command, which is true in Him and in you, because the darkness is passing away and the true light is already shining.

9 The one who says he is in the light but hates his brother is in the darkness until now. 10 The one who loves his brother remains in the light, and there is

---

[a]**1:4** Other mss add *to you*   [b]**1:4** Other mss read *your*   [c]**1:6** Or *not living according to*   [d]**2:2** The word *propitiation* has to do with the removal of divine wrath. Jesus' death is the means that turns God's wrath from the sinner; see 2 Co 5:21.   [e]**2:5** Or *truly completed*

no cause for stumbling in him.ᵃ ¹¹ But the one who hates his brother is in the darkness, walks in the darkness, and doesn't know where he's going, because the darkness has blinded his eyes.

John's Reasons for Writing

¹² I am writing to you, little children,
because your sins have been
   forgiven on account of His name.
¹³ I am writing to you, fathers,
because you have come to know
   the One who is
   from the beginning.
I am writing to you, young men,
because you have had victory
   over the evil one.
¹⁴ I have written to you, children,
because you have come to know
   the Father.
I have written to you, fathers,
because you have come to know
   the One who is
   from the beginning.
I have written to you, young men,
because you are strong,
God's word remains in you,
and you have had victory
   over the evil one.

John Warns about World

¹⁵ Do not love the world or the things that belong toᵇ the world. If anyone loves the world, love for the Father is not in him. ¹⁶ For everything that belongs toᶜ the world—the lust of the flesh, the lust of the eyes, and the pride in one's lifestyle—is not from the Father, but is from the world. ¹⁷ And the world with its lust is passing away, but the one who does God's will remains forever.

Last Hour: "Antichrist Is Coming"

¹⁸ Children, it is the last hour. And as you have heard, "Antichrist is coming," even now many antichrists have come. We know from this that it is the last hour. ¹⁹ They went out from us, but they did not belong to us; for if they had belonged to us, they would have remained with us. However, they went out so that it might be made clear that none of them belongs to us.

²⁰ But you have an anointing from the Holy One, and you all have knowledge.ᵈ ²¹ I have not written to you because you don't know the truth, but because you do know it, and because no lie comes from the truth. ²² Who is the liar, if not the one who denies that Jesus is the •Messiah? He is the antichrist, the one who denies the Father and the Son. ²³ No one who denies the Son can have the Father; he who confesses the Son has the Father as well.

What Must Remain in You

²⁴ What you have heard from the beginning must remain in you. If what you have heard from the beginning remains in you, then you will remain in the Son and in the Father. ²⁵ And this is the promise that He Himself made to us: eternal life. ²⁶ I have written these things to you about those who are trying to deceive you.

²⁷ The anointing you received from Him remains in you, and you don't need anyone to teach you. Instead, His anointing teaches you about all things, and is true and is not a lie; just as it has taught you, remain in Him.

²⁸ So now, little children, remain in Him, so that when He appears we may have boldness and not be ashamed before Him at His coming. ²⁹ If you know that He is righteous, you know this as well: everyone who does what is right has been born of Him.

The Father's Love

3 Look at how great a love[a] the Father has given us, that we should be called God's children. And we are! The reason the world does not know us is that it didn't know Him. [2] Dear friends, we are God's children now, and what we will be has not yet been revealed. We know that when He appears, we will be like Him, because we will see Him as He is. [3] And everyone who has this hope in Him purifies himself just as He is pure.

Test of Sin

[4] Everyone who commits sin also breaks the law;[b] sin is the breaking of law. [5] You know that He was revealed so that He might take away sins,[c] and there is no sin in Him. [6] Everyone who remains in Him does not sin; everyone who sins has not seen Him or known Him.

[7] Little children, let no one deceive you! The one who does what is right is righteous, just as He is righteous. [8] The one who commits sin is of the Devil, for the Devil has sinned from the beginning. The Son of God was revealed for this purpose: to destroy the Devil's works. [9] Everyone who has been born of God does not sin, because His[d] seed remains in him; he is not able to sin, because he has been born of God. [10] This is how God's children—and the Devil's children—are made evident.

Test of Love

Whoever does not do what is right is not of God, especially the one who does not love his brother. [11] For this is the message you have heard from the beginning: we should love one another, [12] unlike Cain, who was of the evil one and murdered[e] his brother. And why did he murder him? Because his works were evil, and his brother's were righteous. [13] Do not be surprised, brothers, if the world hates you. [14] We know that we have passed from death to life because we love our brothers. The one who does not love remains in death. [15] Everyone who hates his brother is a murderer, and you know that no murderer has eternal life residing in him.

What Is Love?

[16] This is how we have come to know love: He laid down His life for us. We should also lay down our lives for our brothers. [17] If anyone has this world's goods and sees his brother in need but shuts off his compassion from him—how can God's love reside in him?

[18] Little children, we must not love in word or speech, but in deed and truth; [19] that is how we will know we are of the truth, and will convince our hearts in His presence, [20] because if our hearts condemn us, God is greater than our hearts and knows all things.

[21] Dear friends, if our hearts do not condemn ⌊us⌋ we have confidence before God, [22] and can receive whatever we ask from Him because we keep His commands and do what is pleasing in His sight. [23] Now this is His command: that we believe in the name of His Son Jesus Christ, and love one another as He commanded us. [24] The one who keeps His commands remains in Him, and He in him. And the way we know that He remains in us is from the Spirit He has given us.

Test the Spirits

4 Dear friends, do not believe every spirit, but test the spirits to determine if they are from God, because

---

[a] **3:1** Or *at what sort of love*   [b] **3:4** Or *also commits iniquity*   [c] **3:5** Other mss read *our sins*   [d] **3:9** God's   [e] **3:12** Or *slaughtered*

many false prophets have gone out into the world. ² This is how you know the Spirit of God: Every spirit who confesses that Jesus Christ has come in the flesh[a] is from God. ³ But every spirit who does not confess Jesus[b] is not from God. This is the spirit of the antichrist; you have heard that he is coming, and he is already in the world now.

⁴ You are from God, little children, and you have conquered them, because <u>the One who is in you is greater than the one who is in the world.</u> ⁵ They are from the world. Therefore what they say is from the world, and the world listens to them. ⁶ We are from God. Anyone who knows God listens to us; anyone who is not from God does not listen to us. From this we know the Spirit of truth and the spirit of deception.

Knowing God through Love

⁷ Dear friends, let us love one another, because love is from God, and everyone who loves has been born of God and knows God. ⁸ The one who does not love does not know God, because <u>God is love.</u> ⁹ God's love was revealed among us in this way:[c] God sent His •One and Only Son into the world so that we might live through Him. ¹⁰ Love consists in this: not that we loved God, but that He loved us and sent His Son to be the[d] propitiation[e] for our sins. ¹¹ Dear friends, if God loved us in this way, we also must love one another. ¹² No one has ever seen God.[f] If we love one another, God remains in[g] us and His love is perfected in us.

¹³ This is how we know that we remain in Him and He in us: He has given

to us from His Spirit. ¹⁴ And we have seen and we testify that the Father has sent the Son as Savior of the world. ¹⁵ Whoever confesses[h] that Jesus is the Son of God—God remains in him and he in God. ¹⁶ And we have come to know and to believe the love that God has for us. <u>God is love, and the one who remains in love remains in God, and God remains in him.</u>

¹⁷ In this, love is perfected with us so that we may have confidence in the day of judgment; for we are as He is in this world. ¹⁸ There is no fear in love; instead, perfect love drives out fear, because fear involves punishment.[i] So the one who fears has not reached perfection in love. ¹⁹ <u>We love[j] because He first loved us.</u>

Keeping God's Love Commands

²⁰ If anyone says, "I love God," yet hates his brother, he is a liar. For the person who does not love his brother whom he has seen cannot love God whom he has not seen.[k] ²¹ And we have this command from Him: the one who loves God must also love his brother.

5 Everyone who believes that Jesus is the •Messiah has been born of God, and everyone who loves the parent also loves his child. ² This is how we know that we love God's children when we love God and obey[l] His commands. ³ For this is what love for God is: to keep His commands. Now His commands are not a burden, ⁴ because whatever has been born of God conquers the world. This is the victory that has conquered the world: our faith. ⁵ And who is the one who conquers the world but the one

---

[a]4:2 Or *confesses Jesus to be the Christ come in the flesh*   [b]4:3 Other mss read *confess that Jesus has come in the flesh*   [c]4:9 Or *revealed in us*   [d]4:10 Or a   [e]4:10 The word *propitiation* has to do with the removal of divine wrath. Jesus' death is the means that turns God's wrath from the sinner; see 2 Co 5:21.   [f]4:12 Since God is an infinite being, no one can see Him in His absolute essential nature; see Ex 33:18-23.   [g]4:12 Or *remains among*   [h]4:15 Or *acknowledges*   [i]4:18 Or *fear has its own punishment* or *torment*   [j]4:19 Other mss add *Him*   [k]4:20 Other mss read *seen, how is he able to love . . . seen?* (as a question)   [l]5:2 Other mss read *keep*

who believes that Jesus is the Son of God?

God's Testimony: Spirit, Water, Blood

[6] Jesus Christ—He is the One who came by water and blood; not by water only, but by water and by blood. And the Spirit is the One who testifies, because the Spirit is the truth. [7] For there are three that testify:[a] [8] the Spirit, the water, and the blood—and these three are in agreement. [9] If we accept the testimony of men, God's testimony is greater, because it is God's testimony that He has given about His Son. [10] (The one who believes in the Son of God has the testimony in himself. The one who does not believe God has made Him a liar, because he has not believed in the testimony that God has given about His Son.) [11] And this is the testimony: God has given us eternal life, and this life is in His Son.

[12] The one who has the Son has life. The one who doesn't have the Son of God does not have life. [13] I have written these things to you who believe in the name of the Son of God, so that you may know that you have eternal life.

Secret to Confidence in Prayer

[14] Now this is the confidence we have before Him: whenever we ask anything according to His will, He hears us. [15] And if we know that He hears whatever we ask, we know that we have what we have asked Him for.

Sin and Death

[16] If anyone sees his brother committing a sin that does not bring death, he should ask, and God[b] will give life to him—to those who commit sin that doesn't bring death. There is sin[c] that brings death. I am not saying he should pray about that. [17] All unrighteousness is sin, and there is sin that does not bring death.

Conclusion

[18] We know that everyone who has been born of God does not sin, but the One[d] who is born of God keeps him,[e] [f] and the evil one does not touch him.

[19] We know that we are of God, and the whole world is under the sway of the evil one.

[20] And we know that the Son of God has come and has given us understanding so that we may know the true One.[g] We are in the true One—that is, in His Son Jesus Christ. He is the true God and eternal life.

[21] Little children, guard yourselves from idols.

[a]**5:7-8** Other mss (the Lat Vg and a few late Gk mss) read *testify in heaven, the Father, the Word, and the Holy Spirit, and these three are One. 8 And there are three who bear witness on earth:* [b]**5:16** Lit *He* [c]**5:16** Or *is a sin* [d]**5:18** *Jesus Christ* [e]**5:18** Other mss read *himself* [f]**5:18** Or *the one who is born of God keeps himself* [g]**5:20** Other mss read *the true God*

2 JOHN

Greeting

The Elder:[a]

To the elect lady[b] and her children, whom I love in truth—and not only I, but also all who have come to know the truth— ² because of the truth that remains in us and will be with us forever.

³ Grace, mercy, and peace will be with us from God the Father and from Jesus Christ, the Son of the Father, in truth and love.

You Must Walk in Love

⁴ I was very glad to find some of your children •walking in truth, in keeping with a command we have received from the Father. ⁵ So now I urge you, lady—not as if I were writing you a new command, but one we have had from the beginning—that we love one another. ⁶ And this is love: that we walk according to His commands. This is the command as you have heard it from the beginning: you must walk in love.[c]

Beware of Deceivers Who Deny Jesus' Humanity

⁷ Many deceivers have gone out into the world; they do not confess the coming of Jesus Christ in the flesh.[d] This is the deceiver and the antichrist. ⁸ Watch yourselves so that you don't lose what we[e] have worked for, but you may receive a full reward. ⁹ Anyone who does not remain in the teaching about Christ, but goes beyond it, does not have God. The one who remains in that teaching, this one has both the Father and the Son. ¹⁰ If anyone comes to you and does not bring this teaching, do not receive him into your home, and don't say, "Welcome," to him; ¹¹ for the one who says, "Welcome," to him shares in his evil works.

Farewell

¹² Though I have many things to write to you, I don't want to do so with paper and ink. Instead, I hope to be with you and talk face to face[f] so that our joy may be complete.

¹³ The children of your elect sister send you greetings.

---

3 JOHN

Greeting

The Elder:

To my dear friend[a] Gaius, whom I love in truth.

[2] Dear friend,[b] I pray that you may prosper in every way and be in good health, just as your soul prospers. [3] For I was very glad when some brothers came and testified to your ⌊faithfulness⌋ to the truth—how you are •walking in the truth. [4] I have no greater joy than this: to hear that my children are walking in the truth.

Gaius Commended

[5] Dear friend,[c] you are showing your faith[d] by whatever you do for the brothers, and this ⌊you are doing⌋ for strangers; [6] they have testified to your love before the church. You will do well to send them on their journey in a manner worthy of God, [7] since they set out for the sake of the name, accepting nothing from pagans. [8] Therefore, we ought to support such men, so that we can be co-workers with[e] the truth.

Slanderous Diotrephes

[9] I wrote something to the church, but Diotrephes, who loves to have first place among them, does not receive us. [10] This is why, if I come, I will remind him of the works he is doing, slandering us with malicious words. And he is not satisfied with that! He not only refuses to welcome the brothers himself, but he even stops those who want to do so and expels them from the church.

Good Demetrius

[11] Dear friend,[f] do not imitate what is evil, but what is good. The one who does good is of God; the one who does evil has not seen God. [12] Demetrius has a ⌊good⌋ testimony from everyone, and from the truth itself. And we also testify for him, and you know that our testimony is true.

Farewell

[13] I have many things to write you, but I don't want to write to you with pen and ink. [14] I hope to see you soon, and we will talk face to face.[g]

Peace be with you. The friends send you greetings. Greet the friends by name.

---

[a]1 Or *my beloved* [b]2 Or *Beloved* [c]5 Or *Beloved* [d]5 Lit *are doing faith* [e]8 Or *co-workers for* [f]11 Or *Beloved*
[g]14 Lit *mouth to mouth*

JUDE

Greeting

Jude, a slave of Jesus Christ, and a brother of James:

To those who are the called, loved[a] by God the Father and kept by Jesus Christ. [2] May mercy, peace, and love be multiplied to you.

Jude's Purpose in Writing

[3] Dear friends, although I was eager to write you about our common salvation, I found it necessary to write and exhort you to contend for the faith that was delivered to the saints once for all. [4] For certain men, who were designated for this judgment long ago, have come in by stealth; they are ungodly, turning the grace of our God into promiscuity and denying our only Master and Lord, Jesus Christ.

Apostates: Past and Present

[5] Now I want to remind you, though you know all these things: the Lord, having first of all[b] saved a people out of Egypt, later destroyed those who did not believe; [6] and He has kept, with eternal chains in darkness for the judgment of the great day, angels who did not keep their own position but deserted their proper dwelling. [7] In the same way, Sodom and Gomorrah and the cities around them committed sexual immorality and practiced perversions,[c] just as they did, and serve as an example by undergoing the punishment of eternal fire.

[8] Nevertheless, these dreamers likewise defile their flesh, despise authority, and blaspheme glorious beings. [9] Yet Michael the archangel, when he was disputing with the Devil in a debate about Moses' body, did not dare bring an abusive condemnation against him, but said, "The Lord rebuke you!" [10] But these people blaspheme anything they don't understand, and what they know by instinct, like unreasoning animals—they destroy themselves with these things. [11] Woe to them! For they have traveled in the way of Cain, have abandoned themselves to the error of Balaam for profit, and have perished in Korah's rebellion.

Features of Contemporary Scoffers

[12] These are the ones who are like dangerous reefs[d] at your love feasts. They feast with you, nurturing only themselves without fear. They are waterless clouds carried along by winds; trees in late autumn—fruitless, twice dead, pulled out by the roots; [13] wild waves of the sea, foaming up their shameful deeds; wandering stars for whom is reserved the blackness of darkness forever!

[14] And Enoch, in the seventh generation from Adam, prophesied about them:

Look! The Lord comes[e]
with thousands of His holy ones
[15] to execute judgment on all,
and to convict them[f]
of all their ungodly deeds
that they have done
in an ungodly way,
and of all the harsh things
ungodly sinners
have said against Him.

---

[a]1 Other mss read *sanctified* [b]5 Other mss place *first of all* after *remind you* [c]7 Lit *and went after other flesh*
[d]12 Or *like spots* [e]14 Or *came* [f]15 Lit *convict all*

16 These people are discontented grumblers, •walking according to their desires; their mouths utter arrogant words, flattering people for their own advantage.

17 But you, dear friends, remember the words foretold by the apostles of our Lord Jesus Christ; 18 they told you, "In the end time there will be scoffers walking according to their own ungodly desires." 19 These people create divisions and are merely natural, not having the Spirit.

Exhortation and Benediction

20 But you, dear friends, building yourselves up in your most holy faith and praying in the Holy Spirit, 21 keep yourselves in the love of God, expecting the mercy of our Lord Jesus Christ for eternal life. 22 Have mercy on some who doubt; 23 save others by snatching ⌐them⌐ from the fire; on others have mercy in fear, hating even the garment defiled by the flesh.

24 Now to Him who is able to protect you from stumbling and to make you stand in the presence of His glory, blameless and with great joy, 25 to the only God our Savior, through Jesus Christ our Lord,a be glory, majesty, power, and authority before all time,b now, and forever. •Amen.

REVELATION

Prologue

1 The revelation ofc Jesus Christ that God gave Him to show His •slaves what must quicklyd take place. He sent it and signified ite through His angel to His slave John, 2 who testified to God's word and to the testimonyf about Jesus Christ, in all he saw.g 3 Blessed is the one who reads and blessed are those who hear the words of this prophecy and keeph what is written in it, because the time is near!

4 John:

To the seven churches in the province of Asia.i

Grace and peace to you fromj the One who is, who was, and who is coming; from the seven spiritsk before His throne; 5 and from Jesus Christ, the faithful witness, the firstborn from the dead and the ruler of the kings of the earth.

To Him who loves us and has set us freel from our sins by His blood, 6 and made us a kingdom,m priestsn to His God and Father—to Him be the glory and dominion forever and ever. •Amen.

7 Look! He is coming
   with the clouds,
and every eye will see Him,
   including those who piercedo
   Him.
And all the families of the earthp q
   will mourn over Him.r s
This is certain. Amen.

8 "I am the •Alpha and the Omega," says the Lord God, "the One who is, who was, and who is coming, the Almighty."

---

a25 Other mss omit *through Jesus Christ our Lord*   b25 Other mss omit *before all time*   c1:1 Or *Revelation of*, or *A revelation of*   d1:1 Or *soon*   e1:1 Made it known through symbols   f1:2 Or *witness*   g1:2 Lit *as many as he saw*   h1:3 Or *follow*, or *obey*   i1:4 Lit *churches in Asia;* that is, the Roman province that is now a part of modern Turkey   j1:4 Other mss add *God*   k1:4 Or *the sevenfold Spirit*   l1:5 Other mss read *has washed us*   m1:6 Other mss read *kings and*   n1:6 Or *made us into* (or *to be*) *a kingdom of priests;* see Ex 19:6   o1:7 Or *impaled*   p1:7 Or *All the tribes of the land*   q1:7 Gn 12:3; 28:14; Zch 14:17   r1:7 Or *will wail because of Him*   s1:7 Dn 7:13; Zch 12:10

John's Vision
of Risen Lord

⁹ I, John, your brother and partner in the tribulation, kingdom, and perseverance in Jesus, was on the island called Patmos because of God's word and the testimony about Jesus.ᵃ ¹⁰ I was in the Spiritᵇ ᶜ on the Lord's day,ᵈ and I heard behind me a loud voice like a trumpet ¹¹ saying, "Write on a scrollᵉ what you see and send it to the seven churches: Ephesus, Smyrna, Pergamum, Thyatira, Sardis, Philadelphia, and Laodicea."

¹² I turned to see the voice that was speaking to me. When I turned I saw seven gold lampstands, ¹³ and among the lampstands was One like the •Son of Man,ᶠ dressed in a long robe, and with a gold sash wrapped around His chest. ¹⁴ His head and hair were white like wool—white as snow, His eyes like a fiery flame, ¹⁵ His feet like fine bronze fired in a furnace, and His voice like the sound of cascadingᵍ waters. ¹⁶ In His right hand He had seven stars; from His mouth came a sharp two-edged sword; and His face was shining like the sun at midday.ʰ

¹⁷ When I saw Him, I fell at His feet like a dead man. He laid His right hand on me, and said, "Don't be afraid! I am the First and the Last, ¹⁸ and the Living One. I was dead, but look—I am alive forever and ever, and I hold the keys of death and •Hades. ¹⁹ Therefore write what you have seen, what is, and what will take place after this. ²⁰ The secretⁱ of the seven stars you saw in My right hand, and of the seven gold lampstands, is this: the seven stars are the angelsʲ of the seven churches, and the seven lampstandsᵏ are the seven churches.

THE LETTERS
TO THE SEVEN CHURCHES

Letter to Ephesus

2 "To the angelˡ of the church in Ephesus write:

"The One who holds the seven stars in His right hand and who walks among the seven gold lampstands says: ² I know your works, your labor, and your endurance, and that you cannot tolerate evil. You have tested those who call themselves apostles and are not, and you have found them to be liars. ³ You also possess endurance and have tolerated ⸢many things⸣ because of My name, and have not grown weary. ⁴ But I have this against you: <u>you have abandoned the love ⸢you had⸣ at first</u>. ⁵ Remember then how far you have fallen; repent, and do the works you did at first. Otherwise, I will come to youᵐ and remove your lampstand from its place—unless you repent. ⁶ Yet you do have this: you hate the practices of the Nicolaitans, which I also hate.

⁷ "Anyone who has an ear should listen to what the Spirit says to the churches. I will give the victor the right to eat from the tree of life, which is inⁿ the paradise of God.

Letter to Smyrna

⁸ "To the angel of the church in Smyrna write:

"The First and the Last, the One who was dead and came to life, says: ⁹ I know yourᵒ tribulation and poverty, yet you are rich. ⸢I know⸣ the slander of those who say they are Jews and are not, but are a •synagogue of Satan. ¹⁰ Don't be afraid of what you are about to suffer. Look, the Devil is about to throw some

---

ᵃ**1:9** Lit the witness of Jesus   ᵇ**1:10** Lit I became in the Spirit or in spirit   ᶜ**1:10** John was brought by God's Spirit into a realm of spiritual vision.   ᵈ**1:10** Sunday   ᵉ**1:11** Or book   ᶠ**1:13** Or like a son of man   ᵍ**1:15** Lit many   ʰ**1:16** Lit like the sun shines in its power   ⁱ**1:20** Or mystery   ʲ**1:20** Or messengers   ᵏ**1:20** Other mss add that you saw   ˡ**2:1** Or messenger here and elsewhere   ᵐ**2:5** Other mss add quickly   ⁿ**2:7** Other mss read in the midst of   ᵒ**2:9** Other mss add works and

of you into prison to test you, and you will have tribulation for 10 days. Be faithful until death, and I will give you the crown[a] of life.

11 "Anyone who has an ear should listen to what the Spirit says to the churches. The victor will never be harmed by the second death.

Letter to Pergamum

12 "To the angel of the church in Pergamum write:

"The One who has the sharp, two-edged sword says: 13 I know[b] where you live—where Satan's throne is! And you are holding on to My name and did not deny your faith in Me,[c] even in the days of Antipas, My faithful witness, who was killed among you, where Satan lives. 14 But I have a few things against you. You have some there who hold to the teaching of Balaam, who taught Balak to place a stumbling block[d] in front of the sons of Israel: to eat meat sacrificed to idols and to commit sexual immorality.[e] 15 In the same way, you also have those who hold to the teaching of the Nicolaitans.[f] 16 Therefore repent! Otherwise, I will come to you quickly and fight against them with the sword of My mouth.

17 "Anyone who has an ear should listen to what the Spirit says to the churches. I will give the victor some of the hidden manna.[g] I will also give him a white stone, and on the stone a new name is inscribed that no one knows except the one who receives it.

Letter to Thyatira

18 "To the angel of the church in Thyatira write:

"The Son of God, the One whose eyes are like a fiery flame, and whose feet are like fine bronze says: 19 I know your works—your love, faithfulness,[h] service, and endurance. Your last works are greater than the first. 20 But I have this against you: you tolerate the woman Jezebel, who calls herself a prophetess, and teaches and deceives My slaves to commit sexual immorality[e] and to eat meat sacrificed to idols. 21 I gave her time to repent, but she does not want to repent of her sexual immorality.[i] 22 Look! I will throw her into a sickbed, and those who commit adultery with her into great tribulation, unless they repent of her[j] practices. 23 I will kill her children with the plague.[k] Then all the churches will know that I am the One who examines minds[l] and hearts, and I will give to each of you according to your works. 24 I say to the rest of you in Thyatira, who do not hold this teaching, who haven't known the deep things[m] of Satan—as they say—I do not put any other burden on you. 25 But hold on to what you have until I come. 26 The victor and the one who keeps My works to the end: I will give him authority over the nations—

27 　**and He will shepherd[n] them**
　　with an iron scepter;
　He will shatter them
　　like pottery[o]—

just as I have received ⌊this⌋ from My Father. 28 I will also give him the morning star.

29 "Anyone who has an ear should listen to what the Spirit says to the churches.

Letter to Sardis

3 "To the angel of the church in Sardis write:

"The One who has the seven spirits of God and the seven stars says: I know your works; you have a reputation[a] for being alive, but you are dead. [2] Be alert and strengthen[b] what remains, which is about to die, for I have not found your works complete before My God. [3] Remember therefore what you have received and heard; keep it, and repent. But if you are not alert, I will come[c] like a thief, and you have no idea at what hour I will come against you.[d] [4] But you have a few people[e] in Sardis who have not defiled[f] their clothes, and they will walk with Me in white, because they are worthy. [5] In the same way, the victor will be dressed in white clothes, and I will never erase his name from the book of life, but will acknowledge his name before My Father and before His angels.

[6] "Anyone who has an ear should listen to what the Spirit says to the churches.

Letter to Philadelphia

[7] "To the angel of the church in Philadelphia write:

"The Holy One, the True One, the One who has the key of David, who opens and no one will close, and closes and no one opens says: [8] I know your works. Because you have limited strength, have kept My word, and have not denied My name, look, I have placed before you an open door that no one is able to close. [9] Take note! I will make those from the •synagogue of Satan, who claim to be Jews and are not, but are lying—note this—I will make them come and bow down at your feet, and they will

know that I have loved you. [10] Because you have kept My command to endure,[g] I will also keep you from the hour of testing that is going to come over the whole world to test those who live on the earth. [11] I am coming quickly. Hold on to what you have, so that no one takes your crown. [12] The victor: I will make him a pillar in the sanctuary of My God, and he will never go out again. I will write on him the name of My God, and the name of the city of My God—the new Jerusalem, which comes down out of heaven from My God—and My new name.

[13] "Anyone who has an ear should listen to what the Spirit says to the churches.

Letter to Laodicea

[14] "To the angel of the church in Laodicea write:

"The •Amen, the faithful and true Witness, the Originator[h] of God's creation says: [15] I know your works, that you are neither cold nor hot. I wish that you were cold or hot. [16] So, because you are lukewarm, and neither hot nor cold, I am going to vomit[i] you out of My mouth. [17] Because you say, 'I'm rich; I have become wealthy, and need nothing,' and you don't know that you are wretched, pitiful, poor, blind, and naked, [18] I advise you to buy from Me gold refined in the fire so that you may be rich, and white clothes so that you may be dressed and your shameful nakedness not be exposed, and ointment to spread on your eyes so that you may see. [19] As many as I love, I rebuke and discipline. So be committed[j] and repent. [20] Listen! I stand at the door and knock. If anyone hears My voice and opens the door, I will come in to him and have dinner with him, and

---

a3:1 Lit have a name b3:2 Other mss read guard c3:3 Other mss add upon you d3:3 Or upon you e3:4 Lit few names f3:4 Or soiled g3:10 Lit My word of endurance h3:14 Or Ruler, or Source, or Beginning i3:16 Or spit j3:19 Or be zealous

he with Me. ²¹ The victor: I will give him the right to sit with Me on My throne, just as I also won the victory and sat down with My Father on His throne.

²² "Anyone who has an ear should listen to what the Spirit says to the churches."

Throne Room of Heaven

4 After this I looked, and there in heaven was an open door. The first voice that I had heard speaking to me like a trumpet said, "Come up here, and I will show you what must take place after this."

² Immediately I was in the Spirit,^a and there in heaven a throne was set. One was seated on the throne, ³ and the One seated^b looked like jasper^c and carnelian^d stone. A rainbow that looked like an emerald surrounded the throne. ⁴ Around that throne were 24 thrones, and on the thrones sat 24 elders dressed in white clothes, with gold crowns on their heads. ⁵ From the throne came flashes of lightning, rumblings, and thunder. Burning before the throne were seven fiery torches, which are the seven spirits of God. ⁶ Also before the throne was something like a sea of glass, similar to crystal. In the middle^e and around the throne were four living creatures covered with eyes in front and in back. ⁷ The first living creature was like a lion; the second living creature was like a calf; the third living creature had a face like a man; and the fourth living creature was like a flying eagle. ⁸ Each of the four living creatures had six wings; they were covered with eyes around and inside. Day and night they never stop,^f saying:

"Holy, Holy, Holy"

Holy, holy, holy,^g
Lord God, the Almighty,
who was, who is,
    and who is coming.

⁹ Whenever the living creatures give glory, honor, and thanks to the One seated on the throne, the One who lives forever and ever, ¹⁰ the 24 elders fall down before the One seated on the throne, worship the One who lives forever and ever, cast their crowns before the throne, and say:

¹¹   Our Lord and God,^h
    You are worthy to receive
    glory and honor and power,
    because You have created
      all things,
    and because of Your will
    they exist and were created.

Worthy Lamb Takes Scroll

5 Then I saw in the right hand of the One seated on the throne a scroll with writing on the inside and on the back, sealed with seven seals. ² I also saw a mighty angel proclaiming in a loud voice, "Who is worthy to open the scroll and break its seals?" ³ But no one in heaven or on earth or under the earth was able to open the scroll or even to look in it. ⁴ And I cried and cried because no one was found worthy to openⁱ the scroll or even to look in it.

⁵ Then one of the elders said to me, "Stop crying. Look! The Lion from the tribe of Judah, the Root of David, has been victorious so that He may open the scroll and^j its seven seals." ⁶ Then I saw one like a slaughtered lamb standing between^k the throne and the four living

^a**4:2** Lit *I became in the Spirit* or *in spirit*   ^b**4:3** Other mss omit *and the One seated*   ^c**4:3** A precious stone   ^d**4:3** A translucent red gem   ^e**4:6** Lit *In the middle of the throne*   ^f**4:8** Or *they never rest*   ^g**4:8** Other mss read *holy* 9 times   ^h**4:11** Other mss add *the Holy One*; other mss read *O Lord*   ⁱ**5:4** Other mss add *and read*   ^j**5:5** Other mss add *loose*   ^k**5:6** Or *standing in the middle of*

creatures and among the elders. He had seven horns and seven eyes, which are the seven spirits of God sent into all the earth. [7] He came and took ⌊the scroll⌋[a] out of the right hand of the One seated on the throne.

Why Lamb Is Worthy

[8] When He took the scroll, the four living creatures and the 24 elders fell down before the Lamb. Each one had a harp and gold bowls filled with incense, which are the prayers of the saints. [9] And they sang a new song:

> You are worthy to take the scroll
>   and to open its seals;
> because You were slaughtered,
>   and You redeemed[b] ⌊people⌋[c]
>   for God by Your blood
> from every tribe and language
>   and people and nation.
> [10] You made them a kingdom[d]
>   and priests to our God,
>   and they will reign on the earth.

Elders, Angels, and Creatures Worship

[11] Then I looked, and heard the voice of many angels around the throne, and also of the living creatures, and of the elders. Their number was countless thousands, plus thousands of thousands. [12] They said with a loud voice:

> The Lamb who was slaughtered
>   is worthy
> to receive power and riches
>   and wisdom and strength
>   and honor and glory
>   and blessing!

[13] I heard every creature in heaven, on earth, under the earth, on the sea, and everything in them say:

> Blessing and honor and glory
>   and dominion
> to the One seated on the throne,
>   and to the Lamb, forever and ever!

[14] The four living creatures said, "•Amen," and the elders fell down and worshiped.

Lamb Opens First Seal on Scroll

6 Then I saw[e] the Lamb open one of the seven[f] seals, and I heard one of the four living creatures say with a voice like thunder, "Come!"[g] [h] [2] I looked, and there was a white horse. The horseman on it had a bow; a crown was given to him, and he went out as a victor to conquer.[i]

Lamb Opens Second Seal

[3] When He opened the second seal, I heard the second living creature say, "Come!"[g] [h] [4] Then another horse went out, a fiery red one, and its horseman was empowered[j] to take peace from the earth, so that people would slaughter one another. And a large sword was given to him.

Lamb Opens Third Seal

[5] When He opened the third seal, I heard the third living creature say, "Come!"[g] [h] And I looked, and there was a black horse. The horseman on it had a balance scale in his hand. [6] Then I heard something like a voice among the four living creatures say, "A quart of wheat for a •denarius, and three quarts of barley for a denarius—but do not harm the olive oil and the wine."

Lamb Opens Fourth Seal

[7] When He opened the fourth seal, I heard the voice of the fourth living

---

[a]**5:7** Other mss include *the scroll*   [b]**5:9** Or *purchased*   [c]**5:9** Other mss read *us*   [d]**5:10** Other mss read *them kings*
[e]**6:1** Lit *saw when*   [f]**6:1** Other mss omit *seven*   [g]**6:1,3,5** Other mss add *and see*   [h]**6:1,3,5** Or *Go!*   [i]**6:2** Lit *went out conquering and in order to conquer*   [j]**6:4** Or *was granted*; lit *was given*

creature say, "Come!"ᵃ ᵇ ⁸ And I looked, and there was a pale greenᶜ horse. The horseman on it was named Death, and •Hades was following after him. Authority was given to themᵈ over a fourth of the earth, to kill by the sword, by famine, by plague, and by the wild animals of the earth.

Lamb Opens Fifth Seal

⁹ When He opened the fifth seal, I saw under the altar the souls of those slaughtered because of God's word and the testimony they had.ᵉ ¹⁰ They cried out with a loud voice: "O Lord,ᶠ holy and true, how long until You judge and avenge our blood from those who live on the earth?" ¹¹ So a white robe was given to each of them, and they were told to rest a little while longer until ⌊the number of⌋ their fellow slaves and their brothers, who were going to be killed just as they had been, would be completed.

Lambs Opens Sixth Seal

¹² Then I saw Him openᵍ the sixth seal. A violent earthquake occurred; the sun turned black like sackcloth made of goat hair; the entire moonʰ became like blood; ¹³ the starsⁱ of heaven fell to the earth as a fig tree drops its unripe figs when shaken by a high wind; ¹⁴ the sky separated like a scroll being rolled up; and every mountain and island was moved from its place.

¹⁵ Then the kings of the earth, the nobles, the military commanders, the rich, the powerful, and every slave and free person hid in the caves and among the rocks of the mountains. ¹⁶ And they said to the mountains and to the rocks, "Fall on us and hide us from the face of the One seated on the throne and from the wrath of the Lamb, ¹⁷ because the great day of Theirʲ wrath has come! And who is able to stand?"

Sealed of Israel

7 After this I saw four angels standing at the four corners of the earth, restraining the four winds of the earth so that no wind could blow on the earth or on the sea or on any tree. ² Then I saw another angel rise up from the east, who had the seal of the living God. He cried out in a loud voice to the four angels who were empoweredᵏ to harm the earth and the sea: ³ "Don't harm the earth or the sea or the trees until we seal the slaves of our God on their foreheads." ⁴ And I heard the number of those who were sealed:

144,000 sealed from every tribe
  of the sons of Israel:
⁵ 12,000 sealed from the tribe
  of Judah,
  12,000ˡ from the tribe of Reuben,
  12,000 from the tribe of Gad,
⁶ 12,000 from the tribe of Asher,
  12,000 from the tribe of Naphtali,
  12,000 from the tribe of Manasseh,
⁷ 12,000 from the tribe of Simeon,
  12,000 from the tribe of Levi,
  12,000 from the tribe of Issachar,
⁸ 12,000 from the tribe of Zebulun,
  12,000 from the tribe of Joseph,
  12,000 sealed from the tribe
  of Benjamin.

Multitude from Great Tribulation

⁹ After this I looked, and there was a vast multitude from every nation, tribe, people, and language, which no one could number, standing before the

---

ᵃ**6:7** Other mss add *and see*   ᵇ**6:7** Or *Go!*   ᶜ**6:8** Or *a greenish gray*   ᵈ**6:8** Other mss read *him*   ᵉ**6:9** Other mss add *about the Lamb*   ᶠ**6:10** Or *Master*   ᵍ**6:12** Lit *I saw when He opened*   ʰ**6:12** Or *the full moon*   ⁱ**6:13** Perhaps meteors   ʲ**6:17** Other mss read *His*   ᵏ**7:2** Lit *angels to whom it was given*   ˡ**7:5-8** Other mss add *sealed* after each number

throne and before the Lamb. They were robed in white with palm branches in their hands. [10] And they cried out in a loud voice:

> Salvation belongs to our God,
> who is seated on the throne,
> and to the Lamb!

[11] All the angels stood around the throne, the elders, and the four living creatures, and they fell on their faces before the throne and worshiped God, [12] saying:

> •Amen! Blessing and glory
> and wisdom
> and thanksgiving and honor
> and power and strength,
> be to our God forever and ever.
> Amen.

[13] Then one of the elders asked me, "Who are these people robed in white, and where did they come from?"

[14] I said to him, "Sir,[a] you know."

Then he told me:

> These are the ones coming out
> of the great tribulation.
> They washed their robes
> and made them white
> in the blood of the Lamb.
> [15] For this reason they are
> before the throne of God,
> and they serve Him day and night
> in His sanctuary.
> The One seated on the throne
> will shelter[b] them:
> [16] no longer will they hunger;
> no longer will they thirst;
> no longer will the sun strike them,
> or any heat.
> [17] Because the Lamb who is
> at the center of the throne
> will shepherd them;

> He will guide them to springs
> of living waters,
> and God will wipe away every tear
> from their eyes.

Lamb Opens Seventh Seal

8 When He opened the seventh seal, there was silence in heaven for about half an hour. [2] Then I saw the seven angels who stand in the presence of God; seven trumpets were given to them. [3] Another angel, with a gold incense burner, came and stood at the altar. He was given a large amount of incense to offer with the prayers of all the saints on the gold altar in front of the throne. [4] The smoke of the incense, with the prayers of the saints, went up in the presence of God from the angel's hand. [5] The angel took the incense burner, filled it with fire from the altar, and hurled it to the earth; there were thunders, rumblings, lightnings, and an earthquake. [6] And the seven angels who had the seven trumpets prepared to blow them.

The First Trumpet

[7] The first ɪangelɪ[c] blew his trumpet, and hail and fire, mixed with blood, were hurled to the earth. So a third of the earth was burned up, a third of the trees were burned up, and all the green grass was burned up.

The Second Trumpet

[8] The second angel blew his trumpet, and something like a great mountain ablaze with fire was hurled into the sea. So a third of the sea became blood, [9] a third of the living creatures in the sea died, and a third of the ships were destroyed.

---

[a] **7:14** Lit *My lord*   [b] **7:15** Or *will spread His tent over*   [c] **8:7** Other mss include *angel*

The Third Trumpet

[10] The third angel blew his trumpet, and a great star, blazing like a torch, fell from heaven. It fell on a third of the rivers and springs of water. [11] The name of the star is Wormwood,[a] and a third of the waters became wormwood. So, many of the people died from the waters, because they had been made bitter.

The Fourth Trumpet

[12] The fourth angel blew his trumpet, and a third of the sun was struck, a third of the moon, and a third of the stars, so that a third of them were darkened. A third of the day was without light, and the night as well.

[13] I looked, and I heard an eagle,[b] flying in mid-heaven,[c] saying in a loud voice, "Woe! Woe! Woe to those who live on the earth, because of the remaining trumpet blasts that the three angels are about to sound!"

The Fifth Trumpet

9 The fifth angel blew his trumpet, and I saw a star that had fallen from heaven to earth. The key to the shaft of the •abyss was given to him. [2] He opened the shaft of the abyss, and smoke came up out of the shaft like smoke from a great[d] furnace so that the sun and the air were darkened by the smoke from the shaft. [3] Then out of the smoke locusts came to the earth, and power[e] was given to them like the power that scorpions have on the earth. [4] They were told not to harm the grass of the earth, or any green plant, or any tree, but only people who do not have God's seal on their foreheads. [5] They were not permitted to kill them, but were to torment ⌊them⌋ for five months; their torment is like the torment caused by a scorpion when it strikes a man. [6] In those days people will seek death and will not find it; they will long to die, but death will flee from them.

[7] The appearance of the locusts was like horses equipped for battle. On their heads were something like gold crowns; their faces were like men's faces; [8] they had hair like women's hair; their teeth were like lions' teeth; [9] they had chests like iron breastplates; the sound of their wings was like the sound of chariots with many horses rushing into battle; [10] and they had tails with stingers, like scorpions, so that with their tails they had the power[e] to harm people for five months. [11] They had as their king[f] the angel of the abyss; his name in Hebrew is Abaddon,[g] and in Greek he has the name Apollyon.[h] [12] The first woe has passed. There are still two more woes to come after this.

The Sixth Trumpet

[13] The sixth angel blew his trumpet. From the four[i] horns of the gold altar that is before God, I heard a voice [14] say to the sixth angel who had the trumpet, "Release the four angels bound at the great river Euphrates." [15] So the four angels who were prepared for the hour, day, month, and year were released to kill a third of the human race. [16] The number of mounted troops was 200 million;[j] I heard their number. [17] This is how I saw the horses in my vision: The horsemen had breastplates that were fiery red, hyacinth blue, and sulfur yellow. The heads of the horses were like lions' heads, and from their mouths came fire, smoke, and sulfur. [18] A third of the human race was killed by these three

---

[a] **8:11** *Wormwood* is absinthe, a bitter herb.   [b] **8:13** Other mss read *angel*   [c] **8:13** Very high   [d] **9:2** Other mss omit *great*   [e] **9:3,10** Or *authority*   [f] **9:11** Or *as king over them*   [g] **9:11** Or *destruction*   [h] **9:11** Or *destroyer*   [i] **9:13** Other mss omit *four*   [j] **9:16** Other mss read *100 million*

plagues—by the fire, the smoke, and the sulfur that came from their mouths. [19] For the power of the horses is in their mouths and in their tails, because their tails, like snakes, have heads, and they inflict injury with them.

[20] The rest of the people, who were not killed by these plagues, did not repent of the works of their hands to stop worshiping demons and idols of gold, silver, bronze, stone, and wood, which are not able to see, hear, or walk. [21] And they did not repent of their murders, their sorceries,[a] their sexual immorality, or their thefts.

The Mighty Angel and Small Scroll

10 Then I saw another mighty angel coming down from heaven, surrounded by a cloud, with a rainbow over his head.[b] His face was like the sun, his legs[c] were like fiery pillars, [2] and he had a little scroll opened in his hand. He put his right foot on the sea, his left on the land, [3] and he cried out with a loud voice like a roaring lion. When he cried out, the seven thunders spoke with their voices. [4] And when the seven thunders spoke, I was about to write. Then I heard a voice from heaven, saying, "Seal up what the seven thunders said, and do not write it down!"

[5] Then the angel that I had seen standing on the sea and on the land raised his right hand to heaven. [6] He swore an oath by the One who lives forever and ever, who created heaven and what is in it, the earth and what is in it, and the sea and what is in it: "There will no longer be an interval of time,[d] [7] but in the days of the sound of the seventh angel, when

he will blow his trumpet, then God's hidden plan[e] will be completed, as He announced to His servants[f] the prophets."

John Eats Small Scroll

[8] Now the voice that I heard from heaven spoke to me again and said, "Go, take the scroll that lies open in the hand of the angel who is standing on the sea and on the land."

[9] So I went to the angel and asked him to give me the little scroll. He said to me, "Take and eat it; it will be bitter in your stomach, but it will be as sweet as honey in your mouth."

[10] Then I took the little scroll from the angel's hand and ate it. It was as sweet as honey in my mouth, but when I ate it, my stomach became bitter. [11] And I was told,[g] "You must prophesy again about[h] many peoples, nations, languages, and kings."

The Two Witnesses

11 Then I was given a measuring reed like a rod,[i] with these words: "Go[j] and measure God's sanctuary and the altar, and ⌊count⌋ those who worship there. [2] But exclude the courtyard outside the sanctuary. Don't measure it, because it is given to the nations,[k] and they will trample the holy city for 42 months. [3] I will empower[l] my two witnesses, and they will prophesy for 1,260 days,[m] dressed in sackcloth."[n] [4] These are the two olive trees and the two lampstands that stand before the Lord[o] of the earth. [5] If anyone wants to harm them, fire comes from their mouths and consumes their enemies; if anyone wants to harm them, he must be killed in this way. [6] These men

have the power to close the sky so that it does not rain during the days of their prophecy. They also have power over the waters to turn them into blood, and to strike the earth with any plague whenever they want.

Witnesses Martyred

7 When they finish their testimony, the beast[a] that comes up out of the •abyss will make war with them, conquer them, and kill them. 8 Their dead bodies[b] will lie in the public square[c] of the great city, which is called, prophetically,[d] Sodom and Egypt, where also their Lord was crucified. 9 And representatives from[e] the peoples, tribes, languages, and nations will view their bodies for three and a half days and not permit their bodies to be put into a tomb. 10 Those who live on the earth will gloat over them and celebrate and send gifts to one another, because these two prophets tormented those who live on the earth.

Witnesses Resurrected

11 But after the three and a half days, the breath[f] of life from God entered them, and they stood on their feet. So great fear fell on those who saw them. 12 Then they heard[g] a loud voice from heaven saying to them, "Come up here." They went up to heaven in a cloud, while their enemies watched them. 13 At that moment a violent earthquake took place, a tenth of the city fell, and 7,000 people were killed in the earthquake. The survivors were terrified and gave glory to the God of heaven. 14 The second woe has passed. Take note: the third woe is coming quickly!

The Seventh Trumpet

15 The seventh angel blew his trumpet, and there were loud voices in heaven saying:

The kingdom of the world
　has become the ⌊kingdom⌋
of our Lord and of His •Messiah,
and He will reign forever and ever!

16 The 24 elders, who were seated before God on their thrones, fell on their faces and worshiped God, 17 saying:

We thank You, Lord God,
　the Almighty, who is
　and who was,[h]
because You have taken
　Your great power and have begun
　to reign.
18 The nations were angry,
　but Your wrath has come.
The time has come for the dead
　to be judged,
and to give the reward
　to Your servants the prophets,
to the saints, and to those who fear
　Your name, both small and great,
and the time has come to destroy
　those who destroy the earth.

19 God's sanctuary in heaven was opened, and the ark of His covenant[i] appeared in His sanctuary. There were lightnings, rumblings, thunders, an earthquake,[j] and severe hail.

Woman, Child, and Dragon

12 A great sign[k] appeared in heaven: a woman clothed with the sun, with the moon under her feet, and a crown of 12 stars on her head. 2 She was pregnant and cried out in labor and agony to give birth. 3 Then another sign[l] appeared in

---

[a]11:7 Or wild animal　[b]11:8 Lit Their corpse　[c]11:8 Or lie on the broad street　[d]11:8 Or spiritually, or symbolically　[e]11:9 Lit And from　[f]11:11 Or spirit　[g]11:12 Other mss read Then I heard　[h]11:17 Other mss add and who is to come　[i]11:19 Other mss read ark of the covenant of the Lord　[j]11:19 Other mss omit an earthquake　[k]12:1 Or great symbolic display; see Rv 12:3　[l]12:3 Or another symbolic display

heaven: There was a great fiery red dragon having seven heads and 10 horns, and on his heads were seven diadems.[a] [4] His tail swept away a third of the stars in heaven and hurled them to the earth. And the dragon stood in front of the woman who was about to give birth, so that when she did give birth he might devour her child. [5] But she gave birth to a Son—a male who is going to shepherd[b] all nations with an iron scepter—and her child was caught up to God and to His throne. [6] The woman fled into the wilderness, where she had a place prepared by God, to be fed there[c] for 1,260 days.

Dragon Thrown Out of Heaven

[7] Then war broke out in heaven: Michael and his angels fought against the dragon. The dragon and his angels also fought, [8] but he could not prevail, and there was no place for them in heaven any longer. [9] So the great dragon was thrown out—the ancient serpent, who is called the Devil[d] and Satan,[e] the one who deceives the whole world. He was thrown to earth, and his angels with him.

[10] Then I heard a loud voice in heaven say:

The salvation and the power
　and the kingdom of our God
and the authority of His •Messiah
　have now come,
because the accuser of our brothers
　has been thrown out:
the one who accuses them
　before our God day and night.
[11] They conquered him by the blood
　of the Lamb

and by the word of their testimony,
　for they did not love their lives
　　in the face of death.
[12] Therefore rejoice, O heavens,
　and you who dwell in them!
Woe to the earth and the sea,
　for the Devil has come down to you
　with great fury,
　because he knows he has
　　a short time.

The Woman Persecuted

[13] When the dragon saw that he had been thrown to earth, he persecuted the woman who gave birth to the male. [14] The woman was given two wings of a great eagle, so that she could fly from the serpent's presence to her place in the wilderness, where she was fed for a time, times, and half a time.[f] [15] From his mouth the serpent spewed water like a river after the woman, to sweep her away in a torrent. [16] But the earth helped the woman: the earth opened its mouth and swallowed up the river that the dragon had spewed from his mouth. [17] So the dragon was furious with the woman and left to wage war against the rest of her offspring[g]—those who keep the commandments of God and have the testimony about Jesus. [18] He[h] stood on the sand of the sea.[i]

Beast from the Sea

13 And I saw a beast coming up out of the sea. He[j] had 10 horns and seven heads. On his horns were 10 diadems, and on his heads were blasphemous names.[k] [2] The beast I saw was like a leopard, his feet were like a bear's, and his mouth was like a lion's mouth. The

[a]**12:3** Or crowns　[b]**12:5** Or rule　[c]**12:6** Lit God, that they might feed her there　[d]**12:9** Gk diabolos, meaning slanderer　[e]**12:9** Hb word meaning adversary　[f]**12:14** An expression occurring in Dn 7:25; 12:7 that means 3½ years or 42 months (Rv 11:2; 13:5) or 1,260 days (Rv 11:3)　[g]**12:17** Or seed　[h]**12:18** Other mss read I. "He" is apparently a reference to the dragon.　[i]**12:18** Some translations put Rv 12:18 either in Rv 12:17 or Rv 13:1.　[j]**13:1** The beasts in Rv 13:1,11 are customarily referred to as "he" or "him" rather than "it." The Gk word for a beast (therion) is grammatically neuter.　[k]**13:1** Other mss read heads was a blasphemous name

dragon gave him his power, his throne,
and great authority. 3 One of his heads appeared to be fatally wounded,[a] but his fatal
wound was healed. The whole earth was
amazed and followed the beast.[b] 4 They
worshiped the dragon because he gave authority to the beast. And they worshiped
the beast, saying, "Who is like the beast?
Who is able to wage war against him?"

Blasphemy from Beast

5 A mouth was given to him to speak
boasts and blasphemies. He was also
given authority to act[c] [d] for 42 months.
6 He began to speak[e] blasphemies against
God: to blaspheme His name and His
dwelling—those who dwell in heaven.
7 And he was permitted to wage war
against the saints and to conquer them.
He was also given authority over every
tribe, people, language, and nation.

Worship of Beast

8 All those who live on the earth will
worship him, everyone whose name was
not written from the foundation of the
world in the book[f] of life of the Lamb
who was slaughtered.[g]
9 If anyone has an ear, he should listen:

10 If anyone is destined for captivity,
into captivity he goes.
If anyone is to be killed[h] with a sword,
with a sword he will be killed.

Here is the endurance and the faith of
the saints.[i]

Second Beast from Earth

11 Then I saw another beast coming up
out of the earth; he had two horns like a
lamb,[j] but he sounded like a dragon.
12 He exercises all the authority of the
first beast on his behalf and compels the
earth and those who live on it to worship the first beast, whose fatal wound
was healed. 13 He also performs great
signs, even causing fire to come down
from heaven to earth before people.
14 He deceives those who live on the
earth because of the signs that he is permitted to perform on behalf of the beast,
telling those who live on the earth to
make an image[k] of the beast who had the
sword wound yet lived. 15 He was permitted to give a spirit[l] to the image of
the beast, so that the image of the beast
could both speak and cause whoever
would not worship the image of the
beast to be killed. 16 And he requires everyone—small and great, rich and poor,
free and slave—to be given a mark[m] on
his[n] right hand or on his[n] forehead, 17 so
that no one can buy or sell unless he has
the mark: the beast's name or the number of his name.

Number 666

18 Here is wisdom:[o] The one who has
understanding must calculate[p] the number of the beast, because it is the number of a man.[q] His number is 666.[r]

Lamb and the 144,000

14 Then I looked, and there on
Mount Zion stood the Lamb, and
with Him were 144,000 who had His
name and His Father's name written on
their foreheads. 2 I heard a sound[s] from
heaven like the sound of cascading waters and like the rumbling of loud thunder. The sound I heard was also like
harpists playing on their harps. 3 They

[a]**13:3** Lit *be slain to death* [b]**13:3** Lit *amazed after the beast* [c]**13:5** Other mss read *wage war* [d]**13:5** Or *to rule* [e]**13:6** Lit *He opened his mouth in* [f]**13:8** Or *scroll* [g]**13:8** Or *written in the book of life of the Lamb who was slaughtered from the foundation of the world* [h]**13:10** Other mss read *anyone kills* [i]**13:10** Or *This calls for the endurance and faith of the saints.* [j]**13:11** Or *ram* [k]**13:14** Or *statue*, or *likeness* [l]**13:15** Or *give breath*, or *give life* [m]**13:16** Or *stamp*, or *brand* [n]**13:16** Lit *their* [o]**13:18** Or *This calls for wisdom* [p]**13:18** Or *count*, or *figure out* [q]**13:18** Or *is a man's number*, or *is the number of a person* [r]**13:18** One Gk ms plus other ancient evidence read *616* [s]**14:2** Or *voice*

sang[a] a new song before the throne and before the four living creatures and the elders, but no one could learn the song except the 144,000 who had been redeemed[b] from the earth. [4] These are the ones not defiled with women, for they have kept their virginity. These are the ones who follow the Lamb wherever He goes. They were redeemed[c][b] from the human race as the •firstfruits for God and the Lamb. [5] No lie was found in their mouths; they are blameless.

Proclamation of Three Angels

[6] Then I saw another angel flying in mid-heaven, having the eternal gospel to announce to the inhabitants of the earth—to every nation, tribe, language, and people. [7] He spoke with a loud voice: "Fear God and give Him glory, because the hour of His judgment has come. Worship the Maker of heaven and earth, the sea and springs of water."

[8] A second angel[d] followed, saying: "It has fallen, Babylon the Great has fallen,[e] who made all nations drink the wine of her sexual immorality,[f] which brings wrath."

[9] And a third angel[g] followed them and spoke with a loud voice: "If anyone worships the beast and his image and receives a mark on his forehead or on his hand, [10] he will also drink the wine of God's wrath, which is mixed full strength in the cup of His anger. He will be tormented with fire and sulfur in the sight of the holy angels and in the sight of the Lamb, [11] and the smoke of their torment will go up forever and ever. There is no rest[h] day or night for those who worship the beast and his image, or anyone who receives the mark of his name. [12] Here is the endurance[i][j] of the saints, who keep the commandments of God and the faith in Jesus."[k]

[13] Then I heard a voice from heaven saying, "Write: Blessed are the dead who die in the Lord from now on."

"Yes," says the Spirit, "let them rest from their labors, for their works follow them!"

Angels Harvest Earth

[14] Then I looked, and there was a white cloud, and One like the Son of Man[l] was seated on the cloud, with a gold crown on His head and a sharp sickle in His hand. [15] Another angel came out of the sanctuary, crying out in a loud voice to the One who was seated on the cloud, "Use your sickle and reap, for the time to reap has come, since the harvest of the earth is ripe." [16] So the One seated on the cloud swung His sickle over the earth, and the earth was harvested.

[17] Then another angel who also had a sharp sickle came out of the sanctuary in heaven. [18] Yet another angel, who had authority over fire, came from the altar, and he called with a loud voice to the one who had the sharp sickle, "Use your sharp sickle and gather the clusters of grapes from earth's vineyard, because its grapes have ripened." [19] So the angel swung his sickle toward earth and gathered the grapes from earth's vineyard, and he threw them into the great winepress of God's wrath. [20] Then the press was trampled outside the city, and blood flowed out of the press up to the horses' bridles for about 180 miles.[m]

---

[a]**14:3** Other mss add *as it were*   [b]**14:3,4** Or *purchased*   [c]**14:4** Other mss add *by Jesus*   [d]**14:8** Lit *Another angel, a second*   [e]**14:8** Other mss omit the second *has fallen*   [f]**14:8** Or *wine of her passionate immorality*   [g]**14:9** Lit *Another angel, a third*   [h]**14:11** Lit *They have no rest*   [i]**14:12** Or *This calls for the endurance of the saints*   [j]**14:12** This is what the endurance of the saints means   [k]**14:12** Or *and faith in Jesus,* or *their faith in,* or *faithfulness to Jesus*   [l]**14:14** Or *like a son of man*   [m]**14:20** Lit *1,600 stadia*

Praise on Sea of Glass

15 Then I saw another great and awe-inspiring sign[a] in heaven: seven angels with the seven last plagues, for with them, God's wrath will be completed. [2] I also saw something like a sea of glass mixed with fire, and those who had won the victory from the beast, his image,[b] and the number of his name, were standing on the sea of glass with harps from God.[c] [3] They sang the song of God's servant Moses, and the song of the Lamb:

> Great and awe-inspiring are
>   Your works, Lord God,
>   the Almighty;
> righteous and true are Your ways,
>   King of the Nations.
> [4] Lord, who will not fear and glorify
>   Your name?
> Because You alone are holy,
> because all the nations will come
>   and worship before You,
> because Your righteous acts
> have been revealed.

Seven Angels, Seven Plagues

[5] After this I looked, and the heavenly sanctuary—the tabernacle of testimony—was opened. [6] Out of the sanctuary came the seven angels with the seven plagues, dressed in clean, bright linen, with gold sashes wrapped around their chests. [7] One of the four living creatures gave the seven angels <u>seven gold bowls filled with the wrath of God</u> who lives forever and ever. [8] Then the sanctuary was filled with smoke from God's glory and from His power, and no one could enter the sanctuary until the seven plagues of the seven angels were completed.

Pouring Out First Bowl

16 Then I heard a loud voice from the sanctuary saying to the seven angels, "Go and pour out the seven[d] bowls of God's wrath on the earth." [2] The first went and poured out his bowl on the earth, and severely painful sores[e] broke out on the people who had the mark of the beast and who worshiped his image.

Pouring Out Second Bowl

[3] The second[f] poured out his bowl into the sea. It turned to blood like a dead man's, and all life[g] in the sea died.

Pouring Out Third Bowl

[4] The third[f] poured out his bowl into the rivers and the springs of water, and they became blood. [5] I heard the angel of the waters say:

> You are righteous, who is
>   and who was, the Holy One,
>   for You have decided these things.
> [6] Because they poured out the blood
>   of the saints and the prophets,
> You also gave them blood to drink;
>   they deserve it!

[7] Then I heard someone from the altar say:

> Yes, Lord God, the Almighty,
> true and righteous are
>   Your judgments.

Pouring Out Fourth Bowl

[8] The fourth[f] poured out his bowl on the sun. He[h] was given the power[i] to burn people with fire, [9] and people were burned by the intense heat. So <u>they blasphemed the name of God</u> who had the power[i] over these plagues, and they did not repent and give Him glory.

[a]**15:1** Or *and awesome symbolic display*   [b]**15:2** Other mss add *his mark*   [c]**15:2** Or *harps of God*; that is, harps belonging to the service of God   [d]**16:1** Other mss omit *seven*   [e]**16:2** Lit *and a severely painful sore*   [f]**16:3,4,8** Other mss add *angel*   [g]**16:3** Lit *and every soul of life*   [h]**16:8** Or *It*   [i]**16:8,9** Or *authority*

Pouring Out Fifth Bowl

[10] The fifth[a] poured out his bowl on the throne of the beast, and his kingdom was plunged into darkness. People[b] gnawed their tongues from pain [11] and blasphemed the God of heaven because of their pains and their sores, yet they did not repent of their actions.

Pouring Out Sixth Bowl

[12] The sixth[a] poured out his bowl on the great river Euphrates, and its water was dried up to prepare the way for the kings from the east. [13] Then I saw three unclean spirits like frogs ⌊coming⌋ from the dragon's mouth, from the beast's mouth, and from the mouth of the false prophet. [14] For they are spirits of demons performing signs, who travel to the kings of the whole world to assemble them for the battle of the great day of God, the Almighty.

[15] "Look, I am coming like a thief. Blessed is the one who is alert and remains clothed[c] so that he may not go naked, and they see his shame."

[16] So they assembled them at the place called in Hebrew Armagedon.[d] [e]

Pouring Out Seventh Bowl

[17] Then the seventh[a] poured out his bowl into the air,[f] and a loud voice came out of the sanctuary,[g] from the throne, saying, "It is done!" [18] There were lightnings, rumblings, and thunders. And a severe earthquake occurred like no other since man has been on the earth— so great was the quake. [19] The great city split into three parts, and the cities of the nations[h] fell. Babylon the Great was remembered in God's presence; He gave her the cup filled with the wine of His fierce anger. [20] Every island fled, and the mountains disappeared.[i] [21] Enormous hailstones, each weighing about 100 pounds,[j] fell from heaven on the people, and they[k] blasphemed God for the plague of hail because that plague was extremely severe.

Woman and Scarlet Beast

17 Then one of the seven angels who had the seven bowls came and spoke with me: "Come, I will show you the judgment of the notorious prostitute[l] who sits on many[m] waters. [2] The kings of the earth committed sexual immorality with her, and those who live on the earth became drunk on the wine of her sexual immorality." [3] So he carried me away in the Spirit[n] to a desert. I saw a woman sitting on a scarlet beast that was covered[o] with blasphemous names, having seven heads and 10 horns. [4] The woman was dressed in purple and scarlet, adorned with gold, precious stones, and pearls. She had a gold cup in her hand filled with everything vile and with the impurities of her[p] prostitution. [5] On her forehead a cryptic name was written:

> BABYLON THE GREAT THE
> MOTHER OF PROSTITUTES
> AND OF THE VILE THINGS
> OF THE EARTH

[6] Then I saw that the woman was drunk on the blood of the saints and on the blood of the witnesses to Jesus. When I saw her, I was utterly astounded.

---

[a]**16:10,12,17** Other mss add *angel*   [b]**16:10** Lit *They*   [c]**16:15** Or *and guards his clothes*   [d]**16:16** Other mss read *Armageddon*; other mss read *Harmegedon*; other mss read *Mageddon*; other mss read *Magedon*
[e]**16:16** Traditionally *the hill of Megiddo*, a great city that guarded the pass between the coast and the valley of Jezreel or Esdraelon; see Jdg 5:19; 2 Kg 9:27   [f]**16:17** Or *on the air*   [g]**16:17** Other mss add *of heaven*   [h]**16:19** Or *the Gentile cities*   [i]**16:20** Lit *mountains were not found*   [j]**16:21** Lit *about a talent*; talents varied in weight upwards from 75 pounds   [k]**16:21** Lit *people*   [l]**17:1** Traditionally, *the great whore*   [m]**17:1** Or *by many*   [n]**17:3** Or *in spirit*   [o]**17:3** Lit *was filled*   [p]**17:4** Other mss read *of earth's*

Meaning of Woman and Beast

7 Then the angel said to me, "Why are you astounded? I will tell you the secret meaning[a] of the woman and of the beast, with the seven heads and the 10 horns, that carries her. 8 The beast that you saw was, and is not, and is about to come up from the •abyss and go to destruction. Those who live on the earth whose names were not written in the book of life from the foundation of the world will be astounded when they see the beast that was, and is not, and will be present ⌊again⌋.

9 "Here is the mind with wisdom:[b] the seven heads are seven mountains on which the woman is seated. 10 They are also seven kings:[c] five have fallen, one is, the other has not yet come, and when he comes, he must remain for a little while. 11 The beast that was and is not, is himself the eighth, yet is of the seven and goes to destruction. 12 The 10 horns you saw are 10 kings who have not yet received a kingdom, but they will receive authority as kings with the beast for one hour. 13 These have one purpose, and they give their power and authority to the beast. 14 These will make war against the Lamb, but the Lamb will conquer them because He is Lord of lords and King of kings. Those with Him are called and elect and faithful."

15 He also said to me, "The waters you saw, where the prostitute was seated, are peoples, multitudes, nations, and languages. 16 The 10 horns you saw, and the beast, will hate the prostitute. They will make her desolate and naked, devour her flesh, and burn her up with fire. 17 For God has put it into their hearts to carry out His plan by having one purpose, and to give their kingdom[d] to the beast until God's words are accomplished. 18 And the woman you saw is the great city that has an empire[e] over the kings of the earth."

Fall of Babylon the Great

18 After this I saw another angel with great authority coming down from heaven, and the earth was illuminated by his splendor. 2 He cried in a mighty voice:

> It has fallen,[f] Babylon the Great
>   has fallen!
> She has become a dwelling
>   for demons,
> a haunt[g] for every unclean spirit,
> a haunt[g] for every unclean bird,
> and a haunt[g] for every unclean
>   and despicable beast.[h]
> 3 For all the nations have drunk[i]
>   the wine of her sexual immorality,
>   which brings wrath.
> The kings of the earth
>   have committed
>   sexual immorality with her,
> and the merchants of the earth
>   have grown wealthy
>   from her excessive luxury.

Heavenly Voice Says Flee!

4 Then I heard another voice from heaven:

> Come out of her, My people,
> so that you will not share
>   in her sins,
> or receive any of her plagues.
> 5 For her sins are piled up[j] to heaven,
>   and God has remembered
>   her crimes.
> 6 Pay her back the way she also paid,

---

a17:7 Lit the mystery   b17:9 Or This calls for the mind with wisdom   c17:10 Some editors or translators put They are also seven kings: in v. 9.   d17:17 Or sovereignty   e17:18 Or has sovereignty or rulership   f18:2 Other mss omit It has fallen   g18:2 Or prison   h18:2 Other mss omit the words and a haunt for every unclean beast. The words and despicable then refer to the bird of the previous line.   i18:3 Other mss read have collapsed; other mss read have fallen   j18:5 Or sins have reached up

and double it
according to her works.
In the cup in which she mixed,
mix a double portion for her.
7 As much as she glorified herself
and lived luxuriously,
give her that much torment
and grief.
Because she says in her heart,
'I sit as queen;
I am not a widow,
and I will never see grief,'
8 therefore her plagues will come
in one day[a]—
death, and grief, and famine.
She will be burned up with fire,
because the Lord God
who judges her is mighty.

World Mourns Babylon's Fall

9 The kings of the earth who have committed sexual immorality and lived luxuriously with her will weep and mourn over her when they see the smoke of her burning. 10 They stand far off in fear of her torment, saying:

Woe, woe, the great city,
Babylon, the mighty city!
For in a single hour[a]
your judgment has come.

11 The merchants of the earth will also weep and mourn over her, because no one buys their merchandise any longer— 12 merchandise of gold, silver, precious stones, and pearls; fine fabrics of linen, purple, silk, and scarlet; all kinds of fragrant wood products; objects of ivory; objects of expensive wood, brass,[b] iron, and marble; 13 cinnamon, spice,[c] [d] incense, myrrh,[e] and frankincense; wine, olive oil, fine wheat flour, and grain; cattle and sheep; horses and carriages; and human bodies and souls.[f] [g]

14 The fruit you craved has left you.
All your splendid
and glamorous things are gone;
they will never find them again.

15 The merchants of these things, who became rich from her, will stand far off in fear of her torment, weeping and mourning, 16 saying:

Woe, woe, the great city,
clothed in fine linen, purple,
and scarlet,
adorned with gold, precious stones,
and pearls;
17 because in a single hour[a]
such fabulous wealth
was destroyed!

And every shipmaster, seafarer, the sailors, and all who do business by sea, stood far off 18 as they watched the smoke from her burning and kept crying out: "Who is like the great city?" 19 They threw dust on their heads and kept crying out, weeping, and mourning:

Woe, woe, the great city,
where all those who have ships
on the sea
became rich from her wealth;
because in a single hour[a]
she was destroyed.
20 Rejoice over her, heaven, and you
saints, apostles, and prophets,
because God has executed
your judgment on her![h]

Finality of Babylon's Fall

21 Then a mighty angel picked up a stone like a large millstone and threw it into the sea, saying:

[a]18:8,10,17,19 Suddenly   [b]18:12 Or bronze, or copper   [c]18:13 Other mss omit spice   [d]18:13 Or amomum, an aromatic plant   [e]18:13 Or perfume   [f]18:13 Or carriages; and slaves, namely, human beings   [g]18:13 Slaves; "bodies" was the Gk way of referring to slaves; "souls of men" was the Hb way.   [h]18:20 Or God pronounced on her the judgment she passed on you; see Rv 18:6

In this way, Babylon the great city
  will be thrown down violently
  and never be found again.
22 The sound of harpists, musicians,
    flutists, and trumpeters
  will never be heard in you again;
  no craftsman of any trade
  will ever be found in you again;
  the sound of a mill
  will never be heard in you again;
23 the light of a lamp will never shine
    in you again;
  and the voice of a groom and bride
  will never be heard in you again.
  ⌊All this will happen⌋
  because your merchants
    were the nobility of the earth,
  because all the nations
    were deceived by your sorcery,[a]
24 and the blood of prophets
    and saints,
  and all those slaughtered on earth,
    was found in you.[b]

Heaven Exults over Babylon

19 After this I heard something like
the loud voice of a vast multitude
in heaven, saying:

Hallelujah![c]
Salvation, glory, and power belong
  to our God,
2 because His judgments are true[d]
    and righteous,
  because He has judged
    the notorious prostitute
  who corrupted the earth
    with her sexual immorality;
  and He has avenged the blood
    of His servants that was
    on her hands.

3 A second time they said:

Hallelujah![e]
Her smoke ascends forever
  and ever!

4 Then the 24 elders and the four living creatures fell down and worshiped
God, who is seated on the throne, saying:

•Amen! Hallelujah![e]

5 A voice came from the throne, saying:

Praise our God,
  all you His servants,
    you who fear Him,
  both small and great!

Marriage of Lamb Announced

6 Then I heard something like the
voice of a vast multitude, like the sound
of cascading waters, and like the rumbling of loud thunder, saying:

Hallelujah[e] —because
  our Lord God, the Almighty,
  has begun to reign!
7 Let us be glad, rejoice,
  and give Him glory,
  because the marriage of the Lamb
    has come,
  and His wife has prepared herself.
8 She was permitted to wear
  fine linen, bright and pure.

For the fine linen represents the righteous acts of the saints.

9 Then he[f] said to me, "Write: Blessed
are those invited to the marriage feast of
the Lamb!" He also said to me, "These
words of God are true." 10 Then I fell at
his feet to worship him, but he said to
me, "Don't do that! I am a fellow •slave
with you and your brothers who have

a18:23 Ancient sorcery or witchcraft often used spells and drugs. Here the term may be non-literal, that is, Babylon drugged the nations with her beauty and power. b18:24 Lit in her c19:1 Lit Praise Yahweh; the Gk word is transliterated hallelujah from a Hb expression of praise and is used in many places in the OT, such as Ps 106:1. d19:2 Valid; see Jn 8:16; 19:35 e19:3,4,6 See note at Rv 19:1 f19:9 Probably an angel; see Rv 17:1; 22:8-9

the testimony about[a] Jesus. Worship God, because the testimony about[a] Jesus is the spirit of prophecy."

Rider on a White Horse

[11] Then I saw heaven opened, and there was a white horse! Its rider is called Faithful and True, and in righteousness He judges and makes war. [12] His eyes were like a fiery flame, and on His head were many crowns. He had a name written that no one knows except Himself. [13] He wore a robe stained with blood,[b] and His name is called the Word of God. [14] The armies that were in heaven followed Him on white horses, wearing pure white linen. [15] From His mouth came a sharp[c] sword, so that with it He might strike the nations. He will shepherd[d] them with an iron scepter. He will also trample the winepress of the fierce anger of God, the Almighty. [16] And on His robe and on His thigh He has a name written:

> **KING OF KINGS AND LORD OF LORDS**

Beast and His Armies Defeated

[17] Then I saw an angel standing in the sun, and he cried out in a loud voice, saying to all the birds flying in midheaven, "Come, gather together for the great supper of God, [18] so that you may eat the flesh of kings, the flesh of commanders, the flesh of mighty men, the flesh of horses and of their riders, and the flesh of everyone, both free and •slave, small and great."

[19] Then I saw the beast, the kings of the earth, and their armies gathered together to wage war against the rider on the horse and against His army. [20] But the beast was taken prisoner, and along with him the false prophet, who had performed signs on his authority,[e] by which he deceived those who accepted the mark of the beast and those who worshiped his image. Both of them were thrown alive into the lake of fire that burns with sulfur. [21] The rest were killed with the sword that came from the mouth of the rider on the horse, and all the birds were filled with their flesh.

Satan Bound

20 Then I saw an angel coming down from heaven with the key to the •abyss and a great chain in his hand. [2] He seized the dragon, that ancient serpent who is the Devil and Satan,[f] and bound him for 1,000 years. [3] He threw him into the abyss, closed it, and put a seal on it so that he would no longer deceive the nations until the 1,000 years were completed. After that, he must be released for a short time.

Saints Reign with the Messiah

[4] Then I saw thrones, and people seated on them who were given authority to judge. ⌊I⌋ also ⌊saw⌋ the souls of those who had been beheaded[g] because of their testimony about Jesus and because of God's word, who had not worshiped the beast or his image, and who had not accepted the mark on their foreheads or their hands. They came to life and reigned with the •Messiah for 1,000 years. [5] The rest of the dead did not come to life until the 1,000 years were completed. This is the first resurrection. [6] Blessed and holy is the one who shares in the first resurrection! The second

[a]**19:10** Or *testimony to* [b]**19:13** Or *a robe dipped in* [c]**19:15** Other mss add *double-edged* [d]**19:15** Or *rule* [e]**19:20** Lit *signs before him* [f]**20:2** Other mss add *who deceives the whole world* [g]**20:4** All who had given their lives for their faith in Christ

death has no power[a] over these, but they will be priests of God and the Messiah, and they will reign with Him for 1,000 years.

Satanic Rebellion Crushed

[7] When the 1,000 years are completed, Satan will be released from his prison [8] and will go out to deceive the nations at the four corners of the earth, Gog and Magog, to gather them for battle. Their number is like the sand of the sea. [9] They came up over the surface of the earth and surrounded the encampment of the saints, the beloved city. Then fire came down from heaven[b] and consumed them. [10] The Devil who deceived them was thrown into the lake of fire and sulfur where the beast and the false prophet are, and they will be tormented day and night forever and ever.

Great White Throne Judgment

[11] Then I saw a great white throne and One seated on it. Earth and heaven fled from His presence, and no place was found for them. [12] I also saw the dead, the great and the small, standing before the throne, and books were opened. Another book was opened, which is the book of life, and the dead were judged according to their works by what was written in the books. [13] Then the sea gave up its dead, and Death and •Hades gave up their dead; all[c] were judged according to their works. [14] Death and Hades were thrown into the lake of fire. This is the second death, the lake of fire.[d] [15] And anyone not found written in the book of life was thrown into the lake of fire.

New Heaven, New Earth

21 Then I saw a new heaven and a new earth, for the first heaven and the first earth had passed away, and the sea existed no longer. [2] I also saw the Holy City, new Jerusalem, coming down out of heaven from God, prepared like a bride adorned for her husband.

[3] Then I heard a loud voice from the throne:[e]

Look! God's dwelling[f] is
    with men,
and He will live with them.
They will be His people,
and God Himself will be with them
    and be their God.[g]
[4] He will wipe away every tear
    from their eyes.
Death will exist no longer;
grief, crying, and pain will exist
    no longer,
because the previous things[h]
    have passed away.

John Commanded to Write

[5] Then the One seated on the throne said, "Look! I am making everything new." He also said, "Write, because these words[i] are faithful and true." [6] And He said to me, "It is done! I am the •Alpha and the Omega, the Beginning and the End. I will give to the thirsty from the spring of living water as a gift. [7] The victor will inherit these things, and I will be his God, and he will be My son. [8] But the cowards, unbelievers,[j] vile, murderers, sexually immoral, sorcerers, idolaters, and all liars—their share will be in the lake that burns with fire and sulfur, which is the second death."

---

[a]**20:6** Or *authority*   [b]**20:9** Other mss add *from God*   [c]**20:13** Lit *each*   [d]**20:14** Other mss omit *the lake of fire*   [e]**21:3** Other mss read *from heaven*   [f]**21:3** Or *tent,* or *tabernacle*   [g]**21:3** Other mss omit *and be their God*   [h]**21:4** Or *the first things*   [i]**21:5** Other mss add *of God*   [j]**21:8** Other mss add *the sinful*

The New Jerusalem

⁹ Then one of the seven angels, who had held the seven bowls filled with the seven last plagues, came and spoke with me: "Come, I will show you the bride, the wife of the Lamb." ¹⁰ He then carried me away in the Spiritᵃ to a great and high mountain and showed me the holy city, Jerusalem, coming down out of heaven from God, ¹¹ arrayed with God's glory. Her radiance was like a very precious stone, like a jasper stone, bright as crystal. ¹² ₍The city₎ had a massive high wall, with 12 gates. Twelve angels were at the gates; ₍on the gates₎, names were inscribed, the names of the 12 tribes of the sons of Israel. ¹³ There were three gates on the east, three gates on the north, three gates on the south, and three gates on the west. ¹⁴ The city wall had 12 foundations, and on them were the 12 names of the Lamb's 12 apostles.

¹⁵ The one who spoke with me had a gold measuring rod to measure the city, its gates, and its wall. ¹⁶ The city is laid out in a square; its length and width are the same. He measured the city with the rod at 12,000 *stadia*.ᵇ Its length, width, and height are equal. ¹⁷ Then he measured its wall, 144 •cubits according to human measurement, which the angel used. ¹⁸ The building material of its wall was jasper, and the city was pure gold like clear glass.

¹⁹ The foundations of the city wall were adorned with every kind of precious stone:

the first foundation jasper,
the second sapphire,
the third chalcedony,
the fourth emerald,
²⁰ the fifth sardonyx,
the sixth carnelian,
the seventh chrysolite,
the eighth beryl,
the ninth topaz,
the tenth chrysoprase,
the eleventh jacinth,
the twelfth amethyst.

²¹ The 12 gates are 12 pearls; each individual gate was made of a single pearl. The broad streetᶜ of the city was pure gold, like transparent glass.

Sanctuary: Lord God and Lamb

²² I did not see a sanctuary in it, because the Lord God the Almighty and the Lamb are its sanctuary. ²³ The city does not need the sun or the moon to shine on it, because God's glory illuminates it, and its lamp is the Lamb. ²⁴ The nationsᵈ will walk in its light, and the kings of the earth will bring their glory into it.ᵉ ²⁵ Each day its gates will never close because it will never be night there. ²⁶ They will bring the glory and honor of the nations into it.ᶠ ²⁷ Nothing profane will ever enter it: no one who does what is vile or false, but only those written in the Lamb's book of life.

Tree of Life

22 Then he showed me the riverᵍ of living water, sparkling like crystal, flowing from the throne of God and of the Lamb ² down the middle of the broad street ₍of the city₎. On both sides of the river was the tree of lifeʰ bearing 12 kinds of fruit, producing its fruit every month. The leaves of the tree are for healing the nations, ³ and there will no longer be any curse. The throne of God and of the Lamb will be in the city,ⁱ and His servants will serve Him. ⁴ They will

---

ᵃ**21:10** Or *in spirit* ᵇ**21:16** A *stadion* (sg) equals about 600 feet; the total is about 1,400 miles. ᶜ**21:21** Or *The public square* ᵈ**21:24** Other mss add *of those who are saved* ᵉ**21:24** Other mss read *will bring to Him the nations' glory and honor* ᶠ**21:26** Other mss add *in order that they might go in* ᵍ**22:1** Other mss read *pure river* ʰ**22:2** Or *was a tree of life*, or *was a tree that gives life* ⁱ**22:3** Lit *in it*

see His face, and His name will be on their foreheads. ⁵ Night will no longer exist, and people will not need lamplight or sunlight, because the Lord God will give them light. And they will reign forever and ever.

"I Am Coming Quickly!"

⁶ Then he said to me, "These words are faithful and true. And the Lord, the God of the spirits of the prophets,ᵃ has sent His angel to show His servants what must quickly take place."ᵇ

⁷ "Look, I am coming quickly! Blessed is the one who keeps the prophetic words of this book."

⁸ I, John, am the one who heard and saw these things. When I heard and saw them, I fell down to worship at the feet of the angel who had shown them to me. ⁹ But he said to me, "Don't do that! I am a fellow •slave with you, your brothers the prophets, and those who keep the words of this book. Worship God." ¹⁰ He also said to me, "Don't seal the prophetic words of this book, because the time is near. ¹¹ Let the unrighteous go on in unrighteousness; let the filthy go on being made filthy; let the righteous go on in righteousness; and let the holy go on being made holy."

¹² "Look! I am coming quickly, and My reward is with Me to repay each person according to what he has done. ¹³ I am the •Alpha and the Omega, the First and the Last, the Beginning and the End.

¹⁴ "Blessed are those who wash their robes,ᶜ so that they may have the right to the tree of life and may enter the city by the gates. ¹⁵ Outside are the dogs, the sorcerers, the sexually immoral, the murderers, the idolaters, and everyone who loves and practices lying.

¹⁶ "I, Jesus, have sent My angel to attest these things to youᵈ for the churches. I am the Root and the Offspring of David, the Bright Morning Star."

John's Testimony and Warning

¹⁷ Both the Spirit and the bride say, "Come!" Anyone who hears should say, "Come!" And the one who is thirsty should come. Whoever desires should take the living water as a gift.

¹⁸ I testify to everyone who hears the prophetic words of this book: If anyone adds to them, God will add to him the plagues that are written in this book. ¹⁹ And if anyone takes away from the words of this prophetic book, God will take away his share of the tree of life and the holy city, written in this book.

²⁰ He who testifies about these things says, "Yes, I am coming quickly." •Amen! Come, Lord Jesus!

²¹ The grace of the Lord Jesusᵉ be with all the saints.ᶠ Amen.ᵍ

ᵃ**22:6** Other mss read *God of the holy prophets*   ᵇ**22:6** Or *soon*   ᶜ**22:14** Other mss read *who keep His commandments*   ᵈ**22:16** *you* (pl in Gk)   ᵉ**22:21** Other mss add *Christ*   ᶠ**22:21** Other mss omit *the saints*   ᵍ**22:21** Other mss omit *Amen.*

HOLMAN CSB BULLET NOTES

Holman CSB Bullet Notes are one of the unique features of the Holman Christian Standard Bible®. These notes explain frequently used biblical words or terms. These "bullet" words (for example: •abyss) are normally marked with a bullet only on their first occurrence in a chapter of the biblical text. However, certain important or easily misunderstood terms, such as •Jews or •slaves, will have more than one bullet per chapter. Other frequently used words, like •gate, are marked with bullets only where the use of the word fits the definitions given below. A few words in footnotes, like •acrostic, also have a bullet.

Abaddon	Either the grave or the realm of the dead
Abba	The Aramaic word for "father"
abyss	The *bottomless pit* or *the depths* (of the sea); the prison for Satan and the demons
acrostic	A device in Hebrew poetry in which each verse begins with a successive letter of the Hebrew alphabet
advocate	(see "Counselor/advocate")
Almighty	(see "God Almighty")
Alpha and Omega	The first and last letters of the Greek alphabet; it is used to refer to God the Father in Rv 1:8 and 21:6, and to Jesus, God the Son, in Rv 22:13.
Amen	The transliteration of a Hebrew word signifying that something is certain, valid, truthful, or faithful; it is often used at the end of biblical songs, hymns, and prayers.
Arabah	The section of the Great Rift in Palestine, extending from the Jordan Valley and the Dead Sea to the Gulf of Aqabah. The Hebrew word can also be translated as "plain," referring to any plain or to any part of the Arabah.
Asaph	A musician appointed by David to oversee the music used in worship at the Temple; 12 psalms are attributed to Asaph.
Asherah pole(s)	(see "Asherah(s)")
Asherah(s)	A Canaanite fertility goddess, who was the mother of the god Baal; also the wooden poles associated with the worship of her
Ashtoreth(s)	A Canaanite goddess of fertility, love, and war, who was the daughter of Asherah and consort of Baal; the plural form of her name in Hebrew is *Ashtaroth*.
Asia	A Roman province that is now part of modern Turkey; it did not refer to the modern continent of Asia.

asleep	A term used in reference to those who have died
atone/atonement	A theological term for God's provision to deal with human sin. In the OT, it primarily means purification. In some contexts forgiveness, pardon, expiation, propitiation, or reconciliation is included. The basis of atonement is substitutionary sacrifice offered in faith. The OT sacrifices were types and shadows of the great and final sacrifice of Jesus on the cross.
Baal	A fertility god who was the main god of the Canaanite religion and the god of rain and thunderstorms; also the Hebrew word meaning "lord," "master," "owner," or "husband"
Beelzebul	A term of slander, which was variously interpreted "lord of flies," "lord of dung," or "ruler of demons"; 2 Kg 1:2; Mk 3:22
burnt offering(s)	Or *holocaust*, an offering completely burned to ashes; it was used in connection with worship, seeking God's favor, expiating sin, or averting judgment.
cause the downfall of/ causes to sin	The Greek word *skandalizo* has a root meaning of "snare" or "trap," but has no real English counterpart.
centurion	A Roman officer who commanded about 100 soldiers
Cephas	The Aramaic word for *rock*; it is parallel to the Greek word *petros* from which the English name Peter is derived; Jn 1:42; 1 Co 1:12.
cherubim	A class of winged angels, associated with the throne of God, who function as guardians and who prevented Adam and Eve from returning to the garden of Eden
chief priest(s)	A group of Jewish temple officers that included the highpriest, captain of the temple, temple overseers, and treasurers
company/regiment	Or *cohort*, a Roman military unit that numbered as many as 600 men
completely destroy	(see "set apart for destruction/completely destroy")
Counselor/advocate	The Greek word *parakletos* means one called alongside to help, counsel, or protect; it is used of the Holy Spirit in Jn and in 1 Jn.
cubit	An OT measurement of distance that equaled about 18 inches
Cush/Cushite	The lands of the Nile in southern Egypt, including Nubia and Northern Sudan; the people who lived in that region
Decapolis	Originally a federation of 10 Gentile towns east of the Jordan River

denarius	A small silver Roman coin, which was equal to a day's wage for a common laborer
divination	An attempt to foresee future events or discover hidden knowledge by means of physical objects such as water, arrows, flying birds, or animal livers
engaged	Jewish engagement was a binding agreement that could only be broken by divorce.
ephod	A vestlike garment, extending below the waist and worn under the breastpiece, which was used by both the priests and the high priest
everyone/human race	Literally, *sons of man* or *sons of Adam*
family redeemer	A family member who had certain obligations of marriage, redeeming an estate, and punishment of a wrongdoer
fear(s) God or the LORD/ the fear of the LORD	No single English word conveys every aspect of the word *fear* in this phrase. The meaning includes worshipful submission, reverential awe, and obedient respect to the covenant-keeping God of Israel.
firstfruits	The agricultural products harvested first and given to God as an offering; also the first of more products to come
fellowship sacrifice(s) or offering(s)	An animal offering was given to maintain and strengthen a person's relationship with God. It was not required as a remedy for impurity or sin but was an expression of thanksgiving for various blessings. An important function of this sacrifice was to provide meat for the priests and the participants in the sacrifice; it was also called the *peace offering* or the *sacrifice of well-being.*
gate(s)	The center for community discussions, political meetings, and trying of court cases
Gittith	Perhaps an instrument, musical term, tune from Gath, or song for the grape harvest
God Almighty	The Hebrew word is *El Shaddai*; *El* = "God," but the meaning of *Shaddai* is disputed; traditionally it is translated "Almighty".
grain offering(s)	An offering given along with animal sacrifices or given by itself. A portion was burnt and the priests and participant ate the remainder.
Hades	The Greek word for the place of the dead; it corresponds to the Hebrew word *Sheol.*
Hallelujah!	Or *Praise the LORD!;* it literally means *Praise Yah!* (a shortened form of *Yahweh*)

headquarters/palace	The Latin word *Praetorium* was used by Greek writers for the residence of the Roman governor; it may also refer to military headquarters, the imperial court, or the emperor's guard.
Hebrew	Or *Aramaic*; the translation of this word is debated since some claim Aramaic was commonly spoken in Palestine during NT times. More recently others claim that Hebrew was the spoken language.
hell/hellfire	Greek *Gehenna*; Aramaic for Valley of Hinnom on the south side of Jerusalem; it was formerly a place of human sacrifice and in NT times a place for the burning of garbage; the place of final judgment for those rejecting Christ.
Herod	The name of the Idumean family ruling Palestine from 37 B.C. to A.D. 95; the main rulers from this family mentioned in the NT are:
Herod I	(37 B.C.–4 B.C.) also known as Herod the Great; built the great temple in Jerusalem and massacred the male babies in Bethlehem
Herod Antipas	(4 B.C.–A.D. 39) son of Herod the Great; ruled one-fourth of his father's kingdom (Galilee and Perea); killed John the Baptist and mocked Jesus
Agrippa I	(A.D. 37–44) grandson of Herod the Great; beheaded James the apostle and imprisoned Peter
Agrippa II	(A.D. 52–c. 95) great-grandson of Herod the Great; heard Paul's defense
Herodians	Political supporters of Herod the Great and his family
Higgaion	Perhaps a musical notation, a device denoting a pause in an instrumental interlude, or a murmuring harp tone
high place(s)	An ancient place of worship most often associated with pagan religions, usually built on an elevated location
horn	A symbol of power based on the strength of animal horns
Hosanna	A term of praise derived from the Hebrew word for *save*
Hosts/hosts	Military forces consisting of God's angels, sometimes including the sun, moon, and stars, and occasionally, Israel
human race	(see "everyone")
I assure you	This is a phrase used only by Jesus to testify to the certainty and importance of His words; in Mt, Mk and Lk it is literally *Amen, I say to you*, and in Jn it is literally *Amen, amen, I say to you*.
Jew(s)	In Jn the term *Jews* usually indicates those in Israel who were opposed to Jesus, particularly the Jewish authorities in Jerusalem who led the nation.

Leviathan	Or *twisting one*; a mythological sea serpent or dragon associated with the chaos at creation. Sometimes it is applied to an animal such as a crocodile.
life/soul	The Greek word *psyche* can be translated life or soul.
mankind	Literally *sons of man* or *sons of Adam*
Mary Magdalene	Or *Mary of Magdala*; Magdala was probably on the western shore of the Sea of Galilee, north of Tiberias.
Maskil	From a Hebrew word meaning *to be prudent or to have insight*; possibly a contemplative, instructive, or wisdom psalm
men	Literally *sons of man* or *sons of Adam*
mercy seat	Or *place of atonement*; the gold lid on the ark of the covenant, first used in the tabernacle and later in the temple
Messiah	Or *the Christ*; the Greek word *Christos* means "the anointed one".
Miktam	A musical term of uncertain meaning, possibly denoting a plaintive style
Milcom	An Ammonite god who was the equivalent of Baal, the Canaanite storm god
Molech	A Canaanite god associated with death and the underworld. The worship ritual of passing someone through the fire is connected with him. This ritual could have been either fire-walking or child sacrifice.
Most High	The Hebrew word is *Elyon*. It is often used with other names of God, such as *El (God)* or *Yahweh (Lord)*; it is used to refer to God as the supreme being.
Mount of Olives	A mountain east of Jerusalem, across the Kidron Valley
Mystery	Transliteration of the Greek word *mysterion*; a secret hidden in the past but now revealed
Nazarene	A person from Nazareth; growing up in Nazareth was an aspect of the Messiah's humble beginnings; Jn 1:46.
Negev	An arid region in the southern part of Israel; the Hebrew word means "south".
offend	(see "cause the downfall of/cause to sin")
offspring/seed	This term is used literally or metaphorically to refer to plants or grain, sowing or harvest, male reproductive seed, human children or physical descendants, and also to spiritual children or to Christ (Gl 3:16).

One and Only	Or *one of a kind*, or *incomparable*, or *only begotten*; the Greek word can refer to someone's only child such as in Lk 7:12; 8:42; 9:38. It can also refer to someone's special child as in Heb 11:17.
oracle	A prophetic speech of a threatening or menacing character, often against the nations
overseer(s)	Or *elder(s)*, or *bishop(s)*
palace	(see "headquarters/palace")
Passover	The Israelite festival celebrated on the fourteenth day of the first month in the early spring. It was a celebration of the deliverance of the Israelites from Egypt, commemorating the final plague on Egypt when the firstborn were killed.
people	Literally *sons of man* or *sons of Adam*
perverted men	(see "wicked men/perverted men")
Pharisee(s)	In Judaism a religious sect that followed the whole written and oral law
Pilate	Pontius Pilate was governor of the province of Judea A.D. 26–36.
Pit	Either the grave or the realm of the dead
proconsul	The chief Roman government official in a senatorial province who presided over Roman court hearings
proselyte	A person from another race or religion who went through a prescribed ritual to become a Jew
Rabbi	The Hebrew word *Rabbi* means *my great one*; it is used of a recognized teacher of the Scriptures.
Rabshakeh	The title of a high-ranking Assyrian official who was the chief cupbearer to the king
Rahab	Or *boisterous one*, a mythological sea serpent or dragon defeated at the time of creation. Scripture sometimes uses the name metaphorically to describe Egypt.
Red Sea	Literally *Sea of Reeds*
regiment	(see "company/regiment")
restitution offering(s)	An offering that was a penalty for unintentional sins, primarily in relation to the tabernacle or temple; traditionally *trespass* or *guilt offering*
sackcloth	Garment made of poor quality material and worn as a sign of grief and mourning

sacred bread	Literally *bread of presentation*; 12 loaves, representing the 12 tribes of Israel, put on the table in the holy place in the tabernacle, and later in the temple. The priests ate the previous week's loaves; Ex 25:30; 29:32; Lv 24:5-9.
Sadducee(s)	In Judaism a religious sect that followed primarily the first 5 books of the OT (Torah or Pentateuch)
Samaritan(s)	People of mixed, Gentile/Jewish ancestry who lived between Galilee and Judea and were hated by the Jews
Sanhedrin	The supreme council of Judaism with 70 members, patterned after Moses' 70 elders
scribe(s)	A professional group in Judaism that copied the law of Moses and interpreted it, especially in legal cases
seed	(see "offspring/seed")
Selah	A Hebrew word whose meaning is uncertain; various interpretations include: (1) a musical notation, (2) a pause for silence, (3) a signal for worshipers to fall prostrate on the ground, (4) a term for the worshipers to call out, and (5) a word meaning "forever"
set apart for destruction/ completely destroy	In Canaan or its neighboring countries, this was the destruction during war of a city, its inhabitants, and their possessions, including livestock.
shekel(s)	In the OT the *shekel* is a measurement of weight that came to be used as money, either gold or silver.
Sheminith	A musical term meaning instruments or on the *instrument of eight strings*
Sheol	A Hebrew word for either the grave or the realm of the dead
Shinar	A land in Mesopotamia, including ancient Sumer and Babylon; modern Iraq
sin offering(s)	Or *purification offering*; the *sin offering* was the most important OT sacrifice for cleansing from impurities. It provided purification from sin and certain forms of ceremonial uncleanness.
slave	The strong Greek word *doulos* cannot be accurately translated in English by "servant" or "bond servant"; the HCSB translates this word as "slave," not out of insensitivity to the legitimate concerns of modern English speakers, but out of a commitment to accurately convey the brutal reality of the Roman empire's inhumane institution as well as the ownership called for by Christ.
Son of Man	The most frequent title Jesus used for Himself; Dn 7:13
song of ascents	Probably the songs pilgrims sang as they traveled the roads going up to worship in Jerusalem; Pss 120–134

soul	(see "life/soul")
stumble	(see "cause the downfall of/cause to sin")
synagogue	A place where the Jewish people met for prayer, worship and teaching of the Scriptures
tabernacle	Or *tent*, or *shelter*; terms used for temporary housing
take offense	(see "cause the downfall of/cause to sin")
tassel	Fringe put on the clothing of devout Jews to remind them to keep the law; Nm 15:37-41
temple complex	In the Jerusalem temple, the complex included the sanctuary (the holy place and the holy of holies), at least 4 courtyards (for priests, Jewish men, Jewish women, and Gentiles), numerous gates, and several covered walkways.
testimony	A reference to either the Mosaic law in general or to a specific section of the law, the Ten Commandments, which were written on stone tablets and placed in the ark of the covenant (also called the ark of the testimony)
Topheth	A place of human sacrifice outside Jerusalem in the Hinnom Valley; Jr 7:31-32; see "hell/hellfire"
Unleavened Bread	A seven-day festival celebrated in conjunction with the Passover; Ex 12:1-20
Urim & Thummim	Two objects used by Israelite priests to determine God's will
wadi	A seasonal stream that flows only in the rainy season
walk	A term often used in a figurative way to mean "way of life" or "behavior"
wicked men/perverted men	Literally *sons of Belial*; the basic meaning of *Belial* in Hebrew is "worthless".
wise men	The Greek word is *magoi*; the English word "Magi" is based on a Persian word. They were eastern sages who observed the heavens for signs and omens.
woman	When used in direct address, "Woman" was not a term of disrespect but of honor.
world	The organized Satanic system that is opposed to God and hostile to Jesus and His followers. The non-Christian culture including governments, educational systems, and businesses
wormwood	A small shrub used as a medicinal herb, noted for its bitter taste
Yah	(see "Yahweh")
Yahweh	Or *The Lord*; the personal name of God in Hebrew; "Yah" is the shortened form of the name.

TOPICAL CONCORDANCE

Angels
Are ministering spirits. Ps 68:17; Lk 16:22;
Ac 12:7-11; 27:23; Heb 1:7,14.
Not to be worshiped. Col 2:18; Rv 19:10;
22:8-9.
Rejoice over every repentant sinner.
Lk 15:7,10.

Anger
Be slow to. Pr 15:18; 16:32; 19:11; Ti 1:7;
Jms 1:19.
Characteristic of fools. Pr 12:16; 14:29; 27:3.
Pray without. 1Tm 2:8.
A work of sinful nature. Gl 5:20.

Anxiety
The cure for. Mt 6:25-34; Php 2:28;
1Pt 5:7.
Prevented. Ps 121:4; 1Pt 5:7.

Appearance
Can be deceiving. Mt 23:27-28.
Do not judge by. Jms 2:2-4.
Inner versus outward. 1Sm 16:7; 1Pt 3:1-6.

Assurance
Abundant in the understanding of the gospel.
Col 2:2; 1Th 1:5.
Confirmed by love. 1Jn 3:14,19; 4:18.
Eternal life. Rm 8:28-39; 1Th 1:5; 1Jn 5:13.
Give diligence to attain. 2Pt 1:10-11.
In Christ. Jn 6:39; 17:12; 18:9.
Made full by hope. Heb 6:19.
Produced by faith. Eph 3:12; 2Tm 1:12;
Heb 10:22.

Baptism
Jesus was baptized. Mt 3:13-16.
The Ethiopian eunuch. Ac 8:36.
A sign of repentance and sins forgiven.
Mk 1:4; Ac 2:38.
Shows identification with Jesus Christ.
Rm 6:3-8.
A command for all believers. Mt 28:18-20.

Belief
In Christ. Jn 3:16; 14:1; 20:31; Ac 8:37.
In God required. 2Ch 20:20.
Making all things possible. Mk 9:23.
Of devils. Jms 2:19.
Producing healing. Mt 9:22.

Bible
Inspired by God. Jr 36:1-2; 2Tm 3:14-17.
Inspired by the Holy Spirit. Ac 1:16; 2Pt 1:21.
Points to Christ. Jn 5:39; Ac 18:28.
An unerring guide. 2Pt 1:19.
Sharp as a sword. Eph 6:17; Heb 4:12.
Received message, not from men, but from
God. 1Th 2:13.
Everything should be tested against. Is 8:20;
Ac 17:11.
Warning against those who add to or take
from. Dt 4:2; Rv 22:18-19.

Body
Is the temple of Holy Spirit. 1Co 6:19.
Will be resurrected. 1Co 15:12-58.

Born Again
Prophesied. Ezk 11:19; 36:26.
All believers are. Jn 3:3-9; 1Pt 1:23; 1Jn 2:29;
3:9; 4:7; 5:1,4,18.

Capital Punishment
For murder. Gn 9:5-6; Ex 21:12; Nm 35:33.
Warning against putting innocent to death.
Ex 23:7.

Celibacy (see also *Sex*)
Teaching concerning.
Mt 9:10-12; 1Co7:1-9, 25-26, 32-39.
Wrongly insisted on. 1Tm 4:1-3.

Children
Gifts from God. Gn 33:5; Ps 127:3.
Should obey parents. Ex 20:12; Pr 6:20;
Eph 6:1.
Should take care of parents. 1Tm 5:4.
Should be treated with respect. Eph 6:4.

Christ (see *Jesus the Christ*)

Church
Christ will build. Mt 16:18.
Commission of. Mt 28:18-20.
Is the bride of Christ. Rv 19:7-8.
Christ is the head. Col 1:18.
Is like a body. 1Co 12:12-13.

Circumcision
Abolished by the gospel. Gl 2:3-5;
Eph 2:11,15; Php 3:3; Col 2:11; 3:11.
Described. Gn 17:9-11; Ex 4:25.
Without faith, vain. Rm 3:30; Gl 5:6.
Without obedience, vain. Rm 2:25; 1Co 7:19.

Contentment
With wages and possessions. Lk 3:14;
Heb 13:5.
With food and clothing. 1Tm 6:8.
With godliness is great gain. Ps 37:16;
1Tm 6:6.

Counselor
A title of Christ. Is 9:6.
A role of the Spirit. Jn 14:16,26; 15:26; 16:7.

Courage
Commanded. Dt 31:6; Jos 1:7; Is 41:10.

Covenant
Abraham's. Gn 12:1-3; 15:7-18; 17:2-14;
1Ch 16:16-17; Lk 1:72-75; Ac 3:25;
Gl 3:16.
Isaac's. Gn 17:19,21; 26:3-4.
Jacob's. Gn 28:13-14.
Israel's. Ex 6:4; Ac 3:25.
David's. 2Sm 23:5; Ps 89:3-4.
New. Jr 31:31-33; Rm 11:27; Heb 8:8-10,13.

Creation
By Christ. Jn 1:3,10; Col 1:16.
By God. Gn 1:1; 2:4-5; Pr 26:10.
For God's pleasure. Pr 16:4; Rv 4:11.
Glorifies God. Neh 9:6; Pss 19:1; 136:3-9;
145:10; 148:5.

Crown
A reward. 1Co 9:25; 2Tm 2:5; 4:8; Jms 1:12;
1Pt 5:4; Rv 3:11.
Symbolism. Rv 4:4,10; 6:2; 9:7; 12:1,3; 13:1;
14:14; 19:12.
Of thorns. Mt 27:29; Jn 19:5.

Crucifixion
Of Christ. Mt 27:32-56.
Symbolism. Rm 6:6; Gl 2:20.

Dancing
Praising God with. Ex 15:20; 2Sm 6:14;
Ps 150:4.
Examples of sinful. Ex 32:19,25; Mt 14:6.

Death
A consequence of sin. Gn 2:17; Rm 5:12-14;
6:23.
Christ delivers from the fear of. Heb 2:15.
Conquered by Christ. Rm 6:9; Rv 1:18.
Everyone will experience. Jb 30:23;
1Co 15:22; 1Tm 6:7; Heb 9:27.
For believers, a passage to God. 2Co 5:1-8;
Php 1:21-24.
For believers, a place of rest. Jb 3:17;
Lk 16:22,25; Php 1:23; Rv 14:13.
Precious in God's sight. Ps 116:15.

Debt
Borrower is slave of lender. Pr 22:7.
Owe no one anything. Rm 13:8.

Demons
Jesus casts out. Mt 17:14-21; Lk 4:31-36.
Disciples cast out. Mk 16:17; Lk 10:17-20;
Ac 5:16.
Paul casts out. Ac 16:16-18; 19:12.

Devil
Assumes the form of an angel of light.
2Co 11:14.
Believers should resist. Jms 4:7; 1Pt 5:9.
Ultimately defeated. Gn 3:15; 2Pt 2:4; Jd 6;
Rv 20:10.
Is our adversary. Jb 1:6-12; Zch 3:1; 1Th 2:18.
Subtle. 2Co 11:3,13.

Discipleship
Cost of. Mt 16:24-28.
Tests of. Mt 10:32-39; Lk 14:26-27,33;
Jn 21:15-19.

Discipling
Commanded. Dt 6:6-7; Mt 28:18-20;
2Tm 2:2.

Disease (see also *Healing*)
Relationship to sin. Ps 107:17; Mt 9:1-8;
Mk 2:1-12; Ac 12:20-25; Rm 1:26-27;
1Co 11:27-34; Jms 5:14-16.

Divorce
Jesus' teaching concerning. Mt 19:1-10;
Mk 10:2-12.

Doubt (see also *Assurance*)
God's help in. Ps 73:13-17; Is 40:27-28.
Jesus' response to. Mt 11:1-19; Mk 9:14-29;
Jn 20:24-29.

Drugs
Honor God with body. Rm 12:1; 1Co 6:19-20.
Mind should stay alert. Eph 5:18; 1Pt 1:13;
1Th 5:6.

Drunkenness
Avoid those given to. Pr 23:20; 1Co 5:11.
To be avoided. Pr 23:29-35; Lk 21:34;
Rm 13:13; Eph 5:18.
Results in punishment. Is 28:1-3;
Mt 24:49-51; 1Co 6:10; Gl 5:21.

Earth
Believers will inherit. Ps 25:13; Mt 5:5.

Is the Lord's. 1Co 10:26.
Not to be flooded again. 2Pt 3:6-7.
To be renewed. 2Pt 3:13.
Eagerly longs for redemption. Rm 8:19-22.

Edification
All to be done for. 2Co 12:19; Eph 4:29.
Described. Eph 4:12-16.
Gospel as the instrument of. Ac 20:32.
Love leads to. 1Co 8:1.

Education
Of children in God's Word. Dt 6:7; Ps 78:1-8;
    Eph 6:4; 2Tm 3:15-16.
In the pastoral ministry. 1Tm 4:11.

Election
Of Israel. Dt 7:6; Is 45:4.
Of believers. Ps 65:4; Is 65:9; Jn 6:44; 13:18;
    Ac 13:48; 22:14; Rm 8:28-30; 9:11-16;
    Eph 1:4-6,11; 2:10; 1Th 1:4; 2Th 2:13;
    1Pt 1:2.
Should be evidenced by diligence. 2Pt 1:10.
Should lead to godliness. Col 3:12.

Encouragement
Exhorted. 1Th 4:18; 5:11; Ti 2:15;
    Heb 3:13; 10:25.
Through fellow believers. Ac 14:22;
    15:31-32; Rm 1:12.
Through God's Word. Rm 15:4.
Through the Spirit. Ac 9:31.

Enemies
Should be loved. Mt 5:44.
Should be prayed for. Ac 7:60.
Christ forgave. Lk 23:34.
God delivers from. Dt 32:35; Pss 18:48; 61:3.

Equality
Among believers. Gn 13:8; Mt 23:8.
In Christ. Gl 3:28.
Under God. Pr 22:2.
In justice. Pr 24:23.
In salvation. Jn 3:16; Rm 5:18-21.
In sin and guilt. Rm 3:10-19; 5:12-21.

Eternal life
May have assurance of. 1Jn 5:13.
To know God and Christ is. Jn 17:3.
To those who believe in Christ.
    Jn 3:15-16; 6:40,47.

Evangelism
Commanded by Christ. Mt 28:18-20.

Excuses
Adam and Eve to the Lord. Gn 3:12-13.

A disciple to Jesus. Mt 8:21.
Felix to Paul. Ac 24:25.
Humanity to God. Rm 1:20.
Moses to the Lord. Ex 4:1-14.
Saul to the Lord. 1Sm 15:13-15.

Fairness
God's. 2Ch 19:7; Pss 98:9; 99:4; Ezk 18:29;
    Rm 3:3-6.
In business. Lv 19:36; Dt 25:15; Pr 11:1;
    1Tm 5:18.
In legal judgment. Ex 23:3; Dt 1:17; 16:19;
    Pr 29:14.
In treatment of slaves. Col 4:1.
Through wisdom. Pr 8:15.
Lacking. Ps 82:2-4; Is 59:9-11; Mc 3:9;
    Hab 1:4.

Faith
Demonstrated by a pagan soldier. Lk 7:1-10.
All things should be done in. Rm 14:22;
    Heb 11:6.
Have full assurance of. 2Tm 1:12; Heb 10:22.
The gift of God. Rm 12:3; Eph 2:8; 6:23;
    Php 1:29.
Christ the source and perfecter of. Heb 12:2.
Proof of things not seen. Heb 11:1.
Examine whether you are in. 2Co 13:5.
A gift of the Holy Spirit. 1Co 12:9.
Right with God by. Gn 15:6; Rm 4:16.
Necessary in prayer. Mt 21:22; Jms 1:6.
Produces confidence. 1Pt 2:6.
Scripture designed to produce. Jn 20:31;
    2Tm 3:14-16.
The wicked often profess. Ac 8:9-24.

Family
Believers' families blessed. Ps 128:3-6.
Honoring God in. Dt 6:6-7; Jos 24:15;
    Eph 5:22–6:9.
Jesus' family. Mk 3:31-35.
Paul's family. Ac 23:16.
Timothy's family. 2Tm 1:5.
Church leaders' families. 1Tm 3:1-13.

Fasting
Expected of Christians. Mt 6:16; 9:15.
Along with prayer, when seeking God's grace.
    1Sm 7:5-6; Neh 1:4; Dn 9:3;
    Ac 13:3; 14:23.
Wrong way and right way compared.
    Is 58:3-12; Zch 7:5-10; Mt 6:16-18.

Father
God in heaven. Mt 6:9; 23:9.

Duties of godly. Dt 6:6-7; Eph 6:4.
To be honored. Ex 20:12; Pr 23:22;
Eph 6:2; Col 3:17.

Fear

Of God, advantages of. Pr 9:10; 15:16; 19:23;
2Co 7:1.
Godly delivered from. Ps 27:1; Pr 1:33;
1Jn 4:16-18.

Fellowship

Blessings of. 1Jn 1:7.
In Christ. Mt 18:20; 1Co 1:9; Rv 3:20.
In the Holy Spirit. 2Co 13:14.

Flattery

Beware of. Pss 5:9; 12:3; Pr 29:5; Rm 16:18;
Jd 16.

Flood

Noah's. Gn 6–8.
Came suddenly and unexpectedly.
Mt 24:38-39.
Whole earth affected by. Gn 7:23; 2Pt 3:5-6.
Noah warned of. Gn 6:13; Heb 11:7.
Wicked warned of. 1Pt 3:19-20; 2Pt 2:5.

Forgiveness

Of sins, from God. Ex 34:6-7; Ps 103:1-4;
Dn 9:9.
Of sins, through Christ. Ac 4:11-12; 1Jn 2:12.
Of each other. Mt 6:14-15; 18:21-35;
Mk 11:25; Eph 4:32; Jms 2:13.

Freedom

Result of truth. Jn 8:32.
From condemnation. Rm 8:1,33-39.
From sin's power. Rm 8:2-4; Rv 1:5.

Friends

Constancy of. Pr 17:17; 18:24.
David and Jonathan. 1Sm 18:1-4; 20:1-29.
Jesus called His disciples. Jn 15:13-15.

Gambling

Can result in destructive life-style. 1Tm 6:9.
Harms the poor and families. Pr 14:23;
1Tm 5:8.
Poor example for those who may become
addicted. 1Co 8:13; Rm 14:21.
Stems from covetousness. Lk 12:15;
1Tm 6:10.

Genders, Relationship between (see also Male and Female; Women in Roles of Responsibility)

Subject to one another. Eph 5:21.

Male and female in image of God.
Gn 1:26-27; 5:1-2.
Equal as regards salvation. Ac 10:34;
Rm 2:9-11; Gl 3:28.
One flesh in marriage. Gn 2:24.
Partnership in childrearing. Pr 1:8; Eph 6:1-4;
Col 3:20.
Woman a suitable helper of man. Gn 2:18.

Genealogies

Of Patriarchs. Gn 4:16-22; 5; 10; 11:10-32;
22:20-24; 25:1-4,12-16; 35:23-26; 36;
Ru 4:18-20; 1Ch 1–9.
Of Christ. Mt 1:1-17; Lk 3:23-38.
No spiritual value. Mt 3:9; 1Tm 1:4; Ti 3:9.

Giving

Blessings connected with. Ps 41:1; Pr 22:9;
28:27; Ec 11:1-2; Is 58:10; Ac 20:35.
Encouraged. Lk 6:38; 2Co 8:1-12.
Toward enemies. Pr 25:21.

God

Is all knowing. Is 55:9; Dn 2:20; Rm 11:33.
Is all powerful. Jr 32:27; Lk 1:37; Rv 1:8.
Is faithful. Ps 89:24,33; Is 49:7; Lm 3:23;
1Co 1:9; 1Th 5:24; 2Th 3:3; 2Tm 2:13.
Is good. Pss 25:8; 119:68.
Is holy. 1Sm 2:2; Is 57:15; 1Pt 1:15-16.
Is judge. Ps 9:7; Jms 4:12.
Is just. Dt 32:4; Ezk 18:25; Rm 3:26; 9:14.
Is kind. Rm 2:4.
Is knowable. Jr 31:34; Eph 1:17.
Is love. Dt 7:8; Jr 31:3; Hs 11:4; 1Jn 4:16.
Is our Father. Hs 1:10; Mt 6:9; Rm 8:15.
Is sovereign. Ex 18:11; Dt 10:14; 2Kg 19:15;
Pss 24:1; 115:3; 135:6; 146:10; Is 40:23;
45:23; Lm 3:37; Dn 4:35; Rm 9:16;
Col 2:13.
Is spirit. Jn 4:24.
Is to be glorified. 1Ch 16:28-29; Is 42:12;
Dn 5:23; Rm 1:21; 1Co 6:20.
Is unchanging. Ps 102:26-27; Jms 1:17.

Gospel

Predicted. Is 41:27; 52:7; 61:1-3.
Described. 1Co 15:1-4.
Brings peace. Lk 2:10-14.
Veiled to the lost. 2Co 4:3.
There is only one. Gl 1:8.
Must be believed. Mk 1:15; Heb 4:2.
The power of God for salvation. Rm 1:16;
1Co 1:18; 1Th 1:5.
Produces hope. 1Co 1:23.

Grace
Came by Christ. Jn 1:17; Rm 5:15.
Believers should grow in. 2Pt 3:18.
God's work completed in believers by.
2Th 1:11-12.
Justifies sinners. Ps 51:1-12; Rm 5:1-21.
Not to be abused. Rm 3:8; 6:1,15; 2Co 6:1;
Jd 4.
Salvation by. Ac 15:11; Eph 2:1-10; Ti 2:11.

Hate
Embitters life. Pr 15:17.
Of neighbors, prohibited. Lv 19:17; 1Jn 3:15.
Of evil, condoned. Pss 97:10; 119:104;
139:21; Pr 8:13.
Believers should expect. Mt 10:22;
Jn 15:18-19.
Return good for. Mt 5:44.

Healing
Comes from God. Ex 15:26; Ps 103:3.
Proof that Jesus is the Messiah. Mt 11:5.
Son of a royal official. Jn 4:46-54.

Heaven
Believers rewarded in. Is 65:17-25; Mt 5:12;
1Pt 1:4; Rv 21:1-7.
Jesus entered. Ac 3:21; Heb 6:20.
God's dwelling place. Pss 11:4; 115:3;
Is 66:1; Mt 6:9.
Believers names are written in. Lk 10:20;
Heb 12:23.
Wicked are excluded from. Gl 5:21; Eph 5:5;
Rv 22:15.

Hell
The beast, false prophet, and the Devil
thrown into. Rv 19:20; 20:10.
Body suffers in. Mt 5:29; 10:28.
Everlasting fire. Is 1:28-31; 66:24; Mt 3:12;
25:41,46.
Destruction, away from God's presence.
2Th 1:9.
Strive to keep others from. Mt 18:14; Jd 23.

Holiness
God's, as standard. Lv 19:2; Eph 5:1.
Believers called to. Lv 11:45; 20:7; Lk 1:74-
75; Rm 6:13,19; 8:29; 12:1; Eph 1:4; 5:8;
1Th 4:7; Heb 12:14; 1Pt 1:14-16.

Holy Spirit
Believers receive. 1Jn 2:20.
Guides into all truth. Is 30:21; Ezk 36:27;
Jn 16:13; 1Jn 2:27.
Baptism of, through Christ. Ti 3:6.

Communicates joy. Rm 14:17; Gl 5:22;
1Th 1:6.
Given by the Father. Neh 9:20; Ezk 36:27;
Jl 2:28; Jn 14:15-18.
Gives the new birth. Jn 3:5-6.
Called God. Ac 5:3-4.
Convinces of sin. Neh 9:30; Mc 3:8;
Jn 16:8-11.
Lives in believers. Is 59:21; Hg 2:5; Jn 14:16-
17; 1Co 3:16; 6:19; Eph 5:18; 1Pt 4:14.
Blasphemy against is unpardonable.
Zch 7:12-13; Mt 12:31-32; 1Jn 5:16.
Can be grieved. Is 63:10; Eph 4:30;
1Th 5:19.
Believers sealed by. 2Co 1:22;
Eph 1:13; 4:30.

Homosexuality
Prohibited. Lv 18:22; 20:13.
Condemned. Gn 18:20-21; 19:4-7;
Rm 1:26-27; 1Co 6:9; 1Tm 1:8-10.

Honesty (see also *Integrity; Lying; Truth*)
Commanded. Dt 25:13; Lv 19:35; Pr 11:1;
12:22; Am 8:4-7; Zch 8:16; 2Co 4:2.
Necessary in speaking. Ps 101:7; Pr 12:19;
17:20; Mt 5:33-37; Eph 4:25; Rv 22:15.

Hope
In God. Ps 39:7; Ti 1:2; 1Pt 1:21.
Be ready to give a reason for. 1Pt 3:15.
Believers enjoy. Rm 5:2; 12:12; Ti 2:13.
Leads to patience. Rm 8:25; 1Th 1:3.

Hospitality
Commanded. Rm 12:13; 1Tm 3:2; 5:10;
Ti 1:8; 1Pt 4:9.
To enemies. 2Kg 6:22-23; Rm 12:20.
To the poor. Is 58:7; Lk 14:13-14.
To strangers. Heb 13:2.

Humility
Afflictions intended to produce. Lv 26:41;
Dt 8:3.
Averts punishment. 2Ch 7:14; 12:6-7.
Before honor. Pr 15:33.
Brings wisdom. Pr 11:2; Mt 11:25.
Christ's example. Mt 11:29; Jn 13:14-15;
Php 2:5-8.
In believers. Mc 6:8; Rm 12:16; Eph 4:1-2;
Php 2:3; Col 3:12; 1Pt 5:5.

Husband
To love wife. Gn 2:23-24; Eph 5:25-30;
Col 3:19.
To respect wife. 1Pt 3:7.

Should have only one wife. Mt 19:3-9; Mk 10:6-8; 1Co 7:2-4; 1Tm 3:12.

Idolatry

Forbidden by the law. Ex 20:4-5; Dt 4:15-19.
Provokes God. Dt 31:20; Is 65:3; Jr 25:6.
Ridiculed. Is 44:10-20; 45:20; Jr 10:3-5;
Hab 2:18-19; 1Co 12:2.
Not gods. Jr 5:7; Gl 4:8.
Nothing. Is 41:24; 1Co 8:4.
Believers should avoid. Ex 34:16;
Dt 7:3-5,26; Ac 14:15; 1Co 10:14,19-21.

Image of God

Man created in. Gn 1:26-27; 5:1; 9:5;
Jms 3:9.
Christ as. Col 1:15; Heb 1:3.

Immortality

David's hope. 2Sm 12:23.
Jesus' promise of. Jn 6:39-58.

Incest (see also Sex)

Forbidden. Gn 19:31-36; 38:16-18; Lv 18:6-
18; 2Sm 13:14; 1Co 5:1; Mt 14:3-4.

Integrity (see also Honesty)

Required. Dt 6:5.
Characterizes righteous men. Nm 16:15;
Jb 27:5; Pss 25:21; 26:11; Pr 11:3.

Intercession (see also Prayer)

Should be made for everyone. Nm 14:19;
Jb 42:8-10; Jn 17:1-26; Ac 7:60; Rm
8:26,34; Eph 6:18; 1Tm 2:1; Heb 7:25;
1Jn 2:1.

Intolerance, Religious

Proper. Ex 22:20; Dt 13; 17:1-7; 1Kg 18:40;
2Kg 10:18-30; 2Ch 15:12-13.
Improper. Nm 11:24-30; Mk 9:38-39;
Ac 4:1-3; 13:50; 17:5; 18:13; 21:28-31;
22:22.

Jealousy

God's righteous. Ex 20:5; 1Kg 14:22;
Ps 78:58;1Co 10:22.
Consequences of man's. Gn 4:4-8; 37:4-
8,18,28; Mt 2:16-18.

Jesus the Christ

Pre-existence. Jn 1:1-18; Col 1:16; Heb 1:2.
Genealogy traced through Joseph. Mt 1:1-17.
Genealogy traced through Mary. Lk 3:23-38.
Birth of. Mt 1:18-25; Lk 2:1-20.
Circumcision and naming of. Lk 2:21.
Childhood. Lk 2:41-52.
Baptism. Mt 3:13-17.

Tempted by Satan. Mt 4:1-11; Mk 1:12-13;
Lk 4:1-13.
Calls His first disciples. Jn 1:35-51.
Mission. Lk 4:16-21.
Manner of relating to people. Mt 12:18-21.
Sinless. Jn 8:46; 2Co 5:21; Heb 4:14-16.
Forgives sins. Col 3:13; Mk 2:7,10-11.
One with the Father. Jn 10:30,38; 12:45;
14:7-10; 17:10.
Fully God. Col 2:9; Heb 1:3.
Eternally the same. Heb 1:12; 13:8.
Fully human. Jn 1:14; Heb 2:14.
Humility of attitude rewarded. Php 2:5-11.
The only mediator between God and man.
1Tm 2:5.

Joy

Commanded of believers. Ps 32:11; Zch 9:9;
Php 3:1.
Despite difficulties. Hab 3:17-18; Mt 5:11-12;
Jms 1:2; 1Pt 1:6.
Over sinners who repent. Lk 15.
In fellowship. 2Tm 1:4; 1Jn 1:3-4; 2Jn 12.
A fruit of the Spirit. Gl 5:22.

Judgment

By God for words spoken. Nm 14:29;
Mt 12:36.
Of Christians. Rm 14:10; 2Co 5:10;
Jms 2:12-13.
After death. Heb 9:27.
Not by outward appearances. Jn 7:24.
Will be righteous. Neh 9:33; Ps 98:9;
Dn 9:14; Ac 17:31.

Kindness

An attribute of God. Ru 2:20; Hs 11:4;
Eph 2:7; Ti 3:4-7.
A quality of believers. Col 3:12; 2Pt 1:7;
1Co 13:4.

Knowledge

Fear of the Lord is the beginning of. Pr 1:7.
Of God among all human beings. Rm 1:20.
Jesus' disciples have. Lk 8:10; Col 2:2-3.
Every disciple's goal. Php 3:10; Col 1:9;
2Pt 3:18.
Of salvation. Lk 1:77; 1Jn 5:13.
Needed to guide zeal. Rm 10:2-3.

Law

1. Ceremonial: Israel's worship. Lv 7:37-38;
Heb 9:1-7.
2. Civil: Israel's justice. Ex 21:1.

3. Moral: universal, timeless. Ex 20:1-17; Dt 6:5; Mt 22:37-39.

Jesus fulfills. Mt 5:17-20; Gl 3:24-25.

Jesus' interpretation of. Mt 12:9-14; Mk 2:23-28.

Man's sinful nature and the law. Rm 7:7-25.

Lawsuits

To be avoided. Pr 25:8-10; Mt 5:25-26; 1Co 6:1-8.

Laziness

Characteristics of. Pr 18:9; 26:13-16.

Consequences of. Pr 6:6-9; 10:26; 12:24; 15:19; 19:15; 20:4; 21:25; 24:30-34; Ec 10:18; 2Th 3:10.

Contrasted with diligence. Pr 13:4.

Love

Covers sin. Pr 10:12.

For God. Dt 6:5; Mt 22:36-40.

Described. 1Co 13:4-7.

Fulfills the law. Rm 13:8; Gl 5:6.

God is. 1Jn 4:7-8,16.

Marks the child of God. Jn 13:35; 1Jn 2:15; 4:7.

Lust (see also *Sex*)

Condemned. Pr 5:15-20; Php 4:8.

Must be controlled by God. Rm 13:14; Gl 5:17.

Same as committing adultery. Jb 31:1; Mt 5:27-28.

Leads to trouble. 2Sm 11:2-5; Pr 5:3-5; 6:25-35; Jms 1:14-15.

Results in perverted sexual behavior. 2Sm 13:1-18; Rm 1:26-27.

Lying (see also *Honesty*)

A characteristic of unbelief. 1Th 2:9; 1Tm 4:2; 1Jn 2:4.

The Devil is the father of. Jn 8:44.

Forbidden. Lv 19:11; Pr 12:22; Zch 1:16; Col 3:9.

Punished. Pss 5:6; 120:3-4; Pr 19:5; Rv 21:8.

Magic (see also *Occult*)

Forbidden. Dt 13:1-18; 18:9-14.

Male and Female (see also *Genders*)

Mutual love. 1Co 7:3-4; Col 3:19; Ti 2:4.

Different roles. Gn 3:16-19; 1Co 14:34-35; Eph 5:22-33; Col 3:18-19; 1Tm 2:11; Ti 2:2-5; 1Pt 3:1-7.

Mankind

Made in God's image. Gn 1:26-27; Jms 3:9.

More valuable than animals. Gn 1:28; 9:3-6; Ps 8:4-8; Mt 10:31; 12:11-12.

All sinned. Ps 14:1-3; Rm 3:23.

Object of God's love. Jn 3:16.

Marriage (see also *Sex*)

Jesus blesses. Jn 2:1-11.

Honorable for all. 1Tm 4:3; Heb 13:4.

Not believer with unbeliever. Dt 7:3-4; 1Co 7:39; 2Co 6:14.

Should be permanent. Pr 5:15-19; Mal 2:14; Mt 19:6; 1Co 7:39.

Illustrates Christ and the church. Eph 5:22-32.

Materialism

Insufficient. Lk 12:15; 1Pt 1:18-19.

Root of all evil. 1Tm 6:10.

Makes entry into God's kingdom difficult. Mk 10:23-25.

Meditation

On the Lord. Pss 1:1-2; 63:6-7; 119:148; 143:5.

On what is good. Php 4:8.

Mercy

Denunciations against those lacking. Mt 18:23-35; Jms 2:13.

Encouraged. 2Kg 6:21-23; Pr 14:21; Mt 5:7; Lk 6:36; Rm 12:20-21.

Mind

Love God with. Mt 22:36-40.

Renewed, key to spirituality. Rm 12:2; Eph 4:23.

Use while praying or singing. 1Co 14:15-16.

Miracles

Purpose is to encourage belief. Ex 4:1-5; Mk 16:20; Jn 20:30-31.

Insufficient to produce conversion. Ps 106:7; Lk 16:31.

Jesus proved to be the Messiah by. Mt 11:4-6; Lk 7:20-22; Jn 5:36.

Performed by false prophets. Ex 7:12; Dt 13:1-3; Mt 24:24; 2Th 2:9; Rv 19:20.

Missions

All believers are called to. Mt 28:18-20; Mk 16:15.

Principle of. 2Co 5:14-15.

Obligations to engage in. Lk 10:2; Ac 4:19-20; Rm 1:13-15; 10:14-15; 1Co 9:16.

Modesty

Of women. 1Tm 2:9.

Money

Must choose between God or money. Mt 6:24.

Cannot rescue. Pr 11:4; Ezk 7:19; Zph 1:18.

Use your money to benefit others. Lk 16:9.

Love of is root of all evil. 1Tm 6:9-10.

Morality

Exalts a nation. Pr 14:34.

Sermon on the Mount. Mt 5–7.

Ten Commandments. Ex 20:1-17.

The heart of religion. Am 5:21,24; Mc 6:6-8; Ti 2:7; 1Jn 2:29.

Mother

To be honored and cared for. Pr 23:22; Jn 19:27; Eph 6:2.

Murder

Hatred is. Mt 5:21-22; 1Jn 3:15.

God despises. Gn 4:11; 9:6; Ex 20:13; Pr 6:16-17.

Punished by death. Gn 9:5-6; Ex 21:12; Nm 35:16,30.

Music

Used in the temple. 1Ch 16:4-6; 23:5-6; 25:1; 2Ch 29:25.

Used by Christians. Eph 5:19.

Neighbor

Care for. Pr 3:28-29; Mt 25:34-46.

Love as you love yourself. Lv 19:18; Lk 10:25-37; Rm 13:8-10; Gl 5:13-15; Jms 2:8.

New Creation

Christ brings about. Rm 6:4; 2Co 5:14-17; Gl 6:14-15.

Will transform the entire universe. Rm 8:18-21; 2Pt 3:7-13; Rv 21:1-8.

Oaths

Permitted. Is 65:16; Jr 12:16; Heb 6:16.

False, condemned. Lv 6:3; Zch 5:4; Ml 3:5.

Forbidden in the name of idol or created thing. Jos 23:7; Mt 5:34-36; Jms 5:12.

Rash. Lv 5:4; Nm 30:2; Dt 23:21-22; Ec 5:5.

Occult (see also *Magic*)

Denounced by God. Lv 19:26,31; Dt 18:9-14.

Severe punishment for. Ex 22:18; Lv 20:27; Dt 13:5; Gl 5:20-21.

Saul and the medium. 1Sm 28:7-25.

Girl involved with. Ac 16:16.

Books of, destroyed. Ac 19:19.

Pain

None in heaven. Rv 21:4.

Presence in hell. Lk 16:24; Rv 16:10.

Parables

Why Jesus spoke in. Mt 13:10-17.

Paradise

Place of glorified spirits. Lk 23:43; 2Co 12:4; Rv 2:7.

Patience

Waiting for God. Pss 37:7; 40:1.

Believers receive from God. Col 1:11.

Toward others. 1Th 5:14.

Running the race with. Heb 12:1.

Peace

Believers have. Ps 85:8; Is 26:3; 53:5; 57:2; Ezk 34:25; Jn 14:27; Rm 5:1; Php 4:6-7; Col 1:19-20.

Wicked do not know. Is 48:22; 59:8; Jr 6:14; Rm 3:17.

Persecution

Christ's followers will have. Mt 16:21-26; 2Tm 3:12.

God will deliver from. Dn 3:25,28; 2Co 1:10; 4:9; 2Tm 3:11.

Perseverance (see *Assurance*)

Poor

Jesus preached to. Lk 4:18.

God cares for. 1Sm 2:8; Pss 35:10; 68:10; Is 41:17.

Do not despise. Dt 15:7; Pr 14:21,31; Jms 2:2-17.

Praise (see also *Worship; Singing*)

Continuous. Pss 35:28; 71:6.

Christ is worthy of. Rv 5:1-14.

Prayer (see also *Intercession*)

Jesus' way. Mt 6:5-13.

Acceptable through Christ. Jn 14:13-14.

Husband and wife relationship important for. 1Pt 3:7.

At all times. Ps 88:1; 1Th 5:17; 1Tm 5:5.

Regarding everything. Php 4:6.

For others. 1Tm 2:1; Jms 5:13-18; 1Jn 5:16.

Preaching

Purpose of. 2Tm 4:1-4.

Predestination

Of the crucifixion. Acts 4:28.

Of salvation. Rm 8:28-33; 9:11-29; 11:5-8; 1Co 2:7; Eph 1:5,11.

Pride
Warnings against. 1Sm 2:3; Pr 21:4; 1Co 8:1-2; 10:12.

God sees and judges. Is 2:12; Zph 2:10-11; Lk 1:51.

Prophecy
Blessing for those who listen. 1Th 5:20; Rv 1:3; 22:7.

Does not come by human will. Jr 1:5; Am 7:14-15; 2Pt 1:20-21.

Racism
Rejected since all are from one man. Gn 9:18-19; Ac 17:26.

No racial distinction in the law. Lv 24:22; Dt 24:17.

No racial distinction in Christ. Gl 3:28-29; Eph 2:19; Rv 5:9-10.

Rape (see also Sex)
Forbidden. Dt 22:25-28.

Redemption
Is by the blood of Christ. Heb 9:12; 1Pt 1:18-19; Rv 5:9.

Repentance
Given by God. Ac 11:18; 2Tm 2:25.

Godly grief produces. Ezr 9:6-9; Jr 31:19; Zch 12:10; 2Co 7:10.

Commanded. Ezk 18:30-32; Mk 1:15; Ac 17:30.

Results in changed behavior. 2Ch 6:26; Lk 3:7-14; 2Co 7:11.

Resurrection
OT doctrine of. Jb 19:26; Pss 16:10; 49:15; Is 26:19; Dn 12:2; Hs 13:14.

Of Jesus, the historical event. Mt 28:5-10.

Preached by the Apostles. Ac 4:2.

Of the body. Is 26:19; 1Co 15:42-45.

First principle of the gospel. 1Co 15:1-19.

Revenge
Law of. Ex 21:23-25.

Prohibited. Lv 19:18; Rm 12:17-19; 1Th 5:15; 1Pt 3:9.

Righteousness
Our own does not save. Ti 3:5.

God gives. Ps 24:5; Is 61:10.

Given through Christ. Rm 3:21-26; Php 3:4-11.

Sabbath
Grounds of its institution. Gn 2:2-3; Ex 20:11.

Made for man. Mk 2:27.

Works of mercy lawful on. Mt 12:12; Lk 13:16; Jn 9:14.

Salvation
From God. Ps 3:8; Is 45:21-22; Jr 3:23.

In Jesus alone. Ac 4:11-12; Rm 10:9.

Gospel is power of God to. Rm 1:16; 1Co 1:21.

Sanctification
Through Christ. Rm 8:29-30; 1Co 1:2,30; Heb 10:10; 13:12.

Through the Word of God. Jn 17:17,19; Eph 5:26.

Satan (see Devil)

Second Coming of Christ
Jesus predicted. Mt 25:31; Jn 14:3.

In same way as He ascended into heaven. Dn 7:13; Ac 1:9-11.

Will complete salvation of believers. Heb 9:28.

Time of, unknown and sudden. Mt 24:36,44; Mk 13:32-37; Lk 12:40; 1Th 5:1-11; 2Th 1:3-12; 2Pt 3:10-13.

Self-esteem
Cautions regarding. Rm 12:3; 2Co 10:7-13; Gl 6:1-3; Php 2:3.

Self-confidence in Christ. Rm 8:1; 2Co 3:5; Php 3:4-7; 4:13.

Sex (see also Celibacy; Homosexuality; Incest; Lust; Marriage; Rape)
Prohibited outside marriage. Sg 2:7; 1Co 6:15-20; Heb 13:4.

Blessed within marriage. Sg 4:1–5:1.

Not to be withheld in marriage. 1Co 7:3-5.

Sin
Begins in the mind. Mt 5:27-28; Jms 1:14-15.

All have committed. Rm 3:23.

Confession leads to forgiveness. 2Sm 12:13; Ps 32:5; 1Jn 1:9.

God helps believers resist. Ps 119:11; 1Co 10:13.

Christ's blood removes. Mt 26:28; Eph 1:7; 1Jn 1:7.

Singing (see also Music; Worship)
Commanded. 1Ch 16:9; Ps 100:2; Eph 5:19; Col 3:16; Jms 5:13.

From God. Ps 40:3.

Stealing
Prohibited. Ex 20:15.

From the poor, specially forbidden. Pr 22:22.
Do honest work instead. Eph 4:28.

Talent (Ability)
Differs in individuals. Mt 25:15.
Given by God. 1Co 12:4.
To be used. 1Tm 4:14; Rm 12:6.

Tax
Jesus paid. Mt 17:24-27.

Thankfulness
Commanded. Ps 50:14; Php 4:6.
Accompanies prayer. Php 4:6; Col 4:2.
In all things. Eph 5:20; 1Th 5:18; 1Tm 4:4-5.

Tithe
Preceded law. Gn 14:20; Heb 7:6.
Given to the Levites for their services. Nm 18:21,24; Neh 10:37.
Punishment for withholding. Ml 3:8.

Trinity
There is only one God. Dt 4:39; 6:4; 1Co 8:4,6; Eph 4:5-6.
Christ and his Father are one. Jn 10:30.
The Holy Spirit is the Spirit of God and of Christ. Rm 8:9,14; 1Co 3:16.
Reference to. Rm 8:9; 1Co 12:3-6; Eph 4:4-6; 2Th 2:13-14; Ti 3:4-6; 1Pt 1:2; Jd 20-21.
Evident at Jesus' baptism. Mt 3:16-17.
To be baptized in the name of. Mt 28:18-20.
The apostolic benediction. 2Co 13:13.

Truth (see also Honesty)
Leaders should be men of. Ex 18:21; Pr 20:28.
The Holy Spirit guides believers into. Jn 14:17; 16:13.
The Word of God is. Dn 10:21; Jn 17:17.

Unbelief
Is sin. Jn 16:8-11.
Questions truthfulness of God. 2Kg 17:13-15; Ps 106:24; 1Jn 5:10.

Vegetarianism
In Creation. Gn 2:16; Is 11:7; 65:25.
Tolerance for. Rm 14:1-3.

Vows (see Oaths)

Widows
Cared for. Dt 10:18; Ps 68:5; Ac 6:1.
Allowed to marry again. Rm 7:3; 1Co 7:39.

Paul's commandments concerning. 1Co 7:8-9; 1Tm 5:3-16.

Wife
A helper like him. Gn 2:18-23.
A capable. Pr 31:10-31.
A blessing to her husband. Pr 12:4; 31:10,12.
Submissive to her husband. 1Co 11:3-12; Eph 5:22-33.
Win unbelieving husband by her life. 1Pt 3:1-2.

Women in Roles of Responsibility
Miriam. Ex 15:20; Mc 6:4.
Deborah. Jdg 4–5.
Huldah. 2Kg 22:12-20.
Virtuous woman. Pr 31:10-31.
Mary. Mt 28:1-10.
Phoebe. Rm 16:1.
Priscilla. Rm 16:3-4.

Work
Believers should. Pr 10:4; 13:4,11; Eph 6:5-8; 2Th 3:10-12.

Works
Can not save. Rm 3:20; Gl 2:16; Eph 2:8-9; 2Tm 1:9; Ti 3:5.
Are the fruit of true faith. Mt 3:8; Eph 2:10; Jms 2:14-26.

Worship
With fear and reverence. Pss 5:7; 96:9; Is 6:1-7.
With music. Pss 57:7-8; 150.
With a new song. Pss 33:3; 96:1; 98:1; 149:1; Is 42:10; Rv 5:9; 14:3.
With dance. 2Sm 6:14-16; Ps 149:3.
Bowing down. 1Ch 29:20; Ps 95:6; Mt 2:11.
Authentic. Jn 4:19-26.

Youth
Examples of. 1Sm 2:11; 17:1-54.
Should be an example. 1Tm 4:12.

Zeal
Sometimes not according to knowledge. Ac 21:20; Rm 10:2; Gl 1:14.
Sometimes wrongly directed. 2Sm 21:2; Ac 22:3-4; Php 3:6.
Stimulates others to do good. 2Co 9:2.